SELECTED
FEDERAL TAXATION
STATUTES AND REGULATIONS

1983 EDITION

Selected and edited

by

MICHAEL D. ROSE
Professor of Law, The Ohio State University

ST. PAUL, MINN.
WEST PUBLISHING CO.
1983

Sel.Prov.I.R.C.Reg.—1
1983 Pamph.

PREFACE

———

This pamphlet is for student use. It contains selected and edited provisions of the Internal Revenue Code (Title 26 of the United States Code) and the Treasury Regulations (Title 26 of the Code of Federal Regulations).

The aim of the pamphlet is to provide a reasonably compact, convenient, and economical set of materials. Thus, it is not a complete source of the Internal Revenue Code and Treasury Regulations. The entire text of the Code and Regulations is approximately 8,000 pages, the bulk of which students do not use.

This edition reflects the Internal Revenue Code provisions amended, added, and repealed by the Tax Equity and Fiscal Responsibility Act of 1982 as well as the Subchapter S Revision Act of 1982.

MICHAEL D. ROSE

Columbus, Ohio
November 1982.

*

SUMMARY OF CONTENTS

	Page
INTERNAL REVENUE TITLE	1
Income Taxes	1
Estate Tax	504
Gift Tax	540
Generation-Skipping Transfer Tax	551
Procedure and Administration	562
TREASURY REGULATIONS	609
Income Taxes	609
Estate Tax	1138
Gift Tax	1205
Procedure and Administration	1233
TOPICAL INDEX	1241

*

SELECTED FEDERAL TAXATION
STATUTES & REGULATIONS
1983 EDITION

*

Sel.Prov.I.R.C.Reg.
1983 Pamph.

INTERNAL REVENUE TITLE

Subtitle
- A. Income taxes.
- B. Estate and gift taxes.
- C. Employment taxes.*
- D. Miscellaneous excise taxes.*
- E. Alcohol, tobacco, and certain other excise taxes.*
- F. Procedure and administration.
- G. The Joint Committee on Taxation.*
- H. Financing of presidential election campaigns.*
- I. Trust Fund Code.*

SUBTITLE A—INCOME TAXES

Chapter
1. Normal taxes and surtaxes.
2. Tax on self-employment income.*
3. Withholding of tax on nonresident aliens and foreign corporations and tax-free covenant bonds.*
4. Rules applicable to recovery of excessive profits on government contracts.*
5. Tax on transfers to avoid income tax.
6. Consolidated returns.

CHAPTER 1—NORMAL TAXES AND SURTAXES

Subchapter
- A. Determination of tax liability.
- B. Computation of taxable income.
- C. Corporate distributions and adjustments.
- D. Deferred compensation, etc.
- E. Accounting periods and methods of accounting.
- F. Exempt organizations.
- G. Corporations used to avoid income tax on shareholders.
- H. Banking institutions.*
- I. Natural resources.
- J. Estates, trust, beneficiaries, and decedents.
- K. Partners and partnerships.
- L. Insurance companies.*
- M. Regulated investment companies and real estate investment trusts.*
- N. Tax based on income from sources within or without the United States.*
- O. Gain or loss on disposition of property.
- P. Capital gains and losses.
- Q. Readjustment of tax between years and special limitations.
- [R. Repealed]
- S. Election of certain small business corporations as to taxable status.

* Omitted entirely.

Subchapter
T. Cooperatives and their patrons.*
U. General stock ownership plans.*
V. Title 11 cases.*

SUBCHAPTER A—DETERMINATION OF TAX LIABILITY

Part
I. Tax on individuals.
II. Tax on corporations.
III. Changes in rates during a taxable year.*
IV. Credits against tax.
[V. Repealed]
VI. Minimum tax for tax preferences.

PART I—TAX ON INDIVIDUALS

§ 1.   Tax imposed

(a) **Married individuals filing joint returns and surviving spouses.**—There is hereby imposed on the taxable income of every married individual (as defined in section 143) who makes a single return jointly with his spouse under section 6013, and every surviving spouse (as defined in section 2(a)), a tax determined in accordance with the following tables:

(1) For taxable years beginning in 1982.—

If taxable income is:	The tax is:
Not over $3,400	No tax.
Over $3,400 but not over $5,500	12% of the excess over $3,400.
Over $5,500 but not over $7,600	$252, plus 14% of the excess over $5,500.
Over $7,600 but not over $11,900	$546, plus 16% of the excess over $7,600.
Over $11,900 but not over $16,000	$1,234, plus 19% of the excess over $11,900.
Over $16,000 but not over $20,200	$2,013, plus 22% of the excess over $16,000.
Over $20,200 but not over $24,600	$2,937, plus 25% of the excess over $20,200.
Over $24,600 but not over $29,900	$4,037, plus 29% of the excess over $24,600.
Over $29,900 but not over $35,200	$5,574, plus 33% of the excess over $29,900.
Over $35,200 but not over $45,800	$7,323, plus 39% of the excess over $35,200.
Over $45,800 but not over $60,000	$11,457, plus 44% of the excess over $45,800.
Over $60,000 but not over $85,600	$17,705, plus 49% of the excess over $60,000.
Over $85,600	$30,249, plus 50% of the excess over $85,600.

(2) For taxable years beginning in 1983.—

If taxable income is:	The tax is:
Not over $3,400	No tax.
Over $3,400 but not over $5,500	11% of the excess over $3,400.
Over $5,500 but not over $7,600	$231, plus 13% of the excess over $5,500.
Over $7,600 but not over $11,900	$504, plus 15% of the excess over $7,600.
Over $11,900 but not over $16,000	$1,149, plus 17% of the excess over $11,900.
Over $16,000 but not over $20,200	$1,846, plus 19% of the excess over $16,000.
Over $20,200 but not over $24,600	$2,644, plus 23% of the excess over $20,200.
Over $24,600 but not over $29,900	$3,656, plus 26% of the excess over $24,600.
Over $29,900 but not over $35,200	$5,034, plus 30% of the excess over $29,900.
Over $35,200 but not over $45,800	$6,624, plus 35% of the excess over $35,200.
Over $45,800 but not over $60,000	$10,334, plus 40% of the excess over $45,800.
Over $60,000 but not over $85,600	$16,014, plus 44% of the excess over $60,000.
Over $85,600 but not over $109,400	$27,278, plus 48% of the excess over $85,600.
Over $109,400	$38,702, plus 50% of the excess over $109,400.

* Omitted entirely.

(3) For taxable years beginning after 1983.—

If taxable income is:	The tax is:
Not over $3,400	No tax.
Over $3,400 but not over $5,500	11% of the excess over $3,400.
Over $5,500 but not over $7,600	$231, plus 12% of the excess over $5,500.
Over $7,600 but not over $11,900	$483, plus 14% of the excess over $7,600.
Over $11,900 but not over $16,000	$1,085, plus 16% of the excess over $11,900.
Over $16,000 but not over $20,200	$1,741, plus 18% of the excess over $16,000.
Over $20,200 but not over $24,600	$2,497, plus 22% of the excess over $20,200.
Over $24,600 but not over $29,900	$3,465, plus 25% of the excess over $24,600.
Over $29,900 but not over $35,200	$4,790, plus 28% of the excess over $29,900.
Over $35,200 but not over $45,800	$6,274, plus 33% of the excess over $35,200.
Over $45,800 but not over $60,000	$9,772, plus 38% of the excess over $45,800.
Over $60,000 but not over $85,600	$15,168, plus 42% of the excess over $60,000.
Over $85,600 but not over $109,400	$25,920, plus 45% of the excess over $85,600.
Over $109,400 but not over $162,400	$36,630, plus 49% of the excess over $109,400.
Over $162,400	$62,600, plus 50% of the excess over $162,400.

(b) Heads of households.—There is hereby imposed on the taxable income of every individual who is the head of a household (as defined in section 2(b)) a tax determined in accordance with the following tables:

(1) For taxable years beginning in 1982.—

If taxable income is:	The tax is:
Not over $2,300	No tax.
Over $2,300 but not over $4,400	12% of the excess over $2,300.
Over $4,400 but not over $6,500	$252, plus 14% of the excess over $4,400.
Over $6,500 but not over $8,700	$546, plus 16% of the excess over $6,500.
Over $8,700 but not over $11,800	$898, plus 20% of the excess over $8,700.
Over $11,800 but not over $15,000	$1,518, plus 22% of the excess over $11,800.
Over $15,000 but not over $18,200	$2,222, plus 23% of the excess over $15,000.
Over $18,200 but not over $23,500	$2,958, plus 28% of the excess over $18,200.
Over $23,500 but not over $28,800	$4,442, plus 32% of the excess over $23,500.
Over $28,800 but not over $34,100	$6,138, plus 38% of the excess over $28,800.
Over $34,100 but not over $44,700	$8,152, plus 41% of the excess over $34,100.
Over $44,700 but not over $60,600	$12,498, plus 49% of the excess over $44,700.
Over $60,600	$20,289, plus 50% of the excess over $60,600.

(2) For taxable years beginning in 1983.—

If taxable income is:	The tax is:
Not over $2,300	No tax.
Over $2,300 but not over $4,400	11% of the excess over $2,300.
Over $4,400 but not over $6,500	$231, plus 13% of the excess over $4,400.
Over $6,500 but not over $8,700	$504, plus 15% of the excess over $6,500.
Over $8,700 but not over $11,800	$834, plus 18% of the excess over $8,700.
Over $11,800 but not over $15,000	$1,392, plus 19% of the excess over $11,800.
Over $15,000 but not over $18,200	$2,000, plus 21% of the excess over $15,000.
Over $18,200 but not over $23,500	$2,672, plus 25% of the excess over $18,200.
Over $23,500 but not over $28,800	$3,997, plus 29% of the excess over $23,500.
Over $28,800 but not over $34,100	$5,534, plus 34% of the excess over $28,800.
Over $34,100 but not over $44,700	$7,336, plus 37% of the excess over $34,100.
Over $44,700 but not over $60,600	$11,258, plus 44% of the excess over $44,700.
Over $60,600 but not over $81,800	$18,254, plus 48% of the excess over $60,600.
Over $81,800	$28,430, plus 50% of the excess over $81,800.

(3) For taxable years beginning after 1983.—

If taxable income is:	The tax is:
Not over $2,300	No tax.
Over $2,300 but not over $4,400	11% of the excess over $2,300.
Over $4,400 but not over $6,500	$231, plus 12% of the excess over $4,400.
Over $6,500 but not over $8,700	$483, plus 14% of the excess over $6,500.
Over $8,700 but not over $11,800	$791, plus 17% of the excess over $8,700.
Over $11,800 but not over $15,000	$1,318, plus 18% of the excess over $11,800.
Over $15,000 but not over $18,200	$1,894, plus 20% of the excess over $15,000.
Over $18,200 but not over $23,500	$2,534, plus 24% of the excess over $18,200.
Over $23,500 but not over $28,800	$3,806, plus 28% of the excess over $23,500.
Over $28,800 but not over $34,100	$5,290, plus 32% of the excess over $28,800.
Over $34,100 but not over $44,700	$6,986, plus 35% of the excess over $34,100.
Over $44,700 but not over $60,600	$10,696, plus 42% of the excess over $44,700.
Over $60,600 but not over $81,800	$17,374, plus 45% of the excess over $60,600.
Over $81,800 but not over $108,300	$26,914, plus 48% of the excess over $81,800.
Over $108,300	$39,634, plus 50% of the excess over $108,300.

(c) Unmarried individuals (other than surviving spouses and heads of households).—There is hereby imposed on the taxable income of every individual (other than a surviving spouse as defined in section 2(a) or the head of a household as defined in section 2(b) who is not a married individual (as defined in section 143) a tax determined in accordance with the following tables:

(1) For taxable years beginning in 1982.—

If taxable income is:	The tax is:
Not over $2,300	No tax.
Over $2,300 but not over $3,400	12% of the excess over $2,300.
Over $3,400 but not over $4,400	$132, plus 14% of the excess over $3,400.
Over $4,400 but not over $6,500	$272, plus 16% of the excess over $4,400.
Over $6,500 but not over $8,500	$608, plus 17% of the excess over $6,500.
Over $8,500 but not over $10,800	$948, plus 19% of the excess over $8,500.
Over $10,800 but not over $12,900	$1,385, plus 22% of the excess over $10,800.
Over $12,900 but not over $15,000	$1,847, plus 23% of the excess over $12,900.
Over $15,000 but not over $18,200	$2,330, plus 27% of the excess over $15,000.
Over $18,200 but not over $23,500	$3,194, plus 31% of the excess over $18,200.
Over $23,500 but not over $28,800	$4,837, plus 35% of the excess over $23,500.
Over $28,800 but not over $34,100	$6,692, plus 40% of the excess over $28,800.
Over $34,100 but not over $41,500	$8,812, plus 44% of the excess over $34,100.
Over $41,500	$12,068, plus 50% of the excess over $41,500.

(2) For taxable years beginning in 1983.—

If taxable income is:	The tax is:
Not over $2,300	No tax.
Over $2,300 but not over $3,400	11% of the excess over $2,300.
Over $3,400 but not over $4,400	$121, plus 13% of the excess over $3,400.
Over $4,400 but not over $8,500	$251, plus 15% of the excess over $4,400.
Over $8,500 but not over $10,800	$866, plus 17% of the excess over $8,500.
Over $10,800 but not over $12,900	$1,257, plus 19% of the excess over $10,800.
Over $12,900 but not over $15,000	$1,656, plus 21% of the excess over $12,900.
Over $15,000 but not over $18,200	$2,097, plus 24% of the excess over $15,000.
Over $18,200 but not over $23,500	$2,865, plus 28% of the excess over $18,200.
Over $23,500 but not over $28,800	$4,349, plus 32% of the excess over $23,500.
Over $28,800 but not over $34,100	$6,045, plus 36% of the excess over $28,800.
Over $34,100 but not over $41,500	$7,953, plus 40% of the excess over $34,100.
Over $41,500 but not over $55,300	$10,913, plus 45% of the excess over $41,500.
Over $55,300	$17,123, plus 50% of the excess over $55,300.

(3) For taxable years beginning after 1983.—

If taxable income is:	The tax is:
Not over $2,300	No tax.
Over $2,300 but not over $3,400	11% of the excess over $2,300.
Over $3,400 but not over $4,400	$121, plus 12% of the excess over $3,400.
Over $4,400 but not over $6,500	$241, plus 14% of the excess over $4,400.
Over $6,500 but not over $8,500	$535, plus 15% of the excess over $6,500.
Over $8,500 but not over $10,800	$835, plus 16% of the excess over $8,500.
Over $10,800 but not over $12,900	$1,203, plus 18% of the excess over $10,800.
Over $12,900 but not over $15,000	$1,581, plus 20% of the excess over $12,900.
Over $15,000 but not over $18,200	$2,001, plus 23% of the excess over $15,000.
Over $18,200 but not over $23,500	$2,737, plus 26% of the excess over $18,200.
Over $23,500 but not over $28,800	$4,115, plus 30% of the excess over $23,500.
Over $28,800 but not over $34,100	$5,705, plus 34% of the excess over $28,800.
Over $34,100 but not over $41,500	$7,507, plus 38% of the excess over $34,100.
Over $41,500 but not over $55,300	$10,319, plus 42% of the excess over $41,500.
Over $55,300 but not over $81,800	$16,115, plus 48% of the excess over $55,300.
Over $81,800	$28,835, plus 50% of the excess over $81,800.

(d) Married individuals filing separate returns.—There is hereby imposed on the taxable income of every married individual (as defined in section 143) who does not make a single return jointly with his spouse under section 6013 a tax determined in accordance with the following tables:

(1) For taxable years beginning in 1982.—

If taxable income is:	The tax is:
Not over $1,700	No tax.
Over $1,700 but not over $2,750	12% of the excess over $1,700.
Over $2,750 but not over $3,800	$126, plus 14% of the excess over $2,750.
Over $3,800 but not over $5,950	$273, plus 16% of the excess over $3,800.
Over $5,950 but not over $8,000	$617, plus 19% of the excess over $5,950.
Over $8,000 but not over $10,100	$1,006, plus 22% of the excess over $8,000.
Over $10,100 but not over $12,300	$1,468, plus 25% of the excess over $10,100.
Over $12,300 but not over $14,950	$2,018, plus 29% of the excess over $12,300.
Over $14,950 but not over $17,600	$2,787, plus 33% of the excess over $14,950.
Over $17,600 but not over $22,900	$3,661, plus 39% of the excess over $17,600.
Over $22,900 but not over $30,000	$5,728, plus 44% of the excess over $22,900.
Over $30,000 but not over $42,800	$8,852, plus 49% of the excess over $30,000.
Over $42,800	$15,124, plus 50% of the excess over $42,800.

(2) For taxable years beginning in 1983.—

If taxable income is:	The tax is:
Not over $1,700	No tax.
Over $1,700 but not over $2,750	11% of the excess over $1,700.
Over $2,750 but not over $3,800	$115, plus 13% of the excess over $2,750.
Over $3,800 but not over $5,950	$252, plus 15% of the excess over $3,800.
Over $5,950 but not over $8,000	$574, plus 17% of the excess over $5,950.
Over $8,000 but not over $10,100	$923, plus 19% of the excess over $8,000.
Over $10,100 but not over $12,300	$1,322, plus 23% of the excess over $10,100.
Over $12,300 but not over $14,950	$1,828, plus 26% of the excess over $12,300.
Over $14,950 but not over $17,600	$2,517, plus 30% of the excess over $14,950.
Over $17,600 but not over $22,900	$3,312, plus 35% of the excess over $17,600.
Over $22,900 but not over $30,000	$5,167, plus 40% of the excess over $22,900.
Over $30,000 but not over $42,800	$8,007, plus 44% of the excess over $30,000.
Over $42,800 but not over $54,700	$13,639, plus 48% of the excess over $42,800.
Over $54,700	$19,351, plus 50% of the excess over $54,700.

(3) For taxable years beginning after 1983.—

If taxable income is:	The tax is:
Not over $1,700	No tax.
Over $1,700 but not over $2,750	11% of the excess over $1,700.
Over $2,750 but not over $3,800	$115, plus 12% of the excess over $2,750.
Over $3,800 but not over $5,950	$241, plus 14% of the excess over $3,800.
Over $5,950 but not over $8,000	$542, plus 16% of the excess over $5,950.
Over $8,000 but not over $10,100	$870, plus 18% of the excess over $8,000.
Over $10,100 but not over $12,300	$1,248, plus 22% of the excess over $10,100.
Over $12,300 but not over $14,950	$1,732, plus 25% of the excess over $12,300.
Over $14,950 but not over $17,600	$2,395, plus 28% of the excess over $14,950.
Over $17,600 but not over $22,900	$3,137, plus 33% of the excess over $17,600.
Over $22,900 but not over $30,000	$4,886, plus 38% of the excess over $22,900.
Over $30,000 but not over $42,800	$7,584, plus 42% of the excess over $30,000.
Over $42,800 but not over $54,700	$12,960, plus 45% of the excess over $42,800.
Over $54,700 but not over $81,200	$18,315, plus 49% of the excess over $54,700.
Over $81,200	$31,300, plus 50% of the excess over $81,200.

(e) Estates and trusts.—There is hereby imposed on the taxable income of every estate and trust taxable under this subsection a tax determined in accordance with the following tables:

(1) For taxable years beginning in 1982.—

If taxable income is:	The tax is:
Not over $1,050	12% of taxable income.
Over $1,050 but not over $2,100	$126, plus 14% of the excess over $1,050.
Over $2,100 but not over $4,250	$273, plus 16% of the excess over $2,100.
Over $4,250 but not over $6,300	$617, plus 19% of the excess over $4,250.
Over $6,300 but not over $8,400	$1,006, plus 22% of the excess over $6,300.
Over $8,400 but not over $10,600	$1,468, plus 25% of the excess over $8,400.
Over $10,600 but not over $13,250	$2,018, plus 29% of the excess over $10,600.
Over $13,250 but not over $15,900	$2,787, plus 33% of the excess over $13,250.
Over $15,900 but not over $21,200	$3,661, plus 39% of the excess over $15,900.
Over $21,200 but not over $28,300	$5,728, plus 44% of the excess over $21,200.
Over $28,300 but not over $41,100	$8,852, plus 49% of the excess over $28,300.
Over $41,100	$15,124, plus 50% of the excess over $41,100.

(2) For taxable years beginning in 1983.—

If taxable income is:	The tax is:
Not over $1,050	11% of taxable income.
Over $1,050 but not over $2,100	$115, plus 13% of the excess over $1,050.
Over $2,100 but not over $4,250	$252, plus 15% of the excess over $2,100.
Over $4,250 but not over $6,300	$574, plus 17% of the excess over $4,250.
Over $6,300 but not over $8,400	$923, plus 19% of the excess over $6,300.
Over $8,400 but not over $10,600	$1,322, plus 23% of the excess over $8,400.
Over $10,600 but not over $13,250	$1,828, plus 26% of the excess over $10,600.
Over $13,250 but not over $15,900	$2,517, plus 30% of the excess over $13,250.
Over $15,900 but not over $21,200	$3,312, plus 35% of the excess over $15,900.
Over $21,200 but not over $28,300	$5,167, plus 40% of the excess over $21,200.
Over $28,300 but not over $41,100	$8,007, plus 44% of the excess over $28,300.
Over $41,100 but not over $53,000	$13,639, plus 48% of the excess over $41,100.
Over $53,000	$19,351, plus 50% of the excess over $53,000.

(3) For taxable years beginning after 1983.—

If taxable income is:	The tax is:
Not over $1,050	11% of taxable income.
Over $1,050 but not over $2,100	$115, plus 12% of the excess over $1,050.
Over $2,100 but not over $4,250	$241, plus 14% of the excess over $2,100.
Over $4,250 but not over $6,300	$542, plus 16% of the excess over $4,250.
Over $6,300 but not over $8,400	$870, plus 18% of the excess over $6,300.
Over $8,400 but not over $10,600	$1,248, plus 22% of the excess over $8,400.
Over $10,600 but not over $13,250	$1,732, plus 25% of the excess over $10,600.
Over $13,250 but not over $15,900	$2,395, plus 28% of the excess over $13,250.
Over $15,900 but not over $21,200	$3,137, plus 33% of the excess over $15,900.
Over $21,200 but not over $28,300	$4,886, plus 38% of the excess over $21,200.
Over $28,300 but not over $41,100	$7,584, plus 42% of the excess over $28,300.
Over $41,100 but not over $53,000	$12,960, plus 45% of the excess over $41,100.
Over $53,000 but not over $79,500	$18,315, plus 49% of the excess over $53,000.
Over $79,500	$31,300, plus 50% of the excess over $79,500.

(f) Adjustments in tax tables so that inflation will not result in tax increases.—

    (1) In general.—Not later than December 15 of 1984 and each subsequent calendar year, the Secretary shall prescribe tables which shall apply in lieu of the tables contained in paragraph (3) of subsections (a), (b), (c), (d), and (e) with respect to taxable years beginning in the succeeding calendar year.

    (2) Method of prescribing tables.—The table which under paragraph (1) is to apply in lieu of the table contained in paragraph (3) of subsection (a), (b), (c), (d), or (e), as the case may be, with respect to taxable years beginning in any calendar year shall be prescribed—

        (A) by increasing—

            (i) the maximum dollar amount on which no tax is imposed under such table, and

            (ii) the minumum and maximum dollar amounts for each rate bracket for which a tax is imposed under such table,

by the cost-of-living adjustment for such calendar year,

        (B) by not changing the rate applicable to any rate bracket as adjusted under subparagraph (A)(ii), and

        (C) by adjusting the amounts setting forth the tax to the extent necessary to reflect the adjustments in the rate brackets.

    If any increase determined under subparagraph (A) is not a multiple of $10, such increase shall be rounded to the nearest multiple of $10 (or if such increase is a multiple of $5, such increase shall be increased to the next highest multiple of $10).

    (3) Cost-of-living adjustment.—For purposes of paragraph (2), the cost-of-living adjustment for any calendar year is the percentage (if any) by which—

        (A) the CPI for the preceding calendar year, exceeds

        (B) the CPI for the calendar year 1983.

    (4) CPI for any calendar year.—For purposes of paragraph (3), the CPI for any calendar year is the average of the Consumer Price Index as of the close of the 12–month period ending on September 30 of such calendar year.

    (5) Consumer price index.—For purposes of paragraph (4), the term "Consumer Price Index" means the last Consumer Price Index for all-urban consumers published by the Department of Labor.

§ 2.   Definitions and special rules

(a) Definition of surviving spouse.—

(1) In general.—For purposes of section 1, the term "surviving spouse" means a taxpayer—

    (A) whose spouse died during either of his two taxable years immediately preceding the taxable year, and

    (B) who maintains as his home a household which constitutes for the taxable year the principal place of abode (as a member of such household) of a dependent (i) who (within the meaning of section 152) is a son, stepson, daughter, or stepdaughter of the taxpayer, and (ii) with respect to whom the taxpayer is entitled to a deduction for the taxable year under section 151.

For purposes of this paragraph, an individual shall be considered as maintaining a household only if over half of the cost of maintaining the household during the taxable year is furnished by such individual.

(2) Limitations.—Notwithstanding paragraph (1), for purposes of section 1 a taxpayer shall not be considered to be a surviving spouse—

    (A) if the taxpayer has remarried at any time before the close of the taxable year, or

    (B) unless, for the taxpayer's taxable year during which his spouse died, a joint return could have been made under the provisions of section 6013 (without regard to subsection (a) (3) thereof).

. . . . .

(b) Definition of head of household.—

(1) In general.—For purposes of this subtitle, an individual shall be considered a head of a household if, and only if, such individual is not married at the close of his taxable year, is not a surviving spouse (as defined in subsection (a)), and either—

    (A) maintains as his home a household which constitutes for such taxable year the principal place of abode, as a member of such household, of—

        (i) a son, stepson, daughter, or stepdaughter of the taxpayer, or a descendant of a son or daughter of the taxpayer, but if such son, stepson, daughter, stepdaughter, or descendant is married at the close of the taxpayer's taxable year, only if the taxpayer is entitled to a deduction for the taxable year for such person under section 151, or

        (ii) any other person who is a dependent of the taxpayer, if the taxpayer is entitled to a deduction for the taxable year for such person under section 151, or

    (B) maintains a household which constitutes for such taxable year the principal place of abode of the father or mother of the taxpayer, if the taxpayer is entitled to a deduction for the taxable year for such father or mother under section 151.

For purposes of this paragraph, an individual shall be considered as maintaining a household only if over half of the cost of maintaining the household during the taxable year is furnished by such individual.

(2) Determination of status.—For purposes of this subsection—

    (A) a legally adopted child of a person shall be considered a child of such person by blood;

(B) an individual who is legally separated from his spouse under a decree of divorce or of separate maintenance shall not be considered as married;

(C) a taxpayer shall be considered as not married at the close of his taxable year if at any time during the taxable year his spouse is a nonresident alien; and

(D) a taxpayer shall be considered as married at the close of his taxable year if his spouse (other than a spouse described in subparagraph (C)) died during the taxable year.

(3) **Limitations.**—Notwithstanding paragraph (1), for purposes of this subtitle a taxpayer shall not be considered to be a head of a household—

(A) if at any time during the taxable year he is a nonresident alien; or

(B) by reason of an individual who would not be a dependent for the taxable year but for—

(i) paragraph (9) of section 152(a), or

(ii) subsection (c) of section 152.

(c) **Certain married individuals living apart.**—For purposes of this part, an individual shall be treated as not married at the close of the taxable year if such individual is so treated under the provisions of section 143(b).

. . . . .

§ 3.   Tax tables for individuals

(a) Imposition of tax table tax.—

(1) **In general.**—In lieu of the tax imposed by section 1, there is hereby imposed for each taxable year on the tax table income of every individual whose tax table income for such year does not exceed the ceiling amount, a tax determined under tables, applicable to such taxable year, which shall be prescribed by the Secretary and which shall be in such form as he determines appropriate. In the tables so prescribed, the amounts of tax shall be computed on the basis of the rates prescribed by section 1.

(2) **Ceiling amount defined.**—For purposes of paragraph (1), the term "ceiling amount" means, with respect to any taxpayer, the amount (not less than $20,000) determined by the Secretary for the tax rate category in which such taxpayer falls.

(3) **Certain taxpayers with large number of exemptions.**—The Secretary may exclude from the application of this section taxpayers in any tax rate category having more than the number of exemptions for that category determined by the Secretary.

(4) **Tax table income defined.**—For purposes of this section, the term "tax table income" means adjusted gross income—

(A) reduced by the sum of—

(i) the excess itemized deductions, and

(ii) the direct charitable deduction, and

(B) increased (in the case of an individual to whom section 63(e) applies) by the unused zero bracket amount.

(5) Section may be applied on the basis of taxable income.—The Secretary may provide that this section shall be applied for any taxable year on the basis of taxable income in lieu of tax table income.

(b) Section inapplicable to certain individuals.—This section shall not apply to—

    (1) an individual to whom section 1301 (relating to income averaging) applies for the taxable year,

    (2) an individual making a return under section 443(a)(1) for a period of less than 12 months on account of a change in annual accounting period, and

    (3) an estate or trust.

(c) Tax treated as imposed by section 1.—For purposes of this title, the tax imposed by this section shall be treated as tax imposed by section 1.

(d) Taxable income.—Whenever it is necessary to determine the taxable income of an individual to whom this section applies, the taxable income shall be determined under section 63.

          ·   ·   ·

PART II—TAX ON CORPORATIONS

§ 11.   Tax imposed

(a) Corporations in general.—A tax is hereby imposed for each taxable year on the taxable income of every corporation.

(b) Amount of tax.—The amount of the tax imposed by subsection (a) shall be the sum of—

    (1) 15 percent (16 percent for taxable years beginning in 1982) of so much of the taxable income as does not exceed $25,000;

    (2) 18 percent (19 percent for taxable years beginning in 1982) of so much of the taxable income as exceeds $25,000 but does not exceed $50,000;

    (3) 30 percent of so much of the taxable income as exceeds $50,000 but does not exceed $75,000;

    (4) 40 percent of so much of the taxable income as exceeds $75,000 but does not exceed $100,000; plus

    (5) 46 percent of so much of the taxable income as exceeds $100,000.

PART IV—CREDITS AGAINST TAX

Subpart
    A. Credits allowable.
    B. Rules for computing credit for investment in certain depreciable property.
    C. Rules for computing credit for expenses of work incentive program.*
    D. Rules for computing credit for employment of certain new employees.*

* Omitted entirely.

SUBPART A—CREDITS ALLOWABLE

§ 37.   Credit for the elderly

(a) General rule.—In the case of an individual who has attained age 65 before the close of the taxable year, there shall be allowed as a credit against the tax imposed by this chapter for the taxable year an amount equal to 15 percent of such individual's section 37 amount for such taxable year.

(b) Section 37 amount.—For purposes of subsection (a)—

    (1) In general.—An individual's section 37 amount for the taxable year is the applicable initial amount determined under paragraph (2), reduced as provided in paragraph (3) and in subsection (c).

    (2) Initial amount.—The initial amount is—

        (A) $2,500 in the case of a single individual,

        (B) $2,500 in the case of a joint return where only one spouse is eligible for the credit under subsection (a),

        (C) $3,750 in the case of a joint return where both spouses are eligible for the credit under subsection (a), or

        (D) $1,875 in the case of a married individual filing a separate return.

    (3) Reduction.—The reduction under this paragraph is an amount equal to the sum of the amounts received by the individual (or, in the case of a joint return, by either spouse) as a pension or annuity—

        (A) under title II of the Social Security Act,

        (B) under the Railroad Retirement Act of 1935 or 1937, or

        (C) otherwise excluded from gross income.

No reduction shall be made under this paragraph for any amount excluded from gross income under section 72 (relating to annuities), 101 (relating to life insurance proceeds), 104 (relating to compensation for injuries or sickness), 105 (relating to amounts received under accident and health plans), 120 (relating to amounts received under qualified group legal services plans), 402 (relating to taxability of beneficiary of employees' trust), 403 (relating to taxation of employee annuities), or 405 (relating to qualified bond purchase plans).

(c) Limitations.—

    (1) Adjusted gross income limitation.—If the adjusted gross income of the taxpayer exceeds—

        (A) $7,500 in the case of a single individual,

        (B) $10,000 in the case of a joint return, or

        (C) $5,000 in the case of a married individual filing a separate return,

the section 37 amount shall be reduced by one-half of the excess of the adjusted gross income over $7,500, $10,000, or $5,000, as the case may be.

    (2) Limitation based on amount of tax.—The amount of the credit allowed by this section for the taxable year shall not exceed the amount of the tax imposed by this chapter for such taxable year.

. . . .

§ 38. Investment in certain depreciable property

(a) **General rule.**—There shall be allowed, as a credit against the tax imposed by this chapter, the amount determined under subpart B of this part.

(b) **Regulations.**—The Secretary shall prescribe such regulations as may be necessary to carry out the purposes of this section and subpart B.

§ 41. Contributions to candidates for public office

(a) **General rule.**—In the case of an individual, there shall be allowed, subject to the limitations of subsection (b), as a credit against the tax imposed by this chapter for the taxable year, an amount equal to one-half of all political contributions and all newsletter fund contributions, payment of which is made by the taxpayer within the taxable year.

(b) **Limitations.—**

(1) **Maximum credit.**—The credit allowed by subsection (a) for a taxable year shall not exceed $50 ($100 in the case of a joint return under section 6013).

(2) **Application with other credits.**—The credit allowed by subsection (a) shall not exceed the amount of the tax imposed by this chapter for the taxable year reduced by the sum of the credits allowable under section 33 (relating to foreign tax credit), section 37 (relating to credit for the elderly), and section 38 (relating to investment in certain depreciable property).

(3) **Verification.**—The credit allowed by subsection (a) shall be allowed, with respect to any political contribution or newsletter fund contribution, only if such contribution is verified in such manner as the Secretary shall prescribe by regulations.

(c) **Definitions.**—For purposes of this section—

(1) **Political contribution.**—The term "political contribution" means a contribution or gift of money to—

(A) an individual who is a candidate for nomination or election to any Federal, State, or local elective public office in any primary, general, or special election, for use by such individual to further his candidacy for nomination or election to such office;

(B) any committee, association, or organization (whether or not incorporated) organized and operated exclusively for the purpose of influencing, or attempting to influence, the nomination or election of one or more individuals who are candidates for nomination or election to any Federal, State, or local elective public office, for use by such committee, association, or organization to further the candidacy of such individual or individuals for nomination or election to such office;

(C) the national committee of a national political party;

(D) the State committee of a national political party as designated by the national committee of such party; or

(E) a local committee of a national political party as designated by the State committee of such party designated under subparagraph (D).

(2) Candidate.—The term "candidate" means, with respect to any Federal, State, or local elective public office, an individual who—

(A) publicly announces before the close of the calendar year following the calendar year in which the contribution or gift is made that he is a candidate for nomination or election to such office; and

(B) meets the qualifications prescribed by law to hold such office.

. . . . .

§ 43. Earned income

(a) Allowance of credit.—In the case of an eligible individual, there is allowed as a credit against the tax imposed by this subtitle for the taxable year an amount equal to 10 percent of so much of the earned income for the taxable year as does not exceed $5,000.

(b) Limitation.—The amount of the credit allowable to a taxpayer under subsection (a) for any taxable year shall not exceed the excess (if any) of—

(1) $500, over

(2) 12.5 percent of so much of the adjusted gross income (or, if greater, the earned income) of the taxpayer for the taxable year as exceeds $6,000.

(c) Definitions.—For purposes of this section—

(1) Eligible individual.—

(A) In general.—The term "eligible individual" means an individual who, for the taxable year—

(i) is married (within the meaning of section 143) and is entitled to a deduction under section 151 for a child (within the meaning of section 151(e) (3)),

(ii) is a surviving spouse (as determined under section 2(a)), or

(iii) is a head of a household (as determined under subsection (b) of section 2 without regard to subparagraphs (A) (ii) and (B) of paragraph (1) of such subsection).

(B) Child must reside with taxpayer in the United States.—An individual shall be treated as satisfying clause (i) of subparagraph (A) only if the child has the same principal place of abode as the individual and such abode is in the United States. An individual shall be treated as satisfying clause (ii) or (iii) of subparagraph (A) only if the household in question is in the United States.

. . . . .

(2) Earned income.—

(A) The term "earned income" means—

(i) wages, salaries, tips, and other employee compensation, plus

(ii) the amount of the taxpayer's net earnings from self-employment for the taxable year (within the meaning of section 1402(a)).

(B) For purposes of subparagraph (A)—

(i) the earned income of an individual shall be computed without regard to any community property laws,

(ii) no amount received as a pension or annuity shall be taken into account, and

. . . . .

(d) **Married individuals.**—In the case of an individual who is married (within the meaning of section 143), this section shall apply only if a joint return is filed for the taxable year under section 6013.

. . . . .

§ 44A. Expenses for household and dependent care services necessary for gainful employment

(a) **Allowance of credit.**—

(1) **In general.**—In the case of an individual who maintains a household which includes as a member one or more qualifying individuals (as defined in subsection (c)(1)), there shall be allowed as a credit against the tax imposed by this chapter for the taxable year an amount equal to the applicable percentage of the employment-related expenses (as defined in subsection (c)(2)) paid by such individual during the taxable year.

(2) **Applicable percentage defined.**—For purposes of paragraph (1), the term "applicable percentage" means 30 percent reduced (but not below 20 percent) by 1 percentage point for each $2,000 (or fraction thereof) by which the taxpayer's adjusted gross income for the taxable year exceeds $10,000.

(b) **Application with other credits.**—The credit allowed by subsection (a) shall not exceed the amount of the tax imposed by this chapter for the taxable year reduced by the sum of the credits allowable under—

(1) section 33 (relating to foreign tax credit),

(2) section 37 (relating to credit for the elderly),

(3) section 38 (relating to investment in certain depreciable property),

(4) section 40 (relating to expenses of work incentive programs),

(5) section 41 (relating to contributions to candidates for public office),

. . . . .

(c) **Definitions of qualifying individual and employment-related expenses.** —For purposes of this section—

(1) **Qualifying individual.**—The term "qualifying individual" means—

(A) a dependent of the taxpayer who is under the age of 15 and with respect to whom the taxpayer is entitled to a deduction under section 151(e),

(B) a dependent of the taxpayer who is physically or mentally incapable of caring for himself, or

(C) the spouse of the taxpayer, if he is physically or mentally incapable of caring for himself.

(2) Employment-related expenses.—

(A) In general.—The term "employment-related expenses" means amounts paid for the following expenses, but only if such expenses are incurred to enable the taxpayer to be gainfully employed for any period for which there are 1 or more qualifying individuals with respect to the taxpayer:

(i) expenses for household services, and

(ii) expenses for the care of a qualifying individual.

(B) Exception.—Employment-related expenses described in subparagraph (A) which are incurred for services outside the taxpayer's household shall be taken into account only if incurred for the care of—

(i) a qualifying individual described in paragraph (1)(A), or

(ii) a qualifying individual (not described in paragraph (1)(A)) who regularly spends at least 8 hours each day in the taxpayer's household.

(C) Dependent care centers.—Employment-related expenses described in subparagraph (A) which are incurred for services provided outside the taxpayer's houshold by a dependent care center (as defined in subparagraph (D)) shall be taken into account only if—

(i) such center complies with all applicable laws and regulations of a State or unit of local government, and

(ii) the requirements of subparagraph (B) are met.

(D) Dependent care center defined.—For purposes of this paragraph, the term "dependent care center" means any facility which—

(i) provides care for more than six individuals (other than individuals who reside at the facility), and

(ii) receives a fee, payment, or grant for providing services for any of the individuals (regardless of whether such facility is operated for profit).

(d) Dollar limit on amount creditable.—The amount of the employment-related expenses incurred during any taxable year which may be taken into account under subsection (a) shall not exceed—

(1) $2,400 if there is 1 qualifying individual with respect to the taxpayer for such taxable year, or

(2) $4,800 if there are 2 or more qualifying individuals with respect to the taxpayer for such taxable year.

(e) Earned income limitation.—

(1) In general.—Except as otherwise provided in this subsection, the amount of the employment-related expenses incurred during any taxable year which may be taken into account under subsection (a) shall not exceed—

(A) in the case of an individual who is not married at the close of such year, such individual's earned income for such year, or

(B) in the case of an individual who is married at the close of such year, the lesser of such individual's earned income or the earned income of his spouse for such year.

(2) Special rule for spouse who is a student or incapable of caring for himself.—In the case of a spouse who is a student or a qualifying individual described in subsection (c) (1) (C), for purposes of paragraph (1), such spouse shall be deemed for each month during which such spouse is a full-time student at an educational institution, or is such a qualifying individual, to be gainfully employed and to have earned income of not less than—

(A) $200 if subsection (d) (1) applies for the taxable year, or

(B) $400 if subsection (d) (2) applies for the taxable year.

In the case of any husband and wife, this paragraph shall apply with respect to only one spouse for any one month.

(f) Special rules.—For purposes of this section—

(1) Maintaining household.—An individual shall be treated as maintaining a household for any period only if over half the cost of maintaining the household for such period is furnished by such individual (or, if such individual is married during such period, is furnished by such individual and his spouse).

(2) Married couples must file joint return.—If the taxpayer is married at the close of the taxable year, the credit shall be allowed under subsection (a) only if the taxpayer and his spouse file a joint return for the taxable year.

(3) Marital status.—An individual legally separated from his spouse under a decree of divorce or of separate maintenance shall not be considered as married.

(4) Certain married individuals living apart.—If—

(A) an individual who is married and who files a separate return—

(i) maintains as his home a household which constitutes for more than one-half of the taxable year the principal place of abode of a qualifying individual, and

(ii) furnishes over half of the cost of maintaining such household during the taxable year, and

(B) during the last 6 months of such taxable year such individual's spouse is not a member of such household,

such individual shall not be considered as married.

(5) Special dependency test in case of divorced parents, etc.—If—

(A) a child (as defined in section 151(e) (3)) who is under the age of 15 or who is physically or mentally incapable of caring for himself receives over half of his support during the calendar year from his parents who are divorced or legally separated under a decree of divorce or separate maintenance or who are separated under a written separation agreement, and

(B) such child is in the custody of one or both of his parents for more than one-half of the calendar year,

in the case of any taxable year beginning in such calendar year such child shall be treated as being a qualifying individual described in subparagraph (A) or (B) of subsection (c) (1), as the case may be, with respect to that parent who has custody for a longer period during such calendar year than the other parent, and shall not be treated as being a qualifying individual with respect to such other parent.

(6) Payments to related individuals.—No credit shall be allowed under subsection (a) for any amount paid by the taxpayer to an individual—

(A) with respect to whom, for the taxable year, a deduction under section 151(e) (relating to deduction for personal exemptions for dependents) is allowable either to the taxpayer or his spouse, or

(B) who is a child of the taxpayer (within the meaning of section 151(e) (3)) who has not attained the age of 19 at the close of the taxable year.

For purposes of this paragraph, the term "taxable year" means the taxable year of the taxpayer in which the service is performed.

(7) Student.—The term "student" means an individual who during each of 5 calendar months during the taxable year is a full-time student at an educational organization.

(8) Educational organization.—The term "educational organization" means an educational organization described in section 170(b) (1) (A) (ii).

(g) Regulations.—The Secretary shall prescribe such regulations as may be necessary to carry out the purposes of this section.

§ 44C.   Residential energy credit

(a) General rule.—In the case of an individual, there shall be allowed as a credit against the tax imposed by this chapter for the taxable year an amount equal to the sum of—

(1) the qualified energy conservation expenditures, plus

(2) the qualified renewable energy source expenditures.

(b) Qualified expenditures.—For purposes of subsection (a)—

(1) Energy conservation.—In the case of any dwelling unit, the qualified energy conservation expenditures are 15 percent of so much of the energy conservation expenditures made by the taxpayer during the taxable year with respect to such unit as does not exceed $2,000.

. . . . .

(c) Definitions and special rules.—For purposes of this section—

(1) Energy conservation expenditures.—The term "energy conservation expenditure" means an expenditure made on or after April 20, 1977, by the taxpayer for insulation or any other energy-conserving component (or for the original installation of such insulation or other component) installed in or on a dwelling unit—

(A) which is located in the United States,

(B) which is used by the taxpayer as his principal residence, and

(C) the construction of which was substantially completed before April 20, 1977.

. . . . .

(3) Insulation.—The term "insulation" means any item—

(A) which is specifically and primarily designed to reduce when installed in or on a dwelling (or water heater) the heat loss or gain of such dwelling (or water heater),

(B) the original use of which begins with the taxpayer,

(C) which can reasonably be expected to remain in operation for at least 3 years, and

(D) which meets the performance and quality standards (if any) which—

    (i) have been prescribed by the Secretary by regulations, and

    (ii) are in effect at the time of the acquisition of the item.

(4) Other energy-conserving component.—The term "other energy-conserving component" means any item (other than insulation)—

    (A) which is—

        (i) a furnace replacement burner designed to achieve a reduction in the amount of fuel consumed as a result of increased combustion efficiency,

        (ii) a device for modifying flue openings designed to increase the efficiency of operation of the heating system,

        (iii) an electrical or mechanical furnace ignition system, which replaces a gas pilot light,

        (iv) a storm or thermal window or door for the exterior of the dwelling,

        (v) an automatic energy-saving setback thermostat,

        (vi) caulking or weatherstripping of an exterior door or window,

        (vii) a meter which displays the cost of energy usage, or

        (viii) an item of the kind which the Secretary specifies by regulations as increasing the energy efficiency of the dwelling,

    (B) the original use of which begins with the taxpayer,

    (C) which can reasonably be expected to remain in operation for at least 3 years, and

    (D) which meets the performance and quality standards (if any) which—

        (i) have been prescribed by the Secretary by regulations, and

        (ii) are in effect at the time of the acquisition of the item.

· · · · ·

(f) Termination.—This section shall not apply to expenditures made after December 31, 1985.

§ 44F.   Credit for increasing research activities

(a) General rule.—There shall be allowed as a credit against the tax imposed by this chapter for the taxable year an amount equal to 25 percent of the excess (if any) of—

    (1) the qualified research expenses for the taxable year, over

    (2) the base period research expenses.

(b) Qualified research expenses.—For purposes of this section—

    (1) Qualified research expenses.—The term "qualified research expenses" means the sum of the following amounts which are paid or incurred by the taxpayer during the taxable year in carrying on any trade or business of the taxpayer—

        (A) in-house research expenses, and

        (B) contract research expenses.

(2) In-house research expenses.—

(A) In general.—The term "in-house research expenses" means—

(i) any wages paid or incurred to an employee for qualified services performed by such employee,

(ii) any amount paid or incurred for supplies used in the conduct of qualified research, and

(iii) any amount paid or incurred to another person for the right to use personal property in the conduct of qualified research.

(B) Qualified services.—The term "qualified services" means services consisting of—

(i) engaging in qualified research, or

(ii) engaging in the direct supervision or direct support of research activities which constitute qualified research.

If substantially all of the services performed by an individual for the taxpayer during the taxable year consists of services meeting the requirements of clause (i) or (ii), the term "qualified services" means all of the services performed by such individual for the taxpayer during the taxable year.

(C) Supplies.—The term "supplies" means any tangible property other than—

(i) land or improvements to land, and

(ii) property of a character subject to the allowance for depreciation.

(D) Wages.—

(i) In general.—The term "wages" has the meaning given such term by section 3401(a).

(ii) Self-employed individuals and owner-employees.—In the case of an employee (within the meaning of section 401(c)(1)), the term "wages" includes the earned income (as defined in section 401(c)(2)) of such employee.

(iii) Exclusion for wages to which new jobs or WIN credit applies.—The term "wages" shall not include any amount taken into account in computing the credit under section 40 or 44B.

(3) Contract research expenses.—

(A) In general.—The term "contract research expenses" means 65 percent of any amount paid or incurred by the taxpayer to any person (other than an employee of the taxpayer) for qualified research.

(B) Prepaid amounts.—If any contract research expenses paid or incurred during any taxable year are attributable to qualified research to be conducted after the close of such taxable year, such amount shall be treated as paid or incurred during the period during which the qualified research is conducted.

(c) Base period research expenses.—For purposes of this section—

(1) In general.—The term "base period research expenses" means the average of the qualified research expenses for each year in the base period.

(2) Base period.—

(A) In general.—For purposes of this subsection, the term "base period" means the 3 taxable years immediately preceding the taxable year for which the determination is being made (hereinafter in this subsection referred to as the "determination year").

(B) Transitional rules.—Subparagraph (A) shall be applied—

(i) by substituting "first taxable year" for "3 taxable years" in the case of the first determination year ending after June 30, 1981, and

(ii) by substituting "2" for "3" in the case of the second determination year ending after June 30, 1981.

(3) Minimum base period research expenses.—In no event shall the base period research expenses be less than 50 percent of the qualified research expenses for the determination year.

(d) Qualified research.—For purposes of this section the term "qualified research" has the same meaning as the term research or experimental has under section 174, except that such term shall not include—

(1) qualified research conducted outside the United States,

(2) qualified research in the social sciences or humanities, and

(3) qualified research to the extent funded by any grant, contract, or otherwise by another person (or any governmental entity).

(e) Credit available with respect to certain basic research by colleges, universities, and certain research organizations.—

(1) In general.—65 percent of any amount paid or incurred by a corporation (as such term is defined in section 170(e)(4)(D)) to any qualified organization for basic research to be performed by such organization shall be treated as contract research expenses. The preceding sentence shall apply only if the amount is paid or incurred pursuant to a written research agreement between the corporation and the qualified organization.

(2) Qualified organization.—For purposes of this subsection, the term "qualified organization" means—

(A) any educational organization which is described in section 170(b)(1)(A)(ii) and which is an institution of higher education (as defined in section 3304(f)), and

(B) any other organization which—

(i) is described in section 501(c)(3) and exempt from tax under section 501(a),

(ii) is organized and operated primarily to conduct scientific research, and

(iii) is not a private foundation.

(3) Basic research.—The term "basic research" means any original investigation for the advancement of scientific knowledge not having a specific commercial objective, except that such term shall not include—

(A) basic research conducted outside the United States, and

(B) basic research in the social sciences or humanities.

. . . . .

SUBPART B—RULES FOR COMPUTING CREDIT FOR INVESTMENT IN CERTAIN DEPRECIABLE PROPERTY

§ 46. Amount of credit

(a) General rule.—

(1) First-in-first-out rule.—The amount of the credit allowed by section 38 for the taxable year shall be an amount equal to the sum of—

(A) the investment credit carryovers carried to such taxable year,

(B) the amount of the credit determined under paragraph (2) for such taxable year, plus

(C) the investment credit carrybacks carried to such taxable year.

(2) Amount of credit.—

(A) In general.—The amount of the credit determined under this paragraph for the taxable year shall be an amount equal to the sum of the following percentages of the qualified investment (as determined under subsections (c) and (d)):

(i) the regular percentage,

(ii) in the case of energy property, the energy percentage,

(iii) the employee plan percentage, and

(iv) in the case of that portion of the basis of any property which is attributable to qualified rehabilitation expenditures, the rehabilitation percentage.

(B) Regular percentage.—For purposes of this paragraph, the regular percentage is 10 percent.

. . . . .

(F) Rehabilitation percentage.—For purposes of this paragraph—

(i) In General—

In the case of qualified rehabilitation expenditures with respect to a:	The rehabilitation percentage is:
30-year building	15
40-year building	20
Certified historic structure	25.

(ii) Regular and energy percentages not to apply.—The regular percentage and the energy percentage shall not apply to that portion of the basis of any property which is attributable to qualified rehabilitation expenditures.

(iii) Definitions.—

(I) 30-year building.—The term "30-year building" means a qualified rehabilitated building other than a 40-year building and other than a certified historic structure.

(II) 40-year building.—The term "40-year building" means any building (other than a certified historic structure) which would meet the requirements of section 48(g)(1)(B) if "40" were substituted for "30" each place it appears in subparagraph (B) thereof.

(III) **Certified historic structure.**—The term "certified historic structure" has the meaning given to such term by section 48(g)(3).

(3) **Limitation based on amount of tax.**—Notwithstanding paragraph (1), the credit allowed by section 38 for the taxable year shall not exceed—

(A) so much of the liability for tax for the taxable year as does not exceed $25,000, plus

(B) 85 percent of so much of the liability for tax for the taxable year as exceeds $25,000:

(4) **Liability for tax.**—For purposes of paragraph (3), the liability for tax for the taxable year shall be the tax imposed by this chapter for such year, reduced by the sum of the credits allowable under—

(A) section 33 (relating to foreign tax credit), and

(B) section 37 (relating to credit for the elderly).

For purposes of this paragraph, any tax imposed for the taxable year by section 56 (relating to corporate minimum tax), section 72(m)(5)(B) (relating to 10 percent tax on premature distributions to owner-employees), section 72(q)(1) (relating to 5-percent tax on premature distributions under annuity contracts), section 402(e) (relating to tax on lump sum distributions), section 408(f) (relating to additional tax on income from certain retirement accounts), section 531 (relating to accumulated earnings tax), section 541 (relating to personal holding company tax), or section 1374 (relating to tax on certain capital gains of S corporations), and any additional tax imposed for the taxable year by section 1351(d)(1) (relating to recoveries of foreign expropriation losses) shall not be considered tax imposed by this chapter for such year.

(5) **Married individuals.**—In the case of a husband or wife who files a separate return, the amount specified under subparagraphs (A) and (B) of paragraph (3) shall be $12,500 in lieu of $25,000. This paragraph shall not apply if the spouse of the taxpayer has no qualified investment for, and no unused credit carryback or carryover to, the taxable year of such spouse which ends within or with the taxpayer's taxable year.

(6) **Controlled groups.**—In the case of a controlled group, the $25,000 amount specified under paragraph (3) shall be reduced for each component member of such group by apportioning $25,000 among the component members of such group in such manner as the Secretary shall by regulations prescribe. For purposes of the preceding sentence, the term "controlled group" has the meaning assigned to such term by section 1563(a).

. . . . .

(b) **Carryback and carryover of unused credits.**—

(1) **In general.**—If the sum of the amount of the investment credit carryovers to the taxable year under subsection (a) (1) (A) plus the amount determined under subsection (a) (1) (B) for the taxable year exceeds the amount of the limitation imposed by subsection (a) (3) for such taxable year (hereinafter in this subsection referred to as the "unused credit year"), such

excess attributable to the amount determined under subsection (a) (1) (B) shall be—

(A) an investment credit carryback to each of the 3 taxable years preceding the unused credit year, and

(B) an investment credit carryover to each of the 7 taxable years following the unused credit year,

and, subject to the limitations imposed by paragraphs (2) and (3), shall be taken into account under the provisions of subsection (a) (1) in the manner provided in such subsection. The entire amount of the unused credit for an unused credit year shall be carried to the earliest of the 10 taxable years to which (by reason of subparagraphs (A) and (B)) such credit may be carried and then to each of the other 9 taxable years to the extent, because of the limitations imposed by paragraphs (2) and (3), such unused credit may not be taken into account under subsection (a) (1) for a prior taxable year to which such unused credit may be carried. In the case of an unused credit for an unused credit year ending before January 1, 1971, which is an investment credit carryover to a taxable year beginning after December 31, 1970 (determined without regard to this sentence), this paragraph shall be applied—

(C) by substituting "10 taxable years" for "7 taxable years" in subparagraph (B), and by substituting "13 taxable years" for "10 taxable years", and "12 taxable years" for "9 taxable years" in the preceding sentence, and

(D) by carrying such an investment credit carryover to a later taxable year (than the taxable year to which it would, but for this subparagraph, be carried) to which it may be carried if, because of the amendments made by section 802(b) (2) of the Tax Reform Act of 1976, carrying such carryover to the taxable year to which it would, but for this subparagraph, be carried would cause a portion of an unused credit from an unused credit year ending after December 31, 1970 to expire.

In the case of an unused credit for an unused credit year ending after December 31, 1973, this paragraph shall be applied by substituting "15" for "7" in subparagraph (B), and by substituting "18" for "10", and "17" for "9" in the second sentence.

(2) **Limitation on carrybacks.**—The amount of the unused credit which may be taken into account under subsection (a) (1) for any preceding taxable year shall not exceed the amount by which the limitation imposed by subsection (a) (3) for such taxable year exceeds the sum of—

(A) the amounts determined under subparagraphs (A) and (B) of subsection (a) (1) for such taxable year, plus

(B) the amounts which (by reason of this subsection) are carried back to such taxable year and are attributable to taxable years preceding the unused credit year.

(3) **Limitation on carryovers.**—The amount of the unused credit which may be taken into account under subsection (a) (1) (A) for any succeeding taxable year shall not exceed the amount by which the limitation imposed by subsection (a) (3) for such taxable year exceeds the sum of the amounts which, by reason of this subsection, are carried to such taxable year and are attributable to taxable years preceding the unused credit year.

(c) Qualified investment.—

(1) **In general.**—For purposes of this subpart, the term "qualified investment" means, with respect to any taxable year, the aggregate of—

(A) the applicable percentage of the basis of each new section 38 property (as defined in section 48(b)) placed in service by the taxpayer during such taxable year, plus

(B) the applicable percentage of the cost of each used section 38 property (as defined in section 48(c) (1)) placed in service by the taxpayer during such taxable year.

(2) **Applicable percentage in certain cases.**—Except as provided in paragraphs (3), (6), and (7), the applicable percentage for purposes of paragraph (1) for any property shall be determined under the following table:

If the useful life is—	The applicable percentage is—
3 years or more but less than 5 years	33⅓
5 years or more but less than 7 years	66⅔
7 years or more	100

For purposes of this subpart, the useful life of any property shall be the useful life used in computing the allowance for depreciation under section 167 for the taxable year in which the property is placed in service.

(7) **Applicable percentage for recovery property.**—Notwithstanding paragraph (2), the applicable percentage for purposes of paragraph (1) shall be—

(A) in the case of 15-year public utility, 10-year, or 5-year property (within the meaning of section 168(c)), 100 percent, and

(B) in the case of 3-year property (within the meaning of section 168(c)), 60 percent.

. . . . .

(8) **Limitation to amount at risk.—**

(A) **In general.**—In the case of new or used section 38 property which—

(i) is placed in service during the taxable year by a taxpayer described in section 465(a)(1), and

(ii) is used in connection with an activity with respect to which any loss is subject to limitation under section 465,

the basis of such property for purposes of paragraph (1) shall not exceed the amount the taxpayer is at risk with respect to such property as of the close of such taxable year.

(B) **Amount at risk.—**

(i) **In general.**—Except as provided in clause (ii), the term "at risk" has the same meaning given such term by section 465(b) (without regard to paragraph (5) thereof).

(ii) **Certain financing.**—In the case of a taxpayer who at all times is at risk (determined without regard to this clause) in an amount

24

equal to at least 20 percent of the basis (determined under section 168(d)(1)(A)(i)) of property described in subparagraph (A) and who acquired such property from a person who is not a related person, such taxpayer shall for purposes of this paragraph be considered at risk with respect to any amount borrowed in connection with such property (other than convertible debt) to the extent that such amount—

(I) is borrowed from a qualified person, or

(II) represents a loan from any Federal, State, or local government or instrumentality thereof, or is guaranteed by, any Federal, State, or local government.

(C) **Special rule for partnerships and subchapter S corporations.**—In the case of any partnership or S corporation, any amount treated as at risk under subparagraph (B)(ii) shall be allocated among the partners or shareholders (and treated as an amount at risk with respect to such persons) in the same manner as the credit allowable by section 38.

(D) **Qualified person.**—For purposes of this paragraph, the term "qualified person" means any person—

(i) which—

(I) is an institution described in clause (i), (ii), or (iii) of subparagraph (A) or subparagraph (B) of section 128(c)(2) or an insurance company to which subchapter L applies, or

(II) is a pension trust qualified under section 401(a) or a person not described in subclause (I) and which is actively and regularly engaged in the business of lending money,

(ii) which is not a related person with respect to the taxpayer,

(iii) which is not a person who receives a fee with respect to the taxpayer's investment in property described in subparagraph (A) or a related person to such person, and

(iv) which is not a person from which the taxpayer acquired the property described in subparagraph (A) or a related person to such person.

(E) **Related person.**—For purposes of this paragraph, the term "related person" has the same meaning as such term is used in section 168(e)(4), except that in applying section 168(e)(4)(D)(i) in the case of a person described in subparagraph (D)(i)(II) of this paragraph, sections 267(b) and 707(b)(1) shall be applied by substituting "0 percent" for "50 percent".

(e) **Limitations with respect to certain persons.**—

. . . .

(3) **Noncorporate lessors.**—A credit shall be allowed by section 38 to a person which is not a corporation with respect to property of which such person is the lessor only if—

(A) the property subject to the lease has been manufactured or produced by the lessor, or

(B) the term of the lease (taking into account options to renew) is less than 50 percent of the useful life of the property, and for the period consisting of the first 12 months after the date on which the property is transferred to the lessee the sum of the deductions with respect to such property which are allowable to the lessor solely by reason of section 162 (other than rents and reimbursed amounts with respect to such property) exceeds 15 percent of the rental income produced by such property.

In the case of property of which a partnership is the lessor, the credit otherwise allowable under section 38 with respect to such property to any partner which is a corporation shall be allowed notwithstanding the first sentence of this paragraph. For purposes of this paragraph, an S corporation shall be treated as a person which is not a corporation. This paragraph shall not apply with respect to any property which is treated as section 38 property by reason of section 48(a)(1)(E). For purposes of subparagraph (B), in the case of any recovery property (within the meaning of section 168), the useful life shall be the present class life for such property (as defined in section 168(g)(2)).

. . . .

§ 47.   Certain dispositions, etc., of section 38 property

(a) **General rule.**—Under regulations prescribed by the Secretary—

(1) **Early disposition, etc.**—If during any taxable year any property is disposed of, or otherwise ceases to be section 38 property with respect to the taxpayer, before the close of the useful life which was taken into account in computing the credit under section 38, then the tax under this chapter for such taxable year shall be increased by an amount equal to the aggregate decrease in the credits allowed under section 38 for all prior taxable years which would have resulted solely from substituting, in determining qualified investment, for such useful life the period beginning with the time such property was placed in service by the taxpayer and ending with the time such property ceased to be section 38 property.

. . . .

(b) **Section not to apply in certain cases.**—Subsection (a) shall not apply to—

(1) a transfer by reason of death,

(2) a transaction to which section 381(a) applies, or

. . . .

For purposes of subsection (a), property shall not be treated as ceasing to be section 38 property with respect to the taxpayer by reason of a mere change in the form of conducting the trade or business so long as the property is retained in such trade or business as section 38 property and the taxpayer retains a substantial interest in such trade or business.

(c) **Special rule.**—Any increase in tax under subsection (a) shall not be treated as tax imposed by this chapter for purposes of determining the amount of any credit allowable under subpart A.

. . . .

§ 48.   Definitions; special rules

(a) **Section 38 property.**—

(1) **In general.**—Except as provided in this subsection, the term "section 38 property" means—

(A) tangible personal property (other than an air conditioning or heating unit), or

(B) other tangible property (not including a building and its structural components) but only if such property—

(i) is used as an integral part of manufacturing, production, or extraction or of furnishing transportation, communications, electrical energy, gas, water, or sewage disposal services, or

(ii) constitutes a research facility used in connection with any of the activities referred to in clause (i), or

(iii) constitutes a facility used in connection with any of the activities referred to in clause (i) for the bulk storage of fungible commodities (including commodities in a liquid or gaseous state), or

(C) elevators and escalators, but only if—

(i) the construction, reconstruction, or erection of the elevator or escalator is completed by the taxpayer after June 30, 1963, or

(ii) the elevator or escalator is acquired after June 30, 1963, and the original use of such elevator or escalator commences with the taxpayer and commences after such date, or

(D) single purpose agricultural or horticultural structures; or

(E) in the case of a qualified rehabilitated building, that portion of the basis which is attributable to qualified rehabilitation expenditures (within the meaning of subsection (g)), or

(F) in the case of qualified timber property (within the meaning of section 194(c)(1)), that portion of the basis of such property constituting the amortizable basis acquired during the taxable year (other than that portion of such amortizable basis attributable to property which otherwise qualifies as section 38 property) and taken into account under section 194 (after the application of section 194(b)(1)), or

(G) a storage facility used in connection with the distribution of petroleum or any primary product of petroleum.

Such term includes only recovery property (within the meaning of section 168 without regard to any useful life) and any other property with respect to which depreciation (or amortization in lieu of depreciation) is allowable and having a useful life (determined as of the time such property is placed in service) of 3 years or more. The preceding sentence shall not apply to property described in subparagraph (F) and, for purposes of this subpart, the useful life of such property shall be treated as its normal growing period.

(2) Property used outside the United States.—

(A) **In general.**—Except as provided in subparagraph (B), the term "section 38 property" does not include property which is used predominantly outside the United States.

(B) **Exceptions.**—Subparagraph (A) shall not apply to—

(i) any aircraft which is registered by the Administrator of the Federal Aviation Agency and which is operated to and from the United States or is operated under contract with the United States;

(ii) rolling stock which is used within and without the United States and which is—

(I) of a domestic railroad corporation providing transportation subject to subchapter I of chapter 105 of title 49, or

(II) of a United States person (other than a corporation described in subclause (I)) but only if the rolling stock is not leased to one or more foreign persons for periods aggregating more than 12 months in any 24-month period;

(iii) any vessel documented under the laws of the United States which is operated in the foreign or domestic commerce of the United States;

(iv) any motor vehicle of a United States person (as defined in section 7701(a) (30)) which is operated to and from the United States;

* * * *

(3) **Property used for lodging.**—Property which is used predominantly to furnish lodging or in connection with the furnishing of lodging shall not be treated as section 38 property. The preceding sentence shall not apply to—

(A) nonlodging commercial facilities which are available to persons not using the lodging facilities on the same basis as they are available to persons using the lodging facilities,

(B) property used by a hotel or motel in connection with the trade or business of furnishing lodging where the predominant portion of the accommodations is used by transients,

(C) coin-operated vending machines and coin-operated washing machines and dryers, and

(D) a certified historic structure to the extent of that portion of the basis which is attributable to qualified rehabilitation expenditures.

(4) **Property used by certain tax-exempt organizations.**—Property used by an organization (other than a cooperative described in section 521) which is exempt from the tax imposed by this chapter shall be treated as section 38 property only if such property is used predominantly in an unrelated trade or business the income of which is subject to tax under section 511. If the property is debt-financed property (as defined in section 514(c)), the basis or cost of such property for purposes of computing qualified investment under section 46(c) shall include only that percentage of the basis or cost which is the same percentage as is used under section 514(b), for the year the property is placed in service, in computing the amount of gross income to be taken into account during such taxable year with respect to such property. If any qualified rehabilitated building is used by the tax-exempt organization pursuant to a lease, this paragraph shall not apply to that portion of the basis of such building which is attributable to qualified rehabilitation expenditures.

(5) **Property used by governmental units.**—Property used by the United States, any State or political subdivision thereof, any international organization (other than the International Telecommunications Satellite Consortium or any successor organization), or any agency or instrumentality of any of the foregoing shall not be treated as section 38 property. For purposes of the preceding sentence, the International Telecommunications Satellite Consortium, the International Maritime Satellite Organization, and any successor organization of such Consortium or Organization shall not be treated as an international organization. If any qualified rehabilitated building is used by the governmental unit pursuant to a lease, this paragraph shall not apply to that portion of the basis of such building which is attributable to qualified rehabilitation expenditures.

(6) **Livestock.**—Livestock (other than horses) acquired by the taxpayer shall be treated as section 38 property, except that if substantially identical livestock is sold or otherwise disposed of by the taxpayer during the one-year period beginning 6 months before the date of such acquisition and if section 47(a) (relating to certain dispositions, etc., of section 38 property) does not apply to such sale or other disposition, then, unless such sale or other disposition constitutes an involuntary conversion (within the meaning of section 1033), the cost of the livestock acquired shall, for purposes of this subpart, be reduced by an amount equal to the amount realized on such sale or other disposition. Horses shall not be treated as section 38 property.

. . . .

(b) New section 38 property.—For purposes of this subpart, the term "new section 38 property" means section 38 property—

(1) the construction, reconstruction, or erection of which is completed by the taxpayer after December 31, 1961, or

(2) acquired after December 31, 1961, if the original use of such property commences with the taxpayer and commences after such date.

In applying section 46(c) (1) (A) in the case of property described in paragraph (1), there shall be taken into account only that portion of the basis which is properly attributable to construction, reconstruction, or erection after December 31, 1961. For purposes of determining whether section 38 property subject to a lease is new section 38 property, such property shall be treated as originally placed in service not earlier than the date such property is used under the lease but only if such property is leased within 3 months after such property is placed in service.

(c) Used section 38 property.—

(1) In general.—For purposes of this subpart, the term "used section 38 property" means section 38 property acquired by purchase after December 31, 1961, which is not new section 38 property. Property shall not be treated as "used section 38 property" if, after its acquisition by the taxpayer, it is used by a person who used such property before such acquisition (or by a person who bears a relationship described in section 179(d) (2) (A) or (B) to a person who used such property before such acquisition).

(2) Dollar limitation.—

(A) In general.—The cost of used section 38 property taken into account under section 46(c)(1)(B) for any taxable year shall not exceed $150,000 ($125,000 for taxable years beginning in 1981, 1982, 1983, or 1984). If such cost exceeds $150,000 (or $125,000 as the case may be), the taxpayer shall select (at such time and in such manner as the Secretary shall by regulations prescribe) the items to be taken into account, but only to the extent of an aggregate cost of $150,000 (or $125,000). Such a selection, once made, may be changed only in the manner, and to the extent, provided by such regulations.

(B) Married individuals.—In the case of a husband or wife who files a separate return, the limitation under subparagraph (A) shall be $75,000 ($62,500 for taxable years beginning in 1981, 1982, 1983, or 1984). This subparagraph shall not apply if the spouse of the taxpayer has no used section 38 property which may be taken into account as qualified investment for the taxable year of such spouse which ends within or with the taxpayer's taxable year.

(C) **Controlled groups.**—In the case of a controlled group, the amount specified under subparagraph (A) shall be reduced for each component member of the group by apportioning such amount among the component members of such group in accordance with their respective amounts of used section 38 property which may be taken into account.

(D) **Partnerships and S corporations.**—In the case of a partnership, the limitation contained in subparagraph (A) shall apply with respect to the partnership and with respect to each partner. A similar rule shall apply in the case of an S corporation and its shareholders.

(3) **Definitions.**—For purposes of this subsection—

(A) **Purchase.**—The term "purchase" has the meaning assigned to such term by section 179(d) (2).

(B) **Cost.**—The cost of used section 38 property does not include so much of the basis of such property as is determined by reference to the adjusted basis of other property held at any time by the person acquiring such property. If property is disposed of (other than by reason of its destruction or damage by fire, storm, shipwreck, or other casualty, or its theft) and used section 38 property similar or related in service or use is acquired as a replacement therefor in a transaction to which the preceding sentence does not apply, the cost of the used section 38 property acquired shall be its basis reduced by the adjusted basis of the property replaced. The cost of used section 38 property shall not be reduced with respect to the adjusted basis of any property disposed of if, by reason of section 47, such disposition involved an increase of tax or a reduction of the unused credit carrybacks or carryovers described in section 46(b).

(C) **Controlled group.**—The term "controlled group" has the meaning assigned to such term by section 1563(a), except that the phrase "more than 50 percent" shall be substituted for the phrase "at least 80 percent" each place it appears in section 1563(a) (1).

(d) **Certain leased property.**—

(1) **General rule.**—A person (other than a person referred to in section 46(e) (1)) who is a lessor of property may (at such time, in such manner, and subject to such conditions as are provided by regulations prescribed by the Secretary) elect with respect to any new section 38 property (other than property described in paragraph (4)) to treat the lessee as having acquired such property for an amount equal to—

(A) except as provided in subparagraph (B), the fair market value of such property, or

(B) if the property is leased by a corporation which is a component member of a controlled group (within the meaning of section 46(a) (6)) to another corporation which is a component member of the same controlled group, the basis of such property to the lessor.

(2) **Special rule for certain short term leases.**—

(A) **In general.**—A person (other than a person referred to in section 46(e) (1)) who is a lessor of property described in paragraph (4) may (at such time, in such manner, and subject to such conditions as are provided by regulations prescribed by the Secretary) elect with respect to such property to treat the lessee as having acquired a portion of such property for the amount determined under subparagraph (B).

(B) Determination of lessee's investment.—The amount for which a lessee of property described in paragraph (4) shall be treated as having acquired a portion of such property is an amount equal to a fraction, the numerator of which is the term of the lease and the denominator of which is the class life of the property leased (determined under section 167(m)), of the amount for which the lessee would be treated as having acquired the property under paragraph (1).

(C) Determination of lessor's qualified investment.—The qualified investment of a lessor of property described in paragraph (4) in any such property with respect to which he has made an election under this paragraph is an amount equal to his qualified investment in such property (as determined under section 46(c)) multiplied by a fraction equal to the excess of one over the fraction used under subparagraph (B) to determine the lessee's investment in such property.

(3) Limitations.—The elections provided by paragraphs (1) and (2) may be made with respect to property which would be new section 38 property if acquired by the lessee. For purposes of the preceding sentence and section 46(c), the useful life of property in the hands of the lessee is the useful life of such property in the hands of the lessor. If a lessor makes the election provided by paragraph (1) with respect to any property, the lessee shall be treated for all purposes of this subpart as having acquired such property. If a lessor makes the election provided by paragraph (2) with respect to any property, the lessee shall be treated for all purposes of this subpart as having acquired a fractional portion of such property equal to the fraction determined under paragraph (2) (B) with respect to such property.

(4) Property to which paragraph (2) applies.—Paragraph (2) shall apply only to property which—

(A) is new section 38 property,

(B) has a class life (determined under section 167(m)) in excess of 14 years,

(C) is leased for a period which is less than 80 percent of its class life, and

(D) is not leased subject to a net lease (within the meaning of section 57(c) (1) (B)).

(5) Coordination with basis adjustment.—In the case of any property with respect to which an election is made under this subsection—

(A) subsection (q) (other than paragraph (4)) shall not apply with respect to such property,

(B) the lessee of such property shall include ratably in gross income over the shortest recovery period which could be applicable under section 168 with respect to such property an amount equal to 50 percent of the amount of the credit allowable under section 38 to the lessee with respect to such property, and

(C) in the case of a disposition of such property to which section 47 applies, this paragraph shall be applied in accordance with regulations prescribed by the Secretary.

[(e) Repealed.]

(f) Estates and trusts.—In the case of an estate or trust—

(1) the qualified investment for any taxable year shall be apportioned between the estate or trust and the beneficiaries on the basis of the income of the estate or trust allocable to each,

(2) any beneficiary to whom any investment has been apportioned under paragraph (1) shall be treated (for purposes of this subpart) as the taxpayer with respect to such investment, and such investment shall not (by reason of such apportionment) lose its character as an investment in new section 38 property or used section 38 property, as the case may be, and

(3) the $25,000 amount specified under subparagraphs (A) and (B) of section 46(a) (3) applicable to such estate or trust shall be reduced to an amount which bears the same ratio to $25,000 as the amount of the qualified investment allocated to the estate or trust under paragraph (1) bears to the entire amount of the qualified investment.

(g) Special rules for qualified rehabilitated buildings.—For purposes of this subpart—

(1) Qualified rehabilitated building defined.—

(A) In general.—The term "qualified rehabilitated building" means any building (and its structural components)—

(i) which has been substantially rehabilitated,

(ii) which was placed in service before the beginning of the rehabilitation, and

(iii) 75 percent or more of the existing external walls of which are retained in place as external walls in the rehabilitation process.

(B) 30 years must have elapsed since construction.—In the case of a building other than a certified historic structure, a building shall not be a qualified rehabilitated building unless there is a period of at least 30 years between the date the physical work on the rehabilitation began and the date the building was first placed in service.

(C) Substantially rehabilitated defined.—

(i) In general.—For purposes of subparagraph (A)(i), a building shall be treated as having been substantially rehabilitated only if the qualified rehabilitation expenditures during the 24-month period ending on the last day of the taxable year exceed the greater of—

(I) the adjusted basis of such property, or

(II) $5,000.

The adjusted basis of the property shall be determined as of the beginning of the first day of such 24-month period, or of the holding period of the property (within the meaning of section 1250(e)), whichever is later.

(ii) Special rule for phased rehabilitation.—In the case of any rehabilitation which may reasonably be expected to be completed in phases set forth in architectural plans and specifications completed before the rehabilitation begins, clause (i) shall be applied by substituting "60-month period" for "24-month period".

(iii) Lessees.—The Secretary shall prescribe by regulation rules for applying this provision to lessees.

(D) Reconstruction.—Rehabilitation includes reconstruction.

(2) Qualified rehabilitation expenditure defined.—

(A) In general.—The term "qualified rehabilitation expenditure" means any amount properly chargeable to capital account which is incurred after December 31, 1981—

(i) for property (or additions or improvements to property) which have a recovery period (within the meaning of section 168) of 15 years, and

(ii) in connection with the rehabilitation of a qualified rehabilitated building.

(B) Certain expenditures not included.—The term "qualified rehabilitation expenditure" does not include—

(i) Accelerated methods of depreciation may not be used.—Any expenditures with respect to which an election has not been made under section 168(b)(3) (to use the straight-line method of depreciation).

(ii) Cost of acquisition.—The cost of acquiring any building or interest therein.

(iii) Enlargements.—Any expenditure attributable to the enlargement of an existing building.

(iv) Certified historic structure, etc.—Any expenditure attributable to the rehabilitation of a certified historic structure or a building in a registered historic district, unless the rehabilitation is a certified rehabilitation (within the meaning of subparagraph (C)). The preceding sentence shall not apply to a building in a registered historic district if—

(I) such building was not a certified historic structure,

(II) the Secretary of the Interior certified to the Secretary that such building is not of historic significance to the district, and

(III) if the certification referred to in subclause (II) occurs after the beginning of the rehabilitation of such building, the taxpayer certifies to the Secretary that, at the beginning of such rehabilitation, he in good faith was not aware of the requirements of subclause (II).

(v) Expenditures of lessee.—Any expenditure of a lessee of a building if, on the date the rehabilitation is completed, the remaining term of the lease (determined without regard to any renewal periods) is less than 15 years.

(C) Certified rehabilitation.—For purposes of subparagraph (B), the term "certified rehabilitation" means any rehabilitation of a certified historic structure which the Secretary of the Interior has certified to the Secretary as being consistent with the historic character of such property or the district in which such property is located.

(3) Certified historic structure defined.—

(A) In general.—The term "certified historic structure" means any building (and its structural components) which—

(i) is listed in the National Register, or

(ii) is located in a registered historic district and is certified by the Secretary of the Interior to the Secretary as being of historic significance to the district.

(B) Registered historic district.—The term "registered historic district" means—

(i) any district listed in the National Register, and

(ii) any district—

(I) which is designated under a statute of the appropriate State or local government, if such statute is certified by the Secretary of the Interior to the Secretary as containing criteria which will substantially achieve the purpose of preserving and rehabilitating buildings of historic significance to the district, and

(II) which is certified by the Secretary of the Interior to the Secretary as meeting substantially all of the requirements for the listing of districts in the National Register.

(4) Property treated as new section 38 property.—Property which is treated as section 38 property by reason of subsection (a)(1)(E) shall be treated as new section 38 property.

. . . .

(p) Single purpose agricultural or horticultural structure defined.—For purposes of this section—

(1) In general.—The term "single purpose agricultural or horticultural structure" means—

(A) a single purpose livestock structure, and

(B) a single purpose horticultural structure.

(2) Single purpose livestock structure.—The term "single purpose livestock structure" means any enclosure or structure specifically designed, constructed, and used—

(A) for housing, raising, and feeding a particular type of livestock and their produce, and

(B) for housing the equipment (including any replacements) necessary for the housing, raising, and feeding referred to in subparagraph (A).

(3) Single purpose horticultural structure.—The term "single purpose horticultural structure" means—

(A) a greenhouse specifically designed, constructed, and used for the commercial production of plants, and

(B) a structure specifically designed, constructed and used for the commercial production of mushrooms.

(4) Structures which include work space.—An enclosure or structure which provides work space shall be treated as a single purpose agricultural or horticultural structure only if such work space is solely for—

(A) the stocking, caring for, or collecting of livestock or plants (as the case may be) or their produce,

(B) the maintenance of the enclosure or structure, and

(C) the maintenance or replacement of the equipment or stock enclosed or housed therein.

(5) Special rule for applying section 47.—For purposes of section 47, any single purpose agricultural or horticultural structure shall be treated as meeting the requirements of this subsection for any period during which such structure is held for the use under which it qualified under this subsection.

(6) Livestock.—The term "livestock" includes poultry.

(q) Basis Adjustment to Section 38 Property.—

(1) In general.—For purposes of this subtitle, if a credit is determined under section 46(a)(2) with respect to section 38 property, the basis of such property shall be reduced by 50 percent of the amount of the credit so determined.

(2) Certain dispositions.—If during any taxable year there is a recapture amount determined with respect to any section 38 property the basis of which was reduced under paragraph (1), the basis of such property (immediately before the event resulting in such recapture) shall be increased by an amount equal to 50 percent of such recapture amount. For purposes of the preceding sentence, the term "recapture amount" means any increase in tax (or adjustment in carrybacks or carryovers) determined under section 47.

(3) Special rule for qualified rehabilitated buildings.—In the case of any credit determined under section 46(a)(2) for any qualified rehabilitation expenditure in connection with a qualified rehabilitated building other than a certified historic structure, paragraphs (1) and (2) shall be applied without regard to the phrase "50 percent of".

(4) Election of reduced credit in lieu of basis adjustment for regular percentage.—

(A) In general.—If the taxpayer elects to have this paragraph apply with respect to any recovery property—

(i) paragraphs (1) and (2) shall not apply to so much of the credit determined under section 46(a)(2) with respect to such property as is attributable to the regular percentage set forth in section 46(a)(2)(B); and

(ii) the amount of the credit allowable under section 38 with respect to such property shall be determined under subparagraph (B).

(B) Reduction in credit.—In the case of any recovery property to which an election under subparagraph (A) applies—

(i) solely for the purposes of applying the regular percentage, the applicable percentage under subsection (c) or (d) of section 46 shall be deemed to be 100 percent, and

(ii) notwithstanding section 46(a)(2)(B), the regular percentage shall be—

(I) 8 percent in the case of recovery property other than 3-year property, or

(II) 4 percent in the case of recovery property which is 3-year property.

For purposes of the preceding sentence, RRB replacement property (within the meaning of section 168(f)(3)(B)) shall be treated as property which is not 3-year property.

(C) Time and manner of making election.—

(i) In general.—An election under this subsection with respect to any property shall be made on the taxpayer's return of the tax imposed by this chapter for the taxpayer's taxable year in which such property is placed in service (or in the case of property to which an election under section 46(d) applies, for the first taxable year for which qualified progress expenditures were taken into account with respect to such property).

(ii) Revocable only with consent.—An election under this subsection with respect to any property, once made, may be revoked only with the consent of the Secretary.

(5) Recapture of reductions.—

(A) In general.—For purposes of sections 1245 and 1250, any reduction under this subsection shall be treated as a deduction allowed for depreciation.

(B) Special rule for section 1250.—For purposes of section 1250(b), the determination of what would have been the depreciation adjustments under the straight line method shall be made as if there had been no reduction under this section.

. . . . .

PART VI—MINIMUM TAX FOR TAX PREFERENCES

§ 55. Alternative minimum tax for taxpayers other than corporations

(a) Tax imposed.—In the case of a taxpayer other than a corporation, there is imposed (in addition to any other tax imposed by this subtitle) a tax equal to the excess (if any) of—

(1) an amount equal to 20 percent of so much of the alternative minimum taxable income as exceeds the exemption amount, over

(2) the regular tax for the taxable year.

(b) Alternative minimum taxable income.—For purposes of this title, the term "alternative minimum taxable income" means the adjusted gross income (determined without regard to the deduction allowed by section 172) of the taxpayer for the taxable year—

(1) reduced by the sum of—

(A) the alternative tax net operating loss deduction, plus

(B) the alternative tax itemized deductions, plus

(C) any amount included in income under section 667, and

(2) increased by the amount of items of tax preference.

(c) Credits.—

(1) In general.—For purposes of determining any credit allowable under subpart A of part IV of this subchapter (other than the foreign tax credit allowed under section 33(a))—

(A) the tax imposed by this section shall not be treated as a tax imposed by this chapter, and

(B) the amount of the foreign tax credit allowed by section 33(a) shall be determined without regard to this section.

. . . . .

(d) Alternative tax net operating loss deduction defined.—For purposes of this section—

(1) In general.—The term "alternative tax net operating loss deduction" means the net operating loss deduction allowable for the taxable year under section 172, except that in determining the amount of such deduction—

(A) in the case of taxable years beginning after December 31, 1982, section 172(b)(2) shall be applied by substituting "alternative minimum taxable income" for "taxable income" each place it appears, and

(B) the net operating loss (within the meaning of section 172(c)) for any loss year shall be adjusted as provided in paragraph (2).

(2) Adjustments to net operating loss computation.—

(A) Post-1982 loss years.—In the case of a loss year beginning after December 31, 1982, the net operating loss for such year under section 172(c) shall—

(i) be reduced by the amount of the items of tax preference arising in such year which are taken into account in computing the net operating loss, and

(ii) be computed by taking into account only itemized deductions which are alternative tax itemized deductions for the taxable year and which are otherwise described in section 172(c).

(B) Pre-1983 years.—In the case of loss years beginning before January 1, 1983, the amount of the net operating loss which may be carried over to taxable years beginning after December 31, 1982, for purposes of subparagraph (A), shall be equal to the amount which may be carried from the loss year to the first taxable year of the taxpayer beginning after December 31, 1982.

(e) Alternative tax itemized deductions.—For purposes of this section—

(1) In general.—The term "alternative tax itemized deductions" means an amount equal to the sum of any amount allowable as a deduction for the taxable year (other than a deduction allowable in computing adjusted gross income) under—

(A) section 165(a) for losses described in subsection (c)(3) or (d) of section 165,

(B) section 170 (relating to charitable deductions),

(C) section 213 (relating to medical deductions),

(D) this chapter for qualified interest, or

(E) section 691(c) (relating to deduction for estate tax).

(2) Amounts which may be carried over.—No amount shall be taken into account under paragraph (1) to the extent such amount may be carried to another taxable year for purposes of the regular tax.

(3) Qualified interest.—The term "qualified interest" mean the sum of—

(A) any qualified housing interest, and

(B) any amount allowed as a deduction for interest (other than qualified housing interest) to the extent such amount does not exceed the qualified net investment income of the taxpayer for the taxable year.

(4) Qualified housing interest.—

(A) In general.—The term "qualified housing interest" means interest which is paid or accrued during the taxable year on indebtedness which is incurred in acquiring, constructing, or substantially rehabilitating any property which—

(i) is the principal residence (within the meaning of section 1034) of the taxpayer at the time such interest accrues or is paid, or

(ii) is a qualified dwelling used by the taxpayer (or any member of his family within the meaning of section 267(c)(4)) during the taxable year.

(B) **Qualified dwelling.**—The term "qualified dwelling" means any—

(i) house,

(ii) apartment,

(iii) condominium, or

(iv) mobile home not used on a transient basis (within the meaning of section 7701(a)(19)(C)(v)),

including all structures or other property appurtenant thereto.

(C) **Special rule for indebtedness incurred before July 1, 1982.**—The term "qualified housing interest" includes interest paid or accrued on indebtedness which—

(i) was incurred by the taxpayer before July 1, 1982, and

(ii) is secured by property which, at the time such indebtedness was incurred, was—

(I) the principal residence (within the meaning of section 1034) of the taxpayer, or

(II) a qualified dwelling used by the taxpayer (or any member of his family (within the meaning of section 267(c)(4))).

(5) **Qualified net investment income.**—For purposes of this subsection—

(A) **In general.**—The term "qualified net investment income" means the excess of—

(i) qualified investment income, over

(ii) qualified investment expenses.

(B) **Qualified investment income.**—The term "qualified investment income" means the sum of—

(i) investment income (within the meaning of section 163(d)(3)(B) other than clause (ii) thereof),

(ii) any net capital gain attributable to the disposition of property held for investment, and

(iii) the amount of items of tax preference described in paragraph (1) of section 57(a).

(C) **Qualified investment expenses.**—The term "qualified investment expenses" means the deductions directly connected with the production of qualified investment income to the extent that—

(i) such deductions are allowable in computing adjusted gross income, and

(ii) such deductions are not items of tax preference.

(6) **Special rules for estates and trusts.—**

(A) **In general.**—In the case of an estate or trust, the alternative tax itemized deductions for any taxable year includes [sic] the deductions allowable under sections 642(c), 651(a), and 661(a).

(B) Determination of adjusted gross income.—The adjusted gross income of an estate or trust shall be computed in the same manner as in the case of an individual, except that the deductions for costs paid or incurred in connection with the administration of the estate or trust shall be treated as allowable in arriving at adjusted gross income.

(7) Limitation on medical deduction.—In applying subparagraph (C) of paragraph (1), the amount allowable as a deduction under section 213 shall be determined by substituting "10 percent" for "5 percent" in section 213(a).

(8) Treatment of interests in limited partnerships and subchapter s corporations.—

(A) Certain interest treated as not allowable in computing adjusted gross income.—Any amount allowable as a deduction for interest on indebtedness incurred or continued to purchase or carry a limited business interest shall be treated as not allowable in computing adjusted gross income.

(B) Income treated as qualified investment income.—Any income derived from a limited business interest shall be treated as qualified investment income.

(C) Limited business interest.—The term "limited business interest" means an interest—

(i) as a limited partner in a partnership, or

(ii) as a shareholder in an S corporation if the taxpayer does not actively participate in the management of such corporation.

(f) Other definitions.—For purposes of this section—

(1) Exemption amount.—The term "exemption amount" means—

(A) $40,000 in the case of—

(i) a joint return, or

(ii) a surviving spouse (as defined in section 2(a)),

(B) $30,000 in the case of an individual who—

(i) is not a married individual (as defined in section 143), and

(ii) is not a surviving spouse (as so defined), and

(C) $20,000 in the case of—

(i) a married individual (as so defined) who files a separate return, or

(ii) an estate or trust.

(2) Regular tax.—The term "regular tax" means the taxes imposed by this chapter for the taxable year (computed without regard to this section and without regard to the taxes imposed by sections 72(m)(5)(B), 72(q), 402(e), 408(f), 409(c), and 667(b)) reduced by the sum of the credits allowable under subpart A of part IV of this subchapter (other than under sections 31, 39, and 43). For purposes of this paragraph, the amount of the credits allowable under such subpart shall be determined without regard to this section.

§ 56. Corporate minimum tax

(a) General rule.—In addition to the other taxes imposed by this chapter, there is hereby imposed for each taxable year, with respect to the income of every corporation, a tax equal to 15 percent of the amount by which the sum of the items of tax preference exceeds the greater of—

(1) $10,000, or

(2) the regular tax deduction for the taxable year (as determined under subsection (c)).

(b) Deferral of tax liability in case of certain net operating losses.—

(1) **In general.**—If for any taxable year a corporation—

(A) has a net operating loss any portion of which (under section 172) remains as a net operating loss carryover to a succeeding taxable year, and

(B) has items of tax preference in excess of $10,000,

then an amount equal to the lesser of the tax imposed by subsection (a) or 15 percent of the amount of the net operating loss carryover described in subparagraph (A) shall be treated as tax liability not imposed for the taxable year, but as imposed for the succeeding taxable year or years pursuant to paragraph (2).

(2) **Year of liability.**—In any taxable year in which any portion of the net operating loss carryover attributable to the excess described in paragraph (1) (B) reduces taxable income, the amount of tax liability described in paragraph (1) shall be treated as tax liability imposed in such taxable year in an amount equal to 15 percent of such reduction.

(3) **Priority of application.**—For purposes of paragraph (2), if any portion of the net operating loss carryover described in paragraph (1) (A) is not attributable to the excess described in paragraph (1) (B), such portion shall be considered as being applied in reducing taxable income before such other portion.

(c) Regular tax deduction defined.—For purposes of this section, the term "regular tax deduction" means an amount equal to one-half of (or in the case of a corporation, an amount equal to) the taxes imposed by this chapter for the taxable year (computed without regard to this part and without regard to the taxes imposed by sections 531 and 541), reduced by the sum of the credits allowable under subpart A of part IV other than under sections 39 and 44G. For purposes of the preceding sentence, the amount of the credit allowable under section 38 shall be determined without regard to the employee plan percentage set forth in section 46(a)(2)(E).

.   .   .   .   .

§ 57. Items of tax preference

(a) In general.—For purposes of this part, the items of tax preference are—

(1) **Exclusion of interest and dividends.**—Any amount excluded from gross income for the taxable year under section 116 or 128.

(2) **Accelerated depreciation on real property.**—With respect to each section 1250 property (as defined in section 1250(c)), the amount by which the deduction allowable for the taxable year for exhaustion, wear and tear, obsolescence, or amortization exceeds the depreciation deduction which would have been allowable for the taxable year had the taxpayer depreciated the

property under the straight line method for each taxable year of its useful life (determined without regard to section 167(k)) for which the taxpayer has held the property.

(3) Accelerated depreciation on leased personal property.—With respect to each item of section 1245 property (as defined in section 1245(a) (3)) which is subject to a lease, the amount by which—

(A) the deduction allowable for the taxable year for depreciation or amortization, exceeds

(B) the deduction which would have been allowable for the taxable year had the taxpayer depreciated the property under the straight-line method for each taxable year of its useful life for which the taxpayer has held the property.

For purposes of subparagraph (B), useful life shall be determined as if section 167(m) (1) (relating to asset depreciation range) did not include the last sentence thereof.

. . . . .

(8) Depletion.—With respect to each property (as defined in section 614), the excess of the deduction for depletion allowable under section 611 for the taxable year over the adjusted basis of the property at the end of the taxable year (determined without regard to the depletion deduction for the taxable year).

(9) Capital gains.—

(A) Individuals.—In the case of a taxpayer other than a corporation, an amount equal to the net capital gain deduction for the taxable year determined under section 1202.

(B) Corporations.—In the case of a corporation having a net capital gain for the taxable year, an amount equal to the product obtained by multiplying the net capital gain by a fraction the numerator of which is the highest rate of tax specified in section 11(b), minus the alternative tax rate under section 1201(a), for the taxable year, and the denominator of which is the highest rate of tax specified in section 11(b) for the taxable year. In the case of a corporation to which section 1201(a) does not apply, the amount under this subparagraph shall be determined under regulations prescribed by the Secretary in a manner consistent with the preceding sentence.

(C) Preference reduction for timber.—In the case of a corporation, the amount of the tax preference under subparagraph (B) shall be reduced (but not below zero) by the sum of—

(i) one-third of the corporation's timber preference income (as defined in subsection (e)), plus

(ii) $20,000,

but in no event shall this reduction exceed the amount of timber preference income.

(D) Principal residence.—For purposes of subparagraph (A), gain from the sale or exchange of a principal residence (within the meaning of section 1034) shall not be taken into account.

. . . . .

(11) Intangible drilling costs.—

(A) In general.—With respect to all oil, gas, and geothermal properties of the taxpayer, the amount (if any) by which the amount of the excess intangible drilling costs arising in the taxable year is greater than the amount of the net income of the taxpayer from oil, gas, and geothermal properties for the taxable year.

(B) Excess intangible drilling costs.—For purposes of subparagraph (A), the amount of the excess intangible drilling costs arising in the taxable year is the excess of—

(i) the intangible drilling and development costs described in section 263(c) paid or incurred in connection with oil, gas, and geothermal wells (other than costs incurred in drilling a nonproductive well) allowable under this chapter for the taxable year, over

(ii) the amount which would have been allowable for the taxable year if such costs had been capitalized and straight line recovery of intangibles (as defined in subsection (d)) had been used with respect to such costs.

(C) Net income from oil, gas, and geothermal properties.—For purposes of subparagraph (A), the amount of the net income of the taxpayer from oil, gas, and geothermal properties for the taxable year is the excess of—

(i) the aggregate amount of gross income (within the meaning of section 613(a)) from all oil, gas, and geothermal properties of the taxpayer received or accrued by the taxpayer during the taxable year, over

(ii) the amount of any deductions allocable to such properties reduced by the excess described in subparagraph (B) for such taxable year.

(D) Paragraph applied separately with respect to geothermal properties and oil and gas properties.—This paragraph shall be applied separately with respect to—

(i) all oil and gas properties which are not described in clause (ii), and

(ii) all properties which are geothermal deposits (as defined in section 613(e) (3)).

(12) Accelerated cost recovery deduction.—

(A) In general.—With respect to each recovery property (other than 15-year real property) which is subject to a lease, the amount (if any) by which the deduction allowed under section 168(a) for the taxable year exceeds the deduction which would have been allowable for the taxable year had the property been depreciated using the straight-line method (with a half-year convention and without regard to salvage value) and a recovery period determined in accordance with the following table:

In the case of:	The recovery period is:
3-year property	5 years.
5-year property	8 years.
10-year property	15 years.
15-year public utility property	22 years.

42

(B) 15-year real property.—With respect to each recovery property which is 15-year real property, the amount (if any) by which the deduction allowed under section 168(a) for the taxable year exceeds the deduction which would have been allowable for the taxable year had the property been depreciated using a 15-year period and the straight-line method (without regard to salvage value).

(C) Paragraphs (2) and (3) shall not apply.—Paragraphs (2) and (3) shall not apply to recovery property.

(D) Definitions.—For purposes of this paragraph, the terms "3-year property", "5-year property", "10-year property", "15-year public utility property", "15-year real property", and "recovery property", shall have the same meanings given such terms under section 168.

Paragraphs (1), (3), (5), (6), (11), and (12)(A) shall not apply to a corporation other than a personal holding company (as defined in section 542).

(b) Application with section 291.—

(1) In general.—In the case of any item of tax preference of a corporation described in—

(A) paragraph (4) or (7) of subsection (a), or

(B) paragraph (8) of subsection (a) (but only to the extent such item is allocable to a deduction for depletion for iron ore and coal (including lignite)),

only 71.6 percent of the amount of such item of tax preference (determined without regard to this subsection) shall be taken into account as an item of tax preference.

(2) Certain capital gains.—In determining the net capital gain of any corporation for purposes of paragraph (9)(B) of subsection (a), there shall be taken into account only 71.6 percent of any gain from the sale or exchange of section 1250 property which is equal to 85 percent of the excess determined under section 291(a)(1) with respect to such property.

. . . .

(c) Net leases.—

(1) In general.—For purposes of this section, property shall be considered to be subject to a net lease for a taxable year if—

(A) for such taxable year the sum of the deductions of the lessor with respect to such property which are allowable solely by reason of section 162 (other than rents and reimbursed amounts with respect to such property) is less than 15 percent of the rental income produced by such property, or

(B) the lessor is either guaranteed a specified return or is guaranteed in whole or in part against loss of income.

(2) Multiple leases of single parcel of real property.—If a parcel of real property of the taxpayer is leased under two or more leases, paragraph (1) (A) shall, at the election of the taxpayer, be applied by treating all leased portions of such property as subject to a single lease.

(3) Elimination of 15-percent test after 5 years in case of real property.—At the election of the taxpayer, paragraph (1) (A) shall not apply with respect to real property of the taxpayer which has been in use for more than 5 years.

(4) Elections.—An election under paragraph (2) or (3) shall be made at such time and in such manner as the Secretary prescribes by regulations.

(d) Straight line recovery of intangibles defined.—For purposes of paragraph (11) of subsection (a)—

(1) In general.—The term "straight line recovery of intangibles", when used with respect to intangible drilling and development costs for any well, means (except in the case of an election under paragraph (2)) ratable amortization of such costs over the 120-month period beginning with the month in which production from such well begins.

(2) Election.—If the taxpayer elects, at such time and in such manner as the Secretary may by regulations prescribe, with respect to the intangible drilling and development costs for any well, the term "straight line recovery of intangibles" means any method which would be permitted for purposes of determining cost depletion with respect to such well and which is selected by the taxpayer for purposes of subsection (a) (11).

(e) Timber preference income defined.—For purposes of this part, the term "timber preference income" means the sum of—

(1) the gains referred to in section 631(a) and section 631(b),

(2) long-term capital gains on timber, and

(3) gains on the sale of timber included in paragraph 1231(b) (1),

multiplied by the fraction determined in paragraph 57(a) (9) (B).

§ 58.   Rules for application of this part

(a) Married individuals filing separate returns.—In the case of a married individual who files a separate return for the taxable year, section 56 shall be applied by substituting $5,000 for $10,000 each place it appears. In the case of a married individual who files a separate return for the taxable year, the amount determined under paragraph (1) of section 55(a) shall be an amount equal to one-half of the amount which would be determined under such paragraph if the amount of the individual's alternative minimum taxable income were multiplied by 2.

(b) Members of controlled groups.—In the case of a controlled group of corporations (as defined in section 1563(a)), the $10,000 amount specified in section 56 shall be divided among the component members of such group in proportion to their respective regular tax deductions (within the meaning of section 56(c)) for the taxable year.

(c) Estates and trusts.—In the case of an estate or trust, the items of tax preference for any taxable year shall be apportioned between the estate or trust and the beneficiaries in accordance with regulations prescribed by the Secretary.

(d) Certain capital gains of S corporations.—If for a taxable year of an S corporation a tax is imposed on the income of such corporation under section 1374, such corporation shall be subject to the tax imposed by section 56, but computed only with reference to the item of tax preference set forth in section 57(a)(9)(B) to the extent attributable to gains subject to the tax imposed by section 1374.

. . . . .

(h) Regulations to include tax benefit rule.—The Secretary shall prescribe regulations under which items of tax preference shall be properly adjusted where the tax treatment giving rise to such items will not result in the reduction of the taxpayer's tax under this subtitle for any taxable years.

(i) Optional 10-year writeoff of certain tax preferences.—

(1) In general.—For purposes of this title, in the case of an individual, any qualified expenditure to which an election under this paragraph applies shall be allowed as a deduction ratably over the 10-year period beginning with the taxable year in which such expenditure was made.

(2) Qualified expenditure.—For purposes of this subsection, the term "qualified expenditure" means any amount which, but for an election under this subsection, would have been allowable as a deduction for the taxable year in which paid or incurred under—

(A) section 173 (relating to circulation expenditures),

(B) section 174(a) (relating to research and experimental expenditures),

(C) section 263(c) (relating to intangible drilling and development expenditures),

(D) section 616(a) (relating to development expenditures), or

(E) section 617 (relating to deduction of certain mining exploration expenditures).

(3) Other sections not applicable.—Except as provided in this subsection, no deduction shall be allowed under any other section for any qualified expenditure to which an election under this subsection applies.

(4) Special election for intangible drilling and development costs not allocable to limited business interest.—

(A) In general.—In the case of any nonlimited partnership intangible drilling costs to which an election under this paragraph applies—

(i) the applicable percentage of such costs (adjusted as provided in section 48(q)) shall be allowed as a deduction for the taxable year in which paid or incurred and for each of the 4 succeeding taxable years, and

(ii) such costs shall be treated, for purposes of determining the amount of the credit allowable under section 38 for the taxable year in which paid or incurred, as qualified investment (within the meaning of subsections (c) and (d) of section 46) with respect to property placed in service during such year.

(B) Applicable percentage.—For purposes of subparagraph (A), the term "applicable percentage" means the percentage determined in accordance with the following table:

Taxable Year:	Applicable percentage:
1	15
2	22
3	21
4	21
5	21.

(C) **Nonlimited intangible drilling costs.**—For purposes of this paragraph, the term "nonlimited intangible drilling costs" means any qualified expenditure described in paragraph (2)(C) of an individual which is not allocable to a limited business interest (as defined in section 55(e)(8)(C)) of such individual.

(5) **Election.**—

(A) **In general.**—An election may be made under this subsection with respect to any qualified expenditure.

(B) **Revocable only with consent.**—An election under this subsection with respect to any qualified expenditure may be revoked only with the consent of the Secretary.

(C) **Time and manner.**—An election under this subsection shall be made at such time and in such manner as the Secretary shall by regulations prescribe.

(D) **Partners and shareholders of S corporations.**—In the case of a partnership, any election under this subsection shall be made separately by each partner with respect to the partner's allocable share of any qualified expenditure. A similar rule shall apply in the case of an S corporation and its shareholders.

(6) **Dispositions.**—

(A) **Oil, gas, and geothermal property.**—In the case of any disposition of any oil, gas, or geothermal property to which section 1254 applies (determined without regard to this section)—

(i) any deduction under paragraph (1) or (4)(A) with respect to costs which are allocable to such property shall, for purposes of section 1254, be treated as a deduction allowable under section 263(c), and

(ii) in the case of any credit allowable under section 38 by reason of paragraph (4)(B) which is allocable to such property, such disposition shall, for purposes of section 47, be treated as a disposition of section 38 recovery property which is not 3-year property.

(B) **Application of section 617(d).**—In the case of any disposition of mining property to which section 617(d) applies (determined without regard to this subsection), any amount allowable as a deduction under paragraph (1) which is allocable to such property shall, for purposes of section 617(d), be treated as a deduction allowable under section 617(a).

(7) **Amounts to which election apply [applies] not treated as tax preference.**—Any qualified expenditure to which an election under paragraph (1) or (4) applies shall not be treated as an item of tax preference under section 57(a).

SUBCHAPTER B—COMPUTATION OF TAXABLE INCOME

Part
   I. Definition of gross income, adjusted gross income, taxable income, etc.
  II. Items specifically included in gross income.
 III. Items specifically excluded from gross income.
 IV. Determination of marital status.
  V. Deductions for personal exemptions.
 VI. Itemized deductions for individuals and corporations.
VII. Additional itemized deductions for individuals.
VIII. Special deductions for corporations.
 IX. Items not deductible.
  X. Terminal railroad corporations and their shareholders.*

PART I—DEFINITION OF GROSS INCOME, ADJUSTED GROSS INCOME, TAXABLE INCOME, ETC.

§ 61.   Gross income defined

(a) General definition.—Except as otherwise provided in this subtitle, gross income means all income from whatever source derived, including (but not limited to) the following items:

(1) Compensation for services, including fees, commissions, and similar items;

(2) Gross income derived from business;

(3) Gains derived from dealings in property;

(4) Interest;

(5) Rents;

(6) Royalties;

(7) Dividends;

(8) Alimony and separate maintenance payments;

(9) Annuities;

(10) Income from life insurance and endowment contracts;

(11) Pensions;

(12) Income from discharge of indebtedness;

(13) Distributive share of partnership gross income;

(14) Income in respect of a decedent; and

(15) Income from an interest in an estate or trust.

. . . .

* Omitted entirely.

§ 62.   Adjusted gross income defined

For purposes of this subtitle, the term "adjusted gross income" means, in the case of an individual, gross income minus the following deductions:

(1) Trade and business deductions.—The deductions allowed by this chapter (other than by part VII of this subchapter) which are attributable to a trade or business carried on by the taxpayer, if such trade or business does not consist of the performance of services by the taxpayer as an employee.

(2) Trade and business deductions of employees.—

    (A) Reimbursed expenses.—The deductions allowed by part VI (sec. 161 and following) which consist of expenses paid or incurred by the taxpayer, in connection with the performance by him of services as an employee, under a reimbursement or other expense allowance arrangement with his employer.

    (B) Expenses for travel away from home.—The deductions allowed by part VI (sec. 161 and following) which consist of expenses of travel, meals, and lodging while away from home, paid or incurred by the taxpayer in connection with the performance by him of services as an employee.

    (C) Transportation expenses.—The deductions allowed by part VI (sec. 161 and following) which consist of expenses of transportation paid or incurred by the taxpayer in connection with the performance by him of services as an employee.

    (D) Outside salesmen.—The deductions allowed by part VI (sec. 161 and following) which are attributable to a trade or business carried on by the taxpayer, if such trade or business consists of the performance of services by the taxpayer as an employee and if such trade or business is to solicit, away from the employer's place of business, business for the employer.

(3) Long-term capital gains.—The deduction allowed by section 1202.

(4) Losses from sale or exchange of property.—The deductions allowed by part VI (sec. 161 and following) as losses from the sale or exchange of property.

(5) Deductions attributable to rents and royalties.—The deductions allowed by part VI (sec. 161 and following), by section 212 (relating to expenses for production of income), and by section 611 (relating to depletion) which are attributable to property held for the production of rents or royalties.

(6) Certain deductions of life tenants and income beneficiaries of property.—In the case of a life tenant of property, or an income beneficiary of property held in trust, or an heir, legatee, or devisee of an estate, the deduction for depreciation allowed by section 167 and the deduction allowed by section 611.

(7) Pension, profit-sharing, annuity, and bond purchase plans of self-employed individuals.—In the case of an individual who is an employee within the meaning of section 401(c) (1), the deductions allowed by section 404 and section 405(c) to the extent attributable to contributions made on behalf of such individual.

(8) Moving expense deduction.—The deduction allowed by section 217.

(9) [Repealed.]

(10) **Retirement savings.**—The deduction allowed by section 219 (relating to deduction of certain retirement savings).

(11) **Certain portion of lump-sum distributions from pension plans taxed under section 402(e).**—The deduction allowed by section 402(e) (3).

(12) **Penalties forfeited because of premature withdrawal of funds from time savings accounts or deposits.**—The deductions allowed by section 165 for losses incurred in any transaction entered into for profit, though not connected with a trade or business to the extent that such losses include amounts forfeited to a bank, mutual savings bank, savings and loan association, building and loan association, cooperative bank or homestead association as a penalty for premature withdrawal of funds from a time savings account, certificate of deposit, or similar class of deposit.

(13) **Alimony.**—The deduction allowed by section 215.

(14) **Reforestation expenses.**—The deduction allowed by section 194.

(15) **Certain required repayments of supplemental unemployment compensation benefits.**—The deduction allowed by section 165 for the repayment to a trust described in paragraph (9) or (17) of section 501(c) of supplemental unemployment compensation benefits received from such trust if such repayment is required because of the receipt of trade readjustment allowances under section 231 or 232 of the Trade Act of 1974 (19 U.S.C. 2291 and 2292).

(16) **Deduction for two-earner married couples.**—The deduction allowed by section 221.

Nothing in this section shall permit the same item to be deducted more than once.

§ 63.   Taxable income defined

(a) **Corporations.**—For purposes of this subtitle, in the case of a corporation, the term "taxable income" means gross income minus the deductions allowed by this chapter.

(b) **Individuals.**—For purposes of this subtitle, in the case of an individual, the term "taxable income" means adjusted gross income—

(1) reduced by the sum of—

(A) the excess itemized deductions,

(B) the deductions for personal exemptions provided by section 151, and

(C) the direct charitable deduction, and

(2) increased (in the case of an individual for whom an unused zero bracket amount computation is provided by subsection (e)) by the unused zero bracket amount (if any).

(c) **Excess itemized deductions.**—For purposes of this subtitle, the term "excess itemized deductions" means the excess (if any) of—

(1) the itemized deductions, over

(2) the zero bracket amount.

(d) Zero bracket amount.—For purposes of this subtitle, the term "zero bracket amount" means—

(1) $3,400 in the case of—

(A) a joint return under section 6013, or

(B) a surviving spouse (as defined in section 2(a)),

(2) $2,300 in the case of an individual who is not married and who is not a surviving spouse (as so defined),

(3) $1,700 in the case of a married individual filing a separate return, or

(4) zero in any other case.

(e) Unused zero bracket amount.—

(1) Individuals for whom computation must be made.—A computation for the taxable year shall be made under this subsection for the following individuals:

(A) a married individual filing a separate return where either spouse itemizes deductions,

. . . .

(D) an individual with respect to whom a deduction under section 151(e) is allowable to another taxpayer for a taxable year beginning in the calendar year in which the individual's taxable year begins.

(2) Computation.—For purposes of this subtitle, an individual's unused zero bracket amount for the taxable year is an amount equal to the excess (if any) of—

(A) the zero bracket amount, over

(B) the itemized deductions.

In the case of an individual referred to in paragraph (1) (D), if such individual's earned income (as defined in section 911(d)(2)) exceeds the itemized deductions, such earned income shall be substituted for the itemized deductions in subparagraph (B).

(f) Itemized deductions.—For purposes of this subtitle, the term "itemized deductions" means the deductions allowable by this chapter other than—

(1) the deductions allowable in arriving at adjusted gross income,

(2) the deductions for personal exemptions provided by section 151, and

(3) the direct charitable deduction.

(g) Election to itemize.—

(1) In general.—Unless an individual makes an election under this subsection for the taxable year, no itemized deduction shall be allowed for the taxable year. For purposes of this subtitle, the determination of whether a deduction is allowable under this chapter shall be made without regard to the preceding sentence.

(2) Who may elect.—Except as provided in paragraph (3), an individual may make an election under this subsection for the taxable year only if such individual's itemized deductions exceed the zero bracket amount.

(3) Certain individuals treated as electing to itemize.—An individual who has an unused zero bracket amount (as determined under subsection (e) (2)) shall be treated as having made an election under this subsection for the taxable year.

(4) Time and manner of election.—Any election under this subsection shall be made on the taxpayer's return, and the Secretary shall prescribe the manner of signifying such election on the return.

(5) Change of treatment.—Under regulations prescribed by the Secretary, a change of treatment with respect to the zero bracket amount and itemized deductions for any taxable year may be made after the filing of the return for such year. If the spouse of the taxpayer filed a separate return for any taxable year corresponding to the taxable year of the taxpayer, the change shall not be allowed unless, in accordance with such regulations—

(A) the spouse makes a change of treatment with respect to the zero bracket amount and itemized deductions, for the taxable year covered in such separate return, consistent with the change of treatment sought by the taxpayer, and

(B) the taxpayer and his spouse consent in writing to the assessment, within such period as may be agreed on with the Secretary, of any deficiency, to the extent attributable to such change of treatment, even though at the time of the filing of such consent the assessment of such deficiency would otherwise be prevented by the operation of any law or rule of law.

This paragraph shall not apply if the tax liability of the taxpayer's spouse, for the taxable year corresponding to the taxable year of the taxpayer, has been compromised under section 7122.

(h) Marital status.—For purposes of this section, marital status shall be determined under section 143.

(i) Direct charitable deduction.—For purposes of this section, the term "direct charitable deduction" means that portion of the amount allowable under section 170(a) which is taken as a direct charitable deduction for the taxable year under section 170(i).

§ 64. Ordinary income defined

For purposes of this subtitle, the term "ordinary income" includes any gain from the sale or exchange of property which is neither a capital asset nor property described in section 1231(b). Any gain from the sale or exchange of property which is treated or considered, under other provisions of this subtitle, as "ordinary income" shall be treated as gain from the sale or exchange of property which is neither a capital asset nor property described in section 1231(b).

§ 65. Ordinary loss defined

For purposes of this subtitle, the term "ordinary loss" includes any loss from the sale or exchange of property which is not a capital asset. Any loss from the sale or exchange of property which is treated or considered, under other provisions of this subtitle, as "ordinary loss" shall be treated as loss from the sale or exchange of property which is not a capital asset.

§ 66. Treatment of community income where spouses live apart

(a) General rule.—If—

(1) 2 individuals are married to each other at any time during a calendar year;

51

(2) such individuals—

(A) live apart at all times during the calendar year, and

(B) do not file a joint return under section 6013 with each other for a taxable year beginning or ending in the calendar year;

(3) one or both of such individuals have earned income for the calendar year which is community income; and

(4) no portion of such earned income is transferred (directly or indirectly) between such individuals before the close of the calendar year,

then, for purposes of this title, any community income of such individuals for the calendar year shall be treated in accordance with the rules provided by section 879(a).

(b) Definitions.—For purposes of this section—

(1) **Earned income.**—The term "earned income" has the meaning given to such term by section 911(b).

(2) **Community income.**—The term "community income" means income which, under applicable community property laws, is treated as community income.

(3) **Community property laws.**—The term "community property laws" means the community property laws of a State, a foreign country, or a possession of the United States.

PART II—ITEMS SPECIFICALLY INCLUDED IN GROSS INCOME

§ 71. Alimony and separate maintenance payments

(a) General rule.—

(1) **Decree of divorce or separate maintenance.**—If a wife is divorced or legally separated from her husband under a decree of divorce or of separate maintenance, the wife's gross income includes periodic payments (whether or not made at regular intervals) received after such decree in discharge of (or attributable to property transferred, in trust or otherwise, in discharge of) a legal obligation which, because of the marital or family relationship, is imposed on or incurred by the husband under the decree or under a written instrument incident to such divorce or separation.

(2) **Written separation agreement.**—If a wife is separated from her husband and there is a written separation agreement executed after the date of the enactment of this title, the wife's gross income includes periodic payments (whether or not made at regular intervals) received after such agreement is executed which are made under such agreement and because of the marital or family relationship (or which are attributable to property transferred, in trust or otherwise, under such agreement and because of such relationship). This paragraph shall not apply if the husband and wife make a single return jointly.

(3) **Decree for support.**—If a wife is separated from her husband, the wife's gross income includes periodic payments (whether or not made at regular intervals) received by her after the date of the enactment of this title from her husband under a decree entered after March 1, 1954, requiring the husband to make the payments for her support or maintenance. This paragraph shall not apply if the husband and wife make a single return jointly.

(b) Payments to support minor children.—Subsection (a) shall not apply to that part of any payment which the terms of the decree, instrument, or agreement fix, in terms of an amount of money or a part of the payment, as a sum which is payable for the support of minor children of the husband. For purposes of the preceding sentence, if any payment is less than the amount specified in the decree, instrument, or agreement, then so much of such payment as does not exceed the sum payable for support shall be considered a payment for such support.

(c) Principal sum paid in installments.—

    (1) General rule.—For purposes of subsection (a), installment payments discharging a part of an obligation the principal sum of which is, either in terms of money or property, specified in the decree, instrument, or agreement shall not be treated as periodic payments.

    (2) Where period for payment is more than 10 years.—If, by the terms of the decree, instrument, or agreement, the principal sum referred to in paragraph (1) is to be paid or may be paid over a period ending more than 10 years from the date of such decree, instrument, or agreement, then (notwithstanding paragraph (1)) the installment payments shall be treated as periodic payments for purposes of subsection (a), but (in the case of any one taxable year of the wife) only to the extent of 10 percent of the principal sum. For purposes of the preceding sentence, the part of any principal sum which is allocable to a period after the taxable year of the wife in which it is received shall be treated as an installment payment for the taxable year in which it is received.

(d) Rule for husband in case of transferred property.—The husband's gross income does not include amounts received which, under subsection (a), are (1) includible in the gross income of the wife, and (2) attributable to transferred property.

. . . .

§ 72.   Annuities; certain proceeds of endowment and life insurance contracts

(a) General rule for annuities.—Except as otherwise provided in this chapter, gross income includes any amount received as an annuity (whether for a period certain or during one or more lives) under an annuity, endowment, or life insurance contract.

(b) Exclusion ratio.—Gross income does not include that part of any amount received as an annuity under an annuity, endowment, or life insurance contract which bears the same ratio to such amount as the investment in the contract (as of the annuity starting date) bears to the expected return under the contract (as of such date). This subsection shall not apply to any amount to which subsection (d) (1) (relating to certain employee annuities) applies.

(c) Definitions.—

    (1) Investment in the contract.—For purposes of subsection (b), the investment in the contract as of the annuity starting date is—

        (A) the aggregate amount of premiums or other consideration paid for the contract, minus

        (B) the aggregate amount received under the contract before such date, to the extent that such amount was excludable from gross income under this subtitle or prior income tax laws.

(2) Adjustment in investment where there is refund feature.—If—

(A) the expected return under the contract depends in whole or in part on the life expectancy of one or more individuals;

(B) the contract provides for payments to be made to a beneficiary (or to the estate of an annuitant) on or after the death of the annuitant or annuitants; and

(C) such payments are in the nature of a refund of the consideration paid,

then the value (computed without discount for interest) of such payments on the annuity starting date shall be subtracted from the amount determined under paragraph (1). Such value shall be computed in accordance with actuarial tables prescribed by the Secretary. For purposes of this paragraph and of subsection (e) (2) (A), the term "refund of the consideration paid" includes amounts payable after the death of an annuitant by reason of a provision in the contract for a life annuity with minimum period of payments certain, but (if part of the consideration was contributed by an employer) does not include that part of any payment to a beneficiary (or to the estate of the annuitant) which is not attributable to the consideration paid by the employee for the contract as determined under paragraph (1) (A).

(3) Expected return.—For purposes of subsection (b), the expected return under the contract shall be determined as follows:

(A) Life expectancy.—If the expected return under the contract, for the period on and after the annuity starting date, depends in whole or in part on the life expectancy of one or more individuals, the expected return shall be computed with reference to actuarial tables prescribed by the Secretary.

(B) Installment payments.—If subparagraph (A) does not apply, the expected return is the aggregate of the amounts receivable under the contract as an annuity.

(4) Annuity starting date.—For purposes of this section, the annuity starting date in the case of any contract is the first day of the first period for which an amount is received as an annuity under the contract; except that if such date was before January 1, 1954, then the annuity starting date is January 1, 1954.

(d) Employees' annuities.—

(1) Employee's contributions recoverable in 3 years.—Where—

(A) part of the consideration for an annuity, endowment, or life insurance contract is contributed by the employer, and

(B) during the 3-year period beginning on the date on which an amount is first received under the contract as an annuity, the aggregate amount receivable by the employee under the terms of the contract is equal to or greater than the consideration for the contract contributed by the employee,

then all amounts received as an annuity under the contract shall be excluded from gross income until there has been so excluded an amount equal to the consideration for the contract contributed by the employee. Thereafter all amounts so received under the contract shall be included in gross income.

(2) **Special rules for application of paragraph (1).**—For purposes of paragraph (1)—

(A) if the employee died before any amount was received as an annuity under the contract, the words "receivable by the employee" shall be read as "receivable by a beneficiary of the employee"; and

(B) any contribution made with respect to the contract while the employee is an employee within the meaning of section 401(c) (1) which is not allowed as a deduction under section 404 shall be treated as consideration for the contract contributed by the employee.

. . . . .

(g) **Rules for transferee where transfer was for value.**—Where any contract (or any interest therein) is transferred (by assignment or otherwise) for a valuable consideration, to the extent that the contract (or interest therein) does not, in the hands of the transferee, have a basis which is determined by reference to the basis in the hands of the transferor, then—

(1) for purposes of this section, only the actual value of such consideration, plus the amount of the premiums and other consideration paid by the transferee after the transfer, shall be taken into account in computing the aggregate amount of the premiums or other consideration paid for the contract;

(2) for purposes of subsection (c) (1) (B), there shall be taken into account only the aggregate amount received under the contract by the transferee before the annuity starting date, to the extent that such amount was excludable from gross income under this subtitle or prior income tax laws; and

(3) the annuity starting date is January 1, 1954, or the first day of the first period for which the transferee received an amount under the contract as an annuity, whichever is the later.

For purposes of this subsection, the term "transferee" includes a beneficiary of, or the estate of, the transferee.

(h) **Option to receive annuity in lieu of lump sum.**—If—

(1) a contract provides for payment of a lump sum in full discharge of an obligation under the contract, subject to an option to receive an annuity in lieu of such lump sum;

(2) the option is exercised within 60 days after the day on which such lump sum first became payable; and

(3) part or all of such lump sum would (but for this subsection) be includible in gross income by reason of subsection (e) (1),

then, for purposes of this subtitle, no part of such lump sum shall be considered as includible in gross income at the time such lump sum first became payable.

[(i) Repealed. Pub.L. 94–455, Title XIX, § 1951(b) (1) (A), Oct. 4, 1976, 90 Stat. 1836]

(j) **Interest.**—Notwithstanding any other provision of this section, if any amount is held under an agreement to pay interest thereon, the interest payments shall be included in gross income.

(k) **Payments in discharge of alimony.**—

(1) **In general.**—This section shall not apply to so much of any payment under an annuity, endowment, or life insurance contract (or any interest

therein) as is includible in the gross income of the wife under section 71 or section 682 (relating to income of an estate or trust in case of divorce, etc.).

. . . . .

(m) Special rules applicable to employee annuities and distributions under employee plans.—

[(1) Repealed. Pub.L. 93–406, Title II, § 2001(h) (2), Sept. 2, 1974, 88 Stat. 957]

(2) Computation of consideration paid by the employee.—In computing—

(A) the aggregate amount of premiums or other consideration paid for the contract for purposes of subsection (c) (1) (A) (relating to the investment in the contract),

(B) the consideration for the contract contributed by the employee for purposes of subsection (d) (1) (relating to employee's contributions recoverable in 3 years), and

(C) the aggregate premiums or other consideration paid for purposes of subsection (e) (1) (B) (relating to certain amounts not received as an annuity),

any amount allowed as a deduction with respect to the contract under section 404 which was paid while the employee was an employee within the meaning of section 401(c) (1) shall be treated as consideration contributed by the employer, and there shall not be taken into account any portion of the premiums or other consideration for the contract paid while the employee was an owner-employee which is properly allocable (as determined under regulations prescribed by the Secretary) to the cost of life, accident, health, or other insurance.

(3) Life insurance contracts.—

(A) This paragraph shall apply to any life insurance contract—

(i) purchased as a part of a plan described in section 403(a), or

(ii) purchased by a trust described in section 401(a) which is exempt from tax under section 501(a) if the proceeds of such contract are payable directly or indirectly to a participant in such trust or to a beneficiary of such participant.

(B) Any contribution to a plan described in subparagraph (A) (i) or a trust described in subparagraph (A) (ii) which is allowed as a deduction under section 404, and any income of a trust described in subparagraph (A) (ii), which is determined in accordance with regulations prescribed by the Secretary to have been applied to purchase the life insurance protection under a contract described in subparagraph (A), is includible in the gross income of the participant for the taxable year when so applied.

(C) In the case of the death of an individual insured under a contract described in subparagraph (A), an amount equal to the cash surrender value of the contract immediately before the death of the insured shall be treated as a payment under such plan or a distribution by such trust, and the excess of the amount payable by reason of the death of the insured over such cash surrender value shall not be includible in gross income under this section and shall be treated as provided in section 101.

. . . . .

(p) Loans treated as distributions.—For purposes of this section—

(1) Treatment as distributions.—

(A) Loans.—If during any taxable year a participant or beneficiary receives (directly or indirectly) any amount as a loan from a qualified employer plan, such amount shall be treated as having been received by such individual as a distribution under such plan.

(B) Assignments or pledges.—If during any taxable year a participant or beneficiary assigns (or agrees to assign) or pledges (or agrees to pledge) any portion of his interest in a qualified employer plan, such portion shall be treated as having been received by such individual as a loan from such plan.

(2) Exception for certain loans.—

(A) General rule.—Paragraph (1) shall not apply to any loan to the extent that such loan (when added to the outstanding balance of all other loans from such plan whether made on, before, or after August 13, 1982), does not exceed the lesser of—

(i) $50,000, or

(ii) ½ of the present value of the nonforfeitable accrued benefit of the employee under the plan (but not less than $10,000).

(B) Requirement that loan be repayable within 5 years.—

(i) In general.—Subparagraph (A) shall not apply to any loan unless such loan, by its terms, is required to be repaid within 5 years.

(ii) Exception for home loans.—Clause (i) shall not apply to any loan used to acquire, construct, reconstruct, or substantially rehabilitate any dwelling unit which within a reasonable time is to be used (determined at the time the loan is made) as a principal residence of the participant or a member of the family (within the meaning of section 267(c)(4)) of the participant.

(C) Related employers and related plans.—For purposes of this paragraph—

(i) the rules of subsections (b), (c), and (m) of section 414 shall apply, and

(ii) all plans of an employer (determined after the application of such subsections) shall be treated as 1 plan.

(3) Qualified employer plan, etc.—For purposes of this subsection, the term "qualified employer plan" means any plan which was (or was determined to be) a qualified employer plan (as defined in section 219(e)(3) without regard to subparagraph (D) thereof). For purposes of this subsection, such term includes any government plan (as defined in section 219(e)(4)).

(4) Special rules for loans, etc., from certain contracts.—For purposes of this subsection, any amount received as a loan under a contract purchased under a qualified employer plan (and any assignment or pledge with respect to such a contract) shall be treated as a loan under such employer plan.

(q) 5-percent penalty for premature distributions from annuity contracts.—

(1) Imposition of penalty.—

(A) In general.—If any taxpayer receives any amount under an annuity contract, the taxpayer's tax under this chapter for the taxable year in which such amount is received shall be increased by an amount equal to 5 percent of the portion of such amount includible in gross income which is properly allocable to any investment in the annuity contract made during the 10-year period ending on the date such amount was received by the taxpayer.

(B) Allocation on first-in, first-out basis.—For purposes of subparagraph (A), the amount includible in gross income shall be allocated to the earliest investment in the contract with respect to which amounts have not been previously fully allocated under this paragraph.

(2) Subsection not to apply to certain distributions.—This subsection shall not apply to any distribution—

(A) made on or after the date on which the taxpayer attains age 59½,

(B) made to a beneficiary (or to the estate of an annuitant) on or after the death of an annuitant,

(C) attributable to the taxpayer's becoming disabled within the meaning of subsection (m)(7),

(D) which is one of a series of substantially equal periodic payments made for the life of a taxpayer or over a period extending for at least 60 months after the annuity starting date,

(E) from a plan, contract, account, trust, or annuity described in subsection (e)(5)(D), or

(F) allocable to investment in the contract before August 14, 1982.

. . . . .

§ 73. Services of child

(a) Treatment of amounts received.—Amounts received in respect of the services of a child shall be included in his gross income and not in the gross income of the parent, even though such amounts are not received by the child.

(b) Treatment of expenditures.—All expenditures by the parent or the child attributable to amounts which are includible in the gross income of the child (and not of the parent) solely by reason of subsection (a) shall be treated as paid or incurred by the child.

(c) Parent defined.—For purposes of this section, the term "parent" includes an individual who is entitled to the services of a child by reason of having parental rights and duties in respect of the child.

. . . . .

§ 74. Prizes and awards

(a) General rule.—Except as provided in subsection (b) and in section 117 (relating to scholarships and fellowship grants), gross income includes amounts received as prizes and awards.

(b) Exception.—Gross income does not include amounts received as prizes and awards made primarily in recognition of religious, charitable, scientific, educational, artistic, literary, or civic achievement, but only if—

(1) the recipient was selected without any action on his part to enter the contest or proceeding; and

(2) the recipient is not required to render substantial future services as a condition to receiving the prize or award.

§ 79.   Group-term life insurance purchased for employees

(a) **General rule.**—There shall be included in the gross income of an employee for the taxable year an amount equal to the cost of group-term life insurance on his life provided for part or all of such year under a policy (or policies) carried directly or indirectly by his employer (or employers); but only to the extent that such cost exceeds the sum of—

(1) the cost of $50,000 of such insurance, and

(2) the amount (if any) paid by the employee toward the purchase of such insurance.

(b) **Exceptions.**—Subsection (a) shall not apply to—

(1) the cost of group-term life insurance on the life of an individual which is provided under a policy carried directly or indirectly by an employer after such individual has terminated his employment with such employer and either has reached the retirement age with respect to such employer or is disabled (within the meaning of section 72(m) (7)).

(2) the cost of any portion of the group-term life insurance on the life of an employee provided during part or all of the taxable year of the employee under which—

(A) the employer is directly or indirectly the beneficiary, or

(B) a person described in section 170(c) is the sole beneficiary, for the entire period during such taxable year for which the employee receives such insurance, and

(3) the cost of any group-term life insurance which is provided under a contract to which section 72(m) (3) applies.

. . . . .

(d) **Nondiscrimination requirements.**—

(1) **In general.**—In the case of a discriminatory group-term life insurance plan, paragraph (1) of subsection (a) shall not apply with respect to any key employee.

(2) **Discriminatory group-term life insurance plan.**—For purposes of this subsection, the term "discriminatory group-term life insurance plan" means any plan of an employer for providing group-term life insurance unless—

(A) the plan does not discriminate in favor of key employees as to eligibility to participate, and

(B) the type and amount of benefits available under the plan do not discriminate in favor of participants who are key employees.

(3) **Nondiscriminatory eligibility classification.**—

(A) **In general.**—A plan does not meet requirements of subparagraph (A) of paragraph (2) unless—

(i) such plan benefits 70 percent or more of all employees of the employer,

(ii) at least 85 percent of all employees who are participants under the plan are not key employees,

(iii) such plan benefits such employees as qualify under a classification set up by the employer and found by the Secretary not to be discriminatory in favor of key employees, or

(iv) in the case of a plan which is part of a cafeteria plan, the requirements of section 125 are met.

(B) Exclusion of certain employees.—For purposes of subparagraph (A), there may be excluded from consideration—

(i) employees who have not completed 3 years of service;

(ii) part-time or seasonal employees;

(iii) employees not included in the plan who are included in a unit of employees covered by an agreement between employee representatives and one or more employers which the Secretary finds to be a collective bargaining agreement, if the benefits provided under the plan were the subject of good faith bargaining between such employee representatives and such employer or employers; and

(iv) employees who are nonresident aliens and who receive no earned income (within the meaning of section 911(d)(2)) from the employer which constitutes income from sources within the United States (within the meaning of section 861(a)(3)).

(4) Nondiscriminatory benefits.—A plan does not meet the requirements of paragraph (2)(B) unless all benefits available to participants who are key employees are available to all other participants.

(5) Special rule.—A plan shall not fail to meet the requirements of paragraph (2)(B) merely because the amount of life insurance on behalf of the employees under the plan bears a uniform relationship to the total compensation or the basic or regular rate of compensation of such employees.

(6) Key employee defined.—For purposes of this subsection, the term "key employee" has the meaning given to such term by paragraph (1) of section 416(i), except that subparagraph (A)(iv) of such paragraph shall be applied by not taking into account employees described in paragraph (3)(B) who are not participants in the plan.

(7) Certain controlled groups, etc.—All employees who are treated as employed by a single employer under subsection (b), (c), or (m) of section 414 shall be treated as employed by a single employer for purposes of this section.

§ 82. Reimbursement for expenses of moving

There shall be included in gross income (as compensation for services) any amount received or accrued, directly or indirectly, by an individual as a payment for or reimbursement of expenses of moving from one residence to another residence which is attributable to employment or self-employment.

§ 83. Property transferred in connection with performance of services

(a) General rule.—If, in connection with the performance of services, property is transferred to any person other than the person for whom such services are performed, the excess of—

(1) the fair market value of such property (determined without regard to any restriction other than a restriction which by its terms will never lapse) at the first time the rights of the person having the beneficial interest in such

property are transferable or are not subject to a substantial risk of forfeiture, whichever occurs earlier, over

(2) the amount (if any) paid for such property,

shall be included in the gross income of the person who performed such services in the first taxable year in which the rights of the person having the beneficial interest in such property are transferable or are not subject to a substantial risk of forfeiture, whichever is applicable. The preceding sentence shall not apply if such person sells or otherwise disposes of such property in an arm's length transaction before his rights in such property become transferable or not subject to a substantial risk of forfeiture.

(b) Election to include in gross income in year of transfer.—

(1) In general.—Any person who performs services in connection with which property is transferred to any person may elect to include in his gross income, for the taxable year in which such property is transferred, the excess of—

(A) the fair market value of such property at the time of transfer (determined without regard to any restriction other than a restriction which by its terms will never lapse), over

(B) the amount (if any) paid for such property.

If such election is made, subsection (a) shall not apply with respect to the transfer of such property, and if such property is subsequently forfeited, no deduction shall be allowed in respect of such forfeiture.

(2) Election.—An election under paragraph (1) with respect to any transfer of property shall be made in such manner as the Secretary prescribes and shall be made not later than 30 days after the date of such transfer. Such election may not be revoked except with the consent of the Secretary.

(c) Special rules.—For purposes of this section—

(1) Substantial risk of forfeiture.—The rights of a person in property are subject to a substantial risk of forfeiture if such person's rights to full enjoyment of such property are conditioned upon the future performance of substantial services by any individual.

(2) Transferability of property.—The rights of a person in property are transferable only if the rights in such property of any transferee are not subject to a substantial risk of forfeiture.

(3) Sales which may give rise to suit under section 16(b) of the Securities and Exchange Act of 1934.—So long as the sale of property at a profit could subject a person to suit under section 16(b) of the Securities and Exchange Act of 1934, such person's rights in such property are—

(A) subject to a substantial risk of forfeiture, and

(B) not transferable.

(d) Certain restrictions which will never lapse.—

(1) Valuation.—In the case of property subject to a restriction which by its terms will never lapse, and which allows the transferee to sell such property only at a price determined under a formula, the price so determined shall be deemed to be the fair market value of the property unless established to the contrary by the Secretary, and the burden of proof shall be on the Secretary with respect to such value.

(2) Cancellation.—If, in the case of property subject to a restriction which by its terms will never lapse, the restriction is canceled, then, unless the taxpayer establishes—

(A) that such cancellation was not compensatory, and

(B) that the person, if any, who would be allowed a deduction if the cancellation were treated as compensatory, will treat the transaction as not compensatory, as evidenced in such manner as the Secretary shall prescribe by regulations,

the excess of the fair market value of the property (computed without regard to the restrictions) at the time of cancellation over the sum of—

(C) the fair market value of such property (computed by taking the restriction into account) immediately before the cancellation, and

(D) the amount, if any, paid for the cancellation,

shall be treated as compensation for the taxable year in which such cancellation occurs.

(e) Applicability of section.—This section shall not apply to—

(1) a transaction to which section 421 applies,

(2) a transfer to or from a trust described in section 401(a) or a transfer under an annuity plan which meets the requirements of section 404(a) (2),

(3) the transfer of an option without a readily ascertainable fair market value, or

(4) the transfer of property pursuant to the exercise of an option with a readily ascertainable fair market value at the date of grant.

(f) Holding period.—In determining the period for which the taxpayer has held property to which subsection (a) applies, there shall be included only the period beginning at the first time his rights in such property are transferable or are not subject to a substantial risk of forfeiture, whichever occurs earlier.

. . . .

(h) Deduction by employer.—In the case of a transfer of property to which this section applies or a cancellation of a restriction described in subsection (d), there shall be allowed as a deduction under section 162, to the person for whom were performed the services in connection with which such property was transferred, an amount equal to the amount included under subsection (a), (b), or (d) (2) in the gross income of the person who performed such services. Such deduction shall be allowed for the taxable year of such person in which or with which ends the taxable year in which such amount is included in the gross income of the person who performed such services.

. . . .

§ 84.   Transfer of appreciated property to political organization

(a) General rule.—If—

(1) any person transfers property to a political organization, and

(2) the fair market value of such property exceeds its adjusted basis,

then for purposes of this chapter the transferor shall be treated as having sold such property to the political organization on the date of the transfer, and the transferor shall be treated as having realized an amount equal to the fair market value of such property on such date.

(b) Basis of property.—In the case of a transfer of property to a political organization to which subsection (a) applies, the basis of such property in the hands of the political organization shall be the same as it would be in the hands of the transferor, increased by the amount of gain recognized to the transferor by reason of such transfer.

(c) Political organization defined.—For purposes of this section, the term "political organization" has the meaning given to such term by section 527(e)(1).

§ 85.   Unemployment compensation

(a) In general.—If the sum for the taxable year of the adjusted gross income of the taxpayer (determined without regard to this section, section 105(d), and section 221) and the unemployment compensation exceeds the base amount, gross income for the taxable year includes unemployment compensation in an amount equal to the lesser of—

(1) one-half of the amount of the excess of such sum over the base amount, or

(2) the amount of the unemployment compensation.

(b) Base amount defined.—For purposes of this section, the term "base amount" means—

(1) except as provided in paragraphs (2) and (3), $12,000,

(2) $18,000, in the case of a joint return under section 6013, or

(3) zero, in the case of a taxpayer who—

(A) is married at the close of the taxable year (within the meaning of section 143) but does not file a joint return for such year, and

(B) does not live apart from his spouse at all times during the taxable year.

(c) Unemployment compensation defined.—For purposes of this section, the term "unemployment compensation" means any amount received under a law of the United States or of a State which is in the nature of unemployment compensation.

PART III—ITEMS SPECIFICALLY EXCLUDED FROM GROSS INCOME

§ 101.   Certain death benefits

(a) Proceeds of life insurance contracts payable by reason of death.—

(1) **General rule.**—Except as otherwise provided in paragraph (2), subsection (d), and subsection (f), gross income does not include amounts received (whether in a single sum or otherwise) under a life insurance contract, if such amounts are paid by reason of the death of the insured.

(2) **Transfer for valuable consideration.**—In the case of a transfer for a valuable consideration, by assignment or otherwise, of a life insurance contract or any interest therein, the amount excluded from gross income by paragraph (1) shall not exceed an amount equal to the sum of the actual value of such consideration and the premiums and other amounts subsequently paid by the transferee. The preceding sentence shall not apply in the case of such a transfer—

(A) if such contract or interest therein has a basis for determining gain or loss in the hands of a transferee determined in whole or in part by reference to such basis of such contract or interest therein in the hands of the transferor, or

(B) if such transfer is to the insured, to a partner of the insured, to a partnership in which the insured is a partner, or to a corporation in which the insured is a shareholder or officer.

(b) Employees' death benefits.—

(1) General rule.—Gross income does not include amounts received (whether in a single sum or otherwise) by the beneficiaries or the estate of an employee, if such amounts are paid by or on behalf of an employer and are paid by reason of the death of the employee.

(2) Special rules for paragraph (1).—

(A) $5,000 limitation.—The aggregate amounts excludable under paragraph (1) with respect to the death of any employee shall not exceed $5,000.

(B) Nonforfeitable rights.—Paragraph (1) shall not apply to amounts with respect to which the employee possessed, immediately before his death, a nonforfeitable right to receive the amounts while living. This subparagraph shall not apply to a lump sum distribution (as defined in section 402(e) (4))—

(i) by a stock bonus, pension, or profit-sharing trust described in section 401(a) which is exempt from tax under section 501(a),

(ii) under an annuity contract under a plan described in section 403(a), or

(iii) under an annuity contract purchased by an employer which is an organization referred to in section 170(b) (1) (A) (ii) or (vi) or which is a religious organization (other than a trust) and which is exempt from tax under section 501(a), but only with respect to that portion of such total distributions payable which bears the same ratio to the amount of such total distributions payable which is (without regard to this subsection) includible in gross income, as the amounts contributed by the employer for such annuity contract which are excludable from gross income under section 403(b) bear to the total amounts contributed by the employer for such annuity contract.

(C) Joint and survivor annuities.—Paragraph (1) shall not apply to amounts received by a surviving annuitant under a joint and survivor's annuity contract after the first day of the first period for which an amount was received as an annuity by the employee (or would have been received if the employee had lived).

(D) Other annuities.—In the case of any amount to which section 72 (relating to annuities, etc.) applies, the amount which is excludable under paragraph (1) (as modified by the preceding subparagraphs of this paragraph) shall be determined by reference to the value of such amount as of the day on which the employee died. Any amount so excludable under paragraph (1) shall, for purposes of section 72, be treated as additional consideration paid by the employee. Paragraph (1) shall not apply in the case of an annuity under chapter 73 of title 10 of the United States Code if the member or former member of the uniformed services by reason of whose death such annuity is payable died after attaining retirement age.

(3) Treatment of self-employed individuals.—For purposes of this subsection—

(A) Self-employed individual not considered employee.—Except as provided in subparagraph (B), the term "employee" does not include a self-employed individual described in section 401(c)(1).

(B) Special rule for certain lump sum distributions.—In the case of any lump sum distribution described in the second sentence of paragraph (2)(B), the term "employee" includes a self-employed individual described in section 401(c)(1).

(c) Interest.—If any amount excluded from gross income by subsection (a) or (b) is held under an agreement to pay interest thereon, the interest payments shall be included in gross income.

(d) Payment of life insurance proceeds at a date later than death.—

(1) General rule.—The amounts held by an insurer with respect to any beneficiary shall be prorated (in accordance with such regulations as may be prescribed by the Secretary) over the period or periods with respect to which such payments are to be made. There shall be excluded from the gross income of such beneficiary in the taxable year received—

(A) any amount determined by such proration, and

(B) in the case of the surviving spouse of the insured, that portion of the excess of the amounts received under one or more agreements specified in paragraph (2) (A) (whether or not payment of any part of such amounts is guaranteed by the insurer) over the amount determined in subparagraph (A) of this paragraph which is not greater than $1,000 with respect to any insured.

Gross incomes includes, to the extent not excluded by the preceding sentence, amounts received under agreements to which this subsection applies.

(2) Amount held by an insurer.—An amount held by an insurer with respect to any beneficiary shall mean an amount to which subsection (a) applies which is—

(A) held by any insurer under an agreement provided for in the life insurance contract, whether as an option or otherwise, to pay such amount on a date or dates later than the death of the insured, and

(B) is equal to the value of such agreement to such beneficiary

(i) as of the date of death of the insured (as if any option exercised under the life insurance contract were exercised at such time), and

(ii) as discounted on the basis of the interest rate and mortality tables used by the insurer in calculating payments under the agreement.

(3) Surviving spouse.—For purposes of this subsection, the term "surviving spouse" means the spouse of the insured as of the date of death, including a spouse legally separated but not under a decree of absolute divorce.

(4) Application of subsection.—This subsection shall not apply to any amount to which subsection (c) is applicable.

(e) Alimony, etc., payments.—

(1) In general.—This section shall not apply to so much of any payment as is includible in the gross income of the wife under section 71 (relating to alimony) or section 682 (relating to income of an estate or trust in case of divorce, etc.).

§ 102. Gifts and inheritances

(a) General rule.—Gross income does not include the value of property acquired by gift, bequest, devise, or inheritance.

(b) Income.—Subsection (a) shall not exclude from gross income—

(1) the income from any property referred to in subsection (a); or

(2) where the gift, bequest, devise, or inheritance is of income from property, the amount of such income.

Where, under the terms of the gift, bequest, devise, or inheritance, the payment, crediting, or distribution thereof is to be made at intervals, then, to the extent that it is paid or credited or to be distributed out of income from property, it shall be treated for purposes of paragraph (2) as a gift, bequest, devise, or inheritance of income from property. Any amount included in the gross income of a beneficiary under subchapter J shall be treated for purposes of paragraph (2) as a gift, bequest, devise, or inheritance of income from property.

§ 103. Interest on certain governmental obligations

(a) General rule.—Gross income does not include interest on—

(1) the obligations of a State, a Territory, or a possession of the United States, or any political subdivision of any of the foregoing, or of the District of Columbia; and

(2) qualified scholarship funding bonds.

(b) Industrial development bonds.—

(1) Subsection (a) (1) or (2) not to apply.—Except as otherwise provided in this subsection, any industrial development bond shall be treated as an obligation not described in subsection (a) (1) or (2).

(2) Industrial development bond.—For purposes of this section, the term "industrial development bond" means any obligation—

(A) which is issued as part of an issue all or a major portion of the proceeds of which are to be used directly or indirectly in any trade or business carried on by any person who is not an exempt person (within the meaning of paragraph (3)), and

(B) the payment of the principal or interest on which (under the terms of such obligation or any underlying arrangement) is, in whole or in major part—

(i) secured by any interest in property used or to be used in a trade or business or in payments in respect of such property, or

(ii) to be derived from payments in respect of property, or borrowed money, used or to be used in a trade or business.

(3) Exempt person.—For purposes of paragraph (2) (A), the term "exempt person" means—

(A) a governmental unit, or

(B) an organization described in section 501(c) (3) and exempt from tax under section 501(a) (but only with respect to a trade or business carried on by such organization which is not an unrelated trade or business, determined by applying section 513(a) to such organization).

. . . .

(5) Industrial parks.—Paragraph (1) shall not apply to any obligation issued as part of an issue substantially all of the proceeds of which are to be used for the acquisition or development of land as the site for an industrial park. For purposes of the preceding sentence, the term "development of land" includes the provision of water, sewage, drainage, or similar facilities, or of transportation, power, or communication facilities, which are incidental to use of the site as an industrial park, but, except with respect to such facilities, does not include the provision of structures or buildings.

(6) Exemption for certain small issues.—

    (A) In general.—Paragraph (1) shall not apply to any obligation issued as part of an issue the aggregate authorized face amount of which is $1,000,000 or less and substantially all of the proceeds of which are to be used (i) for the acquisition, construction, reconstruction, or improvement of land or property of a character subject to the allowance for depreciation, or (ii) to redeem part or all of a prior issue which was issued for purposes described in clause (i) or this clause.

. . . .

(j) Obligations must be in registered form to be tax-exempt.—

(1) In general.—Nothing in subsection (a) or in any other provision of law shall be construed to provide an exemption from Federal income tax for Interest on any registration-required obligation unless the obligation is in registered form.

(2) Registration-required obligation.—The term "registration-required obligation" means any obligation other than an obligation which—

    (A) is not of a type offered to the public,

    (B) has a maturity (at issue) of not more than 1 year, or

    (C) is described in section 163(f)(2)(B).

(3) Special rules.—

    (A) Book entries permitted.—For purposes of paragraph (1), a book entry obligation shall be treated as in registered form if the right to the principal of, and stated interest on, such obligation may be transferred only through a book entry consistent with regulations prescribed by the Secretary.

    (B) Nominees.—The Secretary shall prescribe such regulations as may be necessary to carry out the purpose of paragraph (1) where there is a nominee or chain of nominees.

(k) Public approval for industrial development bonds.—

(1) In general.—Notwithstanding subsection (b), an industrial development bond shall be treated as an obligation not described in subsection (a) unless the requirements of paragraph (2) of this subsection are satisfied.

(2) Public approval requirement.—

    (A) In general.—An obligation shall satisfy the requirements of this paragraph if such obligation is issued as a part of an issue which has been approved by—

        (i) the governmental unit—

            (I) which issued such obligation, or

            (II) on behalf of which such obligation was issued, and

(ii) each governmental unit having jurisdiction over the area in which any facility, with respect to which financing is to be provided from the proceeds of such issue, is located (except that if more than 1 governmental unit within a State has jurisdiction over the entire area within such State in which such facility is located, only 1 such unit need approve such issue).

(B) Approval by a governmental unit.—For purposes of subparagraph (A), an issue shall be treated as having been approved by any governmental unit if such issue is approved—

(i) by the applicable elected representative of such governmental unit after a public hearing following reasonable public notice, or

(ii) by voter referendum of such governmental unit.

(C) Special rules for approval of facility.—If there has been public approval under subparagraph (A) of the plan of financing a facility, such approval shall constitute approval under subparagraph (A) for any issue—

(i) which is issued pursuant to such plan within 3 years after the date of the first issue pursuant to the approval, and

(ii) all or substantially all of the proceeds of which are to be used to finance such facility or to refund previous financing under such plan.

(D) Refunding obligations.—No approval under subparagraph (A) shall be necessary with respect to any obligation which is issued to refund an obligation approved under subparagraph (A) (or treated as approved under subparagraph (C)) unless the maturity date of such obligation is later than the maturity date of the obligation to be refunded.

(E) Applicable elected representative.—For purposes of this paragraph—

(i) In general.—The term "applicable elected representative" means with respect to any governmental unit—

(I) an elected legislative body of such unit, or

(II) the chief elected executive officer, the chief elected State legal officer of the executive branch, or any other elected official of such unit designated for purposes of this paragraph by such chief elected executive officer or by State law.

(ii) No applicable elected representative.—If (but for this clause) a governmental unit has no applicable elected representative, the applicable elected representative for purposes of clause (i) shall be the applicable elected representative of the governmental unit—

(I) which is the next higher governmental unit with such a representative, and

(II) from which the authority of the governmental unit with no such representative is derived.

(*l***) Information reporting requirements for certain bonds.**—

(1) In general.—Notwithstanding subsection (b), any industrial development bond or any other obligation which is issued as part of an issue all or a major portion of the proceeds of which are to be used directly or indirectly—

(A) to finance loans to individuals for educational expenses, or

(B) by an organization described in section 501(c)(3) which is exempt from taxation by reason of section 501(a),

shall be treated as an obligation not described in paragraph (1) or (2) of subsection (a) unless such bond satisfies the requirements of paragraph (2).

(2) **Information reporting requirement.**—An obligation satisfies the requirement of this paragraph if the issuer submits to the Secretary, not later than the 15th day of the 2nd calendar month after the close of the calendar quarter in which the obligation is issued, a statement concerning the issue of which the obligation is a part which contains—

(A) the name and address of the issuer,

(B) the date of issue, the amount of lendable proceeds of the issue, and the stated interest rate, term, and face amount of each obligation which is part of the issue,

(C) where required, the name of the applicable elected representative who approved the issue, or a description of the voter referendum by which the issue was approved,

(D) the name, address, and employer identification number of—

(i) each initial principal user of any facilities provided with the proceeds of the issue,

(ii) the common parent of any affiliated group of corporations (within the meaning of section 1504(a)) of which such initial principal user is a member and

(iii) if the issue is treated as a separate issue under subsection (b)(6)(K), any person treated as a principal user under subsection (b)(6)(L), and

(E) a description of any property to be financed from the proceeds of the issue.

(3) **Extension of time.**—The Secretary may grant an extension of time for the filing of any statement required under paragraph (2) if there is reasonable cause for the failure to file such statement in a timely fashion.

. . . . .

§ 104.   Compensation for injuries or sickness

(a) **In general.**—Except in the case of amounts attributable to (and not in excess of) deductions allowed under section 213 (relating to medical, etc., expenses) for any prior taxable year, gross income does not include—

(1) amounts received under workmen's compensation acts as compensation for personal injuries or sickness;

(2) the amount of any damages received (whether by suit or agreement) on account of personal injuries or sickness;

(3) amounts received through accident or health insurance for personal injuries or sickness (other than amounts received by an employee, to the extent such amounts (A) are attributable to contributions by the employer which were not includible in the gross income of the employee, or (B) are paid by the employer);

(4) amounts received as a pension, annuity, or similar allowance for personal injuries or sickness resulting from active service in the armed forces

of any country or in the Coast and Geodetic Survey or the Public Health Service, or as a disability annuity payable under the provisions of section 808 of the Foreign Service Act of 1980; and

(5) amounts received by an individual as disability income attributable to injuries incurred as a direct result of a violent attack which the Secretary of State determines to be a terrorist attack and which occurred while such individual was an employee of the United States engaged in the performance of his official duties outside the United States.

For purposes of paragraph (3), in the case of an individual who is, or has been, an employee within the meaning of section 401(c) (1) (relating to self-employed individuals), contributions made on behalf of such individual while he was such an employee to a trust described in section 401(a) which is exempt from tax under section 501(a), or under a plan described in section 403(a), shall, to the extent allowed as deductions under section 404, be treated as contributions by the employer which were not includible in the gross income of the employee.

(b) Termination of application of subsection (a) (4) in certain cases.—

(1) In general.—Subsection (a) (4) shall not apply in the case of any individual who is not described in paragraph (2).

(2) Individuals to whom subsection (a) (4) continues to apply.—An individual is described in this paragraph if—

(A) on or before September 24, 1975, he was entitled to receive any amount described in subsection (a) (4),

(B) on September 24, 1975, he was a member of any organization (or reserve component thereof) referred to in subsection (a) (4) or under a binding written commitment to become such a member,

(C) he receives an amount described in subsection (a) (4) by reason of a combat-related injury, or

(D) on application therefor, he would be entitled to receive disability compensation from the Veterans' Administration.

(4) Amount excluded to be not less than veterans' disability compensation.—In the case of any individual described in paragraph (2), the amounts excludable under subsection (a) (4) for any period with respect to any individual shall not be less than the maximum amount which such individual, on application therefor, would be entitled to receive as disability compensation from the Veterans' Administration.

. . . .

§ 105.   Amounts received under accident and health plans

(a) Amounts attributable to employer contributions.—Except as otherwise provided in this section, amounts received by an employee through accident or health insurance for personal injuries or sickness shall be included in gross income to the extent such amounts (1) are attributable to contributions by the employer which were not includible in the gross income of the employee, or (2) are paid by the employer.

(b) Amounts expended for medical care.—Except in the case of amounts attributable to (and not in excess of) deductions allowed under section 213 (relating to medical, etc., expenses) for any prior taxable year, gross income does not include amounts referred to in subsection (a) if such amounts are paid, directly or indirectly, to the taxpayer to reimburse the taxpayer for expenses incurred by him for the medical care (as defined in section 213(d)) of the taxpayer, his spouse, and his dependents (as defined in section 152).

(c) Payments unrelated to absence from work.—Gross income does not include amounts referred to in subsection (a) to the extent such amounts—

(1) constitute payment for the permanent loss or loss of use of a member or function of the body, or the permanent disfigurement, of the taxpayer, his spouse, or a dependent (as defined in section 152), and

(2) are computed with reference to the nature of the injury without regard to the period the employee is absent from work.

(d) Certain disability payments.—

(1) In general.—In the case of a taxpayer who—

(A) has not attained age 65 before the close of the taxable year, and

(B) retired on disability and, when he retired, was permanently and totally disabled,

gross income does not include amounts referred to in subsection (a) if such amounts constitute wages or payments in lieu of wages for a period during which the employee is absent from work on account of permanent and total disability.

(2) Limitation.—This subsection shall not apply to the extent that the amounts referred to in paragraph (1) exceed a weekly rate of $100.

(3) Phaseout over $15,000.—If the adjusted gross income of the taxpayer for the taxable year (determined without regard to this subsection and section 221) exceeds $15,000, the amount which but for this paragraph would be excluded under this subsection for the taxable year shall be reduced by an amount equal to the excess of the adjusted gross income (as so determined) over $15,000.

(4) Permanent and total disability defined.—For purposes of this subsection, an individual is permanently and totally disabled if he is unable to engage in any substantial gainful activity by reason of any medically determinable physical or mental impairment which can be expected to result in death or which has lasted or can be expected to last for a continuous period of not less than 12 months. An individual shall not be considered to be permanently and totally disabled unless he furnishes proof of the existence thereof in such form and manner, and at such times, as the Secretary may require.

(5) Special rules for married couples.—

(A) Married couple must file joint return.—Except in the case of a husband and wife who live apart at all times during the taxable year, if the taxpayer is married at the close of the taxable year, the exclusion provided by this subsection shall be allowed only if the taxpayer and his spouse file a joint return for the taxable year.

(B) Application of paragraphs (2) and (3).—In the case of a joint return—

(i) paragraph (2) shall be applied separately with respect to each spouse, but

(ii) paragraph (3) shall be applied with respect to their combined adjusted gross income.

(C) Determination of marital status.—For purposes of this subsection, marital status shall be determined under section 143(a).

(D) Joint return defined.—For purposes of this subsection, the term "joint return" means the joint return of a husband and wife made under section 6013.

(6) Coordination with section 72.—In the case of an individual described in subparagraphs (A) and (B) of paragraph (1), for purposes of section 72 the annuity starting date shall not be deemed to occur before the beginning of the taxable year in which the taxpayer attains age 65, or before the beginning of an earlier taxable year for which the taxpayer makes an irrevocable election not to seek the benefits of this subsection for such year and all subsequent years.

(e) Accident and health plans.—For purposes of this section and section 104—

(1) amounts received under an accident or health plan for employees, and

(2) amounts received from a sickness and disability fund for employees maintained under the law of a State or the District of Columbia,

shall be treated as amounts received through accident or health insurance.

(f) Rules for application of section 213.—For purposes of section 213(a) (relating to medical, dental, etc., expenses) amounts excluded from gross income under subsection (c) or (d) shall not be considered as compensation (by insurance or otherwise) for expenses paid for medical care.

(g) Self-employed individual not considered an employee.—For purposes of this section, the term "employee" does not include an individual who is an employee within the meaning of section 401(c) (1) (relating to self-employed individuals).

(h) Amount paid to highly compensated individuals under a discriminatory self-insured medical expense reimbursement plan.—

(1) In general.—In the case of amounts paid to a highly compensated individual under a self-insured medical reimbursement plan which does not satisfy the requirements of paragraph (2) for a plan year, subsection (b) shall not apply to such amounts to the extent they constitute an excess reimbursement of such highly compensated individual.

(2) Prohibition of discrimination.—A self-insured medical reimbursement plan satisfies the requirements of this paragraph only if—

(A) the plan does not discriminate in favor of highly compensated individuals as to eligibility to participate; and

(B) the benefits provided under the plan do not discriminate in favor of participants who are highly compensated individuals.

(3) Nondiscriminatory eligibility classifications.—

(A) **In general.**—A self-insured medical reimbursement plan does not satisfy the requirements of subparagraph (A) of paragraph (2) unless such plan benefits—

(i) 70 percent or more of all employees, or 80 percent or more of all the employees who are eligible to benefit under the plan if 70 percent or more of all employees are eligible to benefit under the plan; or

(ii) such employees as qualify under a classification set up by the employer and found by the Secretary not to be discriminatory in favor of highly compensated individuals.

(B) **Exclusion of certain employees.**—For purposes of subparagraph (A), there may be excluded from consideration—

(i) employees who have not completed 3 years of service;

(ii) employees who have not attained age 25;

(iii) part-time or seasonal employees;

(iv) employees not included in the plan who are included in a unit of employees covered by an agreement between employee representatives and one or more employers which the Secretary finds to be a collective bargaining agreement, if accident and health benefits were the subject of good faith bargaining between such employee representatives and such employer or employers; and

(v) employees who are nonresident aliens and who receive no earned income (within the meaning of section 911(d)(2)) from the employer which constitutes income from sources within the United States (within the meaning of section 861(a) (3)).

(4) Nondiscriminatory benefits.—A self-insured medical reimbursement plan does not meet the requirements of subparagraph (B) of paragraph (2) unless all benefits provided for participants who are highly compensated individuals are provided for all other participants.

(5) Highly compensated individual defined.—For purposes of this subsection, the term "highly compensated individual" means an individual who is—

(A) one of the 5 highest paid officers,

(B) a shareholder who owns (with the application of section 318) more than 10 percent in value of the stock of the employer, or

(C) among the highest paid 25 percent of all employees (other than employees described in paragraph (3) (B) who are not participants).

(6) Self-insured medical reimbursement plan.—The term "self-insured medical reimbursement plan" means a plan of an employer to reimburse employees for expenses referred to in subsection (b) for which reimbursement is not provided under a policy of accident and health insurance.

(7) Excess reimbursement of highly compensated individual.—For purposes of this section, the excess reimbursement of a highly compensated individual which is attributable to a self-insured medical reimbursement plan is—

(A) in the case of a benefit available to highly compensated individuals but not to all other participants (or which otherwise fails to satisfy the requirements of paragraph (2)(B)), the amount reimbursed under the plan to the employee with respect to such benefit, and

(B) in the case of benefits ([1] other than benefits described in subparagraph (A) paid to a highly compensated individual by a plan which fails to satisfy the requirements of paragraph (2), the total amount reimbursed to the highly compensated individual for the plan year multiplied by a fraction—

(i) the numerator of which is the total amount reimbursed to all participants who are highly compensated individuals under the plan for the plan year, and

(ii) the denominator of which is the total amount reimbursed to all employees under the plan for such plan year.

In determining the fraction under subparagraph (B), there shall not be taken into account any reimbursement which is attributable to a benefit described in subparagraph (A).

(8) Certain controlled groups, etc.—All employees who are treated as employed by a single employer under subsection (b), (c), or (m) of section 414 shall be treated as employed by a single employer for purposes of this section.

(9) Regulations.—The Secretary shall prescribe such regulations as may be necessary to carry out the provisions of this section.

(10) Time of inclusion.—Any amount paid for a plan year that is included in income by reason of this subsection shall be treated as received or accrued in the taxable year of the participant in which the plan year ends.

1 So in original. No closing parenthesis.

§ 106. Contributions by employer to accident and health plans

Gross income does not include contributions by the employer to accident or health plans for compensation (through insurance or otherwise) to his employees for personal injuries or sickness.

§ 107. Rental value of parsonages

In the case of a minister of the gospel, gross income does not include—

(1) the rental value of a home furnished to him as part of his compensation; or

(2) the rental allowance paid to him as part of his compensation, to the extent used by him to rent or provide a home.

§ 108. Income from discharge of indebtedness

(a) Exclusion from gross income.—

(1) In general.—Gross income does not include any amount which (but for this subsection) would be includible in gross income by reason of the discharge (in whole or in part) of indebtedness of the taxpayer if—

(A) the discharge occurs in a title 11 case,

(B) the discharge occurs when the taxpayer is insolvent, or

(C) the indebtedness discharged is qualified business indebtedness.

(2) Coordination of exclusions.—

(A) Title 11 exclusion takes precedence.—Subparagraphs (B) and (C) of paragraph (1) shall not apply to a discharge which occurs in a title 11 case.

(B) Insolvency exclusion takes precedence over qualified business exclusion.—Subparagraph (C) of paragraph (1) shall not apply to a discharge to the extent that the taxpayer is insolvent.

(3) Insolvency exclusion limited to amount of insolvency.—In the case of a discharge to which paragraph (1)(B) applies, the amount excluded under paragraph (1)(B) shall not exceed the amount by which the taxpayer is insolvent.

(b) Reduction of tax attributes in title 11 case or insolvency.—

(1) In general.—The amount excluded from gross income under subparagraph (A) or (B) of subsection (a)(1) shall be applied to reduce the tax attributes of the taxpayer as provided in paragraph (2).

(2) Tax attributes affected; order of reduction.—Except as provided in paragraph (5), the reduction referred to in paragraph (1) shall be made in the following tax attributes in the following order:

(A) NOL.—Any net operating loss for the taxable year of the discharge, and any net operating loss carryover to such taxable year.

(B) **Certain credit carryovers.**—Any carryover to or from the taxable year of the discharge of an amount for purposes of determining the amount of a credit allowable under—

(i) section 38 (relating to investment in certain depreciable property),

(ii) section 40 (relating to expenses of work incentive programs),

(iii) section 44B (relating to credit for employment of certain new employees), or

(iv) section 44E (relating to alcohol used as a fuel).

For purposes of clause (i), there shall not be taken into account any portion of a carryover which is attributable to the employee plan credit (within the meaning of section 48(*o*)(3)).

(C) **Capital loss carryovers.**—Any net capital loss for the taxable year of the discharge, and any capital loss carryover to such taxable year under section 1212.

(D) **Basis reduction.**—

(i) **In general.**—The basis of the property of the taxpayer.

. . . . .

(3) Amount of reduction.—

(A) **In general.**—Except as provided in subparagraph (B), the reductions described in paragraph (2) shall be one dollar for each dollar excluded by subsection (a).

(B) **Credit carryover reduction.**—The reductions described in subparagraphs (B) and (E) of paragraph (2) shall be 50 cents for each dollar excluded by subsection (a).

(4) Ordering rules.—

(A) **Reductions made after determination of tax for year.**—The reductions described in paragraph (2) shall be made after the determination of the tax imposed by this chapter for the taxable year of the discharge.

(B) **Reductions under subparagraph (A) or (C) of paragraph (2).**—The reductions described in subparagraph (A) or (C) of paragraph (2) (as the case may be) shall be made first in the loss for the taxable year of the discharge and then in the carryovers to such taxable year in the order of the taxable years from which each such carryover arose.

(C) **Reductions under subparagraphs (B) and (E) of paragraph (2).**—The reductions described in subparagraphs (B) and (E) of paragraph (2) shall be made in the order in which carryovers are taken into account under this chapter for the taxable year of the discharge.

(5) Election to apply reduction first against depreciable property.—

(A) **In general.**—The taxpayer may elect to apply any portion of the reduction referred to in paragraph (1) to the reduction under section 1017 of the basis of the depreciable property of the taxpayer.

(B) **Limitation.**—The amount to which an election under subparagraph (A) applies shall not exceed the aggregate adjusted bases of the depreciable property held by the taxpayer as of the beginning of the taxable year following the taxable year in which the discharge occurs.

(C) Other tax attributes not reduced.—Paragraph (2) shall not apply to any amount to which an election under this paragraph applies.

(c) Tax treatment of discharge of qualified business indebtedness.—In the case of a discharge of qualified business indebtedness—

(1) Basis reduction.—

(A) In general.—The amount excluded from gross income under subparagraph (C) of subsection (a)(1) shall be applied to reduce the basis of the depreciable property of the taxpayer.

. . . . .

(2) Limitation.—The amount excluded under subparagraph (C) of subsection (a)(1) shall not exceed the aggregate adjusted bases of the depreciable property held by the taxpayer as of the beginning of the taxable year following the taxable year in which the discharge occurs (determined after any reductions under subsection (b)).

(d) Meaning of terms; special rules relating to subsections (a), (b), and (c).—

(1) Indebtedness of taxpayer.—For purposes of this section, the term "indebtedness of the taxpayer" means any indebtedness—

(A) for which the taxpayer is liable, or

(B) subject to which the taxpayer holds property.

(2) Title 11 case.—For purposes of this section, the term "title 11 case" means a case under title 11 of the United States Code (relating to bankruptcy), but only if the taxpayer is under the jurisdiction of the court in such case and the discharge of indebtedness is granted by the court or is pursuant to a plan approved by the court.

(3) Insolvent.—For purposes of this section, the term "insolvent" means the excess of liabilities over the fair market value of assets. With respect to any discharge, whether or not the taxpayer is insolvent, and the amount by which the taxpayer is insolvent, shall be determined on the basis of the taxpayer's assets and liabilities immediately before the discharge.

(4) Qualified business indebtedness.—Indebtedness of the taxpayer shall be treated as qualified business indebtedness if (and only if)—

(A) the indebtedness was incurred or assumed—

(i) by a corporation, or

(ii) by an individual in connection with property used in his trade or business, and

(B) such taxpayer makes an election under this paragraph with respect to such indebtedness.

(5) Depreciable property.—The term "depreciable property" has the same meaning as when used in section 1017.

(6) Subsections (a), (b), and (c) to be applied at partner level or S corporation shareholder level.—In the case of a partnership, subsections (a), (b), and (c) shall be applied at the partner level. In the case of an S corporation, subsections (a), (b), and (c) shall be applied at the shareholder level.

(7) Reductions of tax attributes in title 11 cases of individuals to be made by estate.—In any case under chapter 7 or 11 of title 11 of the United States Code to which section 1398 applies, for purposes of paragraphs (1) and (5) of subsection (b) the estate (and not the individual) shall be treated as the taxpayer. The preceding sentence shall not apply for purposes of applying section 1017 to property transferred by the estate to the individual.

(8) Time for making election, etc.—

(A) Time.—An election under paragraph (4) of this subsection or under paragraph (5) of subsection (b) shall be made on the taxpayer's return for the taxable year in which the discharge occurs or at such other time as may be permitted in regulations prescribed by the Secretary.

(B) Revocation only with consent.—An election referred to in subparagraph (A), once made, may be revoked only with the consent of the Secretary.

(C) Manner.—An election referred to in subparagraph (A) shall be made in such manner as the Secretary may by regulations prescribe.

. . . . .

(e) General rules for discharge of indebtedness (including discharges not in title 11 cases or insolvency).—For purposes of this title—

(1) No other insolvency exception.—Except as otherwise provided in this section, there shall be no insolvency exception from the general rule that gross income includes income from the discharge of indebtedness.

(2) Income not realized to extent of lost deductions.—No income shall be realized from the discharge of indebtedness to the extent that payment of the liability would have given rise to a deduction.

(3) Adjustments for unamortized premium and discount.—The amount taken into account with respect to any discharge shall be properly adjusted for unamortized premium and unamortized discount with respect to the indebtedness discharged.

(4) Acquisition of indebtedness by person related to debtor.—

(A) Treated as acquisition by debtor.—For purposes of determining income of the debtor from discharge of indebtedness, to the extent provided in regulations prescribed by the Secretary, the acquisition of outstanding indebtedness by a person bearing a relationship to the debtor specified in section 267(b) or 707(b)(1) from a person who does not bear such a relationship to the debtor shall be treated as the acquisition of such indebtedness by the debtor. Such regulations shall provide for such adjustments in the treatment of any subsequent transactions involving the indebtedness as may be appropriate by reason of the application of the preceding sentence.

(B) Members of family.—For purposes of this paragraph, sections 267(b) and 707(b)(1) shall be applied as if section 267(c)(4) provided that the family of an individual consists of the individual's spouse, the individual's children, grandchildren, and parents, and any spouse of the individual's children or grandchildren.

(C) Entities under common control treated as related.—For purposes of this paragraph, two entities which are treated as a single employer under subsection (b) or (c) of section 414 shall be treated as bearing a relationship to each other which is described in section 267(b).

(5) Purchase-money debt reduction for solvent debtor treated as price reduction.—If—

(A) the debt of a purchaser of property to the seller of such property which arose out of the purchase of such property is reduced,

(B) such reduction does not occur—

(i) in a title 11 case, or

(ii) when the purchaser is insolvent, and

(C) but for this paragraph, such reduction would be treated as income to the purchaser from the discharge of indebtedness,

then such reduction shall be treated as a purchase price adjustment.

(6) Indebtedness contributed to capital.—For purposes of determining income of the debtor from discharge of indebtedness, if a debtor corporation acquires its indebtedness from a shareholder as a contribution to capital—

(A) section 118 shall not apply, but

(B) such corporation shall be treated as having satisfied the indebtedness with an amount of money equal to the shareholder's adjusted basis in the indebtedness.

(7) Recapture of gain on subsequent sale of stock.—

(A) **In general.**—If a creditor acquires stock of a debtor corporation in satisfaction of such corporation's indebtedness, for purposes of section 1245—

(i) such stock (and any other property the basis of which is determined in whole or in part by reference to the adjusted basis of such stock) shall be treated as section 1245 property, and

(ii) the aggregate amount allowed to the creditor—

(I) as deductions under subsection (a), (b), or (c) of section 166 (by reason of the worthlessness or partial worthlessness of the indebtedness), or

(II) as an ordinary loss on the exchange,

shall be treated as an amount allowed as a deduction for depreciation.

The amount determined under clause (ii) shall be reduced by the amount (if any) included in the creditor's gross income on the exchange.

(B) **Taxpayers on reserve method.**—In the case of a taxpayer to whom subsection (c) of section 166 (relating to reserve for bad debts) applies, the amount determined under clause (ii) of subparagraph (A) shall be the aggregate charges to the reserve resulting from the worthlessness or partial worthlessness of the indebtedness.

(C) **Special rule for cash basis taxpayers.**—In the case of any creditor who computes his taxable income under the cash receipts and disbursements method, proper adjustment shall be made in the amount taken into account under clause (ii) of subparagraph (A) for any amount which was not included in the creditor's gross income but which would have been included in such gross income if such indebtedness had been satisfied in full.

(D) **Stock of parent corporation.**—For purposes of this paragraph, stock of a corporation in control (within the meaning of section 368(c)) of the debtor corporation shall be treated as stock of the debtor corporation.

(E) **Treatment of successor corporation.**—For purposes of this paragraph, the term "debtor corporation" includes a successor corporation.

(F) **Partnership rule.**—Under regulations prescribed by the Secretary, rules similar to the rules of subparagraphs (A), (B), (C), (D), and (E) of this paragraph shall apply with respect to the indebtedness of a partnership.

(8) **Stock for debt exception not to apply in de minimis cases.**—For purposes of determining income of the debtor from discharge of indebtedness, the stock for debt exception shall not apply—

(A) to the issuance of nominal or token shares, or

(B) with respect to an unsecured creditor, where the ratio of the value of the stock received by such unsecured creditor to the amount of his indebtedness cancelled or exchanged for stock in the workout is less than 50 percent of a similar ratio computed for all unsecured creditors participating in the workout.

. . . . .

§ 109. Improvements by lessee on lessor's property

Gross income does not include income (other than rent) derived by a lessor of real property on the termination of a lease, representing the value of such property attributable to buildings erected or other improvements made by the lessee.

§ 111. Recovery of bad debts, prior taxes, and delinquency amounts

(a) **General rule.**—Gross income does not include income attributable to the recovery during the taxable year of a bad debt, prior tax, or delinquency amount, to the extent of the amount of the recovery exclusion with respect to such debt, tax, or amount.

(b) **Definitions.**—For purposes of subsection (a)—

(1) **Bad debt.**—The term "bad debt" means a debt on account of the worthlessness or partial worthlessness of which a deduction was allowed for a prior taxable year.

(2) **Prior tax.**—The term "prior tax" means a tax on account of which a deduction or credit was allowed for a prior taxable year.

(3) **Delinquency amount.**—The term "delinquency amount" means an amount paid or accrued on account of which a deduction or credit was allowed for a prior taxable year and which is attributable to failure to file return with respect to a tax, or pay a tax, within the time required by the law under which the tax is imposed, or to failure to file return with respect to a tax or pay a tax.

(4) **Recovery exclusion.**—The term "recovery exclusion", with respect to a bad debt, prior tax, or delinquency amount, means the amount, determined in

accordance with regulations prescribed by the Secretary, of the deductions or credits allowed, on account of such bad debt, prior tax, or delinquency amount, which did not result in a reduction of the taxpayer's tax under this subtitle (not including the accumulated earnings tax imposed by section 531 or the tax on personal holding companies imposed by section 541) or corresponding provisions of prior income tax laws (other than subchapter E of chapter 2 of the Internal Revenue Code of 1939, relating to World War II excess profits tax), reduced by the amount excludable in previous taxable years with respect to such debt, tax, or amount under this section.

(c) **Special rules for accumulated earnings tax and for personal holding company tax.**—In applying subsections (a) and (b) for the purpose of determining the accumulated earnings tax under section 531 or the tax under section 541 (relating to personal holding companies)—

(1) a recovery exclusion allowed for purposes of this subtitle (other than section 531 or section 541) shall be allowed whether or not the bad debt, prior tax, or delinquency amount resulted in a reduction of the tax under section 531 or the tax under section 541 for the prior taxable year; and

(2) where a bad debt, prior tax, or delinquency amount was not allowable as a deduction or credit for the prior taxable year for purposes of this subtitle other than of section 531 or section 541 but was allowable for the same taxable year under section 531 or section 541, then a recovery exclusion shall be allowable if such bad debt, prior tax, or delinquency amount did not result in a reduction of the tax under section 531 or the tax under section 541.

(d) **Increase in carryover treated as yielding tax benefit.**—For purposes of paragraph (4) of subsection (b), an increase in a carryover which has not expired shall be treated as a reduction in tax.

§ 113.   Mustering-out payments for members of the Armed Forces

Gross income does not include amounts received during the taxable year as mustering-out payments with respect to service in the Armed Forces of the United States.

§ 115.   Income of states, municipalities, etc.

Gross income does not include—

(1) income derived from any public utility or the exercise of any essential governmental function and accruing to a State or any political subdivision thereof, or the District of Columbia; or

(2) income accruing to the government of any possession of the United States, or any political subdivision thereof.

§ 116.   Partial exclusion of dividends received by individuals

(a) **Exclusion from gross income.**—

(1) **In general.**—Gross income does not include amounts received by an individual as dividends from domestic corporations.

(2) **Maximum dollar amount.**—The aggregate amount excluded under subsection (a) for any taxable year shall not exceed $100 ($200 in the case of a joint return under section 6013).

. . . . .

§ 117.   Scholarships and fellowship grants

(a) General rule.—In the case of an individual, gross income does not include—

    (1) any amount received—

        (A) as a scholarship at an educational organization described in section 170(b) (1) (A) (ii), or

        (B) as a fellowship grant,

including the value of contributed services and accommodations; and

    (2) any amount received to cover expenses for—

        (A) travel,

        (B) research,

        (C) clerical help, or

        (D) equipment,

which are incident to such a scholarship or to a fellowship grant, but only to the extent that the amount is so expended by the recipient.

(b) Limitations.—

    (1) Individuals who are candidates for degrees.—In the case of an individual who is a candidate for a degree at an educational organization described in section 170(b) (1) (A) (ii), subsection (a) shall not apply to that portion of any amount received which represents payment for teaching, research, or other services in the nature of part-time employment required as a condition to receiving the scholarship or the fellowship grant. If teaching, research, or other services are required of all candidates (whether or not recipients of scholarships or fellowship grants) for a particular degree as a condition to receiving such degree, such teaching, research, or other services shall not be regarded as part-time employment within the meaning of this paragraph.

    (2) Individuals who are not candidates for degrees.—In the case of an individual who is not a candidate for a degree at an educational organization described in section 170(b) (1) (A) (ii), subsection (a) shall apply only if the condition in subparagraph (A) is satisfied and then only within the limitations provided in subparagraph (B).

        (A) Conditions for exclusion.—The grantor of the scholarship or fellowship grant is—

            (i) an organization described in section 501(c) (3) which is exempt from tax under section 501(a),

            (ii) a foreign government,

            (iii) an international organization, or a binational or multinational educational and cultural foundation or commission created or continued pursuant to the Mutual Educational and Cultural Exchange Act of 1961, or

            (iv) the United States, or an instrumentality or agency thereof, or a State, or a possession of the United States, or any political subdivision thereof, or the District of Columbia.

        (B) Extent of exclusion.—The amount of the scholarship or fellowship grant excluded under subsection (a) (1) in any taxable year shall be limited to an amount equal to $300 times the number of months for which the recipient received amounts under the scholarship or fellowship grant during such taxable year, except that no exclusion shall be allowed under subsection (a) after the recipient has been entitled to exclude under this section for a period of 36 months (whether or not consecutive) amounts received as a scholarship or fellowship grant while not a candidate for a degree at an educational organization described in section 170(b) (1) (A) (ii).

(c) Federal grants for tuition and related expenses not includable merely because there is requirement of future service as federal employee.—

    (1) In general.—If—

      (A) an amount received by an individual under a Federal program would be excludable under subsections (a) and (b) as a scholarship or fellowship grant but for the fact that the individual is required to perform future service as a Federal employee, and

      (B) the individual establishes that, in accordance with the terms of the grant, such amount was used for qualified tuition and related expenses,

gross income shall not include such amount.

    (2) Qualified tuition and related expenses defined.—For purposes of this subsection—

      (A) In general.—The term "qualified tuition and related expenses" means—

        (i) tuition and fees required for the enrollment or attendance of a student at an institution of higher education, and

        (ii) fees, books, supplies, and equipment required for courses of instruction at an institution of higher education.

      (B) Institution of higher education.—The term "institution of higher education" means an educational institution in any State which—

        (i) admits as regular students only individuals having a certificate of graduation from a high school, or the recognized equivalent of such a certificate,

        (ii) is legally authorized within such State to provide a program of education beyond high school,

        (iii) provides an educational program for which it awards a bachelor's or higher degree, provides a program which is acceptable for full credit toward such a degree, or offers a program of training to prepare students for gainful employment in a recognized health profession, and

        (iv) is a public or other nonprofit institution.

    (3) Service as Federal employee.—For purposes of this subsection, service in a health manpower shortage area shall be treated as service as a Federal employee.

§ 118.   Contributions to the capital of a corporation

    (a) General rule.—In the case of a corporation, gross income does not include any contribution to the capital of the taxpayer.

    (b) Contributions in aid of construction.—

    (1) General rule.—For purposes of this section, the term "contribution to the capital of the taxpayer" includes any amount of money or other property received from any person (whether or not a shareholder) by a regulated public utility which provides electric energy, gas (through a local distribution system or transportation by pipeline), water, or sewerage disposal services if—

(A) such amount is a contribution in aid of construction,

(B) where the contribution is in property which is other than electric energy, gas, steam, water, or sewerage disposal facilities, such amount meets the requirements of the expenditure rule of paragraph (2), and

(C) such amounts (or any property acquired or constructed with such amounts) are not included in the taxpayer's rate base for rate-making purposes.

(2) **Expenditure rule.**—An amount meets the requirements of this paragraph if—

(A) an amount equal to such amount is expended for the acquisition or construction of tangible property described in section 1231(b)—

(i) which was the purpose motivating the contribution, and

(ii) which is used predominantly in the trade or business of furnishing electric energy, gas, steam, water, or sewerage disposal services,

(B) the expenditure referred to in subparagraph (A) occurs before the end of the second taxable year after the year in which such amount was received, and

(C) accurate records are kept of the amounts contributed and expenditures made on the basis of the project for which the contribution was made and on the basis of the year of contribution or expenditure.

(3) **Definitions.**—For purposes of this section—

(A) **Contribution in aid of construction.**—The term "contribution in aid of construction" shall be defined by regulations prescribed by the Secretary; except that such term shall not include amounts paid as customer connection fees (including amounts paid to connect the customer's line to an electric line, a gas main, a steam line, or a main water or sewer line and amounts paid as service charges for starting or stopping services).

(B) **Predominantly.**—The term "predominantly" means 80 percent or more.

. . . .

(4) **Disallowance of deductions and investment credit; adjusted basis.** —Notwithstanding any other provision of this subtitle, no deduction or credit shall be allowed for, or by reason of, the expenditure which constitutes a contribution in aid of construction to which this subsection applies. The adjusted basis of any property acquired with contributions in aid of construction to which this subsection applies shall be zero.

. . . .

§ 119.   Meals or lodging furnished for the convenience of the employer

(a) **Meals and lodging furnished to employee, his spouse, and his dependents, pursuant to employment.**—There shall be excluded from gross income of an employee the value of any meals or lodging furnished to him, his spouse, or any of his dependents by or on behalf of his employer for the convenience of the employer, but only if—

(1) in the case of meals, the meals are furnished on the business premises of the employer, or

(2) in the case of lodging, the employee is required to accept such lodging on the business premises of his employer as a condition of his employment.

(b) Special rules.—For purposes of subsection (a)—

(1) Provisions of employment contract or state statute not to be determinative.—In determining whether meals or lodging are furnished for the convenience of the employer, the provisions of an employment contract or of a State statute fixing terms of employment shall not be determinative of whether the meals or lodging are intended as compensation.

(2) Certain factors not taken into account with respect to meals.—In determining whether meals are furnished for the convenience of the employer, the fact that a charge is made for such meals, and the fact that the employee may accept or decline such meals, shall not be taken into account.

(3) Certain fixed charges for meals.—

(A) In general.—If—

(i) an employee is required to pay on a periodic basis a fixed charge for his meals, and

(ii) such meals are furnished by the employer for the convenience of the employer,

there shall be excluded from the employee's gross income an amount equal to such fixed charge.

(B) Application of subparagraph (A).—Subparagraph (A) shall apply—

(i) whether the employee pays the fixed charge out of his stated compensation or out of his own funds, and

(ii) only if the employee is required to make the payment whether he accepts or declines the meals.

. . . . .

§ 120. Amounts received under qualified group legal services plans

(a) Exclusion by employee for contributions and legal services provided by employer.—Gross income of an employee, his spouse, or his dependents, does not include—

(1) amounts contributed by an employer on behalf of an employee, his spouse, or his dependents under a qualified group legal services plan (as defined in subsection (b)); or

(2) the value of legal services provided, or amounts paid for legal services, under a qualified group legal services plan (as defined in subsection (b)) to, or with respect to, an employee, his spouse, or his dependents.

(b) Qualified group legal services plan.—For purposes of this section, a qualified group legal services plan is a separate written plan of an employer for the exclusive benefit of his employees or their spouses or dependents to provide such employees, spouses, or dependents with specified benefits consisting of personal legal services through prepayment of, or provision in advance for, legal fees in whole or in part by the employer, if the plan meets the requirements of subsection (c).

(c) Requirements.—

(1) Discrimination.—The contributions or benefits provided under the plan shall not discriminate in favor of employees who are officers, shareholders, self-employed individuals, or highly compensated.

(2) **Eligibility.**—The plan shall benefit employees who qualify under a classification set up by the employer and found by the Secretary not to be discriminatory in favor of employees who are described in paragraph (1). For purposes of this paragraph, there shall be excluded from consideration employees not included in the plan who are included in a unit of employees covered by an agreement which the Secretary of Labor finds to be a collective bargaining agreement between employee representatives and one or more employers, if there is evidence that group legal services plan benefits were the subject of good faith bargaining between such employee representatives and such employer or employers.

(3) **Contribution limitation.**—Not more than 25 percent of the amounts contributed under the plan during the year may be provided for the class of individuals who are shareholders or owners (or their spouses or dependents), each of whom (on any day of the year) owns more than 5 percent of the stock or of the capital or profits interest in the employer.

(4) **Notification.**—The plan shall give notice to the Secretary, in such manner as the Secretary may by regulations prescribe, that it is applying for recognition of the status of a qualified group legal services plan.

(5) **Contributions.**—Amounts contributed under the plan shall be paid only (A) to insurance companies, or to organizations or persons that provide personal legal services, or indemnification against the cost of personal legal services, in exchange for a prepayment or payment of a premium, (B) to organizations or trusts described in section 501(c) (20), (C) to organizations described in section 501(c) which are permitted by that section to receive payments from an employer for support of one or more qualified group legal services plan or plans, except that such organizations shall pay or credit the contribution to an organization or trust described in section 501(c) (20), (D) as prepayments to providers of legal services under the plan, or (E) a combination of the above.

. . . .

(e) **Termination.**—This section shall not apply to taxable years ending after December 31, 1984.

§ 121. One-time exclusion of gain from sale of principal residence by individual who has attained age 55

(a) **General rule.**—At the election of the taxpayer, gross income does not include gain from the sale or exchange of property if—

(1) the taxpayer has attained the age of 55 before the date of such sale or exchange, and

(2) during the 5-year period ending on the date of the sale or exchange, such property has been owned and used by the taxpayer as his principal residence for periods aggregating 3 years or more.

(b) **Limitations.—**

(1) **Dollar limitation.**—The amount of the gain excluded from gross income under subsection (a) shall not exceed $125,000 ($62,500 in the case of a separate return by a married individual).

(2) **Application to only 1 sale or exchange.**—Subsection (a) shall not apply to any sale or exchange by the taxpayer if an election by the taxpayer or his

spouse under subsection (a) with respect to any other sale or exchange is in effect.

(3) Additional election if prior sale was made on or before July 26, 1978. —In the case of any sale or exchange after July 26, 1978, this section shall be applied by not taking into account any election made with respect to a sale or exchange on or before such date.

(c) Election.—An election under subsection (a) may be made or revoked at any time before the expiration of the period for making a claim for credit or refund of the tax imposed by this chapter for the taxable year in which the sale or exchange occurred, and shall be made or revoked in such manner as the Secretary shall by regulations prescribe. In the case of a taxpayer who is married, an election under subsection (a) or a revocation thereof may be made only if his spouse joins in such election or revocation.

(d) Special rules.—

    (1) Property held jointly by husband and wife.—For purposes of this section, if—

        (A) property is held by a husband and wife as joint tenants, tenants by the entirety, or community property,

        (B) such husband and wife make a joint return under section 6013 for the taxable year of the sale or exchange, and

        (C) one spouse satisfies the age, holding, and use requirements of subsection (a) with respect to such property,

then both husband and wife shall be treated as satisfying the age, holding, and use requirements of subsection (a) with respect to such property.

    (2) Property of deceased spouse.—For purposes of this section, in the case of an unmarried individual whose spouse is deceased on the date of the sale or exchange of property, if—

        (A) the deceased spouse (during the 5-year period ending on the date of the sale or exchange) satisfied the holding and use requirements of subsection (a) (2) with respect to such property, and

        (B) no election by the deceased spouse under subsection (a) is in effect with respect to a prior sale or exchange,

then such individual shall be treated as satisfying the holding and use requirements of subsection (a) (2) with respect to such property.

    (3) Tenant-stockholder in cooperative housing corporation.—For purposes of this section, if the taxpayer holds stock as a tenant-stockholder (as defined in section 216) in a cooperative housing corporation (as defined in such section), then—

        (A) the holding requirements of subsection (a) (2) shall be applied to the holding of such stock, and

        (B) the use requirements of subsection (a) (2) shall be applied to the house or apartment which the taxpayer was entitled to occupy as such stockholder.

    (4) Involuntary conversions.—For purposes of this section, the destruction, theft, seizure, requisition, or condemnation of property shall be treated as the sale of such property.

    (5) Property used in part as principal residence.—In the case of property only a portion of which, during the 5-year period ending on the date of the sale or exchange, has been owned and used by the taxpayer as his principal residence for periods aggregating 3 years or more, this section shall apply with respect to so much of the gain from the sale or exchange of such property as is determined, under regulations prescribed by the Secretary, to be attributable to the portion of the property so owned and used by the taxpayer.

(6) **Determination of marital status.**—In the case of any sale or exchange, for purposes of this section—

(A) the determination of whether an individual is married shall be made as of the date of the sale or exchange; and

(B) an individual legally separated from his spouse under a decree of divorce or of separate maintenance shall not be considered as married.

(7) **Application of sections 1033 and 1034.**—In applying sections 1033 (relating to involuntary conversions) and 1034 (relating to sale or exchange of residence), the amount realized from the sale or exchange of property shall be treated as being the amount determined without regard to this section, reduced by the amount of gain not included in gross income pursuant to an election under this section.

§ 123.　Amounts received under insurance contracts for certain living expenses

(a) **General rule.**—In the case of an individual whose principal residence is damaged or destroyed by fire, storm, or other casualty, or who is denied access to his principal residence by governmental authorities because of the occurrence or threat of occurrence of such a casualty, gross income does not include amounts received by such individual under an insurance contract which are paid to compensate or reimburse such individual for living expenses incurred for himself and members of his household resulting from the loss of use or occupancy of such residence.

(b) **Limitation.**—Subsection (a) shall apply to amounts received by the taxpayer for living expenses incurred during any period only to the extent the amounts received do not exceed the amount by which—

(1) the actual living expenses incurred during such period for himself and members of his household resulting from the loss of use or occupancy of their residence, exceed

(2) the normal living expenses which would have been incurred for himself and members of his household during such period.

§ 127.　Educational assistance programs

(a) **General rule.**—Gross income of an employee does not include amounts paid or expenses incurred by the employer for educational assistance to the employee if the assistance is furnished pursuant to a program which is described in subsection (b).

(b) **Educational assistance program.—**

(1) **In general.**—For purposes of this section an educational assistance program is a separate written plan of an employer for the exclusive benefit of his employees to provide such employees with educational assistance. The program must meet the requirements of paragraphs (2) through (6) of this subsection.

(2) **Eligibility.**—The program shall benefit employees who qualify under a classification set up by the employer and found by the Secretary not to be discriminatory in favor of employees who are officers, owners, or highly compensated, or their dependents. For purposes of this paragraph, there shall be excluded from consideration employees not included in the program who are included in a unit of employees covered by an agreement which the Secretary of Labor finds to be a collective bargaining agreement between employee representatives and one or more employers, if there is evidence that educational assistance benefits were the subject of good faith bargaining between such employee representatives and such employer or employers.

(3) **Principal shareholders or owners.**—Not more than 5 percent of the amounts paid or incurred by the employer for educational assistance during the year may be provided for the class of individuals who are shareholders or owners (or their spouses or dependents), each of whom (on any day of the year) owns more than 5 percent of the stock or of the capital or profits interest in the employer.

(4) **Other benefits as an alternative.**—A program must not provide eligible employees with a choice between educational assistance and other remuneration includible in gross income. For purposes of this section, the business practices of the employer (as well as the written program) will be taken into account.

(5) **No funding required.**—A program referred to in paragraph (1) is not required to be funded.

(6) **Notification of employees.**—Reasonable notification of the availability and terms of the program must be provided to eligible employees.

(c) **Definitions; special rules.**—For purposes of this section—

(1) **Educational assistance.**—The term "educational assistance" means—

(A) the payment, by an employer, of expenses incurred by or on behalf of an employee for education of the employee (including, but not limited to, tuition, fees, and similar payments, books, supplies, and equipment), and

(B) the provision, by an employer, of courses of instruction for such employee (including books, supplies, and equipment),

but does not include payment for, or the provision of, tools or supplies which may be retained by the employee after completion of a course of instruction, or meals, lodging, or transportation. The term "educational assistance" also does not include any payment for, or the provision of any benefits with respect to, any course or other education involving sports, games, or hobbies.

(2) **Employee.**—The term "employee" includes, for any year, an individual who is an employee within the meaning of section 401(c) (1) (relating to self-employed individuals).

(3) **Employer.**—An individual who owns the entire interest in an unincorporated trade or business shall be treated as his own employer. A partnership shall be treated as the employer of each partner who is an employee within the meaning of paragraph (2).

. . . .

(6) **Relationship to current law.**—This section shall not be construed to affect the deduction or inclusion in income of amounts (not within the exclusion under this section) which are paid or incurred, or received as reimbursement, for educational expenses under section 117, 162 or 212.

(7) Disallowance of excluded amounts as credit or deduction.—No deduction or credit shall be allowed under any other section of this chapter for any amount excluded from income by reason of this section.

(d) Termination.—This section shall not apply to taxable years beginning after December 31, 1983.

PART IV—DETERMINATION OF MARITAL STATUS

§ 143.   Determination of marital status

(a) General rule.—For purposes of part V—

(1) The determination of whether an individual is married shall be made as of the close of his taxable year; except that if his spouse dies during his taxable year such determination shall be made as of the time of such death; and

(2) An individual legally separated from his spouse under a decree of divorce or of separate maintenance shall not be considered as married.

(b) Certain married individuals living apart.—For purposes of part V, if—

(1) an individual who is married (within the meaning of subsection (a)) and who files a separate return maintains as his home a household which constitutes for more than one-half of the taxable year the principal place of abode of a dependent (A) who (within the meaning of section 152) is a son, stepson, daughter, or stepdaughter of the individual, and (B) with respect to whom such individual is entitled to a deduction for the taxable year under section 151,

(2) such individual furnishes over half of the cost of maintaining such household during the taxable year, and

(3) during the entire taxable year such individual's spouse is not a member of such household,

such individual shall not be considered as married.

PART V—DEDUCTIONS FOR PERSONAL EXEMPTIONS

§ 151.   Allowance of deductions for personal exemptions

(a) Allowance of deductions.—In the case of an individual, the exemptions provided by this section shall be allowed as deductions in computing taxable income.

(b) Taxpayer and spouse.—An exemption of $1,000 for the taxpayer; and an additional exemption of $1,000 for the spouse of the taxpayer if a joint return is not made by the taxpayer and his spouse, and if the spouse, for the calendar year in which the taxable year of the taxpayer begins, has no gross income and is not the dependent of another taxpayer.

(c) Additional exemption for taxpayer or spouse aged 65 or more.—

(1) **For taxpayer.**—An additional exemption of $1,000 for the taxpayer if he has attained the age of 65 before the close of his taxable year.

(2) **For spouse.**—An additional exemption of $1,000 for the spouse of the taxpayer if a joint return is not made by the taxpayer and his spouse, and if the spouse has attained the age of 65 before the close of such taxable year, and, for the calendar year in which the taxable year of the taxpayer begins, has no gross income and is not the dependent of another taxpayer.

(d) Additional exemption for blindness of taxpayer or spouse.—

(1) For taxpayer.—An additional exemption of $1,000 for the taxpayer if he is blind at the close of his taxable year.

. . . .

(2) For spouse.—An additional exemption of $1,000 for the spouse of the taxpayer if a separate return is made by the taxpayer, and if the spouse is blind and, for the calendar year in which the taxable year of the taxpayer begins, has no gross income and is not the dependent of another taxpayer. For purposes of this paragraph, the determination of whether the spouse is blind shall be made as of the close of the taxable year of the taxpayer; except that if the spouse dies during such taxable year such determination shall be made as of the time of such death.

(3) Blindness defined.—For purposes of this subsection, an individual is blind only if his central visual acuity does not exceed 20/200 in the better eye with correcting lenses, or if his visual acuity is greater than 20/200 but is accompanied by a limitation in the fields of vision such that the widest diameter of the visual field subtends an angle no greater than 20 degrees.

(e) Additional exemption for dependents.—

(1) In general.—An exemption of $1,000 for each dependent (as defined in section 152)—

    (A) whose gross income for the calendar year in which the taxable year of the taxpayer begins is less than $1,000, or

    (B) who is a child of the taxpayer and who (i) has not attained the age of 19 at the close of the calendar year in which the taxable year of the taxpayer begins, or (ii) is a student.

(2) Exemption denied in case of certain married dependents.—No exemption shall be allowed under this subsection for any dependent who has made a joint return with his spouse under section 6013 for the taxable year beginning in the calendar year in which the taxable year of the taxpayer begins.

(3) Child defined.—For purposes of paragraph (1) (B), the term "child" means an individual who (within the meaning of section 152) is a son, stepson, daughter, or stepdaughter of the taxpayer.

(4) Student defined.—For purposes of paragraph (1) (B) (ii), the term "student" means an individual who during each of 5 calendar months during the calendar year in which the taxable year of the taxpayer begins—

    (A) is a full-time student at an educational organization described in section 170(b) (1) (A) (ii); or

    (B) is pursuing a full-time course of institutional on-farm training under the supervision of an accredited agent of an educational organization described in section 170(b) (1) (A) (ii) or of a State or political subdivision of a State.

§ 152.   Dependent defined

(a) General definition.—For purposes of this subtitle, the term "dependent" means any of the following individuals over half of whose support, for the calendar year in which the taxable year of the taxpayer begins, was received from the taxpayer (or is treated under subsection (c) or (e) as received from the taxpayer):

(1) A son or daughter of the taxpayer, or a descendant of either,

(2) A stepson or stepdaughter of the taxpayer,

(3) A brother, sister, stepbrother, or stepsister of the taxpayer,

(4) The father or mother of the taxpayer, or an ancestor of either,

(5) A stepfather or stepmother of the taxpayer,

(6) A son or daughter of a brother or sister of the taxpayer,

(7) A brother or sister of the father or mother of the taxpayer,

(8) A son-in-law, daughter-in-law, father-in-law, mother-in-law, brother-in-law, or sister-in-law of the taxpayer, or

(9) An individual (other than an individual who at any time during the taxable year was the spouse, determined without regard to section 143, of the taxpayer) who, for the taxable year of the taxpayer, has as his principal place of abode the home of the taxpayer and is a member of the taxpayer's household.

(b) **Rules relating to general definition.**—For purposes of this section—

(1) The terms "brother" and "sister" include a brother or sister by the halfblood.

(2) In determining whether any of the relationships specified in subsection (a) or paragraph (1) of this subsection exists, a legally adopted child of an individual (and a child who is a member of an individual's household, if placed with such individual by an authorized placement agency for legal adoption by such individual), or a foster child of an individual (if such child satisfies the requirements of subsection (a) (9) with respect to such individual), shall be treated as a child of such individual by blood.

(3) The term "dependent" does not include any individual who is not a citizen or national of the United States unless such individual is a resident of the United States or of a country contiguous to the United States. The preceding sentence shall not exclude from the definition of "dependent" any child of the taxpayer legally adopted by him, if, for the taxable year of the taxpayer, the child has as his principal place of abode the home of the taxpayer and is a member of the taxpayer's household, and if the taxpayer is a citizen or national of the United States.

(4) A payment to a wife which is includible in the gross income of the wife under section 71 or 682 shall not be treated as a payment by her husband for the support of any dependent.

(5) An individual is not a member of the taxpayer's household if at any time during the taxable year of the taxpayer the relationship between such individual and the taxpayer is in violation of local law.

(c) **Multiple support agreements.**—For purposes of subsection (a), over half of the support of an individual for a calendar year shall be treated as received from the taxpayer if—

(1) no one person contributed over half of such support;

(2) over half of such support was received from persons each of whom, but for the fact that he did not contribute over half of such support, would have been entitled to claim such individual as a dependent for a taxable year beginning in such calendar year;

(3) the taxpayer contributed over 10 percent of such support; and

(4) each person described in paragraph (2) (other than the taxpayer) who contributed over 10 percent of such support files a written declaration (in such manner and form as the Secretary may by regulations prescribe) that he will not claim such individual as a dependent for any taxable year beginning in such calendar year.

(d) **Special support test in case of students.**—For purposes of subsection (a), in the case of any individual who is—

(1) a son, stepson, daughter, or stepdaughter of the taxpayer (within the meaning of this section), and

(2) a student (within the meaning of section 151(e) (4)),

amounts received as scholarships for study at an educational organization described in section 170(b) (1) (A) (ii) shall not be taken into account in determining whether such individual received more than half of his support from the taxpayer.

(e) **Support test in case of child of divorced parents, etc.—**

(1) **General rule.**—If—

(A) a child (as defined in section 151(e) (3)) receives over half of his support during the calendar year from his parents who are divorced or legally separated under a decree of divorce or separate maintenance, or who are separated under a written separation agreement, and

(B) such child is in the custody of one or both of his parents for more than one-half of the calendar year,

such child shall be treated, for purposes of subsection (a), as receiving over half of his support during the calendar year from the parent having custody for a greater portion of the calendar year unless he is treated, under the provisions of paragraph (2), as having received over half of his support for such year from the other parent (referred to in this subsection as the parent not having custody).

(2) **Special rule.**—The child of parents described in paragraph (1) shall be treated as having received over half of his support during the calendar year from the parent not having custody if—

(A) (i) the decree of divorce or of separate maintenance, or a written agreement between the parents applicable to the taxable year beginning in such calendar year, provides that the parent not having custody shall be entitled to any deduction allowable under section 151 for such child, and

(ii) such parent not having custody provides at least $600 for the support of such child during the calendar year, or

(B) (i) the parent not having custody provides $1,200 or more for the support of such child (or if there is more than one such child, $1,200 or more for each of such children) for the calendar year, and

(ii) the parent having custody of such child does not clearly establish that he provided more for the support of such child during the calendar year than the parent not having custody.

For the purposes of this paragraph, amounts expended for the support of a child or children shall be treated as received from the parent not having custody to the extent that such parent provided amounts for such support.

(3) **Itemized statement required.**—If a taxpayer claims that paragraph (2) (B) applies with respect to a child for a calendar year and the other parent claims that paragraph (2) (B) (i) is not satisfied or claims to have provided more for the support of such child during such calendar year than the taxpayer, each parent shall be entitled to receive, under regulations to be prescribed by the Secretary, an itemized statement of the expenditures upon which the other parent's claim of support is based.

(4) **Exception for multiple-support agreement.**—The provisions of this subsection shall not apply in any case where over half of the support of the child is treated as having been received from a taxpayer under the provisions of subsection (c).

(5) **Regulations.**—The Secretary shall prescribe such regulations as may be necessary to carry out the purposes of this subsection.

PART VI—ITEMIZED DEDUCTIONS FOR INDIVIDUALS AND CORPORATIONS

§ 161.　Allowance of deductions

In computing taxable income under section 63, there shall be allowed as deductions the items specified in this part, subject to the exceptions provided in part IX (sec. 261 and following, relating to items not deductible).

§ 162.　Trade or business expenses

(a) **In general.**—There shall be allowed as a deduction all the ordinary and necessary expenses paid or incurred during the taxable year in carrying on any trade or business, including—

(1) a reasonable allowance for salaries or other compensation for personal services actually rendered;

(2) traveling expenses (including amounts expended for meals and lodging other than amounts which are lavish or extravagant under the circumstances) while away from home in the pursuit of a trade or business; and

(3) rentals or other payments required to be made as a condition to the continued use or possession, for purposes of the trade or business, of property to which the taxpayer has not taken or is not taking title or in which he has no equity.

For purposes of the preceding sentence, the place of residence of a Member of Congress (including any Delegate and Resident Commissioner) within the State, congressional district, or possession which he represents in Congress shall be considered his home but amounts expended by such Members within each taxable year for living expenses shall not be deductible for income tax purposes in excess of $3,000.

(b) **Charitable contributions and gifts excepted.**—No deduction shall be allowed under subsection (a) for any contribution or gift which would be allowable as a deduction under section 170 were it not for the percentage limitations, the dollar limitations, or the requirements as to the time of payment, set forth in such section.

(c) **Illegal bribes, kickbacks, and other payments.**—

(1) **Illegal payments to government officials or employees.**—No deduction shall be allowed under subsection (a) for any payment made, directly or indirectly, to an official or employee of any government, or of any agency or

instrumentality of any government, if the payment constitutes an illegal bribe or kickback or, if the payment is to an official or employee of a foreign government, the payment is unlawful under the Foreign Corrupt Practices Act of 1977. The burden of proof in respect of the issue, for the purposes of this paragraph, as to whether a payment constitutes an illegal bribe or kickback (or is unlawful under the Foreign Corrupt Practices Act of 1977) shall be upon the Secretary to the same extent as he bears the burden of proof under section 7454 (concerning the burden of proof when the issue relates to fraud).

(2) Other illegal payments.—No deduction shall be allowed under subsection (a) for any payment (other than a payment described in paragraph (1)) made, directly or indirectly, to any person, if the payment constitutes an illegal bribe, illegal kickback, or other illegal payment under any law of the United States, or under any law of a State (but only if such State law is generally enforced), which subjects the payor to a criminal penalty or the loss of license or privilege to engage in a trade or business. For purposes of this paragraph, a kickback includes a payment in consideration of the referral of a client, patient, or customer. The burden of proof in respect of the issue, for purposes of this paragraph, as to whether a payment constitutes an illegal bribe, illegal kickback, or other illegal payment shall be upon the Secretary to the same extent as he bears the burden of proof under section 7454 (concerning the burden of proof when the issue relates to fraud).

(3) Kickbacks, rebates, and bribes under medicare and medicaid.—No deduction shall be allowed under subsection (a) for any kickback, rebate, or bribe made by any provider of services, supplier, physician, or other person who furnishes items or services for which payment is or may be made under the Social Security Act, or in whole or in part out of Federal funds under a State plan approved under such Act, if such kickback, rebate, or bribe is made in connection with the furnishing of such items or services or the making or receipt of such payments. For purposes of this paragraph, a kickback includes a payment in consideration of the referral of a client, patient, or customer.

. . . . . .

(e) Appearances, etc., with respect to legislation.—

(1) In general.—The deduction allowed by subsection (a) shall include all the ordinary and necessary expenses (including, but not limited to, traveling expenses described in subsection (a) (2) and the cost of preparing testimony) paid or incurred during the taxable year in carrying on any trade or business—

(A) in direct connection with appearances before, submission of statements to, or sending communications to, the committees, or individual members, of Congress or of any legislative body of a State, a possession of the United States, or a political subdivision of any of the foregoing with respect to legislation or proposed legislation of direct interest to the taxpayer, or

(B) in direct connection with communication of information between the taxpayer and an organization of which he is a member with respect to legislation or proposed legislation of direct interest to the taxpayer and to such organization,

and that portion of the dues so paid or incurred with respect to any organization of which the taxpayer is a member which is attributable to the expenses of the activities described in subparagraphs (A) and (B) carried on by such organization.

(2) Limitation.—The provisions of paragraph (1) shall not be construed as allowing the deduction of any amount paid or incurred (whether by way of contribution, gift, or otherwise)—

(A) for participation in, or intervention in, any political campaign on behalf of any candidate for public office, or

(B) in connection with any attempt to influence the general public, or segments thereof, with respect to legislative matters, elections, or referendums.

(f) Fines and penalties.—No deduction shall be allowed under subsection (a) for any fine or similar penalty paid to a government for the violation of any law.

(g) Treble damage payments under the antitrust laws.—If in a criminal proceeding a taxpayer is convicted of a violation of the antitrust laws, or his plea of guilty or nolo contendere to an indictment or information charging such a violation is entered or accepted in such a proceeding, no deduction shall be allowed under subsection (a) for two-thirds of any amount paid or incurred—

(1) on any judgment for damages entered against the taxpayer under section 4 of the Act entitled "An Act to supplement existing laws against unlawful restraints and monopolies, and for other purposes", approved October 15, 1914 (commonly known as the Clayton Act), on account of such violation or any related violation of the antitrust laws which occurred prior to the date of the final judgment of such conviction, or

(2) in settlement of any action brought under such section 4 on account of such violation or related violation.

. . . . . .

§ 163.   Interest

(a) General rule.—There shall be allowed as a deduction all interest paid or accrued within the taxable year on indebtedness.

(b) Installment purchases where interest charge is not separately stated.—

(1) General rule.—If personal property or educational services are purchased under a contract—

(A) which provides that payment of part or all of the purchase price is to be made in installments, and

(B) in which carrying charges are separately stated but the interest charge cannot be ascertained,

then the payments made during the taxable year under the contract shall be treated for purposes of this section as if they included interest equal to 6 percent of the average unpaid balance under the contract during the taxable year. For purposes of the preceding sentence, the average unpaid balance is the sum of the unpaid balance outstanding on the first day of each month beginning during the taxable year, divided by 12. For purposes of this paragraph, the term "educational services" means any service (including lodging) which is purchased from an educational organization described in section 170(b) (1) (A) (ii) and which is provided for a student of such organization.

(2) Limitation.—In the case of any contract to which paragraph (1) applies, the amount treated as interest for any taxable year shall not exceed the aggregate carrying charges which are properly attributable to such taxable year.

(c) Redeemable ground rents.—For purposes of this subtitle, any annual or periodic rental under a redeemable ground rent (excluding amounts in redemption thereof) shall be treated as interest on an indebtedness secured by a mortgage.

(d) Limitation on interest on investment indebtedness.—

(1) **In general.**—In the case of a taxpayer other than a corporation, the amount of investment interest (as defined in paragraph (3) (D)) otherwise allowable as a deduction under this chapter shall be limited, in the following order, to—

(A) $10,000 ($5,000, in the case of a separate return by a married individual), plus

(B) the amount of the net investment income (as defined in paragraph (3) (A)), plus the amount (if any) by which the deductions allowable under this section (determined without regard to this subsection) and sections 162, 164(a) (1) or (2), or 212 attributable to property of the taxpayer subject to a net lease exceeds the rental income produced by such property for the taxable year.

In the case of a trust, the $10,000 amount specified in subparagraph (A) shall be zero.

(2) **Carryover of disallowed investment interest.**—The amount of disallowed investment interest for any taxable year shall be treated as investment interest paid or accrued in the succeeding taxable year.

(3) **Definitions.**—For purposes of this subsection—

(A) **Net investment income.**—The term "net investment income" means the excess of investment income over investment expenses. If the taxpayer has investment interest for the taxable year to which this subsection (as in effect before the Tax Reform Act of 1976) applies, the amount of the net investment income taken into account under this subsection shall be the amount of such income (determined without regard to this sentence) multiplied by a fraction the numerator of which is the excess of the investment interest for the taxable year over the investment interest to which such prior provision applies, and the denominator of which is the investment interest for the taxable year.

(B) **Investment income.**—The term "investment income" means—

(i) the gross income from interest, dividends, rents, and royalties,

(ii) the net short-term capital gain attributable to the disposition of property held for investment, and

(iii) any amount treated under sections 1245, 1250, and 1254 as ordinary income,

but only to the extent such income, gain, and amounts are not derived from the conduct of a trade or business.

(C) **Investment expenses.**—The term "investment expenses" means the deductions allowable under sections 162, 164(a) (1) or (2), 166, 167, 171, 212, or 611 directly connected with the production of investment income. For purposes of this subparagraph, the deduction allowable under section 167 with respect to any property may be treated as the amount which would have been allowable had the taxpayer depreciated the property under the straight line method for each taxable year of its useful life for which the taxpayer has held the property, and the deduction allowable under section 611 with respect to any property may be treated as the amount which would have been allowable had the taxpayer determined the deduction under section 611 without regard to section 613 for each taxable year for which the taxpayer has held the property.

(D) Investment interest.—The term "investment interest" means interest paid or accrued on indebtedness incurred or continued to purchase or carry property held for investment.

(E) Disallowed investment interest.—The term "disallowed investment interest" means with respect to any taxable year, the amount not allowable as a deduction solely by reason of the limitation in paragraph (1).

(4) Special rules.—

(A) Property subject to net lease.—For purposes of this subsection, property subject to a lease shall be treated as property held for investment, and not as property used in a trade or business, for a taxable year, if—

(i) for such taxable year the sum of the deductions of the lessor with respect to such property which are allowable solely by reason of section 162 (other than rents and reimbursed amounts with respect to such property) is less than 15 percent of the rental income produced by such property, or

(ii) the lessor is either guaranteed a specified return or is guaranteed in whole or in part against loss of income.

(B) Construction interest.—For purposes of this subsection, interest paid or accrued on indebtedness incurred or continued in the construction of property to be used in a trade or business shall not be treated as investment interest.

(5) Exceptions.—This subsection shall not apply with respect to investment interest, investment income, and investment expenses attributable to a specific item of property, if the indebtedness with respect to such property—

(A) is for a specified term, and

(B) was incurred before December 17, 1969, or is incurred after December 16, 1969, pursuant to a written contract or commitment which, on such date and at all times thereafter prior to the incurring of such indebtedness, is binding on the taxpayer.

For taxable years beginning after December 31, 1975, this paragraph shall be applied on an allocation basis rather than a specific item basis.

(6) Real property leases.—For purposes of paragraph (4) (A)—

(A) if a parcel of real property of the taxpayer is leased under two or more leases, paragraph (4) (A) (i) shall, at the election of the taxpayer, be applied by treating all leased portions of such property as subject to a single lease; and

(B) at the election of the taxpayer, paragraph (4) (A) (i) shall not apply with respect to real property of the taxpayer which has been in use for more than 5 years.

An election under subparagraph (A) or (B) shall be made at such time and in such manner as the Secretary prescribes by regulations.

(7) Special rule where taxpayer owns 50 percent or more of enterprise.—

(A) General rule.—In the case of any 50 percent owned corporation or partnership, the $10,000 figure specified in paragraph (1) shall be increased by the lesser of—

(i) $15,000, or

(ii) the interest paid or accrued during the taxable year on investment indebtedness incurred or continued in connection with the acquisition of the interest in such corporation or partnership.

In the case of a separate return by a married individual, $7,500 shall be substituted for the $15,000 figure in clause (1).

(B) Ownership requirements.—This paragraph shall apply with respect to indebtedness only if the taxpayer, his spouse, and his children own 50 percent or more of the total value of all classes of stock of the corporation or 50 percent or more of all capital interests in the partnership, as the case may be.

(e) Original issue discount.—

(1) In general.—In the case of any bond issued after July 1, 1982, by an issuer (other than a natural person), the portion of the original issue discount with respect to such bond which is allowable as a deduction to the issuer for any taxable year shall be equal to the aggregate daily portions of the original issue discount for days during such taxable year.

(2) Definitions and special rules.—For purposes of this section—

(A) Bond.—The term "bond" has the meaning given to such term by section 1232A(c)(1).

(B) Daily portions.—The daily portion of the original issue discount for any day shall be determined under section 1232A(a) (without regard to paragraphs (2)(B) and (6) thereof and without regard to the second sentence of section 1232(b)(1)).

(f) Denial of deduction for interest on certain obligations not in registered form.—

(1) In general.—Nothing in subsection (a) or in any other provision of law shall be construed to provide a deduction for interest on any registration-required obligation unless such obligation is in registered form.

(2) Registration-required obligation.—For purposes of this section—

(A) In general.—The term "registration-required obligation" means any obligation (including any obligation issued by a governmental entity) other than an obligation which—

(i) is issued by a natural person,

(ii) is not of a type offered to the public,

(iii) has a maturity (at issue) of not more than 1 year, or

(iv) is described in subparagraph (B).

(B) Certain obligations not included.—An obligation is described in this subparagraph if—

(i) there are arrangements reasonably designed to ensure that such obligation will be sold (or resold in connection with the original issue) only to a person who is not a United States person, and

(ii) in the case of an obligation not in registered form—

(I) interest on such obligation is payable only outside the United States and its possessions, and

(II) on the face of such obligation there is a statement that any United States person who holds such obligation will be subject to limitations under the United States income tax laws.

(C) Authority to include other obligations.—Clauses (ii) and (iii) of subparagraph (A), and subparagraph (B), shall not apply to any obligation if—

(i) such obligation is of a type which the Secretary has determined by regulations to be used frequently in avoiding Federal taxes, and

(ii) such obligation is issued after the date on which the regulations referred to in clause (i) take effect.

(3) Book entries permitted, etc.—For purposes of this subsection, rules similar to the rules of section 103(j)(3) shall apply.

. . . . .

§ 164.   Taxes

(a) General rule.—Except as otherwise provided in this section, the following taxes shall be allowed as a deduction for the taxable year within which paid or accrued:

(1) State and local, and foreign, real property taxes.

(2) State and local personal property taxes.

(3) State and local, and foreign, income, war profits, and excess profits taxes.

(4) State and local general sales taxes.

(5) The windfall profit tax imposed by section 4986.

In addition, there shall be allowed as a deduction State and local, and foreign, taxes not described in the preceding sentence which are paid or accrued within the taxable year in carrying on a trade or business or an activity described in section 212 (relating to expenses for production of income).

(b) Definitions and special rules.—For purposes of this section—

(1) Personal property taxes.—The term "personal property tax" means an ad valorem tax which is imposed on an annual basis in respect of personal property.

(2) General sales taxes.—

(A) In general.—The term "general sales tax" means a tax imposed at one rate in respect of the sale at retail of a broad range of classes of items.

(B) Special rules for food, etc.—In the case of items of food, clothing, medical supplies, and motor vehicles—

(i) the fact that the tax does not apply in respect of some or all of such items shall not be taken into account in determining whether the tax applies in respect of a broad range of classes of items, and

(ii) the fact that the rate of tax applicable in respect of some or all of such items is lower than the general rate of tax shall not be taken into account in determining whether the tax is imposed at one rate.

(C) Items taxed at different rates.—Except in the case of a lower rate of tax applicable in respect of an item described in subparagraph (B), no deduction shall be allowed under this section for any general sales tax imposed in respect of an item at a rate other than the general rate of tax.

(D) Compensating use taxes.—A compensating use tax in respect of an item shall be treated as a general sales tax. For purposes of the preceding sentence, the term "compensating use tax" means, in respect of any item, a tax which—

(i) is imposed on the use, storage, or consumption of such item, and

(ii) is complementary to a general sales tax, but only if a deduction is allowable under subsection (a) (4) in respect of items sold at retail in the taxing jurisdiction which are similar to such item.

(E) Special rule for motor vehicles.—In the case of motor vehicles, if the rate of tax exceeds the general rate, such excess shall be disregarded and the general rate shall be treated as the rate of tax.

(3) State or local taxes.—A State or local tax includes only a tax imposed by a State, a possession of the United States, or a political subdivision of any of the foregoing, or by the District of Columbia.

(4) Foreign taxes.—A foreign tax includes only a tax imposed by the authority of a foreign country.

(5) Separately stated general sales taxes.—If the amount of any general sales tax is separately stated, then, to the extent that the amount so stated is paid by the consumer (otherwise than in connection with the consumer's trade or business) to his seller, such amount shall be treated as a tax imposed on, and paid by, such consumer.

(c) Deduction denied in case of certain taxes.—No deduction shall be allowed for the following taxes:

(1) Taxes assessed against local benefits of a kind tending to increase the value of the property assessed; but this paragraph shall not prevent the deduction of so much of such taxes as is properly allocable to maintenance or interest charges.

(2) Taxes on real property, to the extent that subsection (d) requires such taxes to be treated as imposed on another taxpayer.

(d) Apportionment of taxes on real property between seller and purchaser.—

(1) General rule.—For purposes of subsection (a), if real property is sold during any real property tax year, then—

(A) so much of the real property tax as is properly allocable to that part of such year which ends on the day before the date of the sale shall be treated as a tax imposed on the seller, and

(B) so much of such tax as is properly allocable to that part of such year which begins on the date of the sale shall be treated as a tax imposed on the purchaser.

(2) Special rules.—

(A) In the case of any sale of real property, if—

(i) a taxpayer may not, by reason of his method of accounting, deduct any amount for taxes unless paid, and

(ii) the other party to the sale is (under the law imposing the real property tax) liable for the real property tax for the real property tax year,

then for purposes of subsection (a) the taxpayer shall be treated as having paid, on the date of the sale, so much of such tax as, under paragraph (1) of this subsection, is treated as imposed on the taxpayer. For purposes of the preceding sentence, if neither party is liable for the tax, then the party holding the property at the time the tax becomes a lien on the property shall be considered liable for the real property tax for the real property tax year.

(B) In the case of any sale of real property, if the taxpayer's taxable income for the taxable year during which the sale occurs is computed under an accrual method of accounting, and if no election under section 461(c) (relating to the accrual of real property taxes) applies, then, for purposes of subsection (a), that portion of such tax which—

(i) is treated, under paragraph (1) of this subsection, as imposed on the taxpayer, and

(ii) may not, by reason of the taxpayer's method of accounting, be deducted by the taxpayer for any taxable year,

shall be treated as having accrued on the date of the sale.

(e) Taxes of shareholder paid by corporation.—Where a corporation pays a tax imposed on a shareholder on his interest as a shareholder, and where the shareholder does not reimburse the corporation, then—

(1) the deduction allowed by subsection (a) shall be allowed to the corporation; and

(2) no deduction shall be allowed the shareholder for such tax.

§ 165. Losses

(a) General rule.—There shall be allowed as a deduction any loss sustained during the taxable year and not compensated for by insurance or otherwise.

(b) Amount of deduction.—For purposes of subsection (a), the basis for determining the amount of the deduction for any loss shall be the adjusted basis provided in section 1011 for determining the loss from the sale or other disposition of property.

(c) Limitation on losses of individuals.—In the case of an individual, the deduction under subsection (a) shall be limited to—

(1) losses incurred in a trade or business;

(2) losses incurred in any transaction entered into for profit, though not connected with a trade or business; and

(3) except as provided in subsection (h), losses of property not connected with a trade or business, if such losses arise from fire, storm, shipwreck, or other casualty, or from theft.

(d) Wagering losses.—Losses from wagering transactions shall be allowed only to the extent of the gains from such transactions.

(e) Theft losses.—For purposes of subsection (a), any loss arising from theft shall be treated as sustained during the taxable year in which the taxpayer discovers such loss.

(f) Capital losses.—Losses from sales or exchanges of capital assets shall be allowed only to the extent allowed in sections 1211 and 1212.

(g) Worthless securities.—

    (1) General rule.—If any security which is a capital asset becomes worthless during the taxable year, the loss resulting therefrom shall, for purposes of this subtitle, be treated as a loss from the sale or exchange, on the last day of the taxable year, of a capital asset.

    (2) Security defined.—For purposes of this subsection, the term "security" means—

        (A) a share of stock in a corporation;

        (B) a right to subscribe for, or to receive, a share of stock in a corporation; or

        (C) a bond, debenture, note, or certificate, or other evidence of indebtedness, issued by a corporation or by a government or political subdivision thereof, with interest coupons or in registered form.

    (3) Securities in affiliated corporation.—For purposes of paragraph (1), any security in a corporation affiliated with a taxpayer which is a domestic corporation shall not be treated as a capital asset. For purposes of the preceding sentence, a corporation shall be treated as affiliated with the taxpayer only if—

        (A) stock possessing at least 80 percent of the voting power of all classes of its stock and at least 80 percent of each class of its nonvoting stock is owned directly by the taxpayer, and

        (B) more than 90 percent of the aggregate of its gross receipts for all taxable years has been from sources other than royalties, rents (except rents derived from rental of properties to employees of the corporation in the ordinary course of its operating business), dividends, interest (except interest received on deferred purchase price of operating assets sold), annuities, and gains from sales or exchanges of stocks and securities.

In computing gross receipts for purposes of the preceding sentence, gross receipts from sales or exchanges of stocks and securities shall be taken into account only to the extent of gains therefrom. As used in subparagraph (A), the term "stock" does not include nonvoting stock which is limited and preferred as to dividends.

(h) Casualty and theft losses.—

    (1) General rule.—Any loss of an individual described in subsection (c)(3) shall be allowed for any taxable year only to the extent that—

        (A) the amount of loss to such individual arising from each casualty, or from each theft, exceeds $100, and

        (B) the aggregate amount of all such losses sustained by such individual during the taxable year (determined after application of subparagraph (A)) exceeds 10 percent of the adjusted gross income of the individual.

(2) Special rules.—

(A) Joint returns.—For purposes of the $100 and 10 percent limitations described in paragraph (1), a husband and wife making a joint return for the taxable year shall be treated as one individual.

(B) Coordination with estate tax.—No loss described in subsection (c)(3) shall be allowed if, at the time of filing the return, such loss has been claimed for estate tax purposes in the estate tax return.

(i) Disaster losses.—

(1) Election to take deduction for preceding year.—Notwithstanding the provisions of subsection (a), any loss attributable to a disaster occurring in an area subsequently determined by the President of the United States to warrant assistance by the Federal Government under the Disaster Relief Act of 1974 may, at the election of the taxpayer, be taken into account for the taxable year immediately preceding the taxable year in which the disaster occurred.

(2) Year of loss.—If an election is made under this subsection, the casualty resulting in the loss shall be treated for purposes of this title as having occurred in the taxable year for which the deduction is claimed.

(3) Amount of loss.—The amount of the loss taken into account in the preceding taxable year by reason of paragraph (1) shall not exceed the uncompensated amount determined on the basis of the facts existing at the date the taxpayer claims the loss.

(j) Denial of deduction for losses on certain obligations not in registered form.—

(1) In general.—Nothing in subsection (a) or in any other provision of law shall be construed to provide a deduction for any loss sustained on any registration-required obligation unless such obligation is in registered form (or the issuance of such obligation was subject to tax under section 4701).

(2) Definitions.—For purposes of this subsection—

(A) Registration-required obligation.—The term "registration-required obligation" has the meaning given to such term by section 163(f)(2) except that clause (iv) of subparagraph (A), and subparagraph (B), of such section shall not apply.

(B) Registered form.—The term "registered form" has the same meaning as when used in section 163(f).

(3) Exceptions.—The Secretary may, by regulations, provide that this subsection and subsection (d) of section 1232 shall not apply with respect to obligations held by any person if—

(A) such person holds such obligations in connection with a trade or business outside the United States,

(B) such person holds such obligations as a broker dealer (registered under Federal or State law) for sale to customers in the ordinary course of his trade or business,

(C) such person complies with reporting requirements with respect to ownership, transfers, and payments as the Secretary may require, or

(D) such person promptly surrenders the obligations to the issuer for the issuance of a new obligation in registered form, but only if such obligations are held under arrangements provided in regulations or otherwise which are designed to assure that such obligations are not delivered to any United States person other than a person described in subparagraph (A), (B), or (C).

§ 166. Bad debts

(a) General rule.—

(1) Wholly worthless debts.—There shall be allowed as a deduction any debt which becomes worthless within the taxable year.

(2) Partially worthless debts.—When satisfied that a debt is recoverable only in part, the Secretary may allow such debt, in an amount not in excess of the part charged off within the taxable year, as a deduction.

(b) Amount of deduction.—For purposes of subsection (a), the basis for determining the amount of the deduction for any bad debt shall be the adjusted basis provided in section 1011 for determining the loss from the sale or other disposition of property.

(c) Reserve for bad debts.—In lieu of any deduction under subsection (a), there shall be allowed (in the discretion of the Secretary) a deduction for a reasonable addition to a reserve for bad debts.

(d) Nonbusiness debts.—

(1) General rule.—In the case of a taxpayer other than a corporation—

(A) subsections (a) and (c) shall not apply to any nonbusiness debt; and

(B) where any nonbusiness debt becomes worthless within the taxable year, the loss resulting therefrom shall be considered a loss from the sale or exchange, during the taxable year, of a capital asset held for not more than 1 year.

(2) Nonbusiness debt defined.—For purposes of paragraph (1), the term "nonbusiness debt" means a debt other than—

(A) a debt created or acquired (as the case may be) in connection with a trade or business of the taxpayer; or

(B) a debt the loss from the worthlessness of which is incurred in the taxpayer's trade or business.

(e) Worthless securities.—This section shall not apply to a debt which is evidenced by a security as defined in section 165(g) (2) (C).

(f) Reserve for certain guaranteed debt obligations.—

(1) Allowance of deduction.—In the case of a taxpayer who is a dealer in property, in lieu of any deduction under subsection (a), there shall be allowed (in the discretion of the Secretary) for any taxable year ending after October 21, 1965, a deduction—

(A) for a reasonable addition to a reserve for bad debts which may arise out of his liability as a guarantor, endorser, or indemnitor of debt obligations arising out of the sale by him of real property or tangible personal property (including related services) in the ordinary course of his trade or business; and

(B) for the amount of any reduction in the suspense account required by paragraph (4) (B) (i).

(2) Deduction disallowed in other cases.—Except as provided in paragraph (1), no deduction shall be allowed to a taxpayer for any addition to a reserve for bad debts which may arise out of his liability as guarantor, endorser, or indemnitor of debt obligations.

- - - - -

§ 167. Depreciation

(a) General rule.—There shall be allowed as a depreciation deduction a reasonable allowance for the exhaustion, wear and tear (including a reasonable allowance for obsolescence)—

(1) of property used in the trade or business, or

(2) of property held for the production of income.

In the case of recovery property (within the meaning of section 168), the deduction allowable under section 168 shall be deemed to constitute the reasonable allowance provided by this section, except with respect to that portion of the basis of such property to which subsection (k) applies.

(b) Use of certain methods and rates.—For taxable years ending after December 31, 1953, the term "reasonable allowance" as used in subsection (a) shall include (but shall not be limited to) an allowance computed in accordance with regulations prescribed by the Secretary, under any of the following methods:

(1) the straight line method,

(2) the declining balance method, using a rate not exceeding twice the rate which would have been used had the annual allowance been computed under the method described in paragraph (1),

(3) the sum of the years-digits method, and

(4) any other consistent method productive of an annual allowance which, when added to all allowances for the period commencing with the taxpayer's use of the property and including the taxable year, does not, during the first two-thirds of the useful life of the property, exceed the total of such allowances which would have been used had such allowances been computed under the method described in paragraph (2).

Nothing in this subsection shall be construed to limit or reduce an allowance otherwise allowable under subsection (a).

(c) Limitations on use of certain methods and rates.—Paragraphs (2), (3), and (4) of subsection (b) shall apply only in the case of property (other than intangible property) described in subsection (a) with a useful life of 3 years or more—

(1) the construction, reconstruction, or erection of which is completed after December 31, 1953, and then only to that portion of the basis which is properly attributable to such construction, reconstruction, or erection after December 31, 1953, or

(2) acquired after December 31, 1953, if the original use of such property commences with the taxpayer and commences after such date.

(d) Agreement as to useful life on which depreciation rate is based.—Where, under regulations prescribed by the Secretary, the taxpayer and the Secretary have, after August 16, 1954, entered into an agreement in writing specifically dealing with the useful life and rate of depreciation of any property, the rate so agreed upon shall be binding on both the taxpayer and the Secretary in the absence of facts or circumstances not taken into consideration in the adoption of such agreement. The responsibility of establishing the existence of such facts and circumstances shall rest with the party initiating the modification. Any change in the agreed rate and useful life specified in the agreement shall not be effective for taxable years before the taxable year in which notice in writing by certified mail or registered mail is served by the party to the agreement initiating such change. This subsection shall not apply with respect to recovery property defined in section 168.

(e) **Change in method.—**

(1) **Change from declining balance method.**—In the absence of an agreement under subsection (d) containing a provision to the contrary, a taxpayer may at any time elect in accordance with regulations prescribed by the Secretary to change from the method of depreciation described in subsection (b) (2) to the method described in subsection (b) (1).

(2) **Change with respect to section 1245 property.**—A taxpayer may, on or before the last day prescribed by law (including extensions thereof) for filing his return for his first taxable year beginning after December 31, 1962, and in such manner as the Secretary shall by regulations prescribe, elect to change his method of depreciation in respect of section 1245 property (as defined in section 1245(a) (3)) from any declining balance or sum of the years-digits method to the straight line method. An election may be made under this paragraph notwithstanding any provision to the contrary in an agreement under subsection (d).

(3) **Change with respect to section 1250 property.**—A taxpayer may, on or before the last day prescribed by law (including extensions thereof) for filing his return for his first taxable year beginning after December 31, 1975, and in such manner as the Secretary shall by regulation prescribe, elect to change his method of depreciation in respect of section 1250 property (as defined in section 1250(c)) from any declining balance or sum of the years-digits method to the straight line method. An election may be made under this paragraph notwithstanding any provision to the contrary in an agreement under subsection (d).

(f) **Salvage value.—**

(1) **General rule.**—Under regulations prescribed by the Secretary, a taxpayer may, for purposes of computing the allowance under subsection (a) with respect to personal property, reduce the amount taken into account as salvage value by an amount which does not exceed 10 percent of the basis of such property (as determined under subsection (g) as of the time as of which such salvage value is required to be determined).

(2) **Personal property defined.**—For purposes of this subsection, the term "personal property" means depreciable personal property (other than livestock) with a useful life of 3 years or more acquired after October 16, 1962.

(g) **Basis for depreciation.**—The basis on which exhaustion, wear and tear, and obsolescence are to be allowed in respect of any property shall be the adjusted basis provided in section 1011 for the purpose of determining the gain on the sale or other disposition of such property.

(h) **Life tenants and beneficiaries of trusts and estates.**—In the case of property held by one person for life with remainder to another person, the deduction shall be computed as if the life tenant were the absolute owner of the property and shall be allowed to the life tenant. In the case of property held in trust, the allowable deduction shall be apportioned between the income beneficiaries and the trustee in accordance with the pertinent provisions of the instrument creating the trust, or, in the absence of such provisions, on the basis of the trust income allocable to each. In the case of an estate, the allowable deduction shall be apportioned between the estate and the heirs, legatees, and devisees on the basis of the income of the estate allocable to each.

[(i) Repealed. Pub.L. 95–600, Title III, § 312(c) (4), Nov. 6, 1978, 92 Stat. 2826]

(j) Special rules for section 1250 property.—

    (1) General rule.—Except as provided in paragraphs (2) and (3), in the case of section 1250 property, subsection (b) shall not apply and the term "reasonable allowance" as used in subsection (a) shall include an allowance computed in accordance with regulations prescribed by the Secretary, under any of the following methods:

        (A) the straight line method,

        (B) the declining balance method, using a rate not exceeding 150 percent of the rate which would have been used had the annual allowance been computed under the method described in subparagraph (A), or

        (C) any other consistent method productive of an annual allowance which, when added to all allowances for the period commencing with the taxpayer's use of the property and including the taxable year, does not, during the first two-thirds of the useful life of the property, exceed the total of such allowances which would have been used had such allowances been computed under the method described in subparagraph (B).

Nothing in this paragraph shall be construed to limit or reduce an allowance otherwise allowable under subsection (a) except where allowable solely by reason of paragraph (2), (3), or (4) of subsection (b).

    (2) Residential rental property.—

        (A) In general.—Paragraph (1) of this subsection shall not apply, and subsection (b) shall apply in any taxable year, to a building or structure—

            (i) which is residential rental property located within the United States or any of its possessions, or located within a foreign country if a method of depreciation for such property comparable to the method provided in subsection (b) (2) or (3) is provided by the laws of such country, and

            (ii) the original use of which commences with the taxpayer.

In the case of residential rental property located within a foreign country, the original use of which commences with the taxpayer, if the allowance for depreciation provided under the laws of such country for such property is greater than that provided under paragraph (1) of this subsection, but less than that provided under subsection (b), the allowance for depreciation under subsection (b) shall be limited to the amount provided under the laws of such country.

        (B) Definition.—For purposes of subparagraph (A), a building or structure shall be considered to be residential rental property for any taxable year only if 80 percent or more of the gross rental income from such building or structure for such year is rental income from dwelling units (within the meaning of subsection (k) (3) (C)). For purposes of the preceding sentence, if any portion of such building or structure is occupied by the taxpayer, the gross rental income from such building or structure shall include the rental value of the portion so occupied.

(C) **Change in method of depreciation.**—Any change in the computation of the allowance for depreciation for any taxable year, permitted or required by reason of the application of subparagraph (A), shall not be considered a change in a method of accounting.

(3) **Property constructed, etc., before July 25, 1969.**—Paragraph (1) of this subsection shall not apply, and subsection (b) shall apply, in the case of property—

(A) the construction, reconstruction, or erection of which was begun before July 25, 1969, or

(B) for which a written contract entered into before July 25, 1969, with respect to any part of the construction, reconstruction, or erection or for the permanent financing thereof, was on July 25, 1969, and at all times thereafter, binding on the taxpayer.

(4) **Used section 1250 property.**—Except as provided in paragraph (5), in the case of section 1250 property acquired after July 24, 1969, the original use of which does not commence with the taxpayer, the allowance for depreciation under this section shall be limited to an amount computed under—

(A) the straight line method, or

(B) any other method determined by the Secretary to result in a reasonable allowance under subsection (a), not including—

(i) any declining balance method,

(ii) the sum of the years-digits method, or

(iii) any other method allowable solely by reason of the application of subsection (b) (4) or paragraph (1) (C) of this subsection.

(5) **Used residential rental property.**—In the case of section 1250 property which is residential rental property (as defined in paragraph (2) (B)) acquired after July 24, 1969, having a useful life of 20 years or more, the original use of which does not commence with the taxpayer, the allowance for depreciation under this section shall be limited to an amount computed under—

(A) the straight line method,

(B) the declining balance method, using a rate not exceeding 125 percent of the rate which would have been used had the annual allowance been computed under the method described in subparagraph (A), or

(C) any other method determined by the Secretary to result in a reasonable allowance under subsection (a), not including—

(i) the sum of the years-digits method,

(ii) any declining balance method using a rate in excess of the rate permitted under subparagraph (B), or

(iii) any other method allowable solely by reason of the application of subsection (b) (4) or paragraph (1) (C) of this subsection.

(6) Special rules.—

(A) Under regulations prescribed by the Secretary, rules similar to the rules provided in paragraphs (5), (9), (10), and (13) of section 48(h) shall be applied for purposes of paragraphs (3), (4), and (5) of this subsection.

(B) For purposes of paragraphs (2), (4), and (5), if section 1250 property which is not property described in subsection (a) when its original use commences, becomes property described in subsection (a) after July 24, 1969, such property shall not be treated as property the original use of which commences with the taxpayer.

(C) Paragraphs (4) and (5) shall not apply in the case of section 1250 property acquired after July 24, 1969, pursuant to a written contract for the acquisition of such property or for the permanent financing thereof, which was, on July 24, 1969, and at all times thereafter, binding on the taxpayer.

(k) Depreciation of expenditures to rehabilitate low-income rental housing.—

(1) 60-month rule.—The taxpayer may elect, in accordance with regulations prescribed by the Secretary, to compute the depreciation deduction provided by subsection (a) attributable to rehabilitation expenditures incurred with respect to low-income rental housing after July 24, 1969, and before January 1, 1984, under the straight line method using a useful life of 60 months and no salvage value. Such method shall be in lieu of any other method of computing the depreciation deduction under subsection (a), and in lieu of any deduction for amortization, for such expenditures.

(2) Limitations.—

(A) Except as provided in subparagraph (B), the aggregate amount of rehabilitation expenditures paid or incurred by the taxpayer with respect to any dwelling unit in any low-income rental housing which may be taken into account under paragraph (1) shall not exceed $20,000.

(B) The aggregate amount of rehabilitation expenditures paid or incurred by the taxpayer with respect to any dwelling unit in any low-income rental housing which may be taken into account under paragraph (1) may exceed $20,000, but shall not exceed $40,000, if the rehabilitation is conducted pursuant to a program certified by the Secretary of Housing and Urban Development, or his delegate, or by the government of a State or political subdivision of the United States and if:

(i) the certification of development costs is required;

(ii) the tenants occupy units in the property as their principal residence and the program provides for sale of the units to tenants demonstrating home ownership responsibility; and

(iii) the leasing and sale of such units are pursuant to a program in which the sum of the taxable income, if any, from leasing of each such unit, for the entire period of such leasing, and the amount realized from sale or other disposition of a unit, if sold, normally does not exceed the excess of the taxpayer's cost basis for such unit of property, before adjustment under section 1016 for deductions under section 167, over the net tax benefits realized by the taxpayer, consisting of the tax benefits from such deductions under section 167 minus the tax incurred on such taxable income from leasing, if any.

(C) Rehabilitation expenditures paid or incurred by the taxpayer in any taxable year with respect to any dwelling unit in any low-income rental housing shall be taken into account under paragraph (1) only if over a period of two consecutive years, including the taxable year, the aggregate amount of such expenditures exceeds $3,000.

(3) **Definitions.**—For purposes of this subsection—

(A) **Rehabilitation expenditures.**—The term "rehabilitation expenditures" means amounts chargeable to capital account and incurred for property or additions or improvements to property (or related facilities) with a useful life of 5 years or more, in connection with the rehabilitation of an existing building for low-income rental housing; but such term does not include the cost of acquisition of such building or any interest therein.

(B) **Low-income rental housing.**—The term "low-income rental housing" means any building the dwelling units in which are held for occupancy on a rental basis by families and individuals of low or moderate income, as determined by the Secretary in a manner consistent with the Leased Housing Program under section 8 of the United States Housing Act of 1937 pursuant to regulations prescribed under this subsection.

(C) **Dwelling unit.**—The term "dwelling unit" means a house or an apartment used to provide living accommodations in a building or structure, but does not include a unit in a hotel, motel, inn, or other establishment more than one-half of the units in which are used on a transient basis.

(D) **Rehabilitation expenditures incurred.**—Rehabilitation expenditures incurred pursuant to a binding contract entered into before January 1, 1984, and rehabilitation expenditures incurred with respect to low-income rental housing the rehabilitation of which has begun before January 1, 1984, shall be deemed incurred before January 1, 1984.

. . . . .

(m) **Class lives.**—

(1) **In general.**—In the case of a taxpayer who has made an election under this subsection for the taxable year, the term "reasonable allowance" as used in subsection (a) means (with respect to property which is placed in service during the taxable year and which is included in any class for which a class life has been prescribed) only an allowance based on the class life prescribed by the Secretary which reasonably reflects the anticipated useful life of that class of property to the industry or other group. The allowance so prescribed may (under regulations prescribed by the Secretary) permit a variance from any class life by not more than 20 percent (rounded to the nearest half year) of such life.

(2) **Certain first-year conventions not permitted.**—No convention with respect to the time at which assets are deemed placed in service shall be permitted under this section which generally would provide greater depreciation allowances during the taxable year in which the assets are placed in service than would be permitted if all assets were placed in service ratably throughout the year and if depreciation allowances were computed without regard to any convention.

(3) **Making of election.**—An election under this subsection for any taxable year shall be made at such time, in such manner, and subject to such conditions as may be prescribed by the Secretary by regulations.

(4) Termination.—This subsection shall not apply with respect to recovery property (within the meaning of section 168) placed in service after December 31, 1980.

. . . . .

§ 168.   Accelerated cost recovery system

(a) Allowance of deduction.—There shall be allowed as a deduction for any taxable year the amount determined under this section with respect to recovery property.

(b) Amount of deduction.—

(1) In general.—Except as otherwise provided in this section, the amount of the deduction allowable by subsection (a) for any taxable year shall be the aggregate amount determined by applying to the unadjusted basis of recovery property the applicable percentage determined in accordance with the following table:

If the recovery year is:	The applicable percentage for the class of property is:			
	3-year	5-year	10-year	15-year public utility
1	25	15	8	5
2	38	22	14	10
3	37	21	12	9
4		21	10	8
5		21	10	7
6			10	7
7			9	6
8			9	6
9			9	6
10			9	6
11				6
12				6
13				6
14				6
15				6.

(2) 15-year real property.—

(A) In general.—In the case of 15-year real property, the applicable percentage shall be determined in accordance with a table prescribed by the Secretary. In prescribing such table, the Secretary shall—

(i) assign to the property a 15-year recovery period, and

(ii) assign percentages generally determined in accordance with use of the 175 percent declining balance method (200 percent declining balance method in the case of low-income housing), switching to the method described in section 167(b)(1) at a time to maximize the deduction allowable under subsection (a).

For purposes of this subparagraph the applicable percentage in the taxable year in which the property is placed in service shall be determined on the basis of the number of months in such year during which the property was in service. For purposes of this subparagraph the term "low-income housing" means property described in clause (i), (ii), (iii), or (iv) of section 1250(a)(1)(B).

(B) Special rule for year of disposition.—In the case of a disposition of 15-year real property, the deduction allowable under subsection (a) for the taxable year in which the disposition occurs shall reflect only the months during such year the property was in service.

(3) Election of different recovery percentage.—

(A) In general.—Except as provided in subsection (f)(2), in lieu of any applicable percentage under paragraphs (1) and (2), the taxpayer may elect, with respect to one or more classes of recovery property placed in service during the taxable year, the applicable percentage determined by use of the straight line method over the recovery period elected by the taxpayer in accordance with the following table:

In the case of:	The taxpayer may elect a recovery period of:
3-year property	3, 5, or 12 years.
5-year property	5, 12, or 25 years.
10-year property	10, 25, or 35 years.
15-year real property	15, 35, or 45 years.
15-year public utility property	15, 35, or 45 years.

(B) Operating rules.—

(i) In general.—Except as provided in clause (ii), the taxpayer may elect under subparagraph (A) only a single percentage for property in any class of recovery property placed in service during the taxable year. The percentage so elected shall apply to all property in such class placed in service during such taxable year and shall apply throughout the recovery period elected for such property.

(ii) Real property.—In the case of 15-year real property the taxpayer shall make the election under subparagraph (A) on a property-by-property basis.

(iii) Convention.—Under regulations prescribed by the Secretary, the half-year convention shall apply to any election with respect to any recovery property (other than 15-year real property) with respect to which an election is made under this paragraph.

(c) Recovery property.—For purposes of this title—

(1) Recovery property defined.—Except as provided in subsection (e), the term "recovery property" means tangible property of a character subject to the allowance for depreciation—

(A) used in a trade or business, or

(B) held for the production of income.

(2) Classes of recovery property.—Each item of recovery property shall be assigned to one of the following classes of property:

(A) 3-year property.—The term "3-year property" means section 1245 class property—

(i) with a present class life of 4 years or less; or

(ii) used in connection with research and experimentation.

(B) 5-year property.—The term "5-year property" means recovery property which is section 1245 class property and which is not 3-year property, 10-year property, or 15-year public utility property.

(C) 10-year property.—The term "10-year property" means—

(i) public utility property (other than section 1250 class property or 3-year property) with a present class life of more than 18 years but not more than 25 years; and

(ii) section 1250 class property with a present class life of 12.5 years or less.

(D) 15-year real property.—The term "15-year real property" means section 1250 class property which does not have a present class life of 12.5 years or less.

(E) 15-year public utility property.—The term "15-year public utility property" means public utility property (other than section 1250 class property or 3-year property) with a present class life of more than 25 years.

(d) Unadjusted basis; adjustments.—

(1) Unadjusted basis defined.—

(A) In general.—For purposes of this section, the term "unadjusted basis" means the excess of—

(i) the basis of the property determined under part II of subchapter O of chapter 1 for purposes of determining gain (determined without regard to the adjustments described in paragraph (2) or (3) of section 1016(a)), over

(ii) the sum of—

(I) that portion of the basis for which the taxpayer properly elects amortization (including the deduction allowed under section 167(k)) in lieu of depreciation, and

(II) that portion of the basis which the taxpayer properly elects to treat as an expense under section 179.

(B) Time for taking basis into account.—

(i) In general.—The unadjusted basis of property shall be first taken into account under subsection (b) for the taxable year in which the property is placed in service.

(ii) Redeterminations.—The Secretary shall by regulation provide for the method of determining the deduction allowable under subsection (a) for any taxable year (and succeeding taxable years) in which the basis is redetermined (including any reduction under section 1017).

(2) Dispositions.—

(A) Mass asset accounts.—In lieu of recognizing gain or loss under this chapter, a taxpayer who maintains one or more mass asset accounts of recovery property may, under regulations prescribed by the Secretary, elect to include in income all proceeds realized on the disposition of such property.

(B) Adjustment to basis.—Except as provided under regulations prescribed by the Secretary under subsection (f)(7), if any recovery property (other than 15-year real property or property with respect to which an election under subparagraph (A) is made) is disposed of, the unadjusted basis of such property shall cease to be taken into account in determining any recovery deduction allowable under subsection (a) as of the beginning of the taxable year in which such disposition occurs.

(C) Disposition includes retirement.—For purposes of this subparagraph, the term "disposition" includes retirement.

(e) Property excluded from application of section.—For purposes of this section—

(1) Property placed in service before January 1, 1981.—The term "recovery property" does not include property placed in service by the taxpayer before January 1, 1981.

(2) Certain methods of depreciation.—The term "recovery property" does not include property if—

(A) the taxpayer elects to exclude such property from the application of this section, and

(B) for the first taxable year for which a deduction would (but for this election) be allowable under this section with respect to such property in the hands of the taxpayer, the property is properly depreciated under the unit-of-production method or any method of depreciation not expressed in a term of years (other than the retirement-replacement-betterment method).

. . . . .

(4) Certain transactions in property placed in service before 1981.—

(A) Section 1245 class property.—The term "recovery property" does not include section 1245 class property acquired by the taxpayer after December 31, 1980, if—

(i) the property was owned or used at any time during 1980 by the taxpayer or a related person,

(ii) the property is acquired from a person who owned such property at any time during 1980, and, as part of the transaction, the user of such property does not change,

(iii) the taxpayer leases such property to a person (or a person related to such person) who owned or used such property at any time during 1980, or

(iv) the property is acquired in a transaction as part of which the user of such property does not change and the property is not recovery property in the hands of the person from which the property is so acquired by reason of clause (ii) or (iii).

For purposes of this subparagraph and subparagraph (B), property shall not be treated as owned before it is placed in service. For purposes of this subparagraph, whether the user of property changes as part of a transaction shall be determined in accordance with regulations prescribed by the Secretary.

(B) Section 1250 class property.—The term "recovery property" does not include section 1250 class property acquired by the taxpayer after December 31, 1980, if—

(i) such property was owned by the taxpayer or by a related person at any time during 1980;

(ii) the taxpayer leases such property to a person (or a person related to such person) who owned such property at any time during 1980; or

(iii) such property is acquired in an exchange described in section 1031, 1033, 1038, or 1039 to the extent that the basis of such property includes an amount representing the adjusted basis of other property owned by the taxpayer or a related person during 1980.

(C) Certain nonrecognition transactions.—The term "recovery property" does not include property placed in service by the transferor or distributor before January 1, 1981, which is acquired by the taxpayer after December 31, 1980, in a transaction described in section 332, 351, 361, 371(a), 374(a), 721, or 731 (or such property acquired from the transferee or acquiring corporation in a transaction described in such section), to the extent that the basis of the property is determined by reference to the basis of the property in the hands of the transferor or distributor. In the case of property to which this subparagraph applies, rules similar to the rules described in section 381(c)(6) shall apply.

(D) Related person defined.—Except as provided in subparagraph (E), for purposes of this paragraph a person (hereinafter referred to as the related person) is related to any person if—

(i) the related person bears a relationship to such person specified in section 267(b) or section 707(b)(1), or

(ii) the related person and such person are engaged in trades or businesses under common control (within the meaning of subsections (a) and (b) of section 52).

For purposes of clause (i), in applying section 267(b) and section 707(b)(1) "10 percent" shall be substituted for "50 percent". The determination of whether a person is related to another person shall be made as of the time the taxpayer acquires the property involved.

(E) Liquidation of subsidiary, etc.—For purposes of this paragraph, a corporation is not a related person to the taxpayer—

(i) if such corporation is a distributing corporation in a transaction to which section 334(b)(2)(B) applies and the stock of such corporation referred to in such subparagraph (B) was acquired by the taxpayer by purchase after December 31, 1980, or

(ii) if such corporation is liquidated in a liquidation to which section 331(a) applies and the taxpayer (or a related person) by himself or together with 1 or more other persons acquires the stock of the liquidated corporation by purchase (meeting the requirements of section 334(b)(2)(B)) after December 31, 1980.

A similar rule shall apply in the case of a deemed liquidation under section 338.

(F) Antiavoidance rule.—The term "recovery property" does not include property acquired by the taxpayer after December 31, 1980, which, under regulations prescribed by the Secretary, is acquired in a transaction one of the principal purposes of which is to avoid the principles of paragraph (1) and this paragraph.

(G) Reduction in unadjusted basis.—In the case of an acquisition of property described in subparagraph (B) or (C), the unadjusted basis of the property under subsection (d) shall be reduced to the extent that such property acquired is not recovery property.

(f) Special rules for application of this section.—For purposes of this section—

(1) Components of section 1250 class property.—

(A) In general.—Except as otherwise provided in this paragraph—

(i) the deduction allowable under subsection (a) with respect to any component (which is section 1250 class property) of a building shall be computed in the same manner as the deduction allowable with respect to such building, and

(ii) the recovery period for such component shall begin on the later of—

(I) the date such component is placed in service, or

(II) the date on which the building is placed in service.

(B) Transitional rule.—In the case of any building placed in service by the taxpayer before January 1, 1981, for purposes of applying subparagraph (A) to components of such buildings placed in service after December 31, 1980, the deduction allowable under subsection (a) with respect to such components shall be computed in the same manner as the deduction allowable with respect to the first such component placed in service after December 31, 1980. For purposes of the preceding sentence, the method of computing the deduction allowable with respect to such first component shall be determined as if it were a separate building.

(C) Exception for substantial improvements.—

(i) In general.—For purposes of this paragraph, a substantial improvement shall be treated as a separate building.

(ii) Substantial improvement.—For purposes of clause (i), the term "substantial improvement" means the improvements added to capital account with respect to any building during any 24-month period, but only if the sum of the amounts added to such account during such period equals or exceeds 25 percent of the adjusted basis of the building (determined without regard to the adjustments provided in paragraphs (2) and (3) of section 1016(a)) as of the first day of such period.

(iii) Improvements must be made after building in service for 3 years.—For purposes of this paragraph, the term "substantial improvement" shall not include any improvement made before the date 3 years after the building was placed in service.

. . . . .

(4) Manner and time for making elections.—

(A) In general.—Any election under this section shall be made for the taxable year in which the property is placed in service.

(B) Made on return.—Any election under this section shall be made on the taxpayer's return of the tax imposed by this chapter for the taxable year concerned.

(C) Revocation only with consent.—Any election under this section, once made, may be revoked only with the consent of the Secretary.

(5) Short taxable years.—In the case of a taxable year that is less than 12 months, the amount of the deduction under this section shall be an amount which bears the same relationship to the amount of the deduction, determined without regard to this paragraph, as the number of months in the short taxable year bears to 12. In such case, the amount of the deduction for subsequent taxable years shall be appropriately adjusted in accordance with regulations prescribed by the Secretary. The determination of when a taxable year begins shall be made in accordance with regulations prescribed by the Secretary. This paragraph shall not apply to any deduction with respect to any property for the first taxable year of the lessor for which an election under paragraph (8) is in effect with respect to such property.

(6) Leasehold improvements.—For purposes of determining whether a leasehold improvement which is recovery property shall be amortized over the term of the lease, the recovery period (taking into account any election under paragraph (2)(C) of this subsection or under subsection (b)(3) with respect to such property) of such property shall be taken into account in lieu of its useful life.

(7) Special rule for acquisitions and dispositions in nonrecognition transactions.—Notwithstanding any other provision of this section, the deduction allowed under this section in the taxable year in which recovery property is acquired or is disposed of in a transaction in which gain or loss is not recognized in whole or in part shall be determined in accordance with regulations prescribed by the Secretary.

(8) Special rule for leases.—

(A) In general.—In the case of an agreement with respect to qualified leased property, if all of the parties to the agreement characterize such agreement as a lease and elect to have the provisions of this paragraph apply with respect to such agreement, and if the requirements of subparagraph (B) are met, then, except as provided in subsection (i), for purposes of this subtitle—

(i) such agreement shall be treated as a lease entered into by the parties (and any party which is a corporation described in subparagraph (B)(i)(I) shall be deemed to have entered into the lease in the course of carrying on a trade or business), and

(ii) the lessor shall be treated as the owner of the property and the lessee shall be treated as the lessee of the property.

(B) Certain requirements must be met.—The requirements of this subparagraph are met if—

(i) the lessor is—

(I) a corporation (other than an S corporation or a personal holding company (within the meaning of section 542(a))) which is not a related person with respect to the lessee,

(II) a partnership all of the partners of which are corporations described in subclause (I), or

(III) a grantor trust with respect to which the grantor and all beneficiaries of the trust are described in subclause (I) or (II),

(ii) the minimum investment of the lessor—

(I) at the time the property is first placed in service under the lease, and

(II) at all times during the term of the lease,

is not less than 10 percent of the adjusted basis of such property, and

(iii) the term of the lease (including any extensions) does not exceed the greater of—

(I) 120 percent of the present class life of the property, or

(II) the period equal to the recovery period determined with respect to such property under subsection (i)(2).

(C) No other factors taken into account.—If the requirements of subparagraphs (A) and (B) are met with respect to any transaction described in subparagraph (A), no other factors shall be taken into account in making a determination as to whether subparagraph (A) (i) or (ii) applies with respect to such transaction.

(D) Qualified leased property defined.—For purposes of this section—

(i) In general.—The term "qualified leased property" means recovery property—

(I) which is new section 38 property of the lessor, which is leased within 3 months after such property was placed in service, and which, if acquired by the lessee, would have been new section 38 property of the lessee, or

(II) which was new section 38 property of the lessee, which is leased within 3 months after such property is placed in service by the lessee, and with respect to which the adjusted basis of the lessor does not exceed the adjusted basis of the lessee at the time of the lease.

(ii) Only 45 percent of the lessee's property may be treated as qualified.— The cost basis of all safe harbor lease property (determined without regard to this clause)—

(I) which is placed in service during any calendar year, and

(II) with respect to which the taxpayer is a lessee,

shall not exceed an amount equal to the 45 percent of the cost basis of the taypayer's qualified base property placed in service during such calendar year.

(iii) Allocation of disqualified basis.—The cost basis not treated as qualified leased property under clause (ii) shall be allocated to safe harbor lease property for such calendar year (determined without regard to clause (ii)) in reverse order to when the agreement described in subparagraph (A) with respect to such property was entered into.

(iv) Certain property may not be treated as qualified leased property.—The term "qualified leased property" shall not include recovery property—

(I) which is a qualified rehabilitated building (within the meaning of section 48(g)(1)),

(II) which is public utility property (within the meaning of section 167(*l*)(3)(A)),

(III) which is property with respect to which a deduction is allowable by reason of section 291(b),

(IV) with respect to which the lessee of the property (other than property described in clause (v)) under the agreement described in subparagraph (A) is a nonqualified tax-exempt organization, or

(V) property with respect to which the user of such property is a person (other than a United States person) not subject to United States tax on income derived from the use of such property.

(v) Qualified mass commuting vehicles included.—The term "qualified leased property" includes recovery property which is a qualifed mass commuting vehicle (as defined in section 103(b)(9)) which is financed in whole or in part by obligations the interest on which is excludable under section 103(a).

(vi) Qualified base property.—For purposes of this subparagraph, the term "qualified base property" means property placed in service during any calendar year which—

(I) is new section 38 property of the taxpayer,

(II) is safe harbor lease property (not described in subclause (I)) with respect to which the taxpayer is the lessee, or

(III) is designated leased property (other than property described in subclause (I) or (II)) with respect to which the taxpayer is the lessee.

Any designated leased property taken into account by any lessee under the preceding sentence shall not be taken into account by the lessor in determining the lessor's qualified base property. The lessor shall provide the lessee with such information with respect to the cost basis of such property as is necessary to carry out the purposes of this clause.

(vii) Definition of designated leased property.—For purposes of this subparagraph, the term "designated leased property" means property—

(I) which is new section 38 property,

(II) which is subject to a lease with respect to which the lessor of the property is treated (without regard to this paragraph) as the owner of the property for Federal tax purposes,

(III) with respect to which the term of the lease to which such property is subject is more than 50 percent of the present class life (or, if no present class life, the recovery period used in subsection (i)(2)) of such property, and

(IV) which the lessee designates on his return as designated leased property.

(viii) Definition; special rule.—For purposes of this subparagraph—

(I) New section 38 property.—The term "new section 38 property" has the meaning given such term by section 48(b).

(II) Property placed in service.—For purposes of this title (other than clause (i)), any property described in clause (i) to which subparagraph (A) applies shall be deemed originally placed in service not earlier than the date such property is used under the lease.

(E) Minimum investment.—

(i) In general.—For purposes of subparagraph (A), the term "minimum investment" means the amount the lessor has at risk with respect to the property (other than financing from the lessee or a related party of the lessee).

(ii) Special rule for purchase requirement.—For purposes of clause (i), an agreement between the lessor and lessee requiring either or both parties to purchase or sell the qualified leased property at some price (whether or not fixed in the agreement) at the end of the lease term shall not affect the amount the lessor is treated as having at risk with respect to the property.

(F) Characterization by parties.—For purposes of this paragraph, any determination as to whether a person is a lessor or lessee or property is leased shall be made on the basis of the characterization of such person or property under the agreement described in subparagraph (A).

(G) Regulations.—The Secretary shall prescribe such regulations as may be necessary to carry out the purposes of this paragraph, including (but not limited to) regulations consistent with such purposes which limit the aggregate amount of (and timing of) deductions and credits in respect of qualified leased property to the aggregate amount (and the timing) allowable without regard to this paragraph.

(H) Definitions.—For purposes of this paragraph—

(i) Related person.—A person is related to another person if both persons are members of the same affiliated group (within the meaning of subsection (a) of section 1504 and determined without regard to subsection (b) of section 1504).

(ii) Nonqualified tax-exempt organization.—

(I) In general.—The term "nonqualified tax-exempt organization" means, with respect to any agreement to which subparagraph (A) applies, any organization (or predecessor organization which was engaged in substantially similar activities) which was exempt from taxation under this title at any time during the 5-year period ending on the date such agreement was entered into.

(II) Special rule for farmers' cooperatives.—The term "nonqualified tax-exempt organization" shall not include any farmers' cooperative organization described in section 521 whether or not exempt from taxation under section 521.

(III) Special rule for property used in unrelated trade or business.—An organization shall not be treated as a nonqualified tax-exempt organization with respect to any property if such property is used in an unrelated trade or business (within the meaning of section 513) of such organization which is subject to tax under section 511.

(I) Transitional rules for certain transactions.—

(i) In general.—Except as provided in clause (ii), clause (ii) of subparagraph (D) shall not apply to any transitional safe harbor lease property (within the meaning of section 208(d)(3) of the Tax Equity and Fiscal Responsibility Act of 1982).

(ii) Special rules.—For purposes of subparagraph (D)(ii)—

(I) Determination of qualified base property.—The cost basis of property described in clause (i) (and other property placed in service during 1982 to which subparagraph (D)(ii) does not apply) shall be taken into account in determining the qualified base property of the taxpayer for the taxable year in which such property was placed in service.

(II) Reduction in qualified leased property.—The cost basis of property which may be treated as qualified leased property under subparagraph (D)(ii) for the taxable year in which such property was placed in service (determined without regard to this subparagraph) shall be reduced by the cost basis of the property taken into account under subclause (I).

(J) Coordination with at risk rules.—

(i) In general.—For purposes of section 465, in the case of property placed in service after the date of the enactment of this subparagraph, if—

(I) an activity involves the leasing of section 1245 property which is safe harbor lease property, and

(II) the lessee of such property (as determined under this paragraph) would, but for this paragraph, be treated as the owner of such property for purposes of this title,

then the lessor (as so determined) shall be considered to be at risk with respect to such property in an amount equal to the amount the lessee is considered at risk with respect to such property (determined under section 465 without regard to this paragraph).

(ii) Subparagraph not to apply to certain service corporations.—Clause (i) shall not apply to any lessor which is a corporation the principal function of which is the performance of services in the field of health, law, engineering, architecture, accounting, actuarial science, performing arts, athletics, or consulting.

(iii) Special rule for property placed in service before date of enactment of this subparagraph.—This subparagraph shall apply to property placed in service before the date of enactment of this subparagraph if the provisions of section 465 did not apply to the lessor before such date but become applicable to such lessor after such date.

. . . . .

(9) Salvage value.—No salvage value shall be taken into account in determining the deduction allowable under subsection (a).

(10) Transferee bound by transferor's period and method in certain cases.—

(A) In general.—In the case of recovery property transferred in a transaction described in subparagraph (B), the transferee shall be treated as the transferor for purposes of computing the deduction allowable under subsection (a) with respect to so much of the basis in the hands of the transferee as does not exceed the adjusted basis in the hands of the transferor.

(B) Transfers covered.—The transactions described in this subparagraph are—

(i) a transaction described in section 332, 351, 361, 371(a), 374(a), 721, or 731;

(ii) an acquisition (other than described in clause (i)) from a related person (as defined in subparagraph (D) of subsection (e)(4)); and

(iii) an acquisition followed by a leaseback to the person from whom the property is acquired.

(C) Property reacquired by the taxpayer.—Under regulations prescribed by the Secretary, recovery property which is disposed of and then reacquired by the taxpayer shall be treated for purposes of computing the deduction allowable under subsection (a) as if such property had not been disposed of.

(D) Exception.—This paragraph shall not apply to any transaction to which subsection (e)(4) applies.

. . . . .

(h) Special rules for recovery property classes.—For purposes of this section—

(1) Certain horses.—The term "3-year property" includes—

(A) any race horse which is more than 2 years old at the time such horse is placed in service; or

(B) any other horse which is more than 12 years old at such time.

(2) Railroad tank cars.—The term "10-year property" includes railroad tank cars.

(3) Manufactured homes.—The term "10-year property" includes manufactured homes.

(4) Qualified coal utilization property.—The term "10-year property" includes qualified coal utilization property which is not 3-year property, 5-year property, or 10-year property (determined without regard to this paragraph).

(5) Application with other classes.—Any property which is treated as included in a class or property by reason of this subsection shall not be treated as property included in any other class.

(i) Limitations relating to leases of qualified leased property.—For purposes of this subtitle, in the case of safe harbor lease property, the following limitations shall apply:

(1) Lessor may not reduce tax liability by more than 50 percent.—

(A) In general.—The aggregate amount allowable as deductions or credits for any taxable year which are allocable to all safe harbor lease property with respect to which the taxpayer is the lessor may not reduce the liability for tax of the taxpayer for such taxable year (determined without regard to safe harbor lease items) by more than 50 percent of such liability.

(B) Carryover of amounts not allowable as deductions or credits.—Any amount not allowable as a deduction or credit under subparagraph (A)—

(i) may be carried over to any subsequent taxable year, and

(ii) shall be treated as a deduction or credit allocable to safe harbor lease property in such subsequent taxable year.

(C) Allocation among deductions and credits.—The Secretary shall prescribe regulations for determining the amount—

(i) of any deduction or credit allocable to safe harbor lease property for any taxable year to which subparagraph (A) applies, and

(ii) of any carryover of any such deduction or credit under subparagraph (B) to any subsequent taxable year.

(D) Liability for tax and safe harbor lease items defined.—For purposes of this paragraph—

(i) Liability for tax defined.—Except as provided in this subparagraph, the term "liability for tax" means the tax imposed by this chapter, reduced by the sum of the credits allowable under subpart A of part IV of subchapter A of this chapter.

(ii) Safe harbor lease items defined.—The term "safe harbor lease items" means any of the following items which are properly allocable to safe harbor lease property with respect to which the taxpayer is the lessor:

(I) Any deduction or credit allowable under this chapter (other than any deduction for interest).

(II) Any rental income received by the taxpayer from any lessee of such property.

(III) Any interest allowable as a deduction under this chapter on indebtedness of the taxpayer (or any related person within the meaning of subsection (e)(4)(D)) which is paid or incurred to the lessee of such property (or any person so related to the lessee).

(iii) Certain taxes not included.—The term "tax imposed by this chapter" shall not include any tax treated as not imposed by this chapter under the last sentence of section 53(a) (other than the tax imposed by section 56).

(2) Method of cost recovery.—The deduction allowable under subsection (a) with respect to any safe harbor lease property shall be determined by using the 150 percent declining balance method, switching to the straight-line method at a time to maximize the deduction (with a half-year convention in the first recovery year and without regard to salvage value) and a recovery period determined in accordance with the following table:

In the case of:	The recovery period is:
3-year property	5 years.
5-year property	8 years.
10-year property	15 years.

(3) Investment credit allowed only over 5-year period.—In the case of any credit which would otherwise be allowable under section 38 with respect to any safe harbor lease property for any taxable year (determined without regard to this paragraph), only 20 percent of the amount of such credit shall be allowable in such taxable year and 20 percent of such amount shall be allowable in each of the succeeding 4 taxable years.

(4) No carrybacks of credit or net operating loss allocable to elected qualified leased property.—

    (A) Credit carrybacks.—In determining the amount of any credit allowable under subpart A of part IV of subchapter A of this chapter which may be carried back to any preceding taxable year—

        (i) the liability for tax for the taxable year from which any such credit is to be carried shall be reduced first by any credit not properly allocable to safe harbor lease property, and

        (ii) no credit which is properly allocable to safe harbor lease property shall be taken into account in determining the amount of any credit which may be carried back.

    (B) Net operating loss carrybacks.—The net operating loss carryback provided in section 172(b) for any taxable year shall be reduced by that portion of the amount of such carryback which is properly allocable to the items described in paragraph (1)(D)(ii) with respect to all safe harbor lease property with respect to which the taxpayer is the lessor.

(5) Limitation on deduction for interest paid by the lessor to the lessee.—In the case of interest described in paragraph (1)(D)(ii)(III), the amount allowable as a deduction for any taxable year with respect to such interest shall not exceed the amount which would have been computed if the rate of interest under the agreement were equal to the rate of interest in effect under section 6621 at the time the agreement was entered into.

(6) Computation of taxable income of lessee for purposes of percentage depletion.—

    (A) In general.—For purposes of section 613 or 613A, the taxable income of any taxpayer who is a lessee of any safe harbor lease property shall be computed as if the taxpayer was the owner of such property, except that the amount of the deduction under subsection (a) of this section shall be determined after application of paragraph (2) of this subsection.

    (B) Coordination with crude oil windfall profit tax.—Section 4988(b)(3)(A) shall be applied without regard to subparagraph (A).

(7) Transitional rule for application of paragraph (1) to certain transactions.—In the case of any deduction or credit with respect to—

    (A) any transitional safe harbor lease property (within the meaning of section 208(d)(3) of the Tax Equity and Fiscal Responsibility Act of 1982), or

    (B) any other safe harbor lease property placed in service during 1982 and to which paragraph (1) does not apply,

paragraph (1) shall not operate to disallow any such deduction or credit for the taxable year for which such deduction or credit would otherwise be allowable but deductions and credits with respect to such property shall be taken into account first in determining whether any deduction or credit is allowable under paragraph (1) with respect to any other safe harbor lease property.

(8) Safe harbor lease property.—For purposes of this section, the term "safe harbor lease property" means qualified leased property with respect to which an election under section 168(f)(8) is in effect.

. . . . .

§ 169.   Amortization of pollution control facilities

(a) Allowance of deduction.—Every person, at his election, shall be entitled to a deduction with respect to the amortization of the amortizable basis of any certified pollution control facility (as defined in subsection (d)), based on a period of 60 months. Such amortization deduction shall be an amount, with respect to each month of such period within the taxable year, equal to the amortizable basis of the pollution control facility at the end of such month divided by the number of months (including the month for which the deduction is computed) remaining in the period. Such amortizable basis at the end of the month shall be computed without regard to the amortization deduction for such month. The amortization deduction provided by this section with respect to any month shall be in lieu of the depreciation deduction with respect to such pollution control facility for such month provided by section 167. The 60-month period shall begin, as to any pollution control facility, at the election of the taxpayer, with the month following the month in which such facility was completed or acquired, or with the succeeding taxable year.

. . . . .

§ 170.   Charitable, etc., contributions and gifts

(a) Allowance of deduction.—

(1) General rule.—There shall be allowed as a deduction any charitable contribution (as defined in subsection (c)) payment of which is made within the taxable year. A charitable contribution shall be allowable as a deduction only if verified under regulations prescribed by the Secretary.

(2) Corporations on accrual basis.—In the case of a corporation reporting its taxable income on the accrual basis, if—

(A) the board of directors authorizes a charitable contribution during any taxable year, and

(B) payment of such contribution is made after the close of such taxable year and on or before the 15th day of the third month following the close of such taxable year,

then the taxpayer may elect to treat such contribution as paid during such taxable year. The election may be made only at the time of the filing of the return for such taxable year, and shall be signified in such manner as the Secretary shall by regulations prescribe.

(3) Future interests in tangible personal property.—For purposes of this section, payment of a charitable contribution which consists of a future interest in tangible personal property shall be treated as made only when all intervening interests in, and rights to the actual possession or enjoyment of, the property have expired or are held by persons other than the taxpayer or those standing in a relationship to the taxpayer described in section 267(b). For purposes of the preceding sentence, a fixture which is intended to be severed from the real property shall be treated as tangible personal property.

(b) Percentage limitations.—

(1) Individuals.—In the case of an individual, the deduction provided in subsection (a) shall be limited as provided in the succeeding subparagraphs.

(A) **General rule.**—Any charitable contribution to—

(i) a church or a convention or association of churches,

(ii) an educational organization which normally maintains a regular faculty and curriculum and normally has a regularly enrolled body of pupils or students in attendance at the place where its educational activities are regularly carried on,

(iii) an organization the principal purpose or functions of which are the providing of medical or hospital care or medical education or medical research, if the organization is a hospital, or if the organization is a medical research organization directly engaged in the continuous active conduct of medical research in conjunction with a hospital, and during the calendar year in which the contribution is made such organization is committed to spend such contributions for such research before January 1 of the fifth calendar year which begins after the date such contribution is made,

(iv) an organization which normally receives a substantial part of its support (exclusive of income received in the exercise or performance by such organization of its charitable, educational, or other purpose or function constituting the basis for its exemption under section 501(a)) from the United States or any State or political subdivision thereof or from direct or indirect contributions from the general public, and which is organized and operated exclusively to receive, hold, invest, and administer property and to make expenditures to or for the benefit of a college or university which is an organization referred to in clause (ii) of this subparagraph and which is an agency or instrumentality of a State or political subdivision thereof, or which is owned or operated by a State or political subdivision thereof or by an agency or instrumentality of one or more States or political subdivisions,

(v) a governmental unit referred to in subsection (c) (1),

(vi) an organization referred to in subsection (c) (2) which normally receives a substantial part of its support (exclusive of income received in the exercise or performance by such organization of its charitable, educational, or other purpose or function constituting the basis for its exemption under section 501(a)) from a governmental unit referred to in subsection (c) (1) or from direct or indirect contributions from the general public,

(vii) a private foundation described in subparagraph (D), or

(viii) an organization described in section 509(a) (2) or (3),

shall be allowed to the extent that the aggregate of such contributions does not exceed 50 percent of the taxpayer's contribution base for the taxable year.

(B) Other contributions.—Any charitable contribution other than a charitable contribution to which subparagraph (A) applies shall be allowed to the extent that the aggregate of such contributions does not exceed the lesser of—

(i) 20 percent of the taxpayer's contribution base for the taxable year, or

(ii) the excess of 50 percent of the taxpayer's contribution base for the taxable year over the amount of charitable contributions allowable under subparagraph (A) (determined without regard to subparagraph (C)).

(C) Special limitation with respect to contributions of certain capital gain property.—

(i) In the case of charitable contributions of capital gain property to which subsection (e) (1) (B) does not apply, the total amount of contributions of such property which may be taken into account under subsection (a) for any taxable year shall not exceed 30 percent of the taxpayer's contribution base for such year. For purposes of this subsection, contributions of capital gain property to which this paragraph applies shall be taken into account after all other charitable contributions.

(ii) If charitable contributions described in subparagraph (A) of capital gain property to which clause (i) applies exceeds 30 percent of the taxpayer's contribution base for any taxable year, such excess shall be treated, in a manner consistent with the rules of subsection (d) (1), as a charitable contribution of capital gain property to which clause (i) applies in each of the 5 succeeding taxable years in order of time.

(iii) At the election of the taxpayer (made at such time and in such manner as the Secretary prescribes by regulations), subsection (e) (1) shall apply to all contributions of capital gain property (to which subsection (e) (1) (B) does not otherwise apply) made by the taxpayer during the taxable year. If such an election is made, clauses (i) and (ii) shall not apply to contributions of capital gain property made during the taxable year, and, in applying subsection (d) (1) for such taxable year with respect to contributions of capital gain property made in any prior contribution year for which an election was not made under this clause, such contributions shall be reduced as if subsection (e) (1) had applied to such contributions in the year in which made.

(iv) For purposes of this subparagraph, the term "capital gain property" means, with respect to any contribution, any capital asset the sale of which at its fair market value at the time of the contribution would have resulted in gain which would have been long-term capital gain. For purposes of the preceding sentence, any property which is property used in the trade or business (as defined in section 1231(b)) shall be treated as a capital asset.

. . . .

(E) Contribution base defined.—For purposes of this section, the term "contribution base" means adjusted gross income (computed without regard to any net operating loss carryback to the taxable year under section 172).

(2) Corporations.—In the case of a corporation, the total deductions under subsection (a) for any taxable year shall not exceed 10 percent of the taxpayer's taxable income computed without regard to—

(A) this section,

(B) part VII (except section 248),

(C) any net operating loss carryback to the taxable year under section 172,

(D) Section 922 (special deduction for Western Hemisphere trade corporations), and

(E) any capital loss carryback to the taxable year under section 1212(a) (1).

(c) Charitable contribution defined.—For purposes of this section, the term "charitable contribution" means a contribution or gift to or for the use of—

(1) A State, a possession of the United States, or any political subdivision of any of the foregoing, or the United States or the District of Columbia, but only if the contribution or gift is made for exclusively public purposes.

(2) A corporation, trust, or community chest, fund, or foundation—

(A) created or organized in the United States or in any possession thereof, or under the law of the United States, any State, the District of Columbia, or any possession of the United States;

(B) organized and operated exclusively for religious, charitable, scientific, literary, or educational purposes, or to foster national or international amateur sports competition (but only if no part of its activities involve the provision of athletic facilities or equipment), or for the prevention of cruelty to children or animals;

(C) no part of the net earnings of which inures to the benefit of any private shareholder or individual; and

(D) which is not disqualified for tax exemption under section 501(c) (3) by reason of attempting to influence legislation, and which does not participate in, or intervene in (including the publishing or distributing of statements), any political campaign on behalf of any candidate for public office.

A contribution or gift by a corporation to a trust, chest, fund, or foundation shall be deductible by reason of this paragraph only if it is to be used within the United States or any of its possessions exclusively for purposes specified in subparagraph (B). Rules similar to the rules of section 501(j) shall apply for purposes of this paragraph.

(3) A post or organization of war veterans, or an auxiliary unit or society of, or trust or foundation for, any such post or organization—

(A) organized in the United States or any of its possessions, and

(B) no part of the net earnings of which inures to the benefit of any private shareholder or individual.

(4) In the case of a contribution or gift by an individual, a domestic fraternal society, order, or association, operating under the lodge system, but only if such contribution or gift is to be used exclusively for religious, charitable, scientific, literary, or educational purposes, or for the prevention of cruelty to children or animals.

(5) A cemetery company owned and operated exclusively for the benefit of its members, or any corporation chartered solely for burial purposes as a cemetery corporation and not permitted by its charter to engage in any business not necessarily incident to that purpose, if such company or corporation is not operated for profit and no part of the net earnings of such company or corporation inures to the benefit of any private shareholder or individual.

For purposes of this section, the term "charitable contribution" also means an amount treated under subsection (g) as paid for the use of an organization described in paragraph (2), (3), or (4).

(d) Carryovers of excess contributions.—

(1) Individuals.—

(A) **In general.**—In the case of an individual, if the amount of charitable contributions described in subsection (b) (1) (A) payment of which is made within a taxable year (hereinafter in this paragraph referred to as the "contribution year") exceeds 50 percent of the taxpayer's contribution base for such year, such excess shall be treated as a charitable contribution described in subsection (b) (1) (A) paid in each of the 5 succeeding taxable years in order of time, but, with respect to any such succeeding taxable year, only to the extent of the lesser of the two following amounts:

(i) the amount by which 50 percent of the taxpayer's contribution base for such succeeding taxable year exceeds the sum of the charitable contributions described in subsection (b) (1) (A) payment of which is made by the taxpayer within such succeeding taxable year (determined without regard to this subparagraph) and the charitable contributions described in subsection (b) (1) (A) payment of which was made in taxable years before the contribution year which are treated under this subparagraph as having been paid in such succeeding taxable year; or

(ii) in the case of the first succeeding taxable year, the amount of such excess, and in the case of the second, third, fourth, or fifth succeeding taxable year, the portion of such excess not treated under this subparagraph as a charitable contribution described in subsection (b) (1) (A) paid in any taxable year intervening between the contribution year and such succeeding taxable year.

(B) Special rule for net operating loss carryovers.—In applying subparagraph (A), the excess determined under subparagraph (A) for the contribution year shall be reduced to the extent that such excess reduces taxable income (as computed for purposes of the second sentence of section 172(b) (2)) and increases the net operating loss deduction for a taxable year succeeding the contribution year.

(2) Corporations.—

(A) In general.—Any contribution made by a corporation in a taxable year (hereinafter in this paragraph referred to as the "contribution year") in excess of the amount deductible for such year under subsection (b) (2) shall be deductible for each of the 5 succeeding taxable years in order of time, but only to the extent of the lesser of the two following amounts: (i) the excess of the maximum amount deductible for such succeeding taxable year under subsection (b) (2) over the sum of the contributions made in such year plus the aggregate of the excess contributions which were made in taxable years before the contribution year and which are deductible under this subparagraph for such succeeding taxable year; or (ii) in the case of the first succeeding taxable year, the amount of such excess contribution, and in the case of the second, third, fourth, or fifth succeeding taxable year, the portion of such excess contribution not deductible under this subparagraph for any taxable year intervening between the contribution year and such succeeding taxable year.

(B) Special rule for net operating loss carryovers.—For purposes of subparagraph (A), the excess of—

(i) the contributions made by a corporation in a taxable year to which this section applies, over

(ii) the amount deductible in such year under the limitation in subsection (b) (2), shall be reduced to the extent that such excess reduces taxable income (as computed for purposes of the second sentence of section 172(b) (2)) and increases a net operating loss carryover under section 172 to a succeeding taxable year.

(e) Certain contributions of ordinary income and capital gain property.—

(1) **General rule.**—The amount of any charitable contribution of property otherwise taken into account under this section shall be reduced by the sum of—

(A) the amount of gain which would not have been long-term capital gain if the property contributed had been sold by the taxpayer at its fair market value (determined at the time of such contribution), and

(B) in the case of a charitable contribution—

(i) of tangible personal property, if the use by the donee is unrelated to the purpose or function constituting the basis for its exemption under section 501 (or, in the case of a governmental unit, to any purpose or function described in subsection (c)), or

(ii) to or for the use of a private foundation (as defined in section 509(a)), other than a private foundation described in subsection (b) (1) (D),

40 percent (²⁸/₄₆, in the case of a corporation) of the amount of gain which would have been long-term capital gain if the property contributed had been sold by the taxpayer at its fair market value (determined at the time of such contribution).

For purposes of applying this paragraph (other than in the case of gain to which section 617(d) (1), 1245(a), 1250(a), 1251(c), 1252(a), or 1254(a) applies), property which is property used in the trade or business (as defined in section 1231(b)) shall be treated as a capital asset.

(2) **Allocation of basis.**—For purposes of paragraph (1), in the case of a charitable contribution of less than the taxpayer's entire interest in the property contributed, the taxpayer's adjusted basis in such property shall be allocated between the interest contributed and any interest not contributed in accordance with regulations prescribed by the Secretary.

(3) **Special rule for certain contributions of inventory and other property.—**

(A) **Qualified contributions.**—For purposes of this paragraph, a qualified contribution shall mean a charitable contribution of property described in paragraph (1) or (2) of section 1221, by a corporation (other than a corporation which is an S corporation) to an organization which is described in section 501(c)(3) and is exempt under section 501(a) (other than a private foundation, as defined in section 509(a), which is not an operating foundation, as defined in section 4942(j)(3)), but only if—

(i) the use of the property by the donee is related to the purpose or function constituting the basis for its exemption under section 501 and the property is to be used by the donee solely for the care of the ill, the needy, or infants;

(ii) the property is not transferred by the donee in exchange for money, other property, or services;

(iii) the taxpayer receives from the donee a written statement representing that its use and disposition of the property will be in accordance with the provisions of clauses (i) and (ii); and

(iv) in the case where the property is subject to regulation under the Federal Food, Drug, and Cosmetic Act, as amended, such property must fully satisfy the applicable requirements of such Act and regulations promulgated thereunder on the date of transfer and for one hundred and eighty days prior thereto.

(B) Amount of reduction.—The reduction under paragraph (1) (A) for any qualified contribution (as defined in subparagraph (A)) shall be no greater than the sum of—

(i) one-half of the amount computed under paragraph (1) (A) (computed without regard to this paragraph), and

(ii) the amount (if any) by which the charitable contribution deduction under this section for any qualified contribution (computed by taking into account the amount determined in clause (i), but without regard to this clause) exceeds twice the basis of such property.

(C) This paragraph shall not apply to so much of the amount of the gain described in paragraph (1) (A) which would be long-term capital gain but for the application of sections 617, 1245, 1250, 1251, or 1252.

(4) Special rule for contributions of scientific property used for research.—

(A) Limit on reduction.—In the case of a qualified research contribution, the reduction under paragraph (1) (A) shall be no greater than the amount determined under paragraph (3) (B).

(B) Qualified research contributions.—For purposes of this paragraph, the term "qualified research contribution" means a charitable contribution by a corporation of tangible personal property described in paragraph (1) of section 1221, but only if—

(i) the contribution is to an educational organization which is described in subsection (b) (1) (A) (ii) of this section and which is an institution of higher education (as defined in section 3304(f)),

(ii) the property is constructed by the taxpayer,

(iii) the contribution is made not later than 2 years after the date the construction of the property is substantially completed,

(iv) the original use of the property is by the donee,

(v) the property is scientific equipment or apparatus substantially all of the use of which by the donee is for research or experimentation (within the meaning of section 174), or for research training, in the United States in physical or biological sciences,

(vi) the property is not transferred by the donee in exchange for money, other property, or services, and

(vii) the taxpayer receives from the donee a written statement representing that its use and disposition of the property will be in accordance with the provisions of clauses (v) and (vi).

(C) Construction of property by taxpayer.—For purposes of this paragraph, property shall be treated as constructed by the taxpayer only if the cost of the parts used in the construction of such property (other than parts manufactured by the taxpayer or a related person) do not exceed 50 percent of the taxpayer's basis in such property.

(D) **Corporation.**—For purposes of this paragraph, the term "corporation" shall not include—

(i) an S corporation,

(ii) a personal holding company (as defined in section 542), and

(iii) a service organization (as defined in section 414(m) (3)).

(f) Disallowance of deduction in certain cases and special rules.—

(1) In general.—No deduction shall be allowed under this section for a contribution to or for the use of an organization or trust described in section 508(d) or 4948(c) (4) subject to the conditions specified in such sections.

(2) Contributions of property placed in trust.—

(A) Remainder interest.—In the case of property transferred in trust, no deduction shall be allowed under this section for the value of a contribution of a remainder interest unless the trust is a charitable remainder annuity trust or a charitable remainder unitrust (described in section 664), or a pooled income fund (described in section 642(c) (5)).

(B) Income interests, etc.—No deduction shall be allowed under this section for the value of any interest in property (other than a remainder interest) transferred in trust unless the interest is in the form of a guaranteed annuity or the trust instrument specifies that the interest is a fixed percentage distributed yearly of the fair market value of the trust property (to be determined yearly) and the grantor is treated as the owner of such interest for purposes of applying section 671. If the donor ceases to be treated as the owner of such an interest for purposes of applying section 671, at the time the donor ceases to be so treated, the donor shall for purposes of this chapter be considered as having received an amount of income equal to the amount of any deduction he received under this section for the contribution reduced by the discounted value of all amounts of income earned by the trust and taxable to him before the time at which he ceases to be treated as the owner of the interest. Such amounts of income shall be discounted to the date of the contribution. The Secretary shall prescribe such regulations as may be necessary to carry out the purposes of this subparagraph.

(C) Denial of deduction in case of payments by certain trusts.—In any case in which a deduction is allowed under this section for the value of an interest in property described in subparagraph (B), transferred in trust, no deduction shall be allowed under this section to the grantor or any other person for the amount of any contribution made by the trust with respect to such interest.

(D) Exception.—This paragraph shall not apply in a case in which the value of all interests in property transferred in trust are deductible under subsection (a).

(3) Denial of deduction in case of certain contributions of partial interests in property.—

(A) In general.—In the case of a contribution (not made by a transfer in trust) of an interest in property which consists of less than the taxpayer's entire interest in such property, a deduction shall be allowed under this section only to the extent that the value of the interest contributed would be allowable as a deduction under this section if such interest had been transferred in trust. For purposes of this subparagraph, a contribution by a taxpayer of the right to use property shall be treated as a contribution of less than the taxpayer's entire interest in such property.

(B) Exceptions.—Subparagraph (A) shall not apply to—

(i) a contribution of a remainder interest in a personal residence or farm,

(ii) a contribution of an undivided portion of the taxpayer's entire interest in property, and

(iii) a qualified conservation contribution.

(4) Valuation of remainder interest in real property.—For purposes of this section, in determining the value of a remainder interest in real property, depreciation (computed on the straight line method) and depletion of such property shall be taken into account, and such value shall be discounted at a rate of 6 percent per annum, except that the Secretary may prescribe a different rate.

(5) Reduction for certain interest.—If, in connection with any charitable contribution, a liability is assumed by the recipient or by any other person, or if a charitable contribution is of property which is subject to a liability, then, to the extent necessary to avoid the duplication of amounts, the amount taken into account for purposes of this section as the amount of the charitable contribution—

(A) shall be reduced for interest (i) which has been paid (or is to be paid) by the taxpayer, (ii) which is attributable to the liability, and (iii) which is attributable to any period after the making of the contribution, and

(B) in the case of a bond, shall be further reduced for interest (i) which has been paid (or is to be paid) by the taxpayer on indebtedness incurred or continued to purchase or carry such bond, and (ii) which is attributable to any period before the making of the contribution.

The reduction pursuant to subparagraph (B) shall not exceed the interest (including interest equivalent) on the bond which is attributable to any period before the making of the contribution and which is not (under the taxpayer's method of accounting) includible in the gross income of the taxpayer for any taxable year. For purposes of this paragraph, the term "bond" means any bond, debenture, note, or certificate or other evidence of indebtedness.

(6) Deductions for out-of-pocket expenditures.—No deduction shall be allowed under this section for an out-of-pocket expenditure made by any person on behalf of an organization described in subsection (c) (other than an organization described in section 501(h) (5) (relating to churches, etc.)) if the expenditure is made for the purpose of influencing legislation (within the meaning of section 501(c) (3)).

(g) Amounts paid to maintain certain students as members of taxpayer's household.—

(1) In general.—Subject to the limitations provided by paragraph (2), amounts paid by the taxpayer to maintain an individual (other than a dependent, as defined in section 152, or a relative of the taxpayer) as a member of his household during the period that such individual is—

(A) a member of the taxpayer's household under a written agreement between the taxpayer and an organization described in paragraph (2), (3), or (4) of subsection (c) to implement a program of the organization to provide educational opportunities for pupils or students in private homes, and

(B) a full-time pupil or student in the twelfth or any lower grade at an educational organization described in section 170(b) (1) (A) (ii) located in the United States,

shall be treated as amounts paid for the use of the organization.

(2) **Limitations.—**

(A) **Amount.—**Paragraph (1) shall apply to amounts paid within the taxable year only to the extent that such amounts do not exceed $50 multiplied by the number of full calendar months during the taxable year which fall within the period described in paragraph (1). For purposes of the preceding sentence, if 15 or more days of a calendar month fall within such period such month shall be considered as a full calendar month.

(B) **Compensation or reimbursement.—**Paragraph (1) shall not apply to any amount paid by the taxpayer within the taxable year if the taxpayer receives any money or other property as compensation or reimbursement for maintaining the individual in his household during the period described in paragraph (1).

(3) **Relative defined.—**For purposes of paragraph (1), the term "relative of the taxpayer" means an individual who, with respect to the taxpayer, bears any of the relationships described in paragraphs (1) through (8) of section 152(a).

(4) **No other amount allowed as deduction.—**No deduction shall be allowed under subsection (a) for any amount paid by a taxpayer to maintain an individual as a member of his household under a program described in paragraph (1) (A) except as provided in this subsection.

(h) **Qualified conservation contribution.—**

(1) **In general.—**For purposes of subsection (f)(3)(B)(iii), the term "qualified conservation contribution" means a contribution—

(A) of a qualified real property interest,

(B) to a qualified organization,

(C) exclusively for conservation purposes.

(2) **Qualified real property interest.—**For purposes of this subsection, the term "qualified real property interest" means any of the following interests in real property:

(A) the entire interest of the donor other than a qualified mineral interest,

(B) a remainder interest, and

(C) a restriction (granted in perpetuity) on the use which may be made of the real property.

(3) **Qualified organization.—**For purposes of paragraph (1), the term "qualified organization" means an organization which—

(A) is described in clause (v) or (vi) of subsection (b)(1)(A), or

(B) is described in section 501(c)(3) and—

(i) meets the requirements of section 509(a)(2), or

(ii) meets the requirements of section 509(a)(3) and is controlled by an organization described in subparagraph (A) or in clause (i) of this subparagraph.

(4) **Conservation purpose defined.—**

(A) **In general.—**For purposes of this subsection, the term "conservation purpose" means—

    (i) the preservation of land areas for outdoor recreation by, or the education of, the general public,

    (ii) the protection of a relatively natural habitat of fish, wildlife, or plants, or similar ecosystem,

    (iii) the preservation of open space (including farmland and forest land) where such preservation is—

        (I) for the scenic enjoyment of the general public, or

        (II) pursuant to a clearly delineated Federal, State, or local governmental conservation policy,

and will yield a significant public benefit, or

    (iv) the preservation of an historically important land area or a certified historic structure.

(B) Certified historic structure.—For purposes of subparagraph (A)(iv), the term "certified historic structure" means any building, structure, or land area which—

    (i) is listed in the National Register, or

    (ii) is located in a registered historic district (as defined in section 191(d)(2)) and is certified by the Secretary of the Interior to the Secretary as being of historic significance to the district.

A building, structure, or land area satisfies the preceding sentence if it satisfies such sentence either at the time of the transfer or on the due date (including extensions) for filing the transferor's return under this chapter for the taxable year in which the transfer is made.

    (5) Exclusively for conservation purposes.—For purposes of this subsection—

    (A) Conservation purpose must be protected.—A contribution shall not be treated as exclusively for conservation purposes unless the conservation purpose is protected in perpetuity.

    (B) No surface mining permitted.—In the case of a contribution of any interest where there is a retention of a qualified mineral interest, subparagraph (A) shall not be treated as met if at any time there may be extraction or removal of minerals by any surface mining method.

    (6) Qualified mineral interest.—For purposes of this subsection, the term "qualified mineral interest" means—

    (A) subsurface oil, gas, or other minerals, and

    (B) the right to access to such minerals.

(i) Rule for nonitemization of deductions.—

    (1) In general.—In the case of an individual who does not itemize his deductions for the taxable year, the applicable percentage of the amount allowable under subsection (a) for the taxable year shall be taken into account as a direct charitable deduction under section 63.

(2) Applicable percentage.—For purposes of paragraph (1), the applicable percentage shall be determined under the following table:

For taxable years beginning in—	The applicable percentage is—
1982, 1983 or 1984	25
1985	50
1986 or thereafter	100.

(3) Limitation for taxable years beginning before 1985.—In the case of a taxable year beginning before 1985, the portion of the amount allowable under subsection (a) to which the applicable percentage shall be applied—

(A) shall not exceed $100 for taxable years beginning in 1982 or 1983, and

(B) shall not exceed $300 for taxable years beginning in 1984.

In the case of a married individual filing a separate return, the limit under subparagraph (A) shall be $50, and the limit under subparagraph (B) shall be $150.

(4) Termination.—The provisions of this subsection shall not apply to contributions made after December 31, 1986.

. . . . .

§ 172. Net operating loss deduction

(a) Deduction allowed.—There shall be allowed as a deduction for the taxable year an amount equal to the aggregate of (1) the net operating loss carryovers to such year, plus (2) the net operating loss carrybacks to such year. For purposes of this subtitle, the term "net operating loss deduction" means the deduction allowed by this subsection.

(b) Net operating loss carrybacks and carryovers.—

(1) Years to which loss may be carried.—

(A) Except as provided in subparagraphs (D), (E), (F), (G), (H) and (I), a net operating loss for any taxable year shall be a net operating loss carryback to each of the 3 taxable years preceding the taxable year of such loss.

(B) Except as provided in subparagraphs (C), (D), and (E), a net operating loss for any taxable year ending after December 31, 1955, shall be a net operating loss carryover to each of the 5 taxable years following the taxable year of such loss. Except as provided in subparagraphs (C), (D), (E), (F), (G), and (I), a net operating loss for any taxable year ending after December 31, 1975, shall be a net operating loss carryover to each of the 15 taxable years following the taxable year of such loss.

. . . . .

(2) Amount of carrybacks and carryovers.—Except as provided in subsection (g), the entire amount of the net operating loss for any taxable year (hereinafter in this section referred to as the "loss year") shall be carried to the earliest of the taxable years to which (by reason of paragraph (1)) such loss may be carried. The portion of such loss which shall be carried to each of the other taxable years shall be the excess, if any, of the amount of such loss over the sum of the taxable income for each of the prior taxable years to which such loss may be carried. For purposes of the preceding sentence, the taxable income for any such prior taxable year shall be computed—

(A) with the modifications specified in subsection (d) other than paragraphs (1), (4), and (6) thereof; and

(B) by determining the amount of the net operating loss deduction—

(i) without regard to the net operating loss for the loss year or for any taxable year thereafter, and

(ii) without regard to that portion, if any, of a net operating loss for a taxable year attributable to a foreign expropriation loss, if such portion may not, under paragraph (1) (D), be carried back to such prior taxable year,

and the taxable income so computed shall not be considered to be less than zero. . . . . .

(3) Special rules.—

(C) Any taxpayer entitled to a carryback period under paragraph (1) may elect to relinquish the entire carryback period with respect to a net operating loss for any taxable year ending after December 31, 1975. Such election shall be made in such manner as may be prescribed by the Secretary, and shall be made by the due date (including extensions of time) for filing the taxpayer's return for the taxable year of the net operating loss for which the election is to be in effect. Such election, once made for any taxable year, shall be irrevocable for that taxable year.

(c) Net operating loss defined.—For purposes of this section, the term "net operating loss" means the excess of the deductions allowed by this chapter over the gross income. Such excess shall be computed with the modifications specified in subsection (d).

(d) Modifications.—The modifications referred to in this section are as follows:

(1) Net operating loss deduction.—No net operating loss deduction shall be allowed.

(2) Capital gains and losses of taxpayers other than corporations.—In the case of a taxpayer other than a corporation—

(A) the amount deductible on account of losses from sales or exchanges of capital assets shall not exceed the amount includible on account of gains from sales or exchanges of capital assets; and

(B) the deduction for long-term capital gains provided by section 1202 shall not be allowed.

(3) Deduction for personal exemptions.—No deduction shall be allowed under section 151 (relating to personal exemptions). No deduction in lieu of any such deduction shall be allowed.

(4) Nonbusiness deductions of taxpayers other than corporations.—In the case of a taxpayer other than a corporation, the deductions allowable by this chapter which are not attributable to a taxpayer's trade or business shall be allowed only to the extent of the amount of the gross income not derived from such trade or business. For purposes of the preceding sentence—

(A) any gain or loss from the sale or other disposition of—

(i) property, used in the trade or business, of a character which is subject to the allowance for depreciation provided in section 167, or

(ii) real property used in the trade or business,

shall be treated as attributable to the trade or business;

(B) the modifications specified in paragraphs (1), (2) (B), and (3) shall be taken into account;

(C) any deduction allowable under section 165(c) (3) (relating to casualty losses) shall not be taken into account; and

(D) any deduction allowed under section 404 or section 405(c) to the extent attributable to contributions which are made on behalf of an individual who is an employee within the meaning of section 401(c) (1) shall not be treated as attributable to the trade or business of such individual.

. . . .

(e) Law applicable to computations.—In determining the amount of any net operating loss carryback or carryover to any taxable year, the necessary computations involving any other taxable year shall be made under the law applicable to such other taxable year.

(f) [Repealed.]

§ 174.   Research and experimental expenditures

(a) Treatment as expenses.—

(1) In general.—A taxpayer may treat research or experimental expenditures which are paid or incurred by him during the taxable year in connection with his trade or business as expenses which are not chargeable to capital account. The expenditures so treated shall be allowed as a deduction.

(2) When method may be adopted.—

(A) Without consent.—A taxpayer may, without the consent of the Secretary, adopt the method provided in this subsection for his first taxable year—

(i) which begins after December 31, 1953, and ends after August 16, 1954, and

(ii) for which expenditures described in paragraph (1) are paid or incurred.

(B) With consent.—A taxpayer may, with the consent of the Secretary, adopt at any time the method provided in this subsection.

(3) Scope.—The method adopted under this subsection shall apply to all expenditures described in paragraph (1). The method adopted shall be adhered to in computing taxable income for the taxable year and for all subsequent taxable years unless, with the approval of the Secretary, a change to a different method is authorized with respect to part or all of such expenditures.

(b) Amortization of certain research and experimental expenditures.—

(1) In general.—At the election of the taxpayer, made in accordance with regulations prescribed by the Secretary, research or experimental expenditures which are—

(A) paid or incurred by the taxpayer in connection with his trade or business,

(B) not treated as expenses under subsection (a), and

(C) chargeable to capital account but not chargeable to property of a character which is subject to the allowance under section 167 (relating to allowance for depreciation, etc.) or section 611 (relating to allowance for depletion),

may be treated as deferred expenses. In computing taxable income, such deferred expenses shall be allowed as a deduction ratably over such period of not less than 60 months as may be selected by the taxpayer (beginning with the month in which the taxpayer first realizes benefits from such expenditures). Such deferred expenses are expenditures properly chargeable to capital account for purposes of section 1016(a) (1) (relating to adjustments to basis of property).

(2) **Time for and scope of election.**—The election provided by paragraph (1) may be made for any taxable year beginning after December 31, 1953, but only if made not later than the time prescribed by law for filing the return for such taxable year (including extensions thereof). The method so elected, and the period selected by the taxpayer, shall be adhered to in computing taxable income for the taxable year for which the election is made and for all subsequent taxable years unless, with the approval of the Secretary, a change to a different method (or to a different period) is authorized with respect to part or all of such expenditures. The election shall not apply to any expenditure paid or incurred during any taxable year before the taxable year for which the taxpayer makes the election.

(c) **Land and other property.**—This section shall not apply to any expenditure for the acquisition or improvement of land, or for the acquisition or improvement of property to be used in connection with the research or experimentation and of a character which is subject to the allowance under section 167 (relating to allowance for depreciation, etc.) or section 611 (relating to allowance for depletion); but for purposes of this section allowances under section 167, and allowances under section 611, shall be considered as expenditures.

(d) **Exploration expenditures.**—This section shall not apply to any expenditure paid or incurred for the purpose of ascertaining the existence, location, extent, or quality of any deposit of ore or other mineral (including oil and gas).

. . . . .

§ 175.   Soil and water conservation expenditures

(a) **In general.**—A taxpayer engaged in the business of farming may treat expenditures which are paid or incurred by him during the taxable year for the purpose of soil or water conservation in respect of land used in farming, or for the prevention of erosion of land used in farming, as expenses which are not chargeable to capital account. The expenditures so treated shall be allowed as a deduction.

(b) **Limitation.**—The amount deductible under subsection (a) for any taxable year shall not exceed 25 percent of the gross income derived from farming during the taxable year. If for any taxable year the total of the expenditures treated as expenses which are not chargeable to capital account exceeds 25 percent of the gross income derived from farming during the taxable year, such excess shall be deductible for succeeding taxable years in order of time; but the amount deductible under this section for any one such succeeding taxable year (including the expenditures actually paid or incurred during the taxable year) shall not exceed 25 percent of the gross income derived from farming during the taxable year.

. . . . .

§ 177.   Trademark and trade name expenditures

(a) **Election to amortize.**—Any trademark or trade name expenditure paid or incurred during a taxable year beginning after December 31, 1955, may, at the election of the taxpayer (made in accordance with regulations prescribed by the Secretary), be treated as a deferred expense. In computing taxable income, all expenditures paid or incurred during the taxable year which are so treated shall be allowed as a deduction ratably over such period of not less than 60 months (beginning with the first month in such taxable year) as may be selected by the taxpayer in making such election. The expenditures so treated are expenditures properly chargeable to capital account for purposes of section 1016(a) (1) (relating to adjustments to basis of property).

(b) **Trademark and trade name expenditures defined.**—For purposes of subsection (a), the term "trademark or trade name expenditure" means any expenditure which—

    (1) is directly connected with the acquisition, protection, expansion, registration (Federal, State, or foreign), or defense of a trademark or trade name;

    (2) is chargeable to capital account; and

    (3) is not part of the consideration paid for a trademark, trade name, or business.

(c) **Time for and scope of election.**—The election provided by subsection (a) shall be made within the time prescribed by law (including extensions thereof) for filing the return for the taxable year during which the expenditure is paid or incurred. The period selected by the taxpayer under subsection (a) with respect to the expenditures paid or incurred during the taxable year which are treated as deferred expenses shall be adhered to in computing his taxable income for the taxable year for which the election is made and all subsequent years.

. . . . .

§ 178.   Depreciation or amortization of improvements made by lessee on lessor's property

(a) **General rule.**—Except as provided in subsection (b), in determining the amount allowable to a lessee as a deduction for any taxable year for exhaustion, wear and tear, obsolescence, or amortization—

    (1) in respect of any building erected (or other improvement made) on the leased property, if the portion of the term of the lease (excluding any period for which the lease may subsequently be renewed, extended, or continued pursuant to an option exercisable by the lessee) remaining upon the completion of such building or other improvement is less than 60 percent of the useful life of such building or other improvement, or

    (2) in respect of any cost of acquiring the lease, if less than 75 percent of such cost is attributable to the portion of the term of the lease (excluding any

period for which the lease may subsequently be renewed, extended, or continued pursuant to an option exercisable by the lessee) remaining on the date of its acquisition,

the term of the lease shall be treated as including any period for which the lease may be renewed, extended, or continued pursuant to an option exercisable by the lessee, unless the lessee establishes that (as of the close of the taxable year) it is more probable that the lease will not be renewed, extended, or continued for such period than that the lease will be so renewed, extended, or continued.

(b) Related lessee and lessor.—

    (1) General rule.—If a lessee and lessor are related persons (as determined under paragraph (2)) at any time during the taxable year then, in determining the amount allowable to the lessee as a deduction for such taxable year for exhaustion, wear and tear, obsolescence, or amortization in respect of any building erected (or other improvement made) on the leased property, the lease shall be treated as including a period of not less duration than the remaining useful life of such improvement.

    (2) Related persons defined.—For purposes of paragraph (1), a lessor and lessee shall be considered to be related persons if—

        (A) the lessor and the lessee are members of an affiliated group (as defined in section 1504), or

        (B) the relationship between the lessor and lessee is one described in subsection (b) of section 267, except that, for purposes of this subparagraph, the phrase "80 percent or more" shall be substituted for the phrase "more than 50 percent" each place it appears in such subsection.

For purposes of determining the ownership of stock in applying subparagraph (B), the rules of subsection (c) of section 267 shall apply, except that the family of an individual shall include only his spouse, ancestors, and lineal descendants.

(c) Reasonable certainty test.—In any case in which neither subsection (a) nor subsection (b) applies, the determination as to the amount allowable to a lessee as a deduction for any taxable year for exhaustion, wear and tear, obsolescence, or amortization—

    (1) in respect of any building erected (or other improvement made) on the leased property, or

    (2) in respect of any cost of acquiring the lease,

shall be made with reference to the term of the lease (excluding any period for which the lease may subsequently be renewed, extended, or continued pursuant to an option exercisable by the lessee), unless the lease has been renewed, extended, or continued or the facts show with reasonable certainty that the lease will be renewed, extended, or continued.

§ 179.   Election to expense certain depreciable business assets

(a) Treatment as expenses.—A taxpayer may elect to treat the cost of any section 179 property as an expense which is not chargeable to capital account. Any cost so treated shall be allowed as a deduction for the taxable year in which the section 179 property is placed in service.

(b) Dollar limitation.—

(1) In general.—The aggregate cost which may be taken into account under subsection (a) for any taxable year shall not exceed the following applicable amount:

If the taxable year begins in:	The applicable amount is:
1981	$0
1982	5,000
1983	5,000
1984	7,500
1985	7,500
1986 or thereafter	10,000

(2) Married individuals filing separately.—In the case of a husband and wife filing separate returns for a taxable year, the applicable amount under paragraph (1) shall be equal to 50 percent of the amount otherwise determined under paragraph (1).

(c) Election.—

(1) In general.—An election under this section for any taxable year shall—

(A) specify the items of section 179 property to which the election applies and the portion of the cost of each of such items which is to be taken into account under subsection (a), and

(B) be made on the taxpayer's return of the tax imposed by this chapter for the taxable year.

Such election shall be made in such manner as the Secretary may by regulations prescribe.

(2) Election irrevocable.—Any election made under this section, and any specification contained in any such election, may not be revoked except with the consent of the Secretary.

(d) Definitions and special rules.—

(1) Section 179 property.—For purposes of this section, the term "section 179 property" means any recovery property which is section 38 property and which is acquired by purchase for use in a trade or business.

(2) Purchase defined.—For purposes of paragraph (1), the term "purchase" means any acquisition of property, but only if—

(A) the property is not acquired from a person whose relationship to the person acquiring it would result in the disallowance of losses under section 267 or 707(b) (but, in applying section 267(b) and (c) for purposes of this section, paragraph (4) of section 267(c) shall be treated as providing that the family of an individual shall include only his spouse, ancestors, and lineal descendants),

(B) the property is not acquired by one component member of a controlled group from another component member of the same controlled group, and

(C) the basis of the property in the hands of the person acquiring it is not determined—

(i) in whole or in part by reference to the adjusted basis of such property in the hands of the person from whom acquired, or

(ii) under section 1014(a) (relating to property acquired from a decedent).

(3) **Cost.**—For purposes of this section, the cost of property does not include so much of the basis of such property as is determined by reference to the basis of other property held at any time by the person acquiring such property.

(4) **Section not to apply to estates and trusts.**—This section shall not apply to estates and trusts.

(5) **Section not to apply to certain noncorporate lessors.**—This section shall not apply to any section 179 property purchased by any person described in section 46(e) (3) unless the credit under section 38 is allowable with respect to such person for such property (determined without regard to this section).

(6) **Dollar limitation of controlled group.**—For purposes of subsection (b) of this section—

(A) all component members of a controlled group shall be treated as one taxpayer, and

(B) the Secretary shall apportion the dollar limitation contained in subsection (b) (1) among the component members of such controlled group in such manner as he shall by regulations prescribe.

(7) **Controlled group defined.**—For purposes of paragraphs (2) and (6), the term "controlled group" has the meaning assigned to it by section 1563(a), except that, for such purposes, the phrase "more than 50 percent" shall be substituted for the phrase "at least 80 percent" each place it appears in section 1563(a) (1).

(8) **Dollar limitation in case of partnerships and S corporations.**—In the case of a partnership, the dollar limitation contained in subsection (b) (1) shall apply with respect to the partnership and with respect to each partner. A similar rule shall apply in the case of an S corporation and its shareholders.

(9) **Coordination with section 38.**—No credit shall be allowed under section 38 with respect to any amount for which a deduction is allowed under subsection (a).

(e) **Regulations.**—The Secretary shall prescribe such regulations as may be necessary to carry out the purposes of this section.

§ 180.   Expenditures by farmers for fertilizer, etc.

(a) **In general.**—A taxpayer engaged in the business of farming may elect to treat as expenses which are not chargeable to capital account expenditures (otherwise chargeable to capital account) which are paid or incurred by him during the taxable year for the purchase or acquisition of fertilizer, lime, ground limestone, marl, or other materials to enrich, neutralize, or condition land used in farming, or for the application of such materials to such land. The expenditures so treated shall be allowed as a deduction.

. . . . .

§ 182.   Expenditures by farmers for clearing land

(a) **In general.**—A taxpayer engaged in the business of farming may elect to treat expenditures which are paid or incurred by him during the taxable year in the clearing of land for the purpose of making such land suitable for use in farming as expenses which are not chargeable to capital account. The expenditures so treated shall be allowed as a deduction.

(b) Limitation.—The amount deductible under subsection (a) for any taxable year shall not exceed whichever of the following amounts is the lesser:

    (1) $5,000, or

    (2) 25 percent of the taxable income derived from farming during the taxable year.

For purposes of paragraph (2), the term "taxable income derived from farming" means the gross income derived from farming reduced by the deductions allowed by this chapter (other than by this section) which are attributable to the business of farming.

        .   .   .   .

§ 183.   Activities not engaged in for profit

(a) General rule.—In the case of an activity engaged in by an individual or an S corporation, if such activity is not engaged in for profit, no deduction attributable to such activity shall be allowed under this chapter except as provided in this section.

(b) Deductions allowable.—In the case of an activity not engaged in for profit to which subsection (a) applies, there shall be allowed—

    (1) the deductions which would be allowable under this chapter for the taxable year without regard to whether or not such activity is engaged in for profit, and

    (2) a deduction equal to the amount of the deductions which would be allowable under this chapter for the taxable year only if such activity were engaged in for profit, but only to the extent that the gross income derived from such activity for the taxable year exceeds the deductions allowable by reason of paragraph (1).

(c) Activity not engaged in for profit defined.—For purposes of this section, the term "activity not engaged in for profit" means any activity other than one with respect to which deductions are allowable for the taxable year under section 162 or under paragraph (1) or (2) of section 212.

(d) Presumption.—If the gross income derived from an activity for 2 or more of the taxable years in the period of 5 consecutive taxable years which ends with the taxable year exceeds the deductions attributable to such activity (determined without regard to whether or not such activity is engaged in for profit), then, unless the Secretary establishes to the contrary, such activity shall be presumed for purposes of this chapter for such taxable year to be an activity engaged in for profit. In the case of an activity which consists in major part of the breeding, training, showing, or racing of horses, the preceding sentence shall be applied by substituting the period of 7 consecutive taxable years for the period of 5 consecutive taxable years.

(e) Special rule.—

    (1) In general.—A determination as to whether the presumption provided by subsection (d) applies with respect to any activity shall, if the taxpayer so elects, not be made before the close of the fourth taxable year (sixth taxable year, in the case of an activity described in the last sentence of such subsection) following the taxable year in which the taxpayer first engages in the activity. For purposes of the preceding sentence, a taxpayer shall be treated as not having engaged in an activity during any taxable year beginning before January 1, 1970.

(2) Initial period.—If the taxpayer makes an election under paragraph (1), the presumption provided by subsection (d) shall apply to each taxable year in the 5-taxable year (or 7-taxable year) period beginning with the taxable year in which the taxpayer first engages in the activity, if the gross income derived from the activity for 2 or more of the taxable years in such period exceeds the deductions attributable to the activity (determined without regard to whether or not the activity is engaged in for profit).

(3) Election.—An election under paragraph (1) shall be made at such time and manner, and subject to such terms and conditions, as the Secretary may prescribe.

(4) Time for assessing deficiency attributable to activity.—If a taxpayer makes an election under paragraph (1) with respect to an activity, the statutory period for the assessment of any deficiency attributable to such activity shall not expire before the expiration of 2 years after the date prescribed by law (determined without extensions) for filing the return of tax under chapter 1 for the last taxable year in the period of 5 taxable years (or 7 taxable years) to which the election relates. Such deficiency may be assessed notwithstanding the provisions of any law or rule of law which would otherwise prevent such an assessment.

§ 189.   Amortization of real property construction period interest and taxes

(a) Capitalization of construction period interest and taxes.—Except as otherwise provided in this section or in section 266 (relating to carrying charges), no deduction shall be allowed for real property construction period interest and taxes.

(b) Amortization of amounts charged to capital account.—Any amount paid or accrued which would (but for subsection (a)) be allowable as a deduction for the taxable year shall be allowable for such taxable year and each subsequent amortization year in accordance with the following table:

If the amount is paid or accrued in a taxable year beginning in—		The percentage of such amount allowable for each amortization year shall be the following percentage of such amount
Nonresidential real property	Residential real property (other than low-income housing)	
1976	. . . .	see subsection (f)
. . . .	1978	25
1977	1979	20
1978	1980	16⅔
1979	1981	14²⁄₇
1980	1982	12½
1981	1983	11⅑
after 1981	after 1983	10

(c) Amortization year.—

(1) In general.—For purposes of this section, the term "amortization year" means the taxable year in which the amount is paid or accrued, and each taxable year thereafter (beginning with the taxable year after the taxable year in which paid or accrued or, if later, the taxable year in which the real property is ready to be placed in service or is ready to be held for sale) until the full amount has been allowable as a deduction (or until the property is sold or exchanged).

(2) **Rules for sales and exchanges.**—For purposes of paragraph (1)—

(A) **Proportion of percentage allowed.**—For the amortization year in which the property is sold or exchanged, a proportionate part of the percentage allowable for such year (determined without regard to the sale or exchange) shall be allowable. If the real property is subject to an allowance for depreciation, the proportion shall be determined in accordance with the convention used for depreciation purposes with respect to such property. In the case of all other real property, under regulations prescribed by the Secretary, the proportion shall be based on that proportion of the amortization year which elapsed before the sale or exchange.

(B) **Unamortized balance.**—In the case of a sale or exchange of the property, the portion of the amount not allowable shall be treated as an adjustment to basis under section 1016 for purposes of determining gain or loss.

(C) **Certain exchanges.**—An exchange or transfer after which the property received has a basis determined in whole or in part by reference to the basis of the property to which the amortizable construction period interest and taxes relate, shall not be treated as an exchange.

(d) **Certain property excluded.**—This section shall not apply to any—

(1) low-income housing,

(2) residential real property (other than low income housing) acquired, constructed, or carried by a corporation other than an S corporation, a personal holding company (within the meaning of section 542), or a foreign personal holding company (within the meaning of section 552), or

(3) real property acquired, constructed, or carried if such property is not, and cannot reasonably [be] expected to be, held in a trade or business, or in an activity conducted for profit.

(e) **Definitions.**—For purposes of this section—

(1) **Real property construction period interest and taxes.**—The term "real property construction period interest and taxes" means all—

(A) interest paid or accrued on indebtedness incurred or continued to acquire, construct, or carry real property, and

(B) real property taxes,

to the extent such interest and taxes are attributable to the construction period for such property and would be allowable as a deduction under this chapter for the taxable year in which paid or accrued (determined without regard to this section). The Secretary shall prescribe regulations which provide for the allocation of interest to real property under construction.

· · · · ·

§ 195.   Start-up expenditures

(a) **Election to amortize.**—Start-up expenditures may, at the election of the taxpayer, be treated as deferred expenses. Such deferred expenses shall be allowed as a deduction ratably over such period of not less than 60 months as may be selected by the taxpayer (beginning with the month in which the business begins).

(b) Start-up expenditures.—For purposes of this section, the term "start-up expenditure" means any amount—

(1) paid or incurred in connection with—

(A) investigating the creation or acquisition of an active trade or business, or

(B) creating an active trade or business, and

(2) which, if paid or incurred in connection with the expansion of an existing trade or business (in the same field as the trade or business referred to in paragraph (1)), would be allowable as a deduction for the taxable year in which paid or incurred.

(c) Election.—

(1) Time for making election.—An election under subsection (a) shall be made not later than the time prescribed by law for filing the return for the taxable year in which the business begins (including extensions thereof).

(2) Scope of election.—The period selected under subsection (a) shall be adhered to in computing taxable income for the taxable year for which the election is made and all subsequent taxable years.

(3) Manner of making election.—An election under subsection (a) shall be made in such manner as the Secretary shall by regulations prescribe.

(d) Business beginning.—For purposes of this section, an acquired trade or business shall be treated as beginning when the taxpayer acquires it.

§ 196. Deduction for certain unused investment credits

(a) Allowance of deductions.—If—

(1) the amount of the credit determined under section 46(a)(2) for any taxable year exceeds the limitation provided by section 46(a)(3) for such taxable year, and

(2) the amount of such excess has not, after the application of section 46(b), been allowed to the taxpayer as a credit under section 38 for any taxable year,

then an amount equal to 50 percent of the amount of such excess (to the extent attributable to property the basis of which is reduced under section 48(q)) not so allowed as a credit shall be allowed to the taxpayer as a deduction for the first taxable year following the last taxable year in which such excess could under section 46(b) have been allowed as a credit.

(b) Taxpayers dying or ceasing to exist.—If a taxpayer dies or ceases to exist prior to the first taxable year following the last taxable year in which the excess described in subsection (a) could under section 46(b) have been allowed as a credit, the amount described in subsection (a), or the proper portion thereof, shall, under regulations prescribed by the Secretary, be allowed to the taxpayer as a deduction for the taxable year in which such death or cessation occurs.

(c) Special rule for qualified rehabilitated buildings.—In the case of any credit to which section 48(q)(3) applies, subsection (a) shall be applied without regard to the phrase "50 percent of".

PART VII—ADDITIONAL ITEMIZED DEDUCTIONS FOR INDIVIDUALS

§ 211. Allowance of deductions

In computing taxable income under section 63, there shall be allowed as deductions the items specified in this part, subject to the exceptions provided in part IX (section 261 and following, relating to items not deductible).

§ 212. Expenses for production of income

In the case of an individual, there shall be allowed as a deduction all the ordinary and necessary expenses paid or incurred during the taxable year—

(1) for the production or collection of income;

(2) for the management, conservation, or maintenance of property held for the production of income; or

(3) in connection with the determination, collection, or refund of any tax.

§ 213. Medical, dental, etc., expenses

(a) Allowance of deduction.—There shall be allowed as a deduction the expenses paid during the taxable year, not compensated for by insurance or otherwise, for medical care of the taxpayer, his spouse, or a dependent (as defined in section 152), to the extent that such expenses exceed 5 percent of adjusted gross income.

(b) Limitation with respect to medicine and drugs.—An amount paid during the taxable year for medicine or a drug shall be taken into account under subsection (a) only if such medicine or drug is a prescribed drug or is insulin.

(c) Special rule for decedents.—

(1) **Treatment of expenses paid after death.**—For purposes of subsection (a), expenses for the medical care of the taxpayer which are paid out of his estate during the 1-year period beginning with the day after the date of his death shall be treated as paid by the taxpayer at the time incurred.

(2) **Limitation.**—Paragraph (1) shall not apply if the amount paid is allowable under section 2053 as a deduction in computing the taxable estate of the decedent, but this paragraph shall not apply if (within the time and in the manner and form prescribed by the Secretary) there is filed—

(A) a statement that such amount has not been allowed as a deduction under section 2053, and

(B) a waiver of the right to have such amount allowed at any time as a deduction under section 2053.

(d) Definitions.—For purposes of this section—

(1) The term "medical care" means amounts paid—

(A) for the diagnosis, cure, mitigation, treatment, or prevention of disease, or for the purpose of affecting any structure or function of the body,

(B) for transportation primarily for and essential to medical care referred to in subparagraph (A), or

(C) for insurance (including amounts paid as premiums under part B of title XVIII of the Social Security Act [sections 1395j–1395w of Title 42],

148

relating to supplementary medical insurance for the aged) covering medical care referred to in subparagraphs (A) and (B).

(2) Prescribed drug.—The term "prescribed drug" means a drug or biological which requires a prescription of a physician for its use by an individual.

(3) Physician.—The term "physician" has the meaning given to such term by section 1861(r) of the Social Security Act (42 U.S.C. 1395x(r)).

(4) In the case of an insurance contract under which amounts are payable for other than medical care referred to in subparagraphs (A) and (B) of paragraph (1)—

(A) no amount shall be treated as paid for insurance to which paragraph (1) (C) applies unless the charge for such insurance is either separately stated in the contract, or furnished to the policyholder by the insurance company in a separate statement,

(B) the amount taken into account as the amount paid for such insurance shall not exceed such charge, and

(C) no amount shall be treated as paid for such insurance if the amount specified in the contract (or furnished to the policyholder by the insurance company in a separate statement) as the charge for such insurance is unreasonably large in relation to the total charges under the contract.

(5) Subject to the limitations of paragraph (2), premiums paid during the taxable year by a taxpayer before he attains the age of 65 for insurance covering medical care (within the meaning of subparagraphs (A) and (B) of paragraph (1)) for the taxpayer, his spouse, or a dependent after the taxpayer attains the age of 65 shall be treated as expenses paid during the taxable year for insurance which constitutes medical care if premiums for such insurance are payable (on a level payment basis) under the contract for a period of 10 years or more or until the year in which the taxpayer attains the age of 65 (but in no case for a period of less than 5 years).

(6) The determination of whether an individual is married at any time during the taxable year shall be made in accordance with the provisions of section 6013(d) (relating to determination of status as husband and wife).

(e) Exclusion of amounts allowed for care of certain dependents.—Any expense allowed as a credit under section 44A shall not be treated as an expense paid for medical care.

§ 215.   Alimony, etc., payments

(a) General rule.—In the case of a husband described in section 71, there shall be allowed as a deduction amounts includible under section 71 in the gross income of his wife, payment of which is made within the husband's taxable year. No deduction shall be allowed under the preceding sentence with respect to any payment if, by reason of section 71(d) or 682, the amount thereof is not includible in the husband's gross income.

§ 216.   Deduction of taxes, interest, and business depreciation by cooperative housing corporation tenant-stockholder

(a) Allowance of deduction.—In the case of a tenant-stockholder (as defined in subsection (b) (2)), there shall be allowed as a deduction amounts (not otherwise deductible) paid or accrued to a cooperative housing corporation within the taxable year, but only to the extent that such amounts represent the tenant-stock-holder's proportionate share of—

    (1) the real estate taxes allowable as a deduction to the corporation under section 164 which are paid or incurred by the corporation on the houses or apartment building and on the land on which such houses (or building) are situated, or

    (2) the interest allowable as a deduction to the corporation under section 163 which is paid or incurred by the corporation on its indebtedness contracted—

        (A) in the acquisition, construction, alteration, rehabilitation, or maintenance of the houses or apartment building, or

        (B) in the acquisition of the land on which the houses (or apartment building) are situated.

. . . . .

§ 217.   Moving expenses

(a) Deduction allowed.—There shall be allowed as a deduction moving expenses paid or incurred during the taxable year in connection with the commencement of work by the taxpayer as an employee or as a self-employed individual at a new principal place of work.

(b) Definition of moving expenses.—

    (1) In general.—For purposes of this section, the term "moving expenses" means only the reasonable expenses—

        (A) of moving household goods and personal effects from the former residence to the new residence,

        (B) of traveling (including meals and lodging) from the former residence to the new place of residence,

        (C) of traveling (including meals and lodging), after obtaining employment, from the former residence to the general location of the new principal place of work and return, for the principal purpose of searching for a new residence,

        (D) of meals and lodging while occupying temporary quarters in the general location of the new principal place of work during any period of 30 consecutive days after obtaining employment, or

        (E) constituting qualified residence sale, purchase, or lease expenses.

    (2) Qualified residence sale, etc., expenses.—For purposes of paragraph (1) (E), the term "qualified residence sale, purchase, or lease expenses" means only reasonable expenses incident to—

        (A) the sale or exchange by the taxpayer or his spouse of the taxpayer's former residence (not including expenses for work performed on such residence in order to assist in its sale) which (but for this subsection and subsection (e)) would be taken into account in determining the amount realized on the sale or exchange,

        (B) the purchase by the taxpayer or his spouse of a new residence in the general location of the new principal place of work which (but for this subsection and subsection (e)) would be taken into account in determining—

           (i) the adjusted basis of the new residence, or

           (ii) the cost of a loan (but not including any amounts which represent payments or prepayments of interest),

(C) the settlement of an unexpired lease held by the taxpayer or his spouse on property used by the taxpayer as his former residence, or

(D) the acquisition of a lease by the taxpayer or his spouse on property used by the taxpayer as his new residence in the general location of the new principal place of work (not including amounts which are payments or prepayments of rent).

(3) Limitations.—

(A) Dollar limits.—The aggregate amount allowable as a deduction under subsection (a) in connection with a commencement of work which is attributable to expenses described in subparagraph (C) or (D) of paragraph (1) shall not exceed $1,500. The aggregate amount allowable as a deduction under subsection (a) which is attributable to qualified residence sale, purchase, or lease expenses shall not exceed $3,000, reduced by the aggregate amount so allowable which is attributable to expenses described in subparagraph (C) or (D) of paragraph (1).

(B) Husband and wife.—If a husband and wife both commence work at a new principal place of work within the same general location, subparagraph (A) shall be applied as if there was only one commencement of work. In the case of a husband and wife filing separate returns, subparagraph (A) shall be applied by substituting "$750" for "$1,500", and by substituting "$1,500" for "$3,000".

(C) Individuals other than taxpayer.—In the case of any individual other than the taxpayer, expenses referred to in subparagraphs (A) through (D) of paragraph (1) shall be taken into account only if such individual has both the former residence and the new residence as his principal place of abode and is a member of the taxpayer's household.

(c) Conditions for allowance.—No deduction shall be allowed under this section unless—

(1) the taxpayer's new principal place of work—

(A) is at least 35 miles farther from his former residence than was his former principal place of work, or

(B) if he had no former principal place of work, is at least 35 miles from his former residence, and

(2) either—

(A) during the 12-month period immediately following his arrival in the general location of his new principal place of work, the taxpayer is a full-time employee, in such general location, during at least 39 weeks, or

(B) during the 24-month period immediately following his arrival in the general location of his new principal place of work, the taxpayer is a full-time employee or performs services as a self-employed individual on a full-time basis, in such general location, during at least 78 weeks, of which not less than 39 weeks are during the 12-month period referred to in subparagraph (A).

For purposes of paragraph (1), the distance between two points shall be the shortest of the more commonly traveled routes between such two points.

(d) Rules for application of subsection (c) (2).—

(1) The condition of subsection (c) (2) shall not apply if the taxpayer is unable to satisfy such condition by reason of—

(A) death or disability, or

(B) involuntary separation (other than for willful misconduct) from the service of, or transfer for the benefit of, an employer after obtaining full-time employment in which the taxpayer could reasonably have been expected to satisfy such condition.

(2) If a taxpayer has not satisfied the condition of subsection (c) (2) before the time prescribed by law (including extensions thereof) for filing the return for the taxable year during which he paid or incurred moving expenses which would otherwise be deductible under this section, but may still satisfy such condition, then such expenses may (at the election of the taxpayer) be deducted for such taxable year notwithstanding subsection (c) (2).

(3) If—

(A) for any taxable year moving expenses have been deducted in accordance with the rule provided in paragraph (2), and

(B) the condition of subsection (c) (2) cannot be satisfied at the close of a subsequent taxable year,

then an amount equal to the expenses which were so deducted shall be included in gross income for the first such subsequent taxable year.

(e) Denial of double benefit.—The amount realized on the sale of the residence described in subparagraph (A) of subsection (b) (2) shall not be decreased by the amount of any expenses described in such subparagraph which are allowed as a deduction under subsection (a), and the basis of a residence described in subparagraph (B) of subsection (b) (2) shall not be increased by the amount of any expenses described in such subparagraph which are allowed as a deduction under subsection (a). This subsection shall not apply to any expenses with respect to which an amount is included in gross income under subsection (d) (3).

(f) Rules for self-employed individuals.—

(1) Definition.—For purposes of this section, the term "self-employed individual" means an individual who performs personal services—

(A) as the owner of the entire interest in an unincorporated trade or business, or

(B) as a partner in a partnership carrying on a trade or business.

(2) Rule for application of subsections (b) (1) (C) and (D).—For purposes of subparagraphs (C) and (D) of subsection (b) (1), an individual who commences work at a new principal place of work as a self-employed individual shall be treated as having obtained employment when he has made substantial arrangements to commence such work.

(g) Rules for members of the Armed Forces of the United States.—In the case of a member of the Armed Forces of the United States on active duty who moves pursuant to a military order and incident to a permanent change of station—

(1) the limitations under subsection (c) shall not apply;

(2) any moving and storage expenses which are furnished in kind (or for which reimbursement or an allowance is provided, but only to the extent of the expenses paid or incurred) to such member, his spouse, or his dependents, shall not be includible in gross income, and no reporting with respect to such expenses shall be required by the Secretary of Defense or the Secretary of Transportation, as the case may be; and

(3) if moving and storage expenses are furnished in kind (or if reimbursement or an allowance for such expenses is provided) to such member's spouse and his dependents with regard to moving to a location other than the one to which such member moves (or from a location other than the one from which such member moves), this section shall apply with respect to the moving expenses of his spouse and dependents—

(A) as if his spouse commenced work as an employee at a new principal place of work at such location;

(B) for purposes of subsection (b) (3), as if such place of work was within the same general location as the member's new principal place of work, and

(C) without regard to the limitations under subsection (c).

· · · ·

(j) **Regulations.**—The Secretary shall prescribe such regulations as may be necessary to carry out the purposes of this section.

§ 219.   Retirement savings

(a) **Allowance of deduction.**—In the case of an individual, there shall be allowed as a deduction an amount equal to the qualified retirement contributions of the individual for the taxable year.

(b) **Maximum amount of deduction.**—

(1) **In general.**—The amount allowable as a deduction under subsection (a) to any individual for any taxable year shall not exceed the lesser of—

(A) $2,000, or

(B) an amount equal to the compensation includible in the individual's gross income for such taxable year.

(2) **Special rules for employer contributions under simplified employee pensions.**—

(A) **Limitation.**—If there is an employer contribution on behalf of the employee to a simplified employee pension, an employee shall be allowed as a deduction under subsection (a) (in addition to the amount allowable under paragraph (1)) an amount equal to the lesser of—

(i) 15 percent of the compensation from such employer includible in the employee's gross income for the taxable year (determined without regard to the employer contribution to the simplified employee pension), or

(ii) the amount contributed by such employer to the simplified employee pension and included in gross income (but not in excess of $15,000).

(B) **Certain limitations do not apply to employer contribution.** —Paragraph (1) of this subsection and paragraph (1) of subsection (d) shall not apply with respect to the employer contribution to a simplified employee pension.

(C) **Special rule for applying subparagraph (A) (ii).**—In the case of an employee who is an officer, shareholder, or owner-employee described in section 408(k) (3), the $15,000 amount specified in subparagraph (A) (ii) shall be reduced by the amount of tax taken into account with respect to such individual under subparagraph (D) of section 408(k) (3).

(3) Special rule for individual retirement plans.—If the individual has paid any qualified voluntary employee contributions for the taxable year, the amount of the qualified retirement contributions (other than employer contributions to a simplified employee pension) which are paid for the taxable year to an individual retirement plan and which are allowable as a deduction under subsection (a) for such taxable year shall not exceed—

(A) the amount determined under paragraph (1) for such taxable year, reduced by

(B) the amount of the qualified voluntary employee contributions for the taxable year.

(4) Certain divorced individuals.—

(A) In general.—In the case of an individual to whom this paragraph applies, the limitation of paragraph (1) shall not be less than the lesser of—

(i) $1,125, or

(ii) the sum of the amount referred to in paragraph (1) (B) and any qualifying alimony received by the individual during the taxable year.

(B) Qualifying alimony.—For purposes of this paragraph, the term "qualifying alimony" means amounts includible in the individual's gross income under paragraph (1) of section 71(a) (relating to decree of divorce or separate maintenance).

(C) Individuals to whom paragraph applies.—This paragraph shall apply to an individual if—

(i) an individual retirement plan was established for the benefit of the individual at least 5 years before the beginning of the calendar year in which the decree of divorce or separate maintenance was issued, and

(ii) for at least 3 of the former spouse's most recent 5 taxable years ending before the taxable year in which the decree was issued, such former spouse was allowed a deduction under subsection (c) (or the corresponding provisions of prior law) for contributions to such individual retirement plan.

(c) Special rules for certain married individuals.—

(1) In general.—In the case of any individual with respect to whom a deduction is otherwise allowable under subsection (a)—

(A) who files a joint return under section 6013 for a taxable year, and

(B) whose spouse has no compensation (determined without regard to section 911) for such taxable year,

there shall be allowed as a deduction any amount paid in cash for the taxable year by or on behalf of the individual to an individual retirement plan established for the benefit of his spouse.

(2) Limitation.—The amount allowable as a deduction under paragraph (1) shall not exceed the excess of—

(A) the lesser of—

(i) $2,250, or

(ii) an amount equal to the compensation includible in the individual's gross income for the taxable year, over

(B) the amount allowed as a deduction under subsection (a) for the taxable year.

In no event shall the amount allowable as a deduction under paragraph (1) exceed $2,000.

(d) Other limitations and restrictions.—

(1) Individuals who have attained age 70½.—No deduction shall be allowed under this section with respect to any qualified retirement contribution which is made for a taxable year of an individual if such individual has attained age 70½ before the close of such taxable year.

(2) Recontributed amounts.—No deduction shall be allowed under this section with respect to a rollover contribution described in section 402(a) (5), 402(a) (7), 403(a) (4), 403(b) (8), 405(d) (3), 408(d) (3), or 409(b) (3) (C).

(3) Amounts contributed under endowment contract.—In the case of an endowment contract described in section 408(b), no deduction shall be allowed under this section for that portion of the amounts paid under the contract for the taxable year which is properly allocable, under regulations prescribed by the Secretary, to the cost of life insurance.

(4) Denial of deduction for amount contributed to inherited annuities or accounts.—No deduction shall be allowed under this section with respect to any amount paid to an inherited individual retirement account or individual retirement annuity (within the meaning of section 408(d)(3)(C)(ii)).

(e) Definition of retirement savings contributions, etc.—For purposes of this section—

(1) Qualified retirement contribution.—The term "qualified retirement contribution" means—

(A) any qualified voluntary employee contribution paid in cash by the individual for the taxable year, and

(B) any amount paid in cash for the taxable year by or on behalf of such individual for his benefit to an individual retirement plan.

For purposes of the preceding sentence, the term "individual retirement plan" includes a retirement bond described in section 409 only if the bond is not redeemed within 12 months of its issuance.

(2) Qualified voluntary employee contribution.—

(A) In general.—The term "qualified voluntary employee contribution" means any voluntary contribution—

(i) which is made by an individual as an employee under a qualified employer plan or government plan, which plan allows an employee to make contributions which may be treated as qualified voluntary employee contributions under this section, and

(ii) with respect to which the individual has not designated such contribution as a contribution which should not be taken into account under this section.

(B) Voluntary contribution.—For purposes of subparagraph (A), the term "voluntary contribution" means any contribution which is not a mandatory contribution (within the meaning of section 411(c) (2) (C)).

(C) Designation.—For purposes of determining whether or not an individual has made a designation described in subparagraph (A) (ii) with respect to any contribution during any calendar year under a qualified employer plan or government plan, such individual shall be treated as having made such designation if he notifies the plan administrator of such plan, not later than the earlier of—

    (i) April 15 of the succeeding calendar year, or

    (ii) the time prescribed by the plan administrator,

that the individual does not want such contribution taken into account under this section. Any designation or notification referred to in the preceding sentence shall be made in such manner as the Secretary shall by regulations prescribe and, after the last date on which such designation or notification may be made, shall be irrevocable for such taxable year.

    (3) Qualified employer plan.—The term "qualified employer plan" means—

        (A) a plan described in section 401(a) which includes a trust exempt from tax under section 501(a),

        (B) an annuity plan described in section 403(a),

        (C) a qualified bond purchase plan described in section 405(a),

        (D) a simplified employee pension (within the meaning of section 408(k)), and

        (E) a plan under which amounts are contributed by an individual's employer for an annuity contract described in section 403(b).

    (4) Government plan.—The term "government plan" means any plan, whether or not qualified, established and maintained for its employees by the United States, by a State or political subdivision thereof, or by an agency or instrumentality of any of the foregoing.

    (5) Payments for certain plans.—The term "amounts paid to an individual retirement plan" includes amounts paid for an individual retirement annuity or a retirement bond.

(f) Other definitions and special rules.—

    (1) Compensation.—For purposes of this section, the term "compensation" includes earned income as defined in section 401(c)(2).

    (2) Married individuals.—The maximum deduction under subsections (b) and (c) shall be computed separately for each individual, and this section shall be applied without regard to any community property laws.

    (3) Time when contributions deemed made.—

        (A) Individual retirement plans.—For purposes of this section, a taxpayer shall be deemed to have made a contribution to an individual retirement plan on the last day of the preceding taxable year if the contribution is made on account of such taxable year and is made not later than the time prescribed by law for filing the return for such taxable year (including extensions thereof).

        (B) Qualified employer or government plans.—For purposes of this section, if a qualified employer or government plan elects to have the provisions of this subparagraph apply, a taxpayer shall be deemed to have made a voluntary contribution to such plan on the last day of the preceding calendar year (if, without regard to this paragraph, such contribution may be made on such date) if the contribution is made by

April 15 of the calendar year or such earlier time as is provided by the plan administrator.

(4) Reports.—The Secretary shall prescribe regulations which prescribe the time and the manner in which reports to the Secretary and plan participants shall be made by the plan administrator of a qualified employer or government plan receiving qualified voluntary employee contributions.

(5) Employer payments.—For purposes of this title, any amount paid by an employer to an individual retirement plan shall be treated as payment of compensation to the employee (other than a self-employed individual who is an employee within the meaning of section 401(c)(1)) includible in his gross income in the taxable year for which the amount was contributed, whether or not a deduction for such payment is allowable under this section to the employee.

(6) Excess contributions treated as contribution made during subsequent year for which there is an unused limitation.—

(A) In general.—If for the taxable year the maximum amount allowable as a deduction under this section for contributions to an individual retirement plan exceeds the amount contributed, then the taxpayer shall be treated as having made an additional contribution for the taxable year in an amount equal to the lesser of—

(i) the amount of such excess, or

(ii) the amount of the excess contributions for such taxable year (determined under section 4973(b)(2) without regard to subparagraph (C) thereof).

(B) Amount contributed.—For purposes of this paragraph, the amount contributed—

(i) shall be determined without regard to this paragraph, and

(ii) shall not include any rollover contribution.

(C) Special rule where excess deduction was allowed for closed year.—Proper reduction shall be made in the amount allowable as a deduction by reason of this paragraph for any amount allowed as a deduction under this section for a prior taxable year for which the period for assessing deficiency has expired if the amount so allowed exceeds the amount which should have been allowed for such prior taxable year.

. . . . .

§ 221. Deduction for two-earner married couples

(a) Deduction allowed.—

(1) In general.—In the case of a joint return under section 6013 for the taxable year, there shall be allowed as a deduction an amount equal to 10 percent of the lesser of—

(A) $30,000, or

(B) the qualified earned income of the spouse with the lower qualified earned income for such taxable year.

(2) Special rule for 1982.—In the case of a taxable year beginning during 1982, paragraph (1) shall be applied by substituting "5 percent" for "10 percent".

(b) Qualified earned income defined.—

    (1) In general.—For purposes of this section, the term "qualified earned income" means an amount equal to the excess of—

        (A) the earned income of the spouse for the taxable year, over

        (B) an amount equal to the sum of the deductions described in paragraphs (1), (2), (7), (9), (10), and (15) of section 62 to the extent such deductions are properly allocable to or chargeable against earned income described in subparagraph (A).

The amount of qualified earned income shall be determined without regard to any community property laws.

    (2) Earned income.—For purposes of paragraph (1), the term "earned income" means income which is earned income within the meaning of section 911(d)(2) or 401(c)(2)(C), except that—

        (A) such term shall not include any amount—

            (i) not includible in gross income,

            (ii) received as a pension or annuity,

            (iii) paid or distributed out of an individual retirement plan (within the meaning of section 7701(a)(37)),

            (iv) received as deferred compensation, or

            (v) received for services performed by an individual in the employ of his spouse (within the meaning of section 3121(b)(3)(A)), and

        (B) section 911(d)(2)(B) shall be applied without regard to the phrase "not in excess of 30 percent of his share of net profits of such trade or business".

· · · · ·

PART VIII—SPECIAL DEDUCTIONS FOR CORPORATIONS

§ 241.   Allowance of special deductions

    In addition to the deductions provided in part VI (sec. 161 and following), there shall be allowed as deductions in computing taxable income the items specified in this part.

§ 243.   Dividends received by corporations

    (a) General rule.—In the case of a corporation, there shall be allowed as a deduction an amount equal to the following percentages of the amount received as dividends from a domestic corporation which is subject to taxation under this chapter:

    (1) 85 percent, in the case of dividends other than dividends described in paragraph (2) or (3);

    (2) 100 percent, in the case of dividends received by a small business investment company operating under the Small Business Investment Act of 1958 (15 U.S.C. 661 and following); and

    (3) 100 percent, in the case of qualifying dividends (as defined in subsection (b) (1)).

(b) Qualifying dividends.—

(1) **Definition.**—For purposes of subsection (a) (3), the term "qualifying dividends" means dividends received by a corporation which, at the close of the day the dividends are received, is a member of the same affiliated group of corporations (as defined in paragraph (5)) as the corporation distributing the dividends, if—

(A) such affiliated group has made an election under paragraph (2) which is effective for the taxable years of its members which include such day, and either

(B) such dividends are distributed out of earnings and profits of a taxable year of the distributing corporation ending after December 31, 1963—

(i) on each day of which the distributing corporation and the corporation receiving the dividends were members of such affiliated group, and

(ii) for which an election under section 1562 (relating to election of multiple surtax exemptions) is not effective, or

.   .   .   .   .

(2) **Election.**—An election under this paragraph shall be made for an affiliated group by the common parent corporation, and shall be made for any taxable year of the common parent corporation at such time and in such manner as the Secretary by regulations prescribes. Such election may not be made for an affiliated group for any taxable year of the common parent corporation for which an election under section 1562 is effective. Each corporation which is a member of such group at any time during its taxable year which includes the last day of such taxable year of the common parent corporation must consent to such election at such time and in such manner as the Secretary by regulations prescribes. An election under this paragraph shall be effective—

(A) for the taxable year of each member of such affiliated group which includes the last day of the taxable year of the common parent corporation with respect to which the election is made, and

(B) for the taxable year of each member of such affiliated group which ends after the last day of such taxable year of the common parent corporation but which does not include such date, unless the election is terminated under paragraph (4).

(3) **Effect of election.**—If an election by an affiliated group is effective with respect to a taxable year of the common parent corporation, then under regulations prescribed by the Secretary—

(A) no member of such affiliated group may consent to an election under section 1562 for such taxable year,

(B) the members of such affiliated group shall be treated as one taxpayer for purposes of making the election under section 901(a) (relating to allowance of foreign tax credit), and

(C) the members of such affiliated group shall be limited to one—

(i) $250,000 minimum accumulated earnings credit under section 535(c) (2) or (3),

(ii) $400,000 limitation for certain exploration expenditures under section 617(h) (1),

. . . . .

(4) **Termination.**—An election by an affiliated group under paragraph (2) shall terminate with respect to the taxable year of the common parent corporation and with respect to the taxable years of the members of such affiliated group which include the last day of such taxable year of the common parent corporation if—

(A) **Consent of members.**—Such affiliated group files a termination of such election (at such time and in such manner as the Secretary by regulations prescribes) with respect to such taxable year of the common parent corporation, and each corporation which is a member of such affiliated group at any time during its taxable year which includes the last day of such taxable year of the common parent corporation consents to such termination, or

(B) **Refusal by new member to consent.**—During such taxable year of the common parent corporation such affiliated group includes a member which—

(i) was not a member of such group during such common parent corporation's immediately preceding taxable year, and

(ii) such member files a statement that it does not consent to the election at such time and in such manner as the Secretary by regulations prescribes.

(5) **Definition of affiliated group.**—For purposes of this subsection, the term "affiliated group" has the meaning assigned to it by section 1504(a), except that for such purposes sections 1504(b) (2), 1504(b) (4), and 1504(c) shall not apply.

. . . . .

§ 246. Rules applying to deductions for dividends received

(a) **Deduction not allowed for dividends from certain corporations.**—The deductions allowed by sections 243, 244, and 245 shall not apply to any dividend from a corporation which, for the taxable year of the corporation in which the distribution is made, or for the next preceding taxable year of the corporation, is a corporation exempt from tax under section 501 (relating to certain charitable, etc., organizations) or section 521 (relating to farmers' cooperative associations).

(b) **Limitation on aggregate amount of deductions.**—

(1) **General rule.**—Except as provided in paragraph (2), the aggregate amount of the deductions allowed by sections 243(a) (1), 244(a), and 245 shall not exceed 85 percent of the taxable income computed without regard to the deductions allowed by sections 172, 243(a) (1), 244(a), 245, and 247, and without regard to any capital loss carryback to the taxable year under section 1212(a) (1).

(2) **Effect of net operating loss.**—Paragraph (1) shall not apply for any taxable year for which there is a net operating loss (as determined under section 172).

. . . . .

§ 248.   Organizational expenditures

(a) Election to amortize.—The organizational expenditures of a corporation may, at the election of the corporation (made in accordance with regulations prescribed by the Secretary), be treated as deferred expenses. In computing taxable income, such deferred expenses shall be allowed as a deduction ratably over such period of not less than 60 months as may be selected by the corporation (beginning with the month in which the corporation begins business).

(b) Organizational expenditures defined.—The term "organizational expenditures" means any expenditure which—

(1) is incident to the creation of the corporation;

(2) is chargeable to capital account; and

(3) is of a character which, if expended incident to the creation of a corporation having a limited life, would be amortizable over such life.

(c) Time for and scope of election.—The election provided by subsection (a) may be made for any taxable year beginning after December 31, 1953, but only if made not later than the time prescribed by law for filing the return for such taxable year (including extensions thereof). The period so elected shall be adhered to in computing the taxable income of the corporation for the taxable year for which the election is made and all subsequent taxable years. The election shall apply only with respect to expenditures paid or incurred on or after August 16, 1954.

PART IX—ITEMS NOT DEDUCTIBLE

§ 261.   General rule for disallowance of deductions

In computing taxable income no deduction shall in any case be allowed in respect of the items specified in this part.

§ 262.   Personal, living, and family expenses

Except as otherwise expressly provided in this chapter, no deduction shall be allowed for personal, living, or family expenses.

§ 263.   Capital expenditures

(a) General rule.—No deduction shall be allowed for—

(1) Any amount paid out for new buildings or for permanent improvements or betterments made to increase the value of any property or estate. This paragraph shall not apply to—

(A) expenditures for the development of mines or deposits deductible under section 616,

(B) research and experimental expenditures deductible under section 174,

(C) soil and water conservation expenditures deductible under section 175,

(D) expenditures by farmers for fertilizer, etc., deductible under section 180,

(E) expenditures by farmers for clearing land deductible under section 182,

(F) expenditures for removal of architectural and transportation barriers to the handicapped and elderly which the taxpayer elects to deduct under section 190,

(G) expenditures for tertiary injectants with respect to which a deduction is allowed under section 193, or

(H) expenditures for which a deduction is allowed under section 179.

(2) Any amount expended in restoring property or in making good the exhaustion thereof for which an allowance is or has been made.

. . . . .

(c) Intangible drilling and development costs in the case of oil and gas wells. —Notwithstanding subsection (a), regulations shall be prescribed by the Secretary under this subtitle corresponding to the regulations which granted the option to deduct as expenses intangible drilling and development costs in the case of oil and gas wells and which were recognized and approved by the Congress in House Concurrent Resolution 50, Seventy-ninth Congress. Such regulations shall also grant the option to deduct as expenses intangible drilling and development costs in the case of wells drilled for any geothermal deposit (as defined in section 613(e)(3)) to the same extent and in the same manner as such expenses are deductible in the case of oil and gas wells. This subsection shall not apply with respect to any costs to which any deduction is allowed under section 58(i) or 291.

. . . . .

(g) Certain interest and carrying costs in the case of straddles.—

(1) General rule.—No deduction shall be allowed for interest and carrying charges properly allocable to personal property which is part of a straddle (as defined in section 1092(c)). Any amount not allowed as a deduction by reason of the preceding sentence shall be chargeable to the capital account with respect to the personal property to which such amount relates.

(2) Interest and carrying charges defined.—For purposes of paragraph (1), the term "interest and carrying charges" means the excess of—

(A) the sum of—

(i) interest on indebtedness incurred or continued to purchase or carry the personal property, and

(ii) amounts paid or incurred to insure, store, or transport the personal property, over

(B) the sum of—

(i) the amount of interest (including original issue discount) includible in gross income for the taxable year with respect to the property described in subparagraph (A), and

(ii) any amount treated as ordinary income under section 1232(a)(4)(A) with respect to such property for the taxable year.

(3) Exception for hedging transactions.—This subsection shall not apply in the case of any hedging transaction (as defined in section 1256(e)).

§ 264.   Certain amounts paid in connection with insurance contracts

(a) General rule.—No deduction shall be allowed for—

(1) Premiums paid on any life insurance policy covering the life of any officer or employee, or of any person financially interested in any trade or

business carried on by the taxpayer, when the taxpayer is directly or indirectly a beneficiary under such policy.

(2) Any amount paid or accrued on indebtedness incurred or continued to purchase or carry a single premium life insurance, endowment, or annuity contract.

(3) Except as provided in subsection (c), any amount paid or accrued on indebtedness incurred or continued to purchase or carry a life insurance, endowment, or annuity contract (other than a single premium contract or a contract treated as a single premium contract) pursuant to a plan of purchase which contemplates the systematic direct or indirect borrowing of part or all of the increases in the cash value of such contract (either from the insurer or otherwise).

Paragraph (2) shall apply in respect of annuity contracts only as to contracts purchased after March 1, 1954. Paragraph (3) shall apply only in respect of contracts purchased after August 6, 1963.

(b) Contracts treated as single premium contracts.—For purposes of subsection (a) (2), a contract shall be treated as a single premium contract—

(1) if substantially all the premiums on the contract are paid within a period of 4 years from the date on which the contract is purchased, or

(2) if an amount is deposited after March 1, 1954, with the insurer for payment of a substantial number of future premiums on the contract.

(c) Exceptions.—Subsection (a) (3) shall not apply to any amount paid or accrued by a person during a taxable year on indebtedness incurred or continued as part of a plan referred to in subsection (a) (3)—

(1) if no part of 4 of the annual premiums due during the 7-year period (beginning with the date the first premium on the contract to which such plan relates was paid) is paid under such plan by means of indebtedness,

(2) if the total of the amounts paid or accrued by such person during such taxable year for which (without regard to this paragraph) no deduction would be allowable by reason of subsection (a) (3) does not exceed $100,

(3) if such amount was paid or accrued on indebtedness incurred because of an unforeseen substantial loss of income or unforeseen substantial increase in his financial obligations, or

(4) if such indebtedness was incurred in connection with his trade or business.

For purposes of applying paragraph (1), if there is a substantial increase in the premiums on a contract, a new 7-year period described in such paragraph with respect to such contract shall commence on the date the first such increased premium is paid.

§ 265. Expenses and interest relating to tax-exempt income

No deduction shall be allowed for—

(1) Expenses.—Any amount otherwise allowable as a deduction which is allocable to one or more classes of income other than interest (whether or not any amount of income of that class or classes is received or accrued) wholly exempt from the taxes imposed by this subtitle, or any amount otherwise allowable under section 212 (relating to expenses for production of income) which is allocable to interest (whether or not any amount of such interest is received or accrued) wholly exempt from the taxes imposed by this subtitle.

(2) **Interest.**—Interest on indebtedness incurred or continued to purchase or carry obligations the interest on which is wholly exempt from the taxes imposed by this subtitle, or to purchase or carry obligations or shares, or to make deposits or other investments, the interest on which is described in section 116(c) to the extent such interest is excludable from gross income under section 116, or to purchase or to carry any certificate to the extent the interest on such certificate is excludable under section 128. In applying the preceding sentence to a financial institution (other than a bank) which is a face-amount certificate company registered under the Investment Company Act of 1940 (15 U.S.C. 80a–1 and following) and which is subject to the banking laws of the State in which such institution is incorporated, interest on face-amount certificates (as defined in section 2(a) (15) of such Act) issued by such institution, and interest on amounts received for the purchase of such certificates to be issued by such institution, shall not be considered as interest on indebtedness incurred or continued to purchase or carry obligations the interest on which is wholly exempt from the taxes imposed by this subtitle, to the extent that the average amount of such obligations held by such institution during the taxable year (as determined under regulations prescribed by the Secretary) does not exceed 15 percent of the average of the total assets held by such institution during the taxable year (as so determined).

. . . . . .

§ 266.   Carrying charges

No deduction shall be allowed for amounts paid or accrued for such taxes and carrying charges as, under regulations prescribed by the Secretary, are chargeable to capital account with respect to property, if the taxpayer elects, in accordance with such regulations, to treat such taxes or charges as so chargeable.

§ 267.   Losses, expenses, and interest with respect to transactions between related taxpayers

(a) **Deductions disallowed.**—No deduction shall be allowed—

(1) **Losses.**—In respect of losses from sales or exchanges of property (other than losses in cases of distributions in corporate liquidations), directly or indirectly, between persons specified within any one of the paragraphs of subsection (b).

(2) **Unpaid expenses and interest.**—In respect of expenses, otherwise deductible under section 162 or 212, or of interest, otherwise deductible under section 163,—

(A) If within the period consisting of the taxable year of the taxpayer and 2½ months after the close thereof (i) such expenses or interest are not paid, and (ii) the amount thereof is not includible in the gross income of the person to whom the payment is to be made; and

(B) If, by reason of the method of accounting of the person to whom the payment is to be made, the amount thereof is not, unless paid, includible in the gross income of such person for the taxable year in which or with which the taxable year of the taxpayer ends; and

(C) If, at the close of the taxable year of the taxpayer or at any time within 2½ months thereafter, both the taxpayer and the person to whom the payment is to be made are persons specified within any one of the paragraphs of subsection (b).

(b) Relationships.—The persons referred to in subsection (a) are:

(1) Members of a family, as defined in subsection (c) (4);

(2) An individual and a corporation more than 50 percent in value of the outstanding stock of which is owned, directly or indirectly, by or for such individual;

(3) Two corporations more than 50 percent in value of the outstanding stock of each of which is owned, directly or indirectly, by or for the same individual, if either one of such corporations, with respect to the taxable year of the corporation preceding the date of the sale or exchange was, under the law applicable to such taxable year, a personal holding company or a foreign personal holding company;

(4) A grantor and a fiduciary of any trust;

(5) A fiduciary of a trust and a fiduciary of another trust, if the same person is a grantor of both trusts;

(6) A fiduciary of a trust and a beneficiary of such trust;

(7) A fiduciary of a trust and a beneficiary of another trust, if the same person is a grantor of both trusts;

(8) A fiduciary of a trust and a corporation more than 50 percent in value of the outstanding stock of which is owned, directly or indirectly, by or for the trust or by or for a person who is a grantor of the trust;

(9) A person and an organization to which section 501 (relating to certain educational and charitable organizations which are exempt from tax) applies and which is controlled directly or indirectly by such person or (if such person is an individual) by members of the family of such individual;

(10) An S corporation and a partnership if the same persons own—

    (A) more than 50 percent in value of the outstanding stock of the S corporation, and

    (B) more than 50 percent of the capital interest, or the profits interest, in the partnership;

(11) An S corporation and another S corporation if the same persons own more than 50 percent in value of the outstanding stock of each corporation; or

(12) An S corporation and a C corporation, if the same individual owns more than 50 percent in value of the outstanding stock of each corporation.

(c) Constructive ownership of stock.—For purposes of determining, in applying subsection (b), the ownership of stock—

(1) Stock owned, directly or indirectly, by or for a corporation, partnership, estate, or trust shall be considered as being owned proportionately by or for its shareholders, partners, or beneficiaries;

(2) An individual shall be considered as owning the stock owned, directly or indirectly, by or for his family;

(3) An individual owning (otherwise than by the application of paragraph (2)) any stock in a corporation shall be considered as owning the stock owned, directly or indirectly, by or for his partner;

(4) The family of an individual shall include only his brothers and sisters (whether by the whole or half blood), spouse, ancestors, and lineal descendants; and

(5) Stock constructively owned by a person by reason of the application of paragraph (1) shall, for the purpose of applying paragraph (1), (2), or (3), be treated as actually owned by such person, but stock constructively owned by an individual by reason of the application of paragraph (2) or (3) shall not be treated as owned by him for the purpose of again applying either of such paragraphs in order to make another the constructive owner of such stock.

(d) Amount of gain where loss previously disallowed.—If—

(1) in the case of a sale or exchange of property to the taxpayer a loss sustained by the transferor is not allowable to the transferor as a deduction by reason of subsection (a) (1) (or by reason of section 24(b) of the Internal Revenue Code of 1939); and

(2) after December 31, 1953, the taxpayer sells or otherwise disposes of such property (or of other property the basis of which in his hands is determined directly or indirectly by reference to such property) at a gain,

then such gain shall be recognized only to the extent that it exceeds so much of such loss as is properly allocable to the property sold or otherwise disposed of by the taxpayer. This subsection applies with respect to taxable years ending after December 31, 1953. This subsection shall not apply if the loss sustained by the transferor is not allowable to the transferor as a deduction by reason of section 1091 (relating to wash sales) or by reason of section 118 of the Internal Revenue Code of 1939.

. . . . .

(f) Special rules for unpaid expenses and interest of S corporations.—

(1) In general.—In the case of any amount paid or incurred by an S corporation, if—

(A) by reason of the method of accounting of the person to whom the payment is to be made, the amount thereof is not (unless paid) includible in the gross income of such person, and

(B) at the close of the taxable year of the S corporation for which (but for this paragraph) the amount would be deductible under section 162, 212, or 163, both the S corporation and the person to whom the payment is to be paid are persons specified in one of the paragraphs of subsection (b).

then no deduction shall be allowed in respect of expenses otherwise deductible under section 162 or 212, or of interest otherwise deductible under section 163, before the day as of which the amount thereof is includible in the gross income of the person to whom the payment is made.

(2) Certain shareholders, etc., treated as related persons.—For purposes of applying paragraph (1)—

(A) an S corporation,

(B) any person who owns, directly or indirectly, 2 percent or more in value of the outstanding stock of such corporation, and

(C) any person related (within the meaning of subsection (b) of this section or section 707(b)(1)(A)) to a person described in subparagraph (B),

shall be treated as persons specified in a paragraph of subsection (b).

(3) Subsection (a)(2) not to apply.—Subsection (a)(2) shall not apply to any amount paid or incurred by an S corporation.

§ 268. Sale of land with unharvested crop

Where an unharvested crop sold by the taxpayer is considered under the provisions of section 1231 as "property used in the trade or business", in computing taxable income no deduction (whether or not for the taxable year of the sale and whether for expenses, depreciation, or otherwise) attributable to the production of such crop shall be allowed.

§ 269. Acquisitions made to evade or avoid income tax

(a) In general.—If—

(1) any person or persons acquire, or acquired on or after October 8, 1940, directly or indirectly, control of a corporation, or

(2) any corporation acquires, or acquired on or after October 8, 1940, directly or indirectly, property of another corporation, not controlled, directly or indirectly, immediately before such acquisition, by such acquiring corporation or its stockholders, the basis of which property, in the hands of the acquiring corporation, is determined by reference to the basis in the hands of the transferor corporation,

and the principal purpose for which such acquisition was made is evasion or avoidance of Federal income tax by securing the benefit of a deduction, credit, or other allowance which such person or corporation would not otherwise enjoy, then the Secretary may disallow such deduction, credit, or other allowance. For purposes of paragraphs (1) and (2), control means the ownership of stock possessing at least 50 percent of the total combined voting power of all classes of stock entitled to vote or at least 50 percent of the total value of shares of all classes of stock of the corporation.

(b) Power of Secretary to allow deduction, etc., in part.—In any case to which subsection (a) applies the Secretary is authorized—

(1) to allow as a deduction, credit, or allowance any part of any amount disallowed by such subsection, if he determines that such allowance will not result in the evasion or avoidance of Federal income tax for which the acquisition was made; or

(2) to distribute, apportion, or allocate gross income, and distribute, apportion, or allocate the deductions, credits, or allowances the benefit of which was sought to be secured, between or among the corporations, or properties, or parts thereof, involved, and to allow such deductions, credits, or allowances so distributed, apportioned, or allocated, but to give effect to such allowance only to such extent as he determines will not result in the evasion or avoidance of Federal income tax for which the acquisition was made; or

(3) to exercise his powers in part under paragraph (1) and in part under paragraph (2).

§ 269A. Personal service corporations formed or availed of to avoid or evade income tax

(a) General rule.—If—

(1) substantially all of the services of a personal service corporation are performed for (or on behalf of) 1 other corporation, partnership, or other entity, and

(2) the principal purpose for forming, or availing of, such personal service corporation is the avoidance or evasion of Federal income tax by reducing the income of, or securing the benefit of any expense, deduction, credit, exclusion, or other allowance for, any employee-owner which would not otherwise be available,

then the Secretary may allocate all income, deductions, credits, exclusions, and other allowances between such personal service corporation and its employee-owners, if such allocation is necessary to prevent avoidance or evasion of Federal income tax or clearly to reflect the income of the personal service corporation or any of its employee-owners.

(b) Definitions.—For purposes of this section—

(1) Personal service corporation.—The term "personal service corporation" means a corporation the principal activity of which is the performance of personal services and such services are substantially performed by employee-owners.

(2) Employee-owner.—The term "employee-owner" means any employee who owns, on any day during the taxable year, more than 10 percent of the outstanding stock of the personal service corporation. For purposes of the preceding sentence, section 318 shall apply, except that "5 percent" shall be substituted for "50 percent" in section 318(a)(2)(C).

(3) Related persons.—All related persons (within the meaning of section 103(b)(6)(C)) shall be treated as 1 entity.

§ 271.   Debts owed by political parties, etc.

(a) General rule.—In the case of a taxpayer (other than a bank as defined in section 581) no deduction shall be allowed under section 166 (relating to bad debts) or under section 165(g) (relating to worthlessness of securities) by reason of the worthlessness of any debt owed by a political party.

(b) Definitions.—

(1) Political party.—For purposes of subsection (a), the term "political party" means—

(A) a political party;

(B) a national, State, or local committee of a political party; or

(C) a committee, association, or organization which accepts contributions or makes expenditures for the purpose of influencing or attempting to influence the election of presidential or vice-presidential electors or of any individual whose name is presented for election to any Federal, State, or local elective public office, whether or not such individual is elected.

(2) Contributions.—For purposes of paragraph (1) (C), the term "contributions" includes a gift, subscription, loan, advance, or deposit, of money, or anything of value, and includes a contract, promise, or agreement to make a contribution, whether or not legally enforceable.

(3) Expenditures.—For purposes of paragraph (1) (C), the term "expenditures" includes a payment, distribution, loan, advance, deposit, or gift, of money, or anything of value, and includes a contract, promise, or agreement to make an expenditure, whether or not legally enforceable.

(c) Exception.—In the case of a taxpayer who uses an accrual method of accounting, subsection (a) shall not apply to a debt which accrued as a receivable on a bona fide sale of goods or services in the ordinary course of the taxpayer's trade or business if—

    (1) for the taxable year in which such receivable accrued, more than 30 percent of all receivables which accrued in the ordinary course of the trades and businesses of the taxpayer were due from political parties, and

    (2) the taxpayer made substantial continuing efforts to collect on the debt.

§ 272.   Disposal of coal or domestic iron ore

Where the disposal of coal or iron ore is covered by section 631, no deduction shall be allowed for expenditures attributable to the making and administering of the contract under which such disposition occurs and to the preservation of the economic interest retained under such contract, except that if in any taxable year such expenditures plus the adjusted depletion basis of the coal or iron ore disposed of in such taxable year exceed the amount realized under such contract, such excess, to the extent not availed of as a reduction of gain under section 1231, shall be a loss deductible under section 165(a). This section shall not apply to any taxable year during which there is no income under the contract.

§ 273.   Holders of life or terminable interest

Amounts paid under the laws of a State, the District of Columbia, a possession of the United States, or a foreign country as income to the holder of a life or terminable interest acquired by gift, bequest, or inheritance shall not be reduced or diminished by any deduction for shrinkage (by whatever name called) in the value of such interest due to the lapse of time.

§ 274.   Disallowance of certain entertainment, etc., expenses

(a) Entertainment, amusement, or recreation.—

    (1) In general.—No deduction otherwise allowable under this chapter shall be allowed for any item—

        (A) Activity.—With respect to an activity which is of a type generally considered to constitute entertainment, amusement, or recreation, unless the taxpayer establishes that the item was directly related to, or, in the case of an item directly preceding or following a substantial and bona fide business discussion (including business meetings at a convention or otherwise), that such item was associated with, the active conduct of the taxpayer's trade or business, or

        (B) Facility.—With respect to a facility used in connection with an activity referred to in subparagraph (A).

In the case of an item described in subparagraph (A), the deduction shall in no event exceed the portion of such item which meets the requirements of subparagraph (A).

    (2) Special rules.—For purposes of applying paragraph (1)—

        (A) Dues or fees to any social, athletic, or sporting club or organization shall be treated as items with respect to facilities.

        (B) An activity described in section 212 shall be treated as a trade or business.

        (C) In the case of a club, paragraph (1) (B) shall apply unless the taxpayer establishes that the facility was used primarily for the furtherance of the taxpayer's trade or business and that the item was directly related to the active conduct of such trade or business.

(b) Gifts.—

(1) **Limitation.**—No deduction shall be allowed under section 162 or section 212 for any expense for gifts made directly or indirectly to any individual to the extent that such expense, when added to prior expenses of the taxpayer for gifts made to such individual during the same taxable year, exceeds $25. For purposes of this section, the term "gift" means any item excludable from gross income of the recipient under section 102 which is not excludable from his gross income under any other provision of this chapter, but such term does not include—

(A) an item having a cost to the taxpayer not in excess of $4.00 on which the name of the taxpayer is clearly and permanently imprinted and which is one of a number of identical items distributed generally by the taxpayer,

(B) a sign, display rack, or other promotional material to be used on the business premises of the recipient, or

(C) an item of tangible personal property which is awarded to an employee by reason of length of service, productivity, or safety achievement, but only to the extent that—

(i) the cost of such item to the taxpayer does not exceed $400, or

(ii) such item is a qualified plan award.

(2) **Special rules.—**

(A) In the case of a gift by a partnership, the limitation contained in paragraph (1) shall apply to the partnership as well as to each member thereof.

(B) For purposes of paragraph (1), a husband and wife shall be treated as one taxpayer.

(3) **Qualified plan award.**—For purposes of this subsection—

(A) **In general.**—The term "qualified plan award" means an item which is awarded as part of a permanent, written plan or program of the taxpayer which does not discriminate in favor of officers, shareholders, or highly compensated employees as to eligibility or benefits.

(B) **Average amount of awards.**—An item shall not be treated as a qualified plan award for any taxable year if the average cost of all items awarded under all plans described in subparagraph (A) of the taxpayer during the taxable year exceeds $400.

(C) **Maximum amount per item.**—An item shall not be treated as a qualified plan award under this paragraph to the extent that the cost of such item exceeds $1,600.

(c) Certain foreign travel.—

(1) **In general.**—In the case of any individual who travels outside the United States away from home in pursuit of a trade or business or in pursuit of an activity described in section 212, no deduction shall be allowed under section 162 or section 212 for that portion of the expenses of such travel otherwise allowable under such section which, under regulations prescribed by the Secretary, is not allocable to such trade or business or to such activity.

(2) **Exception.**—Paragraph (1) shall not apply to the expenses of any travel outside the United States away from home if—

(A) such travel does not exceed one week, or

(B) the portion of the time of travel outside the United States away from home which is not attributable to the pursuit of the taxpayer's trade or business or an activity described in section 212 is less than 25 percent of the total time on such travel.

(3) **Domestic travel excluded.**—For purposes of this subsection, travel outside the United States does not include any travel from one point in the United States to another point in the United States.

(d) **Substantiation required.**—No deduction shall be allowed—

(1) under section 162 or 212 for any traveling expense (including meals and lodging while away from home),

(2) for any item with respect to an activity which is of a type generally considered to constitute entertainment, amusement, or recreation, or with respect to a facility used in connection with such an activity, or

(3) for any expense for gifts,

unless the taxpayer substantiates by adequate records or by sufficient evidence corroborating his own statement (A) the amount of such expense or other item, (B) the time and place of the travel, entertainment, amusement, recreation, or use of the facility, or the date and description of the gift, (C) the business purpose of the expense or other item, and (D) the business relationship to the taxpayer of persons entertained, using the facility, or receiving the gift. The Secretary may by regulations provide that some or all of the requirements of the preceding sentence shall not apply in the case of an expense which does not exceed an amount prescribed pursuant to such regulations.

(e) **Specific exceptions to application of subsection (a).**—Subsection (a) shall not apply to—

(1) **Business meals.**—Expenses for food and beverages furnished to any individual under circumstances which (taking into account the surroundings in which furnished, the taxpayer's trade, business, or income-producing activity and the relationship to such trade, business, or activity of the persons to whom the food and beverages are furnished) are of a type generally considered to be conducive to a business discussion.

(2) **Food and beverages for employees.**—Expenses for food and beverages (and facilities used in connection therewith) furnished on the business premises of the taxpayer primarily for his employees.

(3) **Expenses treated as compensation.**—Expenses for goods, services, and facilities, to the extent that the expenses are treated by the taxpayer, with respect to the recipient of the entertainment, amusement, or recreation, as compensation to an employee on the taxpayer's return of tax under this chapter and as wages to such employee for purposes of subchapter A of chapter 24 (relating to withholding of income tax at source on wages).

(4) **Reimbursed expenses.**—Expenses paid or incurred by the taxpayer, in connection with the performance by him of services for another person (whether or not such other person is his employer), under a reimbursement or other expense allowance arrangement with such other person, but this paragraph shall apply—

(A) where the services are performed for an employer, only if the employer has not treated such expenses in the manner provided in paragraph (3), or

(B) where the services are performed for a person other than an employer, only if the taxpayer accounts (to the extent provided by subsection (d)) to such person.

(5) Recreational, etc., expenses for employees.—Expenses for recreational, social, or similar activities (including facilities therefor) primarily for the benefit of employees (other than employees who are officers, shareholders or other owners, or highly compensated employees). For purposes of this paragraph, an individual owning less than a 10-percent interest in the taxpayer's trade or business shall not be considered a shareholder or other owner, and for such purposes an individual shall be treated as owning any interest owned by a member of his family (within the meaning of section 267(c) (4)).

(6) Employee, stockholder, etc., business meetings.—Expenses incurred by a taxpayer which are directly related to business meetings of his employees, stockholders, agents, or directors.

(7) Meetings of business leagues, etc.—Expenses directly related and necessary to attendance at a business meeting or convention of any organization described in section 501(c) (6) (relating to business leagues, chambers of commerce, real estate boards, and boards of trade) and exempt from taxation under section 501(a).

(8) Items available to public.—Expenses for goods, services, and facilities made available by the taxpayer to the general public.

(9) Entertainment sold to customers.—Expenses for goods or services (including the use of facilities) which are sold by the taxpayer in a bona fide transaction for an adequate and full consideration in money or money's worth.

(10) Expenses includible in income of persons who are not employees. —Expenses paid or incurred by the taxpayer for goods, services, and facilities to the extent that the expenses are includible in the gross income of a recipient of the entertainment, amusement, or recreation who is not an employee of the taxpayer as compensation for services rendered or as a prize or award under section 74. The preceding sentence shall not apply to any amount paid or incurred by the taxpayer if such amount is required to be included (or would be so required except that the amount is less than $600) in any information return filed by such taxpayer under part III of subchapter A of chapter 61 and is not so included.

For purposes of this subsection, any item referred to in subsection (a) shall be treated as an expense.

(f) Interest, taxes, casualty losses, etc.—This section shall not apply to any deduction allowable to the taxpayer without regard to its connection with his trade or business (or with his income-producing activity). In the case of a taxpayer which is not an individual, the preceding sentence shall be applied as if it were an individual.

(g) Treatment of entertainment, etc., type facility.—For purposes of this chapter, if deductions are disallowed under subsection (a) with respect to any portion of a facility, such portion shall be treated as an asset which is used for personal, living, and family purposes (and not as an asset used in the trade or business).

(h) Attendance at conventions, etc.—

(1) In general.—In the case of any individual who attends a convention, seminar, or similar meeting which is held outside the North American area, no deduction shall be allowed under section 162 or 212 for expenses allocable to such meeting unless the taxpayer establishes that the meeting is directly related to the active conduct of his trade or business or to an activity described in section 212 and that, after taking into account in the manner provided by regulations prescribed by the Secretary—

(A) the purpose of such meeting and the activities taking place at such meeting,

(B) the purposes and activities of the sponsoring organizations or groups,

(C) the residences of the active members of the sponsoring organization and the places at which other meetings of the sponsoring organization or groups have been held or will be held, and

(D) such other relevant factors as the taxpayer may present,

it is as reasonable for the meeting to be held outside the North American area as within the North American area.

(2) Conventions on cruise ships.—In the case of any individual who attends a convention, seminar, or other meeting which is held on any cruise ship, no deduction shall be allowed under section 162 or 212 for expenses allocable to such meeting.

(3) Definitions.—For purposes of this subsection—

(A) North American area.—The term "North American area" means the United States, its possessions, and the Trust Territory of the Pacific Islands, and Canada and Mexico.

(B) Cruise ship.—The term "cruise ship" means any vessel sailing within or without the territorial waters of the United States.

(4) Subsection to apply to employer as well as to traveler.—

(A) Except as provided in subparagraph (B), this subsection shall apply to deductions otherwise allowable under section 162 or 212 to any person, whether or not such person is the individual attending the convention, seminar, or similar meeting.

(B) This subsection shall not deny a deduction to any person other than the individual attending the convention, seminar, or similar meeting with respect to any amount paid by such person to or on behalf of such individual if includible in the gross income of such individual. The preceding sentence shall not apply if the amount is required to be included in any information return filed by such person under part III of subchapter A of chapter 61 and is not so included.

(i) Regulatory authority.—The Secretary shall prescribe such regulations as he may deem necessary to carry out the purposes of this section, including regulations prescribing whether subsection (a) or subsection (b) applies in cases where both such subsections would otherwise apply.

§ 275. Certain taxes

(a) General rule.—No deduction shall be allowed for the following taxes:

(1) Federal income taxes, including—

(2) Federal war profits and excess profits taxes.

(3) Estate, inheritance, legacy, succession, and gift taxes.

(4) Income, war profits, and excess profits taxes imposed by the authority of any foreign country or possession of the United States, if the taxpayer chooses to take to any extent the benefits of section 901 (relating to the foreign tax credit).

(5) Taxes on real property, to the extent that section 164(d) requires such taxes to be treated as imposed on another taxpayer.

§ 276. Certain indirect contributions to political parties

(a) Disallowance of deduction.—No deduction otherwise allowable under this chapter shall be allowed for any amount paid or incurred for—

(1) advertising in a convention program of a political party, or in any other publication if any part of the proceeds of such publication directly or indirectly inures (or is intended to inure) to or for the use of a political party or a political candidate,

(2) admission to any dinner or program, if any part of the proceeds of such dinner or program directly or indirectly inures (or is intended to inure) to or for the use of a political party or a political candidate, or

(3) admission to an inaugural ball, inaugural gala, inaugural parade, or inaugural concert, or to any similar event which is identified with a political party or a political candidate.

§ 278. Capital expenditures incurred in planting and developing citrus and almond groves; certain capital expenditures of farming syndicates

(a) General rule.—Except as provided in subsection (c), any amount (allowable as a deduction without regard to this section), which is attributable to the planting, cultivation, maintenance, or development of any citrus or almond grove (or part thereof), and which is incurred before the close of the fourth taxable year beginning with the taxable year in which the trees were planted, shall be charged to capital account. For purposes of the preceding sentence, the portion of a citrus or almond grove planted in one taxable year shall be treated separately from the portion of such grove planted in another taxable year.

(b) Farming syndicates.—Except as provided in subsection (c), in the case of any farming syndicate (as defined in section 464(c)) engaged in planting, cultivating, maintaining, or developing a grove, orchard, or vineyard in which fruit or nuts are grown, any amount—

(1) which would be allowable as a deduction but for the provisions of this subsection,

(2) which is attributable to the planting, cultivation, maintenance, or development of such grove, orchard, or vineyard, and

(3) which is incurred in a taxable year before the first taxable year in which such grove, orchard, or vineyard bears a crop or yield in commercial quantities,

shall be charged to capital account.

(c) Exceptions.—Subsections (a) and (b) shall not apply to amounts allowable as deductions (without regard to this section) attributable to a grove, orchard, or vineyard which was replanted after having been lost or damaged (while in the hands of the taxpayer) by reason of freezing temperatures, disease, drought, pests, or casualty.

§ 279. Interest on indebtedness incurred by corporation to acquire stock or assets of another corporation

(a) General rule.—No deduction shall be allowed for any interest paid or incurred by a corporation during the taxable year with respect to its corporate acquisition indebtedness to the extent that such interest exceeds—

(1) $5,000,000, reduced by

(2) the amount of interest paid or incurred by such corporation during such year on obligations (A) issued after December 31, 1967, to provide consideration for an acquisition described in paragraph (1) of subsection (b), but (B) which are not corporate acquisition indebtedness.

(b) Corporate acquisition indebtedness.—For purposes of this section, the term "corporate acquisition indebtedness" means any obligation evidenced by a bond, debenture, note, or certificate or other evidence of indebtedness issued after October 9, 1969, by a corporation (hereinafter in this section referred to as "issuing corporation") if—

(1) such obligation is issued to provide consideration for the acquisition of—

(A) stock in another corporation (hereinafter in this section referred to as "acquired corporation"), or

(B) assets of another corporation (hereinafter in this section referred to as "acquired corporation") pursuant to a plan under which at least two-thirds (in value) of all the assets (excluding money) used in trades and businesses carried on by such corporation are acquired,

(2) such obligation is either—

(A) subordinated to the claims of trade creditors of the issuing corporation generally, or

(B) expressly subordinated in right of payment to the payment of any substantial amount of unsecured indebtedness, whether outstanding or subsequently issued, of the issuing corporation,

(3) the bond or other evidence of indebtedness is either—

(A) convertible directly or indirectly into stock of the issuing corporation, or

(B) part of an investment unit or other arrangement which includes, in addition to such bond or other evidence of indebtedness, an option to acquire, directly or indirectly, stock in the issuing corporation, and

(4) as of a day determined under subsection (c) (1), either—

(A) the ratio of debt to equity (as defined in subsection (c) (2)) of the issuing corporation exceeds 2 to 1, or

(B) the projected earnings (as defined in subsection (c) (3)) do not exceed 3 times the annual interest to be paid or incurred (determined under subsection (c) (4)).

. . . . .

§ 280A.   Disallowance of certain expenses in connection with business use of home, rental of vacation homes, etc.

(a) General rule.—Except as otherwise provided in this section, in the case of a taxpayer who is an individual or an S corporation, no deduction otherwise allowable under this chapter shall be allowed with respect to the use of a dwelling unit which is used by the taxpayer during the taxable year as a residence.

(b) Exception for interest, taxes, casualty losses, etc.—Subsection (a) shall not apply to any deduction allowable to the taxpayer without regard to its connection with his trade or business (or with his income-producing activity).

(c) Exceptions for certain business or rental use; limitation on deductions for such use.—

(1) **Certain business use.**—Subsection (a) shall not apply to any item to the extent such item is allocable to a portion of the dwelling unit which is exclusively used on a regular basis—

(A) the principal place of business for any trade or business of the taxpayer,

(B) as a place of business which is used by patients, clients, or customers in meeting or dealing with the taxpayer in the normal course of his trade or business, or

(C) in the case of a separate structure which is not attached to the dwelling unit, in connection with the taxpayer's trade or business.

In the case of an employee, the preceding sentence shall apply only if the exclusive use referred to in the preceding sentence is for the convenience of his employer.

(2) **Certain storage use.**—Subsection (a) shall not apply to any item to the extent such item is allocable to space within the dwelling unit which is used on a regular basis as a storage unit for the inventory of the taxpayer held for use in the taxpayer's trade or business of selling products at retail or wholesale, but only if the dwelling unit is the sole fixed location of such trade or business.

(3) **Rental use.**—Subsection (a) shall not apply to any item which is attributable to the rental of the dwelling unit or portion thereof (determined after the application of subsection (e)).

(4) **Use in providing day care services.—**

(A) **In general.**—Subsection (a) shall not apply to any item to the extent that such item is allocable to the use of any portion of the dwelling unit on a regular basis in the taxpayer's trade or business of providing day care for children, for individuals who have attained age 65, or for individuals who are physically or mentally incapable of caring for themselves.

(B) Licensing, etc., requirement.—Subparagraph (A) shall apply to items accruing for a period only if the owner or operator of the trade or business referred to in subparagraph (A)—

(i) has applied for (and such application has not been rejected),

(ii) has been granted (and such granting has not been revoked), or

(iii) is exempt from having,

a license, certification, registration, or approval as a day care center or as a family or group day care home under the provisions of any applicable State law. This subparagraph shall apply only to items accruing in periods beginning on or after the first day of the first month which begins more than 90 days after the date of the enactment of the Tax Reduction and Simplification Act of 1977.

(C) Allocation formula.—If a portion of the taxpayer's dwelling unit used for the purposes described in subparagraph (A) is not used exclusively for those purposes, the amount of the expenses attributable to that portion shall not exceed an amount which bears the same ratio to the total amount of the items allocable to such portion as the number of hours the portion is used for such purposes bears to the number of hours the portion is available for use.

(5) Limitation on deductions.—In the case of a use described in paragraph (1), (2), or (4), and in the case of a use described in paragraph (3) where the dwelling unit is used by the taxpayer during the taxable year as a residence, the deductions allowed under this chapter for the taxable year by reason of being attributed to such use shall not exceed the excess of—

(A) the gross income derived from such use for the taxable year, over

(B) the deductions allocable to such use which are allowable under this chapter for the taxable year whether or not such unit (or portion thereof) was so used.

(d) Use as residence.—

(1) In general.—For purposes of this section, a taxpayer uses a dwelling unit during the taxable year as a residence if he uses such unit (or portion thereof) for personal purposes for a number of days which exceeds the greater of—

(A) 14 days, or

(B) 10 percent of the number of days during such year for which such unit is rented at a fair rental.

For purposes of subparagraph (B), a unit shall not be treated as rented at a fair rental for any day for which it is used for personal purposes.

(2) Personal use of unit.—For purposes of this section, the taxpayer shall be deemed to have used a dwelling unit for personal purposes for a day if, for any part of such day, the unit is used—

(A) for personal purposes by the taxpayer or any other person who has an interest in such unit, or by any member of the family (as defined in section 267(c) (4)) of the taxpayer or such other person;

(B) by any individual who uses the unit under an arrangement which enables the taxpayer to use some other dwelling unit (whether or not a rental is charged for the use of such other unit); or

(C) by any individual (other than an employee with respect to whose use section 119 applies), unless for such day the dwelling unit is rented for a rental which, under the facts and circumstances, is fair rental.

The Secretary shall prescribe regulations with respect to the circumstances under which use of the unit for repairs and annual maintenance will not constitute personal use under this paragraph, except that if the taxpayer is engaged in repair and maintenance on a substantially full time basis for any day, such authority shall not allow the Secretary to treat a dwelling unit as being used for personal use by the taxpayer on such day merely because other individuals who are on the premises on such day are not so engaged.

(3) **Rental to family member, etc., for use as principal residence.—**

(A) **In general.—**A taxpayer shall not be treated as using a dwelling unit for personal purposes by reason of a rental arrangement for any period if for such period such dwelling unit is rented, at a fair rental, to any person for use as such person's principal residence.

(B) **Special rules for rental to person having interest in unit.—**

(i) **Rental must be pursuant to shared equity financing agreement.—**Subparagraph (A) shall apply to a rental to a person who has an interest in the dwelling unit only if such rental is pursuant to a shared equity financing agreement.

(ii) **Determination of fair rental.—**In the case of a rental pursuant to a shared equity financing agreement, fair rental shall be determined as of the time the agreement is entered into and by taking into account the occupant's qualified ownership interest.

(C) **Shared equity financing agreement.—**For purposes of this paragraph, the term "shared equity financing agreement" means an agreement under which—

(i) 2 or more persons acquire qualified ownership interests in a dwelling unit, and

(ii) the person (or persons) holding 1 or more of such interests—

(I) is entitled to occupy the dwelling unit for use as a principal residence, and

(II) is required to pay rent to 1 or more other persons holding qualified ownership interests in the dwelling unit.

(D) **Qualified ownership interest.—**For purposes of this paragraph, the term "qualified ownership interest" means an undivided interest for more than 50 years in the entire dwelling unit and appurtenant land being acquired in the transaction to which the shared equity financing agreement relates.

(4) **Rental of principal residence.—**

(A) **In general.—**For purposes of applying subsection (c) (5) to deductions allocable to a qualified rental period, a taxpayer shall not be considered to have used a dwelling unit for personal purposes for any day during the taxable year which occurs before or after a qualified rental period described in subparagraph (B) (i), or before a qualified rental period described in subparagraph (B) (ii), if with respect to such day such unit constitutes the principal residence (within the meaning of section 1034) of the taxpayer.

(B) **Qualified rental period.—**For purposes of subparagraph (A), the term "qualified rental period" means a consecutive period of—

(i) 12 or more months which begins or ends in such taxable year, or

(ii) less than 12 months which begins in such taxable year and at the end of which such dwelling unit is sold or exchanged, and

for which such unit is rented, or is held for rental, at a fair rental.

(e) Expenses attributable to rental.—

(1) In general.—In any case where a taxpayer who is an individual or an S corporation uses a dwelling unit for personal purposes on any day during the taxable year (whether or not he is treated under this section as using such unit as a residence), the amount deductible under this chapter with respect to expenses attributable to the rental of the unit (or portion thereof) for the taxable year shall not exceed an amount which bears the same relationship to such expenses as the number of days during each year that the unit (or portion thereof) is rented at a fair rental bears to the total number of days during such year that the unit (or portion thereof) is used.

(2) Exception for deductions otherwise allowable.—This subsection shall not apply with respect to deductions which would be allowable under this chapter for the taxable year whether or not such unit (or portion thereof) was rented.

(f) Definitions and special rules.—

(1) Dwelling unit defined.—For purposes of this section—

(A) In general.—The term "dwelling unit" includes a house, apartment, condominium, mobile home, boat, or similar property, and all structures or other property appurtenant to such dwelling unit.

(B) Exception.—The term "dwelling unit" does not include that portion of a unit which is used exclusively as a hotel, motel, inn, or similar establishment.

(2) Personal use by shareholders of S corporation.—In the case of an S corporation, sub-paragraphs (A) and (B) of subsection (d)(2) shall be applied by substituting "any shareholder of the S corporation" for "the taxpayer" each place it appears.

(3) Coordination with section 183.—If subsection (a) applies with respect to any dwelling unit (or portion thereof) for the taxable year—

(A) section 183 (relating to activities not engaged in for profit) shall not apply to such unit (or portion thereof) for such year, but

(B) such year shall be taken into account as a taxable year for purposes of applying subsection (d) of section 183 (relating to 5-year presumption).

(4) Coordination with section 162(a)(2), etc.—

(A) In general.—Nothing in this section shall be construed to disallow any deduction allowable under section 162(a)(2) (or any deduction which meets the tests of section 162(a)(2) but is allowable under another provision of this title) by reason of the taxpayer's being away from home in the pursuit of a trade or business (other than the trade or business of renting dwelling units).

(B) Limitation.—The Secretary shall prescribe amounts deductible (without substantiation) pursuant to the last sentence of section 162(a), but nothing in subparagraph (A) or any other provision of this title shall permit such a deduction for any taxable year of amounts in excess of the amounts determined to be appropriate under the circumstances.

(g) Special rule for certain rental use.—Notwithstanding any other provision of this section or section 183, if a dwelling unit is used during the taxable year by the taxpayer as a residence and such dwelling unit is actually rented for less than 15 days during the taxable year, then—

(1) no deduction otherwise allowable under this chapter because of the rental use of such dwelling unit shall be allowed, and

(2) the income derived from such use for the taxable year shall not be included in the gross income of such taxpayer under section 61.

§ 280B. Demolition of certain historic structures

(a) General rule.—In the case of the demolition of a certified historic structure (as defined in section 48(g)(3)(A))—

(1) no deduction otherwise allowable under this chapter shall be allowed to the owner or lessee of such structure for—

(A) any amount expended for such demolition, or

(B) any loss sustained on account of such demolition; and

(2) amounts described in paragraph (1) shall be treated as properly chargeable to capital account with respect to the land on which the demolished structure was located.

(b) Special rule for registered historic districts.—For purposes of this section, any building or other structure located in a registered historic district (as defined in section 48(g)(3)(B)) shall be treated as a certified historic structure unless the Secretary of the Interior has certified that such structure is not a certified historic structure, and that such structure is not of historic significance to the district, and if such certification occurs after the beginning of the demolition of such structure, the taxpayer has certified to the Secretary that, at the time of such demolition, he in good faith was not aware of the certification requirement by the Secretary of the Interior.

(c) Application of section.—This section shall apply with respect to demolitions commencing after June 30, 1976, and before January 1, 1984.

§ 280E. Expenditures in connection with the illegal sale of drugs

No deduction or credit shall be allowed for any amount paid or incurred during the taxable year in carrying on any trade or business if such trade or business (or the activities which comprise such trade or business) consists of trafficking in controlled substances (within the meaning of schedule I and II of the Controlled Substances Act) which is prohibited by Federal law or the law of any State in which such trade or business is conducted.

§ 291. Special rules relating to corporate preference items

(a) 15-percent reduction in certain preference items, etc.—For purposes of this subtitle, in the case of a corporation—

(1) **Section 1250 capital gain treatment.**—In the case of section 1250 property which is disposed of during the taxable year, 15 percent of the excess (if any) of—

(A) the amount which would be treated as ordinary income if such property was section 1245 property or section 1245 recovery property, over

(B) the amount treated as ordinary income under section 1250, shall be treated as gain which is ordinary income and shall be recognized notwithstanding any other provision of this title.

(2) Reduction in percentage depletion.—In the case of iron ore and coal (including lignite), the amount allowable as a deduction under section 613 with respect to any property (as defined in section 614) shall be reduced by 15 percent of the amount of the excess (if any) of—

(A) the amount of the deduction allowable under section 613 for the taxable year (determined without regard to this paragraph), over

(B) the adjusted basis of the property at the close of the taxable year (determined without regard to the depletion deduction for the taxable year).

. . . . . .

(b) Special rules for treatment of intangible drilling costs and mineral exploration and development costs.—For purposes of this subtitle, in the case of a corporation—

(1) In general.—The amount allowable as a deduction for any taxable year (determined without regard to this section)—

(A) under section 263(c) in the case of an integrated oil company, or

(B) under section 616(a) or 617,

shall be reduced by 15 percent.

(2) Special rule for amounts not allowable as deductions under paragraph (1).—

(A) Intangible drilling costs.—The amount not allowable as a deduction under section 263(c) for any taxable year by reason of paragraph (1) shall be allowable as a deduction ratably over the 36-month period beginning with the month in which the costs are paid or incurred.

(B) Mineral exploration and development costs.—In the case of any amount not allowable as a deduction under section 616(a) or 617 for any taxable year by reason of paragraph (1)—

(i) the applicable percentage of the amount not so allowable as a deduction shall be allowable as a deduction for the taxable year in which the costs are paid or incurred and in each of the 4 succeeding taxable years, and

(ii) such costs shall be treated, for purposes of determining the amount of the credit allowable under section 38 for the taxable year in which paid or incurred, as qualified investment (within the meaning of subsections (c) and (d) of section 46) with respect to property placed in service during such year.

(3) Applicable percentage.—For purposes of paragraph (2)(B), the term "applicable percentage" means the percentage determined in accordance with the following table:

Taxable Year:	Applicable Percentage:
1	15
2	22
3	21
4	21
5	21

(4) Dispositions.—

(A) Oil, gas, and geothermal property.—In the case of any disposition of any oil, gas, or geothermal property to which section 1254 applies (determined without regard to this section) any deduction under paragraph (2)(A) with respect to intangible drilling and development costs under section 263(c) which are allocable to such property shall, for purposes of section 1254, be treated as a deduction allowable under section 263(c).

(B) Application of section 617(d).—In the case of any disposition of mining property to which section 617(d) applies (determined without regard to this section), any amount allowable as a deduction under paragraph (2)(B) which is allocable to such property shall, for purposes of section 617(d), be treated as a deduction allowable under section 617(a).

(C) Recapture of investment credit.—In the case of any disposition of any property to which the credit allowable under section 38 by reason of paragraph (2)(B) is allocable, such disposition shall, for purposes of section 47, be treated as a disposition of section 38 recovery property which is not 3-year property.

(5) Integrated oil company defined.—For purposes of this subsection, the term "integrated oil company" means, with respect to any taxable year, any producer (within the meaning of section 4996(a)(1) of crude oil other than an independent producer (within the meaning of section 4992(b)).

(6) Coordination with cost depletion.—The portion of the adjusted basis of any property which is attributable to intangible drilling and development costs or mining exploration and development costs shall not be taken into account for purposes of determining depletion under section 611.

. . . . .

SUBCHAPTER C—CORPORATE DISTRIBUTIONS AND ADJUSTMENTS

Part
I. Distributions by corporations.
II. Corporate liquidations.
III. Corporate organizations and reorganizations.
IV. Insolvency reorganizations.*
V. Carryovers.
VI. Treatment of certain corporate interests as stock or indebtedness.
[VII. Repealed.]

PART I—DISTRIBUTIONS BY CORPORATIONS

Subpart
A. Effects on recipients.
B. Effects on corporation.
C. Definitions; constructive ownership of stock.

* Omitted entirely.

SUBPART A—EFFECTS ON RECIPIENTS

§ 301. Distributions of property

(a) In general.—Except as otherwise provided in this chapter, a distribution of property (as defined in section 317(a)) made by a corporation to a shareholder with respect to its stock shall be treated in the manner provided in subsection (c).

(b) Amount distributed.—

(1) General rule.—For purposes of this section, the amount of any distribution shall be—

(A) Noncorporate distributees.—If the shareholder is not a corporation, the amount of money received, plus the fair market value of the other property received.

(B) Corporate distributees.—If the shareholder is a corporation, unless subparagraph (D) applies, the amount of money received, plus whichever of the following is the lesser:

(i) the fair market value of the other property received; or

(ii) the adjusted basis (in the hands of the distributing corporation immediately before the distribution) of the other property received, increased in the amount of gain recognized to the distributing corporation on the distribution.

. . . . . .

(2) Reduction for liabilities.—The amount of any distribution determined under paragraph (1) shall be reduced (but not below zero) by—

(A) the amount of any liability of the corporation assumed by the shareholder in connection with the distribution, and

(B) the amount of any liability to which the property received by the shareholder is subject immediately before, and immediately after, the distribution.

(3) Determination of fair market value.—For purposes of this section, fair market value shall be determined as of the date of the distribution.

(c) Amount taxable.—In the case of a distribution to which subsection (a) applies—

(1) Amount constituting dividend.—That portion of the distribution which is a dividend (as defined in section 316) shall be included in gross income.

(2) Amount applied against basis.—That portion of the distribution which is not a dividend shall be applied against and reduce the adjusted basis of the stock.

(3) Amount in excess of basis.—

(A) In general.—Except as provided in subparagraph (B), that portion of the distribution which is not a dividend, to the extent that it exceeds the adjusted basis of the stock, shall be treated as gain from the sale or exchange of property.

(B) Distributions out of increase in value accrued before March 1, 1913.—That portion of the distribution which is not a dividend, to the extent that it exceeds the adjusted basis of the stock and to the extent that it is out of increase in value accrued before March 1, 1913, shall be exempt from tax.

(d) Basis.—The basis of property received in a distribution to which subsection (a) applies shall be—

    (1) Noncorporate distributees.—If the shareholder is not a corporation, the fair market value of such property.

    (2) Corporate distributees.—If the shareholder is a corporation, unless paragraph (3) applies, whichever of the following is the lesser:

        (A) the fair market value of such property; or

        (B) the adjusted basis (in the hands of the distributing corporation immediately before the distribution) of such property, increased in the amount of gain recognized to the distributing corporation on the distribution.

. . . .

§ 302.   Distributions in redemption of stock

    (a) General rule.—If a corporation redeems its stock (within the meaning of section 317(b)), and if paragraph (1), (2), (3), or (4) of subsection (b) applies, such redemption shall be treated as a distribution in part or full payment in exchange for the stock.

    (b) Redemptions treated as exchanges.—

    (1) Redemptions not equivalent to dividends.—Subsection (a) shall apply if the redemption is not essentially equivalent to a dividend.

    (2) Substantially disproportionate redemption of stock.—

        (A) In general.—Subsection (a) shall apply if the distribution is substantially disproportionate with respect to the shareholder.

        (B) Limitation.—This paragraph shall not apply unless immediately after the redemption the shareholder owns less than 50 percent of the total combined voting power of all classes of stock entitled to vote.

        (C) Definitions.—For purposes of this paragraph, the distribution is substantially disproportionate if—

            (i) the ratio which the voting stock of the corporation owned by the shareholder immediately after the redemption bears to all of the voting stock of the corporation at such time,

is less than 80 percent of—

            (ii) the ratio which the voting stock of the corporation owned by the shareholder immediately before the redemption bears to all of the voting stock of the corporation at such time.

For purposes of this paragraph, no distribution shall be treated as substantially disproportionate unless the shareholder's ownership of the common stock of the corporation (whether voting or nonvoting) after and before redemption also meets the 80 percent requirement of the preceding sentence. For purposes of the preceding sentence, if there is more than one class of common stock, the determinations shall be made by reference to fair market value.

        (D) Series of redemptions.—This paragraph shall not apply to any redemption made pursuant to a plan the purpose or effect of which is a series of redemptions resulting in a distribution which (in the aggregate) is not substantially disproportionate with respect to the shareholder.

(3) Termination of shareholder's interest.—Subsection (a) shall apply if the redemption is in complete redemption of all of the stock of the corporation owned by the shareholder.

(4) Redemption from noncorporate shareholder in partial liquidation.— Subsection (a) shall apply to a distribution if such distribution is—

(A) in redemption of stock held by a shareholder who is not a corporation, and

(B) in partial liquidation of the distributing corporation.

(5) Application of paragraphs.—In determining whether a redemption meets the requirements of paragraph (1), the fact that such redemption fails to meet the requirements of paragraph (2), (3), or (4) shall not be taken into account. If a redemption meets the requirements of paragraph (3) and also the requirements of paragraph (1), (2), or (4) then so much of subsection (c)(2) as would (but for this sentence) apply in respect of the acquisition of an interest in the corporation within the 10-year period beginning on the date of the distribution shall not apply.

(c) Constructive ownership of stock.—

(1) In general.—Except as provided in paragraph (2) of this subsection, section 318(a) shall apply in determining the ownership of stock for purposes of this section.

(2) For determining termination of interest.—

(A) In the case of a distribution described in subsection (b) (3), section 318(a) (1) shall not apply if—

(i) immediately after the distribution the distributee has no interest in the corporation (including an interest as officer, director, or employee), other than an interest as a creditor,

(ii) the distributee does not acquire any such interest (other than stock acquired by bequest or inheritance) within 10 years from the date of such distribution, and

(iii) the distributee, at such time and in such manner as the Secretary by regulations prescribes, files an agreement to notify the Secretary of any acquisition described in clause (ii) and to retain such records as may be necessary for the application of this paragraph.

If the distributee acquires such an interest in the corporation (other than by bequest or inheritance) within 10 years from the date of the distribution, then the periods of limitation provided in sections 6501 and 6502 on the making of an assessment and the collection by levy or a proceeding in court shall, with respect to any deficiency (including interest and additions to the tax) resulting from such acquisition, include one year immediately following the date on which the distributee (in accordance with regulations prescribed by the Secretary) notifies the Secretary of such acquisition; and such assessment and collection may be made notwithstanding any provision of law or rule of law which otherwise would prevent such assessment and collection.

(B) Subparagraph (A) of this paragraph shall not apply if—

(i) any portion of the stock redeemed was acquired, directly or indirectly, within the 10-year period ending on the date of the distribution by the distributee from a person the ownership of whose stock would (at the time of distribution) be attributable to the distributee under section 318(a), or

(ii) any person owns (at the time of the distribution) stock the ownership of which is attributable to the distributee under section 318(a) and such person acquired any stock in the corporation, directly or indirectly, from the distributee within the 10-year period ending on the date of the distribution, unless such stock so acquired from the distributee is redeemed in the same transaction.

The preceding sentence shall not apply if the acquisition (or, in the case of clause (ii), the disposition) by the distributee did not have as one of its principal purposes the avoidance of Federal income tax.

(C) Special rule for waivers by entities.—

(i) In general.—Subparagraph (A) shall not apply to a distribution to any entity unless—

(I) such entity and each related person meet the requirements of clauses (i), (ii), and (iii) of subparagraph (A), and

(II) each related person agrees to be jointly and severally liable for any deficiency (including interest and additions to tax) resulting from an acquisition described in clause (ii) of subparagraph (A).

In any case to which the preceding sentence applies, the second sentence of subparagraph (A) and subparagraph (B)(ii) shall be applied by substituting "distributee or any related person" for "distributee" each place it appears.

(ii) Definitions.—For purposes of this subparagraph—

(I) the term "entity" means a partnership, estate, trust, or corporation; and

(II) the term "related person" means any person to whom ownership of stock in the corporation is (at the time of the distribution) attributable under section 318(a)(1) if such stock is further attributable to the entity under section 318(a)(3).

(d) Redemptions treated as distributions of property.—Except as otherwise provided in this subchapter, if a corporation redeems its stock (within the meaning of section 317(b)), and if subsection (a) of this section does not apply, such redemption shall be treated as a distribution of property to which section 301 applies.

(e) Partial liquidation defined.—

(1) In general.—For purposes of subsection (b)(4), a distribution shall be treated as in partial liquidation of a corporation if—

(A) the distribution is not essentially equivalent to a dividend (determined at the corporate level rather than at the shareholder level), and

(B) the distribution is pursuant to a plan and occurs within the taxable year in which the plan is adopted or within the succeeding taxable year.

(2) Termination of business.—The distributions which meet the requirements of paragraph (1)(A) shall include (but shall not be limited to) a distribution which meets the requirements of subparagraphs (A) and (B) of this paragraph:

(A) The distribution is attributable to the distributing corporation's ceasing to conduct, or consists of the assets of, a qualified trade or business.

(B) Immediately after the distribution, the distributing corporation is actively engaged in the conduct of a qualified trade or business.

(3) **Qualified trade or business.**—For purposes of paragraph (2), the term "qualified trade or business" means any trade or business which—

(A) was actively conducted throughout the 5-year period ending on the date of the redemption, and

(B) was not acquired by the corporation within such period in a transaction in which gain or loss was recognized in whole or in part.

(4) **Redemption may be pro rata.**—Whether or not a redemption meets the requirements of subparagraphs (A) and (B) of paragraph (2) shall be determined without regard to whether or not the redemption is pro rata with respect to all of the shareholders of the corporation.

(5) **Treatment of certain pass-thru entities.**—For purposes of determining under subsection (b)(4) whether any stock is held by a shareholder who is not a corporation, any stock held by a partnership, estate, or trust shall be treated as if it were actually held proportionately by its partners or beneficiaries.

. . . .

§ 303.   Distributions in redemption of stock to pay death taxes

(a) In general.—A distribution of property to a shareholder by a corporation in redemption of part or all of the stock of such corporation which (for Federal estate tax purposes) is included in determining the gross estate of a decedent, to the extent that the amount of such distribution does not exceed the sum of—

(1) the estate, inheritance, legacy, and succession taxes (including any interest collected as a part of such taxes) imposed because of such decedent's death, and

(2) the amount of funeral and administration expenses allowable as deductions to the estate under section 2053 (or under section 2106 in the case of the estate of a decedent nonresident, not a citizen of the United States),

shall be treated as a distribution in full payment in exchange for the stock so redeemed.

(b) Limitations on application of subsection (a).—

(1) **Period for distribution.**—Subsection (a) shall apply only to amounts distributed after the death of the decedent and—

(A) within the period of limitations provided in section 6501(a) for the assessment of the Federal estate tax (determined without the application of any provision other than section 6501(a)), or within 90 days after the expiration of such period,

(B) if a petition for redetermination of a deficiency in such estate tax has been filed with the Tax Court within the time prescribed in section 6213, at any time before the expiration of 60 days after the decision of the Tax Court becomes final, or

(C) if an election has been made under section 6166 and if the time prescribed by this subparagraph expires at a later date than the time prescribed by subparagraph (B) of this paragraph, within the time determined under section 6166 for the payment of the installments.

(2) Relationship of stock to decedent's estate.—

(A) In general.—Subsection (a) shall apply to a distribution by a corporation only if the value (for Federal estate tax purposes) of all of the stock of such corporation which is included in determining the value of the decedent's gross estate exceeds 35 percent of the excess of—

(i) the value of the gross estate of such decedent, over

(ii) the sum of the amounts allowable as a deduction under section 2053 or 2054.

(B) Special rule for stock in 2 or more corporations.—For purposes of subparagraph (A), stock of 2 or more corporations, with respect to each of which there is included in determining the value of the decedent's gross estate 20 percent or more in value of the outstanding stock, shall be treated as the stock of a single corporation. For purposes of the 20-percent requirement of the preceding sentence, stock which, at the decedent's death, represents the surviving spouse's interest in property held by the decedent and the surviving spouse as community property or as joint tenants, tenants by the entirety, or tenants in common shall be treated as having been included in determining the value of the decedent's gross estate.

(3) Relationship of shareholder to estate tax.—Subsection (a) shall apply to a distribution by a corporation only to the extent that the interest of the shareholder is reduced directly (or through a binding obligation to contribute) by any payment of an amount described in paragraph (1) or (2) of subsection (a).

(4) Additional requirements for distributions made more than 4 years after decedent's death.—In the case of amounts distributed more than 4 years after the date of the decedent's death, subsection (a) shall apply to a distribution by a corporation only to the extent of the lesser of—

(A) the aggregate of the amounts referred to in paragraph (1) or (2) of subsection (a) which remained unpaid immediately before the distribution, or

(B) the aggregate of the amounts referred to in paragraph (1) or (2) of subsection (a) which are paid during the 1-year period beginning on the date of such distribution.

(c) Stock with substituted basis.—If—

(1) a shareholder owns stock of a corporation (referred to in this subsection as "new stock") the basis of which is determined by reference to the basis of stock of a corporation (referred to in this subsection as "old stock"),

(2) the old stock was included (for Federal estate tax purposes) in determining the gross estate of a decedent, and

(3) subsection (a) would apply to a distribution of property to such shareholder in redemption of the old stock,

then, subject to the limitations specified in subsection (b), subsection (a) shall apply in respect of a distribution in redemption of the new stock.

(d) Special rules for generation-skipping transfers.—Under regulations prescribed by the Secretary, where stock in a corporation is subject to tax under section 2601 as a result of a generation-skipping transfer (within the meaning of section 2611(a)), which occurs at or after the death of the deemed transferor (within the meaning of section 2612)—

(1) the stock shall be deemed to be included in the gross estate of the deemed transferor;

(2) taxes of the kind referred to in subsection (a) (1) which are imposed because of the generation-skipping transfer shall be treated as imposed because of the deemed transferor's death (and for this purpose the tax imposed by section 2601 shall be treated as an estate tax);

(3) the period of distribution shall be measured from the date of the generation-skipping transfer; and

(4) the relationship of stock to the decedent's estate shall be measured with reference solely to the amount of the generation-skipping transfer.

§ 304.   Redemption through use of related corporations

(a) Treatment of certain stock purchases.—

(1) Acquisition by related corporation (other than subsidiary).—For purposes of sections 302 and 303, if—

(A) one or more persons are in control of each of two corporations, and

(B) in return for property, one of the corporations acquires stock in the other corporation from the person (or persons) so in control,

then (unless paragraph (2) applies) such property shall be treated as a distribution in redemption of the stock of the corporation acquiring such stock. In any such case, the stock so acquired shall be treated as having been transferred by the person from whom acquired, and as having been received by the corporation acquiring it, as a contribution to the capital of such corporation.

(2) Acquisition by subsidiary.—For purposes of sections 302 and 303, if—

(A) in return for property, one corporation acquires from a shareholder of another corporation stock in such other corporation, and

(B) the issuing corporation controls the acquiring corporation,

then such property shall be treated as a distribution in redemption of the stock of the issuing corporation.

(b) Special rules for application of subsection (a).—

(1) Rule for determinations under section 302(b).—In the case of any acquisition of stock to which subsection (a) of this section applies, determinations as to whether the acquisition is, by reason of section 302(b), to be treated as a distribution in part or full payment in exchange for the stock shall be made by reference to the stock of the issuing corporation. In applying section 318(a) (relating to constructive ownership of stock) with respect to section 302(b) for purposes of this paragraph, sections 318(a) (2) (C) and 318(a) (3) (C) shall be applied without regard to the 50 percent limitation contained therein.

(2) Amount constituting dividend.—

(A) Where subsection (a)(1) applies.—In the case of any acquisition of stock to which paragraph (1) (and not paragraph (2)) of subsection (A) of this section applies, the determination of the amount which is a dividend shall be made as if the property were distributed by the issuing corporation to the acquiring corporation and immediately thereafter distributed by the acquiring corporation.

(B) Where subsection (a) (2) applies.—In the case of any acquisition of stock to which subsection (a) (2) of this section applies, the determination of the amount which is a dividend shall be made as if the property were distributed by the acquiring corporation to the issuing corporation and immediately thereafter distributed by the issuing corporation.

(3) Coordination with section 351.—

(A) Property treated as received in redemption.—Except as otherwise provided in this paragraph, subsection (a) (and not part III) shall apply to any property received in a distribution described in subsection (a).

(B) Certain assumptions of liability, etc.—

(i) In general.—Subsection (a) shall not apply to any liability—

(I) assumed by the acquiring corporation, or
(II) to which the stock is subject,

if such liability was incurred by the transferor to acquire the stock. For purposes of the preceding sentence, the term "stock" means stock referred to in paragraph (1)(B) or (2)(A) of subsection (a).

(ii) Extension of obligations, etc.—For purposes of clause (i), an extension, renewal, or refinancing of a liability which meets the requirements of clause (i) shall be treated as meeting such requirements.

(C) Distributions incident to formation of bank holding companies. —If—

(i) pursuant to a plan, control of a bank is acquired and within 2 years after the date on which such control is acquired, stock constituting control of such bank is transferred to a BHC in connection with its formation,

(ii) incident to the formation of the BHC there is a distribution of property described in subsection (a), and

(iii) the shareholders of the BHC who receive distributions of such property do not have control of such BHC,

then, subsection (a) shall not apply to any securities received by a qualified minority shareholder incident to the formation of such BHC.

(D) Definitions and special rule.—For purposes of subparagraph (C) and this subparagraph—

(i) Qualified minority shareholder.—The term "qualified minority shareholder" means any shareholder who owns less than 10 percent (in value) of the stock of the BHC. For purposes of the preceding sentence, the rules of paragraph (3) of subsection (c) shall apply.

(ii) BHC.—The term "BHC" means a bank holding company (within the meaning of section 2(a) of the Bank Holding Company Act of 1956).

(iii) Special rule in case of BHC's formed before 1985.—In the case of a BHC which is formed before 1985, clause (i) of subparagraph (C) shall not apply.

(c) Control.—

(1) In general.—For purposes of this section, control means the ownership of stock possessing at least 50 percent of the total combined voting power of all classes of stock entitled to vote, or at least 50 percent of the total value of shares of all classes of stock. If a person (or persons) is in control (within the meaning of the preceding sentence) of a corporation which in turn owns at least 50 percent of the total combined voting power of all stock entitled to vote of another corporation, or owns at least 50 percent of the total value of the shares of all classes of stock of another corporation, then such person (or persons) shall be treated as in control of such other corporation.

(2) Stock acquired in the transaction.—For purposes of subsection (a)(1)—

(A) General rule.—Where 1 or more persons in control of the issuing corporation transfer stock of such corporation in exchange for stock of the acquiring corporation, the stock of the acquiring corporation received shall be taken into account in determining whether such person or persons are in control of the acquiring corporation.

(B) Definition of control group.—Where 2 or more persons in control of the issuing corporation transfer stock of such corporation to the acquiring corporation and, after the transfer, the transferors are in control of the acquiring corporation, the person or persons in control of each corporation shall include each of the persons who so transfer stock.

(3) Constructive ownership.—Section 318(a) (relating to the constructive ownership of stock) shall apply for purposes of determining control under this section. For purposes of the preceding sentence, sections 318(a)(2)(C) and 318(a)(3)(C) shall be applied without regard to the 50 percent limitation contained therein.

§ 305.   Distributions of stock and stock rights

(a) General rule.—Except as otherwise provided in this section, gross income does not include the amount of any distribution of the stock of a corporation made by such corporation to its shareholders with respect to its stock.

(b) Exceptions.—Subsection (a) shall not apply to a distribution by a corporation of its stock, and the distribution shall be treated as a distribution of property to which section 301 applies—

(1) Distributions in lieu of money.—If the distribution is, at the election of any of the shareholders (whether exercised before or after the declaration thereof), payable either—

(A) in its stock, or

(B) in property.

(2) **Disproportionate distributions.**—If the distribution (or a series of distributions of which such distribution is one) has the result of—

(A) the receipt of property by some shareholders, and

(B) an increase in the proportionate interests of other shareholders in the assets or earnings and profits of the corporation.

(3) **Distributions of common and preferred stock.**—If the distribution (or a series of distributions of which such distribution is one) has the result of—

(A) the receipt of preferred stock by some common shareholders, and

(B) the receipt of common stock by other common shareholders.

(4) **Distributions on preferred stock.**—If the distribution is with respect to preferred stock, other than an increase in the conversion ratio of convertible preferred stock made solely to take account of a stock dividend or stock split with respect to the stock into which such convertible stock is convertible.

(5) **Distributions of convertible preferred stock.**—If the distribution is of convertible preferred stock, unless it is established to the satisfaction of the Secretary that such distribution will not have the result described in paragraph (2).

(c) **Certain transactions treated as distributions.**—For purposes of this section and section 301, the Secretary shall prescribe regulations under which a change in conversion ratio, a change in redemption price, a difference between redemption price and issue price, a redemption which is treated as a distribution to which section 301 applies, or any transaction (including a recapitalization) having a similar effect on the interest of any shareholder shall be treated as a distribution with respect to any shareholder whose proportionate interest in the earnings and profits or assets of the corporation is increased by such change, difference, redemption, or similar transaction.

(d) **Definitions.**—

(1) **Rights to acquire stock.**—For purposes of this section (other than subsection (e)), the term "stock" includes rights to acquire such stock.

(2) **Shareholders.**—For purposes of subsections (b) and (c), the term "shareholder" includes a holder of rights or of convertible securities.

(e) **Dividend reinvestment in stock of public utilities.**—

(1) **In general.**—Subsection (b) shall not apply to any qualified reinvested dividend.

(2) **Qualified reinvested dividend defined.**—For purposes of this subsection, the term "qualified reinvested dividend" means—

(A) a distribution by a qualified public utility of shares of its qualified common stock to an individual with respect to the common or preferred stock of such corporation pursuant to a plan under which shareholders may elect to receive dividends in the form of stock instead of property, but

(B) only if the shareholder elects to have this subsection apply to such shares.

(3) **Qualified public utility defined.**—

(A) **In general.**—For purposes of this subsection, the term "qualified public utility" means, for any taxable year of the corporation, a domestic corporation which, for the 10-year period ending on the day before the beginning of the taxable year, acquired public utility recovery property having a cost equal to at least 60 percent of the aggregate cost of all tangible property described in section 1245(a)(3) (other than subparagraphs (C) and (D) thereof) acquired by the corporation during such period.

. . . .

(4) Qualified common stock defined.—

(A) In general.—For purposes of this subsection, the term "qualified common stock" means authorized but unissued common stock of the corporation—

(i) which has been designated by the board of directors of the corporation as issued for purposes of this subsection, but

(ii) only if the number of shares to be issued to a shareholder was determined by reference to a value which is not less than 95 percent and not more than 105 percent of the stock's fair market value during the period immediately before the distribution (determined under regulations prescribed by the Secretary).

. . . .

(6) Limitation.—

(A) In general.—In the case of any individual, the aggregate amount of distributions to which this subsection applies for the taxable year shall not exceed $750 ($1,500 in the case of a joint return).

(B) Application of ceiling.—If, but for this subparagraph, a share of stock would, by reason of subparagraph (A), be treated as partly within this subsection and partly outside this subsection, such share shall be treated as outside this subsection.

(7) Basis and holding period.—In the case of stock received as a qualified reinvested dividend—

(A) notwithstanding section 307, the basis shall be zero, and

(B) the holding period shall begin on the date the dividend would (but for this subsection) be includible in income.

(8) Election.—An election under this subsection with respect to any share shall be made on the shareholder's return for the taxable year in which the dividend would (but for this subsection) be includible in income. Any such election, once made, shall be revocable only with the consent of the Secretary.

(9) Dispositions within 1 year of distribution.—Under regulations prescribed by the Secretary—

(A) Disposition of other common stock.—If—

(i) a shareholder receives any qualified reinvested dividend from a corporation, and

(ii) during the period which begins on the record date for the qualified reinvested dividend and ends 1 year after the date of the distribution of such dividend, the shareholder disposes of any common stock of such corporation,

the shareholder shall be treated as having disposed of the stock received as a qualified reinvested dividend (to the extent there remains such stock to which this paragraph has not applied).

(B) Ordinary income treatment.—If any stock received as a qualified reinvested dividend is disposed of within 1 year after the date such stock is distributed, such disposition shall be treated as a disposition of property which is not a capital asset.

(10) No reduction in earnings and profits for distribution of qualified common stock.—The earnings and profits of any corporation shall not be reduced by reason of the distribution of any qualified common stock of such corporation pursuant to a plan under which shareholders may elect to receive dividends in the form of stock instead of property.

. . . .

(12) Termination.—This subsection shall not apply to distributions after December 31, 1985.

. . . .

§ 306.   Dispositions of certain stock

(a) General rule.—If a shareholder sells or otherwise disposes of section 306 stock (as defined in subsection (c))—

(1) Dispositions other than redemptions.—If such disposition is not a redemption (within the meaning of section 317(b))—

(A) The amount realized shall be treated as ordinary income. This subparagraph shall not apply to the extent that—

(i) the amount realized, exceeds

(ii) such stock's ratable share of the amount which would have been a dividend at the time of distribution if (in lieu of section 306 stock) the corporation had distributed money in an amount equal to the fair market value of the stock at the time of distribution.

(B) Any excess of the amount realized over the sum of—

(i) the amount treated under subparagraph (A) as ordinary income, plus

(ii) the adjusted basis of the stock,

shall be treated as gain from the sale of such stock.

(C) No loss shall be recognized.

(2) Redemption.—If the disposition is a redemption, the amount realized shall be treated as a distribution of property to which section 301 applies.

(b) Exceptions.—Subsection (a) shall not apply—

(1) Termination of shareholder's interest.—

(A) Not in redemption.—If the disposition—

(i) is not a redemption;

(ii) is not, directly or indirectly, to a person the ownership of whose stock would (under section 318 (a)) be attributable to the shareholder; and

(iii) terminates the entire stock interest of the shareholder in the corporation (and for purposes of this clause, section 318(a) shall apply).

(B) In redemption.—If the disposition is a redemption and paragraph (3) or (4) of section 302(b) applies.

(2) **Liquidations.**—If the section 306 stock is redeemed in a distribution in complete liquidation to which part II (sec. 331 and following) applies.

(3) **Where gain or loss is not recognized.**—To the extent that, under any provision of this subtitle, gain or loss to the shareholder is not recognized with respect to the disposition of the section 306 stock.

(4) **Transactions not in avoidance.**—If it is established to the satisfaction of the Secretary—

(A) that the distribution, and the disposition or redemption, or

(B) in the case of a prior or simultaneous disposition (or redemption) of the stock with respect to which the section 306 stock disposed of (or redeemed) was issued, that the disposition (or redemption) of the section 306 stock,

was not in pursuance of a plan having as one of its principal purposes the avoidance of Federal income tax.

(c) Section 306 stock defined.—

(1) **In general.**—For purposes of this subchapter, the term "section 306 stock" means stock which meets the requirements of subparagraph (A), (B), or (C) of this paragraph.

(A) **Distributed to seller.**—Stock (other than common stock issued with respect to common stock) which was distributed to the shareholder selling or otherwise disposing of such stock if, by reason of section 305(a), any part of such distribution was not includible in the gross income of the shareholder.

(B) **Received in a corporate reorganization or separation.**—Stock which is not common stock and—

(i) which was received, by the shareholder selling or otherwise disposing of such stock, in pursuance of a plan of reorganization (within the meaning of section 368(a)), or in a distribution or exchange to which section 355 (or so much of section 356 as relates to section 355) applied, and

(ii) with respect to the receipt of which gain or loss to the shareholder was to any extent not recognized by reason of part III, but only to the extent that either the effect of the transaction was substantially the same as the receipt of a stock dividend, or the stock was received in exchange for section 306 stock.

For purposes of this section, a receipt of stock to which the foregoing provisions of this subparagraph apply shall be treated as a distribution of stock.

(C) **Stock having transferred or substituted basis.**—Except as otherwise provided in subparagraph (B), stock the basis of which (in the hands of the shareholder selling or otherwise disposing of such stock) is determined by reference to the basis (in the hands of such shareholder or any other person) of section 306 stock.

(2) **Exception where no earnings and profits.**—For purposes of this section, the term "section 306 stock" does not include any stock no part of the distribution of which would have been a dividend at the time of the distribution if money had been distributed in lieu of the stock.

(3) Certain stock acquired in section 351 exchange.—The term "section 306 stock" also includes any stock which is not common stock acquired in an exchange to which section 351 applied if receipt of money (in lieu of the stock) would have been treated as a dividend to any extent. In the case of such stock, rules similar to the rules of section 304(b)(2) shall apply for purposes of this section.

(4) Application of attribution rules for certain purposes.—For purposes of paragraphs (1)(B)(ii) and (3), section 318(a) shall apply. For purposes of applying the preceding sentence to paragraph (3), sections 318(a)(2)(C) and 318(a)(3)(C) shall be applied without regard to the 50 percent limitation contained therein.

(d) Stock rights.—For purposes of this section—

(1) stock rights shall be treated as stock, and

(2) stock acquired through the exercise of stock rights shall be treated as stock distributed at the time of the distribution of the stock rights, to the extent of the fair market value of such rights at the time of the distribution.

(e) Convertible stock.—For purposes of subsection (c)—

(1) if section 306 stock was issued with respect to common stock and later such section 306 stock is exchanged for common stock in the same corporation (whether or not such exchange is pursuant to a conversion privilege contained in the section 306 stock), then (except as provided in paragraph (2)) the common stock so received shall not be treated as section 306 stock; and

(2) common stock with respect to which there is a privilege of converting into stock other than common stock (or into property), whether or not the conversion privilege is contained in such stock, shall not be treated as common stock.

. . . . .

(g) Change in terms and conditions of stock.—If a substantial change is made in the terms and conditions of any stock, then, for purposes of this section—

(1) the fair market value of such stock shall be the fair market value at the time of the distribution or at the time of such change, whichever such value is higher;

(2) such stock's ratable share of the amount which would have been a dividend if money had been distributed in lieu of stock shall be determined as of the time of distribution or as of the time of such change, whichever such ratable share is higher; and

(3) subsection (c)(2) shall not apply unless the stock meets the requirements of such subsection both at the time of such distribution and at the time of such change.

. . . . .

§ 307.   Basis of stock and stock rights acquired in distributions

(a) General rule.—If a shareholder in a corporation receives its stock or rights to acquire its stock (referred to in this subsection as "new stock") in a distribution to which section 305(a) applies, then the basis of such new stock and of the stock with respect to which it is distributed (referred to in this section as "old stock"), respectively, shall, in the shareholder's hands, be determined by allocating between the old stock and the new stock the adjusted basis of the old stock. Such allocation shall be made under regulations prescribed by the Secretary.

(b) Exception for certain stock rights.—

    (1) In general.—If—

        (A) a corporation distributes rights to acquire its stock to a shareholder in a distribution to which section 305(a) applies, and

        (B) the fair market value of such rights at the time of the distribution is less than 15 percent of the fair market value of the old stock at such time,

then subsection (a) shall not apply and the basis of such rights shall be zero, unless the taxpayer elects under paragraph (2) of this subsection to determine the basis of the old stock and of the stock rights under the method of allocation provided in subsection (a).

    (2) Election.—The election referred to in paragraph (1) shall be made in the return filed within the time prescribed by law (including extensions thereof) for the taxable year in which such rights were received. Such election shall be made in such manner as the Secretary may by regulations prescribe, and shall be irrevocable when made.

. . . . .

SUBPART B—EFFECTS ON CORPORATION

§ 311.   Taxability of corporation on distribution

  (a) General rule.—Except as provided in subsections (b), (c), and (d) of this section and section 453B, no gain or loss shall be recognized to a corporation on the distribution, with respect to its stock, of—

    (1) its stock (or rights to acquire its stock), or

    (2) property.

  (b) LIFO inventory.—

    (1) Recognition of gain.—If a corporation inventorying goods under the method provided in section 472 (relating to last-in, first-out inventories) distributes inventory assets (as defined in paragraph (2) (A)), then the amount (if any) by which—

        (A) the inventory amount (as defined in paragraph (2) (B)) of such assets under a method authorized by section 471 (relating to general rule for inventories), exceeds

        (B) the inventory amount of such assets under the method provided in section 472,

shall be treated as gain to the corporation recognized from the sale of such inventory assets.

    (2) Definitions.—For purposes of paragraph (1)—

        (A) Inventory assets.—The term "inventory assets" means stock in trade of the corporation, or other property of a kind which would properly be included in the inventory of the corporation if on hand at the close of the taxable year.

        (B) Inventory amount.—The term "inventory amount" means, in the case of inventory assets distributed during a taxable year, the amount of such inventory assets determined as if the taxable year closed at the time of such distribution.

(3) Method of determining inventory amount.—For purposes of this subsection, the inventory amount of assets under a method authorized by section 471 shall be determined—

(A) if the corporation uses the retail method of valuing inventories under section 472, by using such method, or

(B) if subparagraph (A) does not apply, by using cost or market, whichever is lower.

(c) Liability in excess of basis.—If—

(1) a corporation distributes property to a shareholder with respect to its stock,

(2) such property is subject to a liability, or the shareholder assumes a liability of the corporation in connection with the distribution, and

(3) the amount of such liability exceeds the adjusted basis (in the hands of the distributing corporation) of such property,

then gain shall be recognized to the distributing corporation in an amount equal to such excess as if the property distributed had been sold at the time of the distribution. In the case of a distribution of property subject to a liability which is not assumed by the shareholder, the amount of gain to be recognized under the preceding sentence shall not exceed the excess, if any, of the fair market value of such property over its adjusted basis.

(d) Appreciated property used to redeem stock.—

(1) In general.—If—

(A) a corporation distributes property (other than an obligation of such corporation) to a shareholder in a redemption (to which subpart A applies) of part or all of his stock in such corporation, and

(B) the fair market value of such property exceeds its adjusted basis (in the hands of the distributing corporation),

then a gain shall be recognized to the distributing corporation in an amount equal to such excess as if the property distributed had been sold at the time of the distribution. Subsections (b) and (c) shall not apply to any distribution to which this subsection applies.

(2) Exceptions and limitations.—Paragraph (1) shall not apply to—

(A) a distribution to a corporate shareholder if the basis of the property distributed is determined under section 301(d)(2);

(B) a distribution to which section 302(b)(4) applies and which is made with respect to qualified stock;

(C) a distribution of stock or an obligation of a corporation if the requirements of paragraph (2) of subsection (e) are met with respect to the distribution;

(D) a distribution to the extent that section 303(a) (relating to distributions in redemption of stock to pay death taxes) applies to such distribution;

(E) a distribution to a private foundation in redemption of stock which is described in section 537(b)(2)(A) and (B); and

(F) a distribution by a corporation to which part I of subchapter M (relating to regulated investment companies) applies, if such distribution is in redemption of its stock upon the demand of the shareholder.

(e) Definitions and special rules for subsection (d)(2).—For purposes of subsection (d)(2) and this subsection—

(1) Qualified stock.—

(A) In general.—The term "qualified stock" means stock held by a person (other than a corporation) who at all times during the lesser of—

(i) the 5-year period ending on the date of distribution, or

(ii) the period during which the distributing corporation (or a predecessor corporation) was in existence,

held at least 10 percent in value of the outstanding stock of the distributing corporation (or predecessor corporation).

(B) Determination of stock held.—Section 318 shall apply in determining ownership of stock under subparagraph (A); except that, in applying section 318(a)(1), the term "family" includes any individual described in section 267(c)(4) and any spouse of any such individual.

(2) Distributions of stock or obligations of controlled corporations.—

(A) Requirements.—A distribution of stock or an obligation of a corporation (hereinafter in this paragraph referred to as the "controlled corporation") meets the requirements of this paragraph if—

(i) such distribution is made with respect to qualified stock,

(ii) substantially all of the assets of the controlled corporation consists of the assets of 1 or more qualified businesses,

(iii) no substantial part of the controlled corporation's nonbusiness assets were acquired from the distributing corporation, in a transaction to which section 351 applied or as a contribution to capital, within the 5-year period ending on the date of the distribution, and

(iv) more than 50 percent in value of the outstanding stock of the controlled corporation is distributed by the distributing corporation with respect to qualified stock.

(B) Definitions.—For purposes of subparagraph (A)—

(i) Qualified business.—The term "qualified business" means any trade or business which—

(I) was actively conducted throughout the 5-year period ending on the date of the distribution, and

(II) was not acquired by any person within such period in a transaction in which gain or loss was recognized in whole or in part.

(ii) Nonbusiness asset.—The term "nonbusiness asset" means any asset not used in the active conduct of a trade or business.

. . . . .

§ 312.   Effect on earnings and profits

(a) General rule.—Except as otherwise provided in this section, on the distribution of property by a corporation with respect to its stock, the earnings and profits of the corporation (to the extent thereof) shall be decreased by the sum of—

(1) the amount of money,

(2) the principal amount of the obligations of such corporation, and

(3) the adjusted basis of the other property,

so distributed.

(b) Certain inventory assets.—

(1) In general.—On the distribution by a corporation, with respect to its stock, of inventory assets (as defined in paragraph (2) (A)) the fair market value of which exceeds the adjusted basis thereof, the earnings and profits of the corporation—

(A) shall be increased by the amount of such excess; and

(B) shall be decreased by whichever of the following is the lesser:

(i) the fair market value of the inventory assets distributed, or

(ii) the earnings and profits (as increased under subparagraph (A)).

(2) Definitions.—

(A) Inventory assets.—For purposes of paragraph (1), the term "inventory assets" means—

(i) stock in trade of the corporation, or other property of a kind which would properly be included in the inventory of the corporation if on hand at the close of the taxable year;

(ii) property held by the corporation primarily for sale to customers in the ordinary course of its trade or business; and

(iii) unrealized receivables or fees, except receivables from sales or exchanges of assets other than assets described in this subparagraph.

(B) Unrealized receivables or fees.—For purposes of subparagraph (A) (iii), the term "unrealized receivables or fees" means, to the extent not previously includible in income under the method of accounting used by the corporation, any rights (contractual or otherwise) to payment for—

(i) goods delivered, or to be delivered, to the extent that the proceeds therefrom would be treated as amounts received from the sale or exchange of property other than a capital asset, or

(ii) services rendered or to be rendered.

(c) Adjustments for liabilities, etc.—In making the adjustments to the earnings and profits of a corporation under subsection (a) or (b), proper adjustment shall be made for—

(1) the amount of any liability to which the property distributed is subject,

(2) the amount of any liability of the corporation assumed by a shareholder in connection with the distribution, and

(3) any gain recognized to the corporation on the distribution.

(d) Certain distributions of stock and securities.—

(1) In general.—The distribution to a distributee by or on behalf of a corporation of its stock or securities, of stock or securities in another corporation, or of property, in a distribution to which this title applies, shall not be considered a distribution of the earnings and profits of any corporation—

(A) if no gain to such distributee from the receipt of such stock or securities, or property, was recognized under this title, or

(B) if the distribution was not subject to tax in the hands of such distributee by reason of section 305(a).

(2) Prior distributions.—In the case of a distribution of stock or securities, or property, to which section 115(h) of the Internal Revenue Code of 1939 (or the corresponding provision of prior law) applied, the effect on earnings and profits of such distribution shall be determined under such section 115(h), or the corresponding provision of prior law, as the case may be.

(3) Stock or securities.—For purposes of this subsection, the term "stock or securities" includes rights to acquire stock or securities.

(e) Special rule for certain redemptions.—In the case of amounts distributed in a redemption to which section 302(a) or 303 applies, the part of such distribution which is properly chargeable to capital account shall not be treated as a distribution of earnings and profits.

(f) Effect on earnings and profits of gain or loss and of receipt of tax-free distributions.—

(1) Effect on earnings and profits of gain or loss.—The gain or loss realized from the sale or other disposition (after February 28, 1913) of property by a corporation—

(A) for the purpose of the computation of the earnings and profits of the corporation, shall (except as provided in subparagraph (B)) be determined by using as the adjusted basis the adjusted basis (under the law applicable to the year in which the sale or other disposition was made) for determining gain, except that no regard shall be had to the value of the property as of March 1, 1913; but

(B) for purposes of the computation of the earnings and profits of the corporation for any period beginning after February 28, 1913, shall be determined by using as the adjusted basis the adjusted basis (under the law applicable to the year in which the sale or other disposition was made) for determining gain.

Gain or loss so realized shall increase or decrease the earnings and profits to, but not beyond, the extent to which such a realized gain or loss was recognized in computing taxable income under the law applicable to the year in which such sale or disposition was made. Where, in determining the adjusted basis used in computing such realized gain or loss, the adjustment to the basis differs from the adjustment proper for the purpose of determining earnings and profits, then the latter adjustment shall be used in determining the increase or decrease above provided. For purposes of this subsection, a loss with respect to which a deduction is disallowed under section 1091 (relating to wash sales of stock or securities), or the corresponding provision of prior law, shall not be deemed to be recognized.

(2) Effect on earnings and profits of receipt of tax-free distributions.—Where a corporation receives (after February 28, 1913) a distribution from a second corporation which (under the law applicable to the year in which the distribution was made) was not a taxable dividend to the shareholders of the second corporation, the amount of such distribution shall not increase the earnings and profits of the first corporation in the following cases:

(A) no such increase shall be made in respect of the part of such distribution which (under such law) is directly applied in reduction of the basis of the stock in respect of which the distribution was made; and

(B) no such increase shall be made if (under such law) the distribution causes the basis of the stock in respect of which the distribution was made to be allocated between such stock and the property received (or such basis would, but for section 307(b), be so allocated).

· · · ·

(h) Allocation in certain corporate separations.—In the case of a distribution or exchange to which section 355 (or so much of section 356 as relates to section 355) applies, proper allocation with respect to the earnings and profits of the distributing corporation and the controlled corporation (or corporations) shall be made under regulations prescribed by the Secretary.

· · · ·

(k) Effect of depreciation on earnings and profits.—

(1) General rule.—For purposes of computing the earnings and profits of a corporation for any taxable year beginning after June 30, 1972, the allowance for depreciation (and amortization, if any) shall be deemed to be the amount which would be allowable for such year if the straight line method of depreciation had been used for each taxable year beginning after June 30, 1972.

(2) Exception.—If for any taxable year beginning after June 30, 1972, a method of depreciation was used by the taxpayer which the Secretary has determined results in a reasonable allowance under section 167(a), and which is not—

(A) a declining balance method,

(B) the sum of the years-digits method, or

(C) any other method allowable solely by reason of the application of subsection (b) (4) or (j) (1) (C) of section 167,

then the adjustment to earnings and profits for depreciation for such year shall be determined under the method so used (in lieu of under the straight line method).

(3) Exception for recovery and section 179 property.—

(A) Recovery property.—Except as provided in subparagraphs (B) and (C), in the case of recovery property (within the meaning of section 168), the adjustment to earnings and profits for depreciation for any taxable year shall be the amount determined under the straight-line method (using a half year convention in the case of property other than the 15-year real property and without regard to salvage value) and using a recovery period determined in accordance with the following table:

In the case of:	The applicable recovery period is:
3-year property	5 years.
5-year property	12 years.
10-year property	25 years.
15-year real property	35 years.
15-year public utility property	35 years.

For purposes of this subparagraph, no adjustment shall be allowed in the year of disposition (except with respect to 15-year real property), and rules similar to the rules under the next to the last sentence of section 168(b)(2)(A) and section 168(b)(2)(B) shall apply.

    (B) Treatment of amounts deductible under section 179.—For purposes of computing the earnings and profits of a corporation, any amount deductible under section 179 shall be allowed as a deduction ratably over the period of 5 years (beginning with the year for which such amount is deductible under section 179).

    (C) Flexibility.—In any case where a different recovery percentage is elected under section 168(b)(3) or (f)(2)(C) based on a recovery period longer than the recovery period provided in subparagraph (A), the adjustment to earnings and profits shall be based on such longer period under rules similar to those provided in subparagraph (A).

. . . .

    (5) Basis adjustment not taken into account.—In computing the earnings and profits of a corporation for any taxable year, the allowance for depreciation (and amortization, if any) shall be computed without regard to any basis adjustment under section 48(q).

(l) Discharge of indebtedness income.—

    (1) Does not increase earnings and profits if applied to reduce basis. —The earnings and profits of a corporation shall not include income from the discharge of indebtedness to the extent of the amount applied to reduce basis under section 1017.

    (2) Reduction of deficit in earnings and profits in certain cases.—If—

        (A) the interest of any shareholder of a corporation is terminated or extinguished in a title 11 or similar case (within the meaning of section 368(a)(3)(A)), and

        (B) there is a deficit in the earnings and profits of the corporation,

then such deficit shall be reduced by an amount equal to the paid-in capital which is allocable to the interest of the shareholder which is so terminated or extinguished.

    (m) No adjustment for interest paid on certain registration-required obligations not in registered form.—The earnings and profits of any corporation shall not be decreased by any interest with respect to which a deduction is not or would not be allowable by reason of section 163(f), unless at the time of issuance the issuer is a foreign corporation that is not a controlled foreign corporation (within the meaning of section 957), a foreign investment company (within the meaning of section 1246(b)), or a foreign personal holding company (within the meaning of section 552) and the issuance did not have as a purpose the avoidance of section 163(f) of this subsection.

SUBPART C—DEFINITIONS; CONSTRUCTIVE OWNERSHIP OF STOCK

§ 316.   Dividend defined

    (a) General rule.—For purposes of this subtitle, the term "dividend" means any distribution of property made by a corporation to its shareholders—

        (1) out of its earnings and profits accumulated after February 28, 1913, or

        (2) out of its earnings and profits of the taxable year (computed as of the close of the taxable year without diminution by reason of any distributions

made during the taxable year), without regard to the amount of the earnings and profits at the time the distribution was made.

Except as otherwise provided in this subtitle, every distribution is made out of earnings and profits to the extent thereof, and from the most recently accumulated earnings and profits. To the extent that any distribution is, under any provision of this subchapter, treated as a distribution of property to which section 301 applies, such distribution shall be treated as a distribution of property for purposes of this subsection.

(b) Special rules.—

(1) Certain insurance company dividends.—The definition in subsection (a) shall not apply to the term "dividend" as used in subchapter L in any case where the reference is to dividends of insurance companies paid to policyholders as such.

(2) Distributions by personal holding companies.—

(A) In the case of a corporation which—

(i) under the law applicable to the taxable year in which the distribution is made, is a personal holding company (as defined in section 542), or

(ii) for the taxable year in respect of which the distribution is made under section 563(b) (relating to dividends paid after the close of the taxable year), or section 547 (relating to deficiency dividends), or the corresponding provisions of prior law, is a personal holding company under the law applicable to such taxable year,

the term "dividend" also means any distribution of property (whether or not a dividend as defined in subsection (a)) made by the corporation to its shareholders, to the extent of its undistributed personal holding company income (determined under section 545 without regard to distributions under this paragraph) for such year.

(B) For purposes of subparagraph (A), the term "distribution of property" includes a distribution in complete liquidation occurring within 24 months after the adoption of a plan of liquidation, but—

(i) only to the extent of the amounts distributed to distributees other than corporate shareholders, and

(ii) only to the extent that the corporation designates such amounts as a dividend distribution and duly notifies such distributees of such designation, under regulations prescribed by the Secretary, but

(iii) not in excess of the sum of such distributees' allocable share of the undistributed personal holding company income for such year, computed without regard to this subparagraph or section 562(b).

. . . . .

§ 317.   Other definitions

(a) Property.—For purposes of this part, the term "property" means money, securities, and any other property; except that such term does not include stock in the corporation making the distribution (or rights to acquire such stock).

(b) Redemption of stock.—For purposes of this part, stock shall be treated as redeemed by a corporation if the corporation acquires its stock from a shareholder in exchange for property, whether or not the stock so acquired is cancelled, retired, or held as treasury stock.

§ 318.　Constructive ownership of stock

(a) **General rule.**—For purposes of those provisions of this subchapter to which the rules contained in this section are expressly made applicable—

(1) **Members of family.**—

(A) **In general.**—An individual shall be considered as owning the stock owned, directly or indirectly, by or for—

(i) his spouse (other than a spouse who is legally separated from the individual under a decree of divorce or separate maintenance), and

(ii) his children, grandchildren, and parents.

(B) **Effect of adoption.**—For purposes of subparagraph (A) (ii), a legally adopted child of an individual shall be treated as a child of such individual by blood.

(2) **Attribution from partnerships, estates, trusts, and corporations.**—

(A) **From partnerships and estates.**—Stock owned, directly or indirectly, by or for a partnership or estate shall be considered as owned proportionately by its partners or beneficiaries.

(B) **From trusts.**—

(i) Stock owned, directly or indirectly, by or for a trust (other than an employees' trust described in section 401(a) which is exempt from tax under section 501(a)) shall be considered as owned by its beneficiaries in proportion to the actuarial interest of such beneficiaries in such trust.

(ii) Stock owned, directly or indirectly, by or for any portion of a trust of which a person is considered the owner under subpart E of part I of subchapter J (relating to grantors and others treated as substantial owners) shall be considered as owned by such person.

(C) **From corporations.**—If 50 percent or more in value of the stock in a corporation is owned, directly or indirectly, by or for any person, such person shall be considered as owning the stock owned, directly or indirectly, by or for such corporation, in that proportion which the value of the stock which such person so owns bears to the value of all the stock in such corporation.

(3) **Attribution to partnerships, estates, trusts, and corporations.**—

(A) **To partnerships and estates.**—Stock owned, directly or indirectly, by or for a partner or a beneficiary of an estate shall be considered as owned by the partnership or estate.

(B) **To trusts.**—

(i) Stock owned, directly or indirectly, by or for a beneficiary of a trust (other than an employees' trust described in section 401(a) which is exempt from tax under section 501(a)) shall be considered as owned by the trust, unless such beneficiary's interest in the trust is a remote contingent interest. For purposes of this clause, a contingent interest of a beneficiary in a trust shall be considered remote if, under the maximum exercise of discretion by the trustee in favor of such beneficiary, the value of such interest, computed actuarially, is 5 percent or less of the value of the trust property.

(ii) Stock owned, directly or indirectly, by or for a person who is considered the owner of any portion of a trust under subpart E of part I of subchapter J (relating to grantors and others treated as substantial owners) shall be considered as owned by the trust.

(C) **To corporations.**—If 50 percent or more in value of the stock in a corporation is owned, directly or indirectly, by or for any person, such corporation shall be considered as owning the stock owned, directly or indirectly, by or for such person.

(4) **Options.**—If any person has an option to acquire stock, such stock shall be considered as owned by such person. For purposes of this paragraph, an option to acquire such an option, and each one of a series of such options, shall be considered as an option to acquire such stock.

(5) **Operating rules.—**

(A) **In general.**—Except as provided in subparagraphs (B) and (C), stock constructively owned by a person by reason of the application of paragraph (1), (2), (3), or (4), shall, for purposes of applying paragraphs (1), (2), (3), and (4), be considered as actually owned by such person.

(B) **Members of family.**—Stock constructively owned by an individual by reason of the application of paragraph (1) shall not be considered as owned by him for purposes of again applying paragraph (1) in order to make another the constructive owner of such stock.

(C) **Partnerships, estates, trusts, and corporations.**—Stock constructively owned by a partnership, estate, trust, or corporation by reason of the application of paragraph (3) shall not be considered as owned by it for purposes of applying paragraph (2) in order to make another the constructive owner of such stock.

(D) **Option rule in lieu of family rule.**—For purposes of this paragraph, if stock may be considered as owned by an individual under paragraph (1) or (4), it shall be considered as owned by him under paragraph (4).

. . . . .

PART II—CORPORATE LIQUIDATIONS

Subpart
A. Effects on recipients.
B. Effects on corporation.
C. Collapsible corporations.
D. Definition.

SUBPART A—EFFECTS ON RECIPIENTS

§ 331.   Gain or loss to shareholders in corporate liquidations

(a) **Distributions in complete liquidation treated as exchanges.**—Amounts received by a shareholder in a distribution in complete liquidation of a corporation shall be treated as in full payment in exchange for the stock.

(b) Nonapplication of section 301.—Section 301 (relating to effects on shareholder of distributions of property) shall not apply to any distribution of property (other than a distribution referred to in paragraph (2) (B) of section 316(b)) in complete liquidation.

. . . .

§ 332.   Complete liquidations of subsidiaries

(a) General rule.—No gain or loss shall be recognized on the receipt by a corporation of property distributed in complete liquidation of another corporation.

(b) Liquidations to which section applies.—For purposes of subsection (a), a distribution shall be considered to be in complete liquidation only if—

(1) the corporation receiving such property was, on the date of the adoption of the plan of liquidation, and has continued to be at all times until the receipt of the property, the owner of stock (in such other corporation) possessing at least 80 percent of the total combined voting power of all classes of stock entitled to vote and the owner of at least 80 percent of the total number of shares of all other classes of stock (except nonvoting stock which is limited and preferred as to dividends); and either

(2) the distribution is by such other corporation in complete cancellation or redemption of all its stock, and the transfer of all the property occurs within the taxable year; in such case the adoption by the shareholders of the resolution under which is authorized the distribution of all the assets of such corporation in complete cancellation or redemption of all its stock shall be considered an adoption of a plan of liquidation, even though no time for the completion of the transfer of the property is specified in such resolution; or

(3) such distribution is one of a series of distributions by such other corporation in complete cancellation or redemption of all its stock in accordance with a plan of liquidation under which the transfer of all the property under the liquidation is to be completed within 3 years from the close of the taxable year during which is made the first of the series of distributions under the plan, except that if such transfer is not completed within such period, or if the taxpayer does not continue qualified under paragraph (1) until the completion of such transfer, no distribution under the plan shall be considered a distribution in complete liquidation.

If such transfer of all the property does not occur within the taxable year, the Secretary may require of the taxpayer such bond, or waiver of the statute of limitations on assessment and collection, or both, as he may deem necessary to insure, if the transfer of the property is not completed within such 3-year period, or if the taxpayer does not continue qualified under paragraph (1) until the completion of such transfer, the assessment and collection of all income taxes then imposed by law for such taxable year or subsequent taxable years, to the extent attributable to property so received. A distribution otherwise constituting a distribution in complete liquidation within the meaning of this subsection shall not be considered as not constituting such a distribution merely because it does not constitute a distribution or liquidation within the meaning of the corporate law under which the distribution is made; and for purposes of this subsection a transfer of property of such other corporation to the taxpayer shall not be considered as not constituting a distribution (or one of a series of distributions) in complete cancellation or redemption of all the stock of such other corporation, merely because the carrying out of the plan involves (A) the transfer under the plan to the taxpayer by such other corporation of property, not attributable to shares owned by the taxpayer, on an exchange described in section 361, and (B) the complete cancellation or redemption under the plan, as a result of exchanges described in section 354, of the shares not owned by the taxpayer.

(c) Special rule for indebtedness of subsidiary to parent.—If—

(1) a corporation is liquidated and subsection (a) applies to such liquidation, and

(2) on the date of the adoption of the plan of liquidation, such corporation was indebted to the corporation which meets the 80 percent stock ownership requirements specified in subsection (b),

then no gain or loss shall be recognized to the corporation so indebted because of the transfer of property in satisfaction of such indebtedness.

§ 333.   Election as to recognition of gain in certain liquidations

(a) General rule.—In the case of property distributed in complete liquidation of a domestic corporation (other than a collapsible corporation to which section 341(a) applies), if—

(1) the liquidation is made in pursuance of a plan of liquidation adopted, and

(2) the distribution is in complete cancellation or redemption of all the stock, and the transfer of all the property under the liquidation occurs within some one calendar month,

then in the case of each qualified electing shareholder (as defined in subsection (c)) gain on the shares owned by him at the time of the adoption of the plan of liquidation shall be recognized only to the extent provided in subsections (e) and (f).

(b) Excluded corporation.—For purposes of this section, the term "excluded corporation" means a corporation which at any time between January 1, 1954, and the date of the adoption of the plan of liquidation, both dates inclusive, was the owner of stock possessing 50 percent or more of the total combined voting power of all classes of stock entitled to vote on the adoption of such plan.

(c) Qualified electing shareholders.—For purposes of this section, the term "qualified electing shareholder" means a shareholder (other than an excluded corporation) of any class of stock (whether or not entitled to vote on the adoption of the plan of liquidation) who is a shareholder at the time of the adoption of such plan, and whose written election to have the benefits of subsection (a) has been made and filed in accordance with subsection (d), but—

(1) in the case of a shareholder other than a corporation, only if written elections have been so filed by shareholders (other than corporations) who at the time of the adoption of the plan of liquidation are owners of stock possessing at least 80 percent of the total combined voting power (exclusive of voting power possessed by stock owned by corporations) of all classes of stock entitled to vote on the adoption of such plan of liquidation; or

(2) in the case of a shareholder which is a corporation, only if written elections have been so filed by corporate shareholders (other than an excluded corporation) which at the time of the adoption of such plan of liquidation are

owners of stock possessing at least 80 percent of the total combined voting power (exclusive of voting power possessed by stock owned by an excluded corporation and by shareholders who are not corporations) of all classes of stock entitled to vote on the adoption of such plan of liquidation.

(d) Making and filing of elections.—The written elections referred to in subsection (c) must be made and filed in such manner as to be not in contravention of regulations prescribed by the Secretary. The filing must be within 30 days after the date of the adoption of the plan of liquidation.

(e) Noncorporate shareholders.—In the case of a qualified electing shareholder other than a corporation—

(1) there shall be recognized, and treated as a dividend, so much of the gain as is not in excess of his ratable share of the earnings and profits of the corporation accumulated after February 28, 1913, such earnings and profits to be determined as of the close of the month in which the transfer in liquidation occurred under subsection (a) (2), but without diminution by reason of distributions made during such month; but by including in the computation thereof all amounts accrued up to the date on which the transfer of all the property under the liquidation is completed; and

(2) there shall be recognized, and treated as short-term or long-term capital gain, as the case may be, so much of the remainder of the gain as is not in excess of the amount by which the value of that portion of the assets received by him which consists of money, or of stock or securities acquired by the corporation after December 31, 1953, exceeds his ratable share of such earnings and profits.

(f) Corporate shareholders.—In the case of a qualified electing shareholder which is a corporation, the gain shall be recognized only to the extent of the greater of the two following—

(1) the portion of the assets received by it which consists of money, or of stock or securities acquired by the liquidating corporation after December 31, 1953; or

(2) its ratable share of the earnings and profits of the liquidating corporation accumulated after February 28, 1913, such earnings and profits to be determined as of the close of the month in which the transfer in liquidation occurred under subsection (a) (2), but without diminution by reason of distributions made during such month; but by including in the computation thereof all amounts accrued up to the date on which the transfer of all the property under the liquidation is completed.

§ 334. Basis of property received in liquidations

(a) General rule.—If property is received in a distribution in complete liquidation (other than a distribution to which section 333 applies), and if gain or loss is recognized on receipt of such property, then the basis of the property in the hands of the distributee shall be the fair market value of such property at the time of the distribution.

(b) Liquidation of subsidiary.—

(1) **Distribution in complete liquidation.**—If property is received by a corporation in a distribution in a complete liquidation to which section 332(a) applies, the basis of the property in the hands of the distributee shall be the same as it would be in the hands of the transferor.

(2) **Transfers to which section 332(c) applies.**—If property is received by a corporation in a transfer to which section 332(c) applies, the basis of the property in the hands of the transferee shall be the same as it would be in the hands of the transferor.

(3) **Distributee defined.**—For purposes of this subsection, the term "distributee" means only the corporation which meets the 80-percent stock ownership requirements specified in section 332(b).

(c) Property received in liquidation under section 333.—If—

(1) property was acquired by a shareholder in the liquidation of a corporation in cancellation or redemption of stock, and

(2) with respect to such acquisition—

(A) gain was realized, but

(B) as the result of an election made by the shareholder under section 333, the extent to which gain was recognized was determined under section 333,

then the basis shall be the same as the basis of such stock cancelled or redeemed in the liquidation, decreased in the amount of any money received by the shareholder, and increased in the amount of gain recognized to him.

SUBPART B—EFFECTS ON CORPORATION

§ 336.   Distributions of property in liquidation

(a) General rule.—Except as provided in subsection (b) of this section and in section 453B (relating to disposition of installment obligations), no gain or loss shall be recognized to a corporation on the distribution of property in complete liquidation.

(b) LIFO inventory.—

(1) **In general.**—If a corporation inventorying goods under the LIFO method distributes inventory assets in complete liquidation, then the LIFO recapture amount with respect to such assets shall be treated as gain to the corporation recognized from the sale of such inventory assets.

(2) **Exception where basis determined under section 334(b).**—Paragraph (1) shall not apply to any liquidation under section 332 for which the basis of property received is determined under section 334(b).

(3) **LIFO recapture amount.**—For purposes of this subsection, the term "LIFO recapture amount" means the amount (if any) by which—

(A) the inventory amount of the inventory assets under the first-in, first-out method authorized by section 471, exceeds

(B) the inventory amount of such assets under the LIFO method.

(4) **Definitions.**—For purposes of this subsection—

(A) **LIFO method.**—The term "LIFO method" means the method authorized by section 472 (relating to last-in, first-out inventories).

(B) **Other definitions.**—The term "inventory assets" has the meaning given to such term by subparagraph (A) of section 311(b)(2), and the term "inventory amount" has the meaning given to such term by subparagraph (B) of section 311(b)(2) (as modified by paragraph (3) of section 311(b)).

§ 337. Gain or loss on sales or exchanges in connection with certain liquidations

(a) **General rule.**—If, within the 12-month period beginning on the date on which a corporation adopts a plan of complete liquidation, all of the assets of the corporation are distributed in complete liquidation, less assets retained to meet claims, then no gain or loss shall be recognized to such corporation from the sale or exchange by it of property within such 12-month period.

(b) **Property defined.**—

(1) **In general.**—For purposes of subsection (a), the term "property" does not include—

(A) stock in trade of the corporation, or other property of a kind which would properly be included in the inventory of the corporation if on hand at the close of the taxable year, and property held by the corporation primarily for sale to customers in the ordinary course of its trade or business,

(B) installment obligations acquired in respect of the sale or exchange (without regard to whether such sale or exchange occurred before, on, or after the date of the adoption of the plan referred to in subsection (a)) of stock in trade or other property described in subparagraph (A) of this paragraph, and

(C) installment obligations acquired in respect of property (other than property described in subparagraph (A)) sold or exchanged before the date of the adoption of such plan of liquidation.

(2) **Nonrecognition with respect to inventory in certain cases.**—Notwithstanding paragraph (1) of this subsection, if substantially all of the property described in subparagraph (A) of such paragraph (1) which is attributable to a trade or business of the corporation is, in accordance with this section, sold or exchanged to one person in one transaction, then for purposes of subsection (a) the term "property" includes—

(A) such property so sold or exchanged, and

(B) installment obligations acquired in respect of such sale or exchange.

(c) **Limitations.**—

(1) **Collapsible corporations and liquidations to which section 333 applies.**—This section shall not apply to any sale or exchange—

(A) made by a collapsible corporation (as defined in section 341(b)), or

(B) following the adoption of a plan of complete liquidation, if section 333 applies with respect to such liquidation.

(2) **Liquidations to which section 332 applies.**—In the case of any sale or exchange following the adoption of a plan of complete liquidation, if section 332 applies with respect to such liquidation, this section shall not apply.

(d) **Special rule for certain minority shareholders.**—If a corporation adopts a plan of complete liquidation, and if subsection (a) does not apply to sales or exchanges of property by such corporation, solely by reason of the application of subsection (c)(2), then for the first taxable year of any shareholder (other than a corporation which meets the 80 percent stock ownership requirement specified in section 332(b) (1)) in which he receives a distribution in complete liquidation—

(1) the amount realized by such shareholder on the distribution shall be increased by his proportionate share of the amount by which the tax imposed by this subtitle on such corporation would have been reduced if subsection (c) (2) had not been applicable, and

(2) for purposes of this title, such shareholder shall be deemed to have paid, on the last day prescribed by law for the payment of the tax imposed by this subtitle on such shareholder for such taxable year, an amount of tax equal to the amount of the increase described in paragraph (1).

(e) Special rule for involuntary conversions.—If—

(1) there is an involuntary conversion (within the meaning of section 1033) of property of a distributing corporation and there is a complete liquidation of such corporation which qualifies under subsection (a),

(2) the disposition of the converted property (within the meaning of clause (ii) of section 1033(a) (2) (E)) occurs during the 60-day period which ends on the day before the first day of the 12-month period, and

(3) such corporation elects the application of this subsection at such time and in such manner as the Secretary may by regulations prescribe,

then for purposes of this section such disposition shall be treated as a sale or exchange occurring within the 12-month period.

(f) Special rule for LIFO inventories.—

(1) In general.—In the case of a corporation inventorying goods under the LIFO method, this section shall apply to gain from the sale or exchange of inventory assets (which under subsection (b)(2) constitute property) only to the extent that such gain exceeds the LIFO recapture amount with respect to such assets.

(2) Definitions.—The terms used in this subsection shall have the same meaning as when used in section 336(b).

. . . . .

(g) Title 11 or similar cases.—If a corporation completely liquidates pursuant to a plan of complete liquidation adopted in a title 11 or similar case (within the meaning of section 368(a)(3)(A))—

(1) for purposes of subsection (a), the term "property" shall not include any item acquired on or after the date of the adoption of the plan of liquidation if such item is not property within the meaning of subsection (b)(2), and

(2) subsection (a) shall apply to sales and exchanges by the corporation of property within the period beginning on the date of the adoption of the plan and ending on the date of the termination of the case.

§ 338. Certain stock purchases treated as asset acquisitions

(a) General rule.—For purposes of this subtitle, if a purchasing corporation makes an election under this section (or is treated under subsection (e) as having made such an election), then, in the case of any qualified stock purchase, the target corporation—

(1) shall be treated as having sold all of its assets at the close of the acquisition date in a single transaction to which section 337 applies, and

(2) shall be treated as a new corporation which pruchased all of the assets referred to in paragraph (1) as of the beginning of the day after the acquisition date.

(b) Price at which deemed sale made.—

(1) **In general.**—For purposes of subsection (a), the assets of the target corporation shall be treated as sold (and purchased) at an amount equal to—

(A) the grossed-up basis of the purchasing corporation's stock in the target corporation on the acquisition date,

(B) properly adjusted under regulations prescribed by the Secretary for liabilities of the target corporation and other relevant items.

(2) **Grossed-up basis.**—For purposes of paragraph (1), the grossed-up basis shall be an amount equal to the basis of the purchasing corporation's stock in the target corporation on the acquisition date multiplied by a fraction—

(A) the numerator of which is 100 percent, and

(B) the denominator of which is the percentage of stock (by value) of the target corporation held by the purchasing corporation on the acquisition date.

(3) **Allocation among assets.**—The amount determined under paragraph (1) shall be allocated among the assets of the target corporation under regulations prescribed by the Secretary.

(c) Special rules.—

(1) **Coordination with section 337 where purchasing corporation holds less than 100 percent of stock.**—If during the 1-year period beginning on the acquisition date the maximum percentage (by value) of stock in the target corporation held by the purchasing corporation is less than 100 percent, then in applying section 337 for purposes of subsection (a)(1), the nonrecognition of gain or loss shall be limited to an amount determined by applying such maximum percentage to such gain or loss. The preceding sentence shall not apply if the target corporation is liquidated during such 1-year period.

(2) **Certain redemptions where election made.**—If, in connection with a qualified stock purchase with respect to which an election is made under this section, the target corporation makes a distribution in complete redemption of all of the stock of a shareholder which qualifies under section 302(b)(3) (determined without regard to the application of section 302(c)(2)(A)(ii)), section 336 shall apply to such distribution as if it were a distribution in complete liquidation.

(d) Purchasing corporation; target corporation; qualified stock purchase. —For purposes of this section—

(1) **Purchasing corporation.**—The term "purchasing corporation" means any corporation which makes a qualified stock purchase of stock of another corporation.

(2) **Target corporation.**—The term "target corporation" means any corporation the stock of which is acquired by another corporation in a qualified stock purchase.

(3) **Qualified stock purchase.**—The term "qualified stock purchase" means any transaction or series of transactions in which stock of 1 corporation possessing—

(A) at least 80 percent of total combined voting power of all classes of stock entitled to vote, and

(B) at least 80 percent of the total number of shares of all other classes of stock (except nonvoting stock which is limited and preferred as to dividends),

is acquired by another corporation by purchase during the 12-month acquisition period.

(e) Deemed election where purchasing corporation acquires asset of target corporation.—

(1) In general.—A purchasing corporation shall be treated as having made an election under this section with respect to any target corporation if, at any time during the consistency period, it acquires any asset of the target corporation (or a target affiliate).

(2) Exceptions.—Paragraph (1) shall not apply with respect to any acquisition by the purchasing corporation if—

(A) such acquisition is pursuant to a sale by the target corporation (or the target affiliate) in the ordinary course of its trade or business,

(B) the basis of the property acquired is determined (in whole or in part) by reference to the adjusted basis of such property in the hands of the person from whom acquired,

(C) such acquisition was before September 1, 1982,

(D) to the extent provided in regulations, the property acquired is located outside the United States, or

(E) such acquisition is described in regulations prescribed by the Secretary.

(3) Anti-avoidance rule.—Whenever necessary to carry out the purpose of this subsection and subsection (f), the Secretary may treat stock acquisitions which are pursuant to a plan and which meet the 80 percent requirements of subparagraphs (A) and (B) of subsection (d)(3) as qualified stock purchases.

(f) Consistency required for all stock acquisitions from same affiliated group.—If a purchasing corporation makes qualified stock purchases with respect to the target corporation and 1 or more target affiliates during any consistency period, then (except as otherwise provided in subsection (e))—

(1) any election under this section with respect to the first such purchase shall apply to each other such purchase, and

(2) no election may be made under this section with respect to the second or subsequent such purchase if such an election was not made with respect to the first such purchase.

(g) Election.—

(1) When made.—Except as otherwise provided in regulations, an election under this section shall be made not later than 75 days after the acquisition date.

(2) Manner.—An election by the purchasing corporation under this section shall be made in such manner as the Secretary shall by regulations prescribe.

(3) Election irrevocable.—An election by a purchasing corporation under this section, once made, shall be irrevocable.

(h) Definitions and special rules.—For purposes of this section—

(1) 12-month acquisition period.—The term "12-month acquisition period" means the 12-month period beginning with the date of the first acquisition by purchase of stock included in a qualified stock purchase.

(2) Acquisition date.—The term "acquisition date" means, with respect to any corporation, the first day on which there is a qualified stock purchase with respect to the stock of such corporation.

(3) Purchase.—

   (A) In general.—The term "purchase" means any acquisition of stock, but only if—

      (i) the basis of the stock in the hands of the purchasing corporation is not determined (I) in whole or in part by reference to the adjusted basis of such stock in the hands of the person from whom acquired, or (II) under section 1014(a) (relating to property acquired from a decedent),

      (ii) the stock is not acquired in an exchange to which section 351 applies, and

      (iii) the stock is not acquired from a person the ownership of whose stock would, under section 318(a) (other than paragraph (4) thereof), be attributed to the person acquiring such stock.

   (B) Deemed purchase of stock of subsidiaries.—If stock in a corporation is acquired by purchase (within the meaning of subparagraph (A)) and, as a result of such acquisition, the corporation making such purchase is treated (by reason of section 318(a)) as owning stock in a 3rd corporation, the corporation making such purchase shall be treated as having purchased such stock in such 3rd corporation. The corporation making such purchase shall be treated as purchasing stock in the 3rd corporation by reason of the preceding sentence on the first day on which the purchasing corporation is considered under section 318(a) as owning such stock.

(4) Consistency period.—

   (A) In general.—Except as provided in subparagraph (B), the term "consistency period" means the period consisting of—

      (i) the 1-year period before the beginning of the 12-month acquisition period for the target corporation,

      (ii) such acquisition period (up to and including the acquisition date), and

      (iii) the 1-year period beginning on the day after the acquisition date.

   (B) Extension where there is plan.—The period referred to in subparagraph (A) shall also include any period during which the Secretary determines that there was in effect a plan to make a qualified stock purchase plus 1 or more other qualified stock purchases (or asset acquisitions described in subsection (e)) with respect to the target corporation or any target affiliate.

(5) Affiliated group.—The term "affiliated group" has the meaning given to such term by section 1504(a) (determined without regard to the exceptions contained in section 1504(b)).

(6) Target affiliate.—

(A) In general.—A corporation shall be treated as a target affiliate of the target corporation if each of such corporations was, at any time during so much of the consistency period as ends on the acquisition date of the target corporation, a member of an affiliated group which had the same common parent.

(B) Certain foreign corporations, etc.—Except as otherwise provided in regulations (and subject to such conditions as may be provided in regulations)—

(i) the term "target affiliate" does not include a foreign corporation, a DISC, a corporation described in section 934(b), or a corporation to which an election under section 936 applies, and

(ii) stock held by a target affiliate in a foreign corporation or a domestic corporation which is a DISC or described in section 1248(e) shall be excluded from the operation of this section.

(7) Acquisitions by purchasing corporation include acquisitions by corporations affiliated with purchasing corporation.—Except as otherwise provided in regulations, an acquisition of stock or assets by any member of an affiliated group which includes a purchasing corporation shall be treated as made by the purchasing corporation.

(i) Regulations.—The Secretary shall prescribe such regulations as may be necessary to ensure that the purposes of this section to require consistency of treatment of stock and asset purchases with respect to a target corporation and its target affiliates (whether by treating all of them as stock purchases or as asset purchases) may not be circumvented through the use of any provision of law or regulations (including the consolidated return regulations).

SUBPART C—COLLAPSIBLE CORPORATIONS

§ 341.   Collapsible corporations

(a) Treatment of gain to shareholders.—Gain from—

(1) the sale or exchange of stock of a collapsible corporation,

(2) a distribution

(A) in complete liquidation of a collapsible corporation if such distribution is treated under this part as in part or full payment in exchange for stock, or

(B) in partial liquidation (within the meaning of section 302(e) of a collapsible corporation if such distribution is treated under section 302(b)(4) as in part or full payment in exchange for the stock, and

(3) a distribution made by a collapsible corporation which, under section 301(c) (3) (A), is treated, to the extent it exceeds the basis of the stock, in the same manner as a gain from the sale or exchange of property,

to the extent that it would be considered (but for the provisions of this section) as gain from the sale or exchange of a capital asset held for more than 1 year shall, except as otherwise provided in this section, be considered as ordinary income.

(b) Definitions.—

(1) **Collapsible corporation.**—For purposes of this section, the term "collapsible corporation" means a corporation formed or availed of principally for the manufacture, construction, or production of property, for the purchase of property which (in the hands of the corporation) is property described in paragraph (3), or for the holding of stock in a corporation so formed or availed of, with a view to—

    (A) the sale or exchange of stock by its shareholders (whether in liquidation or otherwise), or a distribution to its shareholders, before the realization by the corporation manufacturing, constructing, producing, or purchasing the property of a substantial part of the taxable income to be derived from such property, and

    (B) the realization by such shareholders of gain attributable to such property.

(2) **Production or purchase of property.**—For purposes of paragraph (1), a corporation shall be deemed to have manufactured, constructed, produced, or purchased property, if—

    (A) it engaged in the manufacture, construction, or production of such property to any extent,

    (B) it holds property having a basis determined, in whole or in part, by reference to the cost of such property in the hands of a person who manufactured, constructed, produced, or purchased the property, or

    (C) it holds property having a basis determined, in whole or in part, by reference to the cost of property manufactured, constructed, produced, or purchased by the corporation.

(3) **Section 341 assets.**—For purposes of this section, the term "section 341 assets" means property held for a period of less than 3 years which is—

    (A) stock in trade of the corporation, or other property of a kind which would properly be included in the inventory of the corporation if on hand at the close of the taxable year;

    (B) property held by the corporation primarily for sale to customers in the ordinary course of its trade or business;

    (C) unrealized receivables or fees, except receivables from sales of property other than property described in this paragraph; or

    (D) property described in section 1231(b) (without regard to any holding period therein provided), except such property which is or has been used in connection with the manufacture, construction, production, or sale of property described in subparagraph (A) or (B).

In determining whether the 3-year holding period specified in this paragraph has been satisfied, section 1223 shall apply, but no such period shall be deemed to begin before the completion of the manufacture, construction, production, or purchase.

(4) **Unrealized receivables.**—For purposes of paragraph (3) (C), the term "unrealized receivables or fees" means, to the extent not previously includible in income under the method of accounting used by the corporation, any rights (contractual or otherwise) to payment for—

    (A) goods delivered, or to be delivered, to the extent the proceeds therefrom would be treated as amounts received from the sale or exchange of property other than a capital asset, or

    (B) services rendered or to be rendered.

(c) Presumption in certain cases.—

(1) In general.—For purposes of this section, a corporation shall, unless shown to the contrary, be deemed to be a collapsible corporation if (at the time of the sale or exchange, or the distribution, described in subsection (a)) the fair market value of its section 341 assets (as defined in subsection (b) (3)) is—

(A) 50 percent or more of the fair market value of its total assets, and

(B) 120 percent or more of the adjusted basis of such section 341 assets.

Absence of the conditions described in subparagraphs (A) and (B) shall not give rise to a presumption that the corporation was not a collapsible corporation.

(2) Determination of total assets.—In determining the fair market value of the total assets of a corporation for purposes of paragraph (1) (A), there shall not be taken into account—

(A) cash,

(B) obligations which are capital assets in the hands of the corporation, and

(C) stock in any other corporation.

(d) Limitations on application of section.—In the case of gain realized by a shareholder with respect to his stock in a collapsible corporation, this section shall not apply—

(1) unless, at any time after the commencement of the manufacture, construction, or production of the property, or at the time of the purchase of the property described in subsection (b) (3) or at any time thereafter, such shareholder (A) owned (or was considered as owning) more than 5 percent in value of the outstanding stock of the corporation, or (B) owned stock which was considered as owned at such time by another shareholder who then owned (or was considered as owning) more than 5 percent in value of the outstanding stock of the corporation;

(2) to the gain recognized during a taxable year, unless more than 70 percent of such gain is attributable to the property so manufactured, constructed, produced, or purchased; and

(3) to gain realized after the expiration of 3 years following the completion of such manufacture, construction, production, or purchase.

For purposes of paragraph (1), the ownership of stock shall be determined in accordance with the rules prescribed in paragraphs (1), (2), (3), (5), and (6) of section 544(a) (relating to personal holding companies); except that, in addition to the persons prescribed by paragraph (2) of that section, the family of an individual shall include the spouses of that individual's brothers and sisters (whether by the whole or half blood) and the spouses of that individual's lineal descendants.

(e) Exceptions to application of section.—

(1) Sales or exchanges of stock.—For purposes of subsection (a) (1), a corporation shall not be considered to be a collapsible corporation with respect to any sale or exchange of stock of the corporation by a shareholder, if, at the time of such sale or exchange, the sum of—

(A) the net unrealized appreciation in subsection (e) assets of the corporation (as defined in paragraph (5) (A)), plus

(B) if the shareholder owns more than 5 percent in value of the outstanding stock of the corporation, the net unrealized appreciation in assets of the corporation (other than assets described in subparagraph (A)) which would be subsection (e) assets under clauses (i) and (iii) of paragraph (5) (A) if the shareholder owned more than 20 percent in value of such stock, plus

(C) if the shareholder owns more than 20 percent in value of the outstanding stock of the corporation and owns, or at any time during the preceding 3-year period owned, more than 20 percent in value of the outstanding stock of any other corporation more than 70 percent in value of the assets of which are, or were at any time during which such shareholder owned during such 3-year period more than 20 percent in value of the outstanding stock, assets similar or related in service or use to assets comprising more than 70 percent in value of the assets of the corporation, the net unrealized appreciation in assets of the corporation (other than assets described in subparagraph (A)) which would be subsection (e) assets under clauses (i) and (iii) of paragraph (5) (A) if the determination whether the property, in the hands of such shareholder, would be property gain from the sale or exchange of which would under any provision of this chapter be considered in whole or in part as ordinary income, were made—

(i) by treating any sale or exchange by such shareholder of stock in such other corporation within the preceding 3-year period (but only if at the time of such sale or exchange the shareholder owned more than 20 percent in value of the outstanding stock in such other corporation) as a sale or exchange by such shareholder of his proportionate share of the assets of such other corporation, and

(ii) by treating any sale or exchange of property by such other corporation within such 3-year period (but only if at the time of such sale or exchange the shareholder owned more than 20 percent in value of the outstanding stock in such other corporation), gain or loss on which was not recognized to such other corporation under section 337(a), as a sale or exchange by such shareholder of his proportionate share of the property sold or exchanged,

does not exceed an amount equal to 15 percent of the net worth of the corporation. This paragraph shall not apply to any sale or exchange of stock to the issuing corporation or, in the case of a shareholder who owns more than 20 percent in value of the outstanding stock of the corporation, to any sale or exchange of stock by such shareholder to any person related to him (within the meaning of paragraph (8)).

(2) **Distributions in liquidation.**—For purposes of subsection (a) (2), a corporation shall not be considered to be a collapsible corporation with respect to any distribution to a shareholder pursuant to a plan of complete liquidation if, by reason of the application of paragraph (4) of this subsection, section 337(a) applies to sales or exchanges of property by the corporation within the 12-month period beginning on the date of the adoption of such plan, and if, at all times after the adoption of the plan of liquidation, the sum of—

(A) the net unrealized appreciation in subsection (e) assets of the corporation (as defined in paragraph (5) (A)), plus

(B) if the shareholder owns more than 5 percent in value of the outstanding stock of the corporation, the net unrealized appreciation in assets of the corporation described in paragraph (1) (B) (other than assets described in subparagraph (A) of this paragraph), plus

(C) if the shareholder owns more than 20 percent in value of the outstanding stock of the corporation and owns, or at any time during the preceding 3-year period owned, more than 20 percent in value of the outstanding stock of any other corporation more than 70 percent in value of the assets of which are, or were at any time during which such shareholder owned during such 3-year period more than 20 percent in value of the outstanding stock, assets similar or related in service or use to assets comprising more than 70 percent in value of the assets of the corporation, the net unrealized appreciation in assets of the corporation described in paragraph (1) (C) (other than assets described in subparagraph (A) of this paragraph),

does not exceed an amount equal to 15 percent of the net worth of the corporation.

(3) Recognition of gain in certain liquidations.—For purposes of section 333, a corporation shall not be considered to be a collapsible corporation if at all times after the adoption of the plan of liquidation, the net unrealized appreciation in subsection (e) assets of the corporation (as defined in paragraph (5) (B)) does not exceed an amount equal to 15 percent of the net worth of the corporation.

(4) Gain or loss on sales or exchanges in connection with certain liquidations.—For purposes of section 337, a corporation shall not be considered to be a collapsible corporation with respect to any sale or exchange by it of property within the 12-month period beginning on the date of the adoption of a plan of complete liquidation, if—

(A) at all times after the adoption of such plan, the net unrealized appreciation in subsection (e) assets of the corporation (as defined in paragraph (5) (A)) does not exceed an amount equal to 15 percent of the net worth of the corporation,

(B) within the 12-month period beginning on the date of the adoption of such plan, the corporation sells substantially all of the properties held by it on such date, and

(C) following the adoption of such plan, no distribution is made of any property which in the hands of the corporation or in the hands of the distributee is property in respect of which a deduction for exhaustion, wear and tear, obsolescence, amortization, or depletion is allowable.

This paragraph shall not apply with respect to any sale or exchange of property by the corporation to any shareholder who owns more than 20 percent in value of the outstanding stock of the corporation or to any person related to such shareholder (within the meaning of paragraph (8)), if such property in the hands of the corporation or in the hands of such shareholder or related person is property in respect of which a deduction for exhaustion, wear and tear, obsolescence, amortization, or depletion is allowable.

(5) Subsection (e) asset defined.—

(A) For purposes of paragraphs (1), (2), and (4), the term "subsection (e) asset" means, with respect to property held by any corporation—

(i) property (except property used in the trade or business, as defined in paragraph (9)) which in the hands of the corporation is, or, in the hands of a shareholder who owns more than 20 percent in value of the outstanding stock of the corporation, would be, property gain from the sale or exchange of which would under any provision of this chapter be considered in whole or in part as ordinary income;

(ii) property used in the trade or business (as defined in paragraph (9)), but only if the unrealized depreciation on all such property on which there is unrealized depreciation exceeds the unrealized appreciation on all such property on which there is unrealized appreciation;

(iii) if there is net unrealized appreciation on all property used in the trade or business (as defined in paragraph (9)), property used in the trade or business (as defined in paragraph (9)) which, in the hands of a shareholder who owns more than 20 percent in value of the outstanding stock of the corporation, would be property gain from the sale or exchange of which would under any provision of this chapter be considered in whole or in part as ordinary income; and

(iv) property (unless included under clause (i), (ii), or (iii)) which consists of a copyright, a literary, musical, or artistic composition, a letter or memorandum, or similar property, or any interest in any such property, if the property was created in whole or in part by the personal efforts of, or (in the case of a letter, memorandum, or similar property) was prepared, or produced in whole or in part for, any individual who owns more than 5 percent in value of the stock of the corporation.

The determination as to whether property of the corporation in the hands of the corporation is, or in the hands of a shareholder would be, property gain from the sale or exchange of which would under any provision of this chapter be considered in whole or in part as ordinary income shall be made as if all property of the corporation had been sold or exchanged to one person in one transaction.

(B) For purposes of paragraph (3), the term "subsection (e) asset" means, with respect to property held by any corporation, property described in clauses (i), (ii), (iii), and (iv) of subparagraph (A), except that clauses (i) and (iii) shall apply in respect of any shareholder who owns more than 5 percent in value of the outstanding stock of the corporation (in lieu of any shareholder who owns more than 20 percent in value of such stock).

(6) Net unrealized appreciation defined.—

(A) For purposes of this subsection, the term "net unrealized appreciation" means, with respect to the assets of a corporation, the amount by which—

(i) the unrealized appreciation in such assets on which there is unrealized appreciation, exceeds

(ii) the unrealized depreciation in such assets on which there is unrealized depreciation.

(B) For purposes of subparagraph (A) and paragraph (5) (A), the term "unrealized appreciation" means, with respect to any asset, the amount by which—

(i) the fair market value of such asset, exceeds

(ii) the adjusted basis for determining gain from the sale or other disposition of such asset.

(C) For purposes of subparagraph (A) and paragraph (5) (A), the term "unrealized depreciation" means, with respect to any asset, the amount by which—

(i) the adjusted basis for determining gain from the sale or other disposition of such asset, exceeds

(ii) the fair market value of such asset.

(D) For purposes of this paragraph (but not paragraph (5) (A)), in the case of any asset on the sale or exchange of which only a portion of the gain would under any provision of this chapter be considered as ordinary income, there shall be taken into account only an amount of the unrealized appreciation in such asset which is equal to such portion of the gain.

(7) **Net worth defined.**—For purposes of this subsection, the net worth of a corporation, as of any day, is the amount by which—

(A) (i) the fair market value of all its assets at the close of such day, plus

(ii) the amount of any distribution in complete liquidation made by it on or before such day, exceeds

(B) all its liabilities at the close of such day.

For purposes of this paragraph, the net worth of a corporation as of any day shall not take into account any increase in net worth during the one-year period ending on such day to the extent attributable to any amount received by it for stock, or as a contribution to capital or as paid-in surplus, if it appears that there was not a bona fide business purpose for the transaction in respect of which such amount was received.

(8) **Related person defined.**—For purposes of paragraphs (1) and (4), the following persons shall be considered to be related to a shareholder:

(A) If the shareholder is an individual—

(i) his spouse, ancestors, and lineal descendants, and

(ii) a corporation which is controlled by such shareholder.

(B) If the shareholder is a corporation—

(i) a corporation which controls, or is controlled by, the shareholder, and

(ii) if more than 50 percent in value of the outstanding stock of the shareholder is owned by any person, a corporation more than 50 percent in value of the outstanding stock of which is owned by the same person.

For purposes of determining the ownership of stock in applying subparagraphs (A) and (B), the rules of section 267(c) shall apply, except that the family of an individual shall include only his spouse, ancestors, and lineal descendants. For purposes of this paragraph, control means the ownership of stock possessing at least 50 percent of the total combined voting power of all classes of stock entitled to vote or at least 50 percent of the total value of shares of all classes of stock of the corporation.

(9) **Property used in the trade or business.**—For purposes of this subsection, the term "property used in the trade or business" means property

described in section 1231(b), without regard to any holding period therein provided.

(10) Ownership of stock.—For purposes of this subsection (other than paragraph (8)), the ownership of stock shall be determined in the manner prescribed in subsection (d).

(11) Corporations and shareholders not meeting requirements.—In determining whether or not any corporation is a collapsible corporation within the meaning of subsection (b), the fact that such corporation, or such corporation with respect to any of its shareholders, does not meet the requirements of paragraph (1), (2), (3), or (4) of this subsection shall not be taken into account, and such determination, in the case of a corporation which does not meet such requirements, shall be made as if this subsection had not been enacted.

(12) Nonapplication of section 1245(a).—For purposes of this subsection, the determination of whether gain from the sale or exchange of property would under any provision of this chapter be considered as ordinary income shall be made without regard to the application of sections 617(d) (1), 1245(a), 1250(a), 1251(c), 1252(a), and 1254(a).

(f) Certain sales of stock of consenting corporations.—

(1) In general.—Subsection (a) (1) shall not apply to a sale of stock of a corporation (other than a sale to the issuing corporation) if such corporation (hereinafter in this subsection referred to as "consenting corporation") consents (at such time and in such manner as the Secretary may by regulations prescribe) to have the provisions of paragraph (2) apply. Such consent shall apply with respect to each sale of stock of such corporation made within the 6-month period beginning with the date on which such consent is filed.

(2) Recognition of gain.—Except as provided in paragraph (3), if a subsection (f) asset (as defined in paragraph (4)) is disposed of at any time by a consenting corporation (or, if paragraph (3) applies, by a transferee corporation), then the amount by which—

(A) in the case of a sale, exchange, or involuntary conversion, the amount realized, or

(B) in the case of any other disposition, the fair market value of such asset,

exceeds the adjusted basis of such asset shall be treated as gain from the sale or exchange of such asset. Such gain shall be recognized notwithstanding any other provision of this subtitle, but only to the extent such gain is not recognized under any other provision of this subtitle.

(3) Exception for certain tax-free transactions.—If the basis of a subsection (f) asset in the hands of a transferee is determined by reference to its basis in the hands of the transferor by reason of the application of section 332, 351, 361, 371(a), or 374(a), then the amount of gain taken into account by the transferor under paragraph (2) shall not exceed the amount of gain recognized to the transferor on the transfer of such asset (determined without regard to this subsection). This paragraph shall apply only if the transferee—

(A) is not an organization which is exempt from tax imposed by this chapter, and

(B) agrees (at such time and in such manner as the Secretary may by regulations prescribe) to have the provisions of paragraph (2) apply to any disposition by it of such subsection (f) asset.

(4) Subsection (f) asset defined.—For purposes of this subsection—

(A) In general.—The term "subsection (f) asset" means any property which, as of the date of any sale of stock referred to in paragraph (1), is not a capital asset and is property owned by, or subject to an option to acquire held by, the consenting corporation. For purposes of this subparagraph, land or any interest in real property (other than a security interest), and unrealized receivables or fees (as defined in subsection (b) (4)), shall be treated as property which is not a capital asset.

(B) Property under construction.—If manufacture, construction, or production with respect to any property described in subparagraph (A) has commenced before any date of sale described therein, the term "subsection (f) asset" includes the property resulting from such manufacture, construction, or production.

(C) Special rule for land.—In the case of land or any interest in real property (other than a security interest) described in subparagraph (A), the term "subsection (f) asset" includes any improvements resulting from construction with respect to such property if such construction is commenced (by the consenting corporation or by a transferee corporation which has agreed to the application of paragraph (2)) within 2 years after the date of any sale described in subparagraph (A).

(5) 5-year limitation as to shareholder.—Paragraph (1) shall not apply to the sale of stock of a corporation by a shareholder if, during the 5-year period ending on the date of such sale, such shareholder (or any related person within the meaning of subsection (e) (8) (A)) sold any stock of another consenting corporation within any 6-month period beginning on a date on which a consent was filed under paragraph (1) by such other corporation.

(6) Special rule for stock ownership in other corporations.—If a corporation (hereinafter in this paragraph referred to as "owning corporation") owns 5 percent or more in value of the outstanding stock of another corporation on the date of any sale of stock of the owning corporation during a 6-month period with respect to which a consent under paragraph (1) was filed by the owning corporation, such consent shall not be valid with respect to such sale unless such other corporation has (within the 6-month period ending on the date of such sale) filed a valid consent under paragraph (1) with respect to sales of its stock. For purposes of applying paragraph (4) to such other corporation, a sale of stock of the owning corporation to which paragraph (1) applies shall be treated as a sale of stock of such other corporation. In the case of a chain of corporations connected by the 5-percent ownership requirements of this paragraph, rules similar to the rules of the two preceding sentences shall be applied.

(7) Adjustments to basis.—The Secretary shall prescribe such regulations as he may deem necessary to provide for adjustments to the basis of property to reflect gain recognized under paragraph (2).

SUBPART D—DEFINITION

§ 346.   Definition and special rule

(a) Complete liquidation.—For purposes of this subchapter, a distribution shall be treated as in complete liquidation of a corporation if the distribution is one of a series of distributions in redemption of all of the stock of the corporation pursuant to a plan.

(b) Transactions which might reach same result as partial liquidations.—The Secretary shall prescribe such regulations as may be necessary to ensure that the purposes of subsections (a) and (b) of section 222 of the Tax Equity and Fiscal Responsibility Act of 1982 (which repeal the special tax treatment for partial liquidations) may not be circumvented through the use of section 355, 351, 337, or any other provision of law or regulations (including the consolidated return regulations).

PART III—CORPORATE ORGANIZATIONS AND REORGANIZATIONS

Subpart
- A. Corporate organizations.
- B. Effects on shareholders and security holders.
- C. Effects on corporations.
- D. Special rule; definitions.

SUBPART A—CORPORATE ORGANIZATIONS

§ 351.   Transfer to corporation controlled by transferor

(a) General rule.—No gain or loss shall be recognized if property is transferred to a corporation by one or more persons solely in exchange for stock or securities in such corporation and immediately after the exchange such person or persons are in control (as defined in section 368(c)) of the corporation.

(b) Receipt of property.—If subsection (a) would apply to an exchange but for the fact that there is received, in addition to the stock or securities permitted to be received under subsection (a), other property or money, then—

    (1) gain (if any) to such recipient shall be recognized, but not in excess of—

        (A) the amount of money received, plus

        (B) the fair market value of such other property received; and

    (2) no loss to such recipient shall be recognized.

(c) Special rule.—In determining control, for purposes of this section, the fact that any corporate transferor distributes part or all of the stock which it receives in the exchange to its shareholders shall not be taken into account.

(d) Services, certain indebtedness, and accrued interest not treated as property.—For purposes of this section, stock or securities issued for—

    (1) services,

    (2) indebtedness of the transferee corporation which is not evidenced by a security, or

(3) interest on indebtedness of the transferee corporation which accrued on or after the beginning of the transferor's holding period for the debt,

shall not be considered as issued in return for property.

(e) Exceptions.—This section shall not apply to—

(1) Transfer of property to an investment company.—A transfer of property to an investment company.

(2) Title 11 or similar case.—A transfer of property of a debtor pursuant to a plan while the debtor is under the jurisdiction of a court in a title 11 or similar case (within the meaning of section 368(a)(3)(A)), to the extent that the stock or securities received in the exchange are used to satisfy the indebtedness of such debtor.

. . . . .

SUBPART B—EFFECTS ON SHAREHOLDERS AND SECURITY HOLDERS

§ 354.   Exchanges of stock and securities in certain reorganizations

(a) General rule.—

(1) In general.—No gain or loss shall be recognized if stock or securities in a corporation a party to a reorganization are, in pursuance of the plan of reorganization, exchanged solely for stock or securities in such corporation or in another corporation a party to the reorganization.

(2) Limitations.—

(A) Excess principal amount.—Paragraph (1) shall not apply if—

(i) the principal amount of any such securities received exceeds the principal amount of any such securities surrendered, or

(ii) any such securities are received and no such securities are surrendered.

(B) Property attributable to accrued interest.—Neither paragraph (1) nor so much of section 356 as relates to paragraph (1) shall apply to the extent that any stock, securities, or other property received is attributable to interest which has accrued on securities on or after the beginning of the holder's holding period.

. . . . .

(b) Exception.—

(1) In general.—Subsection (a) shall not apply to an exchange in pursuance of a plan of reorganization within the meaning of subparagraph (D) or (G) of section 368(a)(1), unless—

(A) the corporation to which the assets are transferred acquires substantially all of the assets of the transferor of such assets; and

(B) the stock, securities, and other properties received by such transferor, as well as the other properties of such transferor, are distributed in pursuance of the plan of reorganization.

. . . . .

§ 355.   Distribution of stock and securities of a controlled corporation

(a) Effect on distributees.—

(1) General rule.—If—

(A) a corporation (referred to in this section as the "distributing corporation")—

(i) distributes to a shareholder, with respect to its stock, or

(ii) distributes to a security holder, in exchange for its securities,

solely stock or securities of a corporation (referred to in this section as "controlled corporation") which it controls immediately before the distribution,

(B) the transaction was not used principally as a device for the distribution of the earnings and profits of the distributing corporation or the controlled corporation or both (but the mere fact that subsequent to the distribution stock or securities in one or more of such corporations are sold or exchanged by all or some of the distributees (other than pursuant to an arrangement negotiated or agreed upon prior to such distribution) shall not be construed to mean that the transaction was used principally as such a device),

(C) the requirements of subsection (b) (relating to active businesses) are satisfied, and

(D) as part of the distribution, the distributing corporation distributes—

(i) all of the stock and securities in the controlled corporation held by it immediately before the distribution, or

(ii) an amount of stock in the controlled corporation constituting control within the meaning of section 368(c), and it is established to the satisfaction of the Secretary that the retention by the distributing corporation of stock (or stock and securities) in the controlled corporation was not in pursuance of a plan having as one of its principal purposes the avoidance of Federal income tax,

then no gain or loss shall be recognized to (and no amount shall be includible in the income of) such shareholder or security holder on the receipt of such stock or securities.

(2) Non pro rata distributions, etc.—Paragraph (1) shall be applied without regard to the following:

(A) whether or not the distribution is pro rata with respect to all of the shareholders of the distributing corporation,

(B) whether or not the shareholder surrenders stock in the distributing corporation, and

(C) whether or not the distribution is in pursuance of a plan of reorganization (within the meaning of section 368(a) (1) (D)).

(3) Limitations.—

(A) Excess principal amount.—Paragraph (1) shall not apply if—

(i) the principal amount of the securities in the controlled corporation which are received exceeds the principal amount of the securities which are surrendered in connection with such distribution, or

(ii) securities in the controlled corporation are received and no securities are surrendered in connection with such distribution.

(B) Stock acquired in taxable transactions within 5 years treated as boot.—For purposes of this section (other than paragraph (1)(D) of this subsection) and so much of section 356 as relates to this section, stock of a controlled corporation acquired by the distributing corporation by reason of any transaction—

(i) which occurs within 5 years of the distribution of such stock, and

(ii) in which gain or loss was recognized in whole or in part,

shall not be treated as stock of such controlled corporation, but as other property.

(C) Property attributable to accrued interest.—Neither paragraph (1) nor so much of section 356 as relates to paragraph (1) shall apply to the extent that any stock, securities, or other property received is attributable to interest which has accrued on securities on or after the beginning of the holder's holding period.

. . . .

(b) Requirements as to active business.—

(1) In general.—Subsection (a) shall apply only if either—

(A) the distributing corporation, and the controlled corporation (or, if stock of more than one controlled corporation is distributed, each of such corporations), is engaged immediately after the distribution in the active conduct of a trade or business, or

(B) immediately before the distribution, the distributing corporation had no assets other than stock or securities in the controlled corporations and each of the controlled corporations is engaged immediately after the distribution in the active conduct of a trade or business.

(2) Definition.—For purposes of paragraph (1), a corporation shall be treated as engaged in the active conduct of a trade or business if and only if—

(A) it is engaged in the active conduct of a trade or business, or substantially all of its assets consist of stock and securities of a corporation controlled by it (immediately after the distribution) which is so engaged,

(B) such trade or business has been actively conducted throughout the 5-year period ending on the date of the distribution,

(C) such trade or business was not acquired within the period described in subparagraph (B) in a transaction in which gain or loss was recognized in whole or in part, and

(D) control of a corporation which (at the time of acquisition of control) was conducting such trade or business—

(i) was not acquired directly (or through one or more corporations) by another corporation within the period described in subparagraph (B), or

(ii) was so acquired by another corporation within such period, but such control was so acquired only by reason of transactions in which gain or loss was not recognized in whole or in part, or only by reason of such transactions combined with acquisitions before the beginning of such period.

§ 356.   Receipt of additional consideration

(a) Gain on exchanges.—

(1) Recognition of gain.—If—

(A) section 354 or 355 would apply to an exchange but for the fact that

(B) the property received in the exchange consists not only of property permitted by section 354 or 355 to be received without the recognition of gain but also of other property or money,

then the gain, if any, to the recipient shall be recognized, but in an amount not in excess of the sum of such money and the fair market value of such other property.

(2) Treatment as dividend.—If an exchange is described in paragraph (1) but has the effect of the distribution of a dividend (determined with the application of section 318(a)), then there shall be treated as a dividend to each distributee such an amount of the gain recognized under paragraph (1) as is not in excess of his ratable share of the undistributed earnings and profits of the corporation accumulated after February 28, 1913. The remainder, if any, of the gain recognized under paragraph (1) shall be treated as gain from the exchange of property.

(b) Additional consideration received in certain distributions.—If—

(1) section 355 would apply to a distribution but for the fact that

(2) the property received in the distribution consists not only of property permitted by section 355 to be received without the recognition of gain, but also of other property or money,

then an amount equal to the sum of such money and the fair market value of such other property shall be treated as a distribution of property to which section 301 applies.

(c) Loss.—If—

(1) section 354 would apply to an exchange, or section 355 would apply to an exchange or distribution, but for the fact that

(2) the property received in the exchange or distribution consists not only of property permitted by section 354 or 355 to be received without the recognition of gain or loss, but also of other property or money,

then no loss from the exchange or distribution shall be recognized.

(d) Securities as other property.—For purposes of this section—

(1) In general.—Except as provided in paragraph (2), the term "other property" includes securities.

(2) Exceptions.—

(A) Securities with respect to which nonrecognition of gain would be permitted.—The term "other property" does not include securities to the extent that, under section 354 or 355, such securities would be permitted to be received without the recognition of gain.

(B) Greater principal amount in section 354 exchange.—If—

(i) in an exchange described in section 354 (other than subsection (c) or (d) thereof), securities of a corporation a party to the reorganization are surrendered and securities of any corporation a party to the reorganization are received, and

(ii) the principal amount of such securities received exceeds the principal amount of such securities surrendered,

then, with respect to such securities received, the term "other property" means only the fair market value of such excess. For purposes of this subparagraph and subparagraph (C), if no securities are surrendered, the excess shall be the entire principal amount of the securities received.

(C) **Greater principal amount in section 355 transaction.**—If, in an exchange or distribution described in section 355, the principal amount of the securities in the controlled corporation which are received exceeds the principal amount of the securities in the distributing corporation which are surrendered, then, with respect to such securities received, the term "other property" means only the fair market value of such excess.

(e) **Exchanges for section 306 stock.**—Notwithstanding any other provision of this section, to the extent that any of the other property (or money) is received in exchange for section 306 stock, an amount equal to the fair market value of such other property (or the amount of such money) shall be treated as a distribution of property to which section 301 applies.

§ 357. Assumption of liability

(a) **General rule.**—Except as provided in subsections (b) and (c), if—

(1) the taxpayer receives property which would be permitted to be received under section 351, 361, 371, or 374 without the recognition of gain if it were the sole consideration, and

(2) as part of the consideration, another party to the exchange assumes a liability of the taxpayer, or acquires from the taxpayer property subject to a liability,

then such assumption or acquisition shall not be treated as money or other property, and shall not prevent the exchange from being within the provisions of section 351, 361, 371, or 374, as the case may be.

(b) **Tax avoidance purpose.**—

(1) **In general.**—If, taking into consideration the nature of the liability and the circumstances in the light of which the arrangement for the assumption or acquisition was made, it appears that the principal purpose of the taxpayer with respect to the assumption or acquisition described in subsection (a)—

(A) was a purpose to avoid Federal income tax on the exchange, or

(B) if not such purpose, was not a bona fide business purpose,

then such assumption or acquisition (in the total amount of the liability assumed or acquired pursuant to such exchange) shall, for purposes of section 351, 361, 371, or 374 (as the case may be), be considered as money received by the taxpayer on the exchange.

(2) **Burden of proof.**—In any suit or proceeding where the burden is on the taxpayer to prove such assumption or acquisition is not to be treated as money received by the taxpayer, such burden shall not be considered as sustained unless the taxpayer sustains such burden by the clear preponderance of the evidence.

(c) Liabilities in excess of basis.—

    (1) In general.—In the case of an exchange—

        (A) to which section 351 applies, or

        (B) to which section 361 applies by reason of a plan of reorganization within the meaning of section 368(a) (1) (D),

if the sum of the amount of the liabilities assumed, plus the amount of the liabilities to which the property is subject, exceeds the total of the adjusted basis of the property transferred pursuant to such exchange, then such excess shall be considered as a gain from the sale or exchange of a capital asset or of property which is not a capital asset, as the case may be.

    (2) Exceptions.—Paragraph (1) shall not apply to any exchange—

        (A) to which subsection (b)(1) of this section applies,

        (B) to which section 371 or 374 applies, or

        (C) which is pursuant to a plan of reorganization within the meaning of section 368(a)(1)(G) where no former shareholder of the transferor corporation receives any consideration for his stock.

    (3) Certain liabilities excluded.—

        (A) In general.—If a taxpayer transfers, in an exchange to which section 351 applies, a liability the payment of which either—

            (i) would give rise to a deduction, or

            (ii) would be described in section 736(a),

then, for purposes of paragraph (1), the amount of such liability shall be excluded in determining the amount of liabilities assumed or to which the property transferred is subject.

        (B) Exception.—Subparagraph (A) shall not apply to any liability to the extent that the incurrence of the liability resulted in the creation of, or an increase in, the basis of any property.

§ 358.   Basis to distributees

    (a) General rule.—In the case of an exchange to which section 351, 354, 355, 356, 361, 371(b), or 374 applies—

    (1) Nonrecognition property.—The basis of the property permitted to be received under such section without the recognition of gain or loss shall be the same as that of the property exchanged—

        (A) decreased by—

            (i) the fair market value of any other property (except money) received by the taxpayer,

            (ii) the amount of any money received by the taxpayer, and

            (iii) the amount of loss to the taxpayer which was recognized on such exchange, and

        (B) increased by—

            (i) the amount which was treated as a dividend, and

            (ii) the amount of gain to the taxpayer which was recognized on such exchange (not including any portion of such gain which was treated as a dividend).

    (2) Other property.—The basis of any other property (except money) received by the taxpayer shall be its fair market value.

(b) Allocation of basis.—

(1) **In general.**—Under regulations prescribed by the Secretary, the basis determined under subsection (a) (1) shall be allocated among the properties permitted to be received without the recognition of gain or loss.

(2) **Special rule for section 355.**—In the case of an exchange to which section 355 (or so much of section 356 as relates to section 355) applies, then in making the allocation under paragraph (1) of this subsection, there shall be taken into account not only the property so permitted to be received without the recognition of gain or loss, but also the stock or securities (if any) of the distributing corporation which are retained, and the allocation of basis shall be made among all such properties.

. . . .

(c) Section 355 transactions which are not exchanges.—For purposes of this section, a distribution to which section 355 (or so much of section 356 as relates to section 355) applies shall be treated as an exchange, and for such purposes the stock and securities of the distributing corporation which are retained shall be treated as surrendered, and received back, in the exchange.

(d) Assumption of liability.—

(1) **In general.**—Where, as part of the consideration to the taxpayer, another party to the exchange assumed a liability of the taxpayer or acquired from the taxpayer property subject to a liability, such assumption or acquisition (in the amount of the liability) shall, for purposes of this section, be treated as money received by the taxpayer on the exchange.

(2) **Exception.**—Paragraph (1) shall not apply to the amount of any liability excluded under section 357(c) (3).

(e) Exception.—This section shall not apply to property acquired by a corporation by the exchange of its stock or securities (or the stock or securities of a corporation which is in control of the acquiring corporation) as consideration in whole or in part for the transfer of the property to it.

SUBPART C—EFFECTS ON CORPORATION

§ 361. Nonrecognition of gain or loss to corporations

(a) General rule.—No gain or loss shall be recognized if a corporation a party to a reorganization exchanges property, in pursuance of the plan of reorganization, solely for stock or securities in another corporation a party to the reorganization.

(b) Exchanges not solely in kind.—

(1) **Gain.**—If subsection (a) would apply to an exchange but for the fact that the property received in exchange consists not only of stock or securities permitted by subsection (a) to be received without the recognition of gain, but also of other property or money, then—

(A) if the corporation receiving such other property or money distributes it in pursuance of the plan of reorganization, no gain to the corporation shall be recognized from the exchange, but

(B) if the corporation receiving such other property or money does not distribute it in pursuance of the plan of reorganization, the gain, if any, to the corporation shall be recognized, but in an amount not in excess of the sum of such money and the fair market value of such other property so received, which is not so distributed.

(2) Loss.—If subsection (a) would apply to an exchange but for the fact that the property received in exchange consists not only of property permitted by subsection (a) to be received without the recognition of gain or loss, but also of other property or money, then no loss from the exchange shall be recognized.

§ 362.   Basis to corporations

(a) Property acquired by issuance of stock or as paid-in surplus.—If property was acquired on or after June 22, 1954, by a corporation—

(1) in connection with a transaction to which section 351 (relating to transfer of property to corporation controlled by transferor) applies, or

(2) as paid-in surplus or as a contribution to capital,

then the basis shall be the same as it would be in the hands of the transferor, increased in the amount of gain recognized to the transferor on such transfer.

(b) Transfers to corporations.—If property was acquired by a corporation in connection with a reorganization to which this part applies, then the basis shall be the same as it would be in the hands of the transferor, increased in the amount of gain recognized to the transferor on such transfer. This subsection shall not apply if the property acquired consists of stock or securities in a corporation a party to the reorganization, unless acquired by the exchange of stock or securities of the transferee (or of a corporation which is in control of the transferee) as the consideration in whole or in part for the transfer.

(c) Special rule for certain contributions to capital.—

(1) Property other than money.—Notwithstanding subsection (a) (2), if property other than money—

(A) is acquired by a corporation, on or after June 22, 1954, as a contribution to capital, and

(B) is not contributed by a shareholder as such,

then the basis of such property shall be zero.

(2) Money.—Notwithstanding subsection (a) (2), if money—

(A) is received by a corporation, on or after June 22, 1954, as a contribution to capital, and

(B) is not contributed by a shareholder as such,

then the basis of any property acquired with such money during the 12-month period beginning on the day the contribution is received shall be reduced by the amount of such contribution. The excess (if any) of the amount of such contribution over the amount of the reduction under the preceding sentence shall be applied to the reduction (as of the last day of the period specified in the preceding sentence) of the basis of any other property held by the taxpayer. The particular properties to which the reductions required by this paragraph shall be allocated shall be determined under regulations prescribed by the Secretary.

(3) Exception for contributions in aid of construction.—The provisions of this subsection shall not apply to contributions in aid of construction to which section 118(b) applies.

SUBPART D—SPECIAL RULE; DEFINITIONS

§ 368.   Definitions relating to corporate reorganizations

(a) Reorganization.—

(1) In general.—For purposes of parts I and II and this part, the term "reorganization" means—

(A) a statutory merger or consolidation;

(B) the acquisition by one corporation, in exchange solely for all or a part of its voting stock (or in exchange solely for all or a part of the voting stock of a corporation which is in control of the acquiring corporation), of stock of another corporation if, immediately after the acquisition, the acquiring corporation has control of such other corporation (whether or not such acquiring corporation had control immediately before the acquisition);

(C) the acquisition by one corporation, in exchange solely for all or a part of its voting stock (or in exchange solely for all or a part of the voting stock of a corporation which is in control of the acquiring corporation), of substantially all of the properties of another corporation, but in determining whether the exchange is solely for stock the assumption by the acquiring corporation of a liability of the other, or the fact that property acquired is subject to a liability, shall be disregarded;

(D) a transfer by a corporation of all or a part of its assets to another corporation if immediately after the transfer the transferor, or one or more of its shareholders (including persons who were shareholders immediately before the transfer), or any combination thereof, is in control of the corporation to which the assets are transferred; but only if, in pursuance of the plan, stock or securities of the corporation to which the assets are transferred are distributed in a transaction which qualifies under section 354, 355, or 356;

(E) a recapitalization;

(F) a mere change in identity, form, or place of organization of one corporation, however effected; or

(G) a transfer by a corporation of all or part of its assets to another corporation in a title 11 or similar case; but only if, in pursuance of the plan, stock or securities of the corporation to which the assets are transferred are distributed in a transaction which qualifies under section 354, 355, or 356.

(2) Special rules relating to paragraph (1).—

(A) Reorganizations described in both paragraph (1) (C) and paragraph (1) (D).—If a transaction is described in both paragraph (1) (C) and paragraph (1) (D), then, for purposes of this subchapter, such transaction shall be treated as described only in paragraph (1) (D).

(B) Additional consideration in certain paragraph (1) (C) cases. —If—

(i) one corporation acquires substantially all of the properties of another corporation,

(ii) the acquisition would qualify under paragraph (1) (C) but for the fact that the acquiring corporation exchanges money or other property in addition to voting stock, and

(iii) the acquiring corporation acquires, solely for voting stock described in paragraph (1) (C), property of the other corporation having a fair market value which is at least 80 percent of the fair market value of all of the property of the other corporation,

then such acquisition shall (subject to subparagraph (A) of this paragraph) be treated as qualifying under paragraph (1) (C). Solely for the purpose of determining whether clause (iii) of the preceding sentence applies, the amount of any liability assumed by the acquiring corporation, and the amount of any liability to which any property acquired by the acquiring corporation is subject, shall be treated as money paid for the property.

(C) **Transfers of assets or stock to subsidiaries in certain paragraph (1)(A), (1)(B), (1)(C), and (1)(G) cases.**—A transaction otherwise qualifying under paragraph (1)(A), (1)(B), or (1)(C) shall not be disqualified by reason of the fact that part or all of the assets or stock which were acquired in the transaction are transferred to a corporation controlled by the corporation acquiring such assets or stock. A similar rule shall apply to a transaction otherwise qualifying under paragraph (1)(G) where the requirements of subparagraphs (A) and (B) of section 354(b)(1) are met with respect to the acquisition of the assets or stock.

(D) **Use of stock of controlling corporation in paragraph (1)(A) and (1)(G) cases.**—The acquisition by one corporation, in exchange for stock of a corporation (referred to in this subparagraph as "controlling corporation") which is in control of the acquiring corporation, of substantially all of the properties of another corporation shall not disqualify a transaction under paragraph (1)(A) or (1)(G) if—

(i) no stock of the acquiring corporation is used in the transaction, and

(ii) in the case of a transaction under paragraph (1)(A), such transaction would have qualified under paragraph (1)(A) had the merger been into the controlling corporation.

(E) **Statutory merger using voting stock of corporation controlling merged corporation.**—A transaction otherwise qualifying under paragraph (1) (A) shall not be disqualified by reason of the fact that stock of a corporation (referred to in this subparagraph as the "controlling corporation") which before the merger was in control of the merged corporation is used in the transaction, if—

(i) after the transaction, the corporation surviving the merger holds substantially all of its properties and of the properties of the merged corporation (other than stock of the controlling corporation distributed in the transaction); and

(ii) in the transaction, former shareholders of the surviving corporation exchanged, for an amount of voting stock of the controlling corporation, an amount of stock in the surviving corporation which constitutes control of such corporation.

(F) **Certain transactions involving 2 or more investment companies.**—

(i) If immediately before a transaction described in paragraph (1) (other than subparagraph (E) thereof), 2 or more parties to the transaction were investment companies, then the transaction shall not be considered to be a reorganization with respect to any such investment company (and its shareholders and security holders) unless it was a regulated investment company, a real estate investment trust, or a corporation which meets the requirements of clause (ii).

(ii) A corporation meets the requirements of this clause if not more than 25 percent of the value of its total assets is invested in the stock and securities of any one issuer, and not more than 50 percent of the value of its total assets is invested in the stock and securities of 5 or fewer issuers. For purposes of this clause, all members of a controlled group of corporations (within the meaning of section 1563(a)) shall be treated as one issuer.

. . . .

(3) Additional rules relating to title 11 and similar cases.—

(A) Title 11 or similar case defined.—For purposes of this part, the term "title 11 or similar case" means—

(i) a case under title 11 of the United States Code, or

(ii) a receivership, foreclosure, or similar proceeding in a Federal or State court.

(B) Transfer of assets in a title 11 or similar case.—In applying paragraph (1)(G), a transfer of the assets of a corporation shall be treated as made in a title 11 or similar case if and only if—

(i) such corporation is under the jurisdiction of the court in such case, and

(ii) the transfer is pursuant to a plan of reorganization approved by the court.

(C) Reorganizations qualifying under paragraph (1)(G) and another provision.—If a transaction would (but for this subparagraph) qualify both—

(i) under subparagraph (G) of paragraph (1), and

(ii) under any other subparagraph of paragraph (1) or under section 332 or 351,

then, for purposes of this subchapter (other than section 357(c)(1)), such transaction shall be treated as qualifying only under subparagraph (G) of paragraph (1).

. . . .

(E) Application of paragraph (2)(E)(ii).—In the case of a title 11 or similar case, the requirement of clause (ii) of paragraph (2)(E) shall be treated as met if—

(i) no former shareholder of the surviving corporation received any consideration for his stock, and

(ii) the former creditors of the surviving corporation exchanged, for an amount of voting stock of the controlling corporation, debt of the surviving corporation which had a fair market value equal to 80 percent or more of the total fair market value of the debt of the surviving corporation.

(b) Party to a reorganization.—For purposes of this part, the term "a party to a reorganization" includes—

(1) a corporation resulting from a reorganization, and

(2) both corporations, in the case of a reorganization resulting from the acquisition by one corporation of stock or properties of another.

In the case of a reorganization qualifying under paragraph (1) (B) or (1) (C) of subsection (a), if the stock exchanged for the stock or properties is stock of a corporation which is in control of the acquiring corporation, the term "a party to a reorganization" includes the corporation so controlling the acquiring corporation. In the case of a reorganization qualifying under paragraph (1) (A), (1) (B), (1) (C), or (1) (G) of subsection (a) by reason of paragraph (2) (C) of subsection (a), the term "a party to a reorganization" includes the corporation controlling the corporation to which the acquired assets or stock are transferred. In the case of a reorganization qualifying under paragraph (1) (A) or (1) (G) of subsection (a) by reason of paragraph (2) (D) of that subsection, the term "a party to a reorganization" includes the controlling corporation referred to in such paragraph (2) (D). In the case of a reorganization qualifying under subsection (a) (1) (A) by reason of subsection (a) (2) (E), the term "party to a reorganization" includes the controlling corporation referred to in subsection (a) (2) (E).

(c) Control.—For purposes of part I (other than section 304), part II, this part, and part V, the term "control" means the ownership of stock possessing at least 80 percent of the total combined voting power of all classes of stock entitled to vote and at least 80 percent of the total number of shares of all other classes of stock of the corporation.

PART V—CARRYOVERS

§ 381.   Carryovers in certain corporate acquisitions

(a) General rule.—In the case of the acquisition of assets of a corporation by another corporation—

(1) in a distribution to such other corporation to which section 332 (relating to liquidations of subsidiaries) applies, or

(2) in a transfer to which section 361 (relating to nonrecognition of gain or loss to corporations) applies, but only if the transfer is in connection with a reorganization described in subparagraph (A), (C), (D), (F), or (G) of section 368(a) (1),

the acquiring corporation shall succeed to and take into account, as of the close of the day of distribution or transfer, the items described in subsection (c) of the distributor or transferor corporation, subject to the conditions and limitations specified in subsections (b) and (c). For purposes of the preceding sentence, a reorganization shall be treated as meeting the requirements of subparagraph (D) or (G) of section 368(a)(1) only if the requirements of subparagraphs (A) and (B) of section 354(b)(1) are met.

(b) Operating rules.—Except in the case of an acquisition in connection with a reorganization described in subparagraph (F) of section 368(a) (1)—

(1) The taxable year of the distributor or transferor corporation shall end on the date of distribution or transfer.

(2) For purposes of this section, the date of distribution or transfer shall be the day on which the distribution or transfer is completed; except that, under

regulations prescribed by the Secretary, the date when substantially all of the property has been distributed or transferred may be used if the distributor or transferor corporation ceases all operations, other than liquidating activities, after such date.

(3) The corporation acquiring property in a distribution or transfer described in subsection (a) shall not be entitled to carry back a net operating loss or a net capital loss for a taxable year ending after the date of distribution or transfer to a taxable year of the distributor or transferor corporation.

(c) **Items of the distributor or transferor corporation.**—The items referred to in subsection (a) are:

(1) **Net operating loss carryovers.**—The net operating loss carryovers determined under section 172, subject to the following conditions and limitations:

(A) The taxable year of the acquiring corporation to which the net operating loss carryovers of the distributor or transferor corporation are first carried shall be the first taxable year ending after the date of distribution or transfer.

(B) In determining the net operating loss deduction, the portion of such deduction attributable to the net operating loss carryovers of the distributor or transferor corporation to the first taxable year of the acquiring corporation ending after the date of distribution or transfer shall be limited to an amount which bears the same ratio to the taxable income (determined without regard to a net operating loss deduction) of the acquiring corporation in such taxable year as the number of days in the taxable year after the date of distribution or transfer bears to the total number of days in the taxable year.

(C) For the purpose of determining the amount of the net operating loss carryovers under section 172(b) (2), a net operating loss for a taxable year (hereinafter in this subparagraph referred to as the "loss year") of a distributor or transferor corporation which ends on or before the end of a loss year of the acquiring corporation shall be considered to be a net operating loss for a year prior to such loss year of the acquiring corporation. For the same purpose, the taxable income for a "prior taxable year" (as the term is used in section 172(b) (2)) shall be computed as provided in such section; except that, if the date of distribution or transfer is on a day other than the last day of a taxable year of the acquiring corporation—

(i) such taxable year shall (for the purpose of this subparagraph only) be considered to be 2 taxable years (hereinafter in this subparagraph referred to as the "pre-acquisition part year" and the "post-acquisition part year");

(ii) the pre-acquisition part year shall begin on the same day as such taxable year begins and shall end on the date of distribution or transfer;

(iii) the post-acquisition part year shall begin on the day following the date of distribution or transfer and shall end on the same day as the end of such taxable year;

(iv) the taxable income for such taxable year (computed with the modifications specified in section 172(b) (2) (A) but without a net operating loss deduction) shall be divided between the pre-acquisition part year and the post-acquisition part year in proportion to the number of days in each;

(v) the net operating loss deduction for the pre-acquisition part year shall be determined as provided in section 172(b) (2) (B), but without regard to a net operating loss year of the distributor or transferor corporation; and

(vi) the net operating loss deduction for the post-acquisition part year shall be determined as provided in section 172(b) (2) (B).

(2) Earnings and profits.—In the case of a distribution or transfer described in subsection (a)—

(A) the earnings and profits or deficit in earnings and profits, as the case may be, of the distributor or transferor corporation shall, subject to subparagraph (B), be deemed to have been received or incurred by the acquiring corporation as of the close of the date of the distribution or transfer; and

(B) a deficit in earnings and profits of the distributor, transferor, or acquiring corporation shall be used only to offset earnings and profits accumulated after the date of transfer. For this purpose, the earnings and profits for the taxable year of the acquiring corporation in which the distribution or transfer occurs shall be deemed to have been accumulated after such distribution or transfer in an amount which bears the same ratio to the undistributed earnings and profits of the acquiring corporation for such taxable year (computed without regard to any earnings and profits received from the distributor or transferor corporation, as described in subparagraph (A) of this paragraph) as the number of days in the taxable year after the date of distribution or transfer bears to the total number of days in the taxable year.

(3) Capital loss carryover.—The capital loss carryover determined under section 1212, subject to the following conditions and limitations:

(A) The taxable year of the acquiring corporation to which the capital loss carryover of the distributor or transferor corporation is first carried shall be the first taxable year ending after the date of distribution or transfer.

(B) The capital loss carryover shall be a short-term capital loss in the taxable year determined under subparagraph (A) but shall be limited to an amount which bears the same ratio to the capital gain net income (determined without regard to a short-term capital loss attributable to capital loss carryover), if any, of the acquiring corporation in such taxable year as the number of days in the taxable year after the date of distribution or transfer bears to the total number of days in the taxable year.

(C) For purposes of determining the amount of such capital loss carryover to taxable years following the taxable year determined under subparagraph (A), the capital gain net income in the taxable year determined under subparagraph (A) shall be considered to be an amount equal to the amount determined under subparagraph (B).

(4) Method of accounting.—The acquiring corporation shall use the method of accounting used by the distributor or transferor corporation on the date of distribution or transfer unless different methods were used by several distributor or transferor corporations or by a distributor or transferor corporation and the acquiring corporation. If different methods were used, the acquiring corporation shall use the method or combination of methods of computing taxable income adopted pursuant to regulations prescribed by the Secretary.

(5) **Inventories.**—In any case in which inventories are received by the acquiring corporation, such inventories shall be taken by such corporation (in determining its income) on the same basis on which such inventories were taken by the distributor or transferor corporation, unless different methods were used by several distributor or transferor corporations or by a distributor or transferor corporation and the acquiring corporation. If different methods were used, the acquiring corporation shall use the method or combination of methods of taking inventory adopted pursuant to regulations prescribed by the Secretary.

(6) **Method of computing depreciation allowance.**—The acquiring corporation shall be treated as the distributor or transferor corporation for purposes of computing the depreciation allowance under subsections (b), (j), and (k) of section 167 on property acquired in a distribution or transfer with respect to so much of the basis in the hands of the acquiring corporation as does not exceed the adjusted basis in the hands of the distributor or transferor corporation.

[(7) Repealed. June 15, 1955, c. 143, § 2(1), 69 Stat. 134]

(8) **Installment method.**—If the acquiring corporation acquires installment obligations (the income from which the distributor or transferor corporation reports on the installment basis under section 453 or 453A) the acquiring corporation shall, for purposes of section 453 or 453A, be treated as if it were the distributor or transferor corporation.

(9) **Amortization of bond discount or premium.**—If the acquiring corporation assumes liability for bonds of the distributor or transferor corporation issued at a discount or premium, the acquiring corporation shall be treated as the distributor or transferor corporation after the date of distribution or transfer for purposes of determining the amount of amortization allowable or includible with respect to such discount or premium.

(10) **Treatment of certain mining development and exploration expenses of distributor or transferor corporation.**—The acquiring corporation shall be entitled to deduct, as if it were the distributor or transferor corporation, expenses deferred under section 616 (relating to certain development expenditures) if the distributor or transferor corporation has so elected. For the purpose of applying the limitation provided in section 617(h), if, for any taxable year, the distributor or transferor corporation was allowed a deduction under section 617(a), the acquiring corporation shall be deemed to have been allowed such deduction.

(11) **Contributions to pension plans, employees' annuity plans, and stock bonus and profit-sharing plans.**—The acquiring corporation shall be considered to be the distributor or transferor corporation after the date of distribution or transfer for the purpose of determining the amounts deductible under section 404 with respect to pension plans, employees' annuity plans, and stock bonus and profit-sharing plans.

(12) **Recovery of bad debts, prior taxes, or delinquency amounts.**—If the acquiring corporation is entitled to the recovery of bad debts, prior taxes, or delinquency amounts previously deducted or credited by the distributor or transferor corporation, the acquiring corporation shall include in its income such amounts as would have been includible by the distributor or transferor

corporation in accordance with section 111 (relating to the recovery of bad debts, prior taxes, and delinquency amounts).

(13) Involuntary conversions under section 1033.—The acquiring corporation shall be treated as the distributor or transferor corporation after the date of distribution or transfer for purposes of applying section 1033.

(14) Dividend carryover to personal holding company.—The dividend carryover (described in section 564) to taxable years ending after the date of distribution or transfer.

(15) Indebtedness of certain personal holding companies.—The acquiring corporation shall be considered to be the distributor or transferor corporation for the purpose of determining the applicability of subsection (c) of section 545, relating to deduction with respect to payment of certain indebtedness.

(16) Certain obligations of distributor or transferor corporation.—If the acquiring corporation—

    (A) assumes an obligation of the distributor or transferor corporation which, after the date of the distribution or transfer, gives rise to a liability, and

    (B) such liability, if paid or accrued by the distributor or transferor corporation, would have been deductible in computing its taxable income, the acquiring corporation shall be entitled to deduct such items when paid or accrued, as the case may be, as if such corporation were the distributor or transferor corporation. A corporation which would have been an acquiring corporation under this section if the date of distribution or transfer had occurred on or after the effective date of the provisions of this subchapter applicable to a liquidation or reorganization, as the case may be, shall be entitled, even though the date of distribution or transfer occurred before such effective date, to apply this paragraph with respect to amounts paid or accrued in taxable years beginning after December 31, 1953, on account of such obligations of the distributor or transferor corporation. This paragraph shall not apply if such obligations are reflected in the amount of stock, securities, or property transferred by the acquiring corporation to the transferor corporation for the property of the transferor corporation.

(17) Deficiency dividend of personal holding company.—If the acquiring corporation pays a deficiency dividend (as defined in section 547(d)) with respect to the distributor or transferor corporation, such distributor or transferor corporation shall, with respect to such payments, be entitled to the deficiency dividend deduction provided in section 547.

(18) Percentage depletion on extraction of ores or minerals from the waste or residue of prior mining.—The acquiring corporation shall be considered to be the distributor or transferor corporation for the purpose of determining the applicability of section 613(c) (3) (relating to extraction of ores or minerals from the ground).

(19) Charitable contributions in excess of prior years' limitation.—Contributions made in the taxable year ending on the date of distribution or transfer and the 4 prior taxable years by the distributor or transferor corporation in excess of the amount deductible under section 170(b) (2) for such taxable years shall be deductible by the acquiring corporation for its taxable years which begin after the date of distribution or transfer, subject to the limitations imposed in section 170(b) (2). In applying the preceding sentence, each taxable year of the distributor or transferor corporation beginning on or before the date of distribution or transfer shall be treated as a prior taxable year with reference to the acquiring corporation's taxable years beginning after such date.

. . . . . .

(23) Credit under section 38 for investment in certain depreciable property.—The acquiring corporation shall take into account (to the extent proper to carry out the purposes of this section and section 38, and under such regulations as may be prescribed by the Secretary) the items required to be taken into account for purposes of section 38 in respect of the distributor or transferor corporation.

. . . . .

(28) Method of computing recovery allowance for recovery property. —The acquiring corporation shall be treated as the distributor or transferor corporation for purposes of computing the deduction allowable under section 168(a) on property acquired in a distribution or transfer with respect to so much of the basis in the hands of the acquiring corporation as does not exceed the adjusted basis in the hands of the distributor or transferor corporation.

. . . . .

§ 382.   Special limitations on new operating loss carryover

(a) Certain acquisitions of stock of a corporation.—

(1) **In general.**—If—

(A) on the last day of a taxable year of a corporation,

(B) any one or more of the persons described in paragraph (4) (B) own, directly or indirectly, a percentage of the total fair market value of the participating stock or of all the stock of the corporation which exceeds by more than 60 percentage points the percentage of such stock owned by such person or persons at—

(i) the beginning of such taxable year, or

(ii) the beginning of the first or second preceding taxable year, and

(C) such increase in percentage points is attributable to—

(i) a purchase by such person or persons of such stock, or of the stock of another corporation owning stock in such corporation, or of an interest in a partnership or trust owning stock in such corporation,

(ii) an acquisition (by contribution, merger, or consolidation) of an interest in a partnership owning stock in such corporation, or an acquisition (by contribution, merger, or consolidation) by a partnership of such stock,

(iii) an exchange to which section 351 (relating to transfer to corporation controlled by transferor) applies, or an acquisition by a corporation of such stock in an exchange in which section 351 applies to the transferor,

(iv) a contribution to the capital of such corporation,

(v) a decrease in the amount of such stock outstanding or in the amount of stock outstanding of another corporation owning stock in such corporation (except a decrease resulting from a redemption to pay death taxes to which section 303 applies),

(vi) a liquidation of the interest of a partner in a partnership owning stock in such corporation, or

(vii) any combination of the transactions described in clauses (i) through (vi),

then the net operating loss carryover, if any, from such taxable year and the net operating loss carryovers, if any, from prior taxable years to such taxable year and subsequent taxable years of such corporation shall be reduced by the percentage determined under paragraph (2),[1]

(2) Reduction of net operating loss carryover.—The reduction applicable under paragraph (1) shall be the sum of the percentages determined by multiplying—

(A) by three and one-half the increase in percentage points (including fractions thereof) in excess of 60 and up to and including 80, and

(B) by one and one-half the increase in percentage points (including fractions thereof) in excess of 80.

The reduction under this paragraph shall be determined by reference to the increase in percentage points of the total fair market value of the participating stock or of all the stock, whichever increase is greater.

(3) Minimum ownership rule.—Notwithstanding the provisions of paragraph (1), a net operating loss carryover from a taxable year shall not be reduced under this subsection if, at all times during the last half of such taxable year, any of the persons described in paragraph (4) (B) (determined on the last day of the taxable year referred to in paragraph (1) (A)) owned at least 40 percent of the total fair market value of the participating stock and of all the stock of the corporation. For purposes of the preceding sentence, persons owning stock of a corporation on the last day of its first taxable year shall be considered to have owned such stock at all times during the last half of such first taxable year.

(4) Operating rules.—For purposes of this subsection—

(A) Definition of purchase.—The term "purchase" means an acquisition of stock the basis of which is determined by reference to its cost to the holder thereof.

(B) Description of person or persons.—The person or persons referred to in paragraph (1) (B) shall be the 15 persons (or such lesser number as there are persons owning the stock on the last day of the taxable year) who own the greatest percentage of the total fair market value of all the stock on the last day of that year, except that if any other person owns the same percentage of such stock at such time as is owned by one of the 15 persons, that other person shall also be included. If any of the persons are so related that the stock owned by one is attributed to the other under the rules specified in subparagraph (C), such persons shall be considered as only one person solely for the purpose of selecting the 15 persons (more or less) who own the greatest percentage of the total fair market value of all the stock.

(C) **Constructive ownership.**—Section 318 (relating to constructive ownership of stock) shall apply in determining the ownership of stock, except that section 318(a) (2) (C) and 318(a) (3) (C) shall be applied without regard to the 50 percent limitation contained therein.

(D) **Short taxable years.**—If one of the taxable years of the corporation referred to in paragraph (1) (B) is a short taxable year, then such paragraph and paragraph (6) shall be applied by substituting "first, second, or third" for "first or second" each time such phrase occurs.

(5) **Exceptions.**—This subsection shall not apply to a purchase or other acquisition of stock (or of an interest in a partnership or trust owning stock in the corporation)—

(A) from a person whose ownership of stock would be attributed to the holder by application of paragraph (4) (C) to the extent that such stock would be so attributed;

(B) if (and to the extent) the basis thereof is determined under section 1014 or 1023 (relating to property acquired from a decedent), or section 1015(a) or (b) (relating to property acquired by gift or transfers in trust);

(C) by a security holder or creditor in exchange for the relinquishment or extinguishment in whole or part of a claim against the corporation, unless the claim was acquired for the purpose of acquiring such stock;

(D) by one or more persons who were full-time employees of the corporation at all times during the period of 36 months ending on the last day of the taxable year of the corporation (or at all times during the period of the corporation's existence, if shorter);

(E) by a trust described in section 401(a) which is exempt from tax under section 501(a) and which benefits exclusively the employees (or their beneficiaries) of the corporation, including a member of a controlled group of corporations (within the meaning of section 1563(a) determined without regard to section 1563(a) (4) and (e) (3) (C)) which includes such corporation;

(F) by an employee stock ownership plan meeting the requirements of section 301(d) of the Tax Reduction Act of 1975; or

(G) in a recapitalization described in section 368(a) (1) (E).

(6) **Successive applications of subsection.**—If—

(A) a net operating loss carryover is reduced under this subsection at the end of a taxable year of a corporation, and

(B) any person described in paragraph (4) (B) who owns stock of the corporation on the last day of such taxable year does not own, on the last day of the first or second succeeding taxable year of the corporation, a greater percentage of the total fair market value of the participating stock or of all the stock of the corporation than such person owned on the last day of such taxable year,

then, for purposes of applying this subsection as of the end of the first or second succeeding taxable year (as the case may be), stock owned by such person at the end of such succeeding taxable year shall be considered owned by such person at the beginning of the first or second preceding taxable year. Other rules relating to the manner and extent of successive applications of this section in the case of increases in ownership and transfers of stock by the persons described in paragraph (4) (B) shall be prescribed by regulations issued by the Secretary.

(b) Reorganizations.—

    (1) In general.—If one corporation acquires the stock or assets of another corporation in a reorganization described in section 368(a) (1) (A), (B), (C), (D) (but only if the requirements of section 354(b) (1) are met), or (F), and if—

        (A) the acquiring or acquired corporation has a net operating loss for the taxable year which includes the date of the acquisition, or a net operating loss carryover from a prior taxable year to such taxable year, and

        (B) the shareholders (immediately before tne reorganization) of such corporation (the "loss corporation"), as the result of owning stock of the loss corporation, own (immediately after the reorganization) less than 40 percent of the total fair market value of the participating stock or of all the stock of the acquiring corporation,

then the net operating loss carryover (if any) of the loss corporation from the taxable year which includes the date of the acquisition, and the net operating loss carryovers (if any) of the loss corporation from prior taxable years to such taxable year and subsequent taxable years, shall be reduced by the percentage determined under paragraph (2).

    (2) Reduction of net operating loss carryover.—

        (A) Ownership of 20 percent or more.—If such shareholders own less than 40 percent, but not less than 20 percent, of the total fair market value of the participating stock or of all the stock of the acquiring corporation, the reduction applicable under paragraph (1) shall be the percentage equal to the number of percentage points (including fractions thereof) less than 40 percent, multiplied by three and one-half.

        (B) Ownership of less than 20 percent.—If such shareholders own less than 20 percent of the total fair market value of the participating stock or of all the stock of the acquiring corporation, the reduction applicable under paragraph (1) shall be the sum of—

            (i) the percentage that would be determined under subparagraph (A) if the shareholders owned 20 percent of such stock, plus

            (ii) the percentage equal to the number of percentage points (including fractions thereof) of such stock less than 20 percent, multiplied by one and one-half.

The reduction under this paragraph shall be determined by reference to the lesser of the percentage of the total fair market value of the participating stock or of all the stock of the acquiring corporation owned by such shareholders.

    (3) Losses of controlled corporations.—For purposes of this subsection—

        (A) Holding companies.—If, immediately before the reorganization, the acquiring or acquired corporation controls a corporation which has a net operating loss for the taxable year which includes the date of the acquisition, or a net operating loss carryover from a prior taxable year to such taxable year, the acquiring or acquired corporation, as the case may be, shall be treated as the loss corporation (whether or not such corporation is a loss corporation). The reduction, if any, so determined under paragraph (2) shall be applied to the losses of such controlled corporation.

(B) Triangular reorganizations.—Except as otherwise provided in paragraph (5), if the shareholders of the loss corporation (immediately before the reorganization) own, as a result of the reorganization, stock in a corporation controlling the acquiring corporation, such shareholders shall be treated as owning (immediately after the reorganization) a percentage of the total fair market value of the participating stock and of all the stock of the acquiring corporation owned by the controlling corporation equal to the percentage of the total fair market value of the participating stock and of all the stock, respectively, of the controlling corporation owned by such shareholders.

(4) Special rules.—For purposes of applying paragraph (1) (B)—

(A) Certain related transactions.—If, immediately before the reorganization—

(i) one or more shareholders of the loss corporation own stock of such corporation which such shareholder acquired during the 36-month period ending on the date of the acquisition in a transaction described in paragraph (1) or in subsection (a) (1) (C) (unless excepted by subsection (a) (5)), and

(ii) such shareholders own more than 50 percent of the total fair market value of the stock of another corporation a party to the reorganization, or any such shareholder is a corporation controlled by another corporation a party to the reorganization,

then such shareholders shall not be treated as shareholders of the loss corporation with respect to such stock.

(B) Certain prior ownership of loss corporation.—If, immediately before the reorganization, the acquiring or acquired corporation owns stock of the loss corporation, then paragraph (1) (B) shall be applied by treating the shareholders of the loss corporation as owning an additional amount of the total fair market value of the participating stock and of all the stock of the acquiring corporation, as a result of owning stock in the loss corporation, equal to the total fair market value of the participating stock and of all the stock, respectively, of the loss corporation owned (immediately before the reorganization) by the acquiring or acquired corporation. This subparagraph shall not apply to stock of the loss corporation owned by the acquiring or acquired corporation if such stock was acquired by such corporation within the 36-month period ending on the date of the reorganization in a transaction described in subsection (a) (1) (C) (unless excepted by subsection (a) (5)); or to a reorganization described in section 368(a) (1) (B) or (C) to the extent the acquired corporation does not distribute the stock received by it to its own shareholders.

(C) Certain asset acquisitions.—If a loss corporation receives stock of the acquiring corporation in a reorganization described in section 368(a) (1) (C) and does not distribute such stock to its shareholders, paragraph (1) (B) shall be applied by treating the shareholders of the loss corporation as owning (immediately after the reorganization) such undistributed stock in proportion to the fair market value of the stock which such shareholders own in the loss corporation.

(5) Certain stock-for-stock reorganizations.—In the case of a reorganization described in section 368(a) (1) (B) in which the acquired corporation is a loss corporation—

(A) Stock which is exchanged.—Paragraphs (1) (B) and (2) shall be applied by reference to the ownership of stock of the loss corporation (rather than the acquiring corporation) immediately after the reorganization. Shareholders of the loss corporation who exchange stock of the loss corporation shall be treated as owning (immediately after the reorganization) a percentage of the total fair market value of the participating stock and of all the stock of the loss corporation acquired in the exchange by the acquiring corporation which is equal to the percentage of the total fair market value of the participating stock and of all the stock, respectively, of the acquiring corporation owned (immediately after the reorganization) by such shareholders.

(B) Stock which is not exchanged.—Stock of the loss corporation owned by shareholders immediately before the reorganization which was not exchanged in the reorganization shall be taken into account in applying paragraph (1) (B). For purposes of the preceding sentence, the acquiring corporation (or a corporation controlled by the acquiring corporation) shall not be treated as a shareholder of the loss corporation with respect to stock of the loss corporation acquired in a transaction described in paragraph (1), or in subsection (a) (1) (C) (unless excepted by subsection (a) (5)), during the 36-month period ending on the date of the exchange.

(C) Triangular exchanges.—For purposes of applying the rules in this paragraph, if the shareholders of the loss corporation receive stock of a corporation controlling the acquiring corporation, such shareholders shall be treated as owning a percentage of the participating stock and of all the stock of the acquiring corporation owned by the controlling corporation equal to the percentage of the total fair market value of the participating stock and of all the stock, respectively, which such shareholders own of the controlling corporation immediately after the reorganization.

(6) Exceptions.—The limitations in this subsection shall not apply—

(A) if the same persons own substantially all the stock of the acquiring corporation and of the other corporation in substantially the same proportions; or

(B) to a net operating loss carryover from a taxable year if the acquiring or acquired corporation owned at least 40 percent of the total fair market value of the participating stock and of all the stock of the loss corporation at all times during the last half of such taxable year.

For purposes of subparagraph (A), if the acquiring or acquired corporation is controlled by another corporation, the shareholders of the controlling corporation shall be considered as also owning the stock owned by the controlling corporation in that proportion which the total fair market value of the stock which each shareholder owns in the controlling corporation bears to the total fair market value of all the stock in the controlling corporation.

. . . . .

(c) Rules relating to stock.—For purposes of this section—

(1) The term "stock" means all shares of stock, except stock which—

(A) is not entitled to vote,

(B) is fixed and preferred as to dividends and does not participate in corporate growth to any significant extent,

(C) has redemption and liquidation rights which do not exceed the paid-in capital or par value represented by such stock (except for a reasonable redemption premium in excess of such paid-in capital or par value), and

(D) is not convertible into another class of stock.

(2) The term "participating stock" means stock (including common stock) which represents an interest in the earnings and assets of the issuing corporation which is not limited to a stated amount of money or property or percentage of paid-in capital or par value, or by any similar formula.

(3) The Secretary shall prescribe regulations under which—

(A) stock or convertible securities shall be treated as stock or participating stock, or

(B) stock (however denoted) shall not be treated as stock or participating stock,

by reason of conversion and call rights, rights in earnings and assets, priorities and preferences as to distributions of earnings or assets, and similar factors.

1 So in original. A period was probably intended.

§ 383. Special limitations on carryovers of unused investment credits, work incentive program credits, new employee credits, alcohol fuel credits, research credits, employee stock ownership credits, foreign taxes, and capital losses

In the case of a change of ownership of a corporation in the manner described in section 382(a) or (b), the limitations provided in section 382 in such cases with respect to net operating losses shall apply in the same manner, as provided under regulations prescribed by the Secretary, with respect to any unused investment credit of the corporation under section 46(b), to any unused work incentive program credit of the corporation under section 50A(b), to any unused new employee credit of the corporation under section 53(b), to any unused credit of the corporation under section 44E(e)(2), to any unused credit of the corporation under section 44F(g)(2), to any unused credit of the corporation under section 44G(b)(2), to any excess foreign taxes of the corporation under section 904(c), and to any net capital loss of the corporation under section 1212.

PART VI—TREATMENT OF CERTAIN CORPORATE INTERESTS AS STOCK OR INDEBTEDNESS

§ 385. Treatment of certain interests in corporations as stock or indebtedness

(a) **Authority to prescribe regulations.**—The Secretary is authorized to prescribe such regulations as may be necessary or appropriate to determine whether an interest in a corporation is to be treated for purposes of this title as stock or indebtedness.

(b) **Factors.**—The regulations prescribed under this section shall set forth factors which are to be taken into account in determining with respect to a particular factual situation whether a debtor-creditor relationship exists or a corporation-shareholder relationship exists. The factors so set forth in the regulations may include among other factors:

(1) whether there is a written unconditional promise to pay on demand or on a specified date a sum certain in money in return for an adequate consideration in money or money's worth, and to pay a fixed rate of interest,

(2) whether there is subordination to or preference over any indebtedness of the corporation,

(3) the ratio of debt to equity of the corporation,

(4) whether there is convertibility into the stock of the corporation, and

(5) the relationship between holdings of stock in the corporation and holdings of the interest in question.

SUBCHAPTER D—DEFERRED COMPENSATION, ETC.

Part
I. Pension, profit-sharing, stock bonus plans, etc.
II. Certain stock options.

PART I—PENSION, PROFIT-SHARING, STOCK BONUS PLANS, ETC.

Subpart
A. General rule.
B. Special rules.
C. Special rules for multiemployer plans.*

SUBPART A—GENERAL RULE

§ 401.   Qualified pension, profit-sharing, and stock bonus plans

(a) **Requirements for qualification.**—A trust created or organized in the United States and forming part of a stock bonus, pension, or profit-sharing plan of an employer for the exclusive benefit of his employees or their beneficiaries shall constitute a qualified trust under this section—

(1) if contributions are made to the trust by such employer, or employees, or both, or by another employer who is entitled to deduct his contributions under section 404(a) (3) (B) (relating to deduction for contributions to profit-sharing and stock bonus plans), for the purpose of distributing to such employees or their beneficiaries the corpus and income of the fund accumulated by the trust in accordance with such plan;

(2) if under the trust instrument it is impossible, at any time prior to the satisfaction of all liabilities with respect to employees and their beneficiaries under the trust, for any part of the corpus or income to be (within the taxable year or thereafter) used for, or diverted to, purposes other than for the exclusive benefit of his employees or their beneficiaries (but this paragraph shall not be construed, in the case of a multiemployer plan, to prohibit the return of a contribution within 6 months after the plan administrator determines that the contribution was made by a mistake of fact or law ([1] other than a mistake relating to whether the plan is described in section

* Omitted entirely.

401(a) or the trust which is part of such plan is exempt from taxation under section 501(a), or the return of any withdrawal liability payment determined to be an overpayment within 6 months of such determination);

(3) if the plan of which such trust is a part satisfies the requirements of section 410 (relating to minimum participation standards); and

(4) If the contributions or the benefits provided under the plan do not discriminate in favor of employees who are—

    (A) officers,

    (B) shareholders, or

    (C) highly compensated.

For purposes of this paragraph, there shall be excluded from consideration employees described in section 410(b) (3) (A) and (C).

(5) A classification shall not be considered discriminatory within the meaning of paragraph (4) or section 410(b) (without regard to paragraph (1) (A) thereof) merely because it excludes employees the whole of whose remuneration constitutes "wages" under section 3121(a) (1) (relating to the Federal Insurance Contributions Act) or merely because it is limited to salaried or clerical employees. Neither shall a plan be considered discriminatory within the meaning of such provisions merely because the contributions or benefits of or on behalf of the employees under the plan bear a uniform relationship to the total compensation, or the basic or regular rate of compensation, of such employees, or merely because the contributions or benefits based on that part of an employee's remuneration which is excluded from "wages" by section 3121(a) (1) differ from the contributions or benefits based on employee's remuneration not so excluded, or differ because of any retirement benefits created under State or Federal law. For purposes of this paragraph and paragraph (10), the total compensation of an individual who is an employee within the meaning of subsection (c) (1) means such individual's earned income (as defined in subsection (c) (2)), and the basic or regular rate of compensation of such an individual shall be determined, under regulations prescribed by the Secretary, with respect to that portion of his earned income which bears the same ratio to his earned income as the basic or regular compensation of the employees under the plan bears to the total compensation of such employees. For purposes of determining whether two or more plans of an employer satisfy the requirements of paragraph (4) when considered as a single plan, if the amount of contributions on behalf of the employees allowed as a deduction under section 404 for the taxable year with respect to such plans, taken together, bears a uniform relationship to the total compensation, or the basic or regular rate of compensation, of such employees, the plans shall not be considered discriminatory merely because the rights of employees to, or derived from, the employer contributions under the separate plans do not become nonforfeitable at the same rate. For the purposes of determining whether two or more plans of an employer satisfy the requirements of paragraph (4) when considered as a single plan, if the employees' rights to benefits under the separate plans do not become nonforfeitable at the same rate, but the levels of benefits provided by the separate plans satisfy the requirements of regulations prescribed by the Secretary to take account of the differences in such rates, the plans shall not be considered discriminatory merely because of the difference in such rates. For purposes of determining whether one or more plans of an employer satisfy the requirements of paragraph (4) and of section 410(b), an employer

may take into account all simplified employee pensions to which only the employer contributes.

(6) A plan shall be considered as meeting the requirements of paragraph (3) during the whole of any taxable year of the plan if on one day in each quarter it satisfied such requirements.

(7) A trust shall not constitute a qualified trust under this section unless the plan of which such trust is a part satisfies the requirements of section 411 (relating to minimum vesting standards).

(8) A trust forming part of a pension plan shall not constitute a qualified trust under this section unless the plan provides that forfeitures must not be applied to increase the benefits any employee would otherwise receive under the plan.

(9) **Required distributions.—**

(A) **Before death.**—A trust forming part of a plan shall not constitute a qualified trust under this section unless the plan provides that the entire interest of each employee—

(i) either will be distributed to him not later than his taxable year in which he attains age 70½ or, in the case of an employee other than a key employee who is a participant in a top-heavy plan, in which he retires, whichever is the later, or

(ii) will be distributed, commencing not later than such taxable year—

(I) in accordance with regulations prescribed by the Secretary, over the life of such employee or over the lives of such employee and his spouse, or

(II) in accordance with such regulations, over a period not extending beyond the life expectancy of such employee or the life expectancy of such employee and his spouse.

(B) **After death.**—A trust forming part of a plan shall not constitute a qualified trust under this section unless the plan provides that if—

(i) an employee dies before his entire interest has been distributed to him, or

(ii) distribution has been commenced in accordance with subparagraph (A)(ii) to his surviving spouse and such surviving spouse dies before his entire interest has been distributed to such surviving spouse,

his entire interest (or the remaining part of such interest if distribution thereof has commenced) will be distributed within 5 years after his death (or the death of his surviving spouse). The preceding sentence shall not apply if the distribution of the interest of the employee has commenced and such distribution is for a term certain over a period permitted under subparagraph (A)(ii)(II).

(10) **Other requirements.—**

(A) **Plans benefiting owner-employees.**—In the case of any plan which provides contributions or benefits for employees some or all of whom are owner-employees (as defined in subsection (c)(3)), a trust forming part of such plan shall constitute a qualified trust under this section only if the requirements of subsection (d) are also met.

(B) Top-heavy plans.—

(i) In general.—In the case of any top-heavy plan, a trust forming part of such plan shall constitute a qualified trust under this section only if the requirements of section 416 are met.

(ii) Plans which may become top-heavy.—Except to the extent provided in regulations, a trust forming part of a plan (whether or not a top-heavy plan) shall constitute a qualified trust under this section only if such plan contains provisions—

(I) which will take effect if such plan becomes a top-heavy plan, and

(II) which meet the requirements of section 416.

(11) (A) A trust shall not constitute a qualified trust under this section if the plan of which such trust is a part provides for the payment of benefits in the form of an annuity unless such plan provides for the payment of annuity benefits in a form having the effect of a qualified joint and survivor annuity.

(B) Notwithstanding the provisions of subparagraph (A), in the case of a plan which provides for the payment of benefits before the normal retirement age (as defined in section 411(a) (8)), the plan is not required to provide for the payment of annuity benefits in a form having the effect of a qualified joint and survivor annuity during the period beginning on the date on which the employee enters into the plan as a participant and ending on the later of—

(i) the date the employee reaches the earliest retirement age under the plan, or

(ii) the first day of the 120th month beginning before the date on which the employee reaches normal retirement age.

(C) A plan described in subparagraph (B) does not meet the requirements of subparagraph (A) unless, under the plan, a participant has a reasonable period during which he may elect the qualified joint and survivor annuity form with respect to the period beginning on the date on which the period described in subparagraph (B) ends and ending on the date on which he reaches normal retirement age (as defined in section 411(a) (8)) if he continues his employment during that period. A plan does not meet the requirements of this subparagraph unless, in the case of such an election, the payments under the survivor annuity are not less than the payments which would have been made under the joint annuity to which the participant would have been entitled if he made an election described in this subparagraph immediately prior to his retirement and if his retirement had occurred on the day before his death and within the period within which an election can be made.

(D) A plan shall not be treated as not satisfying the requirements of this paragraph solely because the spouse of the participant is not entitled to receive a survivor annuity (whether or not an election described in subparagraph (C) has been made under subparagraph (C)) unless the participant and his spouse have been married throughout the 1-year period ending on the date of such participant's death.

(E) A plan shall not be treated as satisfying the requirements of this paragraph unless, under the plan, each participant has a reasonable period (as described by the Secretary by regulations) before the annuity starting date during which he may elect in writing (after having received a written explanation of the terms and conditions of the joint and survivor annuity and the effect of an election under this subparagraph) not to take such joint and survivor annuity.

(F) A plan shall not be treated as not satisfying the requirements of this paragraph solely because under the plan there is a provision that any election described in subparagraph (C) or (E), and any revocation of any such election, does not become effective (or ceases to be effective) if the participant dies within a period (not in excess of 2 years) beginning on the date of such election or revocation, as the case may be. The preceding sentence does not apply unless the plan provision described in the preceding sentence also provides that such an election or revocation will be given effect in any case in which—

(i) the participant dies from accidental causes,

(ii) a failure to give effect to the election or revocation would deprive the participant's survivor of a survivor annuity, and

(iii) such election or revocation is made before such accident occurred.

(G) For purposes of this paragraph—

(i) the term "annuity starting date" means the first day of the first period for which an amount is received as an annuity (whether by reason of retirement or by reason of disability),

(ii) the term "earliest retirement age" means the earliest date on which, under the plan, the participant could elect to receive retirement benefits, and

(iii) the term "qualified joint and survivor annuity" means an annuity for the life of the participant with a survivor annuity for the life of his spouse which is not less than one-half of, or greater than, the amount of the annuity payable during the joint lives of the participant and his spouse and which is the actuarial equivalent of a single life annuity for the life of the participant.

For purposes of this paragraph, a plan may take into account in any equitable manner (as determined by the Secretary) any increased costs resulting from providing joint and survivor annuity benefits.

(H) This paragraph shall apply only if—

(i) the annuity starting date did not occur before the effective date of this paragraph, and

(ii) the participant was an active participant in the plan on or after such effective date.

(12) A trust shall not constitute a qualified trust under this section unless the plan of which such trust is a part provides that in the case of any merger or consolidation with, or transfer of assets or liabilities to, any other plan after September 2, 1974, each participant in the plan would (if the plan then terminated) receive a benefit immediately after the merger, consolidation, or transfer which is equal to or greater than the benefit he would have been entitled to receive immediately before the merger, consolidation, or transfer (if the plan had then terminated). The preceding sentence does not apply to any multiemployer plan with respect to any transaction to the extent that participants either before or after the transaction are covered under a

multiemployer plan to which title IV of the Employee Retirement Income Security Act of 1974 applies.

(13) A trust shall not constitute a qualified trust under this section unless the plan of which such trust is a part provides that benefits provided under the plan may not be assigned or alienated. For purposes of the preceding sentence, there shall not be taken into account any voluntary and revocable assignment of not to exceed 10 percent of any benefit payment made by any participant who is receiving benefits under the plan unless the assignment or alienation is made for purposes of defraying plan administration costs. For purposes of this paragraph a loan made to a participant or beneficiary shall not be treated as an assignment or alienation if such loan is secured by the participant's accrued nonforfeitable benefit and is exempt from the tax imposed by section 4975 (relating to tax on prohibited transactions) by reason of section 4975(d) (1). This paragraph shall take effect on January 1, 1976 and shall not apply to assignments which were irrevocable on September 2, 1974.

(14) A trust shall not constitute a qualified trust under this section unless the plan of which such trust is a part provides that, unless the participant otherwise elects, the payment of benefits under the plan to the participant will begin not later than the 60th day after the latest of the close of the plan year in which—

(A) the date on which the participant attains the earlier of age 65 or the normal retirement age specified under the plan,

(B) occurs the 10th anniversary of the year in which the participant commenced participation in the plan, or

(C) the participant terminates his service with the employer.

In the case of a plan which provides for the payment of an early retirement benefit, a trust forming a part of such plan shall not constitute a qualified trust under this section unless a participant who satisfied the service requirements for such early retirement benefit, but separated from the service (with any nonforfeitable right to an accrued benefit) before satisfying the age requirement for such early retirement benefit, is entitled upon satisfaction of such age requirement to receive a benefit not less than the benefit to which he would be entitled at the normal retirement age, actuarially, reduced under regulations prescribed by the Secretary.

(15) a trust shall not constitute a qualified trust under this section unless under the plan of which such trust is a part—

(A) in the case of a participant or beneficiary who is receiving benefits under such plan, or

(B) in the case of a participant who is separated from the service and who has nonforfeitable rights to benefits,

such benefits are not decreased by reason of any increase in the benefit levels payable under title II of the Social Security Act or any increase in the wage base under such title II, if such increase takes place after September 2, 1974, or (if later) the earlier of the date of first receipt of such benefits or the date of such separation, as the case may be.

(16) A trust shall not constitute a qualified trust under this section if the plan of which such trust is a part provides for benefits or contributions which exceed the limitations of section 415.

. . . . .

(*l*) Nondiscriminatory coordination of defined contribution plans with OASDI.—

   (1) In general.—Notwithstanding subsection (a)(5), the coordination of a defined contribution plan with OASDI meets the requirements of subsection (a)(4) only if the total contributions with respect to each participant, when increased by the OASDI contributions, bear a uniform relationship—

      (A) to the total compensation of such employee, or

      (B) to the basic or regular rate of compensation of such employee.

   (2) Definitions.—For purposes of paragraph (1)—

      (A) OASDI contributions.—The term "OASDI contributions" means the product of—

         (i) so much of the remuneration paid by the employer to the employee during the plan year as—

            (I) constitutes wages (within the meaning of section 3121(a) without regard to paragraph (1) thereof), and

            (II) does not exceed the contribution and benefit base applicable under OASDI at the beginning of the plan year, multiplied by

         (ii) the rate of tax applicable under section 3111(a) (relating to employer's OASDI tax) at the beginning of the plan year.

In the case of an individual who is an employee within the meaning of subsection (c)(1), the preceding sentence shall be applied by taking into account his earned income (as defined in subsection (c)(2)).

      (B) OASDI.—The term "OASDI" means the system of old-age, survivors, and disability insurance established under title II of the Social Security Act and the Federal Insurance Contributions Act.

      (C) Remuneration.—The term "remuneration" means—

         (i) total compensation, or

         (ii) basic or regular rate of compensation,

whichever is used in determining contributions or benefits under the plan.

   (3) Determination of compensation, etc., of self-employed individuals.—For purposes of this subsection, in the case of an individual who is an employee within the meaning of subsection (c)(1)—

      (A) his total compensation shall include his earned income (as defined in subsection (c)(2)), and

      (B) his basic or regular rate of compensation shall be determined (under regulations prescribed by the Secretary) with respect to that portion of his earned income which bears the same ratio to his earned income as the basic or regular compensation of the employees under the plan (other than employees within the meaning of subsection (c)(1)) bears to the total compensation of such employees.

      .   .   .   .   .   .

---

1 So in original. No closing parenthesis.

§ 402.   Taxability of beneficiary of employees' trust

(a) Taxability of beneficiary of exempt trust.—

(1) General rule.—Except as provided in paragraphs (2) and (4), the amount actually distributed to any distributee by any employees' trust described in section 401(a) which is exempt from tax under section 501(a) shall be taxable to him, in the year in which so distributed, under section 72 (relating to annuities). The amount actually distributed to any distributee shall not include net unrealized appreciation in securities of the employer corporation attributable to the amount contributed by the employee (other than deductible employee contributions within the meaning of section 72(*o*)(5)). Such net unrealized appreciation and the resulting adjustments to basis of such securities shall be determined in accordance with regulations prescribed by the Secretary.

(2) Capital gains treatment for portion of lump sum distributions.—In the case of an employee trust described in section 401(a), which is exempt from tax under section 501(a), so much of the total taxable amount (as defined in subparagraph (D) of subsection (e) (4)) of a lump sum distribution as is equal to the product of such total taxable amount multiplied by a fraction—

    (A) the numerator of which is the number of calendar years of active participation by the employee in such plan before January 1, 1974, and

    (B) the denominator of which is the number of calendar years of active participation by the employee in such plan,

shall be treated as a gain from the sale or exchange of a capital asset held for more than 1 year. For purposes of computing the fraction described in this paragraph and the fraction under subsection (e) (4) (E), the Secretary may prescribe regulations under which plan years may be used in lieu of calendar years. For purposes of this paragraph, in the case of an individual who is an employee without regard to section 401(c) (1), determination of whether or not any distribution is a lump sum distribution shall be made without regard to the requirement that an election be made under subsection (e) (4) (B), but no distribution to any taxpayer other than an individual, estate, or trust may be treated as a lump sum distribution under this paragraph.

. . . .

(5) Rollover amounts.—

    (A) General rule.—If—

        (i) the balance to the credit of an employee in a qualified trust is paid to him in a qualifying rollover distribution,

        (ii) the employee transfers any portion of the property he receives in such distribution to an eligible retirement plan, and

        (iii) in the case of a distribution of property other than money, the amount so transferred consists of the property distributed,

then such distribution (to the extent so transferred) shall not be includible in gross income for the taxable year in which paid.

    (B) Maximum amount which may be rolled over.—In the case of any qualifying rollover distribution, the maximum amount transferred to which subparagraph (A) applies shall not exceed the fair market value of all the property the employee receives in the distribution, reduced by the employee contributions (other than accumulated deductible employee contributions within the meaning of section 75(*o*)(5)).

(C) Transfer must be made within 60 days of receipt.—Subparagraph (A) shall not apply to any transfer of a distribution made after the 60th day following the day on which the employee received the property distributed.

(D) Definitions.—For purposes of this paragraph—

(i) Qualifying rollover distribution.—The term "qualifying rollover distribution" means 1 or more distributions—

(I) within 1 taxable year of the employee on account of a termination of the plan of which the trust is a part or, in the case of a profit-sharing or stock bonus plan, a complete discontinuance of contributions under such plan,

(II) which constitute a lump sum distribution within the meaning of subsection (e) (4) (A) (determined without reference to subparagraphs (B) and (H) of subsection (e) (4)), or

(III) which constitute a distribution of accumulated deductible employee contributions (within the meaning of section 72(*o*)(5)).

(ii) Employee contributions.—The term "employee contributions" means—

(I) the excess of the amounts considered contributed by the employee (determined by applying section 72(f)), over

(II) any amounts theretofore distributed to the employee which were not includible in gross income.

(iii) Qualified trust.—The term "qualified trust" means an employees' trust described in section 401(a) which is exempt from tax under section 501(a).

(iv) Eligible retirement plan.—The term "eligible retirement plan" means—

(I) an individual retirement account described in section 408(a),

(II) an individual retirement annuity described in section 408(b) (other than an endowment contract),

(III) a retirement bond described in section 409,

(IV) a qualified trust, and

(V) an annuity plan described in section 403(a).

(E) Special rules.—

(i) Transfer treated as rollover contribution under section 408. —For purposes of this title, a transfer described in subparagraph (A) to an eligible retirement plan described in subclause (I), (II), or (III) of subparagraph (D) (iv) shall be treated as a rollover contribution described in section 408(d) (3).

(ii) Self-employed individuals and owner-employees.—An eligible retirement plan described in subclause (IV) or (V) of subparagraph (D) (iv) shall not be treated as an eligible retirement plan for the transfer of a distribution if any part of the distribution is attributable to a trust forming part of a plan under which the employee was an employee within the meaning of section 401(c) (1) at the time contributions were made on his behalf under the plan.

. . . . .

(7) Rollover where spouse receives lump-sum distribution at death of employee.—

    (A) General rule.—If—

        (i) any portion of a qualifying rollover distribution attributable to an employee is paid to the spouse of the employee after the employee's death,

        (ii) the spouse transfers any portion of the property which the spouse receives in such distribution to an individual retirement plan, and

        (iii) in the case of a distribution of property other than money, the amount so transferred consists of the property distributed,

then such distribution (to the extent so transferred) shall not be includible in gross income for the taxable year in which paid.

    (B) Certain rules made applicable.—Rules similar to the rules of subparagraphs (B) through (E) of paragraph (5) and of paragraph (6) shall apply for purposes of this paragraph.

    (8) Cash or deferred arrangements.—For purposes of this title, contributions made by an employer on behalf of an employee to a trust which is a part of a qualified cash or deferred arrangement (as defined in section 401(k) (2)) shall not be treated as distributed or made available to the employee nor as contributions made to the trust by the employee merely because the arrangement includes provisions under which the employee has an election whether the contribution will be made to the trust or received by the employee in cash.

  (b) Taxability of beneficiary of nonexempt trust.—Contributions to an employees' trust made by an employer during a taxable year of the employer which ends within or with a taxable year of the trust for which the trust is not exempt from tax under section 501(a) shall be included in the gross income of the employee in accordance with section 83 (relating to property transferred in connection with performance of services), except that the value of the employee's interest in the trust shall be substituted for the fair market value of the property for purposes of applying such section. The amount actually distributed or made available to any distributee by any such trust shall be taxable to him in the year in which so distributed or made available, under section 72 (relating to annuities), except that distributions of income of such trust before the annuity starting date (as defined in section 72(c) (4)) shall be included in the gross income of the employee without regard to section 72(e) (1) (relating to amount not received as annuities). A beneficiary of any such trust shall not be considered the owner of any portion of such trust under subpart E of part I of subchapter J (relating to grantors and others treated as substantial owners).

. . . . .

  (e) Tax on lump sum distributions.—

    (1) Imposition of separate tax on lump sum distributions.—

      (A) Separate tax.—There is hereby imposed a tax (in the amount determined under subparagraph (B)) on the ordinary income portion of a lump sum distribution.

(B) Amount of tax.—The amount of tax imposed by subparagraph (A) for any taxable year shall be an amount equal to the amount of the initial separate tax for such taxable year multiplied by a fraction, the numerator of which is the ordinary income portion of the lump sum distribution for the taxable year and the denominator of which is the total taxable amount of such distribution for such year.

(C) Initial separate tax.—The initial separate tax for any taxable year is an amount equal to 10 times the tax which would be imposed by subsection (c) of section 1 if the recipient were an individual referred to in such subsection and the taxable income were an amount equal to $2,300 plus one-tenth of the excess of—

(i) the total taxable amount of the lump sum distribution for the taxable year, over

(ii) the minimum distribution allowance.

(D) Minimum distribution allowance.—For purposes of this paragraph, the minimum distribution allowance for the taxable year is an amount equal to—

(i) the lesser of $10,000 or one-half of the total taxable amount of the lump sum distribution for the taxable year, reduced (but not below zero) by

(ii) 20 percent of the amount (if any) by which such total taxable amount exceeds $20,000.

(E) Liability for tax.—The recipient shall be liable for the tax imposed by this paragraph.

. . . .

(3) Allowance of deduction.—The ordinary income portion of a lump sum distribution for the taxable year shall be allowed as a deduction from gross income for such taxable year, but only to the extent included in the taxpayer's gross income for such taxable year.

(4) Definitions and special rules.—

(A) Lump sum distribution.—For purposes of this section and section 403, the term "lump sum distribution" means the distribution or payment within one taxable year of the recipient of the balance to the credit of an employee which becomes payable to the recipient—

(i) on account of the employee's death,

(ii) after the employee attains age 59½,

(iii) on account of the employee's separation from the service, or

(iv) after the employee has become disabled (within the meaning of section 72(m) (7))

from a trust which forms a part of a plan described in section 401(a) and which is exempt from tax under section 501 or from a plan described in section 403(a). Clause (iii) of this subparagraph shall be applied only with respect to an individual who is an employee without regard to section 401(c) (1), and clause (iv) shall be applied only with respect to an employee within the meaning of section 401(c) (1). Except for purposes of subsection (a) (2) and section 403(a) (2), a distribution of an annuity contract from a trust or annuity plan referred to in the first sentence of this subparagraph shall be treated as a lump sum distribution. For purposes of this subparagraph, a distribution to two or more trusts shall be treated as a distribution to one recipient. For purposes of this section and section 403, the balance to the credit of the employee does not include the accumulated deductible employee contributions under the plan (within the meaning of section 72(o)(5)).

(B) Election of lump sum treatment.—For purposes of this section and section 403, no amount which is not an annuity contract may be treated as a lump sum distribution under subparagraph (A) unless the taxpayer elects for the taxable year to have all such amounts received during such year so treated at the time and in the manner provided under regulations prescribed by the Secretary. Not more than one election may be made under this subparagraph with respect to any individual after such individual has attained age 59½. No election may be made under this subparagraph by any taxpayer other than an individual, an estate, or a trust. In the case of a lump sum distribution made with respect to an employee to two or more trusts, the election under this subparagraph shall be made by the personal representative of the employee.

(C) Aggregation of certain trusts and plans.—For purposes of determining the balance to the credit of an employee under subparagraph (A)—

(i) all trusts which are part of a plan shall be treated as a single trust, all pension plans maintained by the employer shall be treated as a single plan, all profit-sharing plans maintained by the employer shall be treated as a single plan, and all stock bonus plans maintained by the employer shall be treated as a single plan, and

(ii) trusts which are not qualified trusts under section 401(a) and annuity contracts which do not satisfy the requirements of section 404(a) (2) shall not be taken into account.

(D) Total taxable amount.—For purposes of this section and section 403, the term "total taxable amount" means, with respect to a lump sum distribution, the amount of such distribution which exceeds the sum of—

(i) the amounts considered contributed by the employee (determined by applying section 72(f)), which employee contributions shall be reduced by any amounts theretofore distributed to him which were not includible in gross income, and

(ii) the net unrealized appreciation attributable to that part of the distribution which consists of the securities of the employer corporation so distributed.

(E) Ordinary income portion.—For purposes of this section, the term "ordinary income portion" means, with respect to a lump sum distribution, so much of the total taxable amount of such distribution as is equal to the product of such total taxable amount multiplied by a fraction—

(i) the numerator of which is the number of calendar years of active participation by the employee in such plan after December 31, 1973, and

(ii) the denominator of which is the number of calendar years of active participation by the employee in such plan.

(F) Employee.—For purposes of this subsection and subsection (a) (2), except as otherwise provided in subparagraph (A), the term "employee" includes an individual who is an employee within the meaning of section

401(c) (1) and the employer of such individual is the person treated as his employer under section 401(c) (4).

(G) Community property laws.—The provisions of this subsection, other than paragraph (3), shall be applied without regard to community property laws.

(H) Minimum period of service.—For purposes of this subsection (but not for purposes of subsection (a) (2) or section 403(a) (2) (A)), no amount distributed to an employee from or under a plan may be treated as a lump sum distributed under subparagraph (A) unless he has been a participant in the plan for 5 or more taxable years before the taxable year in which such amounts are distributed.

(I) Amounts subject to penalty.—This subsection shall not apply to amounts described in clause (ii) of subparagraph (A) of section 72(m) (5) to the extent that section 72(m) (5) applies to such amounts.

(J) Unrealized appreciation of employer securities.—In the case of any distribution including securities of the employer corporation which, without regard to the requirement of subparagraph (H), whould be treated as a lump sum distribution under subparagraph (A), there shall be excluded from gross income the net unrealized appreciation attributable to that part of the distribution which consists of securities of the employer corporation so distributed. In the case of any such distribution or any lump sum distribution including securities of the employer corporation, the amount of net unrealized appreciation of such securities and the resulting adjustments to the basis of such securities shall be determined under regulations prescribed by the Secretary. This subparagraph shall not apply to distributions of accumulated deductible employee contributions (within the meaning of section 72(*o*)(5)).

. . . . .

(L) Election to treat pre-1974 participation as post-1973 participation.—For purposes of subparagraph (E), subsection (a) (2), and section 403(a) (2), if a taxpayer elects (at the time and in the manner provided under regulations prescribed by the Secretary), all calendar years of an employee's active participation in all plans in which the employee has been an active participant shall be considered years of active participation by such employee after December 31, 1973. An election made under this subparagraph, once made, shall be irrevocable and shall apply to all lump-sum distributions received by the taxpayer with respect to the employee. This subparagraph shall not apply if the taxpayer received a lump-sum distribution in a previous taxable year of the employee beginning after December 31, 1975, unless no portion of such lump-sum distribution was treated under subsection (a) (2) or section 403(a) (2) as gain from the sale or exchange of a capital asset held for more than 1 year.

§ 403.   Taxation of employee annuities

(a) Taxability of beneficiary under a qualified annuity plan.—

    (1) General rule.—Except as provided in paragraph (2), if an annuity contract is purchased by an employer for an employee under a plan which meets the requirements of section 404(a) (2) (whether or not the employer deducts the amounts paid for the contract under such section), the employee shall include in his gross income the amounts received under such contract for the year received as provided in section 72 (relating to annuities).

(2) Capital gains treatment for certain distributions.—

(A) General rule.—If—

(i) an annuity contract is purchased by an employer for an employee under a plan described in paragraph (1);

(ii) such plan requires that refunds of contributions with respect to annuity contracts purchased under such plan be used to reduce subsequent premiums on the contracts under the plan; and

(iii) a lump sum distribution (as defined in section 402(e) (4) (A)) is paid to the recipient,

so much of the total taxable amount (as defined in section 402(e) (4) (D)) of such distribution as is equal to the product of such total taxable amount multiplied by the fraction described in section 402(a) (2) shall be treated as a gain from the sale or exchange of a capital asset held for more than 1 year. For purposes of this paragraph, in the case of an individual who is an employee without regard to section 401(c) (1), determination of whether or not any distribution is a lump sum distribution shall be made without regard to the requirement that an election be made under subsection (e) (4) (B) of section 402, but no distribution to any taxpayer other than an individual, estate, or trust may be treated as a lump sum distribution under this paragraph.

. . . . .

(3) Self-employed individuals.—For purposes of this subsection, the term "employee" includes an individual who is an employee within the meaning of section 401(c) (1), and the employer of such individual is the person treated as his employer under section 401(c) (4).

(4) Rollover amounts.—

(A) General rule.—If—

(i) the balance to the credit of an employee in an employee annuity described in paragraph (1) is paid to him in a qualifying rollover distribution,

(ii) the employee transfers any portion of the property he receives in such distribution to an eligible retirement plan, and

(iii) in the case of a distribution of property other than money, the amount so transferred consists of the property distributed,

then such distribution (to the extent so transferred) shall not be includible in gross income for the taxable year in which paid.

(B) Certain rules made applicable.—Rules similar to the rules of subparagraphs (B) through (E) of section 402(a) (5) and of paragraphs (6) and (7) of section 402(a) shall apply for purposes of subparagraph (A).

(b) Taxability of beneficiary under annuity purchased by section 501(c) (3) organization or public school.—

(1) General rule.—If—

(A) an annuity contract is purchased—

(i) for an employee by an employer described in section 501(c) (3) which is exempt from tax under section 501(a), or

(ii) for an employee (other than an employee described in clause (i)), who performs services for an educational organization described in section 170(b) (1) (A) (ii), by an employer which is a State, a political subdivision of a State, or an agency or instrumentality of any one or more of the foregoing,

(B) such annuity contract is not subject to subsection (a), and

(C) the employee's rights under the contract are nonforfeitable, except for failure to pay future premiums,

then amounts contributed by such employer for such annuity contract on or after such rights become nonforfeitable shall be excluded from the gross income of the employee for the taxable year to the extent that the aggregate of such amounts does not exceed the exclusion allowance for such taxable year. The employee shall include in his gross income the amounts received under such contract for the year received as provided in section 72 (relating to annuities). For purposes of applying the rules of this subsection to amounts contributed by an employer for a taxable year, amounts transferred to a contract described in this paragraph by reason of a rollover contribution described in paragraph (8) of this subsection or section 408(d) (3) (A) (iii) or 409(b) (3) (C) shall not be considered contributed by such employer.

. . . . .

(8) Rollover amounts.—

(A) General rule.—If—

(i) the balance to the credit of an employee is paid to him in a qualifying distribution,

(ii) the employee transfers any portion of the property he receives in such distribution to an individual retirement plan or to an annuity contract described in paragraph (1), and

(iii) in the case of a distribution of property other than money, the property so transferred consists of the property distributed,

then such distribution (to the extent so transferred) shall not be includible in gross income for the taxable year in which paid.

(B) Qualifying distribution defined.—

(i) In general.—For purposes of subparagraph (A), the term "qualifying distribution" means 1 or more distributions from an annuity contract described in paragraph (1) which would constitute a lump sum distribution within the meaning of section 402(e) (4) (A) (determined without regard to subparagraphs (B) and (H) of section 402(e) (4)) if such annuity contract were described in subsection (a), or 1 or more distributions of accumulated deductible employee contributions (within the meaning of section 72(*o*)(5)).

(ii) Aggregation of annuity contracts.—For purposes of this paragraph, all annuity contracts described in paragraph (1) purchased by an employer shall be treated as a single contract, and section 402(e) (4) (C) shall not apply.

(C) Certain rules made applicable.—Rules similar to the rules of subparagraphs (B), (C), and (E) (i) of section 402(a) (5) and of paragraphs (6) and (7) of section 402(a) shall apply for purposes of subparagraph (A).

. . . . .

(c) Taxability of beneficiary under nonqualified annuities or under annuities purchased by exempt organizations.—Premiums paid by an employer for an annuity contract which is not subject to subsection (a) shall be included in the gross income of the employee in accordance with section 83 (relating to property transferred in connection with performance of services), except that the value of such contract shall be substituted for the fair market value of the property for purposes of applying such section. The preceding sentence shall not apply to that portion of the premiums paid which is excluded from gross income under subsection (b). The amount actually paid or made available to any beneficiary under such contract shall be taxable to him in the year in which so paid or made available under section 72 (relating to annuities).

§ 404. Deduction for contributions of an employer to an employees' trust or annuity plan and compensation under a deferred-payment plan

(a) General rule.—If contributions are paid by an employer to or under a stock bonus, pension, profit-sharing, or annuity plan, or if compensation is paid or accrued on account of any employee under a plan deferring the receipt of such compensation, such contributions or compensation shall not be deductible under section 162 (relating to trade or business expenses) or section 212 (relating to expenses for the production of income); but, if they satisfy the conditions of either of such sections, they shall be deductible under this section, subject, however, to the following limitations as to the amounts deductible in any year:

(1) Pension trusts.—

(A) In general.—In the taxable year when paid, if the contributions are paid into a pension trust, and if such taxable year ends within or with a taxable year of the trust for which the trust is exempt under section 501(a), in an amount determined as follows:

(i) the amount necessary to satisfy the minimum funding standard provided by section 412(a) for plan years ending within or with such taxable year (or for any prior plan year), if such amount is greater than the amount determined under clause (ii) or (iii) (whichever is applicable with respect to the plan),

(ii) the amount necessary to provide with respect to all of the employees under the trust the remaining unfunded cost of their past and current service credits distributed as a level amount, or a level percentage of compensation, over the remaining future service of each such employee, as determined under regulations prescribed by the Secretary, but if such remaining unfunded cost with respect to any 3 individuals is more than 50 percent of such remaining unfunded cost, the amount of such unfunded cost attributable to such individuals shall be distributed over a period of at least 5 taxable years.

(iii) an amount equal to the normal cost of the plan, as determined under regulations prescribed by the Secretary, plus, if past service or other supplementary pension or annuity credits are provided by the plan, an amount necessary to amortize such credits in equal annual payments (until fully amortized) over 10 years, as determined under regulations prescribed by the Secretary.

In determining the amount deductible in such year under the foregoing limitations the funding method and the actuarial assumptions used shall be those used for such year under section 412, and the maximum amount deductible for such year shall be an amount equal to the full funding limitation for such year determined under section 412.

. . . .

(D) **Carryover.**—Any amount paid in a taxable year in excess of the amount deductible in such year under the foregoing limitations shall be deductible in the succeeding taxable years in order of time to the extent of the difference between the amount paid and deductible in each such succeeding year and the maximum amount deductible for such year under the foregoing limitations.

(2) **Employees' annuities.**—In the taxable year when paid, in an amount determined in accordance with paragraph (1), if the contributions are paid toward the purchase of retirement annuities, or retirement annuities and medical benefits as described in section 401(h), and such purchase is a part of a plan which meets the requirements of section 401(a) (3), (4), (5), (6), (7), (8), (9), (11), (12), (13), (14), (15), (16), (19), (20), and (22) and, if applicable, the requirements of section 401(a)(10) and of section 401(d), and if refunds of premiums, if any, are applied within the current taxable year or next succeeding taxable year towards the purchase of such retirement annuities, or such retirement annuities and medical benefits.

(3) **Stock bonus and profit-sharing trusts.**—

(A) **Limits on deductible contributions.**—In the taxable year when paid, if the contributions are paid into a stock bonus or profit-sharing trust, and if such taxable year ends within or with a taxable year of the trust with respect to which the trust is exempt under section 501(a), in an amount not in excess of 15 percent of the compensation otherwise paid or accrued during the taxable year to all employees under the stock bonus or profit-sharing plan. If in any taxable year there is paid into the trust, or a similar trust then in effect, amounts less than the amounts deductible under the preceding sentence, the excess, or if no amount is paid, the amounts deductible, shall be carried forward and be deductible when paid in the succeeding taxable years in order of time, but the amount so deductible under this sentence in any such succeeding taxable year shall not exceed 15 percent of the compensation otherwise paid or accrued during such succeeding taxable year to the beneficiaries under the plan, but the amount so deductible under this sentence in any one succeeding taxable year together with the amount so deductible under the first sentence of this subparagraph shall not exceed 25 percent of the compensation otherwise paid or accrued during such taxable year to the beneficiaries under the plan. In addition, any amount paid into the trust in any taxable year in excess of the amount allowable with respect to such year under the preceding provisions of this subparagraph shall be deductible in the succeeding taxable years in order of time, but the amount so deductible under this sentence in any one such succeeding taxable year together with the amount allowable under the first sentence of this subparagraph shall not exceed 15 percent of the compensation otherwise paid or accrued during such taxable year to the beneficiaries under the plan. The term "stock bonus or profit-sharing trust", as used in this subparagraph, shall not include any trust designed to provide benefits upon retirement and covering a period of years, if under the plan the amounts to be contributed by the employer can be determined actuarially as provided in paragraph (1). If the contributions are made to 2 or more stock bonus or profit-sharing trusts, such trusts shall be considered a single trust for purposes of applying the limitations in this subparagraph.

. . . . .

(5) **Other plans.**—If the plan is not one included in paragraph (1), (2), or (3), in the taxable year in which an amount attributable to the contribution is includible in the gross income of employees participating in the plan, but, in the case of a plan in which more than one employee participates only if separate accounts are maintained for each employee.

(6) **Time when contributions deemed made.**—For purposes of paragraphs (1), (2), and (3), a taxpayer shall be deemed to have made a payment on the last day of the preceding taxable year if the payment is on account of such taxable year and is made not later than the time prescribed by law for filing the return for such taxable year (including extensions thereof).

(7) **Limit on deductions.**—If amounts are deductible under paragraphs (1) and (3), or (2) and (3), or (1), (2), and (3), in connection with two or more trusts, or one or more trusts and an annuity plan, the total amount deductible in a taxable year under such trusts and plans shall not exceed the greater of 25 percent of the compensation otherwise paid or accrued during the taxable year to the beneficiaries of the trusts or plans, or the amount of contributions made to or under the trusts or plans to the extent such contributions do not exceed the amount of employer contributions necessary to satisfy the minimum funding standard provided by section 412 for the plan year which ends with or within such taxable year (or for any prior plan year). In addition, any amount paid into such trust or under such annuity plans in any taxable year in excess of the amount allowable with respect to such year under the preceding provisions of this paragraph shall be deductible in the succeeding taxable years in order of time, but the amount so deductible under this sentence in any one such succeeding taxable year together with the amount allowable under the first sentence of this paragraph shall not exceed 25 percent of the compensation otherwise paid or accrued during such taxable years to the beneficiaries under the trusts or plans. This paragraph shall not have the effect of reducing the amount otherwise deductible under paragraphs (1), (2), and (3), if no employee is a beneficiary under more than one trust or a trust and an annuity plan.

(8) **Self-employed individuals.**—In the case of a plan included in paragraph (1), (2), or (3) which provides contributions or benefits for employees some or all of whom are employees within the meaning of section 401(c) (1), for purposes of this section—

(A) the term "employee" includes an individual who is an employee within the meaning of section 401(c) (1), and the employer of such individual is the person treated as his employer under section 401(c) (4);

(B) the term "earned income" has the meaning assigned to it by section 401(c) (2);

(C) the contributions to such plan on behalf of an individual who is an employee within the meaning of section 401(c) (1) shall be considered to satisfy the conditions of section 162 or 212 to the extent that such contributions do not exceed the earned income of such individual derived from the trade or business with respect to which such plan is established, and to the extent that such contributions are not allocable (determined in accordance with regulations prescribed by the Secretary) to the purchase of life, accident, health, or other insurance; and

(D) any reference to compensation shall, in the case of an individual who is an employee within the meaning of section 401(c) (1), be considered to be a reference to the earned income of such individual derived from the trade or business with respect to which the plan is established.

(9) Plans benefiting self-employed individuals.—In the case of a plan included in paragraph (1), (2), or (3) which provides contributions or benefits for employees some or all of whom are employees within the meaning of section 401(c) (1)—

(A) the limitations provided by paragraphs (1), (2), (3), and (7) on the amounts deductible for any taxable year shall be computed, with respect to contributions on behalf of employees (other than employees within the meaning of section 401(c) (1)), as if such employees were the only employees for whom contributions and benefits are provided under the plan;

(B) the limitations provided by paragraphs (1), (2), (3), and (7) on the amounts deductible for any taxable year shall be computed, with respect to contributions on behalf of employees within the meaning of section 401(c) (1)—

(i) as if such employees were the only employees for whom contributions and benefits are provided under the plan, and

(ii) without regard to the second sentence of paragraph (3); and

(C) the amounts deductible under paragraphs (1), (2), (3), and (7), with respect to contributions on behalf of any employee within the meaning of section 401(c) (1), shall not exceed the applicable limitation provided in subsection (e).

. . . . .

§ 408.   Individual retirement accounts

(a) Individual retirement account.—For purposes of this section, the term "individual retirement account" means a trust created or organized in the United States for the exclusive benefit of an individual or his beneficiaries, but only if the written governing instrument creating the trust meets the following requirements:

(1) Except in the case of a rollover contribution described in subsection (d) (3) in section 402(a)(5), 402(a)(7), 403(a)(4), 403(b)(8), 405(d)(3), or 409(b)(3)(C), no contribution will be accepted unless it is in cash, and contributions will not be accepted for the taxable year in excess of $2,000 on behalf of any individual.

(2) The trustee is a bank (as defined in subsection (n) or such other person who demonstrates to the satisfaction of the Secretary that the manner in which such other person will administer the trust will be consistent with the requirements of this section.

(3) No part of the trust funds will be invested in life insurance contracts.

(4) The interest of an individual in the balance in his account is nonforfeitable.

(5) The assets of the trust will not be commingled with other property except in a common trust fund or common investment fund.

(6) The entire interest of an individual for whose benefit the trust is maintained will be distributed to him not later than the close of his taxable year in which he attains age 70½, or will be distributed, commencing before the close of such taxable year, in accordance with regulations prescribed by the Secretary, over—

(A) the life of such individual or the lives of such individual and his spouse, or

(B) a period not extending beyond the life expectancy of such individual or the life expectancy of such individual and his spouse.

(7) If—

(A) an individual for whose benefit the trust is maintained dies before his entire interest has been distributed to him, or

(B) distribution has been commenced as provided in paragraph (6) to his surviving spouse and such surviving spouse dies before the entire interest has been distributed to such spouse,

the entire interest (or the remaining part of such interest if distribution thereof has commenced) will be distributed within 5 years after his death (or the death of the surviving spouse). The preceding sentence shall not apply if distributions over a term certain commenced before the death of the individual for whose benefit the trust was maintained and the term certain is for a period permitted under paragraph (6).

(b) Individual retirement annuity.—For purposes of this section, the term "individual retirement annuity" means an annuity contract, or an endowment contract (as determined under regulations prescribed by the Secretary), issued by an insurance company which meets the following requirements:

(1) The contract is not transferable by the owner.

(2) Under the contract—

(A) the premiums are not fixed,

(B) the annual premium on behalf of any individual will not exceed $2,000, and

(C) any refund of premiums will be applied before the close of the calendar year following the year of the refund toward the payment of future premiums or the purchase of additional benefits.

(3) The entire interest of the owner will be distributed to him not later than the close of his taxable year in which he attains age 70½, or will be distributed, in accordance with regulations prescribed by the Secretary, over—

(A) the life of such owner or the lives of such owner and his spouse, or

(B) a period not extending beyond the life expectancy of such owner or the life expectancy of such owner and his spouse.

(4) If—

(A) the owner dies before his entire interest has been distributed to him, or

(B) distribution has been commenced as provided in paragraph (3) to his surviving spouse and such surviving spouse dies before the entire interest has been distributed to such spouse,

the entire interest (or the remaining part of such interest if distribution thereof has commenced) will be distributed within 5 years after his death (or the death of his surviving spouse). The preceding sentence shall not apply if distributions over a term certain commenced before the death of the owner and the term certain is for a period permitted under paragraph (3).

(5) The entire interest of the owner is nonforfeitable.

Such term does not include such an annuity contract for any taxable year of the owner in which it is disqualified on the application of subsection (e) or for any subsequent taxable year. For purposes of this subsection, no contract shall be treated as an endowment contract if it matures later than the taxable year in which the individual in whose name such contract is purchased attains age 70½; if it is not for the exclusive benefit of the individual in whose name it is purchased or his beneficiaries; or if the aggregate annual premiums under all such contracts purchased in the name of such individual for any taxable year exceed $2,000.

(c) Accounts established by employers and certain associations of employees. —A trust created or organized in the United States by an employer for the exclusive benefit of his employees or their beneficiaries, or by an association of employees (which may include employees within the meaning of section 401(c) (1)) for the exclusive benefit of its members or their beneficiaries, shall be treated as an individual retirement account (described in subsection (a)), but only if the written governing instrument creating the trust meets the following requirements:

(1) The trust satisfies the requirements of paragraphs (1) through (7) of subsection (a).

(2) There is a separate accounting for the interest of each employee or member (or spouse of an employee or member).

The assets of the trust may be held in a common fund for the account of all individuals who have an interest in the trust.

(d) Tax treatment of distributions.—

(1) **In general.**—Except as otherwise provided in this subsection, any amount paid or distributed out of an individual retirement account or under an individual retirement annuity shall be included in gross income by the payee or distributee, as the case may be, for the taxable year in which the payment or distribution is received. Notwithstanding any other provision of this title (including chapters 11 and 12), the basis [1] any person in such an account or annuity is zero.

(2) **Distributions of annuity contracts.**—Paragraph (1) does not apply to any annuity contract which meets the requirements of paragraphs (1), (3), (4), and (5) of subsection (b) and which is distributed from an individual retirement account. Section 72 applies to any such annuity contract, and for purposes of section 72 the investment in such contract is zero.

(3) **Rollover contribution.**—An amount is described in this paragraph as a rollover contribution if it meets the requirements of subparagraphs (A) and (B).

(A) **In general.**—Paragraph (1) does not apply to any amount paid or distributed out of an individual retirement account or individual retirement annuity to the individual for whose benefit the account or annuity is maintained if—

(i) the entire amount received (including money and any other property) is paid into an individual retirement account or individual retirement annuity (other than an endowment contract) or retirement bond for the benefit of such individual not later than the 60th day after the day on which he receives the payment or distribution;

(ii) the entire amount received (including money and any other property) represents the entire amount in the account or the entire value of the annuity and no amount in the account and no part of the value of the annuity is attributable to any source other than a rollover contribution from an employees' trust described in section 401(a) which is exempt from tax under section 501(a) (other than a trust forming part of a plan under which the individual was an employee within the meaning of section 401(c) (1) at the time contributions were made on his behalf under the plan), or an annuity plan described in section 403(a) (other than a plan under which the individual was an employee within the meaning of section 401(c) (1) at the time contributions were made on his behalf under the plan) and any earnings on such sums and the entire amount thereof is paid into another such trust (for the benefit of such individual) or annuity plan not later than the 60th day on which he receives the payment or distribution; or

(iii) (I) the entire amount received (including money and other property) represents the entire interest in the account or the entire value of the annuity,

(II) no amount in the account and no part of the value of the annuity is attributable to any source other than a rollover contribution from an annuity contract described in section 403(b) and any earnings on such rollover, and

(III) the entire amount thereof is paid into another annuity contract described in section 403(b) (for the benefit of such individual) not later than the 60th day after he receives the payment or distribution.

(B) **Limitation.**—This paragraph does not apply to any amount described in subparagraph (A) (i) received by an individual from an individual retirement account or individual retirement annuity if at any time during the 1-year period ending on the day of such receipt such individual received any other amount described in that subparagraph from an individual retirement account, individual retirement annuity, or a retirement bond which was not includible in his gross income because of the application of this paragraph. Clause (ii) of subparagraph (A) shall not apply to any amount paid or distributed out of an individual retirement account or an individual retirement annuity to which an amount was contributed which was treated as a rollover contribution by section 402(a) (7) (or in the case of an individual retirement annuity, such section as made applicable by section 403(a) (4) (B)).

. . . . .

(4) **Excess contributions returned before due date of return.**—Paragraph (1) does not apply to the distribution of any contribution paid during a

taxable year to an individual retirement account or for an individual retirement annuity to the extent that such contribution exceeds the amount allowable as a deduction under section 219 if—

    (A) such distribution is received on or before the day prescribed by law (including extensions of time) for filing such individual's return for such taxable year,

    (B) no deduction is allowed under section 219 with respect to such excess contribution, and

    (C) such distribution is accompanied by the amount of net income attributable to such excess contribution.

In the case of such a distribution, for purposes of section 61, any net income described in subparagraph (C) shall be deemed to have been earned and receivable in the taxable year in which such excess contribution is made.

(5) Certain distributions of excess contributions after due date for taxable year.—

    (A) In general.—In the case of any individual, if the aggregate contributions (other than rollover contributions) paid for any taxable year to an individual retirement account or for an individual retirement annuity do not exceed $2,250, paragraph (1) shall not apply to the distribution of any such contribution to the extent that such contribution exceeds the amount allowable as a deduction under section 219 for the taxable year for which the contribution was paid—

        (i) if such distribution is received after the date described in paragraph (4),

        (ii) but only to the extent that no deduction has been allowed under section 219 with respect to such excess contribution.

If employer contributions on behalf of the individual are paid for the taxable year to a simplified employee pension, the dollar limitation of the preceding sentence shall be increased by the lesser of the amount of such contributions or $15,000.

    (B) Excess rollover contributions attributable to erroneous information.—If—

        (i) the taxpayer reasonably relies on information supplied pursuant to subtitle F for determining the amount of a rollover contribution, but

        (ii) the information was erroneous,

subparagraph (A) shall be applied by increasing the dollar limit set forth therein by that portion of the excess contribution which was attributable to such information.

    (6) Transfer of account incident to divorce.—The transfer of an individual's interest in an individual retirement account, individual retirement annuity, or retirement bond to his former spouse under a divorce decree or under a written instrument incident to such divorce is not to be considered a taxable transfer made by such individual notwithstanding any other provision of this subtitle, and such interest at the time of the transfer is to be treated as an individual retirement account of such spouse, and not of such individual. Thereafter such account, annuity, or bond for purposes of this subtitle is to be treated as maintained for the benefit of such spouse.

(e) Tax treatment of accounts and annuities.—

(1) **Exemption from tax.—**Any individual retirement account is exempt from taxation under this subtitle unless such account has ceased to be an individual retirement account by reason of paragraph (2) or (3). Notwithstanding the preceding sentence, any such account is subject to the taxes imposed by section 511 (relating to imposition of tax on unrelated business income of charitable, etc. organizations).

(2) **Loss of exemption of account where employee engages in prohibited transaction.—**

(A) **In general.—**If, during any taxable year of the individual for whose benefit any individual retirement account is established, that individual or his beneficiary engages in any transaction prohibited by section 4975 with respect to such account, such account ceases to be an individual retirement account as of the first day of such taxable year. For purposes of this paragraph—

(i) the individual for whose benefit any account was established is treated as the creator of such account, and

(ii) the separate account for any individual within an individual retirement account maintained by an employer or association of employees is treated as a separate individual retirement account.

(B) **Account treated as distributing all its assets.—**In any case in which any account ceases to be an individual retirement account by reason of subparagraph (A) as of the first day of any taxable year, paragraph (1) of subsection (d) applies as if there were a distribution on such first day in an amount equal to the fair market value (on such first day) of all assets in the account (on such first day).

(3) **Effect of borrowing on annuity contract.—**If during any taxable year the owner of an individual retirement annuity borrows any money under or by use of such contract, the contract ceases to be an individual retirement annuity as of the first day of such taxable year. Such owner shall include in gross income for such year an amount equal to the fair market value of such contract as of such first day.

(4) **Effect of pledging account as security.—**If, during any taxable year of the individual for whose benefit an individual retirement account is established, that individual uses the account or any portion thereof as security for a loan, the portion so used is treated as distributed to that individual.

(5) **Purchase of endowment contract by individual retirement account.** —If the assets of an individual retirement account or any part of such assets are used to purchase an endowment contract for the benefit of the individual for whose benefit the account is established—

(A) to the extent that the amount of the assets involved in the purchase are not attributable to the purchase of life insurance, the purchase is treated as a rollover contribution described in subsection (d) (3), and

(B) to the extent that the amount of the assets involved in the purchase are attributable to the purchase of life, health, accident, or other insurance, such amounts are treated as distributed to that individual (but the provisions of subsection (f) do not apply).

(6) Commingling individual retirement account amounts in certain common trust funds and common investment funds.—Any common trust fund or common investment fund of individual retirement account assets which is exempt from taxation under this subtitle does not cease to be exempt on account of the participation or inclusion of assets of a trust exempt from taxation under section 501(a) which is described in section 401(a).

(f) Additional tax on certain amounts included in gross income before age 59½.—

(1) Early distributions from an individual retirement account, etc.—If a distribution from an individual retirement account or under an individual retirement annuity to the individual for whose benefit such account or annuity was established is made before such individual attains age 59½, his tax under this chapter for the taxable year in which such distribution is received shall be increased by an amount equal to 10 percent of the amount of the distribution which is includible in his gross income for such taxable year.

(2) Disqualification cases.—If an amount is includible in gross income for a taxable year under subsection (e) and the taxpayer has not attained age 59½ before the beginning of such taxable year, his tax under this chapter for such taxable year shall be increased by an amount equal to 10 percent of such amount so required to be included in his gross income.

(3) Disability cases.—Paragraphs (1) and (2) do not apply if the amount paid or distributed, or the disqualification of the account or annuity under subsection (e), is attributable to the taxpayer becoming disabled within the meaning of section 72(m) (7).

(g) Community property laws.—This section shall be applied without regard to any community property laws.

(h) Custodial accounts.—For purposes of this section, a custodial account shall be treated as a trust if the assets of such account are held by a bank (as defined in section 401(d) (1)) or another person who demonstrates, to the satisfaction of the Secretary, that the manner in which he will administer the account will be consistent with the requirements of this section, and if the custodial account would, except for the fact that it is not a trust, constitute an individual retirement account described in subsection (a). For purposes of this title, in the case of a custodial account treated as a trust by reason of the preceding sentence, the custodian of such account shall be treated as the trustee thereof.

---

1 So in original. Probably should be "basis of."

SUBPART B—SPECIAL RULES

§ 410.   Minimum participation standards

(a) Participation.—

(1) Minimum age and service conditions.—

(A) General rule.—A trust shall not constitute a qualified trust under section 401(a) if the plan of which it is a part requires, as a condition of participation in the plan, that an employee complete a period of service with the employer or employers maintaining the plan extending beyond the later of the following dates—

(i) the date on which the employee attains the age of 25; or

(ii) the date on which he completes 1 year of service.

(B) Special rules for certain plans.—

(i) In the case of any plan which provides that after not more than 3 years of service each participant has a right to 100 percent of his accrued benefit under the plan which is nonforfeitable (within the meaning of section 411) at the time such benefit accrues, clause (ii) of subparagraph (A) shall be applied by substituting "3 years of service" for "1 year of service".

(ii) In the case of any plan maintained exclusively for employees of an educational institution (as defined in section 170(b) (1) (A) (ii)) by an employer which is exempt from tax under section 501(a) which provides that each participant having at least 1 year of service has a right to 100 percent of his accrued benefit under the plan which is nonforfeitable (within the meaning of section 411) at the time such benefit accrues, clause (i) of subparagraph (A) shall be applied by substituting "30" for "25". This clause shall not apply to any plan to which clause (i) applies.

(2) Maximum age conditions.—A trust shall not constitute a qualified trust under section 401(a) if the plan of which it is a part excludes from participation (on the basis of age) employees who have attained a specified age, unless—

(A) the plan is a—

(i) defined benefit plan, or

(ii) target benefit plan (as defined under regulations prescribed by the Secretary), and

(B) such employees begin employment with the employer after they have attained a specified age which is not more than 5 years before the normal retirement age under the plan.

(3) Definition of year of service.—

(A) **General rule.—**For purposes of this subsection, the term "year of service" means a 12-month period during which the employee has not less than 1,000 hours of service. For purposes of this paragraph, computation of any 12-month period shall be made with reference to the date on which the employee's employment commenced, except that, under regulations prescribed by the Secretary of Labor, such computation may be made by reference to the first day of a plan year in the case of an employee who does not complete 1,000 hours of service during the 12-month period beginning on the date his employment commenced.

· · · · ·

§ 411.   Minimum vesting standards

(a) General rule.—A trust shall not constitute a qualified trust under section 401(a) unless the plan of which such trust is a part provides that an employee's right to his normal retirement benefit is nonforfeitable upon the attainment of normal retirement age (as defined in paragraph (8)) and in addition satisfies the requirements of paragraphs (1) and (2) of this subsection and the requirements of paragraph (2) of subsection (b), and in the case of a defined benefit plan, also satisfies the requirements of paragraph (1) of subsection (b).

(1) Employee contributions.—A plan satisfies the requirements of this paragraph if an employee's rights in his accrued benefit derived from his own contributions are nonforfeitable.

(2) Employer contributions.—A plan satisfies the requirements of this paragraph if it satisfies the requirements of subparagraph (A), (B), or (C).

(A) 10-year vesting.—A plan satisfies the requirements of this subparagraph if an employee who has at least 10 years of service has a nonforfeitable right to 100 percent of his accrued benefit derived from employer contributions.

(B) 5- to 15-year vesting.—A plan satisfies the requirements of this subparagraph if an employee who has completed at least 5 years of service has a nonforfeitable right to a percentage of his accrued benefit derived from employer contributions which percentage is not less than the percentage determined under the following table:

Years of service:	Nonforfeitable percentage
5	25
6	30
7	35
8	40
9	45
10	50
11	60
12	70
13	80
14	90
15 or more	100.

(C) Rule of 45.—

(i) A plan satisfies the requirements of this subparagraph if an employee who is not separated from the service, who has completed at least 5 years of service, and with respect to whom the sum of his age and years of service equals or exceeds 45, has a nonforfeitable right to a percentage of his accrued benefit derived from employer contributions determined under the following table:

If years of service equal or exceed—	and sum of age and service equals or exceeds—	then the nonforfeitable percentage is—
5	45	50
6	47	60
7	49	70
8	51	80
9	53	90
10	55	100.

(ii) Notwithstanding clause (i), a plan shall not be treated as satisfying the requirements of this subparagraph unless any employee who has completed at least 10 years of service has a nonforfeitable right to not less than 50 percent of his accrued benefit derived from employer contributions and to not less than an additional 10 percent for each additional year of service thereafter.

(3) Certain permitted forfeitures, suspensions, etc.—For purposes of this subsection—

(A) Forfeiture on account of death.—A right to an accrued benefit derived from employer contributions shall not be treated as forfeitable solely because the plan provides that it is not payable if the participant dies (except in the case of a survivor annuity which is payable as provided in section 401(a) (11)).

275

(b) Accrued benefit requirements.—

(1) General rules.—

(A) 3-percent method.—A defined benefit plan satisfies the requirements of this paragraph if the accrued benefit to which each participant is entitled upon his separation from the service is not less than—

(i) 3 percent of the normal retirement benefit to which he would be entitled if he commenced participation at the earliest possible entry age under the plan and served continuously until the earlier of age 65 or the normal retirement age specified under the plan, multiplied by

(ii) the number of years (not in excess of 33⅓) of his participation in the plan.

In the case of a plan providing retirement benefits based on compensation during any period, the normal retirement benefit to which a participant would be entitled shall be determined as if he continued to earn annually the average rate of compensation which he earned during consecutive years of service, not in excess of 10, for which his compensation was the highest. For purposes of this subparagraph, social security benefits and all other relevant factors used to compute benefits shall be treated as remaining constant as of the current year for all years after such current year.

(B) 133⅓ percent rule.—A defined benefit plan satisfies the requirements of this paragraph for a particular plan year if under the plan the accrued benefit payable at the normal retirement age is equal to the normal retirement benefit and the annual rate at which any individual who is or could be a participant can accrue the retirement benefits payable at normal retirement age under the plan for any later plan year is not more than 133⅓ percent of the annual rate at which he can accrue benefits for any plan year beginning on or after such particular plan year and before such later plan year. For purposes of this subparagraph—

(i) any amendment to the plan which is in effect for the current year shall be treated as in effect for all other plan years;

(ii) any change in an accrual rate which does not apply to any individual who is or could be a participant in the current year shall be disregarded;

(iii) the fact that benefits under the plan may be payable to certain employees before normal retirement age shall be disregarded; and

(iv) social security benefits and all other relevant factors used to compute benefits shall be treated as remaining constant as of the current year for all years after the current year.

(C) Fractional rule.—A defined benefit plan satisfies the requirements of this paragraph if the accrued benefit to which any participant is entitled upon his separation from the service is not less than a fraction of the annual benefit commencing at normal retirement age to which he would be entitled under the plan as in effect on the date of his separation if he continued to earn annually until normal retirement age the same rate of compensation upon which his normal retirement benefit would be computed under the plan, determined as if he had attained normal retirement age on the date on which any such determination is made (but taking into account no more than the 10 years of service immediately preceding his separation from service). Such fraction shall be a fraction, not exceeding 1, the numerator of which is the total number of his years of participation in the plan (as of the date of his separation from the service) and the denominator of which is the total number of years he would have participated in the plan if he separated from the service at the normal retirement age. For purposes of this subparagraph, social security benefits and all other relevant factors used to compute benefits shall be treated as remaining constant as of the current year for all years after such current year.

(D) Accrual for service before effective date.—Subparagraphs (A), (B), and (C) shall not apply with respect to years of participation before the first plan year to which this section applies, but a defined benefit plan satisfies the requirements of this subparagraph with respect to such years of participation only if the accrued benefit of any participant with respect to such years of participation is not less than the greater of—

(i) his accrued benefit determined under the plan, as in effect from time to time prior to September 2, 1974, or

(ii) an accrued benefit which is not less than one-half of the accrued benefit to which such participant would have been entitled if subparagraph (A), (B), or (C) applied with respect to such years of participation.

(E) First two years of service.—Notwithstanding subparagraphs (A), (B), and (C) of this paragraph, a plan shall not be treated as not satisfying the requirements of this paragraph solely because the accrual of benefits under the plan does not become effective until the employee has two continuous years of service. For purposes of this subparagraph, the term "years of service" has the meaning provided by section 410(a) (3) (A).

(F) Certain insured defined benefit plans.—Notwithstanding subparagraphs (A), (B), and (C), a defined benefit plan satisfies the requirements of this paragraph if such plan—

(i) is funded exclusively by the purchase of insurance contracts, and

(ii) satisfies the requirements of paragraphs (2) and (3) of section 412(i) (relating to certain insurance contract plans),

but only if an employee's accrued benefit as of any applicable date is not less than the cash surrender value his insurance contracts would have on such applicable date if the requirements of paragraphs (4), (5), and (6) of section 412(i) were satisfied.

(G) Accrued benefit may not decrease on account of increasing age or service.—Notwithstanding the preceding subparagraphs, a defined benefit plan shall be treated as not satisfying the requirements of this paragraph if the participant's accrued benefit is reduced on account of any increase in his age or service. The preceding sentence shall not apply to benefits under the plan commencing before entitlement to benefits payable under title II of the Social Security Act which benefits under the plan—

(i) do not exceed such social security benefits, and

(ii) terminate when such social security benefits commence.

(2) **Separate accounting required in certain cases.**—A plan satisfies the requirements of this paragraph if—

(A) in the case of a defined benefit plan, the plan requires separate accounting for the portion of each employee's accrued benefit derived from any voluntary employee contributions permitted under the plan; and

(B) in the case of any plan which is not a defined benefit plan, the plan requires separate accounting for each employee's accrued benefit.

. . . .

§ 412. Minimum funding standards

(a) **General rule.**—Except as provided in subsection (h), this section applies to a plan if, for any plan year beginning on or after the effective date of this section for such plan—

(1) such plan included a trust which qualified (or was determined by the Secretary to have qualified) under section 401(a), or

(2) such plan satisfied (or was determined by the Secretary to have satisfied) the requirements of section 403(a) or 405(a).

A plan to which this section applies shall have satisfied the minimum funding standard for such plan for a plan year if as of the end of such plan year, the plan does not have an accumulated funding deficiency. For purposes of this section and section 4971, the term "accumulated funding deficiency" means for any plan the excess of the total charges to the funding standard account for all plan years (beginning with the first plan year to which this section applies) over the total credits to such account for such years or, if less, the excess of the total charges to the alternative minimum funding standard account for such plan years over the total credits to such account for such years. In any plan year in which a multiemployer plan is in reorganization, the accumulated funding deficiency of the plan shall be determined under section 418B.

(b) **Funding standard account.**—

(1) **Account required.**—Each plan to which this section applies shall establish and maintain a funding standard account. Such account shall be credited and charged solely as provided in this section.

(2) **Charges to account.**—For a plan year, the funding standard account shall be charged with the sum of—

(A) the normal cost of the plan for the plan year,

(B) the amounts necessary to amortize in equal annual installments (until fully amortized)—

(i) in the case of a plan in existence on January 1, 1974, the unfunded past service liability under the plan on the first day of the first plan year to which this section applies, over a period of 40 plan years,

(ii) in the case of a plan which comes into existence after January 1, 1974, the unfunded past service liability under the plan on the first day of the first plan year to which this section applies, over a period of 30 plan years,

(iii) separately, with respect to each plan year, the net increase (if any) in unfunded past service liability under the plan arising from plan amendments adopted in such year, over a period of 30 plan years,

(iv) separately, with respect to each plan year, the net experience loss (if any) under the plan, over a period of 15 plan years, and

(v) separately, with respect to each plan year, the net loss (if any) resulting from changes in actuarial assumptions used under the plan, over a period of 30 plan years,

(C) the amount necessary to amortize each waived funding deficiency (within the meaning of subsection (d) (3)) for each prior plan year in equal annual installments (until fully amortized) over a period of 15 plan years, and

(D) the amount necessary to amortize in equal annual installments (until fully amortized) over a period of 5 plan years any amount credited to the funding standard account under paragraph (3) (D).

(3) **Credits to account.**—For a plan year, the funding standard account shall be credited with the sum of—

(A) the amount considered contributed by the employer to or under the plan for the plan year,

(B) the amount necessary to amortize in equal annual installments (until fully amortized)—

(i) separately, with respect to each plan year, the net decrease (if any) in unfunded past service liability under the plan arising from plan amendments adopted in such year, over a period of 30 plan years,

(ii) separately, with respect to each plan year, the net experience gain (if any) under the plan, over a period of 15 plan years, and

(iii) separately, with respect to each plan year, the net gain (if any) resulting from changes in actuarial assumptions used under the plan, over a period of 30 plan years,

(C) the amount of the waived funding deficiency ([1] within the meaning of subsection (d) (3) for the plan year, and

(D) in the case of a plan year for which the accumulated funding deficiency is determined under the funding standard account if such plan year follows a plan year for which such deficiency was determined under the alternative minimum funding standard, the excess (if any) of any debit balance in the funding standard account (determined without regard to this subparagraph) over any debit balance in the alternative minimum funding standard account.

(4) **Combining and offsetting amounts to be amortized.**—Under regulations prescribed by the Secretary, amounts required to be amortized under paragraph (2) or paragraph (3), as the case may be—

(A) may be combined into one amount under such paragraph to be amortized over a period determined on the basis of the remaining amortization period for all items entering into such combined amount, and

(B) may be offset against amounts required to be amortized under the other such paragraph, with the resulting amount to be amortized over a period determined on the basis of the remaining amortization periods for all items entering into whichever of the two amounts being offset is the greater.

(5) Interest.—The funding standard account (and items therein) shall be charged or credited (as determined under regulations prescribed by the Secretary) with interest at the appropriate rate consistent with the rate or rates of interest used under the plan to determine costs.

. . . . .

(c) Special rules.—

(1) Determinations to be made under funding method.—For purposes of this section, normal costs, accrued liability, past service liabilities, and experience gains and losses shall be determined under the funding method used to determine costs under the plan.

(2) Valuation of assets.—

(A) In general.—For purposes of this section, the value of the plan's assets shall be determined on the basis of any reasonable actuarial method of valuation which takes into account fair market value and which is permitted under regulations prescribed by the Secretary.

(B) Election with respect to bonds.—The value of a bond or other evidence of indebtedness which is not in default as to principal or interest may, at the election of the plan administrator, be determined on an amortized basis running from initial cost at purchase to par value at maturity or earliest call date. Any election under this subparagraph shall be made at such time and in such manner as the Secretary shall by regulations provide, shall apply to all such evidences of indebtedness, and may be revoked only with the consent of the Secretary.

(3) Actuarial assumptions must be reasonable.—For purposes of this section, all costs, liabilities, rates of interest, and other factors under the plan shall be determined on the basis of actuarial assumptions and methods which, in the aggregate, are reasonable (taking into account the experience of the plan and reasonable expectations) and which, in combination, offer the actuary's best estimate of anticipated experience under the plan.

(4) Treatment of certain changes as experience gain or loss.—For purposes of this section, if—

(A) a change in benefits under the Social Security Act or in other retirement benefits created under Federal or State law, or

(B) a change in the definition of the term "wages" under section 3121, or a change in the amount of such wages taken into account under regulations prescribed for purposes of section 401(a) (5),

results in an increase or decrease in accrued liability under a plan, such increase or decrease shall be treated as an experience loss or gain.

(5) Change in funding method or in plan year requires approval.—If the funding method for a plan is changed, the new funding method shall become the funding method used to determine costs and liabilities under the plan only if the change is approved by the Secretary. If the plan year for a plan is changed, the new plan year shall become the plan year for the plan only if the change is approved by the Secretary.

(6) Full funding.—If, as of the close of a plan year, a plan would (without regard to this paragraph) have an accumulated funding deficiency (determined without regard to the alternative minimum funding standard account permitted under subsection (g)) in excess of the full funding limitation—

(A) the funding standard account shall be credited with the amount of such excess, and

(B) all amounts described in paragraphs (2) (B), (C), and (D) and (3) (B) of subsection (b) which are required to be amortized shall be considered fully amortized for purposes of such paragraphs.

(7) **Full funding limitation.**—For purposes of paragraph (6), the term "full funding limitation" means the excess (if any) of—

(A) the accrued liability (including normal cost) under the plan (determined under the entry age normal funding method if such accrued liability cannot be directly calculated under the funding method used for the plan), over

(B) the lesser of the fair market value of the plan's assets or the value of such assets determined under paragraph (2).

(d) **Variance from minimum funding standard.**—

(1) **Waiver in case of substantial business hardship.**—If a employer or in the case of a multiemployer plan, 10 percent or more of the number of employers contributing to or under the plan, are unable to satisfy the minimum funding standard for a plan year without substantial business hardship and if application of the standard would be adverse to the interests of plan participants in the aggregate, the Secretary may waive the requirements of subsection (a) for such year with respect to all or any portion of the minimum funding standard other than the portion thereof determined under subsection (b) (2) (C). The Secretary shall not waive the minimum funding standard with respect to a plan for more than 5 of any 15 consecutive plan years.

(2) **Determination of substantial business hardship.**—For purposes of this section, the factors taken into account in determining substantial business hardship shall include (but shall not be limited to) whether or not—

(A) the employer is operating at an economic loss,

(B) there is substantial unemployment or underemployment in the trade or business and in the industry concerned,

(C) the sales and profits of the industry concerned are depressed or declining, and

(D) it is reasonable to expect that the plan will be continued only if the waiver is granted.

(3) **Waived funding deficiency.**—For purposes of this section, the term "waived funding deficiency" means the portion of the minimum funding standard (determined without regard to subsection (b) (3) (C)) for a plan year waived by the Secretary and not satisfied by employer contributions.

. . . . .

1 So in original. No closing parenthesis.

§ 414.   Definitions and special rules

(a) **Service for predecessor employer.**—For purposes of this part—

(1) in any case in which the employer maintains a plan of a predecessor employer, service for such predecessor shall be treated as service for the employer, and

(2) in any case in which the employer maintains a plan which is not the plan maintained by a predecessor employer, service for such predecessor shall, to the extent provided in regulations prescribed by the Secretary, be treated as service for the employer.

(b) **Employees of controlled group of corporations.**—For purposes of sections 401, 408(k), 410, 411, 415, and 416, all employees of all corporations which are members of a controlled group of corporations (within the meaning of section 1563(a), determined without regard to section 1563(a)(4) and (e)(3)(C)) shall be treated as employed by a single employer. With respect to a plan adopted by more than one such corporation, the minimum funding standard of section 412, the tax imposed by section 4971, and the applicable limitations provided by section 404(a) shall be determined as if all such employers were a single employer, and allocated to each employer in accordance with regulations prescribed by the Secretary.

(c) **Employees of partnerships, proprietorships, etc., which are under common control.**—For purposes of sections 401, 408(k), 410, 411, 415, and 416, under regulations prescribed by the Secretary, all employees of trades or businesses (whether or not incorporated) which are under common control shall be treated as employed by a single employer. The regulations prescribed under this subsection shall be based on principles similar to the principles which apply in the case of subsection (b).

.   .   .   .   .

(i) **Defined contribution plan.**—For purposes of this part, the term "defined contribution plan" means a plan which provides for an individual account for each participant and for benefits based solely on the amount contributed to the participant's account, and any income, expenses, gains and losses, and any forfeitures of accounts of other participants which may be allocated to such participant's account.

(j) **Defined benefit plan.**—For purposes of this part, the term "defined benefit plan" means any plan which is not a defined contribution plan.

.   .   .   .   .

§ 415.   Limitations on benefits and contributions under qualified plans

(a) **General rule.**—

(1) **Trusts.**—A trust which is a part of a pension, profit-sharing, or stock bonus plan shall not constitute a qualified trust under section 401(a) if—

(A) in the case of a defined benefit plan, the plan provides for the payment of benefits with respect to a participant which exceed the limitation of subsection (b),

(B) in the case of a defined contribution plan, contributions and other additions under the plan with respect to any participant for any taxable year exceed the limitation of subsection (c), or

(C) in any case in which an individual is a participant in both a defined benefit plan and a defined contribution plan maintained by the employer, the trust has been disqualified under subsection (g).

. . . . .

(b) Limitation for defined benefit plans.—

(1) **In general.**—Benefits with respect to a participant exceed the limitation of this subsection if, when expressed as an annual benefit (within the meaning of paragraph (2)), such annual benefit is greater than the lesser of—

(A) $90,000, or

(B) 100 percent of the participant's average compensation for his high 3 years.

(2) **Annual benefit.—**

(A) **In general.**—For purposes of paragraph (1), the term "annual benefit" means a benefit payable annually in the form of a straight life annuity (with no ancillary benefits) under a plan to which employees do not contribute and under which no rollover contributions (as defined in sections 402(a) (5), 403(a) (4), 408(d) (3), and 409(b) (3) (C)) are made.

(B) **Adjustment for certain other forms of benefit.**—If the benefit under the plan is payable in any form other than the form described in subparagraph (A), or if the employees contribute to the plan or make rollover contributions (as defined in sections 402(a) (5), 403(a) (4), 408(d) (3) and 409(b) (3) (C)), the determinations as to whether the limitation described in paragraph (1) has been satisfied shall be made, in accordance with regulations prescribed by the Secretary, by adjusting such benefit so that it is equivalent to the benefit described in subparagraph (A). For purposes of this subparagraph, any ancillary benefit which is not directly related to retirement income benefits shall not be taken into account; and that portion of any joint and survivor annuity which constitutes a qualified joint and survivor annuity (as defined in section 401(a) (11) (G) (iii)) shall not be taken into account.

. . . . .

(c) Limitation for defined contribution plans.—

(1) **In general.**—Contributions and other additions with respect to a participant exceed the limitation of this subsection if, when expressed as an annual addition (within the meaning of paragraph (2)) to the participant's account, such annual addition is greater than the lesser of—

(A) $30,000, or

(B) 25 percent of the participant's compensation.

. . . . .

(d) Cost-of-living adjustments.—

(1) **In general.**—The Secretary shall adjust annually—

(A) the $90,000 amount in subsection (b)(1)(A),

(B) the $30,000 amount in subsection (c)(1)(A), and

(C) in the case of a participant who is separated from service, the amount taken into account under subsection (b) (1) (B),

for increases in the cost of living in accordance with regulations prescribed by the Secretary. Such regulations shall provide for adjustment procedures which are similar to the procedures used to adjust benefit amounts under section 215(i)(2)(A) of the Social Security Act.

(2) Base periods.—The base period taken into account—

(A) for purposes of subparagraphs (A) and (B) of paragraph (1) is the calendar quarter beginning October 1, 1984, and

(B) for purposes of subparagraph (C) of paragraph (1) is the last calendar quarter of the calendar year before the calendar year in which the participant is separated from service.

(3) Freeze on adjustment to defined contribution and benefit limits.— The Secretary shall not make any adjustment under subparagraph (A) or (B) of paragraph (1) with respect to any year beginning after December 31, 1982, and before January 1, 1986.

(e) Limitation in case of defined benefit plan and defined contribution plan for same employee.—

(1) In general.—In any case in which an individual is a participant in both a defined benefit plan and a defined contribution plan maintained by the same employer, the sum of the defined benefit plan fraction and the defined contribution plan fraction for any year may not exceed 1.0.

. . . . .

(f) Combining of plans.—

(1) In general.—For purposes of applying the limitations of subsections (b), (c), and (e)—

(A) all defined benefit plans (whether or not terminated) of an employer are to be treated as one defined benefit plan, and

(B) all defined contribution plans (whether or not terminated) of an employer are to be treated as one defined contribution plan.

(2) Annual compensation taken into account for defined benefit plans. —If the employer has more than one defined benefit plan—

(A) subsection (b) (1) (B) shall be applied separately with respect to each such plan, but

(B) in applying subsection (b) (1) (B) to the aggregate of such defined benefit plans for purposes of this subsection, the high 3 years of compensation taken into account shall be the period of consecutive calendar years (not more than 3) during which the individual had the greatest aggregate compensation from the employer.

. . . . .

§ 416.   Special rules for top-heavy plans

(a) General rule.—A trust shall not constitute a qualified trust under section 401(a) for any plan year if the plan of which it is a part is a top-heavy plan for such plan year unless such plan meets—

(1) the vesting requirements of subsection (b),

(2) the minimum benefit requirements of subsection (c), and

(3) the limitation on compensation requirement of subsection (d).

(b) Vesting requirements.—

(1) In general.—A plan satisfies the requirements of this subsection if it satisfies the requirements of either of the following subparagraphs:

(A) 3-year vesting.—A plan satisfies the requirements of this subparagraph if an employee who has completed at least 3 years of service with the employer or employers maintaining the plan has a nonforfeitable right to 100 percent of his accrued benefit derived from employer contributions.

(B) 6-year graded vesting.—A plan satisfies the requirements of this subparagraph if an employee has a nonforfeitable right to a percentage of his accrued benefit derived from employer contributions determined under the following table:

Years of service	The nonforfeitable percentage is:
2	20
3	40
4	60
5	80
6 or more	100

(2) Certain rules made applicable.—Except to the extent inconsistent with the provisions of this subsection, the rules of section 411 shall apply for purposes of this subsection.

(c) Plan must provide minimum benefits.—

(1) Defined benefit plans.—

(A) In general.—A defined benefit plan meets the requirements of this subsection if the accrued benefit derived from employer contributions of each participant who is a non-key employee, when expressed as an annual retirement benefit, is not less than the applicable percentage of the participant's average compensation for years in the testing period.

(B) Applicable percentage.—For purposes of subparagraph (A), the term "applicable percentage" means the lesser of—

(i) 2 percent multiplied by the number of years of service with the employer, or

(ii) 20 percent.

(C) Years of service.—For provisions of this paragraph—

(i) In general.—Except as provided in clause (ii), years of service shall be determined under the rules of paragraphs (4), (5), and (6) of section 411(a).

(ii) Exception for years during which plan was not top-heavy.—A year of service with the employer shall not be taken into account under this paragraph if—

(I) the plan was not a top-heavy plan for any plan year ending during such year of service, or

(II) such year of service was completed in a plan year beginning before January 1, 1984.

(D) Average compensation for high 5 years.—For purposes of this paragraph—

(i) In general.—A participant's testing period shall be the period of consecutive years (not exceeding 5) during which the participant had the greatest aggregate compensation from the employer.

(ii) Year must be included in year of service.—The years taken into account under clause (i) shall be properly adjusted for years not included in a year of service

(iii) Certain years not taken into account.—Except to the extent provided in the plan, a year shall not be taken into account under clause (i) if—

(I) such year ends in a plan year beginning before January 1, 1984, or

(II) such year begins after the close of the last year in which the plan was a top-heavy plan.

(E) Annual retirement benefit.—For purposes of this paragraph, the term "annual retirement benefit" means a benefit payable annually in the form of a single life annuity (with no ancillary benefits) beginning at the normal retirement age under the plan.

(2) Defined contribution plans.—

(A) In general.—A defined contribution plan meets the requirements of the subsection if the employer contribution for the year for each participant who is a non-key employee is not less than 3 percent of such participant's compensation (within the meaning of section 415).

(B) Special rule where maximum contribution less than 3 percent.—

(i) In general.—The percentage referred to in subparagraph (A) for any year shall not exceed the percentage at which contributions are made (or required to be made) under the plan for the year for the key employee for whom such percentage is the highest for the year.

(ii) Determination of percentage.—The determination referred to in clause (i) shall be determined for each key employee by dividing the contributions for such employee by so much of his total compensation for the year as does not exceed $200,000.

(iii) Treatment of aggregation groups.—

(I) For purposes of this subparagraph, all defined contribution plans required to be included in an aggregation group under subsection (g)(2)(A)(i) shall be treated as one plan.

(II) This subparagraph shall not apply to any plan required to be included in an aggregation group if such plan enables a defined benefit plan required to be included in such group to meet the requirements of section 401(a)(4) or 410.

(C) Certain amounts not taken into account.—For purposes of this paragraph, any employer contribution attributable to a salary reduction or similar arrangement shall not be taken into account.

(d) Not more than $200,000 in annual compensation taken into account.—

(1) In general.—A plan meets the requirements of this subsection if the annual compensation of each employee taken into account under the plan does not exceed the first $200,000.

(2) **Cost-of-living adjustments.**—The Secretary shall annually adjust the $200,000 amount contained in paragraph (1) of this subsection and in clause (ii) of subsection (c)(2)(B) in the same manner as he adjusts the dollar amount contained in section 415(c)(1)(A).

(e) **Plan must meet requirements without taking into account social security and similar contributions and benefits.**—A top-heavy plan shall not be treated as meeting the requirement of subsection (b) or (c) unless such plan meets such requirement without taking into account contributions or benefits under chapter 2 (relating to tax on self-employment income), chapter 21 (relating to Federal Insurance Contributions Act), title II of the Social Security Act, or any other Federal or State law.

(f) **Coordination where employer has 2 or more plans.**—The Secretary shall prescribe such regulations as may be necessary or appropriate to carry out the purposes of this section where the employer has 2 or more plans including (but not limited to) regulations to prevent inappropriate omissions or require duplication of minimum benefits or contributions.

(g) **Top-heavy plan defined.**—For purposes of this section—

(1) **In general.**—

(A) **Plans not required to be aggregated.**—Except as provided in subparagraph (B), the term "top-heavy plan" means, with respect to any plan year—

(i) any defined benefit plan if, as of the determination date, the present value of the cumulative accrued benefits under the plan for key employees exceeds 60 percent of the present value of the cumulative accrued benefits under the plan for all employees, and

(ii) any defined contribution plan if, as of the determination date, the aggregate of the accounts of key employees under the plan exceeds 60 percent of the aggregate of the accounts of all employees under such plan.

(B) **Aggregated plans.**—Each plan of an employer required to be included in an aggregation group shall be treated as a top-heavy plan if such group is a top-heavy group.

(2) **Aggregation.**—For purposes of this subsection—

(A) **Aggregation group.**—

(i) **Required aggregation.**—The term "aggregation group" means—

(I) each plan of the employer in which a key employee is a participant, and

(II) each other plan of the employer which enables any plan described in subclause (I) to meet the requirements of section 401(a)(4) or 410.

(ii) **Permissive aggregation.**—The employer may treat any plan not required to be included in an aggregation group under clause (i) as being part of such group if such group would continue to meet the requirements of sections 401(a)(4) and 410 with such plan being taken into account.

(B) Top-heavy group.—The term "top-heavy group" means any aggregation group if—

(i) the sum (as of the determination date) of—

(I) the present value of the cumulative accrued benefits for key employees under all defined benefit plans included in such group, and

(II) the aggregate of the accounts of key employees under all defined contribution plans included in such group,

(ii) exceeds 60 percent of a similar sum determined for all employees.

(3) Distributions during last 5 years taken into account.—For purposes of determining—

(A) the present value of the cumulative accrued benefit for any employee, or

(B) the amount of the account of any employee,

such present value or amount shall be increased by the aggregate distributions made with respect to such employee under the plan during the 5-year period ending on the determination date.

(4) Other special rules.—For purposes of this subsection—

(A) Rollover contributions to plan not taken into account.—Except to the extent provided in regulations, any rollover contribution (or similar transfer) initiated by the employee and made after December 31, 1983, to a plan shall not be taken into account with respect to the transferee plan for purposes of determining whether such plan is a top-heavy plan (or whether any aggregation group which includes such plan is a top-heavy group).

(B) Benefits not taken into account if employee ceases to be key employee.—If any individual is a non-key employee with respect to any plan for any plan year, but such individual was a key employee with respect to such plan for any prior plan year, any accrued benefit for such employee (and the account of such employee) shall not be taken into account.

(C) Determination date.—The term "determination date" means, with respect to any plan year—

(i) the last day of the preceding plan year, or

(ii) in the case of the first plan year of any plan, the last day of such plan year.

(D) Years.—To the extent provided in regulations, this section shall be applied on the basis of any year specified in such regulations in lieu of plan years.

(h) Adjustments in section 415 limits for top-heavy plans.—

(1) In general.—In the case of any top-heavy plan, paragraphs (2)(B) and (3)(B) of section 415(e) shall be applied by substituting "1.0" for "1.25".

(2) Exception where benefits for key employees do not exceed 90 percent of total benefits and additional contributions are made for non-key employees.—Paragraph (1) shall not apply with respect to any top-heavy plan if the requirements of subparagraphs (A) and (B) of this paragraph are met with respect to such plan.

(A) Minimum benefit requirements.—

(i) In general.—The requirements of this subparagraph are met with respect to any top-heavy plan if such plan (and any plan required to be included in an aggregation group with such plan) meets the requirements of subsection (c) as modified by clause (ii).

(ii) Modifications.—For purposes of clause (i)—

(I) paragraph (1)(B) of subsection (c) shall be applied by substituting "3 percent" for "2 percent", and by increasing (but not by more than 10 percentage points) 20 percent by 1 percentage point for each year for which such plan was taken into account under this subsection, and

(II) paragraph (2)(A) shall be applied by substituting "4 percent" for "3 percent".

(B) Benefits for key employees cannot exceed 90 percent of total benefits.—A plan meets the requirements of this subparagraph if such plan would not be a top-heavy plan if "90 percent" were substituted for "60 percent" each place it appears in paragraphs (1)(A) and (2)(B) of subsection (g).

(3) Transition rule.—If, but for this paragraph, paragraph (1) would begin to apply with respect to any top-heavy plan, the application of paragraph (1) shall be suspended with respect to any individual so long at there are no—

(A) employer contributions, forfeitures, or voluntary nondeductible contributions allocated to such individual, or

(B) accruals for such individual under the defined benefit plan.

(4) Coordination with transitional rule under section 415.—In the case of any top heavy plan to which paragraph (1) applies, section 415(e)(6)(B)(i) shall be applied by substituting "$41,500" for "$51,875".

(i) Definitions.—For purposes of this section—

(1) Key employee.—

(A) In general.—The term "key employee" means any participant in an employer plan who, at any time during the plan year or any of the 4 preceding plan years, is—

(i) an officer of the employer,

(ii) 1 of the 10 employees owning (or considered as owning within the meaning of section 318) the largest interests in the employer,

(iii) a 5-percent owner of the employer, or

(iv) a 1-percent owner of the employer having an annual compensation from the employer of more than $150,000.

For purposes of clause (i), no more than 50 employees (or, if lesser, the greater of 3 or 10 percent of the employees) shall be treated as officers.

(B) Percentage owners.—

(i) 5-percent owner.—For purposes of this paragraph, the term "5-percent owner" means—

(I) if the employer is a corporation, any person who owns (or is considered as owning within the meaning of section 318) more than 5 percent of the outstanding stock of the corporation or stock possessing more than 5 percent of the total combined voting power of all stock of the corporation, or

(II) if the employer is not a corporation, any person who owns more than 5 percent of the capital or profits interest in the employer.

(ii) 1-percent owner.—For purposes of this paragraph, the term "1-percent owner" means any person who would be described in clause (i) if "1 percent" were substituted for "5 percent" each place it appears in clause (i).

(iii) Constructive ownership rules.—For purposes of this subparagraph and subparagraph (A)(ii)(II) [(A)(iii)]—

(I) subparagraph (C) of section 318(a)(2) shall be applied by substituting "5 percent" for "50 percent", and

(II) in the case of any employer which is not a corporation, ownership in such employer shall be determined in accordance with regulations prescribed by the Secretary which shall be based on principles similar to the principles of section 318 (as modified by subclause (I)).

(C) Aggregation rules do not apply for purposes of determining 5-percent or 1-percent owners.—The rules of subsections (b), (c), and (m) of section 414 shall not apply for purposes of determining ownership in the employer.

(2) Non-key employee.—The term "non-key employee" means any employee who is not a key employee.

(3) Self-employed individuals.—In the case of a self-employed individual described in section 401(c)(1)—

(A) such individual shall be treated as an employee, and

(B) such individual's earned income (within the meaning of section 401(c)(2)) shall be treated as compensation.

(4) Treatment of employees covered by collective bargaining agreements.—The requirements of subsections (b), (c), and (d) shall not apply with respect to any employee included in a unit of employees covered by an agreement which the Secretary of Labor finds to be a collective bargaining agreement between employee representatives and 1 or more employers if there is evidence that retirement benefits were the subject of good faith bargaining between such employee representatives and such employer or employers.

(5) Treatment of beneficiaries.—The terms "employee" and "key employee" include their beneficiaries.

(6) Treatment of simplified employee pensions.—

(A) Treatment as defined contribution plans.—A simplified employee pension shall be treated as a defined contribution plan.

(B) Election to have determinations based on employer contributions.—In the case of a simplified employee pension, at the election of the employer, paragraphs (1)(A)(ii) and (2)(B) of subsection (g) shall be applied by taking into account aggregate employer contributions in lieu of the aggregate of the accounts of employees.

PART II—CERTAIN STOCK OPTIONS

§ 421. General rules

(a) Effect of qualifying transfer.—If a share of stock is transferred to an individual in a transfer in respect of which the requirements of section 422(a), 422A(a), 423(a), or 424(a) are met—

(1) except as provided in section 422(c) (1), no income shall result at the time of the transfer of such share to the individual upon his exercise of the option with respect to such share;

(2) no deduction under section 162 (relating to trade or business expenses) shall be allowable at any time to the employer corporation, a parent or subsidiary corporation of such corporation, or a corporation issuing or assuming a stock option in a transaction to which section 425(a) applies, with respect to the share so transferred; and

(3) no amount other than the price paid under the option shall be considered as received by any of such corporations for the share so transferred.

. . . .

§ 422A. Incentive stock options

(a) In general.—Section 421(a) shall apply with respect to the transfer of a share of stock to an individual pursuant to his exercise of an incentive stock option if—

(1) no disposition of such share is made by him within 2 years from the date of the granting of the option nor within 1 year after the transfer of such share to him, and

(2) at all times during the period beginning on the date of the granting of the option and ending on the day 3 months before the date of such exercise, such individual was an employee of either the corporation granting such option, a parent or subsidiary corporation of such corporation, or a corporation or a parent or subsidiary corporation of such corporation issuing or assuming a stock option in a transaction to which section 425(a) applies.

(b) Incentive stock option.—For purposes of this part, the term "incentive stock option" means an option granted to an individual for any reason connected with his employment by a corporation, if granted by the employer corporation or its parent or subsidiary corporation, to purchase stock of any of such corporations, but only if—

(1) the option is granted pursuant to a plan which includes the aggregate number of shares which may be issued under options and the employees (or class of employees) eligible to receive options, and which is approved by the stockholders of the granting corporation within 12 months before or after the date such plan is adopted;

(2) such option is granted within 10 years from the date such plan is adopted, or the date such plan is approved by the stockholders, whichever is earlier;

(3) such option by its terms is not exercisable after the expiration of 10 years from the date such option is granted;

(4) the option price is not less than the fair market value of the stock at the time such option is granted;

(5) such option by its terms is not transferable by such individual otherwise than by will or the laws of descent and distribution, and is exercisable, during his lifetime, only by him;

(6) such individual, at the time the option is granted, does not own stock possessing more than 10 percent of the total combined voting power of all classes of stock of the employer corporation or of its parent or subsidiary corporation;

(7) such option by its terms is not exercisable while there is outstanding (within the meaning of subsection (c)(7)) any incentive stock option which was granted, before the granting of such option, to such individual to purchase stock in his employer corporation or in a corporation which (at the time of the granting of such option) is a parent or subsidiary corporation of the employer corporation, or in a predecessor corporation of any of such corporations; and

(8) in the case of an option granted after December 31, 1980, under the terms of the plan the aggregate fair market value (determined as of the time the option is granted) of the stock for which any employee may be granted options in any calendar year (under all such plans of his employer corporation and its parent and subsidiary corporation) shall not exceed $100,000 plus any unused limit carryover to such year.

(c) **Special rules.—**

(1) **Exercise of option when price is less than value of stock.—**If a share of stock is transferred pursuant to the exercise by an individual of an option which would fail to qualify as an incentive stock option under subsection (b) because there was a failure in an attempt, made in good faith, to meet the requirement of subsection (b)(4), the requirement of subsection (b)(4) shall be considered to have been met.

(2) **Certain disqualifying dispositions where amount realized is less than value at exercise.—**If—

(A) an individual who has acquired a share of stock by the exercise of an incentive stock option makes a disposition of such share within the 2-year period described in subsection (a)(1), and

(B) such disposition is a sale or exchange with respect to which a loss (if sustained) would be recognized to such individual,

then the amount which is includible in the gross income of such individual, and the amount which is deductible from the income of his employer corporation, as compensation attributable to the exercise of such option shall not exceed the excess (if any) of the amount realized on such sale or exchange over the adjusted basis of such share.

(3) **Certain transfers by insolvent individuals.—**If an insolvent individual holds a share of stock acquired pursuant to his exercise of an incentive stock option, and if such share is transferred to a trustee, receiver, or other similar fidiciary in any proceeding under title 11 or any other similar insolvency proceeding, neither such transfer, nor any other transfer of such share for the benefit of his creditors in such proceeding, shall constitute a disposition of such share for purposes of subsection (a)(1).

(4) Carryover of unused limit.—

(A) In general.—If—

(i) $100,000 exceeds,

(ii) the aggregate fair market value (determined as of the time the option is granted) of the stock for which an employee was granted options in any calendar year after 1980 (under all plans described in subsection (b) of his employer corporation and its parent and subsidiary corporations),

one-half of such excess shall be unused limit carryover to each of the 3 succeeding calendar years.

(B) Amount carried to each year.—The amount of the unused limit carryover from any calendar year which may be taken into account in any succeeding calendar year shall be the amount of such carryover reduced by the amount of such carryover which was used in prior calendar years.

(C) Special rules.—For purposes of subparagraph (B)—

(i) the amount of options granted during any calendar year shall be treated as first using up the $100,000 limitation of subsection (b)(8), and

(ii) then shall be treated as using up unused limit carryovers to such year in the order of the calendar years in which the carryovers arose.

(5) Permissible provisions.—An option which meets the requirements of subsection (b) shall be treated as an incentive stock option even if—

(A) the employee may pay for the stock with stock of the corporation granting the option,

(B) the employee has a right to receive property at the time of exercise of the option, or

(C) the option is subject to any condition not inconsistent with the provisions of subsection (b).

Subparagraph (B) shall apply to a transfer of property (other than cash) only if section 83 applies to the property so transferred.

(6) Coordination with sections 422 and 424.—Sections 422 and 424 shall not apply to an incentive stock option.

(7) Options outstanding.—For purposes of subsection (b)(7), any incentive stock option shall be treated as outstanding until such option is exercised in full or expires by reason of lapse of time.

(8) 10-percent shareholder rule.—Subsection (b)(6) shall not apply if at the time such option is granted the option price is at least 110 percent of the fair market value of the stock subject to the option and such option by its terms is not exercisable after the expiration of 5 years from the date such option is granted.

(9) Special rule when disabled.—For purposes of subsection (a)(2), in the case of an employee who is disabled (within the meaning of section 105(d)(4)), the 3-month period of subsection (a)(2) shall be 1 year.

SUBCHAPTER E—ACCOUNTING PERIODS AND METHODS OF ACCOUNTING

Part
I. Accounting periods.
II. Methods of accounting.
III. Adjustments.

PART I—ACCOUNTING PERIODS

§ 441.   Period for computation of taxable income

(a) **Computation of taxable income.**—Taxable income shall be computed on the basis of the taxpayer's taxable year.

(b) **Taxable year.**—For purposes of this subtitle, the term "taxable year" means—

(1) the taxpayer's annual accounting period, if it is a calendar year or a fiscal year;

(2) the calendar year, if subsection (g) applies; or

(3) the period for which the return is made, if a return is made for a period of less than 12 months.

(c) **Annual accounting period.**—For purposes of this subtitle, the term "annual accounting period" means the annual period on the basis of which the taxpayer regularly computes his income in keeping his books.

(d) **Calendar year.**—For purposes of this subtitle, the term "calendar year" means a period of 12 months ending on December 31.

(e) **Fiscal year.**—For purposes of this subtitle, the term "fiscal year" means a period of 12 months ending on the last day of any month other than December. In the case of any taxpayer who has made the election provided by subsection (f), the term means the annual period (varying from 52 to 53 weeks) so elected.

. . . . .

(g) **No books kept; no accounting period.**—Except as provided in section 443 (relating to returns for periods of less than 12 months), the taxpayer's taxable year shall be the calendar year if—

(1) the taxpayer keeps no books;

(2) the taxpayer does not have an annual accounting period; or

(3) the taxpayer has an annual accounting period, but such period does not qualify as a fiscal year.

§ 442.   Change of annual accounting period

If a taxpayer changes his annual accounting period, the new accounting period shall become the taxpayer's taxable year only if the change is approved by the Secretary. For purposes of this subtitle, if a taxpayer to whom section 441(g) applies adopts an annual accounting period (as defined in section 441(c)) other than a calendar year, the taxpayer shall be treated as having changed his annual accounting period.

§ 443. Returns for a period of less than 12 months

(a) **Returns for short period.**—A return for a period of less than 12 months (referred to in this section as "short period") shall be made under any of the following circumstances:

(1) **Change of annual accounting period.**—When the taxpayer, with the approval of the Secretary, changes his annual accounting period. In such a case, the return shall be made for the short period beginning on the day after the close of the former taxable year and ending at the close of the day before the day designated as the first day of the new taxable year.

(2) **Taxpayer not in existence for entire taxable year.**—When the taxpayer is in existence during only part of what would otherwise be his taxable year.

(b) **Computation of tax on change of annual accounting period.**—

(1) **General rule.**—If a return is made under paragraph (1) of subsection (a), the taxable income for the short period shall be placed on an annual basis by multiplying the modified taxable income for such short period by 12, dividing the result by the number of months in the short period, and adding the zero bracket amount. The tax shall be the same part of the tax computed on the annual basis as the number of months in the short period is of 12 months.

(2) **Exception.**—

(A) **Computation based on 12-month period.**—If the taxpayer applies for the benefits of this paragraph and establishes the amount of his taxable income for the 12-month period described in subparagraph (B), computed as if that period were a taxable year and under the law applicable to that year, then the tax for the short period, computed under paragraph (1), shall be reduced to the greater of the following:

(i) an amount which bears the same ratio to the tax computed on the taxable income for the 12-month period as the modified taxable income computed on the basis of the short period bears to the modified taxable income for the 12-month period; or

(ii) the tax computed on the sum of the modified taxable income for the short period plus the zero bracket amount.

The taxpayer (other than a taxpayer to whom subparagraph (B) (ii) applies) shall compute the tax and file his return without the application of this paragraph.

(B) **12-month period.**—The 12-month period referred to in subparagraph (A) shall be—

(i) the period of 12 months beginning on the first day of the short period, or

(ii) the period of 12 months ending at the close of the last day of the short period, if at the end of the 12 months referred to in clause (i) the taxpayer is not in existence or (if a corporation) has theretofore disposed of substantially all of its assets.

(C) **Application for benefits.**—Application for the benefits of this paragraph shall be made in such manner and at such time as the regulations prescribed under subparagraph (D) may require; except that the time so prescribed shall not be later than the time (including extensions) for filing the return for the first taxable year which ends on or after the day which is 12 months after the first day of the short period. Such application, in case the return was filed without regard to this paragraph, shall be considered a claim for credit or refund with respect to the amount by which the tax is reduced under this paragraph.

(D) Regulations.—The Secretary shall prescribe such regulations as he deems necessary for the application of this paragraph.

(3) Modified taxable income defined.—For purposes of this subsection the term "modified taxable income" means, with respect to any period, the gross income for such period minus the deductions allowed by this chapter for such period (but, in the case of a short period, only the adjusted amount of the deductions for personal exemptions).

(c) Adjustment in deduction for personal exemption.—In the case of a taxpayer other than a corporation, if a return is made for a short period by reason of subsection (a) (1) and if the tax is not computed under subsection (b) (2), then the exemptions allowed as a deduction under section 151 (and any deduction in lieu thereof) shall be reduced to amounts which bear the same ratio to the full exemptions as the number of months in the short period bears to 12.

. . . . .

PART II—METHODS OF ACCOUNTING

Subpart
    A.   Methods of accounting in general.
    B.   Taxable year for which items of gross income included.
    C.   Taxable year for which deductions taken.
    D.   Inventories.

SUBPART A—METHODS OF ACCOUNTING IN GENERAL

§ 446.   General rule for methods of accounting

(a) General rule.—Taxable income shall be computed under the method of accounting on the basis of which the taxpayer regularly computes his income in keeping his books.

(b) Exceptions.—If no method of accounting has been regularly used by the taxpayer, or if the method used does not clearly reflect income, the computation of taxable income shall be made under such method as, in the opinion of the Secretary, does clearly reflect income.

(c) Permissible methods.—Subject to the provisions of subsections (a) and (b), a taxpayer may compute taxable income under any of the following methods of accounting—

    (1) the cash receipts and disbursements method;

    (2) an accrual method;

    (3) any other method permitted by this chapter; or

    (4) any combination of the foregoing methods permitted under regulations prescribed by the Secretary.

(d) Taxpayer engaged in more than one business.—A taxpayer engaged in more than one trade or business may, in computing taxable income, use a different method of accounting for each trade or business.

(e) Requirement respecting change of accounting method.—Except as otherwise expressly provided in this chapter, a taxpayer who changes the method of accounting on the basis of which he regularly computes his income in keeping his books shall, before computing his taxable income under the new method, secure the consent of the Secretary.

§ 447.   Method of accounting for corporations engaged in farming

(a) General rule.—Except as otherwise provided by law, the taxable income from farming of—

    (1) a corporation engaged in the trade or business of farming, or

    (2) a partnership engaged in the trade or business of farming, if a corporation is a partner in such partnership,

shall be computed on an accrual method of accounting and with the capitalization of preproductive period expenses described in subsection (b). This section shall not apply to the trade or business of operating a nursery or sod farm or to the raising or harvesting of trees (other than fruit and nut trees).

(b) Preproductive period expenses.—

    (1) In general.—For purposes of this section, the term "preproductive period expenses" means any amount which is attributable to crops, animals, or any other property having a crop or yield during the preproductive period of such property.

    (2) Exceptions.—Paragraph (1) shall not apply—

        (A) to taxes and interest, and

        (B) to any amount incurred on account of fire, storm, flood, or other casualty or on account of disease or drought.

    (3) Preproductive period defined.—For purposes of this subsection, the term "preproductive period" means—

        (A) in the case of property having a useful life of more than 1 year which will have more than 1 crop or yield, the period before the disposition of the first such marketable crop or yield, or

        (B) in the case of any other property, the period before such property is disposed of.

For purposes of this section, the use by the taxpayer in the trade or business of farming of any supply produced in such trade or business shall be treated as a disposition.

(c) Exception for small business and family corporations.—For purposes of subsection (a), a corporation shall be treated as not being a corporation if it is—

    (1) an S corporation,

    (2) a corporation of which at least 50 percent of the total combined voting power of all classes of stock entitled to vote, and at least 50 percent of the total number of shares of all other classes of stock of the corporation, are owned by members of the same family, or

    (3) a corporation the gross receipts of which meet the requirements of subsection (e).

(d) **Members of the same family.**—For purposes of subsection (c) (2)—

(1) the members of the same family are an individual, such individual's brothers and sisters, the brothers and sisters of such individual's parents and grandparents, the ancestors and lineal descendants or any of the foregoing, a spouse of any of the foregoing, and the estate of any of the foregoing,

(2) stock owned, directly or indirectly, by or for a partnership or trust shall be treated as owned proportionately by its partners or beneficiaries, and

(3) if 50 percent or more in value of the stock in a corporation (hereinafter in this paragraph referred to as "first corporation") is owned, directly or through paragraph (2), by or for members of the same family, such members shall be considered as owning each class of stock in a second corporation (or a wholly owned subsidiary of such second corporation) owned, directly or indirectly, by or for the first corporation, in that proportion which the value of the stock in the first corporation which such members so own bears to the value of all the stock in the first corporation.

For purposes of paragraph (1), individuals related by the half blood or by legal adoption shall be treated as if they were related by the whole blood.

(e) **Corporations having gross receipts of $1,000,000 or less.**—A corporation meets the requirements of this subsection if, for each prior taxable year beginning after December 31, 1975, such corporation (and any predecessor corporation) did not have gross receipts exceeding $1,000,000. For purposes of the preceding sentence, all corporations which are members of a controlled group of corporations (within the meaning of section 1563(a)) shall be treated as one corporation.

. . . . . .

SUBPART B—TAXABLE YEAR FOR WHICH ITEMS OF GROSS INCOME INCLUDED

§ 451.　　General rule for taxable year of inclusion

(a) **General rule.**—The amount of any item of gross income shall be included in the gross income for the taxable year in which received by the taxpayer, unless, under the method of accounting used in computing taxable income, such amount is to be properly accounted for as of a different period.

(b) **Special rule in case of death.**—In the case of the death of a taxpayer whose taxable income is computed under an accrual method of accounting, any amount accrued only by reason of the death of the taxpayer shall not be included in computing taxable income for the period in which falls the date of the taxpayer's death.

(c) **Special rule for employee tips.**—For purposes of subsection (a), tips included in a written statement furnished an employer by an employee pursuant to section 6053(a) shall be deemed to be received at the time the written statement including such tips is furnished to the employer.

(d) **Special rule for crop insurance proceeds or disaster payments.**—In the case of insurance proceeds received as a result of destruction or damage to crops, a taxpayer reporting on the cash receipts and disbursements method of accounting may elect to include such proceeds in income for the taxable year following the taxable year of destruction or damage, if he establishes that, under his practice, income from such crops would have been reported in a following taxable year. For purposes of the preceding sentence, payments received under the Agricultural

Act of 1949, as amended, as a result of (1) destruction or damage to crops caused by drought, flood, or any other natural disaster, or (2) the inability to plant crops because of such a natural disaster shall be treated as insurance proceeds received as a result of destruction or damage to crops. An election under this subsection for any taxable year shall be made at such time and in such manner as the Secretary prescribes.

. . . . .

§ 453. Installment method

(a) General rule.—Except as otherwise provided in this section, income from an installment sale shall be taken into account for purposes of this title under the installment method.

(b) Installment sale defined.—For purposes of this section—

(1) In general.—The term "installment sale" means a disposition of property where at least 1 payment is to be received after the close of the taxable year in which the disposition occurs.

(2) Exceptions.—The term "installment sale" does not include—

(A) Dealer disposition of personal property.—A disposition of personal property on the installment plan by a person who regularly sells or otherwise disposes of personal property on the installment plan.

(B) Inventories of personal property.—A disposition of personal property of a kind which is required to be included in the inventory of the taxpayer if on hand at the close of the taxable year.

(c) Installment method defined.—For purposes of this section, the term "installment method" means a method under which the income recognized for any taxable year from a disposition is that proportion of the payments received in that year which the gross profit (realized or to be realized when payment is completed) bears to the total contract price.

(d) Election out.—

(1) In general.—Subsection (a) shall not apply to any disposition if the taxpayer elects to have subsection (a) not apply to such disposition.

(2) Time and manner for making election.—Except as otherwise provided by regulations, an election under paragraph (1) with respect to a disposition may be made only on or before the due date prescribed by law (including extensions) for filing the taxpayer's return of the tax imposed by this chapter for the taxable year in which the disposition occurs. Such an election shall be made in the manner prescribed by regulations.

(3) Election revocable only with consent.—An election under paragraph (1) with respect to any disposition may be revoked only with the consent of the Secretary.

(e) Second dispositions by related persons.—

(1) In general.—If—

(A) any person disposes of property to a related person (hereinafter in this subsection referred to as the "first disposition"), and

(B) before the person making the first disposition receives all payments with respect to such disposition, the related person disposes of the property (hereinafter in this subsection referred to as the "second disposition"), then, for purposes of this section, the amount realized with respect to such second disposition shall be treated as received at the time of the second disposition by the person making the first disposition.

(2) 2-year cutoff for property other than marketable securities.—

(A) In general.—Except in the case of marketable securities, paragraph (1) shall apply only if the date of the second disposition is not more than 2 years after the date of the first disposition.

(B) Substantial diminishing of risk of ownership.—The running of the 2-year period set forth in subparagraph (A) shall be suspended with respect to any property for any period during which the related person's risk of loss with respect to the property is substantially diminished by—

(i) the holding of a put with respect to such property (or similar property),

(ii) the holding by another person of a right to acquire the property, or

(iii) a short sale or any other transaction.

(3) Limitation on amount treated as received.—The amount treated for any taxable year as received by the person making the first disposition by reason of paragraph (1) shall not exceed the excess of—

(A) the lesser of—

(i) the total amount realized with respect to any second disposition of the property occurring before the close of the taxable year, or

(ii) the total contract price for the first disposition, over

(B) the sum of—

(i) the aggregate amount of payments received with respect to the first disposition before the close of such year, plus

(ii) the aggregate amount treated as received with respect to the first disposition for prior taxable years by reason of this subsection.

(4) Fair market value where disposition is not sale or exchange.—For purposes of this subsection, if the second disposition is not a sale or exchange, an amount equal to the fair market value of the property disposed of shall be substituted for the amount realized.

(5) Later payments treated as receipt of tax paid amounts.—If paragraph (1) applies for any taxable year, payments received in subsequent taxable years by the person making the first disposition shall not be treated as the receipt of payments with respect to the first disposition to the extent that the aggregate of such payments does not exceed the amount treated as received by reason of paragraph (1).

(6) Exception for certain dispositions.—For purposes of this subsection—

(A) Reacquisitions of stock by issuing corporation not treated as first dispositions.—Any sale or exchange of stock to the issuing corporation shall not be treated as a first disposition.

(B) Involuntary conversions not treated as second dispositions.—A compulsory or involuntary conversion (within the meaning of section 1033) and any transfer thereafter shall not be treated as a second disposition if the first disposition occurred before the threat or imminence of the conversion.

(C) Dispositions after death.—Any transfer after the earlier of—

(i) the death of the person making the first disposition, or

(ii) the death of the person acquiring the property in the first disposition,

and any transfer thereafter shall not be treated as a second disposition.

(7) Exception where tax avoidance not a principal purpose.—This subsection shall not apply to a second disposition (and any transfer thereafter) if it is established to the satisfaction of the Secretary that neither the first disposition nor the second disposition had as one of its principal purposes the avoidance of Federal income tax.

(8) Extension of statute of limitations.—The period for assessing a deficiency with respect to a first disposition (to the extent such deficiency is attributable to the application of this subsection) shall not expire before the day which is 2 years after the date on which the person making the first disposition furnishes (in such manner as the Secretary may by regulations prescribe) a notice that there was a second disposition of the property to which this subsection may have applied. Such deficiency may be assessed notwithstanding the provisions of any law or rule of law which would otherwise prevent such assessment.

(f) Definitions and special rules.—For purposes of this section—

(1) Related person.—Except for purposes of subsections (g) and (h), the term "related person" means a person whose stock would be attributed under section 318(a) (other than paragraph (4) thereof) to the person first disposing of the property.

(2) Marketable securities.—The term "marketable securities" means any security for which, as of the date of the disposition, there was a market on an established securities market or otherwise.

(3) Payment.—Except as provided in paragraph (4), the term "payment" does not include the receipt of evidences of indebtedness of the person acquiring the property (whether or not payment of such indebtedness is guaranteed by another person).

(4) Purchaser evidences of indebtedness payable on demand or readily tradable.—Receipt of a bond or other evidence of indebtedness which—

(A) is payable on demand, or

(B) is issued by a corporation or a government or political subdivision thereof and is readily tradable,

shall be treated as receipt of payment.

(5) Readily tradable defined.—For purposes of paragraph (4), the term "readily tradable" means a bond or other evidence of indebtedness which is issued—

(A) with interest coupons attached or in registered form (other than one in registered form which the taxpayer establishes will not be readily tradable in an established securities market), or

(B) in any other form designed to render such bond or other evidence of indebtedness readily tradable in an established securities market.

(6) Like-kind exchanges.—In the case of any exchange described in section 1031(b)—

(A) the total contract price shall be reduced to take into account the amount of any property permitted to be received in such exchange without recognition of gain,

(B) the gross profit from such exchange shall be reduced to take into account any amount not recognized by reason of section 1031(b), and

(C) the term "payment" shall not include any property permitted to be received in such exchange without recognition of gain.

Similar rules shall apply in the case of an exchange which is described in section 356(a) and is not treated as a dividend.

(7) **Depreciable property.**—The term "depreciable property" means property of a character which (in the hands of the transferee) is subject to the allowance for depreciation provided in section 167.

(g) **Sale of depreciable property to spouse or 80-percent owned entity.**—

(1) **In general.**—In the case of an installment sale of depreciable property between related persons within the meaning of section 1239(b), subsection (a) shall not apply, and, for purposes of this title, all payments to be received shall be deemed received in the year of the disposition.

(2) **Exception where tax avoidance not a principal purpose.**—Paragraph (1) shall not apply if it is established to the satisfaction of the Secretary that the disposition did not have as one of its principal purposes the avoidance of Federal income tax.

(h) **Use of installment method by shareholders in section 337 liquidations.**—

(1) **Receipt of obligations not treated as receipt of payment.**—

(A) **In general.**—If, in connection with a liquidation to which section 337 applies, in a transaction to which section 331 applies the shareholder receives (in exchange for the shareholder's stock) an installment obligation acquired in respect of a sale or exchange by the corporation during the 12-month period set forth in section 337(a), then, for purposes of this section, the receipt of payments under such obligation (but not the receipt of such obligation) by the shareholder shall be treated as the receipt of payment for the stock.

(B) **Obligations attributable to sale of inventory must result from bulk sale.**—Subparagraph (A) shall not apply to an installment obligation described in section 337(b)(1)(B) unless such obligation is also described in section 337(b)(2)(B).

(C) **Special rule where obligor and shareholder are related persons.**—If the obligor of any installment obligation and the shareholder are related persons (within the meaning of section 1239(b)), to the extent such installment obligation is attributable to the disposition by the corporation of depreciable property—

(i) subparagraph (A) shall not apply to such obligation, and

(ii) for purposes of this title, all payments to be received by the shareholder shall be deemed received in the year the shareholder receives the obligation.

(D) **Coordination with subsection (e)(1)(A).**—For purposes of subsection (e)(1)(A), disposition of property by the corporation shall be treated also as disposition of such property by the shareholder.

(E) **Sales by liquidating subsidiary.**—For purposes of subparagraph (A), in any case to which section 337(c)(3) applies, an obligation acquired in respect of a sale or exchange by the selling corporation shall be treated as so acquired by the corporation distributing the obligation to the shareholder.

(2) Distributions received in more than 1 taxable year of shareholder. —If—

(A) paragraph (1) applies with respect to any installment obligation received by a shareholder from a corporation, and

(B) by reason of the liquidation such shareholder receives property in more than 1 taxable year,

then, on completion of the liquidation, basis previously allocated to property so received shall be reallocated for all such taxable years so that the shareholder's basis in the stock of the corporation is properly allocated among all property received by such shareholder in such liquidation.

(i) Application with section 179.—

(1) In general.—In the case of an installment sale of section 179 property, subsection (a) shall not apply, and for purposes of this title, all payments to be received shall be deemed received in the year of disposition.

(2) Limitation.—Paragraph (1) shall apply only to the extent of the amount allowed as a deduction under section 179 with respect to the section 179 property.

(j) Regulations.—

(1) In general.—The Secretary shall prescribe such regulations as may be necessary or appropriate to carry out the provisions of this section.

(2) Selling price not readily ascertainable.—The regulations prescribed under paragraph (1) shall include regulations providing for ratable basis recovery in transactions where the gross profit or the total contract price (or both) cannot be readily ascertained.

§ 453A.   Installment method for dealers in personal property

(a) General rule.—

(1) In general.—Under regulations prescribed by the Secretary, a person who regularly sells or otherwise disposes of personal property on the installment plan may return as income therefrom in any taxable year that proportion of the installment payments actually received in that year which the gross profit, realized or to be realized when payment is completed, bears to the total contract price.

(2) Total contract price.—For purposes of paragraph (1), the total contract price of all sales of personal property on the installment plan includes the amount of carrying charges or interest which is determined with respect to such sales and is added on the books of account of the seller to the established cash selling price of such property. This paragraph shall not apply with respect to sales of personal property under a revolving credit type plan.

(b) Carrying charges not included in total contract price.—If the carrying charges or interest with respect to sales of personal property, the income from which is returned under subsection (a)(1), is not included in the total contract price, payments received with respect to such sales shall be treated as applying first against such carrying charges or interest.

§ 453B.   Gain or loss disposition of installment obligations

(a) General rule.—If an installment obligation is satisfied at other than its face value or distributed, transmitted, sold, or otherwise disposed of, gain or loss shall result to the extent of the difference between the basis of the obligation and—

(1) the amount realized, in the case of satisfaction at other than face value or a sale or exchange, or

(2) the fair market value of the obligation at the time of distribution, transmission, or disposition, in the case of the distribution, transmission, or disposition otherwise than by sale or exchange.

Any gain or loss so resulting shall be considered as resulting from the sale or exchange of the property in respect of which the installment obligation was received.

(b) Basis of obligation.—The basis of an installment obligation shall be the excess of the face value of the obligation over an amount equal to the income which would be returnable were the obligation satisfied in full.

(c) Special rule for transmission at death.—Except as provided in section 691 (relating to recipients of income in respect of decedents), this section shall not apply to the transmission of installment obligations at death.

(d) Effect of distribution in certain liquidations.—

(1) Liquidations to which section 332 applies.—If—

(A) an installment obligation is distributed in a liquidation to which section 332 (relating to complete liquidations of subsidiaries) applies, and

(B) the basis of such obligation in the hands of the distributee is determined under section 334(b)(1),

then no gain or loss with respect to the distribution of such obligation shall be recognized by the distributing corporation.

(2) Liquidations to which section 337 applies.—If—

(A) an installment obligation is distributed by a corporation in the course of a liquidation, and

(B) under section 337 (relating to gain or loss on sales or exchanges in connection with certain liquidations) no gain or loss would have been recognized to the corporation if the corporation had sold or exchanged such installment obligation on the day of such distribution,

then no gain or loss shall be recognized to such corporation by reason of such distribution. The preceding sentence shall not apply to the extent that under paragraph (1) gain to the distributing corporation would be considered as gain to which section 341(f), 617(d)(1), 1245(a), 1250(a), 1251(c), 1252(a), or 1254(a) applies. In the case of any installment obligation which would have met the requirements of subparagraphs (A) and (B) of the first sentence of this paragraph but for section 337(f), gain shall be recognized to such corporation by reason of such distribution only to the extent gain would have been recognized under section 337(f) if such corporation had sold or exchanged such installment obligation on the date of such distribution.

(f) Obligation becomes unenforceable.—For purposes of this section, if any installment obligation is canceled or otherwise becomes unenforceable—

    (1) the obligation shall be treated as if it were disposed of in a transaction other than a sale or exchange, and

    (2) if the obligor and obligee are related persons (within the meaning of section 453(f)(1)), the fair market value of the obligation shall be treated as not less than its face amount.

§ 454.   Obligations issued at discount

    (a) Non-interest-bearing obligations issued at a discount.—If, in the case of a taxpayer owning any non-interest-bearing obligation issued at a discount and redeemable for fixed amounts increasing at stated intervals or owning an obligation described in paragraph (2) of subsection (c), the increase in the redemption price of such obligation occurring in the taxable year does not (under the method of accounting used in computing his taxable income) constitute income to him in such year, such taxpayer may, at his election made in his return for any taxable year, treat such increase as income received in such taxable year. If any such election is made with respect to any such obligation, it shall apply also to all such obligations owned by the taxpayer at the beginning of the first taxable year to which it applies and to all such obligations thereafter acquired by him and shall be binding for all subsequent taxable years, unless on application by the taxpayer the Secretary permits him, subject to such conditions as the Secretary deems necessary, to change to a different method. In the case of any such obligations owned by the taxpayer at the beginning of the first taxable year to which his election applies, the increase in the redemption price of such obligations occurring between the date of acquisition (or, in the case of an obligation described in paragraph (2) of subsection (c), the date of acquisition of the series E bond involved) and the first day of such taxable year shall also be treated as income received in such taxable year.

    (b) Short-term obligations issued on discount basis.—In the case of any obligation—

    (1) of the United States; or

    (2) of a State or a possession of the United States, or any political subdivision of any of the foregoing, or of the District of Columbia,

which is issued on a discount basis and payable without interest at a fixed maturity date not exceeding 1 year from the date of issue, the amount of discount at which such obligation is originally sold shall not be considered to accrue until the date on which such obligation is paid at maturity, sold, or otherwise disposed of.

. . . . .

§ 455.   Prepaid subscription income

    (a) Year in which included.—Prepaid subscription income to which this section applies shall be included in gross income for the taxable years during which the liability described in subsection (d) (2) exists.

    (b) Where taxpayer's liability ceases.—In the case of any prepaid subscription income to which this section applies—

    (1) If the liability described in subsection (d) (2) ends, then so much of such income as was not includible in gross income under subsection (a) for

preceding taxable years shall be included in gross income for the taxable year in which the liability ends.

(2) If the taxpayer dies or ceases to exist, then so much of such income as was not includible in gross income under subsection (a) for preceding taxable years shall be included in gross income for the taxable year in which such death, or such cessation of existence, occurs.

(c) Prepaid subscription income to which this section applies.—

(1) **Election of benefits.**—This section shall apply to prepaid subscription income if and only if the taxpayer makes an election under this section with respect to the trade or business in connection with which such income is received. The election shall be made in such manner as the Secretary may by regulations prescribe. No election may be made with respect to a trade or business if in computing taxable income the cash receipts and disbursements method of accounting is used with respect to such trade or business.

(2) **Scope of election.**—An election made under this section shall apply to all prepaid subscription income received in connection with the trade or business with respect to which the taxpayer has made the election; except that the taxpayer may, to the extent permitted under regulations prescribed by the Secretary, include in gross income for the taxable year of receipt the entire amount of any prepaid subscription income if the liability from which it arose is to end within 12 months after the date of receipt. An election made under this section shall not apply to any prepaid subscription income received before the first taxable year for which the election is made.

(3) **When election may be made.—**

(A) **With consent.**—A taxpayer may, with the consent of the Secretary, make an election under this section at any time.

(B) **Without consent.**—A taxpayer may, without the consent of the Secretary, make an election under this section for his first taxable year in which he receives prepaid subscription income in the trade or business. Such election shall be made not later than the time prescribed by law for filing the return for the taxable year (including extensions thereof) with respect to which such election is made.

(4) **Period to which election applies.**—An election under this section shall be effective for the taxable year with respect to which it is first made and for all subsequent taxable years, unless the taxpayer secures the consent of the Secretary to the revocation of such election. For purposes of this title, the computation of taxable income under an election made under this section shall be treated as a method of accounting.

(d) Definitions.—For purposes of this section—

(1) **Prepaid subscription income.**—The term "prepaid subscription income" means any amount (includible in gross income) which is received in connection with, and is directly attributable to, a liability which extends beyond the close of the taxable year in which such amount is received, and which is income from a subscription to a newspaper, magazine, or other periodical.

(2) **Liability.**—The term "liability" means a liability to furnish or deliver a newspaper, magazine, or other periodical.

(3) **Receipt of prepaid subscription income.**—Prepaid subscription income shall be treated as received during the taxable year for which it is includible in gross income under section 451 (without regard to this section).

(e) Deferral of income under established accounting procedures.—Notwithstanding the provisions of this section, any taxpayer who has, for taxable years prior to the first taxable year to which this section applies, reported his income under an established and consistent method or practice of accounting for prepaid subscription income (to which this section would apply if an election were made) may continue to report his income for taxable years to which this title applies in accordance with such method or practice.

§ 456.   Prepaid dues income of certain membership organizations

(a) Year in which included.—Prepaid dues income to which this section applies shall be included in gross income for the taxable years during which the liability described in subsection (e) (2) exists.

(b) Where taxpayer's liability ceases.—In the case of any prepaid dues income to which this section applies—

(1) If the liability described in subsection (e) (2) ends, then so much of such income as was not includible in gross income under subsection (a) for preceding taxable years shall be included in gross income for the taxable year in which the liability ends.

(2) If the taxpayer ceases to exist, then so much of such income as was not includible in gross income under subsection (a) for preceding taxable years shall be included in gross income for the taxable year in which such cessation of existence occurs.

(c) Prepaid dues income to which this section applies.—

(1) **Election of benefits.**—This section shall apply to prepaid dues income if and only if the taxpayer makes an election under this section with respect to the trade or business in connection with which such income is received. The election shall be made in such manner as the Secretary may by regulations prescribe. No election may be made with respect to a trade or business if in computing taxable income the cash receipts and disbursements method of accounting is used with respect to such trade or business.

(2) **Scope of election.**—An election made under this section shall apply to all prepaid dues income received in connection with the trade or business with respect to which the taxpayer has made the election; except that the taxpayer may, to the extent permitted under regulations prescribed by the Secretary, include in gross income for the taxable year of receipt the entire amount of any prepaid dues income if the liability from which it arose is to end within 12 months after the date of receipt. Except as provided in subsection (d), an election made under this section shall not apply to any prepaid dues income received before the first taxable year for which the election is made.

(3) **When election may be made.**—

(A) **With consent.**—A taxpayer may, with the consent of the Secretary, make an election under this section at any time.

(B) **Without consent.**—A taxpayer may, without the consent of the Secretary, make an election under this section for its first taxable year in which it receives prepaid dues income in the trade or business. Such election shall be made not later than the time prescribed by law for filing the return for the taxable year (including extensions thereof) with respect to which such election is made.

(4) Period to which election applies.—An election under this section shall be effective for the taxable year with respect to which it is first made and for all subsequent taxable years, unless the taxpayer secures the consent of the Secretary to the revocation of such election. For purposes of this title, the computation of taxable income under an election made under this section shall be treated as a method of accounting.

. . . . .

(e) Definitions.—For purposes of this section—

(1) Prepaid dues income.—The term "prepaid dues income" means any amount (includible in gross income) which is received by a membership organization in connection with, and is directly attributable to, a liability to render services or make available membership privileges over a period of time which extends beyond the close of the taxable year in which such amount is received.

(2) Liability.—The term "liability" means a liability to render services or make available membership privileges over a period of time which does not exceed 36 months, which liability shall be deemed to exist ratably over the period of time that such services are required to be rendered, or that such membership privileges are required to be made available.

(3) Membership organization.—The term "membership organization" means a corporation, association, federation, or other organization—

(A) organized without capital stock of any kind, and

(B) no part of the net earnings of which is distributable to any member.

(4) Receipt of prepaid dues income.—Prepaid dues income shall be treated as received during the taxable year for which it is includible in gross income under section 451 (without regard to this section).

SUBPART C—TAXABLE YEAR FOR WHICH DEDUCTIONS TAKEN

§ 461.   General rule for taxable year of deduction

(a) General rule.—The amount of any deduction or credit allowed by this subtitle shall be taken for the taxable year which is the proper taxable year under the method of accounting used in computing taxable income.

(b) Special rule in case of death.—In the case of the death of a taxpayer whose taxable income is computed under an accrual method of accounting, any amount accrued as a deduction or credit only by reason of the death of the taxpayer shall not be allowed in computing taxable income for the period in which falls the date of the taxpayer's death.

(c) Accrual of real property taxes.—

(1) In general.—If the taxable income is computed under an accrual method of accounting, then, at the election of the taxpayer, any real property tax which is related to a definite period of time shall be accrued ratably over that period.

(2) When election may be made.—

(A) Without consent.—A taxpayer may, without the consent of the Secretary, make an election under this subsection for his first taxable year in which he incurs real property taxes. Such an election shall be made not later than the time prescribed by law for filing the return for such year (including extensions thereof).

(B) With consent.—A taxpayer may, with the consent of the Secretary, make an election under this subsection at any time.

(d) Limitation on acceleration of accrual of taxes.—

(1) General rule.—In the case of a taxpayer whose taxable income is computed under an accrual method of accounting, to the extent that the time for accruing taxes is earlier than it would be but for any action of any taxing jurisdiction taken after December 31, 1960, then, under regulations prescribed by the Secretary, such taxes shall be treated as accruing at the time they would have accrued but for such action by such taxing jurisdiction.

(2) Limitation.—Under regulations prescribed by the Secretary, paragraph (1) shall be inapplicable to any item of tax to the extent that its application would (but for this paragraph) prevent all persons (including successors in interest) from ever taking such item into account.

(e) Dividends or interest paid on certain deposits or withdrawable accounts. —Except as provided in regulations prescribed by the Secretary, amounts paid to, or credited to the accounts of, depositors or holders of accounts as dividends or interest on their deposits or withdrawable accounts (if such amounts paid or credited are withdrawable on demand subject only to customary notice to withdraw) by a mutual savings bank not having capital stock represented by shares, a domestic building and loan association, or a cooperative bank shall not be allowed as a deduction for the taxable year to the extent such amounts are paid or credited for periods representing more than 12 months. Any such amount not allowed as a deduction as the result of the application of the preceding sentence shall be allowed as a deduction for such other taxable year as the Secretary determines to be consistent with the preceding sentence.

(f) Contested liabilities.—If—

(1) the taxpayer contests an asserted liability,

(2) the taxpayer transfers money or other property to provide for the satisfaction of the asserted liability,

(3) the contest with respect to the asserted liability exists after the time of the transfer, and

(4) but for the fact that the asserted liability is contested, a deduction would be allowed for the taxable year of the transfer (or for an earlier taxable year),

then the deduction shall be allowed for the taxable year of the transfer. This subsection shall not apply in respect of the deduction for income, war profits, and excess profits taxes imposed by the authority of any foreign country or possession of the United States.

(g) Prepaid interest.—

(1) In general.—If the taxable income of the taxpayer is computed under the cash receipts and disbursements method of accounting, interest paid by the taxpayer which, under regulations prescribed by the Secretary, is properly allocable to any period.—

    (A) with respect to which the interest represents a charge for the use or forbearance of money, and

    (B) which is after the close of the taxable year in which paid, shall be charged to capital account and shall be treated as paid in the period to which so allocable.

    (2) **Exception.**—This subsection shall not apply to points paid in respect of any indebtedness incurred in connection with the purchase or improvement of, and secured by, the principal residence of the taxpayer to the extent that, under regulations prescribed by the Secretary, such payment of points is an established business practice in the area in which such indebtedness is incurred, and the amount of such payment does not exceed the amount generally charged in such area.

§ 464.   Limitations on deductions in case of farming syndicates

    (a) **General rule.**—In the case of any farming syndicate (as defined in subsection (c)), a deduction (otherwise allowable under this chapter) for amounts paid for feed, seed, fertilizer, or other similar farm supplies shall only be allowed for the taxable year in which such feed, seed, fertilizer, or other supplies are actually used or consumed, or, if later, for the taxable year for which allowable as a deduction (determined without regard to this section).

    (b) **Certain poultry expenses.**—In the case of any farming syndicate (as defined in subsection (c))—

    (1) the cost of poultry (including egg-laying hens and baby chicks) purchased for use in a trade or business (or both for use in a trade or business and for sale) shall be capitalized and deducted ratably over the lesser of 12 months or their useful life in the trade or business, and

    (2) the cost of poultry purchased for sale shall be deducted for the taxable year in which the poultry is sold or otherwise disposed of.

    (c) **Farming syndicate defined.**—

    (1) **In general.**—For purposes of this section, the term "farming syndicate" means—

        (A) a partnership or any other enterprise other than a corporation which is not an S corporation engaged in the trade or business of farming, if at any time interests in such partnership or enterprise have been offered for sale in any offering required to be registered with any Federal or State agency having authority to regulate the offering of securities for sale, or

        (B) a partnership or any other enterprise other than a corporation which is not an S corporation engaged in the trade or business of farming, if more than 35 percent of the losses during any period are allocable to limited partners or limited entrepreneurs.

. . . . .

§ 465.   Deductions limited to amount at risk

(a) Limitation to amount at risk.—

  (1) In general.—In the case of—

    (A) an individual, and

    (B) a corporation with respect to which the stock ownership requirement of paragraph (2) of section 542(a) is met,

engaged in an activity to which this section applies, any loss from such activity for the taxable year shall be allowed only to the extent of the aggregate amount with respect to which the taxpayer is at risk (within the meaning of subsection (b)) for such activity at the close of the taxable year.

  (2) Deduction in succeeding year.—Any loss from an activity to which this section applies not allowed under this section for the taxable year shall be treated as a deduction allocable to such activity in the first succeeding taxable year.

  (3) Special rules for applying paragraph (1)(B).—For purposes of paragraph (1)(B)—

    (A) section 544(a)(2) shall be applied as if such section did not contain the phrase "or by or for his partner"; and

    (B) sections 544(a)(4)(A) and 544(b)(1) shall be applied by substituting "the corporation meet the stock ownership requirements of section 542(a)(2)" for "the corporation a personal holding company".

(b) Amounts considered at risk.—

  (1) In general.—For purposes of this section, a taxpayer shall be considered at risk for an activity with respect to amounts including—

    (A) the amount of money and the adjusted basis of other property contributed by the taxpayer to the activity, and

    (B) amounts borrowed with respect to such activity (as determined under paragraph (2)).

  (2) Borrowed amounts.—For purposes of this section, a taxpayer shall be considered at risk with respect to amounts borrowed for use in an activity to the extent that he—

    (A) is personally liable for the repayment of such amounts, or

    (B) has pledged property, other than property used in such activity, as security for such borrowed amount (to the extent of the net fair market value of the taxpayer's interest in such property).

No property shall be taken into account as security if such property is directly or indirectly financed by indebtedness which is secured by property described in paragraph (1).

  (3) Certain borrowed amounts excluded.—For purposes of paragraph (1) (B), amounts borrowed shall not be considered to be at risk with respect to an activity if such amounts are borrowed from any person who—

    (A) has an interest (other than an interest as a creditor) in such activity, or

    (B) has a relationship to the taxpayer specified within any one of the paragraphs of section 267(b).

  (4) Exception.—Notwithstanding any other provision of this section, a taxpayer shall not be considered at risk with respect to amounts protected against loss through nonrecourse financing, guarantees, stop loss agreements, or other similar arrangements.

(5) Amounts at risk in subsequent years.—If in any taxable year the taxpayer has a loss from an activity to which subsection (a) applies, the amount with respect to which a taxpayer is considered to be at risk (within the meaning of subsection (b)) in subsequent taxable years with respect to that activity shall be reduced by that portion of the loss which (after the application of subsection (a)) is allowable as a deduction.

(c) Activities to which section applies.—

(1) Types of activities.—This section applies to any taxpayer engaged in the activity of—

(A) holding, producing, or distributing motion picture films or video tapes,

(B) farming (as defined in section 464(e)),

(C) leasing any section 1245 property (as defined in section 1245(a) (3)),

(D) exploring for, or exploiting, oil and gas resources as a trade or business or for the production of income, or

(E) exploring for, or exploiting, geothermal deposits (as defined in section 613(e) (3)).

(2) Separate activities.—For purposes of this section, a taxpayer's activity with respect to each—

(A) film or video tape,

(B) section 1245 property which is leased or held for leasing,

(C) farm,

(D) oil and gas property (as defined under section 614), or

(E) geothermal property (as determined under section 614),

shall be treated as a separate activity. A partner's interest in a partnership or a shareholder's interest in an S corporation shall be treated as a single activity to the extent that the partnership or the S corporation is engaged in activities described in any subparagraph of this paragraph.

(3) Extension to other activities.—

(A) In general.—In the case of taxable years beginning after December 31, 1978, this section also applies to each activity—

(i) engaged in by the taxpayer in carrying on a trade or business or for the production of income, and

(ii) which is not described in paragraph (1).

(B) Aggregation of activities where taxpayer actively participates in management of trade or business.—Except as provided in subparagraph (C), for purposes of this section, activities described in subparagraph (A) which constitute a trade or business shall be treated as one activity if—

(i) the taxpayer actively participates in the management of such trade or business, or

(ii) such trade or business is carried on by a partnership or an S corporation and 65 percent or more of the losses for the taxable year is allocable to persons who actively participate in the management of the trade or business.

(C) Aggregation or separation of activities under regulations.—The Secretary shall prescribe regulations under which activities described in subparagraph (A) shall be aggregated or treated as separate activities.

(D) Exclusion for real property.—In the case of activities described in subparagraph (A), the holding of real property (other than mineral property) shall be treated as a separate activity, and subsection (a) shall not apply to losses from such activity. For purposes of the preceding sentence, personal property and services which are incidental to making real property available as living accommodations shall be treated as part of the activity of holding such real property.

(E) Application of subsection (b)(3).—In the case of an activity described in subparagraph (A), subsection (b)(3) shall apply only to the extent provided in regulations prescribed by the Secretary.

(4) Exclusion for certain equipment leasing by closely-held corporations.—

    (A) In general.—In the case of a corporation described in subsection (a)(1)(B) actively engaged in equipment leasing—

        (i) the activity of equipment leasing shall be treated as a separate activity, and

        (ii) subsection (a) shall not apply to losses from such activity.

    (B) 50-percent gross receipts test.—For purposes of subparagraph (A), a corporation shall not be considered to be actively engaged in equipment leasing unless 50 percent or more of the gross receipts of the corporation for the taxable year is attributable, under regulations prescribed by the Secretary, to equipment leasing.

    (C) Component members of controlled group treated as a single corporation.—For purposes of subparagraph (A), the component members of a controlled group of corporations shall be treated as a single corporation.

(5) Waiver of controlled group rule where there is substantial leasing activity.—

    (A) In general.—In the case of the component members of a qualified leasing group, paragraph (4) shall be applied—

        (i) by substituting "80 percent" for "50 percent" in subparagraph (B) thereof, and

        (ii) as if paragraph (4) did not include subparagraph (C) thereof.

    (B) Qualified leasing group.—For purposes of this paragraph, the term "qualified leasing group" means a controlled group of corporations which, for the taxable year and each of the 2 immediately preceding taxable years, satisfied each of the following 3 requirements:

        (i) At least 3 employees.—During the entire year, the group had at least 3 full-time employees substantially all of the services of whom were services directly related to the equipment leasing activity of the qualified leasing members.

        (ii) At least 5 separate leasing transactions.—During the year, the qualified leasing members in the aggregate entered into at least 5 separate equipment leasing transactions.

        (iii) At least $1,000,000 equipment leasing receipts.—During the year, the qualified leasing members in the aggregate had at least $1,000,000 in gross receipts from equipment leasing.

The term "qualified leasing group" does not include any controlled group of corporations to which, without regard to this paragraph, paragraph (4) applies.

(C) Qualified leasing member.—For purposes of this paragraph, a corporation shall be treated as a qualified leasing member for the taxable year only if for each of the taxable years referred to in subparagraph (B)—

(i) it is a component member of the controlled group of corporations, and

(ii) it meets the requirements of paragraph (4)(B) (as modified by subparagraph (A)(i) of this paragraph).

(6) Definitions relating to paragraphs (4) and (5).—For purposes of paragraphs (4) and (5)—

(A) Equipment leasing.—The term "equipment leasing" means—

(i) the leasing of equipment which is section 1245 property, and

(ii) the purchasing, servicing, and selling of such equipment.

(B) Leasing of master sound recordings, etc., excluded.—The term "equipment leasing" does not include the leasing of master sound recordings, and other similar contractual arrangements with respect to tangible or intangible assets associated with literary, artistic, or musical properties.

(C) Controlled group of corporations; component member.—The terms "controlled group of corporations" and "component member" have the same meanings as when used in section 1563. The determination of the taxable years taken into account with respect to any controlled group of corporations shall be made in a manner consistent with the manner set forth in section 1563.

(d) Definition of loss.—For purposes of this section, the term "loss" means the excess of the deductions allowable under this chapter for the taxable year (determined without regard to the first sentence of subsection (a)) and allocable to an activity to which this section applies over the income received or accrued by the taxpayer during the taxable year from such activity (determined without regard to subsection (e)(1)(A)).

(e) Recapture of losses where amount at risk is less than zero.—

(1) In general.—If zero exceeds the amount for which the taxpayer is at risk in any activity at the close of any taxable year—

(A) the taxpayer shall include in his gross income for such taxable year (as income from such activity) an amount equal to such excess, and

(B) an amount equal to the amount so included in gross income shall be treated as a deduction allocable to such activity for the first succeeding taxable year.

(2) Limitation.—The excess referred to in paragraph (1) shall not exceed—

(A) the aggregate amount of the reductions required by subsection (b)(5) with respect to the activity by reason of losses for all prior taxable years beginning after December 31, 1978, reduced by

(B) the amounts previously included in gross income with respect to such activity under this subsection.

SUBPART D—INVENTORIES

§ 471.   General rule for inventories

Whenever in the opinion of the Secretary the use of inventories is necessary in order clearly to determine the income of any taxpayer, inventories shall be taken by such taxpayer on such basis as the Secretary may prescribe as conforming as nearly as may be to the best accounting practice in the trade or business and as most clearly reflecting the income.

§ 472.   Last-in, first-out inventories

(a) **Authorization.**—A taxpayer may use the method provided in subsection (b) (whether or not such method has been prescribed under section 471) in inventorying goods specified in an application to use such method filed at such time and in such manner as the Secretary may prescribe. The change to, and the use of, such method shall be in accordance with such regulations as the Secretary may prescribe as necessary in order that the use of such method may clearly reflect income.

(b) **Method applicable.**—In inventorying goods specified in the application described in subsection (a), the taxpayer shall:

(1) Treat those remaining on hand at the close of the taxable year as being: First, those included in the opening inventory of the taxable year (in the order of acquisition) to the extent thereof; and second, those acquired in the taxable year;

(2) Inventory them at cost; and

(3) Treat those included in the opening inventory of the taxable year in which such method is first used as having been acquired at the same time and determine their cost by the average cost method

(c) **Condition.**—Subsection (a) shall apply only if the taxpayer establishes to the satisfaction of the Secretary that the taxpayer has used no procedure other than that specified in paragraphs (1) and (3) of subsection (b) in inventorying such goods to ascertain the income, profit, or loss of the first taxable year for which the method described in subsection (b) is to be used, for the purpose of a report or statement covering such taxable year—

(1) to shareholders, partners, or other proprietors, or to beneficiaries, or

(2) for credit purposes.

(d) **3-year averaging for increases in inventory value.**—The beginning inventory for the first taxable year for which the method described in subsection (b) is used shall be valued at cost. Any change in the inventory amount resulting from the application of the preceding sentence shall be taken into account ratably in each of the 3 taxable years beginning with the first taxable year for which the method described in subsection (b) is first used.

(e) **Subsequent inventories.**—If a taxpayer, having complied with subsection (a), uses the method described in subsection (b) for any taxable year, then such method shall be used in all subsequent taxable years unless—

(1) with the approval of the Secretary a change to a different method is authorized; or,

(2) the Secretary determines that the taxpayer has used for any such subsequent taxable year some procedure other than that specified in para-

graph (1) of subsection (b) in inventorying the goods specified in the application to ascertain the income, profit, or loss of such subsequent taxable year for the purpose of a report or statement covering such taxable year (A) to shareholders, partners, or other proprietors, or beneficiaries, or (B) for credit purposes; and requires a change to a method different from that prescribed in subsection (b) beginning with such subsequent taxable year or any taxable year thereafter.

If paragraph (1) or (2) of this subsection applies, the change to, and the use of, the different method shall be in accordance with such regulations as the Secretary may prescribe as necessary in order that the use of such method may clearly reflect income.

(f) Use of government price indexes in pricing inventory.—The Secretary shall prescribe regulations permitting the use of suitable published governmental indexes in such manner and circumstances as determined by the Secretary for purposes of the method described in subsection (b).

§ 473. Qualified liquidations of LIFO inventories

(a) General rule.—If, for any liquidation year—

(1) there is a qualified liquidation of goods which the taxpayer inventories under the LIFO method, and

(2) the taxpayer elects to have the provisions of this section apply with respect to such liquidation,

then the gross income of the taxpayer for such taxable year shall be adjusted as provided in subsection (b).

(b) Adjustment for replacements.—If the liquidated goods are replaced (in whole or in part) during any replacement year and such replacement is reflected in the closing inventory for such year, then the gross income for the liquidation year shall be—

(1) decreased by an amount equal to the excess of—

(A) the aggregate replacement cost of the liquidated goods so replaced during such year, over

(B) the aggregate cost of such goods reflected in the opening inventory of the liquidation year, or

(2) increased by an amount equal to the excess of—

(A) the aggregate cost reflected in such opening inventory of the liquidated goods so replaced during such year, over

(B) such aggregate replacement cost.

(c) Qualified liquidation defined.—For purposes of this section—

(1) In general.—The term "qualified liquidation" means—

(A) a decrease in the closing inventory of the liquidation year from the opening inventory of such year, but only if

(B) the taxpayer establishes to the satisfaction of the Secretary that such decrease is directly and primarily attributable to a qualified inventory interruption.

(2) Qualified inventory interruption defined.—

(A) **In general.**—The term "qualified inventory interruption" means a regulation, request, or interruption described in subparagraph (B) but only to the extent provided in the notice published pursuant to subparagraph (B).

(B) Determination by Secretary.—Whenever the Secretary, after consultation with the appropriate Federal officers, determines—

(i) that—

(I) any Department of Energy regulation or request with respect to energy supplies, or

(II) any embargo, international boycott, or other major foreign trade interruption,

has made difficult or impossible the replacement during the liquidation year of any class of goods for any class of taxpayers, and

(ii) that the application of this section to that class of goods and taxpayers is necessary to carry out the purposes of this section,

he shall publish a notice of such determinations in the Federal Register, together with the period to be affected by such notice.

(d) Other definitions and special rules.—For purposes of this section—

(1) Liquidation year.—The term "liquidation year" means the taxable year in which occurs the qualified liquidation to which this section applies.

(2) Replacement year.—The term "replacement year" means any taxable year in the replacement period; except that such term shall not include any taxable year after the taxable year in which replacement of the liquidated goods is completed.

(3) Replacement period.—The term "replacement period" means the shorter of—

(A) the period of the 3 taxable years following the liquidation year, or

(B) the period specified by the Secretary in a notice published in the Federal Register with respect to that qualified inventory interruption.

Any period specified by the Secretary under subparagraph (B) may be modified by the Secretary in a subsequent notice published in the Federal Register.

(4) LIFO method.—The term "LIFO method" means the method of inventorying goods described in section 472.

(5) Election.—

(A) In general.—An election under subsection (a) shall be made subject to such conditions, and in such manner and form and at such time, as the Secretary may prescribe by regulation.

(B) Irrevocable election.—An election under this section shall be irrevocable and shall be binding for the liquidation year and for all determinations for prior and subsequent taxable years insofar as such determinations are affected by the adjustments under this section.

(e) Replacement; inventory basis.—For purposes of this chapter—

(1) Replacements.—If the closing inventory of the taxpayer for any replacement year reflects an increase over the opening inventory of such goods for such year, the goods reflecting such increase shall be considered, in the order of their acquisition, as having been acquired in replacement of the goods most recently liquidated (whether or not in a qualified liquidation) and not previously replaced.

(2) Amount at which replacement goods taken into account.—In the case of any qualified liquidation, any goods considered under paragraph (1) as having been acquired in replacement of the goods liquidated in such liquidation shall be taken into purchases and included in the closing inventory of the taxpayer for the replacement year at the inventory cost basis of the goods replaced.

(f) Special rules for application of adjustments.—

    (1) Period of limitations.—If—

        (A) an adjustment is required under this section for any taxable year by reason of the replacement of liquidated goods during any replacement year, and

        (B) the assessment of a deficiency, or the allowance of a credit or refund of an overpayment of tax attributable to such adjustment, for any taxable year, is otherwise prevented by the operation of any law or rule of law (other than section 7122, relating to compromises),

then such deficiency may be assessed, or credit or refund allowed, within the period prescribed for assessing a deficiency or allowing a credit or refund for the replacement year if a notice for deficiency is mailed, or claim for refund is filed, within such period.

    (2) Interest.—Solely for purposes of determining interest on any overpayment or underpayment attributable to an adjustment made under this section, such overpayment or underpayment shall be treated as an overpayment or underpayment (as the case may be) for the replacement year.

(g) Coordination with section 472.—The Secretary shall prescribe such regulations as may be necessary to coordinate the provisions of this section with the provisions of section 472.

§ 474.   Election by certain small businesses to use one inventory pool

(a) In general.—A taxpayer which is an eligible small business and which uses the dollar-value method of pricing inventories under the method provided by section 472(b) may elect to use one inventory pool for any trade or business of such taxpayer.

(b) Eligible small business defined.—For purposes of this section, a taxpayer is an eligible small business for any taxable year if the average annual gross receipts of the taxpayer do not exceed $2,000,000 for the 3-taxable-year period ending with the taxable year.

(c) Special rules.—For purposes of this section—

    (1) Controlled groups.—

        (A) In general.—In the case of a taxpayer which is a member of a controlled group, all persons which are component members of such group at any time during the calendar year shall be treated as one taxpayer for such year for purposes of determining the gross receipts of the taxpayer.

        (B) Controlled group defined.—For purposes of subparagraph (A), persons shall be treated as being members of a controlled group if such persons would be treated as a single employer under the regulations prescribed under section 52(b).

    (2) Election.—

        (A) In general.—The election under this section may be made without the consent of the Secretary and shall be made at such time and in such manner as the Secretary may by regulations prescribe.

(B) Period to which election applies.—The election under this section shall apply—

    (i) to the taxable year for which it is made, and

    (ii) to all subsequent taxable years for which the taxpayer is an eligible small business,

unless the taxpayer secures the consent of the Secretary to the revocation of such election.

    (3) Transitional rules.—In the case of a taxpayer who changes the number of inventory pools maintained by him in a taxable year by reason of an election (or cessation thereof) under this section—

        (A) the inventory pools combined or separated shall be combined or separated in the manner provided by regulations under section 472;

        (B) the aggregate dollar value of the taxpayer's inventory as of the beginning of the first taxable year—

            (i) for which an election under this section is in effect, or

            (ii) after such election ceases to apply,

shall be the same as the aggregate dollar value as of the close of the taxable year preceding the taxable year described in clause (i) or (ii) (as the case may be), and

        (C) the first taxable year for which an election under this section is in effect or after such election ceases to apply (as the case may be) shall be treated as a new base year in accordance with procedures provided by regulations under section 472.

PART III—ADJUSTMENTS

§ 481.   Adjustments required by changes in method of accounting

    (a) General rule.—In computing the taxpayer's taxable income for any taxable year (referred to in this section as the "year of the change")—

    (1) if such computation is under a method of accounting different from the method under which the taxpayer's taxable income for the preceding taxable year was computed, then

    (2) there shall be taken into account those adjustments which are determined to be necessary solely by reason of the change in order to prevent amounts from being duplicated or omitted, except there shall not be taken into account any adjustment in respect of any taxable year to which this section does not apply unless the adjustment is attributable to a change in the method of accounting initiated by the taxpayer.

    (b) Limitation on tax where adjustments are substantial.—

    (1) Three year allocation.—If—

        (A) the method of accounting from which the change is made was used by the taxpayer in computing his taxable income for the 2 taxable years preceding the year of the change, and

(B) the increase in taxable income for the year of the change which results solely by reason of the adjustments required by subsection (a) (2) exceeds $3,000,

then the tax under this chapter attributable to such increase in taxable income shall not be greater than the aggregate increase in the taxes under this chapter (or under the corresponding provisions of prior revenue laws) which would result if one-third of such increase in taxable income were included in taxable income for the year of the change and one-third of such increase were included for each of the 2 preceding taxable years.

(2) Allocation under new method of accounting.—If—

(A) the increase in taxable income for the year of the change which results solely by reason of the adjustments required by subsection (a) (2) exceeds $3,000, and

(B) the taxpayer establishes his taxable income (under the new method of accounting) for one or more taxable years consecutively preceding the taxable year of the change for which the taxpayer in computing taxable income used the method of accounting from which the change is made,

then the tax under this chapter attributable to such increase in taxable income shall not be greater than the net increase in the taxes under this chapter (or under the corresponding provisions of prior revenue laws) which would result if the adjustments required by subsection (a) (2) were allocated to the taxable year or years specified in subparagraph (B) to which they are properly allocable under the new method of accounting and the balance of the adjustments required by subsection (a) (2) was allocated to the taxable year of the change.

(3) Special rules for computations under paragraphs (1) and (2).—For purposes of this subsection—

(A) There shall be taken into account the increase or decrease in tax for any taxable year preceding the year of the change to which no adjustment is allocated under paragraph (1) or (2) but which is affected by a net operating loss (as defined in section 172) or by a capital loss carryback or carryover (as defined in section 1212), determined with reference to taxable years with respect to which adjustments under paragraph (1) or (2) are allocated.

(B) The increase or decrease in the tax for any taxable year for which an assessment of any deficiency, or a credit or refund of any overpayment, is prevented by any law or rule of law, shall be determined by reference to the tax previously determined (within the meaning of section 1314(a)) for such year.

(C) In applying section 7807(b) (1), the provisions of chapter 1 (other than subchapter E, relating to self-employment income) and chapter 2 of the Internal Revenue Code of 1939 shall be treated as the corresponding provisions of the Internal Revenue Code of 1939.

(c) Adjustments under regulations.—In the case of any change described in subsection (a), the taxpayer may, in such manner and subject to such conditions as the Secretary may by regulations prescribe, take the adjustments required by subsection (a) (2) into account in computing the tax imposed by this chapter for the taxable year or years permitted under such regulations.

§ 482.   Allocation of income and deductions among taxpayers

In any case of two or more organizations, trades, or businesses (whether or not incorporated, whether or not organized in the United States, and whether or not affiliated) owned or controlled directly or indirectly by the same interests, the Secretary may distribute, apportion, or allocate gross income, deductions, credits, or allowances between or among such organizations, trades, or businesses, if he determines that such distribution, apportionment, or allocation is necessary in order to prevent evasion of taxes or clearly to reflect the income of any of such organizations, trades, or businesses.

§ 483.   Interest on certain deferred payments

(a) **Amount constituting interest.**—For purposes of this title, in the case of any contract for the sale or exchange of property there shall be treated as interest that part of a payment to which this section applies which bears the same ratio to the amount of such payment as the total unstated interest under such contract bears to the total of the payments to which this section applies which are due under such contract.

(b) **Total unstated interest.**—For purposes of this section, the term "total unstated interest" means, with respect to a contract for the sale or exchange of property, an amount equal to the excess of—

(1) the sum of the payments to which this section applies which are due under the contract, over

(2) the sum of the present values of such payments and the present values of any interest payments due under the contract.

For purposes of paragraph (2), the present value of a payment shall be determined, as of the date of the sale or exchange, by discounting such payment at the rate, and in the manner, provided in regulations prescribed by the Secretary. Such regulations shall provide for discounting on the basis of 6-month brackets and shall provide that the present value of any interest payment due not more than 6 months after the date of the sale or exchange is an amount equal to 100 percent of such payment.

(c) **Payments to which section applies**—

(1) **In general.**—Except as provided in subsection (f), this section shall apply to any payment on account of the sale or exchange of property which constitutes part or all of the sales price and which is due more than 6 months after the date of such sale or exchange under a contract—

(A) under which some or all of the payments are due more than one year after the date of such sale or exchange, and

(B) under which, using a rate provided by regulations prescribed by the Secretary for purposes of this subparagraph, there is total unstated interest.

Any rate prescribed for determining whether there is total unstated interest for purposes of subparagraph (B) shall be at least one percentage point lower than the rate prescribed for purposes of subsection (b) (2).

(2) **Treatment of evidence of indebtedness.**—For purposes of this section, an evidence of indebtedness of the purchaser given in consideration for the sale or exchange of property shall not be considered a payment, and any payment due under such evidence of indebtedness shall be treated as due under the contract for the sale or exchange.

(d) Payments that are indefinite as to time, liability, or amount.—In the case of a contract for the sale or exchange of property under which the liability for, or the amount or due date of, any portion of a payment cannot be determined at the time of the sale or exchange, this section shall be separately applied to such portion as if it (and any amount of interest attributable to such portion) were the only payments due under the contract; and such determinations of liability, amount, and due date shall be made at the time payment of such portion is made.

(e) Change in terms of contract.—If the liability for, or the amount or due date of, any payment (including interest) under a contract for the sale or exchange of property is changed, the "total unstated interest" under the contract shall be recomputed and allocated (with adjustment for prior interest (including unstated interest) payments) under regulations prescribed by the Secretary.

(f) Exceptions and limitations.—

    (1) Sales price of $3,000 or less.—This section shall not apply to any payment on account of the sale or exchange of property if it can be determined at the time of such sale or exchange that the sales price cannot exceed $3,000.

    (2) Carrying charges.—In the case of the purchaser, the tax treatment of amounts paid on account of the sale or exchange of property shall be made without regard to this section if any such amounts are treated under section 163(b) as if they included interest.

    (3) Treatment of seller.—In the case of the seller, the tax treatment of any amounts received on account of the sale or exchange of property shall be made without regard to this section if all of the gain, if any, on such sale or exchange would be considered as ordinary income.

    (4) Sales or exchanges of patents.—This section shall not apply to any payments made pursuant to a transfer described in section 1235(a) (relating to sale or exchange of patents).

    (5) Annuities.—This section shall not apply to any amount the liability for which depends in whole or in part on the life expectancy of one or more individuals and which constitutes an amount received as an annuity to which section 72 applies.

(g) Maximum rate of interest on certain transfers of land between related parties.—

    (1) In general.—In the case of any qualified sale, the maximum interest rate used in determining the total unstated interest rate under the regulations under subsection (b) shall not exceed 7 percent, compounded semiannually.

    (2) Qualified sale.—For purposes of this subsection, the term "qualified sale" means any sale or exchange of land by an individual to a member of such individual's family (within the meaning of section 267(c)(4)).

    (3) $500,000 limitation.—Paragraph (1) shall not apply to any qualified sale between individuals made during any calendar year to the extent that the sales price for such sale (when added to the aggregate sales price for prior qualified sales between such individuals during the calendar year) exceeds $500,000.

    (4) Nonresident alien individuals.—This section shall not apply to any sale or exchange if any party to such sale or exchange is a nonresident alien individual.

SUBCHAPTER F—EXEMPT ORGANIZATIONS

Part
   I. General rule.
  II. Private foundations.*
 III. Taxation of business income of certain exempt organizations.
  IV. Farmers' cooperatives.*
   V. Shipowners' protection and indemnity associations.*
  VI. Political organizations.
 VII. Certain homeowners associations.*

PART I—GENERAL RULE

§ 501.   Exemption from tax on corporations, certain trusts, etc.

(a) Exemption from taxation.—An organization described in subsection (c) or (d) or section 401(a) shall be exempt from taxation under this subtitle unless such exemption is denied under section 502 or 503.

(b) Tax on unrelated business income and certain other activities.—An organization exempt from taxation under subsection (a) shall be subject to tax to the extent provided in parts II, III, and VI of this subchapter, but (notwithstanding parts II, III, and VI of this subchapter) shall be considered an organization exempt from income taxes for the purpose of any law which refers to organizations exempt from income taxes.

(c) List of exempt organizations.—The following organizations are referred to in subsection (a):

(3) Corporations, and any community chest, fund, or foundation, organized and operated exclusively for religious, charitable, scientific, testing for public safety, literary, or educational purposes, or to foster national or international amateur sports competition (but only if no part of its activities involve the provision of athletic facilities or equipment), or for the prevention of cruelty to children or animals, no part of the net earnings of which inures to the benefit of any private shareholder or individual, no substantial part of the activities of which is carrying on propaganda, or otherwise attempting, to influence legislation (except as otherwise provided in subsection (h)), and which does not participate in, or intervene in (including the publishing or distributing of statements), any political campaign on behalf of any candidate for public office.

(4) Civic leagues or organizations not organized for profit but operated exclusively for the promotion of social welfare, or local associations of employees, the membership of which is limited to the employees of a designated person or persons in a particular municipality, and the net earnings of which are devoted exclusively to charitable, educational, or recreational purposes.

(5) Labor, agricultural, or horticultural organizations.

(6) Business leagues, chambers of commerce, real-estate boards, boards of trade, or professional football leagues (whether or not administering a

* Omitted entirely.

pension fund for football players), not organized for profit and no part of the net earnings of which inures to the benefit of any private shareholder or individual.

(7) Clubs organized for pleasure, recreation, and other nonprofitable purposes, substantially all of the activities of which are for such purposes and no part of the net earnings of which inures to the benefit of any private shareholder.

. . . . .

(h) Expenditures by public charities to influence legislation.—

(1) **General rule.**—In the case of an organization to which this subsection applies, exemption from taxation under subsection (a) shall be denied because a substantial part of the activities of such organization consists of carrying on propaganda, or otherwise attempting, to influence legislation, but only if such organization normally—

(A) makes lobbying expenditures in excess of the lobbying ceiling amount for such organization for each taxable year, or

(B) makes grass roots expenditures in excess of the grass roots ceiling amount for such organization for each taxable year.

(2) **Definitions.**—For purposes of this subsection—

(A) **Lobbying expenditures.**—The term "lobbying expenditures" means expenditures for the purpose of influencing legislation (as defined in section 4911(d)).

(B) **Lobbying ceiling amount.**—The lobbying ceiling amount for any organization for any taxable year is 150 percent of the lobbying nontaxable amount for such organization for such taxable year, determined under section 4911.

(C) **Grass roots expenditures.**—The term "grass roots expenditures" means expenditures for the purpose of influencing legislation (as defined in section 4911(d) without regard to paragraph (1) (B) thereof).

(D) **Grass roots ceiling amount.**—The grass roots ceiling amount for any organization for any taxable year is 150 percent of the grass roots nontaxable amount for such organization for such taxable year, determined under section 4911.

(3) **Organizations to which this subsection applies.**—This subsection shall apply to any organization which has elected (in such manner and at such time as the Secretary may prescribe) to have the provisions of this subsection apply to such organization and which, for the taxable year which includes the date the election is made, is described in subsection (c) (3) and—

(A) is described in paragraph (4), and

(B) is not a disqualified organization under paragraph (5).

(4) **Organizations permitted to elect to have this subsection apply.**—An organization is described in this paragraph if it is described in—

(A) section 170(b) (1) (A) (ii) (relating to educational institutions),

(B) section 170(b) (1) (A) (iii) (relating to hospitals and medical research organizations),

(C) section 170(b) (1) (A) (iv) (relating to organizations supporting government schools),

(D) section 170(b) (1) (A) (vi) (relating to organizations publicly supported by charitable contributions),

(E) section 509(a) (2) (relating to organizations publicly supported by admissions, sales, etc.), or

(F) section 509(a) (3) (relating to organizations supporting certain types of public charities) except that for purposes of this subparagraph, section 509(a) (3) shall be applied without regard to the last sentence of section 509(a).

(5) Disqualified organizations.—For purposes of paragraph (3) an organization is a disqualified organization if it is—

(A) described in section 170(b) (1) (A) (i) (relating to churches),

(B) an integrated auxiliary of a church or of a convention or association of churches, or

(C) a member of an affiliated group of organizations (within the meaning of section 4911(f) (2)) if one or more members of such group is described in subparagraph (A) or (B).

. . . . .

(i) Prohibition of discrimination by certain social clubs.—Notwithstanding subsection (a), an organization which is described in subsection (c) (7) shall not be exempt from taxation under subsection (a) for any taxable year if, at any time during such taxable year, the charter, bylaws, or other governing instrument, of such organization or any written policy statement of such organization contains a provision which provides for discrimination against any person on the basis of race, color, or religion. The preceding sentence to the extent it relates to discrimination on the basis of religion shall not apply to—

(1) an auxiliary of a fraternal beneficiary society if such society—

(A) is described in subsection (c)(8) and exempt from tax under subsection (a), and

(B) limits its membership to the members of a particular religion, or

(2) a club which in good faith limits its membership to the members of a particular religion in order to further the teachings or principles of that religion, and not to exclude individuals of a particular race or color.

. . . . .

§ 502.   Feeder organizations

(a) General rule.—An organization operated for the primary purpose of carrying on a trade or business for profit shall not be exempt from taxation under section 501 on the ground that all of its profits are payable to one or more organizations exempt from taxation under section 501.

(b) Special rule.—For purposes of this section, the term "trade or business" shall not include—

(1) the deriving of rents which would be excluded under section 512(b) (3), if section 512 applied to the organization,

(2) any trade or business in which substantially all the work in carrying on such trade or business is performed for the organization without compensation, or

(3) any trade or business which is the selling of merchandise, substantially all of which has been received by the organization as gifts or contributions.

§ 504. Status after organization ceases to qualify for exemption under section 501(c) (3) because of substantial lobbying

(a) **General rule.**—An organization which—

(1) was exempt (or was determined by the Secretary to be exempt) from taxation under section 501(a) by reason of being an organization described in section 501(c) (3), and

(2) is not an organization described in section 501(c) (3) by reason of carrying on propaganda, or otherwise attempting, to influence legislation,

shall not at any time thereafter be treated as an organization described in section 501(c) (4).

(b) **Regulations to prevent avoidance.**—The Secretary shall prescribe such regulations as may be necessary or appropriate to prevent the avoidance of subsection (a), including regulations relating to a direct or indirect transfer of all or part of the assets of an organization to an organization controlled (directly or indirectly) by the same person or persons who control the transferor organization.

(c) **Churches, etc.**—Subsection (a) shall not apply to any organization which is a disqualified organization within the meaning of section 501(h) (5) (relating to churches, etc.) for the taxable year immediately preceding the first taxable year for which such organization is described in paragraph (2) of subsection (a).

PART III—TAXATION OF BUSINESS INCOME OF CERTAIN EXEMPT ORGANIZATIONS

§ 511. Imposition of tax on unrelated business income of charitable, etc., organizations

(a) **Charitable, etc., organizations taxable at corporation rates.**—

(1) **Imposition of tax.**—There is hereby imposed for each taxable year on the unrelated business taxable income (as defined in section 512) of every organization described in paragraph (2) a tax computed as provided in section 11. In making such computation for purposes of this section, the term "taxable income" as used in section 11 shall be read as "unrelated business taxable income".

(2) **Organizations subject to tax.**—

(A) **Organizations described in sections 401(a) and 501(c).**—The tax imposed by paragraph (1) shall apply in the case of any organization (other than a trust described in subsection (b) or an organization described in section 501(c) (1)) which is exempt, except as provided in this part or part II (relating to private foundations), from taxation under this subtitle by reason of section 501(a).

(B) **State colleges and universities.**—The tax imposed by paragraph (1) shall apply in the case of any college or university which is an agency or instrumentality of any government or any political subdivision thereof, or which is owned or operated by a government or any political

326

subdivision thereof, or by any agency or instrumentality of one or more governments or political subdivisions. Such tax shall also apply in the case of any corporation wholly owned by one or more such colleges or universities.

(b) Tax on charitable, etc., trusts.—

(1) **Imposition of tax.**—There is hereby imposed for each taxable year on the unrelated business taxable income of every trust described in paragraph (2) a tax computed as provided in section 1(e). In making such computation for purposes of this section, the term "taxable income" as used in section 1 shall be read as "unrelated business taxable income" as defined in section 512.

(2) **Charitable, etc., trusts subject to tax.**—The tax imposed by paragraph (1) shall apply in the case of any trust which is exempt, except as provided in this part or part II (relating to private foundations), from taxation under this subtitle by reason of section 501(a) and which, if it were not for such exemption, would be subject to subchapter J (sec. 641 and following, relating to estates, trusts, beneficiaries, and decedents).

· · · ·

§ 512.   Unrelated business taxable income

(a) Definition.—For purposes of this title—

(1) **General rule.**—Except as otherwise provided in this subsection, the term "unrelated business taxable income" means the gross income derived by any organization from any unrelated trade or business (as defined in section 513) regularly carried on by it, less the deductions allowed by this chapter which are directly connected with the carrying on of such trade or business, both computed with the modifications provided in subsection (b).

· · · ·

(b) Modifications.—The modifications referred to in subsection (a) are the following:

(1) There shall be excluded all dividends, interest, payments with respect to securities loans (as defined in section 512(a) (5)), and annuities, and all deductions directly connected with such income.

(2) There shall be excluded all royalties (including overriding royalties) whether measured by production or by gross or taxable income from the property, and all deductions directly connected with such income.

(3) In the case of rents—

(A) Except as provided in subparagraph (B), there shall be excluded—

(i) all rents from real property (including property described in section 1245(a) (3) (C)), and

(ii) all rents from personal property (including for purposes of this paragraph as personal property any property described in section 1245(a) (3) (B)) leased with such real property, if the rents attributable to such personal property are an incidental amount of the total rents received or accrued under the lease, determined at the time the personal property is placed in service.

(B) Subparagraph (A) shall not apply—

(i) if more than 50 percent of the total rent received or accrued under the lease is attributable to personal property described in subparagraph (A) (ii), or

(ii) if the determination of the amount of such rent depends in whole or in part on the income or profits derived by any person from the property leased (other than an amount based on a fixed percentage or percentages of receipts or sales).

(C) There shall be excluded all deductions directly connected with rents excluded under subparagraph (A).

(4) Notwithstanding paragraph (1), (2), (3), or (5), in the case of debt-financed property (as defined in section 514) there shall be included, as an item of gross income derived from an unrelated trade or business, the amount ascertained under section 514(a) (1), and there shall be allowed, as a deduction, the amount ascertained under section 514(a) (2).

(5) There shall be excluded all gains or losses from the sale, exchange, or other disposition of property other than—

(A) stock in trade or other property of a kind which would properly be includible in inventory if on hand at the close of the taxable year, or

(B) property held primarily for sale to customers in the ordinary course of the trade or business.

There shall also be excluded all gains on the lapse or termination of options, written by the organization in connection with its investment activities, to buy or sell securities (as defined in section 1236(c)). This paragraph shall not apply with respect to the cutting of timber which is considered, on the application of section 631, as a sale or exchange of such timber.

. . . .

(7) There shall be excluded all income derived from research for (A) the United States, or any of its agencies or instrumentalities, or (B) any State or political subdivision thereof; and there shall be excluded all deductions directly connected with such income.

(8) In the case of a college, university, or hospital, there shall be excluded all income derived from research performed for any person, and all deductions directly connected with such income.

(9) In the case of an organization operated primarily for purposes of carrying on fundamental research the results of which are freely available to the general public, there shall be excluded all income derived from research performed for any person, and all deductions directly connected with such income.

. . . .

§ 513.   Unrelated trade or business

(a) General rule.—The term "unrelated trade or business" means, in the case of any organization subject to the tax imposed by section 511, any trade or business the conduct of which is not substantially related (aside from the need of such organization for income or funds or the use it makes of the profits derived) to the exercise or performance by such organization of its charitable, educational, or other purpose or function constituting the basis for its exemption under section 501 (or, in the case of an organization described in section 511(a) (2) (B), to the exercise or performance of any purpose or function described in section 501(c) (3)), except that such term does not include any trade or business—

(1) in which substantially all the work in carrying on such trade or business is performed for the organization without compensation; or

(2) which is carried on, in the case of an organization described in section 501(c) (3) or in the case of a college or university described in section 511(a) (2) (B), by the organization primarily for the convenience of its members, students, patients, officers, or employees, or, in the case of a local association of employees described in section 501(c) (4) organized before May 27, 1969, which is the selling by the organization of items of work-related clothes and equipment and items normally sold through vending machines, through food dispensing facilities, or by snack bars, for the convenience of its members at their usual places of employment; or

(3) which is the selling of merchandise, substantially all of which has been received by the organization as gifts or contributions.

(b) Special rule for trusts.—The term "unrelated trade or business" means, in the case of—

(1) a trust computing its unrelated business taxable income under section 512 for purposes of section 681; or

(2) a trust described in section 401(a), or section 501(c) (17), which is exempt from tax under section 501(a);

any trade or business regularly carried on by such trust or by a partnership of which it is a member.

(c) Advertising, etc., activities.—For purposes of this section, the term "trade or business" includes any activity which is carried on for the production of income from the sale of goods or the performance of services. For purposes of the preceding sentence, an activity does not lose identity as a trade or business merely because it is carried on within a larger aggregate of similar activities or within a larger complex of other endeavors which may, or may not, be related to the exempt purposes of the organization. Where an activity carried on for profit constitutes an unrelated trade or business, no part of such trade or business shall be excluded from such classification merely because it does not result in profit.

. . . . .

§ 514.   Unrelated debt-financed income

(a) Unrelated debt-financed income and deductions.—In computing under section 512 the unrelated business taxable income for any taxable year—

(1) Percentage of income taken into account.—There shall be included with respect to each debt-financed property as an item of gross income derived from an unrelated trade or business an amount which is the same percentage (but not in excess of 100 percent) of the total gross income derived during the taxable year from or on account of such property as (A) the average acquisition indebtedness (as defined in subsection (c) (7)) for the taxable year with respect to the property is of (B) the average amount (determined under regulations prescribed by the Secretary) of the adjusted basis of such property during the period it is held by the organization during such taxable year.

(2) Percentage of deductions taken into account.—There shall be allowed as a deduction with respect to each debt-financed property an amount determined by applying (except as provided in the last sentence of this paragraph) the percentage derived under paragraph (1) to the sum determined under paragraph (3). The percentage derived under this paragraph shall not be applied with respect to the deduction of any capital loss resulting from the carryback or carryover of net capital losses under section 1212.

(3) **Deductions allowable.**—The sum referred to in paragraph (2) is the sum of the deductions under this chapter which are directly connected with the debt-financed property or the income therefrom, except that if the debt-financed property is of a character which is subject to the allowance for depreciation provided in section 167, the allowance shall be computed only by use of the straight-line method.

(b) **Definition of debt-financed property.**—

(1) **In general.**—For purposes of this section, the term "debt-financed property" means any property which is held to produce income and with respect to which there is an acquisition indebtedness (as defined in subsection (c)) at any time during the taxable year (or, if the property was disposed of during the taxable year, with respect to which there was an acquisition indebtedness at any time during the 12-month period ending with the date of such disposition), except that such term does not include—

(A) (i) any property substantially all the use of which is substantially related (aside from the need of the organization for income or funds) to the exercise or performance by such organization of its charitable, educational, or other purpose or function constituting the basis for its exemption under section 501 (or, in the case of an organization described in section 511(a) (2) (B), to the exercise or performance of any purpose or function designated in section 501(c) (3)), or (ii) any property to which clause (i) does not apply, to the extent that its use is so substantially related;

(B) except in the case of income excluded under section 512(b) (5), any property to the extent that the income from such property is taken into account in computing the gross income of any unrelated trade or business;

(C) any property to the extent that the income from such property is excluded by reason of the provisions of paragraph (7), (8), or (9) of section 512(b) in computing the gross income of any unrelated trade or business; or

(D) any property to the extent that it is used in any trade or business described in paragraph (1), (2), or (3) of section 513(a).

For purposes of subparagraph (A), substantially all the use of a property shall be considered to be substantially related to the exercise or performance by an organization of its charitable, educational, or other purpose or function constituting the basis for its exemption under section 501 if such property is real property subject to a lease to a medical clinic entered into primarily for purposes which are substantially related (aside from the need of such organization for income or funds or the use it makes of the rents derived) to the exercise or performance by such organization of its charitable, educational, or other purpose or function constituting the basis for its exemption under section 501.

(2) **Special rule for related uses.**—For purposes of applying paragraphs (1) (A), (C), and (D), the use of any property by an exempt organization which is related to an organization shall be treated as use by such organization.

PART VI—POLITICAL ORGANIZATIONS

§ 527.   Political organizations

(a) **General rule.**—A political organization shall be subject to taxation under this subtitle only to the extent provided in this section. A political organization shall be considered an organization exempt from income taxes for the purpose of any law which refers to organizations exempt from income taxes.

(b) **Tax imposed.**—

(1) **In general.**—A tax is hereby imposed for each taxable year on the political organization taxable income of every political organization. Such tax shall be computed by multiplying the political organization taxable income by the highest rate of tax specified in section 11(b).

(2) **Alternative tax in case of capital gains.**—If for any taxable year any political organization has a net capital gain, then, in lieu of the tax imposed by paragraph (1), there is hereby imposed a tax (if such a tax is less than the tax imposed by paragraph (1)) which shall consist of the sum of—

(A) a partial tax, computed as provided by paragraph (1), on the political organization taxable income determined by reducing such income by the amount of such gain, and

(B) an amount determined as provided in section 1201(a) on such gain.

(c) **Political organization taxable income defined.**—

(1) **Taxable income defined.**—For purposes of this section, the political organization taxable income of any organization for any taxable year is an amount equal to the excess (if any) of—

(A) the gross income for the taxable year (excluding any exempt function income), over

(B) the deductions allowed by this chapter which are directly connected with the production of the gross income (excluding exempt function income), computed with the modifications provided in paragraph (2).

(2) **Modifications.**—For purposes of this subsection—

(A) there shall be allowed a specific deduction of $100,

(B) no net operating loss deduction shall be allowed under section 172, and

(C) no deduction shall be allowed under part VIII of subchapter B (relating to special deductions for corporations).

(3) **Exempt function income.**—For purposes of this subsection, the term "exempt function income" means any amount received as—

(A) a contribution of money or other property,

(B) membership dues, a membership fee or assessment from a member of the political organization,

(C) proceeds from a political fundraising or entertainment event, or proceeds from the sale of political campaign materials, which are not received in the ordinary course of any trade or business, or

(D) proceeds from the conducting of any bingo game (as defined in section 513(f) (2)),

to the extent such amount is segregated for use only for the exempt function of the political organization.

(d) Certain uses not treated as income to candidate.—For purposes of this title, if any political organization—

(1) contributes any amount to or for the use of any political organization which is treated as exempt from tax under subsection (a) of this section,

(2) contributes any amount to or for the use of any organization described in paragraph (1) or (2) of section 509(a) which is exempt from tax under section 501(a), or

(3) deposits any amount in the general fund of the Treasury or in the general fund of any State or local government,

such amount shall be treated as an amount not diverted for the personal use of the candidate or any other person. No deduction shall be allowed under this title for the contribution or deposit of any amount described in the preceding sentence.

(e) Other definitions.—For purposes of this section—

(1) Political organization.—The term "political organization" means a party, committee, association, fund, or other organization (whether or not incorporated) organized and operated primarily for the purpose of directly or indirectly accepting contributions or making expenditures, or both, for an exempt function.

(2) Exempt function.—The term "exempt function" means the function of influencing or attempting to influence the selection, nomination, election, or appointment of any individual to any Federal, State, or local public office or office in a political organization, or the election of Presidential or Vice-Presidential electors, whether or not such individual or electors are selected, nominated, elected, or appointed.

(3) Contributions.—The term "contributions" has the meaning given to such term by section 271(b) (2).

(4) Expenditures.—The term "expenditures" has the meaning given to such term by section 271(b) (3).

(f) Exempt organization which is not political organization must include certain amounts in gross income.—

(1) In general.—If an organization described in section 501(c) which is exempt from tax under section 501(a) expends any amount during the taxable year directly (or through another organization) for an exempt function (within the meaning of subsection (e) (2)), then, notwithstanding any other provision of law, there shall be included in the gross income of such organization for the taxable year, and shall be subject to tax under subsection (b) as if it constituted political organization taxable income, an amount equal to the lesser of—

(A) the net investment income of such organization for the taxable year, or

(B) the aggregate amount so expended during the taxable year for such an exempt function.

(2) Net investment income.—For purposes of this subsection, the term "net investment income" means the excess of—

(A) the gross amount of income from interest, dividends, rents, and royalties, plus the excess (if any) of gains from the sale or exchange of assets over the losses from the sale or exchange of assets, over

(B) the deductions allowed by this chapter which are directly connected with the production of the income referred to in subparagraph (A).

For purposes of the preceding sentence, there shall not be taken into account items taken into account for purposes of the tax imposed by section 511 (relating to tax on unrelated business income).

. . . .

SUBCHAPTER G—CORPORATIONS USED TO AVOID INCOME TAX ON SHAREHOLDERS

Part
   I. Corporations improperly accumulating surplus.
  II. Personal holding companies.
 III. Foreign personal holding companies.*
  IV. Deduction for dividends paid.

PART I—CORPORATIONS IMPROPERLY ACCUMULATING SURPLUS

§ 531.   Imposition of accumulated earnings tax

In addition to other taxes imposed by this chapter, there is hereby imposed for each taxable year on the accumulated taxable income (as defined in section 535) of every corporation described in section 532, an accumulated earnings tax equal to the sum of—

(1) 27½ percent of the accumulated taxable income not in excess of $100,000, plus

(2) 38½ percent of the accumulated taxable income in excess of $100,000.

§ 532.   Corporations subject to accumulated earnings tax

(a) **General rule.**—The accumulated earnings tax imposed by section 531 shall apply to every corporation (other than those described in subsection (b)) formed or availed of for the purpose of avoiding the income tax with respect to its shareholders or the shareholders of any other corporation, by permitting earnings and profits to accumulate instead of being divided or distributed.

(b) **Exceptions.**—The accumulated earnings tax imposed by section 531 shall not apply to—

(1) a personal holding company (as defined in section 542),

(2) a foreign personal holding company (as defined in section 552), or

(3) a corporation exempt from tax under subchapter F (section 501 and following).

§ 533.   Evidence of purpose to avoid income tax

(a) **Unreasonable accumulation determinative of purpose.**—For purposes of section 532, the fact that the earnings and profits of a corporation are permitted to accumulate beyond the reasonable needs of the business shall be determinative of the purpose to avoid the income tax with respect to shareholders, unless the corporation by the preponderance of the evidence shall prove to the contrary.

* Omitted entirely.

(b) Holding or investment company.—The fact that any corporation is a mere holding or investment company shall be prima facie evidence of the purpose to avoid the income tax with respect to shareholders.

§ 534. Burden of proof

(a) General rule.—In any proceeding before tne Tax Court involving a notice of deficiency based in whole or in part on the allegation that all or any part of the earnings and profits have been permitted to accumulate beyond the reasonable needs of the business, the burden of proof with respect to such allegation shall—

(1) if notification has not been sent in accordance with subsection (b), be on the Secretary, or

(2) if the taxpayer has submitted the statement described in subsection (c), be on the Secretary with respect to the grounds set forth in such statement in accordance with the provisions of such subsection.

(b) Notification by Secretary.—Before mailing the notice of deficiency referred to in subsection (a), the Secretary may send by certified mail or registered mail a notification informing the taxpayer that the proposed notice of deficiency includes an amount with respect to the accumulated earnings tax imposed by section 531.

(c) Statement by taxpayer.—Within such time (but not less than 30 days) after the mailing of the notification described in subsection (b) as the Secretary may prescribe by regulations, the taxpayer may submit a statement of the grounds (together with facts sufficient to show the basis thereof) on which the taxpayer relies to establish that all or any part of the earnings and profits have not been permitted to accumulate beyond the reasonable needs of the business.

§ 535. Accumulated taxable income

(a) Definition.—For purposes of this subtitle, the term "accumulated taxable income" means the taxable income, adjusted in the manner provided in subsection (b), minus the sum of the dividends paid deduction (as defined in section 561) and the accumulated earnings credit (as defined in subsection (c)).

(b) Adjustments to taxable income.—For purposes of subsection (a), taxable income shall be adjusted as follows:

(1) **Taxes.**—There shall be allowed as a deduction Federal income and excess profits taxes and income, war profits, and excess profits taxes of foreign countries and possessions of the United States (to the extent not allowable as a deduction under section 275(a) (4)), accrued during the taxable year or deemed to be paid by a domestic corporation under section 902(a) or 960(a) (1) for the taxable year, but not including the accumulated earnings tax imposed by section 531, the personal holding company tax imposed by section 541, or the taxes imposed by corresponding sections of a prior income tax law.

(2) **Charitable contributions.**—The deduction for charitable contributions provided under section 170 shall be allowed without regard to section 170(b) (2).

(3) **Special deductions disallowed.**—The special deductions for corporations provided in part VIII (except section 248) of subchapter B (section 241 and following, relating to the deduction for dividends received by corporations, etc.) shall not be allowed.

(4) **Net operating loss.**—The net operating loss deduction provided in section 172 shall not be allowed.

(5) **Capital losses.**—There shall be allowed as deductions losses from sales or exchanges of capital assets during the taxable year which are disallowed as deductions under section 1211(a).

(6) **Net capital gains.**—There shall be allowed as a deduction the net capital gain for the taxable year (determined without regard to the capital loss carryback or carryover provided in section 1212) minus the taxes imposed by this subtitle attributable to such net capital gain. The taxes attributable to such net capital gain shall be an amount equal to the difference between—

(A) the taxes imposed by this subtitle (except the tax imposed by this part) for such year, and

(B) such taxes computed for such year without including in taxable income the net capital gain for the taxable year (determined with regard to the capital loss carryback and carryover provided in section 1212).

(7) **Capital loss.**—No allowance shall be made for the capital loss carryback or carryover provided in section 1212.

(c) **Accumulated earnings credit.**—

(1) **General rule.**—For purposes of subsection (a), in the case of a corporation other than a mere holding or investment company the accumulated earnings credit is (A) an amount equal to such part of the earnings and profits for the taxable year as are retained for the reasonable needs of the business, minus (B) the deduction allowed by subsection (b) (6). For purposes of this paragraph, the amount of the earnings and profits for the taxable year which are retained is the amount by which the earnings and profits for the taxable year exceed the dividends paid deduction (as defined in section 561) for such year.

(2) **Minimum credit.**—

(A) **In general.**—The credit allowable under paragraph (1) shall in no case be less than the amount by which $250,000 exceeds the accumulated earnings and profits of the corporation at the close of the preceding taxable year.

(B) **Certain service corporations.**—In the case of a corporation the principal function of which is the performance of services in the field of health, law, engineering, architecture, accounting, actuarial science, performing arts, or consulting, subparagraph (A) shall be applied by substituting "$150,000" for "$250,000".

(3) **Holding and investment companies.**—In the case of a corporation which is a mere holding or investment company, the accumulated earnings credit is the amount (if any) by which $250,000 exceeds the accumulated earnings and profits of the corporation at the close of the preceding taxable year.

(4) **Accumulated earnings and profits.**—For purposes of paragraphs (2) and (3), the accumulated earnings and profits at the close of the preceding

taxable year shall be reduced by the dividends which under section 563(a) (relating to dividends paid after the close of the taxable year) are considered as paid during such taxable year.

. . . . . .

§ 537.   Reasonable needs of the business

(a) **General rule.**—For purposes of this part, the term "reasonable needs of the business" includes—

(1) the reasonably anticipated needs of the business,

(2) the section 303 redemption needs of the business, and

(3) the excess business holdings redemption needs of the business.

(b) **Special rules.**—For purposes of subsection (a)—

(1) **Section 303 redemption needs.**—The term "section 303 redemption needs" means, with respect to the taxable year of the corporation in which a shareholder of the corporation died or any taxable year thereafter, the amount needed (or reasonably anticipated to be needed) to make a redemption of stock included in the gross estate of the decedent (but not in excess of the maximum amount of stock to which section 303(a) may apply).

(2) **Excess business holdings redemption needs.**—The term "excess business holdings redemption needs" means the amount needed (or reasonably anticipated to be needed) to redeem from a private foundation stock which—

(A) such foundation held on May 26, 1969 (or which was received by such foundation pursuant to a will or irrevocable trust to which section 4943(c) (5) applies), and

(B) constituted excess business holdings on May 26, 1969, or would have constituted excess business holdings as of such date if there were taken into account (i) stock received pursuant to a will or trust described in subparagraph (A), and (ii) the reduction in the total outstanding stock of the corporation which would have resulted solely from the redemption of stock held by the private foundation.

(3) **Obligations incurred to make redemptions.**—In applying paragraphs (1) and (2), the discharge of any obligation incurred to make a redemption described in such paragraphs shall be treated as the making of such redemption.

(4) **Product liability loss reserves.**—The accumulation of reasonable amounts for the payment of reasonably anticipated product liability losses (as defined in section 172(i)), as determined under regulations prescribed by the Secretary, shall be treated as accumulated for the reasonably anticipated needs of the business.

(5) **No inference as to prior taxable years.**—The application of this part to any taxable year before the first taxable year specified in paragraph (1) shall be made without regard to the fact that distributions in redemption coming within the terms of such paragraphs were subsequently made.

PART II—PERSONAL HOLDING COMPANIES

§ 541.   Imposition of personal holding company tax

In addition to other taxes imposed by this chapter, there is hereby imposed for each taxable year on the undistributed personal holding company income (as defined in section 545) of every personal holding company (as defined in section 542) a personal holding company tax equal to 50 percent of the undistributed personal holding company income.

§ 542.   Definition of personal holding company

(a) **General rule.**—For purposes of this subtitle, the term "personal holding company" means any corporation (other than a corporation described in subsection (c)) if—

(1) **Adjusted ordinary gross income requirement.**—At least 60 percent of its adjusted ordinary gross income (as defined in section 543(b) (2)) for the taxable year is personal holding company income (as defined in section 543(a)), and

(2) **Stock ownership requirement.**—At any time during the last half of the taxable year more than 50 percent in value of its outstanding stock is owned, directly or indirectly, by or for not more than 5 individuals. For purposes of this paragraph, an organization described in section 401(a), 501(c) (17), or 509(a) or a portion of a trust permanently set aside or to be used exclusively for the purposes described in section 642(c) or a corresponding provision of a prior income tax law shall be considered an individual.

(b) **Corporations filing consolidated returns.**—

(1) **General rule.**—In the case of an affiliated group of corporations filing or required to file a consolidated return under section 1501 for any taxable year, the adjusted ordinary gross income requirement of subsection (a) (1) of this section shall, except as provided in paragraphs (2) and (3), be applied for such year with respect to the consolidated adjusted ordinary gross income and the consolidated personal holding company income of the affiliated group. No member of such an affiliated group shall be considered to meet such adjusted ordinary gross income requirement unless the affiliated group meets such requirement.

(2) **Ineligible affiliated group.**—Paragraph (1) shall not apply to an affiliated group of corporations if—

(A) any member of the affiliated group of corporations (including the common parent corporation) derived 10 percent or more of its adjusted ordinary gross income for the taxable year from sources outside the affiliated group, and

(B) 80 percent or more of the amount described in subparagraph (A) consists of personal holding company income (as defined in section 543).

For purposes of this paragraph, section 543 shall be applied as if the amount described in subparagraph (A) were the adjusted ordinary gross income of the corporation.

(3) **Excluded corporations.**—Paragraph (1) shall not apply to an affiliated group of corporations if any member of the affiliated group (including the

common parent corporation) is a corporation excluded from the definition of personal holding company under subsection (c).

(4) Certain dividend income received by a common parent.—In applying paragraph (2) (A) and (B), personal holding company income and adjusted ordinary gross income shall not include dividends received by a common parent corporation from another corporation if—

(A) the common parent corporation owns, directly or indirectly, more than 50 percent of the outstanding voting stock of such other corporation, and

(B) such other corporation is not a personal holding company for the taxable year in which the dividends are paid.

* * * * *

(c) Exceptions.—The term "personal holding company" as defined in subsection (a) does not include—

(1) a corporation exempt from tax under subchapter F (sec. 501 and following);

(2) a bank as defined in section 581, or a domestic building and loan association within the meaning of section 7701(a) (19);

(3) a life insurance company;

(4) a surety company;

(5) a foreign personal holding company as defined in section 552;

(6) a lending or finance company if—

(A) 60 percent or more of its ordinary gross income (as defined in section 543(b) (1)) is derived directly from the active and regular conduct of a lending or finance business;

(B) the personal holding company income for the taxable year (computed without regard to income described in subsection (d) (3) and income derived directly from the active and regular conduct of a lending or finance business, and computed by including as personal holding company income the entire amount of the gross income from rents, royalties, produced film rents, and compensation for use of corporate property by shareholders) is not more than 20 percent of the ordinary gross income;

(C) the sum of the deductions which are directly allocable to the active and regular conduct of its lending or finance business equals or exceeds the sum of—

(i) 15 percent of so much of the ordinary gross income derived therefrom as does not exceed $500,000, plus

(ii) 5 percent of so much of the ordinary gross income derived therefrom as exceeds $500,000; and

(D) the loans to a person who is a shareholder in such company during the taxable year by or for whom 10 percent or more in value of its outstanding stock is owned directly or indirectly (including, in the case of an individual, stock owned by members of his family as defined in section 544(a) (2)), outstanding at any time during such year do not exceed $5,000 in principal amount;

* * * * *

(9) a corporation which is subject to the jurisdiction of the court in a title 11 or similar case (within the meaning of section 368(a)(3)(A)) unless a major purpose of instituting or continuing such case is the avoidance of the tax imposed by section 541.

(d) Special rules for applying subsection (c) (6).—

(1) Lending or finance business defined.—

(A) In general.—Except as provided in subparagraph (B), for purposes of subsection (c) (6), the term "lending or finance business" means a business of—

(i) making loans,

(ii) purchasing or discounting accounts receivable, notes, or installment obligations,

(iii) rendering services or making facilities available in connection with activities described in clauses (i) and (ii) carried on by the corporation rendering services or making facilities available, or

(iv) rendering services or making facilities available to another corporation which is engaged in the lending or finance business (within the meaning of this paragraph), if such services or facilities are related to the lending or finance business (within such meaning) of such other corporation and such other corporation and the corporation rendering services or making facilities available are members of the same affiliated group (as defined in section 1504).

· · · · ·

§ 543.   Personal holding company income

(a) General rule.—For purposes of this subtitle, the term "personal holding company income" means the portion of the adjusted ordinary gross income which consists of:

(1) Dividends, etc.—Dividends, interest, royalties (other than mineral, oil, or gas royalties or copyright royalties), and annuities. This paragraph shall not apply to—

(A) interest constituting rent (as defined in subsection (b) (3)), and

· · · · ·

(C) dividends to which section 302(b)(4) would apply if the corporation were an individual.

(2) Rents.—The adjusted income from rents; except that such adjusted income shall not be included if—

(A) such adjusted income constitutes 50 percent or more of the adjusted ordinary gross income, and

(B) the sum of—

(i) the dividends paid during the taxable year (determined under section 562),

(ii) the dividends considered as paid on the last day of the taxable year under section 563(c) (as limited by the second sentence of section 563(b)), and

(iii) the consent dividends for the taxable year (determined under section 565), equals or exceeds the amount, if any, by which the personal holding company income for the taxable year (computed without regard to this paragraph and paragraph (6), and computed by including as personal holding company income copyright royalties and the adjusted income from mineral, oil, and gas royalties) exceeds 10 percent of the ordinary gross income.

(3) **Mineral, oil, and gas royalties.**—The adjusted income from mineral, oil, and gas royalties; except that such adjusted income shall not be included if—

(A) such adjusted income constitutes 50 percent or more of the adjusted ordinary gross income,

(B) the personal holding company income for the taxable year (computed without regard to this paragraph, and computed by including as personal holding company income copyright royalties and the adjusted income from rents) is not more than 10 percent of the ordinary gross income, and

(C) the sum of the deductions which are allowable under section 162 (relating to trade or business expenses) other than—

(i) deductions for compensation for personal services rendered by the shareholders, and

(ii) deductions which are specifically allowable under sections other than section 162,

equals or exceeds 15 percent of the adjusted ordinary gross income.

(4) **Copyright royalties.**—Copyright royalties; except that copyright royalties shall not be included if—

(A) such royalties (exclusive of royalties received for the use of, or right to use, copyrights or interests in copyrights on works created in whole, or in part, by any shareholder) constitute 50 percent or more of the ordinary gross income,

(B) the personal holding company income for the taxable year computed—

(i) without regard to copyright royalties, other than royalties received for the use of, or right to use, copyrights or interests in copyrights in works created in whole, or in part, by any shareholder owning more than 10 percent of the total outstanding capital stock of the corporation,

(ii) without regard to dividends from any corporation in which the taxpayer owns at least 50 percent of all classes of stock entitled to vote and at least 50 percent of the total value of all classes of stock and which corporation meets the requirements of this subparagraph and subparagraphs (A) and (C), and

(iii) by including as personal holding company income the adjusted income from rents and the adjusted income from mineral, oil, and gas royalties,

is not more than 10 percent of the ordinary gross income, and

(C) the sum of the deductions which are properly allocable to such royalties and which are allowable under section 162, other than—

(i) deductions for compensation for personal services rendered by the shareholders,

(ii) deductions for royalties paid or accrued, and

(iii) deductions which are specifically allowable under sections other than section 162,

equals or exceeds 25 percent of the amount by which the ordinary gross income exceeds the sum of the royalties paid or accrued and the amounts allowable as deductions under section 167 (relating to depreciation) with respect to copyright royalties.

For purposes of this subsection, the term "copyright royalties" means compensation, however designated, for the use of, or the right to use, copyrights in works protected by copyright issued under title 17 of the United States Code and to which copyright protection is also extended by the laws of any country other than the United States of America by virtue of any international treaty, convention, or agreement, or interests in any such copyrighted works, and includes payments from any person for performing rights in any such copyrighted work and payments (other than produced film rents as defined in paragraph (5) (B)) received for the use of, or right to use, films. For purposes of this paragraph, the term "shareholder" shall include any person who owns stock within the meaning of section 544.

(5) Produced film rents.—

(A) Produced film rents; except that such rents shall not be included if such rents constitute 50 percent or more of the ordinary gross income.

(B) For purposes of this section, the term "produced film rents" means payments received with respect to an interest in a film for the use of, or right to use, such film, but only to the extent that such interest was acquired before substantial completion of production of such film. In the case of a producer who actively participates in the production of the film, such term includes an interest in the proceeds or profits from the film, but only to the extent such interest is attributable to such active participation.

(6) Use of corporate property by shareholder.—

(A) Amounts received as compensation (however designated and from whomever received) for the use of, or the right to use, tangible property of the corporation in any case where, at any time during the taxable year, 25 percent or more in value of the outstanding stock of the corporation is owned, directly or indirectly, by or for an individual entitled to the use of the property (whether such right is obtained directly from the corporation or by means of a sublease or other arrangement).

(B) Subparagraph (A) shall apply only to a corporation which has personal holding company income in excess of 10 percent of its ordinary gross income.

(C) For purposes of the limitation in subparagraph (B), personal holding company income shall be computed—

(i) without regard to subparagraph (A) or paragraph (2),

(ii) by excluding amounts received as compensation for the use of (or right to use) intangible property (other than mineral, oil, or gas royalties or copyright royalties) if a substantial part of the tangible property used in connection with such intangible property is owned by the corporation and all such tangible and intangible property is used in the active conduct of a trade or business by an individual or individuals described in subparagraph (A), and

(iii) by including copyright royalties and adjusted income from mineral, oil, and gas royalties.

(7) Personal service contracts.—

(A) Amounts received under a contract under which the corporation is to furnish personal services; if some person other than the corporation has the right to designate (by name or by description) the individual who is to perform the services, or if the individual who is to perform the services is designated (by name or by description) in the contract; and

(B) amounts received from the sale or other disposition of such a contract.

This paragraph shall apply with respect to amounts received for services under a particular contract only if at some time during the taxable year 25 percent or more in value of the outstanding stock of the corporation is owned, directly or indirectly, by or for the individual who has performed, is to perform, or may be designated (by name or by description) as the one to perform, such services.

(8) Estates and trusts.—Amounts includible in computing the taxable income of the corporation under part I of subchapter J (sec. 641 and following, relating to estates, trusts, and beneficiaries).

(b) Definitions.—For purposes of this part—

(1) Ordinary gross income.—The term "ordinary gross income" means the gross income determined by excluding—

(A) all gains from the sale or other disposition of capital assets,

(B) all gains (other than those referred to in subparagraph (A)) from the sale or other disposition of property described in section 1231(b), and

. . . .

(2) Adjusted ordinary gross income.—The term "adjusted ordinary gross income" means the ordinary gross income adjusted as follows:

(A) Rents.—From the gross income from rents (as defined in the second sentence of paragraph (3) of this subsection) subtract the amount allowable as deductions for—

(i) exhaustion, wear and tear, obsolescence, and amortization of property other than tangible personal property which is not customarily retained by any one lessee for more than three years,

(ii) property taxes,

(iii) interest, and

(iv) rent,

to the extent allocable, under regulations prescribed by the Secretary, to such gross income from rents. The amount subtracted under this subparagraph shall not exceed such gross income from rents.

(B) Mineral royalties, etc.—From the gross income from mineral, oil, and gas royalties described in paragraph (4), and from the gross income from working interests in an oil or gas well, subtract the amount allowable as deductions for—

(i) exhaustion, wear and tear, obsolesence, amortization, and depletion,

(ii) property and severance taxes,

(iii) interest, and

(iv) rent,

to the extent allocable, under regulations prescribed by the Secretary, to such gross income from royalties or such gross income from working interests in oil or gas wells. The amount subtracted under this subparagraph with respect to royalties shall not exceed the gross income from such royalties, and the amount subtracted under this subparagraph with respect to working interests shall not exceed the gross income from such working interests.

(C) **Interest.**—There shall be excluded—

(i) interest received on a direct obligation of the United States held for sale to customers in the ordinary course of trade or business by a regular dealer who is making a primary market in such obligations, and

(ii) interest on a condemnation award, a judgment, and a tax refund.

(D) **Certain excluded rents.**—From the gross income consisting of compensation described in subparagraph (D) of paragraph (3) subtract the amount allowable as deductions for the items described in clauses (i), (ii), (iii), and (iv) of subparagraph (A) to the extent allocable, under regulations prescribed by the Secretary, to such gross income. The amount subtracted under this subparagraph shall not exceed such gross income.

(3) **Adjusted income from rents.**—The term "adjusted income from rents" means the gross income from rents, reduced by the amount subtracted under paragraph (2) (A) of this subsection. For purposes of the preceding sentence, the term "rents" means compensation, however designated, for the use of, or right to use, property, and the interest on debts owed to the corporation, to the extent such debts represent the price for which real property held primarily for sale to customers in the ordinary course of its trade or business was sold or exchanged by the corporation; but such term does not include—

(A) amounts constituting personal holding company income under subsection (a) (6),

(B) copyright royalties (as defined in subsection (a) (4)),

(C) produced film rents (as defined in subsection (a) (5) (B)), or

(D) compensation, however designated, for the use of, or the right to use, any tangible personal property manufactured or produced by the taxpayer, if during the taxable year the taxpayer is engaged in substantial manufacturing or production of tangible personal property of the same type.

(4) **Adjusted income from mineral, oil, and gas royalties.**—The term "adjusted income from mineral, oil, and gas royalties" means the gross income from mineral, oil, and gas royalties (including production payments and overriding royalties), reduced by the amount subtracted under paragraph (2) (B) of this subsection in respect of such royalties.

. . . . .

§ 544.   Rules for determining stock ownership

(a) Constructive ownership.—For purposes of determining whether a corporation is a personal holding company, insofar as such determination is based on stock ownership under section 542(a) (2), section 543(a) (7), section 543(a) (6), or section 543(a) (4)—

(1) Stock not owned by individual.—Stock owned, directly or indirectly, by or for a corporation, partnership, estate, or trust shall be considered as being owned proportionately by its shareholders, partners, or beneficiaries.

(2) Family and partnership ownership.—An individual shall be considered as owning the stock owned, directly or indirectly, by or for his family or by or for his partner. For purposes of this paragraph, the family of an individual includes only his brothers and sisters (whether by the whole or half blood), spouse, ancestors, and lineal descendants.

(3) Options.—If any person has an option to acquire stock, such stock shall be considered as owned by such person. For purposes of this paragraph, an option to acquire such an option, and each one of a series of such options, shall be considered as an option to acquire such stock.

(4) Application of family-partnership and option rules.—Paragraphs (2) and (3) shall be applied—

(A) for purposes of the stock ownership requirement provided in section 542(a) (2), if, but only if, the effect is to make the corporation a personal holding company;

(B) for purposes of section 543(a) (7) (relating to personal service contracts), of section 543(a) (6) (relating to use of property by shareholders), or of section 543(a) (4) (relating to copyright royalties), if, but only if, the effect is to make the amounts therein referred to includible under such paragraph as personal holding company income.

(5) Constructive ownership as actual ownership.—Stock constructively owned by a person by reason of the application of paragraph (1) or (3) shall, for purposes of applying paragraph (1) or (2), be treated as actually owned by such person; but stock constructively owned by an individual by reason of the application of paragraph (2) shall not be treated as owned by him for purposes of again applying such paragraph in order to make another the constructive owner of such stock.

(6) Option rule in lieu of family and partnership rule.—If stock may be considered as owned by an individual under either paragraph (2) or (3) it shall be considered as owned by him under paragraph (3).

(b) Convertible securities.—Outstanding securities convertible into stock (whether or not convertible during the taxable year) shall be considered as outstanding stock—

(1) for purposes of the stock ownership requirement provided in section 542(a) (2), but only if the effect of the inclusion of all such securities is to make the corporation a personal holding company;

(2) for purposes of section 543(a) (7) (relating to personal service contracts), but only if the effect of the inclusion of all such securities is to make the amounts therein referred to includible under such paragraph as personal holding company income;

(3) for purposes of section 543(a) (6) (relating to the use of property by shareholders), but only if the effect of the inclusion of all such securities is to make the amounts therein referred to includible under such paragraph as personal holding company income; and

(4) for purposes of section 543(a) (4) (relating to copyright royalties), but only if the effect of the inclusion of all such securities is to make the amounts therein referred to includible under such paragraph as personal holding company income.

The requirement in paragraphs (1), (2), (3), and (4) that all convertible securities must be included if any are to be included shall be subject to the exception that, where some of the outstanding securities are convertible only after a later date than in the case of others, the class having the earlier conversion date may be included although the others are not included, but no convertible securities shall be included unless all outstanding securities having a prior conversion date are also included.

§ 545.   Undistributed personal holding company income

(a) **Definition.**—For purposes of this part, the term "undistributed personal holding company income" means the taxable income of a personal holding company adjusted in the manner provided in subsections (b), (c), and (d), minus the dividends paid deduction as defined in section 561. In the case of a personal holding company which is a foreign corporation, not more than 10 percent in value of the outstanding stock of which is owned (within the meaning of section 958(a)) during the last half of the taxable year by United States persons, the term "undistributed personal holding company income" means the amount determined by multiplying the undistributed personal holding company income (determined without regard to this sentence) by the percentage in value of its outstanding stock which is the greatest percentage in value of its outstanding stock so owned by United States persons on any one day during such period.

(b) **Adjustments to taxable income.**—For the purposes of subsection (a), the taxable income shall be adjusted as follows:

(1) **Taxes.**—There shall be allowed as a deduction Federal income and excess profits taxes and income, war profits and excess profits taxes of foreign countries and possessions of the United States (to the extent not allowable as a deduction under section 275(a) (4)), accrued during the taxable year or deemed to be paid by a domestic corporation under section 902(a) or 960(a) (1) for the taxable year, but not including the accumulated earnings tax imposed by section 531, the personal holding company tax imposed by section 541, or the taxes imposed by corresponding sections of a prior income tax law.

(2) **Charitable contributions.**—The deduction for charitable contributions provided under section 170 shall be allowed, but in computing such deduction the limitations in section 170(b) (1) (A), (B), and (D) shall apply, and section 170(b) (2) and (d) (1) shall not apply. For purposes of this paragraph, the term "contribution base" when used in section 170(b) (1) means the taxable income computed with the adjustments (other than the 5-percent limitation) provided in section 170(b) (2) and (d) (1) and without deduction of the amount disallowed under paragraph (6) of this subsection.

(3) **Special deductions disallowed.**—The special deductions for corporations provided in part VIII (except section 248) of subchapter B (section 241

and following, relating to the deduction for dividends received by corporations, etc.) shall not be allowed.

(4) Net operating loss.—The net operating loss deduction provided in section 172 shall not be allowed, but there shall be allowed as a deduction the amount of the net operating loss (as defined in section 172(c)) for the preceding taxable year computed without the deductions provided in part VIII (except section 248) of subchapter B.

(5) Net capital gains.—There shall be allowed as a deduction the net capital gain for the taxable year, minus the taxes imposed by this subtitle attributable to such net capital gain. The taxes attributable to such net capital gain shall be an amount equal to the difference between—

　(A) the taxes imposed by this subtitle (except the tax imposed by this part) for such year, and

　(B) such taxes computed for such year without including such excess in taxable income.

(6) Expenses and depreciation applicable to property of the taxpayer. —The aggregate of the deductions allowed under section 162 (relating to trade or business expenses) and section 167 (relating to depreciation), which are allocable to the operation and maintenance of property owned or operated by the corporation, shall be allowed only in an amount equal to the rent or other compensation received for the use of, or the right to use, the property, unless it is established (under regulations prescribed by the Secretary) to the satisfaction of the Secretary—

　(A) that the rent or other compensation received was the highest obtainable, or, if none was received, that none was obtainable;

　(B) that the property was held in the course of a business carried on bona fide for profit; and

　(C) either that there was reasonable expectation that the operation of the property would result in a profit, or that the property was necessary to the conduct of the business.

.　.　.　.　.

§ 547.　Deduction for deficiency dividends

(a) General rule.—If a determination (as defined in subsection (c)) with respect to a taxpayer establishes liability for personal holding company tax imposed by section 541 (or by a corresponding provision of a prior income tax law) for any taxable year, a deduction shall be allowed to the taxpayer for the amount of deficiency dividends (as defined in subsection (d)) for the purpose of determining the personal holding company tax for such year, but not for the purpose of determining interest, additional amounts, or assessable penalties computed with respect to such personal holding company tax.

(b) Rules for application of section.—

(1) Allowance of deduction.—The deficiency dividend deduction shall be allowed as of the date the claim for the deficiency dividend deduction is filed.

(2) Credit or refund.—If the allowance of a deficiency dividend deduction results in an overpayment of personal holding company tax for any taxable year, credit or refund with respect to such overpayment shall be made as if on the date of the determination 2 years remained before the expiration of the period of limitation on the filing of claim for refund for the taxable year to which the overpayment relates. No interest shall be allowed on a credit or refund arising from the application of this section.

(c) Determination.—For purposes of this section, the term "determination" means—

(1) a decision by the Tax Court or a judgment, decree, or other order by any court of competent jurisdiction, which has become final;

(2) a closing agreement made under section 7121; or

(3) under regulations prescribed by the Secretary, an agreement signed by the Secretary and by, or on behalf of, the taxpayer relating to the liability of such taxpayer for personal holding company tax.

(d) Deficiency dividends.—

(1) Definition.—For purposes of this section, the term "deficiency dividends" means the amount of the dividends paid by the corporation on or after the date of the determination and before filing claim under subsection (e), which would have been includible in the computation of the deduction for dividends paid under section 561 for the taxable year with respect to which the liability for personal holding company tax exists, if distributed during such taxable year. No dividends shall be considered as deficiency dividends for purposes of subsection (a) unless distributed within 90 days after the determination.

(2) Effect on dividends paid deduction.—

(A) For taxable year in which paid.—Deficiency dividends paid in any taxable year (to the extent of the portion thereof taken into account under subsection (a) in determining personal holding company tax) shall not be included in the amount of dividends paid for such year for purposes of computing the dividends paid deduction for such year and succeeding years.

(B) For prior taxable year.—Deficiency dividends paid in any taxable year (to the extent of the portion thereof taken into account under subsection (a) in determining personal holding company tax) shall not be allowed for purposes of section 563(b) in the computation of the dividends paid deduction for the taxable year preceding the taxable year in which paid.

(e) Claim required.—No deficiency dividend deduction shall be allowed under subsection (a) unless (under regulations prescribed by the Secretary) claim therefor is filed within 120 days after the determination.

(f) Suspension of statute of limitations and stay of collection.—

(1) Suspension of running of statute.—If the corporation files a claim, as provided in subsection (e), the running of the statute of limitations provided in section 6501 on the making of assessments, and the bringing of distraint or a proceeding in court for collection, in respect of the deficiency and all interest, additional amounts, or assessable penalties, shall be suspended for a period of 2 years after the date of the determination.

(2) Stay of collection.—In the case of any deficiency with respect to the tax imposed by section 541 established by a determination under this section—

(A) the collection of the deficiency and all interest, additional amounts, and assessable penalties shall, except in cases of jeopardy, be stayed until the expiration of 120 days after the date of the determination, and

347

(B) if claim for deficiency dividend deduction is filed under subsection (e), the collection of such part of the deficiency as is not reduced by the deduction for deficiency dividends provided in subsection (a) shall be stayed until the date the claim is disallowed (in whole or in part), and if disallowed in part collection shall be made only with respect to the part disallowed.

No distraint or proceeding in court shall be begun for the collection of an amount the collection of which is stayed under subparagraph (A) or (B) during the period for which the collection of such amount is stayed.

(g) Deduction denied in case of fraud, etc.—No deficiency dividend deduction shall be allowed under subsection (a) if the determination contains a finding that any part of the deficiency is due to fraud with intent to evade tax, or to wilful failure to file an income tax return within the time prescribed by law or prescribed by the Secretary in pursuance of law.

PART IV—DEDUCTION FOR DIVIDENDS PAID

§ 561.   Definition of deduction for dividends paid

(a) General rule.—The deduction for dividends paid shall be the sum of—

(1) the dividends paid during the taxable year,

(2) the consent dividends for the taxable year (determined under section 565), and

(3) in the case of a personal holding company, the dividend carryover described in section 564.

(b) Special rules applicable.—In determining the deduction for dividends paid, the rules provided in section 562 (relating to rules applicable in determining dividends eligible for dividends paid deduction) and section 563 (relating to dividends paid after the close of the taxable year) shall be applicable.

§ 562.   Rules applicable in determining dividends eligible for dividends paid deduction

(a) General rule.—For purposes of this part, the term "dividend" shall, except as otherwise provided in this section, include only dividends described in section 316 (relating to definition of dividends for purposes of corporate distributions).

(b) Distributions in liquidation.—

(1) Except in the case of a personal holding company described in section 542 or a foreign personal holding company described in section 552—

(A) in the case of amounts distributed in liquidation, the part of such distribution which is properly chargeable to earnings and profits accumulated after February 28, 1913, shall be treated as a dividend for purposes of computing the dividends paid deduction, and

(B) in the case of a complete liquidation occurring within 24 months after the adoption of a plan of liquidation, any distribution within such period pursuant to such plan shall, to the extent of the earnings and profits (computed without regard to capital losses) of the corporation for the taxable year in which such distribution is made, be treated as a dividend for purposes of computing the dividends paid deduction.

For purposes of subparagraph (A), a liquidation includes a redemption of stock to which section 302 applies.

(2) In the case of a complete liquidation of a personal holding company, occurring within 24 months after the adoption of a plan of liquidation, the amount of any distribution within such period pursuant to such plan shall be treated as a dividend for purposes of computing the dividends paid deduction, to the extent that such amount is distributed to corporate distributees and represents such corporate distributees' allocable share of the undistributed personal holding company income for the taxable year of such distribution computed without regard to this paragraph and without regard to subparagraph (B) of section 316(b) (2).

(c) Preferential dividends.—The amount of any distribution shall not be considered as a dividend for purposes of computing the dividends paid deduction, unless such distribution is pro rata, with no preference to any share of stock as compared with other shares of the same class, and with no preference to one class of stock as compared with another class except to the extent that the former is entitled (without reference to waivers of their rights by shareholders) to such preference.

(d) Distributions by a member of an affiliated group.—In the case where a corporation which is a member of an affiliated group of corporations filing or required to file a consolidated return for a taxable year is required to file a separate personal holding company schedule for such taxable year, a distribution by such corporation to another member of the affiliated group shall be considered as a dividend for purposes of computing the dividends paid deduction if such distribution would constitute a dividend under the other provisions of this section to a recipient which is not a member of an affiliated group.

§ 563.   Rules relating to dividends paid after close of taxable year

(a) Accumulated earnings tax.—In the determination of the dividends paid deduction for purposes of the accumulated earnings tax imposed by section 531, a dividend paid after the close of any taxable year and on or before the 15th day of the third month following the close of such taxable year shall be considered as paid during such taxable year.

(b) Personal holding company tax.—In the determination of the dividends paid deduction for purposes of the personal holding company tax imposed by section 541, a dividend paid after the close of any taxable year and on or before the 15th day of the third month following the close of such taxable year shall, to the extent the taxpayer elects in its return for the taxable year, be considered as paid during such taxable year. The amount allowed as a dividend by reason of the application of this subsection with respect to any taxable year shall not exceed either—

(1) The undistributed personal holding company income of the corporation for the taxable year, computed without regard to this subsection, or

(2) 20 percent of the sum of the dividends paid during the taxable year, computed without regard to this subsection.

(c) Dividends considered as paid on last day of taxable year.—For the purpose of applying section 562(a), with respect to distributions under subsection (a) or (b) of this section, a distribution made after the close of a taxable year and on or before the 15th day of the third month following the close of the taxable year shall be considered as made on the last day of such taxable year.

§ 564. Dividend carryover

(a) General rule.—For purposes of computing the dividends paid deduction under section 561, in the case of a personal holding company the dividend carryover for any taxable year shall be the dividend carryover to such taxable year, computed as provided in subsection (b), from the two preceding taxable years.

(b) Computation of dividend carryover.—The dividend carryover to the taxable year shall be determined as follows:

(1) For each of the 2 preceding taxable years there shall be determined the taxable income computed with the adjustments provided in section 545 (whether or not the taxpayer was a personal holding company for either of such preceding taxable years), and there shall also be determined for each such year the deduction for dividends paid during such year as provided in section 561 (but determined without regard to the dividend carryover to such year).

(2) There shall be determined for each such taxable year whether there is an excess of such taxable income over such deduction for dividends paid or an excess of such deduction for dividends paid over such taxable income, and the amount of each such excess.

(3) If there is an excess of such deductions for dividends paid over such taxable income for the first preceding taxable year, such excess shall be allowed as a dividend carryover to the taxable year.

(4) If there is an excess of such deduction for dividends paid over such taxable income for the second preceding taxable year, such excess shall be reduced by the amount determined in paragraph (5), and the remainder of such excess shall be allowed as a dividend carryover to the taxable year.

(5) The amount of the reduction specified in paragraph (4) shall be the amount of the excess of the taxable income, if any, for the first preceding taxable year over such deduction for dividends paid, if any, for the first preceding taxable year.

§ 565. Consent dividends

(a) General rule.—If any person owns consent stock (as defined in subsection (f) (1)) in a corporation on the last day of the taxable year of such corporation, and such person agrees, in a consent filed with the return of such corporation in accordance with regulations prescribed by the Secretary, to treat as a dividend the amount specified in such consent, the amount so specified shall, except as provided in subsection (b), constitute a consent dividend for purposes of section 561 (relating to the deduction for dividends paid).

(b) Limitations.—A consent dividend shall not include—

(1) an amount specified in a consent which, if distributed in money, would constitute, or be part of, a distribution which would be disqualified for purposes of the dividends paid deduction under section 562(c) (relating to preferential dividends), or

(2) an amount specified in a consent which would not constitute a dividend (as defined in section 316) if the total amounts specified in consents filed by the corporation had been distributed in money to shareholders on the last day of the taxable year of such corporation.

(c) Effect of consent.—The amount of a consent dividend shall be considered, for purposes of this title—

(1) as distributed in money by the corporation to the shareholder on the last day of the taxable year of the corporation, and

(2) as contributed to the capital of the corporation by the shareholder on such day.

(d) Consent dividends and other distributions.—If a distribution by a corporation consists in part of consent dividends and in part of money or other property, the entire amount specified in the consents and the amount of such money or other property shall be considered together for purposes of applying this title.

. . . . .

(f) Definitions.—

(1) Consent stock.—Consent stock, for purposes of this section, means the class or classes of stock entitled, after the payment of preferred dividends, to a share in the distribution (other than in complete or partial liquidation) within the taxable year of all the remaining earnings and profits, which share constitutes the same proportion of such distribution regardless of the amount of such distribution.

(2) Preferred dividends.—Preferred dividends, for purposes of this section, means a distribution (other than in complete or partial liquidation), limited in amount, which must be made on any class of stock before a further distribution (other than in complete or partial liquidation) of earnings and profits may be made within the taxable year.

SUBCHAPTER I—NATURAL RESOURCES

Part
 I. Deductions.
 II. Exclusions from gross income.*
 III. Sales and exchanges.
 IV. Mineral production payments.
 V. Continental shelf areas.*

PART I—DEDUCTIONS

§ 611.   Allowance of deduction for depletion

(a) General rule.—In the case of mines, oil and gas wells, other natural deposits, and timber, there shall be allowed as a deduction in computing taxable income a reasonable allowance for depletion and for depreciation of improvements, according to the peculiar conditions in each case; such reasonable allowance in all cases to be made under regulations prescribed by the Secretary. For purposes of this part, the term "mines" includes deposits of waste or residue, the extraction of ores or minerals from which is treated as mining under section 613(c). In any case in which it is ascertained as a result of operations or of development work that the recoverable units are greater or less than the prior estimate thereof, then such prior estimate (but not the basis for depletion) shall be

* Omitted entirely.

revised and the allowance under this section for subsequent taxable years shall be based on such revised estimate.

(b) Special rules.—

(1) Leases.—In the case of a lease, the deduction under this section shall be equitably apportioned between the lessor and lessee.

(2) Life tenant and remainderman.—In the case of property held by one person for life with remainder to another person, the deduction under this section shall be computed as if the life tenant were the absolute owner of the property and shall be allowed to the life tenant.

(3) Property held in trust.—In the case of property held in trust, the deduction under this section shall be apportioned between the income beneficiaries and the trustee in accordance with the pertinent provisions of the instrument creating the trust, or, in the absence of such provisions, on the basis of the trust income allocable to each.

(4) Property held by estate.—In the case of an estate, the deduction under this section shall be apportioned between the estate and the heirs, legatees, and devisees on the basis of the income of the estate allocable to each.

- - - - -

§ 612.   Basis for cost depletion

Except as otherwise provided in this subchapter, the basis on which depletion is to be allowed in respect of any property shall be the adjusted basis provided in section 1011 for the purpose of determining the gain upon the sale or other disposition of such property.

§ 613.   Percentage depletion

(a) General rule.—In the case of the mines, wells, and other natural deposits listed in subsection (b), the allowance for depletion under section 611 shall be the percentage, specified in subsection (b), of the gross income from the property excluding from such gross income an amount equal to any rents or royalties paid or incurred by the taxpayer in respect of the property. Such allowance shall not exceed 50 percent of the taxpayer's taxable income from the property (computed without allowance for depletion). For purposes of the preceding sentence, the allowable deductions taken into account with respect to expenses of mining in computing the taxable income from the property shall be decreased by an amount equal to so much of any gain which (1) is treated under section 1245 (relating to gain from disposition of certain depreciable property) as ordinary income, and (2) is properly allocable to the property. In no case shall the allowance for depletion under section 611 be less than it would be if computed without reference to this section.

(b) Percentage depletion rates.—The mines, wells, and other natural deposits, and the percentages, referred to in subsection (a) are as follows:

(1) 22 percent—

(A) sulphur and uranium; and

(B) if from deposits in the United States—anorthosite, clay, laterite, and nephelite syenite (to the extent that alumina and aluminum compounds are extracted therefrom), asbestos, bauxite, celestite, chromite, corundum, fluorspar, graphite, ilmenite, kyanite, mica, olivine, quartz crystals (radio grade), rutile, block steatite talc, and zircon, and ores of the following metals: antimony, beryllium, bismuth, cadmium, cobalt, columbium, lead, lithium, manganese, mercury, molybdenum, nickel, platinum and platinum group metals, tantalum, thorium, tin, titanium, tungsten, vanadium, and zinc.

(2) 15 percent—If from deposits in the United States—

(A) gold, silver, copper, and iron ore, and

(B) oil shale (except shale described in paragraph (5)).

(3) 14 percent—

(A) metal mines (if paragraph (1) (B) or (2) (A) does not apply), rock asphalt, and vermiculite; and

(B) if paragraph (1) (B), (5), or (6) (B) does not apply, ball clay, bentonite, china clay, sagger clay, and clay used or sold for use for purposes dependent on its refractory properties.

(4) 10 percent—asbestos (if paragraph (1) (B) does not apply), brucite, coal, lignite, perlite, sodium chloride, and wollastonite.

(5) 7½ percent—clay and shale used or sold for use in the manufacture of sewer pipe or brick, and clay, shale, and slate used or sold for use as sintered or burned lightweight aggregates.

(6) 5 percent—

(A) gravel, peat, pumice, sand, scoria, shale (except shale described in paragraph (2) (B) or (5)), and stone (except stone described in paragraph (7));

(B) clay used, or sold for use, in the manufacture of drainage and roofing tile, flower pots, and kindred products; and

(C) if from brine wells—bromine, calcium chloride, and magnesium chloride.

(7) 14 percent—all other minerals, including, but not limited to, aplite, barite, borax, calcium carbonates, diatomaceous earth, dolomite, feldspar, fullers earth, garnet, gilsonite, granite, limestone, magnesite, magnesium carbonates, marble, mollusk shells (including clam shells and oyster shells), phosphate rock, potash, quartzite, slate, soapstone, stone (used or sold for use by the mine owner or operator as dimension stone or ornamental stone), thenardite, tripoli, trona, and (if paragraph (1) (B) does not apply) bauxite, flake graphite, fluorspar, lepidolite, mica, spodumene, and talc (including pyrophyllite), except that, unless sold on bid in direct competition with a bona fide bid to sell a mineral listed in paragraph (3), the percentage shall be 5 percent for any such other mineral (other than slate to which paragraph (5) applies) when used, or sold for use, by the mine owner or operator as rip rap, ballast, road material, rubble, concrete aggregates, or for similar purposes. For purposes of this paragraph, the term "all other minerals" does not include—

(A) soil, sod, dirt, turf, water, or mosses;

(B) minerals from sea water, the air, or similar inexhaustible sources; or

(C) oil and gas wells.

For the purposes of this subsection, minerals (other than sodium chloride) extracted from brines pumped from a saline perennial lake within the United States shall not be considered minerals from an inexhaustible source.

(c) Definition of gross income from property.—For purposes of this section—

(1) Gross income from the property.—The term "gross income from the property" means, in the case of a property other than an oil or gas well, and other than a geothermal deposit the gross income from mining.

(2) Mining.—The term "mining" includes not merely the extraction of the ores or minerals from the ground but also the treatment processes considered as mining described in paragraph (4) (and the treatment processes necessary or incidental thereto), and so much of the transportation of ores or minerals (whether or not by common carrier) from the point of extraction from the ground to the plants or mills in which such treatment processes are applied thereto as is not in excess of 50 miles unless the Secretary finds that the physical and other requirements are such that the ore or mineral must be transported a greater distance to such plants or mills.

(3) Extraction of the ores or minerals from the ground.—The term "extraction of the ores or minerals from the ground" includes the extraction by mine owners or operators of ores or minerals from the waste or residue of prior mining. The preceding sentence shall not apply to any such extraction of the mineral or ore by a purchaser of such waste or residue or of the rights to extract ores or minerals therefrom.

(4) Treatment processes considered as mining.—The following treatment processes where applied by the mine owner or operator shall be considered as mining to the extent they are applied to the ore or mineral in respect of which he is entitled to a deduction for depletion under section 611:

(A) in the case of coal—cleaning, breaking, sizing, dust allaying, treating to prevent freezing, and loading for shipment;

(B) in the case of sulfur recovered by the Frasch process—cleaning, pumping to vats, cooling, breaking, and loading for shipment;

(C) in the case of iron ore, bauxite, ball and sagger clay, rock asphalt, and ores or minerals which are customarily sold in the form of a crude mineral product—sorting, concentrating, sintering, and substantially equivalent processes to bring to shipping grade and form, and loading for shipment;

(D) in the case of lead, zinc, copper, gold, silver, uranium, or fluorspar ores, potash, and ores or minerals which are not customarily sold in the form of the crude mineral product—crushing, grinding, and beneficiation by concentration (gravity, flotation, amalgamation, electrostatic, or magnetic), cyanidation, leaching, crystallization, precipitation (but not including electrolytic deposition, roasting, thermal or electric smelting, or refining), or by substantially equivalent processes or combination of processes used in the separation or extraction of the product or products from the ore or the mineral or minerals from other material from the mine or other natural deposit;

(E) the pulverization of talc, the burning of magnesite, the sintering and nodulizing of phosphate rock, the decarbonation of trona, and the furnacing of quicksilver ores;

(F) in the case of calcium carbonates and other minerals when used in making cement—all processes (other than preheating of the kiln feed) applied prior to the introduction of the kiln feed into the kiln, but not including any subsequent process;

(G) in the case of clay to which paragraph (5) or (6) (B) of subsection (b) applies—crushing, grinding, and separating the mineral from waste, but not including any subsequent process;

(H) in the case of oil shale—extraction from the ground, crushing, loading into the retort, and retorting, but not hydrogenation, refining, or any other process subsequent to retorting; and

(I) any other treatment process provided for by regulations prescribed by the Secretary which, with respect to the particular ore or mineral, is not inconsistent with the preceding provisions of this paragraph.

(5) Treatment processes not considered as mining.—Unless such processes are otherwise provided for in paragraph (4) (or are necessary or incidental to processes so provided for), the following treatment processes shall not be considered as "mining": electrolytic deposition, roasting, calcining, thermal or electric smelting, refining, polishing, fine pulverization, blending with other materials, treatment effecting a chemical change, thermal action, and molding or shaping.

(d) Denial of percentage depletion in case of oil and gas wells.—Except as provided in section 613A, in the case of any oil or gas well, the allowance for depletion shall be computed without reference to this section.

(e) Percentage depletion for geothermal deposits.—

(1) In general.—In the case of geothermal deposits located in the United States or in a possession of the United States, for purposes of subsection (a)—

(A) such deposits shall be treated as listed in subsection (b), and

(B) the applicable percentage (determined under the table contained in paragraph (2)) shall be deemed to be the percentage specified in subsection (b).

(2) Applicable percentage.—For purposes of paragraph (1)—

In the case of taxable years beginning in calendar year—	The applicable percentage is—
1978, 1979, or 1980	22
1981	20
1982	18
1983	16
1984 and thereafter	15

(3) Geothermal deposit defined.—For purposes of paragraph (1), the term "geothermal deposit" means a geothermal reservoir consisting of natural heat which is stored in rocks or in an aqueous liquid or vapor (whether or not under pressure). Such a deposit shall in no case be treated as a gas well for purposes of this section or section 613A, and this section shall not apply to a geothermal deposit which is located outside the United States or its possessions.

§ 613A.　Limitations on percentage depletion in case of oil and gas wells

(a) General rule.—Except as otherwise provided in this section, the allowance for depletion under section 611 with respect to any oil or gas well shall be computed without regard to section 613.

(b) Exemption for certain domestic gas wells.—

(1) In general.—The allowance for depletion under section 611 shall be computed in accordance with section 613 with respect to—

    (A) regulated natural gas, and

    (B) natural gas sold under a fixed contract,

and 22 percent shall be deemed to be specified in subsection (b) of section 613 for purposes of subsection (a) of that section.

(2) Natural gas from geopressured brine.—The allowance for depletion under section 611 shall be computed in accordance with section 613 with respect to any qualified natural gas from geopressured brine, and 10 percent shall be deemed to be specified in subsection (b) of section 613 for purposes of subsection (a) of such section.

(c) Exemption for independent producers and royalty owners.—

(1) In general.—Except as provided in subsection (d), the allowance for depletion under section 611 shall be computed in accordance with section 613 with respect to—

    (A) so much of the taxpayer's average daily production of domestic crude oil as does not exceed the taxpayer's depletable oil quantity; and

    (B) so much of the taxpayer's average daily production of domestic natural gas as does not exceed the taxpayer's depletable natural gas quantity;

and the applicable percentage (determined in accordance with the table contained in paragraph (5)) shall be deemed to be specified in subsection (b) of section 613 for purposes of subsection (a) of that section.

(9) Transfer of oil or gas property.—

    (A) In the case of a transfer (including the subleasing of a lease) after December 31, 1974 of an interest (including an interest in a partnership or trust) in any proven oil or gas property, paragraph (1) shall not apply to the transferee (or sublessee) with respect to production of crude oil or natural gas attributable to such interest, and such production shall not be taken into account for any computation by the transferee (or sublessee) under this subsection. A property shall be treated as a proven oil or gas property if at the time of the transfer the principal value of the property has been demonstrated by prospecting or exploration or discovery work.

    (B) Subparagraph (A) shall not apply in the case of—

        (i) a transfer of property at death,

        (ii) the transfer in an exchange to which section 351 applies if following the exchange the tentative quantity determined under the table contained in paragraph (3) (B) is allocated under paragraph (8) between the transferor and transferee,

        (iii) a change of beneficiaries of a trust by reason of the death, birth, or adoption of any vested beneficiary if the transferee was a beneficiary of such trust or is a lineal descendant of the settlor or any other vested beneficiary of such trust, except in the case of any trust where any beneficiary of such trust is a member of the family (as defined in section 267(c) (4)) of a settlor who created inter vivos and testamentary trusts for members of the family and such settlor died within the last six days of the fifth month in 1970, and the law in the jurisdiction in which such trust was created requires all or a portion of the gross or net proceeds of any royalty or other interest in oil, gas, or other mineral representing any percentage depletion allowance to be allocated to the principal of the trust,

(iv) a transfer of property between corporations which are members of the same controlled group of corporations (as defined in paragraph (8) (D) (i)), or

(v) a transfer of property between business entities which are under common control (within the meaning of paragraph (8) (B)) or between related persons in the same family (within the meaning of paragraph (8) (C)), or

(vi) a transfer of property between a trust and related persons in the same family (within the meaning of paragraph (8) (C)) to the extent that the beneficiaries of that trust are and continue to be related persons in the family that transferred the property, and to the extent that the tentative oil quantity is allocated among the members of the family (within the meaning of paragraph (8) (C)).

Clause (iv) or (v) shall apply only so long as the tentative oil quantity determined under the table contained in paragraph (3) (B) is allocated under paragraph (8) between the transferor and transferee.

(10) Transfers by individuals to corporations.—

(A) In general.—Paragraph (9)(A) shall not apply to a transfer by an individual of qualified property to a qualified transferee corporation solely in exchange for stock in such corporation.

(B) 1,000-barrel limit for corporation.—A tentative quantity shall be determined for the qualified transferee corporation under this subsection.

(C) Transferor's tentative quantity reduced.—

(i) In general.—The tentative quantity for the transferor (and his family) for any period shall be reduced by the transferor's pro rata share of the corporation's depletable quantity for such period.

(ii) Pro rata share.—For purposes of clause (i), a transferor's pro rata share for any period shall be—

(I) in the case of production from property to which subparagraph (A) applies, that portion of the corporation's depletable quantity which is allocable to production from such property, and

(II) in the case of production from all other property, that portion of the corporation's depletable quantity which is allocable to the production from such property, multiplied by a fraction the numerator of which is the fair market value of the transferor's stock in the corporation, and the denominator of which is the fair market value of all stock in the corporation.

(iii) Depletable quantity.—For purposes of this paragraph, a corporation's depletable quantity for any period is the lesser of—

(I) such corporation's tentative quantity for such period (determined under paragraphs (3) and (8)), or

(II) such corporation's average daily production for such period.

(D) Qualified transferee corporation defined.—For purposes of this paragraph, the term "qualified transferee corporation" means a corporation all of the outstanding stock of which has been issued to individuals solely in exchange for qualified property held by such individuals.

(E) Qualified property defined.—For purposes of this paragraph, the term "qualified property" means oil or gas property with respect to which—

(i) there has been no prior transfer to which paragraph (9)(A) applied, and

(ii) the transferor has made an election to have this paragraph apply.

The term also includes cash (not to exceed $1,000 in the aggregate) which one or more individuals transfer to the corporation.

(F) Transferor must retain stock during lifetime.—If at any time during his lifetime any transferor disposes of stock in the corporation (other than to a member of his family), then the depletable quantity of the corporation (determined without regard to this subparagraph) shall be reduced (for all periods on or after the date of the disposition) by an amount which bears the same ratio to such quantity as the fair market value of the stock so disposed of bears to the aggregate fair market value of all stock of the corporation on such date of disposition.

(G) Special rules relating to family of transferor.—

(i) In general.—For purposes of this paragraph—

(I) the issuance of stock to a member of the family of the transferor shall be treated as issuance of stock to the transferor, and

(II) during the lifetime of the transferor, stock transferred to a member of the family of the transferor shall be treated as held by the transferor.

If stock described in the preceding sentence ceases to be held by a member of the family of the transferor, the transferor shall be treated as having disposed of such stock at the time of such cessation.

(ii) Family defined.—For purposes of this paragraph, the members of the family of an individual include only his spouse and minor children.

(H) Property subject to liabilities.—For purposes of this paragraph, section 357 shall be applied as if—

(i) references to section 351 include references to subparagraph (A) of this paragraph, and

(ii) the reference in subsection (a)(1) of section 357 to the nonrecognition of gain includes a reference to the nonapplication of paragraph (9)(A) of this subsection.

(I) Election.—A transferor may make an election under this paragraph only in such manner as the Secretary may by regulations prescribe and only on or before the due date (including extensions) for filing the return of the corporation of the taxes imposed by this chapter for the corporation's first taxable year ending after the date of the transfer (or, if later, after the date of the enactment of this paragraph).

(J) Regulations.—The Secretary shall prescribe such regulations as may be necessary to carry out the purposes of this paragraph.

. . . .

(13) Subchapter S corporations.—

(A) Computation of depletion allowance at shareholder level.—In the case of an S corporation, the allowance for depletion with respect to any oil or gas property shall be computed separately by each shareholder.

(B) Allocation of basis.—The S corporation shall allocate to each shareholder his pro rata share of the adjusted basis of the S corporation in each oil or gas property held by the S corporation. The allocation shall be made as of the later of the date of acquisition of the property by the S corporation, or the first day of the first taxable year of the S corporation to which the Subchapter S Revision Act of 1982 applies. Each shareholder shall separately keep records of his share of the adjusted basis in each oil and gas property of the S corporation, adjust such share of the adjusted basis for any depletion taken on such property, and use such adjusted basis each year in the computation of his cost depletion or in the computation of his gain or loss on the disposition of such property by the S corporation. In the case of any distribution of oil or gas property to its shareholders by the S corporation, the corporation's adjusted basis in the property shall be an amount equal to the sum of the shareholders' adjusted bases in such property, as determined under this subparagraph.

(C) Coordination with transfer rule of paragraph (9).—For purposes of paragraph (9)—

(i) an S corporation shall be treated as a partnership, and the shareholders of the S corporation shall be treated as partners, and

(ii) an election by a C corporation to become an S corporation shall be treated as a transfer of all its properties effective on the day on which such election first takes effect.

(D) Coordination with transfer rule of paragraph (10).—For purposes of paragraphs (9) and (10), if an S corporation becomes a C corporation, each shareholder shall be treated as having transferred to such corporation his pro rata share of all the assets of the S corporation.

(d) Limitations on application of subsection (c).—

(1) Limitation based on taxable income.—The deduction for the taxable year attributable to the application of subsection (c) shall not exceed 65 percent of the taxpayer's taxable income (reduced in the case of an individual by the zero bracket amount) for the year computed without regard to—

(A) any depletion on production from an oil or gas property which is subject to the provisions of subsection (c),

(B) any net operating loss carryback to the taxable year under section 172,

(C) any capital loss carryback to the taxable year under section 1212, and

(D) in the case of a trust, any distributions to its beneficiary, except in the case of any trust where any beneficiary of such trust is a member of the family (as defined in section 267(c) (4)) of a settlor who created inter vivos and testamentary trusts for members of the family and such settlor died within the last six days of the fifth month in 1970, and the law in the jurisdiction in which such trust was created requires all or a portion of the gross or net proceeds of any royalty or other interest in oil, gas, or other mineral representing any percentage depletion allowance to be allocated to the principal of the trust.

If an amount is disallowed as a deduction for the taxable year by reason of application of the preceding sentence, the disallowed amount shall be treated as an amount allowable as a deduction under subsection (c) for the following taxable year, subject to the application of the preceding sentence to such taxable year. For purposes of basis adjustments and determining whether cost depletion exceeds percentage depletion with respect to the production from a property, any amount disallowed as a deduction on the application of this paragraph shall be allocated to the respective properties from which the oil or gas was produced in proportion to the percentage depletion otherwise allowable to such properties under subsection (c).

* * * * *

§ 616. Development expenditures

(a) In general.—Except as provided in subsection (b), there shall be allowed as a deduction in computing taxable income all expenditures paid or incurred during the taxable year for the development of a mine or other natural deposit (other than an oil or gas well) if paid or incurred after the existence of ores or minerals in commercially marketable quantities has been disclosed. This section shall not apply to expenditures for the acquisition or improvement of property of a character which is subject to the allowance for depreciation provided in section 167, but allowances for depreciation shall be considered, for purposes of this section, as expenditures.

(b) Election of taxpayer.—At the election of the taxpayer, made in accordance with regulations prescribed by the Secretary, expenditures described in subsection (a) paid or incurred during the taxable year shall be treated as deferred expenses and shall be deductible on a ratable basis as the units of produced ores or minerals benefited by such expenditures are sold. In the case of such expenditures paid or incurred during the development stage of the mine or deposit, the election shall apply only with respect to the excess of such expenditures during the taxable year over the net receipts during the taxable year from the ores or minerals produced from such mine or deposit. The election under this subsection, if made, must be for the total amount of such expenditures, or the total amount of such excess, as the case may be, with respect to the mine or deposit, and shall be binding for such taxable year.

(c) Adjusted basis of mine or deposit.—The amount of expenditures which are treated under subsection (b) as deferred expenses shall be taken into account in computing the adjusted basis of the mine or deposit, except that such amount, and the adjustments to basis provided in section 1016(a) (9), shall be disregarded in determining the adjusted basis of the property for the purpose of computing a deduction for depletion under section 611.

§ 617. Deduction and recapture of certain mining exploration expenditures

(a) Allowance of deduction.—

(1) **General rule.**—At the election of the taxpayer, expenditures paid or incurred during the taxable year for the purpose of ascertaining the existence, location, extent, or quality of any deposit of ore or other mineral, and paid or incurred before the beginning of the development stage of the mine, shall be allowed as a deduction in computing taxable income. This subsection shall apply only with respect to the amount of such expenditures which, but for this subsection, would not be allowable as a deduction for the taxable year. This subsection shall not apply to expenditures for the acquisition or improvement of property of a character which is subject to the allowance for depreciation provided in section 167, but allowances for depreciation shall be considered, for purposes of this subsection, as expenditures paid or incurred. In no case shall this subsection apply with respect to amounts paid or incurred for the purpose of ascertaining the existence, location, extent, or quality of any deposit of oil or gas or of any mineral with respect to which a deduction for percentage depletion is not allowable under section 613.

(2) **Elections.—**

(A) **Method.**—Any election under this subsection shall be made in such manner as the Secretary may by regulations prescribe.

(B) **Time and scope.**—The election provided by paragraph (1) for the taxable year may be made at any time before the expiration of the period prescribed for making a claim for credit or refund of the tax imposed by this chapter for the taxable year. Such an election for the taxable year shall apply to all expenditures described in paragraph (1) paid or incurred by the taxpayer during the taxable year or during any subsequent taxable year. Such an election may not be revoked unless the Secretary consents to such revocation.

(C) **Deficiencies.**—The statutory period for the assessment of any deficiency for any taxable year, to the extent such deficiency is attributable to an election or revocation of an election under this subsection, shall not expire before the last day of the 2-year period beginning on the day after the date on which such election or revocation of election is made; and such deficiency may be assessed at any time before the expiration of such 2-year period, notwithstanding any law or rule of law which would otherwise prevent such assessment.

(b) Recapture on reaching producing stage.—

(1) **Recapture.**—If, in any taxable year, any mine with respect to which expenditures were deducted pursuant to subsection (a) reaches the producing stage, then—

(A) If the taxpayer so elects with respect to all such mines reaching the producing stage during the taxable year, he shall include in gross income for the taxable year an amount equal to the adjusted exploration expenditures with respect to such mines, and the amount so included in income shall be treated for purposes of this subtitle as expenditures which (i) are paid or incurred on the respective dates on which the mines reach the producing stage, and (ii) are properly chargeable to capital account.

(B) If subparagraph (A) does not apply with respect to any such mine, then the deduction for depletion under section 611 with respect to the property shall be disallowed until the amount of depletion which would be allowable but for this subparagraph equals the amount of the adjusted exploration expenditures with respect to such mine.

(2) **Elections.—**

(A) **Method.—**Any election under this subsection shall be made in such manner as the Secretary may by regulations prescribe.

(B) **Time and scope.—**The election provided by paragraph (1) for any taxable year may be made or changed not later than the time prescribed by law for filing the return (including extensions thereof) for such taxable year.

(c) **Recapture in case of bonus or royalty.—**If an election has been made under subsection (a) with respect to expenditures relating to a mining property and the taxpayer receives or accrues a bonus or a royalty with respect to such property, then the deduction for depletion under section 611 with respect to the bonus or royalty shall be disallowed until the amount of depletion which would be allowable but for this subsection equals the amount of the adjusted exploration expenditures with respect to the property to which the bonus or royalty relates.

(d) **Gain from dispositions of certain mining property.—**

(1) **General rule.—**Except as otherwise provided in this subsection, if mining property is disposed of the lower of—

(A) the adjusted exploration expenditures with respect to such property, or

(B) the excess of—

(i) the amount realized (in the case of a sale, exchange, or involuntary conversion), or the fair market value (in the case of any other disposition), over

(ii) the adjusted basis of such property,

shall be treated as ordinary income. Such gain shall be recognized notwithstanding any other provision of this subtitle.

(2) **Disposition of portion of property.—**For purposes of paragraph (1)—

(A) In the case of the disposition of a portion of a mining property (other than an undivided interest), the entire amount of the adjusted exploration expenditures with respect to such property shall be treated as attributable to such portion to the extent of the amount of the gain to which paragraph (1) applies.

(B) In the case of the disposition of an undivided interest in a mining property (or a portion thereof), a proportionate part of the adjusted exploration expenditures with respect to such property shall be treated as attributable to such undivided interest to the extent of the amount of the gain to which paragraph (1) applies.

This paragraph shall not apply to any expenditure to the extent the taxpayer establishes to the satisfaction of the Secretary that such expenditure relates neither to the portion (or interest therein) disposed of nor to any mine, in the property held by the taxpayer before the disposition, which has reached the producing stage.

(3) **Exceptions and limitations.—**Paragraphs (1), (2), and (3) of section 1245(b) (relating to exceptions and limitations with respect to gain from disposition of certain depreciable property) shall apply in respect of this subsection in the same manner and with the same effect as if references in

section 1245(b) to section 1245 or any provision thereof were references to this subsection or the corresponding provisions of this subsection and as if references to section 1245 property were references to mining property.

(4) Application of subsection.—This subsection shall apply notwithstanding any other provision of this subtitle.

(e) Basis of property.—

(1) Basis.—The basis of any property shall not be reduced by the amount of any depletion which would be allowable but for the application of this section.

(2) Adjustments.—The Secretary shall prescribe such regulations as he may deem necessary to provide for adjustments to the basis of property to reflect gain recognized under subsection (d) (1).

.   .   .   .   .

(g) Special rules relating to partnership property.—

(1) Property distributed to partner.—In the case of any property or mine received by the taxpayer in a distribution with respect to part or all of his interest in a partnership, the adjusted exploration expenditures with respect to such property or mine include the adjusted exploration expenditures (not otherwise included under subsection (f) (1)) with respect to such property or mine immediately prior to such distribution, but the adjusted exploration expenditures with respect to any such property or mine shall be reduced by the amount of gain to which section 751(b) applied realized by the partnership (as constituted after the distribution) on the distribution of such property or mine.

(2) Property retained by partnership.—In the case of any property or mine held by a partnership after a distribution to a partner to which section 751(b) applied, the adjusted exploration expenditures with respect to such property or mine shall, under regulations prescribed by the Secretary, be reduced by the amount of gain to which section 751(b) applied realized by such partner with respect to such distribution on account of such property or mine.

.   .   .   .   .

PART III—SALES AND EXCHANGES

§ 631.   Gain or loss in the case of timber, coal, or domestic iron ore

(a) Election to consider cutting as sale or exchange.—If the taxpayer so elects on his return for a taxable year, the cutting of timber (for sale or for use in the taxpayer's trade or business) during such year by the taxpayer who owns, or has a contract right to cut, such timber (providing he has owned such timber or has held such contract right for a period of more than 1 year) shall be considered as a sale or exchange of such timber cut during such year. If such election has been made, gain or loss to the taxpayer shall be recognized in an amount equal to the difference between the fair market value of such timber, and the adjusted basis for depletion of such timber in the hands of the taxpayer. Such fair market value shall be the fair market value as of the first day of the taxable year in which such timber is cut, and shall thereafter be considered as the cost of such cut timber to the taxpayer for all purposes for which such cost is a necessary factor. If a taxpayer makes an election under this subsection, such election shall apply with respect to all timber which is owned by the taxpayer or which the taxpayer has a contract right to cut and shall be binding on the taxpayer for the taxable year for which the election is made and for all subsequent years, unless the Secretary, on showing of undue hardship, permits the taxpayer to revoke his election; such revocation, however, shall preclude any further elections under this subsection except with the consent of the Secretary. For purposes of this subsection and subsection (b), the term "timber" includes evergreen trees which are more than 6 years old at the time severed from the roots and are sold for ornamental purposes.

(b) Disposal of timber with a retained economic interest.—In the case of the disposal of timber held for more than 1 year before such disposal, by the owner thereof under any form or type of contract by virtue of which such owner retains an economic interest in such timber, the difference between the amount realized from the disposal of such timber and the adjusted depletion basis thereof, shall be considered as though it were a gain or loss, as the case may be, on the sale of such timber. In determining the gross income, the adjusted gross income, or the taxable income of the lessee, the deductions allowable with respect to rents and royalties shall be determined without regard to the provisions of this subsection. The date of disposal of such timber shall be deemed to be the date such timber is cut, but if payment is made to the owner under the contract before such timber is cut the owner may elect to treat the date of such payment as the date of disposal of such timber. For purposes of this subsection, the term "owner" means any person who owns an interest in such timber, including a sublessor and a holder of a contract to cut timber.

(c) Disposal of coal or domestic iron ore with a retained economic interest. —In the case of the disposal of coal (including lignite), or iron ore mined in the United States, held for more than 1 year before such disposal, by the owner thereof under any form of contract by virtue of which such owner retains an economic interest in such coal or iron ore, the difference between the amount realized from the disposal of such coal or iron ore and the adjusted depletion basis thereof plus the deductions disallowed for the taxable year under section 272 shall be considered as though it were a gain or loss, as the case may be, on the sale of such coal or iron ore. Such owner shall not be entitled to the allowance for percentage depletion provided in section 613 with respect to such coal or iron ore. This subsection shall not apply to income realized by any owner as a co-adventurer, partner, or principal in the mining of such coal or iron ore, and the word "owner" means any person who owns an economic interest in coal or iron ore in place, including a sublessor. The date of disposal of such coal or iron ore shall be deemed to be the date such coal or iron ore is mined. In determining the gross income, the adjusted gross income, or the taxable income of the lessee, the deductions allowable with respect to rents and royalties shall be determined without regard to the provisions of this subsection. This subsection shall have no application, for purposes of applying subchapter G, relating to corporations used to avoid income tax on shareholders (including the determinations of the amount of the deductions under section 535(b) (6) or section 545(b) (5)). This subsection shall not apply to any disposal of iron ore—

(1) to a person whose relationship to the person disposing of such iron ore would result in the disallowance of losses under section 267 or 707(b), or

(2) to a person owned or controlled directly or indirectly by the same interests which own or control the person disposing of such iron ore.

PART IV—MINERAL PRODUCTION PAYMENTS

§ 636.   Income tax treatment of mineral production payments

(a) Carved-out production payment.—A production payment carved out of mineral property shall be treated, for purposes of this subtitle, as if it were a mortgage loan on the property, and shall not qualify as an economic interest in the mineral property. In the case of a production payment carved out for exploration or development of a mineral property, the preceding sentence shall apply only if and to the extent gross income from the property (for purposes of section 613) would be realized, in the absence of the application of such sentence, by the person creating the production payment.

(b) Retained production payment on sale of mineral property.—A production payment retained on the sale of a mineral property shall be treated, for purposes of this subtitle, as if it were a purchase money mortgage loan and shall not qualify as an economic interest in the mineral property.

(c) Retained production payment on lease of mineral property.—A production payment retained in a mineral property by the lessor in a leasing transaction shall be treated, for purposes of this subtitle, insofar as the lessee (or his successors in interest) is concerned, as if it were a bonus granted by the lessee to the lessor payable in installments. The treatment of the production payment in the hands of the lessor shall be determined without regard to the provisions of this subsection.

. . . . .

SUBCHAPTER J—ESTATES, TRUSTS, BENEFICIARIES, AND DECEDENTS

Part
  I. Estates, trusts, and beneficiaries.
 II. Income in respect of decedents.

PART I—ESTATES, TRUSTS, AND BENEFICIARIES

Subpart
  A. General rules for taxation of estates and trusts.
  B. Trusts which distribute current income only.
  C. Estates and trusts which may accumulate income or which distribute corpus.
  D. Treatment of excess distributions by trusts.
  E. Grantors and others treated as substantial owners.
  F. Miscellaneous.

SUBPART A—GENERAL RULES FOR TAXATION OF ESTATES AND TRUSTS

§ 641.   Imposition of tax

(a) **Application of tax.**—The tax imposed by section 1(e) shall apply to the taxable income of estates or of any kind of property held in trust, including—

(1) income accumulated in trust for the benefit of unborn or unascertained persons or persons with contingent interests, and income accumulated or held for future distribution under the terms of the will or trust;

(2) income which is to be distributed currently by the fiduciary to the beneficiaries, and income collected by a guardian of an infant which is to be held or distributed as the court may direct;

(3) income received by estates of deceased persons during the period of administration or settlement of the estate; and

(4) income which, in the discretion of the fiduciary, may be either distributed to the beneficiaries or accumulated.

(b) **Computation and payment.**—The taxable income of an estate or trust shall be computed in the same manner as in the case of an individual, except as otherwise provided in this part. The tax shall be computed on such taxable income and shall be paid by the fiduciary.

(c) **Exclusion of includible gain from taxable income.**—

(1) **General rule.**—For purposes of this part, the taxable income of a trust does not include the amount of any includible gain as defined in section 644(b) reduced by any deductions properly allocable thereto.

. . . . .

§ 642.   Special rules for credits and deductions

(a) **Credits against tax.**—

. . . . .

(2) **Political contributions.**—An estate or trust shall not be allowed the credit against tax for political contributions provided by section 41.

(b) **Deduction for personal exemption.**—An estate shall be allowed a deduction of $600. A trust which, under its governing instrument, is required to distribute all of its income currently shall be allowed a deduction of $300. All other trusts shall be allowed a deduction of $100. The deductions allowed by this subsection shall be in lieu of the deductions allowed under section 151 (relating to deduction for personal exemption).

(c) **Deduction for amounts paid or permanently set aside for a charitable purpose.**—

(1) **General rule.**—In the case of an estate or trust (other than a trust meeting the specifications of subpart B), there shall be allowed as a deduction in computing its taxable income (in lieu of the deduction allowed by section

170(a), relating to deduction for charitable, etc., contributions and gifts) any amount of the gross income, without limitation, which pursuant to the terms of the governing instrument is, during the taxable year, paid for a purpose specified in section 170(c) (determined without regard to section 170(c) (2) (A)). If a charitable contribution is paid after the close of such taxable year and on or before the last day of the year following the close of such taxable year, then the trustee or administrator may elect to treat such contribution as paid during such taxable year. The election shall be made at such time and in such manner as the Secretary prescribes by regulations.

(2) **Amounts permanently set aside.**—In the case of an estate, and in the case of a trust (other than a trust meeting the specifications of subpart B) required by the terms of its governing instrument to set aside amounts which was—

(A) created on or before October 9, 1969, if—

(i) an irrevocable remainder interest is transferred to or for the use of an organization described in section 170(c), or

(ii) the grantor is at all times after October 9, 1969, under a mental disability to change the terms of the trust; or

(B) established by a will executed on or before October 9, 1969, if—

(i) the testator dies before October 9, 1972, without having republished the will after October 9, 1969, by codicil or otherwise,

(ii) the testator at no time after October 9, 1969, had the right to change the portions of the will which pertain to the trust, or

(iii) the will is not republished by codicil or otherwise before October 9, 1972, and the testator is on such date and at all times thereafter under a mental disability to republish the will by codicil or otherwise,

there shall also be allowed as a deduction in computing its taxable income any amount of the gross income, without limitation, which pursuant to the terms of the governing instrument is, during the taxable year, permanently set aside for a purpose specified in section 170(c), or is to be used exclusively for religious, charitable, scientific, literary, or educational purposes, or for the prevention of cruelty to children or animals, or for the establishment, acquisition, maintenance, or operation of a public cemetery not operated for profit. In the case of a trust, the preceding sentence shall apply only to gross income earned with respect to amounts transferred to the trust before October 9, 1969, or transferred under a will to which subparagraph (B) applies.

(3) **Pooled income funds.**—In the case of a pooled income fund (as defined in paragraph (5)), there shall also be allowed as a deduction in computing its taxable income any amount of the gross income attributable to gain from the sale of a capital asset held for more than 1 year, without limitation, which pursuant to the terms of the governing instrument is, during the taxable year, permanently set aside for a purpose specified in section 170(c).

(4) **Adjustments.**—To the extent that the amount otherwise allowable as a deduction under this subsection consists of gain from the sale or exchange of capital assets held for more than 1 year, proper adjustment shall be made for any deduction allowable to the estate or trust under section 1202 (relating to deduction for excess of capital gains over capital losses). In the case of a

trust, the deduction allowed by this subsection shall be subject to section 681 (relating to unrelated business income).

(5) **Definition of pooled income fund.**—For purposes of paragraph (3), a pooled income fund is a trust—

(A) to which each donor transfers property, contributing an irrevocable remainder interest in such property to or for the use of an organization described in section 170(b) (1) (A) (other than in clauses (vii) or (viii)), and retaining an income interest for the life of one or more beneficiaries (living at the time of such transfer),

(B) in which the property transferred by each donor is commingled with property transferred by other donors who have made or make similar transfers,

(C) which cannot have investments in securities which are exempt from the taxes imposed by this subtitle,

(D) which includes only amounts received from transfers which meet the requirements of this paragraph,

(E) which is maintained by the organization to which the remainder interest is contributed and of which no donor or beneficiary of an income interest is a trustee, and

(F) from which each beneficiary of an income interest receives income, for each year for which he is entitled to receive the income interest referred to in subparagraph (A), determined by the rate of return earned by the trust for such year.

For purposes of determining the amount of any charitable contribution allowable by reason of a transfer of property to a pooled fund, the value of the income interest shall be determined on the basis of the highest rate of return earned by the fund for any of the 3 taxable years immediately preceding the taxable year of the fund in which the transfer is made. In the case of funds in existence less than 3 taxable years preceding the taxable year of the fund in which a transfer is made, the rate of return shall be deemed to be 6 percent per annum, except that the Secretary may prescribe a different rate of return.

.   .   .   .   .

(d) **Net operating loss deduction.**—The benefit of the deduction for net operating losses provided by section 172 shall be allowed to estates and trusts under regulations prescribed by the Secretary.

(e) **Deduction for depreciation and depletion.**—An estate or trust shall be allowed the deduction for depreciation and depletion only to the extent not allowable to beneficiaries under sections 167(h) and 611(b).

(f) **Amortization deductions.**—The benefit of the deductions for amortization provided by sections 169, 184, 187, and 188 shall be allowed to estates and trusts in the same manner as in the case of an individual. The allowable deduction shall be apportioned between the income beneficiaries and the fiduciary under regulations prescribed by the Secretary.

(g) **Disallowance of double deductions.**—Amounts allowable under section 2053 or 2054 as a deduction in computing the taxable estate of a decedent shall not be allowed as a deduction (or as an offset against the sales price of property in determining gain or loss) in computing the taxable income of the estate or of any other person, unless there is filed, within the time and in the manner and form prescribed by the Secretary, a statement that the amounts have not been allowed as deductions under section 2053 or 2054 and a waiver of the right to have such amounts allowed at any time as deductions under section 2053 or 2054. This subsection shall not apply with respect to deductions allowed under part II (relating to income in respect of decedents).

(h) Unused loss carryovers and excess deductions on termination available to beneficiaries.—If on the termination of an estate or trust, the estate or trust has—

(1) a net operating loss carryover under section 172 or a capital loss carryover under section 1212, or

(2) for the last taxable year of the estate or trust deductions (other than the deductions allowed under subsections (b) or (c)) in excess of gross income for such year,

then such carryover or such excess shall be allowed as a deduction, in accordance with regulations prescribed by the Secretary, to the beneficiaries succeeding to the property of the estate or trust.

. . . . .

§ 643.   Definitions applicable to subparts A, B, C, and D

(a) Distributable net income.—For purposes of this part, the term "distributable net income" means, with respect to any taxable year, the taxable income of the estate or trust computed with the following modifications—

(1) Deduction for distributions.—No deduction shall be taken under sections 651 and 661 (relating to additional deductions).

(2) Deduction for personal exemption.—No deduction shall be taken under section 642(b) (relating to deduction for personal exemptions).

(3) Capital gains and losses.—Gains from the sale or exchange of capital assets shall be excluded to the extent that such gains are allocated to corpus and are not (A) paid, credited, or required to be distributed to any beneficiary during the taxable year, or (B) paid, permanently set aside, or to be used for the purposes specified in section 642(c). Losses from the sale or exchange of capital assets shall be excluded, except to the extent such losses are taken into account in determining the amount of gains from the sale or exchange of capital assets which are paid, credited, or required to be distributed to any beneficiary during the taxable year. The deduction under section 1202 (relating to deduction for excess of capital gains over capital losses) shall not be taken into account.

(4) Extraordinary dividends and taxable stock dividends.—For purposes only of subpart B (relating to trusts which distribute current income only), there shall be excluded those items of gross income constituting extraordinary dividends or taxable stock dividends which the fiduciary, acting in good faith, does not pay or credit to any beneficiary by reason of his determination that such dividends are allocable to corpus under the terms of the governing instrument and applicable local law.

(5) Tax-exempt interest.—There shall be included any tax-exempt interest to which section 103 applies, reduced by any amounts which would be deductible in respect of disbursements allocable to such interest but for the provisions of section 265 (relating to disallowance of certain deductions).

. . . . .

(7) Dividends or interest.—There shall be included the amount of any dividends or interest excluded from gross income pursuant to section 116 (relating to partial exclusion of dividends or interest received) or section 128 (relating to interest on certain savings certificates).

If the estate or trust is allowed a deduction under section 642(c), the amount of the modifications specified in paragraphs (5) and (6) shall be reduced to the extent that the amount of income which is paid, permanently set aside, or to be used for the purposes specified in section 642(c) is deemed to consist of items specified in those paragraphs. For this purpose, such amount shall (in the absence of specific provisions in the governing instrument) be deemed to consist of the same proportion of each class of items of income of the estate or trust as the total of each class bears to the total of all classes.

(b) Income.—For purposes of this subpart and subparts B, C, and D, the term "income", when not preceded by the words "taxable", "distributable net", "undistributed net", or "gross", means the amount of income of the estate or trust for the taxable year determined under the terms of the governing instrument and applicable local law. Items of gross income constituting extraordinary dividends or taxable stock dividends which the fiduciary, acting in good faith, determines to be allocable to corpus under the terms of the governing instrument and applicable local law shall not be considered income.

(c) Beneficiary.—For purposes of this part, the term "beneficiary" includes heir, legatee, devisee.

. . . . .

§ 644.   Special rule for gain on property transferred to trust at less than fair market value

(a) Imposition of tax.—

(1) In general.—If—

(A) a trust (or another trust to which the property is distributed) sells or exchanges property at a gain not more than 2 years after the date of the initial transfer of the property in trust by the transferor, and

(B) the fair market value of such property at the time of the initial transfer in trust by the transferor exceeds the adjusted basis of such property immediately after such transfer,

there is hereby imposed a tax determined in accordance with paragraph (2) on the includible gain recognized on such sale or exchange.

(2) Amount of tax.—The amount of the tax imposed by paragraph (1) on any includible gain recognized on the sale or exchange of any property shall be equal to the sum of—

(A) the excess of—

(i) the tax which would have been imposed under this chapter for the taxable year of the transferor in which the sale or exchange of such property occurs had the amount of the includible gain recognized on such sale or exchange, reduced by any deductions properly allocable to such gain, been included in the gross income of the transferor for such taxable year, over

    (ii) the tax actually imposed under this chapter for such taxable year on the transferor, plus

(B) if such sale or exchange occurs in a taxable year of the transferor which begins after the beginning of the taxable year of the trust in which such sale or exchange occurs, an amount equal to the amount determined under subparagraph (A) multiplied by the annual rate established under section 6621.

The determination of tax under clause (i) of subparagraph (A) shall be made by not taking into account any carryback, and by not taking into account any loss or deduction to the extent that such loss or deduction may be carried by the transferor to any other taxable year.

    (3) Taxable year for which tax imposed.—The tax imposed by paragraph (1) shall be imposed for the taxable year of the trust which begins with or within the taxable year of the transferor in which the sale or exchange occurs.

    (4) Tax to be in addition to other taxes.—The tax imposed by this subsection for any taxable year of the trust shall be in addition to any other tax imposed by this chapter for such taxable year.

  (b) Definition of includible gain.—For purposes of this section, the term "includible gain" means the lesser of—

    (1) the gain recognized by the trust on the sale or exchange of any property, or

    (2) the excess of the fair market value of such property at the time of the initial transfer in trust by the transferor over the adjusted basis of such property immediately after such transfer.

  (c) Character of includible gain.—For purposes of subsection (a)—

    (1) The character of the includible gain shall be determined as if the property had actually been sold or exchanged by the transferor, and any activities of the trust with respect to the sale or exchange of the property shall be deemed to be activities of the transferor, and

    (2) the portion of the includible gain subject to the provisions of section 1245 and section 1250 shall be determined in accordance with regulations prescribed by the Secretary.

  (d) Special rules.—

    (1) Short sales.—If the trust sells the property referred to in subsection (a) in a short sale within the 2-year period referred to in such subsection, such 2-year period shall be extended to the date of the closing of such short sale.

    (2) Substituted basis property.—For purposes of this section, in the case of any property held by the trust which has a basis determined in whole or in part by reference to the basis of any other property which was transferred to the trust—

      (A) the initial transfer of such property in trust by the transferor shall be treated as having occurred on the date of the initial transfer in trust of such other property,

(B) subsections (a) (1) (B) and (b) (2) shall be applied by taking into account the fair market value and the adjusted basis of such other property, and

(C) the amount determined under subsection (b) (2) with respect to such other property shall be allocated (under regulations prescribed by the Secretary) among such other property and all properties held by the trust which have a basis determined in whole or in part by reference to the basis of such other property.

(e) Exceptions.—Subsection (a) shall not apply to property—

(1) acquired by the trust from a decedent or which passed to a trust from a decedent (within the meaning of section 1014), or

(2) acquired by a pooled income fund (as defined in section 642(c) (5)), or

(3) acquired by a charitable remainder annuity trust (as defined in section 664(d) (1)) or a charitable remainder unitrust (as defined in sections 664(d) (2) and (3)), or

(4) if the sale or exchange of the property occurred after the death of the transferor.

(f) Special rule for installment sales.—If the trust reports income under section 453 on any sale or exchange to which subsection (a) applies, under regulations prescribed by the Secretary—

(1) subsection (a) (other than the 2-year requirement of paragraph (1) (A) thereof) shall be applied as if each installment were a separate sale or exchange of property to which such subsection applies, and

(2) the term "includible gain" shall not include any portion of an installment received by the trust after the death of the transferor.

SUBPART B—TRUSTS WHICH DISTRIBUTE CURRENT INCOME ONLY

§ 651.   Deduction for trusts distributing current income only

(a) Deduction.—In the case of any trust the terms of which—

(1) provide that all of its income is required to be distributed currently, and

(2) do not provide that any amounts are to be paid, permanently set aside, or used for the purposes specified in section 642(c) (relating to deduction for charitable, etc., purposes),

there shall be allowed as a deduction in computing the taxable income of the trust the amount of the income for the taxable year which is required to be distributed currently. This section shall not apply in any taxable year in which the trust distributes amounts other than amounts of income described in paragraph (1).

(b) Limitation on deduction.—If the amount of income required to be distributed currently exceeds the distributable net income of the trust for the taxable year, the deduction shall be limited to the amount of the distributable net income. For this purpose, the computation of distributable net income shall not include items of income which are not included in the gross income of the trust and the deductions allocable thereto.

§ 652.   Inclusion of amounts in gross income of beneficiaries of trusts distributing current income only

(a) Inclusion.—Subject to subsection (b), the amount of income for the taxable year required to be distributed currently by a trust described in section 651 shall be included in the gross income of the beneficiaries to whom the income is required to be distributed, whether distributed or not. If such amount exceeds the distributable net income, there shall be included in the gross income of each beneficiary an amount which bears the same ratio to distributable net income as the amount of income required to be distributed to such beneficiary bears to the amount of income required to be distributed to all beneficiaries.

(b) Character of amounts.—The amounts specified in subsection (a) shall have the same character in the hands of the beneficiary as in the hands of the trust. For this purpose, the amounts shall be treated as consisting of the same proportion of each class of items entering into the computation of distributable net income of the trust as the total of each class bears to the total distributable net income of the trust, unless the terms of the trust specifically allocate different classes of income to different beneficiaries. In the application of the preceding sentence, the items of deduction entering into the computation of distributable net income shall be allocated among the items of distributable net income in accordance with regulations prescribed by the Secretary.

(c) Different taxable years.—If the taxable year of a beneficiary is different from that of the trust, the amount which the beneficiary is required to include in gross income in accordance with the provisions of this section shall be based upon the amount of income of the trust for any taxable year or years of the trust ending within or with his taxable year.

SUBPART C—ESTATES AND TRUSTS WHICH MAY ACCUMULATE INCOME OR WHICH DISTRIBUTE CORPUS

§ 661.   Deduction for estates and trusts accumulating income or distributing corpus

(a) Deduction.—In any taxable year there shall be allowed as a deduction in computing the taxable income of an estate or trust (other than a trust to which subpart B applies), the sum of—

(1) any amount of income for such taxable year required to be distributed currently (including any amount required to be distributed which may be paid out of income or corpus to the extent such amount is paid out of income for such taxable year); and

(2) any other amounts properly paid or credited or required to be distributed for such taxable year;

but such deduction shall not exceed the distributable net income of the estate or trust. For purposes of paragraph (1), the amount of distributable net income shall be computed without the deduction allowed by section 642(c).

(b) Character of amounts distributed.—The amount determined under subsection (a) shall be treated as consisting of the same proportion of each class of items entering into the computation of distributable net income of the estate or trust as the total of each class bears to the total distributable net income of the estate or trust in the absence of the allocation of different classes of income under the specific terms of the governing instrument. In the application of the preceding sentence, the items of deduction entering into the computation of distributable net income (including the deduction allowed under section 642(c)) shall be allocated among the items of distributable net income in accordance with regulations prescribed by the Secretary.

(c) Limitation on deduction.—No deduction shall be allowed under subsection (a) in respect of any portion of the amount allowed as a deduction under that subsection (without regard to this subsection) which is treated under subsection (b) as consisting of any item of distributable net income which is not included in the gross income of the estate or trust.

§ 662. Inclusion of amounts in gross income of beneficiaries of estates and trusts accumulating income or distributing corpus

(a) Inclusion.—Subject to subsection (b), there shall be included in the gross income of a beneficiary to whom an amount specified in section 661(a) is paid, credited, or required to be distributed (by an estate or trust described in section 661), the sum of the following amounts:

(1) Amounts required to be distributed currently.—The amount of income for the taxable year required to be distributed currently to such beneficiary, whether distributed or not. If the amount of income required to be distributed currently to all beneficiaries exceeds the distributable net income (computed without the deduction allowed by section 642(c), relating to deduction for charitable, etc., purposes) of the estate or trust, then, in lieu of the amount provided in the preceding sentence, there shall be included in the gross income of the beneficiary an amount which bears the same ratio to distributable net income (as so computed) as the amount of income required to be distributed currently to such beneficiary bears to the amount required to be distributed currently to all beneficiaries. For purposes of this section, the phrase "the amount of income for the taxable year required to be distributed currently" includes any amount required to be paid out of income or corpus to the extent such amount is paid out of income for such taxable year.

(2) Other amounts distributed.—All other amounts properly paid, credited, or required to be distributed to such beneficiary for the taxable year. If the sum of—

(A) the amount of income for the taxable year required to be distributed currently to all beneficiaries, and

(B) all other amounts properly paid, credited, or required to be distributed to all beneficiaries

exceeds the distributable net income of the estate or trust, then, in lieu of the amount provided in the preceding sentence, there shall be included in the gross income of the beneficiary an amount which bears the same ratio to distributable net income (reduced by the amounts specified in (A)) as the other amounts properly paid, credited or required to be distributed to the beneficiary bear to the other amounts properly paid, credited, or required to be distributed to all beneficiaries.

(b) Character of amounts.—The amounts determined under subsection (a) shall have the same character in the hands of the beneficiary as in the hands of the estate or trust. For this purpose, the amounts shall be treated as consisting of the same proportion of each class of items entering into the computation of distributable net income as the total of each class bears to the total distributable net income of the estate or trust unless the terms of the governing instrument specifically allocate different classes of income to different beneficiaries. In the application of the preceding sentence, the items of deduction entering into the computation of distributable net income (including the deduction allowed under section 642(c)) shall be allocated among the items of distributable net income in accordance with regulations prescribed by the Secretary. In the application of this subsection to the amount determined under paragraph (1) of subsection (a), distributable net income shall be computed without regard to any portion of the deduction under section 642(c) which is not attributable to income of the taxable year.

(c) **Different taxable years.**—If the taxable year of a beneficiary is different from that of the estate or trust, the amount to be included in the gross income of the beneficiary shall be based on the distributable net income of the estate or trust and the amounts properly paid, credited, or required to be distributed to the beneficiary during any taxable year or years of the estate or trust ending within or with his taxable year.

§ 663. Special rules applicable to sections 661 and 662

(a) **Exclusions.**—There shall not be included as amounts falling within section 661(a) or 662(a)—

(1) **Gifts, bequests, etc.**—Any amount which, under the terms of the governing instrument, is properly paid or credited as a gift or bequest of a specific sum of money or of specific property and which is paid or credited all at once or in not more than 3 installments. For this purpose an amount which can be paid or credited only from the income of the estate or trust shall not be considered as a gift or bequest of a specific sum of money.

(2) **Charitable, etc., distributions.**—Any amount paid or permanently set aside or otherwise qualifying for the deduction provided in section 642(c) (computed without regard to sections 508(d), 681, and 4948(c) (4)).

(3) **Denial of double deduction.**—Any amount paid, credited, or distributed in the taxable year, if section 651 or section 661 applied to such amount for a preceding taxable year of an estate or trust because credited or required to be distributed in such preceding taxable year.

(b) **Distributions in first sixty-five days of taxable year.**—

(1) **General rule.**—If within the first 65 days of any taxable year of a trust, an amount is properly paid or credited, such amount shall be considered paid or credited on the last day of the preceding taxable year.

(2) **Limitation.**—Paragraph (1) shall apply with respect to any taxable year of a trust only if the fiduciary of such trust elects, in such manner and at such time as the Secretary prescribes by regulations, to have paragraph (1) apply for such taxable year.

(c) **Separate shares treated as separate trusts.**—For the sole purpose of determining the amount of distributable net income in the application of sections 661 and 662, in the case of a single trust having more than one beneficiary, substantially separate and independent shares of different beneficiaries in the trust shall be treated as separate trusts. The existence of such substantially separate and independent shares and the manner of treatment as separate trusts, including the application of subpart D, shall be determined in accordance with regulations prescribed by the Secretary.

§ 664. Charitable remainder trusts

(a) **General rule.**—Notwithstanding any other provision of this subchapter, the provisions of this section shall, in accordance with regulations prescribed by the Secretary, apply in the case of a charitable remainder annuity trust and a charitable remainder unitrust.

(b) **Character of distributions.**—Amounts distributed by a charitable remainder annuity trust or by a charitable remainder unitrust shall be considered as having the following characteristics in the hands of a beneficiary to whom is paid the annuity described in subsection (d) (1) (A) or the payment described in subsection (d) (2) (A):

(1) First, as amounts of income (other than gains, and amounts treated as gains, from the sale or other disposition of capital assets) includible in gross income to the extent of such income of the trust for the year and such undistributed income of the trust for prior years;

(2) Second, as a capital gain to the extent of the capital gain of the trust for the year and the undistributed capital gain of the trust for prior years;

(3) Third, as other income to the extent of such income of the trust for the year and such undistributed income of the trust for prior years; and

(4) Fourth, as a distribution of trust corpus.

For purposes of this section, the trust shall determine the amount of its undistributed capital gain on a cumulative net basis.

(c) **Exemption from income taxes.**—A charitable remainder annuity trust and a charitable remainder unitrust shall, for any taxable year, not be subject to any tax imposed by this subtitle, unless such trust, for such year, has unrelated business taxable income (within the meaning of section 512, determined as if part III of subchapter F applied to such trust).

(d) **Definitions.—**

(1) **Charitable remainder annuity trust.**—For purposes of this section, a charitable remainder annuity trust is a trust—

(A) from which a sum certain (which is not less than 5 percent of the initial net fair market value of all property placed in trust) is to be paid, not less often than annually, to one or more persons (at least one of which is not an organization described in section 170(c) and, in the case of individuals, only to an individual who is living at the time of the creation of the trust) for a term of years (not in excess of 20 years) or for the life or lives of such individual or individuals,

(B) from which no amount other than the payments described in subparagraph (A) may be paid to or for the use of any person other than an organization described in section 170(c), and

(C) following the termination of the payments described in subparagraph (A), the remainder interest in the trust is to be transferred to, or for the use of, an organization described in section 170(c) or is to be retained by the trust for such a use.

(2) Charitable remainder unitrust.—For purposes of this section, a charitable remainder unitrust is a trust—

(A) from which a fixed percentage (which is not less than 5 percent) of the net fair market value of its assets, valued annually, is to be paid, not less often than annually, to one or more persons (at least one of which is not an organization described in section 170(c) and, in the case of individuals, only to an individual who is living at the time of the creation of the trust) for a term of years (not in excess of 20 years) or for the life or lives of such individual or individuals,

(B) from which no amount other than the payments described in subparagraph (A) may be paid to or for the use of any person other than an organization described in section 170(c), and

(C) following the termination of the payments described in subparagraph (A), the remainder interest in the trust is to be transferred to, or for the use of, an organization described in section 170(c) or is to be retained by the trust for such a use.

(3) Exception.—Notwithstanding the provisions of paragraphs (2) (A) and (B), the trust instrument may provide that the trustee shall pay the income beneficiary for any year—

(A) the amount of the trust income, if such amount is less than the amount required to be distributed under paragraph (2) (A), and

(B) any amount of the trust income which is in excess of the amount required to be distributed under paragraph (2) (A), to the extent that (by reason of subparagraph (A)) the aggregate of the amounts paid in prior years was less than the aggregate of such required amounts.

(e) Valuation for purposes of charitable contribution.—For purposes of determining the amount of any charitable contribution, the remainder interest of a charitable remainder annuity trust or charitable remainder unitrust shall be computed on the basis that an amount equal to 5 percent of the net fair market value of its assets (or a greater amount, if required under the terms of the trust instrument) is to be distributed each year.

SUBPART D—TREATMENT OF EXCESS DISTRIBUTIONS BY TRUSTS

§ 665.   Definitions applicable to subpart D

(a) Undistributed net income.—For purposes of this subpart, the term "undistributed net income" for any taxable year means the amount by which the distributable net income of the trust for such taxable year exceeds the sum of—

(1) the amounts for such taxable year specified in paragraphs (1) and (2) of section 661(a), and

(2) the amount of taxes imposed on the trust attributable to such distributable net income.

(b) Accumulation distribution.—For purposes of this subpart, the term "accumulation distribution" means, for any taxable year of the trust, the amount by which—

(1) the amounts specified in paragraph (2) of section 661(a) for such taxable year, exceed

(2) distributable net income for such year reduced (but not below zero) by the amounts specified in paragraph (1) of section 661(a).

For purposes of section 667 (other than subsection (c) thereof, relating to multiple trusts), the amounts specified in paragraph (2) of section 661(a) shall not include amounts properly paid, credited, or required to be distributed to a beneficiary from a trust (other than a foreign trust) as income accumulated before the birth of such beneficiary or before such beneficiary attains the age of 21. If the amounts properly paid, credited, or required to be distributed by the trust for the taxable year do not exceed the income of the trust for such year, there shall be no accumulation distribution for such year.

. . . . .

(d) Taxes imposed on the trust.—For purposes of this subpart—

    (1) In general.—The term "taxes imposed on the trust" means the amount of the taxes which are imposed for any taxable year of the trust under this chapter (without regard to this subpart or subpart A of part IV of subchapter A) and which, under regulations prescribed by the Secretary, are properly allocable to the undistributed portions of distributable net income and gains in excess of losses from sales or exchanges of capital assets. The amount determined in the preceding sentence shall be reduced by any amount of such taxes deemed distributed under section 666(b) and (c) or 669(d) and (e) to any beneficiary.

. . . . .

(e) Preceding taxable year.—For purposes of this subpart—

    (1) in the case of a trust (other than a foreign trust created by a United States person), the term "preceding taxable year" does not include any taxable year of the trust—

        (A) which precedes by more than 5 years the taxable year of the trust in which an accumulation distribution is made, if it is made in a taxable year beginning before January 1, 1974, or

        (B) which begins before January 1, 1969, in the case of an accumulation distribution made during a taxable year beginning after December 31, 1973; and

    (2) in the case of a foreign trust created by a United States person, such term does not include any taxable year of the trust to which this part does not apply.

In the case of a preceding taxable year with respect to which a trust qualifies (without regard to this subpart) under the provisions of subpart B, for purposes of the application of this subpart to such trust for such taxable year, such trust shall, in accordance with regulations prescribed by the Secretary, be treated as a trust to which subpart C applies.

§ 666. Accumulation distribution allocated to preceding years

    (a) Amount allocated.—In the case of a trust which is subject to subpart C, the amount of the accumulation distribution of such trust for a taxable year shall be deemed to be an amount within the meaning of paragraph (2) of section 661(a) distributed on the last day of each of the preceding taxable years, commencing with the earliest of such years, to the extent that such amount exceeds the total of any undistributed net income for all earlier preceding taxable years. The amount deemed to be distributed in any such preceding taxable year under the preceding sentence shall not exceed the undistributed net income for such

Ch. 1 ESTATES, TRUSTS, ETC. § 667

preceding taxable year. For purposes of this subsection, undistributed net income for each of such preceding taxable years shall be computed without regard to such accumulation distribution and without regard to any accumulation distribution determined for any succeeding taxable year.

(b) Total taxes deemed distributed.—If any portion of an accumulation distribution for any taxable year is deemed under subsection (a) to be an amount within the meaning of paragraph (2) of section 661(a) distributed on the last day of any preceding taxable year, and such portion of such distribution is not less than the undistributed net income for such preceding taxable year, the trust shall be deemed to have distributed on the last day of such preceding taxable year an additional amount within the meaning of paragraph (2) of section 661(a). Such additional amount shall be equal to the taxes (other than the tax imposed by section 55) imposed on the trust for such preceding taxable year attributable to the undistributed net income. For purposes of this subsection, the undistributed net income and the taxes imposed on the trust for such preceding taxable year attributable to such undistributed net income shall be computed without regard to such accumulation distribution and without regard to any accumulation distribution determined for any succeeding taxable year.

(c) Pro rata portion of taxes deemed distributed.—If any portion of an accumulation distribution for any taxable year is deemed under subsection (a) to be an amount within the meaning of paragraph (2) of section 661(a) distributed on the last day of any preceding taxable year and such portion of the accumulation distribution is less than the undistributed net income for such preceding taxable year, the trust shall be deemed to have distributed on the last day of such preceding taxable year an additional amount within the meaning of paragraph (2) of section 661(a). Such additional amount shall be equal to the taxes (other than the tax imposed by section 55) imposed on the trust for such taxable year attributable to the undistributed net income multiplied by the ratio of the portion of the accumulation distribution to the undistributed net income of the trust for such year. For purposes of this subsection, the undistributed net income and the taxes imposed on the trust for such preceding taxable year attributable to such undistributed net income shall be computed without regard to the accumulation distribution and without regard to any accumulation distribution determined for any succeeding taxable year.

(d) Rule when information is not available.—If adequate records are not available to determine the proper application of this subpart to an amount distributed by a trust, such amount shall be deemed to be an accumulation distribution consisting of undistributed net income earned during the earliest preceding taxable year of the trust in which it can be established that the trust was in existence.

(e) Denial of refund to trusts and beneficiaries.—No refund or credit shall be allowed to a trust or a beneficiary of such trust for any preceding taxable year by reason of a distribution deemed to have been made by such trust in such year under this section.

§ 667. Treatment of amounts deemed distributed by trust in preceding years

(a) General rule.—The total of the amounts which are treated under section 666 as having been distributed by a trust in a preceding taxable year shall be included in the income of a beneficiary of the trust when paid, credited, or required to be distributed to the extent that such total would have been included in the income of such beneficiary under section 662(a) (2) (and, with respect to any tax-exempt interest to which section 103 applies, under section 662(b)) if such total had been paid to such beneficiary on the last day of such preceding taxable year. The tax imposed by this subtitle on a beneficiary for a taxable year in which any such amount is included in his income shall be determined only as provided in this section and shall consist of the sum of—

(1) a partial tax computed on the taxable income reduced by an amount equal to the total of such amounts, at the rate and in the manner as if this section had not been enacted,

(2) a partial tax determined as provided in subsection (b) of this section, and

(3) in the case of a foreign trust, the interest charge determined as provided in section 668.

(b) Tax on distribution.—

(1) In general.—The partial tax imposed by subsection (a) (2) shall be determined—

(A) by determining the number of preceding taxable years of the trust on the last day of which an amount is deemed under section 666(a) to have been distributed,

(B) by taking from the 5 taxable years immediately preceding the year of the accumulation distribution the 1 taxable year for which the beneficiary's taxable income was the highest and the 1 taxable year for which his taxable income was the lowest,

(C) by adding to the beneficiary's taxable income for each of the 3 taxable years remaining after the application of subparagraph (B) an amount determined by dividing the amount deemed distributed under section 666 and required to be included in income under subsection (a) by the number of preceding taxable years determined under subparagraph (A), and

(D) by determining the average increase in tax for the 3 taxable years referred to in subparagraph (C) resulting from the application of such subparagraph.

The partial tax imposed by subsection (a) (2) shall be the excess (if any) of the average increase in tax determined under subparagraph (D), multiplied by the number of preceding taxable years determined under subparagraph (A), over the amount of taxes (other than the amount of taxes described in section 665(d) (2)) deemed distributed to the beneficiary under sections 666(b) and (c).

(2) Treatment of loss years.—For purposes of paragraph (1), the taxable income of the beneficiary for any taxable year shall be deemed not to be less than.—

(A) in the case of a beneficiary who is an individual, the zero bracket amount for such year, or

(B) in the case of a beneficiary who is a corporation, zero.

(3) Certain preceding taxable years not taken into account.—For purposes of paragraph (1), if the amount of the undistributed net income deemed distributed in any preceding taxable year of the trust is less than 25 percent of the amount of the accumulation distribution divided by the number of preceding taxable years to which the accumulation distribution is allocated under section 666(a), the number of preceding taxable years of the trust with

respect to which an amount is deemed distributed to a beneficiary under section 666(a) shall be determined without regard to such year.

(4) Effect of other accumulation distributions.—In computing the partial tax under paragraph (1) for any beneficiary, the income of such beneficiary for each of his prior taxable years shall include amounts previously deemed distributed to such beneficiary in such year under section 666 as a result of prior accumulation distributions (whether from the same or another trust).

(5) Multiple distributions in the same taxable year.—In the case of accumulation distributions made from more than one trust which are includible in the income of a beneficiary in the same taxable year, the distributions shall be deemed to have been made consecutively in whichever order the beneficiary shall determine.

(6) Adjustment in partial tax for estate and generation-skipping transfer taxes attributable to partial tax.—

(A) In general.—The partial tax shall be reduced by an amount which is equal to the pre-death portion of the partial tax multiplied by a fraction—

(i) the numerator of which is that portion of the tax imposed by chapter 11 or 13, as the case may be, which is attributable (on a proportionate basis) to amounts included in the accumulation distribution, and

(ii) the denominator of which is the amount of the accumulation distribution which is subject to the tax imposed by chapter 11 or 13, as the case may be.

(B) Partial tax determined without regard to this paragraph.—For purposes of this paragraph, the term "partial tax" means the partial tax imposed by subsection (a) (2) determined under this subsection without regard to this paragraph.

(C) Pre-death portion.—For purposes of this paragraph, the pre-death portion of the partial tax shall be an amount which bears the same ratio to the partial tax as the portion of the accumulation distribution which is attributable to the period before the date of the death of the decedent or the date of the generation-skipping transfer bears to the total accumulation distribution.

(c) Special rule for multiple trusts.—

(1) In general.—If, in the same prior taxable year of the beneficiary in which any part of the accumulation distribution from a trust (hereinafter in this paragraph referred to as "third trust") is deemed under section 666(a) to have been distributed to such beneficiary, some part of prior distributions by each of 2 or more other trusts is deemed under section 666(a) to have been distributed to such beneficiary, then subsections (b) and (c) of section 666 shall not apply with respect to such part of the accumulation distribution from such third trust.

(2) Accumulation distributions from trust not taken into account unless they equal or exceed $1,000.—For purposes of paragraph (1), an accumulation distribution from a trust to a beneficiary shall be taken into account only if such distribution, when added to any prior accumulation distributions from such trust which are deemed under section 666(a) to have been distributed to such beneficiary for the same prior taxable year of the beneficiary, equals or exceeds $1,000.

. . . . .

§ 668. Interest charge on accumulation distributions from foreign trusts

(a) General rule.—For purposes of the tax determined under section 667(a), the interest charge is an amount equal to 6 percent of the partial tax computed under section 667(b) multiplied by a fraction—

(1) the numerator of which is the sum of the number of taxable years between each taxable year to which the distribution is allocated under section 666(a) and the taxable year of the distribution (counting in each case the taxable year to which the distribution is allocated but not counting the taxable year of the distribution), and

(2) the denominator of which is the number of taxable years to which the distribution is allocated under section 666(a).

(b) Limitation.—The total amount of the interest charge shall not, when added to the total partial tax computed under section 667(b), exceed the amount of the accumulation distribution (other than the amount of tax deemed distributed by section 666(b) or (c)) in respect of which such partial tax was determined.

(c) Special rules.—

(1) Interest charge not deductible.—The interest charge determined under this section shall not be allowed as a deduction for purposes of any tax imposed by this title.

. . . . .

SUBPART E—GRANTORS AND OTHERS TREATED AS SUBSTANTIAL OWNERS

§ 671. Trust income, deductions, and credits attributable to grantors and others as substantial owners

Where it is specified in this subpart that the grantor or another person shall be treated as the owner of any portion of a trust, there shall then be included in computing the taxable income and credits of the grantor or the other person those items of income, deductions, and credits against tax of the trust which are attributable to that portion of the trust to the extent that such items would be taken into account under this chapter in computing taxable income or credits against the tax of an individual. Any remaining portion of the trust shall be subject to subparts A through D. No items of a trust shall be included in computing the taxable income and credits of the grantor or of any other person solely on the grounds of his dominion and control over the trust under section 61 (relating to definition of gross income) or any other provision of this title, except as specified in this subpart.

§ 672. Definitions and rules

(a) Adverse party.—For purposes of this subpart, the term "adverse party" means any person having a substantial beneficial interest in the trust which would be adversely affected by the exercise or nonexercise of the power which he possesses respecting the trust. A person having a general power of appointment over the trust property shall be deemed to have a beneficial interest in the trust.

(b) Nonadverse party.—For purposes of this subpart, the term "nonadverse party" means any person who is not an adverse party.

(c) Related or subordinate party.—For purposes of this subpart, the term "related or subordinate party" means any nonadverse party who is—

(1) the grantor's spouse if living with the grantor;

(2) any one of the following: The grantor's father, mother, issue, brother or sister; an employee of the grantor; a corporation or any employee of a corporation in which the stock holdings of the grantor and the trust are significant from the viewpoint of voting control; a subordinate employee of a corporation in which the grantor is an executive.

For purposes of sections 674 and 675, a related or subordinate party shall be presumed to be subservient to the grantor in respect of the exercise or nonexercise of the powers conferred on him unless such party is shown not to be subservient by a preponderance of the evidence.

(d) Rule where power is subject to condition precedent.—A person shall be considered to have a power described in this subpart even though the exercise of the power is subject to a precedent giving of notice or takes effect only on the expiration of a certain period after the exercise of the power.

§ 673.   Reversionary interests

(a) General rule.—The grantor shall be treated as the owner of any portion of a trust in which he has a reversionary interest in either the corpus or the income therefrom if, as of the inception of that portion of the trust, the interest will or may reasonably be expected to take effect in possession or enjoyment within 10 years commencing with the date of the transfer of that portion of the trust.

[**(b) Repealed.** Pub.L. 91–172, Title II, § 201(c), Dec. 30, 1969, 83 Stat. 560]

(c) Reversionary interest taking effect at death of income beneficiary.—The grantor shall not be treated under subsection (a) as the owner of any portion of a trust where his reversionary interest in such portion is not to take effect in possession or enjoyment until the death of the person or persons to whom the income therefrom is payable.

(d) Postponement of date specified for reacquisition.—Any postponement of the date specified for the reacquisition of possession or enjoyment of the reversionary interest shall be treated as a new transfer in trust commencing with the date on which the postponement is effected and terminating with the date prescribed by the postponement. However, income for any period shall not be included in the income of the grantor by reason of the preceding sentence if such income would not be so includible in the absence of such postponement.

§ 674.   Power to control beneficial enjoyment

(a) General rule.—The grantor shall be treated as the owner of any portion of a trust in respect of which the beneficial enjoyment of the corpus or the income therefrom is subject to a power of disposition, exercisable by the grantor or a nonadverse party, or both, without the approval or consent of any adverse party.

(b) Exceptions for certain powers.—Subsection (a) shall not apply to the following powers regardless of by whom held:

(1) **Power to apply income to support of a dependent.**—A power described in section 677(b) to the extent that the grantor would not be subject to tax under that section.

(2) Power affecting beneficial enjoyment only after expiration of 10-year period.—A power, the exercise of which can only affect the beneficial enjoyment of the income for a period commencing after the expiration of a period such that a grantor would not be treated as the owner under section 673 if the power were a reversionary interest; but the grantor may be treated as the owner after the expiration of the period unless the power is relinquished.

(3) Power exercisable only by will.—A power exercisable only by will, other than a power in the grantor to appoint by will the income of the trust where the income is accumulated for such disposition by the grantor or may be so accumulated in the discretion of the grantor or a nonadverse party, or both, without the approval or consent of any adverse party.

(4) Power to allocate among charitable beneficiaries.—A power to determine the beneficial enjoyment of the corpus or the income therefrom if the corpus or income is irrevocably payable for a purpose specified in section 170(c) (relating to definition of charitable contributions).

(5) Power to distribute corpus.—A power to distribute corpus either—

(A) to or for a beneficiary or beneficiaries or to or for a class of beneficiaries (whether or not income beneficiaries) provided that the power is limited by a reasonably definite standard which is set forth in the trust instrument; or

(B) to or for any current income beneficiary, provided that the distribution of corpus must be chargeable against the proportionate share of corpus held in trust for the payment of income to the beneficiary as if the corpus constituted a separate trust.

A power does not fall within the powers described in this paragraph if any person has a power to add to the beneficiary or beneficiaries or to a class of beneficiaries designated to receive the income or corpus, except where such action is to provide for after-born or after-adopted children.

(6) Power to withhold income temporarily.—A power to distribute or apply income to or for any current income beneficiary or to accumulate the income for him, provided that any accumulated income must ultimately be payable—

(A) to the beneficiary from whom distribution or application is withheld, to his estate, or to his appointees (or persons named as alternate takers in default of appointment) provided that such beneficiary possesses a power of appointment which does not exclude from the class of possible appointees any person other than the beneficiary, his estate, his creditors, or the creditors of his estate, or

(B) on termination of the trust, or in conjunction with a distribution of corpus which is augmented by such accumulated income, to the current income beneficiaries in shares which have been irrevocably specified in the trust instrument.

Accumulated income shall be considered so payable although it is provided that if any beneficiary does not survive a date of distribution which could reasonably have been expected to occur within the beneficiary's lifetime, the share of the deceased beneficiary is to be paid to his appointees or to one or more designated alternate takers (other than the grantor or the grantor's estate) whose shares have been irrevocably specified. A power does not fall within the powers described in this paragraph if any person has a power to add to the beneficiary or beneficiaries or to a class of beneficiaries designated to receive the income or corpus except where such action is to provide for after-born or after-adopted children.

(7) Power to withhold income during disability of a beneficiary.—A power exercisable only during—

    (A) the existence of a legal disability of any current income beneficiary, or

    (B) the period during which any income beneficiary shall be under the age of 21 years,

to distribute or apply income to or for such beneficiary or to accumulate and add the income to corpus. A power does not fall within the powers described in this paragraph if any person has a power to add to the beneficiary or beneficiaries or to a class of beneficiaries designated to receive the income or corpus, except where such action is to provide for after-born or after-adopted children.

(8) Power to allocate between corpus and income.—A power to allocate receipts and disbursements as between corpus and income, even though expressed in broad language.

(c) Exception for certain powers of independent trustees.—Subsection (a) shall not apply to a power solely exercisable (without the approval or consent of any other person) by a trustee or trustees, none of whom is the grantor, and no more than half of whom are related or subordinate parties who are subservient to the wishes of the grantor—

    (1) to distribute, apportion, or accumulate income to or for a beneficiary or beneficiaries, or to, for, or within a class of beneficiaries; or

    (2) to pay out corpus to or for a beneficiary or beneficiaries or to or for a class of beneficiaries (whether or not income beneficiaries).

A power does not fall within the powers described in this subsection if any person has a power to add to the beneficiary or beneficiaries or to a class of beneficiaries designated to receive the income or corpus, except where such action is to provide for after-born or after-adopted children.

(d) Power to allocate income if limited by a standard.—Subsection (a) shall not apply to a power solely exercisable (without the approval or consent of any other person) by a trustee or trustees, none of whom is the grantor or spouse living with the grantor, to distribute, apportion, or accumulate income to or for a beneficiary or beneficiaries, or to, for, or within a class of beneficiaries, whether or not the conditions of paragraph (6) or (7) of subsection (b) are satisfied, if such power is limited by a reasonably definite external standard which is set forth in the trust instrument. A power does not fall within the powers described in this subsection if any person has a power to add to the beneficiary or beneficiaries or to a class of beneficiaries designated to receive the income or corpus except where such action is to provide for after-born or after-adopted children.

§ 675.   Administrative powers

The grantor shall be treated as the owner of any portion of a trust in respect of which—

    (1) Power to deal for less than adequate and full consideration.—A power exercisable by the grantor or a nonadverse party, or both, without the approval or consent of any adverse party enables the grantor or any person to purchase, exchange, or otherwise deal with or dispose of the corpus or the income therefrom for less than an adequate consideration in money or money's worth.

(2) Power to borrow without adequate interest or security.—A power exercisable by the grantor or a nonadverse party, or both, enables the grantor to borrow the corpus or income, directly or indirectly, without adequate interest or without adequate security except where a trustee (other than the grantor) is authorized under a general lending power to make loans to any person without regard to interest or security.

(3) Borrowing of the trust funds.—The grantor has directly or indirectly borrowed the corpus or income and has not completely repaid the loan, including any interest, before the beginning of the taxable year. The preceding sentence shall not apply to a loan which provides for adequate interest and adequate security, if such loan is made by a trustee other than the grantor and other than a related or subordinate trustee subservient to the grantor.

(4) General powers of administration.—A power of administration is exercisable in a nonfiduciary capacity by any person without the approval or consent of any person in a fiduciary capacity. For purposes of this paragraph, the term "power of administration" means any one or more of the following powers: (A) a power to vote or direct the voting of stock or other securities of a corporation in which the holdings of the grantor and the trust are significant from the viewpoint of voting control; (B) a power to control the investment of the trust funds either by directing investments or reinvestments, or by vetoing proposed investments or reinvestments, to the extent that the trust funds consist of stocks or securities of corporations in which the holdings of the grantor and the trust are significant from the viewpoint of voting control; or (C) a power to reacquire the trust corpus by substituting other property of an equivalent value.

§ 676.   Power to revoke

(a) General rule.—The grantor shall be treated as the owner of any portion of a trust, whether or not he is treated as such owner under any other provision of this part, where at any time the power to revest in the grantor title to such portion is exercisable by the grantor or a non-adverse party, or both.

(b) Power affecting beneficial enjoyment only after expiration of 10-year period.—Subsection (a) shall not apply to a power the exercise of which can only affect the beneficial enjoyment of the income for a period commencing after the expiration of a period such that a grantor would not be treated as the owner under section 673 if the power were a reversionary interest. But the grantor may be treated as the owner after the expiration of such period unless the power is relinquished.

§ 677.   Income for benefit of grantor

(a) General rule.—The grantor shall be treated as the owner of any portion of a trust, whether or not he is treated as such owner under section 674, whose income without the approval or consent of any adverse party is, or, in the discretion of the grantor or a nonadverse party, or both, may be—

   (1) distributed to the grantor or the grantor's spouse;

   (2) held or accumulated for future distribution to the grantor or the grantor's spouse; or

(3) applied to the payment of premiums on policies of insurance on the life of the grantor or the grantor's spouse (except policies of insurance irrevocably payable for a purpose specified in section 170(c) (relating to definition of charitable contributions)).

This subsection shall not apply to a power the exercise of which can only affect the beneficial enjoyment of the income for a period commencing after the expiration of a period such that the grantor would not be treated as the owner under section 673 if the power were a reversionary interest; but the grantor may be treated as the owner after the expiration of the period unless the power is relinquished.

(b) Obligations of support.—Income of a trust shall not be considered taxable to the grantor under subsection (a) or any other provision of this chapter merely because such income in the discretion of another person, the trustee, or the grantor acting as trustee or co-trustee, may be applied or distributed for the support or maintenance of a beneficiary (other than the grantor's spouse) whom the grantor is legally obligated to support or maintain, except to the extent that such income is so applied or distributed. In cases where the amounts so applied or distributed are paid out of corpus or out of other than income for the taxable year, such amounts shall be considered to be an amount paid or credited within the meaning of paragraph (2) of section 661(a) and shall be taxed to the grantor under section 662.

§ 678.   Person other than grantor treated as substantial owner

(a) General rule.—A person other than the grantor shall be treated as the owner of any portion of a trust with respect to which:

(1) such person has a power exercisable solely by himself to vest the corpus or the income therefrom in himself, or

(2) such person has previously partially released or otherwise modified such a power and after the release or modification retains such control as would, within the principles of sections 671 to 677, inclusive, subject a grantor of a trust to treatment as the owner thereof.

(b) Exception where grantor is taxable.—Subsection (a) shall not apply with respect to a power over income, as originally granted or thereafter modified, if the grantor of the trust or a transferor (to whom section 679 applies) is otherwise treated as the owner under the provisions of this subpart other than this section.

(c) Obligations of support.—Subsection (a) shall not apply to a power which enables such person, in the capacity of trustee or co-trustee, merely to apply the income of the trust to the support or maintenance of a person whom the holder of the power is obligated to support or maintain except to the extent that such income is so applied. In cases where the amounts so applied or distributed are paid out of corpus or out of other than income of the taxable year, such amounts shall be considered to be an amount paid or credited within the meaning of paragraph (2) of section 661(a) and shall be taxed to the holder of the power under section 662.

(d) Effect of renunciation or disclaimer.—Subsection (a) shall not apply with respect to a power which has been renounced or disclaimed within a reasonable time after the holder of the power first became aware of its existence.

§ 679.   Foreign trusts having one or more United States beneficiaries

(a) Transferor treated as owner.—

(1) **In general.**—A United States person who directly or indirectly transfers property to a foreign trust (other than a trust described in section 404(a)(4) Or[1] section 404A) shall be treated as the owner for his taxable year of the portion of such trust attributable to such property if for such year there is a United States beneficiary of any portion of such trust.

(2) **Exceptions.**—Paragraph (1) shall not apply—

(A) **Transfers by reason of death.**—To any transfer by reason of the death of the transferor.

(B) **Transfers where gain is recognized to transferor.**—To any sale or exchange of the property at its fair market value in a transaction in which all of the gain to the transferor is realized at the time of the transfer and is recognized either at such time or is returned as provided in section 453.

(b) Trusts acquiring United States beneficiaries.—If—

(1) subsection (a) applies to a trust for the transferor's taxable year, and

(2) subsection (a) would have applied to the trust for his immediately preceding taxable year but for the fact that for such preceding taxable year there was no United States beneficiary for any portion of the trust,

then, for purposes of this subtitle, the transferor shall be treated as having income for the taxable year (in addition to his other income for such year) equal to the undistributed net income (at the close of such immediately preceding taxable year) attributable to the portion of the trust referred to in subsection (a).

(c) Trusts treated as having a United States beneficiary.—

(1) **In general.**—For purposes of this section, a trust shall be treated as having a United States beneficiary for the taxable year unless—

(A) under the terms of the trust, no part of the income or corpus of the trust may be paid or accumulated during the taxable year to or for the benefit of a United States person, and

(B) if the trust were terminated at any time during the taxable year, no part of the income or corpus of such trust could be paid to or for the benefit of a United States person.

(2) **Attribution of ownership.**—For purposes of paragraph (1), an amount shall be treated as paid or accumulated to or for the benefit of a United States person if such amount is paid to or accumulated for a foreign corporation, foreign partnership, or foreign trust or estate, and—

(A) in the case of a foreign corporation, more than 50 percent of the total combined voting power of all classes of stock entitled to vote of[2] such corporation is owned (within the meaning of section 958(a)) or is considered to be owned (within the meaning of section 958(b)) by United States shareholders (as defined in section 951(b)),

(B) in the case of a foreign partnership, a United States person is a partner of such partnership, or

(C) in the case of a foreign trust or estate, such trust or estate has a United States beneficiary (within the meaning of paragraph (1)).

1 So in original. Probably should be "or".
2 So in original. Probably should be "if".

388

SUBPART F—MISCELLANEOUS

§ 681.　Limitation on charitable deduction

(a) Trade or business income.—In computing the deduction allowable under section 642(c) to a trust, no amount otherwise allowable under section 642(c) as a deduction shall be allowed as a deduction with respect to income of a taxable year which is allocable to its unrelated business income for such year. For purposes of the preceding sentence, the term "unrelated business income" means an amount equal to the amount which, if such trust were exempt from tax under section 501(a) by reason of section 501(c) (3), would be computed as its unrelated business taxable income under section 512 (relating to income derived from certain business activities and from certain property acquired with borrowed funds).

. . . . .

§ 682.　Income of an estate or trust in case of divorce, etc.

(a) Inclusion in gross income of wife.—There shall be included in the gross income of a wife who is divorced or legally separated under a decree of divorce or of separate maintenance (or who is separated from her husband under a written separation agreement) the amount of the income of any trust which such wife is entitled to receive and which, except for this section, would be includible in the gross income of her husband, and such amount shall not, despite any other provision of this subtitle, be includible in the gross income of such husband. This subsection shall not apply to that part of any such income of the trust which the terms of the decree, written separation agreement, or trust instrument fix, in terms of an amount of money or a portion of such income, as a sum which is payable for the support of minor children of such husband. In case such income is less than the amount specified in the decree, agreement, or instrument, for the purpose of applying the preceding sentence, such income, to the extent of such sum payable for such support, shall be considered a payment for such support.

(b) Wife considered a beneficiary.—For purposes of computing the taxable income of the estate or trust and the taxable income of a wife to whom subsection (a) or section 71 applies, such wife shall be considered as the beneficiary specified in this part. A periodic payment under section 71 to any portion of which this part applies shall be included in the gross income of the beneficiary in the taxable year in which under this part such portion is required to be included.

. . . . .

PART II—INCOME IN RESPECT OF DECEDENTS

§ 691.　Recipients of income in respect of decedents

(a) Inclusion in gross income.—

(1) **General rule.**—The amount of all items of gross income in respect of a decedent which are not properly includible in respect of the taxable period in which falls the date of his death or a prior period (including the amount of all items of gross income in respect of a prior decedent, if the right to receive such amount was acquired by reason of the death of the prior decedent or by

bequest, devise, or inheritance from the prior decedent) shall be included in the gross income, for the taxable year when received, of:

(A) the estate of the decedent, if the right to receive the amount is acquired by the decedent's estate from the decedent;

(B) the person who, by reason of the death of the decedent, acquires the right to receive the amount, if the right to receive the amount is not acquired by the decedent's estate from the decedent; or

(C) the person who acquires from the decedent the right to receive the amount by bequest, devise, or inheritance, if the amount is received after a distribution by the decedent's estate of such right.

(2) Income in case of sale, etc.—If a right, described in paragraph (1), to receive an amount is transferred by the estate of the decedent or a person who received such right by reason of the death of the decedent or by bequest, devise, or inheritance from the decedent, there shall be included in the gross income of the estate or such person, as the case may be, for the taxable period in which the transfer occurs, the fair market value of such right at the time of such transfer plus the amount by which any consideration for the transfer exceeds such fair market value. For purposes of this paragraph, the term "transfer" includes sale, exchange, or other disposition, or the satisfaction of an installment obligation at other than face value, but does not include transmission at death to the estate of the decedent or a transfer to a person pursuant to the right of such person to receive such amount by reason of the death of the decedent or by bequest, devise, or inheritance from the decedent.

(3) Character of income determined by reference to decedent.—The right, described in paragraph (1), to receive an amount shall be treated, in the hands of the estate of the decedent or any person who acquired such right by reason of the death of the decedent, or by bequest, devise, or inheritance from the decedent, as if it had been acquired by the estate or such person in the transaction in which the right to receive the income was originally derived and the amount includible in gross income under paragraph (1) or (2) shall be considered in the hands of the estate or such person to have the character which it would have had in the hands of the decedent if the decedent had lived and received such amount.

(4) Installment obligations acquired from decedent.—In the case of an installment obligation reportable by the decedent on the installment method under section 453 or 453A, if such obligation is acquired by the decedent's estate from the decedent or by any person by reason of the death of the decedent or by bequest, devise, or inheritance from the decedent—

(A) an amount equal to the excess of the face amount of such obligation over the basis of the obligation in the hands of the decedent (determined under section 453B) shall, for the purpose of paragraph (1), be considered as an item of gross income in respect of the decedent; and

(B) such obligation shall, for purposes of paragraphs (2) and (3), be considered a right to receive an item of gross income in respect of the decedent, but the amount includible in gross income under paragraph (2) shall be reduced by an amount equal to the basis of the obligation in the hands of the decedent (determined under section 453B).

(5) Other rules relating to installment obligations.—

(A) In general.—In the case of an installment obligation reportable by the decedent on the installment method under section 453 or 453A, for purposes of paragraph (2)—

(i) the second sentence of paragraph (2) shall be applied by inserting "(other than the obligor)" after "or a transfer to a person",

(ii) any cancellation of such an obligation shall be treated as a transfer, and

(iii) any cancellation of such an obligation occurring at the death of the decedent shall be treated as a transfer by the estate of the decedent (or, if held by a person other than the decedent before the death of the decedent, by such person).

(B) Face amount treated as fair market value in certain cases.—In any case to which the first sentence of paragraph (2) applies by reason of subparagraph (A), if the decedent and the obligor were related persons (within the meaning of section 453(f)(1)), the fair market value of the installment obligation shall be treated as not less than its face amount.

(C) Cancellation includes becoming unenforceable.—For purposes of subparagraph (A), an installment obligation which becomes unenforceable shall be treated as if it were canceled.

(b) Allowance of deductions and credit.—The amount of any deduction specified in section 162, 163, 164, 212, or 611 (relating to deductions for expenses, interest, taxes, and depletion) or credit specified in section 33 (relating to foreign tax credit), in respect of a decedent which is not properly allowable to the decedent in respect of the taxable period in which falls the date of his death, or a prior period, shall be allowed:

(1) Expenses, interest, and taxes.—In the case of a deduction specified in section 162, 163, 164, or 212 and a credit specified in section 33, in the taxable year when paid—

(A) to the estate of the decedent; except that

(B) if the estate of the decedent is not liable to discharge the obligation to which the deduction or credit relates, to the person who, by reason of the death of the decedent or by bequest, devise, or inheritance acquires, subject to such obligation, from the decedent an interest in property of the decedent.

(2) Depletion.—In the case of the deduction specified in section 611, to the person described in subsection (a) (1) (A), (B), or (C) who, in the manner described therein, receives the income to which the deduction relates, in the taxable year when such income is received.

(c) Deduction for estate tax.—

(1) Allowance of deduction.—

(A) General rule.—A person who includes an amount in gross income under subsection (a) shall be allowed, for the same taxable year, as a deduction an amount which bears the same ratio to the estate tax attributable to the net value for estate tax purposes of all the items described in subsection (a) (1) as the value for estate tax purposes of the items of gross income or portions thereof in respect of which such person included the amount in gross income (or the amount included in gross income, whichever is lower) bears to the value for estate tax purposes of all the items described in subsection (a) (1).

(B) Estates and trusts.—In the case of an estate or trust, the amount allowed as a deduction under subparagraph (A) shall be computed by excluding from the gross income of the estate or trust the portion (if any) of the items described in subsection (a) (1) which is properly paid, credited, or to be distributed to the beneficiaries during the taxable year.

(2) Method of computing deduction.—For purposes of paragraph (1)—

(A) The term "estate tax" means the tax imposed on the estate of the decedent or any prior decedent under section 2001 or 2101, reduced by the credits against such tax.

(B) The net value for estate tax purposes of all the items described in subsection (a) (1) shall be the excess of the value for estate tax purposes of all the items described in subsection (a) (1) over the deductions from the gross estate in respect of claims which represent the deductions and credit described in subsection (b). Such net value shall be determined with respect to the provisions of section 421(c) (2), relating to the deduction for estate tax with respect to stock options to which part II of subchapter D applies.

(C) The estate tax attributable to such net value shall be an amount equal to the excess of the estate tax over the estate tax computed without including in the gross estate such net value.

(3) Special rule for generation-skipping transfers.—For purposes of this section—

(A) the tax imposed by section 2601 or any State inheritance tax described in section 2602(c) (5) (B) on any generation-skipping transfer shall be treated as a tax imposed by section 2001 on the estate of the deemed transferor (as defined in section 2612(a);

(B) any property transferred in such a transfer shall be treated as if it were included in the gross estate of the deemed transferor at the value of such property taken into account for purposes of the tax imposed by section 2601; and

(C) under regulations prescribed by the Secretary, any item of gross income subject to the tax imposed under section 2601 shall be treated as income described in subsection (a) if such item is not properly includible in the gross income of the trust on or before the date of the generation-skipping transfer (within the meaning of section 2611(a)) and if such transfer occurs at or after the death of the deemed transferor (as so defined).

(4) Coordination with capital gain deduction, etc.—For purposes of sections 1201, 1202, and 1211, and for purposes of section 57(a) (9), the amount of any gain taken into account with respect to any item described in subsection (a) (1) shall be reduced (but not below zero) by the amount of the deduction allowable under paragraph (1) of this subsection with respect to such item.

(5) Coordination with section 402(e).—For purposes of section 402(e) (other than paragraph (1) (D) thereof), the total taxable amount of any lump sum distribution shall be reduced by the amount of the deduction allowable under paragraph (1) of this subsection which is attributable to the total taxable amount (determined without regard to this paragraph).

(d) Amounts received by surviving annuitant under joint and survivor annuity contract.—

(1) Deduction for estate tax.—For purposes of computing the deduction under subsection (c) (1) (A), amounts received by a surviving annuitant—

(A) as an annuity under a joint and survivor annuity contract where the decedent annuitant died after December 31, 1953, and after the annuity starting date (as defined in section 72(c) (4)), and

(B) during the surviving annuitant's life expectancy period,

shall, to the extent included in gross income under section 72, be considered as amounts included in gross income under subsection (a).

(2) Net value for estate tax purposes.—In determining the net value for estate tax purposes under subsection (c) (2) (B) for purposes of this subsection, the value for estate tax purposes of the items described in paragraph (1) of this subsection shall be computed—

(A) by determining the excess of the value of the annuity at the date of the death of the deceased annuitant over the total amount excludable from the gross income of the surviving annuitant under section 72 during the surviving annuitant's life expectancy period, and

(B) by multiplying the figure so obtained by the ratio which the value of the annuity for estate tax purposes bears to the value of the annuity at the date of the death of the deceased.

(3) Definitions.—For purposes of this subsection—

(A) The term "life expectancy period" means the period beginning with the first day of the first period for which an amount is received by the surviving annuitant under the contract and ending with the close of the taxable year with or in which falls the termination of the life expectancy of the surviving annuitant. For purposes of this subparagraph, the life expectancy of the surviving annuitant shall be determined, as of the date of the death of the deceased annuitant, with reference to actuarial tables prescribed by the Secretary.

(B) The surviving annuitant's expected return under the contract shall be computed, as of the death of the deceased annuitant, with reference to actuarial tables prescribed by the Secretary.

. . . .

SUBCHAPTER K—PARTNERS AND PARTNERSHIPS

Part
  I. Determination of tax liability.
 II. Contributions, distributions, and transfers.
III. Definitions.
[IV. Repealed]

PART I—DETERMINATION OF TAX LIABILITY

§ 701. Partners, not partnership, subject to tax

A partnership as such shall not be subject to the income tax imposed by this chapter. Persons carrying on business as partners shall be liable for income tax only in their separate or individual capacities.

§ 702.   Income and credits of partner

(a) General rule.—In determining his income tax, each partner shall take into account separately his distributive share of the partnership's—

(1) gains and losses from sales or exchanges of capital assets held for not more than 1 year,

(2) gains and losses from sales or exchanges of capital assets held for more than 1 year,

(3) gains and losses from sales or exchanges of property described in section 1231 (relating to certain property used in a trade or business and involuntary conversions),

(4) charitable contributions (as defined in section 170(c)),

(5) dividends or interest with respect to which there is provided an exclusion under section 116 or 128 or a deduction under part VIII of subchapter B,

(6) taxes, described in section 901, paid or accrued to foreign countries and to possessions of the United States,

(7) other items of income, gain, loss, deduction, or credit, to the extent provided by regulations prescribed by the Secretary, and

(8) taxable income or loss, exclusive of items requiring separate computation under other paragraphs of this subsection.

(b) Character of items constituting distributive share.—The character of any item of income, gain, loss, deduction, or credit included in a partner's distributive share under paragraphs (1) through (7) of subsection (a) shall be determined as if such item were realized directly from the source from which realized by the partnership, or incurred in the same manner as incurred by the partnership.

(c) Gross income of a partner.—In any case where it is necessary to determine the gross income of a partner for purposes of this title, such amount shall include his distributive share of the gross income of the partnership.

. . . . .

§ 703.   Partnership computations

(a) Income and deductions.—The taxable income of a partnership shall be computed in the same manner as in the case of an individual except that—

(1) the items described in section 702(a) shall be separately stated, and

(2) the following deductions shall not be allowed to the partnership:

(A) the deductions for personal exemptions provided in section 151,

(B) the deduction for taxes provided in section 164(a) with respect to taxes, described in section 901, paid or accrued to foreign countries and to possessions of the United States,

(C) the deduction for charitable contributions provided in section 170,

(D) the net operating loss deduction provided in section 172,

(E) the additional itemized deductions for individuals provided in part VII of subchapter B (sec. 211 and following), and

(F) the deduction for depletion under section 611 with respect to oil and gas wells.

(b) Elections of the partnership.—Any election affecting the computation of taxable income derived from a partnership shall be made by the partnership, except that any election under—

    (1) section 57(c) (defining net lease),

    (2) subsection (b)(5) or (d)(4) of section 108 (relating to income from discharge of indebtedness),

    (3) section 163(d) (relating to limitation of interest on investment indebtedness),

    (4) section 617 (relating to deduction and recapture of certain mining exploration expenditures), or

    (5) section 901 (relating to taxes of foreign countries and possessions of the United States),

shall be made by each partner separately.

§ 704.   Partner's distributive share

(a) Effect of partnership agreement.—A partner's distributive share of income, gain, loss, deduction, or credit shall, except as otherwise provided in this chapter, be determined by the partnership agreement.

(b) Determination of distributive share.—A partner's distributive share of income, gain, loss, deduction, or credit (or item thereof) shall be determined in accordance with the partner's interest in the partnership (determined by taking into account all facts and circumstances), if—

    (1) the partnership agreement does not provide as to the partner's distributive share of income, gain, loss, deduction, or credit (or item thereof), or

    (2) the allocation to a partner under the agreement of income, gain, loss, deduction, or credit (or item thereof) does not have substantial economic effect.

(c) Contributed property.—

    (1) General rule.—In determining a partner's distributive share of items described in section 702(a), depreciation, depletion, or gain or loss with respect to property contributed to the partnership by a partner shall, except to the extent otherwise provided in paragraph (2) or (3), be allocated among the partners in the same manner as if such property had been purchased by the partnership.

    (2) Effect of partnership agreement.—If the partnership agreement so provides, depreciation, depletion, or gain or loss with respect to property contributed to the partnership by a partner shall, under regulations prescribed by the Secretary, be shared among the partners so as to take account of the variation between the basis of the property to the partnership and its fair market value at the time of contribution.

    (3) Undivided interest.—If the partnership agreement does not provide otherwise, depreciation, depletion, or gain or loss with respect to undivided interests in property contributed to a partnership shall be determined as though such undivided interests had not been contributed to the partnership. This paragraph shall apply only if all the partners had undivided interests in such property prior to contribution and their interests in the capital and profits of the partnership correspond with such undivided interests.

(d) Limitation on allowance of losses.—A partner's distributive share of partnership loss (including capital loss) shall be allowed only to the extent of the adjusted basis of such partner's interest in the partnership at the end of the partnership year in which such loss occurred. Any excess of such loss over such basis shall be allowed as a deduction at the end of the partnership year in which such excess is repaid to the partnership.

(e) Family partnerships.—

(1) **Recognition of interest created by purchase or gift.**—A person shall be recognized as a partner for purposes of this subtitle if he owns a capital interest in a partnership in which capital is a material income-producing factor, whether or not such interest was derived by purchase or gift from any other person.

(2) **Distributive share of donee includible in gross income.**—In the case of any partnership interest created by gift, the distributive share of the donee under the partnership agreement shall be includible in his gross income, except to the extent that such share is determined without allowance of reasonable compensation for services rendered to the partnership by the donor, and except to the extent that the portion of such share attributable to donated capital is proportionately greater than the share of the donor attributable to the donor's capital. The distributive share of a partner in the earnings of the partnership shall not be diminished because of absence due to military service.

(3) **Purchase of interest by member of family.**—For purposes of this section, an interest purchased by one member of a family from another shall be considered to be created by gift from the seller, and the fair market value of the purchased interest shall be considered to be donated capital. The "family" of any individual shall include only his spouse, ancestors, and lineal descendants, and any trusts for the primary benefit of such persons.

.   .   .   .   .

§ 705. Determination of basis of partner's interest

(a) **General rule.**—The adjusted basis of a partner's interest in a partnership shall, except as provided in subsection (b), be the basis of such interest determined under section 722 (relating to contributions to a partnership) or section 742 (relating to transfers of partnership interests)—

(1) increased by the sum of his distributive share for the taxable year and prior taxable years of—

(A) taxable income of the partnership as determined under section 703(a),

(B) income of the partnership exempt from tax under this title, and

(C) the excess of the deductions for depletion over the basis of the property subject to depletion;

(2) decreased (but not below zero) by distributions by the partnership as provided in section 733 and by the sum of his distributive share for the taxable year and prior taxable years of—

(A) losses of the partnership, and

(B) expenditures of the partnership not deductible in computing its taxable income and not properly chargeable to capital account; and

(3) decreased (but not below zero), by the amount of the partner's deduction for depletion under section 611 with respect to oil and gas wells.

(b) Alternative rule.—The Secretary shall prescribe by regulations the circumstances under which the adjusted basis of a partner's interest in a partnership may be determined by reference to his proportionate share of the adjusted basis of partnership property upon a termination of the partnership.

§ 706.   Taxable years of partner and partnership

(a) Year in which partnership income is includible.—In computing the taxable income of a partner for a taxable year, the inclusions required by section 702 and section 707(c) with respect to a partnership shall be based on the income, gain, loss, deduction, or credit of the partnership for any taxable year of the partnership ending within or with the taxable year of the partner.

(b) Adoption of taxable year.—

(1) **Partnership's taxable year.**—The taxable year of a partnership shall be determined as though the partnership were a taxpayer. A partnership may not change to, or adopt, a taxable year other than that of all its principal partners unless it establishes, to the satisfaction of the Secretary, a business purpose therefor.

(2) **Partner's taxable year.**—A partner may not change to a taxable year other than that of a partnership in which he is a principal partner unless he establishes, to the satisfaction of the Secretary, a business purpose therefor.

(3) **Principal partner.**—For the purpose of this subsection, a principal partner is a partner having an interest of 5 percent or more in partnership profits or capital.

(c) Closing of partnership year.—

(1) **General rule.**—Except in the case of a termination of a partnership and except as provided in paragraph (2) of this subsection, the taxable year of a partnership shall not close as the result of the death of a partner, the entry of a new partner, the liquidation of a partner's interest in the partnership, or the sale or exchange of a partner's interest in the partnership.

(2) **Partner who retires or sells interest in partnership.—**

(A) **Disposition of entire interest.**—The taxable year of a partnership shall close—

(i) with respect to a partner who sells or exchanges his entire interest in a partnership, and

(ii) with respect to a partner whose interest is liquidated, except that the taxable year of a partnership with respect to a partner who dies shall not close prior to the end of the partnership's taxable year.

Such partner's distributive share of items described in section 702(a) for such year shall be determined, under regulations prescribed by the Secretary, for the period ending with such sale, exchange, or liquidation.

(B) **Disposition of less than entire interest.**—The taxable year of a partnership shall not close (other than at the end of a partnership's taxable year as determined under subsection (b) (1)) with respect to a partner who sells or exchanges less than his entire interest in the partnership or with respect to a partner whose interest is reduced (whether by entry of a new partner, partial liquidation of a partner's interest, gift, or otherwise), but such partner's distributive share of items described in section 702(a) shall be determined by taking into account his varying interests in the partnership during the taxable year.

§ 707.　　Transactions between partner and partnership

(a) Partner not acting in capacity as partner.—If a partner engages in a transaction with a partnership other than in his capacity as a member of such partnership, the transaction shall, except as otherwise provided in this section, be considered as occurring between the partnership and one who is not a partner.

(b) Certain sales or exchanges of property with respect to controlled partnerships.—

(1) Losses disallowed.—No deduction shall be allowed in respect of losses from sales or exchanges of property (other than an interest in the partnership), directly or indirectly, between—

(A) a partnership and a partner owning, directly or indirectly, more than 50 percent of the capital interest, or the profits interest, in such partnership, or

(B) two partnerships in which the same persons own, directly or indirectly, more than 50 percent of the capital interests or profits interests.

In the case of a subsequent sale or exchange by a transferee described in this paragraph, section 267(d) shall be applicable as if the loss were disallowed under section 267(a) (1).

(2) Gains treated as ordinary income.—In the case of a sale or exchange, directly or indirectly, of property, which in the hands of the transferee, is property other than a capital asset as defined in section 1221—

(A) between a partnership and a partner owning, directly or indirectly, more than 80 percent of the capital interest, or profits interest, in such partnership, or

(B) between two partnerships in which the same persons own, directly or indirectly, more than 80 percent of the capital interests or profits interests,

any gain recognized shall be considered as ordinary income.

(3) Ownership of a capital or profits interest.—For purposes of paragraphs (1) and (2) of this subsection, the ownership of a capital or profits interest in a partnership shall be determined in accordance with the rules for constructive ownership of stock provided in section 267(c) other than paragraph (3) of such section.

(c) Guaranteed payments.—To the extent determined without regard to the income of the partnership, payments to a partner for services or the use of capital shall be considered as made to one who is not a member of the partnership, but only for the purposes of section 61(a) (relating to gross income) and, subject to section 263, for purposes of section 162(a) (relating to trade or business expenses).

§ 708.　Continuation of partnership

(a) General rule.—For purposes of this subchapter, an existing partnership shall be considered as continuing if it is not terminated.

(b) Termination.—

(1) General rule.—For purposes of subsection (a), a partnership shall be considered as terminated only if—

(A) no part of any business, financial operation, or venture of the partnership continues to be carried on by any of its partners in a partnership, or

(B) within a 12-month period there is a sale or exchange of 50 percent or more of the total interest in partnership capital and profits.

(2) Special rules.—

(A) Merger or consolidation.—In the case of the merger or consolidation of two or more partnerships, the resulting partnership shall, for purposes of this section, be considered the continuation of any merging or consolidating partnership whose members own an interest of more than 50 percent in the capital and profits of the resulting partnership.

(B) Division of a partnership.—In the case of a division of a partnership into two or more partnerships, the resulting partnerships (other than any resulting partnership the members of which had an interest of 50 percent or less in the capital and profits of the prior partnership) shall, for purposes of this section, be considered a continuation of the prior partnership.

§ 709.　Treatment of organization and syndication fees

(a) General rule.—Except as provided in subsection (b), no deduction shall be allowed under this chapter to the partnership or to any partner for any amounts paid or incurred to organize a partnership or to promote the sale of (or to sell) an interest in such partnership.

(b) Amortization of organization fees.—

(1) Deduction.—Amounts paid or incurred to organize a partnership may, at the election of the partnership (made in accordance with regulations prescribed by the Secretary), be treated as deferred expenses. Such deferred expenses shall be allowed as a deduction ratably over such period of not less than 60 months as may be selected by the partnership (beginning with the month in which the partnership begins business), or if the partnership is liquidated before the end of such 60-month period, such deferred expenses (to the extent not deducted under this section) may be deducted to the extent provided in section 165.

(2) Organizational expenses defined.—The organizational expenses to which paragraph (1) applies, are expenditures which—

(A) are incident to the creation of the partnership;

(B) are chargeable to capital account; and

(C) are of a character which, if expended incident to the creation of a partnership having an ascertainable life, would be amortized over such life.

PART II—CONTRIBUTIONS, DISTRIBUTIONS, AND TRANSFERS

Subpart
  A. Contributions to a partnership.
  B. Distributions by a partnership.
  C. Transfers of interest in a partnership.
  D. Provisions common to other subparts.

SUBPART A—CONTRIBUTIONS TO A PARTNERSHIP

§ 721. Nonrecognition of gain or loss on contribution

(a) **General rule.**—No gain or loss shall be recognized to a partnership or to any of its partners in the case of a contribution of property to the partnership in exchange for an interest in the partnership.

(b) **Special rule.**—Subsection (a) shall not apply to gain realized on a transfer of property to a partnership which would be treated as an investment company (within the meaning of section 351) if the partnership were incorporated.

§ 722. Basis of contributing partner's interest

The basis of an interest in a partnership acquired by a contribution of property, including money, to the partnership shall be the amount of such money and the adjusted basis of such property to the contributing partner at the time of the contribution increased by the amount (if any) of gain recognized to the contributing partner at such time.

§ 723. Basis of property contributed to partnership

The basis of property contributed to a partnership by a partner shall be the adjusted basis of such property to the contributing partner at the time of the contribution increased by the amount (if any) of gain recognized to the contributing partner at such time.

SUBPART B—DISTRIBUTIONS BY A PARTNERSHIP

§ 731. Extent of recognition of gain or loss on distribution

(a) **Partners.**—In the case of a distribution by a partnership to a partner—

(1) gain shall not be recognized to such partner, except to the extent that any money distributed exceeds the adjusted basis of such partner's interest in the partnership immediately before the distribution, and

(2) loss shall not be recognized to such partner, except that upon a distribution in liquidation of a partner's interest in a partnership where no property other than that described in subparagraph (A) or (B) is distributed to such partner, loss shall be recognized to the extent of the excess of the adjusted basis of such partner's interest in the partnership over the sum of—

(A) any money distributed, and

(B) the basis to the distributee, as determined under section 732, of any unrealized receivables (as defined in section 751(c)) and inventory (as defined in section 751(d) (2)).

Any gain or loss recognized under this subsection shall be considered as gain or loss from the sale or exchange of the partnership interest of the distributee partner.

(b) Partnerships.—No gain or loss shall be recognized to a partnership on a distribution to a partner of property, including money.

(c) Exceptions.—This section shall not apply to the extent otherwise provided by section 736 (relating to payments to a retiring partner or a deceased partner's successor in interest) and section 751 (relating to unrealized receivables and inventory items).

§ 732.   Basis of distributed property other than money

(a) Distributions other than in liquidation of a partner's interest.—

    (1) General rule.—The basis of property (other than money) distributed by a partnership to a partner other than in liquidation of the partner's interest shall, except as provided in paragraph (2), be its adjusted basis to the partnership immediately before such distribution.

    (2) Limitation.—The basis to the distributee partner of property to which paragraph (1) is applicable shall not exceed the adjusted basis of such partner's interest in the partnership reduced by any money distributed in the same transaction.

(b) Distributions in liquidation.—The basis of property (other than money) distributed by a partnership to a partner in liquidation of the partner's interest shall be an amount equal to the adjusted basis of such partner's interest in the partnership reduced by any money distributed in the same transaction.

(c) Allocation of basis.—The basis of distributed properties to which subsection (a) (2) or subsection (b) is applicable shall be allocated—

    (1) first to any unrealized receivables (as defined in section 751(c)) and inventory items (as defined in section 751(d) (2)) in an amount equal to the adjusted basis of each such property to the partnership (or if the basis to be allocated is less than the sum of the adjusted bases of such properties to the partnership, in proportion to such bases), and

    (2) to the extent of any remaining basis, to any other distributed properties in proportion to their adjusted bases to the partnership.

(d) Special partnership basis to transferee.—For purposes of subsections (a), (b), and (c), a partner who acquired all or a part of his interest by a transfer with respect to which the election provided in section 754 is not in effect, and to whom a distribution of property (other than money) is made with respect to the transferred interest within 2 years after such transfer, may elect, under regulations prescribed by the Secretary, to treat as the adjusted partnership basis of such property the adjusted basis such property would have if the adjustment provided in section 743(b) were in effect with respect to the partnership property. The Secretary may by regulations require the application of this subsection in the case of a distribution to a transferee partner, whether or not made within 2 years after the transfer, if at the time of the transfer the fair market value of the partnership property (other than money) exceeded 110 percent of its adjusted basis to the partnership.

(e) Exception.—This section shall not apply to the extent that a distribution is treated as a sale or exchange of property under section 751(b) (relating to unrealized receivables and inventory items).

§ 733.   Basis of distributee partner's interest

In the case of a distribution by a partnership to a partner other than in liquidation of a partner's interest, the adjusted basis to such partner of his interest in the partnership shall be reduced (but not below zero) by—

(1) the amount of any money distributed to such partner, and

(2) the amount of the basis to such partner of distributed property other than money, as determined under section 732.

§ 734.   Optional adjustment to basis of undistributed partnership property

(a) General rule.—The basis of partnership property shall not be adjusted as the result of a distribution of property to a partner unless the election, provided in section 754 (relating to optional adjustment to basis of partnership property), is in effect with respect to such partnership.

(b) Method of adjustment.—In the case of a distribution of property to a partner, a partnership, with respect to which the election provided in section 754 is in effect, shall—

(1) increase the adjusted basis of partnership property by—

(A) the amount of any gain recognized to the distributee partner with respect to such distribution under section 731(a) (1), and

(B) in the case of distributed property to which section 732(a) (2) or (b) applies, the excess of the adjusted basis of the distributed property to the partnership immediately before the distribution (as adjusted by section 732(d)) over the basis of the distributed property to the distributee, as determined under section 732, or

(2) decrease the adjusted basis of partnership property by—

(A) the amount of any loss recognized to the distributee partner with respect to such distribution under section 731(a) (2), and

(B) in the case of distributed property to which section 732(b) applies, the excess of the basis of the distributed property to the distributee, as determined under section 732, over the adjusted basis of the distributed property to the partnership immediately before such distribution (as adjusted by section 732(d)).

(c) Allocation of basis.—The allocation of basis among partnership properties where subsection (b) is applicable shall be made in accordance with the rules provided in section 755.

§ 735.   Character of gain or loss on disposition of distributed property

(a) Sale or exchange of certain distributed property.—

(1) **Unrealized receivables.**—Gain or loss on the disposition by a distributee partner of unrealized receivables (as defined in section 751(c)) distributed by a partnership, shall be considered as ordinary income or as ordinary loss, as the case may be.

(2) **Inventory items.**—Gain or loss on the sale or exchange by a distributee partner of inventory items (as defined in section 751(d) (2)) distributed by a partnership shall, if sold or exchanged within 5 years from the date of the distribution, be considered as ordinary income or as ordinary loss, as the case may be.

(b) **Holding period for distributed property.**—In determining the period for which a partner has held property received in a distribution from a partnership (other than for purposes of subsection (a) (2)), there shall be included the holding period of the partnership, as determined under section 1223, with respect to such property.

§ 736. Payments to a retiring partner or a deceased partner's successor in interest

(a) **Payments considered as distributive share or guaranteed payment.**—Payments made in liquidation of the interest of a retiring partner or a deceased partner shall, except as provided in subsection (b), be considered—

(1) as a distributive share to the recipient of partnership income if the amount thereof is determined with regard to the income of the partnership, or

(2) as a guaranteed payment described in section 707(c) if the amount thereof is determined without regard to the income of the partnership.

(b) **Payments for interest in partnership.**—

(1) **General rule.**—Payments made in liquidation of the interest of a retiring partner or a deceased partner shall, to the extent such payments (other than payments described in paragraph (2)) are determined, under regulations prescribed by the Secretary, to be made in exchange for the interest of such partner in partnership property, be considered as a distribution by the partnership and not as a distributive share or guaranteed payment under subsection (a).

(2) **Special rules.**—For purposes of this subsection, payments in exchange for an interest in partnership property shall not include amounts paid for—

(A) unrealized receivables of the partnership (as defined in section 751(c)), or

(B) good will of the partnership, except to the extent that the partnership agreement provides for a payment with respect to good will.

. . . . .

SUBPART C—TRANSFERS OF INTEREST IN A PARTNERSHIP

§ 741. Recognition and character of gain or loss on sale or exchange

In the case of a sale or exchange of an interest in a partnership, gain or loss shall be recognized to the transferor partner. Such gain or loss shall be considered as gain or loss from the sale or exchange of a capital asset, except as otherwise provided in section 751 (relating to unrealized receivables and inventory items which have appreciated substantially in value).

§ 742.   Basis of transferee partner's interest

The basis of an interest in a partnership acquired other than by contribution shall be determined under part II of subchapter O (sec. 1011 and following).

§ 743.   Optional adjustment to basis of partnership property

(a) **General rule.**—The basis of partnership property shall not be adjusted as the result of a transfer of an interest in a partnership by sale or exchange or on the death of a partner unless the election provided by section 754 (relating to optional adjustment to basis of partnership property) is in effect with respect to such partnership.

(b) **Adjustment to basis of partnership property.**—In the case of a transfer of an interest in a partnership by sale or exchange or upon the death of a partner, a partnership with respect to which the election provided in section 754 is in effect shall—

(1) increase the adjusted basis of the partnership property by the excess of the basis to the transferee partner of his interest in the partnership over his proportionate share of the adjusted basis of the partnership property, or

(2) decrease the adjusted basis of the partnership property by the excess of the transferee partner's proportionate share of the adjusted basis of the partnership property over the basis of his interest in the partnership.

Under regulations prescribed by the Secretary, such increase or decrease shall constitute an adjustment to the basis of partnership property with respect to the transferee partner only. A partner's proportionate share of the adjusted basis of partnership property shall be determined in accordance with his interest in partnership capital and, in the case of an agreement described in section 704(c) (2) (relating to effect of partnership agreement on contributed property), such share shall be determined by taking such agreement into account. In the case of an adjustment under this subsection to the basis of partnership property subject to depletion, any depletion allowable shall be determined separately for the transferee partner with respect to his interest in such property.

(c) **Allocation of basis.**—The allocation of basis among partnership properties where subsection (b) is applicable shall be made in accordance with the rules provided in section 755.

SUBPART D—PROVISIONS COMMON TO OTHER SUBPARTS

§ 751.   Unrealized receivables and inventory items

(a) **Sale or exchange of interest in partnership.**—The amount of any money, or the fair market value of any property, received by a transferor partner in exchange for all or a part of his interest in the partnership attributable to—

(1) unrealized receivables of the partnership, or

(2) inventory items of the partnership which have appreciated substantially in value,

shall be considered as an amount realized from the sale or exchange of property other than a capital asset.

(b) Certain distributions treated as sales or exchanges.—

   (1) General rule.—To the extent a partner receives in a distribution—

      (A) partnership property described in subsection (a) (1) or (2) in exchange for all or a part of his interest in other partnership property (including money), or

      (B) partnership property (including money) other than property described in subsection (a) (1) or (2) in exchange for all or a part of his interest in partnership property described in subsection (a) (1) or (2),

such transaction shall, under regulations prescribed by the Secretary, be considered as a sale or exchange of such property between the distributee and the partnership (as constituted after the distribution).

   (2) Exceptions.—Paragraph (1) shall not apply to—

      (A) a distribution of property which the distributee contributed to the partnership, or

      (B) payments, described in section 736(a), to a retiring partner or successor in interest of a deceased partner.

  (c) Unrealized receivables.—For purposes of this subchapter, the term "unrealized receivables" includes, to the extent not previously includible in income under the method of accounting used by the partnership, any rights (contractual or otherwise) to payment for—

   (1) goods delivered, or to be delivered, to the extent the proceeds therefrom would be treated as amounts received from the sale or exchange of property other than a capital asset, or

   (2) services rendered, or to be rendered.

For purposes of this section and sections 731, 736, and 741, such term also includes mining property (as defined in section 617(f) (2), stock in a DISC (as described in section 992(a)), section 1245 property (as defined in section 1245(a) (3)), stock in certain foreign corporations (as described in section 1248), section 1250 property (as defined in section 1250(c)), farm recapture property (as defined in section 1251(e) (1)), farm land (as defined in section 1252(a)), franchises, trademarks, or trade names (referred to in section 1253(a)), and an oil, gas, or geothermal property (described in section 1254) but only to the extent of the amount which would be treated as gain to which section 617(d) (1), 995(c), 1245(a), 1248(a), 1250(a), 1251(c), 1252(a), 1253(a), or 1254(a) would apply if (at the time of the transaction described in this section or sections 731, 736, or 741, as the case may be) such property had been sold by the partnership at its fair market value.

(d) Inventory items which have appreciated substantially in value.—

   (1) Substantial appreciation.—Inventory items of the partnership shall be considered to have appreciated substantially in value if their fair market value exceeds—

      (A) 120 percent of the adjusted basis to the partnership of such property, and

      (B) 10 percent of the fair market value of all partnership property, other than money.

   (2) Inventory items.—For purposes of this subchapter the term "inventory items" means—

      (A) property of the partnership of the kind described in section 1221(1),

(B) any other property of the partnership which, on sale or exchange by the partnership, would be considered property other than a capital asset and other than property described in section 1231,

(D) any other property held by the partnership which, if held by the selling or distributee partner, would be considered property of the type described in subparagraph (A), (B), or (C).

§ 752.   Treatment of certain liabilities

(a) Increase in partner's liabilities.—Any increase in a partner's share of the liabilities of a partnership, or any increase in a partner's individual liabilities by reason of the assumption by such partner of partnership liabilities, shall be considered as a contribution of money by such partner to the partnership.

(b) Decrease in partner's liabilities.—Any decrease in a partner's share of the liabilities of a partnership, or any decrease in a partner's individual liabilities by reason of the assumption by the partnership of such individual liabilities, shall be considered as a distribution of money to the partner by the partnership.

(c) Liability to which property is subject.—For purposes of this section, a liability to which property is subject shall, to the extent of the fair market value of such property, be considered as a liability of the owner of the property.

(d) Sale or exchange of an interest.—In the case of a sale or exchange of an interest in a partnership, liabilities shall be treated in the same manner as liabilities in connection with the sale or exchange of property not associated with partnerships.

§ 753.   Partner receiving income in respect of decedent

The amount includible in the gross income of a successor in interest of a deceased partner under section 736(a) shall be considered income in respect of a decedent under section 691.

§ 754.   Manner of electing optional adjustment to basis of partnership property

If a partnership files an election, in accordance with regulations prescribed by the Secretary, the basis of partnership property shall be adjusted, in the case of a distribution of property, in the manner provided in section 734 and, in the case of a transfer of a partnership interest, in the manner provided in section 743. Such an election shall apply with respect to all distributions of property by the partnership and to all transfers of interests in the partnership during the taxable year with respect to which such election was filed and all subsequent taxable years. Such election may be revoked by the partnership, subject to such limitations as may be provided by regulations prescribed by the Secretary.

§ 755.   Rules for allocation of basis

(a) General rule.—Any increase or decrease in the adjusted basis of partnership property under section 734(b) (relating to the optional adjustment to the basis of undistributed partnership property) or section 743(b) (relating to the optional adjustment to the basis of partnership property in the case of a transfer of an interest in a partnership) shall, except as provided in subsection (b), be allocated—

(1) in a manner which has the effect of reducing the difference between the fair market value and the adjusted basis of partnership properties, or

(2) in any other manner permitted by regulations prescribed by the Secretary.

(b) Special rule.—In applying the allocation rules provided in subsection (a), increases or decreases in the adjusted basis of partnership property arising from a distribution of, or a transfer of an interest attributable to, property consisting of—

(1) capital assets and property described in section 1231(b), or

(2) any other property of the partnership,

shall be allocated to partnership property of a like character except that the basis of any such partnership property shall not be reduced below zero. If, in the case of a distribution, the adjustment to basis of property described in paragraph (1) or (2) is prevented by the absence of such property or by insufficient adjusted basis for such property, such adjustment shall be applied to subsequently acquired property of a like character in accordance with regulations prescribed by the Secretary.

PART III—DEFINITIONS

§ 761. Terms defined

(a) Partnership.—For purposes of this subtitle, the term "partnership" includes a syndicate, group, pool, joint venture, or other unincorporated organization through or by means of which any business, financial operation, or venture is carried on, and which is not, within the meaning of this title, a corporation or a trust or estate. Under regulations the Secretary may, at the election of all the members of an unincorporated organization, exclude such organization from the application of all or part of this subchapter, if it is availed of—

(1) for investment purposes only and not for the active conduct of a business,

(2) for the joint production, extraction, or use of property, but not for the purpose of selling services or property produced or extracted, or

(3) by dealers in securities for a short period for the purpose of underwriting, selling, or distributing a particular issue of securities,

if the income of the members of the organization may be adequately determined without the computation of partnership taxable income.

(b) Partner.—For purposes of this subtitle, the term "partner" means a member of a partnership.

(c) Partnership agreement.—For purposes of this subchapter, a partnership agreement includes any modifications of the partnership agreement made prior to, or at, the time prescribed by law for the filing of the partnership return for the taxable year (not including extensions) which are agreed to by all the partners, or which are adopted in such other manner as may be provided by the partnership agreement.

(d) Liquidation of a partner's interest.—For purposes of this subchapter, the term "liquidation of a partner's interest" means the termination of a partner's entire interest in a partnership by means of a distribution, or a series of distributions, to the partner by the partnership.

. . . . .

SUBCHAPTER O—GAIN OR LOSS ON DISPOSITION OF PROPERTY

Part
  I. Determination of amount of and recognition of gain or loss.
  II. Basis rules of general application.
  III. Common nontaxable exchanges.
  IV. Special rules.
  V. Changes to effectuate F.C.C. policy.*
  VI. Exchanges in obedience to S.E.C. orders.*
  VII. Wash sales; straddles.
  VIII. Distributions pursuant to Bank Holding Company Act of 1956.*
  [IX. Repealed]

PART I—DETERMINATION OF AMOUNT OF AND RECOGNITION OF GAIN OR LOSS

§ 1001. Determination of amount of and recognition of gain or loss

(a) Computation of gain or loss.—The gain from the sale or other disposition of property shall be the excess of the amount realized therefrom over the adjusted basis provided in section 1011 for determining gain, and the loss shall be the excess of the adjusted basis provided in such section for determining loss over the amount realized.

(b) Amount realized.—The amount realized from the sale or other disposition of property shall be the sum of any money received plus the fair market value of the property (other than money) received. In determining the amount realized—

    (1) there shall not be taken into account any amount received as reimbursement for real property taxes which are treated under section 164(d) as imposed on the purchaser, and

    (2) there shall be taken into account amounts representing real property taxes which are treated under section 164(d) as imposed on the taxpayer if such taxes are to be paid by the purchaser.

(c) Recognition of gain or loss.—Except as otherwise provided in this subtitle, the entire amount of the gain or loss, determined under this section, on the sale or exchange of property shall be recognized.

(d) Installment sales.—Nothing in this section shall be construed to prevent (in the case of property sold under contract providing for payment in installments) the taxation of that portion of any installment payment representing gain or profit in the year in which such payment is received.

(e) Certain term interests.—

    (1) In general.—In determining gain or loss from the sale or other disposition of a term interest in property, that portion of the adjusted basis of such interest which is determined pursuant to section 1014 or 1015 (to the extent that such adjusted basis is a portion of the entire adjusted basis of the property) shall be disregarded.

* Omitted entirely.

(2) **Term interest in property defined.**—For purposes of paragraph (1), the term "term interest in property" means—

    (A) a life interest in property,

    (B) an interest in property for a term of years, or

    (C) an income interest in a trust.

(3) **Exception.**—Paragraph (1) shall not apply to a sale or other disposition which is a part of a transaction in which the entire interest in property is transferred to any person or persons.

. . . .

PART II—BASIS RULES OF GENERAL APPLICATION

§ 1011.   Adjusted basis for determining gain or loss

(a) **General rule.**—The adjusted basis for determining the gain or loss from the sale or other disposition of property, whenever acquired, shall be the basis (determined under section 1012 or other applicable sections of this subchapter and subchapters C (relating to corporate distributions and adjustments), K (relating to partners and partnerships), and P (relating to capital gains and losses)), adjusted as provided in section 1016.

(b) **Bargain sale to a charitable organization.**—If a deduction is allowable under section 170 (relating to charitable contributions) by reason of a sale, then the adjusted basis for determining the gain from such sale shall be that portion of the adjusted basis which bears the same ratio to the adjusted basis as the amount realized bears to the fair market value of the property.

§ 1012.   Basis of property—cost

The basis of property shall be the cost of such property, except as otherwise provided in this subchapter and subchapters C (relating to corporate distributions and adjustments), K (relating to partners and partnerships), and P (relating to capital gains and losses). The cost of real property shall not include any amount in respect of real property taxes which are treated under section 164(d) as imposed on the taxpayer.

§ 1013.   Basis of property included in inventory

If the property should have been included in the last inventory, the basis shall be the last inventory value thereof.

§ 1014.   Basis of property acquired from a decedent

(a) **In general.**—Except as otherwise provided in this section, the basis of property in the hands of a person acquiring the property from a decedent or to whom the property passed from a decedent shall, if not sold, exchanged, or otherwise disposed of before the decedent's death by such person, be—

    (1) the fair market value of the property at the date of the decedent's death, or

(2) in the case of an election under either section 2032 or section 811(j) of the Internal Revenue Code of 1939 where the decedent died after October 21, 1942, its value at the applicable valuation date prescribed by those sections, or

(3) in the case of an election under section 2032A, its value determined under such section.

(b) Property acquired from the decedent.—For purposes of subsection (a), the following property shall be considered to have been acquired from or to have passed from the decedent:

(1) Property acquired by bequest, devise, or inheritance, or by the decedent's estate from the decedent;

(2) Property transferred by the decedent during his lifetime in trust to pay the income for life to or on the order or direction of the decedent, with the right reserved to the decedent at all times before his death to revoke the trust;

(3) In the case of decedents dying after December 31, 1951, property transferred by the decedent during his lifetime in trust to pay the income for life to or on the order or direction of the decedent with the right reserved to the decedent at all times before his death to make any change in the enjoyment thereof through the exercise of a power to alter, amend, or terminate the trust;

(4) Property passing without full and adequate consideration under a general power of appointment exercised by the decedent by will;

. . . . .

(6) In the case of decedents dying after December 31, 1947, property which represents the surviving spouse's one-half share of community property held by the decedent and the surviving spouse under the community property laws of any State, or possession of the United States or any foreign country, if at least one-half of the whole of the community interest in such property was includible in determining the value of the decedent's gross estate under chapter 11 of subtitle B (section 2001 and following, relating to estate tax) or section 811 of the Internal Revenue Code of 1939;

. . . . .

(9) In the case of decedents dying after December 31, 1953, property acquired from the decedent by reason of death, form of ownership, or other conditions (including property acquired through the exercise or non-exercise of a power of appointment), if by reason thereof the property is required to be included in determining the value of the decedent's gross estate under chapter 11 of subtitle B or under the Internal Revenue Code of 1939. In such case, if the property is acquired before the death of the decedent, the basis shall be the amount determined under subsection (a) reduced by the amount allowed to the taxpayer as deductions in computing taxable income under this subtitle or prior income tax laws for exhaustion, wear and tear, obsolescence, amortization, and depletion on such property before the death of the decedent. Such basis shall be applicable to the property commencing on the death of the decedent. This paragraph shall not apply to—

(A) annuities described in section 72;

(B) property to which paragraph (5) would apply if the property had been acquired by bequest; and

(C) property described in any other paragraph of this subsection.

(c) Property representing income in respect of a decedent.—This section shall not apply to property which constitutes a right to receive an item of income in respect of a decedent under section 691.

. . . .

(e) Appreciated property acquired by decedent by gift within 1 year of death.—

(1) In general.—In the case of a decedent dying after December 31, 1981, if—

(A) appreciated property was acquired by the decedent by gift during the 1-year period ending on the date of the decedent's death, and

(B) such property is acquired from the decedent by (or passes from the decedent to) the donor of such property (or the spouse of such donor),

the basis of such property in the hands of such donor (or spouse) shall be the adjusted basis of such property in the hands of the decedent immediately before the death of the decedent.

(2) Definitions.—For purposes of paragraph (1)—

(A) Appreciated property.—The term "appreciated property" means any property if the fair market value of such property on the day it was transferred to the decedent by gift exceeds its adjusted basis.

(B) Treatment of certain property sold by estate.—In the case of any appreciated property described in subparagraph (A) of paragraph (1) sold by the estate of the decedent or by a trust of which the decedent was the grantor, rules similar to the rules of paragraph (1) shall apply to the extent the donor of such property (or the spouse of such donor) is entitled to the proceeds from such sale.

§ 1015.   Basis of property acquired by gifts and transfers in trust

(a) Gifts after December 31, 1920.—If the property was acquired by gift after December 31, 1920, the basis shall be the same as it would be in the hands of the donor or the last preceding owner by whom it was not acquired by gift, except that if such basis (adjusted for the period before the date of the gift as provided in section 1016) is greater than the fair market value of the property at the time of the gift, then for the purpose of determining loss the basis shall be such fair market value. If the facts necessary to determine the basis in the hands of the donor or the last preceding owner are unknown to the donee, the Secretary shall, if possible, obtain such facts from such donor or last preceding owner, or any other person cognizant thereof. If the Secretary finds it impossible to obtain such facts, the basis in the hands of such donor or last preceding owner shall be the fair market value of such property as found by the Secretary as of the date or approximate date at which, according to the best information that the Secretary is able to obtain, such property was acquired by such donor or last preceding owner.

(b) Transfer in trust after December 31, 1920.—If the property was acquired after December 31, 1920, by a transfer in trust (other than by a transfer in trust by a gift, bequest, or devise), the basis shall be the same as it would be in the hands of the grantor increased in the amount of gain or decreased in the amount of loss recognized to the grantor on such transfer under the law applicable to the year in which the transfer was made.

. . . . .

(d) Increased basis for gift tax paid.—

(1) In general.—If—

(A) the property is acquired by gift on or after September 2, 1958, the basis shall be the basis determined under subsection (a), increased (but not above the fair market value of the property at the time of the gift) by the amount of gift tax paid with respect to such gift, or

(B) the property was acquired by gift before September 2, 1958, and has not been sold, exchanged, or otherwise disposed of before such date, the basis of the property shall be increased on such date by the amount of gift tax paid with respect to such gift, but such increase shall not exceed an amount equal to the amount by which the fair market value of the property at the time of the gift exceeded the basis of the property in the hands of the donor at the time of the gift.

(2) Amount of tax paid with respect to gift.—For purposes of paragraph (1), the amount of gift tax paid with respect to any gift is an amount which bears the same ratio to the amount of gift tax paid under chapter 12 with respect to all gifts made by the donor for the calendar year (or preceding calendar period) in which such gift is made as the amount of such gift bears to the taxable gifts (as defined in section 2503(a) but computed without the deduction allowed by section 2521) made by the donor during such calendar year or period. For purposes of the preceding sentence, the amount of any gift shall be the amount included with respect to such gift in determining (for the purposes of section 2503(a)) the total amount of gifts made during the calendar year or period, reduced by the amount of any deduction allowed with respect to such gift under section 2522 (relating to charitable deduction) or under section 2523 (relating to marital deduction).

(3) Gifts treated as made one-half by each spouse.—For purposes of paragraph (1), where the donor and his spouse elected, under section 2513 to have the gift considered as made one-half by each, the amount of gift tax paid with respect to such gift under chapter 12 shall be the sum of the amounts of tax paid with respect to each half of such gift (computed in the manner provided in paragraph (2)).

(4) Treatment as adjustment to basis.—For purposes of section 1016(b), an increase in basis under paragraph (1) shall be treated as an adjustment under section 1016(a).

. . . . .

(6) Special rule for gifts made after December 31, 1976.—

(A) **In general.—**In the case of any gift made after December 31, 1976, the increase in basis provided by this subsection with respect to any gift for the gift tax paid under chapter 12 shall be an amount (not in excess of the amount of tax so paid) which bears the same ratio to the amount of tax so paid as—

(i) the net appreciation in value of the gift, bears to

(ii) the amount of the gift.

(B) **Net appreciation.**—For purposes of paragraph (1), the net appreciation in value of any gift is the amount by which the fair market value of the gift exceeds the donor's adjusted basis immediately before the gift.

§ 1016.   Adjustments to basis

(a) **General rule.**—Proper adjustment in respect of the property shall in all cases be made—

(1) for expenditures, receipts, losses, or other items, properly chargeable to capital account, but no such adjustment shall be made—

(A) for taxes or other carrying charges described in section 266, or

(B) for expenditures described in section 173 (relating to circulation expenditures),

for which deductions have been taken by the taxpayer in determining taxable income for the taxable year or prior taxable years;

(2) in respect of any period since February 28, 1913, for exhaustion, wear and tear, obsolescence, amortization, and depletion, to the extent of the amount—

(A) allowed as deductions in computing taxable income under this subtitle or prior income tax laws, and

(B) resulting (by reason of the deductions so allowed) in a reduction for any taxable year of the taxpayer's taxes under this subtitle (other than chapter 2, relating to tax on self-employment income), or prior income, war-profits, or excess-profits tax laws,

but not less than the amount allowable under this subtitle or prior income tax laws. Where no method has been adopted under section 167 (relating to depreciation deduction), the amount allowable shall be determined under section 167(b)(1).   .   .   .   .

(7) in the case of a residence the acquisition of which resulted, under section 1034, in the nonrecognition of any part of the gain realized on the sale, exchange, or involuntary conversion of another residence, to the extent provided in section 1034(e);

(9) for amounts allowed as deductions as deferred expenses under section 616(b) (relating to certain expenditures in the development of mines) and resulting in a reduction of the taxpayer's taxes under this subtitle, but not less than the amounts allowable under such section for the taxable year and prior years;

[(10) Repealed. Pub.L. 94–455, Title XIX, § 1901(b) (21) (G), Oct. 4, 1976, 90 Stat. 1798]

(11) for deductions to the extent disallowed under section 268 (relating to sale of land with unharvested crops), notwithstanding the provisions of any other paragraph of this subsection;

(14) for amounts allowed as deductions as deferred expenses under section 174(b) (1) (relating to research and experimental expenditures) and resulting in a reduction of the taxpayers' taxes under this subtitle, but not less than the amounts allowable under such section for the taxable year and prior years;

(15) for deductions to the extent disallowed under section 272 (relating to disposal of coal or domestic iron ore), notwithstanding the provisions of any other paragraph of this subsection;

(16) for amounts allowed as deductions for expenditures treated as deferred expenses under section 177 (relating to trademark and trade name expenditures) and resulting in a reduction of the taxpayer's taxes under this subtitle, but not less than the amounts allowable under such section for the taxable year and prior years;

. . . . .

(18) to the extent provided in section 1367 in the case of stock of, and indebtedness owed to, shareholders of an S corporation;

. . . . .

(20) for amounts allowed as deductions for payments made on account of transfers of franchises, trademarks, or trade names under section 1253(d) (2);

. . . . .

(b) Substituted basis.—Whenever it appears that the basis of property in the hands of the taxpayer is a substituted basis, then the adjustments provided in subsection (a) shall be made after first making in respect of such substituted basis proper adjustments of a similar nature in respect of the period during which the property was held by the transferor, donor, or grantor, or during which the other property was held by the person for whom the basis is to be determined. A similar rule shall be applied in the case of a series of substituted bases. The term "substituted basis" as used in this section means a basis determined under any provision of this subchapter and subchapters C (relating to corporate distributions and adjustments), K (relating to partners and partnerships), and P (relating to capital gains and losses), or under any corresponding provision of a prior income tax law, providing that the basis shall be determined—

(1) by reference to the basis in the hands of a transferor, donor, or grantor, or

(2) by reference to other property held at any time by the person for whom the basis is to be determined.

(c) Increase in basis of property on which additional estate tax is imposed.—

(1) Tax imposed with respect to entire interest.—If an additional estate tax is imposed under section 2032A(c)(1) with respect to any interest in property and the qualified heir makes an election under this subsection with respect to the imposition of such tax, the adjusted basis of such interest shall be increased by an amount equal to the excess of—

(A) the fair market value of such interest on the date of the decedent's death (or the alternate valuation date under section 2032, if the executor of the decedent's estate elected the application of such section), over

(B) the value of such interest determined under section 2032A(a).

(2) Partial dispositions.—

(A) In general.—In the case of any partial disposition for which an election under this subsection is made, the increase in basis under paragraph (1) shall be an amount—

(i) which bears the same ratio to the increase which would be determined under paragraph (1) (without regard to this paragraph) with respect to the entire interest, as

(ii) the amount of the tax imposed under section 2032A(c)(1) with respect to such disposition bears to the adjusted tax difference attributable to the entire interest (as determined under section 2032A(c)(2)(B)).

(B) Partial disposition.—For purposes of subparagraph (A), the term "partial disposition" means any disposition or cessation to which subsection (c)(2)(D), (h)(1)(B), or (i)(1)(B) of section 2032A applies.

(3) Time adjustment made.—Any increase in basis under this subsection shall be deemed to have occurred immediately before the disposition or cessation resulting in the imposition of the tax under section 2032A(c)(1).

(4) Special rule in the case of substituted property.—If the tax under section 2032A(c)(1) is imposed with respect to qualified replacement property (as defined in section 2032A(h)(3)(B)) or qualified exchange property (as defined in section 2032A(i)(3)), the increase in basis under paragraph (1) shall be made by reference to the property involuntarily converted or exchanged (as the case may be).

(5) Election.—

(A) In general.—An election under this subsection shall be made at such time and in such manner as the Secretary shall by regulations prescribe. Such an election, once made, shall be irrevocable.

(B) Interest on recaptured amount.—If an election is made under this subsection with respect to any additional estate tax imposed under section 2032A(c)(1), for purposes of section 6601 (relating to interest on underpayments), the last date prescribed for payment of such tax shall be deemed to be the last date prescribed for payment of the tax imposed by section 2001 with respect to the estate of the decedent (as determined for purposes of section 6601).

. . . . .

§ 1017.   Discharge of indebtedness

(a) General rule.—If—

(1) an amount is excluded from gross income under subsection (a) of section 108 (relating to discharge of indebtedness), and

(2) under subsection (b)(2)(D), (b)(5), or (c)(1)(A) of section 108, any portion of such amount is to be applied to reduce basis,

then such portion shall be applied in reduction of the basis of any property held by the taxpayer at the beginning of the taxable year following the taxable year in which the discharge occurs.

(b) Amount and properties determined under regulations.—

(1) In general.—The amount of reduction to be applied under subsection (a) (not in excess of the portion referred to in subsection (a)), and the particular properties the bases of which are to be reduced, shall be determined under regulations prescribed by the Secretary.

(2) Limitation in title 11 case or insolvency.—In the case of a discharge to which subparagraph (A) or (B) of section 108(a)(1) applies, the reduction in basis under subsection (a) of this section shall not exceed the excess of—

    (A) the aggregate of the bases of the property held by the taxpayer immediately after the discharge, over

    (B) the aggregate of the liabilities of the taxpayer immediately after the discharge.

The preceding sentence shall not apply to any reduction in basis by reason of an election under section 108(b)(5).

(3) Certain reductions may only be made in the basis of depreciable property.—

    (A) In general.—Any amount which under subsection (b)(5) or (c)(1)(A) of section 108 is to be applied to reduce basis shall be applied only to reduce the basis of depreciable property held by the taxpayer.

    (B) Depreciable property.—For purposes of this section, the term "depreciable property" means any property of a character subject to the allowance for depreciation, but only if a basis reduction under subsection (a) will reduce the amount of depreciation or amortization which otherwise would be allowable for the period immediately following such reduction.

    (C) Special rule for partnership interests.—For purposes of this section, any interest of a partner in a partnership shall be treated as depreciable property to the extent of such partner's proportionate interest in the depreciable property held by such partnership. The preceding sentence shall apply only if there is a corresponding reduction in the partnership's basis in depreciable property with respect to such partner.

    (D) Special rule in case of affiliated group.—For purposes of this section, if—

        (i) a corporation holds stock in another corporation (hereinafter in this subparagraph referred to as the subsidiary), and

        (ii) such corporations are members of the same affiliated group which file a consolidated return under section 1501 for the taxable year in which the discharge occurs,

then such stock shall be treated as depreciable property to the extent that such subsidiary consents to a corresponding reduction in the basis of its depreciable property.

    (E) Election to treat certain inventory as depreciable property.—

        (i) In general.—At the election of the taxpayer, for purposes of this section, the term "depreciable property" includes any real property which is described in section 1221(1).

        (ii) Election.—An election under clause (i) shall be made on the taxpayer's return for the taxable year in which the discharge occurs or at such other time as may be permitted in regulations prescribed by the Secretary. Such an election, once made, may be revoked only with the consent of the Secretary.

(c) Special rules.—

(1) Reduction not to be made in exempt property.—In the case of an amount excluded from gross income under section 108(a)(1)(A), no reduction in basis shall be made under this section in the basis of property which the debtor treats as exempt property under section 522 of title 11 of the United States Code.

(2) Reductions in basis not treated as dispositions.—For purposes of this title, a reduction in basis under this section shall not be treated as a disposition.

(d) Recapture of reductions.—

(1) In general.—For purposes of sections 1245 and 1250—

(A) any property the basis of which is reduced under this section and which is neither section 1245 property nor section 1250 property shall be treated as section 1245 property, and

(B) any reduction under this section shall be treated as a deduction allowed for depreciation.

(2) Special rule for section 1250.—For purposes of section 1250(b), the determination of what would have been the depreciation adjustments under the straight line method shall be made as if there had been no reduction under this section.

§ 1019.   Property on which lessee has made improvements

Neither the basis nor the adjusted basis of any portion of real property shall, in the case of the lessor of such property, be increased or diminished on account of income derived by the lessor in respect of such property and excludable from gross income under section 109 (relating to improvements by lessee on lessor's property). If an amount representing any part of the value of real property attributable to buildings erected or other improvements made by a lessee in respect of such property was included in gross income of the lessor for any taxable year beginning before January 1, 1942, the basis of each portion of such property shall be properly adjusted for the amount so included in gross income.

PART III—COMMON NONTAXABLE EXCHANGES

§ 1031.   Exchange of property held for productive use or investment

(a) Nonrecognition of gain or loss from exchanges solely in kind.—No gain or loss shall be recognized if property held for productive use in trade or business or for investment (not including stock in trade or other property held primarily for sale, nor stocks, bonds, notes, choses in action, certificates of trust or beneficial interest, or other securities or evidences of indebtedness or interest) is exchanged solely for property of a like kind to be held either for productive use in trade or business or for investment.

(b) Gain from exchanges not solely in kind.—If an exchange would be within the provisions of subsection (a), of section 1035(a), of section 1036(a), or of section 1037(a), if it were not for the fact that the property received in exchange consists not only of property permitted by such provisions to be received without the recognition of gain, but also of other property or money, then the gain, if any, to the recipient shall be recognized, but in an amount not in excess of the sum of such money and the fair market value of such other property.

(c) **Loss from exchanges not solely in kind.**—If an exchange would be within the provisions of subsection (a), of section 1035(a), of section 1036(a), or of section 1037(a), if it were not for the fact that the property received in exchange consists not only of property permitted by such provisions to be received without the recognition of gain or loss, but also of other property or money, then no loss from the exchange shall be recognized.

(d) **Basis.**—If property was acquired on an exchange described in this section, section 1035(a), section 1036(a), or section 1037(a), then the basis shall be the same as that of the property exchanged, decreased in the amount of any money received by the taxpayer and increased in the amount of gain or decreased in the amount of loss to the taxpayer that was recognized on such exchange. If the property so acquired consisted in part of the type of property permitted by this section, section 1035(a), section 1036(a), or section 1037(a), to be received without the recognition of gain or loss, and in part of other property, the basis provided in this subsection shall be allocated between the properties (other than money) received, and for the purpose of the allocation there shall be assigned to such other property an amount equivalent to its fair market value at the date of the exchange. For purposes of this section, section 1035(a), and section 1036(a), where as part of the consideration to the taxpayer another party to the exchange assumed a liability of the taxpayer or acquired from the taxpayer property subject to a liability, such assumption or acquisition (in the amount of the liability) shall be considered as money received by the taxpayer on the exchange.

(e) **Exchanges of livestock of different sexes.**—For purposes of this section, livestock of different sexes are not property of a like kind.

§ 1032.   Exchange of stock for property

(a) **Nonrecognition of gain or loss.**—No gain or loss shall be recognized to a corporation on the receipt of money or other property in exchange for stock (including treasury stock) of such corporation.

. . . . .

§ 1033.   Involuntary conversions

(a) **General rule.**—If property (as a result of its destruction in whole or in part, theft, seizure, or requisition or condemnation or threat or imminence thereof) is compulsorily or involuntarily converted—

(1) **Conversion into similar property.**—Into property similar or related in service or use to the property so converted, no gain shall be recognized.

(2) **Conversion into money.**—Into money or into property not similar or related in service or use to the converted property, the gain (if any) shall be recognized except to the extent hereinafter provided in this paragraph:

(A) **Nonrecognition of gain.**—If the taxpayer during the period specified in subparagraph (B), for the purpose of replacing the property so converted, purchases other property similar or related in service or use to the property so converted, or purchases stock in the acquisition of control of a corporation owning such other property, at the election of the taxpayer the gain shall be recognized only to the extent that the amount realized upon such conversion (regardless of whether such amount is received in one or more taxable years) exceeds the cost of such other property or such stock. Such election shall be made at such time and in such manner as the Secretary may by regulations prescribe. For purposes of this paragraph—

(i) no property or stock acquired before the disposition of the converted property shall be considered to have been acquired for the purpose of replacing such converted property unless held by the taxpayer on the date of such disposition; and

(ii) the taxpayer shall be considered to have purchased property or stock only if, but for the provisions of subsection (b) of this section, the unadjusted basis of such property or stock would be its cost within the meaning of section 1012.

(B) Period within which property must be replaced.—The period referred to in subparagraph (A) shall be the period beginning with the date of the disposition of the converted property, or the earliest date of the threat or imminence of requisition or condemnation of the converted property, whichever is the earlier, and ending—

(i) 2 years after the close of the first taxable year in which any part of the gain upon the conversion is realized, or

(ii) subject to such terms and conditions as may be specified by the Secretary, at the close of such later date as the Secretary may designate on application by the taxpayer. Such application shall be made at such time and in such manner as the Secretary may by regulations prescribe.

(C) Time for assessment of deficiency attributable to gain upon conversion.—If a taxpayer has made the election provided in subparagraph (A), then—

(i) the statutory period for the assessment of any deficiency, for any taxable year in which any part of the gain on such conversion is realized, attributable to such gain shall not expire prior to the expiration of 3 years from the date the Secretary is notified by the taxpayer (in such manner as the Secretary may by regulations prescribe) of the replacement of the converted property or of an intention not to replace, and

(ii) such deficiency may be assessed before the expiration of such 3-year period notwithstanding the provisions of section 6212(c) or the provisions of any other law or rule of law which would otherwise prevent such assessment.

(D) Time for assessment of other deficiencies attributable to election.—If the election provided in subparagraph (A) is made by the taxpayer and such other property or such stock was purchased before the beginning of the last taxable year in which any part of the gain upon such conversion is realized, any deficiency, to the extent resulting from such election, for any taxable year ending before such last taxable year may be assessed (notwithstanding the provisions of section 6212(c) or 6501 or the provisions of any other law or rule of law which would otherwise prevent such assessment) at any time before the expiration of the period within which a deficiency for such last taxable year may be assessed.

(E) Definitions.—For purposes of this paragraph—

(i) **Control.**—The term "control" means the ownership of stock possessing at least 80 percent of the total combined voting power of all classes of stock entitled to vote and at least 80 percent of the total number of shares of all other classes of stock of the corporation.

(ii) **Disposition of the converted property.**—The term "disposition of the converted property" means the destruction, theft, seizure, requisition, or condemnation of the converted property, or the sale or exchange of such property under threat or imminence of requisition or condemnation.

(b) **Basis of property acquired through involuntary conversion.**—If the property was acquired, after February 28, 1913, as the result of a compulsory or involuntary conversion described in subsection (a) (1) or section 112(f) (2) of the Internal Revenue Code of 1939, the basis shall be the same as in the case of the property so converted, decreased in the amount of any money received by the taxpayer which was not expended in accordance with the provisions of law (applicable to the year in which such conversion was made) determining the taxable status of the gain or loss upon such conversion, and increased in the amount of gain or decreased in the amount of loss to the taxpayer recognized upon such conversion under the law applicable to the year in which such conversion was made. This subsection shall not apply in respect of property acquired as a result of a compulsory or involuntary conversion of property used by the taxpayer as his principal residence if the destruction, theft, seizure, requisition, or condemnation of such residence, or the sale or exchange of such residence under threat or imminence thereof, occurred after December 31, 1950, and before January 1, 1954. In the case of property purchased by the taxpayer in a transaction described in subsection (a)(3) [1] which resulted in the nonrecognition of any part of the gain realized as the result of a compulsory or involuntary conversion, the basis shall be the cost of such property decreased in the amount of the gain not so recognized; and if the property purchased consists of more than one piece of property, the basis determined under this sentence shall be allocated to the purchased properties in proportion to their respective costs.

(c) **Property sold pursuant to reclamation laws.**—For purposes of this subtitle, if property lying within an irrigation project is sold or otherwise disposed of in order to conform to the acreage limitation provisions of Federal reclamation laws, such sale or disposition shall be treated as an involuntary conversion to which this section applies.

(d) **Livestock destroyed by disease.**—For purposes of this subtitle, if livestock are destroyed by or on account of disease, or are sold or exchanged because of disease, such destruction or such sale or exchange shall be treated as an involuntary conversion to which this section applies.

(e) **Livestock sold on account of drought.**—For purposes of this subtitle, the sale or exchange of livestock (other than poultry) held by a taxpayer for draft, breeding, or dairy purposes in excess of the number the taxpayer would sell if he followed his usual business practices shall be treated as an involuntary conversion to which this section applies if such livestock are sold or exchanged by the taxpayer solely on account of drought.

(f) **Replacement of livestock with other farm property where there has been environmental contamination.**—For purposes of subsection (a), if, because of soil contamination or other environmental contamination, it is not feasible for the taxpayer to reinvest the proceeds from compulsorily or involuntarily converted livestock in property similar or related in use to the livestock so converted, other property (including real property) used for farming purposes shall be treated as property similar or related in service or use to the livestock so converted.

(g) Condemnation of real property held for productive use in trade or business or for investment.—

(1) Special rule.—For purposes of subsection (a), if real property (not including stock in trade or other property held primarily for sale) held for productive use in trade or business or for investment is (as the result of its seizure, requisition, or condemnation, or threat or imminence thereof) compulsorily or involuntarily converted, property of a like kind to be held either for productive use in trade or business or for investment shall be treated as property similar or related in service or use to the property so converted.

(2) Limitation.—Paragraph (1) shall not apply to the purchase of stock in the acquisition of control of a corporation described in subsection (a) (2) (A).

. . . . . .

(4) Special rule.—In the case of a compulsory or involuntary conversion described in paragraph (1), subsection (a) (2) (B) (i) shall be applied by substituting "3 years" for "2 years".

1 Subsection (a)(3) was redesignated (a)(2).

. . . . . .

§ 1034.   Rollover of gain on sale of principal residence

(a) Nonrecognition of gain.—If property (in this section called "old residence") used by the taxpayer as his principal residence is sold by him and, within a period beginning 2 years before the date of such sale and ending 2 years after such date, property (in this section called "new residence") is purchased and used by the taxpayer as his principal residence, gain (if any) from such sale shall be recognized only to the extent that the taxpayer's adjusted sales price (as defined in subsection (b)) of the old residence exceeds the taxpayer's cost of purchasing the new residence.

(b) Adjusted sales price defined.—

(1) In general.—For purposes of this section, the term "adjusted sales price" means the amount realized, reduced by the aggregate of the expenses for work performed on the old residence in order to assist in its sale.

(2) Limitations.—The reduction provided in paragraph (1) applies only to expenses—

(A) for work performed during the 90-day period ending on the day on which the contract to sell the old residence is entered into;

(B) which are paid on or before the 30th day after the date of the sale of the old residence; and

(C) which are—

(i) not allowable as deductions in computing taxable income under section 63 (defining taxable income), and

(ii) not taken into account in computing the amount realized from the sale of the old residence.

(c) Rules for application of section.—For purposes of this section:

(1) An exchange by the taxpayer of his residence for other property shall be treated as a sale of such residence, and the acquisition of a residence on the exchange of property shall be treated as a purchase of such residence.

(2) A residence any part of which was constructed or reconstructed by the taxpayer shall be treated as purchased by the taxpayer. In determining the taxpayer's cost of purchasing a residence, there shall be included only so much of his cost as is attributable to the acquisition, construction, reconstruction, and improvements made which are properly chargeable to capital account, during the period specified in subsection (a).

(3) If a residence is purchased by the taxpayer before the date of his sale of the old residence, the purchased residence shall not be treated as his new residence if sold or otherwise disposed of by him before the date of the sale of the old residence.

(4) If the taxpayer, during the period described in subsection (a), purchases more than one residence which is used by him as his principal residence at some time within 2 years after the date of the sale of the old residence, only the last of such residences so used by him after the date of such sale shall constitute the new residence. If a principal residence is sold in a sale to which subsection (d) (2) applies within 2 years after the sale of the old residence, for purposes of applying the preceding sentence with respect to the old residence, the principal residence so sold shall be treated as the last residence used during such 2-year period.

(5) **Repealed.** Pub. L. 97–34, Title I, § 122(b)(2), Aug. 13, 1981, 95 Stat. 197.

(d) **Limitation.—**

(1) **In general.**—Subsection (a) shall not apply with respect to the sale of the taxpayer's residence if within 2 years before the date of such sale the taxpayer sold at a gain other property used by him as his principal residence, and any part of such gain was not recognized by reason of subsection (a).

(2) **Subsequent sale connected with commencing work at new place.** —Paragraph (1) shall not apply with respect to the sale of the taxpayer's residence if—

(A) such sale was in connection with the commencement of work by the taxpayer as an employee or as a self-employed individual at a new principal place of work, and

(B) if the residence so sold is treated as the former residence for purposes of section 217 (relating to moving expenses), the taxpayer would satisfy the conditions of subsection (c) of section 217 (as modified by the other subsections of such section).

(e) **Basis of new residence.**—Where the purchase of a new residence results, under subsection (a) or under section 112(n) of the Internal Revenue Code of 1939, in the nonrecognition of gain on the sale of an old residence, in determining the adjusted basis of the new residence as of any time following the sale of the old residence, the adjustments to basis shall include a reduction by an amount equal to the amount of the gain not so recognized on the sale of the old residence. For this purpose, the amount of the gain not so recognized on the sale of the old residence includes only so much of such gain as is not recognized by reason of the cost, up to such time, of purchasing the new residence.

(f) **Tenant-stockholder in a cooperative housing corporation.**—For purposes of this section, section 1016 (relating to adjustments to basis), and section 1223 (relating to holding period), references to property used by the taxpayer as his principal residence, and references to the residence of a taxpayer, shall include stock held by a tenant-stockholder (as defined in section 216, relating to deduction for amounts representing taxes and interest paid to a cooperative housing corporation) in a cooperative housing corporation (as defined in such section) if—

(1) in the case of stock sold, the house or apartment which the taxpayer was entitled to occupy as such stockholder was used by him as his principal residence, and

(2) in the case of stock purchased, the taxpayer used as his principal residence the house or apartment which he was entitled to occupy as such stockholder.

(g) Husband and wife.—If the taxpayer and his spouse, in accordance with regulations which shall be prescribed by the Secretary pursuant to this subsection, consent to the application of paragraph (2) of this subsection, then—

(1) for purposes of this section—

(A) the taxpayer's adjusted sales price of the old residence is the adjusted sales price (of the taxpayer, or of the taxpayer and his spouse) of the old residence, and

(B) the taxpayer's cost of purchasing the new residence is the cost (to the taxpayer, his spouse, or both) of purchasing the new residence (whether held by the taxpayer, his spouse, or the taxpayer and his spouse); and

(2) so much of the gain on the sale of the old residence as is not recognized solely by reason of this subsection, and so much of the adjustment under subsection (e) to the basis of the new residence as results solely from this subsection shall be allocated between the taxpayer and his spouse as provided in such regulations.

This subsection shall apply only if the old residence and the new residence are each used by the taxpayer and his spouse as their principal residence. In case the taxpayer and his spouse do not consent to the application of paragraph (2) of this subsection then the recognition of gain on the sale of the old residence shall be determined under this section without regard to the rules provided in this subsection.

(h) Members of Armed Forces.—The running of any period of time specified in subsection (a) or (c) (other than the 2 years referred to in subsection (c) (4)) shall be suspended during any time that the taxpayer (or his spouse if the old residence and the new residence are each used by the taxpayer and his spouse as their principal residence) serves on extended active duty with the Armed Forces of the United States after the date of the sale of the old residence except that any such period of time as so suspended shall not extend beyond the date 4 years after the date of the sale of the old residence. For purposes of this subsection, the term "extended active duty" means any period of active duty pursuant to a call or order to such duty for a period in excess of 90 days or for an indefinite period.

(i) Special rule for condemnation.—In the case of the seizure, requisition, or condemnation of a residence, or the sale or exchange of a residence under threat or imminence thereof, the provisions of this section, in lieu of section 1033 (relating to involuntary conversions), shall be applicable if the taxpayer so elects. If such election is made, such seizure, requisition, or condemnation shall be treated as the sale of the residence. Such election shall be made at such time and in such manner as the Secretary shall prescribe by regulations.

(j) Statute of limitations.—If the taxpayer during a taxable year sells at a gain property used by him as his principal residence, then—

(1) the statutory period for the assessment of any deficiency attributable to any part of such gain shall not expire before the expiration of 3 years from

the date the Secretary is notified by the taxpayer (in such manner as the Secretary may by regulations prescribe) of—

(A) the taxpayer's cost of purchasing the new residence which the taxpayer claims results in nonrecognition of any part of such gain,

(B) the taxpayer's intention not to purchase a new residence within the period specified in subsection (a), or

(C) a failure to make such purchase within such period; and

(2) such deficiency may be assessed before the expiration of such 3-year period notwithstanding the provisions of any other law or rule of law which would otherwise prevent such assessment.

(k) Individual whose tax home is outside the United States.—The running of any period of time specified in subsection (a) or (c) (other than the 2 years referred to in subsection (c) (4)) shall be suspended during any time that the taxpayer (or his spouse if the old residence and the new residence are each used by the taxpayer and his spouse as their principal residence) has a tax home (as defined in section 911(d)(3)) outside the United States after the date of the sale of the old residence; except that any such period of time as so suspended shall not extend beyond the date 4 years after the date of the sale of the old residence.

. . . . .

§ 1035.   Certain exchanges of insurance policies

(a) General rules.—No gain or loss shall be recognized on the exchange of—

(1) a contract of life insurance for another contract of life insurance or for an endowment or annuity contract; or

(2) a contract of endowment insurance (A) for another contract of endowment insurance which provides for regular payments beginning at a date not later than the date payments would have begun under the contract exchanged, or (B) for an annuity contract; or

(3) an annuity contract for an annuity contract.

(b) Definitions.—For the purpose of this section—

(1) Endowment contract.—A contract of endowment insurance is a contract with a life insurance company as defined in section 801 which depends in part on the life expectancy of the insured, but which may be payable in full in a single payment during his life.

(2) Annuity contract.—An annuity contract is a contract to which paragraph (1) applies but which may be payable during the life of the annuitant only in installments.

(3) Life insurance contract.—A contract of life insurance is a contract to which paragraph (1) applies but which is not ordinarily payable in full during the life of the insured.

. . . . .

§ 1036.   Stock for stock of same corporation

(a) General rule.—No gain or loss shall be recognized if common stock in a corporation is exchanged solely for common stock in the same corporation, or if preferred stock in a corporation is exchanged solely for preferred stock in the same corporation.

. . . . .

§ 1038.   Certain reacquisitions of real property

(a) General rule.—If—

    (1) a sale of real property gives rise to indebtedness to the seller which is secured by the real property sold, and

    (2) the seller of such property reacquires such property in partial or full satisfaction of such indebtedness,

then, except as provided in subsections (b) and (d), no gain or loss shall result to the seller from such reacquisition, and no debt shall become worthless or partially worthless as a result of such reacquisition.

(b) Amount of gain resulting.—

    (1) In general.—In the case of a reacquisition of real property to which subsection (a) applies, gain shall result from such reacquisition to the extent that—

        (A) the amount of money and the fair market value of other property (other than obligations of the purchaser) received, prior to such reacquisition, with respect to the sale of such property, exceeds

        (B) the amount of the gain on the sale of such property returned as income for periods prior to such reacquisition.

    (2) Limitation.—The amount of gain determined under paragraph (1) resulting from a reacquisition during any taxable year beginning after the date of the enactment of this section shall not exceed the amount by which the price at which the real property was sold exceeded its adjusted basis, reduced by the sum of—

        (A) the amount of the gain on the sale of such property returned as income for periods prior to the reacquisition of such property, and

        (B) the amount of money and the fair market value of other property (other than obligations of the purchaser received with respect to the sale of such property) paid or transferred by the seller in connection with the reacquisition of such property.

For purposes of this paragraph, the price at which real property is sold is the gross sales price reduced by the selling commissions, legal fees, and other expenses incident to the sale of such property which are properly taken into account in determining gain or loss on such sale.

    (3) Gain recognized.—Except as provided in this section, the gain determined under this subsection resulting from a reacquisition to which subsection (a) applies shall be recognized, notwithstanding any other provision of this subtitle.

(c) Basis of reacquired real property.—If subsection (a) applies to the reacquisition of any real property, the basis of such property upon such reacquisition shall be the adjusted basis of the indebtedness to the seller secured by such property (determined as of the date of reacquisition), increased by the sum of—

    (1) the amount of the gain determined under subsection (b) resulting from such reacquisition, and

    (2) the amount described in subsection (b) (2) (B).

If any indebtedness to the seller secured by such property is not discharged upon the reacquisition of such property, the basis of such indebtedness shall be zero.

(d) Indebtedness treated as worthless prior to reacquisition.—If, prior to a reacquisition of real property to which subsection (a) applies, the seller has treated indebtedness secured by such property as having become worthless or partially worthless—

(1) such seller shall be considered as receiving, upon the reacquisition of such property, an amount equal to the amount of such indebtedness treated by him as having become worthless, and

(2) the adjusted basis of such indebtedness shall be increased (as of the date of reacquisition) by an amount equal to the amount so considered as received by such seller.

(e) Principal residences.—If—

(1) subsection (a) applies to a reacquisition of real property with respect to the sale of which—

(A) an election under section 121 (relating to one-time exclusion of gain from sale of principal residence by individual who has attained age 55) is in effect, or

(B) gain was not recognized under section 1034 (relating to rollover of gain on sale of principal residence); and

(2) within one year after the date of the reacquisition of such property by the seller, such property is resold by him,

then, under regulations prescribed by the Secretary, subsections (b), (c), and (d) of this section shall not apply to the reacquisition of such property and, for purposes of applying sections 121 and 1034, the resale of such property shall be treated as a part of the transaction constituting the original sale of such property.

* * * * *

(g) Acquisition by estate, etc., of seller.—Under regulations prescribed by the Secretary, if an installment obligation is indebtedness to the seller which is described in subsection (a), and if such obligation is, in the hands of the taxpayer, an obligation with respect to which section 691(a)(4)(B) applies, then—

(1) for purposes of subsection (a), acquisition of real property by the taxpayer shall be treated as reacquisition by the seller, and

(2) the basis of the real property acquired by the taxpayer shall be increased by an amount equal to the deduction under section 691(c) which would (but for this subsection) have been allowable to the taxpayer with respect to the gain on the exchange of the obligation for the real property.

§ 1039. Certain sales of low-income housing projects

(a) Nonrecognition of gain.—If—

(1) a qualified housing project is sold or disposed of by the taxpayer in an approved disposition, and

(2) within the reinvestment period the taxpayer constructs, reconstructs, or acquires another qualified housing project,

then, at the election of the taxpayer, gain from such approved disposition shall be recognized only to the extent that the net amount realized on such approved disposition exceeds the cost of such other qualified housing project. An election under this subsection shall be made at such time and in such manner as the Secretary prescribes by regulations.

(b) Definitions.—For purposes of this section—

(1) Qualified housing project.—The term "qualified housing project" means a project to provide rental or cooperative housing for lower income families—

(A) with respect to which a mortgage is insured under section 221(d) (3) or 236 of the National Housing Act, and

(B) with respect to which the owner is, under such sections or regulations issued thereunder—

(i) limited as to the rate of return on his investment in the project, and

(ii) limited as to rentals or occupancy charges for units in the project.

(2) Approved disposition.—The term "approved disposition" means a sale or other disposition of a qualified housing project to the tenants or occupants of units in such project, or to a cooperative or other nonprofit organization formed solely for the benefit of such tenants or occupants, which sale or disposition is approved by the Secretary of Housing and Urban Development under section 221(d) (3) or 236 of the National Housing Act or regulations issued under such sections.

(3) Reinvestment period.—The reinvestment period, with respect to an approved disposition of a qualified housing project, is the period beginning one year before the date of such approved disposition and ending—

(A) one year after the close of the first taxable year in which any part of the gain from such approved disposition is realized, or

(B) subject to such terms and conditions as may be specified by the Secretary, at the close of such later date as the Secretary may designate on application by the taxpayer. Such application shall be made at such time and in such manner as the Secretary prescribes by regulations.

(4) Net amount realized.—The net amount realized on an approved disposition of a qualified housing project is the amount realized reduced by—

(A) the expenses paid or incurred which are directly connected with such approved disposition, and

(B) the amount of taxes (other than income taxes) paid or incurred which are attributable to such approved disposition.

(c) Special rules.—For purposes of applying subsection (a) (2) with respect to an approved disposition—

(1) no property acquired by the taxpayer before the date of the approved disposition shall be taken into account unless such property is held by the taxpayer on such date, and

(2) no property acquired by the taxpayer shall be taken into account unless, except as provided in subsection (d), the unadjusted basis of such property is its cost within the meaning of section 1012.

(d) Basis of other qualified housing project.—If the taxpayer makes an election under subsection (a) with respect to an approved disposition, the basis of the qualified housing project described in subsection (a) (2) shall be its cost reduced by an amount equal to the amount of gain not recognized by reason of the application of subsection (a).

(e) Assessment of deficiencies.—

(1) Deficiency attributable to gain.—If the taxpayer has made an election under subsection (a) with respect to an approved disposition—

(A) the statutory period for the assessment of any deficiency, for any taxable year in which any part of the gain on such approved disposition is realized, attributable to the gain on such approved disposition shall not expire prior to the expiration of 3 years from the date the Secretary is notified by the taxpayer (in such manner as the Secretary may by regulations prescribe) of the construction, reconstruction, or acquisition of another qualified housing project or of the failure to construct, reconstruct, or acquire another qualified housing project, and

(B) such deficiency may be assessed before the expiration of such 3-year period notwithstanding the provisions of section 6212(c) or the provision of any other law or rule of law which would otherwise prevent such assessment.

(2) Time for assessment of other deficiencies attributable to election.—If a taxpayer has made an election under subsection (a) with respect to an approved disposition and another qualified housing project is constructed, reconstructed, or acquired before the beginning of the last taxable year in which any part of the gain upon such approved disposition is realized, any deficiency, to the extent resulting from such election, for any taxable year ending before such last taxable year may be assessed (notwithstanding the provisions of section 6212(c) or 6501 or the provisions of any other law or rule of law which would otherwise prevent such assessment) at any time before the expiration of the period within which a deficiency for such last taxable year may be assessed.

§ 1040.   Transfer of certain farm, etc., real property

(a) General rule.—If the executor of the estate of any decedent transfers to a qualified heir (within the meaning of section 2032A(e)(1)) any property with respect to which an election was made under section 2032A, then gain on such transfer shall be recognized to the estate only to the extent that, on the date of such exchange, the fair market value of such property exceeds the value of such property for purposes of chapter 11 (determined without regard to section 2032A).

(b) Similar rule for certain trusts.—To the extent provided in regulations prescribed by the Secretary, a rule similar to the rule provided in subsection (a) shall apply where the trustee of a trust (any portion of which is included in the gross estate of the decedent) transfers property with respect to which an election was made under section 2032A.

(c) Basis of property acquired in exchange described in subsection (a) or (b). —The basis of property acquired in an exchange with respect to which gain realized is not recognized by reason of subsection (a) or (b) shall be the basis of such property immediately before the exchange increased by the amount of the gain recognized to the estate or trust on the exchange.

PART IV—SPECIAL RULES

§ 1053.   Property acquired before March 1, 1913

In the case of property acquired before March 1, 1913, if the basis otherwise determined under this subtitle, adjusted (for the period before March 1, 1913) as provided in section 1016, is less than the fair market value of the property as of March 1, 1913, then the basis for determining gain shall be such fair market value. In determining the fair market value of stock in a corporation as of March 1, 1913, due regard shall be given to the fair market value of the assets of the corporation as of that date.

§ 1056.   Basis limitation for player contracts transferred in connection with the sale of a franchise

(a) **General rule.**—If a franchise to conduct any sports enterprise is sold or exchanged, and if, in connection with such sale or exchange, there is a transfer of a contract for the services of an athlete, the basis of such contract in the hands of the transferee shall not exceed the sum of—

    (1) the adjusted basis of such contract in the hands of the transferor immediately before the transfer, plus

    (2) the gain (if any) recognized by the transferor on the transfer of such contract.

For purposes of this section, gain realized by the transferor on the transfer of such contract, but not recognized by reason of section 337(a), shall be treated as recognized to the extent recognized by the transferor's shareholders.

(b) **Exceptions.**—Subsection (a) shall not apply—

    (1) to an exchange described in section 1031 (relating to exchange of property held for productive use or investment), and

    (2) to property in the hands of a person acquiring the property from a decedent or to whom the property passed from a decedent (within the meaning of section 1014(a)).

(c) **Transferor required to furnish certain information.**—Under regulations prescribed by the Secretary, the transfer [1] shall, at the times and in the manner provided in such regulations, furnish to the Secretary and to the transferee the following information:

    (1) the amount which the transferor believes to be the adjusted basis referred to in paragraph (1) of subsection (a),

    (2) the amount which the transferor believes to be the gain referred to in paragraph (2) of subsection (a), and

    (3) any subsequent modification of either such amount.

To the extent provided in such regulations, the amounts furnished pursuant to the preceding sentence shall be binding on the transferor and on the transferee.

(d) **Presumption as to amount allocable to player contracts.**—In the case of any sale or exchange described in subsection (a), it shall be presumed that not more than 50 percent of the consideration is allocable to contracts for the services of athletes unless it is established to the satisfaction of the Secretary that a specified amount in excess of 50 percent is properly allocable to such contracts.

Nothing in the preceding sentence shall give rise to a presumption that an allocation of less than 50 percent of the consideration to contracts for the services of athletes is a proper allocation.

¹ So in original.

§ 1057.   Election to treat transfer to foreign trust, etc., as taxable exchange

In lieu of payment of the tax imposed by section 1491, the taxpayer may elect (for purposes of this subtitle), at such time and in such manner as the Secretary may prescribe, to treat a transfer described in section 1491 as a sale or exchange of property for an amount equal in value to the fair market value of the property transferred and to recognize as gain the excess of—

(1) the fair market value of the property so transferred, over

(2) the adjusted basis (for determining gain) of such property in the hands of the transferor.

PART VII—WASH SALES OF STOCK OR SECURITIES

§ 1091.   Loss from wash sales of stock or securities

(a) **Disallowance of loss deduction.**—In the case of any loss claimed to have been sustained from any sale or other disposition of shares of stock or securities where it appears that, within a period beginning 30 days before the date of such sale or disposition and ending 30 days after such date, the taxpayer has acquired (by purchase or by an exchange on which the entire amount of gain or loss was recognized by law), or has entered into a contract or option so to acquire, substantially identical stock or securities, then no deduction for the loss shall be allowed under section 165(c) (2); nor shall such deduction be allowed a corporation under section 165(a) unless it is a dealer in stocks or securities, and the loss is sustained in a transaction made in the ordinary course of its business.

(b) **Stock acquired less than stock sold.**—If the amount of stock or securities acquired (or covered by the contract or option to acquire) is less than the amount of stock or securities sold or otherwise disposed of, then the particular shares of stock or securities the loss from the sale or other disposition of which is not deductible shall be determined under regulations prescribed by the Secretary.

(c) **Stock acquired not less than stock sold.**—If the amount of stock or securities acquired (or covered by the contract or option to acquire) is not less than the amount of stock or securities sold or otherwise disposed of, then the particular shares of stock or securities the acquisition of which (or the contract or option to acquire which) resulted in the nondeductibility of the loss shall be determined under regulations prescribed by the Secretary.

(d) **Unadjusted basis in case of wash sale of stock.**—If the property consists of stock or securities the acquisition of which (or the contract or option to acquire which) resulted in the nondeductibility (under this section or corresponding provisions of prior internal revenue laws) of the loss from the sale or other disposition of substantially identical stock or securities, then the basis shall be the basis of the stock or securities so sold or disposed of, increased or decreased, as the case may be, by the difference, if any, between the price at which the property was acquired and the price at which such substantially identical stock or securities were sold or otherwise disposed of.

SUBCHAPTER P—CAPITAL GAINS AND LOSSES

Part
  I. Treatment of capital gains.
 II. Treatment of capital losses.
III. General rules for determining capital gains and losses.
 IV. Special rules for determining capital gains and losses.

PART I—TREATMENT OF CAPITAL GAINS

§ 1201.   Alternative tax for corporations

(a) **Corporations.**—If for any taxable year a corporation has a net capital gain, then, in lieu of the tax imposed by sections 11, 511, 821(a) or (c) and 831(a), there is hereby imposed a tax (if such tax is less than the tax imposed by such sections) which shall consist of the sum of—

(1) a tax computed on the taxable income reduced by the amount of the net capital gain, at the rates and in the manner as if this subsection had not been enacted, plus

(2) a tax of 28 percent of the net capital gain.

. . . .

§ 1202.   Deduction for capital gains

(a) **In general.**—If for any taxable year a taxpayer other than a corporation has a net capital gain, 60 percent of the amount of the net capital gain shall be a deduction from gross income.

(b) **Estates and trusts.**—In the case of an estate or trust, the deduction shall be computed by excluding the portion (if any) of the gains for the taxable year from sales or exchanges of capital assets which, under sections 652 and 662 (relating to inclusions of amounts in gross income of beneficiaries of trusts), is includible by the income beneficiaries as gain derived from the sale or exchange of capital assets.

. . . .

PART II—TREATMENT OF CAPITAL LOSSES

§ 1211.   Limitation on capital losses

(a) **Corporations.**—In the case of a corporation, losses from sales or exchanges of capital assets shall be allowed only to the extent of gains from such sales or exchanges.

(b) **Other taxpayers.**—

(1) **In general.**—In the case of a taxpayer other than a corporation, losses from sales or exchanges of capital assets shall be allowed only to the extent

of the gains from such sales or exchanges, plus (if such losses exceed such gains) whichever of the following is smallest:

> (A) the taxable income for the taxable year reduced (but not below zero) by the zero bracket amount,
>
> (B) the applicable amount, or
>
> (C) the sum of—
>
>> (i) the excess of the net short-term capital loss over the net long-term capital gain, and
>>
>> (ii) one-half of the excess of the net long-term capital loss over the net short-term capital gain.

(2) Applicable amount.—For purposes of paragraph (1) (B), the term "applicable amount" means—

> (A) $2,000 in the case of any taxable year beginning in 1977; and
>
> (B) $3,000 in the case of any taxable year beginning after 1977.

In the case of a separate return by a husband or wife, the applicable amount shall be one-half of the amount determined under the preceding sentence.

(3) Computation of taxable income.—For purposes of paragraph (1), taxable income shall be computed without regard to gains or losses from sales or exchanges of capital assets and without regard to the deductions provided in section 151 (relating to personal exemptions) or any deduction in lieu thereof.

§ 1212.   Capital loss carrybacks and carryovers

(a) Corporations.—

(1) In general.—If a corporation has a net capital loss for any taxable year (hereinafter in this paragraph referred to as the "loss year"), the amount thereof shall be—

> (A) a capital loss carryback to each of the 3 taxable years preceding the loss year, but only to the extent—

. . . .

>> (ii) the carryback of such loss does not increase or produce a net operating loss (as defined in section 172(c)) for the taxable year to which it is being carried back;
>
> (B) except as provided in subparagraph (C), a capital loss carryover to each of the 5 taxable years succeeding the loss year; and

. . . .

and shall be treated as a short-term capital loss in each such taxable year. The entire amount of the net capital loss for any taxable year shall be carried to the earliest of the taxable years to which such loss may be carried, and the portion of such loss which shall be carried to each of the other taxable years to which such loss may be carried shall be the excess, if any, of such loss over the total of the capital gain net income for each of the prior taxable years to which such loss may be carried. For purposes of the preceding sentence, the capital gain net income for any such prior taxable year shall be computed without regard to the net capital loss for the loss year or for any taxable year thereafter. In the case of any net capital loss which cannot be carried back in full to a preceding taxable year by reason of clause (ii) of subparagraph (A), the capital gain net income for such prior taxable year shall in no case be treated as greater than the amount of such loss which can be carried back to such preceding taxable year upon the application of such clause (ii).

· · · ·

(b) Other taxpayers.—

(1) **In general.**—If a taxpayer other than a corporation has a net capital loss for any taxable year—

(A) the excess of the net short-term capital loss over the net long-term capital gain for such year shall be a short-term capital loss in the succeeding taxable year, and

(B) the excess of the net long-term capital loss over the net short-term capital gain for such year shall be a long-term capital loss in the succeeding taxable year.

(2) **Special rules.—**

(A) For purposes of determining the excess referred to in paragraph (1) (A), an amount equal to the amount allowed for the taxable year under section 1211(b) (1) (A), (B), or (C) shall be treated as a short-term capital gain in such year.

(B) For purposes of determining the excess referred to in paragraph (1) (B), an amount equal to the sum of—

(i) the amount allowed for the taxable year under section 1211(b) (1) (A), (B), or (C), and

(ii) the excess of the amount described in clause (i) over the net short-term capital loss (determined without regard to this subsection) for such year,

shall be treated as a short-term capital gain in such year.

· · · ·

PART III—GENERAL RULES FOR DETERMINING CAPITAL GAINS AND LOSSES

§ 1221.   Capital asset defined

For purposes of this subtitle, the term "capital asset" means property held by the taxpayer (whether or not connected with his trade or business), but does not include—

(1) stock in trade of the taxpayer or other property of a kind which would properly be included in the inventory of the taxpayer if on hand at the close of the taxable year, or property held by the taxpayer primarily for sale to customers in the ordinary course of his trade or business;

(2) property, used in his trade or business, of a character which is subject to the allowance for depreciation provided in section 167, or real property used in his trade or business;

(3) a copyright, a literary, musical, or artistic composition, a letter or memorandum, or similar property, held by—

(A) a taxpayer whose personal efforts created such property,

(B) in the case of a letter, memorandum, or similar property, a taxpayer for whom such property was prepared or produced, or

(C) a taxpayer in whose hands the basis of such property is determined, for purposes of determining gain from a sale or exchange, in whole or part by reference to the basis of such property in the hands of a taxpayer described in subparagraph (A) or (B);

(4) accounts or notes receivable acquired in the ordinary course of trade or business for services rendered or from the sale of property described in paragraph (1);

(5) a publication of the United States Government (including the Congressional Record) which is received from the United States Government or any agency thereof, other than by purchase at the price at which it is offered for sale to the public, and which is held by—

(A) a taxpayer who so received such publication, or

(B) a taxpayer in whose hands the basis of such publication is determined, for purposes of determining gain from a sale or exchange, in whole or in part by reference to the basis of such publication in the hands of a taxpayer described in subparagraph (A).

§ 1222.   Other terms relating to capital gains and losses

For purposes of this subtitle—

(1) **Short-term capital gain.**—The term "short-term capital gain" means gain from the sale or exchange of a capital asset held for not more than 1 year, if and to the extent such gain is taken into account in computing gross income.

(2) **Short-term capital loss.**—The term "short-term capital loss" means loss from the sale or exchange of a capital asset held for not more than 1 year, if and to the extent that such loss is taken into account in computing taxable income.

(3) **Long-term capital gain.**—The term "long-term capital gain" means gain from the sale or exchange of a capital asset held for more than 1 year, if and to the extent such gain is taken into account in computing gross income.

(4) **Long-term capital loss.**—The term "long-term capital loss" means loss from the sale or exchange of a capital asset held for more than 1 year, if and to the extent that such loss is taken into account in computing taxable income.

(5) **Net short-term capital gain.**—The term "net short-term capital gain" means the excess of short-term capital gains for the taxable year over the short-term capital losses for such year.

(6) Net short-term capital loss.—The term "net short-term capital loss" means the excess of short-term capital losses for the taxable year over the short-term capital gains for such year.

(7) Net long-term capital gain.—The term "net long-term capital gain" means the excess of long-term capital gains for the taxable year over the long-term capital losses for such year.

(8) Net long-term capital loss.—The term "net long-term capital loss" means the excess of long-term capital losses for the taxable year over the long-term capital gains for such year.

(9) Capital gain net income.—The term "capital gain net income" means the excess of the gains from sales or exchanges of capital assets over the losses from such sales or exchanges.

(10) Net capital loss.—The term "net capital loss" means the excess of the losses from sales or exchanges of capital assets over the sum allowed under section 1211. In the case of a corporation, for the purpose of determining losses under this paragraph, amounts which are short-term capital losses under section 1212 shall be excluded.

(11) Net capital gain.—The term "net capital gain" means the excess of the net long-term capital gain for the taxable year over the net short-term capital loss for such year.

For purposes of this subtitle, in the case of futures transactions in any commodity subject to the rules of a board of trade or commodity exchange, the length of the holding period taken into account under this section or under any other section amended by section 1402 of the Tax Reform Act of 1976 shall be determined without regard to the amendments made by subsections (a) and (b) of such section 1402.

§ 1223.   Holding period of property

For purposes of this subtitle—

(1) In determining the period for which the taxpayer has held property received in an exchange, there shall be included the period for which he held the property exchanged if, under this chapter, the property has, for the purpose of determining gain or loss from a sale or exchange, the same basis in whole or in part in his hands as the property exchanged, and, in the case of such exchanges after March 1, 1954, the property exchanged at the time of such exchange was a capital asset as defined in section 1221 or property described in section 1231. For purposes of this paragraph—

(A) an involuntary conversion described in section 1033 shall be considered an exchange of the property converted for the property acquired, and

(B) a distribution to which section 355 (or so much of section 356 as relates to section 355) applies shall be treated as an exchange.

(2) In determining the period for which the taxpayer has held property however acquired there shall be included the period for which such property was held by any other person, if under this chapter such property has, for the purpose of determining gain or loss from a sale or exchange, the same basis in

whole or in part in his hands as it would have in the hands of such other person.

. . . . .

(4) In determining the period for which the taxpayer has held stock or securities the acquisition of which (or the contract or option to acquire which) resulted in the nondeductibility (under section 1091 relating to wash sales) of the loss from the sale or other disposition of substantially identical stock or securities, there shall be included the period for which he held the stock or securities the loss from the sale or other disposition of which was not deductible.

(5) In determining the period for which the taxpayer has held stock or rights to acquire stock received on a distribution, if the basis of such stock or rights is determined under section 307 (or under so much of section 1052(c) as refers to section 113(a) (23) of the Internal Revenue Code of 1939), there shall (under regulations prescribed by the Secretary) be included the period for which he held the stock in the distributing corporation before the receipt of such stock or rights upon such distribution.

(6) In determining the period for which the taxpayer has held stock or securities acquired from a corporation by the exercise of rights to acquire such stock or securities, there shall be included only the period beginning with the date on which the right to acquire was exercised.

(7) In determining the period for which the taxpayer has held a residence, the acquisition of which resulted under section 1034 in the nonrecognition of any part of the gain realized on the sale or exchange of another residence, there shall be included the period for which such other residence had been held as of the date of such sale or exchange. For purposes of this paragraph, the term "sale or exchange" includes an involuntary conversion occurring after December 31, 1950, and before January 1, 1954.

(8) In determining the period for which the taxpayer has held a commodity acquired in satisfaction of a commodity futures contract there shall be included the period for which he held the commodity futures contract if such commodity futures contract was a capital asset in his hands.

. . . . .

(11) In the case of a person acquiring property from a decedent or to whom property passed from a decedent (within the meaning of section 1014(b)), if—

    (A) the basis of such property in the hands of such person is determined under section 1014, and

    (B) such property is sold or otherwise disposed of by such person within 1 year after the decedent's death,

then such person shall be considered to have held such property for more than 1 year.

. . . . .

PART IV—SPECIAL RULES FOR DETERMINING CAPITAL GAINS AND LOSSES

§ 1231.   Property used in the trade or business and involuntary conversions

(a) **General rule.**—If, during the taxable year, the recognized gains on sales or exchanges of property used in the trade or business, plus the recognized gains from the compulsory or involuntary conversion (as a result of destruction in whole or in part, theft or seizure, or an exercise of the power of requisition or condemnation or the threat or imminence thereof) of property used in the trade or business and capital assets held for more than 1 year into other property or money, exceed the recognized losses from such sales, exchanges, and conversions, such gains and losses shall be considered as gains and losses from sales or exchanges of capital assets held for more than 1 year. If such gains do not exceed such losses, such gains and losses shall not be considered as gains and losses from sales or exchanges of capital assets. For purposes of this subsection—

(1) in determining under this subsection whether gains exceed losses, the gains described therein shall be included only if and to the extent taken into account in computing gross income and the losses described therein shall be included only if and to the extent taken into account in computing taxable income, except that section 1211 shall not apply; and

(2) losses (including losses not compensated for by insurance or otherwise) upon the destruction, in whole or in part, theft or seizure, or requisition or condemnation of (A) property used in the trade or business or (B) capital assets held for more than 1 year shall be considered losses from a compulsory or involuntary conversion.

In the case of any involuntary conversion (subject to the provisions of this subsection but for this sentence) arising from fire, storm, shipwreck, or other casualty, or from theft, of any property used in the trade or business or of any capital asset held for more than 1 year, this subsection shall not apply to such conversion (whether resulting in gain or loss) if during the taxable year the recognized losses from such conversions exceed the recognized gains from such conversions.

(b) **Definition of property used in the trade or business.**—For purposes of this section—

(1) **General rule.**—The term "property used in the trade or business" means property used in the trade or business, of a character which is subject to the allowance for depreciation provided in section 167, held for more than 1 year, and real property used in the trade or business, held for more than 1 year, which is not—

(A) property of a kind which would properly be includible in the inventory of the taxpayer if on hand at the close of the taxable year,

(B) property held by the taxpayer primarily for sale to customers in the ordinary course of his trade or business,

(C) a copyright, a literary, musical, or artistic composition, a letter or memorandum, or similar property, held by a taxpayer described in paragraph (3) of section 1221, or

(D) a publication of the United States Government (including the Congressional Record) which is received from the United States Government, or any agency thereof, other than by purchase at the price at which it is offered for sale to the public, and which is held by a taxpayer described in paragraph (5) of section 1221.

(2) Timber, coal, or domestic iron ore.—Such term includes timber, coal, and iron ore with respect to which section 631 applies.

(3) Livestock.—Such term includes—

(A) cattle and horses, regardless of age, held by the taxpayer for draft, breeding, dairy, or sporting purposes, and held by him for 24 months or more from the date of acquisition, and

(B) other livestock, regardless of age, held by the taxpayer for draft, breeding, dairy, or sporting purposes, and held by him for 12 months or more from the date of acquisition.

Such term does not include poultry.

(4) Unharvested crop.—In the case of an unharvested crop on land used in the trade or business and held for more than 1 year, if the crop and the land are sold or exchanged (or compulsorily or involuntarily converted) at the same time and to the same person, the crop shall be considered as "property used in the trade or business."

§ 1232. Bonds and other evidences of indebtedness

(a) General rule.—For purposes of this subtitle, in the case of bonds, debentures, notes, or certificates or other evidences of indebtedness, which are capital assets in the hands of the taxpayer, and which are issued by any corporation, or by any government or political subdivision thereof—

(1) Retirement.—Amounts received by the holder on retirement of such bonds or other evidences of indebtedness shall be considered as amounts received in exchange therefor (except that in the case of bonds or other evidences of indebtedness issued before January 1, 1955, this paragraph shall apply only to those issued with interest coupons or in registered form, or to those in such form on March 1, 1954).

(2) Sale or exchange.—

(A) Corporate bonds issued after May 27, 1969 and government bonds issued after July 1, 1982.—Except as provided in subparagraph (C), on the sale or exchange of bonds or other evidences of indebtedness issued by a corporation after May 27, 1969, or by a government or political subdivision thereof after July 1, 1982, held by the taxpayer more than 1 year, any gain realized shall (except as provided in the following sentence) be considered gain from the sale or exchange of a capital asset held for more than 1 year. If at the time of original issue there was an intention to call the bond or other evidence of indebtedness before maturity, any gain realized on the sale or exchange thereof which does not exceed an amount equal to the original issue discount (as defined in subsection (b)) reduced by the portion of original issue discount previously includible in the gross income of any holder (without regard to subsection (a)(6) or (b)(4) of section 1232A (or the corresponding provisions of prior law)) shall be considered as ordinary income.

(B) Corporate bonds issued on or before May 27, 1969, and government bonds issued on or before July 1, 1982.—Except as provided in subparagraph (C), on the sale or exchange of bonds or other evidences of indebtedness issued by a government or political subdivision thereof after December 31, 1954, and on or before July 1, 1982, or by a corporation after December 31, 1954, and on or before May 27, 1969, held by the taxpayer more than 1 year, any gain realized which does not exceed—

(i) an amount equal to the original issue discount (as defined in subsection (b)), or

(ii) if at the time of original issue there was no intention to call the bond or other evidence of indebtedness before maturity, an amount which bears the same ratio to the original issue discount (as defined in subsection (b)) as the number of complete months that the bond or other evidence of indebtedness was held by the taxpayer bears to the number of complete months from the date of original issue to the date of maturity,

shall be considered as ordinary income. Gain in excess of such amount shall be considered ordinary income held more than 1 year.

(C) **Exceptions.**—This paragraph shall not apply to—

(i) obligations the interest on which is not includible in gross income under section 103 (relating to certain governmental obligations), or

(ii) any holder who has purchased the bond or other evidence of indebtedness at a premium.

(D) **Double inclusion in income not required.**—This section and sections 1232A and 1232B shall not require the inclusion of any amount previously includible in gross income.

(3) **Certain short-term government obligations.**—

(A) **In general.**—On the sale or exchange of any short-term Government obligation, any gain realized which does not exceed an amount equal to the ratable share of the acquisition discount shall be treated as ordinary income. Gain in excess of such amount shall be considered gain from the sale or exchange of a capital asset held less than 1 year.

(B) **Short-term government obligation.**—For purposes of this paragraph, the term "short-term Government obligation" means any obligation of the United States or any of its possessions, or of a State or any political subdivision thereof, or of the District of Columbia which is issued on a discount basis and payable without interest at a fixed maturity date not exceeding 1 year from the date of issue. Such term does not include any obligation the interest on which is not includible in gross income under section 103 (relating to certain governmental obligations).

(C) **Acquisition discount.**—For purposes of this paragraph, the term "acquisition discount" means the excess of the stated redemption price at maturity over the taxpayer's basis for the obligation.

(D) **Ratable share.**—For purposes of this paragraph, the ratable share of the acquisition discount is an amount which bears the same ratio to such discount as—

(i) the number of days which the taxpayer held the obligation, bears to

(ii) the number of days after the date the taxpayer acquired the obligation and up to (and including) the date of its maturity.

(b) **Definitions.**—

(1) **Original issue discount.**—For purposes of subsection (a), the term "original issue discount" means the difference between the issue price and the

stated redemption price at maturity. If the original issue discount is less than one-fourth of 1 percent of the redemption price at maturity multiplied by the number of complete years to maturity, then the issue discount shall be considered to be zero. For purposes of this paragraph, the term "stated redemption price at maturity" means the amount fixed by the last modification of the purchase agreement and includes dividends payable at that time.

(2) **Issue price.**—In the case of issues of bonds or other evidences of indebtedness registered with the Securities and Exchange Commission, the term "issue price" means the initial offering price to the public (excluding bond houses and brokers) at which price a substantial amount of such bonds or other evidences of indebtedness were sold. In the case of privately placed issues of bonds or other evidence of indebtedness, the issue price of each such bond or other evidence of indebtedness is the price paid by the first buyer of such bond increased by the amount, if any, of tax paid under section 4911, as in effect before July 1, 1974 (and not credited, refunded, or reimbursed) on the acquisition of such bond or evidence of indebtedness by the first buyer. For purposes of this paragraph, the terms "initial offering price" and "price paid by the first buyer" include the aggregate payments made by the purchaser under the purchase agreement, including modifications thereof. In the case of a bond or other evidence of indebtedness and an option or other security issued together as an investment unit, the issue price for such investment unit shall be determined in accordance with the rules stated in this paragraph. Such issue price attributable to each element of the investment unit shall be that portion thereof which the fair market value of such element bears to the total fair market value of all the elements in the investment unit. The issue price of the bond or other evidence of indebtedness included in such investment unit shall be the portion so allocated to it. In the case of a bond or other evidence of indebtedness, or an investment unit as described in this paragraph (other than a bond or other evidence of indebtedness or an investment unit issued pursuant to a plan of reorganization within the meaning of section 368(a) (1) or an insolvency reorganization within the meaning of section 371 or 374), which is issued for property and which—

(A) is part of an issue a portion of which is traded on an established securities market, or

(B) is issued for stock or securities which are traded on an established securities market,

the issue price of such bond or other evidence of indebtedness or investment unit, as the case may be, shall be the fair market value of such property. Except in cases to which the preceding sentence applies, the issue price of a bond or other evidence of indebtedness (whether or not issued as a part of an investment unit) which is issued for property (other than money) shall be the stated redemption price at maturity.

(3) **Issue date.**—In the case of issues of bonds or other evidences of indebtedness registered with the Securities and Exchange Commission, the term "date of original issue" means the date on which the issue was first sold to the public at the issue price. In the case of privately placed issues of bonds or other evidences of indebtedness, the term "date of original issue" means the date on which each such bond or other evidence of indebtedness was sold by the issuer.

(d) Denial of capital gain treatment for gains on certain obligations not in registered form.—

(1) In general.—If any registration-required obligation is not in registered form, any gain on the sale or other disposition of such obligation shall be treated as ordinary income (unless the issuance of such obligation was subject to tax under section 4701).

(2) Definitions.—For purposes of this subsection—

(A) Registration-required obligation.—The term "registration-required obligation" has the meaning given to such term by section 163(f)(2) except that clause (iv) of subparagraph (A), and subparagraph (B), of such section shall not apply.

(B) Registered form.—The term "registered form" has the same meaning as when used in section 163(f).

. . . . .

§ 1232A.   Original issue discount

(a) Original issue discount on bonds issued after July 1, 1982, included in income on basis of constant interest rate.—

(3) General rule.—For purposes of this subtitle, there shall be included in the gross income of the holder of any bond having an original issue discount issued after July 1, 1982 (and which is a capital asset in the hands of the holder) an amount equal to the sum of the daily portions of the original issue discount for each day during the taxable year on which such holder held such bond.

(2) Exceptions.—Paragraph (1) shall not apply to—

(A) Natural persons.—Any obligation issued by a natural person.

(B) Tax-exempt obligations.—Any obligation if—

(i) the interest on such obligation is not includible in gross income under section 103, or

(ii) the interest on such obligation is exempt from tax (without regard to the identity of the holder) under any other provision of law.

(C) Short-term government obligations.—Any short-term Government obligation (within the meaning of section 1232(a)(3)).

(D) United States savings bonds.—Any United States saving bond.

(3) Determination of daily portions.—For purposes of paragraph (1), the daily portion of the original issue discount on any bond shall be determined by allocating to each day in any bond period its ratable portion of the increase during such bond period in the adjusted issue price of the bond. For purposes of the preceding sentence, the increase in the adjusted issue price for any bond period shall be an amount equal to the excess (if any) of—

(A) the product of—

(i) the adjusted issue price of the bond at the beginning of such bond period, and

(ii) the yield to maturity (determined on the basis of compounding at the close of each bond period), over

(B) the sum of the amounts payable as interest on such bond during such bond period.

(4) Adjusted issue price.—For purposes of this subsection, the adjusted issue price of any bond at the beginning of any bond period is the sum of—

(A) the issue price of such bond, plus

(B) the adjustments under this subsection to such issue price for all periods before the first day of such bond period.

(5) Bond period.—Except as otherwise provided in regulations prescribed by the Secretary, the term "bond period" means a 1-year period (or the shorter period to maturity) beginning on the day in the calendar year which corresponds to the date of original issue of the bond.

(6) Reduction in case of certain subsequent holders.—For purposes of this subsection, in the case of any purchase of a bond to which this subsection applies after its original issue, the daily portion shall not include an amount (determined at the time of purchase) equal to the excess (if any) of—

(A) the cost of such bond incurred by the purchaser, over

(B) the issue price of such bond, increased by the sum of the daily portions for such bond for all days before the date of purchase (computed without regard to this paragraph),

divided by the number of days beginning on the date of such purchase and ending on the day before the stated maturity date.

(7) Regulation authority.—The Secretary may prescribe regulations providing that where, by reason of varying rates of interest, put or call options, or other circumstances, the inclusion under paragraph (1) for the taxable year does not accurately reflect the income of the holder, the proper amount of income shall be included for such taxable year (and appropriate adjustments shall be made in the amounts included for subsequent taxable years).

(b) Ratable inclusion retained for corporate bonds issued before July 2, 1982.—

(1) General rule.—There shall be included in the gross income of the holder of any bond issued by corporation after May 27, 1969, and before July 2, 1982 (and which is a capital asset in the hands of the holder)—

(A) the ratable monthly portion of original issue discount, multiplied by

(B) the number of complete months (plus any fractional part of a month determined under paragraph (3)) such holder held such bond during the taxable year.

(2) Determination of ratable monthly portion.—Except as provided in paragraph (4), the ratable monthly portion of original issue discount shall equal—

(A) the original issue discount, divided by

(B) the number of complete months from the date of original issue to the stated maturity date of the bond.

(3) Month defined.—For purposes of this subsection, a complete month commences with the date of original issue and the corresponding day of each succeeding calendar month (or the last day of a calendar month in which there is no corresponding day). In any case where a bond is acquired on any day other than a day determined under the preceding sentence, the ratable monthly portion of original issue discount for the complete month (or partial month) in which such acquisition occurs shall be allocated between the transferor and the transferee in accordance with the number of days in such complete (or partial) month each held the bond.

(4) Reduction in case of certain subsequent holders.—For purposes of this subsection, the ratable monthly portion of original issue discount shall not include an amount, determined at the time of any purchase after the original issue of the bond, equal to the excess of—

    (A) the cost of such bond incurred by the holder, over

    (B) the issue price of such bond, increased by the portion of original discount previously includible in the gross income of any holder (computed without regard to this paragraph),

divided by the number of complete months (plus any fractional part of a month) from the date of such purchase to the stated maturity date of such bond.

(c) Definitions and special rules.—

    (1) Bond includes other evidences of indebtedness.—For purposes of this section, the term "bond" means a bond, debenture, note, or certificate or other evidence of indebtedness.

    (2) Purchase defined.—For purposes of this section, the term "purchase" means any acquisition of a bond, but only if the basis of the bond is not determined in whole or in part by reference to the adjusted basis of such bond in the hands of the person from whom acquired, or under section 1014(a) (relating to property acquired from a decedent).

    (3) Original issue discount, etc.—For purposes of this section, the terms "original issue discount", "issue price", and "date of original issue" shall have the respective meanings given to such terms by section 1232(b).

    (4) Exceptions.—This section shall not apply to any holder—

    (A) who has purchased the bond at a premium, or

    (B) which is a life insurance company to which section 818(b) applies.

    (5) Basis adjustments.—The basis of any bond in the hands of the holder thereof shall be increased by the amount included in his gross income pursuant to this section.

§ 1233.   Gains and losses from short sales

(a) Capital assets.—For purposes of this subtitle, gain or loss from the short sale of property shall be considered as gain or loss from the sale or exchange of a capital asset to the extent that the property, including a commodity future, used to close the short sale constitutes a capital asset in the hands of the taxpayer.

(b) Short-term gains and holding periods.—If gain or loss from a short sale is considered as gain or loss from the sale or exchange of a capital asset under subsection (a) and if on the date of such short sale substantially identical property has been held by the taxpayer for not more than 1 year (determined without regard to the effect, under paragraph (2) of this subsection, of such short sale on the holding period), or if substantially identical property is acquired by the taxpayer after such short sale and on or before the date of the closing thereof—

    (1) any gain on the closing of such short sale shall be considered as a gain on the sale or exchange of a capital asset held for not more than 1 year

(notwithstanding the period of time any property used to close such short sale has been held); and

(2) the holding period of such substantially identical property shall be considered to begin (notwithstanding section 1223, relating to the holding period of property) on the date of the closing of the short sale, or on the date of a sale, gift, or other disposition of such property, whichever date occurs first. This paragraph shall apply to such substantially identical property in the order of the dates of the acquisition of such property, but only to so much of such property as does not exceed the quantity sold short.

For purposes of this subsection, the acquisition of an option to sell property at a fixed price shall be considered as a short sale, and the exercise or failure to exercise such option shall be considered as a closing of such short sale.

(c) Certain options to sell.—Subsection (b) shall not include an option to sell property at a fixed price acquired on the same day on which the property identified as intended to be used in exercising such option is acquired and which, if exercised, is exercised through the sale of the property so identified. If the option is not exercised, the cost of the option shall be added to the basis of the property with which the option is identified. This subsection shall apply only to options acquired after August 16, 1954.

(d) Long-term losses.—If on the date of such short sale substantially identical property has been held by the taxpayer for more than 1 year, any loss on the closing of such short sale shall be considered as a loss on the sale or exchange of a capital asset held for more than 1 year (notwithstanding the period of time any property used to close such short sale has been held, and notwithstanding section 1234).

. . . . .

(g) Hedging transactions.—This section shall not apply in the case of a hedging transaction in commodity futures.

§ 1234.   Options to buy or sell

(a) Treatment of gain or loss in the case of the purchaser.—

(1) **General rule.**—Gain or loss attributable to the sale or exchange of, or loss attributable to failure to exercise, an option to buy or sell property shall be considered gain or loss from the sale or exchange of property which has the same character as the property to which the option relates has in the hands of the taxpayer (or would have in the hands of the taxpayer if acquired by him).

(2) **Special rule for loss attributable to failure to exercise option.**—For purposes of paragraph (1), if loss is attributable to failure to exercise an option, the option shall be deemed to have been sold or exchanged on the day it expired.

(3) **Nonapplication of subsection.**—This subsection shall not apply to—

(A) an option which constitutes property described in paragraph (1) of section 1221;

(B) in the case of gain attributable to the sale or exchange of an option, any income derived in connection with such option which, without regard to this subsection, is treated as other than gain from the sale or exchange of a capital asset; and

(C) a loss attributable to failure to exercise an option described in section 1233(c).

(b) Treatment of grantor of option in the case of stock, securities, or commodities.—

(1) **General rule.**—In the case of the grantor of the option, gain or loss from any closing transaction with respect to, and gain on lapse of, an option in property shall be treated as a gain or loss from the sale or exchange of a capital asset held not more than 1 year.

(2) **Definitions.**—For purposes of this subsection—

(A) **Closing transaction.**—The term "closing transaction" means any termination of the taxpayer's obligation under an option in property other than through the exercise or lapse of the option.

(B) **Property.**—The term "property" means stocks and securities (including stocks and securities dealt with on a "when issued" basis), commodities, and commodity futures.

(3) **Nonapplication of subsection.**—This subsection shall not apply to any option granted in the ordinary course of the taxpayer's trade or business of granting options.

§ 1235.   Sale or exchange of patents

(a) General.—A transfer (other than by gift, inheritance, or devise) of property consisting of all substantial rights to a patent, or an undivided interest therein which includes a part of all such rights, by any holder shall be considered the sale or exchange of a capital asset held for more than 1 year, regardless of whether or not payments in consideration of such transfer are—

(1) payable periodically over a period generally coterminous with the transferee's use of the patent, or

(2) contingent on the productivity, use, or disposition of the property transferred.

(b) "Holder" defined.—For purposes of this section, the term "holder" means—

(1) any individual whose efforts created such property, or

(2) any other individual who has acquired his interest in such property in exchange for consideration in money or money's worth paid to such creator prior to actual reduction to practice of the invention covered by the patent, if such individual is neither—

(A) the employer of such creator, nor

(B) related to such creator (within the meaning of subsection (d)).

. . . . .

(d) Related persons.—Subsection (a) shall not apply to any transfer, directly or indirectly, between persons specified within any one of the paragraphs of section

267(b); except that, in applying section 267(b) and (c) for purposes of this section—

(1) the phrase "25 percent or more" shall be substituted for the phrase "more than 50 percent" each place it appears in section 267(b), and

(2) paragraph (4) of section 267(c) shall be treated as providing that the family of an individual shall include only his spouse, ancestors, and lineal descendants.

. . . . .

§ 1236. Dealers in securities

(a) **Capital gains.**—Gain by a dealer in securities from the sale or exchange of any security shall in no event be considered as gain from the sale or exchange of a capital asset unless—

(1) the security was, before the close of the day on which it was acquired (before the close of the following day in the case of an acquisition before January 1, 1982), clearly identified in the dealer's records as a security held for investment or if acquired before October 20, 1951, was so identified before November 20, 1951; and

(2) the security was not, at any time after the close of such day, held by such dealer primarily for sale to customers in the ordinary course of his trade or business.

(b) **Ordinary losses.**—Loss by a dealer in securities from the sale or exchange of any security shall, except as otherwise provided in section 582(c), (relating to bond, etc., losses of banks), in no event be considered as ordinary loss if at any time after November 19, 1951, the security was clearly identified in the dealer's records as a security held for investment.

(c) **Definition of security.**—For purposes of this section, the term "security" means any share of stock in any corporation, certificate of stock or interest in any corporation, note, bond, debenture, or evidence of indebtedness, or any evidence of an interest in or right to subscribe to or purchase any of the foregoing.

. . . . .

§ 1237. Real property subdivided for sale

(a) **General.**—Any lot or parcel which is part of a tract of real property in the hands of a taxpayer other than a corporation shall not be deemed to be held primarily for sale to customers in the ordinary course of trade or business at the time of sale solely because of the taxpayer having subdivided such tract for purposes of sale or because of any activity incident to such subdivision or sale, if—

(1) such tract, or any lot or parcel thereof, had not previously been held by such taxpayer primarily for sale to customers in the ordinary course of trade or business (unless such tract at such previous time would have been covered by this section) and, in the same taxable year in which the sale occurs, such taxpayer does not so hold any other real property; and

(2) no substantial improvement that substantially enhances the value of the lot or parcel sold is made by the taxpayer on such tract while held by the taxpayer or is made pursuant to a contract of sale entered into between the

taxpayer and the buyer. For purposes of this paragraph, an improvement shall be deemed to be made by the taxpayer if such improvement was made by—

(A) the taxpayer or members of his family (as defined in section 267(c) (4)), by a corporation controlled by the taxpayer, or by a partnership which included the taxpayer as a partner; or

(B) a lessee, but only if the improvement constitutes income to the taxpayer; or

(C) Federal, State, or local government, or political subdivision thereof, but only if the improvement constitutes an addition to basis for the taxpayer; and

(3) such lot or parcel, except in the case of real property acquired by inheritance or devise, is held by the taxpayer for a period of 5 years.

(b) Special rules for application of section.—

(1) Gains.—If more than 5 lots or parcels contained in the same tract of real property are sold or exchanged, gain from any sale or exchange (which occurs in or after the taxable year in which the sixth lot or parcel is sold or exchanged) of any lot or parcel which comes within the provisions of paragraphs (1), (2) and (3) of subsection (a) of this section shall be deemed to be gain from the sale of property held primarily for sale to customers in the ordinary course of the trade or business to the extent of 5 percent of the selling price.

(2) Expenditures of sale.—For the purpose of computing gain under paragraph (1) of this subsection, expenditures incurred in connection with the sale or exchange of any lot or parcel shall neither be allowed as a deduction in computing taxable income, nor treated as reducing the amount realized on such sale or exchange; but so much of such expenditures as does not exceed the portion of gain deemed under paragraph (1) of this subsection to be gain from the sale of property held primarily for sale to customers in the ordinary course of trade or business shall be so allowed as a deduction, and the remainder, if any, shall be treated as reducing the amount realized on such sale or exchange.

(3) Necessary improvements.—No improvement shall be deemed a substantial improvement for purposes of subsection (a) if the lot or parcel is held by the taxpayer for a period of 10 years and if—

(A) such improvement is the building or installation of water, sewer, or drainage facilities or roads (if such improvement would except for this paragraph constitute a substantial improvement);

(B) it is shown to the satisfaction of the Secretary that the lot or parcel, the value of which was substantially enhanced by such improvement, would not have been marketable at the prevailing local price for similar building sites without such improvement; and

(C) the taxpayer elects, in accordance with regulations prescribed by the Secretary, to make no adjustment to basis of the lot or parcel, or of any other property owned by the taxpayer, on account of the expenditures for such improvements. Such election shall not make any item deductible which would not otherwise be deductible.

(c) Tract defined.—For purposes of this section, the term "tract of real property" means a single piece of real property, except that 2 or more pieces of real property shall be considered a tract if at any time they were contiguous in the hands of the taxpayer or if they would be contiguous except for the interposition of a road, street, railroad, stream, or similar property. If, following the sale or exchange of any lot or parcel from a tract of real property, no further sales or exchanges of any other lots or parcels from the remainder of such tract are made for a period of 5 years, such remainder shall be deemed a tract.

§ 1239. Gain from sale of depreciable property between certain related taxpayers

(a) Treatment of gain as ordinary income.—In the case of a sale or exchange of property, directly or indirectly, between related persons, any gain recognized to the transferor shall be treated as ordinary income if such property is, in the hands of the transferee, of a character which is subject to the allowance for depreciation provided in section 167.

(b) Related persons.—For purposes of subsection (a), the term "related persons" means—

(1) the taxpayer and the taxpayer's spouse,

(2) the taxpayer and an 80-percent owned entity, or

(3) two 80-percent owned entities.

(c) 80-percent owned entity defined.—

(1) **General rule.**—For purposes of this section, the term "80-percent owned entity" means—

(A) a corporation 80 percent or more in value of the outstanding stock of which is owned (directly or indirectly) by or for the taxpayer, and

(B) a partnership 80 percent or more of the capital interest or profits interest in which is owned (directly or indirectly) by or for the taxpayer.

(2) **Constructive ownership.**—For purposes of subparagraphs (A) and (B) of paragraph (1), the principles of section 318 shall apply, except that—

(A) the members of an individual's family shall consist only of such individual and such individual's spouse, and

(B) paragraphs (2)(C) and (3)(C) of section 318(a) shall be applied without regard to the 50-percent limitation contained therein.

§ 1241. Cancellation of lease or distributor's agreement

Amounts received by a lessee for the cancellation of a lease, or by a distributor of goods for the cancellation of a distributor's agreement (if the distributor has a substantial capital investment in the distributorship), shall be considered as amounts received in exchange for such lease or agreement.

§ 1244. Losses on small business stock

(a) General rule.—In the case of an individual, a loss on section 1244 stock issued to such individual or to a partnership which would (but for this section) be treated as a loss from the sale or exchange of a capital asset shall, to the extent provided in this section, be treated as an ordinary loss.

(b) Maximum amount for any taxable year.—For any taxable year the aggregate amount treated by the taxpayer by reason of this section as an ordinary loss shall not exceed—

(1) $50,000, or

(2) $100,000, in the case of a husband and wife filing a joint return for such year under section 6013.

(c) Section 1244 stock defined.—

(1) In general.—For purposes of this section, the term "section 1244 stock" means common stock in a domestic corporation if—

(A) at the time such stock is issued, such corporation was a small business corporation,

(B) such stock was issued by such corporation for money or other property (other than stock and securities), and

(C) such corporation, during the period of its 5 most recent taxable years ending before the date the loss on such stock was sustained, derived more than 50 percent of its aggregate gross receipts from sources other than royalties, rents, dividends, interests, annuities, and sales or exchanges of stocks or securities.

(2) Rules for application of paragraph (1) (C).—

(A) Period taken into account with respect to new corporations.—For purposes of paragraph (1) (C), if the corporation has not been in existence for 5 taxable years ending before the date the loss on the stock was sustained, there shall be substituted for such 5-year period—

(i) the period of the corporation's taxable years ending before such date, or

(ii) if the corporation has not been in existence for 1 taxable year ending before such date, the period such corporation has been in existence before such date.

(B) Gross receipts from sales of securities.—For purposes of paragraph (1) (C), gross receipts from the sales or exchanges of stock or securities shall be taken into account only to the extent of gains therefrom.

(C) Nonapplication where deductions exceed gross income.—Paragraph (1) (C) shall not apply with respect to any corporation if, for the period taken into account for purposes of paragraph (1) (C), the amount of the deductions allowed by this chapter (other than by sections 172, 243, 244, and 245) exceeds the amount of gross income.

(3) Small business corporation defined.—

(A) In general.—For purposes of this section, a corporation shall be treated as a small business corporation if the aggregate amount of money and other property received by the corporation for stock, as a contribution to capital, and as paid-in surplus, does not exceed $1,000,000. The determination under the preceding sentence shall be made as of the time of the issuance of the stock in question but shall include amounts received for such stock and for all stock theretofore issued.

(B) Amount taken into account with respect to property.—For purposes of subparagraph (A), the amount taken into account with respect to any property other than money shall be the amount equal to the adjusted basis to the corporation of such property for determining gain, reduced by any liability to which the property was subject or which was assumed by the corporation. The determination under the preceding sentence shall be made as of the time the property was received by the corporation.

(d) **Special rules.—**

(1) **Limitations on amount of ordinary loss.—**

(A) **Contributions of property having basis in excess of value.—**If—

(i) section 1244 stock was issued in exchange for property,

(ii) the basis of such stock in the hands of the taxpayer is determined by reference to the basis in his hands of such property, and

(iii) the adjusted basis (for determining loss) of such property immediately before the exchange exceeded its fair market value at such time,

then in computing the amount of the loss on such stock for purposes of this section the basis of such stock shall be reduced by an amount equal to the excess described in clause (iii).

(B) **Increases in basis.—**In computing the amount of the loss on stock for purposes of this section, any increase in the basis of such stock (through contributions to the capital of the corporation, or otherwise) shall be treated as allocable to stock which is not section 1244 stock.

(2) **Recapitalizations, changes in name, etc.—**To the extent provided in regulations prescribed by the Secretary, common stock in a corporation, the basis of which (in the hands of a taxpayer) is determined in whole or in part by reference to the basis in his hands of stock in such corporation which meets the requirements of subsection (c) (1) (other than subparagraph (C) thereof), or which is received in a reorganization described in section 368(a) (1) (F) in exchange for stock which meets such requirements, shall be treated as meeting such requirements. For purposes of paragraphs (1) (C) and (3) (A) of subsection (c), a successor corporation in a reorganization described in section 368(a) (1) (F) shall be treated as the same corporation as its predecessor.

(3) **Relationship to net operating loss deduction.—**For purposes of section 172 (relating to the net operating loss deduction), any amount of loss treated by reason of this section as an ordinary loss shall be treated as attributable to a trade or business of the taxpayer.

(4) **Individual defined.—**For purposes of this section, the term "individual" does not include a trust or estate.

(e) **Regulations.—**The Secretary shall prescribe such regulations as may be necessary to carry out the purposes of this section.

§ 1245.   Gain from dispositions of certain depreciable property

(a) **General rule.—**

(1) **Ordinary income.—**Except as otherwise provided in this section, if section 1245 property is disposed of during a taxable year beginning after

December 31, 1962, or section 1245 recovery property is disposed of after December 31, 1980, the amount by which the lower of—

(A) the recomputed basis of the property, or

(B) (i) in the case of a sale, exchange, or involuntary conversion, the amount realized, or

(ii) in the case of any other disposition, the fair market value of such property,

exceeds the adjusted basis of such property shall be treated as ordinary income. Such gain shall be recognized notwithstanding any other provision of this subtitle.

(2) **Recomputed basis.**—For purposes of this section, the term "recomputed basis" means—

(A) with respect to any property referred to in paragraph (3) (A) or (B), its adjusted basis recomputed by adding thereto all adjustments, attributable to periods after December 31, 1961,

(B) with respect to any property referred to in paragraph (3) (C), its adjusted basis recomputed by adding thereto all adjustments, attributable to periods after June 30, 1963,

(C) with respect to livestock, its adjusted basis recomputed by adding thereto all adjustments attributable to periods after December 31, 1969,

(D) with respect to any property referred to in paragraph (3) (D), its adjusted basis recomputed by adding thereto all adjustments attributable to periods beginning with the first month for which a deduction for amortization is allowed under section 169, 179, 185, 190, 193, or 194, or

(E) with respect to any section 1245 recovery property, the adjusted basis of such property recomputed by adding thereto all adjustments attributable to periods for which a deduction is allowed under section 168(a) (as added by the Economic Recovery Tax Act of 1981) with respect to such property,

reflected in such adjusted basis on account of deductions (whether in respect of the same or other property) allowed or allowable to the taxpayer or to any other person for depreciation, or for amortization under section 168 (as in effect before its repeal by the Tax Reform Act of 1976), 169, 179, 184, 185, 188, 190, 193, 194, or (in the case of property described in paragraph (3) (C)) 191 (as in effect before its repeal by the Econimic Recovery Tax Act of 1981). For purposes of the preceding sentence, if the taxpayer can establish by adequate records or other sufficient evidence that the amount allowed for depreciation, or for amortization under section 168 (as in effect before its repeal by the Tax Reform Act of 1976), 169, 179, 184, 185, 188, 190, 193, 194, or (in the case of property described in paragraph (3) (C)) 191 (as in effect before its repeal by the Economic Recovery Tax Act of 1981) for any period was less than the amount allowable, the amount added for such period shall be the amount allowed. For purposes of this section, any deduction allowable under section 179, 190, 193, or 194 shall be treated as if it were a deduction allowable for amortization.

(3) **Section 1245 property.**—For purposes of this section, the term "section 1245 property" means any property which is or has been property of a character subject to the allowance for depreciation provided in section 167 (or

subject to the allowance of amortization provided in section 185) and is either—

(A) personal property,

(B) other property (not including a building or its structural components) but only if such other property is tangible and has an adjusted basis in which there are reflected adjustments described in paragraph (2) for a period in which such property (or other property)—

(i) was used as an integral part of manufacturing, production, or extraction or of furnishing transportation, communications, electrical energy, gas, water, or sewage disposal services,

(ii) constituted a research facility used in connection with any of the activities referred to in clause (i), or

(iii) constituted a facility used in connection with any of the activities referred to in clause (i) for the bulk storage of fungible commodities (including commodities in a liquid or gaseous state),

(C) an elevator or an escalator,

(D) so much of any real property (other than any property described in subparagraph (B)) which has an adjusted basis in which there are reflected adjustments for amortization under section 169, 179, 185, 188, 190, 193, or 194,

(E) a single purpose agricultural or horticultural structure (as defined in section 48(p)), or

(F) a storage facility used in connection with the distribution of petroleum or any primary product of petroleum.

(4) Special rule for player contracts.—

(A) In general.—For purposes of this section, if a franchise to conduct any sports enterprise is sold or exchanged, and if, in connection with such sale or exchange, there is a transfer of any player contracts, the recomputed basis of such player contracts in the hands of the transferor shall be the adjusted basis of such contracts increased by the greater of—

(i) the previously unrecaptured depreciation with respect to player contracts acquired by the transferor at the time of acquisition of such franchise, or

(ii) the previously unrecaptured depreciation with respect to the player contracts involved in such transfer.

(B) Previously unrecaptured depreciation with respect to initial contracts.—For purposes of subparagraph (A) (i), the term "previously unrecaptured depreciation" means the excess (if any) of—

(i) the sum of the deduction allowed or allowable to the taxpayer transferor for the depreciation attributable to periods after December 31, 1975, of any player contracts acquired by him at the time of acquisition of such franchise, plus the deduction allowed or allowable for losses incurred after December 31, 1975, with respect to such player contracts acquired at the time of such acquisition, over

(ii) the aggregate of the amounts described in clause (i) treated as ordinary income by reason of this section with respect to prior dispositions of such player contracts acquired upon acquisition of the franchise.

(C) Previously unrecaptured depreciation with respect to contracts transferred.—For purposes of subparagraph (A) (ii), the term "previously unrecaptured depreciation" means the amount of any deduction allowed or allowable to the taxpayer transferor for the depreciation of any contracts involved in such transfer.

(D) **Player contract.**—For purposes of this paragraph, the term "player contract" means any contract for the services of an athlete which, in the hands of the taxpayer, is of a character subject to the allowance for depreciation provided in section 167.

(5) **Section 1245 recovery property.**—For purposes of this section, the term "section 1245 recovery property" means recovery property (within the meaning of section 168) other than—

(A) 15-year real property which is residential rental property (as defined in section 167(j)(2)(B)),

(B) 15-year real property which is described in section 168(f)(2),

(C) 15-year real property with respect to which an election under subsection (b)(3) of section 168 to use a different recovery percentage is in effect, and

(D) 15-year real property which is described in clause (i), (ii), (iii), or (iv) of section 1250(a)(1)(B).

If only a portion of a building (or other structure) is section 1245 recovery property, gain from any disposition of such building (or other structure) shall be allocated first to the portion of the building (or other structure) which is section 1245 recovery property (to the extent of the amount which may be treated as ordinary income under this section) and then to the portion of the building or other structure which is not section 1245 recovery property.

(6) **Special rule for qualified leased property.**—In any case in which—

(A) the lessor of qualified leased property (within the meaning of section 168(f)(8)(D)) is treated as the owner of such property for purposes of this subtitle under section 168(f)(8), and

(B) the lessee acquires such property,

the recomputed basis of the lessee under this subsection shall be determined by taking into account any adjustments which would be taken into account in determining the recomputed basis of the lessor.

(b) **Exceptions and limitations.—**

(1) **Gifts.**—Subsection (a) shall not apply to a disposition by gift.

(2) **Transfers at death.**—Except as provided in section 691 (relating to income in respect of a decedent), subsection (a) shall not apply to a transfer at death.

(3) **Certain tax-free transactions.**—If the basis of property in the hands of a transferee is determined by reference to its basis in the hands of the transferor by reason of the application of section 332, 351, 361, 371(a), 374(a), 721, or 731, then the amount of gain taken into account by the transferor under subsection (a) (1) shall not exceed the amount of gain recognized to the transferor on the transfer of such property (determined without regard to this section). Except as provided in paragraph (7), this paragraph shall not apply to a disposition to an organization (other than a cooperative described in section 521) which is exempt from the tax imposed by this chapter.

(4) **Like kind exchanges; involuntary conversions, etc.**—If property is disposed of and gain (determined without regard to this section) is not recognized in whole or in part under section 1031 or 1033, then the amount of

gain taken into account by the transferor under subsection (a) (1) shall not exceed the sum of—

(A) the amount of gain recognized on such disposition (determined without regard to this section), plus

(B) the fair market value of property acquired which is not section 1245 property and which is not taken into account under subparagraph (A).

. . . . .

(6) Property distributed by a partnership to a partner.—

(A) **In general.**—For purposes of this section, the basis of section 1245 property distributed by a partnership to a partner shall be deemed to be determined by reference to the adjusted basis of such property to the partnership.

(B) **Adjustments added back.**—In the case of any property described in subparagraph (A), for purposes of computing the recomputed basis of such property the amount of the adjustments added back for periods before the distribution by the partnership shall be—

(i) the amount of the gain to which subsection (a) would have applied if such property had been sold by the partnership immediately before the distribution at its fair market value at such time, reduced by

(ii) the amount of such gain to which section 751(b) applied.

(7) Transfers to tax-exempt organization where property will be used in unrelated business.—

(A) **In general.**—The second sentence of paragraph (3) shall not apply to a disposition of section 1245 property to an organization described in section 511(a) (2) or 511(b) (2) if, immediately after such disposition, such organization uses such property in an unrelated trade or business (as defined in section 513).

(B) **Later change in use.**—If any property with respect to the disposition of which gain is not recognized by reason of subparagraph (A) ceases to be used in an unrelated trade or business of the organization acquiring such property, such organization shall be treated for purposes of this section as having disposed of such property on the date of such cessation.

(8) Timber property.—In determining, under subsection (a)(2), the recomputed basis of property with respect to which a deduction under section 194 was allowed for any taxable year, the taxpayer shall not take into account adjustments under section 194 to the extent such adjustments are attributable to the amortizable basis of the taxpayer acquired before the 10th taxable year preceding the taxable year in which gain with respect to the property is recognized.

(c) Adjustments to basis.—The Secretary shall prescribe such regulations as he may deem necessary to provide for adjustments to the basis of property to reflect gain recognized under subsection (a).

(d) Application of section.—This section shall apply notwithstanding any other provision of this subtitle.

§ 1250.   Gain from dispositions of certain depreciable realty

(a) General rule.—Except as otherwise provided in this section—

(1) Additional depreciation after December 31, 1975.—

(A) In general.—If section 1250 property is disposed of after December 31, 1975, then the applicable percentage of the lower of—

(i) that portion of the additional depreciation (as defined in subsection (b) (1) or (4)) attributable to periods after December 31, 1975, in respect of the property, or

(ii) the excess of the amount realized (in the case of a sale, exchange, or involuntary conversion), or the fair market value of such property (in the case of any other disposition), over the adjusted basis of such property,

shall be treated as gain which is ordinary income. Such gain shall be recognized notwithstanding any other provision of this subtitle.

(B) Applicable percentage.—For purposes of subparagraph (A), the term "applicable percentage" means—

. . . . .

(iii) in the case of section 1250 property with respect to which a depreciation deduction for rehabilitation expenditures was allowed under section 167(k), 100 percent minus 1 percentage point for each full month in excess of 100 full months after the date on which such property was placed in service;

. . . .

(v) in the case of all other section 1250 property, 100 percent.

. . . .

(2) Additional depreciation after December 31, 1969, and before January 1, 1976.—

(A) In general.—If section 1250 property is disposed of after December 31, 1969, and the amount determined under paragraph (1) (A) (ii) exceeds the amount determined under paragraph (1) (A) (i), then the applicable percentage of the lower of—

(i) that portion of the additional depreciation attributable to periods after December 31, 1969, and before January 1, 1976, in respect of the property, or

(ii) the excess of the amount determined under paragraph (1) (A) (ii) over the amount determined under paragraph (1) (A) (i),

shall also be treated as gain which is ordinary income. Such gain shall be recognized notwithstanding any other provision of this subtitle.

(B) Applicable percentage.—For purposes of subparagraph (A), the term "applicable percentage" means—

(i) in the case of section 1250 property disposed of pursuant to a written contract which was, on July 24, 1969, and at all times thereafter, binding on the owner of the property, 100 percent minus 1 percentage point for each full month the property was held after the date the property was held 20 full months;

. . . . .

(iii) in the case of residential rental property (as defined in section 167(j) (2) (B)) other than that covered by clauses (i) and (ii), 100 percent minus 1 percentage point for each full month the property was held after the date the property was held 100 full months;

(iv) in the case of section 1250 property with respect to which a depreciation deduction for rehabilitation expenditures was allowed under section 167(k), 100 percent minus 1 percentage point for each full month in excess of 100 full months after the date on which such property was placed in service; and

(v) in the case of all other section 1250 property, 100 percent.

Clauses (i), (ii), and (iii) shall not apply with respect to the additional depreciation described in subsection (b) (4).

(3) Additional depreciation before January 1, 1970.—

(A) In general.—If section 1250 property is disposed of after December 31, 1963, and the amount determined under paragraph (1) (A) (ii) exceeds the sum of the amounts determined under paragraphs (1) (A) (i) and (2) (A) (i), then the applicable percentage of the lower of—

(i) that portion of the additional depreciation attributable to periods before January 1, 1970, in respect of the property, or

(ii) the excess of the amount determined under paragraph (1) (A) (ii) over the sum of the amounts determined under paragraphs (1) (A) (i) and (2) (A) (i),

shall also be treated as gain which is ordinary income. Such gain shall be recognized notwithstanding any other provision of this subtitle.

(B) Applicable percentage.—For purposes of subparagraph (A), the term "applicable percentage" means 100 percent minus 1 percentage point for each full month the property was held after the date on which the property was held for 20 full months.

(b) Additional depreciation defined.—For purposes of this section—

(1) In general.—The term "additional depreciation" means, in the case of any property, the depreciation adjustments in respect of such property; except that, in the case of property held more than one year, it means such adjustments only to the extent that they exceed the amount of the depreciation adjustments which would have resulted if such adjustments had been determined for each taxable year under the straight line method of adjustment. For purposes of the preceding sentence, if a useful life (or salvage value) was used in determining the amount allowed as a deduction for any taxable year, such life (or value) shall be used in determining the depreciation adjustments which would have resulted for such year under the straight line method.

(2) Property held by lessee.—In the case of a lessee, in determining the depreciation adjustments which would have resulted in respect of any building erected (or other improvement made) on the leased property, or in respect of any cost of acquiring the lease, the lease period shall be treated as including all renewal periods. For purposes of the preceding sentence—

(A) the term "renewal period" means any period for which the lease may be renewed, extended, or continued pursuant to an option exercisable by the lessee, but

(B) the inclusion of renewal periods shall not extend the period taken into account by more than ⅔ of the period on the basis of which the depreciation adjustments were allowed.

(3) Depreciation adjustments.—The term "depreciation adjustments" means, in respect of any property, all adjustments attributable to periods after December 31, 1963, reflected in the adjusted basis of such property on account of deductions (whether in respect of the same or other property) allowed or allowable to the taxpayer or to any other person for exhaustion, wear and tear, obsolescence, or amortization (other than amortization under section 168 (as in effect before its repeal by the Tax Reform Act of 1976), 169, 185, 188, 190, or 193). For purposes of the preceding sentence, if the taxpayer can establish by adequate records or other sufficient evidence that the amount allowed as a deduction for any period was less than the amount allowable, the amount taken into account for such period shall be the amount allowed.

(4) Additional depreciation attributable to rehabilitation expenditures.—The term "additional depreciation" also means, in the case of section 1250 property with respect to which a depreciation or amortization deduction for rehabilitation expenditures was allowed under section 167(k) or 191 (as in effect before its repeal by the Economic Recovery Tax Act of 1981), the depreciation or amortization adjustments allowed under such section to the extent attributable to such property, except that, in the case of such property held for more than one year after the rehabilitation expenditures so allowed were incurred, it means such adjustments only to the extent that they exceed the amount of the depreciation adjustments which would have resulted if such adjustments had been determined under the straight line method of adjustment without regard to the useful life permitted under section 167(k) or 191 (as in effect before its repeal by the Economic Recovery Tax Act of 1981).

(c) Section 1250 property.—For purposes of this section, the term "section 1250 property" means any real property (other than section 1245 property, as defined in section 1245(a) (3)) which is or has been property of a character subject to the allowance for depreciation provided in section 167.

(d) Exceptions and limitations.—

(1) Gifts.—Subsection (a) shall not apply to a disposition by gift.

(2) Transfers at death.—Except as provided in section 691 (relating to income in respect of a decedent), subsection (a) shall not apply to a transfer at death.

(3) Certain tax-free transactions.—If the basis of property in the hands of a transferee is determined by reference to its basis in the hands of the transferor by reason of the application of section 332, 351, 361, 371(a), 374(a), 721, or 731, then the amount of gain taken into account by the transferor under subsection (a) shall not exceed the amount of gain recognized to the transferor on the transfer of such property (determined without regard to this section). Except as provided in paragraph (9), this paragraph shall not apply to a disposition to an organization (other than a cooperative described in section 521) which is exempt from the tax imposed by this chapter.

(4) Like kind exchanges; involuntary conversions, etc.—

(A) Recognition limit.—If property is disposed of and gain (determined without regard to this section) is not recognized in whole or in part under section 1031 or 1033, then the amount of gain taken into account by the transferor under subsection (a) shall not exceed the greater of the following:

(i) the amount of gain recognized on the disposition (determined without regard to this section), increased as provided in subparagraph (B), or

(ii) the amount determined under subparagraph (C).

(B) Increase for certain stock.—With respect to any transaction, the increase provided by this subparagraph is the amount equal to the fair market value of any stock purchased in a corporation which (but for this paragraph) would result in nonrecognition of gain under section 1033(a) (2) (A).

(C) Adjustment where insufficient section 1250 property is acquired. —With respect to any transaction, the amount determined under this subparagraph shall be the excess of—

(i) the amount of gain which would (but for this paragraph) be taken into account under subsection (a), over

(ii) the fair market value (or cost in the case of a transaction described in section 1033(a) (2)) of the section 1250 property acquired in the transaction.

(D) Basis of property acquired.—In the case of property purchased by the taxpayer in a transaction described in section 1033(a) (2), in applying the last sentence of section 1033(b), such sentence shall be applied—

(i) first solely to section 1250 properties and to the amount of gain not taken into account under subsection (a) by reason of this paragraph, and

(ii) then to all purchased properties to which such sentence applies and to the remaining gain not recognized on the transaction as if the cost of the section 1250 properties were the basis of such properties computed under clause (i).

In the case of property acquired in any other transaction to which this paragraph applies, rules consistent with the preceding sentence shall be applied under regulations prescribed by the Secretary.

(E) Additional depreciation with respect to property disposed of. —In the case of any transaction described in section 1031 or 1033, the additional depreciation in respect of the section 1250 property acquired which is attributable to the section 1250 property disposed of shall be an amount equal to the amount of the gain which was not taken into account under subsection (a) by reason of the application of this paragraph.

. . . . .

(6) Property distributed by a partnership to a partner.—

(A) In general.—For purposes of this section, the basis of section 1250 property distributed by a partnership to a partner shall be deemed to be determined by reference to the adjusted basis of such property to the partnership.

(B) Additional depreciation.—In respect of any property described in subparagraph (A), the additional depreciation attributable to periods before the distribution by the partnership shall be—

(i) the amount of the gain to which subsection (a) would have applied if such property had been sold by the partnership immediately before the distribution at its fair market value at such time and the applicable percentage for the property had been 100 percent, reduced by

(ii) if section 751(b) applied to any part of such gain, the amount of such gain to which section 751(b) would have applied if the applicable percentage for the property had been 100 percent.

(7) Disposition of principal residence.—Subsection (a) shall not apply to a disposition of—

(A) property to the extent used by the taxpayer as his principal residence (within the meaning of section 1034, relating to rollover of gain on sale of principal residence), and

(B) property in respect of which the taxpayer meets the age and ownership requirements of section 121 (relating to one-time exclusion of gain from sale of principal residence by individual who has attained age 55) but only to the extent that he meets the use requirements of such section in respect of such property.

(8) Disposition of qualified low-income housing.—If section 1250 property is disposed of and gain (determined without regard to this section) is not recognized in whole or in part under section 1039, then—

(A) Recognition limit.—The amount of gain recognized by the transferor under subsection (a) shall not exceed the greater of—

(i) the amount of gain recognized on the disposition (determined without regard to this section), or

(ii) the amount determined under subparagraph (B).

(B) Adjustment where insufficient section 1250 property is acquired.—With respect to any transaction, the amount determined under this subparagraph shall be the excess of—

(i) the amount of gain which would (but for this paragraph) be taken into account under subsection (a), over

(ii) the cost of the section 1250 property acquired in the transaction.

(C) Basis of property acquired.—The basis of property acquired by the taxpayer, determined under section 1039(d), shall be allocated—

(i) first to the section 1250 property described in subparagraph (E)(i), in the amount determined under such subparagraph, reduced by the amount of gain not recognized attributable to the section 1250 property disposed of,

(ii) then to any property (other than section 1250 property) to which section 1039 applies, in the amount of its cost, reduced by the amount of gain not recognized except to the extent taken into account under clause (i), and

(iii) then to the section 1250 property described in subparagraph (E) (ii), in the amount determined thereunder, reduced by the amount of gain not recognized except to the extent taken into account under clauses (i) and (ii).

(D) Additional depreciation with respect to property disposed of. —The additional depreciation with respect to any property acquired shall include the additional depreciation with respect to the corresponding section 1250 property disposed of, reduced by the amount of gain recognized attributable to such property.

(E) Property consisting of more than one element.—There shall be treated as a separate element of section 1250 property—

(i) that portion of the section 1250 property acquired the cost of which does not exceed the net amount realized (as defined in section 1039(b)) attributable to the section 1250 property disposed of, reduced by the amount of gain recognized (if any) attributable to such property, and

(ii) that portion of the section 1250 property acquired the cost of which exceeds the net amount realized (as defined in section 1039(b)) attributable to the section 1250 property disposed of.

(F) Allocation rules.—For purposes of this paragraph—

(i) the amount of gain recognized attributable to the section 1250 property disposed of shall be the net amount realized with respect to such property, reduced by the greater of the adjusted basis of the section 1250 property disposed of or the cost of the section 1250 property acquired, but shall not exceed the gain recognized in the transaction, and

(ii) if any section 1250 property is treated as consisting of more than one element by reason of the application of subparagraph (E) to a prior transaction, then the amount of gain recognized, the net amount realized, and the additional depreciation, with respect to each such element shall be allocated in accordance with regulations prescribed by the Secretary.

(9) Transfers to tax-exempt organization where property will be used in unrelated business.—

(A) In general.—The second sentence of paragraph (3) shall not apply to a disposition of section 1250 property to an organization described in section 511(a) (2) or 511(b) (2) if, immediately after such disposition, such organization uses such property in an unrelated trade or business (as defined in section 513).

(B) Later change in use.—If any property with respect to the disposition of which gain is not recognized by reason of subparagraph (A) ceases to be used in an unrelated trade or business of the organization acquiring such property, such organization shall be treated for purposes of this section as having disposed of such property on the date of such cessation.

(10) Foreclosure dispositions.—If any section 1250 property is disposed of by the taxpayer pursuant to a bid for such property at foreclosure or by operation of an agreement or of process of law after there was a default on indebtedness which such property secured, the applicable percentage referred to in paragraph (1) (B), (2) (B), or (3) (B) of subsection (a), as the case may be, shall be determined as if the taxpayer ceased to hold such property on the date of the beginning of the proceedings pursuant to which the disposition occurred, or, in the event there are no proceedings, such percentage shall be determined as if the taxpayer ceased to hold such property on the date, determined under regulations prescribed by the Secretary, on which such operation of an agreement or process of law, pursuant to which the disposition occurred, began.

(11) **Section 1245 recovery property.**—Subsection (a) shall not apply to the disposition of property which is section 1245 recovery property (as defined in section 1245(a)(5)).

(e) **Holding period.**—For purposes of determining the applicable percentage under this section, the provisions of section 1223 shall not apply, and the holding period of section 1250 property shall be determined under the following rules:

(1) **Beginning of holding period.**—The holding period of section 1250 property shall be deemed to begin—

(A) in the case of property acquired by the taxpayer, on the day after the date of acquisition, or

(B) in the case of property constructed, reconstructed, or erected by the taxpayer, on the first day of the month during which the property is placed in service.

(2) **Property with transferred basis.**—If the basis of property acquired in a transaction described in paragraph (1), (2), (3), or (5) of subsection (d) is determined by reference to its basis in the hands of the transferor, then the holding period of the property in the hands of the transferee shall include the holding period of the property in the hands of the transferor.

(3) **Principal residence.**—If the basis of property acquired in a transaction described in paragraph (7) of subsection (d) is determined by reference to the basis in the hands of the taxpayer of other property, then the holding period of the property acquired shall include the holding period of such other property.

(4) **Qualified low-income housing.**—The holding period of any section 1250 property acquired which is described in subsection (d) (8) (E) (i) shall include the holding period of the corresponding element of section 1250 property disposed of.

(f) **Special rules for property which is substantially improved.**—

(1) **Amount treated as ordinary income.**—If, in the case of a disposition of section 1250 property, the property is treated as consisting of more than one element by reason of paragraph (3), then the amount taken into account under subsection (a) in respect of such section 1250 property as ordinary income shall be the sum of the amounts determined under paragraph (2).

(2) **Ordinary income attributable to an element.**—For purposes of paragraph (1), the amount taken into account for any element shall be the sum of a series of amounts determined for the periods set forth in subsection (a), with the amount for any such period being determined by multiplying—

(A) the amount which bears the same ratio to the lower of the amounts specified in clause (i) or (ii) of subsection (a) (1) (A), in clause (i) or (ii) of subsection (a) (2) (A), or in clause (i) or (ii) of subsection (a) (3) (A), as the case may be, for the section 1250 property as the additional depreciation for such element attributable to such period bears to the sum of the additional depreciation for all elements attributable to such period, by

(B) the applicable percentage for such element for such period. For purposes of this paragraph, determinations with respect to any element shall be made as if it were a separate property.

(3) **Property consisting of more than one element.**—In applying this subsection in the case of any section 1250 property, there shall be treated as a separate element—

(A) each separate improvement,

(B) if, before completion of section 1250 property, units thereof (as distinguished from improvements) were placed in service, each such unit of section 1250 property, and

(C) the remaining property which is not taken into account under subparagraphs (A) and (B).

(4) **Property which is substantially improved.**—For purposes of this subsection—

(A) **In general.**—The term "separate improvement" means each improvement added during the 36-month period ending on the last day of any taxable year to the capital account for the property, but only if the sum of the amounts added to such account during such period exceeds the greatest of—

(i) 25 percent of the adjusted basis of the property,

(ii) 10 percent of the adjusted basis of the property, determined without regard to the adjustments provided in paragraphs (2) and (3) of section 1016(a), or

(iii) $5,000.

For purposes of clauses (i) and (ii), the adjusted basis of the property shall be determined as of the beginning of the first day of such 36-month period, or of the holding period of the property (within the meaning of subsection (e)), whichever is the later.

(B) **Exception.**—Improvements in any taxable year shall be taken into account for purposes of subparagraph (A) only if the sum of the amounts added to the capital account for the property for such taxable year exceeds the greater of—

(i) $2,000, or

(ii) one percent of the adjusted basis referred to in subparagraph (A) (ii), determined, however, as of the beginning of such taxable year.

For purposes of this section, if the amount added to the capital account for any separate improvement does not exceed the greater of clause (i) or (ii), such improvement shall be treated as placed in service on the first day, of a calendar month, which is closest to the middle of the taxable year.

(C) **Improvement.**—The term "improvement" means, in the case of any section 1250 property, any addition to capital account for such property after the initial acquisition or after completion of the property.

(g) **Special rules for qualified low-income housing.**—

(1) **Amount treated as ordinary income.**—If, in the case of a disposition of section 1250 property, the property is treated as consisting of more than one element by reason of the application of subsection (d) (8) (E), and gain is recognized in whole or in part, then the amount taken into account under

subsection (a) as ordinary income shall be the sum of the amounts determined under paragraph (2).

(2) **Ordinary income attributable to an element.**—For purposes of paragraph (1), the amount taken into account for any element shall be determined in a manner similar to that provided by subsection (f) (2).

(h) **Adjustments to basis.**—The Secretary shall prescribe such regulations as he may deem necessary to provide for adjustments to the basis of property to reflect gain recognized under subsection (a).

(i) **Application of section.**—This section shall apply notwithstanding any other provision of this subtitle.

§ 1253.   Transfers of franchises, trademarks, and trade names

(a) **General rule.**—A transfer of a franchise, trademark, or trade name shall not be treated as a sale or exchange of a capital asset if the transferor retains any significant power, right, or continuing interest with respect to the subject matter of the franchise, trademark, or trade name.

(b) **Definitions.**—For purposes of this section—

(1) **Franchise.**—The term "franchise" includes an agreement which gives one of the parties to the agreement the right to distribute, sell, or provide goods, services, or facilities, within a specified area.

(2) **Significant power, right, or continuing interest.**—The term "significant power, right, or continuing interest" includes, but is not limited to, the following rights with respect to the interest transferred:

(A) A right to disapprove any assignment of such interest, or any part thereof.

(B) A right to terminate at will.

(C) A right to prescribe the standards of quality of products used or sold, or of services furnished, and of the equipment and facilities used to promote such products or services.

(D) A right to require that the transferee sell or advertise only products or services of the transferor.

(E) A right to require that the transferee purchase substantially all of his supplies and equipment from the transferor.

(F) A right to payments contingent on the productivity, use, or disposition of the subject matter of the interest transferred, if such payments constitute a substantial element under the transfer agreement.

(3) **Transfer.**—The term "transfer" includes the renewal of a franchise, trademark, or trade name.

(c) **Treatment of contingent payments by transferor.**—Amounts received or accrued on account of a transfer, sale, or other disposition of a franchise, trademark, or trade name which are contingent on the productivity, use, or disposition of the franchise, trademark, or trade name transferred shall be treated as amounts received or accrued from the sale or other disposition of property which is not a capital asset.

(d) **Treatment of payments by transferee.**—

(1) **Contingent payments.**—Amounts paid or incurred during the taxable year on account of a transfer, sale, or other disposition of a franchise, trademark, or trade name which are contingent on the productivity, use, or disposition of the franchise, trademark, or trade name transferred shall be

allowed as a deduction under section 162(a) (relating to trade or business expenses).

(2) **Other payments.**—If a transfer of a franchise, trademark, or trade name is not (by reason of the application of subsection (a)) treated as a sale or exchange of a capital asset, any payment not described in paragraph (1) which is made in discharge of a principal sum agreed upon in the transfer agreement shall be allowed as a deduction—

(A) in the case of a single payment made in discharge of such principal sum, ratably over the taxable years in the period beginning with the taxable year in which the payment is made and ending with the ninth succeeding taxable year or ending with the last taxable year beginning in the period of the transfer agreement, whichever period is shorter;

(B) in the case of a payment which is one of a series of approximately equal payments made in discharge of such principal sum, which are payable over—

(i) the period of the transfer agreement, or

(ii) a period of more than 10 taxable years, whether ending before or after the end of the period of the transfer agreement,

in the taxable year in which the payment is made; and

(C) in the case of any other payment, in the taxable year or years specified in regulations prescribed by the Secretary, consistently with the preceding provisions of this paragraph.

(e) **Exception.**—This section shall not apply to the transfer of a franchise to engage in professional football, basketball, baseball, or other professional sport.

§ 1254.   Gain from disposition of interest in oil, gas, or geothermal property

(a) **General rule.**—

(1) **Ordinary income.**—If oil, gas, or geothermal property is disposed of after December 31, 1975, the lower of—

(A) the aggregate amount of expenditures after December 31, 1975, which are allocable to such property and which have been deducted as intangible drilling and development costs under section 263(c) by the taxpayer or any other person and which (but for being so deducted) would be reflected in the adjusted basis of such property, adjusted as provided in paragraph (4), or

(B) the excess of—

(i) the amount realized (in the case of a sale, exchange, or involuntary conversion), or the fair market value of the interest (in the case of any other disposition), over

(ii) the adjusted basis of such interest,

shall be treated as gain which is ordinary income. Such gain shall be recognized notwithstanding any other provision of this subtitle.

(2) **Disposition of portion of property.**—For purposes of paragraph (1)—

(A) In the case of the disposition of a portion of an oil, gas, or geothermal property (other than an undivided interest), the entire amount of the aggregate expenditures described in paragraph (1) (A) with respect to such property shall be treated as allocable to such portion to the extent of the amount of the gain to which paragraph (1) applies.

(B) In the case of the disposition of an undivided interest in an oil, gas, or geothermal property (or a portion thereof), a proportionate part of the expenditures described in paragraph (1) (A) with respect to such property shall be treated as allocable to such undivided interest to the extent of the amount of the gain to which paragraph (1) applies.

This paragraph shall not apply to any expenditures to the extent the taxpayer establishes to the satisfaction of the Secretary that such expenditures do not relate to the portion (or interest therein) disposed of.

(3) Oil, gas, or geothermal property.—The term "oil, gas, or geothermal property" means any property (within the meaning of section 614) with respect to which any expenditures described in paragraph (1) (A) are properly chargeable.

(4) Special rule for paragraph (1) (A).—In applying paragraph (1) (A), the amount deducted for intangible drilling and development costs and allocable to the interest disposed of shall be reduced by the amount (if any) by which the deduction for depletion under section 611 with respect to such interest would have been increased if such costs incurred (after December 31, 1975) had been charged to capital account rather than deducted.

(b) Special rules under regulations.—Under regulations prescribed by the Secretary—

(1) rules similar to the rules of subsection (g) of section 617 and to the rules of subsections (b) and (c) of section 1245 shall be applied for purposes of this section; and

(2) in the case of the sale or exchange of stock in an S corporation, rules similar to the rules of section 751 shall be applied to that portion of the excess of the amount realized over the adjusted basis of the stock which is attributable to expenditures referred to in subsection (a)(1)(A) of this section.

SUBCHAPTER Q—READJUSTMENT OF TAX BETWEEN YEARS AND SPECIAL LIMITATIONS

Part
   I.   Income averaging.
  II.   Mitigation of effect of limitations and other provisions.
[III.   Repealed]
[IV.   Repealed]
  V.   Claim of right.
[VI.   Repealed]
VII.   Recoveries of foreign expropriation losses.*

PART I—INCOME AVERAGING

§ 1301.   Limitation on tax

If an eligible individual has averagable income for the computation year, and if the amount of such income exceeds $3,000, then the tax imposed by section 1 for the computation year which is attributable to averagable income shall be 5 times

* Omitted entirely.

the increase in tax under such section which would result from adding 20 percent of such income to 120 percent of average base period income.

§ 1302.   Definition of averagable income; related definitions

(a) Averagable income.—

(1) In general.—For purposes of this part, the term "averagable income" means the amount by which taxable income for the computation year (reduced as provided in paragraph (2)) exceeds 120 percent of average base period income.

(2) Reductions.—The taxable income for the computation year shall be reduced by—

(A) the amount (if any) to which section 72(m)(5) or (q)(1) applies, and

(B) the amounts included in the income of a beneficiary of a trust under section 667(a).

(b) Average base period income.—For purposes of this part—

(1) In general.—The term "average base period income" means one-fourth of the sum of the base period incomes for the base period.

(2) Base period income.—The base period income for any taxable year is the taxable income for such year—

(A) increased by an amount equal to the excess of—

(i) the amount excluded from gross income under section 911 (relating to citizens or residents of the United States living abroad) and subpart D of part III of subchapter N (sec. 931 and following, relating to income from sources within possessions of the United States), over

(ii) the deductions which would have been properly allocable to or chargeable against such amount but for the exclusion of such amount from gross income; and

(B) decreased by the amounts included in the income of a beneficiary of a trust under section 667(a).

(3) Transitional rule for determining base period income.—The base period income (determined under paragraph (2)) for any taxable year beginning before January 1, 1977, shall be increased by—

(A) $3,200 in the case of a joint return or a surviving spouse (as defined in section 2(a)),

(B) $2,200 in the case of an individual who is not married (within the meaning of section 143) and is not a surviving spouse (as so defined), or

(C) $1,600 in the case of a married individual (within the meaning of section 143) filing a separate return.

For purposes of this paragraph, filing status shall be determined as of the computation year.

(c) Other related definitions.—For purposes of this part—

(1) Computation year.—The term "computation year" means the taxable year for which the taxpayer chooses the benefits of this part.

(2) Base period.—The term "base period" means the 4 taxable years immediately preceding the computation year.

(3) **Base period year.**—The term "base period year" means any of the 4 taxable years immediately preceding the computation year.

(4) **Joint return.**—The term "joint return" means the return of a husband and wife made under section 6013.

§ 1303.   Eligible individuals

(a) **General rule.**—Except as otherwise provided in this section, for purposes of this part the term "eligible individual" means any individual who is a citizen or resident of the United States throughout the computation year.

(c) **Individuals receiving support from others.—**

(1) **In general.**—For purposes of this part, an individual shall not be an eligible individual for the computation year if, for any base period year, such individual (and his spouse) furnished less than one-half of his support.

(2) **Exceptions.**—Paragraph (1) shall not apply to any computation year if—

(A) such year ends after the individual attained age 25 and, during at least 4 of his taxable years beginning after he attained age 21 and ending with his computation year, he was not a full-time student,

(B) more than one-half of the individual's taxable income for the computation year is attributable to work performed by him in substantial part during 2 or more of the base period years, or

(C) the individual makes a joint return for the computation year and not more than 25 percent of the aggregate adjusted gross income of such individual and his spouse for the computation year is attributable to such individual.

In applying subparagraph (C), amounts which constitute earned income (within the meaning of section 911(d)(2)) and are community income under community property laws applicable to such income shall be taken into account as if such amounts did not constitute community income.

(d) **Student defined.**—For purposes of this section, the term "student" means, with respect to a taxable year, an individual who during each of 5 calendar months during such taxable year—

(1) was a full-time student at an educational organization described in section 170(b) (1) (A) (ii); or

(2) was pursuing a full-time course of institutional on-farm training under the supervision of an accredited agent of an educational organization described in section 170(b) (1) (A) (ii) or of a State or political subdivision of a State.

§ 1304.   Special rules

(a) **Taxpayer must choose benefits.**—This part shall apply to the taxable year only if the taxpayer chooses to have the benefits of this part for such taxable year. Such choice may be made or changed at any time before the expiration of the period prescribed for making a claim for credit or refund of the tax imposed by this chapter for the taxable year.

· · · · · ·

(c) Failure of certain married individuals to make joint return, etc.—

(1) Application of subsection.—Paragraphs (2) and (3) of this subsection shall apply in the case of any individual who was married for any base period year or the computation year; except that—

(A) such paragraphs shall not apply in respect of a base period year if—

(i) such individual and his spouse make a joint return, or such individual makes a return as a surviving spouse (as defined in section 2(b)), for the computation year, and

(ii) such individual was not married to any other spouse for such base period year, and

(B) paragraph (3) shall not apply in respect of the computation year if the individual and his spouse make a joint return for such year.

(2) Minimum base period income.—For purposes of this part, the base period income of an individual for any base period year shall not be less than 50 percent of the base period income which would result from combining his income and deductions for such year—

(A) with the income and deductions for such year of the individual who is his spouse for the computation year, or

(B) if greater, with the income and deductions for such year of the individual who was his spouse for such base period year.

(3) Community income attributable to services.—In the case of amounts which constitute earned income (within the meaning of section 911(d)(2)) and are community income under community property laws applicable to such income—

(A) the amount taken into account for any base period year for purposes of determining base period income shall not be less than the amount which would be taken into account if such amounts did not constitute community income, and

(B) the amount taken into account for purposes of determining taxable income for the computation year shall not exceed the amount which would be taken into account if such amounts did not constitute community income.

(4) Marital status.—For purposes of this subsection, section 143(a) shall apply in determining whether an individual is married for any taxable year.

(d) Dollar limitations in case of joint returns.—In the case of a joint return, the $3,000 figure contained in section 1301 shall be applied to the aggregate averagable income.

(e) Treatment of certain other items.—

(1) Section 72(m)(5) or (q)(1).—Section 72(m)(5) (relating to penalties applicable to certain amounts received by owner-employees) or section 72(q)(1) (relating to 5-percent tax on premature distributions under annuity contracts) shall be applied as if this part had not been enacted.

(2) Other items.—Except as otherwise provided in this part, the order and manner in which items of income or limitations on tax shall be taken into account in computing the tax imposed by this chapter on the income of any eligible individual to whom section 1301 applies for any computation year shall be determined under regulations prescribed by the Secretary.

(f) Short taxable years.—In the case of any computation year or base period year which is a short taxable year, this part shall be applied in the manner provided in regulations prescribed by the Secretary.

§ 1305.   Regulations

The Secretary shall prescribe such regulations as may be necessary to carry out the purposes of this part.

PART II—MITIGATION OF EFFECT OF LIMITATIONS AND OTHER PROVISIONS

§ 1311.   Correction of error

(a) General rule.—If a determination (as defined in section 1313) is described in one or more of the paragraphs of section 1312 and, on the date of the determination, correction of the effect of the error referred to in the applicable paragraph of section 1312 is prevented by the operation of any law or rule of law, other than this part and other than section 7122 (relating to compromises), then the effect of the error shall be corrected by an adjustment made in the amount and in the manner specified in section 1314.

(b) Conditions necessary for adjustment.—

(1) Maintenance of an inconsistent position.—Except in cases described in paragraphs (3) (B) and (4) of section 1312, an adjustment shall be made under this part only if—

(A) in case the amount of the adjustment would be credited or refunded in the same manner as an overpayment under section 1314, there is adopted in the determination a position maintained by the Secretary, or

(B) in case the amount of the adjustment would be assessed and collected in the same manner as a deficiency under section 1314, there is adopted in the determination a position maintained by the taxpayer with respect to whom the determination is made,

and the position maintained by the Secretary in the case described in subparagraph (A) or maintained by the taxpayer in the case described in subparagraph (B) is inconsistent with the erroneous inclusion, exclusion, omission, allowance, disallowance, recognition, or nonrecognition, as the case may be.

(2) Correction not barred at time of erroneous action.—

(A) Determination described in section 1312(3) (B).—In the case of a determination described in section 1312(3) (B) (relating to certain exclusions from income), adjustment shall be made under this part only if assessment of a deficiency for the taxable year in which the item is includible or against the related taxpayer was not barred, by any law or rule of law, at the time the Secretary first maintained, in a notice of deficiency sent pursuant to section 6212 or before the Tax Court, that the item described in section 1312(3) (B) should be included in the gross income of the taxpayer for the taxable year to which the determination relates.

(B) Determination described in section 1312(4).—In the case of a determination described in section 1312(4) (relating to disallowance of certain deductions and credits), adjustment shall be made under this part only if credit or refund of the overpayment attributable to the deduction or credit described in such section which should have been allowed to the taxpayer or related taxpayer was not barred, by any law or rule of law, at the time the taxpayer first maintained before the Secretary or before the Tax Court, in writing, that he was entitled to such deduction or credit for the taxable year to which the determination relates.

(3) Existence of relationship.—In case the amount of the adjustment would be assessed and collected in the same manner as a deficiency (except for cases described in section 1312(3) (B)), the adjustment shall not be made with respect to a related taxpayer unless he stands in such relationship to the taxpayer at the time the latter first maintains the inconsistent position in a return, claim for refund, or petition (or amended petition) to the Tax Court for the taxable year with respect to which the determination is made, or if such position is not so maintained, then at the time of the determination.

§ 1312. Circumstances of adjustment

The circumstances under which the adjustment provided in section 1311 is authorized are as follows:

(1) Double inclusion of an item of gross income.—The determination requires the inclusion in gross income of an item which was erroneously included in the gross income of the taxpayer for another taxable year or in the gross income of a related taxpayer.

(2) Double allowance of a deduction or credit.—The determination allows a deduction or credit which was erroneously allowed to the taxpayer for another taxable year or to a related taxpayer.

(3) Double exclusion of an item of gross income.—

(A) Items included in income.—The determination requires the exclusion from gross income of an item included in a return filed by the taxpayer or with respect to which tax was paid and which was erroneously excluded or omitted from the gross income of the taxpayer for another taxable year, or from the gross income of a related taxpayer; or

(B) Items not included in income.—The determination requires the exclusion from gross income of an item not included in a return filed by the taxpayer and with respect to which the tax was not paid but which is includible in the gross income of the taxpayer for another taxable year or in the gross income of a related taxpayer.

(4) Double disallowance of a deduction or credit.—The determination disallows a deduction or credit which should have been allowed to, but was not allowed to, the taxpayer for another taxable year, or to a related taxpayer.

(5) Correlative deductions and inclusions for trusts or estates and legatees, beneficiaries, or heirs.—The determination allows or disallows any of the additional deductions allowable in computing the taxable income of estates or trusts, or requires or denies any of the inclusions in the computation of taxable income of beneficiaries, heirs, or legatees, specified in subparts A to E, inclusive (secs. 641 and following, relating to estates, trusts and beneficiaries) of part I of subchapter J of this chapter, or corresponding provisions of prior internal revenue laws, and the correlative inclusion or deduction, as the case may be, has been erroneously excluded, omitted, or included, or disallowed, omitted, or allowed, as the case may be, in respect of the related taxpayer.

(6) Correlative deductions and credits for certain related corporations. —The determination allows or disallows a deduction (including a credit) in computing the taxable income (or, as the case may be, net income, normal tax net income, or surtax net income) of a corporation, and a correlative deduction or credit has been erroneously allowed, omitted, or disallowed, as the case may be, in respect of a related taxpayer described in section 1313(c) (7).

(7) Basis of property after erroneous treatment of a prior transaction.—

(A) General rule.—The determination determines the basis of property, and in respect of any transaction on which such basis depends, or in respect of any transaction which was erroneously treated as affecting such basis, there occurred, with respect to a taxpayer described in subparagraph (B) of this paragraph, any of the errors described in subparagraph (C) of this paragraph.

(B) Taxpayers with respect to whom the erroneous treatment occurred.—The taxpayer with respect to whom the erroneous treatment occurred must be—

(i) the taxpayer with respect to whom the determination is made,

(ii) a taxpayer who acquired title to the property in the transaction and from whom, mediately or immediately, the taxpayer with respect to whom the determination is made derived title, or

(iii) a taxpayer who had title to the property at the time of the transaction and from whom, mediately or immediately, the taxpayer with respect to whom the determination is made derived title, if the basis of the property in the hands of the taxpayer with respect to whom the determination is made is determined under section 1015(a) (relating to the basis of property acquired by gift).

(C) Prior erroneous treatment.—With respect to a taxpayer described in subparagraph (B) of this paragraph—

(i) there was an erroneous inclusion in, or omission from, gross income,

(ii) there was an erroneous recognition, or nonrecognition, of gain or loss, or

(iii) there was an erroneous deduction of an item properly chargeable to capital account or an erroneous charge to capital account of an item properly deductible.

§ 1313. Definitions

(a) Determination.—For purposes of this part, the term "determination" means—

(1) a decision by the Tax Court or a judgment, decree, or other order by any court of competent jurisdiction, which has become final;

(2) a closing agreement made under section 7121;

(3) a final disposition by the Secretary of a claim for refund. For purposes of this part, a claim for refund shall be deemed finally disposed of by the Secretary—

(A) as to items with respect to which the claim was allowed, on the date of allowance of refund or credit or on the date of mailing notice of disallowance (by reason of offsetting items) of the claim for refund, and

(B) as to items with respect to which the claim was disallowed, in whole or in part, or as to items applied by the Secretary in reduction of the refund or credit, on expiration of the time for instituting suit with respect thereto (unless suit is instituted before the expiration of such time); or

(4) under regulations prescribed by the Secretary, an agreement for purposes of this part, signed by the Secretary and by any person, relating to the liability of such person (or the person for whom he acts) in respect of a tax under this subtitle for any taxable period.

(b) Taxpayer.—Notwithstanding section 7701(a) (14), the term "taxpayer" means any person subject to a tax under the applicable revenue law.

(c) Related taxpayer.—For purposes of this part, the term "related taxpayer" means a taxpayer who, with the taxpayer with respect to whom a determination is made, stood, in the taxable year with respect to which the erroneous inclusion, exclusion, omission, allowance, or disallowance was made, in one of the following relationships:

(1) husband and wife,

(2) grantor and fiduciary,

(3) grantor and beneficiary,

(4) fiduciary and beneficiary, legatee, or heir,

(5) decedent and decedent's estate,

(6) partner, or

(7) member of an affiliated group of corporations (as defined in section 1504).

§ 1314.   Amount and method of adjustment

(a) Ascertainment of amount of adjustment.—In computing the amount of an adjustment under this part there shall first be ascertained the tax previously determined for the taxable year with respect to which the error was made. The amount of the tax previously determined shall be the excess of—

(1) the sum of—

(A) the amount shown as the tax by the taxpayer on his return (determined as provided in section 6211(b) (1), (3), and (4), relating to the definition of deficiency), if a return was made by the taxpayer and an amount was shown as the tax by the taxpayer thereon, plus

(B) the amounts previously assessed (or collected without assessment) as a deficiency, over—

(2) the amount of rebates, as defined in section 6211(b) (2), made.

There shall then be ascertained the increase or decrease in tax previously determined which results solely from the correct treatment of the item which was the subject of the error (with due regard given to the effect of the item in the computation of gross income, taxable income, and other matters under this subtitle). A similar computation shall be made for any other taxable year affected, or treated as affected, by a net operating loss deduction (as defined in section 172) or by a capital loss carryback or carryover (as defined in section 1212), determined with reference to the taxable year with respect to which the error was made. The amount so ascertained (together with any amounts wrongfully collected as additions to the tax or interest, as a result of such error) for each taxable year shall be the amount of the adjustment for that taxable year.

(b) Method of adjustment.—The adjustment authorized in section 1311(a) shall be made by assessing and collecting, or refunding or crediting, the amount thereof in the same manner as if it were a deficiency determined by the Secretary with respect to the taxpayer as to whom the error was made or an overpayment claimed by such taxpayer, as the case may be, for the taxable year or years with respect to which an amount is ascertained under subsection (a), and as if on the date of the determination one year remained before the expiration of the periods of limitation upon assessment or filing claim for refund for such taxable year or years. If, as a result of a determination described in section 1313(a) (4), an adjustment has been made by the assessment and collection of a deficiency or the refund or credit of an overpayment, and subsequently such determination is altered or revoked, the amount of the adjustment ascertained under subsection (a) of this section shall be redetermined on the basis of such alteration or revocation and any overpayment or deficiency resulting from such redetermination shall be refunded or credited, or assessed and collected, as the case may be, as an adjustment under this part. In the case of an adjustment resulting from an increase or decrease in a net operating loss or net capital loss which is carried back to the year of adjustment, interest shall not be collected or paid for any period prior to the close of the taxable year in which the net operating loss or net capital loss arises.

(c) Adjustment unaffected by other items.—The amount to be assessed and collected in the same manner as a deficiency, or to be refunded or credited in the same manner as an overpayment, under this part, shall not be diminished by any credit or set-off based upon any item other than the one which was the subject of the adjustment. The amount of the adjustment under this part, if paid, shall not be recovered by a claim or suit for refund or suit for erroneous refund based upon any item other than the one which was the subject of the adjustment.

. . . . .

PART V—CLAIM OF RIGHT

§ 1341. Computation of tax where taxpayer restores substantial amount held under claim of right

(a) General rule.—If—

(1) an item was included in gross income for a prior taxable year (or years) because it appeared that the taxpayer had an unrestricted right to such item;

(2) a deduction is allowable for the taxable year because it was established after the close of such prior taxable year (or years) that the taxpayer did not have an unrestricted right to such item or to a portion of such item; and

(3) the amount of such deduction exceeds $3,000,

then the tax imposed by this chapter for the taxable year shall be the lesser of the following:

(4) the tax for the taxable year computed with such deduction; or

(5) an amount equal to—

(A) the tax for the taxable year computed without such deduction, minus

(B) the decrease in tax under this chapter (or the corresponding provisions of prior revenue laws) for the prior taxable year (or years) which would result solely from the exclusion of such item (or portion thereof) from gross income for such prior taxable year (or years).

. . . . .

(b) Special rules.—

(1) If the decrease in tax ascertained under subsection (a) (5) (B) exceeds the tax imposed by this chapter for the taxable year (computed without the deduction) such excess shall be considered to be a payment of tax on the last day prescribed by law for the payment of tax for the taxable year, and shall be refunded or credited in the same manner as if it were an overpayment for such taxable year.

(2) Subsection (a) does not apply to any deduction allowable with respect to an item which was included in gross income by reason of the sale or other disposition of stock in trade of the taxpayer (or other property of a kind which would properly have been included in the inventory of the taxpayer if on hand at the close of the prior taxable year) or property held by the taxpayer primarily for sale to customers in the ordinary course of his trade or business. This paragraph shall not apply if the deduction arises out of refunds or repayments with respect to rates made by a regulated public utility (as defined in section 7701(a) (33) without regard to the limitation contained in the last two sentences thereof) if such refunds or repayments are required to be made by the Government, political subdivision, agency, or instrumentality referred to in such section, or by an order of a court, or are made in settlement of litigation or under threat or imminence of litigation.

(3) If the tax imposed by this chapter for the taxable year is the amount determined under subsection (a) (5), then the deduction referred to in subsection (a) (2) shall not be taken into account for any purpose of this subtitle other than this section.

(4) For purposes of determining whether paragraph (4) or paragraph (5) of subsection (a) applies—

(A) in any case where the deduction referred to in paragraph (4) of subsection (a) results in a net operating loss, such loss shall, for purposes of computing the tax for the taxable year under such paragraph (4), be carried back to the same extent and in the same manner as is provided under section 172; and

(B) in any case where the exclusion referred to in paragraph (5) (B) of subsection (a) results in a net operating loss or capital loss for the prior taxable year (or years), such loss shall, for purposes of computing the decrease in tax for the prior taxable year (or years) under such paragraph (5) (B), be carried back and carried over to the same extent and in the same manner as is provided under section 172 or section 1212, except that no carryover beyond the taxable year shall be taken into account.

SUBCHAPTER S—TAX TREATMENT OF S CORPORATIONS AND THEIR SHAREHOLDERS

Part
  I.   In general.
 II.   Tax treatment of shareholders.
III.   Special rules.
IV.   Definitions; miscellaneous.

PART I—IN GENERAL

§ 1361.   S corporation defined

(a) S Corporation defined.—

(1) In general.—For purposes of this title, the term "S corporation" means, with respect to any taxable year, a small business corporation for which an election under section 1362(a) is in effect for such year.

(2) C corporation.—For purposes of this title, the term "C corporation" means, with respect to any taxable year, a corporation which is not an S corporation for such year.

(b) Small business corporation.—

(1) In general.—For purposes of this subchapter, the term "small business corporation" means a domestic corporation which is not an ineligible corporation and which does not—

   (A) have more than 35 shareholders,

   (B) have as a shareholder a person (other than an estate and other than a trust described in subsection (c)(2)) who is not an individual,

   (C) have a nonresident alien as a shareholder, and

   (D) have more than 1 class of stock.

(2) Ineligible corporation defined.—For purposes of paragraph (1), the term "ineligible corporation" means any corporation which is

   (A) a member of an affiliated group (determined under section 1504 without regard to the exceptions contained in subsection (b) thereof),

   (B) a financial institution to which section 585 or 593 applies,

   (C) an insurance company subject to tax under subchapter L,

   (D) a corporation to which an election under section 936 applies, or

   (E) a DISC or former DISC.

(c) Special rules for applying subsection (b).—

(1) Husband and wife treated as 1 shareholder.—For purposes of subsection (b)(1)(A), a husband and wife (and their estates) shall be treated as 1 shareholder.

(2) Certain trusts permitted as shareholders.—

(A) In general.—For purposes of subsection (b)(1)(B), the following trusts may be shareholders:

(i) A trust all of which is treated (under subpart E of part I of subchapter J of this chapter) as owned by an individual who is a citizen or resident of the United States.

(ii) A trust which was described in clause (i) immediately before the death of the deemed owner and which continues in existence after such death, but only for the 60-day period beginning on the day of the deemed owner's death. If a trust is described in the preceding sentence and if the entire corpus of the trust is includible in the gross estate of the deemed owner, the preceding sentence shall be applied by substituting "2-year period" for "60-day period".

(iii) A trust with respect to stock transferred to it pursuant to the terms of a will, but only for the 60-day period beginning on the day on which such stock is transferred to it.

(iv) A trust created primarily to exercise the voting power of stock transferred to it.

This subparagraph shall not apply to any foreign trust.

(B) **Treatment as shareholders.**—For purposes of subsection (b)(1)—

(i) In the case of a trust described in clause (i) of subparagraph (A), the deemed owner shall be treated as the shareholder.

(ii) In the case of a trust described in clause (ii) of subparagraph (A), the estate of the deemed owner shall be treated as the shareholder.

(iii) In the case of a trust described in clause (iii) of subparagraph (A), the estate of the testator shall be treated as the shareholder.

(iv) In the case of a trust described in clause (iv) of subparagraph (A), each beneficiary of the trust shall be treated as a shareholder.

(3) Estate of individual in bankruptcy may be shareholder.—For purposes of subsection (b)(1)(B), the term "estate" includes the estate of an individual in a case under title 11 of the United States Code.

(4) Differences in common stock voting rights disregarded.—For purposes of subsection (b)(1)(D), a corporation shall not be treated as having more than 1 class of stock solely because there are differences in voting rights among the shares of common stock.

(5) Straight debt safe harbor.—

(A) **In general.**—For purposes of subsection (b)(1)(D), straight debt shall not be treated as a second class of stock.

(B) **Straight debt defined.**—For purposes of this paragraph, the term "straight debt" means any written unconditional promise to pay on demand or on a specified date a sum certain in money if—

(i) the interest rate (and interest payment dates) are not contingent on profits, the borrower's discretion, or similar factors,

    (ii) there is no convertibility (directly or indirectly) into stock, and

    (iii) the creditor is an individual (other than a nonresident alien), an estate, or a trust described in paragraph (2).

    (C) **Regulations.**—The Secretary shall prescribe such regulations as may be necessary or appropriate to provide for the proper treatment of straight debt under this subchapter and for the coordination of such treatment with other provisions of this title.

  (6) **Ownership of stock in certain inactive corporations.**—For purposes of subsection (b)(2)(A), a corporation shall not be treated as a member of an affiliated group at any time during any taxable year by reason of the ownership of stock in another corporation if such other corporation—

    (A) has not begun business at any time on or after the date of its incorporation and before the close of such taxable year, and

    (B) does not have taxable income for the period included within such taxable year.

(d) **Special rule for qualified subchapter S trust.—**

  (1) **In general.**—In the case of a qualified subchapter S trust with respect to which a beneficiary makes an election under paragraph (2)—

    (A) such trust shall be treated as a trust described in subsection (c)(2)(A)(i), and

    (B) for purposes of section 678(a), the beneficiary of such trust shall be treated as the owner of that portion of the trust which consists of stock in an S corporation with respect to which the election under paragraph (2) is made.

  (2) **Election.—**

    (A) **In general.**—A beneficiary of a qualified subchapter S trust (or his legal representative) may elect to have this subsection apply.

    (B) **Manner and time of election.—**

      (i) **Separate election with respect to each S corporation.**—An election under this paragraph shall be made separately with respect to each S corporation the stock of which is held by the trust.

      (ii) **Elections with respect to successive income beneficiaries.**—If there is an election under this paragraph with respect to any beneficiary, an election under this paragraph shall be treated as made by each successive beneficiary unless such beneficiary affirmatively refuses to consent to such election.

      (iii) **Time, manner, and form of election.**—Any election, or refusal, under this paragraph shall be made in such manner and form, and at such time, as the secretary may prescribe.

    (C) **Election irrevocable.**—An election under this paragraph, once made, may be revoked only with the consent of the Secretary.

    (D) **Grace period.**—An election under this paragraph shall be effective up to 60 days before the date of the election.

  (3) **Qualified subchapter S trust.**—For purposes of this subsection, the term "qualified subchapter S trust" means a trust—

    (A) which owns stock in 1 or more S corporations,

    (B) all of the income (within the meaning of section 643(b)) of which is distributed) (or required to be distributed) currently to 1 individual who is a citizen or resident of the United States, and

(C) the terms of which require that—

(i) during the life of the current income beneficiary there shall be only 1 income beneficiary of the trust,

(ii) any corpus distributed during the life of the current income beneficiary may be distributed only to such beneficiary,

(iii) the income interest of the current income beneficiary in the trust shall terminate on the earlier of such beneficiary's death or the termination of the trust, and

(iv) upon the termination of the trust during the life of the current income beneficiary, the trust shall distribute all of its assets to such beneficiary.

(4) Trust ceasing to be qualified.—If a qualified subchapter S trust ceases to meet any requirement under paragraph (3), the provisions of this subsection shall not apply to such trust as of the date it ceases to meet such requirements.

§ 1362. Election; revocation; termination

(a) Election.—

(1) In general.—Except as provided in subsection (g), a small business corporation may elect, in accordance with the provisions of this section, to be an S corporation.

(2) All shareholders must consent to election.—An election under this subsection shall be valid only if all persons who are shareholders in such corporation on the day on which such election is made consent to such election.

(b) When made.—

(1) In general.—An election under subsection (a) may be made by a small business corporation for any taxable year—

(A) at any time during the preceding taxable year, or

(B) at any time during the taxable year and on or before the 15th day of the 3d month of the taxable year.

(2) Certain elections made during 1st 2½ months treated as made for next taxable year.—If—

(A) an election under subsection (a) is made for any taxable year during such year and on or before the 15th day of the 3d month of such year, but

(B) either—

(i) on 1 or more days in such taxable year before the day on which the election was made the corporation did not meet the requirements of subsection (b) of section 1361, or

(ii) 1 or more of the persons who held stock in the corporation during such taxable year and before the election was made did not consent to the election,

then such election shall be treated as made for the following taxable year.

(3) Election made after 1st 2½ months treated as made for following taxable year.—If—

(A) a small business corporation makes an election under subsection (a) for any taxable year, and

(B) such election is made after the 15th day of the 3d month of the taxable year and on or before the last day of such taxable year,

then such election shall be treated as made for the following taxable year.

(c) Years for which effective.—An election under subsection (a) shall be effective for the taxable year of the corporation for which it is made and for all succeeding taxable years of the corporation, until such election is terminated under subsection (d).

(d) Termination.—

(1) By revocation.—

(A) In general.—An election under subsection (a) may be terminated by revocation.

(B) More than one-half of shares must consent to revocation.—An election may be revoked only if shareholders holding more than one-half of the shares of stock of the corporation on the day on which the revocation is made consent to the revocation.

(C) When effective.—Except as provided in subparagraph (D)—

(i) a revocation made during the taxable year and on or before the 15th day of the 3d month thereof shall be effective on the 1st day of such taxable year, and

(ii) a revocation made during the taxable year but after such 15th day shall be effective on the 1st day of the following taxable year.

(D) Revocation may specify prospective date.—If the revocation specifies a date for revocation which is on or after the day on which the revocation is made, the revocation shall be effective on and after the date so specified.

(2) By corporation ceasing to be small business corporation.—

(A) In general.—An election under subsection (a) shall be terminated whenever (at any time on or after the 1st day of the 1st taxable year for which the corporation is an S corporation) such corporation ceases to be a small business corporation.

(B) When effective.—Any termination under this paragraph shall be effective on and after the date of cessation.

(3) Where passive interest income exceeds 25 percent of gross receipts for 3 consecutive taxable years and corporation has subchapter C earnings and profits.—

(A) Termination.—

(i) **In general.**—An election under subsection (a) shall be terminated whenever the corporation.—

(I) has subchapter C earnings and profits at the close of each of 3 consecutive taxable years, and

(II) has gross receipts for each of such taxable years more than 25 percent of which are passive investment income.

(ii) **When effective.**—Any termination under this paragraph shall be effective on and after the first day of the first taxable year beginning after the third consecutive taxable year referred to in clause (1).

(iii) **Years taken into account.**—A prior taxable year shall not be taken into account under clause (i) unless—

(I) such taxable year began after December 31, 1981, and

(II) the corporation was an S corporation for such taxable year.

(B) **Subchapter C earnings and profits.**—For purposes of subparagraph (A), the term "subchapter C earnings and profits" means earnings and profits of any corporation for any taxable year with respect to which an election under section 1362(a) (or under section 1372 of prior law) was not in effect.

(C) **Gross receipts from sales of capital assets (other than stocks and securities).**—For purposes of this paragraph, in the case of dispositions of capital assets (other than stock and securities), gross receipts from such dispositions shall be taken into account only to the extent of the capital gain net income therefrom.

(D) **Passive investment income defined.**—For purposes of this paragraph—

(i) **In general.**—Except as otherwise provided in this subparagraph, the term "passive investment income" means gross receipts derived from royalties, rents, dividends, interest, annuities, and sales or exchanges of stock or securities (gross receipts from such sales or exchanges being taken into account for purposes of this paragraph only to the extent of gains therefrom).

(ii) **Exception for interest on notes from sales of inventory.**—The term "passive investment income" shall not include interest on any obligation acquired in the ordinary course of the corporation's trade or business from its sale of property described in section 1221(1).

(iii) **Treatment of certain lending or finance companies.**—If the S corporation meets the requirements of section 542(c)(6) for the taxable year, the term "passive investment income" shall not include gross receipts for the taxable year which are derived directly from the active and regular conduct of a lending or finance business (as defined in section 542(d)(1)).

(iv) **Treatment of certain liquidations.**—Gross receipts derived from sales or exchanges of stock or securities shall not include amounts received by an S corporation which are treated under section 331 (relating to corporate liquidations) as payments in exchange for stock where the S corporation owned more than 50 percent of each class of stock of the liquidating corporation.

(e) **Treatment of S termination year.**—

(1) **In general.**—In the case of an S termination year, for purposes of this title—

(A) **S short year.**—The portion of such year ending before the 1st day for which the termination is effective shall be treated as a short taxable year for which the corporation is an S corporation.

(B) **C short year.**—The portion of such year beginning on such 1st day shall be treated as a short taxable year for which the corporation is a C corporation.

(2) Pro rata allocation.—Except as provided in paragraph (3), the determination of which items are to be taken into account for each of the short taxable years referred to in paragraph (1) shall be made—

(A) first by determining for the S termination year—

(i) the amount of each of the items of income, loss, deduction, or credit described in section 1366(a)(1)(A), and

(ii) the amount of the nonseparately computed income or loss, and

(B) then by assigning an equal portion of each amount determined under subparagraph (A) to each day of the S termination year.

(3) Election to have items assigned to each short taxable year under normal tax accounting rules.—

(A) **In general.**—A corporation may elect to have paragraph (2) not apply.

(B) **All shareholders must consent to election.**—An election under this paragraph shall be valid only if all persons who are shareholders in the corporation at any time during the S termination year consent to such election.

(4) S termination year.—For purposes of this subsection, the term "S termination year" means any taxable year of a corporation (determined without regard to this subsection) in which a termination of an election made under subsection (a) takes effect (other than on the 1st day thereof).

(5) Tax for C short year determined on annualized basis.—

(A) **In general.**—The taxable income for the short year described in subparagraph (B) of paragraph (1) shall be placed on an annual basis by multiplying the taxable income for such short year by the number of days in the S termination year and by dividing the result by the number of days in the short year. The tax shall be the same part of the tax computed on the annual basis as the number of days in such short year is of the number of days in the S termination year.

(B) **Section 443(d)(2) to apply.**—Subsection (d)(2) of section 443 shall apply to the short taxable year described in subparagraph (B) of paragraph (1).

(6) Other special rules.—For purposes of this title—

(A) **Short years treated as 1 year for carryover purposes.**—The short taxable year described in subparagraph (A) of paragraph (1) shall not be taken into account for purposes of determining the number of taxable years to which any item may be carried back or carried forward by the corporation.

(B) **Due date for S year.**—The due date for filing the return for the short taxable year described in subparagraph (A) of paragraph (1) shall be the same as the due date for filing the return for the short taxable year described in subparagraph (B) of paragraph (1) (including extensions thereof).

(f) Inadvertent termination.—If—

(1) an election under subsection (a) by any corporation was terminated under paragraph (2) or (3) of subsection (d),

(2) the Secretary determines that the termination was inadvertent,

(3) no later than a reasonable period of time after discovery of the event resulting in such termination, steps were taken so that the corporation is once more a small business corporation, and

(4) the corporation, and each person who was a shareholder of the corporation at any time during the period specified pursuant to this subsection, agrees to make such adjustments (consistent with the treatment of the corporation as an S corporation) as may be required by the Secretary with respect to such period,

then, notwithstanding the terminating event, such corporation shall be treated as continuing to be an S corporation during the period specified by the Secretary.

(g) Election after termination.—If a small business corporation has made an election under subsection (a) and if such election has been terminated under subsection (d), such corporation (and any successor corporation) shall not be eligible to make an election under subsection (a) for any taxable year before its 5th taxable year which begins after the 1st taxable year for which such termination is effective, unless the Secretary consents to such election.

§ 1363.   Effect of election on corporation

(a) General rule.—Except as otherwise provided in this subchapter and in section 58(d), an S corporation shall not be subject to the taxes imposed by this chapter.

(b) Computation of corporation's taxable income.—The taxable income of an S corporation shall be computed in the same manner as in the case of an individual, except that—

(1) the items described in section 1366(a)(1)(A) shall be separately stated,

(2) the deductions referred to in section 703(a)(2) shall not be allowed to the corporation, and

(3) section 248 shall apply.

(c) Elections of the S corporation.—

(1) In general.—Except as provided in paragraph (2), any election affecting the computation of items derived from an S corporation shall be made by the corporation.

(2) Exceptions.—In the case of an S corporation, elections under the following provisions shall be made by each shareholder separately—

(A) subsection (b)(5) or (d)(4) of section 108 (relating to income from discharge of indebtedness),

(B) section 163(d) (relating to limitation on interest on investment indebtedness),

(C) section 617 (relating to deduction and recapture of certain mining exploration expenditures), and

(D) section 901 (relating to taxes of foreign countries and possessions of the United States).

(d) Distributions of Appreciated Property.—If—

(1) an S corporation makes a distribution of property (other than an obligation of such corporation) with respect to its stock, and

(2) the fair market value of such property exceeds its adjusted basis in the hands of the S corporation,

then, notwithstanding any other provision of this subtitle, gain shall be recognized to the S corporation on the distribution in the same manner as if it had sold such property to the distributee at its fair market value.

PART II—TAX TREATMENT OF SHAREHOLDERS

§ 1366.   Pass-thru of items to shareholders

(a) **Determination of shareholder's tax liability.—**

(1) **In general.**—In determining the tax under this chapter of a shareholder for the shareholder's taxable year in which the taxable year of the S corporation ends (or for the final taxable year of a shareholder who dies before the end of the corporation's taxable year), there shall be taken into account the shareholder's pro rata share of the corporation's—

(A) items of income (including tax-exempt income), loss, deduction, or credit the separate treatment of which could affect the liability for tax of any shareholder, and

(B) nonseparately computed income or loss.

For purposes of the preceding sentence, the items referred to in subparagraph (A) shall include amounts described in paragraph (4) or (6) of section 702(a).

(2) **Nonseparately computed income or loss defined.**—For purposes of this subchapter, the term "nonseparately computed income or loss" means gross income minus the deductions allowed to the corporation under this chapter, determined by excluding all items described in paragraph (1)(A).

(b) **Character passed thru.**—The character of any item included in a shareholder's pro rata share under paragraph (1) of subsection (a) shall be determined as if such item were realized directly from the source from which realized by the corporation, or incurred in the same manner as incurred by the corporation.

(c) **Gross income of a shareholder.**—In any case where it is necessary to determine the gross income of a shareholder for purposes of this title, such gross income shall include the shareholder's pro rata share of the gross income of the corporation.

(d) **Special rules for losses and deductions.—**

(1) **Cannot exceed shareholder's basis in stock and debt.**—The aggregate amount of losses and deductions taken into account by a shareholder under subsection (a) for any taxable year shall not exceed the sum of—

(A) the adjusted basis of the shareholder's stock in the S corporation (determined with regard to paragraph (1) of section 1367(a) for the taxable year), and

(B) the shareholder's adjusted basis of any indebtedness of the S corporation to the shareholder (determined without regard to any adjustment under paragraph (2) of section 1367(b) for the taxable year).

(2) **Indefinite carryover of disallowed losses and deductions.**—Any loss or deduction which is disallowed for any taxable year by reason of paragraph (1) shall be treated as incurred by the corporation in the succeeding taxable year with respect to that shareholder.

(3) **Carryover of disallowed losses and deductions to post-termination transition period.—**

(A) **In general.**—If for the last taxable year of a corporation for which it was an S corporation a loss or deduction was disallowed by reason of paragraph (1), such loss or deduction shall be treated as incurred by the shareholder on the last day of any post-termination transition period.

(B) Cannot exceed shareholder's basis in stock.—The aggregate amount of losses and deductions taken into account by a shareholder under subparagraph (A) shall not exceed the adjusted basis of the shareholder's stock in the corporation (determined at the close of the last day of the post-termination transition period and without regard to this paragraph).

(C) Adjustment in basis of stock.—The shareholder's basis in the stock of the corporation shall be reduced by the amount allowed as a deduction by reason of this paragraph.

(e) Treatment of family group.—If an individual who is a member of the family (within the meaning of section 704(e)(3)) of one or more shareholders of an S corporation renders services for the corporation or furnishes capital to the corporation without receiving reasonable compensation therefor, the Secretary shall make such adjustments in the items taken into account by such individual and such shareholders as may be necessary in order to reflect the value of such services or capital.

(f) Special rules.—

(1) Subsection (a) not to apply to credit allowable under section 39.—Subsection (a) shall not apply with respect to any credit allowable under section 39 (relating to certain uses of gasoline, special fuels, and lubricating oil).

(2) Reduction in pass-thru for tax imposed on capital gain.—If any tax is imposed under section 56 or 1374 for any taxable year on an S corporation, for purposes of subsection (a)—

(A) the amount of the corporation's long-term capital gains for the taxable year shall be reduced by the amount of such tax, and

(B) if the amount of such tax exceeds the amount of such long-term capital gains, the corporation's gains from sales or exchanges of property described in section 1231 shall be reduced by the amount of such excess.

For purposes of the preceding sentence, the term "long-term capital gain" shall not include any gain from the sale or exchange of property described in section 1231.

(3) Reduction in pass-thru for tax imposed on excess net passive income.—If any tax is imposed under section 1375 for any taxable year on an S corporation, for purposes of subsection (a), each item of passive investment income shall be reduced by an amount which bears the same ratio to the amount of such tax as—

(A) the amount of such item, bears to

(B) the total passive investment income for the taxable year.

§ 1367.   Adjustments to basis of stock of shareholders, etc.

(a) **General rule.—**

(1) **Increases in basis.—**The basis of each shareholder's stock in an S corporation shall be increased for any period by the sum of the following items determined with respect to that shareholder for such period:

(A) the items of income described in subparagraph (A) of section 1366(a)(1),

(B) any nonseparately computed income determined under subparagraph (B) of section 1366(a)(1), and

(C) the excess of the deductions for depletion over the basis of the property subject to depletion.

(2) **Decreases in basis.—**The basis of each shareholder's stock in an S corporation shall be decreased for any period (but not below zero) by the sum of the following items determined with respect to the shareholder for such period:

(A) distributions by the corporation which were not includible in the income of the shareholder by reason of section 1368,

(B) the items of loss and deduction described in subparagraph (A) of section 1366(a)(1),

(C) any nonseparately computed loss determined under subparagraph (B) of section 1366(a)(1),

(D) any expense of the corporation not deductible in computing its taxable income and not properly chargeable to capital account, and

(E) the amount of the shareholder's deduction for depletion under section 611 with respect to oil and gas wells.

(b) **Special rules.—**

(1) **Income items.—**An amount which is required to be included in the gross income of a shareholder and shown on his return shall be taken into account under subparagraph (A) or (B) of subsection (a)(1) only to the extent such amount is included in the shareholder's gross income on his return, increased or decreased by any adjustment of such amount in a redetermination of the shareholder's tax liability.

(2) **Adjustments in basis of indebtedness.—**

(A) **Reduction of basis.—**If for any taxable year the amounts specified in subparagraphs (B), (C), (D), and (E) of subsection (a)(2) exceed the amount which reduces the shareholder's basis to zero, such excess shall be applied to reduce (but not below zero) the shareholder's basis in any indebtedness of the S corporation to the shareholder.

(B) **Restoration of basis.—**If for any taxable year there is a reduction under subparagraph (A) in the shareholder's basis in the indebtedness of an S corporation to a shareholder, any net increase (after the application of paragraphs (1) and (2) of subsection (a)) for any subsequent taxable year shall be applied to restore such reduction in basis before any of it may be used to increase the shareholder's basis in the stock of the S corporation.

(3) **Coordination with section 165(g).—**This section and section 1366 shall be applied before the application of section 165(g) to any taxable year of the shareholder or the corporation in which the stock becomes worthless.

§ 1368.   Distributions

(a) General rule.—A distribution of property made by an S corporation with respect to its stock to which (but for this subsection) section 301(c) would apply shall be treated in the manner provided in subsection (b) or (c), whichever applies.

(b) S corporation having no earnings and profits.—In the case of a distribution described in subsection (a) by an S corporation which has no accumulated earnings and profits—

    (1) Amount applied against basis.—The distribution shall not be included in gross income to the extent that it does not exceed the adjusted basis of the stock.

    (2) Amount in excess of basis.—If the amount of the distribution exceeds the adjusted basis of the stock, such excess shall be treated as gain from the sale or exchange of property.

(c) S corporation having earnings and profits.—In the case of a distribution described in subsection (a) by an S corporation which has accumulated earnings and profits—

    (1) Accumulated adjustments account.—That portion of the distribution which does not exceed the accumulated adjustments account shall be treated in the manner provided by subsection (b).

    (2) Dividend.—That portion of the distribution which remains after the application of paragraph (1) shall be treated as a dividend to the extent it does not exceed the accumulated earnings and profits of the S corporation.

    (3) Treatment of remainder.—Any portion of the distribution remaining after the application of paragraph (2) of this subsection shall be treated in the manner provided by subsection (b).

(d) Certain adjustments taken into account.—Subsections (b) and (c) shall be applied by taking into account (to the extent proper)—

    (1) the adjustments to the basis of the shareholder's stock described in section 1367, and

    (2) the adjustments to the accumulated adjustments account which are required by subsection (e)(1).

(e) Definitions and special rules.—For purposes of this section—

    (1) Accumulated adjustments account.—

        (A) In general.—Except as provided in subparagraph (B), the term "accumulated adjustments account" means an account of the S corporation which is adjusted for the S period in a manner similar to the adjustments under section 1367 (except that no adjustment shall be made for income which is exempt from tax under this title and no adjustment shall be made for any expense not deductible in computing the corporation's taxable income and not properly chargeable to capital account).

        (B) Amount of adjustment in the case of redemptions.—In the case of any redemption which is treated as an exchange under section 302(a) or 303(a), the adjustment in the accumulated adjustments account shall be an amount which bears the same ratio to the balance in such account as the number of shares redeemed in such redemption bears to the number of shares of stock in the corporation immediately before such redemption.

(2) S period.—The term "S period" means the most recent continuous period during which the corporation has been an S corporation. Such period shall not include any taxable year beginning before January 1, 1983.

PART III—SPECIAL RULES

§ 1371.   Coordination with subchapter C

(a) Application of subchapter C rules.—

(1) In general.—Except as otherwise provided in this title, and except to the extent inconsistent with this subchapter, subchapter C shall apply to an S corporation and its shareholders.

(2) S corporation as shareholder treated like individual.—For purposes of subchapter C, an S corporation in its capacity as a shareholder of another corporation shall be treated as an individual.

(b) No carryover between C year and S year.—

(1) From C year to S year.—No carryforward, and no carryback, arising for a taxable year for which a corporation is a C corporation may be carried to a taxable year for which such corporation is an S corporation.

(2) No carryover from S year.—No carryforward, and no carryback, shall arise at the corporate level for a taxable year for which a corporation is an S corporation.

(3) Treatment of S year as elapsed year.—Nothing in paragraphs (1) and (2) shall prevent treating a taxable year for which a corporation is an S corporation as a taxable year for purposes of determining the number of taxable years to which an item may be carried back or carried forward.

(c) Earning and profits.—

(1) In general.—Except as provided in paragraphs (2) and (3), no adjustments shall be made to the earnings and profits of an S corporation.

(2) Adjustment for redemptions, liquidations, reorganizations, divisions, etc.—In the case of any transaction involving the application of subchapter C to any S corporation, proper adjustment to any accumulated earnings and profits of the corporation shall be made.

(3) Adjustments in case of distributions treated as dividends under section 1368(c)(2).—Paragraph (1) shall not apply with respect to that portion of a distribution which is treated as a dividend number under section 1368(c)(2).

(d) Coordination with investment credit recapture.—

(1) No recapture by reason of election.—Any election under section 1362 shall be treated as a mere change in the form of conducting a trade or business for purposes of the second sentence of section 47(b).

(2) Corporation continues to be liable.—Notwithstanding an election under section 1362, an S corporation shall continue to be liable for any increase in tax under section 47 attributable to credits allowed for taxable years for which such corporation was not an S corporation.

(e) Cash distributions during post-termination transition period.—Any distribution of money by a corporation with respect to its stock during a post-termination transition period shall be applied against and reduce the adjusted basis of the stock, to the extent that the amount of the distribution does not exceed the accumulated adjustments account.

§ 1372. Partnership rules to apply for fringe benefit purposes

(a) General rule.—For purposes of applying the provisions of this subtitle which relate to employee fringe benefits—

(1) the S corporation shall be treated as a partnership, and

(2) any 2-percent shareholder of the S corporation shall be treated as a partner of such partnership.

(b) 2-Percent shareholder defined.—For purposes of this section, the term "2-percent shareholder" means any person who owns (or is considered as owning within the meaning of section 318) on any day during the taxable year of the S corporation more than 2 percent of the outstanding stock of such corporation or stock possessing more than 2 percent of the total combined voting power of all stock of such corporation.

§ 1373. Foreign income

(a) S corporation treated as partnership, etc.—For purposes of subparts A and F of part III, and part V, of subchapter N (relating to income from sources without the United States)—

(1) an S corporation shall be treated as a partnership, and

(2) the shareholders of such corporation shall be treated as partners of such partnership.

(b) Recapture of overall foreign loss.—For purposes of section 904(f) (relating to recapture of overall foreign loss), the making or termination of an election to be treated as an S corporation shall be treated as a disposition of the business.

§ 1374. Tax imposed on certain capital gains

(a) General rule.—If for a taxable year of an S corporation—

(1) the net capital gain of such corporation exceeds $25,000, and exceeds 50 percent of its taxable income for such year, and

(2) the taxable income of such corporation for such year exceeds $25,000,

there is hereby imposed a tax (computed under subsection (b)) on the income of such corporation.

(b) Amount of tax.—The tax imposed by subsection (a) shall be the lower of—

(1) an amount equal to the tax, determined as provided in section 1201(a), on the amount by which the net capital gain of the corporation for the taxable year exceeds $25,000, or

(2) an amount equal to the tax which would be imposed by section 11 on the taxable income of the corporation for the taxable year if the corporation were not an S corporation.

No credit shall be allowable under part IV of subchapter A of this chapter (other than under section 39) against the tax imposed by subsection (a).

(c) Exceptions.—

(1) **In general.**—Subsection (a) shall not apply to an S corporation for any taxable year if the election under section 1362(a) which is in effect with respect to such corporation for such taxable year has been in effect for the 3 immediately preceding taxable years.

(2) **New corporations.**—Subsection (a) shall not apply to an S corporation if—

    (A) it (and any predecessor corporation) has been in existence for less than 4 taxable years, and

    (B) an election under section 1362(a) has been in effect with respect to such corporation for each of its taxable years.

(3) **Property with substituted basis.**—If—

    (A) but for paragraph (1) or (2), subsection (a) would apply for the taxable year,

    (B) any long-term capital gain is attributable to property acquired by the S corporation during the period beginning 3 years before the first day of the taxable year and ending on the last day of the taxable year, and

    (C) the basis of such property is determined in whole or in part by reference to the basis of any property in the hands of another corporation which was not an S corporation throughout all of the period described in subparagraph (B) before the transfer by such other corporation and during which such other corporation was in existence,

then subsection (a) shall apply for the taxable year, but the amount of the tax determined under subsection (b) shall not exceed a tax, determined as provided in section 1201(a), on the net capital gain attributable to property acquired as provided in subparagraph (B) and having a basis described in subparagraph (C).

(d) **Determination of taxable income.**—For purposes of subsections (a)(2) and (b)(2), taxable income of the corporation shall be determined under section 63(a) without regard to—

    (1) the deduction allowed by section 172 (relating to net operating loss deduction), and

    (2) the deductions allowed by part VIII of subchapter B (other than the deduction allowed by section 248, relating to organization expenditures).

§ 1375. Tax imposed when passive investment income of corporation having subchapter C earnings and profits exceeds 25 percent of gross receipts

(a) **General rule.**—If for the taxable year an S corporation has—

    (1) subchapter C earnings and profits at the close of such taxable year, and

    (2) gross receipts more than 25 percent of which are passive investment income, then there is hereby imposed a tax on the income of such corporation for such taxable year. Such tax shall be computed by multiplying the excess net passive income by the highest rate of tax specified in section 11(b).

(b) **Definitions.**—For purposes of this section—

(1) **Excess net passive income.**—

    (A) **In general.**—Except as provided in subparagraph (B), the term "excess net passive income" means an amount which bears the same ratio to the net passive income for the taxable year as—

        (i) the amount by which the passive investment income for the taxable year exceeds 25 percent of the gross receipts for the taxable year, bears to

        (ii) the passive investment income for the taxable year.

(B) Limitation.—The amount of the excess net passive income for any taxable year shall not exceed the corporation's taxable income for the taxable year (determined in accordance with section 1374(d)).

(2) Net passive income.—The term "net passive income" means—

(A) passive investment income, reduced by

(B) the deductions allowable under this chapter which are directly connected with the production of such income (other than deductions allowable under section 172 and part VIII of subchapter B).

(3) Passive investment income, etc.—The terms "subchapter C earnings and profits", "passive investment income", and "gross receipts" shall have the same respective meanings as when used in paragraph (3) of section 1362(d).

(c) Special rules.—

(1) Disallowance of credit.—No credit shall be allowed under part IV of subchapter A of this chapter (other than section 39) against the tax imposed by subsection (a).

(2) Coordination with section 1374.—If any gain—

(A) is taken into account in determining passive income for purposes of this section, and

(B) is taken into account under section 1374, the amount of such gain taken into account under section 1374 shall be reduced by the portion of the excess net passive income for the taxable year which is attributable (on a pro rata basis) to such gain.

PART IV—DEFINITIONS; MISCELLANEOUS

§ 1377.   Definitions and special rule

(a) Pro rata share.—For purposes of this subchapter—

(1) In general.—Except as provided in paragraph (2), each shareholder's pro rata share of any item for any taxable year shall be the sum of the amounts determined with respect to the shareholder—

(A) by assigning an equal portion of such item to each day of the taxable year, and

(B) then by dividing that portion pro rata among the shares outstanding on such day.

(2) Election to terminate year.—Under regulations prescribed by the Secretary, if any shareholder terminates his interest in the corporation during the taxable year and all persons who are shareholders during the taxable year agree to the application of this paragraph, paragraph (1) shall be applied as if the taxable year consisted of 2 taxable years the first of which ends on the date of the termination.

(b) Post-termination transition period.—

(1) In general.—For purposes of this subchapter, the term "post-termination transition period" means—

(A) the period beginning on the day after the last day of the corporation's last taxable year as an S corporation and ending on the later of—

(i) the day which is 1 year after such last day, or

(ii) the due date for filing the return for such last year as an S corporation (including extensions), and

(B) the 120-day period beginning on the date of a determination that the corporation's election under section 1362(a) had terminated for a previous taxable year.

(2) **Determination defined.**—For purposes of paragraph (1), the term "determination" means—

(A) a court decision which becomes final,

(B) a closing agreement, or

(C) an agreement between the corporation and the Secretary that the corporation failed to qualify as an S corporation.

(c) **Manner of making elections, etc.**—Any election under this subchapter, and any revocation under section 1362(d)(1), shall be made in such manner as the Secretary shall by regulations prescribe.

§ 1378.   Taxable year of S corporation

(a) **General rule.**—For purposes of this subtitle—

(1) an S corporation shall not change its taxable year to any accounting period other than a permitted year, and

(2) no corporation may make an election under section 1362(a) for any taxable year unless such taxable year is a permitted year.

(b) **Permitted year defined.**—For purposes of this section, the term "permitted year" means a taxable year which—

(1) is a year ending December 31, or

(2) is any other accounting period for which the corporation establishes a business purpose to the satisfaction of the Secretary.

(c) **Existing S corporations required to use permitted year after 50-percent shift in ownership.**—

(1) **In general.**—A corporation which is an S corporation for a taxable year which includes December 31, 1982, shall not be treated as an S corporation for any subsequent taxable year beginning after the first day on which more than 50 percent of the stock is newly owned stock unless such subsequent taxable year is a permitted year.

(2) **Newly owned stock.**—For purposes of paragraph (1), the stock held by any person on any day shall be treated as newly owned stock to the extent that—

(A) the percentage of the stock of such corporation owned by such person on such day, exceeds

(B) the percentage of the stock of such corporation owned by such person on December 31, 1982.

(3) **Stock acquired by reason of death, gift from family member, etc.**—

(A) **In general.**—For purposes of paragraph (2), if—

(i) a person acquired stock in the corporation after December 31, 1982, and

(ii) such stock was acquired by such person—

(I) by reason of the death of a qualified transferor,

(II) by reason of a gift from a qualified transferor who is a member of such person's family, or

(III) by reason of a qualified buy-sell agreement from a qualified transferor (or his estate) who was a member of such person's family,

then such stock shall be treated as held on December 31, 1982, by the person described in clause (j).

(B) **Qualified transferor.**—For purposes of subparagraph (A), the term "qualified transferor" means a person—

(i) who held the stock in the corporation (or predecessor stock) on December 31, 1982, or

(ii) who acquired the stock in an acquisition which meets the requirements of subparagraph (A).

(C) **Family.**—For purposes of subparagraph (A), the term "family" has the meaning given such term by section 267(c)(4).

(D) **Qualified buy-sell agreement.**—For purposes of subparagraph (A), the term "qualified buy-sell agreement" means any agreement which—

(i) has been continuously in existence since September 28, 1982, and

(ii) provides that on the death of any party to such agreement, the stock in the S corporation held by such party will be sold to surviving parties to such agreement who were parties to such agreement on September 28, 1982.

§ 1379.   Transitional rules on enactment

(a) **Old elections.**—Any election made under section 1372(a) (as in effect before the enactment of the Subchapter S Revision Act of 1982) shall be treated as an election made under section 1362.

(b) **References to prior law included.**—In applying this subchapter to any taxable year beginning after December 31, 1982, any reference in this subchapter to another provision of this subchapter shall, to the extent not inconsistent with the purposes of this subchapter, include a reference to the corresponding provision as in effect before the enactment of the Subchapter S Revision Act of 1982.

(c) **Distributions of undistributed taxable income.**—If a corporation was an electing small business corporation for the last preenactment year, subsections (f) and (d) of section 1375 (as in effect before the enactment of the Subchapter S Revision Act of 1982) shall continue to apply with respect to distributions of undistributed taxable income for any taxable year beginning before January 1, 1983.

(d) **Carryforwards.**—If a corporation was an electing small business corporation for the last preenactment year and is an S corporation for the 1st postenactment year, any carryforward to the 1st postenactment year which arose in a taxable year for which the corporation was an electing small business corporation shall be treated as arising in the 1st postenactment year.

(e) **Preenactment and postenactment years defined.**—For purposes of this subsection—

(1) **Last preenactment year.**—The term "last preenactment year" means the last taxable year of a corporation which begins before January 1, 1983.

(2) **1st postenactment year.**—The term "1st postenactment year" means the 1st taxable year of a corporation which begins after December 31, 1982.

(a) **Carryover of amounts deductible.**—No amount deductible shall be carried forward under the second sentence of section 404(a)(3)(A) (relating to limits on deductible contributions under stock bonus and profit-sharing trusts) to a taxable year of a corporation with respect to which it is not an electing small business corporation from a taxable year (beginning after December 31, 1970) with respect to which it is an electing small business corporation.

(b) **Shareholder-employee.**—For purposes of this section, the term "shareholder-employee" means an employee or officer of an electing small business corporation who owns (or is considered as owning within the meaning of section 318(a)(1)), on any day during the taxable year of such corporation, more than 5 percent of the outstanding stock of the corporation.

CHAPTER 5—TAX ON TRANSFERS TO AVOID INCOME TAX

§ 1491.   Imposition of tax

There is hereby imposed on the transfer of property by a citizen or resident of the United States, or by a domestic corporation or partnership, or by a [1] estate or trust which is not a foreign estate or trust, to a foreign corporation as paid-in surplus or as a contribution to capital, or to a foreign estate or trust, or to a foreign partnership, an excise tax equal to 35 percent of the excess of—

(1) the fair market value of the properties so transferred, over

(2) the sum of—

    (A) the adjusted basis (for determining gain) of such property in the hands of the transferor, plus

    (B) the amount of the gain recognized to the transferor at the time of the transfer.

1 So in original.

§ 1492.   Nontaxable transfers

The tax imposed by section 1491 shall not apply—

(1) If the transferee is an organization exempt from income tax under part I of subchapter F of chapter 1 (other than an organization described in section 401(a)); or

(2) If before the transfer it has been established to the satisfaction of the Secretary that such transfer is not in pursuance of a plan having as one of its principal purposes the avoidance of Federal income taxes; or

(3) To a transfer described in section 367; or

(4) To a transfer for which an election has been made under section 1057.

§ 1494.   Payment and collection

(a) **Time for payment.**—The tax imposed by section 1491 shall, without assessment or notice and demand, be due and payable by the transferor at the time of the transfer, and shall be assessed, collected, and paid under regulations prescribed by the Secretary.

(b) **Abatement or refund.**—Under regulations prescribed by the Secretary, the tax may be abated, remitted, or refunded if after the transfer it has been established to the satisfaction of the Secretary that such transfer was not in pursuance of a plan having as one of its principal purposes the avoidance of Federal income taxes.

CHAPTER 6—CONSOLIDATED RETURNS

Subchapter
  A. Returns and payment of tax.
  B. Related rules.

SUBCHAPTER A—RETURNS AND PAYMENT OF TAX

§ 1501. Privilege to file consolidated returns

An affiliated group of corporations shall, subject to the provisions of this chapter, have the privilege of making a consolidated return with respect to the income tax imposed by chapter 1 for the taxable year in lieu of separate returns. The making of a consolidated return shall be upon the condition that all corporations which at any time during the taxable year have been members of the affiliated group consent to all the consolidated return regulations prescribed under section 1502 prior to the last day prescribed by law for the filing of such return. The making of a consolidated return shall be considered as such consent. In the case of a corporation which is a member of the affiliated group for a fractional part of the year, the consolidated return shall include the income of such corporation for such part of the year as it is a member of the affiliated group.

§ 1502. Regulations

The Secretary shall prescribe such regulations as he may deem necessary in order that the tax liability of any affiliated group of corporations making a consolidated return and of each corporation in the group, both during and after the period of affiliation, may be returned, determined, computed, assessed, collected, and adjusted, in such manner as clearly to reflect the income-tax liability and the various factors necessary for the determination of such liability, and in order to prevent avoidance of such tax liability.

§ 1503. Computation and payment of tax

[(a) General rule.—]In any case in which a consolidated return is made or is required to be made, the tax shall be determined, computed, assessed, collected, and adjusted in accordance with the regulations under section 1502 prescribed before the last day prescribed by law for the filing of such return.

. . . .

§ 1504. Definitions

(a) Definition of "affiliated group".—As used in this chapter, the term "affiliated group" means one or more chains of includible corporations connected through stock ownership with a common parent corporation which is an includible corporation if—

　　(1) Stock possessing at least 80 percent of the voting power of all classes of stock and at least 80 percent of each class of the nonvoting stock of each of the includible corporations (except the common parent corporation) is owned directly by one or more of the other includible corporations; and

(2) The common parent corporation owns directly stock possessing at least 80 percent of the voting power of all classes of stock and at least 80 percent of each class of the nonvoting stock of at least one of the other includible corporations.

As used in this subsection, the term "stock" does not include nonvoting stock which is limited and preferred as to dividends, employer securities (within the meaning of section 409A(*l*)) while such securities are held under a tax credit employee stock ownership plan, or qualifying employer securities (within the meaning of section 4975(e) (8)) while such securities are held under a [1] employee stock ownership plan which meets the requirements of section 4975(e) (7).

. . . .

---

1 So in original. Probably should be "an".

§ 1505. Cross references

(1) For suspension of running of statute of limitations when notice in respect of a deficiency is mailed to one corporation, see section 6503(a) (1).

(2) For allocation of income and deductions of related trades or businesses, see section 482.

SUBCHAPTER B—RELATED RULES

Part
  I. In general.
  II. Certain controlled corporations.

PART I—IN GENERAL

§ 1551. Disallowance of the benefits of the graduated corporate rates and accumulated earnings credit

(a) In general.—If—

(1) any corporation transfers, on or after January 1, 1951, and on or before June 12, 1963, all or part of its property (other than money) to a transferee corporation,

(2) any corporation transfers, directly or indirectly, after June 12, 1963, all or part of its property (other than money) to a transferee corporation, or

(3) five or fewer individuals who are in control of a corporation transfer, directly or indirectly, after June 12, 1963, property (other than money) to a transferee corporation,

and the transferee corporation was created for the purpose of acquiring such property or was not actively engaged in business at the time of such acquisition, and if after such transfer the transferor or transferors are in control of such transferee corporation during any part of the taxable year of such transferee corporation, then for such taxable year of such transferee corporation the Secretary may (except as may be otherwise determined under subsection (c)) disallow the benefits of the rates contained in section 11(b) which are lower than the highest rate specified in such section, or the accumulated earnings credit provided in paragraph (2) or (3) of section 535(c), unless such transferee corporation shall establish by the clear preponderance of the evidence that the securing of such benefits or credit was not a major purpose of such transfer.

(b) Control.—For purposes of subsection (a), the term "control" means—

(1) With respect to a transferee corporation described in subsection (a) (1) or (2), the ownership by the transferor corporation, its shareholders, or both, of stock possessing at least 80 percent of the total combined voting power of all classes of stock entitled to vote or at least 80 percent of the total value of shares of all classes of the stock; or

(2) With respect to each corporation described in subsection (a) (3), the ownership by the five or fewer individuals described in such subsection of stock possessing—

(A) at least 80 percent of the total combined voting power of all classes of stock entitled to vote or at least 80 percent of the total value of shares of all classes of the stock of each corporation, and

(B) more than 50 percent of the total combined voting power of all classes of stock entitled to vote or more than 50 percent of the total value of shares of all classes of stock of each corporation, taking into account the stock ownership of each such individual only to the extent such stock ownership is identical with respect to each such corporation.

For purposes of this subsection, section 1563(e) shall apply in determining the ownership of stock.

(c) Authority of the Secretary under this section.—The provisions of section 269(b), and the authority of the Secretary under such section, shall, to the extent not inconsistent with the provisions of this section, be applicable to this section.

§ 1552. Earnings and profits

(a) General rule.—Pursuant to regulations prescribed by the Secretary the earnings and profits of each member of an affiliated group required to be included in a consolidated return for such group filed for a taxable year shall be determined by allocating the tax liability of the group for such year among the members of the group in accord with whichever of the following methods the group shall elect in its first consolidated return filed for such a taxable year:

(1) The tax liability shall be apportioned among the members of the group in accordance with the ratio which that portion of the consolidated taxable income attributable to each member of the group having taxable income bears to the consolidated taxable income.

(2) The tax liability of the group shall be allocated to the several members of the group on the basis of the percentage of the total tax which the tax of such member if computed on a separate return would bear to the total amount of the taxes for all members of the group so computed.

(3) The tax liability of the group (excluding the tax increases arising from the consolidation) shall be allocated on the basis of the contribution of each member of the group to the consolidated taxable income of the group. Any tax increases arising from the consolidation shall be distributed to the several members in direct proportion to the reduction in tax liability resulting to such members from the filing of the consolidated return as measured by the difference between their tax liabilities determined on a separate return basis and their tax liabilities based on their contributions to the consolidated taxable income.

(4) The tax liability of the group shall be allocated in accord with any other method selected by the group with the approval of the Secretary.

(b) Failure to elect.—If no election is made in such first return, the tax liability shall be allocated among the several members of the group pursuant to the method prescribed in subsection (a) (1).

PART II—CERTAIN CONTROLLED CORPORATIONS

§ 1561.   Limitations on certain multiple tax benefits in the case of certain controlled corporations

(a) General rule.—The component members of a controlled group of corporations on a December 31 shall, for their taxable years which include such December 31, be limited for purposes of this subtitle to—

(1) amounts in each taxable income bracket in the tax table in section 11(b) which do not aggregate more than the maximum amount in such bracket to which a corporation which is not a component member of a controlled group is entitled,

(2) one $250,000 ($150,000 if any component member is a corporation described in section 535(c) (2) (B)) amount for purposes of computing the accumulated earnings credit under section 535(c) (2) and (3), and

. . . . .

The amounts specified in paragraph (1) shall be divided equally among the component members of such group on such December 31 unless all of such component members consent (at such time and in such manner as the Secretary shall by regulations prescribe) to an apportionment plan providing for an unequal allocation of such amounts. The amounts specified in paragraphs (2), (3), and (4) shall be divided equally among the component members of such group on such December 31 unless the Secretary prescribes regulations permitting an unequal allocation of such amounts.

(b) Certain short taxable years.—If a corporation has a short taxable year which does not include a December 31 and is a component member of a controlled group of corporations with respect to such taxable year, then for purposes of this subtitle—

(1) the amount in each taxable income bracket in the tax table in section 11(b),

(2) the amount to be used in computing the accumulated earnings credit under section 535(c) (2) and (3), and

. . . . .

of such corporation for such taxable year shall be the amount specified in subsection (a)(1), (2), (3), or (4), as the case may be, divided by the number of corporations which are component members of such group on the last day of such taxable year. For purposes of the preceding sentence, section 1563(b) shall be applied as if such last day were substituted for December 31.

§ 1563.   Definitions and special rules

(a) Controlled group of corporations.—For purposes of this part, the term "controlled group of corporations" means any group of—

(1) Parent-subsidiary controlled group.—One or more chains of corporations connected through stock ownership with a common parent corporation if—

(A) stock possessing at least 80 percent of the total combined voting power of all classes of stock entitled to vote or at least 80 percent of the total value of shares of all classes of stock of each of the corporations, except the common parent corporation, is owned (within the meaning of subsection (d) (1)) by one or more of the other corporations; and

(B) the common parent corporation owns (within the meaning of subsection (d) (1)) stock possessing at least 80 percent of the total combined voting power of all classes of stock entitled to vote or at least 80 percent of the total value of shares of all classes of stock of at least one of the other corporations, excluding, in computing such voting power or value, stock owned directly by such other corporations.

(2) Brother-sister controlled group.—Two or more corporations if 5 or fewer persons who are individuals, estates, or trusts own (within the meaning of subsection (d) (2)) stock possessing—

(A) at least 80 percent of the total combined voting power of all classes of stock entitled to vote or at least 80 percent of the total value of shares of all classes of the stock of each corporation, and

(B) more than 50 percent of the total combined voting power of all classes of stock entitled to vote or more than 50 percent of the total value of shares of all classes of stock of each corporation, taking into account the stock ownership of each such person only to the extent such stock ownership is identical with respect to each such corporation.

(3) Combined group.—Three or more corporations each of which is a member of a group of corporations described in paragraph (1) or (2), and one of which—

(A) is a common parent corporation included in a group of corporations described in paragraph (1), and also

(B) is included in a group of corporations described in paragraph (2).

. . . . .

(b) Component member.—

(1) General rule.—For purposes of this part, a corporation is a component member of a controlled group of corporations on a December 31 of any taxable year (and with respect to the taxable year which includes such December 31) if such corporation—

(A) is a member of such controlled group of corporations on the December 31 included in such year and is not treated as an excluded member under paragraph (2), or

(B) is not a member of such controlled group of corporations on the December 31 included in such year but is treated as an additional member under paragraph (3).

(2) Excluded members.—A corporation which is a member of a controlled group of corporations on December 31 of any taxable year shall be treated as an excluded member of such group for the taxable year including such December 31 if such corporation—

(A) is a member of such group for less than one-half the number of days in such taxable year which precede such December 31,

(B) is exempt from taxation under section 501(a) (except a corporation which is subject to tax on its unrelated business taxable income under section 511) for such taxable year,

. . . . .

(E) is a franchised corporation, as defined in subsection (f) (4).

(3) **Additional members.**—A corporation which—

(A) was a member of a controlled group of corporations at any time during a calendar year,

(B) is not a member of such group on December 31 of such calendar year, and

(C) is not described, with respect to such group, in subparagraph (B), (C), (D), or (E) of paragraph (2),

shall be treated as an additional member of such group on December 31 for its taxable year including such December 31 if it was a member of such group for one-half (or more) of the number of days in such taxable year which precede such December 31.

(4) **Overlapping groups.**—If a corporation is a component member of more than one controlled group of corporations with respect to any taxable year, such corporation shall be treated as a component member of only one controlled group. The determination as to the group of which such corporation is a component member shall be made under regulations prescribed by the Secretary which are consistent with the purposes of this part.

(c) **Certain stock excluded.**—

(1) **General rule.**—For purposes of this part, the term "stock" does not include—

(A) nonvoting stock which is limited and preferred as to dividends,

(B) treasury stock, and

(C) stock which is treated as "excluded stock" under paragraph (2).

(2) **Stock treated as "excluded stock".**—

(A) **Parent-subsidiary controlled group.**—For purposes of subsection (a) (1), if a corporation (referred to in this paragraph as "parent corporation") owns (within the meaning of subsections (d) (1) and (e) (4)), 50 percent or more of the total combined voting power of all classes of stock entitled to vote or 50 percent or more of the total value of shares of all classes of stock in another corporation (referred to in this paragraph as "subsidiary corporation"), the following stock of the subsidiary corporation shall be treated as excluded stock—

(i) stock in the subsidiary corporation held by a trust which is part of a plan of deferred compensation for the benefit of the employees of the parent corporation or the subsidiary corporation,

(ii) stock in the subsidiary corporation owned by an individual (within the meaning of subsection (d) (2)) who is a principal stockholder or officer of the parent corporation. For purposes of this clause, the term "principal stockholder" of a corporation means an individual who owns (within the meaning of subsection (d) (2)) 5 percent or more of the total combined voting power of all classes of stock entitled to vote or 5 percent or more of the total value of shares of all classes of stock in such corporation,

(iii) stock in the subsidiary corporation owned (within the meaning of subsection (d) (2)) by an employee of the subsidiary corporation if such stock is subject to conditions which run in favor of such parent (or subsidiary) corporation and which substantially restrict or limit the employee's right (or if the employee constructively owns such stock, the direct owner's right) to dispose of such stock, or

(iv) stock in the subsidiary corporation owned (within the meaning of subsection (d) (2)) by an organization (other than the parent corporation) to which section 501 (relating to certain educational and charitable organizations which are exempt from tax) applies and which is controlled directly or indirectly by the parent corporation or subsidiary corporation, by an individual, estate, or trust that is a principal stockholder (within the meaning of clause (ii)) of the parent corporation, by an officer of the parent corporation, or by any combination thereof.

(B) Brother-sister controlled group.—For purposes of subsection (a) (2), if 5 or fewer persons who are individuals, estates, or trusts (referred to in this subparagraph as "common owners") own (within the meaning of subsection (d) (2)), 50 percent or more of the total combined voting power of all classes of stock entitled to vote or 50 percent or more of the total value of shares of all classes of stock in a corporation, the following stock of such corporation shall be treated as excluded stock—

(i) stock in such corporation held by an employees' trust described in section 401(a) which is exempt from tax under section 501(a), if such trust is for the benefit of the employees of such corporation,

(ii) stock in such corporation owned (within the meaning of subsection (d) (2)) by an employee of the corporation if such stock is subject to conditions which run in favor of any of such common owners (or such corporation) and which substantially restrict or limit the employee's right (or if the employee constructively owns such stock, the direct owner's right) to dispose of such stock. If a condition which limits or restricts the employee's right (or the direct owner's right) to dispose of such stock also applies to the stock held by any of the common owners pursuant to a bona fide reciprocal stock purchase arrangement, such condition shall not be treated as one which restricts or limits the employee's right to dispose of such stock, or

(iii) stock in such corporation owned (within the meaning of subsection (d) (2)) by an organization to which section 501 (relating to certain educational and charitable organizations which are exempt from tax) applies and which is controlled directly or indirectly by such corporation, by an individual, estate, or trust that is a principal stockholder (within the meaning of subparagraph (A) (ii)) of such corporation, by an officer of such corporation, or by any combination thereof.

(d) Rules for determining stock ownership.—

(1) Parent-subsidiary controlled group.—For purposes of determining whether a corporation is a member of a parent-subsidiary controlled group of corporations (within the meaning of subsection (a) (1)), stock owned by a corporation means—

    (A) stock owned directly by such corporation, and

    (B) stock owned with the application of subsection (e) (1).

(2) Brother-sister controlled group.—For purposes of determining whether a corporation is a member of a brother-sister controlled group of corporations (within the meaning of subsection (a) (2)), stock owned by a person who is an individual, estate, or trust means—

    (A) stock owned directly by such person, and

    (B) stock owned with the application of subsection (e).

(e) Constructive ownership.—

    (1) Options.—If any person has an option to acquire stock, such stock shall be considered as owned by such person. For purposes of this paragraph, an option to acquire such an option, and each one of a series of such options, shall be considered as an option to acquire such stock.

    (2) Attribution from partnerships.—Stock owned, directly or indirectly, by or for a partnership shall be considered as owned by any partner having an interest of 5 percent or more in either the capital or profits of the partnership in proportion to his interest in capital or profits, whichever such proportion is the greater.

    (3) Attribution from estates or trusts.—

      (A) Stock owned, directly or indirectly, by or for an estate or trust shall be considered as owned by any beneficiary who has an actuarial interest of 5 percent or more in such stock, to the extent of such actuarial interest. For purposes of this subparagraph, the actuarial interest of each beneficiary shall be determined by assuming the maximum exercise of discretion by the fiduciary in favor of such beneficiary and the maximum use of such stock to satisfy his rights as a beneficiary.

      (B) Stock owned, directly or indirectly, by or for any portion of a trust of which a person is considered the owner under subpart E of part I of subchapter J (relating to grantors and others treated as substantial owners) shall be considered as owned by such person.

      (C) This paragraph shall not apply to stock owned by any employees' trust described in section 401(a) which is exempt from tax under section 501(a).

    (4) Attribution from corporations.—Stock owned, directly or indirectly, by or for a corporation shall be considered as owned by any person who owns (within the meaning of subsection (d)) 5 percent or more in value of its stock in that proportion which the value of the stock which such person so owns bears to the value of all the stock in such corporation.

    (5) Spouse.—An individual shall be considered as owning stock in a corporation owned, directly or indirectly, by or for his spouse (other than a spouse who is legally separated from the individual under a decree of divorce whether interlocutory or final, or a decree of separate maintenance), except in the case of a corporation with respect to which each of the following conditions is satisfied for its taxable year—

      (A) The individual does not, at any time during such taxable year, own directly any stock in such corporation;

(B) The individual is not a director or employee and does not participate in the management of such corporation at any time during such taxable year;

(C) Not more than 50 percent of such corporation's gross income for such taxable year was derived from royalties, rents, dividends, interest, and annuities; and

(D) Such stock in such corporation is not, at any time during such taxable year, subject to conditions which substantially restrict or limit the spouse's right to dispose of such stock and which run in favor of the individual or his children who have not attained the age of 21 years.

(6) Children, grandchildren, parents, and grandparents.—

(A) Minor children.—An individual shall be considered as owning stock owned, directly or indirectly, by or for his children who have not attained the age of 21 years, and, if the individual has not attained the age of 21 years, the stock owned, directly or indirectly, by or for his parents.

(B) Adult children and grandchildren.—An individual who owns (within the meaning of subsection (d) (2), but without regard to this subparagraph) more than 50 percent of the total combined voting power of all classes of stock entitled to vote or more than 50 percent of the total value of shares of all classes of stock in a corporation shall be considered as owning the stock in such corporation owned, directly or indirectly, by or for his parents, grandparents, grandchildren, and children who have attained the age of 21 years.

(C) Adopted child.—For purposes of this section, a legally adopted child of an individual shall be treated as a child of such individual by blood.

(f) Other definitions and rules.—

.   .   .   .

(2) Operating rules.—

(A) In general.—Except as provided in subparagraph (B), stock constructively owned by a person by reason of the application of paragraph (1), (2), (3), (4), (5), or (6) of subsection (e) shall, for purposes of applying such paragraphs, be treated as actually owned by such person.

(B) Members of family.—Stock constructively owned by an individual by reason of the application of paragraph (5) or (6) of subsection (e) shall not be treated as owned by him for purposes of again applying such paragraphs in order to make another the constructive owner of such stock.

(3) Special rules.—For purposes of this section—

(A) If stock may be considered as owned by a person under subsection (e) (1) and under any other paragraph of subsection (e), it shall be considered as owned by him under subsection (e) (1).

(B) If stock is owned (within the meaning of subsection (d)) by two or more persons, such stock shall be considered as owned by the person whose ownership of such stock results in the corporation being a component member of a controlled group. If by reason of the preceding sentence, a corporation would (but for this sentence) become a component member of two controlled groups, it shall be treated as a component member of one controlled group. The determination as to the group of which such corporation is a component member shall be made under regulations prescribed by the Secretary which are consistent with the purposes of this part.

(C) If stock is owned by a person within the meaning of subsection (d) and such ownership results in the corporation being a component member of a controlled group, such stock shall not be treated as excluded stock under subsection (c) (2), if by reason of treating such stock as excluded stock the result is that such corporation is not a component member of a controlled group of corporations.

(4) Franchised corporation.—If—

(A) a parent corporation (as defined in subsection (c) (2) (A)), or a common owner (as defined in subsection (c) (2) (B)), of a corporation which is a member of a controlled group of corporations is under a duty (arising out of a written agreement) to sell stock of such corporation (referred to in this paragraph as "franchised corporation") which is franchised to sell the products of another member, or the common owner, of such controlled group;

(B) such stock is to be sold to an employee (or employees) of such franchised corporation pursuant to a bona fide plan designed to eliminate the stock ownership of the parent corporation or of the common owner in the franchised corporation;

(C) such plan—

(i) provides a reasonable selling price for such stock, and

(ii) requires that a portion of the employee's share of the profits of such corporation (whether received as compensation or as a dividend) be applied to the purchase of such stock (or the purchase of notes, bonds, debentures or other similar evidence of indebtedness of such franchised corporation held by such parent corporation or common owner);

(D) such employee (or employees) owns directly more than 20 percent of the total value of shares of all classes of stock in such franchised corporation;

(E) more than 50 percent of the inventory of such franchised corporation is acquired from members of the controlled group, the common owner, or both; and

(F) all of the conditions contained in subparagraphs (A), (B), (C), (D), and (E) have been met for one-half (or more) of the number of days preceding the December 31 included within the taxable year (or if the taxable year does not include December 31, the last day of such year) of the franchised corporation,

then such franchised corporation shall be treated as an excluded member of such group, under subsection (b) (2), for such taxable year.

SUBTITLE B—ESTATE AND GIFT TAXES

Chapter
11. Estate tax.
12. Gift tax.
13. Tax on certain generation-skipping transfers.

CHAPTER 11—ESTATE TAX

Subchapter
A. Estates of citizens or residents.
B. Estates of nonresidents not citizens.*
C. Miscellaneous.

SUBCHAPTER A—ESTATES OF CITIZENS OR RESIDENTS

Part
I. Tax imposed.
II. Credits against tax.
III. Gross estate.
IV. Taxable estate.

PART I—TAX IMPOSED

§ 2001. Imposition and rate of tax

(a) **Imposition.**—A tax is hereby imposed on the transfer of the taxable estate of every decedent who is a citizen or resident of the United States.

(b) **Computation of tax.**—The tax imposed by this section shall be the amount equal to the excess (if any) of—

(1) a tentative tax computed in accordance with the rate schedule set forth in subsection (c) on the sum of—

(A) the amount of the taxable estate, and

(B) the amount of the adjusted taxable gifts, over

(2) the aggregate amount of tax which would have been payable under chapter 12 with respect to gifts made by the decedent after December 31, 1976, if the rate schedule set forth in subsection (c) (as in effect at the decedent's death) had been applicable at the time of such gifts.

For purposes of paragraph (1) (B), the term "adjusted taxable gifts" means the total amount of the taxable gifts (within the meaning of section 2503) made by the decedent after December 31, 1976, other than gifts which are includible in the gross estate of the decedent.

* Omitted entirely.

504

(c) Rate Schedule.—
    (1) In general.—

If the amount with respect to which the tentative tax to be computed is:	The tentative tax is:
Not over $10,000	18 percent of such amount.
Over $10,000 but not over $20,000	$1,800, plus 20 percent of the excess of such amount over $10,000.
Over $20,000 but not over $40,000	$3,800, plus 22 percent of the excess of such amount over $20,000.
Over $40,000 but not over $60,000	$8,200, plus 24 percent of the excess of such amount over $40,000.
Over $60,000 but not over $80,000	$13,000, plus 26 percent of the excess of such amount over $60,000.
Over $80,000 but not over $100,000	$18,200, plus 28 percent of the excess of such amount over $80,000.
Over $100,000 but not over $150,000	$23,800, plus 30 percent of the excess of such amount over $100,000.
Over $150,000 but not over $250,000	$38,800, plus 32 percent of the excess of such amount over $150,000.
Over $250,000 but not over $500,000	$70,800, plus 34 percent of the excess of such amount over $250,000.
Over $500,000 but not over $750,000	$155,800, plus 37 percent of the excess of such amount over $500,000.
Over $750,000 but not over $1,000,000	$248,300, plus 39 percent of the excess of such amount over $750,000.
Over $1,000,000 but not over $1,250,000	$345,800, plus 41 percent of the excess of such amount over $1,000,000.
Over $1,250,000 but not over $1,500,000	$448,300, plus 43 percent of the excess of such amount over $1,250,000.
Over $1,500,000 but not over $2,000,000	$555,800, plus 45 percent of the excess of such amount over $1,500,000.
Over $2,000,000 but not over $2,500,000	$780,800, plus 49 percent of the excess of such amount over $2,000,000.
Over $2,500,000	$1,025,800, plus 50% of the excess over $2,500,000.

    (2) Phase-in of 50 percent maximum rate.—
        (A) In general.—In the case of decedents dying, and gifts made, before 1985, there shall be substituted for the last item in the schedule contained in paragraph (1) the items determined under this paragraph.
        (B) For 1982.—In the case of decedents dying, and gifts made, in 1982, the substitution under this paragraph shall be as follows:

Over $2,500,000 but not over $3,000,000	$1,025,800, plus 53% of the excess over $2,500,000.
Over $3,000,000 but not over $3,500,000	$1,290,800, plus 57% of the excess over $3,000,000.
Over $3,500,000 but not over $4,000,000	$1,575,800, plus 61% of the excess over $3,500,000.
Over $4,000,000	$1,880,800, plus 65% of the excess over $4,000,000.

(C) For 1983.—In the case of decedents dying, and gifts made, in 1983, the substitution under this paragraph shall be as follows:

Over $2,500,000 but not over $3,000,000	$1,025,800, plus 53% of the excess over $2,500,000.
Over $3,000,000 but not over $3,500,000	$1,290,800, plus 57% of the excess over $3,000,000.
Over $3,500,000	$1,575,800, plus 60% of the excess over $3,500,000.

(D) For 1984.—In the case of decedents dying, and gifts made, in 1984, the substitution under this paragraph shall be as follows:

Over $2,500,000 but not over $3,000,000	$1,025,800, plus 53% of the excess over $2,500,000.
Over $3,000,000	$1,290,800, plus 55% of the excess over $3,000,000.

(d) Adjustment for gift tax paid by spouse.—For purposes of subsection (b) (2), if—

(1) the decedent was the donor of any gift one-half of which was considered under section 2513 as made by the decedent's spouse, and

(2) the amount of such gift is includible in the gross estate of the decedent,

any tax payable by the spouse under chapter 12 on such gift (as determined under section 2012(d)) shall be treated as a tax payable with respect to a gift made by the decedent.

(e) Coordination of sections 2513 and 2035.—If—

(1) the decedent's spouse was the donor of any gift one-half of which was considered under section 2513 as made by the decedent, and

(2) the amount of such gift is includible in the gross estate of the decedent's spouse by reason of section 2035,

such gift shall not be included in the adjusted taxable gifts of the decedent for purposes of subsection (b) (1) (B), and the aggregate amount determined under subsection (b) (2) shall be reduced by the amount (if any) determined under subsection (d) which was treated as a tax payable by the decedent's spouse with respect to such gift.

§ 2002.   Liability for payment

The tax imposed by this chapter shall be paid by the executor.

PART II—CREDITS AGAINST TAX

§ 2010.   Unified credit against estate tax

(a) General rule.—A credit of $192,800 shall be allowed to the estate of every decedent against the tax imposed by section 2001.

(b) Phase-in of credit.—

In the case of decedents dying in:	Subsection (a) shall be applied by substituting for "$192,800" the following amount:
1982	$62,800
1983	79,300
1984	96,300
1985	121,800
1986	155,800

(c) Adjustment to credit for certain gifts made before 1977.—The amount of the credit allowable under subsection (a) shall be reduced by an amount equal to 20 percent of the aggregate amount allowed as a specific exemption under section 2521 (as in effect before its repeal by the Tax Reform Act of 1976) with respect to gifts made by the decedent after September 8, 1976.

(d) Limitation based on amount of tax.—The amount of the credit allowed by subsection (a) shall not exceed the amount of the tax imposed by section 2001.

§ 2011.   Credit for State death taxes

(a) In general.—The tax imposed by section 2001 shall be credited with the amount of any estate, inheritance, legacy, or succession taxes actually paid to any State or the District of Columbia, in respect of any property included in the gross estate (not including any such taxes paid with respect to the estate of a person other than the decedent).

(b) Amount of credit.—The credit allowed by this section shall not exceed the appropriate amount stated in the following table:

If the adjusted taxable estate is:	The maximum tax credit shall be:
Not over $90,000	8/10ths of 1% of the amount by which the taxable estate exceeds $40,000.
Over $90,000 but not over $140,000	$400 plus 1.6% of the excess over $90,000.
Over $140,000 but not over $240,000	$1,200 plus 2.4% of the excess over $140,000.
Over $240,000 but not over $440,000	$3,600 plus 3.2% of the excess over $240,000.
Over $440,000 but not over $640,000	$10,000 plus 4% of the excess over $440,000.
Over $640,000 but not over $840,000	$18,000 plus 4.8% of the excess over $640,000.
Over $840,000 but not over $1,040,000	$27,600 plus 5.6% of the excess over $840,000.
Over $1,040,000 but not over $1,540,000	$38,800 plus 6.4% of the excess over $1,040,000.
Over $1,540,000 but not over $2,040,000	$70,800 plus 7.2% of the excess over $1,540,000.

If the adjusted taxable estate is:	The maximum tax credit shall be:
Over $2,040,000 but not over $2,540,000	$106,800 plus 8% of the excess over $2,040,000.
Over $2,540,000 but not over $3,040,000	$146,800 plus 8.8% of the excess over $2,540,000.
Over $3,040,000 but not over $3,540,000	$190,800 plus 9.6% of the excess over $3,040,000.
Over $3,540,000 but not over $4,040,000	$238,800 plus 10.4% of the excess over $3,540,000.
Over $4,040,000 but not over $5,040,000	$290,800 plus 11.2% of the excess over $4,040,000.
Over $5,040,000 but not over $6,040,000	$402,800 plus 12% of the excess over $5,040,000.
Over $6,040,000 but not over $7,040,000	$522,800 plus 12.8% of the excess over $6,040,000.
Over $7,040,000 but not over $8,040,000	$650,800 plus 13.6% of the excess over $7,040,000.
Over $8,040,000 but not over $9,040,000	$786,800 plus 14.4% of the excess over $8,040,000.
Over $9,040,000 but not over $10,040,000 ...	$930,800 plus 15.2% of the excess over $9,040,000.
Over $10,040,000	$1,082,800 plus 16% of the excess over $10,040,000.

For purposes of this section, the term "adjusted taxable estate" means the taxable estate reduced by $60,000.

(c) **Period of limitations on credit.**—The credit allowed by this section shall include only such taxes as were actually paid and credit therefor claimed within 4 years after the filing of the return required by section 6018, except that—

(1) If a petition for redetermination of a deficiency has been filed with the Tax Court within the time prescribed in section 6213(a), then within such 4-year period or before the expiration of 60 days after the decision of the Tax Court becomes final.

(2) If, under section 6161 or 6166, an extension of time has been granted for payment of the tax shown on the return, or of a deficiency, then within such 4-year period or before the date of the expiration of the period of the extension.

(3) If a claim for refund or credit of an overpayment of tax imposed by this chapter has been filed within the time prescribed in section 6511, then within such 4-year period or before the expiration of 60 days from the date of mailing by certified mail or registered mail by the Secretary to the taxpayer of a notice of the disallowance of any part of such claim, or before the expiration of 60 days after a decision by any court of competent jurisdiction becomes final with respect to a timely suit instituted upon such claim, whichever is later.

Refund based on the credit may (despite the provisions of sections 6511 and 6512) be made if claim therefor is filed within the period above provided. Any such refund shall be made without interest.

(d) **Basic estate tax.**—The basic estate tax and the estate tax imposed by the Revenue Act of 1926 shall be 125 percent of the amount determined to be the maximum credit provided by subsection (b). The additional estate tax shall be the difference between the tax imposed by section 2001 or 2101 and the basic estate tax.

(e) **Limitation in cases involving deduction under section 2053(d).**—In any case where a deduction is allowed under section 2053(d) for an estate, succession, legacy, or inheritance tax imposed by a State or the District of Columbia upon a transfer for public, charitable, or religious uses described in section 2055 or 2106(a) (2), the allowance of the credit under this section shall be subject to the following conditions and limitations:

(1) The taxes described in subsection (a) shall not include any estate, succession, legacy, or inheritance tax for which such deduction is allowed under section 2053(d).

(2) The credit shall not exceed the lesser of—

(A) the amount stated in subsection (b) on a [1] adjusted taxable estate determined by allowing such deduction authorized by section 2053(d), or

(B) that proportion of the amount stated in subsection (b) on a [1] adjusted taxable estate determined without regard to such deduction authorized by section 2053(d) as (i) the amount of the taxes described in subsection (a), as limited by the provisions of paragraph (1) of this subsection, bears to (ii) the amount of the taxes described in subsection (a) before applying the limitation contained in paragraph (1) of this subsection.

(3) If the amount determined under subparagraph (B) of paragraph (2) is less than the amount determined under subparagraph (A) of that paragraph, then for purposes of subsection (d) such lesser amount shall be the maximum credit provided by subsection (b).

(f) Limitation based on amount of tax.—The credit provided by this section shall not exceed the amount of the tax imposed by section 2001, reduced by the amount of the unified credit provided by section 2010.

[1] So in original. Probably should read "an".

§ 2012.   Credit for gift tax

(a) In general.—If a tax on a gift has been paid under chapter 12 (sec. 2501 and following), or under corresponding provisions of prior laws, and thereafter on the death of the donor any amount in respect of such gift is required to be included in the value of the gross estate of the decedent for purposes of this chapter, then there shall be credited against the tax imposed by section 2001 the amount of the tax paid on a gift under chapter 12, or under corresponding provisions of prior laws, with respect to so much of the property which constituted the gift as is included in the gross estate, except that the amount of such credit shall not exceed an amount which bears the same ratio to the tax imposed by section 2001 (after deducting from such tax the credit for State death taxes provided by section 2011 and the unified credit provided by section 2010) as the value (at the time of the gift or at the time of the death, whichever is lower) of so much of the property which constituted the gift as is included in the gross estate bears to the value of the entire gross estate reduced by the aggregate amount of the charitable and marital deductions allowed under sections 2055, 2056, and 2106(a) (2).

(b) Valuation reductions.—In applying, with respect to any gift, the ratio stated in subsection (a), the value at the time of the gift or at the time of the death, referred to in such ratio, shall be reduced—

(1) by such amount as will properly reflect the amount of such gift which was excluded in determining (for purposes of section 2503(a)), or of corresponding provisions of prior laws, the total amount of gifts made during the calendar quarter (or calendar year if the gift was made before January 1, 1971) in which the gift was made;

(2) if a deduction with respect to such gift is allowed under section 2056(a) (relating to marital deduction), then by the amount of such value, reduced as provided in paragraph (1); and

(3) if a deduction with respect to such gift is allowed under sections 2055 or 2106(a) (2) (relating to charitable deduction), then by the amount of such value, reduced as provided in paragraph (1) of this subsection.

(c) **Where gift considered made one-half by spouse.**—Where the decedent was the donor of the gift but, under the provisions of section 2513, or corresponding provisions of prior laws, the gift was considered as made one-half by his spouse—

(1) the term "the amount of the tax paid on a gift under chapter 12", as used in subsection (a), includes the amounts paid with respect to each half of such gift, the amount paid with respect to each being computed in the manner provided in subsection (d); and

(2) in applying, with respect to such gift, the ratio stated in subsection (a), the value at the time of the gift or at the time of the death, referred to in such ratio, includes such value with respect to each half of such gift, each such value being reduced as provided in paragraph (1) of subsection (b).

(d) **Computation of amount of gift tax paid.**—

(1) **Amount of tax.**—For purposes of subsection (a), the amount of tax paid on a gift under chapter 12, or under corresponding provisions of prior laws, with respect to any gift shall be an amount which bears the same ratio to the total tax paid for the calendar quarter (or calendar year if the gift was made before January 1, 1971) in which the gift was made as the amount of such gift bears to the total amount of taxable gifts (computed without deduction of the specific exemption) for such quarter or year.

(2) **Amount of gift.**—For purposes of paragraph (1), the "amount of such gift" shall be the amount included with respect to such gift in determining (for the purposes of section 2503(a), or of corresponding provisions of prior laws) the total amount of gifts made during such quarter or year, reduced by the amount of any deduction allowed with respect to such gift under section 2522, or under corresponding provisions of prior laws (relating to charitable deduction), or under section 2523 (relating to marital deduction).

(e) **Section inapplicable to gifts made after December 31, 1976.**—No credit shall be allowed under this section with respect to the amount of any tax paid under chapter 12 on any gift made after December 31, 1976.

§ 2013.   Credit for tax on prior transfers

(a) **General rule.**—The tax imposed by section 2001 shall be credited with all or a part of the amount of the Federal estate tax paid with respect to the transfer of property (including property passing as a result of the exercise or non-exercise of a power of appointment) to the decedent by or from a person (herein designated as a "transferor") who died within 10 years before, or within 2 years after, the decedent's death. If the transferor died within 2 years of the death of the decedent, the credit shall be the amount determined under subsections (b) and (c). If the transferor predeceased the decedent by more than 2 years, the credit shall be the following percentage of the amount so determined—

(1) 80 percent, if within the third or fourth years preceding the decedent's death;

(2) 60 percent, if within the fifth or sixth years preceding the decedent's death;

(3) 40 percent, if within the seventh or eighth years preceding the decedent's death; and

(4) 20 percent, if within the ninth or tenth years preceding the decedent's death.

(b) Computation of credit.—Subject to the limitation prescribed in subsection (c), the credit provided by this section shall be an amount which bears the same ratio to the estate tax paid (adjusted as indicated hereinafter) with respect to the estate of the transferor as the value of the property transferred bears to the taxable estate of the transferor (determined for purposes of the estate tax) decreased by any death taxes paid with respect to such estate. For purposes of the preceding sentence, the estate tax paid shall be the Federal estate tax paid increased by any credits allowed against such estate tax under section 2012, or corresponding provisions of prior laws, on account of gift tax, and for any credits allowed against such estate tax under this section on account of prior transfers where the transferor acquired property from a person who died within 10 years before the death of the decedent.

(c) Limitation on credit.—

(1) **In general.**—The credit provided in this section shall not exceed the amount by which—

(A) the estate tax imposed by section 2001 or section 2101 (after deducting the credits provided for in sections 2010, 2011, 2012, and 2014) computed without regard to this section, exceeds

(B) such tax computed by excluding from the decedent's gross estate the value of such property transferred and, if applicable, by making the adjustment hereinafter indicated.

If any deduction is otherwise allowable under section 2055 or section 2106(a) (2) (relating to charitable deduction) then, for the purpose of the computation indicated in subparagraph (B), the amount of such deduction shall be reduced by that part of such deduction which the value of such property transferred bears to the decedent's entire gross estate reduced by the deductions allowed under sections 2053 and 2054, or section 2106(a) (1) (relating to deduction for expenses, losses, etc.). For purposes of this section, the value of such property transferred shall be the value as provided for in subsection (d) of this section.

(2) **Two or more transferors.**—If the credit provided in this section relates to property received from 2 or more transferors, the limitation provided in paragraph (1) of this subsection shall be computed by aggregating the value of the property so transferred to the decedent. The aggregate limitation so determined shall be apportioned in accordance with the value of the property transferred to the decedent by each transferor.

(d) Valuation of property transferred.—The value of property transferred to the decedent shall be the value used for the purpose of determining the Federal estate tax liability of the estate of the transferor but—

(1) there shall be taken into account the effect of the tax imposed by section 2001 or 2101, or any estate, succession, legacy, or inheritance tax, on the net value to the decedent of such property;

(2) where such property is encumbered in any manner, or where the decedent incurs any obligation imposed by the transferor with respect to such

property, such encumbrance or obligation shall be taken into account in the same manner as if the amount of a gift to the decedent of such property was being determined; and

(3) if the decedent was the spouse of the transferor at the time of the transferor's death, the net value of the property transferred to the decedent shall be reduced by the amount allowed under section 2056 (relating to marital deductions) as a deduction from the gross estate of the transferor.

(e) Property defined.—For purposes of this section, the term "property" includes any beneficial interest in property, including a general power of appointment (as defined in section 2041).

(f) Treatment of additional tax imposed under section 2032A.—If section 2032A applies to any property included in the gross estate of the transferor and an additional tax is imposed with respect to such property under section 2032A(c) before the date which is 2 years after the date of the decedent's death, for purposes of this section—

(1) the additional tax imposed by section 2032A(c) shall be treated as a Federal estate tax payable with respect to the estate of the transferor; and

(2) the value of such property and the amount of the taxable estate of the transferor shall be determined as if section 2032A did not apply with respect to such property.

(g) Treatment of tax imposed on certain generation-skipping transfers.—If any property was transferred to the decedent in a transfer which is taxable under section 2601 (relating to tax imposed on generation-skipping transfers) and if the deemed transferor (as defined in section 2612) is not alive at the time of such transfer, for purposes of this section—

(1) such property shall be deemed to have passed to the decedent from the deemed transferor;

(2) the tax payable under section 2601 on such transfer shall be treated as a Federal estate tax payable with respect to the estate of the deemed transferor; and

(3) the amount of the taxable estate of the deemed transferor shall be increased by the value of such property as determined for purposes of the tax imposed by section 2601 on the transfer.

§ 2015.   Credit for death taxes on remainders

Where an election is made under section 6163(a) to postpone payment of the tax imposed by section 2001 or 2101, such part of any estate, inheritance, legacy, or succession taxes allowable as a credit under section 2011 or 2014, as is attributable to a reversionary or remainder interest may be allowed as a credit against the tax attributable to such interest, subject to the limitations on the amount of the credit contained in such sections, if such part is paid, and credit therefor claimed, at any time before the expiration of the time for payment of the tax imposed by section 2001 or 2101 as postponed and extended under section 6163.

§ 2016.   Recovery of taxes claimed as credit

If any tax claimed as a credit under section 2011 or 2014 is recovered from any foreign country, any State, any possession of the United States, or the District of Columbia, the executor, or any other person or persons recovering such amount, shall give notice of such recovery to the Secretary at such time and in such manner as may be required by regulations prescribed by him, and the Secretary shall (despite the provisions of section 6501) redetermine the amount of the tax under this chapter and the amount, if any, of the tax due on such redetermination, shall be paid by the executor or such person or persons, as the case may be, on notice and demand. No interest shall be assessed or collected on any amount of tax due on any redetermination by the Secretary, resulting from a refund to the executor of tax claimed as a credit under section 2014, for any period before the receipt of such refund, except to the extent interest was paid by the foreign country on such refund.

PART III—GROSS ESTATE

§ 2031. Definition of gross estate

(a) **General.**—The value of the gross estate of the decedent shall be determined by including to the extent provided for in this part, the value at the time of his death of all property, real or personal, tangible or intangible, wherever situated.

(b) **Valuation of unlisted stock and securities.**—In the case of stock and securities of a corporation the value of which, by reason of their not being listed on an exchange and by reason of the absence of sales thereof, cannot be determined with reference to bid and asked prices or with reference to sales prices, the value thereof shall be determined by taking into consideration, in addition to all other factors, the value of stock or securities of corporations engaged in the same or a similar line of business which are listed on an exchange.

. . . . .

§ 2032. Alternate valuation

(a) **General.**—The value of the gross estate may be determined, if the executor so elects, by valuing all the property included in the gross estate as follows:

(1) In the case of property distributed, sold, exchanged, or otherwise disposed of, within 6 months after the decedent's death such property shall be valued as of the date of distribution, sale, exchange, or other disposition.

(2) In the case of property not distributed, sold, exchanged, or otherwise disposed of, within 6 months after the decedent's death such property shall be valued as of the date 6 months after the decedent's death.

(3) Any interest or estate which is affected by mere lapse of time shall be included at its value as of the time of death (instead of the later date) with adjustment for any difference in its value as of the later date not due to mere lapse of time.

(b) **Special rules.**—No deduction under this chapter of any item shall be allowed if allowance for such item is in effect given by the alternate valuation provided by this section. Wherever in any other subsection or section of this chapter reference is made to the value of property at the time of the decedent's death, such reference shall be deemed to refer to the value of such property used in determining the value of the gross estate. In case of an election made by the executor under this section, then—

(1) for purposes of the charitable deduction under section 2055 or 2106(a) (2), any bequest, legacy, devise, or transfer enumerated therein, and

(2) for the purpose of the marital deduction under section 2056, any interest in property passing to the surviving spouse,

shall be valued as of the date of the decedent's death with adjustment for any difference in value (not due to mere lapse of time or the occurrence or nonoccurrence of a contingency) of the property as of the date 6 months after the decedent's death (substituting, in the case of property distributed by the executor or trustee, or sold, exchanged, or otherwise disposed of, during such 6-month period, the date thereof).

(c) Time of election.—The election provided for in this section shall be exercised by the executor on his return if filed within the time prescribed by law or before the expiration of any extension of time granted pursuant to law for the filing of the return.

§ 2032A.   Valuation of certain farm, etc., real property

(a) Value based on use under which property qualifies.—

(1) General rule.—If—

(A) the decedent was (at the time of his death) a citizen or resident of the United States, and

(B) the executor elects the application of this section and files the agreement referred to in subsection (d) (2),

then, for purposes of this chapter, the value of qualified real property shall be its value for the use under which it qualifies, under subsection (b), as qualified real property.

(2) Limit on aggregate reduction in fair market value.—The aggregate decrease in the value of qualified real property taken into account for purposes of this chapter which results from the application of paragraph (1) with respect to any decedent shall not exceed the applicable limit set forth in the following table:

In the case of decedents dying in:	The applicable limit is:
1981	$600,000
1982	700,000
1983 or thereafter	750,000

(b) Qualified real property.—

(1) In general.—For purposes of this section, the term "qualified real property" means real property located in the United States which was acquired from or passed from the decedent to a qualified heir of the decedent and which, on the date of the decedent's death, was being used for a qualified use by the decedent or a member of the decedent's family, but only if—

(A) 50 percent or more of the adjusted value of the gross estate consists of the adjusted value of real or personal property which—

(i) on the date of the decedent's death, was being used for a qualified use by the decedent or a member of the decedent's family, and

(ii) was acquired from or passed from the decedent to a qualified heir of the decedent.

(B) 25 percent or more of the adjusted value of the gross estate consists of the adjusted value of real property which meets the requirements of subparagraphs (A) (ii) and (C),

(C) during the 8-year period ending on the date of the decedent's death there have been periods aggregating 5 years or more during which—

(i) such real property was owned by the decedent or a member of the decedent's family and used for a qualified use by the decedent or a member of the decedent's family, and

(ii) there was material participation by the decedent or a member of the decedent's family in the operation of the farm or other business, and

(D) such real property is designated in the agreement referred to in subsection (d) (2).

(2) **Qualified use.**—For purposes of this section, the term "qualified use" means the devotion of the property to any of the following:

(A) use as a farm for farming purposes, or

(B) use in a trade or business other than the trade or business of farming.

(3) **Adjusted value.**—For purposes of paragraph (1), the term "adjusted value" means—

(A) in the case of the gross estate, the value of the gross estate for purposes of this chapter (determined without regard to this section), reduced by any amounts allowable as a deduction under paragraph (4) of section 2053(a), or

(B) in the case of any real or personal property, the value of such property for purposes of this chapter (determined without regard to this section), reduced by any amounts allowable as a deduction in respect of such property under paragraph (4) of section 2053(a).

(4) **Decedents who are retired or disabled.—**

(A) **In general.**—If, on the date of the decedent's death, the requirements of paragraph (1)(C)(ii) with respect to the decedent for any property are not met, and the decedent—

(i) was receiving old-age benefits under title II of the Social Security Act for a continuous period ending on such date, or

(ii) was disabled for a continuous period ending on such date,

then paragraph (1)(C)(ii) shall be applied with respect to such property by substituting "the date on which the longer of such continuous periods began" for "the date of the decedent's death" in paragraph (1)(C).

(B) **Disabled defined.**—For purposes of subparagraph (A), an individual shall be disabled if such individual has a mental or physical impairment which renders him unable to materially participate in the operation of the farm or other business.

(C) **Coordination with recapture.**—For purposes of subsection (c)(6)(B)(i), if the requirements of paragraph (1)(C)(ii) are met with respect to any decedent by reason of subparagraph (A), the period ending on the date on which the continuous period taken into account under subparagraph (A) began shall be treated as the period immediately before the decedent's death.

(5) **Special rules for surviving spouses.—**

(A) **In general.**—If property is qualified real property with respect to a decedent (hereinafter in this paragraph referred to as the "first decedent") and such property was acquired from or passed from the first decedent to the surviving spouse of the first decedent, for purposes of applying this subsection and subsection (c) in the case of the estate of such surviving spouse, active management of the farm or other business by the surviving spouse shall be treated as material participation by such surviving spouse in the operation of such farm or business.

(B) **Special rule.**—For the purposes of subparagraph (A), the determination of whether property is qualified real property with respect to the first decedent shall be made without regard to subparagraph (D) of paragraph (1) and without regard to whether an election under this section was made.

(c) **Tax treatment of dispositions and failures to use for qualified use.**—

(1) **Imposition of additional estate tax.**—If, within 10 years after the decedent's death and before the death of the qualified heir—

(A) the qualified heir disposes of any interest in the qualified real property (other than by a disposition to a member of his family), or

(B) the qualified heir ceases to use for the qualified use the qualified real property which was acquired (or passed) from the decedent,

then, there is hereby imposed an additional estate tax.

(2) **Amount of additional tax.**—

(A) **In general.**—The amount of the additional tax imposed by paragraph (1) with respect to any interest shall be the amount equal to the lesser of—

(i) the adjusted tax difference attributable to such interest, or

(ii) the excess of the amount realized with respect to the interest (or, in any case other than a sale or exchange at arm's length, the fair market value of the interest) over the value of the interest determined under subsection (a).

(B) **Adjusted tax difference attributable to interest.**—For purposes of subparagraph (A), the adjusted tax difference attributable to an interest is the amount which bears the same ratio to the adjusted tax difference with respect to the estate (determined under subparagraph (C)) as—

(i) the excess of the value of such interest for purposes of this chapter (determined without regard to subsection (a)) over the value of such interest determined under subsection (a), bears to

(ii) a similar excess determined for all qualified real property.

(C) **Adjusted tax difference with respect to the estate.**—For purposes of subparagraph (B), the term "adjusted tax difference with respect to the estate" means the excess of what would have been the estate tax liability but for subsection (a) over the estate tax liability. For purposes of this subparagraph, the term "estate tax liability" means the tax imposed by section 2001 reduced by the credits allowable against such tax.

. . . .

(4) **Due date.**—The additional tax imposed by this subsection shall become due and payable on the day which is 6 months after the date of the disposition or cessation referred to in paragraph (1).

(5) Liability for tax; furnishing of bond.—The qualified heir shall be personally liable for the additional tax imposed by this subsection with respect to his interest unless the heir has furnished bond which meets the requirements of subsection (e) (11).

(6) Cessation of qualified use.—For purposes of paragraph (1) (B), real property shall cease to be used for the qualified use if—

(A) such property ceases to be used for the qualified use set forth in subparagraph (A) or (B) of subsection (b) (2) under which the property qualified under subsection (b), or

(B) during any period of 8 years ending after the date of the decedent's death and before the date of the death of the qualified heir, there had been periods aggregating more than 3 years during which—

(i) in the case of periods during which the property was held by the decedent, there was no material participation by the decedent or any member of his family in the operation of the farm or other business, and

(ii) in the case of periods during which the property was held by any qualified heir, there was no material participation by such qualified heir or any member of his family in the operation of the farm or other business.

(7) Special rules.—

(A) No tax if use begins within 2 years.—If the date on which the qualified heir begins to use the qualified real property (hereinafter in this subparagraph referred to as the commencement date is before the date 2 years after the decedent's death—

(i) no tax shall be imposed under paragraph (1) by reason of the failure by the qualified heir to so use such property before the commencement date, and

(ii) the 10-year period under paragraph (1) shall be extended by the period after the decedent's death and before the commencement date.

(B) Active management by eligible qualified heir treated as material participation.—For purposes of paragraph (6)(B)(ii), the active management of a farm or other business by—

(i) an eligible qualified heir, or

(ii) a fiduciary of an eligible qualified heir described in clause (ii) or (iii) of subparagraph (C),

shall be treated as material participation by such eligible qualified heir in the operation of such farm or business. In the case of an eligible qualified heir described in clause (ii), (iii), or (iv) of subparagraph (C), the preceding sentence shall apply only during periods during which such heir meets the requirements of such clause.

(C) Eligible qualified heir.—For purposes of this paragraph, the term "eligible qualified heir" means a qualified heir who—

(i) is the surviving spouse of the decedent,

(ii) has not attained the age of 21,

(iii) is disabled (within the meaning of subsection (b)(4)(B)), or

(iv) is a student.

(D) **Student.**—For purposes of subparagrapn (C), an individual shall be treated as a student with respect to periods during any calendar year if (and only if) such individual is a student (within the meaning of section 151(e)(4)) for such calendar year.

(d) Election; agreement.—

(1) **Election.**—The election under this section shall be made on the return of the tax imposed by section 2001. Such election shall be made in such manner as the Secretary shall by regulations prescribe. Such an election, once made, shall be irrevocable.

(2) **Agreement.**—The agreement referred to in this paragraph is a written agreement signed by each person in being who has an interest (whether or not in possession) in any property designated in such agreement consenting to the application of subsection (c) with respect to such property.

(e) Definitions; special rules.—For purposes of this section—

(1) **Qualified heir.**—The term "qualified heir" means, with respect to any property, a member of the decedent's family who acquired such property (or to whom such property passed) from the decedent. If a qualified heir disposes of any interest in qualified real property to any member of his family, such member shall thereafter be treated as the qualified heir with respect to such interest.

(2) **Member of family.**—The term "member of the family" means, with respect to any individual, only—

(A) an ancestor of such individual,

(B) the spouse of such individual,

(C) a lineal descendant of such individual, of such individual's spouse, or of a parent of such individual, or

(D) the spouse of any lineal descendant described in subparagraph (C).

For purposes of the preceding sentence, a legally adopted child of an individual shall be treated as the child of such individual by blood.

(3) **Certain real property included.**—In the case of real property which meets the requirements of subparagraph (C) of subsection (b) (1), residential buildings and related improvements on such real property occupied on a regular basis by the owner or lessee of such real property or by persons employed by such owner or lessee for the purpose of operating or maintaining such real property, and roads, buildings, and other structures and improvements functionally related to the qualified use shall be treated as real property devoted to the qualified use.

(4) **Farm.**—The term "farm" includes stock, dairy, poultry, fruit, furbearing animal, and truck farms, plantations, ranches, nurseries, ranges, greenhouses or other similar structures used primarily for the raising of agricultural or horticultural commodities, and orchards and woodlands.

(5) **Farming purposes.**—The term "farming purposes" means—

(A) cultivating the soil or raising or harvesting any agricultural or horticultural commodity (including the raising, shearing, feeding, caring for, training, and management of animals) on a farm;

(B) handling, drying, packing, grading, or storing on a farm any agricultural or horticultural commodity in its unmanufactured state, but only if the owner, tenant, or operator of the farm regularly produces more than one-half of the commodity so treated; and

(C) (i) the planting, cultivating, caring for, or cutting of trees, or

(ii) the preparation (other than milling) of trees for market.

. . . . .

(7) Method of valuing farms.—

(A) In general.—Except as provided in subparagraph (B), the value of a farm for farming purposes shall be determined by dividing—

(i) the excess of the average annual gross cash rental for comparable land used for farming purposes and located in the locality of such farm over the average annual State and local real estate taxes for such comparable land, by

(ii) the average annual effective interest rate for all new Federal Land Bank loans.

For purposes of the preceding sentence, each average annual computation shall be made on the basis of the 5 most recent calendar years ending before the date of the decedent's death.

(B) Value based on net share rental in certain cases.—

(i) In general.—If there is no comparable land from which the average annual gross cash rental may be determined but there is comparable land from which the average net share rental may be determined, subparagraph (A)(i) shall be applied by substituting "average annual net share rental" for "average annual gross cash rental".

(ii) Net share rental.—For purposes of this paragraph, the term "net share rental" means the excess of—

(I) the value of the produce received by the lessor of the land on which such produce is grown, over

(II) the cash operating expenses of growing such produce which, under the lease, are paid by the lessor.

(C) Exception.—The formula provided by subparagraph (A) shall not be used—

(i) where it is established that there is no comparable land from which the average annual gross cash rental may be determined and that there is no comparable land from which the average net share rental may be determined, or

(ii) where the executor elects to have the value of the farm for farming purposes determined under paragraph (8).

(8) Method of valuing closely held business interest, etc.—In any case to which paragraph (7) (A) does not apply, the following factors shall apply in determining the value of any qualified real property:

(A) The capitalization of income which the property can be expected to yield for farming or closely held business purposes over a reasonable period of time under prudent management using traditional cropping patterns for the area, taking into account soil capacity, terrain configuration, and similar factors,

(B) The capitalization of the fair rental value of the land for farm land or closely held business purposes,

(C) Assessed land values in a State which provides a differential or use value assessment law for farmland or closely held business,

(D) Comparable sales of other farm or closely held business land in the same geographical area far enough removed from a metropolitan or resort area so that nonagricultural use is not a significant factor in the sales price, and

(E) Any other factor which fairly values the farm or closely held business value of the property.

(9) **Property acquired from decedent.**—Property shall be considered to have been acquired from or to have passed from the decedent if—

(A) such property is so considered under section 1014(b) (relating to basis of property acquired from a decedent),

(B) such property is acquired by any person from the estate, or

(C) such property is acquired by any person from a trust (to the extent such property is includible in the gross estate of the decedent).

(10) **Community property.**—If the decedent and his surviving spouse at any time held qualified real property as community property, the interest of the surviving spouse in such property shall be taken into account under this section to the extent necessary to provide a result under this section with respect to such property which is consistent with the result which would have obtained under this section if such property had not been community property.

(11) **Bond in lieu of personal liability.**—If the qualified heir makes written application to the Secretary for determination of the maximum amount of the additional tax which may be imposed by subsection (c) with respect to the qualified heir's interest, the Secretary (as soon as possible, and in any event within 1 year after the making of such application) shall notify the heir of such maximum amount. The qualified heir, on furnishing a bond in such amount and for such period as may be required, shall be discharged from personal liability for any additional tax imposed by subsection (c) and shall be entitled to a receipt or writing showing such discharge.

(12) **Active management.**—The term "active management" means the making of the management decisions of a business (other than the daily operating decisions).

. . . . .

(f) **Statute of limitations.**—If qualified real property is disposed of or ceases to be used for a qualified use, then—

(1) the statutory period for the assessment of any additional tax under subsection (c) attributable to such disposition or cessation shall not expire before the expiration of 3 years from the date the Secretary is notified (in such manner as the Secretary may by regulations prescribe) of such disposition or cessation (or if later in the case of an involuntary conversion or exchange to which subsection (h) or (i) applies, 3 years from the date the Secretary is notified of the replacement of the converted property or of an intention not to replace or of the exchange of property), and

(2) such additional tax may be assessed before the expiration of such 3-year period notwithstanding the provisions of any other law or rule of law which would otherwise prevent such assessment.

(g) Application of this section and section 6324B to interests in partnerships, corporations, and trusts.—The Secretary shall prescribe regulations setting forth the application of this section and section 6324B in the case of an interest in a partnership, corporation, or trust which, with respect to the decedent, is an interest in a closely held business (within the meaning of paragraph (1) of section 6166(b)). For purposes of the preceding sentence, an interest in a discretionary trust all the beneficiaries of which are qualified heirs shall be treated as a present interest.

. . . . .

§ 2033.   Property in which the decedent had an interest

The value of the gross estate shall include the value of all property to the extent of the interest therein of the decedent at the time of his death.

§ 2034.   Dower or curtesy interests

The value of the gross estate shall include the value of all property to the extent of any interest therein of the surviving spouse, existing at the time of the decedent's death as dower or curtesy, or by virtue of a statute creating an estate in lieu of dower or curtesy.

§ 2035.   Adjustments for gifts made within 3 years of decedent's death

(a) Inclusion of gifts made by decedent.—Except as provided in subsection (b), the value of the gross estate shall include the value of all property to the extent of any interest therein of which the decedent has at any time made a transfer, by trust or otherwise, during the 3-year period ending on the date of the decedent's death.

(b) Exceptions.—Subsection (a) shall not apply—

(1) to any bona fide sale for an adequate and full consideration in money or money's worth, and

(2) to any gift to a donee made during a calendar year if the decedent was not required by section 6019 (other than by reason of section 6019(a)(2)) to file any gift tax return for such year with respect to gifts to such donee.

Paragraph (2) shall not apply to any transfer with respect to a life insurance policy.

(c) Inclusion of gift tax on certain gifts made during 3 years before decedent's death.—The amount of the gross estate (determined without regard to this subsection) shall be increased by the amount of any tax paid under chapter 12 by the decedent or his estate on any gift made by the decedent or his spouse after December 31, 1976, and during the 3-year period ending on the date of the decedent's death.

(d) Decedents dying after 1981.—

(1) **In general.**—Except as otherwise provided in this subsection, subsection (a) shall not apply to the estate of a decedent dying after December 31, 1981.

(2) **Exceptions for certain transfers.**—Paragraph (1) shall not apply to a transfer of an interest in property which is included in the value of the gross estate under section 2036, 2037, 2038, 2041, or 2042 or would have been

included under any of such sections if such interest had been retained by the decedent.

(3) **3–year rule retained for certain purposes.**—Paragraph (1) shall not apply for purposes of—

(A) section 303(b) (relating to distributions in redemption of stock to pay death taxes),

(B) section 2032A (relating to special valuation of certain farm, etc., real property),

(C) section 6166 (relating to extension of time for payment of estate tax where estate consists largely of interest in closely held business), and

(D) subchapter C of chapter 64 (relating to lien for taxes).

§ 2036.   Transfers with retained life estate

(a) **General rule.**—The value of the gross estate shall include the value of all property to the extent of any interest therein of which the decedent has at any time made a transfer (except in case of a bona fide sale for an adequate and full consideration in money or money's worth), by trust or otherwise, under which he has retained for his life or for any period not ascertainable without reference to his death or for any period which does not in fact end before his death—

(1) the possession or enjoyment of, or the right to the income from, the property, or

(2) the right, either alone or in conjunction with any person, to designate the persons who shall possess or enjoy the property or the income therefrom.

(b) **Voting rights.**—

(1) **In general.**—For purposes of subsection (a) (1), the retention of the right to vote (directly or indirectly) shares of stock of a controlled corporation shall be considered to be a retention of the enjoyment of transferred property.

(2) **Controlled corporation.**—For purposes of paragraph (1), a corporation shall be treated as a controlled corporation if, at any time after the transfer of the property and during the 3-year period ending on the date of the decedent's death, the decedent owned (with the application of section 318), or had the right (either alone or in conjunction with any person) to vote, stock possessing at least 20 percent of the total combined voting power of all classes of stock.

(3) **Coordination with section 2035.**—For purposes of applying section 2035 with respect to paragraph (1), the relinquishment or cessation of voting rights shall be treated as a transfer of property made by the decedent.

. . . . .

§ 2037.   Transfers taking effect at death

(a) **General rule.**—The value of the gross estate shall include the value of all property to the extent of any interest therein of which the decedent has at any time after September 7, 1916, made a transfer (except in case of a bona fide sale for an adequate and full consideration in money or money's worth), by trust or otherwise, if—

(1) possession or enjoyment of the property can, through ownership of such interest, be obtained only by surviving the decedent, and

(2) the decedent has retained a reversionary interest in the property (but in the case of a transfer made before October 8, 1949, only if such reversionary interest arose by the express terms of the instrument of transfer), and the value of such reversionary interest immediately before the death of the decedent exceeds 5 percent of the value of such property.

(b) Special rules.—For purposes of this section, the term "reversionary interest" includes a possibility that property transferred by the decedent—

(1) may return to him or his estate, or

(2) may be subject to a power of disposition by him,

but such term does not include a possibility that the income alone from such property may return to him or become subject to a power of disposition by him. The value of a reversionary interest immediately before the death of the decedent shall be determined (without regard to the fact of the decedent's death) by usual methods of valuation, including the use of tables of mortality and actuarial principles, under regulations prescribed by the Secretary. In determining the value of a possibility that property may be subject to a power of disposition by the decedent, such possibility shall be valued as if it were a possibility that such property may return to the decedent or his estate. Notwithstanding the foregoing, an interest so transferred shall not be included in the decedent's gross estate under this section if possession or enjoyment of the property could have been obtained by any beneficiary during the decedent's life through the exercise of a general power of appointment (as defined in section 2041) which in fact was exercisable immediately before the decedent's death.

§ 2038.   Revocable transfers

(a) In general.—The value of the gross estate shall include the value of all property—

(1) Transfers after June 22, 1936.—To the extent of any interest therein of which the decedent has at any time made a transfer (except in case of a bona fide sale for an adequate and full consideration in money or money's worth), by trust or otherwise, where the enjoyment thereof was subject at the date of his death to any change through the exercise of a power (in whatever capacity exercisable) by the decedent alone or by the decedent in conjunction with any other person (without regard to when or from what source the decedent acquired such power), to alter, amend, revoke, or terminate, or where any such power is relinquished during the 3-year period ending on the date of the decedent's death.

(2) Transfers on or before June 22, 1936.—To the extent of any interest therein of which the decedent has at any time made a transfer (except in case of a bona fide sale for an adequate and full consideration in money or money's worth), by trust or otherwise, where the enjoyment thereof was subject at the date of his death to any change through the exercise of a power, either by the decedent alone or in conjunction with any person, to alter, amend, or revoke, or where the decedent relinquished any such power during the 3-year period ending on the date of the decedent's death. Except in the case of transfers made after June 22, 1936, no interest of the decedent of which he has made a transfer shall be included in the gross estate under paragraph (1) unless it is includible under this paragraph.

(b) Date of existence of power.—For purposes of this section, the power to alter, amend, revoke, or terminate shall be considered to exist on the date of the decedent's death even though the exercise of the power is subject to a precedent giving of notice or even though the alteration, amendment, revocation, or termination takes effect only on the expiration of a stated period after the exercise of the power, whether or not on or before the date of the decedent's death notice has been given or the power has been exercised. In such cases proper adjustment shall be made representing the interests which would have been excluded from the power if the decedent had lived, and for such purpose, if the notice has not been given or the power has not been exercised on or before the date of his death, such notice shall be considered to have been given, or the power exercised, on the date of his death.

§ 2039. Annuities

(a) General.—The gross estate shall include the value of an annuity or other payment receivable by any beneficiary by reason of surviving the decedent under any form of contract or agreement entered into after March 3, 1931 (other than as insurance under policies on the life of the decedent), if, under such contract or agreement, an annuity or other payment was payable to the decedent, or the decedent possessed the right to receive such annuity or payment, either alone or in conjunction with another for his life or for any period not ascertainable without reference to his death or for any period which does not in fact end before his death.

(b) Amount includible.—Subsection (a) shall apply to only such part of the value of the annuity or other payment receivable under such contract or agreement as is proportionate to that part of the purchase price therefor contributed by the decedent. For purposes of this section, any contribution by the decedent's employer or former employer to the purchase price of such contract or agreement (whether or not to an employee's trust or fund forming part of a pension, annuity, retirement, bonus or profit sharing plan) shall be considered to be contributed by the decedent if made by reason of his employment.

(c) Exemption of annuities under certain trusts and plans.—Subject to the limitation of subsection (g), notwithstanding any other provision of this section or of any provision of law, there shall be excluded from the gross estate the value of an annuity or other payment (other than an amount described in subsection (f)) receivable by any beneficiary (other than the executor) under—

(1) an employees' trust (or under a contract purchased by an employees' trust) forming part of a pension, stock bonus, or profit-sharing plan which, at the time of the decedent's separation from employment (whether by death or otherwise), or at the time of termination of the plan if earlier, met the requirements of section 401(a);

(2) a retirement annuity contract purchased by an employer (and not by an employees' trust) pursuant to a plan which, at the time of decedent's separation from employment (by death or otherwise), or at the time of termination of the plan if earlier, was a plan described in section 403(a);

(3) a retirement annuity contract purchased for an employee by an employer which is an organization referred to in section 170(b) (1) (A) (ii) or (vi), or which is a religious organization (other than a trust), and which is exempt from tax under section 501(a); or

(4) chapter 73 of title 10 of the United States Code.

If such amounts payable after the death of the decedent under a plan described in paragraph (1) or (2), under a contract described in paragraph (3), or under chapter 73 of title 10 of the United States Code are attributable to any extent to payments or contributions made by the decedent, no exclusion shall be allowed for that part of the value of such amounts in the proportion that the total payments or contributions made by the decedent bears to the total payments or contributions made. For purposes of this subsection, contributions or payments made by the decedent's employer or former employer under a trust or plan described in paragraph (1) or (2) shall not be considered to be contributed by the decedent, and contributions or payments made by the decedent's employer or former employer toward the purchase of an annuity contract described in paragraph (3) shall, to the extent excludable from gross income under section 403(b), not be considered to be contributed by the decedent. This subsection shall apply to all decedents dying after December 31, 1953. For purposes of this subsection, contributions or payments on behalf of the decedent while he was an employee within the meaning of section 401(c) (1) made under a trust or plan described in paragraph (1) or (2) shall, to the extent allowable as a deduction under section 404, be considered to be made by a person other than the decedent and, to the extent not so allowable, shall be considered to be made by the decedent. For purposes of this subsection, amounts payable under chapter 73 of title 10 of the United States Code are attributable to payments or contributions made by the decedent only to the extent of amounts deposited by him pursuant to section 1438 or 1452(d) of such title 10. For purposes of this subsection, any deductible employee contributions (within the meaning of paragraph (5) of section 72(o) shall be considered as made by a person other than the decedent.

(d) Exemption of certain annuity interests created by community property laws.—In the case of an employee on whose behalf contributions or payments were made by his employer or former employer under a trust or plan described in subsection (c) (1) or (2), or toward the purchase of a contract described in subsection (c) (3), which under subsection (c) are not considered as contributed by the employee, if the spouse of such employee predeceases him, then, notwithstanding the provisions of this section or of any other provision of law, there shall be excluded from the gross estate of such spouse the value of any interest of such spouse in such trust or plan or such contract, to the extent such interest—

    (1) is attributable to such contributions or payments, and

    (2) arises solely by reason of such spouse's interest in community income under the community property laws of a State.

(e) Exclusion of individual retirement accounts, etc.—Subject to the limitation of subsection (g), notwithstanding any other provision of this section or of any other provision of law, there shall be excluded from the value of the gross estate the value of an annuity receivable by any beneficiary (other than the executor) under—

    (1) an individual retirement account described in section 408(a),

    (2) an individual retirement annuity described in section 408(b), or

    (3) a retirement bond described in section 409(a).

If any payment to an account described in paragraph (1) or for an annuity described in paragraph (2) or a bond described in paragraph (3) was not allowable as a deduction under section 219 and was not a rollover contribution described in section 402(a) (5), 403(a) (4), section 403(b) (8) (but only to the extent such contribution is attributable to a distribution from a contract described in subsection (c) (3)), 405(d)(3), 408(d) (3), or 409(b) (3) (C), the preceding sentence shall not apply to that portion of the value of the amount receivable under such account, annuity, or bond (as the case may be) which bears the same ratio to the total value of the amount so receivable as the total amount which was paid to or for such account, annuity, or bond and which was not allowable as a deduction under section 219 and was not such a rollover contribution bears to the total amount paid to or for such account, annuity, or bond. For purposes of this subsection, the term "annuity" means an annuity contract or other arrangement providing for a series of substantially equal periodic payments to be made to a beneficiary (other than the executor) for his life or over a period extending for at least 36 months after the date of the decedent's death.

(f) Lump sum distributions.—

    (1) In general.—An amount is described in this subsection if it is a lump sum distribution described in section 402(e) (4) (determined without regard to the next to the last sentence of section 402(e) (4) (A)).

    (2) Exception where recipient elects not to take 10-year averaging.—A lump sum distribution described in paragraph (1) shall be treated as not described in this subsection if the recipient elects irrevocably (at such time and in such manner as the Secretary may by regulations prescribe) to treat the distribution as taxable under section 402(a) (without the application of paragraph (2) thereof), except to the extent that section 402(e)(4)(J) applies to such distribution.

    (g) $100,000 limitation on exclusions under subsections (c) and (e).—The aggregate amount excluded from the gross estate of any decedent under subsections (c) and (e) of this section shall not exceed $100,000.

§ 2040.   Joint interests

    (a) General rule.—The value of the gross estate shall include the value of all property to the extent of the interest therein held as joint tenants with right of survivorship by the decedent and any other person, or as tenants by the entirety by the decedent and spouse, or deposited, with any person carrying on the banking business, in their joint names and payable to either or the survivor, except such part thereof as may be shown to have originally belonged to such other person and never to have been received or acquired by the latter from the decedent for less than an adequate and full consideration in money or money's worth: *Provided*, That where such property or any part thereof, or part of the consideration with which such property was acquired, is shown to have been at any time acquired by such other person from the decedent for less than an adequate and full consideration in money or money's worth, there shall be excepted only such part of the value of such property as is proportionate to the consideration furnished by such other person: *Provided further*, That where any property has been acquired by gift, bequest, devise, or inheritance, as a tenancy by the entirety by the decedent and spouse, then to the extent of one-half of the value thereof, or, where so acquired by the decedent and any other person as joint tenants with right of survivorship and their interests are not otherwise specified or fixed by law, then to the extent of the value of a fractional part to be determined by dividing the value of the property by the number of joint tenants with right of survivorship.

    (b) Certain joint interests of husband and wife.—

    (1) Interests of spouse excluded from gross estate.—Notwithstanding subsection (a), in the case of any qualified joint interest, the value included in the gross estate with respect to such interest by reason of this section is one-half of the value of such qualified joint interest.

(2) Qualified joint interest defined.—For purposes of paragraph (1), the term "qualified joint interest" means any interest in property held by the decedent and the decedent's spouse as—

    (A) tenants by the entirety, or

    (B) joint tenants with right of survivorship, but only if the decedent and the spouse of the decedent are the only joint tenants.

§ 2041.   Powers of appointment

(a) In general.—The value of the gross estate shall include the value of all property—

(1) Powers of appointment created on or before October 21, 1942.—To the extent of any property with respect to which a general power of appointment created on or before October 21, 1942, is exercised by the decedent—

    (A) by will, or

    (B) by a disposition which is of such nature that if it were a transfer of property owned by the decedent, such property would be includible in the decedent's gross estate under sections 2035 to 2038, inclusive;

but the failure to exercise such a power or the complete release of such a power shall not be deemed an exercise thereof. If a general power of appointment created on or before October 21, 1942, has been partially released so that it is no longer a general power of appointment, the exercise of such power shall not be deemed to be the exercise of a general power of appointment if—

      (i) such partial release occurred before November 1, 1951, or

      (ii) the donee of such power was under a legal disability to release such power on October 21, 1942, and such partial release occurred not later than 6 months after the termination of such legal disability.

(2) Powers created after October 21, 1942.—To the extent of any property with respect to which the decedent has at the time of his death a general power of appointment created after October 21, 1942, or with respect to which the decedent has at any time exercised or released such a power of appointment by a disposition which is of such nature that if it were a transfer of property owned by the decedent, such property would be includible in the decedent's gross estate under sections 2035 to 2038, inclusive. For purposes of this paragraph (2), the power of appointment shall be considered to exist on the date of the decedent's death even though the exercise of the power is subject to a precedent giving of notice or even though the exercise of the power takes effect only on the expiration of a stated period after its exercise, whether or not on or before the date of the decedent's death notice has been given or the power has been exercised.

(3) Creation of another power in certain cases.—To the extent of any property with respect to which the decedent—

    (A) by will, or

    (B) by a disposition which is of such nature that if it were a transfer of property owned by the decedent such property would be includible in the decedent's gross estate under section 2035, 2036, or 2037,

exercises a power of appointment created after October 21, 1942, by creating another power of appointment which under the applicable local law can be validly exercised so as to postpone the vesting of any estate or interest in such property, or suspend the absolute ownership or power of alienation of such property, for a period ascertainable without regard to the date of the creation of the first power.

(b) Definitions.—For purposes of subsection (a)—

(1) General power of appointment.—The term "general power of appointment" means a power which is exercisable in favor of the decedent, his estate, his creditors, or the creditors of his estate; except that—

(A) A power to consume, invade, or appropriate property for the benefit of the decedent which is limited by an ascertainable standard relating to the health, education, support, or maintenance of the decedent shall not be deemed a general power of appointment.

(B) A power of appointment created on or before October 21, 1942, which is exercisable by the decedent only in conjunction with another person shall not be deemed a general power of appointment.

(C) In the case of a power of appointment created after October 21, 1942, which is exercisable by the decedent only in conjunction with another person—

(i) If the power is not exercisable by the decedent except in conjunction with the creator of the power—such power shall not be deemed a general power of appointment.

(ii) If the power is not exercisable by the decedent except in conjunction with a person having a substantial interest in the property, subject to the power, which is adverse to exercise of the power in favor of the decedent—such power shall not be deemed a general power of appointment. For the purposes of this clause a person who, after the death of the decedent, may be possessed of a power of appointment (with respect to the property subject to the decedent's power) which he may exercise in his own favor shall be deemed as having an interest in the property and such interest shall be deemed adverse to such exercise of the decedent's power.

(iii) If (after the application of clauses (i) and (ii)) the power is a general power of appointment and is exercisable in favor of such other person—such power shall be deemed a general power of appointment only in respect of a fractional part of the property subject to such power, such part to be determined by dividing the value of such property by the number of such persons (including the decedent) in favor of whom such power is exercisable.

For purposes of clauses (ii) and (iii), a power shall be deemed to be exercisable in favor of a person if it is exercisable in favor of such person, his estate, his creditors, or the creditors of his estate.

(2) Lapse of power.—The lapse of a power of appointment created after October 21, 1942, during the life of the individual possessing the power shall be considered a release of such power. The preceding sentence shall apply with respect to the lapse of powers during any calendar year only to the extent that the property, which could have been appointed by exercise of such lapsed powers, exceeded in value, at the time of such lapse, the greater of the following amounts:

(A) $5,000, or

(B) 5 percent of the aggregate value, at the time of such lapse, of the assets out of which, or the proceeds of which, the exercise of the lapsed powers could have been satisfied.

§ 2042.   Proceeds of life insurance

The value of the gross estate shall include the value of all property—

(1) Receivable by the executor.—To the extent of the amount receivable by the executor as insurance under policies on the life of the decedent.

(2) Receivable by other beneficiaries.—To the extent of the amount receivable by all other beneficiaries as insurance under policies on the life of the decedent with respect to which the decedent possessed at his death any of the incidents of ownership, exercisable either alone or in conjunction with any other person. For purposes of the preceding sentence, the term "incident of ownership" includes a reversionary interest (whether arising by the express terms of the policy or other instrument or by operation of law) only if the value of such reversionary interest exceeded 5 percent of the value of the policy immediately before the death of the decedent. As used in this paragraph, the term "reversionary interest" includes a possibility that the policy, or the proceeds of the policy, may return to the decedent or his estate, or may be subject to a power of disposition by him. The value of a reversionary interest at any time shall be determined (without regard to the fact of the decedent's death) by usual methods of valuation, including the use of tables of mortality and actuarial principles, pursuant to regulations prescribed by the Secretary. In determining the value of a possibility that the policy or proceeds thereof may be subject to a power of disposition by the decedent, such possibility shall be valued as if it were a possibility that such policy or proceeds may return to the decedent or his estate.

§ 2043.   Transfers for insufficient consideration

(a) In general.—If any one of the transfers, trusts, interests, rights, or powers enumerated and described in sections 2035 to 2038, inclusive, and section 2041 is made, created, exercised, or relinquished for a consideration in money or money's worth, but is not a bona fide sale for an adequate and full consideration in money or money's worth, there shall be included in the gross estate only the excess of the fair market value at the time of death of the property otherwise to be included on account of such transaction, over the value of the consideration received therefor by the decedent.

(b) Marital rights not treated as consideration.—For purposes of this chapter, a relinquishment or promised relinquishment of dower or curtesy, or of a statutory estate created in lieu of dower or curtesy, or of other marital rights in the decedent's property or estate, shall not be considered to any extent a consideration "in money or money's worth."

§ 2044.   Certain property for which marital deduction was previously allowed

(a) General rule.—The value of the gross estate shall include the value of any property to which this section applies in which the decedent had a qualifying income interest for life.

(b) Property to which this section applies.—This section applies to any property if—

(1) a deduction was allowed with respect to the transfer of such property to the decedent—

      (A) under section 2056 by reason of subsection (b)(7) thereof, or

      (B) under section 2523 by reason of subsection (f) thereof, and

(2) section 2519 (relating to dispositions of certain life estates) did not apply with respect to a disposition by the decedent of part or all of such property.

§ 2045.   Prior interests

Except as otherwise specifically provided by law, sections 2034 to 2042, inclusive, shall apply to the transfers, trusts, estates, interests, rights, powers, and relinquishment of powers, as severally enumerated and described therein, whenever made, created, arising, existing, exercised, or relinquished.

§ 2046.   Disclaimers

For provisions relating to the effect of a qualified disclaimer for purposes of this chapter, see section 2518.

PART IV—TAXABLE ESTATE

§ 2051.   Definition of taxable estate

For purposes of the tax imposed by section 2001, the value of the taxable estate shall be determined by deducting from the value of the gross estate the deductions provided for in this part.

§ 2053.   Expenses, indebtedness, and taxes

(a) **General rule.**—For purposes of the tax imposed by section 2001, the value of the taxable estate shall be determined by deducting from the value of the gross estate such amounts—

(1) for funeral expenses,

(2) for administration expenses,

(3) for claims against the estate, and

(4) for unpaid mortgages on, or any indebtedness in respect of, property where the value of the decedent's interest therein, undiminished by such mortgage or indebtedness, is included in the value of the gross estate,

as are allowable by the laws of the jurisdiction, whether within or without the United States, under which the estate is being administered.

(b) **Other administration expenses.**—Subject to the limitations in paragraph (1) of subsection (c), there shall be deducted in determining the taxable estate amounts representing expenses incurred in administering property not subject to claims which is included in the gross estate to the same extent such amounts would be allowable as a deduction under subsection (a) if such property were subject to claims, and such amounts are paid before the expiration of the period of limitation for assessment provided in section 6501.

(c) **Limitations.—**

(1) **Limitations applicable to subsections (a) and (b).—**

(A) **Consideration for claims.**—The deduction allowed by this section in the case of claims against the estate, unpaid mortgages, or any indebtedness shall, when founded on a promise or agreement, be limited to the extent that they were contracted bona fide and for an adequate and full consideration in money or money's worth; except that in any case in which any such claim is founded on a promise or agreement of the decedent to make a contribution or gift to or for the use of any donee described in section 2055 for the purposes specified therein, the deduction for such claims shall not be so limited, but shall be limited to the extent that it would be allowable as a deduction under section 2055 if such promise or agreement constituted a bequest.

(B) **Certain taxes.**—Any income taxes on income received after the death of the decedent, or property taxes not accrued before his death, or any estate, succession, legacy, or inheritance taxes, shall not be deductible under this section.

(2) **Limitations applicable only to subsection (a).**—In the case of the amounts described in subsection (a), there shall be disallowed the amount by which the deductions specified therein exceed the value, at the time of the decedent's death, of property subject to claims, except to the extent that such deductions represent amounts paid before the date prescribed for the filing of the estate tax return. For purposes of this section, the term "property subject to claims" means property includible in the gross estate of the decedent which, or the avails of which, would under the applicable law, bear the burden of the payment of such deductions in the final adjustment and settlement of the estate, except that the value of the property shall be reduced by the amount of the deduction under section 2054 attributable to such property.

(d) Certain state and foreign death taxes.—

(1) **General rule.**—Notwithstanding the provisions of subsection (c) (1) (B) of this section, for purposes of the tax imposed by section 2001 the value of the taxable estate may be determined, if the executor so elects before the expiration of the period of limitation for assessment provided in section 6501, by deducting from the value of the gross estate the amount (as determined in accordance with regulations prescribed by the Secretary) of—

(A) any estate, succession, legacy, or inheritance tax imposed by a State or the District of Columbia upon a transfer by the decedent for public, charitable, or religious uses described in section 2055 or 2106(a) (2), and

(B) any estate, succession, legacy, or inheritance tax imposed by and actually paid to any foreign country, in respect of any property situated within such foreign country and included in the gross estate of a citizen or resident of the United States, upon a transfer by the decedent for public, charitable, or religious uses described in section 2055.

. . . .

(2) **Condition for allowance of deduction.**—No deduction shall be allowed under paragraph (1) for a State death tax or a foreign death tax specified therein unless the decrease in the tax imposed by section 2001 which results from the deduction provided in paragraph (1) will inure solely for the benefit of the public, charitable, or religious transferees described in section 2055 or section 2106(a) (2). In any case where the tax imposed by section 2001 is equitably apportioned among all the transferees of property included in the gross estate, including those described in sections 2055 and 2106(a) (2) (taking into account any exemptions, credits, or deductions allowed by this chapter), in determining such decrease, there shall be disregarded any decrease in the

Federal estate tax which any transferees other than those described in sections 2055 and 2106(a) (2) are required to pay.

§ 2054.   Losses

For purposes of the tax imposed by section 2001, the value of the taxable estate shall be determined by deducting from the value of the gross estate losses incurred during the settlement of estates arising from fires, storms, shipwrecks, or other casualties, or from theft, when such losses are not compensated for by insurance or otherwise.

§ 2055.   Transfers for public, charitable, and religious uses

(a) In general.—For purposes of the tax imposed by section 2001, the value of the taxable estate shall be determined by deducting from the value of the gross estate the amount of all bequests, legacies, devises, or transfers—

(1) to or for the use of the United States, any State, any political subdivision thereof, or the District of Columbia, for exclusively public purposes;

(2) to or for the use of any corporation organized and operated exclusively for religious, charitable, scientific, literary, or educational purposes, including the encouragement of art, or to foster national or international amateur sports competition (but only if no part of its activities involve the provision of athletic facilities or equipment), and the prevention of cruelty to children or animals, no part of the net earnings of which inures to the benefit of any private stockholder or individual, which is not disqualified for tax exemption under section 501(c) (3) by reason of attempting to influence legislation, and which does not participate in, or intervene in (including the publishing or distributing of statements), any political campaign on behalf of any candidate for public office;

(3) to a trustee or trustees, or a fraternal society, order, or association operating under the lodge system, but only if such contributions or gifts are to be used by such trustee or trustees, or by such fraternal society, order, or association, exclusively for religious, charitable, scientific, literary, or educational purposes, or for the prevention of cruelty to children or animals, such trust, fraternal society, order, or association would not be disqualified for tax exemption under section 501(c) (3) by reason of attempting to influence legislation, and such trustee or trustees, or such fraternal society, order, or association, does not participate in, or intervene in (including the publishing or distributing of statements), any political campaign on behalf of any candidate for public office; or

(4) to or for the use of any veterans' organization incorporated by Act of Congress, or of its departments or local chapters or posts, no part of the net earnings of which inures to the benefit of any private shareholder or individual.

For purposes of this subsection, the complete termination before the date prescribed for the filing of the estate tax return of a power to consume, invade, or appropriate property for the benefit of an individual before such power has been exercised by reason of the death of such individual or for any other reason shall be considered and deemed to be a qualified disclaimer with the same full force and effect as though he had filed such qualified disclaimer. Rules similar to the rules of section 501(j) shall apply for purposes of paragraph (2).

(b) Powers of appointment.—Property includible in the decedent's gross estate under section 2041 (relating to powers of appointment) received by a donee described in this section shall, for purposes of this section, be considered a bequest of such decedent.

(c) Death taxes payable out of bequests.—If the tax imposed by section 2001, or any estate, succession, legacy, or inheritance taxes, are, either by the terms of the will, by the law of the jurisdiction under which the estate is administered, or by the law of the jurisdiction imposing the particular tax, payable in whole or in part out of the bequests, legacies, or devises otherwise deductible under this section, then the amount deductible under this section shall be the amount of such bequests, legacies, or devises reduced by the amount of such taxes.

(d) Limitation on deduction.—The amount of the deduction under this section for any transfer shall not exceed the value of the transferred property required to be included in the gross estate.

(e) Disallowance of deductions in certain cases.—

. . . .

(2) Where an interest in property (other than an interest described in section 170(f) (3) (B)) passes or has passed from the decedent to a person, or for a use, described in subsection (a), and an interest (other than an interest which is extinguished upon the decedent's death) in the same property passes or has passed (for less than an adequate and full consideration in money or money's worth) from the decedent to a person, or for a use, not described in subsection (a), no deduction shall be allowed under this section for the interest which passes or has passed to the person, or for the use, described in subsection (a) unless—

(A) in the case of a remainder interest, such interest is in a trust which is a charitable remainder annuity trust or a charitable remainder unitrust (described in section 664) or a pooled income fund (described in section 642(c) (5)), or

(B) in the case of any other interest, such interest is in the form of a guaranteed annuity or is a fixed percentage distributed yearly of the fair market value of the property (to be determined yearly).

. . . .

(4) Works of art and their copyrights treated as separate properties in certain cases.—

(A) **In general.**—In the case of a qualified contribution of a work of art, the work of art and the copyright on such work of art shall be treated as separate properties for purposes of paragraph (2).

(B) **Work of art defined.**—For purposes of this paragraph, the term "work of art" means any tangible personal property with respect to which there is a copyright under Federal law.

(C) **Qualified contribution defined.**—For purposes of this paragraph, the term "qualified contribution" means any transfer of property to a qualified organization if the use of the property by the organization is related to the purpose or function constituting the basis for its exemption under section 501.

(D) Qualified organization defined.—For purposes of this paragraph, the term "qualified organization" means any organization described in section 501(c)(3) other than a private foundation (as defined in section 509). For purposes of the preceding sentence, a private operating foundation (as defined in section 4942(j)(3)) shall not be treated as a private foundation.

. . . . .

§ 2056.   Bequests, etc., to surviving spouse

(a) Allowance of marital deduction.—For purposes of the tax imposed by section 2001, the value of the taxable estate shall, except as limited by subsections (b), be determined by deducting from the value of the gross estate an amount equal to the value of any interest in property which passes or has passed from the decedent to his surviving spouse, but only to the extent that such interest is included in determining the value of the gross estate.

(b) Limitation in the case of life estate or other terminable interest.—

(1) General rule.—Where, on the lapse of time, on the occurrence of an event or contingency, or on the failure of an event or contingency to occur, an interest passing to the surviving spouse will terminate or fail, no deduction shall be allowed under this section with respect to such interest—

(A) if an interest in such property passes or has passed (for less than an adequate and full consideration in money or money's worth) from the decedent to any person other than such surviving spouse (or the estate of such spouse); and

(B) if by reason of such passing such person (or his heirs or assigns) may possess or enjoy any part of such property after such termination or failure of the interest so passing to the surviving spouse;

and no deduction shall be allowed with respect to such interest (even if such deduction is not disallowed under subparagraphs (A) and (B))—

(C) if such interest is to be acquired for the surviving spouse, pursuant to directions of the decedent, by his executor or by the trustee of a trust.

For purposes of this paragraph, an interest shall not be considered as an interest which will terminate or fail merely because it is the ownership of a bond, note, or similar contractual obligation, the discharge of which would not have the effect of an annuity for life or for a term.

(2) Interest in unidentified assets.—Where the assets (included in the decedent's gross estate) out of which, or the proceeds of which, an interest passing to the surviving spouse may be satisfied include a particular asset or assets with respect to which no deduction would be allowed if such asset or assets passed from the decedent to such spouse, then the value of such interest passing to such spouse shall, for purposes of subsection (a), be reduced by the aggregate value of such particular assets.

(3) Interest of spouse conditional on survival for limited period.—For purposes of this subsection, an interest passing to the surviving spouse shall not be considered as an interest which will terminate or fail on the death of such spouse if—

(A) such death will cause a termination or failure of such interest only if it occurs within a period not exceeding 6 months after the decedent's death, or only if it occurs as a result of a common disaster resulting in the death of the decedent and the surviving spouse, or only if it occurs in the case of either such event; and

(B) such termination or failure does not in fact occur.

(4) **Valuation of interest passing to surviving spouse.**—In determining for purposes of subsection (a) the value of any interest in property passing to the surviving spouse for which a deduction is allowed by this section—

(A) there shall be taken into account the effect which the tax imposed by section 2001, or any estate, succession, legacy, or inheritance tax, has on the net value to the surviving spouse of such interest; and

(B) where such interest or property is encumbered in any manner, or where the surviving spouse incurs any obligation imposed by the decedent with respect to the passing of such interest, such encumbrance or obligation shall be taken into account in the same manner as if the amount of a gift to such spouse of such interest were being determined.

(5) **Life estate with power of appointment in surviving spouse.**—In the case of an interest in property passing from the decedent, if his surviving spouse is entitled for life to all the income from the entire interest, or all the income from a specific portion thereof, payable annually or at more frequent intervals, with power in the surviving spouse to appoint the entire interest, or such specific portion (exercisable in favor of such surviving spouse, or of the estate of such surviving spouse, or in favor of either, whether or not in each case the power is exercisable in favor of others), and with no power in any other person to appoint any part of the interest, or such specific portion, to any person other than the surviving spouse—

(A) the interest or such portion thereof so passing shall, for purposes of subsection (a), be considered as passing to the surviving spouse, and

(B) no part of the interest so passing shall, for purposes of paragraph (1) (A), be considered as passing to any person other than the surviving spouse.

This paragraph shall apply only if such power in the surviving spouse to appoint the entire interest, or such specific portion thereof, whether exercisable by will or during life, is exercisable by such spouse alone and in all events.

(6) **Life insurance or annuity payments with power of appointment in surviving spouse.**—In the case of an interest in property passing from the decedent consisting of proceeds under a life insurance, endowment, or annuity contract, if under the terms of the contract such proceeds are payable in installments or are held by the insurer subject to an agreement to pay interest thereon (whether the proceeds, on the termination of any interest payments, are payable in a lump sum or in annual or more frequent installments), and such installment or interest payments are payable annually or at more frequent intervals, commencing not later than 13 months after the decedent's death, and all amounts, or a specific portion of all such amounts, payable during the life of the surviving spouse are payable only to such spouse, and such spouse has the power to appoint all amounts, or such specific portion, payable under such contract (exercisable in favor of such surviving spouse, or of the estate of such surviving spouse, or in favor of either, whether or not in each case the power is exercisable in favor of others), with no power in any other person to appoint such amounts to any person other than the surviving spouse—

(A) such amounts shall, for purposes of subsection (a), be considered as passing to the surviving spouse, and

(B) no part of such amounts shall, for purposes of paragraph (1) (A), be considered as passing to any person other than the surviving spouse.

This paragraph shall apply only if, under the terms of the contract, such power in the surviving spouse to appoint such amounts, whether exercisable by will or during life, is exercisable by such spouse alone and in all events.

(7) Election with respect to life estate for surviving spouse.—

   (A) In general.—In the case of qualified terminable interest property—

      (i) for purposes of subsection (a), such property shall be treated as passing to the surviving spouse, and

      (ii) for purposes of paragraph (1)(A), no part of such property shall be treated as passing to any person other than the surviving spouse.

   (B) Qualified terminable interest property defined.—For purposes of this paragraph—

      (i) In general.—The term "qualified terminable interest property" means property—

         (I) which passes from the decedent,

         (II) in which the surviving spouse has a qualifying income interest for life, and

         (III) to which an election under this paragraph applies.

      (ii) Qualifying income interest for life.—The surviving spouse has a qualifying income interest for life if—

         (I) the surviving spouse is entitled to all the income from the property, payable annually or at more frequent intervals, and

         (II) no person has a power to appoint any part of the property to any person other than the surviving spouse.

      Subclause (II) shall not apply to a power exercisable only at or after the death of the surviving spouse.

      (iii) Property includes interest therein.—The term "property" includes an interest in property.

      (iv) Specific portion treated as separate property.—A specific portion of property shall be treated as separate property.

      (v) Election.—An election under this paragraph with respect to any property shall be made by the executor on the return of tax imposed by section 2001. Such an election, once made, shall be irrevocable.

(8) Special rule for charitable remainder trusts.—

   (A) In general.—If the surviving spouse of the decedent is the only noncharitable beneficiary of a qualified charitable remainder trust, paragraph (1) shall not apply to any interest in such trust which passes or has passed from the decedent to such surviving spouse.

   (B) Definitions.—For purposes of subparagraph (A)—

      (i) Noncharitable beneficiary.—The term "noncharitable beneficiary" means any beneficiary of the qualified charitable remainder trust other than an organization described in section 170(c).

(ii) Qualified charitable remainder trust.—The term "qualified charitable remainder trust" means a charitable remainder annuity trust or charitable remainder unitrust (described in section 664).

(c) Definition.—For purposes of this section, an interest in property shall be considered as passing from the decedent to any person if and only if—

(1) such interest is bequeathed or devised to such person by the decedent;

(2) such interest is inherited by such person from the decedent;

(3) such interest is the dower or curtesy interest (or statutory interest in lieu thereof) of such person as surviving spouse of the decedent;

(4) such interest has been transferred to such person by the decedent at any time;

(5) such interest was, at the time of the decedent's death, held by such person and the decedent (or by them and any other person) in joint ownership with right of survivorship;

(6) the decedent had a power (either alone or in conjunction with any person) to appoint such interest and if he appoints or has appointed such interest to such person, or if such person takes such interest in default on the release or nonexercise of such power; or

(7) such interest consists of proceeds of insurance on the life of the decedent receivable by such person.

Except as provided in paragraph (5) or (6) of subsection (b), where at the time of the decedent's death it is not possible to ascertain the particular person or persons to whom an interest in property may pass from the decedent, such interest shall, for purposes of subparagraphs (A) and (B) of subsection (b) (1), be considered as passing from the decedent to a person other than the surviving spouse.

SUBCHAPTER C—MISCELLANEOUS

§ 2203. Definition of executor

The term "executor" wherever it is used in this title in connection with the estate tax imposed by this chapter means the executor or administrator of the decedent, or, if there is no executor or administrator appointed, qualified, and acting within the United States, then any person in actual or constructive possession of any property of the decedent.

§ 2204. Discharge of fiduciary from personal liability

(a) General rule.—If the executor makes written application to the Secretary for determination of the amount of the tax and discharge from personal liability therefor, the Secretary (as soon as possible, and in any event within 9 months after the making of such application, or, if the application is made before the return is filed, then within 9 months after the return is filed, but not after the expiration of the period prescribed for the assessment of the tax in section 6501) shall notify the executor of the amount of the tax. The executor, on payment of the amount of which he is notified (other than any amount the time for payment of which is extended under section 6161, 6163, or 6166), and on furnishing any bond which may be required for any amount for which the time for payment is extended, shall be discharged from personal liability for any deficiency in tax thereafter found to be due and shall be entitled to a receipt or writing showing such discharge.

(b) Fiduciary other than the executor.—If a fiduciary (not including a fiduciary in respect of the estate of a nonresident decedent) other than the executor makes written application to the Secretary for determination of the amount of any estate tax for which the fiduciary may be personally liable, and for discharge from personal liability therefor, the Secretary upon the discharge of the executor from personal liability under subsection (a), or upon the expiration of 6 months after the making of such application by the fiduciary, if later, shall notify the fiduciary (1) of the amount of such tax for which it has been determined the fiduciary is liable, or (2) that it has been determined that the fiduciary is not liable for any such tax. Such application shall be accompanied by a copy of the instrument, if any, under which such fiduciary is acting, a description of the property held by the fiduciary, and such other information for purposes of carrying out the provisions of this section as the Secretary may require by regulations. On payment of the amount of such tax for which it has been determined the fiduciary is liable (other than any amount the time for payment of which has been extended under section 6161, 6163, or 6166), and on furnishing any bond which may be required for any amount for which the time for payment has been extended, or on receipt by him of notification of a determination that he is not liable for any such tax, the fiduciary shall be discharged from personal liability for any deficiency in such tax thereafter found to be due and shall be entitled to a receipt or writing evidencing such discharge.

(c) Special lien under section 6324A.—For purposes of the second sentence of subsection (a) and the last sentence of subsection (b), an agreement which meets the requirements of section 6324A (relating to special lien for estate tax deferred under section 6166), shall be treated as the furnishing of bond with respect to the amount for which the time for payment has been extended under section 6166.

(d) Good faith reliance on gift tax returns.—If the executor in good faith relies on gift tax returns furnished under section 6103(e) (3) for determining the decedent's adjusted taxable gifts, the executor shall be discharged from personal liability with respect to any deficiency of the tax imposed by this chapter which is attributable to adjusted taxable gifts which—

(1) are made more than 3 years before the date of the decedent's death, and

(2) are not shown on such returns.

§ 2205.   Reimbursement out of estate

If the tax or any part thereof is paid by, or collected out of, that part of the estate passing to or in the possession of any person other than the executor in his capacity as such, such person shall be entitled to reimbursement out of any part of the estate still undistributed or by a just and equitable contribution by the persons whose interest in the estate of the decedent would have been reduced if the tax had been paid before the distribution of the estate or whose interest is subject to equal or prior liability for the payment of taxes, debts, or other charges against the estate, it being the purpose and intent of this chapter that so far as is practicable and unless otherwise directed by the will of the decedent the tax shall be paid out of the estate before its distribution.

§ 2206.   Liability of life insurance beneficiaries

Unless the decedent directs otherwise in his will, if any part of the gross estate on which tax has been paid consists of proceeds of policies of insurance on the life of the decedent receivable by a beneficiary other than the executor, the executor shall be entitled to recover from such beneficiary such portion of the total tax paid as the proceeds of such policies bear to the taxable estate. If there is more than one such beneficiary, the executor shall be entitled to recover from such beneficiaries in the same ratio. In the case of such proceeds receivable by the surviving spouse of the decedent for which a deduction is allowed under section 2056 (relating to marital deduction), this section shall not apply to such proceeds except as to the amount thereof in excess of the aggregate amount of the marital deductions allowed under such section.

§ 2207.   Liability of recipient of property over which decedent had power of appointment

Unless the decedent directs otherwise in his will, if any part of the gross estate on which the tax has been paid consists of the value of property included in the gross estate under section 2041, the executor shall be entitled to recover from the person receiving such property by reason of the exercise, nonexercise, or release of a power of appointment such portion of the total tax paid as the value of such property bears to the taxable estate. If there is more than one such person, the executor shall be entitled to recover from such persons in the same ratio. In the case of such property received by the surviving spouse of the decedent for which a deduction is allowed under section 2056 (relating to marital deduction), this section shall not apply to such property except as to the value thereof reduced by an amount equal to the excess of the aggregate amount of the marital deductions allowed under section 2056 over the amount of proceeds of insurance upon the life of the decedent receivable by the surviving spouse for which proceeds a marital deduction is allowed under such section.

§ 2207A.   Right of recovery in the case of certain marital deduction property

(a) Recovery with respect to estate tax.—

(1) In general.—If any part of the gross estate consists of property the value of which is includible in the gross estate by reason of section 2044 (relating to certain property for which marital deduction was previously allowed), the decedent's estate shall be entitled to recover from the person receiving the property the amount by which—

(A) the total tax under this chapter which has been paid, exceeds

(B) the total tax under this chapter which would have been payable if the value of such property had not been included in the gross estate.

(2) Decedent may otherwise direct by will.—Paragraph (1) shall not apply if the decedent otherwise directs by will.

(b) Recovery with respect to gift tax.—If for any calendar year tax is paid under chapter 12 with respect to any person by reason of property treated as transferred by such person under section 2519, such person shall be entitled to recover from the person receiving the property the amount by which—

(1) the total tax for such year under chapter 12, exceeds

(2) the total tax which would have been payable under such chapter for such year if the value of such property had not been taken into account for purposes of chapter 12.

(c) More than one recipient of property.—For purposes of this section, if there is more than one person receiving the property, the right of recovery shall be against each such person.

(d) Taxes and interest.—In the case of penalties and interest attributable to additional taxes described in subsections (a) and (b), rules similar to subsections (a), (b), and (c) shall apply.

CHAPTER 12—GIFT TAX

Subchapter
A. Determination of tax liability.
B. Transfers.
C. Deductions.

SUBCHAPTER A—DETERMINATION OF TAX LIABILITY

§ 2501.   Imposition of tax

(a) Taxable transfers.—

   (1) General rule.—A tax, computed as provided in section 2502, is hereby imposed for each calendar year on the transfer of property by gift during such calendar year by any individual, resident or nonresident.

   . . . . .

   (5) Transfers to political organizations.—Paragraph (1) shall not apply to the transfer of money or other property to a political organization (within the meaning of section 527(e) (1)) for the use of such organization.

   . . . . .

§ 2502.   Rate of tax

(a) Computation of tax.—The tax imposed by section 2501 for each calendar year shall be an amount equal to the excess of—

   (1) a tentative tax, computed in accordance with the rate schedule set forth in section 2001(c), on the aggregate sum of the taxable gifts for such calendar year and for each of the preceding calendar periods, over

   (2) a tentative tax, computed in accordance with such rate schedule, on the aggregate sum of the taxable gifts for each of the preceding calendar periods.

(b) Preceding calendar period.—Whenever used in this title in "connection with the gift" tax imposed by this chapter, the term preceding calendar period means—

   (1) calendar years 1932 and 1970 and all calendar years intervening between calendar year 1932 and calendar year 1970,

   (2) the first calendar quarter of calendar year 1971 and all calendar quarters intervening between such calendar quarter and the first calendar quarter of calendar year 1982, and

   (3) all calendar years after 1981 and before the calendar year for which the tax is being computed.

For purposes of paragraph (1), the term "calendar year 1932" includes only that portion of such year after June 6, 1932.

(c) **Tax to be paid by donor.**—The tax imposed by section 2501 shall be paid by the donor.

§ 2503.   Taxable gifts

(a) **General definition.**—The term "taxable gifts" means the total amount of gifts made during the calendar year, less the deductions provided in subchapter C (section 2522 and following).

(b) **Exclusion from gifts.**—In the case of gifts (other than gifts of future interests in property) made to any person by the donor during the calendar year, the first $10,000 of such gifts to such person shall not, for purposes of subsection (a), be included in the total amount of gifts made during such year. Where there has been a transfer to any person of a present interest in property, the possibility that such interest may be diminished by the exercise of a power shall be disregarded in applying this subsection, if no part of such interest will at any time pass to any other person.

(c) **Transfer for the benefit of minor.**—No part of a gift to an individual who has not attained the age of 21 years on the date of such transfer shall be considered a gift of a future interest in property for purposes of subsection (b) if the property and the income therefrom—

(1) may be expended by, or for the benefit of, the donee before his attaining the age of 21 years, and

(2) will to the extent not so expended—

(A) pass to the donee on his attaining the age of 21 years, and

(B) in the event the donee dies before attaining the age of 21 years, be payable to the estate of the donee or as he may appoint under a general power of appointment as defined in section 2514(c).

(d) **Repealed.** Pub.L. 97–34, Title III, § 311(h)(5), Aug. 13, 1981, 95 Stat. 282.

(e) **Exclusion for certain transfers for educational expenses or medical expenses.—**

(1) **In general.**—Any qualified transfer shall not be treated as a transfer of property by gift for purposes of this chapter.

(2) **Qualified transfer.**—For purposes of this subsection, the term "qualified transfer" means any amount paid on behalf of an individual—

(A) as tuition to an educational organization described in section 170(b)(1)(A)(ii) for the education or training of such individual, or

(B) to any person who provides medical care (as defined in section 213(e)) with respect to such individual as payment for such medical care.

§ 2504.   Taxable gifts for preceding calendar periods

(a) **In general.**—In computing taxable gifts for preceding calendar periods for purposes of computing the tax for any calendar year—

(1) there shall be treated as gifts such transfers as were considered to be gifts under the gift tax laws applicable to the calendar period in which the transfers were made,

(2) there shall be allowed such deductions as were provided for under such laws, and

(3) the specific exemption in the amount (if any) allowable under section 2521 (as in effect before its repeal by the Tax Reform Act of 1976) shall be applied in all computations in respect of preceding calendar periods ending before January 1, 1977, for purposes of computing the tax for any calendar year.

(b) Exclusions from gifts for preceding calendar periods.—In the case of gifts made to any person by the donor during preceding calendar periods, the amount excluded, if any, by the provisions of gift tax laws applicable to the periods in which the gifts were made shall not, for purposes of subsection (a), be included in the total amount of the gifts made during such preceding calendar periods.

(c) Valuation of certain gifts for preceding calendar periods.—If the time has expired within which a tax may be assessed under this chapter or under corresponding provisions of prior laws on the transfer of property by gift made during a preceding calendar period, as defined in section 2502(b), and if a tax under this chapter or under corresponding provisions of prior laws has been assessed or paid for such preceding calendar period, the value of such gift made in such preceding calendar period shall, for purposes of computing the tax under this chapter for any calendar year, be the value of such gift which was used in computing the tax for the last preceding calendar period for which a tax under this chapter or under corresponding provisions of prior laws was assessed or paid.

(d) Net gifts.—The term "net gifts" as used in corresponding provisions of prior laws shall be read as "taxable gifts" for purposes of this chapter.

§ 2505.   Unified credit against gift tax

(a) General rule.—In the case of a citizen or resident of the United States, there shall be allowed as a credit against the tax imposed by section 2501 for each calendar year an amount equal to—

(1) $192,800, reduced by

(2) the sum of the amounts allowable as a credit to the individual under this section for all preceding calendar periods.

(b) Phase-in of credit.—

In the case of gifts made in:	Subsection (a)(1) shall be applied by substituting for "$192,800" the following amount:
1982	62,800
1983	79,300
1984	96,300
1985	121,800
1986	155,800

(c) Adjustment to credit for certain gifts made before 1977.—The amount allowable under subsection (a) shall be reduced by an amount equal to 20 percent of the aggregate amount allowed as a specific exemption under section 2521 (as in effect before its repeal by the Tax Reform Act of 1976) with respect to gifts made by the individual after September 8, 1976.

(d) Limitation based on amount of tax.—The amount of the credit allowed under subsection (a) for any calendar year shall not exceed the amount of the tax imposed by section 2501 for such calendar year.

SUBCHAPTER B—TRANSFERS

§ 2511.   Transfers in general

(a) Scope.—Subject to the limitations contained in this chapter, the tax imposed by section 2501 shall apply whether the transfer is in trust or otherwise, whether the gift is direct or indirect, and whether the property is real or personal, tangible or intangible; but in the case of a nonresident not a citizen of the United States, shall apply to a transfer only if the property is situated within the United States.

§ 2512.   Valuation of gifts

(a) If the gift is made in property, the value thereof at the date of the gift shall be considered the amount of the gift.

(b) Where property is transferred for less than an adequate and full consideration in money or money's worth, then the amount by which the value of the property exceeded the value of the consideration shall be deemed a gift, and shall be included in computing the amount of gifts made during the calendar year.

§ 2513.   Gift by husband or wife to third party

(a) Considered as made one-half by each.—

(1) In general.—A gift made by one spouse to any person other than his spouse shall, for the purposes of this chapter, be considered as made one-half by him and one-half by his spouse, but only if at the time of the gift each spouse is a citizen or resident of the United States. This paragraph shall not apply with respect to a gift by a spouse of an interest in property if he creates in his spouse a general power of appointment, as defined in section 2514(c), over such interest. For purposes of this section, an individual shall be considered as the spouse of another individual only if he is married to such individual at the time of the gift and does not remarry during the remainder of the calendar year.

(2) Consent of both spouses.—Paragraph (1) shall apply only if both spouses have signified (under the regulations provided for in subsection (b)) their consent to the application of paragraph (1) in the case of all such gifts made during the calendar year by either while married to the other.

(b) Manner and time of signifying consent.—

(1) Manner.—A consent under this section shall be signified in such manner as is provided under regulations prescribed by the Secretary.

(2) Time.—Such consent may be so signified at any time after the close of the calendar year in which the gift was made, subject to the following limitations—

(A) The consent may not be signified after the 15th day of April following the close of such year, unless before such 15th day no return has been filed for such year by either spouse, in which case the consent may not be signified after a return for such year is filed by either spouse.

(B) The consent may not be signified after a notice of deficiency with respect to the tax for such year has been sent to either spouse in accordance with section 6212(a).

(c) **Revocation of consent.**—Revocation of a consent previously signified shall be made in such manner as is provided under regulations prescribed by the Secretary, but the right to revoke a consent previously signified with respect to a calendar year—

(1) shall not exist after the 15th day of April following the close of such year if the consent was signified on or before such 15th day; and

(2) shall not exist if the consent was not signified until after such 15th day.

(d) **Joint and several liability for tax.**—If the consent required by subsection (a) (2) is signified with respect to a gift made in any calendar year, the liability with respect to the entire tax imposed by this chapter of each spouse for such year shall be joint and several.

§ 2514.　Powers of appointment

(a) **Powers created on or before October 21, 1942.**—An exercise of a general power of appointment created on or before October 21, 1942, shall be deemed a transfer of property by the individual possessing such power; but the failure to exercise such a power or the complete release of such a power shall not be deemed an exercise thereof. If a general power of appointment created on or before October 21, 1942, has been partially released so that it is no longer a general power of appointment, the subsequent exercise of such power shall not be deemed to be the exercise of a general power of appointment if—

(1) such partial release occurred before November 1, 1951, or

(2) the donee of such power was under a legal disability to release such power on October 21, 1942, and such partial release occurred not later than six months after the termination of such legal disability.

(b) **Powers created after October 21, 1942.**—The exercise or release of a general power of appointment created after October 21, 1942, shall be deemed a transfer of property by the individual possessing such power.

(c) **Definition of general power of appointment.**—For purposes of this section, the term "general power of appointment" means a power which is exercisable in favor of the individual possessing the power (hereafter in this subsection referred to as the "possessor"), his estate, his creditors, or the creditors of his estate; except that—

(1) A power to consume, invade, or appropriate property for the benefit of the possessor which is limited by an ascertainable standard relating to the health, education, support, or maintenance of the possessor shall not be deemed a general power of appointment.

(2) A power of appointment created on or before October 21, 1942, which is exercisable by the possessor only in conjunction with another person shall not be deemed a general power of appointment.

(3) In the case of a power of appointment created after October 21, 1942, which is exercisable by the possessor only in conjunction with another person—

(A) if the power is not exercisable by the possessor except in conjunction with the creator of the power—such power shall not be deemed a general power of appointment;

(B) if the power is not exercisable by the possessor except in conjunction with a person having a substantial interest, in the property subject to the power, which is adverse to exercise of the power in favor of the possessor—such power shall not be deemed a general power of appointment. For the purposes of this subparagraph a person who, after the death of the possessor, may be possessed of a power of appointment (with respect to the property subject to the possessor's power) which he may exercise in his own favor shall be deemed as having an interest in the property and such interest shall be deemed adverse to such exercise of the possessor's power;

(C) if (after the application of subparagraphs (A) and (B)) the power is a general power of appointment and is exercisable in favor of such other person—such power shall be deemed a general power of appointment only in respect of a fractional part of the property subject to such power, such part to be determined by dividing the value of such property by the number of such persons (including the possessor) in favor of whom such power is exercisable.

For purposes of subparagraphs (B) and (C), a power shall be deemed to be exercisable in favor of a person if it is exercisable in favor of such person, his estate, his creditors, or the creditors of his estate.

(d) Creation of another power in certain cases.—If a power of appointment created after October 21, 1942, is exercised by creating another power of appointment which, under the applicable local law, can be validly exercised so as to postpone the vesting of any estate or interest in the property which was subject to the first power, or suspend the absolute ownership or power of alienation of such property, for a period ascertainable without regard to the date of the creation of the first power, such exercise of the first power shall, to the extent of the property subject to the second power, be deemed a transfer of property by the individual possessing such power.

(e) Lapse of power.—The lapse of a power of appointment created after October 21, 1942, during the life of the individual possessing the power shall be considered a release of such power. The rule of the preceding sentence shall apply with respect to the lapse of powers during any calendar year only to the extent that the property which could have been appointed by exercise of such lapsed powers exceeds in value the greater of the following amounts:

(1) $5,000, or

(2) 5 percent of the aggregate value of the assets out of which, or the proceeds of which, the exercise of the lapsed powers could be satisfied.

. . . . .

§ 2516.   Certain property settlements

Where husband and wife enter into a written agreement relative to their marital and property rights and divorce occurs within 2 years thereafter (whether or not such agreement is approved by the divorce decree), any transfers of property or interests in property made pursuant to such agreement—

(1) to either spouse in settlement of his or her marital or property rights, or

(2) to provide a reasonable allowance for the support of issue of the marriage during minority,

shall be deemed to be transfers made for a full and adequate consideration in money or money's worth.

§ 2517.   Certain annuities under qualified plans

(a) General rule.—The exercise or nonexercise by an employee of an election or option whereby an annuity or other payment will become payable to any beneficiary at or after the employee's death shall not be considered a transfer for purposes of this chapter if the option or election and annuity or other payment is provided for under—

(1) an employees' trust (or under a contract purchased by an employees' trust) forming part of a pension, stock bonus, or profit-sharing plan which, at the time of such exercise or nonexercise, or at the time of termination of the plan if earlier, met the requirements of section 401(a);

(2) a retirement annuity contract purchased by an employer (and not by an employees' trust) pursuant to a plan which, at the time of such exercise or nonexercise, or at the time of termination of the plan if earlier, was a plan described in section 403(a);

(3) a retirement annuity contract purchased for an employee by an employer which is an organization referred to in section 170(b) (1) (A) (ii) or (vi), or which is a religious organization (other than a trust), and which is exempt from tax under section 501(a);

(4) chapter 73 of title 10 of the United States Code; or

(5) an individual retirement account described in section 408(a) an individual retirement annuity described in section 408(b), or a retirement bond described in section 409(a).

(b) Transfers attributable to employee contributions.—If the annuity or other payment referred to in subsection (a) (other than paragraphs (4) and (5)) is attributable to any extent to payments or contributions made by the employee, then subsection (a) shall not apply to that part of the value of such annuity or other payment which bears the same proportion to the total value of the annuity or other payment as the total payments or contributions made by the employee bear to the total payments or contributions made. For purposes of the preceding sentence, payments or contributions made by the employee's employer or former employer toward the purchase of an annuity contract described in subsection (a) (3) shall, to the extent not excludable from gross income under section 403(b), be considered to have been made by the employee. For purposes of this subsection, contributions or payments on behalf of an individual while he was an employee within the meaning of section 401(c) (1) made under a trust or plan described in paragraph (1) or (2) of subsection (a) shall, to the extent allowable as a deduction under section 404, be considered to be made by a person other than such individual and, to the extent not so allowable, shall be considered to be made by such individual for purposes of this subsection, any deductible employee contributions (within the meaning of paragraph (5) of section 72(o)) shall be considered as made by a person other than the employee.

(c) Exemption of certain annuity interests created by community property laws.—Notwithstanding any other provision of law, in the case of an employee on whose behalf contributions or payments are made—

(1) by his employer or former employer under a trust or plan described in paragraph (1) or (2) of subsection (a), or toward the purchase of a contract described in paragraph (3) of subsection (a), which under subsection (b) are not considered as contributed by the employee, or

(2) by the employee to a retirement plan described in paragraph (5) of subsection (a),

a transfer of benefits attributable to such contributions or payments shall, for purposes of this chapter, not be considered as a transfer by the spouse of the employee to the extent that the value of any interest of such spouse in such contributions or payments or in such trust or plan or such contract—

    (A) is attributable to such contribution or payments, and

    (B) arises solely by reason of such spouse's interest in community income under the community property laws of the State.

(d) Employee defined.—For purposes of this section, the term "employee" includes a former employee. In the case of a retirement plan described in paragraph (5) of subsection (a), such term means the individual for whose benefit the plan was established.

§ 2518.   Disclaimers

(a) General rule.—For purposes of this subtitle, if a person makes a qualified disclaimer with respect to any interest in property, this subtitle shall apply with respect to such interest as if the interest had never been transferred to such person.

(b) Qualified disclaimer defined.—For purposes of subsection (a), the term "qualified disclaimer" means an irrevocable and unqualified refusal by a person to accept an interest in property but only if—

    (1) such refusal is in writing,

    (2) such writing is received by the transferor of the interest, his legal representative, or the holder of the legal title to the property to which the interest relates not later than the date which is 9 months after the later of—

        (A) the day on which the transfer creating the interest in such person is made, or

        (B) the day on which such person attains age 21,

    (3) such person has not accepted the interest or any of its benefits, and

    (4) as a result of such refusal, the interest passes without any direction on the part of the person making the disclaimer and passes either—

        (A) to the spouse of the decedent, or

        (B) to a person other than the person making the disclaimer.

(c) Other rules.—For purposes of subsection (a)—

    (1) Disclaimer of undivided portion of interest.—A disclaimer with respect to an undivided portion of an interest which meets the requirements of the preceding sentence shall be treated as a qualified disclaimer of such portion of the interest.

    (2) Powers.—A power with respect to property shall be treated as an interest in such property.

    (3) Certain transfers treated as disclaimers.—For purposes of subsection (a), a written transfer of the transferor's entire interest in the property—

        (A) which meets requirements similar to the requirements of paragraphs (2) and (3) of subsection (b), and

(B) which is to a person or persons who would have received the property had the transferor made a qualified disclaimer (within the meaning of subsection (b)),

shall be treated as a qualified disclaimer.

§ 2519.   Dispositions of certain life estates

(a) General rule.—Any disposition of all or part of a qualifying income interest for life in any property to which this section applies shall be treated as a transfer of such property.

(b) Property to which this subsection applies.—This section applies to any property if a deduction was allowed with respect to the transfer of such property to the donor—

(1) under section 2056 by reason of subsection (b)(7) thereof, or

(2) under section 2523 by reason of subsection (f) thereof.

SUBCHAPTER C—DEDUCTIONS

§ 2522.   Charitable and similar gifts

(a) Citizens or residents.—In computing taxable gifts for the calendar year, there shall be allowed as a deduction in the case of a citizen or resident the amount of all gifts made during such year to or for the use of—

(1) the United States, any State, or any political subdivision thereof, or the District of Columbia, for exclusively public purposes;

(2) a corporation, or trust, or community chest, fund, or foundation, organized and operated exclusively for religious, charitable, scientific, literary, or educational purposes, or to foster national or international amateur sports competition (but only if no part of its activities involve the provision of athletic facilities or equipment), including the encouragement of art and the prevention of cruelty to children or animals, no part of the net earnings of which inures to the benefit of any private shareholder or individual, which is not disqualified for tax exemption under section 501(c) (3) by reason of attempting to influence legislation, and which does not participate in, or intervene in (including the publishing or distributing of statements), any political campaign on behalf of any candidate for public office;

(3) a fraternal society, order, or association, operating under the lodge system, but only if such gifts are to be used exclusively for religious, charitable, scientific, literary, or educational purposes, including the encouragement of art and the prevention of cruelty to children or animals;

(4) posts or organizations of war veterans, or auxiliary units or societies of any such posts or organizations, if such posts, organizations, units, or societies are organized in the United States or any of its possessions, and if no part of their net earnings inures to the benefit of any private shareholder or individual.

Rules similar to the rules of section 501(j) shall apply for purposes of paragraph (2).

(c) Disallowance of deductions in certain cases.—

(1) No deduction shall be allowed under this section for a gift to of [1] for the use of an organization or trust described in section 508(d) or 4948(c) (4) subject to the conditions specified in such sections.

(2) Where a donor transfers an interest in property (other than an interest described in section 170(f) (3) (B)) to a person, or for a use, described in subsection (a) or (b) and an interest in the same property is retained by the donor, or is transferred or has been transferred (for less than an adequate and full consideration in money or money's worth) from the donor to a person, or for a use, not described in subsection (a) or (b), no deduction shall be allowed under this section for the interest which is, or has been transferred to the person, or for the use, described in subsection (a) or (b), unless—

(A) in the case of a remainder interest, such interest is in a trust which is a charitable remainder annuity trust or a charitable remainder unitrust (described in section 664) or a pooled income fund (described in section 642(c) (5)), or

(B) in the case of any other interest, such interest is in the form of a guaranteed annuity or is a fixed percentage distributed yearly of the fair market value of the property (to be determined yearly).

. . . . .

[1] So in original. Probably should read "or".

§ 2523.   Gift to spouse

(a) Allowance of deduction.—Where a donor who is a citizen or resident transfers during the calendar year by gift an interest in property to a donee who at the time of the gift is the donor's spouse, there shall be allowed as a deduction in computing taxable gifts for the calendar year an amount with respect to such interest equal to its value.

(b) Life estate or other terminable interest.—Where, on the lapse of time, on the occurrence of an event or contingency, or on the failure of an event or contingency to occur, such interest transferred to the spouse will terminate or fail, no deduction shall be allowed with respect to such interest—

(1) if the donor retains in himself, or transfers or has transferred (for less than an adequate and full consideration in money or money's worth) to any person other than such donee spouse (or the estate of such spouse), an interest in such property, and if by reason of such retention or transfer the donor (or his heirs or assigns) or such person (or his heirs or assigns) may possess or enjoy any part of such property after such termination or failure of the interest transferred to the donee spouse; or

(2) if the donor immediately after the transfer to the donee spouse has a power to appoint an interest in such property which he can exercise (either alone or in conjunction with any person) in such manner that the appointee may possess or enjoy any part of such property after such termination or failure of the interest transferred to the donee spouse. For purposes of this paragraph, the donor shall be considered as having immediately after the transfer to the donee spouse such power to appoint even though such power cannot be exercised until after the lapse of time, upon the occurrence of an event or contingency, or on the failure of an event or contingency to occur.

An exercise or release at any time by the donor, either alone or in conjunction with any person, of a power to appoint an interest in property, even though not otherwise a transfer, shall, for purposes of paragraph (1), be considered as a transfer by him. Except as provided in subsection (e), where at the time of the transfer it is impossible to ascertain the particular person or persons who may receive from the donor an interest in property so transferred by him, such interest shall, for purposes of paragraph (1), be considered as transferred to a person other than the donee spouse.

(c) **Interest in unidentified assets.**—Where the assets out of which, or the proceeds of which, the interest transferred to the donee spouse may be satisfied include a particular asset or assets with respect to which no deduction would be allowed if such asset or assets were transferred from the donor to such spouse, then the value of the interest transferred to such spouse shall, for purposes of subsection (a), be reduced by the aggregate value of such particular assets.

(d) **Joint interests.**—If the interest is transferred to the donee spouse as sole joint tenant with the donor or as tenant by the entirety, the interest of the donor in the property which exists solely by reason of the possibility that the donor may survive the donee spouse, or that there may occur a severance of the tenancy, shall not be considered for purposes of subsection (b) as an interest retained by the donor in himself.

(e) **Life estate with power of appointment in donee spouse.**—Where the donor transfers an interest in property, if by such transfer his spouse is entitled for life to all of the income from the entire interest, or all the income from a specific portion thereof, payable annually or at more frequent intervals, with power in the donee spouse to appoint the entire interest, or such specific portion (exercisable in favor of such donee spouse, or of the estate of such donee spouse, or in favor of either, whether or not in each case the power is exercisable in favor of others), and with no power in any other person to appoint any part of such interest, or such portion, to any person other than the donee spouse—

(1) the interest, or such portion, so transferred shall, for purposes of subsection (a) be considered as transferred to the donee spouse, and

(2) no part of the interest, or such portion, so transferred shall, for purposes of subsection (b) (1), be considered as retained in the donor or transferred to any person other than the donee spouse.

This subsection shall apply only if, by such transfer, such power in the donee spouse to appoint the interest, or such portion, whether exercisable by will or during life, is exercisable by such spouse alone and in all events.

(f) **Election with respect to life estate for donee spouse.**—

(1) **In general.**—In the case of qualified terminable interest property—

(A) for purposes of subsection (a), such property shall be treated as transferred to the donee spouse, and

(B) for purposes of subsection (b)(1), no part of such property shall be considered as retained in the donor or transferred to any person other than the donee spouse.

(2) **Qualified terminable interest property.**—For purposes of this subsection, the term "qualified terminable interest property" means any property—

(A) which is transferred by the donor spouse,

(B) in which the donee spouse has a qualifying income interest for life, and

(C) to which an election under this subsection applies.

(3) **Certain rules made applicable.**—For purposes of this subsection, the rules of clauses (ii), (iii), and (iv) of section 2056(b)(7)(B) shall apply.

(4) **Election.**—An election under this subsection with respect to any property shall be made on the return of the tax imposed by section 2501 for the calendar year in which the interest was transferred. Such an election, once made, shall be irrevocable.

(g) Special rule for charitable remainder trusts.—

(1) **In general.**—If, after the transfer, the donee spouse is the only noncharitable beneficiary (other than the donor) of a qualified remainder trust, subsection (b) shall not apply to the interest in such trust which is transferred to the donee spouse.

(2) **Definitions.**—For purposes of paragraph (1), the term "noncharitable beneficiary" and "qualified charitable remainder trust" have the meanings given to such terms by section 2056(b)(8)(B).

§ 2524.   Extent of deductions

The deductions provided in sections 2522 and 2523 shall be allowed only to the extent that the gifts therein specified are included in the amount of gifts against which such deductions are applied.

CHAPTER 13—TAX ON CERTAIN GENERATION–SKIPPING TRANSFERS

Subchapter
  A. Tax imposed.
  B. Definitions and special rules.
  C. Administration.

SUBCHAPTER A—TAX IMPOSED

§ 2601.   Tax imposed

A tax is hereby imposed on every generation-skipping transfer in the amount determined under section 2602.

§ 2602.   Amount of tax

(a) **General rule.**—The amount of the tax imposed by section 2601 with respect to any transfer shall be the excess of—

(1) a tentative tax computed in accordance with the rate schedule set forth in section 2001(c) (as in effect on the date of transfer) on the sum of—

(A) the fair market value of the property transferred determined as of the date of transfer (or in the case of an election under subsection (d), as of the applicable valuation date prescribed by section 2032),

(B) the aggregate fair market value (determined for purposes of this chapter) of all prior transfers of the deemed transferor to which this chapter applied,

551

(C) the amount of the adjusted taxable gifts (within the meaning of section 2001(b), as modified by section 2001(e)) made by the deemed transferor before this transfer, and

(D) if the deemed transferor has died at the same time as, or before, this transfer, the taxable estate of the deemed transferor, over

(2) a tentative tax (similarly computed) on the sum of the amounts determined under subparagraphs (B), (C), and (D) of paragraph (1).

(b) Multiple simultaneous transfers.—If two or more transfers which are taxable under section 2601 and which have the same deemed transferor occur by reason of the same event, the tax imposed by section 2601 on each such transfer shall be the amount which bears the same ratio to—

(1) the amount of the tax which would be imposed by section 2601 if the aggregate of such transfers were a single transfer, as

(2) the fair market value of the property transferred in such transfer bears to the aggregate fair market value of all property transferred in such transfers.

(c) Deductions, credits, etc.—

(1) General rule.—Except as otherwise provided in this subsection, no deduction, exclusion, exemption, or credit shall be allowed against the tax imposed by section 2601.

(2) Charitable deductions allowed.—The deduction under section 2055, 2106(a) (2), or 2522, whichever is appropriate, shall be allowed in determining the tax imposed by section 2601.

(3) Unused portion of unified credit.—If the generation-skipping transfer occurs at the same time as, or after, the death of the deemed transferor, then the portion of the credit under section 2010(a) (relating to unified credit) which exceeds the sum of—

(A) the tax imposed by section 2001, and

(B) the taxes theretofore imposed by section 2601 with respect to this deemed transferor,

shall be allowed as a credit against the tax imposed by section 2601. The amount of the credit allowed by the preceding sentence shall not exceed the amount of the tax imposed by section 2601.

(4) Credit for tax on prior transfers.—The credit under section 2013 (relating to credit for tax on prior transfers) shall be allowed against the tax imposed by section 2601. For purposes of the preceding sentence, section 2013 shall be applied as if so much of the property subject to tax under section 2601 as is not taken into account for purposes of determining the credit allowable by section 2013 with respect to the estate of the deemed transferor passed from the transferor (as defined in section 2013) to the deemed transferor.

(5) Coordination with estate tax.—

(A) Certain expenses attributable to generation-skipping transfer. —If the generation-skipping transfer occurs at the same time as, or after, the death of the deemed transferor, for purposes of this section, the amount taken into account with respect to such transfer shall be reduced—

(i) in the case of a taxable termination, by any item referred to in section 2053 or 2054 to the extent that a deduction would have been allowable under such section for such item if the amount of the trust had been includible in the deemed transferor's gross estate and if the deemed transferor had died immediately before such transfer, or

(ii) in the case of a taxable distribution, by any expense incurred in connection with the determination, collection, or refund of the tax imposed by section 2601 on such transfer.

(B) Credit for State inheritance tax.—If the generation-skipping transfer occurs at the same time as, or after, the death of the deemed transferor, there shall be allowed as a credit against the tax imposed by section 2601 an amount equal to that portion of the estate, inheritance, legacy, or succession tax actually paid to any State or the District of Columbia in respect of any property included in the generation-skipping transfer, but only to the extent of the lesser of—

(i) that portion of such taxes which is levied on such transfer, or

(ii) the excess of the limitation applicable under section 2011(b) if the adjusted taxable estate of the decedent had been increased by the amount of the transfer and all prior generation-skipping transfers to which this subparagraph applied which had the same deemed transferor, over the sum of the amount allowable as a credit under section 2011 with respect to the estate of the decedent plus the aggregate amounts allowable under this subparagraph with respect to such prior generation-skipping transfers.

(d) Alternate valuation.—

(1) In general.—In the case of—

(A) 1 or more generation-skipping transfers from the same trust which have the same deemed transferor and which are taxable terminations occurring at the same time as the death of such deemed transferor (or at the same time as the death of a beneficiary of the trust assigned to a higher generation than such deemed transferor); or

(B) 1 or more generation-skipping transfers from the same trust with different deemed transferors—

(i) which are taxable terminations occurring on the same day; and

(ii) which would, but for section 2613(b) (2), have occurred at the same time as the death of the individuals who are the deemed transferors with respect to the transfers;

the trustee may elect to value all of the property transferred in such transfers in accordance with section 2032.

(2) Special rules.—If the trustee makes an election under paragraph (1) with respect to any generation-skipping transfer, section 2032 shall be applied by taking into account (in lieu of the date of the decedent's death) the following date:

(A) in the case of any generation-skipping transfer described in paragraph (1) (A), the date of the death of the deemed transferor (or beneficiary) described in such paragraph, or

(B) in the case of any generation-skipping transfer described in paragraph (1) (B), the date on which such transfer occurred.

(e) Transfers within 3 years of death of deemed transferor.—Under regulations prescribed by the Secretary, the principles of section 2035 shall apply with respect to transfers made during the 3-year period ending on the date of the deemed transferor's death. In the case of any transfer to which this subsection applies, the amount of the tax imposed by this chapter shall be determined as if the transfer occurred after the death of the deemed transferor and appropriate adjustments shall be made with respect to the amount of any prior transfer which is taken into account under subparagraph (B) or (C) of subsection (a) (1).

§ 2603.   Liability for tax

(a) **Personal liability.—**

    (1) **In general.—**If the tax imposed by section 2601 is not paid, when due then—

        (A) except to the extent provided in paragraph (2), the trustee shall be personally liable for any portion of such tax which is attributable to a taxable termination, and

        (B) the distributee of the property shall be personally liable for such tax to the extent provided in paragraph (3).

    (2) **Limitation of personal liability of trustee who relies on certain information furnished by the Secretary.—**

        (A) **Information with respect to rates.—**The trustee shall not be personally liable for any increase in the tax imposed by section 2601 which is attributable to the application to the transfer of rates of tax which exceeds the rates of tax furnished by the Secretary to the trustee as being the rates at which the transfer may reasonably be expected to be taxed.

        (B) **Amount of remaining exclusion.—**The trustee shall not be personally liable for any increase in the tax imposed by section 2601 which is attributable to the fact that—

            (i) the amount furnished by the Secretary to the trustee as being the amount of the exclusion for a transfer to a grandchild of the grantor of the trust which may reasonably be expected to remain with respect to the deemed transferor, is less than

            (ii) the amount of such exclusion remaining with respect to such deemed transferor.

    (3) **Limitation on personal liability of distributee.—**The distributee of the property shall be personally liable for the tax imposed by section 2601 only to the extent of an amount equal to the fair market value (determined as of the time of the distribution) of the property received by the distributee in the distribution.

(b) **Lien.—**The tax imposed by section 2601 on any transfer shall be a lien on the property transferred until the tax is paid in full or becomes unenforceable by reason of lapse of time.

SUBCHAPTER B—DEFINITIONS AND SPECIAL RULES

§ 2611.   Generation-skipping transfer

(a) **Generation-skipping transfer defined.—**For purposes of this chapter, the terms "generation-skipping transfer" and "transfer" mean any taxable distribution or taxable termination with respect to a generation-skipping trust or trust equivalent.

(b) Generation-skipping trust.—For purposes of this chapter, the term "generation-skipping trust" means any trust having younger generation beneficiaries (within the meaning of section 2613(c) (1)) who are assigned to more than one generation.

(c) Ascertainment of generation.—For purposes of this chapter, the generation to which any person (other than the grantor) belongs shall be determined in accordance with the following rules:

(1) an individual who is a lineal descendent of a grandparent of the grantor shall be assigned to that generation which results from comparing the number of generations between the grandparent and such individual with the number of generations between the grandparent and the grantor,

(2) an individual who has been at any time married to a person described in paragraph (1) shall be assigned to the generation of the person so described and an individual who has been at any time married to the grantor shall be assigned to the grantor's generation,

(3) a relationship by the half blood shall be treated as a relationship by the whole blood,

(4) a relationship by legal adoption shall be treated as a relationship by blood,

(5) an individual who is not assigned to a generation by reason of the foregoing paragraphs shall be assigned to a generation on the basis of the date of such individual's birth, with—

(A) an individual born not more than $12\frac{1}{2}$ years after the date of the birth of the grantor assigned to the grantor's generation,

(B) an individual born more than $12\frac{1}{2}$ years but not more than $37\frac{1}{2}$ years after the date of the birth of the grantor assigned to the first generation younger than the grantor, and

(C) similar rules for a new generation every 25 years,

(6) an individual who, but for this paragraph, would be assigned to more than one generation shall be assigned to the youngest such generation, and

(7) if any beneficiary of the trust is an estate or a trust, partnership, corporation, or other entity (other than an organization described in section 511(a) (2) and other than a charitable trust described in section 511(b) (2)), each individual having an indirect interest or power in the trust through such entity shall be treated as a beneficiary of the trust and shall be assigned to a generation under the foregoing provisions of this subsection.

(d) Generation-skipping trust equivalent.—

(1) In general.—For purposes of this chapter, the term "generation-skipping trust equivalent" means any arrangement which, although not a trust, has substantially the same effect as a generation-skipping trust.

(2) Examples of arrangements to which subsection relates.—Arrangements to be taken into account for purposes of determining whether or not paragraph (1) applies include (but are not limited to) arrangements involving life estates and remainders, estates for years, insurance and annuities, and split interests.

(3) References to trust include references to trust equivalents.—Any reference in this chapter in respect of a generation-skipping trust shall include the appropriate reference in respect of a generation-skipping trust equivalent.

§ 2612.   Deemed transferor

(a) General rule.—For purposes of this chapter, the deemed transferor with respect to a transfer is—

(1) except as provided in paragraph (2), the parent of the transferee of the property who is more closely related to the grantor of the trust than the other parent of such transferee (or if neither parent is related to such grantor, the parent having a closer affinity to the grantor), or

(2) if the parent described in paragraph (1) is not a younger generation beneficiary of the trust but 1 or more ancestors of the transferee is a younger generation beneficiary related by blood or adoption to the grantor of the trust, the youngest of such ancestors.

(b) Determination of relationship.—For purposes of subsection (a), a parent related to the grantor of the trust by blood or adoption is more closely related than a parent related to such grantor by marriage.

§ 2613.   Other definitions

(a) Taxable distribution.—For purposes of this chapter—

(1) In general.—The term "taxable distribution" means any distribution which is not out of the income of the trust (within the meaning of section 643(b)) from a generation-skipping trust to any younger generation beneficiary who is assigned to a generation younger than the generation assignment of any other person who is a younger generation beneficiary. For purposes of the preceding sentence, an individual who at no time has had anything other than a future interest or future power (or both) in the trust shall not be considered as a younger generation beneficiary.

(2) Source of distribution.—If, during the taxable year of the trust, there are distributions out of the income of the trust (within the meaning of section 643(b)) and out of other amounts, for purposes of paragraph (1) the distributions of such income shall be deemed to have been made to the beneficiaries (to the extent of the aggregate distributions made to each such beneficiary during such year) in descending order of generations, beginning with the beneficiaries assigned to the oldest generation.

(3) Payment of tax.—If any portion of the tax imposed by this chapter with respect to any transfer is paid out of the income or corpus of the trust, an amount equal to the portion so paid shall be deemed to be a generation-skipping transfer.

(4) Certain distributions excluded from tax.—The term "taxable distribution" does not include—

(A) any transfer to the extent such transfer is to a grandchild of the grantor of the trust and does not exceed the limitation provided by subsection (b) (6), and

(B) any transfer to the extent such transfer is subject to tax imposed by chapter 11 or 12.

(b) Taxable termination.—For purposes of this chapter—

(1) In general.—The term "taxable termination" means the termination (by death, lapse of time, exercise or nonexercise, or otherwise) of the interest or power in a generation-skipping trust of any younger generation beneficiary who is assigned to any generation older than the generation assignment of any other person who is a younger generation beneficiary of that trust.

Such term does not include a termination of the interest or power of any person who at no time has had anything other than a future interest or future power (or both) in the trust.

(2) Time certain terminations deemed to occur.—

(A) Where 2 or more beneficiaries are assigned to same generation. —In any case where 2 or more younger generation beneficiaries of a trust are assigned to the same generation, except to the extent provided in regulations prescribed by the Secretary, the transfer constituting the termination with respect to each such beneficiary shall be treated as occurring at the time when the last such termination occurs.

(B) Same beneficiary has more than 1 present interest or present power.—In any case where a younger generation beneficiary of a trust has both a present interest and a present power, or more than 1 present interest or present power, in the trust, except to the extent provided in regulations prescribed by the Secretary, the termination with respect to each such present interest or present power shall be treated as occurring at the time when the last such termination occurs.

(C) Unusual order of termination.—

(i) In general.—If—

(I) but for this subparagraph, there would have been a termination (determined after the application of subparagraphs (A) and (B)) of an interest or power of a younger generation beneficiary (hereinafter in this subparagraph referred to as the "younger beneficiary"), and

(II) at the time such termination would have occurred, a beneficiary (hereinafter in this subparagraph referred to as the "older beneficiary") of the trust assigned to a higher generation than the generation of the younger beneficiary has a present interest or power in the trust,

then, except to the extent provided in regulations prescribed by the Secretary, the transfer constituting the termination with respect to the younger beneficiary shall be treated as occurring at the time when the termination of the last present interest or power of the older beneficiary occurs.

(ii) Special rules.—If clause (i) applies with respect to any younger beneficiary—

(I) this chapter shall be applied first to the termination of the interest or power of the older beneficiary as if such termination occurred before the termination of the power or interest of the younger beneficiary; and

(II) the value of the property taken into account for purposes of determining the tax (if any) imposed by this chapter with respect to the termination of the interest or power of the younger beneficiary shall be reduced by the tax (if any) imposed by this chapter with respect to the termination of the interest or power of the older beneficiary.

(D) Special rule.—Subparagraphs (A) and (C) shall also apply where a person assigned to the same generation as, or a higher generation than, the person whose power or interest terminates has a present power or interest immediately after the termination and such power or interest arises as a result of such termination.

(3) Deemed transferees of certain terminations.—Where, at the time of any termination, it is not clear who will be the transferee of any portion of the property transferred, except to the extent provided in regulations prescribed by the Secretary, such portion shall be deemed transferred pro rata to all beneficiaries of the trust in accordance with the amount which each of them would receive under a maximum exercise of discretion on their behalf. For purposes of the preceding sentence, where it is not clear whether discretion will be exercised per stirpes or per capita, it shall be presumed that the discretion will be exercised per stirpes.

(4) Termination of power.—In the case of the termination of any power, the property transferred shall be deemed to be the property subject to the power immediately before the termination (determined without the application of paragraph (2)).

(5) Certain terminations excluded from tax.—The term "taxable termination" does not include—

> (A) any transfer to the extent such transfer is to a grandchild of the grantor of the trust and does not exceed the limitation provided by paragraph (6), and

> (B) any transfer to the extent such transfer is subject to a tax imposed by chapter 11 or 12.

(6) $250,000 limit on exclusion of transfers to grandchildren.—In the case of any deemed transferor, the maximum amount excluded from the terms "taxable distribution" and "taxable termination" by reason of provisions exempting from such terms transfers to the grandchildren of the grantor of the trust shall be $250,000. The preceding sentence shall be applied to transfers from one or more trusts in the order in which such transfers are made or deemed made.

(7) Coordination with subsection (a).—

> **(A) Terminations take precedence over distributions.**—If—

>> (i) the death of an individual or any other occurrence is a taxable termination with respect to any property, and

>> (ii) such occurrence also requires the distribution of part or all of such property in a distribution which would (but for this subparagraph) be a taxable distribution,

> then a taxable distribution shall be deemed not to have occurred with respect to the portion described in clause (i).

> **(B) Certain prior transfers.**—To the extent that—

>> (i) the deemed transferor in any prior transfer of the property of the trust being transferred in this transfer was assigned to the same generation as (or a lower generation than) the generation assignment of the deemed transferor in this transfer,

>> (ii) the transferee in such prior transfer was assigned to the same generation as (or a higher generation than) the generation assignment of the transferee in this transfer, and

>> (iii) such transfers do not have the effect of avoiding tax under this chapter with respect to any transfer,

> the terms "taxable termination" and "taxable distribution" do not include this later transfer.

(c) **Younger generation beneficiary; beneficiary.**—For purposes of this chapter—

(1) **Younger generation beneficiary.**—The term "younger generation beneficiary" means any beneficiary who is assigned to a generation younger than the grantor's generation.

(2) **Time for ascertaining younger generation beneficiaries.**—A person is a younger generation beneficiary of a trust with respect to any transfer only if such person was a younger generation beneficiary of the trust immediately before the transfer (or, in the case of a series of related transfers, only if such person was a younger generation beneficiary of the trust immediately before the first of such transfers).

(3) **Beneficiary.**—The term "beneficiary" means any person who has a present or future interest or power in the trust.

(d) **Interest or power.**—For purposes of this chapter—

(1) **Interest.**—A person has an interest in a trust if such person—

(A) has a right to receive income or corpus from the trust, or

(B) is a permissible recipient of such income or corpus.

(2) **Power.**—The term "power" means any power to establish or alter beneficial enjoyment of the corpus or income of the trust.

(e) **Certain powers not taken into account.**—

(1) **Limited power to appoint among lineal descendants of the grantor.** —For purposes of this chapter, an individual shall be treated as not having any power in a trust if such individual does not have any present or future power in the trust other than a power to dispose of the corpus of the trust or the income therefrom to a beneficiary or a class of beneficiaries who are lineal descendants of the grantor assigned to a generation younger than the generation assignment of such individual.

(2) **Powers of independent trustees.**—

(A) **In general.**—For purposes of this chapter, an individual shall be treated as not having any power in a trust if such individual—

(i) is a trustee who has no interest in the trust (other than as a potential appointee under a power of appointment held by another),

(ii) is not a related or subordinate trustee, and

(iii) does not have any present or future power in the trust other than a power to dispose of the corpus of the trust or the income therefrom to a beneficiary or a class of beneficiaries designated in the trust instrument.

(B) **Related or subordinate trustee defined.**—For purposes of subparagraph (A), the term "related or subordinate trustee" means any trustee who is assigned to a younger generation than the grantor's generation and who is—

(i) the spouse of the grantor or of any beneficiary,

(ii) the father, mother, lineal descendant, brother, or sister of the grantor or of any beneficiary,

(iii) an employee of the grantor or of any beneficiary,

(iv) an employee of a corporation in which the stockholdings of the grantor, the trust, and the beneficiaries of the trust are significant from the viewpoint of voting control,

(v) an employee of a corporation in which the grantor or any beneficiary of the trust is an executive,

(vi) a partner of a partnership in which the interest of the grantor, the trust, and the beneficiaries of the trust are significant from the viewpoint of operating control or distributive share of partnership income, or

(vii) an employee of a partnership in which the grantor or any beneficiary of the trust is a partner.

(f) Effect of adoption.—For purposes of this chapter, a relationship by legal adoption shall be treated as a relationship by blood.

§ 2614.   Special rules

(a) Basis adjustment.—If property is transferred to any person pursuant to a generation-skipping transfer which occurs before the death of the deemed transferor, the basis of such property in the hands of the transferee shall be increased (but not above the fair market value of such property) by an amount equal to that portion of the tax imposed by section 2601 with respect to the transfer which is attributable to the excess of the fair market value of such property over its adjusted basis immediately before the transfer. If property is transferred in a generation-skipping transfer subject to tax under this chapter which occurs at the same time as, or after, the death of the deemed transferor, the basis of such property shall be adjusted in a manner similar to the manner provided under section 1014(a).

. . . . .

(c) Disclaimers.—

For provisions relating to the effect of a qualified disclaimer for purposes of this chapter, see section 2518.

SUBCHAPTER C—ADMINISTRATION

§ 2621.   Administration

(a) General rule.—Insofar as applicable and not inconsistent with the provisions of this chapter—

(1) if the deemed transferor is not alive at the time of the transfer, all provisions of subtitle F (including penalties) applicable to chapter 11 or section 2001 are hereby made applicable in respect of this chapter or section 2601, as the case may be, and

(2) if the deemed transferor is alive at the time of the transfer, all provisions of subtitle F (including penalties) applicable to chapter 12 or section 2501 are hereby made applicable in respect of this chapter or section 2601, as the case may be.

(b) Section 6166 not applicable.—For purposes of this chapter, section 6166 (relating to extension of time for payment of estate tax where estate consists largely of interest in closely held business) shall not apply.

(c) Return requirements.—

(1) **In general.**—The Secretary shall prescribe by regulations the person who is required to make the return with respect to the tax imposed by this

chapter and the time by which any such return must be filed. To the extent practicable, such regulations shall provide that—

(A) the person who is required to make such return shall be—

(i) in the case of a taxable distribution, the distributee, or

(ii) in the case of a taxable termination, the trustee; and

(B) the return shall be filed—

(i) in the case of a generation-skipping transfer occurring before the death of the deemed transferor, on or before the 90th day after the close of the taxable year of the trust in which such transfer occurred, or

(ii) in the case of a generation-skipping transfer occurring at the same time as, or after, the death of the deemed transferor, on or before the 90th day after the last day prescribed by law (including extensions) for filing the return of tax under chapter 11 with respect to the estate of the deemed transferor (or if later, the day which is 9 months after the day on which such generation-skipping transfer occurred).

(2) **Information returns.**—The Secretary may by regulations require the trustee to furnish the Secretary with such information as he determines to be necessary for purposes of this chapter.

§ 2622.　Regulations

The Secretary shall prescribe such regulations as may be necessary or appropriate to carry out the purposes of this chapter, including regulations providing the extent to which substantially separate and independent shares of different beneficiaries in the trust shall be treated as separate trusts.

SUBTITLE F—PROCEDURE AND ADMINISTRATION

Chapter
61. Information and returns.
62. Time and place for paying tax.
63. Assessment.
64. Collection.
65. Abatements, credits, and refunds.*
66. Limitations.
67. Interest.
68. Additions to the tax, additional amounts, and assessable penalties.
69. General provisions relating to stamps.*
70. Jeopardy, receiverships, etc.*
71. Transferees and fiduciaries.
72. Licensing and registration.*
73. Bonds.*
74. Closing agreements and compromises.
75. Crimes, other offenses, and forfeitures.
76. Judicial proceedings.
77. Miscellaneous provisions.
78. Discovery of liability and enforcement of title.
79. Definitions.
80. General Rules.

CHAPTER 61—INFORMATION AND RETURNS

Subchapter
A. Returns and records.
B. Miscellaneous provisions.*

SUBCHAPTER A—RETURNS AND RECORDS

Part
I. Records, statements, and special returns.*
II. Tax returns or statements.
III. Information returns.
IV. Signing and verifying of returns and other documents.*
V. Time for filing returns and other documents.
VI. Extension of time for filing returns.*
VII. Place for filing returns or other documents.*
VIII. Designation of income tax payments to Presidential Election Campaign Fund.*

* Omitted entirely.

PART II—TAX RETURNS OR STATEMENTS

Subpart
A.   General requirement.*
B.   Income tax returns.
C.   Estate and gift tax returns.
D.   Miscellaneous provisions.*

SUBPART B—INCOME TAX RETURNS

§ 6012.   Persons required to make returns of income

(a) General rule.—Returns with respect to income taxes under subtitle A shall be made by the following:

(1) (A) Every individual having for the taxable year a gross income of $1,000 or more, except that a return shall not be required of an individual (other than an individual described in subparagraph (C))—

(i) who is not married (determined by applying section 143), is not a surviving spouse (as defined in section 2(a)), and for the taxable year has a gross income of less than $3,300,

(ii) who is a surviving spouse (as so defined) and for the taxable year has a gross income of less than $4,400, or

(iii) who is entitled to make a joint return under section 6013 and whose gross income, when combined with the gross income of his spouse, is, for the taxable year, less than $5,400, but only if such individual and his spouse, at the close of the taxable year, had the same household as their home.

Clause (iii) shall not apply if for the taxable year such spouse makes a separate return or any other taxpayer is entitled to an exemption for such spouse under section 151(e).

(B) The amount specified in clause (i) or (ii) of subparagraph (A) shall be increased by $1,000 in the case of an individual entitled to an additional personal exemption under section 151(c) (1), and the amount specified in clause (iii) of subparagraph (A) shall be increased by $1,000 for each additional personal exemption to which the individual or his spouse is entitled under section 151(c).

(C) The exception under subparagraph (A) shall not apply to—

. . . . . .

(iii) an individual making a return under section 443(a) (1) for a period of less than 12 months on account of a change in his annual accounting period;

(iv) an individual who has income (other than earned income) of $1,000 or more and who is described in section 63(e) (1) (D); or

(v) an estate or trust.

(2) Every corporation subject to taxation under subtitle A;

(3) Every estate the gross income of which for the taxable year is $600 or more;

* Omitted entirely.

(4) Every trust having for the taxable year any taxable income, or having gross income of $600 or over, regardless of the amount of taxable income;

. . . .

(6) Every political organization (within the meaning of section 527(e) (1)), and every fund treated under section 527(g) as if it constituted a political organization, which has political organization taxable income (within the meaning of section 527(c) (1)) for the taxable year;

. . . .

(9) Every estate of an individual under chapter 7 or 11 of title 11 of the United States Code (relating to bankruptcy) the gross income of which for the taxable year is $2,700 or more.

except that subject to such conditions, limitations, and exceptions and under such regulations as may be prescribed by the Secretary, nonresident alien individuals subject to the tax imposed by section 871 and foreign corporations subject to the tax imposed by section 881 may be exempted from the requirement of making returns under this section.

(b) Returns made by fiduciaries and receivers.—

(1) Returns of decedents.—If an individual is deceased, the return of such individual required under subsection (a) shall be made by his executor, administrator, or other person charged with the property of such decedent.

(2) Persons under a disability.—If an individual is unable to make a return required under subsection (a) or section 6015(a), the return of such individual shall be made by a duly authorized agent, his committee, guardian, fiduciary or other person charged with the care of the person or property of such individual. The preceding sentence shall not apply in the case of a receiver appointed by authority of law in possession of only a part of the property of an individual.

(3) Receivers, trustees and assignees for corporations.—In a case where a receiver, trustee in a case under title 11 of the United States Code, or assignee, by order of a court of competent jurisdiction, by operation of law or otherwise, has possession of or holds title to all or substantially all the property or business of a corporation, whether or not such property or business is being operated, such receiver, trustee, or assignee shall make the return of income for such corporation in the same manner and form as corporations are required to make such returns.

(4) Returns of estates and trusts.—Returns of an estate, a trust, or an estate of an individual under chapter 7 or 11 of title 11 of the United States Code shall be made by the fiduciary thereof.

(5) Joint fiduciaries.—Under such regulations as the Secretary may prescribe, a return made by one of two or more joint fiduciaries shall be sufficient compliance with the requirements of this section. A return made pursuant to this paragraph shall contain a statement that the fiduciary has sufficient knowledge of the affairs of the person for whom the return is made to enable him to make the return, and that the return is, to the best of his knowledge and belief, true and correct.

. . . .

§ 6013.   Joint returns of income tax by husband and wife

(a) Joint returns.—A husband and wife may make a single return jointly of income taxes under subtitle A, even though one of the spouses has neither gross income nor deductions, except as provided below:

. . . .

(2) no joint return shall be made if the husband and wife have different taxable years; except that if such taxable years begin on the same day and end on different days because of the death of either or both, then the joint return may be made with respect to the taxable year of each. The above exception shall not apply if the surviving spouse remarries before the close of his taxable year, nor if the taxable year of either spouse is a fractional part of a year under section 443(a) (1);

(3) in the case of death of one spouse or both spouses the joint return with respect to the decedent may be made only by his executor or administrator; except that in the case of the death of one spouse the joint return may be made by the surviving spouse with respect to both himself and the decedent if no return for the taxable year has been made by the decedent, no executor or administrator has been appointed, and no executor or administrator is appointed before the last day prescribed by law for filing the return of the surviving spouse. If an executor or administrator of the decedent is appointed after the making of the joint return by the surviving spouse, the executor or administrator may disaffirm such joint return by making, within 1 year after the last day prescribed by law for filing the return of the surviving spouse, a separate return for the taxable year of the decedent with respect to which the joint return was made, in which case the return made by the survivor shall constitute his separate return.

. . . .

(c) Treatment of joint return after death of either spouse.—For purposes of sections 21, 443, and 7851(a) (1) (A), where the husband and wife have different taxable years because of the death of either spouse, the joint return shall be treated as if the taxable years of both spouses ended on the date of the closing of the surviving spouse's taxable year.

(d) Special rules.—For purposes of this section—

(1) the status as husband and wife of two individuals having taxable years beginning on the same day shall be determined—

(A) if both have the same taxable year—as of the close of such year; or

(B) if one dies before the close of the taxable year of the other—as of the time of such death;

(2) an individual who is legally separated from his spouse under a decree of divorce or of separate maintenance shall not be considered as married; and

(3) if a joint return is made, the tax shall be computed on the aggregate income and the liability with respect to the tax shall be joint and several.

(e) Spouse relieved of liability in certain cases.—

(1) In general.—Under regulations prescribed by the Secretary, if—

(A) a joint return has been made under this section for a taxable year and on such return there was omitted from gross income an amount properly includable therein which is attributable to one spouse and which is in excess of 25 percent of the amount of gross income stated in the return,

    (B) the other spouse establishes that in signing the return he or she did not know of, and had no reason to know of, such omission, and

    (C) taking into account whether or not the other spouse significantly benefited directly or indirectly from the items omitted from gross income and taking into account all other facts and circumstances, it is inequitable to hold the other spouse liable for the deficiency in tax for such taxable year attributable to such omission,

then the other spouse shall be relieved of liability for tax (including interest, penalties, and other amounts) for such taxable year to the extent that such liability is attributable to such omission from gross income.

    (2) Special rules.—For purposes of paragraph (1)—

      (A) the determination of the spouse to whom items of gross income (other than gross income from property) are attributable shall be made without regard to community property laws, and

      (B) the amount omitted from gross income shall be determined in the manner provided by section 6501(e) (1) (A).

·   ·   ·   ·   ·

SUBPART C—ESTATE AND GIFT TAX RETURNS

§ 6018.   Estate tax returns

(a) Returns by executor.—

    (1) Citizens or residents.—In all cases where the gross estate at the death of a citizen or resident exceeds $600,000, the executor shall make a return with respect to the estate tax imposed by subtitle B.

·   ·   ·   ·   ·

    (3) Phase-in of filing requirement amount.—

In the case of decedents dying in:	Paragraph (1) shall be applied by substituting for "$600,000" the following amount:
1982	$225,000
1983	275,000
1984	325,000
1985	400,000
1986	500,000

·   ·   ·   ·   ·

    (4) Adjustment for certain gifts.—The amount applicable under paragraph (1) and the amount set forth in paragraph (2) shall each be reduced (but not below zero` by the sum of—

      (A) the amount of the adjusted taxable gifts (within the meaning of section 2001(b)) made by the decedent after December 31, 1976, plus

      (B) the aggregate amount allowed as a specific exemption under section 2521 (as in effect before its repeal by the Tax Reform Act of 1976) with respect to gifts made by the decedent after September 8, 1976.

(b) Returns by beneficiaries.—If the executor is unable to make a complete return as to any part of the gross estate of the decedent, he shall include in his return a description of such part and the name of every person holding a legal or beneficial interest therein. Upon notice from the Secretary such person shall in like manner make a return as to such part of the gross estate.

§ 6019.   Gift tax returns

Any individual who in any calendar year makes any transfer by gift other than—

> (1) a transfer which under subsection (b) or (e) of section 2503 is not to be included in the total amount of gifts for such year, or

> (2) a transfer of an interest with respect to which a deduction is allowed under section 2523,

shall make a return for such year with respect to the gift tax imposed by subtitle B.

PART III—INFORMATION RETURNS

Subpart
    A.   Information concerning persons subject to special provisions.
    B.   Information concerning transactions with other persons.
    C.   Information regarding wages paid employees.*
  [D.   Repealed]
    E.   Registration of and information concerning pension, etc., plans.*
    F.   Information concerning income tax return preparers.*

SUBPART A—INFORMATION CONCERNING PERSONS SUBJECT TO SPECIAL PROVISIONS

§ 6031.   Return of partnership income

(a) General rule.—Every partnership (as defined in section 761(a)) shall make a return for each taxable year, stating specifically the items of its gross income and the deductions allowable by subtitle A, and such other information for the purpose of carrying out the provisions of subtitle A as the Secretary may by forms and regulations prescribe, and shall include in the return the names and addresses of the individuals who would be entitled to share in the taxable income if distributed and the amount of the distributive share of each individual.

(b) Copies to partners.—Each partnership required to file a return under subsection (a) for any partnership taxable year shall (on or before the day on which the return for such taxable year was filed) furnish to each person who is a partner at any time during such taxable year a copy of such information shown on such return as may be required by regulations.

§ 6036.   Notice of qualification as executor or receiver

Every receiver, trustee in a case under title 11 of the United States Code, assignee for benefit of creditors, or other like fiduciary, and every executor (as defined in section 2203), shall give notice of his qualification as such to the Secretary in such manner and at such time as may be required by regulations of the Secretary. The Secretary may by regulation provide such exemptions from the requirements of this section as the Secretary deems proper.

    * Omitted entirely.

§ 6037.   Return of S corporation

Every S corporation shall make a return for each taxable year, stating specifically the items of its gross income and the deductions allowable by subtitle A, the names and addresses of all persons owning stock in the corporation at any time during the taxable year, the number of shares of stock owned by each shareholder at all times during the taxable year, the amount of money and other property distributed by the corporation during the taxable year to each shareholder, the date of each such distribution, each shareholder's pro rata share of each item of the corporation for the taxable year, and such other information, for the purpose of carrying out the provisions of subchapter S of chapter 1, as the Secretary may by forms and regulations prescribe. Any return filed pursuant to this section shall, for purposes of chapter 66 (relating to limitations), be treated as a return filed by the corporation under section 6012.

SUBPART B—INFORMATION CONCERNING TRANSACTIONS WITH OTHER PERSONS

§ 6043.   Returns regarding liquidation, dissolution, termination, or contraction

(a) **Corporations.**—Every corporation shall—

(1) Within 30 days after the adoption by the corporation of a resolution or plan for the dissolution of the corporation or for the liquidation of the whole or any part of its capital stock, make a return setting forth the terms of such resolution or plan and such other information as the Secretary shall by forms or regulations prescribe; and

(2) When required by the Secretary, make a return regarding its distributions in liquidation, stating the name and address of, the number and class of shares owned by, and the amount paid to, each shareholder, or, if the distribution is in property other than money, the fair market value (as of the date the distribution is made) of the property distributed to each shareholder.

. . . . .

PART V—TIME FOR FILING RETURNS AND OTHER DOCUMENTS

§ 6072.   Time for filing income tax returns

(a) **General rule.**—In the case of returns under section 6012, 6013, 6017, or 6031 (relating to income tax under subtitle A), returns made on the basis of the calendar year shall be filed on or before the 15th day of April following the close of the calendar year and returns made on the basis of a fiscal year shall be filed on or before the 15th day of the fourth month following the close of the fiscal year, except as otherwise provided in the following subsections of this section.

(b) **Returns of corporations.**—Returns of corporations under section 6012 made on the basis of the calendar year shall be filed on or before the 15th day of March following the close of the calendar year, and such returns made on the basis of a fiscal year shall be filed on or before the 15th day of the third month following the close of the fiscal year. Returns required for a taxable year by section 6011(e)(2) (relating to returns of a DISC) shall be filed on or before the fifteenth day of the ninth month following the close of the taxable year.

. . . . .

§ 6075.   Time for filing estate and gift tax returns

(a) Estate tax returns.—Returns made under section 6018(a) (relating to estate taxes) shall be filed within 9 months after the date of the decedent's death.

(b) Gift tax returns.—

(1) General rule.—Returns made under section 6019 (relating to gift taxes) shall be filed on or before the 15th day of April following the close of the calendar year.

(2) Extension where taxpayer granted extension for filing income tax return.—Any extension of time granted the taxpayer for filing the return of income taxes imposed by subtitle A for any taxable year which is a calendar year shall be deemed to be also an extension of time granted the taxpayer for filing the return under section 6019 for such calendar year.

(3) Coordination with due date for estate tax return.—Notwithstanding paragraphs (1) and (2), the time for filing the return made under section 6019 for the calendar year which includes the date of death of the donor shall not be later than the time (including extensions) for filing the return made under section 6018 (relating to estate tax returns) with respect to such donor.

CHAPTER 62—TIME AND PLACE FOR PAYING TAX

Subchapter
A.   Place and due date for payment of tax.*
B.   Extensions of time for payment.

SUBCHAPTER B—EXTENSIONS OF TIME FOR PAYMENT

§ 6163.   Extension of time for payment of estate tax on value of reversionary or remainder interest in property

(a) Extension permitted.—If the value of a reversionary or remainder interest in property is included under chapter 11 in the value of the gross estate, the payment of the part of the tax under chapter 11 attributable to such interest may, at the election of the executor, be postponed until 6 months after the termination of the precedent interest or interests in the property, under such regulations as the Secretary may prescribe.

(b) Extension for reasonable cause.—At the expiration of the period of postponement provided for in subsection (a), the Secretary may, for reasonable cause, extend the time for payment for a reasonable period or periods not in excess of 3 years from the expiration of the period of postponement provided in subsection (a).

. . . .

* Omitted entirely.

§ 6164.   Extension of time for payment of taxes by corporations expecting carrybacks

(a) **In general.**—If a corporation, in any taxable year, files with the Secretary a statement, as provided in subsection (b), with respect to an expected net operating loss carryback from such taxable year, the time for payment of all or part of any tax imposed by subtitle A for the taxable year immediately preceding such taxable year shall be extended, to the extent and subject to the conditions and limitations hereinafter provided in this section.

§ 6166.   Extension of time for payment of estate tax where estate consists largely of interest in closely held business

(a) **5-year deferral; 10-year installment payment.**—

(1) **In general.**—If the value of an interest in a closely held business which is included in determining the gross estate of a decedent who was (at the date of his death) a citizen or resident of the United States exceeds 35 percent of the adjusted gross estate, the executor may elect to pay part or all of the tax imposed by section 2001 in 2 or more (but not exceeding 10) equal installments.

(2) **Limitation.**—The maximum amount of tax which may be paid in installments under this subsection shall be an amount which bears the same ratio to the tax imposed by section 2001 (reduced by the credits against such tax) as—

(A) the closely held business amount, bears to

(B) the amount of the adjusted gross estate.

(3) **Date for payment of installments.**—If an election is made under paragraph (1), the first installment shall be paid on or before the date selected by the executor which is not more than 5 years after the date prescribed by section 6151(a) for payment of the tax, and each succeeding installment shall be paid on or before the date which is 1 year after the date prescribed by this paragraph for payment of the preceding installment.

(4) **Repealed. Pub. L. 97–34, Title IV, § 422(e)(5)(A), Aug. 13, 1981, 95 Stat. 316.**

(b) **Definitions and special rules.**—

(1) **Interest in closely held business.**—For purposes of this section, the term "interest in a closely held business" means—

(A) an interest as a proprietor in a trade or business carried on as a proprietorship;

(B) an interest as a partner in a partnership carrying on a trade or business, if—

(i) 20 percent or more of the total capital interest in such partnership is included in determining the gross estate of the decedent, or

(ii) such partnership had 15 or fewer partners; or

(C) stock in a corporation carrying on a trade or business if—

(i) 20 percent or more in value of the voting stock of such corporation is included in determining the gross estate of the decedent, or

(ii) such corporation had 15 or fewer shareholders.

(2) **Rules for applying paragraph (1).**—For purposes of paragraph (1)—

(A) **Time for testing.**—Determinations shall be made as of the time immediately before the decedent's death.

(B) **Certain interests held by husband and wife.**—Stock or a partnership interest which—

(i) is community property of a husband and wife (or the income from which is community income) under the applicable community property law of a State, or

(ii) is held by a husband and wife as joint tenants, tenants by the entirety, or tenants in common,

shall be treated as owned by one shareholder or one partner, as the case may be.

(C) **Indirect ownership.**—Property owned, directly or indirectly, by or for a corporation, partnership, estate, or trust shall be considered as being owned proportionately by or for its shareholders, partners, or beneficiaries. For purposes of the preceding sentence, a person shall be treated as a beneficiary of any trust only if such person has a present interest in the trust.

(D) **Certain interests held by members of decedent's family.**—All stock and all partnership interests held by the decedent or by any member of his family (within the meaning of section 267(c)(4)) shall be treated as owned by the decedent.

(3) **Farmhouses and certain other structures taken into account.**—For purposes of the 65-percent requirement of subsection (a) (1), an interest in a closely held business which is the business of farming includes an interest in residential buildings and related improvements on the farm which are occupied on a regular basis by the owner or lessee of the farm or by persons employed by such owner or lessee for purposes of operating or maintaining the farm.

(4) **Value.**—For purposes of this section, value shall be value determined for purposes of chapter 11 (relating to estate tax).

(5) **Closely held business amount.**—For purposes of this section, the term "closely held business amount" means the value of the interest in a closely held business which qualifies under subsection (a) (1).

(6) **Adjusted gross estate.**—For purposes of this section, the term, "adjusted gross estate" means the value of the gross estate reduced by the sum of the amounts allowable as a deduction under section 2053 or 2054. Such sum shall be determined on the basis of the facts and circumstances in existence on the date (including extensions) for filing the return of tax imposed by section 2001 (or, if earlier, the date on which such return is filed).

(7) **Partnership interests and stock which is not readily tradable.**—

(A) **In general.**—If the executor elects the benefits of this paragraph (at such time and in such manner as the Secretary shall by regulations prescribe), then—

(i) for purposes of paragraph (1) (B) (i) or (1) (C) (i) (whichever is appropriate) and for purposes of subsection (c), any capital interest in a partnership and any non-readily-tradable stock which (after the application of paragraph (2)) is treated as owned by the decedent shall be treated as included in determining the value of the decedent's gross estate,

(ii) the executor shall be treated as having selected under subsection (a) (3) the date prescribed by section 6151(a), and

(iii) section 6601(j) (relating to 4-percent rate of interest) shall not apply.

(B) Non-readily-tradable stock defined.—For purposes of this paragraph, the term "non-readily-tradable stock" means stock for which, at the time of the decedent's death, there was no market on a stock exchange or in an over-the-counter market.

(c) Special rule for interests in 2 or more closely held businesses.—For purposes of this section, interests in 2 or more closely held businesses, with respect to each of which there is included in determining the value of the decedent's gross estate 20 percent or more of the total value of each such business, shall be treated as an interest in a single closely held business. For purposes of the 20-percent requirement of the preceding sentence, an interest in a closely held business which represents the surviving spouse's interest in property held by the decedent and the surviving spouse as community property or as joint tenants, tenants by the entirety, or tenants in common shall be treated as having been included in determining the value of the decedent's gross estate.

(d) Election.—Any election under subsection (a) shall be made not later than the time prescribed by section 6075(a) for filing the return of tax imposed by section 2001 (including extensions thereof), and shall be made in such manner as the Secretary shall by regulations prescribe. If an election under subsection (a) is made, the provisions of this subtitle shall apply as though the Secretary were extending the time for payment of the tax.

· · · · ·

(f) Time for payment of interest.—If the time for payment of any amount of tax has been extended under this section—

(1) Interest for first 5 years.—Interest payable under section 6601 of any unpaid portion of such amount attributable to the first 5 years after the date prescribed by section 6151(a) for payment of the tax shall be paid annually.

(2) Interest for periods after first 5 years.—Interest payable under section 6601 on any unpaid portion of such amount attributable to any period after the 5-year period referred to in paragraph (1) shall be paid annually at the same time as, and as a part of, each installment payment of the tax.

· · · · ·

(g) Acceleration of payment.—

(1) Disposition of interest; withdrawal of funds from business.—

(A) If—

(i)(I) any portion of an interest in a closely held business which qualifies under subsection (a)(1) is distributed, sold, exchanged, or otherwise disposed of, or

(II) money and other property attributable to such an interest is withdrawn from such trade or business, and

(ii) the aggregate of such distributions, sales, exchanges, or other dispositions and withdrawals equals or exceeds 50 percent of the value of such interest,

then the extension of time for payment of tax provided in subsection (a) shall cease to apply, and the unpaid portion of the tax payable in installments shall be paid upon notice and demand from the Secretary.

(B) In the case of a distribution in redemption of stock to which section 303 (or so much of section 304 as relates to section 303) applies—

(i) subparagraph (A) (i) does not apply with respect to the stock redeemed; and for purposes of such subparagraph the interest in the closely held business shall be considered to be such interest reduced by the value of the stock redeemed, and

(ii) subparagraph (A) (ii) does not apply with respect to withdrawals of money and other property distributed; and for purposes of such subparagraph the value of the trade or business shall be considered to be such value reduced by the amount of money and other property distributed.

This subparagraph shall apply only if, on or before the date prescribed by subsection (a) (3) for the payment of the first installment which becomes due after the date of the distribution (or, if earlier, on or before the day which is 1 year after the date of the distribution), there is paid an amount of the tax imposed by section 2001 not less than the amount of money and other property distributed.

(C) Subparagraph (A) (i) does not apply to an exchange of stock pursuant to a plan of reorganization described in subparagraph (D), (E), or (F) of section 368(a) (1) nor to an exchange to which section 355 (or so much of section 356 as relates to section 355) applies; but any stock received in such an exchange shall be treated for purposes of subparagraph (A) (i) as an interest qualifying under subsection (a) (1).

(D) Subparagraph (A) (i) does not apply to a transfer of property of the decedent to a person entitled by reason of the decedent's death to receive such property under the decedent's will, the applicable law of descent and distribution, or a trust created by the decedent. A similar rule shall apply in the case of a series of subsequent transfers of the property by reason of death so long as each transfer is to a member of the family (within the meaning of section 267(c)(4)) of the transferor in such transfer.

·   ·   ·   ·

CHAPTER 63—ASSESSMENT

Subchapter
A.   In general.*
B.   Deficiency procedures in the case of income, estate, gift, and certain excise taxes.
C.   Tax treatment of partnership items.
D.   Tax treatment of subchapter S items.*

SUBCHAPTER B—DEFICIENCY PROCEDURES IN THE CASE OF INCOME, ESTATE, GIFT, AND CERTAIN EXCISE TAXES

§ 6211.   Definition of a deficiency

(a) **In general.**—For purposes of this title in the case of income, estate, and gift taxes imposed by subtitles A and B and excise taxes imposed by chapters 41, 42,

* Omitted entirely.

43, 44, and 45 the term "deficiency" means the amount by which the tax imposed by subtitle A or B, or chapter 41, 42, 43, 44, or 45 exceeds the excess of—

(1) the sum of

(A) the amount shown as the tax by the taxpayer upon his return, if a return was made by the taxpayer and an amount was shown as the tax by the taxpayer thereon, plus

(B) the amounts previously assessed (or collected without assessment) as a deficiency, over—

(2) the amount of rebates, as defined in subsection (b) (2), made.

(b) **Rules for application of subsection (a).**—For purposes of this section—

(1) The tax imposed by subtitle A and the tax shown on the return shall both be determined without regard to payments on account of estimated tax, without regard to the credit under section 31, without regard to so much of the credit under section 32 as exceeds 2 percent of the interest on obligations described in section 1451, and without regard to any credits resulting from the collection of amounts assessed under section 6851 (relating to termination assessments).

(2) The term "rebate" means so much of an abatement, credit, refund, or other repayment, as was made on the ground that the tax imposed by subtitle A or B or chapter 41, 42, 43, 44, or 45 was less than the excess of the amount specified in subsection (a) (1) over the rebates previously made.

. . . . .

§ 6212.   Notice of deficiency

(a) **In general.**—If the Secretary determines that there is a deficiency in respect of any tax imposed by subtitles A or B or chapter 41, 42, 43, 44, or 45, he is authorized to send notice of such deficiency to the taxpayer by certified mail or registered mail.

(b) **Address for notice of deficiency.**—

(1) **Income and gift taxes and certain excise taxes.**—In the absence of notice to the Secretary under section 6903 of the existence of a fiduciary relationship, notice of a deficiency in respect of a tax imposed by subtitle A, chapter 12, chapter 41, chapter 42, chapter 43, chapter 44, or chapter 45, if mailed to the taxpayer at his last known address, shall be sufficient for purposes of subtitle A, chapter 12, chapter 41, chapter 42, chapter 43, chapter 44, chapter 45, and this chapter even if such taxpayer is deceased, or is under a legal disability, or, in the case of a corporation, has terminated its existence.

(2) **Joint income tax return.**—In the case of a joint income tax return filed by husband and wife, such notice of deficiency may be a single joint notice, except that if the Secretary has been notified by either spouse that separate residences have been established, then, in lieu of the single joint notice, a duplicate original of the joint notice shall be sent by certified mail or registered mail to each spouse at his last known address.

(3) **Estate tax.**—In the absence of notice to the Secretary under section 6903 of the existence of a fiduciary relationship, notice of a deficiency in respect of a tax imposed by chapter 11, if addressed in the name of the decedent or other person subject to liability and mailed to his last known address, shall be sufficient for purposes of chapter 11 and of this chapter.

(c) Further deficiency letters restricted.—

(1) General rule.—If the Secretary has mailed to the taxpayer a notice of deficiency as provided in subsection (a), and the taxpayer files a petition with the Tax Court within the time prescribed in section 6213(a), the Secretary shall have no right to determine any additional deficiency of income tax for the same taxable year, of gift tax for the same calendar year, of estate tax in respect of the taxable estate of the same decedent, of chapter 41 tax for the same taxable year, of chapter 43 tax for the same taxable year, of chapter 44 tax for the same taxable year, of section 4940 tax for the same taxable year, or of chapter 42 tax (other than under section 4940) with respect to any act (or failure to act) to which such petition relates, or of chapter 45 tax for the same taxable period, except in the case of fraud, and except as provided in section 6214(a) (relating to assertion of greater deficiencies before the Tax Court), in section 6213(b)(1) (relating to mathematical or clerical errors), in section 6851 (relating to termination assessments), or in section 6861(c) (relating to the making of jeopardy assessments).

. . . .

§ 6213. Restrictions applicable to deficiencies; petition to Tax Court

(a) Time for filing petition and restriction on assessment.—Within 90 days, or 150 days if the notice is addressed to a person outside the United States, after the notice of deficiency authorized in section 6212 is mailed (not counting Saturday, Sunday, or a legal holiday in the District of Columbia as the last day), the taxpayer may file a petition with the Tax Court for a redetermination of the deficiency. Except as otherwise provided in section 6851 or section 6861 no assessment of a deficiency in respect of any tax imposed by subtitle A or B, chapter 41, 42, 43, 44, or 45 and no levy or proceeding in court for its collection shall be made, begun, or prosecuted until such notice has been mailed to the taxpayer, nor until the expiration of such 90-day or 150-day period, as the case may be, nor, if a petition has been filed with the Tax Court, until the decision of the Tax Court has become final. Notwithstanding the provisions of section 7421(a), the making of such assessment or the beginning of such proceeding or levy during the time such prohibition is in force may be enjoined by a proceeding in the proper court.

(b) Exceptions to restrictions on assessment.—

(1) Assessments arising out of mathematical or clerical errors.—If the taxpayer is notified that, on account of a mathematical or clerical error appearing on the return, an amount of tax in excess of that shown on the return is due, and that an assessment of the tax has been or will be made on the basis of what would have been the correct amount of tax but for the mathematical or clerical error, such notice shall not be considered as a notice of deficiency for the purposes of subsection (a) (prohibiting assessment and collection until notice of the deficiency has been mailed), or of section 6212(c)(1) (restricting further deficiency letters), or of section 6512(a) (prohibiting credits or refunds after petition to the Tax Court), and the taxpayer shall have no right to file a petition with the Tax Court based on such notice, nor shall such assessment or collection be prohibited by the provisions of subsection (a) of this section. Each notice under this paragraph shall set forth the error alleged and an explanation thereof.

(2) Abatement of assessment of mathematical or clerical errors.—

(A) Request for abatement.—Notwithstanding section 6404(b), a taxpayer may file with the Secretary within 60 days after notice is sent under paragraph (1) a request for an abatement of any assessment specified in such notice, and upon receipt of such request, the Secretary shall abate the assessment. Any reassessment of the tax with respect to which an abatement is made under this subparagraph shall be subject to the deficiency procedures prescribed by this subchapter.

(B) Stay or collection.—In the case of any assessment referred to in paragraph (1), notwithstanding paragraph (1), no levy or proceeding in court for the collection of such assessment shall be made, begun, or prosecuted during the period in which such assessment may be abated under this paragraph.

(3) Assessments arising out of tentative carryback or refund adjustments.—If the Secretary determines that the amount applied, credited, or refunded under section 6411 is in excess of the overassessment attributable to the carryback or the amount described in section 1341(b) (1) with respect to which such amount was applied, credited, or refunded, he may assess without regard to the provisions of paragraph (2) the amount of the excess as a deficiency as if it were due to a mathematical or clerical error appearing on the return.

(4) Assessment of amount paid.—Any amount paid as a tax or in respect of a tax may be assessed upon the receipt of such payment notwithstanding the provisions of subsection (a). In any case where such amount is paid after the mailing of a notice of deficiency under section 6212, such payment shall not deprive the Tax Court of jurisdiction over such deficiency determined under section 6211 without regard to such assessment.

(c) Failure to file petition.—If the taxpayer does not file a petition with the Tax Court within the time prescribed in subsection (a), the deficiency, notice of which has been mailed to the taxpayer, shall be assessed, and shall be paid upon notice and demand from the Secretary.

(d) Waiver of restrictions.—The taxpayer shall at any time (whether or not a notice of deficiency has been issued) have the right, by a signed notice in writing filed with the Secretary, to waive the restrictions provided in subsection (a) on the assessment and collection of the whole or any part of the deficiency.

·   ·   ·   ·   ·

§ 6214.   Determinations by Tax Court

(a) Jurisdiction as to increase of deficiency, additional amounts, or additions to the tax.—Except as provided by section 7463, the Tax Court shall have jurisdiction to redetermine the correct amount of the deficiency even if the amount so redetermined is greater than the amount of the deficiency, notice of which has been mailed to the taxpayer, and to determine whether any additional amount, or addition to the tax should be assessed, if claim therefor is asserted by the Secretary at or before the hearing or a rehearing.

(b) Jurisdiction over other years and quarters.—The Tax Court in redetermining a deficiency of income tax for any taxable year or of gift tax for any calendar year or calendar quarter shall consider such facts with relation to the taxes for other years or calendar quarters as may be necessary correctly to redetermine the amount of such deficiency, but in so doing shall have no jurisdiction to determine whether or not the tax for any other year or calendar quarter has been overpaid or underpaid.

. . . . .

SUBCHAPTER C—TAX TREATMENT OF PARTNERSHIP ITEMS

§ 6221.   Tax treatment determined at partnership level

Except as otherwise provided in this subchapter, the tax treatment of any partnership item shall be determined at the partnership level.

§ 6222.   Partner's return must be consistent with partnership return or secretary notified of inconsistency

(a) **In general.**—A partner shall, on the partner's return, treat a partnership item in a manner which is consistent with the treatment of such partnership item on the partnership return.

(b) **Notification of inconsistent treatment.—**

(1) **In general.**—In the case of any partnership item, if—

(A)(i) the partnership has filed a return but the partner's treatment on his return is (or may be) inconsistent with the treatment of the item on the partnership return, or

(ii) the partnership has not filed a return, and

(B) the partner files with the Secretary a statement identifying the inconsistency,

subsection (a) shall not apply to such item.

(2) **Partner receiving incorrect information.**—A partner shall be treated as having complied with subparagraph (B) of paragraph (1) with respect to a partnership item if the partner—

(A) demonstrates to the satisfaction of the Secretary that the treatment of the partnership item on the partner's return is consistent with the treatment of the item on the schedule furnished to the partner by the partnership, and

(B) elects to have this paragraph apply with respect to that item.

(c) **Effect of failure to notify.**—In any case—

(1) described in paragraph (1)(a)(i) of subsection (b), and

(2) in which the partner does not comply with paragraph (1)(B) of subsection (b),

section 6225 shall not apply to any part of a deficiency attributable to any computational adjustment required to make the treatment of the items by such partner consistent with the treatment of the items on the partnership return.

. . . . .

CHAPTER 64—COLLECTION

Subchapter
- A. General provisions.*
- B. Receipt of payment.*
- C. Lien for taxes.
- D. Seizure of property for collection of taxes.
- E. Collection of State individual income taxes.*

SUBCHAPTER C—LIEN FOR TAXES

§ 6321.   Lien for taxes

If any person liable to pay any tax neglects or refuses to pay the same after demand, the amount (including any interest, additional amount, addition to tax, or assessable penalty, together with any costs that may accrue in addition thereto) shall be a lien in favor of the United States upon all property and rights to property, whether real or personal, belonging to such person.

§ 6322.   Period of lien

Unless another date is specifically fixed by law, the lien imposed by section 6321 shall arise at the time the assessment is made and shall continue until the liability for the amount so assessed (or a judgment against the taxpayer arising out of such liability) is satisfied or becomes unenforceable by reason of lapse of time.

§ 6324.   Special liens for estate and gift taxes

(a) Liens for estate tax.—Except as otherwise provided in subsection (c)—

(1) Upon gross estate.—Unless the estate tax imposed by chapter 11 is sooner paid in full, or becomes unenforceable by reason of lapse of time, it shall be a lien upon the gross estate of the decedent for 10 years from the date of death, except that such part of the gross estate as is used for the payment of charges against the estate and expenses of its administration, allowed by any court having jurisdiction thereof, shall be divested of such lien.

(2) Liability of transferees and others.—If the estate tax imposed by chapter 11 is not paid when due, then the spouse, transferee, trustee (except the trustee of an employees' trust which meets the requirements of section 401(a)), surviving tenant, person in possession of the property by reason of the exercise, nonexercise, or release of a power of appointment, or beneficiary, who receives, or has on the date of the decedent's death, property included in the gross estate under sections 2034 to 2042, inclusive, to the extent of the value, at the time of the decedent's death, of such property, shall be personally liable for such tax. Any part of such property transferred by (or transferred by a transferee of) such spouse, transferee, trustee, surviving tenant, person in possession, or beneficiary, to a purchaser or holder of a security interest shall be divested of the lien provided in paragraph (1) and a like lien shall then attach to all the property of such spouse, transferee, trustee, surviving tenant, person in possession, or beneficiary, or transferee of any such person, except any part transferred to a purchaser or a holder of a security interest.

* Omitted entirely.

(3) **Continuance after discharge of fiduciary.**—The provisions of section 2204 (relating to discharge of fiduciary from personal liability) shall not operate as a release of any part of the gross estate from the lien for any deficiency that may thereafter be determined to be due, unless such part of the gross estate (or any interest therein) has been transferred to a purchaser or a holder of a security interest, in which case such part (or such interest) shall not be subject to a lien or to any claim or demand for any such deficiency, but the lien shall attach to the consideration received from such purchaser or holder of a security interest, by the heirs, legatees, devisees, or distributees.

(b) **Lien for gift tax.**—Except as otherwise provided in subsection (c), unless the gift tax imposed by chapter 12 is sooner paid in full or becomes unenforceable by reason of lapse of time, such tax shall be a lien upon all gifts made during the period for which the return was filed, for 10 years from the date the gifts are made. If the tax is not paid when due, the donee of any gift shall be personally liable for such tax to the extent of the value of such gift. Any part of the property comprised in the gift transferred by the donee (or by a transferee of the donee) to a purchaser or holder of a security interest shall be divested of the lien imposed by this subsection and such lien, to the extent of the value of such gift, shall attach to all the property (including after-acquired property) of the donee (or the transferee) except any part transferred to a purchaser or holder of a security interest.

(c) **Exceptions.**—

(1) The lien imposed by subsection (a) or (b) shall not be valid as against a mechanic's lienor and, subject to the conditions provided by section 6323(b) (relating to protection for certain interests even though noticed filed), shall not be valid with respect to any lien or interest described in section 6323(b).

(2) If a lien imposed by subsection (a) or (b) is not valid as against a lien or security interest, the priority of such lien or security interest shall extend to any item described in section 6323(e) (relating to priority of interest and expenses) to the extent that, under local law, such item has the same priority as the lien or security interest to which it relates.

§ 6324A.   Special lien for estate tax deferred under section 6166

(a) **General rule.**—In the case of any estate with respect to which an election has been made under section 6166, if the executor makes an election under this section (at such time and in such manner as the Secretary shall by regulations prescribe) and files the agreement referred to in subsection (c), the deferred amount (plus any interest, additional amount, addition to tax, assessable penalty, and costs attributable to the deferred amount) shall be a lien in favor of the United States on the section 6166 lien property.

(b) **Section 6166 lien property.**—

(1) **In general.**—For purposes of this section, the term "section 6166 lien property" means interests in real and other property to the extent such interests—

(A) can be expected to survive the deferral period, and

(B) are designated in the agreement referred to in subsection (c).

(2) **Maximum value of required property.**—The maximum value of the property which the Secretary may require as section 6166 lien property with respect to any estate shall be a value which is not greater than the sum of—

(A) the deferred amount, and

(B) the required interest amount.

For purposes of the preceding sentence, the value of any property shall be determined as of the date prescribed by section 6151(a) for payment of the tax imposed by chapter 11 and shall be determined by taking into account any encumbrance such as a lien under section 6324B.

(3) **Partial substitution of bond for lien.**—If the value required as section 6166 lien property pursuant to paragraph (2) exceeds the value of the interests in property covered by the agreement referred to in subsection (c), the Secretary may accept bond in an amount equal to such excess conditioned on the payment of the amount extended in accordance with the terms of such extension.

(c) **Agreement.**—The agreement referred to in this subsection is a written agreement signed by each person in being who has an interest (whether or not in possession) in any property designated in such agreement—

(1) consenting to the creation of the lien under this section with respect to such property, and

(2) designating a responsible person who shall be the agent for the beneficiaries of the estate and for the persons who have consented to the creation of the lien in dealings with the Secretary on matters arising under section 6166 or this section.

(d) **Special rules.**—

(1) **Requirement that lien be filed.**—The lien imposed by this section shall not be valid as against any purchaser, holder of a security interest, mechanic's lien, or judgment lien creditor until notice thereof which meets the requirements of section 6323(f) has been filed by the Secretary. Such notice shall not be required to be refiled.

(2) **Period of lien.**—The lien imposed by this section shall arise at the time the executor is discharged from liability under section 2204 (or, if earlier, at the time notice is filed pursuant to paragraph (1)) and shall continue until the liability for the deferred amount is satisfied or becomes unenforceable by reason of lapse of time.

(3) **Priorities.**—Even though notice of a lien imposed by this section has been filed as provided in paragraph (1), such lien shall not be valid—

(A) **Real property tax and special assessment liens.**—To the extent provided in section 6323(b) (6).

(B) **Real property subject to a mechanic's lien for repairs and improvements.**—In the case of any real property subject to a lien for repair or improvement, as against a mechanic's lienor.

(C) **Real property construction or improvement financing agreement.**—As against any security interest set forth in paragraph (3) of section 6323(c) (whether such security interest came into existence before or after tax lien filing).

Subparagraphs (B) and (C) shall not apply to any security interest which came into existence after the date on which the Secretary filed notice (in a manner similar to notice filed under section 6323(f)) that payment of the deferred amount has been accelerated under section 6166(g).

(4) **Lien to be in lieu of section 6324 lien.**—If there is a lien under this section on any property with respect to any estate, there shall not be any lien under section 6324 on such property with respect to the same estate.

(5) Additional lien property required in certain cases.—If at any time the value of the property covered by the agreement is less than the unpaid portion of the deferred amount and the required interest amount, the Secretary may require the addition of property to the agreement (but he may not require under this paragraph that the value of the property covered by the agreement exceed such unpaid portion). If property having the required value is not added to the property covered by the agreement (or if other security equal to the required value is not furnished) within 90 days after notice and demand therefor by the Secretary, the failure to comply with the preceding sentence shall be treated as an act accelerating payment of the installments under section 6166(g).

(6) Lien to be in lieu of bond.—The Secretary may not require under section 6165 the furnishing of any bond for the payment of any tax to which an agreement which meets the requirements of subsection (c) applies.

§ 6324B.   Special lien for additional estate tax attributable to farm, etc., valuation

(a) General rule.—In the case of any interest in qualified real property (within the meaning of section 2032A(b)), an amount equal to the adjusted tax difference attributable to such interest (within the meaning of section 2032A(c) (2) (B)) shall be a lien in favor of the United States on the property in which such interest exists.

(b) Period of lien.—The lien imposed by this section shall arise at the time an election is filed under section 2032A and shall continue with respect to any interest in the qualified real property—

(1) until the liability for tax under subsection (c) of section 2032A with respect to such interest has been satisfied or has become unenforceable by reason of lapse of time, or

(2) until it is established to the satisfaction of the Secretary that no further tax liability may arise under section 2032A(c) with respect to such interest.

(c) Certain rules and definitions made applicable.—

(1) In general.—The rule set forth in paragraphs (1), (3), and (4) of section 6324A(d) shall apply with respect to the lien imposed by this section as if it were a lien imposed by section 6324A.

(2) Qualified real property.—For purposes of this section, the term "qualified real property" includes qualified replacement property (within the meaning of section 2032A(h)(3)(B)) and qualified exchange property (within the meaning of section 2032A(i)(3)).

(d) Substitution of security for lien.—To the extent provided in regulations prescribed by the Secretary, the furnishing of security may be substituted for the lien imposed by this section.

SUBCHAPTER D—SEIZURE OF PROPERTY FOR COLLECTION OF TAXES

§ 6331.   Levy and distraint

(a) **Authority of Secretary or delegate.**—If any person liable to pay any tax neglects or refuses to pay the same within 10 days after notice and demand, it shall be lawful for the Secretary to collect such tax (and such further sum as shall be sufficient to cover the expenses of the levy) by levy upon all property and rights to property (except such property as is exempt under section 6334) belonging to such person or on which there is a lien provided in this chapter for the payment of such tax. Levy may be made upon the accrued salary or wages of any officer, employee, or elected official, of the United States, the District of Columbia, or any agency or instrumentality of the United States or the District of Columbia, by serving a notice of levy on the employer (as defined in section 3401(d)) of such officer, employee, or elected official. If the Secretary makes a finding that the collection of such tax is in jeopardy, notice and demand for immediate payment of such tax may be made by the Secretary and, upon failure or refusal to pay such tax, collection thereof by levy shall be lawful without regard to the 10-day period provided in this section.

(b) **Seizure and sale of property.**—The term "levy" as used in this title includes the power of distraint and seizure by any means. Except as otherwise provided in subsection (d) (3), a levy shall extend only to property possessed and obligations existing at the time thereof. In any case in which the Secretary may levy upon property or rights to property, he may seize and sell such property or rights to property (whether real or personal, tangible or intangible).

(c) **Successive seizures.**—Whenever any property or right to property upon which levy has been made by virtue of subsection (a) is not sufficient to satisfy the claim of the United States for which levy is made, the Secretary may, thereafter, and as often as may be necessary, proceed to levy in like manner upon any other property liable to levy of the person against whom such claim exists, until the amount due from him, together with all expenses, is fully paid.

(d) **Requirement of notice before levy.**—

(1) **In general.**—Levy may be made under subsection (a) upon the salary or wages or other property of any person with respect to any unpaid tax only after the Secretary has notified such person in writing of his intention to make such levy.

(2) **10-day requirement.**—The notice required under paragraph (1) shall be—

(A) given in person,

(B) left at the dwelling or usual place of business of such person, or

(C) sent by certified or registered mail to such person's last known address,

no less than 10 days before the day of the levy.

(3) **Jeopardy.**—Paragraph (1) shall not apply to a levy if the Secretary has made a finding under the last sentence of subsection (a) that the collection of tax is in jeopardy.

. . . . .

CHAPTER 66—LIMITATIONS

Subchapter
A. Limitations on assessment and collection.
B. Limitations on credit or refund.
C. Mitigation of effect of period of limitations.*
D. Periods of limitation in judicial proceedings.

SUBCHAPTER A—LIMITATIONS ON ASSESSMENT AND COLLECTION

§ 6501.　　Limitations on assessment and collection

(a) General rule.—Except as otherwise provided in this section, the amount of any tax imposed by this title shall be assessed within 3 years after the return was filed (whether or not such return was filed on or after the date prescribed) or, if the tax is payable by stamp, at any time after such tax became due and before the expiration of 3 years after the date on which any part of such tax was paid, and no proceeding in court without assessment for the collection of such tax shall be begun after the expiration of such period.

(b) Time return deemed filed.—

(1) Early return.—For purposes of this section, a return of tax imposed by this title, except tax imposed by chapter 3, 21, or 24, filed before the last day prescribed by law or by regulations promulgated pursuant to law for the filing thereof, shall be considered as filed on such last day.

. . . . .

(c) Exceptions.—

(1) False return.—In the case of a false or fraudulent return with the intent to evade tax, the tax may be assessed, or a proceeding in court for collection of such tax may be begun without assessment, at any time.

(2) Willful attempt to evade tax.—In case of a willful attempt in any manner to defeat or evade tax imposed by this title (other than tax imposed by subtitle A or B), the tax may be assessed, or a proceeding in court for the collection of such tax may be begun without assessment, at any time.

(3) No return.—In the case of failure to file a return, the tax may be assessed, or a proceeding in court for the collection of such tax may be begun without assessment, at any time.

(4) Extension by agreement.—Where, before the expiration of the time prescribed in this section for the assessment of any tax imposed by this title, except the estate tax provided in chapter 11, both the Secretary and the taxpayer have consented in writing to its assessment after such time, the tax may be assessed at any time prior to the expiration of the period agreed upon. The period so agreed upon may be extended by subsequent agreements in writing made before the expiration of the period previously agreed upon.

. . . . .

(d) Request for prompt assessment.—Except as otherwise provided in subsection (c), (e), or (f), in the case of any tax (other than the tax imposed by chapter

---

* Omitted entirely.

11 of subtitle B, relating to estate taxes) for which return is required in the case of a decedent, or by his estate during the period of administration, or by a corporation, the tax shall be assessed, and any proceeding in court without assessment for the collection of such tax shall be begun, within 18 months after written request therefor (filed after the return is made and filed in such manner and such form as may be prescribed by regulations of the Secretary) by the executor, administrator, or other fiduciary representing the estate of such decedent, or by the corporation, but not after the expiration of 3 years after the return was filed. This subsection shall not apply in the case of a corporation unless—

(1) (A) such written request notifies the Secretary that the corporation contemplates dissolution at or before the expiration of such 18-month period, (B) the dissolution is in good faith begun before the expiration of such 18-month period, and (C) the dissolution is completed;

(2) (A) such written request notifies the Secretary that a dissolution has in good faith been begun, and (B) the dissolution is completed; or

(3) a dissolution has been completed at the time such written request is made.

(e) **Substantial omission of items.**—Except as otherwise provided in subsection (c)—

(1) **Income taxes.**—In the case of any tax imposed by subtitle A—

(A) **General rule.**—If the taxpayer omits from gross income an amount properly includible therein which is in excess of 25 percent of the amount of gross income stated in the return, the tax may be assessed, or a proceeding in court for the collection of such tax may be begun without assessment, at any time within 6 years after the return was filed. For purposes of this subparagraph—

(i) In the case of a trade or business, the term "gross income" means the total of the amounts received or accrued from the sale of goods or services (if such amounts are required to be shown on the return) prior to diminution by the cost of such sales or services; and

(ii) In determining the amount omitted from gross income, there shall not be taken into account any amount which is omitted from gross income stated in the return if such amount is disclosed in the return, or in a statement attached to the return, in a manner adequate to apprise the Secretary of the nature and amount of such item.

. . . . .

(2) **Estate and gift taxes.**—In the case of a return of estate tax under chapter 11 or a return of gift tax under chapter 12, if the taxpayer omits from the gross estate or from the total amount of the gifts made during the period for which the return was filed items includible in such gross estate or such total gifts, as the case may be, as exceed in amount 25 percent of the gross estate stated in the return or the total amount of gifts stated in the return, the tax may be assessed, or a proceeding in court for the collection of such tax may be begun without assessment, at any time within 6 years after the return was filed. In determining the items omitted from the gross estate or the total gifts, there shall not be taken into account any item which is omitted from the gross estate or from the total gifts stated in the return if such item is disclosed in the return, or in a statement attached to the return,

in a manner adequate to apprise the Secretary of the nature and amount of such item.

. . . . .

(f) Personal holding company tax.—If a corporation which is a personal holding company for any taxable year fails to file with its return under chapter 1 for such year a schedule setting forth—

(1) the items of gross income and adjusted ordinary gross income, described in section 543, received by the corporation during such year, and

(2) the names and addresses of the individuals who owned, within the meaning of section 544 (relating to rules for determining stock ownership), at any time during the last half of such year more than 50 percent in value of the outstanding capital stock of the corporation,

the personal holding company tax for such year may be assessed, or a proceeding in court for the collection of such tax may be begun without assessment, at any time within 6 years after the return for such year was filed.

. . . . .

§ 6502.   Collection after assessment

(a) Length of period.—Where the assessment of any tax imposed by this title has been made within the period of limitation properly applicable thereto, such tax may be collected by levy or by a proceeding in court, but only if the levy is made or the proceeding begun—

(1) within 6 years after the assessment of the tax, or

(2) prior to the expiration of any period for collection agreed upon in writing by the Secretary and the taxpayer before the expiration of such 6-year period (or, if there is a release of levy under section 6343 after such 6-year period, then before such release).

The period so agreed upon may be extended by subsequent agreements in writing made before the expiration of the period previously agreed upon. The period provided by this subsection during which a tax may be collected by levy shall not be extended or curtailed by reason of a judgment against the taxpayer.

(b) Date when levy is considered made.—The date on which a levy on property or rights to property is made shall be the date on which the notice of seizure provided in section 6335(a) is given.

§ 6503.   Suspension of running of period of limitation

(a) Issuance of statutory notice of deficiency.—

(1) General rule.—The running of the period of limitations provided in section 6501 or 6502 on the making of assessments or the collection by levy or a proceeding in court, in respect of any deficiency as defined in section 6211 (relating to income, estate, gift and certain excise taxes), shall (after the mailing of a notice under section 6212(a)) be suspended for the period during which the Secretary is prohibited from making the assessment or from collecting by levy or a proceeding in court (and in any event, if a proceeding in respect of the deficiency is placed on the docket of the Tax Court, until the decision of the Tax Court becomes final), and for 60 days thereafter.

(2) **Corporation joining in consolidated income tax return.**—If a notice under section 6212(a) in respect of a deficiency in tax imposed by subtitle A for any taxable year is mailed to a corporation, the suspension of the running of the period of limitations provided in paragraph (1) of this subsection shall apply in the case of corporations with which such corporation made a consolidated income tax return for such taxable year.

(b) **Assets of taxpayer in control or custody of court.**—The period of limitations on collection after assessment prescribed in section 6502 shall be suspended for the period the assets of the taxpayer are in the control or custody of the court in any proceeding before any court of the United States or of any State or of the District of Columbia, and for 6 months thereafter.

(c) **Taxpayer outside United States.**—The running of the period of limitations on collection after assessment prescribed in section 6502 shall be suspended for the period during which the taxpayer is outside the United States if such period of absence is for a continuous period of at least 6 months. If the preceding sentence applies and at the time of the taxpayer's return to the United States the period of limitations on collection after assessment prescribed in section 6502 would expire before the expiration of 6 months from the date of his return, such period shall not expire before the expiration of such 6 months.

(d) **Extensions of time for payment of estate tax.**—The running of the period of limitations for collection of any tax imposed by chapter 11 shall be suspended for the period of any extension of time for payment granted under the provisions of section 6161(a) (2) or (b) (2) or under the provisions of section 6163 or 6166.

. . . . .

SUBCHAPTER B—LIMITATIONS ON CREDIT OR REFUND

§ 6511.   Limitations on credit or refund

(a) **Period of limitation on filing claim.**—Claim for credit or refund of an overpayment of any tax imposed by this title in respect of which tax the taxpayer is required to file a return shall be filed by the taxpayer within 3 years from the time the return was filed or 2 years from the time the tax was paid, whichever of such periods expires the later, or if no return was filed by the taxpayer, within 2 years from the time the tax was paid. Claim for credit or refund of an overpayment of any tax imposed by this title which is required to be paid by means of a stamp shall be filed by the taxpayer within 3 years from the time the tax was paid.

(b) **Limitation on allowance of credits and refunds.**—

(1) **Filing of claim within prescribed period.**—No credit or refund shall be allowed or made after the expiration of the period of limitation prescribed in subsection (a) for the filing of a claim for credit or refund, unless a claim for credit or refund is filed by the taxpayer within such period.

(2) **Limit on amount of credit or refund.**—

(A) **Limit where claim filed within 3-year period.**—If the claim was filed by the taxpayer during the 3-year period prescribed in subsection (a), the amount of the credit or refund shall not exceed the portion of the tax paid within the period, immediately preceding the filing of the claim, equal to 3 years plus the period of any extension of time for filing the return. If the tax was required to be paid by means of a stamp, the

amount of the credit or refund shall not exceed the portion of the tax paid within the 3 years immediately preceding the filing of the claim.

(B) Limit where claim not filed within 3-year period.—If the claim was not filed within such 3-year period, the amount of the credit or refund shall not exceed the portion of the tax paid during the 2 years immediately preceding the filing of the claim.

(C) Limit if no claim filed.—If no claim was filed, the credit or refund shall not exceed the amount which would be allowable under subparagraph (A) or (B), as the case may be, if claim was filed on the date the credit or refund is allowed.

(c) Special rules applicable in case of extension of time by agreement.—If an agreement under the provisions of section 6501(c) (4) extending the period for assessment of a tax imposed by this title is made within the period prescribed in subsection (a) for the filing of a claim for credit or refund—

(1) Time for filing claim.—The period for filing claim for credit or refund or for making credit or refund if no claim is filed, provided in subsections (a) and (b) (1), shall not expire prior to 6 months after the expiration of the period within which an assessment may be made pursuant to the agreement or any extension thereof under section 6501(c) (4).

(2) Limit on amount.—If a claim is filed, or a credit or refund is allowed when no claim was filed, after the execution of the agreement and within 6 months after the expiration of the period within which an assessment may be made pursuant to the agreement or any extension thereof, the amount of the credit or refund shall not exceed the portion of the tax paid after the execution of the agreement and before the filing of the claim or the making of the credit or refund, as the case may be, plus the portion of the tax paid within the period which would be applicable under subsection (b) (2) if a claim had been filed on the date the agreement was executed.

(3) Claims not subject to special rule.—This subsection shall not apply in the case of a claim filed, or credit or refund allowed if no claim is filed, either—

(A) prior to the execution of the agreement or

(B) more than 6 months after the expiration of the period within which an assessment may be made pursuant to the agreement or any extension thereof.

(d) Special rules applicable to income taxes.—

(1) Seven-year period of limitation with respect to bad debts and worthless securities.—If the claim for credit or refund relates to an overpayment of tax imposed by subtitle A on account of—

(A) The deductibility by the taxpayer, under section 166 or section 832(c), of a debt as a debt which became worthless, or, under section 165(g), of a loss from worthlessness of a security, or

(B) The effect that the deductibility of a debt or loss described in subparagraph (A) has on the application to the taxpayer of a carryover,

in lieu of the 3-year period of limitation prescribed in subsection (a), the period shall be 7 years from the date prescribed by law for filing the return for the year with respect to which the claim is made. If the claim for credit or refund relates to an overpayment on account of the effect that the deductibility of such a debt or loss has on the application to the taxpayer of a

carryback, the period shall be either 7 years from the date prescribed by law for filing the return for the year of the net operating loss which results in such carryback or the period prescribed in paragraph (2) of this subsection, whichever expires the later. In the case of a claim described in this paragraph the amount of the credit or refund may exceed the portion of the tax paid within the period prescribed in subsection (b) (2) or (c), whichever is applicable, to the extent of the amount of the overpayment attributable to the deductibility of items described in this paragraph.

(2) Special period of limitation with respect to net operating loss or capital loss carrybacks.—

(A) Period of limitation.—If the claim for credit or refund relates to an overpayment attributable to a net operating loss carryback or a capital loss carryback, in lieu of the 3-year period of limitation prescribed in subsection (a), the period shall be that period which ends 3 years after the time prescribed by law for filing the return (including extensions thereof) for the taxable year of the net operating loss or net capital loss which results in such carryback, or the period prescribed in subsection (c) in respect of such taxable year, whichever expires later; except that with respect to an overpayment attributable to the creation of, or an increase in a net operating loss carryback as a result of the elimination of excessive profits by a renegotiation (as defined in section 1481(a) (1) (A)), the period shall not expire before the expiration of the 12th month following the month in which the agreement or order for the elimination of such excessive profits becomes final. In the case of such a claim, the amount of the credit or refund may exceed the portion of the tax paid within the period provided in subsection (b) (2) or (c), whichever is applicable, to the extent of the amount of the overpayment attributable to such carryback.

(B) Applicable rules.—

(i) If the allowance of a credit or refund of an overpayment of tax attributable to a net operating loss carryback or a capital loss carryback is otherwise prevented by the operation of any law or rule of law other than section 7122, relating to compromises, such credit or refund may be allowed or made, if claim therefor is filed within the period provided in subparagraph (A) of this paragraph. If the allowance of an application, credit, or refund of a decrease in tax determined under section 6411(b) is otherwise prevented by the operation of any law or rule of law other than section 7122, such application, credit, or refund may be allowed or made if application for a tentative carryback adjustment is made within the period provided in section 6411(a). In the case of any such claim for credit or refund or any such application for a tentative carryback adjustment, the determination by any court, including the Tax Court, in any proceeding in which the decision of the court has become final, shall be conclusive except with respect to the net operating loss deduction, and the effect of such deduction, or with respect to the determination of a short-term capital loss, and the effect of such short-term capital loss, to the extent that such deduction or short-term capital loss is affected by a carryback which was not an issue in such proceeding.

(ii) A claim for credit or refund for a computation year (as defined in section 1302(c) (1)) shall be determined to relate to an overpay-

ment attributable to a net operating loss carryback or a capital loss carryback, as the case may be, when such carryback relates to any base period year (as defined in section 1302(c) (3)).

. . . .

§ 6513.   Time return deemed filed and tax considered paid

(a) **Early return or advance payment of tax.**—For purposes of section 6511, any return filed before the last day prescribed for the filing thereof shall be considered as filed on such last day. For purposes of section 6511(b) (2) and (c) and section 6512, payment of any portion of the tax made before the last day prescribed for the payment of the tax shall be considered made on such last day. For purposes of this subsection, the last day prescribed for filing the return or paying the tax shall be determined without regard to any extension of time granted the taxpayer and without regard to any election to pay the tax in installments.

(b) **Prepaid income tax.**—For purposes of section 6511 or 6512—

(1) Any tax actually deducted and withheld at the source during any calendar year under chapter 24 shall, in respect of the recipient of the income, be deemed to have been paid by him on the 15th day of the fourth month following the close of his taxable year with respect to which such tax is allowable as a credit under section 31.

(2) Any amount paid as estimated income tax for any taxable year shall be deemed to have been paid on the last day prescribed for filing the return under section 6012 for such taxable year (determined without regard to any extension of time for filing such return).

(3) Any tax withheld at the source under chapter 3 shall, in respect of the recipient of the income, be deemed to have been paid by such recipient on the last day prescribed for filing the return under section 6012 for the taxable year (determined without regard to any extension of time for filing) with respect to which such tax is allowable as a credit under section 1462. For this purpose, any exemption granted under section 6012 from the requirement of filing a return shall be disregarded.

. . . .

§ 6514.   Credits or refunds after period of limitation

(a) **Credits or refunds after period of limitation.**—A refund of any portion of an internal revenue tax shall be considered erroneous and a credit of any such portion shall be considered void—

(1) **Expiration of period for filing claim.**—If made after the expiration of the period of limitation for filing claim therefor, unless within such period claim was filed; or

(2) **Disallowance of claim and expiration of period for filing suit.**—In the case of a claim filed within the proper time and disallowed by the Secretary, if the credit or refund was made after the expiration of the period of limitation for filing suit, unless within such period suit was begun by the taxpayer.

. . . .

(b) Credit after period of limitation.—Any credit against a liability in respect of any taxable year shall be void if any payment in respect of such liability would be considered an overpayment under section 6401(a).

SUBCHAPTER D—PERIODS OF LIMITATION IN JUDICIAL PROCEEDINGS

§ 6531. Periods of limitation on criminal prosecutions

No person shall be prosecuted, tried, or punished for any of the various offenses arising under the internal revenue laws unless the indictment is found or the information instituted within 3 years next after the commission of the offense, except that the period of limitation shall be 6 years—

(1) for offenses involving the defrauding or attempting to defraud the United States or any agency thereof, whether by conspiracy or not, and in any manner;

(2) for the offense of willfully attempting in any manner to evade or defeat any tax or the payment thereof;

(3) for the offense of willfully aiding or assisting in, or procuring, counseling, or advising, the preparation or presentation under, or in connection with any matter arising under, the internal revenue laws, of a false or fraudulent return, affidavit, claim, or document (whether or not such falsity or fraud is with the knowledge or consent of the person authorized or required to present such return, affidavit, claim, or document);

(4) for the offense of willfully failing to pay any tax, or make any return (other than a return required under authority of part III of subchapter A of chapter 61) at the time or times required by law or regulations;

(5) for offenses described in sections 7206(1) and 7207 (relating to false statements and fraudulent documents);

. . . .

§ 6532. Periods of limitation on suits

(a) Suits by taxpayers for refund.—

(1) **General rule.**—No suit or proceeding under section 7422(a) for the recovery of any internal revenue tax, penalty, or other sum, shall be begun before the expiration of 6 months from the date of filing the claim required under such section unless the Secretary renders a decision thereon within that time, nor after the expiration of 2 years from the date of mailing by certified mail or registered mail by the Secretary to the taxpayer of a notice of the disallowance of the part of the claim to which the suit or proceeding relates.

(2) **Extension of time.**—The 2-year period prescribed in paragraph (1) shall be extended for such period as may be agreed upon in writing between the taxpayer and the Secretary.

(3) **Waiver of notice of disallowance.**—If any person files a written waiver of the requirement that he be mailed a notice of disallowance, the 2-year period prescribed in paragraph (1) shall begin on the date such waiver is filed.

(4) Reconsideration after mailing of notice.—Any consideration, reconsideration, or action by the Secretary with respect to such claim following the mailing of a notice by certified mail or registered mail of disallowance shall not operate to extend the period within which suit may be begun.

. . . . .

CHAPTER 67—INTEREST

Subchapter
  A.   Interest on underpayments.
  B.   Interest on overpayments.
  C.   Determination of interest rate.

SUBCHAPTER A—INTEREST ON UNDERPAYMENTS

§ 6601.   Interest on underpayment, nonpayment, or extensions of time for payment, of tax

(a) General rule.—If any amount of tax imposed by this title (whether required to be shown on a return, or to be paid by stamp or by some other method) is not paid on or before the last date prescribed for payment, interest on such amount at an annual rate established under section 6621 shall be paid for the period from such last date to the date paid.

(b) Last date prescribed for payment.—For purposes of this section, the last date prescribed for payment of the tax shall be determined under chapter 62 with the application of the following rules:

(1) Extensions of time disregarded.—The last date prescribed for payment shall be determined without regard to any extension of time for payment.

(2) Installment payments.—In the case of an election under section 6152(a), 6156(a), or 6158(a) to pay the tax in installments—

(A) The date prescribed for payment of each installment of the tax shown on the return shall be determined under section 6152(b), 6156(b), or 6158(a), and

(B) The last date prescribed for payment of the first installment shall be deemed the last date prescribed for payment of any portion of the tax not shown on the return.

For purposes of subparagraph (A), section 6158(a) shall be treated as providing that the date prescribed for payment of each installment shall not be later than the date prescribed for payment of the 1985 installment.

. . . . .

(4) Last date for payment not otherwise prescribed.—In the case of taxes payable by stamp and in all other cases in which the last date for payment is not otherwise prescribed, the last date for payment shall be deemed to be the date the liability for tax arises (and in no event shall be later than the date notice and demand for the tax is made by the Secretary).

(c) Suspension of interest in certain income, estate, gift, and certain excise tax cases.—In the case of a deficiency as defined in section 6211 (relating to

income, estate, gift, and certain excise taxes), if a waiver of restrictions under section 6213(d) on the assessment of such deficiency has been filed, and if notice and demand by the Secretary for payment of such deficiency is not made within 30 days after the filing of such waiver, interest shall not be imposed on such deficiency for the period beginning immediately after such 30th day and ending with the date of notice and demand.

(d) Income tax reduced by carryback or adjustment for certain unused deductions.—

(1) Net operating loss or capital loss carryback.—If the amount of any tax imposed by subtitle A is reduced by reason of a carryback of a net operating loss or net capital loss, such reduction in tax shall not affect the computation of interest under this section for the period ending with the filing date for the taxable year in which the net operating loss or net capital loss arises.

(e) Applicable rules.—Except as otherwise provided in this title—

(1) Interest treated as tax.—Interest prescribed under this section on any tax shall be paid upon notice and demand, and shall be assessed, collected, and paid in the same manner as taxes. Any reference in this title (except subchapter B of chapter 63, relating to deficiency procedures) to any tax imposed by this title shall be deemed also to refer to interest imposed by this section on such tax.

(2) Interest on penalties, additional amounts, or additions to the tax. —Interest shall be imposed under subsection (a) in respect of any assessable penalty, additional amount, or addition to the tax only if such assessable penalty, additional amount, or addition to the tax is not paid within 10 days from the date of notice and demand therefor, and in such case interest shall be imposed only for the period from the date of the notice and demand to the date of payment.

(3) Payments made within 10 days after notice and demand.—If notice and demand is made for payment of any amount, and if such amount is paid within 10 days after the date of such notice and demand, interest under this section on the amount so paid shall not be imposed for the period after the date of such notice and demand.

(j) 4-percent rate on certain portion of estate tax extended under section 6166.—

(1) In general.—If the time for payment of an amount of tax imposed by chapter 11 is extended as provided in section 6166, interest on the 4-percent portion of such amount shall (in lieu of the annual rate provided by subsection (a)) be paid at the rate of 4 percent. For purposes of this subsection, the amount of any deficiency which is prorated to installments payable under section 6166 shall be treated as an amount of tax payable in installments under such section.

(2) 4-percent portion.—For purposes of this subsection, the term "4-percent portion" means the lesser of—

(A) $345,800 reduced by the amount of the credit allowable under section 2010(a); or

(B) the amount of the tax imposed by chapter 11 which is extended as provided in section 6166.

(3) Treatment of payments.—If the amount of tax imposed by chapter 11 which is extended as provided in section 6166 exceeds the 4-percent portion, any payment of a portion of such amount shall, for purposes of computing interest for periods after such payment, be treated as reducing the 4-percent portion by an amount which bears the same ratio to the amount of such payment as the amount of the 4-percent portion (determined without regard to this paragraph) bears to the amount of the tax which is extended as provided in section 6166.

. . . .

SUBCHAPTER B—INTEREST ON OVERPAYMENTS

§ 6611.   Interest on overpayments

(a) Rate.—Interest shall be allowed and paid upon any overpayment in respect of any internal revenue tax at an annual rate established under section 6621.

(b) Period.—Such interest shall be allowed and paid as follows:

(1) Credits.—In the case of a credit, from the date of the overpayment to the due date of the amount against which the credit is taken.

(2) Refunds.—In the case of a refund, from the date of the overpayment to a date (to be determined by the Secretary) preceding the date of the refund check by not more than 30 days, whether or not such refund check is accepted by the taxpayer after tender of such check to the taxpayer. The acceptance of such check shall be without prejudice to any right of the taxpayer to claim any additional overpayment and interest thereon.

(3) Late returns.—Notwithstanding paragraph (1) or (2) in the case of a return of tax which is filed after the last date prescribed for filing such return (determined with regard to extensions), no interest shall be allowed or paid for any day before the date on which the return is filed.

[**(c) Repealed. Pub.L. 85–866, Title I, § 83(c), Sept. 2, 1958, 72 Stat. 1664**]

(d) Advance payment of tax, payment of estimated tax, and credit for income tax withholding.—The provisions of section 6513 (except the provisions of subsection (c) thereof), applicable in determining the date of payment of tax for purposes of determining the period of limitation on credit or refund, shall be applicable in determining the date of payment for purposes of subsection (a).

(e) Income tax refund within 45 days after return is filed.—If any overpayment of tax imposed by subtitle A is refunded within 45 days after the last date prescribed for filing the return of such tax (determined without regard to any extension of time for filing the return) or, in case the return is filed after such last date, is refunded within 45 days after the date the return is filed, no interest shall be allowed under subsection (a) on such overpayment.

(f) Refund of income tax caused by carryback or adjustment for certain unused deductions.—

(1) Net operating loss or capital loss carryback.—For purposes of subsection (a), if any overpayment of tax imposed by subtitle A results from a carryback of a net operating loss or net capital loss, such overpayment shall be deemed not to have been made prior to the filing date for the taxable year in which such net operating loss or net capital loss arises.

. . . . .

SUBCHAPTER C—DETERMINATION OF INTEREST RATE

§ 6621. Determination of rate of interest

(a) **In general.**—The annual rate established under this section shall be such adjusted rate as is established by the Secretary under subsection (b).

(b) **Adjustment of interest rate.—**

(1) **Establishment of adjusted rate.**—If the adjusted prime rate charged by banks (rounded to the nearest full percent)—

(A) during the 6-month period ending on September 30 of any calendar year, or

(B) during the 6-month period ending on March 31 of any calendar year,

differs from the interest rate in effect under this section on either such date, respectively, then the Secretary shall establish, within 15 days after the close of the applicable 6-month period, an adjusted rate of interest equal to such adjusted prime rate.

(2) **Effective date of adjustment.**—Any adjusted rate of interest established under paragraph (1) shall become effective—

(A) on January 1 of the succeeding year in the case of an adjustment attributable to paragraph (1)(A), and

(B) on July 1 of the same year in the case of an adjustment attributable to paragraph (1)(B).

(c) **Definition of prime rate.**—For purposes of subsection (b), the term "adjusted prime rate charged by banks" means the average predominant prime rate quoted by commercial banks to large businesses, as determined by the Board of Governors of the Federal Reserve System.

§ 6622. Interest compounded daily

(a) **General rule.**—In computing the amount of any interest required to be paid under this title or sections 1961(c)(1) or 2411 of title 28, United States Code, by the Secretary or by the taxpayer, or any other amount determined by reference to such amount of interest, such interest and such amount shall be compounded daily.

(b) **Exception for penalty for failure to file estimated tax.**—Subsection (a) shall not apply for purposes of computing the amount of any addition to tax under section 6654 or 6655.

CHAPTER 68—ADDITIONS TO THE TAX, ADDITIONAL AMOUNTS, AND ASSESSABLE PENALTIES

Subchapter
A. Additions to the tax and additional amounts.
B. Assessable penalties.

SUBCHAPTER A—ADDITIONS TO THE TAX AND ADDITIONAL AMOUNTS

§ 6651.   Failure to file tax return or to pay tax

(a) **Addition to the tax.**—In case of failure—

(1) to file any return required under authority of subchapter A of chapter 61 (other than part III thereof), subchapter A of chapter 51 (relating to distilled spirits, wines, and beer), or of subchapter A of chapter 52 (relating to tobacco, cigars, cigarettes, and cigarette papers and tubes), or of subchapter A of chapter 53 (relating to machine guns and certain other firearms), on the date prescribed therefor (determined with regard to any extension of time for filing), unless it is shown that such failure is due to reasonable cause and not due to willful neglect, there shall be added to the amount required to be shown as tax on such return 5 percent of the amount of such tax if the failure is for not more than 1 month, with an additional 5 percent for each additional month or fraction thereof during which such failure continues, not exceeding 25 percent in the aggregate;

(2) to pay the amount shown as tax on any return specified in paragraph (1) on or before the date prescribed for payment of such tax (determined with regard to any extension of time for payment), unless it is shown that such failure is due to reasonable cause and not due to willful neglect, there shall be added to the amount shown as tax on such return 0.5 percent of the amount of such tax if the failure is for not more than 1 month, with an additional 0.5 percent for each additional month or fraction thereof during which such failure continues, not exceeding 25 percent in the aggregate; or

(3) to pay any amount in respect of any tax required to be shown on a return specified in paragraph (1) which is not so shown (including an assessment made pursuant to section 6213(b)), within 10 days of the date of the notice and demand therefor, unless it is shown that such failure is due to reasonable cause and not due to willful neglect, there shall be added to the amount of tax stated in such notice and demand 0.5 percent of the amount of such tax if the failure is for not more than 1 month, with an additional 0.5 percent for each additional month or fraction thereof during which such failure continues, not exceeding 25 percent in the aggregate.

In the case of a failure to file a return of tax imposed by chapter 1 within 60 days of the date prescribed for filing of such return (determined with regard to any extensions of time for filing), unless it is shown that such failure is due to reasonable cause and not due to willful neglect, the addition to tax under paragraph (1) shall not be less than the lesser of $100 or 100 percent of the amount required to be shown as tax on such return.

. . . . .

§ 6653.   Failure to pay tax

(a) **Negligence or intentional disregard of rules and regulations with respect to income, gift, or windfall profit taxes.**—

(1) **In general.**—If any part of any underpayment (as defined in subsection (c)(1)) of any tax imposed by subtitle A, by chapter 12 of subtitle B, or by chapter 45 (relating to windfall profit tax) is due to negligence or intentional disregard of rules or regulations (but without intent to defraud), there shall be added to the tax an amount equal to 5 percent of the underpayment.

(2) Additional amount for portion attributable to negligence, etc.—There shall be added to the tax (in addition to the amount determined under paragraph (1)) an amount equal to 50 percent of the interest payable under section 6601—

(A) with respect to the portion of the underpayment described in paragraph (1) which is attributable to the negligence or intentional disregard referred to in paragraph (1), and

(B) for the period beginning on the last date prescribed by law for payment of such underpayment (determined without regard to any extension) and ending on the date of the assessment of the tax.

(b) Fraud.—

(1) In general.—If any part of an underpayment (as defined in subsection (c)) of tax required to be shown on a return is due to fraud, there shall be added to the tax an amount equal to 50 percent of the underpayment.

(2) Additional amount for portion attributable to fraud.—There shall be added to the tax (in addition to the amount determined under paragraph (1)) an amount equal to 50 percent of the interest payable under section 6601—

(A) with respect to the portion of the underpayment described in paragraph (1) which is attributable to fraud, and

(B) for the period beginning on the last day prescribed by law for payment of such underpayment (determined without regard to any extension) and ending on the date of the assessment of the tax (or, if earlier, the date of the payment of the tax).

(3) No negligence addition when there is addition for fraud.—The addition to tax under this subsection shall be in lieu of any amount determined under subsection (a).

(4) Special rule for joint returns.—In the case of a joint return under section 6013, this subsection shall not apply with respect to the tax of the spouse unless some part of the underpayment is due to the fraud of such spouse.

§ 6659.   Addition to tax in the case of valuation overstatements for purposes of the income tax

(a) Addition to the tax.—If—

(1) an individual, or

(2) a closely held corporation or a personal service corporation,

has an underpayment of the tax imposed by chapter 1 for the taxable year which is attributable to a valuation overstatement, then there shall be added to the tax an amount equal to the applicable percentage of the underpayment so attributable.

(b) Applicable percentage defined.—For purposes of subsection (a), the applicable percentage shall be determined under the following table:

If the valuation claimed is the following percent of the correct valuation—	The applicable percentage is:
150 percent or more but not more than 200 percent	10
More than 200 percent but not more than 250 percent	20
More than 250 percent	30

(c) Valuation overstatement defined.—

(1) In general.—For purposes of this section, there is a valuation overstatement if the value of any property, or the adjusted basis of any property, claimed on any return exceeds 150 percent of the amount determined to be the correct amount of such valuation or adjusted basis (as the case may be).

(2) Property must have been acquired within last 5 years.—This section shall not apply to any property which, as of the close of the taxable year for which there is a valuation overstatement, has been held by the taxpayer for more than 5 years.

(d) Underpayment must be at least $1,000.—This section shall not apply if the underpayment for the taxable year attributable to the valuation overstatement is less than $1,000.

(e) Authority to waive.—The Secretary may waive all or any part of the addition to the tax provided by this section on a showing by the taxpayer that there was a reasonable basis for the valuation or adjusted basis claimed on the return and that such claim was made in good faith.

(f) Other definitions.—For purposes of this section—

(1) Underpayment.—The term "underpayment" has the meaning given to such term by section 6653(c) (1).

(2) Closely held corporation.—The term "closely held corporation" means any corporation described in section 465(a) (1) (C).

(3) Personal service corporation.—The term "personal service corporation" means any corporation which is a service organization (within the meaning of section 414(m) (3)).

SUBCHAPTER B—ASSESSABLE PENALTIES

§ 6672.   Failure to collect and pay over tax, or attempt to evade or defeat tax

(a) General rule.—Any person required to collect, truthfully account for, and pay over any tax imposed by this title who willfully fails to collect such tax, or truthfully account for and pay over such tax, or willfully attempts in any manner to evade or defeat any such tax or the payment thereof, shall, in addition to other penalties provided by law, be liable to a penalty equal to the total amount of the tax evaded, or not collected, or not accounted for and paid over. No penalty shall be imposed under section 6653 for any offense to which this section is applicable.

. . . . .

§ 6673.   Damages assessable for instituting proceedings before the tax court primarily for delay, etc.

Whenever it appears to the Tax Court that proceedings before it have been instituted or maintained by the taxpayer primarily for delay or that the taxpayer's position in such proceedings is frivolous or groundless, damages in an amount not in excess of $5,000 shall be awarded to the United States by the Tax Court in its decision. Damages so awarded shall be assessed at the same time as the deficiency and shall be paid upon notice and demand from the Secretary and shall be collected as a part of the tax.

§ 6698.   Failure to file partnership return

(a) General rule.—In addition to the penalty imposed by section 7203 (relating to willful failure to file return, supply information, or pay tax), if any partnership required to file a return under section 6031 for any taxable year—

    (1) fails to file such return at the time prescribed therefor (determined with regard to any extension of time for filing), or

    (2) files a return which fails to show the information required under section 6031,

such partnership shall be liable for a penalty determined under subsection (b) for each month (or fraction thereof) during which such failure continues (but not to exceed 5 months), unless it is shown that such failure is due to reasonable cause.

(b) Amount per month.—For purposes of subsection (a), the amount determined under this subsection for any month is the product of—

    (1) $50, multiplied by

    (2) the number of persons who were partners in the partnership during any part of the taxable year.

(c) Assessment of penalty.—The penalty imposed by subsection (a) shall be assessed against the partnership.

(d) Deficiency procedures not to apply.—Subchapter B of chapter 63 (relating to deficiency procedures for income, estate, gift, and certain excise taxes) shall not apply in respect of the assessment or collection of any penalty imposed by subsection (a).

CHAPTER 71—TRANSFEREES AND FIDUCIARIES

§ 6901.   Transferred assets

(a) Method of collection.—The amounts of the following liabilities shall, except as hereinafter in this section provided, be assessed, paid, and collected in the same manner and subject to the same provisions and limitations as in the case of the taxes with respect to which the liabilities were incurred:

    (1) Income, estate, and gift taxes.—

        (A) Transferees.—The liability, at law or in equity, of a transferee of property—

            (i) of a taxpayer in the case of a tax imposed by subtitle A (relating to income taxes),

            (ii) of a decedent in the case of a tax imposed by chapter 11 (relating to estate taxes), or

            (iii) of a donor in the case of a tax imposed by chapter 12 (relating to gift taxes),

in respect of the tax imposed by subtitle A or B.

      . . . . .

    (2) Other taxes.—The liability, at law or in equity of a transferee of property of any person liable in respect of any tax imposed by this title (other than a tax imposed by subtitle A or B), but only if such liability arises on the liquidation of a partnership or corporation, or on a reorganization within the meaning of section 368(a).

(b) Liability.—Any liability referred to in subsection (a) may be either as to the amount of tax shown on a return or as to any deficiency or underpayment of any tax.

(c) Period of limitations.—The period of limitations for assessment of any such liability of a transferee or a fiduciary shall be as follows:

(1) Initial transferee.—In the case of the liability of an initial transferee, within 1 year after the expiration of the period of limitation for assessment against the transferor;

(2) Transferee of transferee.—In the case of the liability of a transferee of a transferee, within 1 year after the expiration of the period of limitation for assessment against the preceding transferee, but not more than 3 years after the expiration of the period of limitation for assessment against the initial transferor;

except that if, before the expiration of the period of limitation for the assessment of the liability of the transferee, a court proceeding for the collection of the tax or liability in respect thereof has been begun against the initial transferor or the last preceding transferee, respectively, then the period of limitation for assessment of the liability of the transferee shall expire 1 year after the return of execution in the court proceeding.

(3) Fiduciary.—In the case of the liability of a fiduciary, not later than 1 year after the liability arises or not later than the expiration of the period for collection of the tax in respect of which such liability arises, whichever is the later.

(d) Extension by agreement.—

(1) Extension of time for assessment.—If before the expiration of the time prescribed in subsection (c) for the assessment of the liability, the Secretary and the transferee or fiduciary have both consented in writing to its assessment after such time, the liability may be assessed at any time prior to the expiration of the period agreed upon. The period so agreed upon may be extended by subsequent agreements in writing made before the expiration of the period previously agreed upon. For the purpose of determining the period of limitation on credit or refund to the transferee or fiduciary of overpayments of tax made by such transferee or fiduciary or overpayments of tax made by the transferor of which the transferee or fiduciary is legally entitled to credit or refund, such agreement and any extension thereof shall be deemed an agreement and extension thereof referred to in section 6511(c).

(2) Extension of time for credit or refund.—If the agreement is executed after the expiration of the period of limitation for assessment against the taxpayer with reference to whom the liability of such transferee or fiduciary rises, then in applying the limitations under section 6511(c) on the amount of the credit or refund, the periods specified in section 6511(b) (2) shall be increased by the period from the date of such expiration to the date of the agreement.

(e) Period for assessment against transferor.—For purposes of this section, if any person is deceased, or is a corporation which has terminated its existence, the period of limitation for assessment against such person shall be the period that would be in effect had death or termination of existence not occurred.

(f) Suspension of running of period of limitations.—The running of the period of limitations upon the assessment of the liability of a transferee or fiduciary shall, after the mailing to the transferee or fiduciary of the notice provided for in section 6212 (relating to income, estate, and gift taxes), be suspended for the period during which the Secretary is prohibited from making the assessment in respect of the liability of the transferee or fiduciary (and in any event, if a proceeding in respect of the liability is placed on the docket of the Tax Court, until the decision of the Tax Court becomes final), and for 60 days thereafter.

(g) Address for notice of liability.—In the absence of notice to the Secretary under section 6903 of the existence of a fiduciary relationship, any notice of liability enforceable under this section required to be mailed to such person, shall, if mailed to the person subject to the liability at his last known address, be sufficient for purposes of this title, even if such person is deceased, or is under a legal disability, or, in the case of a corporation, has terminated its existence.

(h) Definition of transferee.—As used in this section, the term "transferee" includes donee, heir, legatee, devisee, and distributee, and with respect to estate taxes, also includes any person who, under section 6324(a) (2), is personally liable for any part of such tax.

. . . . .

§ 6902.   Provisions of special application to transferees

(a) Burden of proof.—In proceedings before the Tax Court the burden of proof shall be upon the Secretary to show that a petitioner is liable as a transferee of property of a taxpayer, but not to show that the taxpayer was liable for the tax.

(b) Evidence.—Upon application to the Tax Court, a transferee of property of a taxpayer shall be entitled, under rules prescribed by the Tax Court, to a preliminary examination of books, papers, documents, correspondence, and other evidence of the taxpayer or a preceding transferee of the taxpayer's property, if the transferee making the application is a petitioner before the Tax Court for the redetermination of his liability in respect of the tax (including interest, additional amounts, and additions to the tax provided by law) imposed upon the taxpayer. Upon such application, the Tax Court may require by subpoena, ordered by the Tax Court or any division thereof and signed by a judge, the production of all such books, papers, documents, correspondence, and other evidence within the United States the production of which, in the opinion of the Tax Court or division thereof, is necessary to enable the transferee to ascertain the liability of the taxpayer or preceding transferee and will not result in undue hardship to the taxpayer or preceding transferee. Such examination shall be had at such time and place as may be designated in the subpoena.

§ 6903.   Notice of fiduciary relationship

(a) Rights and obligations of fiduciary.—Upon notice to the Secretary that any person is acting for another person in a fiduciary capacity, such fiduciary shall assume the powers, rights, duties, and privileges of such other person in respect of a tax imposed by this title (except as otherwise specifically provided and except that the tax shall be collected from the estate of such other person), until notice is given that the fiduciary capacity has terminated.

(b) Manner of notice.—Notice under this section shall be given in accordance with regulations prescribed by the Secretary.

§ 6905.   Discharge of executor from personal liability for decedent's income and gift taxes

(a) Discharge of liability.—In the case of liability of a decedent for taxes imposed by subtitle A or by chapter 12, if the executor makes written application (filed after the return with respect to such taxes is made and filed in such manner and such form as may be prescribed by regulations of the Secretary) for release from personal liability for such taxes, the Secretary may notify the executor of the amount of such taxes. The executor, upon payment of the amount of which he is notified, or 9 months after receipt of the application if no notification is made by the Secretary before such date, shall be discharged from personal liability for any deficiency in such tax thereafter found to be due and shall be entitled to a receipt or writing showing such discharge.

(b) Definition of executor.—For purposes of this section, the term "executor" means the executor or administrator of the decedent appointed, qualified, and acting within the United States.

. . . .

CHAPTER 74—CLOSING AGREEMENTS AND COMPROMISES

§ 7121. Closing agreements

(a) Authorization.—The Secretary is authorized to enter into an agreement in writing with any person relating to the liability of such person (or of the person or estate for whom he acts) in respect of any internal revenue tax for any taxable period.

(b) Finality.—If such agreement is approved by the Secretary (within such time as may be stated in such agreement, or later agreed to) such agreement shall be final and conclusive, and, except upon a showing of fraud or malfeasance, or misrepresentation of a material fact—

(1) the case shall not be reopened as to the matters agreed upon or the agreement modified by any officer, employee, or agent of the United States, and

(2) in any suit, action, or proceeding, such agreement, or any determination, assessment, collection, payment, abatement, refund, or credit made in accordance therewith, shall not be annulled, modified, set aside, or disregarded.

§ 7122. Compromises

(a) Authorization.—The Secretary may compromise any civil or criminal case arising under the internal revenue laws prior to reference to the Department of Justice for prosecution or defense; and the Attorney General or his delegate may compromise any such case after reference to the Department of Justice for prosecution or defense.

(b) Record.—Whenever a compromise is made by the Secretary in any case, there shall be placed on file in the office of the Secretary the opinion of the General Counsel for the Department of the Treasury or his delegate, with his reasons therefor, with a statement of—

(1) The amount of tax assessed,

(2) The amount of interest, additional amount, addition to the tax, or assessable penalty, imposed by law on the person against whom the tax is assessed, and

(3) The amount actually paid in accordance with the terms of the compromise.

Notwithstanding the foregoing provisions of this subsection, no such opinion shall be required with respect to the compromise of any civil case in which the unpaid amount of tax assessed (including any interest, additional amount, addition to the tax, or assessable penalty) is less than $500.

CHAPTER 75—CRIMES, OTHER OFFENSES, AND FORFEITURES

Subchapter
A. Crimes.
B. Other offenses.*
C. Forfeitures.*
D. Miscellaneous penalty and forfeiture provisions.*

SUBCHAPTER A—CRIMES

Part
I. General provisions.
II. Penalties applicable to certain taxes.*

PART I—GENERAL PROVISIONS

§ 7201.   Attempt to evade or defeat tax

Any person who willfully attempts in any manner to evade or defeat any tax imposed by this title or the payment thereof shall, in addition to other penalties provided by law, be guilty of a felony and, upon conviction thereof, shall be fined not more than $100,000 ($500,000 in the case of a corporation), or imprisoned not more than 5 years, or both, together with the costs of prosecution.

§ 7202.   Willful failure to collect or pay over tax

Any person required under this title to collect, account for, and pay over any tax imposed by this title who willfully fails to collect or truthfully account for and pay over such tax shall, in addition to other penalties provided by law, be guilty of a felony and, upon conviction thereof, shall be fined not more than $10,000, or imprisoned not more than 5 years, or both, together with the costs of prosecution.

§ 7203.   Willful failure to file return, supply information, or pay tax

Any person required under this title to pay any estimated tax or tax, or required by this title or by regulations made under authority thereof to make a return (other than a return required under authority of section 6015), keep any records, or supply any information, who willfully fails to pay such estimated tax or tax, make such return, keep such records, or supply such information, at the time or times required by law or regulations, shall, in addition to other penalties provided by law, be guilty of a misdemeanor and, upon conviction thereof, shall be fined not more than $25,000 ($100,000 in the case of a corporation), or imprisoned not more than 1 year, or both, together with the costs of prosecution. . . .

§ 7206.   Fraud and false statements

Any person who—

(1) **Declaration under penalties of perjury.**—Willfully makes and subscribes any return, statement, or other document, which contains or is

* Omitted entirely.

602

verified by a written declaration that it is made under the penalties of perjury, and which he does not believe to be true and correct as to every material matter; or

(2) Aid or assistance.—Willfully aids or assists in, or procures, counsels, or advises the preparation or presentation under, or in connection with any matter arising under, the internal revenue laws, of a return, affidavit, claim, or other document, which is fraudulent or is false as to any material matter, whether or not such falsity or fraud is with the knowledge or consent of the person authorized or required to present such return, affidavit, claim, or document; or

(3) Fraudulent bonds, permits, and entries.—Simulates or falsely or fraudulently executes or signs any bond, permit, entry, or other document required by the provisions of the internal revenue laws, or by any regulation made in pursuance thereof, or procures the same to be falsely or fraudulently executed, or advises, aids in, or connives at such execution thereof; or

(4) Removal or concealment with intent to defraud.—Removes, deposits, or conceals, or is concerned in removing, depositing, or concealing, any goods or commodities for or in respect whereof any tax is or shall be imposed, or any property upon which levy is authorized by section 6331, with intent to evade or defeat the assessment or collection of any tax imposed by this title; or

(5) Compromises and closing agreements.—In connection with any compromise under section 7122, or offer of such compromise, or in connection with any closing agreement under section 7121, or offer to enter into any such agreement, willfully—

    (A) Concealment of property.—Conceals from any officer or employee of the United States any property belonging to the estate of a taxpayer or other person liable in respect of the tax, or

    (B) Withholding, falsifying, and destroying records.—Receives, withholds, destroys, mutilates, or falsifies any book, document, or record, or makes any false statement, relating to the estate or financial condition of the taxpayer or other person liable in respect of the tax;

shall be guilty of a felony and, upon conviction thereof, shall be fined not more than $100,000 ($500,000 in the case of a corporation), or imprisoned not more than 3 years, or both, together with the costs of prosecution.

§ 7207.   Fraudulent returns, statements, or other documents

Any person who willfully delivers or discloses to the Secretary any list, return, account, statement, or other document, known by him to be fraudulent or to be false as to any material matter, shall be fined not more than $10,000 ($50,000 in the case of a corporation), or imprisoned not more than 1 year, or both. Any person required pursuant to subsection (b) or (c) of section 6047 or pursuant to subsection (d) of section 6104 to furnish any information to the Secretary or any other person who willfully furnishes to the Secretary or such other person any information known by him to be fraudulent or to be false as to any material matter shall be fined not more than $10,000 ($50,000 in the case of a corporation), or imprisoned not more than 1 year, or both.

CHAPTER 76—JUDICIAL PROCEEDINGS

Subchapter
    A.   Civil actions by the United States.*
    B.   Proceedings by taxpayers and third parties.
    C.   The Tax Court.*
    D.   Court review of Tax Court decisions.*
    [E.   Repealed]

SUBCHAPTER B—PROCEEDINGS BY TAXPAYERS AND THIRD PARTIES

§ 7421. Prohibition of suits to restrain assessment or collection

(a) Tax.—Except as provided in sections 6212(a) and (c), 6213(a), 6672(b), 6694(c), 7426(a) and (b) (1), and 7429(b), no suit for the purpose of restraining the assessment or collection of any tax shall be maintained in any court by any person, whether or not such person is the person against whom such tax was assessed.

(b) Liability of transferee or fiduciary.—No suit shall be maintained in any court for the purpose of restraining the assessment or collection (pursuant to the provisions of chapter 71) of—

    (1) the amount of the liability, at law or in equity, of a transferee of property of a taxpayer in respect of any internal revenue tax, or

§ 7422. Civil actions for refund

(a) No suit prior to filing claim for refund.—No suit or proceeding shall be maintained in any court for the recovery of any internal revenue tax alleged to have been erroneously or illegally assessed or collected, or of any penalty claimed to have been collected without authority, or of any sum alleged to have been excessive or in any manner wrongfully collected, until a claim for refund or credit has been duly filed with the Secretary, according to the provisions of law in that regard, and the regulations of the Secretary established in pursuance thereof.

(b) Protest or duress.—Such suit or proceeding may be maintained whether or not such tax, penalty, or sum has been paid under protest or duress.

(e) Stay of proceedings.—If the Secretary prior to the hearing of a suit brought by a taxpayer in a district court or the Court of Claims for the recovery of any income tax, estate tax, gift tax, or tax imposed by chapter 41, 42, 43, 44, or 45 (or any penalty relating to such taxes) mails to the taxpayer a notice that a deficiency has been determined in respect of the tax which is the subject matter of taxpayer's suit, the proceedings in taxpayer's suit shall be stayed during the period of time in which the taxpayer may file a petition with the Tax Court for a redetermination of the asserted deficiency, and for 60 days thereafter. If the taxpayer files a petition with the Tax Court, the district court or the Court of

* Omitted entirely.

Claims, as the case may be, shall lose jurisdiction of taxpayer's suit to whatever extent jurisdiction is acquired by the Tax Court of the subject matter of taxpayer's suit for refund. If the taxpayer does not file a petition with the Tax Court for a redetermination of the asserted deficiency, the United States may counterclaim in the taxpayer's suit, or intervene in the event of a suit as described in subsection (c) (relating to suits against officers or employees of the United States), within the period of the stay of proceedings notwithstanding that the time for such pleading may have otherwise expired. The taxpayer shall have the burden of proof with respect to the issues raised by such counterclaim or intervention of the United States except as to the issue of whether the taxpayer has been guilty of fraud with intent to evade tax. This subsection shall not apply to a suit by a taxpayer which, prior to the date of enactment of this title, is commenced, instituted, or pending in a district court or the Court of Claims for the recovery of any income tax, estate, tax, or gift tax (or any penalty relating to such taxes).

. . . . .

CHAPTER 77—MISCELLANEOUS PROVISIONS

§ 7502.   Timely mailing treated as timely filing and paying

(a) General rule.—

(1) **Date of delivery.**—If any return, claim, statement, or other document required to be filed, or any payment required to be made, within a prescribed period or on or before a prescribed date under authority of any provision of the internal revenue laws is, after such period or such date, delivered by United States mail to the agency, officer, or office with which such return, claim, statement, or other document is required to be filed, or to which such payment is required to be made, the date of the United States postmark stamped on the cover in which such return, claim, statement, or other document, or payment, is mailed shall be deemed to be the date of delivery or the date of payment, as the case may be.

(2) **Mailing requirements.**—This subsection shall apply only if—

(A) the postmark date falls within the prescribed period or on or before the prescribed date—

(i) for the filing (including any extension granted for such filing) of the return, claim, statement, or other document, or

(ii) for making the payment (including any extension granted for making such payment), and

(B) the return, claim, statement, or other document, or payment was, within the time prescribed in subparagraph (A), deposited in the mail in the United States in an envelope or other appropriate wrapper, postage prepaid, properly addressed to the agency, officer, or office with which the return, claim, statement, or other document is required to be filed, or to which such payment is required to be made.

(b) Postmarks.—This section shall apply in the case of postmarks not made by the United States Postal Service only if and to the extent provided by regulations prescribed by the Secretary.

(c) Registered and certified mailing.—

(1) **Registered mail.**—For purposes of this section, if any such return, claim, statement, or other document, or payment, is sent by United States registered mail—

(A) such registration shall be prima facie evidence that the return, claim, statement, or other document was delivered to the agency, officer, or office to which addressed, and

(B) the date of registration shall be deemed the postmark date.

(2) Certified mail.—The Secretary is authorized to provide by regulations the extent to which the provisions of paragraph (1) of this subsection with respect to prima facie evidence of delivery and the postmark date shall apply to certified mail.

(d) Exceptions.—This section shall not apply with respect to—

(1) the filing of a document in, or the making of a payment to, any court other than the Tax Court,

(2) currency or other medium of payment unless actually received and accounted for, or

(3) returns, claims, statements, or other documents, or payments, which are required under any provision of the internal revenue laws or the regulations thereunder to be delivered by any method other than by mailing.

· · · · ·

CHAPTER 78—DISCOVERY OF LIABILITY AND ENFORCEMENT OF TITLE

Subchapter
  A. Examination and inspection.
  B. General powers and duties.*
  [C. Repealed]
  D. Possessions.*

SUBCHAPTER A—EXAMINATION AND INSPECTION

§ 7602.   Examination of books and witnesses

(a) Authority to summon, etc.—For the purpose of ascertaining the correctness of any return, making a return where none has been made, determining the liability of any person for any internal revenue tax or the liability at law or in equity of any transferee or fiduciary of any person in respect of any internal revenue tax, or collecting any such liability, the Secretary is authorized—

(1) To examine any books, papers, records, or other data which may be relevant or material to such inquiry;

(2) To summon the person liable for tax or required to perform the act, or any officer or employee of such person, or any person having possession, custody, or care of books of account containing entries relating to the business of the person liable for tax or required to perform the act, or any other person the Secretary may deem proper, to appear before the Secretary at a time and place named in the summons and to produce such books, papers, records, or other data, and to give such testimony, under oath, as may be relevant or material to such inquiry; and

(3) To take such testimony of the person concerned, under oath, as may be relevant or material to such inquiry.

· · · · ·

* Omitted entirely.

CHAPTER 79—DEFINITIONS

§ 7701. Definitions

(a) When used in this title, where not otherwise distinctly expressed or manifestly incompatible with the intent thereof—

(1) **Person.**—The term "person" shall be construed to mean and include an individual, a trust, estate, partnership, association, company or corporation.

(2) **Partnership and partner.**—The term "partnership" includes a syndicate, group, pool, joint venture, or other unincorporated organization, through or by means of which any business, financial operation, or venture is carried on, and which is not, within the meaning of this title, a trust or estate or a corporation; and the term "partner" includes a member in such a syndicate, group, pool, joint venture, or organization.

(3) **Corporation.**—The term "corporation" includes associations, joint-stock companies, and insurance companies.

(4) **Domestic.**—The term "domestic" when applied to a corporation or partnership means created or organized in the United States or under the law of the United States or of any State.

(5) **Foreign.**—The term "foreign" when applied to a corporation or partnership means a corporation or partnership which is not domestic.

(6) **Fiduciary.**—The term "fiduciary" means a guardian, trustee, executor, administrator, receiver, conservator, or any person acting in any fiduciary capacity for any person.

(7) **Stock.**—The term "stock" includes shares in an association, joint-stock company, or insurance company.

(8) **Shareholder.**—The term "shareholder" includes a member in an association, joint-stock company, or insurance company.

. . . .

(17) **Husband and wife.**—As used in sections 71, 152(b) (4), 215, and 682, if the husband and wife therein referred to are divorced, wherever appropriate to the meaning of such sections, the term "wife" shall be read "former wife" and the term "husband" shall be read "former husband"; and, if the payments described in such sections are made by or on behalf of the wife or former wife to the husband or former husband instead of vice versa, wherever appropriate to the meaning of such sections, the term "husband" shall be read "wife" and the term "wife" shall be read "husband."

. . . .

(24) **Fiscal year.**—The term "fiscal year" means an accounting period of 12 months ending on the last day of any month other than December.

(25) **Paid or incurred, paid or accrued.**—The terms "paid or incurred" and "paid or accrued" shall be construed according to the method of accounting upon the basis of which the taxable income is computed under subtitle A.

(26) **Trade or business.**—The term "trade or business" includes the performance of the functions of a public office.

. . . .

(b) Includes and including.—The terms "includes" and "including" when used in a definition contained in this title shall not be deemed to exclude other things otherwise within the meaning of the term defined.

. . . . .

CHAPTER 80—GENERAL RULES

Subchapter
A. Application of internal revenue laws.
B. Effective date and related provisions.*

SUBCHAPTER A—APPLICATION OF INTERNAL REVENUE LAWS

§ 7805.   Rules and regulations

(a) Authorization.—Except where such authority is expressly given by this title to any person other than an officer or employee of the Treasury Department, the Secretary shall prescribe all needful rules and regulations for the enforcement of this title, including all rules and regulations as may be necessary by reason of any alteration of law in relation to internal revenue.

(b) Retroactivity of regulations or rulings.—The Secretary may prescribe the extent, if any, to which any ruling or regulation, relating to the internal revenue laws, shall be applied without retroactive effect.

. . . . .

* Omitted entirely.

TREASURY REGULATIONS

PART 1—INCOME TAXES

§ 1.61–1   Gross income

(a) **General definition.** Gross income means all income from whatever source derived, unless excluded by law. Gross income includes income realized in any form, whether in money, property, or services. Income may be realized, therefore, in the form of services, meals, accommodations, stock, or other property, as well as in cash. Section 61 lists the more common items of gross income for purposes of illustration. For purposes of further illustration, § 1.61–14 mentions several miscellaneous items of gross income not listed specifically in section 61. Gross income, however, is not limited to the items so enumerated.

. . . .

§ 1.61–2   Compensation for services, including fees, commissions, and similar items

(a) **In general.** (1) Wages, salaries, commissions paid salesmen, compensation for services on the basis of a percentage of profits, commissions on insurance premiums, tips, bonuses (including Christmas bonuses), termination or severance pay, rewards, jury fees, marriage fees and other contributions received by a clergyman for services, pay of persons in the military or naval forces of the United States, retired pay of employees, pensions, and retirement allowances are income to the recipients unless excluded by law.

. . . .

(c) **Payment to charitable, etc., organization on behalf of person rendering services.** The value of services is not includible in gross income when such services are rendered directly and gratuitously to an organization described in section 170(c). Where, however, pursuant to an agreement or under-

standing, services are rendered to a person for the benefit of an organization described in section 170(c) and an amount for such services is paid to such organization by the person to whom the services are rendered, the amount so paid constitutes income to the person performing the services.

(d) **Compensation paid other than in cash—(1) In general.** Except as otherwise provided in paragraph (d)(6)(i) of this section (relating to certain property transferred after June 30, 1969), if services are paid for in property, the fair market value of the property taken in payment must be included in income as compensation. If services are paid for in exchange for other services, the fair market value of such other services taken in payment must be included in income as compensation. If the services are rendered at a stipulated price, such price will be presumed to be the fair market value of the compensation received in the absence of evidence to the contrary. For special rules relating to certain options received as compensation, see §§ 1.61–15, 1.83–7, and section 421 and the regulations thereunder. For special rules relating to premiums paid by an employer for an annuity contract which is not subject to section 403(a), see section 403(c) and the regulations thereunder and § 1.83–8(a). For special rules relating to contributions made to an employees' trust which is not exempt under section 501, see section 402(b) and the regulations thereunder and § 1.83–8(a).

(2) **Property transferred to employee or independent contractor.** (i) Except as otherwise provided in section 421 and the regulations thereunder and § 1.61–15 (relating to stock options), and paragraph (d)(6)(i) of this section, if property is transferred by an

employer to an employee or if property is transferred to an independent contractor, as compensation for services, for an amount less than its fair market value, then regardless of whether the transfer is in the form of a sale or exchange, the difference between the amount paid for the property and the amount of its fair market value at the time of the transfer is compensation and shall be included in the gross income of the employee or independent contractor. In computing the gain or loss from the subsequent sale of such property, its basis shall be the amount paid for the property increased by the amount of such difference included in gross income.

(ii) (a) Cost of life insurance on the life of the employee. Generally, life insurance premiums paid by an employer on the life of his employee where the proceeds of such insurance are payable to the beneficiary of such employee are part of the gross income of the employee. However, the amount includible in the employee's gross income is determined with regard to the provisions of section 403 and the regulations thereunder in the case of an individual contract issued after December 31, 1962, or a group contract, which provides incidental life insurance protection and which satisfies the requirements of section 401(g) and § 1.401–9, relating to the nontransferability of annuity contracts. For the special rules relating to the includibility in an employee's gross income of an amount equal to the cost of . . . . which is carried directly or indirectly by his employer, see section 79 and the regulations thereunder. For special rules relating to the exclusion of contributions by an employer to accident and health plans for the employees, see section 106 and the regulations thereunder.

. . . .

(4) Stock and notes transferred to employee or independent contractor. Except as otherwise provided by section 421 and the regulations thereunder and § 1.61–15 (relating to stock options), and paragraph (d)(6)(i) of this section, if a corporation transfers its own stock to an employee or independent contractor as compensation for services, the fair market value of the stock at the time of transfer shall be included in the gross income of the employee or independent contractor. Notes or other evidences of indebtedness received in payment for services constitute income in the amount of their fair market value at the time of the transfer. A taxpayer receiving as compensation a note regarded as good for its face value at maturity, but not bearing interest, shall treat as income as of the time of receipt its fair discounted value computed at the prevailing rate. As payments are received on such a note, there shall be included in income that portion of each payment which represents the proportionate part of the discount originally taken on the entire note.

. . . .

(6) Certain property transferred, premiums paid, and contributions made in connection with the performance of services after June 30, 1969—(i) Exception. Paragraph (d)(1), (2), (4), and (5) of this section and § 1.61–15 do not apply to the transfer of property (as defined in § 1.83–3(e)) after June 30, 1969, unless § 1.61–8 (relating to the applicability of section 83 and transitional rules) applies. If section 83 applies to a transfer of property, and the property is not subject to a restriction that has a significant effect on the fair market value of such property, then the rules contained in paragraph (d) (1), (2), and (4) of this section and § 1.61–15 shall also apply to such transfer to the extent such rules are not inconsistent with section 83.

. . . .

§ 1.61–3　Gross income derived from business

(a) In general. In a manufacturing, merchandising, or mining business, "gross income" means the total sales, less the cost of goods sold, plus any income from investments and from incidental or outside operations or sources. Gross income is determined without subtraction of depletion allowances based on a percentage of income to the extent that it exceeds cost depletion which may be required to be included in the amount of inventoriable costs as provided in § 1.471–11 and without subtraction of selling expenses, losses or other items not ordinarily used in computing costs of goods sold or amounts which are of a type for which a deduction would be disallowed under section 162(c), (f), or (g) in the case of a business expense. The cost of goods sold should be determined in accordance with the method of accounting consistently used by the taxpayer.

. . . .

§ 1.61-4 Gross income of farmers

(a) **Farmers using the cash method of accounting.** A farmer using the cash receipts and disbursements method of accounting shall include in his gross income for the taxable year—

(1) The amount of cash and the value of merchandise or other property received during the taxable year from the sale of livestock and produce which he raised,

(2) The profits from the sale of any livestock or other items which were purchased,

(3) All amounts received from breeding fees, fees from rent of teams, machinery, or land, and other incidental farm income,

(4) All subsidy and conservation payments received which must be considered as income, and

(5) Gross income from all other sources.

The profit from the sale of livestock or other items which were purchased is to be ascertained by deducting the cost from the sales price in the year in which the sale occurs, except that in the case of the sale of purchased animals held for draft, breeding, or dairy purposes, the profits shall be the amount of any excess of the sales price over the amount representing the difference between the cost and the depreciation allowed or allowable (determined in accordance with the rules applicable under section 1016(a) and the regulations thereunder). . . . .

(b) **Farmers using an accrual method of accounting.** A farmer using an accrual method of accounting must use inventories to determine his gross income. His gross income on an accrual method is determined by adding the total of the items described in subparagraphs (1) through (5) of this paragraph and subtracting therefrom the total of the items described in subparagraphs (6) and (7) of this paragraph. These items are as follows:

(1) The sales price of all livestock and other products held for sale and sold during the year;

(2) The inventory value of livestock and products on hand and not sold at the end of the year;

(3) All miscellaneous items of income, such as breeding fees, fees from the rent of teams, machinery, or land, or other incidental farm income;

(4) Any subsidy or conservation payments which must be considered as income;

(5) Gross income from all other sources;

(6) The inventory value of the livestock and products on hand and not sold at the beginning of the year; and

(7) The cost of any livestock or products purchased during the year (except livestock held for draft, dairy, or breeding purposes, unless included in inventory).

All livestock raised or purchased for sale shall be added in the inventory at their proper valuation determined in accordance with the method authorized and adopted for the purpose. Livestock acquired for draft, breeding, or dairy purposes and not for sale may be included in the inventory (see subparagraphs (2), (6), and (7) of this paragraph) instead of being treated as capital assets subject to depreciation, provided such practice is followed consistently from year to year by the taxpayer. When any livestock included in an inventory are sold, their cost must not be taken as an additional deduction in computing taxable income, because such deduction is reflected in the inventory. See the regulations under section 471. . . . .

(c) **Special rules for certain receipts.** In the case of the sale of machinery, farm equipment, or any other property (except stock in trade of the taxpayer, or property of a kind which would properly be included in the inventory of the taxpayer if on hand at the close of the taxable year, or property held by the taxpayer primarily for sale to customers in the ordinary course of his trade or business), any excess of the proceeds of the sale over the adjusted basis of such property shall be included in the taxpayer's gross income for the taxable year in which such sale is made. See, however, section 453 and the regulations thereunder for special rules relating to certain installment sales. If farm produce is exchanged for merchandise, groceries, or the like, the market value of the article received in exchange is to be included in gross income. . . . .

. . . .

§ 1.61–6 Gains derived from dealings in property

(a) **In general.** Gain realized on the sale or exchange of property is included in gross income, unless excluded by law. For this purpose property includes tangible items, such as a building, and intangible items, such as goodwill. Generally, the gain is the excess of the amount realized over the unrecovered cost or other basis for the property sold or exchanged. The specific rules for computing the amount of gain or loss are contained in section 1001 and the regulations thereunder. When a part of a larger property is sold, the cost or other basis of the entire property shall be equitably apportioned among the several parts, and the gain realized or loss sustained on the part of the entire property sold is the difference between the selling price and the cost or other basis allocated to such part. The sale of each part is treated as a separate transaction and gain or loss shall be computed separately on each part. Thus, gain or loss shall be determined at the time of sale of each part and not deferred until the entire property has been disposed of. This rule may be illustrated by the following examples:

Example (1). A, a dealer in real estate, acquires a 10-acre tract for $10,000, which he divides into 20 lots. The $10,000 cost must be equitably apportioned among the lots so that on the sale of each A can determine his taxable gain or deductible loss.

Example (2). B purchases for $25,000 property consisting of a used car lot and adjoining filling station. At the time, the fair market value of the filling station is $15,000 and the fair market value of the used car lot is $10,000. Five years later B sells the filling station for $20,000 at a time when $2,000 has been properly allowed as depreciation thereon. B's gain on this sale is $7,000, since $7,000 is the amount by which the selling price of the filling station exceeds the portion of the cost equitably allocable to the filling station at the time of purchase reduced by the depreciation properly allowed.

(b) **Nontaxable exchanges.** Certain realized gains or losses on the sale or exchange of property are not "recognized", that is, are not included in or deducted from gross income at the time the transaction occurs. Gain or loss from such sales or exchanges is generally recognized at some later time. Examples of such sales or exchanges are the following:

(1) Certain formations, reorganizations, and liquidations of corporations, see sections 331, 333, 337, 351, 354, 355, and 361;

(2) Certain formations and distributions of partnerships, see sections 721 and 731;

(3) Exchange of certain property held for productive use or investment for property of like kind, see section 1031;

(4) A corporation's exchange of its stock for property, see section 1032;

(5) Certain involuntary conversions of property if replaced, see section 1033;

(6) Sale or exchange of residence if replaced, see section 1034;

(7) Certain exchanges of insurance policies and annuity contracts, see section 1035; and

(8) Certain exchanges of stock for stock in the same corporation, see section 1036.

(c) **Character of recognized gain.** Under subchapter P, of chapter 1 of the Code, relating to capital gains and losses, certain gains derived from dealings in property are treated specially, and under certain circumstances the maximum rate of tax on such gains is 25 percent, as provided in section 1201. Generally, the property subject to this treatment is a "capital asset", or treated as a "capital asset". For definition of such assets, see sections 1221 and 1231, and the regulations thereunder. For some of the rules either granting or denying this special treatment, see the following sections and the regulations thereunder:

(1) Transactions between partner and partnership, section 707;

(2) Sale or exchange of property used in the trade or business and involuntary conversions, section 1231;

(3) Payment of bonds and other evidences of indebtedness, section 1232;

(4) Gains and losses from short sales, section 1233;

(5) Options to buy or sell, section 1234;

(6) Sale or exchange of patents, section 1235;

(7) Securities sold by dealers in securities, section 1236;

(8) Real property subdivided for sale, section 1237;

(9) Amortization in excess of depreciation, section 1238;

(10) Gain from sale of certain property between spouses or between an individual and a controlled corporation, section 1239;

. . . .

§ 1.61-8 Rents and royalties

(a) In general. Gross income includes rentals received or accrued for the occupancy of real estate or the use of personal property. For the inclusion of rents in income for the purpose of the retirement income credit, see section 37 and the regulations thereunder. Gross income includes royalties. Royalties may be received from books, stories, plays, copyrights, trademarks, formulas, patents, and from the exploitation of natural resources, such as coal, gas, oil, copper, or timber. Payments received as a result of the transfer of patent rights may under some circumstances constitute capital gain instead of ordinary income. See section 1235 and the regulations thereunder. For special rules for certain income from natural resources, see subchapter I (section 611 and following), chapter 1 of the Code, and the regulations thereunder.

(b) Advance rentals; cancellation payments. Gross income includes advance rentals, which must be included in income for the year of receipt regardless of the period covered or the method of accounting employed by the taxpayer. An amount received by a lessor from a lessee for cancelling a lease constitutes gross income for the year in which it is received, since it is essentially a substitute for rental payments. As to amounts received by a lessee for the cancellation of a lease, see section 1241 and the regulations thereunder.

(c) Expenditures by lessee. As a general rule, if a lessee pays any of the expenses of his lessor such payments are additional rental income of the lessor. If a lessee places improvements on real estate which constitute, in whole or in part, a substitute for rent, such improvements constitute rental income to the lessor. Whether or not improvements made by a lessee result in rental income to the lessor in a particular case depends upon the intention of the parties, which may be indicated either by the terms of the lease or by the surrounding circumstances. For the exclusion from gross income of income (other than rent) derived by a lessor of real property on the termination of a lease, representing the value of such property attributable to buildings erected or other improvements made by a lessee, see section 109 and the regulations thereunder. . . .

§ 1.61-9 Dividends

(a) In general. Except as otherwise specifically provided, dividends are included in gross income under sections 61 and 301. For the principal rules with respect to dividends includible in gross income, see section 316 and the regulations thereunder. As to distributions made or deemed to be made by regulated investment companies, see sections 851 through 855, and the regulations thereunder. As to distributions made by real estate investment trusts, see sections 856 through 858, and the regulations thereunder. See section 116 for the exclusion from gross income of $100 ($50 for dividends received in taxable years beginning before January 1, 1964) of dividends received by an individual, except those from certain corporations. Furthermore, dividends may give rise to a credit against tax under section 34, relating to dividends received by individuals (for dividends received on or before December 31, 1964), and under section 37, relating to retirement income.

(b) Dividends in kind; stock dividends; stock redemptions. Gross income includes dividends in property other than cash, as well as cash dividends. For amounts to be included in gross income when distributions of property are made, see section 301 and the regulations thereunder. A distribution of stock, or rights to acquire stock, in the corporation making the distribution is not a dividend except under the circumstances described in section 305(b). However, the term "dividend" includes a distribution of stock, or rights to acquire stock, in a corporation other than the corporation making the distribution. For determining when distributions in complete liquidation shall be treated as dividends, see section 333 and the regulations thereunder. For rules determining when amounts received in exchanges under section 354 or exchanges and distributions under section 355 shall be treated as dividends, see section 356 and the regulations thereunder.

(c) **Dividends on stock sold.** When stock is sold, and a dividend is both declared and paid after the sale, such dividend is not gross income to the seller. When stock is sold after the declaration of a dividend and after the date as of which the seller becomes entitled to the dividend, the dividend ordinarily is income to the seller. When stock is sold between the time of declaration and the time of payment of the dividend, and the sale takes place at such time that the purchaser becomes entitled to the dividend, the dividend ordinarily is income to him. The fact that the purchaser may have included the amount of the dividend in his purchase price in contemplation of receiving the dividend does not exempt him from tax. Nor can the purchaser deduct the added amount he advanced to the seller in anticipation of the dividend. That added amount is merely part of the purchase price of the stock. In some cases, however, the purchaser may be considered to be the recipient of the dividend even though he has not received the legal title to the stock itself and does not himself receive the dividend. For example, if the seller retains the legal title to the stock as trustee solely for the purpose of securing the payment of the purchase price, with the understanding that he is to apply the dividends received from time to time in reduction of the purchase price, the dividends are considered to be income to the purchaser.

§ 1.61-12 Income from discharge of indebtedness

(a) **In general.** The discharge of indebtedness, in whole or in part, may result in the realization of income. If, for example, an individual performs services for a creditor, who in consideration thereof cancels the debt, the debtor realizes income in the amount of the debt as compensation for his services. A taxpayer may realize income by the payment or purchase of his obligations at less than their face value. In general, if a shareholder in a corporation which is indebted to him gratuitously forgives the debt, the transaction amounts to a contribution to the capital of the corporation to the extent of the principal of the debt.

. . . .

§ 1.61-14 Miscellaneous items of gross income

(a) **In general.** In addition to the items enumerated in section 61(a), there are many other kinds of gross income. For example, punitive damages such as treble damages under the antitrust laws and exemplary damages for fraud are gross income. Another person's payment of the taxpayer's income taxes constitutes gross income to the taxpayer unless excluded by law. Illegal gains constitute gross income. Treasure trove, to the extent of its value in United States currency, constitutes gross income for the taxable year in which it is reduced to undisputed possession.

. . . .

§ 1.62-1 Deductions from adjusted gross income

(a) The term "adjusted gross income" means the gross income computed under section 61 minus such of the deductions allowed by chapter 1 of the Code as are specified in section 62. Adjusted gross income is used as the basis for the determination of the following:

(1) The optional tax if adjusted gross income is less than $5,000 (under section 3);

(2) The amount of the standard deduction (under section 141);

(3) The limitation on the amount of the deduction for charitable contributions (under section 170(b) (1));

(4) The limitation on the amount of the deduction for medical and dental expenses (under section 213); and

(5) In certain cases, the limitation on the deduction for expenses of care of certain dependents (under section 214).

(b) Section 62 merely specifies which of the deductions provided in chapter 1 of the Code shall be allowed in computing adjusted gross income. It does not create any new deductions. The fact that a particular item may be specified in more than one of the paragraphs under section 62 does not permit the item to be twice deducted in computing either adjusted gross income or taxable income.

(c) The deductions specified in section 62 for the purpose of computing adjusted gross income are:

(1) Deductions allowable under chapter 1 of the Code (other than by Part VII (section 211 and following), subchapter B of such chapter) which are attributable to a trade or business carried on by the taxpayer not consisting of services performed as an employee;

(2) Deductions allowable under part VI (section 161 and following), subchapter B, chapter 1 of the Code, which consist of expenses paid or incurred in connection with the performance of services by the taxpayer as an employee under a reimbursement or other expense-allowance arrangement with his employer;

(3) Deductions allowable under part VI which constitute expenses of travel, meals, and lodging while away from home, paid or incurred by the taxpayer in connection with the performance by him of services as an employee;

(4) Transportation expenses (as defined in paragraph (g) of this section) paid or incurred by the taxpayer in connection with the performance by him of services as an employee, allowable as a deduction under part VI;

(5) Deductions allowable by part VI which are attributable to a trade or business carried on by the taxpayer, if such trade or business consists of the performance of services by the taxpayer as an employee and if such trade or business is to solicit, away from the employer's place of business, business for the employer;

(6) The deduction for long-term capital gains allowed by section 1202;

(7) Deductions which are allowable under part VI as losses from the sale or exchange of property;

(8) Deductions allowable under part VI, section 212, and section 611 which are attributable to property held for the production of rents or royalties;

(9) Deductions for depreciation and depletion allowable under sections 167 and 611 to a life tenant of property or to an income beneficiary of property held in trust or to an heir, legatee, or devisee of an estate;

(10) Deductions allowed by sections 404 and 405(c) for contributions on behalf of a self-employed individual;

(11) The deduction for moving expenses allowed by section 217.

(12) The deduction allowed by section 1379(b)(3) to an individual or his beneficiaries upon the termination of rights to receive benefits prior to excludable recovery of amounts which were included in the gross income of a shareholder-employee as excess employer contributions to a pension, etc., plan of an electing small business corporation;

(13) The deduction allowed by section 219 for contributions to an individual retirement account described in section 408(a), for an individual retirement annuity described in section 408 (b), or for a retirement bond described in section 409.

(14) The deduction allowed by section 402(e)(3) for the ordinary income portion of a lump sum distribution.

(15) For taxable years beginning after December 31, 1972, the deduction allowed by section 165 for losses incurred in any transaction entered into for profit though not connected with a trade or business, to the extent that such losses include amounts forfeited to a bank, mutual savings bank, savings and loan association, building and loan association, cooperative bank or homestead association as a penalty for premature withdrawal of funds from a time savings account, certificate of deposit or similar class of deposit.

(16) For taxable years beginning after December 31, 1976, the deduction for alimony and separate maintenance payments allowed by section 215.

(d) For the purpose of the deductions specified in section 62, the performance of personal services as an employee does not constitute the carrying on of a trade or business, except as otherwise expressly provided. The practice of a profession, not as an employee, is considered the conduct of a trade or business within the meaning of such section. To be deductible for the purposes of determining adjusted gross income, expenses must be those directly, and not those merely remotely, connected with the conduct of a trade or business. For example, taxes are deductible in arriving at adjusted gross income only if they constitute expenditures directly attributable to a trade or business or to property from which rents or royalties are derived. Thus, property taxes paid or incurred on real property used in a trade or business are deductible, but State taxes on net income are not deductible even though the taxpayer's income is derived from the conduct of a trade or business.

(e) Traveling expenses paid or incurred by an employee in connection with his employment while away from home which are deductible from gross income under part VI in computing taxable income may be deducted from gross income in computing adjusted gross income. Among the items included in traveling expenses are charges for transportation of persons or baggage, expenditures for meals and lodging, and payments for the use of sample rooms for the display of goods. See section 162 and the regulations thereunder.

(f) (1) Expenses paid or incurred by an employee which are deductible from gross income under part VI in computing taxable income and for which he is reimbursed by the employer under an express agreement for reimbursement or pursuant to an expense allowance arrangement may be deducted from gross income in computing adjusted gross income. Where an employee is reimbursed by his employer in an amount less than his total expense, and the reimbursement is intended to cover all types of deductible expenses, expenses other than those described in section 62 (2) (B), (C), and (D) are taken into account in computing adjusted gross income in an amount which bears the same ratio to the amount of the reimbursement as the total amount of deductible expenses computed without those described in section 62 (2) (B), (C), and (D) bears to the total amount of deductible expenses, including those described in section 62 (2) (B), (C), and (D).

(2) The application of subparagraph (1) of this paragraph may be illustrated by the following example:

Example: S, who is not a full-time outside salesman, received a salary of $20,000 and an expense allowance of $1,200 for the calendar year 1954. He expended $800 for travel, meals, and lodging while away from home, $500 for local transportation expenses and $300 for the entertainment of customers. His adjusted gross income is computed as follows:

Salary		$20,000
Expense allowance		1,200
Gross income		$21,200
Less:		
Travel, meals and lodging while away from home	$800	
Transportation expense	500	
Reimbursed expenses 1	225	
		1,525
Adjusted gross income		$19,675

1 The amount of the reimbursement allocable to entertainment expenses is determined as follows:

Travel, meals, and lodging while away from home	$800
Transportation expense	500
Expenses deductible in arriving at adjusted gross income (whether or not reimbursed)	1,300
Entertainment expense	300
Total expenses	1,600
Deductible for adjusted gross income: 300/1,600 × $1,200 (expense allowance)	225

(g) Transportation expenses paid or incurred by an employee in connection with performance by him of services for his employer are deductible from gross income under part VI in computing adjusted gross income. "Transportation", as used in section 62 (2) (C), is a narrower concept than "travel", as used in section 62 (2) (B), and does not include meals and lodging. The term "transportation expense" includes only the cost of transporting the employee from one place to another in the course of his employment, while he is not away from home in a travel status. Thus, transportation costs may include cab fares, bus fares, and the like, and also a pro rata share of the employee's expenses of operating his automobile, including gas, oil, and depreciation. All transportation expenses must be allowable expenses under part VI (section 161 and following), subchapter B, chapter 1 of the Code, as ordinary and necessary expenses incurred during the taxable year in carrying on a trade or business as an employee. Transportation expenses do not include the cost of commuting to and from work; this cost constitutes a personal, living, or family expense and is not deductible. (See section 262.)

(h) The expenses of an employee attributable to the trade or business carried on as an outside salesman which are allowed by part VI are deductible from gross income in computing adjusted gross income. An outside salesman is an individual who solicits business as a full-time salesman for his employer away from his employer's place of business. The term "outside salesman" does not include a taxpayer whose principal activities consist of service and delivery. For example, a bread driver-salesman or a milk driver-salesman would not be included within the definition. However, an outside salesman may perform incidental inside activities at his employer's place of business, such as writing up and transmitting orders and spending short periods at the employer's place of business to make and receive telephone calls, without losing his classification as an outside salesman.

§ 1.71–1 Alimony and separate maintenance payments; income to wife or former wife

(a) In general. Section 71 provides rules for treatment in certain cases of payments in the nature of or in lieu of alimony or an allowance for support as between spouses who are divorced or separated. For convenience, the payee spouse will hereafter in this section be referred to as the "wife" and the spouse from whom she is divorced or separated as the "husband." See section 7701(a) (17). For rules relative to the deduction by the husband of periodic payments not attributable to transferred property, see section 215 and the regulations thereunder. For rules relative to the taxable status of income of an estate or trust in case of divorce, etc., see section 682 and the regulations thereunder.

(b) Alimony or separate maintenance payments received from the husband— (1) Decree of divorce or separate maintenance. (i) In the case of divorce or legal separation, paragraph (1) of section 71(a) requires the inclusion in the gross income of the wife of periodic payments (whether or not made at regular intervals) received by her after a decree of divorce or of separate maintenance. Such periodic payments must be made in discharge of a legal obligation imposed upon or incurred by the husband because of the marital or family relationship under a court order or decree divorcing or legally separating the husband and wife or a written instrument incident to the divorce status or legal separation status.

(ii) For treatment of payments attributable to property transferred (in trust or otherwise), see paragraph (c) of this section.

(2) Written separation agreement. (i) Where the husband and wife are separated and living apart and do not file a joint income tax return for the taxable year, paragraph (2) of section 71(a) requires the inclusion in the gross income of the wife of periodic payments (whether or not made at regular intervals) received by her pursuant to a written separation agreement executed after August 16, 1954. The periodic payments must be made under the terms of the written separation agreement after its execution and because of the marital or family relationship. Such payments are includible in the wife's gross income whether or not the agreement is a legally enforceable instrument. Moreover, if the wife is divorced or legally separated subsequent to the written separation agree-

ment, payments made under such agreement continue to fall within the provisions of section 71(a) (2).

(ii) For purposes of section 71(a) (2), any written separation agreement executed on or before August 16, 1954, which is altered or modified in writing by the parties in any material respect after that date will be treated as an agreement executed after August 16, 1954, with respect to payments made after the date of alteration or modification.

(iii) For treatment of payments attributable to property transferred (in trust or otherwise), see paragraph (c) of this section.

(3) Decree for support. (i) Where the husband and wife are separated and living apart and do not file a joint income tax return for the taxable year, paragraph (3) of section 71(a) requires the inclusion in the gross income of the wife of periodic payments (whether or not made at regular intervals) received by her after August 16, 1954, from her husband under any type of court order or decree (including an interlocutory decree of divorce or a decree of alimony pendente lite) entered after March 1, 1954, requiring the husband to make the payments for her support or maintenance. It is not necessary for the wife to be legally separated or divorced from her husband under a court order or decree; nor is it necessary for the order or decree for support to be for the purpose of enforcing a written separation agreement.

(ii) For purposes of section 71(a) (3), any decree which is altered or modified by a court order entered after March 1, 1954, will be treated as a decree entered after such date.

(4) Scope of section 71(a). Section 71(a) applies only to payments made because of the family or marital relationship in recognition of the general obligation to support which is made specific by the decree, instrument, or agreement. Thus, section 71(a) does not apply to that part of any periodic payment which is attributable to the repayment by the husband of, for example, a bona fide loan previously made to him by the wife, the satisfaction of which is specified in the decree, instrument, or agreement as a part of the general settlement between the husband and wife.

(5) Year of inclusion. Periodic payments are includible in the wife's income under section 71(a) only for the taxable year in which received by her. As to such amounts, the wife is to be treated as if she makes her income tax returns on the cash receipts and disbursements method, regardless of whether she normally makes such returns on the accrual method. However, if the periodic payments described in section 71(a) are to be made by an estate or trust, such periodic payments are to be included in the wife's taxable year in which they are includible according to the rules as to income of estates and trusts provided in sections 652, 662, and 682, whether or not such payments are made out of the income of such estates or trusts.

(6) Examples. The foregoing rules are illustrated by the following examples in which it is assumed that the husband and wife file separate income tax returns on the calendar year basis:

Example (1). W files suit for divorce from H in 1953. In consideration of W's promise to relinquish all marital rights and not to make public H's financial affairs, H agrees in writing to pay $200 a month to W during her lifetime if a final decree of divorce is granted without any provision for alimony. Accordingly, W does not request alimony and no provision for alimony is made under a final decree of divorce entered December 31, 1953. During 1954, H pays W $200 a month, pursuant to the promise. The $2,400 thus received by W is includible in her gross income under the provisions of section 71 (a) (1). Under section 215, H is entitled to a deduction of $2,400 from his gross income.

Example (2). During 1945, H and W enter into an antenuptial agreement, under which, in consideration of W's relinquishment of all marital rights (including dower) in H's property, and, in order to provide for W's support and household expenses, H promises to pay W $200 a month during her lifetime. Ten years after their marriage, W sues H for divorce but does not ask for or obtain alimony because of the provision already made for her support in the antenuptial agreement. Likewise, the divorce decree is silent as to such agreement and H's obligation to support W. Section 71(a) does not apply to such a case. If, however, the decree were modified so as to refer to the antenuptial agreement, or if reference had been made to the antenuptial agreement in the court's decree or in a written instrument incident to the divorce status, section 71(a) (1) would require the inclusion in W's gross income of the payments received by her after the decree. Similarly, if a written separation agreement were executed after August 16, 1954, and incorporated the payment provisions of the antenuptial agreement, section 71(a) (2) would require the inclusion in W's income of payments received by W after W begins living apart from H, whether or not the divorce decree was subsequently entered and whether or not W was living apart from H when the separation agreement was executed, provided that such payments were made after such agreement was executed and pursuant to its terms. As to including such payments in W's income, if made by a trust created under the antenuptial agreement, regardless of whether referred to in the decree or a later instrument, or created pursuant to the written separation agreement, see section 682 and the regulations thereunder.

. . . .

(c) Alimony and separate maintenance payments attributable to property. (1) (i) In the case of divorce or legal separation, paragraph (1) of section 71(a) requires the inclusion in the gross income of the wife of periodic payments (whether or not made at regular intervals) attributable to property transferred, in trust or otherwise, and received by her after a decree of divorce or of separate maintenance. Such property must have been transferred in discharge of a legal obligation imposed upon or incurred by the husband because of the marital or family relationship under a decree of divorce or separate maintenance or under a written instrument incident to such divorce status or legal separation status.

(ii) Where the husband and wife are separated and living apart and do not file a joint income tax return for the taxable year, paragraph (2) of section 71(a) requires the inclusion in the gross income of the wife of periodic payments (whether or not made at regular intervals) received by her which are attributable to property transferred, in trust or otherwise, under a written separation agreement executed after August 16, 1954. The property must be transferred because of the marital or family relationship. The periodic payments attributable to the property must be received by the wife after the written separation agreement is executed.

(iii) The periodic payments received by the wife attributable to property transferred under subdivisions (i) and (ii) of this subparagraph and includible in her gross income are not to be included in the gross income of the husband.

(2) The full amount of periodic payments received under the circumstances described in section 71(a) (1), (2), and (3) is required to be included in the gross income of the wife regardless of the source of such payments. Thus, it matters not that such payments are attributable to property in trust, to life insurance, endowment, or annuity contracts, or to any other interest in property, or are paid directly or indirectly by the husband from his income or capital. For example, if in order to meet an alimony or separate maintenance obligation of $500 a month the husband purchases or assigns for the benefit of his wife a commercial annuity contract paying such amount, the full $500 a month received by the wife is includible in her income, and no part of such amount is includible in the husband's income or deductible by him. See section 72(k) and the regulations thereunder. Likewise, if property is transferred by the husband, subject to an annual charge of $5,000, payable to his wife in discharge of his alimony or separate maintenance obligation under the divorce or separation decree or written instrument incident to the divorce status or legal separation status or if such property is transferred pursuant to a written separation agreement and subject to a similar annual charge, the $5,000 received annually is, under section 71(a) (1) or (2), includible in the wife's income, regardless of whether such amount is paid out of income or principal of the property.

(3) The same rule applies to periodic payments attributable to property in trust. The full amount of periodic payments to which section 71(a) (1) and (2) applies is includible in the wife's income regardless of whether such payments are made out of trust income. Such periodic payments are to be included in the wife's income under section 71(a) (1) or (2) and are to be excluded from the husband's income even though the income of the trust would otherwise be includible in his income under subpart E, part I, subchapter J, Chapter 1 of the Code, relating to trust income attributable to grantors and others as substantial owners. As to periodic payments received by a wife attributable to property in trust in cases to which section 71(a) (1) or (2) does not apply because the husband's obligation is not specified in the decree or an instrument incident to the divorce status or legal separation status or the property was not transferred under a written separation agreement, see section 682 and the regulations thereunder.

(4) Section 71(a) (1) or (2) does not apply to that part of any periodic payment attributable to that portion of

any interest in property transferred in discharge of the husband's obligation under the decree or instrument incident to the divorce status or legal separation status, or transferred pursuant to the written separation agreement, which interest originally belonged to the wife. It will apply, however, if she received such interest from her husband in contemplation of or as an incident to the divorce or separation without adequate and full consideration in money or money's worth, other than the release of the husband or his property from marital obligations. An example of the first rule is a case where the husband and wife transfer securities, which were owned by them jointly, in trust to pay an annuity to the wife. In this case, the full amount of that part of the annuity received by the wife attributable to the husband's interest in the securities transferred in discharge of his obligation under the decree, or instrument incident to the divorce status or legal separation status, or transferred under the written separation agreement, is taxable to her under section 71(a) (1) or (2), while that portion of the annuity attributable to the wife's interest in the securities so transferred is taxable to her only to the extent it is out of trust income as provided in part I (sections 641 and following), subchapter J, chapter 1 of the Code. If, however, the husband's transfer to his wife is made before such property is transferred in discharge of his obligation under the decree or written instrument, or pursuant to the separation agreement in an attempt to avoid the application of section 71(a) (1) or (2) to part of such payments received by his wife, such transfers will be considered as a part of the same transfer by the husband of his property in discharge of his obligation or pursuant to such agreement. In such a case, section 71(a) (1) or (2) will be applied to the full amount received by the wife. As to periodic payments received under a joint purchase of a commercial annuity contract, see section 72 and the regulations thereunder.

(d) **Periodic and installment payments.** (1) In general, installment payments discharging a part of an obligation the principal sum of which is, in terms of money or property, specified in the decree, instrument, or agreement are not considered "periodic payments" and therefore are not to be included under section 71(a) in the wife's income.

(2) An exception to the general rule stated in subparagraph (1) of this paragraph is provided, however, in cases where such principal sum, by the terms of the decree, instrument, or agreement, may be or is to be paid over a period ending more than 10 years from the date of such decree, instrument, or agreement. In such cases, the installment payment is considered a periodic payment for the purposes of section 71 (a) but only to the extent that the installment payment, or sum of the installment payments, received during the wife's taxable year does not exceed 10 percent of the principal sum. This 10-percent limitation applies to installment payments made in advance but does not apply to delinquent installment payments for a prior taxable year of the wife made during her taxable year.

(3) (i) Where payments under a decree, instrument, or agreement are to be paid over a period ending 10 years or less from the date of such decree, instrument, or agreement, such payments are not installment payments discharging a part of an obligation the principal sum of which is, in terms of money or property, specified in the decree, instrument, or agreement (and are considered periodic payments for the purposes of section 71(a)) only if such payments meet the following two conditions:

(a) Such payments are subject to any one or more of the contingencies of death of either spouse, remarriage of the wife, or change in the economic status of either spouse, and

(b) Such payments are in the nature of alimony or an allowance for support.

(ii) Payments meeting the requirements of subdivision (i) are considered periodic payments for the purposes of section 71(a) regardless of whether—

(a) The contingencies described in subdivision (i) (a) of this subparagraph are set forth in the terms of the decree, instrument, or agreement, or are imposed by local law, or

(b) The aggregate amount of the payments to be made in the absence of the occurrence of the contingencies described in subdivision (i) (a) of this subparagraph is explicitly stated in the decree, instrument, or agreement or may be calculated from the face of the decree, instrument, or agreement, or

(c) The total amount which will be paid may be calculated actuarially.

(4) Where payments under a decree, instrument, or agreement are to be paid over a period ending more than ten years from the date of such decree, instrument, or agreement, but where such payments meet the conditions set forth in subparagraph (3) (i) of this paragraph, such payments are considered to be periodic payments for the purpose of section 71 without regard to the rule set forth in subparagraph (2) of this paragraph. Accordingly, the rules set forth in subparagraph (2) of this paragraph are not applicable to such payments.

(5) The rules as to periodic and installment payments are illustrated by the following examples:

Example (1). Under the terms of a written instrument, H is required to make payments to W which are in the nature of alimony, in the amount of $100 a month for nine years. The instrument provides that if H or W dies the payments are to cease. The payments are periodic.

Example (2). The facts are the same as in example (1) except that the written instrument explicitly provides that H is to pay W the sum of $10,800 in monthly payments of $100 over a period of nine years. The payments are periodic.

Example (3). Under the terms of a written instrument, H is to pay W $100 a month over a period of nine years. The monthly payments are not subject to any of the contingencies of death of H or W, remarriage of W, or change in the economic status of H or W under the terms of the written instrument or by reason of local law. The payments are not periodic.

Example (4). A divorce decree in 1954 provides that H is to pay W $20,000 each year for the next five years, beginning with the date of the decree, and then $5,000 each year for the next ten years. Assuming the wife makes her returns on the calendar year basis, each payment received in the years 1954 to 1958, inclusive, is treated as a periodic payment under section 71(a) (1), but only to the extent of 10 percent of the principal sum of $150,000. Thus, for such taxable years, only $15,000 of the $20,000 received is includible under section 71(a) (1) in the wife's income and is deductible by the husband under section 215. For the years 1959 to 1968, inclusive, the full $5,000 received each year by the wife is includible in her income and is deductible from the husband's income.

(e) Payments for support of minor children. Section 71(a) does not apply to that part of any periodic payment which, by the terms of the decree, instrument, or agreement under section 71(a), is specifically designated as a sum payable for the support of minor children of the husband. The statute prescribes the treatment in cases where an amount or portion is so fixed but the amount of any periodic payment is less than the amount of the periodic payment specified to be made. In such cases, to the extent of the amount which would be payable for the support of such children out of the originally specified periodic payment, such periodic payment is considered a payment for such support. For example, if the husband is by terms of the decree, instrument, or agreement required to pay $200 a month to his divorced wife, $100 of which is designated by the decree, instrument, or agreement to be for the support of their minor children, and the husband pays only $150 to his wife, $100 is nevertheless considered to be a payment by the husband for the support of the children. If, however, the periodic payments are received by the wife for the support and maintenance of herself and of minor children of the husband without such specific designation of the portion for the support of such children, then the whole of such amounts is includible in the income of the wife as provided in section 71(a). Except in cases of a designated amount or portion for the support of the husband's minor children, periodic payments described in section 71(a) received by the wife for herself and any other person or persons are includible in whole in the wife's income, whether or not the amount or portion for such other person or persons is designated.

§ 1.72–1 Introduction

(a) General principle. Section 72 prescribes rules relating to the inclusion in gross income of amounts received under a life insurance, endowment, or annuity contract unless such amounts are specifically excluded from gross income under other provisions of chapter 1 of the Code. In general, these rules provide that amounts subject to the provisions of section 72 are includible in the gross income of the recipient except to the extent that they are considered to represent a reduction or return of premiums or other consideration paid.

(b) Amounts to be considered as a return of premiums. For the purpose of determining the extent to which amounts received represent a reduction or return of premiums or other consideration paid, the provisions of section 72 distinguish between "amounts received as an annuity" and "amounts not received as an annuity". In general, "amounts received as an annuity" are amounts which are payable at regular intervals over a period of more than one full year from the date on which they are deemed to begin, provided the total of the amounts so payable or the period for which they are to be paid can be determined as of that date. See paragraph (b) (2) and (3) of § 1.72-2. Any other amounts to which the provisions of section 72 apply are considered to be "amounts not received as an annuity". See § 1.72-11.

(c) "Amounts received as an annuity." (1) In the case of "amounts received as an annuity" (other than certain employees' annuities described in section 72(d) and in § 1.72-13), a proportionate part of each amount so received is considered to represent a return of premiums or other consideration paid. The proportionate part of each annuity payment which is thus excludable from gross income is determined by the ratio which the investment in the contract as of the date on which the annuity is deemed to begin bears to the expected return under the contract as of that date. See § 1.72-4. . . . . . .

(d) "Amounts not received as an annuity". In the case of "amounts not received as an annuity", if such amounts are received after an annuity has begun and during its continuance, amounts so received are generally includible in the gross income of the recipient. Amounts not received as an annuity which are received at any other time are generally includible in the gross income of the recipient only to the extent that such amounts, when added to all amounts previously received under the contract which were excludable from the gross income of the recipient under the income tax law applicable at the time of receipt, exceed the premiums or other consideration paid (see § 1.72-11). However, if the aggregate of premiums or other consideration paid for the contract includes amounts for which a deduction was allowed under section 404 as contributions on behalf of an owner-employee, the amounts received under the circumstances of the preceding sentence shall be includible in gross income until the amount so included equals the amount for which the deduction was so allowed. . . . . .

(e) Classification of recipients. For the purpose of the regulations under section 72, a recipient shall be considered an "annuitant" if he receives amounts under an annuity contract during the period that the annuity payments are to continue, whether for a term certain or during the continuing life or lives of the person or persons whose lives measure the duration of such annuity. However, a recipient shall be considered a "beneficiary" rather than an "annuitant" if the amounts he receives under a contract are received after the term of the annuity for a life or lives has expired and such amounts are paid by reason of the fact that the contract guarantees that payments of some minimum amount or for some minimum period shall be. made. . . . . .

§ 1.72-2 Applicability of section

(a) Contracts. (1) The contracts under which amounts paid will be subject to the provisions of section 72 include contracts which are considered to be life insurance, endowment, and annuity contracts in accordance with the customary practice of life insurance companies. For the purposes of section 72, however, it is immaterial whether such contracts are entered into with an insurance company. The term "endowment contract" also includes the "face-amount certificates" described in section 72(1). In addition, sections 402 and 403 provide that certain employees' trust and plan distributions are subject to the provisions of section 72, except section 72(e) (3). In such cases the regulations under section 72 shall be applied to all the distributions with respect to a particular employee under each such trust or plan as though such payments were provided under a single contract to which section 72 applied. As used hereafter in these regulations, therefore, the term "contract" shall be considered to include the entire interest of an employee in each trust or plan described in sections 402 and 403 to the extent that distributions thereunder are subject to the provisions of section 72.

(2) If two or more annuity obligations or elements to which section 72

applies are acquired for a single consideration, such as an obligation to pay an annuity to A for his life accompanied by an obligation to pay an annuity to B for his life, there being a single consideration paid for both obligations (whether paid by one or more persons in equal or different amounts, and whether paid in a single sum or otherwise), such annuity elements shall be considered to comprise a single contract for the purpose of the application of section 72 and the regulations thereunder. For rules relating to the allocation of investment in the contract in the case of annuity elements payable to two or more persons, see paragraph (b) of § 1.72-6.

. . . .

(b) Amounts. (1) (i) In general, the amounts to which section 72 applies are any amounts received under the contracts described in paragraph (a) (1) of this section. However, if such amounts are specifically excluded from gross income under other provisions of chapter 1 of the Code, section 72 shall not apply for the purpose of including such amounts in gross income. For example, section 72 does not apply to amounts received under a life insurance contract if such amounts are paid by reason of the death of the insured and are excludable from gross income under section 101(a). See also sections 101(d), relating to proceeds of life insurance paid at a date later than death, and 104(a) (4), relating to compensation for injuries or sickness.

(ii) Section 72 does not exclude from gross income any amounts received under an agreement to hold an amount and pay interest thereon. See paragraph (a) of § 1.72-14. However, section 72 does apply to amounts received by a surviving annuitant under a joint and survivor annuity contract since such amounts are not considered to be paid by reason of the death of an insured. For a special deduction for the estate tax attributable to the inclusion of the value of the interest of a surviving annuitant under a joint and survivor annuity contract in the estate of the deceased primary annuitant, see section 691(d) and the regulations thereunder.

(2) Amounts subject to section 72 in accordance with subparagraph (1) of this paragraph are considered "amounts received as an annuity" only in the event that all of the following tests are met:

(i) They must be received on or after the "annuity starting date" as that term is defined in paragraph (b) of § 1.72-4;

(ii) They must be payable in periodic installments at regular intervals (whether annually, semiannually, quarterly, monthly, weekly, or otherwise) over a period of more than one full year from the annuity starting date; and

(iii) Except as indicated in subparagraph (3) of this paragraph, the total of the amounts payable must be determinable at the annuity starting date either directly from the terms of the contract or indirectly by the use of either mortality tables or compound interest computations, or both, in conjunction with such terms and in accordance with sound actuarial theory. For the purpose of determining whether amounts subject to section 72(d) and § 1.72-13 are "amounts received as an annuity", however, the provisions of subdivision (i) of this subparagraph shall be disregarded. In addition, the term "amounts received as an annuity" does not include amounts received to which the provisions of paragraph (b) or (c) of § 1.72-11 apply, relating to dividends and certain amounts received by a beneficiary in the nature of a refund. If an amount is to be paid periodically until a fund plus interest at a fixed rate is exhausted, but further payments may be made thereafter because of earnings at a higher interest rate, the requirements of subdivision (iii) of this subparagraph are met with respect to the payments determinable at the outset by means of computations involving the fixed interest rate, but any payments received after the expiration of the period determinable by such computations shall be taxable as dividends received after the annuity starting date in accordance with paragraph (b) (2) of § 1.72-11.

(3) (i) Notwithstanding the requirement of subparagraph (2) (iii) of this paragraph, if amounts are to be received for a definite or determinable time (whether for a period certain or for a life or lives) under a contract which provides:

(a) That the amount of the periodic payments may vary in accordance with investment experience (as in certain profit-sharing plans), cost of living indices, or similar fluctuating criteria, or

(b) For specified payments the value of which may vary for income tax purposes, such as in the case of any annuity payable in foreign currency,

each such payment received shall be considered as an amount received as an annuity only to the extent that it does not exceed the amount computed by dividing the investment in the contract, as adjusted for any refund feature, by the number of periodic payments anticipated during the time that the periodic payments are to be made. If payments are to be made more frequently than annually, the amount so computed shall be multiplied by the number of periodic payments to be made during the taxable year for the purpose of determining the total of the amount which may be considered received as an annuity during such year. To this extent, the payments received shall be considered to represent a return of premium or other consideration paid and shall be excludable from gross income in the taxable year in which received. See paragraph (d) (2), and (3) of § 1.72–4. To the extent that the payments received under the contract during the taxable year exceed the total amount thus considered to be received as an annuity during such year, they shall be considered to be amounts not received as an annuity and shall be included in the gross income of the recipient. See section 72(e) and paragraph (b) (2) of § 1.72–11.

, (ii) For purposes of subdivision (i) of this subparagraph, the number of periodic payments anticipated during the time payments are to be made shall be determined by multiplying the number of payments to be made each year (a) by the number of years payments are to be made, or (b) if payments are to be made for a life or lives, by the multiple found by the use of the appropriate tables contained in § 1.72–9, as adjusted in accordance with the table in paragraph (a) (2) of § 1.72–5.

(iii) For an example of the computation to be made in accordance with this subparagraph and a special election

which may be made in a taxable year subsequent to a taxable year in which the total payments received under a contract described in this subparagraph are less than the total of the amounts excludable from gross income in such year under subdivision (i) of this subparagraph, see paragraph (d) (3) of § 1.72–4.

§ 1.72–3 Excludable amounts not income

In general, amounts received under contracts described in paragraph (a) (1) of § 1.72–2 are not to be included in the income of the recipient to the extent that such amounts are excludable from gross income as the result of the application of section 72 and the regulations thereunder.

§ 1.72–4 Exclusion ratio

(a) General rule. (1) (i) To determine the proportionate part of the total amount received each year as an annuity which is excludable from the gross income of a recipient in the taxable year of receipt (other than amounts received under (a) certain employee annuities described in section 72(d) and § 1.72–13, or (b) certain annuities described in section 72(o) and § 1.122–1), an exclusion ratio is to be determined for each contract. In general, this ratio is determined by dividing the investment in the contract as found under § 1.72–6 by the expected return under such contract as found under § 1.72–5. Where a single consideration is given for a particular contract which provides for two or more annuity elements, an exclusion ratio shall be determined for the contract as a whole by dividing the investment in such contract by the aggregate of the expected returns under all the annuity elements provided thereunder. . . . .

(ii) The exclusion ratio for the particular contract is then applied to the total amount received as an annuity during the taxable year by each recipient. See, however, paragraph (e) (3) of § 1.72–5. Any excess of the total amount received as an annuity during the taxable year over the amount determined by the application of the exclusion ratio to such total amount shall be included in the gross income of the recipient for the taxable year of receipt.

(2) The principles of subparagraph (1) may be illustrated by the following example:

Example. Taxpayer A purchased an annuity contract providing for payments of $100 per month for a consideration of $12,650. Assuming that the expected return under this contract is $16,000, the exclusion ratio to be used by A is $\frac{\$12,650}{\$16,000}$, or 79.1 percent (79.06 rounded to the nearest tenth). If 12 such monthly payments are received by A during his taxable year, the total amount he may exclude from his gross income in such year is $949.20 ($1,200 × 79.1 percent). The balance of $250.80 ($1,200 less $949.20) is the amount to be included in gross income. If A instead received only five such payments during the year, he should exclude $395.50 ($500 × 79.1 percent) of the total amounts received. . . . .

(3) The exclusion ratio shall be applied only to amounts received as an annuity within the meaning of that term under paragraph (b) (2) and (3) of § 1.72-2. Where the periodic payments increase in amount after the annuity starting date in a manner not provided by the terms of the contract at such date, the portion of such payments representing the increase is not an amount received as an annuity. For the treatment of amounts not received as an annuity, see section 72(e) and § 1.72-11. For special rules where paragraph (b) (3) of § 1.72-2 applies to amounts received, see paragraph (d) (3) of this section.

(4) After an exclusion ratio has been determined for a particular contract, it shall be applied to any amounts received as an annuity thereunder unless or until one of the following occurs:

(i) The contract is assigned or transferred for a valuable consideration (see section 72(g) and paragraph (a) of § 1.72-10);

(ii) The contract matures or is surrendered, redeemed, or discharged in accordance with the provisions of paragraph (c) or (d) of § 1.72-11;

(iii) The contract is exchanged (or is considered to have been exchanged) in a manner described in paragraph (e) of § 1.72-11.

(b) Annuity starting date. (1) Except as provided in subparagraph (2) of this paragraph, the annuity starting date is the first day of the first period for which an amount is received as an annuity, except that if such date was before January 1, 1954, then the annuity starting date is January 1, 1954. The first day of the first period for which an amount is received as an annuity shall be whichever of the following is the later:

(i) The date upon which the obligations under the contract became fixed, or

(ii) The first day of the period (year, half-year, quarter, month, or otherwise, depending on whether payments are to be made annually, semiannually, quarterly, monthly, or otherwise) which ends on the date of the first annuity payment.

(2) Notwithstanding the provisions of paragraph (b)(1) of this section, the annuity starting date shall be determined in accordance with whichever of the following provisions is appropriate:

(i) In the case of a joint and survivor annuity contract described in section 72(i) and paragraph (b)(3) of § 1.72-5, the annuity starting date is January 1, 1954, or the first day of the first period for which an amount is received as an annuity by the surviving annuitant, whichever is the later;

. . . . .

(d) Exceptions to the general rule. (1) Where the provisions of section 72 would otherwise require an exclusion ratio to be determined, but the investment in the contract (determined under § 1.72-6) is an amount of zero or less, no exclusion ratio shall be determined and all amounts received under such a contract shall be includible in the gross income of the recipient for the purposes of section 72.

(2) Where the investment in the contract is equal to or greater than the total expected return under such contract found under § 1.72-5, the exclusion ratio shall be considered to be 100 percent and all amounts received as an annuity under such contract shall be excludable from the recipient's gross income. . . . .

(3) (i) If a contract provides for payments to be made to a taxpayer in the manner described in paragraph (b) (3) of § 1.72–2, the investment in the contract shall be considered to be equal to the expected return under such contract and the resulting exclusion ratio (100%) shall be applied to all amounts received as an annuity under such contract. For any taxable year, payments received under such a contract shall be considered to be amounts received as an annuity only to the extent that they do not exceed the portion of the investment in the contract which is properly allocable to that year and hence excludable from gross income as a return of premiums or other consideration paid for the contract. The portion of the investment in the contract which is properly allocable to any taxable year shall be determined by dividing the investment in the contract (adjusted for any refund feature in the manner described in paragraph (d) of § 1.72–7, by the applicable multiple (whether for a term certain, life, or lives) which would otherwise be used in determining the expected return for such a contract under § 1.72–5. The multiple shall be adjusted in accordance with the provisions of the table in paragraph (a) (2) of § 1.72–5, if any adjustment is necessary, before making the above computation. If payments are to be made more frequently than annually and the number of payments to be made in the taxable year in which the annuity begins are less than the number of payments to be made each year thereafter, the amounts considered received as an annuity (as otherwise determined under this subdivision) shall not exceed, for such taxable year (including a short taxable year), an amount which bears the same ratio to the portion of the investment in the contract considered allocable to each taxable year as the number of payments to be made in the first year bears to the number of payments to be made in each succeeding year. Thus, if payments are to be made monthly, only seven payments will be made in the first taxable year, and the portion of the investment in the contract allocable to a full year of payments is $600, the amounts considered received as an annuity in the first taxable year cannot exceed $350 ($600 x 7/12). See subdivision (iii) for

an example illustrating the determination of the portion of the investment in the contract allocable to one taxable year of the taxpayer.

(ii) If subdivision (i) of this subparagraph applies to amounts received by a taxpayer and the total amount of payments he receives in a taxable year is less than the total amount excludable for such year under subdivision (i) of this subparagraph, the taxpayer may elect, in a succeeding taxable year in which he receives another payment, to redetermine the amounts to be received as an annuity during the current and succeeding taxable years. This shall be computed in accordance with the provisions of subdivision (i) of this subparagraph except that:

(a) The difference between the portion of the investment in the contract allocable to a taxable year, as found in accordance with subdivision (i) of this paragraph, and the total payments actually received in the taxable year prior to the election shall be divided by the life expectancy of the annuitant (or annuitants), found in accordance with the appropriate table in § 1.72–9 (and adjusted in accordance with paragraph (a) (2) of § 1.72–5), or by the remaining term of a term certain annuity, computed as of the first day of the first period for which an amount is received as an annuity in the taxable year of the election; and

(b) The amount determined under (a) of this subdivision shall be added to the portion of the investment in the contract allocable to each taxable year (as otherwise found). To the extent that the total periodic payments received under the contract in the taxable year of the election or any succeeding taxable year does not equal this total sum, such payments shall be excludable from the gross income of the recipient. To the extent such payments exceed the sum so found, they shall be fully includible in recipient's gross income.

See subdivision (iii) of this paragraph for an example illustrating the redetermination of amounts to be received as an annuity and subdivision (iv) of this subparagraph for the method of making the election provided by this subdivision.

(iii) The application of the principles of this subparagraph may be illustrated by the following example:

Example. Taxpayer A, a 64 year old male, files his return on a calendar year basis and has a life expectancy of 15.6 years on June 30, 1954, the annuity starting date of a contract to which § 1.72–2(b) (3) applies and which he purchased for $20,000. The contract provides for variable annual payments for his life. He receives a payment of $1,000 on June 30, 1955, but receives no other payment until June 30, 1957. He excludes the $1,000 payment from his gross income for the year 1955 since this amount is less than $1,324.50, the amount determined by dividing his investment in the contract ($20,000) by his life expectancy adjusted for annual payments, 15.1 (15.6–0.5), as of the original annuity starting date. Taxpayer A may elect, in his return for the taxable year 1957, to redetermine amounts to be received as an annuity under his contract as of June 30, 1956. For the purpose of determining the extent to which amounts received in 1957 or thereafter shall be considered amounts received as an annuity (to which a 100 percent exclusion ratio shall apply) he shall add $118.63 to the $1,324.50 originally determined to be receivable as an annuity under the contract, making a total of $1,443.13. This is determined by dividing the difference between what was excludable in 1955 and 1956, $2,649 (2 × $1,324.50) and what he actually received in those years ($1,000) by his life expectancy adjusted for annual payments, 13.9 (14.4–0.5), as of his age at his nearest birthday (66) on the first day of the first period for which he received an amount as an annuity in the taxable year of election (June 30, 1956). The result, $1,443.13, is excludable in that year and each year thereafter as an amount received as an annuity to which the 100% exclusion ratio applies. It will be noted that in this example the taxpayer received amounts less than the excludable amounts in two successive years and deferred making his election until the third year, and thus was able to accumulate the portion of the investment in the contract allocable to each taxable year to the extent he failed to receive such portion in both years. Assuming that he received $1,500 in the taxable year of his election, he would include $56.87 in his gross income and exclude $1,443.13 therefrom for that year.

(iv) If the taxpayer chooses to make the election described in subdivision (ii) of this subparagraph, he shall file with his return a statement that he elects to make a redetermination of the amounts excludable from gross income under his annuity contract in accordance with the provisions of paragraph (d) (3) of § 1.72–4. This statement shall also contain the following information:

(a) The original annuity starting date and his age on that date,

(b) The date of the first day of the first period for which he received an amount in the current taxable year,

(c) The investment in the contract originally determined (as adjusted for any refund feature), and

(d) The aggregate of all amounts received under the contract between the date indicated in (a) of this subdivision and the day after the date indicated in (b) of this subdivision to the extent such amounts were excludable from gross income.

He shall include in gross income any amounts received during the taxable year for which the return is made in accordance with the redetermination made under this subparagraph.

· · · · ·

§ 1.72–5 Expected return

(a) Expected return for but one life. (1) If a contract to which section 72 applies provides that one annuitant is to receive a fixed monthly income for life, the expected return is determined by multiplying the total of the annuity payments to be received annually by the multiple shown in Table I of § 1.72–9 under the age (as of annuity starting date) and sex of the measuring life (usually the annuitant's). Thus, where a male purchases a contract providing for an immediate annuity of $100 per month for his life and, as of the annuity starting date (in this case the date of purchase), the annuitant's age at his nearest birthday is 66, the expected return is computed as follows:

Monthly payment of $100 × 12 months
  equals annual payment of $1,200
Multiple shown in Table I, male, age 66 . 14.4
                                         ──────
Expected return ($1,200 × 14.0) $17,280

(2) (i) If payments are to be made quarterly, semiannually, or annually, an adjustment of the applicable multiple shown in Table I may be required. A further adjustment may be required where the interval between the annuity starting date and the date of the first payment is less than the interval between future payments. Neither adjustment shall be made, however, if the payments are to be made more frequently than quarterly. The amount of the adjustment, if any, is to be found in accordance with the following table:

If the number of whole months from the annuity starting date to the first payment date is—	0–1	2	3	4	5	6	7	8	9	10	11	12
And payments under the contract are to be made:												
Annually	+0.5	+0.4	+0.3	+0.2	+0.1	0	0	−0.1	−0.2	−0.3	−0.4	−0.5
Semiannually	+.2	+.1	0	0	−.1	−.2						
Quarterly	+.1	0	−.1									

Thus, for a male, age 66, the multiple found in Table I adjusted for quarterly payments the first of which is to be made one full month after the annuity starting date, is 14.5 (14.4+0.1); for semiannual payments the first of which is to be made six full months from the annuity starting date, the adjusted multiple is 14.2 (14.4−0.2); for annual payments the first of which is to be made one full month from the annuity starting date, the adjusted multiple is 14.9 (14.4+0.5). If the annuitant in the example shown in subparagraph (1) of this paragraph were to receive an annual payment of $1,200 commencing 12 full months after his annuity starting date, the amount of the expected return would be $16,680 ($1,200×13.9 [14.4−0.5]).

. . . .

(3) If the contract provides for fixed payments to be made to an annuitant until death or until the expiration of a specified limited period, whichever occurs earlier, the expected return of such temporary life annuity is determined by multiplying the total of the annuity payments to be received annually by the multiple shown in Table IV of § 1.72–9 for the age (as of the annuity starting date) and sex of the annuitant and the nearest whole number of years in the specified period. For example, if a male annuitant, age 60 (at his nearest birthday), is to receive $60 per month for five years or until he dies, whichever is earlier, the expected return under such a contract is $3,456, computed as follows:

Monthly payments of $60 × 12 months equals annual payment of $720
Multiple shown in Table IV for male, age 60, for term of 5 years 4.8
—
Expected return for 5 year temporary life annuity of $720 per year ($720 × 4.8) .. $3,456

The adjustment provided by subparagraph (2) of this paragraph shall not be made with respect to the multiple found in Table IV.

(4) If the contract provides for payments to be made to an annuitant for his lifetime, but the amount of the annual payments is to be decreased after the expiration of a specified limited period, the expected return is computed by considering the contract as a combination of a whole life annuity for the smaller amount plus a temporary life annuity for an amount equal to the difference between the larger and the smaller amount. For example, if a male annuitant, age 60, is to receive $150 per month for five years or until his earlier death, and is to receive $90 per month for the remainder of his lifetime after such five years, the expected return is computed as if the annuitant's contract consisted of a whole life annuity for $90 per month plus a five year temporary life annuity of $60 per month. In such circumstances, the expected return is computed as follows:

Monthly payments of $90 × 12 months equals annual payment of $1,080
Multiple shown in Table I for male, age 60 .... 18.2
—
Expected return for whole life annuity of $1,080 per year $19,656
Expected return for 5-year temporary life annuity of $720 per year (as found in subparagraph (3) of this paragraph) $3,456
—
Total expected return $23,112

If payments are to be made quarterly, semiannually, or annually, an appropriate adjustment of the multiple found in Table I for the whole life annuity should be made in accordance with subparagraph (2) of this paragraph.

(5) If the contract described in subparagraph (4) of this paragraph provided that the amount of the annual payments to the annuitant were to be increased (instead of decreased) after the expiration of a specified limited period, the expected return would be computed as if the annuitant's contract consisted of a whole life annuity for the larger amount minus a temporary life annuity for an amount equal to the difference between the larger and smaller amount. Thus, if the annuitant described in subparagraph (4) of this paragraph were to receive $90 per month for five years or until his earlier death, and to receive $150 per month for the remainder of his lifetime after such five years, the expected return would be computed by subtracting the expected return under a five year temporary life annuity of $60 per month from the expected return under a whole life annuity of $150 per month. In such circumstances, the expected return is computed as follows:

Monthly payments of $150 × 12 months equals annual payment of	$1,800
Multiple shown in Table I (male, age 60)	18.2

Expected return for annuity for whole life of $1,800 per year	$32,760
Less expected return for 5-year temporary life annuity of $720 per year (as found in subparagraph (3))	$3,456
Net expected return	$29,304

If payments are to be made quarterly, semiannually, or annually, an appropriate adjustment of the multiple found in Table I for the whole life annuity should be made in accordance with subparagraph (2) of this paragraph.

(b) Expected return under joint and survivor and joint annuities. (1) In the case of a joint and survivor annuity contract involving two annuitants which provides the first annuitant with a fixed monthly income for life and, after the death of the first annuitant, provides an identical monthly income for life to a second annuitant, the expected return shall be determined by multiplying the total amount of the payments to be received annually by the multiple obtained from Table II of § 1.72–9 under the ages (as of the annuity starting date) and sexes of the

living annuitants. For example, a husband purchases a joint and survivor annuity contract providing for payments of $100 per month for life, and, after his death, for the same amount to his wife for the remainder of her life. As of the annuity starting date his age at his nearest birthday is 70 and that of his wife at her nearest birthday is 67. The expected return is computed as follows:

Monthly payments of $100 × 12 months equals annual payment of	$1,200
Multiple shown in Table II (male, age 70; female, age 67)	19.7
Expected return ($1,200 × 19.7)	$23,640

If payments are to be made quarterly, semiannually, or annually, an appropriate adjustment of the multiple found in Table II should be made in accordance with paragraph (a) (2) of this section.

(2) If a contract of the type described in subparagraph (1) of this paragraph provides that a different (rather than an identical) monthly income is payable to the second annuitant, the expected return is computed in the following manner. The applicable multiple in Table II is first found as in the example in subparagraph (1) of this paragraph. The multiple applicable to the first annuitant is then found in Table I as though the contract were for a single life annuity. The multiple from Table I is then subtracted from the multiple obtained from Table II and the resulting multiple is applied to the total payments to be received annually under the contract by the second annuitant. The result is the expected return with respect to the second annuitant. The portion of the expected return with respect to payments to be made during the first annuitant's life is then computed by applying the multiple found in Table I to the total annual payments to be received by such annuitant under the contract. The expected returns with respect to each of the annuitants separately are then aggregated to obtain the expected return under the entire contract.

Example. A husband purchases a joint and survivor annuity providing for payments of $100 per month for his life and, after his death, payments to his wife of $50 per month for her life. As of the annuity starting date his age at his nearest birthday is 70 and that of his wife at her nearest birthday is 67.

Multiple from Table II (male, age 70; female, age 67)	19.7
Multiple from Table I (male, age 70) ...	12.1
Difference (multiple applicable to second annuitant)	7.6
Portion of expected return, second annuitant ($600 × 7.6)	$4,560
Portion of expected return, first annuitant ($1,200 × 12.1)	14,520
Expected return under the contract	19,080

The expected return thus found, $19,080, is to be used in computing the amount to be excluded from gross income. Thus, if the investment in the contract in this example is $14,310, the exclusion ratio is $\frac{\$14,310}{\$19,080}$, or 75 percent. The amount excludable from each monthly payment made to the husband is 75 percent of $100, or $75, and the remaining $25 of each payment received by him shall be included in his gross income. After the husband's death, the amount excludable by the second annuitant (the surviving wife) would be 75 percent of each monthly payment of $50, or $37.50, and the remaining $12.50 of each payment shall be included in her gross income.

The same method is used if the payments are to be increased after the death of the first annuitant. Thus, if the payments to be made until the husband's death were $50 per month and his widow were to receive $100 per month thereafter until her death, the 7.6 multiple in the above example would be applied to the $100 payments, yielding an expected return with respect to this portion of the annuity contract of $9,120 ($1,200 x 7.6). An expected return of $7,260 ($600 x 12.1) would be obtained with respect to the payments to be made the husband, yielding a total expected return under the contract of $16,380 ($9,120 plus $7,260). If payments are to be made quarterly, semiannually, or annually, an appropriate adjustment of the multiples found in Tables I and II should be made in accordance with paragraph (a) (2) of this section.

. . . . .

(4) If a contract involving two annuitants provides for fixed monthly payments to be made as a joint life annuity until the death of the first annuitant to die (in other words, only as long as both remain alive), the expected return under such contract shall be determined by multiplying the total of the annuity payments to be received annually under the contract by the multiple obtained from Table IIA of § 1.72-9 under the ages (as of the annuity starting date) and sexes of the annuitants. If, however, payments are to be made under the contract quarterly, semiannually, or annually, an appropriate adjustment of the multiple found in Table IIA shall be made in accordance with paragraph (a) (2) of this section.

(5) If a joint and survivor annuity contract involving two annuitants provides that a specified amount shall be paid during their joint lives and a different specified amount shall be paid to the survivor upon the death of whichever of the annuitants is the first to die, the following preliminary computation shall be made in all cases preparatory to determining the expected return under the contract:

(i) From Table II, obtain the multiple under both of the annuitants' ages (as of the annuity starting date) and their appropriate sexes;

(ii) From Table IIA, obtain the multiple applicable to both annuitants' ages (as of the annuity starting date) and their appropriate sexes;

(iii) Apply the multiple found in subdivision (i) of this subparagraph to the total of the amounts to be received annually after the death of the first to die; and

(iv) Apply the multiple found in subdivision (ii) of this subparagraph to the difference between the total of the amounts to be received annually before and the total of the amounts to be received annually after the death of the first to die.

If the original annual payment is in excess of the annual payment to be made after the death of the first to die, the expected return is the sum of the amounts determined under subdivisions (iii) and (iv) of this subparagraph. This may be illustrated by the following example:

Example. A husband purchases a joint and survivor annuity providing for payments of $100 a month for as long as both he and his wife live, and, after the death of the first to die, payments to the survivor of $75 a month for life. As of the annuity starting date, his age at his nearest birthday is 70 and that of his wife at her nearest birthday is 67. The expected return under the contract is computed as follows:

Multiple from Table II (male, age 70; female, age 67) 19.7

Multiple from Table IIA (male, age 70; female, age 67) 9.3

Portion of expected return ($900 × 19.7 —sum per year after first death) $17,730

Portion of expected return ($300 × 9.3— amount of change in sum at . first death) $2,790

Expected return under the contract $20,520

The total expected return in this example, $20,520, is to be used in computing the amount to be excluded from gross income. Thus, if the investment in the contract is $17,887, the exclusion ratio is $\frac{\$17,887}{\$20,520}$, or 87.2 percent. The amount excludable from each monthly payment made while both are alive is 87.2 percent of $100, or $87.20 and the remaining $12.80 of each payment shall be included in gross income. After the death of the first to die, the amount excludable by the survivor shall be 87.2 percent of each monthly payment of $75, or $65.40, and the remaining $9.60 of each payment shall be included in gross income.

If the original annual payment is less than the annual payment to be made after the death of the first to die, the expected return is the difference between the amounts determined under subdivisions (iii) and (iv) of this subparagraph. If, however, payments are to be made quarterly, semiannually, or annually under the contract, the multiples obtained from both Tables II and IIA shall first be adjusted in a manner prescribed in paragraph (a) (2) of this section.

(6) If a contract provides for the payment of life annuities to two persons during their respective lives and, after the death of one (without regard to which one dies first), provides that the survivor shall receive for life both his own annuity payments and the payments made formerly to the deceased person, the expected return shall be determined in accordance with paragraph (e)(4) of this section.

(7) If paragraph (b) (3) of § 1.72-2 applies to payments provided under a contract and this paragraph applies to such payments, the principles of this paragraph shall be used in making the computations described in paragraph (d) (3) of § 1.72-4. This may be illustrated by the following examples:

Example (1). Taxpayer A, a male age 63, pays $24,000 for a contract which provides that the proceeds (both income and return of capital) from eight units of an investment fund shall be paid monthly to him for his life and that after his death the proceeds from six such units shall be paid monthly to B, a female age 55, for her life, the portion of the investment in the contract allocable to each taxable year of A is $955.20 and that allocable to each taxable year of B is $716.40. This is determined in the following manner:

Multiple from Table II (male, age 63; and female, age 55) 28.1

Number of units to be paid, in effect, as a joint and survivor annuity .... ×6

Number of total annual unit payments anticipatable with respect to the joint and survivor annuity element 168.6

Multiple from Table I (male, age 63) 16.2

Number of units to be paid in effect, as a single life annuity .... ×2

Number of total annual unit payments anticipatable with respect to A alone .. 32.4

Total number of unit payments anticipatable 201

Portion of investment in the contract allocable to unit payments ($24,000 ÷ 201) on an annual basis $119.40

Number of units payable to A while he continues to live .... ×8

Portion of the investment in the contract allocable to each taxable year of A ... $955.20

Portion of investment in the contract allocable to unit payments ($24,000 ÷ 201) on an annual basis $119.40

Number of units payable to B for her life after A's death .... ×6

Portion of the investment in the contract allocable to each taxable year of B ... $716.40

For the purpose of the above computation it is immaterial whether or not A lives to or beyond the life expectancy shown for him in Table I.

Example (2). Assume that Taxpayer A in example (1) receives payments for five years which are at least as large as the portion of the investment in the contract allocable to such years, but in the sixth year he receives a total on only $626.40 rather than the $955.20 allocable to such year. A is 69 and B is 61 at the beginning of the first monthly period for which an amount is payable in the seventh taxable year. A makes the election in that year provided under paragraph (d) (3) of § 1.72-4. The difference between the portion of the investment in the contract allocable to the sixth year and the amount actually received in that year is $328.80 ($955.20 less $626.40). In this case, 139.2 unit payments are anticipatable (on an annual basis), since the appropriate multiple from Table II of § 1.72-9, 23.2, multiplied by the number of units payable, in effect, as a joint and survivor annuity yields this result (6 × 23.2). A's appropriate multiple from Table I of § 1.72-9 for the two units which will cease to be paid at his death is 12.6, and the total number of unit payments anticipatable (on an annual basis) is, therefore, 164.4 (2 × 12.6 plus 139.2). Dividing the difference previously found ($328.80) by the total number of unit payments thus determined (164.4) indicates that A will have an additional allocation of the investment in the contract of $16 to the seventh and every succeeding full taxable year (8 units × $2), and B will have an additional allocation of the investment in the contract of $12 (6 units × $2) to each taxable year in which she receives 12 monthly payments subsequent to the death of A. The total allocable to each taxable year of A is, therefore, $971.20, and that allocable to each taxable year of B will be $728.40.

Example (3). If, in example (2), A had died at the end of the fifth year, in the sixth year B would have received a payment of $469.80 (that portion of the $626.40 that A would have received which is in the same ratio that 6 units bear to 8 units) and would thus have received $246.60 less than the portion of the investment in the contract originally determined to be allocable to each of her taxable years. In these circumstances, B would be entitled to elect to redetermine the portion of the investment in the contract allocable to the taxable year of election and all subsequent years. The new amount allocable thereto would be found by dividing the $246.60 difference by her life expectancy as of the first day of the first period for which she received an amount as an annuity in the seventh year of the annuity contract, and adding the result to her originally determined allocation of $716.40.

(c) Expected return for term certain. In the case of a contract providing for specific periodic payments which are to be paid for a term certain such as a fixed number of months or years, without regard to life expectancy, the expected return is determined by multiplying the fixed number of years or months for which payments are to be made on or after the annuity starting date by the amount of the payment provided in the contract for each such period.

(d) Expected return with respect to amount certain. In the case of contracts involving no life or lives as a measurement of their duration, but under which a determinable total amount is to be paid in installments of lesser amounts paid at periodic intervals, the expected return shall be the total amount guaranteed. If an amount is to be paid periodically until a fund plus interest at a fixed rate is exhausted, but further payments may be made thereafter because of earnings at a higher interest rate, this paragraph shall apply to the total amount anticipatable as a result of the amount of the fund plus the fixed interest thereon. Any amount which may be paid as the result of earnings at a greater interest rate shall be disregarded in determining the expected return. If such an amount is later received, it shall be considered an amount not received as an annuity after the annuity starting date.

. . . .

      . . . .

§ 1.72-6 Investment in the contract

(a) General rule. (1) For the purpose of computing the "investment in the contract", it is first necessary to determine the "aggregate amount of premiums or other consideration paid" for such contract. See section 72(c) (1). This determination is made as of the later of the annuity starting date of the contract or the date on which an amount is first received thereunder as an annuity. The amount so found is then reduced by the sum of the following amounts in order to find the investment in the contract:

(i) The total amount of any return of premiums or dividends received (including unrepaid loans or dividends applied against the principal or interest on such loans) on or before the date on which the foregoing determination is made, and

(ii) The total of any other amounts received with respect to the contract on or before such date which were excludable from the gross income of the recipient under the income tax law applicable at the time of receipt.

Amounts to which subdivision (ii) of this subparagraph applies shall include, for example, amounts considered to be return of premiums or other consideration paid under section 22(b) (2) of the Internal Revenue Code of 1939 and amounts considered to be an employer-provided death benefit under section 22(b) (1) (B) of such Code. For rules relating to the extent to which an employee or his beneficiary may include employer contributions in the aggregate amount of premiums or other consideration paid, see § 1.72-8. If the aggregate amount of premiums or other consideration paid for the contract includes amounts for which deductions were allowed under section 404 as contributions on behalf of a self-employed individual, such amounts shall not be included in the investment in the contract.

(2) For the purpose of subparagraph (1) of this paragraph, amounts received subsequent to the receipt of an amount as an annuity or subsequent to the annuity starting date, whichever is the later, shall be disregarded. See, however, § 1.72–11.

(3) The application of this paragraph may be illustrated by the following examples:

Example (1). In 1950, B purchased an annuity contract for $10,000 which was to provide him with an annuity of $1,000 per year for life. He received $1,000 in each of the years 1950, 1951, 1952, and 1953, prior to the annuity starting date (January 1, 1954). Under the Internal Revenue Code of 1939, $300 of each of these payments (3 percent of $10,000) was includible in his gross income, and the remaining $700 was excludable therefrom during each of the taxable years mentioned. In computing B's investment in the contract as of January 1, 1954, the total amount excludable from his gross income during the years 1950 through 1953 ($2,800) must be subtracted from the consideration paid ($10,000). Accordingly, B's investment in the contract as of January 1, 1954, is $7,200 ($10,000 less $2,800).

Example (2). In 1945, C contracted for an annuity to be paid to him beginning December 31, 1960. In 1945 and in each successive year until 1960, he paid a premium of $5,000. Assuming he receives no payments of any kind under the contract until the date on which he receives the first annual payment as an annuity (December 31, 1960), his investment in the contract as of the annuity starting date (December 31, 1959) will be $75,000 ($5,000 paid each year for the 15 years from 1945 to 1959, inclusive).

Example (3). Assume the same facts as in example (2), except that prior to the annuity starting date C has already received from the insurer dividends of $1,000 each in 1949, 1954, and 1959, such dividends not being includible in his gross income in any of those years. C's investment in the contract, as of the annuity starting date, will then be $72,000 ($75,000 — $3,000).

. . . .

§ 1.72–7 Adjustment in investment where a contract contains a refund feature

(a) Definition of a contract containing a refund feature. A contract to which section 72 applies, contains a refund feature if:

(1) The total amount receivable as an annuity under such contract depends, in whole or in part, on the continuing life of one or more persons,

(2) The contract provides for payments to be made to a beneficiary or the estate of an annuitant on or after the death of the annuitant if a specified amount or a stated number of payments has not been paid to the annuitant or annuitants prior to death, and

(3) Such payments are in the nature of a refund of the consideration paid. See paragraph (c) (1) of § 1.72–11.

(b) Adjustment of investment for the refund feature in the case of a single life annuity. Where a single life annuity contract to which section 72 applies contains a refund feature and the special rule of paragraph (d) of this section does not apply, the investment in the contract shall be adjusted in the following manner:

(1) Determine the number of years necessary for the guaranteed amount to be fully paid by dividing the maximum amount guaranteed as of the annuity starting date by the amount to be received annually under the contract to the extent such amount reduces the guaranteed amount. The number of years should be stated in terms of the nearest whole year, considering for this purpose a fraction of one-half or more as an additional whole year.

(2) Consult Table III of § 1.72–9 for the appropriate percentage under the whole number of years found in subparagraph (1) of this paragraph and the age (as of the annuity starting date) and sex of the annuitant.

(3) Multiply the percentage found in subparagraph (2) of this paragraph by whichever of the following is the smaller: (i) The investment in the contract found in accordance with § 1.72–6 or (ii) the total amount guaranteed as of the annuity starting date.

(4) Subtract the amount found in subparagraph (3) of this paragraph from the investment in the contract found in accordance with § 1.72–6.

The resulting amount is the investment in the contract adjusted for the present value of the refund feature without discount for interest and is to be used in determining the exclusion ratio to be applied to the payments received as an annuity. The percentage found in Table III shall not be adjusted in a manner prescribed in paragraph (a) (2) of

§ 1.72–5. These principles may be illustrated by the following example:

Example. On January 1, 1954, a husband, age 65, purchased for $21,053, an immediate installment refund annuity payable $100 per month for life. The contract provided that in the event the husband did not live long enough to recover the full purchase price, payments were to be made to his wife until the total payments under the contract equaled the purchase price. The investment in the contract adjusted for the purpose of determining the exclusion ratio is computed in the following manner:

Cost of the annuity contract (investment in the contract, unadjusted)	$21,053
Amount to be received annually	$1,200
Number of years for which payment guaranteed ($21,053 divided by $1,200)	17.5
Rounded to nearest whole number of years	18
Percentage located in Table III for age 65 (age of the annuitant as of the annuity starting date) and 18 (the number of whole years) (percent)	30
Subtract value of the refund feature to the nearest dollar (30 percent of $21,053)	6,316
Investment in the contract adjusted for the present value of the refund feature without discount for interest	14,737

If, in the above example, the guaranteed amount had exceeded the investment in the contract, the percentage found in Table III should have been applied to the lesser of these amounts since any excess of the guaranteed amount over the investment in the contract (as found under § 1.72–6) would not have constituted a refund of premiums or other consideration paid. In such a case, however, a different multiple might have been obtained from Table III since the number of years for which payments were guaranteed would have been greater.

. . . .

§ 1.72–9   Tables

The following tables are to be used in connection with computations under section 72 and the regulations thereunder:

TABLE I—ORDINARY LIFE ANNUITIES—ONE LIFE—EXPECTED RETURN MULTIPLES

Male	Female	Multiples	Male	Female	Multiples	Male	Female	Multiples
6	11	65.0	41	46	33.0	76	81	9.1
7	12	64.1	42	47	32.1	77	82	8.7
8	13	63.2	43	48	31.2	78	83	8.3
9	14	62.3	44	49	30.4	79	84	7.8
10	15	61.4	45	50	29.6	80	85	7.5
11	16	60.4	46	51	28.7	81	86	7.1
12	17	59.5	47	52	27.9	82	87	6.7
13	18	58.6	48	53	27.1	83	88	6.3
14	19	57.7	49	54	26.3	84	89	6.0
15	20	56.7	50	55	25.5	85	90	5.7
16	21	55.8	51	56	24.7	86	91	5.4
17	22	54.9	52	57	24.0	87	92	5.1
18	23	53.9	53	58	23.2	88	93	4.8
19	24	53.0	54	59	22.4	89	94	4.5
20	25	52.1	55	60	21.7	90	95	4.2
21	26	51.1	56	61	21.0	91	96	4.0
22	27	50.2	57	62	20.3	92	97	3.7
23	28	49.3	58	63	19.6	93	98	3.5
24	29	48.3	59	64	18.9	94	99	3.3
25	30	47.4	60	65	18.2	95	100	3.1
26	31	46.5	61	66	17.5	96	101	2.9
27	32	45.6	62	67	16.9	97	102	2.7
28	33	44.6	63	68	16.2	98	103	2.5
29	34	43.7	64	69	15.6	99	104	2.3
30	35	42.8	65	70	15.0	100	105	2.1
31	36	41.9	66	71	14.4	101	106	1.9
32	37	41.0	67	72	13.8	102	107	1.7
33	38	40.0	68	73	13.2	103	108	1.5
34	39	39.1	69	74	12.6	104	109	1.3
35	40	38.2	70	75	12.1	105	110	1.2
36	41	37.3	71	76	11.6	106	111	1.0
37	42	36.5	72	77	11.0	107	112	.8
38	43	35.6	73	78	10.5	108	113	.7
39	44	34.7	74	79	10.1	109	114	.6
40	45	33.8	75	80	9.6	110	115	.5
						111	116	0

. . . .

TABLE II—ORDINARY JOINT LIFE AND LAST SURVIVOR ANNUITIES—TWO LIVES—EXPECTED RETURN MULTIPLES

Male		35	36	37	38	39	40	41	42	43	44	45	46	47
Male	**Female**	40	41	42	43	44	45	46	47	48	49	50	51	52
35	40	46.2	45.7	45.3	44.8	44.4	44.0	43.6	43.3	43.0	42.6	42.3	42.0	41.8
36	41	45.7	45.2	44.8	44.3	43.9	43.5	43.1	42.7	42.3	42.0	41.7	41.4	41.1
37	42	45.3	44.8	44.3	43.8-	43.4	42.9	42.5	42.1	41.8	41.4	41.1	40.7	40.4
38	43	44.8	44.3	43.8	43.3	42.9	42.4	42.0	41.6	41.2	40.8	40.5	40.1	39.8
39	44	44.4	43.9	43.4	42.9	42.4	41.9	41.5	41.0	40.6	40.2	39.9	39.5	39.2
40	45	44.0	43.5	42.9	42.4	41.9	41.4	41.0	40.5	40.1	39.7	39.3	38.9	38.6
41	46	43.6	43.1	42.5	42.0	41.5	41.0	40.5	40.0	39.6	39.2	38.8	38.4	38.0
42	47	43.3	42.7	42.1	41.6	41.0	40.5	40.0	39.6	39.1	38.7	38.2	37.8	37.5
43	48	43.0	42.3	41.8	41.2	40.6	40.1	39.6	39.1	38.6	38.2	37.7	37.3	36.9
44	49	42.6	42.0	41.4	40.8	40.2	39.7	39.2	38.7	38.2	37.7	37.2	36.8	36.4
45	50	42.3	41.7	41.1	40.5	39.9	39.3	38.8	38.2	37.7	37.2	36.8	36.3	35.9
46	51	42.0	41.4	40.7	40.1	39.5	38.9	38.4	37.8	37.3	36.8	36.3	35.9	35.4
47	52	41.8	41.1	40.4	39.8	39.2	38.6	38.0	37.5	36.9	36.4	35.9	35.4	35.0

Male		48	49	50	51	52	53	54	55	56	57	58	59	60
Male	**Female**	53	54	55	56	57	58	59	60	61	62	63	64	65
35	40	41.5	41.3	41.0	40.8	40.6	40.4	40.3	40.1	40.0	39.8	39.7	39.6	39.5
36	41	40.8	40.6	40.3	40.1	39.9	39.7	39.5	39.3	39.2	39.0	38.9	38.8	38.6
37	42	40.2	39.9	39.6	39.4	39.2	39.0	38.8	38.6	38.4	38.3	38.1	38.0	37.9
38	43	39.5	39.2	39.0	38.7	38.5	38.3	38.1	37.9	37.7	37.5	37.3	37.2	37.1
39	44	38.9	38.6	38.3	38.0	37.8	37.6	37.3	37.1	36.9	36.8	36.6	36.4	36.3
40	45	38.3	38.0	37.7	37.4	37.1	36.9	36.6	36.4	36.2	36.0	35.9	35.7	35.5
41	46	37.7	37.3	37.0	36.7	36.5	36.2	36.0	35.7	35.5	35.3	35.1	35.0	34.8
42	47	37.1	36.8	36.4	36.1	35.8	35.6	35.3	35.1	34.8	34.6	34.4	34.2	34.1
43	48	36.5	36.2	35.8	35.5	35.2	34.9	34.7	34.4	34.2	33.9	33.7	33.5	33.3
44	49	36.0	35.6	35.3	34.9	34.6	34.3	34.0	33.8	33.5	33.3	33.0	32.8	32.6
45	50	35.5	35.1	34.7	34.4	34.0	33.7	33.4	33.1	32.9	32.6	32.4	32.2	31.9
46	51	35.0	34.6	34.2	33.8	33.5	33.1	32.8	32.5	32.2	32.0	31.7	31.5	31.3
47	52	34.5	34.1	33.7	33.3	32.9	32.6	32.2	31.9	31.6	31.4	31.1	30.9	30.6
48	53	34.0	33.6	33.2	32.8	32.4	32.0	31.7	31.4	31.1	30.8	30.5	30.2	30.0
49	54	33.6	33.1	32.7	32.3	31.9	31.5	31.2	30.8	30.5	30.2	29.9	29.6	29.4
50	55	33.2	32.7	32.3	31.8	31.4	31.0	30.6	30.3	29.9	29.6	29.3	29.0	28.8
51	56	32.8	32.3	31.8	31.4	30.9	30.5	30.1	29.8	29.4	29.1	28.8	28.5	28.2
52	57	32.4	31.9	31.4	30.9	30.5	30.1	29.7	29.3	28.9	28.6	28.2	27.9	27.6
53	58	32.0	31.5	31.0	30.5	30.1	29.6	29.2	28.8	28.4	28.1	27.7	27.4	27.1
54	59	31.7	31.2	30.6	30.1	29.7	29.2	28.8	28.3	27.9	27.6	27.2	26.9	26.6
55	60	31.4	30.8	30.3	29.8	29.3	28.8	28.3	27.9	27.5	27.1	26.7	26.4	26.0
56	61	31.1	30.5	29.9	29.4	28.9	28.4	27.9	27.5	27.1	26.7	26.3	25.9	25.5
57	62	30.8	30.2	29.6	29.1	28.6	28.1	27.6	27.1	26.7	26.2	25.8	25.4	25.1
58	63	30.5	29.9	29.3	28.8	28.2	27.7	27.2	26.7	26.3	25.8	25.4	25.0	24.6
59	64	30.2	29.6	29.0	28.5	27.9	27.4	26.9	26.4	25.9	25.4	25.0	24.6	24.2
60	65	30.0	29.4	28.8	28.2	27.6	27.1	26.5	26.0	25.5	25.1	24.6	24.2	23.8

Table II—Ordinary Joint Life and Last Survivor Annuities—Two Lives—Expected Return Multiples—Continued

Ages														
	Male	61	62	63	64	65	66	67	68	69	70	71	72	73
Male	Female	66	67	68	69	70	71	72	73	74	75	76	77	78
35	40	39.4	39.3	39.2	39.1	39.0	38.9	38.9	38.8	38.8	38.7	38.7	38.6	38.6
36	41	38.5	38.4	38.3	38.2	38.2	38.1	38.0	38.0	37.9	37.9	37.8	37.8	37.7
37	42	37.7	37.6	37.5	37.4	37.3	37.3	37.2	37.1	37.1	37.0	36.9	36.9	36.9
38	43	36.8	36.8	36.7	36.6	36.5	36.4	36.4	36.3	36.2	36.2	36.1	36.0	36.0
39	44	36.2	36.0	35.9	35.8	35.7	35.6	35.5	35.5	35.4	35.3	35.3	35.2	35.2
40	45	35.4	35.3	35.1	35.0	34.9	34.8	34.7	34.6	34.6	34.5	34.4	34.4	34.3
41	46	34.6	34.5	34.4	34.2	34.1	34.0	33.9	33.8	33.8	33.7	33.6	33.5	33.5
42	47	33.9	33.7	33.6	33.5	33.4	33.2	33.1	33.0	33.0	32.9	32.8	32.7	32.7
43	48	33.2	33.0	32.9	32.7	32.6	32.5	32.4	32.3	32.2	32.1	32.0	31.9	31.9
44	49	32.5	32.3	32.1	32.0	31.8	31.7	31.6	31.5	31.4	31.3	31.2	31.1	31.1
45	50	31.8	31.6	31.4	31.3	31.1	31.0	30.8	30.7	30.6	30.5	30.4	30.4	30.3
46	51	31.1	30.9	30.7	30.5	30.4	30.2	30.1	30.0	29.9	29.8	29.7	29.6	29.5
47	52	30.4	30.2	30.0	29.8	29.7	29.5	29.4	29.3	29.1	29.0	28.9	28.8	28.7
48	53	29.8	29.5	29.3	29.2	29.0	28.8	28.7	28.5	28.4	28.3	28.2	28.1	28.0
49	54	29.1	28.9	28.7	28.5	28.3	28.1	28.0	27.8	27.7	27.6	27.5	27.4	27.3
50	55	28.5	28.3	28.1	27.8	27.6	27.5	27.3	27.1	27.0	26.9	26.7	26.6	26.5
51	56	27.9	27.7	27.4	27.2	27.0	26.8	26.6	26.5	26.3	26.2	26.0	25.9	25.8
52	57	27.3	27.1	26.8	26.6	26.4	26.2	26.0	25.8	25.7	25.5	25.4	25.2	25.1
53	58	26.8	26.5	26.2	26.0	25.8	25.6	25.4	25.2	25.0	24.8	24.7	24.6	24.4
54	59	26.2	25.9	25.7	25.4	25.2	25.0	24.7	24.6	24.4	24.2	24.0	23.9	23.8
55	60	25.7	25.4	25.1	24.9	24.6	24.4	24.1	23.9	23.8	23.6	23.4	23.3	23.1
56	61	25.2	24.9	24.6	24.3	24.1	23.8	23.6	23.4	23.2	23.0	22.8	22.6	22.5
57	62	24.7	24.4	24.1	23.8	23.5	23.3	23.0	22.8	22.6	22.4	22.2	22.0	21.9
58	63	24.3	23.9	23.6	23.3	23.0	22.7	22.5	22.2	22.0	21.8	21.6	21.4	21.3
59	64	23.8	23.5	23.1	22.8	22.5	22.2	21.9	21.7	21.5	21.2	21.0	20.9	20.7
60	65	23.4	23.0	22.7	22.3	22.0	21.7	21.4	21.2	20.9	20.7	20.5	20.3	20.1
61	66	23.0	22.6	22.2	21.9	21.6	21.3	21.0	20.7	20.4	20.2	20.0	19.8	19.6
62	67	22.6	22.2	21.8	21.5	21.1	20.8	20.5	20.2	19.9	19.7	19.5	19.2	19.0
63	68	22.2	21.8	21.4	21.1	20.7	20.4	20.1	19.8	19.5	19.2	19.0	18.7	18.5
64	69	21.9	21.5	21.1	20.7	20.3	20.0	19.6	19.3	19.0	18.7	18.5	18.2	18.0
65	70	21.6	21.1	20.7	20.3	19.9	19.6	19.2	18.9	18.6	18.3	18.0	17.8	17.5
66	71	21.3	20.8	20.4	20.0	19.6	19.2	18.8	18.5	18.2	17.9	17.6	17.3	17.1
67	72	21.0	20.5	20.1	19.6	19.2	18.8	18.5	18.1	17.8	17.5	17.2	16.9	16.7
68	73	20.7	20.2	19.8	19.3	18.9	18.5	18.1	17.8	17.4	17.1	16.8	16.5	16.2
69	74	20.4	19.9	19.5	19.0	18.6	18.2	17.8	17.4	17.1	16.7	16.4	16.1	15.8
70	75	20.2	19.7	19.2	18.7	18.3	17.9	17.5	17.1	16.7	16.4	16.1	15.8	15.5
71	76	20.0	19.5	19.0	18.5	18.0	17.6	17.2	16.8	16.4	16.1	15.7	15.4	15.1
72	77	19.8	19.2	18.7	18.2	17.8	17.3	16.9	16.5	16.1	15.8	15.4	15.1	14.8
73	78	19.6	19.0	18.5	18.0	17.5	17.1	16.7	16.2	15.8	15.5	15.1	14.8	14.4

TABLE II—ORDINARY JOINT LIFE AND LAST SURVIVOR ANNUITIES—TWO LIVES—EXPECTED RETURN MULTIPLES—Continued

Ages													
	Male	74	75	76	77	78	79	80	81	82	83	84	85
Male	Female	79	80	81	82	83	84	85	86	87	88	89	90
35	40	38.6	38.5	38.5	38.5	38.4	38.4	38.4	38.4	38.4	38.4	38.3	38.3
36	41	37.7	37.6	37.6	37.6	37.6	37.5	37.5	37.5	37.5	37.5	37.5	37.4
37	42	36.8	36.8	36.7	36.7	36.7	36.7	36.6	36.6	36.6	36.6	36.6	36.6
38	43	36.0	35.9	35.9	35.9	35.8	35.8	35.8	35.8	35.7	35.7	35.7	35.7
39	44	35.1	35.1	35.0	35.0	35.0	34.9	34.9	34.9	34.9	34.8	34.8	34.8
40	45	34.3	34.2	34.2	34.1	34.1	34.1	34.1	34.0	34.0	34.0	34.0	34.0
41	46	33.4	33.4	33.3	33.3	33.3	33.2	33.2	33.2	33.2	33.1	33.1	33.1
42	47	32.8	32.6	32.5	32.5	32.4	32.4	32.4	32.3	32.3	32.3	32.3	32.3
43	48	31.8	31.8	31.7	31.7	31.6	31.6	31.5	31.5	31.5	31.4	31.4	31.4
44	49	31.0	30.9	30.9	30.8	30.8	30.8	30.7	30.7	30.7	30.6	30.6	30.6
45	50	30.2	30.1	30.1	30.0	30.0	29.9	29.9	29.9	29.8	29.8	29.8	29.8
46	51	29.4	29.4	29.3	29.2	29.2	29.2	29.1	29.1	29.0	29.0	29.0	28.9
47	52	28.7	28.6	28.5	28.5	28.4	28.4	28.3	28.3	28.2	28.2	28.2	28.1
48	53	27.9	27.8	27.8	27.7	27.6	27.6	27.5	27.5	27.5	27.4	27.4	27.4
49	54	27.2	27.1	27.0	26.9	26.9	26.8	26.8	26.7	26.7	26.6	26.6	26.6
50	55	26.4	26.3	26.3	26.2	26.1	26.1	26.0	26.0	25.9	25.9	25.9	25.8
51	56	25.7	25.6	25.5	25.5	25.4	25.3	25.3	25.2	25.2	25.1	25.1	25.0
52	57	25.0	24.9	24.8	24.7	24.7	24.6	24.5	24.5	24.4	24.4	24.3	24.3
53	58	24.3	24.2	24.1	24.0	23.9	23.9	23.8	23.7	23.7	23.6	23.6	23.5
54	59	23.6	23.5	23.4	23.3	23.2	23.2	23.1	23.0	23.0	22.9	22.9	22.8
55	60	23.0	22.9	22.8	22.7	22.6	22.5	22.4	22.3	22.3	22.2	22.2	22.1
56	61	22.3	22.2	22.1	22.0	21.9	21.8	21.7	21.6	21.6	21.5	21.5	21.4
57	62	21.7	21.6	21.5	21.3	21.2	21.1	21.1	21.0	20.9	20.8	20.8	20.7
58	63	21.1	21.0	20.8	20.7	20.6	20.5	20.4	20.3	20.2	20.2	20.1	20.0
59	64	20.5	20.4	20.2	20.1	20.0	19.9	19.8	19.7	19.6	19.5	19.4	19.4
60	65	19.9	19.8	19.6	19.5	19.4	19.3	19.1	19.0	19.0	18.9	18.8	18.7
61	66	19.4	19.2	19.1	18.9	18.8	18.7	18.5	18.4	18.3	18.3	18.2	18.1
62	67	18.8	18.7	18.5	18.3	18.2	18.1	18.0	17.8	17.7	17.7	17.6	17.5
63	68	18.3	18.1	18.0	17.8	17.6	17.5	17.4	17.3	17.2	17.1	17.0	16.9
64	69	17.8	17.6	17.4	17.3	17.1	17.0	16.8	16.7	16.6	16.5	16.4	16.3
65	70	17.3	17.1	16.9	16.7	16.6	16.4	16.4	16.2	16.0	15.9	15.8	15.8
66	71	16.9	16.6	16.4	16.3	16.1	15.9	15.8	15.6	15.5	15.5	15.3	15.2
67	72	16.4	16.2	16.0	15.8	15.6	15.4	15.3	15.1	15.0	14.9	14.8	14.7
68	73	16.0	15.7	15.5	15.3	15.1	15.0	14.8	14.6	14.5	14.4	14.3	14.2
69	74	15.6	15.3	15.1	14.9	14.7	14.5	14.3	14.2	14.0	13.9	13.8	13.7
70	75	15.2	14.9	14.7	14.5	14.3	14.1	13.9	13.7	13.6	13.4	13.3	13.2
71	76	14.8	14.5	14.3	14.1	13.8	13.6	13.5	13.3	13.1	13.0	12.8	12.7
72	77	14.5	14.2	13.9	13.7	13.5	13.2	13.0	12.9	12.7	12.5	12.4	12.3
73	78	14.1	13.8	13.6	13.3	13.1	12.9	12.7	12.5	12.3	12.1	12.0	11.8
74	79	13.8	13.5	13.2	13.0	12.7	12.5	12.3	12.1	11.9	11.7	11.6	11.4
75	80	13.5	13.2	12.9	12.6	12.4	12.2	11.9	11.7	11.5	11.4	11.2	11.0
76	81	13.2	12.9	12.6	12.3	12.1	11.8	11.6	11.4	11.2	11.0	10.8	10.7
77	82	13.0	12.6	12.3	12.1	11.8	11.5	11.3	11.1	10.8	10.7	10.5	10.3
78	83	12.7	12.4	12.1	11.8	11.5	11.2	11.0	10.7	10.5	10.3	10.1	10.0
79	84	12.5	12.2	11.8	11.5	11.2	11.0	10.7	10.5	10.2	10.0	9.8	9.6
80	85	12.3	11.9	11.6	11.3	11.0	10.7	10.4	10.2	10.0	10.0	9.5	9.3
81	86	12.1	11.7	11.4	11.1	10.7	10.5	10.2	9.9	9.7	9.5	9.3	9.1
82	87	11.9	11.5	11.2	10.8	10.5	10.2	10.0	9.7	9.4	9.2	9.0	8.8
83	88	11.7	11.4	11.0	10.7	10.3	10.0	9.7	9.5	9.2	9.0	8.7	8.5
84	89	11.6	11.2	10.8	10.5	10.1	9.8	9.5	9.3	9.0	8.7	8.5	8.3
85	90	11.4	11.0	10.7	10.3	10.0	9.6	9.3	9.1	8.8	8.5	8.3	8.1

. . . .

TABLE IIA—ANNUITIES FOR JOINT LIFE ONLY—TWO LIVES—EXPECTED RETURN MULTIPLES

Ages Male		35	36	37	38	39	40	41	42	43	44	45	46	47
Male	Female	40	41	42	43	44	45	46	47	48	49	50	51	52
35	40	30.3	29.9	29.4	29.0	28.5	28.0	27.5	27.0	26.5	26.0	25.5	24.9	24.4
36	41	29.9	29.5	29.0	28.6	28.2	27.7	27.2	26.7	26.2	25.7	25.2	24.7	24.2
37	42	29.4	29.0	28.6	28.2	27.8	27.3	26.9	26.4	25.9	25.5	25.0	24.4	23.9
38	43	29.0	28.6	28.2	27.8	27.4	27.0	26.5	26.1	25.6	25.3	24.7	24.2	23.4
39	44	28.5	28.2	27.8	27.4	27.0	26.6	26.2	25.8	25.3	24.8	24.4	23.9	23.1
40	45	28.0	27.7	27.3	27.0	26.6	26.2	25.8	25.4	25.0	24.5	24.1	23.6	23.1
41	46	27.5	27.2	26.9	26.5	26.2	25.8	25.4	25.0	24.6	24.2	23.8	23.3	22.9
42	47	27.0	26.7	26.4	26.1	25.8	25.4	25.0	24.6	24.2	23.8	23.4	23.0	22.6
43	48	26.5	26.2	25.9	25.6	25.3	25.0	24.6	24.2	23.9	23.5	23.1	22.7	22.3
44	49	26.0	25.7	25.5	25.2	24.8	24.5	24.2	23.8	23.5	23.1	22.7	22.3	21.9
45	50	25.5	25.2	25.0	24.7	24.4	24.1	23.8	23.4	23.1	22.7	22.4	22.0	21.6
46	51	24.9	24.7	24.4	24.2	23.9	23.6	23.3	23.0	22.7	22.3	22.0	21.6	21.2
47	52	24.4	24.2	23.9	23.7	23.4	23.1	22.9	22.6	22.3	21.9	21.6	21.2	20.9

Ages Male		48	49	50	51	52	53	54	55	56	57	58	59	60
Male	Female	53	54	55	56	57	58	59	60	61	62	63	64	65
35	40	23.8	23.3	22.7	22.1	21.6	21.0	20.4	19.8	19.3	18.7	18.1	17.5	17.0
36	41	23.6	23.1	22.5	22.0	21.4	20.8	20.3	19.7	19.1	18.6	18.0	17.4	16.9
37	42	23.4	22.9	22.3	21.8	21.2	20.7	20.1	19.6	19.0	18.4	17.9	17.3	16.8
38	43	23.2	22.6	22.1	21.6	21.1	20.5	20.0	19.4	18.9	18.3	17.8	17.2	16.7
39	44	22.9	22.4	21.9	21.4	20.9	20.3	19.8	19.3	18.7	18.2	17.7	17.1	16.6
40	45	22.7	22.2	21.7	21.2	20.7	20.1	19.6	19.1	18.6	18.0	17.5	17.0	16.5
41	46	22.4	21.9	21.4	20.9	20.4	19.9	19.4	18.9	18.4	17.9	17.4	16.9	16.3
42	47	22.1	21.6	21.2	20.7	20.2	19.7	19.2	18.7	18.2	17.7	17.2	16.7	16.1
43	48	21.8	21.4	20.9	20.5	20.0	19.5	19.0	18.6	18.1	17.6	17.1	16.6	16.1
44	49	21.5	21.1	20.6	20.2	19.8	19.3	18.8	18.4	17.9	17.4	16.9	16.4	15.9
45	50	21.2	20.8	20.4	19.9	19.5	19.1	18.6	18.1	17.7	17.2	16.7	16.3	15.8
46	51	20.9	20.5	20.1	19.7	19.2	18.8	18.4	17.9	17.5	17.0	16.6	16.1	15.6
47	52	20.5	20.1	19.8	19.4	19.0	18.5	18.1	17.7	17.3	16.8	16.4	15.9	15.5
48	53	20.2	19.8	19.4	19.1	18.7	18.3	17.9	17.5	17.0	16.6	16.2	15.7	15.3
49	54	19.8	19.5	19.1	18.8	18.4	18.0	17.6	17.2	16.8	16.4	16.0	15.5	15.1
50	55	19.4	19.1	18.8	18.4	18.1	17.7	17.3	16.9	16.6	16.2	15.8	15.3	14.9
51	56	19.1	18.8	18.4	18.1	17.8	17.4	17.0	16.7	16.3	15.9	15.5	15.1	14.7
52	57	18.7	18.4	18.1	17.8	17.4	17.1	16.8	16.4	16.0	15.7	15.3	14.9	14.5
53	58	18.3	18.0	17.7	17.4	17.1	16.8	16.4	16.1	15.8	15.4	15.1	14.7	14.3
54	59	17.9	17.6	17.3	17.0	16.8	16.4	16.1	15.8	15.5	15.1	14.8	14.4	14.1
55	60	17.5	17.2	16.9	16.7	16.4	16.1	15.8	15.5	15.2	14.9	14.5	14.2	13.9
56	61	17.0	16.8	16.6	16.3	16.0	15.8	15.5	15.2	14.9	14.6	14.3	13.9	13.6
57	62	16.6	16.4	16.2	15.9	15.7	15.4	15.1	14.9	14.6	14.3	14.0	13.7	13.4
58	63	16.2	16.0	15.8	15.5	15.3	15.1	14.8	14.5	14.3	14.0	13.7	13.4	13.1
59	64	15.7	15.5	15.3	15.1	14.9	14.7	14.4	14.2	13.9	13.7	13.4	13.1	12.8
60	65	15.3	15.1	14.9	14.7	14.5	14.3	14.1	13.9	13.6	13.4	13.1	12.8	12.6

TABLE IIA—ANNUITIES FOR JOINT LIFE ONLY—TWO LIVES—EXPECTED RETURN MULTIPLES—Continued

Ages														
	Male	61	62	63	64	65	66	67	68	69	70	71	72	73
Male	Female	66	67	68	69	70	71	72	73	74	75	76	77	78
35	40	16.4	15.8	15.3	14.7	14.2	13.7	13.1	12.6	12.1	11.6	11.1	10.7	10.2
36	41	16.3	15.8	15.2	14.7	14.1	13.6	13.1	12.6	12.1	11.6	11.1	10.6	10.2
37	42	16.2	15.7	15.1	14.6	14.1	13.6	13.0	12.5	12.0	11.5	11.1	10.6	10.1
38	43	16.1	15.6	15.1	14.5	14.0	13.5	13.0	12.5	12.0	11.5	11.0	10.6	10.1
39	44	16.0	15.5	15.0	14.5	13.9	13.4	12.9	12.4	11.9	11.5	11.0	10.5	10.1
40	45	15.9	15.4	14.9	14.4	13.9	13.4	12.9	12.4	11.9	11.4	11.0	10.5	10.0
41	46	15.8	15.3	14.8	14.3	13.8	13.3	12.8	12.3	11.8	11.4	10.9	10.5	10.0
42	47	15.7	15.2	14.7	14.2	13.7	13.2	12.7	12.3	11.8	11.3	10.9	10.4	10.0
43	48	15.6	15.1	14.6	14.1	13.6	13.1	12.7	12.2	11.7	11.3	10.8	10.4	9.9
44	49	15.5	15.0	14.5	14.0	13.5	13.1	12.6	12.1	11.7	11.2	10.8	10.3	9.9
45	50	15.3	14.8	14.4	13.9	13.4	13.0	12.5	12.0	11.6	11.1	10.7	10.3	9.8
46	51	15.2	14.7	14.2	13.8	13.3	12.9	12.4	12.0	11.5	11.1	10.6	10.2	9.8
47	52	15.0	14.6	14.1	13.7	13.2	12.8	12.3	11.9	11.4	11.0	10.6	10.1	9.7
48	53	14.9	14.4	14.0	13.5	13.1	12.6	12.2	11.8	11.3	10.9	10.5	10.1	9.7
49	54	14.7	14.3	13.8	13.4	13.0	12.5	12.1	11.7	11.3	10.8	10.4	10.0	9.6
50	55	14.5	14.1	13.7	13.3	12.8	12.4	12.0	11.6	11.2	10.7	10.3	9.9	9.5
51	56	14.3	13.9	13.5	13.1	12.7	12.3	11.9	11.5	11.1	10.7	10.3	9.9	9.5
52	57	14.1	13.7	13.3	12.9	12.5	12.1	11.7	11.3	10.9	10.6	10.2	9.8	9.4
53	58	13.9	13.6	13.2	12.8	12.4	12.0	11.6	11.2	10.8	10.5	10.1	9.7	9.3
54	59	13.7	13.4	13.0	12.6	12.2	11.9	11.5	11.1	10.7	10.3	10.0	9.6	9.2
55	60	13.5	13.2	12.8	12.4	12.1	11.7	11.3	11.0	10.6	10.2	9.9	9.5	9.1
56	61	13.3	12.9	12.6	12.2	11.9	11.5	11.2	10.8	10.5	10.1	9.8	9.4	9.0
57	62	13.0	12.7	12.4	12.1	11.7	11.4	11.0	10.7	10.3	10.0	9.6	9.3	8.9
58	63	12.8	12.5	12.2	11.9	11.5	11.2	10.9	10.5	10.2	9.8	9.5	9.2	8.8
59	64	12.6	12.3	11.9	11.6	11.3	11.0	10.7	10.4	10.0	9.7	9.4	9.1	8.7
60	65	12.3	12.0	11.7	11.4	11.1	10.8	10.5	10.2	9.9	9.6	9.3	8.9	8.6
61	66	12.0	11.8	11.5	11.2	10.9	10.6	10.3	10.0	9.7	9.4	9.1	8.8	8.5
62	67	11.8	11.5	11.2	11.0	10.7	10.4	10.1	9.8	9.6	9.3	9.0	8.7	8.4
63	68	11.5	11.2	11.0	10.7	10.5	10.2	9.9	9.7	9.4	9.1	8.8	8.5	8.2
64	69	11.2	11.0	10.7	10.5	10.2	10.0	9.7	9.5	9.2	8.9	8.7	8.4	8.1
65	70	10.9	10.7	10.5	10.2	10.0	9.8	9.5	9.3	9.0	8.8	8.5	8.2	8.0
66	71	10.6	10.4	10.2	10.0	9.8	9.5	9.3	9.1	8.8	8.6	8.3	8.1	7.8
67	72	10.3	10.1	9.9	9.7	9.5	9.3	9.1	8.9	8.6	8.4	8.1	7.9	7.7
68	73	10.0	9.8	9.7	9.5	9.3	9.1	8.9	8.6	8.4	8.2	8.0	7.7	7.5
69	74	9.7	9.6	9.4	9.2	9.0	8.8	8.6	8.4	8.2	8.0	7.8	7.6	7.3
70	75	9.4	9.3	9.1	8.9	8.8	8.6	8.4	8.2	8.0	7.8	7.6	7.4	7.2
71	76	9.1	9.0	8.8	8.7	8.5	8.3	8.1	8.0	7.8	7.6	7.4	7.2	7.0
72	77	8.8	8.7	8.5	8.4	8.2	8.1	7.9	7.7	7.6	7.4	7.2	7.0	6.8
73	78	8.5	8.4	8.2	8.1	8.0	7.8	7.7	7.5	7.3	7.2	7.0	6.8	6.7

. . . . .

TABLE III—PERCENT VALUE OF REFUND FEATURE

Ages		Duration of guaranteed amount												
Male	Female	14 years	15 years	16 years	17 years	18 years	19 years	20 years	21 years	22 years	23 years	24 years	25 years	26 years
		Percent	Percent	Percent	Percent	Percent	Percent	Percent	Percent	Percent	Percent	Percent	Percent	Percent
46	51	6	7	7	8	9	9	10	11	12	12	13	14	15
47	52	7	7	8	9	9	10	11	12	12	13	14	15	16
48	53	7	8	8	9	10	11	12	12	13	14	15	16	17
49	54	8	8	9	10	11	11	12	13	14	15	16	17	18
50	55	8	9	10	11	11	12	13	14	15	16	17	18	20
51	56	9	10	10	11	12	13	14	15	16	17	18	20	21
52	57	9	10	11	12	13	14	15	16	17	18	20	21	22
53	58	10	11	12	13	14	15	16	17	19	20	21	22	24
54	59	11	12	13	14	15	16	17	18	20	21	22	24	25
55	60	11	13	14	15	16	17	18	20	21	22	24	25	26
56	61	12	13	15	16	17	18	20	21	22	24	25	27	28
57	62	13	14	16	17	18	20	21	22	24	25	27	28	30
58	63	14	15	17	18	19	21	22	24	25	27	28	30	31
59	64	15	16	18	19	21	22	24	25	27	28	30	31	33
60	65	16	18	19	20	22	24	25	27	28	30	32	33	35
61	66	17	19	20	22	23	25	27	28	30	32	33	35	37
62	67	18	20	22	23	25	27	28	30	32	33	35	37	38
63	68	20	21	23	25	26	28	30	32	33	35	37	39	40
64	69	21	23	24	26	28	30	32	33	35	37	39	41	42
65	70	22	24	26	28	30	32	33	35	37	39	41	42	44
66	71	24	26	28	29	31	33	35	37	39	41	43	44	46
67	72	25	27	29	31	33	35	37	39	41	43	45	46	48
68	73	27	29	31	33	35	37	39	41	43	45	47	48	50
69	74	28	30	33	35	37	39	41	43	45	47	48	50	52
70	75	30	32	34	37	39	41	43	45	47	49	50	52	54
71	76	32	34	36	39	41	43	45	47	49	51	52	54	56
72	77	34	36	38	41	43	45	47	49	51	53	54	56	58
73	78	35	38	40	43	45	47	49	51	53	55	56	58	59
74	79	37	40	42	45	47	49	51	53	55	57	58	60	61
75	80	39	42	44	47	49	51	53	55	57	58	60	62	63
76	81	41	44	46	49	51	53	55	57	59	60	62	63	65
77	82	43	46	48	51	53	55	57	59	61	62	64	65	66
78	83	45	48	50	53	55	57	59	61	62	64	65	67	68
79	84	48	50	53	55	57	59	61	63	64	66	67	68	70
80	85	50	52	55	57	59	61	63	64	66	67	69	70	71
81	86	52	54	57	59	61	63	65	66	68	69	70	72	73
82	87	54	56	59	61	63	65	66	68	69	71	72	73	74
83	88	56	58	61	63	65	66	68	70	71	72	73	74	75
84	89	58	60	63	65	67	68	70	71	73	74	75	76	77
85	90	60	62	65	67	68	70	71	73	74	75	76	77	------

. . . .

§ 1.72-11 Amounts not received as annuity payments

(a) **Introductory.** (1) This section applies to amounts received under a contract to which section 72 applies if either:

(i) Paragraph (b) of § 1.72-2 is inapplicable to such amounts.

(ii) Paragraph (b) of § 1.72-2 is applicable but the annuity payments received differ either in amount, duration, or both, from those originally provided under the contract, or

(iii) Paragraph (b) of § 1.72 is applicable, but such annuity payments are received by a beneficiary after the death of an annuitant (or annuitants) in full discharge of the obligation under the contract and solely because of a guarantee. The payments referred to in subdivision (i) of this subparagraph include all amounts other than "amounts received as an annuity" as that term is defined in paragraph (b) (2) and (3) of § 1.72-2. If such amounts are received as dividends or payments in the nature of dividends, or as a return of premiums, see paragraph (b) of this section. If such amounts are paid in full discharge of the obligation under the contract and are in the nature of a refund of the consideration, see paragraph (c) of this section. If such amounts are paid upon the surrender, redemption, or maturity of the contract, see paragraph (d) of this section. The payments referred to in subdivision (ii) of this subparagraph include all annuity payments which are paid as the result of a modification or an exchange of the annuity obligations originally provided under a contract for different annuity obligations (whether or not such modification or exchange is accompanied by the payment of an amount to which subdivision (i) of this subparagraph applies). If the duration of the new annuity obligations differs from the duration of the old annuity obligations, paragraph (e) of this section applies to the new annuity obligations and paragraph (d) of this section applies to any lump sum payment received. If, however, the duration of the new annuity obligations is the same as the duration of the old obligations, paragraph (f) of this section applies to the new obligations and to any lump sum received in connection therewith. The annuity payments referred to in subdivision (iii) of this subparagraph are annuity payments which are made to a beneficiary after the death of annuitant (or annuitants) in full discharge of the obligations under a contract because of a provision in the contract requiring the payment of a guaranteed amount or minimum number of payments for a fixed period; see paragraph (c) of this section.

(2) The principles of this section apply, to the extent appropriate thereto, to amounts paid which are taxable under section 72 (except, for taxable years beginning before January 1, 1964, section 72(e) (3)) in accordance with sections 402 and 403 and the regulations thereunder. However, if contributions used to purchase the contract include amounts for which a deduction was allowed under section 404 as contributions on behalf of an owner-employee, the rules of this section are modified by the rules of paragraph (b) of § 1.72-17. Further, in applying the provisions of this section, the aggregate premiums or other consideration paid shall not include contributions on behalf of self-employed individuals to the extent that deductions were allowed under section 404 for such contributions. Nor, shall the aggregate of premiums or other consideration paid include amounts used to purchase life, accident, health, or other insurance protection for an owner-employee. See paragraph (b) (4) of § 1.72-16 and paragraph (c) of § 1.72-17. The principles of this section also apply to payments made in the manner described in paragraph (b) (3) (i) of § 1.72-2.

(b) **Amounts received in the nature of dividends or similar distributions.** (1) If dividends (or payments in the nature of dividends or a return of premiums or other consideration) are received under a contract to which section 72 applies and such payments are received before the annuity starting date or before the date on which an amount is first received as an annuity, whichever is the later, such payments are includible in the gross income of the recipient only to the extent that they, taken together with all previous payments received under the contract which were excludable from the gross income of the recipient under the applicable income tax law, exceed the aggregate of premiums or other consideration paid or deemed to have been paid by the recipient. Such payments shall also be subtracted from the consideration paid (or deemed paid) both for the purpose of determining an exclusion ratio to be applied to subsequent amounts paid as an annuity and for the purpose of determining the applicability of section 72(d) and § 1.72–13. relating to employee contributions recoverable in three years.

(2) If dividends or payments in the nature of dividends are paid under a contract to which section 72 applies and such payments are received on or after the annuity starting date or the date on which an amount is first received as an annuity, whichever is later, such payments shall be fully includible in the gross income of the recipient. The receipt of such payments shall not affect the aggregate of premiums or other consideration paid nor the amounts contributed or deemed to have been contributed by an employee as otherwise calculated for purposes of section 72. Since the investment in the contract and the expected return are not affected by a payment which is fully includible in the gross income of the recipient under this rule, the exclusion ratio will not be affected by such payment and will continue to be applied to amounts received as annuity payments in the future as though such payment had not been made. This subparagraph shall apply to amounts received under a contract described in paragraph (b) (3) (i) of § 1.72–2 to the extent that the amounts received exceed the portion of the investment in the contract allocable to each taxable year in accordance with paragraph (d) (3) of § 1.72–4. Hence, such excess is fully includible in the gross income of the recipient.

(c) Amounts received in the nature of a refund of the consideration under a contract and in full discharge of the obligation thereof. (1) Any amount received under a contract to which section 72 applies, if it is at least in part a refund of the consideration paid, including amounts payable to a beneficiary after the death of an annuitant by reason of a provision in the contract for a life annuity with minimum period of payments certain or with a minimum amount which must be paid in any

event, shall be considered an amount received in the nature of a refund of the consideration paid for such contract. If such an amount is in full discharge of an obligation to pay a fixed amount (whether in a lump sum or otherwise) or to pay amounts for a fixed number of years (including amounts described in paragraph (b) (3) (i) of § 1.72–2), it shall be included in the gross income of the recipient only to the extent that it, when added to amounts previously received under the contract which were excludable from gross income under the law applicable at the time of receipt, exceeds the aggregate of premiums or other consideration paid. See section 72(e) (2) (A). This paragraph shall not apply if the total of the amounts to be paid in discharge of the obligation can in any event exceed the total of the annuity payments which would otherwise fully discharge the obligation. For rules to be applied in such a case, see paragraph (e) of this section.

(2) The principles of subparagraph (1) of this paragraph may be illustrated by the following examples:

Example (1). A, a male employee, retired on December 31, 1954, at the age of 60. A life annuity of $75 per month was payable to him beginning January 31, 1955. The annuity contract guaranteed that if A did not live at least ten years, his beneficiary, B, would receive the monthly payments for any balance of the first ten years after A's retirement which remained at the date of A's death. Under section 72, A was deemed to have paid $3,600 toward the cost of the annuity. A lived for five years, receiving a total of $4,500 in annuity payments. After A's death, B began receiving the monthly payments of $75 beginning with the January 31, 1960, payment. B will exclude such payments from his gross income throughout 1960, 1961, and 1962, and will exclude only $18 of the first payment in 1963 from his gross income for that year. Thereafter, B will include the entire amount of all such payments in his gross income for the taxable year of receipt. This result is determined as follows:

A's investment in the contract (unadjusted)	$3,600
Multiple from Table III of § 1.72–9 for male, age 60, where duration of guaranteed amount is 10 years (percent)	11
Subtract value of the refund feature to the nearest dollar (11 percent of $3,600)	396
Investment in the contract adjusted for the present value of the refund feature without discount for interest	$3,204

Aggregate of premiums or other consideration paid 3,600
A's exclusion ratio ($3,204 +
$16,380 [$900 × 18.2]) (percent) 19.6

Subtract amount excludable during five
years A received payments (19.6 percent of $4,500 [$900 × 5]) $882

Remainder of aggregate of premiums or
other consideration paid excludable from
gross income of B under section 72 (e) 2,718

As a result of the above computation, the number of payments to B which will exhaust the
remainder of consideration paid which is excludable from gross income of the recipient is
36⅖ ($2,718 ÷ $75) and B will exclude the payments from his gross income for three years,
then exclude only $18 of the first payment for
the fourth year from his gross income, and
thereafter include the entire amount of all payments he receives in his gross income.

Example (2). The facts are the same as in
example (1), except that B, the beneficiary,
elects to receive $50 per month for his life
in lieu of the payments guaranteed under the
original contractual obligation. Since such
amounts will be received as an annuity and
may, because of the length of time B may live,
exceed the amount guaranteed, they are not
amounts to which this paragraph applies. See
paragraph (e) of this section.

Example (3). The facts are the same as in
example (1), except that B, the beneficiary,
elects to receive the remaining guaranteed
amount in installments which are larger or
smaller than the $75 per month provided until,
under the terms of the contract, the guaranteed
amount is exhausted. The rule of subparagraph
(1) of this paragraph and the computation illustrated in example (1) apply to such installments
since the total of such installments will not exceed the original amount guaranteed to be paid
at A's death in any event.

Example (4). C pays $12,000 for a contract
providing that he is to be paid an annuity of
$1,000 per year for 15 years. His exclusion ratio
is therefore 80 percent ($12,000 ÷ $15,000). He
directs that the annuity is to be paid to D, his
beneficiary, if he should die before the full 15
year period has expired. C dies after 5 years
and D is paid $1,000 in 1960. D will include $200
($1,000 — $800 [80 percent of $1,000]) in his
gross income for the taxable year in which he
receives the $1,000 since section 72(e) and this
section do not apply to the annuity payments
made in accordance with the provisions and
during the term of the contract. D will continue with the same exclusion ratio used by C
(80 percent).

Example (5). In 1954, E paid $50,000 into a
fund and was promised an annual income for
life the amount of which would depend in part
upon the earnings realized from the investment
of the fund in accordance with an agreed formula. The contract also specified that if E should
die before ten years had elapsed, his beneficiary,
F, would be paid the amounts determined annually under the formula until ten payments
had been realized by E and F together. E died
in 1960, having received five payments totalling
$30,000. Assuming that $22,000 of this amount
was properly excludable from E's gross income
prior to his death, F will exclude from his gross
income the payments he receives until the tax-

able year in which his total receipts from the
fund exceeds $28,000 ($50,000 — $22,000). F will
include any excess over the $28,000 in his gross
income for that taxable year. Thereafter, F
will include in his gross income the entire
amount of any payments made to him from the
fund.

(3) For the purpose of applying the
rule contained in subparagraph (1) of
this paragraph, it is immaterial whether
the recipient of the amount received in
full discharge of the obligation is the
same person as the recipient of amounts
previously received under the contract
which were excludable from gross income, except in the case of a contract
transferred for a valuable consideration, with respect to which see paragraph (a) of § 1.72–10. For the limit
on the tax, for taxable years beginning
before January 1, 1964, attributable to
the receipt of a lump sum to which this
paragraph applies, see paragraph (g) of
this section.

. . . . .

§ 1.73–1 Services of child

(a) Compensation for personal services of a child shall, regardless of the
provisions of State law relating to who
is entitled to the earnings of the child,
and regardless of whether the income
is in fact received by the child, be
deemed to be the gross income of the
child and not the gross income of the
parent of the child. Such compensation, therefore, shall be included in
the gross income of the child and shall
be reflected in the return rendered by
or for such child. The income of a
minor child is not required to be included in the gross income of the parent for income tax purposes. For requirements for making the return by
such child, or for such child by his
guardian, or other person charged
with the care of his person or property,
see section 6012.

(b) In the determination of taxable
income or adjusted gross income, as
the case may be, all expenditures made
by the parent or the child attributable
to amounts which are includible in
the gross income of the child and not
of the parent solely by reason of section
73 are deemed to have been paid or incurred by the child. In such determination, the child is entitled to take
deductions not only for expenditures
made on his behalf by his parent which

would be commonly considered as business expenses, but also for other expenditures such as charitable contributions made by the parent in the name of the child and out of the child's earnings.

. . . . .

§ 1.74-1   Prizes and awards

(a) **Inclusion in gross income.**

(1) Section 74(a) requires the inclusion in gross income of all amounts received as prizes and awards, unless such prizes or awards qualify as an exclusion from gross income under subsection (b), or unless such prize or award is a scholarship or fellowship grant excluded from gross income by section 117. Prizes and awards which are includible in gross income include (but are not limited to) amounts received from radio and television giveaway shows, door prizes, and awards in contests of all types, as well as any prizes and awards from an employer to an employee in recognition of some achievement in connection with his employment.

(2) If the prize or award is not made in money but is made in goods or services, the fair market value of the goods or services is the amount to be included in income.

(b) **Exclusion from gross income.** Section 74(b) provides an exclusion from gross income of any amount received as a prize or award, if (1) such prize or award was made primarily in recognition of past achievements of the recipient in religious, charitable, scientific, educational, artistic, literary, or civic fields; (2) the recipient was selected without any action on his part to enter the contest or proceedings; and (3) the recipient is not required to render substantial future services as a condition to receiving the prize or award. Thus, such awards as the Nobel prize and the Pulitzer prize would qualify for the exclusion. Section 74 (b) does not exclude prizes or awards from an employer to an employee in recognition of some achievement in connection with his employment.

(c) **Scholarships and fellowship grants.** See section 117 and the regulations thereunder for provisions relating to scholarships and fellowship grants.

§ 1.82-1   Payments for or reimbursements of expenses of moving from one residence to another residence attributable to employment or self-employment

(a) **Reimbursements in gross income —(1) In general.** Any amount received or accrued, directly or indirectly, by an individual as a payment for or reimbursement of expenses of moving from one residence to another residence attributable to employment or self-employment is includible in gross income under section 82 as compensation for services in the taxable year received or accrued. For rules relating to the year a deduction may be allowed for expenses of moving from one residence to another residence, see section 217 and the regulations thereunder.

(2) **Amounts received or accrued as reimbursement or payment.** For purposes of this section, amounts are considered as being received or accrued by an individual as reimbursement or payment whether received in the form of money, property, or services. A cash basis taxpayer will include amounts in gross income under section 82 when they are received or treated as received by him. Thus, for example, if an employer moves an employee's household goods and personal effects from the employee's old residence to his new residence using the employer's facilities, the employee is considered as having received a payment in the amount of the fair market value of the services furnished at the time the services are furnished by the employer. If the employer pays a mover for moving the employee's household goods and personal effects, the employee is considered as having received the payment at the time the employer pays the mover, rather than at the time the mover moves the employee's household goods and personal effects. Where an employee receives a loan or advance from an employer to enable him to pay his moving expenses, the employee will not be deemed to have received a reimbursement of moving expenses until such time as he accounts to his employer if he is not required to repay such loan or advance and if he makes such accounting within a reasonable time. Such loan or advance will be deemed to be a reimbursement of moving expenses at the time of

such accounting to the extent used by the employee for such moving expenses.

(3) Direct or indirect payments or reimbursements. For purposes of this section amounts are considered as being received or accrued whether received directly (paid or provided to an individual by an employer, a client, a customer, or similar person) or indirectly (paid to a third party on behalf of an individual by an employer, a client, a customer, or similar person). Thus, if an employer pays a mover for the expenses of moving an employee's household goods and personal effects from one residence to another residence, the employee has indirectly received a payment which is includible in his gross income under section 82.

(4) Expenses of moving from one residence to another residence. An expense of moving from one residence to another residence is any expenditure, cost, loss, or similar item paid or incurred in connection with a move from one residence to another residence. Moving expenses include (but are not limited to) any expenditure, cost, loss, or similar item directly or indirectly resulting from the acquisition, sale, or exchange of property, the transportation of goods or property, or travel (by the taxpayer or any other person) in connection with a change in residence. Such expenses include items described in section 217(b) (relating to the definition of moving expenses), irrespective of the dollar limitations contained in section 217(b) (3) and the conditions contained in section 217(c), as well as items not described in section 217(b), such as a loss sustained on the sale or exchange of personal property, storage charges, taxes, or expenses of refitting rugs or draperies.

(5) Attributable to employment or self-employment. Any amount received or accrued from an employer, a client, a customer, or similar person in connection with the performance of services for such employer, client, customer, or similar person, is attributable to employment or self-employment. Thus, for example, if an employer reimburses an employee for a loss incurred on the sale of the employee's house, reimbursement is attributable to the performance of services if made because of the employer-employee relationship. Similarly, if an employer in order to prevent an employee's sustaining a loss on a sale of a house acquires the property from the employee at a price in excess of fair market value, the employee is considered to have received a payment attributable to employment to the extent that such payment exceeds the fair market value of the property.

. . . .

§ 1.83–1 Property transferred in connection with the performance of services

(a) Inclusion in gross income—(1) General rule. Section 83 provides rules for the taxation of property transferred to an employee or independent contractor (or beneficiary thereof) in connection with the performance of services by such employee or independent contractor. In general, such property is not taxable under section 83(a) until it has been transferred (as defined in § 1.83–3(a)) to such person and become substantially vested (as defined in § 1.83–3(b)) in such person. In that case, the excess of—

(i) The fair market value of such property (determined without regard to any lapse restriction, as defined in § 1.83–3(i)) at the time that the property becomes substantially vested, over

(ii) The amount (if any) paid for such property,

shall be included as compensation in the gross income of such employee or independent contractor for the taxable year in which the property becomes substantially vested. Until such property becomes substantially vested, the transferor shall be regarded as the owner of such property, and any income from such property received by the employee or independent contractor (or beneficiary thereof) or the right to the use of such property by the employee or independent contractor constitutes additional compensation and shall be included in the gross income of such employee or independent contractor for the taxable year in which such income is received or such use is made available. This paragraph applies to a transfer of property in connection with the performance of services even though the transferor is not the person for whom such services are performed.

(2) Life insurance. The cost of life insurance protection under a life insurance contract, retirement income contract, endowment contract, or other contract providing life insurance protection is taxable generally under section 61 and the regulations thereunder during the period such contract remains substantially nonvested (as defined in § 1.83–3(b)). The cost of such life insurance protection is the reasonable net premium cost, as determined by the Commissioner, of the current life insurance protection (as defined in § 1.72–16(b)(3)) provided by such contract.

. . . .

(b) Subsequent sale, forfeiture, or other disposition of nonvested property. (1) If substantially nonvested property (that has been transferred in connection with the performance of services) is subsequently sold or otherwise disposed of to a third party in an arm's length transaction while still substantially nonvested, the person who performed such services shall realize compensation in an amount equal to the excess of—

(i) The amount realized on such sale or other disposition, over

(ii) The amount (if any) paid for such property.

Such amount of compensation is includible in his gross income in accordance with his method of accounting. Two preceding sentences also apply when the person disposing of the property has received it in a non-arm's length transaction described in paragraph (c) of this section. In addition, section 83 (a) and paragraph (a) of this section shall thereafter cease to apply with respect to such property.

(2) If substantially nonvested property that has been transferred in connection with the performance of services to the person performing such services is forfeited while still substantially nonvested and held by such person, the difference between the amount paid (if any) and the amount received upon forfeiture (if any) shall be treated as an ordinary gain or loss. This paragraph (b)(2) does not apply to property to which § 1.83–2(a) applies.

(3) This paragraph (b) shall not apply to, and no gain shall be recognized on, any sale, forfeiture, or other disposition described in this paragraph to the extent that any property received in exchange therefor is substantially nonvested. Instead, section 83 and this section shall apply with respect to such property received (as if it were substituted for the property disposed of).

(c) Dispositions of nonvested property not at arm's length. If substantially nonvested property (that has been transferred in connection with the performance of services) is disposed of in a transaction which is not at arm's length and the property remains substantially nonvested, the person who performed such services realizes compensation equal in amount to the sum of any money and the fair market value of any substantially vested property received in such disposition. Such amount of compensation is includible in his gross income in accordance with his method of accounting. However, such amount of compensation shall not exceed the fair market value of the property disposed of at the time of disposition (determined without regard to any lapse restriction), reduced by the amount paid for such property. In addition, section 83 and these regulations shall continue to apply with respect to such property, except that any amount previously includible in gross income under this paragraph (c) shall thereafter be treated as an amount paid for such property. For example, if in 1971 an employee pays $50 for a share of stock which has a fair market value of $100 and is substantially nonvested at that time and later in 1971 (at a time when the property still has a fair market value of $100 and is still substantially nonvested) the employee disposes of, in a transaction not at arm's length, the share of stock to his wife for $10, the employee realizes compensation of $10 in 1971. If in 1972, when the share of stock has a fair market value of $120, it becomes substantially vested, the employee realizes additional compensation in 1972 in the amount of $60 (the $120 fair market value of the stock less both the $50 price paid for the stock and the $10 taxed as compensation in 1971). For purposes of this paragraph, if substantially nonvested property has been transferred to a person other than the person who performed the services, and the transferee dies holding the property while the property is still substantially nonvested and while the person who performed the services is alive, the transfer which results by reason of the death of such transferee is a transfer not at arm's length.

. . . .

(e) Forfeiture after substantial vesting. If a person is taxable under section 83(a) when the property transferred becomes substantially vested and thereafter the person's beneficial interest in such property is nevertheless forfeited pursuant to a lapse restriction, any loss incurred by such person (but not by a beneficiary of such person) upon such forfeiture shall be an ordinary loss to the extent the basis in such property has been increased as a result of the recognition of income by such person under section 83(a) with respect to such property.

(f) Examples. The provisions of this section may be illustrated by the following examples:

Example (1). On November 1, 1978, X corporation sells to E, an employee, 100 shares of X corporation stock at $10 per share. At the time of such sale the fair market value of the X corporation stock is $100 per share. Under the terms of the sale each share of stock is subject to a substantial risk of forfeiture which will not lapse until November 1, 1988. Evidence of this restriction is stamped on the face of E's stock certificates, which are therefore nontransferable (within the meaning of § 1.83-3(d)). Since in 1978 E's stock is substantially nonvested, E does not include any of such amount in his gross income as compensation in 1978. On November 1, 1988, the fair market value of the X corporation stock is $250 per share. Since the X corporation stock becomes substantially vested in 1988, E must include $24,000 (100 shares of X corporation stock × $250 fair market value per share less $10 price paid by E for each share) as compensation for 1988. Dividends paid by X to E on E's stock after it was transferred to E on November 1, 1978, are taxable to E as additional compensation during the period E's stock is substantially nonvested and are deductible as such by X.

Example (2). Assume the facts are the same as in example (1), except that on November 1, 1985, each share of stock of X corporation in E's hands could as a matter of law be transferred to a bona fide purchaser who would not be required to forfeit the stock if the risk of forfeiture materialized. In the event, however, that the risk materializes, E would be liable in damages to X. On November 1, 1985, the fair market value of the X corporation stock is $230

per share. Since E's stock is transferable within the meaning of § 1.83-3(d) in 1985, the stock is substantially vested and E must include $22,000 (100 shares of X corporation stock × $230 fair market value per share less $10 price paid by E for each share) as compensation for 1985.

Example (3). Assume the facts are the same as in example (1) except that, in 1984 E sells his 100 shares of X corporation stock in an arm's length sale to I, an investment company, for $120 per share. At the time of this sale each share of X corporation's stock has a fair market value of $200. Under paragraph (b) of this section, E must include $11,000 (100 shares of X corporation stock × $120 amount realized per share less $10 price paid by E per share) as compensation for 1984 notwithstanding that the stock remains nontransferable and is still subject to a substantial risk of forfeiture at the time of such sale. Under § 1.83-4(b)(2), I's basis in the X corporation stock is $120 per share.

§ 1.83–2 Election to include in gross income in year of transfer

(a) In general. If property is transferred (within the meaning of § 1.83-3 (a)) in connection with the performance of services, the person performing such services may elect to include in gross income under section 83(b) the excess (if any) of the fair market value of the property at the time of transfer (determined without regard to any lapse restriction, as defined in § 1.83–3(i)) over the amount (if any) paid for such property, as compensation for services. The fact that the transferee has paid full value for the property transferred, realizing no bargain element in the transaction, does not preclude the use of the election as provided for in this section. If this election is made, the substantial vesting rules of section 83(a) and the regulations thereunder do not apply with respect to such property, and except as otherwise provided in section 83(d)(2) and the regulations thereunder (relating to the cancellation of a nonlapse restriction), any subsequent appreciation in the value of the property is not taxable as compensation to the person who performed the services. Thus, property with respect to which this election is made shall be includible in gross income as of the time of transfer, even though such property is substantially nonvested (as defined in § 1.83–3(b)) at the time of transfer, and no compensation will be includible in gross income when such property becomes substantially vested (as defined in § 1.83–3(b)). In computing the gain or loss from the subsequent sale or exchange of such property, its basis shall be the amount paid for the property increased by the amount included in gross income under section 83(b). If property for which a section 83(b) election is in effect is forfeited while substantially nonvested, such forfeiture shall be treated as a sale or exchange upon which there is realized a loss equal to the excess (if any) of—

(1) The amount paid (if any) for such property, over,

(2) The amount realized (if any) upon such forfeiture.

If such property is a capital asset in the hands of the taxpayer, such loss shall be a capital loss. A sale or other disposition of the property that is in substance a forfeiture, or is made in contemplation of a forfeiture, shall be treated as a forfeiture under the two immediately preceding sentences.

(b) Time for making election. Except as provided in the following sentence, the election referred to in paragraph (a) of this section shall be filed not later than 30 days after the date the property was transferred (or, if later, January 29, 1970) and may be filed prior to the date of transfer. Any statement filed before February 15, 1970, which was amended not later than February 16, 1970, in order to make it conform to the requirements of paragraph (e) of this section, shall be deemed a proper election under section 83(b).

(c) Manner of making election. The election referred to in paragraph (a) of this section is made by filing one copy of a written statement with the internal revenue office with whom the person who performed the services files his return. In addition, one copy of such statement shall be submitted with this income tax return for the taxable year in which such property was transferred.

. . . . .

(f) Revocability of election. An election under section 83(b) may not be revoked except with the consent of the Commissioner. Consent will be granted only in the case where the transferee is under a mistake of fact as to the underlying transaction and must be requested within 60 days of the date on which the mistake of fact first became known to the person who made the election. In any event, a mistake as to the value, or decline in the value, of the property with respect to which an election under section 83(b) has been made or a failure to perform an act contemplated at the time of transfer of such property does not constitute a mistake of fact.

§ 1.83–3   Meaning and use of certain terms

(a) Transfer—(1) In general. For purposes of section 83 and the regulations thereunder, a transfer of property occurs when a person acquires a beneficial ownership interest in such property (disregarding any lapse restriction, as defined in § 1.83–3(i)).

(2) Option. The grant of an option to purchase certain property does not constitute a transfer of such property. However, see § 1.83–7 for the extent to which the grant of the option itself is subject to section 83. In addition, if the amount paid for the transfer of property is an indebtedness secured by the transferred property, on which there is no personal liability to pay all or a substantial part of such indebtedness, such transaction may be in substance the same as the grant of an option. The determination of the substance of the transaction shall be based upon all the facts and circumstances. The factors to be taken into account include the type of property involved, the extent to which the risk that the property will decline in value has been transferred, and the likelihood that the purchase price will, in fact, be paid. See also § 1.83–4(c) for the treatment of forgiveness of indebtedness that has constituted an amount paid.

(3) Requirement that property be returned. Similarly, no transfer may have occurred where property is transferred under conditions that require its return upon the happening of an event that is certain to occur, such as the termination of employment. In such a case, whether there is, in fact, a transfer depends upon all the facts and circumstances. Factors which indicate that no transfer has occurred are described in paragraph (a)(4), (5), and (6) of this section.

(4) Similarity to option. An indication that no transfer has occurred is the extent to which the conditions relating to a transfer are similar to an option.

(5) Relationship to fair market value. An indication that no transfer has occurred is the extent to which the consideration to be paid the transferee upon surrendering the property does not approach the fair market value of the property at the time of surrender. For purposes of paragraph (a)(5) and (6) of this section, fair market value includes fair market value determined under the rules of § 1.83-5(a)(1), relating to the valuation of property subject to nonlapse restrictions. Therefore, the existence of a nonlapse restriction referred to in § 1.83-5(a)(1) is not a factor indicating no transfer has occurred.

(6) Risk of loss. An indication that no transfer has occurred is the extent to which the transferee does not incur the risk of a beneficial owner that the value of the property at the time of transfer will decline substantially. Therefore, for purposes of this (6), risk of decline in property value is not limited to the risk that any amount paid for the property may be lost.

(7) Examples. The provisions of this paragraph may be illustrated by the following examples:

Example (1). On January 3, 1971, X corporation sells for $500 to S, a salesman of X, 10 shares of stock in X corporation with a fair market value of $1,000. The stock is nontransferable and subject to return to the corporation (for $500) if S's sales do not reach a certain level by December 31, 1971. Disregarding the restriction concerning S's sales (since the restriction is a lapse restriction), S's interest in the stock is that of a beneficial owner and therefore a transfer occurs on January 3, 1971.

Example (2). On November 17, 1972, W sells to E 100 shares of stock in W corporation with a fair market value of $10,000 in exchange for a $10,000 note without personal liability. The note requires E to make yearly payments of $2,000 commencing in 1973. E collects the dividends, votes the stock and pays the interest on the note. However, he makes no payments toward the face amount of the note. Because E has no personal liability on the note, and since E is making no payments towards the face amount of the note, the likelihood of E paying the full purchase price is in substantial doubt. As a result E has not incurred the risks of a beneficial owner that the value of the stock will decline. Therefore, no transfer of the stock has occurred on November 17, 1972, but an option to purchase the stock has been granted to E.

Example (3). On January 3, 1971, X corporation purports to transfer to E, an employee, 100 shares of stock in X corporation. The X stock is subject to the sole restriction that E must sell such stock to X on termination of employment for any reason for an amount which is equal to the excess (if any) of the book value of the X stock at termination of employment over book value on January 3, 1971. The stock is not transferable by E and the restrictions on transfer are stamped on the certificate. Under these facts and circumstances, there is no transfer of the X stock within the meaning of section 83.

Example (4). Assume the same facts as in example (3) except that E paid $3,000 for the stock and that the restriction required E upon termination of employment to sell the stock to M for the total amount of dividends that have been declared on the stock since September 2, 1971, or $3,000 whichever is higher. Again, under the facts and circumstances, no transfer of the X stock has occurred.

Example (5). On July 4, 1971, X corporation purports to transfer to G, an employee, 100 shares of X stock. The stock is subject to the sole restriction that upon termination of employment G must sell the stock to X for the greater of its fair market value at such time or $100, the amount G paid for the stock. On July 4, 1971 the X stock has a fair market value of $100. Therefore, G does not incur the risk of a beneficial owner that the value of the stock at the time of transfer ($100) will decline substantially. Under these facts and circumstances, no transfer has occurred.

(b) Substantially vested and substantially nonvested property. For purposes of section 83 and the regulations thereunder, property is substantially nonvested when it is subject to a substantial risk of forfeiture, within the meaning of paragraph (c) of this section, and is nontransferable, within the meaning of paragraph (d) of this section. Property is substantially vested for such purposes when it is either transferable or not subject to a substantial risk of forfeiture.

(c) Substantial risk of forfeiture—(1) In general. For purposes of section 83 and the regulations thereunder, whether a risk of forfeiture is substantial or not depends upon the facts and circumstances. A substantial risk of forfeiture exists where rights in property that are transferred are conditioned, directly or indirectly, upon the future performance (or refraining from performance) of substantial services by any person, or the occurrence of a condition related to a purpose of the transfer, and the possibility of forfeiture is substantial if such condition is not satisfied.

Property is not transferred subject to a substantial risk of forfeiture to the extent that the employer is required to pay the fair market value of a portion of such property to the employee upon the return of such property. The risk that the value of property will decline during a certain period of time does not constitute a substantial risk of forfeiture. A nonlapse restriction, standing by itself, will not result in a substantial risk of forfeiture.

(2) Illustrations of substantial risks of forfeiture. The regularity of the performance of services and the time spent in performing such services tend to indicate whether services required by a condition are substantial. The fact that the person performing services has the right to decline to perform such services without forfeiture may tend to establish that services are insubstantial. Where stock is transferred to an underwriter prior to a public offering and the full enjoyment of such stock is expressly or impliedly conditioned upon the successful completion of the underwriting, the stock is subject to a substantial risk of forfeiture. Where an employee receives property from an employer subject to a requirement that it be returned if the total earnings of the employer do not increase, such property is subject to a substantial risk of forfeiture. On the other hand, requirements that the property be returned to the employer if the employee is discharged for cause or for committing a crime will not be considered to result in a substantial risk of forfeiture. An enforceable requirement that the property be returned to the employer if the employee accepts a job with a competing firm will not ordinarily be considered to result in a substantial risk of forfeiture unless the particular facts and circumstances indicate to the contrary. Factors which may be taken into account in determining whether a covenant not to compete constitutes a substantial risk of forfeiture are the age of the employee, the availability of alternative employment opportunities, the likelihood of the employee's obtaining such other employment, the degree of skill possessed by the employee, the employee's health, and the practice (if any) of the employer to enforce such covenants. Similarly, rights in property transferred to a retiring employee subject to the sole requirement that it be returned unless he renders consulting services upon the request of his former employer will not be considered subject to a substantial risk of forfeiture unless he is in fact expected to perform substantial services.

(3) Enforcement of forfeiture condition. In determining whether the possibility of forfeiture is substantial in the case of rights in property transferred to an employee of a corporation who owns a significant amount of the total combined voting power or value of all classes of stock of the employer corporation or of its parent corporation, there will be taken into account (i) the employee's relationship to other stockholders and the extent of their control, potential control and possible loss of control of the corporation, (ii) the position of the employee in the corporation and the extent to which he is subordinate to other employees, (iii) the employee's relationship to the officers and directors of the corporation, (iv) the person or persons who must approve the employee's discharge, and (v) past actions of the employer in enforcing the provisions of the restrictions. For example, if an employee would be considered as having received rights in property subject to a substantial risk of forfeiture, but for the fact that the employee owns 20 percent of the single class of stock in the transferor corporation, and if the remaining 80 percent of the class of stock is owned by an unrelated individual (or members of such an individual's family) so that the possibility of the corporation enforcing a restriction on such rights is substantial, then such rights are subject to a substantial risk of forfeiture. On the other hand, if 4 percent of the voting power of all the stock of a corporation is owned by the president of such corporation and the remaining stock is so diversely held by the public that the president, in effect, controls the corporation, then the possibility of the corporation enforcing a restriction on rights in property transferred to the president is not substantial, and such rights are not subject to a substantial risk of forfeiture.

(4) Examples. The rules contained in paragraph (c)(1) of this section may be illustrated by the following examples. In each example it is assumed that, if the conditions on transfer are not satisfied, the forfeiture provision will be enforced.

Example (1). On November 1, 1971, corporation X transfers in connection with the performance of services to E, an employee, 100 shares of corporation X stock for $90 per share. Under the terms of the transfer, E will be subject to a binding commitment to resell the stock to corporation X at $90 per share if he leaves the employment of corporation X for any reason prior to the expiration of a 2-year period from the date of such transfer. Since E must perform substantial services for corporation X and will not be paid more than $90 for the stock, regardless of its value, if he fails to perform such services during such 2-year period, E's rights in the stock are subject to a substantial risk of forfeiture during such period.

Example (2). On November 10, 1971, corporation X transfers in connection with the performance of services to a trust for the benefit of employees, $100x. Under the terms of the trust any child of an employee who is an enrolled full-time student at an accredited educational institution as a candidate for a degree will receive an annual grant of cash for each academic year the student completes as a student in good standing, up to a maximum of four years. E, an employee, has a child who is enrolled as a full-time student at an accredited college as a candidate for a degree. Therefore, E has a beneficial interest in the assets of the trust equalling the value of four cash grants. Since E's child must complete one year of college in order to receive a cash grant, E's interest in the trust assets are subject to a substantial risk of forfeiture to the extent E's child has not become entitled to any grants.

Example (3). On November 25, 1971, corporation X gives to E, an employee, in connection with his performance of services to corporation X, a bonus of 100 shares of corporation X stock. Under the terms of the bonus arrangement E is obligated to return the corporation X stock to corporation X if he terminates his employment for any reason. However, for each year occurring after November 25, 1971, during which E remains employed with corporation X, E ceases to be obligated to return 10 shares of the corporation X stock. Since in each year occurring after November 25, 1971, for which E remains employed he is not required to return 10 shares of corporation X's stock, E's rights in 10 shares each year for 10 years cease to be subject to a substantial risk of forfeiture for each year he remains so employed.

Example (4). (a) Assume the same facts as in example (3) except that for each year occurring after November 25, 1971, for which E remains employed with corporation X, X agrees to pay, in redemption of the bonus shares given to E if he terminates employment for any reason, 10 percent of the fair market value of each share of stock on the date of such termination of employment. Since corporation X will pay E 10 percent of the value of his bonus stock for each of the 10 years after November 25, 1971, in which he remains employed by X, and the risk of a decline in value is not a substantial risk of forfeiture, E's interest in 10 percent of such bonus stock becomes substantially vested in each of those years.

(b) The following chart illustrates the fair market value of the bonus stock and the fair market value of the portion of bonus stock that becomes substantially vested on November 25, for the following years:

Year	Fair market value of	
	All stock	Portion of stock that becomes vested
1972	$200	$20
1973	300	30
1974	150	15
1975	150	15
1976	100	10

If E terminates his employment on July 1, 1977, when the fair market value of the bonus stock is $100, E must return the bonus stock to X, and X must pay, in redemption of the bonus stock, $50 (50 percent of the value of the bonus stock on the date of termination of employment). E has recognized income under section 83(a) and § 1.83-1(a) with respect to 50 percent of the bonus stock, and E's basis in that portion of the stock equals the amount of income recognized, $90. Under § 1.83-1(e), the $40 loss E incurred upon forfeiture ($90 basis less $50 redemption payment) is an ordinary loss.

Example (5). On January 7, 1971, corporation X, a computer service company, transfers to E, 100 shares of corporation X stock for $50. E is a highly compensated salesman who sold X's products in a three-state area since 1960. At the time of transfer each share of X stock has a fair market value of $100. The stock is transferred to E in connection with his termination of employment with X. Each share of X stock is subject to the sole condition that E can keep such share only if he does not engage in competition with X for a 5-year period in the three-state area where E had previously sold X's products. E, who is 45 years old, has no intention of retiring from the work force. In order to earn a salary comparable to his current compensation, while preventing the risk of forfeiture from arising, E will have to expend a substantial amount of time and effort in another industry or market to establish the necessary business contacts. Thus, under these facts and circumstances E's rights in the stock are subject to a substantial risk of forfeiture.

(d) Transferability of property. For purposes of section 83 and the regulations thereunder, the rights of a person in property are transferable if such person can transfer any interest in the property to any person other than the transferor of the property, but only if the rights in such property of such transferee are not subject to a substantial risk of forfeiture. Accordingly, property is transferable if the person performing the services or receiving the property can sell, assign, or pledge (as collateral for a loan, or as security for the performance of an obligation, or for any other purpose) his interest in the property to any person other than the transferor of such property and if the transferee is not required to give up the property or its value in the event the substantial risk of forfeiture materializes. On the other hand, property is not considered to be transferable merely because the person performing the services or receiving the property may designate a beneficiary to receive the property in the event of his death.

(e) Property. For purposes of section 83 and the regulations thereunder, the term "property" includes real and personal property other than money or an unfunded and unsecured promise to pay money in the future. The term also includes a beneficial interest in assets (including money) which are transferred or set aside from the claims of creditors of the transferor, for example, in a trust or escrow account. See, however, § 1.83-8(a) with respect to employee trusts and annuity plans subject to section 402(b) and section 403(c). In the case of a transfer of a life insurance contract, retirement income contract, endowment contract, or other contract providing life insurance protection, only the cash surrender value of the contract is considered to be property. Where rights in a contract providing life insurance protection are substantially nonvested, see § 1.83-1(a)(2) for rules relating to the taxation of the cost of life insurance protection.

(f) Property transferred in connection with the performance of services. Property transferred to an employee or an independent contractor (or beneficiary thereof) in recognition of the performance of, or the refraining from performance of, services is considered transferred in connection with the performance of services within the meaning of section 83. The existence of other persons entitled to buy stock on the same terms and conditions as an employee, whether pursuant to a public or private offering may, however, indicate that in such circumstances a transfer to the employee is not in recognition of the performance of, or the refraining from performance of, services. The transfer of property is subject to sec-

tion 83 whether such transfer is in respect of past, present, or future services.

(g) Amount paid. For purposes of section 83 and the regulations thereunder, the term "amount paid" refers to the value of any money or property paid for the transfer of property to which section 83 applies, and does not refer to any amount paid for the right to use such property or to receive the income therefrom. Such value does not include any stated or unstated interest payments. For rules regarding the calculation of the amount of unstated interest payments, see § 1.483-1 (c). When section 83 applies to the transfer of property pursuant to the exercise of an option, the term "amount paid" refers to any amount paid for the grant of the option plus any amount paid as the exercise price of the option. For rules regarding the forgiveness of indebtedness treated as an amount paid, see § 1.83-4(c).

(h) Nonlapse restriction. For purposes of section 83 and the regulations thereunder, a restriction which by its terms will never lapse (also referred to as a "nonlapse restriction") is a permanent limitation on the transferability of property—

(i) Which will require the transferee of the property to sell, or offer to sell, such property at a price determined under a formula, and

(ii) Which will continue to apply to and be enforced against the transferee or any subsequent holder (other than the transferor).

A limitation subjecting the property to a permanent right of first refusal in a particular person at a price determined under a formula is a permanent nonlapse restriction. Limitations imposed by registration requirements of State or Federal security laws or similar laws imposed with respect to sales or other dispositions of stock or securities are not nonlapse restrictions. An obligation to resell or to offer to sell property transferred in connection with the performance of services to a specific person or persons at its fair market value at the time of such sale is not a nonlapse restriction. See § 1.83-5(c) for examples of nonlapse restrictions.

(i) Lapse restriction. For purposes of section 83 and the regulations thereunder, the term "lapse restriction" means a restriction other than a nonlapse restriction as defined in paragraph (h) of this section, and includes (but is not limited to) a restriction that carries a substantial risk of forfeiture.

§ 1.83-6 Deduction by employer

(a) Allowance of deduction—(1) General rule. In the case of a transfer of property in connection with the performance of services, or a compensatory cancellation of a nonlapse restriction described in section 83(d) and § 1.83-5, a deduction is allowable under sections 162 or 212, to the person for whom such services were performed. The amount of the deduction is equal to the amount includible as compensation in the gross income of the service provider, under section 83(a), (b), or (d)(2), but only to the extent such amount meets the requirements of sections 162 or 212 and the regulations thereunder. Such deduction shall be allowed only for the taxable year of such person in which or with which ends the taxable year of the service provider in which such amount is includible as compensation. For purposes of this paragraph, any amount excluded from gross income under section 79 or section 101(b) or subchapter N shall be considered to have been includible in gross income.

(2) Special rule. If the service provider is an employee of the person for whom services were performed, such deduction is allowed for the taxable year of the employer in which or with which ends the taxable year of the employee in which such amount is includible as compensation, but only if the employer deducts and withholds upon such amount in accordance with section 3402. A deduction will not be disallowed under the preceding sentence if the employer does not withhold and deduct upon amounts excluded from gross income, such as amounts excluded under section 79, section 101(b), or subchapter N.

(3) Exceptions. Where property is substantially vested upon transfer, the deduction shall be allowed to such person in accordance with his method of accounting (in conformity with sections 446 and 461). In the case of a transfer to an employee benefit plan described in § 1.162-10(a) or a transfer to an employees' trust or annuity plan described in section 404(a)(5) and the regulations thereunder, section 83(h) and this section do not apply.

(4) Capital expenditure, etc. No deduction is allowed under section 83(h) to the extent that the transfer of property constitutes a capital expenditure, an item of deferred expense, or an amount properly includible in the value of inventory items. In the case of a capital expenditure, for example, the basis of the property to which such capital expenditure relates shall be increased at the same time and to the same extent as any amount includible in the employee's gross income in respect of such transfer. Thus, for example, no deduction is allowed to a corporation in respect of a transfer of its stock to a promoter upon its organization, notwithstanding that such promoter must include the value of such stock in his gross income in accordance with the rules under section 83.

(b) Recognition of gain or loss. Except as provided in section 1032, at the time of a transfer of property in connection with the performance of services the transferor recognizes gain to the extent that the transferor receives an amount that exceeds the transferor's basis in the property. In addition, at the time a deduction is allowed under section 83(h) and paragraph (a) of this section, gain or loss is recognized to the extent of the difference between (i) the sum of the amount paid plus the amount allowed as a deduction under section 83(h), and (ii) the sum of the taxpayer's basis in the property plus any amount recognized pursuant to the previous sentence.

(c) Forfeitures. If, under section 83(h) and paragraph (a) of this section, a deduction, an increase in basis, or a reduction of gross income was allowable (disregarding the reasonableness of the amount of compensation) in respect of a transfer of property and such property is subsequently forfeited, the amount of such deduction, increase in basis or reduction of gross income shall be includible in the gross income of the person to whom it was allowable for the taxable year of forfeiture. The basis of such property in the hands of the person to whom it is forfeited shall include any such amount includible in the gross income of such person, as well as any amount such person pays upon forfeiture.

(d) **Special rules for transfers by shareholders—(1) Transfers.** If a shareholder of a corporation transfers property to an employee of such corporation or to an independent contractor (or to a beneficiary thereof), in consideration of services performed for the corporation, the transaction shall be considered to be a contribution of such property to the capital of such corporation by the shareholder, and immediately thereafter a transfer of such property by the corporation to the employee or independent contractor under paragraphs (a) and (b) of this section. For purposes of this (1), such a transfer will be considered to be in consideration for services performed for the corporation if either the property transferred is substantially nonvested at the time of transfer or an amount is includible in the gross income of the employee or independent contractor at the time of transfer under § 1.83-1(a)(1) or § 1.83-2(a). In the case of such a transfer, any money or other property paid to the shareholder for such stock shall be considered to be paid to the corporation and transferred immediately thereafter by the corporation to the shareholder as a distribution to which section 302 applies.

(2) **Forfeiture.** If, following a transaction described in paragraph (d)(1) of this section, the transferred property is forfeited to the shareholder, paragraph (c) of this section shall apply both with respect to the shareholder and with respect to the corporation. In addition, the corporation shall in the taxable year of forfeiture be allowed a loss (or realize a gain) to offset any gain (or loss) realized under paragraph (b) of this section. For example, if a shareholder transfers property to an employee of the corporation as compensation, and as a result the shareholder's basis of $200x$ in such property is allocated to his stock in such corporation and such corporation recognizes a short-term capital gain of $800x$, and is allowed a deduction of $1,000x$ on such transfer, upon a subsequent forfeiture of the property to the shareholder, the shareholder shall take $200x$ into gross income, and the corporation shall take $1,000x$ into gross income and be allowed a short-term capital loss of $800x$.

. . . . .

§ 1.83-7   Taxation of nonqualified stock options

(a) **In general.** If there is granted to an employee or independent contractor (or beneficiary thereof) in connection with the performance of services, an option to which section 421 (relating generally to certain qualified and other options) does not apply, section 83(a) shall apply to such grant if the option has a readily ascertainable fair market value (determined in accordance with paragraph (b) of this section) at the time the option is granted. The person who performed such services realizes compensation upon such grant at the time and in the amount determined under section 83(a). If section 83(a) does not apply to the grant of such an option because the option does not have a readily ascertainable fair market value at the time of grant, sections 83(a) and 83(b) shall apply at the time the option is exercised or otherwise disposed of, even though the fair market value of such option may have become readily ascertainable before such time. If the option is exercised, sections 83(a) and 83(b) apply to the transfer of property pursuant to such exercise, and the employee or independent contractor realizes compensation upon such transfer at the time and in the amount determined under section 83(a) or 83(b). If the option is sold or otherwise disposed of in an arm's length transaction, sections 83(a) and 83(b) apply to the transfer of money or other property received in the same manner as sections 83(a) and 83(b) would have applied to the transfer of property pursuant to an exercise of the option.

(b) Readily ascertainable defined— (1) Actively traded on an established market. Options have a value at the time they are granted, but that value is ordinarily not readily ascertainable unless the option is actively traded on an established market. If an option is actively traded on an established market, the fair market value of such option is readily ascertainable for purposes of this section by applying the rules of valuation set forth in § 20.-2031-2.

(2) Not actively traded on an established market. When an option is not actively traded on an established market, it does not have a readily ascertainable fair market value unless its fair market value can otherwise be measured with reasonable accuracy. For purposes of this section, if an option is not actively traded on an established market, the option does not have a readily ascertainable fair market value when granted unless the taxpayer can show that all of the following conditions exist:

(i) The option is transferable by the optionee;

(ii) The option is exerciseable immediately in full by the optionee;

(iii) The option or the property subject to the option is not subject to any restriction or condition (other than a lien or other condition to secure the payment of the purchase price) which has a significant effect upon the fair market value of the option; and

(iv) The fair market value of the option privilege is readily ascertainable in accordance with paragraph (b)(3) of this section.

(3) Option privilege. The option privilege in the case of an option to buy is the opportunity to benefit during the option's exercise period from any increase in the value of property subject to the option during such period, without risking any capital. Similarly, the option privilege in the case of an option to sell is the opportunity to benefit during the exercise period from a decrease in the value of property subject to the option. For example, if at some time during the exercise period of an option to buy, the fair market value of the property subject to the option is greater than the option's exercise price, a profit may be realized by exercising the option and immediately selling the property so acquired for its higher fair market value. Irrespective of whether any such gain may be realized immediately at the time an option is granted, the fair market value of an option to buy includes the value of the right to benefit from any future increase in the value of the property subject to the option (relative to the option exercise price), without risking any capital. Therefore, the fair market value of an option is not merely the difference that may exist at a particular time between the option's exercise price and the value of the property subject to the option, but also includes the value of the option privilege for the remainder of the exercise period. Accordingly, for purposes of this section, in determining whether the fair market value of an option is readily ascertainable, it is necessary to consider whether the value of the entire option privilege can be measured with reasonable accuracy. In determining whether the value of the option privilege is readily ascertainable, and in determining the amount of such value when such value is readily ascertainable, it is necessary to consider—

(i) Whether the value of the property subject to the option can be ascertained;

(ii) The probability of any ascertainable value of such property increasing or decreasing; and

(iii) The length of the period during which the option can be exercised.

. . . .

§ 1.101–1 Exclusion from gross income of proceeds of life insurance contracts payable by reason of death

(a) (1) In general. Section 101(a) (1) states the general rule that the proceeds of life insurance policies, if paid by reason of the death of the insured, are excluded from the gross income of the recipient. Death benefit payments having the characteristics of life insurance proceeds payable by reason of death under contracts, such as workmen's compensation insurance contracts, endowment contracts, or accident and health insurance contracts, are covered by this provision. For provisions relating to death benefits paid by or on behalf of employers, see section 101(b) and § 1.101-2. The exclusion from gross income allowed by section 101(a) applies whether payment is made to the estate of the insured or to any beneficiary (individual, corporation, or partnership) and whether it is made directly or in trust. The extent to which this exclusion applies in cases where life insurance policies have been transferred for a valuable consideration is stated in section 101(a) (2) and in paragraph (b) of this section. In cases where the proceeds of a life insurance policy, payable by reason of the death of the insured, are paid other than in a single sum at the time of such death, the amounts to be excluded from gross income may be affected by the provisions of section 101(c) (relating to amounts held under agreements to pay interest) or section 101(d) (relating to amounts payable at a date later than death). See §§ 1.101-3 and 1.101-4. However, neither section 101(c) nor section 101(d) applies to a single sum payment which does not exceed the amount payable at the time of death even though such amount is actually paid at a date later than death.

. . . .

(b) Transfers of life insurance policies. (1) In the case of a transfer, by assignment or otherwise, of a life insurance policy or any interest therein for a valuable consideration, the amount of the proceeds attributable to such policy or interest which is excludable from the transferee's gross income is generally limited to the sum of (i) the actual value of the consideration for such transfer, and (ii) the premiums and other amounts subsequently paid by the transferee (see section 101(a) (2) and example (1) of subparagraph (5) of this paragraph). However, this limitation on the amount excludable from the transferee's gross income does not apply (except in certain special cases involving a series of transfers), where the basis of the policy or interest transferred, for the purpose of determining gain or loss with respect to the transferee, is determinable, in whole or in part, by reference to the basis of such policy or interest in the hands of the transferor (see sec-

tion 101(a) (2) (A) and examples (2) and (4) of subparagraph (5) of this paragraph). Neither does the limitation apply where the policy or interest therein is transferred to the insured, to a partner of the insured, to a partnership in which the insured is a partner, or to a corporation in which the insured is a shareholder or officer (see section 101(a) (2) (B)). For rules relating to gratuitous transfers, see subparagraph (2) of this paragraph. For special rules with respect to certain cases where a series of transfers is involved, see subparagraph (3) of this paragraph.

(2) In the case of a gratuitous transfer, by assignment or otherwise, of a life insurance policy or any interest therein, as a general rule the amount of the proceeds attributable to such policy or interest which is excludable from the transferee's gross income under section 101(a) is limited to the sum of (i) the amount which would have been excludable by the transferor (in accordance with this section) if no such transfer had taken place, and (ii) any premiums and other amounts subsequently paid by the transferee. See example (6) of subparagraph (5) of this paragraph. However, where the gratuitous transfer in question is made by or to the insured, a partner of the insured, a partnership in which the insured is a partner, or a corporation in which the insured is a shareholder or officer, the entire amount of the proceeds attributable to the policy or interest transferred shall be excludable from the transferee's gross income (see section 101(a) (2) (B) and example (7) of subparagraph (5) of this paragraph).

(3) In the case of a series of transfers, if the last transfer of a life insurance policy or an interest therein is for a valuable consideration—

(i) The general rule is that the final transferee shall exclude from gross income, with respect to the proceeds of such policy or interest therein, only the sum of—

(a) The actual value of the consideration paid by him, and

(b) The premiums and other amounts subsequently paid by him;

(ii) If the final transfer is to the insured, to a partner of the insured, to a partnership in which the insured is a partner, or to a corporation in which the insured is a shareholder or officer, the final transferee shall exclude the entire amount of the proceeds from gross income;

(iii) Except where subdivision (ii) of this subparagraph applies, if the basis of the policy or interest transferred, for the purpose of determining gain or loss with respect to the final transferee, is determinable, in whole or in part, by reference to the basis of such policy or interest therein in the hands of the transferor, the amount of the proceeds which is excludable by the final transferee is limited to the sum of—

(a) The amount which would have been excludable by his transferor if no such transfer had taken place, and

(b) Any premiums and other amounts subsequently paid by the final transferee himself.

(4) For the purposes of section 101 (a) (2) and subparagraphs (1) and (3) of this paragraph, a "transfer for a valuable consideration" is any absolute transfer for value of a right to receive all or a part of the proceeds of a life insurance policy. Thus, the creation, for value, of an enforceable contractual right to receive all or a part of the proceeds of a policy may constitute a transfer for a valuable consideration of the policy or an interest therein. On the other hand, the pledging or assignment of a policy as collateral security is not a transfer for a valuable consideration of such policy or an interest therein, and section 101 is inapplicable to any amounts received by the pledgee or assignee.

(5) The application of this paragraph may be illustrated by the following examples:

Example (1). A pays premiums of $500 for an insurance policy in the face amount of $1,000 upon the life of B, and subsequently transfers the policy to C for $600. C receives the proceeds of $1,000 upon the death of B. The amount which C can exclude from his gross income is limited to $600 plus any premiums paid by C subsequent to the transfer.

Example (2). The X Corporation purchases for a single premium of $500 an insurance policy in the face amount of $1,000 upon the life of A, one of its employees, naming the X Corporation as beneficiary. The X Corporation transfers the policy to the Y Corporation in a tax-free reorganization (the policy having a basis for determining gain or loss in the hands of the Y Corporation determined by reference to its basis in the hands of the X Corporation). The Y Corporation receives the proceeds of $1,000 upon the death of A. The entire $1,000 is to be excluded from the gross income of the Y Corporation.

Example (3). The facts are the same as in example (2) except that, prior to the death of A, the Y Corporation transfers the policy to the Z Corporation for $600. The Z Corporation receives the proceeds of $1,000 upon the death of A. The amount which the Z Corporation can exclude from its gross income is limited to $600 plus any premiums paid by the Z Corporation subsequent to the transfer of the policy to it.

Example (4). The facts are the same as in example (3) except that, prior to the death of A, the Z Corporation transfers the policy to the M Corporation in a tax-free reorganization (the policy having a basis for determining gain or loss in the hands of the M Corporation determined by reference to its basis in the hands of the Z Corporation). The M Corporation receives the proceeds of $1,000 upon the death of A. The amount which the M Corporation can exclude from its gross income is limited to $600 plus any premiums paid by the Z Corporation and the M Corporation subsequent to the transfer of the policy to the Z Corporation.

Example (5). The facts are the same as in example (3) except that, prior to the death of A, the Z Corporation transfers the policy to the N Corporation, in which A is a shareholder. The N Corporation receives the proceeds of $1,000 upon the death of A. The entire $1,000 is to be excluded from the gross income of the N Corporation.

Example (6). A pays premiums of $500 for an insurance policy in the face amount of $1,000 upon his own life, and subsequently transfers the policy to his wife B for $600. B later transfers the policy without consideration to C, who is the son of A and B. C receives the proceeds of $1,000 upon the death of A. The amount which C can exclude from his gross income is limited to $600 plus any premiums paid by B and C subsequent to the transfer of the policy to B.

· · · · ·

§ 1.101–2 Employees' death benefits

(a) In general. (1) Section 101(b) states the general rule that amounts up to $5,000 which are paid to the beneficiaries or the estate of an employee, or former employee, by or on behalf of an employer and by reason of the death of the employee shall be excluded from the gross income of the recipient. This exclusion from gross income applies whether payment is made to the estate of the employee or to any beneficiary (individual, corporation, or partnership), whether it is made directly or in trust, and whether or not it is made pursuant to a contractual obligation of the employer. The exclusion applies whether payment is made in a single sum or otherwise, subject to the provisions of section 101(c), relating to amounts held under an agreement to pay interest thereon (see § 1.101–3). The exclusion from gross income also applies to any amount not actually paid which is otherwise taxable to a beneficiary of an employee because it was made available as a distribution from an employee's trust.

. . . .

(3) The total amount excludable with respect to any employee may not exceed $5,000, regardless of the number of employers or the number of beneficiaries. For allocation of the exclusion among beneficiaries, see paragraph (c) of this section. For rules governing the taxability of benefits payable on the death of an employee under pension, profit-sharing, or stock bonus plans described in section 401(a) and exempt under section 501(a), under annuity plans described in section 403(a), or under annuity contracts to which paragraph (a) or (b) of § 1.403(b)–1 applies, see sections 72(m) (3), 402(a), and 403 and the regulations thereunder.

. . . .

(c) **Allocation of the exclusion.** (1) Where the aggregate payments by or on behalf of an employer or employers as death benefits to the beneficiaries or the estate of a deceased employee exceed $5,000, the $5,000 exclusion shall be apportioned among them in the same proportion as the amount received by or the present value of the amount payable to each bears to the total death benefits paid or payable by or on behalf of the employer or employers.

(2) The application of the rule in subparagraph (1) of this paragraph may be illustrated by the following example:

Example. The M Corporation, the employer of A, a deceased employee who died November 30, 1954, makes payments in 1955 to the beneficiaries of A as follows: $5,000 to W, A's widow, $2,000 to B, the son of A, and $3,000 to C, the daughter of A. No other amounts are paid by any other employer of A to his estate or beneficiaries. By application of the apportionment rule stated above, W, the widow, will exclude $2,500 ($5,000/$10,000, or one-half, of $5,000); B, the son, will exclude $1,000 ($2,000/$10,000, or one-fifth, of $5,000); and C, the daughter, will exclude $1,500 ($3,000/$10,000, or three-tenths, of $5,000).

. . . .

§ 1.101–3   Interest payments

(a) **Applicability of section 101(c).** Section 101(c) provides that if any amount excluded from gross income by section 101(a) (relating to life insurance proceeds) or section 101(b) (relating to employees' death benefits) is held under an agreement to pay interest thereon, the interest payments shall be included in gross income. This provision applies to payments made (either by an insurer or by or on behalf of an employer) of interest earned on any amount so excluded from gross income which is held without substantial diminution of the principal amount during the period when such interest payments are being made or credited to the beneficiaries or estate of the insured or the employee. For example, if a monthly payment is $100, of which $99 represents interest and $1 represents diminution of the principal amount, the principal amount shall be considered held under an agreement to pay interest thereon and the interest payment shall be included in the gross income of the recipient. Section 101(c) applies whether the election to have an amount held under an agreement to pay interest thereon is made by the insured or employee or by his beneficiaries or estate, and whether or not an interest rate is explicitly stated in the agreement. Section 101(d), relating to the payment of life insurance proceeds at a date later than death, shall not apply to any amount to which section 101(c) applies. See section 101(d) (4). However, both section 101(c) and section 101(d) may apply to payments received under a single life insurance contract. For provisions relating to the application of this rule to payments received under a permanent life insurance policy with a family income rider attached, see paragraph (h) of § 1.101–4.

(b) **Determination of "present value".** For the purpose of determining whether section 101(c) or section 101 (d) applies, the present value (at the time of the insured's death) of any amount which is to be paid at a date later than death shall be determined by the use of the interest rate and mortality tables used by the insurer in determining the size of the payments to be made.

§ 1.101–4   **Payment of life insurance proceeds at a date later than death**

(a) **In general.** (1) (i) Section 101 (d) states the provisions governing the exclusion from gross income of amounts (other than those to which section 101 (c) applies) received under a life insurance contract and paid by reason of the death of the insured which are paid to a beneficiary on a date or dates later than the death of the insured. However, if the amounts payable as proceeds of life insurance to which section 101(a) (1) applies cannot in any event exceed the amount payable at the time of the insured's death, such amounts are fully excludable from the gross income of the recipient (or recipients) without regard to the actual time of payment and no further determination need be made under this section. Section 101(d) (1) (A) provides an exclusion from gross income of any amount determined by a proration, under applicable regulations, of "an amount held by an insurer with respect to any beneficiary". The quoted phrase is defined in section 101(d) (2). For the regulations governing the method of computation of this proration, see paragraphs (c) through (f) of this section. The prorated amounts are to be excluded from the gross income of the beneficiary regardless of the taxable year in which they are actually received (see example (2) of subparagraph (2) of this paragraph).

(ii) Section 101(d) (1) (B) provides an additional exclusion where life insurance proceeds are paid to the surviving spouse of an insured. For purposes of this exclusion, the term "surviving spouse" means the spouse of the insured as of the date of death, including a spouse legally separated, but not under a decree of absolute divorce (section 101(d) (3)). To the extent that the total payments, under one or more agreements, made in excess of the amounts determined by proration under section 101(d) (1) (A) do not exceed $1,000 in the taxable year of receipt, they shall be excluded from the gross income of the surviving spouse (whether or not payment of any part of such amounts is guaranteed by the insurer). Amounts excludable under section 101 (d) (1) (B) are not "prorated" amounts.

(2) The principles of this paragraph may be illustrated by the following examples:

Example (1). A surviving spouse elects to receive all of the life insurance proceeds with respect to one insured, amounting to $150,000, in ten annual installments of $16,500 each, based on a certain guaranteed interest rate. The prorated amount is $15,000 ($150,000÷10). As the second payment, the insurer pays $17,850, which exceeds the guaranteed payment by $1,350 as the result of earnings of the insurer in excess of those required to pay the guaranteed installments. The surviving spouse shall include $1,850 in gross income and exclude $16,000—determined in the following manner:

Fixed payment (including guaranteed interest)	$16,500
Excess interest	1,350
Total payment	17,850
Prorated amount	15,000
Excess over prorated amount	2,850
Annual excess over prorated amount excludable under section 101(d) (1) (B)	1,000
Amount includible in gross income	1,850

Example (2). Assume the same facts as in example (1), except that the third and fourth annual installments, totalling $33,000 (2 × $16,500), are received in a single subsequent taxable year of the surviving spouse. The prorated amount of $15,000 of each annual installment, totalling $30,000, shall be excluded even though the spouse receives more than one annual installment in the single subsequent taxable year. However, the surviving spouse is entitled to only one exclusion of $1,000 under section 101 (d) (1) (B) for each taxable year of receipt. The surviving spouse shall include $2,000 in her gross income for the taxable year with respect to the above installment payments ($33,000 less the sum of $30,000 plus $1,000).

. . . .

(b) Amount held by an insurer. (1) For the purpose of the proration referred to in section 101(d) (1), an "amount held by an insurer with respect to any beneficiary" means an amount equal to the present value to such beneficiary (as of the date of death of the insured) of an agreement by the insurer under a life insurance policy (whether as an option or otherwise) to pay such beneficiary an amount or amounts at a date or dates later than the death of the insured (section 101(d) (2)). The present value of such agreement is to be computed as if the agreement under the life insurance policy had been entered into on the date of death of the insured, except that such value shall be determined by the use of the mortality table and interest rate used by the insurer in calculating payments to be made to the beneficiary under such agreement. Where an insurance policy provides an option for the payment of a specific amount upon the death of the insured in full discharge of the contract, such lump sum is the amount held by the insurer with respect to all beneficiaries (or their beneficiaries) under the contract. See, however, paragraph (e) of this section.

(2) In the case of two or more beneficiaries, the "amount held by the insurer" with respect to each beneficiary depends on the relationship of the different benefits payable to such beneficiaries. Where the amounts payable to two or more beneficiaries are independent of each other, the "amount held by the insurer with respect to each beneficiary" shall be determined and prorated over the periods involved independently. Thus, if a certain amount per month is to be paid to A for his life, and, concurrently, another amount per month is to be paid to B for his life, the "amount held by the insurer" shall be determined and prorated for both A and B independently, but the aggregate shall not exceed the total present value of such payments to both. On the other hand, if the obligation to pay B was contingent on his surviving A, the "amount held by the insurer" shall be considered an amount held with respect to both beneficiaries simultaneously. Furthermore, it is immaterial whether B is a named beneficiary or merely the ultimate recipient of payments for a term of years. For the special rules governing the computation of the proration of the "amount held by an insurer" in determining amounts excludable under the provisions of section 101(d), see paragraphs (c) to (f), inclusive, of this section.

(3) Notwithstanding any other provision of this section, if the policy was transferred for a valuable consideration, the total "amount held by an insurer" cannot exceed the sum of the consideration paid plus any premiums or other consideration paid subsequent to the transfer if the provisions of section 101(a) (2) and paragraph (b) of § 1.101–1 limit the excludability of the proceeds to such total.

(c) **Treatment of payments for life to a sole beneficiary.** If the contract provides for the payment of a specified lump sum, but, pursuant to an agreement between the beneficiary and the insurer, payments are to be made during the life of the beneficiary in lieu of such lump sum, the lump sum shall be divided by the life expectancy of the beneficiary determined in accordance with the mortality table used by the insurer in determining the benefits to be paid. However, if payments are to be made to the estate or beneficiary of the primary beneficiary in the event that the primary beneficiary dies before receiving a certain number of payments or a specified total amount, such lump sum shall be reduced by the present value (at the time of the insured's death) of amounts which may be paid by reason of the guarantee, in accordance with the provisions of paragraph (e) of this section, before making this calculation. To the extent that payments received in each taxable year do not exceed the amount found from the above calculation, they are "prorated amounts" of the "amount held by an insurer" and are excludable from the gross income of the beneficiary without regard to whether he lives beyond the life expectancy used in making the calculation. If the contract in question does not provide for the payment of a specific lump sum upon the death of the insured as one of the alternative methods of payment, the present value (at the time of the death of the insured) of the payments to be made to beneficiary, determined in accordance with the interest rate and mortality table used by the insurer in determining the benefits to be paid, shall be used in the above calculation in lieu of a lump sum.

. . . . .

(h) **Applicability of both section 101 (c) and 101(d) to payments under a single life insurance contract—(1) In general.** Section 101(d) shall not apply to interest payments on any amount held by an insurer under an agreement to pay interest thereon (see sections 101 (c) and 101(d) (4) and § 1.101–3). On the other hand, both section 101(c) and section 101(d) may be applicable to payments received under a single life insurance contract, if such payments consist both of interest on an amount held by an insurer under an agreement to pay interest thereon and of amounts held by the insurer and paid on a date or dates later than the death of the insured. One instance when both section 101(c) and section 101(d) may be applicable to payments received under a single life insurance contract is in the case of a permanent life insurance policy with a family income rider attached. A typical family income rider is one which provides additional term insurance coverage for a specified number of years from the register date of the basic policy. Under the policy with such a rider, if the insured dies at any time during the term period, the beneficiary is entitled to receive (i) monthly payments of a specified amount commencing as of the date of death and continuing for the balance of the term period, and (ii) a lump sum payment of the proceeds under the basic policy to be paid at the end of the term period. If the insured dies after the expiration of the term period, the beneficiary receives only the proceeds under the basic policy. If the insured dies before the expiration of the term period, part of each monthly payment received by the beneficiary during the term period consists of interest on the proceeds of the basic policy (such proceeds being retained by the insurer until the end of the term period). The remaining part consists of an installment (principal plus interest) of the proceeds of the terms insurance purchased under the family income rider. The amount of term insurance which is provided under the family income rider is, therefore, that amount which, at the date of the insured's death, will provide proceeds sufficient to fund such remaining part of each monthly payment. Since the proceeds under the basic policy are held by the insurer until the end of the term period, that portion of each monthly payment which consists of interest on such proceeds is interest on an amount held by an insurer under an agreement to pay interest thereon and is includible in gross income under section 101(c). On the other hand, since the remaining portion of each monthly payment consists of an installment payment (principal plus interest) of the proceeds of the term insurance, it is a payment of an amount held by the insurer and paid on a date later than the death of the insured to which section 101(d) and this section applies (including the $1,000 exclusion allowed the surviving spouse under section 101(d) (1) (B)). The proceeds of the basic policy, when received in a lump sum at the end of the term period, are excludable from gross income under section 101(a).

. . . . .

§ 1.102-1 Gifts and inheritances

(a) **General rule.** Property received as a gift, or received under a will or under statutes of descent and distribution, is not includible in gross income, although the income from such property is includible in gross income. An amount of principal paid under a marriage settlement is a gift. However, see section 71 and the regulations thereunder for rules relating to alimony or allowances paid upon divorce or separation. Section 102 does not apply to prizes and awards (see section 74 and § 1.74-1) nor to scholarships and fellowship grants (see section 117 and the regulations thereunder).

(b) **Income from gifts and inheritances.** The income from any property received as a gift, or under a will or statute of descent and distribution shall not be excluded from gross income under paragraph (a) of this section.

(c) **Gifts and inheritances of income.** If the gift, bequest, devise, or inheritance is of income from property, it shall not be excluded from gross income under paragraph (a) of this section. Section 102 provides a special rule for the treatment of certain gifts, bequests, devises, or inheritances which by their terms are to be paid, credited, or distributed at intervals. Except as provided in section 663 (a) (1) and paragraph (d) of this section, to the extent any such gift, bequest, devise, or inheritance is paid, credited, or to be distributed out of income from property, it shall be considered a gift, bequest, devise, or inheritance of income from property. Section 102 provides the same treatment for amounts of income from property which is paid, credited, or to be distributed under a gift or bequest whether the gift or bequest is in terms of a right to payments at intervals (regardless of income) or is in terms of a right to income. To the extent the amounts in either case are paid, credited, or to be distributed at intervals out of income, they are not to be excluded under section 102 from the taxpayer's gross income.

(d) **Effect of subchapter J.** Any amount required to be included in the gross income of a beneficiary under sections 652, 662, or 668 shall be treated for purposes of this section as a gift, bequest, devise, or inheritance of income from property. On the other hand, any amount excluded from the gross income of a beneficiary under section 663 (a) (1) shall be treated for purposes of this section as property acquired by gift, bequest, devise, or inheritance.

(e) Income taxed to grantor or assignor. Section 102 is not intended to tax a donee upon the same income which is taxed to the grantor of a trust or assignor of income under section 61 or sections 671 through 677, inclusive.

§ 1.103–1 Interest upon obligations of a State, territory, etc.

(a) Interest upon obligations of a State, territory, a possession of the United States, the District of Columbia, or any political subdivision thereof (hereinafter collectively or individually referred to as "State or local governmental unit") is not includable in gross income, except as provided under section 103(c) and (d) and the regulations thereunder.

(b) Obligations issued by or on behalf of any State or local governmental unit by constituted authorities empowered to issue such obligations are the obligations of such a unit. However, section 103(a) (1) and this section do not apply to industrial development bonds except as otherwise provided in section 103(c). See section 103(c) and §§ 1.103–7 through 1.103–12 for the rules concerning interest paid on industrial development bonds. See section 103(d) for rules concerning interest paid on arbitrage bonds. Certificates issued by a political subdivision for public improvements (such as sewers, sidewalks, streets, etc.) which are evidence of special assessments against specific property, which assessments become a lien against such property and which the political subdivision is required to enforce, are, for purposes of this section, obligations of the political subdivision even though the obligations are to be satisfied out of special funds and not out of general funds or taxes. The term "political subdivision", for purposes of this section denotes any division of any State or local governmental unit which is a municipal corporation or which has been delegated the right to exercise part of the sovereign power of the unit. As thus defined, a political subdivision of any State or local governmental unit may or may not, for purposes of this section, include special assessment districts so created, such as road, water, sewer, gas, light, reclamation, drainage, irrigation, levee, school, harbor, port improvement, and similar districts and divisions of any such unit.

§ 1.104–1 Compensation for injuries or sickness

(a) In general. Section 104(a) provides an exclusion from gross income with respect to certain amounts described in paragraphs (b), (c), (d) and (e) of this section, which are received for personal injuries or sickness, except to the extent that such amounts are attributable to (but not in excess of) deductions allowed under section 213 (relating to medical, etc., expenses) for any prior taxable year. See section 213 and the regulations thereunder.

(b) Amounts received under workmen's compensation acts. Section 104 (a) (1) excludes from gross income amounts which are received by an employee under a workmen's compensation act (such as the Longshoremen's and Harbor Workers' Compensation Act, 33 U.S.C., c. 18), or under a statute in the nature of a workmen's compensation act which provides compensation to employees for personal injuries or sickness incurred in the course of employment. Section 104(a) (1) also applies to compensation which is paid under a workmen's compensation act to the survivor or survivors of a deceased employee. However, section 104(a) (1) does not apply to a retirement pension or annuity to the extent that it is determined by reference to the employee's age or length of service, or the employee's prior contributions, even though the employee's retirement is occasioned by an occupational injury or sickness. Section 104(a) (1) also does not apply to amounts which are received as compensation for a nonoccupational injury or sickness nor to amounts received as compensation for an occupational injury or sickness to the extent that they are in excess of the amount provided in the applicable workmen's compensation act or acts.

. . . . .

(c) Damages received on account of personal injuries or sickness. Section 104(a) (2) excludes from gross income the amount of any damages received (whether by suit or agreement) on account of personal injuries or sickness. The term "damages received (whether by suit or agreement)" means an amount received (other than workmen's compensation) through prosecution of a legal suit or action based upon tort or tort type rights, or through a settlement agreement entered into in lieu of such prosecution.

(d) Accident or health insurance. Section 104(a) (3) excludes from gross income amounts received through accident or health insurance for personal injuries or sickness (other than amounts received by an employee, to the extent that such amounts (1) are attributable to contributions of the employer which were not includible in the gross income of the employee, or (2) are paid by the employer). Similar treatment is also accorded to amounts received under accident or health plans and amounts received from sickness or disability funds. See section 105(e) and § 1.105–5. If, therefore, an individual purchases a policy accident or health insurance out of his own funds, amounts received thereunder for personal injuries or sickness are excludable from his gross income under section 104(a) (3). See, however, section 213 and the regulations thereunder as to the inclusion in gross income of amounts attributable to deductions allowed under section 213 for any prior taxable year. Section 104(a) (3) also applies to amounts received by an employee for personal injuries or sickness from a fund which is maintained exclusively by employee contributions. Conversely, if an employer is either the sole contributor to such a fund, or is the sole purchaser of a policy of accident or health insurance for his employees (on either a group or individual basis), the exclusion provided under section 104(a) (3) does not apply to any amounts received by his employees through such fund or insurance. If the employer and his employees contribute to a fund or purchase insurance which pays accident or health benefits to employees, section 104(a) (3) does not apply to amounts received thereunder by employees to the extent that such amounts are attributable to the employer's contributions. See § 1.105–1 for rules relating to the determination of the amount attributable to employer contributions. . . . .

§ 1.105–1 Amounts attributable to employer contributions

(a) In general. Under section 105 (a), amounts received by an employee through accident or health insurance for personal injuries or sickness must be included in his gross income to the extent that such amounts (1) are attributable to contributions of the employer which were not includible in the gross income of the employee, or (2) are paid by the employer, unless such amounts are excluded therefrom under section 105(b), (c), or (d). For purposes of this section, the term "amounts received by an employee through an accident or health plan" refers to any amounts received through accident or health insurance, and also to any amounts which, under section 105(e), are treated as being so received. See § 1.105–5. In determining the extent to which amounts received for personal injuries or sickness by an employee through an accident or health plan are subject to the provisions of section 105(a), rather than section 104 (a) (3), the provisions of paragraphs (b), (c), (d), and (e) of this section shall apply. A self-employed individual is not an employee for purposes of section 105 and §§ 1.105–1 through 1.105–5. See paragraph (g) of § 1.72–15. Thus, such an individual will not be treated as an employee with respect to benefits described in section 105 received from a plan in which he participates as an employee within the meaning of section 401(c) (1) at the time he, his spouse, or any of his dependents becomes entitled to receive such benefits.

. . . .

§ 1.105–2 Amounts expended for medical care

Section 105 (b) provides an exclusion from gross income with respect to the amounts referred to in section 105(a) (see § 1.105–1) which are paid, directly or indirectly, to the taxpayer to reimburse him for expenses incurred for the medical care (as defined in section 213(e)) of the taxpayer, his spouse, and his dependents (as defined in section 152). However, the exclusion does not apply to amounts which are attributable to (and not in excess of) deductions allowed under section 213 (relating to medical, etc., expenses) for any prior taxable year. See section 213 and the regulations thereunder. Section 105 (b) applies only to amounts which are paid specifically to reimburse the taxpayer for expenses incurred by him for the prescribed medical care. Thus, section 105(b) does not apply to amounts which the taxpayer would be entitled to receive irrespective of whether or not he incurs expenses for medical care. For example, if under a wage continuation plan the taxpayer is entitled to regular wages during a period of absence from work due to sickness or injury, amounts received under such plan are not excludable from his gross income under section 105(b) even though the taxpayer may have incurred medical expenses during the period of illness. Such amounts may, however, be excludable from his gross income under section 105 (d). See § 1.105–4. If the amounts are paid to the taxpayer solely to reimburse him for expenses which he incurred for the prescribed medical care, section 105 (b) is applicable even though such amounts are paid without proof of the amount of the actual expenses incurred by the taxpayer, but section 105 (b) is not applicable to the extent that such amounts exceed the amount of the actual expenses for such medical care. If the taxpayer incurs an obligation for medical care, payment to the obligee in discharge of such obligation shall constitute indirect payment to the taxpayer as reimbursement for medical care. Similarly, payment to or on behalf of the taxpayer's spouse or dependents shall constitute indirect payment to the taxpayer.

§ 1.105–3 Payments unrelated to absence from work

Section 105(c) provides an exclusion from gross income with respect to the amounts referred to in section 105(a) to the extent that such amounts (a) constitute payments for the permanent loss or permanent loss of use of a member or function of the body, or the permanent disfigurement, of the taxpayer, his spouse, or a dependent (as defined in section 152), and (b) are computed with reference to the nature of the injury without regard to the period the employee is absent from work. Loss of use or disfigurement shall be considered permanent when it may reasonably be expected to continue for the life of the individual. For purposes of section 105 (c), loss or loss of use of a member or function of the body includes the loss or loss of use of an appendage of the body, the loss of an eye, the loss of substantially all of the vision of an eye, and the loss of substantially all of the hearing in one or both ears. The term "disfigurement" shall be given a

reasonable interpretation in the light of all the particular facts and circumstances. Section 105(c) does not apply if the amount of the benefits is determined by reference to the period the employee is absent from work. For example, if an employee is absent from work as a result of the loss of an arm, and under the accident and health plan established by his employer, he is to receive $125 a week so long as he is absent from work for a period not in excess of 52 weeks, section 105(c) is not applicable to such payments. See, however, section 105 (d) and § 1.105–4. However, for purposes of section 105 (c), it is immaterial whether an amount is paid in a lump sum or in installments. Section 105(c) does not apply to amounts which are treated as workmen's compensation under paragraph (b) of § 1.104–1, or to amounts paid by reason of the death of the employee (see section 101).

§ 1.105–5 Accident and health plans

(a) In general. Sections 104(a) (3) and 105(b), (c), and (d) exclude from gross income certain amounts received through accident or health insurance. Section 105(e) provides that for purposes of sections 104 and 105 amounts received through an accident or health plan for employees, and amounts received from a sickness and disability fund for employees maintained under the law of a State, a Territory, or the District of Columbia, shall be treated as amounts received through accident or health insurance. In general, an accident or health plan is an arrangement for the payment of amounts to employees in the event of personal injuries or sickness. A plan may cover one or more employees, and there may be different plans for different employees or classes of employees. An accident or health plan may be either insured or noninsured, and it is not necessary that the plan be in writing or that the employee's rights to benefits under the plan be enforceable. However, if the employee's rights are not enforceable, an amount will be deemed to be received under a plan only if, on the date the employee became sick or injured, the employee was covered by a plan (or a program, policy, or custom having the effect of a plan) providing for the payment of amounts to the employee in the event of personal injuries or sickness, and notice or knowledge of such plan was reasonably available to the employee. It is immaterial who makes payment of the benefits provided by the plan. For example, payment may be made by the employer, a welfare fund, a State sickness or disability benefits fund, an association of employers or employees, or by an insurance company.

(b) Self-employed individuals. Under section 105(g), a self-employed individual is not treated as an employee for purposes of section 105. Therefore, for example, benefits paid under an accident or health plan as referred to in section 105(e) to or on behalf of an individual who is self-employed in the business with respect to which the plan is established will not be treated as received through accident and health insurance for purposes of sections 104(a) (3) and 105.

§ 1.105-11 Self-insured medical reimbursement plan

(a) In general. Under section 105 (a), amounts received by an employee through a self-insured medical reimbursement plan which are attributable to contributions of the employer, or are paid by the employer, are included in the employee's gross income unless such amounts are excludable under section 105(b). For amounts reimbursed to a highly compensated individual to be fully excludable from such individual's gross income under section 105(b), the plan must satisfy the requirements of section 105(h) and this section. Section 105(h) is not satisfied if the plan discriminates in favor of highly compensated individuals as to eligibility to participate or benefits. All or a portion of the reimbursements or payments on behalf of such individuals under a discriminatory plan are not excludable from gross income under section 105 (b). However, benefits paid to participants who are not highly compensated individuals may be excluded from gross income if the requirements of section 105(b) are satisfied, even if the plan is discriminatory.

(b) Self-insured medical reimbursement plan—(1) General rule—

(i) Definition. A self-insured medical reimbursement plan is a separate written plan for the benefit of employees which provides for reimbursement of employee medical expenses referred to in section 105(b). A plan or arrangement is self-insured unless reimbursement is provided under an individual or group policy of accident or health insurance issued by a licensed insurance company or under an arrangement in the nature of a prepaid health care plan that is regulated under federal or state law in a manner similar to the regulation of insurance companies. Thus, for example, a plan of a health maintenance organization, established under the Health Maintenance Organization Act of 1973, would qualify as a prepaid health care plan. In addition, this section applies to a self-insured medical reimbursement plan, determined in accordance with the rules of this section, maintained by an employee organization described in section 501(c)(9).

(ii) Shifting of risk. A plan underwritten by a policy of insurance or a prepaid health care plan that does not involve the shifting of risk to an unrelated third party is considered self-insured for purposes of this section. Accordingly, a cost-plus policy or a policy which in effect merely provides administrative or bookkeeping services is considered self-insured for purposes of this section. However, a plan is not considered self-insured merely because one factor the insurer uses in determining the premium is the employer's prior claims experience.

. . . . .

(2) Other rules. The rules of this section apply to a self-insured portion of an employer's medical plan or arrangement even if the plan is in part underwritten by insurance. For example, if an employer's medical plan reimburses employees for benefits not covered under the insured portion of an overall plan, or for deductible amounts under the insured portions, such reimbursement is subject to the rules of this section. However, a plan which reimburses employees for premiums paid under an insured plan is not subject to this section. In addition, medical expense reimbursements not described in the plan are not paid pursuant to a plan for the benefit of employees, and therefore are not excludable from gross income under section 105 (b). Such reimbursements will not affect the determination of whether or not a plan is discriminatory.

(c) Prohibited discrimination—(1) In general. A self-insured medical reimbursement plan does not satisfy the requirements of section 105(h) and this paragraph for a plan year unless the plan satisfies subparagraphs (2) and (3) of this paragraph. However, a plan does not fail to satisfy the requirements of this paragraph merely because benefits under the plan are offset by benefits paid under a self-insured or insured plan of the employer or another employer, or by benefits paid under Medicare or other Federal or State law or similar foreign law. A self-insured plan may take into account the benefits provided under another plan only to the extent that the type of benefit subject to reimbursement is the same under both plans. For example, an amount reimbursed to an employee for a hospital expense under a medical plan maintained by the employer of the employee's spouse may be offset against the self-insured benefit where the self-insured plan covering the employee provides the same type of hospital benefit.

(2) Eligibility to participate—(i) Percentage test. A plan satisfies the requirements of this subparagraph if it benefits—

(A) Seventy percent or more of all employees, or

(B) Eighty percent or more of all the employees who are eligible to benefit under the plan if 70 percent or more of all employees are eligible to benefit under the plan.

(ii) Classification test. A plan satisfies the requirements of this subparagraph if it benefits such employees as qualify under a classification of employees set up by the employer which is found by the Internal Revenue Service not to be discriminatory in favor of highly compensated individuals. In general, this determination will be made based upon the facts and circumstances of each case, applying the same standards as are applied under section 410 (b)(1)(B) (relating to qualified pension, profit-sharing and stock bonus plans), without regard to the special rules in section 401(a)(5) concerning eligibility to participate.

(iii) Exclusion of certain employees. Under section 105(h)(3), for purposes of this subparagraph (2), there may be excluded from consideration:

(A) Employees who have not completed 3 years of service prior to the beginning of the plan year. For purposes of this section years of service may be determined by any method that is reasonable and consistent. A determination made in the same manner as (and not requiring service in excess of how) a year of service is determined under section 410(a)(3) shall be deemed to be reasonable. For purposes of the 3-year rule, all of an employee's years of service with the employer prior to a separation from service are not taken into account. For purposes of the 3-year rule, an employee's years of service prior to age 25, as a part-time or seasonal employee, as a member of a collective bargaining unit, or as a nonresident alien, as each is described in this subdivision, are not excluded by reason of being so described from counting towards satisfaction of the rule. In addition, if the employer is a predecessor employer (determined in a manner consistent with section 414(a)), service for such predecessor is treated as service for the employer.

(B) Employees who have not attained age 25 prior to the beginning of the plan year.

(C) Part-time employees whose customary weekly employment is less than 35 hours, if other employees in similar work with the same employer (or, if no employees of the employer are in similar work, in similar work in the same industry and location) have substantially more hours, and seasonal employees whose customary annual employment is less than 9 months, if other employees in similar work with the same employer (or, if no employees of the employer are in similar work, in similar work in the same industry and location) have substantially more months. Notwithstanding the preceding sentence, any employee whose customary weekly employment is less than 25 hours or any employee whose customary annual employment is less than 7 months may be considered as a part-time or seasonal employee.

(D) Employees who are included in a unit of employees covered by an agreement between employee representatives and one or more employers which the Commissioner finds to be a collective bargaining agreement, if accident and health benefits were the subject of good faith bargaining between such employee representatives and such employer or employers. For purposes of determining whether such bargaining occurred, it is not material that such employees are not covered by another medical plan or that the plan was not considered in such bargaining.

. . . .

(3) Nondiscriminatory benefits—(i) In general. In general, benefits subject to reimbursement under a plan must not discriminate in favor of highly compensated individuals. Plan benefits will not satisfy the requirements of this subparagraph unless all the benefits provided for participants who are highly compensated individuals are provided for all other participants. In addition, all the benefits available for the dependents of employees who are highly compensated individuals must also be available on the same basis for the dependents of all other employees who are participants. A plan that provides optional benefits to participants will be treated as providing a single benefit with respect to the benefits covered by the option provided that (A) all eligible participants may elect any of the benefits covered by the option and (B) there are either no required employee contributions or the required employee contributions are the same amount. This test is applied to the benefits subject to reimbursement under the plan rather than the actual benefit payments or claims under the plan. The presence or absence of such discrimination will be determined by considering the type of benefit subject to reimbursement provided highly compensated individuals, as well as the amount of the benefit subject to reimbursement. A plan may establish a maximum limit for the amount of reimbursement which may be paid a participant for any single benefit, or combination of benefits. However, any maximum limit attributable to employer contributions must be uniform for all participants and for all dependents of employees who are participants and may not be modified by reason of a participant's age or years of service.

In addition, if a plan covers employees who are highly compensated individuals, and the type or the amount of benefits subject to reimbursement under the plan are in proportion to employee compensation, the plan discriminates as to benefits.

(ii) Discriminatory operation. Not only must a plan not discriminate on its face in providing benefits in favor of highly compensated individuals, the plan also must not discriminate in favor of such employees in actual operation. The determination of whether plan benefits discriminate in operation in favor of highly compensated individuals is made on the basis of the facts and circumstances of each case. A plan is not considered discriminatory merely because highly compensated individuals participating in the plan utilize a broad range of plan benefits to a greater extent than do other employees participating in the plan. In addition, if a plan (or a particular benefit provided by a plan) is terminated, the termination would cause the plan benefits to be discriminatory if the duration of the plan (or benefit) has the effect of discriminating in favor of highly compensated individuals. Accordingly, the prohibited discrimination may occur where the duration of a particular benefit coincides with the period during which a highly compensated individual utilizes the benefit.

(iii) Retired employees. To the extent that an employer provides benefits under a self-insured medical reimbursement plan to a retired employee that would otherwise be excludible from gross income under section 105(b), determined without regard to section 105 (h), such benefits shall not be considered a discriminatory benefit under this paragraph (c). The preceding sentence shall not apply to a retired employee who was a highly compensated individual unless the type, and the dollar limitations, of benefits provided retired employees who were highly compensated individuals are the same for all other retired participants. If this subdivision applies to a retired participant, that individual is not considered an employee for purposes of determining the highest paid 25 percent of all employees under paragraph (d) of this section solely by reason of receiving such plan benefits.

(4) Multiple plans, etc.—(i) General rule. An employer may designate two or more plans as constituting a single plan that is intended to satisfy the requirements of section 105(h)(2) and paragraph (c) of this section, in which case all plans so designated shall be considered as a single plan in determining whether the requirements of such section are satisfied by each of the separate plans. A determination that the combination of plans so designated does not satisfy such requirements does not preclude a determination that one or more of such plans, considered separately, satisfies such requirements. A single plan document may be utilized by an employer for two or more separate plans provided that the employer designates the plans that are to be considered separately and the applicable provisions of each separate plan.

(ii) Other rules. If the designated combined plan discriminates as to eligibility to participate or benefits, the amount of excess reimbursement will be determined under the rules of section 105(h)(7) and paragraph (e) of this section by taking into account all reimbursements made under the combined plan.

(iii) H.M.O. participants. For purposes of section 105(h)(2)(A) and paragraph (c)(2) of this section, a self-insured plan will be deemed to benefit an employee who has enrolled in a health maintenance organization (HMO) that is offered on an optional basis by the employer in lieu of coverage under the self-insured plan if, with respect to that employee, the employer's contributions to the HMO plan equal or exceed those that would be made to the self-insured plan, and if the HMO plan is designated in accordance with subdivision (i) with the self-insured plan as a single plan. For purposes of section 105(h) and this section, except as provided in the preceding sentence, employees covered by, and benefits under, the HMO plan are not treated as part of the self-insured plan.

(d) Highly compensated individuals defined. For purposes of section 105 (h) and this section, the term "highly compensated individual" means an individual who is—

(1) One of the 5 highest paid officers,

(2) A shareholder who owns (with the application of section 318) more than 10 percent in value of the stock of the employer, or

(3) Among the highest paid 25 percent of all employees (including the 5 highest paid officers, but not including employees excludable under paragraph (c)(2)(iii) of this section who are not participants in any self-insured medical reimbursement plan of the employer, whether or not designated as a single plan under paragraph (c)(4) of this section, or in a health maintenance organization plan).

The status of an employee as an officer or stockholder is determined with respect to a particular benefit on the basis of the employee's officer status or stock ownership at the time during the plan year at which the benefit is provided. In calculating the highest paid 25 percent of all employees, the number of employees included will be rounded to the next highest number. For example, if there are 5 employees, the top two are in the highest paid 25 percent. The level of an employee's compensation is determined on the basis of the employee's compensation for the plan year. For purposes of the preceding sentence, fiscal year plans may determine employee compensation on the basis of the calendar year ending within the plan year.

(e) Excess reimbursement of highly compensated individual—(1) In general. For purposes of section 105(h) and this section, a reimbursement paid to a highly compensated individual is an excess reimbursement if it is paid pursuant to a plan that fails to satisfy the requirements of paragraph (c)(2) or (c)(3) for the plan year. The amount reimbursed to a highly compensated individual which constitutes an excess reimbursement is not excludable from such individual's gross income under section 105(b).

(2) Discriminatory benefit. In the case of a benefit available to highly compensated individuals but not to all other participants (or which otherwise discriminates in favor of highly compensated individuals as opposed to other participants), the amount of excess reimbursement equals the total amount reimbursed to the highly compensated individual with respect to the benefit.

(3) **Discriminatory coverage.** In the case of benefits (other than discriminatory benefits described in subparagraph (2)) paid to a highly compensated individual under a plan which fails to satisfy the requirements of paragraph (c)(2) relating to nondiscrimination in eligibility to participate, the amount of excess reimbursement is determined by multiplying the total amount reimbursed to the individual by a fraction. The numerator of the fraction is the total amount reimbursed during that plan year to all highly compensated individuals. The denominator of the fraction is the total amount reimbursed during that plan year to all participants. In computing the fraction and the total amount reimbursed to the individual, discriminatory benefits described in subparagraph (2) are not taken into account. Accordingly, any amount which is included in income by reason of the benefit's not being available to all other participants will not be taken into account.

(4) **Examples.** The provisions of this paragraph are illustrated by the following examples:

Example (1). Corporation M maintains a self-insured medical reimbursement plan which covers all employees. The plan provides the following maximum limits on the amount of benefits subject to reimbursement: $5,000 for officers and $1,000 for all other participants. During a plan year Employee A, one of the 5 highest paid officers, received reimbursements in the amount of $4,000. Because the amount of benefits provided for highly compensated individuals is not provided for all other participants, the plan benefits are discriminatory. Accordingly, Employee A received an excess reimbursement of $3,000 ($4,000 − $1,000) which constitutes a benefit available to highly compensated individuals, but not to all other participants.

Example (2). Corporation N maintains a self-insured medical reimbursement plan which covers all employees. The plan provides a broad range of medical benefits subject to reimbursement for all participants. However, only the 5 highest paid officers are entitled to dental benefits. During the plan year Employee B, one of the 5 highest paid officers, received dental payments under the plan in the amount of $300. Because dental benefits are provided for highly compensated individuals, and not for all other participants, the plan discriminates as to benefits. Accordingly, Employee B received an excess reimbursement in the amount of $300.

Example (3). Corporation O maintains a self-insured medical reimbursement plan which discriminates as to eligibility by covering only the highest paid 40% of all employees. Benefits subject to reimbursement under the plan are the same for all participants. During a plan year Employee C, a highly compensated individual, received benefits in the amount of $1,000. The amount of excess reimbursement paid Employee C during the plan year will be calculated by multiplying the $1,000 by a fraction determined under subparagraph (3).

Example (4). Corporation P maintains a self-insured medical reimbursement plan for its employees. Benefits subject to reimbursement under the plan are the same for all plan participants. However, the plan fails the eligibility tests of section 105(h)(3)(A) and thereby discriminates as to eligibility. During the 1980 plan year Employee D, a highly compensated individual, was hospitalized for surgery and incurred medical expenses of $4,500 which were reimbursed to D under the plan. During that plan year the Corporation P medical plan paid $50,000 in benefits under the plan, $30,000 of which constituted benefits paid to highly compensated individuals. The amount of excess reimbursement not excludable by D under section 105(b) is $2,700.

$$\left(\$4{,}500 \times \frac{30{,}000}{50{,}000} \right)$$

. . . .

(g) **Exception for medical diagnostic procedures—(1) in general.** For purposes of applying section 105(h) and this section, reimbursements paid under a plan for medical diagnostic procedures for an employee, but not a dependent, are not considered to be a part of a plan described in this section. The medical diagnostic procedures include routine medical examinations, blood tests, and X-rays. Such procedures do not include expenses incurred for the treatment, cure or testing of a known illness or disability, or treatment or testing for a physical injury, complaint or specific symptom of a bodily malfunction. For example, a routine dental examination with X-rays is a medical diagnostic procedure, but X-rays and treatment for a specific complaint are not. In addition, such procedures do not include any activity undertaken for exercise, fitness, nutrition, recreation, or the general improvement of health unless they are for medical care as defined in section 213(e). The diagnostic procedures must be performed at a facility which provides no services (directly or indirectly) other than medical, and ancillary, services. For purposes of the preceding sentence, physical proximity between a medical facility and nonmedical facilities will not for that reason alone cause the medical facility not to qualify. For example, an employee's annual physical examination conducted at the employee's personal physician's office is not considered a part of the medical reimbursement plan and therefore is not subject to the nondiscrimination requirements. Accordingly, the amount reimbursed may be excludable from the employee's income if the requirements of section 105(b) are satisfied.

(2) Transportation, etc. expenses. Transportation expenses primarily for an allowable diagnostic procedure are included within the exception described in this paragraph, but only to the extent they are ordinary and necessary. Transportation undertaken merely for the general improvement of health, or in connection with a vacation, is not within the scope of this exception, nor are any incidental expenses for food or lodging; therefore, amounts reimbursed for such expenses may be excess reimbursements under paragraph (e).

(h) Time of inclusion. Excess reimbursements (determined under paragraph (e)) paid to a highly compensated individual for a plan year will be considered as received in the taxable year of the individual in which (or with which) the plan year ends. The particular plan year to which reimbursements relate shall be determined under the plan provisions. In the absence of plan provisions reimbursements shall be attributed to the plan year in which payment is made. For example, under a calendar year plan an excess reimbursement paid to A in 1981 on account of an expense incurred and subject to reimbursement for the 1980 plan year under the terms of the plan will be considered as received in 1980 by A.

(i) Self-insured contributory plan. A medical plan subject to this section may provide for employer and employee contributions. See § 1.105-1(c). The tax treatment of reimbursements attributable to employee contributions is determined under section 104(a)(3). The tax treatment of reimbursements attributable to employer contributions is determined under section 105. The amount of reimbursements which are attributable to contributions of the employer shall be determined in accordance with § 1.105-1(e).

.   .   .   .   .

§ 1.106-1 Contributions by employer to accident and health plans

The gross income of an employee does not include contributions which his employer makes to an accident or health plan for compensation (through insurance or otherwise) to the employee for personal injuries or sickness incurred by him, his spouse, or his dependents, as defined in section 152. The employer may contribute to an accident or health plan either by paying the premium (or a portion of the premium) on a policy of accident or health insurance covering one or more of his employees, or by contributing to a separate trust or fund (including a fund referred to in section 105(e)) which provides accident or health benefits directly or through insurance to one or more of his employees. However, if such insurance policy, trust, or fund provides other benefits in addition to accident or health benefits, section 106 applies only to the portion of the employer's contribution which is allocable to accident or health benefits. See paragraph (d) of § 1.104-1 and §§ 1.105-1 through 1.105-5, inclusive, for regulations relating to exclusion from an employee's gross income of amounts received through accident or health insurance and through accident or health plans.

§ 1.109-1 Exclusion from gross income of lessor of real property of value of improvements erected by lessee

(a) Income derived by a lessor of real property upon the termination, through forfeiture or otherwise, of the lease of such property and attributable to buildings erected or other improvements made by the lessee upon the leased property is excluded from gross income. However, where the facts disclose that such buildings or improvements represent in whole or in part a liquidation in kind of lease rentals, the exclusion from gross income shall not apply to the extent that such buildings or improvements represent such liquidation. The exclusion applies only with respect to the income realized by the lessor upon the termination of the lease and has no application to income, if any, in the form of rent, which may be derived by a lessor during the period of the lease and attributable to buildings erected or other improvements made by the lessee. It has no application to income which may be realized by the lessor upon the termination of the lease but not attributable to the value of such buildings or improvements. Neither does it apply to income derived by the lessor subsequent to the termination of the lease incident to the ownership of such buildings or improvements.

(b) The provisions of this section may be illustrated by the following example:

Example. The A Corporation leased in 1945 for a period of 50 years unimproved real property to the B Corporation under a lease providing that the B Corporation erect on the leased premises an office building costing $500,-000, in addition to paying the A Corporation a lease rental of $10,000 per annum beginning on the date of completion of the improvements, the sum of $100,000 being placed in escrow for payment of the rental. The building was completed on January 1, 1950. The lease provided that all improvements made by the lessee on the leased property would become the absolute property of the A Corporation on the termination of the lease by forfeiture or otherwise and that the lessor would become entitled on such termination to the remainder of the sum, if any, remaining in the escrow fund. The B Corporation forfeited its lease on January 1, 1955, when the improvements had a value of $100,000. Under the provisions of section 109, the $100,000 is excluded from gross income. The amount of $50,000 representing the remainder in the escrow fund is forfeited to the A Corporation and is included in the gross income of that taxpayer. As to the basis of the property in the hands of the A Corporation, see § 1.1019–1.

§ 1.111–1 Recovery of certain items previously deducted or credited

(a) **General.** Section 111 provides that income attributable to the recovery during any taxable year of bad debts, prior taxes, and delinquency amounts shall be excluded from gross income to the extent of the "recovery exclusion" with respect to such items. The rule of exclusion so prescribed by statute applies equally with respect to all other losses, expenditures, and accruals made the basis of deductions from gross income for prior taxable years, including war losses referred to in section 127 of the Internal Revenue Code of 1939, but not including deductions with respect to depreciation, depletion, amortization, or amortizable bond premiums. The term "recovery exclusion" as used in this section means an amount equal to the portion of the bad debts, prior taxes, and delinquency amounts (the items specifically referred to in section 111), and of all other items subject to the rule of exclusion which, when deducted or credited for a prior taxable year, did not result in a reduction of any tax of the taxpayer under subtitle A (other than the accumulated earnings tax imposed by section 531 or the personal holding company tax imposed by section 541) of the Internal Revenue Code of 1954 . . . .

(1) **Section 111 items.** The term "section 111 items" as used in this section means bad debts, prior taxes, delinquency amounts, and all other items subject to the rule of exclusion, for which a deduction or credit was allowed for a prior taxable year. If a bad debt was previously charged against a reserve by a taxpayer on the reserve method of treating bad debts, it was not deducted, and it is therefore not considered a section 111 item. Bad debts, prior taxes, and delinquency amounts are defined in section 111 (b) (1), (2), and (3), respectively. An example of a delinquency amount is interest on delinquent taxes. An example of the other items not expressly referred to in section 111 but nevertheless subject to the rule of exclusion is a loss sustained upon the sale of stock and later recovered, in whole or in part, through an action against the party from whom such stock had been purchased.

(2) **Definition of "recovery."** Recoveries result from the receipt of amounts in respect of the previously deducted or credited section 111 items, such as from the collection or sale of a bad debt, refund or credit of taxes paid, or cancellation of taxes accrued. Care should be taken in the case of bad debts which were treated as only partially worthless in prior years to

distinguish between the item described in section 111, that is, the part of such debt which was deducted, and the part not previously deducted, which is not a section 111 item and is considered the first part collected. The collection of the part not deducted is not considered a "recovery." Furthermore, the term "recovery" does not include the gain resulting from the receipt of an amount on account of a section 111 item which, together with previous such receipts, exceeds the deduction or credit previously allowed for such item. For instance, a $100 corporate bond purchased for $40 and later deducted as worthless is subsequently collected to the extent of $50. The $10 gain (excess of $50 collection over $40 cost) is not a recovery of a section 111 item. Such gain is in no case excluded from gross income under section 111, regardless of whether the $40 recovery is or is not excluded.

(3) Treatment of debt deducted in more than one year by reason of partial worthlessness. In the case of a bad debt deducted in part for two or more prior years, each such deduction of a part of the debt is considered a separate section 111 item. A recovery with respect to such debt is considered first a recovery of those items (or portions thereof), resulting from such debt, for which there are recovery exclusions. If there are recovery exclusions for two or more items resulting from the same bad debt, such items are considered recovered in the order of the taxable years for which they were deducted, beginning with the latest. The recovery exclusion for any such item is determined by considering the recovery exclusion with respect to the prior year for which such item was deducted as being first used to offset all other applicable recoveries in the year in which the bad debt is recovered.

(4) Special provisions as to worthless bonds, etc., which are treated as capital losses. Certain bad debts arising from the worthlessness of securities and certain nonbusiness bad debts are treated as losses from the sale or exchange of capital assets. See sections 165 (g) and 166 (d). The amounts of the deductions allowed for any year under section 1211 on account of such losses for such year are consid-

ered to be section 111 items. Any part of such losses which, under section 1211, is a deduction for a subsequent year through the capital loss carryover (any later receipt of an amount with respect to such deducted loss is a recovery) is considered a section 111 item for the year in which such loss was sustained.

(b) Computation of recovery exclusion—(1) Amount of recovery exclusion allowable for year of recovery. For the year of any recovery, the section 111 items which were deducted or credited for one prior year are considered as a group and the recovery thereon is considered separately from recoveries of any items which were deducted or credited for other years. This recovery is excluded from gross income to the extent of the recovery exclusion with respect to this group of items as (i) determined for the original year for which such items were deducted or credited (see subparagraph (2) of this paragraph) and (ii) reduced by the excludable recoveries in intervening years on account of all section 111 items for such original year. A taxpayer claiming a recovery exclusion shall submit, at the time the exclusion is claimed, the computation of the recovery exclusion claimed for the original year for which the items were deducted or credited, and computations showing the amount recovered in intervening years on account of the section 111 items deducted or credited for the original year.

(2) Determination of recovery exclusion for original year for which items were deducted or credited. (i) The recovery exclusion for the taxable year for which section 111 items were deducted or credited (that is, the "original taxable year") is the portion of the aggregate amount of such deductions and credits which could be disallowed without causing an increase in any tax of the taxpayer imposed under subtitle A (other than the accumulated earnings tax imposed by section 531 or the personal holding company tax imposed by section 541) of the Internal Revenue Code of 1954 or corresponding provisions of prior income tax laws (other than the World War II excess profits tax imposed under subchapter E, chapter 2 of the Internal Revenue Code of 1939). For the purpose of such recovery exclusion, consideration must be given to the effect of net operating loss carryovers and carrybacks or capital loss carryovers.

. . . .

§ 1.117-1 Exclusion of amounts received as a scholarship or fellowship grant

(a) In general. Any amount received by an individual as a scholarship at an educational institution or as a fellowship grant, including the value of contributed services and accommodations, shall be excluded from the gross income of the recipient, subject to the limitations set forth in section 117 (b) and § 1.117-2. The exclusion from gross income of an amount which is a scholarship or fellowship grant is controlled solely by section 117. Accordingly, to the extent that a scholarship or a fellowship grant exceeds the limitations of section 117 (b) and § 1.117-2, it is includible in the gross income of the recipient notwithstanding the provisions of section 102 relating to exclusion from gross income of gifts, or section 74 (b) relating to exclusion from gross income of certain prizes and awards. For definitions, see § 1.117-3.

(b) Exclusion of amounts received to cover expenses. (1) Subject to the limitations provided in subparagraph (2) of this paragraph, any amount received by an individual to cover expenses for travel (including meals and lodging while traveling and an allowance for travel of the individual's family), research, clerical help, or equipment is excludable from gross income provided that such expenses are incident to a scholarship or fellowship grant which is excludable from gross income under section 117(a) (1). If, however, only a portion of a scholarship or fellowship grant is excludable from gross income under section 117(a) (1) because of the part-time employment limitation contained in section 117 (b) (1) or because of the expiration of the 36-month period described in section 117(b) (2) (B), only the amount received to cover expenses incident to such excludable portion is excludable from gross income. The requirement that these expenses be incident to the scholarship or the fellowship grant means that the expenses of travel, research, clerical help, or equipment must be incurred by the individual in order to effectuate the purpose for which the scholarship or the fellowship grant was awarded.

(2) (i) In the case of a scholarship or fellowship grant which is awarded after July 28, 1956, the exclusion provided under subparagraph (1) of this paragraph is not applicable unless the amount received by the individual is specifically designated to cover expenses for travel, research, clerical help, or equipment.

. . . .

(iii) The exclusion provided under subparagraph (1) of this paragraph is applicable only to the extent that the amount received for travel, research, clerical help, or equipment is actually expended for such expenses by the recipient during the term of the scholarship or fellowship grant and within a reasonable time before and after such term.

(3) The portion of any amount received to cover the expenses described in subparagraph (1) of this paragraph which is not actually expended for such expenses within the exclusion period described in subparagraph (2) of this paragraph shall, if not returned to the grantor within this period, be included in the gross income of the recipient for the taxable year in which such exclusion period expires.

§ 1.117-2 Limitations

(a) Individuals who are candidates for degrees—(1) In general. Under the limitations provided by section 117 (b) (1) in the case of an individual who is a candidate for a degree at an educational institution, the exclusion from gross income shall not apply (except as otherwise provided in subparagraph (2) of this paragraph) to that portion of any amount received as payment for teaching, research, or other services in the nature of part-time employment required as a condition to receiving the scholarship or fellowship grant. Payments for such part-time employment shall be included in the gross income of the recipient in an amount determined by reference to the rate of compensation ordinarily paid for similar services performed by an individual who is not the recipient of a scholarship or a fellowship grant. A typical example of employment under this subparagraph is the case of an individual who is required, as a condition to receiving the scholarship or the fellowship grant, to perform part-time teaching services. A requirement that the individual shall furnish periodic reports to the grantor of the scholarship or the fellowship grant for the purpose of keeping the grantor informed as to the general progress of the individual shall not be deemed to constitute the performance of services in the nature of part-time employment.

(2) Exception. If teaching, research, or other services are required of all candidates (whether or not recipients of scholarships or fellowship grants) for a particular degree as a condition to receiving the degree, such teaching, research, or other services on the part of the recipient of a scholarship or fellowship grant who is a candidate for such degree shall not be regarded as part-time employment within the meaning of this paragraph. Thus, if all candidates for a particular education degree are required, as part of their regular course of study or curriculum, to perform part-time practice teaching services, such services are not to be regarded as part-time employment within the meaning of this paragraph.

(b) Individuals who are not candidates for degrees—(1) Conditions for exclusion. In the case of an individual who is not a candidate for a degree at an educational institution, the exclusion from gross income of an amount received as a scholarship or a fellowship grant shall apply (to the extent provided in subparagraph (2) of this paragraph) only if the grantor of the scholarship or fellowship grant is—

(i) An organization described in section 501(c) (3) which is exempt from tax under section 501(a).

(ii) The United States or an instrumentality or agency thereof, or a State, a territory, or a possession of the United States, or any political subdivision thereof, or the District of Columbia, or

(iii) For taxable years beginning after December 31, 1961, a foreign government, an international organization, or a binational or multinational educational and cultural foundation or commission created or continued pursuant to section 103 of the Mutual Educational and Cultural Exchange Act of 1961 (22 U.S.C.A. § 2453).

(2) Extent of exclusion. (i) In the case of an individual who is not a candidate for a degree, the amount received as a scholarship or a fellowship grant which is excludable from gross income under section 117 (a) (1) shall not exceed an amount equal to $300 times the number of months for which the recipient received amounts under the scholarship or fellowship grant during the taxable year. In determining the number of months during the period for which the recipient received amounts under a scholarship or fellowship grant, computation shall be made on the basis of whole calendar months. A whole calendar month means a period of time terminating with the day of the succeeding month numerically corresponding to the day of the month of its beginning, less one, except that if there be no corresponding day of the succeeding month the period terminates with the last day of the succeeding month. For purposes of this computation a fractional part of a calendar month consisting of a period of time including 15 days or more shall be considered to be a whole calendar month and a fractional part of a calendar month consisting of a period of time including 14 days or less shall be disregarded. For example, if an individual receives a fellowship grant on September 13 which is to expire on June 12 of the following year, the grant shall be considered to have extended for a period of 9 months. If in the preceding example the grant expired on June 27, instead of June 12, the grant shall be considered to have extended for a period of 10 months.

(ii) No exclusion shall be allowed under section 117 (a) (1) to an individual who is not a candidate for a degree after the recipient has, as an individual who is not a candidate for a degree, been entitled to an exclusion under that section for a period of 36 months. This limitation applies if the individual has received any amount which was either excluded or excludable from his gross income under section 117 (a) (1) for any prior 36 months, whether or not consecutive. For example, if the individual received a fellowship grant of $7,200 for 3 years (which he elected to receive in 36 monthly installments of $200), his exclusion period would be exhausted even though he did not in any of the 36 months make use of the maximum exclusion. Accordingly, such individual would be entitled to no further exclusion from gross income with respect to any additional grants which he may receive as an individual who is not a candidate for a degree.

(iii) If an individual who is not a candidate for a degree receives amounts from more than one scholarship or fellowship grant during the taxable year, the total amounts received in the taxable year shall be aggregated for the purpose of computing the amount which may be excludable from gross income for such taxable year. If amounts are received from more than one scholarship or fellowship grant during the same month or months within the taxable year, such month or months shall be counted only once for the purpose of determining the number of months for which the individual received such amounts under the scholarships or fellowship grants during the taxable year. For example, if an individual receives a fellowship grant from one source for the months of January to June of the taxable year and also receives a fellowship grant from another source for the months of March through December of the same taxable year, he shall be considered to have received amounts for 12 months of the taxable year. See example (4) in subparagraph (3) of this paragraph for further illustration.

(3) **Examples.** The application of this paragraph may be further illustrated by the following examples, it being assumed that in each example the grantor is a grantor who is described in section 117 (b) (2) (A) and subparagraph (1) of this paragraph:

Example (1). B, an individual who files his return on the calendar year basis, is awarded a post-doctorate fellowship grant in March 1955. The grant is to commence on September 1, 1955, and is to end on May 31, 1956, so that it will extend over a period of 9 months. The amount of the fellowship grant is $4,500 and B receives this amount in monthly installments of $500 on the first day of each month commencing September 1, 1955. During the taxable year 1955, B receives a total of $2,000 with respect to the 4-month period September through December, inclusive. He may exclude $1,200

from gross income in the taxable year 1955 ($300 × 4) and must include the remaining $900 in gross income for that year. For the year 1956, he will exclude $1,500 ($300 × 5) from gross income with respect to the $2,500 which he receives in that year and must include in gross income $1,000.

Example (2). Assume the same facts as in example (1) except that B receives the full amount of the grant ($4,500) on September 1, 1955. Since the amount received in the taxable year 1955 is for the full term of the fellowship grant (9 months), B may exclude $2,700 ($300 × 9) from gross income for the taxable year 1955. The remaining $1,800 must be included in gross income for that year.

Example (3). C, an individual who files his return on the calendar year basis, is awarded a post-doctorate fellowship grant in March 1955. The amount of the grant is $4,500 for a period commencing on September 1, 1955, and ending 24 months thereafter. C receives the full amount of the grant on September 1, 1955. C may exclude from gross income for the taxable year 1955, the full amount of the grant ($4,500) since this amount does not exceed an amount equal to $300 times the number of months (24) for which he received the amount of the grant during that taxable year.

. . . .

§ 1.117-3 Definitions

(a) **Scholarship.** A scholarship generally means an amount paid or allowed to, or for the benefit of, a student, whether an undergraduate or a graduate, to aid such individual in pursuing his studies. The term includes the value of contributed services and accommodations (see paragraph (d) of this section) and the amount of tuition, matriculation, and other fees which are furnished or remitted to a student to aid him in pursuing his studies. The term also includes any amount received in the nature of a family allowance as a part of a scholarship. However, the term does not include any amount provided by an individual to aid a relative, friend, or other individual in pursuing his studies where the grantor is motivated by family or philanthropic considerations. If an educational institution maintains or participates in a plan whereby the tuition of a child of a faculty member of such institution is remitted by any other participating educational institution attended by such child, the amount of the tuition so remitted shall be considered to be an amount received as a scholarship.

(b) **Educational institution.** For definition of "educational institution" section 117 adopts the definition of that term which is prescribed in section 151 (e) (4). Accordingly, for purposes of section 117 the term "educational institution" means only an educational institution which normally maintains a regular faculty and curriculum and normally has a regularly organized body of students in attendance at the place where its educational activities are carried on. See section 151 (e) (4) and regulations thereunder.

(c) Fellowship grant. A fellowship grant generally means an amount paid or allowed to, or for the benefit of, an individual to aid him in the pursuit of study or research. The term includes the value of contributed services and accommodations (see paragraph (d) of this section) and the amount of tuition, matriculation, and other fees which are furnished or remitted to an individual to aid him in the pursuit of study or research. The term also includes any amount received in the nature of a family allowance as a part of a fellowship grant. However, the term does not include any amount provided by an individual to aid a relative, friend, or other individual in the pursuit of study or research where the grantor is motivated by family or philanthropic considerations.

(d) Contributed services and accommodations. The term "contributed services and accommodations" means such services and accommodations as room, board, laundry service, and similar services or accommodations which are received by an individual as a part of a scholarship or fellowship grant.

(e) Candidate for a degree. The term "candidate for a degree" means an individual, whether an undergraduate or a graduate, who is pursuing studies or conducting research to meet the requirements for an academic or professional degree conferred by colleges or universities. It is not essential that such study or research be pursued or conducted at an educational institution which confers such degrees if the purpose thereof is to meet the requirements for a degree of a college or university which does confer such degrees. A student who receives a scholarship for study at a secondary school or other educational institution is considered to be a "candidate for a degree."

§ 1.117-4 Items not considered as scholarships or fellowship grants

The following payments or allowances shall not be considered to be amounts received as a scholarship or a fellowship grant for the purpose of section 117:

. . . .

(c) Amounts paid as compensation for services or primarily for the benefit of the grantor. (1) Except as provided in paragraph (a) of § 1.117-2, any amount paid or allowed to, or on behalf of, an individual to enable him to pursue studies or research, if such amount represents either compensation for past, present, or future employment services or represents payment for services which are subject to the direction or supervision of the grantor.

(2) Any amount paid or allowed to, or on behalf of, an individual to enable him to pursue studies or research primarily for the benefit of the grantor. However, amounts paid or allowed to, or on behalf of, an individual to enable him to pursue studies or research are considered to be amounts received as a scholarship or fellowship grant for the purpose of section 117 if the primary purpose of the studies or research is to further the education and training of the recipient in his individual capacity and the amount provided by the grantor for such purpose does not represent compensation or payment for the services described in subparagraph (1) of this paragraph. Neither the fact that the recipient is required to furnish reports of his progress to the grantor, nor the fact that the results of his studies or research may be of some incidental benefit to the grantor shall, of itself, be considered to destroy the essential character of such amount as a scholarship or fellowship grant.

§ 1.118-1 Contributions to the capital of a corporation

In the case of a corporation, section 118 provides an exclusion from gross income with respect to any contribution of money or property to the capital of the taxpayer. Thus, if a corporation requires additional funds for conducting its business and obtains such funds through voluntary pro rata payments by its shareholders, the amounts so received being credited to its surplus account or to a special account, such amounts do not constitute income, although there is no increase in the outstanding shares of stock of the corporation. In such a case the payments are in the nature of assessments upon, and represent an additional price paid for, the shares of stock held by the individual shareholders, and will be treated as an addition to and as a part of the operating capital of the company. Section 118 also applies to contributions to capital made by persons other than shareholders. For example, the exclusion applies to the value of land or other property contributed to a corporation by a governmental unit or by a civic group for the purpose of inducing the corporation to locate its business in a particular community, or for the purpose of enabling the corporation to expand its operating facilities. However, the exclusion does not apply to any money or property transferred to the corporation in consideration for goods or services rendered, or to subsidies paid for the purpose of inducing the taxpayer to limit production. See section 362 for the basis of property acquired by a corporation through a contribution to its capital by its stockholders or by nonstockholders.

§ 1.119-1 Meals and lodging furnished for the convenience of the employer

(a) Meals—(1) In general. The value of meals furnished to an employee by his employer shall be excluded from the employee's gross income if two tests are met: (i) The meals are furnished on the business premises of the employer, and (ii) the meals are furnished for the convenience of the employer. The question of whether meals are furnished for the convenience of the employer is one of fact to be determined by analysis of all the facts and circumstances in each case. If the tests described in subdivisions (i) and (ii) of this subparagraph are met, the exclusion shall apply irrespective of whether under an employment contract or a statute fixing the terms of employment such meals are furnished as compensation.

(2) Meals furnished without a charge. (i) Meals furnished by an employer without charge to the employee will be regarded as furnished for the convenience of the employer if such meals are furnished for a substantial noncompensatory business reason of the employer. If an employer furnishes meals as a means of providing additional compensation to his employee (and not for a substantial noncompensatory business reason of the employer), the meals so furnished will not be regarded as furnished for the convenience of the employer. Conversely, if the employer furnishes meals to his employee for a substantial noncompensatory business reason, the meals so furnished will be regarded as furnished for the convenience of the employer, even though such meals are also furnished for a compensatory reason. In determining the reason of an employer for furnishing meals, the mere declaration that meals are furnished for a noncompensatory business reason is not sufficient to prove that meals are furnished for the convenience of the employer, but such determination will be based upon an examination of all the surrounding facts and circumstances. In subdivision (ii) of this subparagraph, there are set forth some of the substantial noncompensatory business reasons which occur frequently and which justify the conclusion that meals furnished for such a reason are furnished for the convenience of the employer. In subdivision (iii) of this subparagraph, there are set forth some of the business reasons which are considered to be compensatory and which, in the absence of a substantial noncompensatory business reason, justify the conclusion that meals furnished for such a reason are not furnished for the convenience of the employer. Generally, meals furnished before or after the working hours of the employee will not be regarded as furnished for the convenience of the employer, but see subdivision (ii) (d) and (f) of this subparagraph for some exceptions to this general rule. Meals furnished on nonworking days do not qualify for the exclusion under section 119. If the employee is required to occupy living quarters on the business premises of his employer as a condition of his employment (as defined in paragraph (b) of this section), the exclusion applies to the value of any meal furnished without charge to the employee on such premises.

(ii) (a) Meals will be regarded as furnished for a substantial noncompensatory business reason of the employer when the meals are furnished to the employee during his working hours to have the employee available for emergency call during his meal period. In order to demonstrate that meals are furnished to the employee to have the employee available for emergency call during the meal period, it must be shown that emergencies have actually occurred, or can reasonably be expected to occur, in the employer's business which have resulted, or will result, in the employer calling on the employee to perform his job during his meal period.

(b) Meals will be regarded as furnished for a substantial noncompensatory business reason of the employer when the meals are furnished to the employee during his working hours because the employer's business is such that the employee must be restricted to a short meal period, such as 30 or 45 minutes, and because the employee could not be expected to eat elsewhere in such a short meal period. For example, meals may qualify under this subdivision when the employer is engaged in a business in which the peak workload occurs during the normal lunch hours. However, meals cannot qualify under this subdivision (b) when the reason for restricting the time of the meal period is so that the employee can be let off earlier in the day.

(c) Meals will be regarded as furnished for a substantial noncompensatory business reason of the employer when the meals are furnished to the employee during his working hours because the employee could not otherwise secure proper meals within a reasonable meal period. For example, meals may qualify under this subdivision (c) when there are insufficient eating facilities in the vicinity of the employer's premises.

(d) A meal furnished to a restaurant employee or other food service employee for each meal period in which the employee works will be regarded as furnished for a substantial noncompensatory business reason of the employer, irrespective of whether the meal is furnished during, immediately before, or immediately after the working hours of the employee.

(e) If the employer furnishes meals to employees at a place of business and the reason for furnishing the meals to each of substantially all of the employees who are furnished the meals is a substantial noncompensatory business reason of the employer, the meals furnished to each other employee will also be regarded as furnished for a substantial noncompensatory business reason of the employer.

(f) If an employer would have furnished a meal to an employee during his working hours for a substantial noncompensatory business reason, a meal furnished to such an employee immediately after his working hours because his duties prevented him from obtaining a meal during his working hours will be regarded as furnished for a substantial noncompensatory business reason.

(iii) Meals will be regarded as furnished for a compensatory business reason of the employer when the meals are furnished to the employee to promote the morale or goodwill of the employee, or to attract prospective employees.

(3) Meals furnished with a charge. (i) If an employer provides meals which an employee may or may not purchase, the meals will not be regarded as furnished for the convenience of the employer. Thus, meals for which a charge is made by the employer will not be regarded as furnished for the convenience of the employer if the employee has a choice of accepting the meals and paying for them or of not paying for them and providing his meals in another manner.

(ii) If an employer furnishes an employee meals for which the employee is charged an unvarying amount (for example, by subtraction from his stated compensation) irrespective of whether he accepts the meals, the amount of such flat charge made by the employer for such meals is not, as such, part of the compensation includible in the gross income of the employee; whether the value of the meals so furnished is excludable under section 119 is determined by applying the rules of subparagraph (2) of this paragraph. If meals furnished for an unvarying amount are not furnished for the convenience of the employer in accordance with the rules of subparagraph (2) of this paragraph, the employee shall include in gross income the value of the meals regardless of whether the value exceeds or is less than the amount charged for such meals. In the absence of evidence to the contrary, the value of the meals may be deemed to be equal to the amount charged for them.

(b) Lodging. The value of lodging furnished to an employee by the employer shall be excluded from the employee's gross income if three tests are met:

(1) The lodging is furnished on the business premises of the employer,

(2) The lodging is furnished for the convenience of the employer, and

(3) The employee is required to accept such lodging as a condition of his employment.

The requirement of subparagraph (3) of this paragraph that the employee is required to accept such lodging as a condition of his employment means that he be required to accept the lodging in order to enable him properly to perform the duties of his employment. Lodging will be regarded as furnished to enable the employee properly to perform the duties of his employment when, for example, the lodging is furnished because the employee is required to be available for duty at all times or because the employee could not perform the services required of him unless he is furnished such lodging. If the tests described in subparagraphs (1), (2), and (3) of this paragraph are met, the exclusion shall apply irrespective of whether a charge is made, or whether, under an employment contract or statute fixing the terms of employment, such lodging is furnished as compensation. If the employer furnishes the employee lodging for which the employee is charged an unvarying amount irrespective of whether he accepts the lodging, the amount of the charge made by the employer for such lodging is not, as such, part of the compensation includible in the gross income of the employee; whether the value of the lodging is excludable from gross income under section 119 is determined by applying the other rules of this paragraph. If the tests described in subparagraph (1), (2), and (3) of this paragraph are not met, the employee shall include in gross income the value of the lodging regardless of whether it exceeds or is less than the amount charged. In the absence of evidence to the contrary, the value of the lodging may be deemed to be equal to the amount charged.

(c) Rules. (1) For purposes of this section, the term "business premises of the employer" generally means the place of employment of the employee. For example, meals and lodging furnished in the employer's home to a domestic servant would constitute meals and lodging furnished on the business premises of the employer. Similarly, meals furnished to cowhands while herding their employer's cattle on leased land would be regarded as furnished on the business premises of the employer.

(2) The exclusion provided by section 119 applies only to meals and lodging furnished in kind by an employer to his employee. If the employee has an option to receive additional compensation in lieu of meals or lodging in kind, the value of such meals and lodging is not excluded from gross income. However, the mere fact that an employee, at his option, may decline to accept meals tendered in kind will not of itself require inclusion of the value thereof in gross income. Cash allowances for meals or lodging received by an employee are includible in gross income to the extent that such allowances constitute compensation.

(d) Examples. The provisions of section 119 may be illustrated by the following examples:

Example (1). A waitress who works from 7 a. m. to 4 p. m. is furnished without charge two meals a work day. The employer encourages the waitress to have her breakfast on his business premises before starting work, but does not require her to have breakfast there. She is required, however, to have her lunch on such premises. Since the waitress is a food service employee and works during the normal breakfast and lunch periods, the waitress is permitted to exclude from her gross income both the value of the breakfast and the value of the lunch.

Example (2). The waitress in example (1) is allowed to have meals on the employer's premises without charge on her days off. The waitress is not permitted to exclude the value of such meals from her gross income.

Example (3). A bank teller who works from 9 a. m. to 5 p. m. is furnished his lunch without charge in a cafeteria which the bank maintains on its premises. The bank furnishes the teller such meals in order to limit his lunch period to 30 minutes since the bank's peak work load occurs during the normal lunch period. If the teller had to obtain his lunch elsewhere, it would take him considerably longer than 30 minutes for lunch, and the bank strictly enforces the 30-

minute time limit. The bank teller may exclude from his gross income the value of such meals obtained in the bank cafeteria.

Example (4). Assume the same facts as in example (3), except that the bank charges the bank teller an unvarying rate per meal regardless of whether he eats in the cafeteria. The bank teller is not required to include in gross income such flat amount charged as part of his compensation, and he is entitled to exclude from his gross income the value of the meals he receives for such flat charge.

Example (5). A Civil Service employee of a State is employed at an institution and is required by his employer to be available for duty at all times. The employer furnishes the employee with meals and lodging at the institution without charge. Under the applicable State statute, his meals and lodging are regarded as part of the employee's compensation. The employee would nevertheless be entitled to exclude the value of such meals and lodging from his gross income.

Example (6). An employee of an institution is given the choice of residing at the institution free of charge, or of residing elsewhere and receiving a cash allowance in addition to his regular salary. If he elects to reside at the institution, the value to the employee of the lodging furnished by the employer will be includible in the employee's gross income because his residence at the institution is not required in order for him to perform properly the duties of his employment.

Example (7). A construction worker is employed at a construction project at a remote job site in Alaska. Due to the inaccessibility of facilities for the employees who are working at the job site to obtain food and lodging and the prevailing weather conditions, the employer is required to furnish meals and lodging to the employee at the camp site in order to carry on the construction project. The employee is required to pay $40 a week for the meals and lodging. The weekly charge of $40 is not, as such, part of the compensation includible in the gross income of the employee, and under paragraphs (a) and (b) of this section the value of the meals and lodging is excludable from his gross income.

Example (8). A manufacturing company provides a cafeteria on its premises at which its employees can purchase their lunch. There is no other eating facility located near the company's premises, but the employee can furnish his own meal by bringing his lunch. The amount of compensation which any employee is required to include in gross income is not reduced by the amount charged for the meals, and the meals are not considered to be furnished for the convenience of the employer.

Example (9). A hospital maintains a cafeteria on its premises where all of its 230 employees may obtain a meal during their working hours. No charge is made for these meals. The hospital furnishes such meals in order to have each of 210 of the employees available for any emergencies that may occur, and it is shown that each such employee is at times called upon to perform services during his meal period. Although the hospital does not require such employees to remain on the premises during meal periods, they rarely leave the hospital during their meal period. Since the hospital furnishes meals to each of substantially all of its employees in order to have each of them available for emergency call during his meal period, all of the hospital employees who obtain their meals in the hospital cafeteria may exclude from their gross income the value of such meals.

§ 1.121–1 Gain from sale or exchange of residence of individual who has attained age 55

(a) General rule. Section 121(a) provides that a taxpayer may, under certain circumstances, elect to exclude from gross income gain realized on the sale or exchange of property which was the taxpayer's principal residence. Subject to the other provisions of section 121 and the regulations thereunder, the election may be made only if—

(1) The taxpayer attained the age of 55 before the date of the sale or exchange of the taxpayer's principal residence, and

(2) Except as provided in paragraph (b) of this section, during the 5-year period ending on the date of the sale or exchange of the property the taxpayer owned and used the property as the taxpayer's principal residence for periods aggregating 3 years or more.

(b) Transitional rule. In the case of a sale or exchange of a residence before July 26, 1981, a taxpayer who has attained age 65 on the date of such sale or exchange may elect to have this section applied by substituting "8-year period" for "5-year period" and "5 years" for "3 years" in paragraph (a) of this section and where appropriate in §§ 1.121–4 and 1.121–5.

(c) Ownership and use. The requirements of ownership and use for periods aggregating 3 years or more may be satisfied by establishing ownership and use for 36 full months (or 60 full months if the transitional rule is elected) or for 1,095 days (365 × 3) (or 1,825 days if the transitional rule is elected). In establishing whether a taxpayer has satisfied the requirement of three years of use, short temporary absences such as for vacation or other seasonal absence (although accompanied with rental of the residence) are counted as periods of use.

(d) Examples. The provisions of paragraph (a) are illustrated by the following examples:

Example (1). Taxpayer A owned and used his house as his principal residence since 1966. On January 1, 1980, when he is over 55, A retires and moves to another state with his wife. A leases his house from then until September 30, 1981, when he sells it. A may make an election under section 121(a) with respect to any gain on such sale since he has owned and used the house as his principal residence for 3 years out of the 5 years preceding the sale.

Example (2). Taxpayer B purchased his house in 1971 when he was 65 and lived there with his wife. On July 1, 1977, he moved out and leased the house to a tenant. On September 15, 1979, he sold the house. Although he does not meet the use requirements of section 1.121-1(a), he may elect to use the transitional rule in section 1.121-1(b), since the sale was made before July 26, 1981. Because he owned and used the house as his principal residence for 5 out of the 8 years preceding the sale, under the transitional rule he may elect the section 121 exclusion.

Example (3). Taxpayer C lived with his son and daughter-in-law in a house owned by his son from 1973 through 1979. On January 1, 1980, he purchased this house and on July 31, 1982, he sold it. Although B used the property as his principal residence for more than 3 years, he is not entitled to make an election under section 121(a) in respect of such sale since he did not own the residence for a period aggregating 3 years during the 5 year period ending on the date of the sale.

Example (4). Taxpayer D, a college professor, purchased and moved into a house on January 1, 1980. He used the house as his principal residence continuously to February 1, 1982, on which date he went abroad for a 1-year sabbatical leave. During a portion of the period of leave the property was unoccupied and it was leased during the balance of the period. On March 1, 1983, 1 month after returning from such leave, he sold the house. Since his leave is not considered to be a short temporary absence for purposes of section 121(a), the period of such leave may not be included in determining whether D used the house as his principal residence for periods aggregating 3 years during the 5 year period ending on the date of the sale. Thus, D is not entitled to make an election under section 121(a) since he did not use the residence for the requisite period.

Example (5). Assume the same facts as in example (1) except that during the three summers from 1977 through 1979, A left his residence for a 2-month vacation each year. Although, in the 5 year period preceding the date of sale, the total time spent away from his residence on such vacations (6 months) plus the time spent away from such residence from January 1, 1980, to September 30, 1981 (21 months) exceeds 2 years, he may make an election under section 121(a) since the 2-month vacations are counted as periods of use in determining whether A used the residence for the requisite period.

§ 1.121-2 Limitations

(a) Dollar limitation—(1) Amount excludable. Under section 121(a), an individual may exclude from gross income up to $100,000 of gain from the sale of his or her principal residence ($50,000 in the case of a separate return by a married individual).

(2) Example. The provisions of this paragraph are illustrated by the following example:

Example. Assume that A sells his principal residence for $160,800, that the amount realized is $160,400 (selling price reduced by selling expenses, described in paragraph (b)(4)(i) of § 1.1034-1, of $400); and that A's gain realized from the sale is $107,900 (amount realized reduced by adjusted basis of $52,500). The portion of the gain which is taxable is $7,900 ($107,900) — ($100,000). Thus $100,000 is the portion of the gain excludable from gross income pursuant to an election under section 121(a).

(b) Application to only one sale or exchange. (1) Except as provided in paragraph (c), a taxpayer may not make an election to exclude from gross income gain from the sale or exchange of a principal residence if there is in effect at the time the taxpayer wishes to make such election—

(i) An election made by the taxpayer, under section 121(a), in respect of any other sale or exchange of a residence, or

(ii) An election made by the taxpayer's spouse (such marital status to be determined at the time of the sale or exchange by the taxpayer, see paragraph (f) of § 1.121-5) under the provisions of section 121(a) in respect of any other sale or exchange of a residence (without regard to whether at the time of such sale or exchange such spouse was married to the taxpayer).

If the taxpayer and his spouse, before their marriage each owned and used a separate residence and if (after their marriage) both residences are sold, whether or not in a single transaction, an election under section 121(a) may be made with respect to a sale of either residence (but not with respect to both residences) if, at the time of sale, the age, ownership, and use requirements are met.

(2) The provisions of this paragraph are illustrated by the following examples:

Example (1). While A and B are married, A sells his separately owned residence and makes an election under section 121(a) in respect of such sale. Pursuant to the requirement of section 121(c), B joins in such election. Subsequently, A and B are divorced and B married C. While B and C are married, C sells his residence. C is not entitled to make an election under section 121(a) since an election by B, his spouse, is in effect. It does not matter that B obtained no personal benefit from her election.

Example (2). The facts are the same as in example (1) except that after the sale of C's residence, A and B, pursuant to the provisions of paragraph (c) of § 1.121–4, revoke their election. B and C, subject to the other provisions of this section, may then make an election with respect to any gain realized on the sale of C's residence.

Example (3). The facts are the same as in example (1) except that C marries B after C sells his residence but before he makes an election under section 121(a) with respect to any gain realized on such sale. C, if there is not in effect an election made by him under section 121(a) with respect to a prior sale, may make an election with respect to his sale since B does not have to join with him in such election. (In the case of a sale of property jointly held by husband and wife, see paragraph (a) of § 1.121–5.)

(c) Additional election if prior sale was made on or before July 26, 1978. In the case of any sale or exchange after July 26, 1978, section 121 shall be applied by not taking into account any election made with respect to a sale or exchange on or before such date.

§ 1.121–3   Definitions

(a) Principal residence. The term "principal residence" has the same meaning as in section 1034 (relating to sale or exchange of residence) and the regulations thereunder (see paragraph (c)(3) of § 1.1034–1).

(b) Sale or exchange. A "sale or exchange" of a residence includes the destruction, theft, seizure, requisition, or condemnation of such residence.

(c) Gain realized. The term "gain realized" has the same meaning as in paragraph (b)(5) of § 1.1034–1 (determined without regard to section 121(d)(7) and paragraph (g) of § 1.-121–5).

§ 1.121–4   Election

(a) General rule. A taxpayer may make an election under section 121(a) in respect of a particular sale (or may revoke any such election) at any time before the expiration of the period for making a claim for credit or refund of Federal income tax for the taxable year in which the sale or exchange occurred.

A taxpayer who is married at the time of the sale or exchange—

(1) May not make an election under section 121(a) unless his spouse (at the time of the sale or exchange) joins him in such election, and

(2) May not revoke an election previously made by him unless his spouse (at the time of the sale or exchange) joins him in the revocation.

If the taxpayer's spouse dies after the sale or exchange but before the expiration of the time for making an election under this section (and an election was not made by the husband and wife), the deceased spouse's personal representative (administrator or executor, etc.) must join with the taxpayer in making an election. For purposes of making an election under section 121(a), if no personal representative of the deceased spouse has been appointed at or before the time of making the election, then the surviving spouse shall be considered the personal representative of such deceased spouse. Any election previously made by the taxpayer may be revoked only if the personal representative of the taxpayer's deceased spouse joins in such revocation.

(b) Manner of making election. The election under section 121(a) shall be made in a statement signed by the taxpayer and (where required) by his spouse and attached to the taxpayer's income tax return, when filed, for the taxable year during which the sale or exchange of his residence occurs. (See Form 2119 and the accompanying instructions). The statement shall indicate that the taxpayer elects to exclude from his gross income for such year so much of the gain realized on such sale or exchange as may be excluded under section 121. The statement shall also show—

(1) The adjusted basis of the residence as of the date of disposition;

(2) The date of its acquisition;

(3) The date of its disposition;

(4) The names and social security numbers of the owners of the residence as of the date of sale, the form of such ownership, and the age and marital status (as determined under paragraph (f) of § 1.121–5) of such owner or owners at the time of the sale;

(5) The duration of any absences (other than vacation or other seasonal absence) by such owner or owners during the 5 years (8 years under the transitional rule) preceding the sale; and

(6) Whether any such owner or owners have previously made an election under section 121(a), the date of such election, the taxable year with respect to which such election was made, the district director with whom such election was filed, and, if such election has been revoked, the date of such revocation.

(c) Manner of revoking election. The revocation of an election under section 121(a) shall be made by the taxpayer by filing a signed statement showing his name and social security number and indicating that the taxpayer revokes the election he made under section 121(a). The statement shall also show the taxable year of the taxpayer for which such election was made. The statement shall be signed by the taxpayer and (where required) by his spouse or their personal representatives and filed with the district director with whom the election was filed. In addition, if, at the time the statement is filed, the statutory period for assessment of a deficiency for the taxable year for which the election was made will expire within one year, then, the revocation is not effective unless the taxpayer also consents, in writing, that the statutory period for assessment of any deficiency (to the extent that such deficiency is attributable to the revocation of the election) shall not expire before the expiration of one year after the date the statement was filed with the district director. Such consent must be filed prior to the date of the expiration of the statutory period for assessment for the taxable year for which the election was made.

§ 1.123-1 Exclusion of insurance proceeds for reimbursement of certain living expenses

(a) In general. (1) Gross income does not include insurance proceeds received by an individual on or after January 1, 1969, pursuant to the terms of an insurance contract for indemnification of the temporary increase in living expenses resulting from the loss of use or occupancy of his principal residence, or a part thereof, due to damage or destruction by fire, storm, or other casualty. The term "other casualty" has the same meaning assigned to such term under section 165(c)(3). The exclusion also applies in the case of an individual who is denied access to his principal residence by governmental authorities because of the occurrence (or threat of occurrence) of such a casualty. The amount excludable under this section is subject to the limitation set forth in paragraph (b) of this section.

(2) This exclusion applies to amounts received as reimbursement or compensation for the reasonable and necessary increase in living expenses incurred by the insured and members of his household to maintain their customary standard of living during the loss period.

(3) This exclusion does not apply to an insurance recovery for the loss of rental income. Nor does the exclusion apply to any insurance recovery which compensates for the loss of, or damage to, real or personal property. See section 165(c)(3) relating to casualty losses; section 1231 relating to gain on an involuntary conversion of a capital asset held for more than 1 year (6 months for taxable years beginning before 1977; 9 months for taxable years beginning in 1977); and section 1033 relating to recognition of gain on an involuntary conversion. In the case of property used by an insured partially as a principal residence and partially for other purposes, the exclusion does not apply to the amount of insurance proceeds which compensates for the portion of increased expenses attributable to the nonresidential use of temporary replacement property during the loss period. In the case of denial of access to a principal residence by governmental authority, the exclusion provided by this section does not apply to an insurance recovery received by an individual as reimbursement for living expenses incurred by reason of a governmental condemnation or order not related to a casualty or the threat of a casualty.

(4)(i) Subject to the limitation set forth in paragraph (b), the amount excludable is the amount which is identified by the insurer as being paid exclusively for increased living expenses resulting from the loss of use or occupancy of the principal residence and pursuant to the terms of the insurance contract.

(ii) When a lump-sum insurance settlement includes, but does not specifically identify, compensation for property damage, loss of rental income, and increased living expenses, the amount of such settlement allocable to living expenses shall, in the case of uncontested claims, be that portion of the settlement which bears the same ratio to the total recovery as the amount of claimed increased living expense bears to the total amount of claimed losses and expenses, to the extent not in excess of the coverage limitations specified in the contract for such losses and expenses.

(iii) In the case of a lump-sum settlement involving contested claims, the insured shall establish the amount reasonably allocable to increased living expenses, consistent with the terms of the contract and other facts of the particular case.

(iv) In no event may the amount of a lump-sum settlement which is allocable to increased living expenses exceed the coverage limitation specified in the contract for increased living expenses. Where, however, a coverage limitation is applicable to the total amount payable for increased living expenses and, for example, loss of rental income, the amount of an unitemized settlement which is allocable to increased living expenses may not exceed the portion of the applicable coverage limitation which bears the same ratio to such limitation as the amount of increased living expenses bears to the sum of the amount of such increased living expenses and the amount, if any, of lost rental income.

(5) The portion of any insurance recovery for increased living expenses which exceeds the limitation set forth in paragraph (b) shall be included in gross income under section 61 of the Code.

(b) Limitation—(1) Amount excludable. The amount excludable under this section is limited to amounts received which are not in excess of the amount by which (i) total actual living expenses incurred by the insured and members of his household which result from the loss of use or occupancy of their residence exceed (ii) the total normal living expenses which would have been incurred during the loss period but are not incurred as a result of the loss of use or occupancy of the principal residence. Generally, the excludable amount represents such excess expenses actually incurred by reason of a casualty, or threat thereof, for renting suitable housing and for extraordinary expenses for transportation, food, utilities, and miscellaneous services during the period of repair or replacement of the damaged principal residence or denial of access by governmental authority.

(2) Actual living expenses. For purposes of this section, actual living expenses are the reasonable and necessary expenses incurred as a result of the loss of use or occupancy of the principal residence to maintain the insured and members of his household in accordance with their customary standard of living. Actual living expenses must be of such a nature as to qualify as a reimbursable expense under the terms of the applicable insurance contract without regard to monetary limitations upon coverage. Generally, actual living expenses include the cost during the loss period of temporary housing, utilities furnished at the place of temporary housing, meals obtained at restaurants which customarily would have been prepared in the residence, transportation, and other miscellaneous services. To the extent that the loss of use or occupancy of the principal residence results merely in an increase in the amount expended for items of living expenses normally incurred, such as food and transportation, only the increase in such costs shall be considered as actual living expenses in computing the limitation.

(3) Normal living expenses not incurred. Normal living expenses consist of the same categories of expenses comprising actual living expenses which would have been incurred but are not incurred as a result of the casualty or threat thereof. If the loss of use of the residence results in a decrease in the amount normally expended for a living expense item during the loss period, the item of normal living

expense is considered not to have been incurred to the extent of the decrease for purposes of computing the limitation.

. . . .

§ 1.151-1 Deductions for personal exemptions

(a) **In general.** (1) In computing taxable income, an individual is allowed a deduction for the exemptions specified in section 151. Such exemptions are: (i) The exemptions for an individual taxpayer and spouse (the so-called personal exemptions); (ii) the additional exemptions for a taxpayer attaining the age of 65 years and spouse attaining the age of 65 years (the so-called old-age exemptions); (iii) the additional exemptions for a blind taxpayer and a blind spouse; and (iv) the exemptions for dependents of the taxpayer.

. . . .

(b) **Exemptions for individual taxpayer and spouse (so-called personal exemptions).** Section 151(b) allows an exemption for the taxpayer and an additional exemption for the spouse of the taxpayer if a joint return is not made by the taxpayer and his spouse, and if the spouse, for the calendar year in which the taxable year of the taxpayer begins, has no gross income and is not the dependent of another taxpayer. Thus, a husband is not entitled to an exemption for his wife on his separate return for the taxable year beginning in a calendar year during which she has any gross income (though insufficient to require her to file a return). Since, in the case of a joint return, there are two taxpayers (although under section 6013 there is only one income for the two taxpayers on such return, i. e., their aggregate income), two exemptions are allowed on such return, one for each taxpayer spouse. If in any case a joint return is made by the taxpayer and his spouse, no other person is allowed an exemption for such spouse even though such other person would have been entitled to claim an exemption for such spouse as a dependent if such joint return had not been made.

(c) **Exemptions for taxpayer attaining the age of 65 and spouse attaining the age of 65 (so-called old-age exemptions).** (1) Section 151(c) provides an additional exemption for the taxpayer if he has attained the age of 65 before the close of his taxable year. An additional exemption is also allowed to the taxpayer for his spouse if a joint return is not made by the taxpayer and his spouse and if the spouse has attained the age of 65 before the close of the taxable year of the taxpayer and, for the calendar year in which the taxable year of the taxpayer begins, the spouse has no gross income and is not the dependent of another taxpayer. If a husband and wife make a joint return, an old-age exemption will be allowed as to each taxpayer spouse who has attained the age of 65 before the close of the taxable year for which the joint return is made. The exemptions under section 151(c) are in addition to the exemptions for the taxpayer and spouse under section 151(b).

(2) In determining the age of an individual for the purposes of the exemption for old age, the last day of the taxable year of the taxpayer is the controlling date. Thus, in the event of a separate return by a husband, no additional exemption for old age may be claimed for his spouse unless such spouse has attained the age of 65 on or before the close of the taxable year of the husband. In no event shall the additional exemption for old age be allowed with respect to a spouse who dies before attaining the age of 65 even though such spouse would have attained the age of 65 before the close of the taxable year of the taxpayer. For the purposes of the old-age exemption, an individual attains the age of 65 on the first moment of the day preceding his sixty-fifth birthday. Accordingly, an individual whose sixty-fifth birthday falls on January 1 in a given year attains the age of 65 on the last day of the calendar year immediately preceding.

. . . .

§ 1.161-1 Allowance of deductions

Section 161 provides for the allowance as deductions, in computing taxable income under section 63(a), of the items specified in part VI (section 161 and following), subchapter B, chapter 1 of the Code, subject to the exceptions provided in part IX (section 261 and following), of such subchapter B, relating to items not deductible). Double deductions are not permitted.

Amounts deducted under one provision of the Internal Revenue Code of 1954 cannot again be deducted under any other provision thereof. . . . .

§ 1.162-1 Business expenses

(a) **In general.** Business expenses deductible from gross income include the ordinary and necessary expenditures directly connected with or pertaining to the taxpayer's trade or business, except items which are used as the basis for a deduction or a credit under provisions of law other than section 162. The cost of goods purchased for resale, with proper adjustment for opening and closing inventories, is deducted from gross sales in computing gross income. See paragraph (a) of § 1.61-3. Among the items included in business expenses are management expenses, commissions (but see section 263 and the regulations thereunder), labor, supplies, incidental repairs, operating expenses of automobiles used in the trade or business, traveling expenses while away from home solely in the pursuit of a trade or business (see § 1.162-2), advertising and other selling expenses, together with insurance premiums against fire, storm, theft, accident, or other similar losses in the case of a business, and rental for the use of business property. No such item shall be included in business expenses, however, to the extent that it is used by the taxpayer in computing the cost of property included in its inventory or used in determining the gain or loss basis of its plant, equipment, or other property. See section 1054 and the regulations thereunder. A deduction for an expense paid or incurred after December 30, 1969, which would otherwise be allowable under section 162 shall not be denied on the grounds that allowance of such deduction would frustrate a sharply defined public policy. See section 162(c), (f), and (g) and the regulations thereunder. The full amount of the allowable deduction for ordinary and necessary expenses in carrying on a business is deductible, even though such expenses exceed the gross income derived during the taxable year from such business. . . . .

. . . . .

§ 1.162-2 Traveling expenses

(a) Traveling expenses include travel fares, meals and lodging, and expenses incident to travel such as expenses for sample rooms, telephone and telegraph, public stenographers, etc. Only such traveling expenses as are reasonable and necessary in the conduct of the taxpayer's business and directly attributable to it may be deducted. If the trip is undertaken for other than business purposes, the travel fares and expenses incident to travel are personal expenses and the meals and lodging are living expenses. If the trip is solely on business, the reasonable and necessary traveling expenses, including travel fares, meals and lodging, and expenses incident to travel, are business expenses. For the allowance of traveling expenses as deductions in determining adjusted gross income, see section 62(2) (B) and the regulations thereunder.

(b) (1) If a taxpayer travels to a destination and while at such destination engages in both business and personal activities, traveling expenses to and from such destination are deductible only if the trip is related primarily to the taxpayer's trade or business. If the trip is primarily personal in nature, the traveling expenses to and from the destination are not deductible even though the taxpayer engages in business activities while at such destination. However, expenses while at the destination which are properly allocable to the taxpayer's trade or business are deductible even though the traveling expenses to and from the destination are not deductible.

(2) Whether a trip is related primarily to the taxpayer's trade or business or is primarily personal in nature depends on the facts and circumstances in each case. The amount of time during the period of the trip which is spent on personal activity compared to the amount of time spent on activities directly relating to the taxpayer's trade or business is an important factor in determining whether the trip is primarily personal. If, for example, a taxpayer spends one week while at a destination on activities which are directly related to his trade or business and subsequently spends an additional five weeks for vacation or other personal activities, the trip will be considered primarily personal in nature in the absence of a clear showing to the contrary.

(c) Where a taxpayer's wife accompanies him on a business trip, expenses attributable to her travel are not deductible unless it can be adequately shown that the wife's presence on the trip has a bona fide business purpose. The wife's performance of some incidental service does not cause her expenses to qualify as deductible business expenses. The same rules apply to any other members of the taxpayer's family who accompany him on such a trip.

(d) Expenses paid or incurred by a taxpayer in attending a convention or other meeting may constitute an ordinary and necessary business expense under section 162 depending upon the facts and circumstances of each case. No distinction will be made between self-employed persons and employees. The fact that an employee uses vacation or leave time or that his attendance at the convention is voluntary will not necessarily prohibit the allowance of the deduction. The allowance of deductions for such expenses will depend upon whether there is a sufficient relationship between the taxpayer's trade or business and his attendance at the convention or other meeting so that he is benefiting or advancing the interests of his trade or business by such attendance. If the convention is for political, social or other purposes unrelated to the taxpayer's trade or business, the expenses are not deductible.

(e) Commuters' fares are not considered as business expenses and are not deductible.

. . . . .

§ 1.162–3 Cost of materials

Taxpayers carrying materials and supplies on hand should include in expenses the charges for materials and supplies only in the amount that they are actually consumed and used in operation during the taxable year for which the return is made, provided that the costs of such materials and supplies have not been deducted in determining the net income or loss or taxable income for any previous year. If a taxpayer carries incidental materials or supplies on hand for which no record of consumption is kept or of which physical inventories at the beginning and end of the year are not taken, it will be permissible for the taxpayer to include in his expenses and to deduct from gross income the total cost of such supplies and materials as were purchased during the taxable year for which the return is made, provided the taxable income is clearly reflected by this method.

§ 1.162–4 Repairs

The cost of incidental repairs which neither materially add to the value of the property nor appreciably prolong its life, but keep it in an ordinarily efficient operating condition, may be deducted as an expense, provided the cost of acquisition or production or the gain or loss basis of the taxpayer's plant, equipment, or other property, as the case may be, is not increased by the amount of such expenditures. Repairs in the nature of replacements, to the extent that they arrest deterioration and appreciably prolong the life of the property, shall either be capitalized and depreciated in accordance with section 167 or charged against the depreciation reserve if such an account is kept.

§ 1.162–5 Expenses for education

(a) General rule. Expenditures made by an individual for education (including research undertaken as part of his educational program) which are not expenditures of a type described in paragraph (b) (2) or (3) of this section are deductible as ordinary and necessary business expenses (even though the education may lead to a degree) if the education—

(1) Maintains or improves skills required by the individual in his employment or other trade or business, or

(2) Meets the express requirements of the individual's employer, or the requirements of applicable law or regulations, imposed as a condition to the retention by the individual of an established employment relationship, status, or rate of compensation.

(b) Nondeductible educational expenditures—(1) In general. Educational expenditures described in subparagraphs (2) and (3) of this paragraph are personal expenditures or constitute an inseparable aggregate of personal and capital expenditures and, therefore, are not deductible as ordinary and necessary business expenses even though the education may maintain or improve skills required by the individual in his employment or other trade or business or may meet the express requirements of the individual's employer or of applicable law or regulations.

(2) **Minimum educational requirements.** (i) The first category of nondeductible educational expenses within the scope of subparagraph (1) of this paragraph are expenditures made by an individual for education which is required of him in order to meet the minimum educational requirements for qualification in his employment or other trade or business. The minimum education necessary to qualify for a position or other trade or business must be determined from a consideration of such factors as the requirements of the employer, the applicable law and regulations, and the standards of the profession, trade, or business involved. The fact that an individual is already performing service in an employment status does not establish that he has met the minimum educational requirements for qualification in that employment. Once an individual has met the minimum educational requirements for qualification in his employment or other trade or business (as in effect when he enters the employment or trade or business), he shall be treated as continuing to meet those requirements even though they are changed.

(ii) The minimum educational requirements for qualification of a particular individual in a position in an educational institution is the minimum level of education (in terms of aggregate college hours or degree) which under the applicable laws or regulations, in effect at the time this individual is first employed in such position, is normally required of an individual initially being employed in such a position. If there are no normal requirements as to the minimum level of education required for a position in an educational institution, then an individual in such a position shall be considered to have met the minimum educational requirements for qualification in that position when he becomes a member of the faculty of the educational institution. The determination of whether an individual is a member of the faculty of an educational institution must be made on the basis of the particular practices of the institution. However, an individual will ordinarily be considered to be a member of the faculty of an institution if (a) he has tenure or his years of service are being counted toward obtaining tenure; (b) the institution is making contributions to a retirement plan (other than Social Security or a similar program) in respect of his employment; or (c) he has a vote in faculty affairs.

(iii) The application of this subparagraph may be illustrated by the following examples:

Example (1). General facts: State X requires a bachelor's degree for beginning secondary school teachers which must include 30 credit hours of professional educational courses. In addition, in order to retain his position, a secondary school teacher must complete a fifth year of preparation within 10 years after beginning his employment. If an employing school official certifies to the State Department of Education that applicants having a bachelor's degree and the required courses in professional education cannot be found, he may hire individuals as secondary school teachers if they have completed a minimum of 90 semester hours of college work. However, to be retained in his position, such an individual must obtain his bachelor's degree and complete the required professional educational courses within 3 years after his employment commences. Under these facts, a bachelor's degree, without regard to whether it includes 30 credit hours of professional educational courses, is considered to be the minimum educational requirement for qualification as a secondary school teacher in State X. This is the case notwithstanding the number of teachers who are actually hired without such a degree. The following are examples of the application of these facts in particular situations:

Situation 1. A, at the time he is employed as a secondary school teacher in State X, has a bachelor's degree including 30 credit hours of professional educational courses. After his employment, A completes a fifth college year of education and, as a result, is issued a standard certificate. The fifth college year of education undertaken by A is not education required to meet the minimum educational requirements for qualification as a secondary school teacher. Accordingly, the expenditures for such education are deductible unless the expenditures are for education which is part of a program of study being pursued by A which will lead to qualifying him in a new trade or business.

Situation 2. Because of a shortage of applicants meeting the stated requirements, B, who has a bachelor's degree, is employed as a secondary school teacher in State X even though he has only 20 credit hours of professional educational courses. After his employment, B takes an additional 10 credit hours of professional educational courses. Since these courses do not constitute education required to meet the minimum educational requirements for qualification as a secondary school teacher which is a bachelor's degree and will not lead to qualifying B in a new trade or business, the expenditures for such courses are deductible.

Situation 3. Because of a shortage of applicants meeting the stated requirements, C is employed as a secondary school teacher in State X although he has only 90 semester hours of college work toward his bachelor's degree. After his employment, C undertakes courses leading to a bachelor's degree. These courses (including any courses in professional education) constitute education required to meet the minimum educational requirements for qualification as a secondary school teacher. Accordingly, the expenditures for such education are not deductible.

Situation 4. Subsequent to the employment of A, B, and C, but before they have completed a fifth college year of education, State X changes its requirements affecting secondary school teachers to provide that beginning teachers must have completed 5 college years of preparation. In the cases of A, B, and C, a fifth college year of education is not considered to be education undertaken to meet the minimum educational requirements for qualification as a secondary school teacher. Accordingly, expenditures for a fifth year of college will be deductible unless the expenditures are for education which is part of a program being pursued by A, B, or C which will lead to qualifying him in a new trade or business.

Example (2). D, who holds a bachelor's degree, obtains temporary employment as an instructor at University Y and undertakes graduate courses as a candidate for a graduate degree. D may become a faculty member only if he obtains a graduate degree and may continue to hold a position as instructor only so long as he shows satisfactory progress towards obtaining this graduate degree. The graduate courses taken by D constitute education required to meet the minimum educational requirements for qualification in D's trade or business and, thus, the expenditures for such courses are not deductible.

Example (3). E, who has completed 2 years of a normal 3-year law school course leading to a bachelor of laws degree (LL.B.), is hired by a law firm to do legal research and perform other functions on a full-time basis. As a condition to continued employment, E is required to obtain an LL.B. and pass the State bar examination. E completes his law school education by attending night law school, and he takes a bar review course in order to prepare for the State bar examination. The law courses and bar review course constitute education required to meet the minimum educational requirements for qualification in E's trade or business and, thus, the expenditures for such courses are not deductible.

(3) Qualification for new trade or business. (i) The second category of nondeductible educational expenses within the scope of subparagraph (1) of this paragraph are expenditures made by an individual for education which is part of a program of study being pursued by him which will lead to qualifying him in a new trade or business. In the case of an employee, a change of duties does not constitute a new trade or business if the new duties involve the same general type of work as is involved in the individual's present employment. For this purpose, all teaching and related duties shall be considered to involve the same general type of work. The following are examples of changes in duties

which do not constitute new trades or businesses:

(a) Elementary to secondary school classroom teacher.

(b) Classroom teacher in one subject (such as mathematics) to classroom teacher in another subject (such as science).

(c) Classroom teacher to guidance counselor.

(d) Classroom teacher to principal.

(ii) The application of this subparagraph to individuals other than teachers may be illustrated by the following examples:

Example (1). A, a self-employed individual practicing a profession other than law, for example, engineering, accounting, etc., attends law school at night and after completing his law school studies receives a bachelor of laws degree. The expenditures made by A in attending law school are nondeductible because this course of study qualifies him for a new trade or business.

Example (2). Assume the same facts as in example (1) except that A has the status of an employee rather than a self-employed individual, and that his employer requires him to obtain a bachelor of laws degree. A intends to continue practicing his nonlegal profession as an employee of such employer. Nevertheless, the expenditures made by A in attending law school are not deductible since this course of study qualifies him for a new trade or business.

Example (3). B, a general practitioner of medicine, takes a 2-week course reviewing new developments in several specialized fields of medicine. B's expenses for the course are deductible because the course maintains or improves skills required by him in his trade or business and does not qualify him for a new trade or business.

Example (4). C, while engaged in the private practice of psychiatry, undertakes a program of study and training at an accredited psychoanalytic institute which will lead to qualifying him to practice psychoanalysis. C's expenditures for such study and training are deductible because the study and training maintains or improves skills required by him in his trade or business and does not qualify him for a new trade or business.

(c) Deductible educational expenditures—(1) Maintaining or improving skills. The deduction under the category of expenditures for education which maintains or improves skills required by the individual in his employment or other trade or business includes refresher courses or courses dealing with current developments as well as academic or vocational courses provided the expenditures for the courses are not within either category of nondeductible expenditures described in paragraph (b) (2) or (3) of this section.

(2) Meeting requirements of employer. An individual is considered to have undertaken education in order to meet the express requirements of his employer, or the requirements of applicable law or regulations, imposed as a condition to the retention by the taxpayer of his established employment relationship, status, or rate of compensation only if such requirements are imposed for a bona fide business purpose of the individual's employer. Only the minimum education necessary to the retention by the individual of his established employment relationship, status, or rate of compensation may be considered as undertaken to meet the express requirements of the taxpayer's employer. However, education in excess of such minimum education may qualify as education undertaken in order to maintain or improve the skills required by the taxpayer in his employment or other trade or business (see subparagraph (1) of this paragraph). In no event, however, is a deduction allowable for expenditures for education which, even though for education required by the employer or applicable law or regulations, are within one of the categories of nondeductible expenditures described in paragraph (b) (2) and (3) of this section.

(d) Travel as a form of education. Subject to the provisions of paragraph (b) and (e) of this section, expenditures for travel (including travel while on sabbatical leave) as a form of education are deductible only to the extent such expenditures are attributable to a period of travel that is directly related to the duties of the individual in his employment or other trade or business. For this purpose, a period of travel shall be considered directly related to the duties of an individual in his employment or other trade or business only if the major portion of the activities during such period is of a nature which directly maintains or improves skills required by the individual in such employment or other trade or business. The approval of a travel program by an employer or the fact that travel is accepted by an employer in the fulfillment of its requirements for retention of rate of compensation, status or employment, is not determinative that the required relationship exists between the travel involved and the duties of the individual in his particular position.

(e) Travel away from home. (1) If an individual travels away from home primarily to obtain education the expenses of which are deductible under this section, his expenditures for travel, meals, and lodging while away from home are deductible. However, if as an incident of such trip the individual engages in some personal activity such as sightseeing, social visiting, or entertaining, or other recreation, the portion of the expenses attributable to such personal activity constitutes nondeductible personal or living expenses and is not allowable as a deduction. If the individual's travel away from home is primarily personal, the individual's expenditures for travel, meals and lodging (other than meals and lodging during the time spent in participating in deductible education pursuits) are not deductible.

Whether a particular trip is primarily personal or primarily to obtain education the expenses of which are deductible under this section depends upon all the facts and circumstances of each case. An important factor to be taken into consideration in making the determination is the relative amount of time devoted to personal activity as compared with the time devoted to educational pursuits. The rules set forth in this paragraph are subject to the provisions of section 162(a) (2), relating to deductibility of certain traveling expenses, and section 274(c) and (d), relating to allocation of certain foreign travel expenses and substantiation required, respectively, and the regulations thereunder.

(2) Examples. The application of this subsection may be illustrated by the following examples:

Example (1). A, a self-employed tax practitioner, decides to take a 1-week course in new developments in taxation, which is offered in City X, 500 miles away from his home. His primary purpose in going to X is to take the course, but he also takes a side trip to City Y (50 miles from X for 1 day, takes a sightseeing trip while in X, and entertains some personal friends. A's transportation expenses to City X and return to his home are deductible but his transportation expenses to City Y are not deductible. A's expenses for meals and lodging while away from home will be allocated between his educational pursuits and his personal activities. Those expenses which are entirely personal, such as sightseeing and entertaining friends, are not deductible to any extent.

Example (2). The facts are the same as in example (1) except that A's primary purpose in going to City X is to take a vacation. This purpose is indicated by several factors one of which is the fact that he spends only 1 week attending the tax course and devotes 5 weeks entirely to personal activities. None of A's transportation expenses are deductible and his expenses for meals and lodging while away from home are not deductible to the extent attributable to personal activities. His expenses for meals and lodging allocable to the week attending the tax course are, however, deductible.

Example (3). B, a high school mathematics teacher in New York City, in the summertime travels to a university in California in order to take a mathematics course the expense of which is deductible under this section. B pursues only one-fourth of a full course of study and the remainder of her time is devoted to personal activities the expense of which is not deductible. Absent a showing by B of a substantial nonpersonal reason for taking the course at the university in California, the trip is considered taken primarily for personal reasons and the cost of traveling from New York City to California and return would not be deductible. However, one-fourth of the cost of B's meals and lodging while attending the university in California may be considered properly allocable to deductible educational pursuits and, therefore, is deductible.

§ 1.162–6 Professional expenses

A professional man may claim as deductions the cost of supplies used by him in the practice of his profession, expenses paid or accrued in the operation and repair of an automobile used in making professional calls, dues to professional societies and subscriptions to professional journals, the rent paid or accrued for office rooms, the cost of the fuel, light, water, telephone, etc., used in such offices, and the hire of office assistance. Amounts currently paid or accrued for books, furniture, and professional instruments and equipment, the useful life of which is short, may be deducted.

§ 1.162–7 Compensation for personal services

(a) There may be included among the ordinary and necessary expenses paid or incurred in carrying on any trade or business a reasonable allowance for salaries or other compensation for personal services actually rendered. The test of deductibility in the case of compensation payments is whether they are reasonable and are in fact payments purely for services.

(b) The test set forth in paragraph (a) of this section and its practical application may be further stated and illustrated as follows:

(1) Any amount paid in the form of compensation, but not in fact as the purchase price of services, is not deductible. An ostensible salary paid by a corporation may be a distribution of a dividend on stock. This is likely to occur in the case of a corporation having few shareholders, practically all of whom draw salaries. If in such a case the salaries are in excess of those ordinarily paid for similar services and the excessive payments correspond or bear a close relationship to the stockholdings of the officers or employees, it would seem likely that the salaries are not paid wholly for services rendered, but that the excessive payments are a distribution of earnings upon the stock. An ostensible salary may be in part payment for property. This may occur, for example, where a partnership sells out to a corporation, the former partners agreeing to continue in the service of the corporation. In such a case it may be found that the salaries of the former partners are not merely for services, but in part constitute payment for the transfer of their business.

(2) The form or method of fixing compensation is not decisive as to deductibility. While any form of contingent compensation invites scrutiny as a possible distribution of earnings of the enterprise, it does not follow that payments on a contingent basis are to be treated fundamentally on any basis different from that applying to compensation at a flat rate. Generally speaking, if contingent compensation is paid pursuant to a free bargain between the employer and the individual made before the services are rendered, not influenced by any consideration on the part of the employer other than that of securing on fair and advantageous terms the services of the individual, it should be allowed as a deduction even though in the actual working out of the contract it may prove to be greater than the amount which would ordinarily be paid.

(3) In any event the allowance for the compensation paid may not exceed what is reasonable under all the circumstances. It is, in general, just to assume that reasonable and true compensation is only such amount as would ordinarily be paid for like services by like enterprises under like circumstances. The circumstances to be taken into consideration are those existing at

the date when the contract for services was made, not those existing at the date when the contract is questioned.

.   .   .   .

§ 1.162-8 Treatment of excessive compensation

The income tax liability of the recipient in respect of an amount ostensibly paid to him as compensation, but not allowed to be deducted as such by the payor, will depend upon the circumstances of each case. Thus, in the case of excessive payments by corporations, if such payments correspond or bear a close relationship to stockholdings, and are found to be a distribution of earnings or profits, the excessive payments will be treated as a dividend. If such payments constitute payment for property, they should be treated by the payor as a capital expenditure and by the recipient as part of the purchase price. In the absence of evidence to justify other treatment, excessive payments for salaries or other compensation for personal services will be included in gross income of the recipient.

§ 1.162-9 Bonuses to employees

Bonuses to employees will constitute allowable deductions from gross income when such payments are made in good faith and as additional compensation for the services actually rendered by the employees, provided such payments, when added to the stipulated salaries, do not exceed a reasonable compensation for the services rendered. It is immaterial whether such bonuses are paid in cash or in kind or partly in cash and partly in kind. Donations made to employees and others, which do not have in them the element of compensation or which are in excess of reasonable compensation for services, are not deductible from gross income.

§ 1.162-11 Rentals

(a) Acquisition of a leasehold. If a leasehold is acquired for business purposes for a specified sum, the purchaser may take as a deduction in his return an aliquot part of such sum each year, based on the number of years the lease has to run. Taxes paid by a tenant to or for a landlord for business property are additional rent and constitute a deductible item to the tenant and taxable income to the landlord, the amount of the tax being deductible by the latter. For disallowance of deduction for income taxes paid by a lessee corporation pursuant to a lease arrangement with the lessor corporation, see section 110 and the regulations thereunder. See section 178 and the regulations thereunder for rules governing the effect to be given renewal options in amortizing the costs incurred after July 28, 1958, of acquiring a lease.

(b) Improvements by lessee on lessor's property. (1) The cost to a lessee of erecting buildings or making permanent improvements on property of which he is the lessee is a capital investment, and is not deductible as a business expense. If the estimated useful life in the hands of the taxpayer of the building erected or of the improvements made, determined without regard to the terms of the lease, is longer than the remaining period of the lease, an annual deduction may be made from gross income of an amount equal to the total cost of such improvements divided by the number of years remaining in the term of the lease, and such deduction shall be in lieu of a deduction for depreciation. If, on the other hand, the useful life of such buildings or improvements in the hands of the taxpayer is equal to or shorter than the remaining period of the lease, this deduction shall be computed under the provisions of section 167 (relating to depreciation).

(2) If the lessee began improvements on leased property before July 28, 1958, or if the lessee was on such date and at all times thereafter under a binding legal obligation to make such improvements, the matter of spreading the cost of erecting buildings or making permanent improvements over the term of the original lease, together with the renewal period or periods depends upon the facts in the particular case, including the presence or absence of an obligation of renewal and the relationship between the parties. As a general rule, unless the lease has been renewed or the facts show with reasonable certainty that the lease will be renewed, the cost or other basis of the lease, or the cost of improvements shall be spread only over the number of years the lease has to run without taking into account any right of renewal. The provisions of this subparagraph may be illustrated by the following examples:

Example (1). A subsidiary corporation leases land from its parent at a fair rental for a 25-year period. The subsidiary erects on the land valuable factory buildings having an estimated useful life of 50 years. These facts show with reasonable certainty that the lease will be renewed, even though the lease contains no option of renewal. Therefore, the cost of the buildings shall be depreciated over the estimated useful life of the buildings in accordance with section 167 and the regulations thereunder.

Example (2). A retail merchandising corporation leases land at a fair rental from an unrelated lessor for the longest period that the lessor is willing to lease the land (30 years). The lessee erects on the land a department store having an estimated useful life of 40 years. These facts do not show with reasonable certainty that the lease will be renewed. Therefore, the cost of the building shall be spread over the remaining term of the lease. An annual deduction may be made of an amount equal to the cost of the building divided by the number of years remaining in the term of the lease, and such deduction shall be in lieu of a deduction for depreciation.

. . . .

§ 1.162-12 Expenses of farmers

(a) Farms engaged in for profit. A farmer who operates a farm for profit is entitled to deduct from gross income as necessary expenses all amounts actually expended in the carrying on of the business of farming. The cost of ordinary tools of short life or small cost, such as hand tools, including shovels, rakes, etc., may be deducted. The purchase of feed and other costs connected with raising livestock may be treated as expense deductions insofar as such costs represent actual outlay, but not including the value of farm produce grown upon the farm or the labor of the taxpayer. . . . .

. . . .

§ 1.162-15 Contributions, dues, etc.

(a) Contributions to organizations described in section 170—(1) In general. No deduction is allowable under section 162(a) for a contribution or gift by an individual or a corporation if any part thereof is deductible under section 170. For example, if a taxpayer makes a contribution of $5,000 and only $4,000 of this amount is deductible under section 170(a) (whether because of the percentage limitation under either section 170(b) (1) or (2), the requirement as to time of payment, or both) no deduction is allowable under section 162(a) for the remaining $1,-000.

(2) Scope of limitations. The limitations provided in section 162(b) and this paragraph apply only to payments which are in fact contributions or gifts to organizations described in section 170. For example, payments by a transit company to a local hospital (which is a charitable organization within the meaning of section 170) in consideration of a binding obligation on the part of the hospital to provide hospital services and facilities for the company's employees are not contributions or gifts within the meaning of section 170 and may be deductible under section 162(a) if the requirements of section 162(a) are otherwise satisfied.

(b) Other contributions. Donations to organizations other than those described in section 170 which bear a direct relationship to the taxpayer's business and are made with a reasonable expectation of a financial return commensurate with the amount of the donation may constitute allowable deductions as business expenses, provided the donation is not made for a purpose for which a deduction is not allowable by reason of the provisions of paragraph (b) (1) (i) or (c) of § 1.162—20. For example, a transit company may donate a sum of money to an organization (of a class not referred to in section 170) intending to hold a convention in the city in which it operates, with a reasonable expectation that the holding of such convention will augment its income through a greater number of people using its transportation facilities.

(c) Dues. Dues and other payments to an organization, such as a labor union or a trade association, which otherwise meet the requirements of the regulations under section 162, are deductible in full. For limitations on the deductibility of dues and other payments, see paragraph (b) and (c) of § 1.162-20.

. . . .

§ 1.162-17 Reporting and substantiation of certain business expenses of employees

(a) Introductory. The purpose of the regulations in this section is to provide rules for the reporting of information on income tax returns by taxpayers who pay or incur ordinary and necessary business expenses in connection with the performance of services as an employee and to furnish guidance as to the type of records which will be useful in compiling such information and in its substantiation, if required. The rules prescribed in this section do not apply to expenses paid or incurred for incidentals, such as office supplies for the employer or local transportation in connection with an errand. Employees incurring such incidental expenses are not required to provide substantiation for such amounts. The term "ordinary and necessary business expenses" means only those expenses which are ordinary and necessary in the conduct of the taxpayer's business and are directly attributable to such business. The term does not include nondeductible personal, living or family expenses.

(b) **Expenses for which the employee is required to account to his employer—(1) Reimbursements equal to expenses.** The employee need not report on his tax return (either itemized or in total amount) expenses for travel, transportation, entertainment, and similar purposes paid or incurred by him solely for the benefit of his employer for which he is required to account and does account to his employer and which are charged directly or indirectly to the employer (for example, through credit cards) or for which the employee is paid through advances, reimbursements, or otherwise, provided the total amount of such advances, reimbursements, and charges is equal to such expenses. In such a case the taxpayer need only state in his return that the total of amounts charged directly or indirectly to his employer through credit cards or otherwise and received from the employer as advances or reimbursements did not exceed the ordinary and necessary business expenses paid or incurred by the employee.

(2) **Reimbursements in excess of expenses.** In case the total of amounts charged directly or indirectly to the employer and received from the employer as advances, reimbursements, or otherwise, exceeds the ordinary and necessary business expenses paid or incurred by the employee and the employee is required to and does account to his employer for such expenses, the taxpayer must include such excess in income and state on his return that he has done so.

(3) **Expenses in excess of reimbursements.** If the employee's ordinary and necessary business expenses exceed the total of the amounts charged directly or indirectly to the employer and received from the employer as advances, reimbursements, or otherwise, and the employee is required to and does account to his employer for such expenses, the taxpayer may make the statement in his return required by subparagraph (1) of this paragraph unless he wishes to claim a deduction for such excess. If, however, he wishes to secure a deduction for such excess, he must submit a statement showing the following information as part of his tax return:

(i) The total of any charges paid or borne by the employer and of any other amounts received from the employer for payment of expenses whether by means of advances, reimbursements or otherwise; and

(ii) The nature of his occupation, the number of days away from home on business, and the total amount of ordinary and necessary business expenses paid or incurred by him (including those charged directly or indirectly to the employer through credit cards or otherwise) broken down into such broad categories as transportation, meals and lodging while away from home overnight, entertainment expenses, and other business expenses.

(4) To "account" to his employer as used in this section means to submit an expense account or other required written statement to the employer showing the business nature and the amount of all the employee's expenses (including those charged directly or indirectly to the employer through credit cards or otherwise) broken down into such broad categories as transportation, meals and lodging while away from home overnight, entertainment expenses, and other business expenses. For this purpose, the Commissioner in his discretion may approve reasonable business practices under which mileage, per diem in lieu of subsistence, and similar allowances providing for ordinary and necessary business expenses in accordance with a fixed scale may be regarded as equivalent to an accounting to the employer.

(c) **Expenses for which the employee is not required to account to his em-**

ployer. If the employee is not required to account to his employer for his ordinary and necessary business expenses, e. g., travel, transportation, entertainment, and similar items, or, though required, fails to account for such expenses, he must submit, as a part of his tax return, a statement showing the following information:

(1) The total of all amounts received as advances or reimbursements from his employer in connection with the ordinary and necessary business expenses of the employee, including amounts charged directly or indirectly to the employer through credit cards or otherwise; and

(2) The nature of his occupation, the number of days away from home on business, and the total amount of ordinary and necessary business expenses paid or incurred by him (including those charged directly or indirectly to the employer through credit cards or otherwise) broken down into such broad categories as transportation, meals and lodging while away from home overnight, entertainment expenses, and other business expenses.

(d) Substantiation of items of expense. (1) Although the Commissioner may require any taxpayer to substantiate such information concerning expense accounts as may appear to be pertinent in determining tax liability, taxpayers ordinarily will not be called upon to substantiate expense account information except those in the following categories:

(i) A taxpayer who is not required to account to his employer, or who does not account;

(ii) A taxpayer whose expenses exceed the total of amounts charged to his employer and amounts received through advances, reimbursements or otherwise and who claims a deduction on his return for such excess;

(iii) A taxpayer who is related to his employer within the meaning of section 267 (b); and

(iv) Other taxpayers in cases where it is determined that the accounting procedures used by the employer for the reporting and substantiation of expenses by employees are not adequate.

(2) The Code contemplates that taxpayers keep such records as will be sufficient to enable the Commissioner to correctly determine income tax liability. Accordingly, it is to the advantage of taxpayers who may be called upon to substantiate expense account information to maintain as adequate and detailed records of travel, transportation, entertainment, and similar business expenses as practical since the burden of proof is upon the taxpayer to show that such expenses were not only paid or incurred but also that they constitute ordinary and necessary business expenses. One method for substantiating expenses incurred by an employee in connection with his employment is through the preparation of a daily diary or record of expenditures, maintained in sufficient detail to enable him to readily identify the amount and nature of any expenditure, and the preservation of supporting documents, especially in connection with large or exceptional expenditures. Nevertheless, it is recognized that by reason of the nature of certain expenses or the circumstances under which they are incurred, it is often difficult for an employee to maintain detailed records or to preserve supporting documents for all his expenses. Detailed records of small expenditures incurred in traveling or for transportation, as for example, tips, will not be required.

(3) Where records are incomplete or documentary proof is unavailable, it may be possible to establish the amount of the expenditures by approximations based upon reliable secondary sources of information and collateral evidence. For example, in connection with an item of traveling expense a taxpayer might establish that he was in a travel status a certain number of days but that it was impracticable for him to establish the details of all his various items of travel expense. In such a case rail fares or plane fares can usually be ascertained with exactness and automobile costs approximated on the basis of mileage covered. A reasonable approximation of meals and lodging might be based upon receipted hotel bills or upon average daily rates for such accommodations and meals prevailing in the particular community for comparable accommodations. Since detailed records of incidental items are not required, deductions for these items may be based upon a reasonable approximation. In cases where a taxpayer is called upon to substantiate expense ac-

count information, the burden is on the taxpayer to establish that the amounts claimed as a deduction are reasonably accurate and constitute ordinary and necessary business expenses paid or incurred by him in connection with his trade or business. In connection with the determination of factual matters of this type, due consideration will be given to the reasonableness of the stated expenditures for the claimed purposes in relation to the taxpayer's circumstances (such as his income and the nature of his occupation), to the reliability and accuracy of records in connection with other items more readily lending themselves to detailed record-keeping, and to all of the facts and circumstances in the particular case.

(e) **Applicability.** (1) Except as provided in subparagraph (2) of this paragraph, the provisions of the regulations in this section are supplemental to existing regulations relating to information required to be submitted with income tax returns, and shall be applicable with respect to taxable years beginning after December 31, 1957, notwithstanding any existing regulation to the contrary.

(2) With respect to taxable years ending after December 31, 1962, but only in respect of periods after such date, the provisions of the regulations in this section are superseded by the regulations under section 274(d) to the extent inconsistent therewith. See § 1.274-5.

§ 1.162–18   Illegal bribes and kickbacks

(a) **Illegal payments to government officials or employees—(1) In general.** No deduction shall be allowed under section 162(a) for any amount paid or incurred, directly or indirectly, to an official or employee of any government, or of any agency or other instrumentality of any government, if—

(i) In the case of a payment made to an official or employee of a government other than a foreign government described in subparagraph (3)(ii) or (iii) of this paragraph, the payment constitutes an illegal bribe or kickback, or

(ii) In the case of a payment made to an official or employee of a foreign government described in subparagraph (3)(ii) or (iii) of this paragraph, the

making of the payment would be unlawful under the laws of the United States (if such laws were applicable to the payment and to the official or employee at the time the expenses were paid or incurred).

No deduction shall be allowed for an accrued expense if the eventual payment thereof would fall within the prohibition of this section. The place where the expenses are paid or incurred is immaterial. For purposes of subdivision (ii) of this subparagraph, lawfulness or unlawfulness of the payment under the laws of the foreign country is immaterial.

(2) **Indirect payment.** For purposes of this paragraph, an indirect payment to an individual shall include any payment which inures to his benefit or promotes his interests, regardless of the medium in which the payment is made and regardless of the identity of the immediate recipient or payor. Thus, for example, payment made to an agent, relative, or independent contractor of an official or employee, or even directly into the general treasury of a foreign country of which the beneficiary is an official or employee, may be treated as an indirect payment to the official or employee, if in fact such payment inures or will inure to his benefit or promotes or will promote his financial or other interests. A payment made by an agent or independent contractor of the taxpayer which benefits the taxpayer shall be treated as an indirect payment by the taxpayer to the official or employee.

(3) **Official or employee of a government.** Any individual officially connected with—

(i) The Government of the United States, a State, a territory or possession of the United States, the District of Columbia, or the Commonwealth of Puerto Rico,

(ii) The government of a foreign country, or

(iii) A political subdivision of, or a corporation or other entity serving as an agency or instrumentality of, any of the above,

in whatever capacity, whether on a permanent or temporary basis, and whether or not serving for compensation, shall be included within the term "official or employee of a government", regardless of the place of residence or post of duty of such individual. An independent contractor would not ordinarily be considered to be an official or employee. For purposes of section 162(c) and this paragraph, the term "foreign country" shall include any foreign nation, whether or not such nation has been accorded diplomatic recognition by the United States. Individuals who purport to act on behalf of or as the government of a foreign nation, or an agency or instrumentality thereof, shall be treated under this section as officials or employees of a foreign government, whether or not such individuals in fact control such foreign nation, agency, or instrumentality, and whether or not such individuals are accorded diplomatic recognition. Accordingly, a group in rebellion against an established government shall be treated as officials or employees of a foreign government, as shall officials or employees of the government against which the group is in rebellion.

(4) Laws of the United States. The term "laws of the United States", to which reference is made in paragraph (a)(1)(ii) of this section, shall be deemed to include only Federal statutes, including State laws which are assimilated into Federal law by Federal statute, and legislative and interpretative regulations thereunder. The term shall also be limited to statutes which prohibit some act or acts, for the violation of which there is a civil or criminal penalty.

(5) Burden of proof. In any proceeding involving the issue of whether, for purposes of section 162(c)(1), a payment made to a government official or employee constitutes an illegal bribe or kickback (or would be unlawful under the laws of the United States) the burden of proof in respect of such issue shall be upon the Commissioner to the same extent as he bears the burden of proof in civil fraud cases under section 7454 (i. e., he must prove the illegality of the payment by clear and convincing evidence).

(6) Example. The application of this paragraph may be illustrated by the following example:

Example. X Corp. is in the business of selling hospital equipment in State Y. During 1970, X Corp. employed A who at the time was employed full time by State Y as Superintendent of Hospitals. The purpose of A's employment by X Corp. was to procure for it an improper advantage over other concerns in the making of sales to hospitals in respect of which A, as Superintendent, had authority. X Corp. paid A $5,000 during 1970. The making of this payment was illegal under the laws of State Y. Under section 162(c)(1), X Corp. is precluded from deducting as a trade or business expense the $5,000 paid to A.

(b) Other illegal payments—(1) In general. No deduction shall be allowed under section 162(a) for any payment (other than a payment described in paragraph (a) of this section) made, directly or indirectly, to any person, if the payment constitutes an illegal bribe, illegal kickback, or other illegal payment under the laws of the United States (as defined in paragraph (a)(4) of this section), or under any State law (but only if such State law is generally enforced), which subjects the payor to a criminal penalty or the loss (including a suspension) of license or privilege to engage in a trade or business (whether or not such penalty or loss is actually imposed upon the taxpayer). For purposes of this paragraph, a kickback includes a payment in consideration of the referral of a client, patient, or customer. This paragraph applies only to payments made after December 30, 1969.

(2) State law. For purposes of this paragraph, State law means a statute of a State or the District of Columbia.

(3) Generally enforced. For purposes of this paragaraph, a State law shall be considered to be generally enforced unless it is never enforced or the only persons normally charged with violations thereof in the State (or the District of Columbia) enacting the law are infamous or those whose violations are extraordinarily flagrant. For example, a criminal statute of a State shall be considered to be generally enforced unless violations of the statute which are brought to the attention of appropriate enforcement authorities do not result in any enforcement action in the absence of unusual circumstances.

(4) Burden of proof. In any proceeding involving the issue of whether, for purposes of section 162(c)(2), a payment constitutes an illegal bribe, illegal kickback, or other illegal payment the burden of proof in respect of such issue shall be upon the Commissioner to the same extent as he bears the burden of proof in civil fraud cases under section 7454 (i. e., he must prove the illegality of the payment by clear and convincing evidence).

(5) Example. The application of this paragraph may be illustrated by the following example:

Example. X Corp., a calendar-year taxpayer, is engaged in the ship repair business in State Y. During 1970, repairs on foreign ships accounted for a substantial part of its total business. It was X Corp.'s practice to kick back approximately 10 percent of the repair bill to the captain and chief engineer of all foreign-owned vessels, which kickbacks are illegal under a law of State Y (which is generally enforced) and potentially subject X Corp. to fines. During 1970, X Corp. paid $50,000 in such kickbacks. On X Corp.'s return for 1970, a deduction under section 162 was taken for the $50,000. The deduction of the $50,000 of illegal kickbacks during 1970 is disallowed under section 162(c)(2), whether or not X Corp. is prosecuted with respect to the kickbacks.

(c) Kickbacks, rebates, and bribes under medicare and medicaid. No deduction shall be allowed under section 162(a) for any kickback, rebate, or bribe (whether or not illegal) made on or after December 10, 1971, by any provider of services, supplier, physician, or other person who furnishes items or services for which payment is or may be made under the Social Security Act, as amended, or in whole or in part out of Federal funds under a State plan approved under such Act, if such kickback, rebate, or bribe is made in connection with the furnishing of such items or services or the making or receipt of such payments. For purposes of this paragraph, a kickback includes a payment in consideration of the referral of a client, patient, or customer.

§ 1.162-20 Expenditures attributable to lobbying, political campaigns, attempts to influence legislation, etc., and certain advertising

(a) In general—(1) Scope of section. This section contains rules governing the deductibility or nondeductibility of expenditures for lobbying purposes, for the promotion or defeat of legislation, for political campaign purposes (including the support of or opposition to any candidate for public office) or for carrying on propaganda (including advertising) related to any of the foregoing purposes. . . . . .

(2) Institutional or "good will" advertising. Expenditures for institutional or "good will" advertising which keeps the taxpayer's name before the public are generally deductible as ordinary and necessary business expenses provided the expenditures are related to the patronage the taxpayer might reasonably expect in the future. For example, a deduction will ordinarily be allowed for the cost of advertising which keeps the taxpayer's name before the public in connection with encouraging contributions to such organizations as the Red Cross, the purchase of United States Savings Bonds, or participation in similar causes. In like fashion, expenditures for advertising which presents views on economic, financial, social, or other subjects of a general nature, but which does not involve any of the activities specified in paragraph (b) or (c) of this section for which a deduction is not allowable, are deductible if they otherwise meet the requirements of the regulations under section 162.

(b) Taxable years beginning before January 1, 1963— . . . . .

(c) Taxable years beginning after December 31, 1962—(1) In general. For taxable years beginning after December 31, 1962, certain types of expenses incurred with respect to legislative matters are deductible under section 162(a) if they otherwise meet the requirements of the regulations under section 162. These deductible expenses are described in subparagraph (2) of this paragraph. All other expenditures for lobbying purposes, for the promotion or defeat of legislation . . . ., for political campaign purposes (including the support of or opposition to any candidate for public office), or for carrying on propaganda (including advertising) relating to any of the foregoing purposes are not deductible from gross income for such taxable years. . . . . .

(2) Appearances, etc., with respect to legislation—(i) General rule. Pursuant to the provisions of section 162 (e), expenses incurred with respect to legislative matters which may be deductible are those ordinary and necessary expenses (including, but not limited to, traveling expenses described in section 162(a)(2) and the cost of preparing testimony) paid or incurred by the taxpayer during a taxable year beginning after December 31, 1962, in carrying on any trade or business which are in direct connection with—

(a) Appearances before, submission of statements to, or sending communications to, the committees, or individual members of Congress or of any legislative body of a State, a possession of the United States, or a political subdivision of any of the foregoing with respect to legislation or proposed legislation of direct interest to the taxpayer, or

(b) Communication of information between the taxpayer and an organization of which he is a member with respect to legislation or proposed legislation of direct interest to the taxpayer and to such organization.

For provisions relating to dues paid or incurred with respect to an organization of which the taxpayer is a member, see subparagraph (3) of this paragraph.

(ii) **Legislation or proposed legislation of direct interest to the taxpayer—** (a) **Legislation or proposed legislation.** The term "legislation or proposed legislation" includes bills and resolutions introduced by a member of Congress or other legislative body referred to in subdivision (i) (a) of this subparagraph for consideration by such body as well as oral or written proposals for legislative action submitted to the legislative body or to a committee or member of such body.

(b) **Direct interest—(1) In general.** (i) Legislation or proposed legislation is of direct interest to a taxpayer if the legislation or proposed legislation is of such a nature that it will, or may reasonably be expected to, affect the trade or business of the taxpayer. It is immaterial whether the effect, or expected effect, on the trade or business will be beneficial or detrimental to the trade or business or whether it will be immediate. If legislation or proposed legislation has such a relationship to a trade or business that the expenses of any appearance or communication in connection with the legislation meets the ordinary and necessary test of section 162(a), then such legislation ordinarily meets the direct interest test of section 162(e). However, if the nature of the legislation or proposed legislation is such that the likelihood of its having an effect on the trade or business of the taxpayer is remote or speculative, the legislation or proposed legislation is not of direct interest to the taxpayer. Legislation or proposed legislation which will not affect the trade or business of the taxpayer is not of direct interest to the taxpayer even though such legislation will affect the personal, living, or family activities or expenses of the taxpayer. Legislation or proposed legislation is not of direct interest to a taxpayer merely because it may affect business in general; however, if the legislation or proposed legislation will, or may reasonably be expected to, affect the taxpayer's trade or business it will be of direct interest to the taxpayer even though it also will affect the trade or business of the other taxpayers or business in general. To meet the direct interest test, it is not necessary that all provisions of the legislation or proposed legislation have an effect or expected effect, on the taxpayer's trade or business. The test will be met if one of the provisions of the legislation has the specified effect. Legislation or proposed legislation will be considered to be of direct interest to a membership organization if it is of direct interest to the organization, as such, or if it is of direct interest to one or more of its members.

(ii) Legislation which would increase or decrease the taxes applicable to the trade or business, increase or decrease the operating costs or earnings of the trade or business, or increase or decrease the administrative burdens connected with the trade or business meets the direct interest test. Legislation which would increase the social security benefits or liberalize the right to such benefits meets the direct interest test because such changes in the social security benefits may reasonably be expected to affect the retirement benefits which the employer will be asked to provide his employees or to increase his taxes. Legislation which would impose a retailer's sales tax is of direct interest to a retailer because, although the tax may be passed on to his customers, collection of the tax will impose additional burdens on the retailer, and because the increased cost of his products to the consumer may reduce the demand for them. Legislation which would provide an income tax credit or exclusion for shareholders is of direct interest to a corporation, because those tax benefits may increase the sources of capital available to the corporation. Legislation which would favorably or adversely affect the business of a competitor so as to affect the taxpayer's competitive position is of direct interest to the taxpayer. Legislation which would improve the school system of a community is of direct interest to a membership organization comprised of employers in the community because the improved school system is likely to make the community more attractive to prospective employees of such employers. On the other hand, proposed legislation relating to Presidential succession in the event of the death of the President has only a remote and speculative effect on any trade or business and therefore does not meet the direct interest test. Similarly, if a corporation is represented before a congressional committee to oppose an appropriation bill merely because of a desire to bring increased Government economy with the hope that such economy will eventually cause a reduction in the Federal income tax, the legislation does not meet the direct interest test because any effect it may have upon the corporation's trade or business is highly speculative.

. . . . .

(3) Deductibility of dues and other payments to an organization. If a substantial part of the activities of an organization, such as a labor union or a trade association, consists of one or more of the activities to which this paragraph relates (legislative matters, political campaigns, etc., exclusive of any activity constituting an appearance or communication with respect to legislation or proposed legislation of direct interest to the organization (see subparagraph (2) (ii) (b) (1)), a deduction will be allowed only for such portion of the dues or other payments to the organization as the taxpayer can clearly establish is attributable to activities to which this paragraph does not relate and to any activity constituting an appearance or communication with respect to legislation or proposed legislation of direct interest to the organization. The determination of whether a substantial part of an organization's activities consists of one or more of the activities to which this paragraph relates (exclusive of appearances or communications with respect to legislation or proposed legislation of di-

rect interest to the organization) shall be based on all the facts and circumstances. In no event shall a deduction be allowed for that portion of a special assessment or similar payment (including an increase in dues) made to any organization for any activity to which this paragraph relates if the activity does not constitute an appearance or communication with respect to legislation or proposed legislation of direct interest to the organization. If an organization pays or incurs expenses allocable to legislative activities which meet the tests of subdivisions (i) and (ii) of subparagraph (2) of this paragraph (appearances or communications with respect to legislation or proposed legislation of direct interest to the organization), on behalf of its members, the dues paid by a taxpayer are deductible to the extent used for such activities. Dues paid by a taxpayer will be considered to be used for such an activity, and thus deductible, although the legislation or proposed legislation involved is not of direct interest to the taxpayer, if, pursuant to the provisions of subparagraph (2) (ii) (b) (1) of this paragraph, the legislation or proposed legislation is of direct interest to the organization, as such, or is of direct interest to one or more members of the organization. For other provisions relating to the deductibility of dues and other payments to an organization, such as a labor union or a trade association, see paragraph (c) of § 1.162-15.

(4) Limitations. No deduction shall be allowed under section 162(a) for any amount paid or incurred (whether by way of contribution, gift, or otherwise) in connection with any attempt to influence the general public, or segments thereof, with respect to legislative matters, elections, or referendums. For example, no deduction shall be allowed for any expenses incurred in connection with "grassroot" campaigns or any other attempts to urge or encourage the public to contact members of a legislative body for the purpose of proposing, supporting, or opposing legislation.

§ 1.162-21   Fines and penalties

(a) In general. No deduction shall be allowed under section 162(a) for any fine or similar penalty paid to—
(1) The government of the United States, a State, a territory, or posses-

sion of the United States, the District of Columbia, or the Commonwealth of Puerto Rico;

(2) The government of a foreign country; or

(3) A political subdivision of, or corporation or other entity serving as an agency or instrumentality of, any of the above.

(b) Definition. (1) For purposes of this section a fine or similar penalty includes an amount—

(i) Paid pursuant to conviction or a plea of guilty or *nolo contendere* for a crime (felony or misdemeanor) in a criminal proceeding;

(ii) Paid as a civil penalty imposed by Federal, State, or local law, including additions to tax and additional amounts and assessable penalties imposed by chapter 68 of the Internal Revenue Code of 1954;

(iii) Paid in settlement of the taxpayer's actual or potential liability for a fine or penalty (civil or criminal); or

(iv) Forfeited as collateral posted in connection with a proceeding which could result in imposition of such a fine or penalty.

(2) The amount of a fine or penalty does not include legal fees and related expenses paid or incurred in the defense of a prosecution or civil action arising from a violation of the law imposing the fine or civil penalty, nor court costs assessed against the taxpayer, or stenographic and printing charges. Compensatory damages (including damages under section 4A of the Clayton Act (15 U.S.C. 15a), as amended) paid to a government do not constitute a fine or penalty.

(c) Examples. The application of this section may be illustrated by the following examples:

Example (1). M Corp. was indicted under section 1 of the Sherman Anti-Trust Act (15 U.S.C. 1) for fixing and maintaining prices of certain electrical products. M Corp. was convicted and was fined $50,000. The United States sued M Corp. under section 4A of the Clayton Act (15 U.S.C. 15a) for $100,000, the amount of the actual damages resulting from the price fixing of which M Corp. was convicted. Pursuant to a final judgment entered in the civil action. M Corp. paid the United States $100,000 in damages. Section 162(f) precludes M Corp. from deducting the fine of $50,000 as a trade or business expense. Section 162(f) does not preclude it from deducting the $100,000 paid to the United States as actual damages.

Example (2). N Corp. was found to have violated 33 U.S.C. 1321(b)(3) when a vessel it operated discharged oil in harmful quantities into the navigable waters of the United States. A civil penalty under 33 U.S.C. 1321(b)(6) of $5,000 was assessed against N Corp. with respect to the discharge. N Corp. paid $5,000 to the Coast Guard in payment of the civil penalty. Section 162(f) precludes N Corp. from deducting the $5,000 penalty.

Example (3). O Corp., a manufacturer of motor vehicles, was found to have violated 42 U.S.C. 1857f-2(a)(1) by selling a new motor vehicle which was not covered by the required certificate of conformity. Pursuant to 42 U.S.C. 1857f-4, O Corp. was required to pay, and did pay, a civil penalty to $10,000. In addition, pursuant to 42 U.S.C. 1857f-5a (c)(1), O Corp. was required to expend, and did expend, $500 in order to remedy the nonconformity of that motor vehicle. Section 162(f) precludes O Corp. from deducting the $10,000 penalty as a trade or business expense, but does not preclude it from deducting the $500 which it expended to remedy the nonconformity.

Example (4). P Corp. was the operator of a coal mine in which occurred a violation of a mandatory safety standard prescribed by the Federal Coal Mine Health and Safety Act of 1969 (30 U.S.C. 801 et seq.). Pursuant to 30 U.S.C. 819(a), a civil penalty of $10,000 was assessed against P Corp., and P Corp. paid the penalty. Section 162(f) precludes P Corp. from deducting the $10,000 penalty.

Example (5). Q Corp., a common carrier engaged in interstate commerce by railroad, hauled a railroad car which was not equipped with efficient hand brakes, in violation of 45 U.S.C. 11. Q Corp. was found to be liable for a penalty to $250 pursuant to 45 U.S.C. 13. Q Corp. paid that penalty. Section 162(f) precludes Q Corp. from deducting the $250 penalty.

Example (6). R Corp. owned and operated on the highways of State X a truck weighing in excess of the amount permitted under the law of State X. R Corp. was found to have violated the law and was assessed a fine of $85 which it paid to State X. Section 162(f) precludes R Corp. from deducting the amount so paid.

Example (7). S Corp. was found to have violated a law of State Y which prohibited the emission into the air of particulate matter in excess of a limit set forth in a regulation promulgated under that law. The Environmental Quality Hearing Board of State Y assessed a fine of $500 against S Corp. The fine was payable to State Y, and S Corp. paid it. Section 162(f) precludes S Corp. from deducting the $500 fine.

Example (8). T Corp. was found by a magistrate of City Z to be operating in such city an apartment building which did not conform to a provision of the city housing code requiring operable fire escapes on apartment buildings of that type. Upon the basis of the magistrate's finding, T Corp. was required to pay, and did pay, a fine of $200 to City Z. Section 162(f) precludes T Corp. from deducting the $200 fine.

§ 1.163-1 Interest deduction in general

(a) Except as otherwise provided in sections 264 to 267, inclusive, interest paid or accrued within the taxable year on indebtedness shall be allowed as a deduction in computing taxable income. For rules relating to interest on certain deferred payments, see section 483 and the regulations thereunder.

(b) Interest paid by the taxpayer on a mortgage upon real estate of which he is the legal or equitable owner, even though the taxpayer is not directly liable upon the bond or note secured by such mortgage, may be deducted as interest on his indebtedness. . . . .

* * * *

§ 1.164-1 Deduction for taxes

(a) In general. Only the following taxes shall be allowed as a deduction under this section for the taxable year within which paid or accrued, according to the method of accounting used in computing taxable income:

(1) State and local, and foreign, real property taxes.

(2) State and local personal property taxes.

(3) State and local, and foreign, income, war profits, and excess profits taxes.

(4) State and local general sales taxes.

(5) State and local taxes on the sale of gasoline, diesel fuel, and other motor fuel.

In addition, there shall be allowed as a deduction under this section State and local and foreign taxes not described in subparagraphs (1) through (5) of this paragraph which are paid or accrued within the taxable year in carrying on a trade or business or an activity described in section 212 (relating to expenses for production of income). For example, dealers or investors in securities and dealers or investors in real estate may deduct State stock transfer and real estate transfer taxes, respectively, under section 164, to the extent they are expenses incurred in carrying on a trade or business or an activity for the production of income. In general, taxes are deductible only by the person upon whom they are imposed. However, see § 1.164-5 in the case of certain taxes paid by the consumer. Also, in the case of a qualified State individual income tax (as defined in section 6362 and the regulations thereunder) which is determined by reference to a percentage of the Federal income tax (pursuant to section 6362(c)), an accrual method taxpayer shall use the cash receipts and disbursements method to compute the amount of his deduction therefor. Thus, the deduction under section 164 is in the amount actually paid with respect to the qualified tax, rather than the amount accrued with respect thereto, during the taxable year even though the taxpayer uses the accrual method of accounting for other purposes. . . . .

§ 1.164-3 Definitions and special rules

For purposes of section 164 and § 1.-164-1 to § 1.164-8, inclusive—

(a) State or local taxes. A State or local tax includes only a tax imposed by a State, a possession of the United States, or a political subdivision of any of the foregoing, or by the District of Columbia.

(b) Real property taxes. The term "real property taxes" means taxes imposed on interests in real property and levied for the general public welfare, but it does not include taxes assessed against local benefits. See § 1.164-4.

(c) Personal property taxes. The term "personal property tax" means an ad valorem tax which is imposed on an annual basis in respect of personal property. To qualify as a personal property tax, a tax must meet the following three tests:

(1) The tax must be ad valorem—that is, substantially in proportion to the value of the personal property. A tax which is based on criteria other than value does not qualify as ad valorem. For example, a motor vehicle tax based on weight, model year, and horsepower, or any of these characteristics is not an ad valorem tax. However, a tax which is partly based on value and partly based on other criteria may qualify in part. For example, in the case of a motor vehicle tax of 1 percent of value plus 40 cents per hundredweight, the part of the tax equal to 1 percent of value qualifies as an ad valorem tax and the balance does not qualify.

(2) The tax must be imposed on an annual basis, even if collected more frequently or less frequently.

(3) The tax must be imposed in respect of personal property. A tax may

be considered to be imposed in respect of personal property even if in form it is imposed on the exercise of a privilege. Thus, for taxable y_rs beginning after December 31, 1963, State and local taxes on the registration or licensing of highway motor vehicles are not deductible as personal property taxes unless and to the extent that the tests prescribed in this subparagraph are met. For example, an annual ad valorem tax qualifies as a personal property tax although it is denominated a registration fee imposed for the privilege of registering motor vehicles or of using them on the highways.

(d) Foreign taxes. The term "foreign tax" includes only a tax imposed by the authority of a foreign country. A tax imposed by a political subdivision of a foreign country is considered to be imposed by the authority of that foreign country.

(e) Sales tax. (1) The term "sales tax" means a tax imposed upon persons engaged in selling tangible personal property, or upon the consumers of such property, including persons selling gasoline or other motor vehicle fuels at wholesale or retail, which is a stated sum per unit of property sold or which is measured by the gross sales price or the gross receipts from the sale. The term also includes a tax imposed upon persons engaged in furnishing services which is measured by the gross receipts for furnishing such services.

(2) In general, the term "consumer" means the ultimate user or purchaser; it does not include a purchaser such as a retailer, who acquires the property for resale.

(f) General sales tax. A "general sales tax" is a sales tax which is imposed at one rate in respect of the sale at retail of a broad range of classes of items. No foreign sales tax is deductible under section 164(a) and paragraph (a) (4) of § 1.164-1. To qualify as a general sales tax, a tax must meet the following two tests:

(1) The tax must be a tax in respect of sales at retail. This may include a tax imposed on persons engaged in selling property at retail or furnishing services at retail, for example, if the tax is measured by gross sales price or by gross receipts from sales or services. Rentals qualify as sales at retail

if so treated under applicable State sales tax laws.

(2) The tax must be general—that is, it must be imposed at one rate in respect of the retail sales of a broad range of classes of items. A sales tax is considered to be general although imposed on sales of various classes of items at more than one rate provided that one rate applies to the retail sales of a broad range of classes of items. The term "items" includes both commodities and services.

(g) Special rules relating to general sales taxes. (1) A sales tax which is general is usually imposed at one rate in respect of the retail sales of all tangible personal property with exceptions and additions). However, a sales tax which is selective—that is, a tax which applies at one rate with respect to retail sales of specified classes of items also qualifies as general if the specified classes represent a broad range of classes of items. A selective sales tax which does not apply at one rate to the retail sales of a broad range of classes of items is not general. For example, a tax which applies only to sales of alcoholic beverages, tobacco, admissions, luxury items, and a few other items is not general. Similarly, a tax imposed solely on services is not general. However, a selective sales tax may be deemed to be part of the general sales tax and hence may be deductible, even if imposed by a separate Title, etc., of the State or local law, if imposed at the same rate as the general rate of tax (as defined in subparagraph (4) of this paragraph) which qualifies a tax in the taxing jurisdiction as a general sales tax. For example, if a State has a 5 percent general sales tax and a separate selective sales tax of 5 percent on transient accommodations, the tax on transient accommodations is deductible.

(2) A tax is imposed at one rate only if it is imposed at that rate on generally the same base for all items subject to tax. For example, a sales tax imposed at a 3 percent rate on 100 percent of the sales price of some classes of items and at a 3 percent rate on 50 percent of the sales price of other classes of items would not be imposed at one rate with respect to all such classes. However, a tax is considered to be imposed at one rate although it allows dollar exemptions, if the exemp-

tions are designed to exclude all sales under a certain dollar amount. For example, a tax may be imposed at one rate although it applies to all sales of tangible personal property but applies only to sales amounting to more than 10 cents.

(3) The fact that a sales tax exempts food, clothing, medical supplies, and motor vehicles, or any of them, shall not be taken into account in determining whether the tax applies to a broad range of classes of items. The fact that a sales tax applies to food, clothing, medical supplies, and motor vehicles, or any of them, at a rate which is lower than the general rate of tax (as defined in subparagraph (4) of this paragraph) is not taken into account in determining whether the tax is imposed at one rate on the retail sales of a broad range of classes of items. For purposes of this section, the term "food" means food for human consumption off the premises where sold, and the term "medical supplies" includes drugs, medicines, and medical devices.

(4) Except in the case of a lower rate of tax applicable in respect of food, clothing, medical supplies, and motor vehicles, or any of them, no deduction is allowed for a general sales tax in respect of any item if the tax is imposed on such item at a rate other than the general rate of tax. The general rate of tax is the one rate which qualifies a tax in a taxing jurisdiction as a general sales tax because the tax is imposed at such one rate on a broad range of classes of items. There can be only one general rate of tax in any one taxing jurisdiction. However, a general sales tax imposed at a lower rate or rates on food, clothing, motor vehicles, and medical supplies, or any of them, may nonetheless be deductible with respect to such items. For example, a sales tax which is imposed at 1 percent with respect to food, imposed at 3 percent with respect to a broad range of classes of tangible personal property, and imposed at 4 percent with respect to transient accommodations would qualify as a general sales tax. Taxes paid at the 1 percent and the 3 percent rates are deductible, but tax paid at the 4 percent rate is not deductible. The fact that a sales tax provides for the adjustment of the general rate of tax to reflect the sales tax rate in another taxing jurisdiction shall not be taken into account in determining whether the tax is imposed at one rate on the retail sales of a broad range of classes of items. Moreover, a general sales tax imposed at a lower rate with respect to an item in order to reflect the tax rate in another jurisdiction is also deductible at such lower rate. For example, State E imposes a general sales tax whose general rate is 3 percent. The State E sales tax law provides that in areas bordering on States with general sales taxes, selective sales taxes, or special excise taxes, the rate applied in the adjoining State will be used if such rate is under 3 percent. State F imposes a 2 percent sales tax. The 2 percent sales tax paid by residents of State E in areas bordering on State F is deductible.

. . . .

§ 1.165–1   Losses

(a) **Allowance of deduction.** Section 165(a) provides that, in computing taxable income under section 63, any loss actually sustained during the taxable year and not made good by insurance or some other form of compensation shall be allowed as a deduction subject to any provision of the internal revenue laws which prohibits or limits the amount of the deduction. This deduction for losses sustained shall be taken in accordance with section 165 and the regulations thereunder. For the disallowance of deductions for worthless securities issued by a political party, see § 1.271–1.

(b) **Nature of loss allowable.** To be allowable as a deduction under section 165(a), a loss must be evidenced by closed and completed transactions, fixed by identifiable events, and, except as otherwise provided in section 165(h) and § 1.165–11, relating to disaster losses, actually sustained during the taxable year. Only a bona fide loss is allowable. Substance and not mere form shall govern in determining a deductible loss.

(c) **Amount deductible.** (1) The amount of loss allowable as a deduction under section 165(a) shall not exceed the amount prescribed by § 1.1011–1 as the adjusted basis for determining the loss from the sale or other disposition of the property involved. In the case of each such deduction claimed, therefore, the basis of the property must be properly adjusted as prescribed by § 1.1011–1 for such items as expenditures, receipts, or losses, properly chargeable to capital account, and for such items as depreciation, obsolescence, amortization, and depletion, in order to determine the amount of loss allowable as a deduction. . . . .

(2) The amount of loss recognized upon the sale or exchange of property shall be determined for purposes of section 165(a) in accordance with § 1.1002–1.

(3) A loss from the sale or exchange of a capital asset shall be allowed as a deduction under section 165(a) but only to the extent allowed in section 1211 (relating to limitation on capital losses) and section 1212 (relating to capital loss carrybacks and carryovers), and in the regulations under those sections.

(4) In determining the amount of loss actually sustained for purposes of section 165(a), proper adjustment shall be made for any salvage value and for any insurance or other compensation received.

(d) Year of deduction. (1) A loss shall be allowed as a deduction under section 165(a) only for the taxable year in which the loss is sustained. For this purpose, a loss shall be treated as sustained during the taxable year in which the loss occurs as evidenced by closed and completed transactions and as fixed by identifiable events occurring in such taxable year. For provisions relating to situations where a loss attributable to a disaster will be treated as sustained in the taxable year immediately preceding the taxable year in which the disaster actually occurred, see section 165(h) and § 1.165–11.

(2) (i) If a casualty or other event occurs which may result in a loss and, in the year of such casualty or event, there exists a claim for reimbursement with respect to which there is a reasonable prospect of recovery, no portion of the loss with respect to which reimbursement may be received is sustained, for purposes of section 165, until it can be ascertained with reasonable certainty whether or not such reimbursement will be received. Whether a reasonable prospect of recovery exists with respect to a claim for reimbursement of a loss is a question of fact to be determined upon an examination of all facts and circumstances. Whether or not such reimbursement will be received may be ascertained with reasonable certainty, for example, by a settlement of the claim, by an adjudication of the claim, or by an abandonment of the claim. When a taxpayer claims that the taxable year in which a loss is sustained is fixed by his abandonment of the claim for reimbursement, he must be able to produce objective evidence of his having abandoned the claim, such as the execution of a release.

(ii) If in the year of the casualty or other event a portion of the loss is not covered by a claim for reimbursement with respect to which there is a reasonable prospect of recovery, then such portion of the loss is sustained during the taxable year in which the casualty or other event occurs. For example, if property having an adjusted basis of $10,000 is completely destroyed by fire in 1961, and if the taxpayer's only claim for reimbursement consists of an insurance claim for $8,000 which is settled in 1962, the taxpayer sustains a loss of $2,000 in 1961. However, if the taxpayer's automobile is completely destroyed in 1961 as a result of the negligence of another person and there exists a reasonable prospect of recovery on a claim for the full value of the automobile against such person, the taxpayer does not sustain any loss until the taxable year in which the claim is adjudicated or otherwise settled. If the automobile had an adjusted basis of $5,000 and the taxpayer secures a judgment of $4,000 in 1962, $1,000 is deductible for the taxable year 1962. If in 1963 it becomes reasonably certain that only $3,500 can never be collected on such judgment, $500 is deductible for the taxable year 1963.

(iii) If the taxpayer deducted a loss in accordance with the provisions of this paragraph and in a subsequent taxable year receives reimbursement for such loss, he does not recompute the tax for the taxable year in which the deduction was taken but includes the amount of such reimbursement in his gross income for the taxable year in which received, subject to the provisions of section 111, relating to recovery of amounts previously deducted.

(3) Any loss arising from theft shall be treated as sustained during the taxable year in which the taxpayer discovers the loss (see § 1.165–8, relating to theft losses). However, if in the year of discovery there exists a claim for reimbursement with respect to which there is a reasonable prospect of recovery, no portion of the loss with respect to which reimbursement may be received is sustained, for purposes of section 165, until the taxable year in which it can be ascertained with reasonable certainty whether or not such reimbursement will be received.

. . . .

(e) Limitation on losses of individuals. In the case of an individual, the deduction for losses granted by section 165(a) shall, subject to the provisions of section 165(c) and paragraph (a) of this section, be limited to:

(1) Losses incurred in a trade or business;

(2) Losses incurred in any transaction entered into for profit, though not connected with a trade or business; and

(3) Losses of property not connected with a trade or business and not incurred in any transaction entered into for profit, if such losses arise from fire, storm, shipwreck, or other casualty, or from theft, and if the loss involved has not been allowed for estate tax purposes in the estate tax return. For additional provisions pertaining to the allowance of casualty and theft losses, see §§ 1.165–7, 1.165–8, respectively.

. . . .

§ 1.165–3 Demolition of buildings

(a) Intent to demolish formed at time of purchase. (1) Except as provided in subparagraph (2) of this paragraph, the following rule shall apply when, in the course of a trade or business or in a transaction entered into for profit, real property is purchased with the intention of demolishing either immediately or subsequently the buildings situated thereon: No deduction shall be allowed under section 165(a) on account of the demolition of the old buildings even though any demolition originally planned is subsequently deferred or abandoned. The entire basis of the property so purchased shall, not-

withstanding the provisions of § 1.167 (a)–5, be allocated to the land only. Such basis shall be increased by the net cost of demolition or decreased by the net proceeds from demolition.

(2) (i) If the property is purchased with the intention of demolishing the buildings and the buildings are used in a trade or business or held for the production of income before their demolition, a portion of the basis of the property may be allocated to such buildings and depreciated over the period during which they are so used or held. The fact that the taxpayer intends to demolish the buildings shall be taken into account in making the apportionment of basis between the land and buildings under § 1.167(a)–5. In any event, the portion of the purchase price which may be allocated to the buildings shall not exceed the present value of the right to receive rentals from the buildings over the period of their intended use. The present value of such right shall be determined at the time that the buildings are first used in the trade or business or first held for the production of income. If the taxpayer does not rent the buildings, but uses them in his own trade or business or in the production of his income, the present value of such right shall be determined by reference to the rentals which could be realized during such period of intended use. The fact that the taxpayer intends to rent or use the buildings for a limited period before their demolition shall also be taken into account in computing the useful life in accordance with paragraph (b) of § 1.167(a)–1.

(ii) Any portion of the purchase price which is allocated to the buildings in accordance with this subparagraph shall not be included in the basis of the land computed under subparagraph (1) of this paragraph, and any portion of the basis of the buildings which has not been recovered through depreciation or otherwise at the time of the demolition of the buildings is allowable as a deduction under section 165.

(iii) The application of this subparagraph may be illustrated by the following example:

Example. In January 1958, A purchased land and a building for $60,000 with the intention of demolishing the building. In the following April, A concludes that he will be unable to commence the construction of a proposed new building for a period of more than 3 years. Accordingly, on June 1, 1958, he leased the building for a period of 3 years at an annual rental of $1,200. A intends to demolish the building upon expiration of the lease. A may allocate a portion of the $60,000 basis of the property to the building to be depreciated over the 3-year period. That portion is equal to the present value of the right to receive $3,600 (3 times $1,200). Assuming that the present value of that right determined as of June 1, 1958, is $2,850, A may allocate that amount to the building and, if A files his return on the basis of a taxable year ending May 31, 1959, A may take a depreciation deduction with respect to such building of $950 for such taxable year. The basis of the land to A as determined under subparagraph (1) of this paragraph is reduced by $2,850. If on June 1, 1960, A ceases to rent the building and demolishes it, the balance of the undepreciated portion allocated to the buildings, $950, may be deducted from gross income under section 165.

(3) The basis of any building acquired in replacement of the old buildings shall not include any part of the basis of the property originally purchased even though such part was, at the time of purchase, allocated to the buildings to be demolished for purposes of determining allowable depreciation for the period before demolition.

(b) Intent to demolish formed subsequent to the time of acquisition. (1) Except as provided in subparagraph (2) of this paragraph, the loss incurred in a trade or business or in a transaction entered into for profit and arising from a demolition of old buildings shall be allowed as a deduction under section 165(a) if the demolition occurs as a result of a plan formed subsequent to the acquisition of the buildings demolished. The amount of the loss shall be the adjusted basis of the buildings demolished increased by the net cost of demolition or decreased by the net proceeds from demolition. See paragraph (c) of § 1.165-1 relating to amount deductible under section 165. The basis of any building acquired in replacement of the old buildings shall not include any part of the basis of the property demolished.

(2) If a lessor or lessee of real property demolishes the buildings situated thereon pursuant to a lease or an agreement which resulted in a lease, under which either the lessor was required or the lessee was required or permitted to demolish such buildings, no deduction shall be allowed to the lessor under section 165(a) on account of the demolition of the old buildings. However, the adjusted basis of the demolished buildings, increased by the net cost of demolition or decreased by the net proceeds from demolition, shall be considered as a part of the cost of the lease to be amortized over the remaining term thereof.

(c) Evidence of intention. (1) Whether real property has been purchased with the intention of demolishing the buildings thereon or whether the demolition of the buildings occurs as a result of a plan formed subsequent to their acquisition is a question of fact, and the answer depends upon an examination of all the surrounding facts and circumstances. The answer to the question does not depend solely upon the statements of the taxpayer at the time he acquired the property or demolished the buildings, but such statements, if made, are relevant and will be considered. Certain other relevant facts and circumstances that exist in some cases and the inferences that might reasonably be drawn from them are described in subparagraphs (2) and (3) of this paragraph. The question as to the taxpayer's intention is not answered by any inference that is drawn from any one fact or circumstance but can be answered only by a consideration of all relevant facts and circumstances and the reasonable inferences to be drawn therefrom.

(2) An intention at the time of acquisition to demolish may be suggested by:

(i) A short delay between the date of acquisition and the date of demolition;

(ii) Evidence of prohibitive remodeling costs determined at the time of acquisition;

(iii) Existence of municipal regulations at the time of acquisition which would prohibit the continued use of the buildings for profit purposes;

(iv) Unsuitability of the buildings for the taxpayer's trade or business at the time of acquisition; or

(v) Inability at the time of acquisition to realize a reasonable income from the buildings.

(3) The fact that the demolition occurred pursuant to a plan formed subsequent to the acquisition of the property may be suggested by:

(i) Substantial improvement of the buildings immediately after their acquisition;

(ii) Prolonged use of the buildings for business purposes after their acquisition;

(iii) Suitability of the buildings for investment purposes at the time of acquisition;

(iv) Substantial change in economic or business conditions after the date of acquisition;

(v) Loss of useful value occurring after the date of acquisition;

(vi) Substantial damage to the buildings occurring after their acquisition;

(vii) Discovery of latent structural defects in the buildings after their acquisition;

(viii) Decline in the taxpayer's business after the date of acquisition;

(ix) Condemnation of the property by municipal authorities after the date of acquisition; or

(x) Inability after acquisition to obtain building material necessary for the improvement of the property.

§ 1.165–4 Decline in value of stock

(a) Deduction disallowed. No deduction shall be allowed under section 165(a) solely on account of a decline in the value of stock owned by the taxpayer when the decline is due to a fluctuation in the market price of the stock or to other similar cause. A mere shrinkage in the value of stock owned by the taxpayer, even though extensive, does not give rise to a deduction under section 165(a) if the stock has any recognizable value on the date claimed as the date of loss. No loss for a decline in the value of stock owned by the taxpayer shall be allowed as a deduction under section 165(a) except insofar as the loss is recognized under § 1.1002–1 upon the sale or exchange of the stock and except as otherwise provided in § 1.165–5 with respect to stock which becomes worthless during the taxable year.

. . . . .

(d) Definition. As used in this section, the term "stock" means a share of stock in a corporation or a right to subscribe for, or to receive, a share of stock in a corporation.

§ 1.165–5 Worthless securities

(a) Definition of security. As used in section 165(g) and this section, the term "security" means:

(1) A share of stock in a corporation;

(2) A right to subscribe for, or to receive, a share of stock in a corporation; or

(3) A bond, debenture, note, or certificate, or other evidence of indebtedness to pay a fixed or determinable sum of money, which has been issued with interest coupons or in registered form by a domestic or foreign corporation or by any government or political subdivision thereof.

(b) Ordinary loss. If any security which is not a capital asset becomes wholly worthless during the taxable year, the loss resulting therefrom may be deducted under section 165(a) as an ordinary loss.

(c) Capital loss. If any security which is a capital asset becomes wholly worthless at any time during the taxable year, the loss resulting therefrom may be deducted under section 165(a) but only as though it were a loss from a sale or exchange, on the last day of the taxable year, of a capital asset. See section 165(g) (1). The amount so allowed as a deduction shall be subject to the limitations upon capital losses described in paragraph (c) (3) of § 1.-165–1.

(d) Loss on worthless securities of an affiliated corporation—(1) Deductible as an ordinary loss. If a taxpayer which is a domestic corporation owns any security of a domestic or foreign corporation which is affiliated with the taxpayer within the meaning of subparagraph (2) of this paragraph and such security becomes wholly worthless during the taxable year, the loss resulting therefrom may be deducted under section 165(a) as an ordinary loss in accordance with paragraph (b) of this section. The fact that the security is in fact a capital asset of the taxpayer is immaterial for this purpose, since section 165(g) (3) provides that such security shall be treated as though it were not a capital asset for the purposes of section 165(g) (1). A debt which becomes wholly worthless during the taxable year shall be allowed as an ordinary loss in accordance with the provisions of this subparagraph, to the extent that such debt is a security within the meaning of paragraph (a) (3) of this section.

(2) Affiliated corporation defined. For purposes of this paragraph, a corporation shall be treated as affiliated with the taxpayer owning the security if—

(i) (a) In the case of a taxable year beginning on or after January 1, 1970, the taxpayer owns directly—

(1) Stock possessing at least 80 percent of the voting power of all classes of such corporation's stock, and

(2) At least 80 percent of each class of such corporation's nonvoting stock excluding for purposes of this subdivision (i) (a) nonvoting stock which is limited and preferred as to dividends (see section 1504(a)), or

(b) In the case of a taxable year beginning before January 1, 1970, the taxpayer owns directly at least 95 percent of each class of the stock of such corporation;

(ii) None of the stock of such corporation was acquired by the taxpayer solely for the purpose of converting a capital loss sustained by reason of the worthlessness of any such stock into an ordinary loss under section 165(g) (3), and

(iii) More than 90 percent of the aggregate of the gross receipts of such corporation for all the taxable years during which it has been in existence has been from sources other than royalties, rents (except rents derived from rental of properties to employees of such corporation in the ordinary course of its operating business), dividends, interest (except interest received on the deferred purchase price of operating assets sold), annuities, and gains from sales or exchanges of stocks and securities. For this purpose, the term "gross receipts" means total receipts determined without any deduction for cost of goods sold, and gross receipts from sales or exchanges of stocks and securities shall be taken into account only to the extent of gains from such sales or exchanges.

. . . .

§ 1.165-7 Casualty losses

(a) In general—(1) Allowance of deduction. Except as otherwise provided in paragraphs (b)(4) and (c) of this section, any loss arising from fire, storm, shipwreck, or other casualty is allowable as a deduction under section 165(a) for the taxable year in which the loss is sustained. . . . The manner of determining the amount of a casualty loss allowable as a deduction in computing taxable income under section 63 is the same whether the loss has been incurred in a trade or business or in any transaction entered into for profit, or whether it has been a loss of property not connected with a trade or business and not incurred in any transaction entered into for profit. The amount of a casualty loss shall be determined in accordance with paragraph (b) of this section. For other rules relating to the treatment of deductible casualty losses, see § 1.1231–1, relating to the involuntary conversion of property.

(2) Method of valuation. (i) In determining the amount of loss deductible under this section, the fair market value of the property immediately before and immediately after the casualty shall generally be ascertained by competent appraisal. This appraisal must recognize the effects of any general market decline affecting undamaged as well as damaged property which may occur simultaneously with the casualty, in order that any deduction under this section shall be limited to the actual loss resulting from damage to the property.

(ii) The cost of repairs to the property damaged is acceptable as evidence of the loss of value if the taxpayer shows that (a) the repairs are necessary to restore the property to its condition immediately before the casualty, (b) the amount spent for such repairs is not excessive, (c) the repairs do not care for more than the damage suffered, and (d) the value of the property after the repairs does not as a result of the repairs exceed the value of the property immediately before the casualty.

(3) Damage to automobiles. An automobile owned by the taxpayer, whether used for business purposes or maintained for recreation or pleasure, may be the subject of a casualty loss, including those losses specifically referred to in subparagraph (1) of this paragraph. In addition, a casualty loss occurs when an automobile owned by the taxpayer is damaged and when:

(i) The damage results from the faulty driving of the taxpayer or other person operating the automobile but is not due to the willful act or willful negligence of the taxpayer or of one acting in his behalf, or

(ii) The damage results from the faulty driving of the operator of the vehicle with which the automobile of the taxpayer collides.

. . . .

(6) **Theft losses.** A loss which arises from theft is not considered a casualty loss for purposes of this section. See § 1.165-8, relating to theft losses.

(b) **Amount deductible—(1) General rule.** In the case of any casualty loss whether or not incurred in a trade or business or in any transaction entered into for profit, the amount of loss to be taken into account for the purposes of section 165(a) shall be the lesser of either—

(i) The amount which is equal to the fair market value of the property immediately before the casualty reduced by the fair market value of the property immediately after the casualty; or

(ii) The amount of the adjusted basis prescribed in § 1.1011-1 for determining the loss from the sale or other disposition of the property involved.

However, if property used in a trade or business or held for the production of income is totally destroyed by casualty, and if the fair market value of such property immediately before the casualty is less than the adjusted basis of such property, the amount of the adjusted basis of such property shall be treated as the amount of the loss for purposes of section 165(a).

(2) **Aggregation of property for computing loss.** (i) A loss incurred in a trade or business or in any transaction entered into for profit shall be determined under subparagraph (1) of this paragraph by reference to the single, identifiable property damaged or destroyed. Thus, for example, in determining the fair market value of the property before and after the casualty in a case where damage by casualty has occurred to a building and ornamental

or fruit trees used in a trade or business, the decrease in value shall be measured by taking the building and trees into account separately, and not together as an integral part of the realty, and separate losses shall be determined for such building and trees.

(ii) In determining a casualty loss involving real property and improvements thereon not used in a trade or business or in any transaction entered into for profit, the improvements (such as buildings and ornamental trees and shrubbery) to the property damaged or destroyed shall be considered an integral part of the property, for purposes of subparagraph (1) of this paragraph, and no separate basis need be apportioned to such improvements.

(3) **Examples.** The application of this paragraph may be illustrated by the following examples:

. . . .

Example (2). In 1958 A purchases land containing an office building for the lump sum of $90,000. The purchase price is allocated between the land ($18,000) and the building ($72,-000) for purposes of determining basis. After the purchase A planted trees and ornamental shrubs on the grounds surrounding the building. In 1961 the land, building, trees, and shrubs are damaged by hurricane. At the time of the casualty the adjusted basis of the land is $18,-000 and the adjusted basis of the building is $66,000. At that time the trees and shrubs have an adjusted basis of $1,200. The fair market value of the land and building immediately before the casualty is $18,000 and $70,000, respectively, and immediately after the casualty is $18,000 and $52,000, respectively. The fair market value of the trees and shrubs immediately before the casualty is $2,000 and immediately after the casualty is $400. In 1961 insurance of $5,000 is received to cover the loss to the building. A has no other gains or losses in 1961 subject to section 1231 and § 1.1231-1. The amount of the deduction allowable under section 165(a) with respect to the building for the taxable year 1961 is $13,000, computed as follows:

Value of property immediately before casualty	$70,000
Less: Value of property immediately after casualty	52,000
Value of property actually destroyed ...	18,000
Loss to be taken into account for purposes of section 165(a): Lesser amount of property actually destroyed ($18,000) or adjusted basis of property ($66,000)	$18,000
Less: Insurance received	5,000
Deduction allowable	13,000

The amount of the deduction allowable under section 165(a) with respect to the trees and shrubs for the taxable year 1961 is $1,200, computed as follows:

Value of property immediately before
casualty $2,000
Less: Value of property immediately
after casualty 400
Value of property actually destroyed 1,600

Loss to be taken into account for
purposes of section 165(a): Lesser
amount of property actually destroyed ($1,600) or adjusted basis
of property ($1,200) 1,200

Example (3). Assume the same facts as in
example (2) except that A purchases land containing a house instead of an office building.
The house is used as his private residence.
Since the property is used for personal purposes, no allocation of the purchase price is
necessary for the land and house. Likewise,
no individual determination of the fair market
values of the land, house, trees, and shrubs is
necessary. The amount of the deduction allowable under section 165(a) with respect to the
land, house, trees, and shrubs for the taxable
year 1961 is $14,600, computed as follows:

Value of property immediately be-
fore casualty $90,000
Less: Value of property immediately
after casualty 70,400
Value of property actually destroyed 19,600

Loss to be taken into account for
purposes of section 165(a): Lesser
amount of property actually destroyed ($19,600) or adjusted basis
of property ($91,200) 19,600
Less: Insurance received 5,000
Deduction allowable 14,600

(c) Loss sustained by an estate. A
casualty loss of property not connected
with a trade or business and not incurred in any transaction entered into
for profit which is sustained during the
settlement of an estate shall be allowed
as a deduction under sections 165(a)
and 641(b) in computing the taxable
income of the estate if the loss has not
been allowed under section 2054 in computing the taxable estate of the decedent and if the statement has been filed
in accordance with § 1.642(g)-1. See
section 165(c) (3).

§ 1.165-8 Theft losses

(a) Allowance of deduction. (1) Except as otherwise provided in paragraphs (b) and (c) of this section, any
loss arising from theft is allowable as a
deduction under section 165(a) for the
taxable year in which the loss is sustained. See section 165(c) (3).

(2) A loss arising from theft shall
be treated under section 165(a) as
sustained during the taxable year in
which the taxpayer discovers the loss.
See section 165(e). Thus, a theft loss

is not deductible under section 165(a)
for the taxable year in which the theft
actually occurs unless that is also the
year in which the taxpayer discovers
the loss. However, if in the year of
discovery there exists a claim for reimbursement with respect to which
there is a reasonable prospect of recovery, see paragraph (d) of § 1.165-1.

(c) Amount deductible. The amount
deductible under this section in respect
of a theft loss shall be determined consistently with the manner prescribed in
§ 1.165-7 for determining the amount of
casualty loss allowable as a deduction
under section 165(a). In applying the
provisions of paragraph (b) of § 1.165-
7 for this purpose, the fair market value
of the property immediately after the
theft shall be considered to be zero.
In the case of a loss sustained after December 31, 1963, in a taxable year ending after such date, in respect of property not used in a trade or business or
for income producing purposes, the
amount deductible shall be limited to
that portion of the loss which is in excess of $100. For rules applicable in
applying the $100 limitation, see para-
graph (b) (4) of § 1.165-7. For other
rules relating to the treatment of deductible theft losses, see § 1.1231-1, relating to the involuntary conversion of
property.

(d) Definition. For purposes of this
section the term "theft" shall be deemed to include, but shall not necessarily
be limited to, larceny, embezzlement,
and robbery.

§ 1.165-9 Sale of residential prop-
erty

(a) Losses not allowed. A loss sustained on the sale of residential property purchased or constructed by the
taxpayer for use as his personal residence and so used by him up to the time
of the sale is not deductible under section 165(a).

**(b) Property converted from person-
al use.** (1) If property purchased or
constructed by the taxpayer for use as
his personal residence is, prior to its
sale, rented or otherwise appropriated
to income-producing purposes and is
used for such purposes up to the time
of its sale, a loss sustained on the sale

of the property shall be allowed as a deduction under section 165(a).

(2) The loss allowed under this paragraph upon the sale of the property shall be the excess of the adjusted basis prescribed in § 1.1011-1 for determining loss over the amount realized from the sale. For this purpose, the adjusted basis for determining loss shall be the lesser of either of the following amounts, adjusted as prescribed in § 1.1011-1 for the period subsequent to the conversion of the property to income-producing purposes:

(i) The fair market value of the property at the time of conversion, or

(ii) The adjusted basis for loss, at the time of conversion, determined under § 1.1011-1 but without reference to the fair market value.

* * *

(c) **Examples.** The application of paragraph (b) of this section may be illustrated by the following examples:

Example (1). Residential property is purchased by the taxpayer in 1943 for use as his personal residence at a cost of $25,000, of which $15,000 is allocable to the building. The taxpayer uses the property as his personal residence until January 1, 1952, at which time its fair market value is $22,000, of which $12,000 is allocable to the building. The taxpayer rents the property from January 1, 1952, until January 1, 1955, at which time it is sold for $16,000. On January 1, 1952, the building has an estimated useful life of 20 years. It is assumed that the building has no estimated salvage value and that there are no adjustments in respect of basis other than depreciation, which is computed on the straight-line method. The loss to be taken into account for purposes of section 165(a) for the taxable year 1955 is $4,200, computed as follows:

Basis of property at time of conversion for purposes of this section (that is, the lesser of $25,000 cost or $22,000 fair market value)	$22,000
Less: Depreciation allowable from January 1, 1952, to January 1, 1955 (3 years at 5 percent based on $12,000, the value of the building at time of conversion, as prescribed by § 1.167(g)-1)	1,800
Adjusted basis prescribed in § 1.1011-1 for determining loss on sale of the property	20,200
Less: Amount realized on sale	16,000
Loss to be taken into account for purposes of section 165(a)	4,200

In this example the value of the building at the time of conversion is used as the basis for computing depreciation. See example (2) of this paragraph wherein the adjusted basis of the building is required to be used for such purpose.

Example (2). Residential property is purchased by the taxpayer in 1940 for use as his personal residence at a cost of $23,000, of which $10,000 is allocable to the building. The tax-

payer uses the property as his personal residence until January 1, 1953, at which time its fair market value is $20,000, of which $12,000 is allocable to the building. The taxpayer rents the property from January 1, 1953, until January 1, 1957, at which time it is sold for $17,000. On January 1, 1953, the building has an estimated useful life of 20 years. It is assumed that the building has no estimated salvage value and that there are no adjustments in respect of basis other than depreciation, which is computed on the straight-line method. The loss to be taken into account for purposes of section 165(a) for the taxable year 1957 is $1,000, computed as follows:

Basis of property at time of conversion for purposes of this section (that is, the lesser of $23,000 cost or $20,000 fair market value)	$20,000
Less: Depreciation allowable from January 1, 1953, to January 1, 1957 (4 years at 5 percent based on $10,000, the cost of the building, as prescribed by § 1.167(g)-1)	2,000
Adjusted basis prescribed in § 1.1011-1 for determining loss on sale of the property	18,000
Less: Amount realized on sale	17,000
Loss to be taken into account for purposes of section 165(a)	1,000

§ 1.165-11 Election in respect of losses attributable to a disaster

(a) **In general.** Section 165(h) provides that a taxpayer who has sustained a disaster loss which is allowable as a deduction under section 165(a) may, under certain circumstances, elect to deduct such loss for the taxable year in which the disaster actually occurred.

(b) **Loss subject to election.** The election provided by section 165(h) and paragraph (a) of this section applies only to a loss:

(1) Arising from a disaster resulting in a determination referred to in subparagraph (2) of this paragraph and occurring—

(i) After December 31, 1971, or

(ii) After December 31, 1961, and before January 1, 1972, and during the period following the close of a particular taxable year of the taxpayer and on or before the due date for filing the income tax return for that taxable year (determined without regard to any extension of time granted the taxpayer for filing such return);

(2) Occurring in an area subsequently determined by the President of the United States to warrant assistance by the Federal Government under the Disaster Relief Act of 1974; and

(3) Constituting a loss otherwise allowable as a deduction for the year in

which the loss occurred under section 165(a) and the provisions of §§ 1.165–1 through 1.165–10 which are applicable to such losses.

(c) Amount of loss to which election applies. The amount of the loss to which section 165(h) and this section apply shall be the amount of the loss sustained during the period specified in paragraph (b)(1) of this section computed in accordance with the provisions of section 165 and those provisions of §§ 1.165–1 through 1.165–10 which are applicable to such losses. However, for purposes of making such computation, the period specified in paragraph (b) (1) of this section shall be deemed to be a taxable year.

(d) Scope and effect of election. An election made pursuant to section 165 (h) and this section in respect of a loss arising from a particular disaster shall apply to the entire loss sustained by the taxpayer from such disaster during the period specified in paragraph (b)(1) of this section in the area specified in paragraph (b)(2) of this section. If such an election is made, the disaster to which the election relates will be deemed to have occurred in the taxable year immediately preceding the taxable year in which the disaster actually occurred, and the loss to which the election applies will be deemed to have been sustained in such preceding taxable year.

§ 1.166–1 Bad debts

(a) Allowance of deduction. Section 166 provides that, in computing taxable income under section 63, a deduction shall be allowed in respect of bad debts owed to the taxpayer. For this purpose, bad debts shall, subject to the provisions of section 166 and the regulations thereunder, be taken into account either as—

(1) A deduction in respect of debts which become worthless in whole or in part; or as

(2) A deduction for a reasonable addition to a reserve for bad debts.

(b) Manner of selecting method. (1) A taxpayer filing a return of income for the first taxable year for which he is entitled to a bad debt deduction may select either of the two methods prescribed by paragraph (a) of this section for treating bad debts, but such selection is subject to the approval of the district director upon examination of the return. If the method so select-

ed is approved, it shall be used in returns for all subsequent taxable years unless the Commissioner grants permission to use the other method. A statement of facts substantiating any deduction claimed under section 166 on account of bad debts shall accompany each return of income.

· · · ·

(c) Bona fide debt required. Only a bona fide debt qualifies for purposes of section 166. A bona fide debt is a debt which arises from a debtor-creditor relationship based upon a valid and enforceable obligation to pay a fixed or determinable sum of money. A gift or contribution to capital shall not be considered a debt for purposes of section 166. The fact that a bad debt is not due at the time of deduction shall not of itself prevent its allowance under section 166.

· · · ·

(d) Amount deductible—(1) General rule. Except in the case of a deduction for a reasonable addition to a reserve for bad debts, the basis for determining the amount of deduction under section 166 in respect of a bad debt shall be the same as the adjusted basis prescribed by § 1.1011–1 for determining the loss from the sale or other disposition of property.

· · · ·

(2) Specific cases. Subject to any provision of section 166 and the regulations thereunder which provides to the contrary, the following amounts are deductible as bad debts:

(i) Notes or accounts receivable. (a) If, in computing taxable income, a taxpayer values his notes or accounts receivable at their fair market value when received, the amount deductible as a bad debt under section 166 in respect of such receivables shall be limited to such fair market value even though it is less than their face value.

(b) A purchaser of accounts receivable which become worthless during the taxable year shall be entitled under section 166 to a deduction which is based upon the price he paid for such receivables but not upon their face value.

(ii) Bankruptcy claim. Only the difference between the amount received in distribution of the assets of a bankrupt and the amount of the claim may be deducted under section 166 as a bad debt.

(iii) Claim against decedent's estate. The excess of the amount of the claim over the amount received by a creditor of a decedent in distribution of the assets of the decedent's estate may be considered a worthless debt under section 166.

(e) Prior inclusion in income required. Worthless debts arising from unpaid wages, salaries, fees, rents, and similar items of taxable income shall not be allowed as a deduction under section 166 unless the income such items represent has been included in the return of income for the year for which the deduction as a bad debt is claimed or for a prior taxable year.

(f) Recovery of bad debts. Any amount attributable to the recovery during the taxable year of a bad debt, or of a part of a bad debt, which was allowed as a deduction from gross income in a prior taxable year shall be included in gross income for the taxable year of recovery, except to the extent that the recovery is excluded from gross income under the provisions of § 1.111-1, relating to the recovery of certain items previously deducted or credited. This paragraph shall not apply, however, to a bad debt which was previously charged against a reserve by a taxpayer on the reserve method of treating bad debts.

(g) Worthless securities. (1) Section 166 and the regulations thereunder do not apply to a debt which is evidenced by a bond, debenture, note, or certificate, or other evidence of indebtedness, issued by a corporation or by a government or political subdivision thereof, with interest coupons or in registered form. See section 166(e). For provisions allowing the deduction of a loss resulting from the worthlessness of such a debt, see § 1.165-5.

. . . .

§ 1.166-2   Evidence of worthlessness

(a) General rule. In determining whether a debt is worthless in whole or in part the district director will consider all pertinent evidence, including the value of the collateral, if any, securing the debt and the financial condition of the debtor.

(b) Legal action not required. Where the surrounding circumstances indicate that a debt is worthless and uncollectible and that legal action to enforce payment would in all probability not result in the satisfaction of execution on a judgment, a showing of these facts will be sufficient evidence of the worthlessness of the debt for purposes of the deduction under section 166.

(c) Bankruptcy—(1) General rule. Bankruptcy is generally an indication of the worthlessness of at least a part of an unsecured and unpreferred debt.

(2) Year of deduction. In bankruptcy cases a debt may become worthless before settlement in some instances; and in others, only when a settlement in bankruptcy has been reached. In either case, the mere fact that bankruptcy proceedings instituted against the debtor are terminated in a later year, thereby confirming the conclusion that the debt is worthless, shall not authorize the shifting of the deduction under section 166 to such later year.

. . . .

§ 1.166-3   Partial or total worthlessness

(a) Partial worthlessness—(1) Applicable to specific debts only. A deduction under section 166(a)(2) on account of partially worthless debts shall be allowed with respect to specific debts only.

(2) Charge-off required. (i) If, from all the surrounding and attending circumstances, the district director is satisfied that a debt is partially worthless, the amount which has become worthless shall be allowed as a deduction under section 166(a)(2) but only to the extent charged off during the taxable year.

(ii) If a taxpayer claims a deduction for a part of a debt for the taxable year within which that part of the debt is charged off and the deduction is disallowed for that taxable year, then, in a case where the debt becomes partially worthless after the close of that taxable year, a deduction under section 166(a)(2) shall be allowed for a subsequent taxable year but not in excess of the amount charged off in the prior taxable year plus any amount charged off in the subsequent taxable year. In such instance, the charge-off in the prior taxable year shall, if consistently maintained as such, be sufficient to that extent to meet the charge-off requirement of section 166(a)(2) with respect to the subsequent taxable year.

(iii) Before a taxpayer may deduct a debt in part, he must be able to demonstrate to the satisfaction of the district director the amount thereof which is worthless and the part thereof which has been charged off.

(b) **Total worthlessness.** If a debt becomes wholly worthless during the taxable year, the amount thereof which has not been allowed as a deduction from gross income for any prior taxable year shall be allowed as a deduction for the current taxable year.

§ 1.166-4 Reserve for bad debts

(a) **Allowance of deduction.** A taxpayer who has established the reserve method of treating bad debts and has maintained proper reserve accounts for bad debts or who, in accordance with paragraph (b) of § 1.166-1, adopts the reserve method of treating bad debts may deduct from gross income a reasonable addition to a reserve for bad debts in lieu of deducting specific bad debt items.

(b) **Reasonableness of addition to reserve—(1) Relevant factors.** What constitutes a reasonable addition to a reserve for bad debts shall be determined in the light of the facts existing at the close of the taxable year of the proposed addition. The reasonableness of the addition will vary as between classes of business and with conditions of business prosperity. It will depend primarily upon the total amount of debts outstanding as of the close of the taxable year, including those arising currently as well as those arising in prior taxable years, and the total amount of the existing reserve.

(2) **Correction of errors in prior estimates.** In the event that subsequent realizations upon outstanding debts prove to be more or less than estimated at the time of the creation of the existing reserve, the amount of the excess or inadequacy in the existing reserve shall be reflected in the determination of the reasonable addition necessary in the current taxable year.

(c) **Statement required.** A taxpayer using the reserve method shall file with his return a statement showing—

(1) The volume of his charge sales or other business transactions for the taxable year and the percentage of the reserve to such amount;

(2) The total amount of notes and accounts receivable at the beginning and close of the taxable year;

(3) The amount of the debts which have become wholly or partially worth-

less and have been charged against the reserve account; and

(4) The computation of the addition to the reserve for bad debts.

. . . . .

§ 1.166-5 Nonbusiness debts

(a) **Allowance of deduction as capital loss.** (1) The loss resulting from any nonbusiness debt's becoming partially or wholly worthless within the taxable year shall not be allowed as a deduction under either section 166(a) or section 166(c) in determining the taxable income of a taxpayer other than a corporation. See section 166(d) (1) (A).

(2) If, in the case of a taxpayer other than a corporation, a nonbusiness debt becomes wholly worthless within the taxable year, the loss resulting therefrom shall be treated as a loss from the sale or exchange, during the taxable year, of a capital asset held for not more than 1 year (6 months for taxable years beginning before 1977; 9 months for taxable years beginning in 1977). Such a loss is subject to the limitations provided in section 1211, relating to the limitation on capital losses, and section 1212, relating to the capital loss carryover, and in the regulations under those sections. A loss on a nonbusiness debt shall be treated as sustained only if and when the debt has become totally worthless, and no deduction shall be allowed for a nonbusiness debt which is recoverable in part during the taxable year.

(b) **Nonbusiness debt defined.** For purposes of section 166 and this section, a nonbusiness debt is any debt other than—

(1) A debt which is created, or acquired, in the course of a trade or business of the taxpayer, determined without regard to the relationship of the debt to a trade or business of the taxpayer at the time when the debt becomes worthless; or

(2) A debt, the loss from the worthlessness of which is incurred in the taxpayer's trade or business.

The question whether a debt is a nonbusiness debt is a question of fact in each particular case. The determination of whether the loss on a debt's becoming worthless has been incurred in a trade or business of the taxpayer shall, for this purpose, be made in substantially the same manner for determining whether a loss has been incurred in a trade or business for purposes of section 165(c) (1). For purposes of subparagraph (2) of this paragraph, the character of the debt is to be determined by the relation which the loss resulting from the debt's becoming worthless bears to the trade or business of the taxpayer. If that relation is a proximate one in the conduct of the trade or business in which the taxpayer is engaged at the time the debt becomes worthless, the debt comes within the exception provided by that subparagraph. The use to which the borrowed funds are put by the debtor is of no consequence in making a determination under this paragraph. For purposes of section 166 and this section, a nonbusiness debt does not include a debt described in section 165(g) (2) (C). See § 1.165–5, relating to losses on worthless securities.

. . . . .

(d) Examples. The application of this section may be illustrated by the following examples involving a case where A, an individual who is engaged in the grocery business and who makes his return on the basis of the calendar year, extends credit to B in 1955 on an open account:

Example (1). In 1956 A sells the business but retains the claim against B. The claim becomes worthless in A's hands in 1957. A's loss is not controlled by the nonbusiness debt provisions, since the original consideration has been advanced by A in his trade or business.

Example (2). In 1956 A sells the business to C but sells the claim against B to the taxpayer, D. The claim becomes worthless in D's hands in 1957. During 1956 and 1957, D is not engaged in any trade or business. D's loss is controlled by the nonbusiness debt provsions even though the original consideration has been advanced by A in his trade or business, since the debt has not been created or acquired in connection with a trade or business of D and since in 1957 D is not engaged in a trade or business incident to the conduct of which a loss from the worthlessness of such claim is a proximate result.

Example (3). In 1956 A dies, leaving the business, including the accounts receivable, to his son, C, the taxpayer. The claim against B becomes worthless in C's hands in 1957. C's loss is not controlled by the nonbusiness debt provisions. While C does not advance any consideration for the claim, or create or acquire it in connection with his trade or business, the loss is sustained as a proximate incident to the conduct of the trade or business in which he is engaged at the time the debt becomes worthless.

Example (4). In 1956 A dies, leaving the business to his son, C, but leaving the claim against B to his son, D, the taxpayer. The claim against B becomes worthless in D's hands in 1957. During 1956 and 1957, D is not engaged in any trade or business. D's loss is controlled by the nonbusiness debt provisions even though the original consideration has been advanced by A in his trade or business, since the debt has not been created or acquired in connection with a trade or business of D and since in 1957 D is not engaged in a trade or business incident to the conduct of which a loss from the worthlessness of such claim is a proximate result.

Example (5). In 1956 A dies; and, while his executor, C, is carrying on the business, the claim against B becomes worthless in 1957. The loss sustained by A's estate is not controlled by the nonbusiness debt provisions. While C does not advance any consideration for the claim on behalf of the estate, or create or acquire it in connection with a trade or business in which the estate is engaged, the loss is sustained as a proximate incident to the conduct of the trade or business in which the estate is engaged at the time the debt becomes worthless.

. . . . .

§ 1.166–9 Losses of guarantors, endorsers, and indemnitors incurred, on agreements made after December 31, 1975, in taxable years beginning after such date

(a) Payment treated as worthless business debt. This paragraph applies to taxpayers who, after December 31, 1975, enter into an agreement in the course of their trade or business to act as (or in a manner essentially equivalent to) a guarantor, endorser, or indemnitor of (or other secondary obligor upon) a debt obligation. Subject to the provisions of paragraphs (c), (d), and (e) of this section, a payment of principal or interest made during a taxable year beginning after December 31, 1975, by the taxpayer in discharge of part or all of the taxpayer's obligation as a guarantor, endorser, or indemnitor is treated as a business debt becoming worthless in the taxable year in which the payment is made or in the taxable year described in paragraph (e)(2) of this section. Neither section 163 (relating to interest) nor section 165 (relating to losses) shall apply with respect to such a payment.

(b) Payment treated as worthless nonbusiness debt. This paragraph applies to taxpayers (other than corporations) who, after December 31, 1975, enter into a transaction for profit, but not in the course of their trade or business, to act as (or in a manner essentially equivalent to) a guarantor, endorser, or indemnitor of (or other secondary obligor upon) a debt obligation. Subject to the provisions of paragraphs (c), (d), and (e) of this section, a payment of principal or interests made during a taxable year beginning after December 31, 1975, by the taxpayer in discharge of part or all of the taxpayer's obligation as a guarantor, endorser, or indemnitor is treated as a worthless nonbusiness debt in the taxable year in which the payment is made or in the taxable year described in paragraph (e) (2) of this section. Neither section 163 nor section 165 shall apply with respect to such a payment.

(c) Obligations issued by corporations. No treatment as a worthless debt is allowed with respect to a payment made by the taxpayer in discharge of part or all of the taxpayer's obligation as guarantor, endorser, or indemnitor of an obligation issued by a corporation if—

(1) The taxpayer is considered the primary obligor (see § 1.385-9), or

(2) The payment constitutes a contribution to capital by a shareholder. The rules of this paragraph (c) apply to payments whenever made (see paragraph (f) of this section).

(d) Certain payments treated as worthless debts. A payment in discharge of part or all of taxpayer's agreement to act as guarantor, endorser, or indemnitor of an obligation is to be treated as a worthless debt only if—

(1) The agreement was entered into in the course of the taxpayer's trade or business or a transaction for profit;

(2) There was an enforceable legal duty upon the taxpayer to make the payment (except that legal action need not have been brought against the taxpayer); and

(3) The agreement was entered into before the obligation became worthless (or partially worthless in the case of an agreement entered into in the course of the taxpayer's trade or business). See §§ 1.166-2 and 1.166-3 for rules on worthless and partially worthless debts. For purposes of this paragraph (d)(3), an agreement is considered as entered into before the obligation became worthless (or partially worthless) if there was a reasonable expectation on the part of the taxpayer at the time the

agreement was entered into that the taxpayer would not be called upon to pay the debt (subject to such agreement) without full reimbursement from the issuer of the obligation.

(e) Special rules—(1) Reasonable consideration required. Treatment as a worthless debt of a payment made by a taxpayer in discharge of part or all of the taxpayer's agreement to act as a guarantor, endorser, or indemnitor of an obligation is allowed only if the taxpayer demonstrates that reasonable consideration was received for entering into the agreement. For purposes of this paragraph (e)(1), reasonable consideration is not limited to direct consideration in the form of cash or property. Thus, where a taxpayer can demonstrate that the agreement was given without direct consideration in the form of cash or property but in accordance with normal business practice or for a good faith business purpose, worthless debt treatment is allowed with respect to a payment in discharge of part or all of the agreement if the conditions of this section are met. However, consideration received from a taxpayer's spouse or any individual listed in section 152(a) must be direct consideration in the form of cash or property.

(2) Right of subrogation. With respect to a payment made by a taxpayer in discharge of part or all of the taxpayer's agreement to act as a guarantor, endorser, or indemnitor where the agreement provides for a right of subrogation or other similar right against the issuer, treatment as a worthless debt is not allowed until the taxable year in which the right of subrogation or other similar right becomes totally worthless (or partially worthless in the case of an agreement which arose in the course of the taxpayer's trade or business).

(3) Other applicable provisions. Unless inconsistent with this section, other Internal Revenue laws concerning worthless debts, such as section 111 relating to the recovery of bad debts, apply to any payment which, under the provisions of this section, is treated as giving rise to a worthless debt.

(4) Taxpayer defined. For purposes of this section, except as otherwise provided, the term "taxpayer" means any taxpayer and includes individuals, corporations, partnerships, trusts and estates.

.   .   .   .   .

§ 1.167(a)-1 Depreciation in general

(a) Reasonable allowance. Section 167(a) provides that a reasonable allowance for the exhaustion, wear and tear, and obsolescence of property used in the trade or business or of property held by the taxpayer for the production of income shall be allowed as a depreciation deduction. The allowance is that amount which should be set aside for the taxable year in accordance with a reasonably consistent plan (not necessarily at a uniform rate), so that the aggregate of the amounts set aside, plus the salvage value, will, at the end of the estimated useful life of the depreciable property, equal the cost or other basis of the property as provided in section 167(g) and § 1.167(g)-1. An asset shall not be depreciated below a reasonable salvage value under any method of computing depreciation. However, see section 167(f) and § 1.167(f)-1 for rules which permit a reduction in the amount of salvage value to be taken into account for certain personal property acquired after October 16, 1962. See also paragraph (c) of this section for definition of salvage. The allowance shall not reflect amounts representing a mere reduction in market value. .   .   .   .

(b) Useful life. For the purpose of section 167 the estimated useful life of an asset is not necessarily the useful life inherent in the asset but is the period over which the asset may reasonably be expected to be useful to the taxpayer in his trade or business or in the production of his income. This period shall be determined by reference to his experience with similar property taking into account present conditions and probable future developments. Some of the factors to be considered in determining this period are (1) wear and tear and decay or decline from natural causes, (2) the normal progress of the art, economic changes, inventions, and current developments within the industry and the taxpayer's trade or business, (3) the climatic and other local conditions peculiar to the taxpayer's trade or business, and (4) the taxpayer's policy as to repairs, renewals, and replacements. Salvage value is not a factor for the purpose of determining useful life. If the taxpayer's experience is inadequate, the general experience in the industry may be used until such time as the taxpayer's own experience forms an adequate basis for making the determination. The estimated remaining useful life may be subject to modification by reason of conditions known to exist at the end of the taxable year and shall be redetermined when necessary regardless of the method of computing depreciation. However, estimated remaining useful life shall be redetermined only when the change in the useful life is significant and there is a clear and convincing basis for the redetermination. .   .   .   .

(c) Salvage. (1) Salvage value is the amount (determined at the time of acquisition) which is estimated will be realizable upon sale or other disposition of an asset when it is no longer useful in the taxpayer's trade or business or in the production of his income and is to be retired from service by the taxpayer. Salvage value shall not be changed at any time after the determination made at the time of acquisition merely because of changes in price levels. However, if there is a redetermination of useful life under the rules of paragraph (b) of this section, salvage value may be redetermined based upon facts known at the time of such redetermination of useful life. Salvage, when reduced by the cost of removal, is referred to as net salvage. The time at which an asset is retired from service may vary according to the policy of the taxpayer. If the taxpayer's policy is to dispose of assets which are still in good operating condition, the salvage value may represent a relatively large proportion of the original basis of the asset. However, if the taxpayer customarily uses an asset until its inherent useful life has been substantially exhausted, salvage value may represent no more than junk value. Salvage value must be taken into account in determining the depreciation deduction either by a reduction of the amount subject to depreciation or by a reduction in the rate of depreciation, but in no event shall an asset (or an account) be depreciated below a reasonable salvage value. See, however, paragraph (a) of § 1.167(b)-2 for the treatment of salvage under the declining balance method, and § 1.179-1 for the treatment of salvage in computing the additional first-year depreciation allowance. The taxpayer may use either salvage or net salvage in determining depreciation allowances but such practice must be consistently followed and the treatment of the costs of removal must be consistent with the practice adopted. For specific treatment of salvage value, see §§ 1.167(b)-1, 1.167(b)-2, and 1.167(b)-3. When an asset is retired or disposed of, appropriate adjustments shall be made in the asset and depreciation reserve accounts. For example, the amount of the salvage adjusted for the costs of removal may be credited to the depreciation reserve.

. . . .

§ 1.167(a)-2 Tangible property

The depreciation allowance in the case of tangible property applies only to that part of the property which is subject to wear and tear, to decay or decline from natural causes, to exhaustion, and to obsolescence. The allowance does not apply to inventories or stock in trade, or to land apart from the improvements or physical development added to it. The allowance does not apply to natural resources which are subject to the allowance for depletion provided in section 611. No deduction for depreciation shall be allowed on automobiles or other vehicles used solely for pleasure, on a building used by the taxpayer solely as his residence, or on furniture or furnishings therein, personal effects, or clothing; but properties and costumes used exclusively in a business, such as a theatrical business, may be depreciated.

§ 1.167(a)-3 Intangibles

If an intangible asset is known from experience or other factors to be of use in the business or in the production of income for only a limited period, the length of which can be estimated with reasonable accuracy, such an intangible asset may be the subject of a depreciation allowance. Examples are patents and copyrights. An intangible asset, the useful life of which is not limited, is not subject to the allowance for depreciation. No allowance will be permitted merely because, in the unsupported opinion of the taxpayer, the intangible asset has a limited useful life.

No deduction for depreciation is allowable with respect to goodwill. For rules with respect to organizational expenditures, see section 248 and the regulations thereunder. For rules with respect to trademark and trade name expenditures, see section 177 and the regulations thereunder.

§ 1.167(a)-4 Leased property

Capital expenditures made by a lessee for the erection of buildings or the construction of other permanent improvements on leased property are recoverable through allowances for depreciation or amortization. If the useful life of such improvements in the hands of the taxpayer is equal to or shorter than the remaining period of the lease, the allowances shall take the form of depreciation under section 167. See §§ 1.167(b)-0, 1, 2, 3, and 4 for methods of computing such depreciation allowances. If, on the other hand, the estimated useful life of such property in the hands of the taxpayer, determined without regard to the terms of the lease, would be longer than the remaining period of such lease, the allowances shall take the form of annual deductions from gross income in an amount equal to the unrecovered cost of such capital expenditures divided by the number of years remaining of the term of the lease. Such deductions shall be in lieu of allowances for depreciation. See section 162 and the regulations thereunder. See section 178 and the regulations thereunder for rules governing the effect to be given renewal options in determining whether the useful life of the improvement exceeds the remaining term of the lease where a lessee begins improvements on leased property after July 28, 1958, other than improvements which on such date and at all times thereafter, the lessee was under a binding legal obligation to make. Capital expenditures made by a lessor for the erection of buildings or other improvements shall, if subject to depreciation allowances, be recovered by him over the estimated life of the improvements without regard to the period of the lease.

§ 1.167(a)-5 Apportionment of basis

In the case of the acquisition on or after March 1, 1913, of a combination of depreciable and nondepreciable property for a lump sum, as for example, buildings and land, the basis for depreciation cannot exceed an amount which bears the same proportion to the lump sum as the value of the depreciable property at the time of acquisition bears to the value of the entire property at that time. In the case of property which is subject to both the allowance for depreciation and amortization, depreciation is allowable only with respect to the portion of the depreciable property which is not subject to the allowance for amortization and may be taken concurrently with the allowance for amortization. After the close of the amortization period or after amortization deductions have been discontinued with respect to any such property, the unrecovered cost or other basis of the depreciable portion of such property will be subject to depreciation. For adjustments to basis, see section 1016 and other applicable provisions of law.

§ 1.167(a)-6   Depreciation in special cases

(a) **Depreciation of patents or copyrights.** The cost or other basis of a patent or copyright shall be depreciated over its remaining useful life. Its cost to the patentee includes the various Government fees, cost of drawings, models, attorneys' fees, and similar expenditures. For rules applicable to research and experimental expenditures, see sections 174 and 1016 and the regulations thereunder. If a patent or copyright becomes valueless in any year before its expiration the unrecovered cost or other basis may be deducted in that year.

(b) **Depreciation in case of farmers.** A reasonable allowance for depreciation may be claimed on farm buildings (except a dwelling occupied by the owner), farm machinery, and other physical property but not including land. Livestock acquired for work, breeding, or dairy purposes may be depreciated unless included in an inventory used to determine profits in accordance with section 61 and the regulations thereunder. Such depreciation should be determined with reference to the cost or other basis, salvage value, and the estimated useful life of the livestock. See also section 162 and the regulations

thereunder relating to trade or business expenses, section 165 and the regulations thereunder relating to losses of farmers, and section 175 and the regulations thereunder relating to soil or water conservation expenditures.

§ 1.167(a)-7   Accounting for depreciable property

(a) Depreciable property may be accounted for by treating each individual item as an account, or by combining two or more assets in a single account. Assets may be grouped in an account in a variety of ways. For example, assets similar in kind with approximately the same useful lives may be grouped together. Such an account is commonly known as a group account. Another appropriate grouping might consist of assets segregated according to use without regard to useful life, for example, machinery and equipment, furniture and fixtures, or transportation equipment. Such an account is commonly known as a classified account. A broader grouping, where assets are included in the same account regardless of their character or useful lives, is commonly referred to as a composite account. For example, all the assets used in a business may be included in a single account. Group, classified, or composite accounts may be further broken down on the basis of location, dates of acquisition, cost, character, use, etc.

(b) When group, classified, or composite accounts are used with average useful lives and a normal retirement occurs, the full cost or other basis of the asset retired, unadjusted for depreciation or salvage, shall be removed from the asset account and shall be charged to the depreciation reserve. Amounts representing salvage ordinarily are credited to the depreciation reserve. Where an asset is disposed of for reasons other than normal retirement, the full cost or other basis of the asset shall be removed from the asset account, and the depreciation reserve shall be charged with the depreciation applicable to the retired asset. For rules with respect to losses on normal retirements, see § 1.167(a)-8.

(c) A taxpayer may establish as many accounts for depreciable property as he desires. Depreciation allowances shall be computed separately for each account. Such depreciation preferably should be recorded in a depreciation reserve account; however, in appropriate cases it may be recorded directly in the asset account. Where depreciation reserves are maintained, a separate reserve account shall be maintained for each asset account. The regular books of account or permanent auxiliary records shall show for each account the basis of the property, including adjustments necessary to conform to the requirements of section 1016 and other provisions of law relating to adjustments to basis, and the depreciation allowances for tax purposes. In the event that reserves for book purposes do not correspond with reserves maintained for tax purposes, permanent auxiliary records shall be maintained with the regular books of accounts reconciling the differences in depreciation for tax and book purposes because of different methods of depreciation, bases, rates, salvage, or other factors. Depreciation schedules filed with the income tax return shall show the accumulated reserves computed in accordance with the allowances for income tax purposes.

(d) In classified or composite accounts, the average useful life and rate shall be redetermined whenever additions, retirements, or replacements substantially alter the relative proportion of types of assets in the accounts. See example (2) in paragraph (b) of § 1.167(b)-1 for method of determining the depreciation rate for a classified or composite account.

§ 1.167(a)-9 Obsolescence

The depreciation allowance includes an allowance for normal obsolescence which should be taken into account to the extent that the expected useful life of property will be shortened by reason thereof. Obsolescence may render an asset economically useless to the taxpayer regardless of its physical condition. Obsolescence is attributable to many causes, including technological improvements and reasonably foreseeable economic changes. Among these causes are normal progress of the arts and sciences, supercession or inadequacy brought about by developments in the industry, products, methods,

markets, sources of supply, and other like changes, and legislative or regulatory action. In any case in which the taxpayer shows that the estimated useful life previously used should be shortened by reason of obsolescence greater than had been assumed in computing such estimated useful life, a change to a new and shorter estimated useful life computed in accordance with such showing will be permitted. No such change will be permitted merely because in the unsupported opinion of the taxpayer the property may become obsolete. For rules governing the allowance of a loss when the usefulness of depreciable property is suddenly terminated, see § 1.167(a)-8. If the estimated useful life and the depreciation rates have been the subject of a previous agreement, see section 167(d) and § 1.167(d)-1.

§ 1.167(a)-10 When depreciation deduction is allowable

(a) A taxpayer should deduct the proper depreciation allowance each year and may not increase his depreciation allowances in later years by reason of his failure to deduct any depreciation allowance or of his action in deducting an allowance plainly inadequate under the known facts in prior years. The inadequacy of the depreciation allowance for property in prior years shall be determined on the basis of the allowable method of depreciation used by the taxpayer for such property or under the straight line method if no allowance has ever been claimed for such property. The preceding sentence shall not be construed as precluding application of any method provided in section 167(b) if taxpayer's failure to claim any allowance for depreciation was due solely to erroneously treating as a deductible expense an item properly chargeable to capital account. For rules relating to adjustments to basis, see section 1016 and the regulations thereunder.

(b) The period for depreciation of an asset shall begin when the asset is placed in service and shall end when the asset is retired from service. A proportionate part of one year's depreciation is allowable for that part of the first and last year during which the asset was in service. However, in the case of a multiple asset account, the amount of depreciation may be determined by using what is commonly described as an "averaging convention", that is, by using an assumed timing of additions and retirements. For example, it might be assumed that all additions and retirements to the asset account occur uniformly throughout the taxable year, in which case depreciation is computed on the average of the beginning and ending balances of the asset account for the taxable year. See example (3) under paragraph (b) of § 1.167(b)-1. Among still other averaging conventions which may be used is the one under which it is assumed that all additions and retirements during the first half of a given year were made on the first day of that year and that all additions and retirements during the second half of the year were made on the first day of the following year. Thus, a full year's depreciation would be taken on additions in the first half of the year and no depreciation would be taken on additions in the second half. Moreover, under this convention, no depreciation would be taken on retirements in the first half of the year and a full year's depreciation would be taken on the retirements in the second half. An averaging convention, if used, must be consistently followed as to the account or accounts for which it is adopted, and must be applied to both additions and retirements. In any year in which an averaging convention substantially distorts the depreciation allowance for the taxable year, it may not be used.

§ 1.167(b)-(0) Methods of computing depreciation

(a) In general. Any reasonable and consistently applied method of computing depreciation may be used or continued in use under section 167. Regardless of the method used in computing depreciation, deductions for depreciation shall not exceed such amounts as may be necessary to recover the unrecovered cost or other basis less salvage during the remaining useful life of the property. The reasonableness of any claim for depreciation shall be determined upon the basis of conditions known to exist at the end of the period for which the return is made. It is the responsibility of the taxpayer to establish the reasonableness of the deduction for depreciation claimed. Generally, depreciation deductions so claimed will be changed only where there is a clear and convincing basis for a change.

. . . .

§ 1.167(b)-1 Straight line method

(a) Application of method. Under the straight line method the cost or other basis of the property less its estimated salvage value is deductible in equal annual amounts over the period of the estimated useful life of the property. The allowance for depreciation for the taxable year is determined by dividing the adjusted basis of the property at the beginning of the taxable year, less salvage value, by the remaining useful life of the property at such time. For convenience, the allowance so determined may be reduced to a percentage or fraction. The straight line method may be used in determining a reasonable allowance for depreciation for any property which is subject to depreciation under section 167 and it shall be used in all cases where the taxpayer has not adopted a different acceptable method with respect to such property.

(b) Illustrations. The straight line method is illustrated by the following examples:

Example (1). Under the straight line method items may be depreciated separately:

Year	Item	Cost or other basis less salvage	Useful life	Depreciation allowable		
				1954	1955	1956
			Years			
1954....	Asset A.	$1,600	4	[1] $200	$400	$400
	Asset B.	12,000	40	[1] 150	300	300

[1] In this example it is assumed that the assets were placed in service on July 1, 1954.

Example (2). In group, classified, or composite accounting, a number of assets with the same or different useful lives may be combined into one account, and a single rate of depreciation, i. e., the group, classified, or composite rate used for the entire account. In the case of group accounts, i. e., accounts containing assets which are similar in kind and which have approximately the same estimated useful lives, the group rate is determined from the average of the useful lives of the assets. In the case of classified or composite accounts, the classified or composite rate is generally computed by determining the amount of one year's depreciation for each item or each group of similar items, and by dividing the total depreciation thus obtained by the total cost or other basis of the assets. The average rate so obtained is to be used as long as subsequent additions, retirements, or replacements do not substantially alter the relative proportions of different types of assets in the account. An example of the computation of a classified or composite rate follows:

Cost or other basis	Estimated useful life	Annual depreciation
	Years	
$10,000	5	$2,000
10,000	15	667
20,000		2,667

Average rate is 13.33 percent ($2,667 ÷ $20,000) unadjusted for salvage. Assuming the estimated salvage value is 10 percent of the cost or other basis, the rate adjusted for salvage will be 13.33 percent minus 10 percent of 13.33 percent (13.33% — 1.33%), or 12 percent.

. . . .

§ 1.167(b)-2 Declining balance method

(a) **Application of method.** Under the declining balance method a uniform rate is applied each year to the unrecovered cost or other basis of the property. The unrecovered cost or other basis is the basis provided by section 167(g), adjusted for depreciation previously allowed or allowable, and for all other adjustments provided by section 1016 and other applicable provisions of law. The declining balance rate may be determined without resort to formula. Such rate determined under section 167(b) (2) shall not exceed twice the appropriate straight line rate computed without adjustment for salvage. While salvage is not taken into account in determining the annual allowances under this method, in no event shall an asset (or an account) be depreciated below a reasonable salvage value. However, see section 167(f) and § 1.167(f)-1 for rules which permit a reduction in the amount of salvage value to be taken into account for certain personal property acquired after October 16, 1962. Also, see section 167(c) and § 1.167(c)-1 for restrictions on the use of the declining balance method.

(b) **Illustrations.** The declining balance method is illustrated by the following examples:

Example (1). A new asset having an estimated useful life of 20 years was purchased on January 1, 1954, for $1,000. The normal straight line rate (without adjustment for salvage) is 5 percent, and the declining balance rate at twice the normal straight line rate is 10 percent. The annual depreciation allowances for 1954, 1955, and 1956 are as follows:

Year	Basis	Declining balance rate (percent)	Depreciation allowance
1954	$1,000	10	$100
1955	900	10	90
1956	810	10	81

. . . .

(c) **Change in estimated useful life.** In the declining balance method when a change is justified in the useful life estimated for an account, subsequent computations shall be made as though the revised useful life had been originally estimated. For example, assume that an account has an estimated useful life of ten years and that a declining balance rate of 20 percent is applicable. If, at the end of the sixth year, it is determined that the remaining useful life of the account is six years, computations shall be made as though the estimated useful life was originally determined as twelve years. Accordingly, the applicable depreciation rate will be 16⅔ percent. This rate is thereafter applied to the unrecovered cost or other basis.

§ 1.167(b)-3 Sum of the years-digits method

(a) **Applied to a single asset—(1) General rule.** Under the sum of the years-digits method annual allowances for depreciation are computed by applying changing fractions to the cost or other basis of the property reduced by estimated salvage. The numerator of the fraction changes each year to a number which corresponds to the remaining useful life of the asset (including the year for which the allowance is being computed), and the denominator which remains constant is the sum of all the years digits corresponding to the estimated useful life of the asset. See section 167(c) and

§ 1.167(c)–1 for restrictions on the use of the sum of the years-digits method.

(i) Illustrations. Computation of depreciation allowances on a single asset under the sum of the years-digits method is illustrated by the following examples:

Example (1). A new asset having an estimated useful life of five years was acquired on January 1, 1954, for $1,750. The estimated salvage is $250. For a taxpayer filing his returns on a calendar year basis, the annual depreciation allowances are as follows:

Year	Cost or other basis less salvage	Fraction [1]	Allowable depreciation	Depreciation reserve
1954	$1,500	$5/15$	$500	$500
1955	1,500	$4/15$	400	900
1956	1,500	$3/15$	300	1,200
1957	1,500	$2/15$	200	1,400
1958	1,500	$1/15$	100	1,500

Unrecovered value (salvage) $250

[1] The denominator of the fraction is the sum of the digits representing the years of useful life, i. e., 5, 4, 3, 2, and 1, or 15.

(ii) Change in useful life. Where in the case of a single asset, a change is justified in the useful life, subsequent computations shall be made as though the remaining useful life at the beginning of the taxable year of change were the useful life of a new asset acquired at such time and with a basis equal to the unrecovered cost or other basis of the asset at that time. For example, assume that a new asset with an estimated useful life of ten years is purchased in 1954. At the time of making out his return for 1959, the taxpayer finds that the asset has a remaining useful life of seven years from January 1, 1959. Depreciation for 1959 should then be computed as though 1959 were the first year of the life of an asset estimated to have a useful life of seven years, and the allowance for 1959 would be 7/28 of the unrecovered cost or other basis of the asset after adjustment for salvage.

(2) Remaining life—(i) Application. Under the sum of the years-digits method, annual allowances for depreciation may also be computed by applying changing fractions to the unrecovered cost or other basis of the asset reduced by estimated salvage. The numerator of the fraction changes each year to a number which corresponds to the remaining useful life of the asset (including the year for which the allowance is being computed), and the denominator changes each year to a number which represents the sum of the digits corresponding to the years of estimated remaining useful life of the asset.

. . . .

§ 1.167(c)–1 Limitations on methods of computing depreciation under section 167(b) (2), (3), and (4)

(a) In general. (1) Section 167(c) provides limitations on the use of the declining balance method described in section 167(b) (2), the sum of the years-digits method described in section 167(b) (3), and certain other methods authorized by section 167(b) (4). These methods are applicable only to tangible property having a useful life of three years or more. If construction, reconstruction, or erection by the taxpayer began before January 1, 1954, and was completed after December 31, 1953, these methods apply only to that portion of the basis of the property which is properly attributable to such construction, reconstruction, or erection after December 31, 1953. Property is considered as constructed, reconstructed, or erected by the taxpayer if the work is done for him in accordance with his specifications. The portion of the basis of such property attributable to construction, reconstruction, or erection after December 31, 1953, consists of all costs of the property allocable to the period after December 31, 1953, including the cost or other basis of materials entering into such work. It is not necessary that such materials be acquired after December 31, 1953, or that they be new in use. If construction or erection by the taxpayer began after December 31, 1953, the entire cost or other basis of such construction or erection qualifies for these methods of depreciation. In the case of reconstruction of property, these methods do not apply to any part of the adjusted basis of such property on December 31, 1953. For purposes of this section, construction, reconstruction, or erection by the taxpayer begins when physical work is started on such construction, reconstruction, or erection.

(2) If the property was not constructed, reconstructed, or erected by the taxpayer, these methods apply only if it was acquired after December 31, 1953, and if the original use of the property commences with the taxpayer and commences after December 31, 1953. For the purpose of the preceding sentence, property shall be deemed to be acquired when reduced to physical possession, or control. The term "original use" means the first use to which the property is put, whether or not such use corresponds to the use of such property by the taxpayer. For example, a reconditioned or rebuilt machine acquired after December 31, 1953, will not be treated as being put to original use by the taxpayer even though it is put to a different use, nor will a horse acquired for breeding purposes be treated as being put to original use by the taxpayer if prior to the purchase the horse was used for racing purposes. See §§ 1.167(b)-2, 1.167(b)-3, and 1.167(b)-4 for application of the various methods.

(3) Assets having an estimated average useful life of less than three years shall not be included in a group, classified, or composite account to which the methods described in §§ 1.-167(b)-2, 1.167(b)-3, and 1.167(b)-4 are applicable. However, an incidental retirement of an asset from such an account prior to the expiration of a useful life of three years will not prevent the application of these methods to such an account.

. . . . .

(6) Except in the cases described in subparagraphs (4) and (5) of this paragraph, the methods of depreciation described in §§ 1.167(b)-2, 1.167(b)-

3, and 1.167(b)-4 are not applicable to property in the hands of a distributee, vendee, transferee, donee, or grantee unless the original use of the property begins with such person and the conditions required by section 167(c) and this section are otherwise met. For example, these methods of depreciation may not be used by a corporation with respect to property which it acquires from an individual or partnership in exchange for its stock. Similarly, if an individual or partnership receives property in a distribution upon dissolution of a corporation, these methods of depreciation may not be used with respect to property so acquired by such individual or partnership. As a further example, these methods of depreciation may not be used by a partnership with respect to contributed property, nor by a partner with respect to partnership property distributed to him. Moreover, where a partnership is entitled to use these depreciation methods, and the optional adjustment to basis of partnership property provided by section 743 is applicable, (i) in the case of an increase in the adjusted basis of the partnership property under such section, the transferee partner with respect to whom such adjustment is applicable shall not be entitled to use such methods with respect to such increase, and (ii) in the case of a decrease in the adjusted basis of the partnership property under such section, the transferee partner with respect to whom such adjustment is applicable shall include in his income an amount equal to the portion of the depreciation deducted by the partnership which is attributable to such decrease.

. . . . . .

(c) Election to use methods. Subject to the limitations set forth in paragraph (a) of this section, the methods of computing the allowance for depreciation specified in section 167 (b) (2), (3), and (4) may be adopted without permission and no formal election is required. In order for a taxpayer to elect to use these methods for any property described in paragraph (a) of this section, he need only compute depreciation thereon under any of these methods for any taxable year ending after December 31, 1953, in which the property may first be depreciated by him. The election with respect to any property shall not be binding with respect to acquisitions of similar property in the same year or subsequent year which are set up in separate accounts.

. . . .

§ 1.167(f)-1 Reduction of salvage value taken into account for certain personal property

(a) **In general.** For taxable years beginning after December 31, 1961, and ending after October 16, 1962, a taxpayer may reduce the amount taken into account as salvage value in computing the allowance for depreciation under section 167(a) with respect to "personal property" as defined in section 167 (f)(2) and paragraph (b) of this section. The reduction may be made in an amount which does not exceed 10 percent of the basis of the property for determining depreciation, as of the time as of which salvage value is required to be determined (or when salvage value is redetermined), taking into account all adjustments under section 1016 other than (1) the adjustment under section 1016(a)(2) for depreciation allowed or allowable to the taxpayer, and (2) the adjustment under section 1016(a)(19) for a credit earned by the taxpayer under section 38, to the extent such adjustment is reflected in the basis for depreciation. See paragraph (c) of § 1.167(a)-1 for the definition of salvage value, the time for making the determination, the redetermination of salvage value, and the general rules with respect to the treatment of salvage value. See also section 167(g) and § 1.167(g)-1 for basis for depreciation. A reduction of the amount taken into account as salvage value with respect to any property shall not be binding with respect to other property. In no event shall an asset (or an account) be depreciated below a reasonable salvage value after taking into account the reduction in salvage value permitted by section 167(f) and this section.

(b) **Definitions and special rules.** The following definitions and special rules apply for purposes of section 167 (f) and this section.

(1) **Personal property.** The term "personal property" shall include only depreciable—

(i) Tangible personal property (as defined in section 48 and the regulations thereunder) and

(ii) Intangible personal property which has an estimated useful life (determined at the time of acquisition) of 3 years or more and which is acquired after October 16, 1962. Such term shall not include livestock. The term "livestock" includes horses, cattle, hogs, sheep, goats, and mink and other fur-bearing animals, irrespective of the use to which they are put or the purpose for which they are held. The original use of the property need not commence with the taxpayer so long as he acquired it after October 16, 1962; thus, the property may be new or used. For purposes of determining the estimated useful life, the provisions of paragraph (b) of § 1.167(a)-1 shall be applied. For rules determining when property is acquired, see subparagraph (2) of this paragraph. For purposes of determining the types of intangible personal property which are subject to the allowance for depreciation, see § 1.167(a)-3.

(2) **Acquired.** In determining whether property is acquired after October 16, 1962, property shall be deemed to be acquired when reduced to physical possession, or control. Property which has not been used in the taxpayer's trade or business or held for the production of income and which is thereafter converted by the taxpayer to such use shall be deemed to be acquired on the date of such conversion. In addition, property shall be deemed to be acquired if constructed, reconstructed, or erected by the taxpayer. If construction, reconstruction, or erection by the taxpayer began before October 17, 1962, and was completed after October 16, 1962, section 167(f) and this section apply only to that portion of the basis of the property which is properly attributable to such construction, reconstruction, or erection after October 16, 1962. Property is considered as constructed, reconstructed, or erected by the taxpayer if the work is done for him in accordance with his specifications. The portion of the basis of such property attributable to construction, reconstruction, or erection after October 16, 1962, consists of all costs of the property allocable to the period after October 16, 1962, including the cost or other basis of materials entering into such work. It is not necessary that such materials be acquired after October 16, 1962, or that they be new in use. If construction or erection by the taxpayer began after October 16,

1962, the entire cost or other basis of such construction or erection qualifies for the reduction provided for by section 167(f) and this section. In the case of reconstructed property, section 167 (f) and this section do not apply to any part of the adjusted basis of such property on October 16, 1962. For purposes of this section, construction, reconstruction, or erection by the taxpayer begins when physical work is started on such construction, reconstruction, or erection.

. . . .

§ 1.167(g)–1 Basis for depreciation

The basis upon which the allowance for depreciation is to be computed with respect to any property shall be the adjusted basis provided in section 1011 for the purpose of determining gain on the sale or other disposition of such property. In the case of property which has not been used in the trade or business or held for the production of income and which is thereafter converted to such use, the fair market value on the date of such conversion, if less than the adjusted basis of the property at that time, is the basis for computing depreciation.

§ 1.167(h)–1 Life tenants and beneficiaries of trusts and estates

(a) Life tenants. In the case of property held by one person for life with remainder to another person, the deduction for depreciation shall be computed as if the life tenant were the absolute owner of the property so that he will be entitled to the deduction during his life, and thereafter the deduction, if any, shall be allowed to the remainderman.

(b) Trusts. If property is held in trust, the allowable deduction is to be apportioned between the income beneficiaries and the trustee on the basis of the trust income allocable to each, unless the governing instrument (or local law) requires or permits the trustee to maintain a reserve for depreciation in any amount. In the latter case, the deduction is first allocated to the trustee to the extent that income is set aside for a depreciation reserve, and any part of the deduction in excess of the income set aside for the reserve shall be apportioned between the income beneficiaries and the trustee on the basis of the trust income (in excess of the income set aside for the reserve) allocable to each. For example:

(1) If under the trust instrument or local law the income of a trust computed without regard to depreciation is to be distributed to a named beneficiary, the beneficiary is entitled to the deduction to the exclusion of the trustee.

(2) If under the trust instrument or local law the income of a trust is to be distributed to a named beneficiary, but the trustee is directed to maintain a reserve for depreciation in any amount, the deduction is allowed to the trustee (except to the extent that income set aside for the reserve is less than the allowable deduction). The same result would follow if the trustee sets aside income for a depreciation reserve pursuant to discretionary authority to do so in the governing instrument.

No effect shall be given to any allocation of the depreciation deduction which gives any beneficiary or the trustee a share of such deduction greater than his pro rata share of the trust income, irrespective of any provisions in the trust instrument, except as otherwise provided in this paragraph when the trust instrument or local law requires or permits the trustee to maintain a reserve for depreciation.

(c) Estates. In the case of an estate, the allowable deduction shall be apportioned between the estate and the heirs, legatees, and devisees on the basis of income of the estate which is allocable to each.

§ 1.170A–1 Charitable, etc., contributions and gifts; allowance of deduction

(a) In general—(1) Allowance of deduction. Any charitable contribution. as defined in section 170(c), actually paid during the taxable year is allowable as a deduction in computing taxable income, irrespective of the method of accounting employed or of the date on which the contribution is pledged. However, charitable contributions by corporations may under certain circumstances be deductible even though not paid during the taxable year, . . .

(2) Information required in support of deductions—(i) In general. In connection with claims for deductions for charitable contributions, taxpayers shall state in their income tax returns the name of each organization to which a contribution was made and the amount and date of the actual payment of each contribution. If a contribution is made in property other than money, the taxpayer shall state the kind of property contributed, for example, used clothing, paintings, or securities, the method utilized in determining the fair market value of the property at the time the contribution was made, and whether or not the amount of the contribution was reduced under section 170(e). If a taxpayer makes more than one cash contribution to an organization during the taxable year, then in lieu of listing each cash contribution and the date of payment the taxpayer may state the total cash payments made to such organization during the taxable year. . . .

(ii) Contribution by individual of property other than money. If an individual taxpayer makes a charitable contribution of an item of property other than money and claims a deduction in excess of $200 in respect of his contribution of such item, he shall attach to his income tax return the following information with respect to such item:

(a) The name and address of the organization to which the contribution was made.

(b) The date of the actual contribution.

(c) A description of the property in sufficient detail to identify the particular property contributed, including in the case of tangible property the physical condition of the property at the time of contribution, and, in the case of securities, the name of the issuer, the type of security, and whether or not such security is regularly traded on a stock exchange or in an over-the-counter market.

(d) The manner of acquisition, as, for example, by purchase, gift, bequest, inheritance, or exchange, and the approximate date of acquisition of the property by the taxpayer or, if the property was created, produced, or manufactured by or for the taxpayer, the approximate date the property was substantially completed.

(e) The fair market value of the property at the time the contribution was made, the method utilized in determining the fair market value, and, if the valuation was determined by appraisal, a copy of the signed report of the appraiser.

(f) The cost or other basis, adjusted as provided by section 1016, of property, other than securities, held by the taxpayer for a period of less than 5 years immediately preceding the date on which the contribution was made and, when the information is available, of property, other than securities, held for a period of 5 years or more preceding the date on which the contribution was made.

(g) In the case of property to which section 170(e) applies, the cost or other basis, adjusted as provided by section 1016, the reduction by reason of section 170(e)(1) in the amount of the charitable contribution otherwise taken into account, and the manner in which such reduction was determined.

(h) The terms of any agreement or understanding entered into by or on behalf of the taxpayer which relates to the use, sale, or disposition of the property contributed, as, for example, the terms of any agreement or understanding which—

(1) Restricts temporarily or permanently the donee's right to dispose of the donated property,

(2) Reserves to, or confers upon, anyone other than the donee organization or other than an organization participating with such organization in cooperative fund raising, any right to the income from such property, to the possession of the property, including the right to vote securities, to acquire such property by purchase or otherwise, or to designate the person to have such income, possession, or right to acquire, or

(3) Earmarks contributed property for a particular charitable use, such as the use of donated furniture in the reading room of the donee organization's library.

(i) The total amount claimed as a deduction for the taxable year due to the contribution of the property and, if less than the entire interest in the property is contributed during the taxable year, the amount claimed as a deduction in any prior year or years for contributions of other interests in such property, the name and address of each organization to which any such contribution was made, the place where any such property which is tangible property is located or kept, and the name of any person, other than the organization to which the property giving rise to the deduction was contributed, having actual possession of the property.

. . . . .

(b) Time of making contribution. Ordinarily, a contribution is made at the time delivery is effected. The unconditional delivery or mailing of a check which subsequently clears in due course will constitute an effective contribution on the date of delivery or mailing. If a taxpayer unconditionally delivers or mails a properly endorsed stock certificate to a charitable donee or the donee's agent, the gift is completed on the date of delivery or, if such certificate is received in the ordinary course of the mails, on the date of mailing. If the donor delivers the stock certificate to his bank or broker as the donor's agent, or to the issuing corporation or its agent, for transfer into the name of the donee, the gift is completed on the date the stock is transferred on the books of the corporation.

. . . .

(c) Value of a contribution in property. (1) If a charitable contribution is made in property other than money, the amount of the contribution is the fair market value of the property at the time of the contribution reduced as provided in section 170(e) (1) . . . .

(2) The fair market value is the price at which the property would change hands between a willing buyer and a willing seller, neither being under any compulsion to buy or sell and both having reasonable knowledge of relevant facts. If the contribution is made in property of a type which the taxpayer sells in the course of his business, the fair market value is the price which the taxpayer would have received if he had sold the contributed property in the usual market in which he customarily sells, at the time and place of the contribution and, in the case of a contribution of goods in quantity, in the quantity contributed. The usual market of a manufacturer or other producer consists of the wholesalers or other distributors to or through whom he customarily sells, but if he sells only at retail the usual market consists of his retail customers.

(3) If a donor makes a charitable contribution of property, such as stock in trade, at a time when he could not reasonably have been expected to realize its usual selling price, the value of the gift is not the usual selling price but is the amount for which the quantity of property contributed would have been sold by the donor at the time of the contribution.

(4) Any costs and expenses pertaining to the contributed property which were incurred in taxable years preceding the year of contribution and are properly reflected in the opening inventory for the year of contribution must be removed from inventory and are not a part of the cost of goods sold for purposes of determining gross income for the year of contribution. Any costs and expenses pertaining to the contributed property which are incurred in the year of contribution and would, under the method of accounting used, be properly reflected in the cost of goods sold for such year are to be treated as part of the cost of goods sold for such year. If costs and expenses incurred in producing or acquiring the contributed property are, under the method of accounting used, properly deducted under section 162 or other section of the Code, such costs and expenses will be allowed as deductions for the taxable year in which they are paid or incurred, whether or not such year is the year of the contribution. Any such costs and expenses which are treated as part of the cost of goods sold for the year of contribution, and any such costs and expenses which are properly deducted under section 162 or other section of the Code, are not to be treated under any section of the Code as resulting in any basis for the contributed property. Thus, for example, the contributed property has no basis for purposes of determining under section 170(e) (1) (A) and paragraph (a) of § 1.170A–4 the

amount of gain which would have been recognized if such property had been sold by the donor at its fair market value at the time of its contribution. The amount of any charitable contribution for the taxable year is not to be reduced by the amount of any costs or expenses pertaining to the contributed property which was properly deducted under section 162 or other section of the Code for any taxable year preceding the year of the contribution. This subparagraph applies only to property which was held by the taxpayer for sale in the course of a trade or business. . . . .

(5) Transfers of property to an organization described in section 170(c) which bear a direct relationship to the taxpayer's trade or business and which are made with a reasonable expectation of financial return commensurate with the amount of the transfer may constitute allowable deductions as trade or business expenses rather than as charitable contributions. See section 162 and the regulations thereunder.

. . . . .

(e) Transfers subject to a condition or power. If as of the date of a gift a transfer for charitable purposes is dependent upon the performance of some act or the happening of a precedent event in order that it might become effective, no deduction is allowable unless the possibility that the charitable transfer will not become effective is so remote as to be negligible. If an interest in property passes to, or is vested in, charity on the date of the gift and the interest would be defeated by the subsequent performance of some act or the happening of some event, the possibility of occurrence of which appears on the date of the gift to be so remote as to be negligible, the deduction is allowable. For example, A transfers land to a city government for as long as the land is used by the city for a public park. If on the date of the gift the city does plan to use the land for a park and the possibility that the city will not use the land for a public park is so remote as to be negligible, A is entitled to a deduction under section 170 for his charitable contribution.

. . . . .

(g) Contributions of services. No deduction is allowable under section 170 for a contribution of services. However, unreimbursed expenditures made incident to the rendition of services to an organization contributions to which are deductible may constitute a deductible contribution. For example, the cost of a uniform without general utility which is required to be worn in performing donated services is deductible. Similarly, out-of-pocket transportation expenses necessarily incurred in performing donated services are deductible. Reasonable expenditures for meals and lodging necessarily incurred while away from home in the course of performing donated services also are deductible. For the purposes of this paragraph, the phrase "while away from home" has the same meaning as that phrase is used for purposes of section 162 and the regulations thereunder.

. . . .

§ 1.170A-4   Reduction in amount of charitable contributions of certain appreciated property

(a) Amount of reduction. Section 170(e) (1) requires that the amount of the charitable contribution which would be taken into account under section 170(a) without regard to section 170(e) shall be reduced before applying the percentage limitations under section 170(b)—

(1) In the case of a contribution by an individual or by a corporation of ordinary income property, as defined in paragraph (b) (1) of this section, by the amount of gain (hereinafter in this section referred to as ordinary income) which would have been recognized as gain which is not long-term capital gain if the property had been sold by the donor at its fair market value at the time of its contribution to the charitable organization,

(2) In the case of a contribution by an individual of section 170(e) capital gain property, as defined in paragraph (b) (2) of this section, by 50 percent of the amount of gain (hereinafter in this section referred to as long-term capital gain) which would have been recognized as long-term capital gain if the property had been sold by the donor at its fair market value at the time of its contribution to the charitable organization, and

(3) In the case of a contribution by a corporation of section 170(e) capital gain property, as defined in paragraph (b) (2) of this section, by 62½ percent of the amount of gain (hereinafter in this section referred to as long-term capital gain) which would have been recognized as long-term capital gain if the property had been sold by the donor at its fair market value at the time of its contribution to the charitable organization.

Section 170(e) (1) and this paragraph do not apply to reduce the amount of the charitable contribution where, by reason of the transfer of the contributed property, ordinary income or capital gain is recognized by the donor in the same taxable year in which the contribution is made. Thus, where income or gain is recognized under section 453 (d) upon the transfer of an installment obligation to a charitable organization, or under section 454(b) upon the transfer of an obligation issued at a discount to such an organization, or upon the assignment of income to such an organization, section 170(e) (1) and this paragraph do not apply if recognition of the income or gain occurs in the same taxable year in which the contribution is made. Section 170(e) (1) and this paragraph apply to a charitable contribution of an interest in ordinary income property or section 170(e) capital gain property which is described in paragraph (b) of § 1.170A-6, or paragraph (b) of § 1.170A-7. For purposes of applying section 170(e) (1) and this paragraph it is immaterial whether the charitable contribution is made "to" the charitable organization or whether it is made "for the use of" the charitable organization. See § 1.170A-8(a) (2).

(b) Definitions and other rules. For purposes of this section—

(1) Ordinary income property. The term "ordinary income property" means property any portion of the gain on which would not have been long term capital gain if the property had been sold by the donor at its fair market value at the time of its contribution to the charitable organization. Such term includes, for example, property held by the donor primarily for sale to customers in the ordinary course of his trade or business, a work of art created by the donor, a manuscript prepared by the donor, letters and memorandums prepared by or for the donor, a capital asset held by the donor for not more than 1 year (6 months for taxable years beginning before 1977; 9 months for taxable years beginning in 1977), and stock described in section 306(a), 341 (a), or 1248(a) to the extent that, after applying such section, gain on its disposition would not have been long term capital gain. The term does not include an income interest in respect of which a deduction is allowed under section 170 (f)(2)(B) and paragraph (c) of § 1.-170A-6.

(2) Section 170(e) capital gain property. The term "section 170(e) capital gain property" means property any portion of the gain on which would have been treated as long-term capital gain if the property had been sold by the donor at its fair market value at the time of its contribution to the charitable organization and which—

(i) Is contributed to or for the use of a private foundation, as defined in section 509(a) and the regulations thereunder, other than a private foundation described in section 170(b) (1) (E),

(ii) Constitutes tangible personal property contributed to or for the use of a charitable organization, other than a private foundation to which subdivision (i) of this subparagraph applies, which is put to an unrelated use by the charitable organization within the meaning of subparagraph (3) of this paragraph, or

(iii) Constitutes property not described in subdivision (i) or (ii) of this subparagraph which is 30-percent capital gain property to which an election under paragraph (d) (2) of § 1.170A-8 applies.

For purposes of this subparagraph a fixture which is intended to be severed from real property shall be treated as tangible personal property.

(3) Unrelated use—(i) In general. The term "unrelated use" means a use which is unrelated to the purpose or function constituting the basis of the charitable organization's exemption under section 501 or, in the case of a contribution of property to a governmental unit, the use of such property by such unit for other than exclusively public purposes. For example, if a painting contributed to an educational institution is used by that organization for educational purposes by being placed in its library for display and study by art students, the use is not an unrelated use; but if the painting is sold and the proceeds used by the organization for educational purposes, the use of the property is an unrelated use. If furnishings contributed to a charitable organization are used by it in its offices and buildings in the course of carrying out its functions, the use of the property is not an unrelated use. If a set or collection of items of tangible personal property is contributed to a charitable organization or governmental unit, the use of the set or collection is not an unrelated use if the donee sells or otherwise disposes of only an insubstantial portion of the set or collection. The use by a trust of tangible personal property contributed to it for the benefit of a charitable organization is an unrelated use if the use by the trust is one which would have been unrelated if made by the charitable organization.

(ii) **Proof of use.** For purposes of applying subparagraph (2) (ii) of this paragraph, a taxpayer who makes a charitable contribution of tangible personal property to or for the use of a charitable organization or governmental unit may treat such property as not being put to an unrelated use by the donee if—

(a) He establishes that the property is not in fact put to an unrelated use by the donee, or

(b) At the time of the contribution or at the time the contribution is treated as made, it is reasonable to anticipate that the property will not be put to an unrelated use by the donee. In the case of a contribution of tangible personal property to or for the use of a museum, if the object donated is of a general type normally retained by such museum or other museums for museum purposes, it will be reasonable for the donor to anticipate, unless he has actual knowledge to the contrary, that the object will not be put to an unrelated use by the donee, whether or not the object is later sold or exchanged by the donee.

(4) **Property used in trade or business.** For purposes of applying subparagraphs (1) and (2) of this paragraph, property which is used in the trade or business, as defined in section 1231(b), shall be treated as a capital asset, except that any gain in respect of such property which would have been recognized if the property had been sold by the donor at its fair market value at the time of its contribution to the charitable organization shall be treated as ordinary income to the extent that such gain would have constituted ordinary income by reason of the application of section 617(d) (1), 1245 (a), 1250(a), ...

. . . .

(c) **Allocation of basis and gain—(1) In general.** Except as provided in subparagraph (2) of this paragraph—

(i) If a taxpayer makes a charitable contribution of less than his entire interest in appreciated property, whether or not the transfer is made in trust, as, for example, in the case of a transfer of appreciated property to a pooled income fund described in section 642(c) (5) and § 1.642(c)-5, and is allowed a deduction under section 170 for a portion of the fair market value of such property, then for purposes of applying the reduction rules of section 170(e) (1) and this section to the contributed portion of the property the taxpayer's adjusted basis in such property at the time of the contribution shall be allocated under section 170(e) (2) between the contributed portion of the property and the noncontributed portion.

(ii) The adjusted basis of the contributed portion of the property shall be that portion of the adjusted basis of the entire property which bears the same ratio to the total adjusted basis as the fair market value of the contributed portion of the property bears to the fair market value of the entire property.

(iii) The ordinary income and the long-term capital gain which shall be taken into account in applying section 170(e) (1) and paragraph (a) of this section to the contributed portion of the property shall be the amount of gain which would have been recognized as ordinary income and long-term capital gain if such contributed portion had been sold by the donor at its fair market value at the time of its contribution to the charitable organization.

(2) **Bargain sale.** (i) If there is a bargain sale of property to the charitable organization and if section 1011(b)

and § 1.1011–2 apply, then for purposes of applying the reduction rules of section 170(e) (1) and this section to the contributed portion of the property there shall be allocated under section 1011(b) to the contributed portion of the property the portion of the adjusted basis which is not allocated under section 1011(b) to the noncontributed portion of the property for purposes of determining gain from the bargain sale. The portion of the adjusted basis which is so allocated to the contributed portion of the property shall be that portion of the adjusted basis of the entire property which bears the same ratio to the total adjusted basis as the fair market value of the contributed portion of the property bears to the fair market value of the entire property. For purposes of applying section 170(e) (1) and paragraph (a) of this section to the contributed portion of the property in such a case, there shall be allocated to the contributed portion the amount of gain which is not recognized on the bargain sale but which would have been recognized as ordinary income or long-term capital gain if such contributed portion had been sold by the donor at its fair market value at the time of its contribution to the charitable organization.

(ii) If there is a bargain sale of property to the charitable organization and if section 1011(b) and § 1.1011–2 do not apply, the taxpayer's adjusted basis of the entire property shall be allocated to the noncontributed portion of the property in accordance with paragraph (e) of § 1.1001–1 for purposes of determining gain from the sale. In such case, no portion of the adjusted basis shall be allocated to the contributed portion of the property.

(iii) The term "bargain sale", as used in this subparagraph, means a transfer of property which is in part a sale or exchange of the property and in part a charitable contribution, as defined in section 170(c), of the property.

(3) Ratio of ordinary income and capital gain. For purposes of applying subparagraphs (1) (iii) and (2) (i) of this paragraph, the amount of ordinary income (or long-term capital gain) which would have been recognized if the contributed portion of the property had been sold by the donor at its fair market value at the time of its contribution shall be that amount which bears the same ratio to the ordinary income (or long-term capital gain) which would have been recognized if the entire property had been sold by the donor at its fair market value at the time of its contribution as (i) the fair market value of the contributed portion at such time bears to (ii) the fair market value of the entire property at such time. In the case of a bargain sale, the fair market value of the contributed portion for purposes of subdivision (i) is the amount determined by subtracting from the fair market value of the entire property the amount realized on the sale.

· · · ·

(d) Illustrations. The application of this section may be illustrated by the following examples:

Example (1). (a) On July 1, 1970, C, an individual, makes the following charitable contributions, all of which are made to a church except in the case of the stock (as indicated):

Property	Fair market value	Adjusted basis	Recognized gain if sold
Ordinary income property	$50,000	$35,000	$15,000
Property which, if sold, would produce long-term capital gain:			
(1) Stock held more than 6 months contributed to—			
(i) A church	25,000	21,000	4,000
(ii) A private foundation not described in section 170(b) (1) (E)	15,000	10,000	5,000
(2) Tangible personal property held more than 6 months (put to unrelated use by church)	12,000	6,000	6,000
Total	102,000	72,000	30,000

(b) After making the reductions required by paragraph (a) of this section, the amount of charitable contributions allowed (before application of section 170(b) limitations) is as follows:

Property	Fair market value	Reduction	Contribution allowed
Ordinary income property	$50,000	$15,000	$35,000
Property which, if sold, would produce long-term capital gain:			

Property	Fair market value	Reduction	Contribution allowed
(1) Stock contributed to—			
(i) The church	25,000	......	25,000
(ii) The private foundation	15,000	2,500	12,500
(2) Tangible personal property	12,000	3,000	9,000
Total	102,000	20,500	81,500

(c) If C were a corporation, rather than an individual, the amount of charitable contributions allowed (before application of section 170(b) limitation) would be as follows:

Property	Fair market value	Reduction	Contribution allowed
Ordinary income property	$50,000	$15,000	$35,000
Property which, if sold, would produce long-term capital gain:			
(1) Stock contributed to—			
(i) The church	25,000	......	25,000
(ii) The private foundation	15,000	3,125	11,875
(2) Tangible personal property	12,000	3,750	8,250
Total	102,000	21,875	80,125

. . . . .

§ 1.170A-5 Future interests in tangible personal property

(a) In general. (1) A contribution consisting of a transfer of a future interest in tangible personal property shall be treated as made only when all intervening interests in, and rights to the actual possession or enjoyment of the property—

(i) Have expired, or

(ii) Are held by persons other than the taxpayer or those standing in a relationship to the taxpayer described in section 267(b) and the regulations thereunder, relating to losses, expenses, and interest with respect to transactions between related taxpayers.

(2) Section 170(a)(3) and this section have no application in respect of a transfer of an undivided present interest in property. For example, a contribution of an undivided one-quarter interest in a painting with respect to which the donee is entitled to possession during 3 months of each year shall be treated as made upon the receipt by the donee of a formally executed and acknowledged deed of gift. However, the period of initial possession by the

donee may not be deferred in time for more than 1 year.

(3) Section 170(a)(3) and this section have no application in respect of a transfer of a future interest in intangible personal property or in real property. However, a fixture which is intended to be severed from real property shall be treated as tangible personal property. For example, a contribution of a future interest in a chandelier which is attached to a building is considered a contribution which consists of a future interest in tangible personal property if the transferor intends that it be detached from the building at or prior to the time when the charitable organization's right to possession or enjoyment of the chandelier is to commence.

(4) For purposes of section 170(a)(3) and this section, the term "future interest" has generally the same meaning as it has when used in section 2503 and § 25.2503-3 of this chapter (Gift Tax Regulations); it includes reversions, remainders, and other interests or estates, whether vested or contingent, and whether or not supported by a particular interest or estate, which are limited to commence in use, possession, or enjoyment at some future date or time. The term "future interest" includes situations in which a donor purports to give tangible personal property to a charitable organization, but has an understanding, arrangement, agreement, etc., whether written or oral, with the charitable organization which has the effect of reserving to, or retaining in, such donor a right to the use, possession, or enjoyment of the property.

(5) In the case of a charitable contribution of a future interest to which section 170(a)(3) and this section apply, the other provisions of section 170 and the regulations thereunder are inapplicable to the contribution until such time as the contribution is treated as made under section 170(a)(3).

(b) Illustrations. The application of this section may be illustrated by the following examples:

Example (1). On December 31, 1970, A, an individual who reports his income on the calendar year basis, conveys by deed of gift to a museum title to a painting, but reserves to himself the right to the use, possession, and enjoyment of the painting during his lifetime. It is assumed that there was no intention to avoid the application of section 170(f)(3)(A) by the conveyance. At the time of the gift the value of the painting is $90,000. Since the contribution consists of a future interest in tangible personal property in which the donor has retained an intervening interest, no contribution is considered to have been made in 1970.

Example (2). Assume the same facts as in example (1) except that on December 31, 1971, A relinquishes all of his right to the use, possession, and enjoyment of the painting and delivers the painting to the museum. Assuming that the value of the painting has increased to $95,000, A is treated as having made a charitable contribution of $95,000 in 1971 for which a deduction is allowable without regard to section 170(f)(3)(A).

Example (3). Assume the same facts as in example (1) except A dies without relinquishing his right to the use, possession, and enjoyment of the painting. Since A did not relinquish his right to the use, possession, and enjoyment of the property during his life, A is treated as not having made a charitable contribution of the painting for income tax purposes.

. . . .

§ 1.170A-6 Charitable contributions in trust

(a) **In general.** (1) No deduction is allowed under section 170 for the fair market value of a charitable contribution of any interest in property which is less than the donor's entire interest in the property and which is transferred in trust unless the transfer meets the requirements of paragraph (b) or (c) of this section. If the donor's entire interest in the property is transferred in trust and is contributed to a charitable organization described in section 170 (c), a deduction is allowed under section 170. Thus, if on July 1, 1972, property is transferred in trust with the requirement that the income of the trust be paid for a term of 20 years to a church and thereafter the remainder be paid to an educational organization described in section 170(b)(1)(A), a deduction is allowed for the value of such property. See section 170(f)(2) and (3)(B), and paragraph (b)(1) of § 1.170A-7.

(2) A deduction is allowed without regard to this section for a contribution of a partial interest in property if such interest is the taxpayer's entire interest in the property, such as an income interest or a remainder interest. If, however, the property in which such partial interest exists was divided in order to

create such interest and thus avoid section 170(f)(2), the deduction will not be allowed. Thus, for example, assume that a taxpayer desires to contribute to a charitable organization the reversionary interest in certain stocks and bonds which he owns. If the taxpayer transfers such property in trust with the requirement that the income of the trust be paid to his son for life and that the reversionary interest be paid to himself and immediately after creating the trust contributes the reversionary interest to a charitable organization, no deduction will be allowed under section 170 for the contribution of the taxpayer's entire interest consisting of the reversionary interest in the trust.

(b) **Charitable contribution of a remainder interest in trust—(1) In general.** No deduction is allowed under section 170 for the fair market value of a charitable contribution of a remainder interest in property which is less than the donor's entire interest in the property and which the donor transfers in trust unless the trust is—

(i) A pooled income fund described in section 642(c)(5) and § 1.642(c)-5,

(ii) A charitable remainder annuity trust described in section 664(d)(1) and § 1.664-2, or

(iii) A charitable remainder unitrust described in section 664(d)(2) and § 1.664-3.

(2) **Value of a remainder interest.** The fair market value of a remainder interest in a pooled income fund shall be computed under § 1.642(c)-6. The fair market value of a remainder interest in a charitable remainder annuity trust shall be computed under § 1.664-2. The fair market value of a remainder interest in a charitable remainder unitrust shall be computed under § 1.664-4. However, in some cases a reduction in the amount of a charitable contribution of the remainder interest may be required. See section 170(e) and § 1.170A-4.

(c) **Charitable contribution of an income interest in trust—(1) In general.** No deduction is allowed under section 170 for the fair market value of a charitable contribution of an income interest in property which is less than the donor's entire interest in the property and which the donor transfers in trust unless the income interest is either a guaranteed annuity interest or a unitrust interest, as defined in paragraph (c)(2) of this section, and the grantor is treated as the owner of such interest for purposes of applying section 671, relating to grantors and others treated as substantial owners. See section 4947(a)(2) for the application to such income interests in trust of the provisions relating to private foundations and section 508(e) for rules relating to provisions required in the governing instruments.

(2) **Definitions.** For purposes of this paragraph—

(i) **Guaranteed annuity interest.** (A) An income interest is a "guaranteed annuity interest", only if it is an irrevocable right pursuant to the governing instrument of the trust to receive a guaranteed annuity. A guaranteed annuity is an arrangement under which a determinable amount is paid periodically, but not less often than annually, for a specified term or for the life or lives of an individual or individuals, each of whom must be living at the date of transfer and can be ascertained at such date. For example, the annuity may be paid for the life of A plus a term of years. An amount is determinable if the exact amount which must be paid under the conditions specified in the governing instrument of the trust can be ascertained as of the date of transfer. For example, the amount to be paid may be a stated sum for a term, or for the life of an individual, at the expiration of which it may be changed by a specified amount, but it may not be redetermined by reference to a fluctuating index such as the cost of living index. In further illustration, the amount to be paid may be expressed in terms of a fraction or percentage of the cost of living index on the date of transfer.

(B) An income interest is a guaranteed annuity interest only if it is a guaranteed annuity interest in every respect. For example, if the income interest is the right to receive from a trust each year a payment equal to the lesser of a sum certain or a fixed percentage of the net fair market value of the trust assets, determined annually, such interest is not a guaranteed annuity interest.

(C) Where a charitable interest is in the form of a guaranteed annuity interest, the governing instrument of the trust may provide that income of the trust which is in excess of the amount required to pay the guaranteed annuity interest shall be paid to or for the use of a charitable organization. Nevertheless, the amount of the deduction under section 170(f)(2)(B) shall be limited to the fair market value of the guaranteed annuity interest as determined under paragraph (c)(3) of this section. For a rule relating to treatment by the grantor of any contribution made by the trust in excess of the amount required to pay the guaranteed annuity interest, see paragraph (d)(2)(ii) of this section.

(D) If the present value on the date of transfer of all the income interests for a charitable purpose exceeds 60 percent of the aggregate fair market value of all amounts in the trust (after the payment of liabilities), the income interest will not be considered a guaranteed annuity interest unless the governing instrument of the trust prohibits both the acquisition and the retention of assets which would give rise to a tax under section 4944 if the trustee had acquired such assets. The requirement in this subdivision (D) for a prohibition in the governing instrument against the retention of assets which would give rise to a tax under section 4944 if the trustee had acquired the assets shall not apply to a transfer in trust made on or before May 21, 1972.

(E) An income interest consisting of an annuity transferred in trust after May 21, 1972, will not be considered a guaranteed annuity interest if any amount other than an amount in payment of a guaranteed annuity interest may be paid by the trust for a private purpose before the expiration of all the income interests for a charitable purpose, unless such amount for a private purpose is paid from a group of assets which, pursuant to the governing instrument of the trust, are devoted exclusively to private purposes and to which section 4947(a)(2) is inapplicable by reason of section 4947(a)(2)(B). The exception in the immediately preceding sentence with respect to any guaranteed annuity for a private purpose shall apply only if the obligation to pay the annuity for a charitable purpose begins as of the date of creation of the trust and the obligation to pay the guaranteed annuity for a private purpose does not precede in point of time the obligation to pay the annuity for a charitable purpose and only if the governing instrument of the trust does not provide for any preference or priority in respect of any payment of the guaranteed annuity for a private purpose as opposed to any payment of any annuity for a charitable purpose. For purposes of this subdivision (E), an amount is not paid for a private purpose if it is paid for an adequate and full consideration in money or money's worth. . . . .

Example. In 1975, E transfers $75,000 in trust with the requirement that an annuity of $5,000 a year, payable annually at the end of each year, be paid to B, an individual, for a period of 5 years and thereafter an annuity of $5,000 a year, payable annually at the end of each year, be paid to M Charity for a period of 5 years. The remainder is to be paid to C, an individual. No deduction is allowed under subparagraph (1) of this paragraph with respect to the charitable annuity because it is not a "guaranteed annuity interest" within the meaning of this subdivision.

. . . . .

(ii) Unitrust interest. (A) An income interest is a "unitrust interest" only if it is an irrevocable right pursuant to the governing instrument of the trust to receive payment, not less often than annually, of a fixed percentage of the net fair market value of the trust assets, determined annually. In computing the net fair market value of the trust assets, all assets and liabilities shall be taken into account without regard to whether particular items are taken into account in determining the income of the trust. The net fair market value of the trust assets may be determined on any one date during the year or by taking the average of valuations made on more than one date during the year, provided that the same valuation date or dates and valuation methods are used each year. Where the governing instrument of the trust does not specify the valuation date or dates, the trustee shall select such date or dates and shall indicate his selection on the first return on Form 1041 which the trust is required to file. Payments under a unitrust interest may be paid for a specified term or for the life or lives of an individual or individuals, each of whom must be living at the date of transfer and can be ascertained at such date. For example, the uni-

trust interest may be paid for the life of A plus a term of years.

(B) An income interest is a unitrust interest only if it is a unitrust interest in every respect. For example, if the income interest is the right to receive from a trust each year a payment equal to the lesser of a sum certain or a fixed percentage of the net fair market value of the trust assets, determined annually, such interest is not a unitrust interest.

(C) Where a charitable interest is in the form of a unitrust interest, the governing instrument of the trust may provide that income of the trust which is in excess of the amount required to pay the unitrust interest shall be paid to or for the use of a charitable organization. Nevertheless, the amount of the deduction under section 170(f)(2)(B) shall be limited to the fair market value of the unitrust interest as determined under paragraph (c)(3) of this section. For a rule relating to treatment by the grantor of any contribution made by the trust in excess of the amount required to pay the unitrust interest, see paragraph (d)(2)(ii) of this section.

(D) An income interest in the form of a unitrust interest will not be considered a unitrust interest if any amount other than an amount in payment of a unitrust interest may be paid by the trust for a private purpose before the expiration of all the income interests for a charitable purpose, unless such amount for a private purpose is paid from a group of assets which, pursuant to the governing instrument of the trust, are devoted exclusively to private purposes and to which section 4947(a)(2) is inapplicable by reason of section 4947(a)(2)(B). The exception in the immediately preceding sentence with respect to any unitrust interest for a private purpose shall apply only if the obligation to pay the unitrust interest for a charitable purpose begins as of the date of creation of the trust and the obligation to pay the unitrust interest for a private purpose does not precede in point of time the obligation to pay the unitrust interest for a charitable purpose and only if the governing instrument of the trust does not provide for any preference or priority in respect of any payment of the unitrust interest for a private purpose as opposed to any payments of any unitrust interest for a charitable purpose.

For purposes of this subdivision (D), an amount is not paid for a private purpose if it is paid for an adequate and full consideration in money or money's worth. See § 53.4947-1(c) o1 this chapter (Foundation Excise Tax Regulations) for rules relating to the inapplicability of section 4947(a)(2) to segregated amounts in a split-interest trust.

· · · · ·

(3) Valuation of income interest. (i) The deduction allowed by section 170(f)(2)(B) for a charitable contribution of a guaranteed annuity interest is limited to the fair market value of such interest on the date of contribution, as computed under § 20.2031-10 of this chapter (Estate Tax Regulations).

(ii) The deduction allowed under section 170(f)(2)(B) for a charitable contribution of a unitrust interest is limited to the fair market value of the unitrust interest on the date of contribution. The fair market value of the unitrust interest shall be determined by subtracting the present value of all interests in the transferred property other than the unitrust interest from the fair market value of the transferred property.

(iii) If by reason of all the conditions and circumstances surrounding a transfer of an income interest in property in trust it appears that the charity may not receive the beneficial enjoyment of the interest, a deduction will be allowed under paragraph (c) (1) of this section only for the minimum amount it is evident the charity will receive. The application of this subdivision may be illustrated by the following examples:

Example (1). In 1972, B transfers $20,000 in trust with the requirement that M Church be paid a guaranteed annuity interest (as defined in subparagraph (2)(i) of this paragraph) of $4,000, payable annually at the end of each year for 9 years, and that the residue revert to himself. Since the fair market value of an annuity of $4,000 a year for a period of 9 years, as determined under Table B in § 20.2031-10(f) of this chapter, is $27,206.80 ($4,000 × 6.8017), it appears that M will not receive the beneficial enjoyment of the income interest. Accordingly, even though B is treated as the owner of the trust under section 673, he is allowed a deduction under subparagraph (1) of this paragraph for only $20,000, which is the minimum amount it is evident M will receive.

Example (2). In 1975, C transfers $40,000 in trust with the requirement that D, an individual, and X Charity be paid simultaneously guaranteed annuity interests (as defined in subparagraph (2)(i) of this paragraph) of $5,000 a year each, payable annually at the end of each year, for a period of 5 years and that the remainder be paid to C's children. The fair market value of two annuities of $5,000 each a year for a period of 5 years is $42,124 ([$5,000 × 4.2124] × 2), as determined under Table B in § 20.2031-10(f) of this chapter. The trust instrument provides that in the event the trust fund is insufficient to pay both annuities in a given year, the trust fund will be evenly divided between the charitable and private annuitants. The deduction under subparagraph (1) of this paragraph with respect to the charitable annuity will be limited to $20,000, which is the minimum amount it is evident X will receive.

· · · ·

(4) Recapture upon termination of treatment as owner. If for any reason the donor of an income interest in property ceases at any time before the termination of such interest to be treated as the owner of such interest for purposes of applying section 671, as for example, where he dies before the termination of such interest, he shall for purposes of this chapter be considered as having received, on the date he ceases to be so treated, an amount of income equal to (i) the amount of any deduction he was allowed under section 170 for the contribution of such interest reduced by (ii) the discounted value of all amounts which were required to be, and actually were, paid with respect to such interest under the terms of trust to the charitable organization before the time at which he ceases to be treated as the owner of the interest. The discounted value of the amounts described in subdivision (ii) of this subparagraph shall be computed by treating each such amount as a contribution of a remainder interest after a term of years and valuing such amount as of the date of contribution of the income interest by the donor, such value to be determined under § 20.2031-10 of this chapter consistently with the manner in which the fair market value of the income interest which was determined pursuant to subparagraph (3) (i) of this paragraph. The application of this subparagraph will not be construed to disallow a deduction to the trust for amounts paid by the trust to the charitable organization after the time at which the donor ceased to be treated as the owner of the trust.

· · · ·

(d) Denial of deduction for certain contributions by a trust. (1) If by reason of section 170(f)(2)(B) and paragraph (c) of this section a charitable contributions deduction is allowed under section 170 for the fair market value of an income interest transferred in trust, neither the grantor of the income interest, the trust, nor any other person shall be allowed a deduction under section 170 or any other section for the amount of any charitable contribution made by the trust with respect to, or in fulfillment of, such income interest.

(2) Section 170(f)(2)(C) and subparagraph (1) of this paragraph shall not be construed, however, to—

(i) Disallow a deduction to the trust, pursuant to section 642(c)(1) and the regulations thereunder, for amounts paid by the trust after the grantor ceases to be treated as the owner of the income interest for purposes of applying section 671 and which are not taken into account in determining the amount of recapture under paragraph (c)(4) of this section, or

(ii) Disallow a deduction to the grantor under section 671 and § 1.671-2(c) for a charitable contribution made by the trust in excess of the contribution required to be made by the trust under the terms of the trust instrument with respect to, or in fulfillment of, the income interest.

. . . . .

§ 1.170A-7 Contributions not in trust of partial interests in property

(a) In general. (1) In the case of a charitable contribution, not made by a transfer in trust, of any interest in property which consists of less than the donor's entire interest in such property, no deduction is allowed under section 170 for the value of such interest unless the interest is an interest described in paragraph (b) of this section. See section 170(f)(3)(A). For purposes of this section, a contribution of the right to use property which the donor owns, for example, a rent-free lease, shall be treated as a contribution of less than the taxpayer's entire interest in such property.

(2)(i) A deduction is allowed without regard to this section for a contribution of a partial interest in property if such interest is the taxpayer's entire interest in the property, such as an income interest or a remainder interest. Thus, if securities are given to A for life, with the remainder over to B, and B makes a charitable contribution of his remainder interest to an organization described in section 170(c), a deduction is allowed under section 170 for the present value of B's remainder interest in the securities. If, however, the property in which such partial interest exists was divided in order to create such interest and thus avoid section 170(f)(3)(A), the deduction will not be allowed. Thus, for example, assume that a taxpayer desires to contribute to a charitable organization an income interest in property held by him, which is not of a type described in paragraph (b)(2) of this section. If the taxpayer transfers the remainder interest in such property to his son and immediately thereafter contributes the income interest to a charitable organization, no deduction shall be allowed under section 170 for the contribution of the taxpayer's entire interest consisting of the retained income interest. In further illustration, assume that a taxpayer desires to contribute to a charitable organization the reversionary interest in certain stocks and bonds held by him, which is not of a type described in paragraph (b)(2) of this section. If the taxpayer grants a life estate in such property to his son and immediately thereafter contributes the reversionary interest to a charitable organization, no deduction will be allowed under section 170 for the contribution of the taxpayer's entire interest consisting of the reversionary interest.

(ii) A deduction is allowed without regard to this section for a contribution of a partial interest in property if such contribution constitutes part of a charitable contribution not in trust in which all interests of the taxpayer in the property are given to a charitable organization described in section 170(c). Thus, if on March 1, 1971, an income interest in property is given not in trust to a church and the remainder interest in the property is given not in trust to an educational organization described in section 170(b)(1)(A), a deduction is allowed for the value of such property.

(3) A deduction shall not be disallowed under section 170(f)(3)(A) and

this section merely because the interest which passes to, or is vested in, the charity may be defeated by the performance of some act or the happening of some event, if on the date of the gift it appears that the possibility that such act or event will occur is so remote as to be negligible. See paragraph (e) of § 1.170A-1.

(b) Contributions of certain partial interests in property for which a deduction is allowed. A deduction is allowed under section 170 for a contribution not in trust of a partial interest which is less than the donor's entire interest in property and which qualifies under one of the following subparagraphs:

(1) Undivided portion of donor's entire interest. (i) A deduction is allowed under section 170 for the value of a charitable contribution not in trust of an undivided portion of a donor's entire interest in property. An undivided portion of a donor's entire interest in property must consist of a fraction or percentage of each and every substantial interest or right owned by the donor in such property and must extend over the entire term of the donor's interest in such property and in other property into which such property is converted. For example, assuming that in 1967 B has been given a life estate in an office building for the life of A and that B has no other interest in the office building, B will be allowed a deduction under section 170 for his contribution in 1972 to charity of a one-half interest in such life estate in a transfer which is not made in trust. Such contribution by B will be considered a contribution of an undivided portion of the donor's entire interest in property. In further illustration, assuming that in 1968 C has been given the remainder interest in a trust created under the will of his father and C has no other interest in the trust, C will be allowed a deduction under section 170 for his contribution in 1972 to charity of a 20-percent interest in such remainder interest in a transfer which is not made in trust. Such contribution by C will be considered a contribution of an undivided portion of the donor's entire interest in property. If a taxpayer owns 100 acres of land and makes a contribution of 50 acres to a charitable organization, the charitable contribution is allowed as a deduction under sec-

tion 170. A deduction is allowed under section 170 for a contribution of property to a charitable organization whereby such organization is given the right, as a tenant in common with the donor, to possession, dominion, and control of the property for a portion of each year appropriate to its interest in such property. However, for purposes of this subparagraph a charitable contribution in perpetuity of an interest in property not in trust where the donor transfers some specific rights and retains other substantial rights will not be considered a contribution of an undivided portion of the donor's entire interest in property to which section 170(f) (3) (A) does not apply. Thus, for example, a deduction is not allowable for the value of an immediate and perpetual gift not in trust of an interest in original historic motion picture films to a charitable organization where the donor retains the exclusive right to make reproductions of such films and to exploit such reproductions commercially.

(ii) For purposes of this subparagraph a charitable contribution of an open space easement in gross in perpetuity shall be considered a contribution of an undivided portion of the donor's entire interest in property to which section 170(f) (3) (A) does not apply. For this purpose an easement in gross is a mere personal interest in, or right to use, the land of another; it is not supported by a dominant estate but is attached to, and vested in, the person to whom it is granted. Thus, for example, a deduction is allowed under section 170 for the value of a restrictive easement gratuitously conveyed to the United States in perpetuity whereby the donor agrees to certain restrictions on the use of his property, such as, restrictions on the type and height of buildings that may be erected, the removal of trees, the erection of utility lines, the dumping of trash, and the use of signs.

(2) Partial interests in property which would be deductible in trust. A deduction is allowed under section 170 for the value of a charitable contribution not in trust of a partial interest in property which is less than the donor's entire interest in the property and which would be deductible under section 170(f) (2) and § 1.170A-6 if such interest had been transferred in trust.

(3) Contribution of a remainder interest in a personal residence. A deduction is allowed under section 170 for the value of a charitable contribution not in trust of an irrevocable remainder interest in a personal residence which is not the donor's entire interest in such property. Thus, for example, if a taxpayer contributes not in trust to an organization described in section 170 (c) a remainder interest in a personal residence and retains an estate in such property for life or for a term of years, a deduction is allowed under section 170 for the value of such remainder interest not transferred in trust. For purposes of section 170(f) (3) (B) (i) and this subparagraph, the term "personal residence" means any property used by the taxpayer as his personal residence even though it is not used as his principal residence. For example, the taxpayer's vacation home may be a personal residence for purposes of this subparagraph. The term "personal residence" also includes stock owned by a taxpayer as a tenant-stockholder in a cooperative housing corporation (as those terms are defined in section 216(b) (1) and (2)) if the dwelling which the taxpayer is entitled to occupy as such stockholder is used by him as his personal residence.

(4) Contribution of a remainder interest in a farm. A deduction is allowed under section 170 for the value of a charitable contribution not in trust of an irrevocable remainder interest in a farm which is not the donor's entire interest in such property. Thus, for example, if a taxpayer contributes not in trust to an organization described in section 170(c) a remainder interest in a farm and retains an estate in such farm for life or for a term of years, a deduction is allowed under section 170 for the value of such remainder interest not transferred in trust. For purposes of section 170(f) (3) (B) (i) and this subparagraph, the term "farm" means any land used by the taxpayer or his tenant for the production of crops, fruits, or other agricultural products or for the sustenance of livestock. The term "livestock" includes cattle, hogs, horses, mules, donkeys, sheep, goats, captive fur-bearing animals, chickens, turkeys, pigeons, and other poultry. A farm includes the improvements thereon.

(c) Valuation of a partial interest in property. The amount of the deduction under section 170 in the case of a charitable contribution of a partial interest in property to which paragraph (b) of this section applies is the fair market value of the partial interest at the time of the contribution. See § 1.-170A–1(c). The fair market value of such partial interest must be determined in accordance with § 20.2031–10 of this chapter (Estate Tax Regulations), except that, in the case of a charitable contribution of a remainder interest in real property which is not transferred in trust, the fair market value of such interest must be determined in accordance with section 170 (f) (4) and § 1.170A–12. In the case of a charitable contribution of a remainder interest in the form of a remainder interest in a pooled income fund, a charitable remainder annuity trust, or a charitable remainder unitrust, the fair market value of the remainder interest must be determined as provided in paragraph (b) (2) of § 1.-170A–6. However, in some cases a reduction in the amount of a charitable contribution of the remainder interest may be required. See section 170(e) and paragraph (a) of § 1.170A–4.

(d) Illustrations. The application of this section may be illustrated by the following examples:

Example (1). A, an individual owning a 10-story office building, donates the rent-free use of the top floor of the building for the year 1971 to a charitable organization. Since A's contribution consists of a partial interest to which section 170(f) (3) (A) applies, he is not entitled to a charitable contributions deduction for the contribution of such partial interest.

Example (2). In 1971, B contributes to a charitable organization an undivided one-half interest in 100 acres of land, whereby as tenants in common they share in the economic benefits from the property. The present value of the contributed property is $50,000. Since B's contribution consists of an undivided portion of his entire interest in the property to which section 170(f) (3) (B) applies, he is allowed a deduction in 1971 for his charitable contribution of $50,000.

Example (3). In 1971, D loans $10,000 in cash to a charitable organization and does not require the organization to pay any interest for the use of the money. Since D's contribution consists of a partial interest to which section 170(f) (3) (A) applies, he is not entitled to a charitable contributions deduction for the contribution of such partial interest.

. . . . .

§ 1.174–1 Research and experimental expenditures; in general

Section 174 provides two methods for treating research or experimental expenditures paid or incurred by the taxpayer in connection with his trade or business. These expenditures may be treated as expenses not chargeable to capital account and deducted in the year in which they are paid or incurred (see § 1.174–3), or they may be deferred and amortized (see § 1.174–4). Research or experimental expenditures which are neither treated as expenses nor deferred and amortized under section 174 must be charged to capital account. The expenditures to which section 174 applies may relate either to a general research program or to a particular project. See § 1.174–2 for the definition of research and experimental expenditures. The term "paid or incurred", as used in section 174 and in §§ 1.174–1 to 1.174–4, inclusive, is to be construed according to the method of accounting used by the taxpayer in computing taxable income. See section 7701(a) (25).

§ 1.174–2 Definition of research and experimental expenditures

(a) In general. (1) The term "research or experimental expenditures", as used in section 174, means expenditures incurred in connection with the taxpayer's trade or business which represent research and development costs in the experimental or laboratory sense. The term includes generally all such costs incident to the development of an experimental or pilot model, a plant process, a product, a formula, an invention, or similar property, and the improvement of already existing property of the type mentioned. The term does not include expenditures such as those for the ordinary testing or inspection of materials or products for quality control or those for efficiency surveys, management studies, consumer surveys, advertising, or promotions. However, the term includes the costs of obtaining a patent, such as attorneys' fees expended in making and perfecting a patent application. On the other hand, the term does not include the costs of acquiring another's patent, model, production or process, nor does it include expenditures paid or incurred for re-search in connection with literary, historical, or similar projects.

(2) The provisions of this section apply not only to costs paid or incurred by the taxpayer for research or experimentation undertaken directly by him but also to expenditures paid or incurred for research or experimentation carried on in his behalf by another person or organization (such as a research institute, foundation, engineering company, or similar contractor). However, any expenditures for research or experimentation carried on in the taxpayer's behalf by another person are not expenditures to which section 174 relates, to the extent that they represent expenditures for the acquisition or improvement of land or depreciable property, used in connection with the research or experimentation, to which the taxpayer acquires rights of ownership.

.   .   .   .

§ 1.183–1 Activities not engaged in for profit

(a) In general. Section 183 provides rules relating to the allowance of deductions in the case of activities (whether active or passive in character) not engaged in for profit by individuals and electing small business corporations, creates a presumption that an activity is engaged in for profit if certain requirements are met, and permits the taxpayer to elect to postpone determination of whether such presumption applies until he has engaged in the activity for at least 5 taxable years, or, in certain cases, 7 taxable years. Whether an activity is engaged in for profit is determined under section 162 and section 212(1) and (2) except insofar as section 183(d) creates a presumption that the activity is engaged in for profit. If deductions are not allowable under sections 162 and 212(1) and (2), the deduction allowance rules of section 183(b) and this section apply. Pursuant to section 641(b), the taxable income of an estate or trust is computed in the same manner as in the case of an individual, with certain exceptions not here relevant. Accordingly, where an estate or trust engages in an activity or activities which are not for profit, the rules of section 183 and this section apply in computing the allowable deductions of such trust or estate. No inference is to be drawn from the provisions of section 183 and the regulations thereunder that any activity of a corporation (other than an electing small business corporation) is or is not a business or engaged in for profit. For rules relating to the deductions that may be taken into account by taxable membership organizations which are operated primarily to furnish services, facilities, or goods to members, see section 277 and the regulations thereunder. For the definition of an activity not engaged in for profit, see § 1.183-2. For rules relating to the election contained in section 183(e), see § 1.183-3.

(b) Deductions allowable—(1) Manner and extent. If an activity is not engaged in for profit, deductions are allowable under section 183(b) in the following order and only to the following extent:

(i) Amounts allowable as deductions during the taxable year under chapter 1 of the Code without regard to whether the activity giving rise to such amounts was engaged in for profit are allowable to the full extent allowed by the relevant sections of the Code, determined after taking into account any limitations or exceptions with respect to the allowability of such amounts. For example, the allowability-of-interest expenses incurred with respect to activities not engaged in for profit is limited by the rules contained in section 163 (d).

(ii) Amounts otherwise allowable as deductions during the taxable year under chapter 1 of the Code, but only if such allowance does not result in an adjustment to the basis of property, determined as if the activity giving rise to such amounts was engaged in for profit, are allowed only to the extent the gross income attributable to such activity exceeds the deductions allowed or allowable under subdivision (i) of this subparagraph.

(iii) Amounts otherwise allowable as deductions for the taxable year under chapter 1 of the Code which result in (or if otherwise allowed would have resulted in) an adjustment to the basis of property, determined as if the activity giving rise to such deductions was engaged in for profit, are allowed only to the extent the gross income attributable to such activity exceeds the

deductions allowed or allowable under subdivisions (i) and (ii) of this subparagraph. Deductions falling within this subdivision include such items as depreciation, partial losses with respect to property, partially worthless debts, amortization, and amortizable bond premium.

. . . .

(c) Presumption that activity is engaged in for profit—(1) In general. If for—

(i) Any 2 of 7 consecutive taxable years, in the case of an activity which consists in major part of the breeding, training, showing, or racing of horses, or

(ii) Any 2 of 5 consecutive taxable years, in the case of any other activity, the gross income derived from an activity exceeds the deductions attributable to such activity which would be allowed or allowable if the activity were engaged in for profit, such activity is presumed, unless the Commissioner establishes to the contrary, to be engaged in for profit. For purposes of this determination the deduction permitted by section 1202 shall not be taken into account. Such presumption applies with respect to the second profit year and all years subsequent to the second profit year within the 5- or 7-year period beginning with the first profit year. This presumption arises only if the activity is substantially the same activity for each of the relevant taxable years, including the taxable year in question. If the taxpayer does not meet the requirements of section 183(d) and this paragraph, no inference that the activity is not engaged in for profit shall arise by reason of the provisions of section 183. For purposes of this paragraph, a net operating loss deduction is not taken into account as a deduction. For purposes of this subparagraph a short taxable year constitutes a taxable year.

. . . .

(3) Activity which consists in major part of the breeding, training, showing, or racing of horses. For purposes of this paragraph an activity consists in major part of the breeding, training, showing, or racing of horses for the taxable year if the average of the portion of expenditures attributable to breeding, training, showing, and racing of horses for the 3 taxable years preceding the taxable year (or, in the case of an activity which has not been conducted by the taxpayer for 3 years, for so long as it has been carried on by him) was at least 50 percent of the total expenditures attributable to the activity for such prior taxable years.

. . . .

(d) Activity defined—(1) Ascertainment of activity. In order to determine whether, and to what extent, section 183 and the regulations thereunder apply, the activity or activities of the taxpayer must be ascertained. For instance, where the taxpayer is engaged in several undertakings, each of these may be a separate activity, or several undertakings may constitute one activity. In ascertaining the activity or activities of the taxpayer, all the facts and circumstances of the case must be taken into account. Generally, the most significant facts and circumstances in making this determination are the degree of organizational and economic interrelationship of various undertakings, the business purpose which is (or might be) served by carrying on the various undertakings separately or together in a trade or business or in an investment setting, and the similarity of various undertakings. Generally, the Commissioner will accept the characterization by the taxpayer of several undertakings either as a single activity or as separate activities. The taxpayer's characterization will not be accepted, however, when it appears that his characterization is artificial and cannot be reasonably supported under the facts and circumstances of the case. If the taxpayer engages in two or more separate activities, deductions and income from each separate activity are not aggregated either in determining whether a particular activity is engaged in for profit or in applying section 183. Where land is purchased or held primarily with the intent to profit from increase in its value, and the taxpayer also engages in farming on such land, the farming and the holding of the land will ordinarily be considered a single activity only if the farming activity reduces the net cost of carrying the land for its appreciation in value. Thus, the farming and holding of the land will be considered a single activity only if the income derived from farming exceeds the deductions attributable to the farming activity which are not directly attributable to the holding of the land (that is, deductions other than those directly attributable to the holding of the land such as interest on a mortgage secured by the land, annual property taxes attributable to the land and improvements, and depreciation of improvements to the land).

(2) Rules for allocation of expenses. If the taxpayer is engaged in more than one activity, an item of deduction or income may be allocated between two or more of these activities. Where property is used in several activities, and one or more of such activities is determined not to be engaged in for profit, deductions relating to such property must be allocated between the various activities on a reasonable and consistently applied basis.

. . . .

(e) Gross income from activity not engaged in for profit defined. For purposes of section 183 and the regulations thereunder, gross income derived from an activity not engaged in for profit includes the total of all gains from the sale, exchange, or other disposition of property, and all other gross receipts derived from such activity. Such gross income shall include, for instance, capital gains, and rents received for the use of property which is held in connection with the activity. The taxpayer may determine gross income from any activity by subtracting the cost of goods sold from the gross receipts so long as he consistently does so and follows generally accepted methods of accounting in determining such gross income.

. . . .

§ 1.183–2 Activity not engaged in for profit defined

(a) In general. For purposes of section 183 and the regulations thereunder, the term "activity not engaged in for profit" means any activity other than one with respect to which deductions are allowable for the taxable year under section 162 or under paragraph (1) or (2) of section 212. Deductions are allowable under section 162 for expenses of carrying on activities which constitute a trade or business of the taxpayer and under section 212 for expenses incurred in connection with activities engaged in for the production or collection of income or for the management, conservation, or maintenance of property held for the production of income. Except as provided in section 183 and § 1.-183-1, no deductions are allowable for expenses incurred in connection with activities which are not engaged in for profit. Thus, for example, deductions are not allowable under section 162 or 212 for activities which are carried on primarily as a sport, hobby, or for recreation. The determination whether an activity is engaged in for profit is to be made by reference to objective standards, taking into account all of the facts and circumstances of each case. Although a reasonable expectation of profit is not required, the facts and circumstances must indicate that the taxpayer entered into the activity, or continued the activity, with the objective of making a profit. In determining whether such an objective exists, it may be sufficient that there is a small chance of making a large profit. Thus it may be found that an investor in a wildcat oil well who incurs very substantial expenditures is in the venture for profit even though the expectation of a profit might be considered unreasonable. In determining whether an activity is engaged in for profit, greater weight is given to objective facts than to the taxpayer's mere statement of his intent.

(b) Relevant factors. In determining whether an activity is engaged in for profit, all facts and circumstances with respect to the activity are to be taken into account. No one factor is determinative in making this determination. In addition, it is not intended that only the factors described in this paragraph are to be taken into account in making the determination, or that a determination is to be made on the basis that the number of factors (whether or not listed in this paragraph) indicating a lack of profit objective exceeds the number of factors indicating a profit objective, or vice versa. Among the factors which should normally be taken into account are the following:

(1) Manner in which the taxpayer carries on the activity. The fact that the taxpayer carries on the activity in a businesslike manner and maintains complete and accurate books and records may indicate that the activity is engaged in for profit. Similarly, where an activity is carried on in a manner substantially similar to other activities of the same nature which are profitable, a profit motive may be indicated. A change of operating methods, adoption of new techniques or abandonment of unprofitable methods in a manner consistent with an intent to improve profitability may also indicate a profit motive.

(2) The expertise of the taxpayer or his advisors. Preparation for the activity by extensive study of its accepted business, economic, and scientific practices, or consultation with those who are expert therein, may indicate that the taxpayer has a profit motive where the taxpayer carries on the activity in accordance with such practices. Where a taxpayer has such preparation or procures such expert advice, but does not carry on the activity in accordance with such practices, a lack of intent to derive profit may be indicated unless it appears that the taxpayer is attempting to develop new or superior techniques which may result in profits from the activity.

(3) The time and effort expended by the taxpayer in carrying on the activity. The fact that the taxpayer devotes much of his personal time and effort to carrying on an activity, particularly if the activity does not have substantial personal or recreational aspects, may indicate an intention to derive a profit. A taxpayer's withdrawal from another occupation to devote most of his energies to the activity may also be evidence that the activity is engaged in for profit. The fact that the taxpayer devotes a limited amount of time to an activity does not necessarily indicate a lack of profit motive where the taxpayer employs competent and qualified persons to carry on such activity.

(4) Expectation that assets used in activity may appreciate in value. The term "profit" encompasses appreciation in the value of assets, such as land, used in the activity. Thus, the taxpayer may intend to derive a profit from the operation of the activity, and may also intend that, even if no profit from current operations is derived, an overall profit will result when appreciation in the value of land used in the activity is realized since income from the activity together with the appreciation of land will exceed expenses of operation. See, however, paragraph (d) of § 1.183-1 for definition of an activity in this connection.

(5) The success of the taxpayer in carrying on other similar or dissimilar activities. The fact that the taxpayer has engaged in similar activities in the past and converted them from unprofitable to profitable enterprises may indicate that he is engaged in the present activity for profit, even though the activity is presently unprofitable.

(6) The taxpayer's history of income or losses with respect to the activity. A series of losses during the initial or start-up stage of an activity may not necessarily be an indication that the activity is not engaged in for profit. However, where losses continue to be sustained beyond the period which customarily is necessary to bring the operation to profitable status such continued losses, if not explainable, as due to customary business risks or reverses, may be indicative that the activity is not being engaged in for profit. If losses are sustained because of unforeseen or fortuitous circumstances which are beyond the control of the taxpayer, such as drought, disease, fire, theft, weather damages, other involuntary conversions, or depressed market conditions, such losses would not be an indication that the activity is not engaged in for profit. A series of years in which net income was realized would of course be strong evidence that the activity is engaged in for profit.

(7) The amount of occasional profits, if any, which are earned. The amount of profits in relation to the amount of losses incurred, and in relation to the amount of the taxpayer's investment and the value of the assets used in the activity, may provide useful criteria in determining the taxpayer's intent. An occasional small profit from an activity generating large losses, or from an activity in which the taxpayer has made a large investment, would not generally be determinative that the activity is engaged in for profit. However, substantial profit, though only occasional, would generally be indicative that an activity is engaged in for profit, where the investment or losses are comparatively small. Moreover, an opportunity to earn a substantial ultimate profit in a highly speculative venture is ordinarily sufficient to indicate that the activity is engaged in for profit even though losses or only occasional small profits are actually generated.

(8) The financial status of the taxpayer. The fact that the taxpayer does not have substantial income or capital from sources other than the activity may indicate that an activity is engaged in for profit. Substantial income from sources other than the activity (particularly if the losses from the activity generate substantial tax benefits) may indicate that the activity is not engaged in for profit especially if there are personal or recreational elements involved.

(9) Elements of personal pleasure or recreation. The presence of personal motives in carrying on of an activity may indicate that the activity is not engaged in for profit, especially where there are recreational or personal elements involved. On the other hand, a profit motivation may be indicated where an activity lacks any appeal other than profit. It is not, however, necessary that an activity be engaged in with the exclusive intention of deriving a profit or with the intention of maximizing profits. For example, the availability of other investments which would yield a higher return, or which would be more likely to be profitable, is not evidence that an activity is not engaged in for profit. An activity will not be treated as not engaged in for profit merely because the taxpayer has purposes or motivations other than solely to make a profit. Also, the fact that the taxpayer derives personal pleasure from engaging in the activity is not sufficient to cause the activity to be classified as not engaged in for profit if the activity is in fact engaged in for profit as evidenced by other factors whether or not listed in this paragraph.

(c) Examples. The provisions of this section may be illustrated by the following examples:

Example (1). The taxpayer inherited a farm from her husband in an area which was becoming largely residential, and is now nearly all so. The farm had never made a profit before the taxpayer inherited it, and the farm has since had substantial losses in each year. The decedent from whom the taxpayer inherited the farm was a stockbroker, and he also left the taxpayer substantial stock holdings which yield large income from dividends. The taxpayer lives on an area of the farm which is set aside exclusively for living purposes. A farm manager is employed to operate the farm, but modern methods are not used in operating the farm. The taxpayer was born and raised on a farm, and expresses a strong preference for living on a farm. The taxpayer's activity of farming, based on all the facts and circumstances, could be found not to be engaged in for profit.

Example (2). The taxpayer is a wealthy individual who is greatly interested in philosophy. During the past 30 years he has written and published at his own expense several pamphlets, and he has engaged in extensive lecturing activity, advocating and disseminating his ideas. He has made a profit from these activities in only occasional years, and the profits in those years were small in relation to the amounts of the losses in all other years. The taxpayer has very sizeable income from securities (dividends and capital gains) which constitutes the principal source of his livelihood. The activity of lecturing, publishing pamphlets, and disseminating his ideas is not an activity engaged in by the taxpayer for profit.

Example (3). The taxpayer, very successful in the business of retailing soft drinks, raises dogs and horses. He began raising a particular breed of dogs many years ago in the belief that the breed was in danger of declining, and he has raised and sold the dogs in each year since. The taxpayer recently began raising and racing thoroughbred horses. The losses from the taxpayer's dog and horse activities have increased in magnitude over the years, and he has not made a profit on these operations during any of the last 15 years. The taxpayer generally sells the dogs only to friends, does not advertise the dogs for sale, and shows the dogs only infrequently. The taxpayer races his horses only at the "prestige" tracks at which he combines his racing activities with social and recreational activities. The horse and dog operations are conducted at a large residential property on which the taxpayer also lives, which includes substantial living quarters and attractive recreational facilities for the taxpayer and his family. Since (i) the activity of raising dogs and horses and racing the horses is of a sporting and recreational nature, (ii) the taxpayer has substantial income from his business activities of retailing soft drinks, (iii) the horse and dog operations are not conducted in a businesslike manner, and (iv) such operations have a continuous record of losses, it could be determined that the horse and dog activities of the taxpayer are not engaged in for profit.

Example (4). The taxpayer inherited a farm of 65 acres from his parents when they died 6 years ago. The taxpayer moved to the farm from his house in a small nearby town, and he operates it in the same manner as his parents operated the farm before they died. The taxpayer is employed as a skilled machine operator in a nearby factory, for which he is paid approximately $8,500 per year. The farm has not been profitable for the past 15 years because of rising costs of operating farms in general, and because of the decline in the price of the produce of this farm in particular. The taxpayer consults the local agent of the State agricultural service from time-to-time, and the suggestions of the agent have generally been followed. The manner in which the farm is operated by the taxpayer is substantially similar to the manner in which farms of similar size, and which grow similar crops in the area are operated. Many of these other farms do not make profits. The taxpayer does much of the required labor around the farm himself,

such as fixing fences, planting, crops, etc. The activity of farming could be found, based on all the facts and circumstances, to be engaged in by the taxpayer for profit.

Example (5). A, an independent oil and gas operator, frequently engages in the activity of searching for oil on undeveloped and unexplored land which is not near proven fields. He does so in a manner substantially similar to that of others who engage in the same activity. The chances, based on the experience of A and others who engaged in this activity, are strong that A will not find a commercially profitable oil deposit when he drills on land not established geologically to be proven oil bearing land. However, on the rare occasions that these activities do result in discovering a well, the operator generally realizes a very large return from such activity. Thus, there is a small chance that A will make a large profit from his oil exploration activity. Under these circumstances, A is engaged in the activity of oil drilling for profit.

. . . . .

§ 1.212–1 Nontrade or nonbusiness expenses

(a) An expense may be deducted under section 212 only if—

(1) It has been paid or incurred by the taxpayer during the taxable year (i) for the production or collection of income which, if and when realized, will be required to be included in income for Federal income tax purposes, or (ii) for the management, conservation, or maintenance of property held for the production of such income, or (iii) in connection with the determination, collection, or refund of any tax; and

(2) It is an ordinary and necessary expense for any of the purposes stated in subparagraph (1) of this paragraph.

(b) The term "income" for the purpose of section 212 includes not merely income of the taxable year but also income which the taxpayer has realized in a prior taxable year or may realize in subsequent taxable years; and is not confined to recurring income but applies as well to gains from the disposition of property. For example, if defaulted bonds, the interest from which if received would be includible in income, are purchased with the expectation of realizing capital gain on their resale, even though no current yield thereon is anticipated, ordinary and necessary expenses thereafter paid or incurred in connection with such bonds are deductible. Similarly, ordinary and necessary expenses paid or incurred in the management, conservation, or maintenance of a building devoted to rental purposes are deductible notwithstanding that there is actually no income therefrom in the taxable year, and regardless of the manner in which or the purpose for which the property in question was acquired. Expenses paid or incurred in managing, conserving, or maintaining property held for investment may be deductible under section 212 even though the property is not currently productive and there is no likelihood that the property will be sold at a profit or will otherwise be productive of income and even though the property is held merely to minimize a loss with respect thereto.

. . . .

(d) Expenses, to be deductible under section 212, must be "ordinary and necessary". Thus, such expenses must be reasonable in amount and must bear a reasonable and proximate relation to the production or collection of taxable income or to the management, conservation, or maintenance of property held for the production of income.

(e) A deduction under section 212 is subject to the restrictions and limitations in part IX (section 261 and following), subchapter B, chapter 1 of the Code, relating to items not deductible. Thus, no deduction is allowable under section 212 for any amount allocable to the production or collection of one or more classes of income which are not includible in gross income, or for any amount allocable to the management, conservation, or maintenance of property held for the production of income which is not included in gross income. See section 265. Nor does section 212 allow the deduction of any expenses which are disallowed by any of the provisions of subtitle A of the Code, even though such expenses may be paid or incurred for one of the purposes specified in section 212.

(f) Among expenditures not allowable as deductions under section 212 are the following: Commuter's expenses; expenses of taking special courses or training; expenses for improving personal appearance; the cost of rental of a safe-deposit box for storing jewelry and other personal effects; expenses such as those paid or incurred in seeking employment or in placing oneself in a position to begin rendering personal services for compensation, campaign expenses of a candidate for public office, bar examination fees and other expenses paid or incurred in securing admission to the bar, and corresponding fees and expenses paid or incurred by physicians, dentists, accountants, and other taxpayers for securing the right to practice their respective professions. See, however, section 162 and the regulations thereunder.

(g) Fees for services of investment counsel, custodial fees, clerical help, office rent, and similar expenses paid or incurred by a taxpayer in connection with investments held by him are deductible under section 212 only if (1) they are paid or incurred by the taxpayer for the production or collection of income or for the management, conservation, or maintenance of investments held by him for the production of income; and (2) they are ordinary and necessary under all the circumstances, having regard to the type of investment and to the relation of the taxpayer to such investment.

(h) Ordinary and necessary expenses paid or incurred in connection with the management, conservation, or maintenance of property held for use as a residence by the taxpayer are not deductible. However, ordinary and necessary expenses paid or incurred in connection with the management, conservation, or maintenance of property held by the taxpayer as rental property are deductible even though such property was formerly held by the taxpayer for use as a home.

(i) Reasonable amounts paid or incurred by the fiduciary of an estate or trust on account of administration expenses, including fiduciaries' fees and expenses of litigation, which are ordinary and necessary in connection with the performance of the duties of administration are deductible under section 212, notwithstanding that the estate or trust is not engaged in a trade or business, except to the extent that such expenses are allocable to the production or collection of tax-exempt income. But see section 642(g) and the regulations thereunder for disallowance of such deductions to an estate where such items are allowed as a deduction under section 2053 or 2054 in computing the net estate subject to the estate tax.

(j) Reasonable amounts paid or incurred for the services of a guardian or committee for a ward or minor, and other expenses of guardians and committees which are ordinary and necessary, in connection with the production or collection of income inuring to the ward or minor, or in connection with the management, conservation, or maintenance of property, held for the production of income, belonging to the ward or minor, are deductible.

(k) Expenses paid or incurred in defending or perfecting title to property, in recovering property (other than investment property and amounts of income which, if and when recovered, must be included in gross income), or in developing or improving property, constitute a part of the cost of the property and are not deductible expenses. Attorneys' fees paid in a suit to quiet title to lands are not deductible; but if the suit is also to collect accrued rents thereon, that portion of such fees is deductible which is properly allocable to the services rendered in collecting such rents. Expenses paid or incurred in protecting or asserting one's right to property of a decedent as heir or legatee, or as beneficiary under a testamentary trust, are not deductible.

(l) Expenses paid or incurred by an individual in connection with the determination, collection, or refund of any tax, whether the taxing authority be Federal, State, or municipal, and whether the tax be income, estate, gift, property, or any other tax, are deductible. Thus, expenses paid or incurred by a taxpayer for tax counsel or expenses paid or incurred in connection with the preparation of his tax returns or in connection with any proceedings involved in determining the extent of his tax liability or in contesting his tax liability are deductible.

(m) An expense (not otherwise deductible) paid or incurred by an individual in determining or contesting a liability asserted against him does not become deductible by reason of the fact that property held by him for the production of income may be required to be used or sold for the purpose of satisfying such liability.

(n) Capital expenditures are not allowable as nontrade or nonbusiness expenses. The deduction of an item otherwise allowable under section 212 will not be disallowed simply because the taxpayer was entitled under subtitle A of the Code to treat such item as a capital expenditure, rather than to deduct it as an expense. For example, see section 266. Where, however, the item may properly be treated only as a capital expenditure or where it was properly so treated under an option granted in subtitle A of the Code, no deduction is allowable under section 212; and this is true regardless of whether any basis adjustment is allowed under any other provision of the Code.

(o) The provisions of section 212 are not intended in any way to disallow expenses which would otherwise be allowable under section 162 and the regulations thereunder. Double deductions are not permitted. Amounts deducted under one provision of the Internal Revenue Code of 1954 cannot again be deducted under any other provision thereof.

(p) Frustration of public policy. The deduction of a payment will be disallowed under section 212 if the payment is of a type for which a deduction would be disallowed under section 162 (c), (f), or (g) and the regulations thereunder in the case of a business expense.

§ 1.213–1 Medical, dental, etc., expenses

(a) Allowance of deduction. (1) Section 213 permits a deduction of payments for certain medical expenses (including expenses for medicine and drugs). Except as provided in paragraph (d) of this section (relating to special rule for decedents) a deduction is allowable only to individuals and only with respect to medical expenses actually paid during the taxable year, regardless of when the incident or event which occasioned the expenses occurred and regardless of the method of accounting employed by the taxpayer in making his income tax return. Thus, if the medical expenses are incurred but not paid during the taxable year, no deduction for such expenses shall be allowed for such year.

. . . .

(e) Definitions—(1) General. (i) The term "medical care" includes the diagnosis, cure, mitigation, treatment, or prevention of disease. Expenses paid for "medical care" shall include those paid for the purpose of affecting any structure or function of the body or for transportation primarily for and essential to medical care. See subparagraph (4) of this paragraph for provisions relating to medical insurance.

(ii) Amounts paid for operations or treatments affecting any portion of the body, including obstetrical expenses and expenses of therapy or X-ray treatments, are deemed to be for the purpose of affecting any structure or function of the body and are therefore paid for medical care. Amounts expended for illegal operations or treatments are not deductible. Deductions for expenditures for medical care allowable under section 213 will be confined strictly to expenses incurred primarily for the prevention or alleviation of a physical or mental defect or illness. Thus, payments for the following are payments for medical care: hospital services, nursing services (including nurses' board where paid by the taxpayer), medical, laboratory, surgical, dental and other diagnostic and healing services, X-rays, medicine and drugs (as defined in subparagraph (2) of this paragraph, subject to the 1-percent limitation in paragraph (b) of this section), artificial teeth or limbs, and ambulance hire. However, an expenditure which is merely beneficial to the general health of an individual, such as an expenditure for a vacation, is not an expenditure for medical care.

(iii) Capital expenditures are generally not deductible for Federal income tax purposes. See section 263 and the regulations thereunder. However, an expenditure which otherwise qualifies as a medical expense under section 213 shall not be disqualified merely because it is a capital expenditure. For purposes of section 213 and this paragraph, a capital expenditure made by the taxpayer may qualify as a medical expense, if it has as its primary purpose the medical care (as defined in subdivisions (i) and (ii) of this subparagraph) of the taxpayer, his spouse, or his dependent. Thus, a capital expenditure which is related only to the sick person and is not related to permanent improvement or betterment of property, if it otherwise qualifies as an expenditure for medical care, shall be deductible; for example, an expenditure for eye glasses, a seeing eye dog, artificial teeth and limbs, a wheel chair, crutches, an inclinator or an air conditioner which is detachable from the property and purchased only for the use of a sick person, etc. Moreover, a capi-

tal expenditure for permanent improvement or betterment of property which would not ordinarily be for the purpose of medical care (within the meaning of this paragraph) may, nevertheless, qualify as a medical expense to the extent that the expenditure exceeds the increase in the value of the related property, if the particular expenditure is related directly to medical care. Such a situation could arise, for example, where a taxpayer is advised by a physician to install an elevator in his residence so that the taxpayer's wife who is afflicted with heart disease will not be required to climb stairs. If the cost of installing the elevator is $1,000 and the increase in the value of the residence is determined to be only $700, the difference of $300, which is the amount in excess of the value enhancement, is deductible as a medical expense. If, however, by reason of this expenditure, it is determined that the value of the residence has not been increased, the entire cost of installing the elevator would qualify as a medical expense. Expenditures made for the operation or maintenance of a capital asset are likewise deductible medical expenses if they have as their primary purpose the medical care (as defined in subdivisions (i) and (ii) of this subparagraph) of the taxpayer, his spouse, or his dependent. Normally, if a capital expenditure qualifies as a medical expense, expenditures for the operation or maintenance of the capital asset would also qualify provided that the medical reason for the capital expenditure still exists. The entire amount of such operation and maintenance expenditures qualifies, even if none or only a portion of the original cost of the capital asset itself qualified.

(iv) Expenses paid for transportation primarily for and essential to the rendition of the medical care are expenses paid for medical care. However, an amount allowable as a deduction for "transportation primarily for and essential to medical care" shall not include the cost of any meals and lodging while away from home receiving medical treatment. For example, if a doctor prescribes that a taxpayer go to a warm climate in order to alleviate a specific chronic ailment, the cost of meals and lodging while there would not be deductible. On the other hand, if the travel is undertaken merely for the general improvement of a taxpayer's health, neither the cost of transportation nor the cost of meals and lodging would be deductible. If a doctor prescribes an operation or other medical care, and the taxpayer chooses for purely personal considerations to travel to another locality (such as a resort area) for the operation or the other medical care, neither the cost of transportation nor the cost of meals and lodging (except where paid as part of a hospital bill) is deductible.

(v) The cost of in-patient hospital care (including the cost of meals and lodging therein) is an expenditure for medical care. The extent to which expenses for care in an institution other than a hospital shall constitute medical care is primarily a question of fact which depends upon the condition of the individual and the nature of the services he receives (rather than the nature of the institution). A private establishment which is regularly engaged in providing the types of care or services outlined in this subdivision shall be considered an institution for purposes of the rules provided herein. In general, the following rules will be applied:

(a) Where an individual is in an institution because his condition is such that the availability of medical care (as defined in subdivisions (i) and (ii) of this subparagraph) in such institution is a principal reason for his presence there, and meals and lodging are furnished as a necessary incident to such care, the entire cost of medical care and meals and lodging at the institution, which are furnished while the individual requires continual medical care, shall constitute an expense for medical care. For example, medical care includes the entire cost of institutional care for a person who is mentally ill and unsafe when left alone. While ordinary education is not medical care, the cost of medical care includes the cost of attending a special school for a mentally or physically handicapped individual, if his condition is such that the resources of the institution for alleviating such mental or physical handicap are a principal reason for his presence there. In such a case, the cost of attending such a special school will include the cost of meals and lodging, if supplied, and the cost of ordinary education furnished which is incidental to the special services furnished by the school. Thus, the cost of medical care includes the cost of attending a special school designed to compensate for or overcome a physical handicap, in order to qualify the individual for future normal education or for normal living, such as a school for the teaching of braille or lip reading. Similarly, the cost of care and supervision, or of treatment and training, of a mentally retarded or physically handicapped individual at an institution is within the meaning of the term "medical care".

(b) Where an individual is in an institution, and his condition is such that the availability of medical care in such institution is not a principal reason for his presence there, only that part of the cost of care in the institution as is attributable to medical care (as defined in subdivisions (i) and (ii) of this subparagraph) shall be considered as a cost of medical care; meals and lodging at the institution in such a case are not considered a cost of medical care for purposes of this section. For example, an individual is in a home for the aged for personal or family considerations and not because he requires medical or nursing attention. In such case, medical care consists only of that part of the cost for care in the home which is attributable to medical care or nursing attention furnished to him; his meals and lodging at the home are not considered a cost of medical care.

(c) It is immaterial for purposes of this subdivision whether the medical care is furnished in a Federal or State institution or in a private institution.

(vi) See section 262 and the regulations thereunder for disallowance of deduction for personal, living, and family expenses not falling within the definition of medical care.

. . . .

(3) **Status as spouse or dependent.** In the case of medical expenses for the care of a person who is the taxpayer's spouse or dependent, the deduction under section 213 is allowable if the status of such person as "spouse" or "dependent" of the taxpayer exists either at the time the medical services were rendered or at the time the expenses were paid. In determining whether such status as "spouse" exists, a taxpayer who is legally separated from his spouse under a decree of separate maintenance is not considered as married. Thus, payments

made in June 1956 by A, for medical services rendered in 1955 to B, his wife, may be deducted by A for 1956 even though, before the payments were made, B may have died or in 1956 secured a divorce. Payments made in July 1956 by C, for medical services rendered to D in 1955 may be deducted by C for 1956 even though C and D were not married until June 1956.

. . . . .

(g) **Reimbursement for expenses paid in prior years.** (1) Where reimbursement, from insurance or otherwise, for medical expenses is received in a taxable year subsequent to a year in which a deduction was claimed on account of such expenses, the reimbursement must be included in gross income in such subsequent year to the extent attributable to (and not in excess of) deductions allowed under section 213 for any prior taxable year. See section 104, relating to compensation for injuries or sickness, and section 105(b), relating to amounts expended for medical care, and the regulations thereunder, with regard to amounts in excess of or not attributable to deductions allowed.

(2) If no medical expense deduction was taken in an earlier year, for example, if the standard deduction under section 141 was taken for the earlier year, the reimbursement received in the taxable year for the medical expense of the earlier year is not includible in gross income.

. . . . .

(h) **Substantiation of deductions.** In connection with claims for deductions under section 213, the taxpayer shall furnish the name and address of each person to whom payment for medical expenses was made and the amount and date of the payment thereof in each case. If payment was made in kind, such fact shall be so reflected. Claims for deductions must be substantiated, when requested by the district director, by a statement or itemized invoice from the individual or entity to which payment for medical expenses was made showing the nature of the service rendered, and to or for whom rendered; the nature of any other item of expense and for whom incurred and for what specific purpose, the amount paid therefor and the date of the payment thereof; and by such other information as

the district director may deem necessary.

§ 1.215–1 Periodic alimony, etc., payments

(a) A deduction is allowable under section 215 with respect to periodic payments in the nature of, or in lieu of, alimony or an allowance for support actually paid by the taxpayer during his taxable year and required to be included in the income of the payee wife or former wife, as the case may be, under section 71. As to the amounts required to be included in the income of such wife or former wife, see section 71 and the regulations thereunder. For definition of "husband" and "wife" see section 7701(a) (17).

(b) The deduction under section 215 is allowed only to the obligor spouse. It is not allowed to an estate, trust, corporation, or any other person who may pay the alimony obligation of such obligor spouse. The obligor spouse, however, is not allowed a deduction for any periodic payment includible under section 71 in the income of the wife or former wife, which payment is attributable to property transferred in discharge of his obligation and which, under section 71(d) or section 682, is not includible in his gross income.

(c) The following examples, in which both H and W file their income tax returns on the basis of a calendar year, illustrate cases in which a deduction is or is not allowed under section 215:

Example (1). Pursuant to the terms of a decree of divorce, H, in 1956, transferred securities valued at $100,000 in trust for the benefit of W, which fully discharged all his obligations to W. The periodic payments made by the trust to W are required to be included in W's income under section 71. Such payments are stated in section 71(d) not to be includible in H's income and, therefore, under section 215 are not deductible from his income.

Example (2). A decree of divorce obtained by W from H incorporated a previous agreement of H to establish a trust, the trustees of which were instructed to pay W $5,000 a year for the remainder of her life. The court retained jurisdiction to order H to provide further payments if necessary for the support of W. In 1956 the trustee paid to W $4,000 from the income of the trust and $1,000 from the corpus of the trust. Under the provisions of sections 71 and 682(b), W would include $5,000 in her income for 1956. He would not include any part of the $5,000 in his income nor take a deduction therefor. If H had paid the $1,000 to W pursuant to court order rather than allowing the trustees to pay it out of corpus, he would have been entitled to a deduction of $1,000 under the provisions of section 215.

. . . . .

§ 1.217-2 Deduction for moving expenses paid or incurred in taxable years beginning after December 31, 1969

(a) Allowance of deduction—(1) In general. Section 217(a) allows a deduction from gross income for moving expenses paid or incurred by the taxpayer during the taxable year in connection with his commencement of work as an employee or as a self-employed individual at a new principal place of work. For purposes of this section, amounts are considered as being paid or incurred by an individual whether goods or services are furnished to the taxpayer directly (by an employer, a client, a customer, or similar person) or indirectly (paid to a third party on behalf of the taxpayer by an employer, a client, a customer, or similar person). A cash basis taxpayer will treat moving expenses as being paid for purposes of section 217 and this section in the year in which the taxpayer is considered to have received such payment under section 82 and § 1.82-1. No deduction is allowable under section 162 for any expenses incurred by the taxpayer in connection with moving from one residence to another residence unless such expenses are deductible under section 162 without regard to such change in residence. To qualify for the deduction under section 217 the expenses must meet the definition of the term "moving expenses" provided in section 217(b) and the taxpayer must meet the conditions set forth in section 217(c). The term "employee" as used in this section has the same meaning as in § 31.3401(c)-1 of this chapter (Employment Tax Regulations). The term "self-employed individual" as used in this section is defined in paragraph (f)(1) of this section.

(2) Expenses paid in a taxable year other than the taxable year in which reimbursement representing such expenses is received. In general, moving expenses are deductible in the year paid or incurred. If a taxpayer who uses the cash receipts and disbursements method of accounting receives reimbursement for a moving expense in a taxable year other than the taxable year the taxpayer pays such expense, he may elect to deduct such expense in the taxable year that he receives such reimbursement, rather than the taxable year when he paid such expense in any case where—

(i) The expense is paid in a taxable year prior to the taxable year in which the reimbursement is received, or

(ii) The expense is paid in the taxable year immediately following the taxable year in which the reimbursement is received, provided that such expense is paid on or before the due date prescribed for filing the return (determined with regard to any extension of time for such filing) for the taxable year in which the reimbursement is received.

An election to deduct moving expenses in the taxable year that the reimbursement is received shall be made by claiming the deduction on the return, amended return, or claim for refund for the taxable year in which the reimbursement is received.

(3) Commencement of work. (i) To be deductible the moving expenses must be paid or incurred by the taxpayer in connection with his commencement of work at a new principal place of work (see paragraph (c)(3) of this section for a discussion of the term "principal place of work"). Except for those expenses described in section 217(b)(1) (C) and (D) it is not necessary for the taxpayer to have made arrangements to work prior to his moving to a new location; however, a deduction is not allowable unless employment or self-employment actually does occur. The term "commencement" includes (a) the beginning of work by a taxpayer as an employee or as a self-employed individual for the first time or after a substantial period of unemployment or part-time employment, (b) the beginning of work by a taxpayer for a different employer or in the case of a self-employed individual in a new trade or business.

or (c) the beginning of work by a taxpayer for the same employer or in the case of a self-employed individual in the same trade or business at a new location. To qualify as being in connection with the commencement of work, the move must bear a reasonable proximity both in time and place to such commencement at the new principal place of work. In general, moving expenses incurred within 1 year of the date of the commencement of work are considered to be reasonably proximate in time to such commencement. Moving expenses incurred after the 1-year period may be considered reasonably proximate in time if it can be shown that circumstances existed which prevented the taxpayer from incurring the expenses of moving within the 1-year period allowed. Whether circumstances existed which prevented the taxpayer from incurring the expenses of moving within the period allowed is dependent upon the facts and circumstances of each case. The length of the delay and the fact that the taxpayer may have incurred part of the expenses of the move within the 1-year period allowed shall be taken into account in determining whether expenses incurred after such period are allowable. In general, a move is not considered to be reasonably proximate in place to the commencement of work at the new principal place of work where the distance between the taxpaper's new residence and his new principal place of work exceeds the distance between his former residence and his new principal place of work. A move to a new residence which does not satisfy this test may, however, be considered reasonably proximate in place to the commencement of work if the taxpayer can demonstrate, for example, that he is required to live at such residence as a condition of employment or that living at such residence will result in an actual decrease in commuting time or expense. For example, assume that in 1977 A is transferred by his employer to a new principal place of work and the distance between his former residence and his new principal place of work is 35 miles greater than was the distance between his former residence and his former principal place of work. However, the distance between his new residence and his new principal place of work is 10 miles greater than was the distance between his former residence and his new principal place of work. Although the minimum distance requirement of section 217(c)(1) is met the expenses of moving to the new residence are not considered as incurred in connection with A's commencement of work at his new principal place of work since the new residence is not proximate in place to the new place of work. If, however, A can demonstrate, for example, that he is required to live at such new residence as a condition of employment or if living at such new residence will result in an actual decrease in commuting time or expense, the expenses of the move may be considered as incurred in connection with A's commencement of work at his new principal place of work.

(ii) The provisions of subdivision (i) of this subparagraph may be illustrated by the following examples:

Example (1). Assume that A is transferred by his employer from Boston, Mass., to Washington, D. C. A moves to a new residence in Washington, D. C., and commences work on February 1, 1971. A's wife and his two children remain in Boston until June 1972 in order to allow A's children to complete their grade school education in Boston. On June 1, 1972, A sells his home in Boston and his wife and children move to the new residence in Washington, D. C. The expenses incurred on June 1, 1972, in selling the old residence and in moving A's family, their household goods, and personal effects to the new residence in Washington are allowable as a deduction although they were incurred 16 months after the date of the commencement of work by A since A has moved to and established a new residence in Washington, D. C., and thus incurred part of the total expenses of the move prior to the expiration of the 1-year period.

Example (2). Assume that A is transferred by his employer from Washington, D. C., to Baltimore, Md. A commences work on January 1, 1971, in Baltimore. A commutes from his residence in Washington to his new principal place of work in Baltimore for a period of 18 months. On July 1, 1972, A decides to move to and establish a new residence in Baltimore. None of the moving expenses otherwise allowable under section 217 may be deducted since A neither incurred the expenses within 1 year nor has shown circumstances under which he was prevented from moving within such period.

(b) Definition of moving expenses— (1) In general. Section 217(b) defines the term "moving expenses" to mean only the reasonable expenses (i) of moving household goods and personal effects from the taxpayer's former residence to his new residence, (ii) of traveling (including meals and lodging) from the taxpayer's former residence to his new place of residence, (iii) of traveling (including meals and lodging), after obtaining employment, from the taxpayer's former residence to the general location of his new principal place of work and return, for the principal purpose of searching for a new residence, (iv) of meals and lodging while occupying temporary quarters in the general location of the new principal place of work during any period of 30 consecutive days after obtaining employment, or (v) of a nature constituting qualified residence sale, purchase, or lease expenses. Thus, the test of deductibility is whether the expenses are reasonable and are incurred for the items set forth in subdivisions (i) through (v) of this subparagraph.

(2) Reasonable expenses. (i) The term "moving expenses" includes only those expenses which are reasonable under the circumstances of the particular move. Expenses paid or incurred in excess of a reasonable amount are not deductible. Generally, expenses paid or incurred for movement of household goods and personal effects or for travel (including meals and lodging) are reasonable only to the extent that they are paid or incurred for such movement or travel by the shortest and most direct route available from the former residence to the new residence by the conventional mode or modes of transportation actually used and in the shortest period of time commonly required to travel the distance involved by such mode. Thus, if moving or travel arrangements are made to provide a circuitous route for scenic, stopover, or other similar reasons, additional expenses resulting therefrom are not deductible since they are not reasonable nor related to the commencement of work at the new principal place of work. In addition, expenses paid or incurred for meals and lodging while traveling from the former residence to the new place of residence or to the general location of the new principal place of work and return or occupying temporary quarters in the general location of the new principal place of work are reasonable only if under the facts and circumstances involved such expenses are not lavish or extravagant.

(ii) The application of this subparagraph may be illustrated by the following example:

Example. A, an employee of the M Company works and maintains his residence in Boston, Mass. Upon receiving orders from his employer that he is to be transferred to M's Los Angeles, Calif., office, A motors to Los Angeles with his family with stopovers at various cities between Boston and Los Angeles to visit friends and relatives. In addition, A detours into Mexico for sightseeing. Because of the stopovers and tour into Mexico, A's travel time and distance are increased over what they would have been had he proceeded directly to Los Angeles. To the extent that A's route of travel between Boston and Los Angeles is in a generally southwesterly direction it may be said that he is traveling by the shortest and most direct route available by motor vehicle. Since A's excursion into Mexico is away from the usual Boston-Los Angeles route, the portion of the expenses paid or incurred attributable to such excursion is not deductible. Likewise, that portion of the expenses attributable to A's delay en route in visiting personal friends and sightseeing are not deductible.

(3) Expense of moving household goods and personal effects. Expenses of moving household goods and personal effects include expenses of transporting such goods and effects from the taxpayer's former residence to his new residence, and expenses of packing, crating, and in-transit storage and insurance for such goods and effects. Such expenses also include any costs of connecting or disconnecting utilities required because of the moving of household goods, appliances, or personal effects. Expenses of storing and insuring household goods and personal effects constitute in-transit expenses if incurred within any consecutive 30-day period after the day such goods and effects are moved from the taxpayer's former residence and prior to delivery at the taxpayer's new residence. Expenses paid or incurred in moving household goods and personal effects to the taxpayer's new residence from a place other than his former residence are allowable, but only to the extent that such expenses do not exceed the amount which would be allowable had such goods and effects been moved from the taxpayer's former residence. Expenses of moving household goods and personal effects do not include, for example, storage charges (other than in-transit), costs incurred in the acquisition of property, costs incurred and losses sustained in the disposition of property, penalties for breaking leases, mortgage penalties, expenses of refitting rugs or draperies, losses sustained on the disposal of memberships in clubs, tuition fees, and similar items. The above expenses may, however, be described in other provisions of section 217(b) and if so a deduction may be allowed for them subject to the allowable dollar limitations.

(4) **Expenses of traveling from the former residence to the new place of residence.** Expenses of traveling from the former residence to the new place of residence include the cost of transportation and of meals and lodging en route (including the date of arrival) from the taxpayer's former residence to his new place of residence. Expenses of meals and lodging incurred in the general location of the former residence within 1 day after the former residence is no longer suitable for occupancy because of the removal of household goods and personal effects shall be considered as expenses of traveling for purposes of this subparagraph. The date of arrival is the day the taxpayer secures lodging at the new place of residence, even if on a temporary basis. Expenses of traveling from the taxpayer's former residence to his new place of residence do not include, for example, living or other expenses following the date of arrival at the new place of residence and while waiting to enter the new residence or waiting for household goods to arrive, expenses in connection with house or apartment hunting, living expenses preceding date of departure for the new place of residence (other than expenses of meals and lodging incurred within 1 day after the former residence is no longer suitable for occupancy), expenses of trips for purposes of selling property, expenses of trips to the former residence by the taxpayer pending the move by his family to the new place of residence, or any allowance for depreciation. The above expenses may, however, be described in other provisions of section 217(b) and if so a deduction may be allowed for them subject to the allowable dollar limitations. The deduction for traveling expenses from the former residence to the new place of residence is allowable for only one trip made by the taxpayer and members of his household; however, it is not necessary that the taxpayer and all members of his household travel together or at the same time.

(5) **Expenses of traveling for the principal purpose of looking for a new residence.** Expenses of traveling, after obtaining employment, from the former residence to the general location of the new principal place of work and return, for the principal purpose of searching for a new residence include the cost of transportation and meals and lodging during such travel and while at the general location of the new place of work for the principal purpose of searching for a new residence. However, such expenses do not include, for example, expenses of meals and lodging of the taxpayer and members of his household before departing for the new principal place of work, expenses for trips for purposes of selling property, expenses of trips to the former residence by the taxpayer pending the move by his family to the place of residence, or any allowance for depreciation. The above expenses may, however, be described in other provisions of section 217(b) and if so a deduction may be allowed for them. The deduction for expenses of traveling for the principal purpose of looking for a new residence is not limited to any number of trips by the taxpayer and by members of his household. In addition, the taxpayer and all members of his household need not travel together or at the same time. Moreover, a trip need not result in acquisition of a lease of property or purchase of property. An employee is considered to have obtained employment in the general location of the new principal place of work after he has obtained a contract or agreement of employment. A self-employed individual is considered to have obtained employment when he has made substantial arrangements to commence work at the new principal place of work (see paragraph (f) (2) of this section for a discussion of the term "made substantial arrangements to commence to work").

(6) **Expenses of occupying temporary quarters.** Expenses of occupying temporary quarters include only the cost of meals and lodging while occupying temporary quarters in the general location of the new principal place of work during any period of 30 consecutive days after the taxpayer has obtained employment in such general location. Thus, expenses of occupying temporary quarters do not include, for

example, the cost of entertainment, laundry, transportation, or other personal, living family expenses, or expenses of occupying temporary quarters in the general location of the former place of work. The 30 consecutive day period is any one period of 30 consecutive days which can begin, at the option of the taxpayer, on any day after the day the taxpayer obtains employment in the general location of the new principal place of work.

(7) Qualified residence sale, purchase, or lease expenses. Qualified residence sale, purchase, or lease expenses (hereinafter "qualified real estate expenses") are only reasonable amounts paid or incurred for any of the following purposes:

(i) Expenses incident to the sale or exchange by the taxpayer or his spouse of the taxpayer's former residence which, but for section 217(b) and (e), would be taken into account in determining the amount realized on the sale or exchange of the residence. These expenses include real estate commissions, attorneys' fees, title fees, escrow fees, so called "points" or loan placement charges which the seller is required to pay, State transfer taxes and similar expenses paid or incurred in connection with the sale or exchange. No deduction, however, is permitted under section 217 and this section for the cost of physical improvements intended to enhance salability by improving the condition or appearance of the residence.

(ii) Expenses incident to the purchase by the taxpayer or his spouse of a new residence in the general location of the new principal place of work which, but for section 217(b) and (e), would be taken into account in determining either the adjusted basis of the new residence or the cost of a loan. These expenses include attorneys' fees, escrow fees, appraisal fees, title costs, so-called "points" or loan placement charges not representing payments or prepayments of interest, and similar expenses paid or incurred in connection with the purchase of the new residence. No deduction, however, is permitted under section 217 and this section for any portion of real estate taxes or insurance, so-called "points" or loan placement charges which are, in essence, prepayments of interest, or the purchase price of the residence.

(iii) Expenses incident to the settlement of an unexpired lease held by the taxpayer or his spouse on property used by the taxpayer as his former residence. These expenses include consideration paid to a lessor to obtain a release from a lease, attorneys' fees, real estate commissions, or similar expenses incident to obtaining a release from a lease or to obtaining an assignee or a sublessee such as the difference between rent paid under a primary lease and rent received under a sublease. No deduction, however, is permitted under section 217 and this section for the cost of physical improvement intended to enhance marketability of the leasehold by improving the condition or appearance of the residence.

(iv) Expenses incident to the acquisition of a lease by the taxpayer or his spouse. These expenses include the cost of fees or commissions for obtaining a lease, a sublease, or an assignment of an interest in property used by the taxpayer as his new residence in the general location of the new principal place of work. No deduction, however, is permitted under section 217 and this section for payments or prepayments of rent or payments representing the cost of a security or other similar deposit.

Qualified real estate expenses do not include losses sustained on the disposition of property or mortgage penalties, to the extent that such penalties are otherwise deductible as interest.

(8) Residence. The term "former residence" refers to the taxpayer's principal residence before his departure for his new principal place of work. The term "new residence" refers to the taxpayer's principal residence within the general location of his new principal place of work. Thus, neither term includes other residences owned or maintained by the taxpayer or members of his family or seasonal residences such as a summer beach cottage. Whether or not property is used by the taxpayer as his principal residence depends upon all the facts and circumstances in each case. Property used by the taxpayer as his principal residence may include a houseboat, a housetrailer, or similar dwelling. The term "new place of residence" generally includes the area within which the taxpayer might reasonably be expected to commute to his new principal place of work.

. . . .

(c) Conditions for allowance—(1) In general. Section 217(c) provides two conditions which must be satisfied in order for a deduction of moving expenses to be allowed under section 217 (a). The first is a minimum distance condition prescribed by section 217(c) (1), and the second is a minimum period of employment condition prescribed by section 217(c) (2).

. . . .

(3) Principal place of work. (i) A taxpayer's "principal place of work" usually is the place where he spends most of his working time. The principal place of work of a taxpayer who performs services as an employee is his employer's plant, office, shop, store, or other property. The principal place of work of a taxpayer who is self-employed is the plant, office, shop, store, or other property which serves as the center of his business activities. However, a taxpayer may have a principal place of work even if there is no one place where he spends a substantial portion of his working time. In such case, the taxpayer's principal place of work is the place where his business activities are centered—for example, because he reports there for work, or is required either by his employer or the nature of his employment to "base" his employment there. Thus, while a member of a railroad crew may spend most of his working time aboard a train, his principal place of work is his home terminal, station, or other such central point where he reports in, checks out, or receives instructions. The principal place of work of a taxpayer who is employed by a number of employers on a relatively short-term basis, and secures employment by means of a union hall system (such as a construction or building trades worker) would be the union hall.

(ii) Where a taxpayer has more than one employment (i. e., the taxpayer is employed by more than one employer, or is self-employed in more than one trade or business, or is an employee and is self-employed at any particular time) his principal place of work is determined with reference to his principal employment. The location of a taxpayer's principal place of work is a question of fact determined on the basis of the particular circumstances in each case. The more important factors to be considered in making this determination are (a) the total time ordinarily spent by the taxpayer at each place, (b) the degree of the taxpayer's business activity at each place, and (c) the relative significance of the financial return to the taxpayer from each place.

(iii) Where a taxpayer maintains inconsistent positions by claiming a deduction for expenses of meals and lodging while away from home (incurred in the general location of the new principal place of work) under section 162 (relating to trade or business expenses) and by claiming a deduction under this section for moving expenses incurred in connection with the commencement of work at such place of work, it will be a question of facts and circumstances as to whether such new place of work will be considered a principal place of work, and accordingly, which category of deductions he will be allowed.

. . . .

(d) Rules for application of section 217(c) (2)—(1) Inapplicability of minimum period of employment condition in certain cases. Section 217(d) (1) provides that the minimum period of employment condition of section 217(c) (2) does not apply in the case of a taxpayer who is unable to meet such condition by reason of—

(i) Death or disability, or

(ii) Involuntary separation (other than for willful misconduct) from the service of an employer or separation by reason of transfer for the benefit of an employer after obtaining full-time employment in which the taxpayer could reasonably have been expected to satisfy such condition.

For purposes of subdivision (i) of this paragraph disability shall be determined according to the rules in section 72(m) (7) and § 1.72–17(f). Subdivision (ii) of this subparagraph applies only where the taxpayer has obtained full-time employment in which he could reasonably have been expected to satisfy the minimum period of employment condition. A taxpayer could reasonably have been expected to satisfy the minimum period of employment condition if at the time he commences work at the new principal place of work he could have been expected, based upon the facts known to him at such time, to satisfy such condition. Thus, for example, if the taxpayer at the time of transfer was not advised by his employer that he planned to transfer him within 6 months to another principal place of work, the taxpayer could, in the absence of other factors, reasonably have been expected to satisfy the minimum employment period condition at the time of the first transfer. On the other hand, a taxpayer could not reasonably have been expected to satisfy the minimum employment condition if at the time of the commencement of the move he knew that his employer's retirement age policy would prevent his satisfying the minimum employment period condition.

(2) Election of deduction before minimum period of employment condition is satisfied. (i) Paragraph (2) of section 217(d) provides a rule which applies where a taxpayer paid or incurred, in a taxable year, moving expenses which would be deductible in that taxable year except that the minimum period of employment condition of section 217(c) (2) has not been satisfied before the time prescribed by law for filing the return for such taxable year. The rule provides that where a taxpayer has paid or incurred moving expenses and as of the date prescribed by section 6072 for filing his return for such taxable year (determined with regard to extensions of time for filing) there remains unexpired a sufficient portion of the 12-month or the 24-month period so that it is still possible for the taxpayer to satisfy the applicable period of employment condition, the taxpayer may elect to claim a deduction for such moving expenses on the return for such taxable year. The election is exercised by taking the deduction on the return.

(ii) Where a taxpayer does not elect to claim a deduction for moving expenses on the return for the taxable year in which such expenses were paid or incurred in accordance with subdivision (i) of this subparagraph and the applicable minimum period of employment condition of section 217(c) (2) (as

well as all other requirements of section 217) is subsequently satisfied, the taxpayer may file an amended return or a claim for refund for the taxable year such moving expenses were paid or incurred on which he may claim a deduction under section 217.

(iii) The application of this subparagraph may be illustrated by the following examples:

Example (1). A is transferred by his employer from Boston, Massachusetts, to Cleveland, Ohio. He begins working there on November 1, 1970. Moving expenses are paid by A in 1970 in connection with this move. On April 15, 1971, when he files his income tax return for the year 1970, A has been a full-time employee in Cleveland for approximately 24 weeks. Although he has not satisfied the 39-week employment condition at this time, A may elect to claim his 1970 moving expenses on his 1970 income tax return as there is still sufficient time remaining before November 1, 1971, to satisfy such condition.

Example (2). Assume the same facts as in example (1), except that on April 15, 1971, A has voluntarily left his employer and is looking for other employment in Cleveland. A may not be sure he will be able to meet the 39-week employment condition by November 1, 1971. Thus, he may if he wishes wait until such condition is met and file an amended return claiming as a deduction the expenses paid in 1970. Instead of filing an amended return A may file a claim for refund based on a deduction for such expenses. If A fails to meet the 39-week employment condition on or before November 1, 1971, no deduction is allowable for such expenses.

Example (3). B is a self-employed accountant. He moves from Rochester, N. Y., to New York, N. Y., and begins to work there on December 1, 1970. Moving expenses are paid by B in 1970 and 1971 in connection with this move. On April 15, 1971, when he files his income tax return for the year 1970, B has been performing services as a self-employed individual on a full-time basis in New York City for approximately 20 weeks. Although he has not satisfied the 78-week employment condition at this time, A may elect to claim his 1970 moving expenses on his 1970 income tax return as there is still sufficient time remaining before December 1, 1972, to satisfy such condition. On April 15, 1972, when he files his income tax return for the year 1971, B has been performing services as a self-employed individual on a full-time basis in New York City for approximately 72 weeks. Although he has not met the 78-week employment condition at this time, B may elect to claim his 1971 moving expenses on his 1971 income tax return as there is still sufficient time remaining before December 1, 1972, to satisfy such requirement.

(3) Recapture of deduction. Paragraph (3) of section 217(d) provides a rule which applies where a taxpayer has deducted moving expenses under the election provided in section 217(d) (2) prior to satisfying the applicable minimum period of employment condition and such condition cannot be satisfied at the close of a subsequent taxable year. In such cases an amount equal to the expenses deducted must be included in the taxpayer's gross income for the taxable year in which the taxpayer is no longer able to satisfy such minimum period of employment condition. Where the taxpayer has deducted moving expenses under the election provided in section 217(d) (2) for the taxable year and subsequently files an amended return for such year on which he does not claim the deduction, such expenses are not treated as having been deducted for purposes of the recapture rule of the preceding sentence.

. . . . .

§ 1.248–1 Election to amortize organizational expenditures

(a) In general. (1) Section 248(a) provides that a corporation may elect for any taxable year beginning after December 31, 1953, to treat its organizational expenditures, as defined in subsection (b) of section 248 and in paragraph (b) of this section, as deferred expenses. A corporation which exercises such election must, at the time it makes the election, select a period of not less than 60 months, beginning with the month in which it began business, over which it will amortize its organizational expenditures. The period selected by the corporation may be equal to or greater, but not less, than 60 months, but in any event it must begin with the month in which the corporation began business. The organizational expenditures of the corporation which are treated as deferred expenses under the provisions of section 248 and this section shall then be allowed as a deduction in computing taxable income ratably over the period selected by the taxpayer. The period selected by the taxpayer in making its election may not be subsequently changed but shall be adhered to in computing taxable income for the taxable year for which the election is made and all subsequent taxable years.

(2) If a corporation exercises the election provided in section 248(a), such election shall apply to all of its expenditures which are organizational expenditures within the meaning of subsection (b) of section 248 and paragraph (b) of this section. The election shall apply, however, only with respect to expenditures incurred before the end of the taxable year in which the corporation begins business (without regard to whether the corporation files its returns on the accrual or cash method of accounting or whether the expenditures are paid in the taxable year in which they are incurred), if such expenditures are paid or incurred on or after August 16, 1954 (the date of enactment of the Internal Revenue Code of 1954).

(3) The deduction allowed under section 248 must be spread over a period beginning with the month in which the corporation begins business. The determination of the date the corporation begins business presents a question of fact which must be determined in each case in light of all the circumstances of the particular case. The words "begins business," however, do not have the same meaning as "in existence." Ordinarily, a corporation begins business when it starts the business operations for which it was organized; a corporation comes into existence on the date of its incorporation. Mere organizational activities, such as the obtaining of the corporate charter, are not alone sufficient to show the beginning of business. If the activities of the corporation have advanced to the extent necessary to establish the nature of its business operations, however, it will be deemed to have begun business. For example, the acquisition of operating assets which are necessary to the type of business contemplated may constitute the beginning of business.

(b) Organizational expenditures defined. (1) Section 248(b) defines the term "organizational expenditures." Such expenditures, for purposes of section 248 and this section, are those expenditures which are directly incident to the creation of the corporation. An expenditure, in order to qualify as an organizational expenditure, must be (i) incident to the creation of the corporation, (ii) chargeable to the capital account of the corporation, and (iii) of a character which, if expended incident to the creation of a corporation having a limited life, would be amortizable over such life. An expenditure which fails to meet each of these three tests may not be considered an organizational expenditure for purposes of section 248 and this section.

(2) The following are examples of organizational expenditures within the meaning of section 248 and this section: legal services incident to the organization of the corporation, such as drafting the corporate charter, by-laws, minutes of organizational meetings, terms of original stock certificates, and the like; necessary accounting services; expenses of temporary directors and of organizational meetings of directors or stockholders; and fees paid to the State of incorporation.

(3) The following expenditures are not organizational expenditures within the meaning of section 248 and this section:

(i) Expenditures connected with issuing or selling shares of stock or other securities, such as commissions, professional fees, and printing costs. This is so even where the particular issue of stock to which the expenditures relate is for a fixed term of years;

(ii) Expenditures connected with the transfer of assets to a corporation.

(4) Expenditures connected with the reorganization of a corporation, unless directly incident to the creation of a corporation, are not organizational expenditures within the meaning of section 248 and this section.

(c) **Time and manner of making election.** The election provided by section 248(a) and paragraph (a) of this section shall be made in a statement attached to the taxpayer's return for the taxable year in which it begins business. Such taxable year must be one which begins after December 31, 1953. The return and statement must be filed not later than the date prescribed by law for filing the return (including any extensions of time) for the taxable year in which the taxpayer begins business. The statement shall set forth the description and amount of the expenditures involved, the date such expenditures were incurred, the month in which the corporation began business, and the number of months (not less than 60 and beginning with the month in which the taxpayer began business) over which such expenditures are to be deducted ratably.

§ 1.262–1 Personal, living, and family expenses

(a) **In general.** In computing taxable income, no deduction shall be allowed, except as otherwise expressly provided in chapter 1 of the Code, for personal, living, and family expenses.

(b) **Examples of personal, living, and family expenses.** Personal, living, and family expenses are illustrated in the following examples:

(1) Premiums paid for life insurance by the insured are not deductible. See also section 264 and the regulations thereunder.

(2) The cost of insuring a dwelling owned and occupied by the taxpayer as a personal residence is not deductible.

(3) Expenses of maintaining a household, including amounts paid for rent, water, utilities, domestic service, and the like, are not deductible. A taxpayer who rents a property for residential purposes, but incidentally conducts business there (his place of business being elsewhere) shall not deduct any part of the rent. If, however, he uses part of the house as his place of business, such portion of the rent and other similar expenses as is properly attributable to such place of business is deductible as a business expense.

(4) Losses sustained by the taxpayer upon the sale or other disposition of property held for personal, living, and family purposes are not deductible. But see section 165 and the regulations thereunder for deduction of losses sustained to such property by reason of casualty, etc.

(5) Expenses incurred in traveling away from home (which include transportation expenses, meals, and lodging) and any other transportation expenses are not deductible unless they qualify as expenses deductible under section 162, § 1.162–2, and paragraph (d) of § 1.162–5 (relating to trade or business expenses), section 170 and paragraph (a) (2) of § 1.170–2 or paragraph (g) of § 1.170A–1 (relating to charitable contributions), section 212 and § 1.212–1 (relating to expenses for production of income), section 213(e) and paragraph (e) of § 1.213–1 (relating to medical expenses) or section 217(a) and paragraph (a) of § 1.217–1 (relating to moving expenses). The taxpayer's costs of commuting to his place of business or employment are personal expenses and do not qualify as deductible expenses. The costs of the taxpayer's lodging not incurred in traveling away from home are personal expenses and are not deductible unless they qualify as deductible expenses under sec-

tion 217. Except as permitted under section 162, 212, or 217, the costs of the taxpayer's meals not incurred in traveling away from home are personal expenses.

(6) Amounts paid as damages for breach of promise to marry, and attorney's fees and other costs of suit to recover such damages, are not deductible.

(7) Generally, attorney's fees and other costs paid in connection with a divorce, separation, or decree for support are not deductible by either the husband or the wife. However, the part of an attorney's fee and the part of the other costs paid in connection with a divorce, legal separation, written separation agreement, or a decree for support, which are properly attributable to the production or collection of amounts includible in gross income under section 71 are deductible by the wife under section 212.

(8) The cost of equipment of a member of the armed services is deductible only to the extent that it exceeds nontaxable allowances received for such equipment and to the extent that such equipment is especially required by his profession and does not merely take the place of articles required in civilian life. For example, the cost of a sword is an allowable deduction in computing taxable income, but the cost of a uniform is not. However, amounts expended by a reservist for the purchase and maintenance of uniforms which may be worn only when on active duty for training for temporary periods, when attending service school courses, or when attending training assemblies are deductible except to the extent that nontaxable allowances are received for such amounts.

(9) Expenditures made by a taxpayer in obtaining an education or in furthering his education are not deductible unless they qualify under section 162 and § 1.162-5 (relating to trade or business expenses).

. . . .

§ 1.263(a)-1 Capital expenditures; in general

(a) Except as otherwise provided in chapter 1 of the Code, no deduction shall be allowed for—

(1) Any amount paid out for new buildings or for permanent improvements or betterments made to increase the value of any property or estate, or

(2) Any amount expended in restoring property or in making good the exhaustion thereof for which an allowance is or has been made in the form of a deduction for depreciation, amortization, or depletion.

(b) In general, the amounts referred to in paragraph (a) of this section include amounts paid or incurred (1) to add to the value, or substantially prolong the useful life, of property owned by the taxpayer, such as plant or equipment, or (2) to adapt property to a new or different use. Amounts paid or incurred for incidental repairs and maintenance of property are not capital expenditures within the meaning of subparagraphs (1) and (2) of this paragraph. See section 162 and § 1.162-4.

. . . . .

§ 1.263(a)-2 Examples of capital expenditures

The following paragraphs of this section include examples of capital expenditures:

(a) The cost of acquisition, construction, or erection of buildings, machinery and equipment, furniture and fixtures, and similar property having a useful life substantially beyond the taxable year.

(b) Amounts expended for securing a copyright and plates, which remain the property of the person making the payments.

(c) The cost of defending or perfecting title to property.

(d) The amount expended for architect's services.

(e) Commissions paid in purchasing securities. Commissions paid in selling securities are an offset against the selling price, except that in the case of dealers in securities such commissions may be treated as an ordinary and necessary business expense.

(f) Amounts assessed and paid under an agreement between bondholders or shareholders of a corporation to be used in a reorganization of the corporation or voluntary contributions by shareholders to the capital of the corporation for any corporate purpose. Such amounts are capital investments and are not deductible. See section 118 and § 1.118-1.

(g) A holding company which guarantees dividends at a specified rate on the stock of a subsidiary corporation for the purpose of securing new capital for the subsidiary and increasing the value of its stockholdings in the subsidiary shall not deduct amounts paid in carrying out this guaranty in computing its taxable income, but such payments are capital expenditures to be added to the cost of its stock in the subsidiary.

(h) The cost of good will in connection with the acquisition of the assets of a going concern is a capital expenditure. . . . .

§ 1.263(a)-3   Election to deduct or capitalize certain expenditures

(a) Under certain provisions of the Code, taxpayers may elect to treat capital expenditures as deductible expenses or as deferred expenses, or to treat deductible expenses as capital expenditures.

(b) The sections referred to in paragraph (a) of this section include:

(1) Section 173 (circulation expenditures).

(2) Section 174 (research and experimental expenditures).

(3) Section 175 (soil and water conservation expenditures).

(4) Section 177 (trademark and trade name expenditures).

(5) Section 180 (expenditures by farmers for fertilizer, lime, etc.).

(6) Section 182 (expenditures by farmers for clearing land).

(7) Section 248 (organizational expenditures of a corporation).

(8) Section 266 (carrying charges).

(9) Section 615 (exploration expenditures).

(10) Section 616 (development expenditures).

§ 1.266-1   Taxes and carrying charges chargeable to capital account and treated as capital items

(a) In general. In accordance with section 266, items enumerated in paragraph (b) (1) of this section may be capitalized at the election of the taxpayer. Thus, taxes and carrying charges with respect to property of the type described in this section are chargeable to capital account at the election of the taxpayer, notwithstanding that they are otherwise expressly deductible under provisions of subtitle A of the Code. No deduction is allowable for any items so treated.

(b) Taxes and carrying charges. (1) The taxpayer may elect, as provided in paragraph (c) of this section, to treat the items enumerated in this subparagraph which are otherwise expressly deductible under the provisions of subtitle A of the Code as chargeable to capital account either as a component of original cost or other basis, for the purposes of section 1012, or as an adjustment to basis, for the purposes of section 1016(a) (1). The items thus chargeable to capital account are—

(i) In the case of unimproved and unproductive real property: Annual taxes, interest on a mortgage, and other carrying charges.

(ii) In the case of real property, whether improved or unimproved and whether productive or unproductive:

‹ (a) Interest on a loan (but not theoretical interest of a taxpayer using his own funds),

(b) Taxes of the owner of such real property measured by compensation paid to his employees,

(c) Taxes of such owner imposed on the purchase of materials, or on the storage, use, or other consumption of materials, and

(d) Other necessary expenditures, paid or incurred for the development of the real property or for the construction of an improvement or additional improvement to such real property, up to the time the development or construction work has been completed. The development or construction work with respect to which such items are incurred may relate to unimproved and unproductive real estate whether the construction work will make the property productive of income subject to tax (as in the case of a factory) or not (as in the case of a personal residence), or may relate to property already improved or productive (as in the case of a plant addition or improvement, such as the construction of another floor on a factory or the installation of insulation therein).

(iii) In the case of personal property:

(a) Taxes of an employer measured by compensation for services rendered in transporting machinery or other fixed assets to the plant or installing them therein,

(b) Interest on a loan to purchase such property or to pay for transporting or installing the same, and

(c) Taxes of the owner thereof imposed on the purchase of such property or on the storage, use, or other consumption of such property,

paid or incurred up to the date of installation or the date when such property is first put into use by the taxpayer, whichever date is later.

(iv) Any other taxes and carrying charges with respect to property, otherwise deductible, which in the opinion of the Commissioner are, under sound accounting principles, chargeable to capital account.

(2) The sole effect of section 266 is to permit the items enumerated in subparagraph (1) of this paragraph to be chargeable to capital account notwithstanding that such items are otherwise expressly deductible under the provisions of subtitle A of the Code. An item not otherwise deductible may not be capitalized under section 266.

(3) In the absence of a provision in this section for treating a given item as a capital item, this section has no effect on the treatment otherwise accorded such item. Thus, items which are otherwise deductible are deductible notwithstanding the provisions of this section, and items which are otherwise treated as capital items are to be so treated. Similarly, an item not otherwise deductible is not made deductible by this section. Nor is the absence of a provision in this section for treating a given item as a capital item to be construed as withdrawing or modifying the right now given to the taxpayer under any other provisions of subtitle A of the Code, or of the regulations thereunder, to elect to capitalize or to deduct a given item.

(c) **Election to charge taxes and carrying charges to capital account.** (1) If for any taxable year there are two or more items of the type described in paragraph (b) (1) of this section, which relate to the same project to which the election is applicable, the taxpayer may elect to capitalize any one or more of such items even though he does not elect to capitalize the remaining items or to capitalize items of the same type relating to other projects. However, if expenditures for several items of the same type are incurred with respect to a single project, the election to capitalize must, if exercised, be exercised as to all items of that type. For purposes of this section, a "project" means, in the case of items described in paragraph (b) (1) (ii) of this section, a particular development of, or construction of an improvement to, real property, and in the case of items described in paragraph (b) (1) (iii) of this section, the transportation and installation of machinery or other fixed assets.

(2) (i) An election with respect to an item described in paragraph (b) (1) (i) of this section is effective only for the year for which it is made.

(ii) An election with respect to an item described in—

(a) Paragraph (b) (1) (ii) of this section is effective until the development or construction work described in that subdivision has been completed;

(b) Paragraph (b) (1) (iii) of this section is effective until the later of either the date of installation of the property described in that subdivision, or the date when such property is first put into use by the taxpayer;

(c) Paragraph (b) (1) (iv) of this section is effective as determined by the Commissioner.

Thus, an item chargeable to capital account under this section must continue to be capitalized for the entire period described in this subdivision applicable to such election although such period may consist of more than one taxable year.

(3) If the taxpayer elects to capitalize an item or items under this section, such election shall be exercised by filing with the original return for the year for which the election is made a statement indicating the item or items (whether with respect to the same project or to different projects) which the taxpayer elects to treat as chargeable to capital account. . . . .

(d) The following examples are illustrative of the application of the provisions of this section:

Example (1). In 1956 and 1957 A pays annual taxes and interest on a mortgage on a piece of real property. During 1956, the property is vacant and unproductive, but throughout 1957 A operates the property as a parking lot. A may capitalize the taxes and mortgage interest paid in 1956, but not the taxes and mortgage interest paid in 1957.

Example (2). In February 1957, B began the erection of an office building for himself. B in 1957, in connection with the erection of the building, paid $6,000 social security taxes, which in his 1957 return he elected to capitalize. B must continue to capitalize the social security taxes paid in connection with the erection of the building until its completion.

Example (3). Assume the same facts as in example (2) except that in November 1957, B also begins to build a hotel. In 1957 B pays $3,000 social security taxes in connection with the erection of the hotel. B's election to capitalize the social security taxes paid in erecting the office building started in February 1957 does not bind him to capitalize the social security taxes paid in erecting the hotel; he may deduct the $3,000 social security taxes paid in erecting the hotel.

Example (4). In 1957, M Corporation began the erection of a building for itself, which will take three years to complete. M Corporation in 1957 paid $4,000 social security taxes and $8,000 interest on a building loan in connection with this building. M Corporation may elect to capitalize the social security taxes although it deducts the interest charges.

Example (5). C purchases machinery in 1957 for use in his factory. He pays social security taxes on the labor for transportation and installation of the machinery, as well as interest on a loan to obtain funds to pay for the machinery and for transportation and installation costs. C may capitalize either the social security taxes or the interest, or both, up to the date of installation or until the machinery is first put into use by him, whichever date is later.

(e) Allocation. If any tax or carrying charge with respect to property is in part a type of item described in paragraph (b) of this section and in part a type of item or items with respect to which no election to treat as a capital item is given, a reasonable proportion of such tax or carrying charge, determined in the light of all the facts and circumstances in each case, shall be allocated to each item. The rule of this paragraph may be illustrated by the following example:

Example. N Corporation, the owner of a factory in New York on which a new addition is under construction, in 1957 pays its general manager, B, a salary of $10,000 and also pays a New York State unemployment insurance tax of $81 on B's salary. B spends nine-tenths of his time in the general business of the firm and the remaining one-tenth in supervising the construction work. N Corporation treats as expenses $9,000 of B's salary, and charges the remaining $1,000 to capital account. N Corporation may elect to capitalize $8.10 of the $81 New York State unemployment insurance tax paid in 1957 since such tax is deductible under section 164.

§ 1.267(a)-1 Deductions disallowed

(a) Losses. Except in cases of distributions in corporate liquidations,

no deduction shall be allowed for losses arising from direct or indirect sales or exchanges of property between persons who, on the date of the sale or exchange, are within any one of the relationships specified in section 267(b). See § 1.267(b)-1.

(b) Unpaid expenses and interest. (1) No deduction shall be allowed a taxpayer for trade or business expenses otherwise deductible under section 162, for expenses for production of income otherwise deductible under section 212, or for interest otherwise deductible under section 163—

(i) If, at the close of the taxpayer's taxable year within which such items are accrued by the taxpayer or at any time within 2½ months thereafter, both the taxpayer and the payee are persons within any one of the relationships specified in section 267(b) (see § 1.267(b)-1); and

(ii) If the payee is on the cash receipts and disbursements method of accounting with respect to such items of gross income for his taxable year in which or with which the taxable year of accrual by the debtor-taxpayer ends; and

(iii) If, within the taxpayer's taxable year within which such items are accrued by the taxpayer and 2½ months after the close thereof, the amount of such items is not paid and the amount of such items is not otherwise (under the rules of constructive receipt) includible in the gross income of the payee.

(2) The provisions of section 267(a) (2) and this paragraph do not otherwise affect the general rules governing the allowance of deductions under an accrual method of accounting. For example, if the accrued expenses or interest are paid after the deduction has become disallowed under section 267(a) (2), no deduction would be allowable for the taxable year in which payment is made, since an accrual item is deductible only in the taxable year in which it is properly accruable.

(3) The expenses and interest specified in section 267(a) (2) and this paragraph shall be considered as paid for purposes of that section to the extent of the fair market value on the date of issue of notes or other instruments of similar effect received in payment of such expenses or interest if such notes or other instruments were issued in

such payment by the taxpayer within his taxable year or within 2½ months after the close thereof. The fair market value on the date of issue of such notes or other instruments of similar effect is includible in the gross income of the payee for the taxable year in which he receives the notes or other instruments.

(4) The provisions of this paragraph may be illustrated by the following example:

Example. A, an individual, is the holder and owner of an interest-bearing note of the M Corporation, all the stock of which was owned by him on December 31, 1956. A and the M Corporation make their income tax returns for a calendar year. The M Corporation uses an accrual method of accounting. A uses a combination of accounting methods permitted under section 446(c) (4) in which he uses the cash receipts and disbursements method in respect of items of gross income. The M Corporation does not pay any interest on the note to A during the calendar year 1956 or within 2½ months after the close of that year, nor does it credit any interest to A's account in such a manner that it is subject to his unqualified demand and thus is constructively received by him. M Corporation claims a deduction for the year 1956 for the interest accruing on the note in that year. Since A is on the cash receipts and disbursements method in respect of items of gross income, the interest is not includible in his return for the year 1956. Under the provisions of section 267(a) (2) and this paragraph, no deduction for such interest is allowable in computing the taxable income of the M Corporation for the taxable year 1956 or for any other taxable year. However, if the interest had actually been paid to A on or before March 15, 1957, or if it had been made available to A before that time (and thus had been constructively received by him), the M Corporation would be allowed to deduct the amount of the payment in computing its taxable income for 1956.

(c) **Scope of section.** Section 267 (a) requires that deductions for losses or unpaid expenses or interest described therein be disallowed even though the transaction in which such losses, expenses, or interest were incurred was a bona fide transaction. However, section 267 is not exclusive. No deduction for losses or unpaid expenses or interest arising in a transaction which is not bona fide will be allowed even though section 267 does not apply to the transaction.

§ 1.267(b)–1 Relationships

(a) **In general.** (1) The persons referred to in section 267(a) and § 1.-267(a)–1 are specified in section 267(b).

(2) Under section 267(b) (3), it is not necessary that either of the two corporations be a personal holding company or a foreign personal holding company for the taxable year in which the sale or exchange occurs or in which the expenses or interest are properly accruable, but either one of them must be such a company for the taxable year next preceding the taxable year in which the sale or exchange occurs or in which the expenses or interest are accrued.

(3) Under section 267(b) (9), the control of certain educational and charitable organizations exempt from tax under section 501 includes any kind of control, direct or indirect, by means of which a person in fact controls such an organization, whether or not the control is legally enforceable and regardless of the method by which the control is exercised or exercisable. In the case of an individual, control possessed by the individual's family, as defined in section 267(c) (4) and paragraph (a) (4) of § 1.267(c)–1, shall be taken into account.

(b) **Partnerships.** (1) Since section 267 does not include members of a partnership and the partnership as related persons, transactions between partners and partnerships do not come within the scope of section 267. Such transactions are governed by section 707 for the purposes of which the partnership is considered to be an entity separate from the partners. See section 707 and § 1.707–1. Any transaction described in section 267(a) between a partnership and a person other than a partner shall be considered as occurring between the other person and the members of the partnership separately. Therefore, if the other person and a partner are within any one of the relationships specified in section 267(b), no deductions with respect to such transactions between the other person and the partnership shall be allowed—

(i) To the related partner to the extent of his distributive share of partnership deductions for losses or unpaid expenses or interest resulting from such transactions, and

(ii) To the other person to the extent the related partner acquires an interest in any property sold to or exchanged with the partnership by such other person at a loss, or to the extent of the related partner's distributive share of the unpaid expenses or interest payable to the partnership by the other person as a result of such transaction.

(2) The provisions of this paragraph may be illustrated by the following examples:

Example (1). A, an equal partner in the ABC partnership, personally owns all the stock of M Corporation. B and C are not related to A. The partnership and all the partners use an accrual method of accounting, and are on a calendar year. M Corporation uses the cash receipts and disbursements method of accounting and is also on a calendar year. During 1956 the partnership borrowed money from M Corporation and also sold property to M Corporation, sustaining a loss on the sale. On December 31, 1956, the partnership accrued its interest liability to the M Corporation and on April 1, 1957 (more than 2½ months after the close of its taxable year), it paid the M Corporation the amount of such accrued interest. Applying the rules of this paragraph, the transactions are considered as occurring between M Corporation and the partners separately. The sale and interest transactions considered as occurring between A and the M Corporation fall within the scope of section 267(a) and (b), but the transactions considered as occurring between partners B and C and the M Corporation do not. The latter two partners may, therefore, deduct their distributive shares of partnership deductions for the loss and the accrued interest. However, no deduction shall be allowed to A for his distributive shares of these partnership deductions. Furthermore, A's adjusted basis for his partnership interest must be decreased by the amount of his distributive share of such deductions. See section 705(a)(2).

Example (2). Assume the same facts as in example (1) of this subparagraph except that the partnership and all the partners use the cash receipts and disbursements method of accounting, and that M Corporation uses an accrual method. Assume further, that during 1956 M Corporation borrowed money from the partnership and that on a sale of property to the partnership during that year M Corporation sustained a loss. On December 31, 1956, the M Corporation accrued its interest liability on the borrowed money and on April 1, 1957 (more than 2½ months after the close of its taxable year) it paid the accrued interest to the partnership. The corporation's deduction for the accrued interest is not allowed to the extent of A's distributive share (one-third) of such interest income. M Corporation's deduction for the loss on the sale of the property to the partnership is not allowed to the extent of A's one-third interest in the purchased property.

§ 1.267(c)-1 Constructive ownership of stock

(a) In general. (1) The determination of stock ownership for purposes of section 267(b) shall be in accordance with the rules in section 267(c).

(2) For an individual to be considered under section 267(c)(2) as constructively owning the stock of a corporation which is owned, directly or indirectly, by or for members of his family it is not necessary that he own stock in the corporation either directly or indirectly. On the other hand, for an individual to be considered under section 267(c)(3) as owning the stock of a corporation owned either actually, or constructively under section 267(c)(1), by or for his partner, such individual must himself actually own, or constructively own under section 267(c)(1), stock of such corporation.

(3) An individual's constructive ownership, under section 267(c)(2) or (3), of stock owned directly or indirectly by or for a member of his family, or by or for his partner, is not to be considered as actual ownership of such stock, and the individual's constructive ownership of the stock is not to be attributed to another member of his family or to another partner. However, an individual's constructive ownership, under section 267(c)(1), of stock owned directly or indirectly by or for a corporation, partnership, estate, or trust shall be considered as actual ownership of the stock, and the individual's ownership may be attributed to a member of his family or to his partner.

(4) The family of an individual shall include only his brothers and sisters, spouse, ancestors, and lineal descendants. In determining whether any of these relationships exist, full effect shall be given to a legal adoption. The term "ancestors" includes parents and grandparents, and the term "lineal descendants" includes children and grandchildren.

(b) Examples. The application of section 267(c) may be illustrated by the following examples:

Example (1). On July 1, 1957, A owned 75 percent, and AW, his wife, owned 25 percent, of the outstanding stock of the M Corporation. The M Corporation in turn owned 80 percent of the outstanding stock of the O Corporation. Under section 267(c)(1), A and AW are each considered as owning an amount of the O Corporation stock actually owned by M Corporation in proportion to their respective ownership of M Corporation stock. Therefore, A constructively owns 60 percent (75 percent of 80 percent) of the O Corporation stock and AW constructively owns 20 percent (25 percent of 80 percent) of such stock. Under the family ownership rule of section 267(c)(2), an individual is considered as constructively owning the stock actually owned by his spouse. A and AW, therefore, are each considered as constructively owning the M Corporation stock actually owned by the other. For the purpose of applying this family ownership rule, A's and AW's constructive ownership of O Corporation stock is considered as actual ownership under section 267 (c) (5). Thus, A constructively owns the 20 percent of the O Corporation stock constructively owned by AW, and AW constructively owns the 60 percent of the O Corporation stock constructively owned by A. In addition, the family ownership rule may be applied to make AWF, AW's father, the constructive owner of the 25 percent of the M Corporation stock actually owned by AW. As noted above, AW's con-

structive ownership of 20 percent of the O Corporation stock is considered as actual ownership for purposes of applying the family ownership rule, and AWF is thereby considered the constructive owner of this stock also. However, AW's constructive ownership of the stock constructively and actually owned by A may not be considered as actual ownership for the purpose of again applying the family ownership rule to make AWF the constructive owner of these shares. The ownership of the stock in the M and O Corporations may be tabulated as follows:

Person	Stock ownership in M Corporation		Total under Section 267	Stock ownership in O Corporation		Total under Section 267
	Actual	Constructive		Actual	Constructive	
	Percent	*Percent*	*Percent*	*Percent*	*Percent*	*Percent*
A	75	25	100	None	60 / 20	80
AW (A's wife)	25	75	100	None	20 / 60	80
AWF (AW's father)	None	25	25	None	20	20
M Corporation				80	None	80
O Corporation	None	None	None			

Assuming that the M Corporation and the O Corporation make their income tax returns for calendar years, and that there was no distribution in liquidation of the M or O Corporation, and further assuming that either corporation was a personal holding company under section 542 for the calendar year 1956, no deduction is allowable with respect to losses from sales or exchanges of property made on July 1, 1957, between the two corporations. Moreover, whether or not either corporation was a personal holding company, no loss would be allowable on a sale or exchange between A or AW and either corporation. A deduction would be allowed, however, for a loss sustained in an arm's length sale or exchange between A and AWF, and between AWF and the M or O Corporation.

Example (2). On June 15, 1957, all of the stock of the N Corporation was owned in equal proportions by A and his partner, AP. Except in the case of distributions in liquidation by the N Corporation, no deduction is allowable with respect to losses from sales or exchanges of property made on June 15, 1957, between A and the N Corporation or AP and the N Corporation since each partner is considered as owning the stock owned by the other; therefore, each is considered as owning more than 50 percent in value of the outstanding stock of the N Corporation.

Example (3). On June 7, 1957, A owned no stock in X Corporation, but his wife, AW, owned 20 percent in value of the outstanding stock of X, and A's partner, AP, owned 60 percent in value of the outstanding stock of X. The partnership firm of A and AP owned no stock in X Corporation. The ownership of AW's stock is attributed to A, but not that of AP since A does not own any X Corporation stock either actually, or constructively under section 267(c) (1). A's constructive ownership of AW's stock is not the ownership required for the attribution of AP's stock. Therefore, deductions

for losses from sales or exchanges of property made on June 7, 1957, between X Corporation and A or AW are allowable since neither person owned more than 50 percent in value of the outstanding stock of X, but deductions for losses from sales or exchanges between X Corporation and AP would not be allowable by section 267(a) (except for distributions in liquidation of X Corporation).

§ 1.267(d)-1 Amount of gain where loss previously disallowed

(a) General rule. (1) If a taxpayer acquires property by purchase or exchange from a transferor who, on the transaction, sustained a loss not allowable as a deduction by reason of section 267(a) (1) (or by reason of section 24(b) of the Internal Revenue Code of 1939), then any gain realized by the taxpayer on a sale or other disposition of the property after December 31, 1953, shall be recognized only to the extent that the gain exceeds the amount of such loss as is properly allocable to the property sold or otherwise disposed of by the taxpayer.

(2) The general rule is also applicable to a sale or other disposition of property by a taxpayer when the basis of such property in the taxpayer's hands is determined directly or indirectly by reference to other property acquired by the taxpayer from a transferor through a sale or exchange in which a loss sustained by the transferor was not allowable. Therefore, section 267(d) applies to a sale or oth-

er disposition of property after a series of transactions if the basis of the property acquired in each transaction is determined by reference to the basis of the property transferred, and if the original property was acquired in a transaction in which a loss to a transferor was not allowable by reason of section 267(a) (1) . . . .

(3) The benefit of the general rule is available only to the original transferee but does not apply to any original transferee (e. g., a donee) who acquired the property in any manner other than by purchase or exchange.

(4) The application of the provisions of this paragraph may be illustrated by the following examples:

Example (1). H sells to his wife, W, for $500, certain corporate stock with an adjusted basis for determining loss to him of $800. The loss of $300 is not allowable to H by reason of section 267(a) (1) and paragraph (a) of § 1.267 (a)-1. W later sells this stock for $1,000. Although W's realized gain is $500 ($1,000 minus $500, her basis), her recognized gain under section 267(d) is only $200, the excess of the realized gain of $500 over the loss of $300 not allowable to H. In determining capital gain or loss W's holding period commences on the date of the sale from H to W.

Example (2). Assume the same facts as in example (1) except that W later sells her stock for $300 instead of $1,000. Her recognized loss is $200 and not $500 since section 267(d) applies only to the nonrecognition of gain and does not affect basis.

Example (3). Assume the same facts as in example (1) except that W transfers her stock as a gift to X. The basis of the stock in the hands of X for the purpose of determining gain, under the provisions of section 1015, is the same as W's, or $500. If X later sells the stock for $1,000 the entire $500 gain is taxed to him.

Example (4). H sells to his wife, W, for $5,500, farmland, with an adjusted basis for determining loss to him of $8,000. The loss of $2,500 is not allowable to H by reason of section 267(a) (1) and paragraph (a) of § 1.267 (a)-1. W exchanges the farmland, held for investment purposes, with S, an unrelated individual, for two city lots, also held for investment purposes. The basis of the city lots in the hands of W ($5,500) is a substituted basis determined under section 1031(d) by reference to the basis of the farmland. Later W sells the city lots for $10,000. Although W's realized gain is $4,500 ($10,000 minus $5,500), her recognized gain under section 267(d) is only $2,000, the excess of the realized gain of $4,500 over the loss of $2,500 not allowable to H.

(b) Determination of basis and gain with respect to divisible property—(1) Taxpayer's basis. When the taxpayer acquires divisible property or property that consists of several items or classes of items by a purchase or exchange on which loss is not allowable to the trans-

feror, the basis in the taxpayer's hands of a particular part, item, or class of such property shall be determined (if the taxpayer's basis for that part is not known) by allocating to the particular part, item, or class a portion of the taxpayer's basis for the entire property in the proportion that the fair market value of the particular part, item, or class bears to the fair market value of the entire property at the time of the taxpayer's acquisition of the property.

(2) Taxpayer's recognized gain. Gain realized by the taxpayer on sales or other dispositions after December 31, 1953, of a part, item, or class of the property shall be recognized only to the extent that such gain exceeds the amount of loss attributable to such part, item, or class of property not allowable to the taxpayer's transferor on the latter's sale or exchange of such property to the taxpayer.

(3) Transferor's loss not allowable. (i) The transferor's loss on the sale or exchange of a part, item, or class of the property to the taxpayer shall be the excess of the transferor's adjusted basis for determining loss on the part, item, or class of the property over the amount realized by the transferor on the sale or exchange of the part, item, or class. The amount realized by the transferor on the part, item, or class shall be determined (if such amount is not known) in the same manner that the taxpayer's basis for such part, item, or class is determined. See subparagraph (1) of this paragraph.

(ii) If the transferor's basis for determining loss on the part, item, or class cannot be determined, the transferor's loss on the particular part, item, or class transferred to the taxpayer shall be determined by allocating to the part, item, or class a portion of his loss on the entire property in the proportion that the fair market value of such part, item, or class bears to the fair market value of the entire property on the date of the taxpayer's acquisition of the entire property.

(4) Examples. The application of the provisions of this paragraph may be illustrated by the following examples:

Example (1). During 1953, H sold class A stock which had cost him $1,100, and common stock which had cost him $2,000, to his wife W for a lump sum of $1,500. Under section 24 (b) (1) (A) of the 1939 Code, the loss of $1,600 on the transaction was not allowable to H. At the time the stocks were purchased by W, the fair market value of class A stock was $900 and the fair market value of common stock was $600. In 1954, W sold the class A stock for $2,500. W's recognized gain is determined as follows:

Amount realized by W on sale of class
A stock $2,500
Less: Basis allocated to class A stock—
$900/$1,500 × $1,500 900

Realized gain on transaction 1,600
Less: Loss sustained by H on sale
of class A stock to W not al-
lowable as a deduction:
Basis to H of class A stock $1,100
Amount realized by H on class
A stock—$900/$1,500 × $1,500 .. 900

Unallowable loss to H on sale
of class A stock 200

Recognized gain on sale of class
A stock by W 1,400

Example (2). Assume the same facts as those stated in example (1) of this subparagraph except that H originally purchased both classes of stock for a lump sum of $3,100. The unallowable loss to H on the sale of all the stock to W is $1,600 ($3,100 minus $1,500). An exact determination of the unallowable loss sustained by H on sale to W of class A stock cannot be made because H's basis for class A stock cannot be determined. Therefore, a determination of the unallowable loss is made by allocating to class A stock a portion of H's loss on the entire property transferred to W in the proportion that the fair market value of class A stock at the time acquired by W ($900) bears to the fair market value of both classes of stock at that time ($1,500). The allocated portion is $900/$1,500 × $1,600, or $960. W's recognized gain is, therefore, $640 (W's realized gain of $1,600 minus $960).

(c) Special rules. (1) Section 267 (d) does not affect the basis of property for determining gain. Depreciation and other items which depend on such basis are also not affected.

(2) The provisions of section 267(d) shall not apply if the loss sustained by the transferor is not allowable to the transferor as a deduction by reason of section 1091, or section 118 of the Internal Revenue Code of 1939, which relate to losses from wash sales of stock or securities.

(3) In determining the holding period in the hands of the transferee of property received in an exchange with a transferor with respect to whom a loss on the exchange is not allowable by reason of section 267, section 1223 (2) does not apply to include the period during which the property was held by the transferor. In determining such holding period, however, section 1223 (1) may apply to include the period during which the transferee held the property which he exchanged where, for example, he exchanged a capital asset in a transaction which, as to him, was nontaxable under section 1031 and the property received in the exchange has the same basis as the property exchanged.

§ 1.269–1 Meaning and use of terms

As used in section 269 and §§ 1.269–2 through 1.269–6—

(a) Allowance. The term "allowance" refers to anything in the internal revenue laws which has the effect of diminishing tax liability. The term includes, among other things, a deduction, a credit, an adjustment, an exemption, or an exclusion.

(b) Evasion or avoidance. The phrase "evasion or avoidance" is not limited to cases involving criminal penalties, or civil penalties for fraud.

(c) Control. The term "control" means the ownership of stock possessing at least 50 percent of the total combined voting power of all classes of stock entitled to vote, or at least 50 percent of the total value of shares of all classes of stock of the corporation. For control to be "acquired on or after October 8, 1940", it is not necessary that all of such stock be acquired on or after October 8, 1940. Thus, if A, on October 7, 1940, and at all times thereafter, owns 40 percent of the stock of X Corporation and acquires on October 8, 1940, an additional 10 percent of such stock, an acquisition within the meaning of such phrase is made by A on October 8, 1940. Similarly, if B, on October 7, 1940, owns certain assets and transfers on October 8, 1940, such assets to a newly organized Y Corporation in exchange for all the stock of Y Corporation, an acquisition within the meaning of such phrase is made by B on October 8, 1940. If, under the facts stated in the preceding sentence, B is a corporation, all of whose stock is owned by Z Corporation, then an acquisition within the meaning of such phrase is also made by Z Corporation on October 8, 1940, as well as by the shareholders of Z Corporation taken as a group on such date, and by any of such shareholders if such shareholders as a group own 50 percent of the stock of Z on such date.

(d) Person. The term "person" includes an individual, a trust, an estate, a partnership, an association, a company, or a corporation.

§ 1.269-2 Purpose and scope of section 269

(a) General. Section 269 is designed to prevent in the instances specified therein the use of sections of the Internal Revenue Code providing deductions, credits, or allowances in evading or avoiding Federal income tax. See § 1.269-3.

(b) Disallowance of deduction, credit, or other allowance. Under the Code, an amount otherwise constituting a deduction, credit, or other allowance becomes unavailable as such under certain circumstances. Characteristic of such circumstances are those in which the effect of the deduction, credit, or other allowance would be to distort the liability of the particular taxpayer when the essential nature of the transaction or situation is examined in the light of the basic purpose or plan which the deduction, credit, or other allowance was designed by the Congress to effectuate. The distortion may be evidenced, for example, by the fact that the transaction was not undertaken for reasons germane to the conduct of the business of the taxpayer, by the unreal nature of the transaction such as its sham character, or by the unreal or unreasonable relation which the deduction, credit, or other allowance bears to the transaction. The principle of law making an amount unavailable as a deduction, credit, or other allowance in cases in which the effect of making an amount so available would be to distort the liability of the taxpayer, has been judicially recognized and applied in several cases. Included in these cases are Gregory v. Helvering (1935) (293 U.S. 465; Ct.D. 911, C.B. XIV-1, 193); Griffiths v. Helvering (1939) (308 U.S. 355; Ct.D. 1431, C.B. 1940-1, 136); Higgins v. Smith (1940) (308 U.S. 473; Ct. D. 1434, C.B. 1940-1, 127); and J. D. & A. B. Spreckles Co. v. Commissioner (1940) (41 B.T.A. 370). In order to give effect to such principle, but not in limitation thereof, several provisions of the Code, for example, section 267 and section 270, specify with some particu-larity instances in which disallowance of the deduction, credit, or other allowance is required. Section 269 is also included in such provisions of the Code. The principal of law and the particular sections of the Code are not mutually exclusive and in appropriate circumstances they may operate together or they may operate separately. See, for example, § 1.269-6.

§ 1.269-3 Instances in which section 269(a) disallows a deduction, credit, or other allowance

(a) Instances of disallowance. Section 269 specifies two instances in which a deduction, credit, or other allowance is to be disallowed. These instances, described in paragraphs (1) and (2) of section 269(a), are those in which—

(1) Any person or persons acquire, or acquired on or after October 8, 1940, directly or indirectly, control of a corporation, or

(2) Any corporation acquires, or acquired on or after October 8, 1940, directly or indirectly, property of another corporation (not controlled, directly or indirectly, immediately before such acquisition by such acquiring corporation or its stockholders), the basis of which property in the hands of the acquiring corporation is determined by reference to the basis in the hands of the transferor corporation.

In either instance the principal purpose for which the acquisition was made must have been the evasion or avoidance of Federal income tax by securing the benefit of a deduction, credit, or other allowance which such other person, or persons, or corporation, would not otherwise enjoy. If this requirement is satisfied, it is immaterial by what method or by what conjunction of events the benefit was sought. Thus, an acquiring person or corporation can secure the benefit of a deduction, credit, or other allowance within the meaning of section 269 even though it is the acquired corporation that is entitled to such deduction, credit, or other allowance in the determination of its tax. If the purpose to evade or avoid Federal income tax exceeds in importance any other purpose, it is the principal purpose. This does not mean that only those acquisitions fall within the provisions of section 269 which would not have been made if the evasion or avoidance purpose was not present. The determination of the purpose for which an acquisition was made requires a scrutiny of the entire circumstances in which the transaction or course of conduct occured, in connection with the tax result claimed to arise therefrom.

.   .   .   .   .

(b) Acquisition of control; transactions indicative of purpose to evade or avoid tax. If the requisite acquisition of control within the meaning of paragraph (1) of section 269(a) exists, the transactions set forth in the following subparagraphs are among those which, in the absence of additional evidence to the contrary, ordinarily are indicative that the principal purpose for acquiring control was evasion or avoidance of Federal income tax:

(1) A corporation or other business enterprise (or the interest controlling such corporation or enterprise) with large profits acquires control of a corporation with current, past, or prospective credits, deductions, net operating losses, or other allowances and the acquisition is followed by such transfers or other action as is necessary to bring the deduction, credit, or other allowance into conjunction with the income (see further § 1.269–6). This subparagraph may be illustrated by the following example:

Example. Individual A acquires all of the stock of L Corporation which has been engaged in the business of operating retail drug stores. At the time of the acquisition, L Corporation has net operating loss carryovers aggregating $100,000 and its net worth is $100,000. After the acquisition, L Corporation continues to engage in the business of operating retail drug stores but the profits attributable to such business after the acquisition are not sufficient to absorb any substantial portion of the net operating loss carryovers. Shortly after the acquisition, individual A causes to be transferred to L Corporation the assets of a hardware business previously controlled by A which business produces profits sufficient to absorb a substantial portion of L Corporation's net operating loss carryovers. The transfer of the profitable business, which has the effect of using net operating loss carryovers to offset gains of a business unrelated to that which produced the losses, indicates that the principal purpose for which the acquisition of control was made is evasion or avoidance of Federal income tax.

(2) A person or persons organize two or more corporations instead of a single corporation in order to secure the benefit of multiple surtax exemptions (see section 11(c)) or multiple minimum ac-

cumulated earnings credits (see section 535(c) (2) and (3)).

(3) A person or persons with high earning assets transfer them to a newly organized controlled corporation retaining assets producing net operating losses which are utilized in an attempt to secure refunds.

(c) Acquisition of property; transactions indicative of purpose to evade or avoid tax. If the requisite acquisition of property within the meaning of paragraph (2) of section 269(a) exists, the transactions set forth in the following subparagraphs are among those which, in the absence of additional evidence to the contrary, ordinarily are indicative that the principal purpose for acquiring such property was evasion or avoidance of Federal income tax:

(1) A corporation acquires property having in its hands an aggregate carryover basis which is materially greater than its aggregate fair market value at the time of such acquisition and utilizes the property to create tax-reducing losses or deductions.

(2) A subsidiary corporation, which has sustained large net operating losses in the operation of business X and which has filed separate returns for the taxable years in which the losses were sustained, acquires high earning assets, comprising business Y, from its parent corporation. The acquisition occurs at a time when the parent would not succeed to the net operating loss carryovers of the subsidiary if the subsidiary were liquidated, and the profits of business Y are sufficient to offset a substantial portion of the net operating loss carryovers attributable to business X (see further example (3) of § 1.269–6).

§ 1.274–1 Disallowance of certain entertainment, gift and travel expenses

Section 274 disallows in whole, or in part, certain expenditures for entertainment, gifts and travel which would otherwise be allowable under chapter 1 of the Code. The requirements imposed by section 274 are in addition to the requirements for deductibility imposed by other provisions of the Code. If a deduction is claimed for an expenditure for entertainment, gifts, or travel, the taxpayer must first establish that it is otherwise allowable as a deduction under chapter 1 of the Code before the provisions of section 274 become applicable. An expenditure for entertainment, to the extent it is lavish or extravagant, shall not be allowable as a deduction. The taxpayer should then substantiate such an expenditure in accordance with the rules under section 274(d). See § 1.274-5. Section 274 is a disallowance provision exclusively, and does not make deductible any expense which is disallowed under any other provision of the Code. Similarly, section 274 does not affect the includability of an item in, or the excludability of an item from, the gross income of any taxpayer.

. . . .

§ 1.274-2 Disallowance of deductions for certain expenses for entertainment, amusement, or recreation

(a) General rules—(1) Entertainment activity. Except as provided in this section, no deduction otherwise allowable under chapter 1 of the Code shall be allowed for any expenditure with respect to entertainment unless the taxpayer establishes—

(i) That the expenditure was directly related to the active conduct of the taxpayer's trade or business, or

(ii) In the case of an expenditure directly preceding or following a substantial and bona fide business discussion (including business meetings at a convention or otherwise), that the expenditure was associated with the active conduct of the taxpayer's trade or business. Such deduction shall not exceed the portion of the expenditure directly related to (or in the case of an expenditure described in subdivision (ii) of this subparagraph, the portion of the expenditure associated with) the active conduct of the taxpayer's trade or business.

. . . .

(b) Definitions—(1) Entertainment defined—(i) In general. For purposes of this section, the term "entertainment" means any activity which is of a type generally considered to constitute entertainment, amusement, or recreation, such as entertaining at night clubs, cocktail lounges, theaters, country clubs, golf and athletic clubs, sporting events, and on hunting, fishing, vacation and similar trips, including such activity relating solely to the taxpayer or the taxpayer's family. The term "entertainment" may include an activity, the cost of which is claimed as a business expense by the taxpayer, which satisfies the personal, living, or family needs of any individual, such as providing, food and beverages, a hotel suite, or an automobile to a business customer or his family. The term "entertainment" does not include activities which, although satisfying personal, living, or family needs of an individual, are clearly not regarded as constituting entertainment, such as (a) supper money provided by an employer to his employee working overtime, (b) a hotel room maintained by an employer for lodging of his employees while in business travel status, or (c) an automobile used in the active conduct of trade or business even though used for routine personal purposes such as commuting to and from work. On the other hand, the providing of a hotel room or an automobile by an employer to his employee who is on vacation would constitute entertainment of the employee.

(ii) Objective test. An objective test shall be used to determine whether an activity is of a type generally considered to constitute entertainment. Thus, if an activity is generally considered to be entertainment, it will constitute entertainment for purposes of this section and section 274(a) regardless of whether the expenditure can also be described otherwise, and even though the expenditure relates to the taxpayer alone. This objective test precludes arguments such as that "entertainment" means only entertainment of others or that an expenditure for entertainment should be characterized as an expenditure for advertising or public relations. However, in applying this test the taxpayer's trade or business shall be considered. Thus, although attending a theatrical performance would generally be considered entertainment, it would not be so considered in the case of a professional theater critic, attending in his professional capacity. Similarly, if a manufacturer of dresses conducts a fashion show to introduce his products to a group of store buyers, the show would not be generally considered to constitute entertainment. However, if an appliance distributor conducts a fashion show for the wives of his retailers, the fashion show would be generally considered to constitute entertainment.

(iii) Special definitional rules—(a) In general. Except as otherwise provided in (b) or (c) of this subdivision, any expenditure which might generally be considered either for a gift or entertainment, or considered either for travel or entertainment, shall be considered an expenditure for entertainment rather than for a gift or travel.

(b) Expenditures deemed gifts. An expenditure described in (a) of this subdivision shall be deemed for a gift to which this section does not apply if it is:

(1) An expenditure for packaged food or beverages transferred directly or indirectly to another person intended for consumption at a later time.

(2) An expenditure for tickets of admission to a place of entertainment transferred to another person if the taxpayer does not accompany the recipient to the entertainment unless the taxpayer treats the expenditure as entertainment. The taxpayer may change his treatment of such an expenditure as either a gift or entertainment at any time within the period prescribed for assessment of tax as provided in section 6501 of the Code and the regulations thereunder.

(3) Such other specific classes of expenditure generally considered to be for a gift as the Commissioner, in his discretion, may prescribe.

(c) Expenditures deemed travel. An expenditure described in (a) of this subdivision shall be deemed for travel to which this section does not apply if it is:

(1) With respect to a transportation type facility (such as an automobile or an airplane), even though used on other occasions in connection with an activity of a type generally considered to constitute entertainment, to the extent the facility is used in pursuit of a trade or business for purposes of transportation not in connection with entertainment.

See also paragraph (e) (3) (iii) (b) of this section for provisions covering non-entertainment expenditures with respect to such facilities.

(2) Such other specific classes of expenditure generally considered to be for travel as the Commissioner, in his discretion, may prescribe.

(2) Other definitions—(i) Expenditure. The term "expenditure" as used in this section shall include expenses paid or incurred for goods, services, facilities, and items (including items such as losses and depreciation).

(ii) Expenses for production of income. For purposes of this section, any reference to "trade or business" shall include any activity described in section 212.

(iii) Business associate. The term "business associate" as used in this section means a person with whom the taxpayer could reasonably expect to engage or deal in the active conduct of the taxpayer's trade or business such as the taxpayer's customer, client, supplier, employee, agent, partner, or professional adviser, whether established or prospective.

(c) Directly related entertainment— (1) In general. Except as otherwise provided in paragraph (d) of this section (relating to associated entertainment) or under paragraph (f) of this section (relating to business meals and other specific exceptions), no deduction shall be allowed for any expenditure for entertainment unless the taxpayer establishes that the expenditure was directly related to the active conduct of his trade or business within the meaning of this paragraph.

(2) Directly related entertainment defined. Any expenditure for entertainment, if it is otherwise allowable as a deduction under chapter 1 of the Code, shall be considered directly related to the active conduct of the taxpayer's trade or business if it meets the requirements of any one of subparagraphs (3), (4), (5), or (6) of this paragraph.

(3) Directly related in general. Except as provided in subparagraph (7) of this paragraph, an expenditure for entertainment shall be considered directly related to the active conduct of the taxpayer's trade or business if it is established that it meets all of the requirements of subdivisions (i), (ii), (iii) and (iv) of this subparagraph.

(i) At the time the taxpayer made the entertainment expenditure (or committed himself to make the expenditure), the taxpayer had more than a general expectation of deriving some income or other specific trade or business benefit (other than the goodwill of the person or persons entertained) at some indefinite future time from the making of the expenditure. A taxpayer, however, shall not be required to show that income or other business benefit actually resulted from each and every expenditure for which a deduction is claimed.

(ii) During the entertainment period to which the expenditure related, the taxpayer actively engaged in a business meeting, negotiation, discussion, or other bona fide business transaction, other than entertainment, for the purpose of obtaining such income or other specific trade or business benefit (or, at the time the taxpayer made the expenditure or committed himself to the expenditure, it was reasonable for the taxpayer to expect that he would have done so, although such was not the case solely for reasons beyond the taxpayer's control).

(iii) In light of all the facts and circumstances of the case, the principal character or aspect of the combined business and entertainment to which the expenditure related was the active conduct of the taxpayer's trade or business (or at the time the taxpayer made the expenditure or committed himself to the expenditure, it was reasonable for the taxpayer to expect that the active conduct of trade or business would have been the principal character or aspect of the entertainment, although such was not the case solely for reasons beyond the taxpayer's control). It is not necessary that more time be devoted to business than to entertainment to meet this requirement. The active conduct of trade or business is considered not to be the principal character or aspect of combined business and entertainment activity on hunting or fishing trips or on yachts and other pleasure boats unless the taxpayer clearly establishes to the contrary.

(iv) The expenditure was allocable to the taxpayer and a person or persons with whom the taxpayer engaged in the active conduct of trade or business during the entertainment or with whom the taxpayer establishes he would have engaged in such active conduct of trade or business if it were not for circumstances beyond the taxpayer's control. For expenditures closely connected with directly related entertainment, see paragraph (d) (4) of this section.

(4) **Expenditures in clear business setting.** An expenditure for entertainment shall be considered directly related to the active conduct of the taxpayer's trade or business if it is established that the expenditure was for entertainment occurring in a clear business setting directly in furtherance of the taxpayer's trade or business. Generally, entertainment shall not be considered to have occurred in a clear business setting unless the taxpayer clearly establishes that any recipient of the entertainment would have reasonably known that the taxpayer had no significant motive, in incurring the expenditure, other than directly furthering his trade or business. Objective rather than subjective standards will be determinative. Thus, entertainment which occurred under any circumstances described in subparagraph (7) (ii) of this paragraph ordinarily will not be considered as occurring in a clear business setting. Such entertainment will generally be considered to be socially rather than commercially motivated. Expenditures made for the furtherance of a taxpayer's trade or business in providing a "hospitality room" at a convention (described in paragraph (d) (3) (i) (b) of this section) at which goodwill is created through display or discussion of the taxpayer's products, will, however, be treated as directly related. In addition, entertainment of a clear business nature which occurred under circumstances where there was no meaningful personal or social relationship between the taxpayer and the recipients of the entertainment may be considered to have occurred in a clear business setting. For example, entertainment of business representatives and civic leaders at the opening of a new hotel or theatrical production, where the clear purpose of the taxpayer is to obtain business publicity rather than to create

or maintain the goodwill of the recipients of the entertainment, would generally be considered to be in a clear business setting. Also, entertainment which has the principal effect of a price rebate in connection with the sale of the taxpayer's products generally will be considered to have occurred in a clear business setting. Such would be the case, for example, if a taxpayer owning a hotel were to provide occasional free dinners at the hotel for a customer who patronized the hotel.

(5) **Expenditures for services performed.** An expenditure shall be considered directly related to the active conduct of the taxpayer's trade or business if it is established that the expenditure was made directly or indirectly by the taxpayer for the benefit of an individual (other than an employee), and if such expenditure was in the nature of compensation for services rendered or was paid as a prize or award which is required to be included in gross income under section 74 and the regulations thereunder. For example, if a manufacturer of products provides a vacation trip for retailers of his products who exceed sales quotas as a prize or award which is includible in gross income, the expenditure will be considered directly related to the active conduct of the taxpayer's trade or business.

. . . .

(7) **Expenditures generally considered not directly related.** Expenditures for entertainment, even if connected with the taxpayer's trade or business, will generally be considered not directly related to the active conduct of the taxpayer's trade or business, if the entertainment occurred under circumstances where there was little or no possibility of engaging in the active conduct of trade or business. The following circumstances will generally be considered circumstances where there was little or no possibility of engaging in the active conduct of a trade or business:

(i) The taxpayer was not present;
(ii) The distractions were substantial, such as—

(a) A meeting or discussion at night clubs, theaters, and sporting events, or during essentially social gatherings such as cocktail parties, or

(b) A meeting or discussion, if the taxpayer meets with a group which includes persons other than business associates, at places such as cocktail lounges, country clubs, golf and athletic clubs, or at vacation resorts.

An expenditure for entertainment in any such case is considered not to be directly related to the active conduct of the taxpayer's trade or business unless the taxpayer clearly establishes to the contrary.

(d) **Associated entertainment—(1) In general.** Except as provided in paragraph (f) of this section (relating to business meals and other specific exceptions) and subparagraph (4) of this paragraph (relating to expenditures closely connected with directly related entertainment), any expenditure for entertainment which is not directly related to the active conduct of the taxpayer's trade or business will not be allowable as a deduction unless—

(i) It was associated with the active conduct of trade or business as defined in subparagraph (2) of this paragraph, and

(ii) The entertainment directly preceded or followed a substantial and bona fide business discussion as defined in subparagraph (3) of this paragraph.

(2) **Associated entertainment defined.** Generally, any expenditure for entertainment, if it is otherwise allowable under chapter 1 of the Code, shall be considered associated with the active conduct of the taxpayer's trade or business if the taxpayer establishes that he had a clear business purpose in making the expenditure, such as to obtain new business or to encourage the continuation of an existing business relationship. However, any portion of an expenditure allocable to a person who was not closely connected with a person who engaged in the substantial and bona fide business discussion (as defined in subparagraph (3) (i) of this paragraph) shall not be considered associated with the active conduct of the taxpayer's trade or business. The por-

tion of an expenditure allocable to the spouse of a person who engaged in the discussion will, if it is otherwise allowable under chapter 1 of the Code, be considered associated with the active conduct of the taxpayer's trade or business.

(3) Directly preceding or following a substantial and bona fide business discussion defined—(i) Substantial and bona fide business discussion—(a) In general. Whether any meeting, negotiation or discussion constitutes a "substantial and bona fide business discussion" within the meaning of this section depends upon the facts and circumstances of each case. It must be established, however, that the taxpayer actively engaged in a business meeting, negotiation, discussion or other bona fide business transaction, other than entertainment, for the purpose of obtaining income or other specific trade or business benefit. In addition, it must be established that such a business meeting, negotiation, discussion, or transaction was substantial in relation to the entertainment. This requirement will be satisfied if the principal character or aspect of the combined entertainment and business activity was the active conduct of business. However, it is not necessary that more time be devoted to business than to entertainment to meet this requirement

(b) Meetings at conventions, etc. Any meeting officially scheduled in connection with a program at a convention or similar general assembly, or at a bona fide trade or business meeting sponsored and conducted by business or professional organizations, shall be considered to constitute a substantial and bona fide business discussion within the meaning of this section provided—

(1) Expenses necessary to taxpayer's attendance. The expenses necessary to the attendance of the taxpayer at the convention, general assembly, or trade or business meeting, were ordinary and necessary within the meaning of section 162 or 212;

(2) Convention program. The organization which sponsored the convention, or trade or business meeting had scheduled a program of business activities (including committee meetings or presentation of lectures, panel discussions, display of products, or other similar activities), and that such program was the principal activity of the convention, general assembly, or trade or business meeting.

(ii) Directly preceding or following. Entertainment which occurs on the same day as a substantial and bona fide business discussion (as defined in subdivision (i) of this subparagraph) will be considered to directly precede or follow such discussion. If the entertainment and the business discussion do not occur on the same day, the facts and circumstances of each case are to be considered, including the place, date and duration of the business discussion, whether the taxpayer or his business associates are from out of town, and, if so, the date of arrival and departure, and the reasons the entertainment did not take place on the day of the business discussion. For example, if a group of business associates comes from out of town to the taxpayer's place of business to hold a substantial business discussion, the entertainment of such business guests and their wives on the evening prior to, or on the evening of the day following, the business discussion would generally be regarded as directly preceding or following such discussion.

(4) Expenses closely connected with directly related entertainment. If any portion of an expenditure meets the requirements of paragraph (c) (3) of this section (relating to directly related entertainment in general), the remaining portion of the expenditure, if it is otherwise allowable under chapter 1 of the Code, shall be considered associated with the active conduct of the taxpayer's trade or business to the extent allocable to a person or persons closely connected with a person referred to in paragraph (c) (3) (iv) of this section. The spouse of a person referred to in paragraph (c) (3) (iv) of this section will be considered closely connected to such a person for purposes of this subparagraph. Thus, if a taxpayer and his wife entertain a business customer and the customer's wife under circumstances where the entertainment of the customer is considered directly related to the active conduct of the taxpayer's trade or business (within the meaning of paragraph (c) (3) of this section) the portion of the expenditure allocable to both wives will be considered associated with the active conduct of the taxpayer's trade or business under this subparagraph.

.   .   .   .

§ 1.274–3 Disallowance of deduction for gifts

(a) **In general.** No deduction shall be allowed under section 162 or 212 for any expense for a gift made directly or indirectly by a taxpayer to any individual to the extent that such expense, when added to prior expenses of the taxpayer for gifts made to such individual during the taxpayer's taxable year, exceeds $25.

(b) **Gift defined—(1) In general.** Except as provided in subparagraph (2) of this paragraph the term "gift", for purposes of this section, means any item excludable from the gross income of the recipient under section 102 which is not excludable from his gross income under any other provision of chapter 1 of the Code. Thus, a payment by an employer to a deceased employee's widow is not a gift, for purposes of this section, to the extent that payment constitutes an employee's death benefit excludable by the recipient under section 101(b). Similarly, a scholarship which is excludable from a recipient's gross income under section 117, and a prize or award which is excludable from a recipient's gross income under section 74(b), are not subject to the provisions of this section.

(2) **Items not treated as gifts.** The term "gift", for purposes of this section, does not include the following:

(i) An item having a cost to the taxpayer not in excess of $4.00 on which the name of the taxpayer is clearly and permanently imprinted and which is one of a number of identical items distributed generally by such a taxpayer.

(ii) A sign, display rack, or other promotional material to be used on the business premises of the recipient, or

(iii) An item of tangible personal property having a cost to the taxpayer not in excess of $100 which is awarded to an employee by reason of length of service or for safety achievement.

The deductibility of the expense of any of the items described in this subparagraph is not governed by this section and the taxpayer need not take such items into account in determining whether the $25 limitation on gifts to any individual has been exceeded. The fact that such items are excepted from the applicability of this section has no effect in determining whether the value of such items is includible in the gross income of the recipient.

(c) **Expense for a gift.** For purposes of this section, the term "expense for a gift" means the cost of the gift to the taxpayer, other than incidental costs such as for customary engraving on jewelry, or for packaging, insurance, and mailing or other delivery. A related cost will be considered "incidental" only if it does not add substantial value to the gift. Although the cost of customary gift wrapping will be considered an incidental cost, the purchase of an ornamental basket for packaging fruit will not be considered an incidental cost of packaging if the basket has a value which is substantial in relation to the value of the fruit.

.   .   .   .

§ 1.274–5 Substantiation requirements

(a) **In general.** No deduction shall be allowed for any expenditure or item with respect to—

(1) Traveling away from home (including meals and lodging) deductible under section 162 or 212,

(2) Any activity which is of a type generally considered to constitute entertainment, amusement, or recreation, or with respect to a facility used in connection with such an activity, including the items specified in section 274(e), or

(3) Gifts defined in section 274, unless the taxpayer substantiates such expenditure as provided in paragraph

(c) of this section. This limitation supersedes with respect to any such expenditure the doctrine of Cohan v. Commissioner (C.C.A.2d 1930) 39 F.2d 540. The decision held that where the evidence indicated a taxpayer incurred deductible travel or entertainment expense but the exact amount could not be determined, the court should make a close approximation and not disallow the deduction entirely. Section 274(d) contemplates that no deduction shall be allowed a taxpayer for such expenditures on the basis of such approximations or unsupported testimony of the taxpayer. For purposes of this section, the term "entertainment" means entertainment, amusement, or recreation, and use of a facility therefor; and the term "expenditure" includes expenses and items (including items such as losses and depreciation).

(b) Elements of an expenditure—(1) In general. Section 274(d) and this section contemplate that no deduction shall be allowed for any expenditure for travel, entertainment, or a gift unless the taxpayer substantiates the following elements for each such expenditure:

(i) Amount;

(ii) Time and place of travel or entertainment (or use of a facility with respect to entertainment), or date and description of a gift;

(iii) Business purpose; and

(iv) Business relationship to the taxpayer of each person entertained using an entertainment facility or receiving a gift.

(2) Travel. The elements to be proved with respect to an expenditure for travel are—

(i) Amount. Amount of each separate expenditure for traveling away from home, such as cost of transportation or lodging, except that the daily cost of the traveler's own breakfast, lunch, and dinner and of expenditures incidental to such travel may be aggregated, if set forth in reasonable categories, such as for meals, for gasoline and oil, and for taxi fares;

(ii) Time. Dates of departure and return for each trip away from home, and number of days away from home spent on business;

(iii) Place. Destinations or locality of travel, described by name of city or town or other similar designation; and

(iv) Business purpose. Business reason for travel or nature of the business benefit derived or expected to be derived as a result of travel.

(3) Entertainment in general. Elements to be proved with respect to an expenditure for entertainment are—

(i) Amount. Amount of each separate expenditure for entertainment, except that such incidental items as taxi fares or telephone calls may be aggregated on a daily basis;

(ii) Time. Date of entertainment;

(iii) Place. Name, if any, address or location, and designation of type of entertainment, such as dinner or theater, if such information is not apparent from the designation of the place;

(iv) Business purpose. Business reason for the entertainment or nature of business benefit derived or expected to be derived as a result of the entertainment and, except in the case of business meals described in section 274(e)(1), the nature of any business discussion or activity;

(v) Business relationship. Occupation or other information relating to the person or persons entertained, including name, title, or other designation, sufficient to establish business relationship to the taxpayer.

(4) Entertainment directly preceding or following a substantial and bona fide business discussion. If a taxpayer claims a deduction for entertainment directly preceding or following a substantial and bona fide business discussion on the ground that such entertainment was associated with the active conduct of the taxpayer's trade or business, the elements to be proved with respect to such expenditure, in addition to those enumerated in subparagraph (3) (i), (ii), (iii), and (v) of this paragraph, are—

(i) Time. Date and duration of business discussion;

(ii) Place. Place of business discussion;

(iii) Business purpose. Nature of business discussion, and business reason for the entertainment or nature of business benefit derived or expected to be derived as the result of the entertainment;

(iv) Business relationship. Identification of those persons entertained who participated in the business discussion.

(5) Gifts. Elements to be proved with respect to an expenditure for a gift are—

(i) Amount. Cost of the gift to the taxpayer;

(ii) Time. Date of the gift;

(iii) Description. Description of the gift;

(iv) Business purpose. Business reason for the gift or nature of business benefit derived or expected to be derived as a result of the gift; and

(v) Business relationship. Occupation or other information relating to the recipient of the gift, including name, title, or other designation, sufficient to establish business relationship to the taxpayer.

(c) Rules for substantiation—(1) In general. A taxpayer must substantiate each element of an expenditure (described in paragraph (b) of this section) by adequate records or by sufficient evidence corroborating his own statement except as otherwise provided in this section. Section 274(d) contemplates that a taxpayer will maintain and produce such substantiation as will constitute clear proof of an expenditure for travel, entertainment, or gifts referred to in section 274. A record of the elements of an expenditure made at or near the time of the expenditure, supported by sufficient documentary evidence, has a high degree of credibility not present with respect to a statement prepared subsequent thereto when generally there is a lack of accurate recall. Thus, the corroborative evidence required to support a statement not made at or near the time of the expenditure must have a high degree of probative value to elevate such statement and evidence to the level of credibility reflected by a record made at or near the time of the expenditure supported by sufficient documentary evidence. The substantiation requirements of section 274(d) are designed to encourage taxpayers to maintain the records, together with documentary evidence, as provided in subparagraph (2) of this paragraph. To obtain a deduction for an expenditure for travel, entertainment, or gifts, a taxpayer must substantiate, in accordance with the provisions of this paragraph, each element of such an expenditure.

(2) Substantiation by adequate records—(i) In general. To meet the "adequate records" requirements of section 274(d), a taxpayer shall maintain an account book, diary, statement of expense or similar record (as provided in subdivision (ii) of this subparagraph) and documentary evidence (as provided in subdivision (iii) of this subparagraph) which, in combination, are sufficient to establish each element of an expenditure specified in paragraph (b) of this section. It is not necessary to record information in an account book, diary, statement of expense or similar record which duplicates information reflected on a receipt so long as such account book and receipt complement each other in an orderly manner.

(ii) Account book, diary, etc. An account book, diary, statement of expense or similar record must be prepared or maintained in such manner that each recording of an element of an expenditure is made at or near the time of the expenditure.

(a) Made at or near the time of the expenditure. For purposes of this section, the phrase "made at or near the time of the expenditure" means the elements of an expenditure are recorded at a time when, in relation to the making of an expenditure, the taxpayer has full present knowledge of each element of the expenditure, such as the amount, time, place and business purpose of the expenditure and business relationship to the taxpayer of any person entertained. An expense account statement which is a transcription of an account book, diary, or similar record prepared or maintained in accordance with the provisions of this subdivision shall be considered a record prepared or maintained in the manner prescribed in the preceding sentence if such expense account statement is submitted by an employee to his employer or by an independent contractor to his client or customer in the regular course of good business practice.

(b) Substantiation of business purpose. In order to constitute an adequate record of business purpose within the meaning of section 274(d) and this subparagraph, a written statement of business purpose generally is required. However, the degree of substantiation necessary to establish business purpose will vary depending upon the facts and circumstances of each case. Where the business purpose of an expenditure is evident from the surrounding facts and circumstances, a written explanation of such business purpose will not be required. For example, in the case of a salesman calling on customers on an established sales route, a written explanation of the business purpose of such travel ordinarily will not be required. Similarly, in the case of a business meal described in section 274(e) (1), if the business purpose of such meal is evident from the business relationship to the taxpayer of the persons entertained and other surrounding circumstances, a written explanation of such business purpose will not be required.

.   .   .   .   .

(iii) Documentary evidence. Documentary evidence, such as receipts, paid bills, or similar evidence sufficient to support an expenditure shall be required for—

(a) Any expenditure for lodging while traveling away from home, and

(b) Any other expenditure of $25 or more, except, for transportation charges, documentary evidence will not be required if not readily available.

provided, however, that the Commissioner, in his discretion, may prescribe rules waiving such requirements in circumstances where he determines it is impracticable for such documentary evidence to be required. Ordinarily, documentary evidence will be considered adequate to support an expenditure if it includes sufficient information to establish the amount, date, place, and the essential character of the expenditure. For example, a hotel receipt is sufficient to support expenditures for business travel if it contains the following: name, location, date, and separate amounts for charges such as for lodging, meals, and telephone. Similarly, a restaurant receipt is sufficient to support an expenditure for a business meal if it contains the following: name and location of the restaurant, the date and amount of the expenditure, and, if a charge is made for an item other than meals and beverages, an indication that such is the case. A document may be indicative of only one (or part of one) element of an expenditure. Thus, a cancelled check, together with a bill from the payee, ordinarily would establish the element of cost. In contrast, a cancelled check drawn payable to a named payee would not by itself support a business expenditure without other evidence showing that the check was used for a certain business purpose.

(iv) Retention of documentary evidence. The Commissioner may, in his discretion, prescribe rules under which an employer may dispose of documentary evidence submitted to him by employees who are required to, and do, make an adequate accounting to the employer (within the meaning of paragraph (e) (4) of this section) if the employer maintains adequate accounting procedures with respect to such employees (within the meaning of paragraph (e) (5) of this section).

(v) Substantial compliance. If a taxpayer has not fully substantiated a particular element of an expenditure, but the taxpayer establishes to the satisfaction of the district director that he has substantially complied with the "adequate records" requirements of this subparagraph with respect to the expenditure, the taxpayer may be permitted to establish such element by evidence which the district director shall deem adequate.

(3) Substantiation by other sufficient evidence. If a taxpayer fails to establish to the satisfaction of the district director that he has substantially complied with the "adequate records" requirements of subparagraph (2) of this paragraph with respect to an element of an expenditure, then, except as otherwise provided in this paragraph, the taxpayer must establish such element—

(i) By his own statement, whether written or oral, containing specific information in detail as to such element; and

(ii) By other corroborative evidence sufficient to establish such element. If such element is the description of a gift, or the cost, time, place, or date of an expenditure, the corroborative evidence shall be direct evidence, such as a statement in writing or the oral testimony of persons entertained or other witness setting forth detailed information about such element, or the documentary evidence described in subparagraph (2) of this paragraph. If such element is either the business relationship to the taxpayer of persons entertained or the business purpose of an expenditure, the corroborative evidence may be circumstantial evidence.

(4) **Substantiation in exceptional circumstances.** If a taxpayer establishes that, by reason of the inherent nature of the situation in which an expenditure was made—

(i) He was unable to obtain evidence with respect to an element of the expenditure which conforms fully to the "adequate records" requirements of subparagraph (2) of this paragraph,

(ii) He is unable to obtain evidence with respect to such element which conforms fully to the "other sufficient evidence" requirements of subparagraph (3) of this paragraph, and

(iii) He has presented other evidence, with respect to such element, which possesses the highest degree of probative value possible under the circumstances, such other evidence shall be considered to satisfy the substantiation requirements of section 274(d) and this paragraph.

(5) **Loss of records due to circumstances beyond control of taxpayer.** Where the taxpayer establishes that the failure to produce adequate records is due to the loss of such records through circumstances beyond the taxpayer's control, such as destruction by fire, flood, earthquake, or other casualty, the taxpayer shall have a right to substantiate a deduction by reasonable reconstruction of his expenditures.

. . . . .

§ 1.301–1 Rules applicable with respect to distributions of money and other property

(a) **General.** Section 301 provides the general rule for treatment of distributions on or after June 22, 1954, of property by a corporation to a shareholder with respect to its stock. The term "property" is defined in section 317(a). Such distributions, except as otherwise provided in this chapter, shall be treated as provided in section 301(c). Under section 301(c), distributions may be included in gross income, applied against and reduce the adjusted basis of the stock, treated as gain from the sale or exchange of property, or (in the case of certain distributions out of increase in value accrued before March 1, 1913) may be exempt from tax. The amount of the distributions to which section 301 applies is determined in accordance with the provisions of section 301(b). The basis of property received in a distribution to which section 301 applies is determined in accordance with the provisions of section 301(d). Accordingly, except as otherwise provided in this chapter, a distribution on or after June 22, 1954, of property by a corporation to a shareholder with respect to its stock shall be included in gross income to the extent the amount distributed is considered a dividend under section 316. For examples of distributions treated otherwise, see sections 116, 301(c)(2), 301(c)(3)(B), 301(e), 302(b), 303, and 305. See also part II (relating to distributions in partial or complete liquidation), part III (relating to corporate organizations and reorganizations), and part IV (relating to insolvency reorganizations), subchapter C, chapter 1 of the Code.

(b) **Time of inclusion in gross income and of determination of fair market value.** A distribution made by a corporation to its shareholders shall be included in the gross income of the distributees when the cash or other property is unqualifiedly made subject to their demands. However, if such distribution is a distribution other than in cash, the fair market value of the property shall be determined as of the date of distribution without regard to whether such date is the same as that on which the distribution is includible in gross income. For example, if a corporation distributes a taxable dividend in property (the adjusted basis of which exceeds its fair market value on December 31, 1955) on December 31, 1955, which is received by, or unqualifiedly made subject to the demand of, its shareholders on January 2, 1956, the amount to be included in the gross income of the shareholders will be the fair market value of such property on

December 31, 1955, although such amount will not be includible in the gross income of the shareholders until January 2, 1956.

(c) Application of section to shareholders. Section 301 is not applicable to an amount paid by a corporation to a shareholder unless the amount is paid to the shareholder in his capacity as such.

(d) Distributions to corporate shareholders. (1) If the shareholder is a corporation, the amount of any distribution to be taken into account under section 301(c) shall be:

(i) The amount of money distributed,

(ii) An amount equal to the fair market value of any property distributed which consists of any obligations of the distributing corporation, stock of the distributing corporation treated as property under section 305(b), or rights to acquire such stock treated as property under section 305(b), plus

(iii) In the case of a distribution not described in subdivision (iv) of this subparagraph, an amount equal to (a) the fair market value of any other property distributed or, if lesser, (b) the adjusted basis of such other property in the hands of the distributing corporation (determined immediately before the distribution and increased for any gain recognized to the distributing corporation under section 311(b), (c), or (d), or under section 341(f), 617(d), 1245(a), 1250(a), 1251(c), or 1252(a)), or

(iv) In the case of a distribution made after November 8, 1971, to a shareholder which is a foreign corporation, an amount equal to the fair market value of any other property distributed, but only if the distribution received by such shareholder is not effectively connected with the conduct of a trade or business in the United States by such shareholder.

(2) In the case of a distribution the amount of which is determined by reference to the adjusted basis described in subparagraph (1)(iii)(b) of this paragraph:

(i) That portion of the distribution which is a dividend under section 301 (c)(1) may not exceed such adjusted basis, or

(ii) If the distribution is not out of earnings and profits, the amount of the reduction in basis of the shareholder's stock, and the amount of any gain resulting from such distribution, are to be determined by reference to such adjusted basis of the property which is distributed.

. . . .

(e) Adjusted basis. In determining the adjusted basis of property distributed in the hands of the distributing corporation immediately before the distribution for purposes of section 301(b) (1)(B)(ii), (b)(1)(C)(i), and (d)(2) (B), the basis to be used shall be the basis for determining gain upon a sale or exchange.

(f) Examples. The application of this section (except paragraph (n)) may be illustrated by the following examples:

Example (1). On January 1, 1955, A, an individual owned all of the stock of Corporation M with an adjusted basis of $2,000. During 1955, A received distributions from Corporation M totaling $30,000, consisting of $10,000 in cash and listed securities having a basis in the hands of Corporation M and a fair market value on the date distributed of $20,000. Corporation M's taxable year is the calendar year. As of December 31, 1954, Corporation M had earnings and profits accumulated after February 28, 1913, in the amount of $26,000, and it had no earnings and profits and no deficit for 1955. Of the $30,000 received by A, $26,000 will be treated as an ordinary dividend; the remaining $4,-000 will be applied against the adjusted basis of his stock; the $2,000 in excess of the adjusted basis of his stock will either be treated as gain from the sale or exchange of property (under section 301(c)(3)(A)) or, if out of increase in value accrued before March 1, 1913, will (under section 301(c)(3)(B)) be exempt from tax. If A subsequently sells his stock in Corporation M, the basis for determining gain or loss on the sale will be zero.

Example (2). The facts are the same as in Example 1 with the exceptions that the shareholder of Corporation M is Corporation W and that the securities which were distributed had an adjusted basis to Corporation M of $15,000. The distribution received by Corporation W totals $25,000 consisting of $10,000 in cash and securities with an adjusted basis of $15,000. The total $25,000 will be treated as a dividend to Corporation W since the earnings and profits of Corporation M ($26,000) are in excess of the amount of the distribution.

Example (3). Corporation X owns timber land which it acquired prior to March 1, 1913, at a cost of $50,000 with $5,000 allocated as the separate cost of the land. On March 1, 1913, this property had a fair market value of $150,-000 of which $135,000 was attributable to the timber and $15,000 to the land. All of the timber was cut prior to 1955 and the full appreciation in the value thereof, $90,000 ($135,000—$45,000), realized through depletion allowances based on March 1, 1913, value. None of this surplus from realized appreciation had been distributed. In 1955, Corporation X sold the land for $20,000 thereby realizing a gain of $15,000. Of this gain, $10,000 is due to realized appreciation in value which accrued before March 1, 1913 ($15,000—$5,000). Of the gain of $15,000, $5,000 is taxable. Therefore, at December 31, 1955, Corporation X had a surplus from realized appreciation in the amount of $100,000. It had no accumulated earnings and profits and no deficit at January 1, 1955. The net earnings for 1955 (including the $5,000 gain on the sale of the land) were $20,000. During 1955, Corporation X distributed $75,000 to its stockholders. Of this amount, $20,000 will be treated as a dividend. The remaining $55,000, which is a distribution of realized appreciation, will be applied against and reduce the adjusted basis of the shareholders' stock. If any part of the $55,000 is in excess of the adjusted basis of a shareholder's stock, such part will be exempt from tax.

(g) Reduction for liabilities. For the purpose of section 301(a), the amount of any distribution shall be reduced by—

(1) The amount of any liability of the corporation assumed by the shareholder in connection with the distribution, and

(2) The amount of any liability to which the property received by the shareholder is subject immediately before and immediately after the distribution.

Such reduction, however, shall not cause the amount of the distribution to be reduced below zero.

(h) Basis. The basis of property received in the distribution to which section 301 applies shall be—

(1) If the shareholder is not a corporation, the fair market value of such property;

(2) If the shareholder is a corporation—

(i) In the case of a distribution of the obligations of the distributing corporation or of the stock of such corporation or rights to acquire such stock (if such stock or rights are treated as property under section 305(b)), the fair market value of such obligations, stock, or rights;

(ii) In the case of the distribution of any other property, except as provided in subdivision (iii) (relating to certain distributions by a foreign corporation) or subdivision (iv) (relating to certain distributions to foreign corporate distributees) of this subparagraph, whichever of the following is the lesser—

(a) The fair market value of such property; or

(b) The adjusted basis (in the hands of the distributing corporation immediately before the distribution) of such property increased in the amount of gain to the distributing corporation which is recognized under section 311(b) (relating to distributions of LIFO inventory), section 311(c) (relating to distributions of property subject to liabilities in excess of basis), section 311(d) (relating to appreciated property used to redeem stock), section 341(f) (relating to certain sales of stock of consenting corporations), section 617(d) (relating to gain from dispositions of certain mining property), section 1245(a) or 1250(a) (relating to gain from dispositions of certain depreciable property), section 1251(c) (relating to gain from disposition of farm recapture property), or section 1252(a) (relating to gain from disposition of farm land);

(iii) In the case of the distribution by a foreign corporation of any other property after December 31, 1962, in a distribution not described in subdivision (iv) of this subparagraph, the amount determined under paragraph (n) of this section;

. . . .

(i) [Reserved]

(j) Transfers for less than fair market value. If property is transferred by a corporation to a shareholder which is not a corporation for an amount less than its fair market value in a sale or exchange, such shareholder shall be treated as having received a distribution to which section 301 applies. In such case, the amount of the distribution shall be the difference between the amount paid for the property and its fair market value. If property is transferred in a sale or exchange by a corporation to a shareholder which is a corporation, for an amount less than its fair market value and also less than its adjusted basis, such shareholder shall be treated as having received a distribution to which section 301 applies, and—

(1) Where the fair market value of the property equals or exceeds its adjusted basis in the hands of the distributing corporation the amount of the distribution shall be the excess of the adjusted basis (increased by the amount of gain recognized under section 311(b), (c), or (d), or under section 341(f), 617(d), 1245(a), 1250(a), 1251(c), or 1252(a) to the distributing

corporation) over the amount paid for the property;

(2) Where the fair market value of the property is less than its adjusted basis in the hands of the distributing corporation, the amount of the distribution shall be the excess of such fair market value over the amount paid for the property.

If property is transferred in a sale or exchange after December 31, 1962, by a foreign corporation to a shareholder which is a corporation for an amount less than the amount which would have been computed under paragraph (n) of this section if such property had been received in a distribution to which section 301 applied, such shareholder shall be treated as having received a distribution to which section 301 applies, and the amount of the distribution shall be the excess of the amount which would have been computed under paragraph (n) of this section with respect to such property over the amount paid for the property. Notwithstanding the preceding provisions of this paragraph, if property is transferred in a sale or exchange after November 8, 1971, by a corporation to a shareholder which is a foreign corporation, for an amount less than its fair market value, and if paragraph (d)(1)(iv) of this section would apply if such property were received in a distribution to which section 301 applies, such shareholder shall be treated as having received a distribution to which section 301 applies and the amount of the distribution shall be the difference between the amount paid for the property and its fair market value. In all cases, the earnings and profits of the distributing corporation shall be decreased by the excess of the basis of the property in the hands of the distributing corporation over the amount received therefor. In computing gain or loss from the subsequent sale of such property, its basis shall be the amount paid for the property increased by the amount of the distribution.

(k) Application of rule respecting transfers for less than fair market value. The application of paragraph (j) of this section may be illustrated by the following examples:

Example (1). On January 1, 1955, A, an individual shareholder of corporation X, purchased property from that corporation for $20. The fair market value of such property was $100, and its basis in the hands of corporation X was $25. The amount of the distribution

determined under section 301(b) is $80. If A were a corporation, the amount of the distribution would be $5 (assuming that sections 311 (b) and (c), 1245(a), and 1250(a) do not apply), the excess of the basis of the property in the hands of corporation X over the amount received therefor. The basis of such property to corporation A would be $25. If the basis of the property in the hands of corporation X were $10, the corporate shareholder, A, would not receive a distribution. The basis of such property to corporation A would be $20. Whether or not A is a corporation, the excess of the amount paid over the basis of the property in the hands of corporation X ($20 over $10) would be a taxable gain to corporation X.

Example (2). On January 1, 1963, corporation A, which is a shareholder of corporation B (a foreign corporation engaged in business within the United States), purchased one share of corporation X stock from B for $20. The fair market value of the share was $100, and its adjusted basis in the hands of B was $25. Assume that if the share of corporation X stock had been received by A in a distribution to which section 301 applied, the amount of the distribution under paragraph (n) of this section would have been $55. The amount of the distribution under section 301 is $35, i.e., $55 (amount computed under paragraph (n) of this section) minus $20 (amount paid for the property). The basis of such property to A is $55.

(l) Transactions treated as distributions. A distribution to shareholders with respect to their stock is within the terms of section 301 although it takes place at the same time as another transaction if the distribution is in substance a separate transaction whether or not connected in a formal sense. This is most likely to occur in the case of a recapitalization, a reincorporation, or a merger of a corporation with a newly organized corporation having substantially no property. For example, if a corporation having only common stock outstanding, exchanges one share of newly issued common stock and one bond in the principal amount of $10 for each share of outstanding common stock, the distribution of the bonds will be a distribution of property (to the extent of their fair market value) to which section 301 applies, even though the exchange of common stock for common stock may be pursuant to a plan of reorganization under the terms of section 368(a) (1)(E) (recapitalization) and even though the exchange of common stock for common stock may be tax free by virtue of section 354.

(m) Cancellation of indebtedness. The cancellation of indebtedness of a shareholder by a corporation shall be treated as a distribution of property.

* * * *

§ 1.302-1 General

(a) Under section 302(d), unless otherwise provided in subchapter C, chapter 1 of the Code, a distribution in redemption of stock shall be treated as a distribution of property to which section 301 applies if the distribution is not within any of the provisions of section 302(b). A distribution in redemption of stock shall be considered a distribution in part or full payment in exchange for the stock under section 302(a) provided paragraph (1), (2), (3), or (4) of section 302(b) applies. Section 318(a) (relating to constructive ownership of stock) applies to all redemptions under section 302 except that in the termination of a shareholder's interest certain limitations are placed on the application of section 318(a) (1) by section 302(c) (2). The term "redemption of stock" is defined in section 317(b). Section 302 does not apply to that portion of any distribution which qualifies as a distribution in partial liquidation under section 346. For special rules relating to redemption of stock to pay death taxes see section 303. For special rules relating to redemption of section 306 stock see section 306. For special rules relating to redemption of stock in partial or complete liquidation see section 331.

(b) If, in connection with a partial liquidation under the terms of section 346, stock is redeemed in an amount in excess of the amount specified by section 331(a) (2), section 302(b) shall first apply as to each shareholder to which it is applicable without limitation because of section 331(a) (2). That portion of the total distribution which is used in all redemptions from specific shareholders which are within the terms of section 302(a) shall be excluded in determining the application of sections 346 and 331(a) (2). For example, Corporation X has $50,000 which is attributable to the sale of one of two active businesses and which, if distributed in redemption of stock, would qualify as a partial liquidation under the terms of section 346(b). Corporation X distributes $60,000 to its shareholders in redemption of stock, $20,000 of which is in redemption of all of the stock of shareholder A within the meaning of section 302(b) (3). The $20,000 distributed in redemption of the stock of shareholder A will be excluded in determining the application of sections 346 and 331(a) (2). The entire $60,000 will be treated as in part or full payment for stock ($20,000 qualifying under section 302(a) and $40,000 qualifying under sections 346 and 331 (a) (2)).

§ 1.302-2 Redemptions not taxable as dividends

(a) The fact that a redemption fails to meet the requirements of paragraph (2), (3) or (4) of section 302(b) shall not be taken into account in determining whether the redemption is not essentially equivalent to a dividend under section 302(b) (1). See, however, paragraph (b) of this section. For example, if a shareholder owns only nonvoting stock of a corporation which is not section 306 stock and which is limited and preferred as to dividends and in liquidation, and one-half of such stock is redeemed, the distribution will ordinarily meet the requirements of paragraph (1) of section 302(b) but will not meet the requirements of paragraph (2), (3) or (4) of such section. The determination of whether or not a distribution is within the phrase "essentially equivalent to a dividend" (that is, having the same effect as a distribution without any redemption of stock) shall be made without regard to the earnings and profits of the corporation at the time of the distribution. For example, if A owns all the stock of a corporation and the corporation redeems part of his stock at a time when it has no earnings and profits, the distribution shall be treated as a distribution under section 301 pursuant to section 302(d).

(b) The question whether a distribution in redemption of stock of a shareholder is not essentially equivalent to a dividend under section 302(b) (1) depends upon the facts and circumstances of each case. One of the facts to be considered in making this determination is the constructive stock ownership of such shareholder under section 318(a). All distributions in pro rata redemptions of a part of the stock of a corporation generally will be treated as distributions under section 301 if the corporation has only one class of stock outstanding. However, for distributions in partial liquidation, see section 346. The redemption of all of one class of stock (except section 306 stock) either at one time or in a series of redemptions generally will be considered as a distribution under section 301 if all classes of stock outstanding at the time of the redemption are held in the same proportion. Distribution in redemption of stock may be treated as distributions under section 301 regardless of the provisions of the stock certificate and regardless of whether all stock being redeemed was acquired by the stockholders from whom the stock was redeemed by purchase or otherwise. In every case in which a shareholder transfers stock to the corporation which issued such stock in exchange for property, the facts and circumstances shall be reported on his return except as provided in paragraph (d) of § 1.331–1. See sections 346(a) and 6043 for requirements relating to returns by corporations.

(c) In any case in which an amount received in redemption of stock is treated as a distribution of a dividend, proper adjustment of the basis of the remaining stock will be made with respect to the stock redeemed. The following examples illustrate the application of this rule:

Example (1). A, an individual, purchased all of the stock of Corporation X for $100,000. In 1955 the corporation redeems half of the stock for $150,000, and it is determined that this amount constitutes a dividend. The remaining stock of Corporation X held by A has a basis of $100,000.

Example (2). H and W, husband and wife, each own half of the stock of Corporation X. All of the stock was purchased by H for $100,000 cash. In 1950 H gave one-half of the stock to W, the stock transferred having a value in excess of $50,000. In 1955 all of the stock of H is redeemed for $150,000, and it is determined that the distribution to H in redemption of his shares constitutes the distribution of a dividend. Immediately after the transaction, W holds the remaining stock of Corporation X with a basis of $100,000.

Example (3). The facts are the same as in Example (2) with the additional facts that the outstanding stock of Corporation X consists of 1,000 shares and all but 10 shares of the stock of H is redeemed. Immediately after the transaction, H holds 10 shares of the stock of Corporation X with a basis of $50,000, and W holds 500 shares with a basis of $50,000.

§ 1.302–3 Substantially disproportionate redemption

(a) Section 302(b)(2) provides for the treatment of an amount received in redemption of stock as an amount received in exchange for such stock if—

(1) Immediately after the redemption the shareholder owns less than 50 percent of the total combined voting power of all classes of stock as provided in section 302(b)(2)(B),

(2) The redemption is a substantially disproportionate redemption within the meaning of section 302(b)(2)(C), and

(3) The redemption is not pursuant to a plan described in section 302(b)(2)(D).

Section 318(a) (relating to constructive ownership of stock) shall apply both in making the disproportionate redemption test and in determining the percentage of stock ownership after the redemption. The requirements under section 302(b)(2) shall be applied to each shareholder separately and shall be applied only with respect to stock which is issued and outstanding in the hands of the shareholders. Section 302(b)(2) only applies to a redemption of voting stock or to a redemption of both voting stock and other stock. Section 302(b)(2) does not apply to the redemption solely of nonvoting stock (common or preferred). However, if a redemption is treated as an exchange to a particular shareholder under the terms of section 302(b)(2), such section will apply to the simultaneous redemption of nonvoting preferred stock (which is not section 306 stock) owned by such shareholder and such redemption will also be treated as an exchange. Generally, for purposes of this section, stock which does not have voting rights until the happening of an event, such as a default in the payment of dividends on preferred stock, is not voting stock until the happening of the specified event. Subsection 302(b)(2)(D) provides that a redemption will not be treated as substantially disproportionate if made pursuant to a plan the purpose or effect of which is a series of redemptions which result in the aggregate in a distribution which is not substantially disproportionate. Whether or not such a plan exists will be determined from all the facts and circumstances.

(b) The application of paragraph (a) of this section is illustrated by the following example:

Example. Corporation M has outstanding 400 shares of common stock of which A, B, C and D each own 100 shares or 25 percent. No stock is considered constructively owned by A, B, C or D under section 318. Corporation M redeems 55 shares from A, 25 shares from B, and 20 shares from C. For the redemption to be disproportionate as to any shareholder, such shareholder must own after the redemptions less than 20 percent (80 percent of 25 percent) of the 300 shares of stock then outstanding. After the redemptions, A owns 45 shares (15 percent), B owns 75 shares (25 percent), and C owns 80 shares (26⅔ percent). The distribution is disproportionate only with respect to A.

§ 1.302-4 Termination of shareholder's interest

Section 302(b) (3) provides that a distribution in redemption of all of the stock of the corporation owned by a shareholder shall be treated as a distribution in part or full payment in exchange for the stock of such shareholder. In determining whether all of the stock of the shareholder has been redeemed, the general rule of section 302(c) (1) requires that the rules of constructive ownership provided in section 318(a) shall apply. Section 302 (c) (2), however, provides that section 318(a) (1) (relating to constructive ownership of stock owned by members of a family) shall not apply where the specific requirements of section 302(c) (2) are met. The following rules shall be applicable in determining whether the specific requirements of section 302 (c) (2) are met:

(a)(1) The agreement specified in section 302(c)(2)(A)(iii) shall be in the form of a separate statement in duplicate signed by the distributee and attached to the first return filed by the distributee for the taxable year in which the distribution described in section 302(b)(3) occurs. The agreement shall recite that the distributee has not acquired, other than by bequest or inheritance, any interest in the corporation (as described in section 302(c)(2) (A)(i)) since the distribution and that the distributee agrees to notify the district director for the internal revenue district in which the distributee resides of any acquisition, other than by bequest or inheritance, of such an interest in the corporation within 30 days after the acquisition, if the acquisition occurs within 10 years from the date of the distribution.

(2) If the distributee fails to file the agreement specified in section 302(c) (2)(A)(iii) at the time provided in paragraph (a)(1) of this section, then the district director for the internal revenue district in which the distributee resided at the time of filing the first return for the taxable year in which the distribution occurred shall grant a reasonable extension of time for filing such agreement, provided (i) it is established to the satisfaction of the district director that there was reasonable cause for failure to file the agreement within the prescribed time and (ii) a request for such extension is filed within such time as the district director considers reasonable under the circumstances.

(b) The distributee who files an agreement under section 302(c) (2) (A) (iii) shall retain copies of income tax returns and any other records indicating fully the amount of tax which would have been payable had the redemption been treated as a distribution subject to section 301.

(c) If stock of a parent corporation is redeemed, section 302(c) (2) (A), relating to acquisition of an interest in the corporation within 10 years after termination shall be applied with reference to an interest both in the parent corporation and any subsidiary of such parent corporation. If stock of a parent corporation is sold to a subsidiary in a transaction described in section 304, section 302(c) (2) (A) shall be applicable to the acquisition of an interest in such subsidiary corporation or in the parent corporation. If stock of a subsidiary corporation is redeemed, section 302(c) (2) (A) shall be applied with reference to an interest both in such subsidiary corporation and its parent. Section 302(c) (2) (A) shall also be applied with respect to an interest in a corporation which is a successor corporation to the corporation the interest in which has been terminated.

(d) For the purpose of section 302 (c) (2) (A) (i), a person will be considered to be a creditor only if the rights of such person with respect to the corporation are not greater or broader in scope than necessary for the enforcement of his claim. Such claim must not in any sense be proprietary and must not be subordinate to the claims of general creditors. An obligation in the form of a debt may thus constitute a proprietary interest. For example, if under the terms of the instrument the corporation may discharge the principal amount of its obligation to a person by payments, the amount or certainty of which are dependent upon the earnings of the corporation, such a person is not a creditor of the corporation. Furthermore, if under the terms of the instrument the rate of purported interest is dependent upon earnings, the holder of such instrument may not, in some cases, be a creditor.

(e) In the case of a distributee to whom section 302(b) (3) is applicable, who is a creditor after such transaction, the acquisition of the assets of the corporation in the enforcement of the rights of such creditor shall not be considered an acquisition of an interest in the corporation for purposes of section 302(c) (2) unless stock of the corporation, its parent corporation, or, in the case of a redemption of stock of a parent corporation, of a subsidiary of such corporation is acquired.

(f) In determining whether an entire interest in the corporation has been terminated under section 302(b) (3), under all circumstances paragraphs (2), (3), (4), and (5) of section 318(a) (relating to constructive ownership of stock) shall be applicable.

(g) Section 302(c) (2) (B) provides that section 302(c) (2) (A) shall not apply—

(1) If any portion of the stock redeemed was acquired directly or indirectly within the 10-year period ending on the date of the distribution by the distributee from a person, the ownership of whose stock would (at the time of distribution) be attributable to the distributee under section 318(a), or

(2) If any person owns (at the time of the distribution) stock, the ownership of which is attributable to the distributee under section 318(a), such person acquired any stock in the corporation directly or indirectly from the distributee within the 10-year period ending on the date of the distribution, and such stock so acquired from the distributee is not redeemed in the same transaction,

unless the acquisition (described in subparagraph (1) of this paragraph) or the disposition by the distributee (described in subparagraph (2) of this paragraph) did not have as one of its principal purposes the avoidance of Federal income tax. A transfer of stock by the transferor, within the 10-year period ending on the date of the distribution, to a person whose stock would be attributable to the transferor shall not be deemed to have as one of its principal purposes the avoidance of Federal income tax merely because the transferee is in a lower income tax bracket than the transferor.

§ 1.304-2 Acquisition by related corporation (other than subsidiary)

(a) If a corporation, in return for property, acquires stock of another corporation from one or more persons, and the person or persons from whom the stock was acquired were in control of both such corporations before the acquisition, then such property shall be treated as received in redemption of stock of the acquiring corporation. The stock received by the acquiring corporation shall be treated as a contribution to the capital of such corporation. See section 362(a) for determination of the basis of such stock. The transferor's basis for his stock in the acquiring corporation shall be increased by the basis of the stock surrendered by him. (But see below in this paragraph for subsequent reductions of basis in certain cases.) As to each person transferring stock, the amount received shall be treated as a distribution of property under section 302(d), unless as to such person such amount is to be treated as received in exchange for the stock under the terms of section 302(a) or section 303. In applying section 302(b), reference shall be had to the shareholder's ownership of stock in the issuing corporation and not to his ownership of stock in the acquiring corporation (except for purposes of applying section 318(a)). In determining control and applying section 302(b), section 318(a) (relating to the constructive ownership of stock) shall be applied without regard to the 50-percent limitation contained in section 318(a) (2) (C) and (3) (C). A series of redemptions referred to in section 302(b) (2) (D) shall include acquisitions by either of the corporations of stock of the other and stock redemptions by both corporations. If section 302(d) applies to the surrender of stock by a shareholder, his basis for his stock in the acquiring corporation after the transaction (increased as stated above in this paragraph) shall not be decreased except as provided in section 301. If section 302(d) does not apply, the property received shall be treated as received in a distribution in payment in exchange for stock of the acquiring corporation under section 302(a), which stock has a basis equal to the amount by which the shareholder's basis for his stock in the acquiring corporation was increased on account of the contribution to capital as provided for above in this paragraph. Accordingly, such amount shall be applied in reduction of the shareholder's basis for his stock in the acquiring corporation. Thus, the basis of each share of the shareholder's stock in the acquiring corporation will be the same as the basis of such share before the entire transaction. The holding period of the stock which is considered to have been redeemed shall be the same as the holding period of the stock actually surrendered.

(b) In any case in which two or more persons, in the aggregate, control two corporations, section 304(a) (1) will apply to sales by such persons of stock in either corporation to the other (whether or not made simultaneously) provided the sales by each of such persons are related to each other. The determination of whether the sales are related to each other shall be dependent upon the facts and circumstances surrounding all of the sales. For this purpose, the fact that the sales may occur during a period of one or more years (such as in the case of a series of sales by persons who together control each of such corporations immediately prior to the first of such sales and immediately subsequent to the last of such sales) shall be disregarded, provided the other facts and circumstances indicate related transactions.

(c) The application of section 304 (a) (1) may be illustrated by the following examples:

Example (1). Corporation X and corporation Y each have outstanding 200 shares of common stock. One-half of the stock of each corporation is owned by an individual, A, and one-half by another individual, B, who is unrelated to A. On or after August 31, 1964, A sells 30 shares of corporation X stock to corporation Y for $50,000, such stock having an adjusted basis of $10,000 to A. After the sale, A is considered as owning corporation X stock as follows: (i) 70 shares directly, and (ii) 15 shares constructively, since by virtue of his 50-percent ownership of Y he constructively owns 50 percent of the 30 shares owned directly by Y. Since A's percentage of ownership of X's voting stock after the sale (85 out of 200 shares, or 42.5%) is not less than 80 percent of his percentage of ownership of X's voting stock before the sale (100 out of 200 shares, or 50%), the transfer is not "substantially disproportionate" as to him as provided in section 302(b) (2). Under these facts, and assuming that section 302(b) (1) is not applicable, the entire $50,000 is treated as a dividend to A to the extent of the earnings and profits of corporation Y. The basis of the corporation X stock to corporation Y is $10,000, its adjusted basis to A. The amount of $10,000 is added to the basis of the stock of corporation Y in the hands of A.

· · · ·

Example (3). Corporation X and corporation Y each have outstanding 100 shares of common stock. A, an individual, owns one-half the stock of each corporation, B owns one-half the stock of corporation X, and C owns one-half of the stock of corporation Y. A, B, and C are unrelated. A sells 30 shares of the stock of corporation X to corporation Y for $50,000, such stock having an adjusted basis of $10,000 to him. After the sale, A is considered as owning 35 shares of the stock of corporation X (20 shares directly and 15 constructively because one-half of the 30 shares owned by corporation Y are attributed to him). Since before the sale he owned 50 percent of the stock of corporation X and after the sale he owned directly and constructively only 35 percent of such stock, the redemption is substantially disproportionate as to him pursuant to the provisions of section 302(b) (2). He, therefore, realizes a gain of $40,000 ($50,000 minus $10,000). If the stock surrendered is a capital asset, such gain is long-term or short-term capital gain depending on the period of time that such stock was held. The basis to A for the stock of corporation Y is not changed as a result of the entire transaction. The basis to corporation Y for the stock of corporation X is $50,000, i. e., the basis of the transferor ($10,000), increased in the amount of gain recognized to the transferor ($40,000) on the transfer.

Example (4). Corporation X and corporation Y each have outstanding 100 shares of common stock. H, an individual, W, his wife, S, his son, and G, his grandson, each own 25 shares of stock of each corporation. H sells all of his 25 shares of stock of corporation X to corporation Y. Since both before and after the transaction H owned directly and constructively 100 percent of the stock of corporation X, and assuming that section 302(b) (1) is not applicable, the amount received by him for his stock of corporation X is treated as a dividend to him to the extent of the earnings and profits of corporation Y.

§ 1.304–3 Acquisition by a subsidiary

(a) If a subsidiary acquires stock of its parent corporation from a shareholder of the parent corporation, the acquisition of such stock shall be treated as though the parent corporation had redeemed its own stock. For the purpose of this section, a corporation is a parent corporation if it meets the 50 percent ownership requirements of section 304(c). The determination whether the amount received shall be treated as an amount received in payment in exchange for the stock shall be made by applying section 303, or by applying section 302(b) with reference to the stock of the issuing parent corporation. If such distribution would have been treated as a distribution of property (pursuant to section 302(d)) under section 301, the entire amount of the selling price of the stock shall be treated as a dividend to the seller to the extent of the earnings and profits of the parent corporation determined as if the distribution had been made to it of the property that the subsidiary exchanged for the stock. In such cases, the transferor's basis for his remaining stock in the parent corporation will be determined by including the amount of the basis of the stock of the parent corporation sold to the subsidiary.

(b) Section 304(a) (2) may be illustrated by the following example:

Example. Corporation M has outstanding 100 shares of common stock which are owned as follows: B, 75 shares, C, son of B, 20 shares, and D, daughter of B, 5 shares. Corporation M owns the stock of Corporation X. B sells his 75 shares of Corporation M stock to Corporation X. Under section 302 (b) (3) this is a termination of B's entire interest in Corporation M and the full amount received from the sale of his stock will be treated as payment in exchange for this stock, provided he fulfills the requirements of section 302 (c) (2) (relating to an acquisition of an interest in the corporations).

§ 1.305–1 Stock dividends

(a) In general. Under section 305, a distribution made by a corporation to its shareholders in its stock or in rights to acquire its stock is not included in gross income except as provided in section 305(b) and the regulations promulgated under the authority of section 305(c). A distribution made by a corporation to its shareholders in its stock or rights to acquire its stock which would not otherwise be included in gross income by reason of section 305 shall not be so included merely because such distribution was made out of Treasury stock or consisted of rights to acquire Treasury stock. See section 307 for rules as to basis of stock and stock rights acquired in a distribution.

(b) Amount of distribution. (1) In general, where a distribution of stock or rights to acquire stock of a corporation is treated as a distribution of property to which section 301 applies by reason of section 305(b), the amount of the distribution, in accordance with section 301(b) and § 1.301–1, is the fair market value of such stock or rights on the date of distribution. See example (1) of § 1.305–2(b).

(2) Where a corporation which regularly distributes its earnings and profits, such as a regulated investment company, declares a dividend pursuant to which the shareholders may elect to receive either money or stock of the distributing corporation of equivalent value, the amount of the distribution of the stock received by any shareholder electing to receive stock will be considered to equal the amount of the money which could have been received instead. See example (2) of § 1.305–2 (b).

. . . .

(c) Adjustment in purchase price. A transfer of stock (or rights to acquire stock) or an increase or decrease in the conversion ratio or redemption price of stock which represents an adjustment of the price to be paid by the distributing corporation in acquiring property (within the meaning of section 317(a)) is not within the purview of section 305 because it is not a distribution with respect to its stock. For example, assume that on January 1, 1970, pursuant to a reorganization, corporation X acquires all the stock of corporation Y solely in exchange for its convertible preferred class B stock. Under the terms of the class B stock, its conversion ratio is to be adjusted in 1976 under a formula based upon the earnings of corporation Y over the 6-year period ending on December 31, 1975. Such an adjustment in 1976 is not covered by section 305.

. . . .

§ 1.305–2 Distributions in lieu of money

(a) In general. Under section 305 (b)(1), if any shareholder has the right to an election or option with respect to whether a distribution shall be made either in money or any other property, or in stock or rights to acquire stock of the distributing corporation, then, with respect to all shareholders, the distribution of stock or rights to acquire stock is treated as a distribution of property to which section 301 applies regardless of—

(1) Whether the distribution is actually made in whole or in part in stock or in stock rights;

(2) Whether the election or option is exercised or exercisable before or after the declaration of the distribution;

(3) Whether the declaration of the distribution provides that the distribution will be made in one medium unless the shareholder specifically requests payment in the other;

(4) Whether the election governing the nature of the distribution is provided in the declaration of the distribution or in the corporate charter or arises from the circumstances of the distribution; or

(5) Whether all or part of the shareholders have the election.

(b) Examples. The application of section 305(b)(1) may be illustrated by the following examples:

Example (1). (i) Corporation X declared a dividend payable in additional shares of its common stock to the holders of its outstanding common stock on the basis of two additional shares for each share held on the record date but with the provision that, at the election of any shareholder made within a specified period prior to the distribution date, he may receive one additional share for each share held on the record date plus $12 principal amount of securities of corporation Y owned by corporation X. The fair market value of the stock of corporation X on the distribution date was $10 per share. The fair market value of $12 principal amount of securities of corporation Y on the distribution date was $11 but such securities had a cost basis to corporation X of $9.

(ii) The distribution to all shareholders of one additional share of stock of corporation X (with respect to which no election applies) for each share outstanding is not a distribution to which section 301 applies.

(iii) The distribution of the second share of stock of corporation X to those shareholders who do not elect to receive securities of corporation Y is a distribution of property to which section 301 applies, whether such shareholders are individuals or corporations. The amount of the distribution to which section 301 applies is $10 per share of stock of corporation X held on the record date (the fair market value of the stock of corporation X on the distribution date).

(iv) The distribution of securities of corporation Y in lieu of the second share of stock of corporation X to the shareholders of corporation X whether individuals or corporations, who elect to receive such securities, is also a distribution of property to which section 301 applies.

(v) In the case of the individual shareholders of corporation X who elect to receive such securities, the amount of the distribution to which section 301 applies is $11 per share of stock of corporation X held on the record date (the fair market value of the $12 principal amount of securities of corporation Y on the distribution date).

(vi) In the case of the corporate shareholders of corporation X electing to receive such securities, the amount of the distribution to which section 301 applies is $9 per share of stock of corporation X held on the record date (the basis of the securities of corporation Y in the hands of corporation X).

Example (2). On January 10, 1970, corporation X, a regulated investment company, declared a dividend of $1 per share on its common stock payable on February 11, 1970, in cash or in stock of corporation X of equivalent value determined as of January 22, 1970, at the election of the shareholder made on or before January 22, 1970. The amount of the distribution to which section 301 applies is $1 per share whether the shareholder elects to take cash or stock and whether the shareholder is an individual or a corporation. Such amount will also be used in determining the dividend paid deduction of corporation X and the reduction in earnings and profits of corporation X.

§ 1.305–3 Disproportionate distributions

(a) In general. Under section 305 (b)(2), a distribution (including a deemed distribution) by a corporation of its stock or rights to acquire its stock is treated as a distribution of property to which section 301 applies if the distribution (or a series of distributions of which such distribution is one) has the result of (1) the receipt of money or other property by some shareholders, and (2) an increase in the proportionate interests of other shareholders in the assets or earnings and profits of the corporation. Thus, if a corporation has two classes of common stock outstanding and cash dividends are paid on one class and stock dividends are paid on the other class, the stock dividends are treated as distributions to which section 301 applies.

(b) Special rules. (1) As used in section 305(b)(2), the term "a series of distributions" encompasses all distributions of stock made or deemed made by a corporation which have the result of the receipt of cash or property by some shareholders and an increase in the proportionate interests of other shareholders.

(2) In order for a distribution of stock to be considered as one of a series of distributions it is not necessary that such distribution be pursuant to a plan to distribute cash or property to some shareholders and to increase the proportionate interests of other shareholders. It is sufficient if there is an actual or deemed distribution of stock (of which such distribution is one) and as a result of such distribution or distributions some shareholders receive cash or property and other shareholders increase their proportionate interests. For example, if a corporation pays quarterly stock dividends to one class of common shareholders and annual cash dividends to another class of common shareholders the quarterly stock dividends constitute a series of distributions of stock having the result of the receipt of cash or property by some shareholders and an increase in the proportionate interests of other shareholders. This is so whether or not the stock distributions and the cash distributions are steps in an overall plan or

are independent and unrelated. Accordingly, all the quarterly stock dividends are distributions to which section 301 applies.

(3) There is no requirement that both elements of section 305(b)(2) (i. e., receipt of cash or property by some shareholders and an increase in proportionate interests of other shareholders) occur in the form of a distribution or series of distributions as long as the result of a distribution or distributions of stock is that some shareholders' proportionate interests increase and other shareholders in fact receive cash or property. Thus, there is no requirement that the shareholders receiving cash or property acquire the cash or property by way of a corporate distribution with respect to their shares, so long as they receive such cash or property in their capacity as shareholders, if there is a stock distribution which results in a change in the proportionate interests of some shareholders and other shareholders receive cash or property. However, in order for a distribution of property to meet the requirement of section 305(b)(2), such distribution must be made to a shareholder in his capacity as a shareholder, and must be a distribution to which section 301, 356(a)(2), 871(a) (1)(A), 881(a)(1), 852(b), or 857(b) applies. (Under section 305(d)(2), the payment of interest to a holder of a convertible debenture is treated as a distribution of property to a shareholder for purposes of section 305(b)(2).) For example if a corporation makes a stock distribution to its shareholders and, pursuant to a prearranged plan with such corporation, a related corporation purchases such stock from those shareholders who want cash, in a transaction to which section 301 applies by virtue of section 304, the requirements of section 305(b)(2) are satisfied. In addition, a distribution of property incident to an isolated redemption of stock (for example, pursuant to a tender offer) will not cause section 305(b)(2) to apply even though the redemption distribution is treated as a distribution of property to which section 301, 871(a) (1)(A), 881(a)(1), or 356(a)(2) applies.

(4) Where the receipt of cash or property occurs more than 36 months following a distribution or series of distributions of stock, or where a distribution or series of distributions of stock is made more than 36 months following the receipt of cash or property, such distribution or distributions will be presumed not to result in the receipt of cash or property by some shareholders and an increase in the proportionate interest of other shareholders, unless the receipt of cash or property and the distribution or series of distributions of stock are made pursuant to a plan. For example, if, pursuant to a plan, a corporation pays cash dividends to some shareholders on January 1, 1971 and increases the proportionate interests of other shareholders on March 1, 1974, such increases in proportionate interests are distributions to which section 301 applies.

(5) In determining whether a distribution or a series of distributions has the result of a disproportionate distribution, there shall be treated as outstanding stock of the distributing corporation (i) any right to acquire such stock (whether or not exercisable during the taxable year), and (ii) any security convertible into stock of the distributing corporation (whether or not convertible during the taxable year).

(6) In cases where there is more than one class of stock outstanding, each class of stock is to be considered separately in determining whether a shareholder has increased his proportionate interest in the assets or earnings and profits of a corporation. The individual shareholders of a class of stock will be deemed to have an increased interest if the class of stock as a whole has an increased interest in the corporation.

(c) Distributions of cash in lieu of fractional shares. (1) Section 305(b) (2) will not apply if—

(i) A corporation declares a dividend payable in stock of the corporation and distributes cash in lieu of fractional shares to which shareholders would otherwise be entitled, or

(ii) Upon a conversion of convertible stock or securities a corporation distributes cash in lieu of fractional shares to which shareholders would otherwise be entitled,

provided the purpose of the distribution of cash is to save the corporation the trouble, expense, and inconvenience of issuing and transferring fractional shares (or scrip representing fractional shares), or issuing full shares representing the sum of fractional shares, and not to give any particular group of shareholders an increased interest in the assets or earnings and profits of the corporation. For purposes of paragraph (c)(1)(i) of this section, if the total amount of cash distributed in lieu of fractional shares is 5 percent or less of the total fair market value of the stock distributed (determined as of the date of declaration), the distribution shall be considered to be for such valid purpose.

(2) In a case to which subparagraph (1) of this paragraph applies, the transaction will be treated as though the fractional shares were distributed as part of the stock distribution and then were redeemed by the corporation. The treatment of the cash received by a shareholder will be determined under section 302.

(d) **Adjustment in conversion ratio.** (1)(i) Except as provided in subparagraph (2) of this paragraph, if a corporation has convertible stock or convertible securities outstanding (upon which it pays or is deemed to pay dividends or interest in money or other property) and distributes a stock dividend (or rights to acquire such stock) with respect to the stock into which the convertible stock or securities are convertible, an increase in proportionate interest in the assets or earnings and profits of the corporation by reason of such stock dividend shall be considered to have occurred unless a full adjustment in the conversion ratio or conversion price to reflect such stock dividend is made. Under certain circumstances, however, the application of an adjustment formula which in effect provides for a "credit" where stock is issued for consideration in excess of the conversion price may not satisfy the requirement for a "full adjustment." Thus, if under a "conversion price" antidilution formula the formula provides for a "credit" where stock is issued for consideration in excess of the conversion price (in effect as an offset against any decrease in the conversion price which would otherwise be required when stock is subsequently issued for consideration below the conversion price) there may still be an increase in proportionate interest by reason of a stock dividend after application of the formula, since any downward adjustment of the conversion price that would otherwise be required to reflect the stock dividend may be offset, in whole or in part, by the effect of prior sales made at prices above the conversion price. On the other hand, if there were no prior sales

of stock above the conversion price then a full adjustment would occur upon the application of such an adjustment formula and there would be no change in proportionate interest. Similarly, if consideration is to be received in connection with the issuance of stock, such as in the case of a rights offering or a distribution of warrants, the fact that such consideration is taken into account in making the antidilution adjustment will not preclude a full adjustment. See paragraph (b) of the example in this subparagraph for a case where the application of an adjustment formula with a cumulative feature does not result in a full adjustment and where a change in proportionate interest therefore occurs. See paragraph (c) for a case where the application of an adjustment formula with a cumulative feature does result in a full adjustment and where no change in proportionate interest therefore occurs. See paragraph (d) for an application of an antidilution formula in the case of a rights offering. See paragraph (e) for a case where the application of a noncumulative type adjustment formula will in all cases prevent a change in proportionate interest from occurring in the case of a stock dividend, because of the omission of the cumulative feature.

(ii) The principles of this subparagraph may be illustrated by the following example.

Example. (a) Corporation S has two classes of securities outstanding, convertible debentures and common stock. At the time of issuance of the debentures the corporation had 100 shares of common stock outstanding. Each debenture is interest-paying and is convertible into common stock at a conversion price of $2. The debenture's conversion price is subject to reduction pursuant to the following formula:

(Number of common shares outstanding at date of issue of debentures times initial conversion price)

plus

(Consideration received upon issuance of additional common shares)

divided by

(Number of common shares outstanding at date of issue of debentures)

plus

(Number of additional common shares issued)

Under the formula, common stock dividends are treated as an issue of common stock for zero consideration. If the computation results in a figure which is less than the existing conversion price the conversion price is reduced. However, under the formula, the existing conversion price is never increased. The formula works upon a cumulative basis since the numerator includes the consideration received upon the issuance of all common shares subsequent to the issuance of the debentures, and the reduction effected by the formula because of a sale or issuance of common stock below the existing conversion price is thus limited by any prior sales made above the existing conversion price.

(b) In 1972 corporation S sells 100 common shares at $3 per share. In 1973 the corporation declares a stock dividend of 20 shares to all holders of common stock. Under the antidilution formula no adjustment will be made to the conversion price of the debentures to reflect the stock dividend to common stockholders since the prior sale of common stock in excess of the conversion price in 1972 offsets the reduction in the conversion price which would otherwise result, as follows:

$$100 \times \$2 + \$300 \div 100 + 120 = \frac{\$500}{220} = \$2.27$$

Since $2.27 is greater than the existing conversion price of $2 no adjustment is required. As a result, there is an increase in proportionate interest of the common stockholders by reason of the stock dividend and the additional shares of common stock will be treated, pursuant to section 305(b)(2), as a distribution of property to which section 301 applies.

(c) Assume the same facts as above, but instead of selling 100 common shares at $3 per share in 1972, assume corporation S sold no shares. Application of the antidilution formula would give rise to an adjustment in the conversion price as follows:

$$100 \times \$2 + \$0 \div 100 + 20 = \frac{120}{\$200} = \$1.67$$

The conversion price, being reduced from $2 to $1.67, fully reflects the stock dividend distributed to the common stockholders. Hence, the distribution of common stock is not treated under section 305(b)(2) as one to which section 301 applies because the distribution does not increase the proportionate interests of the common shareholders as a class.

(d) Corporation S distributes to its shareholders rights entitling the shareholders to purchase a total of 20 shares at $1 per share. Application of the antidilution formula would produce an adjustment in the conversion price as follows:

$$100 \times \$2 + 20 \times \$1 \div 100 + 20 = \frac{120}{\$220} = \$1.83$$

The conversion price, being reduced from $2 to $1.83, fully reflects the distribution of rights to purchase stock at a price lower than the conversion price. Hence, the distribution of the rights is not treated under section 305(b)(2) as one to which section 301 applies because the distribution does not increase the proportionate interests of the common shareholders as a class.

(e) Assume the same facts as in (b) above, but instead of using a "conversion price" antidilution formula which operates on a cumulative basis, assume corporation S has employed a formula which operates as follows with respect to all stock dividends: The conversion price in effect at the opening of business on the day following the dividend record date is reduced by multiplying such conversion price by a fraction the numerator of which is the number of shares of common stock outstanding at the close of business on the record date and the denominator of which is the sum of such shares so outstanding and the number of shares constituting the stock dividend. Under such a formula the following adjustment would be made to the conversion price upon the declaration of a stock dividend of 20 shares in 1973:

$$200 \div 200 + 20 = \frac{220}{200} \times \$2 = \$1.82$$

The conversion price, being reduced from $2 to $1.82, fully reflects the stock dividend distributed to the common stockholders. Hence, the distribution of common stock is not treated under section 305(b)(2) as one to which section 301 applies because the distribution does not increase the proportionate interests of the common shareholders as a class.

(2)(i) A distributing corporation either must make the adjustment required by subparagraph (1) of this paragraph as of the date of the distribution of the stock dividend, or must elect (in the manner provided in subdivision (iii) of this subparagraph) to make such adjustment within the time provided in subdivision (ii) of this subparagraph.

(ii) If the distributing corporation elects to make such adjustment, such adjustment must be made no later than the earlier of (a) 3 years after the date of the stock dividend, or (b) that date as of which the aggregate stock dividends for which adjustment of the conversion ratio has not previously been made total at least 3 percent of the issued and outstanding stock with respect to which such stock dividends were distributed.

(iii) The election provided by subdivision (ii) of this subparagraph shall be made by filing with the income tax return for the taxable year during which the stock dividend is distributed—

(a) A statement that an adjustment will be made as provided by that subdivision, and

(b) A description of the antidilution provisions under which the adjustment will be made.

. . . .

(e) Examples. The application of section 305(b)(2) to distributions of stock and section 305(c) to deemed distributions of stock may be illustrated by the following examples:

Example (1). Corporation X is organized with two classes of common stock, class A and class B. Each share of stock is entitled to share equally in the assets and earnings and profits of the corporation. Dividends may be paid in stock or in cash on either class of stock without regard to the medium of payment of dividends on the other class. A dividend is declared on the class A stock payable in additional shares of class A stock and a dividend is declared on class B stock payable in cash. Since the class A shareholders as a class will have increased their proportionate interests in the assets and earnings and profits of the corporation and the class B shareholders will have received cash, the additional shares of class A stock are distributions of property to which section 301 applies. This is true even with respect to those shareholders who may own class A stock and class B stock in the same proportion.

Example (2). Corporation Y is organized with two classes of stock, class A common, and class B, which is nonconvertible and limited and preferred as to dividends. A dividend is declared upon the class A stock payable in additional shares of class A stock and a dividend is declared on the class B stock payable in cash. The distribution of class A stock is not one to which section 301 applies because the distribution does not increase the proportionate interests of the class A shareholders as a class.

Example (3). Corporation K is organized with two classes of stock, class A common, and class B, which is nonconvertible preferred stock. A dividend is declared upon the class A stock payable in shares of class B stock and a dividend is declared on the class B stock payable in cash. Since the class A shareholders as a class have an increased interest in the assets and earnings and profits of the corporation, the stock distribution is treated as a distribution to which section 301 applies. If, however, a dividend were declared upon the class A stock payable in a new class of preferred stock that is subordinated in all respects to the class B stock, the distribution would not increase the proportionate interests of the class A shareholders in the assets or earnings and profits of the corporation and would not be treated as a distribution to which section 301 applies.

Example (4). (i) Corporation W has one class of stock outstanding, class A common. The corporation also has outstanding interest paying securities convertible into class A common stock which have a fixed conversion ratio that is not subject to full adjustment in the event stock dividends or rights are distributed to the class A shareholders. Corporation W distributes to the class A shareholders rights to acquire additional shares of class A stock. During the year, interest is paid on the convertible securities.

(ii) The stock rights and convertible securities are considered to be outstanding stock of the corporation and the distribution increases the proportionate interests of the class A shareholders in the assets and earnings and profits of the corporation. Therefore, the distribution is treated as a distribution to which section 301 applies. The same result would follow if, instead of convertible securities, the corporation had outstanding convertible stock. If, however, the conversion ratio of the securities or stock were fully adjusted to reflect the distribution of rights to the class A shareholders, the rights to acquire class A stock would not increase the

proportionate interests of the class A shareholders in the assets and earnings and profits of the corporation and would not be treated as a distribution to which section 301 applies.

Example (5). (i) Corporation S is organized with two classes of stock, class A common and class B convertible preferred. The class B is fully protected against dilution in the event of a stock dividend or stock split with respect to the class A stock; however, no adjustment in the conversion ratio is required to be made until the stock dividends equal 3 percent of the common stock issued and outstanding on the date of the first such stock dividend except that such adjustment must be made no later than 3 years after the date of the stock dividend. Cash dividends are paid annually on the class B stock.

(ii) Corporation S pays a 1 percent stock dividend on the class A stock in 1973. In 1974, another 1 percent stock dividend is paid and in 1975 another 1 percent stock dividend is paid. The conversion ratio of the class B stock is increased in 1975 to reflect the three stock dividends paid on the class A stock. The distributions of class A stock are not distributions to which section 301 applies because they do not increase the proportionate interests of the class A shareholders in the assets and earnings and profits of the corporation.

Example (6). (i) Corporation M is organized with two classes of stock outstanding, class A and class B. Each class B share may be converted, at the option of the holder, into class A shares. During the first year, the conversion ratio is one share of class A stock for each share of class B stock. At the beginning of each subsequent year, the conversion ratio is increased by 0.05 share of class A stock for each share of class B stock. Thus, during the second year, the conversion ratio would be 1.05 shares of class A stock for each share of class B stock, during the third year, the ratio would be 1.10 shares, etc.

(ii) M pays an annual cash dividend on the class A stock. At the beginning of the second year, when the conversion ratio is increased to 1.05 shares of class A stock for each share of class B stock, a distribution of 0.05 shares of class A stock is deemed made under section 305(c) with respect to each share of class B stock, since the proportionate interests of the class B shareholders in the assets or earnings and profits of M are increased and the transaction has the effect described in section 305(b)(2). Accordingly, sections 305(b)(2) and 301 apply to the transaction.

Example (7). (i) Corporation N has two classes of stock outstanding, class A and class B. Each class B share is convertible into class A stock. However, in accordance with a specified formula, the conversion ratio is decreased each time a cash dividend is paid on the class

(a) $\dfrac{100}{955} = 10.47\%$ (percent of C's ownership after redemption);

(b) $\dfrac{100 + x}{1000 + x} = 10.47\%$; $x = 5.25$ (additional shares considered to be distributed to C)).

B stock to reflect the amount of the cash dividend. The conversion ratio is also adjusted in the event that cash dividends are paid on the class A stock to increase the number of class A shares into which the class B shares are convertible to compensate the class B shareholders for the cash dividend paid on the class A stock.

(ii) In 1972, a $1 cash dividend per share is declared and paid on the class B stock. On the date of payment, the conversion ratio of the class B stock is decreased. A distribution of stock is deemed made under section 305(c) to the class A shareholders, since the proportionate interest of the class A shareholders in the assets or earnings and profits of the corporation is increased and the transaction has the effect described in section 305(b)(2). Accordingly, sections 305(b)(2) and 301 apply to the transaction.

(iii) In the following year a cash dividend is paid on the class A stock and none is paid on the class B stock. The increase in conversion rights of the class B shares is deemed to be a distribution under section 305(c) to the class B shareholders since their proportionate interest in the assets or earnings and profits of the corporation is increased and since the transaction has the effect described in section 305(b)(2). Accordingly, sections 305(b)(2) and 301 apply to the transaction.

Example (8). Corporation T has 1,000 shares of stock outstanding. C owns 100 shares. Nine other shareholders each owns 100 shares. Pursuant to a plan for periodic redemptions, T redeems up to 5 percent of each shareholder's stock each year. During the year, each of the nine other shareholders has 5 shares of his stock redeemed for cash. Thus, C's proportionate interest in the assets and earnings and profits of T is increased. Assuming that the cash received by the nine other shareholders is taxable under 301, C is deemed under section 305(c) to have received a distribution under section 305(b)(2) of 5.25 shares of T stock to which section 301 applies. The amount of C's distribution is measured by the fair market value of the number of shares which would have been distributed to C had the corporation sought to increase his interest by 0.47 percentage points (C owned 10 percent of the T stock immediately before the redemption and 10.47 percent immediately thereafter) and the other shareholders continued to hold 900 shares (i. e., Since in computing the amount of additional shares deemed to be distributed to C the redemption of shares is disregarded, the redemption of shares will be similarly disregarded in determining the value of the stock of the corporation which is deemed to be distributed. Thus, in the example, 1,005.25 shares of stock are considered as outstanding after the redemption. The value of each share deemed to be distributed to C is then determined by dividing the 1,005.25 shares into the aggregate fair market value of the actual shares outstanding (955) after the redemption.

Example (9). (i) Corporation O has a stock redemption program under which, instead of paying out earnings and profits to its shareholders in the form of dividends, it redeems the stock of its shareholders up to a stated amount which is determined by the earnings and profits of the corporation. If the stock tendered for redemption exceeds the stated amount, the corporation redeems the stock on a pro rata basis up to the stated amount.

(ii) During the year corporation O offers to distribute $10,000 in redemption of its stock. At the time of the offering, corporation O has 1,000 shares outstanding of which E and F each owns 150 shares and G and H each owns 350 shares. The corporation redeems 15 shares from E and 35 shares from G, F and H continue to hold all of their stock.

(iii) F and H have increased their proportionate interests in the assets and earnings and profits of the corporation. Assuming that the cash E and G receive is taxable, under section 301, F will be deemed under section 305(c) to have received a distribution under section 305(b)(2) of 16.66 shares of stock to which section 301 applies and H will be deemed under section 305(c) to have received a distribution under section 305(b)(2) of 38.86 shares of stock to which section 301 applies. The amount of the distribution to F and H is measured by the number of shares which would have been distributed to F and H had the corporation sought to increase the interest of F by 0.79 percentage points (F owned 15 percent of the stock immediately before the redemption and 15.79 percent immediately thereafter) and the interest of H by 1.84 percentage points (H owned 35 percent of the stock immediately before the redemption and 36.84 percent immediately thereafter) and E and G had continued to hold 150 shares and 350 shares, respectively (i. e.,

(a) $\dfrac{150}{950} + \dfrac{350}{950} = 52.63\%$ (percent of F and H's ownership after redemption);

(b) $\dfrac{500 + y}{1000 + y} = 52.63\%$; $y = 55.52$ (additional shares considered to be distributed to F and H);

(c) (1) $\dfrac{150}{500} \times 55.52 = 16.66$ (shares considered to be distributed to F);

(2) $\dfrac{350}{500} \times 55.52 = 38.86$ (shares considered to be distributed to H)).

Since in computing the amount of additional shares deemed to be distributed to F and H the redemption of shares is disregarded, the redemption of shares will be similarly disregarded in determining the value of the stock of the corporation which is deemed to be distributed. Thus, in the example, 1,055.52 shares of stock are considered as outstanding after the redemption. The value of each share deemed to be distributed to F and H is then determined by dividing the 1,055.52 shares into the aggregate fair market value of the actual shares outstanding (950) after the redemption.

Example (10). Corporation P has 1,000 shares of stock outstanding. T owns 700 shares of the P stock and G owns 300 shares of the P stock. In a single and isolated redemption to which section 301 applies, the corporation redeems 150 shares of T's stock. Since this is an isolated redemption and is not a part of a periodic redemption plan, G is not treated as having received a deemed distribution under section 305(c) to which sections 305(b)(2) and 301 apply even though he has an increased proportionate interest in the assets and earnings and profits of the corporation.

Example (11). Corporation Q is a large corporation whose sole class of stock is widely held. However, the four largest shareholders are officers of the corporation and each owns 8 percent of the outstanding stock. In 1974, in a distribution to which section 301 applies, the corporation redeems 1.5 percent of the stock from each of the four largest shareholders in preparation for their retirement. From 1970 through 1974, the corporation distributes annual stock dividends to its shareholders. No other distributions were made to these shareholders. Since the 1974 redemptions are isolated and are not part of a plan for periodically redeeming the stock of the corporation, the shareholders receiving stock dividends will not be treated as having received a distribution under section 305(b)(2) even though they have an increased proportionate interest in the assets and earnings and profits of the corporation and whether or not the redemptions are treated as distributions to which section 301 applies.

Example (12). Corporation R has 2,000 shares of class A stock outstanding. Five shareholders own 300 shares each and five shareholders own 100 shares each. In preparation for the retirement of the five major shareholders, corporation R, in a single and isolated transaction, has a recapitalization in which each share of class A stock may be exchanged either for five shares of new class B nonconvertible preferred stock plus 0.4 share of new class C common stock, or for two shares of new class C common stock. As a result of the exchanges, each of the five major shareholders receives 1,500 shares of class B nonconvertible preferred stock and 120 shares of class C common stock. The remaining shareholders each receives 200 shares of class C common stock. None of the exchanges are within the purview of section 305.

• • •

§ 1.305-4 Distributions of common and preferred stock

(a) In general. Under section 305 (b)(3), a distribution (or a series of distributions) by a corporation which results in the receipt of preferred stock whether or not convertible into common stock) by some common shareholders and the receipt of common stock by other common shareholders is treated as a distribution of property to which section 301 applies. • • • •

(b) Examples. The application of section 305(b)(3) may be illustrated by the following examples:

Example (1). Corporation X is organized with two classes of common stock, class A and class B. Dividends may be paid in stock or in cash on either class of stock without regard to the medium of payment of dividends on the other class. A dividend is declared on the class A stock payable in additional shares of class A stock and a dividend is declared on class B stock payable in newly authorized class C stock which is nonconvertible and limited and preferred as to dividends. Both the distribution of class A shares and the distribution of new class C shares are distributions to which section 301 applies.

Example (2). Corporation Y is organized with one class of stock, class A common. During the year the corporation declares a dividend on the class A stock payable in newly authorized class B preferred stock which is convertible into class A stock no later than 6 months from the date of distribution at a price that is only slightly higher than the market price of class A stock on the date of distribution. Taking into account the dividend rate, redemption provisions, the marketability of the convertible stock, and the conversion price, it is reasonable to anticipate that within a relatively short period of time some shareholders will exercise their conversion rights and some will not. Since the distribution can reasonably be expected to result in the receipt of preferred stock by some common shareholders and the receipt of common stock by other common shareholders, the distribution

is a distribution of property to which section 301 applies.

§ 1.305-5 Distributions on preferred stock

(a) In general. Under section 305 (b)(4), a distribution by a corporation of its stock (or rights to acquire its stock) made (or deemed made under section 305(c)) with respect to its preferred stock is treated as a distribution of property to which section 301 applies unless the distribution is made with respect to convertible preferred stock to take into account a stock dividend, stock split, or any similar event (such as the sale of stock at less than the fair market value pursuant to a rights offering) which would otherwise result in the dilution of the conversion right. For purposes of the preceding sentence, an adjustment in the conversion ratio of convertible preferred stock made solely to take into account the distribution by a closed end regulated investment company of a capital gain dividend with respect to the stock into which such stock is convertible shall not be considered a "similar event." The term "preferred stock" generally refers to stock which, in relation to other classes of stock outstanding, enjoys certain limited rights and privileges (generally associated with specified dividend and liquidation priorities) but does not participate in corporate growth to any significant extent. The distinguishing feature of "preferred stock" for the purposes of section 305(b)(4) is not its privileged position as such, but that such privileged position is limited, and that such stock does not participate in corporate growth to any significant extent. However, a right to participate which lacks substance will not prevent a class of stock from being treated as preferred stock. Thus, stock which enjoys a priority as to dividends and on liquidation but which is entitled to participate, over and above such priority, with another less privileged class of stock in earnings and profits and upon liquidation, may nevertheless be treated as preferred stock for purposes of section 305 if, taking into account all the facts and circumstances, it is reasonable to anticipate at the time a distribution is made (or is deemed to have been made) with respect to such stock that there is little or no likelihood of such stock actually participating in current and anticipated earnings and upon liquidation beyond its preferred interest.

Among the facts and circumstances to be considered are the prior and anticipated earnings per share, the cash dividends per share, the book value per share, the extent of preference and of participation of each class, both absolutely and relative to each other, and any other facts which indicate whether or not the stock has a real and meaningful probability of actually participating in the earnings and growth of the corporation. The determination of whether stock is preferred for purposes of section 305 shall be made without regard to any right to convert such stock into another class of stock of the corporation. The term "preferred stock", however, does not include convertible debentures.

(b) Redemption premium. (1) If a corporation issues preferred stock which may be redeemed after a specified period of time at a price higher than the issue price, the difference will be considered under the authority of section 305(c) to be a distribution of additional stock on preferred stock which is constructively received by the shareholder over the period of time during which the preferred stock cannot be called for redemption.

(2) Subparagraph (1) of this paragraph shall not apply to the extent that the difference between issue price and redemption price is a reasonable redemption premium. A redemption premium will be considered reasonable if it is in the nature of a penalty for a premature redemption of the preferred stock and if such premium does not exceed the amount the corporation would be required to pay for the right to make such premature redemption under market conditions existing at the time of issuance. Such an amount can be established by comparing call premium rates on comparable stock paying comparable dividends. However, for purposes of this subparagraph, a redemption premium not in excess of 10 percent of the issue price on stock which is not redeemable for 5 years from the date of issue shall be considered reasonable.

· · · · ·

(d) Examples. The application of sections 305(b)(4) and 305(c) may be illustrated by the following examples:

Example (1). (i) Corporation T has outstanding 1,000 shares of $100 par 5-percent cumulative preferred stock and 10,000 shares of no-par common stock. The corporation is 4 years in arrears on dividends to the preferred shareholders. The issue price of the preferred stock is $100 per share. Pursuant to a recapitalization under section 368(a)(1)(E), the preferred shareholders exchange their preferred stock, including the right to dividend arrearages, on the basis of one old preferred share for 1.20 newly authorized class A preferred shares. Immediately following the recapitalization, the new class A shares are traded at $100 per share. The class A shares are entitled to a liquidation preference of $100. The preferred shareholders have increased their proportionate interest in the assets or earnings and profits of corporation T since the fair market value of 1.20 shares of class A preferred stock ($120) exceeds the issue price of the old preferred stock ($100). Accordingly, the preferred shareholders are deemed under section 305(c) to receive a distribution in the amount of $20 on each share of old preferred stock and the distribution is one to which sections 305(b)(4) and 301 apply.

(ii) The same result would occur if the fair market value of the common stock immediately following the recapitalization were $20 per share and each share of preferred stock were exchanged for one share of the new class A preferred stock and one share of common stock.

Example (2). Corporation A, a publicly held company whose stock is traded on a securities exchange (or in the over-the-counter market) has two classes of stock outstanding, common and cumulative preferred. Each share of preferred stock is convertible into .75 shares of common stock. There are no dividend arrearages. At the time of issue of the preferred stock, there was no plan or prearrangement by which it was to be exchanged for common stock. The issue price of the preferred stock is $100 per share. In order to retire the preferred stock, corporation A recapitalizes in a transaction to which section 368(a)(1)(E) applies and each share of preferred stock is exchanged for one share of common stock. Immediately after the recapitalization the common stock has a fair market value of $110 per share. Notwithstanding the fact that the fair market value of the common stock received in the exchange (determined immediately following the recapitalization) exceeds the issue price of the preferred stock surrendered, the recapitalization is not deemed under section 305(c) to result in a distribution to which sections 305(b)(4) and 301 apply since the recapitalization is not pursuant to a plan to periodically increase a shareholder's proportionate interest in the assets or earnings and profits and does not involve dividend arrearages.

Example (3). Corporation V is organized with two classes of stock, 1,000 shares of class A common and 1,000 shares of class B convertible preferred. Each share of class B stock may be converted into two shares of class A stock. Pursuant to a recapitalization under section 368(a)(1)(E), the 1,000 shares of class A stock are surrendered in exchange for 500 shares of new class A common and 500 shares of newly authorized class C common. The conversion right of class B stock is changed to one share of class A stock and one share of class C stock for each share of class B stock. The change in the conversion right is not deemed under section 305(c) to be a distribution on preferred stock to which sections 305(b)(4) and 301 apply.

Example (4). Corporation X issues preferred stock for $100 per share. The stock is redeemable in 5 years or any time thereafter for $110. The redemption price at no time exceeds 10 percent of the issue price. The difference between redemption price and issue price is not deemed under section 305(c) to be a distribution on preferred stock to which sections 305(b)(4) and 301 apply.

Example (5). Corporation W issues preferred stock for $100 per share. The stock pays no dividends but is redeemable at the end of 5 years for $185 with yearly increases thereafter of $15. There are no facts to indicate that a call premium in excess of $10 is reasonable. Since the difference between redemption price and issue price exceeds the reasonable call premium to the extent of $75 that amount is considered to be a distribution of additional stock on preferred stock which is constructively received over the 5-year period. Therefore, the shareholder is deemed under section 305(c) to receive on the last day of each year during the 5-year period a distribution on his preferred stock in an amount equal to 15 percent of the issue price. Each $15 increase in the redemption price thereafter is considered to be a distribution on the preferred stock at the time each such increase becomes effective.

Example (6). Corporation A, a publicly held company whose stock is traded on a securities exchange (or in the over-the-counter market) has two classes of stock outstanding, common and preferred. The preferred stock is nonvoting and nonconvertible, limited and preferred as to dividends, and has a fixed liquidation preference. There are no dividend arrearages. At the time of issue of the preferred stock, there was no plan or prearrangement by which it was to be exchanged for common stock. In order to retire the preferred stock, corporation A recapitalizes in a transaction to which section 368 (a)(1)(E) applies and the preferred stock is exchanged for common stock. The transaction is not deemed to be a distribution under section 305(c) and sections 305(b) and 301 do not apply to the transaction. The same result would follow if the preferred stock was exchanged in any reorganization described in section 3(a)(1) for a new preferred stock having substantially the same market value and having no greater call price or liquidation preference than the old preferred stock, whether the new preferred stock has voting rights or is convertible into common stock of corporation A at a fixed ratio subject to change solely to take account of stock dividends, stock splits, or similar transactions with respect to the stock into which the preferred stock is convertible.

Example (7). Corporation R has only common stock outstanding. Corporation R distributes to the common shareholders on a pro rata basis, newly authorized 2-percent preferred stock. Such stock has a par value of $100 per share and is redeemable at the end of 5 years for $105 per share. At the time of the distribution, the fair market value of the preferred stock is $50 per share. There are no facts to indicate that a call premium in excess of $5 is reasonable. Since the difference between redemption price and issue price (i. e., the fair market value of the preferred stock immediately following its distribution as a stock dividend) exceeds the reasonable call premium to the extent of $50, that amount is considered to be a distribution of additional stock on preferred stock which is constructively received over the 5-year period. Therefore, each shareholder is deemed under section 305(c) to receive each year during the 5-year period a distribution in the amount of $10 on his preferred stock to which sections 305(b)(4) and 301 apply.

Example (8). Corporation Q is organized with 10,000 shares of class A stock and 1,000 shares of class B stock. The terms of the class B stock require that the class B have a preference of $5 per share with respect to dividends and $100 per share with respect to liquidation. In addition, upon a distribution of $10 per share to the class A stock, class B participates equally in any additional dividends. The terms also provide that upon liquidation the class B stock participates equally after the class A stock receives $100 per share. Corporation Q has no accumulated earnings and profits. In 1971 it earned $10,000, the highest earnings in its history. The corporation is in an industry in which it is reasonable to anticipate a growth in earnings of 5 percent per year. In 1971 the book value of corporation Q's assets totalled $100,000. In that year the corporation paid a dividend of $5 per share to the class B stock and $.50 per share to the class A. In 1972 the corporation had no earnings and in lieu of a $5 dividend distributed one share of class B stock for each outstanding share of class B. No distribution was made to the class A stock. Since, in 1972, it was not reasonable to anticipate that the class B stock would participate in the current and anticipated earnings and growth of the corporation beyond its preferred interest, the class B stock is preferred stock and the distribution of class B shares to the class B shareholders is a distribution to which sections 305(b)(4) and 301 apply.

Example (9). Corporation P is organized with 10,000 shares of class A stock and 1,000 shares of class B stock. The terms of the class B stock require that the class B have a preference of $5 per share with respect to dividends and $100 per share with respect to liquidation. In addition, upon a distribution of $5 per share to the class A stock, class B participates equally in any additional dividends. The terms also provide that upon liquidation the class B stock participates equally after the class A receives $100 per share. Corporation P has accumulated earnings and profits of $100,000. In 1971 it earned $75,000. The corporation is in an industry in which it is reasonable to anticipate a growth in earnings of 10 percent per year. In 1971 the book value of corporation P's assets totalled $5 million. In that year the corporation paid a dividend of $5 per share to the class B stock, $5 per share to the class A stock, and it distributed an additional $1 per share to both class A and class B stock. In 1972 the corporation had earnings of $82,500. In that year it paid a dividend of $5 per share to the class B stock and $5 per share to the class A stock. In addition, the corporation declared stock dividends of one share of class B stock for every 10 outstanding shares of class B and one share of class A stock for every 10 outstanding shares of class A. Since, in 1972, it was reasonable to anticipate that both the class B stock and the class A stock would participate in the current and anticipated earnings and growth of the corporation beyond their preferred interests, neither class is preferred stock and the stock dividends are not distributions to which section 305(b)(4) applies.

§ 1.305-6 Distributions of convertible preferred

(a) In general. (1) Under section 305(b)(5), a distribution by a corporation of its convertible preferred stock or rights to acquire such stock made or considered as made with respect to its stock is treated as a distribution of property to which section 301 applies unless the corporation establishes that such distribution will not result in a disproportionate distribution as described in § 1.305-3.

(2) The distribution of convertible preferred stock is likely to result in a disproportionate distribution when both of the following conditions exist: (i) The conversion right must be exercised within a relatively short period of time after the date of distribution of the stock; and (ii) taking into account such factors as the dividend rate, the redemption provisions, the marketability of the convertible stock, and the conversion price, it may be anticipated that some shareholders will exercise their conversion rights and some will not. On the other hand, where the conversion right may be exercised over a period of many years and the dividend rate is consistent with market conditions at the time of distribution of the stock, there is no basis for predicting at what time and the extent to which the stock will be converted and it is unlikely that a disproportionate distribution will result.

(b) Examples. The application of section 305(b)(5) may be illustrated by the following examples:

Example (1). Corporation Z is organized with one class of stock, class A common. During the year the corporation declares a dividend on the class A stock payable in newly authorized class B preferred stock which is convertible into class A stock for a period of 20 years from the date of issuance. Assuming dividend rates are normal in light of existing conditions so that there is no basis for predicting the extent to which the stock will be converted, the circumstances will ordinarily be sufficient to establish that a disproportionate distribution will not result since it is impossible to predict the extent to which the class B stock will be converted into class A stock. Accordingly, the distribution of class B stock is not one to which section 301 applies.

Example (2). Corporation X is organized with one class of stock, class A common. During the year the corporation declares a dividend on the class A stock payable in newly authorized redeemable class C preferred stock which is convertible into class A common stock no later than 4 months from the date of distribution at a price slightly higher than the market price of class A stock on the date of distribution. By prearrangement with corporation Y, corporation Y, an insurance company, agrees to purchase class C stock from any shareholder who does not wish to convert. By reason of this prearrangement, it is anticipated that the shareholders will either sell the class C stock to the insurance company (which expects to retain the shares for investment purposes) or will convert. As a result, some of the shareholders exercise their conversion privilege and receive additional shares of class A stock, while other shareholders sell their class C stock to corporation Y and receive cash. The distribution is a distribution to which section 301 applies since it results in the receipt of property by some shareholders and an increase in the proportionate interests of other shareholders.

§ 1.305-7 Certain transactions treated as distributions

(a) In general. Under section 305 (c), a change in conversion ratio, a change in redemption price, a difference between redemption price and issue price, a redemption which is treated as a distribution to which section 301 applies, or any transaction (including a recapitalization) having a similar effect on the interest of any shareholder may be treated as a distribution with respect to any shareholder whose proportionate interest in the earnings and profits or assets of the corporation is increased by such change, difference, redemption, or similar transaction. In general, such change, difference, redemption, or similar transaction will be treated as a distribution to which sections 305(b) and 301 apply where—

(1) The proportionate interest of any shareholder in the earnings and profits or assets of the corporation deemed to have made such distribution is increased by such change, difference, redemption, or similar transaction; and

(2) Such distribution has the result described in paragraphs (2), (3), (4), or (5) of section 305(b).

Where such change, difference, redemption, or similar transaction is treated as a distribution under the provisions of this section, such distribution will be deemed made with respect to any shareholder whose interest in the earnings and profits or assets of the distributing corporation is increased thereby. Such distribution will be deemed to be a distribution of the stock of such corporation made by the corporation to such shareholder with respect to his stock. Depending upon the facts presented, the distribution may be deemed to be made in common or preferred stock. For example, where a redemption price in excess of a reasonable call premium exists with respect to a class of preferred stock and the other requirements of this section are also met, the distribution will be deemed made with respect to such preferred stock, in stock of the same class. Accordingly, the preferred shareholders are considered under sections 305(b)(4) and 305(c) to have received a distribution of preferred stock to which section 301 applies. See the examples in §§ 1.305-3(e) and 1.305-5(d) for further illustrations of the application of section 305(c).

(b) Antidilution provisions. (1) For purposes of applying section 305(c) in conjunction with section 305(b), a change in the conversion ratio or conversion price of convertible preferred stock (or securities), or in the exercise price of rights or warrants, made pursuant to a bona fide, reasonable, adjustment formula (including, but not limited to, either the so-called "market price" or "conversion price" type of formulas) which has the effect of preventing dilution of the interest of the holders of such stock (or securities) will not be considered to result in a deemed distribution of stock. An adjustment in the conversion ratio or price to compensate for cash or property distributions to other shareholders that are taxable under section 301, 356 (a)(2), 871(a)(1)(A), 881(a)(1), 852 (b), or 857(b) will not be considered as made pursuant to a bona fide adjustment formula.

(2) The principles of this paragraph may be illustrated by the following example:

> **Example.** (i) Corporation U has two classes of stock outstanding, class A and class B. Each class B share is convertible into class A stock. In accordance with a bona fide, reasonable, antidilution provision, the conversion price is adjusted if the corporation transfers class A stock to anyone for a consideration that is below the conversion price.
>
> (ii) The corporation sells class A stock to the public at the current market price but below the conversion price. Pursuant to the antidilution provision, the conversion price is adjusted downward. Such a change in conversion price will not be deemed to be a distribution under section 305(c) for the purposes of section 305(b).

(c) Recapitalizations. (1) A recapitalization (whether or not an isolated transaction) will be deemed to result in a distribution to which section 305 (c) and this section apply if—

(i) It is pursuant to a plan to periodically increase a shareholder's proportionate interest in the assets or earnings and profits of the corporation, or

(ii) A shareholder owning preferred stock with dividends in arrears exchanges his stock for other stock and, as a result, increases his proportionate interest in the assets or earnings and profits of the corporation. An increase in a preferred shareholder's proportion-

ate interest occurs in any case where the fair market value or the liquidation preference, whichever is greater, of the stock received in the exchange (determined immediately following the recapitalization), exceeds the issue price of the preferred stock surrendered.

(2) In a case to which subparagraph (1)(ii) of this paragraph applies, the amount of the distribution deemed under section 305(c) to result from the recapitalization is the lesser of (i) the amount by which the fair market value or the liquidation preference, whichever is greater, of the stock received in the exchange (determined immediately following the recapitalization) exceeds the issue price of the preferred stock surrendered, or (ii) the amount of the dividends in arrears.

(3) For purposes of applying subparagraphs (1) and (2) of this paragraph with respect to stock issued before July 12, 1973, the term "issue price of the preferred stock surrendered" shall mean the greater of the issue price or the liquidation preference (not including dividends in arrears) of the stock surrendered.

* * * * *

§ 1.306-1   General

(a) Section 306 provides, in general, that the proceeds from the sale or redemption of certain stock (referred to as "section 306 stock") shall be treated either as ordinary income or as a distribution of property to which section 301 applies. Section 306 stock is defined in section 306(c) and is usually preferred stock received either as a nontaxable dividend or in a transaction in which no gain or loss is recognized. Section 306(b) lists certain circumstances in which the special rules of section 306(a) shall not apply.

(b)(1) If a shareholder sells or otherwise disposes of section 306 stock (other than by redemption or within the exceptions listed in section 306(b)), the entire proceeds received from such disposition shall be treated as ordinary income to the extent that the fair market value of the stock sold, on the date distributed to the shareholder, would have been a dividend to such shareholder had the distributing corporation distributed cash in lieu of stock. Any excess of the amount received over the sum of the amount treated as ordinary income plus the adjusted basis of the stock disposed of, shall be treated as gain from the sale of a capital asset or noncapital asset as the case may be. No loss shall be recognized. No reduction of earnings and profits results from any disposition of stock other than a redemption. The term "disposition" under section 306(a)(1) includes, among other things, pledges of stock under certain circumstances, particularly where the pledgee can look only to the stock itself as its security.

(2) Section 306(a)(1) may be illustrated by the following examples:

Example (1). On December 15, 1954, A and B owned equally all of the stock of Corporation X which files its income tax return on a calendar year basis. On that date Corporation X distributed pro rata 100 shares of preferred stock as a dividend on its outstanding common stock. On December 15, 1954, the preferred stock had a fair market value of $10,000. On December 31, 1954, the earnings and profits of Corporation X were $20,000. The 50 shares of preferred stock so distributed to A had an allocated basis to him of $10 per share or a total of $500 for the 50 shares. Such shares had a fair market value of $5,000 when issued. A sold the 50 shares of preferred stock on July 1, 1955, for $6,000. Of this amount $5,000 will be treated as ordinary income; $500 ($6,000 minus $5,500) will be treated as gain from the sale of a capital or noncapital asset as the case may be.

Example (2). The facts are the same as in Example 1 except that A sold his 50 shares of preferred stock for $5,100. Of this amount $5,000 will be treated as ordinary income. No loss will be allowed. There will be added back to the basis of the common stock of Corporation X with respect to which the preferred stock was distributed, $400, the allocated basis of $500 reduced by the $100 received.

Example (3). The facts are the same as in example 1 except that A sold 25 of his shares of preferred stock for $2,600. Of this amount $2,500 will be treated as ordinary income. No loss will be allowed. There will be added back to the basis of the common stock of Corporation X with respect to which the preferred stock was distributed, $150, the allocated basis of $250 reduced by the $100 received.

(c) The entire amount received by a shareholder from the redemption of section 306 stock shall be treated as a distribution of property under section 301. See also section 303 (relating to distribution in redemption of stock to pay death taxes).

§ 1.306-2 Exception

(a) If a shareholder terminates his entire stock interest in a corporation—

(1) By a sale or other disposition within the requirements of section 306 (b) (1) (A), or

(2) By redemption under section 302 (b) (3) (through the application of section 306(b) (1) (B)),

the amount received from such disposition shall be treated as an amount received in part or full payment for the stock sold or redeemed. In the case of a sale, only the stock interest need be terminated. In determining whether an entire stock interest has been terminated under section 306(b) (1) (A), all of the provisions of section 318(a) (relating to constructive ownership of stock) shall be applicable. In determining whether a shareholder has terminated his entire interest in a corporation by a redemption of his stock under section 302(b) (3), all of the provisions of section 318(a) shall be applicable unless the shareholder meets the requirements of section 302(c) (2) (relating to termination of all interest in the corporation). If the requirements of section 302(c) (2) are met, section 318(a) (1) (relating to members of a family) shall be inapplicable. Under all circumstances paragraphs (2), (3), (4), and (5) of section 318(a) shall be applicable.

(b) Section 306 (a) does not apply to—

(1) Redemptions of section 306 stock pursuant to a partial or complete liquidation of a corporation to which part II (section 331 and following), subchapter C, chapter 1 of the Code applies.

(2) Exchanges of section 306 stock solely for stock in connection with a reorganization or in an exchange under section 351, 355, or section 1036 (relating to exchanges of stock for stock in the same corporation) to the extent that gain or loss is not recognized to the shareholder as the result of the exchange of the stock (see paragraph (d) of § 1.306-3 relative to the receipt of other property), and

(3) A disposition or redemption, if it is established to the satisfaction of the Commissioner that the distribution, and the disposition or redemption, was not in pursuance of a plan having as one of its principal purposes the avoidance of Federal income tax. However, in the case of a prior or simultaneous disposition (or redemption) of the stock with respect to which the section 306 stock disposed of (or redeemed) was issued, it is not necessary to establish that the distribution was not in pursuance of such a plan. For example, in the absence of such a plan

and of any other facts the first sentence of this subparagraph would be applicable to the case of dividends and isolated dispositions of section 306 stock by minority shareholders. Similarly, in the absence of such a plan and of any other facts, if a shareholder received a distribution of 100 shares of section 306 stock on his holdings of 100 shares of voting common stock in a corporation and sells his voting common stock before he disposes of his section 306 stock, the subsequent disposition of his section 306 stock would not ordinarily be considered a disposition one of the principal purposes of which is the avoidance of Federal income tax.

§ 1.306-3   Section 306 stock defined

(a) For the purpose of subchapter C, chapter 1 of the Code, the term "section 306 stock" means stock which meets the requirements of section 306(c)(1). Any class of stock distributed to a shareholder in a transaction in which no amount is includible in the income of the shareholder or no gain or loss is recognized may be section 306 stock, if a distribution of money by the distributing corporation in lieu of such stock would have been a dividend in whole or in part. However, except as provided in section 306(g), if no part of a distribution of money by the distributing corporation in lieu of such stock would have been a dividend, the stock distributed will not constitute section 306 stock.

(b) For the purpose of section 306, rights to acquire stock shall be treated as stock. Such rights shall not be section 306 stock if no part of the distribution would have been a dividend if money had been distributed in lieu of the rights. When stock is acquired by the exercise of rights which are treated as section 306 stock, the stock acquired is section 306 stock. Upon the disposition of such stock (other than by redemption or within the exceptions listed in section 306(b)), the proceeds received from the disposition shall be treated as ordinary income to the extent that the fair market value of the stock rights, on the date distributed to the shareholder, would have been a dividend to the shareholder had the distributing corporation distributed cash in lieu of stock rights. Any excess of the amount realized over the sum of the amount treated as ordinary income plus the adjusted basis of the stock, shall be treated as gain from the sale of the stock.

(c) Section 306(c)(1)(A) provides that section 306 stock is any stock (other than common issued with respect to common) distributed to the shareholder selling or otherwise disposing thereof if, under section 305(a) (relating to distributions of stock and stock rights) any part of the distribution was not included in the gross income of the distributee.

(d) Section 306(c)(1)(B) includes in the definition of section 306 stock any stock except common stock, which is received by a shareholder in connection with a reorganization under section 368 or in a distribution or exchange under section 355 (or so much of section 356 as relates to section 355) provided the effect of the transaction is substantially the same as the receipt of a stock dividend, or the stock is received in exchange for section 306 stock. If, in a transaction to which section 356 is applicable, a shareholder exchanges section 306 stock for stock and money or other property, the entire amount of such money and of the fair market value of the other property (not limited to the gain recognized) shall be treated as a distribution of property to which section 301 applies. Common stock received in exchange for section 306 stock in a recapitalization shall not be considered section 306 stock. Ordinarily, section 306 stock includes stock which is not common stock received in pursuance of a plan of reorganization (within the meaning of section 368(a)) or received in a distribution or exchange to which section 355 (or so much of section 356 as relates to section 355) applies if cash received in lieu of such stock would have been treated as a dividend under section 356(a)(2) or would have been treated as a distribution to which section 301 applies by virtue of section 356(b) or section 302(d). The application of the preceding sentence is illustrated by the following examples:

Example (1). Corporation A, having only common stock outstanding, is merged in a statutory merger (qualifying as a reorganization under section 368(a)) with Corporation B. Pursuant to such merger, the shareholders of Corporation A received both common and preferred stock in Corporation B. The preferred stock received by such shareholders is section 306 stock.

Example (2). X and Y each own one-half of the 2,000 outstanding shares of preferred stock and one-half of the 2,000 outstanding shares of common stock of Corporation C. Pursuant to a reorganization within the meaning of section 368 (a) (1) (E) (recapitalization) each shareholder exchanges his preferred stock for preferred stock of a new issue which is not substantially different from the preferred stock previously held. Unless the preferred stock exchanged was itself section 306 stock the preferred stock received is not section 306 stock.

(e) Section 306(c) (1) (C) includes in the definition of section 306 stock any stock (except as provided in section 306(c) (1) (B)) the basis of which in the hands of the person disposing of such stock, is determined by reference to section 306 stock held by such shareholder or any other person. Under this paragraph common stock can be section 306 stock. Thus, if a person owning section 306 stock in Corporation A transfers it to Corporation B which is controlled by him in exchange for common stock of Corporation B in a transaction to which section 351 is applicable, the common stock so received by him would be section 306 stock and subject to the provisions of section 306(a) on its disposition. In addition, the section 306 stock transferred is section 306 stock in the hands of Corporation B, the transferee. Section 306 stock transferred by gift remains section 306 stock in the hands of the donee. Stock received in exchange for section 306 stock under section 1036(a) (relating to exchange of stock for stock in the same corporation) or under so much of section 1031 (b) as relates to section 1036(a) becomes section 306 stock and acquires, for purposes of section 306, the characteristics of the section 306 stock exchanged. The entire amount of the fair market value of the other property received in such transaction shall be considered as received upon a disposition (other than a redemption) to which section 306(a) applies. Section 306 stock ceases to be so classified if the basis of such stock is determined by reference to its fair market value on the date of the decedent-stockholder's death or the optional valuation date under section 1014.

(f) If section 306 stock which was distributed with respect to common stock is exchanged for common stock in the same corporation (whether or not such exchange is pursuant to a conversion privilege contained in section 306 stock), such common stock shall not be section 306 stock. This subparagraph applies to exchanges not

coming within the purview of section 306(c) (1) (B). Common stock which is convertible into stock other than common stock or into property, shall not be considered common stock. It is immaterial whether the conversion privilege is contained in the stock or in some type of collateral agreement.

(g) If there is a substantial change in the terms and conditions of any stock, then, for the purpose of this section—

(1) The fair market value of such stock shall be the fair market value at the time of distribution or the fair market value at the time of such change, whichever is higher;

(2) Such stock's ratable share of the amount which would have been a dividend if money had been distributed in lieu of stock shall be determined by reference to the time of distribution or by reference to the time of such change, whichever ratable share is higher; and

(3) Section 306(c) (2) shall be inapplicable if there would have been a dividend to any extent if money had been distributed in lieu of the stock either at the time of the distribution or at the time of such change.

. . . .

§ 1.307-1 General

(a) If a shareholder receives stock or stock rights as a distribution on stock previously held and under section 305 such distribution is not includible in gross income, then, except as provided in section 307(b) and § 1.307-2, the basis of the stock with respect to which the distribution was made shall be allocated between the old and new stocks or rights in proportion to the fair market values of each on the date of distribution. If a shareholder receives stock or stock rights as a distribution on stock previously held and pursuant to section 305 part of the distribution is not includible in gross income, then (except as provided in section 307(b) and § 1.307-2) the basis of the stock with respect to which the distribution is made shall be allocated between (1) the old stock and (2) that part of the new stock or rights which is not includible in gross income, in proportion to the fair market values of each on the date of distribution. The date of distribution in each case shall be the date the stock or the rights are distributed to the stockholder and not the record date. The general rule will apply with respect to stock rights only if such rights are exercised or sold.

(b) The application of paragraph (a) of this section is illustrated by the following example:

Example. A taxpayer in 1947 purchased 100 shares of common stock at $100 per share and in 1954 by reason of the ownership of such stock acquired 100 rights entitling him to subscribe to 100 additional shares of such stock at $90 a share. Immediately after the issuance of the rights, each of the shares of stock in respect of which the rights were acquired had a fair market value, ex-rights, of $110 and the rights had a fair market value of $19 each. The basis of the rights and the common stock for the purpose of determining the basis for gain or loss on a subsequent sale or exercise of the rights or a sale of the old stock is computed as follows:

100 (shares) × $100=$10,000, cost of old stock (stock in respect of which the rights were acquired).

100 (shares) × $110=$11,000, market value of old stock.

100 (rights) × $19=$1,900, market value of rights.

$$\frac{11,000}{12,900} \text{ of } \$10,000 = \$8,527.13, \text{ cost of old stock apportioned to such stock.}$$

$$\frac{1,900}{12,900} \text{ of } \$10,000 = \$1,472.87, \text{ cost of old stock apportioned to rights.}$$

If the rights are sold, the basis for determining gain or loss will be $14.7287 per right. If the rights are exercised, the basis of the new stock acquired will be the subscription price paid therefor ($90) plus the basis of the rights exercised ($14.7287 each) or $104.7287 per share. The remaining basis of the old stock for the purpose of determining gain or loss on a subsequent sale will be $85.2713 per share.

§ 1.307-2　　Exception

The basis of rights to buy stock which are excluded from gross income under section 305(a), shall be zero if the fair market value of such rights on the date of distribution is less than 15 percent of the fair market value of the old stock on that date, unless the shareholder elects to allocate part of the basis of the old stock to the rights as provided in paragraph (a) of § 1.307-1. The election shall be made by a shareholder with respect to all the rights received by him in a particular distribution in respect of all the stock of the same class owned by him in the issuing corporation at the time of such distribution. Such election to allocate basis to rights shall be in the form of a statement attached to the shareholder's return for the year in which the rights are received. This election, once made, shall be irrevocable with respect to the rights for which the election was made. Any shareholder making such an election shall retain a copy of the election and of the tax return with which it was filed, in order to substantiate the use of an allocated basis upon a subsequent disposition of the stock acquired by exercise.

§ 1.311-1　　General

(a) Except as provided in subsections (b), (c), and (d) of section 311, section 453(d) (relating to installment obligations) and such other provisions of the Code as sections 341(f), 617(d), 1245(a), 1250(a), 1251(c), and 1252(a), no gain or loss is recognized to a corporation on the distribution, with respect to its stock, of stock, or rights to acquire its stock, or property (regardless of the fact that such property may have appreciated or depreciated in value since its acquisition by the corporation). However, the proceeds of the sale of property in form made by a shareholder receiving such property in kind from the corporation may be imputed to the corporation if, in substance, the corporation made the sale. Moreover, where property is distributed by a corporation, which distribution is in effect an anticipatory assignment of income, such income may be taxable to the corporation. The term "distributions with respect to its stock" includes distributions made in redemption of stock (other than distributions in complete or partial liquidations). See, however, paragraph (e) of this section for distributions to which section 311 does not apply. For the rule respecting the taxation of a corporation making a distribution of property in partial or complete liquidation, see section 336.

(b) In any case in which a corporation distributes with respect to its stock assets which have been part of an inventory, the value of which has been computed for income tax purposes under the method provided in section 472 (relating to last-in, first-out inventories), such corporation shall—

(1) Compute the amount of its inventory under the method provided in section 472 immediately prior to the distribution and immediately after such distribution;

(2) Compute the difference between the two amounts described in subparagraph (1) of this paragraph;

(3) Compute the amount of its inventory under the method authorized by section 471 (relating to general rule for inventories) immediately prior to the distribution and immediately after such distribution;

(4) Compute the difference between the two amounts determined under subparagraph (3) of this paragraph.

If the amount computed under subparagraph (4) of this paragraph is in excess of the amount computed under subparagraph (2) of this paragraph, then such excess shall, under section 311(b), be included in the income of the corporation for the year in which such distribution occurs. In any case in which a corporation distributes assets which have been a part of an inventory whose value has been computed for income tax purposes under the method provided in section 472, such corporation shall on the date of distribution record a specific statement of the amount of its inventory under each of the applicable methods for use in the determination of the amount of income includible under section 311. Section 311(b) and this paragraph do not apply to any distribution which is governed by section 311(d) (1).

(c) The following example illustrates the application of section 311 (b):

Example. Corporation R, a manufacturing corporation inventorying goods under the method provided in section 472, distributes 200 units of its inventory assets to its shareholders on November 15, 1955. Immediately before the distribution, the corporation held 300 identical inventory units at the following basis determined by reference to the value computed by using the LIFO method and the value computed by using the FIFO method, in the order of acquisition:

Number of units	Basis LIFO	Number of units	Basis FIFO
a. 100	$1,000	100	$4,000
b. 100	2,000	50	2,500
c. 50	1,000	50	2,500
d. 50	2,000	100	6,000

The amount includible in income pursuant to section 311 (b) is $4,000 computed as follows:

(1) Inventory before distribution under FIFO method (a, b, c and d)	$15,000
(2) Inventory under FIFO method immediately after distribution (d)	6,000
(3) Difference (FIFO basis of inventory distributed)	$9,000
(4) Inventory before distribution under LIFO method (a, b, c and d)	$6,000
(5) Inventory under LIFO method immediately after distribution (a)	$1,000
(6) Difference (LIFO basis of inventory distributed)	5,000
(7) Amount includible in income under section 311 (b)	4,000

(d) Section 311(c) provides in general for the inclusion in the income of a corporation, on a distribution of property by such corporation to its shareholders, of an amount equal to the excess of a liability over the basis of the property distributed. Thus, section 311 (c) applies where the property distributed is subject to a liability or where the shareholder assumes a liability of the corporation in connection with the distribution. For example, if property which is a capital asset having an adjusted basis to the distributing corporation of $100 and a fair market value of $1,000 (but subject to a liability of $900) is distributed to a shareholder, such distribution is taxable (as long-term or short-term gain, as the case may be) to the corporation to the extent of the excess of the liability ($900) over the adjusted basis ($100) or $800. However, if in the preceding example the fair market value of the property distributed were $800, the amount taxable to the corporation is limited to the excess of the fair market value of the property ($800) over its adjusted basis ($100) or $700. If the property subject to a liability were not a capital asset in the hands of the distributing corporation, the gain would be taxable as gain from the sale of a noncapital asset. The holding period of assets so distributed shall be determined as if such property were sold on the date of the distribution. Section 311(c) and this paragraph do not apply to any distribution which is governed by section 311(d) (1).

(e) (1) Section 311 is limited to distributions which are made by reason of the corporation-stockholder relationship. Section 311 does not apply to transactions between a corporation and a shareholder in his capacity as debtor, creditor, employee, or vendee, where the fact that such debtor, creditor, employee, or vendee is a shareholder is incidental to the transaction. Thus, if the corporation receives its own stock as consideration upon the sale of property by it, or in satisfaction of indebtedness to it, the gain or loss resulting is to be computed in the same manner as though the payment had been made in any other property.

(2) The following examples illustrate the application of subparagraph (1) of this paragraph:

Example (1). Corporation A has a claim against Corporation B for damages for loss of profits due to patent infringement. Corporation B satisfies such claim by surrendering shares of the stock of Corporation A to Corporation A. The fair market value of such stock is includible in the gross income of Corporation A.

Example (2). Corporation C, a corporation engaged in the manufacture and sale of automobiles, sells an automobile to individual X, and receives in payment therefor shares of the stock of Corporation C. The transaction will be treated in the same manner as if an amount of cash equal to the fair market value of such stock had been received by Corporation C.

§ 1.311–2 Appreciated property used to redeem stock

(a) **In general.** (1) Section 311(d) (1) provides, in general, that gain is recognized to a corporation which distributes appreciated property (other than an obligation of such corporation) to its shareholders after November 30, 1969, in a redemption (as defined in section 317(b) of its stock to which subpart A, part I, subchapter C, chapter 1 of the Code applies, regardless of whether the redemption is treated as a distribution of property to which section 301 applies. Paragraphs (b) through (i) of this section contain exceptions and limitations provided by section 311(d) (2) and section 905(c) of the Tax Reform Act of 1969 to the application of section 311(d) (1). These exceptions and limitations prevent the recognition of gain to a corporation upon a distribution of appreciated property, but do not broaden the general nonrecognition provisions of section 311(a). Thus, for example, if the proceeds of the sale of property in form made by a shareholder, who received such property from a corporation, are imputed to the corporation (see § 1.311–1(a)), the exceptions and limitations of section 311(d) (2) would have no application.

(2) Section 311(d) applies only where there is an actual redemption of stock as a result of the distribution. Thus, section 311(d) does not apply where there is a distribution of appreciated property pro rata among all shareholders and such shareholders do not transfer any of their stock to the distributing corporation in exchange for such property even though the effect of the transaction would have been the same as if there had been actual redemptions. Section 311(d) applies where an acquisition of stock by a corporation is treated under section 304 as a distribution in redemption of the stock of either the acquiring or issuing corporation. Section 311(d) (1) does not apply to a distribution in partial or complete liquidation of a corporation (see sections 331 through 346). In general, the section does not apply to a distribution pursuant to a reorganization to which part III or IV of subchapter C applies or to a distribution of stock or securities of a controlled corporation to which section 355 (or so much of section 356 as relates to section 355) applies. However, if the distribution is in substance a redemption, section 311(d) will apply. Thus, if one class of shareholders exchanges preferred stock for a lesser amount of new preferred stock (having similar rights and privileges) and for other property, the transaction will be considered a redemption for purposes of section 311 (d) rather than a distribution pursuant to a reorganization to which part III or IV of subchapter C would apply.

(3) For purposes of this section, the term "appreciated property" means any property whose fair market value on the date of distribution exceeds its adjusted basis in the hands of the distributing corporation. For purposes of determining the amount of gain which will be recognized under this section, gain realized from the distribution of appreciated property shall not be offset by any loss realized from the distribution of property whose adjusted basis exceeds its fair market value. The amount and nature of gain recognized to a corporation which distributes appreciated property shall be determined as if such property were sold for its fair market value on the date of distribution. The nature of such gain shall be determined by reference to all applicable provisions of law, including section 1245.

§ 1.312–1 Adjustment to earnings and profits reflecting distributions by corporations

(a) In general, on the distribution of property by a corporation with respect to its stock, its earnings and profits (to the extent thereof) shall be decreased by—

(1) The amount of money,

(2) The principal amount of the obligations of such corporation issued in such distribution, and

(3) The adjusted basis of other property.

For special rule with respect to distributions to which section 312 (e) applies, see § 1.312–5.

(b) The adjustment provided in section 312 (a) (3) and (a) (3) of this section with respect to a distribution of property (other than money or its own obligations) shall be made notwithstanding the fact that such property has appreciated or depreciated in value since acquisition.

(c) The application of paragraphs (a) and (b) of this section may be illustrated by the following examples:

Example (1). Corporation A distributes to its sole shareholder property with a value of $10,000 and a basis of $5,000. It has $12,500 in earnings and profits. The reduction in earnings and profits by reason of such distribution is $5,000. Such is the reduction even though the amount of $10,000 is includible in the income of the shareholder (other than a corporation) as a dividend.

Example (2). The facts are the same as in example (1) above except that the property has a basis of $15,000 and the earnings and profits of the corporation are $20,000. The reduction in earnings and profits is $15,000. Such is the reduction even though only the amount of $10,000 is includible in the income of the shareholder as a dividend.

(d) In the case of a distribution of stock or rights to acquire stock a portion of which is includible in income by reason of section 305 (b), the earnings and profits shall be reduced by the fair market value of such portion. No reduction shall be made if a distribution of stock or rights to acquire stock is not includible in income under the provisions of section 305.

(e) No adjustment shall be made in the amount of the earnings and profits of the issuing corporation upon a disposition of section 306 stock unless such disposition is a redemption.

§ 1.312-2 Distribution of inventory assets

Section 312 (b) provides for the increase and the decrease of the earnings and profits of a corporation which distributes, with respect to its stock, inventory assets as defined in section 312 (b) (2), where the fair market value of such assets exceeds their adjusted basis. The rules provided in section 312 (b) (relating to distributions of certain inventory assets) shall be applicable without regard to the method used in computing inventories for the purpose of the computation of taxable income. Section 312 (b) does not apply to distributions described in section 312 (e).

§ 1.312-3 Liabilities

The amount of any reductions in earnings and profits described in section 312(a) or (b) shall be (a) reduced by the amount of any liability to which the property distributed was subject and by the amount of any other liability of the corporation assumed by the shareholder in connection with such distribution, and (b) increased by the amount of gain recognized to the corporation . . . .

§ 1.312-4 Examples of adjustments provided in section 312 (c)

The adjustments provided in section 312 (c) may be illustrated by the following examples:

Example (1). On December 2, 1954, Corporation X distributed to its sole shareholder, A, an individual, as a dividend in kind a vacant lot which was not an inventory asset. On that date, the lot had a fair market value of $5,000 and was subject to a mortgage of $2,000. The adjusted basis of the lot was $3,100. The amount of the earnings and profits was $10,000. The amount of the dividend received by A is $3,000 ($5,000, the fair market value, less $2,000, the amount of the mortgage) and the reduction in the earnings and profits of Corporation X is $1,100 ($3,100, the basis, less $2,000, the amount of mortgage).

Example (2). The facts are the same as in example (1) above with the exception that the amount of the mortgage to which the property was subject was $4,000. The amount of the dividend received by A is $1,000, and there is no reduction in the earnings and profits of the corporation as a result of the distribution (disregarding such reduction as may result from an increase in tax to Corporation X because of gain resulting from the distribution). There is a gain of $900 recognized to Corporation X, the difference between the basis of the property ($3,100) and the amount of the mortgage ($4,000), under section 311 (c) and an increase in earnings and profits of $900.

Example (3). Corporation A, having accumulated earnings and profits of $100,000, distributed in kind to its shareholders, not in liquidation, inventory assets which had a basis to it on the "Lifo" method (section 472) of $46,000 and on the basis of cost or market (section 471) of $50,000. The inventory had a fair market value of $55,000 and was subject to a liability of $35,000. This distribution results in a net decrease in earnings and profits of Corporation A of $11,000, (without regard to any tax on Corporation A) computed as follows:

"Fifo" basis of inventory	$50,000
Less: "Lifo" basis of inventory	46,000
Gain recognized—addition to earnings and profits (section 311 (b))	$4,000
Adjustment to earnings and profits required by section 312 (b) (1) (A):	
Fair market value of inventory ... $55,000	
Less: "Lifo" basis plus adjustment under section 311 (b) ... 50,000	
	5,000
Total increase in earnings and profits	9,000

Decrease in earnings and profits
—under section 312 (b) (1)
(B) (1) $55,000
Less: Liability assumed 35,000

Net amount of distribution (decrease
in earnings) 20,000

Net decrease in earnings and
profits 11,000

§ 1.312–5 Special rule for partial liquidations and certain redemptions

The part of the distribution properly chargeable to capital account within the provisions of section 312(e) shall not be considered a distribution of earnings and profits within the meaning of section 301 for the purpose of determining taxability of subsequent distributions by the corporation.

§ 1.312–6 Earnings and profits

(a) In determining the amount of earnings and profits (whether of the taxable year, or accumulated since February 28, 1913, or accumulated before March 1, 1913) due consideration must be given to the facts, and, while mere bookkeeping entries increasing or decreasing surplus will not be conclusive, the amount of the earnings and profits in any case will be dependent upon the method of accounting properly employed in computing taxable income (or net income, as the case may be). For instance, a corporation keeping its books and filing its income tax returns under subchapter E, chapter 1 of the Code, on the cash receipts and disbursements basis may not use the accrual basis in determining earnings and profits; a corporation computing income on the installment basis as provided in section 453 shall, with respect to the installment transactions, compute earnings and profits on such basis; and an insurance company subject to taxation under section 831 shall exclude from earnings and profits that portion of any premium which is unearned under the provisions of section 832 (b) (4) and which is segregated accordingly in the unearned premium reserve.

(b) Among the items entering into the computation of corporate earnings and profits for a particular period are all income exempted by statute, income not taxable by the Federal Government under the Constitution, as well as all items includible in gross income under section 61 or corresponding provisions of prior revenue acts. Gains and losses within the purview of section 1002 or corresponding provisions of prior revenue acts are brought into the earnings and profits at the time and to the extent such gains and losses are recognized under that section. Interest on State bonds and certain other obligations, although not taxable when received by a corporation, is taxable to the same extent as other dividends when distributed to shareholders in the form of dividends.

(c) (1) In the case of a corporation in which depletion or depreciation is a factor in the determination of income, the only depletion or depreciation deductions to be considered in the computation of the total earnings and profits are those based on cost or other basis without regard to March 1, 1913, value. In computing the earnings and profits for any period beginning after February 28, 1913, the only depletion or depreciation deductions to be considered are those based on (i) cost or other basis, if the depletable or depreciable asset was acquired subsequent to February 28, 1913, or (ii) adjusted cost or March 1, 1913, value, whichever is higher, if acquired before March 1, 1913. Thus, discovery or percentage depletion under all revenue acts for mines and oil and gas wells is not to be taken into consideration in computing the earnings and profits of a corporation. Similarly, where the basis of property in the hands of a corporation is a substituted basis, such basis, and not the fair market value of the property at the time of the acquisition by the corporation, is the basis for computing depletion and depreciation for the purpose of determining earnings and profits of the corporation.

. . . . .

(d) A loss sustained for a year before the taxable year does not affect the earnings and profits of the taxable year. However, in determining the earnings and profits accumulated since February 28, 1913, the excess of a loss sustained for a year subsequent to February 28, 1913, over the undistributed earnings and profits accumulated since February 28, 1913, and before the year for which the loss was sustained, reduces surplus as of March 1, 1913, to the extent of such excess. If the surplus as of March 1, 1913, was sufficient to absorb such excess, distributions to shareholders after the year of the loss are out of earnings and profits accumulated since the year of the loss to the extent of such earnings.

. . . .

§ 1.312-7 Effect on earnings and profits of gain or loss realized after February 28, 1913

(a) In order to determine the effect on earnings and profits of gain or loss realized from the sale or other disposition (after February 28, 1913) of property by a corporation, section 312 (f) (1) prescribed certain rules for—

(1) The computation of the total earnings and profits of the corporation of most frequent application in determining invested capital; and

(2) The computation of earnings and profits of the corporation for any period beginning after February 28, 1913, of most frequent application in determining the source of dividend distributions. Such rules are applicable whenever under any provision of subtitle A of the Code it is necessary to compute either the total earnings and profits of the corporation or the earnings and profits for any period beginning after February 28, 1913. For example, since the earnings and profits accumulated after February 28, 1913, or the earnings and profits of the taxable year, are earnings and profits for a period beginning after February 28, 1913, the determination of either must be in accordance with the regulations prescribed by this section for the ascertainment of earnings and profits for any period beginning after February 28, 1913. Under subparagraph (1) of this paragraph, such gain or loss is determined by using the adjusted basis (under the law applicable to the year in which the sale or other disposition was made) for determining gain, but disregarding value as of March 1, 1913. Under subparagraph (2) of this paragraph, there is used such adjusted basis for determining gain, giving effect to the value as of March 1, 1913, whenever applicable. In both cases the rules are the same as those governing depreciation and depletion in computing earnings and profits (see § 1.312-6). Under both subparagraphs (1) and (2) of this paragraph, the adjusted basis is subject to the limitations of the third sentence of section 312 (f) (1) requiring the use of adjustments proper in determining earnings and profits. The proper adjustments may differ under section 312 (f) (1) (A) and (B) depending upon the basis to which the adjustments are to be made. If the application of

section 312 (f) (1) (B) results in a loss and if the application of section 312 (f) (1) (A) to the same transaction reaches a different result, then the loss under section 312 (f) (1) (B) will be subject to the adjustment thereto required by section 312 (g) (2). . . . .

(b) (1) The gain or loss so realized increases or decreases the earnings and profits to, but not beyond, the extent to which such gain or loss was recognized in computing taxable income (or net income, as the case may be) under the law applicable to the year in which such sale or disposition was made. As used in this paragraph, the term "recognized" has reference to that kind of realized gain or loss which is recognized for income tax purposes by the statute applicable to the year in which the gain or loss was realized. For example, see section 356. A loss (other than a wash sale loss with respect to which a deduction is disallowed under the provisions of section 1091 or corresponding provisions of prior revenue laws) may be recognized though not allowed as a deduction (by reason, for example, of the operation of sections 267 and 1211 and corresponding provisions of prior revenue laws) but the mere fact that it is not allowed does not prevent decrease in earnings and profits by the amount of such disallowed loss. Wash sale losses, however, disallowed under section 1091 and corresponding provisions of prior revenue laws, are deemed nonrecognized losses and do not reduce earnings or profits. The "recognized" gain or loss for the purpose of computing earnings and profits is determined by applying the recognition provisions to the realized gain or loss computed under the provisions of section 312 (f) (1) as distinguished from the realized gain or loss used in computing taxable income (or net income, as the case may be).

(2) The application of subparagraph (1) of this paragraph may be illustrated by the following examples:

Example (1). Corporation X on January 1, 1952, owned stock in Corporation Y which it had acquired from Corporation Y in December 1951, in an exchange transaction in which no gain or loss was recognized. The adjusted basis to Corporation X of the property exchanged by it for the stock in Corporation Y was $30,000. The fair market value of the stock in Corporation Y when received by Corporation X was $930,000. On April 9, 1955, Corporation X made a cash distribution of $900,000 and, except for the possible effect of the transaction in 1951, had no earnings or profits accumulated after February 28, 1913, and had no earnings or profits for the taxable year. The amount of $900,-

000 representing the excess of the fair market value of the stock of Corporation Y over the adjusted basis of the property exchanged therefor was not recognized gain to Corporation X under the provisions of section 112 of the Internal Revenue Code of 1939. Accordingly, the earnings and profits of Corporation X are not increased by $900,000, the amount of the gain realized but not recognized in the exchange, and the distribution was not a taxable dividend. The basis in the hands of Corporation Y of the property acquired by it from Corporation X is $30,000. If such property is thereafter sold by Corporation Y, gain or loss will be computed on such basis of $30,000, and earnings and profits will be increased or decreased accordingly.

. . . . .

(c) (1) The third sentence of section 312(f) (1) provides for cases in which the adjustments, prescribed in section 1016, to the basis indicated in section 312(f) (1) (A) or (B), as the case may be, differ from the adjustments to such basis proper for the purpose of determining earnings or profits. The adjustments provided by such third sentence reflect the treatment provided by § 1.312-6 relative to cases where the deductions for depletion and depreciation in computing taxable income (or net income, as the case may be) differ from the deductions proper for the purpose of computing earnings and profits. The adjustments provided by such third sentence reflect the treatment provided by §§ 1.312-6 and 1.312-15 relative to cases where the deductions for depletion and depreciation in computing taxable income (or net income, as the case may be) differ from the deductions proper for the purpose of computing earnings and profits.

(2) The effect of the third sentence of section 312(f) (1) may be illustrated by the following examples:

Example (1). Corporation X purchased on January 2, 1931, an oil lease at a cost of $10,000. The lease was operated only for the years 1931 and 1932. The deduction for depletion in each of the years 1951 and 1932 amounted to $2,750, of which amount $1,750 represented percentage depletion in excess of depletion based on cost. The lease was sold in 1955 for $15,000. Under section 1016 (a) (2), in determining the gain or loss from the sale of the property, the basis must be adjusted for cost depletion of $1,000 in 1931 and percentage depletion of $2,750 in 1932. However, the adjustment of such basis, proper for the determination of earnings and profits, is $1,000 for each year, or $2,000. Hence, the cost is to be adjusted only to the extent of $2,000, leaving an adjusted basis of $8,000 and the earnings and profits will be increased by $7,000, and not by $8,750. The difference of $1,750 is equal to the amount by which the percentage depletion for the year 1932 ($2,750) exceeds the depletion on cost for that year ($1,000) and has already been applied in the computation of earnings and profits for the year 1932 by taking into account only $1,000 instead

of $2,750 for depletion in the computation of such earnings and profits. (See § 1.316-1.)

Example (2). If, in example (1), above, the property, instead of being sold, is exchanged in a transaction described in section 1031 for like property having a fair market value of $7,750 and cash of $7,250, then the increase in earnings and profits amounts to $7,000, that is, $15,000 ($7,750 plus $7,250) minus the basis of $8,000. However, in computing taxable income of Corporation X, the gain is $8,750, that is, $15,000 minus $6,250 ($10,000 less depletion of $3,750), of which only $7,250 is recognized because the recognized gain cannot exceed the sum of money received in the transaction. See section 1031 (b) and the corresponding provisions of prior revenue laws. If, however, the cash received was only $2,250 and the value of the property received was $12,750, then the increase in earnings and profits would be $2,250, that amount being the gain recognized under section 1031.

Example (3). On January 1, 1973, corporation X purchased for $10,000 a depreciable asset with an estimated useful life of 20 years and no salvage value. In computing depreciation on the asset, corporation X used the declining balance method with a rate twice the straight line rate. On December 31, 1976, the asset was sold for $9,000. Under section 1016(a)(2), the basis of the asset is adjusted for depreciation allowed for the years 1973 through 1976, or a total of $3,439. Thus, X realizes a gain of $2,439 (the excess of the amount realized, $9,000, over the adjusted basis, $6,561). However, the proper adjustment to basis for the purpose of determining earnings and profits is only $2,000, i.e., the total amount which, under § 1.312-15, was applied in the computation of earnings and profits for the years 1973-76. Hence, upon sale of the asset, earnings and profits are increased by only $1,000, i.e., the excess of the amount realized, $9,000, over the adjusted basis for earnings and profits purposes, $8,000.

(d) For adjustment and allocation of the earnings and profits of the transferor as between the transferor and the transferee in cases where the transfer of property by one corporation to another corporation results in the nonrecognition in whole or in part of gain or loss, see § 1.312-10; and see section 381 for earnings and profits of successor corporations in certain transactions.

§ 1.312-10   Allocation of earnings in certain corporate separations

(a) If one corporation transfers part of its assets constituting an active trade or business to another corporation in a transaction to which section 368 (a) (1) (D) applies and immediately thereafter the stock and securities of the controlled corporation are distributed in a distribution or exchange to which section 355 (or so much of section 356 as relates to section 355) applies, the earnings and profits of the distributing corporation immediately before the transaction shall be allocated between the distributing corporation and the controlled corporation. In the case of a newly created controlled corporation, such allocation generally shall be made in proportion to the fair market value of the business or businesses (and interests in any other properties) retained by the distributing corporation and the business or businesses (and interests in any other properties) of the controlled corporation immediately after the transaction. In a proper case, allocation shall be made between the distributing corporation and the controlled corporation in proportion to the net basis of the assets transferred and of the assets retained or by such other method as may be appropriate under the facts and circumstances of the case. The term "net basis" means the basis of the assets less liabilities assumed or liabilities to which such assets are subject. The part of the earnings and profits of the taxable year of the distributing corporation in which the transaction occurs allocable to the controlled corporation shall be included in the computation of the earnings and profits of the first taxable year of the controlled corporation ending after the date of the transaction.

(b) If a distribution or exchange to which section 355 applies (or so much of section 356 as relates to section 355) is not in pursuance of a plan meeting the requirements of a reorganization as defined in section 368 (a) (1) (D), the earnings and profits of the distributing corporation shall be decreased by the lesser of the following amounts:

(1) The amount by which the earnings and profits of the distributing corporation would have been decreased if it had transferred the stock of the controlled corporation to a new corporation in a reorganization to which section 368 (a) (1) (D) applied and immediately thereafter distributed the stock of such new corporation or,

(2) The net worth of the controlled corporation. (For this purpose the term "net worth" means the sum of the bases of all of the properties plus cash minus all liabilities.)

If the earnings and profits of the controlled corporation immediately before the transaction are less than the amount of the decrease in earnings and profits of the distributing corporation (including a case in which the controlled corporation has a deficit) the earnings and profits of the controlled corporation, after the transaction, shall be equal to the amount of such decrease. If the earnings and profits of the con-trolled corporation immediately before the transaction are more than the amount of the decrease in the earnings and profits of the distributing corporation, they shall remain unchanged.

(c) In no case shall any part of a deficit of a distributing corporation within the meaning of section 355 be allocated to a controlled corporation.

§ 1.312-11 Effect on earnings and profits of certain other tax-free exchanges, tax-free distributions and tax-free transfers from one corporation to another

(a) If property is transferred by one corporation to another, and, under the law applicable to the year in which the transfer was made, no gain or loss was recognized (or was recognized only to the extent of the property received other than that permitted by such law to be received without the recognition of gain), then proper adjustment and allocation of the earnings and profits of the transferor shall be made as between the transferor and the transferee. Transfers to which the preceding sentence applies include contributions to capital, transfers under section 351, transfers in connection with reorganizations under section 368, transfers in liquidations under section 332 and intercompany transfers during a period of affiliation. However, if, for example, property is transferred from one corporation to another in a transaction under section 351 or as a contribution to capital and the transfer is not followed or preceded by a reorganization, a transaction under section 302(a) involving a substantial part of the transferor's stock, or a total or partial liquidation, then ordinarily no allocation of the earnings and profits of the transferor shall be made. For specific rules as to allocation of earnings and profits in certain reorganizations under section 368 and in certain liquidations under section 332 see section 381 and the regulations thereunder. For allocation of earnings and profits in certain corporate separations see section 312(i) and § 1.312-10.

. . . .

§ 1.312-15 Effect of depreciation on earnings and profits

(a) Depreciation for taxable years beginning after June 30, 1972—(1) In general. Except as provided in subparagraph (2) of this paragraph and paragraph (c) of this section, for purposes of computing the earnings and profits of a corporation (including a real estate investment trust as defined in section 856) for any taxable year beginning after June 30, 1972, the allowance for depreciation (and amortization, if any) shall be deemed to be the amount which would be allowable for such year if the straight line method of depreciation had been used for all property for which depreciation is allowable for each taxable year beginning after June 30, 1972. Thus, for taxable years beginning after June 30, 1972, in determining the earnings and profits of a corporation, depreciation must be computed under the straight line method, notwithstanding that in determining taxable income the corporation uses an accelerated method of depreciation described in subparagraph (A), (B), or (C) of section 312(m) (2) or elects to amortize the basis of property under section 169, 184, 187, or 188, or any similar provision.

(2) **Exception.** (i) If, for any taxable year beginning after June 30, 1972, a method of depreciation is used by a corporation in computing taxable income which the Secretary or his delegate has determined results in a reasonable allowance under section 167(a) and which is not a declining balance method of depreciation (described in § 1.167(b)–2), the sum of the years-digits method (described in § 1.167(b)–3), or any other method allowed solely by reason of the application of subsection (b) (4) or (j) (1) (C) of section 167, then the adjustment to earnings and profits for depreciation for such year shall be determined under the method so used (in lieu of the straight line method).

(ii) The Commissioner has determined that the "unit of production" (see § 1.167(b)–0 (b)), and the "machine hour" methods of depreciation, when properly used under appropriate circumstances, meet the requirements of subdivision (i) of this subparagraph. Thus, the adjustment to earnings and profits for depreciation (for the taxable year for which either of such methods is properly used under appropriate circumstances) shall be determined under whichever of such methods is used to compute taxable income.

(3) **Determinations under straight line method.** (i) In the case of property with respect to which an allowance

for depreciation is claimed in computing taxable income, the determination of the amount which would be allowable under the straight line method shall be based on the manner in which the corporation computes depreciation in determining taxable income. Thus, if an election under § 1.167(a)–11 is in effect with respect to the property, the amount of depreciation which would be allowable under the straight line method shall be determined under § 1.167 (a)–11(g) (3). On the other hand, if property is not depreciated under the provisions of § 1.167(a)–11, the amount of depreciation which would be allowable under the straight line method shall be determined under § 1.167(b)– 1. Any election made under section 167(f), with respect to reducing the amount of salvage value taken into account in computing the depreciation allowance for certain property, or any convention adopted under § 1.167(a)–10 (b) or § 1.167(a)–11(c) (2), with respect to additions and retirements from multiple asset accounts, which is used in computing depreciation for taxable income shall be used in computing depreciation for earnings and profits purposes.

(ii) In the case of property with respect to which an election to amortize is in effect under section 169, 184, 187, or 188, or any similar provision, the amount which would be allowable under the straight line method of depreciation shall be determined under the provisions of § 1.167(b)–1. Thus, the cost or other basis of the property, less its estimated salvage value, is to be deducted in equal annual amounts over the period of the estimated useful life of the property. In computing the amount of depreciation for earnings and profits purposes, a taxpayer may utilize the provisions of section 167(f) (relating to the reduction in the amount of salvage value taken into account in computing the depreciation allowance for certain property) and any convention which could have been adopted for such property under § 1.167(a)–10(b) (relating to additions and retirements from multiple asset accounts).

.   .   .   .   .

(d) **Books and records.** Wherever different methods of depreciation are used for taxable income and earnings and profits purposes, records shall be maintained which show the depreciation taken for earnings and profits purposes each year and which will allow computation of the adjusted basis of the property in each account using the depreciation taken for earnings and profits purposes.

§ 1.316-1 Dividends

(a) (1) The term "dividend" for the purpose of subtitle A of the Code (except when used in subchapter L, chapter 1 of the Code, in any case where the reference is to dividends and similar distributions of insurance companies paid to policyholders as such) comprises any distribution of property as defined in section 317 in the ordinary course of business, even though extraordinary in amount, made by a domestic or foreign corporation to its shareholders out of either—

(i) Earnings and profits accumulated since February 28, 1913, or

(ii) Earnings and profits of the taxable year computed without regard to the amount of the earnings and profits (whether of such year or accumulated since February 28, 1913) at the time the distribution was made.
The earnings and profits of the taxable year shall be computed as of the close of such year, without diminution by reason of any distributions made during the taxable year. For the purpose of determining whether a distribution constitutes a dividend, it is unnecessary to ascertain the amount of the earnings and profits accumulated since February 28, 1913, if the earnings and profits of the taxable year are equal to or in excess of the total amount of the distributions made within such year.

(2) Where a corporation distributes property to its shareholders on or after June 22, 1954, the amount of the distribution which is a dividend to them may not exceed the earnings and profits of the distributing corporation.

(3) The rule of (2) above may be illustrated by the following example:

Example. X and Y, individuals, each own one-half of the stock of Corporation A which has earnings and profits of $10,000. Corporation A distributes property having a basis of $6,000 and a fair market value of $16,000 to its shareholders, each shareholder receiving property with a basis of $3,000 and with a fair market value of $8,000 in a distribution to which section 301 applies. The amount taxable to each shareholder as a dividend under section 301 (c) is $5,000.

(b) (1) In the case of a corporation which, under the law applicable to the taxable year in which a distribution is made, is a personal holding company or which, for the taxable year in respect of which a distribution is made under section 563 (relating to dividends paid within 2½ months after the close of the taxable year), or section 547 (relating to deficiency dividends), or corresponding provisions of a prior income tax law, was under the applicable law a personal holding company, the term "dividend", in addition to the meaning set forth in the first sentence of section 316, also means a distribution to its shareholders as follows: A distribution within a taxable year of the corporation, or of a shareholder, is a dividend to the extent of the corporation's undistributed personal holding company income (determined under section 545 without regard to distributions under section 316(b) (2)) for the taxable year in which, or, in the case of a distribution under section 563 or section 547, the taxable year in respect of which, the distribution was made. This subparagraph does not apply to distributions in partial or complete liquidation of a personal holding company. In the case of certain complete liquidations of a personal holding company see subparagraph (2) of this paragraph.

(2) In the case of a corporation which, under the law applicable to the taxable year in which a distribution is made, is a personal holding company or which, for the taxable year in respect of which a distribution is made under section 563, or section 547, or corresponding provisions of a prior income tax law, was under the applicable law a personal holding company, the term "dividend", in addition to the meaning set forth in the first sentence of section 316, also means, in the case of a complete liquidation occurring within 24 months after the adoption of a plan of liquidation, a distribution of property to its shareholders within such period, but—

(i) Only to the extent of the amounts distributed to distributees other than corporate shareholders, and

(ii) Only to the extent that the corporation designates such amounts as a dividend distribution and duly notifies such distributees in accordance with subparagraph (5) of this paragraph, but

(iii) Not in excess of the sum of such distributees' allocable share of the undistributed personal holding company income for such year (determined under section 545 without regard to sections 562(b) and 316(b) (2) (B)).

Section 316(b) (2) (B) and this subparagraph apply only to distributions made in any taxable year of the distributing corporation beginning after December 31, 1963. The amount designated with respect to a noncorporate distributee may not exceed the amount actually distributed to such distributee. For purposes of determining a noncorporate distributee's gain or loss on liquidation, amounts distributed in complete liquidation to such distributee during a taxable year are reduced by the amounts designated as a dividend with respect to such distributee for such year. For purposes of section 333(e) (1), a shareholder's ratable share of the earnings and profits of the corporation accumulated after February 28, 1913, shall be reduced by the amounts designated as a dividend with respect to such shareholder (even though such designated amounts are distributed during the 1-month period referred to in section 333).

(3) For purposes of subparagraph (2) (iii) of this paragraph—

(i) Except as provided in subdivision (ii) of this subparagraph, the sum of the noncorporate distributees' allocable share of undistributed personal holding company income for the taxable year in which, or in respect of which, the distribution was made (computed without regard to sections 562(b) and 316 (b) (2) (B)) shall be determined by multiplying such undistributed personal holding company income by the ratio which the aggregate value of the stock held by all noncorporate shareholders immediately before the record date of the last liquidating distribution in such year bears to the total value of all stock outstanding on such date. For rules applicable in a case where the distributing corporation has more than one class of stock, see subdivision (iii) of this subparagraph.

(ii) If more than one liquidating distribution was made during the year, and if, after the record date of the first distribution but before the record date of the last distribution, there was a change in the relative shareholdings as between noncorporate shareholders and corporate shareholders, then the sum of the noncorporate distributees' allocable share of undistributed personal

holding company income for the taxable year in which, or in respect of which, the distributions were made (computed without regard to sections 562(b) and 316(b) (2) (B)) shall be determined as follows:

(a) First, allocate the corporation's undistributed personal holding company income among the distributions made during the taxable year by reference to the ratio which the aggregate amount of each distribution bears to the total amount of all distributions during such year;

(b) Second, determine the noncorporate distributees' allocable share of the corporation's undistributed personal holding company income for each distribution by multiplying the amount determined under (a) of this subdivision (ii) for each distribution by the ratio which the aggregate value of the stock held by all noncorporate shareholders immediately before the record date of such distribution bears to the total value of all stock outstanding on such date; and

(c) Last, determine the sum of the noncorporate distributees' allocable share of the corporation's undistributed personal holding company income for all such distributions.

For rules applicable in a case where the distributing corporation has more than one class of stock, see subdivision (iii) of this subparagraph.

(iii) Where the distributing corporation has more than one class of stock—

(a) The undistributed personal holding company income for the taxable year in which, or in respect of which the distribution was made shall be treated as a fund from which dividends may properly be paid and shall be allocated between or among the classes of stock in a manner consistent with the dividend rights of such classes under local law and the pertinent governing instruments, such as, for example, the distributing corporation's articles or certificate of incorporation and bylaws;

(b) The noncorporate distributees' allocable share of the undistributed personal holding company income for each class of stock shall be determined separately in accordance with the rules set forth in subdivisions (i) or (ii) of this subparagraph, as if each class of stock were the only class of stock outstanding; and

(c) The sum of the noncorporate distributees' allocable share of the undistributed personal holding company income for the taxable year in which, or in respect of which, the distribution was made shall be the sum of the noncorporate distributees' allocable share of the undistributed personal holding company income for all classes of stock.

(iv) For purposes of this subparagraph, in any case where the record date of a liquidating distribution cannot be ascertained, the record date of the distribution shall be the date on which the liquidating distribution was actually made.

(4) The amount designated as a dividend to a noncorporate distributee for any taxable year of the distributing corporation may not exceed an amount equal to the sum of the noncorporate distributees' allocable share of undistributed personal holding company income (as determined under subparagraph (3) of this paragraph) for such year multiplied by the ratio which the aggregate value of the stock held by such distributee immediately before the record date of the liquidating distribution or, if the record date cannot be ascertained, immediately before the date on which the liquidating distribution was actually made, bears to the aggregate value of stock outstanding held by all noncorporate distributees on such date. In any case where more than one liquidating distribution is made during the taxable year, the aggregate amount which may be designated as a dividend to a noncorporate distributee for such year may not exceed the aggregate of the amounts determined by applying the principle of the preceding sentence to the amounts determined under subparagraph (3) (ii) (a) and (b) of this paragraph for each distribution. Where the distributing corporation has more than one class of stock, the limitation on the amount which may be designated as a dividend to a noncorporate distributee for any taxable year shall be determined by applying the rules of this subparagraph separately with respect to the noncorporate distributees' allocable share of the undistributed personal holding company income for each class of stock (as determined under subparagraph (3) (iii) (a) and (b) of this paragraph).

(5) A corporation may designate as a dividend to a shareholder all or part of a distribution in complete liquidation described in section 316(b) (2) (B) of this paragraph by:

(i) Claiming a dividends paid deduction for such amount in its return for the year in which, or in respect of which, the distribution is made,

(ii) Including such amount as a dividend in Form 1099 filed in respect of such shareholder pursuant to section 6042(a) and the regulations thereunder and in a written statement of dividend payments furnished to such shareholder pursuant to section 6042(c) and § 1.-6042-4, and

(iii) Indicating on the written statement of dividend payments furnished to such shareholder the amount included in such statement which is designated as a dividend under section 316(b) (2) (B) and this paragraph.

If a corporation complies with the procedure prescribed in the preceding sentence, it satisfies both the designation and notification requirements of section 316(b) (2) (B) (ii) and paragraph (b) (2) (ii) of this section. An amount designated as a dividend shall not be included as a distribution in liquidation on Form 1099L filed pursuant to § 1.6043-2 (relating to returns of information respecting distributions in liquidation). If a corporation designates a dividend in accordance with this subparagraph, it shall attach to the return in which it claims a deduction for such designated dividend a schedule indicating all facts necessary to determine the sum of the noncorporate distributees' allocable share of undistributed personal holding company income (determined in accordance with subparagraph (3) of this paragraph) for the year in which, or in respect of which, the distribution is made.

. . . .

(e) The application of section 316 may be illustrated by the following examples:

Example (1). At the beginning of the calendar year 1955, Corporation M had an operating deficit of $200,000 and the earnings and profits for the year amounted to $100,000. Beginning on March 16, 1955, the corporation made quarterly distributions of $25,000 during the taxable year to its shareholders. Each distribution is a taxable dividend in full, irrespective of the actual or the pro rata amount of the earnings and profits on hand at any of the dates of distribution, since the total distributions made during the year ($100,000) did not exceed the total earnings and profits of the year ($100,000).

. . . .

§ 1.316-2 Sources of distribution in general

(a) For the purpose of income taxation every distribution made by a corporation is made out of earnings and profits to the extent thereof and from the most recently accumulated earnings and profits. In determining the source of a distribution, consideration should be given first, to the earnings and profits of the taxable year; second, to the earnings and profits accumulated since February 28, 1913, only in the case where, and to the extent that, the distributions made during the taxable year are not regarded as out of the earnings and profits of that year; third, to the earnings and profits accumulated before March 1, 1913, only after all the earnings and profits of the taxable year and all the earnings and profits accumulated since February 28, 1913, have been distributed; and, fourth, to sources other than earnings and profits only after the earnings and profits have been distributed.

(b) If the earnings and profits of the taxable year (computed as of the close of the year without diminution by reason of any distributions made during the year and without regard to the amount of earnings and profits at the time of the distribution) are sufficient in amount to cover all the distributions made during that year, then each distribution is a taxable dividend. See § 1.316-1. If the distributions made during the taxable year consist only of money and exceed the earnings and profits of such year, then that propor-

tion of each distribution which the total of the earnings and profits of the year bears to the total distributions made during the year shall be regarded as out of the earnings and profits of that year. The portion of each such distribution which is not regarded as out of earnings and profits of the taxable year shall be considered a taxable dividend to the extent of the earnings and profits accumulated since February 28, 1913, and available on the date of the distribution. In any case in which it is necessary to determine the amount of earnings and profits accumulated since February 28, 1913, and the actual earnings and profits to the date of a distribution within any taxable year (whether beginning before January 1, 1936, or, in the case of an operating deficit, on or after that date) cannot be shown, the earnings and profits for the year (or accounting period, if less than a year) in which the distribution was made shall be prorated to the date of the distribution not counting the date on which the distribution was made.

(c) The provisions of the section may be illustrated by the following example:

Example. At the beginning of the calendar year 1955, Corporation M had $12,000 in earnings and profits accumulated since February 28, 1913. Its earnings and profits for 1955 amounted to $30,000. During the year it made quarterly cash distributions of $15,000 each. Of each of the four distributions made, $7,500 (that portion of $15,000 which the amount of $30,000, the total earnings and profits of the taxable year, bears to $60,000, the total distributions made during the year) was paid out of the earnings and profits of the taxable year; and of the first and second distributions, $7,500 and $4,500, respectively, were paid out of the earnings and profits accumulated after February 28, 1913, and before the taxable year, as follows:

Distributions during 1955		Portion out of earnings and profits of the taxable year	Portion out of earnings accumulated since Feb. 28, 1913, and before the taxable year	Taxable amount of each distribution
Date	Amount			
March 10	$15,000	$7,500	$7,500	$15,000
June 10	15,000	7,500	4,500	12,000
September 10	15,000	7,500	....	7,500
December 10	15,000	7,500	....	7,500
Total amount taxable as dividends				42,000

§ 1.317-1 Property defined

The term "property", for purposes of part 1, subchapter C, chapter 1 of the Code, means any property (including money, securities, and indebtedness to the corporation) other than stock, or rights to acquire stock, in the corporation making the distribution.

§ 1.318-1 Constructive ownership of stock; introduction

(a) For the purposes of certain provisions of chapter 1 of the Code, section 318(a) provides that stock owned by a taxpayer includes stock constructively owned by such taxpayer under the rules set forth in such section. An individual is considered to own the stock owned, directly or indirectly, by or for his spouse (other than a spouse who is legally separated from the individual under a decree of divorce or separate maintenance), and by or for his children, grandchildren, and parents. Under section 318(a) (2) and (3), constructive ownership rules are established for partnerships and partners, estates and beneficiaries, trusts and beneficiaries, and corporations and stockholders. If any person has an option to acquire stock, such stock is considered as owned by such person. The term "option" includes an option to acquire such an option and each of a series of such options.

(b) In applying section 318(a) to determine the stock ownership of any person for any one purpose—

(1) A corporation shall not be considered to own its own stock by reason of section 318(a) (3) (C);

(2) In any case in which an amount of stock owned by any person may be included in the computation more than one time, such stock shall be included only once, in the manner in which it will impute to the person concerned the largest total stock ownership; and

(3) In determining the 50-percent requirement of section 318(a) (2) (C) and (3) (C), all of the stock owned actually and constructively by the person concerned shall be aggregated.

§ 1.318-2 Application of general rules

(a) The application of paragraph (b) of § 1.318-1 may be illustrated by the following examples:

Example (1). H, an individual, owns all of the stock of corporation A. Corporation A is not considered to own the stock owned by H in corporation A.

Example (2). H, an individual, his wife, W, and his son, S, each own one-third of the stock of the Green Corporation. For purposes of determining the amount of stock owned by H, W, or S for purposes of section 318(a) (2) and (3) (C), the amount of stock held by the other members of the family shall be added pursuant to paragraph (b) (3) of § 1.318-1 in applying the 50-percent requirement of such section. H, W, or S, as the case may be, is for this purpose deemed to own 100 percent of the stock of the Green Corporation.

(b) The application of section 318 (a) (1), relating to members of a family, may be illustrated by the following example:

Example. An individual, H, his wife, W, his son, S, and his grandson (S's son), G, own the 100 outstanding shares of stock of a corporation, each owning 25 shares. H, W, and S are each considered as owning 100 shares. G is considered as owning only 50 shares, that is, his own and his father's.

(c) The application of section 318 (a) (2) and (3), relating to partnerships, trusts and corporations, may be illustrated by the following examples:

Example (1). A, an individual, has a 50 percent interest in a partnership. The partnership owns 50 of the 100 outstanding shares of stock of a corporation, the remaining 50 shares being owned by A. The partnership is considered as owning 100 shares. A is considered as owning 75 shares.

Example (2). A testamentary trust owns 25 of the outstanding 100 shares of stock of a corporation. A, an individual, who holds a vested remainder in the trust having a value, computed actuarially equal to 4 percent of the value of the trust property, owns the remaining 75 shares. Since the interest of A in the trust is a vested interest rather than a contingent interest (whether or not remote), the trust is considered as owning 100 shares. A is considered as owning 76 shares.

Example (3). The facts are the same as in (2), above, except that A's interest in the trust is a contingent remainder. A is considered as owning 76 shares. However, since A's interest in the trust is a remote contingent interest, the trust is not considered as owning any of the shares owned by A.

Example (4). A and B, unrelated individuals, own 70 percent and 30 percent, respectively, in value of the stock of Corporation M. Corporation M owns 50 of the 100 outstanding shares of stock of Corporation O, the remaining 50 shares being owned by A. Corporation M is considered as owning 100 shares of Corporation O, and A is considered as owning 85 shares.

Example (5). A and B, unrelated individuals, own 70 percent and 30 percent, respectively, of the stock of corporation M. A, B, and corporation M all own stock of corporation O. Since B owns less than 50 percent in value of the stock of corporation M, neither B nor corporation M constructively owns the stock of corporation O owned by the other. However, for purposes of certain sections of the Code, such as sections 304 and 856(d), the

50-percent limitation of section 318(a) (2) (C) and (3) (C) is disregarded or is reduced to less than 30 percent. For such purposes, B constructively owns his proportionate share of the stock of corporation O owned directly by corporation M, and corporation M constructively owns the stock of corporation O owned by B.

§ 1.318-3 Estates, trusts, and options

(a) For the purpose of applying section 318 (a), relating to estates, property of a decedent shall be considered as owned by his estate if such property is subject to administration by the executor or administrator for the purpose of paying claims against the estate and expenses of administration notwithstanding that, under local law, legal title to such property vests in the decedent's heirs, legatees or devisees immediately upon death. The term "beneficiary" includes any person entitled to receive property of a decedent pursuant to a will or pursuant to laws of descent and distribution. A person shall no longer be considered a beneficiary of an estate when all the property to which he is entitled has been received by him, when he no longer has a claim against the estate arising out of having been a beneficiary, and when there is only a remote possibility that it will be necessary for the estate to seek the return of property or to seek payment from him by contribution or otherwise to satisfy claims against the estate or expenses of administration. When, pursuant to the preceding sentence, a person ceases to be a beneficiary, stock owned by him shall not thereafter be considered owned by the estate, and stock owned by the estate shall not thereafter be considered owned by him. The application of section 318 (a) relating to estates may be illustrated by the following examples:

Example (1). (a) A decedent's estate owns 50 of the 100 outstanding shares of stock of corporation X. The remaining shares are owned by three unrelated individuals, A, B, and C, who together own the entire interest in the estate. A owns 12 shares of stock of corporation X directly and is entitled to 50 percent of the estate. B owns 18 shares directly and has a life estate in the remaining 50 percent of the estate. C owns 20 shares directly and also owns the remainder interest after B's life estate.

(b) If section 318(a) (5) (C) applies (see paragraph (c) (3) of § 1.318-4), the stock of corporation X is considered to be owned as follows: the estate is considered as owning 80 shares, 50 shares directly, 12 shares constructively through A, and 18 shares constructively through B; A is considered as owning 37 shares, 12 shares directly, and 25 shares constructively (50 percent of the 50 shares owned directly by the estate); B is considered as owning 43 shares, 18 shares directly and 25 shares constructively (50 percent of the 50 shares owned directly by the estate); C is considered as owning 20 shares directly and no shares constructively. C is not considered a beneficiary of the estate under section 318(a) since he has no direct present interest in the property held by the estate nor in the income produced by such property.

(c) If section 318(a) (5) (C) does not apply. A is considered as owning nine additional shares (50 percent of the 18 shares owned constructively by the estate through B), and B is considered as owning six additional shares (50 percent of the 12 shares owned constructively by the estate through A).

Example (2). Under the will of A, Blackacre is left to B for life, remainder to C, an unrelated individual. The residue of the estate consisting of stock of a corporation is left to D. B and D are beneficiaries of the estate under section 318 (a). C is not considered a beneficiary since he has no direct present interest in Blackacre nor in the income produced by such property. The stock owned by the estate is considered as owned proportionately by B and D.

(b) For the purpose of section 318 (a) (2) (B) stock owned by a trust will be considered as being owned by its beneficiaries only to the extent of the interest of such beneficiaries in the trust. Accordingly, the interest of income beneficiaries, remainder beneficiaries, and other beneficiaries will be computed on an actuarial basis. Thus, if a trust owns 100 percent of the stock of Corporation A, and if, on an actuarial basis, W's life interest in the trust is 15 percent, Y's life interest is 25 percent, and Z's remainder interest is 60 percent, under this provision W will be considered to be the owner of 15 percent of the stock of Corporation A, Y will be considered to be the owner of 25 percent of such stock, and Z will be considered to be the owner of 60 percent of such stock. The factors and methods prescribed in § 20.2031-7 of this chapter for use in ascertaining the value of an interest in property for estate tax purposes shall be used in determining a beneficiary's actuarial interest in a trust for purposes of this section. See § 20.2031-7 of this chapter for examples illustrating the use of these factors and methods.

(c) The application of section 318 (a) relating to options may be illustrated by the following example:

Example. A and B, unrelated individuals, own all of the 100 outstanding shares of stock of a corporation, each owning 50 shares. A has an option to acquire 25 of B's shares and has an option to acquire a further option to acquire the remaining 25 of B's shares. A is considered as owning the entire 100 shares of stock of the corporation.

§ 1.318-4 Constructive ownership as actual ownership; exceptions

(a) In general. Section 318(a) (5) (A) provides that, except as provided in section 318(a) (5) (B) and (C), stock constructively owned by a person by reason of the application of section 318 (a) (1), (2), (3), or (4) shall be considered as actually owned by such person for purposes of applying section 318 (a) (1), (2), (3), and (4). For example, if a trust owns 50 percent of the stock of corporation X, stock of corporation Y owned by corporation X which is attributed to the trust may be further attributed to the beneficiaries of the trust.

(b) Constructive family ownership. Section 318(a) (5) (B) provides that stock constructively owned by an individual by reason of ownership by a member of his family shall not be considered as owned by him for purposes of making another family member the constructive owner of such stock under section 318(a) (1). For example, if F and his two sons, A and B, each own one-third of the stock of a corporation, under section 318(a) (1), A is treated as owning constructively the stock owned by his father but is not treated as owning the stock owned by B. Section 318(a) (5) (B) prevents the attribution of the stock of one brother through the father to the other brother, an attribution beyond the scope of section 318(a) (1) directly.

(c) Reattribution. (1) Section 318 (a) (5) (C) provides that stock constructively owned by a partnership, estate, trust, or corporation by reason of the application of section 318(a) (3) shall not be considered as owned by it for purposes of applying section 318(a) (2) in order to make another the constructive owner of such stock. For example, if two unrelated individuals are beneficiaries of the same trust, stock held by one which is attributed to the trust under section 318(a) (3) is not reattributed from the trust to the other beneficiary. However, stock constructively owned by reason of section 318 (a) (2) may be reattributed under section 318(a) (3). Thus, for example, if

all the stock of corporations X and Y is owned by A, stock of corporation Z held by X is attributed to Y through A.

(2) Section 318(a) (5) (C) does not prevent reattribution under section 318 (a) (2) of stock constructively owned by an entity under section 318(a) (3) if the stock is also constructively owned by the entity under section 318(a) (4). For example, if individuals A and B are beneficiaries of a trust and the trust has an option to buy stock from A, B is considered under section 318(a) (2) (B) as owning a proportionate part of such stock.

(3) Section 318(a) (5) (C) is effective on and after August 31, 1964, except that for purposes of sections 302 and 304 it does not apply with respect to distributions in payment for stock acquisitions or redemptions if such acquisitions or redemptions occurred before August 31, 1964.

§ 1.331-1 Corporate liquidations

(a) Section 331 contains rules governing the extent to which gain or loss is recognized to a shareholder receiving a distribution in complete or partial liquidation of a corporation. Under section 331(a) (1), it is provided that amounts distributed in complete liquidation of a corporation shall be treated as in full payment in exchange for the stock. Under section 331(a) (2), it is provided that amounts distributed in partial liquidation of a corporation shall be treated as in full or part payment in exchange for the stock. For this purpose, the term "partial liquidation" shall have the meaning ascribed in section 346. If section 331 is applicable to the distribution of property by a corporation, section 301 (relating to the effects on a shareholder of distributions of property) has no application other than to a distribution in complete liquidation to which section 316(b) (2) (B) applies. See paragraph (b) (2) of § 1.316-1.

(b) The gain or loss to a shareholder from a distribution in partial or complete liquidation is to be determined under section 1001 by comparing the amount of the distribution with the cost or other basis of the stock. The gain or loss will be recognized to the extent provided in section 1002 and will be subject to the provisions of parts I, II, and III (section 1201 and following), subchapter P, chapter 1 of the Code.

(c) A liquidation which is followed by a transfer to another corporation of all or part of the assets of the liquidating corporation or which is preceded by such a transfer may, however, have the effect of the distribution of a dividend or of a transaction in which no loss is recognized and gain is recognized only to the extent of "other property." See sections 301 and 356.

(d) In every case in which a shareholder transfers stock in exchange for property to the corporation which issued such stock, the facts and circumstances shall be reported on his return unless the property is part of a distribution made pursuant to a corporate resolution reciting that the distribution is made in liquidation of the corporation and the corporation is completely liquidated and dissolved within one year after the distribution. See section 6043 for requirements relating to returns by corporations.

(e) The provisions of this section may be illustrated by the following example:

Example. A an individual who makes his income tax returns on the calendar year basis, owns 20 shares of stock of the P Corporation, a domestic corporation, 10 shares of which were acquired in 1951 at a cost of $1,500 and the remainder of 10 shares in December 1954 at a cost of $2,900. He receives in April 1955 a distribution of $250 per share in complete liquidation, or $2,500 on the 10 shares acquired in 1951, and $2,500 on the 10 shares acquired in December 1954. The gain of $1,000 on the shares acquired in 1951 is a long-term capital gain to be treated as provided in parts I, II, and III (section 1201 and following), subchapter P, chapter 1 of the Code. The loss of $400 on the shares acquired in 1954 is a short-term capital loss to be treated as provided in parts I, II, and III (section 1201 and following), subchapter P, chapter 1 of the Code.

§ 1.332-1 Distributions in liquidation of subsidiary corporation; general

Under the general rule prescribed by section 331 for the treatment of distributions in liquidation of a corporation, amounts received by one corporation in complete liquidation of another corporation are treated as in full payment in exchange for stock in such other corporation, and gain or loss from the receipt of such amounts is to be determined as provided in section 1001. Section 332 excepts from the general rule property received, under certain specifically described circumstances, by one corporation as a distribution in complete liquidation of the stock of another corporation and provides for the nonrecognition of gain or loss in those cases which meet the statutory requirements. Section 367 places a limitation on the application of section 332 in the case of foreign corporations. See section 334(b) for the basis for determining gain or loss from the subsequent sale of property received upon complete liquidations such as described in this section.

§ 1.332-2 Requirements for nonrecognition of gain or loss

(a) The nonrecognition of gain or loss is limited to the receipt of such property by a corporation which is the actual owner of stock (in the liquidating corporation) possessing at least 80 percent of the total combined voting power of all classes of stock entitled to vote and the owner of at least 80 percent of the total number of shares of all other classes of stock (except nonvoting stock which is limited and preferred as to dividends). The recipient corporation must have been the owner of the specified amount of such stock on the date of the adoption of the plan of liquidation and have continued so to be at all times until the receipt of the property. If the recipient corporation does not continue qualified with respect to the ownership of stock of the liquidating corporation and if the failure to continue qualified occurs at any time prior to the completion of the transfer of all the property, the provisions for the nonrecognition of gain or loss do not apply to any distribution received under the plan.

(b) Section 332 applies only to those cases in which the recipient corporation receives at least partial payment for the stock which it owns in the liquidating corporation. If section 332 is not applicable, see section 165(g) relative to allowance of losses on worthless securities.

(c) To constitute a distribution in complete liquidation within the meaning of section 332, the distribution must be (1) made by the liquidating corporation in complete cancellation or redemption of all of its stock in accordance with a plan of liquidation, or (2) one of a series of distributions in complete cancellation or redemption of all its stock in accordance with a plan of liquidation. Where there is more than one distribution, it is essential that a status of liquidation exist at the time the first distribution is made under the plan and that such status continue until the liquidation is completed. Liquidation is completed when the liquidating corporation and the receiver or trustees in liquidation are finally divested of all the property (both tangible and intangible). A status of liquidation exists when the corporation ceases to be a going concern and its activities are merely for the purpose of winding up its affairs, paying its debts, and distributing any remaining balance to its shareholders. A liquidation may be completed prior to the actual dissolution of the liquidating corporation. However, legal dissolution of the corporation is not required. Nor will the mere retention of a nominal amount of assets for the sole purpose of preserving the corporation's legal existence disqualify the transaction. . . . .

(d) If a transaction constitutes a distribution in complete liquidation within the meaning of the Internal Revenue Code of 1954 and satisfies the requirements of section 332, it is not material that it is otherwise described under the local law. If a liquidating corporation distributes all of its property in complete liquidation and if pursuant to the plan for such complete liquidation a corporation owning the specified amount of stock in the liquidating corporation receives property constituting amounts distributed in complete liquidation within the meaning of the Code and also receives other property attributable to shares not owned by it, the transfer of the property to the recipient corporation shall not be treated, by reason of the receipt of such other property, as not being a distribution (or one of a series of distributions) in complete cancellation or redemption of all of the stock of the liquidating corporation within the meaning of section 332, even though for purposes of those provisions relating to corporate reorganizations the amount received by the recipient corporation in excess of its ratable share is regarded as acquired upon the issuance of its stock or securities in a tax-free exchange as described in section 361 and the cancellation or re-

demption of the stock not owned by the recipient corporation is treated as occurring as a result of a tax-free exchange described in section 354.

(e) The application of these rules may be illustrated by the following example:

Example. On September 1, 1954, the M Corporation had outstanding capital stock consisting of 3,000 shares of common stock, par value $100 a share, and 1,000 shares of preferred stock, par value $100 a share, which preferred stock was limited and preferred as to dividends and had no voting rights. On that date, and thereafter until the date of dissolution of the M Corporation, the O Corporation owned 2,500 shares of common stock of the M Corporation. By statutory merger consummated on October 1, 1954, pursuant to a plan of liquidation adopted on September 1, 1954, the M Corporation was merged into the O Corporation, the O Corporation under the plan issuing stock which was received by the other holders of the stock of the M Corporation. The receipt by the O Corporation of the properties of the M Corporation is a distribution received by the O Corporation in complete liquidation of the M Corporation within the meaning of section 332, and no gain or loss is recognized as the result of the receipt of such properties.

§ 1.332-3 Liquidations completed within one taxable year

If in a liquidation completed within one taxable year pursuant to a plan of complete liquidation, distributions in complete liquidation are received by a corporation which owns the specified amount of stock in the liquidating corporation and which continues qualified with respect to the ownership of such stock until the transfer of all the property within such year is completed (see paragraph (a) of § 1.332-2), then no gain or loss shall be recognized with respect to the distributions received by the recipient corporation. In such case no waiver or bond is required of the recipient corporation under section 332.

§ 1.332-4 Liquidations covering more than one taxable year

(a) If the plan of liquidation is consummated by a series of distributions extending over a period of more than one taxable year, the nonrecognition of gain or loss with respect to the distributions in liquidation shall, in addition to the requirements of § 1.332-2, be subject to the following requirements:

(1) In order for the distribution in liquidation to be brought within the

exception provided in section 332 to the general rule for computing gain or loss with respect to amounts received in liquidation of a corporation, the entire property of the corporation shall be transferred in accordance with a plan of liquidation, which plan shall include a statement showing the period within which the transfer of the property of the liquidating corporation to the recipient corporation is to be completed. The transfer of all the property under the liquidation must be completed within three years from the close of the taxable year during which is made the first of the series of distributions under the plan.

(2) For each of the taxable years which falls wholly or partly within the period of liquidation, the recipient corporation shall, at the time of filing its return, file with the district director of internal revenue a waiver of the statute of limitations on assessment. The waiver shall be executed on such form as may be prescribed by the Commissioner and shall extend the period of assessment of all income and profits taxes for each such year to a date not earlier than one year after the last date of the period for assessment of such taxes for the last taxable year in which the transfer of the property of such liquidating corporation to the controlling corporation may be completed in accordance with section 332. Such waiver shall also contain such other terms with respect to assessment as may be considered by the Commissioner to be necessary to insure the assessment and collection of the correct tax liability for each year within the period of liquidation.

(3) For each of the taxable years which falls wholly or partly within the period of liquidation, the recipient corporation may be required to file a bond, the amount of which shall be fixed by the district director. The bond shall contain all terms specified by the Commissioner, including provisions unequivocally assuring prompt payment of the excess of income and profits taxes (plus penalty, if any, and interest) as computed by the district director without regard to the provisions of sections 332 and 334(b) over such taxes computed with regard to such provisions, regardless of whether such excess may or may not be made the subject of a notice of deficiency under section 6212 and regardless of whether it

may or may not be assessed. Any bond required under section 332 shall have such surety or sureties as the Commissioner may require. However, see 6 U.S.C. 15, providing that where a bond is required by law or regulations, in lieu of surety or sureties there may be deposited bonds or notes of the United States. Only surety companies holding certificates of authority from the Secretary as acceptable sureties on Federal bonds will be approved as sureties. The bonds shall be executed in triplicate so that the Commissioner, the taxpayer, and the surety or the depositary may each have a copy. On and after September 1, 1953, the functions of the Commissioner with respect to such bonds shall be performed by the district director for the internal revenue district in which the return was filed and any bond filed on or after such date shall be filed with such district director.

(b) Pending the completion of the liquidation, if there is a compliance with paragraph (a) (1), (2) and (3) of this section and § 1.332-2 with respect to the nonrecognition of gain or loss, the income and profits tax liability of the recipient corporation for each of the years covered in whole or in part by the liquidation shall be determined without the recognition of any gain or loss on account of the receipt of the distributions in liquidation. In such determination, the basis of the property or properties received by the recipient corporation shall be determined in accordance with section 334(b). However, if the transfer of the property is not completed within the three-year period allowed by section 332 or if the recipient corporation does not continue qualified with respect to the ownership of stock of the liquidating corporation as required by that section, gain or loss shall be recognized with respect to each distribution and the tax liability for each of the years covered in whole or in part by the liquidation shall be recomputed without regard to the provisions of section 332 or section 334(b) and the amount of any additional tax due upon such recomputation shall be promptly paid.

§ 1.332-5   Distributions in liquidation as affecting minority interests

Upon the liquidation of a corporation in pursuance of a plan of complete liquidation, the gain or loss of minority shareholders shall be determined without regard to section 332, since it does not apply to that part of distributions in liquidation received by minority shareholders.

§ 1.332-6 Records to be kept and information to be filed with return

(a) Permanent records in substantial form shall be kept by every corporation receiving distributions in complete liquidation within the exception provided in section 332 showing the information required by this section to be submitted with its return. The plan of liquidation must be adopted by each of the corporations parties thereto; and the adoption must be shown by the acts of its duly constituted responsible officers, and appear upon the official records of each such corporation.

(b) For the taxable year in which the liquidation occurs, or, if the plan of liquidation provides for a series of distributions over a period of more than one year, for each taxable year in which a distribution is received under the plan the recipient must file with its return a complete statement of all facts pertinent to the nonrecognition of gain or loss, including:

(1) A certified copy of the plan for complete liquidation, and of the resolutions under which the plan was adopted and the liquidation was authorized, together with a statement under oath showing in detail all transactions incident to, or pursuant to, the plan.

(2) A list of all the properties received upon the distribution, showing the cost or other basis of such properties to the liquidating corporation at the date of distribution and the fair market value of such properties on the date distributed.

(3) A statement of any indebtedness of the liquidating corporation to the recipient corporation on the date the plan of liquidation was adopted and on the date of the first liquidating distribution. If any such indebtedness was acquired at less than face value, the cost thereof to the recipient corporation must also be shown.

(4) A statement as to its ownership of all classes of stock of the liquidating corporation (showing as to each class the number of shares and percentage owned and the voting power of each share) as of the date of the adoption of the plan of liquidation, and at all times since, to and including the date of the distribution in liquidation. The cost or other basis of such stock and the date or dates on which purchased must also be shown.

§ 1.332-7 Indebtedness of subsidiary to parent

If section 332(a) is applicable to the receipt of the subsidiary's property in complete liquidation, then no gain or loss shall be recognized to the subsidiary upon the transfer of such properties even though some of the properties are transferred in satisfaction of the subsidiary's indebtedness to its parent. However, any gain or loss realized by the parent corporation on such satisfaction of indebtedness, shall be recognized to the parent corporation at the time of the liquidation. For example, if the parent corporation purchased its subsidiary's bonds at a discount and upon liquidation of the subsidiary the parent corporation receives payment for the face amount of such bonds, gain shall be recognized to the parent corporation. Such gain shall be measured by the difference between the cost or other basis of the bonds to the parent and the amount received in payment of the bonds.

§ 1.333-1 Corporate liquidation in some one calendar month

(a) In general. Section 333 provides a special rule, in the case of certain specifically described complete liquidations of domestic corporations occurring within some one calendar month, for the treatment of gain on the shares of stock owned by qualified electing shareholders at the time of the adoption of the plan of liquidation. The effect of such section is in general to postpone the recognition of that portion of a qualified electing shareholder's gain on the liquidation which would otherwise be recognized and which is attributable to appreciation in the value of certain corporate assets unrealized by the corporation at the time such assets are distributed in complete liquidation. Only qualified electing shareholders are entitled to the benefits of section 333. The determination of who is a qualified electing shareholder is to be made under section 333(c). . . . . For the basis of property received on such liquidations, see section 334(c).

Section 333 has no application to gain in respect of stock of a collapsible corporation to which section 341(a) applies.

(b) Type of liquidation. (1) The liquidation must be in pursuance of a plan of liquidation adopted on or after June 22, 1954. The plan must be adopted before the first distribution under the liquidation occurs. The 1954 Code requires that the transfer of all the property, both tangible and intangible, of the corporation to its shareholders shall occur entirely within some one calendar month. This requirement will be considered to have been complied with if cash is set aside under arrangements for the payment, after the close of such month, of unascertained or contingent liabilities and expenses, and such arrangements are made in good faith and the amount set aside is reasonable. It is not necessary that the month in which the transfer occurs must fall within the taxable or calendar year in which the plan of liquidation is adopted. Though it is not necessary that the corporation dissolve in the month of liquidation, it is essential that a status of liquidation exist at the time the first distribution is made under the plan and that such status continue to the date of dissolution of the corporation. A status of liquidation exists when the corporation ceases to be a going concern and its activities are merely for the purpose of winding up its affairs, paying its debts, and distributing any remaining balance to its shareholders.

(2) If a transaction constitutes a distribution in complete liquidation within the meaning of the Code and satisfies the requirements of section 333, it is immaterial that it is otherwise described under the local law.

§ 1.333–2 Qualified electing shareholder

(a) No corporate shareholder may be a qualified electing shareholder if at any time between January 1, 1954, and the date of the adoption of the plan of liquidation, both dates inclusive, it is the owner of stock of the liquidating corporation possessing 50 percent or more of the total combined voting power of all classes of stock entitled to vote upon the adoption of the plan of liquidation. All other shareholders are divided into two groups for the purpose of determining whether they are qualified electing shareholders: (1) shareholders other than corporations, and (2) corporate shareholders.

(b) Any shareholder of either of such two groups, whether or not the stock he owns is entitled to vote on the adoption of the plan of liquidation, is a qualified electing shareholder if:

(1) His written election to be governed by the provisions of section 333, which cannot be withdrawn or revoked . . ., has been made and filed as prescribed in § 1.333–3; and

(2) Like elections have been made and filed by owners of stock possessing at least 80 percent of the total combined voting power of all classes of stock owned by shareholders of the same group at the time of, and entitled to vote upon, the adoption of the plan of liquidation, whether or not the shareholders making such elections actually realize gain upon the cancellation or redemption of such stock upon the liquidation.

(c) The application of this section may be illustrated by the following example:

Example. The R Corporation has outstanding 20 shares of common stock on July 1, 1954, at the time of the adoption of a plan of liquidation within the provisions of section 333, each entitled to one vote upon the adoption of such plan of liquidation. At that time ten of such shares are owned by the S Corporation, two each by the X Corporation and the Y Corporation, one by the Z Corporation, and one each by A, B, C, D, and E, individuals. There are also outstanding at such time two shares of preferred stock, not entitled to vote on liquidation, one share being owned by F, an individual, and one share by the P Corporation. The S Corporation, being a corporate shareholder and the owner of 50 percent of the voting stock, may not be a qualified electing shareholder under any circumstances. In order for any other corporate shareholder to be a qualified electing shareholder, it is necessary that the X Corporation and the Y Corporation file their written elections to be governed by section 333. If this is done, the P Corporation will also be a qualified electing shareholder if it has filed a like election. Similarly, in the case of the individual shareholders, some combination of four of the individual holders of the common stock must have filed their written elections, before any individual shareholder may be considered a qualified electing shareholder, but if this is done, F will also be a qualified electing shareholder if he has filed a like election.

(d) An election to be governed by the provisions of section 333 relates to the treatment of gain realized upon the cancellation or redemption of stock upon liquidation. Such election, therefore, can be made only by or on behalf of the person by whom gains, if any, will be realized. Thus, the shareholder who may make such election must be the actual owner of stock and not a mere record holder, such as a nominee.

(e) A shareholder is entitled to make an election relative to the gain only on stock owned by him at the time of the adoption of the plan of liquidation. The election is personal to the shareholder making it and does not follow such stock into the hands of a transferee.

§ 1.333-3 Making and filing of written elections

An election to be governed by section 333 shall be made on Form 964 (revised) in accordance with the instructions printed thereon and with this section. The original and one copy shall be filed by the shareholder with the district director with whom the final income tax return of the corporation will be filed. The elections must be filed within 30 days after the adoption of the plan of liquidation. Under no circumstances shall section 333 be applicable to any shareholders who fail to file their elections within the 30-day period prescribed. An election shall be considered as timely filed if it is placed in the mail on or before midnight of the 30th day after the adoption of the plan of liquidation, as shown by the postmark on the envelope containing the written election or as shown by other available evidence of the mailing date. Another copy of the election shall be attached to and made a part of the shareholder's income tax return for his taxable year in which the transfer of all the property under the liquidation occurs.

§ 1.333-4 Treatment of gain

(a) Computation of gain. As in the case of shareholders generally, amounts received by qualified electing shareholders are treated as in full payment in exchange for their stock, as provided in section 331 and gain from the receipt of such amounts is determined as provided in section 1001. Gain or loss must be computed separately on each share of stock owned by a qualified electing shareholder at the time of the adoption of the plan of liquidation. The limited recognition and special treatment accorded by section 333 applies only to the gain on such shares of stock upon which gain was realized and not to net gain computed by setting off losses realized on some shares against gain on others. Since section 333 applies only to gain recognized, losses realized on the liquidation will be allowable only in the year of liquidation even though Forms 964 (revised) have been filed by those shareholders who realize only losses. Such filings may be necessary to fulfill the 80 percent requirement (under section 333(c)) so that those shareholders who realize gain may qualify under this section.

(b) Recognition of gain. Pursuant to section 333 only so much of the gain on each share of stock owned by a qualified electing shareholder at the time of the adoption of the plan of liquidation is recognized as does not exceed the greater of the following:

(1) Such share's ratable share of the earnings and profits of the corporation accumulated after February 28, 1913, computed as of the last day of the month of liquidation, without diminution by reason of distributions made during such month, and including in such computation all items of income and expense accrued up to the date on which the transfer of all the property under the liquidation is completed; or

(2) Such share's ratable share of the sum of the amount of money received by such shareholder on shares of the same class and the fair market value of all the stock or securities so received which were acquired by the liquidating corporation after December 31, 1953. The mere replacement after December 31, 1953 of lost or destroyed certificates or instruments acquired on or before December 31, 1953, or the mere conversion of certificates or instruments into certificates or instruments of larger or smaller denominations will not constitute an acquisition within the meaning of the phrase "acquired after December 31, 1953." Nor will such an acquisition result from the issuance after December 31, 1953 of certificates of stock in connection with a subscription made and accepted on or before December 31, 1953.

(c) Treatment of recognized gain. (1) In the case of a qualified electing shareholder other than a corporation, that part of the recognized gain on a share of stock owned at the time of the adoption of the plan of liquidation which is not in excess of his ratable share of the earnings and profits of the liquidating corporation accumulated after February 28, 1913, determined as provided in section 333(e) (1), is treated as a dividend. It retains its character as a dividend for all tax purposes. The remainder of the gain which is recognized is treated as a short-term or long-term capital gain, as the case may be. In the case of a qualified electing shareholder which is a corporation, the entire amount of the gain which is recognized is treated as a short-term or long-term capital gain, as the case may be.

(2) The application of subparagraph (1) of this paragraph may be illustrated by the following example:

Example. (i) X Corporation has only one class of stock outstanding, owned in equal amounts by three shareholders. The basis of the stock owned by each shareholder is $50, each having bought his stock in a single block prior to the date of the adoption of a plan of liquidation conforming to the requirements of section 333. One of the shareholders is an individual; two are corporations. All are "qualified electing shareholders".

(ii) X Corporation has earnings and profits accumulated after February 28, 1913, of $60 (computed as provided in section 333). Its assets consist of (a) cash of $75, (b) stock and securities acquired after December 31, 1953, having a fair market value of $90, and (c) other property having a fair market value of $240. In October 1954, all of these assets are distributed to the shareholders pro rata in complete liquidation of the corporation, as provided in section 333. Each shareholder thus receives $135 in cash and property, and has $85 gain.

(iii) Each shareholder's gain is recognized to the extent of $55 since such amount represents the sum of (a) the cash received by him and (b) the fair market value of the stock and securities received by him which were acquired by the X Corporation after December 31, 1953, and is greater than his ratable share of the earnings and profits ($20). The remainder of each shareholder's gain ($30) is not recognized.

(iv) In the case of the corporate shareholders the entire amount of the recognized gain ($55) is treated as capital gain. In the case of the individual shareholder, $20, being the amount of the shareholder's ratable share of the earnings and profits, is recognized and treated as a dividend, and $35, being the difference between the shareholder's ratable share of the earnings and profits and the sum of the cash and stock and securities received by him, is treated as a short-term or long-term capital gain, as the case may be.

(v) If the basis of each shareholder's stock had been $100, instead of $50, each of the corporate shareholders would be taxed on only $35 as capital gain and the individual shareholder would be taxed on $20 as a dividend and on only $15 as capital gain, since the total amount taxed is limited to the amount of gain realized by the shareholder upon the cancellation or redemption of his stock.

§ 1.333-6   Records to be kept and information to be filed with return

(a) Permanent records in substantial form shall be kept by every qualified electing shareholder receiving distributions in complete liquidation of a domestic corporation. Such shareholder must file with his income tax return for his taxable year in which the liquidation occurs a statement of all facts pertinent to the recognition and treatment of the gain realized by him upon the shares of stock owned by him at the time of the adoption of the plan of liquidation including:

(1) A statement of his stock ownership in the liquidating corporation as of the record date of the distribution, showing the number of shares of each class owned on such date, the cost or other basis of each such share, and the date of acquisition of each such share;

(2) A list of all the property, including money, received upon the distribution, showing the fair market value of each item of such property other than money on the date distributed and stating what items, if any, consist of stock or securities acquired by the liquidating corporation after December 31, 1953, or after December 31, 1962, whichever date is applicable;

(3) A statement of his ratable share of the earnings and profits of the liquidating corporation accumulated after February 28, 1913, computed without diminution by reason of distributions made during the month of liquidation (other than designated dividends under section 316(b) (2) (B));

(5) A copy of such shareholder's written election to be governed by the provisions of section 333. See § 1.333-3.

(b) For information to be filed by the liquidating corporation, see section 6043.

§ 1.334-2   Property received in liquidation under section 333

The basis of assets (other than money) acquired by stockholders in a liquidation upon which the amount of gain recognized was limited under section 333 shall be the same as the basis of the shares of stock redeemed or cancelled, decreased in the amount of any money received and increased in the amount of gain recognized and the amount of the unsecured liabilities assumed by the stockholders. The amount thus arrived at should be allocated to the various assets received on the basis of their net fair market values (the net fair market value of an asset is its fair market value less any specific mortgage or pledge to which it is subject). To that portion of the basis thus determined, for each property against which there is a lien, should be added the amount of such lien. Where more than one property is covered by the same lien, the amount of the lien should be divided among the properties, allocating to each that portion of the lien that the fair market value of such property bears to the total market value of the properties covered by the same lien. Whether the mortgage indebtedness is assumed by the shareholders or the property is taken subject to the mortgage is immaterial. The application of this section may be illustrated by the following example:

Example. The X corporation distributed all its property in complete liquidation during the month of October 1954 pursuant to the provisions of section 333. A, an individual, and a qualifying electing shareholder, received, in cancellation or redemption of 100 shares of stock owned by him at the time of the adoption of the plan of liquidation, $1,000 in cash, property (other than stock or securities acquired by the corporation after December 31, 1953) with a fair market value of $22,000 subject to a lien of $1,000, and stock acquired by the liquidating corporation after December 31, 1953 with a fair market value of $4,000. A, also assumed a $2,000 liability of the liquidating corporation. The basis of the shares owned by A was $120 per share or $12,000. A's ratable share of the earnings and profits of the X corporation accumulated after February 28, 1913 (computed as provided in section 333) was $2,500. His gain is $12,000, but under section 333 only $5,000 of this gain is recognized, $2,500 thereof being taxed as a dividend. The basis of all the property other than money received by A is $19,000, computed as follows:

Adjusted basis of stock cancelled or redeemed	$12,000
Less: money received	1,000
Remainder	11,000
Liability assumed	2,000
Specific lien against property (other than stock)	1,000
Gain recognized	5,000
Basis of property acquired	19,000

The basis, excluding the specific lien attached to the property, ($19,000 less $1,000, $18,000) will be apportioned among the classes of property other than money received as follows: $21,000/$25,000 of $18,000 or $15,120 to the property other than stock; $4,000/$25,000 of $18,000 or $2,880 to the stock. The basis of the property other than stock, $15,120, must be increased by the amount of the specific lien attached thereto, $1,000, making a total basis for such property of $16,120.

§ 1.336–1 General rule on liquidation of corporation

Except as provided in section 453 (d), no gain or loss is recognized to a corporation on the distribution by it of property in kind in partial or complete liquidation (regardless of the fact that such property may have appreciated or depreciated in value since its acquisition by the corporation). However, gain or loss is recognized to a corporation on all sales by it, whether directly or indirectly (as through trustees or a receiver), except as provided in section 337 (relating to sales or exchanges in connection with certain liquidations). . . . .

§ 1.337–1 General

Except as provided in sections 337 (c) and . . ., if a corporation distributes all of its assets in complete liquidation within 12 months after the adoption of a plan of liquidation, . . ., no gain or loss shall be recognized from the sale of property (as defined in section 337(b)) during such 12-month period. For this purpose such sales may be made before the adoption of the plan of liquidation if made on the same day such plan is adopted. All assets (less assets retained to meet claims), both tangible and intangible, must be distributed within the 12-month period. Any assets retained after the expiration of the 12-month period for the payment of claims (including unascertained or contingent liabilities or expenses) must be specifically set apart for that purpose and must be reasonable in amount in relation to the items involved. The 12-month period shall begin on the date of adoption of the plan determined as provided in paragraph (b) of § 1.337-2 and no extension of such period can be granted. See section 453(d) (4) (B) relative to nonrecognition of gain on the distribution of certain installment obligations. Except to the extent provided in section 341(e) (4), sales or exchanges made by a collapsible corporation (as defined in section 341(b)) are excluded from the operation of section 337 by section 337(c). Accordingly, except as provided in section 341(e) (4), section 337 does not apply to any sale or exchange of property whenever the distribution of such property in partial or complete liquidation to the shareholders in lieu of such sale or exchange would have resulted in the taxation of the gain from such distribution in the manner provided in section 341(a) as to any shareholder or would have resulted in the taxation of the gain in such manner, but for the application of section 341(d). Likewise, section 337 does not apply to sales or exchanges made by a corporation if such corporation is liquidated in a transaction to which section 333 is applicable, or in a transaction to which section 332 applies (except to the extent provided in section 337(c) (2) (B)). . . . . .

§ 1.337-2 Sales or exchanges within the scope of section 337

(a) Provided the other conditions of section 337 are met, sales or exchanges which occur on or after the date on which the plan of complete liquidation is adopted and within the 12-month period thereafter are subject to the provisions of such section. The date on which a sale occurs depends primarily upon the intent of the parties to be gathered from the terms of the contract and the surrounding circumstances. In ascertaining whether a sale or exchange occurs on or after the date on which the plan of complete liquidation is adopted, the fact that negotiations for sale may have been commenced, either by the corporation or its shareholders, or both shall be disregarded. Moreover, an executory contract to sell is to be distinguished from a contract of sale. Ordinarily, a sale has not occurred when a contract to sell has been entered into but title and possession of the property have not been transferred and the obligation of the seller to sell or the buyer to buy is conditional.

(b) Ordinarily the date of the adoption of a plan of complete liquidation by a corporation is the date of adoption by the shareholders of the resolution authorizing the distribution of all the assets of the corporation (other than those retained to meet claims) in redemption of all of its stock. Where the corporation sells substantially all of its property of the type defined in section 337 (b) prior to the date of adoption by the shareholders of such resolution, then the date of the adoption of the plan of complete liquidation by such corporation is the date of the adoption by the shareholders of such resolution and gain or loss will be rec-

ognized with respect to such sales. Where no substantial part of the property of the type defined in section 337 (b) has been sold by the corporation prior to the date of adoption by the shareholders of such resolution, the date of the adoption of the plan of complete liquidation by such corporation is the date of adoption by the shareholders of such resolution and no gain or loss will be recognized on sales of such property on or after such date, if all the corporate assets (other than those retained to meet claims) are distributed in liquidation to the shareholders within 12 months after the date of the adoption of such resolution. In all other cases the date of the adoption of the plan of liquidation shall be determined from all the facts and circumstances. Section 337 shall not apply in any case in which all of the corporate assets (other than those retained to meet claims) are not distributed to the shareholders within 12 months after the date of the adoption of a resolution by the shareholders authorizing the distribution of all the corporate assets in redemption of all the corporate stock. A corporation will be considered to have distributed all of its property other than assets retained to meet claims even though it has retained an amount of cash equal to its known liabilities and liquidating expenses plus an amount of cash set aside under arrangements for the payment after the close of the 12-month period of unascertained or contingent liabilities and contingent expenses. Such arrangements for payment must be made in good faith, the amount set aside must be reasonable, and no amount may be set aside to meet claims of shareholders with respect to their stock. If it is established to the satisfaction of the Commissioner that there are shareholders who cannot be located, a distribution in liquidation includes a transfer to a State official, trustee, or other person authorized by law to receive distributions for the benefit of such shareholders. For the purposes of this paragraph "property of the type defined in section 337 (b)" means property upon the sale of which section 337 (a) may provide for the nonrecognition of gain or loss upon sale or exchange during a 12-month period, including property described in subparagraph (A) of section 337 (b) (1) if sold or exchanged at any time under the conditions set forth in section 337 (b) (2) and including installment obligations acquired in respect of such sale or exchange.

§ 1.337-3 Property defined

(a) Except as provided in section 337 (b) (2) and this section, the term "property" as used in section 337 (a) and § 1.337-1 does not include, (1) stock in trade of the corporation, or other property of a kind which would properly be included in the inventory of the corporation if on hand at the close of the taxable year and property held by the corporation primarily for sale to customers in the ordinary course of its trade or business (hereinafter for purposes of section 337 referred to as "inventory"), (2) installment obligations acquired at any time from the sale or exchange of inventory, or (3) installment obligations acquired from the sale or exchange of property (other than inventory) prior to the adoption of the plan of liquidation. With the exceptions listed in this paragraph, the term "property" includes all assets owned by a corporation.

(b) Except as provided in paragraph (c) of this section, if substantially all of the inventory is sold or exchanged to one person in one transaction, then for the purpose of section 337 (a) the term "property" shall include:

(1) The inventory so sold or exchanged, and

(2) Installment obligations acquired in such sale or exchange.

For this purpose, the term "substantially all" means substantially all of the inventory at the time of the sale and includes inventory subject to liabilities, specific or otherwise. Section 337 (b) (2) shall be inapplicable if the inventory so sold is replaced by like inventory, or by a new kind of inventory.

(c) The term "property" in the case of a corporation which is engaged in two or more distinct businesses shall include the inventory of any one of such trades or businesses if substantially all of the inventory attributable to such trade or business is sold or exchanged to one person in one transaction. If installment obligations are received upon such a sale, such obligations are also included within the meaning of the term "property".

(d) This section may be illustrated by the following examples:

Example (1). Corporation A operates a grocery store at one location and a hardware store at another. Neither store handles items similar to those handled by the other. Both stores are served by a common warehouse. Pursuant to a plan of liquidation adopted by the corporation, the grocery store and all of its inventory, including that part of its inventory held in the warehouse, are sold to one person in one transaction. Thereafter, and within 12 months after the adoption of the plan of liquidation, all of the assets of the corporation are distributed to the shareholders. No gain or loss will be recognized upon the sale of all of the assets attributable to the grocery business, including the inventory items.

Example (2). Corporation B operates two department stores, one in the downtown business district and the other in a suburban shopping center. Both handle the same items and are served by a common warehouse which contains an amount of inventory items equal to the total of that in both stores. The part of the inventory in the warehouse which is attributable to each store cannot be clearly determined. Pursuant to a plan of liquidation adopted by the corporation, the assets of the suburban store, including the inventory held in such store, but not including any portion of the inventory held in the warehouse, are sold to one person in one transaction. Thereafter, and within 12 months after the adoption of the plan of liquidation, all of the assets of the corporation are distributed to the shareholders. No gain or loss will be recognized with respect to the sale of the property other than the inventory, but gain or loss will be recognized upon the sale of the inventory.

Example (3). The facts are the same as in example (2) except that the part of the inventory in the warehouse which is attributable to the suburban store can be clearly determined and both the inventory held in the store and that part of the inventory in the warehouse attributable to such store are sold. No gain or loss will be recognized upon the sale of the inventory.

§ 1.337-4 Limitation of gain

(a) Section 337 (c) (2) (B) provides a limitation upon the amount of gain not recognized where a corporation sells or exchanges property pursuant to a plan of complete liquidation (and such property, if distributed, would take the basis of the stock held by the distributee pursuant to the provisions of section 334 (b) (2) (relating to plans of liquidation adopted within 2 years after purchase of the stock)). The amount of gain not recognized shall not be greater than the excess of (1) that portion of the adjusted basis (further adjusted as provided in the second sentence of section 334 (b) (2) and in paragraph (c) of § 1.334-1) of the stock of the liquidating corporation in the hands of its parent corporation allocable to the property sold or exchanged over (2) the adjusted basis of such property in the hands of the liquidating corporation.

(b) Paragraph (a) of this section may be illustrated by the following example:

Example. Corporation A owns more than 80 percent of the stock of Corporation B, which it purchased for $10,000. All of the assets of Corporation B, having a total basis of $4,000 are sold for $12,000. The portion of the realized gain of $8,000 which is not recognized is $6,000, computed as follows:

Basis of stock allocable to property
  sold $10,000
Basis of property sold 4,000
                                            _____
  Excess (not recognized) 6,000

In general, where section 337 (c) (2) (B) is applicable and where the gain realized from the sale of property is greater than the excess of the selling price of the property over the basis of the stock allocable to the property sold, the amount of gain to be recognized from such sale is equal to such excess. In the above example, the $2,000 gain representing the excess of the selling price of $12,000 over the basis of the stock allocable to the property sold ($10,000) would be recognized to the liquidating corporation.

(c) For the purpose of this section only, the basis (adjusted as described in paragraph (a) of this section) of the liquidating corporation's stock in the hands of its parent corporation on the date of the first sale of property, shall be allocated to the assets of the liquidating corporation (unreduced by any amount applicable to minority interests) on the basis of the fair market value of such assets (see paragraph (c) of § 1.334-1), both tangible and intangible, on the date the first property is sold by the liquidating corporation. The allocation then made shall remain unchanged for the purpose of determining recognized gain upon subsequent sales of property by the liquidating corporation unless the stock ownership of the parent corporation changes. In the event of such a change, a new allocation shall be made at the time of the next sale of property thereafter. The new allocation shall be made on the basis of the fair market value of the liquidating corporation's assets on the date of such sale.

§ 1.337-5 Special rules for certain minority shareholders

(a) General. If, with respect to a plan of complete liquidation adopted on or after January 1, 1958, the liqui-

dating corporation fails to qualify for the treatment prescribed by section 337(a) solely by reason of the application of section 337(c) (2) (A), then, for the first taxable year of any shareholder (other than a corporation which meets the 80-percent stock ownership requirement specified in section 332(b) (1)) in which he receives a distribution in complete liquidation, the treatment prescribed by section 337(d) and this section shall be applicable to such shareholder. Since section 337(d) applies only with respect to distributions in complete liquidation under section 331, it does not apply with respect to a distribution which is treated as part of an exchange to which section 354 or 356 applies.

(b) Treatment of minority shareholders. (1) In cases to which section 337(d) and paragraph (a) of this section apply—

(i) The amount realized by the shareholder on the distribution shall be increased by his proportionate share of the amount by which the tax imposed by subtitle A of the Code (income taxes) on the liquidating corporation would have been reduced if section 337(c) (2) (A) had not been applicable (see paragraph (c) of this section for determination of the proportionate share of each shareholder), and

(ii) For purposes of the Code, the shareholder shall be deemed to have paid on the last day prescribed by section 6151 for the payment of the tax (the last day prescribed by section 6072 for the filing of his income tax return) for the taxable year in which he receives the first distribution in complete liquidation (whether the return is filed before, on, or after such last day), an amount of income tax equal to the amount of the increase described in subdivision (i) of this subparagraph.

. . . . .

(c) Determination of each minority shareholder's increase in amount realized. (1) Under section 337(d) and paragraph (b) of this section, the amount realized by each minority shareholder of the liquidating corporation shall be increased by his proportionate share of the amount by which the tax imposed by subtitle A of the Code on the liquidating corporation would have been reduced if section 337(c) (2) (A) had not been applicable. Where the corporation has only the one class of stock outstanding, the increase in the amount realized by each minority shareholder shall be determined by multiplying the reduction in the corporation's tax that would be applicable if section 337(c) (2) (A) did not apply by a fraction, the numerator of which is equal to the sum of all liquidating distributions received by such shareholder and the denominator of which is equal to the sum of all liquidating distributions received by all shareholders. Where the corporation has outstanding preferred stock which is limited to a specified amount on liquidation, as well as common stock, if the holders of the preferred stock received the entire amount to which they are entitled, the fraction described in the preceding sentence shall be applied to determine the increase in the amount realized by the holders of common stock on the liquidation without taking the preferred stock into account. In all other cases, in determining the increase in the amount realized by each minority shareholder, consideration must be given to the extent to which different classes of stock are entitled to participate in the assets of the corporation on liquidation.

(2) If two or more minority shareholders receive distributions in liquidation with respect to the same stock (e. g., if a minority shareholder sells his stock after receiving one of a series of distributions in complete liquidation), the increase in the amount realized by the minority shareholder who surrenders the stock in liquidation shall be determined as though he received all the distributions in liquidation with respect to such stock and shall then be divided between himself and the shareholder who has already received distributions in liquidation with respect to the same stock. This division must be in proportion to the amount each minority shareholder received in liquidation with respect to such stock.

* * * * *

(e) **Illustrations.** The application of this section may be illustrated by the following examples:

Example (1). (i) Assume that corporation S, having only common stock outstanding, is owned 90 percent by corporation P (which has owned the S stock for 3 years) and 10 percent by individual A (a calendar year taxpayer), and that the sole assets of corporation S are two buildings, each having a fair market value of $100,000 and a basis to the corporation of $50,-000. Assume further that A's basis for his stock is $10,000. On August 1, 1958, corporation S adopts a plan of complete liquidation. On September 1, 1958, corporation S sells building No. 1 for $100,000 and, during October 1958, the corporation makes a pro rata distribution of building No. 2 and the proceeds of the sale of building No. 1 (less $12,500 retained to pay the tax on such sale at the rate of 25 percent).

(ii) Under section 337(d) and this section, the amount realized by A on the distribution is increased by $1,250, A's proportionate share (10 percent) of the amount by which the tax imposed on corporation S upon such sale would have been reduced ($12,500) if section 337(a) had been applicable. Thus, the tax imposed on A with respect to the complete liquidation is computed as follows: The amount realized by A is $18,750 ($10,000 for A's one-tenth interest in building No. 2, plus $8,750 representing A's proportionate share of the $100,000 received by corporation S on the sale of building No. 1 less the tax imposed on corporation S upon such sale) plus $1,250 (the increase in the amount realized), or $20,000. Since A's basis for his stock is $10,-000, the tax imposed on A with respect to the complete liquidation (assuming A's gain is taxed at a rate of 25 percent) is $2,500. Under section 337(d) and this section, A shall be deemed to have paid $1,250 in tax. Accordingly, A will be left with $17,500 in property and money ($18,750 minus $1,250).

Example (2). (i) Assume all the facts set forth in example (1) and the following additional facts: Corporation S has outstanding 1,000 shares of $100 par value preferred stock, the holders of which are entitled to receive full par value on liquidation, after which the common shareholders receive the balance of the assets. Individual A owns 10 percent of the preferred stock, with a basis to him of $10,000, as well as 10 percent of the common stock. Corporation S has, in addition to its two buildings, $100,000 in cash which it distributes in full payment in exchange for the outstanding preferred stock.

(ii) Individual A receives $10,000 in exchange for his preferred stock and recognizes no gain or loss on this portion of the liquidation. Under section 337(d) and this section, A is accorded the same treatment described in example (1) with respect to his common stock as though it were the only stock outstanding. Thus, with respect to his common stock the amount realized by A on the distribution is increased by $1,250, and the tax deemed paid by him is $1,250. Accordingly, after credit, A will be left with $27,500 in property and money ($10,000 on his preferred stock and $17,500 on his common stock).

Example (3). (i) Assume the same facts as in example (1) except that on August 2 1958, corporation S makes a pro rata distribution of building No. 2 as a first distribution in complete liquidation. Assume further that on August 15, 1958, individual A sells his stock to B, and that on October 1, 1958, building No. 1 is sold and final distribution in liquidation is made of $87,500 ($100,000 sales proceeds less $12,500 retained to pay tax, assuming a 25-percent rate).

(ii) Under section 337(d) and this section, the increase in the amount realized by B shall first be determined as though he had received all the distributions in liquidation with respect to such stock. Then the increase in the amount realized ($1,250) is divided between A and B in proportion to the amount each shareholder received in liquidation with respect to such stock. Thus, A's share of the increase in the amount realized is $666.67 ($1,250×10,000/18,750) and B's share is $583.33 ($1,250× 8,750/18,750). A is deemed to have paid tax in the amount of $666.67 and B is deemed to have paid tax in the amount of $583.33.

. . . . .

§ 1.337-6   Information to be filed

(a) **Cases to which section 337(a) applies.** In cases to which section 337 (a) applies, there must be attached to the return of the liquidating corporation the following information:

(1) A copy of the minutes of the stockholders' meeting at which the plan of liquidation was formally adopted, including a copy of the plan of liquidation.

(2) A statement of the assets sold after the adoption of the plan of liquidation, including the dates of such sales. If section 337(c) (2) (B), relating to limited nonrecognition of gain on sales by subsidiaries, is applicable, this statement must include a computation of the total gain and of the gain not recognized under section 337.

(3) Information as to the date of the final liquidating distribution.

(4) A statement of the assets, if any, retained to pay liabilities and the nature of the liabilities.

. . . . .

§ 1.341-1   Collapsible corporations; in general

Subject to the limitations contained in § 1.341-4 and the exceptions contained in § 1.341-6 and § 1.341-7(a). the entire gain from (a) the actual sale or exchange of stock of a collapsible corporation, (b) amounts distributed in a complete or partial liquidation of a collapsible corporation which are treated, under section 331, as payment in exchange for stock, and (c) a distribution made by a collapsible corporation which, under section 301(c)(3), is treated, to the extent it exceeds the basis of the stock, in the same manner as a gain from the sale or exchange of property, shall be considered as ordinary income.

§ 1.341-2   Definitions

(a) **Determination of collapsible corporation.** (1) A collapsible corporation is defined by section 341(b) (1) to be a corporation formed or availed of

principally (i) for the manufacture, construction, or production of property, (ii) for the purchase of property which (in the hands of the corporation) is property described in section 341(b) (3), or (iii) for the holding of stock in a corporation so formed or availed of, with a view to (a) the sale or exchange of stock by its shareholders (whether in liquidation or otherwise), or a distribution to its shareholders, prior to the realization by the corporation manufacturing, constructing, producing, or purchasing the property of a substantial part of the taxable income to be derived from such property, and (b) the realization by such shareholders of gain attributable to such property. See § 1.341-5 for a description of the facts which will ordinarily be considered sufficient to establish whether or not a corporation is a collapsible corporation under the rules of this section. See paragraph (d) of § 1.341-5 for examples of the application of section 341.

(2) Under section 341(b) (1) the corporation must be formed or availed of with a view to the action therein described, that is, the sale or exchange of its stock by its shareholders, or a distribution to them prior to the realization by the corporation manufacturing, constructing, producing, or purchasing the property of a substantial part of the taxable income to be derived from such property, and the realization by the shareholders of gain attributable to such property. This requirement is satisfied in any case in which such action was contemplated by those persons in a position to determine the policies of the corporation, whether by reason of their owning a majority of the voting stock of the corporation or otherwise. The requirement is satisfied whether such action was contemplated, unconditionally, conditionally, or as a recognized possibility. If the corporation was so formed or availed of, it is immaterial that a particular shareholder was not a shareholder at the time of the manufacture, construction, production, or purchase of the property, or if a shareholder at such time, did not share in such view. Any gain of such a shareholder on his stock in the corporation shall be treated in the same manner as gain of a shareholder who did share in such view. The existence of a bona fide business reason for doing business in the corporate form

does not, by itself, negate the fact that the corporation may also have been formed or availed of with a view to the action described in section 341(b).

(3) A corporation is formed or availed of with a view to the action described in section 341(b) if the requisite view existed at any time during the manufacture, production, construction, or purchase referred to in that section. Thus, if the sale, exchange, or distribution is attributable solely to circumstances which arose after the manufacture, construction, production, or purchase (other than circumstances which reasonably could be anticipated at the time of such manufacture, construction, production, or purchase), the corporation shall, in the absence of compelling facts to the contrary, be considered not to have been so formed or availed of. However, if the sale, exchange or distribution is attributable to circumstances present at the time of the manufacture, construction, production, or purchase, the corporation shall, in the absence of compelling facts to the contrary, be considered to have been so formed or availed of.

(4) The property referred to in section 341(b) is that property or the aggregate of those properties with respect to which the requisite view existed. In order to ascertain the property or properties as to which the requisite view existed, reference shall be made to each property as to which, at the time of the sale, exchange, or distribution referred to in section 341(b) there has not been a realization by the corporation manufacturing, constructing, producing, or purchasing the property of a substantial part of the taxable income to be derived from such property. However, where any such property is a unit of an integrated project involving several properties similar in kind, the determination whether the requisite view existed shall be made only if a substantial part of the taxable income to be derived from the project has not been realized at the time of the sale, exchange, or distribution, and in such case the determination shall be made by reference to the aggregate of the properties constituting the single project.

(5) A corporation shall be deemed to have manufactured, constructed, produced, or purchased property if it (i) engaged in the manufacture, construction, or production of property to any extent, or (ii) holds property having a basis determined, in whole or in part, by reference to the cost of such property in the hands of a person who manufactured, constructed, produced, or purchased the property, or (iii) holds property having a basis determined, in whole or in part, by reference to the cost of property manufactured, constructed, produced, or purchased by the corporation. Thus, under subdivision (i) of this subparagraph, for example, a corporation need not have originated nor have completed the manufacture, construction, or production of the property. Under subdivision (ii) of this subparagraph, for example, if an individual were to transfer property constructed by him to a corporation in exchange for all of the capital stock of such corporation, and such transfer qualifies under section 351, then the corporation would be deemed to have constructed the property, since the basis of the property in the hands of the corporation would, under section 362 be determined by reference to the basis of the property in the hands of the individual. Under subdivision (iii) of this subparagraph, for example, if a corporation were to exchange property constructed by it for property of like kind constructed by another person, and such exchange qualifies under section 1031(a), then the corporation would be deemed to have constructed the property received by it in the exchange, since the basis of the property received by it in the exchange would, under section 1031(d), be determined by reference to the basis of the property constructed by the corporation.

(6) In determining whether a corporation is a collapsible corporation by reason of the purchase of property, it is immaterial whether the property is purchased from the shareholders of the corporation or from persons other than such shareholders. The property, however, must be property which, in the hands of the corporation, is property of a kind described in section 341(b) (3). The determination whether property is of a kind described in section 341(b) (3) shall be made without regard to the fact that the corporation is formed or availed of with a view to the action described in section 341(b) (1).

(7) Section 341 is applicable whether the shareholder is an individual, a trust, an estate, a partnership, a company, or a corporation.

(b) Section 341 assets. For the purposes of this section, the term "section 341 assets" means the following listed property if held for less than 3 years:

(1) Stock in trade of the corporation, or other property of a kind which would properly be included in the inventory of the corporation if on hand at the close of the taxable year.

(2) Property held primarily for sale to customers in the ordinary course of a trade or business.

(3) Property used in a trade or business as defined in section 1231(b) and held for less than 3 years, except property that is or has been used in connection with the manufacture, construction, production or sale of property described in subparagraphs (1) and (2) of this paragraph.

(4) Unrealized receivables or fees pertaining to property listed in this paragraph. The term "unrealized receivables or fees" means any rights (contractual or otherwise) to payment for property listed in subparagraphs (1), (2), and (3) of this paragraph which has been delivered or is to be delivered and rights to payments for services rendered or to be rendered, to the extent such rights have not been included in the income of the corporation under the method of accounting used by it. In determining whether the assets referred to in this paragraph have been held for 3 years, the time such assets were held by a transferor shall be taken into consideration (section 1223). However, no such period shall begin before the date the manufacture, construction, production, or purchase of such assets is completed.

§ 1.341–3 Presumptions

(a) Unless shown to the contrary a corporation shall be considered to be a collapsible corporation if at the time of the transactions described in § 1.341–1 the fair market value of the section 341 assets held by it constitutes 50 percent or more of the fair market value of its total assets and the fair market value of the section 341 assets is 120 percent or more of the adjusted basis of such assets. In determining the fair market value of the total assets, cash, obligations which are capital assets in the hands of the corporation, governmental obligations, and stock in any other corporation shall not be taken into consideration. The failure of a cor-

poration to meet the requirements of this paragraph, shall not give rise to the presumption that the corporation was not a collapsible corporation.

(b) The following example will illustrate the application of this section:

Example. A corporation, filing its income tax returns on the accrual basis, on July 31, 1955, owned assets with the following fair market values: Cash, $175,000; note receivable held for investment, $130,000; stocks of other corporations, $545,000; rents receivable, $15,000; and a building constructed by the corporation in 1953 and held thereafter as rental property, $750,000. The adjusted basis of the building on that date was $600,000. The only debt outstanding was a $500,000 mortgage on the building. On July 31, 1955, the corporation liquidated and distributed all of its assets to its shareholders. In computing whether the fair market value of the section 341 assets (only the building) is 50 percent or more of the fair market value of the total assets, the cash, note receivable, and stocks of other corporations are not taken into account in determining the value of the total assets, with the result that the fair market value of the total assets was $765,000 ($750,000 (building) plus $15,000 (rents receivable)). Therefore, the value of the building is 98 percent of the total assets ($750,000÷$765,000). The value of the building is also 125 percent of the adjusted basis of the building ($750,000÷$600,000). In view of the above facts, there arises a presumption that the corporation is a collapsible corporation.

§ 1.341–4 Limitations on application of section

(a) General. This section shall apply only to the extent that the recognized gain of a shareholder upon his stock in a collapsible corporation would be considered, but for the provisions of this section, as gain from the sale or exchange of a capital asset held for more than 1 year (6 months for taxable years beginning before 1977; 9 months for taxable years beginning in 1977). Thus, if a taxpayer sells at a gain stock of a collapsible corporation which he had held for six months or less, this section would not, in any event, apply to such gain. Also, if it is determined, under provisions of law other than section 341, that a sale or exchange at a gain of stock of a collapsible corporation which has been held for more than 1 year (6 months for taxable years beginning before 1977; 9 months for taxable years beginning in 1977) results in ordinary income rather than long-term capital gain, then this section (including the limitations contained herein) has no application whatsoever to such gain.

(b) Stock ownership rules. (1) This section shall apply in the case of gain realized by a shareholder upon his stock in a collapsible corporation only if the shareholder, at any time after the actual commencement of the manufacture, construction, or production of the property, or at the time of the purchase of the property described in section 341(b) (3) or at any time thereafter, (i) owned, or was considered as owning, more than 5 percent in value of the outstanding stock of the corporation, or (ii) owned stock which was considered as owned at such time by another shareholder who then owned, or was considered as owning, more than 5 percent in value of the outstanding stock of the corporation.

(2) The ownership of stock shall be determined in accordance with the rules prescribed by section 544(a) (1), (2), (3), (5), and (6), except that, in addition to the persons prescribed by section 544(a) (2), the family of an individual shall include the spouses of that individual's brothers and sisters, whether such brothers and sisters are by the whole or the half blood, and the spouses of that individual's lineal descendants.

(3) For the purpose of this limitation, treasury stock shall not be considered as outstanding stock.

(4) It is possible, under this limitation, that a shareholder in a collapsible corporation may have gain upon his stock in that corporation treated differently from the gain of another shareholder in the same collapsible corporation.

(c) **Seventy-percent rule.** (1) This section shall apply to the gain recognized during a taxable year upon the stock in a collapsible corporation only if more than 70 percent of such gain is attributable to the property referred to in section 341(b) (1). If more than 70 percent of such gain is so attributable, then all of such gain is subject to this section, and, if 70 percent or less of such gain is so attributable, then none of such gain is subject to this section.

(2) For the purpose of this limitation, the gain attributable to the property referred to in section 341(b) (1) is the excess of the recognized gain of the shareholder during the taxable year upon his stock in the collapsible corporation over the recognized gain which the shareholder would have if the property had not been manufactured, constructed, produced, or purchased. In the case of gain on a distribution in partial liquidation or a distribution de-scribed in section 301(c) (3) (A), the gain attributable to the property shall not be less than an amount which bears the same ratio to the gain on such distribution as the gain which would be attributable to the property if there had been a complete liquidation at the time of such distribution bears to the total gain which would have resulted from such complete liquidation.

(3) Gain may be attributable to the property referred to in section 341(b) (1) even though such gain is represented by an appreciation in the value of property other than that manufactured, constructed, produced, or purchased. Where, for example, a corporation owns a tract of land and the development of one-half of the tract increases the value of the other half, the gain attributable to the developed half of the tract includes the increase in the value of the other half.

(4) The following example will illustrate the application of the 70 percent rule:

Example: On January 2, 1954, A formed the Z Corporation and contributed $1,000,000 cash in exchange for all of the stock thereof. The Z Corporation invested $400,000 in one project for the purpose of building and selling residential houses. As of December 31, 1954, the residential houses in this project were all sold, resulting in a profit of $100,000 (after taxes). Simultaneously with the development of the first project and in connection with a second and separate project the Z Corporation invested $600,000 in land for the purpose of subdividing such land into lots suitable for sale as home sites and distributing such lots in liquidation before the realization by the corporation of a substantial part of the taxable income to be realized from this second project. As of December 31, 1954, Corporation Z had derived $60,000 in profits (after taxes) from the sale of some of the lots. On January 2, 1955, the Z Corporation made a distribution in complete liquidation to shareholder A who received:

(i) $560,000 in cash and notes, and

(ii) Lots having a fair market value of $940,-000. The gain recognized to shareholder A upon the liquidation is $500,000 ($1,500,000 minus $1,000,000). The gain which would have been recognized to A if the second project had not been undertaken is $100,000 ($1,100,000 minus $1,000,000). Therefore, the gain attributable to the second project which is property referred to in section 341 (b) (1), is $400,000 ($500,000 minus $100,000). Since this gain ($400,000) is more than 70 percent of the entire gain ($500,-000) recognized to A on the liquidation, the entire gain so recognized is gain subject to section 341 (a).

(d) **Three-year rule.** This section shall not apply to that portion of the gain of a shareholder that is realized more than three years after the actual completion of the manufacture, construction, production, or purchase of the property referred to in section 341 (b) (1) to which such portion is attributable. However, if the actual completion of the manufacture, construction, production, or purchase of all of such property occurred more than 3 years before the date on which the gain is realized, this section shall not apply to any part of the gain realized.

§ 1.341-5   Application of section

(a) Whether or not a corporation is a collapsible corporation shall be determined under the rules of §§ 1.341-2 and §§ 1.341-3 on the basis of all the facts and circumstances in each particular case. The following paragraphs of this section set forth those facts which will ordinarily be considered sufficient to establish that a corporation is or is not a collapsible corporation. The facts set forth in the following paragraphs of this section are not exclusive of other facts which may be controlling in any particular case. For example, if the facts in paragraph (b) of this section, but not the facts in paragraph (c) of this section, are present, the corporation may nevertheless not be a collapsible corporation if there are other facts which clearly establish that the regulations of §§ 1.341-2 and §§ 1.341-3 are not satisfied. Similarly, if the facts in paragraph (c) of this section are present, the corporation may nevertheless be a collapsible corporation if there are other facts which clearly establish that the corporation was formed or availed of in the manner described in §§ 1.341-2 and 1.341-3 or if the facts in paragraph (c) of this section are not significant by reason of other facts, such as the fact that the corporation is subject to the control of persons other than those who were in control immediately prior to the manufacture, construction, production, or purchase of the property. See § 1.341-4 for provisions which make section 341 inapplicable to certain shareholders of collapsible corporations.

(b) The following facts will ordinarily be considered sufficient (except as otherwise provided in paragraph (a) of this section and paragraph (c) of this section) to establish that a corporation is a collapsible corporation:

(1) A shareholder of the corporation sells or exchanges his stock, or receives a liquidating distribution, or a distribution described in section 301 (c) (3) (A),

(2) Upon such sale, exchange, or distribution, such shareholder realizes gain attributable to the property described in subparagraphs (4) and (5) of this paragraph, and

(3) At the time of the manufacture, construction, production, or purchase of the property described in subparagraphs (4) and (5) of this paragraph, such activity was substantial in relation to the other activities of the corporation which manufactured, constructed, produced, or purchased such property.

The property referred to in subparagraphs (2) and (3) of this paragraph is that property or the aggregate of those properties which meet the following two requirements:

(4) The property is manufactured, constructed, or produced by the corporation or by another corporation stock of which is held by the corporation, or is property purchased by the corporation or by such other corporation which (in the hands of the corporation holding such property) is property described in section 341 (b) (3), and

(5) At the time of the sale, exchange, or distribution described in subparagraph (1) of this paragraph, the corporation which manufactured, constructed, produced, or purchased such property has not realized a substantial part of the taxable income to be derived from such property.

In the case of property which is a unit of an integrated project involving several properties similar in kind. the rules of this subparagraph shall be applied to the aggregate of the properties constituting the single project rather than separately to such unit. Under the rules of this subparagraph, a corporation shall be considered a collapsible corporation by reason of holding stock in other corporations which manufactured, constructed, produced, or purchased the property only if the activity of the corporation in holding stock in such other corporations is substantial in relation to the other activities of the corporation.

(c) The absence of any of the facts set forth in paragraph (b) of this section or the presence of the following facts will ordinarily be considered sufficient (except as otherwise provided in paragraph (a) of this section) to establish that a corporation is not a collapsible corporation:

(1) In the case of a corporation subject to paragraph (b) of this section only by reason of the manufacture, construction, production, or purchase (either by the corporation or by another corporation the stock of which is held by the corporation) of property which is property described in section 341(b) (3) (A) and (B), the amount (both in quantity and value) of such property is not in excess of the amount which is normal—

(i) For the purpose of the business activities of the corporation which manufactured, constructed, produced, or purchased the property if such corporation has a substantial prior business history involving the use of such property and continues in business, or

(ii) For the purpose of an orderly liquidation of the business if the corporation which manufactured, constructed, produced, or purchased such property has a substantial prior business history involving the use of such property and is in the process of liquidation.

(2) In the case of a corporation subject to paragraph (b) of this section with respect to the manufacture, construction, or production (either by the corporation or by another corporation the stock of which is held by the corporation) of property, the amount of the unrealized taxable income from such property is not substantial in relation to the amount of the taxable income realized (after the completion of a material part of such manufacture, construction, or production, and prior to the sale, exchange, or distribution referred to in paragraph (b) (1) of this section) from such property and from other property manufactured, constructed, or produced by the corporation.

(d) The following examples will illustrate the application of this section:

Example (1). (i) On January 2, 1954, A formed the W Corporation and contributed $50,000 cash in exchange for all of the stock thereof. The W Corporation borrowed $900,000 from a bank and used $800,000 of such sum in the construction of an apartment house on land which it purchased for $50,000. The apartment house was completed on December 31, 1954. On December 31, 1954, the corporation, having determined that the fair market value of the apartment house, separate and apart from the land, was $900,000, made a distribution (per-

mitted under the applicable State law) to A of $100,000. At this time, the fair market value of the land was $50,000. As of December 31, 1954, the corporation has not realized any earnings and profits. In 1955, the corporation began the operation of the apartment house and received rentals therefrom. The corporation has since continued to own and operate the building. The corporation reported on the basis of the calendar year and cash receipts and disbursements.

(ii) Since A received a distribution and realized a gain attributable to the building constructed by the corporation, since, at the time of such distribution, the corporation has not realized a substantial part of the taxable income to be derived from such building, and since the construction of the building was a substantial activity of the corporation, the W Corporation is considered a collapsible corporation under paragraph (b) of § 1.341–5. The provisions of section 341 (d) do not prohibit the application of section 341 (a). Therefore, the distribution, if and to the extent that it may be considered long-term capital gain rather than ordinary income without regard to section 341, will be considered ordinary income under section 341 (a).

(iii) In the event of the existence of additional facts and circumstances in the above case, the corporation, notwithstanding the above facts, might not be considered a collapsible corporation. See § 1.342–2 and paragraph (a) of § 1.341–5.

Example (2). (i) On January 2, 1954, B formed X Corporation and became its sole shareholder. In August 1954, the corporation completed construction of an office building. It immediately sold this building at a gain of $50,000, included this entire gain in its return for 1954, and distributed this entire gain (less taxes) to B. In June 1955, the corporation completed construction of a second office building. In August 1955, B sold the entire stock of X Corporation at a gain of $12,000, which gain is attributable to the second building.

(ii) X Corporation is a collapsible corporation under section 341 (b) for the following reasons: The gain realized through the sale of the stock of X Corporation was attributable to the second office building; the construction of that building was a substantial activity of X Corporation during the time of construction and, at the time of sale, the corporation had not realized a substantial part of the taxable income to be derived from such building. Since the provisions of section 341 (d) do not prohibit the application of section 341 (a) to B, the gain of $12,000 to B is, accordingly, considered ordinary income.

Example (3). The facts are the same as in example (2), except that the following facts are shown: B was the president of the X Corporation and active in the conduct of its business. The second building was constructed as the first step in a project of the X Corporation for the development for rental purposes of a large suburban center involving the construction of several buildings by the corporation. The sale of the stock by B was caused by his retiring from all business activity as a result of illness arising after the second building was constructed. Under these additional facts, the corporation is not considered a collapsible corporation. See § 1.341–2 and paragraph (a) of § 1.341–5.

Example (4). (i) On January 2, 1948, C formed the Y Corporation and became the sole shareholder thereof. The Y Corporation has been engaged solely in the business of producing motion pictures and licensing their exhibition. On January 2, 1955, C sold all of the stock of the Y Corporation at a gain. The Y Corporation has produced one motion picture each year since its organization and before January 2, 1955, it has realized a substantial part of the taxable income to be derived from each of its motion pictures except the last one made in 1954. This last motion picture was completed September 1, 1954. As of January 2, 1955, no license had been made for its exhibition. The fair market value on January 2, 1955, of this last motion picture exceeds the cost of its production by $50,000. A material part of the production of this last picture was completed on January 1, 1954, and between that date and January 2, 1955, the corporation had realized taxable income of $500,000 from other motion pictures produced by it. The corporation has consistently distributed to its shareholder its taxable income when received (after adjustment for taxes).

(ii) Although the corporation is within paragraph (b) of this section with respect to the production of property, the amount of the unrealized income from such property ($50,000) is not substantial in relation to the amount of the income realized, after the completion of a material part of the production of such property and prior to sale of the stock, from such property and other property produced by the corporation ($500,000). Accordingly, the Y Corporation is within paragraph (c) (2) of this section, and is not considered a collapsible corporation.

Example (5). The facts are the same as in example (4) except that C sold all of his stock to D on February 1, 1954. On January 2, 1955, D sold all of the Y Corporation stock at a gain, the gain being attributable to the picture completed September 1, 1954, and not released by the corporation for exhibition. In view of the change of control of the corporation, the provisions of paragraph (c) (2) of this section are not significant at the time of the sale by D, and the Y Corporation would be considered a collapsible corporation on January 2, 1955. See § 1.341-2 and paragraph (a) of § 1.341-5.

§ 1.341-6   Exceptions to application of section

(a) In general—(1) Transactions excepted. Section 341(e) excepts 4 types of transactions from the application of the collapsible corporation provisions. These exceptions, where applicable, eliminate the necessity of determining whether a corporation is a collapsible corporation within the meaning of section 341(b) or whether any of the limitations of section 341(d) are applicable. Under section 341(e) (1) and (2), there are 2 exceptions which are designed to allow the shareholders of a corporation either to sell or exchange their stock or to receive distributions in certain complete liquidations without having any gain considered under section 341(a)

(1) or (2) as gain from the sale or exchange of property which is not a capital asset. Under section 341(e) (3), a third exception is designed to permit the shareholders of a corporation to make use of section 333, relating to elections as to recognition of gain in certain complete liquidations occurring within one calendar month. Under section 341(e) (4), the fourth exception permits a corporation to make use of section 337, relating to nonrecognition of gain or loss on sales or exchanges of property by a corporation following the adoption of a plan of complete liquidation. Section 341(e) does not apply to distributions in partial liquidation or in redemption of stock (other than any such distribution pursuant to a plan of complete liquidation), or to distributions described in section 301 (c) (3) (A). . . . .

(4) General corporate test. No exception provided in section 341(e) applies unless a general corporate test and, where applicable, a specific shareholder test are satisfied. Under the general corporate test no taxpayer may utilize the provisions of section 341(e) unless the net increase in value (called "net unrealized appreciation") in the corporation's "subsection (e) assets" does not exceed 15 percent of the corporation's net worth. Subsection (e) assets are, in general, those assets of the corporation which, if sold at a gain by the corporation or by any actual or constructive shareholder who is considered to own more than 20 percent in value of the outstanding stock, would result in the realization of ordinary income. See paragraph (b) of this section for the definition of subsection (e) assets, and paragraph (h) of this section for definition of net unrealized appreciation. This subparagraph may be illustrated by the following examples:

Example (1). X Corporation is in the business of selling whiskey. The net unrealized appreciation in its whiskey is $20,000 and the net worth of the corporation is $100,000. Since the corporation's whiskey is a subsection (e) asset and since the net unrealized appreciation in subsection (e) assets ($20,000) exceeds 15 percent of net worth ($15,000), the general corporate test is not satisfied and section 341(e) is inapplicable to the corporation or its shareholders.

Example (2). Assume the same facts as in example (1) except that X Corporation is not in the business of selling whiskey. Assume further that an actual shareholder who owns more than 20 percent in value of the outstanding X stock (or a person who is considered to own such actual shareholder's stock, such as his spouse) is in the business of selling whiskey. The result is the same as in example (1).

(5) **Specific shareholder test.** Even if the general corporate test is met, a shareholder selling or exchanging his stock or receiving a distribution with respect to his stock (referred to as a "specific shareholder") who is considered to own more than 5 percent in value of the outstanding stock of the corporation may not utilize the benefits of the exception in section 341(e) (1) (or the exception in section 341(e) (2)) unless he satisfies the applicable specific shareholder test. In general, the specific shareholder test is satisfied if the net unrealized appreciation in subsection (e) assets of the corporation, plus the net unrealized appreciation in certain other assets of the corporation which would be subsection (e) assets in respect of the specific shareholder under the following circumstances, does not exceed 15 percent of the corporation's net worth:

(i) If the specific shareholder is considered to own more than 5 percent but not more than 20 percent in value of the outstanding stock, he must take into account the net unrealized appreciation in assets of the corporation which would be subsection (e) assets if he was considered to own more than 20 percent in value of the outstanding stock (see paragraph (c) (3) (i) of this section);

(ii) In addition, if the specific shareholder is considered to own more than 20 percent in value of the outstanding stock, he must also take into account the net unrealized appreciation in assets of the corporation which would be subsection (e) assets under section 341(e) (5) (A) (i) and (iii) if his ownership within the preceding 3 years of stock in certain "related" corporations were taken into account in the manner prescribed in paragraphs (c) (3) (ii) and (d) of this section.

. . . .

§ 1.341-7 Certain sales of stock of consenting corporations

(a) **In general.**—(1) Under section 341(f)(1), if a corporation consents (in the manner provided in paragraph (b) of this section) to the application of section 341(f)(2) with respect to dispositions by it of its subsection (f) assets (as defined in paragraph (g) of this section), then section 341(a)(1) does not apply to any sales of stock of such consenting corporation (other than a sale to such corporation) made by any of its shareholders within the 6-month period beginning on the date on which such consent is filed.

(2) For purposes of section 341(f) (1) and (5)—(i) The term "sale" means a sale or exchange of stock at a gain. but only if such gain would be recognized as long-term capital gain were section 341 not a part of the Code. Thus, a sale or exchange of stock is not a "sale" within the meaning of section 341(f)(1) and (5) if there is no gain on the transaction, or if the sale or exchange gives rise to ordinary income under a provision of the Code other than section 341, or if gain on the transaction is not recognized under any provision of subtitle A of the Code.

(ii) A sale of stock in a corporation does not include any disposition of such stock by a shareholder if, by reason of section 341(d)(1), section 341(a) could not have applied to that disposition. (Under section 341(d)(1), section 341 (a) does not apply except to more-than-5-percent shareholders.) Except as otherwise provided in paragraph (a)(2) (i) of this section, the term "sale" includes a disposition of stock in a corporation by a more-than-5-percent shareholder described in section 341 (d)(1), even though section 341(a) did not apply to the disposition because the corporation was not collapsible or by reason of the application of section 341(d)(2),(3), or (e).

(3) A corporation which consents to the application of section 341(f)(2) does not thereby become noncollapsible, and the fact that a corporation consents to the application of section 341(f)(2) does not affect the determination as to whether it is a collapsible corporation.

(4) For limitation on the application of section 341(f)(1) see section 341(f) (5) and (6) and paragraphs (h) and (j) of this section.

(b) **Statement of consent.**—(1) The consent of a corporation referred to in paragraph (a)(1) or (j)(1) of this section shall be given by means of a statement, signed by any officer who is duly authorized to act on behalf of the consenting corporation stating that the corporation consents to have the provisions of section 341(f)(2) apply to any dispositions by it of its subsection (f) assets. The statement shall be filed with the district director having jurisdiction over the income tax return of the consenting corporation for the taxable year during which the statement is filed.

(2)(i) The statement shall contain the name, address, and employer identification number of any corporation 5 percent or more in value of the outstanding stock of which is owned directly by the consenting corporation, and of any other corporation connected to the consenting corporation through a chain of stock ownership described in paragraph (j)(4) of this section. The statement shall also indicate whether such 5-percent-or-more corporation (or such "connected" corporation) has consented, within the 6-month period ending on the date on which the statement is filed, to the application of section 341(f)(2) with respect to any dispositions of its subsection (f) assets (see paragraph (j) of this section), and, if so, the district director with whom such consent was filed and the date on which such consent was filed.

(ii) If, during the 6-month period beginning on the date on which the statement is filed, the consenting corporation becomes the owner of 5 percent or more in value of the outstanding stock of another corporation or becomes connected to another corporation through a chain of stock ownership described in paragraph (j)(4) of this section, then the consenting corporation shall, within 5 days after such occurrence, notify the district director with whom it filed the statement of the name, address and employer identification number of such corporation.

(3) A consent under section 341(f)(1) may be filed at any time and there is no limit as to the number of such consents that may be filed. If a consent is filed by a corporation under section 341(f)(1) and if a shareholder sells stock (i) in such corporation, or (ii) in another corporation a sale of whose stock is treated under section 341(f)(6) as a sale of stock in such corporation, at any time during the applicable 6-month period, then the consent cannot thereafter be revoked or withdrawn by the corporation. However, a consent may be revoked or withdrawn at any time prior to a sale during the applicable 6-month period. If no

sale is made during such period, the consent will have no effect on the corporation. See paragraph (g) of this section.

(c) **Consenting corporation.**—(1) A consenting corporation at the time that it files a consent under section 341(f)(1) shall notify its shareholders that such consent is being filed. In addition, the consenting corporation shall, at the request of any shareholder, promptly supply the shareholder with a copy of the consent.

(2) A consenting corporation shall maintain records adequate to permit identification of its subsection (F) assets.

(d) **Shareholders of consenting corporation.**—(1) A shareholder who sells stock in a consenting corporation within the 6-month period beginning on the date on which the consent is filed shall—

(i) Notify the corporation, within 5 days after such sale, of the date on which such sale is made, and

(ii) Attach a copy of the corporation's consent to the shareholder's income tax return for the taxable year in which the sale is made.

(2) If the sale of stock in a consenting corporation is treated under section 341(f)(6) as the sale of stock in any other corporation, the consenting corporation shall notify such other corporation, within 5 days after receiving notification of a sale of its stock, of the date on which such sale was made.

(e) **Recognition of gain under section 341(f)(2).**—(1) Under section 341(f)(2), if a subsection (f) asset (as defined in paragraph (g) of this section) is disposed of at any time by a consenting corporation, then, except as provided in section 341(f)(3) and paragraph (f) of this section, the amount by which—

(i) The amount realized (in the case of a sale, exchange, or involuntary conversion), or

(ii) The fair market value of such asset (in the case of any other disposition),

exceeds the adjusted basis of such asset is treated as gain from the sale or exchange of such asset. Such gain is recognized notwithstanding any contrary non-recognition provision of subtitle A of the Code, but only to the extent such gain is not recognized under any other provision of subtitle A of the Code (for example, section 1245(a)(1) or 1250(a)). Gain recognized under section 341(f)(2) with respect to a disposition of a subsection (f) asset has the same character (i. e., ordinary income or capital gain) that such gain would have if it arose from a sale of such asset.

(2) The nonrecognition provisions of subtitle A of the Code which section 341(f)(2) overrides include, but are not limited to, sections 311(a), 332(c), 336, 337, 351, 361, 371(a), 374(a), 721, 1031, 1033, 1071, and 1081.

(3) In the case of a foreign corporation which files a statement of consent pursuant to paragraph (b) of this section, such statement, in addition to the information required in paragraph (b) of this section, shall also contain a declaration that the corporation consents that any gain upon the disposition of a subsection (f) asset which would otherwise be recognized under section 341(f)(2) will, for purposes of section 882(a)(2), be considered as gross income which is effectively connected with the conduct of a trade or business which is conducted through a permanent establishment within the United States.

· · · ·

§ 1.351–1 Transfer to corporation controlled by transferor

(a) (1) Section 351(a) provides, in general, for the nonrecognition of gain or loss upon the transfer by one or more persons of property to a corporation solely in exchange for stock or securities in such corporation, if immediately after the exchange, such person or persons are in control of the corporation to which the property was transferred. As used in section 351, the phrase "one or more persons" includes individuals, trusts, estates, partnerships, associations, companies, or corporations (see section 7701(a) (1)). To be in control of the transferee corporation, such person or persons must own immediately after the transfer stock possessing at least 80 percent of the total combined voting power of all classes of stock entitled to vote and at least 80 percent of the total number of shares of all other classes of stock of such corporation (see section 368(c)). In determining control under this section, the fact that any corporate transferor distributes

part or all of the stock which it receives in the exchange to its shareholders shall not be taken into account. The phrase "immediately after the exchange" does not necessarily require simultaneous exchanges by two or more persons, but comprehends a situation where the rights of the parties have been previously defined and the execution of the agreement proceeds with an expedition consistent with orderly procedure. For purposes of this section—

(i) Stock or securities issued for services rendered or to be rendered to or for the benefit of the issuing corporation will not be treated as having been issued in return for property, and

(ii) Stock or securities issued for property which is of relatively small value in comparison to the value of the stock and securities already owned (or to be received for services) by the person who transferred such property, shall not be treated as having been issued in return for property if the primary purpose of the transfer is to qualify under this section the exchanges of property by other persons transferring property.

For the purpose of section 351, stock rights or stock warrants are not included in the term "stock or securities."

(2) The application of section 351 (a) is illustrated by the following examples:

Example (1). C owns a patent right worth $25,000 and D owns a manufacturing plant worth $75,000. C and D organize the R Corporation with an authorized capital stock of $100,000. C transfers his patent right to the R Corporation for $25,000 of its stock and D transfers his plant to the new corporation for $75,000 of its stock. No gain or loss to C or D is recognized.

Example (2). B owns certain real estate which cost him $50,000 in 1930, but which has a fair market value of $200,000 in 1955. He transfers the property to the N Corporation in 1955 for 78 percent of each class of stock of the corporation having a fair market value of $200,-000, the remaining 22 percent of the stock of the corporation having been issued by the corporation in 1940 to other persons for cash. B realized a taxable gain of $150,000 on this transaction.

Example (3). E, an individual, owns property with a basis of $10,000 but which has a fair market value of $18,000. E also had rendered services valued at $2,000 to Corporation F. Corporation F has outstanding 100 shares of common stock all of which are held by G. Corporation F issues 400 shares of its common stock (having a fair market value of $20,000) to E in exchange for his property worth $18,000 and in compensation for the services he has rendered worth $2,000. Since immediately after the transaction, E owns 80 percent of the outstanding stock of Corporation F, no gain is recognized upon the exchange of the property for the stock. However, E realized $2,000 of ordinary income as compensation for services rendered to Corporation F.

(b) (1) Where property is transferred to a corporation by two or more persons in exchange for stock or securities, as described in paragraph (a) of this section, it is not required that the stock and securities received by each be substantially in proportion to his interest in the property immediately prior to the transfer. However, where the stock and securities received are received in disproportion to such interest, the entire transaction will be given tax effect in accordance with its true nature, and in appropriate cases the transaction may be treated as if the stock and securities had first been received in proportion and then some of such stock and securities had been used to make gifts (section 2501 and following), to pay compensation (section 61(a) (1)), or to satisfy obligations of the transferor of any kind.

(2) The application of paragraph (b) (1) of this section may be illustrated as follows:

Example (1). Individuals A and B, father and son, organize a corporation with 100 shares of common stock to which A transfers property worth $8,000 in exchange for 20 shares of stock, and B transfers property worth $2,000 in exchange for 80 shares of stock. No gain or loss will be recognized under section 351. However, if it is determined that A in fact made a gift to B, such gift will be subject to tax under section 2501 and following. Similarly, if B had rendered services to A (such services having no relation to the assets transferred or to the business of the corporation) and the disproportion in the amount of stock received constituted the payment of compensation by A to B, B will be taxable upon the fair market value of the 60 shares of stock received as compensation for services rendered, and A will realize gain or loss upon the difference between the basis to him of the 60 shares and their fair market value at the time of the exchange.

Example (2). Individuals C and D each transferred, to a newly organized corporation, property having a fair market value of $4,500 in exchange for the issuance by the corporation of 45 shares of its capital stock to each transferor. At the same time, the corporation issued to E, an individual, 10 shares of its capital stock in payment for organizational and promotional services rendered by E for the benefit of the corporation. E transferred no property to the corporation. C and D were under no obligation to pay for E's services. No gain or loss is recognized to C or D. E received compensation taxable as ordinary income to the extent of the fair market value of the 10 shares of stock received by him.   • • • •

§ 1.351-2   Receipt of property

(a) If an exchange would be within the provisions of section 351(a) if it were not for the fact that the property received in exchange consists not only of property permitted by such subsection to be received without the recognition of gain, but also of other property or money, then the gain, if any, to the recipient shall be recognized, but in an amount not in excess of the sum of such money and the fair market value of such other property. No loss to the recipient shall be recognized.

(b) See section 357 and the regulations pertaining to that section for applicable rules as to the treatment of liabilities as "other property" in cases subject to section 351, where another party to the exchange assumes a liability, or acquires property subject to a liability.

(c) See sections 358 and 362 and the regulations pertaining to those sections for applicable rules with respect to the determination of the basis of stock, securities, or other property received in exchanges subject to section 351.

(d) See part I (section 301 and following), subchapter C, chapter 1 of the Code, and the regulations thereunder for applicable rules with respect to the taxation of dividends where a distribution by a corporation of its stock or securities in connection with an exchange subject to section 351(a) has the effect of the distribution of a taxable dividend.

§ 1.351-3   Records to be kept and information to be filed

(a) Every person who received the stock or securities of a controlled corporation, or other property as part of the consideration, in exchange for property under section 351, shall file with his income tax return for the taxable year in which the exchange is consummated a complete statement of all facts pertinent to such exchange, including—

(1) A description of the property transferred, or of his interest in such property, together with a statement of the cost or other basis thereof, adjusted to the date of transfer.

(2) With respect to stock of the controlled corporation received in the exchange, a statement of—

(i) The kind of stock and preferences, if any;

(ii) The number of shares of each class received; and

(iii) The fair market value per share of each class at the date of the exchange.

(3) With respect to securities of the controlled corporation received in the exchange, a statement of—

(i) The principal amount and terms; and

(ii) The fair market value at the date of exchange.

(4) The amount of money received, if any.

(5) With respect to other property received—

(i) A complete description of each separate item;

(ii) The fair market value of each separate item at the date of exchange; and

(iii) In the case of a corporate shareholder, the adjusted basis of the other property in the hands of the controlled corporation immediately before the distribution of such other property to the corporate shareholder in connection with the exchange.

(6) With respect to liabilities of the transferors assumed by the controlled corporation, a statement of—

(i) The nature of the liabilities;

(ii) When and under what circumstances created;

(iii) The corporate business reason for assumption by the controlled corporation; and

(iv) Whether such assumption eliminates the transferor's primary liability.

(b) Every such controlled corporation shall file with its income tax return for the taxable year in which the exchange is consummated—

(1) A complete description of all the property received from the transferors.

(2) A statement of the cost or other basis thereof in the hands of the transferors adjusted to the date of transfer.

(3) The following information with respect to the capital stock of the controlled corporation—

(i) The total issued and outstanding capital stock immediately prior to and immediately after the exchange, with a complete description of each class of stock;

(ii) The classes of stock and number of shares issued to each transferor in the exchange, and the number of shares of each class of stock owned by each transferor immediately prior to and immediately after the exchange, and

(iii) The fair market value of the capital stock as of the date of exchange which was issued to each transferor.

(4) The following information with respect to securities of the controlled corporation—

(i) The principal amount and terms of all securities outstanding immediately prior to and immediately after the exchange,

(ii) The principal amount and terms of securities issued to each transferor in the exchange, with a statement showing each transferor's holdings of securities of the controlled corporation immediately prior to and immediately after the exchange,

(iii) The fair market value of the securities issued to the transferors on the date of the exchange, and

(iv) A statement as to whether the securities issued in the exchange are subordinated in any way to other claims against the controlled corporation.

(5) The amount of money, if any, which passed to each of the transferors in connection with the transaction.

(6) With respect to other property which passed to each transferor—

(i) A complete description of each separate item;

(ii) The fair market value of each separate item at the date of exchange, and

(iii) In the case of a corporate transferor, the adjusted basis of each separate item in the hands of the controlled corporation immediately before the distribution of such other property to the corporate transferor in connection with the exchange.

(7) The following information as to the transferor's liabilities assumed by the controlled corporation in the exchange—

(i) The amount and a description thereof,

(ii) When and under what circumstances created, and

(iii) The corporate business reason or reasons for assumption by the controlled corporation.

(c) Permanent records in substantial form shall be kept by every taxpayer who participates in the type of exchange described in section 351, showing the information listed above, in order to facilitate the determination of gain or loss from a subsequent disposition of stock or securities and other property, if any, received in the exchange.

§ 1.354-1   Exchanges of stock and securities in certain reorganizations

(a) Section 354 provides that under certain circumstances no gain or loss is recognized to a shareholder who surrenders his stock in exchange for other stock or to a security holder who surrenders his securities in exchange for stock. Section 354 also provides that under certain circumstances a security holder may surrender securities and receive securities in the same principal amount or in a lesser principal amount without the recognition of gain or loss to him. The exchanges to which section 354 applies must be pursuant to a plan of reorganization as provided in section 368(a) and the stock and securities surrendered as well as the stock and securities received must be those of a corporation which is a party to the reorganization. Section 354 does not apply to exchanges pursuant to a reorganization described in section 368 (a) (1) (D) unless the transferor corporation—

(1) Transfers all or substantially all of its assets to a single corporation, and

(2) Distributes all of its remaining properties (if any) and the stock, securities and other properties received in the exchange to its shareholders or security holders in pursuance of the plan of reorganization. The fact that properties retained by the transferor corporation, or received in exchange for the properties transferred in the reorganization, are used to satisfy existing liabilities not represented by securities and which were incurred in the ordinary course of business before the reorganization does not prevent the application of section 354 to an exchange pursuant to a plan of reorganization defined in section 368(a) (1) (D).

(b) Except in the case described in subsection (c), section 354 is not applicable to an exchange of stock or securities if a greater principal amount of securities is received than the principal amount of securities the recipient surrenders, or if securities are received and the recipient surrenders no securities. See, however, section 356 and regulations pertaining to such section. See also section 306 with respect to the receipt of preferred stock in a transaction to which section 354 is applicable.

.   .   .   .

(d) The rules of section 354 may be illustrated by the following examples:

Example (1). Pursuant to a reorganization under section 368 (a) to which Corporations T and W are parties, A, a shareholder in Corporation T, surrenders all his common stock in Corporation T in exchange for common stock of Corporation W. No gain or loss is recognized to A.

Example (2). Pursuant to a reorganization under section 368 (a) to which Corporations X and Y (which are not railroad corporations) are parties, B, a shareholder in Corporation X, surrenders all his stock in X for stock and securities in Y. Section 354 does not apply to this exchange. See, however, section 356.

Example (3). C, a shareholder in Corporation Z (which is not a railroad corporation), surrenders all his stock in Corporation Z in exchange for securities in Corporation Z. Whether or not this exchange is in connection with a recapitalization under section 368 (a) (1) (E), section 354 does not apply. See, however, section 302.

(e) For the purpose of section 354, stock rights or stock warrants are not included in the term "stock or securities".

§ 1.355-1   Distribution of stock and securities of controlled corporation

(a) Application of section. Section 355 provides for the separation, without recognition of gain or loss to the shareholders and security holders, of two or more existing businesses formerly operated, directly or indirectly, by a single corporation. It applies only to the separation of existing businesses which have been in active operation for at least five years, and which, in general, have been owned for at least five years by the corporation making the distribution of stock or of stock and securities. Section 355 does not apply to the division of a single business.

For the purpose of section 355, stock rights or stock warrants are not included in the term "stock and securities".

(b) Types of separations. Section 355 is concerned with two general types of separations of businesses. The first is the distribution of the stock of an existing corporation. The second is the distribution of the stock of a new corporation which stock was received in exchange for the assets of a business previously operated by the distributing corporation. In both cases, this section contemplates the continued operation of the businesses existing prior to the separation.

(c) Active business. Section 355 is not applicable unless the controlled corporation and the distributing corporation are each engaged in the active conduct of a trade or business. For specific rules in this connection see section 355(b) (1) and (2). Without regard to such rules, for purposes of section 355, a trade or business consists of a specific existing group of activities being carried on for the purpose of earning income or profit from only such group of activities, and the activities included in such group must include every operation which forms a part of, or a step in, the process of earning income or profit from such group. Such group of activities ordinarily must include the collection of income and the payment of expenses. It does not include—

(1) The holding for investment purposes of stock, securities, land or other property, including casual sales thereof (whether or not the proceeds of such sales are reinvested),

(2) The ownership and operation of land or buildings all or substantially all of which are used and occupied by the owner in the operation of a trade or business, or

(3) A group of activities which, while a part of a business operated for profit, are not themselves independently producing income even though such activities would produce income with the addition of other activities or with large increases in activities previously incidental or insubstantial.

(d) Examples. The following examples illustrate the application of the rules described in paragraph (c) of this section:

Example (1). Corporation A is engaged in the manufacture and sale of soap and detergents and owns investment securities. It proposes to place the investment securities in a new corporation and distribute the stock of such new corporation to its shareholders. The holding of investment securities does not constitute a trade or business.

Example (2). Corporation B is engaged in the business of manufacturing and selling hats in its own factory building. It proposes to transfer the factory building to a new corporation and distribute the stock of such new corporation to its shareholders. The activities in connection with the manufacturing of hats constitute a trade or business; but the operation of the factory building does not.

Example (3). Corporation C, a bank, owns an eleven-story downtown office building, the ground floor of which is occupied by it in the conduct of its banking business and the remaining ten floors of which it rents to various tenants. The ten floors are rented, managed and maintained by the real estate department of the bank. It is proposed to transfer the building to a new corporation and distribute the stock of such new corporation to the bank's shareholders. The activities in connection with banking constitute a trade or business as do also the activities in connection with the rental of the building.

Example (4). Corporation D, a bank, owns a two-story building in a suburban area, the ground floor and approximately one-half of the second floor of which is occupied by it in the conduct of its banking business. The remainder of the second floor is rented as storage space to a neighboring retail merchant. It is proposed to transfer the building to a new corporation and distribute the stock of such new corporation to the bank's shareholders. With respect to the rental of part of the second floor of its building, the bank is not engaged in the active conduct of a trade or business, such activity being only incidental to its banking business.

Example (5). Corporation E is engaged in the manufacture and sale of wood products. In connection with such manufacturing, it maintains a research department for its own use. It proposes to transfer the research department to a new corporation after which it will engage the services of the new corporation on a contract basis. The activities of the research department do not constitute a trade or business.

Example (6). Corporation F owns and rents an office building and owns vacant land. It proposes to transfer the vacant land to a new corporation and distribute the stock of such new corporation to its shareholders. The holding of the vacant land does not constitute a trade or business.

Example (7). Corporation G owns land on which it engages in the ranching business. Oil has been discovered in the area and it is apparent that oil may be found under the land on which the ranching activities are maintained. Corporation G has engaged in no activities in connection with the mineral rights. It proposes to transfer the mineral rights to a new corporation and distribute the stock of such new corporation to shareholders. Corporation G is not engaged in an active trade or business with respect to the mineral rights.

Example (8). Corporation H manufactures and sells ice cream at a plant in State X and at a plant in State Y. Corporation H proposes to transfer the plant and related activities in State Y to a new corporation and distribute the stock of such new corporation to its shareholders. The activities in each State constitute a trade or business.

Example (9). Corporation I manufactures and sells ice cream in State X. It purchases land and constructs a new plant in State Y. After manufacturing and selling operations have commenced at the new plant, it proposes to transfer it to a new corporation and distribute the stock of such new corporation to its shareholders. The activities at the new plant constitute a trade or business which, however, has been in existence only since such activities began.

Example (10). Corporation J has owned and operated a men's retail clothing store in the downtown area of the City of R for seven years and has also owned and operated a men's retail clothing store in the suburban area of the City of R for nine years. The manager of each store directs its operations and makes the necessary purchases. No common warehouse is maintained. Corporation J proposes to transfer the store building, fixtures, and inventory of the suburban store to a new corporation and distribute the stock of such new corporation to the shareholders of Corporation J. The activities of each store constitute a trade or business which has been in existence for more than five years.

Example (11). Corporation K processes and sells meat products. It is proposed to separate the selling from the manufacturing activities by forming a separate corporation, L, to handle sales. Corporation K will transfer to Corporation L certain physical assets pertaining to the sales function plus cash for working capital in exchange for the capital stock of Corporation L which will be distributed to the shareholders of Corporation K. Since the manufacturing and selling operations constitute only one integrated business, neither Corporation K nor Corporation L will be continuing the active conduct of a trade or business formerly conducted by Corporation K.

Example (12). Corporation M is engaged in the manufacture and sale of steel and steel products. In addition, Corporation M owns and operates a coal mine for the sole purpose of supplying its coal requirements in the manufacture of steel. It is proposed to transfer the coal mine to a new corporation and distribute the stock of such new corporation to the shareholders of Corporation M. The activities of Corporation M in connection with the operation of the coal mine do not constitute a trade or business, since such activities are not themselves independently producing income although a part of the business operated for profit.

Example (13). Corporation N manufactures steel containers for oil and oil products at a plant in State X and at a plant in State Y. Pursuant to a sales contract with Corporation O, Corporation N sells its entire product to Corporation O. Corporation N proposes to transfer the plant and related activities in State Y, together with that portion of the sales contract with Corporation O applicable to the sales

of that plant to a new corporation and distribute the stock of such new corporation to its shareholders. The activities in each State constitute a trade or business before and after the transfer to the new corporation.

Example (14). Corporation P manufactures and sells steel containers for oil and oil products at a plant in State X and at a plant in State Y. Corporation P makes all of its sales through its wholly-owned subsidiary pursuant to a sales contract, by virtue of which the subsidiary acts either as principal or sales agent for Corporation P. Corporation P proposes to transfer the plant and related activities in State Y, together with that portion of the sales contract applicable to the sales of that plant to a new corporation and distribute the stock of such new corporation to its shareholders. The activities in each State constitute a trade or business before and after the transfer to the new corporation.

Example (15). Corporation Q manufactures electrical products at a plant in State X and at a plant in State Y. The sales of the electrical products produced by each plant are made by the corporation's sales office located at the plant in State X. Corporation Q proposes to transfer the plant and related activities in State Y, together with that portion of the facilities and personnel of the sales office allocable to the sales of the plant in State Y to a new corporation and distribute the stock of such new corporation to its shareholders. The activities in each state constitute a trade or business before and after the transfer to the new corporation.

Example (16). Corporation R manufactures and sells automobiles and operates an executive dining room primarily for the convenience of its executives. The dining room is managed and operated as a separate unit and the executives are charged for their meals. Corporation R derives a profit from the operation of the dining room. The activities connected with the executive dining room do not constitute a trade or business.

(e) Businesses operated by one corporation. For further examples of businesses operated by one corporation, see paragraph (d) of § 1.337–3.

§ 1.355–2   Limitations

(a) Property distributed. The property distributed must consist solely of stock or stock and securities of a controlled corporation. If additional property (including an excess principal amount of securities received over securities surrendered) is received, see section 356.

(b) Distribution of earnings and profits. (1) The transaction must not have been used principally as a device for the distribution of the earnings and profits of the distributing corporation or of the controlled corporation or of both. If, pursuant to an arrangement negotiated or agreed upon prior to the distribution of stock or securities of the controlled corporation, part or all of the stock or securities of either corporation are sold or exchanged after the distribution, such sale or exchange will be evidence that the transaction was used principally as a device for the distribution of the earnings and profits of the distributing corporation or of the controlled corporation, or both. However, if the rules respecting continuity of interest contained in paragraph (c) of this section are not met, section 355 will not apply. If a sale of such stock or securities is made after the distribution and is not pursuant to an arrangement negotiated or agreed upon prior to the distribution, the mere fact of such sale is not determinative that the transaction was used principally as a device for the distribution of earnings and profits, but such fact will be evidence that the transaction was used principally as such a device.

(2) A sale is pursuant to an arrangement agreed upon prior to the distribution when enforcible rights to buy or to sell exist before such distribution. In any case in which a sale or exchange was discussed by the buyer and the seller before the distribution, but enforcible rights to buy or to sell did not exist before such distribution, the question whether an arrangement was negotiated within the meaning of section 355(a) (1) (B) shall be determined from all the facts and circumstances.

(3) In determining whether a transaction was used principally as a device for the distribution of the earnings and profits of the distributing corporation or of the controlled corporation or both, consideration will be given to all of the facts and circumstances of the transaction. In particular, consideration will be given to the nature, kind and amount of the assets of both corporations (and corporations controlled by them) immediately after the transaction. The fact that at the time of the transaction substantially all of the assets of each of the corporations involved are and have been used in the active conduct of trades or businesses which meet the requirements of section 355(b) will be considered evidence that the transaction was not used principally as such a device.

(c) **Business purpose.** The distribution by a corporation of stock or securities of a controlled corporation to its shareholders with respect to its own stock or to its security holders in exchange for its own securities will not qualify under section 355 where carried out for purposes not germane to the business of the corporation. The principal reason for this requirement is to limit the application of section 355 to certain specified distributions or exchanges with respect to the stock or securities of controlled corporations incident to such readjustment of corporate structures as is required by business exigencies and which, in general, effect only a readjustment of continuing interests in property under modified corporate forms. Section 355 contemplates a continuity of the entire business enterprise under modified corporate forms and a continuity of interest in all or part of such business enterprise on the part of those persons who, directly or indirectly, were the owners of the enterprise prior to the distribution or exchange. All the requisites of business and corporate purposes described under § 1.368 must be met to exempt a transaction from the recognition of gain or loss under this section.

(d) **Stock and securities distributed.** The distributing corporation must distribute:

(1) All of the stock and securities of the controlled corporation which it owns, or

(2) At least an amount of the stock which constitutes control as defined in section 368(c). In such case all, or any part, of the securities of the controlled corporation may be distributed.

Where a part of either the stock or securities is retained under subparagraph (2) of this paragraph, it must be established to the satisfaction of the Commissioner that such retention was not in pursuance of a plan having as one of its principal purposes the avoidance of Federal income tax. Ordinarily, the business reasons (as distinguished from the desire to make a distribution of the earnings and profits) which support a distribution of stock and securities of a controlled corporation under paragraph (c) of this section will require the distribution of all of the stock and securities. If the distribution of all of the stock and securities of a controlled corporation would be treated to any extent as a distribution of "other property" under section 356, this fact does not tend to establish that the retention of any of such stock and securities is not in pursuance of a plan having as one of its principal purposes the avoidance of Federal income tax.

(e) Principal amount of securities. (1) Section 355(a) (1) is not applicable if the principal amount of securities received exceeds the principal amount of securities surrendered or if securities are received and no securities are surrendered. In such cases, see section 356.

(2) If only stock is received in a transaction to which section 355 is applicable, the principal amount of securities surrendered, if any, and the par or stated value of stock is not relevant to the application of such section. For example: All of the stock of Corporation A is owned by X, an individual, and securities in the principal amount of $100,000 which were issued by Corporation A are owned by Y, an individual. Corporation A distributes all of the stock of a controlled corporation to Y in exchange for his securities. The par or stated value of the stock of the controlled corporation is $150,000. No gain or loss is recognized to Y upon the receipt of the stock of the controlled corporation.

(f) Period of ownership. (1) For the purposes of determining whether gain or loss will be recognized upon a distribution, stock of a controlled corporation acquired (in a transaction in which gain or loss is recognized, in whole or in part) within five years of the date of the distribution of such stock is treated as "other property." Section 355 does not apply to a transaction which includes a distribution of such stock. See section 356. The stock so acquired is "stock", however, for the purpose of the requirements respecting the distribution of stock of such controlled corporation provided in section 355(a) (1) (D).

(2) Subparagraph (1) of this paragraph may be illustrated by the following example:

Example. Corporation A has held 85 of the 100 outstanding shares of the stock of Corporation B for more than five years on the date of distribution. Six months before such date, it purchased 10 shares of such stock. If all of the stock of the controlled corporation owned by Corporation A is distributed, section 355 is not applicable to such distribution since the 10 shares would represent "other property." See, however, section 356. If, however, for proper business reasons it is decided to retain some of the stock of Corporation B, then the determination of the amount of such stock which must be distributed under section 355 (a) (1) (D) in order to constitute a distribution to which section 355 is applicable must be made by reference to all of the stock of the controlled corporation including the 10 shares acquired six months before such date and the 5 shares owned by others. Similarly, if, by the use of any agency, the distributing corporation acquires stock of the controlled corporation within five years of the date of distribution, for example, where another subsidiary purchases such stock, such stock will be treated as "other property." If Corporation A had held only 75 of the 100 outstanding shares of stock of Corporation B for more than five years on the date of distribution and had purchased the remaining 25 shares six months before such date, neither section 355 nor section 356 would be applicable.

(g) Active businesses. The rules of section 355(b) and § 1.355-4, relating to active businesses, must be satisfied.

§ 1.355-3 Non pro rata distributions, etc.

(a) The rule of section 355(a) (1) prescribing that gain or loss will not be recognized applies whether or not the distribution is pro rata with respect to the interests of all the shareholders in the distributing corporation provided all other requirements of section 355 are satisfied. For example, if two individuals, A and B, own all of the stock of Corporation X which operates two active businesses, one business may be transferred to a new corporation in exchange for all of its stock and such stock distributed to either A or B in exchange for all of his stock of Corporation X. Similarly, if, in the above example, only a part of the stock of the new corporation is transferred to one of the shareholders in exchange for all of his stock of Corporation X and the balance of such stock is distributed to the other shareholder (whether or not such other shareholder surrenders stock in Corporation X), no gain or loss will be recognized. The same rule will be applicable if the stock of an existing controlled corporation is distributed to the shareholders even though such distribution is not pursuant to a plan of reorganization. Section 355 does not apply, however, if the substance of the transaction is merely an exchange between shareholders or security holders of stock or securities in one corporation for stock or securities in another corporation. For example, if two individuals, C and D, each own directly fifty percent of the stock of Corporation M and fifty percent of the stock of Corporation N, section 355 would not apply to a transaction in which C and D transfer all of their stock in Corporation M and Corporation N to a new corporation, P, for all of the stock of Corporation P, and Corporation P then distributes the stock of Corporation M to C and the stock of Corporation N to D.

(b) The stock of the controlled corporation which is distributed may consist of either common or preferred stock. See, however, section 306 with respect to the receipt of preferred stock in a transaction to which section 355 is applicable.

(c) The rule of section 355(a) (1) prescribing that gain or loss will not be recognized applies whether or not the shareholder surrenders stock in the distributing corporation and whether or not the distribution is in pursuance of a plan of reorganization (within the meaning of section 368(a) (1) (D)).

§ 1.355-4 Active conduct of a trade or business

(a) A distribution of stock or securities of a controlled corporation is subject to section 355(a) only, if:

(1) The distributing corporation and the controlled corporation are each engaged in the active conduct of a trade or business immediately after the distribution of stock or securities of the controlled corporation; or

(2) Immediately before the distribution the distributing corporation had no assets other than stock or securities in the controlled corporations and each of the controlled corporations is engaged in the active conduct of a trade or business immediately after the distribution. In connection with the requirement of "no assets" a de minimis rule is applicable.

(3) These rules are illustrated by the following examples:

Example (1). Corporation A, prior to the distribution, operates an active business and owns all of the stock of Corporation B which also is engaged in the active conduct of a business. Corporation A distributes all of the stock of Corporation B to its shareholders, and both continue the operations of their separate businesses. The active business requirement of section 355 (b) (1) (A) is satisfied.

Example (2). The facts are the same as in example 1, except that Corporation A transfers all of its assets except the stock of Corporation B to a new corporation in exchange for all of its stock and transfers the stock of both controlled corporations to its shareholders. The active business requirement of section 355 (b) (1) (B) is satisfied.

(b) (1) Section 355(b) (2) provides rules for determining whether any corporation is treated as engaged in the active conduct of a trade or business for purposes of ascertaining whether the distributing corporation and the controlled corporation meet the requirements of section 355(b) (1). Under section 355(b) (2) (A), a corporation is treated as engaged in the active conduct of a trade or business if it is itself engaged in such a trade or business or if substantially all of its assets consist of the stock and securities of a corporation or corporations controlled by it (immediately after the distribution) each of which is engaged in the active conduct of a trade or business. Regardless of whether the determination is based upon a corporation's own conduct of a trade or business or on the basis of its ownership of the stock of a corporation or corporations which conduct a trade or business, such trade or business must have been actively conducted for the five-year period ending on the date of distribution of the stock and securities of the controlled corporation the stock of which was distributed as provided in section 355(b) (2) (B). Furthermore, such trade or business must not have been acquired by either corporation during such five-year period unless it was acquired in a transaction in which gain or loss was not recognized (section 355(b) (2) (C)). In addition, under section 355 (b) (2) (D), such business must not have been indirectly acquired during such five-year period by means of the acquisition of control of another corporation in a transaction in which gain or loss was recognized. Thus, section 355(b) (2) (D) requires that during the five-year period during which the trade or business must be actively conducted, such business cannot have been acquired, directly or indirectly, through another corporation by such other corporation or any of its predecessors in interest in a transaction in which gain or loss was recognized in whole or in part.

(2) Subparagraph (1) of this paragraph may be illustrated by the following example:

Example. In 1956, Corporation B, having cash and other liquid assets and engaged in only one active business purchases all of the stock of Corporation A, also engaged in a single active business. Later in the same year, Corporation B in a "downstairs" statutory merger merges into Corporation A. In 1958, Corporation A places the assets of the active business formerly operated by Corporation B in a new subsidiary X. A distribution of the stock of Corporation X to the stockholders of Corporation A is not within the terms of section 355, since one of the active businesses had, in effect, been purchased less than five years prior to the distribution.

(3) For the purpose of determining whether such trade or business has been actively conducted throughout the five-year period described in section 355(b) (2), the fact that during such five-year period such trade or business underwent change (for example, by the addition of new or the dropping of old products, changes in production capacity, and the like) shall be disregarded provided the changes are not of such a character as to constitute the acquisition of a new or different business.

§ 1.355-5 Records to be kept and information to be filed

(a) Every corporation that makes a distribution of stock or securities of a controlled corporation, as described in section 355, shall attach to its return for the year of the distribution a detailed statement setting forth such data as may be appropriate in order to show compliance with the provisions of such section.

(b) Every taxpayer who receives a distribution of stock or securities of a corporation that was controlled by a corporation in which he holds stock or securities shall attach to his return for the year in which such distribution is received a detailed statement setting forth such data as may be appropriate in order to show the applicability of section 355. Such statement shall include, but shall not be limited to, a description of the stock and securities surrendered (if any) and received, and the names and addresses of all of the corporations involved in the transaction.

§ 1.356-1 Receipt of additional consideration in connection with an exchange

(a) If in any exchange to which the provisions of section 354 or section 355 would apply except for the fact that there is received by the shareholders or the security holders other property (in addition to property permitted to be received without recognition of gain by such sections) or money, then—

(1) The gain, if any, to the taxpayer shall be recognized in an amount not in excess of the sum of the money and the fair market value of the other property, but,

(2) The loss, if any, to the taxpayer from the exchange or distribution shall not be recognized to any extent.

(b) If the distribution of such other property or money by or on behalf of a corporation has the effect of the distribution of a dividend, then there shall be chargeable to each distributee (either an individual or a corporation)—

(1) As a dividend, such an amount of the gain recognized as is not in excess of the distributee's ratable share of the undistributed earnings and profits of the corporation accumulated after February 28, 1913, and

(2) As a gain from the exchange of property, the remainder of the gain so recognized.

(c) This section may be illustrated by the following examples:

Example (1). In an exchange to which the provisions of section 356 apply and to which section 354 would apply but for the receipt of property not permitted to be received without the recognition of gain or loss, A (either an individual or a corporation), received the following in exchange for a share of stock having an adjusted basis to him of $85:

One share of stock worth	$100
Cash	25
Other property (basis $25) fair market value	50
Total fair market value of consideration received	175
Adjusted basis of stock surrendered in exchange	85
Total gain	90
Gain to be recognized, limited to cash and other property received	$75
A's pro rata share of earnings and profits accumulated after February 28, 1913 (taxable dividend)	30
Remainder to be treated as a gain from the exchange of property	45

Example (2). If, in example (1), A's stock had an adjusted basis to him of $200, he would have realized a loss of $25 on the exchange, which loss would not be recognized.

(d) Section 301(b) (1) (B) and section 301(d) (2) do not apply to a distribution of "other property" to a corporate shareholder if such distribution is within the provisions of section 356.

(e) See paragraph (1) of § 1.301-1 for certain transactions which are not within the scope of section 356.

§ 1.356-2 Receipt of additional consideration not in connection with an exchange

(a) If, in a transaction to which section 355 would apply except for the fact that a shareholder (individual or corporate) receives property permitted by section 355 to be received without the recognition of gain, together with other property or money, without the surrender of any stock or securities of the distributing corporation, then the sum of the money and the fair market value of the other property as of the date of the distribution shall be treated as a distribution of property to which the rules of section 301 (other than section 301(b) and section 301(d)) apply. See section 358 for determination of basis of such other property.

(b) Paragraph (a) of this section may be illustrated by the following examples:

Example (1). Individuals A and B each own 50 of the 100 outstanding shares of common stock of Corporation X. Corporation X owns all of the stock of Corporation Y, 100 shares. Corporation X distributes to each shareholder 50 shares of the stock of Corporation Y plus $100 cash without requiring the surrender of any shares of its own stock. The $100 cash received by each is treated as a distribution of property to which the rules of section 301 apply.

Example (2). If, in the above example, Corporation X distributes 50 shares of stock of Corporation Y to A and 30 shares of such stock plus $100 cash to B without requiring the surrender of any of its own stock, the amount of cash received by B is treated as a distribution of property to which the rules of section 301 apply.

§ 1.356-3 Rules for treatment of securities as "other property"

(a) As a general rule, for purposes of section 356, the term "other property" includes securities. However, it does not include securities permitted under section 354 or section 355 to be received tax free. Thus, when securities are surrendered in a transaction to which section 354 or section 355 is applicable, the characterization of the securities received as "other property" does not include securities received where the principal amount of such securities does not exceed the principal amount of securities surrendered in the transaction. If a greater principal amount of securities is received in an exchange described in section 354 (other than subsection (c) thereof) or section 355 over the principal amount of securities surrendered, the term "other property" includes the fair market value of such excess principal amount as of the date of the exchange. If no securities are surrendered in exchange, the term "other property" includes the fair market value, as of the date of receipt, of the entire principal amount of the securities received.

(b) The following examples illustrate the application of the above rules:

Example (1). A, an individual, exchanged 100 shares of stock for 100 shares of stock and a security in the principal amount of $1,000 with a fair market value of $990. The amount of $990 is treated as "other property."

Example (2). B, an individual, exchanged 100 shares of stock and a security in the principal amount of $1,000 for 300 shares of stock and a security in the principal amount of $1,500. The security had a fair market value on the date of receipt of $1,575. The fair market value of the excess principal amount, or $525, is treated as "other property."

Example (3). C, an individual, exchanged a security in the principal amount of $1,000 for 100 shares of stock and a security in the principal amount of $900. No part of the security received is treated as "other property."

Example (4). D, an individual, exchanged a security in the principal amount of $1,000 for 100 shares of stock and a security in the principal amount of $1,200 with a fair market value of $1,100. The fair market value of the excess principal amount, or $183.33, is treated as "other property."

Example (5). E, an individual, exchanged a security in the principal amount of $1,000 for another security in the principal amount of $1,200 with a fair market value of $1,080. The fair market value of the excess principal amount, or $180, is treated as "other property."

Example (6). F, an individual, exchanged a security in the principal amount of $1,000 for two different securities each in the principal amount of $750. One of the securities had a fair market value of $750, the other had a fair market value of $600. One-third of the fair market value of each security ($250 and $200) is treated as "other property."

§ 1.356-4 Exchanges for section 306 stock

If, in a transaction to which section 356 is applicable, other property or money is received in exchange for section 306 stock, an amount equal to the fair market value of the property plus the money, if any, shall be treated as a distribution of property to which section 301 is applicable. The determination of whether section 306 stock is surrendered for other property (including money) is a question of fact to be decided under all of the circumstances of each case. Ordinarily, the other property (including money) received will first be treated as received in exchange for any section 306 stock owned by a shareholder prior to such transaction. For example, if a shareholder who owns a share of common stock (having a basis to him of $100) and a share of preferred stock which is section 306 stock (having a basis to him of $100) surrenders both shares in a transaction to which section 356 is applicable for one share of common stock having a fair market value of $80 and one $100 bond having a fair market value of $100, the bond will be deemed received in exchange for the section 306 stock and it will be treated as a distribution to which section 301 is applicable to the extent of its entire fair market value ($100).

§ 1.356-5 Transactions involving gift or compensation

With respect to transactions described in sections 354, 355, or 356, but which—

(a) Result in a gift, see section 2501 and following, and the regulations pertaining thereto, or

(b) Have the effect of the payment of compensation, see section 61(a) (1), and the regulations pertaining thereto.

§ 1.357-1 Assumption of liability

(a) **General rule.** Section 357(a) does not affect the rule that liabilities assumed are to be taken into account for the purpose of computing the amount of gain or loss realized under section 1001 upon an exchange. Section 357(a) provides, subject to the exceptions and limitations specified in section 357(b) and (c) that:

(1) Liabilities assumed are not to be treated as "other property or money" for the purpose of determining the amount of realized gain which is to be recognized under section 351, 361, 371, or 374, if the transactions would, but for the receipt of "other property or money" have been exchanges of the type described in any one of such sections; and

(2) If the only type of consideration received by the transferor in addition to that permitted to be received by sections 351, 361, 371, or 374, consists of an assumption of liabilities, the transaction, if otherwise qualified, will be deemed to be within the provisions of section 351, 361, 371, or 374.

(b) **Application of general rule.** The application of paragraph (a) of this section may be illustrated by the following example:

Example. A, an individual, transfers to a controlled corporation property with an adjusted basis of $10,000 in exchange for stock of the corporation with a fair market value of $8,000, $3,000 cash, and the assumption by the corporation of indebtedness of A amounting to $4,000. A's gain is $5,000, computed as follows:

Stock received, fair market value	$8,000
Cash received	3,000
Liability assumed by transferee	4,000
Total consideration received	15,000
Less: Adjusted basis of property transferred	10,000
Gain realized	5,000

Assuming that the exchange falls within section 351 as a transaction in which the gain to be recognized is limited to "other property or money" received, the gain recognized to A will be limited to the $3,000 cash received, since, under the general rule of section 357 (a), the assumption of the $4,000 liability does not constitute "other property."

(c) **Tax avoidance purpose.** The benefits of section 357(a) do not extend to any exchange involving an assumption of liabilities where it appears that the principal purpose of the taxpayer with respect to such assumption was to avoid Federal income tax on the exchange, or, if not such purpose, was not a bona fide business purpose. In such cases, the total amount of liabilities assumed or acquired pursuant to such exchange (and not merely a particular liability with respect to which the tax avoidance purpose existed) shall, for the purpose of determining the amount of gain to be recognized upon the exchange in which the liabilities are assumed or acquired, be treated as money received by the taxpayer upon the exchange. Thus, if in the example set forth in paragraph (b) of this section, the principal purpose of the assumption of the $4,000 liability was to avoid tax on the exchange, or was not a bona fide business purpose, then the amount of gain recognized would be $5,000. In any suit or proceeding where the burden is on the taxpayer to prove that an assumption of liabilities is not to be treated as "other property or money" under section 357, which is the case if the Commissioner determines that the taxpayer's purpose with respect thereto was a purpose to avoid Federal income tax on the exchange or was not a bona fide business purpose, and the taxpayer contests such determination by litigation, the taxpayer must sustain such burden by the clear preponderance of the evidence. Thus, the taxpayer must prove his case by such a clear preponderance of all the evidence that the absence of a purpose to avoid Federal income tax on the exchange, or the presence of a bona fide business purpose, is unmistakable.

§ 1.357-2 Liability in excess of basis

(a) Section 357(c) provides in general that in an exchange to which section 351 (relating to a transfer to a corporation controlled by the transferor) is applicable, or to which section 361 (relating to the nonrecognition of gain or loss to corporations) is applicable by reason of a section 368(a) (1) (D) reorganization, if the sum of the amount of liabilities assumed plus the amount of liabilities to which the property is subject exceeds the total of the adjusted basis of the property transferred pursuant to such exchange, then such excess shall be considered as a gain from the sale or exchange of a capital asset or of property which is not a capital asset as the case may be. Thus, if an individual transfers, under section 351, properties having a total basis in his hands of $20,000, one of which has a basis of $10,000 but is subject to a mortgage of $30,000, to a corporation controlled by him, such individual will be subject to tax with respect to $10,000, the excess of the amount of the liability over the total adjusted basis of all the properties in his hands. The same result will follow whether or not the liability is assumed by the transferee. The determination of whether a gain resulting from the transfer of capital assets is long-term or short-term capital gain shall be made by reference to the holding period to the transferor of the assets transferred. An exception to the general rule of section 357(c) is made (1) for any exchange as to which under section 357 (b) (relating to assumption of liabilities for tax-avoidance purposes) the entire amount of the liabilities is treated as money received . . . .

(b) The application of paragraph (a) of this section may be illustrated by the following examples:

Example (1). If all such assets transferred are capital assets and if half the assets (ascertained by reference to their fair market value at the time of the transfer) have been held for less than 1 year (6 months for taxable years beginning before 1977; 9 months for taxable years beginning in 1977) and the remaining half for more than 1 year (6 months for taxable years beginning before 1977; 9 months for taxable years beginning in 1977), half the excess of the amount of the liability over the total of the adjusted basis of the property transferred pursuant to the exchange shall be treated as short-term capital gain, and the remaining half shall be treated as long-term capital gain.

Example (2). If half of the assets (ascertained by reference to their fair market value at the time of the transfer) transferred are capital assets and half are assets other than capital assets, then half of the excess of the amount of the liability over the total of the adjusted basis of the property transferred pursuant to the exchange shall be treated as capital gain, and the remaining half shall be treated as gain from the sale or exchange of assets other than capital assets.

§ 1.358-1 Basis to distributees

(a) In the case of an exchange or distribution to which section 354, 355, or 371(b) applies in which, under the law applicable to the year in which the exchange is made, only nonrecognition property is received, the sum of the basis of all of the stock and securities in the corporation whose stock and securities are exchanged or with respect to which the distribution is made, held immediately after the transaction, plus the basis of all stock and securities received in the transaction shall be the same as the basis of all the stock and securities in such corporation held immediately before the transaction allocated in the manner described in § 1.358-2. In the case of an exchange to which section 351 or 361 applies in which, under the law applicable to the year in which the exchange was made, only nonrecognition property is received, the basis of all the stock and securities received in the exchange shall be the basis of all property exchanged therefor. If in an exchange or distribution to which section 351, 356, 361, or 371 (b) applies both nonrecognition property and "other property" are received, the basis of all the property except "other property" held after the transaction shall be determined as described in the preceding two sentences decreased by the sum of the money and the fair market value of the "other property" (as of the date of the transaction) and increased by the sum of the amount treated as a dividend (if any) and the amount of the gain recognized on the exchange, but the term "gain" as here used does not include any portion of the recognized gain that was treated as a dividend. In any case in which a taxpayer transfers property with respect to which loss is recognized, such loss shall be reflected in determining the basis of the property received in the exchange. The basis of the "other property" is its fair market value as of the date of the transaction.

(b) The application of paragraph (a) of this section may be illustrated by the following example:

Example. A purchased a share of stock in Corporation X in 1935 for $150. Since that date he has received distributions out of other than earnings and profits (as defined in section 316) totalling $60, so that his adjusted basis for the stock is $90. In a transaction qualifying under section 356, A exchanged this share for one share in Corporation Y, worth $100, cash in the amount of $10, and other property with a fair market value of $30. The exchange had the effect of the distribution of a dividend. A's ratable share of the earnings and profits of Corporation X accumulated after February 28, 1913, was $5. A realized a gain of $50 on the exchange, but the amount recognized is limited to $40, the sum of the cash received and the fair market value of the other property. Of the gain recognized, $5 is taxable as a dividend, and $35 as a gain from the exchange of property. The basis to A of the one share of stock of Corporation Y is $90, that is, the adjusted basis of the one share of stock of Corporation X ($90), decreased by the sum of the cash received ($10) and the fair market value of the other property received ($30) and increased by the sum of the amount treated as a dividend ($5) and the amount treated as a gain from the exchange of property ($35). The basis of the other property received is $30.

§ 1.358-2   Allocation of basis among nonrecognition property

(a) (1) As used in this paragraph the term "stock" means stock which is not "other property" under section 356 or 371(b), stock with respect to which a distribution is made, and, in the case of a surrender of part of the stock of a particular class, the retained part of such stock. The term "securities" means securities (including, where appropriate, fractional parts of securities) which are not "other property" under section 356 or 371(b) and in the case of a surrender of part of the securities of a particular class, the retained part of such securities. Stock, or securities, as the case may be, which differ either because they are in different corporations or because the rights attributable to them differ (although they are in the same corporation) are considered different classes of stock or securities, as the case may be, for purposes of this section.

(2) If as the result of an exchange or distribution under the terms of sec-

tion 354, 355, 356 or 371(b) a shareholder who owned stock of only one class before the transaction owns stock of two or more classes after the transaction, then the basis of all the stock held before the transaction (as adjusted under § 1.358-1) shall be allocated among the stock of all classes (whether or not such stock was received in the transaction) held immediately after the transaction in proportion to the fair market values of the stock of each class.

(3) If as the result of an exchange under the terms of section 354, 355, 356 or 371(b) a security holder who owned only securities, all of one class, before the transaction, owns securities or stock of more than one class, or owns both stock and securities, then the basis of all the securities held before the transaction (as adjusted under § 1.358-1) shall be allocated among all the stock and securities (whether or not received in the transaction) held immediately after the transaction in proportion to the fair market values of the stock of each class and the securities of each class.

(4) In every case in which, before the transactions, a person owned stock of more than one class or securities of more than one class or owned both stock and securities, a determination must be made, upon the basis of all the facts, of the stock or securities received with respect to stock and securities of each class held (whether or not surrendered). The allocation described in subparagraph (2) of this paragraph shall be separately made as to the stock of each class with respect to which there is an exchange or distribution and the allocation described in subparagraph (3) of this paragraph shall be separately made with respect to the securities of each class, part or all of which are surrendered in the exchange.

(5) Notwithstanding the provisions of subparagraphs (2), (3) and (4) of this paragraph, in any case in which a plan of recapitalization under section 368(a) (1) (E) provides that each holder of stock or securities of a particular class shall have an option to surrender some or none of such stock or securities in exchange for stock or securities, and a shareholder or security holder exchanges an identifiable part of his stock or securities, the basis of the part of the stock or securities re-

tained shall remain unchanged and shall not be taken into account in determining the basis of the stock or securities received.

(b) (1) As used in this paragraph the term "stock" refers only to stock which is not "other property" under section 351 or 361 and the term "securities" refers only to securities which are not "other property" under section 351 or 361.

(2) If in an exchange to which section 351 or 361 applies property is transferred to a corporation and the transferor receives stock or securities of more than one class or receives both stock and securities, then the basis of the property transferred (as adjusted under § 1.358-1) shall be allocated among all of the stock and securities received in proportion to the fair market values of the stock of each class and the securities of each class.

(c) The application of paragraphs (a) and (b) of this section may be illustrated by the following examples:

Example (1). A, an individual, owns stock in Corporation X with an adjusted basis of $1,000. In a transaction qualifying under section 356 (so far as such section relates to section 354), he exchanged this stock for 20 shares of stock of Corporation Y worth $1,200 and securities of Corporation Y worth $400. A realizes a gain of $600 of which $400 is recognized. The adjusted basis in A's hands of each share of the stock of Corporation Y is $50 determined by allocating the basis of the stock of Corporation X ratably to the stock of Corporation Y received in the exchange. The securities of Corporation Y have a basis in the hands of A of $400.

Example (2). B, an individual, owns a security in the principal amount of $10,000 with a basis of $5,000. In a transaction to which section 354 is applicable, he exchanges this security for four securities in the principal amount of $750 each, worth $800 each, four securities in the principal amount of $750 each, worth $600 each, class A common stock worth $1,000, and class B common stock worth $400. B realizes a gain of $2,000 none of which is recognized. The basis of his original security, $5,000, will be allocated 32/70ths to the four securities worth $800, 24/70ths to the four securities worth $600, 10/70ths to the class A common stock, and 4/70ths to the class B common stock.

Example (3). C, an individual, owns stock of Corporation Y with a basis of $5,000 and owns a security issued by Corporation Y in the principal amount of $5,000 with a basis of $5,000. In a transaction to which section 354 is applicable, he exchanges the stock of Corporation Y for stock of Corporation Z with a value of $6,000, and he exchanges the security of Corporation Y for stock of Corporation Z worth $1,500 and a security of Corporation Z in the principal amount of $4,500 worth $4,500. No gain is recognized to C on either exchange.

The basis of the stock of Corporation Z received for the stock of Corporation Y is $5,000. The bases of the stock and security of Corporation Z received in exchange for the security of Corporation Y are $1,250 and $3,750, respectively.

Example (4). D, an individual, owns stock in Corporation M with a basis of $15,000, worth $40,000, and owns a security issued by Corporation M in the principal amount of $5,000 with a basis of $4,000. In a transaction qualifying under section 356 (so far as such section relates to section 355), he exchanges the security of Corporation M for a security of Corporation O (a controlled corporation) in the principal amount of $5,000, worth $5,000, and exchanges one-half of his stock of Corporation M for stock of Corporation O worth $15,000 and a security of Corporation O in the principal amount of $5,000, worth $5,000. All of the stock and securities of Corporation O are distributed pursuant to the transaction. D realizes a gain of $12,500 on the exchange of the stock of Corporation M for the stock and security of Corporation O of which $5,000 is recognized. D also realizes a gain of $1,000 on the exchange of a security of Corporation M for a security of Corporation O, none of which is recognized. The basis of his stock of Corporation M held before the transaction is allocated 20/35ths to the stock of Corporation M held after the transaction and 15/35ths to the stock of Corporation O. The basis of the security of Corporation O received in exchange for his security of Corporation M is $4,000, the basis of the security of Corporation M exchanged. The basis of the security of Corporation O received with respect to D's stock of Corporation M is $5,000, its fair market value.

§ 1.358-3 Treatment of assumption of liabilities

(a) For purposes of section 358, where a party to the exchange assumes a liability of a distributee or acquires from him property subject to a liability, the amount of such liability is to be treated as money received by the distributee upon the exchange, whether or not the assumption of liabilities resulted in a recognition of gain or loss to the taxpayer under the law applicable to the year in which the exchange was made.

(b) The application of paragraph (a) of this section may be illustrated by the following examples:

Example (1). A, an individual, owns property with an adjusted basis of $100,000 on which there is a purchase money mortgage of $25,000. On December 1, 1954, A organizes Corporation X to which he transfers the property in exchange for all the stock of Corporation X and the assumption by Corporation X of the mortgage. The capital stock of Corporation X has a fair market value of $150,000. Under sections 351 and 357, no gain or loss is recognized to A. The basis in A's hands of the stock of Corporation X is $75,000, computed as follows:

Adjusted basis of property transferred $100,000

Less: Amount of money received
(amount of liabilities assumed) ...... -25,000

Basis of Corporation X stock
to A 75,000

Example (2). A, an individual, owns property with an adjusted basis of $25,000 on which there is a mortgage of $50,000. On December 1, 1954, A organizes Corporation X to which he transfers the property in exchange for all the stock of Corporation X and the assumption by Corporation X of the mortgage. The stock of Corporation X has a fair market value of $50,000. Under sections 351 and 357, gain is recognized to A in the amount of $25,000. The basis in A's hands of the stock of Corporation X is zero, computed as follows:

Adjusted basis of property transferred $25,000
Less: Amount of money received
(amount of liabilities) .... -50,000
Plus: Amount of gain recognized to
taxpayer 25,000

Basis of Corporation X stock
to A 0

§ 1.361-1 Nonrecognition of gain or loss to corporations

Section 361 provides the general rule that no gain or loss shall be recognized if a corporation, a party to a reorganization, exchanges property in pursuance of the plan of reorganization solely for stock or securities in another corporation, a party to the reorganization. This provision includes only stock and securities received in connection with a reorganization defined in section 368(a). It also includes nonvoting stock and securities in a corporation, a party to a reorganization, received in a transaction to which section 368(a) (1) (C) is applicable only by reason of section 368(a) (2) (B).

§ 1.362-1 Basis to corporations

(a) In general. Section 362 provides, as a general rule, that if property was acquired on or after June 22, 1954, by a corporation (1) in connection with a transaction to which section 351 (relating to transfer of property to corporation controlled by transferor) applies, (2) as paid-in surplus or as a contribution to capital, or (3) in connection with a reorganization to which Part III, subchapter C, Chapter 1 of the code applies, then the basis shall be the same as it would be in the hands of the transferor, increased in the amount of gain recognized to the transferor on such transfer. (See also § 1.362-2.)

(b) Exceptions. (1) In the case of a plan of reorganization adopted after October 22, 1968, section 362 does not apply if the property acquired in connection with such reorganization consists of stock or securities in a corporation a party to the reorganization, unless acquired by the exchange of stock or securities of the transferee (or of a corporation which is in control of the transferee) as the consideration in whole or in part for the transfer.

(2) In the case of a plan of reorganization adopted before October 23, 1968, section 362 does not apply if the property acquired in connection with such reorganization consists of stock or securities in a corporation a party to the reorganization, unless acquired by the issuance of stock or securities of the transferee (or, in the case of transactions occurring after December 31, 1963, of a corporation which is in control of the transferee) as the consideration in whole or in part for the transfer. The term "issuance of stock or securities" includes any transfer of stock or securities, including stock or securities which were purchased or were acquired as a contribution to capital.

§ 1.362-2 Certain contributions to capital

The following regulations shall be used in the application of section 362 (c):

(a) Property deemed to be acquired with contributed money shall be that property, if any, the acquisition of which was the purpose motivating the contribution;

(b) In the case of an excess of the amount of money contributed over the cost of the property deemed to be acquired with such money (as defined in paragraph (a) of this section) such excess shall be applied to the reduction of the basis (but not below zero) of other properties held by the corporation, on the last day of the 12-month period beginning on the day the contribution is received, in the following order—

(1) All property of a character subject to an allowance for depreciation (not including any properties as to which a deduction for amortization is allowable),

(2) Property with respect to which a deduction for amortization is allowable,

(3) Property with respect to which a deduction for depletion is allowable under section 611 but not under section 613, and

(4) All other remaining properties. The reduction of the basis of each of the properties within each of the above categories shall be made in proportion to the relative bases of such properties.

(c) With the consent of the Commissioner, the taxpayer may, however, have the basis of the various units of property within a particular category adjusted in a manner different from the general rule set forth in paragraph (b) of this section. Variations from such rule may, for example, involve adjusting the basis of only certain units of the taxpayer's property within a given category. A request for variations from the general rule should be filed by the taxpayer with its return for the taxable year for which the transfer of the property has occurred.

§ 1.368-1 Purpose and scope of exception of reorganization exchanges

(a) **Reorganizations.** As used in the regulations under parts I, II, and III (section 301 and following), subchapter C, chapter 1 of the Code, the terms "reorganization" and "party to a reorganization" mean only a reorganization or a party to a reorganization as defined in subsections (a) and (b) of section 368 . . . .

(b) **Purpose.** Under the general rule, upon the exchange of property, gain or loss must be accounted for if the new property differs in a material particular, either in kind or in extent, from the old property. The purpose of the reorganization provisions of the Code is to except from the general rule certain specifically described exchanges incident to such readjustments of corporate structures made in one of the particular ways specified in the Code, as are required by business exigencies and which effect only a readjustment of continuing interest in property under modified corporate forms. Requisite to a reorganization under the Code are a continuity of the business enterprise under the modified corporate form, and (except as provided in section 368(a)(1)(D))

a continuity of interest therein on the part of those persons who, directly or indirectly, were the owners of the enterprise prior to the reorganization. The continuity of business enterprise requirement is described in paragraph (d) of this section. The Code recognizes as a reorganization the amalgamation (occurring in a specified way) of two corporate enterprises under a single corporate structure if there exists among the holders of the stock and securities of either of the old corporations the requisite continuity of interest in the new corporation, but there is not a reorganization if the holders of the stock and securities of the old corporation are merely the holders of short-term notes in the new corporation. In order to exclude transactions not intended to be included, the specifications of the reorganization provisions of the law are precise. Both the terms of the specifications and their underlying assumptions and purposes must be satisfied in order to entitle the taxpayer to the benefit of the exception from the general rule. Accordingly, under the Code, a short-term purchase money note is not a security of a party to a reorganization, an ordinary dividend is to be treated as an ordinary dividend, and a sale is nevertheless to be treated as a sale even though the mechanics of a reorganization have been set up.

(c) **Scope.** The nonrecognition of gain or loss is prescribed for two specifically described types of exchanges, viz: The exchange that is provided for in section 354(a)(1) in which stock or securities in a corporation, a party to a reorganization, are, in pursuance of a plan of reorganization, exchanged for the stock or securities in a corporation, a party to the same reorganization; and the exchange that is provided for in section 361(a) in which a corporation, a party to a reorganization, exchanges property, in pursuance of a plan of reorganization, for stock or securities in another corporation, a party to the same reorganization. Section 368 (a)(1) limits the definition of the term "reorganization" to six kinds of transactions and excludes all others. From its context, the term "a party to a reorganization" can only mean a party to a transaction specifically defined as a reorganization by section 368(a). Certain rules respecting boot received in either of the two types of exchanges provided for in section 354(a) (1) and section 361(a) are prescribed in sections 356, 357, and 361(b). A special rule respecting a transfer of property with a liability in excess of its basis is prescribed in section 357(c). Under section 367 a limitation is placed on all these provisions by providing that except under specified conditions foreign corporations shall not be deemed within their scope. The provisions of the Code referred to in this paragraph are inapplicable unless there is a plan of reorganization. A plan of reorganization must contemplate the bona fide execution of one of the transactions specifically described as a reorganization in section 368(a) and for the bona fide consummation of each of the requisite acts under which nonrecognition of gain is claimed. Such transaction and such acts must be an ordinary and necessary incident of the conduct of the enterprise and must provide for a continuation of the enterprise. A scheme, which involves an abrupt departure from normal reorganization procedure in connection with a transaction on which the imposition of tax is imminent, such as a mere device that puts on the form of a corporate reorganization as a disguise for concealing its real character, and the object and accomplishment of which is the consummation of a preconceived plan having no business or corporate purpose, is not a plan of reorganization.

(d) Continuity of business enterprise —(1) Effective date. (i) This paragraph (d) applies to acquisitions occurring after January 30, 1981.

(ii) For an asset acquisition, the date of acquisition is the date of transfer. To determine the date of transfer, see § 1.381(b)–1(b).

(iii) For a stock acquisition, the date of acquisition is the date on which the exchange of stock occurs. If all stock is not exchanged on the same date, the date of exchange is the date the exchange of all stock under the plan of reorganization is complete.

(2) General rule. Continuity of business enterprise requires that the acquiring corporation (P) either (i) continue the acquired corporation's (T's) historic business or (ii) use a significant portion of T's historic business assets in a business. The application of this general rule to certain transactions, such as mergers of holding companies, will depend on all facts and circumstances. The policy underlying this general rule, which is to ensure that reorganizations are limited to readjustments of continuing interests in property under modified corporate form, provides the guidance necessary to make these facts and circumstances determinations.

(3) Business continuity. (i) The continuity of business enterprise requirement is satisfied if P continues T's historic business. The fact P is in the same line of business as T tends to establish the requisite continuity, but is not alone sufficient.

(ii) If T has more than one line of business, continuity of business enterprise requires only that P continue a significant line of business.

(iii) In general, a corporation's historic business is the business it has conducted most recently. However, a corporation's historic business is not one the corporation enters into as part of a plan of reorganization.

(iv) All facts and circumstances are considered in determining the time when the plan comes into existence and in determining whether a line of business is "significant".

(4) Asset continuity. (i) The continuity of business enterprise requirement is satisfied if P uses a significant portion of T's historic business assets in a business.

(ii) A corporation's historic business assets are the assets used in its historic business. Business assets may include stock and securities and intangible operating assets such as good will, patents, and trademarks, whether or not they have a tax basis.

(iii) In general, the determination of the portion of a corporation's assets considered "significant" is based on the relative importance of the assets to operation of the business. However, all other facts and circumstances, such as the net fair market value of those assets, will be considered.

(5) Examples. The following examples illustrate this paragraph (d).

Example (1). T conducts three lines of business: manufacture of synthetic resins, manufacture of chemicals for the textile industry, and distribution of chemicals. The three lines of business are approximately equal in value. On July 1, 1981, *T* sells the synthetic resin and chemicals distribution businesses to a third party for cash and marketable securities. On December 31, 1981, *T* transfers all of its assets to *P* solely for *P* voting stock. *P* continues the chemical manufacturing business without interruption. The continuity of business enterprise requirement is met. Continuity of business enterprise requires only that *P* continue one of *T*'s three significant lines of business.

Example (2). *P* manufactures computers and *T* manufactures components for computers. *T* sells all of its output to *P*. On January 1, 1981, *P* decides to buy imported components only. On March 1, 1981, *T* merges into *P*. *P* continues buying imported components but retains *T*'s equipment as a backup source of supply. The use of the equipment as a backup source of supply constitutes use of a significant portion of *T*'s historic business assets, thus establishing continuity of business enterprise. *P* is not required to continue *T*'s business.

Example (3). *T* is a manufacturer of boys' and men's trousers. On January 1, 1978, as part of a plan of reorganization, *T* sold all of its assets to a third party for cash and purchased a highly diversified portfolio of stocks and bonds. As part of the plan *T* operates an investment business until July 1, 1981. On that date, the plan of reorganization culminates in a transfer by *T* of all its assets to *P*, a regulated investment company, solely in exchange for *P* voting stock. The continuity of business enterprise requirement is not met. *T*'s investment activity is not its historic business, and the stocks and bonds are not *T*'s historic business assets.

Example (4). *T* manufactures children's toys and *P* distributes steel and allied products. On January 1, 1981, *T* sells all of its assets to a third party for $100,000 cash and $900,000 in notes. On March 1, 1981, *T* merges into *P*. Continuity of business enterprise is lacking. The use of the sales proceeds in *P*'s business is not sufficient.

Example (5). *T* manufactures farm machinery and *P* operates a lumber mill. *T* merges into *P*. *P* disposes of *T*'s assets immediately after the merger as part of the plan of reorganization. *P* does not continue *T*'s farm machinery manufacturing business. Continuity of business enterprise is lacking.

§ 1.368-2 Definition of terms

(a) The application of the term "reorganization" is to be strictly limited to the specific transactions set forth in section 368(a). The term does not embrace the mere purchase by one corporation of the properties of another corporation, for it imports a continuity of interest on the part of the transferor or its shareholders in the properties transferred. If the properties are transferred for cash and deferred payment obligations of the transferee evidenced by short-term notes, the transaction is a sale and not an exchange in which gain or loss is not recognized.

(b) (1) In order to qualify as a reorganization under section 368(a)(1)(A) the transaction must be a merger or consolidation effected pursuant to the corporation laws of the United States or a State or territory, or the District of Columbia.

(2) In order for the transaction to qualify under section 368(a)(1)(A) by reason of the application of section 368(a)(2)(D), one corporation (the acquiring corporation) must acquire substantially all of the properties of another corporation (the acquired corporation) partly or entirely in exchange for stock of a corporation which is in control of the acquiring corporation (the controlling corporation), provided that (i) the transaction would have qualified under section 368(a)(1)(A) if the merger had been into the controlling corporation, and (ii) no stock of the acquiring corporation is used in the transaction. The foregoing test of whether the transaction would have qualified under section 368(a)(1)(A) if the merger had been into the controlling corporation means that the general requirements of a reorganization under section 368(a)(1)(A) (such as a business purpose, continuity of business enterprise, and continuity of interest) must be met in addition to the special requirements of section 368(a)(2)(D). Under this test, it is not relevant whether the merger into the controlling corporation could have been effected pursuant to State or Federal corporation law. The term "substantially all" has the same meaning as it has in section 368(a)(1)(C). Although no stock of the acquiring corporation can be used in the transaction, there is no prohibition (other than the continuity of interest requirement) against using other property, such as cash or securities, of either the acquiring corporation or the parent or both. In addition, the controlling corporation may assume liabilities of the acquired corporation without disqualifying the transaction under section 368(a)(2)(D), and for purposes of section 357(a) the controlling corporation is considered a party to the exchange. For example, if the controlling corporation agrees to substitute its stock for stock of the acquired corporation under an outstanding employee stock option agreement, this assumption of liability will not prevent the transaction from qualifying as a reorganization under

section 368(a)(2)(D) and the assumption of liability is not treated as money or other property for purposes of section 361(b). Section 368(a)(2)(D) applies whether or not the controlling corporation (or the acquiring corporation) is formed immediately before the merger, in anticipation of the merger, or after preliminary steps have been taken to merge directly into the controlling corporation. Section 368(a)(2)(D) applies only to statutory mergers occurring after October 22, 1968.

(c) In order to qualify as a "reorganization" under section 368(a)(1)(B), the acquisition by the acquiring corporation of stock of another corporation must be in exchange solely for all or a part of the voting stock of the acquiring corporation (or, in the case of transactions occurring after December 31, 1963, solely for all or a part of the voting stock of a corporation which is in control of the acquiring corporation), and the acquiring corporation must be in control of the other corporation immediately after the transaction. If, for example, corporation X in one transaction exchanges nonvoting preferred stock or bonds in addition to all or a part of its voting stock in the acquisition of stock of corporation Y, the transaction is not a reorganization under section 368(a)(1)(B). Nor is a transaction a reorganization described in section 368(a)(1)(B) if stock is acquired in exchange for voting stock both of the acquiring corporation and of a corporation which is in control of the acquiring corporation. The acquisition of stock of another corporation by the acquiring corporation solely for its voting stock (or solely for voting stock of a corporation which is in control of the acquiring corporation) is permitted tax-free even though the acquiring corporation already owns some of the stock of the other corporation. Such an acquisition is permitted tax-free in a single transaction or in a series of transactions taking place over a relatively short period of time such as 12 months. For example, corporation A purchased 30 percent of the common stock of corporation W (the only class of stock outstanding) for cash in 1939. On March 1, 1955, corporation A offers to exchange its own voting stock for all the stock of corporation W tendered within 6 months from the date of the offer. Within the 6-months' period corporation A acquires an additional 60 percent of stock of corporation W solely for its own voting stock, so that it owns 90 percent of the stock of corporation W. No gain or loss is recognized with respect to the exchanges of stock of corporation A for stock of corporation W. For this purpose, it is immaterial whether such exchanges occurred before corporation A acquired control (80 percent) of corporation W or after such control was acquired. If corporation A had acquired 80 percent of the stock of corporation W for cash in 1939, it could likewise acquire some or all of the remainder of such stock solely in exchange for its own voting stock without recognition of gain or loss.

(d) In order to qualify as a reorganization under section 368(a)(1)(C), the transaction must be one described in subparagraph (1) or (2) of this paragraph:

(1) One corporation must acquire substantially all the properties of another corporation solely in exchange for all or a part of its own voting stock, or solely in exchange for all or a part of the voting stock of a corporation which is in control of the acquiring corporation. For example, Corporation P owns all the stock of Corporation A. All the properties of Corporation W are transferred to Corporation A either solely in exchange for voting stock of Corporation P or solely in exchange for less than 80 percent of the voting stock of Corporation A. Either of such transactions constitutes a reorganization under section 368(a)(1)(C). However, if the properties of Corporation W are acquired in exchange for voting stock of both Corporation P and Corporation A, the transaction will not constitute a reorganization under section 368(a)(1)(C). In determining whether the exchange meets the requirement of "solely for voting stock", the assumption by the acquiring corporation of liabilities of the transferor corporation, or the fact that property acquired from the transferor corporation is subject to a liability, shall be disregarded. Though such an assumption does not prevent an exchange from being solely for voting stock for the purposes of the definition of a reorganization contained in section 368(a)(1)(C), it may in some cases, however, so alter the character of the transaction as to place the transaction outside the purposes and assumptions

of the reorganization provisions. Section 368(a) (1) (C) does not prevent consideration of the effect of an assumption of liabilities on the general character of the transaction but merely provides that the requirement that the exchange be solely for voting stock is satisfied if the only additional consideration is an assumption of liabilities.

(2) One corporation:

(i) Must acquire substantially all of the properties of another corporation in such manner that the acquisition would qualify under (1) above, but for the fact that the acquiring corporation exchanges money, or other property in addition to such voting stock, and

(ii) Must acquire solely for voting stock (either of the acquiring corporation or of a corporation which is in control of the acquiring corporation) properties of the other corporation having a fair market value which is at least 80 percent of the fair market value of all the properties of the other corporation.

(3) For the purposes of subparagraph (2) (ii) only, a liability assumed or to which the properties are subject is considered money paid for the properties. For example, Corporation A has properties with a fair market value of $100,000 and liabilities of $10,000. In exchange for these properties, Corporation Y transfers its own voting stock, assumes the $10,000 liabilities, and pays $8,000 in cash. The transaction is a reorganization even though a part of the properties of Corporation A is acquired for cash. On the other hand, if the properties of Corporation A worth $100,000 were subject to $50,000 in liabilities, an acquisition of all the properties, subject to the liabilities, for any consideration other than solely voting stock would not qualify as a reorganization under this section since the liabilities alone are in excess of 20 percent of the fair market value of the properties. If the transaction would qualify under either subparagraph (1) or (2) of this paragraph and also under section 368(a) (1) (D), such transaction shall not be treated as a reorganization under section 368(a) (1) (C).

(e) A "recapitalization", and therefore a reorganization, takes place if, for example:

(1) A corporation with $200,000 par value of bonds outstanding, instead of paying them off in cash, discharges them by issuing preferred shares to the bondholders;

(2) There is surrendered to a corporation for cancellation 25 percent of its preferred stock in exchange for no par value common stock;

(3) A corporation issues preferred stock, previously authorized but unissued, for outstanding common stock;

(4) An exchange is made of a corporation's outstanding preferred stock, having certain priorities with reference to the amount and time of payment of dividends and the distribution of the corporate assets upon liquidation, for a new issue of such corporation's common stock having no such rights;

(5) An exchange is made of an amount of a corporation's outstanding preferred stock with dividends in arrears for other stock of the corporation. However, if pursuant to such an exchange there is an increase in the proportionate interest of the preferred shareholders in the assets or earnings and profits of the corporation, then under § 1.305-7(c)(2), an amount equal to the lesser of (i) the amount by which the fair market value or liquidation preference, whichever is greater, of the stock received in the exchange (determined immediately following the recapitalization) exceeds the issue price of the preferred stock surrendered, or (ii) the amount of the dividends in arrears, shall be treated under section 305 (c) as a deemed distribution to which sections 305(b)(4) and 301 apply.

(f) The term "a party to a reorganization" includes a corporation resulting from a reorganization, and both corporations, in a transaction qualifying as a reorganization where one corporation acquires stock or properties of another corporation. A corporation remains a party to the reorganization although it transfers all or part of the assets acquired to a controlled subsidiary. A corporation controlling an acquiring corporation is a party to the reorganization when the stock of such controlling corporation is used in the acquisition of properties. Both corporations are parties to the reorganization if, under statutory authority, Corporation A is merged into Corporation B. All three of the corporations are parties to the reorganization if, pursuant to statutory authority, Corporation C and Corporation D are consolidated into Corporation E. Both corporations are parties to the reorganization if Corporation F transfers substantially all its assets to Corporation G in exchange for all or a part of the voting stock of Corporation G. All three corporations are parties to the reorganization if Corporation H transfers substantially all its assets to Corporation K in exchange for all or a part of the voting stock of Corporation L, which is in control of Corporation K. Both corporations are parties to the reorganization if Corporation M transfers all or part of its assets to Corporation N in exchange for all or a part of the stock and securities of Corporation N, but only if (1) immediately after such transfer, Corporation M, or one or more of its shareholders (including persons who were shareholders immediately before such transfer), or any combination thereof, is in control of Corporation N, and (2) in pursuance of the plan, the stock and securities of Corporation N are transferred or distributed by Corporation M in a transaction in which gain or loss is not recognized under section 354 or 355, or is recognized only to the extent provided in section 356. Both Corporation O and Corporation P, but not Corporation S, are parties to the reorganization if Corporation O acquires stock of Corporation P from Corporation S in exchange solely for a part of the voting stock of Corporation O, if (1) the stock of Corporation P does not constitute substantially all of the assets of Corporation S, (2) Corporation S is not in control of Corporation O immediately after the acquisition, and (3) Corporation O is in control of Corporation P immediately after the acquisition.

(g) The term "plan of reorganization" has reference to a consummated transaction specifically defined as a reorganization under section 368(a). The term is not to be construed as broadening the definition of "reorganization" as set forth in section 368(a), but is to be taken as limiting the nonrecognition of gain or loss to such exchanges or distributions as are directly a part of the transaction specifically described as a reorganization in section 368(a). Moreover, the transaction, or series of transactions, embraced in a plan of reorganization must not only come within the specific language of section 368(a), but the readjustments involved in the exchanges or distributions effected in the consummation thereof must be undertaken for reasons germane to the continuance of the business of a corporation a party to the reorganization. Section 368(a) contemplates genuine corporate reorganizations which are designed to effect a readjustment of continuing interests under modified corporate forms.

(h) As used in section 368, as well as in other provisions of the Internal Revenue Code, if the context so requires, the conjunction "or" denotes both the conjunctive and the disjunctive, and the singular includes the plural. For example, the provisions of the statute are complied with if "stock and securities" are received in exchange as well as if "stock or securities" are received.

§ 1.368–3 Records to be kept and information to be filed with returns

(a) The plan of reorganization must be adopted by each of the corporations parties thereto; and the adoption must be shown by the acts of its duly constituted responsible officers, and appear upon the official records of the corporation. Each corporation, a party to a reorganization, shall file as a part of its return for its taxable year within which the reorganization occurred a complete statement of all facts pertinent to the nonrecognition of gain or loss in connection with the reorganization, including:

(1) A copy of the plan of reorganization, together with a statement, executed under the penalties of perjury, showing in full the purposes thereof and in detail all transactions incident to, or pursuant to, the plan.

(2) A complete statement of the cost or other basis of all property, including all stock or securities, transferred incident to the plan.

(3) A statement of the amount of stock or securities and other property or money received from the exchange, including a statement of all distributions or other disposition made thereof. The amount of each kind of stock or securities and other property received shall be stated on the basis of the fair market value thereof at the date of the exchange.

(4) A statement of the amount and nature of any liabilities assumed upon

the exchange, and the amount and nature of any liabilities to which any of the property acquired in the exchange is subject.

(b) Every taxpayer, other than a corporation a party to the reorganization, who receives stock or securities and other property or money upon a tax-free exchange in connection with a corporate reorganization shall incorporate in his income tax return for the taxable year in which the exchange takes place a complete statement of all facts pertinent to the nonrecognition of gain or loss upon such exchange including:

(1) A statement of the cost or other basis of the stock or securities transferred in the exchange, and

(2) A statement in full of the amount of stock or securities and other property or money received from the exchange, including any liabilities assumed upon the exchange, and any liabilities to which property received is subject. The amount of each kind of stock or securities and other property (other than liabilities assumed upon the exchange) received shall be set forth upon the basis of the fair market value thereof at the date of the exchange.

(c) Permanent records in substantial form shall be kept by every taxpayer who participates in a tax-free exchange in connection with a corporate reorganization showing the cost or other basis of the transferred property and the amount of stock or securities and other property or money received (including any liabilities assumed on the exchange, or any liabilities to which any of the properties received were subject), in order to facilitate the determination of gain or loss from a subsequent disposition of such stock or securities and other property received from the exchange.

§ 1.385-1 Stock or indebtedness

(a) Effective date—(1) In general. The regulations under section 385 apply to instruments (as defined in § 1.385-3(c)) and preferred stock issued after 90 days after publication of the final revisions to the section 385 regulations in the Federal Register, or, if later, December 31, 1982, and to loans described in § 1.385-7 and guaranteed loans made after 90 days after publication of the final revisions to the section 385 regulations in the Federal Register, or, if later, December 31, 1982.

(2) Exceptions. The regulations under section 385 do not apply to—

(i) Instruments issued pursuant to a plan of reorganization filed on or before December 29, 1980, in a proceeding under the Federal bankruptcy laws (Title 11, U.S.C.) or under the Regional Rail Reorganization Act of 1973 [45 U.S.C.A. § 701 et seq.], or

(ii) Instruments, loans described in § 1.385-7, guaranteed loans, or preferred stock issued or made pursuant to a written contract which is binding on December 29, 1980, and at all times thereafter.

(b) Scope—(1) In general. The regulations under section 385 contain rules under which certain interests in corporations are treated as stock or indebtedness. All other interests (such as bank deposits, insurance policies, claims for wages, and trade accounts payable) are outside the scope of the regulations. Any interest outside the scope of the regulations will be treated as stock or indebtedness under applicable principles of law without reference to the regulations.

(2) Similar distinctions. Certain other sections of the Internal Revenue Code make distinctions that are similar to (but not the same as) the one between stock and indebtedness. Section 385 does not necessarily govern these distinctions. Thus, for example, an interest in an organization may be treated as indebtedness under section 385, but the net profits of the organization may, by reason of the indebtedness, inure to the benefit of the holder within the meaning of section 501(c). Similarly, section 385 does not affect the treatment of a loan as an ownership interest within the meaning of section 48(k)(1)(C) (relating to the investment credit for movies). See § 1.48-8(a)(4)(iii).

(c) Authority. Sections 1.385-1 through 1.385-10 are prescribed under the authority of section 385. In addition, certain provisions in these sections derive additional authority under section 7805, because they interpret other sections of the Internal Revenue Code, including section 301 (relating to distributions of property), section 1012 (relating to basis), and section 1232 (relating to original issue discount).

* * * * *

§ 1.385–2   Summary

(a) **Instruments issued proportionately—(1) Straight debt instruments.** Straight debt instruments (as defined in § 1.385–3(f)) issued proportionately to the issuing corporation's shareholders are ordinarily treated as indebtedness. Exceptions may apply where the issuing corporation has excessive debt (see § 1.385–6(f)), or where the instruments are not issued for money (see § 1.385–6(d) or are payable on demand (see § 1.385–6(l)). Additionally, straight debt instruments initially treated as debt may be reclassified as stock where there is a failure to pay interest or principal when due (see § 1.385–6(k) and (l)(3)) or where there is a change in terms (see § 1.385–6(j)).

(2) **Hybrid instruments.** Hybrid instruments (e. g., income bonds or convertible debentures) are treated as stock if they are issued proportionately (see § 1.385–6(c)).

(b) **Instruments not issued proportionately—(1) Straight debt instruments.** Straight debt instruments not issued proportionately are ordinarily treated as indebtedness.

(2) **Hybrid instruments.** Hybrid instruments not issued proportionately are treated as stock if their equity features are predominant (see § 1.385–5). Otherwise, they are generally treated in the same manner as straight debt instruments.

(c) **Ancillary rules—(1) In general.** In addition to the primary rules described in paragraphs (a) and (b) of this section, the regulations under section 385 also contain a variety of significant ancillary rules. These rules are subordinate in the sense that they do not apply directly to treat any interest as stock or indebtedness. However, they are essential to the working of the regulations.

(2) **Adjustment of interest rate.** If instruments issued to shareholders do not carry a reasonable rate of interest, then a contribution to the capital of the corporation or a corporate distribution to the shareholder is imputed under § 1.385–3(a). This ordinarily results in the creation of either original issue discount (see section 1232) or amortizable bond premium (see § 1.61–12(c) (2)). This result ensures that the holders take a reasonable amount into income as interest received, and that the issuing corporation takes a reasonable deduction for interest paid on the instruments each year.

(3) **Reasonable rate of interest.** Section 1.385–6(e) contains rules for determining whether a rate of interest is reasonable. These rules are significant—

(i) Where instruments are issued proportionately to shareholders other than in exchange for money (see § 1.385–6(d));

(ii) Where instruments are held proportionately and there is a change in terms (see § 1.385–6(j)) or nonpayment of principal (see § 1.385–6(l)(3));

(iii) Where instruments held proportionately are payable on demand (see § 1.385–6(l));

(iv) Where loans of money made to a corporation by persons other than independent creditors are not evidenced by an instrument (see § 1.385–7); and

(v) In determining the fair market value of an instrument (see § 1.385–3 (b)(2)).

(4) **Debt-to-equity ratio.** Paragraphs (g) and (h) of § 1.385–6 contain rules for determining a corporation's debt-to-equity ratio. These rules are significant in determining—

(i) Whether a rate of interest is presumptively reasonable (see § 1.385–6(e) (2)); and

(ii) Whether a corporation has excessive debt (see § 1.385–6(f)).

(5) **Fair market value.** Section 1.385–3(b) contains rules for determining the fair market value of an instrument. These rules are significant in determining—

(i) Whether a contribution to capital or corporate distribution is imputed under § 1.385–3(a); and

(ii) Whether the equity features of a hybrid instrument are predominant (see § 1.385–5).

(d) **Safe harbor.** In general, the regulations under section 385 provide a safe harbor for a straight debt instrument (as defined in § 1.385–3(f)) issued by a corporation whenever all of the following conditions are satisfied:

(1) **Principal and interest.** The instrument has a fixed maturity date and provides for annual payments of interest at (i) the rate in effect under

section 6621, (ii) the prime rate in effect at any local commercial bank, (iii) a rate determined from time to time by the Secretary taking into consideration the average yield on outstanding marketable obligations of the United States of comparable maturity, or (iv) any rate in between.

(2) Debt-to-equity ratio. The debt-to-equity ratio of the corporation does not exceed 1:1.

(3) Paid when due. All principal and interest on the instrument are paid when due.

If a straight debt instrument falls within the safe harbor, then it will be treated as indebtedness when issued, no orginal issue discount or bond premium will be imputed with respect to it, and (assuming its terms are not changed) it will not be subsequently reclassified as stock.

. . . .

(f) Cautionary note. This section is merely a summary of the regulations under section 385, and is subject in all respects to the more complete rules contained in §§ 1.385-3 through 1.385-10.

§ 1.385-3 Preliminary rules

(a) Excessive or inadequate consideration—(1) Excessive consideration. If a corporation issues an instrument to a shareholder, then (whether the instrument is treated as stock or indebtedness) the excess of—

(i) The consideration paid, over

(ii) The fair market value of the instrument, is a contribution to capital.

(2) Inadequate consideration. (i) If a corporation issues an instrument to a shareholder and the instrument is treated as indebtedness, then the excess of—

(A) The fair market value of the instrument, over

(B) The consideration paid,

is a distribution to which section 301 applies. See § 1.301-1(d), (j) and (k).

(ii) If a corporation issues an instrument to a shareholder and the instrument is treated as stock, then the amount determined under paragraph (a)(2)(i) of this section is treated as a distribution of stock to which section 305 applies.

(3) Illustrations. The following examples illustrate the application of this paragraph (a) and related provisions:

Example (1). Corporation S is organized in 1985 for the purpose of constructing, owning, and operating a professional office building. Fifteen persons, all medical doctors, subscribe for the capital stock of S at $100 a share. On January 1, 1988, the doctors agree to advance $300 to S for each share of stock subscribed. These advances are represented by 19-year, 7-percent debentures in the principal amount of $300 each. Assume that the debentures are treated as indebtedness under § 1.385-4(a) (relating to instruments generally), and that the fair market value of each debenture is $246. Based on these facts, $54 of each $300 advance is treated as a contribution to capital. Therefore, the doctors' basis in each debenture is $246, and there is an original issue discount of $54 on each debenture. See section 1232.

Example (2). The facts are the same as in example (1), except that the doctors pay $200 for each debenture. Based on these facts, the doctors are treated as receiving a $46 distribution to which section 301 applies on each share of stock. Therefore, the doctors' basis in each debenture is $246 (see § 1.301-1(j)), and there is an original issue discount of $54 on each debenture.

Example (3). The facts are the same as in example (1), except that the debentures bear interest at 9 percent a year. Assume that the fair market value of each 9-percent debenture is $300. Based on these facts, the doctors are not treated as making a contribution to capital or as receiving a distribution to which section 301 applies. Therefore, the doctors' basis in each debenture is $300, and there is no original issue discount on the debentures.

Example (4). The facts are the same as in example (1), except that S issues the debentures together with the capital stock in 1985, and the doctors pay $400 for each unit consisting of one debenture and one share of stock. Based on these facts, the doctors' basis in each debenture is $246 (see § 1.1012-1(d)), their basis in each share of stock is $154, and the original issue discount on each debenture is $54 (see § 1.1232-3(b)(2)(ii)).

Example (5). Individuals A and B each own ½ the common stock of corporation M, which is the only class of stock outstanding. On January 1, 1982, M issues two 12-percent $1,000 notes, one to A and one to B, each for $1,000 in cash. Assume that the fair market value of each note is $1,250 and that the notes are treated as indebtedness under § 1.385-4(a) (relating to instruments generally). Based on these facts, on January 1, 1982, A and B each receive a $250 distribution to which section 301 applies. Thus, each note has a basis of $1,250 and is issued at a premium of $250 (see section 171(b) and § 1.61-12(c)(2)).

Example (6). The facts are the same as in example (5), except that interest on the notes is payable only at the discretion of M's board of directors, and the notes are treated as preferred stock under § 1.385-6(c) (relating to hybrid instruments held proportionately). Based on these facts, on January 1, 1982, A and B each receive a $250 distribution of preferred stock on common stock.

(b) Fair market value. The following rules apply for purposes of the regulations under section 385:

(1) In general. (i) The fair market value of an instrument is the price at which it would change hands between a willing buyer and a willing seller, neither being under any compulsion to buy or to sell and both having reasonable knowledge of all relevant facts.

(ii) The fair market value of an instrument may be determined by using present value and standard bond tables. See § 1.1232-3(b)(2)(ii)(d) for examples in which the fair market values of instruments are determined by the use of these tables.

(iii)(A) In determining the fair market value of an instrument (or the reasonableness of an interest rate), the Commissioner may disregard a noncommercial term of the instrument if the principal purpose of the inclusion of the term is to increase or decrease the fair market value of the instrument (or a reasonable rate of interest for the instrument). See also section 482.

(B) The following example illustrates the application of this subdivision (iii):

Example. N, a nonresident alien of the United States and a resident of country Q is the sole shareholder of domestic corporation W. On January 1, 1987, W issues a $100,000, 28-percent debenture to N in exchange for $100,000. Under provision P of the debenture, an action to enforce the terms of the debenture can be maintained only in the village court of village V, located in Q. Assume that the principal purpose of the inclusion of provision P is to reduce the fair market value of the debenture. Based on these facts, the Commissioner may disregard provision P in determining the fair market value of the debenture.

(2) Rules of convenience. (i) On the day of issue, the fair market value of a straight debt instrument is considered to be equal to the face amount if—

(A) The stated annual rate of interest on the instrument is reasonable (within the meaning of § 1.385-6(e)), and

(B) The consideration paid for the instrument is equal to the face amount.

(ii) Notwithstanding any other provision of this paragraph (b), if an instrument is registered with the Securities and Exchange Commission and sold to the public for money, then the fair market value of the instrument on the day of issue is the issue price (as defined in section 1232(b)(2)).

(3) Examples. The following examples illustrate the application of paragraph (b)(2) of this section:

Example (1). On March 1, 1985, corporation M issues a $1,000 8-percent, 5-year note at par. Assume that on that date, 10 to 12 percent is the range of rates of interest paid to independent creditors on similar instruments issued by corporations of the same general size and in the same general industry, geographic location, and financial condition; that the rate of interest in effect under section 6621 is 6 percent; that the interest rate for 5-year obligations determined by the Secretary pursuant to § 1.385-6 (e)(2)(i) is 7 percent; and that the prime rate at local commercial banks is 9 percent. Also assume that M's debt-to-equity ratio at the end of the taxable year is 1:2. Based on these facts, any rate between 6 and 12 percent is a reasonable rate of interest within the meaning of § 1.385-6(e). In particular, 8 percent is a reasonable rate of interest, and the fair market value of the note is therefore considered to be $1,000.

Example (2). The facts are the same as in example (1) except that M's debt-to-equity ratio at the end of the taxable year is 2:1. Based on these facts, paragraph (b)(2)(i) of this section does not apply.

Example (3). The facts are the same as in example (2) except that the note provides for annual payments of interest at a rate of 11 percent. Since 11 percent is within the range of rates of interest paid to independent creditors on similar instruments issued by corporations of the same general size and in the same general industry, geographic location, and financial condition, the fair market value of the note is considered to be $1,000.

(c) Instrument. The term "instrument" means any bond, note, debenture, or similar written evidence of an obligation.

(d) Obligation. The term "obligation" means an interest in a corporation that is treated as indebtedness under applicable nontax law.

(e) Hybrid instrument. The term "hybrid instrument" means an instrument that is convertible into stock or one (such as an income bond or a participating bond) that provides for any contingent payment to the holder (other than a call premium).

(f) Straight debt instrument. The term "straight debt instrument" means any instrument other than a hybrid instrument.

§ 1.385-4 Instruments generally

(a) General rule. Except as otherwise provided in the regulations under section 385, all instruments (as defined in § 1.385-3(c)) are treated as indebtedness for all purposes of the Internal Revenue Code. For exceptions, see §

1.385–5 (relating to certain hybrid instruments) and § 1.385–6 (relating to proportionality).

(b) Operating rules—(1) In general. The regulations under section 385 determine the status of each instrument (i. e., as stock or indebtedness) at the time the instrument is issued. Except as provided in paragraphs (j), (k), and (l) of § 1.385–6 (relating to proportionality), the status of an instrument can never change. Thus, for example, the status of an instrument is not affected by a mere change in ownership.

(2) Special rule. Under § 1.385–6 (j), (k), and (l), the status of an instrument can change from indebtedness to stock (e. g., in the event of a failure to pay interest when due).

(c) Effect of classification—(1) In general. (i) If an instrument is treated as stock under section 385, then the instrument is treated as preferred stock for all purposes of the Internal Revenue Code. In particular, all payments of "interest" on the instrument are treated as distributions to which section 301 applies, and all payments of "principal" are treated as distributions in redemption of stock. Such preferred stock is considered to have the same terms (e. g., voting rights) as the instrument has under applicable local law. Each class of instruments classified as preferred stock is treated as a separate class of preferred stock. See § 1.1371–1 for the effect on an election made under Subchapter S. Also see § 1.992–1(d)(2) for an exception to this rule.

(ii) If an instrument becomes stock under § 1.385–6(j), (k), or (l), then the instrument is treated as having been exchanged (without recognition of gain or loss) for preferred stock in a recapitalization to which section 368(a)(1)(E) applies.

(2) Illustrations. The following examples illustrate the application of this paragraph (c):

Example (1). On January 1, 1982, corporation X issues a $100,000 note to A. The note is due on January 1, 1992, and pays interest at a rate of 10 percent a year. Assume that at first the note is treated as indebtedness under paragraph (a) of this section. However, on January 1, 1987, the note becomes stock under § 1.385–6 (k) (relating to nonpayment of interest). A is treated as having exchanged the note for preferred stock on January 1, 1987, in a recapitalization to which section 368(a)(1)(E) applies. Moreover, A does not recognize gain or loss merely because the note is reclassified.

Example (2). The facts are the same as in example (1). In addition, on July 1, 1988, A receives $15,000 in interest on the note. The entire $15,000 payment is treated as a distribution to which section 301 applies.

Example (3). Individuals B and C each own 50 percent of the stock of corporation Y. On January 1, 1990, Y distributes one convertible debenture each to B and C as a dividend. Assume that the convertible debentures are treated as stock under § 1.385–6(c) (relating to hybrid instruments). Also assume that Y has accumulated earnings and profits of $5 million at the time of the distribution. Based on these facts, the debentures are treated as section 306 stock unless their distribution is taxable under section 305(b)(5).

Example (4). Individual D is a shareholder in corporation Z. On January 1, 1990, D buys a 20-year, $10,000 subordinated income bond from Z. D transfers $10,000 to Z for the bond, and the bond is treated as stock under § 1.385–5 (relating to hybrid instruments). On January 1, 1990, the fair market value of the bond is $8,000. Based on these facts, D has made a contribution of $2,000 to the capital of Z on January 1, 1990, and has paid $8,000 for the bond. See § 1.385–3(a)(1). In addition, because the bond is treated as preferred stock, section 305 (c) and § 1.305–5(b) may apply to the $2,000 difference between the purchase price and the redemption price.

§ 1.385–5 Certain hybrid instruments

(a) In general. A hybrid instrument is treated as stock if, on the day of issue—

(1) The fair market value of the instrument without its equity features is less than

(2) Fifty percent of the actual fair market value of the instrument (with those features).

(b) Equity features. The equity features of an instrument are the right to convert it into stock and the right to contingent payments (other than a call premium).

(c) Special rule. Paragraph (a) of this section shall be applied by substituting "Forty-five percent" for "Fifty percent" if clear and convincing evidence shows that, on the day of issue, both the issuer and holder reasonably believe that—

(1) The fair market value of the instrument without its equity features is not less than

(2) Fifty percent of the actual fair market value of the instrument (with those features).

(d) Meaning of terms. The following rules apply for purposes of the regulations under section 385:

(1) Contingent payment. The term "contingent payment" means any payment other than a fixed payment of principal or interest.

(2) Fixed payments; interest. An instrument provides for fixed payments of interest if both of the following conditions are satisfied:

(i) Interest at a definitely ascertainable rate is due on definitely ascertainable dates.

(ii) Except as provided in paragraph (d)(5) of this section, the holder's right to receive interest when due (or within 90 days thereafter) cannot be impaired without the holder's consent.

(3) Fixed payments; principal. An instrument provides for the fixed payment of principal if both of the following conditions are satisfied:

(i) A definitely ascertainable principal sum is payable on demand or due on definitely ascertainable dates.

(ii) Except as provided in paragraph (d)(5) of this section, the holder's right to receive principal when due cannot be impaired without the holder's consent.

(4) Definitely ascertainable. (i) A rate of interest is definitely ascertainable if it is applied to a definitely ascertainably principal sum and if it is—

(A) An invariable rate, or

(B) A variable rate determined according to an external standard that is not subject to the borrower's control and that is not related to the success or failure of the borrower's business or activities.

(ii) A principal sum is definitely ascertainable if it is—

(A) An invariable sum, or

(B) A variable sum determined according to an external standard that is not subject to the borrower's control and that is not related to the success or failure of the borrower's business or activities.

A principal sum is not variable simply because it is within the borrower's control to prepay all or a portion of the principal sum.

(5) Exceptions. The classification of a payment as fixed is not affected by the fact that:

(i) The instrument is issued under an indenture that satisfies the requirements of section 316 of the Trust Indenture Act of 1939 (15 U.S.C. § 77ppp);

(ii) A holder's right to receive interest or principal may be impaired by the operation of the Federal bankruptcy laws (Title 11, U.S.C.), the Railroad Modification Act (47 U.S.C. § 20b), or a similar provision of law; or

(iii) A holder's right to receive interest or principal may be impaired in the event of the insolvency of the issuing corporation (either in the sense that the corporation is not able to pay its debts as they become due or in the sense that its liabilities exceed its assets).

(6) Illusory contingencies. For purposes of this paragraph (d), the Commissioner may disregard a contingency where there is no reasonably foreseeable circumstance in which it could affect the likelihood of payment.

(7) Certain guarantees. If—

(i) A payment does not satisfy the requirements of paragraph (d)(2) or (3) of this section, but

(ii) The payment is guaranteed (directly or indirectly) by any person, then (depending on the facts and circumstances) the Commissioner may treat the payment as fixed. See example (5) of § 1.385–10(c).

. . . .

(e) Illustrations. The following examples illustrate the application of this section. It is assumed that § 1.-385–6 does not apply to the instruments described in these examples.

Example (1). (a) On July 1, 1987, corporation J issues subordinated income debenture bonds in the principal amount of $1,000 each. The bonds pay interest at the rate of 8 percent a year. However, interest is payable only if earned. The bonds are due on December 31, 2006. Based on these facts, each bond provides for a fixed payment of $1,000 in principal on December 31, 2006, but for contingent payments of interest.

(b) Assume that the fair market value of the 8-percent subordinated income debenture bonds is $1,000 each. The bonds without their equity features would be $1,000 noninterest-bearing subordinated debenture bonds due on December 31, 2006. Assume that the fair market value of such instruments would be $261 each. Based on these facts, the subordinated income debenture bonds are treated as stock because the fair market value of each debenture bond without its equity features (i. e., $261) is less than 50 percent of its actual fair market value (i. e., $1,000/2 = $500).

Example (2). (a) On March 1, 1988, corporation M issues 6-percent subordinated income debentures in the principal amount of $1,000 each due on March 1, 2038. Annual payment of interest is mandatory if net income is available and optional otherwise. Accumulated interest must be paid in all events at maturity. Based on these facts, each debenture provides for fixed payments of $1,000 in principal and $3,000 in simple interest on March 1, 2038.

(b) Assume that the fair market value of the 6-percent subordinated income debentures is $1,000 each. The debentures without their equity features would provide for the payment of $4,000 (total principal and interest) on March 1, 2038, and would be subordinated to the general creditors of M. Assume that the fair market value of such instruments would be $265 each. Based on these facts, the income debentures are treated as stock because the fair market value of each income debenture without its equity features (i. e., $265) is less than 50 percent of its actual fair market value (i. e., $1,000/2 = $500).

Example (3). (a) On February 7, 1987, corporation P issues written obligations called "debenture preference stock" in the principal amount of $50 each. The debenture preference stock bears interest at 6 percent a year. In addition, at the discretion of the board of directors of P, the holders of the debenture preference stock may share in the profits of P after a dividend of $6 has been paid on each share of P's common stock. The debenture preference stock matures on December 31, 2017, except that the maturity may be extended from time to time (but in no event beyond December 31, 2037) at the discretion of P's board of directors. Based on these facts, the debenture preference stock provides for fixed payments of interest at a rate of 6 percent and a fixed payment of $50 in principal on December 31, 2037.

(b) Assume that the fair market value of the debenture preference stock is $50 each. The debenture preference stock without its equity features would be 6-percent nonparticipating debentures due on December 31, 2037. Assume that the fair market value of such instruments would be $20.12 each. Based on these facts, the debenture preference stock is treated as stock because its fair market value without equity features (i. e., $20.12) is less than 50 percent of its actual fair market value (i. e., $50/2 = $25).

Example (4). (a) On December 1, 1989, corporation T issues variable interest notes in the principal amount of $1,000 each. The notes pay interest at a rate that may vary between 2 percent and 10 percent, depending on the earnings of T. The board of directors of T may, in its discretion, defer all payments of interest until the notes mature on December 1, 2014, and may subordinate the notes to other debts of T. Based on these facts, each note provides for fixed payments of $1,000 in principal and $500 in interest (i. e., 2 percent × $1,000 × 25 years) on December 1, 2014.

(b) Assume that the fair market value of the variable interest notes is $1,000 each. The notes without their equity features would provide for the payment of $1,500 (total principal and interest) on December 1, 2014, and would be subject to subordination at the discretion of the board of directors of T. Assume that the fair market value of such instruments would be $219 each. Based on these facts, the variable interest notes

are treated as stock because the fair market value of each note without its equity features i. e., $219) is less than 50 percent of its actual fair market value (i. e., $1,000/2 = $500).

Example (5). (a) on April 1, 1984, corporation U issues inflation provision notes in the principal amount of $557,700. The notes pay interest at a fixed rate of 6 percent on a fluctuating maturity value, and are due on April 1, 1994. The maturity value is determined according to the Consumer's Price Index, published monthly by the Bureau of Labor Statistics. Based on these facts, the inflation provision notes provide for fixed payments of both principal and interest. See paragraph (d)(4)(i)(A) and (ii)(B) of this section.

(b) The inflation provision notes are treated as indebtedness because they are straight debt instruments.

Example (6). (a) Corporation W owns a tract of land and is building 350 houses there. On August 15, 1985, P lends $300,000 to W pursuant to written agreement. The agreement provides that W will pay $175,000 to P "in lieu of interest," with $500 payable on the sale of each house. In addition, W is obligated to return P's $300,000 investment on demand at any time after December 31, 1990. The loan is secured by the general credit of W, and the written agreement contains appropriate protective provisions. Based on these facts, the written agreement provides for the fixed payment of $300,000 in principal and for contingent payment of $175,000.

(b) Assume that the fair market value of the obligation to P is $300,000. The obligation without its equity features would be a noninterest-bearing note for $300,000 due on December 31, 1990. Assume that the fair market value of such a note would be $170,000. Based on these facts, the obligation to P is treated as indebtedness because its fair market value without equity features (i. e., $170,000) is not less than 50 percent of its actual fair market value (i. e., $300,000/2 = $150,000).

Example (7). (a) On May 1, 1982, corporation X issues subordinated debentures due on May 1, 1992, in the principal amount of $1,000 each. Interest is payable annually at the fixed rate of 7 percent a year. Additional interest, which is contingent on the new profits of X, is payable at a maximum rate of 1 percent a year. Default in payment of interest, while not accelerating the maturity of the debenture, gives rise to a cause of action which the debenture holder may maintain against X for nonpayment of interest. Based on these facts, each debenture provides for a fixed $1,000 payment of principal and for fixed payments of interest at the rate of 7 percent a year.

(b) Assume that the fair market value of the subordinated debentures is $1,000 each. The debentures without their equity features would be 7 percent subordinated debentures with no provision for additional interest. Assume that the fair market value of such debentures would be $949 each. Based on these facts, the subordinated debentures issued by X are treated as indebtedness because the fair market value of each debenture without its equity features (i. e., $949) is not less than 50 percent of its actual fair market value (i. e., $1,000/2 = $500).

Example (8). (a) Corporation Z owns a large tract of land and is engaged in the business of developing, subdividing, and selling the land. On January 25, 1986, Z issues noninterest-bearing debenture bonds having a face value of $500,000 and a maturity date of January 25, 2011. The retirement of the bonds will be secured by the deposit of 10 percent of Z's gross receipts into a special bank account. However, if Z is liquidated after all of its lands have been sold, it will have no further obligation to retire any of the outstanding bonds unless the 10 percent payments have not been made as required. Based on these facts, the bonds do not provide for fixed payments of either principal or interest.

(b) The debenture bonds without their equity features would pay neither principal nor interest. Such instruments would be worthless. Therefore, the debenture bonds are treated as stock.

Example (9). (a) On August 1, 1983, U, an industrial corporation, issues debentures in the principal amount of $1,000 each. The debentures pay interest at a fixed rate of 8 percent, are due on August 1, 1993, and provide for the payment of principal and interest in German marks at the exchange rate in effect on August 1, 1983. Based on these facts, the debentures provide for fixed payments of both principal and interest. See paragraph (d)(4)(i)(B) and (ii)(B) of this section.

(b) The debentures are treated as indebtedness because they are straight debt instruments.

Example (10). (a) On September 1, 1984, corporation W issues floating rate notes in the principal amount of $100,000. The notes pay interest at 3 percentage points above the prime rate and are due on September 1, 1994. Based on these facts, the floating rate notes provide for fixed payments of both principal and interest. See paragraph (d)(4)(i)(B) and (ii)(A) of this section.

(b) The floating rate notes are treated as indebtedness because they are straight debt instruments.

Example (11). (a) A and B each own 50 percent of the only class of stock of corporation X. In addition to the outstanding stock, X has outstanding debentures held by independent creditors. On January 1, 1988, X redeems all of A's stock in exchange for a 10-year note with a principal amount of $500,000. Under the terms of the note, interest on outstanding principal is payable annually at a rate of 10 percent. Under applicable local law, the note is treated as indebtedness. However, under local law, each payment of principal and interest is subject to the restriction that no payment may be made at a time when the corporation is (or would be rendered) insolvent (i. e., unable to pay its debts as they become due). The insolvency restriction does not affect the classification of the principal or interest payments as fixed payments. See paragraph (d)(5)(iii) of this section. Therefore, the note provides for fixed payments of both principal and interest.

(b) The note is treated as indebtedness because it is a straight debt instrument. The result would be the same if, under local law, payments could not be made when X's liabilities exceeded its assets.

Example (12). (a) The facts are the same as in example (11) except that, under local law, the payments of principal and interest on the note are subject to the additional restriction that each payment can only be made out of X's earned surplus. Based on these facts, the note does not provide for fixed payments of principal or interest.

(b) The note without its equity features would pay neither principal nor interest. Such an instrument would be worthless. Therefore, the note is treated as stock.

Example (13). (a) On January 1, 1990, corporation Y issues 10,000 shares of $100 par value cumulative preferred stock. The preferred stock provides for an $8 dividend, payable annually, and for mandatory redemption beginning on January 1, 1996. Twenty percent of the preferred stock (selected by lot) must be redeemed on January 1 of each of 1996, 1997, 1998, 1999, and 2000. The redemption price is $100 plus all accrued but unpaid dividends. Annual dividends are payable only out of Y's earned surplus but mandatory redemption payments (including all accrued but unpaid dividends) are payable out of all "legally available funds." Under applicable local law, this means that the preferred stockholders have an absolute right to compel mandatory redemption payments subject to only two restrictions. First, mandatory redemption payments are not permitted if Y is (or would be rendered) insolvent (i. e., not able to pay its debts as they become due). Second, mandatory redemption payments are not permitted if they would impair Y's capital (i. e., if the fair market value of Y's remaining assets would be less than the sum of Y's liabilities and the liquidation value of other classes of preferred stock that are senior or equal in rank). Based on these facts, the preferred stock is treated as an instrument. See example (2) of § 1.385-10(c). Each share of preferred stock provides for fixed payments of $29.60 on January 1, 1996 ($20 redemption payment + ($8 dividend × 6)/5), $31.20 on January 1, 1997 ($20 + ($8 × 7)/5), $32.80 on January 1, 1998 ($20 + ($8 × 8)/5), $34.40 on January 1, 1999 ($20 + ($8 × 9)/5), and $36.00 on January 1, 2000 ($20 + ($8 × 10)/5).

(b) Assume that the fair market value of a share of preferred stock is $100. The preferred stock without its equity features would provide for the payment on January 1 of 1996, 1997, 1998, 1999, and 2000, respectively of $29.60, $31.20, $32.80, $34.40 and $36. Assume that the fair market value of an instrument providing for such payments would be $66.35. Based on these facts, the preferred stock is treated as indebtedness because the fair market value of each share of preferred stock without its equity features (i. e., $66.35) is not less than 50 percent of its actual fair market value (i. e., $100/2 = $50).

Example (14). (a) R is a corporation in the business of purchasing and operating office buildings and other commercial real property. On January 1, 1990, R purchases an office building from unrelated corporation S for a purchase price of $20 million. R pays $5 million in cash and issues a 15 year, 12-percent note for the remaining $15 million of the purchase price. The note is secured by a first mortgage on the office building but is otherwise nonrecourse with respect to R. The fair market value of the office building is $20 million and it is customary under the circumstances for the purchase of the building to be financed on a nonrecourse basis. Based on these facts, the note provides for fixed payments of principal and interest.

(b) The note is treated as indebtedness because it is a straight debt instrument.

. . . .

§ 1.385-6 Proportionality

(a) In general—(1) Scope. This section applies to a class of instruments if holdings of stock and the instruments are substantially proportionate. This section affects hybrid instruments, instruments not issued for money, instruments that are payable on demand, and certain other instruments where there is a change in terms or a failure to pay principal or interest, or where a corporation's debt-to-equity ratio is excessive.

(2) Proportionality. (i) Substantial proportionality is determined from all relevant facts and circumstances, including family or other relationships described in section 318(a).

(ii) Stock constructively owned under section 318(a)(4) (relating to options) is taken into account to the extent it is reasonable to expect, at the time of the determination, that the options may be exercised.

(3) Exceptions. (i) This section does not apply if a corporation's stock and instruments are widely held and the instruments are separately traded and readily marketable.

(ii) This section does not apply to any instrument held by an independent creditor (as defined in § 1.385-6(b)).

(4) To classes treated as one. Depending on the facts and circumstances, two or more classes of instruments may be considered together. For example:
(i) If—
(A) Two or more classes of instruments are issued pursuant to a plan, and

(B) Holdings of stock and the instruments will be substantially proportionate on completion of the plan,

then this section applies to each instrument immediately after it is issued.
(ii) If (regardless of whether issued pursuant to a plan)—
(A) Subsequent to their issuance, two or more classes of instruments are treated as a single class, and

(B) Considered as a single class, holdings of stock and such class are substantially proportionate,

then this section applies to each class beginning at the time of such treatment.

(5) One class treated as two. If two portions of a class of instruments are treated differently (e. g., interest is paid on one portion but not on the other), then each portion is treated as a separate class beginning at the time of such treatment.

(6) Illustrations. The following examples illustrate the application of this paragraph (a):

Example (1). A and B each own 50 percent of the stock of corporation X. In addition, A owns 40 percent of a class of debentures issued by X, and B owns the remaining 60 percent. Based on these facts, holdings of the debentures and holdings of stock in X are substantially proportionate, and this section applies to the debentures. The result would be the same if the debentures owned by B were owned by B's spouse.

Example (2). A, B, and C each own 100 shares of common stock in corporation Y. Y has no other stock of any class outstanding. However, Y does have outstanding subordinated 8-percent debentures in the principal amount of $100,000. A owns $40,000 of the debentures, B owns $30,000, C owns $20,000 and an independent creditor owns the remaining $10,000. Based on these facts, holdings of the debentures and holdings of stock in Y are substantially proportionate, and this section applies to the debentures held by A, B and C. However, this section does not apply to the debentures held by the independent creditor.

Example (3). The facts are the same as in example (2), except that A, B, and C each own $10,000 of debentures, and the independent creditor owns $70,000. Based on these facts, the holdings of stock and debentures are not substantially proportionate. Therefore, this section does not apply to the debentures upon their issuance.

Example (4). A, B, and C each own ⅓ of the common stock of corporation Z. Pursuant to a plan, Z issues $100,000 of 10-year, 8-percent debentures to A, $100,000 of 12-year, 8½ percent debentures to B, and $100,000 of 15-year, 9-percent debentures to C. Based on these facts, upon completion of the plan, holdings of the debentures and Z's stock are substantially proportionate. Therefore, this section applies to the debentures.

Example (5). Corporation P owns all the stock of corporations S and T. In addition, S owns 85 percent of a class of debentures issued by T. Based on these facts, holdings of the T stock and debentures are substantially proportionate. Therefore, this section applies to the debentures.

Example (6). Corporation V has more than 100,000 shareholders. On January 1, 1990, V issues $10 of debentures on each share of stock as a dividend. The stock and debentures are traded separately on a national securities exchange. Based on these facts, this section does not apply to the debentures.

Example (7). A and B each own 50 percent of the common stock of corporation W. In addition, W has outstanding $100,000 of 6-percent debentures owned entirely by A. Based on these facts, this section does not apply to the debentures.

Example (8). A owns all 100 shares of stock in corporation Y. A also owns 50 percent of a class of senior debentures issued by Y, and B owns the remaining 50 percent. In addition, B owns all of a class of junior debentures issued by Y, which are convertible into a total of 100 shares of Y stock of the same class as that held by A. Further, it is reasonable to expect that B may ultimately exercise the conversion privilege. Based on these facts, holdings of stock in Y and the senior debentures are treated as substantially proportionate under paragraph (a)(2) of this section. Consequently, this section applies to the senior debentures. However, holdings of Y stock and the junior debentures are not substantially proportionate.

Example (9) A owns all 100 shares of stock of corporation U. In addition, B owns $100,000 of convertible debentures issued by U. The debentures are convertible into 1,000 shares of U's common stock. Assume that it is reasonable to expect that B may ultimately exercise the conversion privilege. Based on these facts, B is treated as owning 1,000 shares of U common stock, and holdings of the convertible debentures and stock in U are substantially proportionate. Therefore, this section applies, and the convertible debentures are treated as stock under paragraph (c) (relating to hybrid instruments).

Example (10). Corporation M is a large manufacturing company whose products are sold through independent dealers. In order to assist individuals who do not have enough capital to become dealers, M has established a dealer investment plan. Pursuant to the dealer investment plan, M and unrelated individual I organize corporation D on January 1, 1982. M transfers $900,000 to D in exchange for 10-percent notes in the principal amount of $500,000 and 400 shares of class A stock. I transfers $100,000 to D in exchange for 1,000 shares of class B stock. The class B stock is nonvoting until all the Class A shares are redeemed for $1,000 each. At least 70 percent of D's earnings and profits must be used each year to retire the notes and to redeem the class A stock. I had no control over the redemption of stock and no right to have his stock redeemed while any of the class A stock is outstanding. M's investment will thus be systematically eliminated, and I will become the sole owner of D. Because the plan is akin to a security arrangement (see example (14) of § 1.305-3(e)), holdings of the stock and notes are not substantially proportionate. Therefore, this section does not apply to the notes. However, for purposes of section 1232 (relating to original issue discount), the issue price of the notes is equal to their fair market value. See § 1.1232-3(b)(2)(ii) (relating to investment units).

Example (11). Corporation S is a small business investment company operating under the Small Business Investment Act of 1958 (15 U.S.C. 661 and following). Individual J is an electrical engineer. On January 1, 1983, S and J, who are otherwise unrelated, form corporation X to manufacture high technology electrical components. X has a total authorized capital of 2,000 shares of common stock. S transfers $810,000 to X for 9-percent subordinated debentures in the principal amount of $800,000, 100 shares of common stock, and warrants to acquire an additional 900 shares of common stock at $100 a share. J transfers $100,000 to X for 1,000 shares of common stock. Based on these facts, holdings of the stock and debentures are not substantially proportionate. Therefore, this section does not apply to the subordinated debentures. However, for purposes of section 1232 (relating to original issue discount), the issue price of the debentures is equal to their fair market value. See § 1.1232-3(b)(2)(ii) (relating to investment units).

Example (12). Corporation T is a medium-sized supplier of computer software. Individual K is the manager of T's military applications division. On January 1, 1984, K forms corporation Y to acquire the assets of T's military applications division. K transfers $100,000 to Y for all 100 shares of Y's outstanding common stock. In addition, Y obtains financing from the following sources: $2 million from a small business investment company for 8-percent junior subordinated debentures and warrants to acquire 100 shares of common stock, $3 million from an insurance company for 14-percent senior subordinated debentures, and $2,500,000 from a bank for 10-percent secured notes. K is not otherwise related to T, the small business investment company, the insurance company, or the bank. Based on these facts, there is no substantial proportionality between holdings of stock and any class or classes of instruments. Therefore, this section does not apply to any of the instruments. However, for purposes of section 1232 (relating to original issue discount), the issue price of the junior subordinated debentures is equal to their fair market value. See § 1.1232-3(b)(2)(ii) (relating to investment units).

Example (13). A is the sole shareholder of corporation X. On January 1, 1987, X issues $50,000 of Class B debentures to A and $50,000 of Class B debentures to independent creditor K. Based on these facts, holdings of the X stock and the Class B debentures are not substantially proportionate. However, on January 1, 1989, A voluntarily under paragraph (a)(5) of this section, A's debentures are treated as a separate class beginning on January 1, 1989. Thus, they may be treated as stock under paragraph (j) of this section (relating to a change in terms). The result would be the same if, on January 1, 1989, X missed an interest payment due on A's debentures, but made the payment on K's debentures. In this event, A's debentures might be treated as stock under paragraph (k) of this section (relating to nonpayment of interest).

Example (14). (a) A and B each own 50 percent of the stock of corporation Z, a calendar year taxpayer. Pursuant to a plan, Z issues $100,000 of Class A convertible debentures to A on January 1, 1983 and issues $100,000 of Class B convertible debentures to B on January 1, 1985. Based on these facts, the two classes of debentures are considered together. Therefore, holdings of the debentures and the

STOCK OR INDEBTEDNESS § 1.385-6

stock are substantially proportionate and each class of debentures is treated as stock upon issuance under section 1.385–6(c) (relating to hybrid instruments issued proportionately).

(b) The facts are the same as in (a) except that the two classes of debentures are not issued pursuant to a plan. Based on these facts, this section does not apply to either class of debentures upon their issuance.

(c) The facts are the same as in (b) except that Z fails to pay interest on the debentures accrued during 1989. Based on these facts, this section applies to the two classes of debentures as of January 1, 1989 and the debentures may be treated as stock under paragraph (k) of this section (relating to nonpayment of interest). See paragraph (a)(4)(ii) of this section.

Example (15). E owns all of the common stock of corporation X. In addition, F (who is unrelated to E) owns all of the preferred stock of X. The preferred stock is an 8-percent non-participating nonconvertible, nonvoting preferred stock. Further, E owns a class of debentures issued by X. Based on these facts, holdings of the X stock and debentures are substantially proportionate, and this section applies to the debentures. However, if F owned all of the debentures, this section would not apply.

(7) Special rule. (i) If, pursuant to an agreement or arrangement—

(A) The terms of an instrument issued to a shareholder are not fixed at arm's length or the instrument is not enforced according to its terms, and

(B) There are related, compensating non-arm's length transactions, then the Commissioner may treat holdings of the instrument and the corporation's stock as substantially proportionate.

(ii) The following examples illustrate the application of this subparagraph (7):

Example (1). A and B each own 50 percent of the common stock of corporation X. On January 1, 1985, A lends $500,000 to X in exchange for a 10-year, 10-percent $500,000 note. B is the general manager of X. During 1987, pursuant to an arrangement between A and B, X does not pay the $50,000 of interest on A's note and X pays B $50,000 less compensation than B would be entitled to under B's employment contract with X. Based on these facts, holdings of X's stock and the note will be treated as substantially proportionate. Therefore, this section applies to the note and the note may be reclassified as stock under paragraph (k) of this section (relating to nonpayment of interest).

Example (2). C and D each own 50 percent of the stock of corporation Y. On January 1, 1987, C leases a townhouse to Y for a ten-year term. Y agrees to pay an annual rent of $10,000 and additional rent equal to 20 percent of the net annual rentals from the townhouse. Also on January 1, 1987, as part of the same arrangement, D lends $100,000 to Y in exchange for a 10-year debenture. Ten percent annual interest is payable on the debenture. In addition, the holder of the debenture is entitled to

contingent annual interest equal to 20 percent of the net annual rentals from the townhouse. Based on these facts, holdings of the debenture and Y's stock shall be treated as substantially proportionate. Accordingly, the debenture will be treated as stock under paragraph (c) of this section (relating to hybrid instruments issued proportionately).

(b) Independent creditor—(1) In general. For purposes of the regulations under section 385, all relevant facts and circumstances must be taken into account in determining whether a creditor is independent.

(2) Safe harbor. In applying this section to a class of instruments issued by a corporation, a creditor is deemed to be independent if—

(i) Stock owned by the corporation would not be attributed to the creditor under the constructive ownership rules of section 318(a) (as modified by subparagraph (3) of this paragraph (b)), and

(ii) The creditor's holdings of stock and instruments issued by the corporation are not substantially proportionate.

(3) Constructive ownership. For purposes of subparagraph (2)(i) of this paragraph (b)—

(i) The constructive ownership rules of section 318(a) shall be applied by substituting "5 percent" for "50 percent" in sections 318(a)(2)(C) and 318(a)(3)(C), and

(ii) In determining whether any person owns 5 percent or more of the stock of a corporation, stock constructively owned by an unrelated person under section 318(a)(4) (relating to options) is not taken into account.

(4) Illustrations. The following examples illustrate the application of this paragraph (b):

Example (1). Individual C owns (actually or under the constructive ownership rules of section 318(a) as modified by paragraph (b)(3) of this section) 5 percent or more in value of the stock of corporation Y. Based on these facts, stock owned by Y is attributed to C under the constructive ownership rules of section 318(a) as modified by paragraph (b)(3) of this section. Consequently, C does not come within the safe harbor of paragraph (b)(2) of this section with respect to instruments issued by Y.

Example (2). Individual A owns all 100 outstanding shares of stock and an option to acquire an additional 1,000 shares of stock in corporation X. Individual B owns an option to acquire 10 shares of stock in X. Applying the constructive ownership rules of section

875

318(a) as modified by paragraph (b)(3) of this section, B is considered to own 10 out of 110 outstanding shares of stock in X. Therefore, B does not come within the safe harbor of paragraph (b)(2) of this section. The result would be the same if the option owned by B were owned by B's spouse.

Example (3). Corporation Y obtains a $100,000 loan from C, an unrelated commercial bank. As a condition for making a loan, C obtains the right to designate one of Y's directors. Based on these facts, C is an independent creditor of Y.

Example (4). Individual E owns 96 percent of the stock of corporation Z, and individual F owns the remaining 4 percent. In addition, E owns 96.2 percent of a class of debentures issued by Z, and F owns the remaining 3.8 percent. Because F's own holdings of Z stock and debentures are substantially proportionate, F does not come within the safe harbor of paragraph (b)(2) of this section.

(c) Hybrid instruments—(1) In general. If this section applies to a hybrid instrument immediately after it is issued, then the instrument is treated as stock.

(2) Hybrid instrument. For the definition of the term "hybrid instrument", see § 1.385-3(e).

(3) Illustration. The following example illustrates the application of this paragraph (c):

Example. Corporation X's only outstanding stock is 100 shares of common stock. Individual A owns 50 shares, individual B owns 30 shares, and individual C owns 20 shares. On January 1, 1990, X issues $100,000 of convertible debentures. Sixty thousand dollars of the convertible debentures are issued to A, $25,000 are issued to B, and the remaining $15,000 is issued to C. Based on these facts, the convertible debentures are treated as stock.

(d) Instruments not issued for money —(1) In general. An instrument issued by a corporation is treated as stock if—

(i) This section applies to the instrument immediately after it is issued,

(ii) The stated annual rate of interest on the instrument is not reasonable (within the meaning of paragraph (e) of this section), and

(iii) The issuance of the instrument does not give rise to original issue discount under section 1232(a)(3) or amortizable bond premium under § 1-61-12(c)(2).

(2) Special rule. For purposes of this paragraph (d), the reasonableness of a rate of interest is determined on the day an instrument is issued.

(3) Exception. (i) This paragraph (d) does not apply to an instrument that is issued in exchange for an equal or greater principal amount of indebtedness of the issuing corporation if—

(A) An independent creditor holding the outstanding indebtedness would, in the exercise of ordinary diligence, have agreed to the exchange, and

(B) The issuing corporation would, in the exercise of ordinary diligence, have agreed to make the exchange with an independent creditor holding the outstanding indebtedness.

(ii) For purposes of subdivision (i) of this subparagraph (3), the principal amount of indebtedness includes interest accrued but unpaid up until the date of the exchange, but only to the extent that such interest is paid with principal in the exchange.

(4) Illustrations. The following examples illustrate the application of this paragraph (d):

Example (1). J organizes corporation W on December 10, 1985 to operate a distributorship of radios, television sets, and other types of electrical appliances. On the same day, J transfers certain franchises and other assets to W in exchange for all of W's capital stock and $100,000 of 10-year, 9-percent debenture bonds. Assume that on December 10, 1985, 9 percent is not a reasonable rate of interest (within the meaning of paragraph (e) of this section). Based on these facts, the debenture bonds are treated as stock.

Example (2). Corporation X operates a wholesale electrical supply business. In the course of a recapitalization on December 30, 1990, X issues 2,100 Class B debentures to L in exchange for X common stock. Immediately after the recapitalization, L holds 90 percent of the common stock of X. The principal amount of each Class B debenture is $100, and each debenture pays $50 a year in interest. Assume that on December 30, 1990, 50 percent is not a reasonable rate of interest (within the meaning of paragraph (e) of this section). Based on these facts, the Class B debentures issued to L are treated as stock.

Example (3). On January 1, 1987, individuals A, B, and C transfer a tract of undeveloped land and $4,500 in cash to newly formed corporation X. In exchange, each receives 100 shares of stock and a 2-year, 10-percent promissory note for $110,000. Assume that 10 percent is not a reasonable rate of interest (within the meaning of paragraph (e) of this section). Based on these facts, the promissory notes are treated as stock for all purposes of the Internal Revenue Code. In particular, the notes are not treated as "other property" within the meaning of section 351(b). Thus, no gain or loss is recognized on the transfer of the land to X (see section 351), and X's basis in the land is the same as it was in the hands of A, B, and C (see section 362(a)(1)).

Example (4). B is the sole shareholder of corporation Y. On January 1, 1990, Y issues a $30,000, 10-percent note to B in exchange for $30,000. The note is due on January 1, 2000 and is treated as indebtedness under § 1.385-4 (a). Interest on the note is paid according to its terms through 1999. During 1999, Y encounters business difficulties. On December 11, 1999, Y issues a new note to B in exchange for the outstanding note. The terms of the new note are identical to those of the outstanding note except that the new note is due on January 1, 2002 and is subordinated to a new bank loan being made at the time of the exchange. Assume that an independent creditor holding the outstanding note would, in the exercise of ordinary diligence, have agreed to exchange the outstanding note for the new note. Assume also that Y would, in the exercise of ordinary diligence, have agreed to the exchange even if the outstanding note were held by an independent creditor. Based on these facts, this paragraph (d) does not apply to the new note. However, the new note is subject to paragraphs (j), (k), and (l) of this section.

(e) Reasonable rate of interest—(1) In general. The annual rate of interest on an instrument issued by a corporation is reasonable if it is within the normal range of rates paid to independent creditors on similar instruments by corporations of the same general size and in the same general industry, geographic location, and financial condition on the date the determination is made.

(2) Rule of convenience. For purposes of the regulations under section 385, an annual rate of interest on an instrument is considered to be reasonable if—

(i) On the date the determination is made, (A) it is equal to the rate in effect under section 6621, the prime rate in effect any local commercial bank, or a rate determined from time to time by the Secretary taking into consideration the average yield on outstanding marketable obligations of the United States of comparable maturity or (B) it is in between any two of the rates described in subdivision (A) of this subdivision (i), and

(ii) At the end of the taxable year in which the determination is made, the debt-to-equity ratio of the issuing corporation is not greater than 1:1.

(3) Exception. Paragraph (e)(2) of this section does not apply to an instrument that evidences a nonrecourse liability.

(4) Local commercial bank. The term "local commercial bank" includes any commercial bank at which the issuing corporation ordinarily does business.

(5) Illustrations. The following examples illustrate the application of this paragraph (e):

Example (1). Individual A is the sole shareholder of corporation X. On January 1, 1990, A lends $100,000 to X in exchange for a 10-percent note. At about the same time, a local commercial bank lends $100,000 to X in exchange for a 10-percent note with approximately the same terms. The bank loan is personally guaranteed by A. However, the guarantee is required pursuant to the bank's normal lending practice as a substitute for detailed covenants, and the bank loan was made principally on X's credit (and not A's). Based on these facts, 10 percent is a reasonable rate of interest.

Example (2). A is the sole shareholder of corporation X. On July 1, 1989, A lends $100,000 to X in exchange for an 8-year note bearing annual interest at 10 percent. On December 31, 1989, X's debt-to-equity ratio, computed in accordance with the principles of paragraphs (g) and (h) of this section, is 1:1. On July 1, 1989, the section 6621 rate is 12 percent; the prime rate is 14 percent; and the interest rate for 10-year obligations determined by the Secretary pursuant to paragraph (e)(2)(i) of this section is 10 percent. Based on these facts, the rate of interest on the note is considered to be reasonable.

. . . .

(f) Excessive debt—(1) In general. If, immediately after an instrument is issued by a corporation—

(i) **This section applies to the instrument, and**

(ii) **The corporation's debt is excessive,**

then the instrument is treated as stock.

(2) Excessive debt. The corporation's debt is "excessive" if (i) all of the instrument's terms and conditions and (ii) the corporation's financial structure, taken together, would not be satisfactory to a bank, insurance company or similar lending institution which makes ordinary commercial loans. For this purpose, the corporation's size, industry, geographic location, and financial condition must be taken into account.

(3) Safe harbor. A corporation's debt is not excessive if—

(i) The corporation's outside ratio is less than or equal to 10:1, and

(ii) The corporation's inside ratio is less than or equal to 3:1.

(4) Ratios. The corporation's outside ratio is the debt-to-equity ratio determined under paragraphs (g) and (h) of this section. Its inside ratio is determined in the same manner by excluding liabilities to independent creditors (except in computing stockholders' equity). Both ratios are determined at the end of the taxable year in which the instrument is issued.

(5) **Exception.** This paragraph (f) does not apply to instruments issued in exchange for an equal or greater principal amount of indebtedness. For purposes of the preceding sentence, the principal amount of indebtedness includes interest accrued but unpaid up until the date of the exchange, but only to the extent that such interest is paid with principal in the exchange.

(6) **Illustrations.** The following examples illustrate the application of this paragraph (f):

Example (1). A, a nonresident alien, forms corporation X on December 31, 1982. X uses the calendar year as the taxable year. A transfers $1 million to X on December 31, 1982 for $200,000 of common stock and $800,000 of 22–percent subordinated notes. In addition, X borrows $200,000 from an unrelated commercial bank. Thus, X's inside debt-to-equity ratio (determined under paragraph (f)(4) of this section) is greater than 3:1 (i. e., $800,000: $200,000 = 4:1). Assume that a financial institution (such as a commercial bank) which makes ordinary commercial loans normally would lend X a maximum of between 1 and 1½ times A's equity investment under the terms and conditions of the subordinated notes. Assume further, however, that a lender engaged in the business of making high risk loans would lend X four times A's equity investment under the terms and conditions of the subordinate notes. Based on these facts, the subordinated notes are treated as stock.

Example (2). Individual B forms corporation Y on December 31, 1982. Y uses the calendar year as the taxable year. On December 31, 1982, Y acquires rental property from an unrelated third party for $100,000. It obtains the $100,000 from the following sources: $10,000 from B for common stock, $10,000 from C on a second mortgage note, and $80,000 from D on a first mortgage note. Assume that C and D are B's father and mother. Also assume that the terms and conditions of the mortgage notes and Y's financial structure would be satisfactory to financial institutions (such as commercial banks) which make ordinary commercial loans. Based on these facts, the mortgage notes are not treated as stock under this paragraph (f).

(g) **Debt-to-equity ratio.** The following rules apply for purposes of the regulations under section 385:

(1) **In general.** The debt-to-equity ratio of a corporation is the ratio that—

(i) The corporation's liabilities (excluding trade accounts payable, accrued operating expenses and taxes, and other similar items) bears to

(ii) The stockholders' equity.

(2) **Stockholders' equity.** The stockholders' equity in a corporation is the excess of—

(i) The adjusted basis of its assets (less reserves for bad debts, if applicable, and other similar asset offsets) over

(ii) Its liabilities (including liabilities excluded under paragraph (g)(1)(i) of this section).

(3) **Operating rules.** Except as provided in paragraph (g)(5) of this section, the adjusted basis of a corporation's assets and the amount of its liabilities are determined—

(i) In accordance with the tax accounting principles properly used by the corporation in determining taxable income; and

(ii) Without regard to the treatment of any interest as stock or indebtedness by reason of section 385, except that preferred stock is considered a liability if it is treated as indebtedness under the regulations under section 385.

(4) **Illustrations.** The following examples illustrate the application of this paragraph (g):

Example (1). On December 31, 1990, corporation M has assets with an adjusted basis of $150,000 and liabilities of $100,000. The stockholders' equity in M is $50,000 (i. e., $150,000–$100,000). Assume that M has no trade accounts payable, accrued taxes and operating expenses, etc., and that the special rules in paragraph (g)(5) of this section do not apply. Based on these facts, the debt-to-equity ratio of corporation M on December 31, 1990 is 2:1 (i. e., $100,000:$50,000).

Example (2). On December 31, 1990, corporation N has assets with an adjusted basis of $150,000. In addition, N has liabilities of $100,000, including $30,000 of trade accounts payable, accrued taxes and operating expenses, etc. The stockholders' equity in N is $50,000 (i. e., $150,000–$100,000). Assume that the special rules in paragraph (g)(5) of this section do not apply. Based on these facts, N has a debt-to-equity ratio on December 31, 1990 of 7:5 (i. e., $70,000:$50,000).

Example (3). On December 31, 1982, foreign corporation F organizes domestic corporation D to acquire and operate a coal mine. D uses the calendar year as the taxable year. Assume that F transfers $10 million to D on December 31, 1982, in exchange for $5 million of 28-percent, 25-year debentures and 100 shares of common stock. Also assume that the interest rate generally paid on similar debentures issued to independent creditors by corporations of the same general size and in the same general industry, geographical location, and financial condition is approximately 14 percent and that 28 percent is higher than the 3 rates described in paragraph (e)(2)(i) of this section (relating to the reasonable rate of interest rule of convenience). Based on these facts, the fair market value of the debentures is approximately $9.8 million. Therefore, the balance sheet of D on December 31, 1981 is approximately as follows:

Assets—$10 million cash. Liabilities and stockholders' equity—$5.0 million debentures; $4.8 million bond premium; $9.8 million total liabilities; $0.2 million stockholders' equity = $10.0 million.

Accordingly, D has a debt-to-equity ratio of approximately 49:1 (i. e., $9.8 million: $0.2 million).

(5) **Special rules.** (i) In the case of a corporation that uses the cash method of accounting, the adjusted basis of trade accounts receivable shall be deemed to be equal to the face amount of the receivables (less an appropriate reserve for uncollectibles).

(ii)(A) In determining the debt-to-equity ratio of a corporation at the end of a taxable year, the stockholders' equity shall be increased by the amount of any net operating loss (determined without regard to sections 1211(a) and 1212) sustained by the corporation during the taxable year.

(B) The following example illustrates the application of this subdivision (ii):

Example. On January 1, 1985, individual A organizes corporation T and transfers $100,000 to it for $50,000 of stock and a $50,000 note. At the end of T's first taxable year, T has assets with an adjusted basis of $120,000 and liabilities of $80,000, including $30,000 of trade accounts payable, accrued taxes and operating expenses, etc. T also has a net operating loss (determined without regard to sections 1211(a) and 1212) for the taxable year of $10,000. Based on these facts, T's stockholders' equity at the end of the taxable year is $50,000 (i. e., ($120,000–$80,000) + $10,000). Consequently, T's debt-to-equity ratio is 1:1 (i .e., $50,000:$50,000).

(iii) In determining the debt-to-equity ratio of a corporation that is a bank (as defined in section 581) or is primarily engaged in a lending or finance business (as defined in section 279(c)(5)), adjustments shall be made in accordance with the principles of section 279(c)(5)(A).

(iv) In determining the debt-to-equity ratio of an insurance company (as defined in § 1.801–1(b)), insurance reserves shall be treated in the same manner as trade accounts payable.

(v) A liability is treated in the same manner as a trade account payable if it is—

(A) Incurred under a commercial financing agreement (such as an automobile "floorplan" agreement) to buy an item of inventory,

(B) Secured by the item, and

(C) Due on (or before) sale of the item.

(vi)(A) The debt-to-equity ratio shall be computed without regard to distortions created by a temporary contribution to equity or any similar contrivance.

(B) The following example illustrates the application of this subdivision (vi):

Example. Individual A organizes corporation X on December 31, 1985. X uses the calendar year as the taxable year. A contributes $100,000 in cash and property with a basis of $20,000 to X in exchange for 1,000 shares of common stock and a 10-percent note worth $20,000. On January 4, 1986, X redeems 900 shares of stock for $90,000 in cash. Based on these facts, X's debt-to-equity ratio on December 31, 1985 is determined by not treating the $90,000 paid in redemption of stock on January 4, 1986 as an asset of X. Therefore, the debt-to-equity ratio is 2:1 (i. e., $20,000:$10,000).

(h) **Affiliated groups—(1) In general.** For purposes of the regulations under section 385, the debt-to-equity ratio of a member of an affiliated group of corporations (within the meaning of section 279(g)) is determined in accordance with paragraph (g) of this section and this subparagraph (1). If one includible corporation ("X") owns stock in another includible corporation ("Y"), then X's debt-to-equity ratio is determined as follows:

(i) X is treated as having a ratable share of Y's assets and liabilities. This ratable share is determined by dividing—

(A) The fair market value of the Y stock owned by X, by

(B) The fair market value of all of Y's stock.

(ii) X's investments in Y and Y's liabilities to X are eliminated. In addition, any other duplication in the amount of X's money and other assets and liabilities resulting from the application of this subparagraph (1)(for example, resulting from Y's ownership of stock in X) is eliminated.

(2) **Illustrations.** The following examples illustrate the application of this paragraph (h):

Example (1). Corporations P and S–1 comprise an affiliated group, P owning all the stock of S–1. On December 31, 1985, P's only asset is stock in S–1, and P has no liabilities. In addition, S–1 has assets with an adjusted basis of $200,000 and liabilities of $150,000. Assume that S–1 has no trade accounts payable, accrued taxes and operating expenses, etc. and that the special rules in paragraph (g)(5) of this section do not apply. Based on these facts, P is treated as having assets with an adjusted basis of $200,000 and liabilities of $150,000. Therefore, P's debt-to-equity ration is 3:1 (i. e., $150,000:-$50,000).

Example (2). The facts are the same as in example (1), except that S–1's liabilities include a $50,000 note payable to P, and P's assets consist of this note and the S–1 stock. Eliminating this note, S–1's liabilities are only $100,000. Based on these facts, P is treated as having liabilities of $100,000 and assets with an adjusted basis of $200,000. Therefore, P's debt-to-ratio is 1:1 (i. e., $100,000:$100,000).

Example (3). (a) The facts are the same as in example (1), except that S–1's assets include 80 percent of the one class of stock of corporation S–2, which also is a member of the affiliated group. S–1's adjusted basis in the stock of S–2 is $15,000. In addition, S–2 has assets with an adjusted basis of $50,000 and no liabilities.

(b) Based on these facts, S–1 is treated as having $40,000 (i. e., 80 percent of $50,000) of S–2's assets instead of the S–2 stock. Therefore, S–1 is treated as having assets with an adjusted basis of $225,000 and liabilities of $150,-000. Thus, S–1's debt-to-equity ratio is 2:1 (i. e., $150,000:$75,000).

(i) [Reserved]

(j) Change in terms—(1) In general. If—

(i) The holder agrees to postpone the maturity date or otherwise to make a substantial change in the terms of an instrument,

(ii) The instrument is treated as indebtedness under the regulations under section 385, and

(iii) This section applies to the instrument on the day of agreement,

then (for purposes of the regulations under section 385) the instrument is treated as newly issued in exchange for property on the day of agreement. Thus, beginning on the day of agreement the instrument may be treated as stock under paragraph (c) of this section (relating to hybrid instruments), paragraph (d) of this section (relating to certain instruments not issued for money), paragraph (f) of this section (relating to excessive debt), or paragraph (l) of this section (relating to instruments payable on demand). However, the exceptions to paragraphs (d) and (f) of this section may apply to the constructive exchange. See paragraphs (d)(3) and (f)(5) of this section.

(2) Substantial. For purposes of this paragraph (j), each change in the terms of an instrument is substantial if the fair market value of the instrument could be materially affected by that change. Thus, for example, subordination (however effected) or a change in interest rate is ordinarily a substantial change. On the other hand, a mere substitution of collateral need not be a substantial change. In addition, prepayment will not be considered a substantial change in terms.

(3) Day of agreement. For purposes of this paragraph (j), the "day of agreement" is the day the issuer and the holder enter into a binding contract to change the terms of an instrument.

(4) Illustrations. The following examples illustrate the application of this paragraph (j):

Example (1). A is the sole shareholder of corporation X. On January 1, 1990, X issues a $10,000 9-percent note to A for $10,000 in cash. The note is due on January 1, 2000, and is treated as indebtedness under § 1.385-4(a). However, on December 10, 1995, A and X agree to extend the maturity of the note until January 1, 2015. Assume that under the terms of the agreement the note will continue to pay 9-percent interest, and that on December 10, 1995, 9-percent is not a reasonable rate of interest (within the meaning of paragraph (e) of this section) for a note due on January 1, 2015. Also assume that an independent creditor holding the note would not, in the exercise of ordinary diligence, have agreed to the extension of maturity and that, therefore, the exception of paragraph (d)(3) of this section is not applicable. Based on these facts, the note would be treated as stock under paragraph (d) of this section if it were newly issued in exchange for property on December 10, 1995. Therefore, the note is reclassified as stock on December 10, 1995.

Example (2). A is the sole shareholder of corporation X. X issues a $20,000, 10-percent note to A for $20,000 in cash on January 1, 2005. The note is due on January 1, 2007, and is treated as indebtedness under § 1.385-4(a). On December 10, 2005, A and X agree to extend the maturity of the note until January 1, 2037, and to increase the interest rate from 10 to 11 percent. For purposes of this paragraph (j), both changes in terms made on December 10, 2005 are substantial because both could materially affect the fair market value of the note. The result is the same even if the two changes are mutually offsetting in the sense that, taken together, they have no material effect on the fair market value of the note.

Example (3). B is the sole shareholder of corporation Y. On January 1, 1990, Y issues a $30,000, 10-percent note to B in exchange for

$30,000. The note is due on January 1, 2000 and is treated as indebtedness under § 1.385-4 (a). Interest on the note is paid according to its terms through 1999. During 1999, Y encounters business difficulties. On December 11, 1999, B agrees to extend the note until January 1, 2002 and also agrees to subordinate the note to a new bank loan being made at this time. Based on these facts, the note is treated (for purposes of the regulations under section 385) as newly issued in exchange for an equal principal amount of indebtedness. Assume that an independent creditor holding the note would, in the exercise of ordinary diligence, have agreed to both the extension of maturity and the subordination to the new bank loan. Assume also that Y would, in the exercise of ordinary diligence, have agreed to the extension and the subordination even if the note were held by an independent creditor. Based on these additional facts, the note continues to be treated as indebtedness notwithstanding the extension of maturity and the subordination to the new bank loan. See paragraph (d)(3) and example (4) of paragraph (d) (4) of this section. However, the note continues to be subject to this paragraph (j) and to paragraphs (k) and (l) of this section.

(k) Nonpayment of interest—(1) In general. If—

(i) A corporation fails to pay all or part of the interest due and payable on an instrument during a taxable year,

(ii) This section applies to the instrument on the last day of the taxable year, and

(iii) The owner of the instrument fails to exercise the ordinary diligence of an independent creditor,

then the instrument is treated as stock beginning on the later of the first day of the taxable year during which the failure to pay occurs on the first day on which this section applied to the instrument.

(2) Illustrations. The following examples illustrate the application of paragraph (k)(1) of this section:

Example (1). N is the sole shareholder of corporation Y. On January 1, 1986, Y issues $100,000 of 10-year, 10-percent debentures. Eighty thousand dollars of the debentures are issued to N and are treated as indebtedness under § 1.385-4(a). The remaining debentures are issued to independent creditors. Y pays all interest accrued on the debentures semiannually until 1991. Because of adverse business conditions, Y does not pay the interest accrued in 1991 on either the debentures held by N or the debentures held by the independent creditors. Both N and the independent creditors decide not to bring suit against Y in the hope that conditions will improve and that Y will be able to meet its obligations. Based on these facts, the debentures held by N continue to be treated as indebtedness because N has not failed to exercise the ordinary diligence of an independent creditor.

Example (2). (a) M is the sole shareholder of X, a corporation that uses the calendar year as the taxable year. On January 1, 1985, X issues $100,000 of 10-year, 9-percent debentures. Ten thousand dollars of the debentures are issued to M and are treated as indebtedness under § 1.385-4(a). The remaining debentures are issued to independent creditors. X pays all interest accrued on the debentures semiannually until 1990. Because of adverse business conditions, X does not pay the interest accrued in 1990 on the debentures held by M. However, X continues to pay interest on the debentures held by the independent creditors. Based on these facts, the debentures held by M are treated as a separate class of instruments beginning on January 1, 1990. See paragraph (a)(5) of this section. Since the debentures held by M are treated as a separate class of instruments, the holdings of M's debentures and the stock of X are substantially proportionate as of January 1, 1990.

(b) M has failed to take the steps that a reasonably diligent independent creditor would take to secure payment of interest. Based on these facts, the debentures held by M are treated as stock beginning on January 1, 1990. However, the debentures held by the independent creditors are not affected.

Example (3). L owns 80 percent of the stock of Z, a corporation that uses the calendar year as the taxable year. On January 1, 1985, Z issues $200,000 of 10-year, 10-percent unsecured notes to L. Z pays all interest accrued on the notes semiannually until 1990. Because of adverse business conditions, Z does not pay the interest accrued in 1990 on the notes. On February 1, 1991, L agrees to postpone $10,000 of the interest accrued in 1990 until the notes mature on January 1, 1995. In addition, Z agrees to pledge certain collateral as security for the debentures. Taking into account Z's prior record of paying all interest accrued until 1990, the pledge of collateral, and all other relevant facts and circumstances, it is assumed that L has exercised the ordinary diligence of an independent creditor. Based on these facts, the notes continue to be treated as indebtedness.

(3) Failure to pay. For purposes of this section, a corporation fails to pay interest on an instrument during a taxable year of the corporation if the interest is not actually paid within 90 days after the end of the year. For this purpose, payment of interest with property other than money will be considered actual payment, but only to the extent of the fair market value of such property. For example, payment of interest with a note will be considered actual payment, but only to the extent of the fair market value of the note.

(4) Special rule. (i) For purposes of this paragraph (k), interest accrued while this section does not apply to the instrument is disregarded.

(ii) The following example illustrates the application of this subparagraph (4):

Example. Individual A owns all the stock of X, a corporation that uses the calendar year as the taxable year. On January 1, 1982, X issues $10,000 of 8-percent debentures to B, an independent creditor. The debentures are treated as indebtedness under § 1.385-4(a) (relating to instruments generally). Interest on the debentures is payable semiannually on January 1 and July 1 of each year. X fails to make the $400 payment of interest due on July 1, 1986, and A then buys the debentures from B. X actually pays the $400 interest due on January 1, 1987, but A forgives the $400 payment that was due on July 1, 1986. Based on these facts, the debentures are not treated as stock under this paragraph (k). There is no requirement that interest accrued while B held the debentures must be paid. However, X may have income under § 1.61-12(a) (relating to discharge of indebtedness).

(l) Payable on demand—(1) Initial classification. If immediately after it is issued—

(i) This section applies to an instrument,

(ii) By its terms, the instrument is payable on demand, and

(iii) The stated annual rate of interest on the instrument is not reasonable (within the meaning of paragraph (e) of this section),

then the instrument is treated as stock.

(2) Reclassification. If for any taxable year (or portion thereof)—

(i) Either by its terms or by operation of paragraph (l)(3) of this section, an instrument is payable on demand,

(ii) This section applies to the instrument, and

(iii) The issuing corporation fails to pay interest on the instrument at a reasonable rate,

then the instrument is treated as stock beginning on the first day of that taxable year (or portion thereof). For purposes of this subparagraph (2), a rate of interest is considered reasonable if it is reasonable (within the meaning of paragraph (e) of this section) as of any day of the taxable year.

(3) Nonpayment of principal. If—

(i) The issuing corporation fails to make a scheduled payment of principal on an instrument within 90 days after the payment is due, and

(ii) The holder of the instrument fails to exercise the ordinary diligence of an independent creditor,

then, for purposes of this paragraph (l) the instrument is considered to be payable on demand beginning on the day after the day the principal is due.

(4) Exceptions. (i) This paragraph (l) does not apply to an instrument that is actually retired within 6 months after the day of issue provided that the sum of—

(A) The outstanding principal amount of all such instruments, plus

(B) The outstanding balance of all loans described in § 1.385-7(a)(2)(i),

does not exceed $25,000 on the day of issue. For this purpose, an instrument is not considered to be actually retired if it is reissued, renewed, or offset in any manner.

(ii)(A) If a failure to pay interest on an instrument at a reasonable rate results solely from a failure to pay interest when due, then paragraph (l)(2) of this section does not apply. See, however, paragraph (k) of this section (relating to nonpayment of interest when due).

(B) The following example illustrates the application of this subdivision (ii):

Example. Individual A owns 100 percent of the stock of corporation X. On January 1, 1990, X issues a 14-percent demand note to A. X uses the calendar year as its taxable year. Assume that 14 percent is a reasonable rate of interest (within the meaning of paragraph (e) of this section) on January 1, 1990, but that X fails to pay any part of the interest due on the note for the taxable year 1990. Based on these facts, paragraph (l)(2) of this section does not apply. However, if A has failed to exercise the ordinary diligence of an independent creditor, the note will be treated as stock under paragraph (k) of this section.

(5) Illustrations. The following examples illustrate the application of this paragraph (l) and related provisions:

Example (1). J and N operate a partnership that distributes beer. On April 1, 1989, J and N organize corporation T and transfer the assets of the partnership to the corporation. In exchange for the assets of the partnership, J and N each receive half of the common stock of T and an 8-percent demand note for $45,000. Assume that 8 percent is not a reasonable rate of interest (within the meaning of paragraph (e) of this section) on any day during 1989. Based on these facts, the demand notes are treated as stock.

Example (2). On August 24, 1986, F organizes corporation G to own and operate an outdoor amusement business. G uses the calendar year as its taxable year. On August 25, 1986, F transfers trucking equipment, mechanical rides, and other assets to G in exchange for all the capital stock of G and a 6-percent note for $200,000. The note is due on August 25, 1990, and is classified as indebtedness under § 1.385-4 (a). However, G does not pay the principal within 90 days after it is due, and F does not pursue such payment with the ordinary diligence of an independent creditor. Based on these facts, beginning on August 26, 1990, the note is considered to be payable on demand. Assume that during 1990 the lowest reasonable rate of interest on a demand note issued by G (taking into account the financial condition of G) is 12 percent a year, and that under applicable local law the note continues to pay 6 percent interest after maturity. Based on these facts, the note is treated as stock on August 26, 1990.

Example (3). The facts are the same as in example (2) except that G agrees to pay 12-percent interest on the note. In addition, assume that 12 percent is a reasonable rate of interest on August 26, 1990. Based on these facts, the note is not treated as stock under this paragraph (l).

Example (4). The facts are the same as in example (3), except that G issues a 12-percent demand note for $200,000 to F in payment for the 6-percent note due on August 25, 1990. Based on these facts, the 6-percent note is not treated as stock. In addition, the 12-percent note may be treated as indebtedness under § 1.385-4(a).

．．．．

§ 1.385-7 Certain other obligations

(a) Scope—(1) In general. This section applies to any loan of money (e. g., a cash advance) made to a corporation unless—

(i) The loan is made by an independent creditor (within the meaning of § 1.385-6(b)), or

(ii) The loan is evidenced by an instrument within six months after the day the loan is made.

(For treatment of the instrument as stock or indebtedness, see §§ 1.385-4 through 1.385-6).

(2) Exception. (i) This section does not apply to a loan repaid within six months after the day it is made but only to the extent that the outstanding balance of such loan, reduced by the outstanding balance of prior qualifying loans, does not exceed $25,000. For this purpose, a prior loan is "qualifying" if—

(A) It is described in paragraph (a) (1) of this section, and

(B) This section does not apply to the prior loan by reason of this paragraph (a)(2).

(ii) For purposes of paragraph (a) (2)(i)(A) of this section, a loan is not considered to be actually repaid if it is renewed or offset in any manner.

(b) Initial classification—(1) In general. Except as provided in paragraph (b)(2) of this section, a loan to which this section applies is treated as indebtedness.

(2) Exception. A loan to which this section applies is treated as a contribution to capital if the debtor corporation has excessive debt when the loan is made (under the principles of § 1.385-6(f)).

(c) Reclassification—(1) In general. If a loan is treated as indebtedness under paragraph (b)(1) of this section and if the debtor corporation fails to pay interest on the loan at a reasonable rate during any taxable year, then the loan is reclassified as a contribution to capital as of the later of the first day of the taxable year or the date of the loan. For purposes of this subparagraph (1), a rate is considered reasonable if it is reasonable (under the principles of § 1.385-6(e)) as of any day of the taxable year.

(2) Special rule. For purposes of paragraph (c)(1) of this section, a corporation is not considered to pay interest on a loan during a taxable year unless the interest is actually paid within 90 days after the end of the year. For this purpose, payment of interest with property other than money will be considered actual payment, but only to the extent of the fair market value of such property. For example, payment of interest with a note will be considered actual payment, but only to the extent of the fair market value of the note.

(d) Effect of this section—(1) Initial classification. If a loan is treated as a contribution to capital under paragraph (b)(2) of this section, then all payments of principal and interest on the loan are treated as distributions to which section 301 applies.

(2) Reclassification. If a loan is reclassified as a contribution to capital under paragraph (c) of this section, then all payments of principal and interest made on the loan after the beginning of the year of reclassification are treated as distributions to which section 301 applies. In addition, once a loan is reclassified under paragraph

(c) of this section, its status as a contribution to capital can never change.

(e) Illustrations. The following examples illustrate the application of this section:

Example (1). Corporation M uses the calendar year as the taxable year. A is the sole shareholder of M. On March 1, 1968, A advances $73,000 to M, and M establishes an account payable to A in the amount of $73,000. The account payable is entered on the books of M but is not evidenced by an instrument. The account payable is not repaid within six months. In addition, M has excessive debt within the meaning of § 1.385-6(f). Based on these facts, the account payable is classified as a contribution to capital.

Example (2). The facts are the same as in example (1), except that M does not have excessive debt. The account payable is classified as indebtedness. However, if M fails to pay (before April 1, 1987) interest at a reasonable rate on the account payable for the last 10 months of 1986, the account payable will be reclassified as a contribution to capital (effective retroactively to March 1, 1986).

Example (3). Corporation X, which has excessive debt, uses the calendar year as the taxable year. On January 1, 1985, X's sole shareholder advances $60,000 to X. The advance is entered on the books of X but is not evidenced by an instrument. X repays $40,000 of the advance on April 1, 1985 and the remaining $20,000 on October 1, 1985. Based on these facts, this section does not apply to $25,000 of the advance that was repaid on April 1, 1985. The remaining $35,000 is treated as a contribution to capital. Therefore, $15,000 of the amount repaid on April 1 and the entire $20,000 repaid on October 1, are treated as distributions to which section 301 applies.

Example (4). (a) Corporation Y, which has excessive debt, uses the calendar year as the taxable year. A is the sole shareholder of Y. On January 1, 1990, A advances $100,000 to Y. Y repays the advance on August 1, 1990. Based on these facts, the $100,000 advance is treated as a contribution to capital.

(b) On June 1, 1990, A advances an additional $20,000 to Y. The $20,000 advance is also repaid on August 1, 1990. Based on these facts, this section does not apply to the advance of $20,000.

(c) On July 1, 1990, A advances another $10,000 to Y. The $10,000 advance is repaid on July 15, 1990. The $20,000 advance described in (b) is a prior qualifying loan with respect to the $10,000 advance (although this cannot be determined until August 1, 1990). Therefore, this section does not apply to $5,000 (i. e., $25,000-$20,000) of the advance made on July 1, 1990. However, the remaining $5,000 of this advance is treated as a contribution to capital.

Example (5). Corporations S and T are wholly-owned subsidiaries of corporation P. On January 1, 1990, S makes a non-interest bearing advance of $50,000 to T. The advance is entered on the books of T but it is not evidenced by an instrument and it is not repaid within 6 months. Based on these facts, S is treated as distributing $50,000 to P, and P is then treated as contributing this amount to the capital of T.

§ 1.385–9 Guaranteed loans

(a) In general. If—

(1) A shareholder in a corporation guarantees a loan made to the corporation (either directly or indirectly, e. g., by pledging collateral), and

(2) Under relevant legal principles (applied without reference to the regulations under section 385), the loan is treated as made to the shareholder, then the shareholder is treated as making a contribution to the capital of the corporation.

(b) Illustrations. The following examples illustrate the application of this section:

Example (1). On September 25, 1982, J organizes corporation N and acquires all of its capital stock. In addition, J guarantees a note for $600,000 issued by N on September 28, 1982. Assume that under the principles of *Plantation Patterns, Inc. v. Commissioner*, 462 F.2d 712 (5th Cir. 1972), cert. denied, 409 U.S. 1076 (1972), aff'g T.C. Memo. Dec. 1970–82 (1970), and other relevant case law, the note is properly treated as an obligation of J. Based on these facts, J is treated as making a $600,000 contribution to the capital of N.

Example (2). The facts are the same as in example (1). In addition, N pays $33,000 in interest and $100,000 in principal on the note on September 28, 1983. The total $133,000 in payments is treated as a distribution from N to J to which section 301 applies. Thus, N is not allowed a deduction for interest paid under section 163. However, J is allowed a deduction of $33,000 for interest paid.

Example (3). The facts are the same as in example (1). In addition, N defaults and J is required to pay $500,000 in principal on the note. Because J is treated as the primary obligor on the note (and not merely as a guarantor), the $500,000 payment will in no circumstances be treated as a loss from a loan or as a contribution to the capital of N.

Example (4). The facts are the same as in example (1), except that J does not guarantee the note issued by N until September 28, 1983. Assume that this note is properly treated as an obligation of J beginning on September 28, 1983. Also assume that on that date a principal balance of $400,000 is due on the note. Based on these facts, J is treated as making a $400,000 contribution to the capital of N on September 28, 1983.

§ 1.385–10 Certain preferred stock

(a) In general. Preferred stock is treated as stock if it does not provide for fixed payments (as defined in §

1.385–5(d)) in the nature of either principal or interest. On the other hand, preferred stock is treated as an instrument if it provides for fixed payments in the nature of principal or interest. Accordingly, preferred stock treated as an instrument is classified as indebtedness under § 1.385–4(a) (relating to instruments generally) unless it is classified as stock under § 1.385–5 (relating to hybrid instruments) or § 1.365–6 (relating to proportionality). See example (13) of § 1.385–5(e).

(b) Rule of convenience. Notwithstanding paragraph (a) of this section, preferred stock is treated as stock (and not as an instrument) if it satisfies each of the following conditions:

(1) The preferred stock is denominated preferred stock and is treated as preferred stock under applicable nontax law.

(2) The excess (if any) of the preferred stock's redemption price over its issue price is a reasonable redemption premium under § 1.305–5.

(3) Current dividends on the preferred stock are contingent (e. g., payable only out of earned surplus or only at the board of directors' discretion).

(4) The right to receive dividend payments and payments in redemption of the preferred stock may not be enforced under applicable nontax law if either (i) the issuing corporation is insolvent or would be rendered insolvent by such payments or (ii) the making of such payments would impair the issuing corporation's capital (i. e., the fair market value of the remaining assets of the issuing corporation would be less than the sum of its liabilities and the liquidation value of its other classes of preferred stock that are senior or equal in rank).

(5) Default in the making of a dividend payment or a payment in redemption of the preferred stock does not entitle the holder to accelerate redemption payments.

(6) The preferred stock has a term (during which the holder cannot compel redemption) of at least 10 years. In the case of an issue of preferred stock which provides for redemption over a period of years, the term shall be the weighted average life of the issue.

(c) Illustrations. The following examples illustrate the application of this section:

Example (1). On August 8, 1985, corporation D issues 500 shares of $100 par value, 6-percent preferred stock. Dividends on the preferred stock are cumulative, and D may not pay dividends on its common stock or repurchase shares of common stock so long as dividends on the preferred stock are in arrears. However, dividends on the preferred stock are payable only if declared by D's board of directors. In addition, the preferred stock is callable after August 8, 1990 for $100 a share at the discretion of D's board of directors. Thus, the holders of the preferred stock cannot compel D to redeem or purchase the stock. Based on these facts the preferred stock does not provide for fixed payments in the nature of principal or interest. Therefore, the preferred stock is treated as stock.

Example (2). On February 2, 1984, corporation E issues 500 shares of cumulative Class A sinking fund preferred stock. The Class A preferred stock provides for quarterly dividends, payable out of E's earnings, and for sinking fund payments, which must be used by E to redeem the preferred stock on specified dates. The weighted average life of the preferred stock issue is less than 10 years. Under E's articles of incorporation, sinking fund payments must be made out of all "legally available funds." Under applicable local law, this means that the preferred stockholders have an absolute right to compel the sinking fund payments subject to only two restrictions. First, sinking fund payments are not permitted if E is insolvent (i. e., not able to pay its debts as they become due) or would be rendered insolvent by the payment. Second, sinking fund payments are not permitted if they would impair E's capital. The first restriction is not a contingency that prevents the payments from being considered fixed. See § 1.385–5(d)(5)(iii). The second restriction is, in effect, a subordination provision in that it merely prevents preferential treatment of the Class A preferred stock over equal or more senior issues of preferred stock. Based on these facts, the Class A preferred stock provides for fixed payments in the nature of principal. Therefore, the Class A preferred stock is treated as an instrument. Assuming that sinking fund payments must include all accrued and unpaid dividends, the Class A preferred stock also provides for fixed payments in the nature of interest. For this purpose, the dividends are considered to be fixed at the time they become part of a sinking fund payment. See example (13) of § 1.385–5(e).

Example (3). The facts are the same as in example (2) except that the weighted average life of the preferred stock issue is more than 10 years. Additionally, the preferred stock is treated as preferred stock under applicable nontax law; the issue price of the preferred stock is equal to its redemption price; and default in the making of a dividend payment does not entitle the holders of the preferred stock to accelerate sinking fund payments. Based on these facts, the Class A preferred stock is treated as stock under paragraph (b) of this section. The result would be the same if, under applicable local law, E would be considered insolvent (and therefore sinking fund payments would not be permitted) if its liabilities exceeded its assets (rather than if E were not able to pay its debts as they became due).

Example (4). F is a large, stable, and consistently profitable corporation. On March 21, 1985, F issues 50,000 shares of $100 par value, 9-percent sinking fund preferred stock. Dividends and sinking fund payments, which begin five years after issuance, are mandatory to the extent of retained earnings. In addition, dividends are cumulative, but they are payable only out of retained earnings. Based on these facts, the preferred stock does not provide for fixed payments in the nature of either principal or interest. Therefore, the preferred stock is treated as stock.

Example (5). The facts are the same as in example (1). In addition, corporation G, which owns all the common stock of D, unconditionally guarantees timely payment of all dividends on the preferred stock. Further, G guarantees that the preferred stock will be called for redemption by August 8, 2005. Based on these facts, the preferred stock is treated as an instrument. See § 1.385-5(d)(7).

Example (6). H, a closely-held corporation, issues 1,000 shares of $100 par value, 12-percent preferred stock on January 1, 1984. Dividends are cumulative but are payable only out of earned surplus. The preferred stock is subject to mandatory redemption after 9 years at a redemption price of $100 per share plus accrued but unpaid dividends. However, the accrued but unpaid dividends are payable, upon redemption, only out of earned surplus plus unrealized appreciation of H's assets (but not out of capital or capital surplus). Based on these facts, the preferred stock does not provide for fixed payments in the nature of interest but does provide for fixed payments in the nature of principal. Therefore, the preferred stock is treated as an instrument.

§ 1.401-1   Qualified pension, profit-sharing, and stock bonus plans

. . . .

(b) **General rules.** (1) (i) A pension plan within the meaning of section 401 (a) is a plan established and maintained by an employer primarily to provide systematically for the payment of definitely determinable benefits to his employees over a period of years, usually for life, after retirement. Retirement benefits generally are measured by, and based on, such factors as years of service and compensation received by the employees. The determination of the amount of retirement benefits and the contributions to provide such benefits are not dependent upon profits. Benefits are not definitely determinable if funds arising from forfeitures on termination of service, or other reason, may be used to provide increased benefits for the remaining participants (see § 1.401-7, relating to the treatment of forfeitures under a qualified pension plan). A plan designed to provide benefits for employees or their beneficiaries to be paid upon retirement or over a period of years after retirement will, for the purposes of section 401(a), be considered a pension plan if the employer contributions under the plan can be determined actuarially on the basis of definitely determinable benefits, or, as in the case of money purchase pension plans, such contributions are fixed without being geared to profits. A pension plan may provide for the payment of a pension due to disability and may also provide for the payment of incidental death benefits through insurance or otherwise. However, a plan is not a pension plan if it provides for the payment of benefits not customarily included in a pension plan such as layoff benefits or benefits for sickness, accident, hospitalization, or medical expenses (except medical benefits described in section 401(h) as defined in paragraph (a) of § 1.401-14).

(ii) A profit-sharing plan is a plan established and maintained by an employer to provide for the participation in his profits by his employees or their beneficiaries. The plan must provide a definite predetermined formula for allocating the contributions made to the plan among the participants and for distributing the funds accumulated under the plan after a fixed number of years, the attainment of a stated age, or upon the prior occurrence of some event such as layoff, illness, disability, retirement, death, or severance of employment. A formula for allocating the contributions among the participants is definite if, for example, it provides for an allocation in proportion to the basic compensation of each participant. A plan (whether or not it contains a definite predetermined formula for determining the profits to be shared with the employees) does not qualify under section 401(a) if the contributions to the plan are made at such times or in such amounts that the plan in operation discriminates in favor of officers, shareholders, persons whose principal duties consist in supervising the work of other employees, or highly compensated employees. For the rules with respect to discrimination, see §§ 1.401–3 and 1.401–4. A profit-sharing plan within the meaning of section 401 is primarily a plan of deferred compensation, but the amounts allocated to the account of a participant may be used to provide for him or his family incidental life or accident or health insurance.

(iii) A stock bonus plan is a plan established and maintained by an employer to provide benefits similar to those of a profit-sharing plan, except that the contributions by the employer are not necessarily dependent upon profits and the benefits are distributable in stock of the employer company. For the purpose of allocating and distributing the stock of the employer which is to be shared among his employees or their beneficiaries, such a plan is subject to the same requirements as a profit-sharing plan.

. . . .

(2) The term "plan" implies a permanent as distinguished from a temporary program. Thus, although the employer may reserve the right to change or terminate the plan, and to discontinue contributions thereunder, the abandonment of the plan for any reason other than business necessity within a few years after it has taken effect will be evidence that the plan from its inception was not a bona fide program for the exclusive benefit of employees in general. Especially will this be true if, for example, a pension plan is abandoned soon after pensions have been fully funded for persons in favor of whom discrimination is prohibited under section 401(a). The permanency of the plan will be indicated by all of the surrounding facts and circumstances, including the likelihood of the employer's ability to continue contributions as provided under the plan. In the case of a profit-sharing plan, other than a profit-sharing plan which covers employees and owner-employees (see section 401(d) (2) (B)), it is not necessary that the employer contribute every year or that he contribute the same amount or contribute in accordance with the same ratio every year. However, merely making a single or occasional contribution out of profits for employees does not establish a plan of profit-sharing. To be a profit-sharing plan, there must be recurring and substantial contributions out of profits for the employees. In the event a plan is abandoned, the employer should promptly, notify the district director stating the circumstances which led to the discontinuance of the plan.

(3) If the plan is so designed as to amount to a subterfuge for the distribution of profits to shareholders, it will not qualify as a plan for the exclusive benefit of employees even though other employees who are not shareholders are also included under the plan. The plan must benefit the employees in general, although it need not provide benefits for all of the employees. Among the employees to be benefited may be persons who are officers and shareholders. However, a plan is not for the exclusive benefit of employees in general if, by any device whatever, it discriminates either in eligibility requirements, contributions, or benefits in favor of employees who are officers, shareholders, persons whose principal duties consist in supervising the work of other employees, or the highly compensated employees. See section 401(a) (3), (4), and (5). Similarly, a stock bonus or profit-sharing plan is not a plan for the exclusive benefit of employees in general if the funds therein may be used to relieve the employer from contributing to a pension plan operating concurrently and covering the same employees. All of the surrounding and attendant circumstances and the details of the plan will be indicative of whether it is a bona fide stock bonus, pension, or profit-sharing plan for the exclusive benefit of employees in general. The law is concerned not only with the form of a plan but also with its effects in operation. For example, section 401(a) (5) specifies certain provisions which of themselves are not discriminatory. However, this does not mean that a plan containing these provisions may not be discriminatory in actual operation.

(4) A plan is for the exclusive benefit of employees or their beneficiaries even though it may cover former employees as well as present employees and employees who are temporarily on leave, as, for example, in the Armed Forces of the United States. A plan covering only former employees may qualify under section 401(a) if it complies with the provisions of section 401 (a) (3) (B), with respect to coverage, and section 401(a) (4), with respect to contributions and benefits, as applied to all of the former employees. The term

"beneficiaries" of an employee within the meaning of section 401 includes the estate of the employee, dependents of the employee, persons who are the natural objects of the employee's bounty, and any persons designated by the employee to share in the benefits of the plan after the death of the employee.

(5) (i) No specific limitations are provided in section 401(a) with respect to investments which may be made by the trustees of a trust qualifying under section 401(a). Generally, the contributions may be used by the trustees to purchase any investments permitted by the trust agreement to the extent allowed by local law. However, such a trust will be subject to tax under section 511 with respect to any "unrelated business taxable income" (as defined in section 512) realized by it from its investments.

. . . .

§ 1.441-1 Period for computation of taxable income

(a) **Computation of taxable income.** Taxable income shall be computed and a return shall be made for a period known as the "taxable year." For rules relating to methods of accounting, the taxable year for which items of gross income are included and deductions are taken, inventories, and adjustments, see parts II and III (section 446 and following), subchapter E, chapter 1 of the Code, and the regulations thereunder.

(b) **Taxable year.** (1) The term "taxable year" means—

(i) The taxpayer's annual accounting period, if it is a calendar year or a fiscal year;

(ii) The calendar year, if section 441 (g) (relating to taxpayers who keep no books or have no accounting period) applies; or

(iii) The period for which the return is made, if the return is made under section 443 for a period of less than 12 months, referred to as a "short period."

(2) A taxable year may not cover a period of more than 12 calendar months except in the case of a 52-53-week taxable year. See § 1.441-2.

(3) A new taxpayer in his first return may adopt any taxable year which meets the requirements of section 441 and this section without obtaining prior approval. The first taxable year of a new taxpayer must be adopted on or before the time prescribed by law (not including extensions) for the filing of the return for such taxable year. However, for rules applicable to the adoption of a taxable year by a partnership, see paragraph (b) (2) of § 1.442-1, section 706(b), and paragraph (b) of § 1.706-1. . . . .

(4) After a taxpayer has adopted a calendar or a fiscal year, he must use it in computing his taxable income and making his returns for all subsequent years unless prior approval is obtained from the Commissioner to make a change or unless a change is otherwise permitted under the internal revenue laws or regulations. See section 442 and § 1.442-1. For rules applicable to changes in taxable years of partners and partnerships, see also section 706 (b) and paragraph (b) of § 1.706-1.

(c) **Annual accounting period.** The term "annual accounting period" means the annual period (calendar year or fiscal year) on the basis of which the taxpayer regularly computes his income in keeping his books.

(d) **Calendar year.** The term "calendar year" means a period of 12 months ending on December 31. A taxpayer who has not established a fiscal year must make his return on the basis of a calendar year.

(e) **Fiscal year.** (1) The term "fiscal year" means—

(i) A period of 12 months ending on the last day of any month other than December, or

(ii) The 52-53-week annual accounting period, if such period has been elected by the taxpayer.

(2) A fiscal year will be recognized only if it is established as the annual accounting period of the taxpayer and only if the books of the taxpayer are kept in accordance with such fiscal year.

. . . .

(g) **No books kept; no accounting period.** Except in the case of a short period under section 443, the taxpayer's taxable year shall be the calendar year if—

(1) The taxpayer keeps no books;

(2) The taxpayer does not have an annual accounting period (as defined in section 441(c) and paragraph (c) of this section); or

(3) The taxpayer has an annual accounting period, but such period does not qualify as a fiscal year (as defined in section 441(e) and paragraph (e) of this section).

For the purposes of subparagraph (1) of this paragraph, the keeping of books does not require that records be bound. Records which are sufficient to reflect income adequately and clearly on the basis of an annual accounting period will be regarded as the keeping of books. A taxpayer whose taxable year is required to be a calendar year under section 441(g) and this paragraph may not adopt a fiscal year without obtaining prior approval from the Commissioner since such adoption is treated as a change of annual accounting period. See section 442 and paragraph (a) (2) of § 1.442-1.

§ 1.442-1 Change of annual accounting period

(a) **Manner of effecting such change. (1) In general.** If a taxpayer wishes to change his annual accounting period (as defined in section 441(c)) and adopt a new taxable year (as defined in section 441(b)), he must obtain prior approval from the Commissioner by application, as provided in paragraph (b) of this section, or the change must be authorized under the Income Tax Regulations. A new taxpayer who adopts an annual accounting period as provided in section 441 and §§ 1.-441-1 or 1.441-2 need not secure the permission of the Commissioner under section 442 and this section. However, see subparagraph (2) of this paragraph. For adoption of and changes to or from a 52-53-week taxable year, see section 441(f) and § 1.441-2; for adoption of and changes in the taxable years of partners and partnerships, see paragraph (b) (2) of this section, section 706(b) and paragraph (b) of § 1.706-1; for special rules relating to certain corporations, subsidiary corporations, and newly married couples, see paragraphs (c), (d), and (e), respectively, of this section. . . . .

(2) **Taxpayers to whom section 441 (g) applies.** Section 441 (g) provides that if a taxpayer keeps no books, does not have an annual accounting period, or has an accounting period which does not meet the requirements for a fiscal year, his taxable year shall be the calendar year. If section 441(g) applies to a taxpayer, the adoption of a fiscal year will be treated as a change in his annual accounting period under section 442. Therefore, such fiscal year can become the taxpayer's taxable year only with the approval of the Commissioner. Approval of any such change will be denied unless the taxpayer agrees in his application to establish and maintain accurate records of his taxable income for the short period involved in the change and for the fiscal year proposed. The keeping of records which adequately and clearly reflect income for the taxable year constitutes the keeping of books within the meaning of section 441(g) and paragraph (g) of § 1.441-1.

(b) **Prior approval of the Commissioner—(1) In general.** In order to secure prior approval of a change of a taxpayer's annual accounting period, the taxpayer must file an application on Form 1128 with the Commissioner of Internal Revenue, Washington, D. C. 20224, to effect the change of accounting period. If the short period involved in the change ends after December 31, 1973, such form shall be filed on or before the 15th day of the second calendar month following the close of such short period; if such short period ends before January 1, 1974, such form shall be filed on or before the last day of the first calendar month following the close of such short period. Approval will not be granted unless the taxpayer and the Commissioner agree to the terms, conditions, and adjustments under which the change will be effected. In general, a change of annual accounting period will be approved where the taxpayer establishes a substantial business purpose for making the change. In determining whether a taxpayer has established a substantial business purpose for making the change, consideration will be given to all the facts and circumstances relating to the change, including the tax consequences resulting therefrom. Among the nontax factors that will be considered in determining whether a substantial business purpose has been established is the effect of the change on the taxpayer's annual cycle of business activity. The agreement between the taxpayer and the Commissioner under which the change will be effected shall, in appropriate cases, provide terms, conditions, and adjustments necessary to prevent a substantial distortion of income which otherwise would result from the change. The following are examples of effects of the change which would substantially distort income: (i) Deferral of a substantial portion of the taxpayer's income, or shifting of a substantial portion of deductions, from one year to another so as to reduce substantially the taxpayer's tax liability; (ii) causing a similar deferral or shifting in the case of any other person, such as a partner, a beneficiary, or a shareholder in an electing small business corporation as defined in section 1371(b); or (iii) creating a short period in which there is either (a) a substantial net operating loss, or (b) in the case of an electing small business corporation, a substantial portion of amounts treated as long-term capital gain. Even though a substantial business purpose is not established, the Commissioner in appropriate cases may permit a husband or wife to change his or her taxable year in order to secure the benefits of section 1(a) (relating to tax in case of a joint return). . . .

(2) **Partnerships and partners.** (i) A newly-formed partnership may adopt a taxable year which is the same as the taxable year of all its principal partners (or is the same taxable year to which its principal partners who do not have such taxable year concurrently change) without securing prior approval from the Commissioner. If all its principal partners are not on the same taxable year, a newly-formed partnership may adopt a calendar year without securing prior approval from the Commissioner. If a newly-formed partnership wishes to adopt a taxable year that does not qualify under the preceding two sentences, the adoption of such year requires the prior approval of the Commissioner in accordance with section 706(b) (1) and paragraph (b) of § 1.706–1. An existing partnership may change its taxable year without securing prior approval from the Commissioner if all its principal partners have the same taxable year to which the partnership changes, or if all its principal partners who do not

have such a taxable year concurrently change to such taxable year. In any other case, an existing partnership may not change its taxable year unless it secures the prior approval of the Commissioner in accordance with paragraph (b) (1) of this section and section 706 (b) (1) and paragraph (b) of § 1.706–1.

(ii) A partner may change his taxable year only if he secures the prior approval of the Commissioner in accordance with paragraph (b) (1) of this section.

. . . .

§ 1.443–1 Returns for periods of less than 12 months

(a) **Returns for short period.** A return for a short period, that is, for a taxable year consisting of a period of less than 12 months, shall be made under any of the following circumstances:

(1) **Change of annual accounting period.** In the case of a change in the annual accounting period of a taxpayer, a separate return must be filed for the short period of less than 12 months beginning with the day following the close of the old taxable year and ending with the day preceding the first day of the new taxable year. However, such a return is not required for a short period of six days or less, or 359 days or more, resulting from a change from or to a 52–53-week taxable year. See section 441(f) and § 1.441–2. The computation of the tax for a short period required to effect a change of annual accounting period is described in paragraph (b) of this section. In general, a return for a short period resulting from a change of annual accounting period shall be filed and the tax paid within the time prescribed for filing a return for a taxable year of 12 months ending on the last day of the short period. For rules applicable to a subsidiary corporation which becomes a member of an affiliated group which files a consolidated return, see § 1.1502–76.

(2) **Taxpayer not in existence for entire taxable year.** If a taxpayer is not in existence for the entire taxable year, a return is required for the short period during which the taxpayer was in existence. For example, a corpora-

tion organized on August 1 and adopting the calendar year as its annual accounting period is required to file a return for the short period from August 1 to December 31, and returns for each calendar year thereafter. Similarly, a dissolving corporation which files its returns for the calendar year is required to file a return for the short period from January 1 to the date it goes out of existence. Income for the short period is not required to be annualized if the taxpayer is not in existence for the entire taxable year, and, in the case of a taxpayer other than a corporation, the deduction under section 151 for personal exemptions (or deductions in lieu thereof) need not be reduced under section 443(c). In general, the requirements with respect to the filing of returns and the payment of tax for a short period where the taxpayer has not been in existence for the entire taxable year are the same as for the filing of a return and the payment of tax for a taxable year of 12 months ending on the last day of the short period. Although the return of a decedent is a return for the short period beginning with the first day of his last taxable year and ending with the date of his death, the filing of a return and the payment of tax for a decedent may be made as though the decedent had lived throughout his last taxable year.

§ 1.446-1 General rule for methods of accounting

(a) General rule. (1) Section 446 (a) provides that taxable income shall be computed under the method of accounting on the basis of which a taxpayer regularly computes his income in keeping his books. The term "method of accounting" includes not only the over-all method of accounting of the taxpayer but also the accounting treatment of any item. Examples of such over-all methods are the cash receipts and disbursements method, an accrual method, combinations of such methods, and combinations of the foregoing with various methods provided for the accounting treatment of special items. These methods of accounting for special items include the accounting treatment prescribed for research and experimental expenditures, soil and water conservation expenditures, de-

preciation, net operating losses, etc. Except for deviations permitted or required by such special accounting treatment, taxable income shall be computed under the method of accounting on the basis of which the taxpayer regularly computes his income in keeping his books. For requirement respecting the adoption or change of accounting method, see section 446(e) and paragraph (e) of this section.

(2) It is recognized that no uniform method of accounting can be prescribed for all taxpayers. Each taxpayer shall adopt such forms and systems as are, in his judgment, best suited to his needs. However, no method of accounting is acceptable unless, in the opinion of the Commissioner, it clearly reflects income. A method of accounting which reflects the consistent application of generally accepted accounting principles in a particular trade or business in accordance with accepted conditions or practices in that trade or business will ordinarily be regarded as clearly reflecting income, provided all items of gross income and expense are treated consistently from year to year.

(3) Items of gross income and expenditures which are elements in the computation of taxable income need not be in the form of cash. It is sufficient that such items can be valued in terms of money. For general rules relating to the taxable year for inclusion of income and for taking deductions, see sections 451 and 461, and the regulations thereunder.

(4) Each taxpayer is required to make a return of his taxable income for each taxable year and must maintain such accounting records as will enable him to file a correct return. See section 6001 and the regulations thereunder. Accounting records include the taxpayer's regular books of account and such other records and data as may be necessary to support the entries on his books of account and on his return, as for example, a reconciliation of any differences between such books and his return. The following are among the essential features that must be considered in maintaining such records:

(i) In all cases in which the production, purchase, or sale of merchandise of any kind is an income-producing factor, merchandise on hand (including finished goods, work in process, raw materials, and supplies) at the beginning and end of the year shall be taken into account in computing the taxable income of the year. (For rules relating to computation of inventories, see sections 471 and 472, and the regulations thereunder.)

(ii) Expenditures made during the year shall be properly classified as between capital and expense. For example, expenditures for such items as plant and equipment, which have a useful life extending substantially beyond the taxable year, shall be charged to a capital account and not to an expense account.

(iii) In any case in which there is allowable with respect to an asset a deduction for depreciation, amortization, or depletion, any expenditures (other than ordinary repairs) made to restore the asset or prolong its useful life shall be added to the asset account or charged against the appropriate reserve.

(b) **Exceptions.** (1) If the taxpayer does not regularly employ a method of accounting which clearly reflects his income, the computation of taxable income shall be made in a manner which, in the opinion of the Commissioner, does clearly reflect income.

(2) A taxpayer whose sole source of income is wages need not keep formal books in order to have an accounting method. Tax returns, copies thereof, or other records may be sufficient to establish the use of the method of accounting used in the preparation of the taxpayer's income tax returns.

(c) **Permissible methods—(1) In general.** Subject to the provisions of paragraphs (a) and (b) of this section, a taxpayer may compute his taxable income under any of the following methods of accounting:

(i) **Cash receipts and disbursements method.** Generally, under the cash receipts and disbursements method in the computation of taxable income, all items which constitute gross income (whether in the form of cash, property, or services) are to be included for the taxable year in which actually or constructively received. Expenditures are to be deducted for the taxable year in which actually made. For rules relating to constructive receipt, see § 1.451-2. For treatment of an expenditure attributable to more than one tax-

able year, see section 461(a) and paragraph (a) (1) of § 1.461-1.

(ii) **Accrual method.** Generally, under an accrual method, income is to be included for the taxable year when all the events have occurred which fix the right to receive such income and the amount thereof can be determined with reasonable accuracy. Under such a method, deductions are allowable for the taxable year in which all the events have occurred which establish the fact of the liability giving rise to such deduction and the amount thereof can be determined with reasonable accuracy. The method used by the taxpayer in determining when income is to be accounted for will be acceptable if it accords with generally accepted accounting principles, is consistently used by the taxpayer from year to year, and is consistent with the Income Tax Regulations. For example, a taxpayer engaged in a manufacturing business may account for sales of his product when the goods are shipped, when the product is delivered or accepted, or when title to the goods passes to the customer, whether or not billed, depending upon the method regularly employed in keeping his books.

(iii) **Other permissible methods.** Special methods of accounting are described elsewhere in chapter 1 of the Code and the regulations thereunder. For example, see the following sections and the regulations thereunder: Sections 61 and 162, relating to the crop method of accounting; section 453, relating to the installment method; section 451, relating to the long-term contract methods. In addition, special methods of accounting for particular items of income and expense are provided under other sections of chapter 1. For example, see section 174, relating to research and experimental expenditures, and section 175, relating to soil and water conservation expenditures.

(iv) **Combinations of the foregoing methods.** (a) In accordance with the following rules, any combination of the foregoing methods of accounting will be permitted in connection with a trade or business if such combination clearly reflects income and is consistently used. Where a combination of methods of accounting includes any special methods, such as those referred to in subdivision (iii) of this subparagraph, the taxpayer must comply with the requirements relating to such special methods. A taxpayer using an accrual method of accounting with respect to purchases and sales may use the cash method in computing all other items of income and expense. However, a taxpayer who uses the cash method of accounting in computing gross income from his trade or business shall use the cash method in computing expenses of such trade or business. Similarly, a taxpayer who uses an accrual method of accounting in computing business expenses shall use an accrual method in computing items affecting gross income from his trade or business.

(b) A taxpayer using one method of accounting in computing items of income and deductions of his trade or business may compute other items of income and deductions not connected with his trade or business under a different method of accounting.

(2) **Special rules.** (i) In any case in which it is necessary to use an inventory the accrual method of accounting must be used with regard to purchases and sales unless otherwise authorized under subdivision (ii) of this subparagraph.

(ii) No method of accounting will be regarded as clearly reflecting income unless all items of gross profit and deductions are treated with consistency from year to year. The Commissioner may authorize a taxpayer to adopt or change to a method of accounting permitted by this chapter although the method is not specifically described in the regulations in this part if, in the opinion of the Commissioner, income is clearly reflected by the use of such method. Further, the Commissioner may authorize a taxpayer to continue the use of a method of accounting consistently used by the taxpayer, even though not specifically authorized by the regulations in this part if, in the opinion of the Commissioner, income is clearly reflected by the use of such method. See section 446(a) and paragraph (a) of this section, which require that taxable income shall be computed under the method of accounting on the basis of which the taxpayer regularly computes his income in keeping his books, and section 446(e) and paragraph (e) of this section, which require the prior approval of the Commissioner

in the case of changes in accounting method.

(d) **Taxpayer engaged in more than one business.** (1) Where a taxpayer has two or more separate and distinct trades or businesses, a different method of accounting may be used for each trade or business, provided the method used for each trade or business clearly reflects the income of that particular trade or business. For example, a taxpayer may account for the operations of a personal service business on the cash receipts and disbursements method and of a manufacturing business on an accrual method, provided such businesses are separate and distinct and the methods used for each clearly reflect income. The method first used in accounting for business income and deductions in connection with each trade or business, as evidenced in the taxpayer's income tax return in which such income or deductions are first reported, must be consistently followed thereafter.

(2) No trade or business will be considered separate and distinct for purposes of this paragraph unless a complete and separable set of books and records is kept for such trade or business.

(3) If, by reason of maintaining different methods of accounting, there is a creation or shifting of profits or losses between the trades or businesses of the taxpayer (for example, through inventory adjustments, sales, purchases, or expenses) so that income of the taxpayer is not clearly reflected, the trades or businesses of the taxpayer will not be considered to be separate and distinct.

(e) **Requirement respecting the adoption or change of accounting method.** (1) A taxpayer filing his first return may adopt any permissible method of accounting in computing taxable income for the taxable year covered by such return. See section 446(c) and paragraph (c) of this section for permissible methods. Moreover, a taxpayer may adopt any permissible method of accounting in connection with each separate and distinct trade or business, the income from which is reported for the first time. See section

446(d) and paragraph (d) of this section. See also section 446(a) and paragraph (a) of this section.

(2) (i) Except as otherwise expressly provided in chapter 1 of the Code and the regulations thereunder, a taxpayer who changes the method of accounting employed in keeping his books shall, before computing his income upon such new method for purposes of taxation, secure the consent of the Commissioner. Consent must be secured whether or not such method is proper or is permitted under the Internal Revenue Code or the regulations thereunder.

(ii) (a) A change in the method of accounting includes a change in the overall plan of accounting for gross income or deductions or a change in the treatment of any material item used in such overall plan. Although a method of accounting may exist under this definition without the necessity of a pattern of consistent treatment of an item, in most instances a method of accounting is not established for an item without such consistent treatment. A material item is any item which involves the proper time for the inclusion of the item in income or the taking of a deduction. Changes in method of accounting include a change from the cash receipts and disbursement method to an accrual method, or vice versa, a change involving the method or basis used in the valuation of inventories (see sections 471 and 472 and the regulations thereunder), a change from the cash or accrual method to a long-term contract method, or vice versa (see § 1.451-3), a change involving the adoption, use or discontinuance of any other specialized method of computing taxable income, such as the crop method, and a change where the Internal Revenue Code and regulations thereunder specifically require that the consent of the Commissioner must be obtained before adopting such a change.

(b) A change in method of accounting does not include correction of mathematical or posting errors, or errors in the computation of tax liability (such as errors in computation of the foreign tax credit, net operating loss, percentage depletion or investment credit). Also, a change in method of accounting does not include adjustment of any item of income or deduction which does not involve the proper time for the inclusion of the item of income or the taking of a deduction. For example, corrections of items that are deducted as interest or salary, but which are in fact payments of dividends, and of items that are deducted as business expenses, but which are in fact personal expenses, are not changes in method of accounting. In addition, a change in the method of accounting does not include an adjustment with respect to the addition to a reserve for bad debts or an adjustment in the useful life of a depreciable asset. Although such adjustments may involve the question of the proper time for the taking of a deduction, such items are traditionally corrected by adjustments in the current and future years. For the treatment of the adjustment of the addition to a bad debt reserve, see the regulations under section 166 of the Code; for the treatment of a change in the useful life of a depreciable asset, see the regulations under section 167(b) of the Code. A change in the method of accounting also does not include a change in treatment resulting from a change in underlying facts. On the other hand, for example, a correction to require depreciation in lieu of a deduction for the cost of a class of depreciable assets which had been consistently treated as an expense in the year of purchase involves the question of the proper timing of an item, and is to be treated as a change in method of accounting.

(c) A change in an overall plan or system of identifying or valuing items in inventory is a change in method of accounting. Also a change in the treatment of any material item used in the overall plan for identifying or valuing items in inventory is a change in method of accounting.

(iii) A change in the method of accounting may be illustrated by the following examples:

Example (1). Although the sale of merchandise is an income producing factor, and therefore inventories are required, a taxpayer in the retail jewelry business reports his income on the cash receipts and disbursements method of accounting. A change from the cash receipts and disbursements method of accounting to the accrual method of accounting is a change in the overall plan of accounting and thus is a change in method of accounting.

Example (2). A taxpayer in the wholesale dry goods business computes its income and expenses on the accrual method of accounting and files its Federal income tax returns on such basis except for real estate taxes which have been reported on the cash receipts and disbursements method of accounting. A change in the treatment of real estate taxes from the cash receipts and disbursements method to the accrual method is a change in method of accounting because such change is a change in the treatment of a material item within his overall accounting practice.

. . . . .

Example (5). A taxpayer values inventories at cost. A change in the basis for valuation of inventories from cost to the lower of cost or market is a change in an overall practice of valuing items in inventory. The change, therefore, is a change of method of accounting for inventories.

. . . .

(3) (i) Except as otherwise provided under the authority of subdivision (ii) of this subparagraph, in order to secure the Commissioner's consent to a change of a taxpayer's method of accounting, the taxpayer must file an application on Form 3115 with the Commissioner of Internal Revenue, Washington, D.C. 20224, within 180 days after the beginning of the taxable year in which it is desired to make the change. The taxpayer shall, to the extent applicable, furnish (a) all information requested on such form, disclosing in detail all classes of items which would be treated differently under the new method of accounting and showing all amounts which would be duplicated or omitted as a result of the proposed change and (b) the taxpayer's computation of the adjustments to take into account such duplications or omissions. The Commissioner may require such other information as may be necessary in order to determine whether the proposed change will be permitted. Permission to change a taxpayer's method of accounting will not be granted unless the taxpayer and the Commissioner agree to the terms, conditions, and adjustments under which the change will be effected. See section 481 and the regulations thereunder, relating to certain adjustments required by such changes, section 472 and the regulations thereunder, relating to changes to and from the last-in, first-out method of inventorying goods, and section 453 and the regulations thereunder, relating to certain adjustments required by a change from an accrual method to the installment method.

(ii) Notwithstanding the provisions of subdivision (i) of this subparagraph,

the Commissioner may prescribe administrative procedures, subject to such limitations, terms, and conditions as he deems necessary to obtain his consent, to permit taxpayers to change their accounting practices or methods to an acceptable treatment consistent with applicable regulations. Limitations, terms, and conditions, as may be prescribed in such administrative procedures by the Commissioner, shall include those necessary to prevent the omission or duplication of items includible in gross income or deductions.

§ 1.451-1 General rule for taxable year of inclusion

(a) General rule. Gains, profits, and income are to be included in gross income for the taxable year in which they are actually or constructively received by the taxpayer unless includible for a different year in accordance with the taxpayer's method of accounting. Under an accrual method of accounting, income is includible in gross income when all the events have occurred which fix the right to receive such income and the amount thereof can be determined with reasonable accuracy. Therefore, under such a method of accounting if, in the case of compensation for services, no determination can be made as to the right to such compensation or the amount thereof until the services are completed, the amount of compensation is ordinarily income for the taxable year in which the determination can be made. Under the cash receipts and disbursements method of accounting, such an amount is includible in gross income when actually or constructively received. Where an amount of income is properly accrued on the basis of a reasonable estimate and the exact amount is subsequently determined, the difference, if any, shall be taken into account for the taxable year in which such determination is made. To the extent that income is attributable to the recovery of bad debts for accounts charged off in prior years, it is includible in the year of recovery in accordance with the taxpayer's method of accounting, regardless of the date when the amounts were charged off. For treatment of bad debts and bad debt recoveries, see sections 166 and 111 and the regulations thereunder. For rules relating to the treatment of amounts received in crop shares, see section 61 and the regulations thereunder. For the year in which a partner must include his distributive share of partnership income, see section 706(a) and paragraph (a) of § 1.706-1. If a taxpayer ascertains that an item should have been included in gross income in a prior taxable year, he should, if within the period of limitation, file an amended return and pay any additional tax due. Similarly, if a taxpayer ascertains that an item was improperly included in gross income in a prior taxable year, he should, if within the period of limitation, file claim for credit or refund of any overpayment of tax arising therefrom.

(b) **Special rule in case of death.** (1) A taxpayer's taxable year ends on the date of his death. See section 443 (a) (2) and paragraph (a) (2) of § 1.443-1. In computing taxable income for such year, there shall be included only amounts properly includible under the method of accounting used by the taxpayer. However, if the taxpayer used an accrual method of accounting, amounts accrued only by reason of his death shall not be included in computing taxable income for such year. If the taxpayer uses no regular accounting method, only amounts actually or constructively received during such year shall be included. (For rules relating to the inclusion of partnership income in the return of a decedent partner, see subchapter K, chapter 1 of the Code, and the regulations thereunder.)

(2) If the decedent owned an installment obligation the income from which was taxable to him under section 453, no income is required to be reported in the return of the decedent by reason of the transmission at death of such obligation. See section 453(d) (3). For the treatment of installment obligations acquired by the decedent's estate or by any person by bequest, devise, or inheritance from the decedent, see section 691(a) (4) and the regulations thereunder.

.   .   .   .   .

§ 1.451-2 Constructive receipt of income

(a) **General rule.** Income although not actually reduced to a taxpayer's possession is constructively received by him in the taxable year during which it is credited to his account, set apart for him, or otherwise made available so that he may draw upon it at any time, or so that he could have drawn upon it during the taxable year if notice of intention to withdraw had been given. However, income is not constructively received if the taxpayer's control of its receipt is subject to substantial limitations or restrictions. Thus, if a corporation credits its employees with bonus stock, but the stock is not available to such employees until some future date, the mere crediting on the books of the corporation does not constitute receipt. In the case of interest, dividends, or other earnings (whether or not credited) payable in respect of any deposit or account in a bank, building and loan association, savings and loan association, or similar institution, the following are not substantial limitations or restrictions on the taxpayer's control over the receipt of such earnings:

(1) A requirement that the deposit or account, and the earnings thereon, must be withdrawn in multiples of even amounts;

(2) The fact that the taxpayer would, by withdrawing the earnings during the taxable year, receive earnings that are not substantially less in comparison with the earnings for the corresponding period to which the taxpayer would be entitled had he left the account on deposit until a later date (for example, if an amount equal to three months' interest must be forfeited upon withdrawal or redemption before maturity of a one year or less certificate of deposit, time deposit, bonus plan, or other deposit arrangement then the earnings payable on premature withdrawal or redemption would be substantially less when compared with the earnings available at maturity);

(3) A requirement that the earnings may be withdrawn only upon a withdrawal of all or part of the deposit or account. However, the mere fact that such institutions may pay earnings on withdrawals, total or partial, made during the last three business days of any calendar month ending a regular quarterly or semiannual earnings period at

the applicable rate calculated to the end of such calendar month shall not constitute constructive receipt of income by any depositor or account holder in any such institution who has not made a withdrawal during such period;

(4) A requirement that a notice of intention to withdraw must be given in advance of the withdrawal. In any case when the rate of earnings payable in respect of such a deposit or account depends on the amount of notice of intention to withdraw that is given, earnings at the maximum rate are constructively received during the taxable year regardless of how long the deposit or account was held during the year or whether, in fact, any notice of intention to withdraw is given during the year However, if in the taxable year of withdrawal the depositor or account holder receives a lower rate of earnings because he failed to give the required notice of intention to withdraw, he shall be allowed an ordinary loss in such taxable year in an amount equal to the difference between the amount of earnings previously included in gross income and the amount of earnings actually received. See section 165 and the regulations thereunder.

(b) Examples of constructive receipt. Amounts payable with respect to interest coupons which have matured and are payable but which have not been cashed are constructively received in the taxable year during which the coupons mature, unless it can be shown that there are no funds available for payment of the interest during such year. Dividends on corporate stock are constructively received when unqualifiedly made subject to the demand of the shareholder. However, if a dividend is declared payable on December 31 and the corporation followed its usual practice of paying the dividends by checks mailed so that the shareholders would not receive them until January of the following year, such dividends are not considered to have been constructively received in December. Generally, the amount of dividends or interest credited on savings bank deposits or to shareholders of organizations such as building and loan associations or cooperative banks is income to the depositors or shareholders for the taxable year when credited. However, if any portion of such dividends or interest is not subject to withdrawal at the time credited, such portion is not constructively received and does not constitute income to the depositor or shareholder until the taxable year in which the portion first may be withdrawn. Accordingly, if, under a bonus or forfeiture plan, a portion of the dividends or interest is accumulated and may not be withdrawn until the maturity of the plan, the crediting of such portion to the account of the shareholder or depositor does not constitute constructive receipt. In this case, such credited portion is income to the depositor or shareholder in the year in which the plan matures. However, in the case of certain deposits made after December 31, 1970, in banks, domestic building and loan associations, and similar financial institutions, the ratable inclusion rules of section 1232(a) (3) apply. See § 1.1232–3A. Accrued interest on unwithdrawn insurance policy dividends is gross income to the taxpayer for the first taxable year during which such interest may be withdrawn by him.

§ 1.451–5 Advance payments for goods and long-term contracts

(a) Advance payment defined. (1) For purposes of this section, the term "advance payment" means any amount which is received in a taxable year by a taxpayer using an accrual method of accounting for purchases and sales or a long-term contract method of accounting (described in § 1.451–3), pursuant to, and to be applied against, an agreement:

(i) For the sale or other disposition in a future taxable year of goods held by the taxpayer primarily for sale to customers in the ordinary course of his trade or business, or

(ii) For the building, installing, constructing or manufacturing by the taxpayer of items where the agreement is not completed within such taxable year.

(2) For purposes of subparagraph (1) of this paragraph:

(i) The term "agreement" includes (a) a gift certificate that can be redeemed for goods, and (b) an agreement which obligates a taxpayer to perform activities described in subparagraph (1) (i) or (ii) of this paragraph and which also contains an obligation to perform services that are to be performed as an integral part of such activities; and

(ii) Amounts due and payable are considered "received".

(3) If a taxpayer (described in subparagraph (1) of this paragraph) receives an amount pursuant to, and to be applied against, an agreement that not only obligates the taxpayer to perform the activities described in subparagraph (1) (i) and (ii) of this paragraph, but also obligates the taxpayer to perform services that are not to be performed as an integral part of such activities, such amount will be treated as an "advance payment" (as defined in subparagraph (1) of this paragraph) only to the extent such amount is properly allocable to the obligation to perform the activities described in subparagraph (1) (i) and (ii) of this paragraph. The portion of the amount not so allocable will not be considered an "advance payment" to which this section applies. If, however, the amount not so allocable is less than 5 percent of the total contract price, such amount will be treated as so allocable except that such treatment can not result in delaying the time at which the taxpayer would otherwise accrue the amounts attributable to the activities described in subparagraph (1) (i) and (ii) of this paragraph.

(b) **Taxable year of inclusion.** (1) Advance payments must be included in income either—

(i) In the taxable year of receipt; or

(ii) Except as provided in paragraph (c) of this section,

(a) In the taxable year in which properly accruable under the taxpayer's method of accounting for tax purposes if such method results in including advance payments in gross receipts no later than the time such advance payments are included in gross receipts for purposes of all of his reports (including consolidated financial statements) to shareholders, partners, beneficiaries, other proprietors, and for credit purposes, or

(b) If the taxpayer's method of accounting for purposes of such reports results in advance payments (or any portion of such payments) being included in gross receipts earlier than for tax purposes, in the taxable year in which includible in gross receipts pursuant to his method of accounting for purposes of such reports.

(2) This paragraph may be illustrated by the following examples:

Example (1). S, a retailer who uses for tax purposes and for purposes of the reports referred to in subparagraph (1)(ii)(a) of this paragraph, an accrual method of accounting under which it accounts for its sales of goods when the goods are shipped, receives advance payments for such goods. Such advance payments must be included in gross receipts for tax purposes either in the taxable year the payments are received or in the taxable year such goods are shipped (except as provided in paragraph (c) of this section).

Example (2). T, a manufacturer of household furniture, is a calendar year taxpayer who uses an accrual method of accounting pursuant to which income is accrued when furniture is shipped for purposes of its financial reports (referred to in subparagraph (1)(ii)(a) of this paragraph) and an accrual method of accounting pursuant to which the income is accrued when furniture is delivered and accepted for tax purposes. See § 1.446-1(c)(1)(ii). In 1974, T receives an advance payment of $8,000 from X with respect to an order of furniture to be manufactured for X for a total price of $20,000. The furniture is shipped to X in December 1974, but it is not delivered to and accepted by X until January 1975. As a result of this contract, T must include the entire advance payment in its gross income for tax purposes in 1974 pursuant to subparagraph (1)(ii)(b) of this paragraph. T must include the remaining $12,000 of the gross contract price in its gross income in 1975 for tax purposes.

(3) In the case of a taxpayer accounting for advance payments for tax purposes pursuant to a long-term contract method of accounting under § 1.451-3, or of a taxpayer accounting for advance payments with respect to a long-term contract pursuant to an accrual method of accounting referred to in the succeeding sentence, advance payments shall be included in income in the taxable year in which property included in gross receipts pursuant to such method of accounting (without regard to the financial reporting requirement contained in subparagraph (1)(ii)(a) or (b) of this paragraph). An accrual method of accounting to which the preceding sentence applies shall consist of any method of accounting under which the income is accrued when, and costs are accumulated until, the subject matter of the contract is shipped, delivered, or accepted.

. . . . .

§ **1.453-1 Installment method of reporting income**

. . . .

(b) Income to be reported. (1) Persons permitted to use the installment method of accounting prescribed in section 453 may return as income from installment sales in any taxable year that proportion of the installment payments actually received in that year which the gross profit realized or to be realized when the property is paid for bears to the total contract price. In the case of dealers in personal property, for this purpose, gross profit means sales less cost of goods sold. See § 1.453-2 for rules applicable to the computation of income of dealers in personal property reporting on the installment method. In the case of sales of real estate and casual sales of personal property, gross profit means the selling price less the adjusted basis as defined in section 1011 and the regulations thereunder. Gross profit, in the case of a sale of real estate by a person other than a dealer and a casual sale of personal property, is reduced by commissions and other selling expenses for purposes of determining the proportion of installment payments returnable as income. For rules applicable in determining "selling price" and the use of certain other terms, see also paragraph (c) of § 1.453-4.

(2) For purposes of section 453, any total unstated interest (as defined in section 483(b) under a contract for the sale or exchange of property, payments on account of which are subject to the application of section 483, shall not be included as a part of the selling price or the total contract price. . . . .

. . . . .

§ 1.453-4 Sale of real property involving deferred periodic payments

. . . .

(c) Determination of "selling price". In the sale of mortgaged property the amount of the mortgage, whether the property is merely taken subject to the mortgage or whether the mortgage is assumed by the purchaser, shall, for the purpose of determining whether a sale is on the installment plan, be included as a part of the "selling price"; and for the purpose of determining the payments and the total contract price as those terms are used in section 453, and §§ 1.453-1 through 1.453-7, the amount of such mortgage shall be in-cluded only to the extent that it exceeds the basis of the property. The term "payments" does not include amounts received by the vendor in the year of sale from the disposition to a third person of notes given by the vendee as part of the purchase price which are due and payable in subsequent years. Commissions and other selling expenses paid or incurred by the vendor shall not reduce the amount of the payments, the total contract price, or the selling price.

§ 1.453-6 Deferred-payment sale of real property not on installment method

(a) Value of obligations. (1) In transactions included in paragraph (b) (2) of § 1.453-4, that is, sales of real property involving deferred payments in which the payments received during the year of sale exceed 30 percent of the selling price, the obligations of the purchaser received by the vendor are to be considered as an amount realized to the extent of their fair market value in ascertaining the profit or loss from the transaction. Such obligations, however, are not considered in determining whether the payments during the year of sale exceed 30 percent of the selling price.

(2) If the obligations received by the vendor have no fair market value, the payments in cash or other property having a fair market value shall be applied against and reduce the basis of the property sold and, if in excess of such basis, shall be taxable to the extent of the excess. Gain or loss is realized when the obligations are disposed of or satisfied, the amount thereof being the difference between the reduced basis as provided in the preceding sentence and the amount realized therefor. Only in rare and extraordinary cases does property have no fair market value.

. . . .

§ 1.453-9 Gain or loss on disposition of installment obligations

(a) In general. Subject to the exceptions contained in section 453(d) (4) and paragraph (c) of this section, the entire amount of gain or loss resulting from any disposition or satisfaction of installment obligations, computed in accordance with section 453(d), is recognized in the taxable year of such disposition or satisfaction and shall be considered as resulting from the sale or exchange of the property in respect of which the installment obligation was received by the taxpayer.

(b) **Computation of gain or loss.** (1) The amount of gain or loss resulting under paragraph (a) of this section is the difference between the basis of the obligation and (i) the amount realized, in the case of satisfaction at other than face value or in the case of a sale or exchange, or (ii) the fair market value of the obligation at the time of disposition, if such disposition is other than by sale or exchange.

(2) The basis of an installment obligation shall be the excess of the face value of the obligation over an amount equal to the income which would be returnable were the obligation satisfied in full.

(3) The application of subparagraphs (1) and (2) of this paragraph may be illustrated by the following examples:

Example (1). In 1960 the M Corporation sold a piece of unimproved real estate to B for $20,000. The company acquired the property in 1948 at a cost of $10,000. During 1960 the company received $5,000 cash and vendee's notes for the remainder of the selling price, or $15,000, payable in subsequent years. In 1962, before the vendee made any further payments, the company sold the notes for $13,000 in cash. The corporation makes its returns on the calendar year basis. The income to be reported for 1962 is $5,500, computed as follows:

Proceeds of sale of notes	$13,000
Selling price of property	$20,000
Cost of property	10,000
Total profit	10,000
Total contract price	20,000

Percent of profit, or proportion of each payment returnable as income, $10,000 divided by $20,000, 50 percent.

Face value of notes	15,000
Amount of income returnable were the notes satisfied in full, 50 percent of $15,000	7,500
Basis of obligation—excess of face value of notes over amount of income returnable were the notes satisfied in full	7,500
Taxable income to be reported for 1962	5,500

Example (2). Suppose in example (1) the M Corporation, instead of selling the notes, distributed them in 1962 to its shareholders as a dividend, and at the time of such distribution, the fair market value of the notes was $14,000. The income to be reported for 1962 is $6,500, computed as follows:

Fair market value of notes	$14,000
Basis of obligation—excess of face value of notes over amount of income returnable were the notes satisfied in full (computed as in example (1))	7,500
Taxable income to be reported for 1962	6,500

. . . .

§ 15A.453–0   **Taxable years affected**

(a) **In general.** Except as otherwise provided, the provisions of § 15a.453–1 (a) through (e) generally apply to installment method reporting for sales of real property and casual sales of personal property occurring after October 19, 1980. See 26 CFR § 1.453–1 (rev. as of April 1, 1980) for the provisions relating to installment method reporting for sales of real property and casual sales before October 20, 1980 (except as provided in paragraph (b) of this section) and for provisions relating to installment sales by dealers in personal property occurring before October 20, 1980.

(b) **Certain limitations.** The provisions of prior law (section 453(b) of the Internal Revenue Code of 1954, in effect as of October 18, 1980) which required that the buyer receive no more than 30 percent of the selling price in the taxable year of the installment sale and that at least two payments be received shall not apply to reporting for casual installment sales of personal property and installment sales of real property occurring in a taxable year ending after October 19, 1980.

§ 15A.453–1   **Installment method reporting for sales of real property and casual sales of personal property**

(a) **In general.** Unless the taxpayer otherwise elects in the manner prescribed in paragraph (d)(3) of this section, income from a sale of real property or a casual sale of personal property, where any payment is to be received in a taxable year after the year of sale, is to be reported on the installment method.

(b) **Installment sale defined—(1) In general.** The term "installment sale" means a disposition of property (except as provided in paragraph (b)(4) of this section) where at least one payment is to be received after the close of the taxable year in which the disposition occurs. The term "installment sale" includes dispositions from which payment is to be received in a lump sum in a taxable year subsequent to the year of sale. For purposes of this paragraph, the taxable year in which payments are to be received is to be determined without regard to section 453(e) (relating to related party sales), section (f)(3) (relating to the definition of a "payment") and section (g) (relating to sales of depreciable property to a spouse or 80-percent-owned entity).

(2) **Installment method defined**—(i) In general. Under the installment method, the amount of any payment which is income to the taxpayer is that portion of the installment payment received in that year which the gross profit realized or to be realized bears to the total contract price (the "gross profit ratio"). See paragraph (c) of this section for rules describing installment method reporting of contingent payment sales.

(ii) Selling price defined. The term "selling price" means the gross selling price without reduction to reflect any existing mortgage or other encumbrance on the property (whether assumed or taken subject to by the buyer) and, for installment sales in taxable years ending after October 19, 1980, without reduction to reflect any selling expenses. Neither interest, whether stated or unstated, nor original issue discount is considered to be a part of the selling price. See paragraph (c) of this section for rules describing installment method reporting of contingent payment sales.

(iii) Contract price defined. The term "contract price" means the total contract price equal to selling price reduced by that portion of any qualifying indebtedness (as defined in paragraph (b)(2)(iv) of this section), assumed or taken subject to by the buyer, which does not exceed the seller's basis in the property (adjusted, for installment sales in taxable years ending after October 19, 1980, to reflect commissions and other selling expenses as provided in paragraph (b)(2)(v) of this section). See paragraph (c) of this section for rules describing installment method reporting of contingent payment sales.

(iv) **Qualifying indebtedness**. The term "qualifying indebtedness" means a mortgage or other indebtedness encumbering the property and indebtedness, not secured by the property but incurred or assumed by the purchaser incident to the purchaser's acquisition, holding, or operation in the ordinary course of business or investment, of the property. The term "qualifying indebtedness" does not include an obligation of the taxpayer incurred incident to the disposition of the property (e.g., legal fees relating to the taxpayer's sale of the property) or an obligation functionally unrelated to the acquisition, holding, or operating of the property (e.g., the taxpayer's medical bill). Any obligation created subsequent to the taxpayer's acquisition of the property and incurred or assumed by the taxpayer or placed as an encumbrance on the property in contemplation of disposition of the property is not qualifying indebtedness if the arrangement results in accelerating recovery of the taxpayer's basis in the installment sale.

(v) Gross profit defined. The term "gross profit" means the selling price less the adjusted basis as defined in section 1011 and the regulations thereunder. For sales in taxable years ending after October 19, 1980, in the case of sales of real property by a person other than a dealer and casual sales of personal property, commissions and other selling expenses shall be added to basis for purposes of determining the proportion of payments which is gross profit attributable to the disposition. Such additions to basis will not be deemed to affect the taxpayer's holding period in the transferred property.

(3) **Payment**—(i) In general. Except as provided in paragraph (e) of this section (relating to purchaser evidences of indebtedness payable on demand or readily tradable), the term "payment" does not include the receipt of evidences of indebtedness of the person acquiring the property ("installment obligation"), whether or not payment of such indebtedness is guaranteed by a third party (including a government agency). A standby letter of credit (as defined in paragraph (b)(3)(iii) of this section) shall be treated as a third party guarantee. Payments include amounts actually or constructively received in the taxable year under an installment obligation. Receipt of an evidence of indebtedness which is secured directly or indirectly by cash or a cash equivalent, such as a bank certificate of deposit or a treasury note, will be treated as the receipt of payment.

Payment may be received in cash or other property, including foreign currency, marketable securities, and evidences or indebtedness which are payable on demand or readily tradable. However, for special rules relating to the receipt of certain property with respect to which gain is not recognized, see paragraph (f) of this section (relating to transactions described in sections 351, 356(a) and 1031). Except as provided in § 15a.453-2 of these regulations (relating to distributions of installment obligations in corporate liquidations described in section 337), payment includes receipt of an evidence of indebtedness of a person other than the person acquiring the property from the taxpayer. For purposes of determining the amount of payment received in the taxable year, the amount of qualifying indebtedness (as defined in paragraph (b)(2)(iv) of this section) assumed or taken subject to by the person acquiring the property shall be included only to the extent that it exceeds the basis of the property (determined after adjustment to reflect selling expenses). For purposes of the preceding sentence, an arrangement under which the taxpayer's liability on qualifying indebtedness is eliminated incident to the disposition (e.g., a novation) shall be treated as an assumption of the qualifying indebtedness. If the taxpayer sells property to a creditor of the taxpayer and indebtedness of the taxpayer is cancelled in consideration of the sale, such cancellation shall be treated as payment. To the extent that cancellation is not in consideration of the sale, see §§ 1.61-12 (b)(1) and 1.1001-2(a)(2) relating to discharges of indebtedness. If the taxpayer sells property which is encumbered by a mortgage or other indebtedness on which the taxpayer is not personally liable, and the person acquiring the property is the obligee, the taxpayer shall be treated as having received payment in the amount of such indebtedness.

. . . . .

(5) **Examples.** The following examples illustrate installment method reporting under this section:

Example (1). In 1980, A, a calendar year taxpayer, sells Blackacre, an unencumbered capital asset in A's hands, to B for $100,000: $10,000 down and the remainder payable in equal annual installments over the next 9 years, together with adequate stated interest. A's basis in Blackacre, exclusive of selling expenses, is $38,000. Selling expenses paid by A are $2,000. Therefore, the gross profit is $60,000 ($100,000 selling price—$40,000 basis inclusive of selling expenses). The gross profit ratio is ⅗ (gross profit of $60,000 divided by $100,000 contract price). Accordingly, $6,000 (⅗ of $10,000) of each $10,000 payment received is gain attributable to the sale and $4,000 ($10,000—$6,000) is recovery of basis. The interest received in addition to principal is ordinary income to A.

Example (2). C sells Whiteacre to D for a selling price of $160,000. Whiteacre is encumbered by a longstanding mortgage in the principal amount of $60,000. D will assume or take subject to the $60,000 mortgage and pay the remaining $100,000 in 10 equal annual installments together with adequate stated interest. C's basis in Whiteacre is $90,000. There are no selling expenses. The contract price is $100,000, the $160,000 selling price reduced by the mortgage of $60,000 assumed or taken subject to. Gross profit is $70,000 ($160,000 selling price less C's basis of $90,000). C's gross profit ratio is 7/10 (gross profit of $70,000 divided by $100,000 contract price). Thus, $7,000 (7/10 of $10,000) of each $10,000 annual payment is gain attributable to the sale, and $3,000 ($10,000—$7,000) is recovery of basis.

Example (3). The facts are the same as in example (2), except that C's basis in the land is $40,000. In the year of the sale C is deemed to have received payment of $20,000 ($60,000—$40,000, the amount by which the mortgage D assumed or took subject to exceeds C's basis). Since basis is fully recovered in the year of sale, the gross profit ratio is 1 ($120,000/$120,000) and C will report 100% of the $20,000 deemed payment in the year of sale and each $10,000 annual payment as gain attributable to the sale.

Example (4). E sells Blackacre, an unencumbered capital gain property in E's hands, to F on January 2, 1981. F makes a cash down payment of $500,000 and issues a note to E obliging F to pay an additional $500,000 on the fifth anniversary date. The note does not require a payment of interest. In determining selling price, section 483 will apply to recharacterize as interest a portion of the $500,000 future payment. Assume that under section 483 and the applicable regulations $193,045 is treated as total unstated interest, and the selling price is $806,955 ($1 million less unstated interest). Assuming E's basis (including selling expenses) in Blackacre is $200,000, gross profit is $606,955 ($806,955—$200,000) and the gross profit ratio is 75.21547%. Accordingly, of the $500,000 cash down payment received by E in 1981, $376,077 (75.21547% of $500,000) is gain attributable to the sale and $123,923 is recovery of basis ($500,000—$376,077).

. . . . .

(c) Contingent payment sales—(1) In general. Unless the taxpayer otherwise elects in the manner prescribed in paragraph (d)(3) of this section, contingent payment sales are to be reported on the installment method. As used in this section, the term "contingent payment sale" means a sale or other disposition of property in which the aggregate selling price cannot be determined by the close of the taxable year in which such sale of other disposition occurs. The term "contingent payment sale" does not include transactions with respect to which the installment obligation represents, under applicable principles of tax law, a retained interest in the property which is the subject of the transaction, an interest in a joint venture or a partnership, an equity interest in a corporation or similar transactions, regardless of the existence of a stated maximum selling price or a fixed payment term.

. . . .

This paragraph prescribes the rules to be applied in allocating the taxpayer's basis (including selling expenses except for selling expenses of dealers in real estate) to payments received and to be received in a contingent payment sale. The rules are designed appropriately to distinguish contingent payment sales for which a maximum selling price is determinable, sales for which a maximum selling price is not determinable but the time over which payments will be received is determinable, and sales for which neither a maximum selling price nor a definite payment term is determinable. In addition, rules are prescribed under which, in appropriate circumstances, the taxpayer will be permitted to recover basis under an income forecast computation.

. . . .

(d) Election not to report an installment sale on the installment method— (1) In general. An installment sale is to be reported on the installment method unless the taxpayer elects otherwise in accordance with the rules set forth in paragraph (d)(3) of this section.

(2) Treatment of an installment sale when a taxpayer elects not to report on the installment method—(i) In general. A taxpayer who elects not to report an installment sale on the installment method must recognize gain on the sale in accordance with the taxpayer's method of accounting. The fair market value of an installment obligation shall be determined in accordance with paragraph (d) (2)(ii) and (iii) of this section. In making such determination, any provision of contract or local law restricting the transferability of the installment obligation shall be disregarded. Receipt of an installment obligation shall be treated as a receipt of property, in an amount equal to the fair market value of the installment obligation, whether or not such obligation is the equivalent of cash. An installment obligation is considered to be property and is subject to

valuation, as provided in paragraph (d) (2)(ii) and (iii) of this section, without regard to whether the obligation is embodied in a note, an executory contract, or any other instrument, or is an oral promise enforceable under local law.

(ii) Fixed amount obligations. (A) A fixed amount obligation means an installment obligation the amount payable under which is fixed. Solely for the purpose of determining whether the amount payable under an installment obligation is fixed, the provisions of section 483 and any "payment recharacterization" arrangement (as defined in paragraph (c)(2)(ii) of this section) shall be disregarded. If the fixed amount payable is stated in identified, fungible units of property the value of which will or may vary over time in relation to the United States dollar (e.g., foreign currency, ounces of gold, or bushels of wheat), such units shall be converted to United States dollars at the rate of exchange or dollar value on the date the installment sale is made. A taxpayer using the cash receipts and disbursements methods of accounting shall treat as an amount realized in the year of sale the fair market value of the installment obligation. In no event will the fair market value of the installment obligation be considered to be less than the fair market value of the property sold (minus any other consideration received by the taxpayer on the sale). A taxpayer using the accrual method of accounting shall treat as an amount realized in the year of sale the total amount payable under the installment obligation. For this purpose, neither interest (whether stated or unstated) nor original issue discount is considered to be part of the amount payable. If the amount payable is otherwise fixed, but because the time over which payments may be made is contingent, a portion of the fixed amount will or may be treated as internal interest (as defined in paragraph (c)(2)(ii) of this section), the amount payable shall be determined by applying the price interest recomputation rule (described in paragraph (c)(2)(ii) of this section). Under no circumstances will an installment sale for a fixed amount obligation be considered an "open" transaction. For purposes of this (ii), remote or incidental contingencies are not to be taken into account.

(B) The following examples illustrate the provisions of paragraph (d)(2) of this section.

Example (1). A, an accrual method taxpayer, owns all of the stock of X corporation with a basis of $20 million. On July 1, 1981, A sells the stock of X corporation to B for $60 million payable on June 15, 1992. The agreement also provides that, against this fixed amount, B shall make annual prepayments (on June 15) equal to 5% of the net profits of X earned in the immediately preceding fiscal year beginning with the fiscal year ending March 31, 1982. Thus, the first prepayment will be made on June 15, 1982. No stated interest is payable under the agreement and thus the unstated interest provisions of section 483 are applicable. Under section 483, no part of any payment made on June 15, 1982 (which is within one year following the July 1, 1981 sale date), will be treated as unstated interest. Under the price interest recomputation rule, it is presumed that the entire $60 million fixed amount will be paid on June 15, 1982. Accordingly, if A elects not to report the transaction on the installment method, in 1981 A must report $60 million as the amount realized on the sale and must report $40 million as gain on the sale in that year.

Example (2). The facts are the same as in example (1) except that A uses the cash receipts and disbursements method of accounting. In 1981 A must report as an amount realized on the sale the fair market value of the installment obligation and must report as gain on the sale in 1981 the excess of that amount realized over A's basis of $20 million. In no event will the fair market value of the installment obligation be considered to be less than the fair market value of the stock of X. In determining the fair market value of the installment obligation, any contractual or legal restrictions on the transferability of the installment obligation, and any remote or incidental contingencies otherwise affecting the amount payable or time of payments under the installment obligation, shall be disregarded.

(iii) *Contingent payment obligations.* Any installment obligation which is not a fixed amount obligation (as defined in paragraph (d)(2)(ii) of this section) is a contingent payment obligation. If an installment obligation contains both a fixed amount component and a contingent payment component, the fixed amount component shall be treated under the rules of paragraph (d)(2)(ii) of this section and the contingent amount component shall be treated under the rules of this (iii). The fair market value of a contingent payment obligation shall be determined by disregarding any restrictions on transfer imposed by agreement or under local law. The fair market value of a contingent payment obligation may be ascertained from, and in no event shall be considered to be less than, the fair market value of the property sold (less the amount of any other consideration received in the sale). Only in those rare and extraordinary cases involving sales for a contingent payment obligation in which the fair market value of the obligation (determinable under the preceding sentences) cannot reasonably be ascertained will the taxpayer be entitled to assert that the transaction is "open." Any such transaction will be carefully scrutinized to determine whether a sale in fact has taken place. A taxpayer using the cash receipts and disbursements method of accounting must report as an amount realized in the year of sale the fair market value of the contingent payment obligation. A taxpayer using the accrual method of accounting must report an amount realized in the year of sale determined in accordance with that method of accounting, but in no event less than the fair market value of the contingent payment obligation.

(3) **Time and manner for making election**—(i) *In general.* An election under paragraph (d)(1) or this section must be made on or before the due date prescribed by law (including extensions) for filing the taxpayer's return for the taxable year in which the installment sale occurs. The election must be made in the manner prescribed by the appropriate forms for the taxpayer's return for the taxable year of the sale. A taxpayer who reports an amount realized equal to the selling price including the full face amount of any installment obligation on the tax return filed for the taxable year in which the installment sale occurs will be considered to have made an effective election under paragraph (d)(1) of this section. A cash method taxpayer receiving an obligation the fair market value of which is less than the face value must make the election in the manner prescribed by appropriate instructions for the return filed for the taxable year of the sale.

(ii) *Election made after the due date.* Elections after the time specified in paragraph (d)(3)(i) of this section will be permitted only in those rare circumstances when the Internal Revenue Service concludes that the taxpayer had good cause for failing to make a timely election. A recharacterization of a transaction as a sale in a taxable year subsequent to the taxable year in which the transaction occurred (e.g., a transaction initially reported as a lease later is determined to have been an installment sale) will not justify a late election. No conditional elections will be permitted. . . .

(4) **Revoking an election.** Generally, an election made under paragraph (d)(1) is irrevocable. An election may be re-

voked only with the consent of the Internal Revenue Service. A revocation is retroactive. A revocation will not be permitted when one of its purposes is the avoidance of federal income taxes, or when the taxable year in which any payment was received has closed.

. . . . .

§ 1.455-1 Treatment of prepaid subscription income

Effective with respect to taxable years beginning after December 31, 1957, section 455 permits certain taxpayers to elect with respect to a trade or business in connection with which prepaid subscription income is received, to include such income in gross income for the taxable years during which a liability exists to furnish or deliver a newspaper, magazine, or other periodical. If a taxpayer does not elect to treat prepaid subscription income under the provisions of section 455, such income is includible in gross income for the taxable year in which received by the taxpayer, unless under the method or practice of accounting used in computing taxable income such amount is to be properly accounted for as of a different period.

§ 1.461-1 General rule for taxable year of deduction

(a) General rule—(1) Taxpayer using cash receipts and disbursements method. Under the cash receipts and disbursements method of accounting, amounts representing allowable deductions shall, as a general rule, be taken into account for the taxable year in which paid. Further, a taxpayer using this method may also be entitled to certain deductions in the computation of taxable income which do not involve cash disbursements during the taxable year, such as the deductions for depreciation, depletion, and losses under sections 167, 611, and 165, respectively. If an expenditure results in the creation of an asset having a useful life which extends substantially beyond the close of the taxable year, such an expenditure may not be deductible, or may be deductible only in part, for the taxable year in which made. An example is an expenditure for the construction of improvements by the lessee on leased property where the estimated life of the improvements is in excess of the remain-

ing period of the lease. In such a case, in lieu of the allowance for depreciation provided by section 167, the basis shall be amortized ratably over the remaining period of the lease. See section 178 and the regulations thereunder for rules governing the effect to be given renewal options in determining whether the useful life of the improvements exceeds the remaining term of the lease where a lessee begins improvements on leased property after July 28, 1958, other than improvements which on such date and at all times thereafter, the lessee was under a binding legal obligation to make. See section 263 and the regulations thereunder for rules relating to capital expenditures.

(2) Taxpayer using an accrual method. Under an accrual method of accounting, an expense is deductible for the taxable year in which all the events have occurred which determine the fact of the liability and the amount thereof can be determined with reasonable accuracy. However, any expenditure which results in the creation of an asset having a useful life which extends substantially beyond the close of the taxable year may not be deductible, or may be deductible only in part, for the taxable year in which incurred. While no accrual shall be made in any case in which all of the events have not occurred which fix the liability, the fact that the exact amount of the liability which has been incurred cannot be determined will not prevent the accrual within the taxable year of such part thereof as can be computed with reasonable accuracy. For example, A renders services to B during the taxable year for which A claims $10,000. B admits the liability to A for $5,000 but contests the remainder. B may accrue only $5,000 as an expense for the taxable year in which the services were rendered. In the case of certain contested liabilities in respect of which a taxpayer transfers money or other property to provide for the satisfaction of the contested liability, see § 1.461-2. Where a deduction is properly accrued on the basis of a computation made with reasonable accuracy and the exact amount is subsequently determined in a later taxable year, the difference, if any, between such amounts shall be taken into account for the later taxable year in which such determination is made.

(3) Other factors which determine when deductions may be taken. (i)

Each year's return should be complete in itself, and taxpayers shall ascertain the facts necessary to make a correct return. The expenses, liabilities, or loss of one year cannot be used to reduce the income of a subsequent year. A taxpayer may not take advantage in a return for a subsequent year of his failure to claim deductions in a prior taxable year in which such deductions should have been properly taken under his method of accounting. If a taxpayer ascertains that a deduction should have been claimed in a prior taxable year, he should, if within the period of limitation, file a claim for credit or refund of any overpayment of tax arising therefrom. Similarly, if a taxpayer ascertains that a deduction was improperly claimed in a prior taxable year, he should, if within the period of limitation, file an amended return and pay any additional tax due. However, in a going business there are certain overlapping deductions. If these overlapping items do not materially distort income, they may be included in the years in which the taxpayer consistently takes them into account.

(ii) Where there is a dispute and the entire liability is contested, judgments on account of damages for patent infringement, personal injuries or other causes, or other binding adjudications, including decisions of referees and boards of review under workmen's compensation laws, are deductions from gross income when the claim is finally adjudicated or is paid, depending upon the taxpayer's method of accounting. However, see subparagraph (2) of this paragraph.

(iii) For special rules relating to certain deductions, see the following sections and the regulations thereunder: Section 1481, relating to accounting for amounts repaid in connection with renegotiation of a government contract; section 1341, relating to the computation of tax where the taxpayer repays a substantial amount received under a claim of right in a prior taxable year; section 165(e), relating to losses resulting from theft; and section 165(h), relating to an election of the year of deduction of disaster losses.

. . . . .

(b) **Special rule in case of death.** A taxpayer's taxable year ends on the date of his death. See section 443(a) (2) and paragraph (a) (2) of § 1.443–1. In computing taxable income for such year, there shall be deducted only amounts properly deductible under the method of accounting used by the taxpayer. However, if the taxpayer used an accrual method of accounting, no deduction shall be allowed for amounts accrued only by reason of his death. For rules relating to the inclusion of items of partnership deduction, loss, or credit in the return of a decedent partner, see subchapter K, chapter 1 of the Code, and the regulations thereunder.

. . . . .

§ **1.461–2 Timing of deductions in certain cases where asserted liabilities are contested**

(a) General rule—(1) Taxable year of deduction. If—

(i) The taxpayer contests an asserted liability,

(ii) The taxpayer transfers money or other property to provide for the satisfaction of the asserted liability,

(iii) The contest with respect to the asserted liability exists after the time of the transfer, and

(iv) But for the fact that the asserted liability is contested, a deduction would be allowed for the taxable year of the transfer (or, in the case of an accrual method taxpayer, for an earlier taxable year for which such amount would be accruable),

then the deduction with respect to the contested amount shall be allowed for the taxable year of the transfer.

(2) **Exception.** Subparagraph (1) of this paragraph shall not apply in respect of the deduction for income, war profits, and excess profits taxes imposed by the authority of any foreign country or possession of the United States, including a tax paid in lieu of a tax on income, war profits, or excess profits otherwise generally imposed by any foreign country or by any possession of the United States.

(3) **Refunds includible in gross income.** If any portion of the contested amount which is deducted under sub-

paragraph (1) of this paragraph for the taxable year of transfer is refunded when the contest is settled, such portion is includible in gross income except as provided in § 1.111–1, relating to recovery of certain items previously deducted or credited. Such refunded amount is includible in gross income for the taxable year of receipt, or for an earlier taxable year if properly accruable for such earlier year.

(4) Examples. The provisions of this paragraph are illustrated by the following examples:

Example (1). X Corporation, which uses an accrual method of accounting, in 1964 contests $20 of a $100 asserted real property tax liability but pays the entire $100 to the taxing authority. In 1968, the contest is settled and X receives a refund of $5. X deducts $100 for the taxable year 1964, and includes $5 in gross income for the taxable year 1968 (assuming § 1.111–1 does not apply to such amount). If in 1964 X pays only $80 to the taxing authority, X deducts only $80 for 1964. The result would be the same if X Corporation used the cash method of accounting.

Example (2). Y Corporation makes its return on the basis of a calendar year and uses an accrual method of accounting. Y's real property taxes are assessed and become a lien on December 1, but are not payable until March 1 of the following year. On December 10, 1964, Y contests $20 of the $100 asserted real property tax which was assessed and became a lien on December 1, 1964. On March 1, 1965, Y pays the entire $100 to the taxing authority. In 1968, the contest is settled and Y receives a refund of $5. Y deducts $80 for the taxable year 1964, deducts $20 for the taxable year 1965, and includes $5 in gross income for the taxable year 1968 (assuming § 1.111–1 does not apply to such amount).

(b) Contest of asserted liability—(1) Asserted liability. For purposes of paragraph (a) (1) of this section, the term "asserted liability" means an item with respect to which, but for the existence of any contest in respect of such item, a deduction would be allowable under an accrual method of accounting. For example, a notice of a local real estate tax assessment and a bill received for services may represent asserted liabilities.

(2) Definition of the term "contest". Any contest which would prevent accrual of a liability under section 461(a) shall be considered to be a contest in determining whether the taxpayer satisfies paragraph (a) (1) (i) of this sec-

tion. A contest arises when there is a bona fide dispute as to the proper evaluation of the law or the facts necessary to determine the existence or correctness of the amount of an asserted liability. It is not necessary to institute suit in a court of law in order to contest an asserted liability. An affirmative act denying the validity or accuracy, or both, of an asserted liability to the person who is asserting such liability, such as including a written protest with payment of the asserted liability, is sufficient to commence a contest. Thus, lodging a protest in accordance with local law is sufficient to contest an asserted liability for taxes. It is not necessary that the affirmative act denying the validity or accuracy, or both, of an asserted liability be in writing if, upon examination of all the facts and circumstances, it can be established to the satisfaction of the Commissioner that a liability has been asserted and contested.

(3) Example. The provisions of this paragraph are illustrated by the following example:

Example: O Corporation makes its return on the basis of a calendar year and uses an accrual method of accounting. O receives a large shipment of typewriter ribbons from S Company on January 30, 1964, which O pays for in full on February 10, 1964. Subsequent to their receipt, several of the ribbons prove defective because of inferior materials used by the manufacturer. On August 9, 1964, O orally notifies S and demands refund of the full purchase price of the ribbons. After negotiations prove futile and a written demand is rejected by S, O institutes an action for the full purchase price. For purposes of paragraph (a) (1) (i) of this section, S has asserted a liability against O which O contests on August 9, 1964. O deducts the contested amount for 1964.

(c) Transfer to provide for the satisfaction of an asserted liability—(1) In general. A taxpayer may provide for the satisfaction of an asserted liability by transferring money or other property beyond his control (i) to the person who is asserting the liability, (ii) to an escrowee or trustee pursuant to a written agreement (among the escrowee or trustee, the taxpayer, and the person who is asserting the liability) that the money or other property be delivered in accordance with the settlement of the contest, or (iii) to an escrowee or trustee pursuant to an order of the United

States, any State or political subdivision thereof, or any agency or instrumentality of the foregoing, or a court that the money or other property be delivered in accordance with the settlement of the contest. A taxpayer may also provide for the satisfaction of an asserted liability by transferring money or other property beyond his control to a court with jurisdiction over the contest. Purchasing a bond to guarantee payment of the asserted liability, an entry on the taxpayer's books of account, and a transfer to an account which is within the control of the taxpayer are not transfers to provide for the satisfaction of an asserted liability. In order for money or other property to be beyond the control of a taxpayer, the taxpayer must relinquish all authority over such money or other property.

(2) **Examples.** The provisions of this paragraph are illustrated by the following examples:

Example (1). M Corporation contests a $5,000 liability asserted against it by L Company for services rendered. To provide for the contingency that it might have to pay the liability, M establishes a separate bank account in its own name. M then transfers $5,000 from its general account to such separate account. Such transfer does not qualify as a transfer to provide for the satisfaction of an asserted liability because M has not transferred the money beyond its control.

Example (2). M Corporation contests a $5,000 liability asserted against it by L Company for services rendered. To provide for the contingency that it might have to pay the liability, M transfers $5,000 to an irrevocable trust pursuant to a written agreement among the trustee, M (the taxpayer), and L (the person who is asserting the liability) that the money shall be held until the contest is settled and then disbursed in accordance with the settlement. Such transfer qualifies as a transfer to provide for the satisfaction of an asserted liability.

(d) **Contest exists after transfer.** In order for a contest with respect to an asserted liability to exist after the time of transfer, such contest must be pursued subsequent to such time. Thus, the contest must have been neither settled nor abandoned at the time of the transfer. A contest may be settled by a decision, judgment, decree, or other order of any court of competent jurisdiction which has become final, or by written or oral agreement between the parties. For example, Z Corporation, which uses an accrual method of ac-

counting, in 1964 contests a $100 asserted liability. In 1967 the contested liability is settled as being $80 which Z accrues and deducts for such year. In 1968 Z pays the $80. Section 461(f) does not apply to Z with respect to the transfer because a contest did not exist after the time of such transfer.

(e) **Deduction otherwise allowed—** (1) **In general.** The existence of the contest with respect to an asserted liability must prevent (without regard to section 461(f)) and be the only factor preventing a deduction for the taxable year of the transfer (or, in the case of an accrual method taxpayer, for an earlier taxable year for which such amount would be accruable) to provide for the satisfaction of such liability. Nothing in section 461(f) or this section shall be construed to give rise to a deduction since section 461(f) and this section relate only to the timing of deductions which are otherwise allowable under the Code.

(2) **Example.** The provisions of this paragraph are illustrated by the following example:

Example. A, an individual, makes a gift of certain property to B, an individual. A pays the entire amount of gift tax assessed against him but contests his liability for such tax. Section 275(a) (3) provides that gift taxes are not deductible. A does not satisfy the requirement of paragraph (a) (1) (iv) of this section since a deduction would not be allowed for the taxable year of the transfer even if A did not contest his liability for such tax.

· · · ·

§ 1.471-1 Need for inventories

In order to reflect taxable income correctly, inventories at the beginning and end of each taxable year are necessary in every case in which the production, purchase, or sale of merchandise is an income-producing factor. The inventory should include all finished or partly finished goods and, in the case of raw materials and supplies, only those which have been acquired for sale or which will physically become a part of merchandise intended for sale, in which class fall containers, such as kegs, bottles, and cases, whether returnable or not, if title thereto will pass to the purchaser of the product to be sold therein. Merchandise should be included in the inventory only if title thereto is vested in the taxpayer. Accordingly, the seller should include in his inventory goods under contract for sale but not yet segregated and applied to the contract and goods out upon consignment, but should exclude from inventory goods sold (including containers), title to which has passed to the purchaser. A purchaser should include in inventory merchandise purchased (including containers), title to which has passed to him, although such merchandise is in transit or for other reasons has not been reduced to physical possession, but should not include goods ordered for future delivery, transfer of title to which has not yet been effected. (But see § 1.472–1.)

§ 1.471–2 Valuation of inventories

(a) Section 471 provides two tests to which each inventory must conform:

(1) It must conform as nearly as may be to the best accounting practice in the trade or business, and

(2) It must clearly reflect the income.

(b) It follows, therefore, that inventory rules cannot be uniform but must give effect to trade customs which come within the scope of the best accounting practice in the particular trade or business. In order to clearly reflect income, the inventory practice of a taxpayer should be consistent from year to year, and greater weight is to be given to consistency than to any particular method of inventorying or basis of valuation so long as the method or basis used is in accord with §§ 1.471–1 through 1.471–11.

(c) The bases of valuation most commonly used by business concerns and which meet the requirements of section 471 are (1) cost and (2) cost or market, whichever is lower. (For inventories by dealers in securities, see § 1.471–5.) Any goods in an inventory which are unsalable at normal prices or unusable in the normal way because of damage, imperfections, shop wear, changes of style, odd or broken lots, or other similar causes, including second-hand

goods taken in exchange, should be valued at bona fide selling prices less direct cost of disposition, whether subparagraph (1) or (2) of this paragraph is used, or if such goods consist of raw materials or partly finished goods held for use or consumption, they shall be valued upon a reasonable basis, taking into consideration the usability and the condition of the goods, but in no case shall such value be less than the scrap value. Bona fide selling price means actual offering of goods during a period ending not later than 30 days after inventory date. The burden of proof will rest upon the taxpayer to show that such exceptional goods as are valued upon such selling basis come within the classifications indicated above, and he shall maintain such records of the disposition of the goods as will enable a verification of the inventory to be made.

.   .   .   .   .

(f) The following methods, among others, are sometimes used in taking or valuing inventories, but are not in accord with the regulations in this part:

(1) Deducting from the inventory a reserve for price changes, or an estimated depreciation in the value thereof.

(2) Taking work in process, or other parts of the inventory, at a nominal price or at less than its proper value.

(3) Omitting portions of the stock on hand.

(4) Using a constant price or nominal value for so-called normal quantity of materials or goods in stock.

(5) Including stock in transit, shipped either to or from the taxpayer, the title to which is not vested in the taxpayer.

.   .   .   .   .

§ 1.471–3 Inventories at cost

Cost means:
(a) In the case of merchandise on hand at the beginning of the taxable year, the inventory price of such goods.

(b) In the case of merchandise purchased since the beginning of the taxable year, the invoice price less trade or other discounts, except strictly cash discounts approximating a fair interest rate, which may be deducted or not at the option of the taxpayer, provided a consistent course is followed. To this net invoice price should be added transportation or other necessary charges incurred in acquiring possession of the goods.

(c) In the case of merchandise produced by the taxpayer since the beginning of the taxable year, (1) the cost of raw materials and supplies entering into or consumed in connection with the product, (2) expenditures for direct labor, and (3) indirect production costs incident to and necessary for the production of the particular article, including in such indirect production costs an appropriate portion of management expenses, but not including any cost of selling or return on capital, whether by way of interest or profit. See § 1.471-11 for more specific rules regarding the treatment of indirect production costs.

(d) In any industry in which the usual rules for computation of cost of production are inapplicable, costs may be approximated upon such basis as may be reasonable and in conformity with established trade practice in the particular industry. Among such cases are: (1) Farmers and raisers of livestock (see § 1.471-6); (2) miners and manufacturers who by a single process or uniform series of processes derive a product of two or more kinds, sizes, or grades, the unit cost of which is substantially alike (see § 1.471-7); and (3) retail merchants who use what is known as the "retail method" in ascertaining approximate cost (see § 1.471-8).

Notwithstanding the other rules of this section, cost shall not include an amount which is of a type for which a deduction would be disallowed under section 162(c), (f), or (g) and the regulations thereunder in the case of a business expense.

§ 1.471-4 Inventories at cost or market, whichever is lower

(a) Under ordinary circumstances and for normal goods in an inventory, 'market" means the current bid price prevailing at the date of the inventory for the particular merchandise in the volume in which usually purchased by the taxpayer, and is applicable in the cases—

(1) Of goods purchased and on hand, and

(2) Of basic elements of cost (materials, labor, and burden) in goods in process of manufacture and in finished goods on hand; exclusive, however, of goods on hand or in process of manufacture for delivery upon firm sales contracts (i. e., those not legally subject to cancellation by either party) at fixed prices entered into before the date of the inventory, under which the taxpayer is protected against actual loss, which goods must be inventoried at cost.

(b) Where no open market exists or where quotations are nominal, due to inactive market conditions, the taxpayer must use such evidence of a fair market price at the date or dates nearest the inventory as may be available, such as specific purchases or sales by the taxpayer or others in reasonable volume and made in good faith, or compensation paid for cancellation of contracts for purchase commitments. Where the taxpayer in the regular course of business has offered for sale such merchandise at prices lower than the current price as above defined, the inventory may be valued at such prices less direct cost of disposition, and the correctness of such prices will be determined by reference to the actual sales of the taxpayer for a reasonable period before and after the date of the inventory. Prices which vary materially from the actual prices so ascertained will not be accepted as reflecting the market.

(c) Where the inventory is valued upon the basis of cost or market, whichever is lower, the market value of each article on hand at the inventory date shall be compared with the cost of the article, and the lower of such values shall be taken as the inventory value of the article.

§ 1.471-11 Inventories of manufacturers

(a) Use of full absorption method of inventory costing.—In order to conform as nearly as may be possible to the best accounting practices and to clearly reflect income (as required by section 471 of the Code), both direct and indirect production costs must be taken into account in the computation of inventoriable costs in accordance with the "full absorption" method of inventory costing. Under the full absorption method of inventory costing production costs must be allocated to goods produced during the taxable year, whether sold during the taxable year or in inventory at the close of the taxable year determined in accordance with the taxpayer's method of identifying goods in inventory. Thus, the taxpayer must include as inventoriable costs all direct production costs and, to the extent provided by paragraphs (c) and (d) of this section, all indirect production costs. For purposes of this section, the term "financial reports" means financial reports (including consolidated financial statements) to shareholders, partners, beneficiaries or other proprietors and for credit purposes.

(b) Production costs—(1) In general. Costs are considered to be production costs to the extent that they are incident to and necessary for production or manufacturing operations or processes. Production costs include direct production costs and fixed and variable indirect production costs.

(2) Direct production costs. (i) Costs classified as "direct production costs" are generally those costs which are incident to and necessary for production or manufacturing operations or processes and are components of the cost of either direct material or direct labor. Direct material costs include the cost of those materials which become an integral part of the specific product and those materials which are consumed in the ordinary course of manufacturing and can be identified or associated with particular units or groups of units of that product. See § 1.471–3 for the elements of direct material costs. Direct labor costs include the cost of labor which can be identified or associated with particular units or groups of units of a specific product. The elements of direct labor costs include such items as basic compensation, overtime pay, vacation and holiday pay, sick leave pay

(other than payments pursuant to a wage continuation plan under section 105(d)), shift differential, payroll taxes and payments to a supplemental unemployment benefit plan paid or incurred on behalf of employees engaged in direct labor. For the treatment of rework labor, scrap, spoilage costs, and any other costs not specifically described as direct production costs see § 1.471–11(c)(2).

(ii) Under the full absorption method, a taxpayer must take into account all items of direct production cost in his inventoriable costs. Nevertheless, a taxpayer will not be treated as using an incorrect method of inventory costing if he treats any direct production costs as indirect production costs, provided such costs are allocated to the taxpayer's ending inventory to the extent provided by paragraph (d) of this section. Thus, for example, a taxpayer may treat direct labor costs as part of indirect production costs (for example, by use of the conversion cost method), provided all such costs are allocated to ending inventory to the extent provided by paragraph (d) of this section.

(3) Indirect production costs—(i) In general. The term "indirect production costs" includes all costs which are incident to and necessary for production or manufacturing operations or processes other than direct production costs (as defined in subparagraph (2) of this paragraph). Indirect production costs may be classified as to kind or type in accordance with acceptable accounting principles so as to enable convenient identification with various production or manufacturing activities or functions and to facilitate reasonable groupings of such costs for purposes of determining unit product costs.

(ii) Fixed and variable classifications. For purposes of this section, fixed indirect production costs are generally those costs which do not vary significantly with changes in the amount of goods produced at any given level of production capacity. These fixed costs may include, among other costs, rent and property taxes on buildings and machinery incident to and necessary for manufacturing operations or processes.

On the other hand, variable indirect production costs are generally those costs which do vary significantly with changes in the amount of goods produced at any given level of production capacity. These variable costs may include, among other costs, indirect materials, factory janitorial supplies, and utilities. Where a particular cost contains both fixed and variable elements, these elements should be segregated into fixed and variable classifications to the extent necessary under the taxpayer's method of allocation, such as for the application of the practical capacity concept (as described in paragraph (d) (4) of this section).

(c) **Certain indirect production costs —(1) General rule.** Except as provided in subparagraph (3) of this paragraph, in order to determine whether indirect production costs referred to in paragraph (b) of this section must be included in a taxpayer's computation of the amount of inventoriable costs, three categories of costs have been provided in subparagraph (2) of this paragraph. Costs described in subparagraph (2)(i) of this paragraph must be included in the taxpayer's computation of the amount of inventoriable costs, regardless of their treatment by the taxpayer in his financial reports. Costs described in subparagraph(2)(ii) of this paragraph need not enter into the taxpayer's computation of the amount of inventoriable costs, regardless of their treatment by the taxpayer in his financial reports. Costs described in subparagraph (2)(iii) of this paragraph must be included in or excluded from the taxpayer's computation of the amount of inventoriable costs in accordance with the treatment of such costs by the taxpayer in his financial reports and generally accepted accounting principles. For the treatment of indirect production costs described in subparagraph (2) of this paragraph in the case of a taxpayer who is not using comparable methods of accounting for such costs for tax and financial reporting, see subparagraph (3) of this paragraph. After a taxpayer has determined which costs must be treated as indirect production costs includible in the computation of the amount of inventoriable costs, such costs must be allocated to a taxpayer's ending inventory in a man-

ner prescribed by paragraph (d) of this section.

(2) **Includibility of certain indirect production costs—(i) Indirect production costs included in inventoriable costs.** Indirect production costs which must enter into the computation of the amount of inventoriable costs (regardless of their treatment by a taxpayer in his financial reports) include:

(a) Repair expenses,

(b) Maintenance,

(c) Utilities, such as heat, power and light,

(d) Rent,

(e) Indirect labor and production supervisory wages, including basic compensation, overtime pay, vacation and holiday pay, sick leave pay (other than payments pursuant to a wage continuation plan under section 105(d)), shift differential, payroll taxes and contributions to a supplemental unemployment benefit plan.

(f) Indirect materials and supplies,

(g) Tools and equipment not capitalized, and

(h) Costs of quality control and inspection,

to the extent, and only to the extent, such costs are incident to and necessary for production or manufacturing operations or processes.

(ii) **Costs not included in inventoriable costs.** Costs which are not required to be included for tax purposes in the computation of the amount of inventoriable costs (regardless of their treatment by a taxpayer in his financial reports) include:

(a) Marketing expenses,

(b) Advertising expenses,

(c) Selling expenses,

(d) Other distribution expenses,

(e) Interest,

(f) Research and experimental expenses including engineering and product development expenses,

(g) Losses under section 165 and the regulations thereunder,

(h) Percentage depletion in excess of cost depletion,

(i) Depreciation and amortization reported for Federal income tax purposes in excess of depreciation reported by the taxpayer in his financial reports,

(j) Income taxes attributable to income received on the sale of inventory,

(k) Pension contributions to the extent that they represent past services cost,

(l) General and administrative expenses incident to and necessary for the taxpayer's activities as a whole rather than to production or manufacturing operations or processes, and

(m) Salaries paid to officers attributable to the performance of services which are incident to and necessary for the taxpayer's activities· taken as a whole rather than to production or manufacturing operations or processes. Notwithstanding the preceding sentence, if a taxpayer consistently includes in his computation of the amount of inventoriable costs any of the costs described in the preceding sentence, a change in such method of inclusion shall be considered a change in method of accounting within the meaning of sections 446, 481, and paragraph (e)(4) of this section.

(iii) Indirect production costs includible in inventoriable costs depending upon treatment in taxpayer's financial reports. In the case of costs listed in this subdivision, the inclusion or exclusion of such costs from the amount of inventoriable costs for purposes of a taxpayer's financial reports shall determine whether such costs must be included in or excluded from the computation of inventoriable costs for tax purposes, but only if such treatment is not inconsistent with generally accepted accounting principles. In the case of costs which are not included in subdivision (i) or (ii) of this subparagraph, nor listed in this subdivision, whether such costs must be included in or excluded from the computation of inventoriable costs for tax purposes depends upon the extent to which such costs are similar to costs included in subdivision (i) or (ii), and if such costs are dissimilar to costs in subdivision (i) or (ii), such costs shall be treated as included in or excludable from the amount of inventoriable costs in accordance with this subdivision.

The costs listed in this subdivision are:

(a) Taxes. Taxes otherwise allowable as a deduction under section 164 (other than State and local and foreign income taxes) attributable to assets incident to and necessary for production or manufacturing operations or processes. Thus, for example, the cost of State and local property taxes imposed on a factory or other production facility and any State and local taxes imposed on inventory must be included in or excluded from the computation of the amount of inventoriable costs for tax purposes depending upon their treatment by a taxpayer in his financial reports.

(b) Depreciation and depletion. Depreciation reported in financial reports and cost depletion on assets incident to and necessary for production or manufacturing operations or processes. In computing cost depletion under this section, the adjusted basis of such assets shall be reduced by cost depletion and not by percentage depletion taken thereon.

(c) Employee benefits. Pension and profit-sharing contributions representing current service costs otherwise allowable as a deduction under section 404, and other employee benefits incurred on behalf of labor incident to and necessary for production or manufacturing operations or processes. These other benefits include workmen's compensation expenses, payments under a wage continuation plan described in section 105(d), amounts of a type which would be includible in the gross income of employees under non-qualified pension, profit-sharing and stock bonus

913

plans, premiums on life and health insurance and miscellaneous benefits provided for employees such as safety, medical treatment, cafeteria, recreational facilities, membership dues, etc., which are otherwise allowable as deductions under chapter 1 of the Code.

(d) **Costs attributable to strikes, rework labor, scrap and spoilage.** Costs attributable to rework labor, scrap and spoilage which are incident to and necessary for production or manufacturing operations or processes and costs attributable to strikes incident to production or manufacturing operation or processes.

(e) **Factory administrative expenses.** Administrative costs of production (but not including any cost of selling or any return on capital) incident to and necessary for production or manufacturing operations or processes.

(f) **Officers' salaries.** Salaries paid to officers attributable to services performed incident to and necessary for production or manufacturing operations or processes.

(g) **Insurance costs.** Insurance costs incident to and necessary for production or manufacturing operations or processes such as insurance on production machinery and equipment.

A change in the taxpayer's treatment in his financial reports of costs described in this subdivision which results in a change in treatment of such costs for tax purposes shall constitute a change in method of accounting within the meaning of sections 446 and 481 to which paragraph (e) applies.

(3) **Exception.** In the case of a taxpayer whose method of accounting for production costs in his financial reports is not comparable to his method of accounting for such costs for tax purposes (such as a taxpayer using the prime cost method for purposes of financial reports), the following rules apply:

(i) **Indirect production costs included in inventoriable costs.** Indirect production costs which must enter into the computation of the amount of inventoriable costs (to the extent, and

only to the extent, such costs are incident to and necessary for production or manufacturing operations or processes) include:

(a) Repair expenses,

(b) Maintenance,

(c) Utilities, such as heat, power and light,

(d) Rent,

(e) Indirect labor and production supervisory wages, including basic compensation, overtime pay, vacation and holiday pay, sick leave pay (other than payments pursuant to a wage continuation plan under section 105(d)), shift differential, payroll taxes and contributions to a supplemental unemployment benefit plan,

(f) Indirect materials and supplies,

(g) Tools and equipment not capitalized,

(h) Costs of quality control and inspection,

(i) Taxes otherwise allowable as a deduction under section 164 (other than State and local and foreign income taxes),

(j) Depreciation and amortization reported for financial purposes and cost depletion,

(k) Administrative costs of production (but not including any cost of selling or any return on capital) incident to and necessary for production or manufacturing operations or processes,

(l) Salaries paid to officers attributable to services performed incident to and necessary for production or manufacturing operations or processes, and

(m) Insurance costs incident to and necessary for production or manufacturing operations or processes such as insurance on production machinery and equipment.

(ii) **Costs not included in inventoriable costs.** Costs which are not required to be included in the computation of the amount of inventoriable costs include:

(a) Marketing expenses,

(b) Advertising expenses,

914

(c) Selling expenses,

(d) Other distribution expenses,

(e) Interest,

(f) Research and experimental expenses including engineering and product development expenses,

(g) Losses under section 165 and the regulations thereunder,

(h) Percentage depletion in excess of cost depletion,

(i) Depreciation reported for Federal income tax purposes in excess of depreciation reported by the taxpayer in his financial reports,

(j) Income taxes attributable to income received on the sale of inventory,

(k) Pension and profit-sharing contributions representing either past service costs or representing current service costs otherwise allowable as a deduction under section 404, and other employee benefits incurred on behalf of labor. These other benefits include workmen's compensation expenses, payments under a wage continuation plan described in section 105(d), amounts of a type which would be includible in the gross income of employees under nonqualified pension, profit-sharing and stock bonus plans, premiums on life and health insurance and miscellaneous benefits provided for employees such as safety, medical treatment, cafeteria, recreational facilities, membership dues, etc., which are otherwise allowable as deductions under chapter 1 of the Code,

(l) Cost attributable to strikes, rework labor, scrap and spoilage,

(m) General and administrative expenses incident to and necessary for the taxpayer's activities as a whole rather than to production or manufacturing operations or processes, and

(n) Salaries paid to officers attributable to the performance of services which are incident to and necessary for the taxpayer's activities as a whole rather than to production or manufacturing operations or processes.

. . . . .

§ 1.472–1 Last-in, first-out inventories

(a) Any taxpayer permitted or required to take inventories pursuant to the provisions of section 471, and pursuant to the provisions of §§ 1.471–1 to 1.471–9, inclusive, may elect with respect to those goods specified in his application and properly subject to inventory to compute his opening and closing inventories in accordance with the method provided by section 472, this section, and § 1.472–2. Under this last-in, first-out (LIFO) inventory method, the taxpayer is permitted to treat those goods remaining on hand at the close of the taxable year as being:

(1) Those included in the opening inventory of the taxable year, in the order of acquisition and to the extent thereof, and

(2) Those acquired during the taxable year.

The LIFO inventory method is not dependent upon the character of the business in which the taxpayer is engaged, or upon the identity or want of identity through commingling of any of the goods on hand, and may be adopted by the taxpayer as of the close of any taxable year.

(b) If the LIFO inventory method is used by a taxpayer who regularly and consistently, in a manner similar to hedging on a futures market, matches purchases with sales, then firm purchases and sales contracts (i. e., those not legally subject to cancellation by either party) entered into at fixed prices on or before the date of the inventory may be included in purchases or sales, as the case may be, for the purpose of determining the cost of goods sold and the resulting profit or loss, provided that this practice is regularly and consistently adhered to by the taxpayer and provided that, in the opinion of the Commissioner, income is clearly reflected thereby.

(c) A manufacturer or processor who has adopted the LIFO inventory method as to a class of goods may elect to have such method apply to the raw materials only (including those included in goods in process and in finished goods) expressed in terms of appropriate units. If such method is adopted, the adjustments are confined to costs of the raw material in the inventory and the cost of the raw material in goods in process and in finished goods produced by such manufacturer or processor and reflected in the inventory. The provisions of this paragraph may be illustrated by the following examples:

Example (1). Assume that the opening inventory had 10 units of raw material, 10 units of goods in process, and 10 units of finished goods, and that the raw material cost was 6 cents a unit, the processing cost 2 cents a unit, and overhead cost 1 cent a unit. For the purposes of this example, it is assumed that the entire amount of goods in process was 50 percent processed.

OPENING INVENTORY

	Raw material	Goods in process	Finished goods
Raw material.......	$0.60	$0.60	$0.60
Processing cost.....	....	.10	.20
Overhead...........	....	.05	.10

In the closing inventory there are 20 units of raw material, 6 units of goods in process, and 8 units of finished goods and the costs were: Raw material 10 cents, processing cost 4 cents, and overhead 1 cent.

CLOSING INVENTORY

[Based on cost and prior to adjustment]

	Raw material	Goods in process	Finished goods
Raw material......	$2.00	$0.60	$0.80
Processing costs....	....	.12	.32
Overhead...........	....	.03	.08
Total..........	2.00	.75	1.20

There were 30 units of raw material in the opening inventory and 34 units in the closing inventory. The adjustment to the closing inventory would be as follows:

CLOSING INVENTORY AS ADJUSTED

	Raw material	Goods in process	Finished goods
Raw material:			
20 at 6 cents......	$1.20	....	....
6 at 6 cents.......	....	$0.36	....
4 at 6 cents.......	....	....	$0.24
4 at 10 cents[1].....	....	....	.40
Processing costs....	....	.12	.32
Overhead...........	....	.03	.08
Total...........	1.20	.51	1.04

[1] This excess is subject to determination of price under section 472(b) (1) and § 1.472-2. If the excess falls in goods in process, the same adjustment is applicable.
The only adjustment to the closing inventory is the cost of the raw material; the processing costs and overhead cost are not changed.

Example (2). Assume that the opening inventory had 5 units of raw material, 10 units of goods in process, and 20 units of finished goods, with the same prices as in example (1), and that the closing inventory had 20 units of raw material, 20 units of goods in process, and 10 units of finished goods, with raw material costs as in the closing inventory in example (1). The

adjusted closing inventory would be as follows in so far as the raw material is concerned:

Raw material, 20 at 6 cents............ $1.20
Goods in process:
    15 at 6 cents............................ .90
    5 at 10 cents[1]........................... .50

Finished goods:
    None at 6 cents......................... .00
    10 at 10 cents[1]........................ 1.00

[1] This excess is subject to determination of price under section 472(b) (1) and § 1.472-2. The 20 units of raw material in the raw state plus 15 units of raw material in goods in process make up the 35 units of raw material that were contained in the opening inventory.

(d) For the purposes of this section, raw material in the opening inventory must be compared with similar raw material in the closing inventory. There may be several types of raw materials, depending upon the character, quality, or price, and each type of raw material in the opening inventory must be compared with a similar type in the closing inventory.

. . . .

§ 1.472–2   Requirements incident to adoption and use of LIFO inventory method

. . . .

(e) LIFO conformity requirement— (1) In general. The taxpayer must establish to the satisfaction of the Commissioner that the taxpayer, in ascertaining the income, profit, or loss for the taxable year for which the LIFO inventory method is first used, or for any subsequent taxable year, for credit purposes or for purposes of reports to shareholders, partners, or other proprietors, or to beneficiaries, has not used any inventory method other than that referred to in § 1.472–1 or at variance with the requirement referred to in § 1.472–2(c). See paragraph (e)(2) of this section for rules relating to the meaning of the term "taxable year" as used in this paragraph. The following are not considered at variance with the requirement of this paragraph:

(i) The taxpayer's use of an inventory method other than LIFO for purposes of ascertaining information reported as a supplement to or explanation of the taxpayer's primary presentation of the taxpayer's income, profit, or loss for a taxable year in credit statements or financial reports (including preliminary and unaudited financial reports). See paragraph (e)(3) of this section for rules relating to the reporting of supplemental and explanatory information ascertained by the use of an inventory method other than LIFO.

(ii) The taxpayer's use of an inventory method other than LIFO to ascertain the value of the taxpayer's inventory of goods on hand for purposes of reporting the value of such inventories as assets. See paragraph (e)(4) of this section for rules relating to such disclosures.

(iii) The taxpayer's use of an inventory method other than LIFO for purposes of ascertaining information reported in internal management reports. See paragraph (e)(5) of this section for rules relating to such reports.

(iv) The taxpayer's use of an inventory method other than LIFO for purposes of issuing reports or credit statements covering a period of operations that is less than the whole of a taxable year for which the LIFO method is used for Federal income tax purposes. See paragraph (e)(6) of this section for rules relating to series of interim reports.

(v) The taxpayer's use of the lower of LIFO cost or market method to value LIFO inventories for purposes of financial reports and credit statements. However, except as provided in paragraph (e)(7) of this section, a taxpayer may not use market value in lieu of cost to value inventories for purposes of financial reports or credit statements.

(vi) The taxpayer's use of a costing method or accounting method to ascertain income, profit, or loss for credit purposes or for purposes of financial reports if such costing method or accounting method is neither inconsistent with the inventory method referred to in § 1.472-1 nor at variance with the requirement referred to in § 1.472-2(c), regardless of whether such costing method or accounting method is used by the taxpayer for Federal income tax purposes. See paragraph (e)(8) of this section for examples of such costing methods and accounting methods.

(vii) For credit purposes or for purposes of financial reports, the taxpay-

er's treatment of inventories, after such inventories have been acquired in a transaction to which section 351 applies from a transferor that used the LIFO method with respect to such inventories, as if such inventories had the same acquisition dates and costs as in the hands of the transferor.

(viii) For credit purposes or for purposes of financial reports relating to a taxable year, the taxpayer's determination of income, profit, or loss for the taxable year by valuing inventories in accordance with the procedures described in section 472(b)(1) and (3), notwithstanding that such valuation differs from the valuation of inventories for Federal income tax purposes because the taxpayer either—

(A) Adopted such procedures for credit or financial reporting purposes beginning with an accounting period other than the taxable year for which the LIFO method was first used by the taxpayer for Federal income tax purposes, or

(B) With respect to such inventories treated a business combination for credit or financial reporting purposes in a manner different from the treatment of the business combination for Federal income tax purposes.

. . . . .

§ 1.472-3 Time and manner of making election

(a) The LIFO inventory method may be adopted and used only if the taxpayer files with his income tax return for the taxable year as of the close of which the method is first to be used a statement of his election to use such inventory method. The statement shall be made on Form 970 pursuant to the instructions printed with respect thereto and to the requirements of this section, or in such other manner as may be acceptable to the Commissioner. Such statement shall be accompanied by an analysis of all inventories of the taxpayer as of the beginning and as of the end of the taxable year for which the LIFO inventory method is proposed first to be used, and also as of the beginning of the prior taxable year. In the case of a manufacturer, this analysis shall show in detail the manner in which costs are computed with respect to raw materials, goods in process, and finished goods, segregating the products (whether in process or finished goods) into natural groups on the basis of either (1) similarity in factory processes through which they pass, or (2) similarity of raw materials used, or (3) similarity in style, shape, or use of finished products. Each group of products shall be clearly described.

(b) The taxpayer shall submit for the consideration of the Commissioner in connection with the taxpayer's adoption or use of the LIFO inventory method such other detailed information with respect to his business or accounting system as may be at any time requested by the Commissioner.

(c) As a condition to the taxpayer's use of the LIFO inventory method, the Commissioner may require that the method be used with respect to goods other than those specified in the taxpayer's statement of election if, in the opinion of the Commissioner, the use of such method with respect to such other goods is essential to a clear reflection of income.

(d) Whether or not the taxpayer's application for the adoption and use of the LIFO inventory method should be approved, and whether or not such method, once adopted, may be continued, and the propriety of all computations incidental to the use of such method, will be determined by the Commissioner in connection with the examination of the taxpayer's income tax returns.

§ 1.472–4 Adjustments to be made by taxpayer

A taxpayer may not change to the LIFO method of taking inventories unless, at the time he files his application for the adoption of such method, he agrees to such adjustments incident to the change to or from such method, or incident to the use of such method, in the inventories of prior taxable years or otherwise, as the district director upon the examination of the taxpayer's returns may deem necessary in order that the true income of the taxpayer will be clearly reflected for the years involved.

§ 1.481–5 Adjustments taken into account with consent

(a) In addition to the methods of allocation described in section 481(b), the adjustments required by section 481(a) may be taken into account in computing the tax under chapter 1 for such taxable years, in such manner and subject to such conditions as may be agreed upon between the Commissioner and the taxpayer. See section 481(c). Requests for approval of a method of allocation differing from those described in section 481(b) shall be addressed to the Commissioner of Internal Revenue, Attention: T:R, Washington 25, D.C., and shall set forth in detail the facts and circumstances upon which the taxpayer bases his request. Permission will be granted only if the taxpayer and the Commissioner agree to the terms and conditions under which the allocation is to be effected.

(b) The agreement shall be in writing and shall be signed by the Commissioner and the taxpayer. It shall set forth the items to be adjusted, the amount of the adjustments, the taxable year or years for which the adjustments are to be taken into account, and the amount of the adjustments allocable to each such year. The agreement shall be binding on the parties except upon a showing of fraud, malfeasance, or misrepresentation of a material fact.

§ 1.482–1 Allocation of income and deductions among taxpayers

(a) Definitions. When used in this section and in § 1.482–2—

(1) The term "organization" includes any organization of any kind, whether it be a sole proprietorship, a partnership, a trust, an estate, an association, or a corporation (as each is defined or understood in the Internal Revenue Code or the regulations thereunder), irrespective of the place where organized, where operated, or where its trade or business is conducted, and regardless of whether domestic or foreign, whether exempt, whether affiliated, or whether a party to a consolidated return.

(2) The term "trade" or "business" includes any trade or business activity of any kind, regardless of whether or where organized, whether owned indi-

vidually or otherwise, and regardless of the place where carried on.

(3) The term "controlled" includes any kind of control, direct or indirect, whether legally enforceable, and however exercisable or exercised. It is the reality of the control which is decisive, not its form or the mode of its exercise. A presumption of control arises if income or deductions have been arbitrarily shifted.

(4) The term "controlled taxpayer" means any one of two or more organizations, trades, or businesses owned or controlled directly or indirectly by the same interests.

(5) The terms "group" and "group of controlled taxpayers" mean the organizations, trades, or businesses owned or controlled by the same interests.

(6) The term "true taxable income" means, in the case of a controlled taxpayer, the taxable income—(or, as the case may be, any item or element affecting taxable income) which would have resulted to the controlled taxpayer, had it in the conduct of its affairs (or, as the case may be, in the particular contract, transaction, arrangement, or other act) dealt with the other member or members of the group at arm's length. It does not mean the income, the deductions, the credits, the allowances, or the item or element of income, deductions, credits, or allowances, resulting to the controlled taxpayer by reason of the particular contract, transaction, or arrangement, the controlled taxpayer, or the interests controlling it, chose to make (even though such contract, transaction, or arrangement be legally binding upon the parties thereto).

(b) Scope and purpose. (1) The purpose of section 482 is to place a controlled taxpayer on a tax parity with an uncontrolled taxpayer, by determining, according to the standard of an uncontrolled taxpayer, the true taxable income from the property and business of a controlled taxpayer. The interests controlling a group of controlled taxpayers are assumed to have complete power to cause each controlled taxpayer so to conduct its affairs that its transactions and accounting records truly reflect the taxable income from the property and business of each of the controlled taxpayers. If, however, this

has not been done, and the taxable incomes are thereby understated, the district director shall intervene, and, by making such distributions, apportionments, or allocations as he may deem necessary of gross income, deductions, credits, or allowances, or of any item or element affecting taxable income, between or among the controlled taxpayers constituting the group, shall determine the true taxable income of each controlled taxpayer. The standard to be applied in every case is that of an uncontrolled taxpayer dealing at arm's length with another uncontrolled taxpayer.

(2) Section 482 and this section apply to the case of any controlled taxpayer, whether such taxpayer makes a separate or a consolidated return. If a controlled taxpayer makes a separate return, the determination is of its true separate taxable income. If a controlled taxpayer is a party to a consolidated return, the true consolidated taxable income of the affiliated group and the true separate taxable income of the controlled taxpayer are determined consistently with the principles of a consolidated return.

(3) Section 482 grants no right to a controlled taxpayer to apply its provisions at will, nor does it grant any right to compel the district director to apply such provisions. It is not intended (except in the case of the computation of consolidated taxable income under a consolidated return) to effect in any case such a distribution, apportionment, or allocation of gross income, deductions, credits, or allowances, or any item of gross income, deductions, credits, or allowances, as would produce a result equivalent to a computation of consolidated taxable income under subchapter A, chapter 6 of the Code.

(c) Application. Transactions between one controlled taxpayer and another will be subjected to special scrutiny to ascertain whether the common control is being used to reduce, avoid, or escape taxes. In determining the true taxable income of a controlled taxpayer, the district director is not restricted to the case of improper accounting, to the case of a fraudulent, colorable, or sham transaction, or to the case of a device designed to reduce or avoid tax by shifting or distorting income, deductions, credits, or allowances. The authority to determine true taxable income extends to any case in which either by inadvertence or design the taxable income, in whole or in part, of a controlled taxpayer, is other than it would have been had the taxpayer in the conduct of his affairs been an uncontrolled taxpayer dealing at arm's length with another uncontrolled taxpayer.

(d) Method of allocation. (1) The method of allocating, apportioning, or distributing income, deductions, credits, and allowances to be used by the district director in any case, including the form of the adjustments and the character and source of amounts allocated, shall be determined with reference to the substance of the particular transactions or arrangements which result in the avoidance of taxes or the failure to clearly reflect income. The appropriate adjustments may take the form of an increase or decrease in gross income, increase or decrease in deductions (including depreciation), increase or decrease in basis of assets (including inventory), or any other adjustment which may be appropriate under the circumstances. See § 1.482–2 for specific rules relating to methods of allocation in the case of several types of business transactions.

(2) Whenever the district director makes adjustments to the income of one member of a group of controlled taxpayers (such adjustments being referred to in this paragraph as "primary" adjustments) he shall also make appropriate correlative adjustments to the income of any other member of the group involved in the allocation. The correlative adjustment shall actually be made if the U.S. income tax liability of the other member would be affected for any pending taxable year. Thus, if the district director makes an allocation of income, he shall not only increase the income of one member of the group, but shall decrease the income of the other member if such adjustment would have an effect on the U.S. income tax liability of the other member for any pending taxable year. For the purposes of this subparagraph, a "pending taxable year" is any taxable year with respect to which the U.S. income tax return of the other member has been filed by the time the alloca-

tion is made, and with respect to which a credit or refund is not barred by the operation of any law or rule of law. If a correlative adjustment is not actually made because it would have no effect on the U.S. income tax liability of the other member involved in the allocation for any pending taxable year, such adjustment shall nevertheless be deemed to have been made for the purpose of determining the U.S. income tax liability of such member for a later taxable year, or for the purposes of determining the U.S. income tax liability of any person for any taxable year. The district director shall furnish to the taxpayer with respect to which the primary adjustment is made a written statement of the amount and nature of the correlative adjustment which is deemed to have been made. For purposes of this subparagraph, a primary adjustment shall not be considered to have been made (and therefore a correlative adjustment is not required to be made) until the first occurring of the following events with respect to the primary adjustment:

(i) The date of assessment of the tax following execution by the taxpayer of a Form 870 (Waiver of Restrictions on Assessment and Collection of Deficiency in Tax and Acceptance of Overassessment) with respect to such adjustment.

(ii) Acceptance of a Form 870–AD (Offer of Waiver of Restriction on Assessment and Collection of Deficiency in Tax and Acceptance of Overassessment),

(iii) Payment of the deficiency,

(iv) Stipulation in the Tax Court of the United States, or

(v) Final determination of tax liability by offer-in-compromise, closing agreement, or court action.

The principles of this subparagraph may be illustrated by the following examples in each of which it is assumed that X and Y are members of the same group of controlled entities and that they regularly compute their incomes on the basis of a calendar year:

Example (1). Assume that in 1968 the district director proposes to adjust X's income for 1966 to reflect an arm's length rental charge for Y's use of X's tangible property in 1966; that X consents to an assessment reflecting such adjustment by executing a Waiver, Form 870; and that an assessment of the tax with respect to such adjustment is made in 1968. The primary adjustment is therefore considered to have been made in 1968. Assume further that both X and Y are United States corporations and that Y had net operating losses in 1963, 1964, 1965, 1966, and 1967. Although a correlative adjustment would not have an effect on Y's U. S. income tax liability for any pending taxable year, an adjustment increasing Y's net operating loss for 1966 shall be deemed to have been made for the purposes of determining Y's U. S. income tax liability for 1968 or a later taxable year to which the increased operating loss may be carried. The district director shall notify X in writing of the amount and nature of the adjustment which is deemed to have been made to Y.

Example (2). Assume that X and Y are United States corporations; that X is in the business of rendering engineering services; that in 1968 the district director proposes to adjust X's income for 1966 to reflect an arm's length fee for the rendition of engineering services by X in 1966 relating to the construction of Y's factory; that X consents to an assessment reflecting such adjustment by executing a Waiver, Form 870; and that an assessment of the tax with respect to such adjustment is made in 1968. Assume further that fees for such services would properly constitute a capital expenditure by Y, and that Y does not place the factory in service until 1969. Although a correlative adjustment (increase in basis) would not have an effect on Y's U. S. income tax liability for a pending taxable year, an adjustment increasing the basis of Y's assets for 1966 shall be deemed to have been made in 1968 for the purpose of computing allowable depreciation or gain or loss on disposition for 1969 and any future taxable year. The district director shall notify X in writing of the amount and nature of the adjustment which is deemed to have been made to Y.

* * * *

(3) In making distributions, apportionments, or allocations between two members of a group of controlled entities with respect to particular transactions, the district director shall consider the effect upon such members of an arrangement between them for reimbursement within a reasonable period before or after the taxable year if the taxpayer can establish that such an arrangement in fact existed during the taxable year under consideration. The district director shall also consider the effect of any other nonarm's length transaction between them in the taxable year which, if taken into account, would result in a set off against any allocation which would otherwise be made, provided the taxpayer is able to establish with reasonable specificity that the transaction was not at arm's length and the amount of the appropriate arm's length charge. For purposes of the preceding sentence, the term arm's length refers to the amount which was charged or would have been charged in independent transactions with unrelated parties under the same or similar circumstances considering all the relevant facts and without regard to the rules found in § 1.482-2 by which certain charges are deemed to be equal to arm's length. For example, assume that one member of a group performs services which benefit a second member, which would in itself require an allocation to reflect an arm's length charge for the performance of such services. Assume further that the first member can establish that during the same taxable year the second member engages in other nonarm's length transactions which benefit the first member, such as by selling products to the first member at a discount, or purchasing products from the first member at a premium, or paying royalties to the first member in an excessive amount. In such case, the value of the benefits received by the first member as a result of the other activities will be set-off against the allocation which would otherwise be made. If the effect of the set-off is to change the characterization or source of the income or deductions, or otherwise distort taxable income, in such a manner as to affect the United States tax liability of any member, allocations will be made to reflect the correct amount of each category of income or deductions. In order to establish that a set-off to the adjustments proposed by the district director is appropriate, the taxpayer must notify the district director of the basis of any claimed set-off at any time before the expiration of the period ending 30 days after the date of a letter by which the district director transmits an examination report notifying the taxpayer of proposed adjustments or before July 16, 1968, whichever is later. The principles of this subparagraph may be illustrated by the following examples, in each of which it is assumed that P and S are calendar year corporations and are both members of the same group of controlled entities:

Example (1). P performs services in 1966 for the benefit of S in connection with S's manufacture and sale of a product. S does not pay P for such services in 1966, but in consideration for such services, agrees in 1966 to pay P a percentage of the amount of sales of the product in 1966 through 1970. In 1966 it appeared this agreement would provide adequate consideration for the services. No allocation will be made with respect to the services performed by P.

Example (2). P renders services to S in connection with the construction of S's factory. An arm's length charge for such services, determined under paragraph (b) of § 1.482-2, would be $100,000. During the same taxable year P makes available to S a machine to be used in such construction. P bills S $125,000 for the services, but does not bill for the use of the machine. No allocation will be made with respect to the excessive charge for services or the undercharge for the machine if P can establish that the excessive charge services was equal to an arm's length charge for the use of the machine, and if the taxable income and income tax liabilities of P and S are not distorted.

Example (3). Assume the same facts as in example (2), except that, if P had reported $25,000 as rental income and $25,000 less service income, it would have been subject to the tax on personal holding companies. Allocations will be made to reflect the correct amounts of rental income and service income.

(4) If the members of a group of controlled taxpayers engage in transactions with one another, the district director may distribute, apportion, or allocate income, deductions, credits, or allowances to reflect the true taxable income of the individual members under the standards set forth in this section and in § 1.482-2 notwithstanding the fact that the ultimate income anticipated from a series of transactions may not be realized or is realized during a later period. For example, if one member of a controlled group sells a product at less than an arm's length price to a second member of the group in one taxable year and the second member resells the product to an unrelated party in the next taxable year, the district director may make an appropriate allocation to reflect an arm's length price for the sale of the product in the first taxable year, notwithstanding that the second member of the group had not realized any gross income from the resale of the product in the first year. Similarly, if one member of a group lends money to a second member of the group in a taxable year, the district director may make an appropriate allocation to reflect an arm's length charge for interest during such taxable year even if the second member does not realize income during such year. The provisions of this subparagraph apply even if the gross income contemplated from a series of transactions is never, in fact, realized by the other members.

(5) Section 482 may, when necessary to prevent the avoidance of taxes or to clearly reflect income, be applied in circumstances described in sections of the Code (such as section 351) providing for nonrecognition of gain or loss. See, for example, "National Securities Corporation v. Commissioner of Internal Revenue", 137 F.2d 600 (3d Cir. 1943), cert. denied 320 U.S. 794 (1943).

(6) If payment or reimbursement for the sale, exchange, or use of property, the rendition of services, or the advance of other consideration among members of a group of controlled entities was prevented, or would have been prevented, at the time of the transaction because of currency or other restrictions imposed under the laws of any foreign country, any distributions, apportionments, or allocations which may be made under section 482 with respect to such transactions may be treated as deferrable income or deductions, providing the taxpayer has, for the year to which the distributions, apportionments, or allocations relate, elected to use a method of accounting in which the reporting of deferrable income is deferred until the income ceases to be deferrable income. Under such method of accounting, referred to in this section as the deferred income method of accounting, any payments or reimbursements which were prevented or would have been prevented, and any deductions attributable directly or indirectly to such payments or reimbursements, shall be deferred until they cease to be deferrable under such method of accounting. If such method of accounting has not been elected with respect to the taxable year to which the allocations under section 482 relate, the taxpayer may elect such method with respect to such allocations (but not with respect to other deferrable income) at any time before the first occurring of the following events with respect to the allocations:

(i) Execution by the taxpayer of Form 870 (Waiver of Restrictions on Assessment and Collection of Deficiency in Tax and Acceptance of Overassessment);

(ii) Expiration of the period ending 30 days after the date of a letter by which the district director transmits an examination report notifying the taxpayer of proposed adjustments reflecting such allocations or before July 16, 1968, whichever is later; or

(iii) Execution of a closing agreement or offer-in-compromise.

The principles of this subparagraph may be illustrated by the following example in which it is assumed that X, a domestic corporation, and Y, a foreign corporation, are members of the same group of controlled entities:

Example. X. which is in the business of rendering a certain type of service to unrelated parties, renders such services for the benefit of Y in 1965. The direct and indirect costs allocable to such services are $60,000, and an arm's length charge for such services is $100,000. Assume that the district director proposes to increase X's income by $100,000, but that the country in which Y is located would have blocked payment in 1965 for such services. If, prior to the first occurring of the events described in subdivisions (i), (ii), or (iii) of this subparagraph, X elects to use the deferred income method of accounting with respect to such allocation, the $100,000 allocation and the $60,000 of costs are deferrable until such amounts cease to be deferrable under X's method of accounting.

§ 1.482-2 Determination of taxable income in specific situations

(a) Loans or advances—(1) In general. Where one member of a group of controlled entities makes a loan or advance directly or indirectly to, or otherwise becomes a creditor of, another member of such group, and charges no interest, or charges interest at a rate which is not equal to an arm's length rate as defined in subparagraph (2) of this paragraph, the district director may make appropriate allocations to reflect an arm's length interest rate for the use of such loan or advance.

(2) Arm's length interest rate—(i) In general. For the purposes of this paragraph, the arm's length interest rate shall be the rate of interest which was charged, or would have been charged at the time the indebtedness arose, in independent transactions with or between unrelated parties under similar circumstances. All relevant factors will be considered, including the amount and duration of the loan, the security involved, the credit standing of the borrower, and the interest rate prevailing at the situs of the lender or creditor for comparable loans.

. . . .

(iii) Safe haven rule for certain loans and advances. (A) Paragraph (a)(2)(iii) of this section applies to interest paid or accrued—

(1) Pursuant to a loan or advance (other than a loan or advance entered into pursuant to a binding contract entered into prior to August 29, 1980), which was entered into on or after July 1, 1981, and

(2) On or after July 1, 1981, pursuant to a demand loan or advance.

(B) If a creditor was not regularly engaged in the business of making loans or advances of the same general type as the loan or advance in question to unrelated parties, the arm's length rate of interest to which paragraph (a)(2)(iii) of this section applies for purposes of this paragraph—

(1) The rate of interest actually charged if at least 11, but not in excess of 13, percent per annum simple interest, or

(2) 12 percent per annum simple interest if no interest was charged or if the rate of interest charged was less than 11, or in excess of 13 percent per annum simple interest, unless the taxpayer establishes a more appropriate rate under the standards set forth in paragraph (a)(2)(i) of this section. For purposes of the preceding sentence, if the rate actually charged is greater than 13 percent per annum simple interest and less than the rate determined under the standards set forth in paragraph (a)(2)(i) of this section, or if the rate actually charged is less than 11 percent per annum simple interest and greater than the rate determined under the standards set forth in paragraph (a)(2)(i) of the section, then the rate actually charged shall be deemed to be a more appropriate rate under the standards set forth in paragraph (a)(2)(i) of this section.

. . . .

(3) Loans or advances to which subparagraph (1) applies. Subparagraph (1) of this paragraph applies to all forms of bona fide indebtedness and includes:

(i) Loans or advances of money or other consideration (whether or not evidenced by a written instrument), and

(ii) Indebtedness arising in the ordinary course of business out of sales, leases, or the rendition of services by or between members of the group, or any other similar extension of credit. Subparagraph (1) of this paragraph does not apply to alleged indebtedness which was in fact a contribution of capital or a distribution by a corporation with respect to its shares. The interest period shall commence at the date the indebtedness arises, except that with respect to indebtedness described in subdivision (ii) of this subparagraph that is not evidenced by a written instrument requiring payment of interest, the interest period shall not commence until a date 6 months after the date the indebtedness arises, or until a later date if the taxpayer is able to demonstrate that either it or others in its industry, as a regular trade practice, permit comparable balances in the case of similar transactions with unrelated parties to remain outstanding for a longer period without charging interest. For the purpose of determining the period of time for which a balance is outstanding, payments or credits shall be applied against the earliest balance outstanding, unless the taxpayer applies such payments or credits in some other order on its books in accordance with an agreement or understanding of the parties if the taxpayer can demonstrate that either it or others in its industry, as a regular trade practice, enter into such agreements or understandings.

(4) **Relation to section 1232.** In determining the rate of interest actually charged on a loan or advance evidenced by a written instrument there is taken into account—

(i) Any original issue discount included in income by the lender under section 1232(a)(3), or

(ii) Any bond premium deducted by the lender under § 1.61–12(c)(2).

(5) **Relation to section 385.** If a taxpayer is subject both to section 482 and to section 385 with respect to a loan, then the sections will be applied in the following order.

(i) First, sections 385 and 1232 (and the regulations under such sections and under § 1.61–12(c)(2)) are applied to determine:

(A) Whether the loan is treated as stock or indebtedness;

(B) Whether a capital contribution or a distribution under section 301 is imputed; and

(C) Whether there is original issue discount or bond premium.

(ii) Second, section 482 is applied. The fact that a stated rate of interest on a loan falls within the safe haven of paragraph (a)(2)(iii) of this section does not preclude the application of section 385 to such loan. However, the interest rate actually charged (within the meaning of paragraph (a)(4) of this section) after application of sections 385 and 1232 will ordinarily be considered an arm's length interest rate for purposes of section 482. If a loan is classified as stock under section 385, then subparagraph (1) of this paragraph (a) is inapplicable.

. . . .

(7) **Relation to section 483.** If a taxpayer is subject to section 482 and to section 483 with respect to the appropriateness of an interest rate used in a transaction, then section 482 and section 483 will be applied in the following order:

(i) First, section 483 is applied to determine whether there is unstated interest on the contract, and if so, to impute interest.

(ii) Second, section 482 is applied to determine whether the interest rate used in the contract exceeds the arm's length interest rate as defined in paragraph (a)(2) of this section, and if so, to make appropriate allocations to reflect an arm's length interest rate. Section 482 will not be used to impute interest if the interest rate used in the contract is less than this arm's length interest rate.

(iii) Third, paragraphs (b), (c), (d) or (e) of this section, if applicable, may be used to make other appropriate allocations to reflect an arm's length transaction based on the interest rate as adjusted in the situations described in paragraph (a)(7)(i) or (ii) of this section. For example, assume the case of a deferred-payment sale of tangible property at no interest between two organizations that are controlled by the same interests, and assume that section 483 is applied to treat some portion of the principal payments as interests, and therefore to reduce the sales price of the property. If, after this recharacterization of principal as interest, the recomputed sales price does not reflect an arm's length sales price under the principles of paragraph (e) of this section, the district director may make other appropriate allocations (other than an interest rate adjustment) under that paragraph (e) to reflect an arm's length sales price for such sale.

(b) Performance of services for another—(1) General rule. Where one member of a group of controlled entities performs marketing, managerial, administrative, technical, or other services for the benefit of, or on behalf of another member of the group without charge, or at a charge which is not equal to an arm's length charge as defined in subparagraph (3) of this paragraph, the district director may make appropriate allocations to reflect an arm's length charge for such services.

(2) Benefit test. (i) Allocations may be made to reflect arm's length charges with respect to services undertaken for the joint benefit of the members of a group of controlled entities, as well as with respect to services performed by one member of the group exclusively for the benefit of another member of the group. Any allocations made shall be consistent with the relative benefits intended from the services, based upon the facts known at the time the services were rendered, and shall be made even if the potential benefits anticipated are not realized. No allocations shall be made if the probable benefits to the other members were so indirect or remote that unrelated parties would not have charged for such services. In general, allocations may be made if the service, at the time it was performed, related to the carrying on of an activity by another member or was intended to benefit another member, either in the member's overall operations or in its day-to-day activities. The principles of this subdivision may be illustrated by the following examples in each of which it is assumed that X and Y are corporate members of the same group of controlled entities:

Example (1). X's International Division engages in a wide range of sales promotion activities. Although most of these activities are undertaken exclusively for the benefit of X's international operations, some are intended to jointly benefit both X and Y and others are undertaken exclusively for the benefit of Y. The district director may make an allocation to reflect an arm's length charge with respect to the activities undertaken for the joint benefit of X and Y consistent with the relative benefits intended as well as with respect to the services performed exclusively for the benefit of Y.

Example (2). X operates an international airline, and Y owns and operates hotels in several cities which are serviced by X. X, in conjunction with its advertising of the airline, often pictures Y's hotels and mentions Y's name. Although such advertising was primarily intended to benefit X's airline operations, it was reasonable to anticipate that there would be substantial benefits to Y resulting from patronage by travelers who responded to X's advertising. Since an unrelated hotel operator would have been charged for such advertising, the district director may make an appropriate allocation to reflect an arm's length charge consistent with the relative benefits intended.

Example (3). Assume the same facts as in Example (2) except that X's advertising neither mentions nor pictures Y's hotels. Although it is reasonable to anticipate that increased air travel attributable to X's advertising will result in some benefit to Y due to increased patronage by air travelers, the district director will not make an allocation with respect to such advertising since the probable benefit to Y was so indirect and remote that an unrelated hotel operator would not have been charged for such advertising.

(ii) Allocations will generally not be made if the service is merely a duplication of a service which the related party has independently performed or is performing for itself. In this connection, the ability to independently perform the service (in terms of qualification and availability of personnel) shall be taken into account. The principles of this subdivision may be illustrated by the following examples, in each of which it is assumed that X and Y are corporate members of the same group of controlled entities:

Example (1). At the request of Y, the financial staff of X makes an analysis to determine the amount and source of the borrowing needs of Y. Y does not have personnel qualified to make the analysis, and it does not undertake the same analysis. The district director may make an appropriate allocation to reflect an arm's length charge for such analysis.

Example (2). Y, which has a qualified financial staff, makes an analysis to determine the amount and source of its borrowing needs. Its report, recommending a loan from a bank, is submitted to X. X's financial staff reviews the analysis to determine whether X should advise Y to reconsider its plan. No allocation should be made with respect to X's review.

(3) **Arm's length charge.** For the purpose of this paragraph an arm's length charge for services rendered shall be the amount which was charged or would have been charged for the same or similar services in independent transactions with or between unrelated parties under similar circumstances considering all relevant facts. However, except in the case of services which are an integral part of the business activity of either the member rendering the services or the member receiving the benefit of the services (as described in subparagraph (7) of this paragraph), the arm's length charge shall be deemed equal to the costs or deductions incurred with respect to such services by the member or members rendering such services unless the taxpayer establishes a more appropriate charge under the standards set forth in the first sentence of this subparagraph. Where costs or deductions are a factor in applying the provisions of this paragraph adequate books and records must be maintained by taxpayers to permit verification of such costs or deductions by the Internal Revenue Service.

. . . .

(c) **Use of tangible property—(1) General rule.** Where possession, use, or occupancy of tangible property owned or leased by one member of a group of controlled entities (referred to in this paragraph as the owner) is transferred by lease or other arrangement to another member of such group (referred to in this paragraph as the user) without charge or at a charge which is not equal to an arm's length rental charge (as defined in subdivision (i) of subparagraph (2) of this paragraph), the district director may make appropriate allocations to properly reflect such arm's length charge. Where possession, use, or occupancy of only a portion of such property is transferred, the determination of the arm's length charge and the allocation shall be made with reference to the portion transferred.

(2) **Arm's length charge.** (i) For the purposes of this paragraph, an arm's length rental charge shall be the amount of rent which was charged, or would have been charged for the use of the same or similar property, during the time it was in use, in independent transactions with or between unrelated parties under similar circumstances considering the period and location of the use, the owner's investment in the property or rent paid for the property, expenses of maintaining the property, the type of property involved, its condition, and all other relevant facts. If neither the owner nor the user was engaged in the trade or business of renting property, the arm's length rental charge for the taxable year shall be deemed to be equal to the amount specified in subdivision (ii) or (iii) of this subparagraph, whichever is appropriate, unless the taxpayer establishes a more appropriate charge under the standards set forth in the first sentence of this subdivision. For purposes of this subdivision, an owner or user shall be considered to be in the trade or business of renting property if it engages in the trade or business of renting property of the same general type as the property in question to unrelated parties. An owner or user will not be considered to be engaged in the trade or business of renting property of the same general type solely on the basis of casual or infrequent rentals of property which is predominantly used in its trade or business.

. . . .

(d) **Transfer or use of intangible property—(1) In general.** (i) Except as otherwise provided in subparagraph (4) of this paragraph, where intangible property or an interest therein is transferred, sold, assigned, loaned, or otherwise made available in any manner by one member of a group of controlled entities (referred to in this paragraph as the transferor) to another member of the group (referred to in this paragraph as the transferee) for other than an arm's length consideration, the district director may make appropriate allocations to reflect an arm's length consideration for such property or its use.

Subparagraph (2) of this paragraph provides rules for determining the form and amount of an appropriate allocation, subparagraph (3) of this paragraph provides a definition of "intangible property", and subparagraph (4) of this paragraph provides rules with respect to certain cost-sharing arrangements in connection with the development of intangible property. For purposes of this paragraph, an interest in intangible property may take the form of the right to use such property.

. . . .

(e) Sales of tangible property—(1) In general. (i) Where one member of a group of controlled entities (referred to in this paragraph as the "seller") sells or otherwise disposes of tangible property to another member of such group (referred to in this paragraph as the "buyer") at other than an arm's length price (such a sale being referred to in this paragraph as a "controlled sale"), the district director may make appropriate allocations between the seller and the buyer to reflect an arm's length price for such sale or disposition. An arm's length price is the price that an unrelated party would have paid under the same circumstances for the property involved in the controlled sale. Since unrelated parties normally sell products at a profit, an arm's length price normally involves a profit to the seller.

. . . .

§ 1.483-1 Computation of interest on certain deferred payments

(a) Computation of amount constituting interest—(1) General rule. For all purposes of the Internal Revenue Code, in the case of any contract for the sale or exchange of property, there shall be treated as interest that part of a payment to which section 483 applies (see paragraph (b) of this section) which bears the same ratio to the amount of such payment as the total unstated interest (as defined in paragraph (c) of this section) under such contract bears to the total of the payments to which section 483 applies which are due under such contract. Thus, the amount to be treated as interest under section 483 is determined by multiplying each payment to which such section applies by a fraction, the numerator of which is the total unstated interest under the contract, and the denominator of which is the total of all the payments to which section 483 applies which are due under such contract. The effect of this ratio is to allocate the total unstated interest on a pro rata basis among the total payments to which section 483 applies. Accordingly, the total amount to be treated as interest for a taxable year with respect to a contract under which there are payments which include unstated interest is an amount equal to the unstated interest allocated to the payments under the contract for such year plus any stated interest reportable under the contract for such year. See paragraph (b) (2) of this section for rules relating to allocation of contract price, payments, and stated interest; paragraph (e) of this section for rules relating to indefinite payments; paragraph (f) of this section for rules relating to changes in terms of contract; and paragraph (b) of § 1.483-2 for exceptions and limitations to the application of section 483.

(2) Examples. The provisions of this paragraph may be illustrated by the following examples:

Example (1). On December 31, 1963, A sells property to B under a contract which provides that B is to make three payments of $2,000 each, such payments being due, respectively, at the end of each year for the next 3 years. No interest is provided for in the contract. Assume that section 483 applies to each of the payments, and that the total unstated interest under the contract is $559.88. The portion of each $2,000 payment which is treated as interest is $186.63

$$\left(\$2,000 \times \frac{\$559.88}{\$6000.00} \right).$$

. . . .

(b) Payments to which section 483 applies—(1) In general. Except as provided in subparagraph (4) of this paragraph, section 483 applies to any payment made after December 31, 1963, on account of the sale or exchange of property occurring after June 30, 1963, which payment constitutes part or all of the sales price and which is due more than 6 months after the date of such sale or exchange under a contract—

(i) Under which one or more of the payments are due more than 1 year after the date of such sale or exchange, and

(ii) Under which there is "total unstated interest" (within the meaning of paragraph (d) of this section).

For purposes of the preceding sentence, the term "sales price" does not include any interest payments provided for in the contract. The term "sale or exchange" includes any transaction treated as a sale or exchange for purposes of the Code. For purposes of section 483, a payment may be made in cash, stock or securities, or other property (except as provided in subparagraph (5) of this paragraph). Section 483 does not apply to any deferred payments under a contract under which all of the payments are due no more than 1 year after the date of the sale or exchange. Section 483 does not apply to a distribution in complete liquidation of a corporation, regardless of whether the corporation is liquidated in one distribution or in a series of distributions. For special rules relating to the time a sale or exchange takes place in the case of a disposal of timber, coal, or domestic iron ore, which qualifies under section 631 (relating to gain or loss in the case of timber, coal, or domestic iron ore), see that section and the regulations thereunder. See paragraph (e) of this section for special rules relating to indefinite payments, and paragraph (f) of this section for rules relating to the effect of a late payment on the determination of the due date of such payment. Section 483 may apply whether the contract providing for deferred payments is expressed (whether written or oral) or implied. In general, for purposes of section 483, all sales or exchanges involving deferred payments are considered as made under a contract.

(2) **Allocation of contract price, payments, and stated interest.** If payments are due under a contract both for the sale or exchange of property to which section 483 applies (for example, capital assets) and for either the sale or exchange of property to which such section does not apply (for example, the transfer of patents described in section 1235(a)) or services rendered or to be rendered, the parties to the contract may agree at the time of the sale

or exchange on a reasonable determination of the portion of the contract price and the stated interest (if any), and of each payment due under the contract, which is allocable to each such type of property and to services. However, if the parties do not so agree on a reasonable determination of the allocation of the contract price, or the stated interest (if any), or each payment due under the contract, the district director shall make such reasonable determination.

(3) **Effect of other provisions of law.** If there is total unstated interest under a contract, a portion of each payment to which section 483 applies shall be treated as interest to the extent provided in such section, notwithstanding that some other provision of law (for example, section 1245, relating to gain from dispositions of certain depreciable property) would, without regard to section 483, treat a portion of the payment as ordinary income or in some other manner. In such a case, section 483 shall apply first and the other provision of law shall apply only to the remainder of the payment not treated as interest under section 483. For example, if a portion of a payment is treated as interest under section 483 and such portion would otherwise be treated as gain from the sale or exchange of property which is not a capital asset under section 1232(a) (2) (B) (relating to corporate bonds issued on or before May 27, 1969, and Government bonds), section 483 shall apply first and section 1232(a) (2) (B) shall apply only to the remainder of the payment after the interest portion has been determined. In such case, in order to avoid a double inclusion in income, for purposes of section 1232(b) the "stated redemption price at maturity" shall be reduced by any amount treated as interest under section 483. If, however, with respect to an evidence of indebtedness issued by a corporation after May 27, 1969, any amount of original issue discount is ratably includible in the gross income of the holder under section 1232(a) (3), there will be no unstated interest to which section 483 applies since paragraph (d) (3) of this section provides for a zero test rate of interest for determining whether there is total unstated interest with respect to such an evidence of indebtedness.

. . . .

(5) Evidence of indebtedness. For purposes of section 483, an evidence of indebtedness (whether or not negotiable and whether or not includible in gross income) of the purchaser given in consideration for the sale or exchange of property is not a payment, and any payment due under such evidence of indebtedness shall be treated as due under the contract for the sale or exchange.

. . . .

(c) Total unstated interest—(1) In general. For purposes of paragraph (a) of this section (that is, for purposes of determining the portion of a payment to which section 483 applies which is to be treated as interest), the term "total unstated interest" means, with respect to a contract for the sale or exchange of property, an amount equal to the excess of—

(i) The sum of the payments to which section 483 applies which are due under the contract (within the meaning of paragraph (b) of this section), over

(ii) The sum of the present values of such payments and the present values of any stated interest payments due under the contract.

(2) Present value of a payment—(i) In general. The present value of any interest payment due under the contract not more than 6 months after the date of the sale or exchange is an amount equal to 100 percent of such payment. The present value of any other interest payment, and of any payment to which section 483 applies, which is due under the contract shall be determined by discounting such payment at the interest rate prescribed by paragraph (c)(2)(ii) of this section, from the nearest date (to the date such payment is actually due under the contract) which marks a 6-month interval from the date of the sale or exchange. For purposes of computing the present value of a payment at such rate, column (b) of the appropriate table set forth in paragraph (g)(2) of this section shall be used.

(ii) Prescribed interest rates.

(A) For payments on account of a sale or exchange of property entered into before July 24, 1975, as well as a sale or exchange of property pursuant to a binding written contract (including an irrevocable written option) entered into before such date, the interest rate prescribed by paragraph (c)(2)(ii)(A) shall be 5 percent per annum compounded semiannually. (See paragraph (c)(4) of this section for special rules where there has been a substantial change in the terms of a binding written contract entered into before July 24, 1975.)

(B) For payments on account of a sale or exchange of property entered into on or after July 24, 1975, and before July 1, 1981, except a sale or exchange entered into pursuant to a binding written contract (including an irrevocable written option) entered into before July 24, 1975, the interest rate prescribed by paragraph (c)(2)(ii)(B) of this section shall be 7 percent per annum compounded semiannually. For payments on account of a sale or exchange of property entered into on or after July 1, 1981, pursuant to a binding written contract (including an irrevocable written option) entered into after July 23, 1975, and before September 29, 1980, the interest rate prescribed by paragraph (c)(2)(ii)(B) of this section shall be 7 percent per annum compounded semiannually. (See paragraph (c)(5) of this section for special rules where there has been a substantial change in the terms of a binding written contract entered into after July 23, 1975 and before September 29, 1980.)

(C) For payments on account of a sale or exchange of property entered into on or after July 1, 1981, except a sale or exchange entered into pursuant to a binding written contract (including an irrevocable written option) entered into before September 29, 1980, the interest rate described by paragraph (c)(2)(ii)(C) of this section shall be 10 percent per annum compounded semiannually. (See paragraph (c)(5) of this section for special rules where there has been a substantial change in the terms of a binding written contract entered into before September 29, 1980.)

. . . .

(d) Test of whether there is total unstated interest under a contract—(1) In general—(i) How to apply prescrib-

ed test rate. Except as provided in paragraph (d)(2) and (3) of this section for purposes of determining whether section 483 applies to payments under a contract (that is, for purposes of paragraph (b)(1)(ii) of this section), the determination of whether there is total unstated interest under a contract shall be made in accordance with the method for computing total unstated interest provided in paragraph (c) of this section, except that column (a) of the appropriate table contained in paragraph (g)(2) of this section (which provides for discounting payments at the appropriate test rate prescribed by paragraph (d)(1)(ii) of this section) shall be used to determine the present value of a payment. If, after applying the appropriate test rate, there is total unstated interest (regardless of amount) with respect to a contract, section 483 applies to the payments described in paragraph (b) of this section which are due under the contract. In such case, the amount of total unstated interest under the contract which is includible in or deductible from income must be computed by using the higher interest rate prescribed in paragraph (c) of this section, and then allocating such amount among the payments due under the contract in the manner provided in paragraph (a) of this section.

(ii) Prescribed test rates. (A) For payments on account of a sale or exchange of property entered into before July 24, 1975, as well as a sale or exchange of property entered into pursuant to a binding written contract (including an irrevocable written option) entered into before such date, the test prescribed by paragraph (d)(1)(ii)(A) of this section shall be 4 percent per annum simple interest. (See paragraph (c)(4) of this section for special rules where there has been a substantial change in the terms of a binding written contract entered into before July 24, 1975.)

(B) For payments on account of a sale or exchange of property entered into on or after July 24, 1975, and before July 1, 1981, except a sale or exchange entered into pursuant to a binding written contract (including an irrevocable written option) entered into before July 24, 1975, the test rate prescribed by paragraph (d)(1)(ii)(B) of this section shall be 6 percent per annum simple interest. For payments on account of a sale or exchange of property entered into on or after July 1, 1981, pursuant to a binding written contract (including an irrevocable written option) entered into after July 23, 1975, and before September 29, 1980, the test rate prescribed by paragraph (d)(1)(ii)(B) of this section shall be 6 percent per annum simple interest. (See paragraph (c)(5) of this section for special rules where there has been a substantial change in the terms of a contract entered into after July 23, 1975 and before September 29, 1980.

(C) For payments on account of a sale or exchange of property entered into on or after July 1, 1981, except a sale or exchange entered into pursuant to a binding written contract (including an irrevocable written option) entered into before September 29, 1980, the test rate prescribed by paragraph (d)(1)(ii)(C) of this section shall be 9 percent per annum simple interest. (See paragraph (c)(5) of this section for special rules where there has been a substantial change in the terms of a contract entered into before September 29, 1980).

(2) Alternative test where contract rate is at least that prescribed in paragraph (d)(1)(ii) of this section. The method provided in paragraph (d)(1) of this section for determining whether there is total unstated interest need not be used in the case of a contract which provides for interest at a rate of at least that prescribed in paragraph (d)(1)(ii) of this section, payable on each installment of principal at the time such installment is payable. For purposes of paragraph (b)(1)(ii) of this section, there is no total unstated interest under such a contract and, therefore, section 483 does not apply to payments under such a contract. For purposes of this paragraph, simple interest means straight interest computed on the principal amount of a payment from the time of the sale or exchange to the time the payment is required to be made. As an illustration of the meaning of simple interest, if a contract provides for payments totaling $6,000 in 3 equal installments of $2,000

plus 4 percent per annum simple interest, such installments of principal and interest being due 1, 2, and 3 years, respectively, from the date of the sale, the amount of interest due with the first installment is $80 ($2,000 × 0.04 × 1), the amount of interest due with the second installment is $160 ($2,000 × 0.04 × 2), and the amount of interest due with the third installment is $240 ($2,000 × 0.04 × 3).

(3) Test rate for certain obligations. The test rate of interest for determining whether there is total unstated interest shall be zero in the case of—

(i) A contract under which the purchaser is the United States, a State, or any other governmental body described in section 103 (relating to interest on certain governmental obligations), and under which the deferred payments are made pursuant to an obligation to which section 103 applies, or

(ii) An evidence of indebtedness which is issued after May 27, 1969, by a corporation in an exchange for property (other than money) which results under paragraph (b)(2)(iii) of § 1.-1232–3 in creating original issue discount subject to ratable inclusion under section 1232(a)(3) in the holder's gross income.

. . . . .

(g) Present value tables—(1) Computation of present value. If the purpose of the present value computation is to determine under paragraph (d) of this section whether there is total unstated interest under a contract, column (a) of the appropriate table set forth in paragraph (g)(2) of this section shall be used. For the rules relating to certain governmental obligations, see paragraph (d)(3) of this section. If the purpose of the present value computation is to determine under paragraph (c) of this section the amount of total unstated interest under a contract to be included in or deducted from income (that is, after it has already been determined by using column (a) of the appropriate table that the contract contains total unstated interest), column (b) of the appropriate table set forth in paragraph (g)(2) of this section shall be used. If a contract provides for deferred payments for a period in excess of 60 years, the factor (or factors) necessary may be obtained upon request to the Commissioner of Internal Revenue, Washington, D. C. 20224. In general, such request must be accompanied by a copy of the contract (or the proposed contract) and other relevant instruments.

(2) Tables. The following tables shall be used for computing the present value of a payment to which section 483 applies and the present value of any interest payment due under a contract:

Table VII—Present Value of Deferred Payment

(Applicable to contracts entered into on or after July 1, 1981, to which paragraphs (c)(2)(ii)(C) and (d)(1)(ii)(C) of this section apply.)

(col. (a) 9 percent simple interest—col. (b) 10 percent interest, compounded semiannually.)

Number of months deferred		Col. (a)	Col. (b)	Number of months deferred		Col. (a)	Col. (b)	Number of months deferred		Col. (a)	Col. (b)
More than	But not more than	Present value of $1 at 9 percent simple interest	Present value of $1 at 10 percent compounded semi-annually	More than	But not more than	Present value of $1 at 9 percent simple interest	Present value of $1 at 10 percent compounded semi-annually	More than	But not more than	Present value of $1 at 9 percent simple interest	Present value of $1 at 10 percent compounded semi-annually
0	6	1.00000	1.00000	237	243	.35714	.14205	477	483	.21739	.02018
6	9	.95694	.95238	243	249	.35149	.13528	483	489	.21529	.01922
9	15	.91743	.90703	249	255	.34602	.12884	489	495	.21322	.01830
15	21	.88106	.86384	255	261	.34072	.12270	495	501	.21119	.01743
21	27	.84746	.82270	261	267	.33557	.11686	501	507	.20921	.01660
27	33	.81633	.78353	267	273	.33058	.11130	507	513	.20725	.01581
33	39	.78740	.74622	273	279	.32573	.10600	513	519	.20534	.01506
39	45	.76068	.71068	279	285	.32103	.10095	519	525	.20346	.01434
45	51	.73529	.67684	285	291	.31646	.09614	525	531	.20161	.01366
51	57	.71174	.64461	291	297	.31201	.09156	531	537	.19980	.01301
57	63	.68966	.61391	297	303	.30769	.08720	537	543	.19802	.01239
63	69	.66890	.58468	303	309	.30349	.08305	543	549	.19627	.01180
69	75	.64935	.55684	309	315	.29940	.07910	549	555	.19455	.01124
75	81	.63091	.53032	315	321	.29542	.07533	555	561	.19286	.01070
81	87	.61350	.50507	321	327	.29155	.07174	561	567	.19120	.01019
87	93	.59701	.48102	327	333	.28777	.06833	567	573	.18957	.00971
93	99	.58140	.45811	333	339	.28409	.06507	573	579	.18797	.00924
99	105	.56657	.43630	339	345	.28050	.06197	579	585	.18639	.00880
105	111	.55249	.41552	345	351	.27701	.05902	585	591	.18484	.00838
111	117	.53908	.39573	351	357	.27360	.05621	591	597	.18332	.00798
117	123	.52632	.37689	357	363	.27027	.05354	597	603	.18182	.00760
123	129	.51414	.35894	363	369	.26702	.05099	603	609	.18034	.00724
129	135	.50251	.34185	369	375	.26385	.04856	609	615	.17889	.00690
135	141	.49140	.32557	375	381	.26076	.04625	615	621	.17746	.00657
141	147	.48077	.31007	381	387	.25773	.04404	621	627	.17606	.00626
147	153	.47059	.29530	387	393	.25478	.04195	627	633	.17467	.00596
153	159	.46083	.28124	393	399	.25189	.03995	633	639	.17331	.00567
159	165	.45147	.26785	399	405	.24907	.03805	639	645	.17197	.00540
165	171	.44248	.25509	405	411	.24631	.03623	645	651	.17065	.00515
171	177	.43384	.24295	411	417	.24361	.03451	651	657	.16935	.00490
177	183	.42553	.23138	417	423	.24096	.03287	657	663	.16807	.00467
183	189	.41754	.22036	423	429	.23838	.03130	663	669	.16681	.00445
189	195	.40984	.20987	429	435	.23585	.02961	669	675	.16556	.00423
195	201	.40241	.19987	435	441	.23337	.02839	675	681	.16434	.00403
201	207	.39526	.19035	441	447	.23095	.02704	681	687	.16313	.00384
207	213	.38835	.18129	447	453	.22857	.02575	687	693	.16194	.00366
213	219	.38168	.17266	453	459	.22624	.02453	693	699	.16077	.00348
219	225	.37523	.16444	459	465	.22396	.02336	699	705	.15962	.00332
225	231	.36900	.15661	465	471	.22173	.02225	705	711	.15848	.00316
231	237	.36298	.14915	471	477	.21954	.02119	711	717	.15736	.00301
								717	723	.15625	.00287

Table IX—Present Value of Annuity Certain: $1 Every 12 Months

(Applicable to contracts entered into on or after July 1, 1981, to which paragraphs (c)(2)(ii)(C) of this section apply).

(col. (a) 4 percent simple interest—col. (b) 5 percent interest, compounded semiannually)

Number of years final payment deferred	Col. (a) Present value at 9 percent simple interest	Col. (b) Present value at 10 percent compounded semi-annually	Number of years final payment deferred	Col. (a) Present value at 9 percent simple interest	Col. (b) Present value at 10 percent compounded semi-annually
1.0	0.91743	0.90703			
2.0	1.76489	1.72973	31.0	14.44296	9.28236
3.0	2.55229	2.47595	32.0	14.70071	9.32640
4.0	3.28758	3.15279	33.0	14.95260	9.36635
5.0	3.97724	3.76670	34.0	15.19691	9.40259
			35.0	15.43987	9.43545
6.0	4.62659	4.32354	36.0	15.67572	9.46526
7.0	5.24009	4.82861	37.0	15.90667	9.49230
8.0	5.82149	5.28672	38.0	16.13291	9.51683
9.0	6.37398	5.70224	39.0	16.35464	9.53907
10.0	6.90030	6.07913	40.0	16.57203	9.55925
11.0	7.40261	6.42096	41.0	16.78525	9.57755
12.0	7.88358	6.73104	42.0	16.99446	9.5945
13.0	8.34441	7.01229	43.0	17.19980	9.60921
14.0	8.78689	7.26738	44.0	17.40141	9.82286
15.0	9.21242	7.49875	45.0	17.59943	9.63525
16.0	9.62228	7.70862	46.0	17.79396	9.64648
17.0	10.01752	7.89896	47.0	17.98518	9.65668
18.0	10.39920	8.07163	48.0	18.17315	9.66592
19.0	10.76820	8.22824	49.0	18.35799	9.67430
20.0	11.12534	8.37029	50.0	18.53961	9.68191
21.0	11.47136	8.49913	51.0	18.71870	9.68880
22.0	11.80693	8.61599	52.0	18.89476	9.69506
23.0	12.13266	8.72198	53.0	19.06807	9.70074
24.0	12.44912	8.81813	54.0	19.23872	9.70588
25.0	12.75681	8.90533	55.0	19.40679	9.71055
26.0	13.05621	8.96443	56.0	19.57235	9.71479
27.0	13.34776	9.05617	57.0	19.73548	9.71863
28.0	13.63185	9.12124	58.0	19.89625	9.72211
29.0	13.90886	9.18026	59.0	20.05473	9.72527
30.0	14.17913	9.23380	60.0	20.21096	9.72814

. . . . .

§ 1.531–1 Imposition of tax

Section 531 imposes (in addition to the other taxes imposed upon corporations by chapter 1 of the Code) a graduated tax on the accumulated taxable income of every corporation described in section 532 and § 1.532–1. In the case of an affiliated group which makes or is required to make a consolidated return, see § 1.1502–2(d). All of the taxes on corporations under chapter 1 of the Code are treated as one tax for purposes of assessment, collection, payment, period of limitations, etc. See section 535 and §§ 1.535–1, 1.535–2, and 1.535–3 for the definition and determination of accumulated taxable income.

§ 1.532–1 Corporations subject to accumulated earnings tax

(a) General rule. (1) The tax imposed by section 531 applies to any domestic or foreign corporation (not specifically excepted under section 532(b) and paragraph (b) of this section) formed or availed of to avoid or prevent the imposition of the individual income tax on its shareholders, or on the shareholders of any other corporation, by permitting earnings and profits to accumulate instead of dividing or distributing them. See section 533 and § 1.533–1, relating to evidence of purpose to avoid income tax with respect to shareholders.

(2) The tax imposed by section 531 may apply if the avoidance is accomplished through the formation or use of one corporation or a chain of corporations. For example, if the capital stock of the M Corporation is held by the N Corporation, the earnings and profits of the M Corporation would not be returned as income subject to the individual income tax until such earnings and profits of the M Corporation were distributed to the N Corporation and distributed in turn by the N Corporation to its shareholders. If either the M Corporation or the N Corporation was formed or is availed of for the purpose of avoiding or preventing the imposition of the individual income tax upon the shareholders of the N Corporation, the accumulated taxable income of the corporation so formed or availed of (M or N, as the case may be) is subject to the tax imposed by section 531.

(b) Exceptions. The accumulated earnings tax imposed by section 531 does not apply to a personal holding company (as defined in section 542), to a foreign personal holding company (as defined in section 552), or to a corporation exempt from tax under subchapter F, chapter 1 of the Code.

. . . .

§ 1.533–1 Evidence of purpose to avoid income tax

(a) In general. (1) The Commissioner's determination that a corporation was formed or availed of for the purpose of avoiding income tax with respect to shareholders is subject to disproof by competent evidence. Section 533(a) provides that the fact that earnings and profits of a corporation are permitted to accumulate beyond the reasonable needs of the business shall be determinative of the purpose to avoid the income tax with respect to shareholders unless the corporation, by the preponderance of the evidence, shall prove to the contrary. The burden of proving that earnings and profits have been permitted to accumulate beyond the reasonable needs of the business may be shifted to the Commissioner under section 534. See §§ 1.534–1 through 1.534–4. Section 533 (b) provides that the fact that the taxpayer is a mere holding or investment company shall be prima facie evidence of the purpose to avoid income tax with respect to shareholders.

(2) The existence or nonexistence of the purpose to avoid income tax with respect to shareholders may be indicated by circumstances other than the conditions specified in section 533. Whether or not such purpose was present depends upon the particular circumstances of each case. All circumstances which might be construed as evidence of the purpose to avoid income tax with respect to shareholders cannot be outlined, but among other things, the following will be considered:

(i) Dealings between the corporation and its shareholders, such as withdrawals by the shareholders as personal loans or the expenditure of funds by the corporation for the personal benefit of the shareholders,

(ii) The investment by the corporation of undistributed earnings in assets having no reasonable connection with the business of the corporation (see § 1.537–3), and

(iii) The extent to which the corporation has distributed its earnings and profits.

The fact that a corporation is a mere holding or investment company or has an accumulation of earnings and profits in excess of the reasonable needs of the business is not absolutely conclusive against it if the taxpayer satisfies the Commissioner that the corporation was neither formed nor availed of for the purpose of avoiding income tax with respect to shareholders.

(b) General burden of proof and statutory presumptions. The Commissioner may determine that the taxpayer was formed or availed of to avoid income tax with respect to shareholders through the medium of permitting earnings and profits to accumulate. In the case of litigation involving any such determination (except where the burden of proof is on the Commissioner under section 534), the burden of proving such determination wrong by a preponderance of the evidence, together with the corresponding burden of first going forward with the evidence, is on the taxpayer under principles applicable to income tax cases generally. For the burden of proof in a proceeding before the Tax Court with respect to the allegation that earnings and profits have been permitted to accumulate beyond the reasonable needs of the business, see section 534 and §§ 1.534–2 through 1.534–4. For a definition of a holding or investment company, see paragraph (c) of this section. For determination of the reasonable needs of the business, see section 537 and §§ 1.537–1 through 1.537–3. If the taxpayer is a mere holding or investment company, and the Commissioner therefore determines that the corporation was formed or availed of for the purpose of avoiding income tax with respect to shareholders, then section 533 (b) gives further weight to the presumption of correctness already arising from the Commissioner's determination by expressly providing an additional presumption of the existence of a purpose to avoid income tax with respect to shareholders. Further, if it is established (after complying with section 534 where applicable) that

earnings and profits were permitted to accumulate beyond the reasonable needs of the business and the Commissioner has therefore determined that the corporation was formed or availed of for the purpose of avoiding income tax with respect to shareholders, then section 533(a) adds still more weight to the Commissioner's determination. Under such circumstances, the existence of such an accumulation is made determinative of the purpose to avoid income tax with respect to shareholders unless the taxpayer proves to the contrary by the preponderance of the evidence.

(c) Holding or investment company. A corporation having practically no activities except holding property and collecting the income therefrom or investing therein shall be considered a holding company within the meaning of section 533(b). If the activities further include, or consist substantially of, buying and selling stocks, securities, real estate, or other investment property (whether upon an outright or marginal basis) so that the income is derived not only from the investment yield but also from profits upon market fluctuations, the corporation shall be considered an investment company within the meaning of section 533(b).

. . . .

§ 1.533–2 Statement required

The corporation may be required to furnish a statement of its accumulated earnings and profits, the payment of dividends, the name and address of, and number of shares held by, each of its shareholders, the amounts that would be payable to each of the shareholders if the income of the corporation were distributed, and other information required under section 6042.

§ 1.534–1 Burden of proof as to unreasonable accumulations generally

For purposes of applying the presumption provided for in section 533 (a) and in determining the extent of the accumulated earnings credit under section 535(c) (1), the burden of proof with respect to an allegation by the Commissioner that all or any part of the earnings and profits of the corporation have been permitted to accumulate beyond the reasonable needs of the business may vary under section 534 as between litigation in the Tax Court and that in any other court. In case of a proceeding in a court other than the Tax Court, see paragraph (b) of § 1.533-1.

§ 1.534-2 Burden of proof as to unreasonable accumulations in cases before the Tax Court

(a) Burden of proof on Commissioner. Under the general rule provided in section 534(a), in any proceeding before the Tax Court involving a notice of deficiency based in whole or in part on the allegation that all or any part of the earnings and profits have been permitted to accumulate beyond the reasonable needs of the business, the burden of proof with respect to such allegation is upon the Commissioner if—

(1) A notification, as provided for in section 534(b) and paragraph (c) of this section, has not been sent to the taxpayer; or

(2) A notification, as provided for in section 534(b) and paragraph (c) of this section, has been sent to the taxpayer and, in response to such notification, the taxpayer has submitted a statement, as provided in section 534 (c) and paragraph (d) of this section, setting forth the ground or grounds (together with facts sufficient to show the basis thereof) on which it relies to establish that all or any part of its earnings and profits have not been permitted to accumulate beyond the reasonable needs of the business. However, the burden of proof in the latter case is upon the Commissioner only with respect to the relevant ground or grounds set forth in the statement submitted by the taxpayer, and only if such ground or grounds are supported by facts (contained in the statement) sufficient to show the basis thereof.

(b) Burden of proof on the taxpayer. The burden of proof in a Tax Court proceeding with respect to an allegation that all or any part of the earnings and profits have been permitted to accumulate beyond the reasonable needs of the business is upon the taxpayer if—

(1) A notification, as provided for in section 534(b) and paragraph (c) of

this section, has been sent to the taxpayer and the taxpayer has not submitted a statement, in response to such notification, as provided in section 534 (c) and paragraph (d) of this section; or

(2) A statement has been submitted by the taxpayer in response to such notification, but the ground or grounds on which the taxpayer relies are not relevant to the allegation or, if relevant, the statement does not contain facts sufficient to show the basis thereof.

. . . .

(d) Statement by taxpayer. (1) A taxpayer who has received a notification, as provided in section 534(b) and paragraph (c) of this section, that the proposed notice of deficiency includes an amount with respect to the accumulated earnings tax imposed by section 531, may, under section 534(c), submit a statement that all or any part of the earnings and profits of the corporation have not been permitted to accumulate beyond the reasonable needs of the business. Such statement shall set forth the ground or grounds (together with facts sufficient to show the basis thereof) on which the taxpayer relies to establish that there has been no accumulation of earnings and profits beyond the reasonable needs of the business. See paragraphs (a) and (b) of this section for rules concerning the effect of the statement with respect to burden of proof. See §§ 1.537-1 to 1.537-3, inclusive, relating to reasonable needs of the business.

(2) The taxpayer's statement, under section 534(c) and this paragraph, must be submitted to the Internal Revenue office which issued the notification (referred to in section 534(b) and paragraph (c) of this section) within 60 days after the mailing of such notification. If the taxpayer is unable, for good cause, to submit the statement within such 60-day period, an additional period not exceeding 30 days may be granted upon receipt in the Internal Revenue office concerned (before the expiration of the 60-day period provided herein) of a request from the taxpayer, setting forth the reasons for such request. See section 534(d) and § 1.534-3 with respect to a statement in the case of a jeopardy assessment.

§ 1.535-1 Definition

(a) The accumulated earnings tax is imposed by section 531 on the accumulated taxable income. Accumulated taxable income is the taxable income of the corporation with the adjustments prescribed by section 535(b) and § 1.-535-2, minus the sum of the dividends paid deduction and the accumulated earnings credit. See section 561 and the regulations thereunder, relating to the definition of the deduction for dividends paid, and section 535(c) and § 1.-535-3, relating to the accumulated earnings credit.

. . . .

§ 1.535-2 Adjustments to taxable income

(a) Taxes—(1) United States taxes. In computing accumulated taxable income for any taxable year, there shall be allowed as a deduction the amount by which Federal income and excess profits taxes accrued during the taxable year exceed the credit provided by section 33 (relating to taxes of foreign countries and possessions of the United States), except that no deduction shall be allowed for (i) the accumulated earnings tax imposed by section 531 (or a corresponding section of a prior law), (ii) the personal holding company tax imposed by section 541 (or a corresponding section of a prior law), and (iii) the excess profits tax imposed by subchapter E, chapter 2 of the Internal Revenue Code of 1939, for taxable years beginning after December 31, 1940. The deduction is for taxes accrued during the taxable year, regardless of whether the corporation uses an accrual method of accounting, the cash receipts and disbursements method, or any other allowable method of accounting. In computing the amount of taxes accrued, an unpaid tax which is being contested is not considered accrued until the contest is resolved.

. . . .

§ 1.535-3 Accumulated earnings credit

(a) In general. As provided in section 535(a) and § 1.535-1, the accumulated earnings credit, provided by section 535(c), reduces taxable income in computing accumulated taxable income. In the case of a corporation, not a mere holding or investment company, the accumulated earnings credit is determined as provided in paragraph (b) of this section and, in the case of a holding or investment company, as provided in paragraph (c) of this section.

(b) Corporation which is not a mere holding or investment company—(1) General rule. (i) In the case of a corporation, not a mere holding or investment company, the accumulated earnings credit is the amount equal to such part of the earnings and profits of the taxable year which is retained for the reasonable needs of the business, minus the deduction allowed by section 535 (b) (6) (see paragraph (f) of § 1.535-2, relating to the deduction for long-term capital gains). In no event shall the accumulated earnings credit be less than the minimum credit provided for in section 535(c) (2) and subparagraph (2) of this paragraph. The amount of the earnings and profits for the taxable year retained is the amount by which the earnings and profits for the taxable year exceed the dividends paid deduction for such taxable year. See section 561 and §§ 1.561-1 and 1.-561-2, relating to the deduction for dividends paid.

(ii) In determining whether any amount of the earnings and profits of the taxable year has been retained for the reasonable needs of the business, the accumulated earnings and profits of prior years will be taken into consideration. Thus, for example, if such accumulated earnings and profits of prior years are sufficient for the reasonable needs of the business, then any earnings and profits of the current taxable year which are retained will not be considered to be retained for the reasonable needs of the business. See section 537 and §§ 1.537-1 and 1.537-2.

. . . .

(d) Accumulated earnings and profits. For the purposes of determining the minimum credit provided by section 535(c) (2) and paragraph (b) (2) of this section, and the credit provided by section 535(c) (3) and paragraph (c) of this section, dividends paid after the close of any taxable year which are considered paid during such taxable year, shall be deducted from the earnings and profits accumulated at the close of such taxable year. See section 563 and §§ 1.563–1 and 1.563–3, relating to dividends paid after the close of the taxable year.

§ 1.537–1 Reasonable needs of the business

(a) **In general.** The term "reasonable needs of the business" includes (1) the reasonably anticipated needs of the business, (2) the section 303 redemption needs of the business, as defined in paragraph (c) of this section, and (3) the excess business holdings redemption needs of the business as described in paragraph (d) of this section. See paragraph (e) of this section for additional rules relating to the section 303 redemption needs and the excess business holdings redemption needs of the business. An accumulation of the earnings and profits (including the undistributed earnings and profits of prior years) is in excess of the reasonable needs of the business if it exceeds the amount that a prudent businessman would consider appropriate for the present business purposes and for the reasonably anticipated future needs of the business. The need to retain earnings and profits must be directly connected with the needs of the corporation itself and must be for bona fide business purposes. For purposes of this paragraph the section 303 redemption needs of the business and the excess business holdings redemption needs of the business are deemed to be directly connected with the needs of the business and for a bona fide business purpose. See § 1.537–3 for a discussion of what constitutes the business of the corporation. The extent to which earnings and profits have been distributed by the corporation may be taken into account in determining whether or not retained earnings and profits exceed the reasonable needs of the business. See § 1.537–2, relating to grounds for accumulation of earnings and profits.

(b) **Reasonable anticipated needs.** (1) In order for a corporation to justify an accumulation of earnings and profits for reasonably anticipated future needs, there must be an indication that the future needs of the business require such accumulation, and the corporation must have specific, definite, and feasible plans for the use of such accumulation. Such an accumulation need not be used immediately, nor must the plans for its use be consummated within a short period after the close of the taxable year, provided that such accumulation will be used within a reasonable time depending upon all the facts and circumstances relating to the future needs of the business. Where the future needs of the business are uncertain or vague, where the plans for the future use of an accumulation are not specific, definite, and feasible, or where the execution of such a plan is postponed indefinitely, an accumulation cannot be justified on the grounds of reasonably anticipated needs of the business.

(2) Consideration shall be given to reasonably anticipated needs as they exist on the basis of the facts at the close of the taxable year. Thus, subsequent events shall not be used for the purpose of showing that the retention of earnings or profits was unreasonable at the close of the taxable year if all the elements of reasonable anticipation are present at the close of such taxable year. However, subsequent events may be considered to determine whether the taxpayer actually intended to consummate or has actually consummated the plans for which the earnings and profits were accumulated. In this connection, projected expansion or investment plans shall be reviewed in the light of the facts during each year and as they exist as of the close of the taxable year. If a corporation has justified an accumulation for future needs by plans never consummated, the amount of such an accumulation shall be taken into account in determining the reasonableness of subsequent accumulations.

(c) **Section 303 redemption needs of the business.** (1) The term "section 303 redemption needs" means, with respect to the taxable year of the corporation in which a shareholder of the corporation died or any taxable year thereafter, the amount needed (or reasonably anticipated to be needed) to redeem stock included in the gross estate of such shareholder but not in excess of the amount necessary to effect a distribution to which section 303 applies. For purposes of this paragraph, the term "shareholder" includes an individual in whose gross estate stock of the corporation is includable upon his death for Federal estate tax purposes.

(2) This paragraph applies to a corporation to which section 303(c) would apply if a distribution described therein were made.

(3) If stock included in the gross estate of a decedent is stock of two or more corporations described in section 303(b) (2) (B), the amount needed by each such corporation for section 303 redemption purposes under this section shall, unless the particular facts and circumstances indicate otherwise, be that amount which bears the same ratio to the amount described in section 303(a) as the fair market value of such corporation's stock included in the gross estate of such decedent bears to the fair market value of all of the stock of such corporations included in the gross estate. For example, facts and circumstances indicating that the allocation prescribed by this subparagraph is not required would include notice given to the corporations by the executor or administrator of the decedent's estate that he intends to request the redemption of stock of only one of such corporations or the redemption of stock of such corporations in a ratio which is unrelated to the respective fair market values of the stock of the corporations included in the decedent's gross estate.

§ 1.537-2 Grounds for accumulation of earnings and profits

(a) In general. Whether a particular ground or grounds for the accumulation of earnings and profits indicate that the earnings and profits have been accumulated for the reasonable needs of the business or beyond such needs is dependent upon the particular circumstances of the case. Listed below in paragraphs (b) and (c) of this section are some of the grounds which may be used as guides under ordinary circumstances.

(b) Reasonable accumulation of earnings and profits. Although the following grounds are not exclusive, one or more of such grounds, if supported by sufficient facts, may indicate that the earnings and profits of a corporation are being accumulated for the reasonable needs of the business provided the general requirements under §§ 1.-537-1 and 1.537-3 are satisfied:

(1) To provide for bona fide expansion of business or replacement of plant;

(2) To acquire a business enterprise through purchasing stock or assets;

(3) To provide for the retirement of bona fide indebtedness created in connection with the trade or business, such as the establishment of a sinking fund for the purpose of retiring bonds issued by the corporation in accordance with contract obligations incurred on issue;

(4) To provide necessary working capital for the business, such as, for the procurement of inventories; or

(5) To provide for investments or loans to suppliers or customers if necessary in order to maintain the business of the corporation.

(c) Unreasonable accumulations of earnings and profits. Although the following purposes are not exclusive, accumulations of earnings and profits to meet any one of such objectives may indicate that the earnings and profits of a corporation are being accumulated beyond the reasonable needs of the business:

(1) Loans to shareholders, or the expenditure of funds of the corporation for the personal benefit of the shareholders;

(2) Loans having no reasonable relation to the conduct of the business made to relatives or friends of shareholders, or to other persons;

(3) Loans to another corporation, the business of which is not that of the taxpayer corporation, if the capital stock of such other corporation is owned, directly or indirectly, by the shareholder or shareholders of the taxpayer corporation and such shareholder or shareholders are in control of both corporations;

(4) Investments in properties, or securities which are unrelated to the activities of the business of the taxpayer corporation; or

(5) Retention of earnings and profits to provide against unrealistic hazards.

§ 1.537-3 Business of the corporation

(a) The business of a corporation is not merely that which it has previously carried on but includes, in general, any line of business which it may undertake.

(b) If one corporation owns the stock of another corporation and, in effect, operates the other corporation, the business of the latter corporation may be considered in substance, although not in legal form, the business of the first corporation. However, investment by a corporation of its earnings and profits in stock and securities of another corporation is not, of itself, to be regarded as employment of the earnings and profits in its business. Earnings and profits of the first corporation put into the second corporation through the purchase of stock or securities or otherwise, may, if a subsidiary relationship is established, constitute employment of the earnings and profits in its own business. Thus, the business of one corporation may be regarded as including the business of another corporation if such other corporation is a mere instrumentality of the first corporation; that may be established by showing that the first corporation owns at least 80 percent of the voting stock of the second corporation. If the taxpayer's ownership of stock is less than 80 percent in the other corporation, the determination of whether the funds are employed in a business operated by the taxpayer will depend upon the particular circumstances of the case. Moreover, the business of one corporation does not include the business of another corporation if such other corporation is a personal holding company, an investment company, or a corporation not engaged in the active conduct of a trade or business.

§ 1.541-1 Imposition of tax

(a) Section 541 imposes a graduated tax upon corporations classified as personal holding companies under section 542. This tax, if applicable, is in addition to the tax imposed upon corporations generally under section 11. Unless specifically excepted under section 542(c) the tax applies to domestic and foreign corporations and, to the extent provided by section 542(b), to an affiliated group of corporations filing a consolidated return. Corporations classified as personal holding companies are exempt from the accumulated earnings tax imposed under section 531 but are not exempt from other income taxes imposed upon corporations, generally, under any other provisions of the Code. Unlike the accumulated earnings tax imposed under section 531, the personal holding company tax imposed by section 541 applies to all personal holding companies as defined in section 542, whether or not they were formed or availed of to avoid income tax upon shareholders. See section 6501(f) and § 301.6501(f)-1 of this chapter (Regulations on Procedure and Administration) with respect to the period of limitation on assessment of personal holding company tax upon failure to file a schedule of personal holding company income.

. . . . .

§ 1.542-2 Gross income requirement

To meet the gross income requirement it is necessary that at least 80 percent of the total gross income of the corporation for the taxable year be personal holding company income as defined in section 543 and §§ 1.543-1 and 1.543-2. For the definition of "gross income" see section 61 and §§ 1.61-1 through 1.61-14. Under such provisions gross income is not necessarily synonymous with gross receipts. Further, in the case of transactions in stocks and securities and in commodities transactions, gross income for personal holding company tax purposes shall include only the excess of gains over losses from such transactions. See section 543(b), paragraph (b) (5) and (6) of § 1.543-1 and § 1.543-2.

§ 1.543-1 Personal holding company income

(a) General rule. The term "personal holding company income" means the portion of the gross income which consists of the classes of gross income described in paragraph (b) of this section. See section 543(b) and § 1.543-2 for special limitations on gross income and personal holding company income in cases of gains from stocks', securities', and commodities' transactions.

(b) Definitions—(1) Dividends. The term "dividends" includes dividends as defined in section 316 and amounts required to be included in gross income under section 551 and §§ 1.551-1—1.551-2 (relating to foreign personal holding company income taxed to United States shareholders).

(2) Interest. The term "interest" means any amounts, includible in gross income, received for the use of money loaned. However, (i) interest which

constitutes "rent" shall not be classified as interest but shall be classified as "rents" (see subparagraph (10) of this paragraph) . . . . shall not be included in personal holding company income.

(3) Royalties (other than mineral, oil, or gas royalties or certain copyright royalties). The term "royalties" (other than mineral, oil, or gas royalties or certain copyright royalties) includes amounts received for the privilege of using patents, copyrights, secret processes and formulas, good will, trade marks, trade brands, franchises, and other like property. It does not, however, include rents.
. . . .

(4) Annuities. The term "annuities" includes annuities only to the extent includible in the computation of gross income. See section 72 and §§ 1.72-1—1.72-14 for rules relating to the inclusion of annuities in gross income.

(5) Gains from the sale or exchange of stock or securities. (i) Except in the case of regular dealers in stocks or securities as provided in subdivision (ii) of this subparagraph, gross income and personal holding company income include the amount by which the gains exceed the losses from the sale or exchange of stock or securities. See section 543(b) (1) and § 1.543-2 for provisions relating to this limitation. For this purpose, there shall be taken into account all those gains includible in gross income (including gains from liquidating dividends and other distributions from capital) and all those losses deductible from gross income which are considered under chapter 1 of the Code to be gains or losses from the sale or exchange of stock or securities. The term "stock or securities" as used in section 543(a) (2) and this subparagraph includes shares or certificates of stock, stock rights or warrants, or interest in any corporation (including any joint stock company, insurance company, association, or other organization classified as a corporation by the Code, certificates of interest or participation in any profit-sharing agreement, or in any oil, gas, or other mineral property, or lease, collateral trust certificates, voting trust certificates, bonds, debentures, certificates of

indebtedness, notes, car trust certificates, bills of exchange, obligations issued by or on behalf of a State, Territory, or political subdivision thereof.

(ii) In the case of "regular dealers in stock or securities" there shall not be included gains or losses derived from the sale or exchange of stock or securities made in the normal course of business. The term "regular dealer in stock or securities" means a corporation with an established place of business regularly engaged in the purchase of stock or securities and their resale to customers. However, such corporations shall not be considered as regular dealers with respect to stock or securities which are held for investment. See section 1236 and § 1.1236-1.

(6) Gains from futures transactions in commodities. Gross income and personal holding company income include the amount by which the gains exceed the losses from futures transactions in any commodity on or subject to the rules of a board of trade or commodity exchange. See § 1.543-2 for provisions relating to this limitation. In general, for the purpose of determining such excess, there are included all gains and losses on futures contracts which are speculative. However, for the purpose of determining such excess, there shall not be included gains or losses from cash transactions, or gains or losses by a producer, processor, merchant, or handler of the commodity, which arise out of bona fide hedging transactions reasonably necessary to the conduct of its business in the manner in which such business is customarily and usually conducted by others. See section 1233 and § 1.1233-1.

(7) Estates and trusts. Under section 543(a) (4) personal holding company income includes amounts includible in computing the taxable income of the corporation under part I, subchapter J of the Code (relating to estates, trusts, and beneficiaries) ; and any gain derived by the corporation from the sale or other disposition of any interest in an estate or trust.

(8) Personal service contracts. (i) Under section 543(a) (5) amounts received under a contract under which the corporation is to furnish personal services, as well as amounts received from the sale or other disposition of such contract, shall be included as personal holding company income if—

(a) Some person other than the corporation has the right to designate (by name or by description) the individual who is to perform the services, or if the individual who is to perform the services is designated (by name or by description) in the contract; and

(b) At any time during the taxable year 25 percent or more in value of the outstanding stock of the corporation is owned, directly or indirectly, by or for the individual who has performed, is to perform, or may be designated (by name or by description) as the one to perform, such services. For this purpose, the amount of stock outstanding and its value shall be determined in accordance with the rules set forth in the last two sentences of paragraph (b) and in paragraph (c) of § 1.542–3. It should be noted that the stock ownership requirement of section 543(a) (5) and this subparagraph relates to the stock ownership at any time during the taxable year. For rules relating to the determination of stock ownership, see section 544 and §§ 1.544–1 through 1.544–7.

(ii) If the contract, in addition to requiring the performance of services by a 25-percent stockholder who is designated or who could be designated (as specified in section 543(a) (5) and subdivision (i) of this subparagraph), requires the performance of services by other persons which are important and essential, then only that portion of the amount received under such contract which is attributable to the personal services of the 25-percent stockholder shall constitute personal holding company income. Incidental personal services of other persons employed by the corporation to facilitate the performance of the services by the 25-percent stockholder, however, shall not constitute important or essential services. Under section 482 gross income, deductions, credits, or allowances between or among organizations, trades, or businesses may be allocated if it is determined that allocation is necessary in order to prevent evasion of taxes or clearly to reflect the income of any such organizations, trades, or businesses.

(iii) The application of section 543 (a) (5) and this subparagraph may be illustrated by the following examples:

Example (1). A, whose profession is that of an actor, owns all of the outstanding capital stock of the M Corporation. The M Corporation entered into a contract with A under which A was to perform personal services for the person or persons whom the M Corporation might designate, in consideration of which A was to receive $10,000 a year from the M Corporation. The M Corporation entered into a contract with the O Corporation in which A was designated to perform personal services for the O Corporation in consideration of which the O Corporation was to pay the M Corporation $500,000 a year. The $500,000 received by the M Corporation from the O Corporation constitutes personal holding company income.

Example (2). Assume the same facts as in example (1), except that, in addition to A's contract with the M Corporation, B, whose profession is that of a dancer and C, whose profession is that of a singer, were also under contract to the M Corporation to perform personal services for the person or persons whom the M Corporation might designate, in consideration of which they were each to receive $25,000 a year from the M Corporation. Neither B nor C were stockholders of the M Corporation. The contract entered into by the M Corporation with the O Corporation, in addition to designating that A was to perform personal services for the O Corporation, designated that B and C were also to perform personal services for the O Corporation. Although the O Corporation particularly desired the services of A for an entertainment program it planned, it also desired the services of B and C, who were prominent in their fields, to provide a good supporting cast for the program. The services of B and C required under the contract are determined to be important and essential; therefore, only that portion of the $500,000 received by the M Corporation which is attributable to the personal services of A constitutes personal holding company income. The same result would obtain although the dancer and the singer required by the contract were not designated by name but the contract gave the M Corporation discretion to select and provide the services of a singer and a dancer for the program and such services were provided.

Example (3). The N Corporation is engaged in engineering. Its entire outstanding capital stock is owned by four individuals. The N Corporation entered into a contract with the R Corporation to perform engineering services in consideration of which the R Corporation was to pay the N Corporation $50,000. The individual who was to perform the services was not designated (by name or by description) in the contract and no one but the N Corporation had the right to designate (by name or by description) such individual. The $50,000 received by the N Corporation from the R Corporation does not constitute personal holding company income.

(9) **Compensation for use of property.** Under section 543(a) (6) amounts received as compensation for the use of, or right to use, property of the corporation shall be included as personal holding company income if, at any time during the taxable year, 25 percent or more in value of the outstanding stock of the corporation is owned, directly or indirectly, by or for an individual entitled to the use of the property. Thus, if a shareholder who

meets the stock ownership requirement of section 543(a) (6) and this subparagraph uses, or has the right to use, a yacht, residence, or other property owned by the corporation, the compensation to the corporation for such use. or right to use, the property constitutes personal holding company income. This is true even though the shareholder may acquire the use of, or the right to use, the property by means of a sublease or under any other arrangement involving parties other than the corporation and the shareholder. However, if the personal holding company income of the corporation (after excluding any such income described in section 543(a) (6) and this subparagraph, relating to compensation for use of property, and after excluding any such income described in section 543(a) (7) and subparagraph (10) of this paragraph, relating to rents) is not more than 10 percent of its gross income, compensation for the use of property shall not constitute personal holding company income. For purposes of the preceding sentence, in determining whether personal holding company income is more than 10 percent of gross income, copyright royalties constitute personal holding company income, regardless of whether such copyright royalties are excluded from personal holding company income under section 543(a) (9) and subparagraph (12) (ii) of this paragraph. For purposes of applying section 543(a) (6) and this subparagraph, the amount of stock outstanding and its value shall be determined in accordance with the rules set forth in the last two sentences of paragraph (b) and in paragraph (c) of § 1.542-3. It should be noted that the stock ownership requirement of section 543(a) (6) and this subparagraph relates to the stock outstanding at any time during the entire taxable year. For rules relating to the determination of stock ownership, see section 544 and §§ 1.-544-1 through 1.544-7.

(10) Rents (including interest constituting rents). Rents which are to be included as personal holding company income consist of compensation (however designated) for the use, or right to use, property of the corporation. The term "rents" does not include amounts includible in personal holding company income under section 543(a) (6) and subparagraph (9) of this paragraph. The amounts considered as rents include charter fees, etc., for the use of, or the right to use, property, as well as interest on debts owed to the corporation (to the extent such debts represent the price for which real property held primarily for sale to customers in the ordinary course of the corporation's trade or business was sold or exchanged by the corporation). However, if the amount of the rents includible under section 543(a) (7) and this subparagraph constitutes 50 percent or more of the gross income of the corporation, such rents shall not be considered to be personal holding company income.

(11) Mineral, oil, or gas royalties. (i) The income from mineral, oil, or gas royalties is to be included as personal holding company income, unless (a) the aggregate amount of such royalties constitutes 50 percent or more of the gross income of the corporation for the taxable year and (b) the aggregate amount of deductions allowable under section 162 (other than compensation for personal services rendered by the shareholders of the corporation) equals 15 percent or more of the gross income of the corporation for the taxable year.

(ii) The term "mineral, oil, or gas royalties" means all royalties, including overriding royalties and, to the extent not treated as loans under section 636, mineral production payments, received from any interest in mineral, oil, or gas properties. The term "mineral" includes those minerals which are included within the meaning of the term "minerals" in the regulations under section 611.

(iii) The first sentence of subdivision (ii) of this subparagraph shall apply to overriding royalties received from the sublessee by the operating company which originally leased and developed the natural resource property in respect of which such overriding royalties are paid, and to mineral, oil, or gas production payments, only with respect to amounts received after September 30, 1958.

(12) Copyright royalties—(i) In general. The income from copyright royalties constitutes, generally, personal holding company income. However, for taxable years beginning after December 31, 1959, those copyright royalties which come within the definition of "copyright royalties" in section 543(a) (9) and subdivision (iv) of this subparagraph shall be excluded from personal holding company income only if the conditions set forth in subdivision (ii) of this subparagraph are satisfied.

(ii) Exclusion from personal holding company income. For taxable years beginning after December 31, 1959, copyright royalties (as defined in section 543(a) (9) and subdivision (iv) of this subparagraph) shall be excluded from personal holding company income only if the conditions set forth in (a), (b), and (c) of this subdivision are met.

(a) Such copyright royalties for the taxable year must constitute 50 percent or more of the corporation's gross income. For this purpose, copyright royalties shall be computed by excluding royalties received for the use of, or the right to use, copyrights or interests in copyrights in works created, in whole or in part, by any person who, at any time during the corporation's taxable year, is a shareholder.

(b) Personal holding company income for the taxable year must be 10 percent or less of the corporation's gross income. For this purpose, personal holding company income shall be computed by excluding (1) copyright royalties (except that there shall be included royalties received for the use of, or the right to use, copyrights or interests in copyrights in works created, in whole or in part, by any shareholder owning, at any time during the corporation's taxable year, more than 10 percent in value of the outstanding stock of the corporation), and (2) dividends from any corporation in which the taxpayer owns, on the date the taxpayer becomes entitled to the dividends, at least 50 percent of all classes of stock entitled to vote and at least 50 percent of the total value of all classes of stock, provided the corporation which pays the dividends meets the requirements of subparagraphs (A), (B), and (C) of section 543(a) (9).

(c) The aggregate amount of the deductions allowable under section 162 must constitute 50 percent or more of the corporation's gross income for the taxable year. For this purpose, the de-

ductions allowable under section 162 shall be computed by excluding deductions for compensation for personal services rendered by, and deductions for copyright and other royalties to, shareholders of the corporation.

(iii) Determination of stock value and stock ownership. For purposes of section 543(a) (9) and this subparagraph, the following rules shall apply:

(a) The amount and value of the outstanding stock of a corporation shall be determined in accordance with the rules set forth in the last two sentences of paragraph (b) and in paragraph (c) of § 1.542-3.

(b) The ownership of stock shall be determined in accordance with the rules set forth in section 544 and §§ 1.544-1 through 1.544-7.

(c) Any person who is considered to own stock within the meaning of section 544 and §§ 1.544-1 through 1.544-7 shall be a shareholder.

(iv) Copyright royalties defined. For purposes of section 543(a) (9) and this subparagraph, the term "copyright royalties" means compensation, however designated, for the use of, or the right to use, copyrights in works protected by copyright issued under Title 17 of the United States Code (other than by reason of section 2 or 6 thereof), and to which copyright protection is also extended by the laws of any foreign country as a result of any international treaty, convention, or agreement to which the United States is a signatory. Thus, "copyright royalties" includes not only royalties from sources within the United States under protection of United States laws relating to statutory copyrights but also royalties from sources within a foreign country with respect to United States statutory copyrights protected in such foreign country by any international treaty, convention, or agreement to which the United States is a signatory. The term "copyright royalties" includes compensation for the use of, or right to use, an interest in any such copyrighted works as well as payments from any person for performing rights in any such copyrighted works.

(v) Compensation which is rent. Section 543(a) (9) and subdivisions (i) through (iv) of this subparagraph shall not apply to compensation which is "rent" within the meaning of the second sentence of section 543(a)(7).

§ 1.545-2 Adjustments to taxable income

(a) Taxes—(1) General rule. (i) In computing undistributed personal holding company income for any taxable year, there shall be allowed as a deduction the amount by which Federal income and excess profits taxes accrued during the taxable year exceed the credit provided by section 33 (relating to taxes of foreign countries and possessions of the United States), and the income, war profits, and excess profits taxes of foreign countries and possessions of the United States accrued during the taxable year (to the extent provided by subparagraph (3) of this paragraph), except that no deduction shall be allowed for (a) the accumulated earnings tax imposed by section 531 (or a corresponding section of a prior law), (b) the personal holding company tax imposed by section 541 (or a corresponding section of a prior law), and (c) the excess profits tax imposed by subchapter E, chapter 2 of the Internal Revenue Code of 1939, for taxable years beginning after December 31, 1940. The deduction is for taxes for the taxable year, determined under the accrual method of accounting, regardless of whether the corporation uses an accrual method of accounting, the cash receipts and disbursement method, or any other allowable method of accounting. In computing the amount of taxes accrued, an unpaid tax which is being contested is not considered accrued until the contest is resolved.

. . . . .

§ 1.547-1 General rule

Section 547 provides a method under which, by virtue of dividend distributions, a corporation may be relieved from the payment of a deficiency in the personal holding company tax imposed by section 541 (or by a corresponding provision of a prior income tax law), or may be entitled to a credit or refund of a part or all of any such deficiency which has been paid. The method provided by section 547 is to allow an additional deduction for a dividend distribution (which meets the requirements of this section) in computing undistributed personal holding company income for the taxable year for which a deficiency in personal holding company tax is determined. The additional deduction for deficiency dividends will not, however, be allowed for the purpose of determining interest, additional amounts, or assessable penalties, computed with respect to the personal holding company tax prior to the allowance of the additional deduction for deficiency dividends. Such amounts remain payable as if section 547 had not been enacted.

§ 1.547-2 Requirements for deficiency dividends

(a) In general. There are certain requirements which must be fulfilled before a deduction is allowed for a deficiency dividend under section 547 and this section. These are—

(1) The taxpayer's liability for personal holding company tax shall be determined only in the manner provided in section 547(c) and paragraph (b)(1) of this section.

(2) The deficiency dividend shall be paid by the corporation on, or within 90 days after, the date of such determination and prior to the filing of a claim under section 547(e) and paragraph (b)(2) of this section for deduction for deficiency dividends. This claim must be filed within 120 days after such determination.

(3) The deficiency dividend must be of such a nature as would have permitted its inclusion in the computation of a deduction for dividends paid under section 561 for the taxable year with respect to which the liability for personal holding company tax exists, if it had been distributed during such year. See section 562 and §§ 1.562-1 through 1.562-3. In this connection, it should be noted that under section 316 (b)(2), the term "dividend" means (in addition to the usual meaning under section 316(a)) any distribution of property (whether or not a dividend as defined in section 316(a)) made by a corporation to its shareholders, to the extent of its undistributed personal holding company income (determined under section 545 and §§ 1.545-1 and 1.545-2 without regard to section 316 (b)(2)) for the taxable year in respect of which the distribution is made.

(b) Special rules—(1) Nature and details of determination. (i) A determination of a taxpayer's liability for personal holding company tax shall, for the purposes of section 547, be established in the manner specified in section 547(c) and this subparagraph.

(ii) The date of determination by a decision of the Tax Court of the United States is the date upon which such decision becomes final, as prescribed in section 7481.

(iii) The date upon which a judgment of a court becomes final, which is the date of the determination in such cases, must be determined upon the basis of the facts in the particular case. Ordinarily, a judgment of a United States district court becomes final upon the expiration of the time allowed for taking an appeal, if no such appeal is duly taken within such time; and a judgment of the United States Court of Claims becomes final upon the expiration of the time allowed for filing a petition for certiorari if no such petition is duly filed within such time.

(iv) The date of determination by a closing agreement, made under section 7121, is the date such agreement is approved by the Commissioner.

(v) A determination under section 547(c) (3) may be made by an agreement signed by the district director or such other official to whom authority to sign the agreement is delegated, and by or on behalf of the taxpayer. The agreement shall set forth the total amount of the liability for personal holding company tax for the taxable year or years. An agreement under this subdivision which is signed by the district director (or such other official to whom authority to sign the agreement is delegated) on or after July 15, 1963, shall be sent to the taxpayer at his last known address by either registered or certified mail. If registered mail is used for such purpose, the date of registration shall be treated as the date of determination; if certified mail is used for such purpose, the date of the postmark on the sender's receipt for such mail shall be treated as the date of determination. However, if a dividend is paid by the corporation before such registration or postmark date but

on or after the date such agreement is signed by the district director or such other official to whom authority to sign the agreement is delegated, the date of determination shall be such date of signing. The date of determination with respect to an agreement which is signed by the district director (or such other official to whom authority to sign the agreement is delegated) before July 15, 1963, shall be the date of the postmark on the cover envelope in which such agreement is sent by ordinary mail, except that if a dividend is paid by the corporation before such postmark date but on or after the date such agreement is signed by the district director or such other official to whom authority to sign the agreement is delegated, the date of determination shall be such date of signing.

(2) Claim for deduction—(i) Contents of claim. A claim for deduction for a deficiency dividend shall be made with the requisite declaration, on Form 976 and shall contain the following information:

(a) The name and address of the corporation;

(b) The place and date of incorporation;

(c) The amount of the deficiency determined with respect to the tax imposed by section 541 (or a corresponding provision of a prior income tax law) and the taxable year or years involved; the amount of the unpaid deficiency or, if the deficiency has been paid in whole or in part, the date of payment and the amount thereof; a statement as to how the deficiency was established, if unpaid; or if paid in whole or in part, how it was established that any portion of the amount paid was a deficiency at the time when paid and, in either case whether it was by an agreement under section 547(c) (3), by a closing agreement under section 7121, or by a decision of the Tax Court or court judgment and the date thereof; if established by a final judgment in a suit against the United States for refund, the date of payment of the deficiency, the date the claim for refund was filed, and the date the suit was brought; if established by a Tax Court decision or court judgment, a copy thereof shall be attached, together with an explanation of how the decision became final; if established by an agreement under section 547(c) (3), a copy of such agreement shall be attached;

(d) The amount and date of payment of the dividend with respect to which the claim for the deduction for deficiency dividends is filed;

(e) A statement setting forth the various classes of stock outstanding, the name and address of each shareholder, the class and number of shares held by each on the date of payment of the dividend with respect to which the claim is filed, and the amount of such dividend paid to each shareholder;

(f) The amount claimed as a deduction for deficiency dividends; and

(g) Such other information as may be required by the claim form.

(ii) Filing of claim and corporate resolution. The claim together with a certified copy of the resolution of the board of directors or other authority, authorizing the payment of the dividend with respect to which the claim is filed, shall be filed with the district director of internal revenue for the internal revenue district in which the return is filed

. . .

§ 1.561-1 Deduction for dividends paid

(a) The deduction for dividends paid is applicable in determining accumulated taxable income under section 535, undistributed personal holding company income under section 545, undistributed foreign personal holding company income under section 556, investment company taxable income under section 852, and real estate investment trust taxable income under section 857. The deduction for dividends paid includes—

(1) The dividends paid during the taxable year;

(2) The consent dividends for the taxable year, determined as provided in section 565; and

(3) In the case of a personal holding company, the dividend carryover computed as provided in section 564.

(b) For dividends for which the dividends paid deduction is allowable, see section 562 and § 1.562-1. As to when dividends are considered paid, see § 1.561-2.

§ 1.561-2 When dividends are considered paid

(a) In general. (1) A dividend will be considered as paid when it is received by the shareholder. A deduction for dividends paid during the taxable year will not be permitted unless the shareholder receives the dividend during the taxable year for which the deduction is claimed. See section 563 for special rule with respect to dividends paid after the close of the taxable year.

(2) If a dividend is paid by check and the check bearing a date within the taxable year is deposited in the mails, in a cover properly stamped and addressed to the shareholder at his last known address, at such time that in the ordinary handling of the mails the check would be received by the shareholder within the taxable year, a presumption arises that the dividend was paid to the shareholder in such year.

(3) The payment of a dividend during the taxable year to the authorized agent of the shareholder will be deemed payment of the dividend to the shareholder during such year.

(4) If a corporation, instead of paying the dividend directly to the shareholder, credits the account of the shareholder on the books of the corporation with the amount of the dividend, the deduction for a dividend paid will not be permitted unless it be shown to the satisfaction of the Commissioner that such crediting constituted payment of the dividend to the shareholder within the taxable year.

(5) A deduction will not be permitted for the amount of a dividend credited during the taxable year upon an obligation of the shareholder to the corporation unless it is shown to the satisfaction of the Commissioner that such crediting constituted payment of the dividend to the shareholder within the taxable year.

(6) If the dividend is payable in obligations of the corporation, they should be entered or registered in the taxable year on the books of the corporation, in the name of the shareholder (or his nominee or transferee), and, in the case of obligations payable to bearer, should be received in the taxable year by the shareholder (or his nominee or transferee) to constitute payment of the dividend within the taxable year.

(7) In the case of a dividend from which the tax has been deducted and withheld as required by chapter 3 (section 1441 and following), of the Code the dividend is considered as paid when such deducting and withholding occur.

(b) Methods of accounting. The determination of whether a dividend has been paid to the shareholder by the corporation during its taxable year is in no way dependent upon the method of accounting regularly employed by the corporation in keeping its books or upon the method of accounting upon the basis of which the taxable income of the corporation is computed.

(c) Records. Every corporation claiming a deduction for dividends paid shall keep such permanent records as are necessary (1) to establish that the dividends with respect to which such deduction is claimed were actually paid during the taxable year and (2) to supply the information required to be filed with the income tax return of the corporation. Such corporation shall file with its return (i) a copy of the dividend resolution; and (ii) a concise statement of the pertinent facts relating to the payment of the dividend, clearly specifying (a) the medium of payment and (b) if not paid in money, the fair market value and adjusted basis (or face value, if paid in its own obligations) on the date of distribution of the property distributed and the manner in which such fair market value and adjusted basis were determined. Canceled dividend checks and receipts obtained from shareholders acknowledging payment of dividends paid otherwise than by check need not be filed with the return but shall be kept by the corporation as a part of its records.

§ 1.562–1 Dividends for which the dividends paid deduction is allowable

(a) General rule. Except as otherwise provided in section 562(b) and (d), the term "dividend", for purposes of determining dividends eligible for the dividends paid deduction, refers only to a dividend described in section 316 (relating to definition of dividends for purposes of corporate distributions). No distribution, however, which

is preferential within the meaning of section 562(c) and § 1.562–2 shall be eligible for the dividends paid deduction. Moreover, when computing the dividends paid deduction with respect to a U.S. person (as defined in section 957(d)), no distribution which is excluded from the gross income of a foreign corporation under section 959(b) with respect to such person or from gross income of such person under section 959(a) shall be eligible for such deduction. Further, for purposes of the dividends paid deduction, the term "dividend" does not include a distribution in liquidation unless the distribution is treated as a dividend under section 316(b) (2) and paragraph (b) (2) of § 1.316–1, or under section 333 (e) (1) and paragraph (c) of § 1.333–4 or paragraph (c) (2), (d) (1) (ii), or (d) (2) of § 1.333–5, or qualifies under section 562(b) and paragraph (b) of this section. If a dividend is paid in property (other than money) the amount of the dividends paid deduction with respect to such property shall be the adjusted basis of the property in the hands of the distributing corporation at the time of the distribution. See paragraph (b) (2) of this section for special rules with respect to liquidating distributions by personal holding companies occurring during a taxable year of the distributing corporation beginning after December 31, 1963. Also see section 563 for special rules with respect to dividends paid after the close of the taxable year.

. . . . .

§ 1.562–2 Preferential dividends

(a) Section 562(c) imposes a limitation upon the general rule that a corporation is entitled to a deduction for dividends paid with respect to all dividends which it actually pays during the taxable year. Before a corporation may be entitled to any such deduction with respect to a distribution regardless of the medium in which the distribution is made, every shareholder of the class of stock with respect to which the distribution is made must be treated the same as every other shareholder of that class, and no class of stock may be treated otherwise than in accordance with its dividend rights as a class. The limitation imposed by section 562(c) is unqualified, except in the case of an actual distribution made in connection with a consent distribution (see section 565), if the entire distribution composed of such actual distribution and consent distribution is not preferential. The existence of a preference is sufficient to prohibit the deduction regardless of the fact (1) that such preference is authorized by all the shareholders of the corporation or (2) that the part of the distribution received by the shareholder benefited by the preference is taxable to him as a dividend. A corporation will not be entitled to a deduction for dividends paid with respect to any distribution upon a class of stock if there is distributed to any shareholder of such class (in proportion to the number of shares held by him) more or less than his pro rata part of the distribution as compared with the distribution made to any other shareholder of the same class. Nor will a corporation be entitled to a deduction for dividends paid in the case of any distribution upon a class of stock if there is distributed upon such class of stock more or less than the amount to which it is entitled as compared with any other class of stock. A preference exists if any rights to preference inherent in any class of stock are violated. The disallowance, where any preference in fact exists, extends to the entire amount of the distribution and not merely to a part of such distribution. As used in this section, the term "distribution" includes a dividend as defined in subchapter C, chapter 1 of the Code, and a distribution in liquidation referred to in section 562(b).

(b) The application of the provisions of section 562(c) may be illustrated by the following examples:

Example (1). A, B, C, and D are the owners of all the shares of class A common stock in the M Corporation, which makes its income tax returns on a calendar year basis. With the consent of all the shareholders, the M Corporation on July 15, 1954, declared a dividend of $5 a share payable in cash on August 1, 1954, to A. On September 15, 1954, it declared a dividend of $5 a share payable in cash on October 1, 1954, to B, C, and D. No allowance for dividends paid for the taxable year 1954 is permitted to the M Corporation with respect to any part of the dividends paid on August 1, 1954, and October 1, 1954.

Example (2). The N Corporation, which makes its income tax returns on the calendar year basis, has a capital of $100,000 (consisting of 1,000 shares of common stock of a par value of $100) and earnings or profits accumulated after February 28, 1913, in the amount of $50,000. In the year 1954, the N Corporation distributes $7,500 in cancellation of 50 shares of the stock owned by three of the four shareholders of the corporation. No deduction for

dividends paid is permissible under section 562(c) and paragraph (a) of this section with respect to such distribution.

Example (3). The P Corporation has two classes of stock outstanding, 10 shares of cumulative preferred, owned by E, entitled to $5 per share and on which no dividends have been paid for two years, and 10 shares of common, owned by F. On December 31, 1954, the corporation distributes a dividend of $125, $50 to E, and $75 to F. The corporation is entitled to no deduction for any part of such dividend paid, since there has been a preference to F. If, however, the corporation had distributed $100 to E and $25 to F, it would have been entitled to include $125 as a dividend paid deduction.

§ 1.563–1 Accumulated earnings tax

In the determination of the dividends paid deduction for purposes of the accumulated earnings tax imposed by section 531, a dividend paid after the close of any taxable year and on or before the 15th day of the third month following the close of such taxable year shall be considered as paid during such taxable year, and shall not be included in the computation of the dividends paid deduction for the year of payment. However, the rule provided in section 563(a) is not applicable to dividends paid during the first two and one-half months of the first taxable year of the corporation subject to tax under chapter 1 of the Internal Revenue Code of 1954.

§ 1.565–1 General rule

(a) **Consent dividends.** The dividends paid deduction, as defined in section 561, includes the consent dividends for the taxable year. A consent dividend is a hypothetical distribution (as distinguished from an actual distribution) which any person, who owns consent stock on the last day of the taxable year of the corporation, agrees to treat as a dividend subject to the limitations in section 565(b) and § 1.565.2. The amount of the distribution must be specified by such person in a consent (or consents) filed at the time and in the manner specified in paragraph (b) of this section.

(b) **Making and filing of consents.** (1) A consent shall be made on Form 972 in accordance with this section and the instructions on the form issued therewith. It may be made only by or on behalf of a person who was the actual owner on the last day of the corporation's taxable year of any class of consent stock, that is, the person who would have been required to include in gross income any dividends on such stock actually distributed on the last day of such year. Form 972 shall contain or be verified by a written declaration that it is made under the penalties of perjury. In the consent such person must agree to include in his gross income for his taxable year in which or with which the taxable year of the corporation ends a specific amount as a taxable dividend.

(2) See § 1.565-2 for rules as to when all or a portion of the amount so specified will be disregarded for tax purposes.

(3) A consent may be filed at any time not later than the due date of the corporation's income tax return for the taxable year for which the dividends paid deduction is claimed. With such return, and not later than the due date thereof, the corporation must file Forms 972 duly executed by each consenting shareholder, and a return on Form 973 showing by classes the stock outstanding on the first and last days of the taxable year, the dividend rights of such stock, distributions made during the taxable year to shareholders, and giving all the other information required by the form. Form 973 shall contain or be verified by a written declaration that it is made under the penalties of perjury.

(c) **Taxability of amounts specified in consents.** (1) Once a shareholder's consent is filed, the full amount specified therein shall be included in his gross income as a taxable dividend, except as otherwise provided in section 565(b) and § 1.565-2. Where the shareholder is taxable on a dividend only if received from sources within the United States, the amount specified in the consent of such shareholder shall be treated as a dividend from such sources in the same manner as if the dividend had been paid in money to the shareholder on the last day of the corporation's taxable year. See paragraph (b) of this section, relating to the making and filing of consents, and section 565 (e) and § 1.565-5, with respect to the payment requirements in the case of nonresident aliens and foreign corporations.

(2) Except as provided in section 565 (b) and § 1.565-2, the ground upon which a consent dividends deduction is denied the corporation does not affect the taxability of a shareholder whose consent has been filed for the amount specified in his consent. Thus, he is taxable on the full amount so specified even though a consent dividends deduction may be denied the corporation or may be of less value to it because, for example, (i) it is determined that it is not a corporation subject to part I, II, or III, subchapter G, chapter 1 of the Code, (ii) although subject to part II, subchapter G, chapter 1 of the Code, its taxable income (as adjusted under section 545(b) and § 1.545-2) is less than the total of the consent dividends, or (iii) in the case of nonresident aliens or foreign corporations, payment has not been made as required by section 565(e) and § 1.565-5.

§ 1.565-2 Limitations

(a) Amounts specified in consents are not treated as consent dividends to the extent that they would constitute a preferential dividend, or would not constitute a dividend (as defined in section 316), if distributed in money to shareholders on the last day of the taxable year of the corporation. If any portion of an amount specified in a consent is not treated as a consent dividend under section 565(b) and this section, it is disregarded for all tax purposes. For example, it is not taxable to the consenting shareholder, and paragraph (c) of § 1.565-1 is not applicable to such portion of the amount specified in the consent.

(b) (1) A preferential distribution is an actual distribution, or a consent distribution, or a combination of the two, which involves a preference to one or more shares of stock as compared with other shares of the same class or to one class of stock as compared with any other class of stock. See section 562(c) and § 1.562-2.

(2) The application of section 565 (b) (1) may be illustrated by the following examples:

Example (1). The X Corporation, which makes its income tax returns on the calendar year basis, has 200 shares of stock outstanding, owned by A and B in equal amounts. On December 15, 1954, the corporation distributes $600 to B and $100 to A. As a part of the same distribution A executes a consent to include $500 in his gross income as a taxable dividend though such amount is not distributed to him. The X Corporation assuming the other requirements of section 565 have been complied with is entitled to a consent dividends deduction of $500. Although the consent dividend is deemed to have been paid on December 31, 1954, the last day of the taxable year of the corporation, they constitute a single nonpreferential distribution of $1,200.

Example (2). The Y Corporation, which makes its income tax returns on the calendar year basis, has one class of consent stock outstanding, owned in equal amounts by A, B, and C. On December 15, 1954, the corporation makes a distribution in cash of $5,000 each to A and B, and $3,000 to C. The distribution is preferential. If A and B each receive a distribution in cash of $5,000 and C consents to include $3,000 in gross income as a taxable dividend, the combined actual and consent distribution is preferential. Similarly, if no one receives a distribution in cash, but A and B each consents to include $5,000 as a taxable dividend in gross income and C agrees to include only $3,000, the consent distribution is preferential.

Example (3). The Z Corporation, which makes its income tax returns on the calendar year basis, has only two classes of stock outstanding, each class being consent stock and consisting of 500 shares. Class A, with a par value of $40 per share, is entitled to two-thirds of any distribution of earnings and profits. Class B, with a par value of $20 per share, is entitled to one-third of any distribution of earnings and profits. On December 15, 1954, there is distributed on the class B stock $2 per share, or $1,000, and shareholders of the class A stock consent to include in gross income amounts equal to $2 per share, or $1,000. The distribution is preferential, inasmuch as the class B stock has received more than its pro rata share of the combined amounts of the actual distributions and the consent distributions.

(c) (1) An additional limitation under section 565(b) is that the amounts specified in consents which may be treated as consent dividends cannot exceed the amounts which would constitute a dividend (as defined in section 316) if the corporation had distributed the total specified amounts in money to shareholders on the last day of the taxable year of the corporation. If only a portion of such total would constitute a dividend, then only a corresponding portion of each specified amount is treated as a consent dividend.

(2) The application of section 565 (b) (2) may be illustrated by the following example:

Example. The X Corporation, which makes its income tax returns on the calendar year basis, has only one class of stock outstanding, owned in equal amounts by A and B. It makes no distributions during the taxable year 1954. Its earnings and profits for the calendar year 1954 amount to $8,000, there being at the beginning of such year no accumulated earnings or profits. A and B execute proper consents to include $5,000 each in their gross income as a dividend received by them on December 31, 1954. The sum of the amount specified in the consents executed by A and B is $10,000, but if $10,000 had actually been distributed by the X Corporation on December 31, 1954, only $8,000 would have constituted a dividend under section 316 (a). The amount which could be considered as consent dividends in computing the dividends paid deduction for purposes of the accumulated earnings tax is limited to $8,000, or $4,000 of the $5,000 specified in each consent. The remaining $1,000 in each consent is disregarded for all tax purposes. In the case of a personal holding company, the amount which could be considered as consent dividends in computing the dividends paid deduction for purposes of the personal holding company tax is $10,000 (assuming that the undistributed personal holding company income, determined without regard to distributions under section 316 (b) (2), is equal to at least that amount). In that event, A and B would each include $5,000 in gross income as a dividend received on December 31, 1954.

§ 1.565-3 Effect of consent

(a) The amount of the consent dividend shall be considered, for all purposes of the Code, as if it were distributed in money by the corporation to the shareholder on the last day of the taxable year of the corporation, received by the shareholder on such day, and immediately contributed by the shareholder as paid-in capital to the corporation on such day. Thus, the amount of the consent dividend will be treated by the shareholder as a dividend. The shareholder will be entitled to the dividends received credit under section 34 (for dividends received on or before December 31, 1964) and the exclusion under section 116, or to the dividends received deduction under section 243, with respect to such consent dividend. The basis of the shareholder's consent stock in a corporation will be increased by the amount thus treated in his hands as a dividend which he is considered as having contributed to the corporation as paid-in capital. The amount of the consent dividend will also be treated as a dividend received from sources within the United States in the same manner as if the dividend had been paid in money to the shareholders. Among other effects of the consent dividend, the earnings and profits of the corporation will be decreased by the amount of the consent dividends. Moreover, if the shareholder is a corporation, its accumulated earnings and profits will be increased by the amount of the consent dividend with respect to which it makes a consent.

. . . . .

§ 1.565-6   Definitions

(a) **Consent stock.** (1) The term "consent stock" includes what is generally known as common stock. It also includes participating preferred stock, the participation rights of which are unlimited.

(2) The definition of consent stock may be illustrated by the following example:

Example. If in the case of the X Corporation there is only one class of stock outstanding, it would all be consent stock. If, on the other hand, there were two classes of stock, class A and class B, and class A was entitled to 6 percent before any distribution could be made on class B, but class B was entitled to everything distributed after class A had received its 6 percent, only class B stock would be consent stock. Similarly, if class A, after receiving its 6 percent, was to participate equally or in some fixed proportion with class B until it had received a second 6 percent, after which class B alone was entitled to any further distributions, only class B stock would be consent stock. The same result would follow if the order of preferences were class A 6 percent, then class B 6 percent, then class A a second 6 percent, either alone or in conjunction with class B, then class B the remainder. If, however, class A stock is entitled to ultimate participation without limit as to amount, then it, too, may be consent stock. For example, if class A is to receive 3 percent and then share equally or in some fixed proportion with class B in the remainder of the earnings or profits distributed, both class A stock and class B stock are consent stock.

. . . . .

§ 1.641(a)-0   Scope of Subchapter J

(a) **In general.** Subchapter J (sections 641 and following), Chapter 1 of the Code, deals with the taxation of income of estates and trusts and their beneficiaries, and of income in respect of decedents. Part I of Subchapter J contains general rules for taxation of estates and trusts (Subpart A), specific rules relating to trusts which distribute current income only (Subpart B), estates and trusts which may accumulate income or which distribute corpus (Subpart C), treatment of excess distributions by trusts (Subpart D), grantors and other persons treated as substantial owners (Subpart E), and miscellaneous provisions relating to limitations on charitable deductions, income of an estate or trust in case of divorce, and taxable years to which the provisions of Subchapter J are applicable (Subpart F). Part I has no application to any organization which is not to be classified for tax purposes as a trust under the classification rules of §§ 301.7701-2, 301.7701-3, and 301.7701-4 of this chapter (Regulations on Procedure and Administration). Part II of Subchapter J relates to the treatment of income in respect of decedents. However, the provisions of Subchapter J do not apply to employee trusts subject to Subchapters D and F, Chapter 1 of the Code, and common trust funds subject to Subchapter H, Chapter 1 of the Code.

(b) **Scope of subparts A, B, C, and D.** Subparts A, B, C, and D (section 641 and following), part I, subchapter J, chapter 1 of the Code, relate to the taxation of estates and trusts and their beneficiaries. These subparts have no application to any portion of the corpus or income of a trust which is to be regarded, within the meaning of the Code, as that of the grantor or others treated as its substantial owners. See subpart E (section 671 and following), part I, subchapter J, chapter 1 of the Code, and the regulations thereunder for rules for the treatment of any portion of a trust where the grantor (or another person) is treated as the substantial owner. So-called alimony trusts are treated under subparts A, B, C, and D, except to the extent otherwise provided in section 71 or section 682. These subparts have no application to beneficiaries of non-exempt employees' trusts. See section 402(b) and the regulations thereunder.

(c) **Multiple trusts.** Multiple trusts that have—

(1) No substantially independent purposes (such as independent dispositive purposes),

(2) The same grantor and substantially the same beneficiary, and

(3) The avoidance or mitigation of (a) the progressive rates of tax (including mitigation as a result of deferral of tax) or (b) the minimum tax for tax preferences imposed by section 56 as their principal purpose,
shall be consolidated and treated as one trust for the purposes of subchapter J.

§ 1.641(b)-1   Computation and payment of tax; deductions and credits of estates and trusts

Generally, the deductions and credits allowed to individuals are also allowed to estates and trusts. However, there are special rules for the computation of certain deductions and for the allocation between the estate or trust and the beneficiaries of certain credits and deductions. See section 642 and the regulations thereunder. In addition, an estate or trust is allowed to deduct, in computing its taxable income, the deductions provided by sections 651 and 661 and regulations thereunder, relating to distributions to beneficiaries.

§ 1.641(b)-2 Filing of returns and payment of the tax

(a) The fiduciary is required to make and file the return and pay the tax on the taxable income of an estate or of a trust. Liability for the payment of the tax on the taxable income of an estate attaches to the person of the executor or administrator up to and after his discharge if, prior to distribution and discharge, he had notice of his tax obligations or failed to exercise due diligence in ascertaining whether or not such obligations existed. For the extent of such liability, see section 3467 of the Revised Statutes, as amended by section 518 of the Revenue Act of 1934 (31 U.S.C. 192). Liability for the tax also follows the assets of the estate distributed to heirs, devisees, legatees, and distributees, who may be required to discharge the amount of the tax due and unpaid to the extent of the distributive shares received by them. See section 6901. The same considerations apply to trusts.

(b) The estate of an infant, incompetent, or other person under a disability, or, in general, of an individual or corporation in receivership or a corporation in bankruptcy is not a taxable entity separate from the person for whom the fiduciary is acting, in that respect differing from the estate of a deceased person or of a trust. See section 6012(b) (2) and (3) for provisions relating to the obligation of the fiduciary with respect to returns of such persons.

§ 1.641(b)-3 Termination of estates and trusts

(a) The income of an estate of a deceased person is that which is received by the estate during the period of administration or settlement. The period of administration or settlement is the period actually required by the administrator or executor to perform the ordinary duties of administration, such as the collection of assets and the payment of debts, taxes, legacies, and bequests, whether the period required is longer or shorter than the period specified under the applicable local law for the settlement of estates. For example, where an executor who is also named as trustee under a will fails to obtain his discharge as executor, the period of administration continues only until the duties of administration are complete and he actually assumes his duties as trustee, whether or not pursuant to a court order. However, the period of administration of an estate cannot be unduly prolonged. If the administration of an estate is unreasonably prolonged, the estate is considered terminated for Federal income tax purposes after the expiration of a reasonable period for the performance by the executor of all the duties of administration. Further, an estate will be considered as terminated when all the assets have been distributed except for a reasonable amount which is set aside in good faith for the payment of unascertained or contingent liabilities and expenses (not including a claim by a beneficiary in the capacity of beneficiary).

(b) Generally, the determination of whether a trust has terminated depends upon whether the property held in trust has been distributed to the persons entitled to succeed to the property upon termination of the trust rather than upon the technicality of whether or not the trustee has rendered his final accounting. A trust does not automatically terminate upon the happening of the event by which the duration of the trust is measured. A reasonable time is permitted after such event for the trustee to perform the duties necessary to complete the administration of the trust. Thus, if under the terms of the governing instrument, the trust is to terminate upon the death of the life beneficiary and the corpus is to be distributed to the remainderman, the trust continues after the death of the life beneficiary for a period reasonably necessary to a proper winding up of the affairs of the trust. However, the winding up of a trust cannot be unduly postponed and if the distribution of the trust corpus is unreasonably delayed, the trust is considered terminated for Federal income tax purposes after the expiration of a reasonable period for the trustee to complete the administration of the trust. Further, a trust will be considered as terminated when all the assets have been distributed except for a reasonable amount which is set aside in good faith for the payment of unascertained or contingent liabilities and expenses (not including a claim by a beneficiary in the capacity of beneficiary).

(c) (1) Except as provided in subparagraph (2) of this paragraph, during the period between the occurrence of an event which causes a trust to terminate and the time when the trust is considered as terminated under this section, whether or not the income and the excess of capital gains over capital losses of the trust are to be considered as amounts required to be distributed currently to the ultimate distributee for the year in which they are received depends upon the principles stated in § 1.-651(a)-2. See § 1.663 et seq. for application of the separate share rule.

(2) (i) Except in cases to which the last sentence of this subdivision applies, for taxable years of a trust ending before September 1, 1957, subparagraph (1) of this paragraph shall not apply and the rule of subdivision (ii) of this subparagraph shall apply unless the trustee elects to have subparagraph (1) of this paragraph apply. Such election shall be made by the trustee in a statement filed on or before April 15, 1959, with the district director with whom such trust's return for any such taxable year was filed. The election provided by this subdivision shall not be available if the treatment given the income and the excess of capital gains over capital losses for taxable years for which returns have been filed was consistent with the provisions of subparagraph (1) of this paragraph.

(ii) The rule referred to in subdivision (i) of this subparagraph is as follows: During the period between the occurrence of an event which causes a trust to terminate and the time when a trust is considered as terminated under this section, the income and the excess of capital gains over capital losses of the trust are in general considered as amounts required to be distributed for the year in which they are received. For example, a trust instrument provides for the payment of income to A during her life, and upon her death for the payment of the corpus to B. The trust reports on the basis of the calendar year. A dies on November 1, 1955, but no distribution is made to B until January 15, 1956. The income of the trust and the excess of capital gains over capital losses for the entire year 1955, to the extent not paid, credited, or required to be distributed to A or A's estate, are treated under sections 661 and 662 as amounts required to be distributed to B for the year 1955.

(d) If a trust or the administration or settlement of an estate is considered terminated under this section for Federal income tax purposes (as for instance, because administration has been unduly prolonged), the gross income, deductions, and credits of the estate or trust are, subsequent to the termination, considered the gross income, deductions, and credits of the person or persons succeeding to the property of the estate or trust.

§ 1.642(c)-1 Unlimited deduction for amounts paid for a charitable purpose

(a) In general. (1) Any part of the gross income of an estate or trust which, pursuant to the terms of the governing instrument is paid (or treated under paragraph (b) of this section as paid) during the taxable year for a purpose specified in section 170(c) shall be allowed as a deduction to such estate or trust in lieu of the limited charitable contributions deduction authorized by section 170(a). In applying this paragraph without reference to paragraph (b) of this section, a deduction shall be allowed for an amount paid during the taxable year in respect of gross income received in a previous taxable year, but only if no deduction was allowed for any previous taxable year for the amount so paid.

(2) In determining whether an amount is paid for a purpose specified in section 170(c)(2) the provisions of section 170(c)(2)(A) shall not be taken into account. Thus, an amount paid to a corporation, trust, or community chest, fund, or foundation otherwise described in section 170(c)(2) shall be considered paid for a purpose specified in section 170(c) even though the corporation, trust, or community chest,

fund, or foundation is not created or organized in the United States, any State, the District of Columbia, or any possession of the United States.

(3) See section 642(c)(6) and § 1.642 (c)-4 for disallowance of a deduction under this section to a trust which is, or is treated under section 4947(a)(1) as though it were, a private foundation (as defined in section 509(a) and the regulations hereunder) and not exempt from taxation under section 501(a).

(b) Election to treat contributions as paid in preceding taxable year—(1) In general. For purposes of determining the deduction allowed under paragraph (a) of this section, the fiduciary (as defined in section 7701(a)(6)) of an estate or trust may elect under section 642(c)(1) to treat as paid during the taxable year (whether or not such year begins before January 1, 1970) any amount of gross income received during such taxable year or any preceding taxable year which is otherwise deductible under such paragraph and which is paid after the close of such taxable year but on or before the last day of the next succeeding taxable year of the estate or trust. The preceding sentence applies only in the case of payments actually made in a taxable year which is a taxable year beginning after December 31, 1969. No election shall be made, however, in respect of any amount which was deducted for any previous taxable year or which is deducted for the taxable year in which such amount is paid.

(2) Time for making election. The election under subparagraph (1) of this paragraph shall be made not later than the time, including extensions thereof, prescribed by law for filing the income tax return for the succeeding taxable year. Such election shall, except as provided in subparagraph (4) of this paragraph, become irrevocable after the last day prescribed for making it. Having made the election for any taxable year, the fiduciary may, within the time prescribed for making it, revoke the election without the consent of the Commissioner.

(3) Manner of making the election. The election shall be made by filing with the income tax return (or an amended return) for the taxable year in which the contribution is treated as paid a statement which—

(i) States the name and address of the fiduciary,

(ii) Identifies the estate or trust for which the fiduciary is acting,

(iii) Indicates that the fiduciary is making an election under section 642 (c)(1) in respect of contributions treated as paid during such taxable year,

(iv) Gives the name and address of each organization to which any such contribution is paid, and

(v) States the amount of each contribution and date of actual payment or, if applicable, the total amount of contributions paid to each organization during the succeeding taxable year, to be treated as paid in the preceding taxable year.

(4) Revocation of certain elections with consent. An application to revoke with the consent of the Commissioner any election made on or before June 8, 1970, must be in writing and must be filed not later than September 2, 1975. No consent will be granted to revoke an election for any taxable year for which the assessment of a deficiency is prevented by the operation of any law or rule of law. If consent to revoke the election is granted, the fiduciary must attach a copy of the consent to the return (or amended return) for each taxable year affected by the revocation. The application must be addressed to the Commissioner of Internal Revenue, Washington, D. C. 20224, and must indicate—

(i) The name and address of the fiduciary and the estate or trust for which he was acting,

(ii) The taxable year for which the election was made,

(iii) The office of the district director, or the service center, where the return (or amended return) for the year of election was filed, and

(iv) The reason for revoking the election.

§ 1.642(c)-2 Unlimited deduction for amounts permanently set aside for a charitable purpose

(a) Estates. Any part of the gross income of an estate which pursuant to the terms of the will—

(1) Is permanently set aside during the taxable year for a purpose specified in section 170(c), or

(2) Is to be used (within or without the United States or any of its possessions), exclusively for religious, charitable, scientific, literary, or educational purposes, or for the prevention of cruelty to children or animals, or for the establishment, acquisition, maintenance, or operation of a public cemetery not operated for profit,

shall be allowed as a deduction to the estate in lieu of the limited charitable contributions deduction authorized by section 170(a).

(b) Certain trusts—(1) In general. Any part of the gross income of a trust to which either subparagraph (3) or (4) of this paragraph applies, that by the terms of the governing instrument—

(i) Is permanently set aside during the taxable year for a purpose specified in section 170(c), or

(ii) Is to be used (within or without the United States or any of its possessions) exclusively for religious, charitable, scientific, literary, or educational purposes, or for the prevention of cruelty to children or animals, or for the establishment, acquisition, maintenance, or operation of a public cemetery not operated for profit,

shall be allowed, subject to the limitation provided in subparagraph (2) of this paragraph, as a deduction to the trust in lieu of the limited charitable contributions deduction authorized by section 170(a). The preceding sentence applied only to a trust which is required by the terms of its governing instrument to set amounts aside. See section 642(c)(6) and § 1.642(c)-4 for disallowance of a deduction under this section to a trust which is, or is treated under section 4947(a)(1) as though it were, a private foundation (as defined in section 509(a) and the regulations thereunder) that is not exempt from taxation under section 501(a).

(2) Limitation of deduction. Subparagraph (1) of this paragraph applies only to the gross income earned by a trust with respect to amounts transferred to the trust under a will executed on or before October 9, 1969, and satisfying the requirements of subparagraph (4) of this paragraph or transferred to the trust on or before October 9, 1969. For such purposes, any income, gains, or losses, which are derived at any time from the amounts so transferred to the trust shall also be taken into account in applying subparagraph

(1) of this paragraph. If any such amount so transferred to the trust is invested or reinvested at any time, any asset received by the trust upon such investment or reinvestment shall also be treated as an amount which was so transferred to the trust. In the case of a trust to which this paragraph applies which contains (i) amounts transferred pursuant to transfers described in the first sentence of this subparagraph and (ii) amounts transferred pursuant to transfers not so described, subparagraph (1) of this paragraph shall apply only if the amounts described in subdivision (i) of this subparagraph, together with all income, gains, and losses derived therefrom, are separately accounted for from the amounts described in subdivision (ii) of this subparagraph, together with all income, gains, and losses derived therefrom. Such separate accounting shall be carried out consistently with the principles of paragraph (c)(4) of § 53.4947-1 of this chapter (Foundation Excise Tax Regulations), relating to accounting for segregated amounts of split-interest trusts.

(3) Trusts created on or before October 9, 1969. A trust to which this subparagraph applies is a trust, testamentary or otherwise, which was created on or before October 9, 1969, and which qualifies under either subdivision (i) or (ii) of this subparagraph.

(i) Transfer of irrevocable remainder interest to charity. To qualify under this subdivision the trust must have been created under the terms of an instrument granting an irrevocable remainder interest in such trust to or for the use of an organization described in section 170(c). If the instrument granted a revocable remainder interest but the power to revoke such interest terminated on or before October 9, 1969, without the remainder interest having been revoked, the remainder interest will be treated as irrevocable for purposes of the preceding sentence.

(ii) Grantor under a mental disability to change terms of trust. (A) To qualify under this subdivision (ii) the trust must have been created by a grantor who was at all times after October 9, 1969, under a mental disability to change the terms of the trust. The term "mental disability" for this purpose means mental incompetence to change the terms of the trust, whether or not there has been an adjudication of mental incompetence and whether or not there has been an appointment of a committee, guardian, fiduciary, or other person charged with the care of the person or property of the grantor.

(B) If the grantor has not been adjudged mentally incompetent, the trustee must obtain from a qualified physician a certificate stating that the grantor of the trust has been mentally incompetent at all times after October 9, 1969, and that there is no reasonable probability that the grantor's mental capacity will ever improve to the extent that he will be mentally competent to change the terms of the trust. A copy of this certification must be filed with the first return on which a deduction is claimed by reason of this subdivision (ii) and subparagraph (1) of this paragraph. Thereafter, a statement referring to such medical opinion must be attached to any return for a taxable year for which such a deduction is claimed and during which the grantor's mental incompetence continues. The original certificate must be retained by the trustee of the trust.

(C) If the grantor has been adjudged mentally incompetent, a copy of the judgment or decree, and any modification thereof, must be filed with the first return on which a deduction is claimed by reason of this subdivision (ii) and subparagraph (1) of this paragraph. Thereafter, a statement referring to such judgment or decree must be attached to any return for a taxable year for which such a deduction is claimed and during which the grantor's mental incompetence continues. A copy of such judgment or decree must also be retained by the trustee of the trust.

(D) This subdivision (ii) applies even though a person charged with the care of the person or property of the grantor has the power to change the terms of the trust.

(c) Pooled income funds. Any part of the gross income of a pooled income fund to which § 1.642(c)-5 applies for the taxable year that is attributable to net long-term capital gain (as defined in section 1222(7)) which, pursuant to the terms of the governing instrument. is permanently set aside during the taxable year for a purpose specified in section 170(c) shall be allowed as a deduction to the fund in lieu of the limited charitable contributions deduction authorized by section 170(a). No de-

duction shall be allowed under this paragraph for any portion of the gross income of such fund which is (1) attributable to income other than net long-term capital gain or (2) earned with respect to amounts transferred to such fund before August 1, 1969. However, see paragraph (b) of this section for a deduction (subject to the limitations of such paragraph) for amounts permanently set aside by a pooled income fund which meets the requirements of that paragraph. The principles of paragraph (b)(2) of this section with respect to investment, reinvestment, and separate accounting shall apply under this paragraph in the case of amounts transferred to the fund after July 31, 1969.

(d) Disallowance of deduction for certain amounts not deemed to be permanently set aside for charitable purposes. No amount will be considered to be permanently set aside, or to be used, for a purpose described in paragraph (a) or (b)(1) of this section unless under the terms of the governing instrument and the circumstances of the particular case the possibility that the amount set aside, or to be used, will not be devoted to such purpose or use is so remote as to be negligible. Thus, for example, where there is possibility of the invasion of the corpus of a charitable remainder trust, as defined in § 1.664-1(a)(1)(ii), in order to make payment of the annuity amount or unitrust amount, no deduction will be allowed under paragraph (a) of this section in respect of any amount set aside by an estate for distribution to such a charitable remainder trust.

For treatment of distributions by an estate to a charitable remainder trust, see paragraph (a)(5)(iii) of § 1.664-1.

§ 1.642(d)-1 Net operating loss deduction

The net operating loss deduction allowed by section 172 is available to estates and trusts generally, with the following exceptions and limitations:

(a) In computing gross income and deductions for the purposes of section 172, a trust shall exclude that portion of the income and deductions attributable to the grantor or another person under sections 671 through 678 (relating to grantors and others treated as substantial owners).

(b) An estate or trust shall not, for the purposes of section 172, avail itself of the deductions allowed by section 642(c) (relating to charitable contributions deductions) and sections 651 and 661 (relating to deductions for distributions).

§ 1.642(g)-1 Disallowance of double deductions; in general

Amounts allowable under section 2053(a) (2) (relating to administration expenses) or under section 2054 (relating to losses during administration) as deductions in computing the taxable estate of a decedent are not allowed as deductions in computing the taxable income of the estate unless there is filed a statement, in duplicate, to the effect that the items have not been allowed as deductions from the gross estate of the decedent under section 2053 or 2054 and that all rights to have such items allowed at any time as deductions under section 2053 or 2054 are waived. The statement should be filed with the return for the year for which the items are claimed as deductions or with the district director for the internal revenue district in which the return was filed, for association with the return. The statement may be filed at any time before the expiration of the statutory period of limitation applicable to the taxable year for which the deduction is sought. Allowance of a deduction in computing an estate's taxable income is not precluded by claiming a deduction in the estate tax return, so long as the estate tax deduction is not finally allowed and the statement is filed. However, after a statement is filed under section 642(g) with respect to a particular item or portion of an item, the item cannot thereafter be allowed as a deduction for estate tax purposes since the waiver operates as a relinquishment of the right to have the deduction allowed at any time under section 2053 or 2054.

§ 1.642(g)-2 Deductions included

It is not required that the total deductions, or the total amount of any deduction, to which section 642(g) is applicable be treated in the same way. One deduction or portion of a deduction may be allowed for income tax purposes if the appropriate statement is filed, while another deduction or portion is allowed for estate tax purposes. Section 642(g) has no application to deductions for taxes, interest, business expenses, and other items accrued at the date of a decedent's death so that they are allowable as a deduction under section 2053(a) (3) for estate tax purposes as claims against the estate, and are also allowable under section 691 (b) as deductions in respect of a decedent for income tax purposes. However, section 642(g) is applicable to deductions for interest, business expenses, and other items not accrued at the date of the decedent's death so that they are allowable as deductions for estate tax purposes only as administration expenses under section 2053(a) (2). Although deductible under section 2053(a) (3) in determining the value of the taxable estate of a decedent, medical, dental, etc., expenses of a decedent which are paid by the estate of the decedent are not deductible in computing the taxable income of the estate. See section 213(d) and the regulations thereunder for rules relating to the deductibility of such expenses in computing the taxable income of the decedent.

§ 1.642(h)-1 Unused loss carryovers on termination of an estate or trust

(a) If, on the final termination of an estate or trust, a net operating loss carryover under section 172 or a capital loss carryover under section 1212 would be allowable to the estate or trust in a taxable year subsequent to the taxable year of termination but for the termination, the carryover or carryovers are allowed under section 642(h) (1) to the beneficiaries succeeding to the property of the estate or trust. See § 1.641 (b)-3 for the determination of when an estate or trust terminates.

(b) The net operating loss carryover and the capitol loss carryover are the same in the hands of a beneficiary as in the estate or trust, except that the capital loss carryover in the hands of a beneficiary which is a corporation is a short-term loss irrespective of whether it would have been a long-term or short-term capital loss in the hands of the estate or trust. The net operating loss carryover and the capital loss carryover are taken into account in computing taxable income, adjusted gross income, and the tax imposed by section 56 (relating to the minimum tax for tax preferences). The first taxable year of the beneficiary to which the loss shall be carried over is the taxable year of the beneficiary in which or with which the estate or trust terminates. However, for purposes of determining the number of years to which a net operating loss, or a capital loss under paragraph (a) of § 1.1212-1, may be carried over by a beneficiary, the last taxable year of the estate or trust (whether or not a short taxable year) and the first taxable year of the beneficiary to which a loss is carried over each constitute a taxable year, and, in the case of a beneficiary of an estate or trust that is a corporation, capital losses carried over by the estate or trust to any taxable year of the estate or trust beginning after December 31, 1963, shall be treated as if they were incurred in the last taxable year of the estate or trust (whether or not a short taxable year). For the treatment of the net operating loss carryover when the last taxable year of the estate or trust is the last taxable year to which such loss can be carried over, see § 1.642(h)-2.

(c) The application of this section may be illustrated by the following examples:

Example (1). A trust distributes all of its assets to A, the sole remainderman, and terminates on December 31, 1954, when it has a capital loss carryover of $10,000 attributable to transactions during the taxable year 1952. A, who reports on the calendar year basis, otherwise has ordinary income of $10,000 and capital gains of $4,000 for the taxable year 1954. A would offset his capital gains of $4,000 against the capital loss of the trust and, in addition, deduct under section 1211(b) $1,000 on his return for the taxable year 1954. The balance of the capital loss carryover of $5,000 may be carried over only to the years 1955 and 1956, in accordance with paragraph (a) of § 1.1212-1 and the rules of this section.

Example (2). A trust distributes all of its assets, one-half to A, an individual, and one-half to X, a corporation, who are the sole remaindermen, and terminates on December 31, 1966, when it has a short-term capital loss carryover of $20,000 attributable to short-term transactions during the taxable years 1964, 1965, and 1966, and a long-term capital loss carryover

of $12,000 attributable to long-term transactions during such years. A, who reports on the calendar year basis, otherwise has ordinary income of $15,000, short-term capital gains of $4,000 and long-term capital gains of $6,000, for the taxable year 1966. A would offset his short-term capital gains of $4,000 against his share of the short-term capital loss carryover of the trust, $10,000 (one-half of $20,000), and, in addition deduct under section 1211(b) $1,000 (treated as a short-term gain for purposes of computing capital loss carryovers) on his return for the taxable year 1966. A would also offset his long-term capital gains of $6,000 against his share of the long-term capital loss carryover of the trust, $6,000 (one-half of $12,000). The balance of A's share of the short-term capital loss carryover, $5,000, may be carried over as a short-term capital loss carryover to the succeeding taxable year and treated as a short-term capital loss incurred in such succeeding taxable year in accordance with paragraph (b) of § 1.1212-1. X, which also reports on the calendar year basis, otherwise has capital gains of $4,000 for the taxable year 1966. X would offset its capital gains of $4,000 against its share of the capital loss carryovers of the trust, $16,000 (the sum of one-half of each the short-term carryover and the long-term carryover of the trust), on its return for the taxable year 1966. The balance of X's share, $12,000, may be carried over as a short-term capital loss only to the years 1967, 1968, 1969, and 1970, in accordance with paragraph (a) of § 1.1212-1 and the rules of this section.

§ 1.642(h)-3 Meaning of "beneficiaries succeeding to the property of the estate or trust"

(a) The phrase "beneficiaries succeeding to the property of the estate or trust" means those beneficiaries upon termination of the estate or trust who bear the burden of any loss for which a carryover is allowed, or of any excess of deductions over gross income for which a deduction is allowed, under section 642(h).

(b) With reference to an intestate estate, the phrase means the heirs and next of kin to whom the estate is distributed, or if the estate is insolvent, to whom it would have been distributed if it had not been insolvent. If a decedent's spouse is entitled to a specified dollar amount of property before any distribution to other heirs and next of kin, and if the estate is less than that amount, the spouse is the beneficiary succeeding to the property of the estate or trust to the extent of the deficiency in amount.

(c) In the case of a testate estate, the phrase normally means the residuary beneficiaries (including a residuary trust), and not specific legatees or devisees, pecuniary legatees, or other nonresiduary beneficiaries. However, the phrase does not include the recipient of a specific sum of money even though it is payable out of the residue, except to the extent that it is not payable in full. On the other hand, the phrase includes a beneficiary (including a trust) who is not strictly a residuary beneficiary but whose devise or bequest is determined by the value of the decedent's estate as reduced by the loss or deductions in question. Thus the phrase includes:

(1) A beneficiary of a fraction of a decedent's net estate after payment of debts, expenses, etc.;

(2) A nonresiduary legatee or devisee, to the extent of any deficiency in his legacy or devise resulting from the insufficiency of the estate to satisfy it in full;

(3) A surviving spouse receiving a fractional share of an estate in fee under a statutory right of election, to the extent that the loss or deductions are taken into account in determining the share. However, the phrase does not include a recipient of dower or curtesy, or any income beneficiary of the estate or trust from which the loss or excess deduction is carried over.

(d) The principles discussed in paragraph (c) of this section are equally applicable to trust beneficiaries. A remainderman who receives all or a fractional share of the property of a trust as a result of the final termination of the trust is a beneficiary succeeding to the property of the trust. For example, if property is transferred to pay the income to A for life and then to pay $10,000 to B and distribute the balance of the trust corpus to C, C and not B is considered to be the succeeding beneficiary except to the extent that the trust corpus is insufficient to pay B $10,000.

§ 1.643(a)-0 Distributable net income; deduction for distributions; in general

The term "distributable net income" has no application except in the taxation of estates and trusts and their beneficiaries. It limits the deductions allowable to estates and trusts for amounts paid, credited, or required to be distributed to beneficiaries and is used to determine how much of an amount paid, credited, or required to be distributed to a beneficiary will be includible in his gross income. It is also used to determine the character of distributions to the beneficiaries. Distributable net income means for any taxable year, the taxable income (as defined in section 63) of the estate or trust, computed with the modifications set forth in §§ 1.643(a)-1 through 1.-643(a)-7.

§ 1.643(a)-1 Deduction for distributions

The deduction allowable to a trust under section 651 and to an estate or trust under section 661 for amounts paid, credited, or required to be distributed to beneficiaries is not allowed in the computation of distributable net income.

§ 1.643(a)-2 Deduction for personal exemption

The deduction for personal exemption under section 642(b) is not allowed in the computation of distributable net income.

§ 1.643(a)-3 Capital gains and losses

(a) Except as provided in § 1.643 (a)-6, gains from the sale or exchange of capital assets are ordinarily excluded from distributable net income, and are not ordinarily considered as paid, credited, or required to be distributed to any beneficiary unless they are:

(1) Allocated to income under the terms of the governing instrument or local law by the fiduciary on its books or by notice to the beneficiary,

(2) Allocated to corpus and actually distributed to beneficiaries during the taxable year, or

(3) Utilized (pursuant to the terms of the governing instrument or the practice followed by the fiduciary) in determining the amount which is distributed or required to be distributed. However, if capital gains are paid, permanently set aside, or to be used for the purposes specified in section 642(c), so that a charitable deduction is allowed under that section in respect of the gains, they must be included in the computation of distributable net income.

(b) Losses from the sale or exchange of capital assets are excluded in computing distributable net income except to the extent that they enter into the determination of any capital gains that are paid, credited, or required to be distributed to any beneficiary during the taxable year (but see § 1.642(h)-1 with respect to capital loss carryovers in the year of final termination of an estate or trust).

. . . .

(d) The application of this section may be illustrated by the following examples:

Example (1). A trust is created to pay the income to A for life, with a discretionary power in the trustee to invade principal for A's benefit. In the taxable year, $10,000 is realized from the sale of securities at a profit, and $10,000 in excess of income is distributed to A. The capital gain is not allocated to A by the trustee. During the taxable year the trustee received and paid out $5,000 of dividends. No other cash was received or on hand during the taxable year. The capital gain will not ordinarily be included in distributable net income. However, if the trustee follows a regular practice of distributing the exact net proceeds of the sale of trust property, capital gains will be included in distributable net income.

Example (2). The result in example (1) would have been the same if the trustee had been directed to pay an annuity of $15,000 a year to A (instead of being directed to pay the income to A with a discretionary power to distribute principal).

Example (3). The trustee of a trust containing Blackacre and other property is directed to hold Blackacre for ten years, and then sell it and distribute its proceeds to A. Any capital gain realized from the sale of Blackacre will be included in distributable net income.

Example (4). A trust instrument directs that the income shall be paid to A, and that the principal shall be distributed to A when he reaches age 35. All capital gains realized in the year of termination will be included in distributable net income. (See § 1.641(b)-3 for the determination of the year of final termination and the taxability of capital gains realized after the terminating event and before final distribution).

Example (5). If in example (4) the trustee had been directed to distribute half of the principal to A when he reached 35, the capital gain would be included in distributable net income (and in the distribution to A) to the extent the capital gain is allocable to A under the governing instrument and local law. Thus, if the trust assets consisted entirely of 100 shares of corporation M stock and the trustee sold half the shares and distributed the proceeds to A, the entire capital gain would normally be considered as allocated to A. On the other hand, if the trustee sold all the shares and distributed half the proceeds to A, half the capital gain would be considered as allocable to A.

Example (6). If in example (4) the trustee had been directed to pay $10,000 to B before making distribution to A, no portion of the

capital gains would be allocable to B since the distribution to B is a gift of a specific sum of money within the meaning of section 663(a) (1).

§ 1.643(a)-5   Tax-exempt interest

(a) There is included in distributable net income any tax-exempt interest excluded from gross income under section 103, reduced by disbursements allocable to such interest which would have been deductible under section 212 but for the provisions of section 265 (relating to disallowance of deductions allocable to tax-exempt income).

(b) If the estate or trust is allowed a charitable contributions deduction under section 642(c), the amounts specified in paragraph (a) of this section and § 1.643(a)-6 are reduced by the portion deemed to be included in income paid, permanently set aside, or to be used for the purposes specified in section 642(c). If the governing instrument specifically provides as to the source out of which amounts are paid, permanently set aside, or to be used for such charitable purposes, the specific provisions control. In the absence of specific provisions in the governing instrument, an amount to which section 642(c) applies is deemed to consist of the same proportion of each class of the items of income of the estate or trust as the total of each class bears to the total of all classes.

. . . .

§ 1.643(b)-1   Definition of "income"

For purposes of subparts A through D, part I, subchapter J, chapter 1 of the Code, the term "income", when not preceded by the words "taxable", "distributable net", "undistributed net", or "gross", means the amount of income of an estate or trust for the taxable year determined under the terms of its governing instrument and applicable local law. Trust provisions which depart fundamentally from concepts of local law in the determination of what constitutes income are not recognized for this purpose. For example, if a trust instrument directs that all the trust income shall be paid to A, but defines ordinary dividends and interest as corpus, the trust will not be considered one which under its governing instrument is required to distribute all its income currently for purposes of section 642(b) (relating to the personal exemption) and section 651 (relating to "simple" trusts).

§ 1.643(b)-2   Dividends allocated to corpus

Extraordinary dividends or taxable stock dividends which the fiduciary, acting in good faith, determines to be allocable to corpus under the terms of the governing instrument and applicable local law are not considered "income" for purposes of Subpart A, B, C, or D, Part I, Subchapter J, Chapter 1 of the Code. . . . .

§ 1.643(c)-1   Definition of "beneficiary"

An heir, legatee, or devisee (including an estate or trust) is a beneficiary. A trust created under a decedent's will is a beneficiary of the decedent's estate. The following persons are treated as beneficiaries:

(a) Any person with respect to an amount used to discharge or satisfy that person's legal obligation as that term is used in § 1.662(a)-4.

(b) The grantor of a trust with respect to an amount applied or distributed for the support of a dependent under the circumstances specified in section 677(b) out of corpus or out of other than income for the taxable year of the trust.

(c) The trustee or cotrustee of a trust with respect to an amount applied or distributed for the support of a dependent under the circumstances specified in section 678(c) out of corpus or out of other than income for the taxable year of the trust.

§ 1.651(a)-1   Simple trusts; deduction for distributions; in general

Section 651 is applicable only to a trust the governing instruments of which:

(a) Requires that the trust distribute all of its income currently for the taxable year, and

(b) Does not provide that any amounts may be paid, permanently set aside, or used in the taxable year for the charitable, etc., purposes specified in section 642(c),

and does not make any distribution other than of current income. A trust to which section 651 applies is referred to in this part as a "simple" trust. Trusts subject to section 661 are referred to as "complex" trusts. A trust may be a simple trust for one year and a complex trust for another year. It should be noted that under section 651 a trust qualifies as a simple trust in a taxable year in which it is required to distribute all its income currently and makes no other distributions, whether or not distributions of current income are in fact made. On the other hand a trust is not a complex trust by reason of distributions of amounts other than income unless such distributions are in fact made during the taxable year, whether or not they are required in that year.

§ 1.651(a)-2   Income required to be distributed currently

(a) The determination of whether trust income is required to be distributed currently depends upon the terms of the trust instrument and the applicable local law. For this purpose, if the trust instrument provides that the trustee in determining the distributable income shall first retain a reserve for depreciation or otherwise make due allowance for keeping the trust corpus intact by retaining a reasonable amount of the current income for that purpose, the retention of current income for that purpose will not disqualify the trust from being a "simple" trust. The fiduciary must be under a duty to distribute the income currently even if, as a matter of pratical necessity, the income is not distributed until after the close of the trust's taxable year. For example: Under the terms of the trust instrument, all of the income is currently distributable to A. The trust reports on the calendar year basis and as a matter of practical necessity makes distribution to A of each quarter's income on the fifteenth day of the month following the close of the quarter. The distribution made by the trust on January 15, 1955, of the income for the fourth quarter of 1954 does not disqualify the trust for treatment in 1955 under section 651, since the income is required to be distributed currently. However, if the terms of a trust require that none of the income be distributed until after the year of its receipt by the trust, the income of the trust is not required to be distributed currently and the trust is not a simple trust. For definition of the term "income" see section 643(b) and § 1.643(b)-1.

(b) It is immaterial, for purposes of determining whether all the income is required to be distributed currently, that the amount of income allocated to a particular beneficiary is not specified in the instrument. For example, if the fiduciary is required to distribute all the income currently, but has discretion to "sprinkle" the income among a class of beneficiaries, or among named beneficiaries in such amount as he may see fit, all the income is required to be distributed currently, even though the amount distributable to a particular beneficiary is unknown until the fiduciary has exercised his discretion.

(c) If in one taxable year of a trust its income for that year is required or permitted to be accumulated, and in another taxable year its income for the year is required to be distributed currently (and no other amounts are distributed), the trust is a simple trust for the latter year. For example, a trust under which income may be accumulated until a beneficiary is 21 years old, and thereafter must be distributed currently, is a simple trust for taxable years beginning after the beneficiary reaches the age of 21 years in which no other amounts are distributed.

§ 1.651(a)-3 Distribution of amounts other than income

(a) A trust does not qualify for treatment under section 651 for any taxable year in which it actually distributes corpus. For example, a trust which is required to distribute all of its income currently would not qualify as a simple trust under section 651 in the year of its termination since in that year actual distributions of corpus would be made.

(b) A trust, otherwise qualifying under section 651, which may make a distribution of corpus in the discretion of the trustee, or which is required under the terms of its governing instrument to make a distribution of corpus upon the happening of a specified event, will be disqualified for treatment under section 651 only for the taxable year in which an actual distribution of corpus is made. For example: Under the terms of a trust, which is required to distribute all of its income currently, half of the corpus is to be distributed to beneficiary A when he becomes 30 years of age. The trust reports on the calendar year basis. On December 28, 1954, A becomes 30 years of age and the trustee distributes half of the corpus of the trust to him on January 3, 1955. The trust will be disqualified for treatment under section 651 only for the taxable year 1955, the year in which an actual distribution of corpus is made.

(c) See section 661 and the regulations thereunder for the treatment of trusts which distribute corpus or claim the charitable contributions deduction provided by section 642(c).

§ 1.651(b)-1 Deduction for distributions to beneficiaries

In computing its taxable income, a simple trust is allowed a deduction for the amount of income which is required under the terms of the trust instrument to be distributed currently to beneficiaries. If the amount of income required to be distributed currently exceeds the distributable net income, the deduction allowable to the trust is limited to the amount of the distributable net income. For this purpose the amount of income required to be distributed currently, or distributable net income, whichever is applicable, does not include items of trust income (adjusted for deductions allocable thereto) which are not included in the gross income of the trust. For determination of the character of the income required to be distributed currently, see § 1.652(b)-2. Accordingly, for the purposes of determining the deduction allowable to the trust under section 651, distributable net income is computed without the modifications specified in paragraphs (5), (6), and (7) of section 643(a), relating to tax-exempt interest, foreign income, and excluded dividends. For example: Assume that the distributable net income of a trust as computed under section 643 (a) amounts to $99,000 but includes nontaxable income of $9,000. Then distributable net income for the purpose of determining the deduction allowable under section 651 is $90,000 ($99,000 less $9,000 nontaxable income).

§ 1.652(a)-1 Simple trusts; inclusion of amounts in income of beneficiaries

Subject to the rules in §§ 1.652(a)-2 and 1.652(b)-1, a beneficiary of a simple trust includes in his gross income for the taxable year the amounts of income required to be distributed to him for such year, whether or not distributed. Thus, the income of a simple trust is includible in the beneficiary's gross income for the taxable year in which the income is required to be distributed currently even though, as a matter of practical necessity, the income is not distributed until after the close of the taxable year of the trust. See § 1.642 (a) (3)-2 with respect to time of receipt of dividends. See § 1.652(c)-1 for treatment of amounts required to be distributed where a beneficiary and the trust have different taxable years. The term "income required to be distributed currently" includes income required to be distributed currently which is in fact used to discharge or satisfy any person's legal obligation as that term is used in § 1.662(a)-4.

§ 1.652(a)-2 Distributions in excess of distributable net income

If the amount of income required to be distributed currently to beneficiaries exceeds the distributable net income of the trust (as defined in section 643(a)), each beneficiary includes in his gross income an amount equivalent to his proportionate share of such distributable net income. Thus, if beneficiary A is to receive two-thirds of the trust income and B is to receive one-third, and the income required to be distributed currently is $99,000, A will receive $66,000 and B, $33,000. However, if the distributable net income, as determined under section 643(a) is only $90,000, A will include two-thirds ($60,000) of that sum in his gross income, and B will include one-third ($30,000) in his gross income. See §§ 1.652(b)-1 and 1.652(b)-2, however, for amounts which are not includible in the gross income of a beneficiary because of their tax-exempt character.

§ 1.652(b)-1 Character of amounts

In determining the gross income of a beneficiary, the amounts includible under § 1.652(a)-1 have the same character in the hands of the beneficiary as in the hands of the trust. For example, to the extent that the amounts specified in § 1.652(a)-1 consist of income exempt from tax under section 103, such amounts are not included in the beneficiary's gross income. Sim-

ilarly, dividends distributed to a beneficiary retain their original character in the beneficiary's hands for purposes of determining the availability to the beneficiary of the dividends received credit under section 34 (for dividends received on or before December 31, 1964) and the dividend exclusion under section 116. Also, to the extent that the amounts specified in § 1.652(a)-1 consist of "earned income" in the hands of the trust under the provisions of section 1348 such amount shall be treated under section 1348 as "earned income" in the hands of the beneficiary. Similarly, to the extent such amounts consist of an amount received as a part of a lump sum distribution from a qualified plan and to which the provisions of section 72(n) would apply in the hands of the trust, such amount shall be treated as subject to such section in the hands of the beneficiary except where such amount is deemed under section 666(a) to have been distributed in a preceding taxable year of the trust and the partial tax described in section 668(a) (2) is determined under section 668(b) (1) (B). The tax treatment of amounts determined under § 1.652(a)-1 depends upon the beneficiary's status with respect to them not upon the status of the trust. Thus, if a beneficiary is deemed to have received foreign income of a foreign trust, the includibility of such income in his gross income depends upon his taxable status with respect to that income.

§ 1.652(b)-2 Allocation of income items

(a) The amounts specified in § 1.652 (a)-1 which are required to be included in the gross income of a beneficiary are treated as consisting of the same proportion of each class of items entering into distributable net income of the trust (as defined in section 643(a)) as the total of each class bears to such distributable net income, unless the terms of the trust specifically allocate different classes of income to different beneficiaries, or unless local law requires such an allocation. For example: Assume that under the terms of the governing instrument, beneficiary A is to receive currently one-half of the trust income and beneficiaries B and C are each to receive currently one-quarter, and the distributable net income of the trust (after allocation of expenses) consists of dividends of $10,000, taxable interest of $10,000, and tax-exempt interest of $4,000. A will be deemed to have received $5,000 of dividends, $5,000 of taxable interest, and $2,000 of tax-exempt interest; B and C will each be deemed to have received $2,500 of dividends, $2,500 of taxable interest, and $1,000 of tax-exempt interest. However, if the terms of the trust specifically allocate different classes of income to different beneficiaries, entirely or in part, or if local law requires such an allocation, each beneficiary will be deemed to have received those items of income specifically allocated to him.

(b) The terms of the trust are considered specifically to allocate different classes of income to different beneficiaries only to the extent that the allocation is required in the trust instrument, and only to the extent that it has an economic effect independent of the income tax consequences of the allocation. For example:

(1) Allocation pursuant to a provision in a trust instrument granting the trustee discretion to allocate different classes of income to different beneficiaries is not a specific allocation by the terms of the trust.

(2) Allocation pursuant to a provision directing the trustee to pay all of one income to A, or $10,000 out of the income to A, and the balance of the income to B, but directing the trustee first to allocate a specific class of income to A's share (to the extent there is income of that class and to the extent it does not exceed A's share) is not a specific allocation by the terms of the trust.

(3) Allocation pursuant to a provision directing the trustee to pay half the class of income (whatever it may be) to A, and the balance of the income to B, is a specific allocation by the terms of the trust.

§ 1.652(b)-3 Allocation of deductions

Items of deduction of a trust that enter into the computation of distributable net income are to be allocated among the items of income in accordance with the following principles:

(a) All deductible items directly attributable to one class of income (except dividends excluded under section 116) are allocated thereto. For example, repairs to, taxes on, and other expenses directly attributable to the maintenance of rental property or the collection of rental income are allocated to rental income. See § 1.642(e)-1 for treatment of depreciation of rental property. Similarly, all expenditures directly attributable to a business carried on by a trust are allocated to the income from such business. If the deductions directly attributable to a particular class of income exceed that income, the excess is applied against other classes of income in the manner provided in paragraph (d) of this section.

(b) The deductions which are not directly attributable to a specific class of income may be allocated to any item of income (including capital gains) included in computing distributable net income, but a portion must be allocated to nontaxable income (except dividends excluded under section 116) pursuant to section 265 and the regulations thereunder. For example, if the income of a trust is $30,000 (after direct expenses), consisting equally of $10,000 of dividends, tax-exempt interest, and rents, and income commissions amount to $3,000, one-third ($1,000) of such commissions should be allocated to tax-exempt interest, but the balance of $2,000 may be allocated to the rents or dividends in such proportions as the trustee may elect. The fact that the governing instrument or applicable local law treats certain items of deduction as attributable to corpus or to income not included in distributable net income does not affect allocation under this paragraph. For instance, if in the example set forth in this paragraph the trust also had capital gains which are allocable to corpus under the terms of the trust instrument, no part of the deductions would be allocable thereto since the capital gains are excluded from the computation of distributable net income under section 643(a)(3).

(c) Examples of expenses which are considered as not directly attributable to a specific class of income are trustee's commissions, the rental of safe deposit boxes, and State income and personal property taxes.

(d) To the extent that any items of deduction which are directly attributable to a class of income exceed that class of income, they may be allocated to any other class of income (including capital gains) included in distributable net income in the manner provided in paragraph (b) of this section, except that any excess deductions attributable to tax-exempt income (other than dividends excluded under section 116) may not be offset against any other class of income. See section 265 and the regulations thereunder. Thus, if the trust has rents, taxable interest, dividends, and tax-exempt interest, and the deductions directly attributable to the rents exceed the rental income, the excess may be allocated to the taxable interest or dividends in such proportions as the fiduciary may elect. However, if the excess deductions are attributable to the tax-exempt interest, they may not be allocated to either the rents, taxable interest, or dividends.

§ 1.661(a)-1 Estates and trusts accumulating income or distributing corpus; general

Subpart C, part I, subchapter J, chapter 1, of the Code, is applicable to all decedents' estates and their beneficiaries, and to trusts and their beneficiaries other than trusts subject to the provisions of subpart B of such part I (relating to trusts which distribute current income only, or "simple" trusts). A trust which is required to distribute amounts other than income during the taxable year may be subject to subpart B, and not subpart C, in the absence of an actual distribution of amounts other than income during the taxable year. See §§ 1.651(a)-1 and 1.651(a)-3. A trust to which subpart C is applicable is referred to as a "complex" trust in this part. Section 661 has no application to amounts excluded under section 663(a).

§ 1.661(a)-2 Deduction for distributions to beneficiaries

(a) In computing the taxable income of an estate or trust there is allowed under section 661(a) as a deduction for distributions to beneficiaries the sum of:

(1) The amount of income for the taxable year which is required to be distributed currently, and

(2) Any other amounts properly paid or credited or required to be distributed for such taxable year.

However, the total amount deductible under section 661(a) cannot exceed the distributable net income as computed under section 643(a) and as modified by section 661(c). See § 1.661(c)-1.

(b) The term "income required to be distributed currently" includes any amount required to be distributed which may be paid out of income or corpus (such as an annuity), to the extent it is paid out of income for the taxable year. See § 1.651(a)-2 which sets forth additional rules which are applicable in determining whether income of an estate or trust is required to be distributed currently.

(c) The term "any other amounts properly paid or credited or required to be distributed" includes all amounts properly paid, credited, or required to be distributed by an estate or trust during the taxable year other than income required to be distributed currently. Thus, the term includes the payment of an annuity to the extent it is not paid out of income for the taxable year, and a distribution of property in kind (see paragraph (f) of this section). However, see section 663(a) and regulations thereunder for distributions which are not included. Where the income of an estate or trust may be accumulated or distributed in the discretion of the fiduciary, or where the fiduciary has a power to distribute corpus to a beneficiary, any such discretionary distribution would qualify under section 661(a)(2). The term also includes an amount applied or distributed for the support of a dependent of a grantor or of a trustee or cotrustee under the circumstances described in section 677(b) or section 678(c) out of corpus or out of other than income for the taxable year.

(d) The terms "income required to be distributed currently" and "any other amounts properly paid or credited or required to be distributed" also include any amount used to discharge or satisfy any person's legal obligation as that term is used in § 1.662(a)-4.

(e) The terms "income required to be distributed currently" and "any other amounts properly paid or credited or required to be distributed" include amounts paid, or required to be paid, during the taxable year pursuant to a court order or decree or under local law, by a decedent's estate as an allowance or award for the support of the decedent's widow or other dependent for a limited period during the administration of the estate. The term "any other amounts properly paid or credited or required to be distributed" does not include the value of any interest in real estate owned by a decedent, title to which under local law passes directly from the decedent to his heirs or devisees.

(f) If property is paid, credited, or required to be distributed in kind:

(1) No gain or loss is realized by the trust or estate (or the other beneficiaries) by reason of the distribution, unless the distribution is in satisfaction of a right to receive a distribution in a specific dollar amount or in specific property other than that distributed.

(2) In determining the amount deductible by the trust or estate and includible in the gross income of the beneficiary the property distributed in kind is taken into account at its fair market value at the time it was distributed, credited, or required to be distributed.

(3) The basis of the property in the hands of the beneficiary is its fair market value at the time it was paid, credited, or required to be distributed, to the extent such value is included in the gross income of the beneficiary. To the extent that the value of property distributed in kind is not included in the gross income of the beneficiary, its basis in the hands of the beneficiary is governed by the rules in sections 1014 and 1015 and the regulations thereunder. For this purpose, if the total value of cash and property distributed, credited, or required to be distributed in kind to a beneficiary in any taxable year exceeds the amount includible in his gross income for that year, the value of the property other than cash is normally considered as includible in his gross income only to the extent that the amount includible exceeds the cash paid, credited, or required to be distributed to the beneficiary in that year. Further, to the extent that the value of different items of property other than cash is includible in the gross income of a beneficiary in accordance with the preceding sentence, a pro rata portion of the total value of each item of property distributed, credited, or required to be distributed is normally considered as includible in the beneficiary's gross income.

§ 1.661(c)-2 Illustration of the provisions of section 661

The provisions of section 661 may be illustrated by the following example:

Example. (a) Under the terms of a trust, which reports on the calendar year basis, $10,000 a year is required to be paid out of income to a designated charity. The balance of the income may, in the trustee's discretion, be accumulated or distributed to beneficiary A. Expenses are allocable against income and the trust instrument requires a reserve for depreciation. During the taxable year 1955 the trustee contributes $10,000 to charity and in his discretion distributes $15,000 of income to A. The trust has the following items of income and expense for the taxable year 1955:

Dividends	$10,000
Partially tax-exempt interest	10,000
Fully tax-exempt interest	10,000
Rents	20,000
Rental expenses	2,000
Depreciation of rental property	3,000
Trustee's commissions	5,000

(b) The income of the trust for fiduciary accounting purposes is $40,000, computed as follows:

Dividends		$10,000
Partially tax-exempt interest		10,000
Fully tax-exempt interest		10,000
Rents		20,000
Total		50,000
Less:		
Rental expenses	$2,000	
Depreciation	3,000	
Trustee's commissions	5,000	
		10,000
Income as computed under section 643(b)		40,000

(c) The distributable net income of the trust as computed under section 643(a) is $30,000, determined as follows:

Rents			$20,000
Dividends			10,000
Partially tax-exempt interest			10,000
Fully tax-exempt interest		$10,000	
Less:			
Expenses allocable thereto (10,000/50,000 × $5,000)	$1,000		
Charitable contributions allocable thereto (10,000/50,000 × $10,000)	2,000		
		3,000	
			7,000
Total			47,000
Deductions:			
Rental expenses		$2,000	
Depreciation of rental property		3,000	
Trustee's commissions ($5,000 less $1,000 allocated to tax-exempt interest)		4,000	
Charitable contributions ($10,000 less $2,000 allocated to tax-exempt interest)		8,000	
			17,000
Distributable net income (section 643(a))			30,000

(d) The character of the amounts distributed under section 661(a), determined in accordance with the rules prescribed in §§ 1.661(b)-1 and 1.661(b)-2 is shown by the following table (for the purpose of this allocation, it is assumed that the trustee elected to allocate the trustee's commissions to rental income except for the amount required to be allocated to tax-exempt interest):

	Rental income	Taxable dividends	Excluded dividends	Partially tax-exempt interest	Tax-exempt interest	Total
Trust income	$20,000	$9,950	$50	$10,000	$10,000	$50,000
Less:						
Charitable contributions.....	4,000	2,000	....	2,000	2,000	10,000
Rental expenses	2,000	....	....	....	....	2,000
Depreciation	3,000	....	....	....	....	3,000
Trustee's commissions	4,000	....	....	....	1,000	5,000
Total deductions	13,000	2,000	0	2,000	3,000	20,000
Distributable net income........	7,000	7,950	50	8,000	7,000	30,000
Amounts deemed distributed under section 661(a) before applying the limitation of section 661(c)	3,500	3,975	25	4,000	3,500	15,000

In the absence of specific provisions in the trust instrument for the allocation of different classes of income, the charitable contribution is deemed to consist of a pro rata portion of the gross amount of each item of income of the trust (except the dividends excluded under section 116) and the trust is deemed to have distributed to A a pro rata portion (one-half) of each item of income included in distributable net income.

(e) The taxable income of the trust is $11,375 computed as follows:

```
Rental income .......................... $20,000
Dividends ($10,000 less $50 exclusion) ..   9,950
Partially tax-exempt interest ..........  10,000
                                          -------
    Gross income ...................      39,950
```

Deductions:

```
    Rental expenses ................  $2,000
    Depreciation of rental property .  3,000
    Trustee's commissions ........     4,000
    Charitable contributions .......   8,000
    Distributions to A ...........    11,475
    Personal exemption ..........        100
                                      ------
                                              28,575
                                              ------
    Taxable income ................           11,375
```

In computing the taxable income of the trust no deduction is allowable for the portions of the charitable contributions deduction ($2,000) and trustee's commissions ($1,000) which are treated under section 661(b) as attributable to the tax-exempt interest excludable from gross income. Also, of the dividends of $4,000 deemed to have been distributed to A under section 661(a), $25 (25/50ths of $50) is deemed to have been distributed from the excluded dividends and is not an allowable deduction to the trust. Accordingly, the deduction allowable under section 661 is deemed to be composed of $3,500 rental income, $3,975 of dividends, and $4,000 partially tax-exempt interest. No deduction is allowable for the portion of tax-exempt interest or for the portion of the excluded dividends deemed to have been distributed to the beneficiary.

(f) The trust is entitled to the credit allowed by section 34 with respect to dividends of $5,975 ($9,950 less $3,975 distributed to A) included in gross income. Also, the trust is allowed the credit provided by section 35 with respect to partially tax-exempt interest of $6,000 ($10,000 less $4,000 deemed distributed to A) included in gross income.

(g) Dividends of $4,000 allocable to A are to be aggregated with his other dividends (if any) for purposes of the dividend exclusion under section 116 and the dividend received credit under section 34.

§ 1.662(a)-1 Inclusion of amounts in gross income of beneficiaries of estates and complex trusts; general

There is included in the gross income of a beneficiary of an estate or complex trust the sum of:

(1) Amounts of income required to be distributed currently to him, and

(2) All other amounts properly paid, credited, or required to be distributed to him

by the estate or trust. The preceding sentence is subject to the rules contained in § 1.662(a)-2 (relating to currently distributable income), § 1.662(a)-3 (relating to other amounts distributed), and §§ 1.662(b)–1 and 1.662(b)–2 (relating to character of amounts). Section 662 has no application to amounts excluded under section 663(a).

§ 1.662(a)–2 Currently distributable income

(a) There is first included in the gross income of each beneficiary under section 662(a)(1) the amount of income for the taxable year of the estate or trust required to be distributed currently to him, subject to the provisions of paragraph (b) of this section. Such amount is included in the beneficiary's gross income whether or not it is actually distributed.

(b) If the amount of income required to be distributed currently to all beneficiaries exceeds the distributable net income (as defined in section 643 (a) but computed without taking into account the payment, crediting, or setting aside of an amount for which a charitable contributions deduction is allowable under section 642(c)) of the estate or trust, then there is included in the gross income of each beneficiary an amount which bears the same ratio to distributable net income (as so computed) as the amount of income required to be distributed currently to the beneficiary bears to the amount required to be distributed currently to all beneficiaries.

(c) The phrase "the amount of income for the taxable year required to be distributed currently" includes any amount required to be paid out of income or corpus to the extent the amount is satisfied out of income for the taxable year. Thus, an annuity required to be paid in all events (either out of income or corpus) would qualify as income required to be distributed currently to the extent there is income (as defined in section 643(b)) not paid, credited, or required to be distributed to other beneficiaries for the taxable year. If an annuity or a portion of an annuity is deemed under this paragraph to be income required to be distributed currently, it is treated in all respects in the same manner as an amount of income actually required to be distributed currently. The phrase "the amount of income for the taxable year required to be distributed currently" also includes any amount required to be paid during

the taxable year in all events (either out of income or corpus) pursuant to a court order or decree or under local law, by a decedent's estate as an allowance or award for the support of the decedent's widow or other dependent for a limited period during the administration of the estate to the extent there is income (as defined in section 643(b)) of the estate for the taxable year not paid, credited, or required to be distributed to other beneficiaries.

(d) If an annuity is paid, credited, or required to be distributed tax free, that is, under a provision whereby the executor or trustee will pay the income tax of the annuitant resulting from the receipt of the annuity, the payment of or for the tax by the executor or trustee will be treated as income paid, credited, or required to be distributed currently to the extent it is made out of income.

(e) The application of the rules stated in this section may be illustrated by the following examples:

Example (1). (1) Assume that under the terms of the trust instrument $5,000 is to be paid to X charity out of income each year; that $20,000 of income is currently distributable to A; and that an annuity of $12,000 is to be paid to B out of income or corpus. All expenses are charges against income and capital gains are allocable to corpus. During the taxable year the trust had income of $30,000 (after the payment of expenses) derived from taxable interest and made the payments to X charity and distributions to A and B as required by the governing instrument.

(2) The amounts treated as distributed currently under section 662(a)(1) total $25,000 ($20,000 to A and $5,000 to B). Since the charitable contribution is out of income, the amount of income available for B's annuity is only $5,-000. The distributable net income of the trust computed under section 643(a) without taking into consideration the charitable contributions deduction of $5,000 as provided by section 661 (a)(1), is $30,000. Since the amounts treated as distributed currently of $25,000 do not exceed the distributable net income (as modified) of $30,000, A is required to include $20,000 in his gross income and B is required to include $5,000 in his gross income under section 662(a) (1).

Example (2). Assume the same facts as in paragraph (1) of example (1), except that the trust has, in addition, $10,000 of administration expenses, commissions, etc., chargeable to corpus. The amounts treated as distributed currently under section 662(a)(1) total $25,000 ($20,000 to A and $5,000 to B), since trust income under section 643(b) remains the same as in example (1). Distributable net income of the trust computed under section 643(a) but without taking into account the charitable contributions deduction of $5,000 as provided by section 662(a)(1) is only $20,000. Since the amounts treated as distributed currently of

$25,000 exceed the distributable net income (as so computed) of $20,000, A is required to include $16,000 (20,000/25,000 of $20,000) in his gross income and B is required to include $4,000 (5,000/25,000 of $20,000) in his gross income under section 662(a) (1). Because A and B are beneficiaries of amounts of income required to be distributed currently, they do not benefit from the reduction of distributable net income by the charitable contributions deduction.

§ 1.662(a)-3 Other amounts distributed

(a) There is included in the gross income of a beneficiary under section 662(a) (2) any amount properly paid, credited, or required to be distributed to the beneficiary for the taxable year, other than (1) income required to be distributed currently, as determined under § 1.662(a)-2, (2) amounts excluded under section 663(a) and the regulations thereunder, and (3) amounts in excess of distributable net income (see paragraph (c) of this section). An amount which is credited or required to be distributed is included in the gross income of a beneficiary whether or not it is actually distributed.

(b) Some of the payments to be included under paragraph (a) of this section are: (1) A distribution made to a beneficiary in the discretion of the fiduciary; (2) a distribution required by the terms of the governing instrument upon the happening of a specified event; (3) an annuity which is required to be paid in all events but which is payable only out of corpus; (4) a distribution of property in kind (see paragraph (f) of § 1.661(a)-2); (5) an amount applied or distributed for the support of a dependent of a grantor or a trustee or cotrustee under the circumstances specified in section 677(b) or section 678(c) out of corpus or out of other than income for the taxable year; and (6) an amount required to be paid during the taxable year pursuant to a court order or decree or under local law, by a decedent's estate as an allowance or award for the support of the decedent's widow or other dependent for a limited period during the administration of the estate which is payable only out of corpus of the estate under the order or decree or local law.

(c) If the sum of the amounts of income required to be distributed currently (as determined under § 1.662(a)-2) and other amounts properly paid, credited, or required to be distributed (as determined under paragraph (a) of this section) exceeds distributable net income (as defined in section 643(a)), then such other amounts properly paid, credited, or required to be distributed are included in gross income of the beneficiary but only to the extent of the excess of such distributable net income over the amounts of income required to be distributed currently. If the other amounts are paid, credited, or required to be distributed to more than one beneficiary, each beneficiary includes in gross income his proportionate share of the amount includible in gross income pursuant to the preceding sentence. The proportionate share is an amount which bears the same ratio to distributable net income (reduced by amounts of income required to be distributed currently) as the other amounts (as determined under paragraphs (a) and (d) of this section) distributed to the beneficiary bear to the other amounts distributed to all beneficiaries. For treatment of excess distributions by trusts, see sections 665 to 668, inclusive, and the regulations thereunder.

(d) The application of the rules stated in this section may be illustrated by the following example:

Example. The terms of a trust require the distribution annually of $10,000 of income to A. If any income remains, it may be accumulated or distributed to B, C, and D in amounts in the trustee's discretion. He may also invade corpus for the benefit of A, B, C, or D. In the taxable year, the trust has $20,000 of income after the deduction of all expenses. Distributable net income is $20,000. The trustee distributes $10,000 of income to A. Of the remaining $10,000 of income, he distributes $3,000 each to B, C, and D, and also distributes an additional $5,000 to A. A includes $10,000 in income under section 662(a) (1). The "other amounts distributed" amount to $14,000, includible in the income of the recipients to the extent of $10,000, distributable net income less the income currently distributable to A. A will include an additional $3,571 (5,000/14,000 × $10,000) in income under this section, and B, C, and D will each include $2,143 (3,000/14,000 × $10,000).

§ 1.662(a)-4 Amounts used in discharge of a legal obligation

Any amount which, pursuant to the terms of a will or trust instrument, is used in full or partial discharge or satisfaction of a legal obligation of any person is included in the gross income of such person under section 662(a) (1) or (2), whichever is applicable, as though directly distributed to him as a beneficiary, except in cases to which section 71 (relating to alimony payments) or section 682 (relating to income of a trust in case of divorce, etc.) applies. The term "legal obligation" includes a legal obligation to support another person if, and only if, the obligation is not affected by the adequacy of the dependent's own resources. For example, a parent has a "legal obligation" within the meaning of the preceding sentence to support his minor child if under local law property or income from property owned by the child cannot be used for his support so long as his parent is able to support him. On the other hand, if under local law a mother may use the resources of a child for the child's support in lieu of supporting him herself, no obligation of support exists within the meaning of this paragraph, whether or not income is actually used for support. Similarly, since under local law a child ordinarily is obligated to support his parent only if the parent's earnings and resources are insufficient for the purpose, no obligation exists whether or not the parent's earnings and resources are sufficient. In any event, the amount of trust income which is included in the gross income of a person obligated to support a dependent is limited by the extent of his legal obligation under local law. In the case of a parent's obligation to support his child, to the extent that the parent's legal obligation of support, including education, is determined under local law by the family's station in life and by the means of the parent, it is to be determined without consideration of the trust income in question.

§ 1.662(c)-4 Illustration of the provisions of sections 661 and 662

The provisions of sections 661 and 662 may be illustrated in general by the following example:

Example. (a) Under the terms of a testamentary trust one-half of the trust income is to be distributed currently to W, the decedent's wife, for her life. The remaining trust income may, in the trustee's discretion, either be paid to D, the grantor's daughter, paid to designated charities, or accumulated. The trust is to terminate at the death of W and the principal will then be payable to D. No provision is made in the trust instrument with respect to depreciation of rental property. Capital gains are allocable to the principal account under the applicable local law. The trust and both beneficiaries file returns on the calendar year basis. The records of the fiduciary show the following items of income and deduction for the taxable year 1955:

Rents	$50,000
Dividends of domestic corporations	50,000
Tax-exempt interest	20,000
Partially tax-exempt interest	10,000
Capital gains (long term)	20,000
Depreciation of rental property	10,000
Expenses attributable to rental income	15,400
Trustee's commissions allocable to income account	2,800
Trustee's commissions allocable to principal account	1,100

(b) The income for trust accounting purposes is $111,800, and the trustee distributes one-half ($55,900) to W and in his discretion makes a contribution of one-quarter ($27,950) to charity X and distributes the remaining one-quarter ($27,950) to D. The total of the distributions to beneficiaries is $83,850, consisting of (1) income required to be distributed currently to W of $55,900 and (2) other amounts properly paid or credited to D of $27,950. The income for trust accounting purposes of $111,800 is determined as follows:

Rents		$50,000
Dividends		50,000
Tax-exempt interest		20,000
Partially tax-exempt interest		10,000
Total		130,000
Less:		
Rental expenses	$15,400	
Trustee's commissions allocable to income account	2,800	
		18,200
Income as computed under section 643(b)		111,800

(c) The distributable net income of the trust as computed under section 643(a) is $82,750, determined as follows:

Rents		$50,000
Dividends		50,000
Partially tax-exempt interest		10,000
Tax-exempt interest	$20,000	
Less:		
Trustee's commissions allocable thereto (20,000/130,000 of $3,900)	$ 600	
Charitable contributions allocable thereto (20,000/130,000 of $27,950)	4,300	
		4,900
		15,100
Total		125,100
Deductions:		
Rental expenses	$15,400	
Trustee's commissions ($3,900 less $600 allocated to tax-exempt interest)	3,300	
Charitable deduction ($27,950 less $4,300 attributable to tax-exempt interest)	23,650	
		42,350
Distributable net income		82,750

In computing the distributable net income of $82,750, the taxable income of the trust was computed with the following modifications: No deductions were allowed for distributions to beneficiaries and for personal exemption of the trust (section 643(a) (1) and (2)); capital gains were excluded and no deduction under section 1202 (relating to the 50 percent deduction for long-term capital gains) was taken into account (section 643(a) (3)); and the tax-exempt interest (as adjusted for expenses and charitable contributions) and the dividend exclusion of $50 were included (section 643(a) (5) and (7)).

(d) Inasmuch as the distributable net income of $82,750 as determined under section 643(a) is less than the sum of the amounts distributed to W and D of $83,850, the deduction allowable to the trust under section 661(a) is such distributable net income as modified under section 661 (c) to exclude therefrom the items of income not included in the gross income of the trust, as follows:

Distributable net income	$82,750

Less:

Tax-exempt interest (as adjusted for expenses and the charitable contributions)	$15,100	
Dividend exclusion allowable under section 116	50	
		15,150
Deduction allowable under section 661(a)		67,600

(e) For the purpose of determining the character of the amounts deductible under section 642(c) and section 661(a), the trustee elected to offset the trustee's commissions (other than the portion required to be allocated to tax-exempt interest) against the rental income. The following table shows the determination of the character of the amounts deemed distributed to beneficiaries and contributed to charity:

	Rents	Taxable dividends	Excluded dividends	Tax-exempt interest	Partially tax-exempt interest	Total
Trust income	$50,000	$49,950	$50	$20,000	$10,000	$130,000
Less:						
Charitable contribution.......	10,750	10,750	....	4,300	2,150	27,950
Rental expenses.................	15,400	....	....	....	....	15,400
Trustee's commissions........	3,300	....	....	600	....	3,900
Total deductions............	29,450	10,750	0	4,900	2,150	47,250
Amounts distributable to beneficiaries	20,550	39,200	50	15,100	7,850	82,750

The character of the charitable contribution is determined by multiplying the total charitable contribution ($27,950) by a fraction consisting of each item of trust income, respectively, over the total trust income, except that no part of the dividends excluded from gross income are deemed included in the charitable contribution. For example, the charitable contribution is deemed to consist of rents of $10,750 (50,000/130,-000 × $27,950).

(f) The taxable income of the trust is $9,900 determined as follows:

Rental income	$50,000
Dividends ($50,000 less $50 exclusion) ...	49,950
Partially tax-exempt interest	10,000
Capital gains	20,000
Gross income	129,950

Deductions:

Rental expenses	$15,400
Trustee's commissions	3,300
Charitable contributions	23,650
Capital gain deduction	10,000
Distributions to beneficiaries ..	67,600
Personal exemption	100
	120,050
Taxable income	9,900

(g) In computing the amount includible in W's gross income under section 662(a) (1), the $55,900 distribution to her is deemed to be composed of the following proportions of the items of income deemed to have been distributed to the beneficiaries by the trust (see paragraph (e) of this example):

Rents (20,550/82,750 × $55,900)	$13,882
Dividends (39,250/82,750 × $55,900)	26,515
Partially tax-exempt interest (7,850/82,750 × $55,900)	5,303
Tax-exempt interest (15,100/82,750 × $55,900)	10,200
Total	55,900

Accordingly, W will exclude $10,200 of tax-exempt interest from gross income and will receive the credits and exclusion for dividends received and for partially tax-exempt interest provided in sections 34, 116, and 35, respectively, with respect to the dividends and partially tax-exempt interest deemed to have been distributed to her, her share of the dividends being aggregated with other dividends received by her for purposes of the dividend credit and exclusion. In addition, she may deduct a share of the depreciation deduction proportionate to the trust income allocable to her; that is, one-half of the total depreciation deduction, or $5,000.

(h) Inasmuch as the sum of the amount of income required to be distributed currently to W ($55,900) and the other amounts properly paid, credited, or required to be distributed to D ($27,950) exceeds the distributable net income ($82,750) of the trust as determined under section 643(a), D is deemed to have received $26,850 ($82,750 less $55,900) for income tax purposes. The character of the amounts deemed distributed to her is determined as follows:

Rents (20,550/82,750 × $26,850) **$6,668**
Dividends (39,250/82,750 × $26,850) 12,735
Partially tax-exempt interest (7,850/82,750 × $26,850) 2,547
Tax-exempt interest (15,100/82,750 × $26,850) 4,900
                                                    ————
    Total 26,850

Accordingly, D will exclude $4,900 of tax-exempt interest from gross income and will receive the credits and exclusion for dividends received and for partially tax-exempt interest provided in sections 34, 116, and 35, respectively, with respect to the dividends and partially tax-exempt interest deemed to have been distributed to her, her share of the dividends being aggregated with other dividends received by her for purposes of the dividend credit and exclusion. In addition, she may deduct a share of the depreciation deduction proportionate to the trust income allocable to her; that is, one-fourth of the total depreciation deduction, or $2,500.

(i) [Reserved.]

(j) The remaining $2,500 of the depreciation deduction is allocated to the amount distributed to charity X and is hence nondeductible by the trust, W, or D. (See § 1.642(e)-1.)

§ 1.663(a)-1 Special rules applicable to sections 661 and 662; exclusions; gifts, bequests, etc.

(a) In general. A gift or bequest of a specific sum of money or of specific property, which is required by the specific terms of the will or trust instrument and is properly paid or credited to a beneficiary, is not allowed as a deduction to an estate or trust under section 661 and is not included in the gross income of a beneficiary under section 662, unless under the terms of the will or trust instrument the gift or bequest is to be paid or credited to the recipient in more than three installments. Thus, in order for a gift or bequest to be excludable from the gross income of the recipient, (1) it must qualify as a gift or bequest of a specific sum of money or of specific property (see paragraph (b) of this section), and (2) the terms of the governing instrument must not provide for its payment in more than three installments (see paragraph (c) of this section). The date when the estate came into existence or the date when the trust was created is immaterial.

(b) Definition of a gift or bequest of a specific sum of money or of specific property. (1) In order to qualify as a gift or bequest of a specific sum of

money or of specific property under section 663(a), the amount of money or the identity of the specific property must be ascertainable under the terms of a testator's will as of the date of his death, or under the terms of an inter vivos trust instrument as of the date of the inception of the trust. For example, bequests to a decedent's son of the decedent's interest in a partnership and to his daughter of a sum of money equal to the value of the partnership interest are bequests of specific property and of a specific sum of money, respectively. On the other hand, a bequest to the decedent's spouse of money or property, to be selected by the decedent's executor, equal in value to a fraction of the decedent's "adjusted gross estate" is neither a bequest of a specific sum of money or of specific property. The identity of the property and the amount of money specified in the preceding sentence are dependent both on the exercise of the executor's discretion and on the payment of administration expenses and other charges, neither of which are facts existing on the date of the decedent's death. It is immaterial that the value of the bequest is determinable after the decedent's death before the bequest is satisfied (so that gain or loss may be realized by the estate in the transfer of property in satisfaction of it).

(2) The following amounts are not considered as gifts or bequests of a sum of money or of specific property within the meaning of this paragraph:

(i) An amount which can be paid or credited only from the income of an estate or trust, whether from the income for the year of payment or crediting, or from the income accumulated from a prior year;

(ii) An annuity, or periodic gifts of specific property in lieu of or having the effect of an annuity;

(iii) A residuary estate or the corpus of a trust; or

(iv) A gift or bequest paid in a lump sum or in not more than three installments, if the gift or bequest is required to be paid in more than three installments under the terms of the governing instrument.

(3) The provisions of subparagraphs (1) and (2) of this paragraph may be illustrated by the following examples,

in which it is assumed that the gift or bequest is not required to be made in more than three installments (see paragraph (c)):

Example (1). Under the terms of a will, a legacy of $5,000 was left to A, 1,000 shares of X company stock was left to W, and the balance of the estate was to be divided equally between W and X. No provision was made in the will for the disposition of income of the estate during the period of administration. The estate had income of $25,000 during the taxable year 1954, which was accumulated and added to corpus for estate accounting purposes. During the taxable year, the executor paid the legacy of $5,000 in a lump sum to A and transferred the X company stock to W. No other distributions to beneficiaries were made during the taxable year. The distributions to A and W qualify as exclusions within the meaning of section 663(a) (1).

Example (2). Under the terms of a will, the testator's estate was to be divided equally between A and B. No provision was made in the will for the disposition of income of the estate during the period of administration. The estate had income of $50,000 for the taxable year 1954. In accordance with an agreement among the beneficiaries that part of the assets of the estate would be distributed in kind to the beneficiaries, stock in corporation X was distributed to A during 1954. The fair market value of the stock was $40,000 on the date of distribution. No other distribution was made during the year. The distribution does not qualify as an exclusion within the meaning of section 663(a) (1), since it is not a specific gift to A required by the terms of the will. Accordingly, the fair market value of the property ($40,000) represents a distribution within the meaning of section 661(a) and section 662(a) (see paragraph (c) of § 1.661(a)–2).

Example (3). Under the terms of a trust instrument, income is to be accumulated during the minority of A. Upon A's reaching the age of 21, $10,000 is to be distributed to B out of income or corpus. Also at that time, $10,000 is to be distributed to C out of the accumulated income and the remainder of the accumulations are to be paid to A. A is then to receive all the income until he is 25, when the trust is to terminate. Only the distribution to B would qualify for exclusion under section 663(a) (1).

(4) A gift or bequest of a specific sum of money or of specific property is not disqualified under this paragraph solely because its payment is subject to a condition. For example, provision for a payment by a trust to beneficiary A of $10,000 when he reaches age 25, and $10,000 when he reaches age 30, with payment over to B of any amount not paid to A because of his death, is a gift to A of a specific sum of money payable in two installments, within the meaning of this paragraph, even though the exact amount payable to A cannot be ascertained with certainty under the terms of the trust instrument.

(c) Installment payments. (1) In determining whether a gift or bequest of a specific sum of money or of specific property, as defined in paragraph (b) of this section, is required to be paid or credited to a particular beneficiary in more than three installments—

(i) Gifts or bequests of articles for personal use (such as personal and household effects, automobiles, and the like) are disregarded.

(ii) Specifically devised real property, the title to which passes directly from the decedent to the devisee under local law, is not taken into account, since it would not constitute an amount paid, credited, or required to be distributed under section 661 (see paragraph (e) of § 1.661(a)–2).

(iii) All gifts and bequests under a decedent's will (which are not disregarded pursuant to subdivisions (i) and (ii) of this subparagraph) for which no time of payment or crediting is specified, and which are to be paid or credited in the ordinary course of administration of the decedent's estate, are considered as required to be paid or credited in a single installment.

(iv) All gifts and bequests (which are not disregarded pursuant to subdivisions (i) and (ii) of this subparagraph) payable at any one specified time under the terms of the governing instrument are taken into account as a single installment.

For purposes of determining the number of installments paid or credited to a particular beneficiary, a decedent's estate and a testamentary trust shall each be treated as a separate entity.

(2) The application of the rules stated in subparagraph (1) of this paragraph may be illustrated by the following examples:

Example (1). (i) Under the terms of a decedent's will, $10,000 in cash, household furniture, a watch, an automobile, 100 shares of X company stock, 1,000 bushels of grain, 500 head of cattle, and a farm (title to which passed directly to A under local law) are bequeathed or devised outright to A. The will also provides for the creation of a trust for the benefit of A, under the terms of which there are required to be distributed to A, $10,000 in cash and 100 shares of Y company stock when he reaches 25 years of age, $25,000 in cash and 200 shares of Y company stock when he reaches 30 years of age, and $50,000 in cash and 300 shares of Y company stock when he reaches 35 years of age.

(ii) The furniture, watch, automobile, and the farm are excluded in determining whether any gift or bequest is required to be paid or credited to A in more than three installments. These items qualify for the exclusion under section 663(a) (1) regardless of the treatment of the other items of property bequeathed to A.

(iii) The $10,000 in cash, the shares of X Company stock, the grain, the cattle and the assets required to create the trust, to be paid or credited by the estate to A and the trust are considered as required to be paid or credited in a single installment to each, regardless of the manner of payment or distribution by the executor, since no time of payment or crediting is specified in the will. The $10,000 in cash and shares of Y Company stock required to be distributed by the trust to A when he is 25 years old are considered as required to be paid or distributed as one installment under the trust. Likewise, the distributions to be made by the trust to A when he is 30 and 35 years old are each considered as one installment under the trust. Since the total number of installments to be made by the estate does not exceed three, all of the items of money and property distributed by the estate qualify for the exclusion under section 663(a) (1). Similarly, the three distributions by the trust qualify.

Example (2). Assume the same facts as in example (1), except that another distribution of a specified sum of money is required to be made by the trust to A when he becomes 40 years old. This distribution would also qualify as an installment, thus making four installments in all under the trust. None of the gifts to A under the trust would qualify for the exclusion under section 663(a) (1). The situation as to the estate, however, would not be changed.

Example (3). A trust instrument provides that A and B are each to receive $75,000 in installments of $25,000, to be paid in alternate years. The trustee distributes $25,000 to A in 1954, 1956, and 1958, and to B in 1955, 1957, and 1959. The gifts to A and B qualify for exclusion under section 663(a) (1), although a total of six payments is made. The gifts of $75,000 to each beneficiary are to be separately treated.

§ 1.663(c)-1 Separate shares treated as separate trusts; in general

(a) If a single trust has more than one beneficiary, and if different beneficiaries have substantially separate and independent shares, their shares are treated as separate trusts for the sole purpose of determining the amount of distributable net income allocable to the respective beneficiaries under sections 661 and 662. Application of this rule will be significant in, for example, situations in which income is accumulated for beneficiary A but a distribution is made to beneficiary B of both income and corpus in an amount exceeding the share of income that would be distributable to B had there been separate trusts. In the absence of a separate share rule B would be taxed on income which is accumu-

lated for A. The division of distributable net income into separate shares will limit the tax liability of B. Section 663(c) does not affect the principles of applicable law in situations in which a single trust instrument creates not one but several separate trusts, as opposed to separate shares in the same trust within the meaning of this section.

(b) The separate share rule does not permit the treatment of separate shares as separate trusts for any purpose other than the application of distributable net income. It does not, for instance, permit the treatment of separate shares as separate trusts for purposes of:

(1) The filing of returns and payment of tax,

(2) The exclusion of dividends under section 116,

(3) The deduction of personal exemption under section 642(b), and

(4) The allowance to beneficiaries succeeding to the trust property of excess deductions and unused net operating loss and capital loss carryovers on termination of the trust under section 642(h).

(c) The separate share rule may be applicable even though separate and independent accounts are not maintained and are not required to be maintained for each share on the books of account of the trust, and even though no physical segregation of assets is made or required.

(d) Separate share treatment is not elective. Thus, if a trust is properly treated as having separate and independent shares, such treatment must prevail in all taxable years of the trust unless an event occurs as a result of which the terms of the trust instrument and the requirements of proper administration require different treatment.

§ 1.663(c)-2 Computation of distributable net income

The amount of distributable net income for any share under section 663(c) is computed for each share as if each share constituted a separate trust. Accordingly, any deduction or any loss which is applicable solely to one separate share of the trust is not available to any other share of the same trust.

§ 1.663(c)-3 Applicability of separate share rule

(a) The applicability of the separate share rule provided by section 663(c) will generally depend upon whether distributions of the trust are to be made in substantially the same manner as if separate trusts had been created. Thus, if an instrument directs a trustee to divide the testator's residuary estate into separate shares (which under applicable law do not constitute separate trusts) for each of the testator's children and the trustee is given discretion, with respect to each share, to distribute or accumulate income or to distribute principal or accumulated income, or to do both, separate shares will exist under section 663(c). In determining whether separate shares exist, it is immaterial whether the principal and any accumulated income of each share is ultimately distributable to the beneficiary of such share, to his descendants, to his appointees under a general or special power of appointment, or to any other beneficiaries (including a charitable organization) designated to receive his share of the trust and accumulated income upon termination of the beneficiary's interest in the share. Thus, a separate share may exist if the instrument provides that upon the death of the beneficiary of the share, the share will be added to the shares of the other beneficiaries of the trust.

(b) Separate share treatment will not be applied to a trust or portion of a trust subject to a power to:

(1) Distribute, apportion, or accumulate income, or

(2) Distribute corpus

to or for one or more beneficiaries within a group or class of beneficiaries, unless payment of income, accumulated income, or corpus of a share of one beneficiary cannot affect the proportionate share of income, accumulated income, or corpus of any shares of the other beneficiaries, or unless substantially proper adjustment must thereafter be made (under the governing instrument) so that substantially separate and independent shares exist.

(c) A share may be considered as separate even though more than one beneficiary has an interest in it. For example, two beneficiaries may have equal, disproportionate, or indeterminate interests in one share which is separate and independent from another share in which one or more beneficiaries have an interest. Likewise, the same person may be a beneficiary of more than one separate share.

(d) Separate share treatment may be given to a trust or portion of a trust otherwise qualifying under this section if the trust or portion of a trust is subject to a power to pay out to a beneficiary of a share (of such trust or portion) an amount of corpus in excess of his proportionate share of the corpus of the trust if the possibility of exercise of the power is remote. For example, if the trust is subject to a power to invade the entire corpus for the health, education, support, or maintenance of A, separate share treatment is applied if exercise of the power requires consideration of A's other income which is so substantial as to make the possibility of exercise of the power remote. If instead it appears that A and B have separate shares in a trust, subject to a power to invade the entire corpus for the comfort, pleasure, desire, or happiness of A, separate share treatment shall not be applied.

(e) The separate share rule may also be applicable to successive interests in point of time, as for instance in the case of a trust providing for a life estate to A and a second life estate or outright remainder to B. In such a case, in the taxable year of a trust in which a beneficiary dies items of income and deduction properly allocable under trust accounting principles to the period before a beneficiary's death are attributed to one share, and those allocable to the period after the beneficiary's death are attributed to the other share. Separate share treatment is not available to a succeeding interest, however, with respect to distributions which would otherwise be deemed distributed in a taxable year of the earlier interest under the throwback provisions of subpart D (section 665 and following), part I, subchapter J, chapter 1 of the Code. The application of this paragraph may be illustrated by the following example:

Example. A trust instrument directs that the income of a trust is to be paid to A for her life. After her death income may be distributed to B or accumulated. A dies on June 1, 1956. The trust keeps its books on the basis of the calendar year. The trust instrument permits invasions of corpus for the benefit of A and B, and an invasion of corpus was in fact made for A's benefit in 1956. In determining the distributable net income of the trust for the purpose of determining the amounts includible in A's income, income and deductions properly allocable to the period before A's death are treated as income and deductions of a separate share, and for that purpose no account is taken of income and deductions allocable to the period after A's death.

(f) Separate share treatment is not applicable to an estate.

§ 1.663(c)-4 Example

Section 663(c) may be illustrated by the following example:

Example. (a) A single trust was created in 1940 for the benefit of A, B, and C, who were aged 6, 4, and 2, respectively. Under the terms of the instrument, the trust income is required to be divided into three equal shares. Each beneficiary's share of the income is to be accumulated until he becomes 21 years of age. When a beneficiary reaches the age of 21, his share of the income may thereafter be either accumulated or distributed to him in the discretion of the trustee. The trustee also has discretion to invade corpus for the benefit of any beneficiary to the extent of his share of the trust estate, and the trust instrument requires that the beneficiary's right to future income and corpus will be proportionately reduced. When each beneficiary reaches 35 years of age, his share of the trust estate shall be paid over to him. The interest in the trust estate of any beneficiary dying without issue and before he has attained the age of 35 is to be equally divided between the other beneficiaries of the trust. All expenses of the trust are allocable to income under the terms of the trust instrument.

(b) No distributions of income or corpus were made by the trustee prior to 1955, although A became 21 years of age on June 30, 1954. During the taxable year 1955, the trust has income from royalties of $20,000 and expenses of $5,000. The trustee in his discretion distributes $12,000 to A. Both A and the trust report on the calendar year basis.

(c) The trust qualifies for the separate share treatment under section 663(c) and the distributable net income must be divided into three parts for the purpose of determining the amount deductible by the trust under section 661 and the amount includible in A's gross income under section 662.

(d) The distributable net income of each share of the trust is $5,000 ($6,667 less $1,667). Since the amount ($12,000) distributed to A during 1955 exceeds the distributable net income of $5,000 allocated to his share, the trust is deemed to have distributed to him $5,000 of 1955 income and $7,000 of amounts other than 1955 income. Accordingly, the trust is allowed a deduction of $5,000 under section 661. The taxable income of the trust for 1955 is $9,900, computed as follows:

Royalties $20,000

Deductions:
Expenses $5,000
Distribution to A 5,000
Personal exemption 100
_____
10,100

Taxable income 9,900

(e) In accordance with section 662, A must include in his gross income for 1955 an amount equal to the portion ($5,000) of the distributable net income of the trust allocated to his share. Also, the excess distribution of $7,000 made by the trust is subject to the throwback provisions of subpart D (section 665 and following), part I, subchapter J, chapter 1 of the Code, and the regulations thereunder.

§ 1.665(d)-1A Taxes imposed on the trust

(a) **In general.** (1) For purposes of subpart D, the term "taxes imposed on the trust" means the amount of Federal income taxes properly imposed for any taxable year on the trust that are attributable to the undistributed portions of distributable net income and gains in excess of losses from the sales or exchanges of capital assets. Except as provided in paragraph (c)(2) of this section, the minimum tax for tax preferences imposed by section 56 is not a tax attributable to the undistributed portions of distributable net income and gains in excess of losses from the sales or exchanges of capital assets. See section 56 and the regulations thereunder.

(2) In the case of a trust that has received an accumulation distribution from another trust, the term "taxes imposed on the trust" also includes the amount of taxes deemed distributed under §§ 1.666(b)-1A, 1.666(c)-1A, 1.669(d)-1A, and 1.669(e)-1A (whichever are applicable) as a result of such accumulation distribution, to the extent that they were taken into account under paragraphs (b)(2) or (c)(1)(vi) of § 1.668(b)-1A and (b)(2) or (c)(1)(vi) of § 1.669(b)-1A in computing the partial tax on such accumulation distribution. For example, assume that trust A, a calendar year trust, makes an accumulation distribution in 1975 to trust B, also on the calendar year basis, in connection with which $500 of taxes are deemed under § 1.666(b)-1A to be distributed to trust B. The partial tax on the accumulation distribution is computed under paragraph (b) of § 1.668(b)-1A (the exact method) to be $600 and all of the $500 is used under paragraph (b)(2) of § 1.668(b)-1A to reduce the partial tax to $100. The taxes imposed on trust B for 1975 will, in addition to the $100 partial tax, also include the $500 used to reduce the partial tax.

(b) **Taxes imposed on the trust attributable to undistributed net income.** (1) For the purpose of subpart D, the term "taxes imposed on the trust attributable to the undistributed net income" means the amount of Federal income taxes for the taxable year properly allocable to the undistributed portion of the distributable net income for such taxable year. This amount is (i) an amount that bears the same relationship to the total taxes of the trust for the year (other than the minimum tax for tax preferences imposed by section 56), computed after the allowance of credits under section 642(a), as (a) the taxable income of the trust, other than the capital gains not included in distributable net income less their share of section 1202 deduction, bears to (b) the total taxable income of the trust for such year or, (ii) if the alternative tax computation under section 1201(b) is used and there are no net short-term gains, an amount equal to such total taxes less the amount of the alternative tax imposed on the trust and attributable to the capital gain. Thus, for the purposes of subpart D, in determining the amount of taxes imposed on the trust attributable to the undistributed net income, that portion of the taxes paid by the trust attributable to capital gain allocable to corpus is excluded. The rule stated in this subparagraph may be illustrated by the following example, which assumes that the alternative tax computation is not used:

Example. (1) Under the terms of a trust, which reports on the calendar year basis, the income may be accumulated or distributed to A in the discretion of the trustee and capital gains are allocable to corpus. During the taxable year 1974, the trust had income of $20,000 from royalties, long-term capital gains of $10,-000, and expenses of $2,000. The trustee in his discretion made a distribution of $10,000 to A. The taxes imposed on the trust for such year attributable to the undistributed net income are $2,319, determined as shown below.

(2) The distributable net income of the trust computed under section 643(a) is $18,000 (royalties of $20,000 less expenses of $2,000). The total taxes paid by the trust are $3,787, computed as follows:

Royalties	$20,000
Capital gain allocable to corpus	10,000
Gross income	30,000

Deductions:

Expenses	$ 2,000
Distributions to A	10,000
Capital gain deduction	5,000
Personal exemption	100
	17,100
Taxable income	12,900
Total income taxes	3,787

(3) Taxable income other than capital gains less the section 1202 deduction is $7,900 ($12,900

—($10,000—$5,000)). Therefore, the amount of taxes imposed on the trust attributable to the undistributed net income is $2,319, computed as follows:

$3,787 (total taxes) × $7,900 (taxable income other than capital gains not included in d.n.i. less the 1202 deduction) divided by $12,900 (taxable income) ... $2,319

. . . .

§ 1.665(e)–1A   Preceding taxable year

. . . .

(b) Simple trusts. A taxable year of a trust during which the trust was a simple trust (that is, was subject to subpart B) for the entire year shall not be considered a "preceding taxable year" unless during such year the trust received "outside income" or unless the trustee did not distribute all of the income of the trust that was required to be distributed currently for such year. In such event, undistributed net income for such year shall not exceed the greater of the "outside income" or income not distributed during such year. For purposes of this paragraph, the term "outside income" means amounts that are included in distributable net income of the trust for the year but that are not "income" of the trust as that term is defined in § 1.643(b)–1. Some examples of "outside income" are:

(1) Income taxable to the trust under section 691;

(2) Unrealized accounts receivable that were assigned to the trust; and

(3) Distributions from another trust that include distributable net income or undistributed net income of such other trust.

The term "outside income," however, does not include amounts received as distributions from an estate, other than income specified in (1) and (2), for which the estate was allowed a deduction under section 661(a). The application of this paragraph may be illustrated by the following examples:

Example (1). By his will D creates a trust for his widow W. The terms of the trust require that the income be distributed currently (i. e., it is a simple trust), and authorize the trustee to make discretionary payments of corpus to W. Upon W's death the trust corpus is to be distributed to D's then living issue. The executor of D's will makes a $10,000 distribution of corpus to the trust that carries out estate income consisting of dividends and interest to the trust under section 662(a) (2). The trust reports this income as its only income on its income tax return for its taxable year in which ends the taxable year of the estate in which the $10,000 distribution was made, and pays a tax thereon of $2,106. Thus, the trust has undistributed net income of $7,894 ($10,000 - $2,106). Several years later the trustee makes a discretionary corpus payment of $15,000 to W. This payment is an accumulation distribution under section 665(b). However, since the trust had no "outside income" in the year of the estate distribution, such year is not a preceding taxable year. Thus, W is not treated as receiving undistributed net income of $7,894 and taxes thereon of $2,106 for the purpose of including the same in her gross income under section 668. The result would be the same if the invasion power were not exercised and the accumulation distribution occurred as a result of the distribution of the corpus to D's issue upon the death of W.

Example (2). Trust A, a simple trust on the calendar year basis, received in 1972 extraordinary dividends or taxable stock dividends that the trustee in good faith allocated to corpus, but that are determined in 1974 to have been currently distributable to the beneficiary. See section 643(a) (4) and § 1.643(a)-4. Trust A would qualify for treatment under subpart C for 1974, the year of distribution of the extraordinary dividends or taxable stock dividends, because the distribution is not out of income of the current taxable year and is treated as an other amount properly paid or credited or required to be distributed for such taxable year within the meaning of section 661 (a) (2). Also, the distribution in 1974 qualifies as an accumulation distribution for the purposes of subpart D. For purposes only of such subpart D, trust A would be treated as subject to the provisions of such subpart C for 1972, the preceding taxable year in which the extraordinary or taxable stock dividends were received, and, in computing undistributed net income for 1972, the extraordinary or taxable stock dividends would be included in distributable net income under section 643(a). The rule stated in the preceding sentence would also apply if the distribution in 1974 was made out of corpus without regard to a determination that the extraordinary dividends or taxable stock dividends in question were currently distributable to the beneficiary.

§ 1.666(a)-1A   Amount allocated

(a) In general. In the case of a trust that is subject to subpart C of part I of subchapter J of chapter 1 of the Code (relating to estates and trusts that may accumulate income or that distribute corpus), section 666(a) prescribes rules for determining the taxable years from which an accumulation distribution will be deemed to have been made and the extent to which the accumulation distribution is considered to consist of undistributed net income. In general, an accumulation distribution made in taxable years beginning after December 31, 1969, is deemed to have been made first from the earliest preceding taxable year of the trust for which there is undistributed net income. An accumulation distribution made in a taxable year beginning before January 1, 1970, is deemed to have been made first from the most recent preceding taxable year of the trust for which there is undistributed net income. . . . .

(b) Distributions by domestic trusts—(1) Taxable years beginning after December 31, 1973. An accumulation distribution made by a trust (other than a foreign trust created by a U. S. person) in any taxable year beginning after December 31, 1973, is allocated to the preceding taxable years of the trust (defined in § 1.665(e)-1A(a) (1) (ii) as those beginning after December 31, 1968) according to the amount of undistributed net income of the trust for such years. For this purpose, an accumulation distribution is first to be allocated to the earliest such preceding taxable year in which there is undistributed net income and shall then be allocated, beginning with the next earliest, to any remaining preceding taxable years of the trust. The portion of the accumulation distribution allocated to the earliest preceding taxable year is the amount of the undistributed net income for that preceding taxable year. The portion of the accumulation distribution allocated to any preceding taxable year subsequent to the earliest such preceding taxable year is the excess of the accumulation distribution over the aggregate of the undistributed net income for all earlier preceding taxable years. See paragraph (d) of this section for adjustments to undistributed net income for prior distributions. The provisions of this subparagraph may be illustrated by the following example:

Example. In 1977, a domestic trust reporting on the calendar year basis makes an accumulation distribution of $33,000. Therefore, years before 1969 are ignored. In 1969, the trust had $6,000 of undistributed net income; in 1970, $4,000; in 1971, none; in 1972, $7,000; in 1973, $5,000; in 1974, $8,000; in 1975, $6,000; and $4,000 in 1976. The accumulation distribution is deemed distributed $6,000 in 1969, $4,000 in 1970, none in 1971, $7,000 in 1972, $5,000 in 1973, $8,000 in 1974, and $3,000 in 1975.

§ 1.666(b)-1A Total taxes deemed distributed

(a) If an accumulation distribution is deemed under § 1.666(a)-1A to be distributed on the last day of a preceding taxable year and the amount is not less than the undistributed net income for such preceding taxable year, then an additional amount equal to the "taxes imposed on the trust attributable to the undistributed net income" (as defined in § 1.665(d)-1A(b)) for such preceding taxable year is also deemed distributed under section 661(a) (2). For example, a trust has undistributed net income of $8,000 for the taxable year 1974. The taxes imposed on the trust attributable to the undistributed net income are $3,032. During the taxable year 1977, an accumulation distribution of $8,000 is made to the beneficiary, which is deemed under § 1.666(a)-1A to have been distributed on the last day of 1974. The 1977 accumulation distribution is not less than the 1974 undistributed net income. Accordingly, the taxes of $3,032 imposed on the trust attributable to the undistributed net income for 1974 are also deemed to have been distributed on the last day of 1974. Thus, a total of $11,032 will be deemed to have been distributed on the last day of 1974.

(b) For the purpose of paragraph (a) of this section, the undistributed net income of any preceding taxable year and the taxes imposed on the trust for such preceding taxable year attributable to such undistributed net income are computed after taking into account any accumulation distributions of taxable years intervening between such preceding taxable year and the taxable year. See paragraph (d) of § 1.666(a)-1A.

§ 1.666(c)-1A Pro rata portion of taxes deemed distributed

(a) If an accumulation distribution is deemed under § 1.666(a)-1A to be distributed on the last day of a preceding txable year and the amount is less than the undistributed net income for such preceding taxable year, then an additional amount is also deemed distributed under section 661(a) (2). The additional amount is equal to the "taxes imposed on the trust attributable to the undistributed net income" (as defined in § 1.665(a)-1A(b)) for such preceding taxable year, multiplied by a fraction, the numerator of which is the amount of the accumulation distribution allocated to such preceding taxable year and the denominator of which is the undistributed net income for such preceding taxable year. . . . .

(b) For the purpose of paragraph (a) of this section, the undistributed net income of any preceding taxable year and the taxes imposed on the trust for such preceding taxable year attributable to such undistributed net income are computed after taking into account any accumulation distributions of any taxable years intervening between such preceding taxable year and the taxable year. . . . . .

§ 1.671-1 Grantors and others treated as substantial owners; scope

(a) Subpart E (section 671 and following), part I, subchapter J, chapter 1 of the Code, contains provisions taxing income of a trust to the grantor or another person under certain circumstances even though he is not treated as a beneficiary under subparts A through D (section 641 and following) of such part I. Sections 671 and 672 contain general provisions relating to the entire subpart. Sections 673 through 677 define the circumstances under which income of a trust is taxed to a grantor. These circumstances are in general as follows:

(1) If the grantor has retained a reversionary interest in the trust, within specified time limits (section 673);

(2) If the grantor or a nonadverse party has certain powers over the beneficial interests under the trust (section 674);

(3) If certain administrative powers over the trust exist under which the grantor can or does benefit (section 675);

(4) If the grantor or a nonadverse party has a power to revoke the trust or return the corpus to the grantor (section 676); or

(5) If the grantor or a nonadverse party has the power to distribute income to or for the benefit of the grantor or the grantor's spouse (section 677).

Under section 678, income of a trust is taxed to a person other than the grantor to the extent that he has the sole power to vest corpus or income in himself.

(b) Sections 671 through 677 do not apply if the income of a trust is taxable to a grantor's spouse under section 71 or 682 (relating respectively to alimony and separate maintenance payments, and the income of an estate or trust in the case of divorce, etc.).

(c) Except as provided in subpart E, income of a trust is not included in computing the taxable income and credits of a grantor or another person solely on the grounds of his dominion and control over the trust. However, the provisions of subpart E do not apply in situations involving an assignment of future income, whether or not the assignment is to a trust. Thus, for example, a person who assigns his right to future income under an employment contract may be taxed on that income even though the assignment is to a trust over which the assignor has retained none of the controls specified in sections 671 through 677. Similarly, a bondholder who assigns his right to interest may be taxed on interest payments even though the assignment is to an uncontrolled trust. Nor are the rules as to family partnerships affected by the provisions of subpart E even though a partnership interest is held in trust. Likewise, these sections have no application in determining the right of a grantor to deductions for payments to a trust under a transfer and leaseback arrangement. In addition, the limitation of the last sentence of section 671 does not prevent any person from being taxed on the income of a trust when it is used to discharge his legal obligation. See § 1.662(a)-4. He is then treated as a beneficiary under subparts A through D or treated as an owner under section 677 because the income is distributed for his benefit, and not because of his dominion or control over the trust.

. . . .

§ 1.671-2 Applicable principles

(a) Under section 671 a grantor or another person includes in computing his taxable income and credits those items of income, deduction, and credit against tax which are attributable to or included in any portion of a trust of which he is treated as the owner. Sections 673 through 678 set forth the rules for determining when the grantor or another person is treated as the owner of any portion of a trust. The rules for determining the items of income, deduction, and credit against tax that are attributable to or included in a portion of the trust are set forth in § 1.671-3.

(b) Since the principle underlying subpart E (section 671 and following), part I, subchapter J, chapter 1 of the Code, is in general that income of a trust over which the grantor or another person has retained substantial dominion or control should be taxed to the grantor or other person rather than to the trust which receives the income or to the beneficiary to whom the income may be distributed, it is ordinarily immaterial whether the income involved constitutes income or corpus for trust accounting purposes. Accordingly, when it is stated in the regulations under subpart E that "income" is attributed to the grantor or another person, the reference, unless specifically limited, is to income determined for tax purposes and not to income for trust accounting purposes. When it is intended to emphasize that income for trust accounting purposes (determined in accordance with the provisions set forth in § 1.643(b)-1, is meant, the phrase "ordinary income" is used.

(c) An item of income, deduction, or credit included in computing the taxable income and credits of a grantor or another person under section 671 is treated as if it had been received or paid directly by the grantor or other person (whether or not an individual). For example, a charitable contribution made by a trust which is attributed to the grantor (an individual) under sections 671 through 677 will be aggregated with his other charitable contributions to determine their deductibility under the limitations of section 170(b) (1). Likewise, dividends received by a trust from sources in a particular foreign country which are attributed to a grantor or another person under subpart E will be aggregated with his other income from sources within that country to determine whether the taxpayer is subject to the limitations of section 904 with respect to credit for the tax paid to that country.

(d) Items of income, deduction, and credit not attributed to or included in any portion of a trust of which the grantor or another person is treated as the owner under subpart E are subject to the provisions of subparts A through D (section 641 and following), of such part I

(e) The term "grantor" as used in the regulations under subpart E includes a corporation.

§ 1.671-3 Attribution or inclusion of income, deductions, and credits against tax

(a) When a grantor or another person is treated under subpart E (section 671 and following) as the owner of any portion of a trust, there are included in computing his tax liability those items of income, deduction, and credit against tax attributable to or included in that portion. For example:

(1) If a grantor or another person is treated as the owner of an entire trust (corpus as well as ordinary income), he takes into account in computing his income tax liability all items of income, deduction, and credit (including capital gains and losses) to which he would have been entitled had the trust not been in existence during the period he is treated as owner.

(2) If the portion treated as owned consists of specific trust property and its income, all items directly related to that property are attributable to the portion. Items directly related to trust property not included in the portion treated as owned by the grantor or other person are governed by the provisions of subparts A through D (section 641 and following), part I, subchapter J, chapter 1 of the Code. Items that relate both to the portion treated as owned by the grantor and to the balance of the trust must be apportioned in a manner that is reasonable in the light of all the circumstances of each case, including the terms of the governing instrument, local law, and the practice of the trustee if it is reasonable and consistent.

(3) If the portion of a trust treated as owned by a grantor or another person consists of an undivided fractional interest in the trust, or of an interest represented by a dollar amount, a pro rata share of each item of income, deduction, and credit is normally allocated to the portion. Thus, where the portion owned consists of an interest in or a right to an amount

of corpus only, a fraction of each item (including items allocated to corpus, such as capital gains) is attributed to the portion. The numerator of this fraction is the amount which is subject to the control of the grantor or other person and the denominator is normally the fair market value of the trust corpus at the beginning of the taxable year in question. The share not treated as owned by the grantor or other person is governed by the provisions of subparts A through D. See the last three sentences of paragraph (c) of this section for the principles applicable if the portion treated as owned consists of an interest in part of the ordinary income in contrast to an interest in corpus alone.

(b) If a grantor or another person is treated as the owner of a portion of a trust, that portion may or may not include both ordinary income and other income allocable to corpus. For example—

(1) Only ordinary income is included by reason of an interest in or a power over ordinary income alone. Thus, if a grantor is treated under section 673 as an owner by reason of a reversionary interest in ordinary income only, items of income allocable to corpus will not be included in the portion he is treated as owning. Similarly, if a grantor or another person is treated under sections 674–678 as an owner of a portion by reason of a power over ordinary income only, items of income allocable to corpus are not included in that portion. (See paragraph (c) of this section to determine the treatment of deductions and credits when only ordinary income is included in the portion.)

(2) Only income allocable to corpus is included by reason of an interest in or a power over corpus alone, if satisfaction of the interest or an exercise of the power will not result in an interest in or the exercise of a power over ordinary income which would itself cause that income to be included. For example, if a grantor has a reversionary interest in a trust which is not such as to require that he be treated as an owner under section 673, he may nevertheless be treated as an owner under section 677(a) (2) since any income allocable to corpus is accumulated for future distribution to him, but items of income included in determining ordinary income are not included in the portion he is treated as owning. Similarly, he may

have a power over corpus which is such that he is treated as an owner under section 674 or 676(a), but ordinary income will not be included in the portion he owns, if his power can only affect income received after a period of time such that he would not be treated as an owner of the income if the power were a reversionary interest. (See paragraph (c) of this section to determine the treatment of deductions and credits when only income allocated to corpus is included in the portion.)

(3) Both ordinary income and other income allocable to corpus are included by reason of an interest in or a power over both ordinary income and corpus, or an interest in or a power over corpus alone which does not come within the provisions of subparagraph (2) of this paragraph. For example, if a grantor is treated under section 673 as the owner of a portion of a trust by reason of a reversionary interest in corpus, both ordinary income and other income allocable to corpus are included in the portion. Further, a grantor includes both ordinary income and other income allocable to corpus in the portion he is treated as owning if he is treated under section 674 or 676 as an owner because of a power over corpus which can affect income received within a period such that he would be treated as an owner under section 673 if the power were a reversionary interest. Similarly, a grantor or another person includes both ordinary income and other income allocable to corpus in the portion he is treated as owning if he is treated as an owner under section 675 or 678 because of a power over corpus.

(c) If only income allocable to corpus is included in computing a grantor's tax liability, he will take into account in that computation only those items of income, deduction, and credit which would not be included under subparts A through D in the computation of the tax liability of the current income beneficiaries if all distributable net income had actually been distributed to those beneficiaries. On the other hand, if the grantor or another person is treated as an owner solely because of his interest in or power over ordinary income alone, he will take into account in computing his tax lia-

bility those items which would be included in computing the tax liability of a current income beneficiary, including expenses allocable to corpus which enter into the computation of distributable net income. If the grantor or other person is treated as an owner because of his power over or right to a dollar amount of ordinary income, he will first take into account a portion of those items of income and expense entering into the computation of ordinary income under the trust instrument or local law sufficient to produce income of the dollar amount required. There will then be attributable to him a pro rata portion of other items entering into the computation of distributable net income under subparts A through D, such as expenses allocable to corpus, and a pro rata portion of credits of the trust. For examples of computations under this paragraph see paragraph (g) of § 1.677(a)-1.

§ 1.672(a)-1 Definition of adverse party

(a) Under section 672(a) an adverse party is defined as any person having a substantial beneficial interest in a trust which would be adversely affected by the exercise or nonexercise of a power which he possesses respecting the trust. A trustee is not an adverse party merely because of his interest as trustee. A person having a general power of appointment over the trust property is deemed to have a beneficial interest in the trust. An interest is a substantial interest if its value in relation to the total value of the property subject to the power is not insignificant.

(b) Ordinarily, a beneficiary will be an adverse party, but if his right to share in the income or corpus of a trust is limited to only a part, he may be an adverse party only as to that part. Thus, if A, B, C, and D are equal income beneficiaries of a trust and the grantor can revoke with A's consent, the grantor is treated as the owner of a portion which represents three-fourths of the trust; and items of income, deduction, and credit attributable to that portion are included in determining the tax of the grantor.

(c) The interest of an ordinary income beneficiary of a trust may or may not be adverse with respect to the exercise of a power over corpus. Thus, if the income of a trust is payable to A for life, with a power (which is not a general power of appointment) in A to appoint the corpus to the grantor either during his life or by will, A's interest is adverse to the return of the corpus to the grantor during A's life, but is not adverse to a return of the corpus after A's death. In other words, A's interest is adverse as to ordinary income but is not adverse as to income allocable to corpus. Therefore, assuming no other relevant facts exist, the grantor would not be taxable on the ordinary income of the trust under sections 674, 676, or 677, but would be taxable under section 677 on income allocable to corpus (such as capital gains), since it may in the discretion of a nonadverse party be accumulated for future distribution to the grantor. Similarly, the interest of a contingent income beneficiary is adverse to a return of corpus to the grantor before the termination of his interest but not to a return of corpus after the termination of his interest.

(d) The interest of a remainderman is adverse to the exercise of any power over the corpus of a trust, but not to the exercise of a power over any income interest preceding his remainder. For example, if the grantor creates a trust which provides for income to be distributed to A for 10 years and then for the corpus to go to X if he is then living, a power exercisable by X to revest corpus in the grantor is a power exercisable by an adverse party; however, a power exercisable by X to distribute part or all of the ordinary income to the grantor may be a power exercisable by a nonadverse party (which would cause the ordinary income to be taxed to the grantor).

§ 1.672(b)-1   Nonadverse party

A "nonadverse party" is any person who is not an adverse party.

§ 1.672(c)-1   Related or subordinate party

Section 672(c) defines the term "related or subordinate party". The term, as used in sections 674(c) and 675(3), means any nonadverse party who is the grantor's spouse if living with the grantor; the grantor's father, mother, issue, brother or sister; an employee of the grantor; a corporation or any employee of a corporation in which the stock holdings of the grantor and the trust are significant from the viewpoint of voting control; or a subordinate employee of a corporation in which the grantor is an executive. For purposes of sections 674(c) and 675(3), these persons are presumed to be subservient to the grantor in respect of the exercise or nonexercise of the powers conferred on them unless shown not to be subservient by a preponderance of the evidence.

§ 1.672(d)-1   Power subject to condition precedent

Section 672(d) provides that a person is considered to have a power described in subpart E (section 671 and following), part I, subchapter J, Chapter 1 of the Code, even though the exercise of the power is subject to a precedent giving of notice or takes effect only after the expiration of a certain period of time. However, although a person may be considered to have such a power, the grantor will nevertheless not be treated as an owner by reason of the power if its exercise can only affect beneficial enjoyment of income received after the expiration of a period of time such that, if the power were a reversionary interest, he would not be treated as an owner under section 673. See sections 674(b) (2), 676(b), and the last sentence of section 677(a). Thus, for example, if a grantor creates a trust for the benefit of his son and retains a power to revoke which takes effect only after the expiration of 2 years from the date of exercise, he is treated as an owner from the inception of the trust. However, if the grantor retains a power to revoke, exercisable at any time, which can only affect the beneficial enjoyment of the ordinary income of a trust received after the expiration of 10 years commencing with the date of the transfer in trust, or after the death of the income beneficiary, the power does not cause him to be treated as an owner with respect to ordinary income during the first 10 years of the trust or during the income beneficiary's life, as the case may be. See section 676(b).

§ 1.673(a)-1 Reversionary interests; income payable to beneficiaries other than certain charitable organizations; general rule

(a) Under section 673(a), a grantor, in general, is treated as the owner of any portion of a trust in which he has a reversionary interest in either the corpus or income if, as of the inception of that portion of the trust, the grantor's interest will or may reasonably be expected to take effect in possession or enjoyment within 10 years commencing with the date of transfer of that portion of the trust. However, the following types of reversionary interests are excepted from the general rule of the preceding sentence:

(1) A reversionary interest after the death of the income beneficiary of a trust (see paragraph (b) of this section); and

. . . .

Even though the duration of the trust may be such that the grantor is not treated as its owner under section 673, and therefore is not taxed on the ordinary income, he may nevertheless be treated as an owner under section 677 (a) (2) if he has a reversionary interest in the corpus. In the latter case, items of income, deduction, and credit allocable to corpus, such as capital gains and losses, will be included in the portion he owns. See § 1.671-3 and the regulations under section 677. See § 1.673(d)-1 with respect to a postponement of the date specified for reacquisition of a reversionary interest.

(b) Section 673(c) provides that a grantor is not treated as the owner of any portion of a trust by reason of section 673 if his reversionary interest in the portion is not to take effect in possession or enjoyment until the death of the person or persons to whom the income of the portion is payable, regardless of the life expectancies of the income beneficiaries. If his reversionary interest is to take effect on or after the death of an income beneficiary or upon the expiration of a specific term of years, whichever is earlier, the grantor is treated as the owner if the specific term of years is less than 10 years (but not if the term is 10 years or longer).

(c) Where the grantor's reversionary interest in a portion of a trust is to take effect in possession or enjoyment by reason of some event other than the expiration of a specific term of years or the death of the income beneficiary, the grantor is treated as the owner of the portion if the event may reasonably be expected to occur within 10 years from the date of transfer of that portion, but he is not treated as the owner under section 673 if the event may not reasonably be expected to occur within 10 years from that date. For example, if the reversionary interest in any portion of a trust is to take effect on or after the death of the grantor (or any person other than the person to whom the income is payable) the grantor is treated under section 673 as the owner of the portion if the life expectancy of the grantor (or other person) is less than 10 years on the date of transfer of the portion, but not if the life expectancy is 10 years or longer. If the reversionary interest in any portion is to take effect on or after the death of the grantor (or any person other than the person to whom the income is payable) or upon the expiration of a specific term of years, whichever is earlier, the grantor is treated as the owner of the portion if on the date of transfer of the portion either the life expectancy of the grantor (or other person) or the specific term is less than 10 years; however, if both the life expectancy and the specific term are 10 years or longer the grantor is not treated as the owner of the portion under section 673. Similarly, if the grantor has a reversionary interest in any portion which will take effect at the death of the income beneficiary or the grantor, whichever is earlier, the grantor is not treated as an owner of the portion unless his life expectancy is less than 10 years.

(d) It is immaterial that a reversionary interest in corpus or income is subject to a contingency if the reversionary interest may, taking the contingency into consideration, reasonably be expected to take effect in possession or enjoyment within 10 years. For example, the grantor is taxable where the trust income is to be paid to the grantor's son for 3 years, and the corpus is then to be returned to the grantor if he survives that period, or to be paid to the grantor's son if he is already deceased.

(e) See section 671 and §§ 1.671-2 and 1.671-3 for rules for treatment of items of income, deduction, and credit when a person is treated as the owner of all or only a portion of a trust.

§ 1.673(d)-1   Postponement of date specified for reacquisition

Any postponement of the date specified for the reacquisitior of possession or enjoyment of any reversionary interest is considered a new transfer in trust commencing with the date on which the postponement is effected and terminating with the date prescribed by the postponement. However, the grantor will not be treated as the owner of any portion of a trust for any taxable year by reason of the foregoing sentence if he would not be so treated in the absence of any postponement. The rules contained in this section may be illustrated by the following example:

Example. G places property in trust for the benefit of his son B. Upon the expiration of 12 years or the earlier death of B the property is to be paid over to G or his estate. After the expiration of 9 years G extends the term of the trust for an additional 2 years. G is considered to have made a new transfer in trust for a term of 5 years (the remaining 3 years of the original transfer plus the 2-year extension). However, he is not treated as the owner of the trust under section 673 for the first 3 years of the new term because he would not be so treated if the term of the trust had not been extended. G is treated as the owner of the trust, however, for the remaining 2 years.

§ 1.674(a)-1   Power to control beneficial enjoyment; scope of section 674

(a) Under section 674, the grantor is treated as the owner of a portion of trust if the grantor or a nonadverse party has a power, beyond specified limits, to dispose of the beneficial enjoyment of the income or corpus, whether the power is a fiduciary power, a power of appointment, or any other power. Section 674(a) states in general terms that the grantor is treated as the owner in every case in which he or a nonadverse party can affect the beneficial enjoyment of a portion of a trust, the limitations being set forth as exceptions in subsections (b), (c),

and (d) of section 674. These exceptions are discussed in detail in §§ 1.674 (b)-1 through 1.674(d)-1. Certain limitations applicable to sections 674(b), (c), and (d) are set forth in § 1.674 (d)-2. Section 674(b) describes powers which are excepted regardless of who holds them. Section 674(c) describes additional powers of trustees which are excepted if at least half the trustees are independent, and if the grantor is not a trustee. Section 674 (d) describes a further power which is excepted if it is held by trustees other than the grantor or his spouse (if living with the grantor).

(b) In general terms thc grantor is treated as the owner of a portion of a trust if he or a nonadverse party or both has a power to dispose of the beneficial enjoyment of the corpus or income unless the power is one of the following:

(1) Miscellaneous powers over either ordinary income or corpus. (i) A power that can only affect the beneficial enjoyment of income (including capital gains) received after a period of time such that the grantor would not be treated as an owner under section 673 if the power were a reversionary interest (section 674(b) (2));

(ii) A testamentary power held by anyone (other than a testamentary power held by the grantor over accumulated income) (section 674(b) (3));

(iii) A power to choose between charitable beneficiaries or to affect the manner of their enjoyment of a beneficial interest (section 674(b) (4));

(iv) A power to allocate receipts and disbursements between income and corpus (section 674(b) (8)).

(2) Powers of distribution primarily affecting only one beneficiary. (i) A power to distribute corpus to or for a current income beneficiary, if the distribution must be charged against the share of corpus from which the beneficiary may receive income (section 674 (b) (5) (B));

(ii) A power to distribute income to or for a current income beneficiary or to accumulate it either (a) if accumulated income must either be payable to the beneficiary from whom it was withheld or as described in paragraph (b) (6) of § 1.674(b)-1 (section 674(b) (6)); (b) if the power is to apply income to the support of a dependent of the grantor, and the income is not so applied (section 674(b) (1)); or (c) if the beneficiary is under 21 or under a legal disability and accumulated income is added to corpus (section 674(b)(7)).

(3) Powers of distribution affecting more than one beneficiary. A power to distribute corpus or income to or among one or more beneficiaries or to accumulate income, either (i) if the power is held by a trustee or trustees other than the grantor, at least half of whom are independent (section 674 (c)), or (ii) if the power is limited by a reasonably definite standard in the trust instrument, and in the case of a power over income, if in addition the power is held by a trustee or trustees other than the grantor and the grantor's spouse living with the grantor (sections 674(b) (5) (A) and (d)). (These powers include both powers to "sprinkle" income or corpus among current beneficiaries, and powers to shift income or corpus between current beneficiaries and remaindermen; however, certain of the powers described under subparagraph (2) of this paragraph can have the latter effect incidentally.)

(c) See section 671 and §§ 1.671-2 and 1.671-3 for rules for the treatment of income, deductions, and credits when a person is treated as the owner of all or only a portion of a trust.

§ 1.674(b)-1 Excepted powers exercisable by any person

(a) Paragraph (b) (1) through (8) of this section sets forth a number of powers which may be exercisable by any person without causing the grantor to be treated as an owner of a trust under section 674(a). Further, with the exception of powers described in paragraph (b) (1) of this section, it is immaterial whether these powers are held in the capacity of trustee. It makes no difference under section 674 (b) that the person holding the power is the grantor, or a related or subordinate party (with the qualifications noted in paragraph (b) (1) and (3) of this section).

(b) The exceptions referred to in paragraph (a) of this section are as follows (see, however, the limitations set forth in § 1.674(d)-2):

(1) Powers to apply income to support of a dependent. Section 674(b) (1) provides, in effect, that regardless of the general rule of section 674(a),

the income of a trust will not be considered as taxable to the grantor merely because in the discretion of any person (other than a grantor who is not acting as a trustee or cotrustee) it may be used for the support of a beneficiary whom the grantor is legally obligated to support, except to the extent that it is in fact used for that purpose. See section 677(b) and the regulations thereunder.

(2) Powers affecting beneficial enjoyment only after a period. Section 674 (b) (2) provides an exception to section 674(a) if the exercise of a power can only affect the beneficial enjoyment of the income of a trust received after a period of time which is such that a grantor would not be treated as an owner under section 673 if the power were a reversionary interest. See §§ 1.673(a)-1 and 1.673(b)-1. For example, if a trust created on January 1, 1955, provides for the payment of income to the grantor's son, and the grantor reserves the power to substitute other beneficiaries of income or corpus in lieu of his son on or after January 1, 1965, the grantor is not treated under section 674 as the owner of the trust with respect to ordinary income received before January 1, 1965. But the grantor will be treated as an owner on and after that date unless the power is relinquished. If the beginning of the period during which the grantor may substitute beneficiaries is postponed, the rules set forth in § 1.673(d)-1 are applicable in order to determine whether the grantor should be treated as an owner during the period following the postponement.

(3) Testamentary powers. Under paragraph (3) of section 674(b) a power in any person to control beneficial enjoyment exercisable only by will does not cause a grantor to be treated as an owner under section 674 (a). However, this exception does not apply to income accumulated for testamentary disposition by the grantor or to income which may be accumulated for such distribution in the discretion of the grantor or a nonadverse party, or both, without the approval or consent of any adverse party. For example, if a trust instrument provides that the income is to be accumulated during the grantor's life and that the grantor may appoint the accumulated income by will, the grantor is treated as the owner of the trust. Moreover, if a trust instrument provides that the income is payable to another person for his life, but the grantor has a testamentary power of appointment over the remainder, and under the trust instrument and local law capital gains are added to corpus, the grantor is treated as the owner of a portion of the trust and capital gains and losses are included in that portion. (See § 1.671–3.)

. . . .

(5) Powers to distribute corpus. Paragraph (5) of section 674(b) provides an exception to section 674(a) for powers to distribute corpus, subject to certain limitations, as follows:

(i) If the power is limited by a reasonably definite standard which is set forth in the trust instrument, it may extend to corpus distributions to any beneficiary or beneficiaries or class of beneficiaries (whether income beneficiaries or remaindermen) without causing the grantor to be treated as an owner under section 674. See section 674(b) (5) (A). It is not required that the standard consist of the needs and circumstances of the beneficiary. A clearly measurable standard under which the holder of a power is legally accountable is deemed a reasonably definite standard for this purpose. For instance, a power to distribute corpus for the education, support, maintenance, or health of the beneficiary; for his reasonable support and comfort; or to enable him to maintain his accustomed standard of living; or to meet an emergency, would be limited by a reasonably definite standard. However, a power to distribute corpus for the pleasure, desire, or happiness of a beneficiary is not limited by a reasonably definite standard. The entire context of a provision of a trust instrument granting a power must be considered in determining whether the power is limited by a reasonably definite standard. For example, if a trust instrument provides that the determination of the trustee shall be conclusive with respect to the exercise or nonexercise of a power, the power is not limited by a reasonably definite standard. However, the fact that the governing instrument is phrased in discretionary terms is not in itself an indication that no reasonably definite standard exists.

(ii) If the power is not limited by a reasonably definite standard set forth in the trust instrument, the exception applies only if distributions of corpus may be made solely in favor of current income beneficiaries, and any corpus distribution to the current income beneficiary must be chargeable against the proportionate part of corpus held in trust for payment of income to that beneficiary as if it constituted a separate trust (whether or not physically segregated). See section 674(b) (5) (B).

(iii) This subparagraph may be illustrated by the following examples:

Example (1). A trust instrument provides for payment of the income to the grantor's two brothers for life, and for payment of the corpus to the grantor's nephews in equal shares. The grantor reserves the power to distribute corpus to pay medical expenses that may be incurred by his brothers or nephews. The grantor is not treated as an owner by reason of this power because section 674(b) (5) (A) excepts a power, exercisable by any person, to invade corpus for any beneficiary, including a remainderman, if the power is limited by a reasonably definite standard which is set forth in the trust instrument. However, if the power were also exercisable in favor of a person (for example, a sister) who was not otherwise a beneficiary of the trust, section 674(b) (5) (A) would not be applicable.

Example (2). The facts are the same as in example (1) except that the grantor reserves the power to distribute any part of the corpus to his brothers or to his nephews for their happiness. The grantor is treated as the owner of the trust. Paragraph (5) (A) of section 674 (b) is inapplicable because the power is not limited by a reasonably definite standard. Paragraph (5) (B) is inapplicable because the power to distribute corpus permits a distribution of corpus to persons other than current income beneficiaries.

Example (3). A trust instrument provides for payment of the income to the grantor's two adult sons in equal shares for 10 years, after which the corpus is to be distributed to his grandchildren in equal shares. The grantor reserves the power to pay over to each son up to one-half of the corpus during the 10-year period, but any such payment shall proportionately reduce subsequent income and corpus payments made to the son receiving the corpus. Thus, if one-half of the corpus is paid to one son, all the income from the remaining half is thereafter payable to the other son. The grantor is not treated as an owner under section 674(a) by reason of this power because it qualifies under the exception of section 674(b) (5) (B).

(6) Powers to withhold income temporarily. (i) Section 674(b) (6) excepts a power which, in general, enables the holder merely to effect a postponement in the time when the ordinary income is enjoyed by a current income beneficiary. Specifically, there is excepted a power to distribute or apply ordinary income to or for a current income beneficiary or to accumulate the income, if the accumulated income must ultimately be payable either:

(a) To the beneficiary from whom it was withheld, his estate, or his appointees (or persons designated by name, as a class, or otherwise as alternate takers in default of appointment) under a power of appointment held by the beneficiary which does not exclude from the class of possible appointees any person other than the beneficiary, his estate, his creditors, or the creditors of his estate (section 674(b) (6) (A));

(b) To the beneficiary from whom it was withheld, or if he does not survive a date of distribution which could reasonably be expected to occur within his lifetime, to his appointees (or alternate takers in default of appointment) under any power of appointment, general or special, or if he has no power of appointment to one or more designated alternate takers (other than the grantor or the grantor's estate) whose shares have been irrevocably specified in the trust instrument (section 674(b) (6) (A) and the flush material following); or

(c) On termination of the trust, or in conjunction with a distribution of corpus which is augmented by the accumulated income, to the current income beneficiaries in shares which have been irrevocably specified in the trust instrument, or if any beneficiary does not survive a date of distribution which would reasonably be expected to occur within his lifetime, to his appointees (or alternate takers in default of appointment) under any power of appointment, general or special, or if he has no power of appointment to one or more designated alternate takers (other than the grantor or the grantor's estate) whose shares have been irrevocably specified in the trust instrument (section 674(b) (6) (B) and the flush material following).

(In the application of (a) of this subdivision, if the accumulated income of a trust is ultimately payable to the estate of the current income beneficiary, or is ultimately payable to his appointees, or takers in default of appointment, under a power of the type described in (a) of this subdivision, it need not be payable to the beneficiary from whom it was withheld under any circumstances. Furthermore, if a trust otherwise qualifies for the exception in (a) of this subdivision the trust income will not be considered to be taxable to the grantor under section 677 by reason of the existence of the power of appointment referred to in (a) of this subdivision.) In general, the exception in section 674(b) (6) is not applicable if the power is in substance one to shift ordinary income from one beneficiary to another. Thus, a power will not qualify for this exception if ordinary income may be distributed to beneficiary A, or may be added to corpus which is ultimately payable to beneficiary B, a remainderman who is not a current income beneficiary. However, section 674(b) (6) (B), and (c) of this subdivision, permit a limited power to shift ordinary income among current income beneficiaries, as illustrated in example (1) of this subparagraph.

(ii) The application of section 674 (b) (6) may be illustrated by the following examples:

Example (1). A trust instrument provides that the income shall be paid in equal shares to the grantor's two adult daughters but the grantor reserves the power to withhold from either beneficiary any part of that beneficiary's share of income and to add it to the corpus of the trust until the younger daughter reaches the age of 30 years. When the younger daughter reaches the age of 30, the trust is to terminate and the corpus is to be divided equally between the two daughters or their estates. Although exercise of this power may permit the shifting of accumulated income from one beneficiary to the other (since the corpus with the accumulations is to be divided equally) the power is excepted under section 674(b) (6) (B) and subdivision (i) (c) of this subparagraph.

Example (2). The facts are the same as in example (1), except that the grantor of the trust reserves the power to distribute accumulated income to the beneficiaries in such shares as he chooses. The combined powers are not excepted by section 674(b) (6) (B) since income accumulated pursuant to the first power is neither required to be payable only in conjunction with a corpus distribution nor required to be payable in shares specified in the trust instrument. See, however, section 674 (c) and § 1.674(c)-1 for the effect of such a power if it is exercisable only by independent trustees.

Example (3). A trust provides for payment of income to the grantor's adult son with the grantor retaining the power to accumulate the income until the grantor's death, when all accumulations are to be paid to the son. If the son predeceases the grantor, all accumulations are, at the death of the grantor, to be paid to his daughter, or if she is not living, to alternate takers (which do not include the grantor's estate) in specified shares. The power is excepted under section 674(b) (6) (A) since the date of distribution (the date of the grantor's death) may, in the usual case, reasonably be expected to occur during the beneficiary's (the son's) lifetime. It is not necessary that the accumulations be payable to the son's estate or his appointees if he should predecease the grantor for this exception to apply.

(7) Power to withhold income during disability. Section 674(b) (7) provides an exception for a power which, in general, will permit ordinary income to be withheld during the legal disability of an income beneficiary or while he is under 21. Specifically, there is excepted a power, exercisable only during the existence of a legal disability of any current income beneficiary or the period during which any income beneficiary is under the age of 21 years, to distribute or apply ordinary income to or for that beneficiary or to accumulate the income and add it to corpus. To qualify under this exception it is not necessary that the income ultimately be payable to the income beneficiary from whom it was withheld, his estate, or his appointees; that is, the accumulated income may be added to corpus and ultimately distributed to others. For example, the grantor is not treated as an owner under section 674 if the income of a trust is payable to his son for life, remainder to his grandchildren, although he reserves the power to accumulate income and add it to corpus while his son is under 21.

(8) Powers to allocate between corpus and income. Paragraph (8) of section 674(b) provides that a power to allocate receipts and disbursements between corpus and income, even though expressed in broad language, will not cause the grantor to be treated as an owner under the general rule of section 674(a).

§ 1.674(c)–1   Excepted powers exercisable only by independent trustees

Section 674(c) provides an exception to the general rule of section 674(a) for certain powers that are exercisable by independent trustees. This exception is in addition to those provided for under section 674(b) which may be held by any person including an independent trustee. The powers to which section 674(c) apply are powers (a) to distribute, apportion, or accumulate income to or for a beneficiary or beneficiaries, or to, for, or within a class of beneficiaries, or (b) to pay out corpus to or for a beneficiary or beneficiaries or to or for a class of beneficiaries (whether or not income beneficiaries). In order for such a power to fall within the exception of section 674(c) it must be exercisable solely (without the approval or consent of any other person) by a trustee or trustees none of whom is the grantor and no more than half of whom are related or subordinate parties who are subservient to the wishes of the grantor. (See section 672(c) for definitions of these terms.) An example of the application of section 674(c) is a trust whose income is payable to the grantor's three adult sons with power in an independent trustee to allocate without restriction the amounts of income to be paid to each son each year. Such a power does not cause the grantor to be treated as the owner of the trust. See, however, the limitations set forth in § 1.674 (d)–2.

§ 1.674(d)–1   Excepted powers exercisable by any trustee other than grantor or spouse

Section 674(d) provides an additional exception to the general rule of section 674(a) for a power to distribute, apportion, or accumulate income to or for a beneficiary or beneficiaries or to, for, or within a class of beneficiaries, whether or not the conditions of section 674(b) (6) or (7) are satisfied, if the power is solely exercisable (without the approval or consent of any other person) by a trustee or trustees none of whom is the grantor or spouse living with the grantor, and if the power is limited by a reasonably definite external standard set forth in the trust instrument (see paragraph (b) (5) of § 1.674(b)–1 with respect to what constitutes a reasonably definite standard). See, however, the limitations set forth in § 1.674(d)–2.

§ 1.674(d)–2   Limitations on exceptions in section 674(b), (c), and (d)

(a) Power to remove trustee. A power in the grantor to remove, substitute, or add trustees (other than a power exercisable only upon limited conditions which do not exist during the taxable year, such as the death or resignation of, or breach of fiduciary duty by, an existing trustee) may prevent a trust from qualifying under section 674(c) or (d). For example, if a grantor has an unrestricted power to remove an independent trustee and substitute any person including himself as trustee, the trust will not qualify under section 674(c) or (d). On the other hand if the grantor's power to remove, substitute, or add trustees is limited so that its exercise could not alter the trust in a manner that would disqualify it under section 674(c) or (d), as the case may be, the power itself does not disqualify the trust. Thus, for example, a power in the grantor to remove or discharge an independent trustee on the condition that he substitute another independent trustee will not prevent a trust from qualifying under section 674(c).

(b) Power to add beneficiaries. The exceptions described in sections 674(b) (5), (6), and (7), (c) and (d) are not applicable if any person has a power to add to the beneficiary or beneficiaries or to a class of beneficiaries designated to receive the income or corpus, except where the action is to provide for after-born or after-adopted children. This limitation does not apply to a power held by a beneficiary to substitute other beneficiaries to succeed to his interest in the trust (so that he would be an adverse party as to the exercise or nonexercise of that power). For example, the limitation does not apply to a power in a beneficiary of a nonspendthrift trust to assign his interest. Nor does the limitation apply to a power held by any person which would qualify as an exception under section 674(b) (3) (relating to testamentary powers).

§ 1.675-1 Administrative powers

(a) General rule. Section 675 provides in effect that the grantor is treated as the owner of any portion of a trust if under the terms of the trust instrument or circumstances attendant on its operation administrative control is exercisable primarily for the benefit of the grantor rather than the bene-ficiaries of the trust. If a grantor retains a power to amend the administrative provisions of a trust instrument which is broad enough to permit an amendment causing the grantor to be treated as the owner of a portion of the trust under section 675, he will be treated as the owner of the portion from its inception. See section 671 and §§ 1.671-2 and 1.671-3 for rules for treatment of items of income, deduction, and credit when a person is treated as the owner of all or only a portion of a trust.

(b) Prohibited controls. The circumstances which cause administrative controls to be considered exercisable primarily for the benefit of the grantor are specifically described in paragraphs (1) through (4) of section 675 as follows:

(1) The existence of a power, exercisable by the grantor or a nonadverse party, or both, without the approval or consent of any adverse party, which enables the grantor or any other person to purchase, exchange, or otherwise deal with or dispose of the corpus or the income of the trust for less than adequate consideration in money or money's worth. Whether the existence of the power itself will constitute the holder an adverse party will depend on the particular circumstances.

(2) The existence of a power exercisable by the grantor or a nonadverse party, or both, which enables the grantor to borrow the corpus or income of the trust, directly or indirectly, without adequate interest or adequate security. However, this paragraph does not apply where a trustee (other than the grantor acting alone) is authorized under a general lending power to make loans to any person without regard to interest or security. A general lending power in the grantor, acting alone as trustee, under which he has power to determine interest rates and the adequacy of security is not in itself an indication that the grantor has power to borrow the corpus or income without adequate interest or security.

(3) The circumstance that the grantor has directly or indirectly borrowed the corpus or income of the trust and has not completely repaid the loan, including any interest, before the beginning of the taxable year. The preceding sentence does not apply to a loan which provides for adequate interest and adequate security, if it is

made by a trustee other than the grantor or a related or subordinate trustee subservient to the grantor. See section 672(c) for definition of "a related or subordinate party".

(4) The existence of certain powers of administration exercisable in a non-fiduciary capacity by any nonadverse party without the approval or consent of any person in a fiduciary capacity. The term "powers of administration" means one or more of the following powers:

(i) A power to vote or direct the voting of stock or other securities of a corporation in which the holdings of the grantor and the trust are significant from the viewpoint of voting control;

(ii) A power to control the investment of the trust funds either by directing investments or reinvestments, or by vetoing proposed investments or reinvestments, to the extent that the trust funds consist of stocks or securities of corporations in which the holdings of the grantor and the trust are significant from the viewpoint of voting control; or

(iii) A power to reacquire the trust corpus by substituting other property of an equivalent value.

If a power is exercisable by a person as trustee, it is presumed that the power is exercisable in a fiduciary capacity primarily in the interests of the beneficiaries. This presumption may be rebutted only by clear and convincing proof that the power is not exercisable primarily in the interests of the beneficiaries. If a power is not exercisable by a person as trustee, the determination of whether the power is exercisable in a fiduciary or a nonfiduciary capacity depends on all the terms of the trust and the circumstances surrounding its creation and administration.

(c) **Authority of trustee.** The mere fact that a power exercisable by a trustee is described in broad language does not indicate that the trustee is authorized to purchase, exchange, or otherwise deal with or dispose of the trust property or income for less than an adequate and full consideration in money or money's worth, or is authorized to lend the trust property or income to the grantor without adequate interest. On the other hand, such authority may be indicated by the actual administration of the trust.

§ 1.676(a)-1 Power to revest title to portion of trust property in grantor; general rule

If a power to revest in the grantor title to any portion of a trust is exercisable by the grantor or a nonadverse party, or both, without the approval or consent of an adverse party, the grantor is treated as the owner of that portion, except as provided in section 676(b) (relating to powers affecting beneficial enjoyment of income only after the expiration of certain periods of time). If the title to a portion of the trust will revest in the grantor upon the exercise of a power by the grantor or a nonadverse party, or both, the grantor is treated as the owner of that portion regardless of whether the power is a power to revoke, to terminate, to alter or amend, or to appoint. See section 671 and §§ 1.671-2 and 1.671-3 for rules for treatment of items of income, deduction, and credit when a person is treated as the owner of all or only a portion of a trust.

§ 1.676(b)-1 Powers exercisable only after a period of time

Section 676(b) provides an exception to the general rule of section 676(a) when the exercise of a power can only affect the beneficial enjoyment of the income of a trust received after the expiration of a period of time which is such that a grantor would not be treated as an owner under section 673 if the power were a reversionary interest. See §§ 1.673(a)-1 and 1.673(b)-1. Thus, for example, a grantor is excepted from the general rule of section 676(a) with respect to ordinary income if exercise of a power to revest corpus in him cannot affect the beneficial enjoyment of the income received within 10 years after the date of transfer of that portion of the trust. It is immaterial for this purpose that the power is vested at the time of the transfer. However, the grantor is subject to the general rule of section 676(a) after the expiration of the period unless the power is relinquished. Thus, in the above example, the grantor may be treated as the owner and be taxed on all income in the eleventh and succeeding years if exercise of the power can affect beneficial enjoyment of income received in those years. If the beginning of the period during which the grantor may revest is postponed, the rules set forth in § 1.673(d)-1 are applicable to determine whether the grantor should be treated as an owner during the period following the postponement.

§ 1.677(a)-1 Income for benefit of grantor; general rule

(a) (1) Scope. Section 677 deals with the treatment of the grantor of a trust as the owner of a portion of the trust because he has retained an interest in the income from that portion. For convenience, "grantor" and "spouse" are generally referred to in the masculine and feminine genders, respectively, but if the grantor is a woman the reference to "grantor" is to her and the reference to "spouse" is to her husband. Section 677 also deals with the treatment of the grantor of a trust as the owner of a portion of the trust because the income from property transferred in trust after October 9, 1969, is, or may be, distributed to his spouse or applied to the payment of premiums on policies of insurance on the life of his spouse. However, section 677 does not apply when the income of a trust is taxable to a grantor's spouse under section 71 (relating to alimony and separate maintenance payments) or section 682 (relating to income of an estate or trust in case of divorce, etc.). See section 671-1(b).

. . . .

(b) Income for benefit of grantor or his spouse; general rule—(1) Property transferred in trust prior to October 10, 1969. . . . .

(2) Property transferred in trust after October 9, 1969. With respect to property transferred in trust after October 9, 1969, the grantor is treated, under section 677, in any taxable year as the owner (whether or not he is treated as an owner under section 674) of a portion of a trust of which the income for the taxable year or for a period not within the exception described in paragraph (e) of this section is, or in the discretion of the grantor, or his spouse, or a nonadverse party, or any combination thereof (without the approval or consent of any adverse party other than the grantor's spouse) may be:

(i) Distributed to the grantor or the grantor's spouse;

(ii) Held or accumulated for future distribution to the grantor or the grantor's spouse; or

(iii) Applied to the payment of premiums on policies of insurance on the life of the grantor or the grantor's spouse, except policies of insurance irrevocably payable for a charitable purpose specified in section 170(c).

With respect to the treatment of a grantor as the owner of a portion of a trust solely because its income is, or may be, distributed or held or accumulated for future distributions to a beneficiary who is his spouse or applied to the payment of premiums for insurance on the spouse's life, section 677(a) applies to the income of a trust solely during the period of the marriage of the grantor to a beneficiary. In the case of divorce or separation, see sections 71 and 682 and the regulations thereunder.

(c) Constructive distribution; cessation of interest. Under section 677 the grantor is treated as the owner of a portion of a trust if he has retained any interest which might, without the approval or consent of an adverse party, enable him to have the income from that portion, distributed to him at some time, either actually or constructively (subject to the exception described in paragraph (e) of this section). In the case of a transfer in trust after October 9, 1969, the grantor is also treated as the owner of a portion of a trust if he has granted or retained any interest which might, without the approval or consent of an adverse party (other than the grantor's spouse), enable his spouse to have the income from the portion at some time, whether or not within the grantor's lifetime, distributed to the spouse either actually or constructively. See paragraph (b) (2) of this section for additional rules relating to the income of a trust prior to the grantor's marriage to a beneficiary. Constructive distribution to the grantor or to his spouse includes payment on behalf of the grantor or his spouse to another in obedience to his or her direction and payment of premiums upon policies of insurance on the grantor's or his spouse's, life (other than policies of insurance irrevocably payable for charitable purposes specified in section 170 (c)). If the grantor (in the case of property transferred prior to Oct. 10, 1969) or the grantor and his spouse (in the case of property transferred after Oct. 9, 1969) are divested permanently and completely of every interest described in this paragraph, the grantor is not treated as an owner under section 677 after that divesting. The word "interest" as used in this paragraph does not include the possibility that the grantor or his spouse might receive back from a beneficiary an interest in a trust by inheritance. Further, with respect to transfers in trust prior to October 10, 1969, the word "interest" does not include the possibility that the grantor might receive back from a beneficiary an interest in a trust as a surviving spouse under a statutory right of election or a similar right.

(d) Discharge of legal obligation of grantor or his spouse. Under section 677 a grantor is, in general, treated as the owner of a portion of a trust whose income is, or in the discretion of the grantor or a nonadverse party, or both, may be applied in discharge of a legal obligation of the grantor (or his spouse in the case of property transferred in trust by the grantor after October 9, 1969). However, see § 1.677(b)-1 for special rules for trusts whose income may not be applied for the discharge of any legal obligation of the grantor or the grantor's spouse other than the support or maintenance of a beneficiary (other than the grantor's spouse) whom the grantor or grantor's spouse is legally obligated to support.

(e) Exception for certain discretionary rights affecting income. The last sentence of section 677(a) provides that a grantor shall not be treated as the owner when a discretionary right can only affect the beneficial enjoyment of the income of a trust received after a period of time during which a grantor would not be treated as an owner under section 673 if the power were a reversionary interest. See §§ 1.673 (a)-1 and 1.673(b)-1. For example, if the ordinary income of a trust is payable to B for 10 years and then in the grantor's discretion income or corpus may be paid to B or to the grantor (or his spouse in the case of property transferred in trust by the grantor after October 9, 1969), the grantor is not treated as an owner with respect to the ordinary income under section 677 during the first 10 years. He will be treat-

ed as an owner under section 677 after the expiration of the 10-year period unless the power is relinquished. If the beginning of the period during which the grantor may substitute beneficiaries is postponed, the rules set forth in § 1.673(d)-1 are applicable in determining whether the grantor should be treated as an owner during the period following the postponement.

(f) Accumulation of income. If income is accumulated in any taxable year for future distribution to the grantor (or his spouse in the case of property transferred in trust by the grantor after Oct. 9, 1969), section 677 (a) (2) treats the grantor as an owner for that taxable year. The exception set forth in the last sentence of section 677(a) does not apply merely because the grantor (or his spouse in the case of property transferred in trust by the grantor after Oct. 9, 1969) must await the expiration of a period of time before he or she can receive or exercise discretion over previously accumulated income of the trust, even though the period is such that the grantor would not be treated as an owner under section 673 if a reversionary interest were involved. Thus, if income (including capital gains) of a trust is to be accumulated for 10 years and then will be, or at the discretion of the grantor, or his spouse in the case of property transferred in trust after October 9, 1969, or a nonadverse party, may be, distributed to the grantor (or his spouse in the case of property transferred in trust after Oct. 9, 1969), the grantor is treated as the owner of the trust from its inception. If income attributable to transfers after October 9, 1969 is accumulated in any taxable year during the grantor's lifetime for future distribution to his spouse, section 677 (a) (2) treats the grantor as an owner for that taxable year even though his spouse may not receive or exercise discretion over such income prior to the grantor's death.

(g) Examples. The application of section 677(a) may be illustrated by the following examples:

Example (1). G creates an irrevocable trust which provides that the ordinary income is to be payable to him for life and that on his death the corpus shall be distributed to B, an unrelated person. Except for the right to receive income, G retains no right or power which would cause him to be treated as an owner under sections 671 through 677. Under the applicable local law capital gains must be applied to corpus. During the taxable year 1970 the trust has the following items of gross income and deductions:

Dividends $5,000
Capital gain 1,000
Expenses allocable to income 200
Expenses allocable to corpus 100

Since G has a right to receive income he is treated as an owner of a portion of the trust under section 677. Accordingly, he should include the $5,000 of dividends, $200 income expense, and $100 corpus expense in the computation of his taxable income for 1970. He should not include the $1,000 capital gain since that is not attributable to the portion of the trust that he owns. See § 1.671-3(b). The tax consequences of the capital gain are governed by the provisions of subparts A, B, C, and D (section 641 and following), part I, subchapter J, chapter 1 of the Code. Had the trust sustained a capital loss in any amount the loss would likewise not be included in the computation of G's taxable income, but would also be governed by the provisions of such subparts.

Example (2). G creates a trust which provides that the ordinary income is payable to his adult son. Ten years and one day from the date of transfer or on the death of his son, whichever is earlier, corpus is to revert to G. In addition, G retains a discretionary right to receive $5,000 of ordinary income each year. (Absent the exercise of this right all the ordinary income is to be distributed to his son.) G retained no other right or power which would cause him to be treated as an owner under subpart E (section 671 and following). Under the terms of the trust instrument and applicable local law capital gains must be applied to corpus. During the taxable year 1970 the trust had the following items of income and deductions:

Dividends $10,000
Capital gain 2,000
Expenses allocable to income 400
Expenses allocable to corpus 200

Since the capital gain is held or accumulated for future distributions to G, he is treated under section 677(a)(2) as an owner of a portion of the trust to which the gain is attributable. See § 1.671-3(b).

Therefore, he must include the capital gain in the computation of his taxable income. (Had the trust sustained a capital loss in any amount, G would likewise include that loss in the computation of his taxable income.) In addition, because of G's discretionary right (whether exercised or not) he is treated as the owner of a portion of the trust which will permit a distribution of income to him of $5,000. Accordingly, G includes dividends of $5,208.33 and income expenses of $208.33 in computing his taxable income, determined in the following manner:

Total dividends $10,000.00
Less: Expenses allocable to income .. 400.00

Distributable income of the trust 9,600.00

Portion of dividends attributable to G (5,000/9,600 × $10,000) 5,208.33
Portion of income expenses attributable to G (5,000/9,600 × $400) 208.33

Amount of income subject to discretionary right 5,000.00

In accordance with § 1.671-3(c), G also takes into account $104.17 (5,000/9,600 × $200) of corpus expenses in computing his tax liability. The portion of the dividends and expenses of the trust not attributable to G are governed by the provisions of Subparts A through D.

§ 1.677(b)-1 Trusts for support

(a) Section 677(b) provides that a grantor is not treated as the owner of a trust merely because its income may in the discretion of any person other than the grantor (except when he is acting as trustee or cotrustee) be applied or distributed for the support or maintenance of a beneficiary (other than the grantor's spouse in the case of income from property transferred in trust after October 9, 1969), such as the child of the grantor, whom the grantor or his spouse is legally obligated to support. If income of the current year of the trust is actually so applied or distributed the grantor may be treated as the owner of any portion of the trust under section 677 to that extent, even though it might have been applied or distributed for other purposes. In the case of property transferred to a trust before October 10, 1969, for the benefit of the grantor's spouse, the grantor may be treated as the owner to the extent income of the current year is actually applied for the support or maintenance of his spouse.

(b) If any amount applied or distributed for the support of a beneficiary, including the grantor's spouse in the case of property transferred in trust before October 10, 1969, whom the grantor is legally obligated to support is paid out of corpus or out of income other than income of the current year, the grantor is treated as a beneficiary of the trust, and the amount applied or distributed is considered to be an amount paid within the meaning of section 661(a)(2), taxable to the grantor under section 662. Thus, he is subject to the other relevant portions of subparts A through D (section 641 and following), part I, subchapter J, chapter 1 of the Code. Accordingly, the grantor may be taxed on an accumulation distribution or a capital gain distribution under subpart D (section 665 and following) of such part I. Those provisions are applied on the basis that the grantor is the beneficiary.

(c) For the purpose of determining the items of income, deduction, and credit of a trust to be included under this section in computing the grantor's tax liability, the income of the trust for the taxable year of distribution will be deemed to have been first distributed. For example, in the case of a trust reporting on the calendar year basis, a distribution made on January 1, 1956, will be deemed to have been made out of ordinary income of the trust for the calendar year 1956 to the extent of the income for that year even though the trust had received no income as of January 1, 1956. Thus, if a distribution of $10,000 is made on January 1, 1956, for the support of the grantor's dependent, the grantor will be treated as the owner of the trust for 1956 to that extent. If the trust received dividends of $5,000 and incurred expenses of $1,000 during that year but subsequent to January 1, he will take into account dividends of $5,000 and expenses of $1,000 in computing his tax liability for 1956. In addition, the grantor will be treated as a beneficiary of the trust with respect to the $6,000 ($10,000 less distributable income of $4,000 (dividends of $5,000 less expenses of $1,000)) paid out of corpus or out of other than income of the current year. See paragraph (b) of this section.

(d) The exception provided in section 677(b) relates solely to the satisfaction of the grantor's legal obligation to support or maintain a beneficiary. Consequently, the general rule of section 677(a) is applicable when in the discretion of the grantor or nonadverse parties income of a trust may be applied in discharge of a grantor's obligations other than his obligation of support or maintenance falling within section 677(b). Thus, if the grantor creates a trust the income of which may in the discretion of a nonadverse party be applied in the payment of the grantor's debts, such as the payment of his rent or other household expenses, he is treated as an owner of the trust regardless of whether the income is actually so applied.

(e) The general rule of section 677 (a), and not section 677(b), is applicable if discretion to apply or distribute income of a trust rests solely in the grantor, or in the grantor in conjunction with other persons, unless in either case the grantor has such discretion as trustee or cotrustee.

(f) The general rule of section 677 (a), and not section 677(b), is applicable to the extent that income is required, without any discretionary determination, to be applied to the support of a beneficiary whom the grantor is legally obligated to support.

§ 1.678(a)–1 Person other than grantor treated as substantial owner; general rule

(a) Where a person other than the grantor of a trust has a power exercisable solely by himself to vest the corpus or the income of any portion of a testamentary or inter vivos trust in himself, he is treated under section 678 (a) as the owner of that portion, except as provided in section 678(b) (involving taxation of the grantor) and section 678(c) (involving an obligation of support). The holder of such a power also is treated as an owner of the trust even though he has partially released or otherwise modified the power so that he can no longer vest the corpus or income in himself, if he has retained such control of the trust as would, if retained by a grantor, subject the grantor to treatment as the owner under sections 671 to 677, inclusive. See section 671 and §§ 1.671–2 and 1.–671–3 for rules for treatment of items of income, deduction, and credit where a person is treated as the owner of all or only a portion of a trust.

(b) Section 678(a) treats a person as an owner of a trust if he has a power exercisable solely by himself to apply the income or corpus for the satisfaction of his legal obligations, other than an obligation to support a dependent (see § 1.678(c)–1) subject to the limitation of section 678(b). Section 678 does not apply if the power is not exercisable solely by himself. However, see § 1.662(a)–4 for principles applicable to income of a trust which, pursuant to the terms of the trust instrument, is used to satisfy the obligations of a person other than the grantor.

§ 1.678(c)–1 Trusts for support

(a) Section 678(a) does not apply to a power which enables the holder, in the capacity of trustee or cotrustee, to apply the income of the trust to the support or maintenance of a person whom the holder is obligated to support, except to the extent the income is so applied. See paragraphs (a), (b), and (c) of § 1.677(b)-1 for applicable principles where any amount is applied for the support or maintenance of a person whom the holder is obligated to support.

(b) The general rule in section 678 (a) (and not the exception in section 678(c)) is applicable in any case in which the holder of a power exercisable solely by himself is able, in any capacity other than that of trustee or co-trustee, to apply the income in discharge of his obligation of support or maintenance.

(c) Section 678(c) is concerned with the taxability of income subject to a power described in section 678(a). It has no application to the taxability of income which is either required to be applied pursuant to the terms of the trust instrument or is applied pursuant to a power which is not described in section 678(a), the taxability of such income being governed by other provisions of the Code. See § 1.662 (a)-4.

§ 1.691(a)-1 Income in respect of a decedent

(a) Scope of section 691. In general, the regulations under section 691 cover: (1) The provisions requiring that amounts which are not includible in gross income for the decedent's last taxable year or for a prior taxable year be included in the gross income of the estate or persons receiving such income to the extent that such amounts constitute "income in respect of a decedent"; (2) the taxable effect of a transfer of the right to such income; (3) the treatment of certain deductions and credit in respect of a decedent which are not allowable to the decedent for the taxable period ending with his death or for a prior taxable year; (4) the allowance to a recipient of income in respect of a decedent of a deduction for estate taxes attributable to the inclusion of the value of the right to such income in the decedent's estate; (5) special provisions with respect to installment obligations acquired from a decedent and with respect to the allowance of a deduction for estate taxes to a surviving annuitant under a joint and survivor annuity contract; and (6) special provisions relating to installment obliga-

tions transmitted at death when prior law applied to the transmission.

(b) General definition. In general, the term "income in respect of a decedent" refers to those amounts to which a decedent was entitled as gross income but which were not properly includible in computing his taxable income for the taxable year ending with the date of his death or for a previous taxable year under the method of accounting employed by the decedent. See the regulations under section 451. Thus, the term includes—

(1) All accrued income of a decedent who reported his income by use of the cash receipts and disbursements method;

(2) Income accrued solely by reason of the decedent's death in case of a decedent who reports his income by use of an accrual method of accounting; and

(3) Income to which the decedent had a contingent claim at the time of his death.

See sections 736 and 753 and the regulations thereunder for "income in respect of a decedent" in the case of a deceased partner.

(c) Prior decedent. The term "income in respect of a decedent" also includes the amount of all items of gross income in respect of a prior decedent, if (1) the right to receive such amount was acquired by the decedent by reason of the death of the prior decedent or by bequest, devise, or inheritance from the prior decedent and if (2) the amount of gross income in respect of the prior decedent was not properly includible in computing the decedent's taxable income for the taxable year ending with the date of his death or for a previous taxable year. See example (2) of paragraph (b) of § 1.691(a)-2.

(d) Items excluded from gross income. Section 691 applies only to the amount of items of gross income in respect of a decedent, and items which are excluded from gross income under subtitle A of the Code are not within the provisions of section 691.

· · · ·

§ 1.691(a)-2 Inclusion in gross income by recipients

(a) Under section 691(a)(1), income in respect of a decedent shall be included in the gross income, for the taxable year when received, of—

(1) The estate of the decedent, if the right to receive the amount is acquired by the decedent's estate from the decedent;

(2) The person who, by reason of the death of the decedent, acquires the right to receive the amount, if the right to receive the amount is not acquired by the decedent's estate from the decedent; or

(3) The person who acquires from the decedent the right to receive the amount by bequest, devise, or inheritance, if the amount is received after a distribution by the decedent's estate of such right.

These amounts are included in the income of the estate or of such persons when received by them whether or not they report income by use of the cash receipts and disbursements method.

(b) The application of paragraph (a) of this section may be illustrated by the following examples, in each of which it is assumed that the decedent kept his books by use of the cash receipts and disbursements method.

Example (1). The decedent was entitled at the date of his death to a large salary payment to be made in equal annual installments over five years. His estate, after collecting two installments, distributed the right to the remaining installment payments to the residuary legatee of the estate. The estate must include in its gross income the two installments received by it, and the legatee must include in his gross income each of the three installments received by him.

Example (2). A widow acquired, by bequest from her husband, the right to receive renewal commissions on life insurance sold by him in his lifetime, which commissions were payable over a period of years. The widow died before having received all of such commissions, and her son inherited the right to receive the rest of the commissions. The commissions received by the widow were includible in her gross income. The commissions received by the son were not includible in the widow's gross income but must be included in the gross income of the son.

Example (3). The decedent owned a Series E United States savings bond, with his wife as co-owner or beneficiary, but died before the payment of such bond. The entire amount of interest accruing on the bond and not includible in income by the decedent, not just the amount accruing after the death of the decedent, would be treated as income to his wife when the bond is paid.

Example (4). A, prior to his death, acquired 10,000 shares of the capital stock of the X Corporation at a cost of $100 per share. During his lifetime, A had entered into an agreement with X Corporation whereby X Corporation agreed to purchase and the decedent agreed that his executor would sell the 10,000 shares of X Corporation stock owned by him at the book value of the stock at the date of A's death.

Upon A's death, the shares are sold by A's executor for $500 a share pursuant to the agreement. Since the sale of stock is consummated after A's death, there is no income in respect of a decedent with respect to the appreciation in value of A's stock to the date of his death. If, in this example, A had in fact sold the stock during his lifetime but payment had not been received before his death, any gain on the sale would constitute income in respect of a decedent when the proceeds were received.

. . . .

§ 1.691(a)-3   Character of gross income

(a) The right to receive an amount of income in respect of a decedent shall be treated in the hands of the estate, or by the person entitled to receive such amount by bequest, devise, or inheritance from the decedent or by reason of his death, as if it had been acquired in the transaction by which the decedent (or a prior decedent) acquired such right, and shall be considered as having the same character it would have had if the decedent (or a prior decedent) had lived and received such amount. The provisions of section 1014(a), relating to the basis of property acquired from a decedent, do not apply to these amounts in the hands of the estate and such persons. See section 1014(c).

. . . .

§ 1.691(a)-4   Transfer of right to income in respect of a decedent

(a) Section 691(a) (2) provides the rules governing the treatment of income in respect of a decedent (or a prior decedent) in the event a right to receive such income is transferred by the estate or person entitled thereto by bequest, devise, or inheritance, or by reason of the death of the decedent. In general, the transferor must include in his gross income for the taxable period in which the transfer occurs the amount of the consideration, if any, received for the right or the fair market value of the right at the time of the transfer, whichever is greater. Thus, upon a sale of such right by the estate or person entitled to receive it, the fair market value of the right or the amount received upon the sale, whichever is greater, is included in the gross income of the vendor. Similarly, if such right is disposed of by gift, the fair market value of the right at the time of the gift must be included in the gross income of the donor. In the case of a satisfaction of an installment obligation at other than face value, which is likewise considered a transfer under section 691(a) (2), see § 1.691(a)-5.

(b) If the estate of a decedent or any person transmits the right to income in respect of a decedent to another who would be required by section 691(a) (1) to include such income when received in his gross income, only the transferee will include such income when received in his gross income. In this situation, a transfer within the meaning of section 691(a) (2) has not occurred. This paragraph may be illustrated by the following:

(1) If a person entitled to income in respect of a decedent dies before receiving such income, only his estate or other person entitled to such income by bequest, devise, or inheritance from the latter decedent, or by reason of the death of the latter decedent, must include such amount in gross income when received.

(2) If a right to income in respect of a decedent is transferred by an estate to a specific or residuary legatee, only the specific or residuary legatee must include such income in gross income when received.

(3) If a trust to which is bequeathed a right of a decedent to certain payments of income terminates and transfers the right to a beneficiary, only the beneficiary must include such income in gross income when received.

If the transferee described in subparagraphs (1), (2), and (3) of this paragraph transfers his right to receive the amounts in the manner described in paragraph (a) of this section, the principles contained in paragraph (a) are applied to such transfer. On the other hand, if the transferee transmits his right in the manner described in this paragraph, the principles of this paragraph are again applied to such transfer.

§ 1.691(b)-1 Allowance of deductions and credit in respect of decedents

(a) Under section 691(b) the expenses, interest, and taxes described in sec-

tions 162, 163, 164, and 212 for which the decedent (or a prior decedent) was liable, which were not properly allowable as a deduction in his last taxable year or any prior taxable year, are allowed when paid—

(1) As a deduction by the estate; or

(2) If the estate was not liable to pay such obligation, as a deduction by the person who by bequest, devise, or inheritance from the decedent or by reason of the death of the decedent acquires, subject to such obligation, an interest in property of the decedent (or the prior decedent).

Similar treatment is given to the foreign tax credit provided by section 33. For the purposes of subparagraph (2) of this paragraph, the right to receive an amount of gross income in respect of a decedent is considered property of the decedent; on the other hand, it is not necessary for a person, otherwise within the provisions of subparagraph (2) of this paragraph, to receive the right to any income in respect of a decedent. Thus, an heir who receives a right to income in respect of a decedent (by reason of the death of the decedent) subject to an income tax imposed by a foreign country during the decedent's life, which tax must be satisfied out of such income, is entitled to the credit provided by section 33 when he pays the tax. If a decedent who reported income by use of the cash receipts and disbursements method owned real property on which accrued taxes had become a lien, and if such property passed directly to the heir of the decedent in a jurisdiction in which real property does not become a part of a decedent's estate, the heir, upon paying such taxes, may take the same deduction under section 164 that would be allowed to the decedent if, while alive, he had made such payment.

(b) The deduction for percentage depletion is allowable only to the person (described in section 691(a) (1)) who receives the income in respect of the decedent to which the deduction relates, whether or not such person receives the property from which such income is derived. Thus, an heir who (by reason of the decedent's death) receives income derived from sales of units of mineral by the decedent (who reported income by use of the cash receipts and disbursements method) shall be allowed the deduction for percentage depletion, computed on the gross income from such number of units as if the heir had the same economic interest in the property as the decedent. Such heir need not also receive any interest in the mineral property other than such income. If the decedent did not compute his deduction for depletion on the basis of percentage depletion, any deduction for depletion to which the decedent was entitled at the date of his death would be allowable in computing his taxable income for his last taxable year, and there can be no deduction in respect of the decedent by any other person for such depletion.

§ 1.701–1 Partners, not partnership, subject to tax

Partners are liable for income tax only in their separate capacities. Partnerships as such are not subject to the income tax imposed by subtitle A but are required to make returns of income under the provisions of section 6031 and the regulations thereunder. For definition of the terms "partner" and "partnership", see sections 761 and 7701 (a) (2), and the regulations thereunder.

§ 1.702–1 Income and credits of partner

(a) **General rule.** Each partner is required to take into account separately in his return his distributive share, whether or not distributed, of each class or item of partnership income, gain, loss, deduction, or credit described in subparagraphs (1) through (9) of this paragraph. (For the taxable year in which a partner includes his distributive share of partnership taxable income, see section 706(a) and § 1.706–1 (a). Such distributive share shall be determined as provided in section 704 and § 1.704–1). Accordingly, in determining his income tax:

(1) Each partner shall take into account, as part of his gains and losses from sales or exchanges of capital assets held for not more than 1 year (6 months for taxable years beginning before 1977; 9 months for taxable years beginning in 1977), his distributive share of the combined net amount of such gains and losses of the partnership.

(2) Each partner shall take into account, as part of his gains and losses from sales or exchanges of capital assets held for more than 1 year (6 months for taxable years beginning before 1977; 9 months for taxable years beginning in 1977), his distributive share of the combined net amount of such gains and losses of the partnership.

(3) Each partner shall take into account, as part of his gains and losses from sales or exchanges of property described in section 1231 (relating to property used in the trade or business and involuntary conversions), his distributive share of the combined net amount of such gains and losses of the partnership. The partnership shall not combine such items with items set forth in subparagraph (1) or (2) of this paragraph.

(4) Each partner shall take into account, as part of the charitable contributions paid by him, his distributive share of each class of charitable contributions paid by the partnership within the partnership's taxable year. Section 170 determines the extent to which such amount may be allowed as a deduction to the partner. For the definition of the term "charitable contribution", see section 170(c).

(5) Each partner shall take into account, as part of the dividends received by him from domestic corporations, his distributive share of dividends received by the partnership, with respect to which the partner is entitled to a credit under section 34 (for dividends received on or before December 31, 1964), an exclusion under section 116, or a deduction under part VIII, subchapter B, chapter 1 of the Code.

.   .   .   .

(8) (i) Each partner shall take into account separately, as part of any class of income, gain, loss, deduction, or credit, his distributive share of the following items: recoveries of bad debts, prior taxes, and delinquency amounts (section 111); gains and losses from wagering transactions (section 165(d)); soil and water conservation expenditures (section 175); nonbusiness expenses as described in section 212; medical, dental, etc., expenses (section 213); expenses for care of certain dependents (section 214); alimony, etc., payments (section 215); amounts representing taxes and interest paid to co-

operative housing corporations (section 216); intangible drilling and developments costs (section 263(c)); pre-1970 exploration expenditures (section 615); certain mining exploration expenditures (section 617); income, gain, or loss to the partnership under section 751(b); and any items of income, gain, loss, deduction, or credit subject to a special allocation under the partnership agreement which differs from the allocation of partnership taxable income or loss generally.

(ii) Each partner must also take into account separately his distributive share of any partnership item which if separately taken into account by any partner would result in an income tax liability for that partner different from that which would result if that partner did not take the item into account separately. Thus, if any partner would qualify for the retirement income credit under section 37 if the partnership pensions and annuities, interest, rents, dividends, and earned income were separately stated, such items must be separately stated for all partners. Under section 911 (a), if any partner is a bona fide resident of a foreign country who may exclude from his gross income the part of his distributive share which qualifies as earned income as defined in section 911 (b), the earned income of the partnership for all partners must be separately stated. Similarly, all relevant items of income or deduction of the partnership must be separately stated for all partners in determining the applicability of section 270 (relating to "hobby losses") and the recomputation of tax thereunder for any partner.

(iii) Each partner shall aggregate the amount of his separate deductions or exclusions and his distributive share of partnership deductions or exclusions separately stated in determining the amount allowable to him of any deduction or exclusion under subtitle A of the Code as to which a limitation is imposed. For example, partner A has individual domestic exploration expenditures of $300,000. He is also a member of the AB partnership which in 1971 in its first year of operation has foreign exploration expenditures of $400,000. A's distributable share of this item is $200,000. However, the total amount of his distributable share that A can deduct as exploration expenditures under section

617(a) is limited to $100,000 in view of the limitation provided in section 617 (h). Therefore, the excess of $100,000 ($200,000 minus $100,000) is not deductible by A.

(9) Each partner shall also take into account separately his distributive share of the taxable income or loss of the partnership, exclusive of items requiring separate computations under subparagraphs (1) through (8) of this paragraph. For limitation on allowance of a partner's distributive share of partnership losses, see section 704 (d) and paragraph (d) of § 1.704-1.

(b) **Character of items constituting distributive share.** The character in the hands of a partner of any item of income, gain, loss, deduction, or credit described in section 702 (a) (1) through (8) shall be determined as if such item were realized directly from the source from which realized by the partnership or incurred in the same manner as incurred by the partnership. For example, a partner's distributive share of gain from the sale of depreciable property used in the trade or business of the partnership shall be considered as gain from the sale of such depreciable property in the hands of the partner.

(c) **Gross income of a partner.** (1) Where it is necessary to determine the amount or character of the gross income of a partner, his gross income shall include the partner's distributive share of the gross income of the partnership, that is, the amount of gross income of the partnership from which was derived the partner's distributive share of partnership taxable income or loss (including items described in section 702 (a) (1) through (8)). For example, a partner is required to include his distributive share of partnership gross income:

(i) In computing his gross income for the purpose of determining the necessity of filing a return (section 6012 (a));

(ii) In determining the application of the provisions permitting the spreading of income for services rendered over a 36-month period (section 1301, as in effect for taxable years beginning before January 1, 1964);

(iii) In computing the amount of gross income received from sources within possessions of the United States (section 931); and

(iv) In determining a partner's "gross income from farming" (sections 175 and 6073).

(2) In determining the applicability of the 6-year period of limitation on assessment and collection provided in section 6501 (e) (relating to omission of more than 25 percent of gross income), a partner's gross income includes his distributive share of partnership gross income (as described in section 6501 (e) (1) (A) (i)). In this respect, the amount of partnership gross income from which was derived the partner's distributive share of any item of partnership income, gain, loss, deduction, or credit (as included or disclosed in the partner's return) is considered as an amount of gross income stated in the partner's return for the purposes of section 6501 (e). For example, A, who is entitled to one-fourth of the profits of the ABCD partnership, which has $10,000 gross income and $2,000 taxable income, reports only $300 as his distributive share of partnership profits. A should have shown $500 as his distributive share of profits, which amount was derived from $2,500 of partnership gross income. However, since A included only $300 on his return without explaining in the return the difference of $200, he is regarded as having stated in his return only $1,500 ($300/$500 of $2,500) as gross income from the partnership.

(d) Partners in community property States. If separate returns are made by a husband and wife domiciled in a community property State, and only one spouse is a member of the partnership, the part of his or her distributive share of any item or items listed in paragraph (a) (1) through (9) of this section which is community property, or which is derived from community property, should be reported by the husband and wife in equal proportions.

§ 1.702-2 Net operating loss deduction of partner

For the purpose of determining a net operating loss deduction under section 172, a partner shall take into account his distributive share of items of income, gain, loss, deduction, or credit of the partnership. The character of any such item shall be determined as if such item were realized directly from the source from which realized by the partnership, or incurred in the same manner as incurred by the partnership. See section 702(b) and paragraph (b) of § 1.702–1. To the extent necessary to determine the allowance under section 172(d) (4) of the nonbusiness deductions of a partner (arising from both partnership and nonpartnership sources), the partner shall separately take into account his distributive share of the deductions of the partnership which are not attributable to a trade or business and combine such amount with his nonbusiness deductions from nonpartnership sources. Such partner shall also separately take into account his distributive share of the gross income of the partnership not derived from a trade or business and combine such amount with his nonbusiness income from nonpartnership sources. See section 172 and the regulations thereunder.

§ 1.703–1 Partnership computations

(a) Income and deductions. (1) The taxable income of a partnership shall be computed in the same manner as the taxable income of an individual, except as otherwise provided in this section. A partnership is required to state separately in its return the items described in section 702 (a) (1) through (7) and, in addition, to attach to its return a statement setting forth separately those items described in section 702 (a) (8) which the partner is required to take into account separately in determining his income tax. See paragraph (a) (8) of § 1.702–1. The partnership is further required to compute and to state separately in its return:

(i) As taxable income under section 702 (a) (9), the total of all other items of gross income (not separately stated) over the total of all other allowable deductions (not separately stated), or

(ii) As loss under section 702 (a) (9), the total of all other allowable deductions (not separately stated) over the total of all other items of gross income (not separately stated).

The taxable income or loss so computed shall be accounted for by the partners in accordance with their partnership agreement.

(2) The partnership is not allowed the following deductions:

(i) The standard deduction provided in section 141.

(ii) The deduction for personal exemptions provided in section 151.

(iii) The deduction provided in section 164 (a) for taxes, described in section 901, paid or accrued to foreign countries or possessions of the United States. Each partner's distributive share of such taxes shall be accounted for separately by him as provided in section 702 (a) (6).

(iv) The deduction for charitable contributions provided in section 170. Each partner is considered as having paid within his taxable year his distributive share of any contribution or gift, payment of which was actually made by the partnership within its taxable year ending within or with the partner's taxable year. This item shall be accounted for separately by the partners as provided in section 702 (a) (4). See also paragraph (b) of § 1.702-1.

(v) The net operating loss deduction provided in section 172. See § 1.702-2.

(vi) The additional itemized deductions for individuals provided in part VII, subchapter B, chapter 1 of the Code, as follows: expenses for production of income (section 212); medical, dental, etc., expenses (section 213); expenses for care of certain dependents (section 214); alimony, etc., payments (section 215); and amounts representing taxes and interest paid to cooperative housing corporation (section 216). However, see paragraph (a) (8) of § 1.702-1.

(vii) The deduction for capital gains provided by section 1202 and the deduction for capital loss carryover provided by section 1212.

(b) Elections of the partnership— (1) General rule. Any elections (other than those described in subparagraph (2) of this paragraph) affecting the computation of income derived from a partnership shall be made by the partnership. For example, elections of methods of accounting, of computing depreciation, of treating soil and water conservation expenditures, and the option to deduct as expenses intangible drilling and development costs, shall be made by the partnership and not by the partners separately. All partnership elections are applicable to all partners equally, but any election made by a partnership shall not apply to any partner's nonpartnership interests.

. . . .

§ 1.704-1 Partner's distributive share

(a) Effect of partnership agreement. A partner's distributive share of any item or class of items of income, gain, loss, deduction, or credit of the partnership shall be determined by the partnership agreement, unless otherwise provided by section 704 and paragraphs (b) through (e) of this section. For definition of partnership agreement see section 761 (c).

(b) Distributive share determined by income or loss ratio. (1) If the partnership agreement makes no specific provision for the manner of sharing one or more items or classes of items, a partner's distributive share of such items shall be determined in accordance with the provisions of the partnership agreement for the division of the general profits or losses (that is, the taxable income or loss of the partnership as described in section 702 (a) (9)). In applying this rule, the manner in which the net profit or loss (computed after excluding any item subject to a recognized special allocation) is actually credited on the partnership books to the accounts of the partners will generally determine each partner's share of taxable income or loss as described in section 702 (a) (9).

(2) If the principal purpose of any provision in the partnership agreement determining a partner's distributive share of a particular item is to avoid or evade the Federal income tax, the provision shall be disregarded and the partners' distributive shares of that item shall be determined in accordance with the ratio in which the partners divide the general profits or losses of the partnership (as described in section 702 (a) (9)). In determining whether the principal purpose of any provision in the partnership agreement for a special allocation is the avoidance or evasion of Federal income tax, the provision must be considered in relation to all the surrounding facts and circumstances. Among the relevant circum-

stances are the following: Whether the partnership or a partner individually has a business purpose for the allocation; whether the allocation has "substantial economic effect", that is, whether the allocation may actually affect the dollar amount of the partners' shares of the total partnership income or loss independently of tax consequences; whether related items of income, gain, loss, deduction, or credit from the same source are subject to the same allocation; whether the allocation was made without recognition of normal business factors and only after the amount of the specially allocated item could reasonably be estimated; the duration of the allocation; and the overall tax consequences of the allocation. The application of the provisions of this subparagraph may be illustrated by the following examples:

Example (1). The provisions of a partnership agreement for a year in which the partnership incurs losses on the sale of depreciable property used in the trade or business are amended to allocate such losses to one partner who has no such gains individually. An equivalent amount of partnership loss or deduction of a different character is allocated to other partners who individually have gains from the sale of depreciable property used in the trade or business. Since the purpose and effect of this allocation is solely to reduce the taxes of certain partners without actually affecting their shares of partnership income, such allocation will not be recognized. Under section 704(b)(2), those items will be allocated to all the partners in accordance with the provisions of the partnership agreement for sharing partnership income or loss generally.

Example (2). The provisions of a partnership agreement allocate to a partner who is a resident of a foreign country a percentage of the profit derived from operations conducted by him within such country, which percentage is greater than his distributive share of partnership income generally. Such allocation has substantial economic effect and will be recognized in the absence of other circumstances showing that the principal purpose was tax avoidance or evasion.

Example (3). Rather than impair the credit standing of the AB partnership by a distribution, the partners agree to invest surplus partnership funds in an equal dollar amount of municipal bonds and corporate stock. The partners further agree that A is to receive all the interest income and gain or loss from tax-exempt bonds and B is to receive all the dividend income and gain or loss from corporate stock. Such allocation has substantial economic effect and will be recognized in the absence of other circumstances showing that the principal purpose was tax avoidance or evasion. On the other hand, under an agreement with respect to partnership CD, it is provided that C's distributive share of income shall be the first $10,000 of tax-exempt income, and D's distributive share of income shall be the first $10,000 of dividend income, the balances to be divided

equally. Since the principal purpose of this provision is to allocate tax-exempt interest to C, who is in a higher income tax bracket than D, it will be disregarded. Each partner's distributive share of such interest and dividends will then be allocated in accordance with the provisions of the partnership agreement for sharing partnership income or loss generally.

Example (4). KL is a brokerage partnership with assets consisting of securities with a basis of $20,000 and a value of $50,000. M makes a $25,000 cash contribution to the partnership in order to become an equal partner. Subsequently, when the value of the securities has appreciated to $74,000, they are sold. Of the $54,000 taxable gain on the sale of the securities, $24,000 (appreciation in value occurring after M became a partner) is allocated in equal shares to K, L, and M, in accordance with the ratio for sharing profits and losses generally. The $30,000 balance is allocated to K and L in the profit and loss ratio existing before M became a partner. This latter allocation attributes to K and L the appreciation in value of the securities occurring before M became a partner, even though the cash proceeds are a partnership asset in which all three partners share equally. This allocation has substantial economic effect and will be recognized in the absence of other circumstances showing that the principal purpose of the allocation was tax avoidance or evasion.

Example (5). G and H, each of whom is engaged as a sole proprietor in the business of developing and marketing electronic devices, enter into a partnership agreement to develop and market electronic devices. H contributes $2,500 cash and agrees to devote his full-time services to the partnership. G contributes $100,000 cash and agrees to obtain a loan for the partnership of any additional capital needed. The partnership agreement provides that the full amount of any research and experimental expenditures and any interest on partnership loans are to be charged to G. It also provides that G's distributive share is to be 90 percent of partnership income or loss computed without reduction by such research and experimental expenditures and such interest, until all loans have been repaid and G has received through his 90 percent share of income an amount equal to the full amount of such research and experimental expenditures, of such interest, and his share of any partnership operating losses. During this time H's distributive share will be 10 percent. Thereafter, G and H will share profits and losses equally. Since all of the research and experimental expenditures and interest specially allocated to G are in fact borne by G, the allocation will be recognized in the absence of other circumstances showing that its principal purpose was tax avoidance or evasion.

(c) Contributed property—(1) In general. Where property has actually been contributed by a partner to a partnership (so as to become partnership property as among the partners and not merely property subject to the claims of partnership creditors), section 704 (c) and this paragraph provide rules for determining a partner's distributive share of depreciation, depletion, or gain or loss with respect to such contributed property. These rules do not apply to property, only the use of which is permitted the partnership by the partner who owns it. Section 704 (c) and this paragraph provide certain alternatives in determining the partners' distributive shares of such items in order to account for precontribution appreciation or diminution in value of the property contributed. When the partnership agreement is silent as to the treatment of such items with respect to contributed property (and if such property is not an undivided interest as described in section 704 (c) (3)), depreciation, depletion, or gain or loss with respect to such property shall be treated in the same manner as though such items arose with respect to property purchased by the partnership. The application of this provision may be illustrated by the following examples:

Example (1). A and B form an equal partnership. A contributes $1,000 cash and B contributes inventory with an adjusted basis to him of $800 and a fair market value of $1,000. Under section 723, the basis of the inventory to the partnership is also $800. During the year, the inventory is sold for $1,100. There is no provision in the partnership agreement for treatment of items with respect to contributed property. Under section 704(c) (1), the $300 profit on the sale of the inventory is treated as if it were gain on property that had been purchased by the partnership and subsequently sold. Therefore, each partner's distributive share of such profit on the inventory is $150.

Example (2). C and D form an equal partnership. C contributes machinery worth $10,000 with an adjusted basis to him of $4,000. D contributes $10,000 cash. Under the provisions of section 722, the basis of C's partnership interest is $4,000 and the basis of D's interest is $10,000. There is no provision in the partnership agreement relating to contributed property. If the contributed property depreciates at an annual rate of 10 percent, the partnership will have an annual depreciation deduction of $400, which will result in a reduction of $200 in each partner's distributive share of partnership income. Thus, at the end of the first year, the adjusted basis of the contributed property will be $3,600. If the partnership has no other taxable income or loss for that year, each partner will have a deduction of $200, representing his distributive share of partnership loss for the year. C's adjusted basis for his interest will be $3,800 ($4,000, the original basis of his interest, reduced by $200); D's adjusted basis will be $9,800 ($10,000, reduced by $200).

. . . . .

(2) Effect of partnership agreement. (i) If the partners so provide in the partnership agreement, depreciation, depletion, or gain or loss with respect to contributed property may be allocat-

ed among the partners in a manner which takes into account all or any portion of the difference between the adjusted basis and the fair market value of contributed property at the time of contribution. The allocation may apply to all contributed property or to specific items. The appreciation or diminution in value represented by the difference between the adjusted basis and the fair market value of contributed property at the time of contribution may thus be attributed to the contributing partner upon a subsequent sale or exchange of the property by the partnership. Such appreciation or diminution also may be used in allocating the allowable depreciation or depletion with respect to such property among the contributing partner and the noncontributing partners. In any case, however, the total depreciation, depletion, or gain or loss allocated to the partners is limited to a "ceiling" which cannot exceed the amount of gain or loss realized by the partnership or the depreciation or depletion allowable to it. The application of this subdivision may be illustrated by the following examples:

Example (1). Assume that partners C and D, in examples (2) and (3) of subparagraph (1) of this paragraph, agree under section 704(c) (2) to attribute to C, the contributor of the machinery, the potential gain of $6,000 represented by the difference between its adjusted basis of $4,000 and its fair market value of $10,000. With his contribution of $10,000 cash, D has, in effect, purchased an undivided one-half interest in the property for $5,000. Since the property depreciates at an annual rate of 10 percent, D would have been entitled to a depreciation deduction of $500 per year. However, since under the "ceiling" approach the partnership is allowed only $400 per year (10 percent of $4,000), no more than $400 may be allocated between the partners, i. e., the partnership cannot allocate $500 of depreciation to D and thereby treat C as if C had received an additional $100 of income. Therefore, the partners allocate the $400 deduction for depreciation entirely to D and none to C, the contributor. At the end of the first year, the adjusted basis of the contributed property will be $3,600. Since the $400 deduction is allocated entirely to D, if the partnership has no other taxable income or loss, C will have no income or loss, and D will have a deduction of $400. C's basis for his interest will remain $4,000. D's adjusted basis for his interest will be $9,600 ($10,000, the original basis of his interest, reduced by the deduction of $400).

Example (2). Assume that the partners in example (1) of this subdivision also agree under section 704(c) (2) that, upon a sale of the contributed property, the portion of the proceeds attributable to the excess of the fair market value of the property at date of contribution (less accumulated depreciation on such value) over its basis at date of contribution (less accumulated depreciation on such basis) shall result in gain to the contributing partner only. If the property is sold at the beginning of the second year of partnership operation for $9,000, the partnership gain of $5,400 ($9,000, the amount realized, less the adjusted basis of $3,-600) must be allocated to the partners under the terms of the agreement. The fair market value of the property as depreciated is $9,000 ($10,000, the value on contribution, less $1,000, the accumulated depreciation on such value). Under section 704(c)(2) and the terms of the partnership agreement, the $5,400 difference between $9,000, the fair market value as depreciated, and $3,600, the adjusted basis of the property, represents the portion of the gain to be allocated to C. None of this gain is allocated to D. (If the property were sold for more than $9,000, the portion of the gain in excess of $5,-400 would be allocated equally between the partners in accordance with their agreement for sharing gains. If the property were sold for less than $9,000, the entire gain would be allocated to C and nothing to D.) If the partnership and partners engaged in no other transactions that year, C will report a gain of $5,400, and D, no income or loss. C's adjusted basis for his interest will then be $9,400 ($4,000, his original basis, increased by the gain of $5,400). D's adjusted basis will be $9,600 ($10,000, his original basis, less $400 depreciation deduction in the first partnership year). If the partnership is then terminated, and its assets consisting of $19,000 in cash are distributed to the partners pro rata in liquidation of their interests, C will have a capital gain of $100 ($9,500, the amount received, less $9,400, the adjusted basis of his interest). D will have a capital loss of $100 (the excess of D's adjusted basis, $9,600, over the amount received, $9,500).

(ii) For the effect of an agreement under section 704 (c) (2) on undivided interests in property contributed to the partnership where the partners' interests in the capital and profits of the partnership do not correspond with such undivided interests, see subparagraph (3) (ii) of this paragraph.

(3) Undivided interests. (i) Section 704 (c) (3) provides a special rule for the allocation of depreciation, depletion, or gain or loss with respect to undivided interests in property contributed by the partners to a partnership where the partnership agreement does not provide otherwise. This provision applies only to property contributed to a partnership by all of its partners and only where the relative undivided interests of the partners in the property prior to the contribution are in the same ratio as their interests in the capital and in the profits of the partnership (except for depreciation, depletion, or gain or loss with respect to the contributed undivided interest) after the contribution. Where these conditions are met, depreciation, depletion, or gain or loss with respect to the

undivided interests in contributed property shall be determined in the same manner as though such undivided interests continued to be held by the partners outside the partnership. The rule stated in section 704 (c) (3) applies only to the case where persons actually contribute undivided interests to a partnership. The provisions of this subdivision may be illustrated by the following examples:

Example (1). A and B are tenants in common owning undivided one-half interests in improved real estate consisting of land on which a factory is situated. They each contribute their respective undivided interests in the real estate to a partnership in which the profits are to be divided equally and, because the partners have equal shares in the capital, the assets will be divided equally on dissolution. A's basis for his undivided one-half interest is $4,000, of which $1,000 is allocable to the land and $3,000 to the factory. B's basis for his undivided one-half interest is $10,000, of which $3,000 is allocable to the land and $7,000 to the factory. The partnership agreement contains no provisions as to the allocation of depreciation or gain or loss on disposition of the property by the partnership. The factory depreciates at a rate of 5 percent a year. The annual partnership allowance for depreciation of $500 (5 percent of $10,000) will be allocated between the partners by allowing A a deduction of $150 (5 percent of $3,000, his basis for his undivided interest in the factory), and by allowing B a deduction of $350 (5 percent of $7,000, his basis for his undivided interest in the factory). At the end of the first year of partnership operation, A's adjusted basis for his undivided interest in the factory is $2,850 ($3,000 less $150), and B's adjusted basis is $6,650 ($7,000 less $350).

Example (2). If, in example (1) of this subdivision, the partnership at the end of the first year's operation sells the factory and land for $12,000, each partner's share of the gain or loss would be determined as follows: Since the undivided interests in the factory and the land are to be treated as though held by the partners outside the partnership, A's share of the proceeds of the sale is $6,000. His adjusted basis in the contributed property is $3,850 ($1,000 for the land and $2,850 for the factory). Therefore, his gain from the sale is $2,150. Since B's share of the proceeds is also $6,000, and his adjusted basis in the contributed property is $9,650 ($3,-000 for the land and $6,650 for the factory), his loss is $3,650.

Example (3). Assume the same facts as in examples (1) and (2) of this subdivision, except that A and B do not enter into a partnership agreement. Assume further that they are found to be a partnership for income tax purposes because of their joint business activity, but that the factory and the land are not actually contributed by them to the partnership. Although A and B have permitted the partnership to use such properties, they continue to own the factory and the land in their individual capacities (as tenants in common), and the same tax consequences result as in examples (1) and (2) of this subdivision.

(ii) The allocation illustrated in subdivision (i) of this subparagraph will not be affected by the contribution, either at the time of the original contribution or subsequent thereto, of additional property not held as undivided interests if the partners' respective interests in the capital and in the profits of the partnership (except for depreciation, depletion, or gain or loss with respect to the contributed undivided interests) remain the same as their undivided interests in the property previously contributed to the partnership. If the partners' interests in the capital and profits of the partnership are changed from their undivided interests in the property previously contributed to the partnership, the method of allocation of depreciation, depletion, or gain or loss with respect to such property no longer applies. Such a change of the partner's interests in capital and profits may result from a modification of the agreement, or from a change in a partner's respective interest in capital either as a result of a further contribution or as a result of a distribution. (However, drawings made throughout the year against profits, and loans will be disregarded.) Where such a change takes place, the partners may agree under section 704 (c) (2) that depreciation, depletion, or gain or loss with respect to the property formerly held as undivided interests shall continue to be allocated in the same manner as prior to the change. These provisions may be illustrated by the following examples:

Example (1). C and D are tenants in common, each owning an undivided one-half interest in certain unimproved land. Each contributes his respective undivided interest in the land to a partnership in which each has an equal interest in capital and profits. C's basis for his one-half interest is $4,000; D's basis is $10,000. The fair market value of the land is $20,000. Subsequently, C contributes $5,000 cash to his share of partnership capital. As a result of C's additional contribution, he now has a 60-percent interest in partnership capital and D, a 40-percent interest, although profits and losses still are to be shared equally. Since the interests of the partners in the capital and profits of the partnership no longer correspond to their undivided interests in the land, the method of allocation prescribed by section 704(c) (3) no longer applies. Therefore, if the land is sold for $12,000, the partnership will have a loss of $2,000 ($14,000 partnership basis minus $12,-000). Since the partnership agreement contains no special allocation for gain or loss with respect to contributed property, the $2,000 loss is allocated as if such property had been purchased by the partnership, i. e., $1,000 to each partner.

Example (2). Assume in example (1) of this subdivision that the partners agree that, because of C's additional contribution of $5,000

cash, he is to have a 60-percent interest in partnership capital. Profits and losses still are to be shared equally, except that gain or loss with respect to the land is, under section 704 (c) (2), to continue to be allocated in the same manner as it had been allocated under section 704(c) (3) prior to the additional contribution. The land is sold for $12,000. C's share of the proceeds is $6,000. His basis for the land is $4,000. Therefore, he has a $2,000 gain. D's loss is $4,000 ($10,000 basis less $6,000 proceeds).

(d) Limitation on allowance of losses. (1) A partner's distributive share of partnership loss will be allowed only to the extent of the adjusted basis (before reduction by current year's losses) of such partner's interest in the partnership at the end of the partnership taxable year in which such loss occurred. A partner's share of loss in excess of his adjusted basis at the end of the partnership taxable year will not be allowed for that year. However, any loss so disallowed shall be allowed as a deduction at the end of the first succeeding partnership taxable year, and subsequent partnership taxable years, to the extent that the partner's adjusted basis for his partnership interest at the end of any such year exceeds zero (before reduction by such loss for such year).

(2) In computing the adjusted basis of a partner's interest for the purpose of ascertaining the extent to which a partner's distributive share of partnership loss shall be allowed as a deduction for the taxable year, the basis shall first be increased under section 705 (a) (1) and decreased under section 705 (a) (2), except for losses of the taxable year and losses previously disallowed. If the partner's distributive share of the aggregate of items of loss specified in section 702 (a) (1), (2), (3), (8), and (9) exceeds the basis of the partner's interest computed under the preceding sentence, the limitation on losses under section 704 (d) must be allocated to his distributive share of each such loss. This allocation shall be determined by taking the proportion that each loss bears to the total of all such losses. For purposes of the preceding sentence, the total losses for the taxable year shall be the sum of his distributive share of losses for the current year and his losses disallowed and carried forward from prior years.

(3) For the treatment of certain liabilities of the partner or partnership, see section 752 and § 1.752-1.

(4) The provisions of this paragraph may be illustrated by the following examples:

Example (1). At the end of the partnership taxable year 1955, partnership AB has a loss of $20,000. Partner A's distributive share of this loss is $10,000. At the end of such year, A's adjusted basis for his interest in the partnership (not taking into account his distributive share of the loss) is $6,000. Under section 704(d), A's distributive share of partnership loss is allowed to him (in his taxable year within or with which the partnership taxable year ends) only to the extent of his adjusted basis of $6,000. The $6,000 loss allowed for 1955 decreases the adjusted basis of A's interest to zero. Assume that, at the end of partnership taxable year 1956, A's share of partnership income has increased the adjusted basis of A's interest in the partnership to $3,000 (not taking into account the $4,000 loss disallowed in 1955). Of the $4,000 loss disallowed for the partnership taxable year 1955, $3,000 is allowed A for the partnership taxable year 1956, thus again decreasing the adjusted basis of his interest to zero. If, at the end of partnership taxable year 1957, A has an adjusted basis of his interest of at least $1,000 (not taking into account the disallowed loss of $1,000), he will be allowed the $1,000 loss previously disallowed.

Example (2). At the end of partnership taxable year 1955, partnership CD has a loss of $20,000. Partner C's distributive share of this loss is $10,000. The adjusted basis of his interest in the partnership (not taking into account his distributive share of such loss) is $6,000. Therefore, $4,000 of the loss is disallowed. At the end of partnership taxable year 1956, the partnership has no taxable income or loss, but owes $8,000 to a bank for money borrowed. Since C's share of this liability is $4,000, the basis of his partnership interest is increased from zero to $4,000. (See sections 752 and 722, and §§ 1.752-1 and 1.722-1.) C is allowed the $4,000 loss, disallowed for the preceding year under section 704(d), for his taxable year within or with which partnership taxable year 1956 ends.

Example (3). At the end of partnership taxable year 1955, partner C has the following distributive share of partnership items described in section 702(a): long-term capital loss, $4,000; short-term capital loss, $2,000; income as described in section 702(a) (9), $4,000. Partner C's adjusted basis for his partnership interest at the end of 1955, before adjustment for any of the above items, is $1,000. As adjusted under section 705(a) (1) (A), C's basis is increased from $1,000 to $5,000 at the end of the year. C's total distributive share of partnership loss is $6,000. Since without regard to losses, C has a basis of only $5,000, C is allowed only $5,000/$6,-000 of each loss, that is, $3,333 of his long-term capital loss, and $1,667 of his short-term capital loss. C must carry forward to succeeding taxable years $667 as a long-term capital loss and $333 as a short-term capital loss.

(e) Family partnerships—(1) In general—(i) Introduction. The production of income by a partnership is attributable to the capital or services, or both, contributed by the partners. The provisions of subchapter K, chapter 1 of the Code, are to be read in the light of their relationship to section 61, which requires, inter alia, that income be taxed to the person who earns it through his own labor and skill and the utilization of his own capital.

(ii) Recognition of donee as partner. With respect to partnerships in which capital is a material income-producing factor, section 704 (e) (1) provides that a person shall be recognized as a partner for income tax purposes if he owns a capital interest in such a partnership whether or not such interest is derived by purchase or gift from any other person. If a capital interest in a partnership in which capital is a material income-producing factor is created by gift, section 704 (e) (2) provides that the distributive share of the donee under the partnership agreement shall be includible in his gross income, except to the extent that such distributive share is determined without allowance of reasonable compensation for services rendered to the partnership by the donor, and except to the extent that the portion of such distributive share attributable to donated capital is proportionately greater than the share of the donor attributable to the donor's capital. For rules of allocation in such cases, see subparagraph (3) of this paragraph.

(iii) Requirement of complete transfer to donee. A donee or purchaser of a capital interest in a partnership is not recognized as a partner under the principles of section 704 (e) (1) unless such interest is acquired in a bona fide transaction, not a mere sham for tax avoidance or evasion purposes, and the donee or purchaser is the real owner of such interest. To be recognized, a transfer must vest dominion and control of the partnership interest in the transferee. The existence of such dominion and control in the donee is to be determined from all the facts and circumstances. A transfer is not recognized if the transferor retains such incidents of ownership that the transferee has not acquired full and complete ownership of the partnership interest. Transactions between members of a family will be closely scrutinized, and the circumstances, not only at the time of the purported transfer but also during the periods preceding and following it, will be taken into consideration in determining the bona fides or lack of bona fides of the purported gift or sale. A partnership may be recognized for income tax purposes as to some partners but not as to others.

(iv) **Capital as a material income-producing factor.** For purposes of section 704 (e) (1), the determination as to whether capital is a material income-producing factor must be made by reference to all the facts of each case. Capital is a material income-producing factor if a substantial portion of the gross income of the business is attributable to the employment of capital in the business conducted by the partnership. In general, capital is not a material income-producing factor where the income of the business consists principally of fees, commissions, or other compensation for personal services performed by members or employees of the partnership. On the other hand, capital is ordinarily a material income-producing factor if the operation of the business requires substantial inventories or a substantial investment in plant, machinery, or other equipment.

(v) **Capital interest in a partnership.** For purposes of section 704 (e), a capital interest in a partnership means an interest in the assets of the partnership, which is distributable to the owner of the capital interest upon his withdrawal from the partnership or upon liquidation of the partnership. The mere right to participate in the earnings and profits of a partnership is not a capital interest in the partnership.

(2) **Basic tests as to ownership—(i) In general.** Whether an alleged partner who is a donee of a capital interest in a partnership is the real owner of such capital interest, and whether the donee has dominion and control over such interest, must be ascertained from all the facts and circumstances of the particular case. Isolated facts are not determinative; the reality of the donee's ownership is to be determined in the light of the transaction as a whole. The execution of legally sufficient and irrevocable deeds or other instruments of gift under State law is a factor to be taken into account but is not determinative of ownership by the donee for the purposes of section 704 (e). The reality of the transfer and of the donee's ownership of the property attributed to him are to be ascertained from the conduct of the parties with respect to the alleged gift and not by any mechanical or formal test. Some of the more important factors to be considered in determining whether the donee has acquired ownership of the capital interest in a partnership are indicated in subdivisions (ii) to (x), inclusive, of this subparagraph.

(ii) **Retained controls.** The donor may have retained such controls of the interest which he has purported to transfer to the donee that the donor should be treated as remaining the substantial owner of the interest. Controls of particular significance include, for example, the following:

(a) Retention of control of the distribution of amounts of income or restrictions on the distributions of amounts of income (other than amounts retained in the partnership annually with the consent of the partners, including the donee partner, for the reasonable needs of the business). If there is a partnership agreement providing for a managing partner or partners, then amounts of income may be retained in the partnership without the acquiescence of all the partners if such amounts are retained for the reasonable needs of the business.

(b) Limitation of the right of the donee to liquidate or sell his interest in the partnership at his discretion without financial detriment.

(c) Retention of control of assets essential to the business (for example, through retention of assets leased to the alleged partnership).

(d) Retention of management powers inconsistent with normal relationships among partners. Retention by the donor of control of business management or of voting control, such as is common in ordinary business relationships, is not by itself to be considered as inconsistent with normal relationships among partners, provided the donee is free to liquidate his interest at his discretion without financial detriment. The donee shall not be considered free to liquidate his interest unless, considering all the facts, it is evident that the donee is independent of the donor and has such maturity and understanding of his rights as to be capable of deciding to exercise, and capable of exercising, his right to withdraw his capital interest from the partnership.

The existence of some of the indicated controls, though amounting to less than substantial ownership retained by the donor, may be considered along with other facts and circumstances as tending to show the lack of reality of the partnership interest of the donee.

(iii) **Indirect controls.** Controls inconsistent with ownership by the donee may be exercised indirectly as well as directly, for example, through a separate business organization, estate, trust, individual, or other partnership. Where such indirect controls exist, the reality of the donee's interest will be determined as if such controls were exercisable directly.

(iv) **Participation in management.** Substantial participation by the donee in the control and management of the business (including participation in the major policy decisions affecting the business) is strong evidence of a donee partner's exercise of dominion and control over his interest. Such participation presupposes sufficient maturity and experience on the part of the donee to deal with the business problems of the partnership.

(v) **Income distributions.** The actual distribution to a donee partner of the entire amount or a major portion of his distributive share of the business income for the sole benefit and use of the donee is substantial evidence of the reality of the donee's interest, provided the donor has not retained controls inconsistent with real ownership by the donee. Amounts distributed are not considered to be used for the donee's sole benefit if, for example, they are deposited, loaned, or invested in such manner that the donor controls or can control the use or enjoyment of such funds.

(vi) **Conduct of partnership business.** In determining the reality of the donee's ownership of a capital interest in a partnership, consideration shall be given to whether the donee is actually treated as a partner in the operation of the business. Whether or not the donee has been held out publicly as a partner in the conduct of the business, in relations with customers, or with creditors or other sources of financing, is of primary significance. Other factors of significance in this connection include:

(a) Compliance with local partnership, fictitious names, and business registration statutes.

(b) Control of business bank accounts.

(c) Recognition of the donee's rights in distributions of partnership property and profits.

(d) Recognition of the donee's interest in insurance policies, leases, and other business contracts and in litigation affecting business.

(e) The existence of written agreements, records, or memoranda, contemporaneous with the taxable year or years concerned, establishing the nature of the partnership agreement and the rights and liabilities of the respective partners.

(f) Filing of partnership tax returns as required by law.

However, despite formal compliance with the above factors, other circumstances may indicate that the donor has retained substantial ownership of the interest purportedly transferred to the donee.

(vii) **Trustees as partners.** A trustee may be recognized as a partner for income tax purposes under the principles relating to family partnerships generally as applied to the particular facts of the trust-partnership arrangement. A trustee who is unrelated to and independent of the grantor, and who participates as a partner and receives distribution of the income distributable to the trust, will ordinarily be recognized as the legal owner of the partnership interest which he holds in trust unless the grantor has retained controls inconsistent with such ownership. However, if the grantor is the trustee, or if the trustee is amenable to the will of the grantor, the provisions of the trust instrument (particularly as to whether the trustee is subject to the responsibilities of a fiduciary), the provisions of the partnership agreement, and the conduct of the parties must all be taken into account in determining whether the trustee in a fiduciary capacity has become the real owner of the partnership interest. Where the grantor (or person amenable to his will) is the trustee, the trust may be recognized as a partner only if the grantor (or such other person) in his participation in the affairs of the partnership actively represents and protects the interests of the beneficiaries in accordance with the obligations of a fiduciary and does not subordinate such interests to the interests of the grantor. Furthermore, if the grantor (or person amenable to his will) is the trustee, the following factors will be given particular consideration:

(a) Whether the trust is recognized as a partner in business dealings with customers and creditors, and

(b) Whether, if any amount of the partnership income is not properly retained for the reasonable needs of the business, the trust's share of such amount is distributed to the trust annually and paid to the beneficiaries or reinvested with regard solely to the interests of the beneficiaries.

(viii) Interests (not held in trust) of minor children. Except where a minor child is shown to be competent to manage his own property and participate in the partnership activities in accordance with his interest in the property, a minor child generally will not be recognized as a member of a partnership unless control of the property is exercised by another person as fiduciary for the sole benefit of the child, and unless there is such judicial supervision of the conduct of the fiduciary as is required by law. The use of the child's property or income for support for which a parent is legally responsible will be considered a use for the parent's benefit. "Judicial supervision of the conduct of the fiduciary" includes filing of such accountings and reports as are required by law of the fiduciary who participates in the affairs of the partnership on behalf of the minor. A minor child will be considered as competent to manage his own property if he actually has sufficient maturity and experience to be treated by disinterested persons as competent to enter business dealings and otherwise to conduct his affairs on a basis of equality with adult persons, notwithstanding legal disabilities of the minor under State law.

(ix) Donees as limited partners. The recognition of a donee's interest in a limited partnership will depend, as in the case of other donated interests, on whether the transfer of property is real and on whether the donee has acquired dominion and control over the interest purportedly transferred to him. To be recognized for Federal income tax purposes, a limited partnership must be organized and conducted in accordance with the requirements of the applicable State limited-partnership law. The absence of services and participation in management by a donee in a limited partnership is immaterial if the limited partnership meets all the other requirements prescribed in this paragraph. If the limited partner's right to transfer or liquidate his interest is subject to substantial restrictions (for example, where the interest of the limited partner is not assignable in a real sense or where such interest may be required to be left in the business for a long term of years), or if the general partner retains any other control which substantially limits any of the rights which would ordinarily be exercisable by unrelated limited partners in normal business relationships, such restrictions on the right to transfer or liquidate, or retention of other control, will be considered evidence strong as to the lack of reality of ownership by the donee.

(x) Motive. If the reality of the transfer of interest is satisfactorily established, the motives for the transaction are generally immaterial. However, the presence or absence of a tax-avoidance motive is one of many factors to be considered in determining the reality of the ownership of a capital interest acquired by gift.

(3) Allocation of family partnership income—(i) In general. (a) Where a capital interest in a partnership in which capital is a material income-producing factor is created by gift, the donee's distributive share shall be includible in his gross income, except to the extent that such share is determined without allowance of reasonable compensation for services rendered to the partnership by the donor, and except to the extent that the portion of such distributive share attributable to donated capital is proportionately greater than the distributive share attributable to the donor's capital. For the purpose of section 704, a capital interest in a partnership purchased by one member of a family from another shall be considered to be created by gift from the seller, and the fair market value of the purchased interest shall be considered to be donated capital. The "family" of any individual, for the purpose of the preceding sentence, shall include only his spouse, ancestors, and lineal descendants, and any trust for the primary benefit of such persons.

(b) To the extent that the partnership agreement does not allocate the partnership income in accordance with (a) of this subdivision, the distributive shares of the partnership income of the donor and donee shall be reallocated by making a reasonable allowance for the services of the donor and by attributing the balance of such income (other than a reasonable allowance for the services, if any, rendered by the donee) to the partnership capital of the donor and donee. The portion of income, if any, thus attributable to partnership capital for the taxable year shall be allocated between the donor and donee in accordance with their respective interests in partnership capital.

(c) In determining a reasonable allowance for services rendered by the partners, consideration shall be given to all the facts and circumstances of the business, including the fact that some of the partners may have greater managerial responsibility than others. There shall also be considered the amount that would ordinarily be paid in order to obtain comparable services from a person not having an interest in the partnership.

(d) The distributive share of partnership income, as determined under (b) of this subdivision, of a partner who rendered services to the partnership before entering the Armed Forces of the United States shall not be diminished because of absence due to military service. Such distributive share shall be adjusted to reflect increases or decreases in the capital interest of the absent partner. However, the partners may by agreement allocate a smaller share to the absent partner due to his absence.

(ii) Special rules. (a) The provisions of subdivision (i) of this subparagraph, relating to allocation of family partnership income, are applicable where the interest in the partnership is created by gift, indirectly or directly. Where the partnership interest is created indirectly, the term "donor" may include persons other than the nominal transferor. This rule may be illustrated by the following examples:

Example (1). A father gives property to his son who shortly thereafter conveys the property to a partnership consisting of the father and the son. The partnership interest of the son may be considered created by gift and the father may be considered the donor of the son's partnership interest.

Example (2). A father, the owner of a business conducted as a sole proprietorship, transfers the business to a partnership consisting of his wife and himself. The wife subsequently conveys her interest to their son. In such case, the father, as well as the mother, may be considered the donor of the son's partnership interest.

Example (3). A father makes a gift to his son of stock in the family corporation. The corporation is subsequently liquidated. The son later contributes the property received in the liquidation of the corporation to a partnership consisting of his father and himself. In such case, for purposes of section 704, the son's partnership interest may be considered created by gift and the father may be considered the donor of his son's partnership interest.

(b) The allocation rules set forth in section 704 (e) and subdivision (i) of this subparagraph apply in any case in which the transfer or creation of the partnership interest has any of the substantial characteristics of a gift. Thus, allocation may be required where transfer of a partnership interest is made between members of a family (including collaterals) under a purported purchase agreement, if the characteristics of a gift are ascertained from the terms of the purchase agreement, the terms of any loan or credit arrangements made to finance the purchase, or from other relevant data.

(c) In the case of a limited partnership, for the purpose of the allocation provisions of subdivision (i) of this subparagraph, consideration shall be given to the fact that a general partner, unlike a limited partner, risks his credit in the partnership business.

(4) Purchased interest—(i) In general. If a purported purchase of a capital interest in a partnership does not meet the requirements of subdivision (ii) of this subparagraph, the ownership by the transferee of such capital interest will be recognized only if it qualifies under the requirements applicable to a transfer of a partnership interest by gifts. In a case not qualifying under subdivision (ii) of this subparagraph, if payment of any part of the purchase price is made out of partnership earnings, the transaction may be regarded in the same light as a purported gift subject to deferred enjoyment of income. Such a transaction may be lacking in reality either as a gift or as a bona fide purchase.

(ii) Tests as to reality of purchased interests. A purchase of a capital interest in a partnership, either directly or by means of a loan or credit extended by a member of the family, will be recognized as bona fide if:

(a) It can be shown that the purchase has the usual characteristics of an arm's-length transaction, considering all relevant factors, including the terms of the purchase agreement (as to price, due date of payment, rate of interest, and security, if any) and the terms of any loan or credit arrangement collateral to the purchase agreement; the credit standing of the purchaser (apart from relationship to the seller) and the capacity of the purchaser to incur a legally binding obligation; or

(b) It can be shown, in the absence of characteristics of an arm's-length transaction, that the purchase was genuinely intended to promote the success of the business by securing participation of the purchaser in the business or by adding his credit to that of the other participants.

However, if the alleged purchase price or loan has not been paid or the obligation otherwise discharged, the factors indicated in (a) and (b) of this subdivision shall be taken into account only as an aid in determining whether a bona fide purchase or loan obligation existed.

§ 1.705–1 Determination of basis of partner's interest

(a) General rule. (1) Section 705 and this section provide rules for determining the adjusted basis of a partner's interest in a partnership. A partner is required to determine the adjusted basis of his interest in a partnership only when necessary for the determination of his tax liability or that of any other person. The determination of the adjusted basis of a partnership interest is ordinarily made as of the end of a partnership taxable year. Thus, for example, such year-end determination is necessary in ascertaining the extent to which a partner's distributive share of partnership losses may be allowed. See section 704 (d). However, where there has been a sale or exchange of all or a part of a partnership interest or a liquidation of a partner's entire interest in a partnership, the adjusted basis of the partner's interest should be determined as of the date of sale or exchange or liquidation. The adjusted basis of a partner's interest in a partnership is determined without regard to any amount shown in the partnership books as the partner's "capital", "equity", or similar account. For example, A contributes property with an adjusted basis to him of $400 (and a value of $1,000) to a partnership. B contributes $1,000 cash. While under their agreement each may have a "capital account" in the partnership of $1,000, the adjusted basis of A's interest is only $400 and B's interest $1,000.

(2) The original basis of a partner's interest in a partnership shall be determined under section 722 (relating to contributions to a partnership) or section 742 (relating to transfers of partnership interests). Such basis shall be increased under section 722 by any further contributions to the partnership and by the sum of the partner's distributive share for the taxable year and prior taxable years of—

(i) Taxable income of the partnership as determined under section 703 (a),

(ii) Tax-exempt receipts of the partnership, and

(iii) The excess of the deductions for depletion over the basis of the depletable property.

(3) The basis shall be decreased (but not below zero) by distributions from the partnership as provided in section 733 and by the sum of the partner's distributive share for the taxable year and prior taxable years of—

(i) Partnership losses (including capital losses), and

(ii) Partnership expenditures which are not deductible in computing partnership taxable income or loss and which are not capital expenditures.

(4) For the effect of liabilities in determining the amount of contributions made by a partner to a partnership or the amount of distributions made by a partnership to a partner, see section 752 and § 1.752–1, relating to the treatment of certain liabilities. In determining the basis of a partnership interest on the effective date of subchapter K, chapter 1 of the Code, or any of the sections thereof, the partner's share of partnership liabilities on that date shall be included.

(b) Alternative rule. In certain cases, the adjusted basis of a partner's interest in a partnership may be determined by reference to the partner's share of the adjusted basis of partnership property which would be distributable upon termination of the partnership. The alternative rule may be used to determine the adjusted basis of a partner's interest where circumstances are such that the partner cannot practicably apply the general rule set forth in section 705 (a) and paragraph (a) of this section, or where, from a consideration of all the facts, it is, in the opinion of the Commissioner, reasonable to conclude that the result produced will not vary substantially from the result obtainable under the general rule. Where the alternative rule is used, adjustments may be necessary in determining the adjusted basis of a partner's interest in a partnership. Adjustments would be required, for example, in order to reflect in a partner's share of the adjusted basis of partnership property any significant discrepancies arising as a result of contributed property, transfers of partnership interests, or distributions of property to the partners. The operation of the alternative rules may be illustrated by the following examples:

Example (1). The ABC partnership, in which A, B, and C are equal partners, owns various properties with a total adjusted basis of $1,500 and has earned and retained an additional $1,500. The total adjusted basis of partnership property is thus $3,000. Each partner's share in the adjusted basis of partnership property is one-third of this amount, or $1,000. Under the alternative rule, this amount represents each partner's adjusted basis for his partnership interest.

Example (2). Assume that partner A in example (1) of this paragraph sells his partnership interest to D for $1,250 at a time when the partnership property with an adjusted basis of $1,500 had appreciated in value to $3,000, and when the partnership also had $750 in cash. The total adjusted basis of all partnership property is $2,250 and the value of such property is $3,750. D's basis for his partnership interest is his cost, $1,250. However, his one-third share of the adjusted basis of partnership property is only $750. Therefore, for the purposes of the alternative rule, D has an adjustment of $500 in determining the basis of his interest. This amount represents the difference between the cost of his partnership interest and his share of partnership basis at the time of his purchase. If the partnership subsequently earns and retains an additional $1,500, its property will have an adjusted basis of $3,750. D's adjusted basis for his interest under the alternative rule is $1,750, determined by adding $500, his basis adjustment to $1,250 (his one-third share of the $3,750 adjusted basis of partnership property). If the partnership distributes $250 to each partner in a current distribution, D's adjusted basis for his interest will be $1,500 ($1,000, his one-third share of the remaining basis of partner-

ship property, $3,000, plus his basis adjustment of $500).

Example (3). Assume that BCD partnership in example (2) of this paragraph continues to operate. In 1960, D proposes to sell his partnership interest and wishes to evaluate the tax consequences of such sale. It is necessary, therefore, to determine the adjusted basis of his interest in the partnership. Assume further that D cannot determine the adjusted basis of his interest under the general rule. The balance sheet of the BCD partnership is as follows:

Assets	Adjusted basis per books	Market value
Cash	$3,000	$3,000
Receivables	4,000	4,000
Depreciable property	5,000	5,000
Land held for investment...	18,000	30,000
Total	30,000	42,000

Liabilities and capital	Per books
Liabilities	$6,000
Capital accounts:	
B	4,500
C	4,500
D	15,000
Total	30,000

The $15,000 representing the amount of D's capital account does not reflect the $500 basis adjustment arising from D's purchase of his interest. See example (2) of this paragraph. The adjusted basis of D's partnership interest determined under the alternative rule is as follows:

D's share of the adjusted basis of partnership property (reduced by the amount of liabilities) at time of proposed sale................	$15,000
D's share of partnership liabilities (under the partnership agreement liabilities are shared equally)	2,000
D's basis adjustment from example (2).......	500
Adjusted basis of D's interest at the time of proposed sale, as determined under alternative rule	17,500

§ 1.706–1 Taxable years of partner and partnership

(a) Year in which partnership income is includible. (1) In computing his taxable income for a taxable year, a partner is required to include his distributive share of partnership items set forth in section 702 for any partnership year ending within or with his taxable year. A partner shall also include in his taxable income for a taxable year "guaranteed payments" under section 707 (c) which are made to him in a partnership taxable year ending within or with his taxable year. The provisions of this subparagraph may be illustrated by the following example:

Example. Partner A reports his income for a calendar year, while the partnership of which he is a member reports its income for a fiscal year ending May 31. During the partnership taxable year ending May 31, 1956, A received guaranteed payments of $1,200 for services and for the use of capital. Of this amount, $700 was received by A between June 1 and December 31, 1955, and the remaining $500 was received by him between January 1 and May 31, 1956. This entire $1,200 received by A is includible in his taxable income for the calendar year 1956 (together with his distributive share of partnership items set forth in section 702 for the partnership taxable year ending May 31, 1956).

(2) If a partner receives distributions under section 731 or sells or exchanges all or part of his partnership interest, any gain or loss arising therefrom does not constitute partnership income and is includible in the partner's gross income for his taxable year in which the payment is made. See sections 451 and 461.

(b) Adoption or change in taxable year—(1) Partnership taxable year. (i) The taxable year of a partnership shall be determined as though the partnership were a taxpayer.

(ii) A newly formed partnership may adopt a taxable year which is the same as the taxable year of all its principal partners (or the same as the taxable year to which all of its principal partners are concurrently changing) without securing prior approval from the Commissioner, or it may adopt a calendar year without securing prior approval from the Commissioner if all its principal partners are not on the same taxable year. In any other case, a newly formed partnership must secure prior approval from the Commissioner for the adoption of a taxable year.

(iii) An existing partnership may not change its taxable year without securing prior approval from the Commissioner, unless all its principal partners have the same taxable year to which the partnership changes, or unless all its principal partners concurrently change to such taxable year.

(2) Partner's taxable year. A partner may not change his taxable year without securing prior approval from the Commissioner. See section 442 and the regulations thereunder.

(3) Principal partner. For the purpose of this paragraph, a principal partner is a partner having an interest of 5 percent or more in partnership profits or capital.

(4) Application for approval—(i) Change. Application for a change in a taxable year shall be filed on Form 1128 with the Commissioner of Internal Revenue, Washington, D. C. 20224. If the short period involved in the change ends after December 31, 1973, such form shall be filed on or before the 15th day of the second calendar month following the close of such short period; if such short period ends before January 1, 1974, such form shall be filed on or before the last day of the first calendar month following the close of such short period.

(ii) Adoption. Where a newly formed partnership is required to secure prior approval from the Commissioner for the adoption of a taxable year, the partnership shall file an application on Form 1128 with the Commissioner on or before the last day of the month following the close of the taxable year to be adopted. The partnership shall modify Form 1128 to the extent necessary to indicate that it is an application for adoption of a taxable year.

(iii) Business purpose. Where prior approval is required under this paragraph, the applicant must establish a business purpose to the satisfaction of the Commissioner. For example, partnership AB, which is on a calendar year, is engaged in a business which has a natural business year (the annual accounting period encompassing all related income and expenses) ending on September 30th. The intention of the partnership to make its tax year coincide with such natural business year constitutes a sufficient business purpose.

(5) Returns—(i) Partner. A partner who changes his taxable year shall make his return for a short period in accordance with section 443, and shall attach to the return a copy of the letter from the Commissioner granting approval for the change of taxable year.

(ii) Partnership. (a) A partnership which changes its taxable year shall make its return for a short period in accordance with section 443, but shall not annualize the partnership taxable income. The partnership shall attach to the return either a copy of the letter from the Commissioner granting approval of the change of taxable year, or a statement indicating that the partnership is changing its taxable year to the same taxable year as that of all its principal partners or to the same taxable year as that to which all its principal partners are concurrently changing.

(b) Any newly formed partnership shall file with its first return either:

(1) A copy of the letter from the Commissioner approving the adoption of a partnership taxable year which is not the same as the taxable year of all its principal partners; or

(2) A statement indicating that the taxable year it has adopted is the same as the taxable year of all its principal partners, or that all its principal partners are concurrently changing to the taxable year it has adopted; or

(3) A statement that all its principal partners are not on the same taxable year and that it is adopting a calendar year without prior approval.

. . . .

(c) Closing of partnership year—(1) General rule. Section 706 (c) and this paragraph provide rules governing the closing of partnership years. The closing of a partnership taxable year or a termination of a partnership for Federal income tax purposes is not necessarily governed by the "dissolution", "liquidation", etc., of a partnership under State or local law. The taxable year of a partnership shall not close as the result of the death of a partner, the entry of a new partner, the liquidation of a partner's entire interest in the partnership (as defined in section 761 (d)), or the sale or exchange of a partner's interest in the partnership, except in the case of a termination of a partnership and except as provided in subparagraph (2) of this paragraph. In the case of termination, the partnership taxable year closes for all partners as of the date of termination. See section 708(b) and paragraph (b) of § 1.708–1.

(2) Partner who retires or sells interest in partnership—(i) Disposition of entire interest. A partnership taxable year shall close with respect to a partner who sells or exchanges his entire interest in a partnership, and with respect to a partner whose entire interest is liquidated. However, a partnership taxable year with respect to a partner who dies shall not close prior to the end of such partnership taxable year, or the time when such partner's interest (held by his estate or other successor) is liquidated or sold or exchanged, whichever is earlier. See subparagraph (3) of this paragraph.

(ii) Inclusions in taxable income. In the case of a sale, exchange, or liquidation of a partner's entire interest in a partnership, the partner shall include in his taxable income for his taxable year within or with which his membership in the partnership ends, his distributive share of items described in section 702(a), and any guaranteed payments under section 707 (c), for his partnership taxable year ending with the date of such sale, exchange, or liquidation. In order to avoid an interim closing of the partnership books, such partner's distributive share of items described in section 702 (a) may, by agreement among the partners, be estimated by taking his pro rata part of the amount of such items he would have included in his taxable income had he remained a partner until the end of the partnership taxable year. The proration may be based on the portion of the taxable year that has elapsed prior to the sale, exchange, or liquidation, or may be determined under any other method that is reasonable. Any partner who is the transferee of such partner's interest shall include in his taxable income, as his distributive share of items described in section 702 (a) with respect to the acquired interest, the pro rata part (determined by the method used by the transferor partner) of the amount of such items he would have included had he been a partner from the beginning of the taxable year of the partnership. The application of this subdivision may be illustrated by the following example:

Example. Assume that a partner selling his partnership interest on June 30, 1955, has an adjusted basis for his interest of $5,000 on that date; that his pro rata share of partnership income up to June 30 is $15,000; and that he sells his interest for $20,000. Under the provisions of section 706(c) (2), the partnership year with respect to him closes at the time of the sale. The $15,000 is includible in his income as his distributive share and, under section 705, it increases the basis of his partnership interest to $20,000, which is also the selling price of his interest. Therefore, no gain is realized on the sale of his partnership interest. The purchaser of this partnership interest shall include in his income as his distributive share his pro rata part of partnership income for the remainder of the partnership taxable year.

(3) Partner who dies. (i) When a partner dies, the partnership taxable year shall not close with respect to such partner prior to the end of the partnership taxable year. The partnership taxable year shall continue both for

the remaining partners and the decedent partner. Where the death of a partner results in the termination of the partnership, the partnership taxable year shall close for all partners on the date of such termination under section 708(b) (1) (A). See also paragraph (b) (1) (i) (b) of § 1.708–1 for the continuation of a 2-member partnership under certain circumstances after the death of a partner. However, if the decedent partner's estate or other successor sells or exchanges its entire interest in the partnership, or if its entire interest is liquidated, the partnership taxable year with respect to the estate or other successor in interest shall close on the date of such sale or exchange, or the date of completion of the liquidation.

(ii) The last return of a decedent partner shall include only his share of partnership taxable income for any partnership taxable year or years ending within or with the last taxable year for such decedent partner (i. e., the year ending with the date of his death). The distributive share of partnership taxable income for a partnership taxable year ending after the decedent's last taxable year is includible in the return of his estate or other successor in interest. If the estate or other successor in interest of a partner continues to share in the profits or losses of the partnership business, the distributive share thereof is includible in the taxable year of the estate or other successor in interest within or with which the taxable year of the partnership ends. See also paragraph (a) (1) (ii) of § 1.736–1. Where the estate or other successor in interest receives distributions, any gain or loss on such distributions is includible in its gross income for its taxable year in which the distribution is made.

(iii) If a partner (or a retiring partner), in accordance with the terms of the partnership agreement, designates a person to succeed to his interest in the partnership after his death, such designated person shall be regarded as a successor in interest of the deceased for purposes of this chapter. Thus, where a partner designates his widow as the successor in interest, her distributive share of income for the taxable year of the partnership ending within or with her taxable year may be included in a joint return in accord-

ance with the provisions of sections 2 and 6013 (a) (2) and (3).

(iv) If, under the terms of an agreement existing at the date of death of a partner, a sale or exchange of the decedent partner's interest in the partnership occurs upon that date, then the taxable year of the partnership with respect to such decedent partner shall close upon the date of death. See section 706 (c) (2) (A) (i). The sale or exchange of a partnership interest does not, for the purpose of this rule, include any transfer of a partnership interest which occurs at death as a result of inheritance or any testamentary disposition.

(v) To the extent that any part of a distributive share of partnership income of the estate or other successor in interest of a deceased partner is attributable to the decedent for the period ending with the date of his death, such part of the distributive share is income in respect of the decedent under section 691. See section 691 and the regulations thereunder.

(vi) The provisions of this subparagraph may be illustrated by the following examples:

Example (1). B has a taxable year ending December 31 and is a member of partnership ABC, the taxable year of which ends on June 30. B dies on October 31, 1955. His estate (which as a new taxpayer may, under section 441 and the regulations thereunder, adopt any taxable year) adopts a taxable year ending October 31. The return of the decedent for the period January 1 to October 31, 1955, will include only his distributive share of taxable income of the partnership for its taxable year ending June 30, 1955. The distributive share of taxable income of the partnership for its taxable year ending June 30, 1956, arising from the interest of the decedent, will be includible in the return of the estate for its taxable year ending October 31, 1956. That part of the distributive share attributable to the decedent for the period ending with the date of his death (July 1 through October 31, 1955) is income in respect of a decedent under section 691.

Example (2). Assume the same facts as in example (1) of this subdivision, except that, prior to B's death, B and D had agreed that, upon B's death, D would purchase B's interest for $10,000. When B dies on October 31, 1955, the partnership taxable year beginning July 1, 1955, closes with respect to him. Therefore, the return for B's last taxable year (January 1 to October 31, 1955) will include his distributive share of taxable income of the partnership for its taxable year ending June 30, 1955, plus his distributive share of partnership taxable income for the period July 1 to October 31, 1955. See subdivision (iv) of this subparagraph.

Example (3). H is a member of a partnership having a taxable year ending December 31. Both H and his wife W are on a calendar year and file joint returns. H dies on March 31, 1955. Administration of the estate is completed and the estate, including the partnership interest, is distributed to W as legatee on November 30, 1955. Such distribution by the estate is not a sale or exchange of H's partnership interest. No part of the taxable income of the partnership for the taxable year ending December 31, 1955, which is allocable to H, will be included in H's taxable income for his last taxable year (January 1 through March 31, 1955) or in the taxable income of H's estate for the taxable year April 1 through November 30, 1955. The distributive share of partnership taxable income for the full calendar year that is allocable to H will be includible in the taxable income of W for her taxable year ending December 31, 1955, and she may file a joint return under sections 2 and 6013(a) (3). That part of the distributive share attributable to the decedent for the period ending with the date of his death (January 1 through March 31, 1955) is income in respect of a decedent under section 691.

. . . . .

(4) **Disposition of less than entire interest.** If a partner sells or exchanges a part of his interest in a partnership, or if the interest of a partner is reduced, the partnership taxable year shall continue to its normal end. In such case, the partner's distributive share of items which he is required to include in his taxable income under the provisions of section 702 (a) shall be determined by taking into account his varying interests in the partnership during the partnership taxable year in which such sale, exchange, or reduction of interest occurred.

(5) **Transfer of interest by gift.** The transfer of a partnership interest by gift does not close the partnership taxable year with respect to the donor. However, the income up to the date of gift attributable to the donor's interest shall be allocated to him under section 704 (e) (2).

§ 1.707-1 Transactions between partner and partnership

(a) **Partner not acting in capacity as partner.** A partner who engages in a transaction with a partnership other than in his capacity as a partner shall be treated as if he were not a member of the partnership with respect to such transaction. Such transactions include, for example, loans of money or property by the partnership to the partner or by the partner to the partnership, the sale of property by the partner to the partnership, the purchase of property by the partner from the partnership, and the rendering of services by the partnership to the partner or by the partner to the partnership. Where a partner retains

the ownership of property but allows the partnership to use such separately owned property for partnership purposes (for example, to obtain credit or to secure firm creditors by guaranty, pledge, or other agreement) the transaction is treated as one between a partnership and a partner not acting in his capacity as a partner. However, transfers of money or property by a partner to a partnership as contributions, or transfers of money or property by a partnership to a partner as distributions, are not transactions included within the provisions of this section. In all cases, the substance of the transaction will govern rather than its form. See paragraph (c) (3) of § 1.731-1.

(b) **Certain sales or exchanges of property with respect to controlled partnerships—(1) Losses disallowed.** (i) No deduction shall be allowed for a loss on a sale or exchange of property (other than an interest in the partnership), directly or indirectly, between a partnership and a partner who owns, directly or indirectly, more than 50 percent of the capital interest or profits interest in such partnership. A loss on a sale or exchange of property, directly or indirectly, between two partnerships in which the same persons own, directly or indirectly, more than 50 percent of the capital interest or profits interest in each partnership shall not be allowed.

(ii) If a gain is realized upon the subsequent sale or exchange by a transferee of property with respect to which a loss was disallowed under the provisions of subdivision (i) of this subparagraph, section 267 (d) (relating to amount of gain where loss previously disallowed) shall apply as though the loss were disallowed under section 267 (a) (1).

(2) **Gains treated as ordinary income.** Any gain recognized upon the sale or exchange, directly or indirectly, of property which, in the hands of the transferee immediately after the transfer, is property other than a capital asset, as defined in section 1221, shall be ordinary income if the transaction is between a partnership and a partner who owns, directly or indirectly, more than 80 percent of the capital interest or profits interest in the partnership. This rule also applies where such a transaction is between partnerships in which the same persons

own, directly or indirectly, more than 80 percent of the capital interest or profits interest in each partnership. The term "property other than a capital asset" includes (but is not limited to) trade accounts receivable, inventory, stock in trade, and depreciable or real property used in the trade or business.

(3) **Ownership of a capital or profits interest.** In determining the extent of the ownership by a partner, as defined in section 761(b), of his capital interest or profits interest in a partnership, the rules for constructive ownership of stock provided in section 267 (c) (1), (2), (4), and (5) shall be applied for the purpose of section 707(b) and this paragraph. Under these rules, ownership of a capital or profits interest in a partnership may be attributed to a person who is not a partner as defined in section 761(b) in order that another partner may be considered the constructive owner of such interest under section 267(c). However, section 707(b) (1) (A) does not apply to a constructive owner of a partnership interest since he is not a partner as defined in section 761(b). For example, where trust T is a partner in the partnership ABT, and AW, A's wife, is the sole beneficiary of the trust, the ownership of a capital and profits interest in the partnership by T will be attributed to AW only for the purpose of further attributing the ownership of such interest to A. See section 267(c) (1) and (5). If A, B, and T are equal partners, then A will be considered as owning more than 50 percent of the capital and profits interest in the partnership, and losses on transactions between him and the partnership will be disallowed by section 707(b) (1) (A). However, a loss sustained by AW on a sale or exchange of property with the partnership would not be disallowed by section 707, but will be disallowed to the extent provided in paragraph (b) of § 1.267(b)-1. See section 267(a) and (b), and the regulations thereunder.

(c) **Guaranteed payments.** Payments made by a partnership to a partner for services or for the use of capital are considered as made to a person who is not a partner, to the extent such payments are determined without regard to the income of the partnership. However, a partner must include such payments as ordinary income for his taxable year within or with which ends the partnership taxable year in which the partnership deducted such payments as paid or accrued under its method of accounting. See section 706 (a) and paragraph (a) of § 1.706-1. Guaranteed payments are considered as made to one who is not a member of the partnership only for the purposes of section 61(a) (relating to gross income) and section 162 (a) (relating to trade or business expenses). They do not constitute an interest in partnership profits for purposes of sections 706 (b) (3), 707 (b), and 708 (b). For the purposes of other provisions of the internal revenue laws, guaranteed payments are regarded as a partner's distributive share of ordinary income. Thus, a partner who receives guaranteed payments for a period during which he is absent from work because of personal injuries or sickness is not entitled to exclude such payments from his gross income under section 105 (d). Similarly, a partner who receives guaranteed payments is not regarded as an employee of the partnership for the purposes of withholding of tax at source, deferred compensation plans, etc. The provisions of this paragraph may be illustrated by the following examples:

Example (1). Under the ABC partnership agreement, partner A is entitled to a fixed annual payment of $10,000 for services, without regard to the income of the partnership. His distributive share is 10 percent. After deducting the guaranteed payment, the partnership has $50,000 ordinary income. A must include $15,000 as ordinary income for his taxable year within or with which the partnership taxable year ends ($10,000 guaranteed payment plus $5,000 distributive share).

Example (2). Partner C in the CD partnership is to receive 30 percent of partnership income as determined before taking into account any guaranteed payments, but not less than $10,000. The income of the partnership is $60,000, and C is entitled to $18,000 (30 percent of $60,000) as his distributive share. No part of this amount is a guaranteed payment. However, if the partnership had income of $20,000 instead of $60,000, $6,000 (30 percent of $20,000) would be partner C's distributive share, and the remaining $4,000 payable to C would be a guaranteed payment.

Example (3). Partner X in the XY partnership is to receive a payment of $10,000 for services, plus 30 percent of the taxable income or loss of the partnership. After deducting the payment of $10,000 to partner X, the XY partnership as a loss of $9,000. Of this amount, $2,700 (30 percent of the loss) is X's distributive share of partnership loss and, subject to section 704(d), is to be taken into account by him in his return. In addition, he must report as ordinary income the guaranteed payment of $10,000 made to him by the partnership.

Example (4). Assume the same facts as in example (3) of this paragraph except that, instead of a $9,000 loss, the partnership has $30,000 in capital gains and no other items of income or deduction except the $10,000 paid X as a guaranteed payment. Since the items of partnership income or loss must be segregated under section 702(a), the partnership has a $10,000 ordinary loss and $30,000 in capital gains. X's 30 percent distributive shares of these amounts are $3,000 ordinary loss and $9,000 capital gain. In addition, X has received a $10,000 guaranteed payment which is ordinary income to him.

§ 1.708-1 Continuation of partnership

(a) **General rule.** For purposes of subchapter K, chapter 1 of the Code, an existing partnership shall be considered as continuing if it is not terminated.

(b) **Termination—(1) General rule.** (i) A partnership shall terminate when the operations of the partnership are discontinued and no part of any business, financial operation, or venture of the partnership continues to be carried on by any of its partners in a partnership. For example, on November 20, 1956, A and B, each of whom is a 20-percent partner in partnership ABC, sell their interests to C, who is a 60-percent partner. Since the business is no longer carried on by any of its partners in a partnership, the ABC partnership is terminated as of November 20, 1956. However, where partners DEF agree on April 30, 1957, to dissolve their partnership, but carry on the business through a winding up period ending September 30, 1957, when all remaining assets, consisting only of cash, are distributed to the partners, the partnership does not terminate because of cessation of business until September 30, 1957.

(a) Upon the death of one partner in a 2-member partnership, the partnership shall not be considered as terminated if the estate or other successor in interest of the deceased partner continues to share in the profits or losses of the partnership business.

(b) For the continuation of a partnership where payments are being made under section 736 (relating to payments to a retiring partner or a deceased partner's successor in interest), see paragraph (a) (6) of § 1.736-1.

(ii) A partnership shall terminate when 50 percent or more of the total interest in partnership capital and profits is sold or exchanged within a period of 12 consecutive months. Such sale or exchange includes a sale or exchange to another member of the partnership. However, a disposition of a partnership interest by gift (including assignment to a successor in interest), bequest, or inheritance, or the liquidation of a partnership interest, is not a sale or exchange for purposes of this subparagraph. Furthermore, the contribution of property to a partnership does not constitute such a sale or exchange. See, however, paragraph (c) (3) of § 1.731-1. Fifty percent or more of the total interest in partnership capital and profits means 50 percent or more of the total inerest in partnership capital plus 50 percent or more of the total interest in partnership profits. Thus, the sale of a 30-percent interest in partnership capital and a 60-percent interest in partnership profits is not the sale or exchange of 50 percent or more of the total interest in partnership capital and profits. If one or more partners sell or exchange interests aggregating 50 percent or more of the total interest in partnership capital and 50 percent or more of the total interest in partnership profits within a period of 12 consecutive months, such sale or exchange is considered as being within the provisions of this subparagraph.

When interests are sold or exchanged on different dates, the percentages to be added are determined as of the date of each sale. For example, with respect to the ABC partnership, the sale by A on May 12, 1956, of a 30-percent interest in capital and profits to D, and the sale by B on March 27, 1957, of a 30-percent interest in capital and profits to E, is a sale of a 50-percent or more interest. Accordingly, the partnership is terminated as of March 27, 1957. However, if, on March 27, 1957, D instead of B, sold his 30-percent interest in capital and profits to E, there would be no termination since only one 30-percent interest would have been sold or exchanged within a 12-month period.

(iii) For purposes of subchapter K, chapter 1 of the Code, a partnership taxable year closes with respect to all partners on the date on which the partnership terminates. See section 706(c)

(1) and paragraph (c) (1) of § 1.706–1. The date of termination is:

(a) For purposes of section 708 (b) (1) (A), the date on which the winding up of the partnership affairs is completed.

(b) For purposes of section 708 (b) (1) (B), the date of the sale or exchange of a partnership interest which, of itself or together with sales or exchanges in the preceding 12 months, transfers an interest of 50 percent or more in both partnership capital and profits.

(iv) If a partnership is terminated by a sale or exchange of an interest, the following is deemed to occur: The partnership distributes its properties to the purchaser and the other remaining partners in proportion to their respective interests in the partnership properties; and, immediately thereafter, the purchaser and the other remaining partners contribute the properties to a new partnership, either for the continuation of the business or for its dissolution and winding up. In the latter case, the new partnership terminates in accordance with subdivision (i) of this subparagraph. See sections 731 and 732 and §§ 1.731–1 and 1.732–1. For election of basis adjustments by the purchaser and other remaining partners, see sections 732 (d) and 743 (b) and paragraph (d) of § 1.732–1 and paragraph (b) of § 1.743–1.

(2) Special rules—(i) Merger or consolidation. If two or more partnerships merge or consolidate into one partnership, the resulting partnership shall be considered a continuation of the merging or consolidating partnership the members of which own an interest of more than 50 percent in the capital and profits of the resulting partnership. If the resulting partnership can, under the preceding sentence, be considered a continuation of more than one of the merging or consolidating partnerships, it shall, unless the Commissioner permits otherwise, be considered the continuation of that partnership which is credited with the contribution of the greatest dollar value of assets to the resulting partnership. Any other merging or consolidating partnerships shall be considered as terminated. If the members of none of the merging or consolidating partnerships have an interest of more than 50 percent in the capital and profits of the resulting partnership, all of the merged or consolidated partnerships are terminated, and a new partnership results. The taxable years of such merging or consolidating partnerships which are considered terminated shall be closed in accordance with the provisions of section 706 (c), and such partnerships shall file their returns for a taxable year ending upon the date of termination, i. e., the date of merger or consolidation. The resulting partnership shall file a return for the taxable year of the merging or consolidating partnership that is considered as continuing. The return shall state that the resulting partnership is a continuation of such merging or consolidating partnership and shall include the names and addresses of the merged or consolidated partnerships. The respective distributive shares of the partners for the periods prior to and subsequent to the date of merger or consolidation shall be shown as a part of the return. The provisions of this subdivision may be illustrated by the following example:

Example. Partnership AB, in whose capital and profits A and B each own a 50-percent interest, and partnership CD, in whose capital and profits C and D each own a 50-percent interest, merge on September 30, 1955, and form partnership ABCD. Partners A, B, C, and D are on a calendar year; partnership AB is also on a calendar year; and partnership CD is on a fiscal year ending June 30th. After the merger, the partners have capital and profits interests as follows: A, 30 percent; B, 30 percent; C, 20 percent; and D, 20 percent. Since A and B together own an interest of more than 50 percent in the capital and profits of partnership ABCD, such partnership shall be considered a continuation of partnership AB and shall continue to file returns on a calendar year basis. Since C and D own an interest of less than 50 percent in the capital and profits of partnership ABCD, the taxable year of partnership CD closes as of September 30, 1955, the date of the merger, and CD partnership is terminated as of that date. Partnership ABCD is required to file a return for the taxable year January 1 to December 31, 1955, indicating thereon that, until September 30, 1955, it was partnership AB. Partnership CD is required to file a return for its final taxable year, July 1 through September 30, 1955.

(ii) Division of a partnership. Upon the division of a partnership into two or more partnerships, any resulting partnership or partnerships shall be considered a continuation of the prior partnership if its members had an interest of more than 50 percent in the capital and profits of the prior partnership. Any other resulting partnership will not be considered a continuation of the prior partnership but will be considered a new partnership. If the members of none of the resulting partnerships owned an interest of more than 50 percent in the capital and profits of the divided partnership, the divided partnership is terminated. Where members of a partnership which has been divided into two or more partnerships do not become members of a resulting partnership which is considered a continuation of the prior partnership, such partner's interests shall be considered liquidated as of the date of the division. The resulting partnership that is regarded as continuing shall file a return for the taxable year of the partnership that has been divided. The return shall state that the partnership is a continuation of the divided partnership and shall set forth separately the respective distributive shares of the partners for the periods prior to and subsequent to the date of division. The provisions of this subdivision may be illustrated by the following example:

Example. Partnership ABCD is in the real estate and insurance business. A owns a 40-percent interest, and B, C, and D each owns a 20-percent interest, in the capital and profits of the partnership. The partnership and the partners report their income on a calendar year. They agree to separate the real estate and insurance business as of November 1, 1955, and to form two partnerships; partnership AB to take over the real estate business, and partnership CD to take over the insurance business. Since members of resulting partnership AB owned more than a 50-percent interest in the capital and profits of partnership ABCD (A, 40 percent, and B, 20 percent), partnership AB shall be considered a continuation of partnership ABCD. Partnership AB is required to file a return for the taxable year January 1 to December 31, 1955, indicating thereon that until November 1, 1955, it was partnership ABCD. In forming partnership CD, partners C and D may contribute the property distributed to them in liquidation of their entire interests in divided partnership ABCD. Partnership CD will be required to file a return for the taxable year it adopts pursuant to section 706(b) and § 1.706-1(b).

§ 1.721-1 Nonrecognition of gain or loss on contribution

(a) No gain or loss shall be recognized either to the partnership or to any of its partners upon a contribution of property, including installment obligations, to the partnership in exchange for a partnership interest. This rule applies whether the contribution is made to a partnership in the process of formation or to a partnership which is already formed and operating. Section 721 shall not apply to a transaction between a partnership and a partner not acting in his capacity as a part-

ner since such a transaction is governed by section 707. Rather than contributing property to a partnership, a partner may sell property to the partnership or may retain the ownership of property and allow the partnership to use it. In all cases, the substance of the transaction will govern, rather than its form. See paragraph (c) (3) of § 1.731-1. Thus, if the transfer of property by the partner to the partnership results in the receipt by the partner of money or other consideration, including a promissory obligation fixed in amount and time for payment, the transaction will be treated as a sale or exchange under section 707 rather than as a contribution under section 721. For the rules governing the treatment of liabilities to which contributed property is subject, see section 752 and § 1.752-1.

(b) (1) Normally, under local law, each partner is entitled to be repaid his contributions of money or other property to the partnership (at the value placed upon such property by the partnership at the time of the contribution) whether made at the formation of the partnership or subsequent thereto. To the extent that any of the partners gives up any part of his right to be repaid his contributions (as distinguished from a share in partnership profits) in favor of another partner as compensation for services (or in satisfaction of an obligation), section 721 does not apply. The value of an interest in such partnership capital so transferred to a partner as compensation for services constitutes income to the partner under section 61. The amount of such income is the fair market value of the interest in capital so transferred, either at the time the transfer is made for past services, or at the time the services have been rendered where the transfer is conditioned on the completion of the transferee's future services. The time when such income is realized depends on all the facts and circumstances, including any substantial restrictions or conditions on the compensated partner's right to withdraw or otherwise dispose of such interest. To the extent that an interest in capital representing compensation for services rendered by the decedent prior to his death is transferred after his death to the decedent's successor in interest, the fair market value of such interest is income in respect of a decedent under section 691.

(2) To the extent that the value of such interest is: (i) compensation for services rendered to the partnership, it is a guaranteed payment for services under section 707(c); (ii) compensation for services rendered to a partner, it is not deductible by the partnership, but is deductible only by such partner to the extent allowable under this chapter.

§ 1.722-1 Basis of contributing partner's interest

The basis to a partner of a partnership interest acquired by a contribution of property, including money, to the partnership shall be the amount of money contributed plus the adjusted basis at the time of contribution of any property contributed. If the acquisition of an interest in partnership capital results in taxable income to a partner, such income shall constitute an addition to the basis of the partner's interest. See paragraph (b) of § 1.721-1. If the contributed property is subject to indebtedness or if liabilities of the partner are assumed by the partnership, the basis of the contributing partner's interest shall be reduced by the portion of the indebtedness assumed by the other partners, since the partnership's assumption of his indebtedness is treated as a distribution of money to the partner. Conversely, the assumption by the other partners of a portion of the contributor's indebtedness is treated as a contribution of money by them. See section 752 and § 1.752-1. The provisions of this section may be illustrated by the following examples:

Example (1). A acquired a 20-percent interest in a partnership by contributing property. At the time of A's contribution, the property had a fair market value of $10,000, an adjusted basis to A of $4,000, and was subject to a mortgage of $2,000. Payment of the mortgage was assumed by the partnership. The basis of A's interest in the partnership is $2,400, computed as follows:

Adjusted basis to A of property contributed.. $4,000
Less portion of mortgage assumed by other partners which must be treated as a distribution (80 percent of $2,000) 1,600
Basis of A's interest........................ 2,400

Example (2). If, in example (1) of this section, the property contributed by A was subject to a mortgage of $6,000, the basis of A's interest would be zero, computed as follows:

Adjusted basis to A of property contributed.. $4,000
Less portion of mortgage assumed by other partners which must be treated as a distribution (80 percent of $6,000).................. 4,800
(800)

Since A's basis cannot be less than zero, the $800 in excess of basis, which is considered as a distribution of money under section 752(b), is treated as capital gain from the sale or exchange or a partnership interest. See section 731(a).

§ 1.723-1 Basis of property contributed to partnership

The basis to the partnership of property contributed to it by a partner is the adjusted basis of such property to the contributing partner at the time of the contribution. Since such property has the same basis in the hands of the partnership as it had in the hands of the contributing partner, the holding period of such property for the partnership includes the period during which it was held by the partner. See section 1223(2). For elective adjustments to the basis of partnership property arising from distributions or transfers of partnership interests, see sections 732(d), 734(b), and 743(b).

§ 1.731-1 Extent of recognition of gain or loss on distribution

(a) Recognition of gain or loss to partner—(1) Recognition of gain. (i) Where money is distributed by a partnership to a partner, no gain shall be recognized to the partner except to the extent that the amount of money distributed exceeds the adjusted basis of the partner's interest in the partnership immediately before the distribution. This rule is applicable both to current distributions (i. e., distributions other than in liquidation of an entire interest) and to distributions in liquidation of a partner's entire interest in a partnership. Thus, if a partner with a basis for his interest of $10,-000 receives a distribution of cash of $8,000 and property with a fair market value of $3,000, no gain is recognized to him. If $11,000 cash were distributed, gain would be recognized to the extent of $1,000. No gain shall be recognized to a distributee partner with respect to a distribution of property (other than money) until he sells or otherwise disposes of such property, except to the extent otherwise provided by section 736 (relating to payments to a retiring partner or a deceased partner's successor in interest) and section 751 (relating to unrealized receivables and inventory items). See section 731 (c) and paragraph (c) of this section.

(ii) For the purposes of sections 731 and 705, advances or drawings of money or property against a partner's distributive share of income shall be treated as current distributions made on the last day of the partnership taxable year with respect to such partner.

(2) **Recognition of loss.** Loss is recognized to a partner only upon liquidation of his entire interest in the partnership, and only if the property distributed to him consists solely of money, unrealized receivables (as defined in section 751(c)), and inventory items (as defined in section 751(d)(2)). The term "liquidation of a partner's interest", as defined in section 761(d), is the termination of the partner's entire interest in the partnership by means of a distribution or a series of distributions. Loss is recognized to the distributee partner in such cases to the extent of the excess of the adjusted basis of such partner's interest in the partnership at the time of the distribution over the sum of—

(i) Any money distributed to him, and

(ii) The basis to the distributee, as determined under section 732, of any unrealized receivables and inventory items that are distributed to him.

If the partner whose interest is liquidated receives any property other than money, unrealized receivables, or inventory items, then no loss will be recognized.

. . . .

(3) **Character of gain or loss.** Gain or loss recognized under section 731(a) on a distribution is considered gain or loss from the sale or exchange of the partnership interest of the distributee partner, that is, capital gain or loss.

(b) **Gain or loss recognized by partnership.** A distribution of property (including money) by a partnership to a partner does not result in recognized gain or loss to the partnership under section 731. However, recognized gain or loss may result to the partnership from certain distributions which, under section 751(b), must be treated as a sale or exchange of property between the distributee partner and the partnership.

(c) **Exceptions.** (1) Section 731 does not apply to the extent otherwise provided by—

(i) Section 736 (relating to payments to a retiring partner or to a deceased partner's successor in interest) and

(ii) Section 751 (relating to unrealized receivables and inventory items). For example, payments under section 736(a), which are considered as a distributive share or guaranteed payment, are taxable as such under that section.

(2) The receipt by a partner from the partnership of money or property under an obligation to repay the amount of such money or to return such property does not constitute a distribution subject to section 731 but is a loan governed by section 707(a). To the extent that such an obligation is canceled, the obligor partner will be considered to have received a distribution of money or property at the time of cancellation.

(3) If there is a contribution of property to a partnership and within a short period:

(i) Before or after such contribution other property is distributed to the contributing partner and the contributed property is retained by the partnership, or

(ii) After such contribution the contributed property is distributed to another partner,

such distribution may not fall within the scope of section 731. Section 731 does not apply to a distribution of property, if, in fact, the distribution was made in order to effect an exchange of property between two or more of the partners or between the partnership and a partner. Such a transaction shall be treated as an exchange of property.

§ 1.732-1 Basis of distributed property other than money

(a) **Distributions other than in liquidation of a partner's interest.** The basis of property (other than money) received by a partner in a distribution from a partnership, other than in liquidation of his entire interest, shall be its adjusted basis to the partnership immediately before such distribution. However, the basis of the property to the partner shall not exceed the adjusted basis of the partner's interest in the partnership, reduced by the amount of any money distributed to him in the same transaction. The provisions of this paragraph may be illustrated by the following examples:

Example (1). Partner A, with an adjusted basis of $15,000 for his partnership interest, receives in a current distribution property having an adjusted basis of $10,000 to the partnership immediately before distribution, and $2,000 cash. The basis of the property in A's hands will be $10,000. Under sections 733 and 705, the basis of A's partnership interest will be reduced by the distribution to $3,000 ($15,000, less $2,000 cash, less $10,000, the basis of the distributed property to A).

Example (2). Partner R has an adjusted basis of $10,000 for his partnership interest. He receives a current distribution of $4,000 cash and property with an adjusted basis to the partnership of $8,000. The basis of the distributed property to partner R is limited to $6,000 ($10,-000, the adjusted basis of his interest, reduced by $4,000, the cash distributed).

(b) Distribution in liquidation. Where a partnership distributes property (other than money) in liquidation of a partner's entire interest in the partnership, the basis of such property to the partner shall be an amount equal to the adjusted basis of his interest in the partnership reduced by the amount of any money distributed to him in the same transaction. Application of this rule may be illustrated by the following example:

Example. Partner B, with a partnership interest having an adjusted basis to him of $12,-000, retires from the partnership and receives cash of $2,000, and real property with an adjusted basis to the partnership of $6,000 and a fair market value of $14,000. The basis of the real property to B is $10,000 (B's basis for his partnership interest, $12,000, reduced by $2,000, the cash distributed).

(c) Allocation of basis among properties distributed to a partner. (1) Under section 732(a) (2) or (b), the basis to be allocated to properties distributed to a partner shall be allocated first to any unrealized receivables (as defined in section 751(c)) and inventory items (as defined in section 751 (d) (2)) included in the distribution. However, such receivables or inventory items may not take a higher basis in the hands of the partner than their common adjusted basis to the partnership immediately before the distribution, unless such distribution is treated as a sale or exchange under section 751(b), or unless the distributee partner has a special basis adjustment for the distributed property under sections 732(d) or 743(b). Any basis not allocated to unrealized receivable or inventory items shall be allocated to any

other properties distributed to the partner in the same transaction, in proportion to the bases of such other properties in the hands of the partnership before distribution. The provisions of this subparagraph may be illustrated by the following example:

Example. Partner A, whose partnership interest in partnership ABC has an adjusted basis of $15,000, receives as a distribution in liquidation of his entire interest inventory items having a basis to the partnership of $6,000. In addition, he receives cash of $5,000, and two parcels of real property with adjusted bases to the partnership of $6,000 and $2,000, respectively. Basis in the amount of $10,000 ($15,000 basis, less $5,-000 cash received) is allocated $6,000 to inventory items, and $3,000 (6,000/8,000 x $4,000) and $1,000 (2,000/8,000 x $4,000), respectively, to the two parcels of real property.

(2) If the adjusted basis to the partnership of the unrealized receivables and inventory items distributed to a partner is greater than the partner's adjusted basis of his interest (reduced by the amount of money distributed to him in the same transaction), the amount of the basis to be allocated to such unrealized receivables and inventory items shall be allocated in proportion to the adjusted bases of such properties in the hands of the partnership. If the basis of the partner's interest to be allocated upon a distribution in liquidation of his entire interest is in excess of the adjusted basis to the partnership of the unrealized receivables and inventory items distributed, and if there is no other property distributed to which such excess can be allocated, the distributee partner sustains a capital loss under section 731(a) (2) to the extent of the unallocated basis of his partnership interest. . . . .

. . . .

(d) Special partnership basis to transferee under section 732(d). (1) (i) A transfer of a partnership interest occurs upon a sale or exchange of an interest or upon the death of a partner. Section 732(d) provides a special rule for the determination of the basis of property distributed to a transferee partner who acquired any part of his partnership interest in a transfer with respect to which the election under section 754 (relating to the optional adjustment to basis of partnership property) was not in effect.

(ii) Where an election under section 754 is in effect, see section 743(b) and paragraph (b) of § 1.743–1 and § 1.732–2.

(iii) If a transferee partner receives a distribution of property (other than money) from the partnership within 2 years after he acquired his interest or part thereof in the partnership by a transfer with respect to which the election under section 754 was not in effect, he may elect to treat as the adjusted partnership basis of such property the adjusted basis such property would have if the adjustment provided in section 743(b) were in effect.

(iv) If an election under section 732 (d) is made upon a distribution of property to a transferee partner, the amount of the adjustment with respect to the transferee partner is not diminished by any depletion or depreciation of that portion of the basis of partnership property which arises from the special basis adjustment under section 732(d), since depletion or depreciation on such portion for the period prior to distribution is allowed or allowable only if the optional adjustment under section 743(b) is in effect.

(v) If property is distributed to a transferee partner who elects under section 732(d), and if such property is not the same property which would have had a special basis adjustment, then such special basis adjustment shall apply to any like property received in the distribution, provided that the transferee, in exchange for the property distributed, has relinquished his interest in the property with respect to which he would have had a special basis adjustment. This rule applies whether the property in which the transferee has relinquished his interest is retained or disposed of by the partnership.   .   .   .   .

.   .   .   .

(2) A transferee partner who wishes to elect under section 732(d) shall make the election with his tax return—

(i) For the year of the distribution, if the distribution includes any property subject to the allowance for depreciation, depletion, or amortization, or

(ii) For any taxable year no later than the first taxable year in which the basis of any of the distributed property is pertinent in determining his income tax, if the distribution does not include any such property subject to the allowance for depreciation, depletion or amortization.

(3) A taxpayer making an election under section 732(d) shall submit with the return in which the election is made a schedule setting forth the following:

(i) That under section 732(d) he elects to adjust the basis of property received in a distribution; and

(ii) The computation of the special basis adjustment for the property distributed and the properties to which the adjustment has been allocated. For rules of allocation, see section 755.

(4) A partner who acquired any part of his partnership interest in a transfer to which the election provided in section 754 was not in effect, is required to apply the special basis rule contained in section 732(d) to a distribution to him, whether or not made within 2 years after the transfer, if at the time of his acquisition of the transferred interest—

(i) The fair market value of all partnership property (other than money) exceeded 110 percent of its adjusted basis to the partnership,

(ii) An allocation of basis under section 732(c) upon a liquidation of his interest immediately after the transfer of the interest would have resulted in a shift of basis from property not subject to an allowance for depreciation, depletion, or amortization, to property subject to such an allowance, and

(iii) A special basis adjustment under section 743(b) would change the basis to the transferee partner of the property actually distributed.

.   .   .   .

(e) Exception. When a partnership distributes unrealized receivables (as defined in section 751(c)) or substantially appreciated inventory items (as defined in section 751(d)) in exchange for any part of a partner's interest in other partnership property (including money), or, conversely, partnership property (including money) other than unrealized receivables or substantially appreciated inventory items in exchange for any part of a partner's interest in the partnership's unrealized receivables or substantially appreciated inventory items, the distribution will be treated as a sale or exchange of property under the provisions of section 751(b). In such case, section

732 (including subsection (d) thereof) applies in determining the partner's basis of the property which he is treated as having sold to or exchanged with the partnership (as constituted after the distribution). The partner is considered as having received such property in a current distribution and paragraph (b) of § 1.751–1. However, section 732 does not apply in determining the basis of that part of property actually distributed to a partner which is treated as received by him in a sale or exchange under section 751(b). Consequently, the basis of such property shall be its cost to the partner.

§ 1.732–2 Special partnership basis of distributed property

(a) **Adjustments under section 734 (b).** In the case of a distribution of property to a partner, the partnership bases of the distributed properties shall reflect any increases or decreases to the basis of partnership property which have been made previously under section 734(b) (relating to the optional adjustment to basis of undistributed partnership property) in connection with previous distributions.

(b) **Adjustments under section 743 (b).** In the case of a distribution of property to a partner who acquired any part of his interest in a transfer as to which an election under section 754 was in effect, then, for the purposes of section 732 (other than subsection (d) thereof), the adjusted partnership bases of the distributed property shall take into account, in addition to any adjustments under section 734(b), the transferee's special basis adjustment for the distributed property under section 743(b). The application of this paragaraph may be illustrated by the following example:

Example. Partner D acquired his interest in partnership ABD from a previous partner. Since the partnership had made an election under section 754, a special basis adjustment with respect to D is applicable to the basis of partnership property in accordance with section 743(b). One of the assets of the partnership at the time D acquired his interest was property X, which is later distributed to D in a current distribution. Property X has an adjusted basis to the partnership of $1,000 and with respect to D it has a special basis adjustment of $500. Therefore, for purposes of section 732(a) (1), the adjusted basis of such property to the partnership with respect to D immediately before its distribution is $1,-500. However, if property X is distributed to partner A, a nontransferee partner, its adjust-

ed basis to the partnership for purposes of section 732(a) (1) is only $1,000. In such case, D's $500 special basis adjustment may shift over to other property. See paragraph (b) (2) (ii) of § 1.743–1.

(c) **Adjustments to basis of distributed inventory and unrealized receivables.** Under section 732, the basis to be allocated to distributed properties shall be allocated first to any unrealized receivables and inventory items. If the distributee partner is a transferee of a partnership interest and has a special basis adjustment for unrealized receivables or inventory items under either section 743(b) or section 732(d), then the partnership adjusted basis immediately prior to distribution of any unrealized receivables or inventory items distributed to such partner shall be determined as follows: If the distributee partner receives his entire share of the fair market value of the inventory items or unrealized receivables of the partnership, the adjusted basis of such distributed property to the partnership, for the purposes of section 732, shall take into account the entire amount of any special basis adjustment which the distributee partner may have for such assets. If the distributee partner receives less than his entire share of the fair market value of partnership inventory items or unrealized receivables, then, for purposes of section 732, the adjusted basis of such distributed property to the partnership shall take into account the same proportion of the distributee's special basis adjustment for unrealized receivables or inventory items as the value of such items distributed to him bears to his entire share of the total value of all such items of the partnership. The provisions of this paragraph may be illustrated by the following example:

Example. Partner C acquired his 40-percent interest in partnership AC from a previous partner. Since the partnership had made an election under section 754, C has a special basis adjustment to partnership property under section 743(b). C retires from the partnership when the adjusted basis of his partnership interest is $3,000. He receives from the partnership in liquidation of his entire interest, $1,000 cash, certain capital assets, depreciable property, and certain inventory items and unrealized receivables. C has a special basis adjustment of $800 with respect to partnership inventory items and of $200 with respect to unrealized receivables. The common partnership basis for the inventory items distributed to him is $500 and for the unrealized receivables is zero. If the value of inventory items and the unrealized receivables distributed to C in his 40 percent share of the total value of all partnership inventory items and unrealized receivables, then, for purposes of section 732, the adjusted basis of such property in C's hands will be $1,300 for the inventory items ($500 plus $800) and $200 for the unrealized receivables (zero plus $200). The remaining basis of $500, which constitutes the basis of the capital assets and depreciable property distributed to C, is determined as follows: $3,000 (total basis) less $1,000 cash, or $2,000 (the amount to be allocated to the basis of all distributed property), less $1,500 ($800 and $200 special basis adjustments, plus $500 common partnership basis, the amount allocated to inventory items and unrealized receivables). However, if the value of the inventory items and unrealized receivables distributed to C consisted of only 20 percent of the total fair market value of such property (i. e., only one-half of C's 40-percent share), then only one-half of C's special basis adjustment of $800 for partnership inventory items and $200 for unrealized receivables would be taken into account. In that case, the basis of the inventory items in C's hands would be $650 ($250, the common partnership basis for inventory items distributed to him, plus $400, one-half of C's special basis adjustment for inventory items). The basis of the unrealized receivables in C's hands would be $100 (zero plus $100, one-half of C's special basis adjustment for unrealized receivables).

§ 1.733–1 Basis of distributee partner's interest

In the case of a distribution by a partnership to a partner other than in liquidation of a partner's entire interest, the adjusted basis to such partner of his interest in the partnership shall be reduced (but not below zero) by the amount of any money distributed to such partner and by the amount of the basis to him of distributed property other than money as determined under section 732 and §§ 1.732–1 and 1.732–2.

§ 1.734–1 Optional adjustment to basis of undistributed partnership property

(a) General rule. A partnership shall not adjust the basis of partnership property as the result of a distribution of property to a partner, unless the election provided in section 754 (relating to optional adjustment to basis of partnership property) is in effect.

(b) Method of adjustment—(1) Increase in basis. Where an election under section 754 is in effect and a distribution of partnership property is made, whether or not in liquidation of the partner's entire interest in the

partnership, the adjusted basis of the remaining partnership assets shall be increased by—

(i) The amount of any gain recognized under section 731(a) (1) to the distributee partner, or

(ii) The excess of the adjusted basis to the partnership immediately before the distribution of any property distributed (including adjustments under section 743(b) or section 732(d) when applied) over the basis under section 732 (including such special basis adjustments) of such property to the distributee partner.

The provisions of this subparagraph may be illustrated by the following examples:

Example (1). Partner A has a basis of $10,000 'for his one-third interest in partnership ABC. The partnership has no liabilities and has assets consisting of cash of $11,000 and property with a partnership basis of $19,000 and a value of $22,000. A receives $11,000 in cash in liquidation of his entire interest in the partnership. He has a gain of $1,000 under section 731 (a) (1). If the election under section 754 is in effect, the partnership basis for the property becomes $20,000 ($19,000 plus $1,000).

Example (2). Partner D has a basis of $10,000 for his one-third interest in partnership DEF. The partnership balance sheet before the distribution shows the following:

Assets

	Adjusted basis	Value
Cash	$4,000	$4,000
Property X	11,000	11,000
Property Y	15,000	18,000
Total	30,000	33,000

Liabilities and Capital

Liabilities	$0	$0
Capital:		
D	10,000	11,000
E	10,000	11,000
F	10,000	11,000
Total	30,000	33,000

In liquidation of his entire interest in the partnership, D received property X with a partnership basis of $11,000. D's basis for property X is $10,000 under section 732(b). Where the election under section 754 is in effect, the excess of $1,000 (the partnership basis before the distribution less D's basis for property X after distribution) is added to the basis of property Y. The basis of property Y becomes $16,000 ($15,000 plus $1,000). If the distribution is made to a transferee partner who elects under section 732(d), see § 1.734-2.

(2) Decrease in basis. Where the election provided in section 754 is in

effect and a distribution is made in liquidation of a partner's entire interest, the partnership shall decrease the adjusted basis of the remaining partnership property by—

(i) The amount of loss, if any, recognized under section 731(a) (2) to the distributee partner, or

(ii) The excess of the basis of the distributed property to the distributee, as determined under section 732 (including adjustments under section 743 (b) or section 732(d) when applied) over the adjusted basis of such property to the partnership (including such special basis adjustments) immediately before such distribution.

The provisions of this subparagraph may be illustrated by the following examples:

Example (1). Partner G has a basis of $11,000 for his one-third interest in partnership GHI. Partnership assets consist of cash of $10,000 and property with a basis of $23,000 and a value of $20,000. There are no partnership liabilities. In liquidation of his entire interest in the partnership, G receives $10,000 in cash. He has a loss of $1,000 under section 731(a) (2). If the election under section 754 is in effect, the partnership basis for the property becomes $22,000 ($23,000 less $1,000).

Example (2). Partner J has a basis of $11,000 for his one-third interest in partnership JKL. The partnership balance sheet before the distribution shows the following:

ASSETS

	Adjusted basis	Value
Cash	$5,000	$5,000
Property X	10,000	10,000
Property Y	18,000	15,000
Total	33,000	30,000

LIABILITIES AND CAPITAL

	Adjusted basis	Value
Liabilities	$0	$0
Capital:		
J	11,000	10,000
K	11,000	10,000
L	11,000	10,000
Total	33,000	30,000

In liquidation of his entire interest in the partnership, J receives property X with a partnership basis of $10,000. J's basis for property X under section 732(b) is $11,000. Where the election under section 754 is in effect, the excess of

$1,000 ($11,000 basis of property X to J, the distributee, less its $10,000 adjusted basis to the partnership immediately before the distribution) decreases the basis of property Y in the partnership. Thus, the basis of property Y becomes $17,000 ($18,000 less $1,000). If the distribution is made to a transferee partner who elects under section 732(d), see § 1.734-2.

(c) Allocation of basis. For allocation among the partnership properties of basis adjustments under section 734(b) and paragraph (b) of this section, see section 755 and § 1.755-1.

(d) Returns. A partnership which must adjust the basis of partnership properties under section 734 shall attach a statement to the partnership return for the year of the distribution setting forth the computation of the adjustment and the partnership properties to which the adjustment has been allocated.

§ 1.734–2 Adjustment after distribution to transferee partner

(a) In the case of a distribution of property by the partnership to a partner who has obtained all or part of his partnership interest by transfer, the adjustments to basis provided in section 743(b) and section 732(d) shall be taken into account in applying the rules under section 734(b). For determining the adjusted basis of distributed property to the partnership immediately before the distribution where there has been a prior transfer of a partnership interest with respect to which the election provided in section 754 or section 732(d) is in effect, see §§ 1.732-1 and 1.732-2.

(b) (1) If a transferee partner, in liquidation of his entire partnership interest, receives a distribution of property (including money) with respect to which he has no special basis adjustment, in exchange for his interest in property with respect to which he has a special basis adjustment, and does not utilize his entire special basis adjustment in determining the basis of the distributed property to him under section 732, the unused special basis adjustment of the distributee shall be applied as an adjustment to the partnership basis of the property retained by the partnership and as to which the distributee did not use his special basis adjustment. The provisions of this subparagraph may be illustrated by the following example:

Example. Upon the death of his father, partner S acquires by inheritance a half-interest in partnership ACS. Partners A and C each have a one-quarter interest. The assets of the partnership consist of $10,000 cash and land used in farming worth $10,000 with a basis of $1,000 to the partnership. Since the partnership had made the election under section 754 at the time of transfer, partner S had a special basis adjustment of $4,500 under section 743(b) with respect to his undivided half-interest in the real estate. The basis of S's partnership interest, in accordance with section 742, is $10,000. S retires from the partnership and receives $10,000 in cash in exchange for his entire interest. Since S has received no part of the real estate, his special basis adjustment of $4,500 will be allocated to the real estate, the remaining partnership property, and will increase its basis to the partnership to $5,500.

* * * * *

§ 1.735-1   Character of gain or loss on disposition of distributed property

(a) Sale or exchange of distributed property—(1) Unrealized receivables. Any gain realized or loss sustained by a partner on a sale or exchange or other disposition of unrealized receivables (as defined in paragraph (c) (1) of § 1.751–1) received by him in a distribution from a partnership shall be considered gain or loss from the sale or exchange of property other than a capital asset.

(2) Inventory items. Any gain realized or loss sustained by a partner on a sale or exchange of inventory items (as defined in section 751(d) (2)) received in a distribution from a partnership shall be considered gain or loss from the sale or exchange of property other than a capital asset if such inventory items are sold or exchanged within 5 years from the date of the distribution by the partnership. The character of any gain or loss from a sale or exchange by the distributee partner of such inventory items after 5 years from the date of distribution shall be determined as of the date of such sale or exchange by reference to the character of the assets in his hands at that date (inventory items, capital assets, property used in a trade or business, etc.).

(b) Holding period for distributed property. A partner's holding period for property distributed to him by a partnership shall include the period such property was held by the part-

nership. The provisions of this paragraph do not apply for the purpose of determining the 5-year period described in section 735(a) (2) and paragraph (a) (2) of this section. If the property has been contributed to the partnership by a partner, then the period that the property was held by such partner shall also be included. See section 1223(2). For a partnership's holding period for contributed property, see § 1.723–1.

* * * * *

§ 1.736-1   Payments to a retiring partner or a deceased partner's successor in interest

(a) Payments considered as distributive share or guaranteed payment. (1) (i) Section 736 and this section apply only to payments made to a retiring partner or to a deceased partner's successor in interest in liquidation of such partner's entire interest in the partnership. See section 761(d). Section 736 and this section do not apply if the estate or other successor in interest of a deceased partner continues as a partner in its own right under local law. Section 736 and this section apply only to payments made by the partnership and not to transactions between the partners. Thus, a sale by partner A to partner B of his entire one-fourth interest in partnership ABCD would not come within the scope of section 736.

(ii) A partner retires when he ceases to be a partner under local law. However, for the purposes of subchapter K, chapter 1 of the Code, a retired partner or a deceased partner's successor will be treated as a partner until his interest in the partnership has been completely liquidated.

(2) When payments (including assumption of liabilities treated as a distribution of money under section 752) are made to a withdrawing partner, that is, a retiring partner or the estate or other successor in interest of a deceased partner, the amounts paid may represent several items. In part, they may represent the fair market value at the time of his death or retirement of the withdrawing partner's interest in all the assets of the partnership (including inventory) unreduced by partnership liabilities. Also, part of such payments may be attributable to his

interest in unrealized receivables and part to an arrangement among the partners in the nature of mutual insurance. When a partnership makes such payments, whether or not related to partnership income, to retire the withdrawing partner's entire interest in the partnership, the payments must be allocated between (i) payments for the value of his interest in assets, except unrealized receivables and, under some circumstances, good will (section 736(b)), and (ii) other payments (section 736(a)). The amounts paid for his interest in assets are treated in the same manner as a distribution in complete liquidation under sections 731, 732, and, where applicable, 751. See paragraph (b) (4) (ii) of § 1.751-1. The remaining partners are allowed no deduction for these payments since they represent either a distribution or a purchase of the withdrawing partner's capital interest by the partnership (composed of the remaining partners).

(3) Under section 736(a), the portion of the payments made to a withdrawing partner for his share of unrealized receivables, good will (in the absence of an agreement to the contrary), or otherwise not in exchange for his interest in assets under the rules contained in paragraph (b) of this section will be considered either—

(i) A distributive share of partnership income, if the amount of payment is determined with regard to income of the partnership; or

(ii) A guaranteed payment under section 707(c), if the amount of the payment is determined without regard to income of the partnership.

(4) Payments, to the extent considered as a distributive share of partnership income under section 736(a) (1), are taken into account under section 702 in the income of the withdrawing partner and thus reduce the amount of the distributive shares of the remaining partners. Payments, to the extent considered as guaranteed payments under section 736(a) (2), are deductible by the partnership under section 162(a) and are taxable as ordinary income to the recipient under section 61(a). See section 707(c).

(5) The amount of any payments under section 736(a) shall be included in the income of the recipient for his taxable year with or within which ends the partnership taxable year for which the payment is a distributive share, or in which the partnership is entitled to deduct such amount as a guaranteed payment. On the other hand, payments under section 736(b) shall be taken into account by the recipient for his taxable year in which such payments are made. See paragraph (b) (4) of this section.

(6) A retiring partner or a deceased partner's successor in interest receiving payments under section 736 is regarded as a partner until the entire interest of the retiring or deceased partner is liquidated. Therefore, if one of the members of a 2-man partnership retires under a plan whereby he is to receive payments under section 736, the partnership will not be considered terminated, nor will the partnership year close with respect to either partner, until the retiring partner's entire interest is liquidated, since the retiring partner continues to hold a partnership interest in the partnership until that time. Similarly, if a partner in a 2-man partnership dies, and his estate or other successor in interest receives payments under section 736, the partnership shall not be considered to have terminated upon the death of the partner but shall terminate as to both partners only when the entire interest of the decedent is liquidated. See section 708(b).

(b) Payments for interest in partnership. (1) Payments made in liquidation of the entire interest of a retiring partner or deceased partner shall, to the extent made in exchange for such partner's interest in partnership property (except for unrealized receivables and good will as provided in subparagraphs (2) and (3) of this paragraph), be considered as a distribution by the partnership (and not as a distributive share or guaranteed payment under section 736(a)). Generally, the valuation placed by the partners upon a partner's interest in partnership property in an arm's length agreement will be regarded as correct. If such valuation reflects only the partner's net interest in the property (i. e., total assets less liabilities), it must be adjusted so that both the value of the partner's interest in property and the basis for his interest take into account the partner's share of partnership liabilities. Gain or loss with respect to distributions under section 736(b) and this paragraph will be recognized to the distributee to the extent provided in section 731 and, where applicable, section 751.

(2) Payments made to a retiring partner or to the successor in interest of a deceased partner for his interest in unrealized receivables of the partnership in excess of their partnership basis, including any special basis adjustment for them to which such partner is entitled, shall not be considered as made in exchange for such partner's interest in partnership property. Such payments shall be treated as payments under section 736(a) and paragraph (a) of this section. For definition of unrealized receivables, see section 751 (c).

(3) For the purposes of section 736 (b) and this paragraph, payments made to a retiring partner or to a successor in interest of a deceased partner in exchange for the interest of such partner in partnership property shall not include any amount paid for the partner's share of good will of the partnership in excess of its partnership basis, including any special basis adjustments for it to which such partner is entitled, except to the extent that the partnership agreement provides for a reasonable payment with respect to such good will. Such payments shall be considered as payments under section 736(a). To the extent that the partnership agreement provides for a reasonable payment with respect to good will, such payments shall be treated under section 736(b) and this paragraph. Generally, the valuation placed upon good will by an arm's length agreement of the partners, whether specific in amount or determined by a formula, shall be regarded as correct.

(4) Payments made to a retiring partner or to a successor in interest of a deceased partner for his interest in inventory shall be considered as made in exchange for such partner's interest in partnership property for the purposes of section 736(b) and this paragraph. However, payments for an interest in substantially appreciated inventory items, as defined in section 751 (d), are subject to the rules provided in section 751(b) and paragraph (b) of § 1.751-1. The partnership basis in inventory items as to a deceased partner's successor in interest does not change

because of the death of the partner unless the partnership has elected the optional basis adjustment under section 754. But see paragraph (b) (3) (iii) § 1.751-1.

(5) Where payments made under section 736 are received during the taxable year, the recipient must segregate that portion of each such payment which is determined to be in exchange for the partner's interest in partnership property and treated as a distribution under section 736(b) from that portion treated as a distributive share or guaranteed payment under section 736(a). Such allocation shall be made as follows—

(i) If a fixed amount (whether or not supplemented by any additional amounts) is to be received over a fixed number of years, the portion of each payment to be treated as a distribution under section 736(b) for the taxable year shall bear the same ratio to the total fixed agreed payments for such year (as distinguished from the amount actually received) as the total fixed agreed payments under section 736(b) bear to the total fixed agreed payments under section 736(a) and (b). The balance, if any, of such amount received in the same taxable year shall be treated as a distributive share or a guaranteed payment under section 736(a) (1) or (2). However, if the total amount received in any one year is less than the amount considered as a distribution under section 736(b) for that year, then any unapplied portion shall be added to the portion of the payments for the following year or years which are to be treated as a distribution under section 736(b). For example, retiring partner W who is entitled to an annual payment of $6,000 for 10 years for his interest in partnership property, receives only $3,500 in 1955. In 1956, he receives $10,000. Of this amount, $8,500 ($6,000 plus $2,500 from 1955) is treated as a distribution under section 736(b) for 1956; $1,500, as a payment under section 736(a).

(ii) If the retiring partner or deceased partner's successor in interest receives payments which are not fixed in amount, such payments shall first be treated as payments in exchange for his interest in partnership property under section 736(b) to the extent of the value of that interest and, thereafter, as payments under section 736 (a).

(iii) In lieu of the rules provided in subdivisions (i) and (ii) of this subparagraph, the allocation of each annual payment between section 736(a) and (b) may be made in any manner to which all the remaining partners and the withdrawing partner or his successor in interest agree, provided that the total amount allocated to property under section 736(b) does not exceed the fair market value of such property at the date of death or retirement.

(6) Except to the extent section 751 (b) applies, the amount of any gain or loss with respect to payments under section 736(b) for a retiring or deceased partner's interest in property for each year of payment shall be determined under section 731. However, where the total of section 736(b) payments is a fixed sum, a retiring partner or a deceased partner's successor in interest may elect (in his tax return for the first taxable year for which he receives such payments), to report and to measure the amount of any gain or loss by the difference between—

(i) The amount treated as a distribution under section 736(b) in that year, and

(ii) The portion of the adjusted basis of the partner for his partnership interest attributable to such distribution (i. e., the amount which bears the same proportion to the partner's total adjusted basis for his partnership interest as the amount distributed under section 736(b) in that year bears to the total amount to be distributed under section 736(b)).

A recipient who elects under this subparagraph shall attach a statement to his tax return for the first taxable year for which he receives such payments, indicating his election and showing the computation of the gain included in gross income.

. . . .

§ 1.741-1 Recognition and character of gain or loss on sale or exchange

(a) The sale or exchange of an interest in a partnership shall, except to the extent section 751(a) applies, be treated as the sale or exchange of a capital asset, resulting in capital gain or loss measured by the difference between the amount realized and the adjusted basis of the partnership interest, as determined under section 705. For treatment of selling partner's distributive share up to date of sale, see section 706(c) (2). Where the provisions of section 751 require the recognition of ordinary income or loss with respect to a portion of the amount realized from such sale or exchange, the amount realized shall be reduced by the amount attributable under section 751 to unrealized receivables and substantially appreciated inventory items, and the adjusted basis of the transferor partner's interest in the partnership shall be reduced by the portion of such basis attributable to such unrealized receivables and substantially appreciated inventory items. See section 751 and § 1.751–1.

(b) Section 741 shall apply whether the partnership interest is sold to one or more members of the partnership or to one or more persons who are not members of the partnership. Section 741 shall also apply even though the sale of the partnership interest results in a termination of the partnership under section 708(b). Thus, the provisions of section 741 shall be applicable (1) to the transferor partner in a 2-man partnership when he sells his interest to the other partner, and (2) to all the members of a partnership when they sell their interests to one or more persons outside the partnership.

(c) See section 351 for nonrecognition of gain or loss upon transfer of a partnership interest to a corporation controlled by the transferor.

(d) For rules relating to the treatment of liabilities on the sale or exchange of interests in a partnership see §§ 1.752–1 and 1.1001–2.

§ 1.742–1 Basis of transferee partner's interest

The basis to a transferee partner of an interest in a partnership shall be determined under the general basis rules for property provided by part II (section 1011 and following), subchapter O, chapter 1 of the Code. Thus, the basis of a purchased interest will be its cost. The basis of a partnership interest acquired from a decedent is the fair market value of the interest at the date of his death or at the alternate valuation date, increased by his estate's or other successor's share of partnership liabilities, if any, on that date, and reduced to the extent that such value is attributable to items constituting income in respect of a decedent (see section 753 and paragraph (c) (3) (v) of § 1.706–1 and paragraph (b) of § 1.753–1) under section 691. See section 1014 (c). For basis of contributing partner's interest, see section 722. The basis so determined is then subject to the adjustments provided in section 705.

§ 1.743–1 Optional adjustment to basis of partnership property

(a) General rule. The basis of partnership property shall not be adjusted as the result of a transfer of an interest in a partnership, either by sale or exchange or as a result of the death of a partner, unless the election provided by section 754 (relating to optional adjustment to basis of partnership property) is in effect with respect to the partnership. However, whether or not the election provided in section 754 is in effect, the basis of partnership property shall not be adjusted as the result of a contribution of property, including money, to the partnership.

(b) Adjustment to basis of partnership property—(1) Determination of adjustment. In the case of a transfer of an interest in a partnership, either by sale or exchange or as a result of the death of a partner, a partnership as to which the election under section 754 is in effect shall:

(i) Increase the adjusted basis of partnership property by the excess of the transferee's basis for his partnership interest over his share of the adjusted basis to the partnership of all partnership property, or

(ii) Decrease the adjusted basis of partnership property by the excess of the transferee partner's share of the adjusted basis of all partnership property over his basis for his partnership interest.

The amount of the increase or decrease constitutes an adjustment affecting the basis of partnership property with respect to the transferee partner only. Thus, for purposes of

depreciation, depletion, gain or loss, and distributions, the transferee partner will have a special basis for those partnership properties which are adjusted under section 743(b) and this paragraph. This special basis is his share of the common partnership basis (i. e., the adjusted basis of such properties to the partnership without regard to any special basis adjustments of any transferee) plus or minus his special basis adjustments. A partner's share of the adjusted basis of partnership property is equal to the sum of his interest as a partner in partnership capital and surplus, plus his share of partnership liabilities. Where an agreement with respect to contributed property is in effect under section 704(c) (2), such agreement shall be taken into account in determining a partner's share of the adjusted basis of partnership property. Generally, if a partner's interest in partnership capital and profits is one-third, his share of the adjusted basis of partnership property will be one-third of such basis. The provisions of this paragraph may be illustrated by the following examples:

Example (1). A is a member of partnership ABC in which the partners have equal interests in capital and profits. The partnership has made the election under section 754, relating to the optional adjustment to the basis of partnership property. A sells his interest to P for $22,-000. The balance sheet of the partnership at the date of sale shows the following:

ASSETS

	Adjusted basis per books	Market value
Cash	$5,000	$5,000
Accounts receivable	10,000	10,000
Inventory	20,000	21,000
Depreciable assets	20,000	40,000
Total	55,000	76,000

LIABILITIES AND CAPITAL

	Adjusted basis per books	Value
Liabilities	$10,000	$10,000
Capital:		
A	15,000	22,000
B	15,000	22,000
C	15,000	22,000
Total	55,000	76,000

The amount of the adjustment under section 743(b) is the difference between the basis of the transferee's interest in the partnership and his share of the adjusted basis of partnership property. Under section 742, the basis of P's interest is $25,333 (the cash paid for A's interest, $22,000, plus $3,333, P's share of partnership liabilities). P's share of the adjusted basis of partnership property is $18,333, i. e., $15,000 plus $3,333. The amount to be added to the basis of partnership property is, therefore, $7,000, the difference between $25,333 and $18,333. This amount will be allocated to partnership properties in accordance with the rules set forth in section 755 and § 1.755-1.

Example (2). D is a member of partnership DEF in which the partners have equal interests in profits, but not in capital. The partnership has made the election under section 754. D dies and his interest passes to W, his widow. The balance sheet of the partnership at the date of D's death shows the following:

ASSETS

	Adjusted basis per books	Market value
Cash	$7,000	$7,000
Accounts receivable	10,000	10,000
Inventory	20,000	24,000
Depreciable assets	20,000	40,000
Total	57,000	81,000

LIABILITIES AND CAPITAL

	Adjusted basis per books	Value
Liabilities	$10,000	$10,000
Capital:		
D	18,000	26,000
E	15,000	23,000
F	14,000	22,000
Total	57,000	81,000

The amount of the adjustment under section 743(b) is the difference between the basis of the transferee's interest in the partnership and her share of the adjusted basis of partnership property. Under section 742, the basis of W's interest is $29,333 (the fair market value of D's interest at his death, $26,000, plus $3,333, his share of partnership liabilities). W's share of the adjusted basis of partnership property is $21,333 (i. e., $18,000 plus $3,333, per share of partnership liabilities). The amount to be added to the basis of partnership property is, therefore, $8,000, the difference between $29,333 and $21,333. This amount will be allocated to partnership properties in accordance with the rules set forth in section 755 and § 1.755-1.

Note that in examples (1) and (2) of this subparagraph the amount of the adjustment does not depend upon the adjusted basis to the transferor for his interest in partnership capital.

(2) Determination of partner's share of adjusted basis of partnership property. (i) Under the provisions of section 743(b), a partner's share of the adjusted basis of partnership property shall be determined by taking in-to account the effect of any partnership agreement with respect to contributed property as described in section 704(c) (2), or the effect of the contribution of undivided interests under section 704(c) (3). This rule may be illustrated by the following examples:

Example (1). A, B, and C form partnership ABC, to which A contributes land worth $1,000 (property X) with an adjusted basis to him of $400, and B and C each contributes $1,000 cash. Each partner has $1,000 credited to him on the books of the partnership as his capital contribution. The partners share in profits equally. During the partnership's first taxable year, property X appreciates in value to $1,300. A sells his one-third interest in the partnership to D for $1,100, when the election under section 754 is in effect. No agreement under section 704 (c) (2) is in effect. The adjusted basis of the partnership property is increased with respect to D by the excess of his basis for his partnership interest, $1,100, over his share of the adjusted basis of partnership property, $800 (⅓ of $2,400, the total adjusted basis of partnership property). The amount of the adjustment, therefore, is $300 ($1,100 minus $800), which is an increase in the basis of partnership property with respect to D only. This special basis adjustment will be allocated to property X. (See section 755 and § 1.755-1.) If property X is sold for $1,600, the gain to the partnership is $1,200 ($1,600 received, less the adjusted common partnership basis of $400 for property X). Thus, each partner's distributive share of the gain on the sale is $400. However, D's recognized gain is only $100 (his $400 distributive share of the gain, reduced by $300, his special basis adjustment with respect to property X). If D purchased his interest from B or C, the partners who contributed cash, D's adjustment under section 743(b) would also be $300, computed in exactly the same manner as in the case of a purchase from A.

Example (2). Assume that partnership ABC described in example (1) of this subdivision has an agreement under section 704(c) (2) with respect to property X, stating that upon the sale of that property any gain, to the extent attributable to the precontribution appreciation of $600 (the difference between its value, $1,000, and its basis, $400, at the time of the contribution) is to be allocated entirely to A, who contributed property X. Upon the purchase of A's interest by D for $1,100, the computation of D's special basis would differ from that indicated in example (1) of this subdivision as follows: Under the partnership agreement, A's share of the $2,400 adjusted basis of partnership property is only $400 (his basis for property X prior to its contribution to the partnership), and B's and C's share is $1,000 each (the amount of the cash investment of each). The amount of the increase to D in the adjusted basis of partnership property under section 743(b) (1) is $700 (the excess of $1,100, D's cost basis for his interest, over $400, A's share of the adjusted basis of partnership property to which D succeeds). This amount constitutes an adjustment to the basis of partnership property with respect to D only. If X is sold by the partnership for $1,600, the gain is $1,200 ($1,600 received less the adjusted common partnership basis of $400). Under the partnership agreement, $600 of this gain, which is attributable to precontribution appreciation in value, is allocable to D, who is A's successor. The remaining $600 gain is not subject to the agreement and is allocable to the partners equally, $200 each. D's distributive share of the partnership gain is thus $600 plus $200, or $800. However, D has a special basis adjustment of $700 under section 743(b) (1), which reduces his gain from $800 to $100. B and C each has a gain of $200, which is unaffected by the transfer of A's interest to D.

Example (3). Assume the same facts as in example (2) of this subdivision, except that D has purchased his interest from B instead of from A. His special basis adjustment for partnership property in this case differs from that where he had purchased his interest from A, because of the effect of the agreement under section 704(c) (2). In this case, D is a successor to B, whose share of the adjusted basis of partnership property is $1,000, instead of A, whose share is only $400. As a result, the adjustment under section 743(b) (1) is the excess of D's cost basis for his interest, $1,100, over his share of the adjusted basis of partnership property, $1,000, or $100. In this case, if property X is sold for $1,600, the partnership gain is $1,200 ($1,600 less the adjusted partnership basis of $400). Of this gain, $600, representing precontribution appreciation, is allocable to A under the partnership agreement. The remaining $600 is allocable in the amount of $200 to each partner. Since D as a transferee has a special basis adjustment of $100 under section 743(b) (1), his gain is reduced from $200 to $100.

(ii) If a partner receives a distribution of property with respect to which another partner has a special basis adjustment, the distributee shall not take into account the special basis adjustment of the other partner. However, the partner with the special basis adjustment will reallocate it under section 755 to remaining partnership property of a like kind or, if he receives a distribution of like property, to such distributed property. If a partner receives a distribution of property with respect to which he has a special basis adjustment, such basis adjustment will be taken into account when relevant under section 732. See paragraph (b) of § 1.732–2. If, at the time a partner receives property (whether or not he has a special basis adjustment with respect to such property), he relinquishes his interest in other property of a like kind with respect to which he has a special basis adjustment, the adjusted basis to the partnership of the distributed property shall include his special basis adjustment for the property in which he relinquished his interest. For the purposes of the preceding sentence, a partner will be considered as having relinquished his interest in any remaining partnership properties when his interest has been completely liquidated; however, when a partner receives a distribution not in liquidation, he will be considered as relinquishing his interest only in property distributed to other partners. For the purposes of this subdivision, like property means property of the same class, that is, stock in trade, property used in the trade or business, capital assets, etc. For certain adjustments to the basis of remaining partnership property after a distribution to a transferee partner, see paragraph (b) of § 1.734–2. The provisions of this subdivision may be illustrated by the following examples:

Example (1). C is a transferee partner in partnership BC. The partnership owns, among other assets, X, a depreciable asset with a common basis to the partnership of $1,000 and a special basis adjustment to C of $200, and Y, another depreciable asset with a common basis of $800 and a special basis adjustment to C of $300. B and C agree that B will receive a distribution of property Y, and C will receive a distribution of property X, with all other property to remain in the partnership. With respect to B, the partnership basis of property Y is $800, the common partnership basis. Y will, therefore, have a basis of $800 in B's hands under section 732(a) which provides for the use of a carryover basis in the case of current distributions. With respect to C, however, the partnership basis of property X is $1,500, the common partnership basis of $1,000, plus C's special basis adjustment of $200 for property X, plus C's additional special basis adjustment of $300 for property Y, in which he has relinquished his interest.

Example (2). (a) Partner D acquired his one-third interest in partnership BCD for $14,000 from a previous partner when an election under section 754 was in effect. Therefore, under section 743(b), D has a special basis adjustment for certain partnership property. Assume that at the time of the distribution in paragraph (b) of this example, the partnership assets consist of cash and rental property and that such assets and D's special basis adjustments under section 743(b) are as follows:

Item	Fair market value	Common partnership basis	D's share	D's special basis adjustment	Partnership basis to D
Cash	$12,000	$12,000	$4,000	....	$4,000
House:					
U	9,000	1,200	400	....	400
V	6,000	4,500	1,500	....	1,500
W	8,000	1,500	500	....	500
X	9,000	4,800	1,600	$2,000	3,600
Y	9,000	6,000	2,000	....	2,000
Z	7,000	3,000	1,000	1,000	2,000
Total	60,000	33,000	11,000	3,000	14,000

(b) Assume further that D receives $4,000 in cash and houses Y and Z in complete liquidation of his interest in partnership BCD. In determining the basis to D of houses Y and Z under section 732(b) and (c), D must allocate $10,000 basis ($14,000 basis for his interest, less $4,000 cash received) to houses Y and Z in proportion to their adjusted bases to the partnership. For purposes of section 732(c), the adjusted basis of house Y is $7,200 ($6,000 common partnership basis, plus $1,200, allocated share of D's special basis adjustment of $2,000 for house X, in which D relinquished his interest). The adjusted basis of house Z is $4,800 ($3,000 common partnership basis, plus $1,000, D's special basis for house Z, plus $800, allocated share of D's special basis of $2,000 for house X, in which D relinquished his interest). Under the rule of this subdivision, 6,000/10,000 of the $2,000 special basis adjustment for X is allocated to Y and 4,000/10,000 of such amount to Z. Therefore, $6,000 basis (7,200/12,000 of $10,000) is allocated to house Y and $4,000 basis (4,800/12,000 of $10,000) to house Z.

(c) Since houses Y and Z had $12,000 basis to the partnership, as computed in paragraph (b) of this example, and only $10,000 basis to D, as determined under section 732, the partnership, under section 734(b) (1) (B), must increase the basis of remaining partnership property (houses U, V, W, and X) by $2,000 (excess of $12,000 over $10,000). For allocation of this amount, see section 755 and § 1.755-1.

(iii) Where an adjustment is made under section 743(b) to the basis of partnership property subject to depletion, any depletion allowable shall be determined separately for each partner, including the transferee partner, based on his interest in such property. See paragraph (a) (8) of § 1.702-1. This rule may be illustrated by the following example:

Example. A, B, and C each contributes $5,000 cash to form partnership ABC, which purchases oil property for $15,000. C subsequently sells his partnership interest to D for $100,000 when the election under section 754 is in effect. D has a special basis adjustment for the oil property of $95,000 (the difference between D's basis, $100,000, and his share of the basis of partnership property, $5,000). Assume that the depletion allowance computed under the percentage method would be $21,000 for the taxable year so that each partner would be entitled to $7,000 as his share of the deduction for depletion. However,

under the cost depletion method, at an assumed rate of 10 percent, the allowance with respect to D's one-third interest which has a basis to him of $100,000 ($5,000, plus his special basis adjustment of $95,000) is $10,000, although the cost depletion allowance with respect to the one-third interest of A and B in the oil property, each of which has a basis of $5,000, is only $500. For partners A and B, the percentage depletion is greater than cost depletion and each will deduct $7,000 based on the percentage depletion method. However, as to D, the transferee partner, the cost depletion method results in a greater allowance and D will, therefore, deduct $10,000 based on cost depletion. See section 613(a).

(iv) Where there has been more than one transfer of partnership interests, the last transferee's special basis adjustment, if any, under section 743(b) shall be determined by reference to the partnership common basis for its property without regard to any prior transferee's special basis adjustment. For example, A, B, and C form a partnership. A and B each contributes $1,000 cash and C contributes land with a basis and value of $1,000. When the land has appreciated in value to $1,300, A sells his interest to D for $1,100 (⅓ of $3,300, the value of the partnership property). The election under section 754 is in effect; therefore, D has a special basis adjustment of $100 with respect to the land under section 743(b). After the land has further appreciated in value to $1,600, D sells his interest to E for $1,200 (⅓ of $3,600, the value of the partnership property). Under section 743(b), E has a special basis adjustment of $200. This amount is determined without regard to any special basis adjustment that D may have had in the partnership assets.

(3) Returns. A transferee partner who has a special basis adjustment under section 743(b) shall attach a statement to his income tax return for the first taxable year in which the basis of any partnership property subject to

the adjustment is pertinent in determining his income tax, showing the computation of the adjustment and the partnership properties to which the adjustment has been allocated.

(c) **Allocation of basis.** For the allocation of basis among partnership properties where section 743(b) applies, see section 755 and § 1.755-1.

§ 1.751-1 Unrealized receivables and inventory items

(a) **Sale or exchange of interest in a partnership—(1) Character of amount realized.** To the extent that money or property received by a partner in exchange for all or part of his partnership interest is attributable to his share of the value of partnership unrealized receivables or substantially appreciated inventory items, the money or fair market value of the property received shall be considered as an amount realized from the sale or exchange of property other than a capital asset. The remainder of the total amount realized on the sale or exchange of the partnership interest is realized from the sale or exchange of a capital asset under section 741. For definition of "unrealized receivables" and "inventory items which have appreciated substantially in value", see section 751(c) and (d). Unrealized receivables and substantially appreciated inventory items are hereafter in this section referred to as "section 751 property". See paragraph (e) of this section.

(2) **Determination of gain or loss.** The income or loss realized by a partner upon the sale or exchange of his interest in section 751 property is the difference between (i) the portion of the total amount realized for the partnership interest allocated to section 751 property, and (ii) the portion of the selling partner's basis for his entire interest allocated to such property. Generally, the portion of the total amount realized which the seller and the purchaser allocate to section 751 property in an arm's length agreement will be regarded as correct. The portion of the partner's adjusted basis for his partnership interest to be allocated to section 751 property shall be an amount equal to the basis such property would have had under section 732 (including subsection (d) thereof) if

the selling partner had received his share of such properties in a current distribution made immediately before the sale. See §§ 1.732-1 and 1.732-2. Such basis shall reflect the rules of section 704(c) (3), if applicable, or any agreement under section 704(c) (2). Any gain or loss recognized which is attributable to section 751 property will be ordinary gain or loss. The difference between the remainder, if any, of the partner's adjusted basis for his partnership interest and the balance, if any, of the amount realized is the transferor's capital gain or loss on the sale of his partnership interest.

(3) **Statement required.** A transferor partner selling or exchanging any part of his interest in a partnership which has any section 751 property at the time of sale or exchange shall submit with his income tax return for the taxable year in which the sale or exchange occurs a statement setting forth separately the following information:

(i) The date of the sale or exchange, the amount of the transferor partner's adjusted basis for his partnership interest, and the portion thereof attributable to section 751 property under section 732; and

(ii) The amount of any money and the fair market value of any other property received or to be received for the transferred interest in the partnership, and the portion thereof attributable to section 751 property.

(iii) If the transferor partner computes his adjusted basis for section 751 property under the provisions of section 732(d), he must also include in the statement the information required by paragraph (d) (3) of § 1.732-1.

(iv) If the transferor partner has a special basis adjustment under section 743(b), he must also include in the statement the computation of his special basis adjustment and the partnership properties to which the adjustment has been allocated.

(b) **Certain distributions treated as sales or exchanges—(1) In general.** (i) Certain distributions to which section 751(b) applies are treated in part as sales or exchanges of property between the partnership and the distributee partner, and not as distributions to which sections 731 through 736 apply. A distribution treated as a sale or exchange under section 751(b) is not subject to the provisions of section 707(b). Section 751(b) applies whether or not the distribution is in liquidation of the distributee partner's entire interest in the partnership. However, section 751(b) applies only to the extent that a partner either receives section 751 property in exchange for his relinquishing any part of his interest in other property, or receives other property in exchange for his relinquishing any part of his interest in section 751 property.

(ii) Section 751(b) does not apply to a distribution to a partner which is not in exchange for his interest in other partnership property. Thus, section 751(b) does not apply to the extent that a distribution consists of the distributee partner's share of section 751 property or his share of other property. Similarly, section 751(b) does not apply to current drawings or to advances against the partner's distributive share, or to a distribution which is, in fact, a gift or payment for services or for the use of capital. In determining whether a partner has received only his share of either section 751 property or of other property, his interest in such property remaining in the partnership immediately after a distribution must be taken into account. For example, the section 751 property in partnership ABC has a fair market value of $100,000 in which partner A has an interest of 30 percent, or $30,000. If A receives $20,000 of section 751 property in a distribution, and continues to have a 30-percent interest in the $80,000 of section 751 property remaining in the partnership after the distribution, only $6,000 ($30,000 minus $24,000 (30 percent of $80,000)) of the section 751 property received by him will be considered to be his share of such property. The remaining $14,000 ($20,000 minus $6,000) received is in excess of his share.

(iii) If a distribution is, in part, a distribution of the distributee partner's share of section 751 property, or of other property (including money) and, in part, a distribution in exchange of such properties, the distribution shall be divided for the purpose of applying section 751(b). The rules of section 751(b) shall first apply to the part of the distribution treated as a sale or exchange of such properties, and then the rules of sections 731 through 736 shall apply to the part of the distribution not treated as a sale or exchange. See paragraph (b) (4) (ii) of this section for treatment of payments under section 736(a).

(2) Distribution of section 751 property (unrealized receivables or substantially appreciated inventory items). (i) To the extent that a partner receives section 751 property in a distribution in exchange for any part of his interest in partnership property (including money) other than section 751 property, the transaction shall be treated as a sale or exchange of such properties between the distributee partner and the partnership (as constituted after the distribution).

(ii) At the time of the distribution, the partnership (as constituted after the distribution) realizes ordinary income or loss on the sale or exchange of the section 751 property. The amount of the income or loss to the partnership will be measured by the difference between the adjusted basis to the partnership of the section 751 property considered as sold to or exchanged with the partner, and the fair market value of the distributee partner's interest in other partnership property which he relinquished in the exchange. In computing the partners' distributive shares of such ordinary income or loss, the income or loss shall be allocated only to partners other than the distributee and separately taken into account under section 702 (a) (8).

(iii) At the time of the distribution, the distributee partner realizes gain or loss measured by the difference between his adjusted basis for the property relinquished in the exchange (including any special basis adjustment which he may have) and the fair market value of the section 751 property received by him in exchange for his interest in other property which he has relinquished. The distributee's adjusted basis for the property relinquished is the basis such property would have had under section 732 (including subsection (d) thereof) if the distributee partner had received such property in a current distribution immediately before the actual distribution which is treated wholly or partly as a sale or exchange under section

751(b). The character of the gain or loss to the distributee partner shall be determined by the character of the property in which he relinquished his interest.

(3) **Distribution of partnership property other than section 751 property.** (i) To the extent that a partner receives a distribution of partnership property (including money) other than section 751 property in exchange for any part of his interest in section 751 property of the partnership, the distribution shall be treated as a sale or exchange of such properties between the distributee partner and the partnership (as constituted after the distribution).

(ii) At the time of the distribution, the partnership (as constituted after the distribution) realizes gain or loss on the sale or exchange of the property other than section 751 property. The amount of the gain to the partnership will be measured by the difference between the adjusted basis to the partnership of the distributed property considered as sold to or exchanged with the partner, and the fair market value of the distributee partner's interest in section 751 property which he relinquished in the exchange. The character of the gain or loss to the partnership is determined by the character of the distributed property treated as sold or exchanged by the partnership. In computing the partners' distributive shares of such gain or loss, the gain or loss shall be allocated only to partners other than the distributee and separately taken into account under section 702(a) (8).

(iii) At the time of the distribution, the distributee partner realizes ordinary income or loss on the sale or exchange of the section 751 property. The amount of the distributee partner's income or loss shall be measured by the difference between his adjusted basis for the section 751 property relinquished in the exchange (including any special basis adjustment which he may have), and the fair market value of other property (including money) received by him in exchange for his interest in the section 751 property which he has relinquished. The distributee partner's adjusted basis for the section 751 property relinquished is the basis such property would have had under section 732 (including subsection (d) thereof) if the distributee

partner had received such property in a current distribution immediately before the actual distribution which is treated wholly or partly as a sale or exchange under section 751(b).

(4) **Exceptions.** (i) Section 751(b) does not apply to the distribution to a partner of property which the distributee partner contributed to the partnership. The distribution of such property is governed by the rules set forth in sections 731 through 736, relating to distributions by a partnership.

(ii) Section 751(b) does not apply to payments made to a retiring partner or to a deceased partner's successor in interest to the extent that, under section 736(a), such payments constitute a distributive share of partnership income or guaranteed payments. Payments to a retiring partner or to a deceased partner's successor in interest for his interest in unrealized receivables of the partnership in excess of their partnership basis, including any special basis adjustment for them to which such partner is entitled, constitute payments under section 736(a) and, therefore, are not subject to section 751(b). However, payments under section 736(b) which are considered as made in exchange for an interest in partnership property are subject to section 751(b) to the extent that they involve an exchange of substantially appreciated inventory items for other property. Thus, payments to a retiring partner or to a deceased partner's successor in interest under section 736 must first be divided between payments under section 736(a) and section 736(b). The section 736(b) payments must then be divided, if there is an exchange of substantially appreciated inventory items for other property, between the payments treated as a sale or exchange under section 751(b) and payments treated as a distribution under sections 731 through 736. See subparagraph (1) (iii) of this paragraph, and section 736 and § 1.736–1.

(5) **Statement required.** A partnership which distributes section 751 property to a partner in exchange for his interest in other partnership property, or which distributes other property in exchange for any part of the partner's interest in section 751 property, shall submit with its return for the year of the distribution a statement showing

the computation of any income, gain, or loss to the partnership under the provisions of section 751(b) and this paragraph. The distributee partner shall submit with his return a statement showing the computation of any income, gain, or loss to him. Such statement shall contain information similar to that required under paragraph (a) (3) of this section.

(c) Unrealized receivables. (1) The term "unrealized receivables", as used in subchapter K, chapter 1 of the Code, means any rights (contractual or otherwise) to payment for—

(i) Goods delivered or to be delivered (to the extent that such payment would be treated as received for property other than a capital asset), or

(ii) Services rendered or to be rendered,

to the extent that income arising from such rights to payment was not previously includible in income under the method of accounting employed by the partnership. Such rights must have arisen under contracts or agreements in existence at the time of sale or distribution, although the partnership may not be able to enforce payment until a later time. For example, the term includes trade accounts receivable of a cash method taxpayer, and rights to payment for work or goods begun but incomplete at the time of the sale or distribution.

(2) The basis for such unrealized receivables shall include all costs or expenses attributable thereto paid or accrued but not previously taken into account under the partnership method of accounting.

(3) In determining the amount of the sale price attributable to such unrealized receivables, or their value in a distribution treated as a sale or exchange, any arm's length agreement between the buyer and the seller, or between the partnership and the distributee partner, will generally establish the amount or value. In the absence of such an agreement, full account shall be taken not only of the estimated cost of completing performance of the contract or agreement, but also of the time between the sale or distribution and the time of payment.

(4) (i) With respect to any taxable year of a partnership beginning after December 31, 1962, the term "unrealized receivables," for purposes of this section and sections 731, 736, 741, and 751, also includes "potential section 1245 income." With respect to each item of partnership section 1245 property (as defined in sec. 1245(a) (3)), "potential section 1245 income" is the amount which would be treated as gain to which section 1245(a) (1) would apply if (at the time of the transaction described in section 731, 736, 741, or 751, as the case may be) the item of section 1245 property were sold by the partnership at its fair market value. See paragraph (e) (1) of § 1.1245-1. For example, if a partnership would recognize under section 1245(a) (1) gain of $600 upon a sale of one item of section 1245 property and gain of $300 upon a sale of its only other item of such property, the potential section 1245 income of the partnership would be $900.

(ii) With respect to any taxable year of a partnership ending after December 31, 1963, the term "unrealized receivables," for purposes of this section and sections 731, 736, 741, and 751, also includes "potential section 1250 income." With respect to each item of partnership section 1250 property (as defined in section 1250(c)), "potential section 1250 income" is the amount which would be treated as gain to which section 1250(a) would apply if (at the time of the transaction described in section 731, 736, 741, or 751, as the case may be) the item of section 1250 property were sold by the partnership at its fair market value. See paragraph (f) (1) of § 1.1250-1.

(iii) For purposes of determining potential section 1245 income or potential section 1250 income, any arm's-length agreement between the buyer and seller, or between the partnership and distributee partner, will generally establish the fair market value of section 1245 property or section 1250 property (as the case may be).

(5) For purposes of subtitle A of the Code, the basis of potential section 1245 income and of potential section 1250 income is zero.

(6) (i) If (at the time of the transaction referred to in subparagraph (4) of this paragraph) a partnership holds section 1245 (or 1250) property and if (a) a partner had a special basis adjustment under section 743(b) in respect of the property, or (b) the basis

under section 732 of the property if distributed to the partner would reflect a special basis adjustment under section 732(d), or (c) on the date a partner acquires his partnership interest by way of a sale or exchange (or upon death of another partner) the partnership owned the property and an election under section 754 was in effect with respect to the partnership, then the partner's share of the potential section 1245 (or 1250) income of the partnership in respect of the property shall be determined under subdivision (ii) of this subparagraph.

(ii) The partner's share of the potential section 1245 (or 1250) income of the partnership in respect of the property to which this subdivision applies shall be that amount of gain which the partner would recognize under paragraph (e) (3) of § 1.1245-1 (or paragraph (f) of § 1.1250-1) upon a sale of the property by the partnership, except that, for purposes of this subparagraph (a) the items which are allocated under (or in a manner consistent with the principles provided in) paragraph (e) (3) (ii) of § 1.1245-1 shall be allocated to the partner in the same manner as his share of partnership property is determined, and (b) the amount of a special basis adjustment under section 732(d) shall be treated as if it were the amount of a special basis adjustment under section 743(b).

(d) **Inventory items which have substantially appreciated in value—(1) Substantial appreciation.** Partnership inventory items shall be considered to have appreciated substantially in value if, at the time of the sale or distribution, the total fair market value of all the inventory items of the partnership exceeds 120 percent of the aggregate adjusted basis for such property in the hands of the partnership (without regard to any special basis adjustment of any partner) and, in addition, exceeds 10 percent of the fair market value of all partnership property other than money. The terms "inventory items which have appreciated substantially in value" or "substantially appreciated inventory items" refer to the aggregate of all partnership inventory items. These terms do not refer to specific partnership inventory items or to specific groups of such items. For example, any distribution of inventory items by a partnership the inventory items of which as a whole are substantially appreciated in value shall be a distribution of substantially appreciated inventory items for the purposes of section 751(b), even though the specific inventory items distributed may not be appreciated in value. Similarly, if the aggregate of partnership inventory items are not substantially appreciated in value, a distribution of specific inventory items, the value of which is more than 120 percent of their adjusted basis, will not constitute a distribution of substantially appreciated inventory items. For the purpose of this paragraph, the "fair market value" of inventory items has the same meaning as "market" value in the regulations under section 471, relating to general rule for inventories.

(2) **Inventory items.** The term "inventory items" as used in subchapter K, chapter 1 of the Code, includes the following types of property:

(i) Stock in trade of the partnership, or other property of a kind which would properly be included in the inventory of the partnership if on hand at the close of the taxable year, or property held by the partnership primarily for sale to customers in the ordinary course of its trade or business. See section 1221(1).

(ii) Any other property of the partnership which, on sale or exchange by the partnership, would be considered property other than a capital asset and other than property described in section 1231. Thus, accounts receivable acquired in the ordinary course of business for services or from the sale of stock in trade constitute inventory items (see section 1221(4)), as do any unrealized receivables.

(iii) Any other property retained by the partnership which, if held by the partner selling his partnership interest or receiving a distribution described in section 751(b), would be considered property described in subdivisions (i) or (ii) of this subparagraph. Property actually distributed to the partner does not come within the provisions of section 751(d) (2) (C) and this subdivision.

(e) **Section 751 property and other property.** For the purposes of this section, "section 751 property" means unrealized receivables or substantially appreciated inventory items, and "other property" means all property (including money) except section 751 property.

• • • •

(g) Examples. Application of the provisions of section 751 may be illustrated by the following examples:

Example (1). C buys B's interest in personal service partnership AB for $15,000, when the balance sheet of the firm (reflecting a cash receipts and disbursements method of accounting) is as follows:

ASSETS

	Adjusted basis per books	Market value
Cash	$3,000	$3,000
Loans receivable	10,000	10,000
Other assets	7,000	7,000
Unrealized receivables	0	12,000
Total	20,000	32,000

LIABILITIES AND CAPITAL

	Per books	Value
Liabilities	$2,000	$2,000
Capital:		
A	9,000	15,000
B	9,000	15,000
Total	20,000	32,000

Section 751(a) applies to the sale. The total amount realized by B is $16,000, consisting of the cash received, $15,000, plus $1,000, B's share of the partnership liabilities assumed by C. See section 752. B's undivided half interest in the partnership property includes a half-interest in the partnership's unrealized receivables which are worth $12,000. Consequently, $6,000 of the $16,000 realized by B shall be considered received in exchange for B's interest in the partnership attributable to its unrealized receivables. The remaining $10,000 realized by B is in exchange for a capital asset. B's basis for his partnership interest is $10,000 ($9,000, plus $1,000, B's share of partnership liabilities). No portion of this basis is attributable to B's share of the unrealized receivables of the partnership since such property has a zero basis in the hands of the partnership; therefore, B has a basis of zero for the unrealized receivables because the partnership basis for such receivables would have carried over to him under section 732 had they been distributed to him. The difference between the zero basis and the $6,000 B realized for the unrealized receivables is ordinary income to him. The entire $10,000 of B's basis is the basis for his interest in partnership property other than unrealized receivables and is applied against the remaining $10,000 ($16,000 minus $6,000) received from the sale of his interest. Therefore, B has no capital gain or loss. (If B's basis for his interest in partnership

property, other than unrealized receivables, were $9,000, he would realize capital gain of $1,000. If his basis were $11,000, he would sustain a capital loss of $1,000.)

Example (2). (a) Facts. Partnership ABC makes a distribution to partner C in liquidation of his entire one-third interest in the partnership. At the time of the distribution, the balance sheet of the partnership, which uses the accrual method of accounting, is as follows:

ASSETS

	Adjusted basis per books	Market value
Cash	$15,000	$15,000
Accounts receivable	9,000	9,000
Inventory	21,000	30,000
Depreciable property	42,000	48,000
Land	9,000	9,000
Total	96,000	111,000

LIABILITIES AND CAPITAL

	Per books	Value
Current liabilities	$15,000	$15,000
Mortgage payable	21,000	21,000
Capital:		
A	20,000	25,000
B	20,000	25,000
C	20,000	25,000
Total	96,000	111,000

The distribution received by C consists of $10,000 cash and depreciable property with a fair market value of $15,000 and an adjusted basis to the partnership of $15,000.

(b) Presence of section 751 property. The partnership has no unrealized receivables, but the dual test provided in section 751(d) (1) must be applied to determine whether the inventory items of the partnership, in the aggregate, have appreciated substantially in value. The fair market value of all partnership inventory items, $39,000 (inventory $30,000, and accounts receivable $9,000), exceeds 120 percent of the $30,000 adjusted basis of such items to the partnership. The fair market value of the inventory items, $39,000, also exceeds 10 percent of the fair market value of all partnership property other than money (10 percent of $96,000 or $9,600). Therefore, the partnership inventory items have substantially appreciated in value.

(c) The properties exchanged. Since C's entire partnership interest is to be liquidated, the provisions of section 736 are applicable. No part of the payment, however, is considered as a distributive share or as a guaranteed payment under section 736(a) because the entire payment is made for C's interest in partnership property. Therefore, the entire payment is for an interest in partnership property under section 736(b), and, to the extent applicable, subject to the rules of section 751. In the distribution, C received his share of cash ($5,000) and $15,000 in depreciable property ($1,000 less than his $16,000 share). In addition, he received other partnership property ($5,000 cash and $12,000 liabilities assumed, treated as money distributed under section 752(b)) in exchange for his interest in accounts receivable ($3,000), inventory ($10,000), land ($3,000), and the balance of his interest in depreciable property ($1,000). Section 751(b) applies only to the extent of the exchange of other property for section 751 property (i. e., inventory items, which include trade accounts receivable). The section 751 property exchanged has a fair market value of $13,000 ($3,000 in accounts receivable and $10,000 in inventory). Thus, $13,000 of the total amount C received is considered as received for the sale of section 751 property.

(d) Distributee partner's tax consequences. C's tax consequences on the distribution are as follows:

(1) The section 751(b) sale or exchange. C's share of the inventory items is treated as if he received them in a current distribution, and his basis for such items is $10,000 ($7,000 for inventory and $3,000 for accounts receivable) as determined under paragraph (b) (3) (iii) of this section. Then C is considered as having sold his share of inventory items to the partnership for $13,000. Thus, on the sale of his share of inventory items, C realizes $3,000 of ordinary income.

(2) The part of the distribution not under section 751(b). Section 751(b) does not apply to the balance of the distribution. Before the distribution, C's basis for his partnership interest was $32,000 ($20,000 plus $12,000, his share of partnership liabilities). See section 752(a). This basis is reduced by $10,000, the basis attributed to the section 751 property treated as distributed to C and sold by him to the partnership. Thus, C has a basis of $22,000 for the remainder of his partnership interest. The total distribution to C was $37,000 ($22,000 in cash and liabilities assumed, and $15,000 in depreciable property). Since C received no more than his share of the depreciable property, none of the depreciable property constitutes proceeds of the sale under section 751(b). C did receive more than his share of money. Therefore, the sale proceeds, treated separately in subparagraph (1) of this paragraph of this example, must consist of money and therefore must be deducted from the money distribution. Consequently, in liquidation of the balance of C's interest, he receives depreciable property and $9,000 in money ($22,000 less $13,000). Therefore, no gain or loss is recognized to C on the distribution. Under section 732(b), C's basis for the depreciable property is $13,000 (the remaining basis of his partnership interest, $22,000, reduced by $9,000, the money received in the distribution).

(e) Partnership's tax consequences. The tax consequences to the partnership on the distribution are as follows:

(1) The section 751(b) sale or exchange. The partnership consisting of the remaining members has no ordinary income on the distribution since it did not give up any section 751 property in the exchange. Of the $22,000 money distributed (in cash and the assumption of C's share of liabilities), $13,000 was paid to acquire

C's interest in inventory ($10,000 fair market value) and in accounts receivable ($3,000). Since under section 751(b) the partnership is treated as buying these properties, it has a new cost basis for the inventory and accounts receivable acquired from C. Its basis for C's share of inventory and accounts receivable is $13,000, the amount which the partnership is considered as having paid C in the exchange. Since the partnership is treated as having distributed C's share of inventory and accounts receivable to him, the partnership must decrease its basis for inventory and accounts receivable ($30,000) by $10,000, the basis of C's share treated as distributed to him, and then increase the basis for inventory and accounts receivable by $13,000 to reflect the purchase prices of the items acquired. Thus, the basis of the partnership inventory is increased from $21,000 to $24,000 in the transaction. (Note that the basis of property acquired in a section 751(b) exchange is determined under section 1012 without regard to any elections of the partnership. See paragraph (e) of § 1.732-1.) Further, the partnership realizes no capital gain or loss on the portion of the distribution treated as a sale under section 751(b) since, to acquire C's interest in the inventory and accounts receivable, it gave up money and assumed C's share of liabilities.

(2) The part of the distribution not under section 751(b). In the remainder of the distribution to C which was not in exchange for C's interest in section 751 property, C received only other property as follows: $15,000 in depreciable property (with a basis to the partnership of $15,000) and $9,000 in money ($22,000 less $13,000 treated under subparagraph (1) of this paragraph of this example). Since this part of the distribution is not an exchange of section 751 property for other property, section 751(b) does not apply. Instead, the provisions which apply are sections 731 through 736, relating to distributions by a partnership. No gain or loss is recognized to the partnership on the distribution. (See section 731(b).) Further, the partnership makes no adjustment to the basis of remaining depreciable property unless an election under section 754 is in effect. (See section 734(a).) Thus, the basis of the depreciable property before the distribution, $42,000, is reduced by the basis of the depreciable property distributed, $15,000, leaving a basis for the depreciable property in the partnership of $27,000. However, if an election under section 754 is in effect, the partnership must make the adjustment required under section 734 (b) as follows: Since the adjusted basis of the distributed property to the partnership had been $15,000, and is only $13,000 in C's hands (see paragraph (d) (2) of this example), the partnership will increase the basis of the depreciable property remaining in the partnership by $2,000 (the excess of the adjusted basis to the partnership of the distributed depreciable property immediately before the distribution over its basis to the distributee). Whether or not an election under section 754 is in effect, the basis for each of the remaining partner's partnership interests will be $38,000 ($20,000 original contribution, plus $12,000, each partner's original share of the liabilities, plus $6,000, the share of C's liabilities each assumed).

(f) Partnership trial balance. A trial balance of the AB partnership after the distribution in liquidation of C's entire interest would reflect the results set forth in the schedule below. Column I shows the amounts to be reflected in the records if an election is in effect under section 754 with respect to an optional adjustment under section 734 (b) to the basis of undistributed partnership property.

Column II shows the amounts to be reflected in the records where an election under section 754 is not in effect. Note that in column II, the total bases for the partnership assets do not equal the total of the bases for the partnership interests.

	I		II	
	Sec. 754, Election in effect		Sec. 754, Election not in effect	
	Basis	Fair market value	Basis	Fair market value
Cash	$5,000	$5,000	$5,000	$5,000
Accounts receivable	9,000	9,000	9,000	9,000
Inventory	24,000	30,000	24,000	30,000
Depreciable property	29,000	33,000	27,000	33,000
Land	9,000	9,000	9,000	9,000
	76,000	86,000	74,000	86,000
Current liabilities	15,000	15,000	15,000	15,000
Mortgage	21,000	21,000	21,000	21,000
Capital:				
A	20,000	25,000	20,000	25,000
B	20,000	25,000	20,000	25,000
	76,000	86,000	76,000	86,000

Example (3). (a) Facts. Assume that the distribution to partner C in example (2) of this paragraph in liquidation of his entire interest in partnership ABC consists of $5,000 in cash and $20,000 worth of partnership inventory with a basis of $14,000.

(b) Presence of section 751 property. For the same reason as stated in paragraph (b) of example (2), the partnership inventory items have substantially appreciated in value.

(c) The properties exchanged. In the distribution, C received his share of cash ($5,000) and his share of appreciated inventory items ($13,000). In addition, he received appreciated inventory with a fair market value of $7,000 (and with an adjusted basis to the partnership of $4,900) and $12,000 in money (liabilities assumed). C has relinquished his interest in $16,000 of depreciable property and $3,000 of land. Although C relinquished his interest in $3,000 of accounts receivable, such accounts receivable are inventory items and, therefore, that exchange was not an exchange of section 751 property for other property. Section 751 (b) applies only to the extent of the exchange of other property for section 751 property (i. e., depreciable property or land for inventory items). Assume that the partners agree that the $7,000 of inventory in excess of C's share was received by him in exchange for $7,000 of depreciable property.

(d) Distributee partner's tax consequences. C's tax consequence on the distributions are as follows:

(1) The section 751 (b) sale or exchange. C is treated as if he had received his 7/16ths share of the depreciable property in a current distribution. His basis for that share is $6,125 (42,000/48,000 of $7,000), as determined under paragraph (b) (2) (iii) of this section.

Then C is considered as having sold his 7/16ths share of depreciable property to the partnership for $7,000, realizing a gain of $875.

(2) The part of the distribution not under section 751 (b). Section 751(b) does not apply to the balance of the distribution. Before the distribution, C's basis for his partnership interest was $32,000 ($20,000, plus $12,000, his share of partnership liabilities). See section 752 (a). This basis is reduced by $6,125, the basis of property treated as distributed to C and sold by him to the partnership. Thus, C will have a basis of $25,875 for the remainder of his partnership interest. Of the $37,000 total distribution to C, $30,000 ($17,000 in money, including liabilities assumed, and $13,000 in inventory) is not within section 751 (b). Under section 732 (b), C's basis for the inventory with a fair market value of $13,000 (which had an adjusted basis to the partnership of $9,100) is limited to $8,875, the amount of the remaining basis for his partnership interest, $25,875, reduced by $17,000, the money received. Thus, C's total aggregate basis for the inventory received is $15,875 ($7,000 plus $8,875), and not its $14,000 basis in the hands of the partnership.

(e) Partnership's tax consequences. The tax consequences to the partnership on the distribution are as follows:

(1) The section 751 (b) sale or exchange. The partnership consisting of the remaining members has $2,100 of ordinary income on the sale of the $7,000 of inventory which had a basis to the partnership of $4,900 (21,000/30,000 of $7,000). This $7,000 of inventory was paid to acquire 7/16ths of C's interest in the depreciable property. Since, under section 751 (b), the partnership is treated as buying this property from C, it has a new cost basis for such property. Its basis for the depreciable property is $42,875 ($42,000 less $6,125, the basis of the 7/19ths share considered as distributed to C, plus $7,000, the partnership purchase price for this share).

(2) **The part of the distribution not under section 751 (b).** In the remainder of the distribution to C which was not a sale or exchange of section 751 property for other property, the partnership realizes no gain or loss. See section 731 (b). Further, under section 734 (a), the partnership makes no adjustment to the basis of the accounts receivable or the 9/19ths interest in depreciable property which C relinquished. However, if an election under section 754 is in effect, the partnership must make the adjustment required under section 734 (b) since the adjusted basis to the partnership of the inventory distributed had been $9,100, and C's basis for such inventory after distribution is only $8,875. The basis of the inventory remaining in the partnership must be increased by $225. Whether or not an election under section 754 is in effect, the basis for each of the remaining partnership interests will be $39,050 ($20,000 original contribution, plus $12,000, each partner's original share of the liabilities, plus $6,000, the share of C's liabilities now assumed, plus $1,050, each partner's share of ordinary income realized by the partnership upon that part of the distribution treated as a sale or exchange).

Example (4). (a) Facts. Assume the same facts as in example (3) of this paragraph, except that the partners did not identify the property which C relinquished in exchange for the $7,000 of inventory which he received in excess of his share.

(b) **Presence of section 751 property.** For the same reasons stated in paragraph (b) of example (2) of this paragraph, the partnership inventory items have substantially appreciated in value.

(c) **The properties exchanged.** The analysis stated in paragraph (c) of example (3) of this paragraph is the same in this example, except that, in the absence of a specific agreement among the partners as to the properties exchanged, C will be presumed to have sold to the partnership a proportionate amount of each property in which he relinquished an interest. Thus, in the absence of an agreement, C has received $7,000 of inventory in exchange for his release of 7/19ths of the depreciable property and 7/19ths of the land. ($7,000, fair market value of property released, over $19,000, the sum of the fair market values of C's interest in the land and C's interest in the depreciable property.)

(d) **Distributee partner's tax consequences.** C's tax consequences on the distribution are as follows:

(1) **The section 751 (b) sale or exchange.** C is treated as if he had received his 7/19ths shares of the depreciable property and land in a current distribution. His basis for those shares is $6,263 (51,000/57,000 of $7,000, their fair market value), as determined under paragraph (b) (2) (iii) of this section. Then C is considered as having sold his 7/19ths shares of depreciable property and land to the partnership for $7,000, realizing a gain of $737.

(2) **The part of the distribution not under section 751 (b).** Section 751 (b) does not ap-

ply to the balance of the distribution. Before the distribution C's basis for his partnership interest was $32,000 ($20,000 plus $12,000, his share of partnership liabilities). See section 752 (a). This basis is reduced by $6,263, the bases of C's shares of depreciable property and land treated as distributed to him and sold by him to the partnership. Thus, C will have a basis of $25,737 for the remainder of his partnership interest. Of the total $37,000 distributed to C, $30,000 ($17,000 in money, including liabilities assumed, and $13,000 in inventory) is not within section 751 (b). Under section 732 (b), C's basis for the inventory (with a fair market value of $13,000 and an adjusted basis to the partnership of $9,100) is limited to $8,737, the amount of the remaining basis for his partnership interest ($25,737 less $17,000, money received. Thus, C's total aggregate basis for the inventory he received is $15,737 ($7,000 plus $8,737), and not the $14,000 basis it had in the hands of the partnership.

(e) **Partnership's tax consequences.** The tax consequences to the partnership on the distribution are as follows:

(1) **The section 751 (b) sale or exchange.** The partnership consisting of the remaining members has $2,100 of ordinary income on the sale of $7,000 of inventory which had a basis to the partnership of $4,900 (21,000/30,000 of $7,000). This $7,000 of inventory was paid to acquire 7/19ths of C's interest in the depreciable property and land. Since, under section 751 (b), the partnership is treated as buying this property from C, it has a new cost basis for such property. The bases of the depreciable property and land would be $42,737 and $9,000, respectively. The basis for the depreciable property is computed as follows: The common partnership basis of $42,000 is reduced by the $5,158 (42,000/48,000 of $5,895) for C's 7/19ths interest constructively distributed and increased by $5,895 (16,000/19,000 of $7,000), the part of the purchase price allocated to the depreciable property. The basis of the land would be computed in the same way. The $9,000 original partnership basis is reduced by $1,105 basis (9,000/9,000 of $1,105) of land constructively distributed to C, and increased by $1,105 (3,000/19,000 of $7,000), the portion of the purchase price allocated to the land.

(2) **The part of the distribution not under section 751 (b).** In the remainder of the distribution to C which was not a sale or exchange of section 751 property for other property, the partnership realizes no gain or loss. See section 731 (b). Further, under section 734 (a), the partnership makes no adjustment to the basis of the accounts receivable or the 12/19ths interests in depreciable property and land which C relinquished. However, if an election under section 754 is in effect, the partnership must make the adjustment required under section 734 (b) since the adjusted basis to the partnership of the inventory distributed had been $9,100 and C's basis for such inventory after the distribution is only $8,737. The basis of the inventory remaining in the partnership must be increased by the difference of $363. Whether or not an election under section 754 is in effect, the basis for each of the remaining partnership interests will be $39,050 ($20,000 original contribution plus $12,000, each partner's original share of the liabilities, plus $6,000, the share of C's liabilities

assumed, plus $1,050, each partner's share of ordinary income realized by the partnership upon the part of the distribution treated as a sale or exchange).

Example (5). (a) Facts. Assume that partner C in example (2) of this paragraph agrees to reduce his interest in capital and profits from one-third to one-fifth for a current distribution consisting of $5,000 in cash, and $7,500 of accounts receivable with a basis to the partnership of $7,500. At the same time, the total liabilities of the partnership are not reduced.

Therefore, after the distribution, C's share of the partnership liabilities has been reduced by $4,800 from $12,000 (⅓ of $36,000) to $7,200 (⅕ of $36,000).

(b) Presence of section 751 property. For the same reasons as stated in paragraph (b) of example (2) of this paragraph, the partnership inventory items have substantially appreciated in value.

(c) The properties exchanged. C's interest in the fair market value of the partnership properties before and after the distribution can be illustrated by the following table:

Item	C's interest Fair Market Value		C received		C relinquished
	One-third before	One-fifth after	Distribution of share	In excess of share	
Cash	$5,000	$2,000	$3,000	$2,000	....
Liabilities assumed	(12,000)	(7,200)	....	4,800	....
Inventory items:					
Accounts receivable	3,000	300	2,700	4,800	....
Inventory	10,000	6,000	....	....	$4,000
Depreciable property	16,000	9,600	....	....	6,400
Land	3,000	1,800	....	....	1,200
Total	25,000	12,500	5,700	11,600	11,600

Although C relinquished his interest in $4,000 of inventory and received $4,800 of accounts receivable, both items constitute section 751 property and C has received only $800 of accounts receivable for $800 worth of depreciable property or for an $800 undivided interest in land. In the absence of an agreement identifying the properties exchanged, it is presumed C received $800 for proportionate shares of his interests in both depreciable property and land. To the extent that inventory was exchanged for accounts receivable, or to the extent cash was distributed for the release of C's interest in the balance of the depreciable property and land, the transaction does not fall within section 751 (b) and is a current distribution under section 732 (a). Thus, the remaining $6,700 of accounts receivable are received in a current distribution.

(d) Distributee partner's tax consequences. C's tax consequences on the distribution are as follows:

(1) The section 751 (b) sale or exchange. Assuming that the partners paid $800 worth of accounts receivable for $800 worth of depreciable property, C is treated as if he received the depreciable property in a current distribution, and his basis for the $800 worth of de-

preciable property is $700 (42,000/48,000 of $800, its fair market value), as determined under paragraph (b) (2) (iii) of this section. Then C is considered as having sold his $800 share of depreciable property to the partnership for $800. On the sale of the depreciable property, C realizes a gain of $100. If, on the other hand, the partners had agreed that C exchanged an $800 interest in the land for $800 worth of accounts receivable, C would realize no gain or loss, because under paragraph (b) (2) (iii) of this section his basis for the land sold would be $800. In the absence of an agreement, the basis for the depreciable property and land (which C is considered as having received in a current distribution and then sold back to the partnership) would be $716 (51,000/57,000 of $800). In that case, on the sale of the balance of the $800 share of depreciable property and land, C would realize $84 of gain ($800 less $716).

(2) The part of the distribution not under section 751 (b). Section 751 (b) does not apply to the balance of the distribution. Under section 731, C does not realize either gain or loss on the balance of the distribution. The adjustments to the basis of C's interest are illustrated in the following table:

	If accounts receivable received for depreciable property	If accounts receivable received for land	If there is no agreement
Original basis for C's interest.......	$32,000	$32,000	$32,000
Less basis of property distributed prior to sec. 751 (b) sale or exchange	-700	-800	-716
	31,300	31,200	31,284
Less money received in distribution	-9,800	-9,800	-9,800
	21,500	21,400	21,484
Less basis of property received in a current distribution under sec. 732	-6,700	-6,700	-6,700
Resulting basis for C's interest......	14,800	14,700	14,784

C's basis for the $7,500 worth of accounts receivable which he received in the distribution will be $7,500, composed of $800 for the portion purchased in the section 751 (b) exchange, plus $6,700, the basis carried over under section 732 (a) for the portion received in the current distribution.

(e) **Partnership's tax consequences.** The tax consequences to the partnership on the distribution are as follows:

(1) **The section 751 (b) sale or exchange.** The partnership realizes no gain or loss in the section 751 sale or exchange because it had a basis of $800 for the accounts receivable for which it received $800 worth of other property. If the partnership agreed to purchase $800 worth of depreciable property, the partnership basis of depreciable property becomes $42,100 ($42,000 less $700 basis of property constructively distributed to C, plus $800, price of property purchased). If the partnership purchased land with the accounts receivable, there would be no change in the basis of the land to the partnership because the basis of land distributed was equal to its purchase price. If there were no agreement, the basis of the depreciable property and land would be $51,084 (depreciable property, $42,084 and land $9,000). The basis for the depreciable property is computed as follows: The common partnership basis of $42,000 is reduced by the $590 basis (42,000/48,000 of $674) for C's $674 interest constructively distributed, and increased by $674 (6,400/7,600 of $800), the part of the purchase price allocated to the depreciable property. The basis of the land would be computed in the same way. The $9,000 original partnership basis is reduced by $126 basis (9,000/9,000 of $126) of the land constructively distributed to C, and increased by $126 (1,200/7,600 of $800), the portion of the purchase price allocated to the land.

(2) **The part of the distribution not under section 751 (b).** The partnership will realize no gain or loss in the balance of the distribution under section 731. Since the property in C's hands after the distribution will have the same basis it had in the partnership, the basis of partnership property remaining in the partnership after the distribution will not be ad-

justed (whether or not an election under 754 is in effect).

Example (6). (a) **Facts.** Partnership ABC distributes to partner C, in liquidation of his entire one-third interest in the partnership, a machine which is section 1245 property with a recomputed basis (as defined in section 1245 (a)(2)) of $18,000. At the time of the distribution, the balance sheet of the partnership is as follows:

ASSETS

	Adjusted basis per books	Market value
Cash	$3,000	$3,000
Machine (section 1245 property)	9,000	15,000
Land	18,000	27,000
Total	30,000	45,000

LIABILITIES AND CAPITAL

	Per books	Value
Liabilities	$0	$0
Capital :		
A	10,000	15,000
B	10,000	15,000
C	10,000	15,000
Total	30,000	45,000

(b) **Presence of section 751 property.** The section 1245 property is an unrealized receivable of the partnership to the extent of the potential section 1245 income in respect of the property. Since the fair market value of the property ($15,000) is lower than its recomputed basis ($18,000), the excess of the fair market value over its adjusted basis ($9,000), or $6,000, is the potential section 1245 income of the partnership in respect of the property. The partnership has no other section 751 property.

(c) The properties exchanged. In the distribution C received his share of section 751 property (potential section 1245 income of $2,000, i. e., ⅓ of $6,000) and his share of section 1245 property (other than potential section 1245 income) with a fair market value of $3,000, i. e., ⅓ of ($15,000 minus $6,000), and an adjusted basis of $3,000, i. e., ⅓ of $9,000. In addition he received $4,000 of section 751 property (consisting of $4,000 ($6,000 minus $2,000) of potential section 1245 income) and section 1245 property (other than potential section 1245 income) with a fair market value of $6,000 ($9,000 minus $3,000) and an adjusted basis of $6,000 ($9,000 minus $3,000). C relinquished his interest in $1,000 of cash and $9,000 of land. Assume that the partners agree that the $4,000 of section 751 property in excess of C's share was received by him in exchange for $4,000 of land.

(d) Distributee partner's tax consequences. C's tax consequences on the distributions are as follows:

(1) The section 751(b) sale or exchange. C is treated as if he received in a current distribution 4/9ths of his share of the land with a basis of $2,667 (18,000/27,000×$4,000). Then C is considered as having sold his 4/9ths share of the land to the partnership for $4,000, realizing a gain of $1,333. C's basis for the remainder of his partnership interest after the current distribution is $7,333, i. e., the basis of his partnership interest before the current distribution ($10,000) minus the basis of the land treated as distributed to him ($2,667).

(2) The part of the distribution not under section 751(b). Of the $15,000 total distribution to C, $11,000 ($2,000 of potential section 1245 income and $9,000 section 1245 property other than potential section 1245 income) is not within section 751(b). Under section 732 (b) and (c), C's basis for his share of potential section 1245 income is zero (see paragraph (c) (5) of this section) and his basis for $9,000 of section 1245 property (other than potential section 1245 income) is $7,333, i. e., the amount of the remaining basis for his partnership interest ($7,333) reduced by the basis for his share of potential section 1245 income (zero). Thus C's total aggregate basis for the section 1245 property (fair market value of $15,000) distributed to him is $11,333 ($4,000 plus $7,333). For an illustration of the computation of his recomputed basis for the section 1245 property immediately after the distribution, see example (2) of paragraph (f) (3) of § 1.1245-4.

(e) Partnership's tax consequences. The tax consequences to the partnership on the distribution are as follows:

(1) The section 751(b) sale or exchange. Upon the sale of $4,000 potential section 1245 income, with a basis of zero, for 4/9ths of C's interest in the land, the partnership consisting of the remaining members has $4,000 ordinary income under sections 751(b) and 1245(a) (1). See section 1245(b) (3) and (6) (A). The partnership's new basis for the land is $19,333, i. e., $18,000, less the basis of the 4/9ths share considered as distributed to C ($2,667), plus the partnership purchase price for this share ($4,000).

(2) The part of the distribution not under section 751(b). The analysis under this subparagraph should be made in accordance with the principles illustrated in paragraph (e) (2) of examples (3), (4), and (5) of this paragraph.

§ 1.752-1 Treatment of certain liabilities

(a) Increase in partner's liabilities. (1) Where the liabilities of a partnership are increased, and each partner's share of such liabilities is thereby increased, the amount of each partner's increase shall be treated as a contribution of money by that partner to the partnership. For example, partnership AB borrows $1,000. If A and B are equal partners, the basis of the partnership interest of each is increased by $500 since each is considered under section 752(a) to have contributed that amount of money to the partnership.

(2) Any increase in a partner's individual liabilities because of the assumption by him of partnership liabilities shall also be considered as a contribution of money by him to the partnership. For example, equal partnership AB owns real property with an adjusted basis to the partnership of $1,000, a fair market value of $800, and which is subject to a mortgage of $400 which the partnership has not assumed. The mortgage is considered as a liability of the partnership under section 752(c). Since A and B each share one-half thereof, under section 752(a) the liability of each has been increased $200. Under section 722 such $200 increase is reflected in the basis of each partner for his interest. The real property is distributed by the partnership to A. Under the provisions of section 733(2), there is a net decrease of $800 in A's basis for his partnership interest. This amount is computed as follows: The basis of A's partnership interest is decreased in the distribution by $1,000 (the partnership basis for the distributed property) and further decreased under section 752(b) by $200 (the decrease in A's share of partnership liabilities) and increased under section 752(a) by $400 (the increase in A's individual liability by reason of section 752(c)). Conversely, the basis of B's partnership interest is decreased by $200 since the distribution of the real property to A resulted in a decrease in B's share of the partnership liability under section 752(b).

(b) Decrease in partner's liabilities.
(1) Where the liabilities of a partnership are decreased, and each partner's share of such liabilities is thereby decreased, the amount of the decrease shall be treated as a distribution of money to the partner by the partnership. For example, partnership AB, in which A and B are equal partners, repays an obligation of $10,000. The repayment reduces each partner's share of partnership liabilities by $5,000 and is considered a distribution of money which reduces the basis of each partner's interest in the partnership by that amount. For the effect of a discharge of indebtedness on the basis of partnership property, see sections 108 and 1017.

(2) Where a partnership assumes the separate liabilities of a partner or a liability to which property owned by such partner is subject (see paragraph (c) of this section), the amount of the decrease in such partner's liabilities is treated as a distribution of money by the partnership to such partner. For example, partner A contributes property with a basis of $1,000 to partnership ABC in exchange for a one-third interest in the partnership. The property is subject to a mortgage of $150. (It is immaterial whether the mortgage is assumed by the partnership. See section 752(c).) The basis of A's partnership interest is $900, computed as follows: $1,000, A's basis for the contributed property, reduced by $100, two-thirds of A's original liability of $150 now attributable to partners B and C and reflected in their bases under the provisions of paragraph (a) of this section.

(c) Liability to which property is subject. Where property subject to a liability is contributed by a partner to a partnership, or distributed by a partnership to a partner, the amount of the liability, to an extent not exceeding the fair market value of the property at the time of the contribution or distribution, shall be considered as a liability assumed by the transferee. For example, A contributes property with a basis to him of $1,000 to equal partnership AB. The property is subject to a mortgage of $2,500 and its value exceeds $2,500. Under paragraph (b) of this section, A will be treated as receiving a distribution in money of $1,250, one-half of the liability of $2,500 assumed by the partnership. Since the basis of A's partnership interest is $1,000 (the basis of the property contributed by him), the distribution to him of $1,250 results in his realizing a capital gain of $250 under section 731 (a). A's basis for his partnership interest is zero. Although as a partner A has a $1,250 share of the $2,500 partnership liability, this $1,250 is not added to the basis of A's partnership interest since it does not represent an increase in liabilities as to him.

(d) Sale or exchange of a partnership interest. Where there is a sale or exchange of an interest in a partnership, liabilities shall be treated in the same manner as liabilities in connection with the sale or exchange of property not associated with partnerships. For example, if a partner sells his interest in a partnership for $750 cash and at the same time transfers to the purchaser his share of partnership liabilities amounting to $250, the amount realized by the seller on the transaction is $1,000.

(e) Partner's share of partnership liabilities. A partner's share of partnership liabilities shall be determined in accordance with his ratio for sharing losses under the partnership agreement. In the case of a limited partnership, a limited partner's share of partnership liabilities shall not exceed the difference between his actual contribution credited to him by the partnership and the total contribution which he is obligated to make under the limited partnership agreement. However, where none of the partners have any personal liability with respect to a partnership liability (as in the case of a mortgage on real estate acquired by the partnership without the assumption by the partnership or any of the partners of any liability on the mortgage), then all partners, including limited partners, shall be considered as sharing such liability under section 752 (c) in the same proportion as they share the profits. The provisions of this paragraph may be illustrated by the following example:

Example. G is a general partner and L is a limited partner in partnership GL. Each makes equal contributions of $20,000 cash to the partnership upon its formation. Under the terms of the partnership agreement, they are to share profits equally but L's liabilities are limited to the extent of his contribution. Subsequently, the partnership pays $10,000 for real property which is subject to a mortgage of $5,000. Neither the partnership nor any of the partners assume any liability on the mortgage. The basis of such property to the partnership is $15,000. The basis of G and L for their partnership interests is increased by $2,500 each, since each partner's share of the partnership liability (the $5,000 mortgage) has increased by that amount. However, if the partnership had assumed the mortgage so that G had become personally liable thereunder, G's basis for his interest would have been increased by $5,000 and L's basis would remain unchanged.

(f) Limitation. In determining the amount of liabilities for the purposes of section 752 and this section, the amount of an indebtedness is to be taken into account only once, even though a partner (in addition to his liability for such indebtedness as a partner) may be separately liable therefor in a capacity other than as a partner.

§ 1.753-1 Partner receiving income in respect of decedent

(a) Income in respect of a decedent under section 736(a). All payments coming within the provisions of section 736(a) made by a partnership to the estate or other successor in interest of a deceased partner are considered income in respect of the decedent under section 691. The estate or other successor in interest of a deceased partner shall be considered to have received income in respect of a decedent to the extent that amounts are paid by a third person in exchange for rights to future payments from the partnership under section 736(a). When a partner who is receiving payments under section 736(a) dies, section 753 applies to any remaining payments under section 736(a) made to his estate or other successor in interest.

(b) Other income in respect of a decedent. When a partner dies, the entire portion of the distributive share which is attributable to the period ending with the date of his death and which is taxable to his estate or other successor constitutes income in respect of a decedent under section 691. This rule applies even though that part of the distributive share for the period before death which the decedent withdrew is not included in the value of the decedent's partnership interest for estate tax purposes. See paragraph (c) (3) of § 1.706-1.

§ 1.754-1 Time and manner of making election to adjust basis of partnership property

(a) In general. A partnership may adjust the basis of partnership property under sections 734(b) and 743(b) if it files an election in accordance with the rules set forth in paragraph (b) of this section. An election may not be filed to make the adjustments provided in either section 734(b) or section 743(b) alone, but such an election must apply to both sections. An election made under the provisions of this section shall apply to all property distributions and transfers of partnership interests taking place in the partnership taxable year for which the election is made and in all subsequent partnership taxable years unless the election is revoked pursuant to paragraph (c) of this section.

(b) Time and method of making election. (1) An election under section 754 and this section to adjust the basis of partnership property under sections 734(b) and 743(b), with respect to a distribution of property to a partner or a transfer of an interest in a partnership, shall be made in a written statement filed with the partnership return for the taxable year during which the distribution or transfer occurs. For the election to be valid, the return must be filed not later than the time prescribed by paragraph (e) of § 1.6031-1 (including extensions thereof) for filing the return for such taxable year (or before August 23, 1956, whichever is later). Notwithstanding the preceding two sentences, if a valid election has been made under section 754 and this section for a preceding taxable year and not revoked pursuant to paragraph (c) of this section, a new election is not required to be made. The statement required by this subparagraph shall (i) set forth the name and address of the partnership making the election, (ii) be signed by any one of the partners, and (iii) contain a declaration that the partnership elects under section 754 to apply the provisions of section 734(b) and section 743(b). For rules regarding extensions of time for filing elections, see § 1.9100-1.

(2) The principles of this paragraph may be illustrated by the following example:

Example. A, a U.S. citizen, is a member of partnership ABC, which has not previously made an election under section 754 to adjust the basis of partnership property. The partnership and the partners use the calendar year as the taxable year. A sells his interest in the partnership to D on January 1, 1971. The partnership may elect under section 754 and this section to adjust the basis of partnership property under sections 734(b) and 743(b). Unless an extension of time to make the election is obtained under the provisions of § 1.9100-1, the election must be made in a written statement filed with the partnership return for 1971 and must contain the information specified in subparagraph (1) of this paragraph. Such return must be filed by April 17, 1972 (unless an extension of time for filing the return is obtained). The election will apply to all distributions of property to a partner and transfers of an interest in the partnership occurring in 1971 and subsequent years, unless revoked pursuant to paragraph (c) of this section.

(c) Revocation of election. A partnership having an election in effect under this section may revoke such election with the approval of the district director for the internal revenue district in which the partnership return is required to be filed. A partnership which wishes to revoke such an election shall file with the district director for the internal revenue district in which the partnership return is required to be filed an application setting forth the grounds on which the revocation is desired. The application shall be filed not later than 30 days after the close of the partnership taxable year with respect to which revocation is intended to take effect and shall be signed by any one of the partners. Examples of situations which may be considered sufficient reason for approving an application for revocation include a change in the nature of the partnership business, a substantial increase in the assets of the partnership, a change in the character of partnership assets, or an increased frequency of retirements or shifts of partnership interests, so that an increased administrative burden would result to the partnership from the election. However, no application for revocation of an election shall be approved when the purpose of the revocation is primarily to avoid stepping down the basis of partnership assets upon a transfer or distribution.

§ 1.755–1   Rules for allocation of basis

(a) General rule. (1) (i) A partnership which has elected under section 754 must adjust the basis of partnership property under the provisions of section 734(b) (relating to the optional adjustment to the basis of undistributed partnership property) and section 743(b) (relating to the optional adjustment to the basis of partnership property where a partnership interest is transferred). The amount of the increase or decrease (as determined in those sections) in the adjusted basis of the partnership property shall first be divided, under paragraph (b) of this section, between the two classes of property described in section 755(b). Then, the portion of the increase or decrease allocated to each class shall be further allocated to the bases of the properties within the class in a manner which will reduce the difference between the fair market value and the adjusted basis of partnership properties. In the alternative, any increase or decrease may be allocated in any other manner approved by the district director under subparagraph (2) of this paragraph.

(ii) If there is an increase in basis to be allocated to partnership assets, such increase must be allocated only to assets whose values exceed their bases and in proportion to the difference between the value and basis of each. No increase shall be made to the basis of any asset the adjusted basis of which equals or exceeds its fair market value.

(iii) If there is a decrease in basis to be allocated to partnership assets, such decrease must be allocated to assets whose bases exceed their value and in proportion to the difference between the basis and value of each. No decrease shall be made to the basis of any asset, the fair market value of which equals or exceeds its adjusted basis.

(iv) The application of the rules with respect to the allocation of an adjustment in basis under subdivisions (ii) and (iii) of this subparagraph requires that a portion of such adjustment be allocated to partnership good will, to the extent that good will exists and is reflected in the value of the property distributed, the price at which the partnership interest is sold, or the basis of the partnership interest determined under section 1014, in accordance with the difference between such value of the good will and its adjusted basis at the time of the transaction.

(2) If a partnership (or a partner electing under section 732(d)) desires to adjust the basis of assets under section 734(b) or 743(b) in a manner other than that prescribed in subparagraph (1) of this paragraph, it must file an application for permission to use such method with the district director no later than 30 days after the close of the partnership taxable year in which the proposed adjustment is to be made. The application must describe the proposed adjustments in detail and set forth the reasons for the desired use of the other method. Under section 755(a) (2), the district director may permit the partnership to increase the bases of some partnership properties and decrease the bases of other partnership properties under section 734(b) or 743(b). Each increase or decrease to the basis of an asset must reduce or eliminate the difference between such basis and the value of the asset. The net amount of all such adjustments must equal the amount of the adjustment under section 734(b) or 743(b). Adjustments that both increase and decrease the basis of partnership assets will be permitted by the district director only upon a satisfactory showing of the values for partnership assets used by the parties to determine the price at which a partnership interest was sold, the value of the decedent's partnership interest at date of death (or at the alternate valuation date, if used), or the amount of a distribution.

(b) **Special rules.** For the purposes of applying section 755, all partnership property shall be classified into two categories: capital assets and property described in section 1231(b) (certain property used in the trade or business), or any other property of the partnership.

(1) **Distributions.** (i) Where there is a distribution of partnership property resulting in an adjustment to the basis of undistributed partnership property under section 734(b) (1) (B) or (b) (2) (B), such adjustment must be allocated to remaining partnership property of a character similar to that of the distributed property with respect to which the adjustment arose. Thus, when the partnership adjusted basis of distributed capital assets and section 1231(b) property immediately prior to distribution exceeds the basis of such property to the distributee part-

ner (as determined under section 732), the basis of the undistributed capital assets and section 1231(b) property remaining in the partnership shall be increased by an amount equal to such excess. Conversely, when the basis to the distributee partner (as determined under section 732) of distributed capital assets and section 1231(b) property exceeds the partnership adjusted basis of such property immediately prior to the distribution, the basis of the undistributed capital assets and section 1231(b) property remaining in the partnership shall be decreased by an amount equal to such excess. Similarly, where there is a distribution of partnership property other than capital assets and section 1231(b) property, and the basis of such other property to the distributee partner (as determined under section 732) is not the same as the partnership adjusted basis of such property immediately prior to distribution, the adjustment shall be made only to undistributed property of the same category remaining in the partnership.

(ii) Where there is a distribution resulting in an adjustment under section 734(b) (1) (A) or (b) (2) (A) to the basis of undistributed partnership property, such adjustment must be allocated only to capital assets or section 1231(b) property.

(2) **Transfers.** Where there is a basis adjustment under section 743(b) arising from a transfer of an interest in a partnership by sale or exchange or upon the death of a partner, the amount of the adjustment shall be allocated between the two classes of property described in section 755(b) and then the amount allocated to each class shall be further allocated under the rules of paragraph (a) (1) of this section. Thus, to the extent that an amount paid by a purchaser of a partnership interest (or the basis of the partnership interest to the estate or other successor in interest of a deceased partner) is attributable to the value of capital assets and section 1231(b) property, any difference between the amount so attributable and the transferee partner's share of the partnership basis of such property shall constitute a special basis adjustment with respect to partnership capital assets and section 1231(b) property. Similarly, any such difference attributable

to any other property of the partnership shall constitute a special basis adjustment with respect to such property.

(3) Limitation on decrease of basis. Where a decrease in the basis of partnership assets is required under section 734(b) (2) and the amount of the decrease exceeds the adjusted basis to the partnership of property of the required character, the basis of such property shall be reduced to zero (but not below zero), and the balance of the decrease in basis shall be made when the partnership subsequently acquires property of a like character to which an adjustment can be made.

(4) Carryover of adjustment. Where, in the case of a distribution, an increase or decrease required under paragraph (a) of this section in the basis of undistributed partnership property cannot be made because the partnership owns no property of the character required to be adjusted, or because the adjustment has been limited under subparagraph (3) of this paragraph, the adjustment shall be made when the partnership subsequently acquires property of a like character to which an adjustment can be made.

(c) Examples. The provisions of this section may be illustrated by the following examples:

Example (1). Assume that partnership ABC has three assets: X, a capital asset with an adjusted basis of $1,000 and a value of $1,500; Y, a depreciable asset with an adjusted basis of $1,000 and a value of $900; and Z, inventory items with an adjusted basis of $700 and a value of $600. A sells his interest to D (when an election under 754 is in effect) for $1,000 (⅓ of $3,000, the total value of partnership assets). D's share of the adjusted basis of partnership property is $900 (⅓ of $2,700). Therefore, under section 743 (b), D has a special basis adjustment of $100 ($1,000 minus $900). This adjustment must be allocated entirely to property X, since such allocation will have the effect of reducing the difference between the value and basis of such asset. Therefore, D has a special basis adjustment of $100 with respect to property X, which now has a special basis to him of $1,100. No part of the adjustment is made to depreciable property Y or inventory items Z, since any such adjustment would increase the difference between the basis and value of each such asset.

Example (2). Assume the same facts as in example (1) of this paragraph, except that capital asset X has a value of $1,500, depreciable property Y has a value of $1,100, and inventory items Z have a value of only $400. Therefore, under section 743 (b), D has a special basis adjustment of $100, the excess of D's basis for his interest in the partnership ($1,000) over his share of the adjusted basis of partnership property ($900). This $100 adjustment must be allocated entirely to capital asset X and depreciable property Y in proportion to the difference between the value and basis of each since such allocation has the effect of reducing the difference between the value and basis of each such asset. Therefore, D has a special basis adjustment of $83 ($500/$600 of $100) with respect to capital asset X, which now has a special basis to him of $1,083, and of $17 ($100/$600 of $100) with respect to depreciable property Y, which now has a special basis to him of $1,017. No part of the adjustment is made to inventory items Z, since any such adjustment would increase the difference between the basis of such asset and its value.

Example (3). Assume that partnership EFG has three assets: X, a capital asset with an adjusted basis of $1,000 and a value of $1,500; Y, a depreciable asset with an adjusted basis of $1,000 and a value of $700; and Z, inventory items with an adjusted basis of $700 and a value of $800. E sells his interest to H (when an election under section 754 is in effect) for $1,000 (⅓ of $3,000, the total value of the partnership assets). H's share of the adjusted basis of partnership is $900 (⅓ of $2,700). Therefore, H has a special basis adjustment of $100 ($1,000 minus $900) under section 743 (b). Since, of the total $300 difference between the value and the adjusted basis of all partnership property, $200 ($500, appreciation in value of X, minus $300, depreciation in value of Y) is attributable to the class of capital assets and depreciable property, and $100 (appreciation in value of inventory items Z) to the class of other property, H's special basis adjustment of $100 must be allocated ⅔ to capital assets and depreciable property and ⅓ to other property (inventory). The $67 increase (⅔ of $100) to be allocated to capital assets and depreciable property must further be allocated so as to reduce the difference between the value and basis of such assets. This can be done only by allocating the entire $67 increase to capital asset X (the basis of which is less than its value), and no part of the increase to depreciable property Y (the basis of which exceeds its value). Therefore, H has a special basis adjustment of $67 for capital asset X, which now has a special basis to him of $1,067; he has no special basis adjustment for depreciable property Y. H also has a special basis adjustment of $33 (⅓ of $100) for inventory items Z, the special basis of which is now $733.

§ 1.761-1   Terms defined

(a) Partnership. The term "partnership" includes a syndicate, group, pool, joint venture, or other unincorporated organization through or by means of which any business, financial operation, or venture is carried on, and which is not a corporation or a trust or estate within the meaning of the Code. The term "partnership" is broader in scope than the common law meaning of partnership, and may include groups not commonly called partnerships. See section 7701(a)(2). See regulations under section 7701(a) (1), (2), and (3) for the description of those unincorporated organizations taxable as corporations or trusts. A joint undertaking merely to share expenses is not a partnership. For example, if two or more persons jointly construct a ditch merely to drain surface water from their properties, they are not partners. Mere coownership of property which is maintained, kept in repair, and rented or leased does not constitute a partnership. For example, if an individual owner, or tenants in common, of farm property lease it to a farmer for a cash rental or a share of the crops, they do not necessarily create a partnership thereby. Tenants in common, however, may be partners if they actively carry on a trade, business, financial operation, or venture and divide the profits thereof. For example, a partnership exists if coowners of an apartment building lease space and in addition provide services to the occupants either directly or through an agent. For rules relating to the exclusion of certain partnerships from the application of all or part of subchapter K of chapter 1 of the Code, see § 1.761-2.

. . . .

(c) Partnership agreement. For the purposes of subchapter K, a partnership agreement includes the original agreement and any modifications thereof agreed to by all the partners or adopted in any other manner provided by the partnership agreement. Such agreement or modifications can be oral or written. A partnership agreement may be modified with respect to a particular taxable year subsequent to the close of such taxable year, but not later than the date (not including any extension of time) prescribed by law for the filing of the partnership return. As to any matter on which the partnership agreement, or any modification thereof, is silent, the provisions of local law shall be considered to constitute a part of the agreement.

(d) Liquidation of partner's interest. The term "liquidation of a partner's interest" means the termination of a partner's entire interest in a partnership by means of a distribution, or a series of distributions, to the partner by the partnership. A series of distributions will come within the meaning of this term whether they are made in one year or in more than one year. Where a partner's interest is to be liquidated by a series of distributions, the interest will not be considered as liquidated un-

til the final distribution has been made. For the basis of property distributed in one liquidating distribution, or in a series of distributions in liquidation, see section 732(b). A distribution which is not in liquidation of a partner's entire interest, as defined in this paragraph, is a current distribution. Current distributions, therefore, include distributions in partial liquidation of a partner's interest, and distributions of the partner's distributive share. See paragraph (a) (1) (ii) of § 1.731-1.

§ 1.1001-1 Computation of gain or loss

(a) General rule. Except as otherwise provided in subtitle A of the Code, the gain or loss realized from the conversion of property into cash, or from the exchange of property for other property differing materially either in kind or in extent, is treated as income or as loss sustained. The amount realized from a sale or other disposition of property is the sum of any money received plus the fair market value of any property (other than money) received. The fair market value of property is a question of fact, but only in rare and extraordinary cases will property be considered to have no fair market value. The general method of computing such gain or loss is prescribed by section 1001(a) through (d) which contemplates that from the amount realized upon the sale or exchange there shall be withdrawn a sum sufficient to restore the adjusted basis prescribed by section 1011 and the regulations thereunder (i. e., the cost or other basis adjusted for receipts, expenditures, losses, allowances, and other items chargeable against and applicable to such cost or other basis). The amount which remains after the adjusted basis has been restored to the taxpayer constitutes the realized gain. If the amount realized upon the sale or exchange is insufficient to restore to the taxpayer the adjusted basis of the property, a loss is sustained to the extent of the difference between such adjusted basis and the amount realized. The basis may be different depending upon whether gain or loss is being computed. For example, see section 1015(a) and the regulations thereunder. Section 1001(e) and paragraph (f) of this section prescribe the method of computing gain or loss upon the sale or other disposition of a term interest in property the adjusted basis (or a portion) of which is determined pursuant, or by reference, to section 1014 (relating to the basis of property acquired from a decedent) or section 1015 (relating to the basis of property acquired by gift or by a transfer in trust).

(b) Real estate taxes as amounts received. (1) Section 1001 (b) and section 1012 state rules applicable in making an adjustment upon a sale of real property with respect to the real property taxes apportioned between seller and purchaser under section 164 (d). Thus, if the seller pays (or agrees to pay) real property taxes attributable to the real property tax year in which the sale occurs, he shall not take into account, in determining the amount realized from the sale under section 1001 (b), any amount received as reimbursement for taxes which are treated under section 164(d) as imposed upon the purchaser. Similarly, in computing the cost of the property under section 1012, the purchaser shall not take into account any amount paid to the seller as reimbursement for real property taxes which are treated under section 164 (d) as imposed upon the purchaser. These rules apply whether or not the contract of sale calls for the purchaser to reimburse the seller for such real property taxes paid or to be paid by the seller.

(2) On the other hand, if the purchaser pays (or is to pay) an amount representing real property taxes which are treated under section 164 (d) as imposed upon the seller, that amount shall be taken into account both in determining the amount realized from the sale under section 1001 (b) and in computing the cost of the property under section 1012. It is immaterial whether or not the contract of sale specifies that the sale price has been reduced by, or is in any way intended to reflect, the taxes allocable to the seller. See also paragraph (b) of § 1.1012–1.

(3) Subparagraph (1) of this paragraph shall not apply to a seller who, in a taxable year prior to the taxable year of sale, pays an amount representing real property taxes which are treated under section 164(d) as imposed on the purchaser, if such seller has elected to capitalize such amount in accordance with section 266 and the regulations

thereunder (relating to election to capitalize certain carrying charges and taxes).

(4) The application of this paragraph may be illustrated by the following examples:

Example (1). Assume that the contract price on the sale of a parcel of real estate is $50,000 and that real property taxes thereon in the amount of $1,000 for the real property tax year in which occurred the date of sale were previously paid by the seller. Assume further that $750 of the taxes are treated under section 164 (d) as imposed upon the purchaser and that he reimburses the seller in that amount in addition to the contract price. The amount realized by the seller is $50,000. Similarly, $50,000 is the purchaser's cost. If, in this example, the purchaser made no payment other than the contract price of $50,000, the amount realized by the seller would be $49,250, since the sales price would be deemed to include $750 paid to the seller in reimbursement for real property taxes imposed upon the purchaser. Similarly, $49,250 would be the purchaser's cost.

Example (2). Assume that the purchaser in example (1) above paid all of the real property taxes. Assume further that $250 of the taxes are treated under section 164(d) as imposed upon the seller. The amount realized by the seller is $50,250. Similarly, $50,250 is the purchaser's cost, regardless of the taxable year in which the purchaser makes actual payment of the taxes.

. . . .

(c) Other rules. (1) Even though property is not sold or otherwise disposed of, gain is realized if the sum of all the amounts received which are required by section 1016 and other applicable provisions of subtitle A of the Code to be applied against the basis of the property exceeds such basis. Except as otherwise provided in section 301 (c) (3) (B) with respect to distributions out of increase in value of property accrued prior to March 1, 1913, such gain is includible in gross income under section 61 as "income from whatever source derived". On the other hand, a loss is not ordinarily sustained prior to the sale or other disposition of the property, for the reason that until such sale or other disposition occurs there remains the possibility that the taxpayer may recover or recoup the adjusted basis of the property. Until some identifiable event fixes the actual sustaining of a loss and the amount thereof, it is not taken into account.

(2) The provisions of subparagraph (1) of this paragraph may be illustrated by the following example:

Example. A, an individual on a calendar year basis, purchased certain shares of stock subsequent to February 28, 1913, for $10,000. On January 1, 1954, A's adjusted basis for the stock had been reduced to $1,000 by reason of receipts and distributions described in sections 1016(a) (1) and 1016(a) (4). He received in 1954 a further distribution of $5,000, being a distribution covered by section 1016(a) (4), other than a distribution out of increase of value of property accrued prior to March 1, 1913. This distribution applied against the adjusted basis as required by section 1016(a) (4) exceeds that basis by $4,000. The $4,000 excess is a gain realized by A in 1954 and is includible in gross income in his return for that calendar year. In computing gain from the stock, as in adjusting basis, no distinction is made between items of receipts or distributions described in section 1016. If A sells the stock in 1955 for $5,000, he realizes in 1955 a gain of $5,000, since the adjusted basis of the stock for the purpose of computing gain or loss from the sale is zero.

(d) Installment sales. In the case of property sold on the installment plan, special rules for the taxation of the gain are prescribed in section 453.

(e) Transfers in part a sale and in part a gift. (1) Where a transfer of property is in part a sale and in part a gift, the transferor has a gain to the extent that the amount realized by him exceeds his adjusted basis in the property. However, no loss is sustained on such a transfer if the amount realized is less than the adjusted basis. For the determination of basis of property in the hands of the transferee, see § 1.1015–4. For the allocation of the adjusted basis of property in the case of a bargain sale to a charitable organization, see § 1.1011–2.

(2) Examples. The provisions of subparagraph (1) may be illustrated by the following examples:

Example (1). A transfers property to his son for $60,000. Such property in the hands of A has an adjusted basis of $30,000 (and a fair market value of $90,000). A's gain is $30,000, the excess of $60,000, the amount realized, over the adjusted basis, $30,000. He has made a gift of $30,000, the excess of $90,000, the fair market value, over the amount realized, $60,000.

Example (2). A transfers property to his son for $30,000. Such property in the hands of A has an adjusted basis of $60,000 (and a fair market value of $90,000). A has no gain or loss, and has made a gift of $60,000, the excess of $90,000, the fair market value, over the amount realized, $30,000.

Example (3). A transfers property to his son for $30,000. Such property in A's hands has an adjusted basis of $30,000 (and a fair market value of $60,000). A has no gain and has made a gift of $30,000, the excess of $60,000, the fair market value, over the amount realized, $30,000.

Example (4). A transfers property to his son for $30,000. Such property in A's hands has an adjusted basis of $90,000 (and a fair market value of $60,000). A has sustained no loss, and has made a gift of $30,000, the excess of $60,000, the fair market value, over the amount realized, $30,000.

(f) Sale or other disposition of a term interest in property—(1) General rule. Except as otherwise provided in subparagraph (3) of this paragraph, for purposes of determining gain or loss from the sale or other disposition after October 9, 1969, of a term interest in property (as defined in subparagraph (2) of this paragraph) a taxpayer shall not take into account that portion of the adjusted basis of such interest which is determined pursuant, or by reference, to section 1014 (relating to the basis of property acquired from a decedent) or section 1015 (relating to the basis of property acquired by gift or by a transfer in trust) to the extent that such adjusted basis is a portion of the adjusted uniform basis of the entire property (as defined in § 1.1014–5). Where a term interest in property is transferred to a corporation in connection with a transaction to which section 351 applies and the adjusted basis of the term interest (i) is determined pursuant to section 1014 or 1015 and (ii) is also a portion of the adjusted uniform basis of the entire property, a subsequent sale or other disposition of such term interest by the corporation will be subject to the provisions of section 1001(e) and this paragraph to the extent that the basis of the term interest so sold or otherwise disposed of is determined by reference to its basis in the hands of the transferor as provided by section 362 (a). See subparagraph (2) of this paragraph for rules relating to the characterization of stock received by the transferor of a term interest in property in connection with a transaction to which section 351 applies. That portion of the adjusted uniform basis of the entire property which is assignable to such interest at the time of its sale or other disposition shall be determined under the rules provided in § 1.1014–5. Thus, gain or loss realized from a sale or other disposition of a term interest in property shall be determined by comparing the amount of the proceeds of such sale with that part of the adjusted basis of such interest which is not a portion of the adjusted uniform basis of the entire property.

(2) Term interest defined. For purposes of section 1001(e) and this paragraph, a "term interest in property" means—

(i) A life interest in property,

(ii) An interest in property for a term,

(iii) An income interest in a trust.

Generally, subdivisions (i), (ii), and (iii) refer to an interest, present or future, in the income from property or the right to use property which will terminate or fail on the lapse of time, on the occurrence of an event or contingency, or on the failure of an event or contingency to occur. Such divisions do not refer to remainder or reversionary interests in the property itself or other interests in the property which will ripen into ownership of the entire property upon termination or failure of a preceding term interest. A "term interest in property" also includes any property received upon a sale or other disposition of a life interest in property, an interest in property for a term of years, or an income interest in a trust by the original holder of such interest, but only to the extent that the adjusted basis of the property received is determined by reference to the adjusted basis of the term interest so transferred.

(3) Exception. Paragraph (1) of section 1001(e) and subparagraph (1) of this paragraph shall not apply to a sale or other disposition of a term interest in property as a part of a single transaction in which the entire interest in the property is transferred to a third person or to two or more other persons, including persons who acquire such entire interest as joint tenants, tenants by the entirety, or tenants in common. See § 1.1014–5 for computation of gain or loss upon such a sale or other disposition where the property has been acquired from a decedent or by gift or transfer in trust.

. . . . .

§ 1.1001–2   Discharge of liabilities

(a) Inclusion in amount realized—(1) In general. Except as provided in paragraph (a)(2) and (3) of this section, the amount realized from a sale or other disposition of property includes the amount of liabilities from which the transferor is discharged as a result of the sale or disposition.

(2) Discharge of indebtedness. The amount realized on a sale or other disposition of property that secures a recourse liability does not include amounts that are (or would be if realized and recognized) income from the

discharge of indebtedness under section 61(a)(12). For situations where amounts arising from the discharge of indebtedness are not realized and recognized, see section 108 and § 1.61–12(b)(1).

(3) Liability incurred on acquisition. In the case of a liability incurred by reason of the acquisition of the property, this section does not apply to the extent that such liability was not taken into account in determining the transferor's basis for such property.

(4) Special rules. For purposes of this section—

(i) The sale or other disposition of property that secures a nonrecourse liability discharges the transferor from the liability;

(ii) The sale or other disposition of property that secures a recourse liability discharges the transferor from the the liability if another person agrees to pay the liability (whether or not the transferor is in fact released from liability);

(iii) A disposition of property includes a gift of the property or a transfer of the property in satisfaction of liabilities to which it is subject;

(iv) Contributions and distributions of property between a partner and a partnership are not sales or other dispositions of property; and

(v) The liabilities from which a transferor is discharged as a result of the sale or disposition of a partnership interest include the transferor's share of the liabilities of the partnership.

(b) Effect of fair market value of security. The fair market value of the security at the time of sale or disposition is not relevant for purposes of determining under paragraph (a) of this section the amount of liabilities from which the taxpayer is discharged or treated as discharged. Thus, the fact that the fair market value of the property is less than the amount of the liabilities it secures does not prevent the full amount of those liabilities from being treated as money received from the sale or other disposition of the property. However, see paragraph (a)(2) of this section for a rule relating to certain income from discharge of indebtedness.

(c) Examples. The provisions of this section may be illustrated by the following examples. In each example assume the taxpayer uses the cash receipts and disbursements method of accounting, makes a return on the basis of the calendar year, and sells or disposes of all property which is security for a given liability.

Example (1). In 1976 A purchases an asset for $10,000. A pays the seller $1,000 in cash and signs a note payable to the seller for $9,000. A is personally liable for repayment with the seller having full recourse in the event of default. In addition, the asset which was purchased is pledged as security. During the years 1976 and 1977, A takes depreciation deductions on the asset in the amount of $3,100. During this same time period A reduces the outstanding principal on the note of $7,600. At the beginning of 1978 A sells the asset. The buyer pays A $1,600 in cash and assumes personal liability for the $7,600 outstanding liability. A becomes secondarily liable for repayment of the liability. A's amount realized is $9,200 ($1,600 + $7,600). Since A's adjusted basis in the asset is $6,900 ($10,000 — $3,100) A realizes a gain of $2,300 ($9,200 — $6,900).

Example (2). Assume the same facts as in example (1) except that A is not personally liable on the $9,000 note given to the seller and in the event of default the seller's only recourse is to the asset. In addition, on the sale of the asset by A, the purchaser takes the asset subject to the liability. Nevertheless, A's amount realized is $9,200 and A's gain realized is $2,300 on the sale.

Example (3). In 1975 L becomes a limited partner in partnership GL. L contributes $10,000 in cash to GL and L's distributive share of partnership income and loss is 10 percent. L is not entitled to receive any guaranteed payments. In 1978 M purchases L's entire interest in partnership GL. At the time of the sale L's adjusted basis in the partnership interest is $20,000. At that time L's proportionate share of liabilities, of which no partner has assumed personal liability, is $15,000. M pays $10,000 in cash for L's interest in the partnership. Under section 752(d) and this section, L's share of partnership liabilities, $15,000, is treated as money received. Accordingly, L's amount realized on the sale of the partnership interest is $25,000 ($10,000 + $15,000). L's gain realized on the sale is $5,000 ($25,000 — $20,000).

Example (4). In 1976 B becomes a limited partner in partnership BG. In 1978 B contributes B's entire interest in BG to a charitable organization described in section 170(c). At the time of the contribution all of the partnership liabilities are liabilities for which neither B nor G has assumed any personal liability and B's proportionate share of which is $9,000. The charitable organization does not pay any cash or other property to B, but takes the partnership interest subject to the $9,000 of liabilities. Assume that the contribution is treated as a bargain sale to a charitable organization and that under section 1011(b) $3,000 is determined to be the portion of B's basis in the partnership interest allocable to the sale. Under section 752(d) and this section, the $9,000 of liabilities is treated by B as money received, thereby making B's amount realized $9,000. B's gain realized is $6,000 ($9,000 — $3,000).

Example (5). In 1975 C, an individual, creates T, an irrevocable trust. Due to certain powers expressly retained by C, T is a "grantor trust" for purposes of subpart E of part 1 of subchapter J of the Code and therefore C is treated as the owner of the entire trust. T purchases an interest in P, a partnership. C, as owner of T, deducts the distributive share of partnership losses attributable to the partnership interest held by T. In 1978, when the adjusted basis of the partnership interest held by T is $1,200, C renounces the powers previously and expressly retained that initially resulted in T being classified as a grantor trust. Consequently, T ceases to be a grantor trust and C is no longer considered to be the owner of the trust. At the time of the renunciation all of P's liabilities are liabilities on which none of the partners have assumed any personal liability and the proportionate share of which of the interest held by T is $11,000. Since prior to the renunciation C was the owner of the entire trust, C was considered the owner of all the trust property for Federal income tax purposes, including the partnership interest. Since C was considered to be the owner of the partnership interest, C not T, was considered to be the partner in P during the time T was a "grantor trust". However, at the time C renounced the powers that gave rise to T's classification as a grantor trust, T no longer qualified as a grantor trust with the result that C was no longer considered to be the owner of the trust and trust property for Federal income tax purposes. Consequently, at that time, C is considered to have transferred ownership of the interest in P to T, now a separate taxable entity, independent of its grantor C. On the transfer, C's share of partnership liabilities ($11,000) is treated as money received. Accordingly, C's amount realized is $11,000 and C's gain realized is $9,800 ($11,000 — $1,200).

Example (6). In 1977 D purchases an asset for $7,500. D pays the seller $1,500 in cash and signs a note payable to the seller for $6,000. D is not personally liable for repayment but pledges as security the newly purchased asset. In the event of default, the seller's only recourse is to the asset. During the years 1977 and 1978 D takes depreciation deductions on the asset totaling $4,200 thereby reducing D's basis in the asset to $3,300 ($7,500 — $4,200). In 1979 D transfers the asset to a trust which is not a "grantor trust" for purposes of subpart E of part 1 of subchapter J of the Code. Therefore D is not treated as the owner of the trust. The trust takes the asset subject to the liability and in addition pays D $750 in cash. Prior to the transfer D had reduced the amount outstanding on the liability to $4,700. D's amount realized on the transfer is $5,450 ($4,700 + $750). Since D's adjusted basis is $3,300, D's gain realized is $2,150 ($5,450 — $3,300).

Example (7). In 1974 E purchases a herd of cattle for breeding purposes. The purchase price is $20,000 consisting of $1,000 cash and a $19,000 note. E is not personally liable for repayment of the liability and the seller's only recourse in the event of default is to the herd of cattle. In 1977 E transfers the herd back to the original seller thereby satisfying the indebtedness pursuant to a provision in the original sales agreement. At the time of the transfer the fair market value of the herd is $15,000 and the remaining principal balance on the note is $19,000. At that time E's adjusted basis in the herd is $16,500 due to a deductible loss incurred when a portion of the herd died as a result of disease. As a result of the indebtedness being satisfied, E's amount realized is

$19,000 notwithstanding the fact that the fair market value of the herd was less than $19,000. E's realized gain is $2,500 ($19,000 − $16,500).

Example (8). In 1980, F transfers to a creditor an asset with a fair market value of $6,000 and the creditor discharges $7,500 of indebtedness for which F is personally liable. The amount realized on the disposition of the asset is its fair market value ($6,000). In addition, F has income from the discharge of indebtedness of $1,500 ($7,500 − $6,000).

§ 1.1002–1 Sales or exchanges

(a) General rule. The general rule with respect to gain or loss realized upon the sale or exchange of property as determined under section 1001 is that the entire amount of such gain or loss is recognized except in cases where specific provisions of subtitle A of the Code provide otherwise.

(b) Strict construction of exceptions from general rule. The exceptions from the general rule requiring the recognition of all gains and losses, like other exceptions from a rule of taxation of general and uniform application, are strictly construed and do not extend either beyond the words or the underlying assumptions and purposes of the exception. Nonrecognition is accorded by the Code only if the exchange is one which satisfies both (1) the specific description in the Code of an excepted exchange, and (2) the underlying purpose for which such exchange is excepted from the general rule. The exchange must be germane to, and a necessary incident of, the investment or enterprise in hand. The relationship of the exchange to the venture or enterprise is always material, and the surrounding facts and circumstances must be shown. As elsewhere, the taxpayer claiming the benefit of the exception must show himself within the exception.

(c) Certain exceptions to general rule. Exceptions to the general rule are made, for example, by sections 351 (a), 354, 361(a), 371(a) (1), 371(b) (1), 721, 1031, 1035 and 1036. These sections describe certain specific exchanges of property in which at the time of the exchange particular differences exist between the property parted with and the property acquired, but such differences are more formal than substantial. As to these, the Code provides that such differences shall not be deemed controlling, and that gain or loss shall not be recognized at the time

of the exchange. The underlying assumption of these exceptions is that the new property is substantially a continuation of the old investment still unliquidated; and, in the case of reorganizations, that the new enterprise, the new corporate structure, and the new property are substantially continuations of the old still unliquidated.

(d) Exchange. Ordinarily, to constitute an exchange, the transaction must be a reciprocal transfer of property, as distinguished from a transfer of property for a money consideration only.

§ 1.1011–1 Adjusted basis

The adjusted basis for determining the gain or loss from the sale or other disposition of property is the cost or other basis prescribed in section 1012 or other applicable provisions of subtitle A of the Code, adjusted to the extent provided in sections 1016, 1017, and 1018 or as otherwise specifically provided for under applicable provisions of internal revenue laws.

§ 1.1011–2 Bargain sale to a charitable organization

(a) In general. (1) If for the taxable year a charitable contributions deduction is allowable under section 170 by reason of a sale or exchange of property, the taxpayer's adjusted basis of such property for purposes of determining gain from such sale or exchange must be computed as provided in section 1011(b) and paragraph (b) of this section. If after applying the provisions of section 170 for the taxable year, including the percentage limitations of section 170(b), no deduction is allowable under that section by reason of the sale or exchange of the property, section 1011(b) does not apply and the adjusted basis of the property is not required to be apportioned pursuant to paragraph (b) of this section. In such case the entire adjusted basis of the property is to be taken into account in determining gain from the sale or exchange, as provided in § 1.1001–1(e). In ascertaining whether or not a charitable contributions deduction is allowable under section 170 for the taxable year for such purposes, that section is to be applied without regard to this section and the amount by which the contributed portion of the property must be reduced under section 170(e)

(1) is the amount determined by taking into account the amount of gain which would have been ordinary income or long-term capital gain if the entire property had been sold by the donor at its fair market value at the time of the sale or exchange.

(2) If in the taxable year there is a sale or exchange of property which gives rise to a charitable contribution which is carried over under section 170 (b) (1) (D) (ii) or section 170(d) to a subsequent taxable year or is postponed under section 170(a) (3) to a subsequent taxable year, section 1011(b) and paragraph (b) of this section must be applied for purposes of apportioning the adjusted basis of the property for the year of the sale or exchange, whether or not such contribution is allowable as a deduction under section 170 in such subsequent year.

(3) If property is transferred subject to an indebtedness, the amount of the indebtedness must be treated as an amount realized for purposes of determining whether there is a sale or exchange to which section 1011(b) and this section apply, even though the transferee does not agree to assume or pay the indebtedness.

(4) (i) Section 1011(b) and this section apply where property is sold or exchanged in return for an obligation to pay an annuity and a charitable contributions deduction is allowable under section 170 by reason of such sale or exchange.

(ii) If in such case the annuity received in exchange for the property is nonassignable, or is assignable but only to the charitable organization to which the property is sold or exchanged, and if the transferor is the only annuitant or the transferor and a designated survivor annuitant or annuitants are the only annuitants, any gain on such exchange is to be reported as provided in example (8) in paragraph (c) of this section. In determining the period over which gain may be reported as provided in such example, the life expectancy of the survivor annuitant may not be taken into account. The fact that the transferor may retain the right to revoke the survivor's annuity or relinquish his own right to the annuity will not be considered, for purposes of this subdivision, to make the annuity assignable to someone other than the charitable organization. Gain on an exchange of the type described in this subdivision pursuant to an agreement which is entered into after December 19, 1969, and before May 3, 1971, may be reported as provided in example (8) in paragraph (c) of this section, even though the annuity is assignable.

(iii) In the case of an annuity to which subdivision (ii) of this subparagraph applies, the gain unreported by the transferor with respect to annuity payments not yet due when the following events occur is not required to be included in gross income of any person where—

(a) The transferor dies before the entire amount of gain has been reported and there is no surviving annuitant, or

(b) The transferor relinquishes the annuity to the charitable organization. If the transferor dies before the entire amount of gain on a two-life annuity has been reported, the unreported gain is required to be reported by the surviving annuitant or annuitants with respect to the annuity payments received by them.

(b) **Apportionment of adjusted basis.** For purposes of determining gain on a sale or exchange to which this paragraph applies, the adjusted basis of the property which is sold or exchanged shall be that portion of the adjusted basis of the entire property which bears the same ratio to the adjusted basis as the amount realized bears to the fair market value of the entire property. The amount of such gain which shall be treated as ordinary income (or long-term capital gain) shall be that amount which bears the same ratio to the ordinary income (or long-term capital gain) which would have been recognized if the entire property had been sold by the donor at its fair market value at the time of the sale or exchange as the amount realized on the sale or exchange bears to the fair market value of the entire property at such time. The terms "ordinary income" and "long-term capital gain", as used in this section, have the same meaning as they have in paragraph (a) of § 1.170A–4. For determining the portion of the adjusted basis, ordinary income, and long-term capital gain allocated to the contributed portion of the property for purposes of applying section 170(e) (1) and paragraph (a) of § 1.170A–4 to the contributed portion of the property, and for determining the donee's basis in such contributed portion, see paragraph (c) (2) and (4) of § 1.170A–4. For determining the holding period of such contributed portion, see section 1223(2) and the regulations thereunder.

(c) Illustrations. The application of this section may be illustrated by the following examples, which are supplemented by other examples in paragraph (d) of § 1.170A–4:

Example (1). In 1970, A, a calendar-year individual taxpayer, sells to a church for $4,000 stock held for more than 6 months which has an adjusted basis of $4,000 and a fair market value of $10,000. A's contribution base for 1970, as defined in section 170(b) (1) (F), is $100,000, and during that year he makes no other charitable contributions. Thus, A makes a charitable contribution to the church of $6,000 ($10,000 value — $4,000 amount realized). Without regard to this section, A is allowed a deduction under section 170 of $6,000 for his charitable contribution to the church, since there is no reduction under section 170(e) (1) with respect to the long-term capital gain. Accordingly, under paragraph (b) of this section the adjusted basis for determining gain on the bargain sale is $1,600 ($4,000 adjusted basis × $4,000 amount realized/$10,000 value of property). A has a recognized long-term capital gain of $2,400 ($4,000 amount realized — $1,600 adjusted basis) on the bargain sale.

Example (2). The facts are the same as in example (1) except that A also makes a charitable contribution in 1970 of $50,000 cash to the church. By reason of section 170(b) (1) (A), the deduction allowed under section 170 for 1970 is $50,000 for the amount of cash contributed to the church; however, the $6,000 contribution of property is carried over to 1971 under section 170(d). Under paragraphs (a) (2) and (b) of this section the adjusted basis for determining gain on the bargain sale in that year is $1,600 ($4,000 × $4,000/$10,000). A has a recognized long-term capital gain for 1970 of $2,400 ($4,000 — $1,600) on the sale.

. . . .

Example (7). In 1970, C, a calendar-year individual taxpayer, sells to a church for $4,000 tangible personal property used in his business for more than 6 months which has an adjusted basis of $4,000 and a fair market value of $10,000. Thus, C makes a charitable contribution to the church of $6,000 ($10,000 value — $4,000 amount realized). C's contribution base for 1970, as defined in section 170(b) (1) (F), is $100,000 and during such year he makes no other charitable contributions. If C had sold the property at its fair market value at the time of its contribution, it is assumed that under section 1245 $4,000 of the gain of $6,000 ($10,000 value — $4,000 adjusted basis) would have been treated as ordinary income. Thus, there would have been long-term capital gain of $2,000. It is also assumed that the church does not put the property to an unrelated use, as defined in paragraph (b) (3) of § 1.170A–4. Since without regard to this section C is allowed a deduction under section 170 of $2,000

($6,000 gift — $4,000 ordinary income), under paragraph (b) of this section the adjusted basis for determining gain on the bargain sale is $1,600 ($4,000 adjusted basis × $4,000 amount realized/$10,000 value of property). Accordingly, C has a recognized gain of $2,400 ($4,000 amount realized — $1,600 adjusted basis) on the bargain sale, consisting of ordinary income of $1,600 ($4,000 ordinary income × $4,000 amount realized/$10,000 value of property) and of long-term capital gain of $800 ($2,000 long-term gain × $4,000 amount realized/$10,000 value of property). After applying section 1011(b) and paragraphs (a) and (c) (2) (i) of § 1.170A–4, C is allowed a charitable contributions deduction for 1970 of $3,600 ($6,000 gift — [$4,000 ordinary income × $6,000 value of gift/$10,000 value of property]).

Example (8). (a) On January 1, 1970, A, a male of age 65, transfers capital assets consisting of securities held for more than 6 months to a church in exchange for a promise by the church to pay A a nonassignable annuity of $5,000 per year for life. The annuity is payable monthly with the first payment to be made on February 1, 1970. A's contribution base for 1970, as defined in section 170(b) (1) (F), is $200,000, and during that year he makes no other charitable contributions. On the date of transfer the securities have a fair market value of $100,000 and an adjusted basis to A of $20,000.

(b) The present value of the right of a male age 65 to receive a life annuity of $5,000 per annum, payable in equal installments at the end of each monthly period, is $59,755 ($5,000 × 11.469 + 0.482]), determined in accordance with section 101(b) of the Code, paragraph (e) (1) (iii) (b) (2) of § 1.101–2, and section 3 of Rev. Rul. 62–216, C.B. 1962–2, 30. Thus, A makes a charitable contribution to the church of $40,245 ($100,000 — $59,755). Without regard to this section, A is allowed a deduction under section 170 of $40,245 for his charitable contribution to the church, since the property contributed is not section 170(e) capital gain property within the meaning of paragraph (b) (3) of § 1.170A–4 and no reduction of the contribution is made under section 170(e) (1).

(c) Under paragraph (b) of this section, the adjusted basis for determining gain on the bargain sale is $11,951 ($20,000 × $59,755/$100,000). Accordingly, A has a recognized long-term capital gain of $47,804 ($59,755 — $11,951) on the bargain sale. Such gain is to be reported by A ratably over the period of years measured by the expected return multiple under the contract, but only from that portion of the annual payments which is a return of his investment in the contract under section 72 of the Code. For such purposes, the investment in the contract is $59,755, that is, the present value of the annuity.

(d) The computation and application of the exclusion ratio, the gain, and the ordinary annuity income are as follows, determined by using the expected return multiple of 15.0 applicable under Table I of § 1.72–9:

A's expected return (annual payments of $5,000 × 15) $75,000.00

Exclusion ratio ($59,755 investment in contract divided by expected return of $75,000) 79.7%

Annual exclusion (annual payments of $5,000 × 79.7%) $3,985.00

Ordinary annuity income
($5,000 — $3,985) $1,015.00

Long-term capital gain per year
($47,804/15) with respect to the an-
nual exclusion $3,186.93

(e) The exclusion ratio of 79.7 percent applies throughout the life of the contract. During the first 15 years of the annuity, A is required to report ordinary income of $1,015 and long-term capital gain of $3,186.93 with respect to the annuity payments he receives. After the total long-term capital gain of $47,804 has been reported by A, he is required to report only ordinary income of $1,015.00 per annum with respect to the annuity payments he receives.

. . . .

§ 1.1012–1 Basis of property

(a) **General rule.** In general, the basis of property is the cost thereof. The cost is the amount paid for such property in cash or other property. This general rule is subject to exceptions stated in subchapter O (relating to gain or loss on the disposition of property), subchapter C (relating to corporate distributions and adjustments), subchapter K (relating to partners and partnerships), and subchapter P (relating to capital gains and losses), chapter 1 of the Code.

(b) **Real estate taxes as part of cost.** In computing the cost of real property, the purchaser shall not take into account any amount paid to the seller as reimbursement for real property taxes which are treated under section 164(d) as imposed upon the purchaser. This rule applies whether or not the contract of sale calls for the purchaser to reimburse the seller for such real estate taxes paid or to be paid by the seller. On the other hand, where the purchaser pays (or assumes liability for) real estate taxes which are treated under section 164(d) as imposed upon the seller, such taxes shall be considered part of the cost of the property. It is immaterial whether or not the contract of sale specifies that the sale price has been reduced by, or is in any way intended to reflect, real estate taxes allocable to the seller under section 164(d). For illustrations of the application of this paragraph, see paragraph (b) of § 1.1001–1.

(c) **Sale of stock—(1) In general.** If shares of stock in a corporation are sold or transferred by a taxpayer who purchased or acquired lots of stock on different dates or at different prices, and the lot from which the stock was sold or transferred cannot be adequately identified, the stock sold or transferred shall be charged against the earliest of such lots purchased or acquired in order to determine the cost or other basis of such stock and in order to determine the holding period of such stock for purposes of subchapter P, chapter 1 of the Code. If, on the other hand, the lot from which the stock is sold or transferred can be adequately identified, the rule stated in the preceding sentence is not applicable. As to what constitutes "adequate identification", see subparagraphs (2), (3), and (4) of this paragraph.

(2) **Identification of stock.** An adequate identification is made if it is shown that certificates representing shares of stock from a lot which was purchased or acquired on a certain date or for a certain price were delivered to the taxpayer's transferee. Except as otherwise provided in subparagraph (3) or (4) of this paragraph, such stock certificates delivered to the transferee constitute the stock sold or transferred by the taxpayer. Thus, unless the requirements of subparagraph (3) or (4) of this paragraph are met, the stock sold or transferred is charged to the lot to which the certificates delivered to the transferee belong, whether or not the taxpayer intends, or instructs his broker or other agent, to sell or transfer stock from a lot purchased or acquired on a different date or for a different price.

(3) **Identification on confirmation document.** (i) Where the stock is left in the custody of a broker or other agent, an adequate identification is made if—

(a) At the time of the sale or transfer, the taxpayer specifies to such broker or other agent having custody of the stock the particular stock to be sold or transferred, and

(b) Within a reasonable time thereafter, confirmation of such specification is set forth in a written document from such broker or other agent.

Stock identified pursuant to this subdivision is the stock sold or transferred by the taxpayer, even though stock certificates from a different lot are delivered to the taxpayer's transferee.

(ii) Where a single stock certificate represents stock from different lots, where such certificate is held by the taxpayer rather than his broker or other agent, and where the taxpayer sells a part of the stock represented by such certificate through a broker or other agent, an adequate identification is made if—

(a) At the time of the delivery of the certificate to the broker or other agent, the taxpayer specifies to such broker or other agent the particular stock to be sold or transferred, and

(b) Within a reasonable time thereafter, confirmation of such specification is set forth in a written document from such broker or agent.

Where part of the stock represented by a single certificate is sold or transferred directly by the taxpayer to the purchaser or transferee instead of through a broker or other agent, an adequate identification is made if the taxpayer maintains a written record of the particular stock which he intended to sell or transfer.

. . . .

§ 1.1012–2   Transfers in part a sale and in part a gift

For rules relating to basis of property acquired in a transfer which is in part a gift and in part a sale, see § 1.-170A–4(c), § 1.1011–2(b), and § 1.1015–4.

. . . .

§ 1.1014–1   Basis of property acquired from a decedent

(a) General rule. The purpose of section 1014 is, in general, to provide a basis for property acquired from a decedent which is equal to the value placed upon such property for purposes of the Federal estate tax. Accordingly, the general rule is that the basis of property acquired from a decedent is the fair market value of such property at the date of the decedent's death, or, if the decedent's executor so elects, at the alternate valuation date prescribed in section 2032, or in section 811(j) of the Internal Revenue Code of 1939. Property acquired from a decedent includes, principally, property acquired by bequest, devise, or inheritance, and, in the case of decedents dying after December 31, 1953, property required to be included in determining the value of the decedent's

gross estate under any provision of the Internal Revenue Code of 1954 or the Internal Revenue Code of 1939. The general rule governing basis of property acquired from a decedent, as well as other rules prescribed elsewhere in this section, shall have no application if the property is sold, exchanged, or otherwise disposed of before the decedent's death by the person who acquired the property from the decedent. . . . .

§ 1.1014–3   Other basis rules

(a) Fair market value. For purposes of this section and § 1.1014–1, the value of property as of the date of the decedent's death as appraised for the purpose of the Federal estate tax or the alternate value as appraised for such purpose, whichever is applicable, shall be deemed to be its fair market value. If no estate tax return is required to be filed under section 6018 (or under section 821 or 864 of the Internal Revenue Code of 1939), the value of the property appraised as of the date of the decedent's death for the purpose of State inheritance or transmission taxes shall be deemed to be its fair market value and no alternate valuation date shall be applicable.

. . . .

(c) Reinvestments by a fiduciary. The basis of property acquired after the death of the decedent by a fiduciary as an investment is the cost or other basis of such property to the fiduciary, and not the fair market value of such property at the death of the decedent. For example, the executor of an estate purchases stock of X company at a price of $100 per share with the proceeds of the sale of property acquired from a decedent. At the date of the decedent's death the fair market value of such stock was $98 per share. The basis of such stock to the executor or to a legatee, assuming the stock is distributed, is $100 per share.

(d) Reinvestments of property transferred during life. Where property is transferred by a decedent during life and the property is sold, exchanged, or otherwise disposed of before the decedent's death by the person who acquired the property from the decedent, the general rule stated in paragraph (a) of § 1.1014–1 shall not apply to such property. However, in such a case, the basis of any property acquired by such donee in exchange for the original property, or of any property acquired by the donee through reinvesting the proceeds of the sale of the original property, shall be the fair market value of the property thus acquired at the date of the decedent's death (or applicable alternate valuation date) if the property thus acquired is properly included in the decedent's gross estate for Federal estate tax purposes. These rules also apply to property acquired by the donee in any further exchanges or in further reinvestments. For example, on January 1, 1956, the decedent made a gift of real property to a trust for the benefit of his children, reserving to himself the power to revoke the trust at will. Prior to the decedent's death, the trustee sold the real property and invested the proceeds in stock of the Y company at $50 per share. At the time of the decedent's death, the value of such stock was $75 per share. The corpus of the trust was required to be included in the decedent's gross estate owing to his reservation of the power of revocation. The basis of the Y company stock following the decedent's death is $75 per share. Moreover, if the trustee sold the Y company stock before the decedent's death for $65 a share and reinvested the proceeds in Z company stock which increased in value to $85 per share at the time of the decedent's death, the basis of the Z company stock following the decedent's death would be $85 per share.

. . . .

§ 1.1014-4 Uniformity of basis; adjustment to basis

(a) In general. (1) The basis of property acquired from a decedent, as determined under section 1014(a), is uniform in the hands of every person having possession or enjoyment of the property at any time under the will or other instrument or under the laws of descent and distribution. The principle of uniform basis means that the basis of the property (to which proper adjustments must, of course, be made) will be the same, or uniform, whether the property is possessed or enjoyed by the executor or administrator, the heir, the legatee or devisee, or the trustee or beneficiary of a trust created by a will or an inter vivos trust. In determining the amount allowed or allowable to a taxpayer in computing taxable income as deductions for depreciation or depletion under section 1016(a) (2), the uniform basis of the property shall at all times be used and adjusted. The sale, exchange, or other disposition by a life tenant or remainderman of his interest in property will, for purposes of this section, have no effect upon the uniform basis of the property in the hands of those who acquired it from the decedent. Thus, gain or loss on sale of trust assets by the trustee will be determined without regard to the prior sale of any interest in the property. Moreover, any adjustment for depreciation shall be made to the uniform basis of the property without regard to such prior sale, exchange, or other disposition.

(2) Under the law governing wills and the distribution of the property of decedents, all titles to property acquired by bequest, devise, or inheritance relate back to the death of the decedent, even though the interest of the person taking the title was, at the date of death of the decedent, legal, equitable, vested, contingent, general, specific, residual, conditional, executory, or otherwise. Accordingly, there is a common acquisition date for all titles to property acquired from a decedent within the meaning of section 1014, and, for this reason, a common or uniform basis for all such interests. For example, if distribution of personal property left by a decedent is not made until one year after his death, the basis of such property in the hands of the legatee is its fair market value at the time when the decedent died, and not when the legatee actually received the property. If the bequest is of the residue to trustees in trust, and the executors do not distribute the residue to such trustees until five years after the death of the decedent, the basis of each piece of property left by the decedent and thus received, in the hands of the trustees, is its fair market value at the time when the decedent dies. If the bequest is to trustees in trust to pay to A during his lifetime the income of the property bequeathed, and after his death to distribute such property to the survivors of a class, and upon A's death the property is distributed to the taxpayer as the sole survivor, the basis of such property, in the hands of the taxpayer, is its fair market value at the time when the decedent died.

The purpose of the Code in prescribing a general uniform basis rule for property acquired from a decedent is, on the one hand, to tax the gain, in respect of such property, to him who realizes it (without regard to the circumstances that at the death of the decedent it may have been quite uncertain whether the taxpayer would take or gain anything); and, on the other hand, not to recognize as gain any element of value resulting solely from the circumstance that the possession or enjoyment of the taxpayer was postponed. Such postponement may be, for example, until the administration of the decedent's estate is completed, until the period of the possession or enjoyment of another has terminated, or until an uncertain event has happened. It is the increase or decrease in the value of property reflected in a sale or other disposition which is recognized as the measure of gain or loss.

(3) The principles stated in subparagraphs (1) and (2) of this paragraph do not apply to property transferred by an executor, administrator or trustee, to an heir, legatee, devisee or beneficiary under circumstances such that the transfer constitutes a sale or exchange. In such a case, gain or loss must be recognized by the transferor to the extent required by the revenue laws, and the transferee acquires a basis equal to the fair market value of the property on the date of the transfer. Thus, for example, if the trustee of a trust created by will transfers to a beneficiary, in satisfaction of a specific bequest of $10,000, securities which had a fair market value of $9,000 on the date of the decedent's death (the applicable valuation date) and $10,000 on the date of the transfer, the trust realizes a taxable gain of $1,000 and the basis of the securities in the hands of the beneficiary would be $10,000. As a further example, if the executor of an estate transfers to a trust property worth $200,000, which had a fair market value of $175,000 on the date of the decedent's death (the applicable valuation date), in satisfaction of the decedent's bequest in trust for the benefit of his wife of cash or securities to be selected by the executor in an amount sufficient to utilize the marital deduction to the maximum extent authorized by law (after taking into consideration any other property qualifying for the marital deduction), capital gain in the amount of $25,000 would be realized by the estate and the basis of the property in the hands of the trustees would be $200,000. If, on the other hand, the decedent bequeathed a fraction of his residuary estate to a trust for the benefit of his wife, which fraction will not change regardless of any fluctuations in value of property in the decedent's estate after his death, no gain or loss would be realized by the estate upon transfer of property to the trust, and the basis of the property in the hands of the trustee would be its fair market value on the date of the decedent's death or on the alternate valuation date.

(b) **Multiple interests.** Where more than one person has an interest in property acquired from a decedent, the basis of such property shall be determined and adjusted without regard to the multiple interests. The basis for computing gain or loss on the sale of any one of such multiple interests shall be determined under § 1.1014-5. Thus, the deductions for depreciation and for depletion allowed or allowable, under sections 167 and 611, to a legal life tenant as if the life tenant were the absolute owner of the property, constitute an adjustment to the basis of the property not only in the hands of the life tenant, but also in the hands of the remainderman and every other person to whom the same uniform basis is applicable. Similarly, the deductions allowed or allowable under sections 167 and 611, both to the trustee and to the trust beneficiaries, constitute an adjustment to the basis of the property not only in the hands of the trustee, but also in the hands of the trust beneficiaries and every other person to whom the uniform basis is applicable. See, however, section 262. Similarly, adjustments in respect of capital expenditures or losses, tax-free distributions, or other distributions applicable in reduction of basis, or other items for which the basis is adjustable are made without regard to which one of the persons to whom the same uniform basis is applicable makes the capital expenditures or sustains the capital losses, or to whom the tax-free or other distributions are made, or to whom the deductions are allowed or allowable. See § 1.1014-6 for adjustments in respect of property acquired from a decedent prior to his death.

(c) Records. The executor or other legal representative of the decedent, the fiduciary of a trust under a will, the life tenant and every other person to whom a uniform basis under this section is applicable, shall maintain records showing in detail all deductions, distributions, or other items for which adjustment to basis is required to be made by sections 1016 and 1017, and shall furnish to the district director such information with respect to those adjustments as he may require.

§ 1.1014-5 Gain or loss

(a) Sale or other disposition of a life interest, remainder interest, or other interest in property acquired from a decedent. (1) Except as provided in paragraph (b) of this section with respect to the sale or other disposition after October 9, 1969, of a term interest in property, gain or loss from a sale or other disposition of a life interest, remainder interest, or other interest in property acquired from a decedent is determined by comparing the amount of the proceeds with the amount of that part of the adjusted uniform basis which is assignable to the interest so transferred. The adjusted uniform basis is the uniform basis of the entire property adjusted to the date of sale or other disposition of any such interest as required by sections 1016 and 1017. The uniform basis is the unadjusted basis of the entire property determined immediately after the decedent's death under the applicable sections of part II of subchapter O of chapter 1 of the Code.

(2) Except as provided in paragraph (b) of this section, the proper measure of gain or loss resulting from a sale or other disposition of an interest in property acquired from a decedent is so much of the increase or decrease in the value of the entire property as is reflected in such sale or other disposition. Hence, in ascertaining the basis of a life interest, remainder interest, or other interest which has been so transferred, uniform basis rule contem-

plates that proper adjustments will be made to reflect the change in relative value of the interests on account of the passage of time.

(3) The factors set forth in the tables contained in § 20.2031-7 or § 20.2031-10, whichever is applicable, of Part 20 of this chapter (Estate Tax Regulations) shall be used in the manner provided therein in determining the basis of the life interest, the remainder interest, or the term certain interest in the property on the date such interest is sold. The basis of the life interest, the remainder interest, or the term certain interest is computed by multiplying the uniform basis (adjusted to the time of the sale) by the appropriate factor. In the case of the sale of a life interest or a remainder interest, the factor used is the factor (adjusted where appropriate) which appears in the life interest or the remainder interest column of the table opposite the age (on the date of the sale) of the person at whose death the life interest will terminate. In the case of the sale of a term certain interest, the factor used is the factor (adjusted where appropriate) which appears in the term certain column of the table opposite the number of years remaining (on the date of sale) before the term certain interest will terminate.

(b) Sale or other disposition of certain term interests. In determining gain or loss from the sale or other disposition after October 9, 1969, of a term interest in property (as defined in paragraph (f) (2) of § 1.1001-1) the adjusted basis of which is determined pursuant, or by reference, to section 1014 (relating to the basis of property acquired from a decedent) or section 1015 (relating to the basis of property acquired by gift or by a transfer in trust), that part of the adjusted uniform basis assignable under the rules of paragraph (a) of this section to the interest sold or otherwise disposed of shall be disregarded to the extent and in the manner provided by section 1001 (e) and paragraph (f) of § 1.1001-1.

(c) Illustrations. The application of this section may be illustrated by the following examples, in which references are made to the actuarial tables contained in Part 20 of this chapter (Estate Tax Regulations):

Example (1). Securities worth $500,000 at the date of decedent's death on January 1, 1971, are bequeathed to his wife, W, for life, with remainder over to his son, S. W is 48 years of age when the life interest is acquired. The estate does not elect the alternate valuation allowed by section 2032. By reference to Table A(2) in paragraph (f) of § 20.2031-10, the life estate factor for age 48, female, is found to be 0.77488 and the remainder factor for such age is found to be 0.22512. Therefore, the present value of the portion of the uniform basis assigned to W's life interest is $387,440 ($500,000 × 0.77488), and the present value of the portion of the uniform basis assigned to S's remainder interest is $112,560 ($500,000 × 0.22512). W sells her life interest to her nephew, A, on February 1, 1971, for $370,000, at which time W is still 48 years of age. Pursuant to section 1001(e), W realizes no loss; her gain is $370,000, the amount realized from the sale. A has a basis of $370,000 which he can recover by amortization deductions over W's life expectancy.

Example (2). The facts are the same as in example (1) except that W retains the life interest for 12 years, until she is 60 years of age, and then sells it to A on February 1, 1983, when the fair market value of the securities has increased to $650,000. By reference to Table A(2) in paragraph (f) of § 20.2031-10, the life estate factor for age 60, female, is found to be 0.63226 and the remainder factor for such age is found to be 0.36774. Therefore, the present value on February 1, 1983, of the portion of the uniform basis assigned to W's life interest is $316,130 ($500,000 × 0.63226) and the present value on that date of the portion of the uniform basis assigned to S's remainder interest is $183,870 ($500,000 × 0.36774). W sells her life interest for $410,969, that being the commuted value of her remaining life interest in the securities as appreciated ($650,000 × 0.63226). Pursuant to section 1001(e), W's gain is $410,969, the amount realized. A has a basis of $410,969 which he can recover by amortization deductions over W's life expectancy.

Example (3). Unimproved land having a fair market value of $18,800 at the date of the decedent's death on January 1, 1970, is devised to A, a male, for life, with remainder over to B, a female. The estate does not elect the alternate valuation allowed by section 2032. On January 1, 1971, A sells his life interest to S for $12,500. S is not related to A or B. At the time of the sale, A is 39 years of age. By reference to Table A(1) in paragraph (f) of § 20.2031-10, the life estate factor for age 39, male, is found to be 0.79854. Therefore, the present value of the portion of the uniform basis assigned to A's life interest is $15,012.55 ($18,800 × 0.79854). This portion is disregarded under section 1001(e). A realizes no loss; his gain is $12,500, the amount realized. S has a basis of $12,500 which he can recover by amortization deductions over A's life expectancy.

Example (4). The facts are the same as in example (3) except that on January 1, 1971, A and B jointly sell the entire property to S for $25,000 and divide the proceeds equally between them. A and B are not related, and there is no element of gift or compensation in the transaction. By reference to Table A(1) in paragraph (f) of § 20.2031-10, the remainder factor for age 39, male, is found to be 0.20146. There-

fore, the present value of the uniform basis assigned to B's remainder interest is $3,787.45 ($18,800 × 0.20146). On the sale A realizes a loss of $2,512.55 ($15,012.55 less $12,500), the portion of the uniform basis assigned to his life interest not being disregarded by reason of section 1001(e) (3). B's gain on the sale is $8,712.55 ($12,500 less $3,787.45). S has a basis in the entire property of $25,000, no part of which, however, can be recovered by amortization deductions over A's life expectancy.

. . . .

§ 1.1014-6 Special rule for adjustments to basis where property is acquired from a decedent prior to his death

(a) In general. (1) The basis of property described in section 1014(b) (9) which is acquired from a decedent prior to his death shall be adjusted for depreciation, obsolescence, amortization, and depletion allowed the taxpayer on such property for the period prior to the decedent's death. Thus, in general, the adjusted basis of such property will be its fair market value at the decedent's death, or the applicable alternate valuation date, less the amount allowed (determined with regard to section 1016(a) (2) (B)) to the taxpayer as deductions for exhaustion, wear and tear, obsolescence, amortization and depletion for the period held by the taxpayer prior to the decedent's death. The deduction allowed for a taxable year in which the decedent dies shall be an amount properly allocable to that part of the year prior to his death. For a discussion of the basis adjustment required by section 1014(b) (9) where property is held in trust, see paragraph (c) of this section.

. . . . .

§ 1.1015-1 Basis of property acquired by gift after December 31, 1920

(a) General rule. (1) In the case of property acquired by gift after December 31, 1920 (whether by a transfer in trust or otherwise), the basis of the property for the purpose of determining gain is the same as it would be in the hands of the donor or the last preceding owner by whom it was not acquired by gift. The same rule applies in determining loss unless the basis (adjusted for the period prior to the date of gift in accordance with sections 1016 and 1017) is greater than the fair market value of the property at the time of the gift. In such case, the basis for determining loss is the fair market value at the time of the gift.

(2) The provisions of subparagraph (1) of this paragraph may be illustrated by the following example:

Example. A acquires by gift income-producing property which has an adjusted basis of $100,000 at the date of gift. The fair market value of the property at the date of gift is $90,000. A later sells the property for $95,000. In such case there is neither gain nor loss. The basis for determining loss is $90,000; therefore, there is no loss. Furthermore, there is no gain, since the basis for determining gain is $100,000.

* * * *

(b) **Uniform basis; proportionate parts of.** Property acquired by gift has a single or uniform basis although more than one person may acquire an interest in such property. The uniform basis of the property remains fixed subject to proper adjustment for items under sections 1016 and 1017. However, the value of the proportionate parts of the uniform basis represented, for instance, by the respective interests of the life tenant and remainderman are adjustable to reflect the change in the relative values of such interest on account of the lapse of time. The portion of the basis attributable to an interest at the time of its sale or other disposition shall be determined under the rules provided in § 1.1014–5. In determining gain or loss from the sale or other disposition after October 9, 1969, of a term interest in property (as defined in § 1.1001–1(f) (2)) the adjusted basis of which is determined pursuant, or by reference, to section 1015, that part of the adjusted uniform basis assignable under the rules of § 1.1014–5(a) to the interest sold or otherwise disposed of shall be disregarded to the extent and in the manner provided by section 1001(e) and § 1.1001–1(f).

(c) **Time of acquisition.** The date that the donee acquires an interest in property by gift is when the donor relinquishes dominion over the property and not necessarily when title to the property is acquired by the donee. Thus, the date that the donee acquires an interest in property by gift where he is a successor in interest, such as in the case of a remainderman of a life estate or a beneficiary of the distribution of the corpus of a trust, is the date such interests are created by the donor

and not the date the property is actually acquired.

* * * *

(e) **Fair market value.** For the purposes of this section, the value of property as appraised for the purpose of the Federal gift tax, or, if the gift is not subject to such tax, its value as appraised for the purpose of a State gift tax, shall be deemed to be the fair market value of the property at the time of the gift.

* * * *

(g) **Records.** To insure a fair and adequate determination of the proper basis under section 1015, persons making or receiving gifts of property should preserve and keep accessible a record of the facts necessary to determine the cost of the property and, if pertinent, its fair market value as of March 1, 1913, or its fair market value as of the date of the gift.

§ 1.1015–4 Transfers in part a gift and in part a sale

(a) **General rule.** Where a transfer of property is in part a sale and in part a gift, the unadjusted basis of the property in the hands of the transferee is the sum of—

(1) Whichever of the following is the greater:

(i) The amount paid by the transferee for the property, or

(ii) The transferor's adjusted basis for the property at the time of the transfer, and

(2) The amount of increase, if any, in basis authorized by section 1015(d) for gift tax paid (see § 1.1015–5).

For determining loss, the unadjusted basis of the property in the hands of the transferee shall not be greater than the fair market value of the property at the time of such transfer. For determination of gain or loss of the transferor, see § 1.1001–1(e) and § 1.1011–2. For special rule where there has been a charitable contribution of less than a taxpayer's entire interest in property, see section 170(e) (2) and § 1.170A–4(c).

(b) **Examples.** The rule of paragraph (a) of this section is illustrated by the following examples:

Example (1). If A transfers property to his son for $30,000, and such property at the time of the transfer has an adjusted basis of $30,000 in A's hands (and a fair market value of $60,-

000), the unadjusted basis of the property in the hands of the son is $30,000.

Example (2). If A transfers property to his son for $60,000, and such property at the time of transfer has an adjusted basis of $30,000 in A's hands (and a fair market value of $90,000), the unadjusted basis of such property in the hands of the son is $60,000.

Example (3). If A transfers property to his son for $30,000, and such property at the time of transfer has an adjusted basis in A's hands of $60,000 (and a fair market value of $90,000), the unadjusted basis of such property in the hands of the son is $60,000.

Example (4). If A transfers property to his son for $30,000 and such property at the time of transfer has an adjusted basis of $90,000 in A's hands (and a fair market value of $60,000), the unadjusted basis of the property in the hands of the son is $90,000. However, since the adjusted basis of the property in A's hands at the time of the transfer was greater than the fair market value at that time, for the purpose of determining any loss on a later sale or other disposition of the property by the son its unadjusted basis in his hands is $60,000.

§ 1.1016–2 Items properly chargeable to capital account

(a) The cost or other basis shall be properly adjusted for any expenditure, receipt, loss, or other item, properly chargeable to capital account, including the cost of improvements and betterments made to the property. No adjustment shall be made in respect of any item which, under any applicable provision of law or regulation, is treated as an item not properly chargeable to capital account but is allowable as a deduction in computing net or taxable income for the taxable year. For example, in the case of oil and gas wells no adjustment may be made in respect of any intangible drilling and development expense allowable as a deduction in computing net or taxable income. See the regulations under section 263 (c).

(b) The application of the foregoing provisions may be illustrated by the following example:

Example. A, who makes his returns on the calendar year basis, purchased property in 1941 for $10,000. He subsequently expended $6,000 for improvements. Disregarding, for the purpose of this example, the adjustments required for depreciation, the adjusted basis of the property is $16,000. If A sells the property in 1954 for $20,000, the amount of his gain will be $4,000.

* * * *

§ 1.1016–3 Exhaustion, wear and tear, obsolescence, amortization, and depletion for periods since February 28, 1913

(a) In general—(1) Adjustment where deduction is claimed. (i) For taxable periods beginning on or after January 1, 1952, the cost or other basis of property shall be decreased for exhaustion, wear and tear, obsolescence, amortization, and depletion by the greater of the following two amounts: (a) the amount allowed as deductions in computing taxable income, to the extent resulting in a reduction of the taxpayer's income taxes, or (b) the amount allowable for the years involved. See paragraph (b) of this section. Where the taxpayer makes an appropriate election the above rule is applicable for periods since February 28, 1913, and before January 1, 1952. See paragraph (d) of this section. For rule for such periods where no election is made, see paragraph (c) of this section.

(ii) The determination of the amount properly allowable for exhaustion, wear and tear, obsolescence, amortization, and depletion shall be made on the basis of facts reasonably known to exist at the end of the taxable year. A taxpayer is not permitted to take advantage in a later year of his prior failure to take any such allowance or his taking an allowance plainly inadequate under the known facts in prior years. In the case of depreciation, if in prior years the taxpayer has consistently taken proper deductions under one method, the amount allowable for such prior years shall not be increased even though a greater amount would have been allowable under another proper method. For rules governing losses on retirement of depreciable property, including rules for determining basis, see § 1.167(a)–8. This subdivision may be illustrated by the following example:

Example. An asset was purchased January 1, 1950, at a cost of $10,000. The useful life of the asset is 10 years. It has no salvage value. Depreciation was deducted and allowed for 1950 to 1954 as follows:

1950	$500
1951	.....
1952	1,000
1953	1,000
1954	1,000
Total amount allowed	3,500

The correct reserve as of December 31, 1954, is computed as follows:

Dec. 31:

1950 ($10,000 ÷ 10)	$1,000
1951 ($9,000 ÷ 9)	1,000
1952 ($8,000 ÷ 8)	1,000
1953 ($7,000 ÷ 7)	1,000
1954 ($6,000 ÷ 6)	1,000
Reserve Dec. 31, 1954	5,000

Depreciation for 1955 is computed as follows:

Cost	$10,000
Reserve as of December 31, 1954	5,000
Unrecovered cost	5,000
Depreciation allowable for 1955 ($5,000 ÷ 5)	1,000

(2) **Adjustment for amount allowable where no depreciation deduction claimed.** (i) If the taxpayer has not taken a depreciation deduction either in the taxable year or for any prior taxable year, adjustments to basis of the property for depreciation allowable shall be determined by using the straight-line method of depreciation. (See § 1.1016-4 for adjustments in the case of persons exempt from income taxation.)

(ii) For taxable years beginning after December 31, 1953, and ending after August 16, 1954, if the taxpayer with respect to any property has taken a deduction for depreciation properly under one of the methods provided in section 167(b) for one or more years but has omitted the deduction in other years, the adjustment to basis for the depreciation allowable in such a case will be the deduction under the method which was used by the taxpayer with respect to that property. Thus, if A acquired property in 1954 on which he properly computed his depreciation deduction under the method described in section 167(b) (2) (the declining-balance method) for the first year of its useful life but did not take a deduction in the second and third year of the asset's life, the adjustment to basis for depreciation allowable for the second and third year will be likewise computed under the declining-balance method.

. . . . .

§ 1.1017-1 **Adjusted basis; discharge of indebtedness; general rule**

(a) In addition to the adjustments provided in section 1016 and the regulations thereunder which are required to be made with respect to the cost or other basis of property, and except as otherwise provided in section 372(a), 373(b) (2), or 1018, a further adjustment shall be made in any case in which there shall have been an exclusion from gross income under section 108(a) on account of a discharge of indebtedness during the taxable year.

Such further adjustments shall, except as otherwise provided in § 1.1017-2, be made in the following manner and order (but in the case of an individual, subparagraphs (1) to (4), inclusive, of this paragraph, shall apply only to property used in any trade or business of such individual):

(1) In the case of indebtedness incurred to purchase specific property (other than inventory or notes or accounts receivable), whether or not a lien is placed against such property securing the payment of all or part of such indebtedness, which indebtedness shall have been discharged, the cost or other basis of such property shall be decreased by an amount equal to the amount excluded from gross income under section 108(a) and attributable to the discharge of the indebtedness so incurred with respect to such property;

(2) In the case of specific property (other than inventory or notes or accounts receivable) against which, at the time of the discharge of the indebtedness, there is a lien (other than a lien securing indebtedness incurred to purchase such property) the cost or other basis of such property shall be decreased by an amount equal to the amount excluded from gross income under section 108(a) and attributable to the discharge of the indebtedness secured by such lien;

(3) Any excess of the total amount excluded from gross income under section 108(a) over the sum of the adjustments made under subparagraphs (1) and (2) of this paragraph shall next be applied to reduce the cost or other basis of all the property of the debtor (other than inventory and notes and accounts receivable) as follows: The cost or other basis of each unit of property shall be decreased in an amount equal to such proportion of such excess as the adjusted basis (without reference to this section) of each such unit of property bears to the sum of adjusted bases (without reference to this section) of all the property of the debtor other than inventory and notes and accounts receivable;

(4) Any excess of the total amount excluded from gross income under section 108(a) over the sum of the adjustments made under subparagraphs (1), (2), and (3) of this paragraph shall next be applied to reduce the cost or

other basis of inventory and notes and accounts receivable, as follows: The cost or other basis of inventory or notes or accounts receivable, as the case may be, shall be decreased in an amount equal to such proportion of such excess as the adjusted basis of inventory, notes receivable or accounts receivable, as the case may be, bears to the sum of the adjusted bases of such inventory and notes and accounts receivable;

(5) In the case of an individual, any excess of the total amount excluded from gross income under section 108 (a) over the sum of the adjustments made under subparagraphs (1), (2), (3), and (4) of this paragraph shall next be applied to reduce the cost or other basis of his property held for the production of income, as follows: The cost or other basis of each unit of such property shall be decreased in an amount equal to such proportion of such excess as the adjusted basis (without reference to this section) of each such unit of property bears to the sum of the adjusted bases (without reference to this section) of all of such property of the debtor; and

(6) In the case of an individual, any excess of the total amount excluded from gross income under section 108 (a) over the sum of the adjustments made under subparagraphs (1), (2), (3), (4), and (5) of this paragraph shall next be applied to reduce the cost or other basis of his property other than property used in any trade or business and property held for the production of income, as follows: The cost or other basis of each unit of such property shall be decreased in an amount equal to such proportion of such excess as the adjusted basis (without reference to this section) of each such unit of property bears to the sum of the adjusted bases (without reference to this section) of all of such property of the debtor.

In the application of subparagraphs (1), (2), (3), (4), (5) and (6) of this paragraph, no decrease in the cost or other basis of any property shall exceed the amount of adjusted basis of such property without reference to this section.

. . . . .

§ 1.1031(a)-1 Property held for productive use in trade or business or for investment

(a) Section 1031(a) provides an exception from the general rule requiring the recognition of gain or loss upon the sale or exchange of property. . . . . Under section 1031(a), no gain or loss is recognized if property held for productive use in trade or business or for investment is exchanged solely for property of a like kind to be held either for productive use in trade or business or for investment. Under section 1031(a), property held for productive use in trade or business may be exchanged for property held for investment. Similarly property held for investment may be exchanged for property held for productive use in trade or business. However, section 1031(a) provides that property held for productive use in trade or business or for investment does not include stock in trade or other property held primarily for sale, nor stocks, bonds, notes, choses in action, certificates of trust or beneficial interest, or other securities or evidences of indebtedness or interest. A transfer is not within the provisions of section 1031(a) if as part of the consideration the taxpayer receives money or property which does not meet the requirements of section 1031(a), but the transfer, if otherwise qualified, will be within the provisions of section 1031(b). Similarly, a transfer is not within the provisions of section 1031(a) if as part of the consideration the other party to the exchange assumes a liability of the taxpayer (or acquires property from the taxpayer that is subject to a liability), but the transfer, if otherwise qualified, will be within the provisions of section 1031 (b). A transfer of property meeting the requirements of section 1031(a) may be within the provisions of section 1031(a) even though the taxpayer transfers in addition property not meeting the requirements of section 1031(a) or money. However, the nonrecognition treatment provided by section 1031(a) does not apply to the property transferred which does not meet the requirements of section 1031(a).

(b) As used in section 1031(a), the words "like kind" have reference to the nature or character of the property and not to its grade or quality. One kind or class of property may not, under that section, be exchanged for property of a different kind or class. The fact that any real estate involved is improved or unimproved is not material, for that fact relates only to the grade or quality of the property and not to its kind or class. Unproductive real estate held by one other than a dealer for future use or future realization of the increment in value is held for investment and not primarily for sale.

(c) No gain or loss is recognized if (1) a taxpayer exchanges property held for productive use in his trade or business, together with cash, for other property of like kind for the same use, such as a truck for a new truck or a passenger automobile for a new passenger automobile to be used for a like purpose; or (2) a taxpayer who is not a dealer in real estate exchanges city real estate for a ranch or farm, or exchanges a leasehold of a fee with 30 years or more to run for real estate, or exchanges improved real estate for unimproved real estate; or (3) a taxpayer exchanges investment property and cash for investment property of a like kind.

. . . .

§ 1.1031(b)-1 Receipt of other property or money in tax-free exchange

(a) If the taxpayer receives other property (in addition to property permitted to be received without recognition of gain) or money—

(1) In an exchange described in section 1031(a) of property held for investment or productive use in trade or business for property of like kind to be held either for productive use or for investment,

(2) In an exchange described in section 1035(a) of insurance policies or annuity contracts,

(3) In an exchange described in section 1036(a) of common stock for common stock, or preferred stock for preferred stock, in the same corporation and not in connection with a corporate reorganization, or

. . . .

(b) The application of this section may be illustrated by the following examples:

Example (1). A, who is not a dealer in real estate, in 1954 exchanges real estate held for investment, which he purchased in 1940 for $5,000, for other real estate (to be held for productive use in trade or business) which has a fair market value of $6,000, and $2,000 in cash. The gain from the transaction is $3,000, but is recognized only to the extent of the cash received of $2,000.

. . . . .

(c) Consideration received in the form of an assumption of liabilities (or a transfer subject to a liability) is to be treated as "other property or money" for the purposes of section 1031(b). Where, on an exchange described in section 1031(b), each party to the exchange either assumes a liability of the other party or acquires property subject to a liability, then, in determining the amount of "other property or money" for purposes of section 1031(b), consideration given in the form of an assumption of liabilities (or a receipt of property subject to a liability) shall be offset against consideration received in the form of an assumption of liabilities (or a transfer subject to a liability). See § 1.1031(d)-2, examples (1) and (2).

§ 1.1031(d)-1 Property acquired upon a tax-free exchange

(a) If, in an exchange of property solely of the type described in section 1031, section 1035(a), section 1036(a), or section 1037(a), no part of the gain or loss was recognized under the law applicable to the year in which the exchange was made, the basis of the property acquired is the same as the basis of the property transferred by the taxpayer with proper adjustments to the date of the exchange. If additional consideration is given by the taxpayer in the exchange, the basis of the property acquired shall be the same as the property transferred increased by the amount of additional consideration given (see section 1016 and the regulations thereunder).

(b) If, in an exchange of properties of the type indicated in section 1031, section 1035(a), section 1036(a), or section 1037(a), gain to the taxpayer was recognized under the provisions of section 1031(b) or a similar provision of a prior revenue law, on account of the receipt of money in the transaction, the basis of the property acquired is the basis of the property transferred (adjusted to the date of the exchange), decreased by the amount of money received and increased by the amount of gain recognized on the exchange. The application of this paragraph may be illustrated by the following example:

Example. A, an individual in the moving and storage business, in 1954 transfers one of his moving trucks with an adjusted basis in his hands of $2,500 to B in exchange for a truck (to be used in A's business) with a fair market value of $2,400 and $200 in cash. A realizes a gain of $100 upon the exchange, all of which is recognized under section 1031(b). The basis of the truck acquired by A is determined as follows:

Adjusted basis of A's former truck	$2,500
Less: Amount of money received	200
Difference	2,300
Plus: Amount of gain recognized	100
Basis of truck acquired by A	2,400

(c) If, upon an exchange of properties of the type described in section 1031, section 1035(a), section 1036(a), or section 1037(a), the taxpayer received other property (not permitted to be received without the recognition of gain) and gain from the transaction was recognized as required under section 1031(b), or a similar provision of a prior revenue law, the basis (adjusted to the date of the exchange) of the property transferred by the taxpayer, decreased by the amount of any money received and increased by the amount of gain recognized, must be allocated to and is the basis of the properties (other than money) received on the exchange. For the purpose of the allocation of the basis of the properties received, there must be assigned to such other property an amount equivalent to its fair market value at the date of the exchange. The application of this paragraph may be illustrated by the following example:

Example. A, who is not a dealer in real estate, in 1954 transfers real estate held for investment which he purchased in 1940 for $10,000 in exchange for other real estate (to be held for investment) which has a fair market value of $9,000, an automobile which has a fair market value of $2,000, and $1,500 in cash. A realizes a gain of $2,500, all of which is recognized under section 1031(b). The basis of the property received in exchange is the basis of the real estate A transfers ($10,000) decreased by the amount of money received ($1,500) and increased in the amount of gain that was recognized ($2,500), which results in a basis for the property received of $11,000. This basis of $11,000 is allocated between the automobile and the real estate received by A, the basis of the automobile being its fair market value at the date of the exchange, $2,000, and the basis of the real estate received being the remainder, $9,000.

(d) Section 1031(c) and, with respect to section 1031 and section 1036 (a), similar provisions of prior revenue laws provide that no loss may be recognized on an exchange of properties of a type described in section 1031, section 1035(a), section 1036(a), or section 1037(a), although the taxpayer receives other property or money from the transaction. However, the basis of the property or properties (other than money) received by the taxpayer is the basis (adjusted to the date of the exchange) of the property transferred, decreased by the amount of money received. This basis must be allocated to the properties received, and for this purpose there must be allocated to such other property an amount of such basis equivalent to its fair market value at the date of the exchange.

(e) If, upon an exchange of properties of the type described in section 1031, section 1035(a), section 1036(a), or section 1037(a), the taxpayer also exchanged other property (not permitted to be transferred without the recognition of gain or loss) and gain or loss from the transaction is recognized under section 1002 or a similar provision of a prior revenue law, the basis of the property acquired is the total basis of the properties transferred (adjusted to the date of the exchange) increased by the amount of gain and decreased by the amount of loss recognized on the other property. For purposes of this rule, the taxpayer is deemed to have received in exchange for such other property an amount equal to its fair market value on the date of the exchange. The application of this paragraph may be illustrated by the following example:

Example. A exchanges real estate held for investment plus stock for real estate to be held for investment. The real estate transferred has an adjusted basis of $10,000 and a fair market value of $11,000. The stock transferred has an adjusted basis of $4,000 and a fair market value of $2,000. The real estate acquired has a fair market value of $13,000. A is deemed to have received a $2,000 portion of the acquired real estate in exchange for the stock, since $2,000 is the fair market value of the stock at the time of the exchange. A $2,000 loss is recognized under section 1002 on the exchange of the stock for real estate. No gain or loss is recognized on the exchange of the real estate since the property received is of the type permitted to be received without recognition of gain or loss. The basis of the real estate acquired by A is determined as follows:

Adjusted basis of real estate transferred	$10,000
Adjusted basis of stock transferred	4,000
	14,000

Less: Loss recognized on transfer of
stock 2,000

Basis of real estate acquired upon
the exchange 12,000

§ 1.1031(d)-2 Treatment of assumption of liabilities

For the purposes of section 1031(d), the amount of any liabilities of the taxpayer assumed by the other party to the exchange (or of any liabilities to which the property exchanged by the taxpayer is subject) is to be treated as money received by the taxpayer upon the exchange, whether or not the assumption resulted in a recognition of gain or loss to the taxpayer under the law applicable to the year in which the exchange was made. The application of this section may be illustrated by the following examples:

Example (1). B, an individual, owns an apartment house which has an adjusted basis in his hands of $500,000, but which is subject to a mortgage of $150,000. On September 1, 1954, he transfers the apartment house to C, receiving in exchange therefor $50,000 in cash and another apartment house with a fair market value on that date of $600,000. The transfer to C is made subject to the $150,000 mortgage. B realizes a gain of $300,000 on the exchange, computed as follows:

Value of property received $600,000
Cash 50,000
Liabilities subject to which old property was transferred 150,000

Total consideration received .. 800,000
Less: Adjusted basis of property transferred 500,000

Gain realized 300,000

Under section 1031(b), $200,000 of the $300,000 gain is recognized. The basis of the apartment house acquired by B upon the exchange is $500,000, computed as follows:
Adjusted basis of property transferred $500,000
Less: Amount of money received:
Cash $50,000
Amount of liabilities subject to which property was transferred 150,000

200,000

Difference 300,000
Plus: Amount of gain recognized upon the exchange 200,000

Basis of property acquired upon the exchange 500,000

Example (2). (a) D, an individual, owns an apartment house. On December 1, 1955, the apartment house owned by D has an adjusted basis in his hands of $100,000, a fair market value of $220,000, but is subject to a mortgage of $80,000. E, an individual, also owns an apartment house. On December 1, 1955, the apartment house owned by E has an adjusted basis

of $175,000, a fair market value of $250,000, but is subject to a mortgage of $150,000. On December 1, 1955, D transfers his apartment house to E, receiving in exchange therefor $40,000 in cash and the apartment house owned by E. Each apartment house is transferred subject to the mortgage on it.

(b) D realizes a gain of $120,000 on the exchange, computed as follows:

Value of property received $250,000
Cash 40,000
Liabilities subject to which old property was transferred 80,000

Total consideration received ... 370,000
Less:
Adjusted basis of property transferred $100,000
Liabilities to which new property is subject 150,000

250,000

Gain realized 120,000

For purposes of section 1031(b), the amount of "other property or money" received by D is $40,000. (Consideration received by D in the form of a transfer subject to a liability of $80,000 is offset by consideration given in the form of a receipt of property subject to a $150,000 liability. Thus, only the consideration received in the form of cash, $40,000, is treated as "other property or money" for purposes of section 1031(b).) Accordingly, under section 1031(b), $40,000 of the $120,000 gain is recognized. The basis of the apartment house acquired by D is $170,000, computed as follows:

Adjusted basis of property transferred $100,000
Liabilities to which new property is subject 150,000

Total 250,000
Less: Amount of money received:
Cash $40,000
Amount of liabilities subject to which property was transferred 80,000

120,000

Difference 130,000
Plus: Amount of gain recognized upon the exchange 40,000

Basis of property acquired upon the exchange 170,000

(c) E realizes a gain of $75,000 on the exchange, computed as follows:
Value of property received $220,000
Liabilities subject to which old property was transferred 150,000

Total consideration received ... 370,000
Less:
Adjusted basis of property transferred $175,000
Cash 40,000

Liabilities to which new property is subject 80,000

295,000

Gain realized 75,000

For purposes of section 1031(b), the amount of "other property or money" received by E is $30,000. (Consideration received by E in the form of a transfer subject to a liability of $150,-000 is offset by consideration given in the form of a receipt of property subject to an $80,000 liability and by the $40,000 cash paid by E. Although consideration received in the form of cash or other property is not offset by consideration given in the form of an assumption of liabilities or a receipt of property subject to a liability, consideration given in the form of cash or other property is offset against consideration received in the form of an assumption of liabilities or a transfer of property subject to a liability.) Accordingly, under section 1031(b), $30,000 of the $75,000 gain is recognized. The basis of the apartment house acquired by E is $175,000, computed as follows:

Adjusted basis of property transferred	$175,000
Cash	40,000
Liabilities to which new property is subject	80,000
Total	295,000
Less: Amount of money received: Amount of liabilities subject to which property was transferred $150,000	
	150,000
Difference	145,000
Plus: Amount of gain recognized upon the exchange	30,000
Basis of property acquired upon the exchange	175,000

§ 1.1032–1 Disposition by a corporation of its own capital stock

(a) The disposition by a corporation of shares of its own stock (including treasury stock) for money or other property does not give rise to taxable gain or deductible loss to the corporation regardless of the nature of the transaction or the facts and circumstances involved. For example, the receipt by a corporation of the subscription price of shares of its stock upon their original issuance gives rise to neither taxable gain nor deductible loss, whether the subscription or issue price be equal to, in excess of, or less than, the par or stated value of such stock. Also, the exchange or sale by a corporation of its own shares for money or other property does not result in taxable gain or deductible loss, even though the corporation deals in such shares as it might in the shares of another corporation. A transfer by a corporation of shares of its own stock (including treasury stock) as compensation for services is considered, for purposes of section 1032(a), as a disposition by the corporation of such shares for money or other property.

(b) Section 1032(a) does not apply to the acquisition by a corporation of shares of its own stock except where the corporation acquires such shares in exchange for shares of its own stock (including treasury stock). See paragraph (e) of § 1.311–1, relating to treatment of acquisitions of a corporation's own stock. Section 1032(a) also does not relate to the tax treatment of the recipient of a corporation's stock.

(c) Where a corporation acquires shares of its own stock in exchange for shares of its own stock (including treasury stock) the transaction may qualify not only under section 1032(a), but also under section 368(a)(1)(E) (recapitalization) or section 305(a) (distribution of stock and stock rights).

(d) For basis of property acquired by a corporation in connection with a transaction to which section 351 applies or in connection with a reorganization, see section 362. For basis of property acquired by a corporation in a transaction to which section 1032 applies but which does not qualify under any other nonrecognition provision, see section 1012.

§ 1.1033(a)–1 Involuntary conversions; nonrecognition of gain

(a) **In general.** Section 1033 applies to cases where property is compulsorily or involuntarily converted. An "involuntary conversion" may be the result of the destruction of property in whole or in part, the theft of property, the seizure of property, the requisition or condemnation of property, or the threat or imminence of requisition or condemnation of property. An "involuntary conversion" may be a conversion into similar property or into money or into dissimilar property. Section 1033 provides that, under certain specified circumstances, any gain which is realized from an involuntary conversion shall not be recognized. In cases where property is converted into other property similar or related in service or use to the converted property, no gain shall be recognized regardless of when the disposition of the converted property occurred and regardless of whether or not the taxpayer elects to have the gain not recognized. In other types of involuntary conversion cases, however, the proceeds arising from the disposition of the converted property must (within the time limits specified) be reinvested in similar property in order to avoid recognition of any gain realized. Section 1033 applies only with respect to gains; losses from involuntary conversions are recognized or not recognized without regard to this section.

(b) Special rules. For rules relating to the application of section 1033 to involuntary conversions of a principal residence with respect to which an election has been made under section 121 (relating to gain from sale or exchange of residence of individual who has attained age 65), see paragraph (g) of § 1.121-5. For rules applicable to involuntary conversions of a principal residence occurring before January 1, 1951, see § 1.1033(a)-3. For rules applicable to involuntary conversions of a principal residence occurring after December 31, 1950, and before January 1, 1954, see paragraph (h)(1) of § 1.-1034-1. For rules applicable to involuntary conversions of a personal residence occurring after December 31, 1953, see § 1.1033(a)-3. For special rules relating to the election to have section 1034 apply to certain involuntary conversions of a principal residence occurring after December 31, 1957, see paragraph (h)(2) of § 1.-1034-1. For special rules relating to certain involuntary conversions of real property held either for productive use in trade or business or for investment and occurring after December 31, 1957, see § 1.1033(g)-1. See also special rules applicable to involuntary conversions of property sold pursuant to reclamation laws, livestock destroyed by disease, and livestock sold on account of drought provided in §§ 1.1033(c)-1, 1.1033(d)-1, and 1.1033(e)-1, respectively. For rules relating to basis of property acquired through involuntary conversions, see § 1.1033(b)-1. For determination of the period for which the taxpayer has held property acquired as a result of certain involuntary conversions, see section 1223 and regulations issued thereunder. For treatment of gains from involuntary conversions as capital gains in certain cases, see section 1231(a) and regulations issued thereunder. For portion of war loss recoveries treated as gain on involuntary conversion, see section 1332(b)(3) and regulations issued thereunder.

§ 1.1033(a)-2 Involuntary conversion into similar property, into money or into dissimilar property

(a) In general. The term "disposition of the converted property" means the destruction, theft, seizure, requisition, or condemnation of the converted property, or the sale or exchange of such property under threat or imminence of requisition or condemnation.

(b) Conversion into similar property. If property (as a result of its destruction in whole or in part, theft, seizure, or requisition or condemnation or threat or imminence thereof) is compulsorily or involuntarily converted only into property similar or related in service or use to the property so converted, no gain shall be recognized. Such nonrecognition of gain is mandatory.

(c) Conversion into money or into dissimilar property. (1) If property (as a result of its destruction in whole or in part, theft, seizure, or requisition or condemnation or threat or imminence thereof) is compulsorily or involuntarily converted into money or into property not similar or related in service or use to the converted property, the gain, if any, shall be recognized, at the election of the taxpayer, only to the extent that the amount realized upon such conversion exceeds the cost of other property purchased by the taxpayer which is similar or related in service or use to the property so converted, or the cost of stock of a corporation owning such other property which is purchased by the taxpayer in the acquisition of control of such corporation, if the taxpayer purchased such other property, or such stock, for the purpose of replacing the property so converted and during the period specified in subparagraph (3) of this paragraph. For the purposes of section 1033, the term "control" means the ownership of stock possessing at least 80 percent of the total combined voting power of all classes of stock entitled to vote and at least 80 percent of the total number of shares of all other classes of stock of the corporation.

(2) All of the details in connection with an involuntary conversion of property at a gain (including those relating to the replacement of the converted property, or a decision not to replace, or the expiration of the period for replacement) shall be reported in the return for the taxable year or years in which any of such gain is realized. An election to have such gain recognized only to the extent provided in subparagraph (1) of this paragraph shall be made by including such gain in gross income for such year or years only to such extent. If, at the time of filing such a return, the period within which the converted property must be replaced has expired, or if such an election is not desired, the gain should be included in gross income for such year or years in the regular manner. A failure to so include such gain in gross income in the regular manner shall be deemed to be an election by the taxpayer to have such gain recognized only to the extent provided in subparagraph (1) of this paragraph even though the details in connection with the conversion are not reported in such return. If, after having made an election under section 1033(a)(2), the converted property is not replaced within the required period of time, or replacement is made at a cost lower than was anticipated at the time of the election, or a decision is made not to replace, the tax liability for the year or years for which the election was made shall be recomputed. Such recomputation should be in the form of an "amended return". If a decision is made to make an election under section 1033(a)(2) after the filing of the return and the payment of the tax for the year or years in which any of the gain on an involuntary conversion is realized and before the expiration of the period within which the converted property must be replaced, a claim for credit or refund for such year or years should be filed. If the replacement of the converted property occurs in a year or years in which none of the gain on the conversion is realized, all of the details in connection with such replacement shall

be reported in the return for such year or years.

(3) The period referred to in subparagraphs (1) and (2) of this paragraph is the period of time commencing with the date of the disposition of the converted property, or the date of the beginning of the threat or imminence of requisition or condemnation of the converted property, whichever is earlier, and ending 2 years (or, in the case of a disposition occurring before Dec. 31, 1969, 1 year) after the close of the first taxable year in which any part of the gain upon the conversion is realized, or at the close of such later date as may be designated pursuant to an application of the taxpayer. Such application shall be made prior to the expiration of 2 years (or, in the case of a disposition occurring before Dec. 31, 1969, 1 year) after the close of the first taxable year in which any part of the gain from the conversion is realized, unless the taxpayer can show to the satisfaction of the district director—

(i) Reasonable cause for not having filed the application within the required period of time, and

(ii) The filing of such application was made within a reasonable time after the expiration of the required period of time. The application shall contain all of the details in connection with the involuntary conversion. Such application shall be made to the district director for the internal revenue district in which the return is filed for the first taxable year in which any of the gain from the involuntary conversion is realized. No extension of time shall be granted pursuant to such application unless the taxpayer can show reasonable cause for not being able to replace the converted property within the required period of time.

See section 1033(g)(4) and § 1.-1033(g)–1 for the circumstances under which, in the case of the conversion of real property held either for productive use in trade or business or for investment, the 2-year period referred to in this paragraph (c)(3) shall be extended to 3 years.

(4) Property or stock purchased before the disposition of the converted

property shall be considered to have been purchased for the purpose of replacing the converted property only if such property or stock is held by the taxpayer on the date of the disposition of the converted property. Property or stock shall be considered to have been purchased only if, but for the provisions of section 1033(b), the unadjusted basis of such property or stock would be its cost to the taxpayer within the meaning of section 1012. If the taxpayer's unadjusted basis of the replacement property would be determined, in the absence of section 1033(b), under any of the exceptions referred to in section 1012, the unadjusted basis of the property would not be its cost within the meaning of section 1012. For example, if property similar or related in service or use to the converted property is acquired by gift and its basis is determined under section 1015, such property will not qualify as a replacement for the converted property.

(5) If a taxpayer makes an election under section 1033(a)(2), any deficiency, for any taxable year in which any part of the gain upon the conversion is realized, which is attributable to such gain may be assessed at any time before the expiration of three years from the date the district director with whom the return for such year has been filed is notified by the taxpayer of the replacement of the converted property or of an intention not to replace, or of a failure to replace, within the required period, notwithstanding the provisions of section 6212(c) or the provisions of any other law or rule of law which would otherwise prevent such assessment. If replacement has been made, such notification shall contain all of the details in connection with such replacement. Such notification should be made in the return for the taxable year or years in which the replacement occurs, or the intention not to replace is formed, or the period for replacement expires, if this return is filed with such district director. If this return is not filed with such district director, then such notification shall be made to such district director at the time of filing this return. If the taxpayer so desires, he may, in either event, also notify such district director before the filing of such return.

(6) If a taxpayer makes an election under section 1033(a)(2) and the replacement property or stock was purchased before the beginning of the last taxable year in which any part of the gain upon the conversion is realized, any deficiency, for any taxable year ending before such last taxable year, which is attributable to such election may be assessed at any time before the expiration of the period within which a deficiency for such last taxable year may be assessed, notwithstanding the provisions of section 6212(c) or 6501 or the provisions of any law or rule of law which would otherwise prevent such assessment.

(7) If the taxpayer makes an election under section 1033(a)(2), the gain upon the conversion shall be recognized to the extent that the amount realized upon such conversion exceeds the cost of the replacement property or stock, regardless of whether such amount is realized in one or more taxable years.

(8) The proceeds of a use and occupancy insurance contract, which by its terms insured against actual loss sustained of net profits in the business, are not proceeds of an involuntary conversion but are income in the same manner that the profits for which they are substituted would have been.

(9) There is no investment in property similar in character and devoted to a similar use if—

(i) The proceeds of unimproved real estate, taken upon condemnation proceedings, are invested in improved real estate.

(ii) The proceeds of conversion of real property are applied in reduction of indebtedness previously incurred in the purchase of a leasehold.

(iii) The owner of a requisitioned tug uses the proceeds to buy barges.

(10) If, in a condemnation proceeding, the Government retains out of the award sufficient funds to satisfy special assessments levied against the remaining portion of the plot or parcel of real estate affected for benefits accruing in connection with the condemnation, the amount so retained shall be deducted from the gross award in

determining the amount of the net award.

(11) If, in a condemnation proceeding, the Government retains out of the award sufficient funds to satisfy liens (other than liens due to special assessments levied against the remaining portion of the plot or parcel of real estate affected for benefits accruing in connection with the condemnation) and mortgages against the property, and itself pays the same, the amount so retained shall not be deducted from the gross award in determining the amount of the net award. If, in a condemnation proceeding, the Government makes an award to a mortgagee to satisfy a mortgage on the condemned property, the amount of such award shall be considered as a part of the "amount realized" upon the conversion regardless of whether or not the taxpayer was personally liable for the mortgage debt. Thus, if a taxpayer has acquired property worth $100,000 subject to a $50,000 mortgage (regardless of whether or not he was personally liable for the mortgage debt) and, in a condemnation proceeding, the Government awards the taxpayer $60,000 and awards the mortgagee $50,000 in satisfaction of the mortgage, the entire $110,000 is considered to be the "amount realized" by the taxpayer.

(12) An amount expended for replacement of an asset in excess of the recovery for loss, represents a capital expenditure and is not a deductible loss for income tax purposes.

§ 1.1033(b)-1   Basis of property acquired as a result of an involuntary conversion

(a) The provisions of the first sentence of section 1033(b) may be illustrated by the following example:

Example. A's vessel which has an adjusted basis of $100,000 is destroyed in 1950 and A receives in 1951 insurance in the amount of $200,-000. If A invests $150,000 in a new vessel, taxable gain to the extent of $50,000 would be recognized. The basis of the new vessel is $100,000; that is, the adjusted basis of the old vessel ($100,000) minus the money received by the taxpayer which was not expended in the acquisition of the new vessel ($50,000) plus the amount of gain recognized upon the conversion ($50,000). If any amount in excess of the proceeds of the conversion is expended in the acquisition of the new property, such amount may be added to the basis otherwise determined.

(b) The provisions of the last sentence of section 1033(b) may be illustrated by the following example:

Example. A taxpayer realizes $22,000 from the involuntary conversion of his barn in 1955; the adjusted basis of the barn to him was $10,000, and he spent in the same year $20,000 for a new barn which resulted in the nonrecognition of $10,000 of the $12,000 gain on the conversion. The basis of the new barn to the taxpayer would be $10,000—the cost of the new barn ($20,000) less the amount of the gain not recognized on the conversion ($10,000). The basis of the new barn would not be a substituted basis in the hands of the taxpayer within the meaning of section 1016(b)(2). If the replacement of the converted barn had been made by the purchase of two smaller barns which, together, were similar or related in service or use to the converted barn and which cost $8,000 and $12,000, respectively, then the basis of the two barns would be $4,000 and $6,000, respectively, the total basis of the purchased property ($10,000) allocated in proportion to their respective costs (8,000/20,000 of $10,000 or $4,000; and 12,000/20,000 of $10,000, or $6,000).

§ 1.1033(g)-1   Condemnation of real property held for productive use in trade or business or for investment

(a) Special rule in general. This section provides special rules for applying section 1033 with respect to certain dispositions, occurring after December 31, 1957, of real property held either for productive use in trade or business or for investment (not including stock in trade or other property held primarily for sale). For this purpose, disposition means the seizure, requisition, or condemnation (but not destruction) of the converted property, or the sale or exchange of such property under threat or imminence of seizure, requisition, or condemnation. In such cases, for purposes of applying section 1033, the replacement of such property with property of like kind to be held either for productive use in trade or business or for investment shall be treated as property similar or related in service or use to the property so converted. For principles in determining whether the replacement property is property of like kind, see paragraph (b) of § 1.1031(a)-1.

.   .   .   .   .

§ 1.1034-1 Sale or exchange of residence

(a) **Nonrecognition of gain; general statement.** Section 1034 provides rules for the nonrecognition of gain in certain cases where a taxpayer sells one residence after December 31, 1953, and buys or builds, and uses as his principal residence, another residence within specified time limits before or after such sale. In general, if the taxpayer invests in a new residence an amount at least as large as the adjusted sales price of his old residence, no gain is recognized on the sale of the old residence (see paragraph (b) of this section for definitions of "adjusted sales price", "new residence", and "old residence"). On the other hand, if the new residence costs the taxpayer less than the adjusted sales price of the old residence, gain is recognized to the extent of the difference. Thus, if an amount equal to or greater than the adjusted sales price of an old residence is invested in a new residence, according to the rules stated in section 1034, none of the gain (if any) realized from the sale shall be recognized. If an amount less than such adjusted sales price is so invested, gain shall be recognized, but only to the extent provided in section 1034. If there is no investment in a new residence, section 1034 is inapplicable and all of the gain shall be recognized. Whenever, as a result of the application of section 1034, any or all of the gain realized on the sale of an old residence is not recognized, a corresponding reduction must be made in the basis of the new residence. The provisions of section 1034 are mandatory, so that the taxpayer cannot elect to have gain recognized under circumstances where this section is applicable. Section 1034 applies only to gains; losses are recognized or not recognized without regard to the provisions of this section. Section 1034 affects only the amount of gain recognized, and not the amount of gain realized (see also section 1001 and the regulations issued thereunder). Any gain realized upon disposition of other property in exchange for the new residence is not affected by section 1034. For special rules relating to the sale or exchange of a principal residence by a taxpayer who has attained age 65, see section 121 and paragraph (g) of § 1.121-5. For special rules relating to a case where real property with respect to the sale of which gain is not recognized under this section is reacquired by the seller in partial or full satisfaction of the indebtedness arising from such sale and resold by him within 1 year after the date of such reacquisition, see § 1.1038-2.

(b) **Definitions.** The following definitions of frequently used terms are applicable for purposes of section 1034 (other definitions and detailed explanations appear in subsequent paragraphs of this regulation):

(1) "Old residence" means property used by the taxpayer as his principal residence which is the subject of a sale by him after December 31, 1953 (section 1034(a); for detailed explanation see paragraph (c) (3) of this section).

(2) "New residence" means property used by the taxpayer as his principal residence which is the subject of a purchase by him (section 1034(a); for detailed explanation and limitations see paragraph (c) (3) and (d) (1) of this section).

(3) "Adjusted sales price" means the amount realized reduced by the fixing-up expenses (section 1034(b) (1); for special rule applicable in some cases to husband and wife, see paragraph (f) of this section).

(4) "Amount realized" is to be computed by subtracting

(i) The amount of the items which, in determining the gain from the sale of the old residence, are properly an offset against the consideration received upon the sale (such as commissions and expenses of advertising the property for sale, of preparing the deed, and of other legal services in connection with the sale); from

(ii) The amount of the consideration so received, determined (in accordance with section 1001(b) and regulations issued thereunder) by adding to the sum of any money so received, the fair market value of the property (other than money) so received. If, as part of the consideration for the sale, the purchaser either assumes a liability of the taxpayer or acquires the old residence subject to a liability (whether or not the taxpayer is personally liable on the debt), such assumption or acquisition, in the amount of the liability, shall be treated as money received by the taxpayer in computing the "amount realized."

(5) "Gain realized" is the excess (if any) of the amount realized over the adjusted basis of the old residence (see also section 1001(a) and regulations issued thereunder).

(6) "Fixing-up expenses" means the aggregate of the expenses for work performed (in any taxable year, whether beginning before, on, or after January 1, 1954) on the old residence in order to assist in its sale, provided that such expenses (i) are incurred for work performed during the 90-day period ending on the day on which the contract to sell the old residence is entered into; and (ii) are paid on or before the 30th day after the date of the sale of the old residence; and (iii) are neither (a) allowable as deductions in computing taxable income under section 63(a), nor (b) taken into account in computing the amount realized from the sale of the old residence (section 1034(b) (2) and (3)). "Fixing-up expenses" does not include expenditures which are properly chargeable to capital account and which would, therefore, constitute adjustments to the basis of the old residence (see section 1016 and regulations issued thereunder).

(7) "Cost of purchasing the new residence" means the total of all amounts which are attributable to the acquisition, construction, reconstruction, and improvements constituting capital expenditures, made during the period beginning 18 months (one year in the case of a sale of an old residence prior to January 1, 1975) before the date of sale of. the old residence and ending either (i) 18 months (one year in the case of a sale of an old residence prior to January 1, 1975) after such date in the case of a new residence purchased but not constructed by the taxpayer, or (ii) two years (18 months in the case of a sale of an old residence prior to Jan-

uary 1, 1975) after such date in the case of a new residence the construction of which was commenced by the taxpayer before the expiration of 18 months (one year in the case of a sale of an old residence prior to January 1, 1975) after such date (section 1034(a), (c)(2) and (c)(5); for detailed explanation, see paragraph (c)(4) of this section; for special rule applicable in some cases to husband and wife, see paragraph (f) of this section; see also paragraph (b)(9) of this section for definition of "purchase").

(8) "Sale" (of a residence) means a sale or an exchange (of a residence) for other property which occurs after December 31, 1953, an involuntary conversion (of a residence) which occurs after December 31, 1950, and before January 1, 1954, or certain involuntary conversions where the disposition of the property occurs after December 31, 1957, in respect of which a proper election is made under section 1034(i) (2) (see sections 1034(c) (1), 1034(i) (1) (A), and 1034(i) (2); for detailed explanation concerning involuntary conversions, see paragraph (h) of this section).

(9) "Purchase" (of a residence) means a purchase or an acquisition (of a residence) on the exchange of property or the partial or total construction or reconstruction (of a residence) by the taxpayer (section 1034(c) (1) and (2)). However, the mere improvement of a residence, not amounting to reconstruction, does not constitute "purchase" of a residence.

(c) Rules for application of section 1034—.   .   .   .

(3) Property used by the taxpayer as his principal residence. (i) Whether or not property is used by the taxpayer as his residence, and whether or not property is used by the taxpayer as his principal residence (in the case of a taxpayer using more than one property as a residence), depends upon all the facts and circumstances in each case, including the good faith of the taxpayer. The mere fact that property is, or has been, rented is not determinative that such property is not used by the taxpayer as his principal residence.

For example, if the taxpayer purchases his new residence before he sells his old residence, the fact that he temporarily rents out the new residence during the period before he vacates the old residence may not, in the light of all the facts and circumstances in the case, prevent the new residence from being considered as property used by the taxpayer as his principal residence. Property used by the taxpayer as his principal residence may include a houseboat, a house trailer, or stock held by a tenant-stockholder in a co-operative housing corporation (as those terms are defined in section 216 (b) (1) and (2)), if the dwelling which the taxpayer is entitled to occupy as such stockholder is used by him as his principal residence (section 1034(f)). Property used by the taxpayer as his principal residence does not include personal property such as a piece of furniture, a radio, etc., which, in accordance with the applicable local law, is not a fixture.

(ii) Where part of a property is used by the taxpayer as his principal residence and part is used for other purposes, an allocation must be made to determine the application of this section. If the old residence is used only partially for residential purposes, only that part of the gain allocable to the residential portion is not to be recognized under this section and only an amount allocable to the selling price of such portion need be invested in the new residence in order to have the gain allocable to such portion not recognized under this section. If the new residence is used only partially for residential purposes only so much of its cost as is allocable to the residential portion may be counted as the cost of purchasing the new residence.

(4) Cost of purchasing new residence. (i) The taxpayer's cost of purchasing the new residence includes not only cash but also any indebtedness to which the property purchased is subject at the time of purchase whether or not assumed by the taxpayer (including purchase-money mortgages, etc.) and the face amount of any liabilities of the taxpayer which are part of the consideration for the purchase. Commissions and other purchasing expenses paid or incurred by the taxpayer on the purchase of the new residence are to be included in determining such cost. In the case of an acquisition of a residence upon an exchange which is considered as a "purchase" under this section, the fair market value of the new residence on the date of the exchange shall be considered as the taxpayer's cost of purchasing the new residence. Where any part of the new residence is acquired by the taxpayer other than by "purchase", the value of such part is not to be included in determining the taxpayer's cost of the new residence (see paragraph (b) (9) of this section for definition of "purchase"). For example, if the taxpayer acquires a residence by gift or inheritance, and spends $20,000 in reconstructing such residence, only such $20,000 may be treated as his cost of purchasing the new residence.

(ii) The taxpayer's cost of purchasing the new residence includes only so much of such cost as is attributable to acquisition, construction, reconstruction, or improvements made within the period of three years or 42 months (two years or 30 months in the case of a sale of an old residence prior to January 1, 1975), as the case may be, in which the purchase and use of the new residence must be made in order to have gain on the sale of the old residence not recognized under this section. Thus, if the construction of the new residence is begun three years before the date of sale of the old residence and completed on the date of sale of the old residence, only that portion of the cost which is attributable to the last 18 months (last year in the case of a sale of an old residence prior to January 1, 1975) of such construction constitutes the taxpayer's cost of purchasing the new residence, for purposes of section 1034. Furthermore, the taxpayer's cost of purchasing the new residence includes only such amounts as are properly chargeable to capital account rather than to current expense. As to what constitutes capital expenditures, see section 263.

(iii) The provisions of this subparagraph may be illustrated by the following example:

Example. M began the construction of a new residence on January 15, 1974, and completed it on October 14, 1974. The cost of $45,000 was incurred ratably over the 9-month period of construction. On December 14, 1975, M sold his old residence and realized a gain. In determining the extent to which the realized gain is not to be recognized under section 1034, M's cost of constructing the new residence shall include only the $20,000 which was attributable to the June 15—October 14, 1974, period (4 months at $5,000). The $25,000 balance of the cost of constructing the new residence was not attributable to the period begining 18 months before the date of the sale of the old residence and ending two years after such date and, under section 1034, is not properly a part of M's cost of constructing the new residence.

. . . . .

§ 1.1036-1 Stock for stock of the same corporation

(a) Section 1036 permits the exchange, without the recognition of gain or loss, of common stock for common stock, or of preferred stock for preferred stock, in the same corporation. Section 1036 applies even though voting stock is exchanged for nonvoting stock or nonvoting stock is exchanged for voting stock. It is not limited to an exchange between two individual stockholders; it includes a transaction between a stockholder and the corporation. However, a transaction between a stockholder and the corporation may qualify not only under section 1036(a), but also under section 368(a)(1)(E) (recapitalization) or section 305(a) (distribution of stock and stock rights). The provisions of section 1036(a) do not apply if stock is exchanged for bonds, or preferred stock is exchanged for common stock, or common stock is exchanged for preferred stock, or common stock in one corporation is exchanged for common stock in another corporation. See paragraph (l) of § 1.-301-1 for certain transactions treated as distributions under section 301. See paragraph (e)(5) of § 1.368-2 for certain transactions which result in deemed distributions under section 305(c) to which sections 305(b)(4) and 301 apply.

. . . . .

§ 1.1091-1 Losses from wash sales of stock or securities

(a) A taxpayer cannot deduct any loss claimed to have been sustained from the sale or other disposition of stock or securities if, within a period beginning 30 days before the date of such sale or disposition and ending 30 days after such date (referred to in this section as the 61-day period), he has acquired (by purchase or by an exchange upon which the entire amount of gain or loss was recognized by law), or has entered into a contract or option so to acquire, substantially identical stock or securities. However, this prohibition does not apply (1) in the case of a taxpayer, not a corporation, if the sale or other disposition of stock or securities is made in connection with the taxpayer's trade or business, or (2) in the case of a corporation, a dealer in stock or securities, if the sale or other disposition of stock or securities is made in the ordinary course of its business as such dealer.

(b) Where more than one loss is claimed to have been sustained within the taxable year from the sale or other disposition of stock or securities, the provisions of this section shall be applied to the losses in the order in which the stock or securities the disposition of which resulted in the respective losses were disposed of (beginning with the earliest disposition). If the order of disposition of stock or securities disposed of at a loss on the same day cannot be determined, the stock or securities will be considered to have been disposed of in the order in which they were originally acquired (beginning with the earliest acquisition).

(c) Where the amount of stock or securities acquired within the 61-day period is less than the amount of stock or securities sold or otherwise disposed of, then the particular shares of stock or securities the loss from the sale or other disposition of which is not deductible shall be those with which the stock or securities acquired are matched in accordance with the following rule: The stock or securities acquired will be matched in accordance with the order of their acquisition (beginning with the earliest acquisition) with an equal number of the shares of stock or securities sold or otherwise disposed of.

(d) Where the amount of stock or securities acquired within the 61-day period is not less than the amount of stock or securities sold or otherwise disposed of, then the particular shares of stock or securities the acquisition of which resulted in the nondeductibility of the loss shall be those with which the stock or securities disposed of are matched in accordance with the following rule: The stock or securities sold or otherwise disposed of will be matched with an equal number of the shares of stock or securities acquired in accordance with the order of acquisition (beginning with the earliest acquisition) of the stock or securities acquired.

(e) The acquisition of any share of stock or any security which results in the nondeductibility of a loss under the provisions of this section shall be disregarded in determining the deductibility of any other loss.

(f) The word "acquired" as used in this section means acquired by purchase or by an exchange upon which the entire amount of gain or loss was recognized by law, and comprehends cases where the taxpayer has entered into a contract or option within the 61-day period to acquire by purchase or by such an exchange.

(g) For purposes of determining under this section the 61-day period applicable to a short sale of stock or securities, the principles of paragraph (a) of § 1.1233-1 for determining the consummation of a short sale shall generally apply except that the date of entering into the short sale shall be deemed to be the date of sale if, on the date of entering into the short sale, the taxpayer owns (or on or before such date has entered into a contract or option to acquire) stock or securities identical to those sold short and subsequently delivers such stock or securities to close the short sale.

(h) The following examples illustrate the application of this section:

Example (1). A, whose taxable year is the calendar year, on December 1, 1954, purchased 100 shares of common stock in the M Company for $10,000 and on December 15, 1954, purchased 100 additional shares for $9,000. On January 3, 1955, he sold the 100 shares purchased on December 1, 1954, for $9,000. Because of the provisions of section 1091, no loss from the sale is allowable as a deduction.

Example (2). A, whose taxable year is the calendar year, on September 21, 1954, purchased 100 shares of the common stock of the M Company for $5,000. On December 21, 1954, he purchased 50 shares of substantially identical stock for $2,750, and on December 27, 1954, he purchased 25 additional shares of such stock for $1,125. On January 3, 1955, he sold for $4,000 the 100 shares purchased on September 21, 1954. There is an indicated loss of $1,000 on the sale of the 100 shares. Since, within the 61-day period, A purchased 75 shares of substantially

identical stock, the loss on the sale of 75 of the shares ($3,750 - $3,000, or $750) is not allowable as a deduction because of the provisions of section 1091. The loss on the sale of the remaining 25 shares ($1,250 — $1,000, or $250) is deductible subject to the limitations provided in sections 267 and 1211. The basis of the 50 shares purchased December 21, 1954, the acquisition of which resulted in the nondeductibility of the loss ($500) sustained on 50 of the 100 shares sold on January 3, 1955, is $2,500 (the cost of 50 of the shares sold on January 3, 1955) + $750 (the difference between the purchase price ($2,750) of the 50 shares acquired on December 21, 1954, and the selling price ($2,000) of 50 of the shares sold on January 3, 1955), or $3,250. Similarly, the basis of the 25 shares purchased on December 27, 1954, the acquisition of which resulted in the nondeductibility of the loss ($250) sustained on 25 of the shares sold on January 3, 1955, is $1,250 + $125, or $1,375. See § 1.1091-2.

. . . .

§ 1.1091-2 Basis of stock or securities acquired in "wash sales"

(a) **In general.** The application of section 1091(d) may be illustrated by the following examples:

Example (1). A purchased a share of common stock of the X Corporation for $100 in 1935, which he sold January 15, 1955, for $80. On February 1, 1955, he purchased a share of common stock of the same corporation for $90. No loss from the sale is recognized under section 1091. The basis of the new share is $110; that is, the basis of the old share ($100) increased by $10, the excess of the price at which the new share was acquired ($90) over the price at which the old share was sold ($80).

Example (2). A purchased a share of common stock of the Y Corporation for $100 in 1935, which he sold January 15, 1955, for $80. On February 1, 1955, he purchased a share of common stock of the same corporation for $70. No loss from the sale is recognized under section 1091. The basis of the new share is $90; that is, the basis of the old share ($100) decreased by $10, the excess of the price at which the old share was sold ($80) over the price at which the new share was acquired ($70).

. . . .

§ 1.1221-1 Meaning of terms

(a) The term "capital assets" includes all classes of property not specifically excluded by section 1221. In determining whether property is a "capital asset", the period for which held is immaterial.

(b) Property used in the trade or business of a taxpayer of a character which is subject to the allowance for depreciation provided in section 167 and real property used in the trade or business of a taxpayer is excluded from the term "capital assets". Gains and losses from the sale or exchange of such property are not treated as gains and losses from the sale or exchange of capital assets, except to the extent provided in section 1231. See § 1.1231-1. Property held for the production of income, but not used in a trade or business of the taxpayer, is not excluded from the term "capital assets" even though depreciation may have been allowed with respect to such property under section 23(1) of the Internal Revenue Code of 1939 before its amendment by section 121(c) of the Revenue Act of 1942 (56 Stat. 819). However, gain or loss upon the sale or exchange of land held by a taxpayer primarily for sale to customers in the ordinary course of his business, as in the case of a dealer in real estate, is not subject to the provisions of subchapter P (section 1201 and following), chapter 1 of the Code.

(c)(1) A copyright, a literary, musical, or artistic composition, and similar property are excluded from the term "capital assets" if held by a taxpayer whose personal efforts created such property, or if held by a taxpayer in whose hands the basis of such property is determined, for purposes of determining gain from a sale or exchange, in whole or in part by reference to the basis of such property in the hands of a taxpayer whose personal efforts created such property. For purposes of this subparagraph, the phrase "similar property" includes for example, such property as a theatrical production, a radio program, a newspaper cartoon strip, or any other property eligible for copyright protection (whether under statute or common law), but does not include a patent or an invention, or a design which may be protected only under the patent law and not under the copyright law.

(2) In the case of sales and other dispositions occurring after July 25, 1969, a letter, a memorandum, or similar property is excluded from the term "capital asset" if held by (i) a taxpayer whose personal efforts created such property, (ii) a taxpayer for whom such property was prepared or produced, or (iii) a taxpayer in whose hands the basis of such property is determined, for purposes of determining gain from a sale or exchange, in whole or in part by reference to the basis of such property in the hands of a taxpayer described in subdivision (i) or

(ii) of this subparagraph. In the case of a collection of letters, memorandums, or similar property held by a person who is a taxpayer described in subdivision (i), (ii), or (iii) of this subparagraph as to some of such letters, memorandums, or similar property but not as to others, this subparagraph shall apply only to those letters, memorandums, or similar property as to which such person is a taxpayer described in such subdivision. For purposes of this subparagraph, the phrase "similar property" includes, for example, such property as a draft of a speech, a manuscript, a research paper, an oral recording of any type, a transcript of an oral recording, a transcript of an oral interview or of dictation, a personal or business diary, a log or journal, a corporate archive, including a corporate charter, office correspondence, a financial record, a drawing, a photograph, or a dispatch. A letter, memorandum, or property similar to a letter or memorandum, addressed to a taxpayer shall be considered as prepared or produced for him. This subparagraph does not apply to property, such as a corporate archive, office correspondence, or a financial record, sold or disposed of as part of a going business if such property has no significant value separate and apart from its relation to and use in such business; it also does not apply to any property to which subparagraph (1) of this paragraph applies (i. e., property to which section 1221 (3) applied before its amendment by section 514(a) of the Tax Reform Act of 1969 (83 Stat. 643)).

(3) For purposes of this paragraph, in general property is created in whole or in part by the personal efforts of a taxpayer if such taxpayer performs literary, theatrical, musical, artistic, or other creative or productive work which affirmatively contributes to the creation of the property, or if such taxpayer directs and guides others in the performance of such work. A taxpayer, such as corporate executive, who merely has administrative control of writers, actors, artists, or personnel and who does not substantially engage in the direction and guidance of such persons in the performance of their work, does not create property by his personal efforts. However, for purposes of subparagraph (2) of this paragraph, a letter or memorandum, or property similar to a letter or memo-

randum, which is prepared by personnel who are under the administrative control of a taxpayer, such as a corporate executive, shall be deemed to have been prepared or produced for him whether or not such letter, memorandum, or similar property is reviewed by him.

(4) For the application to section 1231 to the sale or exchange of property to which this paragraph applies, see § 1.1231-1. For the application of section 170 to the charitable contribution of property to which this paragraph applies, see section 170(e) and the regulations thereunder.

(d) Section 1221(4) excludes from the definition of "capital asset" accounts or notes receivable acquired in the ordinary course of trade or business for services rendered or from the sale of stock in trade or inventory or property held for sale to customers in the ordinary course of trade or business. Thus, if a taxpayer acquires a note receivable for services rendered, reports the fair market value of the note as income, and later sells the note for less than the amount previously reported, the loss is an ordinary loss. On the other hand, if the taxpayer later sells the note for more than the amount originally reported, the excess is treated as ordinary income.

(e) Obligations of the United States or any of its possessions, or of a State or Territory, or any political subdivision thereof, or of the District of Columbia, issued on or after March 1, 1941, on a discount basis and payable without interest at a fixed maturity date not exceeding one year from the date of issue, are excluded from the term "capital assets."

· · · ·

§ 1.1223-1 Determination of period for which capital assets are held

(a) The holding period of property received in an exchange by a taxpayer includes the period for which the property which he exchanged was held by him, if the property received has the same basis in whole or in part for determining gain or loss in the hands of the taxpayer as the property exchanged. However, this rule shall apply, in the case of exchanges after March 1, 1954, only if the property exchanged was at the time of the exchange a capital asset in the hands of the taxpayer or property used in his trade or business as defined in section 1231(b). For the purposes of this paragraph the term "exchange" includes the following transactions: (1) An involuntary conversion described in section 1033, and (2) a distribution to which section 355 (or so much of section 356 as relates to section 355) applies. Thus, if property acquired as the result of a compulsory or involuntary conversion of other property of the taxpayer has under section 1033(c) the same basis in whole or in part in the hands of the taxpayer as the property so converted, its acquisition is treated as an exchange and the holding period of the newly acquired property shall include the period during which the converted property was held by the taxpayer. Thus, also, where stock of a controlled corporation is received by a taxpayer pursuant to a distribution to which section 355 (or so much of section 356 as relates to section 355) applies, the distribution is treated as an exchange and the period for which the taxpayer has held the stock of the controlled corporation shall include the period for which he held the stock of the distributing corporation with respect to which such distribution was made.

(b) The holding period of property in the hands of a taxpayer shall include the period during which the property was held by any other person, if such property has the same basis in whole or in part in the hands of the taxpayer for determining gain or loss from a sale or exchange as it would have in the hands of such other person. For example, the period for which property acquired by gift after December 31, 1920, was held by the donor must be included in determining the period for which the property was held by the taxpayer if, under the provisions of section 1015, such property has, for the purpose of determining gain or loss from the sale or exchange, the same basis in the hands of the taxpayer as it would have in the hands of the donor.

· · · ·

(d) If the acquisition of stock or securities resulted in the nondeductibility (under section 1091, relating to wash sales) of the loss from the sale or other disposition of substantially identical stock or securities, the holding period of the newly acquired securities shall include the period for which the taxpayer held the securities with respect to which the loss was not allowable.

(e) The period for which the taxpayer has held stock, or stock subscription rights, received on a distribution shall be determined as though the stock dividend, or stock right, as the case may be, were the stock in respect of which the dividend was issued if the basis for determining gain or loss upon the sale or other disposition of such stock dividend or stock right is determined under section 307. If the basis of stock received by a taxpayer pursuant to a spin-off is determined under so much of section 1052(c) as refers to section 113(a) (23) of the Internal Revenue Code of 1939, and such stock is sold or otherwise disposed of in a taxable year which is subject to the Internal Revenue Code of 1954, the period for which the taxpayer has held the stock received in such spin-off shall include the period for which he held the stock of the distributing corporation with respect to which such distribution was made.

(f) The period for which the taxpayer has held stock or securities issued to him by a corporation pursuant to the exercise by him of rights to acquire such stock or securities from the corporation will, in every case and whether or not the receipt of taxable gain was recognized in connection with the distribution of the rights, begin with and include the day upon which the rights to acquire such stock or securities were exercised. A taxpayer will be deemed to have exercised rights received from a corporation to acquire stock or securities therein where there is an expression of assent to the terms of such rights made by the taxpayer in the manner requested or authorized by the corporation.

(g) The period for which the taxpayer has held a residence, the acquisition of which resulted under the provisions of section 1034 in the nonrecognition of any part of the gain realized on the sale or exchange of another residence, shall include the period for which such other residence

had been held as of the date of such sale or exchange. See § 1.1034–1. For purposes of this paragraph, the term "sale or exchange" includes an involuntary conversion occurring after December 31, 1950, and before January 1, 1954.

(h) If a taxpayer accepts delivery of a commodity in satisfaction of a commodity futures contract, the holding period of the commodity shall include the period for which the taxpayer held the commodity futures contract, if such futures contract was a capital asset in his hands.

(i) If shares of stock in a corporation are sold from lots purchased at different dates or at different prices and the identity of the lots cannot be determined, the rules prescribed by the regulations under section 1012 for determining the cost or other basis of such stocks so sold or transferred shall also apply for the purpose of determining the holding period of such stock.

. . . .

§ 1.1231–1   Gains and losses from the sale or exchange of certain property used in the trade or business

(a) In general. Section 1231 provides that, subject to the provisions of paragraph (e) of this section, a taxpayer's gains and losses from the disposition (including involuntary conversion) of assets described in that section as "property used in the trade or business" and from the involuntary conversion of capital assets held for more than 1 year (6 months for taxable years beginning before 1977; 9 months for taxable years beginning in 1977) shall be treated as long-term capital gains and losses if the total gains exceed the total losses. If the total gains do not exceed the total losses, all such gains and losses are treated as ordinary gains and losses. Therefore, if the taxpayer has no gains subject to section 1231, a recognized loss from the condemnation (or from a sale or exchange under threat of condemnation) of even a capital asset held for more than 1 year (6 months for taxable years beginning before 1977; 9 months for taxable years beginning in 1977) is an ordinary loss.

Capital assets subject to section 1231 treatment include only capital assets involuntarily converted. The non-capital assets subject to section 1231 treatment are (1) depreciable business property and business real property held for more than 1 year (6 months for taxable years beginning before 1977; 9 months for taxable years beginning in 1977), other than stock in trade and certain copyrights and artistic property and, in the case of sales and other dispositions occurring after July 25, 1969, other than a letter, memorandum, or property similar to a letter or memorandum; (2) timber, coal, and iron ore, which do not otherwise meet the requirements of section 1231, but with respect to which section 631 applies; and (3) certain livestock and unharvested crops. See paragraph (c) of this section.

(b) Treatment of gains and losses. For the purpose of applying section 1231, a taxpayer must aggregate his recognized gains and losses from—

(1) The sale, exchange, or involuntary conversion of property used in the trade or business (as defined in section 1231(b)), and

(2) The involuntary conversion (but not sale or exchange) of capital assets held for more than 1 year (6 months for taxable years beginning before 1977; 9 months for taxable years beginning in 1977).

If the gains to which section 1231 applies exceed the losses to which the section applies, the gains and losses are treated as long-term capital gains and losses and are subject to the provisions of parts I and II (section 1201 and following), subchapter P, chapter 1 of the Code, relating to capital gains and losses. If the gains to which section 1231 applies do not exceed the losses to which the section applies, the gains and losses are treated as ordinary gains and losses. Therefore, in the latter case, a loss from the involuntary conversion of a capital asset held for more than 1 year (6 months for taxable years beginning before 1977; 9 months for taxable years beginning in 1977) is treated as an ordinary loss and is not subject to the limitation on capital losses in section 1211. The phrase "involuntary conversion" is defined in paragraph (e) of this section.

·   ·   ·

(d) Extent to which gains and losses are taken into account. All gains and losses to which section 1231 applies must be taken into account in determining whether and to what extent the gains exceed the losses. For the purpose of this computation, the provisions of section 1211 limiting the deduction of capital losses do not apply, and no losses are excluded by that section. With that exception, gains are included in the computations under section 1231 only to the extent that they are taken into account in computing gross income, and losses are included only to the extent that they are taken into account in computing taxable income. The following are examples of gains and losses not included in the computations under section 1231:

(1) Losses of a personal nature which are not deductible by reason of section 165 (c) or (d), such as losses from the sale of property held for personal use;

(2) Losses which are not deductible under section 267 (relating to losses with respect to transactions between related taxpayers) or section 1091 (relating to losses from wash sales);

(3) Gain on the sale of property (to which section 1231 applies) reported for any taxable year on the installment method under section 453, except to the extent the gain is to be reported under section 453 for the taxable year; and

(4) Gains and losses which are not recognized under section 1002, such as those to which sections 1031 through 1036, relating to common nontaxable exchanges, apply.

(e) Involuntary   conversion—(1) General rule. For purposes of section 1231, the terms "compulsory or involuntary conversion" and "involuntary conversion" of property mean the conversion of property into money or other property as a result of complete or partial destruction, theft or seizure, or an exercise of the power of requisition or condemnation, or the threat or imminence thereof. Losses upon the complete or partial destruction, theft, seizure, requisition, or condemnation of property are treated as losses upon an involuntary conversion whether or not there is a conversion of the property into other property or money and whether or not the property is uninsured, partially insured, or totally insured. For example, if a capital asset held for more than 1 year (6 months for taxable years beginning before 1977; 9 months for taxable years beginning in 1977), with an adjusted basis of $400, but not held for the production of income, is stolen, and the loss which is sustained in the taxable year 1956 is not compensated for by insurance or otherwise, section 1231 applies to the $400 loss. For certain exceptions to this subparagraph, see subparagraphs (2) and (3) of this paragraph.

.   .   .   .   .

(3) **Exclusion of gains and losses from certain involuntary conversions.** Notwithstanding the provisions of subparagraph (1) of this paragraph, if for any taxable year beginning after December 31, 1969, the recognized losses from the involuntary conversion as a result of fire, storm, shipwreck, or other casualty, or from theft, of any property used in the trade or business or of any capital asset held for more than 1 year (6 months for taxable years beginning before 1977; 9 months for taxable years beginning in 1977) exceed the recognized gains from the involuntary conversion of any such property as a result of fire, storm, shipwreck, or other casualty, or from theft, such gains and losses are not gains and losses to which section 1231 applies and shall not be taken into account in applying the provisions of this section. The net loss, in effect, will be treated as an ordinary loss. This subparagraph shall apply whether such property is uninsured, partially insured, or totally insured and, in the case of a capital asset held for more than 1 year (6 months for taxable years beginning before 1977; 9 months for taxable years beginning in 1977), whether the property is property used in the trade or business, property held for the production of income, or a personal asset.

.   .   .   .   .

§ 1.1235-1   Sale or exchange of patents

(a) **General rule.** Section 1235 provides that a transfer (other than by gift, inheritance, or devise) of all substantial rights to a patent, or of an undivided interest in all such rights to a patent, by a holder to a person other than a related person constitutes the sale or exchange of a capital asset held for more than 1 year (6 months for taxable years beginning before 1977; 9 months for taxable years beginning in 1977), whether or not payments therefor are—

(1) **Payable periodically** over a period generally coterminous with the transferee's use of the patent, or

(2) **Contingent** on the productivity, use, or disposition of the property transferred.

(b) **Scope of section 1235.** If a transfer is not one described in paragraph (a) of this section, section 1235 shall be disregarded in determining whether or not such transfer is the sale or exchange of a capital asset. For example, a transfer by a person other than a holder or a transfer by a holder to a related person is not governed by section 1235. The tax consequences of such transfers shall be determined under other provisions of the internal revenue laws.

(c) **Special rules—(1) Payments for infringement.** If section 1235 applies to the transfer of all substantial rights to a patent (or an undivided interest therein), amounts received in settlement of, or as the award of damages in, a suit for compensatory damages for infringement of the patent shall be considered payments attributable to a transfer to which section 1235 applies to the extent that such amounts relate to the interest transferred.   .   .   .

(2) **Payments to an employee.** Payments received by an employee as compensation for services rendered as an employee under an employment contract requiring the employee to transfer to the employer the rights to any invention by such employee are not attributable to a transfer to which section 1235 applies. However, whether payments received by an employee from his employer (under an employment contract or otherwise) are attributable to the transfer by the employee of all substantial rights to a patent (or an undivided interest therein) or are compensation for services rendered the employer by the employee is a question of fact. In determining which is the case, consideration shall be given not only to all the facts and circumstances of the employment relationship but also to whether the amount of such payments depends upon the production, sale, or use by, or the value to, the employer of the patent rights transferred by the employee. If it is determined that payments are attributable to

the transfer of patent rights, and all other requirements under section 1235 are met, such payments shall be treated as proceeds derived from the sale of a patent.

(3) **Successive transfers.** The applicability of section 1235 to transfers of undivided interest in patents, or to successive transfers of such rights, shall be determined separately with respect to each transfer. For example, X, who is a holder, and Y, who is not a holder, transfer their respective two-thirds and one-third undivided interests in a patent to Z. Assume the transfer by X qualifies under section 1235 and that X in a later transfer acquires all the rights with respect to Y's interest, including the rights to payments from Z. One-third of all the payments thereafter received by X from Z are not attributable to a transfer to which section 1235 applies.

(d) **Payor's treatment of payments in a transfer under section 1235.** Payments made by the transferee of patent rights pursuant to a transfer satisfying the requirements of section 1235 are payments of the purchase price for the patent rights and are not the payment of royalties.

. . . .

§ 1.1235–2 Definition of terms

For the purposes of section 1235 and § 1.1235–1—

(a) **Patent.** The term "patent" means a patent granted under the provisions of title 35 of the United States Code, or any foreign patent granting rights generally similar to those under a United States patent. It is not necessary that the patent or patent application for the invention be in existence if the requirements of section 1235 are otherwise met.

(b) **All substantial rights to a patent.** (1) The term "all substantial rights to a patent" means all rights (whether or not then held by the grantor) which are of value at the time the rights to the patent (or an undivided interest therein) are transferred. The term "all substantial rights to a patent" does not include a grant of rights to a patent—

(i) Which is limited geographically within the country of issuance;

(ii) Which is limited in duration by the terms of the agreement to a period less than the remaining life of the patent;

(iii) Which grants rights to the grantee, in fields of use within trades or industries, which are less than all the rights covered by the patent, which exist and have value at the time of the grant; or

(iv) Which grants to the grantee less than all the claims or inventions covered by the patent which exist and have value at the time of the grant.

The circumstances of the whole transaction, rather than the particular terminology used in the instrument of transfer, shall be considered in determining whether or not all substantial rights to a patent are transferred in a transaction.

(2) Rights which are not considered substantial for purposes of section 1235 may be retained by the holder. Examples of such rights are:

(i) The retention by the transferor of legal title for the purpose of securing performance or payment by the transferee in a transaction involving transfer of an exclusive license to manufacture, use, and sell for the life of the patent;

(ii) The retention by the transferor of rights in the property which are not inconsistent with the passage of ownership, such as the retention of a security interest (such as a vendor's lien), or a reservation in the nature of a condition subsequent (such as a provision for forfeiture on account of nonperformance).

(3) Examples of rights which may or may not be substantial, depending upon the circumstances of the whole transaction in which rights to a patent are transferred, are:

(i) The retention by the transferor of an absolute right to prohibit sublicensing or subassignment by the transferee;

(ii) The failure to convey to the transferee the right to use or to sell the patent property.

(4) The retention of a right to terminate the transfer at will is the retention of a substantial right for the purposes of section 1235.

(c) **Undivided interest.** A person owns an "undivided interest" in all substantial rights to a patent when he owns the same fractional share of each and every substantial right to the patent. It does not include, for example, a right to the income from a patent, or a license limited geographically, or a license which covers some, but not all, of the valuable claims or uses covered by the patent. A transfer limited in duration by the terms of the instrument to a period less than the remaining life of the patent is not a transfer of an undivided interest in all substantial rights to a patent.

(d) Holder. (1) The term "holder" means any individual—

(i) Whose efforts created the patent property and who would qualify as the "original and first" inventor, or joint inventor, within the meaning of title 35 of the United States Code, or

(ii) Who has acquired his interest in the patent property in exchange for a consideration paid to the inventor in money or money's worth prior to the actual reduction of the invention to practice (see paragraph (e) of this section), provided that such individual was neither the employer of the inventor nor related to him (see paragraph (f) of this section). The requirement that such individual is neither the employer of the inventor nor related to him must be satisfied at the time when the substantive rights as to the interest to be acquired are determined, and at the time when the consideration in money or money's worth to be paid is definitely fixed. For example, if prior to the actual reduction to practice of an invention an individual who is neither the employer of the inventor nor related to him agrees to pay the inventor a sum of money definitely fixed as to amount in return for an undivided one-half interest in rights to a patent and at a later date, when such individual has become the employer of the inventor, he pays the definitely fixed sum of money pursuant to the earlier agreement, such individual will not be denied the status of a holder because of such employment relationship.

(2) Although a partnership cannot be a holder, each member of a partnership who is an individual may qualify as a holder as to his share of a patent owned by the partnership. For example, if an inventor who is a member of a partnership composed solely of individuals uses partnership property in the development of his invention with the understanding that the patent when issued will become partnership property, each of the inventor's partners during this period would qualify as a holder. If, in this example, the partner-

ship were not composed solely of individuals, nevertheless, each of the individual partners' distributive shares of income attributable to the transfer of all substantial rights to the patent or an undivided interest therein, would be considered proceeds from the sale or exchange of a capital asset held for more than 1 year (6 months for taxable years beginning before 1977; 9 months for taxable years beginning in 1977).

(3) An individual may qualify as a holder whether or not he is in the business of making inventions or in the business of buying and selling patents.

(e) Actual reduction to practice. For the purposes of determining whether an individual is a holder under paragraph (d) of this section, the term "actual reduction to practice" has the same meaning as it does under section 102(g) of title 35 of the United States Code. Generally, an invention is reduced to actual practice when it has been tested and operated successfully under operating conditions. This may occur either before or after application for a patent but cannot occur later than the earliest time that commercial exploitation of the invention occurs.

* * * * *

§ 1.1236-1   Dealers in securities

(a) Capital gains. Section 1236 (a) provides that gain realized by a dealer in securities from the sale or exchange of a security (as defined in paragraph (c) of this section) shall not be considered as gain from the sale or exchange of a capital asset unless—

(1) The security is, before the expiration of the thirtieth day after the date of its acquisition, clearly identified in the dealer's records as a security held for investment or, if acquired before October 20, 1951, was so identified before November 20, 1951; and

(2) The security is not held by the dealer primarily for sale to customers in the ordinary course of his trade or business at any time after the identification referred to in subparagraph (1) of this paragraph has been made.

Unless both of these requirements are met, the gain is considered as gain from the sale of assets held by the dealer primarily for sale to customers in the course of his business.

(b) Ordinary losses. Section 1236 (b) provides that a loss sustained by a dealer in securities from the sale or exchange of a security shall not be considered a loss from the sale or exchange of property which is not a capital asset if at any time after November 19, 1951, the security has been clearly identified in the dealer's records as a security held for investment. Once a security has been identified after November 19, 1951, as being held by the dealer for investment, it shall retain that character for purposes of determining loss on its ultimate disposition, even though at the time of its disposition the dealer holds it primarily for sale to his customers in the ordinary course of his business. However, section 1236 has no application to the extent that section 582 (c) applies to losses of banks.

(c) Definitions—(1) Security. For the purposes of this section, the term "security" means any share of stock in any corporation, any certificate of stock or interest in any corporation, any note, bond, debenture, or other evidence of indebtedness, or any evidence of any interest in, or right to subscribe to or purchase, any of the foregoing.

(2) Dealer in securities. For definition of a "dealer in securities", see the regulations under section 471.

(d) Identification of security in dealer's records. (1) A security is clearly identified in the dealer's records as a security held for investment when there is an accounting separation of the security from other securities, as by making appropriate entries in the dealer's books of account to distinguish the security from inventories and to designate it as an investment and by (i) indicating with such entries, to the extent feasible, the individual serial number of, or other characteristic symbol imprinted upon, the individual security, or (ii) adopting any other method of identification satisfactory to the Commissioner.

(2) In computing the 30-day period prescribed by section 1236 (a), the first day of the period is the day following the date of acquisition. Thus, in the case of a security acquired on March 18, 1957, the 30-day period expires at midnight on April 17, 1957.

§ 1.1237-1 Real property subdivided for sale

(a) General rule—(1) Introductory. This section provides a special rule for determining whether the taxpayer holds real property primarily for sale to customers in the ordinary course of his business under section 1221 (1). This rule is to permit taxpayers qualifying under it to sell real estate from a single tract held for investment without the income being treated as ordinary income merely because of subdividing the tract or of active efforts to sell it. The rule is not applicable to dealers in real estate or to corporations, except a corporation making such sales in a taxable year beginning after December 31, 1954, if such corporation qualifies under the provisions of paragraph (c) (5) (iv) of this section.

(2) When subdividing and selling activities are to be disregarded. When its conditions are met, section 1237 provides that if there is no other substantial evidence that a taxpayer holds real estate primarily for sale to customers in the ordinary course of his business, he shall not be considered a real estate dealer holding it primarily for sale merely because he has (i) subdivided the tract into lots (or parcels) and (ii) engaged in advertising, promotion, selling activities or the use of sales agents in connection with the sale of lots in such subdivision. Such subdividing and selling activities shall be disregarded in determining the purpose for which the taxpayer held real property sold from a subdivision whenever it is the only substantial evidence indicating that the taxpayer has ever held the real property sold primarily for sale to customers in the ordinary course of his business.

(3) When subdividing and selling activities are to be taken into account. When other substantial evidence tends to show that the taxpayer held real property for sale to customers in the ordinary course of his business, his activities in connection with the subdivision and sale of the property sold shall be taken into account in determining the purpose for which the taxpayer held both the subdivided property and any other real property. For example, such other evidence may consist of the taxpayer's selling activities in connection with other property in prior years during which he was engaged in subdividing or selling activities with respect to the subdivided tract, his intention in prior years (or at the time of acquiring the property subdivided) to hold the tract primarily for sale in his business, his subdivision of other tracts in the same year, his holding other real property for sale to customers in the same year, or his construction of a permanent real estate office which he could use in selling other real property. On the other hand, if the only evidence of the taxpayer's purpose in holding real property consisted of not more than one of the following, in the year in question, such fact would not be considered substantial other evidence:

(i) Holding a real estate dealer's license;

(ii) Selling other real property which was clearly investment property;

(iii) Acting as a salesman for a real estate dealer, but without any financial interest in the business; or

(iv) Mere ownership of other vacant real property without engaging in any selling activity whatsoever with respect to it.

If more than one of the above exists, the circumstances may or may not constitute substantial evidence that the taxpayer held real property for sale in his business, depending upon the particular facts in each case.

(4) **Section 1237 not exclusive.** (i) The rule in section 1237 is not exclusive in its application. Section 1237 has no application in determining whether or not real property is held by a taxpayer primarily for sale in his business if any requirement under the section is not met. Also, even though the conditions of section 1237 are met, the rules of section 1237 are not applicable if without regard to section 1237 the real property sold would not have been considered real property held primarily for sale to customers in the ordinary course of his business. Thus, the district director may at all times conclude from convincing evidence that the taxpayer held the real property solely as an investment. Furthermore, whether or not the conditions of section 1237 are met, the section has no application to losses realized upon the sale of realty from subdivided property.

(ii) If, owing solely to the application of section 1237, the real property sold is deemed not to have been held primarily for sale in the ordinary course of business, any gain realized upon such sale shall be treated as ordinary income to the extent provided in section 1237

(b) (1) and (2) and paragraph (e) of this section. Any additional gain realized upon the sale shall be treated as gain arising from the sale of a capital asset or, if the circumstances so indicate, as gain arising from the sale of real property used in the trade or business as defined in section 1231(b) (1). For the relationship between sections 1237 and 1231, see paragraph (f) of this section.

(5) **Principal conditions of qualification.** Before section 1237 applies, the taxpayer must meet three basic conditions, more fully explained later: He cannot have held any part of the tract at any time previously for sale in the ordinary course of his business, nor in the year of sale held any other real estate for sale to customers; he cannot make substantial improvements on the tract which increase the value of the lot sold substantially; and he must have owned the property 5 years, unless he inherited it. However, the taxpayer may make certain improvements if they are necessary to make the property marketable if he elects neither to add their cost to the basis of the property, or of any other property, nor to deduct the cost as an expense, and he has held the property at least 10 years. If the requirements of section 1237 are met, gain (but not more than 5 percent of the selling price of each lot) shall be treated as ordinary income in and after the year in which the sixth lot or parcel is sold.

. . . . .

§ 1.1239-1 Gain from sale or exchange of depreciable property between certain related taxpayers after October 4, 1976

(a) **In general.** In the case of a sale or exchange of property, directly or indirectly, between related persons after October 4, 1976 (other than a sale or exchange made under a binding contract entered into on or before that date), any gain recognized by the transferor shall be treated as ordinary income if such property is, in the hands of the transferee, subject to the allowance for depreciation provided in section 167. This rule also applies to property which would be subject to the allowance for depreciation provided in section 167 except that the purchaser has elected a different form of deduction, such as those allowed under sections 169, 188, and 191.

. . . .

(c) Rules of construction—(1) Husband and wife. For purposes of paragraph (b)(1), if on the date of the sale or exchange a taxpayer is legally separated from his spouse under an interlocutory decree of divorce, the taxpayer and his spouse shall not be treated as husband and wife, provided the sale or exchange is made pursuant to the decree and the decree subsequently becomes final. Thus, if pursuant to an interlocutory decree of divorce, an individual transfers depreciable property to his spouse and, because of this section, the gain recognized on the transfer of the property is treated as ordinary income, the individual may, if the interlocutory decree becomes final after his tax return has been filed, file a claim for a refund.

(2) Sales between commonly controlled corporations. In general, in the case of a sale or exchange of depreciable property between related corporations (within the meaning of paragraph (b)(3) of this section), gain which is treated as ordinary income by reason of this section shall be taxable to the transferor corporation rather than to a controlling shareholder. However, such gain shall be treated as ordinary income taxable to a controlling shareholder rather than the transferor corporation if the transferor corporation is used by a controlling shareholder as a mere conduit to make a sale to another controlled corporation, or the entity of the corporate transferor is otherwise properly disregarded for tax purposes. Sales between two or more corporations that are related within the meaning of paragraph (b)(3) of this section may also be subject to the rules of section 482 (relating to allocation of income between or among organizations, trades, or businesses which are commonly owned or controlled), and to rules requiring constructive dividend treatment to the controlling shareholder in appropriate circumstances.

(3) Ownership of stock. For purposes of determining the ownership of stock under this section, the constructive ownership rules of section 318 shall be applied, except that section 318(a) (2)(C) (relating to attribution of stock ownership from a corporation) and section 318(a)(3)(C) (relating to attribution of stock ownership to a corporation) shall be applied without regard to the 50-percent limitation contained therein. The application of the constructive ownership rules of section 318 to section 1239 is illustrated by the following examples:

Example (1). A, an individual, owns 79 percent of the stock (by value) of Corporation X, and a trust for A's children owns the remaining 21 percent of the stock. A's children are deemed to own the stock owned for their benefit by the trust in proportion to their actuarial interests in the trust (section 318(a)(2)(B)). A, in turn, constructively owns the stock so deemed to be owned by his children (section 318(a) (1)(A)(ii)). Thus, A is treated as owning all the stock of Corporation X, and any gain A recognizes from the sale of depreciable property to Corporation X is treated under section 1239 as ordinary income.

Example (2). Y Corporation owns 100 percent in value of the stock of Z Corporation. Y Corporation sells depreciable property at a gain to Z Corporation. P and his daughter, D, own 80 percent in value of the Y Corporation stock. Under the constructive ownership rules of section 318, as applied to section 1239, P and D are each considered to own the stock in Z Corporation owned by Y Corporation. Also, P and D are each considered to own the stock in Y Corporation owned by the other. As a result, both P and D constructively own 80 percent or more in value of the stock of both Y and Z Corporations. Thus, the sale between Y and Z is governed by section 1239 and produces ordinary income to Y.

§ 1.1241-1 Cancellation of lease or distributor's agreement

(a) In general. Section 1241 provides that proceeds received by lessees or distributors from the cancellation of leases or of certain distributorship agreements are considered as amounts received in exchange therefor. Section 1241 applies to leases of both real and personal property. Distributorship agreements to which section 1241 applies are described in paragraph (c) of this section. Section 1241 has no application in determining whether or not a cancellation not qualifying under that section is a sale or exchange. Further, section 1241 has no application in determining whether or not a lease or a distributorship agreement is a capital asset, even though its cancellation qualifies as an exchange under section 1241.

(b) Definition of "cancellation". The term "cancellation" of a lease or a distributor's agreement, as used in section

1241, means a termination of all the contractual rights of a lessee or distributor with respect to particular premises or a particular distributorship, other than by the expiration of the lease or agreement in accordance with its terms. A payment made in good faith for a partial cancellation of a lease or a distributorship agreement is recognized as an amount received for cancellation under section 1241 if the cancellation relates to a severable economic unit, such as a portion of the premises covered by a lease, a reduction in the unexpired term of a lease or distributorship agreement, or a distributorship in one of several areas or of one of several products. Payments made for other modifications of leases or distributorship agreements, however, are not recognized as amounts received for cancellation under section 1241.

(c) Amounts received upon cancellation of a distributorship agreement. Section 1241 applies to distributorship agreements only if they are for marketing or marketing and servicing of goods. It does not apply to agreements for selling intangible property or for rendering personal services as, for example, agreements establishing insurance agencies or agencies for the brokerage of securities. Further, it applies to a distributorship agreement only if the distributor has made a substantial investment of capital in the distributorship. The substantial capital investment must be reflected in physical assets such as inventories of tangible goods, equipment, machinery, storage facilities, or similar property. An investment is not considered substantial for purposes of section 1241 unless it consists of a significant fraction or more of the facilities for storing, transporting, processing, or otherwise dealing with the goods distributed, or consists of a substantial inventory of such goods. The investment required in the maintenance of an office merely for clerical operations is not considered substantial for purposes of this section. Furthermore, section 1241 shall not apply unless a substantial amount of the capital or assets needed for carrying on the operations of a distributorship are acquired by the distributor and actually used in carrying on the distributorship at some time before the cancellation of the distributorship agreement. It is immaterial for the purposes of section 1241 whether the distributor acquired the assets used in performing the functions of the distributorship before or after beginning his operations under the distributorship agreement. It is also immaterial whether the distributor is a retailer, wholesaler, jobber, or other type of distributor. The application of this paragraph may be illustrated by the following examples:

Example (1). Taxpayer is a distributor of various food products. He leases a warehouse including cold storage facilities and owns a number of motor trucks. In 1955 he obtains the exclusive rights to market certain frozen food products in his State. The marketing is accomplished by using the warehouse and trucks acquired before he entered into the agreement and entails no additional capital. Payments received upon the cancellation of the agreement are treated under section 1241 as though received upon the sale or exchange of the agreement.

Example (2). Assume that the taxpayer in example (1) entered into an exclusive distributorship agreement with the producer under which the taxpayer merely solicits orders through his staff of salesmen, the goods being shipped direct to the purchasers. Payments received upon the cancellation of the agreement would not be treated under section 1241 as though received upon the sale or exchange of the agreement.

Example (3). Taxpayer is an exclusive distributor for M city of certain frozen food products which he distributes to frozen-food freezer and locker customers. The terms of his distributorship do not make it necessary for him to have any substantial investment in inventory. Taxpayer rents a loading platform for a nominal amount, but has no warehouse space. Orders for goods from customers are consolidated by the taxpayer and forwarded to the producer from time to time. Upon receipt of these goods, taxpayer allocates them to the individual orders of customers and delivers them immediately by truck. Although it would require a fleet of fifteen or twenty trucks to carry out this operation, the distributor uses only one truck of his own and hires cartage companies to deliver the bulk of the merchandise to the customers. Payments received upon the cancellation of the distributorship agreement in such a case would not be considered received upon the sale or exchange of the agreement under section 1241 since the taxpayer does not have facilities for the physical handling of more than a small fraction of the goods involved in carrying on the distributorship and, therefore, does not have a substantial capital investment in the distributorship. On the other hand, if the taxpayer had acquired and used a substantial number of the trucks necessary for the deliveries to his customers, payments received upon the cancellation of the agreement would be considered received in exchange therefor under section 1241.

§ 1.1244(a)-1 Loss on small business stock treated as ordinary loss

(a) In general. Subject to certain conditions and limitations, section 1244 provides that a loss on the sale or exchange (including a transaction treated as a sale or exchange, such as worthlessness) of "section 1244 stock" which would otherwise be treated as a loss from the sale or exchange of a capital asset shall be treated as a loss from the sale or exchange of an asset which is not a capital asset (referred to in this section and §§ 1.1244(b)-1 to 1.1244 (e)-1, inclusive, as an "ordinary loss"). Such a loss shall be allowed as a deduction from gross income in arriving at adjusted gross income. The requirements that must be satisfied in order that stock may be considered section 1244 stock are described in §§ 1.1244 (c)-1 and 1.1244(c)-2. These requirements relate to the stock itself and the corporation issung such stock. In addition, the taxpayer who claims an ordinary loss deduction pursuant to section 1244 must satisfy the requirements of paragraph (b) of this section.

(b) Taxpayers entitled to ordinary loss. The allowance of an ordinary loss deduction for a loss of section 1244 stock is permitted only to the following two classes of taxpayers:

(1) An individual sustaining the loss to whom the stock was issued by a small business corporation, or

(2) An individual who is a partner in a partnership at the time the partnership acquired the stock in an issuance from a small business corporation and whose distributive share of partnership items reflects the loss sustained by the partnership. The ordinary loss deduction is limited to the lesser of the partner's distributive share at the time of the issuance of the stock or the partner's distributive share at the time the loss is sustained. In order to claim a deduction under section 1244 the individual, or the partnership, sustaining the loss must have continuously held the stock from the date of issuance. A corporation, trust, or estate is not entitled to ordinary loss treatment under section 1244 regardless of how the stock was acquired. An individual who acquires stock from a shareholder by purchase, gift, devise, or in any other manner is not entitled to an ordinary loss under section 1244 with respect to this stock. Thus, ordinary loss treatment is not available to a partner to whom the stock is distributed by the partnership. Stock acquired through an investment banking firm, or other person, participating in the sale of an issue may qualify for ordinary loss treatment only if the stock is not first issued to the firm or person. Thus, for example, if the firm acts as a selling agent for the issuing corporation the stock may qualify. On the other hand, stock purchased by an investment firm and subsequently resold does not qualify as section 1244 stock in the hands of the person acquiring the stock from the firm.

(c) Examples. The provisions of paragraph (b) of this section may be illustrated by the following examples:

Example (1). A and B, both individuals, and C, a trust, are equal partners in a partnership to which a small business corporation issues section 1244 stock. The partnership sells the stock at a loss. A's and B's distributive share of the loss may be treated as an ordinary loss pursuant to section 1244, but C's distributive share of the loss may not be so treated.

Example (2). The facts are the same as in example (1) except that the section 1244 stock is distributed by the partnership to partner A and he subsequently sells the stock at a loss. Section 1244 is not applicable to the loss since A did not acquire the stock by issuance from the small business corporation.

§ 1.1244(b)-1 Annual limitation

(a) In general. Subsection (b) of section 1244 imposes a limitation on the aggregate amount of loss that for any taxable year may be treated as an ordinary loss by a taxpayer by reason of that section. In the case of a partnership, the limitation is determined separately as to each partner. Any amount of loss in excess of the applicable limitation is treated as loss from the sale or exchange of a capital asset.

(b) Amount of loss—(1) Taxable years beginning after December 31, 1978. For any taxable year beginning after December 31, 1978, the maximum amount that may be treated as an ordinary loss under section 1244 is—

(i) $50,000, or

(ii) $100,000, if a husband and wife file a joint return under section 6013.

These limitations on the maximum amount of ordinary loss apply whether the loss or losses are sustained on pre-November 1978 stock (as defined in § 1.1244(c)-1(a)(1)), post-November 1978 stock (as defined in § 1.1244(c)-1 (a)(2)), or on any combination of pre-November 1978 stock and post-November 1978 stock. The limitation referred to in (ii) applies to a joint return whether the loss or losses are sustained by one or both spouses.

. . . . .

§ 1.1244(c)-1 Section 1244 stock defined

(a) **In general.** For purposes of §§ 1.1244(a)-1 to 1.1244(e)-1, inclusive—

(1) The term "pre-November 1978 stock" means stock issued after June 30, 1958, and on or before November 6, 1978.

(2) The term "post-November 1978 stock" means stock issued after November 6, 1978.

In order that stock may qualify as section 1244 stock, the requirements described in paragraphs (b) through (e) of this section must be satisfied. In addition, the requirements of paragraph (f) of this section must be satisfied in the case of pre-November 1978 stock. Whether these requirements have been met is determined at the time the stock is issued, except for the requirement in paragraph (e) of this section. Whether the requirement in paragraph (e) of this section, relating to gross receipts of the corporation, has been satisfied is determined at the time a loss is sustained. Therefore, at the time of issuance it cannot be said with certainty that stock will qualify for the benefits of section 1244.

(b) **Common stock.** Only common stock, either voting or nonvoting, in a domestic corporation may qualify as section 1244 stock. For purposes of section 1244, neither securities of the corporation covertible into common stock nor common stock convertible into other securities of the corporation are treated as common stock. An increase in the basis of outstanding stock as a result of a contribution to capital is not treated as an issuance of stock under section 1244. For definition of domestic corporation, see section 7701 (a)(4) and the regulations under that section.

(c) **Small business corporation.** At the time the stock is issued (or, in the case of pre-November 1978 stock, at the time of adoption of the plan described in paragraph (f)(1) of this section) the corporation must be a "small business corporation". See § 1.1244(c)-2 for the definition of a small business corporation.

(d) **Issued for money or other property.** (1) The stock must be issued to the taxpayer for money or other property transferred by the taxpayer to the corporation. However, stock issued in exchange for stock or securities, including stock or securities of the issuing corporation, cannot qualify as section 1244 stock, except as provided in § 1.1244(d)-3, relating to certain cases where stock is issued in exchange for section 1244 stock. Stock issued for services rendered or to be rendered to, or for the benefit of, the issuing corporation does not qualify as section 1244 stock. Stock issued in consideration for cancellation of indebtedness of the corporation shall be considered issued in exchange for money or other property unless such indebtedness is evidenced by a security, or arises out of the performance of personal services.

(2) The following examples illustrate situations where stock fails to qualify as section 1244 stock as a result of the rules in subparagraph (1) of this paragraph:

Example (1). A taxpayer owns stock of Corporation X issued to him prior to July 1, 1958. Under a plan adopted in 1977, he exchanges his stock for a new issuance of stock of Corporation X. The stock received by the taxpayer in the exchange may not qualify as section 1244 stock even if the corporation has adopted a valid plan and is a small business corporation.

Example (2). A taxpayer owns stock in Corporation X. Corporation X merges into Corporation Y. In exchange for his stock, Corporation Y issues shares of its stock to the taxpayer. The stock in Corporation Y does not qualify as section 1244 stock even if the stock exchanged by the taxpayer did qualify.

Example (3). Corporation X transfers part of its business assets to Corporation Y, a new corporation, and all of the stock of Corporation Y is issued directly to the shareholders of Corporation X. Since the Corporation Y stock was not issued to the shareholders for a transfer by them of money or other property, none of the Corporation Y stock in the hands of the shareholders can qualify.

(e) **Gross receipts.** (1)(i)(a) Except as provided in subparagraph (2) of this paragraph, stock will not qualify under section 1244, if 50 percent or more of the gross receipts of the corporation, for the period consisting of the five most recent taxable years of the corporation ending before the date the loss on such stock is sustained by the shareholders, is derived from royalties, rents, dividends, interest, annuities, and sales or exchanges of stock or securities. If the corporation has not been in existence for five taxable years ending before such date, the percentage test referred to in the preceding sentence applies to the period of the taxable years ending before such date during which the corporation has been in existence; and if the loss is sustained during the first taxable year of the corporation such test applies to the period beginning with the first day of such taxable year and ending on the day before the loss is sustained. The test under this paragraph shall be made on the basis of total gross receipts, except that gross receipts from the sales or exchanges of stock or securities shall be taken into account only to the extent of gains therefrom. The term "gross receipts" as used in section 1244 (c)(1)(C) is not synonymous with "gross income". Gross receipts means the total amount received or accrued under the method of accounting used by the corporation in computing its taxable income. Thus, the total amount of receipts is not reduced by returns and allowances, cost, or deductions. For example, gross receipts will include the total amount received or accrued during the corporation's taxable year from the sale or exchange (including a sale or exchange to which section 337 applies) of any kind of property, from investments, and for services rendered by the corporation. However, gross receipts does not include amounts received in nontaxable sales or exchanges (other than those to which section 337 applies), except to the extent that gain is recognized by the corporation, nor does that term include amounts received as a loan, as a repayment of a loan, as a contribution to capital, or on the issuance by the corporation of its own stock.

(b) The meaning of the term "gross receipts" as used in section 1244(c)(1)(C) may be further illustrated by the following examples:

Example (1). A corporation on the accrual method sells property (other than stock or securities) and receives payment partly in money and partly in the form of a note payable at a future time. The amount of the money and the face amount of the note would be considered gross receipts in the taxable year of the sale and would not be reduced by the adjusted basis of the property, the costs of sale, or any other amount.

Example (2). A corporation has a long-term contract as defined in paragraph (a) of § 1.451-3 with respect to which it reports income according to the percentage-of-completion method as described in paragraph (b) (1) of § 1.451-3. The portion of the gross contract price which corresponds to the percentage of the entire contract which has been

completed during the taxable year shall be included in gross receipts for such year.

Example (3). A corporation which regularly sells personal property on the installment plan elects to report its taxable income from the sale of property (other than stock or securities) on the installment method in accordance with section 453. The installment payments actually received in a given taxable year of the corporation shall be included in gross receipts for such year.

(ii) The term "royalties" as used in subdivision (i) of this subparagraph means all royalties, including mineral, oil, and gas royalties (whether or not the aggregate amount of such royalties constitutes 50 percent or more of the gross income of the corporation for the taxable year), and amounts received for the privilege of using patents, copyrights, secret processes and formulas, good will, trademarks, trade brands, franchises, and other like property. The term "royalties" does not include amounts received upon the disposal of timber, coal, or domestic iron ore with a retained economic interest to which the special rules of section 631(b) and (c) apply or amounts received from the transfer of patent rights to which section 1235 applies. For the definition of "mineral, oil, or gas royalties", see paragraph (b)(11)(ii) and (iii) of § 1.543-1. For purposes of this subdivision, the gross amount of royalties shall not be reduced by any part of the cost of the rights under which they are received or by any amount allowable as a deduction in computing taxable income.

(iii) The term "rents" as used in subdivision (i) of this subparagraph means amounts received for the use of, or right to use, property (whether real or personal) of the corporation, whether or not such amounts constitute 50 percent or more of the gross income of the corporation for the taxable year. The term "rents" does not include payments for the use or occupancy of rooms or other space where significant services are also rendered to the occupant, such as for the use or occupancy of rooms or other quarters in hotels, boarding houses, or apartment houses furnishing hotel services, or in tourist homes, motor courts, or motels. Generally, services are considered rendered to the occupant if they are primarily for his convenience and are other than those usually or customarily rendered in connection with the rental of rooms or other space for occupancy only. The supplying of maid service, for example, constitutes such services; whereas the furnishing of heat and light, the cleaning of public entrances, exits, stairways, and lobbies, the collection of trash, etc., are not considered as services rendered to the occupant. Payments for the use or occupancy of entire private residences or living quarters in duplex or multiple housing units, of offices in an office building, etc., are generally "rents" under section 1244(c)(1)(C). Payments for the parking of automobiles ordinarily do not constitute rents. Payments for the warehousing of goods or for the use of personal property do not constitute rents if significant services are rendered in connection with such payments.

(iv) The term "dividends" as used in subdivision (i) of this subparagraph includes dividends as defined in section 316, amounts required to be included in gross income under section 551 (relating to foreign personal holding company income taxed to United States shareholders), and consent dividends determined as provided in section 565.

(v) The term "interest" as used in subdivision (i) of this subparagraph means any amounts received for the use of money (including tax-exempt interest).

(vi) The term "annuities" as used in subdivision (i) of this subparagraph means the entire amount received as an annuity under an annuity, endowment, or life insurance contract, regardless of whether only part of such amount would be includible in gross income under section 72.

(vii) For purposes of subdivision (i) of this subparagraph, gross receipts from the sales or exchanges of stock or securities are taken into account only to the extent of gains therefrom. Thus, the gross receipts from the sale of a particular share of stock will be the excess of the amount realized over the adjusted basis of such share. If the adjusted basis should equal or exceed the amount realized on the sale or exchange of a certain share of stock, bond, etc., there would be no gross receipts resulting from the sale of such security. Losses on sales or exchanges of stock or securities do not offset gains on the sales or exchanges of other stock or securities for purposes of computing gross receipts from such sales or ex-

changes. Gross receipts from the sale or exchange of stocks and securities include gains received from such sales or exchanges by a corporation even though such corporation is a regular dealer in stocks and securities. For the meaning of the term "stocks or securities", see paragraph (b)(5)(i) of § 1.543-1.

(2) The requirement of subparagraph (1) of this paragraph need not be satisfied if for the applicable period the aggregate amount of deductions allowed to the corporation exceeds the aggregate amount of its gross income. But for this purpose the deductions allowed by section 172, relating to the net operating loss deduction, and by sections 242, 243, 244, and 245, relating to certain special deductions for corporations, shall not be taken into account. Notwithstanding the provisions of this subparagraph and of subparagraph (1) of this paragraph, pursuant to the specific delegation of authority granted in section 1244(e) to prescribe such regulations as may be necessary to carry out the purposes of section 1244, ordinary loss treatment will not be available with respect to stock of a corporation which is not largely an operating company within the five most recent taxable years (or such lesser period as the corporation is in existence) ending before the date of the loss. Thus, for example, assume that a person who is not a dealer in real estate forms a corporation which issues stock to him which meets all the formal requirements of section 1244 stock. The corporation then acquires a piece of unimproved real estate which it holds as an investment. The property declines in value and the stockholder sells his stock at a loss. The loss does not qualify for ordinary loss treatment under section 1244 but must be treated as a capital loss.

(3) In applying subparagraphs (1) and (2) of this paragraph to a successor corporation in a reorganization described in section 368(a)(1)(F), such corporation shall be treated as the same corporation as its predecessor. See paragraph (d)(2) of § 1.1244(d)-3.

. . . .

(g) Gross receipts.   (1) (i) (a) Except as provided in subparagraph (2) of this paragraph, stock will not qualify under section 1244, if 50 percent or more of the gross receipts of the corporation for the period consisting of the five most recent taxable years of the corporation ending before the date the loss on such stock is sustained by the shareholders, is derived from royalties, rents, dividends, interest, annuities, and sales or exchanges of stock or securities. If the corporation has not been in existence for five taxable years ending before such date, the percentage test referred to in the preceding sentence applies to the period of the taxable years ending before such date during which the corporation has been in existence; and if the loss is sustained during the first taxable year of the corporation such test applies to the period beginning with the first day of such taxable year and ending on the day before the loss is sustained. The test under this paragraph shall be made on the basis of total gross receipts, except that gross receipts from the sales or exchanges of stock or securities shall be taken into account only to the extent of gains therefrom. The term "gross receipts" as used in section 1244(c)(1)(E) is not synonymous with "gross income". Gross receipts means the total amount received or accrued under the method of accounting used by the corporation in computing its taxable income. Thus, the total amount of receipts is not reduced by returns and allowances, cost, or deductions. For example, gross receipts will include the total amount received or accrued during the corporation's taxable year from the sale or exchange (including a sale or exchange to which section 337 applies) of any kind of property, from investments, and for services rendered by the corporation. However, gross receipts does not include amounts received in nontaxable sales or exchanges (other than those to which section 337 applies), except to the extent that gain is recognized by the corporation, nor does that term include amounts received as a loan, as a repayment of a loan, as a contribution to capital, or on the issuance by the corporation of its own stock.

(b) The meaning of the term "gross receipts" as used in section 1244(c)(1)(E) may be further illustrated by the following examples:

Example (1). A corporation on the accrual method sells property (other than stock or securities) and receives payment partly in money and partly in the form of a note payable at a future time. The amount of the money and the face amount of the note would be considered gross receipts in the taxable year of the sale and would not be reduced by the adjusted basis of the property, the costs of sale, or any other amount.

Example (2). A corporation has a long-term contract as defined in paragraph (a) of § 1.451-3 with respect to which it reports income according to the percentage-of-completion method as described in paragraph (b)(1) of § 1.451-3. The portion of the gross contract price which corresponds to the percentage of the entire contract which has been completed during the taxable year shall be included in gross receipts for such year.

Example (3). A corpoartion which regularly sells personal property on the installment plan elects to report its taxable income from the sale of property (other than stock or securities) on the installment method in accordance with section 453. The installment payments actually received in a given taxable year of the corporation shall be included in gross receipts for such year.

(ii) The term "royalties" as used in subdivision (i) of this subparagraph means all royalties, including mineral, oil, and gas royalties (whether or not the aggregate amount of such royalties constitutes 50 percent or more of the gross income of the corporation for the taxable year), and amounts received for the privilege of using patents, copyrights, secret processes and formulas, good will, trademarks, trade brands, franchises, and other like property. The term "royalties" does not include amounts received upon the disposal of timber, coal, or domestic iron ore with a retained economic interest to which the special rules of section 631(b) and (c) apply or amounts received from the transfer of patent rights to which section 1235 applies. For the definition of "mineral, oil, or gas royalties", see paragraph (b)(11)(ii) and (iii) of § 1.543-1. For purposes of this subdivision, the gross amount of royalties shall not be reduced by any part of the cost of the rights under which they are received or by any amount allowable as a deduction in computing taxable income.

(iii) The term "rents" as used in subdivision (i) of this subparagraph means amounts received for the use of, or right to use, property (whether real or personal) of the corporation, whether or not such amounts constitute 50 percent or more of the gross income of the corporation for the taxable year. The term "rents" does not include payments for the use or occupancy of rooms or other space where significant services are also rendered to the occupant, such as for the use or occupancy of rooms or other quarters in hotels, boarding houses, or apartment houses furnishing hotel services, or in tourist homes, motor courts, or motels. Generally, services are considered rendered to the occupant if they are primarily for his convenience and are other than those usually or customarily rendered in connection with the rental of rooms or other space for occupancy only. The supplying of maid service, for example, constitutes such services; whereas the furnishing of heat and light, the cleaning of public entrances, exits, stairways, and lobbies, the collection of trash, etc., are not considered as services rendered to the occupant. Payments for the use or occupancy of entire private residences or living quarters in duplex or multiple housing units, of offices in an office building, etc., are generally "rents" under section 1244 (c) (1) (E). Payments for the parking of automobiles ordinarily do not constitute rents. Payments for the warehousing of goods or for the use of personal property do not constitute rents if significant services are rendered in connection with such payments.

(iv) The term "dividends" as used in subdivision (i) of this subparagraph includes dividends as defined in section 316, amounts required to be included in gross income under section 551 (relating to foreign personal holding company income taxed to United States shareholders), and consent dividends determined as provided in section 565.

(v) The term "interest" as used in subdivision (i) of this subparagraph means any amounts received for the use of money (including tax-exempt interest).

(vi) The term "annuities" as used in subdivision (i) of this subparagraph means the entire amount received as an annuity under an annuity, endowment, or life insurance contract, regardless of whether only part of such amount would be includible in gross income under section 72.

(vii) For purposes of subdivision (i) of this subparagraph, gross receipts from the sales or exchanges of stock or securities are taken into account only to the extent of gains therefrom. Thus, the gross receipts from the sale of a particular share of stock will be the excess of the amount realized over the adjusted basis of such share. If the adjusted basis should equal or ex-ceed the amount realized on the sale or exchange of a certain share of stock, bond, etc., there would be no gross receipts resulting from the sale of such security. Losses on sales or exchanges of stock or securities do not offset gains on the sales or exchanges of other stock or securities for purposes of computing gross receipts from such sales or exchanges. Gross receipts from the sale or exchange of stocks and securities include gains received from such sales or exchanges by a corporation even though such corporation is a regular dealer in stocks and securities. For the meaning of the term "stocks or securities", see paragraph (b) (5) (i) of § 1.543–1.

(2) The requirement of subparagraph (1) of this paragraph need not be satisfied if for the applicable period the aggregate amount of deductions allowed to the corporation exceeds the aggregate amount of its gross income. But for this purpose the deductions allowed by section 172, relating to the net operating loss deduction, and by sections 242, 243, 244, and 245, relating to certain special deductions for corporations, shall not be taken into account. Notwithstanding the provisions of this subparagraph and of subparagraph (1) of this paragraph, pursuant to the specific delegation of authority granted in section 1244(e) to prescribe such regulations as may be necessary to carry out the purposes of section 1244, ordinary loss treatment will not be available with respect to stock of a corporation which is not largely an operating company within the five most recent taxable years (or such lesser period as the corporation is in existence) ending before the date of the loss. Thus, for example, assume that a person who is not a dealer in real estate forms a corporation which issues stock to him which meets all the formal requirements of section 1244 stock. The corporation then acquires a piece of unimproved real estate which it holds as an investment. The property declines in value and the stockholder sells his stock at a loss. The loss does not qualify for ordinary loss treatment under section 1244 but must be treated as a treated as a capital loss.

(3) In applying subparagraphs (1) and (2) of this paragraph to a successor corporation in a reorganization described in section 368(a) (1) (F), such corporation shall be treated as the same

corporation as its predecessor. See paragraph (d) (2) of § 1.1244(d)-3.

(h) Subsequent offering. (1) Even though the plan satisfies the requirements of paragraph (c) of this section, if another offering of stock is made by the corporation subsequent to, or simultaneous with, the adoption of the plan, stock issued pursuant to the plan after such other offering shall not qualify as section 1244 stock. The issuance of stock options, stock rights, or stock warrants, at any time during the period of the plan, which are exercisable with respect to stock other than stock offered under the plan, shall be considered a subsequent offering. Likewise, the issuance of stock other than that offered under the plan shall be considered a subsequent offering. Since stock issued upon exercise of a conversion privilege is stock issued for a security, and stock issued pursuant to a stock option granted in whole or in part for services is not issued for money or other property, the issuance of securities with a conversion privilege and the issuance of such a stock option are subsequent offerings, because the conversion privilege and the stock option are exercisable with respect to stock other than that which may properly be offered under the plan. Stock issued under the plan before a subsequent offering is not disqualified by reason of such subsequent offering. The rule of this paragraph, together with the rule of paragraph (e) of this section, relating to offers prior to the adoption of the plan, limits section 1244 stock to stock issued by the corporation during a period when any stock issued by it must have been issued pursuant to the plan.

(2) Any modification of a plan that changes the offering to include preferred stock, or that increases the amount of stock that may be issued thereunder to such an extent that the requirements of section 1244(c) (1) (B) would not have been satisfied if determined with reference to such amount as of the date such plan was initially adopted, or that extends the period of time during which stock may be issued thereunder to more than two years from the date such plan was initially adopted, shall be considered a subsequent offering, and no stock issued thereafter may qualify. However, a corporation may withdraw a plan and adopt a new plan to issue stock. To determine whether stock issued pursuant to such new plan may qualify, section 1244(c) must be applied with respect to the new plan as of the date of its adoption. For example, amounts received for stock under the prior plan must be taken into account in determining whether the requirements of section 1244(c) (2), relating to definition of small business corporation, are satisfied. In applying the requirements of section 1244(c) (2) (B), reference should be made to equity capital as of the date the new plan is adopted. The same principles apply if the period of the initial plan expires and the corporation adopts a new plan.

§ 1.1244(c)-2 Small business corporation defined

(a) In general. A corporation is treated as a small business corporation if it is a domestic corporation that satisfies the requirements described in paragraph (b) or (c) of this section. The requirements of paragraph (b) of this section apply if a loss is sustained on post-November 1978 stock. The requirements of paragraph (c) of this section apply if a loss is sustained on pre-November 1978 stock. If losses are sustained on both pre-November 1978 stock and post-November 1978 stock in the same taxable year, the requirements of paragraph (b) of this section are applied to the corporation at the time of the issuance of the stock (as required by paragraph (b) in the case of a loss on post-November 1978 stock) in order to determine whether the loss on post-November 1978 stock qualifies as a section 1244 loss, and the requirements of paragraph (c) of this section are applied to the corporation at the time of the adoption of the plan (as required by paragraph (c) in the case of a loss on pre-November 1978 stock) in order to determine whether the loss on pre-November 1978 stock qualifies as a section 1244 loss. For definition of domestic corporation, see section 7701(a)(4) and the regulations under that section.

(b) Post-November 1978 stock—(1) Amount received by corporation for stock. Capital receipts of a small business corporation may not exceed $1,000,000. For purposes of this paragraph the term "capital receipts" means the aggregate dollar amount received by the corporation for its stock, as a contribution to capital, and as paid-in surplus. If the $1,000,000 limitation is exceeded, the rules of subparagraph (2) of this paragraph (b) apply. In making these determinations, (i) property is taken into account at its adjusted basis to the corporation (for determining gain) as of the date received by the corporation, and (ii) this aggregate amount is reduced by the amount of any liability to which the property was subject and by the amount of any liability assumed by the corporation at the time the property was received. Capital receipts are not reduced by distributions to shareholders, even though the distributions may be capital distributions.

(2) Requirement of designation in event $1,000,000 limitation exceeded. (i) If capital receipts exceed $1,000,000, the corporation shall designate as section 1244 stock certain shares of post-November 1978 common stock issued for money or other property in the transitional year. For purposes of this paragraph, the term "transitional year" means the first taxable year in which capital receipts exceed $1,000,000 and in which the corporation issues stock. This designation shall be made in accordance with the rules of subdivision (iii) of this paragraph (b)(2). The amount received for designated stock shall not exceed $1,000,000, less amounts received (i) in exchange for stock in years prior to the transitional year; (ii) as contributions to capital in years prior to the transitional year; and (iii) as paid-in surplus in years prior to the transitional year.

(ii) Post-November 1978 common stock issued for money or other property before the transitional year qualifies as section 1244 stock without affirmative designation by the corporation. Post-November 1978 common stock issued after the transitional year does not qualify as section 1244 stock.

(iii) The corporation shall make the designation required by subdivision (i), of this paragraph (b)(2) not later than the 15th day of the third month following the close of the transitional year. However, in the case of post-November 1978 common stock issued on or before June 2, 1981 the corporation shall make the required designation by August 3, 1981 or by the 15th day of the 3rd month following the close of the transitional

year, whichever is later. The designation shall be made by entering the numbers of the qualifying share certificates on the corporation's records. If the shares do not bear serial numbers or other identifying numbers or letters or are not represented by share certificates, the corporation shall make an alternative designation in writing at the time of issuance, or, in the case of post-November 1978 common stock issued on or before June 2, 1981 by August 3, 1981. This alternative designation may be made in any manner sufficient to identify the shares qualifying for section 1244 treatment. If the corporation fails to make a designation by share certificate number or an alternative written designation as described, the rules of subparagraph (3) of this paragraph (b) apply.

. . . . .

§ 1.1245–1 General rule for treatment of gain from dispositions of certain depreciable property

(a) General. (1) In general, section 1245(a) (1) provides that, upon a disposition of an item of section 1245 property, the amount by which the lower of (i) the "recomputed basis" of the property, or (ii) the amount realized on a sale, exchange, or involuntary conversion (or the fair market value of the property on any other disposition), exceeds the adjusted basis of the property shall be treated as gain from the sale or exchange of property which is neither a capital asset nor property described in section 1231 (that is, shall be recognized as ordinary income). The amount of such gain shall be determined separately for each item of section 1245 property. In general, the term "recomputed basis" means the adjusted basis of property plus all adjustments reflected in such adjusted basis on account of depreciation allowed or allowable for all periods after December 31, 1961. See section 1245(a) (2) and § 1.1245–2. Generally, the ordinary income treatment applies even though in the absence of section 1245 no gain would be recognized under the Code. For example, if a corporation distributes section 1245 property as a dividend, gain may be recognized as ordinary income to the corporation even though, in the absence of section 1245, section 311(a) would preclude any recognition of gain to the corporation. For the definition of "section 1245 property", see section 1245(a) (3) and § 1.1245-3. For exceptions and limitations to the application of section 1245(a) (1), see section 1245(b) and § 1.1245-4.

(2) Section 1245(a) (1) applies to dispositions of section 1245 property in taxable years beginning after December 31, 1962, except that—

(i) In respect of section 1245 property which is an elevator or escalator, section 1245(a) (1) applies to dispositions after December 31, 1963, and

(ii) In respect of section 1245 property which is livestock (described in subparagraph (4) of § 1.1245-3(a)), section 1245(a) (1) applies to dispositions made in taxable years beginning after December 31, 1969, and (iii) [reserved].

(3) For purposes of this section and §§ 1.1245-2 through 1.1245-6, the term "disposition" includes a sale in a sale-and-leaseback transaction and a transfer upon the foreclosure of a security interest, but such term does not include a mere transfer of title to a creditor upon creation of a security interest or to a debtor upon termination of a security interest. Thus, for example, a disposition occurs upon a sale of property pursuant to a conditional sales contract even though the seller retains legal title to the property for purposes of security but a disposition does not occur when the seller ultimately gives up his security interest following payment by the purchaser.

. . . .

(5) In case of a sale, exchange, or involuntary conversion of section 1245 and nonsection 1245 property in one transaction, the total amount realized upon the disposition shall be allocated between the section 1245 property and the nonsection 1245 property in proportion to their respective fair market values. In general, if a buyer and seller have adverse interests as to the allocation of the amount realized between the section 1245 property and the nonsection 1245 property, any arm's length agreement between the buyer and the seller will establish the allocation. In the absence of such an agreement, the allocation shall be made by taking into account the appropriate facts and circumstances. Some of the facts and circumstances which shall be taken into account to the extent appropriate include, but are not limited to, a comparison between the section 1245 property and all the property disposed of in such transaction of (i) the original cost and reproduction cost of construction, erection, or production, (ii) the remaining economic useful life, (iii) state of obsolescence, and (iv) anticipated expenditures to maintain, renovate, or to modernize.

(b) Sale, exchange, or involuntary conversion. (1) In the case of a sale, exchange, or involuntary conversion of section 1245 property, the gain to which section 1245(a) (1) applies is the amount by which (i) the lower of the amount realized upon the disposition of the property or the recomputed basis of the property, exceeds (ii) the adjusted basis of the property.

(2) The provisions of this paragraph may be illustrated by the following examples:

Example (1). On January 1, 1964, Brown purchases section 1245 property for use in his manufacturing business. The property has a basis for depreciation of $3,300. After taking depreciation deductions of $1,300 (the amount allowable), Brown realizes after selling expenses the amount of $2,900 upon sale of the property on January 1, 1969. Brown's gain is $900 ($2,900 amount realized minus $2,000 adjusted basis). Since the amount realized upon disposition of the property ($2,900) is lower than its recomputed basis ($3,300, i. e., $2,000 adjusted basis plus $1,300 in depreciation deductions), the entire gain is treated as ordinary income under section 1245(a) (1) and not as gain from the sale or exchange of property described in section 1231.

Example (2). Assume the same facts as in example (1) except that Brown exchanges the section 1245 property for land which has a fair market value of $3,700, thereby realizing a gain of $1,700 ($3,700 amount realized minus $2,000 adjusted basis). Since the recomputed basis of the property ($3,300) is lower than the amount realized upon its disposition ($3,700), the excess of recomputed basis over adjusted basis, or $1,300, is treated as ordinary income under section 1245(a) (1). The remaining $400 of the gain may be treated as gain from the sale or exchange of property described in section 1231.

(c) Other dispositions. (1) In the case of a disposition of section 1245 property other than by way of a sale, exchange, or involuntary conversion, the gain to which section 1245(a) (1) applies is the amount by which (i) the lower of the fair market value of the property on the date of disposition or the recomputed basis of the property, exceeds (ii) the adjusted basis of the property. If property is transferred by a corporation to a shareholder for an amount less than its fair market value in a sale or exchange, for purposes of applying section 1245 such transfer shall be treated as a disposition other than by way of a sale, exchange, or involuntary conversion.

(2) The provisions of this paragraph may be illustrated by the following examples:

Example (1). X Corporation distributes section 1245 property to its shareholders as a dividend. The property has an adjusted basis of $2,000 to the corporation, a recomputed basis of $3,300, and a fair market value of $3,100. Since the fair market value of the property ($3,100) is lower than its recomputed basis ($3,300), the excess of fair market value over adjusted basis, or $1,100, is treated under section 1245(a) (1) as ordinary income to the corporation even though, in the absence of section 1245, section 311(a) would preclude recognition of gain to the corporation.

Example (2). Assume the same facts as in example (1) except that X Corporation distributes the section 1245 property to its shareholders in complete liquidation of the corporation. Assume further that section 1245(b) (3) does not apply and that the fair market value of the property is $3,800 at the time of the distribution. Since the recomputed basis of the property ($3,300) is lower than its fair market value ($3,800), the excess of recomputed basis over adjusted basis, or $1,300, is treated under section 1245(a) (1) as ordinary income to the corporation even though, in the absence of section 1245, section 336 would preclude recognition of gain to the corporation.

(d) Losses. Section 1245(a) (1) does not apply to losses. Thus, section 1245 (a) (1) does not apply if a loss is realized upon a sale, exchange, or involuntary conversion of property, all of which is considered section 1245 property, nor does the section apply to a disposition of such property other than by way of sale, exchange, or involuntary conversion if at the time of the disposition the fair market value of such property is not greater than its adjusted basis.

. . . . .

§ 1.1245-2   Definition of recomputed basis

(a) General rule—(1) Recomputed basis defined. The term "recomputed basis" means, with respect to any property, an amount equal to the sum of—

(i) The adjusted basis of the property, as defined in section 1011, plus

(ii) The amount of the adjustments reflected in the adjusted basis.

(2) Definition of adjustments reflected in adjusted basis. The term "adjust-

ments reflected in the adjusted basis" means—

(i) With respect to any property other than property described in subdivision (ii), (iii), or (iv) of this subparagraph, the amount of the adjustments attributable to periods after December 31, 1961,

(ii) With respect to an elevator or escalator, the amount of the adjustments attributable to periods after June 30, 1963,

(iii) With respect to livestock (described in subparagraph (4) of § 1.-1245-3(a)), the amount of the adjustments attributable to periods after December 31, 1969, or (iv) [reserved] which are reflected in the adjusted basis of such property on account of deductions allowed or allowable for depreciation or amortization (within the meaning of subparagraph (3) of this paragraph). For cases where the taxpayer can establish that the amount allowed for any period was less than the amount allowable, see subparagraph (7) of this paragraph. . . . . .

(3) Meaning of "depreciation or amortization". (i) For purposes of subparagraph (2) of this paragraph, the term "depreciation or amortization" includes allowances (and amounts treated as allowances) for depreciation (or amortization in lieu thereof), and deductions for amortization of emergency facilities under section 168. Thus, for example, such term includes a reasonable allowance for exhaustion, wear and tear (including a reasonable allowance for obsolescence) under section 167, an additional first-year depreciation allowance for small business under section 179, an expenditure treated as an amount allowed under section 167 by reason of the application of section 182 (d) (2) (B) (relating to expenditures by farmers for clearing land), and a deduction for depreciation of improvements under section 611 (relating to depletion). For further examples, the term "depreciation or amortization" includes periodic deductions referred to in § 1.162-11 in respect of a specified sum paid for the acquisition of a leasehold and in respect of the cost to a lessee of improvements on property of which he is the lessee. However, such term does not include deductions for the periodic payment of rent.

(ii) The provisions of this subparagraph may be illustrated by the following example:

Example. On January 1, 1966, Smith purchases for $1,000, and places in service, an item of property described in section 1245(a) (3) (A). Smith deducts an additional first-year allowance for depreciation under section 179 of $200. Accordingly, the basis of the property for purposes of depreciation is $800 on January 1, 1966. Between that date and January 1, 1974, Smith deducts $640 in depreciation (the amount allowable) with respect to the property, thereby reducing its adjusted basis to $160. Since this adjusted basis reflects deductions for depreciation and amortization (within the meaning of this subparagraph) amounting to $840 ($200 plus $640), the recomputed basis of the property is $1,000 ($160 plus $840).

. . . . .

(7) Depreciation or amortization allowed or allowable. For purposes of determining recomputed basis generally all adjustments (for periods after Dec. 31, 1961, or, in the case of property described in subparagraph (2) (ii), (iii), or (iv) of this paragraph, for periods after the applicable date) attributable to allowed or allowable depreciation or amortization must be taken into account. See section 1016(a) (2) and the regulations thereunder for the meaning of "allowed" and "allowable". However, if a taxpayer can establish by adequate records or other sufficient evidence that the amount allowed for depreciation or amortization for any period was less than the amount allowable for such period, the amount to be taken into account for such period shall be the amount allowed. No adjustment is to be made on account of the tax imposed by section 56 (relating to the minimum tax for tax preferences). See paragraph (b) of this section (relating to records to be kept and information to be filed). For example, assume that in the year 1967 it becomes necessary to determine the recomputed basis of property, the $500 adjusted basis of which reflects adjustments of $1,000 with respect to depreciation deductions allowable for periods after December 31, 1961. If the taxpayer can establish by adequate records or other sufficient evidence that he had been allowed deductions amounting to only $800 for the period, then in determining recomputed basis the amount added to adjusted basis with respect to the $1,000 adjustments to basis for the period will be only $800.

. . . . .

(c) Adjustments reflected in adjusted basis immediately after certain acquisitions—(1) Zero. (i) If on the date a person acquires property his basis for the property is determined solely by reference to its cost (within the meaning of section 1012), then on such date the amount of the adjustments reflected in his adjusted basis for the property is zero.

(ii) If on the date a person acquires property his basis for the property is determined solely by reason of the application of section 301(d) (relating to basis of property received in corporate distribution) or section 334(a) (relating to basis of property received in a liquidation in which gain or loss is recognized), then on such date the amount of the adjustments reflected in his adjusted basis for the property is zero.

(iii) If on the date a person acquires property his basis for the property is determined solely under the rules of section 334(b) (2) or (c) relating to basis of property received in certain corporate liquidations), then on such date the amount of the adjustments reflected in his adjusted basis for the property is zero.

(iv) If as of the date a person acquires property from a decedent such person's basis is determined, by reason of the application of section 1014(a), solely by reference to the fair market value of the property on the date of the decedent's death or on the applicable date provided in section 2032 (relating to alternate valuation date), then on such date the amount of the adjustments reflected in his adjusted basis for the property is zero.

(2) Gifts and certain tax-free transactions. (i) If property is disposed of in a transaction described in subdivision (ii) of this subparagraph, then the amount of the adjustments reflected in the adjusted basis of the property in the hands of a transferee immediately after the disposition shall be an amount equal to—

(a) The amount of the adjustments reflected in the adjusted basis of the property in the hands of the transferor immediately before the disposition, minus

(b) The amount of any gain taken into account under section 1245(a) (1) by the transferor upon the disposition.

(ii) The transactions referred to in subdivision (i) of this subparagraph are—

(a) A disposition which is in part a sale or exchange and in part a gift (see paragraph (a) (3) of § 1.1245–4),

(b) A disposition (other than a disposition to which section 1245(b) (6) (A) applies) which is described in section 1245(b) (3) (relating to certain tax-free transactions), or

(c) An exchange described in paragraph (e) (2) of § 1.1245–4 (relating to transfers described in section 1081(d) (1) (A)).

(iii) The provisions of this subparagraph may be illustrated by the following example:

Example. Jones transfers section 1245 property to a corporation in exchange for stock of the corporation and $1,000 cash in a transaction which qualifies under section 351 (relating to transfer to a corporation controlled by transferor). Before the exchange the amount of the adjustments reflected in the adjusted basis of the property is $3,000. Upon the exchange $1,000 gain is recognized under section 1245(a) (1). Immediately after the exchange, the amount of the adjustments reflected in the adjusted basis of the property in the hands of the corporation is $2,000 (that is, $3,000 minus $1,000).

. . . . .

(4) Property received in a like kind exchange, involuntary conversion, or F. C.C. transaction. (i) If property is acquired in a transaction described in subdivision (ii) of this subparagraph, then immediately after the acquisition (and before applying subparagraph (5) of this paragraph, if applicable) the amount of the adjustments reflected in the adjusted basis of the property acquired shall be an amount equal to—

(a) The amount of the adjustments reflected in the adjusted basis of the property disposed of immediately before the disposition, minus

(b) The sum of (1) the amount of any gain recognized under section 1245 (a) (1) upon the disposition, plus (2) the amount of gain (if any) referred to in subparagraph (5) (ii) of this paragraph.

. . . . .

§ 1.1245–3 Definition of section 1245 property

(a) In general. (1) The term "section 1245 property" means any property (other than livestock excluded by the effective date limitation in subparagraph (4) of this paragraph) which

is or has been property of a character subject to the allowance for depreciation provided in section 167 and which is either—

(i) Personal property (within the meaning of paragraph (b) of this section),

(ii) Property described in section 1245(a) (3) (B) (see paragraph (c) of this section), or

(iii) An elevator or an escalator within the meaning of subparagraph (C) of section 48(a) (1) (relating to the definition of "section 38 property" for purposes of the investment credit), but without regard to the limitations in such subparagraph (C).

(2) If property is section 1245 property under a subdivision of subparagraph (1) of this paragraph, a leasehold of such property is also section 1245 property under such subdivision. Thus, for example, if A owns personal property which is section 1245 property under subparagraph (1) (i) of this paragraph, and if A leases the personal property to B, B's leasehold is also section 1245 property under such provision. For a further example, if C owns and leases to D for a single lump-sum payment of $100,000 property consisting of land and a fully equipped factory building thereon, and if 40 percent of the fair market value of such property is properly allocable to section 1245 property, then 40 percent of D's leasehold is also section 1245 property. A leasehold of land is not section 1245 property.

(3) Even though property may not be of a character subject to the allowance for depreciation in the hands of the taxpayer, such property may nevertheless be section 1245 property if the taxpayer's basis for the property is determined by reference to its basis in the hands of a prior owner of the property and such property was of a character subject to the allowance for depreciation in the hands of such prior owner, or if the taxpayer's basis for the property is determined by reference to the basis of other property which in the hands of the taxpayer was property of a character subject to the allowance for depreciation. Thus, for example, if a father uses an automobile in his trade or business during a period after December 31, 1961, and then gives the automobile to his son as a gift for the son's personal use, the automobile is section 1245 property in the hands of the son.

(4) Section 1245 property includes livestock, but only with respect to taxable years beginning after December 31, 1969. For purposes of section 1245, the term "livestock" includes horses, cattle, hogs, sheep, goats, and mink and other furbearing animals, irrespective of the use to which they are put or the purpose for which they are held.

(b) Personal property defined. The term "personal property" means—

(1) Tangible personal property (as defined in paragraph (c) of § 1.48–1, relating to the definition of "section 38 property" for purposes of the investment credit), and

(2) Intangible personal property.

(c) Property described in section 1245(a) (3) (B). (1) The term "property described in section 1245(a) (3) (B)" means tangible property of the requisite depreciable character other than personal property (and other than a building and its structural components), but only if there are adjustments reflected in the adjusted basis of the property (within the meaning of paragraph (a) (2) of § 1.1245–2) for a period during which such property (or other property)—

(i) Was used as an integral part of manufacturing, production, or extraction, or as an integral part of furnishing transportation, communications, electrical energy, gas, water, or sewage disposal services by a person engaged in a trade or business of furnishing any such service, or

(ii) Constituted a research or storage facility used in connection with any of the foregoing activities.

Thus, even though during the period immediately preceding its disposition the property is not used as an integral part of an activity specified in subdivision (i) of this subparagraph and does not constitute a facility specified in subdivision (ii) of this subparagraph, such property is nevertheless property described in section 1245(a) (3) (B) if, for example, there are adjustments reflected in the adjusted basis of the property for a period during which the property was used as an integral part of manufacturing by the taxpayer or another taxpayer, or for a period during which other property (which was involuntarily converted into, or exchanged in a like kind exchange for, the property) was so used by the taxpayer or another

taxpayer. For rules applicable to involuntary conversions and like kind exchanges, see paragraph (d) (3) of § 1.-1245–4.

· · · ·

§ 1.1245–4 Exceptions and limitations

(a) Exception for gifts—(1) General rule. Section 1245(b) (1) provides that no gain shall be recognized under section 1245(a) (1) upon a disposition by gift. For purposes of this paragraph, the term "gift" means, except to the extent that subparagraph (3) of this paragraph applies, a transfer of property which, in the hands of the transferee, has a basis determined under the provisions of section 1015(a) or (d) (relating to basis of property acquired by gifts). For reduction in amount of charitable contribution in case of a gift of section 1245 property, see section 170 (e) and the regulations thereunder.

· · · ·

(3) Disposition in part a sale or exchange and in part a gift. Where a disposition of property is in part a sale or exchange and in part a gift, the gain to which section 1245(a) (1) applies is the amount by which (i) the lower of the amount realized upon the disposition of the property or the recomputed basis of the property, exceeds (ii) the adjusted basis of the property. For determination of the recomputed basis of the property in the hands of the transferee, see paragraph (c) (2) of § 1.1245–2.

(4) Example. The provisions of subparagraph (3) of this paragraph may be illustrated by the following example:

Example. (i) Smith transfers section 1245 property, which he has held in excess of 1 year (6 months for taxable years beginning before 1977; 9 months for taxable years beginning in 1977), to his son for $60,000. Immediately before the transfer the property in the hands of Smith has an adjusted basis of $30,000, a fair market value of $90,000, and a recomputed basis of $110,000. Since the amount realized upon disposition of the property ($60,000) is lower than its recomputed basis ($110,000), the excess of the amount realized over adjusted basis, or $30,000, is treated as ordinary income under section 1245(a)(1) and not as gain from the sale or exchange of property described in section 1231. Smith has made a gift of $30,000 ($90,000 fair market value minus $60,000 amount realized) to which section 1245 (a)(1) does not apply.

(ii) Immediately before the transfer, the amount of adjustments reflected in the adjusted basis of the property was $80,000. Under paragraph (c)(2) of § 1.1245-2, $50,000 of adjustments are reflected in the adjusted basis of the property immediately after the transfer, that is, $80,00 of such adjustments immediately before the transfer, minus $30,000 gain taken into account under section 1245(a)(1) upon the transfer. Thus, the recomputed basis of the property in the hands of the son is $110,000.

• • • •

(c) **Limitation for certain tax-free transactions—(1) Limitation on amount of gain.** Section 1245(b) (3) provides that upon a transfer of property described in subparagraph (2) of this paragraph, the amount of gain taken into account by the transferor under section 1245(a) (1) shall not exceed the amount of gain recognized to the transferor on the transfer (determined without regard to section 1245). For purposes of this subparagraph, in case of a transfer of both section 1245 property and non-section 1245 property in one transaction, the amount realized from the disposition of the section 1245 property (as determined under paragraph (a) (5) of § 1.1245-1) shall be deemed to consist of that portion of the fair market value of each property acquired which bears the same ratio to the fair market value of such acquired property as the amount realized from the disposition of the section 1245 property bears to the total amount realized. The preceding sentence shall be applied solely for purposes of computing the portion of the total gain (determined without regard to section 1245) which shall be recognized as ordinary income under section 1245(a) (1). For determination of the recomputed basis of the section 1245 property in the hands of the transferee, see paragraph (c) (2) of § 1.1245-2. Section 1245(b) (3) does not apply to a disposition of property to an organization (other than a cooperative described in section 521) which is exempt from the tax imposed by chapter 1 of the Code.

(2) **Transfers covered.** The transfers referred to in subparagraph (1) of this paragraph are transfers of property in which the basis of the property in the hands of the transferee is determined by reference to its basis in the hands of the transferor by reason of the application of any of the following provisions:

(i) Section 332 (relating to distributions in complete liquidation of an 80-percent-or-more controlled subsidiary

corporation). See subparagraph (3) of this paragraph.

(ii) Section 351 (relating to transfer to a corporation controlled by transferor).

(iii) Section 361 (relating to exchanges pursuant to certain corporate reorganizations).

• • • •

(vi) Section 721 (relating to transfers to a partnership in exchange for a partnership interest).

(vii) Section 731 (relating to distributions by a partnership to a partner). For special carryover basis rule, see section 1245(b) (6) (A) and paragraph (f) (1) of this section.

(3) **Complete liquidation of subsidiary.** In the case of a distribution in complete liquidation of an 80-percent-or-more controlled subsidiary to which section 332 applies, the limitation provided in section 1245(b) (3) is confined to instances in which the basis of the property in the hands of the transferee is determined, under section 334(b) (1), by reference to its basis in the hands of the transferor. Thus, for example, the limitation of section 1245(b) (3) may apply in respect of a liquidating distribution of section 1245 property by an 80-percent-or-more controlled corporation to the parent corporation, but does not apply in respect of a liquidating distribution of section 1245 property to a minority shareholder. Section 1245(b) (3) does not apply to a liquidating distribution of property by an 80-percent-or-more controlled subsidiary to its parent if the parent's basis for the property is determined, under section 334(b) (2), by reference to its basis for the stock of the subsidiary.

(4) **Examples.** The provisions of this paragraph may be illustrated by the following examples:

Example (1). Section 1245 property, which is owned by Smith, has a fair market value of $10,000, a recomputed basis of $8,000, and an adjusted basis of $4,000. Smith transfers the property to a corporation in exchange for stock in the corporation worth $9,000 plus $1,000 in cash in a transaction qualifying under section 351. Without regard to section 1245, Smith would recognize $1,000 gain under section 351 (b), and the corporation's basis for the property would be determined under section 362(a) by reference to its basis in the hands of Smith. Since the recomputed basis of the property disposed of ($8,000) is lower than the amount realized ($10,000), the excess of recomputed basis over adjusted basis ($4,000), or $4,000, would be treated as ordinary income under section 1245(a) (1) if the provisions of section 1245(b) (3) did not apply. However, section 1245(b) (3) limits the gain taken into account by Smith under section 1245(a) (1) to $1,000. If, instead, Smith transferred the property to the corporation solely in exchange for stock of the corporation worth $10,000, then, because of the application of section 1245(b) (3), Smith would not take any gain into account under section 1245(a) (1). If, however, Smith transferred the property to the corporation for stock worth $5,000 and $5,000 cash, only $4,000 of the $5,000 gain under section 351(b) would be treated as ordinary income under section 1245(a) (1).

Example (2). Assume the same facts as in example (1) except that Smith contributes the property to a new partnership in which he has a one-half interest. Since, without regard to section 1245, no gain would be recognized to Smith under section 721, and by reason of the application of section 721 the partnership's basis for the property would be determined under section 723 by reference to its basis in the hands of Smith, the application of section 1245(b) (3) results in no gain being taken into account by Smith under section 1245 (a) (1).

* * * * *

§ 1.1245-6 Relation of section 1245 to other sections

(a) General. The provisions of section 1245 apply notwithstanding any other provision of subtitle A of the Code. Thus, unless an exception or limitation under section 1245(b) applies, gain under section 1245(a) (1) is recognized notwithstanding any contrary nonrecognition provision or income characterizing provision. For example, since section 1245 overrides section 1231 (relating to property used in the trade or business), the gain recognized under section 1245(a) (1) upon a disposition will be treated as ordinary income and only the remaining gain, if any, from the disposition may be considered as gain from the sale or exchange of a capital asset if section 1231 is applicable. See example (2) of paragraph (b) (2) of § 1.1245-1. For effect of section 1245 on basis provisions of the Code, see § 1.1245-5.

(b) Nonrecognition sections overridden. The nonrecognition provisions of subtitle A of the Code which section 1245 overrides include, but are not limited to, sections 267(d), 311(a), 336, 337, 501(a), 512(b)(5), and 1039. See section 1245(b) for the extent to which section 1245(a)(1) overrides sections 332, 351, 361, 371(a), 374(a), 721, 731, 1031, 1033, 1071, and 1081(b)(1) and (d)(1)(A). For limitation on amount of adjustments reflected in adjusted basis of property disposed of by an organization exempt from income taxes (within the meaning of section 501(a)), see paragraph (a)(8) of § 1.1245-2.

* * * * *

(d) Installment method. (1) Gain from a disposition to which section 1245 (a) (1) applies may be reported under the installment method if such method is otherwise available under section 453 of the Code. In such case, the income (other than interest) on each installment payment shall be deemed to consist of gain to which section 1245(a) (1) applies until all such gain has been reported, and the remaining portion (if any) of such income shall be deemed to consist of gain to which section 1245(a) (1) does not apply. For treatment of amounts as interest on certain deferred payments, see section 483.

(2) The provisions of this paragraph may be illustrated by the following example:

Example. Jones contracts to sell an item of section 1245 property for $10,000 to be paid in 10 equal payments of $1,000 each, plus a sufficient amount of interest so that section 483 does not apply. He properly elects under section 453 to report under the installment method gain of $2,000 to which section 1245(a) (1) applies and gain of $1,000 to which section 1231 applies. Accordingly, $300 of each of the first 6 installment payments and $200 of the seventh installment payment is ordinary income under section 1245(a) (1), and $100 of the seventh installment payment and $300 of each of the last 3 installment payments is gain under section 1231.

* * * * *

(f) Treatment of gain not recognized under section 1245. Section 1245 does not prevent gain which is not recognized under section 1245 from being considered as gain under another provision of the Code, such as, for example, section 311(c) (relating to liability in excess of basis), section 341(f) (relating to collapsible corporations), section 357 (c) (relating to liabilities in excess of basis), section 1238 (relating to amortization in excess of depreciation), or section 1239 (relating to gain from sale of depreciable property between certain related persons). Thus, for example, if section 1245 property, which has an adjusted basis of $1,000 and a recomputed basis of $1,500, is sold for $1,750 in a transaction to which section 1239 applies, $500 of the gain would be recognized under section 1245(a) (1) and the remaining $250 of the gain would be treated as ordinary income under section 1239.

§ 1.1250-1   Gain from dispositions of certain depreciable realty

(a) **Dispositions after December 31, 1969—(1) Ordinary income.** (i) In general, section 1250(a) (1) provides that, upon a disposition of an item of section 1250 property after December 31, 1969, the applicable percentage of the lower of—

(a) The additional depreciation (as defined in § 1.1250-2) attributable to periods after December 31, 1969 in respect of the property, or

(b) The excess of the amount realized on a sale, exchange, or involuntary conversion (or the fair market value of the property on any other disposition) over the adjusted basis of the property,

shall be treated as gain from the sale or exchange of property which is neither a capital asset nor property described in section 1231 (that is, shall be recognized as ordinary income). The amount of such gain shall be determined separately for each item (see subparagraph (2) (ii) of this paragraph) of section 1250 property. If the amount determined under (b) of this subdivision exceeds the amount determined under (a) of this subdivision, then such excess shall be treated as provided in subdivision (ii) of this subparagraph. For relation of section 1250 to other provisions, see paragraph (c) of this section.

(ii) If the amount determined under subdivision (i) (b) of this subparagraph exceeds the amount determined under subdivision (i) (a) of this subparagraph, then the applicable percentage of the lower of—

(a) The additional depreciation attributable to periods before January 1, 1970, or

(b) Such excess,

shall also be recognized as ordinary income.

(iii) If gain would be recognized upon a disposition of an item of section 1250 property under subdivisions (i) and (ii) of this subparagraph, and if section 1250(d) applies, then the gain recognized shall be considered as recognized first under subdivision (i) of this subparagraph. (See example (3) (i) of paragraph (c) (4) of § 1.1250-3.)

(2) **Meaning of terms.** (i) For purposes of section 1250, the term "disposition" shall have the same meaning as in paragraph (a) (3) of § 1.1245-1. "Section 1250 property" is, in general, depreciable real property other than section 1245 property. See paragraph (e) of this section. See paragraph (d) (1) of this section for meaning of the term "applicable percentage." If, however, the property is considered to have two or more elements with separate periods (for example, because units thereof are placed in service on different dates, improvements are made to the property, or because of the application of paragraph (h) of § 1.1250-3), see the special rules of § 1.1250-5.

(ii) For purposes of applying section 1250, the facts and circumstances of each disposition shall be considered in determining what is the appropriate item of section 1250 property. In general, a building is an item of section 1250 property, but in an appropriate case more than one building may be treated as a single item. For example, if two or more buildings or structures on a single tract or parcel (or contiguous tracts or parcels) of land are operated as an integrated unit (as evidenced by their actual operation, management, financing, and accounting), they may be treated as a single item of section 1250 property. For the manner of determining whether an expenditure shall be treated as an addition to capital account of an item of section 1250 property or as a separate item of section 1250 property, see paragraph (d) (2) (iii) of § 1.1250-5.

(3) **Sale, exchange, or involuntary conversion after December 31, 1969.** (i) In the case of a disposition of section 1250 property by a sale, exchange, or involuntary conversion after December 31, 1969, the gain to which section 1250 (a) (1) applies is the applicable percentage for the property (determined under paragraph (d) (1) of this section) multiplied by the lower of (a) the additional depreciation in respect of the

property attributable to periods after December 31, 1969, or (b) the excess (referred to as "gain realized") of the amount realized over the adjusted basis of the property.

(ii) In addition to gain recognized under section 1250(a) (1) and subdivision (i) of this subparagraph, gain may also be recognized under section 1250 (a) (2) and this subdivision if the gain realized exceeds the additional depreciation attributable to periods after December 31, 1969. In such a case, the amount of gain recognized under section 1250 (a) (2) and this subdivision is the applicable percentage for the property (determined under paragraph (d) (2) of this section) multiplied by the lower of (a) the additional depreciation attributable to periods before January 1, 1970, or (b) the excess (referred to as "remaining gain") of the gain realized over the additional depreciation attributable to periods after December 31, 1969.

. . . . .

(5) Instances of nonapplication. (i) Section 1250(a) (1) does not apply to losses. Thus, section 1250(a) (1) does not apply if a loss is realized upon a sale, exchange, or involuntary conversion of property, all of which is considered section 1250 property, nor does the section apply to a disposition of such property other than by way of sale, exchange, or involuntary conversion if at the time of the disposition the fair market value of such property is not greater than its adjusted basis.

(ii) In general, in the case of section 1250 property with a holding period under section 1223 of more than 1 year, section 1250(a) (1) does not apply if for periods after December 31, 1969, there are no "depreciation adjustments in excess of straight line" (as computed under section 1250(b) and paragraph (b) of § 1.1250–2).

(6) Allocation rules. (i) In the case of a sale, exchange, or involuntary conversion of section 1250 property and non-section 1250 property in one transaction after December 31, 1969, the total amount realized upon the disposition shall be allocated between the section 1250 property and the other property in proportion to their respective fair market values. Such allocation shall be made in accordance with the principles set forth in paragraph (a) (5) of § 1.-1245–1 (relating to allocation between section 1245 property and nonsection 1245 property).

(ii) If an item of section 1250 property has two (or more) applicable percentages because one subdivision of paragraph (d) (1) (i) of this section applies to one portion of the taxpayer's holding period (determined under § 1.-1250–4) and another subdivision of such paragraph applies with respect to another such portion, then the gain realized on a sale, exchange, or involuntary conversion, or the potential gain in the case of any other disposition, shall be allocated to each such portion of the taxpayer's holding period after December 31, 1969, in the same proportion as the additional depreciation with respect to such item for such portion bears to the additional depreciation with respect to such item for the entire holding period after December 31, 1969.

. . . . .

(c) Relation of section 1250 to other provisions—(1) General. The provisions of section 1250 apply notwithstanding any other provision of subtitle A of the Code. See section 1250(i). Thus, unless an exception or limitation under section 1250(d) and § 1.1250–3 applies, gain under section 1250(a) is recognized notwithstanding any contrary nonrecognition provision or income characterizing provision. For example, since section 1250 overrides section 1231 (relating to property used in the trade or business), the gain recognized under section 1250 (a) upon a disposition will be treated as ordinary income and only the remaining gain, if any, from the disposition may be considered as gain from the sale or exchange of a capital asset if section 1231 is applicable. See the example in paragraph (b) (3) (ii) of this section.

(2) Nonrecognition sections overridden. The nonrecognition provisions of subtitle A of the Code which section 1250 overrides include, but are not limited to, sections 267(d), 311(a), 336, 337, 501(a), and 512(b) (5). See section 1250(d) for the extent to which section 1250(a) overrides sections 332, 351, 361, 371(a), 374(a), 721, 731, 1031, 1033, 1039, 1071, and 1081(b) (1) and

(d) (1) (A). For amount of additional depreciation in respect of property disposed of by an organization exempt from income taxes (within the meaning of section 501(a)), see paragraph (d) (6) of § 1.1250-2.

. . . .

(4) Treatment of gain not recognized under section 1250. Section 1250 does not prevent gain which is not recognized under section 1250 from being considered as gain under another provision of the Code, such as, for example, section 1239 (relating to gain from sale of depreciable property between certain related persons). Thus, for example, if section 1250 property which has an adjusted basis of $10,000 is sold for $17,-500 in a transaction to which section 1239 applies, and if $5,000 of the gain would be recognized under section 1250 (a) then the remaining $2,500 of the gain would be treated as ordinary income under section 1239.

. . . .

(6) Installment method. Gain from a disposition to which section 1250(a) applies may be reported under the installment method if such method is otherwise available under section 453 of the Code. In such case, the income (other than interest) on each installment payment shall be deemed to consist of gain to which section 1250(a) applies until all such gain has been reported, and the remaining portion (if any) of such income shall be deemed to consist of other gain. For treatment of amounts as interest on certain deferred payments, see section 483.

(d) Applicable percentage—(1) Definition for purposes of section 1250(a) (1). . . . .

(4) Full month. For purposes of this paragraph, the term "full month" (or "full months") means the period beginning on a date in 1 month and terminating on the date before the corresponding date in the next succeeding month (or in another succeeding month), or, if a particular succeeding month does not have such a corresponding date, terminating on the last day of such particular succeeding month.

(5) Examples. The provisions of this paragraph may be illustrated by the following examples:

Example (1). Property is purchased on January 17, 1959. Under paragraph (b) (1) of § 1.-1250-4, its holding period begins on January 18, 1959, and thus at any time during the period beginning on October 17, 1960, and ending on November 16, 1960, the property is considered held 21 full months and has an applicable percentage under section 1250(a) (2) of 99 percent. On and after January 17, 1969, the property has a holding period of at least 120 full months (10 years) and, therefore, the applicable percentage under section 1250(a) (2) for the property is zero. Accordingly, no gain would be recognized under section 1250(a) (2) upon disposition of the property. If, however, the property consists of two or more elements, see the special rules of § 1.-1250-5.

Example (2). Property is purchased on January 31, 1968. Under paragraph (b) (1) of § 1.-1250-4 its holding period begins on February 1, 1968, and thus at any time during the period beginning on February 29, 1968, and ending on March 30, 1968, the property is considered held 1 full month. At any time during the period beginning on March 31, 1970, and ending on April 29, 1970, the property is considered held 26 full months. At any time during the period beginning on April 30, 1970, and ending on May 30, 1970, the property is considered held 27 full months.

. . . .

(e) Section 1250 property—(1) Definition. The term "section 1250 property" means any real property (other than section 1245 property, as defined in section 1245(a) (3) and § 1.1245-3) which is or has been property of a character subject to the allowance for depreciation provided in section 167. See section 1250(c).

(2) Character of property. For purposes of subparagraph (1) of this paragraph, the term "is or has been property of a character subject to the allowance for depreciation provided in section 167" shall have the same meaning as when used in paragraph (a) (1) and (3) of § 1.1245-3. Thus, if a father uses a house in his trade or business during a period after December 31, 1963, and then gives the house to his son as a gift for the son's personal use, the house is section 1250 property in the hands of the son. For exception to the application of section 1250(a) upon disposition of a principal residence, see section 1250(d) (7).

(3) Real property. (i) For purposes of subparagraph (1) of this paragraph, the term "real property" means any property which is not personal property within the meaning of paragraph (b) of § 1.1245-3. The term section 1250 property includes three types of depreciable real property. The first type is intangible real property. For purposes of this paragraph, a leasehold of land or of section 1250 property is intangible real property, and accordingly such a leasehold is section 1250 property. However, a fee simple interest in land is not depreciable, and therefore is not section 1250 property. The second type is a building or its structural components within the meaning of paragraph (c) of § 1.1245-3. The third type is all other tangible real property except (a) "property described in section 1245(a) (3) (B)" as defined in paragraph (c) (1) of § 1.1245-3 (relating to property used as an integral part of a specified activity or as a specified facility), and (b) property described in section 1245(a) (3) (D). An elevator or escalator (within the meaning of section 1245(a) (3) (C)) is not section 1250 property.

(ii) The provisions of this subparagraph may be illustrated by the following example:

Example. A owns and leases to B for a single lump-sum payment of $100,000 property consisting of land and a fully equipped factory building thereon. If 30 percent of the fair market value of such property is properly allocable to the land, 25 percent to section 1250 property (the building and its structural components), and 45 percent to section 1245 property (the equipment), then 55 percent of B's leasehold is section 1250 property.

(4) Coordination with definition of section 1245 property. (i) Property may lose its character as section 1250 property and become section 1245 property. Thus, for example, if section 1250 property of the third type described in subparagraph (3) (i) (a) of this paragraph is converted to use as an integral part of manufacturing, the property would lose its character as section 1250 property and would become section 1245 property. However, once property in the hands of a taxpayer is section 1245 property, it can never become section 1250 property in the hands of such taxpayer. See also paragraph (a) (4) and (5) of § 1.1245-2.

.   .   .   .

§ 1.1250-2 Additional depreciation defined

(a) In general—(1) Definition for purposes of section 1250(b) (1). Except as otherwise provided in paragraph (e) of this section, for purposes of sec-

tion 1250(b) (1), the term "additional depreciation" means—

(i) In the case of property which at the time of disposition has a holding period under section 1223 of not more than 1 year, the "depreciation adjustments" (as defined in paragraph (d) of this section) in respect of such property for periods after December 31, 1963, and

(ii) In the case of property which at the time of disposition has a holding period under section 1223 of more than 1 year, the depreciation adjustments in excess of straight line for periods after December 31, 1963, computed under paragraph (b) (1) of this section.

.   .   .   .

(b) Computation of depreciation adjustments in excess of straight line—(1) General rule. For purposes of paragraph (a) (1) of this section, depreciation adjustments in excess of straight line shall be, in the case of any property, the excess of (i) the sum of the "depreciation adjustments" (as defined in paragraph (d) of this section) in respect of the property attributable to periods after December 31, 1963, over (ii) the sum such adjustments would have been for such periods if such adjustments had been determined for the entire period the property was held under the straight line method of depreciation (or, if applicable, under the lease-renewal-period provision in paragraph (c) of this section). Depreciation in excess of straight line may arise, for example, if the declining balance method, the sum of the years-digits method, or the units of production method is used, or for another example, if the cost of a leasehold improvement or of a leasehold is depreciated over a period which does not take into account certain renewal periods referred to in paragraph (c) of this section. For computations of depreciation adjustments in excess of straight line (or a deficit therein) both on an annual basis and on the basis of the entire period the property was held, see subparagraph (6) of this paragraph.

.   .   .   .

(3) General rule for computing useful life and salvage value. For purposes of computing under subparagraph

(1) (ii) of this paragraph the sum the depreciation adjustments would have been under the straight line method, if a useful life (or salvage value) was used in determining the amount allowed as a depreciation adjustment for any taxable year, such life (or value) shall be used in determining the amount such depreciation adjustment would have been for such taxable year under the straight line method. If, however, for any taxable year a method of depreciation was used as to which a useful life was not taken into account such as, for example, the units of production method, or as to which salvage value was not taken into account in determining the annual allowances, such as, for example, the declining balance method or the amortization of a leasehold improvement over the term of a lease, then, for the purpose of determining the amount such depreciation adjustment would have been under the straight line method for such taxable year—

(i) There shall be used the useful life (or salvage value) which would have been proper if depreciation had actually been determined under the straight line method throughout the period the property was held, and

(ii) Such useful life (or such salvage value) shall be determined by taking into account for each taxable year the same facts and circumstances as would have been taken into account if the taxpayer had used such method throughout the period the property was held.

. . . . .

(c) Property held by lessee—(1) Amount depreciation would have been. For purposes of paragraph (b) of this section, in case of a leasehold which is section 1250 property, in determining the amount the depreciation adjustments would have been under the straight line method in respect of any building or other improvement (which is section 1250 property) erected or made on the leased property, or in respect of any cost of acquiring the lease, the lease period shall be treated as including all renewal periods. See section 1250(b) (2). For determination of the extent to which a leasehold is section 1250 property, see paragraph (e) (3) of § 1.1250–1.

(2) Renewal period. (i) For purposes of this paragraph, the term "renewal period" means any period for which the lease may be renewed, extended, or continued pursuant to an option or options exercisable by the lessee (whether or not specifically provided for in the lease) except that the inclusion of one or more renewal periods shall not extend the period taken into account by more than two-thirds of the period on the basis of which the depreciation adjustments were allowed.

(ii) In respect of the cost of any building erected (or other improvement made) on the leased property by the lessee, or in respect of the portion of the cost of acquiring a leasehold which is attributable to an existing building (or other improvement) on the leasehold at the time the lessee acquires the leasehold, the inclusion of one or more renewal periods shall not extend the period taken into account to a period which exceeds the useful life remaining, at the time the leasehold is disposed of, of such building (or such other improvement). Determinations under this subdivision shall be made without regard to the proper period under section 167 or 178 for depreciating or amortizing a leasehold acquisition cost or improvement.

(iii) The provisions of this subparagraph may be illustrated by the following example:

Example. Assume that a leasehold improvement with a useful life of 30 years is properly amortized on the basis of a 10-year initial lease term. The lease is renewable for an additional 9 years. The period taken into account is 16⅔ years, that is, 10 years plus two-thirds of 10 years. If, however, the leasehold improvement were disposed of at the end of 12 years, and if its remaining useful life were only 3 years, then the period taken into account would be 15 years.

(d) Depreciation adjustments—(1) General. For purposes of this section, the term "depreciation adjustments" means, in respect of any property, all adjustments reflected in the adjusted basis of such property on account of deductions described in subparagraph (2) of this paragraph allowed or allowable (whether in respect of the same or other property) to the taxpayer or to any other person. For cases where the taxpayer can establish that the amount allowed for any period was less than the amount allowable, see subparagraph (4) of this paragraph. For determination of adjusted basis of property in a multiple asset account, see paragraph (c) (3) of § 1.167(a)–8. The term "depreciation adjustments" as used in this section does not have the same meaning as the term "adjustments reflected in the adjusted basis" as defined in paragraph (a) (2) of § 1.-1245–2.

(2) **Deductions.** The deductions described in this subparagraph are allowances (and amounts treated as allowances) for depreciation or amortization (other than amortization under section 168, 169 (as enacted by section 704(a), Tax Reform Act of 1969 (83 Stat. 667)), or 185). Thus, for example, such deductions include a reasonable allowance for exhaustion, wear, and tear (including a reasonable allowance for obsolesence) under section 167, the periodic deductions referred to in § 1.162–11 in respect of a specified sum paid for the acquisition of a leasehold and in respect of the cost to a lessee of improvements on property of which he is the lessee. However, such deductions do not include deductions for the periodic payment of rent.

(3) **Depreciation of other taxpayers or in respect of other property.** (i) The depreciation adjustments (reflected in the adjusted basis) referred to in subparagraph (1) of this paragraph (a) are not limited to adjustments with respect to the property disposed of, nor to those allowed or allowable to the taxpayer disposing of such property, and (b) except as provided in subparagraph (4) of this paragraph, are taken into account, whether allowed or allowable in respect of the same or other property and whether to the taxpayer or to any other person. For manner of determining the amount of additional depreciation after certain dispositions, see paragraph (e) of this section.

(ii) The provisions of this subparagraph may be illustrated by the following example:

Example. On January 1, 1966, a calendar year taxpayer purchases for $100,000 a building for use in his trade or business. He takes depreciation deductions of $20,000 (the amount allowable), of which $3,000 is additional depreciation, and transfers the building to his son as a gift on January 1, 1968. Since the exception for gifts in section 1250(d) (1) applies, the taxpayer does not recognize gain under section 1250(a) (2). In the son's adjusted basis of $80,000 for

the building there is reflected $3,000 of additional depreciation. On January 1, 1969, after taking a depreciation deduction of $10,000 (the amount allowable), of which $1,000 is additional depreciation, the son sells the building. At the time of the sale the additional depreciation is $4,000 ($3,000 allowed the father plus $1,000 allowed the son).

(4) **Depreciation allowed or allowable.** (i) For purposes of subparagraph (1) of this paragraph, generally all deductions (described in subparagraph (2) of this paragraph) allowed or allowable shall be taken into account. See section 1016(a) (2) and the regulations thereunder for the meaning of "allowed" and "allowable." However, if a taxpayer can establish by adequate records or other sufficient evidence that the amount allowed for any period was less than the amount allowable for such period, the amount to be taken into account for such period shall be the amount allowed. The preceding sentence shall not apply for purposes of computing under paragraph (b) (1) (ii) of this section the amount such deductions would have been under the straight line method.

(ii) The provisions of subdivision (i) of this subparagraph may be illustrated by the following example:

Example. In the year 1969 it becomes necessary to determine the additional depreciation in respect of section 1250 property, the adjusted basis of which reflects a depreciation adjustment of $1,000 with respect to depreciation deductions allowable for the calendar year 1965 under the sum of the years-digits method. Under paragraph (b) (1) (ii) of this section, the depreciation which would have resulted under the straight line method for 1965 is $800. If the taxpayer can establish by adequate records or other sufficient evidence that he did not take, and was not allowed, any deduction for depreciation in respect of the property in 1965, then, for purposes of computing the depreciation adjustments in excess of straight line in respect of the property, the amount to be taken into account for 1965 as allowed or allowable is zero, and the amount to be taken into account in computing deductions which would have resulted under the straight line method in 1965 is $800. Thus, in effect, there is a deficit in additional depreciation for 1965 of $800.

. . . . .

(e) **Additional depreciation immediately after certain acquisitions—(1) Zero.** If on the date a person acquires property his basis for the property is determined solely (i) by reference to its cost (within the meaning of sec. 1012), (ii) by reason of the application of section 301(d) (relating to basis of property received in corporate distribution) or section 334(a) (relating to basis of property received in a liquidation in which gain or loss is recognized), or (iii) under the rules of section 334(b) (2) or (c) (relating to basis of property received in certain corporate liquidations), then on such date the additional depreciation for the property is zero.

(2) Transactions referred to in section 1250(d). In the case of property acquired in a disposition described in section 1250(d) (relating to exceptions and limitations to application of section 1250), additional depreciation shall be computed in accordance with the rules prescribed in § 1.1250-3.

. . . . .

§ 1.1250-3 Exceptions and limitations

(a) Exception for gifts—(1) General rule. Section 1250(d) (1) provides that no gain shall be recognized under section 1250(a) upon a disposition by gift. For purposes of this paragraph, the term "gift" shall have the same meaning as in paragraph (a) of § 1.1245-4. For reduction in amount of charitable contribution in case of a gift of section 1250 property, see section 170(e) and paragraph (c) (3) of § 1.170-1.

(2) Disposition in part a sale or exchange and in part a gift. Where a disposition of property is in part a sale or exchange and in part a gift, the disposition shall be subject to the provisions of § 1.1250-1 and the gain to which section 1250(a) applies, shall be computed under that section.

(3) Treatment of property in hands of transferee. If property is disposed of in a transaction which is a gift—

(i) The additional depreciation for the property in the hands of the transferee immediately after the disposition shall be an amount equal to (a) the amount of the additional depreciation for the property in the hands of the transferor immediately before the disposition, minus (b) the amount of any gain (in case the disposition is in part a sale or exchange and in part a gift) which would have been taken into account under section 1250(a) by the transferor upon the disposition if the applicable percentage had been 100 percent,

(ii) For purposes of computing the applicable percentage, the holding period under section 1250(e) (2) of property received as a gift in the hands of the transferee includes the transferor's holding period,

. . . . .

(c) Limitation for certain tax-free transactions—(1) General. Section 1250(d) (3) provides that upon a transfer of property described in subparagraph (2) of this paragraph, the amount of gain taken into account by the transferor under section 1250(a) shall not exceed the amount of gain recognized to the transferor on the transfer (determined without regard to section 1250). For purposes of this subparagraph, in case of a transfer of both section 1250 property and nonsection 1250 property in one transaction, the amount realized from the disposition of the section 1250 property shall be deemed to consist of that portion of the fair market value of each property acquired which bears the same ratio to the fair market value of such acquired property as the amount realized from the disposition of the section 1250 property bears to the total amount realized. The preceding sentence shall be applied solely for purposes of computing the portion of the total gain (determined without regard to section 1250) which shall be recognized as ordinary income under section 1250(a). Section 1250 (d) (3) does not apply to a disposition of property to an organization (other than a cooperative described in section 521) which is exempt from the tax imposed by chapter 1 of the Code.

(2) Transfers covered. The transfers described in this subparagraph are transfers of property in which the basis of the property in the hands of the transferee is determined by reference to its basis in the hands of the transferor by reason of the application of any of the following provisions:

(i) Section 332 (relating to distributions in complete liquidation of an 80 percent or more controlled subsidiary corporation). For application of section 1250(d) (3) to such a complete liquidation, the principles of paragraph (c) (3) of § 1.1245-4 shall apply.

(ii) Section 351 (relating to transfer to a corporation controlled by transferor).

(iii) Section 361 (relating to exchanges pursuant to certain corporate reorganizations).

. . . .

(vi) Section 721 (relating to transfers to a partnership in exchange for a partnership interest).

(vii) Section 731 (relating to distributions by a partnership to a partner). For special carryover basis rule, see section 1250(d) (6) (A) and paragraph (f) (1) of this section.

(3) Treatment of property in hands of transferee. In the case of a transfer described in subparagraph (2) (other than subdivision (vii) thereof) of this paragraph—

(i) The additional depreciation for the property in the hands of the transferee immediately after the disposition shall be an amount equal to (a) the amount of the additional depreciation for the property in the hands of the transferor immediately before the disposition, minus (b) the amount of additional depreciation necessary to produce an amount equal to the gain taken into account under section 1250(a) by the transferor upon the disposition (taking into account the applicable percentage for the property),

(ii) For purposes of computing applicable percentage, the holding period under section 1250(e) (2) of the property in the hands of the transferee includes the transferor's holding period,

(iii) If the adjusted basis of the property in the hands of the transferee exceeds its adjusted basis immediately before the transfer, the excess is an addition to capital account under paragraph (d) (2) (ii) of § 1.1250-5 (relating to property with 2 or more elements), and

(iv) If the property disposed of consists of 2 or more elements within the meaning of paragraph (c) of § 1.1250-5, see paragraph (e) (1) of § 1.1250-5 for the amount of additional depreciation and the holding period for each element in the hands of the transferee.

(4) Examples. The provisions of this paragraph may be illustrated by the following examples:

Example (1). (i) Green transfers section 1250 property on March 1, 1968, to a corporation, which is not exempt from taxation, in exchange for cash of $9,000 and stock in the corporation worth $91,000, in a transaction qualifying under section 351. Thus, the amount realized is $100,-000 ($9,000 plus $91,000). The property has an applicable percentage under section 1250(a) (2) of 60 percent, an adjusted basis of $40,000, and additional depreciation of $20,000. The gain realized is $60,000, that is, amount realized ($100,000) minus adjusted basis ($40,000). Since the additional depreciation ($20,000) is lower than the gain realized ($60,000), the amount of gain which would be treated as ordinary income under section 1250(a) (2) would be $12,000 (60 percent of $20,000) if the limitation provided in section 1250(d) (3) did not apply. Since under section 351(b) gain in the amount of $9,000 would be recognized to the transferor without regard to section 1250, the limitation provided in section 1250(d) (3) limits the gain taken into account by the transferor under section 1250 (a) (2) to $9,000.

(ii) The amount of additional depreciation for the property in the hands of the transferee immediately after the transfer is $5,000, that is, the amount of additional depreciation before the transfer ($20,000) minus the amount of additional depreciation necessary to produce an amount equal to the gain recognized under section 1250 (a) (2) upon the transfer ($15,000, that is, $9,000 of gain recognized divided by 60 percent, the applicable percentage). (If the property is subsequently disposed of, and for the period after the initial transfer there is additional depreciation in respect of the property, then at the time of the subsequent disposition the additional depreciation will exceed $5,000. If, however, for the period after the initial transfer there was a deficit in additional depreciation, then at the time of the subsequent disposition the additional depreciation would be less than $5,000.)

Example (2). (i) Assume the same facts as in example (1) except that the additional depreciation is $10,000. Since additional depreciation ($10,000) is lower than the gain realized ($60,-000), the amount of gain which would be treated as ordinary income under section 1250(a) (2) would be $6,000 (60 percent of $10,000) if the limitation provided in section 1250(d) (3) did not apply. Since under section 351(b) gain in the amount of $9,000 would be recognized to the transferor without regard to section 1250, the limitation under section 1250(d) (3) does not prevent treatment of the entire $6,000 as ordinary income under section 1250(a) (2). The $3,000 remaining portion of the $9,000 gain may be treated as gain from the sale of property described in section 1231.

(ii) Immediately after the transfer, the amount of additional depreciation is zero, that is, the amount of additional depreciation before the transfer ($10,000) minus the amount of additional depreciation necessary to produce an amount equal to the gain taken into account under section 1250(a) (2) upon the transfer ($10,-000) that is, $6,000 divided by 60 percent.

. . . .

§ 1.1250-4 Holding period.

(a) General. In general, for purposes only of determining the applicable percentage (as defined in sec. 1250(1) (C) and (2) (B)) of section 1250 property, the holding period of the property shall be determined under the rules of section 1250(e) and this section and not under the rules of section 1223. If the property is treated as consisting of two or more elements (within the meaning of paragraph (c) (1) of § 1.1250–5), see paragraph (a) (2) (ii) of § 1.1250–5 for application of this section to determination of holding period of each element. Section 1250(e) does not affect the determination of the amount of additional depreciation in respect of section 1250 property.

(b) Beginning of holding period. (1) For the purpose of determining the applicable percentage, in the case of property acquired by the taxpayer (other than by means of a transaction referred to in paragraph (c) or (d) of this section), the holding period of the property shall begin on the day after the date of its acquisition. See section 1250(e) (1) (A). Thus, for example, if a taxpayer purchases section 1250 property on January 1, 1965, the holding period of the property begins on January 2, 1965. If he sells the property on October 1, 1966, the holding period on the day of the sale is 21 full months, and, accordingly, the applicable percentage is 99 percent. This result would not be changed even if the property initially had been used solely as the taxpayer's residence for a portion of the 21-month period. If, however, the property were sold on September 30, 1966, the holding period would be only 20 full months.

.   .   .   .   .

§ 1.1303–1   Eligible individuals

(a) General rule. Except as otherwise provided in section 1303 and this section, the term "eligible individual" means any individual who is a citizen or resident of the United States throughout the computation year. Such term does not include an estate or trust. If a husband and wife make a joint return under section 6013 for the computation year, both the husband and the wife must be eligible individuals in order to choose the benefits of income averaging.

.   .   .   .   .

(c) Individuals receiving support from others—(1) Self-support rule. Except as provided in section 1303(c)

(2) and subparagraphs (2), (3), and (4) of this paragraph, to be an eligible individual for the computation year under this paragraph, an individual must, together with his spouse, have furnished 50 percent or more of his support during each of his 4-base-period years. For example, H and W are married for the computation year and the 4-base-period years. If H and W have provided more than 50 percent of their support during each of the 4-base-period years, both H and W are eligible individuals for the computation year.

(2) Individuals over 25. Notwithstanding the general rule contained in section 1303(c) (1) and subparagraph (1) of this paragraph, an individual may be an eligible individual for a computation year if—

(i) That year ends after the individual attained age 25, and

(ii) During at least four of his taxable years beginning after he attained age 21 and ending with the computation year, he was not a full-time student.

For the definition of the term "student" as used in this subparagraph, see paragraph (d) (1) of this section.

(3) Major accomplishment rule. Notwithstanding the general rule contained in section 1303(c) (1) and subparagraph (1) of this paragraph, an individual may be an eligible individual for a computation year if more than 50 percent of his taxable income for the computation year is attributable to work performed by him in substantial part during two or more of his 4-base-period years. It is not necessary that the individual perform any of the work in his computation year.

(4) Spouse supported by others. (i) Notwithstanding the general rule contained in section 1303(c) (1) and subparagraph (1) of this paragraph, an individual may be an eligible individual for a computation year if—

(a) Such individual makes a joint return under section 6013 for such year, and

(b) Not more than 25 percent of the aggregate adjusted gross income of such individual and his spouse for such year is attributable to such individual. For example, H and W, who are United States citizens and calendar year taxpayers, were married in August 1970. H supported himself from 1967 to 1971.

W's parents furnished more than 50 percent of her support for each year prior to her marriage. For the taxable year 1971, H and W filed a joint return showing an aggregate adjusted gross income of $10,000, all of which is attributable to H. If H and W are otherwise qualified, they may choose the benefits of income averaging for 1971.

(ii) In applying this subparagraph, to determine the amount of the aggregate adjusted gross income of a husband and wife which is attributable to either of them, amounts of earned income which are community income under community property laws applicable to such income are taken into account as if such amounts did not constitute community income. For the definition of the term "earned income," see section 911(b) and § 1.911-2(b).

(d) Definitions—(1) Student. For purposes of section 1303 and this section, the term "student" means, with respect to a taxable year, an individual who during each of 5 calendar months during such taxable year was a full-time student at an educational institution or was pursuing a full-time course of institutional on-farm training under the supervision of an accredited agent of an educational institution or of a State or political subdivision of a State. An example of "institutional on-farm training" is that authorized by 38 U.S.C.A. § 1652 (formerly section 252 of the Veterans' Readjustment Assistance Act of 1952), as described in section 252 of such act. A full-time student is one who is enrolled for some part of 5 calendar months for the number of hours of courses which is considered to be full-time attendance. The 5 calendar months need not be consecutive. School attendance exclusively at night does not constitute full-time attendance. However, full-time attendance at an educational institution may include some attendance at night in connection with a full-time course of study.

. . . . .

§ 1.1341-1 Restoration of amounts received or accrued under claim of right

(a) In general. (1) If, during the taxable year, the taxpayer is entitled under other provisions of chapter 1 of the Internal Revenue Code of 1954

to a deduction of more than $3,000 because of the restoration to another of an item which was included in the taxpayer's gross income for a prior taxable year (or years) under a claim of right, the tax imposed by chapter 1 of the Internal Revenue Code of 1954 for the taxable year shall be the tax provided in paragraph (b) of this section.

(2) For the purpose of this section "income included under a claim of right" means an item included in gross income because it appeared from all the facts available in the year of inclusion that the taxpayer had an unrestricted right to such item, and "restoration to another" means a restoration resulting because it was established after the close of such prior taxable year (or years) that the taxpayer did not have an unrestricted right to such item (or portion thereof).

(3) For purposes of determining whether the amount of a deduction described in section 1341(a)(2) exceeds $3,000 for the taxable year, there shall be taken into account the aggregate of all such deductions with respect to each item of income (described in section 1341(a)(1)) of the same class.

(b) Determination of tax. (1) Under the circumstances described in paragraph (a) of this section, the tax imposed by chapter 1 of the Internal Revenue Code of 1954 for the taxable year shall be the lesser of—

(i) The tax for the taxable year computed under section 1341(a)(4), that is, with the deduction taken into account, or

(ii) The tax for the taxable year computed under section 1341(a)(5), that is, without taking such deduction into account, minus the decrease in tax (net of any increase in tax imposed by section 56, relating to the minimum tax for tax preferences) (under chapter 1 of the Internal Revenue Code of 1954, under chapter 1 (other than subchapter E) and subchapter E of chapter 2 of the Internal Revenue Code of 1939, or under the corresponding provisions of prior revenue laws) for the prior taxable year (or years) which would result solely from the exclusion from gross income of all or that portion of the income included under a claim of right to which the deduction is attributable. For the purpose of this subdivision, the amount of the decrease in tax is not limited to the amount of the tax for the taxable year. See paragraph (i) of this section where the decrease in tax for the prior taxable year (or years) exceeds the tax for the taxable year.

．．．．

(c) Application to deductions which are capital in nature. Section 1341 and this section shall also apply to a deduction which is capital in nature otherwise allowable in the taxable year. If the deduction otherwise allowable is capital in nature, the determination of whether the taxpayer is entitled to the benefits of section 1341 and this section shall be made without regard to the net capital loss limitation imposed by section 1211. For example, if a taxpayer restores $4,000 in the taxable year and such amount is a long-term capital loss, the taxpayer will, nevertheless, be considered to have met the $3,000 deduction requirement for purposes of applying this section, although the full amount of the loss might not be allowable as a deduction for the taxable year. However, if the tax for the taxable year is computed with the deduction taken into account, the deduction allowable will be subject to the limitation on capital losses provided in section 1211, and the capital loss carryover provided in section 1212.

．．．．

(f) Inventory items, stock in trade, and property held primarily for sale in the ordinary course of trade or business. (1) Except for amounts specified in subparagraphs (2) and (3) of this paragraph the provisions of section 1341 and this section do not apply to deductions attributable to items which were included in gross income by reason of the sale or other disposition of stock in trade of the taxpayer (or other property of a kind which would properly have been included in the inventory of the taxpayer if on hand at the close of the prior taxable year) or property held by the taxpayer primarily for sale to customers in the ordinary course of the taxpayer's trade or business. This section is, therefore, not applicable to sales returns and allowances and similar items.

．．．．

§ 1.1371–1   Definition of small business corporation

．．．．

(g) Classes of stock. A corporation having more than one class of stock does not qualify as a small business corporation. In determining whether a corporation has more than one class of stock, only stock which is issued and outstanding is considered. Therefore, treasury stock and unissued stock of a different class than that held by the shareholders will not disqualify a corporation under section 1371(a)(4). If the outstanding shares of stock of the corporation are not identical with respect to the rights and interest which they convey in the control, profits, and assets of the corporation, then the corporation is considered to have more than one class of stock. Thus, a difference as to voting rights, dividend rights, or liquidation preferences of outstanding stock will disqualify a corporation. However, if two or more groups of shares are identical in every respect except that each group has the right to elect members of the board of directors in a number proportionate to the number of shares in each group, they are considered one class of stock.

．．．．

§ 1.1372–1   Election by small business corporation

(c) Other chapter 1 rules applicable. To the extent that other provisions of chapter 1 of the Code are not inconsistent with those under subchapter S of such chapter and the regulations thereunder, such provisions will apply with respect to both the electing small business corporation and its shareholders in the same manner that they would apply had no election been made. For example:

(1) In general, except as otherwise provided in section 1373(d), taxable income of an electing small business corporation is computed in the same manner that it would have been had no election been made;

(2) Section 301, relating to distributions of property, applies to distributions by an electing small business corporation in the same manner that it would apply had no election been made;

(3) Sections 302, 303, 304, and 331 are applicable in determining whether distributions by an electing small business corporation are to be treated as in exchange for stock;

(4) Section 305 applies to distributions by an electing small business corporation of its own stock;

(5) Section 311 applies to distributions by an electing small business corporation;

(6) Except as provided in sections 1375(d) (1) and (f) (1) and 1377, earnings and profits of an electing small business corporation are computed in the same manner that they would have been computed had no election been made;

(7) Section 316, relating to the definition of a dividend, applies to distributions by an electing small business corporation except as provided in section 1375(d) (1), relating to distributions of previously taxed income, and section 1375(f) (1), relating to distributions of undistributed taxable income (see paragraphs (d) and (e) of § 1.1373–1 for rules relating to allocation of current earnings and profits to distributions during the taxable year); and

(8) Section 341, relating to collapsible corporations, may apply to gain on the sale or exchange of, or a distribution which is in exchange for, stock in an electing small business corporation.

§ 1.1372–3 Shareholders' consent

(a) **In general.** The consent of a shareholder to an election by a small business corporation shall be in the form of a statement signed by the shareholder in which such shareholder consents to the election of the corporation. Such shareholder's consent is binding and may not be withdrawn after a valid election is made by the corporation. Each person who is a shareholder of the electing corporation must consent to the election; thus, where stock of the corporation is owned by a husband and wife as community property (or the income from which is community property), or is owned by tenants in common, joint tenants, or tenants by the entirety, each person having a community interest in such stock and each tenant in common, joint tenant, and tenant by the entirety must consent to the election. The consent of a minor

shall be made by the minor or by his legal guardian, or his natural guardian if no legal guardian has been appointed. The consent of an estate shall be made by the executor or administrator thereof. The statement shall set forth the name and address of the corporation and of the shareholder, the number of shares of stock owned by him, and the date (or dates) on which such stock was acquired. The consents of all shareholders may be incorporated in one statement. The consents of all persons who are shareholders at the time the election is made shall be attached to the election of the corporation.

. . . .

§ 1.1372–4 Termination of election

(a) **In general.** An election under section 1372(a) can be terminated in any one of the five ways described in section 1372(e) (1) through (5) and paragraph (b) of this section. For years affected by termination, see paragraph (c) of this section.

(b) **Methods of termination—(1)**

. . . .

(2) **Revocation.** An election under section 1372(a) may be revoked by the corporation for any taxable year of the corporation after the first taxable year for which the election is effective. A revocation can be made only with the consent of all the persons who are shareholders at the beginning of the day of revocation. Such revocation shall be made by the corporation by filing a statement that the corporation revokes the election made under section 1372(a), which statement shall indicate the first taxable year of the corporation for which the revocation is intended to be effective. The statement shall be signed by any person authorized to sign the return of the corporation under section 6037 and shall be filed with the internal revenue officer with whom the election was filed. In addition, there shall be attached to the statement of revocation a statement of consent, signed by each person who is a shareholder of the corporation at the beginning of the day on which such statement of revocation is filed, in which each such shareholder consents to the revocation by the corporation of the election under section 1372(a). For the time within which a revocation must be made to be effective for a particular taxable year of the cor-

poration, see paragraph (c) of this section.

(3) **Ceases to be small business corporation.** An election under section 1372(a) terminates if at any time after the first day of the first taxable year of the corporation for which the election is effective, or after the day on which the election is made (if such day is later than the first day of the taxable year), the corporation ceases to be a small business corporation as defined in section 1371(a). . . . In the event of a termination under this subparagraph the corporation shall immediately notify the internal revenue officer with whom the election under section 1372(a) was filed. Such notification shall set forth the cause of the termination and the date thereof. . . . If the termination was caused by the issuance of a second class of stock, the notification shall indicate the number of shares of such new class issued and shall describe the differentiating characteristics of the new class of stock.

. . . .

(5) **Passive investment income—(i) In general.** Except as otherwise provided in subdivisions (ii) and (iii) of this subparagraph, an election under section 1372(a) shall terminate if for any taxable year of the corporation the corporation has gross receipts more than 20 percent of which is derived from royalties, rents, dividends, interest, annuities, and sales or exchanges of stock or securities (hereinafter referred to as "passive investment income"), as determined in accordance with the rules of this subparagraph.

(ii) **Taxable years ending after April 14, 1966.** (a) Notwithstanding the provisions of subdivision (i) of this subparagraph, an election under section 1372(a) shall not terminate, under this subparagraph, for any taxable year of the corporation ending after April 14, 1966, if (1) such taxable year is the first taxable year in which the corporation commenced the active conduct of any trade or business or the next succeeding taxable year, and (2) the amount of passive investment income for such taxable year is less than $3,000.

(b) The determination of the first taxable year in which the corporation commenced the active conduct of any trade or business presents a question of fact which must be determined in each case in light of all the circumstances of the particular case. For purposes of this subparagraph, a corporation will be deemed to have commenced the active conduct of a trade or business in the taxable year in which it first engages in activities (other than activities merely incidental to the organization of the corporation) designed or intended to enable it to engage in any business operations. Thus, for example, a corporation organized to operate a restaurant business will be deemed to have commenced the active conduct of a trade or business, for purposes of this subparagraph, in the taxable year in which construction of the restaurant facility is undertaken or real property is purchased or leased by the corporation for such use. However, the mere passive investment of money is not sufficient to constitute the commencement of the active conduct of any trade or business. Each corporation may have only one taxable year of its entire existence which is the first taxable year in which it commenced the active conduct of any trade or business for purposes of this subparagraph. Thus, if a corporation commences the active conduct of any trade or business in a taxable year, and then commences the active conduct of another trade or business in a subsequent taxable year, such subsequent taxable year is not the first taxable year in which the corporation commenced the active conduct of any trade or business, whether or not the corporation was inactive during any period prior to such subsequent taxable year and irrespective of when the election under section 1372(a) was effective.

(c) The provisions of (a) of this subdivision (ii) have no application in respect of any taxable year of the corporation which precedes the first taxable year in which the corporation commenced the active conduct of any trade or business.

(iii) **Taxable years beginning after December 31, 1962, and ending before April 15, 1966—** . . . . .

. . . . .

(iv) **Gross receipts.** (a) The term "gross receipts" as used in section 1372(e) is not synonymous with "gross income". The test under section 1372(e)(4) and (5) shall be made on the basis of total gross receipts, except that, for purposes of section 1372(e)(5), gross receipts from the sales or exchanges of stock or securities shall be taken into account only to the extent of gains therefrom. The term "gross receipts" means the total amount received or accrued under the method of accounting used by the corporation in computing its taxable income. Thus, the total amount of receipts is not reduced by returns and allowances, cost, or deductions. For example, gross receipts will include the total amount received or accrued during the corporation's taxable year from the sale or exchange (including a sale or exchange to which section 337 applies) of any kind of property, from investments, and for services rendered by the corporation. However, gross receipts does not include (1) amounts received in nontaxable sales or exchanges (other than those to which section 337 applies), except to the extent that gain is recognized by the corporation, (2) amounts received as a loan, as a repayment of a loan, as a contribution to capital, or on the issuance by the corporation of its own stock, or (3) certain amounts which are treated under section 331 (relating to corporate liquidations) as payments in exchange for stock (see subdivision (xi) of this subparagraph).

(b) The meaning of the term "gross receipts" as used in section 1372(e) (4) and (5) may be further illustrated by the following examples:

Example (1). A corporation on the accrual method sells property (other than stock or securities) and receives payment partly in money and partly in the form of a note payable at a future time. The amount of the money and the face amount of the note would be considered gross receipts in the taxable year of the sale and would not be reduced by the adjusted basis of the property, the costs of sale, or any other amount.

Example (2). A corporation has a long-term contract as defined in paragraph (a) of § 1.451-3 with respect to which it reports income according to the percentage-of-completion method as described in paragraph (b) (1) of § 1.451-3. The portion of the gross contract price which corresponds to the percentage of the entire contract which has been completed during the taxable year shall be included in gross receipts for such year.

Example (3). A corporation which regularly sells personal property on the installment plan elects to report its taxable income from the sale of property (other than stock or securities) on the installment method in accordance with section 453. The installment payments actually received in a given taxable year of the corporation shall be included in gross receipts for such year.

. . . .

(vi) **Rents.** The term "rents" as used in section 1372(e) (5) means amounts received for the use of, or right to use, property (whether real or personal) of the corporation. The term "rents" does not include payments for the use or occupancy of rooms or other space where significant services are also rendered to the occupant, such as for the use or occupancy of rooms or other quarters in hotels, boarding houses, or apartment houses furnishing hotel services, or in tourist homes, motor courts, or motels. Generally, services are considered rendered to the occupant if they are primarily for his convenience and are other than those usually or customarily rendered in connection with the rental of rooms or other space for occupancy only. The supplying of maid service, for example, constitutes such services; whereas the furnishing of heat and light, the cleaning of public entrances, exits, stairways and lobbies, the collection of trash, etc., are not considered as services rendered to the occupant. Payments for the use or occupancy of entire private residences or living quarters in duplex or multiple housing units, of offices in an office building, etc., are generally "rents" under section 1372(e) (5). Payments for the parking of automobiles ordinarily do not constitute rents. Payments for the warehousing of goods or for the use of personal property do not constitute rents if significant services are rendered in connection with such payments.

. . . .

(x) **Gross receipts from the sale of stock or securities.** For purposes of section 1372(e)(5), gross receipts from the sales or exchanges of stock or securities are taken into account only to the extent of gains therefrom. Thus, the gross receipts from the sale of a particular share of stock will be the excess of the amount realized over the adjusted basis of such share. If the adjusted basis should equal or exceed the amount realized on the sale or exchange of a certain share of stock, bond, etc., there would be no gross receipts resulting from the sale of such security. Losses ou sales or exchanges of stock or securities do not offset gains on the sales or exchanges of other stock or securities for purposes of computing gross receipts from such sales or exchanges. Gross receipts from the sale or exchange of stock and securities include gains received from such sales or exchanges by a corporation even though such corporation is a regular dealer in stocks and securities. However, gross receipts do not include certain amounts which are treated under section 331 (relating to corporate liquidations) as payments in exchange for stock (see subdivision (xi) of this subparagraph). For the meaning of the term "stock or securities", see paragraph (b)(5)(i) of § 1.543-1.

. . . . .

§ 1.1372-5 Election after termination

(a) In general. If a corporation has made a valid election and such election has been terminated, such corporation (or any successor corporation) is not eligible to make a new election for any taxable year prior to its fifth taxable year which begins after the first taxable year for which such termination is effective, unless consent to such new election is given by the Commissioner. The burden will be on the corporation to establish that under the relevant facts the Commissioner should consent to a new election. The fact that more than 50 percent of the stock in the corporation is owned by persons who did not own any stock in the corporation during the first taxable year for which the termination is applicable will tend to establish that consent should be granted. In the absence of such fact, consent will ordinarily be denied unless it can be shown that the event causing the termination was not reasonably within the control of the corporation or shareholders having a substantial interest in the corporation, and was not part of a plan to terminate the election in which plan such shareholders participated.

(b) Successor corporation. The term "successor corporation" as used in section 1372(f) means any corporation—

(1) 50 percent or more of the stock of which is owned, directly or indirectly, by the same persons who, at any time during the first taxable year for which such termination was effective, owned 50 percent or more of the stock of the small business corporation with respect to which the election was terminated, and

(2) (i) Which acquires a substantial portion of the assets of such small business corporation, or

(ii) A substantial portion of the assets of which were assets of such small business corporation.

§ 1.1373-1 Corporation undistributed taxable income taxed to shareholders

(a) In general—(1) Inclusion in gross income. Each person who is a shareholder of an electing small business corporation on the last day of a taxable year of such corporation shall include in his gross income, for his taxable year in which or with which the taxable year of the corporation ends, the amount he would have received as a dividend if on such last day the corporation distributed pro rata to its shareholders an amount of money equal to its undistributed taxable income for the corporation's taxable year. The amount so included in the gross income of the shareholders is treated, for purposes of chapter 1 of the Code, as if it had been distributed as a dividend on the last day of the corporation's taxable year. See, however, section 1375 for special rules applicable to distributions.

(2) Shareholders affected by rule of section 1373. Only those persons who are shareholders of the corporation on the last day of the taxable year of the corporation are required to include in their gross income the amounts specified in section 1373. In determining who are the shareholders of the corporation on the last day of the taxable year for purposes of section 1373, the rules of paragraph (d) (1) of § 1.1371-1 shall apply. If stock is transferred on the last day of the taxable year of the corporation, the transferee (and not the transferor) will be considered the shareholder of such stock for purposes of section 1373. A donee or purchaser of stock in the corporation is not considered a shareholder unless such stock is acquired in a bona fide transaction and the donee or purchaser is the real owner of such stock. The circumstances, not only as of the time of the purported transfer but also during the periods preceding and following it, will be taken into consideration in determining the bona fides of the transfer. Transactions between members of a family will be closely scrutinized.

(b) Determination of amount included by shareholders. To determine the amount each shareholder must include in his gross income as provided in paragraph (a) of this section it is necessary to—

(1) Compute the taxable income of the electing small business corporation for its taxable year in accordance with the provisions of paragraph (c) of this section.

(2) Determine in accordance with paragraph (d) of this section the amount of money distributed as dividends during the taxable year out of earnings and profits of such year.

(3) Determine in accordance with §§ 1.56-1 through 1.56-4 the amount of tax imposed by section 56 for the taxable year.

(4) Determine in accordance with §§ 1.1378-1 through 1.1378-3 the amount of tax imposed by section 1378 for the taxable year.

(5) Subtract the sum of the amounts determined in subparagraphs (2), (3), and (4) of this paragraph from the amount computed in subparagraph (1) of this paragraph. The result is the undistributed taxable income for the taxable year.

(6) Determine in accordance with paragraph (e) of this section the amount that would be treated as a dividend to such shareholder if an amount of money equal to such undistributed taxable income were distributed pro rata to the shareholders of the corporation on the last day of the taxable year of the corporation in a distribution which is not in exchange for stock.

(c) Computation of taxable income. The taxable income of an electing small business corporation is computed in the same manner as it would be computed if no election had been made, with the following exceptions:

(1) The deduction allowed by section 172 (relating to net operating loss deductions) is disregarded, and

(2) The special corporate deductions allowed by part VIII (section 241 and following, except section 248), subchapter B, chapter 1 of the Code, are disregarded.

(d) Determination of dividends in money out of earnings and profits of the taxable year. In applying section 316(a) to distributions by an electing small business corporation, earnings and profits of the taxable year are first allocated to actual distributions of money made during such taxable year (including any distribution which, pursuant to § 1.1375-5, is treated as made on the last day of the taxable year) which are not (1) in exchange for stock, or (2) distributions of the corporation's undistributed taxable income for the immediately preceding taxable year under section 1375(f) and § 1.1375-6. Therefore, such distributions of money are dividends from earnings and profits of the taxable year to the extent of such earnings and profits even though there may be distributions of property other than money during such taxable year or constructive distributions pursuant to section 1373(b) at the end of such taxable year. If such distributions of money made during the taxable year exceed the earnings and profits of such year, then that proportion of each such distribution which the total of the earnings and profits of the year bears to the total of such distributions made during the year shall be regarded as out of the earnings and profits of that year. For purposes of section 1373(c) a distribution of money does not include a distribution of an obligation of the corporation or a distribution of property other than money in satisfaction of a dividend declared in money. See section 1377(b) for special rules relating to computation of earnings and profits of an electing small business corporation for any taxable year.

(e) Dividend resulting from constructive distribution of undistributed taxable income. The amount which would be treated as a dividend if the undistributed taxable income were distributed on the last day of the taxable year is determined in accordance with section 316. In determining the extent to which distributions of an electing small business corporation are out of earnings and profits of the taxable year, the following rules apply:

(1) Earnings and profits of the taxable year are first allocated to certain actual distributions of money as provided in paragraph (d) of this section.

(2) The excess of such earnings and profits over such actual distributions of money is allocated ratably to the constructive distribution of undistributed taxable income and actual distributions of property other than money (taken into account at fair market value for

purposes of this allocation) which are not in exchange for stock, and

(3) The remainder of such earnings and profits is available to be allocated to distributions in exchange for stock of the corporation such as distributions under section 302 or 331.

(f) **When distributions are considered made.** Except as otherwise provided in § 1.1375–5, an actual distribution by an electing small business corporation will be considered to be made only at the time it is received by the shareholder, and earnings and profits of such corporation shall not be reduced with respect to such distribution before such time.

(g) **Examples.** The provisions of this section may be illustrated by the following examples:

Example (1). An electing small business corporation has taxable income and current earnings and profits of $100,000 for its taxable year. During that year it distributes $80,000 in money among its 10 equal shareholders. (Section 1375 (e) or (f) is not applicable with respect to any of such distributions.) The $8,000 received by each shareholder in that year is included in his gross income (for his taxable year in which it was received) as a dividend from current earnings and profits. The undistributed taxable income of the corporation for the taxable year is $20,000 ($100,000 minus $80,000 dividends in money). Since each shareholder would have received a dividend of $2,000 if the undistributed taxable income had been distributed pro rata, that amount must be included as a dividend in the gross income of each shareholder for his taxable year in which or with which the taxable year of the corporation ends.

Example (2). Assume the same facts as in example (1) except that the corporation has only $70,000 of taxable income. The difference between taxable income and current earnings and profits of $100,000 is attributable to the fact that certain deductions allowable in computing taxable income (such as percentage depletion in excess of cost depletion) do not decrease earnings and profits. The distributions of $80,-000 during the taxable year are still included as dividends in the gross income of the shareholders since they are distributions out of earnings and profits. However, there is no amount to be included under section 1373(b) since the corporation has no undistributed taxable income for the taxable year.

Example (3). An electing small business corporation has taxable income and earnings and profits of $10,000 for its taxable year. The corporation has no accumulated earnings and profits as of the beginning of the taxable year. During the taxable year it distributes property other than money with a basis of $10,000 and a fair market value of $20,000. The undistributed taxable income of the corporation is $10,000 since the property distribution does not reduce taxable income for purposes of that computation. However, the current earnings and profits are allocated ratably to the constructive distribution of undistributed taxable income and the distribution of property, taken into account

at fair market value; that is, $3,333 to the constructive distribution and $6,667 to the distribution of property. Therefore, although undistributed taxable income is $10,000, only $3,333 would be treated as a dividend on a distribution of undistributed taxable income, and that is the amount the shareholders include pro rata in gross income pursuant to section 1373 (b). The distribution of property is a dividend only to the extent of $6,667.

Example (4). Assume the facts are the same as in example (3) except that the corporation has accumulated earnings and profits of $20,-000 as of the beginning of the taxable year. The $20,000 accumulated earnings and profits at the beginning of the taxable year are sufficient to cover that portion of the distribution of property which is not out of current earnings and profits ($13,333) and that portion of the constructive distribution which is not out of current earnings and profits ($6,667). Therefore, both distributions of property (at its fair market value) and the corporation's undistributed taxable income will be fully taxable as dividends.

Example (5). An electing small business corporation has taxable income and current earnings and profits of $100,000 for the taxable year. There are no accumulated earnings and profits as of the beginning of the taxable year. During the taxable year the corporation distributes $50,000 in a redemption that qualifies under section 302(a). The undistributed taxable income of the corporation is $100,000. Since the current earnings and profits of $100,-000 are first allocated to the constructive distribution of $100,000, that amount is includible in the gross income of the persons who were shareholders on the last day of the corporation's taxable year.

．　．　．　．　．

§ 1.1374–1 Net operating losses involving electing small business corporations

(a) **Deduction not allowed to corporation.** Under section 1373(d), an electing small business corporation is not allowed a deduction for a net operating loss. Under section 172(h), a net operating loss sustained in taxable years in which a corporation is an electing small business corporation is disregarded in computing the net operating loss deduction of the corporation for taxable years in which it is not an electing small business corporation. In applying section 172(b) (1) and (2) to a net operating loss sustained in a taxable year in which the corporation was not an electing small business corporation, a taxable year in which the corporation was an electing small business corporation is counted as a taxable year to which such net operating loss is carried back or over. However, the taxable income for such year as determined under section 172(b) (2) is treated as if it were zero for purposes of computing the balance of the loss available to the corporation as a carry-back or carryover to other taxable years in which the corporation is not an electing small business corporation

(b) Deduction allowed to shareholders—(1) In general. Under section 1374(a), the net operating loss of an electing small business corporation is allowed as a deduction from gross income of the shareholders of such corporation. Each person who is a shareholder in such corporation at any time during a taxable year of the corporation in which a net operating loss is sustained by the corporation is entitled to a deduction for his pro rata share of such loss. The net operating loss of an electing small business corporation for any taxable year is computed as provided in section 172(c), except that the deductions provided in part VIII (section 241 and following except section 248), subchapter B, chapter 1 of the Code are not allowed.

(2) Year of shareholder in which deduction is allowable. The deduction allowed shareholders by section 1374 (b) is a deduction for the taxable year of the shareholder in which or with which the taxable year of the corporation ends, except that in the case of a shareholder who dies during any taxable year of the corporation which begins after December 31, 1957, with respect to which such corporation is an electing small business corporation, the deduction shall be allowed for the final taxable year of such shareholder (see section 30 of the Revenue Act of 1962 (76 Stat. 1069)).

(3) Pro rata share. A shareholder's pro rata share of the net operating loss of an electing small business corporation is computed as follows:

(i) Divide the corporation's net operating loss by the number of days in the taxable year of the corporation, thus determining the daily net operating loss of the corporation.

(ii) Determine for each day the shareholder's portion of such daily net operating loss by applying to such loss the ratio which the stock owned by the shareholder on that day bears to the total stock outstanding on that day.

(iii) Total the shareholder's daily portions of such daily net operating loss of the corporation for its taxable year.

For purposes of the rule in this subparagraph, shares of stock which are transferred during the year are considered to be held by the transferee (and not the transferor) as of the day of the transfer.

(4) Limitation on deduction—(i) In general. Under section 1374(c) (2), the amount of the net operating loss of the electing small business corporation for any taxable year which may be deducted by any shareholder under section 1374(c) (1) shall not exceed the sum of:

(a) The adjusted basis of the shareholder's stock in the electing small business corporation, and

(b) The adjusted basis of any indebtedness of the corporation to the shareholder.

If a shareholder's pro rata share of the corporation's net operating loss exceeds the limitation imposed by section 1374 (c) (2), such excess is not allowable as a deduction for any taxable year.

(ii) Time for determining basis of stock and indebtedness. The adjusted basis of the stock of, or indebtedness to, the shareholder for purposes of subdivision (i) of this subparagraph is determined as of the close of the taxable year of the corporation, except that—

(a) The adjusted basis of stock which is sold or otherwise disposed of during the taxable year of the corporation is determined as of the close of the day before the day of such sale or other disposition, and

(b) If the shareholder is not a shareholder as of the close of the taxable year of the corporation, the adjusted basis of any indebtedness of the corporation to the shareholder is determined as of the close of the last day in such taxable year on which he was a shareholder.

(iii) Computation of basis of stock and indebtedness. In computing the adjusted basis of stock and indebtedness for purposes of determining how much of a net operating loss may be deducted by a shareholder, any decrease in basis required by section 1376(b) because of such loss shall be disregarded. However, adjustments to the basis of stock and indebtedness under section 1376 for prior years losses of the corporation are to be considered.

§ 1.1375–1 Special rules applicable to capital gains

(a) In general. The amount includable by a shareholder in gross income as dividends received from an electing small business corporation during any taxable year of such corporation shall be treated as long-term capital gain to the extent, if any, of such shareholder's pro rata share of the excess of the corporation's net long-term capital gain over its net short-term capital loss for such taxable year. For this purpose, such excess shall be reduced by the amount of the taxes imposed by sections 56 and 1378 on the income of the corporation for the taxable year, and the amount of such excess so reduced shall not exceed the taxable income (as defined in section 1373(d)) of the corporation for the taxable year. This capital gain treatment applies both to actual distributions of dividends and to amounts treated as dividends pursuant to section 1373(b); however, it applies only to the extent that a dividend is out of earnings and profits of the current taxable year of the corporation. Furthermore, this capital gain treatment applies whether or not the shareholder held any stock in the corporation at the close of the taxable year of the corporation.

(b) Determination of pro rata share. To compute a shareholder's pro rata share of long-term capital gain, it is necessary to determine—

(1) The excess of the corporation's net long-term capital gain over its net short-term capital loss for the taxable year, reduced by the amount of tax, if any, imposed by sections 56 and 1378 on the income of the corporation for such year;

(2) The corporation's taxable income (as defined in section 1373(d)) for the taxable year;

(3) The amount of dividends from earnings and profits of the current taxable year included in such shareholder's gross income, determined in accordance with paragraphs (d) and (e) of § 1.1373–1; and

(4) The amount of dividends from earnings and profits of the current taxable year included in the gross income of all shareholders of the corporation during such taxable year.

The pro rata share is the amount which bears the same ratio to the lesser of the amounts determined in subparagraphs (1) and (2) of this paragraph as the amount determined in subparagraph (3) of this paragraph bears to the amount determined in subparagraph (4) of this paragraph.

(c) Allocation of capital gains to various distributions. If distributions of dividends (including amounts treated as dividends under section 1373(b)) out of the earnings and profits of the taxable year of an electing small business corporation are made to a shareholder at different times during the corporation's taxable year, the amount treated as capital gain to the shareholder pursuant to section 1375(a) shall be allocated ratably to the various distributions of such dividends. Thus, if the taxable year of the corporation includes portions of 2 taxable years of the shareholder, and in both of such years of the shareholder there are distributions treated as dividends out of earnings and profits of the corporation's taxable year, part of the capital gain is allocated to the earlier taxable year of the shareholder and part to the later taxable year. See § 1.1375–5 for rules with respect to certain distributions of money which may be treated as having been made in a preceding taxable year.

(d) Level for determining character of gain. Ordinarily, for purposes of determining whether gain on the sale or exchange of an asset by an electing small business corporation is capital gain, the character of the asset is determined at the corporate level. However, if an electing small business corporation is availed of by any shareholder or group of shareholders owning a substantial portion of the stock of such corporation for the purpose of selling property which in the hands of such shareholder or shareholders would not have been an asset, gain from the sale of which would be capital gain, then the gain on the sale of such property by the corporation shall not be treated as a capital gain. For this purpose, in determining the character of the asset in the hands of the shareholder, the activities of other electing small business corporations in which he is a shareholder shall be taken into consideration.

. . . . .

§ 1.1375–3 Treatment of family groups

(a) In general. Pursuant to section 1375(c), any dividend received by a shareholder from an electing small business corporation (including any amount treated as a dividend under section 1373(b)) may be apportioned or allocated by the Internal Revenue Service between or among shareholders of such corporation who are members of such shareholder's family, if it determines that such apportionment or allocation is necessary in order to reflect the value of services rendered to the corporation by such shareholders. In determining the value of services rendered by a shareholder, consideration shall be given to all the facts and circumstances of the business, including the managerial responsibilities of the shareholder, and the amount that would ordinarily be paid in order to obtain comparable services from a person not having an interest in the corporation. The taxable income of the corporation shall be neither increased nor decreased because of the reallocation of dividends under section 1375(c). The amount reallocated shall be considered a dividend to the shareholder to whom it is reallocated.

(b) Family defined. For purposes of section 1375(c), the family of an individual shall include only his spouse, ancestors, and lineal descendants.

(c) Example. The provisions of section 1375(c) may be illustrated by the following example:

> **Example.** The stock of an electing small business corporation is owned 50 percent by F and 50 percent by S, a minor son of F. For the taxable year, the corporation has $70,000 of taxable income and earnings and profits. During the year, the corporation distributes dividends (including amounts treated as dividends under section 1373(b)) of $35,000 to F and $35,000 to S. Compensation of $10,000 is paid by the corporation to F for services rendered during the year, and no compensation is paid to S, who rendered no services. Based on the relevant facts, a reasonable compensation for the services rendered by F would be $30,000. In the discretion of the Internal Revenue Service, up to $10,000 of the $35,000 dividend received by S may, for tax purposes, be allocated to F.

(d) Effect of waiver of dividends resulting in disproportionate distributions among members of family. If a nonpro rata distribution of dividends is made to members of a family group, the member of such group who receives less than his pro rata share of such distribution will be deemed to have waived his right to dividends to the extent that his distribution is less than his pro rata share, unless he can establish that the distribution was made disproportionately without his consent. In the case of such a waiver, the amount distributed to members of the family group shall be reallocated among all the members of the group in accordance with the number of shares owned by each member.

§ 1.1375–4 Distributions of previously taxed income

(a) In general. Under section 1375 (d) (1), a distribution by an electing small business corporation to a shareholder of all or any portion of his net share of previously taxed income is considered a distribution which is not a dividend. Such a distribution reduces the basis of the shareholder's stock in the corporation in accordance with section 301(c) (2), and, if it exceeds such basis, is subject to the provisions of section 301(c) (3). The earnings and profits of the corporation are not reduced by reason of such a distribution. If an election is terminated under section 1372(e), the corporation may not, during the first taxable year to which the termination applies or during any subsequent taxable year, distribute previously taxed income of taxable years prior to the termination as a nondividend distribution pursuant to this section. (However, see § 1.1375–5 for rules with respect to certain distributions which may be treated as having been made in a preceding taxable year; and see section 1375(f) and § 1.1375–6 for rules with respect to certain distributions which are treated as distributions of a preceding taxable year's undistributed taxable income.)

(b) Source of distribution. Except as provided in paragraph (c) of this section, any actual distribution of money by an electing small business corporation to a shareholder which, but for the operation of this section, would be a dividend out of accumulated earnings and profits shall be considered a distribution of previously taxed income to the extent of the shareholder's net share of previously taxed income immediately before the distribution. Thus, a distribution of property other than money or a distribution in exchange for stock, or a constructive distribution under section 1373(b), is never a distribution of previously taxed income. Since current earnings and profits are first applied to distributions of money which are not (1) in exchange for stock, or (2) distributions of the corporation's undistributed taxable income for the immediately preceding taxable year under section 1375(f) and § 1.1375–6 (see paragraphs (d) and (e) of § 1.1373–1), a distribution of previously taxed income may occur only if during its taxable year the corporation makes such money distributions in excess of its earnings and profits for such taxable year. (See § 1.1375–5 for rules with respect to certain distributions of money which may be treated as having been made in a preceding taxable year.)

(c) **Election.** An electing small business corporation may, with the consent of all of its shareholders, elect to treat distributions which, under this section, would be distributions of previously taxed income, as distributions out of accumulated earnings and profits, if any, rather than as distributions of previously taxed income. For any taxable year for which such election is made, a statement of election shall be filed with a timely return under section 6037 for such year. Such election applies to all distributions during such year which without regard to this paragraph would be distributions of previously taxed income. An election applies only for the year for which it is made, but a new election may be made for any subsequent year.

(d) **Shareholder's net share of previously taxed income.** A shareholder's net share of previously taxed income as of the time of a distribution is—

(1) The sum of the amounts included in the gross income of the shareholder under section 1373(b) for all of his taxable years ending before the distribution, less

(2) The sum of—

(i) The amounts allowable under section 1374(b) as a deduction from gross income of the shareholder for all of his taxable years ending before the distribution,

(ii) The amounts previously distributed to the shareholder during his current taxable year and all of his prior taxable years, which, under section 1375(d)(1), were not considered dividends, and

(iii) The amounts previously distributed to the shareholder during his current taxable year and all his prior taxable years, which, under section 1375 (f), were not considered dividends and were treated as distributions of the corporation's undistributed taxable income for a taxable year of the corporation ending before the beginning of such current taxable year of the shareholder. In computing the sum of the amounts included in gross income under section 1373(b), only the amount included on the shareholder's income tax return for a prior taxable year (increased or decreased by any adjustment of such amount in any redetermination of the shareholder's tax liability) is taken into account, unless the shareholder is not required to file a return for such prior taxable year. The amounts allowable under section 1374(b) as a deduction means all allowable deductions whether or not claimed on the income tax return of the shareholder and whether or not resulting in any tax benefit. If a new election is made subsequent to a termination under section 1372(e) of a prior election, a shareholder's net share of previously taxed income is determined solely by reference to taxable years which are subject to the new election.

(e) **Benefits not transferable.** A shareholder's right to nondividend distributions under this section is personal and cannot in any manner be transferred to another. If a shareholder transfers part but not all of his stock in an electing small business corporation his net share of previously taxed income is not reduced by reason of the transfer and the transferee does not acquire any part of such net share. However, in such a case the transferor's total basis for his stock in the corporation is reduced by the amount of his basis for the stock transferred. A distribution of previously taxed income in excess of the transferor's remaining basis is subject to the provisions of section 301(c) (3). If a shareholder transfers all of his stock in an electing small business corporation, any right which he may have had to nondividend treatment upon the receipt of distributions lapses entirely unless he again becomes a shareholder in the corporation while it is subject to the same election.

(f) **Record requirement.** A record of the net share of previously taxed income of each shareholder shall be maintained by the electing small business corporation. In addition, each shareholder of such corporation shall keep a record of his own net share of previously taxed income and shall make such record available to the corporation for its information.

(g) Examples. The operation of this section may be illustrated by the following examples:

Example (1). (i) Corporation X, of which A (a calendar year taxpayer) is the sole stockholder is an electing small business corporation for its taxable years ended December 31, 1958, 1959, and 1960. For its taxable year 1958 it has a net operating loss of $10,000. For its taxable year 1959 it has undistributed taxable income of $50,000. Assuming that A included in his return the undistributed taxable income for 1959 and assuming that the 1958 net operating loss did not exceed the limitation imposed by section 1374(c) (2), A's net share of previously taxed income as of January 1, 1960, is $40,000.

(ii) Assume the additional fact that for the taxable year 1960 Corporation X has a net operating loss of $40,000, which is fully allowable to A as a deduction. This net operating loss does not affect A's share of previously taxed income for purposes of determining the nature of distributions during 1960, since such net share is reduced only by the deductions allowable for taxable years of the shareholder ending before the distribution. However, in computing his net share of previously taxed income for years subsequent to 1960, A must take the $40,000 deduction for 1960 into account.

(iii) If in 1960, at a time when his net share of previously taxed income is $40,000, A sold his stock in the corporation to B, who was not previously a shareholder, B's net share of previously taxed income as of the date of purchase would be zero. The result would be the same if, for example, B had received the stock by gift or by bequest from A.

Example (2). Corporation Y, an electing small business corporation, is on a fiscal year ending January 31. C, a shareholder in the corporation, is on a calendar year. For its fiscal year ending January 31, 1960, corporation Y has $50,000 of undistributed taxable income, half of which is included in C's gross income for his taxable year 1960. The amount so included does not increase C's net share of previously taxed income for purposes of distributions at any time during 1960, since his net share of previously taxed income is increased only by amounts included in gross income for his taxable years ending before the distribution.

Example (3). Corporation Z, an electing small business corporation, has two equal shareholders, A and B (both calendar year taxpayers), during its taxable year ended December 31, 1960. No election is made under paragraph (c) of this section. As of the beginning of 1960 the corporation has $20,000 of accumulated earnings and profits. For the taxable year 1960, corporation Z has current earnings and profits and taxable income of $8,000. In June 1960, it makes money distributions of $5,000 to A and $5,000 to B, and in November 1960, it distributes the same amount in money to each. Immediately before the distribution in June, A's net share of previously taxed income was $6,000 and B's net share was $4,000. Cur-

rent earnings and profits are allocated ratably to each of the four distributions. (See paragraphs (d) and (e) of § 1.1373-1.) Therefore, each distribution to A and B is a dividend from current earnings and profits to the extent of $2,000. As to the June distribution, the $3,000 distributed to A and B which is not out of current earnings and profits is a distribution of previously taxed income and therefore not a dividend, since immediately before the distribution the net share of each is in excess of $3,000. As to the November distribution, the $3,000 distributed to A which is not out of current earnings and profits is a nondividend distribution since his net share of previously taxed income at that date is $3,000 ($6,000 less $3,000 absorbed by the June distribution); however, the $3,000 distribution to B which is not out of current earnings and profits is a nondividend distribution to the extent of $1,000 and a dividend from accumulated earnings and profits to the extent of $2,000; since his net share of previously taxed income at that date is $1,000 ($4,000 less $3,000 absorbed by the June distribution).

· · · ·

§ 1.1375-6 Distributions of undistributed taxable income

(a) Distributions after April 14, 1966 —(1) In general. Under section 1375 (f), a distribution of money by a corporation after April 14, 1966, is treated, under certain circumstances, as a distribution of the corporation's undistributed taxable income for its taxable year immediately preceding the taxable year in which the distribution is made. A distribution which is so treated shall, for purposes of chapter 1 of the Code, be considered a distribution which is not a dividend. Such a distribution reduces the basis of stock in the corporation in accordance with section 301(c) (2), and, if it exceeds such basis, is subject to the provisions of section 301(c) (3). The earnings and profits of the corporation are not reduced by reason of such a distribution. A distribution may be treated as a nondividend distribution pursuant to section 1375(f) even though the corporation's election was terminated under section 1372(e) for the taxable year during which the distribution is made, if the corporation was an electing small business corporation for its immediately preceding taxable year.

(2) Qualifying distributions. (i) An actual distribution of money by a corporation to a person after April 14, 1966, shall be treated as a distribution of the corporation's undistributed taxable income for its taxable year immediately preceding its taxable year during which the distribution is made, to the extent the distribution does not exceed such person's share of such undistributed taxable income, if—

(a) The corporation was an electing small business corporation for such immediately preceding taxable year.

(b) The distribution is made on or before the 15th day of the third month following the close of such immediately preceding taxable year.

(c) The distribution is made to a person who was a shareholder of the corporation on the last day of such immediately preceding taxable year, and

(d) The distribution is not a distribution in respect of which an election is made under section 1375(e) (see § 1.1375-5).

(ii) The amount of any distribution otherwise described in subdivision (i) of this subparagraph, but which is in excess of the person's share of undistributed taxable income, shall be subject to the rules of paragraphs (d) and (e) of § 1.1373-1 and § 1.1375-4 (if the distributing corporation is an electing small business corporation) or section 301 (if the distributing corporation is not an electing small business corporation). See paragraph (a) of § 1.1375-5 for the treatment of a distribution of money in respect of which an election is made under section 1375(e).

(iii) For purposes of this subparagraph and subparagraph (3) (ii) of this paragraph, a distribution of money does not include a distribution of an obligation of the corporation, a distribution of property other than money in satisfaction of a dividend declared in money, or a distribution in exchange for stock.

(3) Share of undistributed taxable income. For purposes of subparagraph (2) of this paragraph, a person's share of undistributed taxable income for a corporation's taxable year, as of the time a distribution is received, is the excess of—

(i) The amount required, under section 1373(b), to be included in the gross income of such person for his taxable year in which or with which such taxable year of the corporation ends, over

(ii) The sum of all prior distributions of money made to such person after the close of such taxable year of the corporation.

(4) Benefits not transferable. A person's right to nondividend distributions under this section is personal and cannot in any manner be transferred to another. If a shareholder transfers part or all of his stock in a corporation, his share of undistributed taxable income is not reduced by reason of the transfer, and the transferee does not acquire any part of such share. However, in such a case the transferor's total basis for his stock in the corporation is reduced by the amount of his basis for the stock transferred. A distribution of undistributed taxable income in excess of the transferor's remaining basis is subject to the provisions of section 301(c) (3).

(5) Record requirement. A record of each person's share of undistributed taxable income shall be maintained by the electing small business corporation. In addition, each shareholder of such corporation shall keep a record of his own share of undistributed taxable income and shall make such record available to the corporation for its information.

(6) Examples. The operation of this paragraph may be illustrated by the following examples:

Example (1). (a) Corporation X, of which A (a calendar year taxpayer) is the sole shareholder, is an electing small business corporation for its taxable years ending December 31, 1966, and 1967. For its taxable year 1966, it has $20,000 of undistributed taxable income which A must include in his gross income for 1966. For its taxable year 1967, corporation X has $25,000 of taxable income and current earnings and profits. On February 1, 1967, corporation X makes a money distribution of $10,000 to A. This $10,000 distribution is treated as a distribution of the corporation's undistributed taxable income for 1966, and is not a dividend to A. If the corporation makes no further distributions during 1967, its undistributed taxable income for 1967 will be $25,000, and A will include such amount in his gross income for 1967, pursuant to section 1373(b).

(b) Assume the additional fact that A sells one-half of his stock in corporation X to B on January 15, 1968, and B does not consent to the corporation's election under section 1372 (a). Thus, the corporation's election under section 1372(a) is terminated pursuant to section 1372(e) (1), and it is not an electing small business corporation for its taxable year beginning January 1, 1968. The corporation makes a money distribution of $10,000 to A and $10,000 to B on March 1, 1968. The distribution to A is treated as a nondividend distribution of the corporation's undistributed taxable income for its taxable year ending December 31, 1967, even if the corporation has current or accumulated earnings and profits during 1968, and reduces the basis of A's remaining stock in corporation X in accordance with section 301(c) (2). The $10,000 distribution to B is a distribution under section 301(a), and thus a dividend to the extent provided in section 316.

. . . . .

§ 1.1376–1 Adjustment to basis of stock of, and indebtedness to, shareholders; increase in basis of stock

Under section 1376(a), the basis of a shareholder's stock in an electing small business corporation is increased by the amount required to be included in the gross income of such shareholder under section 1373(b), but only to the extent to which such amount is actually included in his gross income in his income tax return (unless under section 6012 (a) (1) the shareholder is not required to file a return), increased or decreased by any adjustment of such amount in any redetermination of the shareholder's tax liability. The effect of this rule is the same as if, on the last day of the corporation's taxable year, such amount had actually been distributed as a dividend and then reinvested by such shareholder. This increase in basis will affect only those shares of stock of the electing small business corporation which the shareholder owned at the end of the corporation's taxable year and is apportioned in equal amounts to each such share. The increase is effective as of such last day, and survives a termination of the corporation's election. See section 1372(b) (2).

§ 1.1376–2 Reduction in basis of stock and indebtedness

(a) Reduction in basis of stock—(1) In general. Under section 1376(b) (1), the basis of a shareholder's stock in an electing small business corporation is reduced by an amount equal to his portion of the corporation's net operating loss for any taxable year attributable to such stock. However, the basis of such stock is not to be reduced below zero.

(2) Amount of reduction in basis of individual shares. (i) The amount of the reduction in the basis of each share of stock shall be that portion of the shareholder's pro rata share of the corporation's net operating loss which is attributable to each such share under the rule in section 1374(c). In the event that the basis reduction applicable to a share of stock under the rule

in the preceding sentence exceeds the basis of such share, the excess shall be applied in reduction of the basis of all other shares of stock owned by the same shareholder in proportion to the basis of such shares remaining after the application of the rule in the preceding sentence.

(ii) The application of this subparagraph may be illustrated by the following example:

Example. A's pro rata share of the corporation's net operating loss for the taxable year is $100. This amount is attributable, under the rule of section 1374(c), to three shares of stock held by A during the taxable year; one of which was owned by him during the entire year and the other two of which were acquired by him in the middle of the year. The amount of the pro rata share of the loss attributable to each share is as follows:

Share No. 1 (owned for entire year)......	$50
Share No. 2 (owned for one-half year)....	25
Share No. 3 (owned for one-half year)....	25

The reduction in basis of share No. 1 is $50, and the reduction in basis of shares No. 2 and No. 3 is $25 each. Assume that the adjusted basis of the three shares of stock prior to this reduction is as follows:

Share No. 1	$40
Share No. 2	45
Share No. 3	35

After the reduction in basis by the amount of the loss attributable to each share, the basis of the shares is as follows:

Share No. 1	$0
Share No. 2	20
Share No. 3	10

The $10 excess of the basis reduction allocable to share No. 1 over the basis of that share is applied to reduce the basis of shares No. 2 and No. 3 in proportion to their remaining basis. Therefore, $6.67 of such excess reduces the basis of share No. 2, and $3.33 of such excess reduces the basis of share No. 3. After this reduction the shares have the following basis:

Share No. 1	$0
Share No. 2	13.33
Share No. 3	6.67

(3) Time of reduction. (i) The reduction in the basis of stock provided under section 1376(b) (1) shall be effective as of the close of the corporation's taxable year in which the net operating loss was incurred as to stock which is held at such time and as of the close of the day before disposition if the stock was disposed of prior to that time.

(ii) The application of this subparagraph may be illustrated by the following example:

Example. Corporation X, an electing small business corporation, is on a calendar year. On June 2, 1960, A, a shareholder in corporation X, sells 50 shares of stock which, without regard to section 1376(b) (1), have a basis of $10,000.

At the end of 1960 it is determined that corporation X has a net operating loss for the year, and $1,000 of A's pro rata share of such loss is attributable to the 50 shares sold in June. The reduction in basis required by section 1376(b)(1) is effective as of the close of June 1, 1960, the day before the sale, and A's basis for purposes of determining gain or loss on the sale is $9,000.

(b) Reduction in basis of indebtedness—(1) In general. Under section 1376(b)(2), the basis of any indebtedness of an electing small business corporation to a shareholder is reduced by an amount equal to the shareholder's portion of the corporation's net operating loss for the taxable year, but only to the extent that such amount exceeds the basis of the shareholder's stock in the corporation. Thus, the amount of the shareholder's portion of the net operating loss is first applied in reduction of the basis of his stock in accordance with the rules of paragraph (a) of this section, and only the remainder, if any, reduces the basis of the indebtedness.

(2) Indebtedness affected by basis reduction. The reduction in the basis of indebtedness provided by section 1376(b)(2) shall apply to the indebtedness to the shareholder as of the close of the corporation's taxable year in which the net operating loss was incurred if the shareholder held stock in the corporation at such time, or, if the shareholder was not a shareholder at such time, then as of the close of the last day on which he was a shareholder.

(3) Amount of reduction in basis of more than one indebtedness. If more than one indebtedness is affected by the basis reduction provided by section 1376(b)(2), the reduction shall be applied to each such indebtedness in proportion to the basis of the various debts.

(4) Time of reduction. The reduction in the basis of indebtedness provided by section 1376(b)(2) shall be effective as of the close of the corporation's taxable year in which the net operating loss was incurred if the shareholder held stock in the corporation at that time, or, if the shareholder was not a shareholder at that time, then as of the last day on which he was a shareholder.

§ 1.1377-1 Reduction of earnings and profits for undistributed taxable income

Section 1377(a) provides that the accumulated earnings and profits of an electing small business corporation as of the close of its taxable year shall be reduced to the extent that its undistributed taxable income for such year is required to be included in the gross income of shareholders under section 1373(b). See section 1375(d) and (f), and the regulations thereunder, for the correlative rules that distributions of previously taxed income, and distributions treated as distributions of undistributed taxable income, do not reduce earnings and profits.

§ 1.1377-2 Current earnings and profits not reduced by any amount not allowable as a deduction

(a) Amounts not deductible. (1) The earnings and profits of an electing small business corporation for any taxable year (but not its accumulated earnings and profits) shall not be reduced by any amount which is not allowable as a deduction in computing its taxable income for such taxable year.

(2) The application of this paragraph may be illustrated by the following examples:

Example (1). Corporation X has $300,000 of accumulated earnings and profits as of the beginning of the taxable year. It would have had earnings and profits of $400,000 for the taxable year (taking into account a net capital loss of $100,000, which amount was not deductible in determining its taxable income) but because it is an electing small business corporation it has earnings and profits of $500,000 for the taxable year. If the corporation makes a dividend distribution during the year in the amount of $500,000, all of such amount will be considered a distribution of current earnings and profits. However, the corporation will have only $200,000 of accumulated earnings and profits as of the beginning of the following taxable year.

Example (2). Assume the same facts as in example (1), except that the corporation does not have any accumulated earnings and profits as of the beginning of the taxable year. The entire $500,000 distribution is a distribution of current earnings and profits. As of the beginning of the year following the taxable year in which the $500,000 distribution was made, the corporation has neither accumulated earnings and profits nor a deficit in accumulated earnings and profits. It would begin such year with its paid-in capital reduced by $100,000.

(b) Computation of earnings and profits. Except as otherwise provided in section 1377, the earnings and profits of the taxable year of an electing small business corporation are computed in the same manner as the earnings and profits of corporations generally. Therefore, such earnings and profits can exceed the taxable income of the corporation, as in the case of a corporation which uses percentage depletion in computing its taxable income or which receives tax-exempt interest on certain governmental obligations.

§ 1.1377–3 Earnings and profits not affected by net operating loss

(a) Net operating loss. Under section 1377(c), the current earnings and profits and the accumulated earnings and profits of an electing small business corporation are not affected by any item of gross income or any deduction taken into account in determining the amount of any net operating loss (computed as provided in section 1374 (c) (1)) of such corporation.

(b) Example. The application of this section may be illustrated by the following example:

Example. At the beginning of its calendar year 1960 corporation X, an electing small business corporation, has accumulated earnings and profits of $50,000. During 1960 the corporation has $5,000 of gross income and deductible expenses of $15,000, which produce a $10,000 net operating loss for the taxable year. If corporation X were not an electing small business corporation, its accumulated earnings and profits as of January 1, 1961, would have been $40,-000. However, since corporation X was an electing small business corporation for 1960, its accumulated earnings and profits are not affected by the income and deductions for 1960 because they are taken into account in determining the net operating loss. Accordingly, the accumulated earnings and profits of corporation X as of January 1, 1961, are $50,000.

§ 1.1377–4 Distributions of undistributed taxable income previously taxed to shareholders

(a) Undistributed taxable income previously taxed. Under section 1377

(d) the current year earnings and profits of an electing small business corporation are computed without regard to section 312(k) (formerly designated as section 312(m) for taxable years beginning before 1977). This rule applies solely for purposes of determining whether a distribution to a shareholder constitutes a distribution of all or any portion of the shareholder's net share of previously taxed income under section 1375(d) and § 1.1375–4. Section 1377 (d) and this section apply to taxable years of an electing small business corporation beginning after December 31, 1975.

(b) Example. The application of this section may be illustrated by the following example:

Example. Corporation M, an electing small business corporation which uses the calendar year as its taxable year, in 1977 has $100 of taxable income, $120 of current earnings and profits the $20 difference between taxable income and current earnings and profits representing the accelerated portion of depreciation which is not deducted for purposes of determining current earnings and profits as a result of section 312(k). On August 12, 1977, the corporation makes a cash distribution of $120 to A, its sole shareholder. At the time of the distribution, A's net share of previously taxed income is $10. Solely for purposes of determining whether the corporation has made a distribution of previously taxed income to A, the corporation's current earnings and profits for 1977 are considered to be $100. Accordingly, $10 of the amount distributed to A is treated as a distribution of previously taxed income (see § 1.1375–4), and $110 of the amount distributed is treated as a distribution of current earnings and profits (determined with regard to section 312(k)) and is taxable as a dividend. The remaining $10 of undistributed current earnings and profits increases accumulated earnings and profits.

§ 20.2031–1 Definition of gross estate; valuation of property

(a) Definition of gross estate. Except as otherwise provided in this paragraph the value of the gross estate of a decedent who was a citizen or resident of the United States at the time of his death is the total value of the interests described in sections 2033 through 2044. . . . . Except as provided in paragraph (c) of this section (relating to the estates of decedents dying after October 16, 1962, and before July 1, 1964), in the case of a decedent dying after October 16, 1962, real property situated outside the United States which comes within the scope of sections 2033 through 2044 is included in the gross estate to the same extent as any other property coming within the scope of those sections. In arriving at the value of the gross estate the interests described in sections 2033 through 2044 are valued as described in this section, §§ 20.2031–2 through 20.2031–9 and § 20.2032–1. The contents of sections 2033 through 2044 are, in general, as follows:

(1) Sections 2033 and 2034 are concerned mainly with interests in property passing through the decedent's probate estate. Section 2033 includes in the decedent's gross estate any interest that the decedent had in property at the time of his death. Section 2034 provides that any interest of the decedent's surviving spouse in the decedent's property, such as dower or curtesy, does not prevent the inclusion of such property in the decedent's gross estate.

(2) Sections 2035 through 2038 deal with interests in property transferred by the decedent during his life under such circumstances as to bring the interests within the decedent's gross estate. Section 2035 includes in the decedent's gross estate property transferred in contemplation of death, even though the decedent had no interest in, or control over, the property at the time of his death. Section 2036 provides for the inclusion of transferred property with respect to which the decedent retained the income or the power to designate who shall enjoy the income. Section 2037 includes in the decedent's gross estate certain transfers under which the beneficial enjoyment of the property could be obtained only by surviving the decedent. Section 2038 provides for the inclusion of transferred property if the decedent had at the time of his death the power to change the beneficial enjoyment of the property. It should be noted that there is considerable overlap in the application of sections 2036 through 2038 with respect to reserved powers, so that transferred property may be includible in the decedent's gross estate in varying degrees under more than one of those sections.

(3) Sections 2039 through 2042 deal with special kinds of property and powers. Sections 2039 and 2040 concern annuities and jointly held property, respectively. Section 2041 deals with powers held by the decedent over the beneficial enjoyment of property not originating with the decedent. Section 2042 concerns insurance under policies on the life of the decedent.

(4) Section 2043 concerns the sufficiency of consideration for transfers made by the decedent during his life. This has a bearing on the amount to be included in the decedent's gross estate under sections 2035 through 2038, and 2041. Section 2044 deals with retroactivity.

(b) Valuation of property in general. The value of every item of property includible in a decedent's gross estate under sections 2031 through 2044 is its fair market value at the time of the decedent's death, except that if the executor elects the alternate valuation method under section 2032, it is the fair market value thereof at the date, and with the adjustments, prescribed in that section. The fair market value is the price at which the property would change hands between a willing buyer and a willing seller, neither being under any compulsion to buy or to sell and both having reasonable knowledge of relevant facts. The fair market value of a particular item of property includible in the decedent's gross estate is not to be determined by a forced sale price. Nor is the fair market value of an item of property to be determined by the sale price of the item in a market other than that in which such item is most commonly sold to the public, taking into account the location of the item wherever appropriate. Thus, in the case of an item of property includible in the decedent's gross estate, which is generally obtained by the public in the retail market, the fair market value of such an item of property is the price at which the item or a comparable item would be sold at retail. For example, the fair market value of an automobile (an article generally obtained by the public in the retail market) includible in the decedent's gross estate is the price for which an automobile of the same or approximately the same description, make, model, age, condition, etc., could be purchased by a member of the general public and not the price for which the particular automobile of the decedent would be purchased by a dealer in used automobiles. Examples of items of property which are generally sold to the public at retail may be found in §§ 20.2031-6 and 20.2031-8. The value is generally to be determined by ascertaining as a basis the fair market value as of the applicable valuation date of each unit of property. For example, in the case of shares of stock or bonds, such unit of property is generally a share of stock or a bond. Livestock, farm machinery, harvested and growing crops must generally be itemized and the value of each item separately returned. Property shall not be returned at the value at which it is assessed for local tax purposes unless that value represents the fair market value as of the applicable valuation date. All relevant facts and elements of value as of the applicable valuation date shall be considered in every case. The value of items of property which were held by the decedent for sale in the course of a business generally should be reflected in the value of the business. For valuation of interests in businesses, see § 20.2031-3. See § 20.2031-2 and §§ 20.-2031-4 through 20.2031-8 for further information concerning the valuation of other particular kinds of property. For certain circumstances under which the sale of an item of property at a price below its fair market value may result in a deduction for the estate, see paragraph (d) (2) of § 20.2053-3.

§ 20.2031-2 Valuation of stocks and bonds

(a) **In general.** The value of stocks and bonds is the fair market value per share or bond on the applicable valuation date.

(b) **Based on selling prices.** (1) In general, if there is a market for stocks or bonds, on a stock exchange, in an over-the-counter market, or otherwise, the mean between the highest and lowest quoted selling prices on the valuation date is the fair market value per share or bond. If there were no sales on the valuation date but there were sales on dates within a reasonable period both before and after the valuation date, the fair market value is determined by taking a weighted average of the means between the highest and lowest sales on the nearest date before and the nearest date after the valuation date. The average is to be weighted inversely by the respective numbers of trading days between the selling dates and the valuation date. If the stocks or bonds are listed on more than one exchange, the records of the exchange where the stocks or bonds are principally dealt in should be employed if such records are available in a generally available listing or publication of general circulation. In the event that such records are not so available and such stocks or bonds are listed on a composite listing of combined exchanges available in a generally available listing or publication of general circulation, the records of such combined exchanges should be employed. In valuing listed securities, the executor should be careful to consult accurate records to obtain values as of the applicable valuation date. If quotations of unlisted securities are obtained from brokers, or evidence as to their sale is obtained from officers of the issuing companies, copies of the letters furnishing such quotations or evidence of sale should be attached to the return.

(2) If it is established with respect to bonds for which there is a market on a stock exchange, that the highest and lowest selling prices are not available for the valuation date in a generally available listing or publication of general circulation but that closing selling prices are so available, the fair market value per bond is the mean between the quoted closing selling price on the valuation date and the quoted

closing selling price on the trading day before the valuation date. If there were no sales on the trading day before the valuation date but there were sales on a date within a reasonable period before the valuation date, the fair market value is determined by taking a weighted average of the quoted closing selling price on the valuation date and the quoted closing selling price on the nearest date before the valuation date. The closing selling price for the valuation date is to be weighted by the number of trading days between the previous selling date and the valuation date. If there were no sales within a reasonable period before the valuation date but there were sales on the valuation date, the fair market value is the closing selling price on such valuation date. If there were no sales on the valuation date but there were sales on dates within a reasonable period both before and after the valuation date, the fair market value is determined by taking a weighted average of the quoted closing selling prices on the nearest date before and the nearest date after the valuation date. The average is to be weighted inversely by the respective numbers of trading days between the selling dates and the valuation date. If the bonds are listed on more than one exchange, the records of the exchange where the bonds are principally dealt in should be employed. In valuing listed securities, the executor should be careful to consult accurate records to obtain values as of the applicable valuation date.

(3) The application of this paragraph may be illustrated by the following examples:

Example (1). Assume that sales of X Company common stock nearest the valuation date (Friday, June 15) occurred two trading days before (Wednesday, June 13) and three trading days after (Wednesday, June 20) and on these days the mean sale prices per share were $10 and $15, respectively. The price of $12 is taken as representing the fair market value of a share of X Company common stock as of the valuation date

$$\frac{(3 \times 10) + (2 \times 15)}{5}$$

Example (2). Assume the same facts as in example (1) except that the mean sale prices per share on June 13 and June 20 were $15 and $10, respectively. The price of $13 is taken as representing the fair market value of a share of X Company common stock as of the valuation date

$$\frac{(3 \times 15) + (2 \times 10)}{5}$$

Example (3). Assume the decedent died on Sunday, October 7, and that Saturday and Sun-

day were not trading days. If sales of X Company common stock occurred on Friday, October 5, at mean sale prices per share of $20 and on Monday, October 8, at mean sale prices per share of $23, the price of $21.50 is taken as representing the fair market value of a share of X Company common stock as of the valuation date

$$\frac{(1 \times 20) + (23 \times 1)}{2}$$

Example (4). Assume that on the valuation date (Tuesday, April 3, 1973) the closing selling price of a listed bond was $25 per bond and that the highest and lowest selling prices are not available in a generally available listing or publication of general circulation for that date. Assume further, that the closing selling price of the same listed bond was $21 per bond on the day before the valuation date (Monday, April 2, 1973). Thus, under paragraph (b)(2) of this section the price of $23 is taken as representing the fair market value per bond as of the valuation date

$$\frac{(25 + 21)}{2}$$

Example (5). Assume the same facts as in example (4) except that there were no sales on the day before the valuation date. Assume further, that there were sales on Thursday, March 29, 1973, and that the closing selling price on that day was $23. The price of $24.50 is taken as representing the fair market value per bond as of the valuation date

$$\frac{((1 \times 23) + (3 \times 25))}{4}$$

Example (6). Assume that no bonds were traded on the valuation date (Friday, April 20). Assume further, that sales of bonds nearest the valuation date occurred two trading days before (Wednesday, April 18) and three trading days after (Wednesday, April 25) the valuation date and that on these two days the closing selling prices per bond were $29 and $22, respectively. The highest and lowest selling prices are not available for these dates in a generally available listing or publication of general circulation. Thus, under paragraph (b)(2) of this section, the price of $26.20 is taken as representing the fair market value of a bond as of the valuation date

$$\frac{((3 \times 29) + (2 \times 22))}{5}$$

(c) Based on bid and asked prices. If the provisions of paragraph (b) of this section are inapplicable because actual sales are not available during a reasonable period beginning before and ending after the valuation date, the fair market value may be determined by taking the mean between the bona fide bid and asked prices on the valuation date, or if none, by taking a weighted average of the means between the bona fide bid and asked prices on the nearest trading date before and the nearest trading date after the valuation date, if both such nearest dates are within a reasonable period. The average is to be determined in the manner described in paragraph (b) of this section.

(d) Based on incomplete selling prices or bid and asked prices. If the provisions of paragraphs (b) and (c) of this section are inapplicable because no actual sale prices or bona fide bid and asked prices are available on a date within a reasonable period before the valuation date, but such prices are available on a date within a reasonable period after the valuation date, or vice versa, then the mean between the highest and lowest available sale prices or bid and asked prices may be taken as the value.

(e) Where selling prices or bid and asked prices do not reflect fair market value. If it is established that the value of any bond or share of stock determined on the basis of selling or bid and asked prices as provided under paragraphs (b), (c), and (d) of this section does not reflect the fair market value thereof, then some reasonable modification of that basis or other relevant facts and elements of value are considered in determining the fair market value. Where sales at or near the date of death are few or of a sporadic nature, such sales alone may not indicate fair market value. In certain exceptional cases, the size of the block of stock to be valued in relation to the number of shares changing hands in sales may be relevant in determining whether selling prices reflect the fair market value of the block of stock to be valued. If the executor can show that the block of stock to be valued is so large in relation to the actual sales on the existing market that it could not be liquidated in a reasonable time without depressing the market, the price at which the block could be sold as such outside the usual market, as through an underwriter, may be a more accurate indication of value that market quotations. Complete data in support of any allowance claimed due to the size of the block of stock being valued shall be submitted with the return. On the other hand, if the block of stock to be valued represents a controlling interest, either actual or effective, in a going business, the price at which other lots change hands may have little relation to its true value.

(f) Where selling prices or bid and asked prices are unavailable. If the provisions of paragraphs (b), (c), and (d) of this section are inapplicable because actual sale prices and bona fide bid and asked prices are lacking, then the fair market value is to be determined by taking the following factors into consideration:

(1) In the case of corporate or other bonds, the soundness of the security, the interest yield, the date of maturity, and other relevant factors; and

(2) In the case of shares of stock, the company's net worth, prospective earning power and dividend-paying capacity, and other relevant factors.

Some of the "other relevant factors" referred to in subparagraphs (1) and (2) of this paragraph are: The good will of the business; the economic outlook in the particular industry; the company's position in the industry and its management; the degree of control of the business represented by the block of stock to be valued; and the values of securities of corporations engaged in the same or similar lines of business which are listed on a stock exchange. However, the weight to be accorded such comparisons or any other evidentiary factors considered in the determination of a value depends upon the facts of each case. In addition to the relevant factors described above, consideration shall also be given to nonoperating assets, including proceeds of life insurance policies payable to or for the benefit of the company, to the extent such nonoperating assets have not been taken into account in the determination of net worth, prospective earning power and dividend-earning capacity. Complete financial and other data upon which the valuation is based should be submitted with the return, including copies of reports of any examinations of the company made by accountants, engineers, or any technical experts as of or near the applicable valuation date.

(g) Pledged securities. The full value of securities pledged to secure an indebtedness of the decedent is included in the gross estate. If the decedent had a trading account with a broker, all securities belonging to the decedent and held by the broker at the date of death must be included at their fair market value as of the applicable valuation date. Securities purchased on margin for the decedent's account and held by a broker must also be returned at their fair market value as of the applicable valuation date. The amount of the decedent's indebtedness to a broker or other person with whom securities were pledged is allowed as a deduction from the gross estate in accordance with the provisions of § 20.2053-1 or § 20.2106-1 (for estates of nonresidents not citizens).

(h) **Securities subject to an option or contract to purchase.** Another person may hold an option or a contract to purchase securities owned by a decedent at the time of his death. The effect, if any, that is given to the option or contract price in determining the value of the securities for estate tax purposes depends upon the circumstances of the particular case. Little weight will be accorded a price contained in an option or contract under which the decedent is free to dispose of the underlying securities at any price he chooses during his lifetime. Such is the effect, for example, of an agreement on the part of a shareholder to purchase whatever shares of stock the decedent may own at the time of his death. Even if the decedent is not free to dispose of the underlying securities at other than the option or contract price, such price will be disregarded in determining the value of the securities unless it is determined under the circumstances of the particular case that the agreement represents a bona fide business arrangement and not a device to pass the decedent's shares to the natural objects of his bounty for less than an adequate and full consideration in money or money's worth.

(i) **Stock sold "ex-dividend."** In any case where a dividend is declared on a share of stock before the decedent's death but payable to stockholders of record on a date after his death and the stock is selling "ex-dividend" on the date of the decedent's death, the amount of the dividend is added to the ex-dividend quotation in determining the fair market value of the stock as of the date of the decedent's death.

§ 20.2031-3   Valuation of interests in businesses

The fair market value of any interest of a decedent in a business, whether a partnership or a proprietorship, is the net amount which a willing purchaser, whether an individual or a corporation, would pay for the interest to a willing seller, neither being under any compulsion to buy or to sell and both having reasonable knowledge of relevant facts.

The net value is determined on the basis of all relevant factors including—

(a) A fair appraisal as of the applicable valuation date of all the assets of the business, tangible and intangible, including good will;

(b) The demonstrated earning capacity of the business; and

(c) The other factors set forth in paragraphs (f) and (h) of § 20.2031-2 relating to the valuation of corporate stock, to the extent applicable.

Special attention should be given to determining an adequate value of the good will of the business in all cases in which the decedent has not agreed, for an adequate and full consideration in money or money's worth, that his interest passes at his death to, for example, his surviving partner or partners. Complete financial and other data upon which the valuation is based should be submitted with the return, including copies of reports of examinations of the business made by accountants, engineers, or any technical experts as of or near the applicable valuation date.

§ 20.2031-4   Valuation of notes

The fair market value of notes, secured or unsecured, is presumed to be the amount of unpaid principal, plus interest accrued to the date of death, unless the executor establishes that the value is lower or that the notes are worthless. However, items of interest shall be separately stated on the estate tax return. If not returned at face value, plus accrued interest, satisfactory evidence must be submitted that the note is worth less than the unpaid amount (because of the interest rate, date of maturity, or other cause), or that the note is uncollectible, either in whole or in part (by reason of the insolvency of the party or parties liable, or for other cause), and that any property pledged or mortgaged as security is insufficient to satisfy the obligation.

§ 20.2031-5   Valuation of cash on hand or on deposit

The amount of cash belonging to the decedent at the date of his death, whether in his possession or in the possession of another, or deposited with a bank, is included in the decedent's gross estate. If bank checks outstanding at the time of the decedent's death and given in discharge of bona fide legal obligations of the decedent incurred for an adequate and full consideration in money or money's worth are subsequently honored by the bank and charged to the decedent's account, the balance remaining in the account may be returned, but only if the obligations are not claimed as deductions from the gross estate.

§ 20.2031-6 Valuation of household and personal effects

(a) **General rule.** The fair market value of the decedent's household and personal effects is the price which a willing buyer would pay to a willing seller, neither being under any compulsion to buy or to sell and both having reasonable knowledge of relevant facts. A room by room itemization of household and personal effects is desirable. All the articles should be named specifically, except that a number of articles contained in the same room, none of which has a value in excess of $100, may be grouped. A separate value should be given for each article named. In lieu of an itemized list, the executor may furnish a written statement, containing a declaration that it is made under penalties of perjury, setting forth the aggregate value as appraised by a competent appraiser or appraisers of recognized standing and ability, or by a dealer or dealers in the class of personalty involved.

(b) **Special rule in cases involving a substantial amount of valuable articles.** Notwithstanding the provisions of paragraph (a) of this section, if there are included among the household and personal effects articles having marked artistic or intrinsic value of a total value in excess of $3,000 (e. g., jewelry, furs, silverware, paintings, etchings, engravings, antiques, books, statuary, vases, oriental rugs, coin or stamp collections), the appraisal of an expert or experts, under oath, shall be filed with the return. The appraisal shall be accompanied by a written statement of the executor containing a declaration that it is made under the penalties of perjury as to the completeness of the itemized list of such property and as to the disinterested character and the qualifications of the appraiser or appraisers.

(c) **Disposition of household effects prior to investigation.** If it is desired to effect distribution or sale of any portion of the household or personal effects of the decedent in advance of an investigation by an officer of the Internal Revenue Service, information to that effect shall be given to the district director. The statement to the district director shall be accompanied by an appraisal of such property, under oath, and by a written statement of the executor, containing a declaration that it is made under the penalties of perjury, regarding the completeness of the list of such property and the qualifications of the appraiser, as heretofore described. If a personal inspection by an officer of the Internal Revenue Service is not deemed necessary, the executor will be so advised. This procedure is designed to facilitate disposition of such property and to obviate future expense and inconvenience to the estate by affording the district director an opportunity to make an investigation should one be deemed necessary prior to sale or distribution.

(d) **Additional rules if an appraisal involved.** If, pursuant to paragraphs (a), (b), and (c) of this section, expert appraisers are employed, care should be taken to see that they are reputable and of recognized competency to appraise the particular class of property involved. In the appraisal, books in sets by standard authors should be listed in separate groups. In listing paintings having artistic value, the size, subject, and artist's name should be stated. In the case of oriental rugs, the size, make, and general condition should be given. Sets of silverware should be listed in separate groups. Groups or individual pieces of silverware should be weighed and the weights given in troy ounces. In arriving at the value of silverware, the appraisers should take into consideration its antiquity, utility, desirability, condition, and obsolescence.

§ 20.2031-8 Valuation of certain life insurance and annuity contracts; valuation of shares in an open-end investment company

(a) **Valuation of certain life insurance and annuity contracts.** (1) The value of a contract for the payment of an annuity, or an insurance policy on the life of a person other than the decedent, issued by a company regularly engaged in the selling of contracts of that character is established through the sale by that company of comparable contracts. An annuity payable under a combination annuity contract and life insurance policy on the decedent's life (e. g., a "retirement income" policy with death benefit) under which there was no insurance element at the time of the decedent's death (see paragraph (d) of § 20.2039-1) is treated like a contract for the payment of an annuity for purposes of this section.

(2) As valuation of an insurance policy through sale of comparable contracts is not readily ascertainable when, at the date of the decedent's death, the contract has been in force for some time and further premium payments are to be made, the value may be approximated by adding to the interpolated terminal reserve at the date of the decedent's death the proportionate part of the gross premium last paid before the date of the decedent's death which covers the period extending beyond that date. If, however, because of the unusual nature of the contract such an approximation is not reasonably close to the full value of the contract, this method may not be used.

(3) The application of this section may be illustrated by the following examples. In each case involving an insurance contract, it is assumed that there are no accrued dividends or outstanding indebtedness on the contract.

Example (1). X purchased from a life insurance company a joint and survivor annuity contract under the terms of which X was to receive payments of $1,200 annually for his life and, upon X's death, his wife was to receive payments of $1,200 annually for her life. Five years after such purchase, when his wife was 50 years of age, X died. The value of the annuity contract at the date of X's death is the amount which the company would charge for an annuity providing for the payment of $1,200 annually for the life of a female 50 years of age.

Example (2). Y died holding the incidents of ownership in a life insurance policy on the life of his wife. The policy was one on which no further payments were to be made to the company (e.g., a single premium policy or a paid-up policy). The value of the insurance policy at the date of Y's death is the amount which the company would charge for a single premium contract of the same specified amount on the life of a person of the age of the insured.

Example (3). Z died holding the incidents of ownership in a life insurance policy on the life of his wife. The policy was an ordinary life policy issued nine years and four months prior to Z's death and at a time when Z's wife was 35 years of age. The gross annual premium is $2,811 and the decedent died four months after the last premium due date. The value of the insurance policy at the date of Z's death is computed as follows:

Terminal reserve at end of tenth year	$14,601.00
Terminal reserve at end of ninth year	12,965.00
Increase	1,636.00
One-third of such increase (Z having died four months following the last preceding premium due date) is	545.33
Terminal reserve at end of ninth year	12,965.00
Interpolated terminal reserve at date of Z's death	13,510.33
Two-thirds of gross premium (⅔ x $2,811)	1,874.00
Value of the insurance policy	15,384.33

(b) Valuation of shares in an open-end investment company. (1) The fair market value of a share in an open-end investment company (commonly known as a "mutual fund") is the public redemption price of a share. In the absence of an affirmative showing of the public redemption price in effect at the time of death, the last public redemption price quoted by the company for the date of death shall be presumed to be the applicable public redemption price. If the alternate valuation method under 2032 is elected, the last public redemption price quoted by the company for the alternate valuation date shall be the applicable redemption price. If there is no public redemption price quoted by the company for the applicable valuation date (e.g., the valuation date is a Saturday, Sunday, or holiday), the fair market value of the mutual fund share is the last public redemption price quoted by the company for the first day preceding the applicable valuation date for which there is a quotation. In any case where a dividend is declared on a share in an open-end investment company before the decedent's death but payable to shareholders of record on a date after his death and the share is quoted "ex-dividend" on the date of the decedent's death, the amount of the dividend is added to the ex-dividend quotation in determining the fair market value of the share as of the date of the decedent's death. As used in this paragraph, the term "open-end investment company" includes only a company which on the applicable valuation date was engaged in offering its shares to the public in the capacity of an open-end investment company.

* * * * *

§ 20.2031-10 Valuation of annuities, life estates, terms for years, remainders, and reversions for estates of decedents dying after December 31, 1970

(a) In general. (1) Except as otherwise provided in this paragraph, for estates of decedents dying after December 31, 1970, the fair market value of annuities, life estates, terms for years, remainders, and reversions is their present value determined under this section. The value of annuities issued by companies regularly engaged in their sale, and of insurance policies on the lives of persons other than the decedent is determined under § 20.2031-8. The fair market value of a remainder interest in a charitable remainder unitrust as defined in § 1.664-3 is its present value determined under § 1.664-4. The fair market value of a life interest or term for years in a charitable remainder unitrust is the fair market value of the property as of the date of valuation less the fair market value of the remainder interest on such date determined under § 1.664-4. The fair market value of interests in a pooled income fund, as defined in § 1.642(c)-5, is their value determined under § 1.642(c)-6. . . . .

(2) The present value of an annuity, life estate, remainder or reversion determined under this section which is dependent on the continuation or termination of the life of one person is computed by the use of Table A(1) or A(2) in paragraph (f) of this section. Table A(1) is to be used when the person upon whose life the interest is based is a male and Table A(2) is to be used when such person is a female. The present value of an annuity, term for years, remainder or reversion dependent on a term certain is computed by the use of Table B in paragraph (f) of this section. If the interest to be valued is dependent upon more than one life or there is a term certain concurrent with one or more lives, see paragraph (e) of this section. For purposes of the computations described in this section, the age of a person is to be taken as the age of that person at his nearest birthday.

(3) In all examples set forth in this section, the decedent is assumed to have died after December 31, 1970.

(b) Annuities—(1) Payable annually at end of year. If an annuity is payable annually at the end of each year during the life of an individual (as, for example, if the first payment is due 1 year after decedent's death), the amount payable annually is multiplied by the figure in column 2 of Table A(1) or A(2), whichever is appropriate, opposite the number of years in column 1 nearest the age of the individual whose life measures the duration of the annuity. If the annuity is payable annually at the end of each year for definite number of years, the amount payable annually is multiplied by the figure in column 2 of Table B opposite the number of years in column 1 representing the duration of the annuity. The application of this subparagraph may be illustrated by the following examples:

Example (1). The decedent received, under the terms of his father's will, an annuity of $10,000 a year payable annually for the life of his elder brother. At the time he died, an annual payment had just been made. The brother at the decedent's death was 40 years 8 months old. By reference to Table A(1) the figure in column 2 opposite 41 years, the number nearest to the brother's actual age, is found to be 12.9934. The present value of the annuity at the date of the decedent's death is, therefore, $129,934 ($10,000×12.9934).

Example (2). The decedent was entitled to receive an annuity of $10,000 a year payable annually throughout a term certain. At the time he died, an annual payment had just been made and five more annual payments were still to be made. By reference to Table B, it is found that the figure in column 2 opposite 5 years is 4.2124. The present value of the annuity is, therefore, $42,124 ($10,000×4.2124).

(2) Payable at the end of semiannual, quarterly, monthly, or weekly periods. If an annuity is payable at the end of semiannual, quarterly, monthly, or weekly periods during the life of an individual (as for example if the first payment is due 1 month after the decedent's death), the aggregate amount to be paid within a year is first multiplied by the figure in column 2 of Table A(1) or A(2), whichever is appropriate, opposite the number of years in column 1 nearest the age of the individual whose life measures the duration of the annuity. The product so obtained is then multiplied by whichever of the following factors is appropriate:

1.0148 for semiannual payments,
1.0222 for quarterly payments,
1.0272 for monthly payments,
1.0291 for weekly payments.

If the annuity is payable at the end of semiannual, quarterly, monthly, or weekly periods for a definite number of years, the aggregate amount to be paid within a year is first multiplied by the figure in column 2 of Table B opposite the number of years in column 1 representing the duration of the annuity. The product so obtained is then multiplied by whichever of the above factors is appropriate. The application of this subparagraph may be illustrated by the following example:

Example. The facts are the same as those contained in example (1) set forth in subparagraph (1) of this paragraph, except that the annuity is payable semiannually. The aggregate annual amount, $10,000, is multiplied by the factor 12.9934, and the product multiplied by 1.0148. The present value of the annuity at the date of the decedent's death is, therefore, $131,857.02 ($10,000×12.9934×1.0148).

(3) Payable at the beginning of annual, semiannual, quarterly, monthly, or weekly periods. (i) If the first payment of an annuity for the life of an individual is due at the beginning of the annual or other payment period rather than at the end (as, for example, if the first payment is to be made immediately after the decedent's death), the value of the annuity is the sum of (a) the first payment plus (b) the present value of a similar annuity, the first payment of which is not to be made until the end of the payment period, determined as provided in subparagraph (1) or (2) of this paragraph. The application of this subdivision may be illustrated by the following example:

Example. The decedent was entitled to receive an annuity of $50 a month during the life of another, a woman. The decedent died on the day a payment was due. At the date of the decedent's death, the person whose life measures the duration of the annuity is 50 years of age. The value of the annuity at the date of the decedent's death is $50 plus the product of $50×12×12.5793 (see Table A(2)) ×1.0272 (see subparagraph (2) of this paragraph). That is, $50 plus $7,752.87, or $7,802.87.

(ii) If the first payment of an annuity for a definite number of years is due at the beginning of the annual or other payment period, the applicable factor is the product of the factor shown in Table B multiplied by whichever of the following factors is appropriate:

    1.0600 for annual payments,
    1.0448 for semiannual payments,
    1.0372 for quarterly payments,
    1.0322 for monthly payments,
    1.0303 for weekly payments.

The application of this subdivision may be illustrated by the following example:

Example. The decedent was the beneficiary of an annuity of $50 a month. On the day a payment was due, the decedent died. There were 300 payments to be made, including the payment due. The value of the annuity as of the date of decedent's death is the product of $50×12×12.7834 (see Table B) ×1.0322, or $7,917.02.

(c) Life estates and terms for years. If the interest to be valued is the right of a person for his life, or for the life of another person, to receive the income of certain property or to use nonincome-producing property, the value of the interest is the value of the property multiplied by the figure in column 3 of Table A(1) or A(2), whichever is appropriate, opposite the number of years nearest to the actual age of the measuring life. If the interest to be valued is the right to receive income of property or to use nonincome-producing property for a term of years, column 3 of Table B is used. The application of this paragraph may be illustrated by the following example:

Example. The decedent or his estate was entitled to receive the income from a fund of $50,000 during the life of his elder brother. Upon the brother's death, the remainder is to go to X. The brother was 31 years 5 months old at the time of decedent's death. By reference to Table A(1) the figure in column 3 opposite 31 years is found to be 0.86117. The present value of decedent's interest is therefore, $43,-058.50 ($50,000×0.86117).

(d) Remainders or reversionary interests. If a decedent had, at the time of his death, a remainder or a reversionary interest in property to take effect after an estate for the life of another, the present value of his interest is obtained by multiplying the value of the property by the figure in column 4 of Table A(1) or A(2), whichever is appropriate, opposite the number of years nearest to the actual age of the person whose life measures the preceding estate. If the remainder or reversion is to take effect at the end of a term for years, column 4 of Table B is used. The application of this paragraph may be illustrated by the following example:

Example. The decedent was entitled to receive certain property worth $50,000 upon the death of his elder sister, to whom the income was bequeathed for life. At the time of the decedent's death, the elder sister was 31 years 5 months old. By reference to Table A(2), the figure in column 4 opposite 31 years is found to be 0.10227. The present value of the remainder interest at the date of decedent's death is, therefore, $5,113.50 ($50,000×0.10227).

(e) **Actuarial computations by the Internal Revenue Service.** If the valuation of the interest involved is dependent upon the continuation or the termination of more than one life or upon a term certain concurrent with one or more lives, a special factor must be used. The factor is to be computed on the basis of interest at the rate of 6 percent a year, compounded annually, and life contingencies determined, as to each male and female life involved, from the values of 1_x that are set forth in columns 2 and 3, respectively, of Table LN of paragraph (f). Table LN contains values of 1_x taken from the life table for total males and the life table for total females appearing as Tables 2 and 3, respectively, in United States Life Tables: 1959–61, published by the Department of Health, Education, and Welfare, Public Health Service, except that for technical reasons Table LN employs graduated data, furnished by that Department, to increase the number of significant figures shown at ages of male lives older than 86 and female lives older than 90. Many such special factors may be found in, or computed with the use of the tables contained in, the publications entitled "Actuarial Values I: Valuation of Last Survivor Charitable Remainders" and "Actuarial Values II: Factors at 6 Percent Involving One and Two Lives." These publications may be purchased from the Superintendent of Documents, U. S. Government Printing Office, Washington, DC 20402. However, if a special factor is required in the case of an actual decedent, the Commissioner will furnish the factor to the executor upon request. The request must be accompanied by a statement of the sex and date of birth of each person, the duration of whose life may affect the value of the interest, and by copies of the relevant instruments.

(f) The following tables shall be used in the application of the provisions of this section:

TABLE A (1)

TABLE, SINGLE LIFE MALE, 6 PERCENT, SHOWING THE PRESENT WORTH OF AN ANNUITY, OF A LIFE INTEREST, AND OF A REMAINDER INTEREST

(1) Age	(2) Annuity	(3) Life estate	(4) Remainder
0	15.6175	0.93705	0.06295
1	16.0362	.96217	.03783
2	16.0283	.96170	.03830
3	16.0089	.96053	.03947
4	15.9841	.95905	.04095
5	15.9553	.95732	.04268
6	15.9233	.95540	.04460
7	15.8885	.95331	.04669

TABLE A(1)—Continued

(1) Age	(2) Annuity	(3) Life estate	(4) Remainder
8	15.8508	.95105	.04895
9	15.8101	.94861	.05139
10	15.7663	.94598	.05402
11	15.7194	.94316	.05684
12	15.6698	.94019	.05981
13	15.6180	.93708	.06292
14	15.5651	.93391	.06609
15	15.5115	.93069	.06931
16	15.4576	.92746	.07254
17	15.4031	.92419	.07581
18	15.3481	.92089	.07911
19	15.2918	.91751	.08249
20	15.2339	.91403	.08597
21	15.1744	.91046	.08954
22	15.1130	.90678	.09328
23	15.0487	.90292	.09702
24	14.9807	.89884	.10116
25	14.9075	.89445	.10555
26	14.8287	.88972	.11028
27	14.7442	.88465	.11535
28	14.6542	.87925	.12075
29	14.5588	.87353	.12647
30	14.4584	.86750	.13250
31	14.3528	.86117	.13883
32	14.2418	.85451	.14549
33	14.1254	.84752	.15248
34	14.0034	.84020	.15980
35	13.8758	.83255	.16745
36	13.7425	.82455	.17545
37	13.6036	.81622	.18378
38	13.4591	.80755	.19245
39	13.3090	.79854	.20146
40	13.1538	.78923	.21077
41	12.9934	.77960	.22040
42	12.8279	.76967	.23033
43	12.6574	.75944	.24056
44	12.4819	.74891	.25109
45	12.3013	.73808	.26192
46	12.1158	.72695	.27305
47	11.9253	.71552	.28448
48	11.7308	.70385	.29615
49	11.5330	.69198	.30802
50	11.3329	.67997	.32003
51	11.1308	.66785	.33215
52	10.9267	.65560	.34440
53	10.7200	.64320	.35680
54	10.5100	.63060	.36940
55	10.2960	.61776	.38224
56	10.0777	.60466	.39534
57	9.8552	.59131	.40869
58	9.6297	.57778	.42222
59	9.4028	.56417	.43583
60	9.1753	.55052	.44948
61	8.9478	.53687	.46313
62	8.7202	.52321	.47679
63	8.4924	.50954	.49046
64	8.2642	.49585	.50415
65	8.0353	.48212	.51788
66	7.8060	.46836	.53164
67	7.5763	.45458	.54542
68	7.3462	.44077	.55923
69	7.1149	.42689	.57311
70	6.8823	.41294	.58706
71	6.6481	.39889	.60111
72	6.4123	.38474	.61526
73	6.1752	.37051	.62949
74	5.9373	.35624	.64376
75	5.6990	.34194	.65806
76	5.4602	.32761	.67239
77	5.2211	.31327	.68673
78	4.9825	.29895	.70105
79	4.7469	.28481	.71519
80	4.5164	.27098	.72902
81	4.2955	.25773	.74227
82	4.0879	.24527	.75473
83	3.8924	.23354	.76646
84	3.7029	.22217	.77783
85	3.5117	.21070	.78930
86	3.3259	.19955	.80045
87	3.1450	.18820	.81130
88	2.9703	.17872	.82178
89	2.8052	.16831	.83169
90	2.6536	.15922	.84078
91	2.5162	.15097	.84903
92	2.3917	.14350	.85650
93	2.2801	.13681	.86319
94	2.1802	.13081	.86919
95	2.0891	.12535	.87465
96	1.9997	.11998	.88002
97	1.9145	.11487	.88513
98	1.8331	.10999	.89001
99	1.7554	.10532	.89468
100	1.6812	.10087	.89913
101	1.6101	.09661	.90339
102	1.5416	.09250	.90750

Table A (1)—Continued

(1) Age	(2) Annuity	(3) Life estate	(4) Remainder
103	1.4744	.08846	.91154
104	1.4065	.08439	.91561
105	1.3334	.08000	.92000
106	1.2452	.07471	.92529
107	1.1196	.06718	.93282
108	.9043	.05426	.94574
109	.4717	.02630	.97170

TABLE A(2)

TABLE, SINGLE LIFE FEMALE, 6 PERCENT, SHOWING THE PRESENT WORTH OF AN ANNUITY, OF A LIFE INTEREST, AND OF A REMAINDER INTEREST

(1) Age	(2) Annuity	(3) Life estate	(4) Remainder
0	15.8972	0.95383	0.04617
1	16.2284	.97370	.02630
2	16.2287	.97372	.02628
3	16.2180	.97308	.02692
4	16.2029	.97217	.02783
5	16.1850	.97110	.02890
6	16.1648	.96989	.03011
7	16.1421	.96853	.03147
8	16.1172	.96703	.03297
9	16.0901	.96541	.03459
10	16.0608	.96365	.03635
11	16.0293	.96176	.03824
12	15.9958	.95975	.04025
13	15.9607	.95764	.04236
14	15.9239	.95543	.04457
15	15.8856	.95314	.04686
16	15.8460	.95076	.04924
17	15.8048	.94829	.05171
18	15.7620	.94572	.05428
19	15.7172	.94303	.05697
20	15.6701	.94021	.05979
21	15.6207	.93724	.06276
22	15.5687	.93412	.06588
23	15.5141	.93085	.06915
24	15.4565	.92739	.07261
25	15.3959	.92375	.07625
26	15.3322	.91993	.08007
27	15.2652	.91591	.08409
28	15.1946	.91168	.08832
29	15.1208	.90725	.09275
30	15.0432	.90259	.09741
31	14.9622	.89773	.10227
32	14.8775	.89265	.10735
33	14.7888	.88733	.11267
34	14.6960	.88176	.11824
35	14.5989	.87593	.12407
36	14.4975	.86985	.13015
37	14.3915	.86349	.13651
38	14.2811	.85687	.14313
39	14.1663	.84998	.15002
40	14.0468	.84281	.15719
41	13.9227	.83536	.16464
42	13.7940	.82764	.17236
43	13.6604	.81962	.18038
44	13.5219	.81131	.18869
45	13.3781	.80269	.19731
46	13.2290	.79374	.20626
47	13.0746	.78448	.21552
48	12.9147	.77488	.22512
49	12.7496	.76498	.23502
50	12.5793	.75476	.24524
51	12.4039	.74423	.25577
52	12.2232	.73339	.26661
53	12.0367	.72220	.27780
54	11.8436	.71062	.28938
55	11.6432	.69859	.30141
56	11.4353	.68612	.31388
57	11.2200	.67320	.32680
58	10.9980	.65988	.34012
59	10.7703	.64622	.35378
60	10.5376	.63226	.36774
61	10.3005	.61803	.38197
62	10.0587	.60359	.39648
63	9.8118	.58871	.41129
64	9.5592	.57355	.42645
65	9.3005	.55803	.44197
66	9.0352	.54211	.45789
67	8.7639	.52583	.47417
68	8.4874	.50924	.49076
69	8.2068	.49241	.50759

TABLE A(2)—Continued

(1) Age	(2) Annuity	(3) Life estate	(4) Remainder
70	7.9234	.47540	.52460
71	7.6371	.45823	.54177
72	7.3480	.44088	.55912
73	7.0568	.42341	.57659
74	6.7645	.40587	.59413
75	6.4721	.38833	.61167
76	6.1788	.37073	.62927
77	5.8845	.35307	.64693
78	5.5910	.33546	.66454
79	5.3018	.31811	.68189
80	5.0195	.30117	.69883
81	4.7482	.28489	.71511
82	4.4892	.26935	.73065
83	4.2398	.25439	.74561
84	3.9927	.23956	.76044
85	3.7401	.22441	.77559
86	3.5016	.21010	.78990
87	3.2790	.19674	.80326
88	3.0719	.18431	.81569
89	2.8808	.17285	.82715
90	2.7068	.16241	.83759
91	2.5502	.15301	.84699
92	2.4116	.14470	.85530
93	2.2901	.13741	.86259
94	2.1839	.13103	.86897
95	2.0891	.12535	.87465
96	1.9997	.11998	.88002
97	1.9145	.11487	.88513
98	1.8331	.10999	.89001
99	1.7554	.10532	.89468
100	1.6812	.10087	.89913
101	1.6101	.09661	.90339
102	1.5416	.09250	.90750
103	1.4744	.08846	.91154
104	1.4065	.08439	.91561
105	1.3334	.08000	.92000
106	1.2452	.07471	.92529
107	1.1196	.06718	.93282
108	.9043	.05426	.94574
109	.4717	.02830	.97170

TABLE B

TABLE SHOWING THE PRESENT WORTH AT 6 PERCENT OF AN ANNUITY FOR A TERM CERTAIN, OF AN INCOME INTEREST FOR A TERM CERTAIN, AND OF A REMAINDER INTEREST POSTPONED FOR A TERM CERTAIN

(1) Number of years	(2) Annuity	(3) Term certain	(4) Remainder
1	0.9434	0.056604	0.943396
2	1.8334	.110004	.889996
3	2.6730	.160381	.839619
4	3.4651	.207906	.792094
5	4.2124	.252742	.747258
6	4.9173	.295039	.704961
7	5.5824	.334943	.665057
8	6.2098	.372588	.627412
9	6.8017	.408102	.591898
10	7.3601	.441605	.558395
11	7.8869	.473212	.526788
12	8.3838	.503031	.496969
13	8.8527	.531161	.468839
14	9.2950	.557699	.442301
15	9.7122	.582735	.417265
16	10.1059	.606354	.393646
17	10.4773	.628636	.371364
18	10.8276	.649656	.350344
19	11.1581	.669487	.330513
20	11.4699	.688195	.311805
21	11.7641	.705845	.294155
22	12.0416	.722495	.277505
23	12.3034	.738203	.261797
24	12.5504	.753021	.246979
25	12.7834	.767001	.232999
26	13.0032	.780190	.219810
27	13.2105	.792632	.207368
28	13.4062	.804370	.195630
29	13.5907	.815443	.184557
30	13.7648	.825890	.174110
31	13.9291	.835745	.164255
32	14.0640	.845043	.154957
33	14.2302	.853814	.146186
34	14.3681	.862088	.137912
35	14.4982	.869895	.130105
36	14.6210	.877259	.122741

TABLE B—Continued

(1) Number of years	(2) Annuity	(3) Term certain	(4) Remainder
37	14.7368	.884207	.115793
38	14.8460	.890761	.109239
39	14.9491	.896944	.103056
40	15.0463	.902778	.097222
41	15.1380	.908281	.091719
42	15.2245	.913473	.086527
43	15.3062	.918370	.081630
44	15.3832	.922991	.077009
45	15.4558	.927350	.072650
46	15.5244	.931462	.068538
47	15.5890	.935342	.064658
48	15.6500	.939002	.060998
49	15.7076	.942454	.057546
50	15.7619	.945712	.054288
51	15.8131	.948785	.051215
52	15.8614	.951684	.048316
53	15.9070	.954418	.045582
54	15.9500	.956999	.043001
55	15.9905	.959433	.040567
56	16.0288	.961729	.038271
57	16.0649	.963895	.036105
58	16.0990	.965939	.034061
59	16.1311	.967867	.032133
60	16.1614	.969686	.030314

TABLE LN
Values of lx

(1) Age x	(2) Total males	(3) Total females
0	100000.	100000.
1	97087.	97744.
2	96911.	97589.
3	96800.	97498.
4	96714.	97429.
5	96643.	97371.
6	96580.	97320.
7	96522.	97277.
8	96469.	97238.
9	96420.	97204.
10	96375.	97173.
11	96333.	97144.
12	96290.	97116.
13	96242.	97086.
14	96182.	97053.
15	96107.	97016.
16	96014.	96973.
17	95905.	96925.
18	95779.	96872.
19	95641.	96815.
20	95491.	96756.
21	95330.	96694.
22	95158.	96629.
23	94981.	96561.
24	94803.	96491.
25	94631.	96418.
26	94466.	96342.
27	94306.	96262.
28	94148.	96179.
29	93990.	96090.
30	93826.	95996.
31	93656.	95894.
32	93479.	95785.
33	93293.	95668.
34	93097.	95543.
35	92889.	95409.
36	92668.	95265.
37	92426.	95110.
38	92166.	94942.
39	91883.	94759.
40	91572.	94560.
41	91230.	94343.
42	90854.	94106.
43	90441.	93848.
44	89988.	93568.
45	89492.	93265.
46	88950.	92938.
47	88359.	92583.
48	87709.	92199.
49	86992.	91781.
50	86199.	91327.
51	85325.	90833.
52	84369.	90297.
53	83333.	89720.
54	82222.	89104.
55	81039.	88451.
56	79783.	87758.
57	78451.	87020.

TABLE LN—Continued
Values of lx

(1) Age x	(2) Total males	(3) Total females
58	77032.	86227.
59	75513.	85367.
60	73887.	84430.
61	72151.	83409.
62	70308.	82302.
63	68361.	81108.
64	66316.	79828.
65	64177.	78462.
66	61947.	77008.
67	59631.	75457.
68	57235.	73798.
69	54770.	72016.
70	52244.	70100.
71	49665.	68047.
72	47040.	65856.
73	44375.	63521.
74	41676.	61035.
75	38950.	58394.
76	36210.	55610.
77	33468.	52693.
78	30732.	49635.
79	28006.	46424.
80	25300.	43063.
81	22619.	39555.
82	19983.	35939.
83	17439.	32290.
84	15045.	28707.
85	12845.	25269.
86	10819.	21877.
87	8979.9	18593.
88	7332.7	15490.
89	5875.8	12628.
90	4608.7	10056.
91	3534.0	7810.9
92	2648.5	5910.7
93	1938.9	4356.1
94	1386.7	3128.5
95	969.97894	2193.0122
96	665.24779	1504.0497
97	446.27929	1008.9868
98	292.53610	661.39091
99	187.17106	423.17250
100	116.76480	263.99194
101	70.944391	160.39721
102	41.934198	94.808454
103	24.086138	54.456022
104	13.428065	30.359329
105	7.2577386	16.408923
106	3.7985839	8.5881608
107	1.9229289	4.3475238
108	0.94040163	2.1261413
109	0.44377201	1.0033181
110	0.	0.

§ 20.2032–1 Alternate valuation

(a) **In general.** In general, section 2032 provides for the valuation of a decedent's gross estate at a date other than the date of the decedent's death. More specifically, if an executor elects the alternate valuation method under section 2032, the property included in the decedent's gross estate on the date of his death is valued as of whichever of the following dates is applicable:

(1) Any property distributed, sold, exchanged, or otherwise disposed of within 6 months (1 year, if the decedent died on or before December 31, 1970) after the decedent's death is valued as of the date on which it is first distributed, sold, exchanged, or otherwise disposed of;

(2) Any property not distributed, sold, exchanged, or otherwise disposed of within 6 months (1 year, if the decedent died on or before December 31,

1970) after the decedent's death is valued as of the date 6 months (1 year, if the decedent died on or before December 31, 1970) after the date of the decedent's death:

(3) Any property, interest, or estate which is affected by mere lapse of time is valued as of the date of the decedent's death, but adjusted for any difference in its value not due to mere lapse of time as of the date 6 months (1 year, if the decedent died on or before December 31, 1970) after the decedent's death, or as of the date of its distribution, sale, exchange, or other disposition, whichever date first occurs.

(b) Method and effect of election. (1) While it is the purpose of section 2032 to permit a reduction in the amount of tax that would otherwise be payable if the gross estate has suffered a shrinkage in its aggregate value in the 6 months (1 year, if the decedent died on or before December 31, 1970) following the decedent's death, the alternate valuation method is not automatic but must be elected. Furthermore, the alternate valuation method may be elected whether or not there has been a shrinkage in the aggregate value of the estate. However, the election is not effective for any purpose unless the value of the gross estate at the time of the decedent's death exceeded $60,000, so that an estate tax return is required to be filed under section 6018.

(2) If the alternate valuation method under section 2032 is to be used, section 2032(c) requires that the executor must so elect on the estate tax return required under section 6018, filed within 9 months (15 months, if the decedent died on or before December 31, 1970) from the date of the decedent's death or within the period of any extension of time granted by the district director under section 6081. In no case may the election be exercised, or a previous election changed, after the expiration of such time. If the election is made, it applies to all the property included in the gross estate, and cannot be applied to only a portion of the property.

(c) Meaning of "distributed, sold, exchanged, or otherwise disposed of". (1) The phrase "distributed, sold, exchanged, or otherwise disposed of" comprehends all possible ways by which property ceases to form a part of the gross estate. For example, money, on hand at the date of the decedent's death which is thereafter used in the payment of funeral expenses, or which is thereafter invested, falls within the term "otherwise disposed of." The term also includes the surrender of a stock certificate for corporate assets in complete or partial liquidation of a corporation pursuant to section 331. The term does not, however, extend to transactions which are mere changes in form. Thus, it does not include a transfer of assets to a corporation in exchange for its stock in a transaction with respect to which no gain or loss would be recognizable for income tax purposes under section 351. Nor does it include an exchange of stock or securities in a corporation for stock or securities in the same corporation or another corporation in a transaction, such as a merger, recapitalization, reorganization or other transaction described in section 368(a) or 355, with respect to which no gain or loss is recognizable for income tax purposes under section 354 or 355.

(2) Property may be "distributed" either by the executor, or by a trustee of property included in the gross estate under sections 2035 through 2038, or section 2041. Property is considered as "distributed" upon the first to occur of the following:

(i) The entry of an order or decree of distribution, if the order or decree subsequently becomes final;

(ii) The segregation or separation of the property from the estate or trust so that it becomes unqualifiedly subject to the demand or disposition of the distributee; or

(iii) The actual paying over or delivery of the property to the distributee.

(3) Property may be "sold, exchanged, or otherwise disposed of" by: (i) The executor; (ii) a trustee or other donee to whom the decedent during his lifetime transferred property included in his gross estate under sections 2035 through 2038, or section 2041; (iii) an heir or devisee to whom title to property passes directly under local law; (iv) a surviving joint tenant or tenant by the entirety; or (v) any other person. If a binding contract for the sale, exchange, or other disposition of property is entered into, the property is considered as sold, exchanged, or otherwise disposed of on

the effective date of the contract, unless the contract is not subsequently carried out substantially in accordance with its terms. The effective date of a contract is normally the date it is entered into (and not the date it is consummated, or the date legal title to the property passes) unless the contract specifies a different effective date.

(d) "Included property" and excluded property". If the executor elects the alternate valuation method under section 2032, all property interests existing at the date of decedent's death which form a part of his gross estate as determined under sections 2033 through 2044 are valued in accordance with the provisions of this section. Such property interests are hereinafter referred to in this section as "included property". Furthermore, such property interests remain "included property" for the purpose of valuing the gross estate under the alternate valuation method even though they change in form during the alternate valuation period by being actually received, or disposed of, in whole or in part, by the estate. On the other hand, property earned or accrued (whether received or not) after the date of the decedent's death and during the alternate valuation period with respect to any property interest existing at the date of the decedent's death, which does not represent a form of "included property" itself or the receipt of "included property" is excluded in valuing the gross estate under the alternate valuation method. Such property is hereinafter referred to in this section as "excluded property". Illustrations of "included property" and "excluded property" are contained in the subparagraphs (1) to (4) of this paragraph:

(1) Interest-bearing obligations. Interest-bearing obligations, such as bonds or notes, may comprise two elements of "included property" at the date of the decedent's death, namely, (i) the principal of the obligation itself, and (ii) interest accrued to the date of death. Each of these elements is to be separately valued as of the applicable valuation date. Interest accrued after the date of death and before the subsequent valuation date constitutes "excluded property". However, any part payment of principal made between the date of death and the subsequent valuation date, or any advance payment of interest for a period after

the subsequent valuation date made during the alternate valuation period which has the effect of reducing the value of the principal obligation as of the subsequent valuation date, will be included in the gross estate, and valued as of the date of such payment.

(2) Leased property. The principles set forth in subparagraph (1) of this paragraph with respect to interest-bearing obligations also apply to leased realty or personalty which is included in the gross estate and with respect to which an obligation to pay rent has been reserved. Both the realty or personalty itself and the rents accrued to the date of death constitute "included property", and each is to be separately valued as of the applicable valuation date. Any rent accrued after the date of death and before the subsequent valuation date is "excluded property". Similarly, the principle applicable with respect to interest paid in advance is equally applicable with respect to advance payments of rent.

(3) Noninterest-bearing obligations. In the case of noninterest-bearing obligations sold at a discount, such as savings bonds, the principal obligation and the discount amortized to the date of death are property interests existing at the date of death and constitute "included property". The obligation itself is to be valued at the subsequent valuation date without regard to any further increase in value due to amortized discount. The additional discount amortized after death and during the alternate valuation period is the equivalent of interest accruing during that period and is, therefore, not to be included in the gross estate under the alternate valuation method.

(4) Stock of a corporation. Shares of stock in a corporation and dividends declared to stockholders of record on or before the date of the decedent's death and not collected at the date of death constitute "included property" of the estate. On the other hand, ordinary dividends out of earnings and profits (whether in cash, shares of the corporation, or other property) declared to stockholders of record after the date of the decedent's death are "excluded property" and are not to be valued under the alternate valuation method. If, however, dividends are declared to stockholders of record after the date of the decedent's death with the effect that the shares of stock at the subsequent valuation date do not reasonably represent the same "included property" of the gross estate as existed at the date of the decedent's death, the dividends are "included property", except to the extent that they are out of earnings of the corporation after the date of the decedent's death. For example, if a corporation makes a distribution in partial liquidation to stockholders of record during the alternate valuation period which is not accompanied by a surrender of a stock certificate for cancellation, the amount of the distribution received on stock included in the gross estate is itself "included property", except to the extent that the distribution was out of earnings and profits since the date of the decedent's death. Similarly, if a corporation, in which the decedent owned a substantial interest and which possessed at the date of the decedent's death accumulated earnings and profits equal to its paid-in capital distributed all of its accumulated earnings and profits as a cash dividend to shareholders of record during the alternate valuation period, the amount of the dividends received on stock includible in the gross estate will be included in the gross estate under the alternate valuation method. Likewise, a stock dividend distributed under such circumstances is "included property".

. . . .

(f) **Mere lapse of time.** In order to eliminate changes in value due only to mere lapse of time, section 2032(a)(3) provides that any interest or estate "affected by mere lapse of time" is included in a decedent's gross estate under the alternate valuation method at its value as of the date of the decedent's death, but with adjustment for any difference in its value as of the subsequent valuation date not due to mere lapse of time. Properties, interests, or estates which are "affected by mere lapse of time" include patents, estates for the life of a person other than the decedent, remainders, reversions, and other like properties, interests, or estates. The phrase "affected by mere lapse of time" has no reference to obligations for the payment of money, whether or not interest-bearing, the value of which changes with the pass-

ing of time. However, such an obligation, like any other property, may become affected by lapse of time when made the subject of a bequest or transfer which itself is creative of an interest or estate so affected. The application of this paragraph is illustrated in subparagraphs (1) and (2) of this paragraph:

(1) **Life estates, remainders, and similar interests.** The values of life estates, remainders, and similar interests are to be obtained by applying the methods prescribed in § 20.2031-7, using (i) the age of each person, the duration of whose life may affect the value of the interest, as of the date of the decedent's death, and (ii) the value of the property as of the alternate date. For example, assume that the decedent or his estate was entitled to receive property upon the death of his elder brother who was entitled to receive the income therefrom for life. At the date of the decedent's death, the property was worth $50,000 and the elder brother was 31 years old. The value of the decedent's remainder interest at the date of his death would, as explained in paragraph (d) of § 20.2031-7, be $14,466 ($50,000 $\times$ 0.28932). If, because of economic conditions, the property declined in value and was worth only $40,000, 6 months (1 year if the decedent died on or before December 31, 1970) after the date of the decedent's death, the value of the remainder interest as of the alternate date would be $11,572.80 ($40,000 $\times$ 0.28932), even though the elder brother may be 32 years old on the alternate date.

. . . .

(g) **Effect of election on deductions.** If the executor elects the alternate valuation method under section 2032, any deduction for administration expenses under section 2053(b) (pertaining to property not subject to claims) or losses under section 2054 (or section 2106(a)(1), relating to estates of nonresidents not citizens) is allowed only to the extent that it is not otherwise in effect allowed in determining the value of the gross estate. Furthermore, the amount of any charitable deduction under section 2055 (or section 2106(a)(2), relating to the estates of nonresidents not citizens) or the amount of any marital deduction under section 2056 is determined by the value of the property with respect to which the deduction is allowed as of the date of the decedent's death, adjusted, however, for any difference in its value as of the date 6 months (1 year, if the decedent died on or before December 31, 1970) after death, or as of the date of its distribution, sale, exchange, or other disposition, whichever first occurs. However, no such adjustment may take into account any difference in value due to lapse of time or to the occurrence or nonoccurrence of a contingency.

§ 20.2033-1 Property in which the decedent had an interest

(a) **In general.** The gross estate of a decedent who was a citizen or resident of the United States at the time of his death includes under section 2033 the value of all property, whether real or personal, tangible or intangible, and wherever situated, beneficially owned by the decedent at the time of his death. (For certain exceptions in the case of real property situated outside the United States, see paragraphs (a) and (c) of § 20.2031-1.) Real property is included whether it came into the possession and control of the executor or administrator or passed directly to heirs or devisees. Various statutory provisions which exempt bonds, notes, bills, and certificates of indebtedness of the Federal Government or its agencies and the interest thereon from taxation are generally not applicable to the estate tax, since such tax is an excise tax on the transfer of property at death and is not a tax on the property transferred.

(b) **Miscellaneous examples.** A cemetery lot owned by the decedent is part of his gross estate, but its value is limited to the salable value of that part of the lot which is not designed for the interment of the decedent and the members of his family. Property subject to homestead or other exemptions under local law is included in the gross estate. Notes or other claims held by the decedent are likewise included even though they are cancelled by the decedent's will. Interest and rents accrued at the date of the decedent's death constitute a part of the gross estate. Similarly, dividends which are payable to the decedent or his estate by reason of the fact that on or before the date of the decedent's death he was a stockholder of record (but which have not been collected at death) constitute a part of the gross estate.

§ 20.2034-1 Dower or curtesy interests

A decedent's gross estate includes under section 2034 any interest in property of the decedent's surviving spouse existing at the time of the decedent's death as dower or curtesy, or any interest created by statute in lieu thereof (although such other interest may differ in character from dower or curtesy). Thus, the full value of property is included in the decedent's gross estate, without deduction of such an interest of the surviving husband or wife, and without regard to when the right to such an interest arose.

§ 20.2035-1 Transactions in contemplation of death

.   .   .   .   .

(b) **Application of other sections.** If a decedent transfers an interest in property or relinquishes a power in contemplation of death, the decedent's gross estate includes the property subject to the interest or power to the extent that it would be included under section 2036, 2037, or 2038 if the decedent had retained the interest or power until his death. If a decedent exercises or releases a general power of appointment in contemplation of death, the property subject to the power is included in the decedent's gross estate to the extent provided in section 2041 and the regulations thereunder.

.   .   .   .   .

(e) **Valuation.** The value of an interest in transferred property includible in a decedent's gross estate under this section is the value of the interest as of the applicable valuation date. In this connection, see sections 2031, 2032, and the regulations thereunder. However, if the transferee has made improvements or additions to the property, any resulting enhancement in the value of the property is not considered in ascertaining the value of the gross estate. Similarly, neither income received subsequent to the transfer nor property purchased with such income is considered.

§ 20.2036-1 Transfers with retained life estate

(a) **In general.** A decedent's gross estate includes under section 2036 the value of any interest in property transferred by the decedent after March 3, 1931, whether in trust or otherwise, except to the extent that the transfer was for an adequate and full consideration in money or money's worth (see § 20.2043-1), if the decedent retained or reserved (1) for his life, or (2) for any period not ascertainable without reference to his death (if the transfer was made after June 6, 1932), or (3) for any period which does not in fact end before his death—

(i) The use, possession, right to the income, or other enjoyment of the transferred property, or

(ii) The right, either alone or in conjunction with any other person or persons, to designate the person or persons who shall possess or enjoy the transferred property or its income (except that, if the transfer was made before June 7, 1932, the right to designate must be retained by or reserved to the decedent alone).

If the decedent retained or reserved an interest or right with respect to all of the property transferred by him, the amount to be included in his gross estate under section 2036 is the value of the entire property, less only the value of any outstanding income interest which is not subject to the decedent's interest or right and which is actually being enjoyed by another person at the time of the decedent's death. If the decedent retained or reserved an interest or right with respect to a part only of the property transferred by him, the amount to be included in his gross estate under section 2036 is only a corresponding proportion of the amount described in the preceding sentence. An interest or right is treated as having been retained or reserved if at the time of the transfer there was an understanding, express or implied, that the interest or right would later be conferred.

(b) **Meaning of terms.** (1) A reservation by the decedent "for any period not ascertainable without reference to his death" may be illustrated by the following examples:

(i) A decedent reserved the right to receive the income from transferred property in quarterly payments, with the proviso that no part of the income between the last quarterly payment and the date of the decedent's death was to be received by the decedent or his estate; and

(ii) A decedent reserved the right to receive the income from transferred property after the death of another person who was in fact enjoying the income at the time of the decedent's death. In such a case, the amount to be included in the decedent's gross estate under this section does not include the value of the outstanding income interest of the other person. It may be noted that if the other person predeceased the decedent, the reservation by the decedent may be considered to be either for his life, or for a period which does not in fact end before his death.

(2) The "use, possession, right to the income, or other enjoyment of the transferred property" is considered as having been retained by or reserved to the decedent to the extent that the use, possession, right to the income, or other enjoyment is to be applied toward the discharge of a legal obligation of the decedent, or otherwise for his pecuniary benefit. The term "legal obligation" includes a legal obligation to support a dependent during the decedent's lifetime.

(3) The phrase "right * * * to designate the person or persons who shall possess or enjoy the transferred property or the income therefrom" includes a reserved power to designate the person or persons to receive the income from the transferred property or to possess or enjoy nonincome-producing property, during the decedent's life or during any other period described in paragraph (a) of this section. With respect to such a power, it is immaterial (i) whether the power was exercisable alone or only in conjunction with another person or persons, whether or not having an adverse interest; (ii) in what capacity the power was exercisable by the decedent or by another person or persons in conjunction with the decedent; and (iii) whether the exercise of the power was subject to a contingency beyond the decedent's control which did not occur before his death (e. g., the death of another person during the decedent's lifetime). The phrase, however, does not include a power over the transferred

property itself which does not affect the enjoyment of the income received or earned during the decedent's life. (See, however, section 2038 for the inclusion of property in the gross estate on account of such a power.) Nor does the phrase apply to a power held solely by a person other than the decedent. But, for example, if the decedent reserved the unrestricted power to remove or discharge a trustee at any time and appoint himself as trustee, the decedent is considered as having the powers of the trustee.

§ 20.2037-1 Transfers taking effect at death

(a) **In general.** A decedent's gross estate includes under section 2037 the value of any interest in property transferred by the decedent after September 7, 1916, whether in trust or otherwise, except to the extent that the transfer was for an adequate and full consideration in money or money's worth (see § 20.2043-1), if—

(1) Possession or enjoyment of the property could, through ownership of the interest, have been obtained only by surviving the decedent,

(2) The decedent had retained a possibility (hereinafter referred to as a "reversionary interest") that the property, other than the income alone, would return to the decedent or his estate or would be subject to a power of disposition by him, and

(3) The value of the reversionary interest immediately before the decedent's death exceeded 5 percent of the value of the entire property.

However, if the transfer was made before October 8, 1949, section 2037 is applicable only if the reversionary interest arose by the express terms of the instrument of transfer and not by operation of law (see paragraph (f) of this section). . . . . .

(b) **Condition of survivorship.** As indicated in paragraph (a) of this section, the value of an interest in transferred property is not included in a decedent's gross estate under section 2037 unless possession or enjoyment of the property could, through ownership of such interest, have been obtained only by surviving the decedent. Thus, property is not included in the decedent's gross estate if, immediately before the decedent's death, possession or enjoyment of the property could have been obtained by any beneficiary either by surviving the decedent or through the occurrence of some other event such as the expiration of a term of years. However, if a consideration of the terms and circumstances of the transfer as a whole indicates that the "other event" is unreal and if the death of the decedent does, in fact, occur before the "other event", the beneficiary will be considered able to possess or enjoy the property only by surviving the decedent. Notwithstanding the foregoing, an interest in transferred property is not includible in a decedent's gross estate under section 2037 if possession or enjoyment of the property could have been obtained by any beneficiary during the decedent's life through the exercise of a general power of appointment (as defined in section 2041) which in fact was exercisable immediately before the decedent's death. See examples (5) and (6) in paragraph (e) of this section.

(c) **Retention of reversionary interest.** (1) As indicated in paragraph (a) of this section, the value of an interest in transferred property is not included in a decedent's gross estate under section 2037 unless the decedent had retained a reversionary interest in the property, and the value of the reversionary interest immediately before the death of the decedent exceeded 5 percent of the value of the property.

(2) For purposes of section 2037, the term "reversionary interest" includes a possibility that property transferred by the decedent may return to him or his estate and a possibility that property transferred by the decedent may become subject to a power of disposition by him. The term is not used in a technical sense, but has reference to any reserved right under which the transferred property shall or may be returned to the grantor. Thus, it encompasses an interest arising either by the express terms of the instrument of transfer or by operation of law. (See, however, paragraph (f) of this section with respect to transfers made before October 8, 1949). The term "reversionary interest" does not include rights to income only, such as the right to receive the income from a trust after the death of another person. (However, see section 2036 for the inclusion of property in the gross estate on account of such rights.) Nor does the term "reversionary interest" include

the possibility that the decedent during his lifetime might have received back an interest in transferred property by inheritance through the estate of another person. Similarly, a statutory right of a spouse to receive a portion of whatever estate a decedent may leave at the time of his death is not a "reversionary interest".

(3) For purposes of this section, the value of the decedent's reversionary interest is computed as of the moment immediately before his death, without regard to whether or not the executor elects the alternate valuation method under section 2032 and without regard to the fact of the decedent's death. The value is ascertained in accordance with recognized valuation principles for determining the value for estate tax purposes of future or conditional interests in property. (See §§ 20.2031–1, 20.-2031–7, and 20.2031–9.) For example, if the decedent's reversionary interest was subject to an outstanding life estate in his wife, his interest is valued according to the actuarial rules set forth in § 20.2031–7. On the other hand, if the decedent's reversionary interest was contingent on the death of his wife without issue surviving and if it cannot be shown that his wife is incapable of having issue (so that his interest is not subject to valuation according to the actuarial rules in § 20.-2031–7), his interest is valued according to the general rules set forth in § 20.2031–1. A possibility that the decedent may be able to dispose of property under certain conditions is considered to have the same value as a right of the decedent to the return of the property under those same conditions.

(4) In order to determine whether or not the decedent retained a reversionary interest in transferred property of a value in excess of 5 percent, the value of the reversionary interest is compared with the value of the transferred property, including interests therein which are not dependent upon survivorship of the decedent. For example, assume that the decedent, A, transferred property in trust with the income payable to B for life and with the remainder payable to C if A predeceases B, but with the property to revert to A if B predeceases A. Assume further that A does, in fact, predecease B. The value of A's reversionary interest immediately before his death is compared with the value of the trust corpus, without

deduction of the value of B's outstanding life estate. If, in the above example, A had retained a reversionary interest in one-half only of the trust corpus, the value of his reversionary interest would be compared with the value of one-half of the trust corpus, again without deduction of any part of the value of B's outstanding life estate.

(d) **Transfers partly taking effect at death.** If separate interests in property are transferred to one or more beneficiaries, paragraphs (a) to (c) of this section are to be separately applied with respect to each interest. For example, assume that the decedent transferred an interest in Blackacre to A which could be possessed or enjoyed only by surviving the decedent, and that the decedent transferred an interest in Blackacre to B which could be possessed or enjoyed only on the occurrence of some event unrelated to the decedent's death. Assume further that the decedent retained a reversionary interest in Blackacre of a value in excess of 5 percent. Only the value of the interest transferred to A is includible in the decedent's gross estate. Similar results would obtain if possession or enjoyment of the entire property could have been obtained only by surviving the decedent, but the decedent had retained a reversionary interest in a part only of such property.

(e) **Examples.** The provisions of paragraphs (a) to (d) of this section may be further illustrated by the following examples. It is assumed that the transfers were made on or after October 8, 1949; for the significance of this date, see paragraphs (f) and (g) of this section:

Example (1). The decedent transferred property in trust with the income payable to his wife for life and, at her death, remainder to the decedent's then surviving children, or if none, to the decedent or his estate. Since each beneficiary can possess or enjoy the property without surviving the decedent, no part of the property is includible in the decedent's gross estate under section 2037, regardless of the value of the decedent's reversionary interest. (However, see section 2033 for inclusion of the value of the reversionary interest in the decedent's gross estate.)

Example (2). The decedent transferred property in trust with the income to be accumulated for the decedent's life, and at his death, principal and accumulated income to be paid to the decedent's then surviving issue, or, if none, to A or A's estate. Since the decedent retained no reversionary interest in the property, no part of the property is includible in the decedent's gross estate, even though possession or enjoyment of the property could be obtained by the issue only by surviving the decedent.

Example (3). The decedent transferred property in trust with the income payable to his wife for life and with the remainder payable to the decedent or, if he is not living at his wife's death, to his daughter or her estate. The daughter cannot obtain possession or enjoyment of the property without surviving the decedent. Therefore, if the decedent's reversionary interest immediately before his death exceeded 5 percent of the value of the property, the value of the property, less the value of the wife's outstanding life estate, is includible in the decedent's gross estate.

Example (4). The decedent transferred property in trust with the income payable to his wife for life and with the remainder payable to his son or, if the son is not living at the wife's death, to the decedent or, if the decedent is not then living, to X or X's estate. Assume that the decedent was survived by his wife, his son, and X. Only X cannot obtain possession or enjoyment of the property without surviving the decedent. Therefore, if the decedent's reversionary interest immediately before his death exceeded 5 percent of the value of the property, the value of X's remainder interest (with reference to the time immediately after the decedent's death) is includible in the decedent's gross estate.

Example (5). The decedent transferred property in trust with the income to be accumulated for a period of 20 years or until the decedent's prior death, at which time the principal and accumulated income was to be paid to the decedent's son if then surviving. Assume that the decedent does, in fact, die before the expiration of the 20-year period. If, at the time of the transfer, the decedent was 30 years of age, in good health, etc., the son will be considered able to possess or enjoy the property without surviving the decedent. If, on the other hand, the decedent was 70 years of age at the time of the transfer, the son will not be considered able to possess or enjoy the property without surviving the decedent. In this latter case, if the value of the decedent's reversionary interest (arising by operation of law) immediately before his death exceeded 5 percent of the value of the property, the value of the property is includible in the decedent's gross estate.

Example (6). The decedent transferred property in trust with the income to be accumulated for his life and, at his death, the principal and accumulated income to be paid to the decedent's then surviving children. The decedent's wife was given the unrestricted power to alter, amend, or revoke the trust. Assume that the wife survived the decedent but did not, in fact, exercise her power during the decedent's lifetime. Since possession or enjoyment of the property could have been obtained by the wife during the decedent's lifetime under the exercise of a general power of appointment, which was, in fact, exercisable immediately before the decedent's death, no part of the property is includible in the decedent's gross estate.

. . . . .

§ 20.2038-1 Revocable transfers

(a) **In general.** A decedent's gross estate includes under section 2038 the value of any interest in property transferred by the decedent, whether in trust or otherwise, if the enjoyment of the interest was subject at the date of the decedent's death to any change through the exercise of a power by the decedent to alter, amend, revoke, or terminate, or if the decedent relinquished such a power in contemplation of death. However, section 2038 does not apply—

(1) To the extent that the transfer was for an adequate and full consideration in money or money's worth (see § 20.2043-1);

(2) If the decedent's power could be exercised only with the consent of all parties having an interest (vested or contingent) in the transferred property, and if the power adds nothing to the rights of the parties under local law; or

(3) To a power held solely by a person other than the decedent. But, for example, if the decedent had the unrestricted power to remove or discharge a trustee at any time and appoint himself trustee, the decedent is considered as having the powers of the trustee. However, this result would not follow if he only had the power to appoint himself trustee under limited conditions which did not exist at the time of his death. (See last two sentences of paragraph (b) of this section.)

Except as provided in this paragraph, it is immaterial in what capacity the power was exercisable by the decedent or by another person or persons in conjunction with the decedent; whether the power was exercisable alone or only in conjunction with another person or persons, whether or not having an adverse interest (unless the transfer was made before June 2, 1924; see paragraph (d) of this section); and at what time or from what source the decedent acquired his power (unless the transfer was made before June 23, 1936; see paragraph (c) of this section). Section 2038 is applicable to any power affecting the time or manner of enjoyment of property or its income, even though the identity of the beneficiary is not affected. For example, section 2038 is applicable to a power reserved by the grantor of a trust to accumulate income or distribute it to A, and to distribute corpus to A, even though the remainder is vested in A or his estate, and no other person has any beneficial interest in the trust. However, only the value of an interest in property subject to a power to which section 2038 applies is included in the decedent's gross estate under section 2038.

(b) Date of existence of power. A power to alter, amend, revoke, or terminate will be considered to have existed at the date of the decedent's death even though the exercise of the power was subject to a precedent giving of notice or even though the alteration, amendment, revocation, or termination would have taken effect only on the expiration of a stated period after the exercise of the power, whether or not on or before the date of the decedent's death notice had been given or the power had been exercised. In determining the value of the gross estate in such cases, the full value of the property transferred subject to the power is discounted for the period required to elapse between the date of the decedent's death and the date upon which the alteration, amendment, revocation, or termination could take effect. In this connection, see especially § 20.2031-7. However, section 2038 is not applicable to a power the exercise of which was subject to a contingency beyond the decedent's control which did not occur before his death (e. g., the death of another person during the decedent's life). See, however, section 2036(a) (2) for the inclusion of property in the decedent's gross estate on account of such a power.

．　．　．　．　．

§ 20.2039-1   Annuities

(a) In general. A decedent's gross estate includes under section 2039(a) and (b) the value of an annuity or other payment receivable by any beneficiary by reason of surviving the decedent under certain agreements or plans to the extent that the value of the annuity or other payment is attributable to contributions made by the decedent or his employer. Section 2039(a) and (b), however, has no application to an amount which constitutes the proceeds of insurance under a policy on the decedent's life. Paragraph (b) of this section describes the agreements or plans to which section 2039(a) and (b) applies; paragraph (c) of this section provides rules for determining the amount includible in the decedent's gross estate; and paragraph (d) of this section distinguishes proceeds of life insurance. The fact that an annuity or

other payment is not includible in a decedent's gross estate under section 2039 (a) and (b) does not mean that it is not includible under some other section of part III of subchapter A of chapter 11. However, see section 2039(c) and (d) and § 20.2039-2 for rules relating to the exclusion from a decedent's gross estate of annuities and other payments under certain "qualified plans".

(b) Agreements or plans to which section 2039(a) and (b) applies. (1) Section 2039(a) and (b) applies to the value of an annuity or other payment receivable by any beneficiary under any form of contract or agreement entered into after March 3, 1931, under which—

(i) An annuity or other payment was payable to the decedent, either alone or in conjunction with another person or persons, for his life or for any period not ascertainable without reference to his death or for any period which does not in fact end before his death, or

(ii) The decedent possessed, for his life or for any period not ascertainable without reference to his death or for any period which does not in fact end before his death, the right to receive such an annuity or other payment, either alone or in conjunction with another person or persons.

The term "annuity or other payment" as used with respect to both the decedent and the beneficiary has reference to one or more payments extending over any period of time. The payments may be equal or unequal, conditional or unconditional, periodic or sporadic. The term "contract or agreement" includes any arrangement, understanding or plan, or any combination of arrangements, understandings or plans arising by reason of the decedent's employment. An annuity or other payment "was payable" to the decedent if, at the time of his death, the decedent was in fact receiving an annuity or other payment, whether or not he had an enforceable right to have payments continued. The decedent "possessed the right to receive" an annuity or other payment if, immediately before his death, the decedent had an enforceable right to receive payments at some time in the future, whether or not, at the time of his death, he had a present right to receive payments. In connection with the preceding sentence, the decedent will be regarded as having had "an enforceable right to receive payments at some time in the future" so long as he had complied with his obligations under the contract or agreement up to the time of his death. For the meaning of the phrase "for his life or for any period not ascertainable without reference to his death or for any period which does not in fact end before his death", see section 2036 and § 20.2036-1.

(2) The application of this paragraph is illustrated and more fully explained in the following examples. In each example: (i) It is assumed that all transactions occurred after March 3, 1931, and (ii) the amount stated to be includible in the decedent's gross estate is determined in accordance with the provisions of paragraph (c) of this section.

Example (1). The decedent purchased an annuity contract under the terms of which the issuing company agreed to pay an annuity to the decedent for his life and, upon his death, to pay a specified lump sum to his designated beneficiary. The decedent was drawing his annuity at the time of his death. The amount of the lump sum payment to the beneficiary is includible in the decedent's gross estate under section 2039(a) and (b).

Example (2). Pursuant to a retirement plan, the employer made contributions to a fund which was to provide the employee, upon his retirement at age 60, with an annuity for life, and which was to provide the employee's wife, upon his death after retirement, with a similar annuity for life. The benefits under the plan were completely forfeitable during the employee's life, but upon his death after retirement, the benefits to the wife were forfeitable only upon her remarriage. The employee had no right to originally designate or to ever change the employer's designation of the surviving beneficiary. The retirement plan at no time met the requirements of section 401(a) (relating to qualified plans). Assume that the employee died at age 61 after the employer started payment of his annuity as described above. The value of the wife's annuity is includible in the decedent's gross estate under section 2039(a) and (b). Includibility in this case is based on the fact that the annuity to the decedent "was payable" at the time of his death. The fact that the decedent's annuity was forfeitable is of no consequence since, at the time of his death, he was in fact receiving payments under the plan. Nor is it important that the decedent had no right to choose the surviving beneficiary. The element of forfeitability in the wife's annuity may be taken into account only with respect to the valuation of the annuity in the decedent's gross estate.

Example (3). Pursuant to a retirement plan, the employer made contributions to a fund which was to provide the employee, upon his retirement at age 60, with an annuity of $100 per month for life, and which was to provide his designated beneficiary, upon the employee's death after retirement, with a similar annuity for life. The plan also provided that (a) upon the employee's separation from service before

retirement, he would have a nonforfeitable right to receive a reduced annuity starting at age 60, and (b) upon the employee's death before retirement, a lump sum payment representing the amount of the employer's contributions credited to the employee's account would be paid to the designated beneficiary. The plan at no time met the requirements of section 401 (a) (relating to qualified plans). Assume that the employee died at age 49 and that the designated beneficiary was paid the specified lump sum payment. Such amount is includible in the decedent's gross estate under section 2039 (a) and (b). Since, immediately before his death, the employee had an enforceable right to receive an annuity commencing at age 60, he is considered to have "possessed the right to receive" an annuity as that term is used in section 2039(a). If, in this example, the employee would not be entitled to any benefits in the event of his separation from service before retirement for any reason other than death, the result would be the same so long as the decedent had complied with his obligations under the contract up to the time of his death. In such case, he is considered to have had, immediately before his death, an enforceable right to receive an annuity commencing at age 60.

Example (4). Pursuant to a retirement plan, the employer made contributions to a fund which was to provide the employee, upon his retirement at age 60, with an annuity for life, and which was to provide his designated beneficiary, upon the employee's death after retirement, with a similar annuity for life. The plan provided, however, that no benefits were payable in the event of the employee's death before retirement. The retirement plan at no time met the requirements of section 401(a) (relating to qualified plans). Assume that the employee died at age 59 but that the employer nevertheless started payment of an annuity in a slightly reduced amount to the designated beneficiary. The value of the annuity is not includible in the decedent's gross estate under section 2039(a) and (b). Since the employee died before reaching the retirement age, the employer was under no obligation to pay the annuity to the employee's designated beneficiary. Therefore, the annuity was not paid under a "contract or agreement" as that term is used in section 2039 (a). If, however, it can be established that the employer has consistently paid an annuity under such circumstances, the annuity will be considered as having been paid under a "contract or agreement".

Example (5). The employer made contributions to a retirement fund which were credited to the employee's individual account. Under the plan, the employee was to receive one-half the amount credited to his account upon his retirement at age 60, and his designated beneficiary was to receive the other one-half upon the employee's death after retirement. If the employee should die before reaching the retirement age, the entire amount credited to his account at such time was to be paid to the designated beneficiary. The retirement plan at no time met the requirements of section 401 (a) (relating to qualified plans). Assume that the employee received one-half the amount credited to his account upon reaching the retirement age and that he died shortly thereafter. Since the employee received all that he was entitled to receive under the plan before his death, no amount was payable to him for his life or for any period not ascertainable without reference to his death, or for any period which did not in fact end before his death. Thus, the amount of the payment to the designated beneficiary is not includible in the decedent's gross estate under section 2039(a) and (b). If, in this example, the employee died before reaching the retirement age, the amount of the payment to the designated beneficiary would be includible in the decedent's gross estate under section 2039(a) and (b). In this latter case, the decedent possessed the right to receive a lump sum payment for a period which did not in fact end before his death.

Example (6). The employer made contributions to two different funds set up under two different plans. One plan was to provide the employee, upon his retirement at age 60, with an annuity for life, and the other plan was to provide the employee's designated beneficiary upon the employee's death, with a similar annuity for life. Each plan was established at a different time and each plan was administered separately in every respect. Neither plan at any time met the requirements of section 401(a) (relating to qualified plans). The value of the designated beneficiary's annuity is includible in the employee's gross estate. All rights and benefits accruing to an employee and to others by reason of the employment (except rights and benefits accruing under certain plans meeting the requirements of section 401(a) (see § 20.2039-2)) are considered together in determining whether or not section 2039(a) and (b) applies. The scope of section 2039(a) and (b) cannot be limited by indirection.

(c) Amount includible in the gross estate. The amount to be included in a decedent's gross estate under section 2039 (a) and (b) is an amount which bears the same ratio to the value at the decedent's death of the annuity or other payment receivable by the beneficiary as the contribution made by the decedent, or made by his employer (or former employer) for any reason connected with his employment, to the cost of the contract or agreement bears to its total cost. In applying this ratio, the value at the decedent's death of the annuity or other payment is determined in accordance with the rules set forth in §§ 20.2031-1, 20.2031-7, 20.2031-8, and 20.2031-9. The application of this paragraph may be illustrated by the following examples:

Example (1). On January 1, 1945, the decedent and his wife each contributed $15,000 to the purchase price of an annuity contract under the terms of which the issuing company agreed to pay an annuity to the decedent and his wife for their joint lives and to continue the annuity to the survivor for his life. Assume that the value of the survivor's annuity at the decedent's death (computed under § 20.2031-8) is $20,000. Since the decedent contributed one-half of the cost of the contract, the amount to be included in his gross estate under section 2039 (a) and (b) is $10,000.

. . . .

(d) Insurance under policies on the life of the decedent. If an annuity or other payment receivable by a beneficiary under a contract or agreement is in substance the proceeds of insurance under a policy on the life of the decedent, section 2039 (a) and (b) does not apply. For the extent to which such an annuity or other payment is includible in a decedent's gross estate, see section 2042 and § 20.2042-1. A combination annuity contract and life insurance policy on the decedent's life (e. g., a "retirement income" policy with death benefits) which matured during the decedent's lifetime so that there was no longer an insurance element under the contract at the time of the decedent's death is subject to the provisions of section 2039 (a) and (b). On the other hand, the treatment of a combination annuity contract and life insurance policy on the decedent's life which did not mature during the decedent's lifetime depends upon the nature of the contract at the time of the decedent's death. The nature of the contract is generally determined by the relation of the reserve value of the policy to the value of the death benefit at the time of the decedent's death. If the decedent dies before the reserve value equals the death benefit, there is still an insurance element under the contract. The contract is therefore considered, for estate tax purposes, to be an insurance policy subject to the provisions of section 2042. However, if the decedent dies after the reserve value equals the death benefit, there is no longer an insurance element under the contract. The contract is therefore considered to be a contract for an annuity or other payment subject to the provisions of section 2039 (a) and (b) or some other section of part III of subchapter A of chapter 11. Notwithstanding the relation of the reserve value to the value of the death benefit, a contract under which the death benefit could never exceed the total premiums paid, plus interest, contains no insurance element.

Example. Pursuant to a retirement plan established January 1, 1945, the employer purchased a contract from an insurance company which was to provide the employee, upon his retirement at age 65, with an annuity of $100 per month for life, and which was to provide his designated beneficiary, upon the employee's death after retirement, with a similar annuity for life. The contract further provided that if the employee should die before reaching the retirement age, a lump sum payment of $20,000 would be paid to his designated beneficiary in lieu of the annuity described above. The plan at no time met the requirements of section 401(a) (relating to qualified plans). Assume that the reserve value of the contract at the retirement age would be $20,000. If the employee died after reaching the retirement age, the death benefit to the designated beneficiary would constitute an annuity, the value of which would be includible in the employee's gross estate under section 2039(a) and (b). If, on the other hand, the employee died before reaching his retirement age, the death benefit to the designated beneficiary would constitute insurance under a policy on the life of the decedent since the reserve value would be less than the death benefit. Accordingly, its includibility would depend upon section 2042 and § 20.2042-1.

§ 20.2039-2 Annuities under "qualified plans" and section 403(b) annuity contracts

(a) Section 2039(c) exclusion. In general, in the case of a decedent dying after December 31, 1953, the value of an annuity or other payment receivable under a plan or annuity contract described in paragraph (b) of this section is excluded from the decedent's gross estate to the extent provided in paragraph (c) of this section. In the case of a plan described in paragraph (b)(1) or (2) of this section (a "qualified plan"), the exclusion is subject to the limitation described in § 20.2039-3 (relating to lump sum distributions paid with respect to a decedent dying after December 31, 1976, and before January 1, 1979) or § 20.2039-4 (relating to lump sum distributions paid with respect to a decedent dying after December 31, 1978).

(b) Plans and annuity contracts to which section 2039(c) applies. Section 2039(c) excludes from a decedent's gross estate, to the extent provided in paragraph (c) of this section, the value of an annuity or other payment receivable by any beneficiary (except the value of an annuity or other payment receivable by or for the benefit of the decedent's estate) under—

(1) An employees' trust (or under a contract purchased by an employees' trust) forming part of a pension, stock bonus, or profit-sharing plan which, at the time of the decedent's separation from employment (whether by death or otherwise), or at the time of the earlier termination of the plan, met the requirements of section 401(a);

(2) A retirement annuity contract purchased by an employer (and not by an employees' trust) pursuant to a plan which, at the time of decedent's separation from employment (by death or otherwise), or at the time of the earlier termination of the plan, was a plan described in section 403(a);

(3) In the case of a decedent dying after December 31, 1957, a retirement annuity contract purchased for an employee by an employer which, for its taxable year in which the purchase occurred, is an organization referred to in section 170(b)(1)(A)(ii) or (vi) or which is a religious organization (other than a trust) and is exempt from tax under 501(a);

(4) In the case of a decedent dying after December 31, 1965, an annuity under chapter 73 of title 10 of the United States Code (10 U.S.C.A. § 1431, et seq.); or

(5) In the case of a decedent dying after December 31, 1962, a bond purchase plan described in section 405.

For the meaning of the term "annuity or other payment", see paragraph (b) of § 20.2039-1. For the meaning of the phrase "receivable by or for the benefit of the decedent's estate", see paragraph (b) of § 20.2042-1. The application of this paragraph may be illustrated by the following examples in each of which it is assumed that the amount stated to be excludable from the decedent's gross estate is determined in accordance with paragraph (c) of this section:

Example (1). Pursuant to a pension plan, the employer made contributions to a trust which was to provide the employee, upon his retirement at age 60, with an annuity for life, and which was to provide his wife, upon the employee's death after retirement, with a similar annuity for life. At the time of the employee's retirement, the pension trust formed part of a plan meeting the requirements of section 401(a). Assume that the employee died at age 61 after the trustee started payment of his annuity as described above. Since the wife's annuity was receivable under a qualified pension plan, no part of the value of such annuity is includible in the decedent's gross estate by reason of the provisions of section 2039(c). If, in this example, the employer provided other benefits under nonqualified plans, the result would be the same since the exclusion under section 2039(c) is confined to the benefits provided for under the qualified plan.

Example (2). Pursuant to a profit-sharing plan, the employer made contributions to a trust which were allocated to the employee's individual account. Under the plan, the employee would, upon retirement at age 60, receive a distribution of the entire amount credited to the account. If the employee should die before reaching retirement age, the amount credited to the account would be distributed to the employee's designated beneficiary. Assume that the employee died before reaching the retirement age and that at such time the plan met the requirements of section 401(a). Since the payment to the designated beneficiary is receivable under a qualified profit-sharing plan, the provisions of section 2039(c) apply. However, if the payment is a lump sum distribution to which § 20.2039-3 or § 20.2039-4 applies, the payment is excludable from the decedent's gross estate only as provided in such section.

Example (3). Pursuant to a pension plan, the employer made contributions to a trust which were used by the trustee to purchase a contract from an insurance company for the benefit of an employee. The contract was to provide the employee, upon retirement at age 65, with an annuity of $100 per month for life, and was to provide the employee's designated beneficiary upon the employee's death after retirement, with a similar annuity for life. The contract further provided that if the employee should die before reaching retirement age, a lump sum payment equal to the greater of (a) $10,000 or (b) the reserve value of the policy would be paid to the designated beneficiary in lieu of the annuity. Assume that the employee died before reaching the retirement age and that at such time the plan met the requirements of section 401(a). Since the payment to the designated beneficiary is receivable under a qualified pension plan, the provisions of section 2039 (c) apply. However, if the payment is a lump sum distribution to which § 20.2039-3 or § 20.-2039-4 applies, the payment is excludable from the decedent's gross estate only as provided in such section. It should be noted that for purposes of the exclusion under section 2039(c) it is immaterial whether or not the payment constitutes the proceeds of life insurance under the principles set forth in § 20.2039-1(d).

Example (4). Pursuant to a profit-sharing plan, the employer made contributions to a trust which were allocated to the employee's individual account. Under the plan, the employee would, upon his retirement at age 60, be given the option to have the amount credited to his account (a) paid to him in a lump sum, (b) used to purchase a joint and survivor annuity for him and his designated beneficiary, or (c) left with the trustee under an arrangement whereby interest would be paid to him for his lifetime with the principal to be paid, at his death, to his designated beneficiary. The plan further provided that, if the third method of settlement were selected, the employee would retain the right to have the principal paid to himself in a lump sum up to the time of his death. At the time of the employee's retirement, the profit-sharing plan met the requirements of section 401(a). Assume that the employee, upon reaching his retirement age, elect-

ed to have the amount credited to his account left with the trustee under the interest arrangement. Assume, further, that the employee did not exercise his right to have such amount paid to him before his death. Under such circumstances, the employee is considered as having constructively received the amount credited to his account upon his retirement. Thus, such amount is not considered as receivable by the designated beneficiary under the profit-sharing plan and the exclusion of section 2039(c) is not applicable.

Example (5). An employer purchased a retirement annuity contract for an employee which was to provide the employee, upon his retirement at age 60, with an annuity for life and which was to provide his wife, upon the employee's death after retirement, with a similar annuity for life. The employer, for its taxable year in which the annuity contract was purchased, was an organization referred to in section 170(b)(1)(A)(ii), and was exempt from tax under section 501(a). The entire amount of the purchase price of the annuity contract was excluded from the employee's gross income under section 403(b). No part of the value of the survivor annuity payable after the employee's death is includible in the decedent's gross estate by reason of the provisions of section 2039(c).

(c) Amounts excludable from the gross estate. (1) The amount to be excluded from a decedent's gross estate under section 2039(c) is an amount which bears the same ratio to the value at the decedent's death of an annuity or other payment receivable by the beneficiary as the employer's contribution (or a contribution made on the employer's behalf) on the employee's account to the plan or towards the purchase of the annuity contract bears to the total contributions on the employee's account to the plan or towards the purchase of the annuity contract. In applying this ratio—

(i) Payments or contributions made by or on behalf of the employer towards the purchase of an annuity contract described in paragraph (b)(3) of this section are considered to include only such payments or contributions as are, or were, excludable from the employee's gross income under section 403(b).

(ii) In the case of a decedent dying before January 1, 1977, payments or contributions made under a plan described in paragraph (b)(1), (2) or (5) of this section on behalf of the decedent for a period for which the decedent was self-employed, within the meaning of section 401(c)(1), with respect to the plan are considered payments or contributions made by the decedent and not by the employer.

(iii) In the case of a decedent dying after December 31, 1976, however, payments or contributions made under a plan described in paragraph (b)(1), (2) or (5) of this section on behalf of the decedent for a period for which the decedent was self-employed, within the meaning of section 401(c)(1), with respect to the plan are considered payments or contributions made by the employer to the extent the payments or contributions are, or were, deductible under section 404 or 405(c). Contributions or payments attributable to that period which are not, or were not, so deductible are considered made by the decedent.

(iv) In the case of a plan described in paragraph (b)(1) or (2) of this section, a rollover contribution described in section 402(a)(5), 403(a)(4), 409(d)(3)(A)(ii) or 409(b)(3)(C) is considered an amount contributed by the employer.

(v) In the case of an annuity contract described in paragraph (b)(3) of this section, a rollover contribution described in section 403(b)(8) is considered an amount contributed by the employer.

(vi) In the case of a plan described in paragraph (b)(1), (2) or (5) of this section, an amount includable in the gross income of an employee under section 1379(b) (relating to shareholder-employee beneficiaries under certain qualified plans) is considered an amount paid or contributed by the decedent.

(vii) Amounts payable under paragraph (b)(4) of this section are attributable to payments or contributions made by the decedent only to the extent of amounts deposited by the decedent pursuant to section 1438 or 1452(d) of Title 10 of the United States Code.

(viii) The value at the decedent's death of the annuity or other payment is determined under the rules of §§ 20.-2031-1 and 20.2031-7 through 20.2031-10.

(d) **Exclusion of certain annuity interests created by community property laws.**—(1) In the case of an employee on whose behalf contributions or payments were made by his employer or former employer under an employees' trust forming part of a pension, stock bonus, or profit-sharing plan described in section 2039(c)(1), under an employee's retirement annuity contract described in section 2039(c)(2), or toward the purchase of an employee's retirement annuity contract described in section 2039(c)(3), which under section 2039(c) are not considered as contributed by the employee, if the spouse of such employee predeceases him, then, notwithstanding the provisions of section 2039 or of any other provision of law, there shall be excluded from the gross estate of such spouse the value of any interest of such spouse in such plan or trust or such contract, to the extent such interest—

(i) Is attributable to such contributions or payments, and

(ii) Arises solely by reason of such spouse's interest in community income under the community property laws of a State.

(2) Section 2039(d) and this paragraph do not provide any exclusion for such spouse's property interest in the plan, trust or contract to the extent it is attributable to the contributions of the employee spouse. Thus, the decedent's community property interest in the plan, trust, or contract which is attributable to contributions made by the employee spouse are includible in the decedent's gross estate. See paragraph (c) of this section.

(3) Section 2039(d) and this paragraph apply to the estate of a decedent who dies on or after October 27, 1972, and to the estate of a decedent who died before October 27, 1972, if the period for filing a claim for credit or refund of an overpayment of the estate tax ends on or after October 27, 1972. Interest will not be allowed or paid on any overpayment of tax resulting from the application of section 2039(d) and this paragraph for any period prior to April 26, 1973.

§ 20.2039-4 Lump sum distributions from "qualified plans;" decedents dying after December 31, 1978

(a) **Limitation on section 2039(c) exclusion.** This section applies in the case of a decedent dying after December 31, 1978. If a lump sum distribution is paid or payable with respect to a decedent under a plan described in § 20.2039-2(b)(1) or (2) (a "qualified plan"), no amount paid or payable with respect to the decedent under the plan is excludable from the decedent's gross estate under § 20.2039-2, unless the recipient of the distribution makes the section 402(a)/403(a) taxation election described in paragraph (c) of this section. For purposes of this section, an amount is payable as a lump sum distribution under a plan if, as of the date the estate tax return is filed (as determined under § 20.2039-3(d)), it is payable as a lump sum distribution at the election of the recipient or otherwise.

(b) "Lump sum distribution" defined; treatment of annuity contracts. For purposes of this section the term "lump sum distribution" means a lump sum distribution defined in section 402(e)(4)(A) that satisfies the requirements of section 402(e)(4)(C), relating to the aggregation of certain trusts and plans. A distribution is a lump sum distribution for purposes of this section without regard to the election described in section 402(e)(4)(B). The distribution of an annuity contract is not a lump sum distribution for purposes of this section, and the limitation described in this section does not apply to an annuity contract distributed under a plan. Accordingly, if the amount payable with respect to a decedent under a plan is paid to a recipient partly by the distribution of an annuity contract, and partly by the distribution of an amount that is a lump sum distribution within the meaning of this paragraph (b), § 20.2039-2 shall apply with respect to the annuity contract without regard to whether the recipient makes the section 402(a)/403(a) taxation election with respect to the remainder of the distribution.

(c) Recipient's section 402(a)/403(a) taxation election. The section 402(a)/403(a) taxation election is the election by the recipient of a lump sum distribution to treat the distribution as—

(1) Taxable under section 402(a), without regard to section 402(a)(2), to the extent includable in gross income (in the case of a distribution under a qualified plan described in § 20.2039-2(b)(1)),

(2) Taxable under section 403(a), without regard to section 403(a)(2), to the extent includable in gross income

(in the case of a distribution under a qualified annuity contract described in § 20.2039-2(b)(2)), or

(3) A rollover contribution, in whole or in part, under section 402(a)(7) (relating to rollovers by a decedent's surviving spouse).

Accordingly, if a recipient makes the election, no portion of the distribution is taxable to the recipient under the 10-year averaging provisions of section 402(e) or as long-term capital gain under section 402(a)(2). However, a recipient's election under this paragraph (c) does not preclude the application of section 402(e)(4)(J) to any securities of the employer corporation included in the distribution.

(d) Method of election. The recipient of a lump sum distribution shall make the section 402(a)/403(a) taxation election by—

(1) Determining the income tax liability on the income tax return (or amended return) for the taxable year of the distribution in a manner consistent with paragraph (c)(1) or (2) of this section, or

(2) Rolling over all or any part of the distribution under section 402(a)(7).

If the date the estate tax return is filed precedes the date on which the recipient makes the section 402(a)/403(a) taxation election with respect to a lump sum distribution, the estate tax return may nevertheless reflect the election, as if the election had been made.

(e) Election irrevocable. If a recipient of a lump sum distribution files an income tax return (or amended return) or makes a rollover contribution that constitutes the section 402(a)/403(a) taxation election described in paragraphs (c) and (d), the election may not be revoked. Accordingly, a subsequent and amended income tax return filed by the recipient that is inconsistent with the prior election will not be given effect for purposes of section 2039 and section 402 or 403.

.   .   .   .   .

§ 20.2039-5 Annuities under individual retirement plans

(a) Section 2039(e) exclusion—(1) In general. In the case of a decedent dying after December 31, 1976, section 2039(e) excludes from the decedent's gross estate, to the extent provided in paragraph (c) of this section, the value of a "qualifying annuity" receivable by a beneficiary under an individual retirement plan. The term "individual retirement plan" means—

(i) An individual retirement account described in section 408(a),

(ii) An individual retirement annuity described in section 408(b), or

(iii) A retirement bond described in section 409(a).

(2) Limitations. (i) Section 2039(e) applies only with respect to the gross estate of a decedent on whose behalf the individual retirement plan was established. Accordingly, section 2039(e) does not apply with respect to the estate of a decedent who was only a beneficiary under the plan.

(ii) Section 2039(e) does not apply to an annuity receivable by or for the benefit of the decedent's estate. For the meaning of the term "receivable by or for the benefit of the decedent's estate," see § 20.2042-1(b).

(b) Qualifying annuity. For purposes of this section, the term "qualifying annuity" means an annuity contract or other arrangement providing for a series of substantially equal periodic payments to be made to a beneficiary for the beneficiary's life or over a period ending at least 36 months after the decedent's death. The term "annuity contract" includes an annuity purchased for a beneficiary and distributed to the beneficiary, if under section 408 the contract is not included in the gross income of the beneficiary upon distribution. The term "other arrangement" includes any arrangement arising by reason of the decedent's participation in the program providing the individual retirement plan. Payments shall be considered "periodic" if under the arrangement or contract (including a distributed contract) payments are to be made to the beneficiary at regular intervals. If the contract or arrangement provides optional payment provisions, not all of which provide for periodic payments, payments shall be considered periodic only if an option providing periodic payments is elected not later than the date the estate tax return is filed (as determined under § 20.2039-3(d)). For this purpose, the right to surrender a contract (including a distributed contract) for a cash surrender value will not be considered an optional payment provision. Payments shall be considered "substantially equal" even though the amounts receivable by the beneficiary may vary. Payments shall not be considered substantially equal, however, if more than 40% of the total amount payable to the beneficiary under the individual retirement plan, determined as of the date of the decedent's death and excluding any postmortem increase, is payable to the beneficiary in any 12-month period.

(c) Amount excludible from gross estate—(1) In general. Except as otherwise described in this paragraph (c), the amount excluded from the decedent's gross estate under section 2039(e) is the entire value of the qualifying annuity (as determined under §§ 20.2031-1 and 20.2031-7 through 20.2031-10) payable under the individual retirement plan.

(2) Excess contribution. In any case in which there exists, on the date of the decedent's death, an excess contribution (as defined in section 4973(b)) with respect to the individual retirement plan, the amount excluded from the value of the decedent's gross estate is determined under the following formula:

$$E = A - A(X \div C - R)$$

Where:

E = the amount excluded from the decedent's gross estate under section 2039(e).

A = the value of the qualifying annuity at the decedent's death (as determined under §§ 20.2031-1 and 20.2031-7 through § 20.2031-10).

X = the amount which is an excess contribution at the decedent's death (as determined under section 4973(b)).

C = the total amount contributed by or on behalf of the decedent to the individual retirement plan, and

R = the total of amounts paid or distributed from the individual retirement plan before the death of the decedent which were either includable in the gross income of the recipient under section 408(d)(1) and represented the payment or distribution of an excess contribution, or were payments or distributions described in section 408(d)(4) or (5) (relating to returned excess contributions).

(3) Certain section 403(b)(8) rollover contributions. This subparagraph (3) applies if the decedent made a rollover contribution to the individual retirement plan under section 403(b)(8), and the contribution was attributable to a distribution under an annuity contract other than an annuity contract described in § 20.2039–2(b)(3). If such a rollover contribution was the only contribution made to the plan, no part of the value of the qualifying annuity payable under the plan is excluded from the decedent's gross estate under section 2039(e). If a contribution other than such a rollover contribution was made to the plan, the amount excluded from the decedent's gross estate is determined under the formula described in subparagraph (2) of this paragraph, except that for purposes of that formula, X includes the amount that was a rollover contribution under section 403(b)(8) attributable to a distribution under an annuity contract not described in § 20.2039–2(b)(3).

(4) Surviving spouse's rollover contribution. This subparagraph (4) applies if the decedent made a rollover contribution to the individual retirement plan under section 402(a)(7), relating to rollovers by a surviving spouse. If the rollover contribution under section 402(a)(7) was the only contribution made by the decedent to the plan, no part of the value of the qualifying annuity payable under the plan is excluded from the decedent's gross estate under section 2039(e). If a contribution other than a rollover contribution under section 402(a)(7) was made by the decedent to the plan, the amount excluded from the decedent's gross estate is determined under the formula described in subparagraph (2) of this paragraph, except that for purposes of that formula, X includes the amount that was a rollover contribution under section 402(a)(7).

· · · · ·

§ 20.2040–1   Joint interests

(a) In general. A decedent's gross estate includes under section 2040 the value of property held jointly at the time of the decedent's death by the decedent and another person or persons with right of survivorship, as follows:

(1) To the extent that the property was acquired by the decedent and the other joint owner or owners by gift, devise, bequest, or inheritance, the decedent's fractional share of the property is included.

(2) In all other cases, the entire value of the property is included except such entire part of the entire value as is attributable to the amount of the consideration in money or money's worth furnished by the other joint owner or owners. See § 20.2043–1 with respect to adequacy of consideration. Such part of the entire value is that portion of the entire value of the property at the decedent's death (or at the alternate valuation date described in section 2032) which the consideration in money or money's worth furnished by the other joint owner or owners bears to the total cost of acquisition and capital additions. In determining the consideration furnished by the other joint owner or owners, there is taken into account only that portion of such consideration which is shown not to be attributable to money or other property acquired by the other joint owner or owners from the decedent for less than a full and adequate consideration in money or money's worth.

The entire value of jointly held property is included in a decedent's gross estate unless the executor submits facts sufficient to show that property was not acquired entirely with consideration furnished by the decedent, or was acquired by the decedent and the other joint owner or owners by gift, bequest, devise, or inheritance.

(b) Meaning of "property held jointly". Section 2040 specifically covers property held jointly by the decedent and any other person (or persons), property held by the decedent and spouse as tenants by the entirety, and a deposit of money, or a bond or other instrument, in the name of the decedent and any other person and payable to either or the survivor. The section applies to all classes of property, whether real or personal, and regardless of when the joint interests were created. Furthermore, it makes no difference that the survivor takes the entire interest in the property by right of survivorship and that no interest therein forms a part of the decedent's estate for purposes of administration. The section has no application to property held by the decedent and any other person (or persons) as tenants in common.

(c) **Examples.** The application of this section may be explained in the following examples in each of which it is assumed that the other joint owner or owners survived the decedent:

(1) If the decedent furnished the entire purchase price of the jointly held property, the value of the entire property is included in his gross estate;

(2) If the decedent furnished a part only of the purchase price, only a corresponding portion of the value of the property is so included;

(3) If the decedent furnished no part of the purchase price, no part of the value of the property is so included;

(4) If the decedent, before the acquisition of the property by himself and the other joint owner, gave the latter a sum of money or other property which thereafter became the other joint owner's entire contribution to the purchase price, then the value of the entire property is so included, notwithstanding the fact that the other property may have appreciated in value due to market conditions between the time of the gift and the time of the acquisition of the jointly held property;

(5) If the decedent, before the acquisition of the property by himself and the other joint owner, transferred to the latter for less than an adequate and full consideration in money or money's worth other income-producing property, the income from which belonged to and became the other joint owner's entire contribution to the purchase price, then the value of the jointly held property less that portion attributable to the income which the other joint owner did furnish is included in the decedent's gross estate;

(6) If the property originally belonged to the other joint owner and the decedent purchased his interest from the other joint owner, only that portion of the value of the property attributable to the consideration paid by the decedent is included;

(7) If the decedent and his spouse acquired the property by will or gift as tenants by the entirety, one-half of the value of the property is included in the decedent's gross estate; and

(8) If the decedent and his two brothers acquired the property by will or gift as joint tenants, one-third of the value of the property is so included.

§ 20.2041-1 Powers of appointment; in general

(a) **Introduction.** A decedent's gross estate includes under section 2041 the value of property in respect of which the decedent possessed, exercised, or released certain powers of appointment. This section contains rules of general application; § 20.2041-2 contains rules specifically applicable to general powers of appointment created on or before October 21, 1942; and § 20.2041-3 sets forth specific rules applicable to powers of appointment created after October 21, 1942.

(b) **Definition of "power of appointment"**—(1) **In general.** The term "power of appointment" includes all powers which are in substance and effect powers of appointment regardless of the nomenclature used in creating the power and regardless of local property law connotations. For example, if a trust instrument provides that the beneficiary may appropriate or consume the principal of the trust, the power to consume or appropriate is a power of appointment. Similarly, a power given to a decedent to affect the beneficial enjoyment of trust property or its income by altering, amending, or revoking the trust instrument or terminating the trust is a power of appointment. If the community property laws of a State confer upon the wife a power of testamentary disposition over property in which she does not have a vested interest she is considered as having a power of appointment. A power in a donee to remove or discharge a trustee and appoint himself may be a power of appointment. For example, if under the terms of a trust instrument, the trustee or his successor has the power to appoint the principal of the trust for the benefit of individuals including himself, and the decedent has the unrestricted power to remove or discharge the trustee at any time and appoint any other person including himself, the decedent is considered as having a power of appointment. However, the decedent is not considered to have a power of appointment if he only had the power to appoint a successor, including himself, under limited conditions which did not exist at the time of his death, without an accompanying unrestricted power of removal. Similarly, a power to amend only the administrative provisions of a trust instrument, which cannot substantially affect the beneficial enjoyment of the trust property or income, is not a power of appointment. The mere power of management, investment, custody of assets, or the power to allocate receipts and disbursements as between income and principal, exercisable in a fiduciary capacity, whereby the holder has no power to enlarge or shift any of the beneficial interests therein except as an incidental consequence of the discharge of such fiduciary duties is not a power of appointment. Further, the right in a beneficiary of a trust to assent to a periodic accounting, thereby relieving the trustee from further accountability, is not a power of appointment if the right of assent does not consist of any power or right to enlarge or shift the beneficial interest of any beneficiary therein.

(2) Relation to other sections. For purposes of §§ 20.2041-1 to 20.2041-3, the term "power of appointment" does not include powers reserved by the decedent to himself within the concept of sections 2036 through 2038. (See §§ 20.2036-1 to 20.2038-1.) No provision of section 2041 or of §§ 20.2041-1 to 20.2041-3 is to be construed as in any way limiting the application of any other section of the Internal Revenue Code or of these regulations. The power of the owner of a property interest already possessed by him to dispose of his interest, and nothing more, is not a power of appointment, and the interest is includible in his gross estate to the extent it would be includible under section 2033 or some other provision of part III of subchapter A of chapter 11. For example, if a trust created by S provides for payment of the income to A for life with power in A to appoint the remainder by will and, in default of such appointment for payment of the income to A's widow, W, for her life and for payment of the remainder to A's estate, the value of A's interest in the remainder is includible in his gross estate under section 2033 regardless of its includibility under section 2041.

(3) Powers over a portion of property. If a power of appointment exists as to part of an entire group of assets or only over a limited interest in property, section 2041 applies only to such part or interest. For example, if a trust created by S provides for the payment of income to A for life, then to W for life; with power in A to appoint the remainder by will and in default of appointment for payment of the remainder to B or his estate, and if A dies before W, section 2041 applies only to the value of the remainder interest excluding W's life estate. If A dies after W, section 2041 would apply to the value of the entire property. If the power were only over one-half the remainder interest, section 2041 would apply only to one-half the value of the amounts described above.

(c) Definition of "general power of appointment"—(1) In general. The term "general power of appointment" as defined in section 2041(b)(1) means any power of appointment exercisable in favor of the decedent, his estate, his creditors, or the creditors of his estate, except (i) joint powers, to the extent provided in §§ 20.2041-2 and 20.-2041-3, and (ii) certain powers limited by an ascertainable standard, to the extent provided in subparagraph (2) of this paragraph. A power of appointment exercisable to meet the estate tax, or any other taxes, debts, or charges which are enforceable against the estate, is included within the meaning of a power of appointment exercisable in favor of the decedent's estate, his creditors, or the creditors of his estate. A power of appointment exercisable for the purpose of discharging a legal obligation of the decedent or for his pecuniary benefit is considered a power of appointment exercisable in favor of the decedent or his creditors. However, for purposes of §§ 20.2041-1 to 20.2041-3, a power of appointment not otherwise considered to be a general power of appointment is not treated as a general power of appointment merely by reason of the fact that an appointee may, in fact, be a creditor of the decedent or his estate. A power of appointment is not a general power if by its terms it is either—

(a) Exercisable only in favor of one or more designated persons or classes other than the decedent or his creditors, or the decedent's estate or the creditors of his estate, or

(b) Expressly not exercisable in favor of the decedent or his creditors, or the decedent's estate or the creditors of his estate.

A decedent may have two powers under the same instrument, one of which is a general power of appointment and the other of which is not. For example, a beneficiary may have a power to withdraw trust corpus during his life, and a testamentary power to appoint the corpus among his descendants. The testamentary power is not a general power of appointment.

(2) Powers limited by an ascertainable standard. A power to consume, invade, or appropriate income or corpus, or both, for the benefit of the decedent which is limited by an ascertainable standard relating to the health, education, support, or maintenance of the decedent is, by reason of section 2041 (b) (1) (A), not a general power of appointment. A power is limited by such a standard if the extent of the holder's duty to exercise and not to exercise the power is reasonably measurable in terms of his needs for health, education, or support (or any combination of them). As used in this subparagraph, the words "support" and "maintenance" are synonymous and their meaning is not limited to the bare necessities of life. A power to use property for the comfort, welfare, or happiness of the holder of the power is not limited by the requisite standard. Examples of powers which are limited by the requisite standard are powers exercisable for the holder's "support," "support in reasonable comfort," "maintenance in health and reasonable comfort," "support in his accustomed manner of living," "education, including college and professional education," "health," and "medical, dental, hospital and nursing expenses and expenses of invalidism." In determining whether a power is limited by an ascertainable standard, it is immaterial whether the beneficiary is required to exhaust his other income before the power can be exercised.

. . . .

(d) Definition of "exercise". Whether a power of appointment is in fact exercised may depend upon local law. For example, the residuary clause of a will may be considered under local law as an exercise of a testamentary power of appointment in the absence of evidence of a contrary intention drawn from the whole of the testator's will. However, regardless of local law, a power of appointment is considered as exercised for purposes of section 2041 even though the exercise is in favor of the taker in default of appointment, and irrespective of whether the appointed interest and the interest in default of appointment are identical or whether the appointee renounces any right to take under the appointment. A power of appointment is also considered as exercised even though the disposition cannot take effect until the occurrence of an event after the exercise takes place, if the exercise is irrevocable and, as of the time of the exercise, the condition was not impossible of occurrence. For example, if property is left in trust to A for life, with a power in B to appoint the remainder by will, and B dies before A, exercising his power by appointing the remainder to C if C survives A, B is considered to have exercised his power if C is living at B's death. On the other hand, a testamentary power of appointment is not considered as exercised if it is exercised subject to the occurrence during the decedent's life of an express or implied condition which did not in fact occur. Thus, if in the preceding example, C dies before B, B's power of appointment would not be considered to have been exercised. Similarly, if a trust provides for income to A for life, remainder as A appoints by will, and A appoints a life estate in the property to B and does not otherwise exercise his power, but B dies before A, A's power is not considered to have been exercised.

(e) Time of creation of power. A power of appointment created by will is, in general considered as created on the date of the testator's death. However, section 2041(b) (3) provides that a power of appointment created by a will executed on or before October 21, 1942, is considered a power created on or before that date if the testator dies before July 1, 1949, without having republished the will, by codicil or otherwise, after October 21, 1942. A power of appointment created by an inter vivos instrument is considered as created on the date the instrument takes effect. Such a power is not considered as created at some future date merely because it is not exercisable on the date the instrument takes effect, or because it is revocable, or because the identity of its holders is not ascertainable until after the date the instrument takes effect. However, if the holder of a power exercises it by creating a second power, the second power is considered as created at the time of the exercise of the first. The application of this paragraph may be illustrated by the following examples:

Example (1). A created a revocable trust before October 22, 1942, providing for payment of income to B for life with remainder as B shall appoint by will. Even though A dies after October 21, 1942, without having exercised his power of revocation, B's power of appointment is considered a power created before October 22, 1942.

Example (2). C created an irrevocable inter vivos trust before October 22, 1942, naming T as trustee and providing for payment of income to D for life with remainder to E. T was given the power to pay corpus to D and the power to appoint a successor trustee. If T resigns after October 21, 1942, and appoints D as successor trustee, D is considered to have a power of appointment created before October 22, 1942.

Example (3). F created an irrevocable inter vivos trust before October 22, 1942, providing for payment of income to G for life with remainder as G shall appoint by will, but in default of appointment income to H for life with remainder as H shall appoint by will. If G died after October 21, 1942, without having exercised his power of appointment, H's power of appointment is considered a power created before October 22, 1942, even though it was only a contingent interest until G's death.

Example (4). If in example (3) above G had exercised his power of appointment by creating a similar power in J, J's power of appointment would be considered a power created after October 21, 1942.

§ 20.2041–3 Powers of appointment created after October 21, 1942

(a) **In general.** (1) Property subject to a power of appointment created after October 21, 1942, is includible in the gross estate of the holder of the power under varying conditions depending on whether the power is (i) general in nature, (ii) possessed at death, or (iii) exercised or released. See paragraphs (b), (c), and (d) of § 20.2041–1 for the definition of various terms used in this section. See paragraph (c) of this section for the rules applicable to determine the extent to which joint powers created after October 21, 1942, are to be treated as general powers of appointment.

(2) If the power is a general power of appointment, the value of an interest in property subject to such a power is includible in a decedent's gross estate under section 2041(a) (2) if either—

(i) The decedent has the power at the time of his death (and the interest exists at the time of his death), or

(ii) The decedent exercised or released the power, or the power lapsed, under the circumstances and to the extent described in paragraph (d) of this section.

(3) If the power is not a general power of appointment, the value of property subject to the power is includible in the holder's gross estate under section 2041(a) (3) only if it is exercised to create a further power under certain circumstances (see paragraph (e) of this section).

(b) **Existence of power at death.** For purposes of section 2041(a) (2), a power of appointment is considered to exist on the date of a decedent's death even though the exercise of the power is subject to the precedent giving of notice, or even though the exercise of the power takes effect only on the expiration of a stated period after its exercise, whether or not on or before the decedent's death notice has been given or the power has been exercised. However, a power which by its terms is exercisable only upon the occurrence during the decedent's lifetime of an event or a contingency which did not in fact take place or occur during such time is not a power in existence on the date of the decedent's death. For example, if a decedent was given a general power of appointment exercisable only after he reached a certain age, only if he survived another person, or only if he died without descendants, the power would not be in existence on the date of the decedent's death if the condition precedent to its exercise had not occurred.

(c) Joint powers created after October 21, 1942. The treatment of a power of appointment created after October 21, 1942, which is exercisable only in conjunction with another person is governed by section 2041(b) (1) (C), which provides as follows:

(1) Such a power is not considered a general power of appointment if it is not exercisable by the decedent except with the consent or joinder of the creator of the power.

(2) Such power is not considered a general power of appointment if it is not exercisable by the decedent except with the consent or joinder of a person having a substantial interest in the property subject to the power which is adverse to the exercise of the power in favor of the decedent, his estate, his creditors, or the creditors of his estate. An interest adverse to the exercise of a power is considered as substantial if its value in relation to the total value of the property subject to the power is not insignificant. For this purpose, the interest is to be valued in accordance with the actuarial principles set forth in § 20.2031-7 or, if it is not susceptible to valuation under those provisions, in accordance with the general principles set forth in § 20.2031-1. A taker in default of appointment under a power has an interest which is adverse to an exercise of the power. A coholder of the power has no adverse interest merely because of his joint possession of the power nor merely because he is a permissible appointee under a power. However, a coholder of a power is considered as having an adverse interest where he may possess the power after the decedent's death and may exercise it at that time in favor of himself, his estate, his creditors, or the creditors of his estate. Thus, for example, if X, Y, and Z held a power jointly to appoint among a group of persons which includes themselves and if on the death of X the power will pass to Y and Z jointly, then Y and Z are considered to have interests adverse to the exercise of the power in favor of X. Similarly, if on Y's death the power will pass to Z, Z is considered to have an interest adverse to the exercise of the power in favor of Y. The application of this subparagraph may be further illustrated by the following additional examples in each of which it is assumed that the value of the interest in question is substantial:

Example (1). The decedent and R were trustees of a trust under the terms of which the income was to be paid to the decedent for life and then to M for life, and the remainder was to be paid to R. The trustees had power to distribute corpus to the decedent. Since R's interest was substantially adverse to an exercise of the power in favor of the decedent the latter did not have a general power of appointment. If M and the decedent were the trustees, M's interest would likewise have been adverse.

Example (2). The decedent and L were trustees of a trust under the terms of which the income was to be paid to L for life and then to M for life, and the remainder was to be paid to the decedent. The trustees had power to distribute corpus to the decedent during L's life. Since L's interest was adverse to an exercise of the power in favor of the decedent, the decedent did not have a general power of appointment. If the decedent and M were the trustees, M's interest would likewise have been adverse.

Example (3). The decedent and L were trustees of a trust under the terms of which the income was to be paid to L for life. The trustees could designate whether corpus was to be distributed to the decedent or to A after L's death. L's interest was not adverse to an exercise of the power in favor of the decedent, and the decedent therefore had a general power of appointment.

(3) A power which is exercisable only in conjunction with another person, and which after application of the rules set forth in subparagraphs (1) and (2) of this paragraph constitutes a general power of appointment, will be treated as though the holders of the power who are permissible appointees of the property were joint owners of property subject to the power. The decedent, under this rule, will be treated as possessed of a general power of appointment over an aliquot share of the property to be determined with reference to the number of joint holders, including the decedent, who (or whose estates or creditors) are permissible appointees. Thus, for example, if X, Y, and Z hold an unlimited power jointly to appoint among a group of persons, including themselves, but on the death of X the power does not pass to Y and Z jointly, then Y and Z are not considered to have interests adverse to the exercise of the power in favor of X. In this case X is considered to possess a general power of appointment as to one-third of the property subject to the power.

(d) Releases, lapses, and disclaimers of general powers of appointment. (1) Property subject to a general power of appointment created after October 21, 1942, is includible in the gross estate of a decedent under section 2041(a) (2) even though he does not have the power at the date of his death, if during his life he exercised or released the power under circumstances such that, if the property subject to the power had been owned and transferred by the decedent, the property would be includible in the decedent's gross estate under section 2035, 2036, 2037, or 2038. Further, section 2041(b) (2) provides that the lapse of a power of appointment is considered to be a release of the power to the extent set forth in subparagraph (3) of this paragraph. A release of a power of appointment need not be formal or express in character. The principles set forth in § 20.2041-2 for determining the application of the pertinent provisions of sections 2035 through 2038 to a particular exercise of a power of appointment are applicable for purposes of determining whether or not an exercise or release of a power of appointment created after October 21, 1942, causes the property to be included in a decedent's gross estate under section 2041(a) (2). If a general power of appointment created after October 21, 1942, is partially released, a subsequent exercise or release of the power under circumstances described in the first sentence of this subparagraph, or its possession at death will nevertheless cause the property subject to the power to be included in the gross estate of the holder of the power.

(3) The failure to exercise a power of appointment created after October 21, 1942, within a specified time, so that the power lapses, constitutes a release of the power. However, section 2041 (b) (2) provides that such a lapse of a power of appointment during any calendar year during the decedent's life is treated as a release for purposes of inclusion of property in the gross estate under section 2041(a) (2) only to the extent that the property which could have been appointed by exercise of the lapsed power exceeds the greater of (i) $5,000 or (ii) 5 percent of the aggregate value, at the time of the lapse, of the assets out of which, or the proceeds of which, the exercise of the lapsed power could have been satisfied. For example, assume that A transferred

$200,000 worth of securities in trust providing for payment of income to B for life with remainder to B's issue. Assume further that B was given a non-cumulative right to withdraw $10,000 a year from the principal of the trust fund (which neither increased nor decreased in value prior to B's death). In such case, the failure of B to exercise his right of withdrawal will not result in estate tax with respect to the power to withdraw $10,000 which lapses each year before the year of B's death. At B's death there will be included in his gross estate the $10,000 which he was entitled to withdraw for the year in which his death occurs less any amount which he may have taken during that year. However, if in the above example B had possessed the right to withdraw $15,000 of the principal annually, the failure to exercise such power in any year will be considered a release of the power to the extent of the excess of the amount subject to withdrawal over 5 percent of the trust fund (in this example, $5,000, assuming that the trust fund is worth $200,000 at the time of the lapse). Since each lapse is treated as though B had exercised dominion over the trust property by making a transfer of principal reserving the income therefrom for his life, the value of the trust property (but only to the extent of the excess of the amount subject to withdrawal over 5 percent of the trust fund) is includible in B's gross estate (unless before B's death he has disposed of his right to the income under circumstances to which sections 2035 through 2038 would not be applicable). The extent to which the value of the trust property is included in the decedent's gross estate is determined as provided in subparagraph (4) of this paragraph.

(4) The purpose of section 2041(b) (2) is to provide a determination, as of the date of the lapse of the power, of the proportion of the property over which the power lapsed which is an exempt disposition for estate tax purposes and the proportion which, if the other requirements of sections 2035 through 2038 are satisfied, will be considered as a taxable disposition. Once the taxable proportion of any disposition at the date of lapse has been determined, the valuation of that proportion as of the date of the decedent's death (or, if the

executor has elected the alternate valuation method under section 2032. the value as of the date therein provided), is to be ascertained in accordance with the principles which are applicable to the valuation of transfers of property by the decedent under the corresponding provisions of sections 2035 through 2038. For example, if the life beneficiary of a trust had a right exercisable only during one calendar year to draw down $50,000 from the corpus of a trust, which he did not exercise, and if at the end of the year the corpus was worth $800,000, the taxable portion over which the power lapsed is $10,000 (the excess of $50,000 over 5 percent of the corpus), or 1/80 of the total value. On the decedent's death, if the total value of the corpus of the trust (excluding income accumulated after the lapse of the power) on the applicable valuation date was $1,200,000, $15,000 (1/80 of $1,200,-000) would be includible in the decedent's gross estate. However, if the total value was then $600,000, only $7,-500 (1/80 of $600,000) would be includible.

(5) If the failure to exercise a power, such as a right of withdrawal, occurs in more than a single year, the proportion of the property over which the power lapsed which is treated as a taxable disposition will be determined separately for each such year. The aggregate of the taxable proportions for all such years, valued in accordance with the above principles, will be includible in the gross estate by reason of the lapse. The includible amount, however, shall not exceed the aggregate value of the assets out of which, or the proceeds of which, the exercise of the power could have been satisfied, valued as of the date of the decedent's death (or, if the executor has elected the alternate valuation method under section 2032, the value as of the date therein provided).

. . . . .

(e) Successive powers. (1) Property subject to a power of appointment created after October 21, 1942, which is not a general power, is includible in the gross estate of the holder of the power under section 2041(a) (3) if the power is exercised, and if both of the following conditions are met:

(i) If the exercise is (a) by will, or (b) by a disposition which is of such nature that if it were a transfer of property owned by the decedent, the property would be includible in the decedent's gross estate under sections 2035 through 2037; and

(ii) If the power is exercised by creating another power of appointment which, under the terms of the instruments creating and exercising the first power and under applicable local law, can be validly exercised so as to (a) postpone the vesting of any estate or interest in the property for a period ascertainable without regard to the date of the creation of the first power, or (b) (if the applicable rule against perpetuities is stated in terms of suspension of ownership or of the power of alienation, rather than of vesting) suspend the absolute ownership or the power of alienation of the property for a period ascertainable without regard to the date of the creation of the first power.

(2) For purposes of the application of section 2041(a) (3), the value of the property subject to the second power of appointment is considered to be its value unreduced by any precedent or subsequent interest which is not subject to the second power. Thus, if a decedent has a power to appoint by will $100,000 to a group of persons consisting of his children and grandchildren and exercises the power by making an outright appointment of $75,000 and by giving one appointee a power to appoint $25,-000, no more than $25,000 will be includible in the decedent's gross estate under section 2041(a) (3). If, however, the decedent appoints the income from the entire fund to a beneficiary for life with power in the beneficiary to appoint the remainder by will, the entire $100,-000 will be includible in the decedent's gross estate under section 2041(a) (3) if the exercise of the second power can validly postpone the vesting of any estate or interest in the property or can suspend the absolute ownership or power of alienation of the property for a period ascertainable without regard to the date of the creation of the first power.

. . . . .

§ 20.2042-1 Proceeds of life insurance

(a) In general. (1) Section 2042 provides for the inclusion in a decedent's gross estate of the proceeds of insurance on the decedent's life (i) receivable by or for the benefit of the estate (see paragraph (b) of this section), and (ii) receivable by other beneficiaries (see paragraph (c) of this section). The term "insurance" refers to life insurance of every description, including death benefits paid by fraternal beneficial societies operating under the lodge system.

(2) Proceeds of life insurance which are not includible in the gross estate under section 2042 may, depending upon the facts of the particular case, be includible under some other section of part III of subchapter A of chapter 11. For example, if the decedent possessed incidents of ownership in an insurance policy on his life but gratuitously transferred all rights in the policy in contemplation of death, the proceeds would be includible under section 2035. Section 2042 has no application to the inclusion in the gross estate of the value of rights in an insurance policy on the life of a person other than the decedent, or the value of rights in a combination annuity contract and life insurance policy on the decedent's life (i. e., a "retirement income" policy with death benefit or an "endowment" policy) under which there was no insurance element at the time of the decedent's death (see paragraph (d) of § 20.2039-1).

(3) Except as provided in paragraph (c)(6), the amount to be included in the gross estate under section 2042 is the full amount receivable under the policy. If the proceeds of the policy are made payable to a beneficiary in the form of an annuity for life or for a term of years, the amount to be included in the gross estate is the one sum payable at death under an option which could have been exercised either by the insured or by the beneficiary, or if no option was granted, the sum used by the insurance company in determining the amount of the annuity.

(b) **Receivable by or for the benefit of the estate.** (1) Section 2042 requires the inclusion in the gross estate of the proceeds of insurance on the decedent's life receivable by the executor or administrator, or payable to the decedent's estate. It makes no difference whether or not the estate is specifically named as the beneficiary

under the terms of the policy. Thus, if under the terms of an insurance policy the proceeds are receivable by another beneficiary but are subject to an obligation, legally binding upon the other beneficiary, to pay taxes, debts, or other charges enforceable against the estate, then the amount of such proceeds required for the payment in full (to the extent of the beneficiary's obligation) of such taxes, debts, or other charges is includible in the gross estate. Similarly, if the decedent purchased an insurance policy in favor of another person or a corporation as collateral security for a loan or other accommodation, its proceeds are considered to be receivable for the benefit of the estate. The amount of the loan outstanding at the date of the decedent's death, with interest accrued to that date, will be deductible in determining the taxable estate. See § 20.2053-4.

(2) If the proceeds of an insurance policy made payable to the decedent's estate are community assets under the local community property law and, as a result, one-half of the proceeds belongs to the decedent's spouse, then only one-half of the proceeds is considered to be receivable by or for the benefit of the decedent's estate.

(c) **Receivable by other beneficiaries.** (1) Section 2042 requires the inclusion in the gross estate of the proceeds of insurance on the decedent's life not receivable by or for the benefit of the estate if the decedent possessed at the date of his death any of the incidents of ownership in the policy, exercisable either alone or in conjunction with any other person. However, if the decedent did not possess any of such incidents of ownership at the time of his death nor transfer them in contemplation of death, no part of the proceeds would be includible in his gross estate under section 2042. Thus, if the decedent owned a policy of insurance on his life and, 4 years before his death, irrevocably assigned his entire interest in the policy to his wife retaining no reversionary interest therein (see subparagraph (3) of this paragraph), the proceeds of the policy would not be includible in his gross estate under section 2042.

(2) For purposes of this paragraph, the term "incidents of ownership" is

not limited in its meaning to ownership of the policy in the technical legal sense. Generally speaking, the term has reference to the right of the insured or his estate to the economic benefits of the policy. Thus, it includes the power to change the beneficiary, to surrender or cancel the policy, to assign the policy, to revoke an assignment, to pledge the policy for a loan, or to obtain from the insurer a loan against the surrender value of the policy, etc. See subparagraph (6) of this paragraph for rules relating to the circumstances under which incidents of ownership held by a corporation are attributable to a decedent through his stock ownership.

(3) The term "incidents of ownership" also includes a reversionary interest in the policy or its proceeds, whether arising by the express terms of the policy or other instrument or by operation of law, but only if the value of the reversionary interest immediately before the death of the decedent exceeded 5 percent of the value of the policy. As used in this subparagraph, the term "reversionary interest" includes a possibility that the policy or its proceeds may return to the decedent or his estate and a possibility that the policy or its proceeds may become subject to a power of disposition by him. In order to determine whether or not the value of a reversionary interest immediately before the death of the decedent exceeded 5 percent of the value of the policy, the principles contained in paragraph (c) (3) and (4) of § 20.-2037-1, insofar as applicable, shall be followed under this subparagraph. In that connection, there must be specifically taken into consideration any incidents of ownership held by others immediately before the decedent's death which would affect the value of the reversionary interest. For example, the decedent would not be considered to have a reversionary interest in the policy of a value in excess of 5 percent if the power to obtain the cash surrender value existed in some other person immediately before the decedent's death and was exercisable by such other person alone and in all events. The terms "reversionary interest" and "incidents of ownership" do not include the possibility that the decedent might receive a policy or its proceeds by inheritance through the estate of another person, or as a surviving spouse under a statutory right of election or a similar right.

(4) A decedent is considered to have an "incident of ownership" in an insurance policy on his life held in trust if, under the terms of the policy, the decedent (either alone or in conjunction with another person or persons) has the power (as trustee or otherwise) to change the beneficial ownership in the policy or its proceeds, or the time or manner of enjoyment thereof, even though the decedent has no beneficial interest in the trust. Moreover, assuming the decedent created the trust, such a power may result in the inclusion in the decedent's gross estate under section 2036 or 2038 of other property transferred by the decedent to the trust if, for example, the decedent has the power to surrender the insurance policy and if the income otherwise used to pay premiums on the policy would become currently payable to a beneficiary of the trust in the event that the policy were surrendered.

(5) As an additional step in determining whether or not a decedent possessed any incidents of ownership in a policy or any part of a policy, regard must be given to the effect of the State or other applicable law upon the terms of the policy. For example, assume that the decedent purchased a policy of insurance on his life with funds held by him and his surviving wife as community property, designating their son as beneficiary but retaining the right to surrender the policy. Under the local law, the proceeds upon surrender would have inured to the marital community. Assuming that the policy is not surrendered and that the son receives the proceeds on the decedent's death, the wife's transfer of her one-half interest in the policy was not considered absolute before the decedent's death. Upon the wife's prior death, one-half of the value of the policy would have been included in her gross estate. Under these circumstances, the power of surrender possessed by the decedent as agent for his wife with respect to one-half of the policy is not, for purposes of this section, an "incident of ownership", and the decedent is, therefore, deemed to possess an incident of ownership in only one-half of the policy.

(6) In the case of economic benefits of a life insurance policy on the decedent's life that are reserved to a corporation of which the decedent is the sole or controlling stockholder, the corporation's incidents of ownership will not be attributed to the decedent through his stock ownership to the extent the proceeds of the policy are payable to the corporation. Any proceeds payable to a third party for a valid business purpose, such as in satisfaction of a business debt of the corporation, so that the net worth of the corporation is increased by the amount of such proceeds, shall be deemed to be payable to the corporation for purposes of the preceding sentence. See § 20.2031-2(f) for a rule providing that the proceeds of certain life insurance policies shall be considered in determining the value of the decedent's stock. Except as hereinafter provided with respect to a group-term life insurance policy, if any part of the proceeds of the policy are not payable to or for the benefit of the corporation, and thus are not taken into account in valuing the decedent's stock holdings in the corporation for purposes of section 2031, any incidents of ownership held by the corporation as to that part of the proceeds will be attributed to the decedent through his stock ownership where the decedent is the sole or controlling stockholder. Thus, for example, if the decedent is the controlling stockholder in a corporation, and the corporation owns a life insurance policy on his life, the proceeds of which are payable to the decedent's spouse, the incidents of ownership held by the corporation will be attributed to the decedent through his stock ownership and the proceeds will be included in his gross estate under section 2042. If in this example the policy proceeds had been payable 40 percent to decedent's spouse and 60 percent to the corporation, only 40 percent of the proceeds would be included in decedent's gross estate under section 2042. For purposes of this subparagraph, the decedent will not be deemed to be the controlling stockholder of a corporation unless, at the time of his death, he owned stock possessing more than 50 percent of the total combined voting power of the corporation. Solely for purposes of the preceding sentence, a decedent shall be considered to be the owner of only the stock with respect to which legal title was held, at the time of his death, by (i) the decedent (or his agent or nominee); the decedent and another person jointly (but only the proportionate number of shares which corresponds to the portion of the total consideration which is considered to be furnished by the decedent for purposes of section 2040 and the regulations thereunder); and (iii) by a trustee of a voting trust (to the extent of the decedent's beneficial interest therein) or any other trust with respect to which the decedent was treated as an owner under subpart E, part I, subchapter J, chapter 1 of the Code immediately prior to his death. In the case of group-term life insurance, as defined in paragraph (b)(1)(i) and (iii) of § 1.79-1 of this chapter (Income Tax Regulations), the power to surrender or cancel a policy held by a corporation shall not be attributed to any decedent through his stock ownership.

§ 20.2043-1 Transfers for insufficient consideration

(a) In general. The transfers, trusts, interests, rights or powers enumerated and described in sections 2035 through 2038 and section 2041 are not subject to the Federal estate tax if made, created, exercised, or relinquished in a transaction which constituted a bona fide sale for an adequate and full consideration in money or money's worth. To constitute a bona fide sale for an adequate and full consideration in money or money's worth, the transfer must have been made in good faith, and the price must have been an adequate and full equivalent reducible to a money value. If the price was less than such a consideration, only the excess of the fair market value of the property (as of the applicable valuation date) over the price received by the decedent is included in ascertaining the value of his gross estate.

(b) Marital rights and support obligations. For purposes of chapter 11, a relinquishment or promised relinquishment of dower, curtesy, or of a statutory estate created in lieu of dower or curtesy, or of other marital rights in the decedent's property or estate, is not to any extent a consideration in "money or money's worth."

§ 20.2053-1 Deductions for expenses, indebtedness, and taxes; in general

(a) **General rule.** In determining the taxable estate of a decedent who was a citizen or resident of the United States at the time of his death, there are allowed as deductions under section 2053 (a) and (b) amounts falling within the following two categories (subject to the limitations contained in this section and in §§ 20.2053-2 through 20.-2053-9):

(1) **First category.** Amounts which are payable out of property subject to claims and which are allowable by the law of the jurisdiction, whether within or without the United States, under which the estate is being administered for—

(i) Funeral expenses;

(ii) Administration expenses;

(iii) Claims against the estate (including taxes to the extent set forth in § 20.2053-6 and charitable pledges to the extent set forth in § 20.2053-5); and

(iv) Unpaid mortgages on, or any indebtedness in respect of, property, the value of the decedent's interest in which is included in the value of the gross estate undiminished by the mortgage or indebtedness.

As used in this subparagraph, the phrase "allowable by the law of the jurisdiction" means allowable by the law governing the administration of decedents' estates. The phrase has no reference to amounts allowable as deductions under a law which imposes a State death tax. See further §§ 20.-2053-2 through 20.2053-7.

(2) **Second category.** Amounts representing expenses incurred in administering property which is included in the gross estate but which is not subject to claims and which—

(i) Would be allowed as deductions in the first category if the property being administered were subject to claims; and

(ii) Were paid before the expiration of the period of limitation for assessment provided in section 6501. See further § 20.2053-8.

(b) **Provisions applicable to both categories—(1) In general.** If the item is not one of those described in paragraph (a) of this section, it is not deductible merely because payment is allowed by the local law. If the amount which may be expended for the particular purpose is limited by the local law no deduction in excess of that limitation is permissible.

(2) **Effect of court decree.** The decision of a local court as to the amount and allowability under local law of a claim or administration expense will ordinarily be accepted if the court passes upon the facts upon which deductibility depends. If the court does not pass upon those facts, its decree will, of course, not be followed. For example, if the question before the court is whether a claim should be allowed, the decree allowing it will ordinarily be accepted as establishing the validity and amount of the claim. However, the decree will not necessarily be accepted even though it purports to decide the facts upon which deductibility depends. It must appear that the court actually passed upon the merits of the claim. This will be presumed in all cases of an active and genuine contest. If the result reached appears to be unreasonable, this is some evidence that there was not such a contest, but it may be rebutted by proof to the contrary. If the decree was rendered by consent, it will be accepted, provided the consent was a bona fide recognition of the validity of the claim (and not a mere cloak for a gift) and was accepted by the court as satisfactory evidence upon the merits. It will be presumed that the consent was of this character, and was so accepted, if given by all parties having an interest adverse to the claimant. The decree will not be accepted if it is at variance with the law of the State; as, for example, an allowance made to an executor in excess of that prescribed by statute. On the other hand, a deduction for the amount of a bona fide indebtedness of the decedent, or of a reasonable expense of administration, will not be denied because no court decree has been entered if the amount would be allowable under local law.

(3) **Estimated amounts.** An item may be entered on the return for deduction though its exact amount is not then known, provided it is ascertainable with reasonable certainty, and will be paid. No deduction may be taken upon the basis of a vague or uncertain estimate. If the amount of a liability was not ascertainable at the time of

final audit of the return by the district director and, as a consequence, it was not allowed as a deduction in the audit, and subsequently the amount of the liability is ascertained, relief may be sought by a petition to the Tax Court or a claim for refund as provided by sections 6213(a) and 6511, respectively.

(c) Provision applicable to first category only. Deductions of the first category (described in paragraph (a) (1) of this section) are limited under section 2053(a) to amounts which would be properly allowable out of property subject to claims by the law of the jurisdiction under which the decedent's estate is being administered. Further, the total allowable amount of deductions of the first category is limited by section 2053(c) (2) to the sum of—

(1) The value of property included in the decedent's gross estate and subject to claims, plus

(2) Amounts paid, out of property not subject to claims against the decedent's estate, within 9 months (15 months in the case of the estate of a decedent dying before January 1, 1971) after the decedent's death (the period within which the estate tax return must be filed under section 6075), or within any extension of time for filing the return granted under section 6081.

The term "property subject to claims" is defined in section 2053(c) (2) as meaning the property includible in the gross estate which, or the avails of which, under the applicable law, would bear the burden of the payment of these deductions in the final adjustment and settlement of the decedent's estate. However, for the purposes of this definition, the value of property subject to claims is first reduced by the amount of any deduction allowed under section 2054 for any losses from casualty or theft incurred during the settlement of the estate attributable to such property. The application of this paragraph may be illustrated by the following examples:

Example (1). The only item in the gross estate is real property valued at $250,000 which the decedent and his surviving spouse held as tenants by the entirety. Under the local law this real property is not subject to claims. Funeral expenses of $1,200 and debts of the decedent in the amount of $1,500 are allowable under local law. Before the prescribed date for filing the estate tax return, the surviving spouse paid the funeral expenses and $1,000 of the debts. The remaining $500 of the debts was paid by

her after the prescribed date for filing the return. The total amount allowable as deductions under section 2053 is limited to $2,200, the amount paid prior to the prescribed date for filing the return.

Example (2). The only two items in the gross estate were a bank deposit of $20,000 and insurance in the amount of $150,000. The insurance was payable to the decedent's surviving spouse and under local law was not subject to claims. Funeral expenses of $1,000 and debts in the amount of $29,000 were allowable under local law. A son was executor of the estate and before the prescribed date for filing the estate tax return he paid the funeral expenses and $9,000 of the debts, using therefor $5,000 of the bank deposit and $5,000 supplied by the surviving spouse. After the prescribed date for filing the return, the executor paid the remaining $20,000 of the debts, using for that purpose the $15,000 left in the bank account plus an additional $5,000 supplied by the surviving spouse. The total amount allowable as deductions under section 2053 is limited to $25,000 ($20,000 of property subject to claims plus the $5,000 additional amount which, before the prescribed date for filing the return, was paid out of property not subject to claims).

(d) Disallowance of double deductions. See section 642(g) and § 1.642 (g)–1 with respect to the disallowance for income tax purposes of certain deductions unless the right to take such deductions for estate tax purposes is waived.

§ 20.2053–2 Deduction for funeral expenses

Such amounts for funeral expenses are allowed as deductions from a decedent's gross estate as (a) are actually expended, (b) would be properly allowable out of property subject to claims under the laws of the local jurisdiction, and (c) satisfy the requirements of paragraph (c) of § 20.2053–1. A reasonable expenditure for a tombstone, monument, or mausoleum, or for a burial lot, either for the decedent or his family, including a reasonable expenditure for its future care, may be deducted under this heading, provided such an expenditure is allowable by the local law. Included in funeral expenses is the cost of transportation of the person bringing the body to the place of burial.

§ 20.2053–3 Deduction for expenses of administering estate

(a) In general. The amounts deductible from a decedent's gross estate as "administration expenses" of the first category (see paragraphs (a) and (c) of § 20.2053–1) are limited to such expenses as are actually and necessarily incurred in the administration of the decedent's estate; that is, in the collection of assets, payment of debts, and distribution of property to the persons entitled to it. The expenses contemplated in the law are such only as attend the settlement of an estate and the transfer of the property of the estate to individual beneficiaries or to a trustee, whether the trustee is the executor or some other person. Expenditures not essential to the proper settlement of the estate, but incurred for the individual benefit of the heirs, legatees, or devisees, may not be taken as deductions. Administration expenses include (1) executor's commissions; (2) attorney's fees; and (3) miscellaneous expenses. Each of these classes is considered separately in paragraphs (b) through (d) of this section.

(b) Executor's commissions. (1) The executor or administrator, in filing the estate tax return, may deduct his commissions in such an amount as has actually been paid, or in an amount which at the time of filing the estate tax return may reasonably be expected to be paid, but no deduction may be taken if no commissions are to be collected. If the amount of the commissions has not been fixed by decree of the proper court, the deduction will be allowed on the final audit of the return, to the extent that all three of the following conditions are satisfied:

(i) The district director is reasonably satisfied that the commissions claimed will be paid;

(ii) The amount claimed as a deduction is within the amount allowable by the laws of the jurisdiction in which the estate is being administered; and

(iii) It is in accordance with the usually accepted practice in the jurisdiction to allow such an amount in estates of similar size and character.

If the deduction is disallowed in whole or in part on final audit, the disallowance will be subject to modification as the facts may later require. If the deduction is allowed in advance of payment and payment is thereafter waived, it shall be the duty of the executor to notify the district director and to pay the resulting tax, together with interest.

(2) A bequest or devise to the executor in lieu of commissions is not de-ductible. If, however, the decedent fixed by his will the compensation payable to the executor for services to be rendered in the administration of the estate, deduction may be taken to the extent that the amount so fixed does not exceed the compensation allowable by the local law or practice.

(3) Except to the extent that a trustee is in fact performing services with respect to property subject to claims which would normally be performed by an executor, amounts paid as trustees' commissions do not constitute expenses of administration under the first category, and are only deductible as expenses of the second category to the extent provided in § 20.2053–8.

(c) Attorney's fees. (1) The executor or administrator, in filing the estate tax return, may deduct such an amount of attorney's fees as has actually been paid, or an amount which at the time of filing may reasonably be expected to be paid. If on the final audit of a return the fees claimed have not been awarded by the proper court and paid, the deduction will, nevertheless, be allowed, if the district director is reasonably satisfied that the amount claimed will be paid and that it does not exceed a reasonable remuneration for the services rendered, taking into account the size and character of the estate and the local law and practice. If the deduction is disallowed in whole or in part on final audit, the disallowance will be subject to modification as the facts may later require.

(2) A deduction for attorneys' fees incurred in contesting an asserted deficiency or in prosecuting a claim for refund should be claimed at the time the deficiency is contested or the refund claim is prosecuted. A deduction for reasonable attorneys' fees actually paid in contesting an asserted deficiency or in prosecuting a claim for refund will be allowed even though the deduction, as such, was not claimed in the estate tax return or in the claim for refund. A deduction for these fees shall not be denied, and the sufficiency of a claim for refund shall not be questioned, solely by reason of the fact that the amount of the fees to be paid was not established at the time that the right to the deduction was claimed.

(3) Attorneys' fees incurred by beneficiaries incident to litigation as to

their respective interests are not deductible if the litigation is not essential to the proper settlement of the estate within the meaning of paragraph (a) of this section. An attorney's fee not meeting this test is not deductible as an administration expense under section 2053 and this section, even if it is approved by a probate court as an expense payable or reimbursable by the estate.

(d) Miscellaneous administration expenses. (1) Miscellaneous administration expenses include such expenses as court costs, surrogates' fees, accountants' fees, appraisers' fees, clerk hire, etc. Expenses necessarily incurred in preserving and distributing the estate are deductible, including the cost of storing or maintaining property of the estate, if it is impossible to effect immediate distribution to the beneficiaries. Expenses for preserving and caring for the property may not include outlays for additions or improvements; nor will such expenses be allowed for a longer period than the executor is reasonably required to retain the property.

(2) Expenses for selling property of the estate are deductible if the sale is necessary in order to pay the decedent's debts, expenses of administration, or taxes, to preserve the estate, or to effect distribution. The phrase "expenses for selling property" includes brokerage fees and other expenses attending the sale, such as the fees of an auctioneer if it is reasonably necessary to employ one. Where an item included in the gross estate is disposed of in a bona fide sale (including a redemption) to a dealer in such items at a price below its fair market value, for purposes of this paragraph there shall be treated as an expense for selling the item whichever of the following amounts is the lesser: (i) The amount by which the fair market value of the property on the applicable valuation date exceeds the proceeds of the sale, or (ii) the amount by which the fair market value of the property on the date of the sale exceeds the proceeds of the sale. The principles used in determining the value at which an item of property is included in the gross estate shall be followed in arriving at the fair market value of the property for purposes of this paragraph. See §§ 20.2031-1 through 20.2031-9.

§ 20.2053-7 Deduction for unpaid mortgages

A deduction is allowed from a decedent's gross estate of the full unpaid amount of a mortgage upon, or of any other indebtedness in respect of, any property of the gross estate, including interest which had accrued thereon to the date of death, provided the value of the property, undiminished by the amount of the mortgage or indebtedness, is included in the value of the gross estate. If the decedent's estate is liable for the amount of the mortgage or indebtedness, the full value of the property subject to the mortgage or indebtedness must be included as part of the value of the gross estate; the amount of the mortgage or indebtedness being in such case allowed as a deduction. But if the decedent's estate is not so liable, only the value of the equity of redemption (or the value of the property, less the mortgage or indebtedness) need be returned as part of the value of the gross estate. In no case may the deduction on account of the mortgage or indebtedness exceed the liability therefor contracted bona fide and for an adequate and full consideration in money or money's worth. See § 20.-2043-1. Only interest accrued to the date of the decedent's death is allowable even though the alternate valuation method under section 2032 is selected. In any case where real property situated outside the United States does not form a part of the gross estate, no deduction may be taken of any mortgage thereon or any other indebtedness in respect thereof.

§ 20.2053-8 Deduction for expenses in administering property not subject to claims

(a) Expenses incurred in administering property included in a decedent's gross estate but not subject to claims fall within the second category of deductions set forth in § 20.2053-1, and may be allowed as deductions if they—

(1) Would be allowed as deductions in the first category if the property being administered were subject to claims; and

(2) Were paid before the expiration of the period of limitation for assessment provided in section 6501.

Usually, these expenses are incurred in connection with the administration of a trust established by a decedent during his lifetime. They may also be incurred in connection with the collection of other assets or the transfer or clearance of title to other property included in a decedent's gross estate for estate tax purposes but not included in his probate estate.

(b) These expenses may be allowed as deductions only to the extent that they would be allowed as deductions under the first category if the property were subject to claims. See § 20.2053-3. The only expenses in administering property not subject to claims which are allowed as deductions are those occasioned by the decedent's death and incurred in settling the decedent's interest in the property or vesting good title to the property in the beneficiaries. Expenses not coming within the description in the preceding sentence but incurred on behalf of the transferees are not deductible.

(c) The principles set forth in paragraphs (b), (c), and (d) of § 20.2053-3 (relating to the allowance of executor's commissions, attorney's fees, and miscellaneous administration expenses of the first category) are applied in determining the extent to which trustee's commissions, attorney's and accountant's fees, and miscellaneous administration expenses are allowed in connection with the administration of property not subject to claims.

(d) The application of this section may be illustrated by the following examples:

Example (1). In 1940, the decedent made an irrevocable transfer of property to the X Trust Company, as trustee. The instrument of transfer provided that the trustee should pay the income from the property to the decedent for the duration of his life and, upon his death, distribute the corpus of the trust among designated beneficiaries. The property was included in the decedent's gross estate under the provisions of section 2036. Three months after the date of death, the trustee distributed the trust corpus among the beneficiaries, except for $6,000 which it withheld. The amount withheld represented $5,000 which it retained as trustee's commissions in connection with the termination of the trust and $1,000 which it had paid to an attorney for representing it in connection with the termination. Both the trustee's commissions and the attorney's fees were allowable under the law of the jurisdiction in which the trust was being administered, were reasonable in amount, and were in accord with local custom. Under these circumstances, the estate is allowed a deduction of $6,000.

Example (2). In 1945, the decedent made an irrevocable transfer of property to Y Trust Company, as trustee. The instrument of transfer provided that the trustee should pay the income from the property to the decedent during his life. If the decedent's wife survived him, the trust was to continue for the duration of her life, with Y Trust Company and the decedent's son as co-trustees, and with income payable to the decedent's wife for the duration of her life. Upon the death of both the decedent and his wife, the corpus is to be distributed among designated remaindermen. The decedent was survived by his wife. The property was included in the decedent's gross estate under the provisions of section 2036. In accordance with local custom, the trustee made an accounting to the court as of the date of the decedent's death. Following the death of the decedent, a controversy arose among the remaindermen as to their respective rights under the instrument of transfer, and a suit was brought in court to which the trustee was made a party. As a part of the accounting, the court approved the following expenses which the trustee had paid within 3 years following the date of death: $10,000, trustee's commissions; $5,000, accountant's fees; $25,000, attorney's fees; and $2,500, representing fees paid to the guardian of a remainderman who was a minor. The trustee's commissions and accountant's fees were for services in connection with the usual issues involved in a trust accounting as also were one-half of the attorney's and guardian's fees. The remainder of the attorney's and guardian's fees were for services performed in connection with the suit brought by the remaindermen. The amount allowed as a deduction is the $28,750 ($10,000, trustee's commissions; $5,000, accountant's fees; $12,500, attorney's fees; and $1,250, guardian's fees) incurred as expenses in connection with the usual issues involved in a trust accounting. The remaining expenses are not allowed as deductions since they were incurred on behalf of the transferees.

. . . . .

§ 20.2054-1 Deduction for losses from casualties or theft

A deduction is allowed for losses incurred during the settlement of the estate arising from fires, storms, shipwrecks, or other casualties, or from theft, if the losses are not compensated for by insurance or otherwise. If the loss is partly compensated for, the excess of the loss over the compensation may be deducted. Losses which are not of the nature described are not deductible. In order to be deductible a loss must occur during the settlement of the estate. If a loss with respect to an asset occurs after its distribution to the distributee it may not be deducted. Notwithstanding the foregoing, no deduction is allowed under this section if the estate has waived its right to take such a deduction pursuant to the provisions of section 642 (g) in order to permit its allowance for income tax purposes. . . . .

§ 20.2055-1 Deduction for transfers for public, charitable, and religious uses; in general

(a) **General rule.** A deduction is allowed under section 2055 (a) from the gross estate of a decedent who was a citizen or resident of the United States at the time of his death for the value of property included in the decedent's gross estate and transferred by the decedent during his lifetime or by will—

(1) To or for the use of the United States, any State, Territory, any political subdivision thereof, or the District of Columbia, for exclusively public purposes;

(2) To or for the use of any corporation or association organized and operated exclusively for religious, charitable, scientific, literary, or educational purposes (including the encouragement of art and the prevention of cruelty to children or animals), if no part of the net earnings of the corporation or association inures to the benefit of any private stockholder or individual (other than as a legitimate object of such purposes), if no substantial part of its activities is carrying on propaganda, or otherwise attempting, to influence legislation, and if, in the case of transfers made after December 31, 1969, it does not participate in, or intervene in (including the publishing or distributing of statements), any political campaign on behalf of any candidate for public office;

(3) To a trustee or trustees, or a fraternal society, order, or association operating under the lodge system, if the transferred property is to be used exclusively for religious, charitable, scientific, literary, or educational purposes (or for the prevention of cruelty to children or animals), if no substantial part of the activities of such transferee is carrying on propaganda, or otherwise attempting, to influence legislation, and if, in the case of transfers made after December 31, 1969, such transferee does not participate in, or intervene in (including the publishing or distributing of statements), any political campaign on behalf of any candidate for public office; or

(4) To or for the use of any veterans' organization incorporated by act of Congress, or of any of its departments, local chapters, or posts, no part of the net earnings of which inures to the benefit of any private shareholder or individual.

The deduction is not limited, in the case of estates of citizens or residents of the United States, to transfers to domestic corporations or associations, or to trustees for use within the United States. Nor is the deduction subject to percentage limitations such as are applicable to the charitable deduction under the income tax. An organization will not be considered to meet the requirements of subparagraph (2) or (3) of this paragraph if such organization engages in any activity which would cause it to be classified as an "action" organization under paragraph (c)(3) of § 1.501(c)(3)-1 of this chapter (Income Tax Regulations). See §§ 20.2055-4 and 20.-2055-5 for rules relating to the disallowance of deductions to trusts and organizations which engage in certain prohibited transactions or whose governing instruments do not contain certain specified requirements.

. . . . .

(c) **Submission of evidence.** In establishing the right of the estate to the deduction authorized by section 2055, the executor should submit the following with the return:

(1) A copy of any instrument in writing by which the decedent made a transfer of property in his lifetime the value of which is required by statute to be included in his gross estate, for which a deduction under section 2055 is claimed. If the instrument is of record the copy should be certified, and if not of record, the copy should be verified.

(2) A written statement by the executor containing a declaration that it is made under penalties of perjury and stating whether any action has been instituted to construe or to contest the decedent's will or any provision thereof affecting the charitable deduction claimed and whether, according to his information and belief, any such action is designed or contemplated.

The executor shall also submit such other documents or evidence as may be requested by the district director.

. . . . .

§ 20.2055-2 Transfers not exclusively for charitable purposes

. . .

(e) Limitation applicable to decedents dying after December 31, 1969— (1) Disallowance of deduction. In general, in the case of decedents dying after December 31, 1969, where an interest in property passes or has passed from the decedent for charitable purposes and an interest (other than an interest which is extinguished upon the decedent's death) in the same property passes or has passed from the decedent for private purposes (for less than an adequate and full consideration in money or money's worth) after October 9, 1969, no deduction is allowed under section 2055 for the value of the interest which passes or has passed for charitable purposes unless the interest in property is a deductible interest described in subparagraph (2) of this paragraph. The principles of section 2056 and the regulations thereunder shall apply for purposes of determining under this subparagraph whether an interest in property passes or has passed from the decedent. If however, as of the date of a decedent's death, a transfer for a private purpose is dependent upon the performance of some act or the happening of a precedent event in order that it might become effective, an interest in property will be considered to pass for a private purpose unless the possibility of occurrence of such act or event is so remote as to be negligible. The application of this subparagraph may be illustrated by the following examples, in each of which it is assumed that the interest in property which passes for private purposes does not pass for an adequate and full consideration in money or money's worth:

Example (1). In 1973, H creates a trust which is to pay the income of the trust to W for her life, the reversionary interest in the trust being retained by H. H predeceases W in 1975. H's will provide that the residue of his estate (including the reversionary interest in the trust) is to be transferred to charity. For purposes of this subparagraph, interests in the same property have passed from H for charitable purposes and for private purposes.

Example (2). In 1973, H creates a trust which is to pay the income of the trust to W for her life and upon termination of the life estate to transfer the remainder to S. S predeceases W in 1975. S's will provides that the residue of his estate (including the remainder interest in the trust) is to be transferred to charity. For purposes of this subparagraph, interests in the same property have not passed from H or S for charitable purposes and for private purposes.

Example (3). H transfers Blackacre to A by gift, reserving the right to the rentals of Blackacre for a term of 20 years. H dies within the 20-year term, bequeathing the right to the remaining rentals to charity. For purposes of this subparagraph the term "property" refers to Blackacre, and the right to rentals from Blackacre consist of an interest in Blackacre. An interest in Blackacre has passed from H for charitable purposes and for private purposes.

Example (4). H bequeaths the residue of his estate in trust for the benefit of A and a charity. An annuity of $5,000 a year is to be paid to charity for 20 years. Upon termination of the 20-year term the corpus is to be distributed to A if living. However, if A should die during the 20-year term, the corpus is to be distributed to charity upon termination of the term. An interest in the residue of the estate has passed from H for charitable purposes. In addition, an interest in the residue of the estate has passed from H for private purposes, unless the possibility that A will survive the 20-year term is so remote as to be negligible.

Example (5). H bequeaths the residue of his estate in trust. Under the terms of the trust an annuity of $5,000 a year is to be paid to charity for 20 years. Upon termination of the term, the corpus is to pass to such of A's children and their issue as A may appoint. However, if A should die during the 20-year term without exercising the power of appointment, the corpus is to be distributed to charity upon termination of the term. Since the possible appointees include private persons, an interest in the residue of the estate is considerd to have passed from H for private purposes.

Example (6). H devises Blackacre to X Charity. Under applicable local law, W, H's widow, is entitled to elect a dower interest in Blackacre. W elects to take her dower interest in Blackacre. For purposes of this subparagraph, interests in the same property have passed from H for charitable purposes and for private purposes. If, however, W does not elect to take her dower interest in Blackacre, then, for purposes of this subparagraph, interests in the same property have not passed from H for charitable purposes and for private purposes.

(2) Deductible interests. A deductible interest for purposes of subparagraph (1) of this paragraph is a charitable interest in property where—

(i) Undivided portion of decedent's entire interest. The charitable interest is an undivided portion, not in trust, of the decedent's entire interest in property. An undivided portion of a decedent's entire interest in property must consist of a fraction or percentage of each and every substantial interest or right owned by the decedent in such property and must extend over the entire term of the decedent's interest in such property and in other property into which such property is converted. For example, if the decedent transferred a life estate in an office building to his wife for her life and retained a reversionary interest in the office building, the devise by the decedent of one-half of that reversionary interest to charity while his wife is still alive will not be considered the transfer of a deductible interest; because an interest in the same property has already passed from the decedent for private purposes, the reversionary interest will not be considered the decedent's entire interest in the property. If, on the other hand, the decedent had been given a life estate in Blackacre for the life of his wife and the decedent had no other interest in Blackacre at any time during his life, the devise by the decedent of one-half of that life estate to charity would be considered the transfer of a deductible interest; because the life estate would be considered the decedent's entire interest in the property, the devise would be of an undivided portion of such entire interest. An undivided portion of a decedent's entire interest in the property includes an interest in property whereby the charity is given the right, as a tenant in common with the decedent's devisee or legatee, to possession, dominion, and control of the property for a portion of each year appropriate to its interest in such property. However, for purposes of this subdivision, a charitable contribution in perpetuity of an interest in property not in trust where the decedent transfers some specific rights to one party and transfers other substantial rights to another party will not be considered a contribution of an undivided portion of the decedent's entire interest in property. Thus, for example, a deduction is not allowable for the value of an immediate and perpetual gift not in trust of an interest in original historic motion picture films to a charitable organization where a private party is granted the exclusive right to make reproductions of such films and to exploit such reproductions commercially. A bequest to charity of an open space easement in gross in perpetuity shall be considered the transfer to charity of an undivided portion of the decedent's entire interest in property. For the definition of an open space easement in gross in perpetuity, see § 1.170 A–7(b)(1)(ii) of this chapter (Income Tax Regulations).

(ii) Remainder interest in personal residence. The charitable interest is a remainder interest, not in trust, in a personal residence. Thus, for example, if the decedent devices to charity a remainder interest in a personal residence and bequeaths to his surviving spouse a life estate in such property, the value of the remainder interest is deductible under section 2055. For purposes of this subdivision, the term "personal residence" means any property which was used by the decedent as his personal residence even though it was not used as his principal residence. For example, a decedent's vacation home may be a personal residence for purposes of this subdivision. The term "personal residence" also includes stock owned by the decedent as a tenant-stockholder in a cooperative housing corporation (as those terms are defined in section 216(b)(1) and (2)) if the dwelling which the decedent was entitled to occupy as such stockholder was used by him as his personal residence.

(iii) Remainder interest in a farm. The charitable interest is a remainder interest, not in trust, in a farm. Thus, for example, if the decedent devises to charity a remainder interest in a farm and bequeaths to his daughter a life estate in such property, the value of the remainder interest is deductible under section 2055. For purposes of this subdivision, the term "farm" means any land used by the decedent or his tenant for the production of crops, fruits, or other agricultural products or for the sustenance of livestock. The term "livestock" includes cattle, hogs, horses, mules, donkeys, sheep, goats, captive fur-bearing animals, chickens, turkeys, pigeons, and other poultry. A farm includes the improvements thereon.

(iv) Charitable remainder trusts and pooled income funds. The charitable interest is a remainder interest in a trust which is a charitable remainder annuity trust, as defin€ in section 664 (d)(1) and § 1.664–2 of this chapter; a charitable remainder unitrust, as defined in section 664(d)(2) and (3) and § 1.664–3 of this chapter; or a pooled income fund, as defined in section 642 (c)(5) and § 1.642(c)–5 of this chapter. The charitable organization to or for the use of which the remainder interest passes must meet the requirements of both section 2055(a) and section 642 (c)(5)(A), section 664(d)(1)(C), or section 664(d)(2)(C), whichever applies. For example, the charitable organization to which the remainder interest in a charitable remainder annuity trust passes may not be a foreign corporation.

(v) **Guaranteed annuity interest.** (a) The charitable interest is a guaranteed annuity interest, whether or not such interest is in trust. For purposes of this subdivision (v), the term "guaranteed annuity interest" means the right pursuant to the instrument of transfer to receive a guaranteed annuity. A guaranteed annuity is an arrangement under which a determinable amount is paid periodically, but not less often than annually, for a specified term or for the life or lives of an individual or individuals, each of whom must be living at the date of death of the decedent and can be ascertained at such date. For example, the annuity may be paid for the life of A plus a term of years. An amount is determinable if the exact amount which must be paid under the conditions specified in the instrument of transfer can be ascertained as of the appropriate valuation date. For example, the amount to be paid may be a stated sum for a term, or for the life of an individual, at the expiration of which it may be changed by a specified amount, but it may not be redetermined by reference to a fluctuating index such as the cost of living index. In further illustration, the amount to be paid may be expressed in terms of a fraction or a percentage of the net fair market value, as finally determined for Federal estate tax purposes, of the residue of the estate on the appropriate valuation date, or it may be expressed in terms of a fraction or percentage of the cost of living index on the appropriate valuation date.

(b) A charitable interest is a guaranteed annuity interest only if it is a guaranteed annuity interest in every respect. For example, if the charitable interest is the right to receive from a trust each year a payment equal to the lesser of a sum certain or a fixed percentage of the net fair market value of the trust assets, determined annually, such interest is not a guaranteed annuity interest.

(c) Where a charitable interest in the form of a guaranteed annuity interest is not in trust, the interest will be considered a guaranteed annuity interest only if it is to be paid by an insurance company or by an organization regularly engaged in issuing annuity contracts.

(d) Where a charitable interest in the form of a guaranteed annuity interest is in trust, the governing instrument of the trust may provide that income of the trust which is in excess of the amount required to pay the guaranteed annuity interest shall be paid to or for the use of a charity. Nevertheless, the amount of the deduction under section 2055 shall be limited to the fair market value of the guaranteed annuity interest as determined under paragraph (f)(2)(iv) of this section.

(e) Where a charitable interest in the form of a guaranteed annuity interest is in trust and the present value, on the appropriate valuation date, of all the income interests for a charitable purpose exceeds 60 percent of the aggregate fair market value of all amounts in such trust (after the payment of estate taxes and all other liabilities), the charitable interest will not be considered a guaranteed annuity interest unless the governing instrument of the trust prohibits both the acquisition and the retention of assets which would give rise to a tax under section 4944 if the trustee had acquired such assets.

．　．　．　．

(vi) **Unitrust interest.** (a) The charitable interest is a unitrust interest, whether or not such interest is in trust. For purposes of this subdivision (vi), the term "unitrust interest" means the right pursuant to the instrument of transfer to receive payment, not less often than annually, of a fixed percentage of the net fair market value, determined annually, of the property which funds the unitrust interest. In computing the net fair market value of the property which funds the unitrust interest, all assets and liabilities shall be taken into account without regard to whether particular items are taken into account in determining the income from the property. The net fair market value of the property which funds the unitrust interest may be determined on any one date during the year or by taking the average of valuations made on more than one date during the year, provided that the same valuation date or dates and valuation methods are used each year. Where the charitable interest is a unitrust interest to be paid by a trust and the governing instrument of the trust does not specify the valuation date or dates, the trustee shall select such date or dates and shall indicate his selection on the first return on Form 1041 which the trust is required to file. Payments under a unitrust interest may be paid for a specified term or for the life or lives of an individual or individuals, each of whom must be living at the date of death of the decedent and can be ascertained at such date. For example, the unitrust interest may be paid for the life of A plus a term of years.

(b) A charitable interest is a unitrust interest only if it is a unitrust interest in every respect. For example, if the charitable interest is the right to receive from a trust each year a payment equal to the lesser of a sum certain or a fixed percentage of the net fair market value of the trust assets, determined annually, such interest is not a unitrust interest.

(c) Where a charitable interest in the form of a unitrust interest is not in trust, the interest will be considered a unitrust interest only if it is to be paid by an insurance company or by an organization regularly engaged in issuing interests otherwise meeting the requirements of a unitrust interest.

(d) Where a charitable interest in the form of a unitrust interest is in trust, the governing instrument of the trust may provide that income of the trust which is in excess of the amount required to pay the unitrust interest shall be paid to or for the use of a charity. Nevertheless, the amount of the deduction under section 2055 shall be limited to the fair market value of

the unitrust interest as determined under paragraph (f)(2)(v) of this section.

. . . .

§ 20.2056(a)-1   Marital deduction; in general

(a) A deduction is allowed under section 2056 from the gross estate of a decedent who was a citizen or resident of the United States at the time of his death for the value of any property interest which passed from the decedent to his surviving spouse, if the interest is a "deductible interest" as defined in § 20.2056(a)-2, and if the total of such interests does not exceed the percentage limitation set forth in §§ 20.2056(c)-1 and 20.2056(c)-2. This deduction is referred to as the "marital deduction". The marital deduction is generally not available if the decedent's gross estate consists exclusively of property held by the decedent and his surviving spouse as community property under the law of any State, Territory, or possession of the United States, or any foreign country. See § 20.2056(c)-2. Except as otherwise provided by a death tax convention with a foreign country, the marital deduction is not allowed in the case of an estate of a nonresident who was not a citizen of the United States at the time of his death. However, if the decedent was a citizen or resident, his estate is not deprived of the right to the marital deduction by reason of the fact that his surviving spouse was neither a resident nor a citizen. For convenience, the surviving spouse is generally referred to in the feminine gender, but if the decedent was a woman the reference is to her surviving husband. . . . . .

. . . .

§ 20.2056(a)-2   Marital deduction; "deductible interests" and "nondeductible interests"

(a) Property interests which passed from a decedent to his surviving spouse fall within two general categories: (1) Those with respect to which the marital deduction is authorized, and (2) those with respect to which the marital deduction is not authorized. These categories are referred to in this section and other sections of the regulations under section 2056 as "deductible interests" and "nondeductible interests", respectively (see paragraph (b) of this section). Subject to the percentage limitation set forth in §§ 20.2056(c)-1 and 20.2056(c)-2, the marital deduction is equal in amount to the aggregate value of the "deductible interests".

(b) An interest passing to a decedent's surviving spouse is a "deductible interest" if it does not fall within one of the following categories of "nondeductible interests":

(1) Any property interest which passed from the decedent to his surviving spouse is a "nondeductible interest" to the extent it is not included in the decedent's gross estate.

(2) If a deduction is allowed under section 2053 (relating to deductions for expenses and indebtedness) by reason of the passing of a property interest from the decedent to his surviving spouse, such interest is, to the extent of the deduction under section 2053, a "nondeductible interest". Thus, a property interest which passed from the decedent to his surviving spouse in satisfaction of a deductible claim of the spouse against the estate is, to the extent of the claim, a "nondeductible interest" (see § 20.2056(b)-4). Similarly, amounts deducted under section 2053 (a)(2) for commissions allowed to the surviving spouse as executor are "nondeductible interests". As to the valuation, for the purpose of the marital deduction, of any property interest which passed from the decedent to his surviving spouse subject to a mortgage or other encumbrance, see § 20.2056(b)-4.

(3) If during settlement of the estate a loss deductible under section 2054 occurs with respect to a property interest, then that interest is, to the extent of the deductible loss, a "nondeductible interest" for the purpose of the marital deduction.

(4) A property interest passing to a decedent's surviving spouse which is a "terminable interest", as defined in § 20.2056(b)-1, is a "nondeductible interest" to the extent specified in that section.

§ 20.2056(b)-1 Marital deduction; limitation in case of life estate or other "terminable interest"

(a) In general. Section 2056(b) provides that no marital deduction is allowed with respect to certain property interests, referred to generally as "terminable interests", passing from a decedent to his surviving spouse. The phrase "terminable interest" is defined in paragraph (b) of this section. However, the fact that an interest in property passing to a decedent's surviving spouse is a "terminable interest" makes it nondeductible only (1) under the circumstances described in paragraph (c) of this section, and (2) if it does not come within one of the exceptions referred to in paragraph (d) of this section.

(b) "Terminable interests". A "terminable interest" in property is an interest which will terminate or fail on the lapse of time or on the occurrence or the failure to occur of some contingency. Life estates, terms for years, annuities, patents, and copyrights are therefore terminable interests. However, a bond, note, or similar contractual obligation, the discharge of which would not have the effect of an annuity or a term for years, is not a terminable interest.

(c) Nondeductible terminable interests. (1) A property interest which constitutes a terminable interest, as defined in paragraph (b) of this section, is nondeductible if—

(i) Another interest in the same property passed from the decedent to some other person for less than an adequate and full consideration in money or money's worth, and

(ii) By reason of its passing, the other person or his heirs or assigns may possess or enjoy any part of the property after the termination or failure of the spouse's interest.

(2) Even though a property interest which constitutes a terminable interest is not nondeductible by reason of the rules stated in subparagraph (1) of this paragraph, such an interest is nondeductible if—

(i) The decedent has directed his executor or a trustee to acquire such an interest for the decedent's surviving spouse (see further paragraph (f) of this section), or

(ii) Such an interest passing to the decedent's surviving spouse may be satisfied out of a group of assets which includes a nondeductible interest (see further § 20.2056(b)-2). In this case, however, full nondeductibility may not result.

(d) Exceptions. A property interest passing to a decedent's surviving spouse is deductible (if it is not otherwise disqualified under § 20.2056(a)–2) even though it is a terminable interest, and even though an interest therein passed from the decedent to another person, if it is a terminable interest only because—

(1) It is conditioned on the spouse's surviving for a limited period, in the manner described in § 20.2056(b)–3;

(2) It is a right to income for life with a general power of appointment, meeting the requirements set forth in § 20.2056(b)–5; or

(3) It consists of life insurance or annuity payments held by the insurer with a general power of appointment in the spouse, meeting the requirements set forth in § 20.2056(b)–6.

(e) Miscellaneous principles. (1) In determining whether an interest passed from the decedent to some other person, it is immaterial whether interests in the same property passed to the decedent's spouse and another person at the same time, or under the same instrument.

(2) In determining whether an interest in the same property passed from the decedent both to his surviving spouse and to some other person, a distinction is to be drawn between "property", as such term is used in section 2056, and an "interest in property". The term "property" refers to the underlying property in which various interests exist; each such interest is not for this purpose to be considered as "property".

(3) Whether or not an interest is nondeductible because it is a terminable interest is to be determined by reference to the property interests which actually passed from the decedent. Subsequent conversions of the property are immaterial for this purpose. Thus, where a decedent bequeathed his estate to his wife for life with remainder to his children, the interest which passed to his wife is a nondeductible interest, even though the wife agrees with the children to take a fractional share of the estate in fee in lieu of the life interest in the whole, or sells the life estate for cash, or acquires the remainder interest of the children either by purchase or gift.

(4) The terms "passed from the decedent", "passed from the decedent to his surviving spouse", and "passed from the decedent to a person other than his surviving spouse" are defined in §§ 20.2056(e)–1 through 20.2056(e)–3.

(f) Direction to acquire a terminable interest. No marital deduction is allowed with respect to a property interest which a decedent directs his executor or a trustee to convert after his death into a terminable interest for his surviving spouse. The marital deduction is not allowed even though no interest in the property subject to the terminable interest passes to another person and even though the interest would otherwise come within the exceptions described in §§ 20.2056(b)–5 and 20.2056(b)–6 (relating to life estates and life insurance and annuity payments with powers of appointment). However, a general investment power, authorizing investments in both terminable interests and other property, is not a direction to invest in a terminable interest.

(g) Examples. The application of this section may be illustrated by the following examples, in each of which it is assumed that the property interest which passed from the decedent to a person other than his surviving spouse did not pass for an adequate and full consideration in money or money's worth:

Example (1). H (the decedent) devised real property to W (his surviving wife) for life, with remainder to A and his heirs. The interest which passed from H to W is a nondeductible interest since it will terminate upon her death and A (or his heirs or assigns) will thereafter possess or enjoy the property.

Example (2). H bequeathed the residue of his estate in trust for the benefit of W and A. The trust income is to be paid to W for life, and upon her death the corpus is to be distributed to A or his issue. However, if A should die without issue, leaving W surviving, the corpus is then to be distributed to W. The interest which passed from H to W is a nondeductible interest since it will terminate in the event of her death if A or his issue survive, and A or his issue will thereafter possess or enjoy the property.

Example (3). H during his lifetime purchased an annuity contract providing for payments to himself for life and then to W for life if she should survive him. Upon the death of the survivor of H and W, the excess, if any, of the cost of the contract over the annuity payments theretofore made was to be refunded to A. The interest which passed from H to W is a nondeductible interest since A may possess or enjoy a part of the property following the termination of the interest of W. If, however, the contract provided for no refund upon the death of the survivor of H and W, or provided that any refund was to go to the estate of the survivor, then the interest which passed from H to W is (to the extent it is included in H's gross estate) a deductible interest.

Example (4). H, in contemplation of death, transferred a residence to A for life with remainder to W provided W survives A, but if W predeceases A, the property is to pass to B and his heirs. If it is assumed that H died during A's lifetime, and the value of the residence was included in determining the value of his gross estate, the interest which passed from H to W is a nondeductible interest since it will terminate if W predeceases A and the property will thereafter be possessed or enjoyed by B (or his heirs or assigns). This result is not affected by B's assignment of his interest during H's lifetime, whether made in favor of W or another person, since the term "assigns" (as used in section 2056(b) (1) (B)) includes such an assignee. However, if it is assumed that A predeceased H, the interest of B in the property was extinguished, and, viewed as of the time of the subsequent death of H, the interest which passed from him to W is the entire interest in the property and, therefore, a deductible interest.

Example (5). H transferred real property to A by gift, reserving the right to the rentals of the property for a term of 20 years. H died within the 20-year term, bequeathing the right to the remaining rentals to a trust for the benefit of W. The terms of the trust satisfy the five conditions stated in § 20.2056(b)-5, so that the property interest which passed in trust is considered to have passed from H to W. However, the interest is a nondeductible interest since it will terminate upon the expiration of the term and A will thereafter possess or enjoy the property.

Example (6). H bequeathed a patent to W and A as tenants in common. In this case, the interest of W will terminate upon the expiration of the term of the patent, but possession or enjoyment of the property by A must necessarily cease at the same time. Therefore, since A's possession or enjoyment cannot outlast the termination of W's interest, the latter is a deductible interest.

Example (7). A decedent bequeathed $100,000 to his wife, subject to a direction to his executor to use the bequest for the purchase of an annuity for the wife. The bequest is a nondeductible interest.

Example (8). Assume that pursuant to local law an allowance for support is payable to the decedent's surviving spouse during the period of the administration of the decedent's estate, but that upon her death or remarriage during such period her right to any further allowance will terminate. Assume further that the surviving spouse is sole beneficiary of the decedent's estate. Under such circumstances, the allowance constitutes a deductible interest since any part of the allowance not receivable by the surviving spouse during her lifetime will pass to her estate under the terms of the decedent's will. If, in this example, the decedent bequeathed only one-third of his residuary estate to his surviving spouse, then two-thirds of the allowance for support would constitute a nondeductible terminable interest.

§ 20.2056(b)-2 Marital deduction; interest in unidentified assets

(a) Section 2056(b) (2) provides that if an interest passing to a decedent's surviving spouse may be satisfied out of assets (or their proceeds) which include a particular asset that would be a nondeductible interest if it passed from the decedent to his spouse, the value of the interest passing to the spouse is reduced, for the purpose of the marital deduction, by the value of the particular asset.

(b) In order for section 2056(b) (2) to apply, two circumstances must coexist, as follows:

(1) The property interest which passed from the decedent to his surviving spouse must be payable out of a group of assets included in the gross estate. Examples of property interests payable out of a group of assets are a general legacy, a bequest of the residue of the decedent's estate or of a portion of the residue, and a right to a share of the corpus of a trust upon its termination.

(2) The group of assets out of which the property interest is payable must include one or more particular assets which, if passing specifically to the surviving spouse, would be nondeductible interests. Therefore, section 2056

(b) (2) is not applicable merely because the group of assets includes a terminable interest, but would only be applicable if the terminable interest were nondeductible under the provisions of § 20.2056 (b)-1.

(c) If both of the circumstances set forth in paragraph (b) of this section are present, the property interest payable out of the group of assets is (except as to any excess of its value over the aggregate value of the particular asset or assets which would not be deductible if passing specifically to the surviving spouse) a nondeductible interest.

(d) The application of this section may be illustrated by the following example:

Example. A decedent bequeathed one-third of the residue of his estate to his wife. The property passing under the decedent's will included a right to the rentals of an office building for a term of years, reserved by the decedent under a deed of the building by way of gift to his son. The decedent did not make a specific bequest of the right to such rentals. Such right, if passing specifically to the wife, would be a nondeductible interest (see example (5) of paragraph (g) of § 20.2056(b)-1. It is assumed that the value of the bequest of one-third of the residue of the estate to the wife was $85,000, and that the right to the rentals was included in the gross estate at a value of $60,000. If the decedent's executor had the right under the decedent's will or local law to assign the entire lease in satisfaction of the bequest, the bequest is a nondeductible interest to the extent of $60,-000. If the executor could only assign a one-third interest in the lease in satisfaction of the bequest, the bequest is a nondeductible interest to the extent of $20,000. If the decedent's will provided that his wife's bequest could not be satisfied with a nondeductible interest, the entire bequest is a deductible interest. If, in this example, the asset in question had been foreign real estate not included in the decedent's gross estate, the results would be the same.

§ 20.2056(b)-3 Marital deduction; interest of spouse conditioned on survival for limited period

(a) In general. Generally, no marital deduction is allowable if the interest passing to the surviving spouse is a terminable interest as defined in paragraph (b) of § 20.2056(b)-1. However, section 2056(b) (3) provides an exception to this rule so as to allow a deduction if (1) the only condition under which it will terminate is the death of the surviving spouse within 6 months after the decedent's death, or her death as a result of a common disaster which also resulted in the decedent's death, and (2) the condition does not in fact occur.

(b) Six months' survival. If the only condition which will cause the interest taken by the surviving spouse to terminate is the death of the surviving spouse and the condition is of such nature that it can occur only within 6 months following the decedent's death, the exception provided by section 2056 (b) (3) will apply, provided the condition does not in fact occur. However, if the condition (unless it relates to death as a result of a common disaster) is one which may occur either within the 6-month period or thereafter, the exception provided by section 2056(b) (3) will not apply.

(c) Common disaster. If a property interest passed from the decedent to his surviving spouse subject to the condition that she does not die as a result of a common disaster which also resulted in the decedent's death, the exception provided by section 2056(b) (3) will not be applied in the final audit of the return if there is still a possibility that the surviving spouse may be deprived of the property interest by operation of the common disaster provision as given effect by the local law.

• • • •

§ 20.2056(b)-4 Marital deduction; valuation of interest passing to surviving spouse

(a) In general. The value, for the purpose of the marital deduction, of any deductible interest which passed from the decedent to his surviving spouse is to be determined as of the date of the decedent's death, except that if the executor elects the alternate valuation method under section 2032 the valuation is to be determined as of the date of the decedent's death but with the adjustment described in paragraph (a) (3) of § 20.2032-1. The marital deduction may be taken only with respect to the net value of any deductible interest which passed from the decedent to his surviving spouse, the same principles being applicable as if the amount of a gift to the spouse were being determined. In determining the value of the interest in property passing to the spouse account must be taken of the effect of any material limitations upon her right to income from the property. An example of a case in which this rule may be applied is a bequest of property in trust for the benefit of the decedent's spouse but the income from the property from the date of the decedent's death until distribution of the property to the trustee is to be used to pay expenses incurred in the administration of the estate.

(b) Property interest subject to an encumbrance or obligation. If a property interest passed from the decedent to his surviving spouse subject to a mortgage or other encumbrance, or if an obligation is imposed upon the surviving spouse by the decedent in connection with the passing of a property interest, the value of the property interest is to be reduced by the amount of the mortgage, other encumbrance, or obligation. However, if under the terms of the decedent's will or under local law the executor is required to discharge, out of other assets of the decedent's estate, a mortgage or other encumbrance on property passing from the decedent to his surviving spouse, or is required to reimburse the surviving spouse for the amount of the mortgage or other encumbrance, the payment or reimbursement constitutes an additional interest passing to the surviving spouse. The passing of a property interest subject to the imposition of an obligation by the decedent does not include a bequest, devise, or transfer in lieu of dower, curtesy, or of a statutory estate created in lieu of dower or curtesy, or of other marital rights in the decedent's property or estate. The passing of a property interest subject to the imposition of an obligation by the decedent does, however, include a bequest, etc., in lieu of the interest of his surviving spouse under community property laws unless such interest was, immediately prior to the decedent's death, a mere expectancy. (As to the circumstances under which the interest of the surviving spouse is regarded as a mere expectancy, see § 20.2056(c)-2.) The following examples are illustrative of property interests which passed from the decedent to his surviving spouse subject to the imposition of an obligation by the decedent:

Example (1). A decedent devised a residence valued at $25,000 to his wife, with a direction that she pay $5,000 to his sister. For the purpose of the marital deduction, the value of the property interest passing to the wife is only $20,000.

Example (2). A decedent devised real property to his wife in satisfaction of a debt owing to her. The debt is a deductible claim under section 2053. Since the wife is obligated to relinquish the claim as a condition to acceptance of the devise, the value of the devise is, for the purpose of the marital deduction, to be reduced by the amount of the claim.

Example (3). A decedent bequeathed certain securities to his wife in lieu of her interest in property held by them as community property under the law of the State of their residence. The wife elected to relinquish her community property interest and to take the bequest. For the purpose of the marital deduction, the value of the bequest is to be reduced by the value of the community property interest relinquished by the wife.

(c) Effect of death taxes. (1) In the determination of the value of any property interest which passed from the decedent to his surviving spouse, there must be taken into account the effect which the Federal estate tax, or any estate, succession, legacy, or inheritance tax, has upon the net value to the surviving spouse of the property interest.

(2) For example, assume that the only bequest to the surviving spouse is $100,000 and the spouse is required to pay a State inheritance tax in the amount of $1,500. If no other death taxes affect the net value of the bequest, the value, for the purpose of the marital deduction, is $98,500.

(3) As another example, assume that a decedent devised real property to his wife having a value for Federal estate tax purposes of $100,000 and also bequeathed to her a nondeductible interest for life under a trust. The State of residence valued the real property at

$90,000 and the life interest at $30,000, and imposed an inheritance tax (at graduated rates) of $4,800 with respect to the two interests. If it is assumed that the inheritance tax on the devise is required to be paid by the wife, the amount of tax to be ascribed to the devise is

$$\frac{90,000}{120,000} \times \$4,800 = \$3,600.$$

Accordingly, if no other death taxes affect the net value of the bequest, the value, for the purpose of the marital deduction, is $100,000 less $3,600, or $96,400.

(4) If the decedent bequeaths his residuary estate, or a portion of it, to his surviving spouse, and his will contains a direction that all death taxes shall be payable out of the residuary estate, the value of the bequest, for the purpose of the marital deduction, is based upon the amount of the residue as reduced pursuant to such direction, if the residuary estate, or a portion of it, is bequeathed to the surviving spouse, and by the local law the Federal estate tax is payable out of the residuary estate, the value of the bequest, for the purpose of the marital deduction, may not exceed its value as reduced by the Federal estate tax. Methods of computing the deduction, under such circumstances, are set forth in supplemental instructions to the estate tax return.

(d) Remainder interests. If the income from property is made payable to another individual for life, or for a term of years, with remainder absolutely to the surviving spouse or to her estate, the marital deduction is based upon the present value of the remainder

.   .   .   .

§ 20.2056(b)−5 Marital deduction; life estate with power of appointment in surviving spouse

(a) In general. Section 2056(b) (5) provides that if an interest in property passes from the decedent to his surviving spouse (whether or not in trust) and the spouse is entitled for life to all the income from the entire interest or all the income from a specific portion of the entire interest, with a power in her to appoint the entire interest or the specific portion, the interest which passes to her is a deductible interest, to the extent that it satisfies all five of the conditions set forth below (see paragraph (b) of this section if one or more of the conditions is satisfied as to only a portion of the interest):

(1) The surviving spouse must be entitled for life to all of the income from the entire interest or a specific portion of the entire interest, or to a specific portion of all the income from the entire interest.

(2) The income payable to the surviving spouse must be payable annually or at more frequent intervals.

(3) The surviving spouse must have the power to appoint the entire interest or the specific portion to either herself or her estate.

(4) The power in the surviving spouse must be exercisable by her alone and (whether exercisable by will or during life) must be exercisable in all events.

(5) The entire interest or the specific portion must not be subject to a power in any other person to appoint any part to any person other than the surviving spouse.

(b) Specific portion; deductible amount. If either the right to income or the power of appointment passing to the surviving spouse pertains only to a specific portion of a property interest passing from the decedent, the marital deduction is allowed only to the extent that the rights in the surviving spouse meet all of the five conditions described in paragraph (a) of this section. While the rights over the income and the power must coexist as to the same interest in property, it is not necessary that the rights over the income or the power as to such interest be in the same proportion. However, if the rights over income meeting the required conditions set forth in paragraph (a) (1) and (2) of this section extend over a smaller share of the property interest than the share with respect to which the power of appointment requirements set forth in paragraph (a) (3) through (5) of this section are satisfied, the deductible interest is limited to the smaller share. Correspondingly, if a power of appointment meeting all the requirements extends to a smaller portion of the property interest than the portion over which the income rights pertain, the deductible interest cannot exceed the value of the portion to which such power of appointment applies. Thus, if the decedent leaves to his surviving spouse the right to receive annually all of the income from a particular property interest and a power of appointment meeting the specifications prescribed in paragraph (a) (3) through (5) of this section as to only one-half of the property interest, then only one-half of the property interest is treated as a deductible interest. Correspondingly, if the income interest of the spouse satisfying the requirements extends to only one-fourth of the property interest and a testamentary power of appointment satisfying the requirements extends to all of the property interest, then only one-fourth of the interest in the spouse qualifies as a deductible interest. Further, if the surviving spouse has no right to income from a specific portion of a property interest but a testamentary power of appointment which meets the necessary conditions over the entire interest, then none of the interest qualifies for the deduction. In addition, if, from the time of the decedent's death, the surviving spouse has a power of appointment meeting all of the required conditions over three-fourths of the entire property interest and the prescribed income rights over the entire interest, but with a power in another person to appoint one-half of the entire interest, the value of the interest in the surviving spouse over only one-half of the property interest will qualify as a deductible interest.

(c) **Definition of "specific portion".** A partial interest in property is not treated as a specific portion of the entire interest unless the rights of the surviving spouse in income and as to the power constitute a fractional or percentile share of a property interest so that such interest or share in the

surviving spouse reflects its proportionate share of the increment or decline in the whole of the property interest to which the income rights and the power relate. Thus, if the right of the spouse to income and the power extent to one-half or a specified percentage of the property, or the equivalent, the interest is considered as a specific portion. On the other hand, if the annual income of the spouse is limited to a specific sum, or if she has a power to appoint only a specific sum out of a larger fund, the interest is not a deductible interest. Even though the rights in the surviving spouse may not be expressed in terms of a definite fraction or percentage, a deduction may be allowable if it is shown that the effect of local law is to give the spouse rights which are identical to those she would have acquired if the size of the share had been expressed in terms of a definite fraction or percentage. The following examples illustrate the application of this and the preceding paragraphs of this section:

Example (1). The decedent transferred to a trustee 500 identical shares of X Company stock. He provided that during the lifetime of the surviving spouse the trustee should pay her annually one-half of the trust income or $6,000, whichever is the larger. The spouse was also given a general power of appointment, exercisable by her last will over the sum of $160,000 or over three-fourths of the trust corpus, whichever should be of larger value. Since there is no certainty that the trust income will not vary from year to year, for purposes of paragraphs (a) and (b) of this section, an annual payment of a specified sum, such as the $6,000 provided for in this case, is not considered as representing the income from a definite fraction or a specific portion of the entire interest if that were the extent of the spouse's interest. However, since the spouse is to receive annually at least one-half of the trust income, she will, for purposes of paragraphs (a) and (b) of this section, be considered as receiving all of the income from one-half of the entire interest in the stock. Inasmuch as there is no certainty that the value of the stock will be the same on the date of the surviving spouse's death as it was on the date of the decedent's death, for purposes of paragraphs (a) and (b) of this section, a specified sum, such as the $160,000 provided for in this case, is not considered to be a definite fraction of the entire interest. However, since the surviving spouse has a general power of appointment over at least three-fourths of the trust corpus, she is considered as having a general power of appointment over three-fourths of the entire interest in the stock.

Example (2). The decedent bequeathed to a trustee an office building and 250 identical shares of Y Company stock. He provided that during the lifetime of the surviving spouse the trustee should pay her annually three-fourths of the trust income. The spouse was given a general power of appointment, exercisable by will, over the office building and 100 shares of the stock. By the terms of the decedent's will the spouse is given all the income from a definite fraction of the entire interest in the office building and in the stock. She also has a general power of appointment over the entire interest in the office building. However, since the amount of property represented by a single share of stock would be altered if the corporation split its stock, issued stock dividends, made a distribution of capital, etc., a power to appoint 100 shares at the time of the surviving spouse's death is not the same necessarily as a power to appoint $100/250$ of the entire interest which the 250 shares represented on the date of the decedent's death. If it is shown in this case that the effect of local law is to give the spouse a general power to appoint not only the 100 shares designated by the decedent but also $100/250$ of any shares or amounts which are distributed by the corporation and included in the corpus, the requirements of this paragraph will be satisfied and the surviving spouse will be considered as having a general power to appoint $100/250$ of the entire interest in the 250 shares.

(d) Definition of "entire interest". Since a marital deduction is allowed for each qualifying separate interest in property passing from the decedent to his surviving spouse (subject to the percentage limitation contained in §§ 20.2056(c)–1 and 20.2056(c)–2 concerning the aggregate amount of the deductions), for purposes of paragraphs (a) and (b) of this section, each property interest with respect to which the surviving spouse received some rights is considered separately in determining whether her rights extend to the entire interest or to a specific portion of the entire interest. A property interest which consists of several identical units of property (such as a block of 250 shares of stock, whether the ownership is evidenced by one or several certificates) is considered one property interest, unless certain of the units are to be segregated and accorded different treatment, in which case each segregated group of items is considered a separate property interest. The bequest of a specified sum of money constitutes the bequest of a separate property interest if immediately following distribution by the executor and thenceforth it, and the investments made with it, must be so segregated or accounted for as to permit its identification as a separate item of property. The application of this paragraph may be illustrated by the following examples:

Example (1). The decedent transferred to a trustee three adjoining farms, Blackacre, Whiteacre, and Greenacre. His will provided that during the lifetime of the surviving spouse the trustee should pay her all of the income from the trust. Upon her death, all of Black-

acre, a one-half interest in Whiteacre, and a one-third interest in Greenacre were to be distributed to the person or persons appointed by her in her will. The surviving spouse is considered as being entitled to all of the income from the entire interest in Blackacre, all of the income from the entire interest in Whiteacre, and all of the income from the entire interest in Greenacre. She also is considered as having a power of appointment over the entire interest in Blackacre, over one-half of the entire interest in Whiteacre, and over one-third of the entire interest in Greenacre.

Example (2). The decedent bequeathed $250,000 to C, as trustee. C is to invest the money and pay all of the income from the investments to W, the decedent's surviving spouse, annually. W was given a general power, exercisable by will, to appoint one-half of the corpus of the trust. Here, immediately following distribution by the executor, the $250,000 will be sufficiently segregated to permit its identification as a separate item, and the $250,000 will constitute an entire property interest. Therefore, W has a right to income and a power of appointment such that one-half of the entire interest is a deductible interest.

Example (3). The decedent bequeathed 100 shares of Z Corporation stock to D, as trustee. W, the decedent's surviving spouse, is to receive all of the income of the trust annually and is given a general power, exercisable by will, to appoint out of the trust corpus the sum of $25,000. In this case the $25,000 is not immediately following distribution, sufficiently segregated to permit its identification as a separate item of property in which the surviving spouse has the entire interest. Therefore, the $25,000 does not constitute the entire interest in a property for the purpose of paragraphs (a) and (b) of this section.

(e) Application of local law. In determining whether or not the conditions set forth in paragraph (a) (1) through (5) of this section are satisfied by the instrument of transfer, regard is to be had to the applicable provisions of the law of the jurisdiction under which the interest passes and, if the transfer is in trust, the applicable provisions of the law governing the administration of the trust. For example, silence of a trust instrument as to the frequency of payment will not be regarded as a failure to satisfy the condition set forth in paragraph (a) (2) of this section that income must be payable to the surviving spouse annually or more frequently unless the applicable law permits payment to be made less frequently than annually. The principles outlined in this paragraph and paragraphs (f) and (g) of this section which are applied in determining whether transfers in trust meet such conditions are equally applicable in ascertaining whether, in the case of interests not in trust, the surviving spouse has the equivalent in rights over income and over the property.

(f) Right to income. (1) If an interest is transferred in trust, the surviving spouse is "entitled for life to all of the income from the entire interest or a specific portion of the entire interest", for the purpose of the condition set forth in paragraph (a) (1) of this section, if the effect of the trust is to give her substantially that degree of beneficial enjoyment of the trust property during her life which the principles of the law of trusts accord to a person who is unqualifiedly designated as the life beneficiary of a trust. Such degree of enjoyment is given only if it was the decedent's intention, as manifested by the terms of the trust instrument and the surrounding circumstances, that the trust should produce for the surviving spouse during her life such an income, or that the spouse should have such use of the trust property as is consistent with the value of the trust corpus and with its preservation. The designation of the spouse as sole income beneficiary for life of the entire interest or a specific portion of the entire interest will be sufficient to qualify the trust unless the terms of the trust and the surrounding circumstances considered as a whole evidence an intention to deprive the spouse of the requisite degree of enjoyment. In determining whether a trust evidences that intention, the treatment required or permitted with respect to individual items must be considered in relation to the entire system provided for the administration of the trust.

(2) If the over-all effect of a trust is to give to the surviving spouse such enforceable rights as will preserve to her the requisite degree of enjoyment, it is immaterial whether that result is effected by rules specifically stated in the trust instrument, or, in their absence, by the rules for the management of the trust property and the allocation of receipts and expenditures supplied by the State law. For example, a provision in the trust instrument for amortization of bond premium by appropriate periodic charges to interest will not disqualify the interest passing in trust even though there is no State law specifically authorizing amortization, or there is a State law denying amortization which is applicable only in the absence of such a provision in the trust instrument.

(3) In the case of a trust, the rules to be applied by the trustee in allocation of receipts and expenses between income and corpus must be considered in relation to the nature and expected productivity of the assets passing in trust, the nature and frequency of occurrence of the expected receipts, and any provisions as to change in the form of investments. If it is evident from the nature of the trust assets and the rules provided for management of the trust that the allocation to income of such receipts as rents, ordinary cash dividends, and interest will give to the spouse the substantial enjoyment during life required by the statute, provisions that such receipts as stock dividends and proceeds from the conversion of trust assets shall be treated as corpus will not disqualify the interest passing in trust. Similarly, provision for a depletion charge against income in the case of trust assets which are subject to depletion will not disqualify the interest passing in trust, unless the effect is to deprive the spouse of the requisite beneficial enjoyment. The same principle is applicable in the case of depreciation, trustees' commissions, and other charges.

(4) Provisions granting administrative powers to the trustee will not have the effect of disqualifying an interest passing in trust unless the grant of powers evidences the intention to deprive the surviving spouse of the beneficial enjoyment required by the statute. Such an intention will not be considered to exist if the entire terms of the instrument are such that the local courts will impose reasonable limitations upon the exercise of the powers. Among the powers which if subject to reasonable limitations will not disqualify the interest passing in trust are the power to determine the allocation or apportionment of receipts and disbursements between income and corpus, the power to apply the income or corpus for the benefit of the spouse, and the power to retain the assets passing to the trust. For example, a power to retain trust assets which consist substantially of unproductive property will not disqualify the interest if the applicable rules for the administration of the trust require, or permit the spouse to require, that the trustee either make the property productive or convert it within a reasonable time. Nor will

such a power disqualify the interest if the applicable rules for administration of the trust require the trustee to use the degree of judgment and care in the exercise of the power which a prudent man would use if he were owner of the trust assets. Further, a power to retain a residence or other property for the personal use of the spouse will not disqualify the interest passing in trust.

(5) An interest passing in trust will not satisfy the condition set forth in paragraph (a) (1) of this section that the surviving spouse be entitled to all the income if the primary purpose of the trust is to safeguard property without providing the spouse with the required beneficial enjoyment. Such trusts include not only trusts which expressly provide for the accumulation of the income but also trusts which indirectly accomplish a similar purpose. For example, assume that the corpus of a trust consists substantially of property which is not likely to be income producing during the life of the surviving spouse and that the spouse cannot compel the trustee to convert or otherwise deal with the property as described in subparagraph (4) of this paragraph. An interest passing to such a trust will not qualify unless the applicable rules for the administration require, or permit the spouse to require, that the trustee provide the required beneficial enjoyment, such as by payments to the spouse out of other assets of the trust.

(6) If a trust is created during the decedent's life, it is immaterial whether or not the interest passing in trust satisfied the conditions set forth in paragraph (a) (1) through (5) of this section prior to the decedent's death. If a trust may be terminated during the life of the surviving spouse, under her exercise of a power of appointment or by distribution of the corpus to her, the interest passing in trust satisfies the condition set forth in paragraph (a) (1) of this section (that the spouse be entitled to all the income) if she (i) is entitled to the income until the trust terminates, or (ii) has the right, exercisable in all events, to have the corpus distributed to her at any time during her life.

(7) An interest passing in trust fails to satisfy the condition set forth in paragraph (a) (1) of this section, that the spouse be entitled to all the income, to the extent that the income is re-quired to be accumulated in whole or in part or may be accumulated in the discretion of any person other than the surviving spouse; to the extent that the consent of any person other than the surviving spouse is required as a condition precedent to distribution of the income; or to the extent that any person other than the surviving spouse has the power to alter the terms of the trust so as to deprive her of her right to the income. An interest passing in trust will not fail to satisfy the condition that the spouse be entitled to all the income merely because its terms provide that the right of the surviving spouse to the income shall not be subject to assignment, alienation, pledge, attachment or claims of creditors.

(8) In the case of an interest passing in trust, the terms "entitled for life" and "payable annually or at more frequent intervals," as used in the conditions set forth in paragraph (a) (1) and (2) of this section, require that under the terms of the trust the income referred to must be currently (at least annually; see paragraph (e) of this section) distributable to the spouse or that she must have such command over the income that it is virtually hers. Thus, the conditions in paragraph (a) (1) and (2) of this section are satisfied in this respect if, under the terms of the trust instrument, the spouse has the right exercisable annually (or more frequently) to require distribution to herself of the trust income, and otherwise the trust income is to be accumulated and added to corpus. Similarly, as respects the income for the period between the last distribution date and the date of the spouse's death, it is sufficient if that income is subject to the spouse's power to appoint. Thus, if the trust instrument provides that income accrued or undistributed on the date of the spouse's death is to be disposed of as if it had been received after her death, and if the spouse has a power of appointment over the trust corpus, the power necessarily extends to the undistributed income.

(9) An interest is not to be regarded as failing to satisfy the conditions set forth in paragraph (a) (1) and (2) of this section (that the spouse be entitled to all the income and that it be payable annually or more frequently) merely because the spouse is not entitled to the income from estate assets for the period before distribution of those assets

by the executor, unless the executor is, by the decedent's will, authorized or directed to delay distribution beyond the period reasonably required for administration of the decedent's estate. As to the valuation of the property interest passing to the spouse in trust where the right to income is expressly postponed, see § 20.2056(b)-4.

(g) Power of appointment in surviving spouse. (1) The conditions set forth in paragraph (a) (3) and (4) of this section, that is, that the surviving spouse must have a power of appointment exercisable in favor of herself or her estate and exercisable alone and in all events, are not met unless the power of the surviving spouse to appoint the entire interest or a specific portion of it falls within one of the following categories:

(i) A power so to appoint fully exercisable in her own favor at any time following the decedent's death (as, for example, an unlimited power to invade); or

(ii) A power so to appoint exercisable in favor of her estate. Such a power, if exercisable during life, must be fully exercisable at any time during life, or, if exercisable by will, must be fully exercisable irrespective of the time of her death (subject in either case to the provisions of § 20.2053(b)-3, relating to interests conditioned on survival for a limited period); or

(iii) A combination of the powers described under subparagraphs (i) and (ii) of this subparagraph. For example, the surviving spouse may, until she attains the age of 50 years, have a power to appoint to herself and thereafter have a power to appoint to her estate. However, the condition that the spouse's power must be exercisable in all events is not satisfied unless irrespective of when the surviving spouse may die the entire interest or a specific portion of it will at the time of her death be subject to one power or the other (subject to the exception in § 20.2053(b)-3, relating to interests contingent on survival for a limited period).

(2) The power of the surviving spouse must be a power to appoint the entire interest or a specific portion of it as unqualified owner (and free of the trust if a trust is involved, or free of the joint tenancy if a joint tenancy is involved) or to appoint the entire interest or a specific portion of it as a part of her estate (and free of the trust if a trust is involved), that is, in effect, to dispose of it to whomsoever she pleases. Thus, if the decedent devised property to a son and the surviving spouse as joint tenants with right of survivorship and under local law the surviving spouse has a power of severance exercisable without consent of the other joint tenant, and by exercising this power could acquire a one-half interest in the property as a tenant in common, her power of severance will satisfy the condition set forth in paragraph (a) (3) of this section that she have a power of appointment in favor of herself or her estate. However, if the surviving spouse entered into a binding agreement with the decedent to exercise the power only in favor of their issue, that condition is not met. An interest passing in trust will not be regarded as failing to satisfy the condition merely because takers in default of the surviving spouse's exercise of the power are designated by the decedent. The decedent may provide that, in default of exercise of the power, the trust shall continue for an additional period.

(3) A power is not considered to be a power exercisable by a surviving spouse alone and in all events as required by paragraph (a) (4) of this section if the exercise of the power in the surviving spouse to appoint the entire interest or a specific portion of it to herself or to her estate requires the joinder or consent of any other person. The power is not "exercisable in all events", if it can be terminated during the life of the surviving spouse by any event other than her complete exercise or release of it. Further, a power is not "exercisable in all events" if it may be exercised for a limited purpose only. For example, a power which is not exercisable in the event of the spouse's remarriage is not exercisable in all events. Likewise, if there are any restrictions, either by the terms of the instrument or under applicable local law, on the exercise of a power to consume property (whether or not held in trust) for the benefit of the spouse, the power is not exercisable in all events. Thus, if a power of invasion is exercisable only for the spouse's support, or only for her limited use, the power is not exercisable in all events. In order for a power of in-

vasion to be exercisable in all events, the surviving spouse must have the unrestricted power exercisable at any time during her life to use all or any part of the property subject to the power, and to dispose of it in any manner, including the power to dispose of it by gift (whether or not she has power to dispose of it by will).

(4) The power in the surviving spouse is exercisable in all events only if it exists immediately following the decedent's death. For example, if the power given to the surviving spouse is exercisable during life, but cannot be effectively exercised before distribution of the assets by the executor, the power is not exercisable in all events. Similarly, if the power is exercisable by will, but cannot be effectively exercised in the event the surviving spouse dies before distribution of the assets by the executor, the power is not exercisable in all events. However, an interest will not be disqualified by the mere fact that, in the event the power is exercised during administration of the estate, distribution of the property to the appointee will be delayed for the period of administration. If the power is in existence at all times following the decedent's death, limitations of a formal nature will not disqualify an interest. Examples of formal limitations on a power exercisable during life are requirements that an exercise must be in a particular form, that it must be filed with a trustee during the spouse's life, that reasonable notice must be given, or that reasonable intervals must elapse between successive partial exercises. Examples of formal limitations on a power exercisable by will are that it must be exercised by a will executed by the surviving spouse after the decedent's death or that exercise must be by specific reference to the power.

(5) If the surviving spouse has the requisite power to appoint to herself or her estate, it is immaterial that she also has one or more lesser powers. Thus, if she has a testamentary power to appoint to her estate, she may also have a limited power of withdrawal or of appointment during her life. Similarly, if she has an unlimited power of withdrawal, she may have a limited testamentary power.

(h) Requirement of survival for a limited period. A power of appointment in the surviving spouse will not

be treated as failing to meet the requirements of paragraph (a) (3) of this section even though the power may terminate, if the only conditions which would cause the termination are those described in paragraph (a) of § 20.-2056(b)–3, and if those conditions do not in fact occur. Thus, the entire interest or a specific portion of it will not be disqualified by reason of the fact that the exercise of the power in the spouse is subject to a condition of survivorship described in § 20.2056(b)–3 if the terms of the condition, that is, the survivorship of the surviving spouse, or the failure to die in a common disaster, are fulfilled.

(j) Existence of a power in another. Paragraph (a) (5) of this section provides that a transfer described in paragraph (a) is nondeductible to the extent that the decedent created a power in the trustee or in any other person to appoint a part of the interest to any person other than the surviving spouse. However, only powers in other persons which are in opposition to that of the surviving spouse will cause a portion of the interest to fail to satisfy the condition set forth in paragraph (a) (5) of this section. Thus, a power in a trustee to distribute corpus to or for the benefit of a surviving spouse will not disqualify the trust. Similarly, a power to distribute corpus to the spouse for the support of minor children will not disqualify the trust if she is legally obligated to support such children. The application of this paragraph may be illustrated by the following examples:

Example (1). Assume that a decedent created a trust, designating his surviving spouse as income beneficiary for life with an unrestricted power in the spouse to appoint the corpus during her life. The decedent further provided that in the event the surviving spouse should die without having exercised the power, the trust should continue for the life of his son with a power in the son to appoint the corpus. Since the power in the son could become exercisable only after the death of the surviving spouse, the interest is not regarded as failing to satisfy the condition set forth in paragraph (a) (5) of this section.

Example (2). Assume that the decedent created a trust, designating his surviving spouse as income beneficiary for life and as donee of a power to appoint by will the entire corpus. The decedent further provided that the trustee could distribute 30 percent of the corpus to the decedent's son when he reached the age of 35 years. Since the trustee has a power to appoint 30 percent of the entire interest for the benefit of a person other than the surviving spouse, only 70 percent of the interest placed in trust satisfied the condition set forth in paragraph (a) (5) of this section. If, in this case, the surviving spouse had a power, exercisable by her will, to appoint only one-half of the corpus as it was constituted at the time of her death, it should be noted that only 35 percent of the interest placed in the trust would satisfy the condition set forth in paragraph (a) (3) of this section.

§ 20.2056(b)-6 Marital deduction; life insurance or annuity payments with power of appointment in surviving spouse

(a) **In general.** Section 2056 (b) (6) provides that an interest in property passing from a decedent to his surviving spouse, which consists of proceeds held by an insurer under the terms of a life insurance, endowment, or annuity contract, is a "deductible interest" to the extent that it satisfied all five of the following conditions (see paragraph (b) of this section if one or more of the conditions is satisfied as to only a portion of the proceeds):

(1) The proceeds, or a specific portion of the proceeds, must be held by the insurer subject to an agreement either to pay the entire proceeds or a specific portion thereof in installments, or to pay interest thereon, and all or a specific portion of the installments or interest payable during the life of the surviving spouse must be payable only to her.

(2) The installments or interest payable to the surviving spouse must be payable annually, or more frequently, commencing not later than 13 months after the decedent's death.

(3) The surviving spouse must have the power to appoint all or a specific portion of the amounts so held by the insurer to either herself or her estate.

(4) The power in the surviving spouse must be exercisable by her alone and (whether exercisable by will or during life) must be exercisable in all events.

(5) The amounts or the specific portion of the amounts payable under such contract must not be subject to a power in any other person to appoint any part thereof to any person other than the surviving spouse.

(b) **Specific portion; deductible interest.** If the right to receive interest or installment payments or the power of appointment passing to the surviving spouse pertains only to a specific portion of the proceeds held by the insurer, the marital deduction is allowed only to the extent that the rights of the surviving spouse in the specific portion meet the five conditions described in paragraph (a) of this section. While the rights to interest, or to receive payment in installments, and the power must coexist as to the proceeds of the same contract, it is not necessary that the rights to each be in the same proportion. If the rights to interest meeting the required conditions set forth in paragraph (a) (1) and (2) of this section extend over a smaller share of the proceeds than the share with respect to which the power of appointment requirements set forth in paragraph (a) (3) through (5) of this section are satisfied, the deductible interest is limited to the smaller share. Similarly, if the portion of the proceeds payable in installments is a smaller portion of the proceeds than the portion to which the power of appointment meeting such requirements relates, the deduction is limited to the smaller portion. In addition, if a power of appointment meeting all the requirements extends to a smaller portion of the proceeds than the portion over which the interest or installment rights pertain, the deductible interest cannot exceed the value of the portion to which such power of appointment applies. Thus, if the contract provides that the insurer is to retain the entire proceeds and pay all of the interest thereon annually to the surviving spouse and if the surviving spouse has a power of appointment meeting the specifications prescribed in paragraph (a) (3) through (5) of this section, as to only one-half of the proceeds held, then only one-half of the proceeds may be treated as a deductible interest. Correspondingly, if the rights of the spouse to receive installment payments or interest satisfying the requirements extend to only one-fourth of the proceeds and a testamentary power of appointment satisfying the requirements of paragraph (a) (3) through (5) of this section extends to all of the proceeds, then only one-fourth of the proceeds qualifies as a deductible interest. Further, if the surviving spouse has no right to installment payments (or interest) over any portion of the proceeds but a testamentary power of appointment which meets the necessary conditions over the entire remaining proceeds, then none of the proceeds qualifies for the deduction. In addition, if, from the time of the decedent's death, the surviving spouse has a power of appointment meeting all of the required conditions over three-fourths of the proceeds and the right to receive interest from the entire proceeds, but with a power in another person to appoint one-half of the entire proceeds, the value of the interest in the surviving spouse over only one-half of the proceeds will qualify as a deductible interest.

(c) Applicable principles. (1) The principles set forth in paragraph (c) of § 20.2056 (b)–5 for determining what constitutes a "specific portion of the entire interest" for the purpose of section 2056 (b) (5) are applicable in determining what constitutes a "specific portion of all such amounts" for the purpose of section 2056 (b) (6). However, the interest in the proceeds passing to the surviving spouse will not be disqualified by the fact that the installment payments or interest to which the spouse is entitled or the amount of the proceeds over which the power of appointment is exercisable may be expressed in terms of a specific sum rather than a fraction or a percentage of the proceeds provided it is shown that such sums are a definite or fixed percentage or fraction of the total proceeds.

(2) The provisions of paragraph (a) of this section are applicable with respect to a property interest which passed from the decedent in the form of proceeds of a policy of insurance upon the decedent's life, a policy of insurance upon the life of a person who predeceased the decedent, a matured endowment policy, or an annuity contract, but only in case the proceeds are to be held by the insurer. With respect to proceeds under any such contract which are to be held by a trustee, with power of appointment in the surviving spouse, see § 20.2056 (b)–5. As to the treatment of proceeds not meeting the requirements of § 20.2056 (b)–5 or of this section, see § 20.2056 (a)–2.

(3) In the case of a contract under which payments by the insurer commenced during the decedent's life, it is immaterial whether or not the conditions in subparagraph (1) through (5) of paragraph (a) of this section were satisfied prior to the decedent's death.

(d) Payments of installments or interest. The conditions in subparagraphs (1) and (2) of paragraph (a) of this section relative to the payments of installments or interest to the surviving spouse are satisfied if, under the terms of the contract, the spouse has the right exercisable annually (or more frequently) to require distribution to herself of installments of the proceeds or a specific portion thereof, as the case may be, and otherwise such proceeds or interest are to be accumulated and held by the insurer pursuant to the terms of the contract. A contract which otherwise requires the insurer to make annual or more frequent payments to the surviving spouse following the decedent's death, will not be disqualified merely because the surviving spouse must comply with certain formalities in order to obtain the first payment. For example, the contract may satisfy the conditions in subparagraphs (1) and (2) of paragraph (a) of this section even though it requires the surviving spouse to furnish proof of death before the first payment is made. The condition in paragraph (a) (1) of this section is satisfied where interest on the proceeds or a specific portion thereof is payable, annually or more frequently, for a term, or until the occurrence of a specified event, following which the proceeds or a specific portion thereof are to be paid in annual or more frequent installments.

(e) Powers of appointment. (1) In determining whether the terms of the contract satisfy the conditions in subparagraph (3), (4), or (5) of paragraph (a) of this section relating to a power of appointment in the surviving spouse or any other person, the principles stated in § 20.2056 (b)–5 are applicable. As stated in § 20.2056 (b)–5, the surviving spouse's power to appoint is "exercisable in all events" only if it is in existence immediately following the decedent's death, subject, however, to the operation of § 20.-2056 (b)–3 relating to interests conditioned on survival for a limited period.

(2) For examples of formal limitations on the power which will not disqualify the contract, see paragraph (g) (4) of § 20.2056 (b)–5. If the power is

exercisable from the moment of the decedent's death, the contract is not disqualified merely because the insurer may require proof of the decedent's death as a condition to making payment to the appointee. If the submission of proof of the decedent's death is a condition to the exercise of the power, the power will not be considered "exercisable in all events" unless in the event the surviving spouse had died immediately following the decedent, her power to appoint would have been considered to exist at the time of her death, within the meaning of section 2041 (a) (2). See paragraph (b) of § 20.2041–3.

(3) It is sufficient for the purposes of the condition in paragraph (a) (3) of this section that the surviving spouse have the power to appoint amounts held by the insurer to herself or her estate if the surviving spouse has the unqualified power, exercisable in favor of herself or her estate, to appoint amounts held by the insurer which are payable after her death. Such power to appoint need not extend to installments or interest which will be paid to the spouse during her life. Further, the power to appoint need not be a power to require payment in a single sum. For example, if the proceeds of a policy are payable in installments, and if the surviving spouse has the power to direct that all installments payable after her death be paid to her estate, she has the requisite power.

(4) It is not necessary that the phrase "power to appoint" be used in the contract. For example, the condition in paragraph (a) (3) of this section that the surviving spouse have the power to appoint amounts held by the insurer to herself or her estate is satisfied by terms of a contract which give the surviving spouse a right which is, in substance and effect, a power to appoint to herself or her estate, such as a right to withdraw the amount remaining in the fund held by the insurer, or a right to direct that any amount held by the insurer under the contract at her death shall be paid to her estate.

§ 20.2056(e)–1 Marital deduction; definition of "passed from the decedent"

(a) The following rules are applicable in determining the person to whom any property interest "passed from the decedent":

(1) Property interests devolving upon any person (or persons) as surviving co-owner with the decedent under any form of joint ownership under which the right of survivorship existed are considered as having passed from the decedent to such person (or persons).

(2) Property interests at any time subject to the decedent's power to appoint (whether alone or in conjunction with any person) are considered as having passed from the decedent to the appointee under his exercise of the power, or, in case of the lapse, release or nonexercise of the power, as having passed from the decedent to the taker in default of exercise.

(3) The dower or curtesy interest (or statutory interest in lieu thereof) of the decedent's surviving spouse is considered as having passed from the decedent to his spouse.

(4) The proceeds of insurance upon the life of the decedent are considered as having passed from the decedent to the person who, at the time of the decedent's death, was entitled to receive the proceeds.

(5) Any property interest transferred during life, bequeathed or devised by the decedent, or inherited from the decedent, is considered as having passed to the person to whom he transferred, bequeathed, or devised the interest, or to the person who inherited the interest from him.

(6) The survivor's interest in an annuity or other payment described in section 2039 (see §§ 20.2039–1 and 20.2039–2) is considered as having passed from the decedent to the survivor only to the extent that the value of such interest is included in the decedent's gross estate under that section. If only a portion of the entire annuity or other payment is included in the decedent's gross estate and the annuity or other payment is payable to more than one beneficiary, then the value of the interest considered to have passed to each beneficiary is that portion of the amount payable to each beneficiary that the amount of the annuity or other payment included in the decedent's gross estate bears to the total value of the annuity or other payment payable to all beneficiaries.

(b) If before the decedent's death the decedent's surviving spouse had merely an expectant interest in property held by her and the decedent under community property laws, that interest is considered as having passed from the decedent to the spouse. As to the circumstances under which the interest of the surviving spouse under community property laws is regarded as merely expectant, see paragraph (d) of § 20.2056(c)-2.

§ 20.2056(e)-2 Marital deduction; definition of "passed from the decedent to his surviving spouse"

(a) In general. In general, the definition stated in § 20.2056(e)-1 is applicable in determining the property interests which "passed from the decedent to his surviving spouse". Special rules are provided, however, for the following:

(1) In the case of certain interests with income for life to the surviving spouse with power of appointment in her (see § 20.2056(b)-5);

(2) In the case of proceeds held by the insurer under a life insurance, endowment, or annuity contract with power of appointment in the surviving spouse (see § 20.2056(b)-6);

(3) In case of the disclaimer of an interest by the surviving spouse or by any other person (see § 20.2056(d)-1);

(4) In case of an election by the surviving spouse (see paragraph (c) of this section); and

(5) In case of a controversy involving the decedent's will, see paragraph (d) of this section.

A property interest is considered as passing to the surviving spouse only if it passed to her as beneficial owner, except to the extent otherwise provided in §§ 20.2056(b)-5 and 20.2056(b)-6 in the case of certain life estates and insurance and annuity contracts with powers of appointment. For this purpose, where a property interest passed from the decedent in trust, such interest is considered to have passed from him to his surviving spouse to the extent of her beneficial interest therein. The deduction may not be taken with respect to a property interest which passed to such spouse merely as trustee, or subject to a binding agreement by the spouse to dispose of the interest in favor of a third person. An allowance or award paid to a surviving spouse pursuant to local law for her support during the administration of the decedent's estate constitutes a property interest passing from the decedent to his surviving spouse. In determining whether or not such an interest is deductible, however, see generally the terminable interest rules of § 20.2056(b)-1 and especially example (8) of paragraph (g) of that section.

(b) Examples. The following illustrate the provisions of paragraph (a) of this section:

(1) A property interest bequeathed in trust by H (the decedent) is considered as having passed from him to W (his surviving spouse)—

(i) If the trust income is payable to W for life and upon her death the corpus is distributable to her executors or administrators;

(ii) If W is entitled to the trust income for a term of years following which the corpus is to be paid to W or her estate;

(iii) If the trust income is to be accumulated for a term of years or for W's life and the augmented fund paid to W or her estate; or

(iv) If the terms of the transfer satisfy the requirements of § 20.2056(b)-5.

(2) If H devised property—

(i) To A for life with remainder absolutely to W or her estate, the remainder interest is considered to have passed from H to W;

(ii) To W for life with remainder to her estate, the entire property is considered as having passed from H to W; or

(iii) Under conditions which satisfy the provisions of § 20.2056(b)-5, the entire property is considered as having passed from H to W.

(3) Proceeds of insurance upon the life of H are considered as having passed from H to W if the terms of the contract—

(i) Meet the requirements of § 20.-2056(b)-6;

(ii) Provide that the proceeds are payable to W in a lump sum;

(iii) Provide that the proceeds are payable in installments to W for life and after her death any remaining installments are payable to her estate;

(iv) Provide that interest on the proceeds is payable to W for life and upon her death the principal amount is payable to her estate; or

(v) Provide that the proceeds are payable to a trustee under an arrangement whereby the requirements of section 2056(b) (5) are satisfied.

(c) Effect of election by surviving spouse. This paragraph contains rules applicable if the surviving spouse may elect between a property interest offered to her under the decedent's will or other instrument and a property interest to which she is otherwise entitled (such as dower, a right in the decedent's estate, or her interest under community property laws) of which adverse disposition was attempted by the decedent under the will or other instrument. If the surviving spouse elects to take against the will or other instrument, then the property interests offered thereunder are not considered as having "passed from the decedent to his surviving spouse" and the dower or other property interest retained by her is considered as having so passed (if it otherwise so qualifies under this section). If the surviving spouse elects to take under the will or other instrument, then the dower or other property interest relinquished by her is not considered as having "passed from the decedent to his surviving spouse" (irrespective of whether it otherwise comes within the definition stated in paragraph (a) of this section) and the interest taken under the will or other instrument is considered as having so passed (if it otherwise so qualifies). As to the valuation of the property interest taken under the will or other instrument, see paragraph (b) of § 20.2056(b)-4.

(d) Will contests. (1) If as a result of a controversy involving the decedent's will, or involving any bequest or devise thereunder, his surviving spouse assigns or surrenders a property interest in settlement of the controversy, the interest so assigned or surrendered is not considered as having "passed from the decedent to his surviving spouse."

(2) If as a result of the controversy involving the decedent's will, or involving any bequest or devise thereunder, a property interest is assigned or surrendered to the surviving spouse, the interest so acquired will be regarded as having "passed from the decedent to his surviving spouse" only if the assignment or surrender was a bona fide recognition of enforceable rights of the surviving spouse in the decedent's estate. Such a bona fide recognition will be presumed where the assignment or surrender was pursuant

to a decision of a local court upon the merits in an adversary proceeding following a genuine and active contest. However, such a decree will be accepted only to the extent that the court passed upon the facts upon which deductibility of the property interests depends. If the assignment or surrender was pursuant to a decree rendered by consent, or pursuant to an agreement not to contest the will or not to probate the will, it will not necessarily be accepted as a bona fide evaluation of the rights of the spouse.

(e) Survivorship. If the order of deaths of the decedent and his spouse cannot be established by proof, a presumption (whether supplied by local law, the decedent's will, or otherwise) that the decedent was survived by his spouse will be recognized as satisfying paragraph (b) (1) of § 20.2056(a)-1, but only to the extent that it has the effect of giving to the spouse an interest in property includible in her gross estate under part III of subchapter A of chapter 11. Under these circumstances, if an estate tax return is required to be filed for the estate of the decedent's spouse, the marital deduction will not be allowed in the final audit of the estate tax return of the decedent's estate with respect to any property interest which has not been finally determined to be includible in the gross estate of his spouse.

§ 20.2056(e)-3 Marital deduction; definition of "passed from the decedent to a person other than his surviving spouse"

The expression "passed from the decedent to a person other than his surviving spouse" refers to any property interest which, under the definition stated in § 20.2056(e)-1 is considered as having "passed from the decedent" and which under the rules referred to in § 20.2056(e)-2 is not considered as having "passed from the decedent to his surviving spouse." Interests which passed to a person other than the surviving spouse include interests so passing under the decedent's exercise, release, or nonexercise of a nontaxable power to appoint. It is immaterial whether the property interest which passed from the decedent to a person other than his surviving spouse is included in the decedent's gross estate. The term "person other than his surviving spouse" includes the possible un-ascertained takers of a property interest, as, for example, the members of a class to be ascertained in the future. As another example, assume that the decedent created a power of appointment over a property interest, which does not come within the purview of § 20.2056(b)–5 or § 20.2056(b)–6. In such a case, the term "person other than his surviving spouse" refers to the possible appointees and possible takers in default (other than the spouse) of such property interest. Whether or not there is a possibility that the "person other than his surviving spouse" (or the heirs or assigns of such person) may possess or enjoy the property following termination or failure of the interest therein which passed from the decedent to his surviving spouse is to be determined as of the time of the decedent's death.

§ 25.2503-3 Future interests in property

(a) No part of the value of a gift of a future interest may be excluded in determining the total amount of gifts made during the calendar quarter (calendar year in the case of gifts made before January 1, 1971). For the definition of "calendar quarter" see § 25.2502-1(c) (1). "Future interest" is a legal term, and includes reversions, remainders, and other interests or estates, whether vested or contingent, and whether or not supported by a particular interest or estate, which are limited to commence in use, possession, or enjoyment at some future date or time. The term has no reference to such contractual rights as exist in a bond, note (though bearing no interest until maturity), or in a policy of life insurance, the obligations of which are to be discharged by payments in the future. But a future interest or interests in such contractual obligations may be created by the limitations contained in a trust or other instrument of transfer used in effecting a gift.

(b) An unrestricted right to the immediate use, possession, or enjoyment of property or the income from property (such as a life estate or term certain) is a present interest in property. An exclusion is allowable with respect to a gift of such an interest (but not in excess of the value of the interest). If a donee has received a present interest in property, the possibility that such interest may be diminished by the transfer of a greater interest in the same property to the donee through the exercise of a power is disregarded in computing the value of the present interest, to the extent that no part of such interest will at any time pass to any other person (see example (4) of paragraph (c) of this section). For an exception to the rule disallowing an exclusion for gifts of future interests in the case of certain gifts to minors, see § 25.2503-4.

(c) The operation of this section may be illustrated by the following examples:

Example (1). Under the terms of a trust created by A the trustee is directed to pay the net income to B, so long as B shall live. The trustee is authorized in his discretion to withhold payments of income during any period he deems advisable and add such income to the trust corpus. Since B's right to receive the income payments is subject to the trustee's discretion, it is not a present interest and no exclusion is allowable with respect to the transfer in trust.

Example (2). C transfers certain insurance policies on his own life to a trust created for the benefit of D. Upon C's death the proceeds of the policies are to be invested and the net income therefrom paid to D during his lifetime. Since the income payments to D will not begin until after C's death the transfer in trust represents a gift of a future interest in property against which no exclusion is allowable.

Example (3). Under the terms of a trust created by E the net income is to be distributed to E's three children in such shares as the trustee, in his uncontrolled discretion, deems advisable. While the terms of the trust provide that all of the net income is to be distributed, the amount of income any one of the three beneficiaries will receive rests entirely within the trustee's discretion and cannot be presently ascertained. Accordingly, no exclusions are allowable with respect to the transfers to the trust.

Example (4). Under the terms of a trust the net income is to be paid to F for life, with the remainder payable to G on F's death. The trustee has the uncontrolled power to pay over the corpus to F at any time. Although F's present right to receive the income may be terminated, no other person has the right to such income interest. Accordingly, the power in the trustee is disregarded in determining the value of F's present interest. The power would not be disregarded to the extent that the trustee during F's life could distribute corpus to persons other than F.

Example (5). The corpus of a trust created by J consists of certain real property, subject to a mortgage. The terms of the trust provide that the net income from the property is to be used to pay the mortgage. After the mortgage is paid in full the net income is to be paid to K during his lifetime. Since K's right to receive the income payments will not begin until after the mortgage is paid in full the transfer in trust represents a gift of a future interest in property against which no exclusion is allowable.

Example (6). L pays premiums on a policy of insurance on his life, all the incidents of ownership in the policy (including the right to surrender the policy) are vested in M. The payment of premiums by L constitutes a gift of a present interest in property.

§ 25.2503-4 Transfer for the benefit of a minor

(a) Section 2503(c) provides that no part of a transfer for the benefit of a donee who has not attained the age of 21 years on the date of the gift will be considered a gift of a future interest in property if the terms of the transfer satisfy all of the following conditions:

(1) Both the property itself and its income may be expended by or for the benefit of the donee before he attains the age of 21 years;

(2) Any portion of the property and its income not disposed of under subparagraph (1) of this paragraph will pass to the donee when he attains the age of 21 years; and

(3) Any portion of the property and its income not disposed of under subparagraph (1) of this paragraph will be payable either to the estate of the donee or as he may appoint under a general power of appointment as defined in section 2514(c) if he dies before attaining the age of 21 years.

(b) Either a power of appointment exercisable by the donee by will or a power of appointment exercisable by the donee during his lifetime will satisfy the conditions set forth in paragraph (a) (3) of this section. However, if the transfer is to qualify for the exclusion under this section, there must be no restrictions of substance (as distinguished from formal restrictions of the type described in paragraph (g) (4) of § 25.2523(e)-1) by the terms of the instrument of transfer on the exercise of the power by the donee. However, if the minor is given a power of appointment exercisable during lifetime or is given a power of appointment exercisable by will, the fact that under the local law a minor is under a disability to exercise an inter vivos power or to execute a will does not cause the transfer to fail to satisfy the conditions of section 2503(c). Further, a transfer does not fail to satisfy the conditions of section 2503(c) by reason of the mere fact that—

(1) There is left to the discretion of a trustee the determination of the amounts, if any, of the income or property to be expended for the benefit of the minor and the purpose for which the expenditure is to be made, provided there are no substantial restrictions under the terms of the trust instrument on the exercise of such discretion;

(2) The donee, upon reaching age 21, has the right to extend the term of the trust; or

(3) The governing instrument contains a disposition of the property or income not expended during the donee's minority to persons other than the donee's estate in the event of the default of appointment by the donee.

(c) A gift to a minor which does not satisfy the requirements of section 2503(c) may be either a present or a future interest under the general rules of § 25.2503-3. Thus, for example, a transfer of property in trust with income required to be paid annually to a minor beneficiary and corpus to be distributed to him upon his attaining the age of 25 is a gift of a present interest with respect to the right to income but is a gift of a future interest with respect to the right to corpus.

§ 25.2511-1   Transfers in general

(a) The gift tax applies to a transfer by way of gift whether the transfer is in trust or otherwise, whether the gift is direct or indirect, and whether the property is real or personal, tangible or intangible. For example, a taxable transfer may be effected by the creation of a trust, the forgiving of a debt, the assignment of a judgment, the assignment of the benefits of an insurance policy, or the transfer of cash, certificates of deposit, or Federal, State or municipal bonds. Statutory provisions which exempt bonds, notes, bills and certificates of indebtedness of the Federal Government or its agencies and the interest thereon from taxation are not applicable to the gift tax, since the gift tax is an excise tax on the transfer, and is not a tax on the subject of the gift.

. . . .

(c) The gift tax also applies to gifts indirectly made. Thus, all transactions whereby property or property rights or interests are gratuitously passed or conferred upon another, regardless of the means or device employed, constitute gifts subject to tax. See further § 25.2512-8. . . .

(d) If a joint income tax return is filed by a husband and wife for a taxable year, the payment by one spouse of all or part of the income tax liability for such year is not treated as resulting in a transfer that is subject to gift tax. The same rule is applicable to the payment of gift tax for a calendar quarter (or calendar year) in the case of a husband and wife who have consented to have the gifts made considered as made half by each of them in accordance with the provisions of section 2513. . . . .

(e) If a donor transfers by gift less than his entire interest in property, the gift tax is applicable to the interest transferred. The tax is applicable, for example, to the transfer of an undivided half interest in property, or to the transfer of a life estate when the grantor retains the remainder interest, or vice versa. However, if the donor's retained interest is not susceptible of measurement on the basis of generally accepted valuation principles, the gift tax is applicable to the entire value of the property subject to the gift. Thus, if a donor, aged 65 years, transfers a life estate in property to A, aged 25 years, with remainder to A's issue, or in default of issue, with reversion to the donor, the gift tax will normally be applicable to the entire value of the property.

(f) If a donor is the owner of only a limited interest in property, and transfers his entire interest, the interest is in every case to be valued by the rules set forth in §§ 25.2512-1 through 25.2512-7. If the interest is a remainder or reversion or other future interest, it is to be valued on the basis of actuarial principles set forth in § 25.2512-5, or if it is not susceptible of valuation in that manner, in accordance with the principles set forth in § 25.2512-1.

(g) (1) Donative intent on the part of the transferor is not an essential element in the application of the gift tax to the transfer. The application of the tax is based on the objective facts of the transfer and the circumstances under which it is made, rather than on the subjective motives of the donor. However, there are certain types of transfers to which the tax is not applicable. It is applicable only to a transfer of a beneficial interest in property. It is not applicable to a transfer of bare legal title to a trustee. A transfer by a trustee of trust property in which he has no beneficial interest does not constitute a gift by the trustee (but such a transfer may constitute a gift by the creator of the trust, if until the transfer he had the power to change the beneficiaries by amending or revoking the trust). The gift tax is not ap-

plicable to a transfer for a full and adequate consideration in money or money's worth, or to ordinary business transactions, described in § 25.2512-8.

(2) If a trustee has a beneficial interest in trust property, a transfer of the property by the trustee is not a taxable transfer if it is made pursuant to a fiduciary power the exercise or non-exercise of which is limited by a reasonably fixed or ascertainable standard which is set forth in the trust instrument. A clearly measurable standard under which the holder of a power is legally accountable is such a standard for this purpose. For instance, a power to distribute corpus for the education, support, maintenance, or health of the beneficiary; for his reasonable support and comfort; to enable him to maintain his accustomed standard of living; or to meet an emergency, would be such a standard. However, a power to distribute corpus for the pleasure, desire, or happiness of a beneficiary is not such a standard. The entire context of a provision of a trust instrument granting a power must be considered in determining whether the power is limited by a reasonably definite standard. For example, if a trust instrument provides that the determination of the trustee shall be conclusive with respect to the exercise or nonexercise of a power, the power is not limited by a reasonably definite standard. However, the fact that the governing instrument is phrased in discretionary terms is not in itself an indication that no such standard exists.

(h) The following are examples of transactions resulting in taxable gifts and in each case it is assumed that the transfers were not made for an adequate and full consideration in money or money's worth:

(1) A transfer of property by a corporation to B is a gift to B from the stockholders of the corporation. If B himself is a stockholder, the transfer is a gift to him from the other stockholders but only to the extent it exceeds B's own interest in such amount as a shareholder. A transfer of property by B to a corporation generally represents gifts by B to the other individual shareholders of the corporation to the extent of their proportionate interests in the corporation However, there may be an exception to this rule, such as a transfer made by an individ-

ual to a charitable, public, political or similar organization which may constitute a gift to the organization as a single entity, depending upon the facts and circumstances in the particular case.

(2) The transfer of property to B if there is imposed upon B the obligation of paying a commensurate annuity to C is a gift to C.

(3) The payment of money or the transfer of property to B in consideration of B's promise to render a service to C is a gift to C, or to both B and C, depending on whether the service to be rendered to C is or is not an adequate and full consideration in money or money's worth for that which is received by B. See section 2512(b) and the regulations thereunder.

(4) If A creates a joint bank account for himself and B (or a similar type of ownership by which A can regain the entire fund without B's consent), there is a gift to B when B draws upon the account for his own benefit, to the extent of the amount drawn without any obligation to account for a part of the proceeds to A. Similarly, if A purchases a United States savings bond registered as payable to "A or B," there is a gift to B when B surrenders the bond for cash without any obligation to account for a part of the proceeds to A.

(5) If A with his own funds purchases property and has the title conveyed to himself and B as joint owners, with rights of survivorship (other than a joint ownership described in example (4)) but which rights may be defeated by either party severing his interest, there is a gift to B in the amount of half the value of the property. However, see § 25.2515-1 relative to the creation of a joint tenancy (or tenancy by the entirety) between husband and wife in real property with rights of survivorship which, unless the donor elects otherwise is not considered as a transfer includible for Federal gift tax purposes at the time of the creation of the joint tenancy. See § 25.2515-2 with respect to determining the extent to which the creation of a tenancy by the entirety constitutes a taxable gift if the donor elects to have the creation of the tenancy so treated. See also § 25.2523(d)-1 with respect to the marital deduction allowed in the case of the

creation of a joint tenancy or a tenancy by the entirety.

(6) If A is possessed of a vested remainder interest in property, subject to being divested only in the event he should fail to survive one or more individuals or the happening of some other event, an irrevocable assignment of all or any part of his interest would result in a transfer includible for Federal gift tax purposes. See especially paragraph (e) of § 25.2512-5 or paragraph (e) of § 25.2512-9, whichever is applicable, for the valuation of an interest of this type.

(7) If A, without retaining a power to revoke the trust or to change the beneficial interests therein, transfers property in trust whereby B is to receive the income for life and at his death the trust is to terminate and the corpus is to be returned to A, provided A survives, but if A predeceases B the corpus is to pass to C, A has made a gift equal to the total value of the property less the value of his retained interest. See paragraph (e) of § 25.2512-5 or paragraph (e) of § 25.2512-9, whichever is applicable, for the valuation of the donor's retained interest.

(8) If the insured purchases a life insurance policy, or pays a premium on a previously issued policy, the proceeds of which are payable to a beneficiary or beneficiaries other than his estate, and with respect to which the insured retains no reversionary interest in himself or his estate and no power to revest the economic benefits in himself or his estate or to change the beneficiaries or their proportionate benefits (or if the insured relinquishes by assignment, by designation of a new beneficiary or otherwise, every such power that was retained in a previously issued policy), the insured has made a gift of the value of the policy, or to the extent of the premium paid, even though the right of the assignee or beneficiary to receive the benefits is conditioned upon his surviving the insured. For the valuation of life insurance policies see § 25.2512-6.

(9) Where property held by a husband and wife as community property is used to purchase insurance upon the husband's life and a third person is revocably designated as beneficiary and under the State law the husband's

death is considered to make absolute the transfer by the wife, there is a gift by the wife at the time of the husband's death of half the amount of the proceeds of such insurance.

(10) If under a pension plan (pursuant to which he has an unqualified right to an annuity) an employee has an option to take either a retirement annuity for himself alone or a smaller annuity for himself with a survivorship annuity payable to his wife, an irrevocable election by the employee to take the reduced annuity in order that an annuity may be paid, after the employee's death, to his wife results in the making of a gift. However, see section 2517 and the regulations thereunder for the exemption from gift tax of amounts attributable to employers' contributions under qualified plans and certain other contracts.

§ 25.2511-2 Cessation of donor's dominion and control

(a) The gift tax is not imposed upon the receipt of the property by the donee, nor is it necessarily determined by the measure of enrichment resulting to the donee from the transfer, nor is it conditioned upon ability to identify the donee at the time of the transfer. On the contrary, the tax is a primary and personal liability of the donor, is an excise upon his act of making the transfer, is measured by the value of the property passing from the donor, and attaches regardless of the fact that the identity of the donee may not then be known or ascertainable.

(b) As to any property, or part thereof or interest therein, of which the donor has so parted with dominion and control as to leave in him no power to change its disposition, whether for his own benefit or for the benefit of another, the gift is complete. But if upon a transfer of property (whether in trust or otherwise) the donor reserves any power over its disposition, the gift may be wholly incomplete, or may be partially complete and partially incomplete, depending upon all the facts in the particular case. Accordingly, in every case of a transfer of property subject to a reserved power, the terms of the power must be examined and its scope determined. For example, if a donor transfers property to another in trust to pay the income to the donor or accumulate it in the discretion of the trustee, and the donor retains a testamentary power to appoint the remainder among his descendants, no portion of the transfer is a completed gift. On the other hand, if the donor had not retained the testamentary power of appointment, but instead provided that the remainder should go to X or his heirs, the entire transfer would be a completed gift. However, if the exercise of the trustee's power in favor of the grantor is limited by a fixed or ascertainable standard (see paragraph (g) (2) of § 25.2511-1), enforceable by or on behalf of the grantor, then the gift is incomplete to the extent of the ascertainable value of any rights thus retained by the grantor.

(c) A gift is incomplete in every instance in which a donor reserves the power to revest the beneficial title to the property in himself. A gift is also incomplete if and to the extent that a reserved power gives the donor the power to name new beneficiaries or to change the interests of the beneficiaries as between themselves unless the power is a fiduciary power limited by a fixed or ascertainable standard. Thus, if an estate for life is transferred but, by an exercise of a power, the estate may be terminated or cut down by the donor to one of less value, and without restriction upon the extent to which the estate may be so cut down, the transfer constitutes an incomplete gift. If in this example the power was confined to the right to cut down the estate for life to one for a term of five years, the certainty of an estate for not less than that term results in a gift to that extent complete.

(d) A gift is not considered incomplete, however, merely because the donor reserves the power to change the manner or time of enjoyment. Thus, the creation of a trust the income of which is to be paid annually to the donee for a period of years, the corpus being distributable to him at the end of the period, and the power reserved by the donor being limited to a right to require that, instead of the income being so payable, it should be accumulated and distributed with the corpus to the donee at the termination of the period, constitutes a completed gift.

(e) A donor is considered as himself having a power if it is exercisable by him in conjunction with any person not having a substantial adverse interest in the disposition of the transferred property or the income therefrom. A trustee, as such, is not a person having an adverse interest in the disposition of the trust property or its income.

(f) The relinquishment or termination of a power to change the beneficiaries of transferred property, occurring otherwise than by the death of the donor (the statute being confined to transfers by living donors), is regarded as the event that completes the gift and causes the tax to apply. For example, if A transfers property in trust for the benefit of B and C but reserves the power as trustee to change the proportionate interests of B and C, and if A thereafter has another person appointed trustee in place of himself, such later relinquishment of the power by A to the new trustee completes the gift of the transferred property, whether or not the new trustee has a substantial adverse interest. The receipt of income or of other enjoyment of the transferred property by the transferee or by the beneficiary (other than by the donor himself) during the interim between the making of the initial transfer and the relinquishment or termination of the power operates to free such income or other enjoyment from the power, and constitutes a gift of such income or of such other enjoyment taxable as of the calendar quarter or calendar year of its receipt. See § 25.2502–1(c)(1) for the definition of calendar quarter. If property is transferred in trust to pay the income to A for life with remainder to B, powers to distribute corpus to A, and to withhold income from A for future distribution to B, are powers to change the beneficiaries of the transferred property.

(g) If a donor transfers property to himself as trustee (or to himself and some other person, not possessing a substantial adverse interest, as trustees), and retains no beneficial interest in the trust property and no power over it except fiduciary powers, the exercise or nonexercise of which is limited by a fixed or ascertainable standard, to change the beneficiaries of the trans-

ferred property, the donor has made a completed gift and the entire value of the transferred property is subject to the gift tax.

(h) If a donor delivers a properly indorsed stock certificate to the donee or the donee's agent, the gift is completed for gift tax purposes on the date of delivery. If the donor delivers the certificate to his bank or broker as his agent, or to the issuing corporation or its transfer agent, for transfer into the name of the donee, the gift is completed on the date the stock is transferred on the books of the corporation.

(i) [Reserved]

(j) If the donor contends that a power is of such nature as to render the gift incomplete, and hence not subject to the tax as of the calendar quarter or calendar year of the initial transfer, the transaction shall be disclosed in the return and evidence showing all relevant facts, including a copy of the instrument of transfer, should be submitted. . . . .

§ 25.2512–1 Valuation of property; in general

Section 2512 provides that if a gift is made in property, its value at the date of the gift shall be considered the amount of the gift. The value of the property is the price at which such property would change hands between a willing buyer and a willing seller, neither being under any compulsion to buy or to sell, and both having reasonable knowledge of relevant facts. The value of a particular item of property is not the price that a forced sale of the property would produce. Nor is the fair market value of an item of property the sale price in a market other than that in which such item is most commonly sold to the public, taking into account the location of the item wherever appropriate. Thus, in the case of an item of property made the subject of a gift, which is generally obtained by the public in the retail market, the fair market value of such an item of property is the price at which the item or a comparable item would be sold at retail. For example, the value of an automobile (an article generally obtained by the public in the retail market) which is the subject of a gift, is the price for which an automobile of the same or approximately the same description, make, model, age, condition, etc., could be purchased by a member of the general public and not the price for which the particular automobile of the donor would be purchased by a dealer in used automobiles. Examples of items of property which are generally sold to the public at retail may be found in § 25.2512-6. The value is generally to be determined by ascertaining as a basis the fair market value at the time of the gift of each unit of the property. For example, in the case of shares of stocks or bonds, such unit of property is generally a share or a bond. Property shall not be returned at the value at which it is assessed for local tax purposes unless that value represents the fair market value thereof on the date of the gift. All relevant facts and elements of value as of the time of the gift shall be considered. Where the subject of a gift is an interest in a business, the value of items of property in the inventory of the business generally should be reflected in the value of the business. . . . .

§ 25.2512-2 Stocks and bonds

(a) In general. The value of stocks and bonds is the fair market value per share or bond on the date of the gift.

(b) Based on selling prices. (1) In general, if there is a market for stocks or bonds, on a stock exchange, in an over-the-counter market or otherwise, the mean between the highest and lowest quoted selling prices on the date of the gift is the fair market value per share or bond. If there were no sales on the date of the gift but there were sales on dates within a reasonable period both before and after the date of the gift, the fair market value is determined by taking a weighted average of the means between the highest and lowest sales on the nearest date before and the nearest date after the date of the gift. The average is to be weighted inversely by the respective numbers of trading days between the selling dates and the date of the gift. If the stocks or bonds are listed on more than one exchange, the records of the exchange where the stocks or bonds are principally dealt in should be employed if such records are available in a generally available listing or publication

of general circulation. In the event that such records are not so available and such stocks or bonds are listed on a composite listing of combined exchanges available in a generally available listing or publication of general circulation, the records of such combined exchanges should be employed. In valuing listed securities, the donor should be careful to consult accurate records to obtain values as of the date of the gift. If quotations of unlisted securities are obtained from brokers, or evidence as to their sale is obtained from the officers of the issuing companies, copies of letters furnishing such quotations or evidence of sale should be attached to the return.

(2) If it is established with respect to bonds for which there is a market on a stock exchange, that the highest and lowest selling prices are not available for the date of the gift in a generally available listing or publication of general circulation but that closing prices are so available, the fair market value per bond is the mean between the quoted closing selling price on the date of the gift and the quoted closing selling price on the trading day before the date of the gift. If there were no sales on the trading day before the date of the gift but there were sales on dates within a reasonable period before the date of the gift, the fair market value is determined by taking a weighted average of the quoted closing selling prices on the date of the gift and the nearest date before the date of the gift. The closing selling price for the date of the gift is to be weighted by the respective number of trading days between the previous selling date and the date of the gift. If there were no sales within a reasonable period before the date of the gift but there were sales on the date of the gift, the fair market value is the closing selling price on the date of the gift. If there were no sales on the date of the gift but there were sales within a reasonable period both before and after the date of the gift, the fair market value is determined by taking a weighted average of the quoted closing selling prices on the nearest date before and the nearest date after the date of the gift. The average is to be weighted inversely by the respective numbers of trading days

1211

between the selling dates and the date of the gift. If the bonds are listed on more than one exchange, the records of the exchange where the bonds are principally dealt in should be employed. In valuing listed securities, the donor should be careful to consult accurate records to obtain values as of the date of the gift.

. . . . .

(c) Based on bid and asked prices. If the provisions of paragraph (b) of this section are inapplicable because actual sales are not available during a reasonable period beginning before and ending after the date of the gift, the fair market value may be determined by taking the mean between the bona fide bid and asked prices on the date of the gift, or if none, by taking a weighted average of the means between the bona fide bid and asked prices on the nearest trading date before and the nearest trading date after the date of the gift, if both such nearest dates are within a reasonable period. The average is to be determined in the manner described in paragraph (b) of this section.

(d) Where selling prices and bid and asked prices are not available for dates both before and after the date of gift. If the provisions of paragraphs (b) and (c) of this section are inapplicable because no actual sale prices or quoted bona fide bid and asked prices are available on a date within a reasonable period before the date of the gift, but such prices are available on a date within a reasonable period after the date of the gift, or vice versa, then the mean between the highest and lowest available sale prices or bid and asked prices may be taken as the value.

(e) Where selling prices or bid and asked prices do not represent fair market value. In cases in which it is established that the value per bond or share of any security determined on the basis of the selling or bid and asked prices as provided under paragraphs (b), (c), and (d) of this section does not represent the fair market value thereof, then some reasonable modification of the value determined on that basis or other relevant facts and elements of value shall be considered in determining fair market value. Where

sales at or near the date of the gift are few or of a sporadic nature, such sales alone may not indicate fair market value. In certain exceptional cases, the size of the block of securities made the subject of each separate gift in relation to the number of shares changing hands in sales may be relevant in determining whether selling prices reflect the fair market value of the block of stock to be valued. If the donor can show that the block of stock to be valued, with reference to each separate gift, is so large in relation to the actual sales on the existing market that it could not be liquidated in a reasonable time without depressing the market, the price at which the block could be sold as such outside the usual market, as through an underwriter, may be a more accurate indication of value than market quotations. Complete data in support of any allowance claimed due to the size of the block of stock being valued should be submitted with the return. On the other hand, if the block of stock to be valued represents a controlling interest, either actual or effective, in a going business, the price at which other lots change hands may have little relation to its true value.

(f) Where selling prices or bid and asked prices are unavailable. If the provisions of paragraphs (b), (c), and (d) of this section are inapplicable because actual sale prices and bona fide bid and asked prices are lacking, then the fair market value is to be determined by taking the following factors into consideration:

(1) In the case of corporate or other bonds, the soundness of the security, the interest yield, the date of maturity, and other relevant factors; and

(2) In the case of shares of stock, the company's net worth, prospective earning power and dividend-paying capacity, and other relevant factors.

Some of the "other relevant factors" referred to in subparagraphs (1) and (2) of this paragraph are: The goodwill of the business; the economic outlook in the particular industry; the company's position in the industry and its management; the degree of control of the business represented by the block of stock to be valued; and the values of securities of corporations engaged in the same or similar lines of business which are listed on a stock exchange. However, the weight to be accorded such comparisons or any other evidentiary factors considered in the determination of a value depends upon the facts of each case. Complete financial and other data upon which the valuation is based should be submitted with the return, including copies of reports of any examinations of the company made by accountants, engineers, or any technical experts as of or near the date of the gift.

§ 25.2512-3 Valuation of interests in businesses

(a) Care should be taken to arrive at an accurate valuation of any interest in a business which the donor transfers without an adequate and full consideration in money or money's worth. The fair market value of any interest in a business, whether a partnership or a proprietorship, is the net amount which a willing purchaser, whether an individual or a corporation, would pay for the interest to a willing seller, neither being under any compulsion to buy or to sell and both having reasonable knowledge of the relevant facts. The net value is determined on the basis of all relevant factors including—

(1) A fair appraisal as of the date of the gift of all the assets of the business, tangible and intangible, including good will;

(2) The demonstrated earning capacity of the business; and

(3) The other factors set forth in paragraph (f) of § 25.2512-2 relating to the valuation of corporate stock, to the extent applicable.

Special attention should be given to determining an adequate value of the good will of the business. Complete financial and other data upon which the valuation is based should be submitted with the return, including copies of reports of examinations of the business made by accountants, engineers, or any technical experts as of or near the date of the gift.

§ 25.2512-4 Valuation of notes

The fair market value of notes, secured or unsecured, is presumed to be the amount of unpaid principal, plus accrued interest to the date of the gift, unless the donor establishes a lower value. Unless returned at face value, plus accrued interest, it must be shown by satisfactory evidence that the note is worth less than the unpaid amount (because of the interest rate, or date of maturity, or other cause), or that the note is uncollectible in part (by reason of the insolvency of the party or parties liable, or for other cause), and that the property, if any, pledged or mortgaged as security is insufficient to satisfy it.

§ 25.2512-6 Valuation of certain life insurance and annuity contracts; valuation of shares in an open-end investment company

(a) Valuation of certain life insurance and annuity contracts. The value of a life insurance contract or of a contract for the payment of an annuity issued by a company regularly engaged in the selling of contracts of that character is established through the sale of the particular contract by the company, or through the sale by the company of comparable contracts. As valuation of an insurance policy through sale of comparable contracts is not readily ascertainable when the gift is of a contract which has been in force for some time and on which further premium payments are to be made, the value may be approximated by adding to the interpolated terminal reserve at the date of the gift the proportionate part of the gross premium last paid before the date of the gift which covers the period extending beyond that date. If, however, because of the unusual nature of the contract such approximation is not reasonably close to the full value, this method may not be used. . . . . .

.   .   .   .

(b) Valuation of shares in an open-end investment company. (1) The fair market value of a share in an open-end investment company (commonly known as a "mutual fund") is the public redemption price of a share. In the absence of an affirmative showing of the public redemption price in effect at the time of the gift, the last public redemption price quoted by the company for the date of the gift shall be presumed to be the applicable public redemption price. If there is no public redemption price quoted by the company for the date of the gift (e.g., the date of the gift is a Saturday, Sunday, or holiday), the fair market value of the mutual fund share is the last public redemption price quoted by the company for the first day preceding the date of the gift for which there is a quotation. As used in this paragraph the term "open-end investment company" includes only a company which on the date of the gift was engaged in offering its shares to the public in the capacity of an open-end investment company.

. . . . .

§ 25.2512-8   Transfers for insufficient consideration

Transfers reached by the gift tax are not confined to those only which, being without a valuable consideration, accord with the common law concept of gifts, but embrace as well sales, exchanges, and other dispositions of property for a consideration to the extent that the value of the property transferred by the donor exceeds the value in money or money's worth of the consideration given therefor. However, a sale, exchange, or other transfer of property made in the ordinary course of business (a transaction which is bona fide, at arm's length, and free from any donative intent), will be considered as made for an adequate and full consideration in money or money's worth. A consideration not reducible to a value in money or money's worth, as love and affection, promise of marriage, etc., is to be wholly disregarded, and the entire value of the property transferred constitutes the amount of the gift. Similarly, a relinquishment or promised relinquishment of dower or curtesy, or of a statutory estate created in lieu of dower or curtesy, or of other marital rights in the spouse's property or estate, shall not be considered to any extent a consideration "in money or money's worth." See, however, section 2516 and the regulations thereunder with respect to certain transfers incident to a divorce.

§ 25.2512-9   Valuation of annuities, life estates, terms for years, remainders, and reversions transferred after December 31, 1970

(a) In general. (1) (i) Except as otherwise provided in this subparagraph, the fair market value of annuities, life estates, terms for years, remainders, and reversions transferred after December 31, 1970, is their present value determined under this section. The value of annuities issued by companies regularly engaged in their sale and of insurance policies issued by companies regularly engaged in their sale is determined under § 25.2512-6. The fair market value of a remainder interest in a charitable remainder unitrust, as defined in § 1.664-3, is its present value determined under § 1.664-4. The fair market value of a life interest or term for years in a charitable remainder unitrust is the fair market value of the property as of the date of transfer less the fair market value of the remainder interest on such date determined under § 1.664-4. The fair market value of interests in a pooled income fund, as defined in § 1.642(c)-5, is their value determined under § 1.642(c)-6. Where the donor transfers property in trust or otherwise and retains an interest therein, the value of the gift is the value of the property transferred less the value of the donor's retained interest. If the donor assigns or relinquishes an annuity, life estate, remainder, or reversion which he holds by virtue of a transfer previously made by himself or another, the value of the gift is the value of the interest transferred. (See § 25.2512-5 with respect to the valuation of annuities, life estates, terms for years, remainders, and reversions transferred on or before Dec. 31, 1970.)

. . . . .

(2) The present value of an annuity, life estate, remainder or reversion determined under this section which is dependent on the continuation or termination of the life of one person is computed by the use of Table A(1) or A(2) in paragraph (f) of this section. Table A(1) is to be used when the person upon whose life the interest is based is a male and Table A(2) is to be used when such person is a female.

The present value of an annuity term for years, remainder or reversion dependent on a term certain is computed by the use of Table B in paragraph (f) of this section. If the interest to be valued is dependent upon more than one life or there is a term certain concurrent with one or more lives, see paragraph (e) of this section. For purposes of the computations described in this section, the age of a person is to be taken as the age of that person at his nearest birthday.

(3) In all examples set forth in this section, the interest is assumed to have been transferred after December 31, 1970.

(b) **Annuities**—(1) **Payable annually at end of year.** If an annuity is payable annually at the end of each year during the life of an individual (as for example if the first payment is due 1 year after the date of the gift), the amount payable annually is multiplied by the figure in column 2 of Table A(1) or A(2), whichever is appropriate, opposite the number of years in column 1 nearest the age of the individual whose life measures the duration of the annuity. If the annuity is payable annually at the end of each year for a definite number of years, the amount payable annually is multiplied by the figure in column 2 of Table B opposite the number of years in column 1 representing the duration of the annuity. The application of this subparagraph may be illustrated by the following examples:

Example (1). The donor, a male, assigns an annuity of $10,000 a year payable annually during his life immediately after an annual payment has been made. The age of the donor on the date of assignment is 40 years and 8 months. By reference to Table A(1), it is found that the figure in column 2 opposite 41 years is 12.9934. The value of the gift is, therefore, $129,934 ($10,000 multiplied by 12.9934).

Example (2). The donor was entitled to receive an annuity of $10,000 a year payable annually at the end of annual periods throughout a term of 20 years; the donor, when 15 years have elapsed, makes a gift thereof to his son. By reference to Table B, it is found that the figure in column 2 opposite 5 years, the unexpired portion of the 20-year period, is 4.2124. The present value of the annuity is, therefore, $42,124 ($10,000 multiplied by 4.2124).

•   •   •   •   •

(c) **Life estates and terms for years.** If the interest to be valued is the right of a person for his life, or for the life of another person, to receive the income

of certain property or to use nonincome-producing property, the value of the interest is the value of the property multiplied by the figure in column 3 of Table A(1) or A(2), whichever is appropriate, opposite the number of years nearest to the actual age of the measuring life. If the interest to be valued is the right to receive income of property or to use nonincome-producing property for a term of years, column 3 of Table B is used. The application of this paragraph may be illustrated by the following example:

Example. The donor, a male, who during his life is entitled to receive the income from property worth $50,000, makes a gift of such interest. The donor is 31 years old on the date of the gift. The value of the gift is $43,058.50 ($50,000×0.86117).

(d) **Remainders or reversionary interests.** If the interest to be valued is a remainder or reversionary interest subject to a life estate, the value of the interest should be obtained by multiplying the value of the property at the date of the gift by the figure in column 4 of Table A(1) or A(2), whichever is appropriate, opposite the number of years nearest the age of the life tenant. If the remainder or reversion is to take effect at the end of a term of years, column 4 of Table B should be used. The application of this paragraph may be illustrated by the following example:

Example. The donor transfers by gift a remainder interest in property worth $50,000, subject to his sister's right to receive the income therefrom for her life. The sister at the date of the gift is 31 years of age. By reference to Table A(2), it is found that the figure in column 4 opposite age 31 is 0.10227. The value of the gift is, therefore, $5,113.50 ($50,000×0.10227).

(e) **Actuarial computations by the Internal Revenue Service.** If the interest to be valued is dependent upon the continuation or termination of more than one life, or there is a term certain concurrent with one or more lives, or if the retained interest of the donor is conditioned upon survivorship, a special factor is necessary. The factor is to be computed on the basis of interest at the rate of 6 percent a year, compounded annually, and life contingencies determined, as to each male and female life involved, from the values of l_x that are set forth in columns 2 and 3, respectively, of Table LN of paragraph (f) of § 20.2031–10. Table LN contains values of l_x taken from the life table for total males and the life table for total females appearing as Tables 2 and 3, respectively, in United States Life Tables: 1959-61, published by the Department of Health, Education, and Welfare, Public Health Service, except that for technical reasons Table LN employs graduated data, furnished by that Department, to increase the number of significant figures shown at ages of male lives older than 86 and female lives older than 90. Many such special factors may be found in, or computed with the use of the tables contained in, the publications entitled "Actuarial Values I: Valuation of Last Survivor Charitable Remainders" and "Actuarial Values II: Factors at 6 Percent Involving One and Two Lives." These publications may be purchased from the Superintendent of Documents, United States Government Printing Office, Washington, DC 20402. However, if a special factor is required in the case of an actual gift, the Commissioner will furnish the factor to the donor upon request. The request must be accompanied by a statement of the sex and date of birth of each person the duration of whose life may affect the value of the interest, and by copies of the relevant instruments.

(f) The following tables shall be used in the application of the provisions of this section:

TABLE A(1)

TABLE. SINGLE LIFE MALE. 6 PERCENT. SHOWING THE PRESENT WORTH OF AN ANNUITY. OF A LIFE INTEREST. AND OF A REMAINDER INTEREST

(1) Age	(2) Annuity	(3) Life estate	(4) Remainder
0	15.6175	0.9305	0.06295
1	16.0362	.96217	.03783
2	16.0283	.96170	.03830
3	16.0089	.96053	.03947
4	15.9841	.95905	.04095
5	15.9553	.95732	.04268
6	15.9233	.95540	.04460
7	15.8885	.95331	.04669
8	15.8508	.95195	.04895
9	15.8101	.94861	.05139
10	15.7663	.94598	.05402
11	15.7194	.94316	.05684
12	15.6698	.94019	.05981
13	15.6180	.93708	.06292
14	15.5651	.93391	.06609
15	15.5115	.93069	.06931
16	15.4576	.92746	.07254
17	15.4031	.02419	.07581
18	15.3481	.92089	.07911
19	15.2918	.91751	.08249
20	15.2339	.91403	.08597
21	15.1744	.91046	.08954
22	15.1130	.90678	.09328
23	15.0487	.90292	.09702

TABLE A(1) —Continued

(1) Age	(2) Annuity	(3) Life estate	(4) Remainder
24	14.9807	.89884	.10116
25	14.9075	.89445	.10555
26	14.8287	.88972	.11028
27	14.7442	.88465	.11535
28	14.6542	.87925	.12075
29	14.5588	.87353	.12647
30	14.4584	.86750	.13250
31	14.3528	.86117	.13883
32	14.2418	.85451	.14549
33	14.1254	.84752	.15248
34	14.0034	.84020	.15980
35	13.8758	.83255	.16745
36	13.7425	.82455	.17545
37	13.6036	.81622	.18378
38	13.4591	.80755	.19245
39	13.3090	.79854	.20146
40	13.1538	.78923	.21077
41	12.9934	.77960	.22040
42	12.8279	.76967	.23033
43	12.6574	.75944	.24056
44	12.4819	.74891	.25109
45	12.3013	.73808	.26192
46	12.1158	.72695	.27305
47	11.9253	.71552	.28448
48	11.7308	.70385	.29615
49	11.5330	.69198	.30802
50	11.3329	.67997	.32003
51	11.1308	.66785	.33215
52	10.9267	.65560	.34440
53	10.7200	.64320	.35680
54	10.5100	.63060	.36940
55	10.2960	.61776	.38224
56	10.0777	.60466	.39534
57	9.8552	.59131	.40869
58	9.6297	.57778	.42222
59	9.4028	.56417	.43583
60	9.1753	.55052	.44948
61	8.9478	.53687	.46313
62	8.7202	.52321	.47679
63	8.4924	.50954	.49046
64	8.2642	.49585	.50415
65	8.0353	.48212	.51788
66	7.8060	.46836	.53164
67	7.5763	.45458	.54542
68	7.3462	.44077	.55923
69	7.1149	.42689	.57311
70	6.8823	.41294	.58706
71	6.6481	.39889	.60111
72	6.4123	.38474	.61526
73	6.1752	.37051	.62949
74	5.9373	.35624	.64376
75	5.6990	.34194	.65806
76	5.4602	.32761	.67239
77	5.2211	.31327	.68673
78	4.9825	.29895	.70105
79	4.7469	.28481	.71519
80	4.5164	.27098	.72902
81	4.2955	.25773	.74227
82	4.0879	.24527	.75473
83	3.8924	.23354	.76646
84	3.7029	.22217	.77783
85	3.5117	.21070	.78930
86	3.3259	.19955	.80045
87	3.1450	.18820	.81130
88	2.9703	.17872	.82178
89	2.8052	.16831	.83169
90	2.6536	.15922	.84078
91	2.5162	.15097	.84903
92	2.3917	.14350	.85650
93	2.2801	.13681	.86319
94	2.1802	.13081	.86919
95	2.0891	.12535	.87465
96	1.9997	.11998	.88002
97	1.9145	.11487	.88513
98	1.8331	.10999	.89001
99	1.7554	.10532	.89468
100	1.6812	.10087	.89913
101	1.6101	.09661	.90339
102	1.5416	.09250	.90750
103	1.4744	.08846	.91154
104	1.4065	.08439	.91561
105	1.3334	.08000	.92000
106	1.2452	.07471	.92529
107	1.1196	.06718	.93282
108	.9043	.05426	.94574
109	.4717	.02830	.97170

TABLE A(2)

TABLE. SINGLE LIFE FEMALE. 6 PERCENT. SHOWING THE
PRESENT WORTH OF AN ANNUITY. OF A LIFE INTEREST.
AND OF A REMAINDER INTEREST

(1) Age	(2) Annuity	(3) Life estate	(4) Remainder
0	15.8972	0.95383	0.04617
1	16.2284	.97370	.02630
2	16.2287	.97372	.02628
3	16.2180	.97308	.02692
4	16.2029	.97217	.02783
5	16.1850	.97110	.02890
6	16.1648	.96989	.03011
7	16.1421	.96853	.03147
8	16.1172	.96703	.03297
9	16.0910	.96541	.03459
10	16.0608	.96365	.03635
11	16.0293	.96176	.03824
12	15.9958	.95975	.04025
13	15.9607	.95764	.04236
14	15.9239	.95543	.04457
15	15.8856	.95314	.04686
16	15.8460	.95076	.04924
17	15.8048	.94829	.05171
18	15.7620	.94572	.05428
19	15.7172	.94303	.05697
20	15.6701	.94021	.05979
21	15.6207	.93724	.06276
22	15.5687	.93412	.06588
23	15.5141	.93085	.06915
24	15.4565	.92739	.07261
25	15.3959	.92375	.07625
26	15.3322	.91993	.08007
27	15.2652	.91591	.08409
28	15.1946	.91168	.08832
29	15.1208	.90725	.09275
30	15.0432	.90259	.09741
31	14.9622	.89773	.10227
32	14.8775	.89265	.10735
33	14.7888	.88733	.11267
34	14.6960	.88176	.11824
35	14.5989	.87593	.12407
36	14.4975	.86985	.13015
37	14.3915	.86349	.13651
38	14.2811	.85687	.14313
39	14.1663	.84998	.15002
40	14.0468	.84281	.15719
41	13.9227	.83536	.16464
42	13.7940	.82764	.17236
43	13.6604	.81962	.18038
44	13.5219	.81131	.18869
45	13.3781	.80269	.19731
46	13.2290	.79374	.20626
47	13.0746	.78448	.21552
48	12.9147	.77488	.22512
49	12.7496	.76498	.23502
50	12.5793	.75476	.24524
51	12.4039	.74423	.25577
52	12.2232	.73339	.26661
53	12.0367	.72220	.27780
54	11.8436	.71062	.28938
55	11.6432	.69859	.30141
56	11.4353	.68612	.31388
57	11.2200	.67320	.32680
58	10.9980	.65988	.34012
59	10.7703	.64622	.35378
60	10.5376	.63226	.36774
61	10.3005	.61803	.38197
62	10.0587	.60352	.39648
63	9.8118	.58871	.41129
64	9.5592	.57355	.42645
65	9.3005	.55803	.44197
66	9.0352	.54211	.45789
67	8.7639	.52583	.47417
68	8.4874	.50924	.49076
69	8.2068	.49241	.50759
70	7.9234	.47540	.52460
71	7.6371	.45823	.54177
72	7.3480	.44088	.55912
73	7.0568	.42341	.57659
74	6.7645	.40587	.59413
75	6.4721	.38833	.61167
76	6.1788	.37073	.62927
77	5.8845	.35307	.64693
78	5.5910	.33546	.66454
79	5.3018	.31811	.68189
80	5.0195	.30117	.69883
81	4.7482	.28489	.71511
82	4.4892	.26935	.73065
83	4.2398	.25439	.74561

TABLE A(2) —Continued

(1) Age	(2) Annuity	(3) Life estate	(4) Remainder
84	3.9927	.23956	.76044
85	3.7401	.22441	.77559
86	3.5016	.21010	.78990
87	3.2790	.19674	.80326
88	3.0719	.18431	.81569
89	2.8808	.17285	.82715
90	2.7058	.16241	.83759
91	2.5502	.15301	.84699
92	2.4116	.14470	.85530
93	2.2901	.13741	.86259
94	2.1839	.13103	.86897
95	2.0891	.12535	.87465
96	1.9997	.11998	.88002
97	1.9145	.11487	.88513
98	1.8331	.10999	.89001
99	1.7554	.10532	.89468
100	1.6812	.10087	.89913
101	1.6101	.09661	.90339
102	1.5416	.09250	.90750
103	1.4744	.08846	.91154
104	1.4065	.08439	.91561
105	1.3334	.08000	.92000
106	1.2452	.07471	.92529
107	1.1196	.06718	.93282
108	.9043	.05426	.94574
109	.4717	.02830	.97170

TABLE B

TABLE SHOWING THE PRESENT WORTH AT 6 PERCENT OF
AN ANNUITY FOR A TERM CERTAIN, OF AN INCOME
INTEREST FOR A TERM CERTAIN, AND OF A REMAINDER
INTEREST POSTPONED FOR A TERM CERTAIN

(1) Number of years	(2) Annuity	(3) Term certain	(4) Remainder
1	0.9434	0.056604	0.943396
2	1.8334	.110004	.889996
3	2.6730	.160381	.839619
4	3.4651	.207906	.792094
5	4.2124	.252742	.747258
6	4.9173	.295039	.704961
7	5.5824	.334943	.665057
8	6.2098	.372588	.627412
9	6.8017	.408102	.591898
10	7.3601	.441605	.558395
11	7.8869	.473212	.526788
12	8.3838	.503031	.496969
13	8.8527	.531161	.468839
14	9.2950	.557699	.442301
15	9.7122	.582735	.417265
16	10.1059	.606354	.393646
17	10.4773	.628636	.371364
18	10.8276	.649656	.350344
19	11.1581	.669487	.330513
20	11.4699	.688195	.311805
21	11.7641	.705845	.294155
22	12.0416	.722495	.277505
23	12.3034	.738203	.261797
24	12.5504	.753021	.246979
25	12.7834	.767001	.232999
26	13.0032	.780190	.219810
27	13.2105	.792632	.207368
28	13.4062	.804370	.195630
29	13.5907	.815443	.184557
30	13.7648	.825890	.174110
31	13.9291	.835745	.164255
32	14.0840	0.845043	0.154957
33	14.2302	.853814	.146186
34	14.3681	.862088	.137912
35	14.4982	.869895	.130105
36	14.6210	.877259	.122741
37	14.7368	.884207	.115793
38	14.8460	.890761	.109239
39	14.9491	.896944	.103056
40	15.0463	.902778	.097222
41	15.1380	.908281	.091719
42	15.2245	.913473	.086527
43	15.3062	.918370	.081630
44	15.3832	.922991	.077009
45	15.4558	.927350	.072650
46	15.5244	.931462	.068538

TABLE B—Continued

TABLE SHOWING THE PRESENT WORTH AT 6 PERCENT OF
AN ANNUITY FOR A TERM CERTAIN, OF AN INCOME
INTEREST FOR A TERM CERTAIN, AND OF A REMAINDER
INTEREST POSTPONED FOR A TERM CERTAIN

(1) Number of years	(2) Annuity	(3) Term certain	(4) Remainder
47	15.5890	.935342	.064658
48	15.6500	.939002	.060998
49	15.7076	.942454	.057546
50	15.7619	.945712	.054288
51	15.8131	.948785	.051215
52	15.8614	.951684	.048316
53	15.9070	.954418	.045582
54	15.9500	.956999	.043001
55	15.9905	.959433	.040567
56	16.0288	.961729	.038271
57	16.0649	.963895	.036105
58	16.0990	.965939	.034061
59	16.1311	.967867	.032133
60	16.1614	.969686	.030314

§ 25.2513-1 Gifts by husband or wife to third party considered as made one-half by each

(a) A gift made by one spouse to a person other than his (or her) spouse may, for the purpose of the gift tax, be considered as made one-half by his spouse, but only if at the time of the gift each spouse was a citizen or resident of the United States. For purposes of this section, an individual is to be considered as the spouse of another individual only if he was married to such individual at the time of the gift and does not remarry during the remainder of the calendar quarter (calendar year with respect to gifts made before January 1, 1971). For the definition of calendar quarter see § 25.-2502-1(c) (1).

(b) The provisions of this section will apply to gifts made during a particular calendar quarter (calendar year with respect to gifts made before January 1, 1971) only if both spouses signify their consent to treat all gifts made to third parties during that calendar quarter (or calendar year) by both spouses while married to each other as having been made one-half by each spouse. As to the manner and time for signifying consent, see § 25.-2513-2. Such consent, if signified with respect to any calendar quarter (or calendar year), is effective with respect to all gifts made to third parties during such calendar quarter or calendar year except as follows:

(1) If the consenting spouses were not married to each other during a portion of the calendar quarter or calendar year, the consent is not effective with respect to any gifts made during such portion of the calendar quarter or calendar year. Where the consent is signified by an executor or administrator of a deceased spouse, the consent is not effective with respect to gifts made by the surviving spouse during the portion of the calendar quarter or calendar year that his spouse was deceased.

(2) If either spouse was a nonresident not a citizen of the United States during any portion of the calendar quarter or calendar year, the consent is not effective with respect to any gift made during that portion of the calendar quarter or calendar year.

(3) The consent is not effective with respect to a gift by one spouse of a property interest over which he created in his spouse a general power of appointment (as defined in section 2514 (c)).

(4) If one spouse transferred property in part to his spouse and in part to third parties, the consent is effective with respect to the interest transferred to third parties only insofar as such interest is ascertainable at the time of the gift and hence severable from the interest transferred to his spouse. See § 25.2512-5 for the principles to be applied in the valuation of annuities, life estates, terms for years, remainders and reversions.

(5) The consent applies alike to gifts made by one spouse alone and to gifts made partly by each spouse, provided such gifts were to third parties and do not fall within any of the exceptions set forth in subparagraphs (1) through (4) of this paragraph. The consent may not be applied only to a portion of the property interest constituting such gifts. For example, a wife may not treat gifts made by her spouse from his separate property to third parties as having been made one-half by her if her spouse does not consent to treat gifts made by her to third parties during the same calendar quarter or calendar year as having been made one-half by him. If the consent is effectively signified on either the husband's return or the wife's return, all gifts made by the spouses to third parties (except as described in subparagraphs (1) through (4) of this paragraph), during the calendar quarter or calendar

year will be treated as having been made one-half by each spouse.

(c) If a husband and wife consent to have the gifts made to third party donees considered as made one-half by each spouse, and only one spouse makes gifts during the calendar quarter (calendar year with respect to gifts made before January 1, 1971), the other spouse is not required to file a gift tax return provided: (1) The total value of the gifts made to each third party donee since the beginning of the calendar year is not in excess of $6,000, and (2) no portion of the property transferred constitutes a gift of a future interest. If a transfer made by either spouse during the calendar quarter (or calendar year) to a third party represents a gift of a future interest in property and the spouses consent to have the gifts considered as made one-half by each, a gift tax return for such calendar quarter (or calendar year) must be filed by each spouse regardless of the value of the transfer. (See § 25.2503-3 for the definition of a future interest.)

. . . .

§ 25.2513-2 Manner and time of signifying consent

(a) (1) Consent to the application of the provisions of section 2513 with respect to a calendar quarter (a calendar year with respect to gifts made before January 1, 1971) shall, in order to be effective, be signified by both spouses. If both spouses file gift tax returns within the time for signifying consent, it is sufficient if—

(i) The consent of the husband is signified on the wife's return, and the consent of the wife is signified on the husband's return;

(ii) The consent of each spouse is signified on his own return; or

(iii) The consent of both spouses is signified on one of the returns.

If only one spouse files a gift tax return within the time provided for signifying consent, the consent of both spouses shall be signified on that return. However, wherever possible, the notice of the consent is to be shown on both returns and it is preferred that the notice be executed in the manner described in subdivision (i) of this subparagraph. The consent may be re-

voked only as provided in § 25.2513-3. If one spouse files more than one gift tax return for a calendar quarter (or a calendar year) on or before the due date of the return, the last return so filed shall, for the purpose of determining whether a consent has been signified, be considered as the return. (See § 25.6075-1 for the due date of a gift tax return.)

(2) Subject to the limitations of paragraph (b) of this section, the consent signified on a return filed for a calendar quarter will be effective for a previous calendar quarter of the same calendar year for which no return was filed because the gifts made during such previous calendar quarter did not exceed the annual exclusion provided by section 2503(b), if the gifts in such previous calendar quarter are listed on that return. Thus, for example, if A gave $2,000 to his son in the first quarter of 1972 (and filed no return because of section 2503(b)) and gave a further $4,000 to such son in the last quarter of the year, A and his spouse could signify consent to the application of section 2513 on the return filed for the fourth quarter and have it apply to the first quarter as well, provided that the $2,000 gift is listed on such return.

(b) (1) With respect to gifts made after December 31, 1970, the consent may be signified at any time following the close of the calendar quarter in which the gift was made, subject to the following limitations:

(i) The consent may not be signified after the 15th day of the second month following the close of such calendar quarter, unless before such 15th day, no return has been filed for such calendar quarter by either spouse, in which case the consent may not be signified after a return for such calendar quarter is filed by either spouse; and

(ii) The consent may not be signified after a notice of deficiency with respect to the tax for such calendar quarter has been sent to either spouse in accordance with section 6212(a).

. . . .

(c) The executor or administrator of a deceased spouse, or the guardian or committee of a legally incompetent spouse, as the case may be, may signify the consent.

(d) If the donor and spouse consent to the application of section 2513, the return or returns for the calendar quarter (calendar year with respect to gifts made before January 1, 1971) must set forth, to the extent provided thereon, information relative to the transfers made by each spouse.

§ 25.2513-3 Revocation of consent

(a) (1) With respect to gifts made after December 31, 1970, if the consent to the application of the provisions of section 2513 for a calendar quarter was effectively signified on or before the 15th day of the second month following the close of such calendar quarter, either spouse may revoke the consent by filing in duplicate a signed statement of revocation, but only if the statement is filed on or before such 15th day of the second month following the close of such calendar quarter. Therefore, a consent that was not effectively signified until after the 15th day of the second month following the close of the calendar quarter to which it applies may not be revoked. (See § 25.2502-1 (c) (1) for the definition of calendar quarter.)

(2) With respect to gifts made before January 1, 1971, if the consent to the application of the provisions of section 2513 for a calendar year was effectively signified on or before the 15th day of April following the close of the calendar year, either spouse may revoke the consent by filing in duplicate a signed statement of revocation, but only if the statement is filed on or before such 15th day of April. Therefore, a consent that was not effectively signified until after the 15th day of April following the close of the calendar year to which it applies may not be revoked.

(b) Except as provided in paragraph (b) of § 301.6091-1 of this chapter (relating to hand-carried documents), the statement referred to in paragraph (a) of this section shall be filed with the internal revenue officer with whom the gift tax return is required to be filed, or with whom the gift tax return would be required to be filed if a return were required.

§ 25.2513-4 Joint and several liability for tax

If consent to the application of the provisions of section 2513 is signified as provided in § 25.2513-2, and not revoked as provided in § 25.2513-3, the liability with respect to the entire gift tax of each spouse for such calendar quarter (calendar year with respect to gifts made before January 1, 1971) is joint and several. See paragraph (d) of § 25.2511-1. . . . .

§ 25.2514-1 Transfers under power of appointment

(a) Introductory. (1) Section 2514 treats the exercise of a general power of appointment created on or before October 21, 1942, as a transfer of property for purposes of the gift tax. The section also treats as a transfer of property the exercise or complete release of a general power of appointment created after October 21, 1942, and under certain circumstances the exercise of a power of appointment (not a general power of appointment) created after October 21, 1942, by the creation of another power of appointment. See paragraph (d) of § 25.2514-3. Under certain circumstances, also, the failure to exercise a power of appointment created after October 21, 1942, within a specified time, so that the power lapses, constitutes a transfer of property. Paragraphs (b) through (e) of this section contain definitions of certain terms used in §§ 25.2514-2 and 25.2514-3. See § 25.2514-2 for specific rules applicable to certain powers created on or before October 21, 1942. See § 25.2514-3 for specific rules applicable to powers created after October 21, 1942.

(b) Definition of "power of appointment"—(1) In general. The term "power of appointment" includes all powers which are in substance and effect powers of appointment received by the donee of the power from another person, regardless of the nomenclature used in creating the power and regardless of local property law connotations. For example, if a trust instrument provides that the beneficiary may appropriate or consume the principal of the trust, the power to consume or appropriate is a power of appointment. Similarly, a power given to a donee to affect the beneficial enjoyment of a trust property or its income by altering, amending or revoking the trust instrument or terminating the trust is a power of appointment. A power in a donee to remove or discharge a trustee and appoint himself may be a power of appointment. For example, if under the terms of a trust instrument, the trustee or his successor has the power to appoint the principal of the trust for the benefit of individuals including himself, and A, another person, has the unrestricted power to remove or discharge the trustee at any time and appoint any other person, including himself, A is considered as having a power of appointment. However, he would not be considered to have a power of appointment if he only had the power to appoint a successor, including himself, under limited conditions which did not exist at the time of exercise, release or lapse of the trustee's power, without an accompanying unrestricted power of removal. Similarly, a power to amend only the administrative provisions of a trust instrument, which cannot substantially affect the beneficial enjoyment of the trust property or income, is not a power of appointment. The mere power of management, investment, custody of assets, or the power to allocate receipts and disbursements as between income and principal, exercisable in a fiduciary capacity, whereby the holder has no power to enlarge or shift any of the beneficial interests therein except as an incidental consequence of the discharge of such fiduciary duties is not a power of appointment. Further, the right in a beneficiary of a trust to assent to a periodic accounting, thereby relieving the trustee from further accountability, is not a power of appointment if the right of assent does not consist of any power or right to enlarge or shift the beneficial interest of any beneficiary therein.

(2) **Relation to other sections.** For purposes of §§ 25.2514-1 through 25.2514-3, the term "power of appointment" does not include powers reserved by a donor to himself. No provision of section 2514 or of §§ 25.2514-1 through 25.2514-3 is to be construed as in any way limiting the application of any other section of the Internal Revenue Code or of these regulations. The power of the owner of a property interest already possessed by him to dispose of his interest, and nothing more, is not a power of appointment, and the interest is includible in the amount of his gifts to the extent it would be includible under section 2511 or other provisions of the Internal Revenue Code. For example, if a trust created by S provides for payment of the income to A for life with power in A to appoint the entire trust property by deed during her lifetime to a class consisting of her children, and a further power to dispose of the entire corpus by will to anyone, including her estate, and A exercises the inter vivos power in favor of her children, she has necessarily made a transfer of her income interest which constitutes a taxable gift under section 2511(a), without regard to section 2514. This transfer also results in a relinquishment of her general power to appoint by will, which constitutes a transfer under section 2514 if the power was created after October 21, 1942.

(3) **Powers over a portion of property.** If a power of appointment exists as to part of an entire group of assets or only over a limited interest in property, section 2514 applies only to such part or interest.

(c) **Definition of "general power of appointment"**—(1) **In general.** The term "general power of appointment" as defined in section 2514(c) means any power of appointment exercisable in favor of the person possessing the power (referred to as the "possessor"), his estate, his creditors, or the creditors of his estate, except (i) joint powers, to the extent provided in §§ 25.-2514-2 and 25.2514-3 and (ii) certain powers limited by an ascertainable standard, to the extent provided in subparagraph (2) of this paragraph. A power of appointment exercisable to meet the estate tax, or any other taxes, debts, or charges which are enforceable against the possessor or his estate, is included within the meaning of a power of appointment exercisable in favor of the possessor, his estate, his creditors, or the creditors of his estate. A power of appointment exercisable for the purpose of discharging a legal obligation of the possessor or for his pecuniary benefit is considered a power of appointment exercisable in favor of the possessor or his creditors. However, for purposes of §§ 25.2514-1 through 25.2514-3, a power of appointment not otherwise considered to be a general power of appointment is not treated as a general power of appointment merely by reason of the fact that an appointee may, in fact, be a creditor of the possessor or his estate. A power of appointment is not a general power if by its terms it is either—

(a) Exercisable only in favor of one or more designated persons or classes other than the possessor or his creditors, or the possessor's estate, or the creditors of his estate, or

(b) Expressly not exercisable in favor of the possessor or his creditors, the possessor's estate, or the creditors of his estate.

A beneficiary may have two powers under the same instrument, one of which is a general power of appointment and the other of which is not. For example, a beneficiary may have a general power to withdraw a limited portion of trust corpus during his life, and a further power exercisable during his lifetime to appoint the corpus among his children. The later power is not a general power of appointment (but its exercise may result in the exercise of the former power; see paragraph (d) of this section).

(2) Powers limited by an ascertainable standard. A power to consume, invade, or appropriate income or corpus, or both, for the benefit of the possessor which is limited by an ascertainable standard relating to the health, education, support, or maintenance of the possessor is, by reason of section 2514(c)(1), not a general power of appointment. A power is limited by such a standard if the extent of the possessor's duty to exercise and not to exercise the power is reasonably measurable in terms of his needs for health, education, or support (or any combination of them). As used in this subparagraph, the words "support" and "maintenance" are synonymous and their meaning is not limited to the bare necessities of life. A power to use property for the comfort, welfare, or happiness of the holder of the power is not limited by the requisite standard. Examples of powers which are limited by the requisite standard are powers exercisable for the holder's "support," "support in reasonable comfort," "maintenance in health and reasonable comfort," "support in his accustomed manner of living," "education, including college and professional education," "health," and "medical, dental, hospital and nursing expenses and expenses of invalidism." In determining whether a power is limited by an ascertainable standard, it is immaterial whether the beneficiary is required to exhaust his other income before the power can be exercised.

· · · · ·

(d) Definition of "exercise." Whether a power of appointment is in fact exercised may depend upon local law. However, regardless of local law, a power of appointment is considered as exercised for purposes of section 2514 even though the exercise is in favor of the taker in default of appointment, and irrespective of whether the appointed interest and the interest in default of appointment are identical, or whether the appointee renounces any right to take under the appointment. A power of appointment is also considered as exercised even though the disposition cannot take effect until the occurrence of an event after the exercise takes place, if the exercise is irrevocable and, as of the time of the exercise, the condition was not impossible of occurrence. For example, if property is left in trust to A for life, with a power in A to appoint the remainder by an instrument filed with the trustee during his life, and A exercises his power by appointing the remainder to B in the event that B survives A, A is considered to have exercised his power if the exercise was irrevocable. Furthermore, if a person holds both a presently exercisable general power of appointment and a presently exercisable nongeneral power of appointment over the same property, the exercise of the nongeneral power is considered the exercise of the general power only to the extent that immediately after the exercise of the nongeneral power the amount of money or property subject to being transferred by the exercise of the general power is decreased. For example, assume A has a noncumulative annual power to withdraw the greater of $5,000 or 5 percent of the value of a trust having a value of $300,000 and a lifetime nongeneral power to appoint all or a portion of the trust corpus to A's child or grandchildren. If A exercises the nongeneral power by appointing $150,000 to A's child, the exercise of the nongeneral power is treated as the exercise of the general power to the extent of $7,500 (maximum exercise of general power before the exercise of the nongeneral power, 5% of $300,000 or $15,000, less maximum exercise of the general power after the exercise of the nongeneral power, 5% of $150,000 or $7,500).

(e) Time of creation of power. A power of appointment created by will is, in general, considered as created on the date of the testator's death. However, section 2514(f) provides that a power of appointment created by a will executed on or before October 21, 1942, is considered a power created on or before that date if the testator dies before July 1, 1949, without having republished the will, by codicil or otherwise, after October 21, 1942. A power of appointment created by an inter vivos instrument is considered as created on the date the instrument takes effect. Such a power is not considered as created at some future date merely because it is not exercisable on the date the instrument takes effect, or because it is revocable, or because the identity of its holders is not ascertainable until after the date the instrument takes effect. However, if the holder of a power exercises it by creating a second power, the second power is considered as created at the time of the exercise of the first. The application of this paragraph may be illustrated by the following examples:

Example (1). A created a revocable trust before October 22, 1942, providing for payment of income to B for life with remainder as B shall appoint by deed or will. Even though A dies after October 21, 1942, without having exercised his power of revocation, B's power of appointment is considered a power created before October 22, 1942.

Example (2). C created an irrevocable inter vivos trust before October 22, 1942, naming T as trustee and providing for payment of income to D for life with remainder to E. T was given the power to pay corpus to D and the power to appoint a successor trustee. If T resigns after October 21, 1942, and appoints D as successor trustee, D is considered to have a power of appointment created before October 22, 1942.

Example (3). F created an irrevocable inter vivos trust before October 22, 1942, providing for payment of income to G for life with remainder as G shall appoint by deed or will, but in default of appointment income to H for life with remainder as H shall appoint by deed or will. If G died after October 21, 1942, without having exercised his power of appointment, H's power of appointment is considered a power created before October 22, 1942, even though it was only a contingent interest until G's death.

Example (4). If in example (3) above G had exercised by will his power of appointment, by creating a similar power in J, J's power of appointment would be considered a power created after October 21, 1942.

§ 25.2514–3 Powers of appointment created after October 21, 1942

(a) In general. The exercise, release, or lapse (except as provided in paragraph (c) of this section) of a general power of appointment created after October 21, 1942, is deemed to be a transfer of property by the individual possessing the power. The exercise of a power of appointment that is not a general power is considered to be a transfer if it is exercised to create a further power under certain circumstances (see paragraph (d) of this section). See paragraph (c) of § 25.2514–1 for the definition of various terms used in this section. See paragraph (b) of this section for the rules applicable to determine the extent to which joint powers created after October 21, 1942, are to be treated as general powers of appointment.

(b) Joint powers created after October 21, 1942. The treatment of a power of appointment created after October 21, 1942, which is exercisable only in conjunction with another person is governed by section 2514(c) (3), which provides as follows:

(1) Such a power is not considered as a general power of appointment if it is not exercisable by the possessor except with the consent or joinder of the creator of the power.

(2) Such power is not considered as a general power of appointment if it is not exercisable by the possessor except with the consent or joinder of a person having a substantial interest in the property subject to the power which is adverse to the exercise of the power in favor of the possessor, his estate, his creditors, or the creditors of his estate.

An interest adverse to the exercise of a power is considered as substantial if its value in relation to the total value of the property subject to the power is not insignificant. For this purpose, the interest is to be valued in accordance with the actuarial principles set forth in § 25.2512–5 or, if it is not susceptible to valuation under those provisions, in accordance with the general principles set forth in § 25.2512–1. A taker in default of appointment under a power has an interest which is adverse to an exercise of the power. A coholder of the power has no adverse interest merely because of his joint possession of the power nor merely because he is a permissible appointee under a power. However, a coholder of a power is considered as having an adverse interest where he may possess the power after the possessor's death and may exercise it at that time in favor of himself, his estate, his creditors, or the creditors of his estate. Thus, for example, if X, Y, and Z held a power jointly to appoint among a group of persons which includes themselves and if on the death of X the power will pass to Y and Z jointly, then Y and Z are considered to have interests adverse to the exercise of the power in favor of X. Similarly, if on Y's death the power will pass to Z, Z is considered to have an interest adverse to the exercise of the power in favor of Y. The application of this subparagraph may be further illustrated by the following examples in each of which it is assumed that the value of the interest in question is substantial:

Example (1). The taxpayer and R are trustees of a trust under which the income is to be paid to the taxpayer for life and then to M for life, and R is remainderman. The trustees have power to distribute corpus to the taxpayer. Since R's interest is substantially adverse to an exercise of the power in favor of the taxpayer, the latter does not have a general power of appointment. If M and the taxpayer were trustees, M's interest would likewise be adverse.

Example (2). The taxpayer and L are trustees of a trust under which the income is to be paid to L for life and then to M for life and the taxpayer is remainderman. The trustees have power to distribute corpus to the taxpayer during L's life. Since L's interest is adverse to an exercise of the power in favor of the taxpayer, the taxpayer does not have a general power of appointment. If the taxpayer and M were trustees, M's interest would likewise be adverse.

Example (3). The taxpayer and L are trustees of a trust under which the income is to be paid to L for life. The trustees can designate whether corpus is to be distributed to the taxpayer or to A after L's death. L's interest is not adverse to an exercise of the power in favor of the taxpayer, and the taxpayer therefore has a general power of appointment.

(3) A power which is exercisable only in conjunction with another person, and which after application of the rules set forth in subparagraphs (1) and (2) of this paragraph, constitutes a general power of appointment, will be treated as though the holders of the power who are permissible appointees of the property were joint owners of property subject to the power. The possessor, under this rule, will be treated as possessed of a general power of appointment over an aliquot share of the property to be determined with reference to the number of joint holders, including the possessor, who (or whose estates or creditors) are permissible appointees. Thus, for example, if X, Y, and Z hold an unlimited power jointly to appoint among a group of persons, including themselves, but on the death of X the power does not pass to Y and Z jointly, then Y and Z are not considered to have interests adverse to the exercise of the power in favor of X. In this case, X is considered to possess a general power of appointment as to one-third of the property subject to the power.

(c) Partial releases, lapses, and disclaimers of general powers created after October 21, 1942. (1) The general principles set forth in § 25.2511–2 for determining whether a donor of property (or of a property right or interest) has divested himself of all or any portion of his interest therein to the extent necessary to effect a completed gift are applicable in determining whether a partial release of a power of appointment constitutes a taxable gift. Thus, if a general power of appointment is partially released so that thereafter the donor may still appoint among a limited class of persons not including himself the partial release does not effect a complete gift, since the possessor of the power has retained the right to designate the ultimate beneficiaries of the property over which he holds the power and since it is only the termination of such control which completes a gift.

(2) If a general power of appointment created after October 21, 1942, was partially released prior to June 1, 1951, so that it no longer represented a general power of appointment, as defined in paragraph (c) of § 25.2514-1, the subsequent exercise, release, or lapse of the partially released power at any time thereafter will not constitute the exercise or release of a general power of appointment. For example, assume that A created a trust in 1943 under which B possessed a general power of appointment. By an instrument executed in 1948 such general power of appointment was reduced in scope by B to an excepted power. The inter vivos exercise in 1955, or in any calendar year or calendar quarter thereafter, of such excepted power is not considered an exercise or release of a general power of appointment for purposes of the gift tax. For the definition of calendar quarter see § 25.2502-1(c)(1).

(3) If a general power of appointment created after October 21, 1942, was partially released after May 31, 1951, the subsequent exercise, release or a lapse of the power at any time thereafter, will constitute the exercise or release of a general power of appointment for gift tax purposes.

(4) A release of a power of appointment need not be formal or express in character. For example, the failure to exercise a general power of appointment created after October 21, 1942, within a specified time so that the power lapses, constitutes a release of the power. In any case where the possessor of a general power of appointment is incapable of validly exercising or releasing a power, by reason of minority, or otherwise, and the power may not be validly exercised or released on his behalf, the failure to exercise or release the power is not a lapse of the power. If a trustee has in his capacity as trustee a power which is considered as a general power of appointment, his resignation or removal as trustee will cause a lapse of his power. However, section 2514(e) provides that a lapse during any calender year is considered as a release so as to be subject to the gift tax only to the extent that the property which could have been appointed by exercise of the lapsed power of appointment exceeds the greater of (i) $5,000, or (ii) 5 percent of the aggregate value, at the time of the lapse, of the assets out of which, or the proceeds of which, the exercise of the lapsed power could be satisfied. For example, if an individual has a noncumulative right to withdraw $10,000 a year from the principal of a trust fund, the failure to exercise this right of withdrawal in a particular year will not constitute a gift if the fund at the end of the year equals or exceeds $200,000. If, however, at the end of the particular year the fund should be worth only $100,000, the failure to exercise the power will be considered a gift to the extent of $5,000, the excess of $10,000 over 5 percent of a fund of $100,000. Where the failure to exercise a power, such as a right of withdrawal, occurs in more than a single year, the value of the taxable transfer will be determined separately for each year.

. . . . .

(d) Creation of another power in certain cases. Paragraph (d) of section 2514 provides that there is a transfer for purposes of the gift tax of the value of property (or of property rights or interests) with respect to which a power of appointment, which is not a general power of appointment, created after October 21, 1942, is exercised by creating another power of appointment which, under the terms of the instruments creating and exercising the first power and under applicable local law, can be validly exercised so as to (1) postpone the vesting of any estate or interest in the property for a period ascertainable without regard to the date of the creation of the first power, or (2) (if the applicable rule against perpetuities is stated in terms of suspension of ownership or of the power of alienation, rather than of vesting) suspend the absolute ownership or the power of alienation of the property for a period ascertainable without regard to the date of the creation of the first power. For the purpose of section 2514(d), the value of the property subject to the second power of appointment is considered to be its value unreduced by any precedent or subsequent interest which is not subject to the second power. Thus, if a donor has a power to appoint $100,000 among a group consisting of his children or grandchildren and during his lifetime exercises the power by making an outright appointment of $75,000 and by giving one appointee a power to appoint $25,000, no more than $25,000 will be considered a gift under section 2514(d). If, however, the donor appoints the income from the entire fund to a beneficiary for life with power in the beneficiary to appoint the remainder, the entire $100,000 will be considered a gift under section 2514(d), if the exercise of the second power can validly postpone the vesting of any estate or interest in the property or can suspend the absolute ownership or power of alienation of the property for a period ascertainable without regard to the date of the creation of the first power.

(e) **Examples.** The application of this section may be further illustrated by the following examples in each of which it is assumed, unless otherwise stated, that S has transferred property in trust after October 21, 1942, with the remainder payable to R at L's death, and that neither L nor R has any interest in or power over the enjoyment of the trust property except as is indicated separately in each example:

Example (1). The income is payable to L for life. L has the power to cause the income to be paid to R. The exercise of the right constitutes the making of a transfer of property under section 2511. L's power does not constitute a power of appointment since it is only a power to dispose of his income interest, a right otherwise possessed by him.

Example (2). The income is to be accumulated during L's life. L has the power to have the income distributed to himself. If L's power is limited by an ascertainable standard (relating to health, etc.) as defined in paragraph (c)(2) of § 25.2514-1, the lapse of such power will not constitute a transfer of property for gift tax purposes. If L's power is not so limited, its lapse or release during L's lifetime may constitute a transfer of property for gift tax purposes. See especially paragraph (c)(4) of § 25.2514-3.

Example (3). The income is to be paid to L for life. L has a power, exercisable at any time, to cause the corpus to be distributed to himself. L has a general power of appointment over the remainder interest, the release of which constitutes a transfer for gift tax purposes of the remainder interest. If in this example L had a power to cause the corpus to be distributed only to X, L would have a power of appointment which is not a general

power of appointment, the exercise or release of which would not constitute a transfer of property for purposes of the gift tax. Although the exercise or release of the nongeneral power is not taxable under this section, see § 25.2514-1(b)(2) for the gift tax consequences of the transfer of the life income interest.

Example (4). The income is payable to L for life. R has the right to cause the corpus to be distributed to L at any time. R's power is not a power of appointment, but merely a right to dispose of his remainder interest, a right already possessed by him. In such a case, the exercise of the right constitutes the making of a transfer of property under section 2511 of the value, if any, of his remainder interest. See paragraph (e) of § 25.2511-1.

Example (5). The income is to be paid to L. R has the right to appoint the corpus to himself at any time. R's general power of appointment over the corpus includes a general power to dispose of L's income interest therein. The lapse or release of R's general power over the income interest during his life may constitute the making of a transfer of property. See especially paragraph (c)(4) of § 25.-2514-3.

§ 25.2516-1 Certain property settlements

(a) Section 2516 provides that transfers of property or interests in property made under the terms of a written agreement between spouses in settlement of their marital or property rights are deemed to be for an adequate and full consideration in money or money's worth and, therefore, exempt from the gift tax (whether or not such agreement is approved by a divorce decree), if the spouses obtain a final decree of divorce from each other within two years after entering into the agreement.

. . . .

§ 25.2516-2 Transfers in settlement of support obligations

Transfers to provide a reasonable allowance for the support of children (including legally adopted children) of a marriage during minority are not subject to the gift tax if made pursuant to an agreement which satisfies the requirements of section 2516.

§ 25.2517-1 Employees' annuities

(a) **In general.** (1) Section 2517 provides an exception to the general rule of section 2511 by exempting from gift tax all or part of the value of certain annuities or other payments for the benefit of employees' surviving beneficiaries. Under the general rule in section 2511, where an employee has an unqualified right to an annuity but takes a lesser annuity with the provision that upon his death a survivor annuity or other payment will be paid to his designated beneficiary, the employee has made a gift to the beneficiary at the time he gives up his power to deprive the beneficiary of the survivor annuity or other payment. See especially § 25.2511-1(h)(10). The making of such a gift by the employee may be accomplished in three principal ways:

(i) By irrevocably electing to take the reduced annuity and designating the individual who is to receive the survivor annuity or other payment. In this case the gift is made at the time the election and designation are irrevocably made.

(ii) By permitting a prior revocable election of a reduced annuity and designation of beneficiary to become irrevocable through failure to revoke during the period during which revocation could be made. In this case the gift is made at the time the prior election and designation become irrevocable.

(iii) By permitting an option to expire under which the employee could, by exercising the option, have defeated the beneficiary's interest in the survivor annuity or other payment, and thereby regain for himself the right to a full annuity. In this case the gift is made at the time the employee permits the option to expire.

The value of the gift is the value, on the date of the gift, of the survivor annuity or other payment, computed in accordance with the principles set forth in §§ 25.2512-1, 25.2512-5, and 25.2512-6. It should be noted that such a gift is a gift of a future interest within the contemplation of § 25.2503-3 and no part thereof may be excluded in determining the total amount of gifts made during the calendar quarter (calendar year with respect to gifts made before January 1, 1971). See § 25.2502-1(c)(1) for the definition of calendar quarter.

(2) Section 2517 exempts from gift tax all or a portion of the value of the annuities or other payments described in subparagraph (1) of this paragraph which otherwise would be considered as gifts by employees to their beneficiaries. See paragraph (b) of this section for a complete description of the annuities and other payments to which the exemption applies. Also see paragraph (c) of this section for the portion of the annuity or other payment which is to be excluded in those cases where the annuity or other payment is attributable to payments or contributions made by both the employee and the employer. In the case of an annuity or other payment payable under an employees' trust or under a retirement annuity contract described in paragraph (b)(1)(i) or (ii) of this section, the exemption applies if the gift would otherwise be considered as having been made on or after January 1, 1955. In the case of an annuity or other payment payable under a retirement annuity contract described in paragraph (b)(1)(iii) of this section, the exclusion applies if the gift would otherwise be considered as having been made on or after January 1, 1958.

(b) **Annuities or other payments to which section 2517 applies.** (1) Except to the extent provided otherwise in paragraph (c) of this section, section 2517 exempts from transfers subject to the gift tax the value of an annuity or other payment which, upon the death of an employee, will become payable to the employee's beneficiary under:

(i) An employees' trust (or under a contract purchased by an employees' trust) forming part of a pension, stock bonus or profit-sharing plan which, at the time of such exercise or nonexercise, or at the time of termination of the plan if earlier, met the requirements of section 401(a);

(ii) A retirement annuity contract purchased by an employer (and not by an employees' trust) pursuant to a plan which, at the time of such exercise or nonexercise, or at the time of termination of the plan if earlier, was a plan described in section 403(a);

(iii) A retirement annuity contract purchased for an employee by an employer which is an organization referred to in section 170(b)(1)(A)(ii) or (vi) or which is a religious organization (other than a trust) and is exempt from tax under section 501(a);

(iv) With respect to calendar years after 1965, an annuity under chapter 73 of title 10 of the United States Code (10 U.S.C. 1431, et seq.);

(v) With respect to transfers made after December 31, 1976, an individual retirement account described in section 408(a), an individual retirement annuity described in section 408(b), or a retirement bond described in section 409(a) (an "individual retirement plan"); or

(vi) With respect to transfers made after December 31, 1962, a bond purchase plan described in section 405.

(2) The term "annuity or other payment" as used in this section, has reference to one or more payments extending over any period of time. The payments may be equal or unequal, conditional or unconditional, periodic or sporadic. For purposes of this section, the term "employee" includes a former employee, and in the case of an individual retirement plan described in subparagraph (1)(v) of this paragraph, means the individual for whose benefit the plan was established or purchased. The application of this paragraph may be illustrated by the following example:

Example. Pursuant to a pension plan, the employer made contributions to a trust which was to provide each employee, upon his retirement at age 60, with an annuity for life, and which contained a provision for designating either before or after retirement, a surviving beneficiary. No contributions under the plan were made by the employee. At the time of designating the surviving beneficiary (January 20, 1955), the pension trust formed part of a plan meeting the requirements of section 401(a). Assume that an employee made an irrevocable election whereby he would receive a lesser annuity, and after his death, annuity payments would be continued to his wife. Since the wife was designated annuitant under a qualified pension plan, no part of the value of such annuity is includible in the total amount of gifts for the calendar year by reason of the provisions of section 2517.

(c) Limitation on amount excludable from gift. (1) In the case of a plan or annuity contract described in paragraph (b)(1)(i), (ii), (iii) or (vi) of this section, if an annuity or other payment payable thereunder is attributable to payments or contributions made by both the employee and the employer, the exclusion is limited to that proportion of the value on the date of the gift (see paragraph (a)(1) of this section) of the annuity or other payment which the employer's contribution (or a contribution made on the employer's behalf) to the plan on the employee's account bears to the total contributions to the plan on the employee's account. In applying this ratio—

(i) Payments or contributions made by the employer toward the purchase of an annuity contract described in paragraph (b)(1)(iii) of this section are considered to be employee contributions to the extent that the contributions are not, or were not, excludable from the employee's gross income under section 403(b).

(ii) For transfers made before January 1, 1977, payments or contributions made to a plan described in paragraph (b)(1)(i), (ii) or (vi) of this section on behalf of an individual for a period for which the individual was self-employed, within the meaning of section 401(c)(1), with respect to the plan are considered payments or contributions made by the employee.

(iii) For transfers made after December 31, 1976, however, payments or contributions made under a plan described in paragraph (b)(1)(i), (ii) or (vi) of this section on behalf of such a self-employed individual are considered employer contributions to the extent that they are, or were, deductible under section 404 or 405(c), and are considered employee contributions to the extent that they are not, or were not, so deductible.

(iv) In the case of a plan described in paragraph (b)(1)(i) or (ii) of this section, a rollover contribution described in section 402(a)(5), 403(a)(4), 408(d)(3)(A)(ii) or 409(b)(3)(C) is considered an amount contributed by the employer.

(v) In the case of an annuity contract described in paragraph (b)(1)(iii) of this section, a rollover contribution described in section 403(b)(8) is considered an amount contributed by the employer.

(vi) In the case of a plan described in paragraph (b)(1)(i), (ii) or (vi) of this section, an amount includable in the gross income of an employee under section 1379(b) (relating to shareholder-beneficiaries under certain plans) is considered an amount paid or contributed by the employee.

(vii) In the case of an annuity described in paragraph (b)(1)(iv) of this section, amounts paid or contributed by the employee include only amounts deposited by the employee under section 1438 or 1452(d) of Title 10 of the United States Code.

. . . .

§ 25.2523(b)-1 Life estate or other terminable interest

(a) **In general.** (1) The provisions of section 2523(b) generally prevent the allowance of the marital deduction with respect to certain property interests (referred to generally as "terminable interests," defined in subparagraph (3) of this paragraph), transferred to the donee spouse under the circumstances described in subparagraph (2) of this paragraph, unless the transfer comes within one of the exceptions set forth in § 25.2523(d)-1, relating to certain joint interests, or § 25.2523(e)-1, relating to certain life estates with powers of appointment.

(2) If a donor transfers a terminable interest in property to the donee spouse, the marital deduction is disallowed with respect to the transfer if the donor spouse also—

(i) Transferred an interest in the same property to another donee (see paragraph (b) of this section), or

(ii) Retained an interest in the same property in himself (see paragraph (c) of this section), or

(iii) Retained a power to appoint an interest in the same property (see paragraph (d) of this section).

Notwithstanding the preceding sentence, the marital deduction is disallowed under these circumstances only if the other donee, the donor, or the possible appointee, may, by reason of the transfer or retention, possess or enjoy any part of the property after the termination or failure of the interest therein transferred to the donee spouse.

(3) For purposes of this section, a distinction is to be drawn between "property," as such term is used in section 2523, and an "interest in property." The "property" referred to is the underlying property in which various interests exist; each such interest is not, for this purpose, to be considered as "property." A "terminable interest" in property is an interest which will terminate or fail on the lapse of time or on the occurrence or failure to occur of some contingency. Life estates, terms for years, annuities, patents, and copyrights are therefore terminable interests. However, a bond, note, or similar contractual obligation, the discharge of which would not have the effect of an annuity or term for years, is not a terminable interest.

(b) **Interest in property which another donee may possess or enjoy.** (1) Section 2523(b) provides that no marital deduction shall be allowed with respect to the transfer to the donee spouse of a "terminable interest" in property, in case—

(i) The donor transferred (for less than an adequate and full consideration in money or money's worth) an interest in the same property to any person other than the donee spouse (or the estate of such spouse), and

(ii) By reason of such transfer, such person (or his heirs or assigns) may possess or enjoy any part of such property after the termination or failure of the interest therein transferred to the donee spouse.

(2) In determining whether the donor transferred an interest in property to any person other than the donee spouse, it is immaterial whether the transfer to the person other than the donee spouse was made at the same time as the transfer to such spouse, or at any earlier time.

(3) Except as provided in § 25.2523 (e)-1, if at the time of the transfer it is impossible to ascertain the particular person or persons who may receive a property interest transferred by the donor, such interest is considered as transferred to a person other than the donee spouse for the purpose of section 2523(b). This rule is particularly applicable in the case of the transfer of a property interest by the donor subject to a reserved power. See § 25.2511-2. Under this rule, any property interest over which the donor reserved a power to revest the beneficial title in himself, or over which the donor reserved the power to name new beneficiaries or to change the interest of the beneficiaries

as between themselves, is for the purpose of section 2523(b), considered as transferred to a "person other than the donee spouse." The following examples illustrate the application of the provisions of this subparagraph:

(i) If a donor transferred property in trust naming his wife as the irrevocable income beneficiary for 10 years, and providing that, upon the expiration of that term, the corpus should be distributed among his wife and children in such proportions as the trustee should determine, the right to the corpus, for the purpose of the marital deduction, is considered as transferred to a "person other than the donee spouse."

(ii) If, in the above example, the donor had provided that, upon the expiration of the 10-year term, the corpus was to be paid to his wife, but also reserved the power to revest such corpus in himself, the right to corpus, for the purpose of the marital deduction, is considered as transferred to a "person other than the donee spouse."

(4) The term "person other than the donee spouse" includes the possible unascertained takers of a property interest, as, for example, the members of a class to be ascertained in the future. As another example, assume that the donor created a power of appointment over a property interest, which does not come within the purview of § 25.2523(e)-1. In such a case, the term "person other than the donee spouse" refers to the possible appointees and takers in default (other than the spouse) of such property interest.

(5) An exercise or release at any time by the donor (either alone or in conjunction with any person) of a power to appoint an interest in property, even though not otherwise a transfer by him is considered as a transfer by him in determining, for the purpose of section 2523(b), whether he transferred an interest in such property to a person other than the donee spouse.

(6) The following examples illustrate the application of this paragraph. In each example it is assumed that the property interest which the donor transferred to a person other than the donee spouse was not transferred for an adequate and full consideration in money or money's worth:

(i) H (the donor) transferred real property to W (his wife) with remainder to A and his heirs. No marital deduction may be taken with respect to the interest transferred to W, since it will terminate upon her death and A (or his heirs or assigns) will thereafter possess or enjoy the property.

(ii) H transferred property for the benefit of W and A. The income was payable to W for life and upon her death the principal was to be distributed to A or his issue. However, if A should die without issue, leaving W surviving, the principal was then to be distributed to W. No marital deduction may be taken with respect to the interest transferred to W, since it will terminate in the event of her death if A or his issue survive, and A or his issue will thereafter possess or enjoy the property.

(iii) H purchased for $100,000 a life annuity for W. If the annuity payments made during the life of W should be less than $100,000, further payments were to be made to A. No marital deduction may be taken with respect to the interest transferred to W, since A may possess or enjoy a part of the property following the termination of W's interest. If, however, the contract provided for no continuation of payments, and provided for no refund upon the death of W, or provided that any refund was to go to the estate of W, then a marital deduction may be taken with respect to the gift.

(iv) H transferred property to A for life with remainder to W provided W survives A, but if W predeceases A, the property is to pass to B and his heirs. No marital deduction may be taken with respect to the interest transferred to W.

(v) H transferred real property to A, reserving the right to the rentals of the property for a term of 20 years. H later transferred the right to the remaining rentals to W. No marital deduction may be taken with respect to the interest since it will terminate upon the expiration of the balance of the 20-year term and A will thereafter possess or enjoy the property.

(vi) H transferred a patent to W and A as tenants in common. In this case, the interest of W will terminate upon the expiration of the term of the patent, but possession and enjoyment of the property by A must necessarily cease at the same time. Therefore, since A's possession or enjoyment cannot outlast the termination of W's interest, the provisions of section 2523(b) do not disallow the marital deduction with respect to the interest.

(c) Interest in property which the donor may possess or enjoy. (1) Section 2523(b) provides that no marital deduction is allowed with respect to the transfer to the donee spouse of a "terminable interest" in property, if—

(i) The donor retained in himself an interest in the same property, and

(ii) By reason of such retention, the donor (or his heirs or assigns) may possess or enjoy any part of the property after the termination or failure of the interest transferred to the donee spouse. . . . .

(2) In general, the principles illustrated by the examples under paragraph (b) of this section are applicable in determining whether the marital deduction may be taken with respect to a property interest transferred to the donee spouse subject to the retention by the donor of an interest in the same property. The application of this paragraph may be further illustrated by the following example:

Example. The donor purchased three annuity contracts for the benefit of his wife and himself. The first contract provided for payments to the wife for life, with refund to the donor in case the aggregate payments made to the wife were less than the cost of the contract. The second contract provided for payments to the donor for life, and then to the wife for life if she survived the donor. The third contract provided for payments to the donor and his wife for their joint lives and then to the survivor of them for life. No marital deduction may be taken with respect to the gifts resulting from the purchases of the contracts since, in the case of each contract, the donor may possess or enjoy a part of the property after the termination or failure of the interest transferred to the wife.

(d) Interest in property over which the donor retained a power to appoint. (1) Section 2523(b) provides that no marital deduction is allowed with respect to the transfer to the donee spouse of a "terminable interest" in property if—

(i) The donor had, immediately after the transfer, a power to appoint an interest in the same property, and

(ii) The donor's power was exercisable (either alone or in conjunction with any person) in such manner that the appointee may possess or enjoy any part of the property after the termination or failure of the interest transferred to the donee spouse.

(2) For the purposes of section 2523 (b), the donor is to be considered as having, immediately after the transfer to the donee spouse, such a power to appoint even though the power cannot be exercised until after the lapse of time, upon the occurrence of an event or contingency, or upon the failure of an event or contingency to occur. It is immaterial whether the power retained by the donor was a taxable power of appointment under section 2514.

(3) The principles illustrated by the examples under paragraph (b) of this section are generally applicable in determining whether the marital deduction may be taken with respect to a property interest transferred to the donee spouse subject to retention by the donor of a power to appoint an interest in the same property. The application of this paragraph may be further illustrated by the following example:

Example. The donor, having a power of appointment over certain property, appointed a life estate to his spouse. No marital deduction may be taken with respect to such transfer, since, if the retained power to appoint the remainder interest is exercised, the appointee thereunder may possess or enjoy the property after the termination or failure of the interest taken by the donee spouse.

§ 25.2523(c)-1 Interest in unidentified assets

(a) Section 2523(c) provides that if an interest passing to a donee spouse may be satisfied out of a group of assets (or their proceeds) which include a particular asset that would be a nondeductible interest if it passed from the donor to his spouse, the value of the interest passing to the spouse is reduced, for the purpose of the marital deduction, by the value of the particular asset.

(b) In order for this section to apply, two circumstances must coexist, as follows:

(1) The property interest transferred to the donee spouse must be payable out of a group of assets. An example of a property interest payable out of a group

of assets is a right to a share of the corpus of a trust upon its termination.

(2) The group of assets out of which the property interest is payable must include one or more particular assets which, if transferred by the donor to the donee spouse, would not qualify for the marital deduction. Therefore, section 2523(c) is not applicable merely because a group of assets includes a terminable interest, but would only be applicable if the terminable interest were nondeductible under the provisions of § 25.2523(b)-1.

(c) If the circumstances in the preceding paragraph are both present, the marital deduction with respect to such property interest may not exceed one-half of the excess, if any, of its value over the aggregate value of the particular asset or assets which, if transferred to the donee spouse, would not qualify for the marital deduction. The application of this section may be illustrated by the following example:

Example. H was absolute owner of a rental property and on July 1, 1950, transferred it to A by gift, reserving the income for a period of 20 years. On July 1, 1955, he created a trust to last for a period of 10 years. H was to receive the income from the trust and at the termination of the trust the trustee is to turn over to H's wife, W, property having a value of $100,000. The trustee has absolute discretion in deciding which properties in the corpus he shall turn over to W in satisfaction of the gift to her. The trustee received two items of property from H. Item (1) consisted of shares of corporate stock. Item (2) consisted of the right to receive the income from the rental property during the unexpired portion of the 20-year term. Assume that at the termination of the trust on July 1, 1965, the value of the right to the rental income for the then unexpired term of 5 years (item (2)) will be $30,000. Since item (2) is a nondeductible interest and the trustee can turn it over to W in partial satisfaction of her gift, only $70,000 of the $100,000 receivable by her on July 1, 1965, will be considered as property with respect to which a marital deduction is allowable. The present value on July 1, 1955, of the right to receive $70,000 at the end of 10 years is $49,624.33 ($70,000 × 0.708919, as found in Table II of § 25.2512-5). The value of the property qualifying for the marital deduction, therefore,

is $49,624.33 and a marital deduction is allowed for one-half of that amount, or $24,812.17.

§ 25.2524-1 Extent of deductions

Under the provisions of section 2524, the charitable deduction provided for in section 2522 and the marital deduction provided for in section 2523 are allowable only to the extent that the gifts, with respect to which those deductions are authorized, are included in the "total amount of gifts" made during the calendar quarter (with respect to gifts made after December 31, 1970) or calendar year (with respect to gifts made before January 1, 1971), computed as provided in section 2503 and § 25.-2503-1 (i. e., the total gifts less exclusions). The following examples (in both of which it is assumed that the donor has previously utilized his entire $30,000 specific exemption provided by section 2521) illustrate the application of the provisions of this section:

Example (1). A donor made transfers by gift to his spouse of $5,000 cash on January 1, 1971, and $1,000 cash on April 5, 1971. The donor made no other transfers during 1971. The first $3,-000 of such gifts for the calendar year is excluded under the provisions of section 2503(b) in determining the "total amount of gifts" made during the first calendar quarter of 1971. The marital deduction for the first calendar quarter of $2,500 (one-half of $5,000) otherwise allowable is limited by section 2524 to $2,000. The amount of taxable gifts is zero ($5,000—$3,000 (annual exclusion)—$2,000 (marital deduction)). For the second calendar quarter of 1971, the marital deduction is $500 (one-half of $1,000); the amount excluded under section 2503(b) is zero because the entire $3,000 annual exclusion was applied against the gift in the first calendar quarter of 1971; and the amount of taxable gifts is $500 ($1,000—$500 (marital deduction)).

Example (2). The only gifts made by a donor to his spouse during calendar year 1969 were a gift of $2,400 in May and a gift of $3,000 in August. The first $3,000 of such gifts is excluded under the provisions of section 2503(b) in determining the "total amount of gifts" made during the calendar year. The marital deduction for 1969 of $2,700 (one-half of $2,400 plus one-half $3,000) otherwise allowable is limited by section 2524 to $2,400. The amount of taxable gifts is zero ($5,400—$3,000 (annual exclusion)—$2,400 (marital deduction)).

§ 301.7701-1 Classification of organizations for tax purposes

(a) Person. The term "person" includes an individual, a corporation, a partnership, a trust or estate, a joint-stock company, an association, or a syndicate, group, pool, joint venture, or other unincorporated organization or group. Such term also includes a guardian, committee, trustee, executor, administrator, trustee in bankruptcy, receiver, assignee for the benefit of creditors, conservator, or any person acting in a fiduciary capacity.

(b) Standards. The Internal Revenue Code prescribes certain categories, or classes, into which various organizations fall for purposes of taxation. These categories, or classes, include associations (which are taxable as corporations), partnerships, and trusts. The tests, or standards, which are to be applied in determining the classification in which an organization belongs (whether it is an association, a partnership, a trust, or other taxable entity) are determined under the Internal Revenue Code. Sections 301.7701-2 to 301.7701-4 set forth these tests, or standards, which are to be applied in determining whether an organization is (1) an association (see § 301.7701-2), (2) a partnership (see § 301.7701-3), or (3) a trust (see § 301.7701-4).

(c) Effect of local law. As indicated in paragraph (b) of this section, the classes into which organizations are to be placed for purposes of taxation are determined under the Internal Revenue Code. Thus, a particular organization might be classified as a trust under the law of one State and a corporation under the law of another State. However, for purposes of the Internal Revenue Code, this organization would be uniformly classed as a trust, an association (and, therefore, taxable as a corporation), or some other entity, depending upon its nature under the classification standards of the Internal Revenue Code. Similarly, the term "partnership" is not limited to the common-law meaning of partnership, but is broader in its scope and includes groups not commonly called partnerships. See § 1.761-1 of this chapter (Income Tax Regulations) and § 301.7701-3. The term "corporation" is not limited to the artificial entity usually known as a corporation, but includes also an association, a trust classed as an association because of its nature or its activities, a joint-stock company, and an insurance company. Although it is the Internal Revenue Code rather than local law which establishes the tests or standards which will be applied in determining the classification in which an organization belongs, local law governs in determining whether the legal relationships which have been established in the formation of an organization are such that the standards are met. Thus, it is local law which must be applied in determining such matters as the legal relationships of the members of the organization among themselves and with the public at large, and the interests of the members of the organization in its assets.

§ 301.7701-2 Associations

(a) Characteristics of corporations. (1) The term "association" refers to an organization whose characteristics require it to be classified for purposes of taxation as a corporation rather than as another type of organization such as a partnership or a trust. There are a number of major characteristics ordinarily found in a pure corporation which, taken together, distinguish it from other organizations. These are: (i) Associates, (ii) an objective to carry on business and divide the gains therefrom, (iii) continuity of life, (iv) centralization of management, (v) liability for corporate debts limited to corporate property, and (vi) free transferability of interests. Whether a particular organization is to be classified as an association must be determined by taking into account the presence or absence of each of these corporate characteristics. The presence or absence of these characteristics will depend upon the facts in each individual case. In addition to the major characteristics set forth in this subparagraph, other factors may be found in some cases which may be significant in classifying an organization as an association, a partnership, or a trust. An organization will be treated as an association if the corporate characteristics are such that the organization more nearly resembles a corporation than a partnership or trust. See Morrissey et al. v. Commissioner (1935) 296 U.S. 344.

(2) Since associates and an objective to carry on business for joint profit are essential characteristics of all organizations engaged in business for profit (other than the so-called one-man corporation and the sole proprietorship), the absence of either of these essential characteristics will cause an arrangement among co-owners of property for the development of such property for the separate profit of each not to be classified as an association. Some of the major characteristics of a corporation are common to trusts and corporations, and others are common to partnerships and corporations. Characteristics common to trusts and corporations are not material in attempting to distinguish between a trust and an association, and characteristics common to partnerships and corporations are not material in attempting to distinguish between an association and a partnership. For example, since centralization of management, continuity of life, free transferability of interests, and limited liability are generally common to trusts and corporations, the determination of whether a trust which has such characteristics is to be treated for tax purposes as a trust or as an association depends on whether there are associates and an objective to carry on business and divide the gains therefrom. On the other hand, since associates and an objective to carry on business and divide the gains therefrom are generally common to both corporations and partnerships, the determination of whether an organization which has such characteristics is to be treated for tax purposes as a partnership or as an association depends on whether there exists centralization of management, continuity of life, free transferability of interests, and limited liability.

(3) An unincorporated organization shall not be classified as an association unless such organization has more corporate characteristics than noncorporate characteristics. In determining whether an organization has more corporate characteristics than noncorporate characteristics, all characteristics common to both types of organizations shall not be considered. For example, if a limited partnership has centralized management and free transferability of interests but lacks continuity of life and limited liability, and if the limited partnership has no other characteristics which are significant in determining its classification, such limited partnership is not classified as an association. Although the limited partnership also has associates and an objective to carry on business and divide the gains therefrom, these characteristics are not considered because they are common to both corporations and partnerships.

. . . .

(b) **Continuity of life.** (1) An organization has continuity of life if the death, insanity, bankruptcy, retirement, resignation, or expulsion of any member will not cause a dissolution of the organization. On the other hand, if the death, insanity, bankruptcy, retirement, resignation, or expulsion of any member will cause a dissolution of the organization, continuity of life does not exist. If the retirement, death, or insanity of a general partner of a limited partnership causes a dissolution of the partnership, unless the remaining general partners agree to continue the partnership or unless all remaining members agree to continue the partnership, continuity of life does not exist. See Glensder Textile Company (1942) 46 B.T.A. 176 (A., C.B. 1942–1, 8).

(2) For purposes of this paragraph, dissolution of an organization means an alteration of the identity of an organization by reason of a change in the relationship between its members as determined under local law. For example, since the resignation of a partner from a general partnership destroys the mutual agency which exists between such partner and his copartners and thereby alters the personal relation between the partners which constitutes the identity of the partnership itself, the resignation of a partner dissolves the partnership. A corporation, however, has a continuing identity which is detached from the relationship between its stockholders. The death, insanity, or bankruptcy of a shareholder or the sale of a shareholder's interest has no effect upon the identity of the corporation and, therefore, does not work a dissolution of the organization. An agreement by which an organization is established may provide that the business will be continued by the remaining

members in the event of the death or withdrawal of any member, but such agreement does not establish continuity of life if under local law the death or withdrawal of any member causes a dissolution of the organization. Thus, there may be a dissolution of the organization and no continuity of life although the business is continued by the remaining members.

(3) An agreement establishing an organization may provide that the organization is to continue for a stated period or until the completion of a stated undertaking or such agreement may provide for the termination of the organization at will or otherwise. In determining whether any member has the power of dissolution, it will be necessary to examine the agreement and to ascertain the effect of such agreement under local law. For example, if the agreement expressly provides that the organization can be terminated by the will of any member, it is clear that the organization lacks continuity of life. However, if the agreement provides that the organization is to continue for a stated period or until the completion of a stated transaction, the organization has continuity of life if the effect of the agreement is that no member has the power to dissolve the organization in contravention of the agreement. Nevertheless, if, notwithstanding such agreement, any member has the power under local law to dissolve the organization, the organization lacks continuity of life. Accordingly, a general partnership subject to a statute corresponding to the Uniform Partnership Act and a limited partnership subject to a statute corresponding to the Uniform Limited Partnership Act both lack continuity of life.

(c) Centralization of management. (1) An organization has centralized management if any person (or any group of persons which does not include all the members) has continuing exclusive authority to make the management decisions necessary to the conduct of the business for which the organization was formed. Thus, the persons who are vested with such management authority resemble in powers and functions the directors of a statutory corporation. The effective operation of a business organization composed of many members generally depends upon the centralization in the hands of a

few of exclusive authority to make management decisions for the organization, and therefore, centralized management is more likely to be found in such an organization than in a smaller organization.

(2) The persons who have such authority may, or may not, be members of the organization and may hold office as a result of a selection by the members from time to time, or may be self-perpetuating in office. See Morrissey et al. v. Commissioner (1935) 296 U.S. 344. Centralized management can be accomplished by election to office, by proxy appointment, or by any other means which has the effect of concentrating in a management group continuing exclusive authority to make management decisions.

(3) Centralized management means a concentration of continuing exclusive authority to make independent business decisions on behalf of the organization which do not require ratification by members of such organization. Thus, there is not centralized management when the centralized authority is merely to perform ministerial acts as an agent at the direction of a principal.

(4) There is no centralization of continuing exclusive authority to make management decisions, unless the managers have sole authority to make such decisions. For example, in the case of a corporation or a trust, the concentration of management powers in a board of directors or trustees effectively prevents a stockholder or a trust beneficiary, simply because he is a stockholder or beneficiary, from binding the corporation or the trust by his acts. However, because of the mutual agency relationship between members of a general partnership subject to a statute corresponding to the Uniform Partnership Act, such a general partnership cannot achieve effective concentration of management powers and, therefore, centralized management. Usually, the act of any partner within the scope of the partnership business binds all the partners; and even if the partners agree among themselves that the powers of management shall be exclusively in a selected few, this agreement will be ineffective as against an outsider who had no notice of it. In addition, limited partnerships subject to a statute corresponding to the Uniform Lim-

ited Partnership Act, generally do not have centralized management, but centralized management ordinarily does exist in such a limited partnership if substantially all the interests in the partnership are owned by the limited partners.

(d) Limited liability. (1) An organization has the corporate characteristic of limited liability if under local law there is no member who is personally liable for the debts of or claims against the organization. Personal liability means that a creditor of an organization may seek personal satisfaction from a member of the organization to the extent that the assets of such organization are insufficient to satisfy the creditor's claim. A member of the organization who is personally liable for the obligations of the organization may make an agreement under which another person, whether or not a member of the organization, assumes such liability or agrees to indemnify such member for any such liability. However, if under local law the member remains liable to such creditors notwithstanding such agreement, there exists personal liability with respect to such member. In the case of a general partnership subject to a statute corresponding to the Uniform Partnership Act, personal liability exists with respect to each general partner. Similarly, in the case of a limited partnership subject to a statute corresponding to the Uniform Limited Partnership Act, personal liability exists with respect to each general partner, except as provided in subparagraph (2) of this paragraph.

(2) In the case of an organization formed as a limited partnership, personal liability does not exist, for purposes of this paragraph, with respect to a general partner when he has no substantial assets (other than his interest in the partnership) which could be reached by a creditor of the organization and when he is merely a "dummy" acting as the agent of the limited partners. Notwithstanding the formation of the organization as a limited partnership, when the limited partners act as the principals of such general partner, personal liability will exist with respect to such limited partners. Also, if a corporation is a general partner, personal liability exists with respect to such general partner when the corporation has substantial assets (other than its inter-

est in the partnership) which could be reached by a creditor of the limited partnership. A general partner may contribute his services, but no capital, to the organization, but if such general partner has substantial assets (other than his interest in the partnership), there exists personal liability. Furthermore, if the organization is engaged in financial transactions which involve large sums of money, and if the general partners have substantial assets (other than their interests in the partnership), there exists personal liability although the assets of such general partners would be insufficient to satisfy any substantial portion of the obligations of the organization. In addition, although the general partner has no substantial assets (other than his interest in the partnership), personal liability exists with respect to such general partner when he is not merely a "dummy" acting as the agent of the limited partners.

(e) Free transferability of interests. (1) An organization has the corporate characteristic of free transferability of interests if each of its members or those members owning substantially all of the interests in the organization have the power, without the consent of other members, to substitute for themselves in the same organization a person who is not a member of the organization. In order for this power of substitution to exist in the corporate sense, the member must be able, without the consent of other members, to confer upon his substitute all the attributes of his interest in the organization. Thus, the characteristic of free transferability of interests does not exist in a case in which each member can, without the consent of other members, assign only his right to share in profits but cannot so assign his rights to participate in the management of the organization. Furthermore, although the agreement provides for the transfer of a member's interest, there is no power of substitution and no free transferability of interest if under local law a transfer of a member's interest results in the dissolution of the old organization and the formation of a new organization.

(2) If each member of an organization can transfer his interest to a person who is not a member of the organization only after having offered such interest to the other members at its fair

market value, it will be recognized that a modified form of free transferability of interests exists. In determining the classification of an organization, the presence of this modified corporate characteristic will be accorded less significance than if such characteristic were present in an unmodified form.

.   .   .   .

(g) Examples. The application of the rules described in this section may be illustrated by the following examples:

Example (1). [Deleted]

Example (2). A group of seven doctors forms a clinic for the purpose of furnishing, for profit, medical and surgical services to the public. They each transfer assets to the clinic, and their agreement provides that except upon complete liquidation of the organization on the vote of three-fourths of its members, no member has any individual interest in its assets. Their agreement also provides that neither the death, insanity, bankruptcy, retirement, resignation, nor expulsion of a member shall cause the dissolution of the organization. However, under the applicable local law, a member who withdraws does have the power to dissolve the organization. While the agreement provides that the management of the clinic is to be vested exclusively in an executive committee of four members elected by all the members, this provision is ineffective as against outsiders who had no notice of it; and therefore, the act of any member within the scope of the organization's business binds the organization insofar as such outsiders are concerned. While the agreement declares that each individual doctor alone is liable for acts of malpractice, members of the clinic are, nevertheless, personally liable for all debts of the clinic including claims based on malpractice. No member has the right, without the consent of all the other members, to transfer his interest to a doctor who is not a member of the clinic. The organization has associates and an objective to carry on business and divide the gains therefrom. However, it does not have the corporate characteristics of continuity of life, centralized management, limited liability, and free transferability of interests. The organization will be classified as a partnership for all purposes of the Internal Revenue Code.

Example (3). A group of twenty-five lawyers forms an organization for the purpose of furnishing, for profit, legal services to the public. Their agreement provides that the organization will dissolve upon the death, insanity, bankruptcy, retirement, or expulsion of a member. While their agreement provides that the management of the organization is to be vested exclusively in an executive committee of five members elected by all the members, this provision is ineffective as against outsiders who had no notice of it; and, therefore, the act of any member within the scope of the organization's business binds the organization insofar as such outsiders are concerned. Members of the organization are personally liable for all debts, or claims against, the organization. No member

has the right, without the consent of all the other members, to transfer his interest to a lawyer who is not a member of the organization. The organization has associates and an objective to carry on business and divide the gains therefrom. However, the four corporate characteristics of limited liability, centralized management, free transferability of interests, and continuity of life are absent in this case. The organization will be classified as a partnership for all purposes of the Internal Revenue Code.

Example (4). A group of twenty-five persons forms an organization for the purpose of engaging in real estate investment activities. Each member has the power to dissolve the organization at any time. The management of the organization is vested exclusively in an executive committee of five members elected by all the members, and under the applicable local law, no one acting without the authority of this committee has the power to bind the organization by his acts. Under the applicable local law, each member is personally liable for the obligations of the organization. Every member has the right to transfer his interest to a person who is not a member of the organization, but he must first advise the organization of the proposed transfer and give it the opportunity on a vote of the majority to purchase the interest at its fair market value. The organization has associates and an objective to carry on business and divide the gains therefrom. While the organization does have the characteristics of centralized management and a modified form of free transferability of interests, it does not have the corporate characteristics of continuity of life and limited liability. Under the circumstances presented, the organization will be classified as a partnership for all purposes of the Internal Revenue Code.

Example (5). A group of twenty-five persons forms an organization for the purpose of engaging in real estate investment activities. Under their agreement, the organization is to have a life of twenty years, and under the applicable local law, no member has the power to dissolve the organization prior to the expiration of that period. The management of the organization is five members elected by all the members, and under the applicable local law no one acting without the authority of this committee has the power to bind the organization by his acts. Under the applicable local law, each member is personally liable for the obligations of the organization. Every member has the right to transfer his interest to a person who is not a member of the organization, but he must first advise the organization of the proposed transfer and give it the opportunity on a vote of the majority to purchase the interest at its fair market value. The organization has associates and an objective to carry on business and divide the gains therefrom. While the organization does not have the corporate characteristic of limited liability, it does have continuity of life, centralized management, and a modified form of free transferability of interests. The organization will be classified as an association for all purposes of the Internal Revenue Code.

Example (6). A group of twenty-five persons forms an organization for purposes of engaging in real estate investment activities. Each member has the power to dissolve the organization at any time. The management of the organization is vested exclusively in an executive committee of five members elected by all the members, and under the applicable local law, no one acting without the authority of this committee has the power to bind the organization by his acts. Under the applicable local law, the liability of each member for the obligations of the organization is limited to paid and subscribed capital. Every member has the right to transfer his interest to a person who is not a member of the organization, but he must first advise the organization of the proposed transfer and give it the opportunity on a vote of the majority to purchase the interest at its fair market value. The organization has associates and an objective to carry on business and divide the gains therefrom. While the organization does not have the characteristic of continuity of life, it does have limited liability, centralized management, and a modified form of free transferability of interests. The organization will be classified as an association for all purposes of the Internal Revenue Code.

Example (7). A group of twenty-five persons forms an organization for the purpose of investing in securities so as to educate the members in principles and techniques of investment practices and to share the income from such investments. While the agreement states that the organization will operate until terminated by a three-fourths vote of the total membership and will not terminate upon the withdrawal or death of any member, under the applicable local law, a member has the power to dissolve the organization at any time. The business of the organization is carried on by the members at regular monthly meetings and buy or sell action may be taken only when voted by a majority of the organization's membership present. Elected officers perform only ministerial functions such as presiding at meetings and carrying out the directions of the members. Members of the organization are personally liable for all debts of, or claims against, the organization. No member may transfer his membership. The organization has associates and an objective to carry on business and divide the gains therefrom. However, the organization does not have the corporate characteristics of limited liability, free transferability of interests, continuity of life, and centralized management. The organization will be treated as a partnership for all purposes of the Internal Revenue Code.

§ 301.7701-3 Partnerships

(a) In general. The term "partnership" is broader in scope than the common law meaning of partnership and may include groups not commonly called partnerships. Thus, the term "partnership" includes a syndicate, group, pool, joint venture, or other unincorporated organization through or by means of which any business, financial operation, or venture is carried on, and which is not a corporation or a trust or estate within the meaning of the Internal Revenue Code of 1954. A joint undertaking merely to share expenses is not a partnership. For example, if two or more persons jointly construct a ditch merely to drain surface water from their properties, they are not partners. Mere co-ownership of property which is maintained, kept in repair, and rented or leased does not constitute a partnership. For example, if an individual owner, or tenants in common, of farm property lease it to a farmer for a cash rental or a share of the crops, they do not necessarily create a partnership thereby. Tenants in common, however, may be partners if they actively carry on a trade, business, financial operation, or venture and divide the profits thereof. For example, a partnership exists if co-owners of an apartment building lease space and in addition provide services to the occupants either directly or through an agent.

(b) Limited partnerships—(1) In general. An organization which qualifies as a limited partnership under State law may be classified for purposes of the Internal Revenue Code as an ordinary partnership or as an association. Such a limited partnership will be treated as an association if, applying the principles set forth in § 301.7701-2, the organization more nearly resembles a corporation than an ordinary partnership or other business entity.

(2) Examples. The principles of this paragraph may be illustrated by the following examples:

Example (1). Three individuals form an organization which qualifies as a limited partnership under the laws of the State in which the organization was formed. The purpose of the organization is to acquire and operate various pieces of commercial and other investment property for profit. Each of the three individuals who are general partners invests $100,000 in the enterprise. Five million dollars of additional capital is raised through contributions of $100,000 or more by each of thirty limited partners. The three general partners are personally capable of assuming a substantial part of the obligations to be incurred by the organization. While a limited partner may assign his right to receive a share of the profits and a return of his contribution, his assignee does not become a substituted limited partner except with the unanimous consent of the general partners. The life of the organization as stated in the certificate is 20 years, but the death, insanity, or retirement of a general partner prior to the expiration of the 20-year period will dissolve the organization. The general partners have exclusive authority to manage the affairs of the organization but can act only upon the unanimous consent of all of them. The organization has associates and an objective to carry on business and divide the gains therefrom, which characterize both partnerships and corporations. While the organization has the corporate characteristic of centralized management, since substantially all of the interests in the organization are owned by the limited partners, it does not have the characteristics of continuity of life, free transferability of interests, or limited liability. The organization will be classified as a partnership for all purposes of the Internal Revenue Code.

Example (2). Three individuals form an organization which qualifies as a limited partnership under the laws of the State in which the organization was formed. The purpose of the organization is to acquire and operate various pieces of commercial and other investment property for profit. The certificate provides that the life of the organization is to be 40 years, unless a general partner dies, becomes insane, or retires during such period. On the occurrence of such death, insanity, or retirement, the remaining general partners may continue the business of the partnership for the balance of the 40-year period under a right so to do stated in the certificate. Each of the three individuals who is a general partner invests $50,000 in the enterprise and has means to satisfy the business obligations of the organization to a substantial extent. Five million dollars of additional capital is raised through the sale of freely transferable interests in amounts of $10,000 or less to limited partners. Nine hundred such interests are sold. The interests of the 900 limited partners are fully transferable, that is, a transferee acquires all the attributes of the transferor's interest in the organization. The general partners have exclusive control over management of the business, their interests are not transferable, and their liability for debts of the organization is not limited to their capital contributions. The organization has associates and an objective to carry on business and divide the gains therefrom. It does not have the corporate characteristics of limited liability and continuity of life. It has centralized management, however, since the three general partners exercise exclusive control over the management of the business, and since substantially all of the interests in the organization are owned by the limited partners. While the interests of the general partners are not transferable, the transferability test of an association is met since substantially all of the interests in the organization are represented by transferable interests. The organization will be classified as a partnership for all purposes of the Internal Revenue Code.

(c) Partnership associations. The laws of a number of States provide for the formation of organizations commonly known as partnership associations. Such a partnership association will be treated as an association if, applying the principles set forth in § 301.7701–2, the organization more nearly resembles a corporation than the other types of business entities.

. . . .

§ 301.7701–4 Trusts

(a) Ordinary trusts. In general, the term "trust" as used in the Internal Revenue Code refers to an arrangement created either by a will or by an inter vivos declaration whereby trustees take title to property for the purpose of protecting or conserving it for the beneficiaries under the ordinary rules applied in chancery or probate courts. Usually the beneficiaries of such a trust do no more than accept the benefits thereof and are not the voluntary planners or creators of the trust arrangement. However, the beneficiaries of such a trust may be the persons who create it and it will be recognized as a trust under the Internal Revenue Code if it was created for the purpose of protecting or conserving the trust property for beneficiaries who stand in the same relation to the trust as they would if the trust had been created by others for them. Generally speaking, an arrangement will be treated as a trust under the Internal Revenue Code if it can be shown that the purpose of the arrangement is to vest in trustees responsibility for the protection and conservation of property for beneficiaries who cannot share in the discharge of this responsibility and, therefore, are not associates in a joint enterprise for the conduct of business for profit.

(b) Business trusts. There are other arrangements which are known as trusts because the legal title to property is conveyed to trustees for the benefit of beneficiaries, but which are not classified as trusts for purposes of the Internal Revenue Code because they are not simply arrangements to protect or conserve the property for the beneficiaries. These trusts, which are often known as business or commercial trusts, generally are created by the beneficiaries simply as a device to carry on a profit-making business which normally would have been carried on through business organizations that are classified as corporations or partnerships under the Internal Revenue Code. However, the fact that the corpus of the trust is not supplied by the beneficiaries is not sufficient reason in itself for classifying the arrangement as an ordinary trust rather than as an association or partnership. The fact that any organization is technically cast in the trust form, by conveying title to property to trustees for the benefit of persons designated as beneficiaries, will not change the real character of the organization if, applying the principles set forth in §§ 301.7701-2 and 301.7701-3, the organization more nearly resembles an association or a partnership than a trust.

(c) Certain investment trusts. An "investment" trust of the type commonly known as a management trust is an association, and a trust of the type commonly known as a fixed investment trust is an association if there is power under the trust agreement to vary the investment of the certificate holders. See Commissioner v. North American Bond Trust (C.C.A.2d 1941) 122 F.2d 545, cert. denied 314 U.S. 701. However, if there is no power under the trust agreement to vary the investment of the certificate holders, such fixed investment trust shall be classified as a trust.

(d) Liquidating trusts. Certain organizations which are commonly known as liquidating trusts are treated as trusts for purposes of the Internal Revenue Code. An organization will be considered a liquidating trust if it is organized for the primary purpose of liquidating and distributing the assets transferred to it, and if its activities are all reasonably necessary to, and consistent with, the accomplishment of that purpose. A liquidating trust is treated as a trust for purposes of the Internal Revenue Code because it is formed with the objective of liquidating particular assets and not as an organization having as its purpose the carrying on of a profit-making business which normally would be conducted through business organizations classified as corporations or partnerships. However, if the liquidation is unreasonably prolonged or if the liquidation purpose becomes so obscured by business activities that the declared purpose of liquidation can be said to be lost or abandoned, the status of the organization will no longer be that of a liquidating trust. Bondholders' protective committees, voting trusts, and other agencies formed to protect the interests of security holders during insolvency, bankruptcy, or corporate reorganization proceedings are analogous to liquidating trusts but if subsequently utilized to further the control or profitable operation of a going business on a permanent continuing basis, they will lose their classification as trusts for purposes of the Internal Revenue Code.

TOPICAL INDEX

(References are to Code Sections)

ESTATE TAX

Administration expenses, deduction from gross estate, § 2053.
Alternate valuation, gross estate, § 2032.
Annuities, § 2039.
Charitable transfers, deduction from gross estate, § 2055.
Claims against estate, deduction from gross estate, § 2053.
Credits against tax,
    Gift tax, § 2012.
    Prior transfers, § 2013.
    Remainders, death tax on, § 2015.
    State death taxes, § 2011.
    Unified, § 2010.
Deductions,
    Charitable transfers, § 2055.
    Expenses, § 2053.
    Indebtedness, § 2053.
    Losses, § 2054.
    Marital, § 2056.
    Taxes, § 2053.
Discharge of fiduciary from personal liability, § 2204.
Disclaimers, § 2046.
Dower or curtesy interests, § 2034.
Election, alternate valuation, gross estate, § 2032.
Executor,
    Defined, § 2203.
    Discharge from personal liability, § 2204.
    Liability for payment, § 2002.
Expenses, deduction from gross estate, § 2053.
Extensions of time for payment, § 6163 et seq.
Farms, valuation, § 2032A.
Funeral expenses, deduction from gross estate, § 2053.
Gift tax, credit, § 2012.
Gifts made within three years of death, § 2035.
Gross estate, § 2031 et seq.
Imposition of tax, § 2001.
Indebtedness, deduction from gross estate, § 2053.
Insufficient consideration, transfers for, § 2043.
Joint interests, § 2040.
Liability,
    Discharge of fiduciary, § 2204.
    For payment, § 2002.
Liens, special, § 6324 et seq.
Life estate, retained, § 2036.
Life insurance,
    Liability of beneficiaries, § 2206.
    Proceeds, gross estate, § 2042.
Losses, deduction from gross estate, § 2054.
Marital deduction, § 2056.
Powers of appointment,
    Liability of recipient, § 2207.
    Proceeds, gross estate, § 2041.
Prior interests, § 2045.
Prior transfers, credit, § 2013.

ESTATE TAX—Continued

Rate of tax, § 2001.

Recovery of marital deduction property, § 2207A.

Remainders, credit for death taxes, § 2015.

Retained life estate, transfers with, § 2036.

Returns, § 6018.

Reversionary interest, § 2037.

Revocable transfers, § 2038.

State death taxes,

    Credit, § 2011.

    Deduction, § 2053.

Surviving spouse, bequests to, § 2056.

Taxable estate, § 2051 et seq.

Taxes, deduction from gross estate, § 2053.

Time for filing return, § 6075.

Transfers for insufficient consideration, § 2043.

Transfers taking effect at death, § 2037.

Transfers with retained life estate, § 2036.

Unified credit, § 2010.

Unpaid mortgages, deduction from gross estate, § 2053.

Valuation, §§ 2031, 2032, 2032A.

GENERATION–SKIPPING TRANSFER TAX

Amount of tax, § 2602.

Deemed transferor, § 2612.

Definitions, § 2611 et seq.

Generation-skipping transfer, § 2611.

Imposition of tax, § 2601.

Liability for tax, § 2603.

Tax imposed, § 2601.

GIFT TAX

Annual exclusion, § 2503.

Annuities under qualified plans, § 2517.

Charitable gifts, § 2522.

Community property, deduction for gift to spouse, § 2523.

Credit against tax, § 2505.

Deductions,

    Charitable, § 2522.

    Marital, § 2523.

Disclaimers, § 2518.

Exclusion, § 2503.

Gift by husband or wife to third party, § 2513.

Imposition of tax, § 2501.

Liens, special, § 6324.

Marital deduction, § 2523.

Minors, transfers for benefit of, § 2503.

Powers of appointment, § 2514.

Property settlement between spouses, § 2516.

Rate of tax, § 2502.

Recovery of marital deduction property, § 2207A.

Returns, § 6019.

Split gifts, § 2513.

Spouse,

    Deduction for gift to, § 2523.

    Gift to third party, § 2513.

    Property settlements, § 2516.

Taxable gifts, § 2503.

Taxable transfers, § 2501.

Time for filing return, § 6075.

Transfers in general, § 2511.

GIFT TAX—Continued
Unified credit, § 2505.
Valuation, § 2512.

INCOME TAXES
Accelerated cost recovery system, § 168.
Accident or health plans,
    Amounts received, § 105.
    Contributions by employer, § 106.
Accounting periods and methods of accounting,
    Accrual method, § 446.
    Adjustments, § 481 et seq.
    Allocation of income and deductions, § 482.
    At risk limitation, § 465.
    Averaging of income, § 1301 et seq.
    Carryovers, net operating loss deduction, § 172.
    Cash receipts and disbursements method, § 446.
    Change of annual accounting period, § 442.
    Claim of right, § 1341.
    Corporations engaged in farming, § 447.
    Deductions, § 461.
    Deferred payments, interest, § 483.
    Discount obligations, § 454.
    Income averaging, § 1301 et seq.
    Installment method, § 453 et seq.
    Inventories, § 471 et seq.
    Methods of accounting, § 446 et seq.
    Period for computation of taxable income, § 441.
    Reserve for bad debts, § 166.
    Short period returns, § 443.
    Taxable year deduction taken, § 461 et seq.
    Taxable year gross income included, § 451 et seq.
Accrual method of accounting, § 446.
Accumulated earnings tax, § 531 et seq.
Acquisitions made to evade or avoid tax, § 269.
Activities not engaged in for profit, § 183.
Adjusted basis, § 1011.
Adjusted gross income defined, § 62.
Adjustments to basis, § 1016.
Alimony and separate maintenance payments,
    Deduction, § 215.
    Gross income, §§ 61, 71.
Allocations of income and deductions, § 482.
Alternative minimum tax for taxpayers other than corporations, § 55.
Alternative tax on capital gains for corporations, § 1201.
Amount realized, § 1001.
Annuities, gross income, §§ 61, 72, 101.
At risk amount,
    Deduction limitation, § 465.
    Investment credit limitation, § 46.
Averaging income, § 1301 et seq.
Awards, gross income, § 74.
Away from home expenses, §§ 162, 274.
Bad debts, deduction, § 166.
Basis,
    Acquired by gift, § 1015.
    Acquired from decedent, § 1014.
    Adjusted basis for determining gain or loss, § 1011.
    Adjustments to, § 1016.
    Cost, § 1012.
    Decedent, property acquired from, § 1014.
    Discharge of indebtedness, § 1017.
    Gifts, § 1015.

TOPICAL INDEX

INCOME TAXES—Continued

Basis—Continued
> Lessee improvements, § 1019.
> Liquidations, property received in, § 334.
> Player contracts transferred in connection with sale of franchise, § 1056.
> Reduction on discharge of indebtedness, § 1017.

Beneficiaries, § 641 et seq.
Bequests, devises, and inheritances, gross income, § 102.
Business expenses, § 162.
Cancellation of lease or distributor's agreement, § 1241.
Candidates for public office, contributions to, credit, § 41.
Capital asset defined, § 1221.
Capital contributions, § 118.
Capital expenditures, § 263.
Capital gains and losses. Gains or losses, post.
Capital loss carrybacks and carryovers, § 1212.
Carrying charges, § 266.
Carryovers,
> Capital losses, § 1212.
> Charitable contributions, § 170.
> Corporate acquisitions, § 381 et seq.
> Net operating loss deduction, § 172.

Carved-out production payments, § 636.
Cash receipts and disbursements method of accounting, § 446.
Casualty losses, § 165.
Charitable contributions, §§ 162, 170.
Charitable remainder trusts, § 664.
Child's services, § 73.
Claim of right, § 1341.
Collapsible corporations, § 341.
Community income of spouses living apart, § 66.
Complete liquidations, § 331 et seq.
Consent dividends, § 565.
Consolidated returns, § 1501 et seq.
Construction period interest and taxes, § 189.
Constructive ownership of stock, § 318.
Contributions of property to partnerships,
> Basis, §§ 722, 723.
> Nonrecognition, § 721.

Contributions to candidates for public office, § 41.
Contributions to capital of corporations,
> Basis, § 362.
> Gross income, exclusion, § 118.
> Nonrecognition, § 1032.

Conventions, § 274.
Corporations,
> Accumulated earnings tax, § 531 et seq.
> Acquisitions made to evade or avoid tax, § 269.
> Allocations of income and deductions, § 482.
> Assumption of liability, § 357.
> Basis of property, §§ 358, 362.
> Carryovers, § 381 et seq.
> Collapsible, § 341.
> Complete liquidations, § 331 et seq.
> Consent dividends, § 565.
> Consolidated returns, § 1501 et seq.
> Constructive ownership of stock, § 318.
> Contribution to capital,
>> Basis, § 362.
>> Gross income, exclusion, § 118.
>> Nonrecognition, § 1032.

Controlled corporations, limitations on multiple benefits, § 1561 et seq.

1244

TOPICAL INDEX

INCOME TAXES—Continued

Corporations—Continued

    Definition, § 7701.

    Distributions, § 301 et seq.

    Dividend defined, § 316.

    Dividend distributions, § 301.

    Dividends paid deduction, § 561 et seq.

    Dividends received deduction, § 243.

    Earnings and profits,

        Dividend defined, § 316.

        Effect on, § 312.

    Indebtedness or stock, § 385.

    Interest on indebtedness incurred to acquire stock or assets, § 279.

    Liquidations, § 331 et seq.

    Minimum tax, § 56.

    Multiple benefits, limitations, § 1561 et seq.

    Net operating loss carryovers, § 382.

    Organization of, § 351 et seq.

    Organizational expenditures, deduction, § 248.

    Personal holding company tax, § 541 et seq.

    Personal service corporations to avoid or evade tax, § 269A.

    Preference items, § 291.

    Redemption of stock, § 302 et seq.

    Reorganizations,

        Assumption of liability, § 357.

        Basis to corporations, § 362.

        Basis to distributees, § 358.

        Defined, § 368.

        Exchange of stock and securities, § 354 et seq.

        Gain or loss, nonrecognition, § 361.

    S corporations, § 1361 et seq.

    Stock or indebtedness, § 385.

    Stock purchases treated as asset acquisitions, § 338.

    Stockholders, post.

    Tax imposed, § 11.

    Taxability of corporation on distribution, § 311 et seq.

Correction of error, § 1311.

Cost basis, § 1012.

Cost depletion, basis for, § 612.

Cost recovery allowances, § 168.

Credits against tax,

    Contributions to candidates for public office, § 41.

    Earned income, § 43.

    Elderly, § 37.

    Energy, residential, § 44C.

    Household and dependent care services, § 44A.

    Investment, §§ 38, 46 et seq.

    Research, § 44F.

    Residential energy, § 44C.

Dealers in securities, § 1236.

Death benefits, § 101.

Death taxes, distributions in redemption of stock to pay, § 303.

Debts,

    Bad, deduction, § 166.

    Discharge of, gross income, §§ 61, 108.

    Interest, deduction, § 163.

    Interest in corporation treated as indebtedness, § 385.

    Interest on indebtedness incurred by corporation to acquire stock or assets, § 279.

Decedents,

    Basis of property acquired from, § 1014.

    Income in respect of, §§ 61, 691.

INCOME TAXES—Continued

Deductions,
    Accelerated cost recovery system, § 168.
    Acquisitions made to evade or avoid tax, § 269.
    Activities not engaged in for profit, § 183.
    Alimony, § 215.
    Allocation, § 482.
    At risk limitation, § 465.
    Bad debts, § 166.
    Business expenses, § 162.
    Capital gains, § 1202.
    Casualty losses, § 165.
    Charitable contributions, §§ 162, 170.
    Compensation for personal services, §§ 83, 162.
    Cooperative housing corporation tenant shareholder, § 216.
    Cost recovery system, § 168.
    Deficiency dividends, § 547.
    Depletion, § 611 et seq.
    Depreciation, §§ 167, 168.
    Development expenditures, § 616.
    Disallowance, general rule, § 261.
    Dividends paid, § 561 et seq.
    Dividends received by corporations, § 243.
    Experimental expenditures, § 174.
    Farming syndicates, § 464.
    Fines and penalties, § 162.
    Homes, business or rental use, § 280A.
    Illegal bribes, kickbacks, and other payments, § 162.
    Illegal sale of drugs, § 280E.
    Interest, §§ 163, 265, 279.
    Itemized deductions, § 161 et seq.
    Items not deductible, § 261 et seq.
    Losses, §§ 165, 172, 267, 1244.
    Meals and lodging, §§ 162, 274.
    Medical and dental expenses, § 213.
    Moving expenses, § 217.
    Net operating loss, § 172.
    Percentage depletion, §§ 613, 613A.
    Personal exemptions, § 151 et seq.
    Production of income expenses, § 212.
    Recovery property, § 168.
    Research and experimental expenditures, § 174.
    Restricted property transferred in connection with services, § 83.
    Retirement savings, § 219.
    Salaries, § 162.
    Soil and water conservation expenditures, § 175.
    Start-up expenditures, § 195.
    Taxes, §§ 164, 275.
    Trade or business expenses, § 162.
    Traveling expenses, §§ 162, 274.
    Two-earner married couples, § 221.
    Vacation homes, § 280A.
Deficiency dividends, deduction, § 547.
Definitions, § 7701.
Dental expenses, deduction, § 213.
Dependent care services credit, § 44A.
Dependent defined, § 152.
Depletion, deductions, § 611 et seq.
Depreciation,
    Deduction, §§ 167, 168.
    Lessee, improvements made on lessor's property, § 178.
    Recapture, §§ 1245, 1250.
Development expenditures, deduction, § 616.

INCOME TAXES—Continued

Disaster losses, § 165.

Discharge of indebtedness, §§ 61, 108, 1017.

Distributable net income, § 643.

Distributive share of partner, § 704.

Distributor's agreement, cancellation of, § 1241.

Dividends,
    Consent dividends, § 565.
    Deduction for dividends paid, § 561 et seq.
    Deduction for dividends received, § 243.
    Deficiency, § 547.
    Defined, § 316.
    Distributions, § 301 et seq.
    Earnings and profits, § 312.
    Exclusion, § 116.
    Received by corporations, § 243.

Divorce,
    Alimony,
        Deduction, § 215.
        Gross income, §§ 61, 71.
    Trusts, § 682.

Earnings and profits,
    Dividend defined, § 316.
    Effect on, § 312.

Educational assistance programs, § 127.

Elderly, credit, § 37.

Employees,
    Accident and health plans, §§ 105, 106.
    Compensation, §§ 83, 162.
    Death benefits, § 101.
    Educational assistance programs, § 127.
    Group-term life insurance, § 79.
    Legal services plans, § 120.
    Meals or lodging, § 119.
    Moving expenses,
        Deduction, § 217.
        Reimbursement for expenses, § 82.
    Pension, profit-sharing, stock bonus plans, § 401 et seq.
    Property transferred in connection with services, § 83.
    Retirement savings, § 219.

Energy credit, residential, § 44C.

Entertainment, amusement, or recreation expenses, § 274.

Error, correction of, § 1311.

Estates, general rules for taxation of, § 641 et seq.

Exclusions from gross income, § 101 et seq.

Exempt organizations,
    Exemption from tax, § 501.
    Feeder organizations, § 502.
    List of, § 501.
    Political organizations, § 527.
    Tax on unrelated business income, § 511.
    Unrelated,
        Business taxable income, § 512.
        Debt-financed income, § 514.
        Trade or business, § 513.

Exemptions, personal, § 151 et seq.

Expenses,
    Entertainment, amusement, or recreation, deduction, § 274.
    Moving, §§ 82, 217.
    Personal, family, or living, § 262.
    Production of income, deduction, § 212.
    Trade or business, deduction, § 162.

Experimental expenditures, deduction, § 174.

TOPICAL INDEX

INCOME TAXES—Continued

Family expenses, § 262.

Family partnerships, § 704.

Farmers and farming,
  Corporations engaged in farming, method of accounting, § 447.
  Farming syndicates,
    Expenditures, § 278.
    Limitations on deductions, § 464.
  Fertilizer expenditures, § 180.
  Groves, capital expenditures, § 278.
  Land clearing expenditures, § 182.
  Soil conservation expenditures, § 175.
  Unharvested crop, sale of land with, § 268.
  Water conservation expenditures, § 175.

Farming syndicates,
  Expenditures, § 278.
  Limitations on deductions, § 464.

Feeder organizations, § 502.

Fellowship grants, gross income, § 117.

Fertilizer expenditures, § 180.

Fiscal year, § 441.

Foreign trusts, §§ 668, 679, 1057, 1491 et seq.

Franchises, transfers of, § 1253.

Gains or losses,
  Adjusted basis for determining, § 1011.
  Amount realized, § 1001.
  Basis, § 1012 et seq.
  Capital asset defined, § 1221.
  Capital gains and losses,
    Alternative tax, § 1201.
    Capital asset defined, § 1221.
    Carrybacks and carryovers, § 1212.
    Deduction for capital gains, § 1202.
    Depreciation recapture, §§ 1245, 1250.
    Holding period, §§ 1222, 1223.
    Limitation on capital losses, § 1211.
    Loss carrybacks and carryovers, § 1212.
    Property used in trade or business, § 1231.
    Treatment, § 1201 et seq.
  Casualty losses, § 165.
  Computation of gain or loss, § 1001.
  Decedents, property acquired from, basis, § 1014.
  Deduction for losses, § 165.
  Determination of amount, § 1001.
  Discharge of indebtedness, reduction of basis, § 1017.
  Gifts, property acquired by, basis, § 1015.
  Holding period of property, §§ 1222, 1223.
  Installment obligations, § 453B.
  Losses, §§ 165, 267, 1244.
  Nonrecognition, common exchanges, § 1031 et seq.
  Real property divided for sale, § 1237.
  Recapture, §§ 1245, 1250, 1254.
  Recognition, § 1001.
  Related taxpayers, §§ 267, 1239.
  Residence, one-time exclusion of gain, § 121.
  Securities dealers, § 1236.
  Short sales, § 1233.
  Small business stock losses, § 1244.

Gifts,
  Basis of property, acquired, § 1015.
  Charitable organization, deduction, § 170.

TOPICAL INDEX

INCOME TAXES—Continued

Gifts—Continued

 Deduction, limitation, § 274.

 Gross income, exclusion, § 102.

Governmental obligations, interest on, § 103.

Grantors treated as substantial owners of trusts, § 671 et seq.

Gross income defined, § 61.

 Excluded items, § 101 et seq.

 Included items, § 71 et seq.

Group-term life insurance, § 79.

Groves, capital expenditures, § 278.

Head of household defined, § 2.

Health plans,

 Amounts received under, § 105.

 Contributions by employer, § 106.

Holding period, §§ 1222, 1223.

Household and dependent care services credit, § 44A.

Illegal sale of drugs, § 280E.

Illness,

 Accident and health insurance, §§ 105, 106.

 Compensation, § 104.

Improvements made by lessee on lessor's property, § 109.

Imputed interest, § 483.

Incentive stock options, § 422A.

Income averaging, § 1301 et seq.

Income in respect of decedents, § 691.

Indebtedness. Debts, ante.

Individual retirement accounts, §§ 219, 408.

Inheritance,

 Basis of property, acquired, § 1014.

 Gross income, exclusion, § 102.

Injuries or sickness, compensation for, § 104.

Installment method, §§ 453, 453A.

Insurance policies, exchanges, § 1035.

Intangible drilling and development costs, § 263.

Interest,

 Construction period, § 189.

 Corporate acquisition indebtedness, § 279.

 Deduction, general rule, § 163.

 Exclusion for interest received, § 103.

 Governmental obligations, interest on, § 103.

 Imputed, § 483.

 Prepaid, § 461.

 Related taxpayers, § 267.

 Tax exempt income, relating to, § 265.

Inventories,

 Basis, § 1013.

 Election to use one inventory pool, § 474.

 General rule, § 471.

 Last-in, first-out, § 472.

 Liquidations of LIFO inventories, § 473.

Investment credit, §§ 38, 46 et seq., 196.

Involuntary conversions, § 1033.

Itemized deductions, § 161 et seq.

 Deductions, ante.

Items of tax preference, § 57.

Joint returns by husbands and wives, § 6013.

Land clearing expenditures, § 182.

Last-in first-out inventories, § 472 et seq.

Leases,

 Cancellation, gain or loss, § 1241.

TOPICAL INDEX

INCOME TAXES—Continued

Leases—Continued

    Improvements by lessees,

        Deduction, depreciation or amortization, § 178.

        Gains or losses, § 1019.

        Gross income, § 109.

    Qualified leased property, § 168.

Legal services plans, § 120.

Life insurance,

    Amounts paid in connection with insurance contracts, § 264.

    Gross income, §§ 61, 72, 101.

    Group-term, § 79.

    Proceeds, § 101.

Like kind exchanges, § 1031.

Liquidations, corporate, § 331 et seq.

Liquidations of LIFO inventories, § 473.

Living expenses, amounts received under insurance contracts, § 123.

Lodging furnished to employees, gross income, § 119.

Losses,

    At risk amounts, § 465.

    Capital, §§ 165, 1211, 1212.

    Casualty, § 165.

    Deduction, § 165.

    Disaster, § 165.

    Limitations on individuals, § 165.

    Net operating, § 172.

    Related taxpayers, § 267.

    Small business stock, § 1244.

    Theft, § 165.

    Wagering, § 165.

    Wash sales, § 1091.

    Worthless securities, § 165.

Meals and lodging, deduction, §§ 162, 274.

Meals furnished employees, gross income, exclusion, § 119.

Medical care and treatment expenses, deduction, § 213.

Mineral production payments, § 636.

Ministers of the gospel, rental value of parsonages, § 107.

Mitigation, § 1311 et seq.

Moving expenses,

    Deductions, § 217.

    Reimbursement, gross income, § 82.

Natural resources, § 611 et seq.

Net operating loss deduction, § 172.

Nonrecognition, common exchanges, § 1031 et seq.

Oil and gas,

    Depletion, § 611 et seq.

    Gain from disposition of interest in, § 1254.

    Intangible drilling and development costs, § 263.

Operating loss deduction, § 172.

Options, § 1234.

Ordinary and necessary expenses, deduction, §§ 162, 212.

Ordinary income defined, § 64.

Ordinary loss defined, § 65.

Organizational expenditures, §§ 248, 709.

Original issue discount, § 1232A.

Parsonages, gross income, § 107.

Partners and partnerships, § 701 et seq.

    Agreement, § 761.

    Allocation of basis, § 755.

    Basis of property,

        Adjusted basis,

            Increase or decrease, § 755.

            Undistributed partnership property, § 734.

            Contributions to partnership, §§ 722, 723.

TOPICAL INDEX

INCOME TAXES—Continued
Partners and partnerships—Continued
Basis of property—Continued
Determination of partner's interest, § 705.
Transferee partner's interest, § 742.
Computations of partnership, § 703.
Continuation of partnership, § 708.
Contributions of property to partnerships, § 721 et seq.
Death of partner,
Gross income of successor in interest, § 753.
Payments to successor in interest, § 736.
Deductions, computation, § 703.
Definition, §§ 761, 7701.
Distributions, § 731 et seq.
Distributive share of partner, § 704.
Division of partnership, § 708.
Family partnership, § 704.
Gross income, § 702.
Guaranteed payment, § 707.
Income and credits of partner, § 702.
Increase or decrease in partner's liabilities, § 752.
Information returns, § 6031.
Inventory items, § 751.
Liquidation of interest, § 761.
Merger or consolidation, § 708.
Organization and syndication fees, § 709.
Partner defined, §§ 761, 7701.
Partners subject to tax, § 701.
Partnership defined, §§ 761, 7701.
Retiring partner, payments in liquidation of interest, § 736.
Syndication and organization fees, § 709.
Taxable years, § 706.
Termination, § 708.
Transactions between partner and partnership, § 707.
Unrealized receivables, § 751.
Patents, sale or exchange, § 1235.
Pension, profit-sharing, stock bonus plans,
Beneficiary, taxability, § 402.
Deduction for contributions of employer, § 404.
Definitions, § 414.
Employee annuities, taxation, § 403.
Individual retirement accounts, § 408.
Limitations on benefits and contributions, § 415.
Minimum,
Funding standards, § 412.
Participation standards, § 410.
Vesting standards, § 411.
Qualification, requirements, § 401.
Retirement savings, § 219.
Top-heavy plans, § 416.
Percentage depletion, §§ 613, 613A.
Personal exemptions, § 151 et seq.
Personal expenses, § 262.
Personal holding companies, § 541 et seq.
Personal injuries,
Accident and health insurance, §§ 105, 106.
Compensation, § 104.
Personal service corporations to avoid or evade tax, § 269A.
Player contracts, basis limitation, § 1056.
Political contributions,
Appreciated property, transfer to political organization, § 84.
Credit, § 41.

TOPICAL INDEX

INCOME TAXES—Continued

Political parties,
    Debts owed by, § 271.
    Indirect contributions to, § 276.
    Transfers of appreciated property to, § 84.
Pollution control facilities, § 169.
Prepaid interest, § 461.
Prizes, gross income, § 74.
Procedure. Procedure and Administration, post.
Production of income expenses, deduction, § 212.
Profit-sharing plans. Pension, profit-sharing, stock bonus plans, ante.
Qualified plans. Pension, profit-sharing, stock bonus plans, ante.
Rates of tax,
    Alternative minimum tax for taxpayers other than corporations, § 55.
    Corporate minimum tax, § 56.
    Tax imposed on,
        Corporations, § 11.
        Estates, § 1.
        Individuals, § 1.
        Trusts, § 1.
Real property,
    Amortization of construction period interest and taxes, § 189.
    Recapture, § 1250.
    Subdivided for sale, § 1237.
    Taxes, deduction, § 164.
Recapture,
    At risk amounts, § 465.
    Gain, §§ 1245, 1250.
    Investment credit, § 47.
    Mining exploration expenditures, § 617.
    Oil, gas, or geothermal property, § 1254.
Recognition, § 1001.
Recovery of bad debts, etc., § 111.
Recovery property, § 168.
Recreation expenses, § 274.
Redemptions of stock, § 302 et seq.
Related taxpayers, transactions between,
    Deductions, § 267.
    Gain from sale of depreciable property, § 1239.
Reorganization defined, § 368.
Research expenditures,
    Credit, § 44F.
    Deduction, § 174.
Reserve for bad debts, § 166.
Residence,
    Business use, § 280A.
    Casualty losses, living expenses from insurance, § 123.
    Disallowance of expenses, § 280A.
    Energy credit, § 44C.
    Moving expenses, § 217.
    Nonrecognition of gain, § 1034.
    One-time exclusion of gain, § 121.
    Vacation home, § 280A.
Restricted property transferred in connection with services, § 83.
Retirement savings, § 219.
Returns, § 6012 et seq.
S corporations, § 1361 et seq.
Scholarships, gross income, § 117.
Separate maintenance payments, gross income, § 71.
Short period returns, § 443.

INCOME TAXES—Continued
Short sales, § 1233.
Sickness or injury, compensation for, § 104.
Soil and water conservation expenditures, § 175.
Start-up expenditures, § 195.
Stockholders,
    Constructive ownership of stock, § 318.
    Controlled corporations, gain or loss, § 355.
    Distributions by corporations, § 301 et seq.
    Dividend defined, § 316.
    Liquidations, § 331 et seq.
    Redemptions, § 302 et seq.
        Death taxes, § 303.
        Defined, § 317.
        Related corporations, § 304.
    Reorganizations, gain or loss, § 354 et seq.
    Stock and stock rights,
        Distributions, § 305.
        Basis, § 307.
    Wash sales, loss from, § 1091.
Subdivided real property, § 1237.
Substantiation, § 274.
Surviving spouse defined, § 2.
Tax imposed,
    Corporations, § 11.
    Estates, § 1.
    Individuals, § 1.
    Trusts, § 1.
Tax preference items, § 57.
Taxable income defined, § 63.
Taxable year, § 441.
Taxes,
    Construction period, § 189.
    Deduction, § 164.
    Federal, § 275.
Tax-exempt income, expenses and interest relating to, § 265.
Tax-free exchanges, common transactions, § 1031 et seq.
Theft losses, deduction, § 165.
Timber, gain or loss, § 631.
Time for filing return, § 6072.
Top-heavy plans, § 416.
Trade names, transfers, § 1253.
Trade or business expenses, § 162.
Trademarks, transfers, § 1253.
Traveling expenses, deduction, §§ 162, 274.
Trusts,
    Accumulation, excess distributions, § 665 et seq.
    Administrative powers, § 675.
    Adverse parties, § 672.
    Beneficial enjoyment, power to control, § 674.
    Beneficiaries, § 641 et seq.
    Charitable remainder, § 664.
    Credits and deductions, special rules, § 642.
    Deductions, § 642 et seq.
    Distributable net income, § 643.
    Distributions,
        Corpus, § 661 et seq.
        Current income, §§ 651, 652.
        Excess, § 665 et seq.
        Net income, § 643.

INCOME TAXES—Continued
Trusts—Continued
 Divorce, § 682.
 Excess distributions, § 665 et seq.
 Foreign, §§ 668, 679, 1057, 1491 et seq.
 Gain on property transferred at less than fair market value, § 644.
 Grantors and others treated as substantial owners, § 671 et seq.
 Imposition of tax, § 641.
 Interest charge on accumulation distributions from foreign trusts, § 668.
 Nonadverse party, § 672.
 Obligations of support, § 677.
 Related or subordinate party, § 672.
 Reversionary interest, § 673.
 Revocable, § 676.
 Spouse, income for benefit of grantor's, § 677.
Two-earner married couples, deduction for, § 221.
Unemployment compensation, § 85.
Unharvested crop, sale of land, § 268.
Unrelated business income of exempt organizations, § 511 et seq.
Unused investment credits, § 196.
Vacation homes, § 280A.
Wagering losses, § 165.
Wash sales, § 1091.
Water conservation expenditures, § 175.
Workmen's compensation, § 104.
Worthless securities, losses, § 165.

PROCEDURE AND ADMINISTRATION
Additions, § 6651 et seq.
 Failure to file return or pay tax, § 6651.
 Failure to pay tax, § 6653.
 Valuation overstatements, § 6659.
Assessable penalties, § 6671 et seq.
Assessment, § 6211 et seq.
Assessment and collection, limitations on, § 6501.
Civil actions for refund, § 7422.
Closing agreements, § 7121.
Collection, § 6321 et seq.
Compromises, § 7122.
Credit or refund, limitations on, § 6511 et seq.
Crimes,
 Attempt to evade or defeat tax, § 7201.
 Fraud and false statements, § 7206.
 Willful failure to file return, supply information, or pay tax, § 7203.
Criminal prosecutions, periods of limitation, § 6531.

Deficiency,
 Defined, § 6211.
 Notice, § 6212.
 Procedures, § 6211 et seq.
Estate tax returns, § 6018.
Examination, § 7602 et seq.
Extensions of time for payment, § 6163 et seq.
Failure to file or pay, § 6651.
Fraud, §§ 6653, 7206.
Gift tax returns, § 6019.
Income tax returns, § 6012 et seq.
Information returns, § 6031 et seq.
Injunctions, prohibition, § 7421.
Innocent spouse, § 6013.
Intentional disregard of rules, § 6653.

TOPICAL INDEX

PROCEDURE AND ADMINISTRATION—Continued
Interest,
    Compounded daily, § 6622.
    Overpayments, § 6611.
    Rate, § 6621.
    Underpayments, § 6601.
Joint returns of income tax, § 6013.
Judicial proceedings, § 7421 et seq.
Levy and distraint, § 6331.
Lien for taxes, § 6321 et seq.
Limitations on assessment and collection, § 6501 et seq.
Limitations on credit or refund, § 6511 et seq.
Negligence, § 6653.
Notice of deficiency, § 6212.
Notice of fiduciary relationship, § 6903.
Partnership items, § 6221, et seq.
Prohibition on suits to restrain assessment or collection, § 7421.
Rate of interest, § 6221.
Refund, civil actions, § 7422.
Restrictions applicable to deficiencies, petition to Tax Court, § 6213.
Returns,
    Consolidated, § 1504 et seq.
    Estate tax, § 6018.
    Extension of time for filing, § 6081.
    Gift tax, § 6019.
    Income tax, § 6012 et seq.
    Information, § 6031 et seq.
    Joint by husband and wife, § 6013.
    Partnership, § 6031.
    S corporation, § 6037.
    Time for filing, §§ 6072, 6075.
Rules and regulations, § 7805.
Small tax cases, § 7463.
Special liens for estate and gift taxes, § 6324 et seq.
Spouse relieved of liability, § 6013.
Suits to restrain assessment or collection prohibited, § 7421.
Third-party summons, special procedures, § 7609.
Time for filing returns,
    Estate and gift tax, § 6075.
    Income tax, § 6072.
Time return deemed filed, § 6513.
Transferees, § 6901 et seq.
Underpayment, § 6653.
Valuation overstatements, § 6659.

†